ARCHBOLD

2015

THIRD SUPPLEMENT TO THE 2015 EDITION

EDITOR

P.J. RICHARDSON, Q.C. (Hon.), LL.M. (LOND.), Dip. Crim. (CANTAB.)
of Gray's Inn and the Inner Temple, Barrister

SUPPLEMENT EDITORS

WILLIAM CARTER, M.A. (OXON.)
of Gray's Inn, Barrister

STEPHEN SHAY, B.A. (OXON.)
of the Middle Temple, Barrister

SWEET & MAXWELL

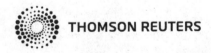

THOMSON REUTERS

Published in 2015 by Sweet & Maxwell, Friars House, 160 Blackfriars Road, London, SE1 8EZ, part of Thomson Reuters (Professional) UK Limited (Company No. 1679046). Registered in England and Wales. Registered office: 2nd Floor, 1 Mark Square, Leonard Street, London EC2A 4EG.

Printed and bound by CPI Group (UK) Ltd, Croydon, CR0 4YY.

Typeset by Sweet & Maxwell, Friars House, 160 Blackfriars Road, London, SE1 8EZ.

For further information on our products and services, visit:

http://www.sweetandmaxwell.co.uk

No natural forests were destroyed to make this product; only farmed timber was used and replanted.

A CIP catalogue record for this book is available from the British Library

ISBN MAINWORK 9780414035928
ISBN THIRD SUPPLEMENT 9780414035959

SERVICE INFORMATION

The Archbold service

Archbold: Criminal Pleading, Evidence and Practice consists of one main text volume (including the tables and index). This volume is re-issued annually, and is updated by cumulative supplements, the e-update service (see below) and *Archbold Review*.

The supplement

Three cumulative supplements, containing updating material for the main volume, are published in each year as part of the service.

This is the third supplement of 2015.

New material is incorporated into this supplement using the same paragraph numbers as appear in the mainwork. All material new to this supplement is marked in the text by a **bold** star in the margin. ★

After consulting the main work on any given subject, reference should always be made to the same paragraph number in the current supplement to check that there have been no new developments since the main text volume was published. The supplement will also track material which has been removed or relocated as part of the re-issue process.

The back cover contains a list of all important developments included in this supplement for the first time and where they can be found.

All references in the text to cases, statutes and statutory instruments are contained in the tables printed at the beginning of this supplement.

Please email smg.archbold@thomson.com with comments/suggestions for any of the Archbold services.

Archbold eBook upgrade

Archbold 2015 is available as an eBook on the iPad, PC and Mac. As a purchaser of *Archbold: Criminal Pleading, Evidence and Practice* 2015, 63rd edition you are also entitled to purchase one copy of the Archbold eBook at a special upgrade price. To find more information about the Archbold eBook please visit the Archbold website www.sweetandmaxwell.co.uk/archbold or contact our customer services team on 0845 600 9355.

Archbold e-update activation code

As a subscriber to Archbold 2015 you have free and unlimited access to the accompanying weekly e-update service and online archive. If you are a new user accessing the service for the first time then please visit www.sweetandmaxwell.co.uk/archbold where you will be asked to complete a simple short registration process, and to enter the following activation code to start receiving updates:

> AB2015

If you are an existing user of the e-update then your access will automatically be updated for the new edition and there is no need to re-register.

TABLE OF CONTENTS

TABLE OF CONTENTS

ABBREVIATIONS OF LEGISLATION

The following abbreviations have been adopted throughout.

AFA	Armed Forces Act
CAA	Criminal Appeal Act
CDA	Crime and Disorder Act
CDDA	Company Directors Disqualification Act
CEMA	Customs and Excise Management Act
CJA	Criminal Justice Act
CJCSA	Criminal Justice and Court Services Act
CJIA	Criminal Justice and Immigration Act
CJPA	Criminal Justice and Police Act
CJPOA	Criminal Justice and Public Order Act
CLA	Criminal Law Act
CPIA	Criminal Procedure and Investigations Act
C(S)A	Crime (Sentences) Act
CYPA	Children and Young Persons Act
DTA	Drug Trafficking Act
DTOA	Drug Trafficking Offences Act
ECHR	European Convention on Human Rights
FSMA	Financial Services and Markets Act
LASPOA	Legal Aid, Sentencing and Punishment of Offenders Act
MCA	Magistrates' Courts Act
MHA	Mental Health Act
PACE	Police and Criminal Evidence
PCA	Proceeds of Crime Act
PCCA	Powers of Criminal Courts Act
PCC(S)A	Powers of Criminal Courts (Sentencing) Act
PJA	Police and Justice Act
RIPA	Regulation of Investigatory Powers Act
RSA	Road Safety Act
RSC	Rules of the Supreme Court (Revision)
RTA	Road Traffic Act
RTOA	Road Traffic Offenders Act
SCA	Serious Crime Act
SOA	Sexual Offences Act
SOCPA	Serious Organised Crime and Police Act
VCRA	Violent Crime Reduction Act
YJCEA	Youth Justice and Criminal Evidence Act

TABLE OF STATUTES

References in bold indicate where legislation is reproduced in full

NORTHERN IRELAND

TABLE OF NON-UK LEGISLATION

TABLE OF EUROPEAN AND INTERNATIONAL TREATIES AND CONVENTIONS

References in bold indicate where legislation is reproduced in full

TABLE OF EUROPEAN DIRECTIVES AND REGULATIONS

TABLE OF STATUTORY INSTRUMENTS

References in bold indicate where legislation is reproduced in full

TABLE OF CASES

TABLE OF EUROPEAN HUMAN RIGHTS CASES

TABLE OF PRACTICE DIRECTIONS

References in bold indicate where legislation is reproduced in full

Chapter 1

THE INDICTMENT

III. SENDINGS FOR TRIAL

B. Principal Provisions

(2) **Sending of cases to the Crown Court**

Crime and Disorder Act 1998, ss.50A, 51–51E

Sending cases to the Crown Court: adults

　With effect from April 12, 2015, the Criminal Justice and Courts Act 2015, s.52(2), amends section 51(2)(b) of the 1998 Act so as to insert "22A(2)(b)," after "21,".　**1-25**

Sending cases to the Crown Court: children and young persons

　In *R. (P.) v. Derby Youth Court*, 179 J.P. 139, DC, it was held that there is no scope for sending young offenders to the Crown Court for trial under section 51A(3)(b) of the 1998 Act where there is evidence before the youth court that the defendant is unfit to stand trial, because the defendant would not be "convicted" and could not therefore be "sentenced" pursuant to section 91 of the PCC(S)A 2000 (§ 5-610 in the main work).　★**1-26**

　As to "it ought to be possible to sentence him in pursuance of subsection (3)" of section 91 in subsection (3)(b), see *R. (DPP) v. South Tyneside Youth Court, post,* § 1-116.　★

D. Mode of Trial for Offences Triable Either Way and Certain Summary Offences

(2) **Procedure**

(a) *Statutory provisions*

Procedure for determining mode of trial of offences triable either way

Magistrates' Court Act 1980, s.22A

Low-value shoplifting to be a summary offence

　With effect from April 12, 2015, the Criminal Justice and Courts Act 2015, s.52(1), amends section 22A of the 1980 Act, so as to substitute subsection (2)(b), as follows—　**1-108a**

　　"(b) the court must proceed in relation to the offence in accordance with section 51(1) of the
　　Crime and Disorder Act 1998.".

Magistrates' Courts Act 1980, ss.24–24D

Jurisdiction to be declined where detention a possibility

　In view of the amendment of the PCC(S)A 2000, s.3B(1) (as to which, see § 5-27 in the main work) by the Criminal Justice and Courts Act 2015, s.53 (as to which, see *post,* § 5-27), it will no longer be necessary to take the prosecution case at its highest when deciding, under section 51A(3)(b) of the CDA 1998 (§ 1-26 in the main work), whether to send a child or young person for trial in the Crown Court on the basis that it "ought to be possible" to sentence him under section 91 of the 2000 Act (*ibid.,* § 5-610): *R. (DPP) v. South Tyneside Youth Court*, unreported, May 20, 2015, DC ([2015] EWHC 1455 (Admin.)) (thus qualifying *R. (W. and M.) v. Oldham Youth Court* (as to which, see the main work)). It was said that while there will be cases in which the alleged offending is so grave that a sentence of or in excess of two years will be a "real prospect" (see *R. (H., A. and O.) v. Southampton Youth Court* (in the main work)) irrespective of particular considerations in relation either to the offence or the offender's role, such cases will be rare; in most cases,　★**1-116** whether there is such a "real prospect" will generally be apparent only when the court has determined the full circumstances of the offence and has a far greater understanding of the position of the offender.

(b) *Procedural rules*

Criminal Procedure Rules 2014 (S.I. 2014 No. 1610), Pt 9

Replacement of 2014 rules by 2015 rules

★**1-117a**   With effect from October 5, 2015, the Criminal Procedure Rules 2015 (S.I. 2015 No. 1490) replace S.I. 2014 No. 1610. Part 9 of the 2014 rules is reproduced (see *post*, Appendix P-71 *et seq.*), with changes of substance to rules 9.9 and 9.13.

Adult defendant: guilty plea

★**1-117i**   With effect from April 6, 2015, the Criminal Procedure (Amendment No. 2) Rules 2015 (S.I. 2015 No. 646), r.6(a), amended rule 9.9(2)(b) of S.I. 2014 No. 1610, so as to substitute "rule 37.11" for "rule 37.10".

Adult defendant: allocation for magistrates' court trial

★**1-117k**   With effect from April 6, 2015, the Criminal Procedure (Amendment No. 2) Rules 2015 (S.I. 2015 No. 646), r.6(b), amended rule 9.11(3)(b)(ii) of S.I. 2014 No. 1610, so as to substitute "rule 37.11" for "rule 37.10".

Young defendant

★**1-117m**   With effect from April 6, 2015, the Criminal Procedure (Amendment No. 2) Rules 2015 (S.I. 2015 No. 646), r.6(c), amended rule 9.13(5)(b) of S.I. 2014 No. 1610, so as to substitute "rule 37.11" for "rule 37.10".

(5) Penalties on summary conviction

Magistrates' Courts Act 1980, s.32

Penalties on summary conviction for offences triable either way

★**1-125**   With effect from March 12, 2015, the Legal Aid, Sentencing and Punishment of Offenders Act 2012 (Fines on Summary Conviction) Regulations 2015 (S.I. 2015 No. 664), amended section 32 of the 1980 Act so as to insert, after subsection (9), a new subsection (10), as follows—

> "(10) Section 85 of the Legal Aid, Sentencing and Punishment of Offenders Act 2012 (removal of limit on certain fines on conviction by magistrates' court) makes provision that affects the application of this section.".

★   With effect from March 12, 2015 (Legal Aid, Sentencing and Punishment of Offenders Act 2012 (Commencement No. 11) Order 2015 (S.I. 2015 No. 504)), section 85(1), (2) and (4) of the 2012 Act were brought into force.

(6) Offences triable either way

Specific offences

Magistrates' Courts Act 1980, s.17, and Sched. 1

★**1-130**   As from a day to be appointed, the Deeds of Arrangement Act 1914 is repealed by the Deregulation Act 2015, s.19, and Sched. 6, para. 1(1), and, in consequence, paragraph 16 of Schedule 1 to the 1980 Act is also repealed by *ibid.*, para. 2(8).

(7) Joinder of certain summary offences in an indictment

Criminal Justice Act 1988, s.40

Power to join in indictment count for common assault etc.

★**1-133**   As from March 20, 2015 (Criminal Justice and Courts Act 2015 (Commencement No. 1, Saving and Transitional Provisions) Order 2015 (S.I. 2015 No. 778)), the Criminal Justice and Courts Act 2015, s.39, and Sched. 10, para. 31, amended section 40(3) of the 1988 Act (see the main work) so as to insert, after paragraph (ab), a new paragraph (ac), as follows—

"(ac) an offence under paragraph 14 or 24 of Schedule 10 to the Criminal Justice and Courts
Act 2015 (assaulting secure college custody officer);".

IV. AGAINST WHOM AN INDICTMENT LIES

C. EXTRADITEES AND REPATRIATED PRISONERS

(1) Introduction

As to the amendment of section 3A of the Repatriation of Prisoners Act 1984 (see the main **1-164**
work), see *post*, § 1-173a.

(2) Legislation

(a) *Extraditees*

Extradition Act 2003, ss.146–150, 151A, 151B

Dealing with person for other offences
   Director of the Serious Fraud Office v. O'Brien is now reported at [2014] A.C. 1246. **1-171**

(b) *Repatriated prisoners*

Repatriation of Prisoners Act 1984, s.3A

Prosecution of other offences
   With effect from December 3, 2014, section 3A of the 1984 Act (see the main work) was **1-173a**
amended by the Criminal Justice and Data Protection (Protocol No. 36) Regulations 2014 (S.I.
2014 No. 3141), reg. 113(1) and (2), so as to substitute the words "the United Kingdom" for the
words "Great Britain" in subsections (1)(a) and (3)(d) (in both places).

V. THE FORM OF AN INDICTMENT

B. DRAWING THE INDICTMENT

(2) Number of counts

For a case considering *R. v. Hartley (Practice Note)* and *R. v. Canavan*; *R. v. Kidd*; *R. v. Shaw* (as ★**1-181**
to both of which, see the main work), see *R. v. A.*, *post*, § 1-225.

C. CONTENTS

(2) Statement and particulars of offence(s) and signature
Criminal Procedure Rules 2014 (S.I. 2014 No. 1610), r.14.2

Form and content of indictment
   With effect from April 6, 2015, rule 14.2(5) of S.I. 2014 No. 1610 is amended by rule 6 of the **1-188**
Criminal Procedure (Amendment) Rules 2015 (S.I. 2015 No. 13), so as to substitute a new sub-
paragraph (a), as follows—
    "(a) any count charging substantially the same offence as one specified in the notice of the of-
    fence or offences for which the defendant was sent for trial; and".

As to the replacement of S.I. 2014 No. 1610, and the incorporation of the amendments made ★
by S.I. 2015 No. 13 (*ante*), see *post*, § 1-299.

Particulars of offence

In *R. v. Clarke (Dean)* [2015] 2 Cr.App.R. 6, CA, it was held that where the particulars of an ★**1-190**
indictment charging conspiracy to rob, contrary to section 1(1) of the CLA 1977 (§ 33-2 in the
main work), averred that the alleged conspirators "... conspired together and with other persons
to rob a dwelling and business of cash and other items", whilst there was no doubt that the indict-

ment was very poorly drafted and ought to have been amended, it had been clear what was alleged and thus the particulars were not so defective as to render it a nullity.

E. Duplicity

(4) Rule 14.2(2) of the Criminal Procedure Rules 2014 (S.I. 2014 No. 1610)

★**1-225**   *R. v. Hartley (Practice Note)* was considered in *R. v. A.* [2015] 2 Cr.App.R.(S.) 12, CA, which gave further guidance as to the use of multiple incident counts pursuant to rule 14.2(2) of the Criminal Procedure Rules 2014 (as to which, see § 1-188 in the main work). It was held that where it is alleged that the defendant repeatedly committed the same offence against the same victim (or victims) over a prolonged period, the prosecution need to ensure that the indictment contains one or more sufficiently broad course of conduct counts, or a mix of individual counts and course of conduct counts, such that the judge would be able to sentence the defendant appropriately on the basis of his criminality as revealed by the counts on which he is convicted. The court said that in most cases it will be unnecessary for the counts to be numerous, but they should be sufficient in number to enable the judge to reflect the seriousness of the offending by reference to the key features of the case, for example, the number of victims, the nature of the offending and the length of time over which it extended. Where, in relation to a "course of conduct" count, the judge had directed the jury that they needed only to be satisfied that there were at least two instances of the commission of the offence, then sentence would have to be passed on the basis of just two instances of the offence. For the suggestion that the judgment – taken as a whole – provides little encouragement for the use of multiple incident counts, and that they are unnecessary and likely only to give rise to confusion (as in this case), see the commentary to the case at CLW/15/16/2.

G. Joinder

(5) Separate trials of counts lawfully joined and of defendants jointly charged

The general approach to severance

1-250   *R. v. Powell (Carl)* is now reported at [2014] 2 Cr.App.R. 31.

VI. TIME FOR COMMENCEMENT OF PROSECUTION

B. Statutory Limitations on the Prosecution of Offences

(1) General time limits

★**1-272**   As from April 13, 2015 (Criminal Justice and Courts Act 2015 (Commencement No. 1, Saving and Transitional Provisions) Order 2015 (S.I. 2015 No. 778)), the Criminal Justice and Courts Act 2015, ss.46(1) to (9) and 47, amended sections 29 and 30 of the CJA 2003 (see the main work). These amendments take account of a new procedure under which non-imprisonable summary offences can be tried by a single justice sitting in private with no oral evidence (provided for by new ss.16A to 16E of the MCA 1980 (as inserted by s.48(1) and (3) of the 2015 Act) (also into force on April 13, 2015)). In particular, the expression "relevant prosecutor" in section 29 is substituted for "public prosecutor". A relevant prosecutor, when issuing a written charge, must now at the same time issue a requisition or "a single justice procedure notice". A new paragraph (c) is inserted at the end of subsection (5) of section 30, to provide that any reference in a prior enactment which is, or includes, a reference to a summons under section 1 of the MCA 1980 (or to a justice of the peace issuing such a summons) is to be read as including a reference to a single justice procedure notice (or to a relevant prosecutor issuing such a notice).

★   With effect from April 6, 2015, Part 7 of the Criminal Procedure Rules 2014 (S.I. 2014 No. 1610) is amended by rule 5 of the Criminal Procedure (Amendment No. 2) Rules 2015 (S.I. 2015 No. 646). These amendments have been incorporated into the Criminal Procedure Rules 2015 (S.I. 2015 No. 1490) (*post*, Appendix P).

C. Commencement of Prosecution

1-276   As to the amendment of section 29 of the CJA 2003 (see the main work), see *ante*, § 1-272.

VII. PREFERRING THE BILL OF INDICTMENT

A. WHEN A BILL OF INDICTMENT MAY BE PREFERRED

Administration of Justice (Miscellaneous Provisions) Act 1933, s.2(1), (2)

With effect from May 26, 2015 (Deregulation Act 2015 (Commencement No. 1 and Transitional and Saving Provisions) Order 2015 (S.I. 2015 No. 994)), the 2015 Act, s.82(1) and (2), amended section 2(2) of the 1933 Act so as to substitute "section 51D(1)" for "section 57D(1)". ★1-277

Indictment based on voluntary bill

An application for a voluntary bill following the dismissal of a charge under Schedule 3, para. 2, to the CDA 1998 (§ 1-36 in the main work), should only be granted where (a) the Crown Court made a basic and substantive error of law that is clear and obvious, (b) new evidence has become available that the prosecution could not put before the court at the time of the dismissal hearing, (c) there was a serious procedural irregularity, or (d) there were other exceptional circumstances, which might include correction of a prosecution mistake or a change of mind by the prosecution; in such circumstances, the power will be used sparingly and its use will depend on the nature of the prosecution's changed position, the reasons for the new approach and the implications for the case as a whole; where changes to the prosecution case have operated to the real prejudice of the accused, it will not be appropriate to grant the application; another exceptional situation might be where the charge was dismissed on a technicality, particularly if it was one that could not reasonably have been anticipated by the prosecution: *Serious Fraud Office v. Evans* [2015] Lloyd's Rep F.C. 59, QBD (Fulford L.J.). Where, however, the prosecution had reformulated their case twice prior to the dismissal ruling (the second time at a reconvened hearing when the judge raised a matter of law after the conclusion of the initial hearing), and where they advanced a fourth possible basis for the charges at the application for the voluntary bill, the application would be refused; the prosecution had failed to approach the case with sufficient analytical precision; instead they were guilty of repeatedly reformulating their case in an attempt to identify a sustainable basis in law for the charges that had been dismissed; it was not in the interests of justice to permit the prosecution to reformulate their case on a legal basis that should, and could, have been presented at the time the case was sent for trial: *ibid.* 1-288

In *Evans v. Serious Fraud Office* [2015] Lloyd's Rep. F.C. 223, Crown Court (at Cardiff) and QBD (Hickinbottom J.), the Serious Fraud Office were ordered to pay the costs of the defendants in relation to the unsuccessful application for a voluntary bill (*ante*) on an indemnity basis, rather than the standard basis. Costs on such basis were only appropriate where the conduct of the paying party was of a nature that took the case out of the norm; unreasonable conduct to a high degree would suffice; here, the application for the voluntary bill had followed conduct in the Crown Court by the prosecution that had been "improper"; the application had then been brought without proper cognisance of the high hurdle a prosecutor has to overcome in relation to a voluntary bill; and, in making it, the prosecution had tried to widen the scope of the case beyond its proper limits. As to this case, see also *post*, § 6-57. ★

Joinder of persons or charges separately sent for trial

Administration of Justice (Miscellaneous Provisions) Act 1933, s.2(3)–(8) and Sched. 2

With effect from May 26, 2015 (Deregulation Act 2015 (Commencement No. 1 and Transitional and Saving Provisions) Order 2015 (S.I. 2015 No. 994)), the 2015 Act, s.82(1), amended section 2(6) of the 1933 Act, so as to substitute "Criminal Procedure Rules" for "Rules", and repealed section 2(6A) of that Act. ★1-296

B. RULES AS TO PROCEDURE

Criminal Procedure Rules 2014 (S.I. 2014 No. 1610), r.14.1

Service of indictment

With effect from April 6, 2015, rule 14.1 of S.I. 2014 No. 1610 is amended by rule 6 of the Criminal Procedure (Amendment) Rules 2015 (S.I. 2015 No. 13), so as to omit "or" at the end of paragraph (1)(c) and paragraph (1)(d). 1-299

★   With effect from October 5, 2015, the Criminal Procedure Rules 2015 (S.I. 2015 No. 1490) replace S.I. 2014 No. 1610, incorporating the amendments made by S.I. 2015 No. 13 (*ante*). Part 14 of the 2014 rules (as so amended) is replaced by Part 10 of the 2015 rules (see *post*, Appendix P-87, P-88).

IX. PROCEEDINGS AGAINST CORPORATIONS AND OTHER BODIES

(2) Deferred prosecutions

Procedural provisions

Criminal Procedure Rules 2014 (S.I. 2014 No. 1610), Pt 12

Replacement of 2014 rules by 2015 rules

★**1-317q**   With effect from October 5, 2015, the Criminal Procedure Rules 2015 (S.I. 2015 No. 1490) replace S.I. 2014 No. 1610. Part 12 of the 2014 rules is replaced by Part 11 of the 2015 rules (see *post*, Appendix P-89 *et seq.*), with minor drafting changes.

XI. POWERS AND DUTIES OF PARTICULAR PROSECUTION AGENCIES

A. CROWN PROSECUTION SERVICE

(2) Functions of Director of Public Prosecutions

Prosecution of Offences Act 1985, s.3

1-326   With effect from October 20, 2014 (Anti-social Behaviour, Crime and Policing Act 2014 (Commencement No. 7, Saving and Transitional Provisions) Order 2014 (S.I. 2014 No. 2590), as amended by the Anti-social Behaviour, Crime and Policing Act 2014 (Commencement No. 7, Saving and Transitional Provisions) (Amendment) Order 2014 (S.I. 2014 No. 2754)), section 181(1) of, and paragraph 5 of Schedule 11 to, the 2014 Act (see the main work) were brought into force; as was the repeal of sections 7 and 8 of the VCRA 2006 by paragraphs 44 and 50 of Schedule 11 to the 2014 Act (as to which, see also the main work).

(7) Bail applications

Prosecution of Offences Act 1985, s.7A

★**1-335**   With effect from March 23, 2015 (Anti-social Behaviour, Crime and Policing Act 2014 (Commencement No. 8, Saving and Transitional Provisions) Order 2015 (S.I. 2015 No. 373)), section 181(1) of, and paragraph 46 of Schedule 11 to, the 2014 Act, were brought into force.

(10) Interpretation of Part I

Prosecution of Offences Act 1985, s.15

★**1-341**   As from April 13, 2015 (Criminal Justice and Courts Act 2015 (Commencement No. 1, Saving and Transitional Provisions) Order 2015 (S.I. 2015 No. 778)), the Criminal Justice and Courts Act 2015, s.50, and Sched. 11, para. 7, amended section 15(1) and (2) of the 1985 Act, so as (i) in subsections (1) and (2)(ba), to substitute "relevant prosecutor" for "public prosecutor", (ii) in subsection (1), to insert ", 'single justice procedure notice'" after "'requisition'", and (iii) to insert, after subsection (2)(ba), a new paragraph (bb), as follows—

> "(bb) where a relevant prosecutor issues a written charge and single justice procedure notice, when the written charge and single justice procedure notice are issued;".

(11) Power of Secretary of State to set time limits in relation to preliminary stages of criminal proceedings

Custody time limits: general and procedure

★**1-348**   It was held in *R. (Campbell-Brown) v. Central Criminal Court* [2015] 1 Cr.App.R. 34, DC, that trials involving defendants remanded in custody should not be listed for trial on a date after the date on which the custody time limit would expire without first considering whether there were grounds for extending the time limit pursuant to section 22(3) of the Prosecution of Offences Act 1985 (§ 1-342 in the main work)). As to this case, see also *post*, § 1-358.

Criteria to be satisfied before extension granted

R. *(Lake and Bennett) v. Northampton Crown Court* was considered in R. *(Campbell-Brown) v. Central*   ★**1-358**
Criminal Court [2015] 1 Cr.App.R. 34, DC, where it was held that it was over-stating the matter to say that the convenience of counsel could never amount to "good and sufficient cause" for extending a time limit (Prosecution of Offences Act 1985, s.22(3)(a)(iii) (§ 1-342 in the main work)). The court said that a trial of a vulnerable defendant who trusted one particular barrister who was well-known to him, or linked fraud trials with common counsel, were examples of cases where the test might be met. As to this case, see also *ante*, § 1-348.

(12) Discontinuance of proceedings in magistrates' courts

Objecting to the discontinuance of proceedings in a magistrates' court

Criminal Procedure Rules 2014 (S.I. 2014 No. 1610), Pt 8

Replacement of 2014 rules by 2015 rules
With effect from October 5, 2015, the Criminal Procedure Rules 2015 (S.I. 2015 No. 1490)   ★**1-361**
replace S.I. 2014 No. 1610. Part 8 of the 2014 rules is replaced by Part 12 of the 2015 rules (see *post*, Appendix P-100 *et seq.*).

B. SERIOUS FRAUD OFFICE

(2) Investigation powers
Criminal Justice Act 1987, s.2

Director's investigation powers
R. *(Rawlinson & Hunter Trustees) v. Central Criminal Court*; R. *(Tchenguiz) v. Director of the Serious*   **1-375**
Fraud Office (as to which, see the main work) was considered in R. *(Mills and Mills) v. Sussex Police and Southwark Crown Court*, *post*, § 15-55, where the court had to decide on the appropriate test to be applied when deciding whether to quash a warrant for material non-disclosure by the applicant for the warrant.

CHAPTER 2

THE CRIMINAL JURISDICTION OF THE CROWN COURT

I. THE CROWN COURT

C. CONSTITUTION

(1) Judges of the Crown Court
Criminal Procedure Rules 2014 (S.I. 2014 No. 1610), r.63.10

Constitution of the Crown Court
As to the renumbering of rule 63.10 of S.I. 2014 No. 1610, see *post*, § 2-180f.   **2-6**
As to the renumbering of rule 63.10 of S.I. 2014 No. 1610, see *post*, § 2-180f.   **2-7**
As to the replacement of S.I. 2014 No. 1610 by the Criminal Procedure Rules 2015 (S.I. 2015   ★
No. 1490), see *post*, § 2-180.

(4) Duties of Crown Court officers
Criminal Procedure Rules 2014 (S.I. 2014 No. 1610), r.38.18

Duty of court officer
As to the replacement of S.I. 2014 No. 1610 by the Criminal Procedure Rules 2015 (S.I. 2015   ★**2-10a**
No. 1490), see *post*, § 4-265a.

II. THE GENERAL JURISDICTION OF THE CROWN COURT

A. GENERAL PRINCIPLES

2-34   *R. v. Rogers* is now reported at [2014] 2 Cr.App.R. 32, *sub nom. R. v. Rogers (Bradley)*.

V. APPELLATE JURISDICTION OF CROWN COURT IN CRIMINAL CASES

B. RIGHTS OF APPEAL TO CROWN COURT

(1) General

Magistrates' Courts Act 1980, s.108

Right of appeal to the Crown Court

★2-161   As from April 13, 2015 (Criminal Justice and Courts Act 2015 (Commencement No. 1, Saving and Transitional Provisions) Order 2015 (S.I. 2015 No. 778)), section 108 of the 1980 Act was amended by the Criminal Justice and Courts Act 2015, s.54(3), and Sched. 12, paras 2 and 4, so as to insert new subsection (5) as follows—

> "(5) Subsection (3) does not prevent an appeal against an order under section 21A of the Prosecution of Offences Act 1985 (criminal courts charge).".

(10) Appeal against drinking banning order

Violent Crime Reduction Act 2006, s.10

Appeals

2-172b   With effect from October 20, 2014 (Anti-social Behaviour, Crime and Policing Act 2014 (Commencement No. 7, Saving and Transitional Provisions) Order 2014 (S.I. 2014 No. 2590), as amended by the Anti-social Behaviour, Crime and Policing Act 2014 (Commencement No. 7, Saving and Transitional Provisions) (Amendment) Order 2014 (S.I. 2014 No. 2754)), section 10(1) of the 2006 Act (see the main work) was repealed by section 181(1) of, and paragraphs 44 and 50 of Schedule 11 to, the 2014 Act, so far as it relates to a drinking banning order made under section 6 of the 2006 Act.

★   With effect from March 23, 2015, the repeal of section 10 of the 2006 Act by section 181(1) of, and paragraphs 44 and 50 of Schedule 11 to, the 2014 Act, took effect for all purposes: Anti-social Behaviour, Crime and Policing Act 2014 (Commencement No. 8, Saving and Transitional Provisions) Order 2015 (S.I. 2015 No. 373).

D. CESSATION AND ABANDONMENT OF RIGHT OF APPEAL

(3) Abandonment of appeal

Criminal Procedure Rules 2014 (S.I. 2014 No. 1610), r.63.8

Abandoning an appeal

2-176   As to the renumbering of rules 63.8 and 63.9 of S.I. 2014 No. 1610, see *post*, § 2-180f.

★   As to the replacement of S.I. 2014 No. 1610 by the Criminal Procedure Rules 2015 (S.I. 2015 No. 1490), see *post*, § 2-180.

F. PROCEDURE

(1) Rules of court

Criminal Procedure Rules 2014 (S.I. 2014 No. 1610), Pt 63

Replacement of 2014 rules by 2015 rules

★2-180   With effect from October 5, 2015, the Criminal Procedure Rules 2015 (S.I. 2015 No. 1490) replace S.I. 2014 No. 1610. Part 63 of the 2014 rules is replaced by Part 34 of the 2015 rules (see *post*, Appendix P-356 *et seq.*). Part 34 incorporates the amendments made to Part 63 of the 2014 rules by S.I. 2015 No. 13 (as to which, see *post*), omits references to drinking banning orders and makes other minor drafting changes.

Hearings and decisions

2-180f   With effect from April 6, 2015, current rules 63.7 to 63.10 of S.I. 2014 No. 1610 are renumbered as rules 63.8 to 63.11, and a new rule 63.7 is inserted, by rule 13 of the Criminal Procedure (Amendment) Rules 2015 (S.I. 2015 No. 13), as follows—

"Application to introduce further evidence
    63.7.—(1) This rule applies where—
      (a) a party wants to introduce evidence that was not introduced by either party in the magistrates' court; and
      (b) one of these Parts applies—
        (i) Part 29 (Measures to assist a witness or defendant to give evidence),
        (ii) Part 34 (Hearsay evidence),
        (iii) Part 35 (Evidence of bad character), or
        (iv) Part 36 (Evidence of a complainant's previous sexual behaviour).
    (2) Such a party must serve the notice or application to introduce evidence required by that Part not more than 14 days after service of the appeal notice.".

As to the replacement of S.I. 2014 No. 1610 by the Criminal Procedure Rules 2015 (S.I. 2015 ★ No. 1490), see *ante*, § 2-180.

Abandoning an appeal
As to the renumbering of rule 63.8 of S.I. 2014 No. 1610, see *ante*, § 2-180f.   **2-180g**
As to the replacement of S.I. 2014 No. 1610 by the Criminal Procedure Rules 2015 (S.I. 2015 ★ No. 1490), see *ante*, § 2-180.

Court's power to vary requirements under this Part
As to the renumbering of rule 63.9 of S.I. 2014 No. 1610, see *ante*, § 2-180f.   **2-180h**
As to the replacement of S.I. 2014 No. 1610 by the Criminal Procedure Rules 2015 (S.I. 2015 ★ No. 1490), see *ante*, § 2-180.

Constitution of the Crown Court
As to the renumbering of rule 63.10 of S.I. 2014 No. 1610, see *ante*, § 2-180f.   **2-181**
As to the replacement of S.I. 2014 No. 1610 by the Criminal Procedure Rules 2015 (S.I. 2015 ★ No. 1490), see *ante*, § 2-180.
As to the renumbering of rule 63.9 of S.I. 2014 No. 1610, see *ante*, § 2-180f.   **2-182**
As to the replacement of S.I. 2014 No. 1610 by the Criminal Procedure Rules 2015 (S.I. 2015 ★ No. 1490), see *ante*, § 2-180.

(2) Applications for leave to appeal against conviction out of time

Where an application was made for an extension of time of nearly eight years to appeal to the ★**2-183** Crown Court against conviction, on a guilty plea, on the basis of legal advice now said to have been erroneous, it was held that the judge had been right to treat the application as an application to vacate an equivocal plea and was entitled to refuse the application on the basis that it was too late to investigate the advice. The factors to be considered included, at least, the reasons for the delay and its length, the apparent strength of the case on its merits, whether there had been substantial injustice, whether the conviction was spent, in an equivocal plea case, the ability to investigate what occurred at the time of the guilty plea, and the practicalities after the lapse of time of there being an effective retrial: *R. v. Khalif* [2015] 4 *Archbold Review* 3, DC.

(8) Change of plea—equivocal plea

(a) *Plea of guilty recorded and magistrates pass sentence*

Procedure

With effect from April 6, 2015, rule 37.9 of the Criminal Procedure Rules 2014 (S.I. 2014 No. ★**2-199a** 1610) was renumbered as rule 37.10 by rule 7(f) of the Criminal Procedure (Amendment No. 2) Rules 2015 (S.I. 2015 No. 646).
With effect from October 5, 2015, the 2014 rules are replaced by the Criminal Procedure Rules ★ 2015 (S.I. 2015 No. 1490). Part 37 of the 2014 rules is replaced by Part 24 of the 2015 rules (*post*, Appendix P-205 *et seq.*), subject to minor changes of substance.

VI. CRIMINAL PROCEDURE RULES

Criminal Procedure Rules 2005–2014

★**2-205**   As to the replacement of the 2014 rules by the Criminal Procedure Rules 2015 (S.I. 2015 No. 1490), with effect from October 5, 2014, see *post*, Appendix P.

Criminal Procedure Rules 2014 (S.I. 2014 No. 1610), Pt 2

Replacement of 2014 rules by 2015 rules

★**2-206**   With effect from October 5, 2015, the Criminal Procedure Rules 2015 (S.I. 2015 No. 1490) replace S.I. 2014 No. 1610. Part 2 of the 2014 rules is reproduced (see *post*, Appendix P-6 *et seq.*) with several changes of substance. In particular, rule 2.4 of the 2014 rules is omitted and reproduced as new rule 46.1 (see *post*, Appendix P-477).

Criminal Procedure Rules 2014 (S.I. 2014 No. 1610), Pt 4

Replacement of 2014 rules by 2015 rules

★**2-207**   With effect from October 5, 2015, the Criminal Procedure Rules 2015 (S.I. 2015 No. 1490) replace S.I. 2014 No. 1610. Part 4 of the 2014 rules is reproduced (see *post*, Appendix P-35 *et seq.*) with several changes of substance.

Documents that must be served by specified methods

★**2-213**   With effect from April 6, 2015, rule 4 of the Criminal Procedure (Amendment No. 2) Rules 2015 (S.I. 2015 No. 646) amended rule 4.7(2)(g) of the Criminal Procedure Rules 2014 (S.I. 2014 No. 1610) by the substitution of "rule 37.16(a)" for "rule 37.15(a)".

2-218a   With effect from February 2, 2015, the preamble to the 2014 rules (as to which, see the main work) was amended by rule 15 of the Criminal Procedure (Amendment) Rules 2015 (S.I. 2015 No. 13), to specify that rules 4.1 and 4.11 (not 4.1 and 4.7) were made under section 12(1) and (3) of the RTOA 1988 (rather than just under subs. (1)). However, this does not affect the question whether new rule 4.7(4) is *ultra vires*. As pointed out in the main work, that provision purports to prescribe the manner in which service of a notice under section 172 of the RTA 1988 (§ 32-185 in the main work) or under section 112 of the Road Traffic Regulation Act 1984 may be effected. Neither section 12 of the 1988 Act, nor any other provision, gives the rule committee such power.

Criminal Procedure Rules 2014 (S.I. 2014 No. 1610), Pt 5

Replacement of 2014 rules by 2015 rules

★**2-219**   With effect from October 5, 2015, the Criminal Procedure Rules 2015 (S.I. 2015 No. 1490) replace S.I. 2014 No. 1610. Part 5 of the 2014 rules is reproduced (see *post*, Appendix P-48 *et seq.*) with several changes of substance.

Criminal Procedure Rules 2014 (S.I. 2014 No. 1610), Pt 75

Replacement of 2014 rules by 2015 rules

★**2-230**   With effect from October 5, 2015, the Criminal Procedure Rules 2015 (S.I. 2015 No. 1490) replace S.I. 2014 No. 1610. Part 75 of the 2014 rules is replaced by Part 44 of the 2015 rules (see *post*, Appendix P-460 *et seq.*).

CHAPTER 3

BAIL, APPEARANCE OF ACCUSED FOR TRIAL, PRESENCE DURING TRIAL

I. BAIL

A. GENERAL

(2) The Bail Act 1976

(a) *Introduction*

European supervision measures

With effect from December 3, 2014, Part 7 of the Criminal Justice and Data Protection (Protocol   **3-9a** No. 36) Regulations 2014 (S.I. 2014 No. 3141) transposed Council Framework Decision 2009/ 829/JHA, which sets out a framework for the mutual recognition of decisions on supervision measures (bail conditions). *Inter alia*, there is provision (a) enabling certain domestic courts to make a request to a competent authority in another member state to monitor the supervision measures in relation to a person granted bail under the 1976 Act (regs 76–84 (*post*, §§ 3-75a *et seq.*)), and (b) a magistrates' court to recognise a decision on supervision measures imposed on a person by a competent authority in another member state, and to take steps to secure the monitoring of those measures (regs 85–94 (not set out in this work)). Regulation 78(2) provides that the requirements that may be imposed on a person under section 3(6) of the 1976 Act (§ 3-13 in the main work) include a requirement that can only be complied with in another member state, and regulation 78(3) modifies sections 3AA, 3AB and 3AC (*ibid.*, §§ 3-16 *et seq.*) of that Act where a court is considering imposing requirements on a person that would involve electronic monitoring of the person in a particular area of another member state. In addition, regulation 88 makes particular provision as to the application of the 1976 Act where a magistrates' court notifies the competent authority in another state that it has decided to recognise a decision on supervision measures; and regulation 91 (which was amended by the Criminal Justice and Data Protection (Protocol No. 36) (Amendment) Regulations 2014 (S.I. 2014 No. 3191) to correct a drafting error) provides for a power of arrest where a magistrates' court is responsible for monitoring supervision measures (and modifies s.128 of the MCA 1980 (§ 3-194 in the main work) for this purpose).

(c) *Text of the Act*

Bail Act 1976, s.3

General provisions

As to the imposition of a requirement under subsection (6) of section 3 of the 1976 Act that   **3-13** may only be complied with in another member state of the European Union, see Chapter 2 of Part 7 of S.I. 2014 No. 3141 (*ante*, § 3-9a; and *post*, §§ 3-75a *et seq.*).

As to the possibility of a person who is "protected" by a bail condition applying for a "protec-   **3-14** tion order", see *post*, § 19-358a.

Conditions of bail

As to the possibility, where a bail condition is a "protection measure" within the Criminal   **3-15** Justice (European Protection Order) (England and Wales) Regulations 2014 (S.I. 2014 No. 3300), of the "protected person" applying to the court that imposed the condition for it to make a "European protection order" as an adjunct to the bail condition, see *post*, §§ 19-358a *et seq.*

Bail Act 1976, s.3AA

Conditions for the imposition of electronic monitoring requirements: children and young persons released on bail other than in extradition proceedings

As to the modification of section 3AA of the 1976 Act where a court is considering imposing   **3-16** requirements on a person that would involve electronic monitoring of the person in a particular area of another member state, see regulation 78(3) of S.I. 2014 No. 3141 (*ante*, § 3-9a; and *post*, § 3-75c).

As to the application of section 3AA where a magistrates' court notifies the competent authority of another member state that it has decided to recognise a decision on supervision measures taken in that member state, see regulation 88 of S.I. 2014 No. 3141.

Bail Act 1976, ss.3AB, 3AC

Conditions for the imposition of electronic monitoring requirements: other persons

3-18   As to the modification of section 3AB of the 1976 Act where a court is considering imposing requirements on a person that would involve electronic monitoring of the person in a particular area of another member state, see regulation 78(3) of S.I. 2014 No. 3141 (*ante*, § 3-9a; and *post*, § 3-75c).

As to the application of section 3AB where a magistrates' court notifies the competent authority of another member state that it has decided to recognise a decision on supervision measures taken in that member state, see regulation 88 of S.I. 2014 No. 3141.

Electronic monitoring: general provisions

3-19   As to the modification of section 3AC of the 1976 Act where a court is considering imposing requirements on a person that would involve electronic monitoring of the person in a particular area of another member state, see regulation 78(3) of S.I. 2014 No. 3141 (*ante*, § 3-9a; and *post*, § 3-75c).

As to the application of section 3AC where a magistrates' court notifies the competent authority of another member state that it has decided to recognise a decision on supervision measures taken in that member state, see regulation 88 of S.I. 2014 No. 3141.

(2A) European supervision orders

Criminal Justice and Data Protection (Protocol No. 36) Regulations 2014
(S.I. 2014 No. 3141), Pt 7, Chap. 2 (regs 76–84)

Interpretation

3-75a   **76.** In this Chapter—

"central authority", in relation to a member State other than the United Kingdom, means an authority designated by the State as a central authority for the purposes of the Framework Decision;

"the central authority for England and Wales" means the Lord Chancellor;

"certificate requesting monitoring under the Framework Decision" means the certificate required by Article 10 of the Framework Decision;

"competent authority", in relation to a member State, means an authority designated by the State as a competent authority for the purposes of the Framework Decision;

"court" means a magistrates' court, the Crown Court, the High Court or the Court of Appeal; and references to a court include a judge of such a court or a justice of the peace and a judge or justice having powers to act in connection with proceedings before such a court;

"the Framework Decision" means Council Framework Decision 2009/829/JHA of 23rd October 2009 on the application, between member States of the European Union, of the principle of mutual recognition to decisions on supervision measures as an alternative to provisional detention;

"notify" means notify in writing (and "notification" is to be read accordingly).

As to Part 7 of S.I. 2014 No. 3141 generally, see *ante*, § 3-9a.

Recognition of supervision measures: requests to other member States

Requests to other member States for monitoring supervision measures

3-75b   **77.**—(1) A court which makes a decision on supervision measures may request a competent authority of a member State other than the United Kingdom ("the executing State") to monitor the supervision measures under the Framework Decision where—

(a) the measures are suitable for monitoring in the executing State, and

(b) the executing State is one to which the request may be made.

(2) To make the request, the court must—

  (a) issue a certificate requesting monitoring under the Framework Decision in respect of the decision on supervision measures, and

  (b) give the following documents to the competent authority or to the central authority of the executing State.

(3) The documents are—

  (a) the decision on supervision measures or a certified copy of it,

  (b) the certificate, and

  (c) a copy of the certificate translated into the official language, or one of the official languages, of the executing State.

(4) But paragraph (3)(c) does not apply if—

  (a) English is an official language of the executing State, or

  (b) the executing State has declared under Article 24 of the Framework Decision that it will accept a certificate translated into English.

(5) A court makes a "decision on supervision measures" if—

  (a) it grants bail in accordance with the Bail Act 1976, as modified by regulation 78, to a person who is charged with an offence, and

  (b) requirements are imposed on the person in accordance with section 3(6) of that Act (general provisions), as so modified, as a condition of bail.

(6) "Supervision measures" means the requirements imposed on the person as a condition of bail.

(7) A supervision measure is "suitable for monitoring in the executing State" if it constitutes—

  (a) a supervision measure of a kind mentioned in Article 8(1) of the Framework Decision (types of supervision measures), or

  (b) a supervision measure of a kind which the executing State has given notice, under Article 8(2) of that Decision, that it is prepared to monitor.

(8) The executing State is "one to which the request may be made" if—

  (a) the person is lawfully and ordinarily resident in the executing State and consents to return to that State with a view to the supervision measures being monitored there under the Framework Decision, or

  (b) the person is not lawfully and ordinarily resident in the executing State but—

    (i) the person asks for the request to be made to a competent authority of the executing State, and

    (ii) the competent authority consents to the making of the request.

(9) In regulations 78 to 84—

"the competent authority of the executing State", in relation to a request under this regulation, means the competent authority to which the request is made;

"decision on supervision measures" and "supervision measures" are to be read in accordance with this regulation;

"the executing State", in relation to a request under this regulation, means the member State of the competent authority to which the request is made.

For section 3(6) of the 1976 Act, see § 3-13 in the main work.

Article 8(1) of the Council Framework Decision lists the following supervision measures: (a) an obligation to inform the competent authority in the executing state of any change of residence, in particular for the purpose of receiving a summons to attend a hearing or a trial in the course of criminal proceedings; (b) an obligation not to enter certain localities, places or defined areas in the issuing or executing state; (c) an obligation to remain at a specified place, where applicable during specified times; (d) an obligation containing limitations on leaving the territory of the executing state; (e) an obligation to report at specified times to a specific authority; and (f) an obligation to avoid contact with specific persons in relation to the offence(s) allegedly committed.

Requirements that may be imposed in connection with a request

78.—(1) This regulation applies where a court is considering making a request under regulation   **3-75c**
77 for a competent authority of a member State other than the United Kingdom to monitor supervision measures under the Framework Decision in relation to the grant of bail to a person who is charged with an offence.

(2) The requirements that may be imposed on the person under section 3(6) of the Bail Act 1976 (general provisions) include requirements which can only be complied with in the other State.

(3) Where the court is considering imposing requirements on the person which would involve electronic monitoring of the person in a particular area in the other State—

    (a)   sections 3AA(4) and 3AB(3) of the Bail Act 1976 (conditions for the imposition of electronic monitoring requirements) have effect as if for references to each local justice area which is a relevant area there were substituted references to that area in the other State, and

    (b)   section 3AC of that Act (electronic monitoring: general provisions) has effect as if subsection (2) were omitted.

For section 3(6) of the 1976 Act, see § 3-13 in the main work. For sections 3AA, 3AB and 3AC of that Act, see *ibid.*, §§ 3-16, 3-18, 3-19 respectively.

Recognition of request

3-75d
    79.—(1) A court which has made a decision on supervision measures ceases to be responsible for monitoring the supervision measures if—

    (a)   the court makes a request under regulation 77 for the competent authority of the executing State to monitor those measures under the Framework Decision, and

    (b)   the competent authority notifies the court that it has decided to recognise the decision on supervision measures under the Framework Decision.

    (2) The fact that the court has ceased to be responsible for monitoring the supervision measures does not affect the court's jurisdiction to take subsequent decisions in relation to the decision on supervision measures, including decisions about—

    (a)   renewal, review or withdrawal of the decision on supervision measures,

    (b)   modification of the supervision measures, and

    (c)   the issue of a warrant for the arrest of the person subject to the decision.

    (3) Where the person subject to the decision on supervision measures is in the executing State, the court may permit the person to attend through a live link any hearing as to whether or not to take a subsequent decision in relation to the decision.

    (4) The person is to be treated as present in court when attending a hearing through a live link by virtue of paragraph (3).

    (5) "Live link" means an arrangement by which a person (when not in the place where a hearing is being held) is able—

    (a)   to see and hear the court during the hearing, and

    (b)   to be seen and heard by the court during the hearing;

(and for this purpose any impairment of eyesight or hearing is to be disregarded).

    (6) Where a subsequent decision relating to a person is a decision to withhold bail, the court making the decision must require the person to surrender to custody in England and Wales at a time appointed by the court.

    (7) The fact that the court has ceased to be responsible for monitoring the supervision measures does not affect any power conferred on a constable by the Bail Act 1976 to arrest without warrant the person subject to the decision on supervision measures.

Power to withdraw certificate

3-75e
    80.—(1) A court which has made a request under regulation 77 for the competent authority of the executing State to monitor supervision measures under the Framework Decision must consider whether to withdraw the certificate requesting monitoring under that Decision if the competent authority informs the court that—

    (a)   the competent authority could refuse to monitor the supervision measures on the ground mentioned in Article 15(1)(h) of that Decision (grounds for non-recognition) but is nevertheless willing to monitor them,

    (b)   the competent authority has taken a decision, in accordance with Article 13 (adaptation of supervision measures) of that Decision, adapting the supervision measures, or

    (c)   there is a maximum period during which, under the law of the executing State, the supervision measures may be monitored.

    (2) But a decision to withdraw the certificate under paragraph (1)(b) or (c) may be made only if monitoring of the supervision measures in the executing State has not yet started.

    (3) If the court withdraws the certificate under this regulation, it must inform the competent authority.

    (4) A decision to withdraw the certificate under this regulation must be taken, and the competent authority must be informed under paragraph (3), no later than 10 days after the day on which the competent authority informs the court as mentioned in paragraph (1).

    (5) This regulation applies where a court informs the competent authority of the executing State under regulation 81(2)(b) that it has renewed a decision on supervision measures, or modified

supervision measures, as it applies where the court makes a request under regulation 77 in relation to the original decision on supervision measures.

Article 15(1)(h) of the Council Framework Decision (see para. (1)(a)) provides that the competent authority in the executing state may refuse to recognise a decision on supervision measures if "(h) it would, in case of breach of the supervision measures, have to refuse to surrender the person concerned in accordance with" Council Framework Decision 2002/584/JHA on the European arrest warrant.

Article 13 of the Council Framework Decision (see para. (1)(b)) provides that, if the nature of the supervision measures is incompatible with the law of the executing state, the competent authority in that state may adapt them in line with the types of supervision measures which apply, under the law of that state, to equivalent offences, and that the adapted measures should correspond as far as possible to those imposed in the issuing state.

Duties where measures being monitored by executing State

81.—(1) This regulation applies in relation to any time when a court which has made a decision on supervision measures— **3-75f**

    (a) has ceased under regulation 79 to be responsible for monitoring the supervision measures, and

    (b) has not yet become responsible under regulation 83 for monitoring them again.

  (2) The court must immediately inform the competent authority of the executing State if—

    (a) legal proceedings are brought in relation to the decision on supervision measures, or

    (b) the court takes a subsequent decision in relation to the decision on supervision measures, as mentioned in regulation 79(2) (a "supervening decision").

  (3) The court must consider whether to take a supervening decision if the competent authority of the executing State notifies the court, using the form set out in Annex II to the Framework Decision, of—

    (a) a breach of the supervision measures, or

    (b) any other finding which could result in the court taking a supervening decision.

  (4) Where the decision on supervision measures provides for the measures to have effect for a specified period, the court must, before the expiry of that period, inform the competent authority of the executing State—

    (a) as to whether the court expects the monitoring of the supervision measures to be necessary for a further period, and

    (b) if so, of the expected length of that period.

  (5) The court must inform the competent authority under paragraph (4)—

    (a) following a request from that authority, or

    (b) if no such request is made, on the initiative of the court.

  (6) If the competent authority of the executing State requests information from the court as to whether monitoring of the supervision measures is still necessary in the circumstances of the case, the court must respond without delay.

  (7) If—

    (a) the law of the executing State requires periodic confirmation of the need to prolong the monitoring of the supervision measures, and

    (b) the competent authority of the executing State requests that confirmation from the court and sets a reasonable time limit for the request to be complied with,

the court must respond within that time limit.

Request to extend maximum period for which measures may be monitored

82.—(1) This regulation applies in relation to any time when a court which has made a decision on supervision measures— **3-75g**

    (a) has ceased under regulation 79 to be responsible for monitoring the supervision measures, and

    (b) has not yet become responsible under regulation 83 for monitoring them again.

  (2) The court may make a request under this regulation if—

    (a) under the law of the executing State, there is a maximum period during which the supervision measures may be monitored,

    (b) the period is due to expire, and

    (c) the court considers that the supervision measures are still needed.

(3) A request under this regulation is a request to the competent authority of the executing State for the period to be extended.

(4) The request must specify the period for which an extension is likely to be needed.

Court becoming responsible again for monitoring measures

3-75h

83.—(1) A court which—

  (a) has made a decision on supervision measures, and

  (b) has ceased under regulation 79 to be responsible for monitoring the supervision measures,

becomes responsible for monitoring them again in any of the following cases.

(2) The first case is where the person subject to the decision on supervision measures becomes lawfully and ordinarily resident in a State other than the executing State.

(3) The second case is where the competent authority of the executing State notifies the court, in accordance with Article 20(2)(c) of the Framework Decision (information from the executing State), that it is not possible, in practice, to monitor the supervision measures.

(4) The third case is where the competent authority of the executing State informs the court that it has decided, in accordance with Article 23 of the Framework Decision (unanswered notices), to stop monitoring the supervision measures.

(5) The fourth case is where—

  (a) the court takes a decision modifying the supervision measures, and

  (b) the competent authority of the executing State informs the court that it has decided, in accordance with Article 18(4)(b) of the Framework Decision (competence to take all subsequent decisions and governing law), to refuse to monitor the modified supervision measures.

(6) The fifth case is where the court—

  (a) withdraws the certificate requesting monitoring under the Framework Decision (whether in accordance with regulation 80 or otherwise), and

  (b) informs the competent authority of the executing State of its withdrawal.

(7) The sixth case is where the court—

  (a) withdraws the decision on supervision measures, and

  (b) informs the competent authority of the executing State of its withdrawal.

(8) The seventh case is where—

  (a) under the law of the executing State, there is a maximum period during which the supervision measures may be monitored, and

  (b) that period expires.

(9) The court must consult the competent authority of the executing State with a view to avoiding as far as possible any interruption in the monitoring of the supervision measures as a result of this regulation.

Consultation and exchange of information

3-75i

84.—(1) A court which is considering making a request under regulation 77 for a competent authority of a member State other than the United Kingdom to monitor supervision measures under the Framework Decision must, unless impracticable, consult the competent authority—

  (a) while preparing the documents mentioned in paragraph (3) of that regulation, or

  (b) at the latest, before giving those documents to the competent authority or to the central authority of that State.

(2) A court which has made a request under regulation 77 for the competent authority of the executing State to monitor supervision measures under the Framework Decision must, unless impracticable, consult the competent authority—

  (a) at such times as it considers necessary, with a view to facilitating the smooth and efficient monitoring of the supervision measures;

  (b) if the competent authority notifies it, in accordance with Article 19(3) of the Framework Decision (obligations of the authorities involved), of a serious breach of those measures.

(3) In consulting under this regulation, the court must co-operate with the competent authority with a view to the exchange of any useful information, including—

  (a) information for verifying the identity and place of residence of the person concerned, and

  (b) relevant information taken from the person's criminal records in accordance with applicable legislation including Part 6 of these regulations.

(4) The court must take due account of any indications communicated by the competent authority as to the risk the person may pose to victims and the general public.

Article 19(3) of the Council Framework Decision provides that the competent authority in the executing state shall immediately notify the competent authority in the issuing state of any breach of a supervision measure, and any other finding which could result in taking any subsequent decision referred to in Article 18(1) (as listed in reg. 79(2)(a), (b) and (c) (*ante*, § 3-75d)).

(6) Place of remand

(b) *Persons under 21 years*

Persons aged 18 to 20

The Criminal Justice and Courts Act 2015, s.38(1), substitutes section 43 of the Prison Act 1952 **3-95** (see the main work). New section 43(1) provides for the detention of young persons (a person who is aged under 18 or who was aged under 18 when convicted of an offence or remanded (s.43(2))) in young offender institutions, secure training centres or secure colleges (a new form of youth detention accommodation with a focus on education). Section 38(1) of the 2015 Act was brought into force with effect from March 20, 2015 (Criminal Justice and Courts Act 2015 (Commencement No. 1, Saving and Transitional Provisions) Order 2015 (S.I. 2015 No. 778) (but the power to provide secure colleges for the detention of persons under 18 for which the new s.43 of the Prison Act 1952 provides is, for the time being limited to males aged 15, 16 or 17). In relation to any time before the coming into force of section 61 of the CJCSA 2000 (abolition of sentence of detention in a young offender institution), section 43(2), as it applies for the purposes of the power under subsection (1) to provide young offender institutions, has effect as if for "18" in each place, there were substituted "21" (s.43(10) and (11)).

Legal Aid, Sentencing and Punishment of Offenders Act 2012, ss.91–94, 96–99, 102, 107

Remands to youth detention accommodation
As from March 20, 2015 (Criminal Justice and Courts Act 2015 (Commencement No. 1, Saving **★3-105** and Transitional Provisions) Order 2015 (S.I. 2015 No. 778)), the Criminal Justice and Courts Act 2015, s.38(3), and Sched. 9, paras 28 and 29, amended section 102(2) of the 2012 Act so as to insert, after paragraph (a), "(aa) a secure college,".

(10) Rules of procedure
Criminal Procedure Rules 2014 (S.I. 2014 No. 1610), Pt 19

Replacement of 2014 rules by 2015 rules
With effect from October 5, 2015, the Criminal Procedure Rules 2015 (S.I. 2015 No. 1490) **★3-118** replace S.I. 2014 No. 1610. Part 19 of the 2014 rules is replaced by Part 14 of the 2015 rules (see *post*, Appendix P-104 *et seq.*), with several changes of substance.

B. Specific Provisions

(1) The police

(a) *The Police and Criminal Evidence Act 1984*

Police and Criminal Evidence Act 1984, s.37

Duties of custody officer before charge
As from a day to be appointed, the Criminal Justice and Courts Act 2015, s.42, amends section **3-141** 37(15) of the 1984 Act, so as to substitute, in the definition of "arrested juvenile", the words "under the age of 18" for the words "under the age of 17".

Police and Criminal Evidence Act 1984, ss.37A–37D

Consultation with the Director of Public Prosecutions
As from April 13, 2015 (Criminal Justice and Courts Act 2015 (Commencement No. 1, Saving **★3-145** and Transitional Provisions) Order 2015 (S.I. 2015 No. 778)), the Criminal Justice and Courts Act 2015, s.18(5), amended section 37B(7) of the 1984 Act, so as to insert, after "such a caution", "(whether because of section 17 of the Criminal Justice and Courts Act 2014 or for any other reason)".

Police and Criminal Evidence Act 1984, s.38

Duties of custody officer in charge

★**3-150**   In *R. (B.G.) v. Chief Constable of West Midlands Constabulary and Birmingham City Council*, 179 J.P. 93, DC, it was held: (i) that subsections 38(6) and (7) of the 1984 Act (§ 3-149 in the main work), only require the custody officer to provide a certificate setting out the relevant "circumstances" in respect of a juvenile who has been detained, rather than to give detailed reasons, and that any failure to produce a certificate would not *ipso facto* render the detention unlawful, and (ii) that section 38 is only engaged when an individual is charged with an offence, and not when he is in custody solely because he has been arrested for breach of his bail conditions (under the Bail Act 1976, s.7 (*ibid.*, § 3-48)).

Police and Criminal Evidence Act 1984, s.40

Review of police detention

3-153   With effect from January 8, 2015, the Police and Criminal Evidence Act 1984 (Remote Reviews of Detention) Regulations 2014 (S.I. 2014 No. 3279) permits the review of detention of persons arrested but not charged, required by section 40(1)(b) of the 1984 Act, to be carried out through the use of video-conferencing facilities by an officer who is not present at the police station where the person is detained.

(2) Magistrates' courts

(i) *Remands*

Magistrates' Courts Act 1980, s.128

Remand in custody or on bail

3-194   As to the modification of section 128 of the 1980 Act where a magistrates' court is responsible for monitoring supervision measures imposed by a competent authority in another member state, see S.I. 2014 No. 3141 (*ante*, § 3-9a).

III. PRESENCE OF THE ACCUSED IN COURT DURING THE TRIAL

A. GENERAL RULE

Proceedings relating to sentence and/or confiscation of assets

3-225   The ambit of the discretion to conduct confiscation proceedings in the absence of the defendant was further considered in *R. v. Ali (Salah)* [2015] 1 W.L.R. 841, CA. It was held, referring to *R. v. Gavin*; *R. v. Tasie* (see the main work), that there was no principle of law that prevented a confiscation order being made in the involuntary absence of the defendant; the question was whether it was fair to do so; and, in answering that question, the reason for his absence (here, he was in hospital on account of mental health problems) was only one factor to be taken into account. In the particular circumstances, it was held that the judge had been entitled to proceed in the defendant's absence where he had taken into account what evidence and information had been placed before him by and on behalf of the defendant (including medical evidence), where an accurate assessment of benefit had been possible without evidence from the defendant, where there were other witnesses who could have been called, and where two of the medical witnesses had said that there was an element of malingering, and all of the medical evidence suggested that resolution of the proceedings would be likely to alleviate some of the stress that was adversely affecting the defendant's mental health. As to this case, see also *post*, §§ 5-828, 5-1050b.

Criminal Practice Direction (Custody and bail) 19E [2013] 1 W.L.R. 3164

★**3-225b**   With effect from April 6, 2015, rule 37.11 of the Criminal Procedure Rules 2014 (S.I. 2014 No. 1610) was renumbered rule 37.12 and was amended by rule 7(f) and (i) of the Criminal Procedure (Amendment No. 2) Rules 2015 (S.I. 2015 No. 646). These amendments are incorporated into the Criminal Procedure Rules 2015 (S.I. 2015 No. 1490), in which Part 37 becomes Part 24 (*post*, Appendix P-205 *et seq.*).

As to the replacement of Part 38 of the 2014 rules, see *post*, § 4-265a.   ★

B. LIMITATIONS

(2) Defendant unruly, obstructive, etc.

With effect from April 6, 2015, a new direction 3L is added, in "General Matters", to the criminal practice directions (*Practice Direction (Criminal Proceedings)* [2013] 1 W.L.R. 3164), on the security of prisoners at court, incorporating guidance issued by Her Majesty's Courts and Tribunals Service and the National Offender Management Service: *Practice Direction (Criminal Proceedings: Various Amendments)* [2015] 1 W.L.R. 1643, Lord Thomas C.J. Paragraphs 3L.5 and 3L.6 make provision in relation to the use of restraints on defendants during court proceedings.   ★**3-232**

Criminal Practice Direction (General matters) 3L [2015] 1 W.L.R. 1643

Security of prisoners at court

3L.1 High-risk prisoners identified to the court as presenting a significant risk of escape, violence in court or danger to those in the court and its environs, and to the public at large, will as far as possible, have administrative and remand appearances listed for disposal by way of live link. They will have priority for the use of video equipment.   ★**3-232a**

3L.2 In all other proceedings that require the appearance in person of a high-risk prisoner, the proceedings will be listed at an appropriately secure court building and in a court with a secure (enclosed or ceiling-high) dock.

3L.3 Where a secure dock or live link is not available the court will be asked to consider an application for additional security measures, which may include: (a) the use of approved restraints (but see below at para. 3L.6); (b) the deployment of additional escort staff; (c) securing the court room for all or part of the proceedings; (d) in exceptional circumstances, moving the hearing to a prison.

3L.4 National Offender Management Service ("NOMS") will be responsible for providing the assessment of the prisoner and it is accepted that this may change at short notice. NOMS must provide notification to the listing officer of all Category A prisoners, those on the escape list and restricted status prisoners or other prisoners who have otherwise been assessed as presenting a significant risk of violence or harm. There is a presumption that all prisoners notified as high-risk will be allocated a hearing by live link and/or secure dock facilities. Where the court cannot provide a secure listing, the reasons should be provided to the establishment so that alternative arrangements can be considered.

Applications for use of approved restraints

3L.5 It is the duty of the court to decide whether a prisoner who appears before them should appear in restraints or not. Their decision must comply with the requirements of the European Convention for the Protection of Human Rights and Fundamental Freedoms, particularly Article 3, which prohibits degrading treatment: see *Raninen v. Finland*, 26 E.H.R.R. 563.   ★**3-232b**

3L.6 No prisoner should be handcuffed in court unless there are reasonable grounds for apprehending that he will be violent or will attempt to escape. If an application is made, it must be entertained by the court and a ruling must be given. The defence should be given the opportunity to respond to the application: proceeding in the absence of the defendant or his representative may give rise to an issue under Article 6.1 of the Convention: *R. v. Rollinson*, 161 JP 107. If an application is to be made *ex parte* then that application should be made *inter partes* and the defence should be given an opportunity to respond.

Additional security measures

3L.7 It may be in some cases that additional dock officers are deployed to mitigate the risk that a prisoner presents. When the nature of the risk is so serious that increased deployment will be insufficient or would in itself be so obtrusive as to prejudice a fair trial, then the court may be required to consider the following measures: (a) reconsider the case for a live link hearing, including transferring the case to a court where the live link is available; (b) transfer the case to an appropriately secure court; (c) the use of approved restraints on the prisoner for all or part of the proceedings; (d) securing the court room for all or part of the proceedings; and (e) the use of (armed) police in the court building.   ★**3-232c**

3L.8 The establishment seeking the additional security measures will submit a court management directions form setting out the evidence of the prisoner's identified risk of escape or violence and requesting the court's approval of security measures to mitigate that risk. This must be sent to the listing officer along with current, specific and credible evidence that the security measures are both necessary and proportionate to the identified risk and that the risk cannot be managed in any other way.

3L.9 If the court is asked to consider transfer of the case, then this must be in accordance with CPD Listing F, paras F.11–F.13 [*post*, Appendix F-19]. The listing officer will liaise with the establishment, prosecution and the defence to ensure the needs of the witnesses are taken into account.

3L.10 The judge who has conduct of the case must deal with any application for the use of restraints or any other security measure and will hear representations from the Crown Prosecution Service and the defence before proceeding. The application will only be granted if: (a) there are good grounds for believing that the prisoner poses a significant risk of trying to escape from the court (beyond the assumed motivation of all prisoners to escape) and/or risk of serious harm towards those persons in court or the public generally should an escape attempt be successful; and (b) where there is no other viable means of preventing escape or serious harm.

High-risk prisoners giving evidence from the witness box

★**3-232d** **3L.11** High-risk prisoners giving evidence from the witness box may pose a significant security risk. In circumstances where such prisoners are required to move from a secure dock to an insecure witness box, an application may be made for the court to consider the use of additional security measures including: (a) the use of approved restraints; (b) the deployment of additional escort staff or police in the courtroom or armed police in the building (the decision to deploy an armed escort is for the chief inspector of the relevant borough: the decision to allow the armed escort in or around the court room is for the Senior Presiding Judge [see *Criminal Practice Direction (General matters) 3M*]); (c) securing the courtroom for all or part of the proceedings; (d) giving evidence from the secure dock; and (e) use of live link if the prisoner is not the defendant.

CHAPTER 4

TRIAL

I. PRELIMINARIES

B. HEARING IN OPEN COURT

(1) European Convention on Human Rights and common law

4-3 For the judgment giving full reasons for the decision in *Re Guardian News and Media Ltd* (as to which, see the main work), see [2015] 1 Cr.App.R. 4, CA. It was held: (i) the Court of Appeal was empowered to consider the *ex parte* materials considered by the judge at first instance and to sit *ex parte* to do so (see *Bank Mellat v. H.M. Treasury (No. 2)* [2014] A.C. 700, SC), for justice to be done; (ii) open justice is both a fundamental principle of the common law and a means of ensuring public confidence in the legal system; exceptions are rare and must be justified on the facts, and any such exceptions must be necessary and proportionate; no more than the minimum departure from open justice will be countenanced; (iii) the United Kingdom's policy is to deal with terrorism, at least in part, through the criminal justice system, and the Crown should not be deterred from prosecuting cases of suspected terrorism by the risk of material, properly secret, becoming public through the trial process; whilst considerations of national security will not by themselves justify a departure from the principle of open justice, open justice must give way to the yet more fundamental principle that the court's paramount object is to do justice; accordingly, where there is a "serious possibility" that an insistence on open justice in the national security context would frustrate the administration of justice, *e.g.*, by deterring the Crown from prosecuting a case where it otherwise should do so, a departure from open justice may be justified; (iv) a hearing *in camera* involves a departure from the principle of open justice, not from natural justice; (v) journalistic presence at a criminal trial fulfils two distinct but related purposes, *viz.* public scrutiny of the proceedings and contemporaneous reporting; whilst the court's decision (see the main work) meant that there would be no contemporaneous reporting, the attendance of accredited journalists meant that the scrutiny function of the media would be preserved throughout the trial (save for the discrete *ex parte* aspects); and (vi) the cumulative effects of holding a criminal trial *in camera* and anonymising the defendants were cause for grave concern; it was difficult to conceive of a situation where both departures from open justice would be justified.

Where the Crown Court sat *in camera* on grounds related to national security to hear sensitive evidence adduced on behalf of the defendant, it was open to the court to order that there should be no communication of the evidence heard *in camera* to anybody who had been, or would have been, excluded from the *in camera* proceedings, and this could include to the staff of the European Court of Human Rights: *R. (Wang Yam) v. Central Criminal Court* [2015] 1 Cr.App.R. 10, DC. Maintaining this restriction in the face of a post-trial application by the defendant for it to be lifted so that he could use the material for the purposes of an application to the Strasbourg court alleging that the reporting restrictions at trial had violated his right to a fair trial, did not interfere with his right of access to a court under Article 6 of the ECHR (§ 16-72 in the main work); the right of access to a supra-national court is not a fundamental common law right, but a matter of treaty obligation; whilst it was true that the Human Rights Act 1998, s.2(1) (*ibid.*, § 16-14), gave effect to the right of access to a court under Article 6, this was only in the context of proceedings before domestic courts: *ibid.* As to this case, see also *post*, §§ 7-11, 16-127, 28-51, 28-56, 28-59.

As to the replacement of Parts 37 and 38 of the Criminal Procedure Rules 2014 (S.I. 2014 No. ★ 1610), see *ante*, § 2-199a, and *post*, § 4-265a, respectively.

Applications to sit in camera, in chambers, or in private

For the judgment giving full reasons for the decision in *Re Guardian News and Media Ltd* (as to **4-6** which, see the main work), see [2015] 1 Cr.App.R. 4, CA.

C. Publicity

(1) General right to publish reports

Re S. (a child) (identification: restrictions on publication) (as to which, see the main work) was **4-15** further considered in *M. (P.N.) v. Times Newspapers Ltd* [2015] 1 Cr.App.R. 1, CA (Civ. Div.), in which the claimant unsuccessfully sought an order to prevent any reporting of his having been named, during the trial of various men for child sex offences, as a person who had been arrested (but not charged) during the course of the investigation.

As to restricting the reporting of proceedings heard *in camera*, see also *R. (Wang Yam) v. Central Criminal Court, ante*, § 4-3.

With effect from April 6, 2015, *Practice Guidance: The Use of Live Text-Based Forms of Communica-* ★ *tion (Including Twitter) from Court for the Purposes of Fair and Accurate Reporting* is revoked and replaced (with no changes of substance) by a new direction 16C on the use of live, text-based communications from the court room, which is inserted into "Preliminary Proceedings" in the criminal practice directions (*Practice Direction (Criminal Proceedings)* [2013] 1 W.L.R. 3164): *Practice Direction (Criminal Proceedings: Various Amendments)* [2015] 1 W.L.R. 1643, Lord Thomas C.J.

(2) Restrictions

(b) *Child or young person as victim, witness or defendant*

Children and Young Persons Act 1933, s.39

Power to prohibit publication

For the Court of Appeal's decision upholding the decision of the Divisional Court (see the main **4-24** work) that an order under section 39 of the 1933 Act expires automatically once the person concerned attains the age of 18, see *R. (J.C.) v. Central Criminal Court (Just for Kids Law intervening)* [2015] 1 W.L.R. 2865, CA (Civ. Div.).

As from April 13, 2015 (Criminal Justice and Courts Act 2015 (Commencement No. 1, Saving ★ and Transitional Provisions) Order 2015 (S.I. 2015 No. 778)), section 39 of the 1933 Act, including the heading (see the main work), was amended by the Criminal Justice and Courts Act 2015, s.79(1) to (8), so as to disapply it in relation to criminal proceedings (superseding the uncommenced amendment of that section in para. 2 of Sched. 2 to the YCJEA 1999 (as to which, see the main work), which is now repealed by s.79(11) of the 2015 Act). There is transitional provision to the effect that the amendment disapplying section 39 in relation to criminal proceedings does not apply in relation to proceedings instituted before the day on which it takes effect, and that, for these purposes, proceedings, other than proceedings on appeal, are instituted when proceedings are instituted for the purposes of Part I of the Prosecution of Offences Act 1985, in accordance with section 15(2) of that Act (§ 1-341 in the main work), and proceedings on appeal are instituted when the notice of appeal is given or the reference under section 9 or 11 of the CAA 1995 is made (s.79(12) and (13)). There is further transitional provision in S.I. 2015 No. 778 (*ante*) (art. 4, and Sched. 2, para. 5), to the effect that the amendments made by section 79 do not apply to the inclusion of matter in a publication before April 13, 2015.

★   It was held in *Aitken v. DPP* (2015) 159(18) S.J. 37, CA ([2015] EWHC 1079 (Admin.)), that the correct interpretation of "any person who publishes" in section 39(2) of the 1933 Act (summary offence of breach of a direction under s.39(1)), is that it refers to any person, natural or legal, who takes such a part in the process of publishing the matter that contravenes the direction or prohibition that it can be properly said of them that they "publish" the matter. The court said that a newspaper's commercial publisher will inevitably be one such person, and, depending on the facts, so might be the editor in charge or the newspaper and the journalist who wrote the matter.

4-25   As to the amendment of section 39 of the 1933 Act (see the main work), see *ante*, § 4-24.

4-26   As to the amendment of section 39 of the 1933 Act (see the main work), see *ante*, § 4-24.

4-27   As to the amendment of section 39 of the 1933 Act (see the main work), see *ante*, § 4-24.

4-28   As to the amendment of section 39 of the 1933 Act (see the main work), see *ante*, § 4-24.

Youth courts

4-29   As to the amendment of section 39 of the 1933 Act (see the main work), see *ante*, § 4-24.

★   The Youth Justice and Criminal Evidence Act 1999 (Commencement No. 14) (England and Wales) Order 2015 (S.I. 2015 No. 818) brought into force, on April 13, 2015, section 48(a) of, and Schedule 2, paras 1 and 3 (except for para. 3(9)) to, the 1999 Act.

Youth Justice and Criminal Evidence Act 1999, ss.44, 45

[Power to restrict reporting of criminal proceedings involving persons under 18

★**4-31**   The Youth Justice and Criminal Evidence Act 1999 (Commencement No. 14) (England and Wales) Order 2015 (S.I. 2015 No. 818) brought into force on April 13, 2015, section 45, insofar as it applies to England and Wales.

★   As to the amendment of the Youth Justice and Criminal Evidence Act 1999 (Application to Service Courts) Order 2009 (S.I. 2009 No. 2083), see *post*, § 4-31a.

★   With effect from immediately after section 78 of the Criminal Justice and Courts Act 2015 comes into force (as to which, see *post*, § 4-31a), the Court Martial and Service Civilian Court (Youth Justice and Criminal Evidence Act 1999) Rules 2009 (S.I. 2009 No. 2100) were amended by the Court Martial and Service Civilian Court (Youth Justice and Criminal Evidence Act 1999) (Amendment) Rules 2015 (S.I. 2015 No. 726) so as to apply them to applications under sections 45 and 45A (see *post*, § 4-31a) of the 1999 Act.

★**4-31a**   As from April 13, 2015 (Criminal Justice and Courts Act 2015 (Commencement No. 1, Saving and Transitional Provisions) Order 2015 (S.I. 2015 No. 778)), the Criminal Justice and Courts Act 2015, s.78(1) and (2), inserted a new section 45A into the 1999 Act.

Youth Justice and Criminal Evidence Act 1999, s.45A

Power to restrict reporting of criminal proceedings for lifetime of witnesses and victims under 18

    45A.—(1) This section applies in relation to—

      (a)   any criminal proceedings in any court (other than a service court) in England and Wales, and

      (b)   any proceedings (whether in the United Kingdom or elsewhere) in any service court.

    (2) The court may make a direction ("a reporting direction") that no matter relating to a person mentioned in subsection (3) shall during that person's lifetime be included in any publication if it is likely to lead members of the public to identify that person as being concerned in the proceedings.

    (3) A reporting direction may be made only in respect of a person who is under the age of 18 when the proceedings commence and who is—

      (a)   a witness, other than an accused, in the proceedings;

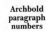

(b)   a person against whom the offence, which is the subject of the proceedings, is alleged to have been committed.

(4) For the purposes of subsection (2), matters relating to a person in respect of whom the reporting direction is made include—

(a)   the person's name,

(b)   the person's address,

(c)   the identity of any school or other educational establishment attended by the person,

(d)   the identity of any place of work of the person, and

(e)   any still or moving picture of the person.

(5) The court may make a reporting direction in respect of a person only if it is satisfied that—

(a)   the quality of any evidence given by the person, or

(b)   the level of co-operation given by the person to any party to the proceedings in connection with that party's preparation of its case,

is likely to be diminished by reason of fear or distress on the part of the person in connection with being identified by members of the public as a person concerned in the proceedings.

(6) In determining whether subsection (5) is satisfied, the court must in particular take into account—

(a)   the nature and alleged circumstances of the offence to which the proceedings relate;

(b)   the age of the person;

(c)   such of the following as appear to the court to be relevant—

(i)   the social and cultural background and ethnic origins of the person,

(ii)   the domestic, educational and employment circumstances of the person, and

(iii)   any religious beliefs or political opinions of the person;

(d)   any behaviour towards the person on the part of—

(i)   an accused,

(ii)   members of the family or associates of an accused, or

(iii)   any other person who is likely to be an accused or a witness in the proceedings.

(7) In determining that question the court must in addition consider any views expressed—

(a)   by the person in respect of whom the reporting restriction may be made, and

(b)   where that person is under the age of 16, by an appropriate person other than an accused.

(8) In determining whether to make a reporting direction in respect of a person, the court must have regard to—

(a)   the welfare of that person,

(b)   whether it would be in the interests of justice to make the direction, and

(c)   the public interest in avoiding the imposition of a substantial and unreasonable restriction on the reporting of the proceedings.

(9) A reporting direction may be revoked by the court or an appellate court.

(10) The court or an appellate court may by direction ("an excepting direction") dispense, to any extent specified in the excepting direction, with the restrictions imposed by a reporting direction.

(11) The court or an appellate court may only make an excepting direction if—

(a)   it is satisfied that it is necessary in the interests of justice to do so, or

(b)   it is satisfied that—

(i)   the effect of the reporting direction is to impose a substantial and unreasonable restriction on the reporting of the proceedings, and

(ii)   it is in the public interest to remove or relax that restriction.

(12) No excepting direction shall be given under subsection (11)(b) by reason only of the fact that the proceedings have been determined in any way or have been abandoned.

(13) In determining whether to make an excepting direction in respect of a person, the court or the appellate court must have regard to the welfare of that person.

(14) An excepting direction—

(a)   may be given at the time the reporting direction is given or subsequently, and

(b)   may be varied or revoked by the court or an appellate court.

(15) For the purposes of this section—

(a)   criminal proceedings in a court other than a service court commence when proceedings are instituted for the purposes of Part 1 of the Prosecution of Offences Act 1985, in accordance with section 15(2) of that Act;

(b)   proceedings in a service court commence when the charge is brought under section 122 of the Armed Forces Act 2006.

(16) In this section—

    (a) "appellate court", in relation to any proceedings in a court, means a court dealing with an appeal (including an appeal by way of case stated) arising out of the proceedings or with any further appeal;

    (b) "appropriate person" has the same meaning as in section 50;

    (c) references to the quality of evidence given by a person are to its quality in terms of completeness, coherence and accuracy (and for this purpose "coherence" refers to a person's ability in giving evidence to give answers which address the questions put to the person and can be understood both individually and collectively);

    (d) references to the preparation of the case of a party to any proceedings include, where the party is the prosecution, the carrying out of investigations into any offence at any time charged in the proceedings.

★   With effect from immediately after section 78 of the Criminal Justice and Courts Act 2015 came into force (as to which, see *ante*), article 13 of the Youth Justice and Criminal Evidence Act 1999 (Application to Service Courts) Order 2009 (S.I. 2009 No. 2083) was amended by the Youth Justice and Criminal Evidence Act 1999 (Application to Service Courts) (Amendment) Order 2015 (S.I. 2015 No. 727), so as to modify the application of section 45A of the 1999 Act (*ante*) to service courts.

★   As to the application of the Court Martial and Service Civilian Court (Youth Justice and Criminal Evidence Act 1999) Rules 2009 (S.I. 2009 No. 2100) to applications under section 45A of the 1999 Act (*ante*), see *ante*, § 4-31.

(c) Certain adult witnesses and victims

Youth Justice and Criminal Evidence Act 1999, s.46

Power to restrict reports about certain adult witnesses in criminal proceedings

★4-33   As to the amendment of the Youth Justice and Criminal Evidence Act 1999 (Application to Service Courts) Order 2009 (S.I. 2009 No. 2083), see *ante*, § 4-31a.

★   As to the amendment of the Court Martial and Service Civilian Court (Youth Justice and Criminal Evidence Act 1999) Rules 2009 (S.I. 2009 No. 2100), see *ante*, § 4-31.

Youth Justice and Criminal Evidence Act 1999, s.47

Restrictions on reporting directions under Chapter 1, 1A or 2

★4-34   As to the amendment of the Youth Justice and Criminal Evidence Act 1999 (Application to Service Courts) Order 2009 (S.I. 2009 No. 2083), see *ante*, § 4-31a.

Offences and defences

★4-35   The Youth Justice and Criminal Evidence Act 1999 (Commencement No. 14) (England and Wales) Order 2015 (S.I. 2015 No. 818) brought sections 49 to 51 of the 1999 Act into force on April 13, 2015 (in so far as they have effect for the purposes of ss.45 (see § 4-31 in the main work and *ante*) and 45A (inserted by s.78 of the Criminal Justice and Courts Act 2015 (see *ante*, § 4-31a)).

★   As from April 13, 2015 (Criminal Justice and Courts Act 2015 (Commencement No. 1, Saving and Transitional Provisions) Order 2015 (S.I. 2015 No. 778)), consequential amendments were made to sections 49 and 50 of the YJCEA 1999 by the Criminal Justice and Courts Act 2015, s.78(1), (3) and (4), to take account of the insertion of new section 45A into the 1999 Act (as to which, see *ante*, § 4-31a). The offence under section 49 is extended to publication of any matter in contravention of a direction under section 45A(2), new subsection (7) of section 49 gives effect to new Schedule 2A (as to which, see *post*) and a new defence is inserted into section 50 (publication with the consent of the person concerned, but no consent can be valid if given by a person under 18).

★   Section 80 of the 2015 Act (which also came into force on April 13, 2015 (as to which, see S.I. 2015 No. 778, *ante*)) introduces Schedule 15, which inserts new Schedules 1A and 2A (*ante*) into the CYPA 1933 and YJCEA 1999 respectively. These make special provision in relation to the liability of providers of information society services for offences under section 39 of the 1933 Act (§ 4-24 in the main work, and *ante*) and 49 of the 1999 Act (see the main work) respectively. The content broadly corresponds to that of the Electronic Commerce Directive (Hatred against Persons on Religious Grounds or the Grounds of Sexual Orientation) Regulations 2010 (S.I. 2010 No. 894) (as to which, see § 29-77 in the main work). There is transitional provision (S.I. 2015 No. 778, art. 4, and Sched. 2, para. 5) in relation to section 80(a) of the 2015 Act, to the effect that the amendment made by it (which relates to the insertion of Sched. 1A into the CYPA 1933) does not apply to the inclusion of matter in a publication before April 13, 2015.

Youth Justice and Criminal Evidence Act 1999, s.52

Decisions as to public interest for purposes of Chapter IV

The Youth Justice and Criminal Evidence Act 1999 (Commencement No. 14) (England and **★4-36** Wales) Order 2015 (S.I. 2015 No. 818) brought section 52 of the 1999 Act into force on April 13, 2015 (in so far as it has effect for the purposes of ss.45 (see § 4-31 in the main work and *ante*) and 45A (inserted by s.78 of the Criminal Justice and Courts Act 2015 (see *ante*, § 4-31a)).

Youth Justice and Criminal Evidence Act 1999, Sched. 7, para. 6

Reporting restrictions: transitional

The Youth Justice and Criminal Evidence Act 1999 (Commencement No. 14) (England and **★4-39** Wales) Order 2015 (S.I. 2015 No. 818) brought paragraphs 1 and 6 of Schedule 7 to the 1999 Act into force on April 13, 2015 (in so far as they have effect for the purposes of s.45 of that Act (see § 4-31 in the main work and *ante*).

(3) **Rules of court**

Criminal Procedure Rules 2014 (S.I. 2014 No. 1610), rr.16.1–16.9

Replacement of 2014 rules by 2015 rules

With effect from October 5, 2015, the Criminal Procedure Rules 2015 (S.I. 2015 No. 1490) **★4-47** replace S.I. 2014 No. 1610. Part 16 of the 2014 rules is replaced by Part 6 of the 2015 rules (see *post*, Appendix P-57 *et seq.*), with minor changes of substance in rules 6.1 and 6.4.

I. ADJOURNMENT OF TRIAL

CPS v. Picton and *Visvaratnam v. Brent Magistrates' Court* (as to both of which, see the main work) **4-71** were distinguished in *DPP v. Radziwilowicz and Wanas*, 178 J.P. 432, DC, where the Divisional Court disapproved of a district judge's decision to refuse a prosecution application for an adjournment on an occasion when the matter had not been listed for trial, but the prosecution had failed to comply with case management directions given at an earlier hearing. It had been inappropriate to discipline the prosecution in this way where the price was that the complainants would be deprived of the opportunity of seeing the case against the defendants pursued in court. The distinction between the instant case and *Picton* and *Visvaratnam* was that in those cases, the matter had been set down for trial on the occasion in question.

For a further case considering an application for an adjournment of a summary trial, see *DPP v. Petrie, post*, § 4-78.

K. LIMITED DISCRETIONARY POWER TO PREVENT PROSECUTION PROCEEDING

(2) **Abuse of process**

(b) *Where it will be impossible to give the defendant a fair trial*

Evidential matters

In *Clay v. South Cambridgeshire JJ.* [2015] R.T.R. 1, DC, the defendant was prosecuted for driv- **4-78** ing without due care and attention (RTA 1988, s.3 (§ 32-58 in the main work)), as a result of a collision between a heavy goods vehicle (which he had been driving) and a car. His solicitor sought access to the car for examination by an accident investigator, and to the tachograph data. The investigating officer had failed to retain this evidence, notwithstanding that there was evidence from witnesses interviewed by him that should have informed him of the need to preserve it (at least until the defendant had had the opportunity to consider whether he needed facilities for inspection). It was held (following the approach in *R. (Ebrahim) v. Feltham Magistrates' Court*; *Mouat v. DPP* (as to which, see the main work) that the trial process could nevertheless accommodate fairly the disadvantage to the defendant; the question whether the defendant could have a fair trial did not logically depend upon whether anyone was at fault in causing the exigency giving rise to the alleged unfairness; and there was a need to apply common sense and proportionality to the question whether it was necessary to retain exhibits.

Where the defendant was charged with driving with excess alcohol (RTA 1988, s.5 (§ 32-89 in the main work)) and where it was accepted that CCTV footage from the police station was required for the trial (the prosecution were not relying on it, but had agreed to produce it at the request of the defence, it being contended that the correct procedures had not been followed and that, in particular, the warning required by s.7(7) (*ibid.*, § 32-126) had not been given), (i) the justices had been entitled, as a robust case management decision, to refuse a prosecution application for an adjournment when, on the day of trial, the CCTV footage supplied by the prosecution had not been suitably formatted and could not be played; although there are instances where the interests of justice require the grant of an adjournment, this should be a course of last rather than first resort; it is essential that parties to proceedings in magistrates' courts should proceed on the basis of a need to get matters right first time; any suggestion of a culture that readily permits an opportunity to correct failures of preparation should be firmly dispelled; (ii) the justices were wrong, however, then to grant a defence application for a stay on grounds of abuse where the prosecution were able to proceed; while the prosecution had been at fault, there was nothing about their failure that began to impinge on the integrity of the criminal justice system such that it would make it unfair to proceed; nor was it the case that the defendant could not have a fair trial; first, nobody having seen the CCTV, it was pure speculation as to whether it would help the defence; secondly, the defendant could properly have made play of the fact that it was missing through no fault of his, and, in this way, the trial process could safely and fairly have dealt with the "hole" in the case arising from the prosecution failure (*R. (Ebrahim) v. Feltham Magistrates Court*; *Mouat v. DPP*, *ante*); thirdly, assuming that, at the conclusion of the evidence, the justices were driven to the view that the interests of justice did require viewing the CCTV footage, they could then have revisited the question of an adjournment; they would still have had to grapple with the difficulty that any assistance to be obtained from it remained speculative; such a course would have been exceptional, but it would have been preferable to a stay: *DPP v. Petrie* [2015] Crim.L.R. 385, DC ([2015] EWHC 48 (Admin.)).

(c) *Where a stay is necessary to protect the integrity of the criminal justice system*

Situations akin to autrefois

4-88   Where the appellant was found in possession of a firearm falling within section 5(1)(aba) of the Firearms Act 1968 (§ 24-24 in the main work) and which was therefore a "prohibited weapon" to which the minimum sentence provisions in section 51A of that Act (*ibid.*, § 5-449) applied on conviction, where he was, at the time, within five years of his release from a detention and training order (thus putting him in breach also of s.21 of the 1968 Act (*ibid.*, § 24-80)), where the CPS advised that he should be charged with offences under section 1(1)(a) and (b) of the 1968 Act (*ibid.*, § 24-4) in respect of his unlicensed possession of the firearm and ammunition (a round of ammunition had been found in the firearm), where he was so charged, and where he pleaded guilty in a magistrates' court (no representations having apparently been made on behalf of the prosecution to the effect that summary trial was unsuitable), and was sentenced to four months' detention in a young offender institution on each charge concurrently, it was not an abuse of process for the CPS 15 days later to institute proceedings against him for offences under sections 5 and 21 of the 1968 Act; whilst the second set of proceedings arose out of the same facts as gave rise to the first, and whilst they involved prosecuting the appellant for more serious charges, there were "special circumstances" (see *Connelly v. DPP* and *R. v. Beedie* (as to which, see the main work, and §§ 4-183, 4-184 in the main work)) that required the prosecution to be continued; no one with responsibility for prosecuting the case had correctly applied their mind to the appropriate charges and how they should be prosecuted; this was not an escalation from minor charges to more serious charges, contrary to the general rule described in *R. v. Elrington* (as to which, see the main work), but a move from misconceived charges to correct charges; whilst serious mistakes were made, there was no bad faith and the mistakes were rectified within a short time; permitting the prosecution to continue did not offend the court's sense of justice and propriety, whereas a stay, far from undermining confidence in the criminal justice system, would have brought it into disrepute: *R. v. Antoine (Jordan)* [2015] 1 Cr.App.R. 8, CA.

Prosecution/investigators contributing to commission of offence

R. v. Palmer is now reported at [2015] Crim.L.R. 153, *sub nom. R. v. Palmer, Gyamfi and Cooke*. **4-97**

N. Pre-Trial Hearings

(1) The court's case management powers and duties

Whilst the Criminal Procedure Rules do not refer explicitly to a power to require the attend- **4-112** ance of appropriate legal representation, it was clear that that was implied by a court's broader case management powers to make directions or orders that would progress the case; and wilful and deliberate disobedience by defence counsel of an order of the Crown Court to attend at a particular time as an act of defiance and in wilful disregard of the authority of the court, would constitute contempt worthy of serious sanction: *Re West (Ian Stuart) (a barrister)* [2014] 2 Cr.App.R. 28, CA. As to this case, see also *post*, §§ 28-52, 28-85, 28-92, 28-98.

It was held in *R. v. Boardman* [2015] 1 Cr.App.R. 33, CA (considering, *inter alia, R. v. Jisl and* ★ *Tekin* (as to which, see the main work)), that a judge had been entitled to exclude evidence (pursuant to the PACE Act 1984, s.78 (§ 15-401 in the main work), and the court's case management powers) that the prosecution intended to rely on, served seven months after the case papers and two days before trial, where their exclusion (and a refusal to adjourn) would have the effect of ending the prosecution. The court did, however, sound some notes of warning: first, if defence solicitors do not alert the court to problems such as the one here when something can be done about it, it would be open to a judge to decide that the consequences of such a failure of duty on the part of the defence should be to reject a complaint of prejudice consequent upon the need for an adjournment; secondly, the Court of Appeal will not support (and, to the contrary, will be extremely critical of) defence attempts to administer interrogatories going beyond a request for disclosure of unused material but, rather, on the face of it, seeking to impose a burden on the police to undertake investigations on their behalf; thirdly, it should not be thought that this decision can be used to create a trap for the prosecution by the over-zealous pursuit of inconsequential material which does not go to the issue, all in the hope that they will fall down and that an application can be made which will have the effect of bringing the prosecution to an end; such conduct is itself an abuse of the process of the court and judges will be assiduous to identify it and impose sanctions on those who seek to manipulate the system.

R. v. L. and *Re W. (Children) (Concurrent criminal and care proceedings)* (as to both of which, see **4-113** the main work) were considered in *A local authority v. D.G.*, *post*, § 12-122.

Criminal Procedure Rules 2014 (S.I. 2014 No. 1610), Pt 1

Replacement of 2014 rules by 2015 rules

With effect from October 5, 2015, the Criminal Procedure Rules 2015 (S.I. 2015 No. 1490) ★**4-114** replace S.I. 2014 No. 1610. Part 1 of the 2014 rules is reproduced (see *post*, Appendix P-3 *et seq.*), with one minor drafting change.

Criminal Procedure Rules 2014 (S.I. 2014 No. 1610), rr.3.1–3.12

Replacement of 2014 rules by 2015 rules

With effect from October 5, 2015, the Criminal Procedure Rules 2015 (S.I. 2015 No. 1490) ★**4-115** replace S.I. 2014 No. 1610. Part 3 of the 2014 rules is reproduced (see *post*, Appendix P-9 *et seq.*), with several changes of substance. Part 3 of the 2015 rules also incorporates the amendments made to the 2014 rules by S.I. 2015 No. 13 (as to which, see *post*, §§ 4-117, 4-120a).

Case preparation and progression

With effect from April 6, 2015, rule 4(a) of the Criminal Procedure (Amendment) Rules 2015 **4-117** (S.I. 2015 No. 13) amends rule 3.9 of the 2014 rules, so as to insert a new paragraph (7) at the end, as follows—

"(7) Where directions for appropriate treatment and questioning are required, the court must—

(a) invite representations by the parties and by any intermediary; and

(b) set ground rules for the conduct of the questioning, which rules may include—

    (i) a direction relieving a party of any duty to put that party's case to a witness or a defendant in its entirety,

    (ii) directions about the manner of questioning,

    (iii) directions about the duration of questioning,

    (iv) if necessary, directions about the questions that may or may not be asked,

    (v) where there is more than one defendant, the allocation among them of the topics about which a witness may be asked, and

    (vi) directions about the use of models, plans, body maps or similar aids to help communicate a question or an answer.".

★   As to the replacement of S.I. 2014 No. 1610 by the Criminal Procedure Rules 2015 (S.I. 2015 No. 1490), see *ante*, § 4-115.

(2) Preliminary hearings and plea and case management hearings

Criminal Procedure Rules 2014 (S.I. 2014 No. 1610), rr.3.13–3.25

Pre-trial hearings: general rules

4-120a   With effect from April 6, 2015, rule 3.13(1)(c) of the 2014 rules is amended by rule 4(b) of the Criminal Procedure (Amendment) Rules 2015 (S.I. 2015 No. 13), so as to omit the word "or" at the end of sub-paragraph (i), to insert the word "or" at the end of sub-paragraph (ii) and to add a sub-paragraph (iii), as follows—

    "(iii)   such a hearing is required to set ground rules for the conduct of the questioning of a witness or defendant.".

★   As to the replacement of S.I. 2014 No. 1610 by the Criminal Procedure Rules 2015 (S.I. 2015 No. 1490), see *ante*, § 4-115.

II. ARRAIGNMENT AND PLEA

B. PLEA

(9) Autrefois acquit and autrefois convict

(b) *A man may not be tried for a crime in respect of which he has previously been acquitted or convicted*

Tainted acquittals

Criminal Procedure Rules 2014 (S.I. 2014 No. 1610), Pt 40

Replacement of 2014 rules by 2015 rules

★**4-200**   With effect from October 5, 2015, the Criminal Procedure Rules 2015 (S.I. 2015 No. 1490) replace S.I. 2014 No. 1610. Part 40 of the 2014 rules is replaced by rules 27.1(1) and 27.2 of the 2015 rules (see *post*, Appendix P-246, P-247), with several changes of substance.

(13) Defendant unfit to plead or take his trial

(a) *Procedure, evidence and burden of proof*

Criminal Procedure Rules 2014 (S.I. 2014 No. 1610), r.38.10

Defendant unfit to plead

★**4-232a**   As to the replacement of S.I. 2014 No. 1610 by the Criminal Procedure Rules 2015 (S.I. 2015 No. 1490), see *post*, § 4-265a.

"did the act or made the omission charged"

★**4-237**   What constitutes "objective evidence", as referred to in *R. v. Antoine* (as to which, see the main work), was considered in *R. v. Wells*; *R. v. Masud*; *R. v. Hone*; *R. v. Kail* [2015] 1 Cr.App.R. 27, CA.

It was held that it would include evidence as to the background to the incident giving rise to the charge, the antecedents of the parties, independent eye-witness evidence, and CCTV, cell site or expert evidence, but would not include the assertions (which need not themselves be obviously delusional) of a defendant who, at the time of speaking, is proved to have been suffering from a mental disorder of a type that undermines his reliability and which itself has precipitated the finding of unfitness to plead. However, the court went on to say that the same approach should not be taken to an interview of a defendant, who, at the time of the interview, was not suffering from psychiatric illness. Where the defendant's disability impacts on his ability to take part in a trial, but he is not otherwise affected by a psychiatric condition such as renders what was said in interview unreliable (whether or not the delusional traits are apparent on the face of the interview), there was no reason why the jury should not hear what was said, albeit with an appropriate warning. It was further held that, in proceedings under section 4A of the Criminal Procedure (Insanity) Act 1964 (§ 4-232 in the main work), (i) where the act alleged against a defendant was that he aided and abetted the commission of an offence by another, there was no need to prove any knowledge on the part of the defendant as to the activities of the alleged principal, and (ii) on a charge of sexual assault (SOA 2003, s.3 (*ibid.*, § 20-29)), an absence of reasonable belief that the complainant was consenting was not a matter about which the jury have to be satisfied (considering, *inter alia*, *R. (Young) v. Central Criminal Court* and *R. v. B. (M.)* (as to both of which, see the main work)).

C. CHANGE OF PLEA

Criminal Procedure Rules 2014 (S.I. 2014 No. 1610), r.38.5

Application to vacate a guilty plea

As to the replacement of S.I. 2014 No. 1610 by the Criminal Procedure Rules 2015 (S.I. 2015 No. 1490), see *post*, § 4-265a. ★4-254

VI. CRIMINAL PROCEDURE RULES: TRIAL AND SENTENCE

Criminal Procedure Rules 2014 (S.I. 2014 No. 1610), Pt 38

Replacement of 2014 rules by 2015 rules

With effect from October 5, 2015, the Criminal Procedure Rules 2015 (S.I. 2015 No. 1490) replace S.I. 2014 No. 1610. Part 38 of the 2014 rules is replaced by Part 25 of the 2015 rules (see *post*, Appendix P-223 *et seq.*), with several changes of substance. ★4-265a

VII. THE JURY

B. QUALIFICATION

Juries Act 1974, s.1

As from a day to be appointed, the Criminal Justice and Courts Act 2015, s.68(1) and (2), amend section 1(1)(a) of the 1974 Act, so as to substitute the words "and aged eighteen or over but under seventy six" for the words from "and" to the end. 4-267

Juries Act 1974, Sched. 1

As from April 13, 2015 (Criminal Justice and Courts Act 2015 (Commencement No. 1, Saving and Transitional Provisions) Order 2015 (S.I. 2015 No. 778)), the Criminal Justice and Courts Act 2015, s.77(1), inserted, after paragraph 6 of Schedule 1 to the 1974 Act, a new paragraph 6A, as follows— 4-269

"6A. A person who at any time in the last ten years has been convicted of—
(a) an offence under section 20A, 20B, 20C or 20D of this Act,
(b) an offence under paragraph 5A, 5B, 5C or 5D of Schedule 6 to the Coroners and Justice Act 2009 (equivalent offences relating to jurors at inquests), or
(c) an offence under paragraph 2, 3, 4 or 5 of Schedule 2A to the Armed Forces Act 2006 (equivalent offences relating to members of the Court Martial).".

Electoral register as basis of jury selection

4-270   The amendment to section 3 of the Juries Act 1974 by the Electoral Administration Act 2006 (as to which, see the main work) is in force: see the Electoral Administration Act 2006 (Commencement No. 2, Transitional and Savings Provisions) Order 2006 (S.I. 2006 No. 3412).

As from a day to be appointed, the Criminal Justice and Courts Act 2015, s.68(1) and (3), amend section 3(1) of the 1974 Act to reflect the change in the upper age limit for jury service from 70 to 75 (as to which, see *ante*, § 4-267).

C. Summoning and Panels

Offences and penalties

4-278   For new offences in relation to jurors, see *post*, §§ 28-41 *et seq.*

D. Attendance, Service, Excusals, Deferral

Criminal Procedure Rules 2014 (S.I. 2014 No. 1610), r.39.1

Appeal against officer's refusal to excuse or postpone jury service

4-289   With effect from February 2, 2015, rule 39.1(1) of S.I. 2014 No. 1610 (the bold centred heading in the main work erroneously refers to the 2013 rules, but the text set out there is the text of the 2014 rules) is amended by rule 8 of the Criminal Procedure (Amendment) Rules 2015 (S.I. 2015 No. 13) to substitute a reference to "the County Court" in lieu of the reference to "a county court".

★   With effect from October 5, 2015, the Criminal Procedure Rules 2015 (S.I. 2015 No. 1490) replace S.I. 2014 No. 1610, incorporating the amendment made by S.I. 2015 No. 13 (*ante*). Part 39 of the 2014 rules is replaced by Part 26 of the 2015 rules (see *post*, Appendix P-241 *et seq.*), with several changes of substance.

Criminal Procedure Rules 2014 (S.I. 2014 No. 1610), r.39.2

Replacement of 2014 rules by 2015 rules

★**4-291**   As to the replacement of S.I. 2014 No. 1610 by the Criminal Procedure Rules 2015 (S.I. 2015 No. 1490), see *ante*, § 4-289.

Criminal Procedure Rules 2014 (S.I. 2014 No. 1610), rr.39.3, 39.4

Replacement of 2014 rules by 2015 rules

★**4-291c**   As to the replacement of S.I. 2014 No. 1610 by the Criminal Procedure Rules 2015 (S.I. 2015 No. 1490), see *ante*, § 4-289.

F. The Judge's Discretion to Stand Jurors Down

4-293   As to police officers as jurors (as to which, see the discussion in the main work), see also § 7-89 in the main work and *post*.

L. Miscellaneous

(2) Direction to jury as to how to approach their role
Criminal Practice Direction (Trial) 39G [2013] 1 W.L.R. 3164

4-325a   For new offences in relation to jurors and their conduct at trial, see *post*, §§ 28-41 *et seq.*

(2A) Surrender of electronic communications devices

★**4-325b**   As from April 13, 2015 (Criminal Justice and Courts Act 2015 (Commencement No. 1, Saving and Transitional Provisions) Order 2015 (S.I. 2015 No. 778)), the Criminal Justice and Courts Act 2015, s.69, inserted a new section 15A into the 1974 Act.

Juries Act 1974, s.15A

Surrender of electronic communications devices

    15A.—(1) A judge dealing with an issue may order the members of a jury trying the issue to surrender any electronic communications devices for a period.

(2) An order may be made only if the judge considers that—

    (a) the order is necessary or expedient in the interests of justice, and

    (b) the terms of the order are a proportionate means of safeguarding those interests.

(3) An order may only specify a period during which the members of the jury are—

    (a) in the building in which the trial is being heard,

    (b) in other accommodation provided at the judge's request,

    (c) visiting a place in accordance with arrangements made by the court, or

    (d) travelling to or from a place mentioned in paragraph (b) or (c).

(4) An order may be made subject to exceptions.

(5) It is a contempt of court for a member of a jury to fail to surrender an electronic communications device in accordance with an order under this section.

(6) Proceedings for a contempt of court under this section may only be instituted on the motion of a court having jurisdiction to deal with it.

(7) In this section, "electronic communications device" means a device that is designed or adapted for a use which consists of or includes the sending or receiving of signals that are transmitted by means of an electronic communications network (as defined in section 32 of the Communications Act 2003).

In connection with section 15A (*ante*), see also section 54A of the Courts Act 2003, which was ★ inserted, as from April 13, 2015 (S.I. 2015 No. 778, *ante*), by section 70(1) and (2) of the 2015 Act, as to the power of court security officers, if ordered to do so by a judge, to search a juror to determine whether or not he has failed to surrender such a device. It also confers a power of seizure if a device is found and the juror refuses to surrender it when asked to do so.

XIV. THE DEFENCE CASE

B. Warning as to Giving of Evidence by Defendant

Criminal Justice and Public Order Act 1994, s.35

A judge had been entitled to give the jury a direction under section 35 of the 1994 Act (§ 4-377   **4-379** in the main work) that they might infer that the defendant's reason for not giving evidence was that he could not give a proper account, or at least not one that would withstand cross-examination, where his reason for not giving evidence was said to be that it would have implicated his co-accused and that he was fearful of the consequences thereof, but where he had already implicated his co-accused in his interviews: *R. v. Rafik* [2015] Crim.L.R. 235, CA (observing that such directions are given day in, day out in cases involving "cut-throat" defences).

L. Expert Evidence as to Defendant's Mental State, I.Q., Etc.

Application

Evidence from a psychologist to the effect that a defendant has a low I.Q. (but greater than 69)   **4-395** and a suggestibility level greater than that of the general population is admissible only in cases involving a defence of duress or confession evidence: *R. v. Jackson-Mason* [2015] 1 Cr.App.R. 6, CA (considering *R. v. Antar*, *The Times*, November 4, 2004, CA). Here, therefore, where the appellant had been one of several vulnerable people used by a gang operating a sophisticated fraud to cash counterfeit benefit cheques, expert evidence as to her suggestibility level was inadmissible. The question was not how easily she allowed herself to be drawn into the plan (which might be relevant to sentence), but what her state of mind at the time was, which had to be decided in the light of all the evidence.

XVI. ARGUMENT AS TO THE RELEVANT LAW

Draft directions provided by judge to jury

It was held in *R. v. Bennett (Anthony)* [2015] 1 Cr.App.R. 16, CA, that the safety of convictions   **★4-418** had not been affected where a judge put a chronology (drafted by himself and not agreed to by the parties), *inter alia*, listing significant events, before the jury to accompany his summing-up.

The court said that whilst the judge would have done better to sum up by reference to the various schedules and other documents that were already before the jury and with which they had become familiar during the trial, his clear warning that they should disregard anything in the chronology that they did not regard as helpful and take into account anything that was relevant but not in the chronology, substantially cured any problems that might otherwise have arisen.

XVII. CLOSING SPEECHES

A. PROSECUTION

(1) Entitlement and timing

Criminal Justice Act 1948, s.42(1)

★**4-424**   It was held in *R. v. Cojan* [2015] Crim.L.R. 376, CA, that the fairness of a trial had not been affected where the prosecution had been allowed to make a closing speech after the accused deliberately dispensed with the services of his legal representatives (and declined an offer of substitute lawyers) part-way through a trial (considering *R. v. Paul* and *R. v. Stovell* (as to both of which, see the main work)).

XVIII. SUMMING UP

K. DEFENDANT'S CHARACTER

(1) Good character

★**4-485**   It was held in *R. v. Ahmed (Aneela)* [2015] 1 Cr.App.R. 21, CA, that where there was conflicting evidence as to the character of the defendant, the discretion whether to give a good character direction, and, if so, in what terms, was that of the trial judge, however, the weight to be given to good character, as directed by the judge, was for the jury. Thus, it was a misdirection to invite the jury to reach their own conclusion as to whether the defendant was of good character (considering *R. v. Aziz* (as to which, see the main work), and *R. v. M. (C.P.) (Practice Note)* (as to which, see *ibid.*, § 4-487)). As to whether there will be any need to refer to this case, in future, however, see *R. v. Hunter (Nigel)*; *R. v. Saruwu (Joseph)*; *R. v. Johnstone (Ian)*; *R. v. Walker (Alan)*; *R. v. Lonsdale (Paul)*, *post*.

★   Comprehensive guidance on good character directions was given in *R. v. Hunter (Nigel)*; *R. v. Saruwu (Joseph)*; *R. v. Johnstone (Ian)*; *R. v. Walker (Alan)*; *R. v. Lonsdale (Paul)* (2015) 159(17) S.J. 37, CA ([2015] EWCA Crim. 631). The court said that the binding principles remained those to be derived from *R. v. Vye*; *R. v. Wise*; *R. v. Stephenson*, and *R. v. Aziz* (and added in a "postscript" (at [103]) that in future there should be no need to rely on anything other than those two judgments and this one). Those principles were, first, that the general rule is that a direction as to the relevance of good character to a defendant's credibility is to be given where a defendant has a good character and has testified or made pre-trial statements; secondly, the general rule is that a direction as to the relevance of good character to the likelihood of a defendant's having committed the offence charged is to be given where a defendant has a good character, whether or not he has testified or made pre-trial answers or statements; thirdly, where defendant A, of good character, is tried jointly with B, who does not have a good character, the first two rules still apply; fourthly, there are exceptions to the general rules, *e.g.*, where a defendant has no previous convictions but has admitted other reprehensible conduct and the judge considers it would be an insult to common sense to give a good character direction; the judge then has a residual discretion to decline to do so; fifthly, a jury must not be misled; and, sixthly, a judge is not obliged to give absurd or meaningless directions (and those cases did not decide that a defendant with no previous convictions is always entitled to a full good character direction, whatever his character or that a defendant with previous convictions is entitled to good character directions/ is entitled to the propensity limb of the good character direction where he has no convictions for offences similar or relevant to those charged/ is entitled to a good character direction where the prosecution do not seek to rely upon his convictions as evidence of guilt or that failure to give an appropriate direction will almost invariably lead to the quashing of a conviction). The court went on to give the following further guidance:

(a) a defendant who is of "absolute good character", having no previous convictions or cautions recorded against him and no other reprehensible conduct alleged, admitted or proven, is entitled to both limbs (credibility and propensity) of the good character direction (and does not have to adduce evidence of positive good character);

(b) where a defendant has previous convictions or cautions recorded that are old, minor and have no relevance to the charge, the judge must make a judgment as to whether or not to treat the defendant as a person of "effective good character"; in fairness to all, a trial judge should be vigilant to ensure that only those defendants who merit an "effective good character" direction are afforded one, and must assess all the circumstances of the offence(s) and the offender, to the extent known, and then decide what fairness to all dictates; the judge should not leave it to the jury to decide whether the defendant is to be treated as of good character; where a judge decides to treat a defendant as of effective good character, he does not have a discretion whether to give the direction and must give both limbs, modified as necessary to reflect the other matters, and thereby ensure the jury are not misled;

(c) where the defence adduce evidence that the defendant has previous convictions that are not old or minor, but are different to the offences charged, the judge has a broad discretion whether to give any part of the good character direction;

(d) where the defendant has no convictions or cautions, but the prosecution rely on other bad character evidence, pursuant to the CJA 2003, s.101 (§ 13-25 in the main work), it is for the good sense of the judge to decide whether to weave a modified good character direction into his bad character directions; again, the judge has a broad discretion and should not do so where the result would offend the absurdity principle;

(e) where the defendant has no convictions or cautions but gives evidence of reprehensible conduct on his part, but the prosecution do not rely on this, the judge has a residual discretion, but the starting point should be that a good character direction should be given unless it would defy common sense to do so; again, the discretion is broad (disapproving *R. v. Gray* and *R. v. D.(P.)* and casting doubt on *R. v. G.* (as to which, see the main work)).

The court added that there could be no fixed rule or principle that a misdirection or non-direction in relation to good character was necessarily or usually fatal to a conviction. Further, as a matter of good practice, the court said that defendants should put the court on notice as early as possible that character and character directions were issues that may need to be resolved. The judge could then decide whether a good character direction would be given and if so the precise terms. This discussion should take place before the evidence is adduced. The defence will thus be better informed before the decision is made whether to adduce the evidence, the Crown could conduct any necessary checks and the judge would have the fullest possible information upon which to rule. The judge should then ensure that the directions given accorded precisely with the ruling. As to this case, see also *post*, § 7-64.

For a case casting doubt on *R. v. G.* (as to which, see the main work), see *R. v. Hunter (Nigel)*; *R. v. Saruwu (Joseph)*; *R. v. Johnstone (Ian)*; *R. v. Walker (Alan)*; *R. v. Lonsdale (Paul)*, *ante*, § 4-485. ★**4-486**

The propositions in the main work as to how a jury should be directed, and as to the consequences of a failure so to direct them, are all now to be read in light of the guidance provided in *R. v. Hunter (Nigel)*; *R. v. Saruwu (Joseph)*; *R. v. Johnstone (Ian)*; *R. v. Walker (Alan)*; *R. v. Lonsdale (Paul)*, *ante*, § 4-485. ★**4-487**

N. DIRECTION CONCERNING NECESSARY "GIVE AND TAKE"

For an example of a case where it was held that a *Watson* direction (*R. v. Watson* [1988] Q.B. 690, 87 Cr.App.R. 1, CA (see the main work)) should not have been given (a jury note did not suggest irretrievable deadlock, and there had not been a prolonged retirement following a majority direction), see *R. v. Malcolm*, unreported, November 18, 2014, CA ([2014] EWCA Crim. 2508) (considering *R. v. Arthur* (as to which, see *ibid.*)). ★**4-492**

XX. VERDICT

H. Verdict for Lesser Offence than that Charged in the Indictment

(2) General statutory provision

Criminal Law Act 1967, s.6(3)–(4)

4-526   For a case considering *R. v. Lahaye* (see the main work), see *R. v. Vaughan*, *post*, § 19-255.

(5) When to leave alternative verdict to jury

4-533   For a case considering *R. v. Foster*; *R. v. Newman*; *R. v. Kempster*; *R. v. Birmingham* and *R. v. Hodson* (as to both of which, see the main work), see *R. v. Vaughan*, *post*, § 19-255.

CHAPTER 5

SENTENCES AND ORDERS ON CONVICTION

I. GENERAL INTERPRETATION

(1) Introduction

(c) *Transitional and saving provisions (2012 Act)*

5-2a   The transitional provisions in the Legal Aid, Sentencing and Punishment of Offenders Act 2012 (Commencement No. 4 and Saving Provisions) Order 2012 (S.I. 2012 No. 2906) were considered in *R. v. Docherty*, *post*, § 5-488.

(2) Legislation

Powers of Criminal Courts (Sentencing) Act 2000, ss.161, 163, 164

Further interpretative provisions

5-6   As from a day to be appointed, the Criminal Justice and Courts Act 2015, s.28(8), and Sched. 5, paras 3 and 8, amend section 164(3) of the 2000 Act so as (i) in paragraph (aa), after "section", to insert "1(2B) or", and (ii) in paragraph (ba), after "section", to insert "139(6B), 139(5B) or".

Criminal Justice Act 2003, ss.176, 305

Interpretation of Part 12

5-8   With effect from February 1, 2015 (Offender Rehabilitation Act 2014 (Commencement No. 2) Order 2015 (S.I. 2015 No. 40)), sections 15, 17, 18 (except to the extent that s.18(5) inserts new para. 16(3) of Sched. 8 to the CJA 2003 (§ 5-350 in the main work) and s.18(8) inserts new para. 14(3) of Sched. 12 (*ibid.*, § 5-576) to that Act) and 21 of, and Schedules 5 to 7 to, the 2014 Act (see the main work) were brought into force.

As from a day to be appointed, the Criminal Justice and Courts Act 2015, s.28(8), and Sched. 5, paras 9 and 16, amend section 305(4) of the 2003 Act so as (i) in paragraph (za), to substitute "section 1(2B) or 1A(5)" for "subsection 5 of section 1A", and "that provision" for "that subsection", and (ii) in paragraph (aa), to substitute "section 139(6B), 139A(5B) or 139AA(7)", for "subsection (7) of section 139AA", and "that provision" for "that subsection".

II. PRELIMINARIES

(1) Procedure following plea of guilty or conviction by court or jury

Criminal Procedure Rules 2014 (S.I. 2014 No. 1610), r.38.16

Replacement of 2014 rules by 2015 rules

★5-11a   As to the replacement of S.I. 2014 No. 1610 by the Criminal Procedure Rules 2015 (S.I. 2015 No. 1490), see *ante*, § 4-265a.

(7) Committal for sentence

Powers of Criminal Courts (Sentencing) Act 2000, ss.3–7

Committal for sentence on indication of guilty plea by child or young person

　As from April 13, 2015 (Criminal Justice and Courts Act 2015 (Commencement No. 1, Saving 　★**5-27**
and Transitional Provisions) Order 2015 (S.I. 2015 No. 778)), the Criminal Justice and Courts Act
2015, s.53(1), amended section 3B of the 2000 Act so as to substitute a new subsection (1), as follows—

　　"(1) This section applies where on the summary trial of an offence mentioned in section 91(1) of
　this Act a person aged under 18 is convicted of the offence.".

　The amendment applies only if the person convicted of the offence first appeared in respect of
the offence (*viz.* when the person first appeared or was brought before a magistrates' court in the
proceedings in which the person was charged with the offence (s.53(4))) after the day on which
the amendment comes into force (s.53(3)).

　As to the effect of this amendment, see *R. (DPP) v. South Tyneside Youth Court*, *ante*, § 1–116.　　★

　With effect from April 13, 2015 (S.I. 2015 No. 778 (*ante*)), section 53(2) of the 2015 Act　　★
substitutes a new heading for section 3B of the 2000 Act, as follows, "Committal for sentence of
young offenders on summary trial of certain serious offences".

Power of Crown Court on committal for sentence under section 6

　As to the commencement of section 85(1), (2) and (4) of the LASPOA 2012 (as to which, see the 　★**5-34**
main work), see *ante*, § 1-125. It should be noted, however, that it may be a moot point whether
section 85(1) would have the effect of lifting the cap in section 7(4)(a) of the 2000 Act. Section 24
of the MCA 1980 (§ 1-110 in the main work) provides that, where a child or young person, is
tried summarily for an indictable offence, the maximum fine is £1,000. Section 85 only bites
where the maximum fine on summary conviction is a fine not exceeding £5,000. Section 7(4)(a)
provides for a maximum fine where the offender was convicted in summary proceedings, committed to the Crown Court to be dealt with, and turns 18 before being dealt with by that court. The
rationale behind the legislation (that wherever the maximum fine for a person dealt with summarily for an offence was capped at £5,000, the cap should be removed) strongly suggests that it
will be removed here, but a literal approach to the legislation might suggest otherwise.

Information to be supplied on committal for sentence, etc.

Criminal Procedure Rules 2014 (S.I. 2014 No. 1610), r.42.10

Replacement of 2014 rules by 2015 rules

　As to the replacement of S.I. 2014 No. 1610 by the Criminal Procedure Rules 2015 (S.I. 2015 　★**5-39**
No. 1490), see *post*, § 5-287.

III. GENERAL PRINCIPLES

A. Purposes of Sentencing

(1) Offenders generally

Criminal Justice Act 2003, s.142

Purposes of sentencing[: offenders aged 18 or over]

　As from a day to be appointed, the Criminal Justice and Courts Act 2015, s.28(8), and Sched. 5,　**5-61**
paras 9 and 10(1) and (2), amend section 142(2)(c) of the 2003 Act, so as to substitute the words
"a provision mentioned in subsection (2A)" for the words from "section 1A(5)" to "detention for
life for certain dangerous offenders)".

　As from a day to be appointed, the 2015 Act, s.28(8), and Sched. 5, paras 9 and 10(1) and (3),
amend section 142 of the 2003 Act, so as to insert, a new subsection (2A), as follows—

　　"(2A) The provisions referred to in subsection (2)(c) are—

    (a) section 1(2B) or 1A(5) of the Prevention of Crime Act 1953 (minimum sentence for certain offences involving offensive weapons);

    (b) section 51A(2) of the Firearms Act 1968 (minimum sentence for certain firearms offences);

    (c) section 139(6B), 139A(5B) or 139AA(7) of the Criminal Justice Act 1988 (minimum sentence for certain offences involving article with blade or point or offensive weapon);

    (d) section 110(2) or 111(2) of the Sentencing Act (minimum sentence for certain drug trafficking and burglary offences);

    (e) section 224A of this Act (life sentence for second listed offence for certain dangerous offenders);

    (f) section 225(2) or 226(2) of this Act (imprisonment or detention for life for certain dangerous offenders);

    (g) section 29(4) or (6) of the Violent Crime Reduction Act 2006 (minimum sentence in certain cases of using someone to mind a weapon).".

(2) Children and young persons

Criminal Justice Act 2003, s.142A

[Purposes etc. of sentencing: offenders under 18

5-66 As from a day to be appointed, the Criminal Justice and Courts Act 2015, s.28(8), and Sched. 5, paras 9 and 11, amend section 142A of the 2003 Act, so as (i) to substitute a new subsection (4)(b), as follows—

    "(b) to an offence the sentence for which falls to be imposed under a provision mentioned in subsection (5), or";

and (ii) to insert a new subsection (5) at the end, as follows—

    "(5) The provisions referred to in subsection (4)(b) are—

      (a) section 1(2B) or 1A(5) of the Prevention of Crime Act 1953 (minimum sentence for certain offences involving offensive weapons);

      (b) section 51A(2) of the Firearms Act 1968 (minimum sentence for certain firearms offences);

      (c) section 139(6B), 139A(5B) or 139AA(7) of the Criminal Justice Act 1988 (minimum sentence for certain offences involving article with blade or point or offensive weapon);

      (d) section 226(2) of this Act (detention for life for certain dangerous offenders);

      (e) section 29(6) of the Violent Crime Reduction Act 2006 (minimum sentence in certain cases of using someone to mind a weapon).".

B. DETERMINING THE SERIOUSNESS OF AN OFFENCE

(2) Factual basis of sentence

(a) *On conviction following plea of not guilty*

Sample counts and specimen charges

★5-84 For a case considering *R. v. Hartley (Practice Note)* and *R. v. Canavan*; *R. v. Kidd*; *R. v. Shaw* (as to both of which, see the main work), see *R. v. A.*, *ante*, § 1-225, in which it was effectively held that if a "multiple incident" count is left to a jury on the basis that they need only be satisfied that there were at least two incidents of the offence, then sentence must be passed on the basis that there were only two incidents.

(b) *Following plea of guilty*

Agreed basis of plea

5-97 In *R. v. Bergin* [2014] 2 Cr.App.R.(S.) 71, CA, it was said that the importance of the prosecuting authority considering with care, and in accordance with their public duty, proposed bases of plea in all cases, whether or not they were realistic and whether or not they could properly form a basis for sentence, could not be over-emphasised. As to this case, see also *post*, § 5-113.

Resolution of disputed issues

5-99 For a case considering whether it would ever be appropriate, in advance of a *Newton* hearing

(*R. v. Newton*, 77 Cr.App.R. 13, CA (as to which, see the main work)), for a judge to indicate what sentence would be passed according to whether or not he found for or against the defendant at the end of the hearing, see *R. v. Martin, post,* § 5-110.

C. REDUCTION IN SENTENCE FOR GUILTY PLEA

Criminal Justice Act 2003, s.144

Reduction in sentences for guilty pleas

As from a day to be appointed, the Criminal Justice and Courts Act 2015, s.28(8), and Sched. 5, **5-107** paras 9 and 12(1) and (2), amend section 144(2) of the 2003 Act, so as to substitute, for the words from "an offence" to "nothing", the following words—

"an offender who—
    (a) is convicted of an offence the sentence for which falls to be imposed under a provision mentioned in subsection (3), and
    (b) is aged 18 or over when convicted,
nothing".

As from a day to be appointed, the Criminal Justice and Courts Act 2015, s.28(8), and Sched. 5, paras 9 and 12(1) and (3), amend section 144(3) of the 2003 Act, so as (i) to substitute the words "section 1(2B) or 1A(5)" for the words "section 1A(6)(a)", and (ii) to substitute the words "section 139(6B), 139A(5B) or 139AA(7)" for the words "section 139AA(8)(a)".

As from a day to be appointed, the Criminal Justice and Courts Act 2015, s.28(8), and Sched. 5, paras 9 and 12(1) and (4), amend section 144(4) of the 2003 Act, so as to substitute, for the words from "an offence" to "nothing", the following words—

"an offender who—
    (a) is convicted of an offence the sentence for which falls to be imposed under a provision mentioned in subsection (5), and
    (b) is aged 16 or 17 when convicted,
nothing".

As from a day to be appointed, the Criminal Justice and Courts Act 2015, s.28(8), and Sched. 5, paras 9 and 12(1) and (5), amend section 144(5) of the 2003 Act, so as (i) to substitute the words "section 1(2B) or 1A(5)" for the words "section 1A(6)(a)", and (ii) to substitute the words "section 139(6B), 139A(5B) or 139AA(7)" for the words "section 139AA(8)(b)".

Advance indication of sentence

In *R. v. Martin* [2014] 2 Cr.App.R.(S.) 21, CA it was held that a sentencing process was flawed **5-110** from the outset where the judge had given unsolicited indications in advance of a *Newton* hearing (*R. v. Newton*, 77 Cr.App.R. 13, CA (see § 5-99 *et seq.* in the main work)) as to what sentences he would pass according to whether or not he found for or against the defendant. The court said that it was difficult to think of any circumstances where a judge would be justified in giving an indication of sentence in advance of a *Newton* hearing. In the particular case, the judge's unequivocal indication that, in the event that he found against the defendant on a *Newton* hearing, the starting point would be 40 months' imprisonment, which would be reduced to 30 months after credit for a plea, could not be avoided even though he had overlooked, when he gave the indication, the need to reduce the discount in the event that he were to find against the defendant.

While *R. v. Goodyear* (as to which, see the main work) recognised that in an appropriate case a ★ judge could remind defence counsel of his right to seek an indication of sentence, that does not include resort to unrecorded conversations in the defendant's absence that were criticised in *R. v. Turner (F.R.)* (as to which, see § 7-96 in the main work) and *Goodyear: Att.-Gen.'s Reference (No. 85 of 2014) (R. v. A.)* [2015] 1 Cr.App.R.(S.) 14, CA. The court reiterated that any indication should be given in open court, with a full recording of the proceedings; and there should be no indication that a plea of guilty could make the difference between an immediate custodial sentence and a suspended sentence.

Extent of discount

Where the appellant pleaded guilty at a plea and case management hearing on a basis that the **5-113** prosecution were prepared to accept, but which the judge regarded as wholly unrealistic, where the prosecution then realised their error and served further evidence, where thereafter the appellant abandoned his previously untruthful, untenable and unrealistic approach and pleaded guilty on a "full facts" basis, whilst every case turns on its own circumstances, the appellant was entitled to the 25 per cent credit that a guilty plea at the plea and case management hearing would normally have attracted; it was the prosecution's approach to the plea that was to blame for the situation that had arisen; if, when the judge had complained about the basis of plea, the prosecution had then conceded the point and acknowledged that it was unrealistic, the appellant's plea on that basis, even though it was ultimately abandoned, may well have justified a further modest diminution in the credit to which he was entitled to reflect the wasted time and costs in obtaining and serving further evidence; here, however, there was little more that the appellant could be expected to do other than to plead guilty on the basis that the prosecution, albeit wrongly, had regarded as acceptable: *R. v. Bergin* [2014] 2 Cr.App.R.(S.) 71, CA. As to this case, see also *ante*, § 5-97.

★   Where the appellant expressed a desire to plead guilty at a preliminary hearing at the Crown Court before the prosecution had prepared the indictment, where the judge indicated that full credit would be available, where more than two months later he entered guilty pleas to various offences at a plea and case management hearing, and a second judge considered the appropriate discount was 20 per cent, as the evidence was overwhelming (ass he had been caught in the act and had no possible defence), he should have been given the full one-third discount; he was perhaps fortunate that the indication had been given, but had the sentencing judge been aware of it, she no doubt would have honoured it: *R. v. Claydon* [2015] 1 Cr.App.R.(S.) 71, CA.

First reasonable opportunity

5-114   It was held in *R. v. Creathorne* [2014] 2 Cr.App.R.(S.) 48, CA, that where a defendant is suffering from amnesia as a consequence of injuries he suffered as a result of the incident that gave rise to the prosecution (here, an allegation of causing death by careless driving), he should not be penalised for delaying his plea of guilty until his legal advisers have seen all the material evidence that they need in order to advise as to plea.

Withholding the discount

★5-115   As to the extent of the discount to be afforded to a defendant who pleads guilty where the evidence is "overwhelming", see *R. v. Walter, R. v. Jenkins* and *R. v. Buckle, post*, Appendix K-352.

E. Mitigation

(3) Selected mitigating factors

Assistance to law enforcement agencies

Criminal Procedure Rules 2014 (S.I. 2014 No. 1610), r.42.11

Replacement of 2014 rules by 2015 rules

★5-135a   As to the replacement of S.I. 2014 No. 1610 by the Criminal Procedure Rules 2015 (S.I. 2015 No. 1490), see *post*, § 5-287.

F. Sentencing Guidelines

Sentencing Council for England and Wales

★5-147   The Sentencing Council for England and Wales has issued a consultation guideline on offences under the Dangerous Dogs Act 1991. The consultation period closed on June 9, 2015, following which a definitive guideline will be issued.

Coroners and Justice Act 2009, ss.121, 125, 126

Sentencing guidelines: duty of court

5-149   As from a day to be appointed, the Criminal Justice and Courts Act 2015, s.28(8), and Sched. 5, para. 17, amend section 125(6) of the Coroners and Justice Act 2009, so as (i) in paragraph (ea), to substitute "sections 1(2B) and" for "section", and "certain offences involving offensive weapon" for "offence of threatening with offensive weapon in public", and (ii) in paragraph (fa), to substitute "sections 139(6B), 139A(5B) and" for "section", and "certain offences involving" for "offence of threatening with".

IV. DISCHARGE AND BINDING OVER

(1) Discharge

Powers of Criminal Courts (Sentencing) Act 2000, s.12

Absolute and conditional discharge

As from April 13, 2015 (Criminal Justice and Courts Act 2015 (Commencement No. 1, Saving and Transitional Provisions) Order 2015 (S.I. 2015 No. 778)), the Criminal Justice and Courts Act 2015, s.28(8), and Sched. 5, paras 3 and 4, amended section 12 of the 2000 Act, so as (i) to substitute the words "a provision mentioned in subsection (1A)" for the words from "section 110(2)" to "2006" in subsection (1), and (ii) to insert after subsection (1), a new subsection (1A), as follows—   ★5-169

"(1A) The provisions referred to in subsection (1) are—
    (a) section 1(2B) or 1A(5) of the Prevention of Crime Act 1953;
    (b) section 51A(2) of the Firearms Act 1968;
    (c) section 139(6B), 139A(5B) or 139AA(7) of the Criminal Justice Act 1988;
    (d) section 110(2) or 111(2) of this Act;
    (e) section 224A, 225(2) or 226(2) of the Criminal Justice Act 2003;
    (f) section 29(4) or (6) of the Violent Crime Reduction Act 2006.".

As from April 13, 2015 (S.I. 2015 No. 778 (*ante*)), the Criminal Justice and Courts Act 2015, s.54(3), and Sched. 12, paras 8 and 9, further amended section 12 of the 2000 Act, so as (i) in subsection (7), to omit "from making an order for costs against the offender or", (ii) in subsection (7), to substitute the words "the offender" for the word "him", and (iii) at the end, to insert a new subsection (8), as follows—   ★

"(8) Nothing in this section shall be construed as preventing a court, on discharging an offender absolutely or conditionally in respect of an offence, from—
    (a) making an order under section 21A of the Prosecution of Offences Act 1985 (criminal courts charge), or
    (b) making an order for costs against the offender.".

Combined with other orders

As to the amendment of section 12 of the PCC(S)A 2000 (see the main work), see *ante*, § 5-169.   **5-174**

V. COMMUNITY SENTENCES

B. GENERAL RESTRICTIONS

Criminal Justice Act 2003, ss.147–151

Community sentence not available where sentence fixed by law etc.

As from a day to be appointed, the Criminal Justice and Courts Act 2015, s.28(8), and Sched. 5, paras 9 and 13, amend section 150(2) of the 2003 Act, so as to substitute new paragraphs (a) and (b), as follows—   **5-250**

"(a) falls to be imposed under section 1(2B) or 1A(5) of the Prevention of Crime Act 1953 (minimum sentence for certain offences involving offensive weapons), or
(b) falls to be imposed under section 139(6B), 139A(5B) or 139AA(7) of the Criminal Justice Act 1988 (minimum sentence for certain offences involving article with blade or point or offensive weapon)".

[Community order or youth rehabilitation order for persistent offender previously fined

As from April 13, 2015 (Criminal Justice and Courts Act 2015 (Commencement No. 1, Saving   ★5-252 and Transitional Provisions) Order 2015 (S.I. 2015 No. 778)), the Criminal Justice and Courts Act 2015, s.54(3), and Sched. 12, paras 12 and 13, amended section 151(5) of the 2003 Act, so as to insert before the words "a compensation order" the words "an order under section 21A of the Prosecution of Offences Act 1985 (criminal courts charge), or".

★ As from a day to be appointed, section 151(5) of the 2003 Act is further amended by the Modern Slavery Act 2015, s.57(1), and Sched. 5, para. 24, so as to insert the words "or a slavery and trafficking reparation order under section 8 of the Modern Slavery Act 2015" after "2013".

C. Community Orders

(1) General

Criminal Justice Act 2003, s.177

Community orders

5-253   As to the commencement of section 15 of, and Schedule 5 to, the Offender Rehabilitation Act 2014 (see the main work), see *ante*, § 5-8.

(2) Definitions

Criminal Justice Act 2003, s.196

Meaning of "relevant order" etc.

5-262   As to the further commencement of section 19 of, and Schedule 6 to, the Offender Rehabilitation Act 2014 (see the main work), see *post*, § 5-598.

(3) Requirements available in the case of all offenders

Criminal Justice Act 2003, ss.199–213

[Rehabilitation activity requirement

5-266a   As to the commencement of section 15 of the Offender Rehabilitation Act 2014 (see the main work), see *ante*, § 5-8.

Activity requirement

5-267   As to the commencement of section 15 of the Offender Rehabilitation Act 2014 (see the main work), see *ante*, § 5-8.

Programme requirement

5-268   With effect from February 1, 2015 (Offender Rehabilitation Act 2014 (Commencement No. 2) Order 2015 (S.I. 2015 No. 40)), section 16 of the 2014 Act (see the main work) was brought into force.

Supervision requirement

5-279   As to the commencement of section 15 of the Offender Rehabilitation Act 2014 (see the main work), see *ante*, § 5-8.

(4) Requirements available only in case of offenders aged under 25

Criminal Justice Act 2003, s.214

Attendance centre requirement

5-280   As to the commencement of section 17 of the Offender Rehabilitation Act 2014 (see the main work), see *ante*, § 5-8.

(6) Provisions applying to relevant orders generally

Criminal Justice Act 2003, ss.216–220

Availability of arrangements in local area

5-284   As to the commencement of sections 15 and 17 of, and Schedule 5 to, the Offender Rehabilitation Act 2014 (see the main work), see *ante*, § 5-8.

[Duty to obtain permission before changing residence

5-286a   As to the commencement (in part) of section 18 of the Offender Rehabilitation Act 2014 (see the main work), see *ante*, § 5-8.

(7) Notification of requirements

Criminal Procedure Rules 2014 (S.I. 2014 No. 1610), r.42.2

Replacement of 2014 rules by 2015 rules

With effect from October 5, 2015, the Criminal Procedure Rules 2015 (S.I. 2015 No. 1490)   ★**5-287** replace S.I. 2014 No. 1610. Part 42 of the 2014 rules is replaced by Part 28 of the 2015 rules (see *post*, Appendix P-253 *et seq.*), with minor changes of substance.

D. YOUTH COMMUNITY ORDERS

Introduction

Attendance centre orders under section 60 of the PCC(S)A 2000 were just one of several "youth   **5-291** community orders" that could be made under that Act. As explained in the main work, however, the sections of the Act that provided for the making of a curfew order (s.37), an exclusion order (s.40A), a supervision order (ss.63, 64 and 67, and Sched. 6) and an action plan order (ss.69–71) were repealed by the CJIA 2008, and these repeals came fully into force on November 30, 2009, except that they continue to apply to offences committed before that date. With the passage of time, it was unlikely that, by the time of publication of the 2013 edition of this work, further reference would need to be made to these provisions. Should it be necessary, however, they can be found in the supplements to the 2012 edition. The position with regard to section 60 is rather different (see the annotations thereto (*post*, § 5-292)).

Powers of Criminal Courts (Sentencing) Act 2000, s.60

Attendance centre orders

60.—(1) Where—   **5-292**

   (a)   (subject to 148, 150 and 156 of the Criminal Justice Act 2003) a person aged under *21* [16] is convicted by or before a court of an offence punishable with imprisonment, or

   (b)   a court [has power or] would have power, but for section 89 below (restrictions on imprisonment of young offenders and defaulters), to commit a person aged under *21* [16] to prison in default of payment of any sum of money or for failing to do or abstain from doing anything required to be done or left undone, *or*

   (c)   *a court has power to commit a person aged at least 21 but under 25 to prison in default of payment of any sum of money,*

the court may, if it has been notified by the Secretary of State that an attendance centre is available for the reception of persons of his description, order him to attend at such a centre, to be specified in the order, for such number of hours as may be so specified.

(2) An order under subsection (1) above is in this Act referred to as an "attendance centre order".

(3) The aggregate number of hours for which an attendance centre order may require a person to attend at an attendance centre shall not be less than 12 except where—

   (a)   he is aged under 14; and

   (b)   the court is of the opinion that 12 hours would be excessive, having regard to his age or any other circumstances.

(4) The aggregate number of hours shall not exceed 12 except where the court is of the opinion, having regard to all the circumstances, that 12 hours would be inadequate, and in that case [shall not exceed 24]—

   (a)   *shall not exceed 24 where the person is aged under 16; and*

   (b)   *shall not exceed 36 where the person is aged 16 or over but under 21 or (where subsection (1)(c) above applies) under 25.*

(5) A court may make an attendance centre order in respect of a person before a previous attendance centre order made in respect of him has ceased to have effect, and may determine the number of hours to be specified in the order without regard—

   (a)   to the number specified in the previous order; or

   (b)   to the fact that order is still in effect.

(6) An attendance centre order shall not be made unless the court is satisfied that the attendance centre to be specified in it is reasonably accessible to the person concerned, having regard to his age, the means of access available to him and any other circumstances.

(7) The times at which a person is required to attend at an attendance centre shall, as for as practicable, be such as to avoid—

41

(a) any conflict with his religious beliefs or with the requirements of any other [youth] community order to which he may be subject; and

(b) any interference with the times, if any, at which he normally works or attends school or any other educational establishment.

(8) The first time at which the person is required to attend at an attendance centre shall be a time at which the centre is available for his attendance in accordance with the notification of the Secretary of State, and shall be specified in the order.

(9) The subsequent times shall be fixed by the officer in charge of the centre, having regard to the person's circumstances.

(10) A person shall not be required under this section to attend at an attendance centre on more than one occasion on any day, or for more than three hours on any occasion.

(11) Where a court makes an attendance centre order, the clerk of the court shall—

(a) deliver or send a copy of the order to the officer in charge of the attendance centre specified in it; and

(b) deliver a copy of the order to the person in respect of whom it is made or send a copy by registered post or the recorded delivery service addressed to his last or usual place of abode.

(12) Where a person ("the defaulter") has been ordered to attend at an attendance centre in default of the payment of any sum of money—

(a) on payment of the whole sum to any person authorised to receive it, the attendance centre order shall cease to have effect;

(b) on payment of a part of the sum to any such person, the total number of hours for which the defaulter is required to attend at the centre shall be reduced proportionately, that is to say by such number of complete hours as bears to the total number the proportion most nearly approximating to, without exceeding, the proportion which the part bears to the whole sum.

[This section is printed as amended by the CJA 2003, s.304, and Sched. 32, para. 102(1), (2)(a) (substitution of references to sections 148, 150 and 156 of the 2003 Act for references to corresponding provisions of the 2000 Act, and substitution of "16" for "21" in subs. (1)(a)), and (4) (substitution of "youth community order" for "community order" in subs. (7)); and as amended, as from a day to be appointed, by the CJCSA 2000, s.74 and Sched. 7, para. 173 (insertion of words in first set of square brackets in subs. (1)(b)); and the CJA 2003, s.304, and Sched. 32, paras 90 and 102(1), and (2)(b) and (c), and (3) (substitution of "16" for "21" in subs. (1)(b), omission of subs. (1)(c) and the word "or" immediately preceding it, substitution of words in square brackets for italicised words in subs. (4)). The amendments to subss. (1)(a) and (7) came into force on April 4, 2005: Criminal Justice Act 2003 (Commencement No. 8 and Transitional and Saving Provisions) Order 2005 (S.I. 2005 No. 950), save that, in the case of persons aged 16 or 17 upon conviction, the substitution of "16" for "21" in subs. (1)(a) and the insertion of the word "youth" before "community order" in subs. (7) have no application in relation to offences committed before November 30, 2009, or in relation to any failure to comply with an order made in respect of an offence committed before that date: *ibid.*, Sched. 2, paras 12 and 13. The whole of this section is repealed as from a day to be appointed (as to which, see §§ 5-1, 5-185, 5-186 in the main work) by the CJIA 2008, ss.6(1) and 149, and Sched. 28, Pt 1. To the extent that this repeal relates to subs. (1)(a), it was brought into force on November 30, 2009: Criminal Justice and Immigration Act 2008 (Commencement No. 13 and Transitory Provision) Order 2009 (S.I. 2009 No. 3074).]

5-293   As to the requirements to be complied with before imposing an attendance centre order, see (for offences committed before April 4, 2005) sections 35 and 36 of the PCC(S)A 2000 (§§ 5-189, 5-190 in the supplements to the 2012 edition) (it being a "community order" within that Act), and (for offences committed after that date) section 148 of the CJA 2003 (§ 5-248 in the main work) (it being a "community sentence" within that Act).

It is not entirely clear whether a court may make attendance centre orders on the same occasion in respect of a number of offences with an aggregate in excess of the limits in subsection (4). It is submitted that the better view is that it cannot; section 60(1) appears to be concerned with defining an *occasion* when an attendance centre order may be made. On any such occasion *one* order may be made. Subsection (5) appears to confirm the correctness of this approach: if it were incorrect, subsection (5) would not be needed.

Section 61 gives effect to Schedule 5 (*post*, §§ 5-365 *et seq.*).

F. Enforcement, etc.

(1) Of community orders
Criminal Justice Act 2003, Sched. 8

Powers of magistrates' court

As from April 13, 2015 (Criminal Justice and Courts Act 2015 (Commencement No. 1, Saving   **★5-345** and Transitional Provisions) Order 2015 (S.I. 2015 No. 778)), the Criminal Justice and Courts Act 2015, s.54(3), and Sched. 12, paras 12 and 15, amended paragraph 9(8) of Schedule 8, so as to substitute for the words "against the sentence", the following words—

"against—
(a) the sentence, and
(b) an order made by the court under section 21A of the Prosecution of Offences Act 1985 (criminal courts charge) when imposing that sentence".

As to the commencement (in part) of section 18 of the Offender Rehabilitation Act 2014 (see   **5-357** the main work), see *ante*, § 5-8.

As to the further commencement of section 19 of, and Schedule 6 to, the Offender Rehabilita-   **5-358** tion Act 2014 (see the main work), see *post*, § 5-598.

(2) Of youth community orders

Curfew, exclusion and supervision orders

As to curfew and exclusion orders, see Schedule 3 to the PCC(S)A 2000 (§§ 5-228 *et seq.* in the   **5-364** supplements to the 2012 edition); and as to supervision orders, see Schedule 7 to that Act (§§ 5-371 *et seq.* in the supplements to the 2012 edition).

Powers of Criminal Courts (Sentencing) Act 2000, Sched. 5

Section 61   SCHEDULE 5

BREACH, REVOCATION AND AMENDMENT OF ATTENDANCE CENTRE ORDERS

Breach of order or attendance centre rules

1.—(1) Where an attendance centre order is in force and it appears on information to a justice   **5-365** that the offender—
(a) has failed to attend in accordance with the order, or
(b) while attending has committed a breach of rules made under section 222(1)(d) or (e) of the Criminal Justice Act 2003 which cannot be adequately dealt with under those rules,
the justice may issue a summons requiring the offender to appear at the place and time specified in the summons or, if the information is in writing and on oath, may issue a warrant for the offender's arrest.

(2) Any summons or warrant issued under this paragraph shall direct the offender to appear or be brought—
(a) before a magistrates' court acting for the petty sessions area in which the offender resides; or
(b) if it is not known where the offender resides, before a magistrates' court acting for the petty sessions area in which is situated the attendance centre which the offender is required to attend by the order or by virtue of an order under paragraph 5(1)(b) below.

2.—(1) If it is proved to the satisfaction of the magistrates' court before which an offender appears or is brought under paragraph 1 above that he has failed without reasonable excuse to attend as mentioned in sub-paragraph (1)(a) of that paragraph or has committed such a breach of rules as is mentioned in sub-paragraph (1)(b) of that paragraph, that court may deal with him in any one of the following ways—
(a) it may impose on him a fine not exceeding £1,000;
(b) where the attendance centre order was made by a magistrates' court, it may deal with him, for the offence in respect of which the order was made, in any way in which he could have

been dealt with for that offence by the court which made the order if the order had not been made; or

    (c) where the order was made by the Crown Court, it may commit him to custody or release him on bail until he can be brought or appear before the Crown Court.

(2) Any exercise by the court of its power under sub-paragraph (1)(a) above shall be without prejudice to the continuation of the order.

(3) A fine imposed under sub-paragraph (1)(a) above shall be deemed, for the purposes of any enactment, to be a sum adjudged to be paid by a conviction.

(4) Where a magistrates' court deals with an offender under sub-paragraph (1)(b) above, it shall revoke the attendance centre order if it is still in force.

(5) In dealing with an offender under sub-paragraph (1)(b) above, a magistrates' court—

    (a) shall take into account the extent to which the offender has complied with the requirements of the attendance centre order; and

    (b) in the case of an offender who has wilfully and persistently failed to comply with those requirements, may impose a custodial sentence notwithstanding anything in section 152(2) of the Criminal Justice Act 2003.

(5A) Where a magistrates' court dealing with an offender under sub-paragraph (1)(a) above would not otherwise have the power to amend the order under paragraph 5(1)(b) below (substitution of different attendance centre), that paragraph has effect as if references to an appropriate magistrates' court were references to the court dealing with an offender.

(6) A person sentenced under sub-paragraph (1)(b) above for an offence may appeal to the Crown Court against the sentence.

(7) A magistrates' court which deals with an offender's case under sub-paragraph (1)(c) above shall send to the Crown Court—

    (a) a certificate signed by a justice of the peace giving particulars of the offender's failure to attend or, as the case may be, the breach of the rules which he has committed; and

    (b) such other particulars of the case as may be desirable;

and a certificate purporting to be so signed shall be admissible as evidence of the failure or the breach before the Crown Court.

3.—(1) Where by virtue of paragraph 2(1)(c) above the offender is brought or appears before the Crown Court and it is proved to the satisfaction of the court—

    (a) that he has failed without reasonable excuse to attend as mentioned in paragraph 1(1)(a) above, or

    (b) that he has committed such a breach of rules as is mentioned in paragraph 1(1)(b) above,

that court may deal with him, for the offence in respect of which the order was made, in any way in which it could have dealt with him for that offence if it had not made the order.

(2) Where the Crown Court deals with an offender under sub-paragraph (1) above, it shall revoke the attendance centre order if it is still in force.

(3) In in dealing with an offender under sub-paragraph (1) above, the Crown Court—

    (a) shall take into account the extent to which the offender has complied with the requirements of the attendance centre order; and

    (b) in the case of an offender who has willfully and persistently failed to comply with those requirements, may impose a custodial sentence notwithstanding anything in section 152(2) of the Criminal Justice Act 2003.

(4) In proceedings before the Crown Court under this paragraph any question whether there has been a failure to attend or a breach of the rules shall be determined by the court and not by the verdict of a jury.

Revocation of order with or without re-sentencing

5-366   4.—(1) Where an attendance centre order is in force in respect of an offender, an appropriate court may, on an application made by the offender or by the officer in charge of the relevant attendance centre, revoke the order.

(2) In sub-paragraph (1) above "an appropriate court" means—

    (a) where the court which made the order was the Crown Court and there is included in the order a direction that the power to revoke the order is reserved to that court, the Crown Court;

    (b) in any other case, either of the following—

        (i) a magistrates' court acting for the petty sessions area in which the relevant attendance centre is situated;

        (ii) the court which made the order.

(3) Any power conferred by this paragraph—

    (a) on a magistrates' court to revoke an attendance centre order made by such a court, or

    (b) on the Crown Court to revoke an attendance centre order made by the Crown Court,

includes power to deal with the offender, for the offence in respect of which the order was made, in any way in which he could have been dealt with for that offence by the court which made the order if the order had not been made.

(4) A person sentenced by a magistrates' court under sub-paragraph (3) above for an offence may appeal to the Crown Court against the sentence.

(5) The proper officer of a court which makes an order under this paragraph revoking an attendance centre order shall—

    (a) deliver a copy of the revoking order to the offender or send a copy by registered post or the recorded delivery service addressed to the offender's last or usual place of abode; and

    (b) deliver or send a copy to the officer in charge of the relevant attendance centre.

(6) In this paragraph "the relevant attendance centre", in relation to an attendance centre order, means the attendance centre specified in the order or substituted for the attendance centre so specified by an order made by virtue of paragraph 5(1)(b) below.

(7) In this paragraph "proper officer" means—

    (a) in relation to a magistrates' court, the justices' chief executive for the court; and

    (b) in relation to the Crown Court, the appropriate officer.

Amendment of order

5-367 5.—(1) Where an attendance centre order is in force in respect of an offender, an appropriate magistrates' court may, on application made by the offender or by the officer in charge of the relevant attendance centre, by order—

    (a) vary the day or hour specified in the order for the offender's first attendance at the relevant attendance centre; or

    (b) substitute for the relevant attendance centre an attendance centre which the court is satisfied is reasonably accessible to the offender, having regard to his age, the means of access available to him and any other circumstances.

(2) In sub-paragraph (1) above "an appropriate magistrates' court" means—

    (a) a magistrates' court acting for the petty sessions area in which the relevant attendance centre is situated; or

    (b) (except where the attendance centre order was made by the Crown Court) the magistrates' court which made the order.

(3) The justices' chief executive for a court which makes an order under this paragraph shall—

    (a) deliver a copy to the offender or send a copy by registered post or the recorded delivery service addressed to the offender's last or usual place of abode; and

    (b) deliver or send a copy—

        (i) if the order is made by virtue of sub-paragraph (1)(a) above, to the officer in charge of the relevant attendance centre; and

        (ii) if it is made by virtue of sub-paragraph (1)(b) above, to the officer in charge of the attendance centre which the order as amended will require the offender to attend.

(4) In this paragraph "the relevant attendance centre" has the meaning given by paragraph 4(6) above.

Orders made on appeal

5-368 6.—(1) Where an attendance centre order has been made on appeal, for the purposes of this Schedule it shall be deemed—

    (a) if it was made on an appeal brought from a magistrates' court, to have been made by that magistrates' court;

    (b) if it was made on an appeal brought from the Crown Court or from the criminal division of the Court of Appeal, to have been made by the Crown Court.

(2) In relation to an attendance centre order made on appeal, paragraphs 2(1)(b) and 4(3) above shall each have effect as if the words "if the order had not been made" were omitted and paragraph 3(1) above shall have effect as if the words "if it had not made the order" were omitted.

Orders for defaulters

5-369 7.—(1) References in this Schedule to an "offender" include a person who has been ordered to attend at an attendance centre for such a default or failure as is mentioned in section 60(1)(b) or (c) of this Act.

(2) Where a person has been ordered to attend at an attendance centre for such a default or failure—

(a) paragraphs 2(1)(b), 3(1) and 4(3) above shall each have effect in relation to the order as if the words ", for the offence in respect of which the order was made," and "for that offence" were omitted; and

(b) paragraphs 2(5)(b) and 3(3)(b) above (which relate to custodial sentences for offences) do not apply.

[This schedule is printed as amended by the CJA 2003, s.304, and Sched. 32, paras 90 and 126; and the Domestic Violence, Crime and Victims Act 2004, s.29, and Sched. 5, para. 6. The whole schedule is repealed as from a day to be appointed (as to which, see §§ 5-1, 5-185, 5-186 in the main work) by the CJIA 2008, ss.6(1) and 149, and Sched. 28, Pt 1.]

5-370   When dealing with an offender under paragraph 3(1), the court must observe any limitations related to his age which applied at the time when he was sentenced: he must be sentenced on the basis of his age when he was originally convicted of the offence for which the attendance centre order was made.

In a case coming within paragraph 4, the failure to attend the attendance centre, or breach of the rules, must be proved to the satisfaction of the Crown Court: the certificate of the magistrates' court is merely evidence.

(4) Procedural rules

Criminal Procedure Rules 2014 (S.I. 2014 No. 1610), Pt 44

Replacement of 2014 rules by 2015 rules

★5-395   With effect from October 5, 2015, the Criminal Procedure Rules 2015 (S.I. 2015 No. 1490) replace S.I. 2014 No. 1610. Part 44 of the 2014 rules is replaced by Part 32 of the 2015 rules (see *post*, Appendix P-282 *et seq.*), with minor drafting changes.

VI. CUSTODIAL SENTENCES

A. MANDATORY LIFE SENTENCE

(2) Legislation

Fixing the minimum term

The whole life starting point

5-406   Four points from *R. v. Jones* (see § 5-404 in the main work) were emphasised in *R. v. Reynolds (Jamie); R. v. Rosser (Anwar), The Times,* December 10, 2014, CA. First, a judge must have regard to the guidance in Schedule 21 to the CJA 2003 (§§ 5-425 *et seq.* in the main work), but each case will depend critically on its particular facts; secondly, where a whole-life order is called for, often, perhaps usually, the case will not be on the borderline; thirdly, the judge should take account of a plea of guilty when deciding whether it is appropriate to order a whole-life term; fourthly, a whole-life order is reserved for the few exceptionally serious offences where the judge is satisfied that the element of just punishment required the imposition of a whole-life order.

In *Hutchinson v. U.K., The Times,* February 5, 2015, the European Court of Human Rights effectively abandoned the position taken by the Grand Chamber in *Vinter v. U.K.* (as to which, see the main work) and accepted the decision of the Court of Appeal in *Att.-Gen.'s Reference (No. 69 of 2013) (R. v. McLoughlin); R. v. Newell,* which, it said, had sufficiently addressed the doubts expressed by the Grand Chamber.

It should be noted, however, that in the earlier chamber decision of *Trabelsi v. Belgium* (2015) 60 E.H.R.R. 21 (not referred to in *Hutchinson*), the court adhered to the line taken in *Vinter,* in relation to an extradition request from the United States of America. *Trabelsi* was then considered by the Divisional Court in *R. (Harkins) v. Secretary of State for the Home Department* [2015] A.C.D. 33, DC (also an extradition case). It was held that whilst the court was bound to take account of the

Strasbourg court's decision, it was not bound to follow it, and, in any event, it did not constitute clear and constant jurisprudence.

The 25-year starting point and taking a knife or other weapon to the scene

R. v. Kelly (as to which, see the main work) emphasises the importance, in cases of similar culpability, of avoiding major differences in sentence based on fine distinctions; thus, if a case is only just within paragraph 5A of Schedule 21 to the 2003 Act (§ 5-426 in the main work), because a knife was taken from a kitchen and used to inflict a fatal wound a short distance outside the door of the premises, this principle may well lead to a minimum term of less than 25 years: *R. v. Dillon* [2015] 1 Cr.App.R.(S.) 62, CA . ★5-410

In *R. v. Beckford* [2014] 2 Cr.App.R.(S.) 34, CA, it was held that a judge had been entitled to find that the case fell within paragraph 5A(2) of Schedule 21 to the 2003 Act, and therefore to take a starting point for the minimum term of 25 years, where the appellant, upon seeing a rival gang member in the street, drove his car onto the footpath and rammed him with sufficient force to cause him to die from his injuries.

Youthfulness/ the prescribed starting points/ disparity

In *R. v. De Silva* [2015] 1 Cr.App.R.(S.) 52, CA, minimum term of 32 years, fixed pursuant to Schedule 21 to the CJA 2003 (§§ 5-425 *et seq.* in the main work) for the murder of the householder during a burglary at night (murder "done for gain" for which the starting point is 30 years (see para. 5)) was reduced to 28 years where the offender had been 19 at the time of the offence. The court said that a minimum term of 32 years for a 19-year-old was a very severe sentence, and perhaps uniquely so; although it was a dreadful crime, the appellant's age was a significant factor in mitigating his culpability; young offenders were more likely to be impulsive and unthinking and to respond to situations with excessive and gratuitous force. ★5-412

Aggravating factors

The aggravating factor in paragraph 10(a) of Schedule 21 to the CJA 2003 (§ 5-427 in the main work) ("a significant degree of planning or premeditation") is not confined to the offence of murder, and it could apply to a case where there had been significant planning by the appellant in relation to a sexual assault on the victim, but where there had been no premeditation or planning of the murder that followed on from that behaviour: *R. v. Minto* [2014] 2 Cr.App.R.(S.) 36, CA. 5-415

Crime (Sentences) Act 1997, s.28

Duty to release certain life prisoners

As from a day to be appointed, the Criminal Justice and Courts Act 2015, s.11(1), amends section 28(7)(c) of the 1997 Act so as to substitute "the requisite custodial period (as defined in section 268 of the Criminal Justice Act 2003)" for "one-half of that sentence". The amendment applies to a person sentenced before the day on which it comes into force as well as to a person sentenced on or after that day (s.11(4) of the 2015 Act). 5-423

Criminal Justice Act 2003, Sched. 21

As from April 13, 2015 (Criminal Justice and Courts Act 2015 (Commencement No. 1, Saving and Transitional Provisions) Order 2015 (S.I. 2015 No. 778)), the Criminal Justice and Courts Act 2015, s.27(1) and (2), amended paragraph 4(2) of Schedule 21 to the 2003 Act, so as to insert, after paragraph (b), new paragraph (ba), as follows— ★5-426

"(ba) the murder of a police officer or prison officer in the course of his or her duty,".

As from April 13, 2015 (S.I. 2015 No. 778 (*ante*)), the Criminal Justice and Courts Act 2015, s.27(1) and (3), amended paragraph 5(2) of Schedule 21 to the 2003 Act, so as to omit paragraph (a). ★

The amendments made to paragraphs 4 and 5 of Schedule 21 to the 2003 Act apply only in relation to an offence committed on or after the day on which they come into force (s.27(4) of the 2015 Act).

Criminal Justice Act 2003, Sched. 22, paras 1, 2, 9 and 10

Section 276

SCHEDULE 22

MANDATORY LIFE SENTENCES: TRANSITIONAL CASES

Interpretation

5-428   1. In this Schedule—

"the commencement date" means the day on which section 269 comes into force;

"the early release provisions" means the provisions of section 28(5) to (8) of the Crime (Sentences) Act 1997;

"existing prisoner" means a person serving one or more mandatory life sentences passed before the commencement date (whether or not he is also serving any other sentence);

"life sentence" means a sentence of imprisonment for life or custody for life passed in England and Wales or by a court-martial outside England and Wales;

"mandatory life sentence" means a life sentence passed in circumstances where the sentence was fixed by law.

Existing prisoners notified by Secretary of State

5-429   2. Paragraph 3 applies in relation to any existing prisoner who, in respect of any mandatory life sentence, has before the commencement date been notified in writing by the Secretary of State (otherwise than in a notice that is expressed to be provisional) either—

(a) of a minimum period which in the view of the Secretary of State should be served before the prisoner's release on licence, or

(b) that the Secretary of State does not intend that the prisoner should ever be released on licence.

Sentences passed on or after commencement date in respect of offences committed before that date

5-430   9. Paragraph 10 applies where—

(a) on or after the commencement date a court passes a life sentence in circumstances where the sentence is fixed by law, and

(b) the offence to which the sentence relates was committed before the commencement date.

10. The court—

(a) may not make an order under subsection (2) of section 269 specifying a part of the sentence which in the opinion of the court is greater than that which, under the practice followed by the Secretary of State before December 2002, the Secretary of State would have been likely to notify as mentioned in paragraph 2(a), and

(b) may not make an order under subsection (4) of section 269 unless the court is of the opinion that, under the practice followed by the Secretary of State before December 2002, the Secretary of State would have been likely to give the prisoner a notification falling within paragraph 2(b).

(3) Practice

Criminal Practice Direction (Sentencing) N [2013] 1 W.L.R. 3164

TRANSITIONAL ARRANGEMENTS FOR SENTENCES WHERE THE OFFENCE WAS COMMITTED
BEFORE 18 DECEMBER 2003

5-432   **N.1** Where the court is passing a sentence of mandatory life imprisonment for an offence committed before 18 December 2003, the court should take a fourth step in determining the minimum term in accordance with section 276 and Schedule 22 …. .

N.2 The purpose of those provisions is to ensure that the sentence does not breach the principle of non-retroactivity by ensuring that a lower minimum term would not have been imposed for the offence when it was committed. Before setting the minimum term the court must check whether the proposed term is greater than that which the Secretary of State would probably have notified under the practice followed by the Secretary of State before December 2002.

N.3 The decision in *Sullivan* … gives detailed guidance as to the correct approach to this practice and judges passing mandatory life sentences where the murder was committed prior to 18 December 2003 are well advised to read that judgment before proceeding.

N.4 The practical result of that judgment is that in sentences where the murder was committed before 31 May 2002, the best guide to what would have been the practice of the Secretary of State is the letter sent to judges by Lord Bingham C.J. on 10th February 1997, the relevant parts of which are set out below.

N.5 The practice of Lord Bingham, as set out in his letter ... was to take 14 years as the period actually to be served for the "average", "normal" or "unexceptional" murder. Examples of factors he outlined as capable, in appropriate cases, of mitigating the normal penalty were:

> youth;
>
> age (where relevant to physical capacity on release or the likelihood of the defendant dying in prison);
>
> intellectual disability or mental disorder;
>
> provocation (in a non-technical sense), or an excessive response to a personal threat;
>
> the absence of an intention to kill;
>
> spontaneity and lack of premeditation (beyond that necessary to constitute the offence: *e.g.* a sudden response to family pressure or to prolonged and eventually insupportable stress);
>
> mercy killing;
>
> a plea of guilty, or hard evidence of remorse or contrition.

N.6 Lord Bingham then listed the following factors as likely to call for a sentence more severe than the norm:

> evidence of a planned, professional, revenge or contract killing;
>
> the killing of a child or a very old or otherwise vulnerable victim;
>
> evidence of sadism, gratuitous violence, or sexual maltreatment, humiliation or degradation before the killing;
>
> killing for gain (in the course of burglary, robbery, blackmail, insurance fraud, *etc.*);
>
> multiple killings;
>
> the killing of a witness or potential witness to defeat the ends of justice;
>
> the killing of those doing their public duty (policemen, prison officers, postmasters, firemen, judges, *etc*);
>
> terrorist or politically motivated killings;
>
> the killing of those doing their public duty (policemen, prison officers, postmasters, firemen, judges, etc);
>
> terrorist or politically motivated killings;
>
> the use of firearms or other dangerous weapons, whether carried for defensive or offensive reasons;
>
> a substantial record of serious violence;
>
> macabre attempts to dismember or conceal the body.

N.7 Lord Bingham further stated that the fact that a defendant was under the influence of drink or drugs at the time of the killing is so common he would be inclined to treat it as neutral. But in the not unfamiliar case in which a couple, inflamed by drink, indulge in a violent quarrel in which one dies, often against a background of long-standing drunken violence, then he would tend to recommend a term somewhat below the norm.

N.8 Lord Bingham went on to say that given the intent necessary for proof of murder, the consequences of taking life and the understandable reaction of relatives to the deceased, a substantial term will almost always be called for, save perhaps in a truly venial case of mercy killing. While a recommendation of a punitive term longer than, say, 30 years will be very rare indeed, there should not be any upper limit. Some crimes will certainly call for terms very well in excess of the norm.

N.9 For the purposes of sentences where the murder was committed after 31 May 2002 and **5-433** before 18 December 2003, the judge should apply the practice statement handed down on 31 May 2002 reproduced at paras N.10 to N.20 below.

N.10 This statement replaces the previous single normal tariff of 14 years by substituting a higher and a normal starting point of respectively 16 (comparable to 32 years) and 12 years (comparable to 24 years). These starting points have then to be increased or reduced because of aggravating or mitigating factors such as those referred to below. It is emphasised that they are no more than starting points.

The normal starting point of 12 years

N.11 Cases falling within this starting point will normally involve the killing of an adult victim, **5-434** arising from a quarrel or loss of temper between two people known to each other. It will not have the characteristics referred to in paragraph N.13. Exceptionally, the starting point may be reduced because of the sort of circumstances described in the next paragraph.

N.12 The normal starting point can be reduced because the murder is one where the offender's culpability is significantly reduced, for example, because: (a) the case came close to the borderline between murder and manslaughter; or (b) the offender suffered from mental disorder, or from a mental disability which lowered the degree of his criminal responsibility for the killing, although not affording a defence of diminished responsibility; or (c) the offender was provoked (in a non-technical sense), such as by prolonged and eventually unsupportable stress; or (d) the case involved an over reaction in self-defence; or (e) the offence was a mercy killing. These factors could justify a reduction to 8/9 years (equivalent to 16/18 years).

The higher starting point of 15/16 years

5-435   **N.13** The higher starting point will apply to cases where the offender's culpability was exceptionally high or the victim was in a particularly vulnerable position. Such cases will be characterised by a feature which makes the crime especially serious, such as: (a) the killing was "professional" or a contract killing; (b) the killing was politically motivated; (c) the killing was done for gain (in the course of a burglary, robbery *etc.*); (d) the killing was intended to defeat the ends of justice (as in the killing of a witness or potential witness); (e) the victim was providing a public service; (f) the victim was a child or was otherwise vulnerable; (g) the killing was racially aggravated; (h) the victim was deliberately targeted because of his or her religion or sexual orientation; (i) there was evidence of sadism, gratuitous violence or sexual maltreatment, humiliation or degradation of the victim before the killing; (j) extensive and/or multiple injuries were inflicted on the victim before death; (k) the offender committed multiple murders.

Variation of the starting point

5-436   **N.14** Whichever starting point is selected in a particular case, it may be appropriate for the trial judge to vary the starting point upwards or downwards, to take account of aggravating or mitigating factors, which relate to either the offence or the offender, in the particular case.

N.15 Aggravating factors relating to the offence can include: (a) the fact that the killing was planned; (b) the use of a firearm; (c) arming with a weapon in advance; (d) concealment of the body, destruction of the crime scene and/or dismemberment of the body; (e) particularly in domestic violence cases, the fact that the murder was the culmination of cruel and violent behaviour by the offender over a period of time.

N.16 Aggravating factors relating to the offender will include the offender's previous record and failures to respond to previous sentences, to the extent that this is relevant to culpability rather than to risk.

N.17 Mitigating factors relating to the offence will include: (a) an intention to cause grievous bodily harm, rather than to kill; (b) spontaneity and lack of pre-meditation.

N.18 Mitigating factors relating to the offender may include: (a) the offender's age; (b) clear evidence of remorse or contrition; (c) a timely plea of guilt.

Very serious cases

5-437   **N.19** A substantial upward adjustment may be appropriate in the most serious cases, for example, those involving a substantial number of murders, or if there are several factors identified as attracting the higher starting point present. In suitable cases, the result might even be a minimum term of 30 years (equivalent to 60 years) which would offer little or no hope of the offender's eventual release. In cases of exceptional gravity, the judge, rather than setting a whole life minimum term, can state that there is no minimum period which could properly be set in that particular case.

N.20 Among the categories of case referred to in paragraph N.13 some offences may be especially grave. These include cases where the victim was performing his duties as a prison officer at the time of the crime or the offence was a terrorist or sexual or sadistic murder or involved a young child. In such a case, a term of 20 years and upwards could be appropriate.

N.21 In following this guidance, judges should bear in mind the conclusion of the court in *Sullivan* that the general effect of both these statements is the same. While Lord Bingham does not identify as many starting points, it is open to the judge to come to exactly the same decision irrespective of which was followed. Both pieces of guidance give the judge a considerable degree of discretion.

5-438   For *Criminal Practice Direction (Sentencing) P* (procedure for announcing the minimum term in open court), see § 5-439 in the main work.

As to the authority referred to in paragraph N.3, see *R. v. Sullivan; R. v. Gibbs; R. v. Elener (Barry) and Elener (Derek)* [2005] 1 Cr.App.R. 3, CA.

B. AUTOMATIC LIFE SENTENCES

Powers of Criminal Courts (Sentencing) Act 2000, s.109

Life sentence for second serious offence

5-440   **109.**—(1) This section applies where—

   (a)   a person is convicted of a serious offence committed after 30th September 1997; and

   (b)   at the time when that offence was committed, he was 18 or over and had been convicted in any part of the United Kingdom of another serious offence.

(2) The court shall impose a life sentence, that is to say—

   (a)   *where the offender is 21 or over when convicted of the offence mentioned in subsection (1)(a) above, a sentence of imprisonment for life,*

   (b)   where he is under 21 at that time, a sentence of custody for life under section 94 above,

[a sentence of imprisonment for life] unless the court is of the opinion that there are exceptional circumstances relating to either of the offences or to the offender which justify its not doing so.

(3) Where the court does not impose a life sentence, it shall state in open court that it is of that opinion and what the exceptional circumstances are.

(4) An offence the sentence for which is imposed under *subsection (2)* above shall not be regarded as an offence the sentence for which is fixed by law.

(5) An offence committed in England and Wales is a serious offence for the purposes of this section if it is any of the following, namely—

   (a)   an attempt to commit murder, a conspiracy to commit murder or an incitement to murder;

   (b)   an offence under section 4 of the Offences Against the Person Act 1861 (soliciting murder);

   (c)   manslaughter;

   (d)   an offence under section 18 of the Offences Against the Person Act 1861 (wounding, or causing grievous bodily harm, with intent);

   (e)   rape or an attempt to commit rape;

   (f)   an offence under section 5 of the Sexual Offences Act 1956 (intercourse with a girl under 13);

   (g)   an offence under section 16 (possession of a firearm with intent to injure), section 17 (use of a firearm to resist arrest) or section 18 (carrying a firearm with criminal intent) of the Firearms Act 1968; and

   (h)   robbery where, at some time during the commission of the offence, the offender had in his possession a firearm or imitation firearm within the meaning of that Act.

(6) An offence committed in Scotland is a serious offence for the purposes of this section if the conviction for it was obtained on indictment in the High Court of Justiciary and it is any of the following, namely—

   (a)   culpable homicide;

   (b)   attempted murder, incitement to commit murder or conspiracy to commit murder;

   (c)   rape or attempted rape;

   (d)   clandestine injury to women or an attempt to cause such injury;

   (e)   sodomy, or an attempt to commit sodomy, where the complainer, that is to say, the person against whom the offence was committed, did not consent;

   (f)   assault where the assault—

      (i)   is aggravated because it was carried out to the victim's severe injury or the danger of the victim's life; or

      (ii)   was carried out with an intention to rape or to ravish the victim;

   (g)   robbery where, at some time during the commission of the offence, the offender had in his possession a firearm or imitation firearm within the meaning of the Firearms Act 1968;

   (h)   an offence under section 16 (possession of a firearm with intent to injure), section 17 (use of a firearm to resist arrest) or section 18 (carrying a firearm with criminal intent) of that Act;

   (i)   lewd, libidinous or indecent behaviour or practices; and

   (j)   an offence under section 5(1) of the Criminal Law (Consolidation) (Scotland) Act 1995 (unlawful intercourse with a girl under 13).

(7) An offence committed in Northern Ireland is a serious offence for the purposes of this section if it is any of the following, namely—

   (a)   an offence falling within any of paragraphs (a) to (e) of subsection (5) above;

   (b)   an offence under section 4 of the Criminal Law Amendment Act 1885 (intercourse with a girl under 14);

   (c)   an offence under Article 17 (possession of a firearm with intent to injure), Article 18(1) (use of a firearm to resist arrest) or Article 19 (carrying a firearm with criminal intent) of the Firearms (Northern Ireland) Order 1981; and

   (d)   robbery where, at some time during the commission of the offence, the offender had in his possession a firearm or imitation firearm within the meaning of that Order.

[This section is printed as amended, as from a day to be appointed, by the CJCSA 2000, s.74, and Sched. 7, para. 189 (substitution of words in square brackets for paras (a) and (b) in subs. (2)). It is repealed, as from April 4, 2005 (Criminal Justice Act 2003 (Commencement No. 8 and Transitional and Saving Provisions) Order 2005 (S.I. 2005 No. 950), by the CJA 2003, s.332, and Sched. 37 Pt 7. For the saving provisions in relation to an offence committed before April 4, 2005, see § 5-2 in the main work.]

Serious offences

5-441   The only attempts which are serious offences are those specifically mentioned: *R. v. Buckland*; *R. v. Newman* [2000] 1 Cr.App.R. 471, CA. Offences under the Firearms Act 1968, s.17(2) are serious offences: *ibid.*; as are offences under sections 16, 17 and 18 of that Act where the firearm was an imitation only: *ibid.*

An offence of robbery is a "serious offence" within section 109(2)(h) if the offence was committed as a joint enterprise where a firearm or imitation was used, even though the offender himself had never had possession of it, provided that there was joint possession of it; where, in relation to the alleged index offence, there is an issue as to whether this was established against the offender, the court must be satisfied that at the earlier hearing the offender admitted, or it was admitted on his behalf, that he was in joint possession of the firearm: *R. v. Flamson* [2002] 2 Cr.App.R.(S.) 48, CA. The court considered that *R. v. Eubank* [2002] 1 Cr.App.R.(S.) 4, CA (§ 24-49 in the main work) had no application to the facts of the case. In *R. v. Murphy* [2003] 1 Cr.App.R.(S.) 39, CA, however, it was held, without reference to *Flamson*, that where there was an issue as to whether the defendant had been in possession of a firearm, the proper way to resolve the issue was, in accordance with *Eubank*, for an appropriate count under the Firearms Act 1968 to be included in the indictment. Where this course had not been adopted, it was not open to the judge to conclude in relation to either the index offence or the fresh offence that it fell within section 109(1)(h); absent an unequivocal admission on the part of the defendant (see *R. v. Benfield*; *R. v. Sobers* [2004] 1 Cr.App.R.(S.) 52, CA).

R. v. Benfield; *R. v. Sobers* was followed in *R. v. Hylands* [2005] 2 Cr.App.R.(S.) 25, CA, where it was said that for an offence of robbery to fall within section 109(5)(h) of the 2000 Act, the qualifying condition relating to a firearm or imitation firearm had to be established either by means of an appropriate count under the Firearms Act 1968 being included in the indictment, or there had to be an unequivocal admission in relation thereto; and this applies where the only issue in relation to the robbery is identity (there being unchallenged evidence before the jury that the robber was in possession of a firearm at the time of the robbery); if there was any doubt about the matter, it was to be resolved in favour of the defendant.

As to whether a conviction at a court-martial in Germany for an offence of wounding with intent to cause grievous bodily harm committed whilst a serving member of the armed forces in Germany may qualify as a "serious offence" within the meaning of section 109(1)(a) of the PC-C(S)A 2000, see *R. v. Sanders, post*, § 5-447.

"exceptional circumstances"

5-442   The meaning of "exceptional circumstances" (s.109(2)) was reconsidered in *R. v. Offen* [2001] 1 W.L.R. 253, CA. Lord Woolf C.J. said that quite apart from the impact of the Human Rights Act 1998, the rationale of the section should be highly relevant in deciding whether or not exceptional circumstances existed. The question whether circumstances were appropriately regarded as "exceptional" must be influenced by the context in which the question was being asked. The policy and intention of Parliament were to protect the public against a person who had committed two serious offences. It therefore could be assumed that the section was not intended to apply to someone in relation to whom it was established that there would be no need for protection in the future. In other words, if the facts showed the statutory assumption was misplaced, then this, in the statutory context, was not the normal situation and in consequence, for the purposes of the section, the position was exceptional. The time that elapsed between the two offences could, but would not necessarily, reflect on whether, after the second serious offence was committed, there was any danger against which the public would need protection. The same was true of two differing offences, and the age of the offender. These were all circumstances which could give rise to the conclusion that what could be normal and not exceptional in a different context was exceptional in this context. If this approach was not adopted, then in the case of the serious offences listed in the section, the gravity of which could vary greatly, the approach to "exceptional circumstances" could be unduly restrictive. The aim of section 2 was not to increase the time offenders spent in prison as a punishment for the offence they had committed, but to provide for an assessment to be made to see whether the offender posed a real risk to the public, in which event his release was deferred. Section 109 established a norm. The norm was that those who commit two serious offences were a danger or risk to the public. If in fact, taking into account all the circumstances relating to a particular offender, he did not create an unacceptable risk to the public, he was an exception to this norm.

Construing section 109 in accordance with the duty imposed on the court by section 3 of the 1998 Act, and taking into account the rationale of the section, gave content to "exceptional circumstances". In the court's judgment, section 109 would not contravene Convention rights if courts applied the section so that it did not result in offenders being sentenced to life imprisonment when they did not constitute a significant risk to the public. Whether there was a significant risk would depend on the evidence which was before the court. If the offender was a significant risk, the court could impose a life sentence under section 109 without contravening the Convention. It would be part of the responsibility of judges to assess the risk to the public that offenders constituted. In many cases the degree of risk that an offender constituted would be established by his record, with or without the assistance of assessments made in reports which were available to the court. If courts needed further assistance, they could call for it when deciding whether a discretionary life sentence should be imposed. There should be no undue difficulty in making a similar assessment when considering whether the court was required to impose an automatic life sentence, although the task would not be straightforward, because of the lack of information as to the first serious offence which will sometimes exist because of the passage of time. This did not mean that the court was approaching the passing of an automatic life sentence as if it was no different from the imposition of a discretionary life sentence. Notwithstanding the interpretation resulting from the application of section 3(1) of the 1998 Act suggested, section 109 would give effect to the intention of Parliament. It would do so, however, in a more just, less arbitrary and more proportionate manner. Section 109 would still mean that a judge was obliged to pass a life sentence in accordance with its terms unless, in all the circumstances, the offender posed no significant risk to the public. There was no such obligation in cases where section 109 did not apply. In addition, if the judge decided not to impose a life sentence under section 109, he would have to give reasons as required by section 109(3). Furthermore, the issue of dangerousness would have to be addressed in every case and a decision made as to whether or not to impose a life sentence.

Offen has since been applied in *R. v. McDonald* [2001] 2 Cr.App.R.(S.) 127, CA (having regard, in particular, to the length of time since the appellant's conviction for his previous "serious" offences (14 years) and to the fact that it was not the appellant but a co-defendant who had produced an imitation firearm in the course of the robbery, although it belonged to the appellant, it would be wrong to conclude that the appellant presented a serious risk of harm to the public so as to justify the imposition of an automatic life sentence); and in *R. v. Kelly (No. 2)* [2002] 1 Cr.App.R.(S.) 85, CA, it was held that the statutory presumption that arises under section 109(2), and which flows from the existence of two qualifying offences remains in place, and has to be displaced by the defendant in any given case; and such displacement may be achieved in a number of ways, including scrutiny of the offending and behaviour pattern, or by positive psychiatric or similar evidence, such evidence being likely to be required if the court is to be persuaded that the presumption cannot apply since the criterion to be established is that there is "no need to protect the public in the future" or "no significant risk to the public".

In *R. v. Baff* [2003] 2 Cr.App.R.(S.) 37, CA, it was said that the use of imitation firearms for the purpose of robbery caused as much fear and alarm to vulnerable members of the public as robbery with a real firearm; and that, if the court were to rule that section 109 did not as a matter of principle apply where the offender limited his offending to robberies with an imitation firearm, it would be creating an exception to an express provision flatly contradicting an aspect of sentencing policy laid down by Parliament.

In *R. v. Richards* [2002] 2 Cr.App.R.(S.) 26, CA, it was held that in considering whether a defendant who qualifies for an automatic life sentence under section 109 presents a significant risk to the public, the judge may take account of a significant risk of the commission of serious offences other than those listed as "serious" in the section itself, for example, burglaries of dwellings or a conspiracy to import hard drugs. For a criticism of this decision, see the commentary in the *Criminal Law Review*. It is inconsistent with the view of the court in *R. v. Fletcher; R. v. Smith* [2002] 1 Cr.App.R.(S.) 82, CA, to the effect that the "danger in point is that of violent or sexual offending."

Richards was not cited in *R. v. Stark* [2002] 2 Cr.App.R.(S.) 104, CA, where there was a high risk of further offences being committed by the appellant, but no significant risk of danger to the public by way of either violent or sexual offences; accordingly, it was held that the case was to be regarded as an exception to the norm, which was that those who committed two serious offences were a danger or risk to the public.

The approach in *R. v. Stark* and *R. v. Fletcher; R. v. Smith* was followed, and that in *Richards* expressly disapproved in *R. v. Magalhaes* [2005] 2 Cr.App.R.(S.) 13, CA.

In *R. v. Frost* [2001] 2 Cr.App.R.(S.) 26, CA, the appellant had been found guilty by a youth court in 1991 of wounding with intent to resist arrest. He was later convicted of wounding with intent to cause grievous bodily harm. The court held that the finding of guilt by the youth court amounted to a "conviction" for the purposes of PCC(S)A 2000, s.109(1), by virtue of the CYPA 1933, s.59. If the appellant had been older and had been subject to a probation order, the "conviction" would have been deemed not to be a conviction by virtue of the PCCA 1973, s.13(1) (*rep.*), but this provision did not apply to a supervision order. The anomaly which resulted from this amounted to an "exceptional circumstance" for the purposes of section 109, and the sentence of life imprisonment was quashed, even though it could not be said that the offender presented no significant risk to the public.

The fact that the offender is mentally ill and eligible for a hospital order does not in itself amount to an "exceptional circumstance" for this purpose: see *R. v. Newman* [2000] 2 Cr.App.R.(S.) 227, CA; *R. v. Drew* [2003] 2 Cr.App.R. 24, HL (where a submission that an automatic life sentence on conviction of wounding with intent constituted inhuman or degrading treatment was rejected; having been transferred administratively to hospital within a few days of the passing of sentence, the appellant was receiving the same treatment as he would have received had he been made subject to a hospital order, and he could not complain of the stigma attaching to the sentence as he had been convicted by a jury, who must therefore have been satisfied as to his intent).

On appeal, the issue is whether the offender created an unacceptable risk to the public at the time when he was sentenced, not at the time when the Court of Appeal is considering the matter: see *R. v. Watkins* [2003] 1 Cr.App.R.(S.) 16, CA; *R. v. Noorkoiv* [2002] 2 Cr.App.R.(S.) 91, CA.

C. Minimum Fixed Term Sentences

(1) Legislation
Powers of Criminal Courts (Sentencing) Act 2000, ss.112–115

Offences under service law

5-447   In *R. v. Sanders* [2007] 1 Cr.App.R.(S.) 74, CA, it was held that the effect of section 114 of the PCC(S)A 2000 was limited to deeming the conviction to have been in England and Wales; it did not deem the offence to have been committed in England and Wales; where, therefore, the appellant had previously been convicted of an offence under section 70 of the Army Act 1955 and the corresponding civil offence had been one of those listed in section 109(5), but the offence had been committed abroad, he was not to be regarded as having previously been convicted of a serious offence, since, under section 109(5), an offence would only be "serious" if committed in England and Wales; section 114 would bite only in relation to convictions under section 70 where the offence occurred in England and Wales. It should be noted that the repeal of the words "a serious offence" in section 114(1)(b) is of no effect where an offender is being dealt with for an offence committed prior to April 4, 2005.

"unjust"

★**5-452**   Where the minimum sentence provisions of section 110 of the PCC(S)A 2000 (§ 5-443 in the main work) are engaged, with the burden being on the defendant to show that such a sentence would be "unjust", sentencing hearings should usually be adjourned to obtain a pre-sentence report: *R. v. Densham* [2015] 1 Cr.App.R.(S.) 37, CA.

The fact that an offender did not receive custodial sentences for the previous drug trafficking convictions that brought him within section 110 of the 2000 Act could not amount to "particular circumstances" within subsection (2) that would make it unjust to impose the minimum sentence required by that section upon his conviction for a third Class A drug trafficking offence: *R. v. Gallone* [2014] 2 Cr.App.R.(S.) 57, CA.

The minimum sentence provisions in section 111 of the 2000 Act (§ 5-444 in the main work) could, however, be avoided as leading to an "unjust" result where the first of the defendant's two previous domestic burglaries were committed by him (now aged 19) when he was 13-years-old at his mother's home when he wasn't living there, and had been dealt with by a supervision order: *R. v. Taylor* [2014] 2 Cr.App.R.(S.) 85, CA.

D. Discretionary Custodial Sentences

(1) General restrictions

(a) *Legislation*

Criminal Justice Act 2003, ss.152, 153

General restrictions on imposing discretionary custodial sentences

As from a day to be appointed, the Criminal Justice and Courts Act 2015, s.28(8), and Sched. 5, **5-458** paras 9 and 14(1) and (2), amend section 152(1)(b) of the 2003 Act, so as to substitute the words "a provision mentioned in subsection (1A)" for the words from "section 1A(5)" to the end.

As from a day to be appointed, the Criminal Justice and Courts Act 2015, s.28(8), and Sched. 5, paras 9 and 14(1) and (3), amend section 152 of the 2003 Act, so as to insert, after subsection (1), a new subsection (1A), as follows—

"(1A) The provisions referred to in subsection (1)(b) are—
(a) section 1(2B) or 1A(5) of the Prevention of Crime Act 1953;
(b) section 51A(2) of the Firearms Act 1968;
(c) section 139(6B), 139A(5B) or 139AA(7) of the Criminal Justice Act 1988;
(d) section 110(2) or 111(2) of the Sentencing Act;
(e) section 224A, 225(2) or 226(2) of this Act;
(f) section 29(4) or (6) of the Violent Crime Reduction Act 2006.".

Length of discretionary custodial sentences: general provision

As from a day to be appointed, the Criminal Justice and Courts Act 2015, s.28(8), and Sched. 5, **5-459** paras 9 and 15, amend section 153 of the 2003 Act, so as (i) in subsection (2), to substitute the words "the provisions listed in subsection (3)" for the words "section 1A(5)" to "this Act", and (ii) after subsection (2), to insert a new subsection (3), as follows—

"(3) The provisions referred to in subsection (2) are—
(a) sections 1(2B) and 1A(5) of the Prevention of Crime Act 1953;
(b) section 51A(2) of the Firearms Act 1968;
(c) sections 139(6B), 139A(5B) and 139AA(7) of the Criminal Justice Act 1988;
(d) sections 110(2) and 111(2) of the Sentencing Act;
(e) sections 226A(4) and 226B(2) of this Act;
(f) section 29(4) or (6) of the Violent Crime Reduction Act 2006.".

(b) *Authorities*

Criminal Practice Direction (Sentencing) H [2013] 1 W.L.R. 3164

Community impact statements

A community impact statement should be limited to expressing the effect of particular crimes ★**5-467a** on a particular community; it most certainly should not be used as a character assassination of the defendant (as where it was suggested that the defendant was, in effect, the "biggest and nastiest drug dealer in the locality"): *R. v. Skelton* [2015] 1 Cr.App.R.(S.) 34, CA.

(c) *Legislation (offences committed before April 4, 2005)*

Powers of Criminal Courts (Sentencing) Act 2000, ss.79, 80

General restrictions on imposing discretionary custodial sentences

5-469   79.—(1) This section applies where a person is convicted of an offence punishable with a custodial sentence other than one—

    (a) fixed by law; or

    (b) falling to be imposed under section 109(2), 110(2) or 111(2) below.

(2) Subject to subsection (3) below, the court shall not pass a custodial sentence on the offender unless it is of the opinion—

    (a) that the offence, or the combination of the offence and one or more offences associated with it, was so serious that only such a sentence can be justified for the offence; or

    (b) where the offence is a violent or sexual offence, that only such a sentence would be adequate to protect the public from serious harm from him.

(3) Nothing in subsection (2) above shall prevent the court from passing a custodial sentence on the offender if he fails to express his willingness to comply with—

    (a) a requirement which is proposed by the court to be included in a community rehabilitation order or supervision order and which requires an expression of such willingness; or

    (b) a requirement which is proposed by the court to be included in a drug treatment and testing order or an order under section 52(4) above (order to provide samples). In relation to an offence committed before 1st October 1997:

(4) Where a court passes a custodial sentence, it shall—

    (a) in a case not falling within subsection (3) above, state in open court that it is of the opinion that either or both of paragraphs (a) and (b) of subsection (2) above apply and why it is of that opinion;.and

    (b) in any case, explain to the offender in open court and in ordinary language why it is passing a custodial sentence on him.

(5) A magistrates' court shall cause a reason stated by it under subsection (4) above to be specified in the warrant of commitment and to be entered in the register.

[This section is printed as amended by the CJCSA 2000, s.74 and Sched. 7, para. 1. It is repealed, as from April 4, 2005 (Criminal Justice Act 2003 (Commencement No. 8 and Transitional and Saving Provisions) Order 2005 (S.I. 2005 No. 950)), by the CJA 2003, s.332, and Sched. 37, Pt 7. As to the saving provision in relation to offences committed before April 4, 2005, see § 5-2 in the main work.]

In relation to an offence committed before October 1, 1997, see the transitional provision in Sched. 11, para. 4(d).

Length of discretionary custodial sentences: general provision

5-470   80.—(1) This section applies where a court passes a custodial sentence other than one fixed by law or falling to be imposed under section 109(2) below.

(2) Subject to sections 110(2) and 111(2) below, the custodial sentence shall be—

    (a) for such term (not exceeding the permitted maximum) as in the opinion of the court is commensurate with the seriousness of the offence, or the combination of the offence and one or more offences associated with it; or

    (b) where the offence is a violent or sexual offence, for such longer term (not exceeding that maximum) as in the opinion of the court is necessary to protect the public from serious harm from the offender.

(3) Where the court passes a custodial sentence for a term longer than is commensurate with the seriousness of the offence, or the combination of the offence and one or more offences associated with it, the court shall—

    (a) state in open court that it is of the opinion that subsection (2)(b) above applies and why it is of that opinion; and

    (b) explain to the offender in open court and in ordinary language why the sentence is for such a term.

(4) A custodial sentence for an indeterminate period shall be regarded for the purposes of subsections (2) and (3) above as a custodial sentence for a term longer than any actual term.

(5) Subsection (3) above shall not apply in any case where the court passes a custodial sentence falling to be imposed under subsection (2) of section 110 or 111 below which is for the minimum term specified in that subsection.

[This section is repealed, as from April 4, 2005 (Criminal Justice Act 2003 (Commencement No. 8 and Transitional and Saving Provisions) Order 2005 (S.I. 2005 No. 950)), by the CJA 2003, s.332, and Sched. 37, Pt 7. As to the saving provision in relation to offences committed before April 4, 2005, see § 5-2 in the main work.]

Powers of Criminal Courts (Sentencing) Act 2000, s.161

Meaning of "associated offence", "sexual offence", "violent offence" and "protecting the public from serious harm"

161.—(1) [*See § 5-2 in the main work.*]   **5-471**

(2) In this Act, "sexual offence" means any of the following—

    (f)   an offence under the Protection of Children Act 1978;

    (fa) an offence under section 3 of the Sexual Offences (Amendment) Act 2000;

    (fa) an offence under any provision of Part 1 of the Sexual Offences Act 2003; except section 52, 53 or 71

    (g)   an offence under section 1 of the Criminal Law Act 1977; of conspiracy to commit any of the offences in paragraphs (a) to (f) above;

    (h)   an offence under section 1 of the Criminal Attempts Act 1981; of attempting to commit any of those offences;

    (i)   an offence of inciting another to commit any of those offences.

(3) In this Act, "violent offence" means an offence which leads, or is intended or likely to lead, to a person's death or to physical injury to a person, and includes an offence which is required to be charged as arson (whether or not it would otherwise fall within this definition).

(4) In this Act any reference, in relation to an offender convicted of a violent or sexual offence, to protecting the public from serious harm from him shall be construed as a reference to protecting members of the public from death or serious personal injury, whether physical or psychological, occasioned by further such offences committed by him.

[Subss. (2) to (4) are printed as amended and repealed in part, by the Sexual Offences (Amendment) Act 2000, s.6(1); and the SOA 2003, ss.139 and 140, and Sched. 6, para. 4 (insertion of second para. (fa) in subs. (2)), and Sched. 7 (repeal of subs. (2)(a)–(e), the failure to repeal the first para. (fa) being accounted for by the draftsman having overlooked the amendment made by the 2000 Act). The amendments effected by the 2003 Act took effect on May 1, 2004 (Sexual Offences Act 2003 (Commencement) Order 2004 (S.I. 2004 No. 874)). For the former provisions, which will continue to apply in relation to offences committed before that date (Interpretation Act 1978, s.16 (Appendix B-16)), see the 2004 edition of this work. Subss. (2) to (4) are repealed, as from April 4, 2005 (Criminal Justice Act 2003 (Commencement No. 8 and Transitional and Saving Provisions) Order 2005 (S.I. 2005 No. 950)), by the CJA 2003, s.332, and Sched. 7. As to the saving provision in relation to offences committed before April 4, 2005, see § 5-2 in the main work.]

"Violent" and "sexual" offences

Whether any particular offence is a violent offence depends on the facts of the individual   **5-472**
offence. An offence which leads to or is intended to lead only to psychological injury is not a "violent offence" but it is not necessary that serious harm should have been caused (see *R. v. Robinson* [1994] 1 W.L.R. 168, CA). Nor does it have to be established that physical injury was a probability: *R. v. Szczerba* [2002] 2 Cr.App.R.(S.) 86, CA.

In *R. v. Cochrane*, 15 Cr.App.R.(S.) 708, CA, it was held that a robbery in which the victim was threatened with a knife was a "violent offence" as the incident could have resulted in injury, either accidentally or if the victim had resisted. See also *R. v. Bibby*, 16 Cr.App.R.(S.) 127, CA. For cases of robbery by persons armed with a firearm, see *R. v. Touriq Khan*, 16 Cr.App.R.(S.) 180, CA, *R. v. Palin*, 16 Cr.App.R.(S.) 888, CA, and *R. v. Baker* [2001] 1 Cr.App.R.(S.) 55, CA. An offence of threatening to kill which does not involve the infliction of physical injury will not normally be a "violent offence": see *R. v. Richart*, 16 Cr.App.R.(S.) 977, CA, *R. v. Ragg* [1996] 1 Cr.App.R.(S.) 176, CA and *R. v. Birch* [2002] 1 Cr.App.R.(S.) 129, CA; but see *R. v. Wilson* [1998] 1 Cr.App.R.(S.) 341, CA.

Attempted arson is "an offence which is required to be charged as arson" and is accordingly a "violent offence" within section 161(3): *R. v. Guirke* [1997] 1 Cr.App.R.(S.) 170, CA.

"Serious harm" (s.161(4) of the Act of 2000)

See § 5-495 in the main work.   **5-473**

The criterion of seriousness

5-474   For discussion of the relevant authorities in relation to section 79(1), see § 5-465 in the main work.

Sentences commensurate with the seriousness of the offence

5-475   For relevant considerations where a court is deciding what term of custody is commensurate with an offence or group of offences, see § 5-466 in the main work.

Longer than normal sentences

5-476   For the definitions of "sexual offence" and "violent offence", see section 161(2) and (3) of the PCC(S)A 2000 (*ante*, § 5-471); and for the authorities in relation thereto, see *ante*, § 5-472. For the construction of references to "protecting the public from serious harm", see section 161(4) of the 2000 Act (*ante*, § 5-471); and the authorities referred to at §§ 5-495 *et seq.* in the main work.

An isolated offence, however serious, will rarely be sufficient to justify a longer than normal sentence under section 80(2)(b), whether the offence is violent or sexual, or both: *R. v. Walsh*, 16 Cr.App.R.(S.) 204, CA; *R. v. Mumtaz Ali*, 16 Cr.App.R.(S.) 692, CA. A longer than commensurate sentence may be passed on an offender with no previous convictions: *R. v. Thomas*, 16 Cr.App.R.(S.) 616, CA.

A court deciding whether to draw the inference that the offender is likely to commit further violent or sexual offences may need to examine the circumstances of the current offence in some detail, going beyond what would be necessary if only a commensurate sentence were in issue: *R. v. Oudkerk*, 16 Cr.App.R.(S.) 172, CA. Equally, if the inference is to be based on a previous conviction, the court may need to examine the circumstances of that offence in detail: *R. v. Samuels*, 16 Cr.App.R.(S.) 856, CA.

An offender may satisfy the requirements of section 80(2)(b) even though the members of the public who are at risk from him are a small group, or possibly an individual: *R. v. Hashi*, 16 Cr.App.R.(S.) 121, CA. Where the offender's behaviour is directed at a small group of people, who can be protected from him by other means, a longer than commensurate sentence may not be justified: *R. v. Nicholas*, 15 Cr.App.R.(S.) 381, CA; *R. v. Swain*, 15 Cr.App.R.(S.) 765, CA; *R. v. L.*, 15 Cr.App.R.(S.) 501, CA.

In many cases the inference of dangerousness will be based in part on psychiatric evidence: *R. v. Lyons*, 15 Cr.App.R.(S.) 460, CA; *R. v. Fawcett*, 16 Cr.App.R.(S.) 55, CA; *R. v. Etchells* [1996] 1 Cr.App.R.(S.) 163, CA.

The principles which should be applied in deciding the length of a longer than commensurate sentence were considered in *R. v. Mansell*, 15 Cr.App.R.(S.) 771, CA; and *R. v. Crow; R. v. Pennington*, 16 Cr.App.R.(S.) 409, CA. Lord Taylor C.J. said that some allowance should usually be made, even in the worst cases, for a plea of guilty. A sentence imposed under section 80(2)(b), whilst long enough to give necessary protection for the public, should still bear a reasonable relationship to the offence for which it was imposed.

This principle was not applied in *R. v. Chapman* [2000] 1 Cr.App.R. 77, CA, where it was said that there was no necessary ratio between the part of the sentence intended to punish and the part intended to protect. There was no objection in principle if the court regarded a sentence of two years as necessary to punish, but an additional term of six or eight years as necessary to protect, making a total term of eight or 10 years. *Chapman* was followed in *R. v. Wilson* [2000] 2 Cr.App.R.(S.) 323, CA, but not apparently in *R. v. De Silva* [2000] 2 Cr.App.R.(S.) 408, CA.

5-477   The question whether a longer than commensurate sentence may properly be imposed to run consecutively to a sentence of imprisonment was considered by the Court of Appeal in *R. v. Everleigh* [2002] 1 Cr.App.R.(S.) 32. The court considered *R. v. King*, 16 Cr.App.R.(S.) 987; *R. v. Walters* [1997] 2 Cr.App.R.(S.) 87; *R. v. Johnson* [1998] 1 Cr.App.R.(S.) 126; *R. v. Cuthbertson and Jenks* [2000] 1 Cr.App.R.(S.) 359; *R. v. Parsons* [2000] 1 Cr.App.R.(S.) 428; *R. v. Blades* [2000] 1 Cr.App.R.(S.) 463; *R. v. Sullivan* [2000] 2 Cr.App.R.(S.) 318; *R. v. Sowden* [2000] 2 Cr.App.R.(S.) 360; *R. v. Wilson* [2000] 2 Cr.App.R.(S.) 323; and *R. v. Ellis* [2001] 1 Cr.App.R.(S.) 43. Accepting that not all of these of authorities could be reconciled, the court held that they showed that it was inappropriate to pass a longer than the normal sentence to run consecutively to another sentence imposed on the same occasion, because a longer than normal sentence is intended in itself to protect the public from serious harm, without the need for any additional penalty in relation to other conduct punishable at the same time. Secondly, there was nothing inappropriate, but on the contrary it might be desirable, for a longer than normal sentence to be passed consecutively either to a sentence passed on an earlier occasion (*Wilson*) or to a period of return to custody ordered under the PCC(S)A 2000, s.116, which was a consequence of a sentence passed on an earlier occasion (*Blades*). As was pointed out in *Blades*, it was important that both the public and the defendant should know that a sentence once passed would have to be served (subject to any reduction which might be appropriate in accordance with *R. v. Taylor* [1998] 1 Cr.App.R.(S.) 312). It was desirable that the sentencing judge, if imposing a consecutive sentence, should make it plain what were the factors which he had taken into consideration in so passing the sentence under section 80(2)(b).

In *R. v. Christie*, 16 Cr.App.R.(S.) 469, CA, it was said to be wrong to add an additional period to the sentence under section 80(2)(b) if the commensurate sentence already incorporated an element for the protection of the public. In *R. v. Campbell* [1997] 1 Cr.App.R.(S.) 119, CA, it was held that if the sentencing guidelines for a particular offence included an element for the protection of the public, the sentencer should decide what was the appropriate sentence, leaving out of account any element for the protection of the public, and should then add the greater element needed for the protection of the public from serious harm under section 80(2)(b). This would avoid the risk of imposing an element of the sentence twice over. In *R. v. Gabbidon and Bramble* [1997] 2 Cr.App.R.(S.) 19, CA, this approach was described as too difficult an exercise in forensic archaeology; it was better that the sentencer simply applied the principle of balance stated by Lord Taylor C.J. in *R. v. Mansell*, 15 Cr.App.R.(S.) 771.

In a case where a longer than normal sentence is passed on one offender and a commensurate sentence on the other, it does not necessarily follow that there is any disparity of sentence, provided that there is evidence of continuing dangerousness on the part of one offender and not in the case of the other: *R. v. Bestwick and Huddlestone*, 16 Cr.App.R.(S.) 168, CA.

A longer than commensurate sentence may be imposed on an offender under section 80(2)(b) even though he does not qualify for a sentence of life imprisonment under the criteria established for that form of sentence: *R. v. Helm*, 16 Cr.App.R.(S.) 834, CA. The enactment of section 80(2)(b) has not reduced the requirements for a life sentence: *R. v. Roche*, 16 Cr.App.R.(S.) 849, CA.

Where a sentencer has in mind the possibility of passing a longer than commensurate sentence, he should warn counsel for the defendant of his intentions and invite submissions on the question: *R. v. Baverstock*, 96 Cr.App.R. 435, CA. This point has been repeated in many cases; it is particularly important when any question arises as to whether the offence is a "violent offence" for the purposes of the Act. Where a court passes a longer than commensurate sentence it is required by the PCC(S)A 2000, s.80(3) to state in open court that it is of the opinion that subsection (2)(b) applies and why it is of that opinion, and explain to the offender in open court and in ordinary language why the sentence is for such a term. Failure to comply with this obligation does not invalidate the sentence: *Baverstock, ante*; *R. v. Thomas*, 16 Cr.App.R.(S.) 616, CA. Even where the nature of the expected future harm is obvious, the sentencer should ensure that he has properly identified what the harm was before he proceeded to sentence, and should point out clearly and in straightforward terms what it was that he considered to be the serious harm in question: *R. v. Bacon*, 16 Cr.App.R.(S.) 1031, CA.

Where a court fails to pass a longer than commensurate sentence where such a sentence should be passed, the resulting sentence may be "unduly lenient" and may be the subject of a reference by the Attorney-General under the CJA 1988, s.36: *Att-Gen.'s Reference (No. 9 of 1994) (R. v. Groves)*, 16 Cr.App.R.(S.) 366, CA. Where a person sentenced to a longer than commensurate sentence persuades the Court of Appeal that the case is not one in which a longer than commensurate sentence should have been passed, the court is not bound to substitute a shorter sentence; its powers are at large, and it may approve the sentence passed as a commensurate sentence if it considers it appropriate to do so: *R. v. Palmer* [1996] 2 Cr.App.R.(S.) 68, CA; and see also *R. v. Henshaw* [1996] 2 Cr.App.R.(S.) 310, CA; and *R. v. Rai and Robinson* [2000] 2 Cr.App.R.(S.) 120, CA.

(2) Imprisonment

(c) *Life sentences and extended sentences for dangerous offenders*

Introduction

A court was not in breach of Article 5 (right to liberty and security (§ 16-53 in the main work)), **5-488** taken with Article 14 (prohibition on discrimination (*ibid.*, § 16-177)), or 7 (prohibition on heavier penalty than that available at time offence committed (*ibid.*, § 16-130)) of the ECHR, where it imposed a sentence of imprisonment for public protection (s.225(3) and (4) of the CJA 2003), rather than the lesser sentence of an "old-style extended sentence" (s.227 of the 2003 Act), where the appellant was convicted before, but sentenced after, the commencement of the repeal of the relevant provisions of the 2003 Act by the LASPOA 2012: *R. v. Docherty* [2014] 2 Cr.App.R.(S.) 76, CA (considering the Legal Aid, Sentencing and Punishment of Offenders Act 2012 (Commencement No. 4 and Saving Provisions) Order 2012 (S.I. 2012 No. 2906) (*ibid.*, § 5-2a), *Att.-Gen.'s Reference (No. 27 of 2013) (R. v. Burinskas)* (*ibid.*, § 5-510), and *Scoppola v. Italy (No. 2)* (*ibid.*, § 16-136)).

Criminal Justice Act 2003, ss.224–229

Life sentence for second listed offence

★**5-495a**   As from April 13, 2015 (Criminal Justice and Courts Act 2015 (Commencement No. 1, Saving and Transitional Provisions) Order 2015 (S.I. 2015 No. 778)), the Criminal Justice and Courts Act 2015, s.5(1), amended section 224A of the 2003 Act, so as to insert at the end, a new subsection (12), as follows—

> "(12) Where an offence is found to have been committed over a period of two or more days, or at some time during a period of two or more days, it must be taken for the purposes of subsections (1)(b) and (4)(a) to have been committed on the last of those days.".

★   The fact that an offender had stayed out of trouble for over a decade since his release from a previous sentence did not make it "unjust" to impose an automatic life sentence under section 224A of the 2003 Act: *R. v. Fernandez* [2015] 1 Cr.App.R.(S.) 35, CA.

Extended sentence for certain violent or sexual offences: persons 18 or over

5-498   With effect from February 1, 2015 (Offender Rehabilitation Act 2014 (Commencement No. 2) Order 2015 (S.I. 2015 No. 40)), sections 8 and 21 of, and Schedule 7 to, the 2014 Act (see the main work) were brought into force.

Extended sentence for certain violent or sexual offences: persons under 18

5-499   As to the commencement of section 8 of the Offender Rehabilitation Act 2014 (see the main work), see *ante*, § 5-498.

Criminal Justice Act 2003, ss.231, 232, 232A

Certificates of conviction

5-502   As from April 13, 2015 (Criminal Justice and Courts Act 2015 (Commencement No. 1, Saving and Transitional Provisions) Order 2015 (S.I. 2015 No. 778)), the Criminal Justice and Courts Act 2015, s.5(2), amended section 232A of the 2003 Act, so as to substitute the words "sections 224A and 226A" for the words "section 224A".

Specified violent and sexual offences

5-503   As from April 13, 2015 (Criminal Justice and Courts Act 2015 (Commencement No. 1, Saving and Transitional Provisions) Order 2015 (S.I. 2015 No. 778)), Schedule 15 to the CJA 2003 was further amended by the Criminal Justice and Courts Act 2015, s.2(1) to (7), so as (i) to add an offence under section 4 of the Explosive Substances Act 1883 (§ 23-72 in the main work) to the list of specified violent offences, (ii) to redraft the paragraphs relating to inchoate offences in Part 1 to include "aiding, abetting, counselling or procuring the commission of an offence specified in the previous paragraphs of this Part", "an attempt to commit such an offence", "conspiracy to commit such an offence", "incitement to commit such an offence", "an offence under Part 2 of the Serious Crime Act 2007 in relation to which an offence specified in the preceding paragraphs of this Part ... is the offence (or one of the offences) which the person intended or believed would be committed", attempt, conspiracy or incitement to commit murder, or an offence under Part 2 of the 2007 Act in relation to which murder is the offence (or one of the offences) which the person intended or believed would be committed, (iii) to replace the reference to the offence of keeping a brothel (SOA 1956, s.33) with a reference to the offence of keeping a brothel used for prostitution (1956

Act, s.33A (*ibid.*, § 20-229), and (iv) at the end of Part 2, to replace the reference to inchoate offences with specific references to "aiding, abetting, counselling or procuring the commission of an
offence specified in this Part", "an attempt to commit such an offence", "conspiracy to commit
such an offence", "incitement to commit such an offence", and "an offence under Part 2 of the
Serious Crime Act 2007 in relation to which an offence specified in this Part ... is the offence (or
one of the offences) which the person intended or believed would be committed".

The amendments apply in relation to a person sentenced for an offence on or after the day on
which they come into force, whenever the offence was committed (2015 Act, s.2(8)). However, section 2(8) is limited in its application to sections 225(1)(a) (§ 5-496 in the main work) and 226(1)(a)
(*ibid.*, § 5-497) of the CJA 2003 and sections 219(1)(b) and 221(1)(b) of the AFA 2006 (2015 Act,
s.2(9)). For the purposes of those provisions of the 2003 and 2006 Acts, the amendments to Part 1
of Schedule 15 consisting of the addition of the reference to section 4 of the 1883 Act and of the
references to inchoate offences in connection with murder apply only in relation to a person
sentenced for an offence that was committed on or after the day on which they come into force
(2015 Act, s.2(10)). Where an offence is found to have been committed over a period of two or
more days, or at some time during a period of two or more days, it must be taken for the
purposes of subsection (10) to have been committed on the last of those days (2015 Act, s.2(11)).

As from April 13, 2015 (S.I. 2015 No. 778 (*ante*)), Part 1 of Schedule 15 to the CJA 2003 was ★
further amended by the Criminal Justice and Courts Act 2015, s.29(4), and Sched. 6, para. 11, so
as to include the new offence under section 3ZC of the RTA 1988 (see *post*, § 32-76a) in the list of
specified violent offences. The amendment has effect only in relation to driving which occurs after
it comes into force (2015 Act, s.29(5)).

With effect from May 3, 2015 (Serious Crime Act 2015 (Commencement No. 1) Regulations ★
2015 (S.I. 2015 No. 820)), Schedule 15 to the 2003 Act was further amended by the SCA 2015,
s.85(1), and Sched. 4, para. 68(1) and (3) to (5), so as to amend the references to sections 48 to 50
of the SOA 2003 to reflect the amendments to those provisions made by section 68 of the 2015
Act (as to which, see *post*, §§ 20-160, 20-167, 20-161). This involves no change of substance.

As from a day to be appointed, Schedule 15 to the 2003 Act is further amended by the SCA ★
2015, s.85(1), and Sched. 4, para. 68(1) and (2), so as to include an offence under section 15A of
the SOA 2003 (as to which, see *post*, § 20-95a) in the list of specified sexual offences.

As from a day to be appointed, Schedule 15 to the CJA 2003 is further amended by the ★
Modern Slavery Act 2015, s.6(1) to (3), so as to insert references to the new offence under section
1 of the 2015 Act (slavery, servitude and forced or compulsory labour) to Part 1, and the new offence under section 2 (human trafficking) to Part 2 if it is committed with a view to sexual
exploitation, and otherwise to Part 1.

Schedule 15B offences (ss.224A(1), (4), 226A(2), 232A(a), 246A)

As from April 13, 2015 (Criminal Justice and Courts Act 2015 (Commencement No. 1, Saving ★**5-505**
and Transitional Provisions) Order 2015 (S.I. 2015 No. 778)), the Criminal Justice and Courts Act
2015, s.3, amended Schedule 15B to the CJA 2003, so as (i) in Part 1, to add references to the offences under the Offences against the Person Act 1861, ss.28 and 29 (§§ 19-288, 19-289 in the
main work), the Explosive Substances Act 1883, ss.2 to 4 (*ibid.*, §§ 23-62 *et seq.*), the Terrorism Act
2000, s.54 (*ibid.*, § 25-63) and the Terrorism Act 2006, s.6 (*ibid.*, § 25-193) (s.3(1) and (2) to (5)),
and (ii) to expand Part 4 (certain offences under the law of Scotland, Northern Ireland or a
member state other than the United Kingdom) to include corresponding service offences in other
member states (s.3(1) and (6) to (8)). For the purposes of section 224A of the CJA 2003 (*ibid.*, §
5-495a) and section 218A of the AFA 2006, these amendments apply only in relation to a person
sentenced for an offence that was committed on or after the day on which they come into force
(s.3(9)). For the purposes of section 226A of the 2003 Act (*ibid.*, § 5-498) and section 219A of the
2006 Act, these amendments apply in relation to a person sentenced for an offence on or after the
day on which they come into force, whenever the offence was committed (s.3(10)). For the
purposes of section 246A of the 2003 Act (*ibid.*, § 5-656), the amendments made by section 3(2) to
(5) of the 2015 Act apply in relation to a person serving an extended sentence imposed on or
after the day on which they come into force, whenever the offence in question was committed
(s.3(11)). Where an offence is found to have been committed over a period of two or more days,
or at some time during a period of two or more days, it must be taken for the purposes of section
3(9) to have been committed on the last of those days (s.3(12)).

★   With effect from May 3, 2015 (Serious Crime Act 2015 (Commencement No. 1) Regulations 2015 (S.I. 2015 No. 820)), Schedule 15B to the 2003 Act was further amended by the SCA 2015, s.85(1), and Sched. 4, para. 69, so as to amend the references to sections 48 to 50 of the SOA 2003 to reflect the amendments to those provisions made by section 68 of the 2015 Act (as to which, see *post*, §§ 20-160, 20-167, 20-161). This involves no change of substance.

★   As from a day to be appointed, Schedule 15B to the CJA 2003 is further amended by the Modern Slavery Act 2015, s.6(1) and (4), so as to insert references to the new offences under sections 1 (slavery, servitude and forced or compulsory labour) and 2 (human trafficking) of the 2015 Act.

Application of principles

5-520   As to *R. v. Terrell* (as to which, see the main work), see *post*, § 20-325.

Fixing the minimum term (life sentences not fixed by law)

Powers of Criminal Courts (Sentencing) Act 2000, s.82A

Determination of tariffs

★**5-531**   As from April 13, 2015 (Criminal Justice and Courts Act 2015 (Commencement No. 1, Saving and Transitional Provisions) Order 2015 (S.I. 2015 No. 778)), the Criminal Justice and Courts Act 2015, s.15(1), substituted section 82A(3)(b) of the 2000 Act, as follows—

> "(b) the effect that the following would have if the court had sentenced the offender to a term of imprisonment—
>> (i) section 240ZA of the Criminal Justice Act 2003 (crediting periods of remand in custody);
>> (ii) section 246 of the Armed Forces Act 2006 (equivalent provision for service courts);
>> (iii) any direction which the court would have given under section 240A of the Criminal Justice Act 2003 (crediting periods of remand on bail subject to certain types of condition);".

This amendment applies in relation to a person sentenced before the day on which it comes into force as well as in relation to a person sentenced on or after that day (2015 Act, s.15(10)).

5-533   As to the further amendment of section 82A of the PCC(S)A 2000 (see the main work), see *ante*, § 5-531.

★   For a case where fixing the minimum term attaching to a discretionary life sentence at other than half the notional determinate term was held to have been justified, see *R. v. Rossi* [2015] 1 Cr.App.R.(S.) 15, CA. For criticism of this approach, see CLW/15/08/13.

(ca) *Special custodial sentence for offenders of particular concern*

★**5-534a**   As from April 13, 2015 (Criminal Justice and Courts Act 2015 (Commencement No. 1, Saving and Transitional Provisions) Order 2015 (S.I. 2015 No. 778)), the Criminal Justice and Courts Act 2015, s.6, and Sched. 1, paras 1 and 2, inserted a new section 236A into the CJA 2003.

Criminal Justice Act 2003, s.236A

Special custodial sentence for certain offenders of particular concern

     236A.—(1) Subsection (2) applies where—
         (a)   a person is convicted of an offence listed in Schedule 18A (whether the offence was committed before or after this section comes into force),
         (b)   the person was aged 18 or over when the offence was committed, and
         (c)   the court does not impose one of the following for the offence—
             (i)   a sentence of imprisonment for life, or
             (ii)   an extended sentence under section 226A.
     (2) If the court imposes a sentence of imprisonment for the offence, the term of the sentence must be equal to the aggregate of—
         (a)   the appropriate custodial term, and
         (b)   a further period of 1 year for which the offender is to be subject to a licence.
     (3) The "appropriate custodial term" is the term that, in the opinion of the court, ensures that the sentence is appropriate.
     (4) The term of a sentence of imprisonment imposed under this section for an offence must not

exceed the term that, at the time the offence was committed, was the maximum term permitted for the offence.

(5) The references in subsections (1)(c) and (2) to a sentence imposed for the offence include a sentence imposed for the offence and one or more offences associated with it.

(6) The Secretary of State may by order amend Schedule 18A by—

    (a) adding offences, or

    (b) varying or omitting offences listed in the Schedule.

(7) An order under subsection (6) may, in particular, make provision that applies in relation to the sentencing of a person for an offence committed before the provision comes into force.

Section 236A applies in relation to the sentencing of a person for an offence after it is brought into force, whether the person was convicted of the offence before or after it was brought into force (2015 Act, s.6(2)(b), and Sched. 1, para. 9(1)). Paragraph 10(1) and (2) of Schedule 1 to the 2015 Act (given effect by s.6(2)(b)) provide that in relation to any time before the coming into force of section 61 of the CJCSA 2000, section 236A applies as if at the end there were inserted, subsection (8), as follows—

"(8) In the case of a person aged under 21, this section applies as if the references to imprisonment were to detention in a young offender institution.".

As from April 13, 2015 (Criminal Justice and Courts Act 2015 (Commencement No. 1, Saving and Transitional Provisions) Order 2015 (S.I. 2015 No. 778)), the Criminal Justice and Courts Act 2015, s.6(1), and Sched. 1, paras 1 and 4, inserted a new Schedule 18A into the CJA 2003. **★5-534b**

Criminal Justice Act 2003, Sched. 18A

SENTENCE UNDER SECTION 236A: OFFENCES

Terrorism offences

1. An offence under section 4 of the Offences against the Person Act 1861 (soliciting murder) that has a terrorist connection.

2. An offence under section 28 of that Act (causing bodily injury by explosives) that has a terrorist connection.

3. An offence under section 29 of that Act (using explosives etc with intent to do grievous bodily harm) that has a terrorist connection.

4. An offence under section 2 of the Explosive Substances Act 1883 (causing explosion likely to endanger life or property) that has a terrorist connection.

5. An offence under section 3 of that Act (attempt to cause explosion, or making or keeping explosive with intent to endanger life or property) that has a terrorist connection.

6. An offence under section 4 of that Act (making or possession of explosive under suspicious circumstances) that has a terrorist connection.

7. An offence under section 54 of the Terrorism Act 2000 (weapons training).

8. An offence under section 56 of that Act (directing terrorist organisation).

9. An offence under section 57 of that Act (possession of article for terrorist purposes).

10. An offence under section 59 of that Act (inciting terrorism overseas).

11. An offence under section 47 of the Anti-terrorism, Crime and Security Act 2001 (use etc of nuclear weapons).

12. An offence under section 50 of that Act (assisting or inducing certain weapons-related acts overseas).

13. An offence under section 113 of that Act (use of noxious substance or thing to cause harm or intimidate).

14. An offence under section 5 of the Terrorism Act 2006 (preparation of terrorist acts).

15. An offence under section 6 of that Act (training for terrorism).

16. An offence under section 9 of that Act (making or possession of radioactive device or material).

17. An offence under section 10 of that Act (use of radioactive device or material for terrorist purposes etc).

18. An offence under section 11 of that Act (terrorist threats relating to radioactive devices etc).

Sexual offences

19. An offence under section 5 of the Sexual Offences Act 2003 (rape of a child under 13).

20. An offence under section 6 of that Act (assault of a child under 13 by penetration).

Accessories and inchoate offences

21.—(1) Aiding, abetting, counselling or procuring the commission of an offence specified in the preceding paragraphs of this Schedule (a "relevant offence").

(2) An attempt to commit a relevant offence.

(3) Conspiracy to commit a relevant offence.

(4) An offence under Part 2 of the Serious Crime Act 2007 in relation to which a relevant offence is the offence (or one of the offences) which the person intended or believed would be committed.

22. An offence in the following list that has a terrorist connection—

(a) an attempt to commit murder,

(b) conspiracy to commit murder, and

(c) an offence under Part 2 of the Serious Crime Act 2007 in relation to which murder is the offence (or one of the offences) which the person intended or believed would be committed.

Abolished offences

23. An offence that—

(a) was abolished before the coming into force of section 236A, and

(b) if committed on the day on which the offender was convicted of the offence, would have constituted an offence specified in the preceding paragraphs of this Schedule.

Meaning of "terrorist connection"

24. For the purposes of this Schedule, an offence has a "terrorist connection" if a court has determined under section 30 of the Counter-Terrorism Act 2008 that the offence has such a connection.

(e) Suspended sentence ("new style")

Criminal Justice Act 2003, ss.189–192

5-549 With effect from February 1, 2015 (Offender Rehabilitation Act 2014 (Commencement No. 2) Order 2015 (S.I. 2015 No. 40)), the 2014 Act (see the main work) was brought into force, so far as it was not already in force, except to the extent that section 18(5) inserts new paragraph 16(3) of Schedule 8 to the CJA 2003 (*ibid.*, § 5-350) and section 18(8) inserts new paragraph 14(3) of Schedule 12 (*ibid.*, § 5-576) to that Act.

Imposition of requirements by suspended sentence order

5-550 As to the commencement of section 15 of, and Schedule 5 to, the Offender Rehabilitation Act 2014 (see the main work), see *ante*, §§ 5-8, 5-549.

Criminal Justice Act 2003, Sched. 12

Further provisions as to order that suspended sentence is to take effect

★5-571 As from April 13, 2015 (Criminal Justice and Courts Act 2015 (Commencement No. 1, Saving and Transitional Provisions) Order 2015 (S.I. 2015 No. 778)), the Criminal Justice and Courts Act 2015, s.54(3), and Sched. 12, paras 12 and 16, amended paragraph 9(3) of Schedule 12 to the 2003 Act, so as (i) to substitute the words "each of the following orders" for the words "any order made by the court under paragraph 8(2)(a) or (b)", and (b) to insert the following text at the end—

"—

(a) an order made by the court under paragraph 8(2)(a) or (b);

(b) an order made by the court under section 21A of the Prosecution of Offences Act 1985 (criminal courts charge) when making an order described in paragraph (a)".

Supplementary

5-581 As to the commencement (in part) of section 18 of the Offender Rehabilitation Act 2014, see *ante*, §§ 5-8, 5-549.

5-582 As to the further commencement of section 19 of, and Schedule 6 to, the Offender Rehabilitation Act 2014, see *post*, § 5-598.

(f) Consecutive sentences

Offences arising out of same transaction

5-588 As to whether a person found to be in possession of an arsenal of firearms on a single occasion could properly receive consecutive sentences on two or more counts of possession of prohibited firearms (Firearms Act 1968, s.5 (§ 24-24 in the main work)), where the total sentence would exceed the statutory maximum for a single offence, see *R. v. Gribbin, post*, § 24-29.

R. v. Noble (as to which, see the main work) was applied to the offence of causing serious injury ★ by dangerous driving in *R. v. Jenkins* [2015] 1 Cr.App.R.(S.) 70, CA.

(3) Detention in young offender institution

Powers of Criminal Courts (Sentencing) Act 2000, ss.96, 97

Term of detention in a young offender institution, and consecutive sentences

As from April 13, 2015 (Criminal Justice and Courts Act 2015 (Commencement No. 1, Saving ★5-595 and Transitional Provisions) Order 2015 (S.I. 2015 No. 778)), the Criminal Justice and Courts Act 2015, s.15(2), amended section 97 of the 2000 Act, so as to (i) in subsection (2), to omit the words "Subject to subsection (3) below,", and (ii) to omit subsection (3).

(4) Detention and training orders

Powers of Criminal Courts (Sentencing) Act 2000, s.100

Offenders under 18: detention and training orders

With effect from a day to be appointed, the Criminal Justice and Courts Act 2015, s.28(8), and 5-597 Sched. 5, paras 3 and 5, amend section 100(1A) of the 2000 Act, so as to substitute new paragraphs (a) and (b), as follows—

> "(a) section 1(2B) or 1A(5) of the Prevention of Crime Act 1953 (minimum sentence for certain offences involving offensive weapons);
> (b) section 139(6B), 139A(5B) or 139AA(7) of the Criminal Justice Act 1988 (minimum sentence for certain offences involving article with blade or point or offensive weapon)".

Powers of Criminal Courts (Sentencing) Act 2000, ss.101, 102

Term of order, consecutive terms and taking account of remands

With effect from February 1, 2015 (Offender Rehabilitation Act 2014 (Commencement No. 2) 5-598 Order 2015 (S.I. 2015 No. 40)), sections 1 to 6, 19 and 21 of, and Schedules 1 to 3, 6 (to the extent that it was not already in force) and 7 to, the 2014 Act (see the main work) were brought into force.

Powers of Criminal Courts (Sentencing) Act 2000, ss.103, 104

The period of supervision

With effect from February 1, 2015 (Offender Rehabilitation Act 2014 (Commencement No. 2) 5-600 Order 2015 (S.I. 2015 No. 40)), sections 6 and 7 of, and Schedule 3 to, the 2014 Act (see the main work) were brought into force.

Powers of Criminal Courts (Sentencing) Act 2000, ss.105–107

Interaction with sentences of detention in a young offender institution

As from April 13, 2015 (Criminal Justice and Courts Act 2015 (Commencement No. 1, Saving ★5-603 and Transitional Provisions) Order 2015 (S.I. 2015 No. 778)), the Criminal Justice and Courts Act 2015, s.15(3), amended section 106(4) of the 2000 Act, so as to substitute the words "Chapter 6 of Part 12 of the Criminal Justice Act 2003 (release, licences, supervision and recall)" for the words "Part II of the Criminal Justice Act 1991 (early release)". The amendment applies in relation to a person sentenced before the day on which it comes into force as well as in relation to a person sentenced on or after that day (2015 Act, s.15(10)).

[Further supervision after end of term of detention and training order

As to the commencement of section 6 of the Offender Rehabilitation Act 2014 (see the main 5-604a work), see *ante*, § 5-600.

Meaning of "youth detention accommodation" and references to terms

As to the commencement of section 7 of, and Schedule 3 to, the Offender Rehabilitation Act 5-605 2014 (see the main work), see *ante*, § 5-600.

As from March 20, 2015 (Criminal Justice and Courts Act 2015 (Commencement No. 1, Saving ★

and Transitional Provisions) Order 2015 (S.I. 2015 No. 778)), the Criminal Justice and Courts Act 2015, s.38(3), and Sched. 9, para. 12, amended section 107(1) of the 2000 Act, so as to insert, after paragraph (a), "(aa) a secure college;".

E. RELEASE ON LICENCE

Introduction

5-616   As to the release on licence of "certain offenders of particular concern" who are given a new "special custodial sentence", see *ante*, § 5-534a; and *post*, § 5-654.

Criminal Justice Act 2003, s.237

Meaning of "fixed-term prisoner" etc.

5-637   As to the commencement of section 2 of the Offender Rehabilitation Act 2014 (see the main work), see *ante*, § 5-598.

★   With effect from April 13, 2015 (Criminal Justice and Courts Act 2015 (Commencement No. 1, Saving and Transitional Provisions) Order 2015 (S.I. 2015 No. 778)), the Criminal Justice and Courts Act 2015, s.6(2)(c), and Sched. 1, paras 14 and 15, amended section 237 of the 2003 Act, so as (i) in subsection (1)(b), to substitute ", 228 or 236A" for "or 228", and (ii) in subsection (1B), to omit "and" at the end of paragraph (c), (iii) to add "and" at the end of paragraph (d), and (iv) to add a new paragraph (e), as follows—

> "(e) references to a sentence under section 236A of this Act include a sentence under that section passed as a result of section 224A of that Act".

Crediting of periods of remand in custody

5-639   Following the coming into force of section 108(1) and (2) of the LASPOA 2012 (which inserted s.240ZA (§ 5-644 in the main work)) into the CJA 2003, where a defendant, following arrest for the index offence, is recalled to prison to continue serving an earlier sentence, his parole licence having been revoked, there is no automatic deduction from any sentence imposed for the index offence for time spent in custody between his arrest and sentencing (so long as he was still serving the previous sentence); Parliament clearly intended that any day in custody should count towards one sentence only; any credit in relation to that time is thus now a matter of discretion for the sentencing judge: *R. v. Kerrigan* [2015] 1 Cr.App.R.(S.) 29, CA.

On a proper construction of section 240ZA of the 2003 Act, time on remand could only be counted against time spent in custody, and could not be credited to reduce time spent on licence; however, subject to subsection (6), time on remand would count towards time spent (or due to be spent) in custody following recall: *R. (Galiazia) v. Governor of Hewell Prison, Secretary of State for Justice and the Crown Court at Warwick* [2015] 1 Cr.App.R.(S.) 13, DC.

Criminal Justice Act 2003, s.240ZA

Time remanded in custody to count as time served: terms of imprisonment and detention

5-644   With effect from February 1, 2015 (Offender Rehabilitation Act 2014 (Commencement No. 2) Order 2015 (S.I. 2015 No. 40)), sections 9 and 21 of, and Schedule 7 to, the 2014 Act (see the main work) were brought into force.

★   With effect from April 13, 2015 (Criminal Justice and Courts Act 2015 (Commencement No. 1, Saving and Transitional Provisions) Order 2015 (S.I. 2015 No. 778)), the Criminal Justice and Courts Act 2015, s.6(2)(c), and Sched. 1, paras 14 and 16, amended section 240ZA(11) of the 2003 Act, so as to substitute ", 228 or 236A" for "or 228".

In relation to section 240ZA of the 2003 Act, see *R. v. Kerrigan* and *R. (Galiazia) v. Governor of Hewell Prison, Secretary of State for Justice and the Crown Court at Warwick, ante*, § 5-639.

Criminal Justice Act 2003, s.240A

Time remanded on bail to count towards time served: terms of imprisonment and detention

5-645   As to the commencement of section 9 of the Offender Rehabilitation Act 2014 (see the main work), see *ante*, § 5-644.

Calculation of credit period

Where a defendant was entitled under section 240A of the CJA 2003 (§ 5-645 in the main **★5-649**
work) to a direction that one-half of the time he had spent on bail subject to a qualifying curfew
should count towards any sentence of imprisonment he received, and the sentencing court failed
to give such direction, and where responsibility for the error and for any delay in seeking leave to
appeal against sentence lay with the court and the legal representatives and not with the defendant, an appropriate extension of time would be granted; it would not be right to refuse an extension by reason only of the proportion that the days subject to qualifying curfew bore to the total
sentence; however, when a defendant, with knowledge of the error, fails to act with due diligence,
the position is likely to be different; and where the passage of time has obscured the entitlement,
the court may refuse relief: *R. v. Thorsby* [2015] 1 Cr.App.R.(S.) 63, CA. The court advised that, in
future, if the Crown Court adopts the practice recommended in *R. v. Hoggard* (as to which, see
the main work, and deriving from that recommended in *R. v. Gordon* (§ 5-1300 in the main
work), and *R. v. Nnaji*; *R. v. Johnson* (see the main work)), appeals should not be necessary, but
that, where it is necessary to seek an extension, the applicant will be expected to present to the
Criminal Appeal Office with his notice and grounds either agreed facts, or evidence as to his
entitlement to credit under section 240A, as to the number of days, and as to when and in what
circumstances he became aware of this entitlement. The court added that, in all well-founded
cases, the prosecution will also have failed in their duty to the sentencing court and the Court of
Appeal will therefore expect them to investigate the complaint promptly and to supply the applicant and the court with a brief written response; this should be done urgently and at a suitably
senior level as such cases directly involve the liberty of the subject.

Criminal Justice Act 2003, ss.242–243A

Duty to release [certain] prisoners serving less than 12 months

With effect from February 1, 2015 (Offender Rehabilitation Act 2014 (Commencement No. 2) **5-652a**
Order 2015 (S.I. 2015 No. 40)), sections 1 and 7 of, and Schedule 3 to, the 2014 Act (see the main
work) were brought into force.

Criminal Justice Act 2003, s.244

Duty to release prisoners

With effect from February 1, 2015 (Offender Rehabilitation Act 2014 (Commencement No. 2) **5-653**
Order 2015 (S.I. 2015 No. 40)), sections 7 and 9 of, and Schedule 3 to, the 2014 Act (see the main
work) were brought into force.

As from April 13, 2015 (Criminal Justice and Courts Act 2015 (Commencement No. 1, Saving **★**
and Transitional Provisions) Order 2015 (S.I. 2015 No. 778)), the Criminal Justice and Courts Act
2015, s.6(1), and Sched. 1, paras 1 and 5, amended section 244(1) of the 2003 Act, so as to insert
", 244A" after "243A".

As from April 13, 2015 (Criminal Justice and Courts Act 2015 (Commencement No. 1, Saving **★5-654**
and Transitional Provisions) Order 2015 (S.I. 2015 No. 778)), the Criminal Justice and Courts Act
2015, s.6(1), and Sched. 1, paras 1 and Sched. 1, paras 1, inserted, after section 244, a new section 244A into the CJA 2003.

Criminal Justice Act 2003, s.244A

Release on licence of prisoners serving sentence under section 236A

244A.—(1) This section applies to a prisoner ("P") who is serving a sentence imposed under section 236A.

(2) The Secretary of State must refer P's case to the Board—

   (a) as soon as P has served the requisite custodial period, and

   (b) where there has been a previous reference of P's case to the Board under this subsection
     and the Board did not direct P's release, not later than the second anniversary of the
     disposal of that reference.

(3) It is the duty of the Secretary of State to release P on licence under this section as soon as—

   (a) P has served the requisite custodial period, and

   (b) the Board has directed P's release under this section.

(4) The Board must not give a direction under subsection (3) unless—

   (a) the Secretary of State has referred P's case to the Board, and

   (b) the Board is satisfied that it is not necessary for the protection of the public that P should
be confined.

  (5) It is the duty of the Secretary of State to release P on licence under this section as soon as P has
served the appropriate custodial term, unless P has previously been released on licence under this
section and recalled under section 254 (provision for the release of such persons being made by sections 255A to 255C).

  (6) For the purposes of this section—

    "the appropriate custodial term" means the term determined as such by the court under section
236A;

    "the requisite custodial period" means—

       (a) in relation to a person serving one sentence, one-half of the appropriate custodial
term, and

       (b) in relation to a person serving two or more concurrent or consecutive sentences, the
period determined under sections 263(2) and 264(2).

Power to release on prisoners on licence before required to do so

★**5-655**   As from April 13, 2015 (Criminal Justice and Courts Act 2015 (Commencement No. 1, Saving
and Transitional Provisions) Order 2015 (S.I. 2015 No. 778)), the Criminal Justice and Courts Act
2015, ss.6(1) and 15(4), and Sched. 1, para. 7, further amended section 246 of the CJA 2003.

Criminal Justice Act 2003, ss.246A, 247, 249

Release on licence of prisoners serving extended sentence under section 226A or 226B

★**5-656**   As from April 13, 2015 (Criminal Justice and Courts Act 2015 (Commencement No. 1, Saving
and Transitional Provisions) Order 2015 (S.I. 2015 No. 778)), the Criminal Justice and Courts Act
2015, s.4, amended section 246A of the 2003 Act, so as (i) in subsection (2), for the words from
"unless" to the end, to substitute new text, as follows—

    "if—

       (a) the sentence was imposed before the coming into force of section 4 of the Criminal Justice
and Courts Act 2014,

       (b) the appropriate custodial term is less than 10 years, and

       (c) the sentence was not imposed in respect of an offence listed in Parts 1 to 3 of Schedule
15B or in respect of offences that include one or more offences listed in those Parts of that
Schedule";

and (ii) in subsection (3), to substitute "In any other case" for "If either or both of those conditions are met".

Duration of licence

5-658   As to the commencement of section 5 of the Offender Rehabilitation Act 2014 (see the main
work), see *ante*, § 5-598.

★**5-658a**   As from April 13, 2015 (Criminal Justice and Courts Act 2015 (Commencement No. 1, Saving
and Transitional Provisions) Order 2015 (S.I. 2015 No. 778)), a new section 255ZA was inserted
into the CJA 2003 by the Criminal Justice and Courts Act 2015, s.12(2).

Criminal Justice Act 2003, s.255ZA

Offence of remaining unlawfully at large after recall

  255ZA.—(1) A person recalled to prison under section 254 or 255 commits an offence if the
person—

    (a) has been notified of the recall orally or in writing, and

    (b) while unlawfully at large fails, without reasonable excuse, to take all necessary steps to
return to prison as soon as possible.

  (2) A person is to be treated for the purposes of subsection (1)(a) as having been notified of the
recall if—

    (a) written notice of the recall has been delivered to an appropriate address, and

    (b) a period specified in the notice has elapsed.

  (3) In subsection (2) "an appropriate address" means—

    (a) an address at which, under the person's licence, the person is permitted to reside or stay,
or

  (b) an address nominated, in accordance with the person's licence, for the purposes of this section.

  (4) A person is also to be treated for the purposes of subsection (1)(a) as having been notified of the recall if—

    (a) the person's licence requires the person to keep in touch in accordance with any instructions given by an officer of a provider of probation services,

    (b) the person has failed to comply with such an instruction, and

    (c) the person has not complied with such an instruction for at least 6 months.

  (5) A person who is guilty of an offence under this section is liable—

    (a) on conviction on indictment to imprisonment for a term not exceeding 2 years or a fine (or both);

    (b) on summary conviction to imprisonment for a term not exceeding 12 months or a fine (or both).

  (6) In relation to an offence committed before section 154(1) comes into force, the reference in subsection (5)(b) to 12 months is to be read as a reference to 6 months.

  (7) In relation to an offence committed before section 85 of the Legal Aid, Sentencing and Punishment of Offenders Act 2012 comes into force, the reference in subsection (5)(b) to a fine is to be read as a reference to a fine not exceeding the statutory maximum.

Section 255ZA applies in relation to a person recalled to prison before or after section 12 of the 2015 Act comes into force: s.12(3) of the 2015 Act.

[Supervision after end of sentence of prisoners serving less than 2 years

  As to the commencement of section 2 of the Offender Rehabilitation Act 2014 (see the main work), see *ante*, § 5-598.   **5-659**

  As from April 13, 2015 (Criminal Justice and Courts Act 2015 (Commencement No. 1, Saving   ★ and Transitional Provisions) Order 2015 (S.I. 2015 No. 778)), the Criminal Justice and Courts Act 2015, s.6(2)(c), and Sched. 1, paras 14 and 18, amended section 256AA(1) of the 2003 Act, so as to insert, after paragraph (b), but before "or", "(ba) the sentence was imposed under section 236A,".

[Supervision requirements under section 256AA

  As to the commencement of section 2 of, and Schedule 1 to, the Offender Rehabilitation Act   **5-660** 2014 (see the main work), see *ante*, § 5-598.

[Breach of supervision requirements imposed under section 256AA

  As to the commencement of section 3 of the Offender Rehabilitation Act 2014 (see the main   **5-661** work), see *ante*, § 5-598.

  As from April 13, 2015 (Criminal Justice and Courts Act 2015 (Commencement No. 1, Saving   ★ and Transitional Provisions) Order 2015 (S.I. 2015 No. 778)), the Criminal Justice and Courts Act 2015, s.54(3), and Sched. 12, paras 12 and 14, amended section 256AC(11) of the 2003 Act, so as to substitute for the words "against the order made by the court", the words—

"against—

    (a) the order made by the court under this section, and

    (b) an order made by the court under section 21A of the Prosecution of Offences Act 1985 (criminal courts charge) when dealing with the person under this section".

Revocation of supervision default order on imposition of further sentence

  As to the commencement of sections 3 and 21 of, and Schedules 2 and 7 to, the Offender   **5-662** Rehabilitation Act 2014 (see the main work), see *ante*, § 5-598.

Post-release supervision of young offenders

  As from April 13, 2015 (Criminal Justice and Courts Act 2015 (Commencement No. 1, Saving   ★**5-663** and Transitional Provisions) Order 2015 (S.I. 2015 No. 778)), the Criminal Justice and Courts Act 2015, s.7(4), and Sched. 2, paras 3 and 6, amended section 256B(7) of the CJA 2003.

  As to the commencement of sections 1 and 4 of the Offender Rehabilitation Act 2014 (see the   **5-664** main work), see *ante*, § 5-598.

Criminal Justice Act 2003, ss.263, 264

Concurrent terms

  As from April 13, 2015 (Criminal Justice and Courts Act 2015 (Commencement No. 1, Saving   ★**5-665** and Transitional Provisions) Order 2015 (S.I. 2015 No. 778)), the Criminal Justice and Courts Act 2015, s.6(2)(c), and Sched. 1, paras 14 and 22, amended section 263(4) of the 2003 Act, so as to substitute ", 228 or 236A" for "or 228".

Consecutive terms

5-666   As to the commencement of section 5 of the Offender Rehabilitation Act 2014 (see the main work), see *ante*, § 5-598.

★   As from April 13, 2015 (Criminal Justice and Courts Act 2015 (Commencement No. 1, Saving and Transitional Provisions) Order 2015 (S.I. 2015 No. 778)), the Criminal Justice and Courts Act 2015, s.6, and Sched. 1, paras 14 and 23, amended section 264 of the 2003 Act so as (i) to substitute subsection (6), as follows—

"(6) In this section 'custodial period' means—
  (a) in relation to an extended sentence imposed under section 226A or 226B, two-thirds of the appropriate custodial term determined by the court under that section,
  (b) in relation to an extended sentence imposed under section 227 or 228, one-half of the appropriate custodial term determined by the court under that section,
  (c) in relation to a sentence imposed under section 236A, one half of the appropriate custodial term determined by the court under that section, and
  (d) in relation to any other sentence, one-half of the sentence.";

and (ii) in subsection (7), to substitute ", 228 or 236A" for "or 228".

[Consecutive terms: supplementary

5-667a   As to the commencement of section 5 of the Offender Rehabilitation Act 2014 (see the main work), see *ante*, § 5-598.

Criminal Justice Act 2003, s.265

Restriction on consecutive sentences for released prisoners

★**5-668**   As from April 13, 2015 (Criminal Justice and Courts Act 2015 (Commencement No. 1, Saving and Transitional Provisions) Order 2015 (S.I. 2015 No. 778)), the Criminal Justice and Courts Act 2015, s.6(2)(c), and Sched. 1, paras 14 and 24, amended section 265(2) of the 2003 Act, so as to substitute ", 228 or 236A" for "or 228".

Criminal Justice Act 2003, s.268

Interpretation of Chapter 6

5-670   As to the commencement of section 7 of, and Schedule 3 to, the Offender Rehabilitation Act 2014 (see the main work), see *ante*, § 5-600.

★   As from April 13, 2015 (Criminal Justice and Courts Act 2015 (Commencement No. 1, Saving and Transitional Provisions) Order 2015 (S.I. 2015 No. 778)), the Criminal Justice and Courts Act 2015, s.14(1) and (2), amended section 268 of the 2003 Act), so as to insert, after subsection (1), a new subsection (1A), as follows—

"(6) In this Chapter, 'the requisite custodial period' means—
  (a) in relation to a person serving an extended sentence imposed under section 226A or 226B, the requisite custodial period for the purposes of section 246A;
  (b) in relation to a person serving an extended sentence imposed under section 227 or 228, the requisite custodial period for the purposes of section 247;
  (c) in relation to a person serving a sentence imposed under section 236A, the requisite custodial period for the purposes of section 244A;
  (d) in relation to any other fixed-term prisoner, the requisite custodial period for the purposes of section 243A or section 244 (as appropriate).".

The amendment applies in relation to a person sentenced before the day on which section 14 of the 2015 Act comes into force as well as in relation to a person sentenced on or after that day (2015 Act, s.14(7)).

As from a day to be appointed, the Criminal Justice and Courts Act 2015, s.8(3), and Sched. 3, paras 4 and 9, further amend section 268 of the 2003 Act so as to insert, at the appropriate place, the words "'recall adjudicator' has the meaning given in section 239A;".

Modifications of Chapter 6 in certain transitional cases

5-670a   As explained in the main work (see § 5-619), the effect of LASPOA 2012 is to apply Chapter 6 of Part 12 of the CJA 2003 to all prisoners regardless of the date of their offence or the date of sentence. However, two new Schedules (20A and 20B) are inserted into the 2003 Act (by the 2012 Act, s.121(5) and (6), and Scheds 16, paras 1 and 3, and 17, paras 1 and 10) for the purpose of preserving the transitional provisions that existed prior to their commencement. These have the effect of modifying Chapter 6 where they apply. It is submitted that they now only have potential relevance to the release date of an offender sentenced after their commencement in one situation, *viz.* where an offender serving a "1991 Act sentence" who has never been released from that sentence (and theoretically also an offender serving a "1967 Act sentence" who has never been released) is sentenced to a consecutive term for a fresh offence (see paras 22 and 33, *post*).

As to the commencement of these provisions of the 2012 Act, see § 5-2a in the main work.

Criminal Justice Act 2003, Sched. 20B, paras 1–3, 7, 8, 18–20, 22, 23, 30, 33

PART 1

Introductory

Interpretation

1.—(1) The following provisions apply for the purposes of this Schedule. **5-670b**

(2) "The commencement date" means the date on which section 121 of the Legal Aid, Sentencing and Punishment of Offenders Act 2012 comes into force.

(3) "The 1967 Act" means the Criminal Justice Act 1967.

(4) "The 1991 Act" means the Criminal Justice Act 1991.

(5) A "section 85 extended sentence" means an extended sentence under section 85 of the Sentencing Act and includes (in accordance with paragraph 1(3) of Schedule 11 to that Act) a sentence under section 58 of the Crime and Disorder Act 1998.

(6) In relation to a section 85 extended sentence, "the custodial term" and "the extension period" have the meaning given by that section.

(7) References to section 86 of the Sentencing Act include (in accordance with paragraph 1(3) of Schedule 11 to that Act) section 44 of the 1991 Act as originally enacted.

(8) A "1967 Act sentence" is a sentence imposed before 1 October 1992.

(9) A "1991 Act sentence" is a sentence which is—

(a) imposed on or after 1 October 1992 but before 4 April 2005, or

(b) imposed on or after 4 April 2005 but before the commencement date and is either—

(i) imposed in respect of an offence committed before 4 April 2005, or

(ii) for a term of less than 12 months.

(10) A "2003 Act sentence" is a sentence which is—

(a) imposed on or after the commencement date, or

(b) imposed on or after 4 April 2005 but before the commencement date and is both—

(i) imposed in respect of an offence committed on or after 4 April 2005, and

(ii) for a term of 12 months or more.

(11) Where an offence is found to have been committed over a period of two or more days, or at some time during a period of two or more days, it is to be taken for the purposes of this Schedule to have been committed on the last of those days.

Explanation of dates

2. The following dates (which are mentioned in this Schedule) are dates on which changes to the **5-670c** law relating to the release and recall of prisoners came into force—

1 October 1992 is the date on which Part 2 of the 1991 Act came into force;

30 September 1998 is the date on which certain provisions of the Crime and Disorder Act 1998 came into force;

4 April 2005 is the date on which this Chapter came into force;

9 June 2008 is the date on which section 26 of the Criminal Justice and Immigration Act 2008 came into force;

14 July 2008 is the date on which certain other provisions of that Act came into force;

2 August 2010 is the date on which section 145 of the Coroners and Justice Act 2009 came into force.

PART 2

Prisoners Serving 1991 Act Sentences, etc.

3.—(1) This Part applies to certain persons serving a 1991 Act sentence. **5-670d**

(2) This Part also applies to a person serving a 2003 Act sentence which is—

(b) an extended sentence imposed under section 227 or 228 before 14 July 2008.

(3) But this Part does not apply to a person who—

(a) has been released on licence under Part 2 of the 1991 Act,

(b) has been recalled to prison, and

(c) (whether or not having returned to custody in consequence of that recall) is unlawfully at large on the commencement date.

★   [Para. 3(2)(a) was repealed by the Criminal Justice and Courts Act 2015, s.15(8).]

Release on licence at one-half of sentence: section 85 extended sentence prisoners

5-670e   7. This paragraph applies to a person if—

(a) the person has been convicted of an offence committed on or after 30 September 1998 but before 4 April 2005,

(b) the person is serving a section 85 extended sentence in respect of that offence,

(c) the person has not previously been released from prison on licence in respect of that sentence, and

(d) paragraph 4 does not apply to the person.

5-670f   8.—(1) As soon as a person to whom paragraph 7 applies has served one-half of the custodial term, it is the duty of the Secretary of State to release the person on licence under this paragraph.

(2) Sub-paragraph (1) applies in place of section 243A or 244, as the case may be (release of prisoners serving less than 12 months, or serving 12 months or more).

It should be noted that paragraph 4 (see para. 7(d)) has no application to a person sentenced after "the commencement date".

Period for which licence to remain in force: section 85 extended sentence prisoners

5-670g   18. This paragraph applies to a person who—

(a) has been convicted of an offence committed on or after 30 September 1998 but before 4 April 2005,

(b) is serving a section 85 extended sentence imposed in respect of that offence, and

(c) has not previously been released from prison on licence in respect of that sentence.

5-670h   19.—(1) Where a person to whom paragraph 18 applies is released on licence and the custodial term is less than 12 months, the licence shall remain in force until the end of the period found by adding—

(a) one-half of the custodial term, and

(b) the extension period.

(2) Where a person to whom paragraph 18 applies is released on licence and the custodial term is 12 months or more, the licence shall remain in force until the end of the period found by adding—

(a) three-quarters of the custodial term, and

(b) the extension period.

(3) Sub-paragraphs (1) and (2) are subject to any revocation under section 254.

(4) Sub-paragraphs (1) to (3) apply in place of section 249 (duration of licence).

Concurrent or consecutive terms

5-670i   20. Paragraphs 21 and 22 apply where a person ("P") is serving two or more sentences of imprisonment imposed on or after 1 October 1992 and—

(a) the sentences were passed on the same occasion, or

(b) where they were passed on different occasions, the person has not been released under Part 2 of the 1991 Act or under this Chapter at any time during the period beginning with the first and ending with the last of those occasions.

5-670j   22.—(1) This paragraph applies where two or more sentences are to be served consecutively on each other and—

(a) one or more of those sentences is a 1991 Act sentence, and

(b) one or more of them is a 2003 Act sentence.

(2) Section 264 does not affect the length of the period which P must serve in prison in respect of the 1991 Act sentence or sentences.

(3) Nothing in this Chapter requires the Secretary of State to release P until P has served a period equal in length to the aggregate of the length of the periods which P must serve in relation to each of the sentences mentioned in sub-paragraph (1).

(3A) If P is subject to supervision requirements under section 256AA (by virtue of section 264(3C)(b)), section 256AA(4)(b) (end of supervision period) applies in relation to P as if the reference to the requisite custodial period were to the period described in sub-paragraph (3) of this paragraph.

(4) If P is also serving one or more 1967 Act sentences, paragraphs 32 and 33 apply instead of this paragraph.

[Sub-para. (3A) was inserted, as from February 1, 2015 (Offender Rehabilitation Act 2014 (Commencement No. 2) Order 2015 (S.I. 2015 No. 40)) by the Offender Rehabilitation Act 2014, s.5(1), (6) and (7). This amendment applies only in relation to any person who falls to be released under Chapter 6 of Part 12 of the 2003 Act on or after the day on which it came into force: 2014 Act, s.21, and Sched. 7, paras 1 and 2.]

PART 3

Prisoners Serving 1967 Act Sentences

23.—(1) This Part applies to certain persons serving a 1967 Act sentence.   **5-670k**

(2) But this Part does not apply to a person who—

    (a) has been released on licence,

    (b) has been recalled to prison, and

    (c) (whether or not having returned to custody in consequence of that recall) is unlawfully at large on the commencement date.

(3) In this Part, references to release under Part 2 of the 1991 Act include release under section 60 of the 1967 Act.

Concurrent or consecutive terms

30. Paragraphs 31 to 33 apply where a person ("P") is serving two or more sentences of imprison-   **5-670l**
ment and—

    (a) the sentences were passed on the same occasion, or

    (b) where they were passed on different occasions, the person has not been released under Part 2 of the 1991 Act or under this Chapter at any time during the period beginning with the first and ending with the last of those occasions.

33.—(1) This paragraph applies where two or more sentences are to be served consecutively on   **5-670m**
each other and—

    (a) one or more of those sentences is a 1967 Act sentence, and

    (b) one or more of them is a 2003 Act sentence.

(2) Section 264 does not affect the length of the period which P must serve in prison in respect of the 1967 Act sentence or sentences.

(3) Nothing in this Chapter requires the Secretary of State to release P until P has served a period equal in length to the aggregate of the length of the periods which P must serve in relation to each of the sentences mentioned in sub-paragraph (1).

(4) If P is subject to supervision requirements under section 256AA (by virtue of section 264(3C)(b)), section 256AA(4)(b) (end of supervision period) applies in relation to P as if the reference to the requisite custodial period were to the period described in sub-paragraph (3) of this paragraph.

[Sub-para. (4) was inserted, as from February 1, 2015 (Offender Rehabilitation Act 2014 (Commencement No. 2) Order 2015 (S.I. 2015 No. 40)) by the Offender Rehabilitation Act 2014, s.5(1), (6) and (8). This amendment applies only in relation to any person who falls to be released under Chapter 6 of Part 12 of the 2003 Act on or after the day on which it came into force: 2014 Act, s.21, and Sched. 7, paras 1 and 2.]

VII. FINES

Criminal Justice Act 2003, ss.163–165

Fixing of fines

  As from April 13, 2015 (Criminal Justice and Courts Act 2015 (Commencement No. 1, Saving   **★5-674**
and Transitional Provisions) Order 2015 (S.I. 2015 No. 778)), the Criminal Justice and Courts Act 2015, s.50, and Sched. 11, para. 23, amended section 164 of the 2003 Act, so as to insert, after subsection (5)(a) but before the "or", a new paragraph (aa), as follows—

    "(aa) an offender has been convicted in the offender's absence in proceedings conducted in accordance with section 16A of the Magistrates' Courts Act 1980 (trial by single justice on the papers),".

Powers of Criminal Courts (Sentencing) Act 2000, ss.139, 140, 142

Power of Crown Court to order search of persons before it

★**5-678**   As from April 13, 2015 (Criminal Justice and Courts Act 2015 (Commencement No. 1, Saving and Transitional Provisions) Order 2015 (S.I. 2015 No. 778)), the Criminal Justice and Courts Act 2015, s.54(3), and Sched. 12, paras 8 and 10, amended section 142(1) of the 2000 Act, so as to insert, after paragraph (b), a new paragraph (ba), as follows—

> "(ba) the Crown Court makes an order against a person under section 21A of the Prosecution of Offences Act 1985 (criminal courts charge),".

Magistrates' Courts Act 1980, ss.36, 75, 82(1), (1A)

Restriction on power to impose imprisonment for default

★**5-682**   As from April 13, 2015 (Criminal Justice and Courts Act 2015 (Commencement No. 1, Saving and Transitional Provisions) Order 2015 (S.I. 2015 No. 778)), the Criminal Justice and Courts Act 2015, s.54(3), and Sched. 12, paras 2 and 3, substituted section 82(1A) of the 1980 Act, as follows—

> "(1A) A magistrates' court may not issue a warrant of commitment in reliance on subsection (1)(c) for a default in paying—
> (a) a charge ordered to be paid under section 21A of the Prosecution of Offences Act 1985 (criminal courts charge), or
> (b) a surcharge ordered to be paid under section 161A of the Criminal Justice Act 2003.".

Criminal Justice Act 1982, s.37

The standard scale of fines for summary offences

★**5-683**   As to the commencement of section 85(1), (2) and (4) of the LASPOA 2012 on March 12, 2015, (see the main work), see *ante*, § 1-125.

★   With effect from March 12, 2015, section 37 of the 1982 Act was amended by the Legal Aid, Sentencing and Punishment of Offenders Act 2012 (Fines on Summary Conviction) Regulations 2015 (S.I. 2015 No. 664), reg. 4(4), and Sched. 5, para. 3, so as to insert a new subsection (4), as follows—

> "(4) Section 85 of the Legal Aid, Sentencing and Punishment of Offenders Act 2012 (removal of limit on certain fines on conviction by magistrates' court) makes provision that affects the application of this section.".

Obtaining financial information

★**5-684a**   In *R. (Natural England) v. Day* [2015] 1 Cr.App.R.(S.) 53, CA, it was said that whereas section 162 of the CJA 2003 Act (§ 5-672 in the main work) enables a court to make a financial circumstances order, a court should, for the purpose of fixing the amount of a fine to be imposed on a wealthy individual, consider making an order requiring a detailed statement of his assets and income; and that it would ordinarily be desirable to require the information to cover five years so that the court can take an informed view.

VIII. COMPENSATION, RESTITUTION AND REPARATION

A. COMPENSATION ORDERS

Powers of Criminal Courts (Sentencing) Act 2000, ss.130–132

Compensation orders against convicted persons

5-691   With effect from a day to be appointed, the Criminal Justice and Courts Act 2015, s.28(8), and Sched. 5, paras 3 and 6, amend section 130 of the 2000 Act, so as (i) in subsection (2), to substitute the words "a provision mentioned in subsection (2ZA)" for the words from "section 110(2)" to "2006", and (ii) to insert after subsection (2), a new subsection (2ZA), as follows—

> "(2ZA) The provisions referred to in subsection (2) are—

   (a) section 1(2B) or 1A(5) of the Prevention of Crime Act 1953;
   (b) section 51A(2) of the Firearms Act 1968;
   (c) section 139(6B), 139A(5B) or 139AA(7) of the Criminal Justice Act 1988;
   (d) section 110(2) or 111(2) of this Act;
   (e) section 224A, 225(2) or 226(2) of the Criminal Justice Act 2003;
   (f) section 29(4) or (6) of the Violent Crime Reduction Act 2006.".

Enforcement and appeals

As from April 13, 2015 (Criminal Justice and Courts Act 2015 (Commencement No. 1, Saving   **★5-693**
and Transitional Provisions) Order 2015 (S.I. 2015 No. 778)), the Criminal Justice and Courts Act
2015, s.83(1), amended section 132(4A) of the 2000 Act, so as to substitute the words "the
Supreme Court" for the words "House of Lords".

Review of compensation orders

As from a day to be appointed, section 133 of the PCC(S)A 2000 is amended by the Modern   **★5-694**
Slavery Act 2015, s.57(1), and Sched. 5, para. 14, so that the text in the main work from "to
satisfy the compensation order and" to the end will read "to satisfy the compensation order and
any or all of a confiscation order, an unlawful profit order under the Prevention of Social Housing Fraud Act 2013, s.4, and a slavery and trafficking reparation order made under the 2015 Act,
s.8, made in the same proceedings".

The means of the offender (s.130(11))

It was held in *R. v. Carrington* [2014] 2 Cr.App.R.(S.) 41, CA, that, having regard to the duty on   **5-704**
a court, under section 130(11) of the 2000 Act (§ 5-591 in the main work), to take into account
the defendant's means in deciding whether to make a compensation order and its amount, (i) a
compensation order may still be an option where a defendant could not make an immediate offer
of payment from his own funds, but could borrow such funds from a third party, but (ii) no order
should be made where the compensation would be funded by a loan, but there was no material
before the court upon which it could be concluded that there were sound prospects that the
defendant would be able to repay the loan.

B. Restitution Orders

Criminal Procedure Rules 2014 (S.I. 2014 No. 1610), r.42.7

Replacement of 2014 rules by 2015 rules

As to the replacement of S.I. 2014 No. 1610 by the Criminal Procedure Rules 2015 (S.I. 2015   **★5-713**
No. 1490), see *ante*, § 5-287.

IX. DEPRIVATION AND CONFISCATION

B. Confiscation under the Drug Trafficking Act 1994

Assessment of benefit

When determining for the purposes of section 2 of the DTA 1994 (confiscation orders) whether   **5-737**
an offender has benefited from an offence of drug trafficking in respect of which he has not been
convicted at trial, the statutory assumptions provided for in section 4(3) are not the only way in
which the Act permits the court to determine the fact (or extent) of such benefit; where those assumptions are not applicable, the court is entitled to rely on other evidence led at trial to show
that one or more offences of drug trafficking (other than those charged) have been committed
(and then to estimate the benefit that must have been obtained from those offences): *R. v. Briggs-
Price* [2009] 1 A.C. 1026, HL. A majority of their Lordships held, however, that a judge should
only rely on evidence of other offences not charged if he was satisfied to the criminal standard
that they had been proved (the minority taking the view that the civil standard was the applicable
standard).

Valuation of property

Where a judge assessed the value of the defendant's proceeds of drug trafficking at £3.2 mil-   **5-738** lion, he was correct in taking the view that he was required by the DTA 1994 to make a confiscation order in that amount, unless the defendant satisfied him (to the civil standard) that his realisable assets were less than that amount; and where the defendant had failed to do so, there was no obligation on the judge to assume that the defendant would have incurred some expenses to be set against that figure, and to make some discount in respect thereof; such approach was misconceived; his task under the statute was to assess the value of the proceeds in accord with the provisions of the statute (which was not the same as profit), and to make an order in that amount unless the value of the realisable assets was less than that amount, and the burden of proof in that regard was on the defendant: *R. v. Versluis* [2005] 2 Cr.App.R.(S.) 26, CA.

"drug trafficking offence"

5-739   Where the defendant was convicted of a conspiracy to convert the proceeds of drug trafficking "or" the proceeds of criminal conduct (the substantive offences being created by the DTA 1994, s.49, and the CJA 1988, s.93C, respectively), this was to be construed as a finding that the agreement was not restricted to the laundering of the proceeds of drug trafficking or to the proceeds of criminal conduct other than drug trafficking, but was an agreement to launder money, whatever its provenance; it was, in effect, an agreement to launder both the proceeds of drug trafficking and the proceeds of other criminal conduct; accordingly, the defendant was properly to be regarded as having been convicted of a "drug trafficking offence" for the purposes of the confiscation provisions of the 1994 Act as the definition of that expression extended to a conspiracy to commit an offence contrary to section 49; and the judge had, therefore, erred in declining to conduct confiscation proceedings under the 1994 Act: *R. v. Suchedina (Att.-Gen.'s Reference (No. 4 of 2003))* [2005] 1 Cr.App.R. 2, CA.

Increase in realisable property

5-740   In *Re Peacock (Secretary of State for the Home Department intervening)* [2012] 2 Cr.App.R.(S.) 81, SC, it was held that the High Court has power, under section 16(2) of the 1994 Act, to certify that the amount that might be realised is greater than the amount taken into account at the time a confiscation order under that Act was made, and to do so by reference to assets honestly acquired since the date of the making of the order. As to the argument that increasing a confiscation order by reference to after-acquired assets would militate against a defendant's reform and rehabilitation, and be likely to discourage him from engaging in lawful and openly profitable employment, the court pointed out that section 16(4) confers a discretion on the Crown Court, rather than obliging it to order an increase in the amount of the confiscation order in parallel with the assessment of the amount of increase in the defendant's realisable property under section 16(2).

Certificate of inadequacy

5-741   It is unambiguously clear from the wording of sections 6 and 8(1) of the 1994 Act that the value of a gift made by a defendant will be included in the amount of a confiscation order and will constitute "realisable property", even though it may not itself be realisable by the defendant because it is no longer in his power or control; and it is implicit in the statutory scheme that, where the value of a gift has been included in the amount of a confiscation order pursuant to section 6(1), it will not then be open to the defendant to seek a certificate of inadequacy under section 17(1) on the basis that he cannot realise or recover that gift; section 17 cannot be used as a device for upsetting an original finding that an item is "realisable property" within section 6(2), and thus to be included in the "amount that might be realised" under section 6(1), and thus within the amount of the confiscation order: *Re L.*, unreported, June 23, 2010, QBD (Hickinbottom J.) ([2010] EWHC 1531 (Admin.)).

Variation of realisable amount

5-742   Where, following the grant of a certificate of inadequacy by the High Court under section 17 of the 1994 Act, the Crown Court had, pursuant to subsection (4) of that section, substituted a nil amount as the amount to be recovered, it was possible, if the defendant thereafter came into funds, for the amount to be varied upwards again if the High Court issued a certificate under section 16(2) that the amount that might be realised was now more than the amount that had been substituted for the original amount; but the Crown Court had a discretion as to whether to accede to an application for the amount to be increased following such certification, and one factor to be taken into account by it in deciding how to exercise its discretion would be whether the state had sat on its hands after significant and clear evidence about the defendant's change in financial circumstances had come to its attention or had unreasonably delayed in re-opening the issue: *R. v. Griffin* [2009] 2 Cr.App.R.(S.) 89, CA.

Restraint orders; payment of legal expenses out of restrained assets

See *Revenue and Customs Prosecution Office v. Briggs-Price and O'Reilly, post,* § 5-761. **5-743**

C. Confiscation under the Criminal Justice Act 1988

Postponement of determinations

In *R. v. Haisman* [2004] 1 Cr.App.R.(S.) 63, CA, it was held that where prosecuting counsel had **5-756** invited the judge to postpone confiscation proceedings and to proceed to sentence, and the judge responded by saying, "If everyone agrees to that, I will do that" and there was no dissent from any counsel to that course, the judge had "manifestly reached a decision" (*R. v. Ross* [2001] 2 Cr.App.R.(S.) 109, CA) to postpone the confiscation proceedings under section 72A of the CJA 1988, with the consequence that the confiscation orders made subsequent to the imposition of sentence were lawful.

In *R. v. Paivarinta-Taylor* [2010] 2 Cr.App.R.(S.) 64, CA, the court said that whereas section 72A(1) of the CJA 1988 enables a court to postpone making a determination as to a defendant's benefit for the purpose of a confiscation order, or as to the amount to be recovered from him under such an order, for such period as it may specify in certain circumstances, and whereas section 72A(9) provides that, in sentencing the defendant at any time during the specified postponement period, the court shall not impose any fine on him, the decision in *R. v. Soneji* [2006] 1 A.C. 340, HL (that where there is a breach of a procedural requirement in a statute, a court should ask itself what Parliament intended should be the consequences and whether it fairly could be taken to have intended total invalidity), remains binding authority, as do *R. v. Ruddick* [2004] 1 Cr.App.R.(S.) 7, CA, *R. v. Simpson* [2003] 2 Cr.App.R. 36, CA, and *R. v. Donohoe* [2007] 1 Cr.App.R.(S.) 88, CA, in so far as they add to the principles identified in *Soneji* as to the correct approach to the consequences of a breach of the procedural provisions relating to confiscation orders under the 1988 Act. Cases such as *R. v. Threapleton* [2002] 2 Cr.App.R.(S.) 46, CA, were decided without reference to *Soneji*, and the Court of Appeal said that they should in future be disregarded when considering the consequences of such a breach. It was held that Parliament could not be taken to have intended that a breach of section 72A(9) would lead to total invalidity, that the imposition of a fine before making a confiscation order would render the fine itself invalid, that, having imposed such a fine, the court could then no longer proceed to consider the making of a confiscation order, or that any confiscation order so made would itself be rendered invalid.

Assessment of benefit/making of assumptions

The assumption provided for in section 72AA(4)(a) of the 1988 Act (*viz.* that any property **5-757** transferred to the defendant since the beginning of the relevant period was received by him "in connection with the commission of offences to which this Part of this Act applies") includes within its scope offences committed by persons other than the defendant; thus it is not sufficient to rebut the presumption to show that the property was obtained by the defendant as a result of somebody else's criminal conduct; but the defendant's knowledge or lack of knowledge would be highly material in deciding whether to apply the safety valve in subsection (5) (assumption not to be made if court is satisfied that there would be a serious risk of injustice): *R. v. Ilyas* [2009] 1 Cr.App.R.(S.) 59, CA. See the commentary by David Thomas Q.C. in the *Criminal Law Review* ([2008] Crim.L.R. 908) for the suggestion that this decision will not carry across to the PCA 2002 regime; and see the commentary in CLW/08/39/9 as to the limitations of the actual decision, and, in particular, for the suggestion that it is out of kilter with the decision of the House of Lords in *R. v. May* (§ 5-1044 in the main work).

Whereas section 72AA of the 1988 Act provided that in certain cases it was to be assumed against the defendant that he had committed offences other than those of which he had been convicted or which he had asked to be taken into consideration, and that this assumed criminal conduct should be included within his "relevant criminal conduct" (the assessed benefit from which would form the basis of any confiscation order, subject only to his realisable assets being insufficient), there was nothing objectionable in imposing on the defendant the burden of showing in the particular case that the assumptions should not be made; the assumptions were founded on his holding of property or expenditure of money, and there was nothing unfair in requiring him to show that the source of his property was legitimate: *R. v. Bagnall and Sharma* [2013] 1 W.L.R. 204, CA.

As to the assessment of benefit under the 1988 Act, see also *R. v. Ahmad (Shakeel) and Ahmad (Syed Mubarak)* (§ 5-1051 in the main work).

Factual basis for making order

5-758   Where an agreement is reached as to the amount of a confiscation order, that agreement will be binding on the defendant unless there are the sort of exceptional circumstances referred to in *R. v. Hirani*, unreported, June 11, 2008, CA ([2008] EWCA Crim. 1463) (save in most exceptional circumstances, a confiscation order based on an agreed amount will not be set aside where the essence of complaint is that, in seeking to secure the best deal available, erroneous advice was given to a party to the agreement; without exhaustively identifying such circumstances, there would need to be a well-founded submission that the whole process was unfair): *R. v. Ayankoya*, unreported, May 24, 2011, CA ([2011] EWCA Crim. 1488). The circumstances had, however, been wholly exceptional where: (i) the defendant had agreed to the amount after being incorrectly informed by his counsel that the judge had ruled that an adjournment to await bank statements supporting his claims would be impossible and that he therefore had a choice of either agreeing the amount or giving evidence without the statements with the inherent risk that a higher amount would result, and (ii) where the bank statements had in fact shown that there was force in the defendant's claims; in these circumstances, the erroneous advice had been of a potentially fundamental nature: *ibid.*

Amount that might be realised

5-759   In *R. v. Blee* [2004] 1 Cr.App.R.(S.) 33, CA, it was held that whereas section 74(3) of the CJA 1988 provides that "the amount that might be realised at the time a confiscation order is made" includes "the total of the values at that time of all gifts caught by this Part of this Act" and whereas section 74(10) provides that a gift is caught by that part of the Act if "(a) it was made by the defendant at any time after the commission of the offence ...; and (b) the court considers it appropriate in all the circumstances to take the gift into account" it follows that the fact that the property held by the donee at the time of the confiscation order is less than the value of the gift does not *per se* preclude the court from taking the full value of the gift into account; the court is given a discretion by section 74(10) and the question for it to decide is whether it is "appropriate" to take the gift into account; if it considers it appropriate to take it into account (in whole or in part), then to the extent that it does so, the value of the gift is to be included in the computation of the amount that might be realised; in exercising the discretion, the court may have regard to the timing of the gift (here, made when the defendant, having been on the run, had decided to surrender), to the fact that it was made to a person from whom the defendant would be likely to be able to receive an equivalent benefit in return, if he wished, and to the fact that whilst the donee currently had assets worth considerably less than the value of the gift, he was in highly paid employment and would be likely again to hold substantial assets; and, where it is said that the gift has been dissipated prior to the confiscation order, this is a matter to be considered under section 74(10), rather than on a subsequent application for a certificate of inadequacy.

As to the approach to be taken where the prosecution allege that the defendant is the beneficial owner of property registered in the name of a third party, see *Revenue and Customs Prosecutions Office v. May* [2010] 3 All E.R. 1173, CA (Civ. Div.) (§ 5-1059 in the main work).

Valuation of property

5-760   In *R. v. Hedges* (2004) 148 S.J. 974, CA, it was held that in making a confiscation order against a defendant whose only realisable asset was the house which he owned jointly with his wife, the correct approach to valuation of his interest in the property had been to determine the market value of the property, then deduct the outstanding mortgage and the reasonable costs of sale before making a confiscation order in respect of half the remaining amount; such an approach properly reflected the intention of section 74(4) of the CJA 1988 and was to be preferred to that of dividing the value of the house and then deducting the remaining mortgage and costs of sale from the defendant's half share, on the basis that he was responsible for payment of the mortgage; whilst it was true that the defendant was in theory liable to repay the whole mortgage, being jointly and severally liable, the reality was that the mortgage and the costs of sale would be discharged out of the proceeds of sale, the net effect of which would be to reduce his share in the value of the house by half the amount of the mortgage and costs of sale.

In *R. v. Ahmed* [2005] 1 All E.R. 128, CA, it was held that where a court concludes that an offender has benefited from relevant criminal conduct (CJA 1988, s.71(1A)), the court has no discretion, in valuing the realisable assets for the purposes of determining the amount of the confiscation order, to exclude from the computation, the value of the defendant's share in the matrimonial home, notwithstanding the probability that the home would have to be sold to meet the confiscation order; the words "the amount appearing to the court" in subsection (6)(b) ("... the sum which an order made by a court under this section requires an offender to pay shall be equal to (a) ...; or (b) the amount appearing to the court to be the amount that might be realised at the time the order is made, whichever is the less") did not give the court a discretion; it merely referred to the valuation process to be carried out under section 74, and section 3 of the Human Rights Act 1998 (§ 16-16 in the main work) did not require it to be read as construing such a discretion on the court on account of the possible interference with innocent third parties' rights under Article 8 of the ECHR (*ibid.*, § 16-137); the court is merely concerned with the arithmetic exercise of computing what is, in effect, a statutory debt; such process does not involve any assessment of the way in which the debt may ultimately be paid; different considerations would apply if the debt is not met and the prosecution determine to take enforcement action; if a court is asked to make an order for the sale of the matrimonial home then the third party's rights under Article 8 would clearly be engaged; and it would be at that stage that the court would have to consider whether or not it would be proportionate to make an order for the sale of the home. In connection with this case, see *Webber v. Webber (CPS intervening)*, § 5-1062 in the main work.

In the earlier case of *R. v. Goodenough* [2005] 1 Cr.App.R.(S.) 88, CA, it was held that where a defendant's only realisable asset was his equity in the matrimonial home, the making of a confiscation order in accordance with the requirements of the 1988 Act for the amount by which he had benefited from his offending (being an amount less than the value of his equity) did not infringe or interfere with his rights under Article 8 or under Article 1 of the First Protocol (right to peaceful enjoyment of possessions); the rights of the defendant's wife might be infringed if the house were to be sold in order to raise the money to pay the amount of the confiscation order, and it would be open to the wife to oppose any application to appoint a receiver to enforce the order.

Restraint orders; payment of legal expenses out of restrained assets

In *Revenue and Customs Prosecution Office v. Briggs-Price and O'Reilly* [2007] L.S. Gazette, June 28, 32, CA (Civ. Div.) ([2007] EWCA Civ. 568) it was held, in relation to the confiscation regimes under the CJA 1988 and the DTA 1994, that the principle in *Customs and Excise Commrs v. Norris* [1991] 2 Q.B. 293, CA (Civ. Div.) (defendant's legal expenses may be met from restrained assets), applies both to legal expenses incurred prior to conviction (and any appeal against conviction) and to legal expenses incurred in connection with the making of a confiscation order and an appeal against such order; there is a discretion in such cases, which will be exercised for a proper and legitimate purpose within the scope of the statutory regime where the released assets are to meet expenses for a prospective appeal which are neither excessive nor improperly incurred (such amount as is released being capable of control by assessment). **5-761**

Restraint orders; appointment of receiver

See *Revenue and Customs Prosecutions Office v. Pigott (Lamb, interested party)* [2010] S.T.C. 1190, CA (Civ. Div.) (§ 5-874 in the main work). **5-762**

Certificate of inadequacy

There is no rule of law that says that, on an application under section 83 of the 1988 Act for a **5-763** certificate of inadequacy, the High Court could not be persuaded that a defendant was unable to pay the outstanding amount by reason of a worsening of his financial circumstances unless he gave full disclosure of what had happened in the meantime to all his assets, including previously unidentified assets (that the Crown Court had found to exist when making the confiscation order); any such rule would trammel the width of section 83 by imposing a restriction which was not in the statute; and it would also be capable of causing not merely hardship, but hardship amounting to injustice; in the case of previously unidentified assets, it is possible that a defendant may genuinely have no idea or only a dim recollection of what originally happened to them; he should be allowed to try to persuade the court, if this be the case, that his identified assets have shrunk in value and that as a result he is not able to pay the amount outstanding: *Glaves v. CPS* [2011] Costs L.R. 556, CA (Civ. Div.) (considering *Telli v. Revenue and Customs Prosecutions Office* (see § 5-1057 in the main work)).

It was held in *Escobar v. DPP* [2009] 1 W.L.R. 64, DC, that when making an order under section 83(4) of the CJA 1988 for the reduction of a sum payable under a confiscation order (following the issue of a certificate of inadequacy), the Crown Court has jurisdiction to fix a time for payment (by way of extension of the original date). The court said that although there is no express power to extend time in section 83, section 75(1) ("(1) Where the Crown Court orders the defendant to pay an amount under this Part ..., sections 139(1) to (4) ... of the Powers of Criminal Courts (Sentencing) Act 2000 (powers of Crown Court in relation to fines and enforcement of Crown Court fines) shall have effect as if that amount were a fine imposed on him by the Crown Court.") operates so as to incorporate section 139(1) of the 2000 Act (§ 5-676 in the main work), which in turn gives the court power to extend the time for payment when it substitutes a lesser sum under section 83. When read as a whole, section 75 is generally concerned to make provision for orders made under section 83 as well as those under other provisions in Part VI, and this is consistent with the natural and grammatical meaning of the relevant provisions, in that the Crown Court is making an order under section 83(4) and the effect of that order is that the defendant has to pay an amount due under Part VI. For the suggestion that the court's conclusion is out of kilter with the legislative structure, see CLW/09/02/5. For the relevant provisions of the PCA 2002, see sections 23 and 39 (§§ 5-824, 5-840 in the main work), neither of which contain any provision for an extension of the time allowed to pay.

Enforcement

5-764   See *Revenue and Customs Prosecutions Office v. May* [2010] 3 All E.R. 1173, CA (Civ. Div.) (§ 5-1059 in the main work).

Presence of the accused

5-765   See *R. v. Spearing* (§ 3-225 in the main work).

D. CONFISCATION UNDER THE PROCEEDS OF CRIME ACT 2002

(1) Summary

Key provisions

Confiscation orders (s.6)

★5-787   As to the amendment of section 6 of the PCA 2002, see *post*, § 5-805.

★   With effect from June 1, 2015 (Serious Crime Act 2015 (Commencement No. 1) Regulations 2015 (S.I. 2015 No. 820)), section 97 of the SOCPA 2005 was amended by the SCA 2015, s.40(1) to (4). The amendments do not affect the summary set out in the main work.

Statements of information (s.16)

★5-794   As to the amendment of section 16 of the 2002 Act, see *post*, § 5-817.

Orders requiring the defendant to provide information (s.18)

★5-796   As to the amendment of section 18 of the 2002 Act, see *post*, § 5-819.

Postponement (s.14)

★5-797   As to the amendment of section 14 of the 2002 Act, see *post*, § 5-814.

The recoverable amount (s.7)
  As to the amendment of section 6 of the PCA 2002, see *post*, § 5-805.   ★**5-798**

Sentencing the defendant for the offence (ss.13-15, 71)
  As to the amendment of section 13 of the 2002 Act, see *post*, § 5-813.   ★**5-801**

(2) Legislation

(a) *Statute*

Proceeds of Crime Act 2002, ss.6–91

Making of order
  With effect from June 1, 2015 (Serious Crime Act 2015 (Commencement No. 1) Regulations   ★**5-805**
2015 (S.I. 2015 No. 820)), section 6(5) of the 2002 Act was amended by the SCA 2015, s.85(1),
and Sched. 4, para. 19, to add the following sentence at the end—

  "Paragraph (b) applies only if, or to the extent that, it would not be disproportionate to require the
defendant to pay the recoverable amount.".

  For a case considering *R. v. Gavin*; *R. v. Tasie* (as to which, see the main work), see *R. v. Ali*   **5-806**
(Salah), *ante*, § 3-225.

Recoverable amount
  With effect from June 1, 2015 (Policing and Crime Act 2009 (Commencement No. 10,   ★**5-807**
Transitional Provision and Savings) Order 2015 (S.I. 2015 No. 983)), the amendments made to
section 7 of the 2002 Act by section 112 of, and paragraphs 99 and 100 of Schedule 7 to, the 2009
Act came into force.

Defendant's benefit
  It was held in *R. v. Chahal* [2014] 2 Cr.App.R.(S.) 35, CA, that the effect of sections 8(4) and   **5-808**
8(5) of the 2002 Act (see the main work) was that where, in one set of proceedings, the Crown
Court, having decided that the defendant had a "criminal lifestyle" and that he had benefited
from his general criminal conduct, made an assessment of his benefit from such conduct and
made a confiscation order pursuant to that assessment, any confiscation order in fresh proceedings had to be confined to benefit obtained subsequent to the date of the first order regardless of
when any criminal conduct occurred.

Determination of extent of defendant's interest in property
  With effect from June 1, 2015 (Serious Crime Act 2015 (Commencement No. 1) Regulations   ★**5-810a**
2015 (S.I. 2015 No. 820)), a new section 10A was inserted into the 2002 Act by the SCA 2015, s.1,
as follows—

  "Determination of extent of defendant's interest in property
    10A.—(1) Where it appears to a court making a confiscation order that—
      (a) there is property held by the defendant that is likely to be realised or otherwise used to
          satisfy the order, and
      (b) a person other than the defendant holds, or may hold, an interest in the property,
    the court may, if it thinks it appropriate to do so, determine the extent (at the time the confiscation
    order is made) of the defendant's interest in the property.
    (2) The court must not exercise the power conferred by subsection (1) unless it gives to anyone
  who the court thinks is or may be a person holding an interest in the property a reasonable opportunity to make representations to it.
    (3) A determination under this section is conclusive in relation to any question as to the extent of
  the defendant's interest in the property that arises in connection with—
      (a) the realisation of the property, or the transfer of an interest in the property, with a view to
          satisfying the confiscation order, or
      (b) any action or proceedings taken for the purposes of any such realisation or transfer.
    (4) Subsection (3)—
      (a) is subject to section 51(8B), and
      (b) does not apply in relation to a question that arises in proceedings before the Court of Ap-
          peal or the Supreme Court.

(5) In this Part, the 'extent' of the defendant's interest in property means the proportion that the value of the defendant's interest in it bears to the value of the property itself.".

Time for payment

★**5-811**   With effect from June 1, 2015 (Serious Crime Act 2015 (Commencement No. 1) Regulations 2015 (S.I. 2015 No. 820)), a new section 11 of the 2002 Act was substituted by the SCA 2015, s.5(1), as follows—

"*Time for payment*

11.—(1) Unless subsection (2) applies, the full amount ordered to be paid under a confiscation order must be paid on the day on which the order is made.

(2) If the court making the confiscation order is satisfied that the defendant is unable to pay the full amount on that day, it may make an order requiring whatever cannot be paid on that day to be paid—

    (a) in a specified period, or

    (b) in specified periods each of which relates to a specified amount.

(3) A specified period—

    (a) must start with the day on which the confiscation order is made, and

    (b) must not exceed three months.

(4) If—

    (a) within any specified period the defendant applies to the Crown Court for that period to be extended, and

    (b) the court is satisfied that, despite having made all reasonable efforts, the defendant is unable to pay the amount to which the specified period relates within that period,

the court may make an order extending the period (for all or any part or parts of the amount in question).

(5) An extended period—

    (a) must start with the day on which the confiscation order is made, and

    (b) must not exceed six months.

(6) An order under subsection (4)—

    (a) may be made after the end of the specified period to which it relates, but

    (b) must not be made after the end of the period of six months starting with the day on which the confiscation order is made.

(7) Periods specified or extended under this section must be such that, where the court believes that a defendant will by a particular day be able—

    (a) to pay the amount remaining to be paid, or

    (b) to pay an amount towards what remains to be paid,

that amount is required to be paid no later than that day.

(8) The court must not make an order under subsection (2) or (4) unless it gives the prosecutor an opportunity to make representations.".

Interest on unpaid sums

★**5-812**   With effect from June 1, 2015 (Serious Crime Act 2015 (Commencement No. 1) Regulations 2015 (S.I. 2015 No. 820)), section 12(1) of the 2002 Act was amended by the SCA 2015, s.85(1), and Sched. 4, para. 20, so as to substitute the words "any amount required to be paid" for "the amount required to be paid", and the words "must pay interest on that amount" for the words "must pay interest on the amount".

★   With effect from June 1, 2015 (S.I. 2015 No. 820 (*ante*)), section 12 of the 2002 Act was further amended by the SCA 2015, s.5(2), so as to substitute a new subsection (3), as follows—

"(3) If—

    (a) an application has been made under section 11(4) for a specified period to be extended,

    (b) the application has not been determined by the court, and

    (c) the period of six months starting with the day on which the confiscation order was made has not ended,

the amount on which interest is payable under this section does not include the amount to which the specified period relates.".

Effect of order on court's other powers

★**5-813**   As from April 13, 2015 (Criminal Justice and Courts Act 2015 (Commencement No. 1, Saving and Transitional Provisions) Order 2015 (S.I. 2015 No. 778)), the Criminal Justice and Courts Act

2015, s.54(3), and Sched. 12, para. 11, amended section 13(3)(a) of the 2002 Act, so as to insert, after "other than", the words "an order under section 21A of the Prosecution of Offences Act 1985 (criminal courts charge) or".

Where both a confiscation and a compensation order are made and a court is considering whether the defendant has sufficient means to satisfy both orders in full (see s.13(5)(b) in the main work), and thus whether to direct that some or all of the compensation should be paid out of sums recovered under the confiscation order (s.13(6)), it will not generally be appropriate to take into account the value of a matrimonial or family home where meeting both orders in full would be likely to require that home to be sold: *R. v. Beaumont* [2015] 1 Cr.App.R.(S.) 1, CA.

With effect from June 1, 2015 (Serious Crime Act 2015 (Commencement No. 1) Regulations ★ 2015 (S.I. 2015 No. 820)), section 13 of the 2002 Act was further amended by the SCA 2015, s.6, so as (i) to substitute, in subsection (3)(a), the words "a priority order" for the words from "an order under section 130" to the end; (ii) to insert a new subsection (3A), as follows—

> "(3A) In this section 'priority order' means any of the following—
> (a) a compensation order under section 130 of the Sentencing Act;
> (b) an order requiring payment of a surcharge under section 161A of the Criminal Justice Act 2003
> (c) an unlawful profit order under section 4 of the Prevention of Social Housing Fraud Act 2013";

(iii) to substitute a new subsection (5), as follows—

> "(5) Subsection (6) applies if—
> (a) the Crown Court makes both a confiscation order and one or more priority orders against the same person in the same proceedings, and
> (b) the court believes the person will not have sufficient means to satisfy all those orders in full.";

and (iv) in subsection (6), to substitute the words "amount payable under the priority order (or orders)" for the words "compensation or amount payable under the unlawful profit order (or both)".

Having become spent as a result of the amendments to section 13 made by section 6 of the ★ 2015 Act (*ante*), paragraph 14 of the schedule to the Prevention of Social Housing Fraud Act 2013 is repealed: 2015 Act, s.85(1), and Sched. 4, para. 89 (into force on the same date as s.6 of the 2015 Act (see *ante*)).

As from a day to be appointed, the Modern Slavery Act 2015, s.57(1), and Sched. 5, para. 15, ★ provides for further amendments to section 13 of the 2002 Act. The draftsman of this Act has, however, acted in ignorance of the amendments already made by the SCA 2015 as these prospective amendments all relate to the 2002 Act as it read prior to its amendment by the SCA. As the Modern Slavery Act amendments clearly cannot be brought into force without further amendment of the legislation, the detail is not set out here, but they relate to subsection (3), subsection (5) and subsection (6).

Orders for securing compliance. with confiscation order

With effect from June 1, 2015 (Serious Crime Act 2015 (Commencement No. 1) Regulations ★**5-813a** 2015 (S.I. 2015 No. 820)), new sections 13A and 13B were inserted into the 2002 Act by the SCA 2015, s.7, as follows—

> *"Orders for securing compliance with confiscation order*
> **13A.**—(1) This section applies where the court makes a confiscation order.
> (2) The court may make such order as it believes is appropriate for the purpose of ensuring that the confiscation order is effective (a 'compliance order').
> (3) The court must consider whether to make a compliance order—
> (a) on the making of the confiscation order, and
> (b) if it does not make a compliance order then, at any later time (while the confiscation order is still in effect) on the application of the prosecutor.
> (4) In considering whether to make a compliance order, the court must, in particular, consider whether any restriction or prohibition on the defendant's travel outside the United Kingdom ought to be imposed for the purpose mentioned in subsection (2).

(5) The court may discharge or vary a compliance order on an application made by—

    (a) the prosecutor;

    (b) any person affected by the order.

Appeals against orders under section 13A

13B.—(1) If on an application under section 13A(3)(b) the Crown Court decides not to make a compliance order, the prosecutor may appeal to the Court of Appeal against the decision.

(2) The following persons may appeal to the Court of Appeal in respect of the Crown Court's decision to make, discharge or vary a compliance order—

    (a) the prosecutor;

    (b) any person affected by the order.

(3) On an appeal under subsection (1) or (2) the Court of Appeal may—

    (a) confirm the decision, or

    (b) make such order as it believes is appropriate.

(4) An appeal lies to the Supreme Court against a decision of the Court of Appeal under subsection (3).

(5) An appeal under subsection (4) lies at the instance of any person who was a party to the proceedings before the Court of Appeal.

(6) On an appeal under subsection (4) the Supreme Court may—

    (a) confirm the decision of the Court of Appeal, or

    (b) make such order as it believes is appropriate.

(7) In this section 'compliance order' means an order made under section 13A.".

★   An order under section 13A may be made in respect of any confiscation order that is made on or after the day on which section 7 of the 2015 Act came into force: 2015 Act, s.86(1).

Postponement

★5-814   With effect from June 1, 2015 (Serious Crime Act 2015 (Commencement No. 1) Regulations 2015 (S.I. 2015 No. 820)), section 14(12) of the 2002 Act was amended by the SCA 2015, s.85(1), and Sched. 4, para. 21, so as to insert a new paragraph (ca), as follows—

    "(ca) made an order under section 161A of the Criminal Justice Act 2003 (orders requiring payment of surcharge);".

★   In *R. v. Guraj* [2015] 3 *Archbold Review* 3, CA ([2015] EWCA Crim. 305), a confiscation order that had been made following a serious breach of section 14 (the initial period of postponement had long expired with no application for an extension having been made) and a serious breach of section 15(2) (the judge had, when sentencing, made a forfeiture order under the Misuse of Drugs Act 1971, s.27, such an order falling within s.13(3)) was quashed, notwithstanding that it had been made within "the permitted period" (see s.14(5)); forfeiture orders should not be made when confiscation proceedings are under way; if they are made in such circumstances, then the prosecution will be held more strictly to the time limits in section 14, as subsection (12) entails that the "balm" of subsection (11) will be unavailable.

Effect of postponement

★5-816   With effect from June 1, 2015 (Serious Crime Act 2015 (Commencement No. 1) Regulations 2015 (S.I. 2015 No. 820)), section 15(2) and (3) of the 2002 Act were amended by the SCA 2015, s.85(1), and Sched. 4, para. 22, so as (i) in subsection (2)(c), to omit the word "or" at the end; (ii) in subsection (2), to insert a new paragraph (ca), as follows—

    "(ca) make an order for the payment of a surcharge under section 161A of the Criminal Justice Act 2003, or";

(iii) in subsection (3)(c), to omit the word "or" at the end; and (iv) in subsection (3), to insert a new paragraph (ca), as follows—

    "(ca) making an order for the payment of a surcharge under section 161A of the Criminal Justice Act 2003, or".

★   For a case considering whether a confiscation order fell to be quashed where there had been a serious breach of section 15(2) of the 2002 Act, see *R. v. Guraj, ante,* § 5-814.

Statement of information

★5-817   With effect from June 1, 2015 (Serious Crime Act 2015 (Commencement No. 1) Regulations

2015 (S.I. 2015 No. 820)), section 16 of the 2002 Act was amended by the SCA 2015, s.2(1), so as to insert new subsections (6A) and (6B), as follows—

"(6A) A statement of information (other than one to which subsection (6B) applies) must include any information known to the prosecutor which the prosecutor believes is or would be relevant for the purpose of enabling the court to decide—
(a) whether to make a determination under section 10A, or
(b) what determination to make (if the court decides to make one).
(6B) If the court has decided to make a determination under section 10A, a further statement of information under subsection (6)(b) must, if the court so orders, include specified information that is relevant to the determination.".

Provision of information by defendant

With effect from June 1, 2015 (Serious Crime Act 2015 (Commencement No. 1) Regulations **★5-819**
2015 (S.I. 2015 No. 820)), section 18 of the 2002 Act was amended by the SCA 2015, s.2(2), so as to insert the words "(including functions under section 10A)" after the word "functions" in subsection (2), and to replace the words "deciding the available amount under section 9," in subsection (6)(b), with the words—

"(b) deciding—
(i) the available amount under section 9, or
(ii) whether to make a determination under section 10A, or what determination to make (if the court decides to make one),".

Provision of information as to defendant's interest in property

With effect from June 1, 2015 (Serious Crime Act 2015 (Commencement No. 1) Regulations **★5-819a**
2015 (S.I. 2015 No. 820)), a new section 18A was inserted into the 2002 Act by the SCA 2015, s.2(3), as follows—

"Provision of information as to defendant's interest in property
18A.—(1) This section applies if the court—
(a) is considering whether to make a determination under section 10A of the extent of the defendant's interest in any property, or
(b) is deciding what determination to make (if the court has decided to make a determination under that section).
In this section 'interested person' means a person (other than the defendant) who the court thinks is or may be a person holding an interest in the property.
(2) For the purpose of obtaining information to help it in carrying out its functions under section 10A the court may at any time order an interested person to give it information specified in the order.
(3) An order under this section may require all or a specified part of the information to be given in a specified manner and before a specified date.
(4) If an interested person fails without reasonable excuse to comply with an order under this section the court may draw such inference as it believes is appropriate.
(5) Subsection (4) does not affect any power of the court to deal with the person in respect of a failure to comply with an order under this section.
(6) If the prosecutor accepts to any extent an allegation made by an interested person—
(a) in giving information required by an order under this section, or
(b) in any other statement given to the court in relation to any matter relevant to a determination under section 10A,
the court may treat the acceptance as conclusive of the matters to which it relates.
(7) For the purposes of this section an allegation may be accepted in a manner ordered by the court.
(8) If the court makes an order under this section it may at any time vary it by making another one.
(9) No information given by a person under this section is admissible in evidence in proceedings against that person for an offence.".

No order made: reconsideration of case

With effect from June 1, 2015 (Serious Crime Act 2015 (Commencement No. 1) Regulations **★5-820**
2015 (S.I. 2015 No. 820)), section 19 of the 2002 Act was amended by the Serious Crime Act 2015, s.85(1), and Sched. 4, para. 23, so as (i) to insert a new paragraph (da) in subsection (7), as follows—

"(da) any order which has been made against the defendant in respect of the offence (or any of the offences) concerned under section 161A of the Criminal Justice Act 2003 (orders requiring payment of surcharge);";

and (ii) in subsection (8), to insert the words ", a surcharge under section 161A of the Criminal Justice Act 2003" after the words "Sentencing Act".

★ As from a day to be appointed, section 19(8) of the 2002 Act is further amended by the Modern Slavery Act 2015, s.57(1), and Sched. 5, para. 16, so as to insert the words "in relation to it" at the end.

No order made: reconsideration of benefit

★**5-821** With effect from June 1, 2015 (Serious Crime Act 2015 (Commencement No. 1) Regulations 2015 (S.I. 2015 No. 820)), section 20 of the 2002 Act was amended by the SCA 2015, s.85(1), and Sched. 4, para. 24, so as (i) in subsection (11) to insert a new paragraph (da), as follows—

"(da) any order which has been made against the defendant in respect of the offence (or any of the offences) concerned under section 161A of the Criminal Justice Act 2003 (orders requiring payment of surcharge);";

and (ii) in subsection (12), to insert the words ", a surcharge under section 161A of the Criminal Justice Act 2003" after the words "Sentencing Act".

★ As from a day to be appointed, section 20(12) of the 2002 Act is further amended by the Modern Slavery Act 2015, s.57(1), and Sched. 5, para. 17, so as to insert the words "in relation to it" at the end.

Order made: reconsideration of benefit

★**5-822** With effect from June 1, 2015 (Serious Crime Act 2015 (Commencement No. 1) Regulations 2015 (S.I. 2015 No. 820)), section 21 of the 2002 Act was amended by the SCA 2015, s.85(1), and Sched. 4, para. 25, so as (i) in subsection (9), to insert a new paragraph (ca), as follows-

"(ca) any order which has been made against the defendant in respect of the offence (or any of the offences) concerned under section 161A of the Criminal Justice Act 2003 (orders requiring payment of surcharge);";

and (ii) in subsection (10), to insert insert ", (ca)" after "(9)(c)".

Order made: reconsideration of available amount

★**5-823** With effect from June 1, 2015 (Serious Crime Act 2015 (Commencement No. 1) Regulations 2015 (S.I. 2015 No. 820)), section 22 of the 2002 Act was amended by the SCA 2015, s.85(1), and Sched. 4, para. 26, so as (i) in subsection (5), to insert a new paragraph (d), as follows—

"(d) any order which has been made against the defendant in respect of the offence (or any of the offences) concerned under section 161A of the Criminal Justice Act 2003 (orders requiring payment of surcharge).";

and (ii) in subsection (6), to insert "or (d)" after "(5)(c)".

Where, following an award of damages in favour of the defendant as a result of a road traffic collision, the Crown Court recalculated the available amount pursuant to an application under section 22 of the PCA 2002 (see the main work) and found an amount that exceeded the relevant amount (see subs. (4)), it would have been appropriate to vary the confiscation order to take account of the general damages but not the special damages (which related to specific expenses that had been incurred): *R. v. John* [2014] 2 Cr.App.R.(S.) 73, CA.

Inadequacy of available amount: variation of order

★**5-824** With effect from June 1, 2015 (Serious Crime Act 2015 (Commencement No. 1) Regulations 2015 (S.I. 2015 No. 820)), section 23(1)(b) of the 2002 Act was amended by the SCA 2015, s.8(1), so as to insert the words "or the prosecutor" after the words "the defendant" in subsection (1)(b).

★ Upon an application by the defendant (under the DTOA 1986, s.14) for a certificate of inadequacy, the fact that an overseas property that he had an interest in was involved in unrelated legal proceedings that prevented sale pending resolution of those proceedings, did not mean that it had a nil value; the crucial question was whether he had proved it was impossible to realise the property, rather than just that a sale would encounter difficulties: *Mundy v. CPS* [2015] Lloyd's Rep. F.C. 109, QBD (Walker J.).

Recovery from estate of deceased defendant impractical: discharge of order
    With effect from June 1, 2015 (Serious Crime Act 2015 (Commencement No. 1) Regulations **★5-826a** 2015 (S.I. 2015 No. 820)), a new section 25A was inserted into the 2002 Act by the SCA 2015, s.8(2), as follows—

> *"Recovery from estate of deceased defendant impractical: discharge of order*
>   **25A.**—(1) This section applies if—
>   (a) a court has made a confiscation order,
>   (b) the defendant dies while the order is not satisfied, and
>   (c) the designated officer for a magistrates' court applies to the Crown Court for the discharge of the order.
>   (2) The court may discharge the order if it appears to the court that—
>   (a) it is not possible to recover anything from the estate of the deceased for the purpose of satisfying the order to any extent, or
>   (b) it would not be reasonable to make any attempt, or further attempt, to recover anything from the estate of the deceased for that purpose.".

    Section 8(3) of the 2015 Act provides that section 25A of the 2002 Act applies to a confiscation **★** order under the CJA 1988 or the DTA 1994 as it applies to one under the 2002 Act.

Defendant absconds after conviction or committal for sentence
    With effect from June 1, 2015 (Serious Crime Act 2015 (Commencement No. 1) Regulations **★5-828** 2015 (S.I. 2015 No. 820)), section 27 of the 2002 Act was amended by the SCA 2015, s.9(1) and (2), so as (i) to substitute a new subsection (2), as follows—

> "(2) The first condition is that a defendant falls within any of the following paragraphs—
>   (a) he absconds and, either before or after doing so, he is convicted of an offence or offences in proceedings before the Crown Court;
>   (b) he absconds after being committed to the Crown Court for sentence in respect of an offence or offences under section 3, 3A, 3B, 3C4, 4A or 6 of the Sentencing Act;
>   (c) he absconds after being committed to the Crown Court in respect of an offence or offences under section 70 below (committal with a view to a confiscation order being considered).";

and (ii) to substitute a new subsection (6) for subsections (6) and (7), as follows—

> "(6) Once the defendant ceases to be an absconder—
>   (a) section 19 has effect as if subsection (1) read—
>   '(1) This section applies if—
>   (a) at a time when the first condition in section 27 was satisfied the court did not proceed under section 6,
>   (b) before the end of the period of six years starting with the day when the defendant ceased to be an absconder, the prosecutor applies to the Crown Court to proceed under section 6, and
>   (c) the court believes it is appropriate for it to do so.';
>   (b) section 20 has effect as if subsection (4) read—
>   '(4) The second condition is that—
>   (a) before the end of the period of six years starting with the day when the defendant ceased to be an absconder, the prosecutor applies to the Crown Court to reconsider whether the defendant has benefited from his general or particular criminal conduct (as the case may be), and
>   (b) the court believes it is appropriate for it to do so.';
>   (c) section 21 has effect as if subsection (1) read—
>   '(1) This section applies if—
>   (a) a court has made a confiscation order,
>   (b) the prosecutor believes that if the court were to find the amount of the defendant's benefit in pursuance of this section it would exceed the relevant amount,
>   (c) before the end of the period of six years starting with the day when the defendant ceased to be an absconder, the prosecutor applies to the Crown Court to proceed under this section, and
>   (d) the court believes it is appropriate for it to do so.';

    (d) the modifications set out in subsection (5)(a) to (d) of this section do not apply to proceedings that take place by virtue of section 19, 20 or 21 (as applied by this subsection).".

★   Having become spent as a result of the amendment made by section 9(1) of the 2015 Act (*ante*), paragraph 75(3) of Schedule 3 to the CJA 2003 is repealed: 2015 Act, s.85(1), and Sched. 4, para. 67 (into force from the same date as s.9 of the 2015 Act (see *ante*)).

★   In *R. v. Ali (Salah)* [2015] 1 W.L.R. 841, CA, the court described a submission that the fact that there was nothing to prevent the assumptions provided for by section 10 of the PCA 2002 (§ 5-810 in the main work) being applied where confiscation proceedings took place in the defendant's absence through illness meant that such a defendant would be in a less favourable position than one who had absconded after conviction because section 27 (see the main work) disapplied section 10 in such a case, as misconceived. The court said that when the absconder returns, the effect of section 27(6) is that the prosecution are able then to proceed against the absconder as if they had not done so in his absence. For a submission that the court misunderstood or misread section 27(6), see CLW/14/45/21. The court was concerned with section 27(6) prior to its replacement by the 2015 Act (as to which, see *ante*). The effect of the new section 27(6)(c), however, is that, upon the defendant ceasing to be an absconder, there may be a reconsideration of benefit under section 21 (without the need for fresh evidence) and the assumptions under section 10 (limited only by s.21(6)) will apply. This certainly will put paid to any argument that an absconder is in a better position than the defendant who is merely absent through illness. As to this case, see also *ante*, § 3-225; and *post*, § 5-1050b.

Defendant neither convicted nor acquitted

★**5-829**   With effect from June 1, 2015 (Serious Crime Act 2015 (Commencement No. 1) Regulations 2015 (S.I. 2015 No. 820)), section 28 of the 2002 Act was amended by the SCA 2015, s.9(3) and (4), so as (i) to substitute the words "three months" for the words "two years" in subsection (2)(c), and (ii) to substitute a new subsection (6), as follows—

    "(6) Once the defendant has ceased to be an absconder—
      (a) section 21 has effect as if subsection (1) read—
        '(1) This section applies if—
        (a) a court has made a confiscation order,
        (b) the prosecutor believes that if the court were to find the amount of the defendant's benefit in pursuance of this section it would exceed the relevant amount,
        (c) before the end of the period of six years starting with the day when the defendant ceased to be an absconder, the prosecutor applies to the Crown Court to proceed under this section, and
        (d) the court believes it is appropriate for it to do so.';
      (b) the modifications set out in subsection (5)(a) to (d) of this section do not apply to proceedings that take place by virtue of section 21 (as applied by this subsection).".

    R. v. Okedare is now reported at [2014] 2 Cr.App.R.(S.) 68.

Appeal by prosecutor

★**5-832**   With effect from June 1, 2015 (Serious Crime Act 2015 (Commencement No. 1) Regulations 2015 (S.I. 2015 No. 820)), section 31 of the 2002 Act was amended by the SCA 2015, s.85(1), and Sched. 4, para. 27, so as (i) to insert "etc." at the end of the heading, and (ii) to insert "10A," after the words "by virtue of section" in subsection (3).

★   With effect from June 1, 2015 (S.I. 2015 No. 820 (*ante*)), section 31 of the 2002 Act was amended by the SCA 2015, s.3(1), so as to insert new subsections (4) to (8), as follows—

    "(4) An appeal lies to the Court of Appeal against a determination, under section 10A, of the extent of the defendant's interest in property.
    (5) An appeal under subsection (4) lies at the instance of—
      (a) the prosecutor;
      (b) a person who the Court of Appeal thinks is or may be a person holding an interest in the property, if subsection (6) or (7) applies.
    (6) This subsection applies if the person was not given a reasonable opportunity to make representations when the determination was made.
    (7) This subsection applies if it appears to the Court of Appeal to be arguable that giving effect to the determination would result in a serious risk of injustice to the person.

(8) An appeal does not lie under subsection (4) where—
   (a) the Court of Appeal believes that an application under section 50 is to be made by the prosecutor for the appointment of a receiver,
   (b) such an application has been made but has not yet been determined, or
   (c) a receiver has been appointed under section 50.".

Court's powers on appeal

With effect from June 1, 2015 (Serious Crime Act 2015 (Commencement No. 1) Regulations 2015 (S.I. 2015 No. 820)), section 32 of the 2002 Act was amended by the SCA 2015, s.3(2), so as to insert a new subsection (2A), as follows—   ★**5-833**

"(2A) On an appeal under section 31(4) the Court of Appeal may—
   (a) confirm the determination, or
   (b) make such order as it believes is appropriate.".

With effect from June 1, 2015 (S.I. 2015 No. 820 (*ante*)), section 32 of the 2002 Act was amended by the SCA 2015, s.85(1), and Sched. 4, para. 28, so as to insert the words ", section 161A of the Criminal Justice Act 2003 (orders requiring payment of surcharge)" after the words "(compensation orders)" in subsection (7).   ★

As from a day to be appointed, section 32 of the 2002 Act was further amended by the Modern Slavery Act 2015, s.57(1), and Sched. 5, para. 18, so as to insert the words "in relation to it" at the end of subsection (7)(b).   ★

Appeal to Supreme Court

With effect from June 1, 2015 (Serious Crime Act 2015 (Commencement No. 1) Regulations 2015 (S.I. 2015 No. 820)), section 33 of the 2002 Act was amended by the SCA 2015, s.3(3), so as (i) to substitute a new subsection (2), as follows—   ★**5-834**

"(2) An appeal under this section lies at the instance of—
   (a) the defendant or the prosecutor (except where paragraph (b) applies);
   (b) if the proceedings in the Court of Appeal were proceedings on an appeal under section 31(4), any person who was a party to those proceedings.".

and (ii) to insert a new subsection (3A), as follows—

"(3A) On an appeal under this section from a decision under section 32(2A) the Supreme Court may—
   (a) confirm the decision of the Court of Appeal, or
   (b) make such order as it believes is appropriate.".

With effect from June 1, 2015 (S.I. 2015 No. 820 (*ante*)), section 33 of the 2002 Act was amended by the SCA 2015, s.85(1), and Sched. 4, para. 29, so as to insert the words ", section 161A of the Criminal Justice Act 2003 (orders requiring payment of surcharge)" after the words "(compensation orders)" in subsection (9).   ★

As from a day to be appointed, section 33 of the 2002 Act (*ante*) is further amended by the Modern Slavery Act 2015, s.57(1), and Sched. 5, para. 19, so as to insert the words "in relation to it" at the end of subsection (9)(b).   ★

Enforcement as fines

With effect from June 1, 2015 (Serious Crime Act 2015 (Commencement No. 1) Regulations 2015 (S.I. 2015 No. 820)), section 35 of the 2002 Act was amended by the SCA 2015, s.85(1), and Sched. 4, para. 30, so as to substitute "139(2), (3)" for "139(2) to (4)" in subsection (2).   ★**5-836**

With effect from June 1, 2015 (S.I. 2015 No. 820 (*ante*)), section 35 of the 2002 Act was amended by the SCA 2015, s.10(1), so as to insert new subsections (2A) to (2C), as follows—   ★

"(2A) Where a court is fixing a term of imprisonment or detention under section 139(2) of the Sentencing Act (as applied by subsection (2) above) in respect of an amount ordered to be paid under a confiscation order, the maximum terms are those specified in the second column of the Table for amounts described in the corresponding entry in the first column.

TABLE

Amount	Maximum term
£10,000 or less	6 months
More than £10,000 but no more than £500,000	5 years
More than £500,000 but no more than £1 million	7 years
More than £1 million	14 years

(2B) In the application of subsection (9) of section 139 of the Sentencing Act by virtue of subsection (2) above, the reference to subsections (2) to (4) of that section is to be read as a reference to—
  (a) subsections (2) and (3) of that section, and
  (b) subsection (2A) above.
(2C) The Secretary of State may by order—
  (a) amend subsection (2A) so as to provide for minimum terms of imprisonment or detention under section 139(2) of the Sentencing Act (as applied by subsection (2) above) in respect of amounts ordered to be paid under a confiscation order;
  (b) amend the Table in subsection (2A) so as to remove, alter or replace any entry (including an entry inserted by virtue of the power in paragraph (a) of this subsection) or to add any entry.".

Conditions of exercise of powers

★**5-841**   With effect from June 1, 2015 (Serious Crime Act 2015 (Commencement No. 1) Regulations 2015 (S.I. 2015 No. 820)), section 40(2)(b) of the 2002 Act was amended by the SCA 2015, s.11(1), so as to substitute the words "are reasonable grounds to suspect" for the words "is reasonable cause to believe".

Restraint orders

★**5-842**   Sections 46(5) (for the purpose of exercising the power to prescribe by regulations), (6) and (7) (and subs. (1), so far as relating thereto) and 47 of the Crime and Courts Act 2013 came into force on March 20, 2015, and section 46 (to the extent that it was not already in force) came into force on June 1, 2015: Crime and Courts Act 2013 (Commencement No. 12) Order 2015 (S.I. 2015 No. 813). As to sections 46 and 47, see the main work.

★   With effect from June 1, 2015 (Serious Crime Act 2015 (Commencement No. 1) Regulations 2015 (S.I. 2015 No. 820)), section 41 of the 2002 Act was amended by the SCA 2015, ss.11(2) and 85(1), and Sched. 4, para. 31, so as to insert new subsections (7A) to (7C) (s.11(2)) and 7D (s.85(1) and Sched. 4, para. 31), as follows—

"(7A) Subsections (7B) and (7C) apply where the Crown Court makes a restraint order (by virtue of the first condition in section 40) as a result of a criminal investigation having been started in England and Wales with regard to an offence.
(7B) The court—
  (a) must include in the order a requirement for the applicant for the order to report to the court on the progress of the investigation at such times and in such manner as the order may specify (a 'reporting requirement'), and
  (b) must discharge the order if proceedings for the offence are not started within a reasonable time (and this duty applies whether or not an application to discharge the order is made under section 42(3)).
(7C) The duty under subsection (7B)(a) does not apply if the court decides that, in the circumstances of the case, a reporting requirement should not be imposed, but the court—
  (a) must give reasons for its decision, and
  (b) may at any time vary the order so as to include a reporting requirement (and this power applies whether or not an application to vary the order is made under section 42(3)).
(7D) In considering whether to make an order under subsection (7), the court must, in particular, consider whether any restriction or prohibition on the defendant's travel outside the United Kingdom ought to be imposed for the purpose mentioned in that subsection.".

★   For regulations made under section 41(5A) and (10) of the 2002 Act (see the main work) prescribing a restriction on the making of a relevant legal aid payment out of assets that are subject to a restraint order, see S.I. 2015 No. 868 (*post*, § 5-846).

Restraint orders

5-844   **Disclosure.** *Barnes v. Eastenders Cash and Carry plc*; *Eastenders Cash and Carry plc v. CPS* is now reported at [2015] A.C. 1.

Legal expenses. As to the commencement of the amendments made to section 41 of the 2002   ★**5-846**
Act by section 46 of the Crime and Courts Act 2013 (as to which, see the main work), see *ante*, §
5-842.

The Restraint Orders (Legal Aid Exception and Relevant Legal Aid Payments) Regulations   ★
2015 (S.I. 2015 No. 868) were made under section 41(5A) and (10) of the 2002 Act, and section
47 of the Crime and Courts Act 2013 (as to all of which, see § 5-842 in the main work). Whereas
the 2013 Act, ss.46 and 47, made provision to enable property that is subject to a restraint order
in accordance with Part 2 of the 2002 Act to be used to make a relevant legal aid payment (as to
which, see s.41(5)), whereas, under section 41 (as amended), every restraint order must be subject
to an exception that enables relevant legal aid payments to be made out of assets restrained by
the order, and whereas the Secretary of State may by regulations restrict the circumstances in
which such payments may be made, Part 2 (reg. 2) of these regulations prescribes such a restriction, so that a relevant legal aid payment may only be made out of realisable property that is
subject to a restraint order where proceedings for an offence to which the relevant legal aid payment relates have resulted in a confiscation order that has been subsequently discharged or
satisfied.

In Part 3 (relevant legal aid payments: continuation of restraint (regs 3-5)), regulation 5 applies   ★
the following provisions of the 2002 Act, with modifications, in relation to restraint orders and
relevant legal aid payments: ss.42(6) (application, discharge and variation (§ 5-848 in the main
work), 47B (conditions for exercise of powers to seize property (*ibid.*, § 5-856)), 47C(1)(a) (power
to seize property (*ibid.*, § 5-857)), 54 (enforcement receivers (*ibid.*, § 5-880)), 63(3)(a) (discharge
and variation of orders relating to management receivers (*ibid.*, § 5-859)), 67D (proceeds of
realisation (*ibid.*, § 5-897)) and 69(2) (powers of court and receiver (*ibid.*, § 5-899)). The effect is
that a restraint order may be maintained after the satisfaction or discharge of an associated
confiscation order, so that relevant legal aid payments may be made out of assets that are still
subject to restraint.

Breach. *Director of the Serious Fraud Office v. O'Brien* is now reported at [2014] A.C. 1246.   **5-846a**

[Restraint orders: power to retain seized property etc.

With effect from November 22, 2014 (Crime and Courts Act 2013 (Commencement No. 11)   **5-847**
Order 2014 (S.I. 2014 No. 3098)), section 55(14) of, and paragraphs 14 and 15 of Schedule 21 to,
the 2013 Act (see the main work) were brought into force.

With effect from June 1, 2015 (Policing and Crime Act 2009 (Commencement No. 10,   ★
Transitional Provision and Savings) Order 2015 (S.I. 2015 No. 983)), the insertion of section 41A
into the 2002 Act by section 52 of the 2009 Act came into force.

Application, discharge and variation

With effect from June 1, 2015 (Serious Crime Act 2015 (Commencement No. 1) Regulations   ★**5-848**
2015 (S.I. 2015 No. 820)), section 42 of the 2002 Act was amended by the SCA 2015, s.12, so as to
insert new subsections (6A) and (6B), as follows—

> "(6A) The duty in subsection (6) to discharge a restraint order on the conclusion of proceedings
> does not apply where—
>> (a) the proceedings are concluded by reason of a defendant's conviction for an offence being
>> quashed,
>> (b) the order is in force at the time when the conviction is quashed, and
>> (c) the Court of Appeal has ordered the defendant to be retried for the offence or the prosecu-
>> tor has applied for such an order to be made.
> (6B) But the court must discharge the restraint order—
>> (a) if the Court of Appeal declines to make an order for the defendant to be retried,
>> (b) if the Court of Appeal orders the defendant to be retried but proceedings for the retrial
>> are not started within a reasonable time, or
>> (c) otherwise, on the conclusion of proceedings for the retrial of the defendant.".

With effect from June 1, 2015 (S.I. 2015 No. 820 (*ante*)), section 42 of the 2002 Act was further   ★
amended by the SCA 2015, s.85(1), and Sched. 4, para. 32, so as (i) to substitute "(8)" for "(7)" in
subsection (4), and (ii) to substitute new subsections (7) and (8) for subsection (7), as follows—

> "(7) If the condition in section 40 which was satisfied was that an investigation was started—

(a) the court must discharge the order if within a reasonable time proceedings for the offence are not started;

(b) otherwise, the court must discharge the order on the conclusion of the proceedings.

(8) If the condition in section 40 which was satisfied was that an application was to be made—

(a) the court must discharge the order if within a reasonable time the application is not made;

(b) otherwise, the court must discharge the order on the conclusion of the application.".

★ As to the application of section 42 of the 2002 Act in relation to restraint orders and relevant legal aid payments, see S.I. 2015 No. 868, *ante*, § 5-846.

Detention of property pending appeal

★5-851 With effect from June 1, 2015 (Policing and Crime Act 2009 (Commencement No. 10, Transitional Provision and Savings) Order 2015 (S.I. 2015 No. 983)), the insertion of section 44A into the 2002 Act by section 52 of the 2009 Act came into force.

Seizure

★5-852 With effect from June 1, 2015 (Policing and Crime Act 2009 (Commencement No. 10, Transitional Provision and Savings) Order 2015 (S.I. 2015 No. 983)), the repeal of section 45 of the 2002 Act by sections 55(1) and (3), and 112(2) of, and Part 4 of Schedule 8 to, the 2009 Act came into force. Section 45 continues to apply, however, in relation to property which, on that date, was subject to the directions of a court made under subsection (2) of that section: S.I. 2015 No. 983, art. 4(1); and section 41A of the 2002 Act (§ 5-847 in the main work) has effect in relation to any such property as if "relevant seizure power" included section 45 of that Act: *ibid.*, art. 4(2).

[Sections 47B to 47S: meaning of "appropriate officer"

5-855 With effect from November 22, 2014 (Policing and Crime Act 2009 (Commencement No. 9) Order 2014 (S.I. 2014 No. 3101)), section 55(1) and (2) of the 2009 Act were brought into force insofar as they insert sections 47A (see the main work), 47G (*ibid.*, § 5-861) and 47S(1) to (5) (*ibid.*, § 5-873) into the 2002 Act, to the extent that they confer a power to make subordinate legislation, and so far as is necessary for the purpose of making regulations, rules of court, orders or codes of practice.

With effect from November 22, 2014 (Crime and Courts Act 2013 (Commencement No. 11) Order 2014 (S.I. 2014 No. 3098)), section 55(3) and (4)(a) of the 2013 Act were brought into force.

★ With effect from June 1, 2015 (Policing and Crime Act 2009 (Commencement No. 10, Transitional Provision and Savings) Order 2015 (S.I. 2015 No. 983)), the insertion of sections 47A to 47S into the 2002 Act (see the main work and *ante*) by section 55(1) and (2) of the 2009 Act (*ibid.*) came fully into force.

For procedural provision in relation to section 47A of the 2002 Act, see *post*, § 5-970.

[Conditions for exercise of powers

★5-856 As to the insertion of section 47B into the 2002 Act, see *ante*, § 5-855.

★ As to the application of section 47B in relation to restraint orders and relevant legal aid payments, see S.I. 2015 No. 868, *ante*, § 5-846.

For procedural provision in relation to section 47B of the 2002 Act, see *post*, § 5-970.

★ As from a day to be appointed, section 47B of the 2002 Act is amended by the SCA 2015, s.13(1), so as to substitute, in subsection (2)(d), the words "are reasonable grounds to suspect" for the words "is reasonable cause to believe".

[Power to seize property

5-857 With effect from November 22, 2014 (Crime and Courts Act 2013 (Commencement No. 11) Order 2014 (S.I. 2014 No. 3098)), section 55(14) of, and paragraphs 14 and 16 of Schedule 21 to, the 2013 Act (see the main work) were brought into force.

★ As to the insertion of section 47C into the 2002 Act, see *ante*, § 5-855.

★ As to the application of section 47C in relation to restraint orders and relevant legal aid payments, see S.I. 2015 No. 868, *ante*, § 5-846.

For procedural provision in relation to section 47C of the 2002 Act, see *post*, § 5-970.

[Search power: premises
As to the insertion of section 47D into the 2002 Act, see *ante*, § 5-855. ★**5-858**
For procedural provision in relation to section 47D of the 2002 Act, see *post*, § 5-970.

[Search power: people
As to the insertion of section 47E into the 2002 Act, see *ante*, § 5-855. ★**5-859**
For procedural provision in relation to section 47E of the 2002 Act, see *post*, § 5-970.

[Search power: vehicles
As to the insertion of section 47C into the 2002 Act, see *ante*, § 5-855. ★**5-860**
For procedural provision in relation to section 47F of the 2002 Act, see *post*, § 5-970.

["Appropriate approval"
As to the insertion of section 47G into the 2002 Act, see *ante*, § 5-855. **5-861**
With effect from November 22, 2014 (Crime and Courts Act 2013 (Commencement No. 11)
Order 2014 (S.I. 2014 No. 3098)), section 55(14) of, and paragraphs 14 and 17 of Schedule 21 to,
the 2013 Act were brought into force.
For procedural provision in relation to section 47G of the 2002 Act, see *post*, § 5-970.
As from a day to be appointed, section 47G(3) of the 2002 Act is amended by the SCA 2015, ★
s.13(2), so as to insert a new paragraph (ab), as follows—

"(ab) in relation to the exercise of a power by a National Crime Agency officer, the Director
General of the National Crime Agency or any other National Crime Agency officer
authorised by the Director General (whether generally or specifically) for this purpose,".

[Exercise of powers without judicial approval
As to the insertion of section 47H into the 2002 Act, see *ante*, § 5-855. ★**5-862**
For procedural provision in relation to section 47H of the 2002 Act, see *post*, § 5-970.

[Report by person appointed under s.47H(4) on exercise of powers
As to the insertion of section 47I into the 2002 Act, see *ante*, § 5-855. ★**5-863**
For procedural provision in relation to section 47I of the 2002 Act, see *post*, § 5-970.

[Initial detention of seized property
As to the insertion of section 47J into the 2002 Act, see *ante*, § 5-855. ★**5-864**
For procedural provision in relation to section 47J of the 2002 Act, see *post*, § 5-970.

[Further detention pending making of restraint order
As to the insertion of section 47K into the 2002 Act, see *ante*, § 5-855. ★**5-865**
For procedural provision in relation to section 47K of the 2002 Act, see *post*, § 5-970.

[Further detention pending variation of restraint order
As to the insertion of section 47L into the 2002 Act, see *ante*, § 5-855. ★**5-866**
For procedural provision in relation to section 47L of the 2002 Act, see *post*, § 5-970.

[Further detention in other cases
With effect from November 22, 2014 (Crime and Courts Act 2013 (Commencement No. 11) **5-867**
Order 2014 (S.I. 2014 No. 3098)), section 55(14) of, and paragraphs 14 and 18 of Schedule 21 to,
the 2013 Act were brought into force.
As to the insertion of section 47M into the 2002 Act, see *ante*, § 5-855. ★
For procedural provision in relation to section 47M of the 2002 Act, see *post*, § 5-970.

[Discharge, variation and lapse of detention order
As to the insertion of section 47N into the 2002 Act, see *ante*, § 5-855. ★**5-868**
For procedural provision in relation to section 47N of the 2002 Act, see *post*, § 5-970.

[Appeals
As to the insertion of section 47O into the 2002 Act, see *ante*, § 5-855. ★**5-869**

For procedural provision in relation to section 47O of the 2002 Act, see *post*, § 5-970.

[Detention of property pending section 47O appeal
★**5-870**   As to the insertion of section 47P into the 2002 Act, see *ante*, § 5-855.
For procedural provision in relation to section 47P of the 2002 Act, see *post*, § 5-970.

[Hearsay evidence in detention order proceedings
★**5-871**   As to the insertion of section 47Q into the 2002 Act, see *ante*, § 5-855.
For procedural provision in relation to section 47Q of the 2002 Act, see *post*, § 5-970.

[Release of property
★**5-872**   As to the insertion of section 47R into the 2002 Act, see *ante*, § 5-855.
For procedural provision in relation to section 47R of the 2002 Act, see *post*, § 5-970.

[Codes of practice
5-873   As to the insertion of section 47S(1) to (5) into the 2002 Act, see *ante*, § 5-855.
For procedural provision in relation to section 47S of the 2002 Act, see *post*, § 5-970.
★   With effect from June 1, 2015, a code of practice made pursuant to section 47S of the 2002 Act was brought into operation by the Proceeds of Crime Act 2002 (Search, Seizure and Detention of Property: Code of Practice) (England and Wales) Order 2015 (S.I. 2015 No. 730).

Management receivers: appointment
5-874   *Barnes v. Eastenders Cash and Carry plc; Eastenders Cash and Carry plc v. CPS* is now reported at [2015] A.C. 1.

Powers
5-875   *Barnes v. Eastenders Cash and Carry plc; Eastenders Cash and Carry plc v. CPS* is now reported at [2015] A.C. 1.

Powers
★**5-877**   With effect from June 1, 2015 (Serious Crime Act 2015 (Commencement No. 1) Regulations 2015 (S.I. 2015 No. 820)), section 51 of the 2002 Act was amended by the SCA 2015, s.4, so as to insert a new subsection (8B), as follows—

"(8B) Representations that a person is entitled to make by virtue of subsection (8) do not include representations that are inconsistent with a determination made under section 10A, unless—
(a) the person was not given a reasonable opportunity to make representations when the determination was made and has not appealed against the determination, or
(b) it appears to the court that there would be a serious risk of injustice to the person if the court was bound by the determination;
and the determination does not bind the court if paragraph (a) or (b) applies.".

Enforcement receivers
★**5-880**   As to the application of section 54 of the 2002 Act in relation to restraint orders and relevant legal aid payments, see S.I. 2015 No. 868, *ante*, § 5-846.

Sums received by justices' chief executive
★**5-881**   With effect from June 1, 2015 (Policing and Crime Act 2009 (Commencement No. 10, Transitional Provision and Savings) Order 2015 (S.I. 2015 No. 983)), the amendments made to section 55 of the 2002 Act by section 58 of the 2009 Act came into force.

★   With effect from June 1, 2015 (Serious Crime Act 2015 (Commencement No. 1) Regulations 2015 (S.I. 2015 No. 820)), section 55(5) of the 2002 Act was amended by the SCA 2015, s.85(1), and Sched. 4, para. 33, so as to substitute the words " an amount payable under a priority order (or orders)" for the words "an amount of compensation or all or part of an amount payable under an unlawful profit order".

★   Having become spent as a result of the amendment made to section 55 by the 2015 Act (*ante*), paragraph 22 of the schedule to the Prevention of Social Housing Fraud Act 2013 (see the main work) is repealed: 2015 Act, s.85(1), and Sched. 4, para. 89 (into force from the same date as the 2015 Act, Sched. 4, para. 33 (*ante*)).

As from a day to be appointed, section 55(5) of the 2002 Act is further amended by the Modern ★
Slavery Act 2015, s.57(1), and Sched. 5, para. 20. As in the case of the amendment of section 13
(*ante*, § 5-813), the draftsman of this Act has acted in ignorance of the amendment already made
by the SCA 2015 as this prospective amendment relates to the 2002 Act as it read prior to its
amendment by the SCA. As the Modern Slavery Act amendment clearly cannot be brought into
force without further amendment of the legislation, the detail is not set out here.

Discharge and variation

As to the application of section 63 of the 2002 Act in relation to restraint orders and relevant ★**5-889**
legal aid payments, see S.I. 2015 No. 868, *ante*, § 5-846.

Seized money

With effect from June 1, 2015 (Serious Crime Act 2015 (Commencement No. 1) Regulations ★**5-893**
2015 (S.I. 2015 No. 820)), section 67 of the 2002 Act was amended by the SCA 2015, s.14(1) to
(3), so as (i) to substitute a new subsection (5) for subsections (4) and (5), as follows—

> "(5) If—
>> (a) a confiscation order is made against a person holding money to which this section applies,
>> and
>> (b) a receiver has not been appointed under section 50 in relation to the money,
> a magistrates' court may order the bank or building society to pay the money to the designated of-
> ficer for the court on account of the amount payable under the confiscation order.";

(ii) to insert new subsections (5A) and (5B), as follows—

> "(5A) A person applying for an order under subsection (5) must give notice of the application to
> the bank or building society with which the account is held.
> (5B) In the case of money held in an account not maintained by the person against whom the
> confiscation order is made, a magistrates' court—
>> (a) may make an order under subsection (5) only if the extent of the person's interest in the
>> money has been determined under section 10A, and
>> (b) must have regard to that determination in deciding what is the appropriate order to
>> make.";

and (iii) to insert new subsections (7A) and (7B), as follows—

> "(7A) The Secretary of State may by order amend this section so that it applies not only to money
> held in an account maintained with a bank or building society but also to—
>> (a) money held in an account maintained with a financial institution of a specified kind, or
>> (b) money that is represented by, or may be obtained from, a financial instrument or product
>> of a specified kind.
> (7B) An order under subsection (7A) may amend this section so that it makes provision about
> realising an instrument or product within subsection (7A)(b) or otherwise obtaining money from it.".

In consequence of the amendment made by section 14(1) of the 2015 Act (new subs. (5) in lieu ★
of subss. (4) and (5)), paragraph 409 of Schedule 8 to the Courts Act 2003 (as to which, see the
main work), is repealed by the 2015 Act, s.85(1), and Sched. 4, para. 61 (into force from the same
date as the 2015 Act, s.14 (*ante*)).

[Sections 47B to 47S: meaning of "appropriate officer"

With effect from June 1, 2015 (Policing and Crime Act 2009 (Commencement No. 10, ★**5-894**
Transitional Provision and Savings) Order 2015 (S.I. 2015 No. 983)), the insertion of sections 67A
to 67D into the 2002 Act by section 58 of the 2009 Act came into force.

With effect from June 1, 2015 (Serious Crime Act 2015 (Commencement No. 1) Regulations ★
2015 (S.I. 2015 No. 820)), section 67A of the 2002 Act was amended by the SCA 2015, s.14(4), so
as to substitute a new subsection (3), for subsections (2) and (3), as follows—

> "(3) If—
>> (a) a confiscation order is made against the person by whom the property is held, and
>> (b) a receiver has not been appointed under section 50 in relation to the property,
> a magistrates' court may by order authorise an appropriate officer to realise the property.".

For procedural provision in relation to section 67A of the 2002 Act, see *post*, §§ 5-969a *et seq.*

[Costs of storage and realisation

As to the insertion of section 67B into the 2002 Act, see *ante*, § 5-894.   ★**5-895**

For procedural provision in relation to section 67B of the 2002 Act, see *post*, §§ 5-969a *et seq.*

[Sections 67A and 67B: appeals

★**5-896**   As to the insertion of section 67C into the 2002 Act, see *ante*, § 5-894.

For procedural provision in relation to section 67C of the 2002 Act, see *post*, §§ 5-969a *et seq.*

[Proceeds of realisation

★**5-897**   As to the insertion of section 67D into the 2002 Act, see *ante*, § 5-894.

★   As to the application of section 67D of the 2002 Act in relation to restraint orders and relevant legal aid payments, see S.I. 2015 No. 868, *ante*, § 5-846.

For procedural provision in relation to section 67D of the 2002 Act, see *post*, §§ 5-969a *et seq.*

Power of court and receiver [etc.]

★**5-899**   With effect from June 1, 2015 (Policing and Crime Act 2009 (Commencement No. 10, Transitional Provision and Savings) Order 2015 (S.I. 2015 No. 983)), the amendments made to section 69 of the 2002 Act by sections 55(1) and (4) and 112(1) of, and paragraphs 66 and 67 of Schedule 7 to, the 2009 Act came into force.

★   As to the application of section 69 of the 2002 Act in relation to restraint orders and relevant legal aid payments, see S.I. 2015 No. 868, *ante*, § 5-846.

Value: the basic rule

5-910   When valuing property, it is not open to the court to accept an arbitrary figure; where property is situated overseas, there must be some evidence as to local property prices, for example from a valuer with experience of the local property market: *R. v. Sheidu* [2014] Crim.L.R. 827, CA.

Free property

★**5-913**   With effect from June 1, 2015 (Policing and Crime Act 2009 (Commencement No. 10, Transitional Provision and Savings) Order 2015 (S.I. 2015 No. 983)), the amendments made to section 82 of the 2002 Act by section 112(1) of, and paragraphs 99 and 101 of Schedule 7 to, the 2009 Act came into force.

Proceedings

★**5-916**   As from April 13, 2015 (Criminal Justice and Courts Act 2015 (Commencement No. 1, Saving and Transitional Provisions) Order 2015 (S.I. 2015 No. 778)), the Criminal Justice and Courts Act 2015, s.50, and Sched. 11, para. 18, amended section 85 of the 2002 Act, so as (i) in subsection (1)(aa), to substitute "relevant prosecutor" for "public prosecutor", and to insert "or single justice procedure notice" after "and requisition", and (ii) in subsection (9), for "relevant", to substitute "public", and to insert ", 'single justice procedure notice'" after "requisition".

★   With effect from June 1, 2015 (Policing and Crime Act 2009 (Commencement No. 10, Transitional Provision and Savings) Order 2015 (S.I. 2015 No. 983)), the amendments made to section 85 of the 2002 Act by section 112(1) of, and paragraphs 66 and 68 of Schedule 7 to, the 2009 Act came into force.

Confiscation orders

★**5-918**   With effect from June 1, 2015 (Policing and Crime Act 2009 (Commencement No. 10, Transitional Provision and Savings) Order 2015 (S.I. 2015 No. 983)), the amendments made to section 87 of the 2002 Act by section 112(1) and (2) of, and paragraphs 66 and 69 of Schedule 7, and Part 4 of Schedule 8, to, the 2009 Act came into force.

★   With effect from June 1, 2015 (Serious Crime Act 2015 (Commencement No. 1) Regulations 2015 (S.I. 2015 No. 820)), section 87 of the 2002 Act was further amended by the SCA 2015, s.5(3), so as to insert a new subsection (1A), as follows—

"(1A) The 'amount payable' under a confiscation order, where part of that amount has been paid, means the amount that remains to be paid.".

[No further possibility of appeal

★**5-919**   With effect from June 1, 2015 (Policing and Crime Act 2009 (Commencement No. 10, Transitional Provision and Savings) Order 2015 (S.I. 2015 No. 983)), the amendments made to section 87A of the 2002 Act by section 112(1) of, and paragraphs 66 and 70 of Schedule 7 to, the 2009 Act came into force.

Procedure on appeal to the Court of Appeal

With effect from June 1, 2015 (Serious Crime Act 2015 (Commencement No. 1) Regulations   ★**5-921**
2015 (S.I. 2015 No. 820)), section 89(4) of the 2002 Act was amended by the SCA 2015, s.85(1), and Sched. 4, para. 34, so as to insert a new paragraph (za) before paragraph (a), as follows—

"(za) section 31(4) (appeals against determinations under section 10A),".

Proceeds of Crime Act 2002, Sched. 2

Slavery

As from a day to be appointed, a new paragraph 3A of Schedule 2 to the 2002 Act is inserted   ★**5-926**
by the Modern Slavery Act 2015, s.7(1) and (2), so as to add the offence under section 1 (slavery, servitude and forced or compulsory labour) of the 2015 Act (as to which, see *post*, § 19-441).

People trafficking

Sub-paragraph 4(3) of Schedule 2 to the 2002 Act ("(3) An offence under section 4 of the   ★**5-927**
Asylum and Immigration (Treatment of Claimants, etc.) Act 2004 (exploitation)") was inserted by section 5(7) of the 2004 Act. The Modern Slavery Act 2015, s.7(1) and (3) will replace both sub-paragraphs (2) and (3) with a new sub-paragraph (4) (referring to the offence of human trafficking, contrary to section 2 of the 2015 Act (as to which, see *post*, § 19-441)), so there will just be sub-paragraphs (1) and (4) when that amendment come into force.

Prostitution and child sex

With effect from May 3, 2015 (Serious Crime Act 2015 (Commencement No. 1) Regulations   ★**5-931**
2015 (S.I. 2015 No. 820)), paragraph 8(b), (c) and (d) of Schedule 2 to the 2002 Act were amended by the SCA 2015, s.85(1), and Sched. 4, para. 58. The amendments effect no change of substance; they simply reflect the amendments to sections 48 to 50 of the SOA 2003 made by section 68 of the 2015 Act (as to which, see *post*, §§ 20-160, 20-167, 20-161).

Financial reporting orders

As to the repeal of section 76 of the SOCPA 2005, see *post*, § 5-1212.   ★**5-935**

(b) *Subordinate legislation*

Commencement

Proceeds of Crime Act 2002 (Commencement No. 5, Transitional Provisions, Savings and Amendment) Order 2003 (S.I. 2003 No. 333)

Citation and interpretation
  1.—(1) [*Citation.*]   **5-937**
  (2) In this Order, "the Act" means the Proceeds of Crime Act 2002.
  (3) Where an offence is found to have been committed over a period of two or more days, or at some time during a period of two or more days, it shall be taken for the purposes of this order to have been committed on the earliest of those days.

Commencement of provisions
  2.—(1) The provisions of the Act listed in column 1 of the Schedule to this Order shall come into   **5-938**
force on 24th March 2003, subject to the transitional provisions and savings contained in this order.
  (2) But where a particular purpose is specified in relation to any such provision in column 2 of that Schedule, the provision concerned shall come into force only for that purpose.

Transitional provisions relating to confiscation orders—England and Wales
  3.—(1) Section 6 of the Act (making of confiscation order) shall not have effect where the offence,   **5-939**
or any of the offences, mentioned in section 6(2) was committed before 24th March 2003.

(2) Section 27 of the Act (defendant convicted or committed absconds) shall not have effect where the offence, or any of the offences, mentioned in section 27(2) was committed before 24th March 2003.

(3) Section 28 of the Act (defendant neither convicted nor acquitted absconds) shall not have effect where the offence, or any of the offences, in respect of which proceedings have been started but not concluded was committed before 24th March 2003.

4. [*Transitional provisions relating to confiscation orders—Northern Ireland.*]

It was held in *R. v. Moulden* [2009] 1 Cr.App.R. 27, CA, that where the respondent appeared before the Crown Court to be dealt with in respect of two indictments, one alleging offences committed before March 24, 2003, and the other alleging offences committed after that date, each indictment represented a separate set of "proceedings" for the purposes of section 6(2)(a) of the 2002 Act (see § 5-805 in the main work) and accordingly, by virtue of article 3(1), the 2002 Act had no application to the pre-March 24, 2003, indictment, but did apply to the post-March 24, 2003, indictment. The judge had, therefore, been correct to apply the confiscation provisions of the CJA 1988 to the one indictment and the confiscation provisions of the 2002 Act to the other indictment, and to reject the prosecution submission that the effect of these provisions was to disapply the 2002 Act in relation to both indictments, thereby triggering the assumptions provided for by section 72AA of the 1988 Act.

Where the defendant pleaded guilty to a count of conspiracy to make false instruments, the particulars of offence alleging that the offence took place "between the 1st day of January 2003 and the 16th day of May 2007", and where his written basis of plea was to the effect that his first admitted act in pursuance of the criminal agreement took place only on October 29, 2003, his offence had begun before March 24, 2003, for the purposes of article 3(1) (having regard to article 1(3)), such that the applicable confiscation provisions were those under Part VI of the CJA 1988, not Part 2 of the PCA 2002, see *R. v. Evwierhowa* [2011] 2 Cr.App.R.(S.) 77, CA.

As to whether, in principle, rental income from criminally-obtained properties could properly be regarded as benefit even though it was derived from properties obtained subject to offences, in respect of which there were convictions, that were committed before the commencement of Part 2 of the 2002 Act, see *R. v. Oyebola*, (§ 5-1049a in the main work).

By virtue of articles 3(1) and 10(1)(e) (*post*, § 5-942), section 16 of the DTA 1994 (increase in realisable property) continues to have effect where an offence mentioned in section 6(2) of the PCA Act 2002 (making of confiscation order (§ 5-805 in the main work)) was committed before March 24, 2003: *Re Peacock (Secretary of State for the Home Department intervening)* [2012] 2 Cr.App.R.(S.) 81, SC. For the suggestion that the court misconstrued the order (albeit reaching the correct result), see CLW/12/08/5.

Transitional provisions relating to restraint orders and enforcement abroad—England and Wales

5-940
5. Sections 41 (restraint orders) and 74 (enforcement abroad) of the Act shall not have effect where—

  (a) the powers in those sections would otherwise be exercisable by virtue of a condition in section 40(2) or (3) of the Act being satisfied; and

  (b) the offence mentioned in section 40(2)(a) or 40(3)(a), as the case may be, was committed before 24th March 2003.

6. [*Transitional provisions relating to restraint orders and enforcement abroad—Northern Ireland.*]

Transitional provisions relating to criminal lifestyle—England and Wales

5-941
7.—(1) This article applies where the court is determining under section 6(4)(a) of the Act whether the defendant has a criminal lifestyle.

(2) Conduct shall not form part of a course of criminal activity under section 75(3)(a) of the Act where any of the three or more offences mentioned in section 75(3)(a) was committed before 24th March 2003.

(3) Where the court is applying the rule in section 75(5) of the Act on the calculation of relevant benefit for the purposes of determining whether or not the test in section 75(2)(b) of the Act is satisfied by virtue of conduct forming part of a course of criminal activity under section 75(3)(a) of the Act, the court must not take into account benefit from conduct constituting an offence mentioned in section 75(5)(c) of the Act which was committed before 24th March 2003.

(4) Conduct shall form part of a course of criminal activity under section 75(3)(b) of the Act, notwithstanding that any of the offences of which the defendant was convicted on at least two

separate occasions in the period mentioned in section 75(3)(b) were committed before 24th March 2003.

(5) Where the court is applying the rule in section 75(5) of the Act on the calculation of relevant benefit for the purposes of determining whether or not the test in section 75(2)(b) of the Act is satisfied by virtue of conduct forming part of a course of criminal activity under section 75(3)(b) of the Act, the court may take into account benefit from conduct constituting an offence committed before 24th March 2003.

(6) Where the court is applying the rule in section 75(6) of the Act on the calculation of relevant benefit for the purposes of determining whether or not the test in section 75(2)(c) of the Act is satisfied, the court must not take into account benefit from conduct constituting an offence mentioned in section 75(6)(b) of the Act which was committed before 24th March 2003.

[This article is printed as substituted by the Proceeds of Crime Act 2002 (Commencement No. 5) (Amendment of Transitional Provisions) Order 2003 (S.I. 2003 No. 531).]

8. [*Transitional provisions relating to criminal lifestyle—Northern Ireland.*]

Transitional provisions relating to particular criminal conduct
9. Conduct which constitutes an offence which was committed before 24th March 2003 is not particular criminal conduct under section 76(3) or 224(3) of the Act.

Savings for England and Wales
10.—(1) Where, under article 3 or 5, a provision of the Act does not have effect, the following **5-942** provisions shall continue to have effect—
- (a) sections 71 to 89 (including Schedule 4) and 102 of the Criminal Justice Act 1988;
- (b) paragraphs 83 and 84 of Schedule 17 to the Housing Act 1988;
- (c) sections 21(3)(e) to (g), 27, 28 and 34 of the Criminal Justice Act 1993;
- (d) paragraph 36 of Schedule 9 to the Criminal Justice and Public Order Act 1994;
- (e) sections 1 to 36 and 41 of the Drug Trafficking Act 1994;
- (f) sections 1 to 10, 15(1) and (3) (including Schedule 1), 16(2), (5) and (6) of the Proceeds of Crime Act 1995;
- (g) section 4(3) of the Private International Law (Miscellaneous Provisions) Act 1995;
- (h) sections 35 to 38 of the Proceeds of Crime (Scotland) Act 1995;
- (i) the Proceeds of Crime (Enforcement of Confiscation Orders made in England and Wales or Scotland) Order (Northern Ireland) 1997 and the Proceeds of Crime (Northern Ireland) Order 1996, so far as necessary for the continued operation of the Proceeds of Crime (Enforcement of Confiscation Orders made in England and Wales or Scotland) Order (Northern Ireland) 1997;
- (j) paragraphs 23 and 36 of Schedule 5 to the Justices of the Peace Act 1997;
- (k) section 83 of, paragraph 114 of Schedule 8 to and paragraph 8 of Schedule 9 to the Crime and Disorder Act 1998;
- (l) paragraphs 139 and 172 of Schedule 13 to the Access to Justice Act 1999;
- (m) paragraphs 105 to 113 and 163 to 173 of Schedule 9 to the Powers of Criminal Courts (Sentencing) Act 2000;
- (n) paragraphs 6(1) to (3) and 10 of Schedule 15 to the Terrorism Act 2000.

(2) Where under article 3 or 5, a provision of the Act does not have effect, the following provisions shall continue to have effect as if they had not been amended by Schedule 11 to the Act—
- (a) section 13(6) of the Criminal Justice (International Co-operation) Act 1990;
- (b) paragraph 17(3) of Schedule 8 to the Terrorism Act 2000.

11. [*Savings for Northern Ireland.*]
12. [*Savings for enforcement of Scottish orders in England, Wales and Northern Ireland.*]
13. [*Savings in relation to external orders.*]
14. [*Amendment of arts 3 and 5 of S.I. 2003 No. 120, §§ 26-4, 26-5 in the main work.*]

Article 2   THE SCHEDULE

Column 1	Column 2
Part 2 (sections 6 to 91, including Schedule 2) (Confiscation: England and Wales).	So far as not already in force.
Part 4 (sections 156 to 239, including Schedule 5) (Confiscation: Northern Ireland).	

5-943

Column 1

Part 9 (sections 417 to 434) (Insolvency *etc.*).

Part 10 (sections 435 to 442) (Information).

Section 444 (External requests and orders).

Section 445 (External investigations).

Section 447 (Interpretation).

Section 456 (Amendments).

Section 457 (Repeals).

In Schedule 11, paragraphs 1, 4, 5, 7, 8, 9, 11, 14(2) and (3), 15, 16, 17(2), (4) and (6), 19(2) and (3), 20, 21, 25(2)(a) and (h) to (j), 26, 27, 28(1) and (2)(e) and (g), 31(2) and (3)(a) to (c), 32, 37 and 39.

In Schedule 12, the following entries; the entry relating to the Criminal Appeal (Northern Ireland) Act 1980; the entry relating to the Police and Criminal Evidence Act 1984; the entry relating to the Criminal Justice Act 1988; the entry relating to the Housing Act 1988; the entry relating to the Police and Criminal Evidence (Northern Ireland) Order 1989; in the entry relating to the Criminal Justice (International Co-operation) Act 1990, the entry in the second column concerning section 13 of that Act; the entry relating to the Criminal Justice (Confiscation) (Northern Ireland) Order 1990; the entry relating to the Criminal Justice Act 1993; the entry relating to the Drug Traficking Act 1994; the entry relating to the Proceeds of Crime Act 1995; in the entry relating to the Criminal Procedure (Consequential Provisions) (Scotland) Act 1995, the entry in the second column concerning Schedule 4 of that Act; the entry relating to the Private International Law (Miscellaneous Provisions) Act 1995; in the entry relating to the Proceeds of Crime (Scotland) Act 1995, the entry in the second column concerning sections 35 to 39 of that Act, the entry in the second column concerning section 40 of that Act and the entry in the second column concerning section 42 of that Act; the entry relating to the Proceeds of Crime (Northern Ireland) Order 1996; the entry relating to the Justices of the Peace Act 1997; in the entry relating to the Crime and Disorder Act 1998, the entry in the second column concerning section 83 of that Act, the entry in the second column concerning Schedule 8 of that Act and the entry in the second

Column 2

So far as not already in force.

Commenced for the purposes of the provisions of Schedule 11 to the Act commenced by this Order.

Commenced for the purposes of the provisions of Schedule 12 to the Act commenced by this Order.

Paragraphs 7, 11, 15, 16, 20, 21 and 39 are commenced except to the extent that they relate to Part 3 of the Act. Paragraph 17(2) is commenced so far as it repeals sections 71 to 89, 94 and 99 to 102 of the Criminal Justice Act 1988. Paragraph 25(2)(a) is commenced so far as it repeals sections 1 to 38 and 41 of the Drug Traficking Act 1994. Paragraph 27 is commenced so far as not already in force. Paragraph 31(2) is commenced so far as it repeals articles 4 to 41 of the Proceeds of Crime (Northern Ireland) Order 1996.

The entry relating to sections 71 to 102 of the Criminal Justice Act 1988 is commenced so far as it repeals sections 71 to 89, 94 and 99 to 102 of that Act. The entries relating to the Criminal Justice Act 1993, the Proceeds of Crime Act 1995 and the Access to Justice Act 1999 are commenced so far as not already in force. The entry relating to sections 1 to 54 of the Drug Traficking Act 1994 is commenced so far as it repeals sections 1 to 38 and 41 of that Act. The entry relating to Parts II and III of the Proceeds of Crime (Northern Ireland) Order 1996 is commenced so far as it repeals articles 4 to 41 of that Order. The entry relating to the Terrorism Act 2000 is commenced so far as it repeals paragraphs 6 and 10 of Schedule 15 to that Act.

Column 1   *Column 2*

column concerning Schedule 9 of that Act; the entry
relating to the Access to Justice Act 1999; the entry
relating to the Powers of Criminal Courts (Sentencing)
Act 2000; the entry relating to the Terrorism Act 2000;
and the entry relating to the Criminal Justice and Police
Act 2001.

Rules of court relating to confiscation, restraint and receivership proceedings

Criminal Procedure Rules 2014 (S.I. 2014 No. 1610), Pt 57

Replacement of 2014 rules by 2015 rules

With effect from October 5, 2015, the Criminal Procedure Rules 2015 (S.I. 2015 No. 1490)   ★**5-944**
replace S.I. 2014 No. 1610. Parts 56 to 61 of the 2014 rules are replaced by Part 33 of the 2015
rules (see *post*, Appendix P-286 *et seq.*). As well as incorporating the amendments to the 2014 rules
made by S.I. 2015 No. 13 (as to which, see *post*, §§ 5-958 *et seq.*, 5-970 *et seq.*), there are several
changes of substance that take account of provisions of the SCA 2015 and the Modern Slavery Act
2015.

Criminal Procedure Rules 2014 (S.I. 2014 No. 1610), Pt 58

Statements in connection with confiscation orders

With effect from April 6, 2015, rule 11(a) of the Criminal Procedure (Amendment) Rules 2015   **5-958**
(S.I. 2015 No. 13) substitutes a new rule 58.1 in the 2014 rules as follows—

"58.1.—(1) This rule applies where—
    (a) the court can make a confiscation order; and
    (b) the prosecutor asks the court to make such an order, or the court decides to make such an
        order on its own initiative.
(2) Within such periods as the court directs—
    (a) if the court so orders, the defendant must give such information, in such manner, as the
        court directs;
    (b) the prosecutor must serve a statement of information relevant to confiscation on the court
        officer and the defendant;
    (c) if the court so directs—
        (i) the defendant must serve a response notice on the court officer and the prosecutor,
           and
        (ii) the parties must identify what is in dispute.
(3) The court may—
    (a) shorten or extend a time limit which it has set;
    (b) vary, discharge or supplement an order which it has made.
(4) A prosecutor's statement of information must—
    (a) identify the maker of the statement and show its date;
    (b) identify the defendant in respect of whom it is served;
    (c) specify the conviction which gives the court power to make the confiscation order, or each
        conviction if more than one;
    (d) if the prosecutor believes the defendant to have a criminal lifestyle, include such matters as
        the prosecutor believes to be relevant in connection with deciding—
        (i) whether the defendant has such a lifestyle,
        (ii) whether the defendant has benefited from his or her general criminal conduct,
        (iii) the defendant's benefit from that conduct, and
        (iv) whether the court should or should not make such assumptions about the defendant's
           property as legislation permits;
    (e) if the prosecutor does not believe the defendant to have a criminal lifestyle, include such
        matters as the prosecutor believes to be relevant in connection with deciding—
        (i) whether the defendant has benefited from his or her particular criminal conduct, and
        (ii) the defendant's benefit from that conduct.
(5) A defendant's response notice must—
    (a) indicate the extent to which the defendant accepts the allegations made in the prosecutor's
        statement of information; and

(b) so far as the defendant does not accept an allegation, give particulars of any matters on which the defendant relies,

in any manner directed by the court.

(6) The court must satisfy itself that there has been explained to the defendant, in terms the defendant can understand (with help, if necessary)—

    (a) that if the defendant accepts to any extent an allegation in a prosecutor's statement of information, then the court may treat that as conclusive for the purposes of deciding whether the defendant has benefited from general or particular criminal conduct, and if so by how much;

    (b) that if the defendant fails in any respect to comply with a direction to serve a response notice, then the court may treat that as acceptance of each allegation to which the defendant has not replied, except the allegation that the defendant has benefited from general or particular criminal conduct; and

    (c) that if the defendant fails without reasonable excuse to comply with an order to give information, then the court may draw such inference as it believes is appropriate.".

★   As to the replacement of S.I. 2014 No. 1610 by the Criminal Procedure Rules 2015 (S.I. 2015 No. 1490), see *ante*, § 5-944.

Postponement of confiscation proceedings

5-959   With effect from April 6, 2015, rule 11(b) of the Criminal Procedure (Amendment) Rules 2015 (S.I. 2015 No. 13) substitutes a new rule 58.2 in the 2014 rules, as follows—

"**58.2.** The court may postpone confiscation proceedings without a hearing.".

★   As to the replacement of S.I. 2014 No. 1610 by the Criminal Procedure Rules 2015 (S.I. 2015 No. 1490), see *ante*, § 5-944.

Application for reconsideration

5-960   With effect from April 6, 2015, rule 11(c)(i) of the Criminal Procedure (Amendment) Rules 2015 (S.I. 2015 No. 13) substitutes a new rule 58.3(1) in the 2014 rules, as follows—

"(1) This rule applies where the prosecutor wants the court, in view of fresh evidence—

    (a) to consider making a confiscation order where the defendant was convicted but no such order was considered;

    (b) to reconsider a decision that the defendant had not benefited from criminal conduct;

    (c) to reconsider a decision about the amount of the defendant's benefit.".

With effect from April 6, 2015, rule 11(c)(ii) of the Criminal Procedure (Amendment) Rules 2015 (S.I. 2015 No. 13) amends rule 58.3(3) of the 2014 rules by substituting the words "served on the court officer" for the words "lodged with the Crown Court".

★   As to the replacement of S.I. 2014 No. 1610 by the Criminal Procedure Rules 2015 (S.I. 2015 No. 1490), see *ante*, § 5-944.

Application for new calculation of available amount

5-961   With effect from April 6, 2015, rule 11(d) of the Criminal Procedure (Amendment) Rules 2015 (S.I. 2015 No. 13) amends rule 58.4 of the 2014 rules, so as (i) to substitute the words "wants the court to make a new calculation of the amount available for confiscation" for the words from "makes an application" to the end of paragraph (1); (ii) to substitute the words "served on the court officer" for the words "lodged with the Crown Court" in paragraph (3); (iii) to omit the words "or under section 50 of the 2002 Act" in paragraph (4)(b); and (iv) to substitute the word "court" for the words "Crown Court" at the end of paragraph (4).

★   As to the replacement of S.I. 2014 No. 1610 by the Criminal Procedure Rules 2015 (S.I. 2015 No. 1490), see *ante*, § 5-944.

Variation of confiscation order due to inadequacy of available amount

5-962   With effect from April 6, 2015, rule 11(e) of the Criminal Procedure (Amendment) Rules 2015 (S.I. 2015 No. 13) amends rule 58.5 of the 2014 rules, so as (i) to substitute the words "wants the court to vary a confiscation order because the amount available is inadequate" for the words from "makes an application" to the end of paragraph (1); (ii) to substitute the words "served on the court officer" for the words "lodged with the Crown Court" in paragraph (3); (iii) to omit the words "or under section 50 of the 2002 Act" in paragraph (4)(c); and (iv) to substitute the word "court" for the words "Crown Court" at the end of paragraph (4).

As to the replacement of S.I. 2014 No. 1610 by the Criminal Procedure Rules 2015 (S.I. 2015 No. 1490), see *ante*, § 5-944. ★

Application by magistrates' court officer to discharge confiscation order

With effect from April 6, 2015, rule 11(f) of the Criminal Procedure (Amendment) Rules 2015 **5-963** (S.I. 2015 No. 13) amends rule 58.6 of the 2014 rules, so as (i) to substitute the words "wants the court to discharge a confiscation order because the amount available is inadequate or the sum outstanding is very small" for the words from "makes an application" to the end of paragraph (1); (ii) to omit the words "appointed under section 50 of the 2002 Act" from paragraph (3)(c); (iii) to omit the words "on him" in paragraph (4) and to insert the words "or she" in that paragraph after the word "he"; (iv) to substitute the word "court" for the words "Crown Court" in paragraph (5) and to insert the word "officer" before the word "must" in that paragraph; and (v) to omit the words "appointed under section 50 of the 2002 Act" from paragraph (5)(d).

As to the replacement of S.I. 2014 No. 1610 by the Criminal Procedure Rules 2015 (S.I. 2015 No. 1490), see *ante*, § 5-944. ★

Application for variation of confiscation order made against an absconder

With effect from April 6, 2015, rule 11(g) of the Criminal Procedure (Amendment) Rules 2015 **5-964** (S.I. 2015 No. 13) amends rule 58.7 of the 2014 rules, so as (i) to substitute the words "wants the court to vary a confiscation order made while the defendant was an absconder" for the words from "makes an application" to the end of paragraph (1); (ii) to omit the words "made against an absconder under section 6 of the 2002 Act as applied by section 28 of the 2002 Act" from paragraph (2)(a); (iii) to substitute the words "the defendant" for the word "he" in paragraph (2)(d); (iv) to substitute the words "served on the court officer" for the words "lodged with the Crown Court" in paragraph (3); and (v) to substitute the word "court" for the words "Crown Court" in paragraph (4).

As to the replacement of S.I. 2014 No. 1610 by the Criminal Procedure Rules 2015 (S.I. 2015 No. 1490), see *ante*, § 5-944. ★

Application for discharge of confiscation order made against an absconder

With effect from April 6, 2015, rule 11(h)(i) of the Criminal Procedure (Amendment) Rules **5-965** 2015 (S.I. 2015 No. 13) substitutes a new paragraph (1) in rule 58.8 of the 2014 rules, as follows—

> "(1) This rule applies where the defendant wants the court to discharge a confiscation order made while the defendant was an absconder and—
> (a) the defendant since has been tried and acquitted of each offence concerned; or
> (b) the prosecution has not concluded or is not to proceed.".

With effect from April 6, 2015, rule 11(h)(ii) to (vi) of the Criminal Procedure (Amendment) Rules 2015 (S.I. 2015 No. 13) amend rule 58.8 of the 2014 rules, so as (i) to omit the words "made under section 28 of the 2002 Act" from paragraph (2)(a); (ii) to insert the words "or she" after the word "he" in paragraph (2)(c); (iii) to substitute the words "that the prosecutor" for the words "given by the prosecutor that he" in paragraph (2)(d)(iii); (iv) to substitute the words "served on the court officer" for the words "lodged with the Crown Court" in paragraph (3); and (v) to substitute the word "court" for the words "Crown Court" in paragraph (4).

With effect from April 6, 2015, rule 11(h)(vii) of the Criminal Procedure (Amendment) Rules 2015 (S.I. 2015 No. 13) substitutes a new paragraph (5) in rule 58.8 of the 2014 rules, as follows—

> "(5) If the court orders the discharge of the confiscation order, the court officer must serve notice on any other court responsible for enforcing the order.".

As to the replacement of S.I. 2014 No. 1610 by the Criminal Procedure Rules 2015 (S.I. 2015 No. 1490), see *ante*, § 5-944. ★

Application for increase in term of imprisonment in default

With effect from April 6, 2015, rule 11(i)(i) of the Criminal Procedure (Amendment) Rules **5-966**

2015 (S.I. 2015 No. 13) substitutes a new paragraph (1) in rule 58.9 of the 2014 rules, as follows—

> "(1) This rule applies where—
>> (a) a court varies a confiscation order; and
>> (b) the prosecutor wants the court in consequence to increase the term of imprisonment to be served in default of payment.".

With effect from April 6, 2015, rule 11(i)(ii) to (v) of the Criminal Procedure (Amendment) Rules 2015 (S.I. 2015 No. 13) amend rule 58.9 of the 2014 rules, so as (i) to substitute the words "the court officer must" for the words "the court must" in paragraph (3); (ii) to substitute the words "any other court" for the words "the magistrates' court" in paragraph (3)(a); (iii) to substitute the word "court" for the words "Crown Court" in paragraph (4), and to insert the word "officer" before the word "must" in that paragraph; and (iv) to substitute the words "any other court" for the words "the magistrates' court" in paragraph (4)(d).

★ As to the replacement of S.I. 2014 No. 1610 by the Criminal Procedure Rules 2015 (S.I. 2015 No. 1490), see *ante*, § 5-944.

Compensation—general

5-967   With effect from April 6, 2015, rule 11(j) of the Criminal Procedure (Amendment) Rules 2015 (S.I. 2015 No. 13) amends rule 58.10 of the 2014 rules, so as (i) to substitute the words "where a person who held realisable property wants the court to award compensation for loss suffered in consequence of anything done in relation to that property in connection with confiscation proceedings" for the words from "to an application" to the end of paragraph (1); (ii) to substitute the words "served on the court officer" for the words "lodged with the Crown Court" in paragraph (3); (iii) to omit the words "under section 72(9) or 302(7A) of the 2002 Act (or if the compensation is payable out of a police fund under section 72(9)(a) or 302(7A), the chief officer of the police force concerned)" from paragraph (4)(b); and (iv) to substitute the word "court" for the words "Crown Court" at the end of paragraph (4).

★ As to the replacement of S.I. 2014 No. 1610 by the Criminal Procedure Rules 2015 (S.I. 2015 No. 1490), see *ante*, § 5-944.

Compensation—confiscation order made against absconder

5-968   With effect from April 6, 2015, rule 11(k)(i) of the Criminal Procedure (Amendment) Rules 2015 (S.I. 2015 No. 13) substitutes a new rule 58.11(1) in the 2014 rules, as follows—

> "(1) This rule applies where—
>> (a) the court varies or discharges a confiscation order made against an absconder;
>> (b) a person who held realisable property suffered loss as a result of the making of that confiscation order; and
>> (c) that person wants the court to award compensation for that loss.".

With effect from April 6, 2015, rule 11(k)(ii) to (v) of the Criminal Procedure (Amendment) Rules 2015 (S.I. 2015 No. 13) amend rule 58.11 of the 2014 rules, so as (i) to omit the words "made under section 28 of the 2002 Act" from paragraph (2)(a); (ii) to omit the words "under section 29 or 30 of the 2002 Act" from paragraph (2)(b); (iii) to substitute the words "served on the court officer" for the words "lodged with the Crown Court" in paragraph (3); and (iv) to substitute the word "court" for the words "Crown Court" in paragraph (4).

★ As to the replacement of S.I. 2014 No. 1610 by the Criminal Procedure Rules 2015 (S.I. 2015 No. 1490), see *ante*, § 5-944.

5-969a   With effect from April 6, 2015, rule 11(l) of the Criminal Procedure (Amendment) Rules 2015 (S.I. 2015 No. 13) inserts rules 58.13 to 58.15 at the end of Part 58 of the 2014 rules, to provide for applications and appeals under the PCA 2002, ss.67A to 67D (§§ 5-894 *et seq.* in the main work).

★ As to the replacement of S.I. 2014 No. 1610 by the Criminal Procedure Rules 2015 (S.I. 2015 No. 1490), see *ante*, § 5-944.

Criminal Procedure Rules 2014 (S.I. 2014 No. 1610), Pt 58, rr.58.13–58.15

Application to realise seized property
   58.13.—(1) This rule applies where—
   (a) property is held by a defendant against whom a confiscation order has been made;

(b)   the property has been seized by or produced to an officer; and

(c)   an officer who is entitled to apply wants a magistrates' court—

    (i)   to make an order under section 67A of the Proceeds of Crime Act 2002 authorising the realisation of the property towards satisfaction of the confiscation order, or

    (ii)   to determine any storage, insurance or realisation costs in respect of the property which may be recovered under section 67B of the 2002 Act.

(2)   Such an officer must—

(a)   apply in writing; and

(b)   serve the application on—

    (i)   the court officer, and

    (ii)   any person whom the applicant believes would be affected by an order.

(3)   The application must—

(a)   specify the property;

(b)   explain—

    (i)   the applicant's entitlement to apply,

    (ii)   how the proposed realisation meets the conditions prescribed by section 67A of the 2002 Act, and

    (iii)   how any storage, etc. costs have been calculated;

(c)   attach any material on which the applicant relies; and

(d)   propose the terms of the order.

(4)   The court may—

(a)   determine the application at a hearing, or without a hearing;

(b)   consider an application made orally instead of in writing;

(c)   consider an application which has not been served on a person likely to be affected by an order.

(5)   If the court authorises the realisation of the property, the applicant must—

(a)   notify any person affected by the order who was absent when it was made; and

(b)   serve on the court officer a list of those so notified.

Appeal about decision on application to realise seized property

58.14.—(1) This rule applies where on an application under rule 58.13 for an order authorising **5-969b**
the realisation of property—

(a)   a magistrates' court decides not to make such an order and an officer who is entitled to apply wants to appeal against that decision to the Crown Court, under section 67C(1) of the Proceeds of Crime Act 2002;

(b)   a magistrates' court makes such an order and a person who is affected by that decision, other than the defendant against whom the confiscation order was made, wants to appeal against it to the Crown Court, under section 67C(2) of the 2002 Act;

(c)   a magistrates' court makes a decision about storage, etc. costs and an officer who is entitled to apply wants to appeal against that decision to the Crown Court, under section 67C(4) of the 2002 Act.

(2)   The appellant must serve an appeal notice—

(a)   on the Crown Court officer and on any other party;

(b)   not more than 21 days after the magistrates' court's decision, or, if applicable, service of notice under rule 58.13(5).

(3)   The appeal notice must—

(a)   specify the decision under appeal;

(b)   where paragraph (1)(a) applies, explain why the property should be realised;

(c)   in any other case, propose the order that the appellant wants the court to make, and explain why.

(4)   Rule 63.10 (constitution of the Crown Court) applies on such an appeal.

Application for direction about surplus proceeds

58.15.—(1) This rule applies where—   **5-969c**

(a)   on an application under rule 58.13, a magistrates' court has made an order authorising an officer to realise property;

(b)   an officer so authorised holds proceeds of that realisation;

(c)   the confiscation order has been fully paid; and

(d)   the officer, or a person who had or has an interest in the property represented by the

proceeds, wants a magistrates' court or the Crown Court to determine under section 67D
of the Proceeds of Crime Act 2002—

    (i) to whom the remaining proceeds should be paid, and

    (ii) in what amount or amounts.

(2) Such a person must—

    (a) apply in writing; and

    (b) serve the application on—

        (i) the court officer, and

        (ii) as appropriate, the officer holding the proceeds, or any person to whom such proceeds
might be paid.

(3) The application must—

    (a) specify the property which was realised;

    (b) explain the applicant's entitlement to apply;

    (c) describe the distribution proposed by the applicant and explain why that is proposed;

    (d) attach any material on which the applicant relies; and

    (e) ask for a hearing, if the applicant wants one, and explain why it is needed.

(4) A person who wants to make representations about the application must—

    (a) serve the representations on—

        (i) the court officer,

        (ii) the applicant, and

        (iii) any other person to whom proceeds might be paid;

    (b) do so as soon as reasonably practicable after service of the application;

    (c) attach any material on which that person relies; and

    (d) ask for a hearing, if that person wants one, and explain why it is needed.

(5) The court—

    (a) must not determine the application unless the applicant and each person on whom it was
served—

        (i) is present, or

        (ii) has had an opportunity to attend or to make representations;

    (b) subject to that, may determine the application—

        (i) at a hearing (which must be in private unless the court otherwise directs), or without a
hearing,

        (ii) in the absence of any party to the application.

Criminal Procedure Rules 2014 (S.I. 2014 No. 1610), Pt 59

Application for restraint order or ancillary order

5-970   With effect from April 6, 2015, Part 59 of S.I. 2014 No. 1610 is renamed "Proceeds of Crime
Act 2002: rules applicable to restraint, seizure and detention proceedings", a new heading
"Restraint proceedings" is inserted at the beginning, and new rules 59.7 to 59.10 are added at the
end (preceded by the heading "Seizure and detention proceedings"), by rule 12 of the Criminal
Procedure (Amendment) Rules 2015 (S.I. 2015 No. 13) to provide for applications and appeals
under sections 47A to 47S of the 2002 Act (§§ 5-855 *et seq.* in the main work), when they come
into force. For the text of the new rules, see *post*, §§ 5-975a *et seq.*

★   As to the replacement of S.I. 2014 No. 1610 by the Criminal Procedure Rules 2015 (S.I. 2015
No. 1490), see *ante*, § 5-944.

5-975a   As to the insertion of new rules 59.7 to 59.10 at the end of Part 59 of the 2014 rules, see *ante*, §
5-970.

Criminal Procedure Rules 2014 (S.I. 2014 No. 1610), Pt 59, rr.59.7–59.10

Application for approval to seize property or to search

    59.7.—(1) This rule applies where an officer who is entitled to apply wants the approval of a
magistrates' court, under section 47G of the Proceeds of Crime Act 2002—

    (a) to seize property, under section 47C of that Act;

    (b) to search premises or a person or vehicle for property to be seized, under section 47D, 47E
or 47F of that Act.

(2) Such an officer must—

    (a) apply in writing; and

    (b) serve the application on the court officer.

(3) The application must—

    (a) (a) explain—

        (i) the applicant's entitlement to apply, and

        (ii) how the proposed seizure meets the conditions prescribed by sections 47B, 47C and, if applicable, 47D, 47E or 47F of the 2002 Act;

    (b) if applicable, specify any premises, person or vehicle to be searched;

    (c) attach any material on which the applicant relies; and

    (d) propose the terms in which the applicant wants the court to give its approval.

(4) The court—

    (a) must determine the application—

        (i) at a hearing, which must be in private unless the court otherwise directs, and

        (ii) in the applicant's presence;

    (b) may consider an application made orally instead of in writing.

Application to extend detention period

59.8.—(1) This rule applies where an officer who is entitled to apply, or the prosecutor, wants a **5-975b** magistrates' court to make an order, under section 47M of the Proceeds of Crime Act 2002, extending the period for which seized property may be detained.

(2) Such an officer or prosecutor must—

    (a) apply in writing; and

    (b) serve the application on—

        (i) the court officer, and

        (ii) any person whom the applicant believes would be affected by an order.

(3) The application must—

    (a) specify—

        (i) the property to be detained, and

        (ii) whether the applicant wants it to be detained for a specified period or indefinitely;

    (b) explain—

        (i) the applicant's entitlement to apply, and

        (ii) how the proposed detention meets the conditions prescribed by section 47M of the 2002 Act;

    (c) attach any material on which the applicant relies; and

    (d) propose the terms of the order.

(4) The court—

    (a) must determine the application—

        (i) at a hearing, which must be in private unless the court otherwise directs, and

        (ii) in the applicant's presence;

    (b) may—

        (i) consider an application made orally instead of in writing,

        (ii) require service of the application on the court officer after it has been heard, instead of before.

(5) If the court extends the period for which the property may be detained, the applicant must—

    (a) notify any person affected by the order who was absent when it was made; and

    (b) serve on the court officer a list of those so notified.

Application to vary or discharge order for extended detention

59.9.—(1) This rule applies where an officer who is entitled to apply, the prosecutor, or a person **5-975c** affected by an order to which rule 59.8 applies, wants a magistrates' court to vary or discharge that order, under section 47N of the Proceeds of Crime Act 2002.

(2) Such a person must—

    (a) apply in writing; and

    (b) serve the application on—

        (i) the court officer, and

        (ii) as appropriate, the applicant for the order, or any person affected by the order.

(3) The application must—

    (a) specify the order and the property detained;

    (b) explain—

      (i)   the applicant's entitlement to apply,

      (ii) why it is appropriate for the order to be varied or discharged,

      (iii) if applicable, on what grounds the court must discharge the order;

  (c) attach any material on which the applicant relies;

  (d) if applicable, propose the terms of any variation; and

  (e) ask for a hearing, if the applicant wants one, and explain why it is needed.

(4) A person who wants to make representations about the application must—

  (a) serve the representations on—

      (i) the court officer, and

      (ii) the applicant;

  (b) do so as soon as reasonably practicable after service of the application;

  (c) attach any material on which that person relies;

  (d) ask for a hearing, if that person wants one, and explain why it is needed.

(5) The court—

  (a) must not determine the application unless the applicant and each person on whom it was served—

      (i) is present, or

      (ii) has had an opportunity to attend or to make representations;

  (b) subject to that, may determine the application—

      (i) at a hearing (which must be in private unless the court otherwise directs), or without a hearing,

      (ii) in the absence of any party to the application.

Appeal about property detention decision

5-975d   **59.10.**—(1) This rule applies where—

  (a) on an application under rule 59.8 for an order extending the period for which property may be detained—

      (i) a magistrates' court decides not to make such an order, and

      (ii) an officer who is entitled to apply for such an order, or the prosecutor, wants to appeal against that decision to the Crown Court under section 47O(1) of the Proceeds of Crime Act 2002;

  (b) on an application under rule 59.9 to vary or discharge an order under rule 59.8—

      (i) a magistrates' court determines the application, and

      (ii) a person who is entitled to apply under that rule wants to appeal against that decision to the Crown Court under section 47O(2) of the 2002 Act.

(2) The appellant must serve an appeal notice—

  (a) on the Crown Court officer and on any other party;

  (b) not more than 21 days after the magistrates' court's decision, or, if applicable, service of notice under rule 59.8(5).

(3) The appeal notice must—

  (a) specify the decision under appeal;

  (b) where paragraph (1)(a) applies, explain why the detention period should be extended;

  (c) where paragraph (1)(b) applies, propose the order that the appellant wants the court to make, and explain why.

(4) Rule 63.10 (constitution of the Crown Court) applies on such an appeal.

Criminal Procedure Rules 2014 (S.I. 2014 No. 1610), Pt 60

Replacement of 2014 rules by 2015 rules

★**5-976**   With effect from October 5, 2015, the Criminal Procedure Rules 2015 (S.I. 2015 No. 1490) replace S.I. 2014 No. 1610. Parts 56 to 61 of the 2014 rules are replaced by Part 33 of the 2015 rules (see *post*, Appendix P-286 *et seq.*). As well as incorporating the amendments to the 2014 rules made by S.I. 2015 No. 13 (as to which, see *ante*, §§ 5-958 *et seq.*, 5-970 *et seq.*), there are several changes of substance that take account of provisions of the SCA 2015 and the Modern Slavery Act 2015.

Criminal Procedure Rules 2014 (S.I. 2014 No. 1610), Pt 61

Replacement of 2014 rules by 2015 rules

★**5-984**   With effect from October 5, 2015, the Criminal Procedure Rules 2015 (S.I. 2015 No. 1490) replace S.I. 2014 No. 1610. Parts 56 to 61 of the 2014 rules are replaced by Part 33 of the 2015 rules (see *post*, Appendix P-286 *et seq.*). As well as incorporating the amendments to the 2014 rules made by S.I. 2015 No. 13 (as to which, see *ante*, §§ 5-958 *et seq.*, 5-970 *et seq.*), there are several changes of substance that take account of provisions of the SCA 2015 and the Modern Slavery Act 2015.

Appeals

Criminal Procedure Rules 2014 (S.I. 2014 No. 1610), Pt 71

Replacement of 2014 rules by 2015 rules
   With effect from October 5, 2015, the Criminal Procedure Rules 2015 (S.I. 2015 No. 1490) **★5-1018** replace S.I. 2014 No. 1610. Parts 71 to 73 of the 2014 rules are replaced by Part 42 of the 2015 rules (see *post*, Appendix P-436 *et seq.*). There are several changes of substance.

Criminal Procedure Rules 2014 (S.I. 2014 No. 1610), Pt 72

Replacement of 2014 rules by 2015 rules
   With effect from October 5, 2015, the Criminal Procedure Rules 2015 (S.I. 2015 No. 1490) **★5-1028** replace S.I. 2014 No. 1610. Parts 71 to 73 of the 2014 rules are replaced by Part 42 of the 2015 rules (see *post*, Appendix P-436 *et seq.*). There are several changes of substance.

Criminal Procedure Rules 2014 (S.I. 2014 No. 1610), Pt 73

Replacement of 2014 rules by 2015 rules
   With effect from October 5, 2015, the Criminal Procedure Rules 2015 (S.I. 2015 No. 1490) **★5-1031** replace S.I. 2014 No. 1610. Parts 71 to 73 of the 2014 rules are replaced by Part 42 of the 2015 rules (see *post*, Appendix P-436 *et seq.*). There are several changes of substance.

(3) Authorities

General approach

   Where the appellant pleaded guilty to four counts of being knowingly concerned in an ar- **5-1045** rangement, knowing or suspecting that the arrangement would facilitate the retention, use or control of criminal property by a co-defendant (PCA 2002, s.328 (§ 26-12 in the main work)), having allowed a co-defendant to deposit cheques obtained fraudulently from an insurance company and payable to the appellant into a bank account in his name, at the moment the cheques cleared the appellant had a chose in action against the bank for the value of the cheques, and he accordingly obtained property to that value for the purposes of the confiscation legislation (see s.76(4) of the 2002 Act (*ibid.*, § 5-907)); the evidence did not support the proposition that the appellant was a mere nominee who had divested himself of all control over the account; nor was the drafting of the counts binding as to who had control of the proceeds of the cheques; the appellant's position was not the equivalent of a courier, as discussed in *R. v. Allpress* (as to which, see the main work): *R. v. Roper* [2015] Lloyd's Rep F.C. 26, CA (considering also *R. v. May* and *R. v. Sivaraman* (as to both of which, see the main work)). No consideration was given to the decisions of the Supreme Court in *R. v. Waya* (§ 5-1042 in the main work), or *R. v. Ahmad*; *R. v. Fields* (§ 5-1046a in the main work). For their suggested potential relevance, see CLW/15/06/10.

Benefit

Property
   General principles. *R. v. Ahmad*; *R. v. Fields* is now reported at [2015] A.C. 299. **★5-1046a**
   Where a judge had found that benefit from particular criminal conduct had been obtained **★** jointly between three defendants, it had not been open to him to make a new finding of separate or several benefit (*vis-à-vis* one of the defendants) in order to achieve what he considered to be a "proportionate" result; to do so would be entirely contrary to the approach laid down in *R. v. Ahmad*; *R. v. Fields*, *ante*: *R. v. Dad (Amer Hussain), Dad (Nadeem) and Dad (Munsif)* [2015] Crim.L.R. 356, CA. The court observed that if a proviso is required to be inserted in a particular confiscation order to the effect that there was not to be more than one recovery in respect of the same

joint benefit, care may need to be given to its drafting; in particular, there may need to be identified on the face of the confiscation order not just the general and particular benefit (as is currently provided for on the standard typed form of confiscation order), but also the sole and joint benefit obtained. As to this case, see also *post*, § 5-1057a.

5-1050b   **Offences committed in connection with the running of a business through a company or otherwise.** Whereas a breach of planning laws is not a criminal offence, but a breach of an enforcement notice served under the Town and Country Planning Act 1990 is (see s.179(2)), any rent or housing benefit derived from letting out flats (in a house that had been converted without planning permission) prior to the expiry of the period for compliance as specified in an enforcement notice, could not constitute a benefit (whether from general or particular criminal conduct) for the purposes of the PCA 2002: *R. v. Ali (Salah)* [2015] 1 W.L.R. 841, CA. As to this case, see also *ante*, §§ 3-225, 5-828.

★5-1050c   Where a property owned by the appellant was occupied by numerous tenants in breach of an enforcement notice under the Town and Country Planning Act 1990, rental income received by a company as his agent was obtained by him "as a result of or in connection with" his criminal conduct for the purposes of section 76(4) of the PCA 2002 (as to which, see § 5-907 in the main work), and a confiscation order for the full amount of the rental income would be upheld; but for his criminal conduct in ignoring the enforcement notice, the rents in the relevant period would not have come into his hands or within his disposition or control; furthermore, the need for proportionality did not dictate that some allowance should be made for expenses incurred; whilst cases where the underlying activity was lawful had to be carefully considered in light of *R. v. Waya* (as to which, see § 5-1042 in the main work), the judge had considered *Waya* and there was no reason to interfere with his order: *Hussain v. Brent LBC* [2015] Lloyd's Rep. F.C. 102, CA (considering *R. v. Sale* (see § 5-1050 in the main work) and *R. v. del Basso*, and distinguishing *Sumal & Sons (Properties) Ltd v. Newham LBC* (as to both of which, see the main work)).

R. v. King is now reported at [2014] 2 Cr.App.R.(S.) 54, *sub nom. R. v. King (Scott)*.

★5-1051   **Offences involving the fraudulent evasion of duty or VAT.** The Supreme Court decision in *R. v. Ahmad*; *R. v. Fields* is now reported at [2015] A.C. 299.

★   Where the defendant had operated a factory producing counterfeit vodka, and pleaded guilty to conspiring to cheat the revenue (in respect of the duty evaded or to be evaded), the sale price or value of the bottles of vodka sold or still held was obtained by him as a result of, or in connection with, the offence to which he pleaded guilty, within section 76(4) of the PCA 2002 Act (§ 5-907 in the main work): *R. v. Eddishaw* [2015] Lloyd's Rep. F.C. 212, CA (considering *R. v. Louca* (as to which, see the main work)).

Pecuniary advantage

★5-1052   With effect from April 1, 2015, the Excise Goods (Holding, Movement and Duty Point) Regulations 2010 (S.I. 2010 No. 593) were further amended by the Excise Goods (Aircraft and Ship's Stores) Regulations 2015 (S.I. 2015 No. 368).

Valuation of benefit

5-1055   Where the defendant pleaded guilty to possessing Class A drugs with intent to supply (Misuse of Drugs Act 1971, s.4(1) (§ 27-28 in the main work)), having been found to be in possession of 169 grammes of cocaine at 80 per cent purity, along with just under three grammes in a wrap at five per cent purity, in valuing his benefit from his criminal conduct under the PCA 2002, the judge had correctly used the retail, rather than wholesale, value of the 169 grammes, based on a finding that they would be cut to a purity of five per cent; the judge's conclusion reflected not simply the potential market value of the drugs, but the actual market value at the time the defendant obtained them (the "market value" of drugs would vary depending on the time at which they had been obtained or the capacity or role of the person obtaining them); this conclusion, on the facts found by the judge, flowed from a "fair and purposive" construction of sections 79 (value: the basic rule) and 80 (value of property obtained from conduct) of the 2002 Act (*ibid.*, §§ 5-910, 5-911): *R. v. Elsayed* [2014] 1 W.L.R. 3916, CA (considering, *inter alia, R. v. Waya* (as to which, see the main work), *R. v. Ascroft* (*ibid.*, § 5-1056) and *R. v. Islam* (*ibid.*, § 5-1049)). For criticism of this decision, see CLW/14/40/3.

"Free property" (s.82), "realisable property" (s.83) and "property" (s.84)

Jointly held property

Where a house was in the defendant's name, but there was a general understanding within his   ★**5-1057a**
family that any profit from the renting out of the house was for the benefit of a non-defendant
brother who was unable to look after his own affairs, it should not have been included within his
realisable assets; the judge had been correct to say that under the relevant statutory provisions a
declaration of trust relating to land ordinarily had to be evidenced in writing, but they did not
displace the applicability, in appropriate circumstances, of the law relating to implied, resulting
and constructive trusts: *R. v. Dad (Amer Hussain), Dad (Nadeem) and Dad (Munsif)* [2015] Crim.L.R.
356, CA. As to this case, see also *ante,* § 5-1046a.

X. DISQUALIFICATION, RESTRICTION, EXCLUSION, ETC., ORDERS

A. BANNING ORDERS UNDER THE FOOTBALL SPECTATORS ACT 1989

(2) Legislation

Banning orders arising out of offences outside England and Wales

With effect from March 11, 2015, the Football Spectators (Corresponding Offences) (Revoca-   **5-1083**
tion) Order 2015 (S.I. 2015 No. 212) revokes the Football Spectators (Corresponding Offences in
the Netherlands) Order 2000 (S.I. 2000 No. 1109) (see the main work).

Football Spectators Act 1989, Sched. 1

With effect from March 2, 2015 (Crime and Courts Act 2013 (Commencement No. 1) (England   **5-1087**
and Wales) Order 2014 (S.I. 2014 No. 3268)), section 56 of, and Schedule 22 to, the 2013 Act (see
the main work) are brought into force.

C. DRINKING BANNING ORDERS

(1) Summary

With effect from October 20, 2014 (Anti-social Behaviour, Crime and Policing Act 2014 (Com-   **5-1093**
mencement No. 7, Saving and Transitional Provisions) Order 2014 (S.I. 2014 No. 2590), as
amended by the Anti-social Behaviour, Crime and Policing Act 2014 (Commencement No. 7, Saving and Transitional Provisions) (Amendment) Order 2014 (S.I. 2014 No. 2754)), sections 22 to
33 of the 2014 Act (see the main work) were brought into force, as was the repeal of sections 6 to
8 and 9(1)(b) and (9) of the VCRA 2006, and of sections 9(7)(b) and 10(1) of that Act, so far as
they relate to a drinking banning order made under section 6 (by s.181(1) of, and Sched. 11,
paras 44 and 50, to, the 2014 Act).

With effect from March 23, 2015, the repeal of sections 1 to 14 of the 2006 Act by section   ★
181(1) of, and paragraphs 44 and 50 of Schedule 11 to, the Anti-social Behaviour, Crime and
Policing Act 2014, took effect for all purposes: Anti-social Behaviour, Crime and Policing Act 2014
(Commencement No. 8, Saving and Transitional Provisions) Order 2015 (S.I. 2015 No. 373).

(2) Legislation

Violent Crime Reduction Act 2006, ss.6–9

Orders on conviction in criminal proceedings

As to the commencement of the repeal of section 6 of the 2006 Act (as to which, see the main   **5-1096**
work), see *ante,* § 5-1093.

Supplementary provision about orders on conviction

As to the commencement of the repeal of section 7 of the 2006 Act (as to which, see the main   **5-1097**
work), see *ante,* § 5-1093.

Variation or discharge of orders under s.6

As to the commencement of the repeal of section 8 of the 2006 Act (as to which, see the main   **5-1098**
work), see *ante,* § 5-1093.

Interim orders

5-1099   As to the commencement of the repeal of section 9 of the 2006 Act (as to which, see the main work), see *ante*, § 5-1093.

Breach of drinking banning orders

★**5-1100**   As to the repeal of section 11 of the VCRA 2006 (as to which, see the main work), see *ante*, § 5-1093.

Approved courses

★**5-1101**   As to the repeal of sections 12 and 13 of the VCRA 2006 (as to which, see the main work), see *ante*, § 5-1093.

Violent Crime Reduction Act, ss.13, 14

Certificates of completion of approved courses

★**5-1102**   As to the commencement of the repeal of section 13 of the 2006 Act (as to which see the main work), see *ante*, § 5-1093.

Interpretation of Chapter 1

★**5-1103**   As to the repeal of section 14 of the VCRA 2006 (as to which, see the main work), see *ante*, § 5-1093.

D. Disqualification from Driving

(1) Legislation

Powers of Criminal Courts (Sentencing) Act 2000, ss.146, 147

Driving disqualification for any offence

★**5-1106**   With effect from June 8, 2015 (Road Safety Act 2006 (Commencement No. 11 and Transitional Provisions) Order 2015 (S.I. 2015 No. 560)), the provisions of the 2006 Act referred to in the main work are brought into force.

At from a day to be appointed, the Criminal Justice and Courts Act 2015, s.28(8), and Sched. 5, paras 3 and 7, amend section 146 of the 2000 Act, so as (i) in subsection (2), to substitute the words "a provision mentioned in subsection (2A)" for the words from "section 110(2)" to "2006", and (ii) to insert after subsection (2), a new subsection (2A), as follows—

"(2A) The provisions referred to in subsection (2) are—
(a) section 1(2B) or 1A(5) of the Prevention of Crime Act 1953;
(b) section 51A(2) of the Firearms Act 1968;
(c) section 139(6B), 139A(5B) or 139AA(7) of the Criminal Justice Act 1988;
(d) section 110(2) or 111(2) of this Act;
(e) section 224A, 225(2) or 226(2) of the Criminal Justice Act 2003;
(f) section 29(4) or (6) of the Violent Crime Reduction Act 2006.".

Powers of Criminal Courts (Sentencing) Act 2000, ss.147A, 147B

Driving disqualification where vehicle used for purposes of crime

★**5-1107**   With effect from June 8, 2015 (Road Safety Act 2006 (Commencement No. 11 and Transitional Provisions) Order 2015 (S.I. 2015 No. 560)), the provisions of the 2006 Act referred to in the main work are brought into force.

[Extension of disqualification where custodial sentence also imposed

5-1108   As from April 13, 2015 (Criminal Justice and Courts Act 2015 (Commencement No. 1, Saving and Transitional Provisions) Order 2015 (S.I. 2015 No. 778)), the Criminal Justice and Courts Act 2015, s.6(2)(c), and Sched. 1, para. 13, amended section 147A(4) of the 2000 Act, so as (i) in paragraph (e), to substitute "the Criminal Justice Act 2003", for "that Act" (in the first place it appears), and (ii) to insert, after paragraph (f), a new paragraph (fa), as follows—

"(fa) in the case of a sentence under section 236A of that Act (special custodial sentence for certain offenders of particular concern), a period equal to half of the term imposed pursuant to section 236A(2)(a) of that Act;".

As from April 13, 2015 (S.I. 2015 No. 778 (*ante*)), the Criminal Justice and Courts Act 2015, ★
s.30(2), further amended section 147A of the 2000 Act so as (i) in subsection (4)(e) and (f), to omit
"calculated after that term has been reduced by any relevant discount", (ii) in subsection (4)(h), to
omit "calculated after that sentence has been reduced by any relevant discount", and (iii) to omit
subsection (6).

Effect of custodial sentence in other cases

With effect from April 13, 2015 (Coroners and Justice Act 2009 (Commencement No. 17) ★**5-1109**
Order 2015 (S.I. 2015 No. 819)), the provisions of the 2009 Act referred to in the main work are
brought into force.

In consequence of the amendments of section 147A of the 2000 Act effected by section 30(2) of ★
the 2015 Act (as to which, see *ante*, § 5-1108), the 2015 Act, s.30(3), repeals paragraph 12 of
Schedule 13 to the LASPOA 2012 (which effected various amendments to s.147A(6)), as from
April 13, 2015 (S.I. 2015 No. 778 (*ante*, § 5-1108)).

(3) Notes on disqualification from driving (s.147)

Relevance to offence

In *R. v. Ketteridge* [2015] 1 Cr.App.R.(S.) 11, CA, a 45-year-old man was driving a jeep on a **5-1111**
motorway; in slow-moving traffic, he drew up alongside a school minibus, and, whilst staring at
the pupils inside (aged 17 and 18), masturbated his exposed penis; five months later and three
days after being committed for trial, he committed a similar offence (repeatedly driving past girls
aged 13 to 16 who were standing at the side of the road). In addition to a sentence of imprisonment (nine months), he was disqualified from driving for 12 months under section 147 of the
PCC(S)A 2000 (§ 5-1107 in the main work). This was justified as a vehicle was used for the
purpose of committing or facilitating the commission of an offence punishable on conviction on
indictment with a term of imprisonment of two years or more; in fixing the length of disqualification, the judge was not bound to ignore the undeniable circumstances of the driving, including
the obvious danger to other road users, notwithstanding that there had been no charge of
dangerous or careless driving: *R. v. Ketteridge* [2015] 1 Cr.App.R.(S.) 11, CA.

(4) Notes on disqualification from driving (ss.147A, 147B)

As to the amendment of section 147A of the 2000 Act (see the main work), see *ante*, § 5-1108. **5-1115**

E. DISQUALIFICATION OF COMPANY DIRECTORS

(1) Legislation
Company Directors Disqualification Act 1986, ss.1, 2

Disqualification orders: general

Section 1(2) of the 1986 Act is amended by the Small Business, Enterprise and Employment Act ★**5-1116**
2015, s.111 and Sched. 7, paras 1 and 2, so as to substitute the words "sections 6 and 8ZA" for the
words "section 6".

Section 111 of, and Schedule 7 to, the 2015 Act came into force on May 26, 2015 (Small Busi- ★
ness, Enterprise and Employment Act 2015 (Commencement No. 1) Regulations 2015 (S.I. 2015
No. 1329)) for the purposes of enabling the exercise of any power to make provision by regulations, rules or order, or to prepare and issue guidance. Otherwise, they come into force on a day
to be appointed.

Disqualification on conviction of indictable offence

Section 2 of the 1986 Act is amended by the Small Business, Enterprise and Employment Act ★**5-1117**
2015, s.111 and Sched. 7, paras 1 and 4 (as to the limited commencement of which, see *ante*, §
5-1116), so as (i) to insert a new subsection (1A), as follows—

"(1A) In subsection (1), 'company' includes overseas company.";

and (ii) to insert a new paragraph (aa) in subsection (2), as follows—

"(aa) in relation to an overseas company not falling within paragraph (a), the High Court or, in
Scotland, the Court of Session, or".

(2) Notes on disqualification of company directors

5-1118   For a case considering the ambit of a civil court's jurisdiction under section 2 of the CDDA 1986 (disqualification on conviction of indictable offence (§ 5-1117 in the main work)), see *Secretary of State for Business, Innovation and Skills v. Weston* [2014] Lloyd's Rep. F.C. 648, Ch D (H.H. Judge Cooke, sitting as a deputy High Court judge).

I. SERIOUS CRIME PREVENTION ORDERS

(1) Summary
Serious Crime Act 2007, Pt 1

★5-1148   As to the amendment of Part 1 of the 2007 Act, see *post*, §§ 5-1151 *et seq.*

(2) Legislation
Serious Crime Act 2007, ss.1, 2, 4, 5

Serious crime prevention orders

★5-1151   As from a day to be appointed, section 1 of the 2007 Act is amended by the SCA 2015, s.46, and Sched. 1, paras 1 and 2. A new subsection (1A) is inserted dealing with the power of "the appropriate court" in Scotland to make a serious crime prevention order, there is a consequential amendment to subsection (3), and subsection (5) is substituted as follows—

> "(5) In this Part—
>> 'appropriate court' means the Court of Session or sheriff;
>> 'serious crime prevention order' means—
>> (a) an order under this section; or
>> (b) an order under section 19 (corresponding order of the Crown Court on conviction).".

Involvement in serious crime: England and Wales orders

★5-1152   As from a day to be appointed, section 2(6) of the 2007 Act is amended by the SCA 2015, s.46, and Sched. 1, paras 1 and 3 (the amendments relate to Scotland).

Involvement in serious crime: Scotland and Northern Ireland orders

★5-1152a   As from a day to be appointed, a new section 2A is inserted into the 2007 Act by the SCA 2015, s.46, and Sched. 1, paras 1 and 4. Section 2A makes provision as to when a person is to be regarded as having been involved in serious crime in Scotland. Section 3, which makes corresponding provision in relation to Northern Ireland, is amended as from a day to be appointed by the 2015 Act, s.46, and Sched. 1, paras 1 and 5.

Involvement in serious crime: supplementary

★5-1153   As from a day to be appointed, section 4 of the 2007 Act is amended by the SCA 2015, s.46, and Sched. 1, paras 1 and 6 (the amendments (inserting new subss. (4A) and (4B)) relate to Scotland).

Type of provision that may be made by orders

★5-1154   As from a day to be appointed, section 5(2) of the 2007 Act is amended by the SCA 2015, s.46, and Sched. 1, paras 1 and 7, so as to insert ", Scotland" after "England and Wales" in both places.

Verification and disclosure of information

★5-1154a   With effect from May 3, 2015 (Serious Crime Act 2015 (Commencement No. 1) Regulations 2015 (S.I. 2015 No. 820)), a new section 5A (verification and disclosure of information) was inserted into the 2007 Act by the SCA 2015, s.50(2). This applies where information is provided to a law enforcement officer in response to an information requirement in a serious crime prevention order, and provides for the officer to disclose the information for specified purposes (including verification of the information and for the prevention, detection prosecution, etc., of crime) and for the disclosure of information to the officer.

Serious Crime Act 2007, ss.6–10

Other exceptions

★5-1156   As from a day to be appointed, section 7 of the 2007 Act is amended by the SCA 2015, s.46, and Sched. 1, paras 1 and 8 (the amendment (inserting new subs. (1A)) relates to Scotland).

Limited class of applicants for making orders

As from a day to be appointed, section 8 of the 2007 Act is amended by the SCA 2015, s.46, and Sched. 1, paras 1 and 9, so as to (i) to omit the word "and" at the end of paragraph (a), and to insert a new paragraph (aa), as follows— ★5-1157

"(aa) in the case of an order in Scotland, the Lord Advocate;".

Right of third parties to make representations

With effect from May 3, 2015 (Serious Crime Act 2015 (Commencement No. 1) Regulations 2015 (S.I. 2015 No. 820)), section 9(4) of the 2007 Act was amended by the SCA 2015, s.85(1), and Sched. 4, para. 76, so as to substitute ", 21 or 22E" for "or 21". ★5-1158

As from a day to be appointed, section 9 of the 2007 Act is further amended by the SCA 2015, s.46, and Sched. 1, paras 1 and 10 (the amendments to subss. (1) to (3), and insertion of new subs. (4A), relate to Scotland). ★

Notice requirements in relation to orders

As from a day to be appointed, section 10(4) of the 2007 Act is amended by the SCA 2015, s.46, and Sched. 1, paras 1 and 11, so as to omit the word "and" at the end of paragraph (a), and to insert a new paragraph (aa), as follows— ★5-1159

"(aa) in relation to a serious crime prevention order in Scotland, the Lord Advocate;".

Serious Crime Act 2007, ss.11–15

Restrictions for legal professional privilege

As from a day to be appointed, section 12 of the 2007 Act is amended by the SCA 2015, s.46, and Sched. 1, paras 1 and 12 (the amendments (inserting the words "in England and Wales or Northern Ireland" in subs. (1) after the word "order" and a new subs. (4A), and substituting the words "subsections (1) and (4A) do not" for the words "subsection (1) does not" in subs. (5)) relate to Scotland). ★5-1161

Restrictions on excluded material and banking information

As from a day to be appointed, section 13(1) of the 2007 Act is amended by the SCA 2015, s.46, and Sched. 1, paras 1 and 13 (the amendments (omitting the word "and" at the end of para. (a), and inserting a new para. (aa)) relate to Scotland). ★5-1162

Serious Crime Act 2007, ss.16–18

Duration of orders

With effect from May 3, 2015 (Serious Crime Act 2015 (Commencement No. 1) Regulations 2015 (S.I. 2015 No. 820)), section 16 of the 2007 Act was amended by the SCA 2015, s.85(1), and Sched. 4, para. 77, so as to insert a new subsection (7), as follows— ★5-1165

"(7) Subsections (2) and (4)(b) have effect subject to section 22E.".

Application to High Court for variation of order

As from a day to be appointed, section 17 of the 2007 Act is amended by the SCA 2015, s.46, and Sched. 1, paras 1 and 14 (the amendments relate to Scotland). ★5-1166

Application to High Court for discharge of order

As from a day to be appointed, section 18 of the 2007 Act is amended by the SCA 2015, s.46, and Sched. 1, paras 1 and 15 (the amendments relate to Scotland). ★5-1167

Serious Crime Act 2007, ss.19–22

Orders by Crown Court on conviction

With effect from May 3, 2015 (Serious Crime Act 2015 (Commencement No. 1) Regulations 2015 (S.I. 2015 No. 820)), section 19 of the 2007 Act was amended by the SCA 2015, s.85(1), and Sched. 4, para. 78, so as (i) to insert a new subsection (2A), as follows— ★5-1168

"(2A) A court that makes an order by virtue of subsection (2) in the case of a person who is already the subject of a serious crime prevention order in England and Wales must discharge the existing order.";

and (ii) to insert a new subsection (4A), as follows—

> "(4A) A court that makes an order by virtue of subsection (4) in the case of a person who is already the subject of a serious crime prevention order in Northern Ireland must discharge the existing order.".

★5-1169   Parliament must have viewed the regime of serious crime prevention orders as adding to the regime of licensed release from custodial sentences, or it would not have been enacted; it is a different regime with different enforcement methods and sanctions; the fact that there could be conditions attaching to a parole licence dealing with the same matters, and that these might last longer than those of a serious crime prevention order, did not mean that in principle such an order should not be made where the offender would in due course be released on licence: *R. v. Hall* [2015] 1 Cr.App.R.(S.) 16, CA (considering *R. v. Hancox and Duffy* (as to which, see the main work)).

Powers of Crown Court to vary orders on breach

★5-1171   With effect from May 3, 2015 (Serious Crime Act 2015 (Commencement No. 1) Regulations 2015 (S.I. 2015 No. 820)), section 21 of the 2007 Act was amended by the SCA 2015, s.85(1), and Sched. 4, para. 79 (to insert "or replace" in the heading after "vary").

★   With effect from May 3, 2015 (S.I. 2015 No. 820 (*ante*)), section 21 of the 2007 Act was further amended by the SCA 2015, s.48, so as (i) in subsection (2), to insert the words "or replace" after the word "vary" and to insert the words ", or the new order" after the words "the order as varied", (ii) to make identical amendments in subsection (4), (iii) in subsection (5), to substitute the words "An order may be varied or replaced under this section" for the words "A variation under this section may be made", (iv) in subsection (6), to insert the words "or new order" after the word "variation", and (v) to insert a new subsection (8), as follows—

> "(8) A reference in this section to replacing a serious crime prevention order is to making a new serious crime prevention order and discharging the existing one.".

Inter-relationship between different types of orders

★5-1172   As from a day to be appointed, the heading to section 22 of the 2007 Act is amended by the SCA 2015, s.46, and Sched. 1, para. 16, so as to add the words "in England and Wales or Northern Ireland".

Scotland

★5-1172a   As from a day to be appointed, new sections 22A to 22D are inserted in the 2007 Act by the SCA 2015, s.46, and Sched. 1, para. 17. These relate to the jurisdiction of the courts in Scotland to make, vary or replace serious crime prevention orders.

Extension of orders pending outcome of criminal proceedings

★5-1172b   With effect from May 3, 2015 (Serious Crime Act 2015 (Commencement No. 1) Regulations 2015 (S.I. 2015 No. 820)), a new section 22E was inserted into the 2007 Act by the SCA 2015, s.49, as follows—

> *Extension of orders pending outcome of criminal proceedings*
> **22E.**—(1) This section applies where a person subject to a serious crime prevention order is charged with—
>> (a) a serious offence, or
>> (b) an offence under section 25 of failing to comply with the serious crime prevention order.
> (2) The relevant applicant authority may make an application under this section to—
>> (a) the Crown Court in England and Wales, in the case of a serious crime prevention order in England and Wales;
>> (b), (c) [*Scotland and Northern Ireland*].
> (3) On an application under this section, the court or sheriff may vary the serious crime prevention order so that it continues in effect until one of the events listed in subsection (4) occurs (if the order would otherwise cease to have effect before then).
> (4) The events are—
>> (a) following the person's conviction of the offence mentioned in subsection (1)—

     (i) the order is varied under section 20 or 21, or under section 22B or 22C, by reference to the offence,

     (ii) a new serious crime prevention order is made under section 19 or 21, or under section 22A or 22C, by reference to the offence, or

     (iii) the court or sheriff deals with the person for the offence without varying the order or making a new one;

  (b) the person is acquitted of the offence;

  (c) the charge is withdrawn;

  (d) in the case of a serious crime prevention order in England and Wales or Northern Ireland—

     (i) proceedings in respect of the charge are discontinued, or

     (ii) an order is made for the charge to lie on the file;

  (e) *[Scotland]*.

  (5) An order may be made under this section only if—

  (a) the serious crime prevention order is still in force, and

  (b) the court or sheriff has reasonable grounds for believing that the order would protect the public by preventing, restricting or disrupting involvement by the person in serious crime.

  (6) In subsection (5)(b) 'serious crime' means—

  (a) serious crime in England and Wales, in the case of a serious crime prevention order in England and Wales;

  (b), (c) *[Scotland and Northern Ireland]*.".

Serious Crime Act 2007, ss.30–34

Other partnerships

  As from a day to be appointed, section 31 of the 2007 Act is amended by the SCA 2015, s.46,   ★**5-1179**
and Sched. 1, paras 1 and 22, so as to insert ", Scotland" after "England and Wales" in subsection (3) in both places and so as to omit subsection (6)(b)(ii).

Unincorporated associations

  As from a day to be appointed, section 32 of the 2007 Act is amended by the SCA 2015, s.46,   ★**5-1180**
and Sched. 1, paras 1 and 23, so as to omit subsection (5)(b)(ii).

Providers of information society services

  As from a day to be appointed, section 34(2)(a) of the 2007 Act is amended by the SCA 2015,   ★**5-1182**
s.46, and Sched. 1, paras 1 and 24, so as to omit "and" at the end of sub-paragraph (i), and to insert a new sub-paragraph (ia), as follows—

  "(ia) in the case of an order in Scotland, serious crime in Scotland;".

Serious Crime Act 2007, ss.35–41

Proceedings in the Crown Court

  With effect from May 3, 2015 (Serious Crime Act 2015 (Commencement No. 1) Regulations   ★**5-1184**
2015 (S.I. 2015 No. 820), section 36(1) of the 2007 Act was amended by the SCA 2015, s.85(1), and Sched. 4, para. 80, so as to substitute ", 21 or 22E" for "or 21".

Compliance with orders: authorised monitors

  As from a day to be appointed, section 39(10) of the 2007 Act is amended by the SCA 2015,   ★**5-1187**
s.46, and Sched. 1, paras 1 and 26, so as to insert, in the definition of "law enforcement agency", a new paragraph (zd), as follows—

  "(zd) the chief constable of the Police Service of Scotland;".

Costs in relation to authorised monitors

  As from a day to be appointed, section 40 of the 2007 Act is amended by the SCA 2015, s.46,   ★**5-1188**
and Sched. 1, paras 1 and 27, so as (i) to vary subsection (5) so that it will read as follows—

  "(5) Any amounts which have not been recovered despite the taking of the reasonable steps are recoverable—

    (a) in England and Wales and Northern Ireland, as if due to the law enforcement agency concerned by virtue of a civil order or judgment,

    (b) *[Scotland]*.";

(ii) to insert a new subsection (6), as follows—

"(6A) Where any amounts required to be paid by virtue of section 39(4) and (5) are, in the case of a serious crime prevention order made under section 22A, not paid within a required period, the unpaid balance from time to time carries interest at the rate payable under a decree of the Court of Session.";

and (iii) to insert a new paragraph (aa) in subsection (9), as follows—

"(aa) in relation to serious crime prevention orders in Scotland, the Scottish Ministers;".

Serious Crime Act 2007, ss.42, 43

Index of defined expressions

★**5-1191**   As from a day to be appointed, section 43 of the 2007 Act is amended by the SCA 2015, s.46, and Sched. 1, paras 1 and 28, to include "appropriate court", "involvement in serious crime: Scotland orders" and "serious offence in Scotland" in the first column and "section 1(5)", "sections 2A, 4 and 31(3)" and "section 2A(2)" in the second column so as to correspond with the new entries in the first column.

Serious offences

★**5-1192**   With effect from May 3, 2015 (Serious Crime Act 2015 (Commencement No. 1) Regulations 2015 (S.I. 2015 No. 820)), Part 1 of Schedule 1 to the SCA 2007 was amended by the SCA 2015, s.47(1) to (4), so as (i) to include an offence under section 6 of the Misuse of Drugs Act 1971 (§ 27-79 in the main work), (ii) to include offences under sections 1(1) (*ibid.*, § 24-4), 2(1) (*ibid.*, § 24-13), 3(1) (*ibid.*, § 24-16), and 5(1), (1A) and (2A) (*ibid.*, §24-24) of the Firearms Act 1968, (iii) to include offences under sections 68 (*ibid.*, § 25-435) and 170 (*ibid.*, § 25-474) of the CEMA 1979, if committed in connection with a firearm or ammunition, and (iv) to include offences under sections 1, 2, 3 (*ibid.*, §§ 23-87 *et seq.*), 3ZA (as to which, see *post*, § 23-89), and 3A (§ 23-89a in the main work) of the Computer Misuse Act 1990.

★   With effect from May 3, 2015 (S.I. 2015 No. 820 (*ante*)), Part 1 of Schedule 1 to the 2007 Act was further amended by the 2015 Act, s.85(1), and Sched. 4, para. 81(1) to (3), so as (i) to amend the references to sections 48 to 50 of the SOA 2003 to reflect the amendments made to those provisions by section 68 of the 2015 Act (as to which, see *post*, §§ 20-160, 20-167, 20-161), and (ii) to include an offence under section 45 of the 2015 Act (as to which, see *post*, § 18-33a).

★   As from a day to be appointed, Part 1 of Schedule 1 to the 2007 Act is further amended by the Modern Slavery Act 2015, s.57(1), and Sched. 5, so as to include references to the offences under subsections 1 and 2 of that Act (as to which, see *post*, §§ 19-441 *et seq.*).

J. ANTI-SOCIAL BEHAVIOUR ORDERS

Crime and Disorder Act 1998, s.1C

Orders on conviction in criminal proceedings

5-1198   With effect from October 20, 2014 (Anti-social Behaviour, Crime and Policing Act 2014 (Commencement No. 7, Saving and Transitional Provisions) Order 2014 (S.I. 2014 No. 2590)), section 181(1) of, and paragraph 24(a) of Schedule 11 to, the 2014 Act (as to which, see the main work) were brought into force to the extent that they repeal, (i) sections 1C, 1CA, 1D(1)(c) and (d) and (6), 1I(1)(b), 1J(1)(c) and 1K(2) of the 1988 Act (see the main work), (ii) the reference to "1C, 1CA" in section 1(1A) of the 1998 Act, (iii) the reference to "1CA" in section 1A(2) of the 1998 Act, (iv) section 1D(2) of the 1998 Act insofar as it relates to a case falling within subsection (1)(c) or (d), and (v) section 1D(4) of the 1998 Act insofar as it relates to a case falling within subsection (1)(c) or (d).

★   With effect from March 23, 2015 (Anti-social Behaviour, Crime and Policing Act 2014 (Commencement No. 8, Saving and Transitional Provisions) Order 2015 (S.I. 2015 No. 373)), the repeal of sections 1 to 1K of the 1998 Act by section 181(1) of, and paragraph 24(a) of Schedule 11 to, the 2014 Act were brought fully into force.

Crime and Disorder Act 1998, s.1(5A), (7), (10), (10A), (10B), (10C), (10D), (10E), (11), (12)

★**5-1199**   As to the commencement of the repeal of section 1 of the 1998 Act (as to which, see the main work), see *ante*, § 5-1198.

Crime and Disorder Act 1998, ss.1A, 1B

Individual support orders

As to the commencement of the repeal of section 1A of the 1998 Act (as to which, see the main   ★**5-1200**
work), see *ante*, § 5-1198.

Individual support orders: explanation, breach, amendment, etc.

As to the commencement of the repeal of section 1B of the 1998 Act (as to which, see the main   ★**5-1201**
work), see *ante*, § 5-1198.

Crime and Disorder Act 1998, ss.1CA, 1D, 1I

Variation and discharge of orders under section 1C

As to the repeal of section 1CA of the 1998 Act (as to which, see the main work), see *ante*, §   **5-1206**
5-1198.

Interim orders

As to the partial repeal of section 1D of the 1998 Act (as to which, see the main work), see *ante*,   **5-1208**
§ 5-1198.

As to the further commencement of the repeal of section 1D of the 1998 Act, see *ante*, § 5-1198.   ★

Special measures for witnesses

As to the partial repeal of section 1I of the 1998 Act (as to which, see the main work), see *ante*, §   **5-1209**
5-1198.

As to the further commencement of the repeal of section 1I of the 1998 Act, see *ante*, § 5-1198.   ★

Review of anti-social behaviour orders

As to the partial repeal of sections 1J and 1K of the CDA 1998 (as to which, see the main work),   **5-1210**
see *ante*, § 5-1198.

As to the further commencement of the repeal of section 1J and 1K of the 1998 Act, see *ante*, §   ★
5-1198.

K. Criminal Behaviour Orders

Anti-Social Behaviour, Crime and Policing Act 2014, ss.22–33

Power to make orders

With effect from October 20, 2014 (Anti-social Behaviour, Crime and Policing Act 2014 (Com-   **5-1210a**
mencement No. 7, Saving and Transitional Provisions) Order 2014 (S.I. 2014 No. 2590)), Part 2
of the 2014 Act (ss.22-33) (see the main work) was brought into force.

In *R. v. Hashi* [2015] 1 Cr.App.R.(S.) 17, CA, it was held that an anti-social behaviour order   ★
could be made where the offending behaviour was not actually witnessed, but where there were
people in the vicinity of someone whose behaviour otherwise crossed the statutory threshold. It is
submitted, in view of the similarity in the language of the relevant legislative provisions (*cf.*
s.1C(2)(a) of the CDA 1998 (§ 5-1198 in the main work) and s.22(3) of the 2014 Act), that the
same approach would be taken to criminal behaviour orders.

Proceedings on an application for an order

As to the commencement of section 23 of the 2014 Act (see the main work), see *ante*, § 5-1210a.   **5-1210b**

Requirements included in orders

As to the commencement of section 24 of the 2014 Act (see the main work), see *ante*, § 5-1210a.   **5-1210c**

Duration of order etc

As to the commencement of section 25 of the 2014 Act (see the main work), see *ante*, § 5-1210a.   **5-1210d**

Interim orders

As to the commencement of section 26 of the 2014 Act (see the main work), see *ante*, § 5-1210a.   **5-1210e**

Variation or discharge of orders

5-1210f   As to the commencement of section 27 of the 2014 Act (see the main work), see *ante*, § 5-1210a.

Review of orders

5-1210g   As to the commencement of section 28 of the 2014 Act (see the main work), see *ante*, § 5-1210a.

Carrying out and participating in reviews

5-1210h   As to the commencement of section 29 of the 2014 Act (see the main work), see *ante*, § 5-1210a.

Breach of order

5-1210i   As to the commencement of section 30 of the 2014 Act (see the main work), see *ante*, § 5-1210a.

Special measures for witnesses

5-1210j   As to the commencement of section 31 of the 2014 Act (see the main work), see *ante*, § 5-1210a.

Guidance

5-1210k   As to the commencement of section 32 of the 2014 Act (see the main work), see *ante*, § 5-1210a.

Saving and transitional provision

5-1210l   As to the commencement of section 33 of the 2014 Act (see the main work), see *ante*, § 5-1210a.

L. FINANCIAL REPORTING ORDERS

(1) Summary

★5-1211   As to the repeal of section 76 of the SOCPA 2005, see *post*, § 5-1212.

(2) Legislation

Serious Organised Crime and Police Act 2005, ss.76–81

Financial reporting orders: making

★5-1212   With effect from May 3, 2015 (Serious Crime Act 2015 (Commencement No. 1) Regulations 2015 (S.I. 2015 No. 820)), section 76 of the 2005 Act was repealed by the SCA 2015, s.50(1)(a). The repeal of section 76, and of sections 79 to 81, so far as they extend to England and Wales, does not apply in the case of a financial reporting order made before section 50(1)(a) came into force: 2015 Act, s.86(7).

★5-1213   As to the repeal of section 76 of the SOCPA 2005, see *ante*, § 5-1212.

★5-1214   As from a day to be appointed, section 77 of the 2005 Act is repealed by the SCA 2015, s.50(1)(b). There is transitional provision that corresponds to that in relation to section 76 (*ante*, § 5-1212): see the 2015 Act, s.86(8).

★5-1215   With effect from May 3, 2015 (Serious Crime Act 2015 (Commencement No. 1) Regulations 2015 (S.I. 2015 No. 820)), section 78 of the 2005 Act was repealed by the SCA 2015, s.50(1)(c). There is transitional provision that corresponds to that in relation to section 76 (*ante*, § 5-1212): see the 2015 Act, s.86(9).

Financial reporting orders: effect

★5-1216   As from a day to be appointed, section 79 of the 2005 Act is repealed by the SCA 2015, s.85(1), and Sched. 4, para. 71. There are transitional provisions: see the 2015 Act, s.86(7), (8) and (9) (*ante*, §§ 5-1212, 5-1214, 5-1215).

Financial reporting orders: variation and revocation

★5-1217   As from a day to be appointed, section 80 of the 2005 Act is repealed by the SCA 2015, s.85(1), and Sched. 4, para. 71. There are transitional provisions: see the 2015 Act, s.86(7), (8) and (9) (*ante*, §§ 5-1212, 5-1214, 5-1215).

Financial reporting orders: verification and disclosure

★5-1218   As from a day to be appointed, section 81 of the 2005 Act is repealed by the SCA 2015, s.85(1), and Sched. 4, para. 71. There are transitional provisions: see the 2015 Act, s.86(7), (8) and (9) (*ante*, §§ 5-1212, 5-1214, 5-1215).

In connection with the repeal of section 81, see the insertion of section 5A into the SCA 2007 ★
by the 2015 Act, s.50(2) (*ante*, § 5-1154a).

M. Procedure

Introduction

With effect from April 6, 2015, (i) Part 50 of the Criminal Procedure Rules 2014 (S.I. 2014 No.   **5-1219**
1610) is renamed "Behaviour orders", and (ii) rules 50.1 (§ 5-1220 in the main work), 50.2 (*ibid.*,
§ 5-1221), 50.4 (*ibid.*, § 5-1223) and 50.5 (*ibid.*, § 5-1224) are amended by rule 9 of the Criminal
Procedure (Amendment) Rules 2015 (S.I. 2015 No. 13), first, to define the scope of the part,
secondly, to omit references to drinking banning orders, following their abolition, and thirdly, to
provide for applications to vary orders by the Director of the Serious Fraud Office.

With effect from October 5, 2015, the Criminal Procedure Rules 2015 (S.I. 2015 No. 1490) ★
replace S.I. 2014 No. 1610. Part 50 of the 2014 rules is replaced by Part 31 of the 2015 rules (see
post, Appendix P-271 *et seq.*). Part 31 incorporates the amendments made to Part 50 of the 2014
rules by S.I. 2015 No. 13 (as to which, see *post*, §§ 5-1220 *et seq.*). In addition, there are several
changes of substance.

Criminal Procedure Rules 2014 (S.I. 2014 No. 1610), Pt 50

When this Part applies

With effect from April 6, 2015, rule 9(a)(i) of the Criminal Procedure (Amendment) Rules 2015   **5-1220**
(S.I. 2015 No. 13) amends rule 50.1 of the 2014 rules, so as to substitute a new paragraph (a), as
follows—

"(a) as well as, or instead of, passing a sentence; and".

As to the replacement of S.I. 2014 No. 1610 by the Criminal Procedure Rules 2015 (S.I. 2015 ★
No. 1490), see *ante*, § 5-1219.

Behaviour orders: general rules

With effect from April 6, 2015, rule 9(b)(i) to (iv) of the Criminal Procedure (Amendment)   **5-1221**
Rules 2015 (S.I. 2015 No. 13) amend rule 50.2 of the 2014 rules, so as (i) to insert the words "unless other legislation otherwise provides" after the word "but" in paragraph (2); (ii) to insert the
word "or" at the end of paragraph (3)(a); (iii) to omit the word "or" at the end of paragraph
(3)(b); and (iv) to omit paragraph (3)(c).

As to the replacement of S.I. 2014 No. 1610 by the Criminal Procedure Rules 2015 (S.I. 2015 ★
No. 1490), see *ante*, § 5-1219.

Evidence to assist the court: special rules

With effect from April 6, 2015, rule 9(c) of the Criminal Procedure (Amendment) Rules 2015   **5-1223**
(S.I. 2015 No. 13) amends rule 50.4 of the 2014 rules, so as (i) to insert the word "or" at the end
of paragraph (1)(b); (ii) to omit the word "or" at the end of paragraph (1)(c); and (iii) to omit
paragraph (1)(d).

As to the replacement of S.I. 2014 No. 1610 by the Criminal Procedure Rules 2015 (S.I. 2015 ★
No. 1490), see *ante*, § 5-1219.

Application to vary or revoke behaviour order

With effect from April 6, 2015, rule 9(d) of the Criminal Procedure (Amendment) Rules 2015   **5-1224**
(S.I. 2015 No. 13) amends rule 50.5 of the 2014 rules, so as (i) to substitute the words "protected
or affected by" for the words "mentioned in" in paragraph (1)(b)(iii); (ii) to omit the word "or" at
the end of paragraph (1)(b)(v); (iii) (ii) to insert the word "or" at the end of paragraph (1)(b)(vi);
and (iv) to insert a new paragraph (1)(b)(vii), as follows—

"(vii) the Director of the Serious Fraud Office".

As to the replacement of S.I. 2014 No. 1610 by the Criminal Procedure Rules 2015 (S.I. 2015 ★
No. 1490), see *ante*, § 5-1219.

XI. ORDERS UNDER THE MENTAL HEALTH ACT 1983

(1) Hospital and guardianship orders

Mental Health Act 1983, s.35

Remand to hospital for report on accused's mental condition

5-1233   R. (M.) v. Kingston Crown Court is now reported at [2015] 1 Cr.App.R. 3.

Mental Health Act 1983, s.38

Interim hospital orders

★**5-1235**   As to the making of an interim order under section 38 of the 1983 Act, see *R. v. Vowles, post*, §
5-1236.

Mental Health Act 1983, s.37

Power of courts to order hospital admission or guardianship

5-1236   As from a day to be appointed, the Criminal Justice and Courts Act 2015, s.28(8), and Sched. 5,
para. 1, amend section 37(1A) of the 1983 Act, so as (i) in paragraph (za), after "section", to insert
"1(2B) or", and (ii) in paragraph (aa), after "section", to insert "139(6B), 139A(5B) or".

★   In *R. v. Vowles* [2015] 2 Cr.App.R.(S.) 6, CA, it was held: (i) where a judge is considering
whether to make a hospital order under section 37 of the 1983 Act, with or without a restriction
order under section 41 (§ 5-1242 in the main work), or, in the alternative, to impose a custodial
sentence, he must carefully consider all the evidence and not feel circumscribed by the psychiatric
opinions; where the conditions in subsection (2)(a) are met, the judge must still consider (subs.
(2)(b)) whether a hospital order is the most suitable disposal; in considering this wider question,
he will invariably have to have regard to, *inter alia* (a) the extent to which the offender needs
treatment, (b) the extent to which the offending is attributable to the mental disorder, (c) the
extent to which punishment is required and (d) the protection of the public including the regime
for deciding release and the regime after release (which may tip the balance in favour of a
hospital order: see *R. v. Teasdale*, unreported, August 15, 2012, CA ([2012] EWCA Crim. 2071));
(ii) where, in light of these considerations, a judge concludes that a hospital order may be an appropriate disposal, he should proceed in the following order; first, as section 45A(1) of the 1983
Act (*ibid.*, § 5-1250) requires, before a hospital order is made, consideration should be given to
whether the mental disorder can appropriately be dealt with by a hospital and limitation direction
under section 45A; if it can, then the judge should make such a direction; if such a direction is
not appropriate, the judge must next consider whether, having regard to the considerations set
out in section 37(2)(b) whether a hospital order would be the most suitable disposal; and it is essential that a judge gives detailed consideration to all the factors encompassed within section
37(2)(b) (*e.g.* where the court is considering a life sentence, if the mental disorder is treatable,
there is no evidence the offender would be in any way dangerous once treated, and the offending
is entirely due to that mental disorder, a hospital order is likely to be the correct disposal); (iii)
the obligation to have regard to other methods of disposal will include having regard to the possibility of transfer to prison for treatment under section 47 of the 1983 Act, and whether that
would, taking into account all the other circumstances, be appropriate; (iv) if the judge concludes
that a hospital order is the most suitable method, then it will generally be desirable to make such
an order without consideration of an interim order under section 38 (*ibid.*, § 5-1235) unless there
is clear evidence that such an order is necessary; a judge should pause long and hard before making an interim order. For criticism of the court's conclusions in relation to points (ii) and (iii), see
CLW/15/11/20.

Inter-relationship with discretionary life sentences

5-1238   In *R. v. Fort* [2014] 2 Cr.App.R.(S.) 24, CA it was held, considering *Att.-Gen.'s Reference (No. 54
of 2011)*, and *R. v. Jenkin* (as to both of which, see the main work), that where an offender who
has been convicted of a serious offence within the meaning of Chapter 5 of Part 12 of the CJA
2003 (*ibid.*, §§ 5-495 *et seq.*), and assessed as dangerous for the purposes of those provisions, satis-

fied the conditions for a hospital order in section 37(2)(a)(i) of the 1983 Act (*ibid.*, § 5-1236), then
a sentence under Chapter 5 of Part 12 of the 2003 Act would be wrong in principle if the court
were satisfied that the reason for the offence was the offender's mental disorder and that he
would not pose a significant risk of serious harm to members of the public occasioned by the commission by him of further specified offences (the test of dangerousness) if his mental illness were
to be cured or substantially alleviated. As to this case, see also *post*, §§ 5-1250, 19-97.

(3) Hospital and limitation directions

Mental Health Act 1983, ss.45A, 45B

Power of higher courts to direct hospital admission

The reference to "a sentence of imprisonment" in section 45A(1)(b) of the 1983 Act (see the   **5-1250**
main work) does not include a custodial sentence imposed on a person under 21: *R. v. Fort* [2014]
2 Cr.App.R.(S.) 24, CA. As to this case, see also *ante*, § 5-1238; and *post*, § 19-97.

In *R. v. Poole* [2015] 1 Cr.App.R.(S.) 2, CA, it was held, in relation to section 45A(3): (i) that a
hospital direction may not be given without also giving a limitation direction, and (ii) a hospital
and limitation direction could be given without the court being satisfied that the conditions for
making a restriction order under section 41 (§ 5-1242 in the main work) were satisfied. As to this
case, see also *post*, §§ 5-1298, 5-1300.

As to section 45A, see also *R. v. Vowles*, *ante*, § 5-1236.   ★

(4) Procedural rules

Criminal Procedure Rules 2014 (S.I. 2014 No. 1610), rr.42.8, 42.9

Replacement of 2014 rules by 2015 rules

As to the replacement of S.I. 2014 No. 1610 by the Criminal Procedure Rules 2015 (S.I. 2015   **★5-1254**
No. 1490), see *ante*, § 5-287.

XII. RECOMMENDATION FOR DEPORTATION

Immigration Act 1971, Sched. 3, paras 2–6

Detention or control pending deportation

With effect from October 20, 2014 (Immigration Act 2014 (Commencement No. 3, Transitional   **5-1264**
and Saving Provisions) Order 2014 (S.I. 2014 No. 2771)), section 73(6) of, and paragraph 9 of
Schedule 9 to, the 2014 Act (see the main work) were brought into force.

The decision of the High Court in *R. (Francis) v. Secretary of State for the Home Department* has   **5-1265**
been upheld in relation to the point dealt with in the main work: see *R. (Francis) v. Secretary of
State for the Home Department (Bail for Immigration Detainees intervening)* [2015] 1 W.L.R 567, CA
(Civ. Div.). It was, however, also held that the purpose of detention under paragraphs 2(1) and
(3) of Schedule 3 to the 1971 Act (§ 5-1261 in the main work) being to facilitate deportation, once
there was no longer any prospect of removal within a reasonable time, detention could not be
justified under those provisions and would become unlawful (applying the principles in *R. v.
Governor of Durham Prison, ex p. Hardial Singh* [1984] 1 W.L.R. 704, DC, to detention under these
provisions).

Criteria for exercise of power to make recommendation

With effect from April 6, 2015, the Immigration (European Economic Area) Regulations 2006   **★5-1268**
(S.I. 2006 No. 1003) were further amended by the Immigration (European Economic Area)
(Amendment) Regulations 2015 (S.I. 2015 No. 694).

XIII. REFERRAL TO YOUTH OFFENDER PANEL

Sections 43 to 45 of the Criminal Justice and Courts Act 2015 relate to referral orders, and   **5-1275**
make a series of amendments to Schedule 1 to the PCC(S)A 2000. The general effect is to provide
greater flexibility where an offender subject to referral is in breach of his contract or commits a

further offence. Thus, where there is a breach, the court before which the offender appears may fine the offender or extend the period for which the contract has effect, instead of having to revoke the referral or to allow it to continue unaffected (s.43); where the offender falls to be dealt with for a further offence, the circumstances in which the court may deal with him by extending the compliance period are relaxed (s.44); and where a court deals with an offender subject to a referral order for a further offence otherwise than by extending the period of compliance or by discharging him, revocation of the referral order is no longer automatic, but is at the discretion of the sentencing court, the test being whether it is in the interests of justice to do so (s.45(1) and (2) (amending para. 14 (see the main work))). Section 45(3) amends section 18 of the 2000 Act by inserting a new subsection (3A) which provides that where a court makes a referral order in respect of an offender who is subject to an earlier referral order, the court may direct that any youth offender contract under the later order is not to take effect until the earlier order is revoked or discharged. The amendments made by section 43 apply only in relation to a person who fails to comply with the terms of a youth offender contract after that section comes into force (s.43(5)). The amendments made by sections 44 and 45 apply in relation to a person dealt with for an offence committed before or after they come into force (ss.44(4), 45(4)).

★   Sections 43 to 45 of the 2015 Act were brought into force on April 13, 2015 (Criminal Justice and Courts Act 2015 (Commencement No. 1, Saving and Transitional Provisions) Order 2015 (S.I. 2015 No. 778).

XIV. ORDERS AGAINST PARENTS OR GUARDIANS

(3) Parenting orders

Crime and Disorder Act 1998, ss.8–10

Parenting orders
5-1282   With effect from October 20, 2014 (Anti-social Behaviour, Crime and Policing Act 2014 (Commencement No. 7, Saving and Transitional Provisions) Order 2014 (S.I. 2014 No. 2590)), section 181(1) of, and paragraph 25 of Schedule 11 to, the 2014 Act (see the main work), were brought into force. There is a saving provision to the effect that, notwithstanding the amendments to sections 8 and 9 of the CDA 1998 effected by paragraphs 25 and 26 (see *post*, § 5-1284) of Schedule 11 to the 2014 Act, those sections, as they were in force immediately before those amendments took effect, continue to apply to an anti-social behaviour order within the meaning of section 1 of that Act: art. 4 (as amended by the Anti-social Behaviour, Crime and Policing Act 2014 (Commencement No. 7, Saving and Transitional Provisions) (Amendment) Order 2014 (S.I. 2014 No. 2754), art. 4).

★   With effect from March 8, 2015 (Anti-social Behaviour, Crime and Policing Act 2014 (Commencement No. 8, Saving and Transitional Provisions) Order 2015 (S.I. 2015 No. 373)), section 181(1) of, and paragraph 55 of Schedule 11 to, the 2014 Act were brought into force.

[Parenting order on breach of anti-social behaviour order
★5-1283   With effect from March 23, 2015 (Anti-social Behaviour, Crime and Policing Act 2014 (Commencement No. 8, Saving and Transitional Provisions) Order 2015 (S.I. 2015 No. 373)), section 181(1) of, and paragraphs 24(c) and 46 of Schedule 11 to, the 2014 Act were brought into force.

Parenting orders: supplemental
5-1284   With effect from October 20, 2014 (Anti-social Behaviour, Crime and Policing Act 2014 (Commencement No. 7, Saving and Transitional Provisions) Order 2014 (S.I. 2014 No. 2590)), section 181(1) of, and paragraph 26 of Schedule 11 to, the 2014 Act (see the main work), were brought into force. It is not apparent why the repeal of section 41 of the Crime and Security Act 2010 (effected by para. 46 of Sched. 11 to the 2014 Act) was not brought into force at the same time, especially bearing in mind that section 41 itself has never been brought into force. For the transitional provision made in connection with the commencement of this amendment, see *ante*, § 5-1283.

★   As to the commencement of section 181(1) of, and paragraph 46 of Schedule 11 to, the Anti-social Behaviour, Crime and Policing Act 2014, see *ante*, § 5-1283.

XV. MISCELLANEOUS MATTERS

B. ALTERATION OF SENTENCE

Criminal Procedure Rules 2014 (S.I. 2014 No. 1610), r.42.4

Variation of sentence

With effect from April 6, 2015, rule 42.4(1)(a) of S.I. 2014 No. 1610 was amended by rule 8 of **★5-1290** the Criminal Procedure (Amendment No. 2) Rules 2015 (S.I. 2015 No. 646) so as to substitute "37.18" for "37.17".

As to the replacement of S.I. 2014 No. 1610 by the Criminal Procedure Rules 2015 (S.I. 2015 **★** No. 1490), see *ante*, § 5-287.

Scope of power

It was open to a judge to rescind, pursuant to section 155 of the PCC(S)A 2000 (§ 5-1289 in the **5-1292** main work), a short custodial sentence (which would probably have led to immediate release having regard to time on remand), and make an order under section 35 of the MHA 1983 (remand to hospital for report on accused's mental condition (*ibid.*, § 5-1233)) later the same day, where he had not had his attention drawn to any material suggesting that the offender had any mental health problems when he passed the original sentence, and where he had subsequently seen a report on the accused's mental condition which complied with the requirements of section 35: *R. v. Catchpole* [2014] 2 Cr.App.R.(S.) 66, CA (considering *R. v. Reynolds* (as to which, see the main work and § 5-530 in the main work)). As to this case, see also, *post*, § 5-1295.

Variation after expiration of relevant time limit

For a case in which the Court of Appeal took a strict approach to what constitutes a "variation **5-1293** of substance" (as to which, see *Commrs of Customs and Excise v. Menocal* in the main work), see *R. v. D.* [2015] 1 Cr.App.R.(S.) 23, CA.

Grounds for alteration

For a further case considering whether new information about an offender's mental condition **5-1294** (as to which, see *R. v. Sodhi* and *R. v. Crozier* in the main work) can be a reason for altering a sentence, see *R. v. Catchpole, ante*, § 5-1292.

Procedure

Where a sentence or order has been rescinded pursuant to section 155 of the PCC(S)A 2000 (§ **5-1295** 5-1289 in the main work), a different judge may deal with the matter when it comes back before the court for final disposal: *R. v. Catchpole* [2014] 2 Cr.App.R.(S.) 66, CA. As to this case, see also *ante*, § 5-1292.

C. DETENTION IN DEFAULT OR FOR CONTEMPT

Powers of Criminal Courts (Sentencing) Act 2000, s.108

With effect from June 1, 2015 (Serious Crime Act 2015 (Commencement No. 1) Regulations **★5-1297** 2015 (S.I. 2015 No. 820)), section 258 of the CJA 2003 was amended by the SCA 2015, s.10(3). There is transitional provision (s.86(2)). It should be noted that section 258 of the 2003 Act was itself brought into force on April 4, 2005: Criminal Justice Act 2003 (Commencement No. 8 and Transitional and Saving Provisions) Order 2005 (S.I. 2005 No. 950).

D. SURCHARGES

Criminal Justice Act 2003, ss.161A, 161B

Court's duty to order payment of surcharge

As from a day to be appointed, section 161A of the 2003 Act is amended by the Modern **★5-1298** Slavery Act 2015, s.57(1), and Sched. 5, para. 25, so as (i) in subsection (3)(a), to substitute the words "one or more of a compensation order, an unlawful profit order and a slavery and trafficking reparation order" for the words from "a" to "both)"; (ii) in subsection (3)(b), to substitute the words "and appropriate amounts under such of those orders as it would be appropriate to make," for the words from "and appropriate compensation" to the end; and (iii) in subsection (5), for the words "this section", to substitute—

"this section—
'slavery and trafficking reparation order' means an order under section 8 of the Modern Slavery Act 2015, and".

The giving of a "direction" under section 45A of the MHA 1983 (§ 5-1250 in the main work) is not an "order" for the purposes of section 161A(4)(b) of the 2003 Act: *R. v. Poole* [2015] 1 Cr.App.R.(S.) 2, CA. As to this case, see also *ante*, § 5-1250; and *post*, § 5-1300.

Transitional cases

5-1300   *R. v. Poole* [2015] 1 Cr.App.R.(S.) 2, CA, concerned an offence of conspiracy to steal that spanned October 1, 2012, the date on which the Criminal Justice Act 2003 (Surcharge) Order 2012 (S.I. 2012 No. 1696) (see the main work) came into force, and article 7 of which stipulates that it does not apply where a court deals with an offence committed before that date, or with two or more offences at least one of which was committed before that date. Adopting the approach in *R. v. Bailey*; *R. v. Kirk*; *R. v. Tote* (as to which, see the main work), it was held that lengthy analysis of the substantive offences and the dates on which they occurred was entirely disproportionate to the time of the court; and that, taking the least punitive disposal (as recommended in *Bailey*), it was appropriate to proceed on the basis that at least part of the offence had taken place before October 1, 2012. It was not, therefore, appropriate to make a victim surcharge order, there being no element of the sentence that included a fine (as required under the old regime). As to this case, see also *ante*, §§ 5-1250, 5-1298.

Chapter 6

COSTS AND LEGAL AID

I. COSTS

B. Prosecution of Offences Act 1985

(1) Award of costs out of central funds

(a) *Defence costs*

Prosecution of Offences Act 1985, ss.16, 16A

Legal costs

6-4   Section 16A (as originally enacted, and as amended) is not incompatible with either a Convention right within the Human Rights Act 1998 or the Bill of Rights 1688: *R. (Henderson) v. Secretary of State for Justice* [2015] 1 Cr.App.R. 29, DC.

Awards by Court of Appeal

6-14   See *R. v. Banfield*, *post*, § 7-165.

Review of order

6-21a   For a case considering *Re Patel (Hitendra) and a Defendant's Costs Order* (see the main work), see *R. v. Banfield*, *post*, § 7-165.

(b) *Prosecution costs*

Amount of award

6-25   In *R. v. Zinga (Costs) (Practice Note)* [2015] 1 Cr.App.R. 2, CA, it was said that, upon an application by a private prosecutor for the payment of his costs out of central funds, pursuant to section

17 of the Prosecution of Offences Act 1985 (§ 6-22 in the main work): (i) in deciding whether the prosecutor had acted reasonably and properly in instructing the solicitors and advocates instructed (see *R. v. Dudley Magistrates' Court, ex p. Power City Stores Ltd* (in the main work)), the court will consider what steps were taken to ensure the terms on which they were instructed were reasonable; in any significant prosecution, the prosecutor would be expected to examine the competition in the relevant market, test it and seek tenders or quotations before instructing any solicitor or advocate; given the changes in the legal market, it would rarely, if ever, be reasonable in such a case to instruct lawyers without taking such steps; (ii) assuming that it was reasonable to instruct those who were instructed, the next issue is the reasonableness of the costs actually incurred; this must be judged by reference first to the proceedings in question (here, resisting an appeal to the Court of Appeal against a confiscation order), secondly, the nature of the issues before the court, thirdly, comparable market rates charged for similar work, and, fourthly, guidance from the Senior Courts Costs Office; (iii) as to the solicitors, it is not the practice of the Court of Appeal, where the issues before the court are of law, unless special circumstances pertain, for solicitors to assist in the preparation of legal argument or to be in attendance; the advocate is expected to do all this work and, given the flexible way the court operates, to liaise directly with the court and to arrange for the filing of all documents; here, in a private prosecution for conspiracy to defraud, the only costs reasonably incurred were of formally instructing counsel, attendances on and correspondence with the other parties to the appeal, and attendances on the private company that brought the action; (iv) as to counsel, it did not follow from the fact that the court had granted the appellant a representation order for leading and junior counsel that such representation was reasonable for the respondent.

(5) Costs against third parties
Prosecution of Offences Act 1985, s.19B

Provision for award of costs against third parties

    Re Applied Language Solutions Ltd (as to which, see the main work) was considered in *R. v. Capita* **6-51** *Translation and Interpreting Ltd*, 179 J.P. 36, CA. The Court of Appeal set aside a third party costs order made against the appellant company, which provided translation services to the courts, on the basis that it had been denied a fair hearing, as a result of the judge refusing to allow it to call a witness to explain its systems because no advance notice of its intention to call such witness had been given. Under the Criminal Procedure Rules it was obliged to make written representations as soon as practicable once it had received notice of a party's intention to apply for a costs order against it, which it had done (see r.76.10 of the 2014 rules (§ 6-118 in the main work)); it was not obliged as a matter of law to serve advance notice of any evidence it wished to call. By not allowing the appellant to call a witness to deal with material put before the court on the day of the hearing by the party seeking the costs order, the judge had denied the appellant a fair hearing.

(6) Supplemental provisions

    As from April 13, 2015 (Criminal Justice and Courts Act 2015 (Commencement No. 1, Saving **6-53a** and Transitional Provisions) Order 2015 (S.I. 2015 No. 778)), the Criminal Justice and Courts Act 2015, s.54(1), inserted a new Part 2A (court costs in criminal cases (ss.21A–21F)) into the 1985 Act, as follows—

Prosecution of Offences Act 1985, ss.21A–21F

PART 2A

COURT COSTS IN CRIMINAL CASES

Criminal courts charge

    21A.—(1) A court mentioned in section 21B must, at the times listed there, order a person convicted of an offence to pay a charge in respect of relevant court costs, subject to—
    (a) subsections (2) and (3), and
    (b) section 21C.
    (2) An order must not be made if the person was under 18 when the offence was committed.
    (3) An order must not be made in a case or class of case prescribed by the Lord Chancellor by regulations.

(4) A court must not take into account the duty under subsection (1) or any order under this section when dealing with a person (other than under this section) for an offence or for a failure to comply with a requirement mentioned in section 21B.

(5) In this section—

"court costs" means costs of providing the judiciary and the rest of the system of courts, but does not include defence or prosecution costs;

"relevant court costs" means court costs incurred in connection with criminal proceedings or proceedings for a failure to comply with a requirement mentioned in section 21B, but does not include costs of providing the Supreme Court or judges of that court.

Section 21A applies only in relation to a person convicted of an offence committed after that section comes into force (s.54(4) of the 2015 Act).

★   In connection with section 21A, see the Prosecution of Offences Act 1985 (Criminal Courts Charge) Regulations 2015 (S.I. 2015 No. 796) (*post*, §§ 6-53g *et seq.*), which (i) prescribe the classes of case in which the criminal courts charge must not be ordered, (ii) make provision for when a court is dealing with an offender in the same proceedings for multiple breaches of orders mentioned in section 21B, (iii) specify the amounts payable in respect of different classes of case, and (iv) specify the period that must have elapsed before a court may remit a criminal courts charge.

Criminal courts charge: courts and times

6-53b   **21B.**—(1) A magistrates' court must make an order under section 21A at the following times—

    (a) when dealing with the person for the offence;

    (b) when dealing with the person under Schedule 8 to the Criminal Justice Act 2003 for failure to comply with any of the requirements of a community order;

    (c) when dealing with the person under Schedule 12 to the Criminal Justice Act 2003 for failure to comply with any of the community requirements of a suspended sentence order;

    (d) when dealing with the person under section 256AC of the Criminal Justice Act 2003 for failure to comply with a supervision requirement imposed under section 256AA of that Act.

(2) The Crown Court must make an order under section 21A at the following times—

    (a) when dealing with the person for the offence;

    (b) when dealing with the person under Schedule 8 to the Criminal Justice Act 2003 for failure to comply with any of the requirements of a community order;

    (c) when dealing with the person under Schedule 12 to the Criminal Justice Act 2003 for failure to comply with any of the community requirements of a suspended sentence order;

    (d) when dismissing an appeal by the person against conviction or sentence for the offence.

(3) The Court of Appeal must make an order under section 21A at the following times—

    (a) when dismissing an appeal under Part 1 of the Criminal Appeal Act 1968 against the person's conviction or sentence for the offence;

    (b) when dismissing an application for leave to bring such an appeal.

Amount of criminal courts charge

6-53c   **21C.**—(1) A charge ordered to be paid under section 21A must be of an amount specified by the Lord Chancellor by regulations.

(2) When specifying amounts under this section, the Lord Chancellor must seek to secure that an amount specified in respect of a class of case does not exceed the relevant court costs reasonably attributable to a case of that class.

(3) In this section "relevant court costs" has the same meaning as in section 21A.

Interest on criminal courts charge

6-53d   **21D.**—(1) The Lord Chancellor may by regulations provide that a person who is ordered to pay a charge under section 21A must pay interest on the charge if or to the extent that it remains unpaid.

(2) The regulations may, in particular—

    (a) make provision about the rate of interest,

    (b) make provision about periods when interest is or is not payable, and

    (c) make provision by reference to a measure or document as amended from time to time.

(3) The regulations may not make provision for a rate of interest that is higher than the rate that the Lord Chancellor considers would maintain the value in real terms of amounts that remain unpaid.

(4) An amount of interest payable under the regulations is to be treated as part of the charge ordered to be paid under section 21A.

Power to remit criminal courts charge

21E.—(1) A magistrates' court may remit the whole or part of a charge ordered to be paid by a **6-53e** person under section 21A, subject to the restrictions in subsections (2) to (4).

(2) It may remit the charge only if—

(a) it is satisfied that the person has taken all reasonable steps to pay it, having regard to the person's personal circumstances, or

(b) it is satisfied that collection and enforcement of the charge is impracticable.

(3) It may not remit the charge at a time when the person is detained in prison.

(4) It may not remit the charge unless each of following [*sic*] has expired—

(a) a specified period beginning with the day on which an order under section 21A was last made in respect of the person;

(b) a specified period beginning with the day on which the person was last convicted of an offence;

(c) where relevant, a specified period beginning with the day on which the person was last released from prison.

(5) Where a court remits a charge under section 21A after an order has been made under section 300(2) of the Criminal Justice Act 2003 (power to impose unpaid work requirement etc on fine defaulter) for default in paying the charge (or the charge and other amounts), the court must—

(a) reduce the total number of hours or days to which the order relates by the same proportion as the amount remitted bears to the total amount in respect of which the order was made, or

(b) if the total number of hours or days would be reduced to nil under paragraph (a), revoke the order.

(6) In calculating a reduction required by subsection (5), any fraction of an hour or day is to be rounded down to the nearest hour or day.

(7) In this section—

"prison" includes any place where a person serving a sentence of detention for an offence is liable to be detained;

"specified period" means a period of a length specified by the Lord Chancellor by regulations.

Regulations under this Part

21F. Regulations under this Part may include transitional, transitory and saving provision. **6-53f**

Prosecution of Offences Act 1985 (Criminal Courts Charge) Regulations 2015
(S.I. 2015 No. 796), regs 1–4

Citation, commencement and interpretation

1.—(1) These regulations may be cited as the Prosecution of Offences Act 1985 (Criminal Courts ★**6-53g** Charge) Regulations 2015 and come into force on 13th April 2015.

(2) In these Regulations—

"the CAA 1968" means the Criminal Appeal Act 1968;

"the MHA 1983" means the Mental Health Act 1983;

"the POA 1985" means the Prosecution of Offences Act 1985;

"the CAA 1995" means the Criminal Appeal Act 1995.

Cases in which the duty to order payment of the criminal courts charge does not apply

2.—(1) An order under section 21A(1) of the POA 1985 (criminal courts charge) must not be made ★**6-53h** against a person ("P") convicted of an offence in the following cases—

(a) where a court deals with P for the offence by making an order discharging P absolutely under section 12 of the Powers of Criminal Courts (Sentencing) Act 2000 (absolute discharge);

(b) where a court deals with P for the offence by making in respect of P an order under section 37(1) of the MHA 1983 (power of courts to order hospital admission or guardianship) or a direction under section 45A(3) of the MHA 1983 (power of higher courts to order hospital admission);

(c) where the Crown Court dismisses an appeal against conviction or sentence for the offence following a reference by the Criminal Cases Review Commission under section 11(1) of the CAA 1995 (cases dealt with summarily in England and Wales);

(d) where the Court of Appeal dismisses an appeal for the offence under Part 1 of the CAA 1968 following a reference by the Criminal Cases Review Commission under section 9(1) of the CAA 1995 (cases dealt with on indictment in England and Wales).

(2) Paragraph (3) applies where a court deals with a person in the same proceedings—

    (a) for an offence; and

    (b) for a failure to comply with a requirement mentioned in section 21B of the POA 1985 (criminal courts charge: courts and times).

(3) An order under section 21A(1) of the POA 1985 must not be made in respect of a failure to comply with a requirement mentioned in section 21B of the POA 1985 .

(4) Paragraph (5) applies where a court deals with a person in the same proceedings for a failure to comply with more than one of the requirements mentioned in section 21B of the POA 1985 and paragraph (3) does not apply.

(5) An order under section 21A(1) of the POA 1985 must not be made—

    (a) where the court deals with the person for a failure to comply with requirements mentioned in section 21B(1)(b), (c) and (d) of the POA 1985, in respect of the failure to comply with requirements mentioned in section 21B(1)(c) or (d);

    (b) where the court deals with the person for a failure to comply with requirements mentioned in section 21B(1)(b) and (c) of the POA 1985, in respect of the failure to comply with requirements mentioned in section 21B(1)(c);

    (c) where the court deals with the person for a failure to comply with requirements mentioned in section 21B(1)(b) and (d) of the POA 1985, in respect of the failure to comply with requirements mentioned in section 21B(1)(d);

    (d) where the court deals with the person for a failure to comply with requirements mentioned in section 21B(1)(c) and (d) of the POA 1985, in respect of the failure to comply with requirements mentioned in section 21B(1)(d);

    (e) where the court deals with the person for a failure to comply with requirements mentioned in section 21B(2)(b) and (c) of the POA 1985, in respect of the failure to comply with requirements mentioned in section 21B(2)(c).

Amount of the criminal courts charge

★6-53i   **3.**—(1) The table in the Schedule, read with the provisions of this regulation, sets out the charge that must be ordered to be paid under section 21A(1) of the POA 1985 by class of case.

(2) Paragraph (3) applies where, following the summary conviction of a person ("P") for an offence, a magistrates' court commits P to the Crown Court for sentence and the Crown Court accordingly deals with P for the offence.

(3) The charge the Crown Court must order to be paid is the amount in column 2 of the table which corresponds to the amount the magistrates' court would have had to order had P not been committed to the Crown Court for sentence.

(4) Paragraph (5) applies where more than one entry in column 1 of the table applies.

(5) The charge the court must order to be paid is the amount in column 2 which corresponds to the entry mentioned in paragraph (4) which results in the highest amount.

(6) Where a person ("P") changes P's plea from not guilty to guilty after the start of a summary or Crown Court trial the charge the court must order to be paid is the amount that would have applied if P had not changed the plea.

(7) For the purposes of paragraph (6)—

    (a) the start of a summary trial is the time when the prosecution opens its case;

    (b) the start of a Crown Court trial is—

        (i) the time when a jury is sworn; or

        (ii) where a trial takes place without a jury, the time when the prosecution opens its case.

Remittal of the criminal courts charge

★6-53j   **4.** The period specified for the purposes of section 21E(4) of the POA 1985 (power to remit criminal courts charge) is—

    (a) where the person liable to pay the charge has made the application to a magistrates' court to remit the charge, two years;

    (b) in any other case, 12 months.

Prosecution of Offences Act 1985 (Criminal Courts Charge) Regulations 2015
(S.I. 2015 No. 796), Sched.

Table

Column 1	Column 2
★6-53k Conviction by a magistrates' court in proceedings conducted in accordance with section 16A of the Magistrates' Courts Act 1980 (trial by single justice on the papers)	£150

Column 1	Column 2
Conviction by a magistrates' court for a summary offence on a guilty plea	£150
Conviction by a magistrates' court at a trial of a summary offence where (a) the defendant did not enter a plea, (b) the trial proceeded in the absence of the defendant, and (c) the court dealt with the case on the papers without reliance on any oral evidence	£150
Conviction by a magistrates' court for an offence triable either-way on a guilty plea	£180
Conviction by a magistrates' court at a trial of a summary offence	£520
Conviction by a magistrates' court at a trial of an offence triable either way	£1000
Conviction by the Crown Court on a guilty plea	£900
Conviction by the Crown Court at a trial on indictment	£1200
Magistrates' court when dealing with a person under section 21B(1)(b), (c) or (d) of the POA 1985	£100
Crown Court when dealing with a person under section 21B(2)(b) or (c) of the POA 1985	£150
Crown Court dismissing an appeal by a person against conviction or sentence	£150
Court of Appeal dismissing an application for leave to bring an appeal under Part 1 of the CAA 1968 against a person's conviction or sentence	£150
Court of Appeal dismissing an appeal under Part 1 of the CAA 1968 against a person's conviction or sentence	£200

C. Costs in Criminal Cases (General) Regulations 1986 (S.I. 1986 No. 1335)

Part II—Costs unnecessarily or improperly incurred (reg. 3)

R. (DPP) v. Sheffield Crown Court is now reported at [2015] 1 Cr.App.R. 23, *sub nom. R. (DPP) v.* **6-57** *Crown Court at Sheffield.*

It was held in *Evans v. Serious Fraud Office* [2015] Lloyd's Rep. F.C. 223, Crown Court (at ★ Cardiff) and QBD (Hickinbottom J.), that the threshold test to be applied when considering the meaning of "as a result of an unnecessary or improper act" in section 19 of the Prosecution of Offences Act 1985 (§ 6-39 in the main work) and Part II of S.I. 1986 No. 1335 (*ibid.*, §§ 6-56, 6-57), was that laid down in *DPP v. Denning* (as to which, see the main work), rather than that in *Ridehalgh v. Horsefield* (as adopted (*obiter*) in *R. (DPP) v. Crown Court at Sheffield* (and as to which, see also the main work)). Further, it was held that, to trigger the jurisdiction, there must have been an act or omission which would not have occurred if the party concerned had conducted his case properly or which could otherwise have been properly avoided. As the procedure was essentially summary, a detailed investigation into, for example, the decision-making process of the prosecution would generally be inappropriate, and orders against a public prosecutor would be rare and restricted to exceptional cases where the prosecution had acted in bad faith or made a clear and stark error. A court should be slow to find that such an error had been made as, generally, a prosecutorial decision would only be improper if it was one that no reasonable prosecutor could have made. Here, however, it was held that the test was met in respect of the prosecution response to the defence giving notice (with reasons) of an application to dismiss in a case of alleged serious fraud (for a summary of the facts, see *Serious Fraud Office v. Evans, ante,* § 1-288). As to this case, see also *ante,* § 1-288.

Part IV—Miscellaneous applications of the Act (reg. 14)

Application of sections 16, 17 and 18 of the Act

With effect from February 1, 2015, the Costs in Criminal Cases (General) (Amendment) Regula- **6-81** tions 2015 (S.I. 2015 No. 12) amend regulation 14(3)(b) of S.I. 1986 No. 1335 so as (i) to substitute the word "any" for the word "either" at the beginning, (ii) to insert new sub-paragraph (ai) before sub-paragraph (i), as follows—

> "(ai)   section 256AC (breach of supervision requirements imposed under section 256AA);";

and (iii) to insert new sub-paragraph (iii) at the end, as follows—

> "(iii)   paragraphs 7 to 9 of Schedule 19A (breach, revocation or amendment of supervision default orders)".

For section 256AC of the CJA 2003, see § 5-661 in the main work; and for Schedule 19A to that Act, see *ibid.*, § 5-662.

D. Miscellaneous Enactments

(1) Senior Courts Act 1981

High Court

6-95   In *Darroch v. Hull and Holderness Magistrates' Court, Media Protection Services Ltd and Football Association Premier League Ltd (Interested parties)*, 179 J.P. 64, DC, the court expressed the *obiter* opinion, having regard to *Murphy v. Media Protection Services Ltd* (as to which, see the main work) and the *Practice Direction (Criminal Proceedings: Costs)* (§§ 6-123 *et seq.* in the main work), that the High Court could make a civil third party costs order under section 51 of the 1981 Act in criminal proceedings. However, it stressed that any such order would be exceptional, and that the court had to be alert to, *inter alia*, the possibility that an application for costs against a non-party was motivated by resentment of an inability to obtain an effective order against a legally aided (or otherwise impecunious) litigant. Refusing to make an order in the particular proceedings, the court pointed out that, whilst the party against whom the order had been sought had stood to benefit financially from a successful prosecution, the proceedings were criminal, with a public, as well as a private, interest.

(12) Criminal Procedure Rules 2014 (S.I. 2014 No. 1610)

Criminal Procedure Rules 2014 (S.I. 2014 No. 1610), Pt 76

Replacement of 2014 rules by 2015 rules

★**6-109**   With effect from October 5, 2015, the Criminal Procedure Rules 2015 (S.I. 2015 No. 1490) replace S.I. 2014 No. 1610. Part 76 of the 2014 rules is replaced by Part 45 of the 2015 rules (see *post*, Appendix P-463 *et seq.*), with minor drafting changes and incorporating the amendment made by S.I. 2015 No. 13 to Part 76 of the 2014 rules (as to which, see *post*, § 6-119).

Assessment and re-assessment

6-119   With effect from February 2, 2015, rule 76.11(2)(a) of S.I. 2014 No. 1610 is amended by rule 14 of the Criminal Procedure (Amendment) Rules 2015 (S.I. 2015 No. 13), so as to substitute the words "Lord Chancellor" for the words "court officer".

★   As to the replacement of S.I. 2014 No. 1610 by the Criminal Procedure Rules 2015 (S.I. 2015 No. 1490), see *ante*, § 6-109.

F. Enforcing Orders as to Costs (and Compensation)

(1) Statute

Administration of Justice Act 1970, s.41

★**6-161**   As from a day to be appointed, the Modern Slavery Act 2015, s.57(1), and Sched. 5, para. 11(1) and (2), amend section 41(8) of the 1970 Act so as to substitute ", 13A or 13B" for "or 13A".

Administration of Justice Act 1970, Sched. 9

6-165   As from April 13, 2015 (Criminal Justice and Courts Act 2015 (Commencement No. 1, Saving and Transitional Provisions) Order 2015 (S.I. 2015 No. 778)), the Criminal Justice and Courts Act 2015, s.54(2)(a), inserted a new paragraph 9A into Schedule 9 to the 1970 Act, as follows—

> "9A. Where a court orders the payment of a charge in respect of relevant court costs under section 21A of the Prosecution of Offences Act 1985.".

As from April 13, 2015 (S.I. 2015 No. 778 (*ante*)), section 54(2)(b) and (c) of the 2015 Act, provide for the re-numbering of paragraph 13 in Part I of Schedule 9 to the 1970 Act as paragraph 12A, and of paragraph 13A as paragraph 12B.

As from a day to be appointed, the Modern Slavery Act 2015, s.57(1), and Sched. 5, para. 11(1) ★ and (3), inserted a new paragraph 13B into Schedule 9 to the 1970 Act, as follows—

"13B. Where under section 8 of the Modern Slavery Act 2015 a court makes a slavery and trafficking reparation order.".

This overlooks the amendments to Schedule 9 made by the Criminal Justice and Courts Act 2015 (*ante*).

II. LEGAL AID

B. PRIMARY LEGISLATION

Legal Aid, Sentencing and Punishment of Offenders Act 2012

Summary

With effect from February 13, 2015, Schedule 1 to the LASPOA 2012 (see the main work) was **6-206** amended by the Counter-Terrorism and Security Act 2015, s.1(2), to make provision for the availability of civil legal aid in respect of proceedings under paragraph 8 of Schedule 1 to the 2015 Act (applications to extend time for which travel documents may be retained).

With effect from June 1, 2015 (Serious Crime Act 2015 (Commencement No. 1) Regulations ★ 2015 (S.I. 2015 No. 820)), Part 1 of Schedule 1 to the 2012 Act was further amended by the SCA 2015, s.85(1), and Sched. 4, para. 87(1), (3) and (4), so as to include legal services provided in relation to proceedings connected with injunctions to restrain drug-dealing activity.

As from a day to be appointed, Part 1 of Schedule 1 to the 2012 Act is further amended by the ★ SCA 2015, s.85(1), and Sched. 4, para. 87(1) and (2), so as to include legal services provided in relation to proceedings connected with female genital mutilation protection orders.

Legal Aid, Sentencing and Punishment of Offenders Act 2012, ss.21–24, 27

Information about financial resources

With effect from the day the Care Act 2014, s.1, comes into force, the Legal Aid (Information ★**6-218** about Financial Resources) Regulations 2013 (S.I. 2013 No. 628) are further amended by the Care Act 2014 (Consequential Amendments) (Secondary Legislation) Order 2015 (S.I. 2015 No. 643).

C. SECONDARY LEGISLATION

Criminal legal aid

Criminal Legal Aid (General) Regulations 2013 (S.I. 2013 No. 9), Pt 3

Criminal proceedings

King's Lynn and West Norfolk Council v. Bunning (Legal Aid Agency, interested party) is now reported ★**6-240** at [2015] 1 W.L.R. 531, *sub nom. King's Lynn and West Norfolk Council v. Bunning*. That case was concerned with contempt in the High Court. It was approved and followed in relation to contempt in the County Court in *Brown v. London Borough of Haringey*, unreported, May 14, 2015, CA (Civ. Div.) ([2015] EWCA Civ. 483).

With effect from March 23, 2015, the Criminal Legal Aid (General) (Amendment) Regulations ★ 2015 (S.I. 2015 No. 326) amended regulation 9 of S.I. 2013 No. 9, so as: (i) to omit paragraphs (d), (e), (o), and (q), (ii) to substitute a new paragraph (f), as follows—

"(f) proceedings in relation to parenting orders made under section 8(1)(b) of the Crime and Disorder Act 1998 where an order under section 22 of the Anti-social Behaviour, Crime and Policing Act 2014 or a sexual harm prevention order under section 103A of the Sexual Offences Act 2003 is made;";

(iii) to substitute a new paragraph (k), as follows—

"(k) proceedings under sections 80, 82, 83 and 84 of the Anti-social Behaviour, Crime and Policing Act 2014 in relation to closure orders made under section 80(5)(a) of that Act where a person has engaged in, or is likely to engage in behaviour that constitutes a criminal offence on the premises;";

(iv) to substitute a new paragraph (n), as follows—

"(n) proceedings under sections 103A, 103E, 103F and 103H of the Sexual Offences Act 2003 in relation to sexual harm prevention orders;";

and (v) to substitute a new paragraph (p), as follows—

"(p) proceedings under sections 122A, 122D, 122E and 122G of the Sexual Offences Act 2003 in relation to sexual risk orders;".

★   For transitional provision in relation to these amendments, see regulation 3 of the amending regulations.

★   With effect from March 24, 2015, the Legal Aid, Community Legal Service and Criminal Defence Service (Amendment) Regulations 2015 (S.I. 2015 No. 838) further amended regulation 9 of S.I. 2013 No. 9 so as to insert, after paragraph (j), a new paragraph (ja) as follows—

"(ja) proceedings in a youth court (or on appeal from such a court) in relation to the breach or potential breach of a provision of an injunction under Part 1 of the Anti-social Behaviour, Crime and Policing Act 2014 where the person who is subject to the injunction is aged under 14;".

Determinations by a court and choice of representative

S.I. 2013 No. 614, regs 4–9

Determinations by the High Court

6-277   *King's Lynn and West Norfolk Council v. Bunning (Legal Aid Agency, interested party)* is now reported at [2015] 1 W.L.R. 531, *sub nom. King's Lynn and West Norfolk Council v. Bunning.*

Financial eligibility (magistrates' courts)

★**6-321**   With effect from the day the Care Act 2014, s.1, comes into force, regulations 11, 20 and 33 of the Criminal Legal Aid (Financial Resources) Regulations 2013 (S.I. 2013 No. 471) are amended by the Care Act 2014 (Consequential Amendments) (Secondary Legislation) Order 2015 (S.I. 2015 No. 643).

Contribution orders (Crown Court)

Summary

★**6-324**   With effect from April 13, 2015, regulation 10(2) of the Criminal Legal Aid (Contribution Orders) Regulations 2013 (S.I. 2013 No. 483) was amended by the Legal Aid, Community Legal Service and Criminal Defence Service (Amendment) Regulations 2015 (S.I. 2015 No. 838).

★   With effect from June 1, 2015, regulation 10(2) of S.I. 2013 No. 483 (*ante*) was further amended by the Criminal Legal Aid (Contribution Orders) (Amendment) Regulations 2015 (S.I. 2015 No. 710).

★   With effect from the day the Care Act 2014, s.1, comes into force, regulation 10(2) of S.I. 2013 No. 483 (*ante*) is further amended by the Care Act 2014 (Consequential Amendments) (Secondary Legislation) Order 2015 (S.I. 2015 No. 643).

★**6-325**   With effect from June 1, 2015, regulations 28 and 32 of the Criminal Legal Aid (Contribution Orders) Regulations 2013 (S.I. 2013 No. 483) were amended by the Criminal Legal Aid (Contribution Orders) (Amendment) Regulations 2015 (S.I. 2015 No. 710).

Criminal Legal Aid (Contribution Orders) Regulations 2013 (S.I. 2013 No. 483), regs 2, 3, 5, 6, 25, 26, 37

Interpretation

★**6-330**   With effect from June 1, 2015, the Criminal Legal Aid (Contribution Orders) (Amendment) Regulations 2015 (S.I. 2015 No. 710) amended regulation 2 of S.I. 2013 No. 483 so as to insert, at the appropriate places, new definitions, as follows—

"'POCA' means the Proceeds of Crime Act 2002;
'POCA restraint order' means a restraint order made under Part 2 of POCA;".

III. DISCIPLINARY JURISDICTION OVER SOLICITORS

In *DLA Piper U.K. LLP v. BDO LLP* [2014] 1 W.L.R. 4425, DC, it was said to be difficult to **6-338** envisage any circumstances in which it would be appropriate for the Crown Court to make an order for costs against solicitors in pursuance of its inherent jurisdiction over solicitors (as to which, see the main work) where it would not be appropriate to make a wasted costs order under section 19A of the Prosecution of Offences Act 1985 (*ibid.*, § 6-40). As to this case, see also *post*, § 7-11.

CHAPTER 7

CRIMINAL APPEAL

II. HIGH COURT JURISDICTION IN CROWN COURT PROCEEDINGS

A. JURISDICTION

(2) Judicial review

(a) *Statute*

Senior Courts Act 1981, ss.29, 31

Application for judicial review

As from April 13, 2015 (Criminal Justice and Courts Act 2015 (Commencement No. 1, Saving ★**7-6** and Transitional Provisions) Order 2015 (S.I. 2015 No. 778)), the Criminal Justice and Courts Act 2015, s.84(1), amended section 31 of the 1981 Act, so as to insert new subsections (2A) to (2C), as follows—

"(2A) The High Court—
    (a) must refuse to grant relief on an application for judicial review, and
    (b) may not make an award under subsection (4) on such an application,
if it appears to the court to be highly likely that the outcome for the applicant would not have been substantially different if the conduct complained of had not occurred.
    (2B) The court may disregard the requirements in subsection (2A)(a) and (b) if it considers that it is appropriate to do so for reasons of exceptional public interest.
    (2C) If the court grants relief or makes an award in reliance on subsection (2B), the court must certify that the condition in subsection (2B) is satisfied.".

The amendment does not apply to an application for judicial review where the claim form was ★ filed before April 13, 2015 (S.I. 2015 No. 778 (*ante*), art. 4, and Sched. 2, para. 6).

As from a day to be appointed, section 85(1) of the 2015 Act amends section 31(3) of the 1981 Act, so as (i) to insert "— (a)" after the second "unless" and (ii) at the end to insert new text, as follows—

    ", and
    (b) the applicant has provided the court with any information about the financing of the application that is specified in rules of court for the purposes of this paragraph".

As from a day to be appointed, section 85(2) of the 2015 Act further amends section 31 of the 1981 Act, so as to insert new subsections (3A) and (3B), as follows—

    "(3A) The information that may be specified for the purposes of subsection (3)(b) includes—
    (a) information about the source, nature and extent of financial resources available, or likely to be available, to the applicant to meet liabilities arising in connection with the application, and

(b) if the applicant is a body corporate that is unable to demonstrate that it is likely to have financial resources available to meet such liabilities, information about its members and about their ability to provide financial support for the purposes of the application.

(3B) Rules of court under subsection (3)(b) that specify information identifying those who are, or are likely to be, sources of financial support must provide that only a person whose financial support (whether direct or indirect) exceeds, or is likely to exceed, a level set out in the rules has to be identified.

This subsection does not apply to rules that specify information described in subsection (3A)(b).".

★ As from April 13, 2015 (S.I. 2015 No. 778 (*ante*)), section 84(2) of the 2015 Act further amends section 31 of the 1981 Act, so as to insert new subsections (3C) to (3F), as follows—

"(3C) When considering whether to grant leave to make an application for judicial review, the High Court—

(a) may of its own motion consider whether the outcome for the applicant would have been substantially different if the conduct complained of had not occurred, and

(b) must consider that question if the defendant asks it to do so.

(3D) If, on considering that question, it appears to the High Court to be highly likely that the outcome for the applicant would not have been substantially different, the court must refuse to grant leave.

(3E) The court may disregard the requirement in subsection (3D) if it considers that it is appropriate to do so for reasons of exceptional public interest.

(3F) If the court grants leave in reliance on subsection (3E), the court must certify that the condition in subsection (3E) is satisfied.".

★ The amendment does not apply to an application for judicial review where the claim form was filed before April 13, 2015 (S.I. 2015 No. 778 (*ante*), art. 4, and Sched. 2, para. 6).

★ As from April 13, 2015 (S.I. 2015 No. 778 (*ante*)), section 84(3) of the 2015 Act further amends section 31 of the 1981 Act, so as to insert a new subsection (8), as follows—

"(8) In this section 'the conduct complained of', in relation to an application for judicial review, means the conduct (or alleged conduct) of the defendant that the applicant claims justifies the High Court in granting relief.".

★ The amendment does not apply to an application for judicial review where the claim form was filed before April 13, 2015 (S.I. 2015 No. 778 (*ante*), art. 4, and Sched. 2, para. 6).

(c) *Matters relating to trial on indictment*

General

7-10 *R. (M.) v. Kingston Crown Court* is now reported at [2015] 1 Cr.App.R. 3.

R. (DPP) v. Sheffield Crown Court is now reported at [2015] 1 Cr.App.R. 3, *sub nom. R. (DPP) v. Crown Court at Sheffield.*

Matters not relating to trial on indictment

7-11 An order for a defendant's solicitors to pay the costs of a party who had successfully resisted an application for a witness summons was not a matter relating to trial on indictment; a distinction could easily be drawn between costs ordered against a party to the trial and costs made against a third party: *DLA Piper U.K. LLP v. BDO LLP* [2014] 1 W.L.R. 4425, DC. As to this case, see also *ante*, § 6-338.

A direction under the Contempt of Court Act 1981, s.11 (§ 28-79 in the main work), is not a matter "relating to trial on indictment" within the Senior Courts Act 1981, s.29(3) (*ibid.*, § 7-4), when given after the conclusion of a trial on indictment and relating to the reporting of part of the proceedings: *R. (Wang Yam) v. Central Criminal Court* [2015] 1 Cr.App.R. 10, DC (considering *R. (Y.) v. Aylesbury Crown Court* (as to which, see the main work)).

7-12 *R. (DPP) v. Sheffield Crown Court* is now reported at [2015] 1 Cr.App.R. 3, *sub nom. R. (DPP) v. Crown Court at Sheffield.*

B. Practice and Procedure

(1) Rules of court

Criminal Procedure Rules 2014 (S.I. 2014 No. 1610), rr.64.2, 64.3

Application to state a case

★7-18 With effect from October 5, 2015, the Criminal Procedure Rules 2015 (S.I. 2015 No. 1490) replace S.I. 2014 No. 1610. Part 64 of the 2014 rules is replaced by Part 35 of the 2015 rules (see *post*, Appendix P-367 *et seq.*).

C. Appeal from High Court

(2) Criminal cause or matter

An application under section 59 of the CJPA 2001 (relating to property that has been seized by the use or purported use of powers that exist in aid of criminal investigations (§ 15-112 in the main work)) is a "criminal cause or matter" within section 18(1)(a) of the Senior Courts Act 1981 (as to which, see the main work), and thus, where a ruling on such an application is subject to a decision of the High Court on an application for judicial review, no appeal lies to the Court of Appeal: *R. (Panesar) v. H.M. Revenue & Customs* [2015] 1 Cr.App.R. 17, CA (Civ. Div.). **7-22**

III. THE COURT OF APPEAL

D. Stare Decisis in the Criminal Division of the Court of Appeal

The decision of the Supreme Court in *F.H.R. European Ventures LLP v. Cedar Capital Partners LLC* is now reported at [2015] A.C. 250. **★7-36**

IV. APPEAL TO COURT OF APPEAL BY THE DEFENDANT

A. Appeal Against Conviction on Indictment

(4) Grounds of appeal

Misdirection

Non-direction

It was held in *R. v. Hunter (Nigel)*; *R. v. Saruwu (Joseph)*; *R. v. Johnstone (Ian)*; *R. v. Walker (Alan)*; *R. v. Lonsdale (Paul)* (2015) 159(17) S.J. 37, CA ([2015] EWCA Crim. 631), that there could be no fixed rule or principle that a misdirection or non-direction in relation to good character would necessarily or usually be fatal to a conviction (considering, *inter alia*, *R. v. Fulcher* and *Jagdeo Singh v. State of Trinidad and Tobago* (as to both of which, see the main work)). As to this case, see also *ante*, § 4-485. **★7-64**

Defects in the indictment

(iv) *Duplicity and other defects of form*

Where the defendant had been subject to a sexual offences prevention order made (in 2007) under the SOA 2003, s.104 (§ 20-324 in the main work), but had never been the subject of a sex offender order under the CDA 1998, an indictment that charged him with breach of a sex offender order, contrary to the 1998 Act, s.2(8), was defective, and and the conviction fell to be quashed; the case was indistinguishable from *R. v. Shields* (as to which, see the main work), where it had been held that the court had no power to substitute a conviction for breach of the sexual offences prevention order, contrary to section 113 of the 2003 Act (§ 20-333 in the main work); that, in the instant case, the appellant had pleaded guilty and that, therefore, the court's powers of substitution were to be found in section 3A of the CAA 1968 (*ibid.*, § 7-105), rather than in section 3 (*ibid.*, § 7-103), made no difference. **7-77**

Miscellaneous

(ii) *Conduct of counsel*

It was held in *R. v. McCook* [2015] Crim.L.R. 350, CA, that it was necessary to go further than the decision in *R. v. A. (E.O.)* (as to which, see the main work), so that in any case where fresh solicitors or counsel are instructed for the purposes of an application for leave to appeal, those **★7-83** solicitors or counsel must go to the solicitors and/ or counsel who acted at trial to check the facts, unless there are, in exceptional circumstances, good and compelling reasons not to do so.

(viii) *Bias*

7-89   In *Armstrong v. U.K.* [2015] Crim.L.R. 447, ECtHR, the court reaffirmed its general approach laid down in *Hanif and Khan v. U.K.* (as to which, see the main work) relating to police officers as jurors. Here, where a jury containing a retired police officer and a serving police officer convicted the applicant of murder, there were a number of safeguards; first, the jurors were among 12 selected randomly from the local population; secondly, they were required to swear an oath or make a solemn affirmation that they would faithfully try the case and give a true verdict according to the evidence; thirdly, they would have been advised to bring any concerns to the trial judge's attention and not to discuss the case with anyone outside the jury; fourthly, they would have received directions from the judge as to how to approach the case and the evidence. More particularly, both jurors had drawn the judge's attention to their professional status at an early stage; the serving officer had also indicated that he recognised a police officer in the courtroom (the "officer in the case" but not a witness); the judge promptly invited submissions from counsel and appropriate investigations were made; questions were put to the juror who was a serving officer to identify the extent of his knowledge of that officer and the police officer witnesses; the applicant was fully involved in those proceedings; following the juror's questioning, defence counsel confirmed he was "quite happy that the juror may continue to serve"; in respect of the retired officer, counsel made it clear he would advise the applicant that the presence of a police officer juror, even a serving one, did not raise concerns, provided he had no knowledge of the case, the parties or any of the police officers involved. In the circumstances, the defence had every opportunity to object to the continued presence of the two men but chose not to; the safeguards were sufficient to ensure the impartiality of the jury in a case where there was no important conflict or clear dispute regarding the police evidence.

(9) Retrials

Criminal Procedure Rules 2014 (S.I. 2014 No. 1610), r.68.14

Renewal or setting aside of order for retrial

★7-115   As to the replacement of S.I. 2014 No. 1610 by the Criminal Procedure Rules 2015 (S.I. 2015 No. 1490), see *post*, § 7-380.

B. Appeal Against Sentence

(1) Who can appeal

Criminal Appeal Act 1968, s.50

Meaning of "sentence"

★7-121   With effect from June 1, 2015 (Serious Crime Act 2015 (Commencement No. 1) Regulations 2015 (S.I. 2015 No. 820)), the SCA 2015, s.85(1), and Sched. 4, para. 3, amended section 50(1) of the 1968 Act so as to insert, at the end of paragraph (ca), the words "(but not a determination under section 10A of that Act)".

★7-122   As to the repeal of section 76 of the SOCPA 2005, see *ante*, § 5-1212.

C. Appeal in Cases of Insanity

Criminal Procedure Rules 2014 (S.I. 2014 No. 1610), r.68.13

Directions about re-admission to hospital on dismissal of appeal

★7-150   As to the replacement of S.I. 2014 No. 1610 by the Criminal Procedure Rules 2015 (S.I. 2015 No. 1490), see *post*, § 7-380.

G. Procedure from Notice of Appeal to Hearing

(2) Right to representation

7-165   Where the applicable legislative regime was the Access to Justice Act 1999 and the Criminal Defence Service (Funding) Order 2007 (S.I. 2007 No. 1174), where the defendant had had the benefit of a representation order at trial, where this had covered the submission of an application for leave to appeal that had been refused by the single judge, where a renewed application to the full court had been successful, where the defendant had been represented by counsel at the renewed application on a private basis, where the full court granted a representation order for the purposes of the appeal but restricted to leading counsel alone, where the defendant's conviction was eventually quashed, and where she made an application for a defendant's costs order to cover, *inter alia*, (a) private costs and disbursements incurred by solicitors and counsel between refusal of leave by the single judge and the grant of leave and a representation order by the full court, and (b) private costs and disbursements incurred by the solicitor after the grant of the representation order limited to leading counsel, it was held in *R. v. Banfield* [2014] Costs L.R. 896, CA, that: as to (a), there were two possibilities; first, to make a retrospective representation order to cover the period between the expiration of the Crown Court order and the grant of the order restricted to leading counsel, such order to be made on terms that all sums paid privately be repaid first; secondly, to make a defendant's costs order under section 16 of the Prosecution of Offences Act 1985 (§ 6-3 in the main work) to cover the same period, but having regard to *Re Patel (Hitendra) and a Defendant's Costs Order* (as to which, see § 6-21a in the main work), such order would not be made without full disclosure of the terms on which the defendant agreed to fund representation, and a detailed examination of the costs claimed; and as to (b), it had long been recognised that there was a ban on "topping up"; this was reflected in article 11 of the 2007 order (prohibition on payments to "representatives" other than by the Lord Chancellor subject to limited exceptions (not applicable here)), and this could not be avoided by maintaining that a solicitor acting otherwise than under a representation order did not fall within the definition of "representative" in the order, and therefore was not covered by the ban. Whilst the court was concerned with the former legislative regime, it made clear that its view was that the same principles applied under the current regime, and it referred, in particular, to the LASPOA 2012, s.28(2), and regulation 9 of the Criminal Legal Aid (Remuneration) Regulations 2013 (S.I. 2013 No. 435) (*post*, Appendix G-16).

(5) Defendant absconding before conviction

R. v. Okedare and related appeals (see the main work) is now reported at [2015] 1 Cr.App.R. 9, **7-169** *sub nom. R. v. Okedare; R. v. Ashraf; R. v. K.; R. v. Hussain.*

(8) Bail pending appeal

Criminal Procedure Rules 2014 (S.I. 2014 No. 1610), rr.68.8, 68.9, 68.10

Application for bail pending appeal or retrial
As to the replacement of S.I. 2014 No. 1610 by the Criminal Procedure Rules 2015 (S.I. 2015 **★7-177** No. 1490), see *post*, § 7-380.

(12) Abandonment of appeal

Criminal Procedure Rules 2014 (S.I. 2014 No. 1610), rr.65.13, 65.14

Abandoning an appeal
As to the replacement of S.I. 2014 No. 1610 by the Criminal Procedure Rules 2015 (S.I. 2015 **★7-185** No. 1490), see *post*, § 7-366.

H. The Hearing

(1) Presence of appellant

Criminal Procedure Rules 2014 (S.I. 2014 No. 1610), rr.68.11, 68.12

Right to attend hearing
As to the replacement of S.I. 2014 No. 1610 by the Criminal Procedure Rules 2015 (S.I. 2015 **★7-194** No. 1490), see *post*, § 7-380.

(3) Appellant who has escaped or absconded

R. v. Okedare and related appeals (see the main work) is now reported at [2015] 1 Cr.App.R. 9, **7-198** *sub nom. R. v. Okedare; R. v. Ashraf; R. v. K.; R. v. Hussain.*

(5) Skeleton arguments and citation of authorities

Criminal Practice Direction (Appeal) 68F [2013] 1 W.L.R. 3164 (as amended by Practice Direction (Criminal Proceedings: Various changes) [2014] 1 W.L.R. 3001)

7-200 The purpose of a skeleton argument is to assist the court by setting out as concisely as practicable the arguments upon which a party intends to rely; it should be concise and both define and confine the area of controversy; it should not include extensive quotations from documents or authorities, and should not normally exceed 25 pages; length obscures the points that are germane to the resolution of an appeal, rather than assisting in their determination: *Tchenguiz v. Director of the Serious Fraud Office (H.M. Procureur for Guernsey intervening)* [2015] 1 W.L.R. 838, CA (Civ. Div.). Whilst this was said in relation to the civil practice directions, it was said in the context of quasi-criminal proceedings and it cannot be doubted that the spirit of what was said applies with equal force to criminal litigation.

(6) Attendance and role of prosecution

Criminal Procedure Rules 2014 (S.I. 2014 No. 1610), r.68.6

Respondent's notice

★**7-202** As to the replacement of S.I. 2014 No. 1610 by the Criminal Procedure Rules 2015 (S.I. 2015 No. 1490), see *post*, § 7-380.

I. NOTIFICATION OF RESULT OF APPEAL AND MATTERS DEPENDING THEREON

(4) Effect of appeal on sentence

★**7-227** For a case repeating what was said in *R. v. Hart; R. v. George; R. v. Clarke; R. v. Brown* and *R. v. Fortean* (as to both of which, see the main work)), in relation to loss of time orders under section 29 (§ 7-225 in the main work) of the CAA 1968 for unmeritorious applications for leave to appeal, see *R. v. Gray* [2015] 1 Cr.App.R.(S.) 27, CA (but adding that the mere fact that the single judge has not "ticked the box" would not protect a defendant against a loss of time order).

V. APPEAL TO COURT OF APPEAL BY THE PROSECUTION

E. RULES OF PROCEDURE

Criminal Procedure Rules 2014 (S.I. 2014 No. 1610), Pt 67

Replacement of 2014 rules by 2015 rules

★**7-265** With effect from October 5, 2015, the Criminal Procedure Rules 2015 (S.I. 2015 No. 1490) replace S.I. 2014 No. 1610. Part 67 of the 2014 rules is replaced by Part 38 of the 2015 rules (see *post*, Appendix P-394 *et seq.*), with minor drafting changes.

Decision to appeal

★**7-266** It was held in *R. v. Quillan* [2015] 2 Cr.App.R. 3, CA, that whether the requirement in rule 67.2(a) of the 2014 rules that an intending appellant should tell the judge "immediately after the ruling" of a decision to appeal had been complied with would depend on the particular facts of each case and its complexity. In that case a delay of one hour was reasonable where the ruling in question had been handed down in writing and consisted of 56 pages.

VI. RETRIAL FOR SERIOUS OFFENCES

B. APPLICATION FOR RETRIAL

Criminal Justice Act 2003, ss.76–83

★**7-282** Where a witness's unavailability to give evidence at trial resulted in the defendant's acquittal, and the witness then became available, his evidence could amount to new evidence for the purposes of a prosecution application for an order under section 76 of the 2003 Act: *R. v. Henry (Duwayne)* [2015] 2 Cr.App.R. 1, CA.

F. Supplementary

Criminal Procedure Rules 2014 (S.I. 2014 No. 1610), Pt 41

Replacement of 2014 rules by 2015 rules
   With effect from October 5, 2015, the Criminal Procedure Rules 2015 (S.I. 2015 No. 1490) ★**7-307a**
replace S.I. 2014 No. 1610. Parts 40 and 41 of the 2014 rules are replaced by Part 27 of the 2015
rules (see *post*, Appendix P-246 *et seq.*). There are necessary drafting changes.

VII. INTERLOCUTORY ETC., APPEALS

C. Procedure

Criminal Procedure Rules 2014 (S.I. 2014 No. 1610), Pt 66

Replacement of 2014 rules by 2015 rules
   With effect from October 5, 2015, the Criminal Procedure Rules 2015 (S.I. 2015 No. 1490) ★**7-315**
replace S.I. 2014 No. 1610. Part 66 of the 2014 rules is replaced by Part 37 of the 2015 rules (see
post, Appendix P-386 *et seq.*), with minor drafting changes.

VIII. MISCELLANEOUS RIGHTS OF APPEAL

A. Appeal in Respect of Orders Restricting Reporting or Public Access

Criminal Procedure Rules 2014 (S.I. 2014 No. 1610), Pt 69

Replacement of 2014 rules by 2015 rules
   With effect from October 5, 2015, the Criminal Procedure Rules 2015 (S.I. 2015 No. 1490) ★**7-326**
replace S.I. 2014 No. 1610. Part 69 of the 2014 rules is replaced by Part 40 of the 2015 rules (see
post, Appendix P-419 *et seq.*), with minor drafting changes.

IX. APPEAL TO THE COURT OF APPEAL: PROCEDURE AND FORMS

A. Procedural Rules

Criminal Procedure Rules 2014 (S.I. 2014 No. 1610), Pt 65

Replacement of 2014 rules by 2015 rules
   With effect from October 5, 2015, the Criminal Procedure Rules 2015 (S.I. 2015 No. 1490) ★**7-366**
replace S.I. 2014 No. 1610. Part 65 of the 2014 rules is replaced by Part 36 of the 2015 rules (see
post, Appendix P-372 *et seq.*), with minor drafting changes.

Criminal Procedure Rules 2014 (S.I. 2014 No. 1610), Pt 68

Replacement of 2014 rules by 2015 rules
   With effect from October 5, 2015, the Criminal Procedure Rules 2015 (S.I. 2015 No. 1490) ★**7-380**
replace S.I. 2014 No. 1610. Part 68 of the 2014 rules is replaced by Part 39 of the 2015 rules (see
post, Appendix P-405 *et seq.*), with minor changes of substance.

X. APPEAL TO THE SUPREME COURT FROM THE COURT OF APPEAL

A. The Appeal

(2) Application for leave to appeal

Criminal Procedure Rules 2014 (S.I. 2014 No. 1610), Pt 74

Replacement of 2014 rules by 2015 rules
   With effect from October 5, 2015, the Criminal Procedure Rules 2015 (S.I. 2015 No. 1490) ★**7-400**
replace S.I. 2014 No. 1610. Part 74 of the 2014 rules is replaced by Part 43 of the 2015 rules (see
post, Appendix P-456 *et seq.*), with minor drafting changes.

XIII. REFERENCES TO THE COURT OF APPEAL BY THE ATTORNEY-GENERAL

B. OF SENTENCES

Criminal Justice Act 1988, s.36

Reviews of sentencing

7-442 As from a day to be appointed, the Criminal Justice and Courts Act 2015, s.28(8), and Sched. 5, para. 2, amend section 36(2)(b) of the 1988 Act, so as (i) in sub-paragraph (zi), after "section", to insert "1(2B) or", and (ii) in sub-paragraph (ia), after "section", to insert "139(6B), 139A(5B) or".

Double jeopardy

7-449 In *Att.-Gen.'s References (Nos 4, 5, 6, 7 and 8 of 2014) (R. v. Deacon)* [2014] 2 Cr.App.R.(S.) 51, CA, it was said that considerations of "double jeopardy" should not feature to any great extent in cases where significant custodial sentences are imposed.

C. PROCEDURE

Criminal Procedure Rules 2014 (S.I. 2014 No. 1610), Pt 70

Replacement of 2014 rules by 2015 rules

★7-453 With effect from October 5, 2015, the Criminal Procedure Rules 2015 (S.I. 2015 No. 1490) replace S.I. 2014 No. 1610. Part 70 of the 2014 rules is replaced by Part 41 of the 2015 rules (see *post*, Appendix P-428 *et seq.*).

CHAPTER 8

ORAL TESTIMONY OF WITNESSES

I. PRELIMINARIES

A. SECURING ATTENDANCE OF WITNESSES, PRODUCTION OF DOCUMENTS, ETC.

(1) Summons to witness to attend Crown Court

Grounds for setting aside witness summons

(v) *Confidentiality, etc., rights of witness or person to whom evidence relates*

8-13 Civil legal aid under the exceptional case funding provisions in section 10 of the LASPOA 2012 is available to a witness who opposes an application for a witness summons seeking production of her medical or other such records: *M. v. Director of Legal Aid Casework* [2014] A.C.D. 124, QBD (Coulson J.). His Lordship had regard to *R. (T.B.) v. Stafford Crown Court* (as to which, see the main work) in saying that such a witness has an unequivocal right to be heard on the application, and commented that it is becoming increasingly common for the CPS to issue witness summonses seeking such records concerning a complainant in an assault or sex case, that they are often made somewhat lazily, in the belief that, if there are some records that may have some relevance, the CPS are fulfilling their obligations to the administration of justice by issuing the summons and then putting the burden of resolving the issues raised onto others. His Lordship said that considerably greater analysis is required before any such summons is issued and that, as a general rule, it is not good enough merely to require the documents on the general basis that they might undermine the prosecution or help the defence.

Setting aside a witness summons—procedure, etc.

Criminal Procedure Rules 2014 (S.I. 2014 No. 1610), Pt 28

Replacement of 2014 rules by 2015 rules

★8-15 With effect from October 5, 2015, the Criminal Procedure Rules 2015 (S.I. 2015 No. 1490) replace S.I. 2014 No. 1610. Part 28 of the 2014 rules is replaced by Part 17 of the 2015 rules (see *post*, Appendix P-136 *et seq.*), with minor drafting changes.

(5) Evidence from overseas

(a) *Service of process*

Crime (International Co-operation) Act 2003, s.3

General requirements for service of process

With effect from October 5, 2015, the Criminal Procedure Rules 2015 (S.I. 2015 No. 1490) ★**8-32** replace the Criminal Procedure Rules 2014 (S.I. 2014 No. 1610). Part 32 of the 2014 rules is replaced by Part 49 of the 2015 rules (*post*, Appendix P-533 *et seq.*), subject to some changes of substance.

III. COMPETENCE AND COMPELLABILITY

(3) Determination of competency

Manner of

For a case considering *Toohey v. Metropolitan Police Commr* (see the main work), see *R. v. H.*, *post*, **8-56** § 8-288.

IV. RULES OF EVIDENCE AND PRACTICE RELATING TO THE QUESTIONING OF WITNESSES

A. GENERAL

(1) Practice rules

Criminal Procedure Rules 2014 (S.I. 2014 No. 1610), r.38.11

Evidence of a witness in person

As to the replacement of S.I. 2014 No. 1610 by the Criminal Procedure Rules 2015 (S.I. 2015 ★**8-70a** No. 1490), see *ante*, § 4-265a.

(2) Special measures directions

Introduction

A court should take every reasonable step to encourage and facilitate the attendance of vulner- **8-71** able witnesses and their participation in the trial process; it was best practice to hold hearings in advance of the trial to ensure its smooth running, to give any special measures directions and to set the ground rules for the treatment of a vulnerable witness; such a hearing should be held, save in exceptional circumstances, in every case involving a vulnerable witness; if there were any doubts on how to proceed, guidance should be sought from those responsible for looking after the witness, or an expert; in general, experts recommended that the judge should introduce himself to the witness in person before any questioning, preferably in the presence of the parties, to put the witness at ease where possible; the hearing should cover, *inter alia*, the general care of the witness, if, when and where the witness was to be shown his video interview, when, where and how the parties (and the judge if identified) intended to introduce themselves to the witness, the length of questioning and frequency of breaks and the nature of the questions to be asked; to avoid any misunderstanding at trial, it would be entirely reasonable for a judge at the hearing to invite defence advocates to reduce their questions to writing in advance; the judge was responsible for controlling questioning and ensuring that vulnerable witnesses and defendants were enabled to give the best evidence they could; therefore, the judge had a duty to intervene if an advocate's questioning was confusing or inappropriate; advocates had to adapt to the witness (not the other way round), and could not insist upon any supposed right "to put one's case" or previous inconsistent statements to a vulnerable witness; if there was a right to "put one's case", it had to be modified for young or vulnerable witnesses; it was perfectly possible to ensure the jury were made aware of the defence case and of significant inconsistencies without intimidating or distressing a witness: *R. v. Lubemba*; *R. v. P. (J.)* [2015] 1 Cr.App.R. 12, CA (drawing particular attention to paras 3D.5 to 3D.7 of *Criminal Practice Direction (General matters) 3D* (§ 8-131e in the main work)). In this connection, see also the amendment to rule 3.9 of the Criminal Procedure Rules 2014 (S.I. 2014 No. 1610), effected by rule 4(a) of the Criminal Procedure (Amendment) Rules 2015 (S.I. 2015 No. 13) (*ante*, § 4-117).

Youth Justice and Criminal Evidence Act 1999, ss.16, 17

Witnesses eligible for assistance on ground of fear or distress about testifying

★8-75   As from a day to be appointed, the Modern Slavery Act 2015, s.46(1) and (2), amend section 17(4) of the 1999 Act so as to substitute "section 1 or 2 of the Modern Slavery Act 2015" for "section 4 of the Asylum and Immigration (Treatment of Claimants, etc.) Act 2004".

Youth Justice and Criminal Evidence Act 1999, ss.23–30

Evidence given in private

★8-86   As from a day to be appointed, the Modern Slavery Act 2015, s.46(1) and (3), amend section 25(4)(a) of the 1999 Act so as to substitute "section 1 or 2 of the Modern Slavery Act 2015" for "section 4 of the Asylum and Immigration (Treatment of Claiments, etc.) Act 2004".

Examination of witness through intermediary

8-94   *R. (O.P.) v. Secretary of State for Justice, Cheltenham Magistrates' Court and CPS (interested parties), Just for Kids Law (intervener)* is now reported at [2015] 1 Cr.App.R. 7, *sub nom. R. (O.P.) v. Secretary of State for Justice.*

Youth Justice and Criminal Evidence Act 1999, ss.31–33

Interpretation of Chapter 1

★8-98   As from a day to be appointed, the Modern Slavery Act 2015, s.46(1) and (4), amend section 33(6)(d) of the 1999 Act so as to substitute "section 1 or 2 of the Modern Slavery Act 2015" for "section 4 of the Asylum and Immigration (Treatment of Claimants, etc.) Act 2004".

Youth Justice and Criminal Evidence Act 1999, ss.33A–33C

Live link directions

★8-99   It was held in *R. v. Rahman* [2015] 1 Cr.App.R. 30, CA, that the fact that a defendant may have a temper and does not like being challenged by authority figures was not a characteristic that demonstrated an impairment of "social functioning" for the purposes of section 33A(4)(a) of the 1999 Act. Further, the court said that, while an expert report was not required to establish such an impairment, a judge had not misdirected himself where he merely observed that if reliance was placed upon a claimed impairment of social functioning, the usual means of establishing this would be via an expert or somebody skilled or experienced in communicating with young people. It was said that a statement from someone as obviously partisan as an accused's mother (as here, where the defendant was 16-years-old) was unlikely to be sufficient on such an issue.

[Examination of accused through intermediary

8-101   *R. (O.P.) v. Secretary of State for Justice, Cheltenham Magistrates' Court and CPS (interested parties), Just for Kids Law (intervener)* is now reported at [2015] 1 Cr.App.R. 7, *sub nom. R. (O.P.) v. Secretary of State for Justice.*

Criminal Procedure Rules 2014 (S.I. 2014 No. 1610), Pt 29

Replacement of 2014 rules by 2015 rules

★8-110   With effect from October 5, 2015, the Criminal Procedure Rules 2015 (S.I. 2015 No. 1490) replace S.I. 2014 No. 1610. Part 29 of the 2014 rules is replaced by Part 18 of the 2015 rules (see *post*, Appendix P-144 *et seq.*), with minor changes of substance.

Vulnerable people in the courts

8-131e   As to paragraphs 3D.5 to 3D.7 of *Criminal Practice Direction (General matters) 3D* (as to which, see the main work), see *R. v. Lubemba*; *R. v. P. (J.)*, *ante*, § 8-71.

B. Examination-In-Chief

(2) Identifying the witness

(a) *Name*

Coroners and Justice Act 2009, ss.86–90

In *R. (B.) v. Westminster Magistrates' Court* [2014] 3 W.L.R. 1336, SC, the Supreme Court held **8-157**
that section 87 of the 2009 Act did not confer power on a judge to make a witness anonymity
order in extradition proceedings.

C. Cross-Examination

(1) General principles

Form of questioning in cross-examination

Vulnerable witnesses
　See *R. v. Lubemba*; *R. v. P. (J.)*, *ante*, § 8-71, where the court suggested that it would be legitimate **8-217a**
for a judge to require advance written notice of questions to be asked of a vulnerable witness in
cross-examination.

(3) Restrictions

(a) *Where defendant acting in person*

Criminal Procedure Rules 2014 (S.I. 2014 No. 1610), Pt 31

Replacement of 2014 rules by 2015 rules
　With effect from October 5, 2015, the Criminal Procedure Rules 2015 (S.I. 2015 No. 1490) ★**8-232**
replace S.I. 2014 No. 1610. Part 31 of the 2014 rules is replaced by Part 23 of the 2015 rules (see
post, Appendix P-197 *et seq.*), with substantial changes to the content.

(b) *In proceedings for sexual offences*

Previous complaints and statements about sexual behaviour

　The restrictions on questions about a complainant's sexual history in section 41 of the YJCEA **8-246**
1999 (§ 8-238 in the main work) do not apply to previous false complaints of sexual assaults;
cross-examination is permitted since such complaints are not about any sexual behaviour of the
complainant within the meaning of section 42(1)(c) (*ibid.*, § 8-239); however, before any such
questions are permissible, the defence must have a proper evidential basis for asserting that any
such statement was, first, made, and, secondly, untrue; the difficulty lies in what constitutes "a
proper evidential basis" (*R. v. M.* (as to which, see the main work)); it is less than a strong factual
foundation for concluding that the previous complaint was false, but there must be some material
from which it could properly be concluded that the complaint was false; the exercise for the judge
is fact-sensitive and will not be assisted by an examination of the facts of other cases; it is an
exercise of judgment rather than discretion, so that it is for the judge to evaluate the matter on
the basis of all the relevant material; the ultimate question is whether the material is capable of
leading to a conclusion that a previous complaint was false: *R. v. All-Hilly* [2014] 2 Cr.App.R. 33,
C.A. (observing that the mere fact that a complaint is made and not pursued does not necessarily
mean that it is false, and that courts should be ready to deploy a degree of understanding of the
position of those who have made sexual allegations).

Criminal Procedure Rules 2014 (S.I. 2014 No. 1610), Pt 36

Replacement of 2014 rules by 2015 rules
　With effect from October 5, 2015, the Criminal Procedure Rules 2015 (S.I. 2015 No. 1490) ★**8-254**
replace S.I. 2014 No. 1610. Part 36 of the 2014 rules is replaced by Part 22 of the 2015 rules (see
post, Appendix P-190 *et seq.*), with minor drafting changes.

(6) As to credit

(c) *Finality of answers*

Exceptions

(iii) *Evidence of reputation for untruthfulness*

8-287   For a case considering *Toohey v. Metropolitan Police Commr* (see the main work), see *R. v. H., post,* § 8-288.

(iv) *Medical evidence relating to reliability of witness's evidence*

8-288   *Toohey v. Metropolitan Police Commr* (see the main work) was considered in *R. v. H.* [2014] Crim.L.R. 905, CA, where the court emphasised that the ultimate question as to the reliability of a witness is always for the tribunal of fact and not for the expert. As to this case, see also *post,* § 10-39.

VI. WITNESS BECOMING ILL

★**8-306**   Where the complainant, in a trial alleging the commission of offences against her when she had been 15 years of age (SOA 2003, s.9 (§ 20-58 in the main work)), was unable to complete her evidence due to the extent of her distress, a judge had properly exercised his discretion to continue with the trial: *R. v. Pipe* [2015] Crim.L.R. 304, CA (considering *R. v. Stretton and McCallion* (as to which, see the main work)). There was no dispute that the complainant was not in a fit state to continue and it was wholly unrealistic to conclude that there could have been a fresh trial; the critical issue was the extent to which the defendant could have a fair trial if it continued with the complainant's evidence having been cut short; the principal defence (that the allegations were fabricated) was fully put to the complainant; there was more than enough material to assist the jury on the critical question as to whether they were sure that the complainant was telling the truth about what she said the defendant had done; the subsidiary issue (the alleged fragile state of the complainant's mental health) was also explored with her in cross-examination; the only element that was cut short was an examination with the complainant of her own medical records, and those (and thus the inconsistencies) were reduced to agreed facts and placed before the jury in writing.

CHAPTER 9

DOCUMENTARY AND REAL EVIDENCE

II. PUBLIC DOCUMENTS

D. CATEGORIES OF PUBLIC DOCUMENTS

(4) Public registers

Newspaper proprietors

★**9-54**   As from May 26, 2015, section 15 of the Newspaper Libel and Registration Act 1881 was repealed by the Deregulation Act 2015, s.107, and Sched. 23, para. 2.

(8) Judicial documents

(g) *Convictions and acquittals*

Police and Criminal Evidence Act 1984, s.73

Proof of convictions and acquittals

9-81   *R. v. E.M.* is now reported at [2014] 2 Cr.App.R. 29, *sub nom. R. v. M. (E.).*

CHAPTER 10

MISCELLANEOUS SOURCES OF EVIDENCE

II. ADMISSIONS

Criminal Justice Act 1967, s.10

As to the replacement of Parts 37 and 38 of the Criminal Procedure Rules 2014 (S.I. 2014 No. 1610), see *ante*, §§ 2-199a and 4-265a, respectively. ★**10-8**

III. DEPOSITIONS AND WRITTEN STATEMENTS

C. WITNESS STATEMENTS

Criminal Justice Act 1967, s.9

Proof by written statement

With effect from May 26, 2015 (Deregulation Act 2015 (Commencement No. 1 and Transitional and Saving Provisions) Order 2015 (S.I. 2015 No. 994)), the 2015 Act, s.80(1) to (4), amended section 9 of the 1967 Act so as: (i) in subsection (2)(d), to substitute the words "within the relevant period" for the words "within seven days from the service of the copy of the statement"; (ii) to insert, after subsection (2), a new subsection (2A) as follows— ★**10-14**

"(2A) For the purposes of subsection (2)(d), 'the relevant period' is—
  (a) such number of days, which may not be less than seven, from the service of the copy of the statement as may be prescribed by Criminal Procedure Rules, or
  (b) if no such number is prescribed, seven days from the service of the copy of the statement.";

and (iii) to omit subsections (3), (3A), (6) and (8).

Criminal Procedure Rules 2014 (S.I. 2014 No. 1610), Pt 27

Replacement of 2014 rules by 2015 rules

With effect from October 5, 2015, the Criminal Procedure Rules 2015 (S.I. 2015 No. 1490) replace S.I. 2014 No. 1610. Part 27 of the 2014 rules is replaced by Part 16 of the 2015 rules (see *post*, Appendix P-132 *et seq*.), with several changes of substance. ★**10-16**

Written statement in evidence

As to the replacement of Parts 37 and 38 of the Criminal Procedure Rules 2014 (S.I. 2014 No. 1610), see *ante*, §§ 2-199a and 4-265a, respectively. ★**10-19**

VI. LETTERS OF REQUEST

Rules of court

As to the replacement of Part 32 of the Criminal Procedure Rules 2014 (S.I. 2014 No. 1610) by Part 49 of the Criminal Procedure Rules 2015 (S.I. 2015 No. 1490), see *ante*, § 8-32. ★**10-34**

VII. EXPERT EVIDENCE

A. LEGISLATION

Criminal Procedure Rules 2014 (S.I. 2014 No. 1610), Pt 33

When this Part applies

In *R. v. H.* [2014] Crim.L.R. 905, CA, it was said that whilst whilst primary legislative reform has not been taken forward following the Law Commission's report (*Expert Evidence in Criminal* **10-39**

Proceedings in England and Wales (2011) (Law Com. No. 325)), real concern about the use of unreliable or inappropriate expert evidence had resulted in the revision of rules 33.1 to 33.4 of the 2014 rules, and the new practice direction (as to which, see § 10-46c in the main work) incorporated the Law Commission's recommended reliability criteria to be considered when ruling on the admissibility of expert evidence. The court advised that, following these and other changes, advocates and the courts must adopt a new and more rigorous approach to the handling of expert evidence; in particular, comment based only on analysis of the evidence, which effectively usurps the task of the jury, is to be avoided; the task of the expert is only to inform a jury of matters of a scientific and medical kind of which they might be unaware, which they ought to take into account when assessing the evidence in the case, in order to decide whether they can be sure about the reliability of a particular witness. As to this case, see also *ante*, § 8-288.

★   With effect from October 5, 2015, the Criminal Procedure Rules 2015 (S.I. 2015 No. 1490) replace S.I. 2014 No. 1610. Part 33 of the 2014 rules is replaced by Part 19 of the 2015 rules (see *post*, Appendix P-170 *et seq.*), with minor changes of substance.

★10-46b   As to the replacement of Parts 37 and 38 of the Criminal Procedure Rules 2014 (S.I. 2014 No. 1610), see *ante*, §§ 2-199a and 4-265a, respectively.

B. OPINION EVIDENCE

Scope

★10-51   Evidence from a clinical psychologist that the confessions of an accused person "are" unreliable was inadmissible: *Pora v. The Queen, The Times,* April 20, 2015, PC ([2015] UKPC 9). The board said that it would have been open to the witness to give evidence of his opinion as to why, by reason of his psychological assessment of the appellant, the latter might have been disposed to make an unreliable confession, but it was not open to him to assert that the confessions were in fact unreliable.

For a case in which the High Court of Australia rejected the evidence of an anatomist of anatomical characteristics that were common to the defendant and to one of the offenders, where his opinion was based on viewing CCTV images of the robbery with which the defendant was charged and images of the defendant taken whilst in custody, see *Honeysett v. The Queen,* unreported, August 13, 2014 ([2014] HCA 29). It was held that his opinion was not based on his undoubted knowledge of anatomy; his evidence gave an unwarranted appearance of science to the prosecution case that the defendant and the offender shared a number of physical characteristics.

CHAPTER 11

HEARSAY EVIDENCE

II. STATUTE

A. CRIMINAL JUSTICE ACT 2003

(1) The basic rules

Criminal Justice Act 2003, ss.114, 115, 133, 134

Hearsay and the right to a fair trial

11-3   For subsequent proceedings in the European Court of Human Rights arising out of the case of *R. v. Horncastle; R. v. Marquis; R. v. Carter* (see the main work), see *Horncastle v. U.K.* (2015) 60 E.H.R.R. 31, in which it was held that the court had to apply the principles set out by the Grand Chamber in *Al-Khawaja v. U.K.* (as to which, see the main work). According to these, it had to decide whether there was a good reason for an absent witness's non-attendance, whether his witness statement was sole or decisive, and, if so, whether there were nonetheless adequate counter-balancing measures, including strong procedural safeguards permitting a fair and proper assessment of the reliability of the evidence; thus the argument that any decisive evidence had to be reliable, or at the very least be shown not to be unreliable to any significant extent, before it could be fairly admitted, had to be rejected. As to reasons for absence, the court said that where a witness had died, there was good reason for this purpose; where absence was the result of fear, a distinction could be drawn between fear attributable to threats or other actions of the defendant (or those acting on his behalf) and a more general fear of what would happen if the witness were to give evidence at trial; in the former case, it was appropriate to allow a statement of that witness to be introduced at trial, even if it was the sole or decisive evidence against the defendant, because to allow the defendant to benefit from the fear he has engendered would be incompatible with the rights of victims and witnesses; as to the latter, the trial court must conduct appropriate inquiries to determine, first, whether or not there were objective grounds for fear, and, secondly, whether those grounds were supported by evidence; in all cases, where no prior examination of the witness has taken place, the admission of a witness statement in lieu of live evidence has to be a measure of last resort; the trial court has to be satisfied that all available alternatives, such as witness anonymity and other special measures, would be inappropriate or impracticable. As far as the sole or decisive rule was concerned, the court held that "decisive" should be narrowly understood as indicating evidence of such significance or importance as was likely to be determinative of the outcome of the case; where the untested evidence of a witness is corroborated by other evidence, the assessment of whether it is decisive will depend on the strength of the supportive evidence; the stronger the corroborative evidence, the less likely that the evidence of the absent witness will be "decisive". In respect of the need for counter-balancing factors where evidence is deemed to be sole or decisive, the court said that the safeguards contained in the CJA 2003, supported by section 78 (§ 15-401 in the main work) of the PACE Act 1984, and the common law (such as proper directions in the summing up), were in principle strong safeguards designed to ensure the fairness of criminal proceedings.

(2) Principal categories of admissibility

(a) *Absent witnesses*

Criminal Justice Act 2003, s.116

Witness cannot be found (s.116(2)(d))

For subsequent proceedings in the European Court of Human Rights in *R. v. Horncastle*; *R. v. Marquis*; *R. v. Carter* (see the main work), see *ante*, § 11-3. **11-21**

A judge had been entitled to find that a case fell within section 116(2)(d) of the 2003 Act (§ 11-15 in the main work) where the witness in question knew of the proceedings, was reluctant to attend (one reason for his professed reluctance being a fear that he would lose his job) and was deliberately lying low (when the police visited his London address during the trial, his girlfriend was present but there was no trace of him): *R. v. M.* [2014] Crim.L.R. 823, CA. The court said that whether or not a case fell within section 116(2)(d) was ultimately a question of fact for the trial judge. As to this case, see also *post*, §§ 13-9, 13-22a.

Witness in fear (s.116(2)(e))

For subsequent proceedings in the European Court of Human Rights in *R. v. Horncastle*; *R. v. Marquis*; *R. v. Carter* (see the main work), see *ante*, § 11-3. **11-22**

(3) Supplementary

(a) *Multiple hearsay*

Criminal Justice Act 2003, s.121

Additional requirements for admissibility of multiple hearsay

Where the applicant's defence to a charge of murder was that he had been present, but that **11-41** the person who had inflicted the fatal stab wound was another person (X), whom he identified, a recording of a telephone conversation allegedly between the defendant's mother and X in which

X appeared to exculpate her son and to discuss handing himself in, which the defence sought to have admitted at trial via a police officer witness (the mother had provided the recording to the police), without calling either X or the mother, was multiple hearsay within section 121 of the 2003 Act (see the main work), and the judge had sustainably decided that admitting it under section 121 would not be in the interests of justice (see s.121(1)(c)); given the extent of contact between the mother and X (extensive phone conversations), and a clear allegation of pressure made by X, it was in the interests of justice for the jury to be put in a position to resolve whether X was in fear, whether he said what the mother wanted to hear to avoid a difficult situation, or whether he was truly admitting an offence; this could not be done without at least one of the mother and X giving evidence: *R. v. Williams,* unreported, September 19, 2014, CA ([2014] EWCA Crim. 1862).

(4) Rules of court
Criminal Procedure Rules 2014 (S.I. 2014 No. 1610), Pt 34

Replacement of 2014 rules by 2015 rules

★**11-52**   With effect from October 5, 2015, the Criminal Procedure Rules 2015 (S.I. 2015 No. 1490) replace S.I. 2014 No. 1610. Part 34 of the 2014 rules is replaced by Part 20 of the 2015 rules (see *post,* Appendix P-179 *et seq.*), with minor drafting changes.

★**11-56**   As to the replacement of Parts 37 and 38 of the Criminal Procedure Rules 2014 (S.I. 2014 No. 1610), see *ante,* §§ 2-199a and 4-265a, respectively.

III. COMMON LAW
(5) Res gestae

(a) *Possibility of concoction or distortion can be disregarded by reason of emotional involvement in events*

Practical considerations

★**11-78**   It had been appropriate to admit transcripts of three 999 calls made by the complainant saying that she had been attacked by her boyfriend, together with her account to the police when they arrived at the scene six minutes after the last call (finding her agitated, upset and with marks to her throat and cheek), under the *res gestae* principle (as preserved by the CJA 2003, s.118(1) (§ 11-70 in the main work)), where she refused to give a statement for fear of further violence, and where the prosecution did not call her to give evidence or tender her for cross-examination; given the clear evidence of recent attempted strangulation, and the complainant's emotional state on the phone and in person, the court had been entitled to dismiss the possibility of concoction or distortion: *Barnaby v. DPP* [2015] 2 Cr.App.R. 4, DC (considering *R. v. Andrews (D.)* (as to which, see the main work)). Whilst a court has a cardinal responsibility to ensure that the defendant receives a fair trial, careful decisions are required if there is a real risk that a domestic abuse victim may suffer further harm following her co-operation with the prosecution; here, the prosecution had not sought to resort to unfair tactics to avoid introducing potentially inconsistent evidence, or because they anticipated the witness being untruthful; instead, they had sensibly recognised the complainant's potentially dangerous position.

CHAPTER 12

PRIVILEGE, PUBLIC INTEREST IMMUNITY AND DISCLOSURE

I. PRIVILEGE
C. LEGAL PROFESSIONAL PRIVILEGE
(1) The nature of legal professional privilege

Litigation privilege

12-7   *Rawlinson and Hunter Trustees S.A. v. Akers* is now reported at [2014] 4 All E.R. 627.

II. PUBLIC INTEREST IMMUNITY

C. THE DECISION AS TO NON-DISCLOSURE

Voluntary disclosure

Public interest immunity is not a private right, but is concerned with maintaining the ★**12-42**
confidentiality of documents that would harm the public interest if they were allowed to enter the
public domain. If the need for confidentiality outweighs the need to promote the administration
of justice, the document must not be disclosed. It follows that, if a document to which public
interest immunity properly attached is disclosed by mistake, and an objection is raised to its use in
the proceedings, it remains necessary for the court to decide, in accordance with established
principles, whether its use should be allowed, regardless of whether the mistake was, or should
reasonably have been, obvious to the recipient: *Rawlinson & Hunter Trustees S.A. (as Trustee of the
Tchenguiz Family Trust) v. Director of the Serious Fraud Office (No. 2); Tchenguiz v. Director of the Serious
Fraud Office* [2015] 1 W.L.R. 797, CA (Civ. Div.).

III. DISCLOSURE

A. PRELIMINARY

Surviving common law

R. (Nunn) v. Chief Constable of Suffolk Police (JUSTICE intervening) is now reported at [2015] A.C. ★**12-49**
225.

B. LEGISLATION

(1) Criminal Procedure and Investigations Act 1996

Criminal Procedure and Investigations Act 1996, ss.7–9

R. (Nunn) v. Chief Constable of Suffolk Police (JUSTICE intervening) is now reported at [2015] A.C. ★**12-75**
225.

Criminal Procedure and Investigations Act 1996, ss.17, 18

As to the commencement of section 85(1) of the LASPOA 2012, see *ante*, § 1-125. ★**12-91**

Criminal Procedure and Investigations Act 1996, s.22

Introduction

As to a further revised code of practice made under section 23 of the 1996 Act, see *post*, Ap- ★**12-96**
pendix A-231.

Code of practice

As to a further revised code of practice made under section 23 of the 1996 Act, see *post*, Ap- ★**12-97**
pendix A-231.

Criminal Procedure and Investigations Act 1996, ss.25–27

Operation and revision of code

As to a further revised code of practice made under section 23 of the 1996 Act, see *post*, Ap- ★**12-98**
pendix A-231.

(2) Rules and regulations

Criminal Procedure Rules 2014 (S.I. 2014 No. 1610), rr.22.1, 22.2, 22.3

Replacement of 2014 rules by 2015 rules

With effect from October 5, 2015, the Criminal Procedure Rules 2015 (S.I. 2015 No. 1490) ★**12-103**
replace S.I. 2014 No. 1610. Part 22 of the 2014 rules is replaced by Part 15 of the 2015 rules (see
post, Appendix P-123 *et seq.*), with minor changes of substance.

Criminal Procedure Rules 2014 (S.I. 2014 No. 1610), rr.22.4–22.9

Defence disclosure

As to the replacement of S.I. 2014 No. 1610 by the Criminal Procedure Rules 2015 (S.I. 2015 ★**12-112**
No. 1490), see *ante*, § 12-103.

Preparation of defence statements

12-122   Where there are concurrent criminal and care proceedings, it is not permissible for those representing the defendant in the criminal proceedings to advise their client not to comply with an order made in the care proceedings to serve a response to the local authority's threshold document or to file a narrative statement, either at all or pending service of the defence statement in the criminal proceedings: *A local authority v. D.G.* [2014] 2 F.L.R. 713, Fam D (Keehan J.) (commenting that any issue about alleged prejudice to the defendant in the criminal proceedings based on him being required to file and serve his response to the threshold document or a narrative statement before the date his criminal defence statement is to be filed and served, or at all, only arises and is only potentially relevant if and when an application is made by the police and/or a co-accused for statements and documents filed in the care proceedings to be disclosed into the linked criminal proceedings).

(4) Sexual offences

Sexual Offences (Protected Material) Act 1997

Introductory

[Meaning of "protected material"

12-129   **1.**—(1) In this Act "protected material", in relation to proceedings for a sexual offence, means a copy (in whatever form) of any of the following material, namely—

    (a) a statement relating to that or any other sexual offence made by any victim of the offence (whether the statement is recorded in writing or in any other form),

    (b) a photograph or pseudo-photograph of any such victim, or

    (c) a report of a medical examination of the physical condition of any such victim,

which is a copy given by the prosecutor to any person under this Act.

(2) For the purposes of subsection (1) a person is, in relation to any proceedings for a sexual offence, a victim of that offence if—

    (a) the charge, summons or indictment by which the proceedings are instituted names that person as a person in relation to whom that offence was committed; or

    (b) that offence can, in the prosecutor's opinion, be reasonably regarded as having been committed in relation to that person;

and a person is, in relation to any such proceedings, a victim of any other sexual offence if that offence can, in the prosecutor's opinion, be reasonably regarded as having been committed in relation to that person.

(3) In this Act, where the context so permits (and subject to subsection (4))—

    (a) references to any protected material include references to any part of any such material; and

    (b) references to a copy of any such material include references to any part of any such copy.

(4) Nothing in this Act—

    (a) so far as it refers to a defendant making any copy of—

        (i) any protected material, or

        (ii) a copy of any such material,

    applies to a manuscript copy which is not a verbatim copy of the whole of that material or copy; or

    (b) so far as it refers to a defendant having in his possession any copy of any protected material, applies to a manuscript copy made by him which is not a verbatim copy of the whole of that material.]

[Meaning of other expressions

12-130   **2.**—(1) In this Act—

    "contracted out prison" means a contracted out prison within the meaning of Part IV of the Criminal Justice Act 1991;

    "defendant", in relation to any proceedings for a sexual offence, means any person charged with that offence (whether or not he has been convicted);

    "governor", in relation to a contracted out prison, means the director of the prison;

    "inform" means inform in writing;

    "legal representative", in relation to a defendant, means a person who, for the purposes of the Legal Services Act 2007, is an authorised person in relation to an activity which constitutes the exercise of a right of audience or the conduct of litigation (within the meaning of that Act) and who is acting for the defendant in connection with any proceedings for the sexual offence in question;

"photograph" and "pseudo-photograph" shall be construed in accordance with section 7(4) and (7) of the Protection of Children Act 1978;

"prison" means any prison, young offender institution or remand centre which is under the general superintendence of, or is provided by, the Secretary of State under the Prison Act 1952, including a contracted out prison;

"proceedings" means (subject to subsection (2)) criminal proceedings;

"the prosecutor", in relation to any proceedings for a sexual offence, means any person acting as prosecutor (whether an individual or a body);

"relevant proceedings", in relation to any material which has been disclosed by the prosecutor under this Act, means any proceedings for the purposes of which it has been so disclosed or any further proceedings for the sexual offence in question;

"sexual offence" means one of the offences listed in the Schedule to this Act.

(2) For the purposes of this Act references to proceedings for a sexual offence include references to—

(a) any appeal or application for leave to appeal brought or made by or in relation to a defendant in such proceedings;

(b) any application made to the Criminal Cases Review Commission for the reference under section 9 or 11 of the Criminal Appeal Act 1995 of any conviction, verdict, finding or sentence recorded or imposed in relation to any such defendant; and

(c) any petition to the Secretary of State requesting him to recommend the exercise of Her Majesty's prerogative of mercy in relation to any such defendant.

(3) In this Act, in the context of the prosecutor giving a copy of any material to any person—

(a) references to the prosecutor include references to a person acting on behalf of the prosecutor; and

(b) where any such copy falls to be given to the defendant's legal representative, references to the defendant's legal representative include references to a person acting on behalf of the defendant's legal representative.]

[The definition of "legal representative" is printed as amended by the Legal Services Act 2007, s.208(1), and Sched 21, para. 123.]

Regulation of disclosures to defendant

[Regulation of disclosures by prosecutor

3.—(1) Where, in connection with any proceedings for a sexual offence, any statement or other **12-131** material falling within any of paragraphs (a) to (c) of section 1(1) would (apart from this section) fall to be disclosed by the prosecutor to the defendant—

(a) the prosecutor shall not disclose that material to the defendant; and

(b) it shall instead be disclosed under this Act in accordance with whichever of subsections (2) and (3) below is applicable.

(2) If—

(a) the defendant has a legal representative, and

(b) the defendant's legal representative gives the prosecutor the undertaking required by section 4 (disclosure to defendant's legal representative),

the prosecutor shall disclose the material in question by giving a copy of it to the defendant's legal representative.

(3) If subsection (2) is not applicable, the prosecutor shall disclose the material in question by giving a copy of it to the appropriate person for the purposes of section 5 (disclosure to unrepresented defendant) in order for that person to show that copy to the defendant under that section.

(4) Where under this Act a copy of any material falls to be given to any person by the prosecutor, any such copy—

(a) may be in such form as the prosecutor thinks fit, and

(b) where the material consists of information which has been recorded in any form, need not be in the same form as that in which the information has already been recorded.

(5) Once a copy of any material is given to any person under this Act by the prosecutor, the copy shall (in accordance with section 1(1)) be protected material for the purposes of this Act.]

[Disclosure to defendant's legal representative

4.—(1) For the purposes of this Act the undertaking which a defendant's legal representative is **12-132**

required to give in relation to any protected material given to him under this Act is an undertaking by him to discharge the obligations set out in subsections (2) to (7).

(2) He must take reasonable steps to ensure—

    (a) that the protected material, or any copy of it, is only shown to the defendant in circumstances where it is possible to exercise adequate supervision to prevent the defendant retaining possession of the material or copy or making a copy of it, and

    (b) that the protected material is not shown and no copy of it is given, and its contents are not otherwise revealed, to any person other than the defendant, except so far as it appears to him necessary to show the material or give a copy of it to any such person—

       (i) in connection with any relevant proceedings, or

       (ii) for the purposes of any assessment or treatment of the defendant (whether before or after conviction).

(3) He must inform the defendant—

    (a) that the protected material is such material for the purposes of this Act,

    (b) that the defendant can only inspect that material, or any copy of it, in circumstances such as are described in subsection (2)(a), and

    (c) that it would be an offence for the defendant—

       (i) to have that material, or any copy of it, in his possession otherwise than while inspecting it or the copy in such circumstances, or

       (ii) to give that material or any copy of it, or otherwise reveal its contents, to any other person.

(4) He must, where the protected material or a copy of it has been shown or given in accordance with subsection (2)(b)(i) or (ii) to a person other than the defendant, inform that person—

    (a) that that person must not give any copy of that material, or otherwise reveal its contents—

       (i) to any other person other than the defendant, or

       (ii) to the defendant otherwise than in circumstances such as are described in subsection (2)(a); and

    (b) that it would be an offence for that person to do so.

(5) He must, where he ceases to act as the defendant's legal representative at a time when any relevant proceedings are current or in contemplation—

    (a) inform the prosecutor of that fact, and

    (b) if he is informed by the prosecutor that the defendant has a new legal representative who has given the prosecutor the undertaking required by this section, give the protected material, and any copies of it in his possession, to the defendant's new legal representative.

(6) He must, at the time of giving the protected material to the new legal representative under subsection (5), inform that person—

    (a) that that material is protected material for the purposes of this Act, and

    (b) of the extent to which—

       (i) that material has been shown by him, and

       (ii) any copies of it have been given by him,

    to any other person (including the defendant).

(7) He must keep a record of every occasion on which the protected material was shown, or a copy of it was given, as mentioned in subsection (6)(b).]

[Disclosure to unrepresented defendant

12-133   **5.**—(1) This section applies where, in accordance with section 3(3), a copy of any material falls to be given by the prosecutor to the appropriate person for the purposes of this section in order for that person to show that copy to the defendant under this section.

(2) Subject to subsection (3), the appropriate person in such a case is—

    (a) if the defendant is detained in a prison, the governor of the prison or any person nominated by the governor for the purposes of this section; and

    (b) otherwise the officer in charge of such police station as appears to the prosecutor to be suitable for enabling the defendant to have access to the material in accordance with this section or any person nominated by that officer for the purposes of this section.

(3) The Secretary of State may by regulations provide that, in such circumstances as are specified in the regulations, the appropriate person for the purposes of this section shall be a person of any description so specified.

(4) The appropriate person shall take reasonable steps to ensure—

    (a) that the protected material, or any copy of it, is only shown to the defendant in circumstances where it is possible to exercise adequate supervision to prevent the defendant retaining possession of the material or copy or making a copy of it,

(b) that, subject to paragraph (a), the defendant is given such access to that material, or a copy of it, as he reasonably requires in connection with any relevant proceedings, and

(c) that that material is not shown and no copy of it is given, and its contents are not otherwise revealed, to any person other than the defendant.

(5) The prosecutor shall, at the time of giving the protected material to the appropriate person, inform him—

(a) that that material is protected material for the purposes of this Act, and

(b) that he is required to discharge the obligations set out in subsection (4) in relation to that material.

(6) The prosecutor shall at that time also inform the defendant—

(a) that that material is protected material for the purposes of this Act,

(b) that the defendant can only inspect that material, or any copy of it, in circumstances such as are described in subsection (4)(a), and

(c) that it would be an offence for the defendant—

   (i) to have that material, or any copy of it, in his possession otherwise than while inspecting it or the copy in such circumstances, or

   (ii) to give that material or any copy of it, or otherwise reveal its contents, to any other person,

as well as informing him of the effect of subsection (7).

(7) If—

(a) the defendant requests the prosecutor in writing to give a further copy of the material mentioned in subsection (1) to some other person, and

(b) it appears to the prosecutor to be necessary to do so—

   (i) in connection with any relevant proceedings, or

   (ii) for the purposes of any assessment or treatment of the defendant (whether before or after conviction),

the prosecutor shall give such a copy to that other person.

(8) The prosecutor may give such a copy to some other person where no request has been made under subsection (7) but it appears to him that in the interests of the defendant it is necessary to do so as mentioned in paragraph (b) of that subsection.

(9) The prosecutor shall, at the time of giving such a copy to a person under subsection (7) or (8), inform that person—

(a) that the copy is protected material for the purposes of this Act,

(b) that he must not give any copy of the protected material or otherwise reveal its contents—

   (i) to any person other than the defendant, or

   (ii) to the defendant otherwise than in circumstances such as are described in subsection (4)(a); and

(c) that it would be an offence for him to do so.

(10) If the prosecutor—

(a) receives a request from the defendant under subsection (7) to give a further copy of the material in question to another person, but

(b) does not consider it to be necessary to do so as mentioned in paragraph (b) of that subsection and accordingly refuses the request,

he shall inform the defendant of his refusal.

(11) [*Making of regulations under subs. (3).*]]

[Further disclosures by prosecutor

12-134

6.—(1) Where—

(a) any material has been disclosed in accordance with section 3(2) to the defendant's legal representative, and

(b) at a time when any relevant proceedings are current or in contemplation the legal representative either—

   (i) ceases to act as the defendant's legal representative in circumstances where section 4(5)(b) does not apply, or

   (ii) dies or becomes incapacitated,

that material shall be further disclosed under this Act in accordance with whichever of section 3(2) or (3) is for the time being applicable.

(2) Where—

(a) any material has been disclosed in accordance with section 3(3), and

(b) at a time when any relevant proceedings are current or in contemplation the defendant acquires a legal representative who gives the prosecutor the undertaking required by section 4,

that material shall be further disclosed under this Act, in accordance with section 3(2), to the defendant's legal representative.]

12-135   [**7.** [*Regulation of disclosures by Criminal Cases Review Commission.*]]

Supplementary

[*Offences*

12-136   **8.**—(1) Where any material has been disclosed under this Act in connection with any proceedings for a sexual offence, it is an offence for the defendant—

(a) to have the protected material, or any copy of it, in his possession otherwise than while inspecting it or the copy in circumstances such as are described in section 4(2)(a) or 5(4)(a), or

(b) to give that material or any copy of it, or otherwise reveal its contents, to any other person.

(2) Where any protected material, or any copy of any such material, has been shown or given to any person in accordance with section 4(2)(b)(i) or (ii) or section 5(7) or (8), it is an offence for that person to give any copy of that material or otherwise reveal its contents—

(a) to any person other than the defendant, or

(b) to the defendant otherwise than in circumstances such as are described in section 4(2)(a) or 5(4)(a).

(3) Subsections (1) and (2) apply whether or not any relevant proceedings are current or in contemplation (and references to the defendant shall be construed accordingly).

(4) A person guilty of an offence under this section is liable—

(a) on summary conviction, to imprisonment for a term not exceeding *six* [12] months or a fine not exceeding the statutory maximum or both;

(b) on conviction on indictment, to imprisonment for a term not exceeding two years or a fine or both.

(5) Where a person is charged with an offence under this section relating to any protected material or copy of any such material, it is a defence to prove that, at the time of the alleged offence, he was not aware, and neither suspected nor had reason to suspect, that the material or copy in question was protected material or (as the case may be) a copy of any such material.

(6) The court before which a person is tried for an offence under this section may (whether or not he is convicted of that offence) make an order requiring him to return any protected material, or any copy of any such material, in his possession to the prosecutor.

(7) Nothing in subsection (1) or (2) shall be taken to apply to—

(a) any disclosure made in the course of any proceedings before a court or in any report of any such proceedings, or

(b) any disclosure made or copy given by a person when returning any protected material, or a copy of any such material, to the prosecutor or the defendant's legal representative;

and accordingly nothing in section 4, or 5 shall be read as precluding the making of any disclosure or the giving of any copy in circumstances falling within paragraph (a) or (as the case may be) paragraph (b) above.]

[In subs. (4)(a), "12" is substituted for "six", as from a day to be appointed, by the CJA 2003, s.282(2) and (3). The increase has no application to offences committed before the substitution takes effect: s.282(4).]

[*Modification and amendment of other enactments*

12-137   **9.**—(1) [*Repealed by CJA 2003, s.332, and Sched. 37, Pt 4.*]

(2) Despite section 20(1) of the Criminal Procedure and Investigations Act 1996 (disclosure provisions of the Act not affected by other statutory duties), section 3(3) to (5) of that Act (manner of disclosure) shall not apply in relation to any disclosure required by section 3, 7 or 9 of that Act if section 3(1) above applies in relation to that disclosure.

(3) [*See ss.17 and 18 of the Criminal Procedure and Investigations Act 1996, §§ 12-88et seq. in the main work*]

(4) [*Inserts subs. 1(6) into the Criminal Procedure and Investigations Act 1996, § 12-56 in the main work.*]]

12-138   [**10.** [*Financial provision.*]]

[*Short title, commencement and extent*

12-139   **11.**—(1) [*Short title.*]

(2) This Act shall come into force on such day as the Secretary of State may appoint by order made by statutory instrument.

(3) Nothing in this Act applies to any proceedings for a sexual offence where the defendant was charged with the offence before the commencement of this Act.

(4) This Act extends to England and Wales only.]

[Section 2   SCHEDULE

SEXUAL OFFENCES FOR PURPOSES OF THIS ACT

5. Any offence under section 1 of the Protection of Children Act 1978 or section 160 of the   **12-140** Criminal Justice Act 1988 (indecent photographs of children).

5A. Any offence under any provision of Part 1 of the Sexual Offences Act 2003 except section 64, 65, 69 or 71.

6. Any offence under section 1 of the Criminal Law Act 1977 of conspiracy to commit any of the offences mentioned in paragraphs 5 and 5A.

7. Any offence under section 1 of the Criminal Attempts Act 1981 of attempting to commit any of those offences.

8. Any offence of inciting another to commit any of those offences.]

[This schedule is printed as amended by the SOA 2003, ss.139 and 140, and Scheds 6, para. 36, and 7. The reference in para. 8 to inciting another to commit an offence has effect as a reference to the offences under Part 2 of the SCA 2007: 2007 Act, s.63(1), and Sched. 6, para. 34.]

(5) Miscellaneous

Initial details of the prosecution case

Criminal Procedure Rules 2014 (S.I. 2014 No. 1610), Pt 10

Replacement of 2014 rules by 2015 rules

With effect from October 5, 2015, the Criminal Procedure Rules 2015 (S.I. 2015 No. 1490)   **★12-142** replace S.I. 2014 No. 1610. Part 10 of the 2014 rules is replaced by Part 8 of the 2015 rules (see *post*, Appendix P-68 *et seq.*), with several changes of substance.

CHAPTER 13

EVIDENCE OF BAD CHARACTER

I. INTRODUCTION

C. INTERPRETATION

Criminal Justice Act 2003, s.112

Interpretation of Chapter 1

In *R. v. M.* [2014] Crim.L.R. 823, CA, the court referred to the fact that in *R. v. Hall-Chung* (as   **13-9** to which, see the main work), it had been held that attempting suicide was not "reprehensible behaviour" within the meaning of section 112 of the 2003 Act (§ 13-8 in the main work), and concluded that the same should apply to self-harming, but it was also held that drinking to excess and taking illegal drugs did amount to such behaviour. As to this case, see also *ante*, § 11-21; and *post*, § 13-22a.

II. PERSONS OTHER THAN DEFENDANTS

(4) Matter in issue (CJA 2003, s.100(1)(b) and (3))

"Substantial probative value"

For a further case emphasising the importance of avoiding satellite litigation where there are   **13-22a** contested allegations of bad character, see *R. v. M.* [2014] Crim.L.R. 823, CA (considering *R. v. Dizaei* (as to which, see the main work) and *R. v. O'Dowd* (as to which, see § 13-67 in the main work)). As to this case, see also *ante*, §§ 11-21, 13-9.

III. DEFENDANTS

A. ADMISSIBILITY

Criminal Justice Act 2003, ss.101, 108

Defendant's bad character

★**13-25**   As to section 101(1)(e) ("... important matter in issue between the defendant and a co-defendant"), see *R. v. Daly*, *post*, § 13-70.

Offences committed by defendant when a child

13-26   There could not be a "near miss" approach to section 108(2) of the 2003 Act, somehow enabling it to be invoked where the defendant was aged 20 at the time of the alleged offences; however, all judges should be sensitive to any attempt to rely on previous convictions for offences committed whilst a child, particularly as a young child: *R. v. Clark (Lucy)*, 178 J.P. 534, CA.

B. THE SEVEN GATEWAYS

(4) Important matter in issue between defendant and prosecution (CJA 2003, ss.101(1)(d), 103)

(a) *Matters in issue*

13-38   For a further decision illustrating that section 101(1)(d) of the 2003 Act (§ 13-37 in the main work) is not only about propensity, and where it was held that the "important matter in issue" (to which the bad character evidence was relevant) was the identity of the offender, not the propensity of the defendant to commit offences of the kind with which he was charged, see *R. v. Richardson*, unreported, August 7, 2014, CA ([2014] EWCA Crim. 1785).

(b) *Evidence that would have been admissible at common law*

The unlikelihood of coincidence

13-42   For a further decision in which evidence was admitted under the "unlikelihood of coincidence" head of admissibility, rather than as evidence of propensity, see *R. v. Richardson*, unreported, August 7, 2014, CA ([2014] EWCA Crim. 1785). The defendant was charged with an offence of wounding with intent (Offences against the Person Act 1861, s.18 (§ 19-251 in the main work)) arising out of an unprovoked attack on a stranger in a street, where the issue was identity, and where there were multiple strands to the prosecution's circumstantial case that the defendant was the offender. It was held that the judge had been entitled to admit evidence of a previous violent assault committed by the defendant, where the earlier assault had also been an unprovoked attack on a stranger and it had taken place in the same street as the offence for which the defendant was being tried. While the court did not express its conclusion in terms of the unlikelihood of coincidence, that undoubtedly was the basis on which it found the evidence to have been relevant and probative.

★   A conviction was unsafe where the issue was identity, where bad character evidence was admitted under section 101(1)(d) of the 2003 Act to rebut coincidence, and where the jury were not told that the only reason the defendant was a suspect and thus put on an identification parade (from which the complainant had identified him) was because he lived in the area in which the offence was committed and he had a previous conviction for a like offence: *R. v. H.* [2015] Crim.L.R. 441, CA.

Practical application

Allegation that prosecution witnesses mistaken or lying

13-57   Evidence that, in 2009, the appellant had been conditionally discharged following his plea of guilty to possessing an indecent photograph of a child (a 49-minute film showing girls aged from seven to 11 years engaged in sexual acts including penetrative sex with an adult), on the unchallenged basis that he had inadvertently downloaded the file while attempting to download an episode of Doctor Who, was admissible at his trial in 2014 on charges of rape and assault by penetration of a child under 10, where the alleged offences had occurred at about the same time as the downloading of the file: *R. v. Wynes*, 179 J.P. 42, CA. The court referred to *R. v. Z.* (as to which, see § 13-61 in the main work) in ruling that, there being no issue estoppel in criminal law, it was open to the jury to go behind the basis of plea, and to take the view that the defendant's possession of the film demonstrated that he had an inappropriate sexual interest in young girls, which might support the prosecution case that the complainant was telling the truth (the defence was that the allegations were lies orchestrated by the complainant's father). No other authorities were referred to, but the circumstances of the case and the court's reasoning have a striking resemblance to those of *R. v. D.; R. v. P.; R. v. U.* (as to which, see the main work).

Non-criminal conduct

R. v. Z. (as to which, see the main work) was considered in *R. v. Wynes*, 179 J.P. 42, CA. **13-61** Evidence was given of prior reprehensible conduct on the part of the defendant that had resulted in a conviction that was founded on a plea entered on an agreed basis that was particularly favourable to the defendant. It was held that it was open to the jury, at the subsequent trial, to go behind the basis of plea. As to this case, see also *ante*, § 13-57.

(c) *Propensity evidence*

Establishing a propensity (s.103(2)–(6))

For a case considering *R. v. O'Dowd* (see the main work), see *R. v. M., ante*, § 13-22a. **13-67**

(5) Important matter in issue between defendant and co-defendant (ss.101(1)(e), 104)

Criminal Justice Act 2003, s.104

It was held in *R. v. Daly*, 179 J.P. 114, CA that a defence by a co-defendant that carried with it ★**13-70** the necessary implication that the defendant was alone guilty of the offence could be an important matter in issue between the defendant and co-defendant so as to engage section 101(1)(e) of the 2003 Act (as to which, see § 13-25 in the main work). The court further held that it was a misreading of section 104(1) of the 2003 Act (as to which, see *ibid.*, § 13-69) to construe it as permitting evidence of bad character under section 101(1)(e) only if the nature or conduct of the defence of the defendant whose character was in issue had been such as to undermine the defence of the defendant who was seeking to adduce the bad character evidence. That restriction only applied where the bad character evidence was being relied on to establish that the co-defendant had a propensity to be untruthful.

IV. PROCEDURE

(5) Rules of court

Criminal Procedure Rules 2014 (S.I. 2014 No. 1610), Pt 35

Replacement of 2014 rules by 2015 rules

With effect from October 5, 2015, the Criminal Procedure Rules 2015 (S.I. 2015 No. 1490) ★**13-111** replace S.I. 2014 No. 1610. Part 35 of the 2014 rules is replaced by Part 21 of the 2015 rules (see *post*, Appendix P-184 *et seq.*), with minor drafting changes.

V. REHABILITATION OF OFFENDERS

(1) Introduction

With effect from February 26, 2015, the Rehabilitation of Offenders Act 1974 (Exceptions) **13-120** Order 1975 (S.I. 1975 No. 1023) was further amended by the Public Contracts Regulations 2015 (S.I. 2015 No. 102).

★ With effect from March 10, 2015, S.I. 1975 No. 1023 (*ante*), was further amended by the Rehabilitation of Offenders Act 1974 (Exceptions) Order 1975 (Amendment) (England and Wales) Order 2015 (S.I. 2015 No. 317).

★ With effect from May 26, 2015, S.I. 1975 No. 1023 (*ante*), was further amended by the Deregulation Act 2015 (Poisons and Explosives Precursors) (Consequential Amendments, Revocations and Transitional Provisions) Order 2015 (S.I. 2015 No. 968).

The decision of the Supreme Court in *R. (T.) v. Chief Constable of Greater Manchester Police (Liberty intervening); R. (B.) v. Secretary of State for the Home Department (Same intervening)* is now reported at [2015] A.C. 49.

(3) Statute

Rehabilitation of Offenders Act 1974, s.1

Rehabilitated persons and spent convictions

★**13-123** As from April 13, 2015 (Criminal Justice and Courts Act 2015 (Commencement No. 1, Saving and Transitional Provisions) Order 2015 (S.I. 2015 No. 778)), the Criminal Justice and Courts Act 2015, s.54(3), and Sched. 12, para. 1, amended section 1(3) of the 1974 Act, so as to insert, at the end, a new paragraph (c), as follows—

"(c) an order under section 21A of the Prosecution of Offences Act 1985 (criminal courts charge)".

CHAPTER 15

INVESTIGATORY POWERS; CONFESSIONS; DISCRETION TO EXCLUDE EVIDENCE, ETC.

I. INVESTIGATORY POWERS

A. POLICE AND CRIMINAL EVIDENCE ACT 1984

(2) Codes of practice

(b) *Commencement*

15-5 A revised Code A came into force on March 19, 2015: Police and Criminal Evidence Act 1984 (Codes of Practice) (Revision of Code A) Order 2015 (S.I. 2015 No. 418). For the full text of the revised code, see *post*, Appendix A-2 *et seq.*

(3) "Reasonable grounds for suspicion"

★**15-15** *R. (Rawlinson & Hunter Trustees) v. Central Criminal Court; R. (Tchenguiz) v. Director of the Serious Fraud Office* (cited in the main work) was followed in *R. (Chatwani) v. National Crime Agency and Birmingham Magistrates' Court*, unreported, May 11, 2015, DC ([2015] EWHC 1283 (Admin.)), where it was said that, particularly in a complex investigation, arresting constables do not have a duty to check the information upon which they are asked by an investigating team to make an arrest; even if the informant is internal and knows that the information he is providing is wrong or misleading, the arresting constable cannot be liable for wrongful arrest if, on the basis of that information, he reasonably suspects the arrestee of having committed an indictable offence. As to this case, see also *post*, § 15-112.

B. STOP AND SEARCH

(2) Criminal Justice and Public Order Act 1994

Criminal Justice and Public Order Act 1994, s.60

Powers to stop and search in anticipation of, or after, violence

15-48 An application by the claimant for permission to appeal from the decision of the civil division

of the Court of Appeal in *R. (Roberts) v. Commr of Police of the Metropolis (Liberty intervening)* has
been allowed: see [2015] 1 W.L.R. 353, SC.

(3) Code of practice

A revised Code A came into force on March 19, 2015: Police and Criminal Evidence Act 1984   **15-51**
(Codes of Practice) (Revision of Code A) Order 2015 (S.I. 2015 No. 418). For the full text of the
revised code, see *post*, Appendix A-2 *et seq.*

C. ENTRY, SEARCH AND SEIZURE

(1) Introduction

With effect from February 18, 2015, the Protection of Freedoms Act 2012 (Code of Practice for   **15-52**
Powers of Entry and Description of Relevant Persons) Order 2015 (S.I. 2015 No. 240), brings into
force on April 6, 2015, the "Powers of Entry Code of Practice" (required by s.47(1) of the 2012
Act (see the main work)). The order also describes "relevant person" for the purposes of section
51 of the 2012 Act (effect of code), as any person exercising a power of entry or associated power,
other than a devolved power of entry or devolved associated power (as to which, see s.47(5)), unless such exercise is subject to a separate code of practice issued (however described) under any
enactment (whenever passed or made).

(2) Statute

Police and Criminal Evidence Act 1984, s.8

Power of justice of the peace to authorise entry and search of premises

R. (Faiseltex Ltd) v. Preston Crown Court (as to which, see the main work) was followed in *R.*   **★15-55**
(Cabot Global Ltd) v. Barkingside Magistrates' Court, unreported, May 20, 2015, DC ([2015] EWHC
1458 (Admin.)), where it was held that the word "material" in section 8(1)(b) of the 1984 Act is
capable of covering a computer and its hard disk, which is a single item or thing, not a container
of a number of things. As to this case, see also *post*, § 15-85.

In *R. (Mills and Mills) v. Sussex Police and Southwark Crown Court* [2014] 2 Cr.App.R. 34, DC,
there was full argument as to the test to be applied in deciding on whether to quash a warrant
where proper disclosure had not been made by the applicant for the warrant. The court disapproved the proposition put forward, *obiter*, in *R. (Rawlinson & Hunter Trustees) v. Central Criminal
Court; R. (Tchenguiz) v. Director of the Serious Fraud Office* [2013] 1 W.L.R. 1634, DC (as to which,
see, in particular, § 1-375 in the main work), that a warrant should only be set aside where the
court was satisfied that the decision would have been different had proper disclosure been made.
It was held that this was wrong in principle and was not in fact supported by the authorities
referred to in that case. The court continued by saying that whilst what was said in that case had
been followed in a number of subsequent cases (*e.g. Zinga v. R.* (as which, see the main work), and
R. (Golfrate Property Management Ltd) v. Southwark Crown Court (Practice Note) (as to which, see § 15-
239 in the main work)), the point had not been argued. The true test that should be applied is
whether the issuing justice might well have refused to issue the warrant if proper disclosure had
been made (*R. (Dulai) v. Chelmsford Magistrates' Court and Essex County Council; R. (Essex County
Council) v. Chelmsford Crown Court and Essex Magistrates' Court, Dulai (interested parties)* (as to which,
see the main work)). If that is the view of the High Court, then it should declare the warrant to
have been unlawfully obtained. Accordingly, in the case before it, the Divisional Court quashed
the warrant because there had been material non-disclosure that might well have led the judge to
issue a warrant which, had there been full candour, he would have refused to issue. Decisions as
to precisely what order to make and the consequences that flowed from the quashing of the warrant were reserved for further argument. It may be noted that the court also re-emphasised the
onerous nature of the duty of disclosure that the law imposes on an applicant for a warrant; he
must "put on his defence hat" and think about what any party affected would be saying to the
court if they were present with an opportunity to address the court.

Police and Criminal Evidence Act 1984, Sched. 1

With effect from May 26, 2015 (Deregulation Act 2015 (Commencement No. 1 and Transitional   **★15-59**
and Saving Provisions) Order 2015 (S.I. 2015 No. 994)), paragraphs 7 to 10 of Schedule 1 to the

1984 Act are amended by the 2015 Act, s.82(3)(a)–(d), so as: (i) in paragraph 7, to insert, after the words "paragraph 4 above", the words "that relates to material that consists of or includes journalistic material"; (ii) in paragraph 8, to substitute, for the words "such an order", the words "an order under paragraph 4 above that relates to material that consists of or includes journalistic material"; (iii) in paragraph 9, to substitute, for the words "Such a notice", the words "Notice of an application for an order under paragraph 4 above that relates to material that consists of or includes journalistic material"; and (iv) in paragraph 10, to substitute, for the words "this Schedule" (in each place where it occurs), the words "paragraph 8".

★**15-60**   With effect from May 26, 2015 (Deregulation Act 2015 (Commencement No. 1 and Transitional and Saving Provisions) Order 2015 (S.I. 2015 No. 994)), a new paragraph 15A is inserted at the end of Schedule 1 to the 1984 Act by the 2015 Act, s.82(3)(e), as follows—

"Procedural rules

15A. Criminal Procedure Rules may make provision about proceedings under this Schedule, other than proceedings for an order under paragraph 4 above that relates to material that consists of or includes journalistic material.".

Police and Criminal Evidence Act 1984, ss.15, 16

Search warrants – safeguards

★**15-85**   As to the further application of, *inter alia*, sections 15 and 16 of the 1984 Act to applications for warrants, and the revocation, in relation to England and Wales, of S.I. 2003 No. 174 (as to which, see the main work), see *post*, § 15-239.

★   For a case illustrating that where there are serious breaches of section 15 (§ 15-84 in the main work) and/ or 16 (*ibid.*, § 15-86) of the 1984 Act, the sanctions will be correspondingly severe, see *R. (Chatwani) v. National Crime Agency and Birmingham Magistrates' Court*, unreported, May 11, 2015, DC ([2015] EWHC 1283 (Admin.)). As to this case, see also *post*, § 15-112.

★   *R. (Glenn & Co. (Essex) Ltd) v. H.M. Commrs for Revenue and Customs* (as to which, see the main work) was followed in *R. (Cabot Global Ltd) v. Barkingside Magistrates' Court*, unreported, May 20, 2015, DC ([2015] EWHC 1458 (Admin.)), where it was held that it was not "practicable" (within the meaning of s.15(6)(b) of the 1984 Act) to specify the items within the computers and mobile telephones to which a search under section 8 of the 1984 Act related; it was unrealistic to expect the officers to take away any relevant material from a computer or other storage device in paper form or on memory sticks; and the police were not obliged to resort to the 1984 Act, ss.19 (§ 15-92 in the main work) and 20 (*ibid.*, § 15-94), or the CJPA 2001, s.50 (*ibid.*, § 15-103), where they had reasonable cause to suspect that a computer would contain incriminating material. As to this case, see also *ante*, § 15-55.

Execution of warrants

★**15-87**   As to serious breaches of section 16 of the 1984 Act (§ 15-86 in the main work), see *R. (Chatwani) v. National Crime Agency and Birmingham Magistrates' Court*, *ante*, § 15-85.

★   In *R. (Chaudhary) v. Bristol Crown Court* [2015] 1 Cr.App.R. 18, DC, it was held that there is no sustainable basis in law for contending that, whenever there has been a more than de minimis breach of section 16(8), the entirety of the entry, search and seizure under the warrant was unlawful; instead, the particular items taken in excess of the warrant's authorisation should be returned, and there may be liability in damages; section 16(8) is concerned with the area of search, not with seizure. As to this case, see also *post*, § 15-112.

Police and Criminal Evidence Act 1984, s.17

Entry for purpose of arrest, etc.

★**15-88**   As from March 20, 2015 (Criminal Justice and Courts Act 2015 (Commencement No. 1, Saving and Transitional Provisions) Order 2015 (S.I. 2015 No. 778)), section 17(cb)(i) of the 1984 Act is amended by the Criminal Justice and Courts Act 2015, s.38(3), and Sched. 9, para. 9, so as to substitute, for the words from "remand centre" to "secure training centre", the words "young offender institution, secure training centre or secure college".

Police and Criminal Evidence Act 1984, s.22

Retention

★**15-99**   Section 22, insofar as it relates to DNA or other biometric material seized by police under section 19 of the 1984 Act (§ 15-92 in the main work), has the same effect as section 63T of the 1984 Act (summarised at § 15-197 in the main work), i.e. the material may not be used other than for criminal law enforcement purposes: *Re Z. (Children) (DNA Profiles: Disclosure)* [2015] 1 Cr.App.R. 28, CA (Civ. Div.).

Criminal Justice and Police Act 2001, ss.53–58

Retention of seized items

As from a day to be appointed, section 57(1) of the 2001 Act is amended by the Consumer Rights Act 2015, s.77(2), and Sched. 6, paras 61 and 62, so as: (i) to omit paragraphs (b), (d) and (g); and (ii) to insert, after paragraph (r), a new paragraph (s), referring to paragraphs 28(7) and 29(8) of Schedule 5 to the Consumer Rights Act 2015. ★**15-110**

Criminal Justice and Police Act 2001, ss.59–62

Application to the appropriate judicial authority

With effect from May 26, 2015 (Deregulation Act 2015 (Commencement No. 1 and Transitional and Saving Provisions) Order 2015 (S.I. 2015 No. 994)), section 59 of the 2001 Act was amended by the 2015 Act, s.82(5), so as to insert, after subsection (12), a new subsection (13), as follows— ★**15-112**

"(13) Criminal Procedure Rules may make provision about proceedings under this section on an application to a judge of the Crown Court in England and Wales.".

In *R. (Panesar) v. H.M. Revenue and Customs* [2015] 1 Cr.App.R. 17, CA (Civ. Div.), it was held that an application under section 59 of the 2001 Act is an application in a "criminal cause or matter" within section 18(1)(a) of the Senior Courts Act 1981 (see generally §§ 7-22 *et seq.* in the main work), and thus the Court of Appeal had no jurisdiction to hear an appeal from the Divisional Court's refusal (summarised in the main work, and now reported at [2015] 1 W.L.R. 2577, *sub nom. R. (Panesar) v. Central Criminal Court; R. (Gill) v. Same*) to accede to an application for judicial review of a decision of the Crown Court on an application under section 59.

R. (Goode) v. Nottingham Crown Court (see the main work) was followed in *R. (Chaudhary) v. Bristol Crown Court* [2015] 1 Cr.App.R. 18, DC (as to this which, see also *ante*, § 15-87), where it was said that it makes no difference whether the warrant is said to be bad on its face or defective for some other reason. ★

A party proposing to make an application under section 59(5)(b) of the 2001 Act (and in parallel judicial review proceedings) owes the court a duty of candour: *R. (Kouyoumjian) v. Hammersmith Magistrates' Court* [2015] Crim.L.R. 455, DC; and see *R. (Chatwani) v. National Crime Agency and Birmingham Magistrates' Court*, unreported, May 11, 2015, DC ([2015] EWHC 1283 (Admin.)) (as to which, see also *ante*, § 15-55), where the Divisional Court ordered the National Crime Agency (which, although held not to have acted in bad faith, had acted with patent and egregious disregard for, or indifference to, the constitutional safeguards within the scheme of the 1984 Act) to deliver up all seized material and to deliver up or destroy all copies or work product derived from that material. The agency had not disputed that the warrants in question should be quashed and the searches and seizures flowing from them should be declared unlawful, but had sought an order from the court that would sanction their retention of the material unlawfully seized pending an application to the Crown Court under section 59. ★

Criminal Justice and Police Act 2001, ss.63–66

Meaning of "appropriate judicial authority"

With effect from June 1, 2015 (Policing and Crime Act 2009 (Commencement No. 10, Transitional Provision and Savings) Order 2015 (S.I. 2015 No. 983), the amendments made to section 64 of the 2001 Act by section 112(1) and (2) of, and paragraph 115 of Schedule 7, and Part 5 of Schedule 8, to, the 2009 Act came into force. There is transitional provision (art. 6(2)). ★**15-117**

Meaning of "legal privilege"

As from a day to be appointed, section 65 of the 2001 Act is amended by the Consumer Rights Act 2015, s.77(2), and Sched. 6, paras 61 and 63, so as: (i) to omit subsections (6) and (8A); (ii) to insert, before subsection (9), a new subsection (8B), as follows— ★**15-118**

"(8B) An item which is, or is comprised in, property which has been seized in exercise or purported exercise of the power of seizure conferred by paragraph 27(1)(b) or 29(1) of Schedule 5 to the Consumer Rights Act 2015 shall be taken for the purposes of this Part to be an item subject to legal privilege if, and only if, the seizure of that item was in contravention of paragraph 27(6) or (as the case may be) 29(6) of that Schedule (privileged documents).";

and (iii) to omit paragraphs (c) and (f) in subsection (9).

General interpretation of Part 2

★**15-119**   As from a day to be appointed, section 66(4) of the 2001 Act is amended by the Consumer Rights Act 2015, s.77(2), and Sched. 6, paras 61 and 64, so as: (i) to omit paragraphs (a), (c), (d), (e), (f), (g), (ma), (q), (r) and (s); (ii) in paragraph (h), to substitute, for the words "29", the words "29(4)"; (iii) in paragraph (o), to substitute, for the words "22", the words "22(4)"; and (iv) to insert, after paragraph (p), a new paragraph (t), as follows—

"(t) Part 4 of Schedule 5 to the Consumer Rights Act 2015".

Powers of seizure (Schedule 1, Parts 1, 2 and 3)

Powers to which section 50 applies (list 1)

★**15-121**   As from a day to be appointed, Schedule 1 to the 2001 Act is amended by the Consumer Rights Act 2015, s.77(2), and Sched. 6, paras 61 and 65, so as: (i) to omit paragraphs 9, 16, 18, 19, 24, 36, 73BA, the first 73G, the second 73J, the second 73K, 73N and 73O (which relates to Northern Ireland); (ii) in paragraph 45, to substitute, for the words "29(4), (5) and (6)", the words "29(4)"; (iii) in the second paragraph 73G, to substitute, for the words "22(4)–(6)", the words "22(4)"; and (iv) to insert, after paragraph 73M, a new paragraph 73P, referring to each of the powers of seizure conferred by paragraphs 27(1)(b), 28(1) and 29(1) of Schedule 5 to the Consumer Rights Act 2015.

Applications under section 59

★**15-125**   See *R. (Kouyoumjian) v. Hammersmith Magistrates' Court, ante,* § 15-112.

E. QUESTIONING AND TREATMENT OF PERSONS

(2) Searches of detained persons

Police and Criminal Evidence Act 1984, ss.53, 54

Searches of detained persons

★**15-156**   There is a lacuna in Code C, Annex A, para. 10 (*post*, A-96), in that it fails to provide for those situations, anticipated by section 54, in which the custody officer wishes to seize clothing that might be used by a detainee to harm himself; Annex A should protect all those in custody whose clothing is removed under a power given by section 54; accordingly, paragraph 11 (the conduct of strip searches) of Annex A is to be taken to apply to a strip search, the sole purpose of which is to remove the detainee's clothes out of a well-grounded fear that they might be used in an attempt at suicide: *Davies (by her mother and litigation friend, Zelda Davies) v. Chief Constable of Merseyside Police, Just for Kids Law intervening,* unreported, February 19, 2015, CA (Civ. Div.) ([2015] EWCA Civ. 114).

(8) Fingerprints, photographs, intimate and other samples

Criminal Justice and Court Services Act 2000, s.70

Interpretation, etc.

15-193   With effect from February 1, 2015 (Offender Rehabilitation Act 2014 (Commencement No. 2) Order 2015 (S.I. 2015 No. 40)), sections 11 and 21 of, and Schedule 7 to, the 2014 Act (see the main work) are brought into force.

For an order under section 70(1) of the 2000 Act, see *post,* § 15-196.

Specification of Class B drugs

15-196   With effect from February 1, 2015, the Criminal Justice (Specified Class B Drugs) Order 2015 (S.I. 2015 No. 9) specifies cannabis and cannabis resin, and amphetamine, its salts and any preparation or other product containing amphetamine or its salts, for the purposes of section 70(1) of the CJCSA 2000 (§ 15-193 in the main work).

Destruction, retention and use of fingerprints, etc.

For a decision of the Supreme Court in which it was held that the policy in Northern Ireland **15-197** (adopted after the decision in *S. v. U.K.* (see § 15-199 in the main work)), and reflecting the current legislation in England and Wales (see s.63I of the 1984 Act in the main work)), of indefinite retention of fingerprints, cellular samples and DNA profiles obtained from those convicted of recordable offences was proportionate, see *Gaughran v Chief Constable of the Police Service of Northern Ireland (Secretary of State for the Home Department intervening)* [2015] 2 W.L.R. 1303, SC.

Police and Criminal Evidence Act 1984, s.64A

Photographing of suspects etc.
With effect from October 20, 2014 (Anti-social Behaviour, Crime and Policing Act 2014 (Com- **15-199** mencement No. 7, Saving and Transitional Provisions) Order 2014 (S.I. 2014 No. 2590)), section 181(1) of, and paragraph 4 of Schedule 11 to, the 2014 Act (see the main work), were brought into force.

(9) Definitions

Police and Criminal Evidence Act 1984, s.65A

"Qualifying offence"
As from a day to be appointed, section 65A(2) of the 1984 Act is amended by the Modern **★15-203** Slavery Act 2015, s.57(1), and Sched. 5, para. 3, so as to insert, after paragraph (r), a new paragraph (s), as follows—

"(s) an offence under section 2 of the Modern Slavery Act 2015 (human trafficking).".

F. Police Act 1997 and Regulation of Investigatory Powers Act 2000

With effect from December 10, 2014, revised codes of practice entitled "Covert Human Intel- **15-206** ligence Sources" and "Covert Surveillance and Property Interference" were brought into force by the Regulation of Investigatory Powers (Covert Human Intelligence Sources: Code of Practice) Order 2014 (S.I. 2014 No. 3119) and the Regulation of Investigatory Powers (Covert Surveillance and Property Interference: Code of Practice) Order 2014 (S.I. 2014 No. 3103) respectively. Both codes are available in the government publications section of www.gov.uk.

G. Drug Trafficking Act 1994

(2) Investigation of offences

Criminal Procedure Rules 2014 (S.I. 2014 No. 1610), r.56.4

Replacement of 2014 rules by 2015 rules
With effect from October 5, 2015, the Criminal Procedure Rules 2015 (S.I. 2015 No. 1490) **★15-212** replace S.I. 2014 No. 1610. Part 56 of the 2014 rules is replaced by Part 33 of the 2015 rules (see *post*, Appendix P-286 *et seq.*), which also reproduces Parts 57 to 61 of the 2014 rules. There are drafting changes to rule 56.4 of the 2014 rules (now r.33.67 of the 2015 rules (*post*, Appendix P-352)).

(3) Prosecution of offences, etc.

Drug Trafficking Act 1994, s.60

Revenue and Customs prosecutions
As from April 13, 2015 (Criminal Justice and Courts Act 2015 (Commencement No. 1, Saving **★15-218** and Transitional Provisions) Order 2015 (S.I. 2015 No. 778)), section 60 of the 1994 Act is amended by the Criminal Justice and Courts Act 2015, s.50, and Sched. 11, para. 15, so as to substitute: (i) in subsection (6), for the words "'public prosecutor'", the words "'relevant prosecutor'"; and (ii) in subsection (6A)(aa), for the words "public prosecutor", the words "relevant prosecutor".

H. PROCEEDS OF CRIME ACT 2002

(2) Statute

Proceeds of Crime Act 2002, ss.341–345

Investigations

★**15-228**   With effect from June 1, 2015, the amendment made to section 341 of the 2002 Act by section 112(1) of, and paragraphs 99 and 110 of Schedule 7 to, the 2009 Act (see the main work) came into force (Policing and Crime Act 2009 (Commencement No. 10, Transitional Provision and Savings) Order 2015 (S.I. 2015 No. 983)); and the amendments made by section 49 of, and paragraphs 1, 2, 24 and 25 of Schedule 19 to, the Crime and Courts Act 2013 (see the main work) also came into force (Crime and Courts Act 2013 (Commencement No. 13 and Savings) Order 2015 (S.I. 2015 No. 964)). There are transitional provisions in relation to the commencement of the 2013 Act provisions.

★   As from a day to be appointed, section 341(1) of the 2002 Act is further amended by the SCA 2015, ss.38(1) and 85(1), and Sched. 4, para. 55, so as: (i) to omit the word "or" at the end of paragraph (a), and (ii) to insert, at the end of subsection (1)—

> "or
>> (c) an offence under section 2 of the Modern Slavery Act 2015 (human trafficking).".

[Orders and warrants sought for civil recovery investigations

★**15-228a**   With effect from June 1, 2015 (Crime and Courts Act 2013 (Commencement No. 13 and Savings) Order 2015 (S.I. 2015 No. 964)), the insertion of section 341A into the 2002 Act by section 49 of, and paragraphs 1 and 3 of Schedule 19 to, the 2013 Act, came into force.

Judges

★**15-230**   With effect from June 1, 2015 (Policing and Crime Act 2009 (Commencement No. 10, Transitional Provision and Savings) Order 2015 (S.I. 2015 No. 983)), the amendments made to section 343 of the 2002 Act by section 66 of the 2009 Act came into force. There is a saving provision (art. 5).

Courts

★**15-231**   With effect from June 1, 2015 (Policing and Crime Act 2009 (Commencement No. 10, Transitional Provision and Savings) Order 2015 (S.I. 2015 No. 983)), the amendments made to section 344 of the 2002 Act by section 66 of the 2009 Act came into force. There is a saving provision (art. 5).

Production orders

★**15-232**   With effect from June 1, 2015 (Crime and Courts Act 2013 (Commencement No. 13 and Savings) Order 2015 (S.I. 2015 No. 964)), the amendment made to section 345 of the 2002 Act by section 49 of, and paragraphs 1 and 4 of Schedule 19 to, the 2013 Act, came into force.

Proceeds of Crime Act 2002, ss.346–369

Requirements for making of production order

★**15-233**   With effect from June 1, 2015 (Crime and Courts Act 2013 (Commencement No. 13 and Savings) Order 2015 (S.I. 2015 No. 964)), section 346 of the 2002 Act was amended by the 2013 Act, s.49, and Sched. 19, para. 5, so as to substitute a new subsection (2)(b), as follows—

> "(b) in the case of a civil recovery investigation—
>> (i) the person the application for the order specifies as being subject to the investigation holds recoverable property or associated property,
>> (ii) that person has, at any time, held property that was recoverable property or associated property at the time, or
>> (iii) the property the application for the order specifies as being subject to the investigation is recoverable property or associated property;".

Government departments

★**15-237**   With effect from June 1, 2015 (Policing and Crime Act 2009 (Commencement No. 10,

Transitional Provision and Savings) Order 2015 (S.I. 2015 No. 983)), the amendments made to section 350 of the 2002 Act by section 66 of the 2009 Act came into force. There is a saving provision (art. 5).

Supplementary

　With effect from June 1, 2015 (Policing and Crime Act 2009 (Commencement No. 10, ★**15-238** Transitional Provision and Savings) Order 2015 (S.I. 2015 No. 983)), the amendments made to section 351 of the 2002 Act by sections 66(1) and (5) and 112(2) of, and Part 5 of Schedule 8 to, the 2009 Act came into force. There is a saving provision (art. 5) in relation to the amendment effected by section 66.

Search and seizure warrants

　With effect from May 26, 2015 (Deregulation Act 2015 (Commencement No. 1 and Transitional ★**15-239** and Saving Provisions) Order 2015 (S.I. 2015 No. 994)), section 352 of the 2002 Act is amended by the 2015 Act, s.82(6), so as to insert, after subsection (7), a new subsection (8), as follows—

　　"(8) Criminal Procedure Rules may make provision about proceedings under this section on an application to a judge entitled to exercise the jurisdiction of the Crown Court in England and Wales.".

　With effect from June 1, 2015 (Crime and Courts Act 2013 (Commencement No. 13 and Sav- ★ ings) Order 2015 (S.I. 2015 No. 964)), the amendment made to section 352 of the 2002 Act by section 49 of, and paragraphs 1 and 6 of Schedule 19 to, the 2013 Act, came into force.

　With effect from June 1, 2015, the Proceeds of Crime Act 2002 (Application of Police and ★ Criminal Evidence Act 1984) Order 2015 (S.I. 2015 No. 759): (i) applies, with modifications, sections 15, 16, 21 and 22 of the PACE Act 1984 (§§ 15-84, 15-86, 15-95 and 15-97 in the main work) to search and seizure warrants obtained under section 352 of the 2002 Act for the purposes of a confiscation, money laundering or detained cash investigation, and to the powers of seizure under those warrants; and (ii) revokes the Proceeds of Crime Act 2002 (Application of Police and Criminal Evidence Act 1984 and Police and Criminal Evidence (Northern Ireland) Order 1989) Order 2003 (S.I. 2003 No. 174)) in relation to England and Wales. There is a saving provision in relation to (ii).

　What was said in *R. (Golfrate Property Management Ltd) v. Southwark Crown Court (Practice Note)* (as to which, see the main work) in relation to the onerous disclosure duties of an applicant for a warrant under sections 352 and 353 of the 2002 Act was repeated in *R. (Mills and Mills) v. Sussex Police and Southwark Crown Court* [2014] 2 Cr.App.R. 34, DC, in which the court also considered the test to be applied in deciding whether to quash a warrant where there had been material non-disclosure. As to this, see *ante*, § 15-55.

Requirements where production order not available

　With effect from June 1, 2015 (Crime and Courts Act 2013 (Commencement No. 13 and Sav- ★**15-240** ings) Order 2015 (S.I. 2015 No. 964)), the amendments made to 353 of the 2002 Act by section 49 of, and paragraphs 1 and 7 of Schedule 19 to, the 2013 Act, came into force.

　As from a day to be appointed, section 353(6)(a) of the 2002 Act is amended by the SCA 2015, ★ s.38(2), so as to insert, after the words "of his benefit from his criminal conduct", the words "or of realisable property available for satisfying a confiscation order made in respect of him".

Further provisions: confiscation and money laundering

　With effect from June 1, 2015 (Policing and Crime Act 2009 (Commencement No. 10, ★**15-242** Transitional Provision and Savings) Order 2015 (S.I. 2015 No. 983)), the amendments made to section 355 of the 2002 Act by section 66 of the 2009 Act came into force. There is a saving provision (art. 5).

　As to the revocation and replacement of S.I. 2003 No. 174 (see the main work) in relation to ★ England and Wales, see *ante*, § 15-239.

Further provisions: civil recovery and detained cash

　With effect from June 1, 2015 (Policing and Crime Act 2009 (Commencement No. 10, ★**15-243** Transitional Provision and Savings) Order 2015 (S.I. 2015 No. 983)), the amendments made to section 356 of the 2002 Act by sections 66(1) and (7) and 112(2) of, and Part 5 of Schedule 8 to, the 2009 Act came into force. There is a saving provision (art. 5) in relation to section 66.

Disclosure orders

15-244   With effect from January 1, 2015, the Proceeds of Crime (Disclosure Orders: Confiscation Investigations) (Specified Person) Order 2014 (S.I. 2014 No. 3207) specifies the Director of the Serious Fraud Office as a "prosecutor" for the purposes of section 357(8)(b) of the 2002 Act.

★   With effect from June 1, 2015 (Crime and Courts Act 2013 (Commencement No. 13 and Savings) Order 2015 (S.I. 2015 No. 964)), the amendment made to section 357 of the 2002 Act by section 49 of, and paragraphs 1 and 8 of Schedule 19 to, the 2013 Act, came into force.

Requirements for making of disclosure order

★**15-245**   With effect from June 1, 2015 (Crime and Courts Act 2013 (Commencement No. 13 and Savings) Order 2015 (S.I. 2015 No. 964)), the amendment made to section 358 of the 2002 Act by section 49 of, and paragraphs 1 and 9 of Schedule 19 to, the 2013 Act, came into force.

Customer information orders

★**15-250**   With effect from June 1, 2015 (Crime and Courts Act 2013 (Commencement No. 13 and Savings) Order 2015 (S.I. 2015 No. 964)), the amendments made to section 363 of the 2002 Act by |section 49 of, and paragraphs 1 and 10 of Schedule 19 to, the 2013 Act, came into force.

Requirements for making of customer information order

★**15-252**   With effect from June 1, 2015 (Crime and Courts Act 2013 (Commencement No. 13 and Savings) Order 2015 (S.I. 2015 No. 964)), the amendments made to section 365 of the 2002 Act by section 49 of, and paragraphs 1 and 11 of Schedule 19 to, the 2013 Act, came into force.

★   In *Ex p. Assets Recovery Agency (Jamaica)* [2015] Lloyds Rep. F.C. 203, PC, where the court was considering Jamaican legislation similar to section 365 of the 2002 Act, it was held: (i) since a person may be convicted of money laundering where nobody has been convicted of the criminal offence(s) that made the property in question "criminal property", it followed that there was no requirement that there should have been a conviction of somebody for the antecedent (or "predicate") offence that had caused the property to be criminal property before a customer information order could be granted in aid of a money laundering investigation; all that is required by subsection (4) is reasonable grounds for suspecting that the person about whom the information is sought has committed a money laundering offence; (ii) it was not necessary, for a customer information order to be granted in aid of a confiscation investigation under subsection (2), that there should have been a conviction; there will frequently be good reason for commencing such an investigation at the same time as the criminal investigation; but the application should not be granted unless its true and dominant purpose is to aid the confiscation investigation, rather than to assist the criminal investigation (*R. v. Southwark Crown Court, ex p. Bowles* [1998] A.C. 641, HL); (iii) applications for such orders are likely to be made *ex parte*, and, as with all *ex parte* applications, there is a duty on the applicant to disclose everything that might point against the grant of the order sought, as well as everything pointing in favour of its grant; this is especially so when the respondent institutions may have little interest beyond ensuring that everything they are required to do is covered by the order of the court; the applicant's duty is to put himself in the place of the person whose affairs are under investigation; (iv) the role of the judge is crucial in scrutinising applications; first, he must ensure that there are reasonable grounds for suspecting that the person specified has benefited from criminal conduct or committed a money laundering offence; this will normally involve requiring the applicant to provide a brief outline of the grounds for such suspicion; secondly, in the case of confiscation investigation, the judge has to be satisfied as to the dominant purpose of the application (*ante*); this will normally mean asking the applicant how far the criminal inquiry has got and why the order sought will help, not that inquiry, but the confiscation inquiry; thirdly, in testing whether the condition in subsection (5) is met, namely that the information sought is likely to be of substantial value to the investigation, the judge is likely to have to ask how it will help; and fourthly, in testing whether the condition in subsection (6) is met, namely that there are reasonable grounds for believing that it is in the public interest for the customer information to be provided, the judge will have to perform a balancing exercise as between the public interest in the detection of money laundering offences and the recovery of the proceeds of crime and the legitimate interests of the individual whose affairs are in question to preserve the privacy of those affairs.

Proceeds of Crime Act 2002, ss.370–379

Account monitoring orders

   With effect from June 1, 2015 (Crime and Courts Act 2013 (Commencement No. 13 and Savings) Order 2015 (S.I. 2015 No. 964)), the amendments made to section 370 of the 2002 Act by section 49 of, and paragraphs 1 and 12 of Schedule 19 to, the 2013 Act, came into force. For the avoidance of doubt, the amendments consist of the insertion of the words in square brackets in subsection (2) and the omission of the italicised words in that subsection.   **★15-257**

Requirements for making of account monitoring order

   With effect from June 1, 2015 (Crime and Courts Act 2013 (Commencement No. 13 and Savings) Order 2015 (S.I. 2015 No. 964)), the amendments made to section 371 of the 2002 Act by section 49 of, and paragraphs 1 and 13 of Schedule 19 to, the 2013 Act, came into force.   **★15-258**

[Evidence overseas

   As to the insertion of section 375A into the 2002 Act, see *post*, § 15-262b.   **★15-262a**

[Evidence overseas: restrictions on use

   With effect from June 1, 2015 (Crime and Courts Act 2013 (Commencement No. 13 and Savings) Order 2015 (S.I. 2015 No. 964)), the insertion of sections 375A and 375B into the 2002 Act by section 49 of, and paragraphs 24 and 26 of Schedule 19 to, the 2013 Act, came fully into force.   **★15-262b**

Code of practice of Secretary of State etc.

   A revised code of practice, in relation to England and Wales, made pursuant to section 377 of the 2002 Act, came into operation on June 1, 2015: Proceeds of Crime Act 2002 (Investigations: Code of Practice) (England and Wales) Order 2015 (S.I. 2015 No. 729).   **★15-263**

Code of practice of Attorney General or Advocate General for Northern Ireland

   A revised code of practice, in relation to England and Wales, made pursuant to section 377A of the 2002 Act, came into operation on June 1, 2015: Proceeds of Crime Act 2002 (Investigative Powers of Prosecutors: Code of Practice) (England and Wales) Order 2015 (S.I. 2015 No. 612).   **★15-264**

Officers

   With effect from June 1, 2015 (Crime and Courts Act 2013 (Commencement No. 13 and Savings) Order 2015 (S.I. 2015 No. 964)), the amendments made to section 378 of the 2002 Act by section 49 of, and paragraphs 24, 27, 29 and 30 of Schedule 19 to, the 2013 Act, came into force.   **★15-265**

Other interpretative provisions

   As from a day to be appointed, section 416 of the 2002 Act is amended by the SCA 2015, s.85(1), and Sched. 4, para. 56, so as to insert, after subsection (3), a new subsection (3A), as follows—   **★15-271**

   "(3A) The expressions "realisable property" and "confiscation order"—
         (a) in the application of this Part to England and Wales, have the same meanings as in Part 2;
         (b), (c) [*Scotland, Northern Ireland*].".

(3) Procedural rules

Criminal Procedure Rules 2014 (S.I. 2014 No. 1610), Pt 6, rr.6.1–6.22, 6.29–6.36

When this part applies

   With effect from February 2, 2015, rule 6.1 of S.I. 2014 No. 1610 is amended by rule 5(a) of the Criminal Procedure (Amendment) Rules 2015 (S.I. 2015 No. 13), so as to substitute a new paragraph (2), as follows—   **15-272**

   "(2) Sections 2 and 4 of this Part apply where, for the purposes of an investigation to which Part 8 of the Proceeds of Crime Act 2002 or the Proceeds of Crime Act 2002 (External Investigations) Order 2014 applies, a Crown Court judge can make, and the Crown Court can vary or discharge—

(a) a production order, under sections 345 and 351 of the 2002 Act or under articles 6 and 12 of the 2014 order;

(b) an order to grant entry, under sections 347 and 351 of the 2002 Act or under articles 8 and 12 of the 2014 order;

(c) a disclosure order, under sections 357 and 362 of the 2002 Act or under articles 16 and 21 of the 2014 order;

(d) a customer information order, under sections 363 and 369 of the 2002 Act or under articles 22 and 28 of the 2014 order;

(e) an account monitoring order, under sections 370, 373 and 375 of the 2002 Act or under articles 29, 32 and 34 of the 2014 order.".

★   With effect from October 5, 2015, the Criminal Procedure Rules 2015 (S.I. 2015 No. 1490) replace S.I. 2014 No. 1610, and incorporate the amendments made to the 2014 rules by S.I. 2015 No. 13 (*ante*). Part 6 of the 2014 rules is replaced by Part 47 of the 2015 rules (see *post*, Appendix P-480 *et seq.*), with minor drafting changes.

Application for an order under the Proceeds of Crime Act 2002

15-285   With effect from February 2, 2015, rule 5(b) of the Criminal Procedure (Amendment) Rules 2015 (S.I. 2015 No. 13) renames the heading to Section 4 of Part 6 of S.I. 2014 No. 1610, the effect of which is to add the word "etc." at the end of the heading.

With effect from February 2, 2015, rule 5(c) of the Criminal Procedure (Amendment) Rules 2015 (S.I. 2015 No. 13) amends rule 6.14 of S.I. 2014 No. 1610 so as (i) to add the word "etc." at the end of the heading, (ii) to substitute a new paragraph (2)(d), as follows—

"(d) in the case of an investigation in the United Kingdom, explain why the applicant thinks that—

(i) the person under investigation has benefited from criminal conduct, in the case of a confiscation investigation, or committed a money laundering offence, in the case of a money laundering investigation, or

(ii) the cash involved is property obtained through unlawful conduct, or is intended to be used in unlawful conduct, in the case of a detained cash investigation;";

(iii) to insert, after paragraph 2(d), a new paragraph (e), as follows—

"(e) in the case of an investigation outside the United Kingdom, explain why the applicant thinks that—

(i) there is an investigation by an overseas authority which relates to a criminal investigation or to criminal proceedings (including proceedings to remove the benefit of a person's criminal conduct following that person's conviction), and

(ii) the investigation is into whether property has been obtained as a result of or in connection with criminal conduct, or into the extent or whereabouts of such property;";

and (iv) to renumber paragraphs (2)(e) and (f) accordingly.

★   As to the replacement of S.I. 2014 No. 1610 by the Criminal Procedure Rules 2015 (S.I. 2015 No. 1490), see *ante*, § 15-272.

Application to punish for contempt of court

15-293   With effect from February 2, 2015, rule 6.22 of S.I. 2014 No. 1610 is amended by rule 5(i) of the Criminal Procedure (Amendment) Rules 2015 (S.I. 2015 No. 13), so as to substitute a new paragraph (1), as follows—

"(1) This rule applies where a person is accused of disobeying—

(a) a production order made under section 345 of the Proceeds of Crime Act 2002 or article 6 of the Proceeds of Crime Act 2002 (External Investigations) Order 2014; or

(b) an account monitoring order made under section 370 of the 2002 Act or article 29 of the 2014 order.".

★   As to the replacement of S.I. 2014 No. 1610 by the Criminal Procedure Rules 2015 (S.I. 2015 No. 1490), see *ante*, § 15-272.

II. CONFESSIONS AND RELATED TOPICS

A. CONFESSIONS

(1) Police and Criminal Evidence Act 1984

(a) *Admissibility*

Police and Criminal Evidence Act 1984, ss.76, 76A

Confessions may be given in evidence for co-accused

Section 76A does not entitle a defendant (D2) in a murder trial to adduce in evidence the   ★**15-312**
interview of another defendant (D3), with a view to using what was said in the interview against a
further defendant (D1), D2's defence being that D1, not D2, had killed the deceased; although
D3's statement in interview, that he had seen D1 beat a man to death, could be seen as adverse to
D3 in that he was admitting presence at the scene, D2 was not relying on that aspect; D3's
description of D1 carrying out a killing was not a confession within the meaning of section 82(1)
of the 1984 Act (§ 15-313 in the main work); and, *obiter*, there is a cogent case for saying that
where a confession is admitted under section 76A of the 1984 Act, it should not be treated as
evidence in the case generally, but only as evidence in favour of the defendant who adduces it,
and not as evidence against any other defendant (apart from the maker of the confession): *R. v.
Sliogeris*, 179 J.P. 156, CA.

(b) *Words and phrases*

**"likely ... to render unreliable any confession which might be made by him in
consequence thereof"**

For subsequent proceedings in the European Court of Human Rights in *R. v. Sherif, Ali (Siraj),*   **15-323**
Ali (Muhedin), Mohammed, Abdurahman and Abdullahi (see the main work) in which it was held, in
relation to the defendant Abdurahman, that there had been no breach of his rights under Article
6 of the ECHR (*ibid.*, § 16-72) by reason of the use at his trial of statements made when he had
initially been treated as a witness when he should have been treated as a suspect, and when he
had been denied access to legal advice, see *Ibrahim v. U.K., The Times*, February 2, 2015, ECtHR
(considering, *inter alia, Salduz v. Turkey* (as to which, see § 16-116 in the main work)). The court
had regard to (a) the fact that he had adopted his statements (a mixture of incriminating and
exculpatory remarks) after he received legal advice, (b) the counter-balancing measures in the
legislative framework (including Code C) and available at trial with a view to ensuring the fairness
of the proceedings, including the judge's ruling on admissibility, and (c) the strength of the other
evidence against him, in ruling that no undue prejudice had been caused to his Article 6 rights by
admitting the statements in evidence despite the denial of access to legal advice and a failure to
caution him. As to this case, which also involved three other applicants who had been tried in
separate proceedings, see also *post*, § 15-430.

B. ACCUSATIONS MADE IN THE PRESENCE OF THE DEFENDANT

(3) Criminal Justice and Public Order Act 1994

Legal advice

Legal advice to remain silent

Where the defence had submitted to a jury that the defendant's decision to follow his solicitor's   **15-369**
advice to remain silent in interview was as reasonable as it would have been to act on a doctor's or
an accountant's professional advice, it was held on appeal that the judge had been entitled to
comment in summing up that a suspect's situation in a police station differed "in important
respects" to that of a person seeking professional advice from a doctor or accountant (*viz.* the
solicitor goes home, but it is the suspect who runs the risk of being charged and who must decide
whether or not to accept the advice): *R. v. Sakyi* [2014] Crim.L.R. 921, CA.

III. DISCRETION TO EXCLUDE EVIDENCE

A. UNDER STATUTE

(1) General

Police and Criminal Evidence Act 1984, s.78

Exclusion of unfair evidence

15-403   In *R. v. Haq*, 178 J.P. 528, CA, the court upheld the trial judge's decision under section 78 to admit in evidence a defendant's incriminating witness statement, which had come into the prosecution's hands innocently by reason of a co-accused's legal representative's oversight. The co-accused had been tried before the trial of the defendant, and the statement had been taken by the solicitors for one of the co-accused when they were considering calling the defendant as a defence witness.

(7) Codes C and H and section 78

(d) *Particular topics: authorities*

Incorrect form of caution

15-430   For subsequent proceedings in the European Court of Human Rights in *R. v. Ibrahim* (see the main work) in which it was held that there had been no violation of three of the applicants' rights under Article 6(1) and (3) of the ECHR (*ibid.*, § 16-72) where statements made in interviews at a time when they were being denied access to legal advice (pursuant to Sched. 8, para. 8, to the Terrorism Act 2000 (*ibid.*, § 25-138)) were admitted at trial, and where the wrong caution was given on some occasions, see *Ibrahim v. U.K.*, *The Times*, February 2, 2015, ECtHR (considering, *inter alia*, *Salduz v. Turkey* (as to which, see § 16-116 in the main work)). The court said that when deciding whether the admission in evidence of a statement made by the defendant when he had been justifiably denied access to legal advice rendered the proceedings unfair, regard should be had to: (a) the applicable legislative framework and any safeguards it contained, (b) the quality of the evidence, including whether the circumstances in which it had been obtained had cast doubt on its reliability or accuracy (improper conduct, notably coercion or ill-treatment, during interrogation and vulnerability of suspects were relevant factors), (c) whether the statement had been promptly retracted and any admissions made in it consistently denied, particularly once legal advice had been obtained, (d) the procedural safeguards applied during the criminal proceedings and, in particular, whether the applicant had been given the opportunity of challenging the authenticity of the evidence and of opposing its use, and (e) the strength of the other evidence in the case. As to this case, which also involved a fourth applicant who had been tried in separate proceedings, see also *ante*, § 15-323.

CHAPTER 16

HUMAN RIGHTS

IV. THE RIGHTS GUARANTEED

B. PROHIBITION OF TORTURE

Scope

★**16-47**   In connection with *Vinter v. U.K.* and *Att.-Gen.'s Reference (No. 69 of 2013) (R. v. McLoughlin); R. v. Newell* (as to both of which, see the main work), see *Hutchinson v. U.K.*, *ante*, § 5-406, *Trabelsi v. Belgium*, *ante*, § 5-406, and *R. (Harkins) v. Secretary of State for the Home Department*, *ante*, § 5-406.

D. Right to Liberty and Security

General

An application by the claimant for permission to appeal from the decision of the civil division of the Court of Appeal in *R. (Roberts) v. Commr of Police of the Metropolis (Liberty intervening)* (see the main work) has been allowed: see [2015] 1 W.L.R. 353, SC.

16-56

E. Right to a Fair Trial

Hearings in camera

See *R. (Wang Yam) v. Central Criminal Court*, *ante*, § 4-3; and *post*, §§ 28-51, 28-79.

16-95

Impartiality

Hanif and Khan v. U.K. (see the main work) was considered in *Armstrong v. U.K.*, *ante*, § 7-89.

16-102

Application of Article 6 to appellate proceedings

A court's refusal to allow the defendant to use sensitive information, which had been put before the court when the court had been sitting *in camera*, for the purposes of an application to the European Court of Human Rights (in which he alleged that reporting restrictions in relation to that information had breached his right to a fair trial under Art. 6 of the ECHR (§ 16-72 in the main work)) did not breach his right of access to the courts: *R. (Wang Yam) v. Central Criminal Court* [2015] 1 Cr.App.R. 10, DC. As to this case, see also *ante*, § 4-3; and *post*, §§ 28-51, 28-56, 28-79.

16-127

F. No Punishment Without Law

Retroactive penalties

As to the repeal of section 76 of the SOCPA 2005, see *ante*, § 5-1212.

★16-134

G. Right to Respect for Private and Family Life

Justification

An application by the claimant for permission to appeal from the decision of the civil division of the Court of Appeal in *R. (Roberts) v. Commr of Police of the Metropolis (Liberty intervening)* (see the main work) has been allowed: see [2015] 1 W.L.R. 353, SC.

16-142

The decision of the Supreme Court in *R. (T.) v. Chief Constable of Greater Manchester Police (Liberty intervening)*; *R. (B.) v. Secretary of State for the Home Department (Same intervening)* is now reported at [2015] A.C. 49.

As to whether a violation of the applicant's rights under Article 8 of the ECHR (§ 16-137 in the main work) was justified where he repeatedly appeared naked in public, see *Gough v. U.K.*, *post*, § 29-44.

The controls on the retention of personal data in police information systems in the United Kingdom are "in accordance with the law" for the purposes of Article 8(2) of the ECHR (§ 16-137 in the main work): *R. (Catt) v. Association of Chief Police Officers of England, Wales and Northern Ireland (Equality and Human Rights Commission intervening)*; *R. (T.) v. Commr of Police of the Metropolis (Secretary of State for the Home Department intervening)* [2015] 2 W.L.R. 664, SC (reversing the decision of the Court of Appeal (as to which, see the main work) in both cases (by a majority (4:1) in the case of the first respondent)).

★

Other issues

R. (Nicklinson) v. Ministry of Justice (C.N.K. Alliance Ltd intervening); *R. (A.M.) v. DPP (Same intervening)* is now reported at [2015] A.C. 657.

★16-152

I. Freedom of Expression

Justification

As to whether a violation of the applicant's rights under Article 10 of the ECHR (§ 16-157 in

16-160

the main work) was justified where he repeatedly appeared naked in public, see *Gough v. U.K.*, *post*, § 29-44.

CHAPTER 17

THE MENTAL ELEMENT IN CRIME

II. SPECIFIC REQUIREMENTS AS TO STATE OF MIND

F. "WILFULLY"

★**17-47**   As to the amendment of section 1 of the CYPA 1933, see *post*, § 19-375.

VI. DURESS

A. AVAILABILITY

★**17-119**   As to duress as a statutory defence that may be available to a defendant who is a victim of human trafficking, see section 45 of the Modern Slavery Act 2015, *post*, § 19-446.

VII. NECESSITY

Availability and scope

★**17-128**   *R. (Nicklinson) v. Ministry of Justice (C.N.K. Alliance Ltd intervening); R. (A.M.) v. DPP (Same intervening)* is now reported at [2015] A.C. 657.

CHAPTER 18

PRINCIPALS AND SECONDARY PARTIES

III. SECONDARY PARTIES

E. COUNTERMAND AND WITHDRAWAL

18-26   For a New Zealand case considering whether (i) the common law's recognition that actions of withdrawal from a "joint enterprise" may excuse a party from criminal liability is because an element of party offending has not been proved or because a true defence to liability as a party has been established, and (ii) what is required before a party can be said to have withdrawn, see *Ahsin and Rameka v. The Queen*, unreported, October 30, 2014, Supreme Court of New Zealand ([2014] NZSC 153).

H. PARTICIPATION IN THE CRIMINAL ACTIVITIES OF AN ORGANISED CRIME GROUP

★**18-33a**   With effect from May 3, 2015 (Serious Crime Act 2015 (Commencement No. 1) Regulations 2015 (S.I. 2015 No. 820)), section 45 of the SCA 2015 created a new offence of participating in the criminal activities of "an organised crime group".

Serious Crime Act 2015, s.45

Offence of participating in activities of organised crime group
    45.—(1) A person who participates in the criminal activities of an organised crime group commits an offence.

174

(2) For this purpose, a person participates in the criminal activities of an organised crime group if the person takes part in any activities that the person knows or reasonably suspects—

    (a) are criminal activities of an organised crime group, or

    (b) will help an organised crime group to carry on criminal activities.

(3) "Criminal activities" are activities within subsection (4) or (5) that are carried on with a view to obtaining (directly or indirectly) any gain or benefit.

(4) Activities are within this subsection if—

    (a) they are carried on in England or Wales, and

    (b) they constitute an offence in England and Wales punishable on conviction on indictment with imprisonment for a term of 7 years or more.

(5) Activities are within this subsection if—

    (a) they are carried on outside England and Wales,

    (b) they constitute an offence under the law in force of the country where they are carried on, and

    (c) they would constitute an offence in England and Wales of the kind mentioned in subsection (4)(b) if the activities were carried on in England and Wales.

(6) "Organised crime group" means a group that—

    (a) has as its purpose, or as one of its purposes, the carrying on of criminal activities, and

    (b) consists of three or more persons who act, or agree to act, together to further that purpose.

(7) For a person to be guilty of an offence under this section it is not necessary—

    (a) for the person to know any of the persons who are members of the organised crime group,

    (b) for all of the acts or omissions comprising participation in the group's criminal activities to take place in England and Wales (so long as at least one of them does), or

    (c) for the gain or benefit referred to in subsection (3) to be financial in nature.

(8) It is a defence for a person charged with an offence under this section to prove that the person's participation was necessary for a purpose related to the prevention or detection of crime.

(9) A person guilty of an offence under this section is liable on conviction on indictment to imprisonment for a term not exceeding 5 years.

CHAPTER 19

OFFENCES AGAINST THE PERSON

I. HOMICIDE

A. MURDER

(4) Defences

(a) *"Loss of control"*

Loss of control

    Daniel v. State of Trinidad and Tobago is now reported at [2014] A.C. 1290.   **19-56a**

Duty of counsel

    For a case considering the assistance advocates should give to a judge in determining whether **★19-61** to leave the partial defence of loss of control to the jury, see *R. v. Gurpinar; R. v. Kojo-Smith and Caton, post,* § 19-62.

Duty of judge

    The approach to be taken by a judge in determining whether to leave the partial defence of **★19-62** loss of control to the jury was considered in *R. v. Gurpinar; R. v. Kojo-Smith and Caton* [2015] 1 Cr.App.R. 31, CA. The court said that a judge should only do so under the terms of section 54(6) of the Coroners and Justice Act 2009 (§ 19-55 in the main work), after consideration of each of the components of the defence under sections 54 and 55. It was held that it was a judge's task to analyse the evidence closely and to be satisfied that there was sufficient evidence in respect of each of the three components of the defence, and he was bound to consider the weight and quality of the evidence in coming to a conclusion. This, the court said, required the judge to undertake a much more rigorous evaluation of the evidence before the defence could be left to the jury than was required under the former law of provocation where only "evidence", as opposed to "sufficient evidence" was required. It was further held that a judge must be assisted by the advocates in this regard. It was generally desirable that the possibility of such an issue arising should be notified to the judge as early as possible in the management of the case, even though it might not form part of the defence case. If, at the conclusion of the evidence, there was a possibility that the judge should leave the issue to the jury when it was not part of the defence case, the judge should receive written submissions so that he may carefully consider whether the evidence is such that the statutory test is met. The court said that in that assessment the judge should have regard to the three components of the defence, undertake a rigorous evaluation of the evidence against those components and set out his conclusion in a reasoned ruling. An appellate court would accord the judge the ambit of judgment open to a trial judge in the evaluation of the evidence and would not readily interfere. Finally, the court said that the test in section 54(6) was clear and that the development of the criminal law was not assisted by continued reference to old cases or further judicial exegesis on the clear statutory words. It should be noted that the court misquoted section 54(6) (which it mistakenly referred to as s.54(4)). For the suggestion that this may have misled the court into exaggerating the significance of the word "sufficient" in the context of the new legislation, see CLW/15/14/9.

(b) *Provocation*

Common law

19-65   At common law, provocation reduced murder to manslaughter; and was available as a potential defence both for a principal and an accessory: *R. v. Marks* [1998] Crim.L.R. 676, CA. It was irrelevant on the issue of guilt in all other crimes.

The jury should be directed that before they have to consider the issue of provocation the Crown must have proved beyond reasonable doubt that all the other elements of murder were present, including the necessary intent: see *Lee Chun-Chuen v. R.* [1963] A.C. 220, PC; and *R. v. Martindale*, 50 Cr.App.R. 273, Ct-MAC.

The law as to provocation immediately prior to October 4, 2010 (as to which, see § 19-54 in the main work) was governed by a blend of common law and statute, *viz.* the Homicide Act 1957, s.3 (*post*, § 19-66).

Homicide Act 1957, s.3

Provocation

19-66   **3.** Where on a charge of murder there is evidence on which the jury can find that the person charged was provoked (whether by things done or by things said or by both together) to lose his self-control, the question whether the provocation was enough to make a reasonable man do as he did shall be left to be determined by the jury; and in determining that question the jury shall take into account everything both done and said according to the effect which, in their opinion, it would have on a reasonable man.

This section altered as well as clarified the common law on this subject.

Duty of judge

19-67   Section 3 involves two questions: (a) is there any evidence of specific provoking conduct of the accused, and (b) is there any evidence that the provocation caused him to lose his self-control? If both questions are answered in the affirmative, the issue of provocation should be left to the jury notwithstanding the fact that in the opinion of the judge no reasonable jury could conclude on the evidence that a reasonable person would have been provoked to lose his self-control: *R. v. Gilbert*, 66 Cr.App.R. 237, CA; *Franco v. R., The Times*, October 11, 2001, PC; notwithstanding that there may be circumstances suggesting that the accused acted in revenge, rather than as a result of a sudden and temporary loss of self-control: *R. v. Baillie* [1995] 2 Cr.App.R. 31, CA; and notwithstanding that the issue has not been raised by the defence: *Bullard v. R.* [1957] A.C. 635, PC; *DPP v. Camplin* [1978] A.C. 705, HL; *R. v. Rossiter*, 95 Cr.App.R. 326, CA; and would prefer it not to be left to the jury: *R. v. Dhillon* [1997] 2 Cr.App.R. 104, CA.

Where, however, there is only a speculative possibility of the accused having acted as a result of provoking conduct, the issue should not be left to the jury: *R. v. Acott* [1997] 2 Cr.App.R. 94, HL (there must be some evidence of specific provoking conduct resulting in a loss of control by the accused; the source of such evidence is immaterial as is reliance thereon by the accused); and *R. v. Evans (John Derek)* [2010] Crim.L.R. 491, CA (§ 19-62 in the main work). Evidence of a loss of self-control is insufficient, for a loss of self-control might be brought on by fear, panic or sheer bad temper, as well as by provoking conduct: *ibid.* Questions put in cross-examination are not evidence: *ibid.* The observations in *Acott* are equally apt when considering whether there is sufficient evidence that a defendant was provoked, as they are when considering whether there was evidence of provoking conduct: *R. v. Miao, The Times,* November 26, 2003, CA. For the issue to be left to the jury, there has to be evidence from which a reasonable jury might conclude that the defendant was or may have been provoked: *R. v. Cambridge,* 99 Cr.App.R. 142, CA. See also *R. v. Jones (Robert James)* [2000] 3 *Archbold News* 2, CA (where the defence is self-defence, with no reliance by the defence on provocation, the judge should not leave provocation to the jury where the evidence of provoking conduct by the deceased, or the evidence that such conduct caused a loss of self-control by the defendant is minimal or fanciful).

In *Daniel v. State of Trinidad and Tobago* [2014] A.C. 1290, PC, it was held that while, in the event of dispute, it is for the judge to rule whether the issue of provocation arises on the evidence in relation to the first, subjective, limb of the test (namely, whether there was provocative behaviour and whether the defendant was in fact provoked by it to lose his self-control and kill in consequence), it is of great importance that judges respect the clear principle that the question as to whether the second, objective, limb of the test for provocation (namely, whether the provocation was such as might cause a reasonable man to act as the accused had) has been met, is a matter for the jury. Provocation has to be left to the jury, it was held, even if it is not the accused's primary case if, taking the evidence at its most favourable to the accused and remembering that the onus of proof is on the prosecution to rebut it, manslaughter by reason of provocation is a conclusion to which a jury might reasonably come. The board added that a judge could not withdraw the issue simply because he would decide the issue against the accused, nor even if he regarded the answer as obvious; but in a case where no jury, properly directed, could possibly find the test met, it is in the interests of a fair trial and of coherent law that an issue that does not arise ought not to be inserted into the jury's deliberations. As to this case, see also *ante,* § 19-56a; and *post,* § 19-75.

Where a judge is obliged to leave provocation to the jury, he should indicate to them, unless it is obvious, what evidence might support the conclusion that the defendant had lost his self-control; this is particularly important where the defence have not raised the issue: *R. v. Stewart* [1996] 1 Cr.App.R. 229, CA. See also *R. v. Humphreys* [1995] 4 All E.R. 1008, CA (similar duty where there is a complex history with several distinct strands of potentially provocative conduct, building up over time until the final encounter).

Where provocation is not left to the jury when it should have been, a conviction for manslaughter will be substituted unless the court is sure that the jury would inevitably have convicted: *R. v. Dhillon, ante,* but an appellate court should be cautious in drawing inferences or making findings about how the jury would have resolved issues which were never before them; and that is particularly so in the context of section 3, since Parliament had gone out of its way, unusually, to stipulate that resolution of the objective issue should be exclusively reserved to the jury; to the extent that an appellate court took it upon itself to decide that issue, it was doing what Parliament had said that the jury should do, and section 3 could not be read as applying only to the trial court: *Franco v. R., ante.*

In *R. v. Van Dongen and Van Dongen* [2005] 2 Cr.App.R. 38, CA, it was held that: (i) section 3 is concerned with provocative conduct, as opposed to merely causative conduct; yet a judgment that particular conduct was no more than causative risks straying into an evaluation of the objective element of the defence, which statute has left to the jury; accordingly, the prudent course for judges to take, in borderline cases, especially if the defence ask for a provocation direction to be given, is to leave the issue to the jury; (ii) where, therefore, in a case in which the defence had been self-defence and/or lack of intent and/or accident, but not provocation, there was evidence of conduct that was capable of being provoking conduct and there was evidence of a loss of self-control, the matter should have been left to the jury, more particularly as defence counsel had sought such a direction; but (iii) the failure to leave it did not mean that the conviction could not be upheld, notwithstanding that the Act specifically provides for the jury to determine the objective issue; *Franco v. R.*, *ante*, was not authority for the proposition that a conviction could not be upheld in such circumstances; whilst it was necessary to be cautious in drawing inferences or making findings about how the jury would have resolved issues which were never before them, the court must not overlook the matter of justice for those concerned with the victim, nor the requirements of a proportionate appellate system, which included that those who were surely and fairly shown to be guilty of murder, and were so found by a jury, should not escape the consequences on gossamer grounds; where, therefore, the unavoidable facts of the case and the necessary logic of the jury's verdict ruled out any possibility of a miscarriage of justice, the conviction should be upheld.

Duty of counsel

19-68   See *R. v. Cox (A.M.)* [1995] 2 Cr.App.R. 513, CA (§ 19-61 in the main work).

Onus of proof

19-69   Once there is evidence from any source, sufficient to be left to the jury on the issue of provocation, the onus remains throughout upon the Crown to prove absence of provocation beyond reasonable doubt: *R. v. McPherson*, 41 Cr.App.R. 213, CCA. As to the necessity for a careful direction on onus of proof, see *R. v. Wheeler*, 52 Cr.App.R. 28, CA (§ 19-48 in the main work).

"Provoked ... to lose his self control"

(i) *Meaning of "provocation"*

19-70   In *R. v. Whitfield*, 63 Cr.App.R. 39 at 42, the Court of Appeal said that the meaning of provocation was still that given to it by Devlin J. in *R. v. Duffy* [1949] 1 All E.R. 932, as cited by Lord Goddard C.J. when giving the judgment of the Court of Criminal Appeal:

> "Provocation is some act, or series of acts, done [or words spoken] [by the dead man to the accused] which would cause in any reasonable person, and actually causes in the accused, a sudden and temporary loss of self-control, rendering the accused so subject to passion as to make him or her for the moment not master of his mind" (at p.932).

The words in the first pair of square brackets were not actually said by Devlin J. but appear in the quotation of him by Lord Lane C.J. as if spoken by him (presumably to take account of the express reference to "things said" in section 3 of the 1957 Act, *ante*, § 19-66); the words in the second pair of square brackets must be ignored in view of the wording of section 3. See also *post*, § 19-73.

(ii) *Loss of self-control must be associated with the act which causes death*

19-71   The point was considered in *R. v. Ibrams and Gregory*, 74 Cr.App.R. 154, CA. Provocation is available only in the case of a sudden and temporary loss of self-control of such a kind as to make the accused for the moment not master of his mind: see *R. v. Duffy* and *R. v. Whitfield, ante*. Circumstances which induce a desire for revenge are inconsistent with provocation, since the conscious formulation of a desire for revenge means that a person has had time to think, to reflect and that would negative a sudden temporary loss of self-control, which is the essence of provocation. But the mere existence of such circumstances does not mean that the judge should not leave the issue to the jury if there is evidence that the accused was in fact provoked; it is for the jury to decide: see *R. v. Baillie* [1995] 2 Cr.App.R. 31, CA.

(iii) *Cumulative provocation*

19-72   Although it is established that a temporary and sudden loss of self-control arising from an act of provocation is essential, it is less clear to what extent previous acts of provocation are admissible. Each case must be considered against the background of its own particular facts: *R. v. Thornton*, 96 Cr.App.R. 112, CA. In *R. v. Brown* [1972] 2 Q.B. 229, 56 Cr.App.R. 564, CA, a direction that the jury had to find provocation in something done on the morning of the killing was approved. In *R. v. Davies (P.)* [1975] Q.B. 691, 60 Cr.App.R. 253, the Court of Appeal described as "too generous" a direction that the jury could review the whole of the deceased's conduct throughout the years preceding death: and see *R. v. Ibrams and Gregory, ante*. In *R. v. Pearson* [1992] Crim.L.R.

193, the Court of Appeal substituted manslaughter for a conviction for murder on the grounds, *inter alia*, that the jury may have been left with the impression that an eight-year history of violent conduct by the deceased towards his younger son was not to be taken into account when considering the case of the elder son, who had spent much of that time away from home.

A general approach can, however, be discerned from the authorities, namely that evidence of previous provocative acts or past conduct, particularly in cases of domestic violence, is admissible in order to place in its appropriate context the reaction of the accused to the alleged provocation on the occasion of the killing: see *R. v. Thornton, ante*, at p. 118. For the proper approach in relation to a history of provocation leading to a post-traumatic stress syndrome or "battered woman syndrome", see *R. v. Ahluwalia*, 96 Cr.App.R. 133, CA, and *R. v. Thornton (No. 2)* [1996] 2 Cr.App.R. 108, CA (a jury might more easily find that there was a sudden loss of self-control triggered even by a minor incident if the defendant had endured abuse over a period, on a last-straw basis).

"Things done or said"

The things done or said may be done or said by the deceased or anyone else: *R. v. Davies (P.), ante*; *R. v. Doughty (S.)*, 83 Cr.App.R. 319, CA.   **19-73**

"Reasonable man"

The "reasonable man" means "an ordinary person of either sex, not exceptionally excitable or **19-74** pugnacious, but possessed of such powers of self-control as everyone is entitled to expect that his fellow citizens will exercise in society as it is today": *per* Lord Diplock in *DPP v. Camplin* [1978] A.C. 705 at 771, HL; means "a man of ordinary self-control": *ibid.*, *per* Lord Simon at p.726. Both formulations were approved by the majority in *Att.-Gen. for Jersey v. Holley* [2005] 2 A.C. 580, PC, in which an enlarged board of nine was assembled for the purpose of considering the conflict between *Camplin* and *Luc Thiet Thuan v. R.* [1997] A.C. 131, PC, on the one hand, and *R. v. Smith (Morgan)* [2001] 1 A.C. 146, HL, on the other, and to "clarify definitively the present state of English law". That it had done so was accepted by the Court of Appeal in *R. v. James; R. v. Karimi* [2006] 1 Cr.App.R. 29.

The majority opinion in *Holley* was that the jury, in deciding whether the defendant lost his self-control and, if he did, whether he did so as a result of provocation, should take the defendant exactly as they find him ("warts and all" (including that he had a violent temperament: see *R. v. Mohammed (Faqir)* [2005] 9 *Archbold News* 3, CA)); but, having assessed the gravity of the provocation to the defendant (for which purpose they must, for example, take account of the fact that he is a homosexual if taunted for his homosexuality, that he is disabled if taunted for being a "cripple", *etc.*), the standard of self-control by which his conduct is to be evaluated is the external standard of a person having and exercising the ordinary powers of self-control to be expected of a person of the defendant's age and sex. The majority ruling in *Smith* was held to be wrong in that section 3 of the 1957 Act adopted a uniform, objective standard; whether the provocative act or words and the defendant's response met the "ordinary person" standard prescribed by the statute is the question the jury must consider, not the altogether looser question (suggested by *Smith*) of whether, having regard to all the circumstances, the jury consider the loss of self-control was sufficiently excusable; the statute, it was said, does not leave each jury free to set whatever standard they consider appropriate. Accordingly, it was held to follow that if the defendant had been taunted by reference to his being an alcoholic or a drug addict, his alcoholism or addiction might be relevant to the jury's consideration of the gravity of the taunt to the defendant, but it would not be relevant to the question whether he exercised ordinary self-control.

Self-induced provocation

The mere fact that the defendant caused a reaction in others which in turn led him to lose his **19-75** self-control does not preclude a successful defence of provocation: *R. v. Johnson (C.)*, 89 Cr.App.R. 148, CA.

In *Edwards v. R.* [1973] A.C. 648, PC, the appellant's case was that the man whom he was blackmailing attacked him with a knife and he thereupon lost his temper and killed him. The relevant ordinance in Hong Kong was in the same terms as section 3 of the Homicide Act 1957, *ante*. The Board said (at p. 658):

"No authority has been cited with regard to what may be called 'self-induced provocation'. On principle it seems reasonable to say that: (1) a blackmailer cannot rely on the predictable results of his own blackmailing conduct as constituting provocation sufficient to reduce his killing of the victim from murder to manslaughter, and the predictable results may include a considerable degree of hostile reaction by the person sought to be blackmailed, for instance vituperous words and even some hostile action such as blows with a fist; (2) but, if the hostile reaction by the person sought to be blackmailed goes to extreme lengths, it might constitute sufficient provocation even for a blackmailer; (3) there would in many cases be a question of degree to be decided by the jury."

In *Daniel v. State of Trinidad and Tobago* [2014] A.C. 1290, PC, it was held that there is no room for any general rule of law that provocation cannot arise because the accused himself generated the provocative conduct in issue. Subject to the proper role of the judge, the issue is for the jury, and the jury should ordinarily be directed that, if they find conduct by the accused which generates the provocative behaviour in question, that conduct will be directly relevant to both the subjective and the objective limbs of provocation. As to the subjective limb, it will go to both (a) the question whether the accused killed as a result of the provocative behaviour relied upon and (b) whether he lost self-control as a result of that behaviour. Generally, the more he generates the reaction of the deceased, the less likely it will be that he lost control and killed as a result of it; he might have been out of control from the outset, but that is not loss of control as a result of the provocative behaviour of the deceased. As to the objective limb, it will go to whether the provocative behaviour was enough to make a reasonable man in the defendant's position do as he did. Generally, the more he has himself generated the provocative behaviour, the less likely it will be that a reasonable man would have killed in consequence of it, but there may be cases where the jury may judge that the provocative behaviour may have induced a similar reaction in a reasonable man, notwithstanding the origins of the dispute between the accused and the deceased. On both limbs of the test of provocation, the extent to which the provocative behaviour relied upon was or was not a predictable result of what the accused did, *i.e.* how far it was to be expected, is itself a jury question and clearly a relevant factor, which the jury should take into account along with all the other circumstances of the killing. As to this case, see also *ante*, §§ 19-56a, 19-67.

Provocation and lies

19-76   Lies and attempts to cover up a killing are not necessarily inconsistent with provocation. In directions about lies, when the issue was murder or manslaughter, the jury should be alerted to the fact that, before they could treat lies as proof of guilt of the offence charged, they had to be sure that there was not some possible explanation which destroyed their potentially probative effect. A failure to give such a direction, coupled with an indication that the jury might regard lies as probative of murder rather than manslaughter, amounted to a material misdirection: *R. v. Richens*, 98 Cr.App.R. 43, CA; *R. v. Taylor* [1998] 7 *Archbold News* 3, CA.

Provocation and good character

19-77   Where there is evidence of the defendant's good character, the judge should direct the jury as to the relevance of that both to credibility and propensity; and, in particular, should remind them that, as a man of good character, the defendant might have been unlikely to indulge in serious violence without first being provoked: *Paria v. R.* [2004] Crim.L.R. 228, PC.

Sentence

19-78   See the guideline issued by the Sentencing Guidelines Council (*post*, K-71 *et seq.*). Of the pre-guideline authorities, see, in particular, *Att.-Gen.'s References (Nos 74, 95 and 118 of 2002) (R. v. Suratan; R. v. Humes; R. v. Wilkinson)* [2003] 2 Cr.App.R.(S.) 42, CA, which is summarised at paragraph 2.1 of the guideline (Appendix K-74).

See also *R. v. Brook (Neil)*, § 5-520 in the main work.

(c) *Diminished responsibility*

Medical evidence

19-94   In *R. v. Brennan* [2015] 1 Cr.App.R. 14, CA, it was held (considering, *inter alia*, *R. v. Matheson*,

R. v. Byrne, R. v. Bailey, Walton v. R., R. v. Sanders (L. J.) and *R. v. Khan (Dawood)* (as to all of which, see the main work), and *R. v. Brown (Robert)* (as to which, see *ibid.*, § 19-86)): (i) where medical evidence supporting a defence of diminished responsibility is uncontradicted, and there is no other evidence that, looked at in the round, is at least capable of rebutting the defence, a charge of murder should be withdrawn from the jury; where an application to withdraw the murder charge is made at the close of evidence, the application should be acceded to if the judge's considered view is that, on the evidence taken as a whole, no properly directed jury could convict; (ii) under section 2 of the Homicide Act 1957 (§ 19-79 in the main work), as amended by the Coroners and Justice Act 2009, s.52, there are essentially four stages to the defence (*viz.* Was the defendant suffering from an abnormality of mental functioning? If so, did it arise from a recognised medical condition? If so, did it substantially impair his ability either to understand the nature of his conduct or to form a rational judgment or to exercise self-control (or any combination)? If so, did it provide an explanation for his conduct?); most, if not all, aspects of the new provisions relate entirely to psychiatric matters; it is both legitimate and helpful, given their structure, for a psychiatrist to express a view on all four issues; and where the expert gives his view on all four matters, there can be no legal or other objection to him, if willing to do so, making explicit his opinion on the "ultimate issue", the more so when this will in any event probably have been implicit from his stated opinion on the four matters; it is difficult to see how the expression of such a view could contravene any principle of deference to the jury as the ultimate decision makers; where the prosecution propose to contest a defence of diminished responsibility, the new provisions in section 2 should be taken as encouragement for them to adduce their own expert evidence to support their stance; (iii) if there are other facts or circumstances that might cast a different light on otherwise uncontradicted defence expert evidence, and the matter is to be left to the jury, one would expect them to be highlighted by prosecuting counsel in discussion with the judge prior to closing speeches, and in due course for them to be specifically identified by the judge in summing up.

Sentence

Att.-Gen.'s Reference (No. 34 of 2014) (R. v. Jenkin) is now reported at [2014] 2 Cr.App.R.(S.) 84. **19-97**
    For an example of a case where a hospital order was held to be appropriate in the case of an offender whose plea of guilty to the manslaughter of his mother on the ground of diminished responsibility had been accepted by the prosecution and who had been assessed as dangerous for the purposes of the provisions of Chapter 5 of Part 12 of the CJA 2003 (§§ 5-495 *et seq.* in the main work), see *R. v. Fort* [2014] 2 Cr.App.R.(S.) 24, CA. As to this case, see also *ante*, §§ 5-1238, 5-1250.

B. Manslaughter

(2) Involuntary manslaughter

(b) *"Unlawful act" manslaughter*

Unlawful acts

For a case considering *R. v. Bristow*, see *R. v. F. (J.) and E. (N.)*, *post*, § 19-120.   ★**19-115**

Recognising the risk of the unlawful act

It was held in *R. v. F. (J.) and E. (N.)* [2015] 2 Cr.App.R. 5, CA, that where the unlawful act   ★**19-120** alleged for a charge of manslaughter was arson of a derelict building, a judge's direction that it had to be proved that the defendant foresaw or contemplated the possibility that some person, or persons might be in the building, went further than was necessary. The court said that the direction appeared to have been derived from the decision in *R. v. Bristow* (as to which, see § 19-115 in the main work), but that that decision did not require the gloss on the well-established law which the judge had introduced. The court reiterated that what was required was proof of an unlawful act (with the *mens rea* appropriate to the unlawful act in question), that it was dangerous and that it inadvertently caused death; and that, in judging whether the act was dangerous, the test is not whether the accused recognised that it was dangerous, but whether all sober and reasonable people would recognise its danger.

(8) Sentence

Involuntary manslaughter

19-134   An extended sentence of 20 years' imprisonment (of which the custodial term was 16 years) for manslaughter was severe but wholly justified where the appellant had subjected the deceased, whom he had met through a lonely hearts column, to a sustained, "grotesque" sexual attack involving anal and vaginal rape (for which he was sentenced to concurrent sentences of 11 years' imprisonment), where he accepted no responsibility and exhibited little if any remorse, but where there was evidence of an initial intention by the deceased to have consensual sex: *R. v. Doblys* [2014] 2 Cr.App.R.(S.) 44, CA.

★   In *R. v. Pisano* [2015] 1 Cr.App.R.(S.) 33, CA, a sentence of 18-and-a-half years' imprisonment was upheld for offences of unlawful act manslaughter, preventing the lawful and decent burial of a body, and inflicting grievous bodily harm in respect of an earlier incident involving the same victim, where the appellant (37), who was living with an older man (62) as a "rent boy", assaulted that man causing death, then left the body in the victim's flat for two months before it was discovered by the police, who had been alerted by the victim's family.

C. CORPORATE MANSLAUGHTER

(1) The offence

Corporate Manslaughter and Corporate Homicide Act 2007, s.1

The offence

19-140   The Sentencing Council for England and Wales has issued a consultation guideline on corporate manslaughter, health and safety and food safety and hygiene offences. The consultation closed on February 18, 2015.

(2) Relevant duty of care

Corporate Manslaughter and Corporate Homicide Act 2007, ss.2–7

Meaning of "relevant duty of care"

★19-141   As from March 20, 2015 (Criminal Justice and Courts Act 2015 (Commencement No. 1, Saving and Transitional Provisions) Order 2015 (S.I. 2015 No. 778)), the Criminal Justice and Courts Act 2015, s.38(3), and Sched. 9, para. 23, amended section 2(7) of the 2007 Act, so as to insert, in the definition of "custodial institution", after "secure training centre," the words "a secure college,".

VI. WOUNDING, CAUSING GRIEVOUS BODILY HARM

(4) Alternative verdicts

19-255   In *R. v. Vaughan* [2014] Crim.L.R. 819, CA, it was said (referring to *R. v. Lahaye* (as to which, see the main work)) that, while there is no universal rule, where there is an allegation of an offence contrary to section 18 of the Offences against the Person Act 1861 (§ 19-251 in the main work), a section 20 count (*ibid.*, § 19-252) should normally be included in the indictment. Where this is not done, the court said (referring to *R. v. Foster*; *R. v. Newman*; *R. v. Kempster*; *R. v. Birmingham* and *R. v. Hodson* (as to both of which, see § 4-533 in the main work)) that it is particularly important to leave an alternative verdict for the consideration of the jury where the offence charged requires proof of a specific intent and the alternative offence does not. In the particular case, where the judge had directed the jury that they could convict the defendant on the basis of excessive self-defence, the failure to leave the alternative section 20 count was held to have been of particular significance.

VIII. MISCELLANEOUS OFFENCES UNDER THE OFFENCES AGAINST THE PERSON ACT 1861

C. ADMINISTERING, ETC., POISON, ETC., SO AS TO ENDANGER LIFE, ETC., OR WITH INTENT TO INJURE, ETC.

(6) Ingredients of the offences

"any other person"

An unborn child does not have legal personality so as to constitute "any other person" for the purposes of section 23 of the Offences against the Person Act 1861 (§ 19-278 in the main work), and thus a mother whose excessive drinking while pregnant caused her child to be born with Foetal Alcohol Spectrum Disorder did not offend against that provision: *Criminal Injuries Compensation Authority v. First-Tier Tribunal (Social Entitlement Chamber)*; *Re C.P.* [2015] 1 Cr.App.R. 19, CA (Civ. Div.) (considering *Att.-Gen.'s Reference (No. 3 of 1994)* (as to which, see *ibid.*, § 19-15)).

19-285a

IX. OFFENCES IN RELATION TO POLICE OFFICERS

A. ASSAULTS

In the execution of duty

Common law

Walker v. Commr of Police of the Metropolis is now reported at [2015] 1 Cr.App.R. 22.

19-331

X. HARASSMENT

A. INTRODUCTION

In *Crawford v. Jenkins* [2015] 1 All E.R. 476, CA (Civ. Div.), it was held that one consequence of the witness immunity rule (*viz.* a statement made to the police by a complainant was part of the process of investigating a crime or a possible crime with a view to a prosecution and was therefore protected by absolute privilege) was that allegations of crime could not be relied on as being part of a course of conduct amounting to harassment, even where they were made maliciously and were known to be false. However, this decision needs to be treated with caution: first, it was decided in the context of a civil claim for harassment; and, secondly, the Supreme Court, whilst refusing permission to appeal on other grounds, conceded that it was arguable that the reasoning of the Court of Appeal was erroneous.

19-337

In connection with the offences under the Protection from Harassment Act 1997, it should be noted that the offence under section 1 of the Malicious Communications Act 1988 (offence of sending letters, etc., with intent to cause distress or anxiety), is amended, as from a day to be appointed, by the Criminal Justice and Courts Act 2015, s.32(1), so as to make it triable either way, with a maximum penalty on conviction on indictment, of two years' imprisonment, or a fine, or both. The amendment applies only in relation to an offence committed on or after the day on which section 32 of the 2015 Act comes into force.

B. STATUTE

Protection from Harassment Act 1997, ss.1, 2

A person may be guilty of harassment of another (and thus be in breach of s.1(1) of the 1997 Act (§ 19-339 in the main work)), where the target of his conduct is a third person: *Levi v. Bates*, *The Times*, May 8, 2015, CA (Civ. Div.) (considering *Dowson v. Northumbria Police* and *Thomas v. News Group Newspapers Ltd* (as to both of which, see § 19-337 in the main work)).

★19-340

Protection from Harassment Act 1997, ss.3–5

Restraining orders on conviction

As to the possibility of making a "European protection order" in conjunction with a restraining order under section 5 of the 1997 Act, see *post*, §§ 19-358a *et seq.*

19-351

Protection from Harassment Act 1997, s.5A

Restraining orders on acquittal

19-353   As to the possibility of making a "European protection order" in conjunction with a restraining order under section 5A of the 1997 Act, see *post*, §§ 19-358a *et seq.*

★   A finding by a jury that a person, who was unfit to plead, pursuant to section 4 (§ 4-321 in the main work) of the Criminal Procedure (Insanity) Act 1964, had done the act charged against him, following a hearing held under section 4A(2) (*ibid.*, § 4-232) of that Act, did not constitute an "acquittal", and therefore did not give the court the power to make a restraining order under section 5A: *R. v. Chinegwundoh* [2015] 1 Cr.App.R. 26, CA.

Controlling or coercive behaviour in an intimate or family relationship

★**19-357a**   As from a day to be appointed, section 76 of the Serious Crime Act 2015 creates a new either-way offence of controlling or coercive behaviour in an intimate or family relationship.

Controlling or coercive behaviour in an intimate or family relationship

    76.—(1) A person (A) commits an offence if—

        (a) A repeatedly or continuously engages in behaviour towards another person (B) that is controlling or coercive,

        (b) at the time of the behaviour, A and B are personally connected,

        (c) the behaviour has a serious effect on B, and

        (d) A knows or ought to know that the behaviour will have a serious effect on B.

    (2) A and B are "personally connected" if—

        (a) A is in an intimate personal relationship with B, or

        (b) A and B live together and—

            (i) they are members of the same family, or

           (ii) they have previously been in an intimate personal relationship with each other.

    (3) But A does not commit an offence under this section if at the time of the behaviour in question—

        (a) A has responsibility for B, for the purposes of Part 1 of the Children and Young Persons Act 1933 (see section 17 of that Act), and

        (b) B is under 16.

    (4) A's behaviour has a "serious effect" on B if—

        (a) it causes B to fear, on at least two occasions, that violence will be used against B, or

        (b) it causes B serious alarm or distress which has a substantial adverse effect on B's usual day-to-day activities.

    (5) For the purposes of subsection (1)(d) A "ought to know" that which a reasonable person in possession of the same information would know.

    (6) For the purposes of subsection (2)(b)(i) A and B are members of the same family if—

        (a) they are, or have been, married to each other;

        (b) they are, or have been, civil partners of each other;

        (c) they are relatives;

        (d) they have agreed to marry one another (whether or not the agreement has been terminated);

        (e) they have entered into a civil partnership agreement (whether or not the agreement has been terminated);

        (f) they are both parents of the same child;

        (g) they have, or have had, parental responsibility for the same child.

    (7) In subsection (6)—

    "civil partnership agreement" has the meaning given by section 73 of the Civil Partnership Act 2004 ;

    "child" means a person under the age of 18 years;

    "parental responsibility" has the same meaning as in the Children Act 1989;

    "relative" has the meaning given by section 63(1) of the Family Law Act 1996.

    (8) In proceedings for an offence under this section it is a defence for A to show that—

        (a) in engaging in the behaviour in question, A believed that he or she was acting in B's best interests, and

        (b) the behaviour was in all the circumstances reasonable.

184

(9) A is to be taken to have shown the facts mentioned in subsection (8) if—

    (a) sufficient evidence of the facts is adduced to raise an issue with respect to them, and

    (b) the contrary is not proved beyond reasonable doubt.

(10) The defence in subsection (8) is not available to A in relation to behaviour that causes B to fear that violence will be used against B.

(11) A person guilty of an offence under this section is liable—

    (a) on conviction on indictment, to imprisonment for a term not exceeding five years, or a fine, or both;

    (b) on summary conviction, to imprisonment for a term not exceeding 12 months, or a fine, or both.

There is transitional provision to the effect that, in relation to an offence committed before the commencement of section 154(1) of the CJA 2003 (§ 5-461 in the main work), the reference to 12 months in section 76(11)(b) is to be read as a reference to six months: 2015 Act, s.86(14)(e). ★

D. European Protection Orders

Introduction

With effect from January 11, 2015, the Criminal Justice (European Protection Order) (England and Wales) Regulations 2014 (S.I. 2014 No. 3300) make provision for "protection measures" in criminal proceedings (*i.e.* measures preventing individuals from entering areas or approaching or contacting a "protected person" which would include restraining orders made under section 5 or 5A of the 1997 Act (§§ 19-350, 19-352 in the main work) and bail conditions) to apply in another EU member state. A protected person can apply to a court (normally a magistrates' court, but, in certain circumstances, the Crown Court) to issue a European protection order if he intends to reside or stay in a different member state and wants to receive equivalent protection to that provided by the domestic protection measure. Where a protection measure is ordered, there is a duty on the court to inform the protected person of the possibility of applying for a protection order. **19-358a**

Criminal Justice (European Protection Order) (England and Wales) Regulations 2014 (S.I. 2014 No. 3300), Pts 1 and 2

Part 1

General

1. [*Citation, commencement and extent*] **19-358b**

Interpretation – general

    2.—(1) In these Regulations—

        "central authority", in relation to a member State other than the United Kingdom, means an authority designated by the State as a central authority for the purposes of the Directive;

        "the central authority for England and Wales" means the Lord Chancellor;

        "competent authority", in relation to a member State other than the United Kingdom, means an authority designated by the State as a competent authority for the purposes of the Directive;

        "the Directive" means Directive 2011/99/EU of the European Parliament and of the Council of 13th December 2011 on the European protection order;

        "notify" means notify in writing (and "notification" is to be read accordingly).

    (2) References in these Regulations to the Crown Court, the High Court, the Court of Appeal or a magistrates' court include references to a judge of such a court or a justice of the peace and a judge or justice having powers to act in connection with proceedings before such a court.

Part 2

Making a European Protection Order in England and Wales: Requests to other Member States to Recognise the Order

Interpretation – Part 2

    3.—(1) In this Part— **19-358c**

"European protection order" has the meaning given by regulation 4(9);

"protected person" means the individual who is the object of the protection given by a protection measure;

"protection measure" means a decision or order of a court in England and Wales when dealing with a criminal cause or matter, in which one or more of the following prohibitions or restrictions are placed on an individual—

    (a) a prohibition from entering certain localities, places or defined areas where the protected person resides or visits;

    (b) a prohibition or restriction of contact with the protected person by any means (including by telephone, post, facsimile transmission or electronic mail);

    (c) a prohibition or restriction preventing the individual from approaching the protected person whether at all or to within a particular distance;

"relevant court", in relation to a protection measure, means—

    (a) if the protection measure was made in the Crown Court and the request for the making of a European protection order is made at the same hearing at which the protection measure is made, the Crown Court; or

    (b) in any other case, a magistrates' court;

"specified information" means the information required by Article 7 of the Directive to be included on the form set out in Annex I to the Directive, except for any information relating to Framework Decision 2008/947/JHA of 27th November 2008 on the application of the principle of mutual recognition to judgments and probation decisions with a view to the supervision of probation measures and alternative sanctions.

(2) References in this Part to "the executing State" are to be construed in accordance with regulation 4(5).

Power of a court to make a European protection order

19-358d   **4.**—(1) This regulation applies where a magistrates' court, the Crown Court, the High Court or the Court of Appeal has made a protection measure.

(2) A relevant court may make an order under this regulation where the following conditions are met.

(3) The first condition is that the protected person requests the making of an order under this regulation in accordance with regulation 5.

(4) The second condition is that the protection measure has not expired.

(5) The third condition is that the court is satisfied that the protected person has decided to reside or stay or is already residing or staying in a member State other than the United Kingdom ("the executing State").

(6) When deciding whether to make an order under this regulation, the relevant court must take into account—

    (a)   the length of the period or periods that the protected person intends to reside or stay in the executing State;

    (b)   the seriousness of the need for protection of the protected person while residing or staying in the executing State;

    (c)   such other matters as it considers appropriate.

(7) An order under this regulation may not have effect for a period longer than the period for which the protection measure has effect.

(8) An order under this regulation may not contain a prohibition or restriction of a kind not mentioned in the definition of "protection measure" in regulation 3(1).

(9) An order under this regulation is referred to in the rest of this Part as a "European protection order".

Applications for a European protection order

19-358e   **5.**—(1) A request for a European protection order may be made to—

    (a)   a relevant court; or

    (b)   the competent authority of the executing State.

(2) Where a request for a European protection order is made to the competent authority of the executing State and transferred by that State to the central authority for England and Wales, it must be treated for the purposes of this regulation as if it were a request made to a magistrates' court under paragraph (1)(a).

(3) A request under paragraph (1) may be made by the protected person or by a guardian or other representative on the protected person's behalf.

Form and content of the European protection order

6. A European protection order must be in the form set out in Annex 1 to the Directive and contain the specified information. **19-358f**

Duty to inform a protected person of the possibility of a European protection order

7. Where a magistrates' court, the Crown Court, the High Court or the Court of Appeal has made a protection measure, it must ensure that the protected person (or, where appropriate, the guardian or representative of the protected person) is— **19-358g**

(a) informed in an appropriate way of the possibility to request a European protection order if the person decides to reside or stay in another member State and of the basic conditions for making such a request; and

(b) advised to submit a request for a European protection order before leaving the United Kingdom.

Duty to inform a protected person about remedies if a request is refused

8. If the relevant court refuses to make a European protection order it must inform the protected person (or, where appropriate, the guardian or representative of the protected person) of any applicable legal remedy that may be available against the decision. **19-358h**

Notifying the executing State of the European protection order

9.—(1) The court which makes a European protection order must notify the competent authority of the executing State of the European protection order by giving the documents specified in paragraph (2) to that authority. **19-358i**

(2) The documents are—

(a) a copy of the form containing the European protection order; and

(b) a copy of the form translated into—

(i) the official language, or one of the official languages, of the executing State; or

(ii) an official language of the European Union if the executing State has declared under Article 17 of the Directive that it will accept a translation in that language.

Renewing, modifying or revoking a protection measure and related European protection order

10.—(1) This regulation applies where a magistrates' court, the Crown Court, the High Court or the Court of Appeal makes a decision renewing, modifying or revoking a protection measure in relation to which a European protection order was made. **19-358j**

(2) The revocation of the protection measure has the effect of revoking the European protection order.

(3) Subject to paragraph (4), if the court modifies one or more of the prohibitions or restrictions placed on an individual under a protection measure, the court must—

(a) amend the European protection order to the like extent; and

(b) complete the form set out in Annex I to the Directive with the specified information.

(4) The modified European protection order may not contain a prohibition or restriction of a kind not mentioned within the definition of "protection measure" in regulation 3(1).

(5) If the court renews a protection measure it—

(a) may amend the European protection order; and

(b) where it does so, must complete the form set out in Annex I to the Directive with the specified information.

(6) The court must, without delay, inform the competent authority of the executing State—

(a) if paragraph (2) applies, that the European protection order is revoked;

(b) if paragraph (3) or (5) applies, of the decision modifying or renewing the protection measure.

(7) Where the court modifies or renews the European protection order, it must send to the competent authority of the executing State—

(a) the modified or renewed order; and

(b) where necessary, a copy of the form translated in accordance with regulation 9(2)(b).

XI. ILL–TREATMENT OR NEGLECT OF PERSONS OF UNSOUND MIND

C. ILL–TREATMENT OR WILFUL NEGLECT BY CARERS OR CARE PROVIDERS

Criminal Justice and Courts Act 2015, ss.20–25

Ill-treatment or wilful neglect: care worker offence

20.—(1) It is an offence for an individual who has the care of another individual by virtue of being a care worker to ill-treat or wilfully to neglect that individual. **19-363f**

(2) An individual guilty of an offence under this section is liable—

    (a) on conviction on indictment, to imprisonment for a term not exceeding 5 years or a fine (or both);

    (b) on summary conviction, to imprisonment for a term not exceeding 12 months or a fine (or both).

(3) "Care worker" means an individual who, as paid work, provides—

    (a) health care for an adult or child, other than excluded health care, or

    (b) social care for an adult,

including an individual who, as paid work, supervises or manages individuals providing such care or is a director or similar officer of an organisation which provides such care.

(4) An individual does something as "paid work" if he or she receives or is entitled to payment for doing it other than—

    (a) payment in respect of the individual's reasonable expenses,

    (b) payment to which the individual is entitled as a foster parent,

    (c) a benefit under social security legislation, or

    (d) a payment made under arrangements under section 2 of the Employment and Training Act 1973 (arrangements to assist people to select, train for, obtain and retain employment).

(5) "Health care" includes—

    (a) all forms of health care provided for individuals, including health care relating to physical health or mental health and health care provided for or in connection with the protection or improvement of public health, and

    (b) procedures that are similar to forms of medical or surgical care but are not provided in connection with a medical condition,

and "excluded health care" has the meaning given in Schedule 4.

(6) "Social care" includes all forms of personal care and other practical assistance provided for individuals who are in need of such care or assistance by reason of age, illness, disability, pregnancy, childbirth, dependence on alcohol or drugs or any other similar circumstances.

(7) References in this section to a person providing health care or social care do not include a person whose provision of such care is merely incidental to the carrying out of other activities by the person.

(8) In this section—

"adult" means an individual aged 18 or over;

"child" means an individual aged under 18;

"foster parent" means—

    (a) a local authority foster parent within the meaning of the Children Act 1989 ,

    (b) a person with whom a child has been placed by a voluntary organisation under section 59(1)(a) of that Act, or

    (c) a private foster parent within the meaning of section 53 of the Safeguarding Vulnerable Groups Act 2006.

(9) In relation to an offence committed before section 154(1) of the Criminal Justice Act 2003 comes into force, the reference in subsection (2)(b) to 12 months is to be read as a reference to 6 months.

(10) In relation to an offence committed before section 85 of the Legal Aid, Sentencing and Punishment of Offenders Act 2012 comes into force, the reference in subsection (2)(b) to a fine is to be read as a reference to a fine not exceeding the statutory maximum.

★   As to the commencement of sections 20 to 25 of the 2015 Act, see *post*, § 19-363k.

Ill-treatment or wilful neglect: care provider offence

19-363g   **21.**—(1) A care provider commits an offence if—

    (a) an individual who has the care of another individual by virtue of being part of the care provider's arrangements ill-treats or wilfully neglects that individual,

    (b) the care provider's activities are managed or organised in a way which amounts to a gross breach of a relevant duty of care owed by the care provider to the individual who is ill-treated or neglected, and

    (c) in the absence of the breach, the ill-treatment or wilful neglect would not have occurred or would have been less likely to occur.

(2) "Care provider" means—

    (a) a body corporate or unincorporated association which provides or arranges for the provision of—

     (i)   health care for an adult or child, other than excluded health care, or

     (ii)   social care for an adult, or

  (b) an individual who provides such care and employs, or has otherwise made arrangements with, other persons to assist him or her in providing such care,

subject to section 22.

(3) An individual is "part of a care provider's arrangements" where the individual—

  (a) is not the care provider, but

  (b) provides health care or social care as part of health care or social care provided or arranged for by the care provider,

including where the individual is not the care provider but supervises or manages individuals providing health care or social care as described in paragraph (b) or is a director or similar officer of an organisation which provides health care or social care as described there.

(4) A "relevant duty of care" means—

  (a) a duty owed under the law of negligence, or

  (b) a duty that would be owed under the law of negligence but for a provision contained in an Act, or an instrument made under an Act, under which liability is imposed in place of liability under that law,

but only to the extent that the duty is owed in connection with providing, or arranging for the provision of, health care or social care.

(5) For the purposes of this section, there is to be disregarded any rule of the common law that has the effect of—

  (a) preventing a duty of care from being owed by one person to another by reason of the fact that they are jointly engaged in unlawful conduct, or

  (b) preventing a duty of care being owed to a person by reason of that person's acceptance of a risk of harm.

(6) A breach of a duty of care by a care provider is a "gross" breach if the conduct alleged to amount to the breach falls far below what can reasonably be expected of the care provider in the circumstances.

(7) In this section—

  (a) references to a person providing health care or social care do not include a person whose provision of such care is merely incidental to the carrying out of other activities by the person, and

  (b) references to a person arranging for the provision of such care do not include a person who makes arrangements under which the provision of such care is merely incidental to the carrying out of other activities.

(8) References in this section to providing or arranging for the provision of health care or social care do not include making payments under—

  (a) regulations under section 57 of the Health and Social Care Act 2001 (direct payments for community services and carers);

  (b) section 12A of the National Health Act 2006 (direct payments for health care);

  (c) section 31 or 32 of the Care Act 2014 (direct payments for care and support);

  (d) regulations under section 50 of the Social Services and Well-being (Wales) Act 2014 (direct payments to meet an adult's needs).

(9) In this section—

"Act" includes an Act or Measure of the National Assembly for Wales;

"adult", "child", "excluded health care", "health care" and "social care" have the same meaning as in section 20.

Care provider offence: excluded care providers

22.—(1) A local authority in England is not a care provider for the purposes of section 21 to the extent that it carries out functions to which Chapter 4 of Part 8 of the Education and Inspections Act 2006 applies. **19-363h**

(2) A person is not a care provider for the purposes of section 21 to the extent that the person carries out a function of a local authority in England mentioned in subsection (1) in respect of which either of the following has effect—

  (a) a direction under section 15(6)(a) of the Local Government Act 1999 (power of Secretary of State to direct functions of a best value authority to be carried out by another person);

  (b) a direction under section 497A(4) or (4A) of the Education Act 1996 (power of Secretary of State to direct certain functions to be carried out by another person).

(3) Where a body corporate has entered into arrangements with a local authority in England

under Part 1 of the Children and Young Persons Act 2008 (social work services for children and young persons), the body is not a care provider for the purposes of section 21 to the extent that it carries out relevant care functions of that authority (as defined in that Part of that Act) under those arrangements.

(4) A local authority in Wales is not a care provider for the purposes of section 21 to the extent that it—

(a) carries out functions under Part 2 of the Childcare Act 2006;

(b) carries out the education functions of the authority (as defined in section 579(1) of the Education Act 1996);

(c) carries out the social services functions of the authority (as defined in the Local Authority Social Services Act 1970), so far as relating to a child.

(5) A person is not a care provider for the purposes of section 21 to the extent that the person carries out a function of a local authority in Wales mentioned in subsection (4) in respect of which any of the following has effect—

(a) a direction under section 29(6)(a) of the Local Government (Wales) Measure 2009 (power of Welsh Ministers to direct certain functions of a Welsh improvement authority to be carried out by another person);

(b) a direction under section 25 or 26 of the School Standards and Organisation (Wales) Act 2013 (powers of Welsh Ministers to direct education functions to be carried out by another person);

(c) a direction under section 154 or 155 of the Social Services and Well–being (Wales) Act 2014 (powers of Welsh Ministers to direct social services functions to be carried out by another person).

(6) A registered adoption society or registered adoption support agency is not a care provider for the purposes of section 21 to the extent that it provides adoption support services (as defined in section 2(6) of the Adoption and Children Act 2002).

(7) In this section, "local authority" means—

(a) in England, a county council, a metropolitan district council, a non–metropolitan district council for an area for which there is no county council, a London borough council, the Council of the Isles of Scilly and (in its capacity as a local authority) the Common Council of the City of London, and

(b) in Wales, a county council or a county borough council.

(8) In this section—

"child" has the same meaning as in section 20;

"registered adoption society" means an adoption society (as defined in section 2 of the Adoption and Children Act 2002) which is a voluntary organisation (as defined in that section) and in respect of which a person is registered under Part 2 of the Care Standards Act 2000;

"registered adoption support agency" means an adoption support agency (as defined in section 8 of the Adoption and Children Act 2002) in respect of which a person is registered under Part 2 of the Care Standards Act 2000.

Care provider offence: penalties

19-363i   **23.**—(1) A person guilty of an offence under section 21 is liable, on conviction on indictment or summary conviction, to a fine.

(2) A court before which a person is convicted of an offence under section 21 may make either or both of the following orders—

(a) a remedial order;

(b) a publicity order;

(whether instead of or as well as imposing a fine).

(3) A "remedial order" is an order requiring the person to take specified steps to remedy one or more of the following—

(a) the breach mentioned in section 21(1)(b) ("the relevant breach");

(b) any matter that appears to the court to have resulted from the relevant breach and to be connected with the ill-treatment or neglect;

(c) any deficiency in the person's policies, systems or practices of which the relevant breach appears to the court to be an indication.

(4) A "publicity order" is an order requiring the person to publicise in a specified manner—

(a) the fact that the person has been convicted of the offence;

(b) specified particulars of the offence;

(c) the amount of any fine imposed;

   (d) the terms of any remedial order made.

  (5) A remedial order—

   (a) may be made only on an application by the prosecution which specifies the terms of the proposed order,

   (b) must be made on such terms as the court considers appropriate having regard to any representations made, and any evidence adduced, in relation to its terms by the prosecution or by or on behalf of the person convicted, and

   (c) must specify a period within which the steps specified in the order must be taken.

  (6) A publicity order must specify a period within which the requirements specified in the order must be complied with.

  (7) A person who fails to comply with a remedial order or a publicity order commits an offence and is liable, on conviction on indictment or summary conviction, to a fine.

  (8) In relation to an offence committed before section 85 of the Legal Aid, Sentencing and Punishment of Offenders Act 2012 comes into force, subsections (1) and (7) have effect as if they provided for a fine on summary conviction not exceeding the statutory maximum.

Care provider offence: application to unincorporated associations

  24.—(1) For the purposes of sections 21 and 23, an unincorporated association is to be treated as **19-363j** owing whatever duties of care it would owe if it were a body corporate.

  (2) Proceedings for an offence under those sections alleged to have been committed by an unincorporated association must be brought in the name of the association (and not in that of any of its members).

  (3) In relation to such proceedings, rules of court relating to the service of documents have effect as if the unincorporated association were a body corporate.

  (4) In proceedings under section 21 or 23 brought against an unincorporated association, the following apply as they apply in relation to a body corporate—

   (a) section 33 of the Criminal Justice Act 1925 (procedure on charge of offence against corporation);

   (b) Schedule 3 to the Magistrates' Courts Act 1980 (provision about corporation charged with offence before a magistrates' court).

  (5) A fine imposed on an unincorporated association on its conviction of an offence under section 21 or 23 is to be paid out of the funds of the association.

Care provider offence: liability for ancillary and other offences

  25.—(1) An individual cannot be guilty of— **19-363k**

   (a) aiding, abetting, counselling or procuring the commission of an offence under section 21, or

   (b) an offence under Part 2 of the Serious Crime Act 2007 (encouraging or assisting crime) by reference to an offence under section 21.

  (2) Where, in the same proceedings, there is—

   (a) a charge under section 21 arising out of a particular set of circumstances, and

   (b) a charge against the same defendant of a relevant offence arising out of some or all of those circumstances,

the defendant may, if the interests of justice so require, be convicted of both offences.

  (3) A person convicted of an offence under section 21 arising out of a particular set of circumstances may, if the interests of justice so require, be charged with a relevant offence arising out of some or all of those circumstances.

  (4) "Relevant offence" means an offence under an Act, or an instrument made under an Act, dealing with—

   (a) health and safety matters, or

   (b) the provision of health care or social care.

  (5) In this section—

  "Act" includes an Act or Measure of the National Assembly for Wales;

  "health care" and "social care" have the same meaning as in section 20.

  Sections 20 to 25 of the 2015 Act came into force on April 13, 2015 (Criminal Justice and ★ Courts Act 2015 (Commencement No. 1, Saving and Transitional Provisions) Order 2015 (S.I. 2015 No. 778)).

XII. FEMALE GENITAL MUTILATION

Female Genital Mutilation Act 2003, ss.1–3

Offence of assisting non-UK person to mutilate overseas a girl's genitalia

★**19-366**   With effect from May 3, 2015, the SCA 2015, s.70(1)(a), amended section 3 of the 2003 Act so as, in subsections (1) and (2)(a), to omit the word "permanent". There is transitional provision to the effect that the amendments apply only in cases where every act or other event proof of which is required for conviction of the offence in question takes place after the provision comes into force (s.86(10)).

Offence of failing to protect girl from risk of genital mutilation

★**19-366a**   With effect from May 3, 2015, a new section 3A was inserted into the 2003 Act by the SCA 2015, s.72(1) and (2), as follows—

"Offence of failing to protect girl from risk of female genital mutilation
    3A.—(1) If a genital mutilation offence is committed against a girl under the age of 16, each person who is responsible for the girl at the relevant time is guilty of an offence.
    This is subject to subsection (5).
    (2) For the purposes of this section a person is 'responsible' for a girl in the following two cases.
    (3) The first case is where the person—
        (a) has parental responsibility for the girl, and
        (b) has frequent contact with her.
    (4) The second case is where the person—
        (a) is aged 18 or over, and
        (b) has assumed (and not relinquished) responsibility for caring for the girl in the manner of a parent.
    (5) It is a defence for the defendant to show that—
        (a) at the relevant time, the defendant did not think that there was a significant risk of a genital mutilation offence being committed against the girl, and could not reasonably have been expected to be aware that there was any such risk, or
        (b) the defendant took such steps as he or she could reasonably have been expected to take to protect the girl from being the victim of a genital mutilation offence.
    (6) A person is taken to have shown the fact mentioned in subsection (5)(a) or (b) if—
        (a) sufficient evidence of the fact is adduced to raise an issue with respect to it, and
        (b) the contrary is not proved beyond reasonable doubt.
    (7) For the purposes of subsection (3)(b), where a person has frequent contact with a girl which is interrupted by her going to stay somewhere temporarily, that contact is treated as continuing during her stay there.
    (8) In this section—
        'genital mutilation offence' means an offence under section 1, 2 or 3 (and for the purposes of subsection (1) the prosecution does not have to prove which section it is);
        'parental responsibility'—
        (a) in England Wales, has the same meaning as in the Children Act 1989;
        (b) in Northern Ireland, has the same meaning as in the Children (Northern Ireland) Order 1995 (S.I. 1995/755 (N.I. 2));
        'the relevant time' means the time when the mutilation takes place.".

★   There is transitional provision to the effect that (i) the reference to an offence under section 1, 2 or 3 in subsection (8) does not include such an offence committed before the coming into force of section 72 of the 2015 Act (2015 Act, s.86(16)), and (ii) in proceedings under section 3A, a defence under subsection (5)(b) may not be negated by reference to steps that the defendant could have taken (but did not) before the coming into force of section 72 of the 2015 Act (2015 Act, s.86(17)).

Extra-territorial acts

★**19-367**   With effect from May 3, 2015, the SCA 2015, s.70(1)(b), amended section 4 of the Female Genital Mutilation Act 2003 so as to omit the word "permanent" in subsection (1). There is transitional provision to the effect that the amendment applies only in cases where every act or other event proof of which is required for conviction of the offence in question takes place after the provision comes into force (s.86(10)).

With effect from the same day, the 2015 Act, s.72(1) and (3), further amended section 4 of the ★ 2003 Act (*ante*), so as (i) in the heading, to substitute "3A" for "3", (ii) in the heading, insert "or omissions" after "acts", and (iii) to insert a new subsection (1A), which provides that an offence under section 3A can be committed wholly or partly outside the United Kingdom by a person who is a United Kingdom national or a United Kingdom resident.

Anonymity of victims

With effect from May 3, 2015, the Serious Crime Act 2015, s.71(1), inserted a new section 4A ★**19-367a** (anonymity of victims) into the Female Genital Mutilation Act 2003. Section 4A gives effect to a new Schedule 1 to the 2003 Act, which is inserted by section 71(2) of the 2015 Act with effect from the same date. Schedule 1 provides for the anonymity of persons against whom a female genital mutilation offence (as defined in Sched. 1, para. 9) is alleged to have been committed. There is transitional provision in relation to Schedule 1 (s.86(15)(b)).

Mode of trial and penalties

With effect from May 3, 2015, the SCA 2015, s.72(1) and (4), amended section 5 of the Female ★**19-368** Genital Mutilation Act 2003 to provide that (i) only the offences under sections 1, 2 and 3 of the 2003 Act are subject to the penalties set out in the main work, and (ii) an offence under new section 3A of the 2003 Act (see *ante*, § 19-366a) is triable either way and punishable on conviction on indictment with seven years' imprisonment or a fine, or both; and on summary conviction for a term not exceeding 12 months' imprisonment, or a fine, or both. There is transitional provision to the effect that, in relation to an offence committed before the commencement of section 154(1) of the CJA 2003 (§ 5-461 in the main work), the reference to 12 months in section 76(11)(b) is to be read as a reference to six months: 2015 Act, s.86(14)(c).

Female genital mutilation protection orders

As from a day to be appointed, new section 5A (female genital mutilation protection orders) is ★**19-368a** inserted into the Female Genital Mutilation Act 2003 by the SCA 2015, s.73(1). Section 5A introduces new Schedule 2 to the 2003 Act (inserted by s.73(2)). Schedule 2 provides for the making of female genital mutilation protection orders (including in criminal proceedings). Paragraph 1 confers power on the High Court and the Family Court to make such an order, and paragraph 3 confers power on a court to make such an order in criminal proceedings for a genital mutilation offence. Breach of a female genital mutilation protection order is an either-way offence (maximum penalty on conviction on indictment, five years' imprisonment, or a fine, or both). There is transitional provision in relation to Schedule 2 (s.86(14)(d) and (15)(a)(iv)).

Duty to notify police of female genital mutilation

As from a day to be appointed, new section 5B is inserted into the Female Genital Mutilation ★**19-368b** Act 2003 by the SCA 2015, s.74. This places a duty on persons who work in a regulated profession (see subss. (2) and (11)) to notify the police if, in the course of their work, they discover (see subss. (2)–(4)) that an act of female genital mutilation appears to have been carried out on a girl aged under 18.

Guidance

As from a day to be appointed, new section 5C is inserted into the Female Genital Mutilation ★**19-368c** Act 2003 by the SCA 2015, s.75. This provides for the Secretary of State to issue guidance about the effect of any provision of the 2003 Act or other matters relating to female genital mutilation.

Definitions

With effect from May 3, 2015, the SCA 2015, s.70(1)(c), substituted subsection 6(3) of the ★**19-369** Female Genital Mutilation Act 2003 to provide "(3) A United Kingdom resident is an individual who is habitually resident in the United Kingdom." There is transitional provision to the effect that the amendment applies only in cases where every act or other event proof of which is required for conviction of the offence in question takes place after the amendment comes into force (s.86(10)).

XIII. OFFENCES RELATING TO CHILDREN AND YOUNG PERSONS

A. OFFENCES RELATING TO THE TREATMENT, CONTROL AND MAINTENANCE OF CHILDREN AND YOUNG PERSONS

(2) Cruelty

(a) *Statute*

Children and Young Persons Act 1933, s.1

Cruelty to persons under sixteen

★**19-375**   With effect from May 3, 2015 (Serious Crime Act 2015 (Commencement No. 1) Regulations 2015 (S.I. 2015 No. 820)), the SCA 2015, s.66, amended section 1 of the 1933 Act so as, in subsection (1), to insert the words "(whether physically or otherwise)" after (i) "ill-treats", and (ii) "ill-treated". There is transitional provision to the effect that the amendments apply only in cases where every act or other event proof of which is required for conviction of the offence in question takes place after they came into force (s.86(10)).

★**19-377**   As to the amendment of section 1 of the 1933 Act, see *ante*, § 19-375.

(d) *Sentence*

19-379   The approach to sentencing for historic child cruelty cases should be that laid down for historic sexual offences in *R. v. H. (J.)* (*post*, Appendix H-12); and where a count alleging child cruelty, contrary to section 1(1) of the CYPA 1933 (§ 19-375 in the main work), straddled September 29, 1988, when the maximum sentence was increased from two to ten years' imprisonment by the CJA 1988, s.45(1), with non-retrospective effect, sentence would have to be passed on the basis of the lower maximum sentence unless it was clear from the way in which the case had been conducted that the offending occurred after the higher maximum came into force (see *R. v. Harries* [2008] 1 Cr.App.R.(S.) 47, CA): *R. v. J.* [2014] 2 Cr.App.R.(S.) 77, CA.

(f) *Ingredients of the offence*

Ill-treat

★**19-386**   As to the amendment of section 1 of the 1933 Act, see *ante*, § 19-375.

C. GENERAL STATUTORY PROVISIONS RELATING TO CHILDREN IN CRIMINAL PROCEEDINGS

Children and Young Persons Act 1933, Sched. 1

★**19-408**   As from a day to be appointed, the Modern Slavery Act 2015, s.57(1), and Sched. 5, para. 1, amend Schedule 1 to the 1933 Act so as (i) in the first entry relating to the SOA 2003, to omit "59A to", (ii) to omit the entry relating to the Asylum and Immigration (Treatment of Claimants, etc.) Act 2004, and (iii) after that entry, to insert "An offence against a child or young person under section 2 of the Modern Slavery Act 2015 (human trafficking), or any attempt to commit such an offence."

Summary of miscellaneous provisions relating to giving evidence, publicity, etc.

19-416   As to the amendment of section 39 of the CYPA 1933 (see the main work), see *ante*, § 4-24.

XIV. FALSE IMPRISONMENT AND KIDNAPPING

(3) Sentence

★**19-423**   It was held in *Att.-Gen.'s References (Nos 92 and 93 of 2014) (R. v. Gibney)* [2015] 1 Cr.App.R.(S.) 44, CA, that *R. v Spence and Thomas* (as to which, see the main work) no longer provided guidance for levels of sentencing in cases of kidnapping and false imprisonment where the victim has been detained, subjected to violence and made the subject of monetary demands. These, the court said, were better reflected in decisions such as *R. v. Ahmed* [2011] 2 Cr.App.R.(S.) 35, CA (sentences of nine years and nine months' and 10 years and six months' imprisonment for a "very grave" offence), and *R. v. Smickele* [2013] 1 Cr.App.R.(S.) 64, CA (sentences of seven and eight years' detention for offenders aged between 16 and 20 (as to which, see also § 5-66 in the main work)). The court gave general guidance on sentencing for such offences and said that close analysis of the facts and circumstances was required. Relevant factors included the length and circumstances of the detention, including the location and any method of restraint, the extent of any violence used, the involvement of weapons, whether demands were made of others, the effect on the victim and others, the extent of planning, the number of offenders involved, the use of torture or humiliation, whether what was done arose from, or was in furtherance of, previous criminal behaviour, and any particular vulnerability of the victim (by reason of age or otherwise). A significant increase in sentencing levels for such offences was demonstrated where sentences of nine years and nine months' imprisonment and 10 years' imprisonment respectively were substituted (on late guilty pleas) where the two respondents had kidnapped another to enforce a drug debt, detained him, and subjected him to violence and monetary demands for about 10 hours.

To similar effect, see *Att.-Gen.'s References (Nos 102 and 103 of 2014) (R. v. Perkins)* [2015] 1 　★
Cr.App.R.(S.) 55, CA (generally speaking, cases involving hostage-taking and ransom demands will attract a starting point of close to 16 years for an adult; others, where such behaviour is absent, will still attract double figures, regardless of the degree of violence).

XV. HUMAN RIGHTS VIOLATIONS

B. Slavery, Servitude And Forced Or Compulsory Labour

Coroners and Justice Act 2009, s.71

Slavery, servitude and forced or compulsory labour
The Modern Slavery Act 2015 received Royal Assent on March 26, 2015. As from a day to be 　★19-437
appointed, the Act replaces the offences under section 71 of the 2009 Act (see the main work), section 4 of the Asylum and Immigration (Treatment of Claimants, etc.) Act 2004 (*ibid.*, § 25-292a), and section 59A of the SOA 2003 (*ibid.*, § 20-179), with three new offences under sections 1 (slavery, servitude and forced or compulsory labour), 2 (human trafficking) and 4 (committing offence with intent to commit offence under section 2). As to the 2015 Act, see *post*, §§ 19-440 *et seq.*

Modern Slavery Act 2015

Introduction

The long title describes it as an Act to make provision about "slavery, servitude and forced or 　★19-440
compulsory labour and ... human trafficking ...". There are 62 sections (in seven parts) and five schedules. As to the offences it replaces, see *ante*, § 19-437.

Offences

Part 1 (ss.1–13) consolidates the current offences of slavery and human trafficking, whilst 　★19-441
increasing the maximum penalties in respect thereof. Section 1 replaces the offence under section 71 (slavery, servitude and forced or compulsory labour) of the Coroners and Justice Act 2009 (§ 19-437 in the main work), with no change in the definition of the offence, but with express provision as to the need to take account of all the circumstances and as to the consent of a person to any of the acts alleged to constitute holding the person in slavery or servitude, or requiring the person to perform forced or compulsory labour, not precluding a determination that the person is being held in slavery or servitude, or required to perform forced or compulsory labour. Under section 2(1), it is an offence to arrange or facilitate (see subss. (3) and (4)) the travel (defined in subs. (5)) of another person with a view to that person being exploited. It is irrelevant whether the victim consents to the travel (subs. (2)). A United Kingdom national commits an offence regardless of where the arranging or facilitating takes place, or where the travel takes place (subs. (6)), and a non-United Kingdom national commits an offence where any part of the arranging or facilitating takes place in the United Kingdom, or the travel consists of arrival in, entry into,

departure from, or travel within, the United Kingdom (subs. (7)). Section 3 makes provision as to when a person is to be regarded as being exploited: there are five headings, *viz.* slavery, etc., sexual exploitation, removal of organs, securing services by force, threats or deception, and securing services of a child or vulnerable person. Section 4 provides that a person commits an offence where he commits any offence with the intention of committing an offence under section 2, including an offence committed by aiding, abetting, counselling or procuring an offence under that section.

The offences under sections 1, 2 and 4 are triable either way, with those contrary to sections 1 and 2 carrying life imprisonment on conviction on indictment as does the offence under section 4, if the index offence is kidnapping or false imprisonment (in which case, it is triable only on indictment); otherwise it carries 10 years' imprisonment.

Section 6 amends the CJA 2003, to add the offence under section 1 to the list of offences in Part 1 of Schedule 15 (§ 5-503 in the main work), the offence under section 2 to Part 2 of Schedule 15 if committed with a view to sexual exploitation, and otherwise to Part 1, and the offences under sections 1 and 2 to Schedule 15B (*ibid.*, § 5-505). Section 7 adds the offences in sections 1 and 2 to the list of offences contained in Schedule 2 (lifestyle offences (*ibid.*, §§ 5-925 *et seq.*)) to the PCA 2002. Section 8(1) provides that the court (see subs. (8)) may make a slavery and trafficking reparation order against a person if he has been convicted of an offence under section 1, 2 or 4, and a confiscation order has been made against the person in respect of the offence. The court may also make such an order if by virtue of section 28 (defendants who abscond during proceedings (*ibid.*, § 5-829)) of the 2002 Act, it has made a confiscation order against a person in respect of an offence under section 1, 2 or 4, and the person is later convicted of the offence (s.8(2)). The court may make a slavery and trafficking reparation order against the person in addition to dealing with him in any other way (subject to s.10(1) (*post*)) (s.8(3)), and may make such an order even if the person has been sentenced for the offence before the confiscation order is made (s.8(4)). In determining whether to make such an order the court must have regard to the defendant's means (s.8(5)). Section 9(1) provides that a slavery and trafficking reparation order is an order requiring the person against whom it is made to pay compensation to the victim of a relevant offence (see subs. (2)) for any harm resulting from that offence, and the total amount of compensation payable under the order must not exceed the amount the person is required to pay under the confiscation order (subs. (4)). Section 10 contains supplemental provision in relation in particular to the relationship with compensation orders, the provisions of the 2002 Act relating to variation of confiscation orders and the effect of appeals. Under section 11, when a person is convicted on indictment of a human trafficking offence (under s.2) the court may order the forfeiture of a land vehicle, ship or aircraft used or intended to be used in connection with the offence of which the person is convicted. Section 12 provides that a constable or senior immigration officer may detain a relevant land vehicle, ship or aircraft (see subs. (2)) where a person has been arrested for an offence under section 2. Section 13 is an interpretation provision for Part 1.

Prevention orders (Pt 2 (ss.14–34))

Slavery and trafficking prevention orders (ss.14–22)

★**19-442**   Section 14(1) provides that a court may make a slavery and trafficking prevention order against a defendant where it deals with him in respect of a conviction for a slavery or human trafficking offence (an offence listed in Sched. 1 (subs. (4)), a finding that the defendant is not guilty of a slavery or human trafficking offence by reason of insanity, or a finding that the defendant is under a disability and has done the act charged against him in respect of such an offence. The court may make the order only if it is satisfied that there is a risk that the defendant may commit a slavery or human trafficking offence, and it is necessary to make the order for the purpose of protecting persons generally, or particular persons, from the physical or psychological harm that would be likely to occur if the defendant committed such an offence (subs. (2)). Under section 15, on application by a chief officer of police, an immigration officer, or the Director General of the National Crime Agency, a magistrates' court may make a slavery and trafficking prevention order against a person where it is satisfied that he is a "relevant offender" (see s.16 (*post*)), and since he first became a relevant offender, he has acted in a way that means that the condition in subsection (3) (which corresponds to s.14(2)) is met. A relevant offender includes a person convicted, etc., or cautioned for a slavery or human trafficking offence in the United Kingdom (s.16(2)), and also persons convicted, etc., in relation to an equivalent offence outside the United Kingdom (s.16(3)–(5)). Section 17 deals with the effect of slavery and trafficking prevention orders, subsection (1) providing that such an order is an order prohibiting the defendant from doing anything described in it; but the only prohibitions that may be included are those that the court is satisfied are necessary for the purpose of protecting persons generally, or particular persons, from the physical or psychological harm that would be likely to occur if the defendant committed a slavery or human trafficking offence (s.17(2)). Under section 18, a prohibition on foreign travel (see subs. (2)) contained in an order must be for a fixed period of not more than five years (though that may be extended for a further period (of no more than five years each time) under s.20 (subs. (3)). A person prohibited from travelling to any country must surrender all his passports to the police (s.18(4)). Section 19 makes provision for an order to include notification requirements (as to name and address, change of name or address, etc.), section 20 provides for the variation, renewal and discharge of an order, section 21 makes provision for interim orders and section 22 concerns appeals.

Slavery and trafficking risk orders (ss.23–29)

Under section 23(1), a magistrates' court may make a slavery and trafficking risk order against ★**19-443**
a defendant on an application by a chief officer of police, an immigration officer, or the Director General of the National Crime Agency, where it is satisfied that the defendant has acted in a way that means that there is a risk that he will commit a slavery or human trafficking offence, and it is necessary to make the order for the purpose of protecting persons generally, or particular persons, from the physical or psychological harm which would be likely to occur if the defendant committed such an offence (s.23(2)). Sections 24 (effect of slavery and trafficking risk orders), 25 (prohibitions on foreign travel), 26 (requirement to provide name and address), 27 (variation, renewal and discharge), 28 (interim slavery and trafficking risk orders) and 29 (appeals) make further provision in relation thereto (similar to that made in respect of slavery and trafficking prevention orders).

Offences and supplementary provision (ss.30–34)

Section 30(1) provides that a person who, without reasonable excuse, does anything that he is ★**19-444**
prohibited from doing by any order under the preceding provisions of this part or under equivalent Northern Irish legislation commits an either-way offence (maximum penalty on conviction on indictment, five years' imprisonment (subs. (3)). Under section 30(2), a person commits an offence if, without reasonable excuse, he fails to comply with a requirement imposed under section 18(4) or 25(4) (requirement to surrender passports), or section 19(1), 21(6), 26(1) or 28(6) (requirement to provide name and address) (penalty as for subs. (1) (subs. (3)). Section 31 concerns cross-border enforcement. Section 34 concerns interpretation for Part 2.

Maritime enforcement (Pt 3 (ss.35–39))

Under section 35(1), an English and Welsh constable or an enforcement officer may exercise ★**19-445**
the powers set out in Part 1 of Schedule 2 (for the purpose of preventing, detecting, investigating or prosecuting an offence under s.1 or 2, and in accordance with the rest of this section (subs. (2))) in relation to a United Kingdom ship in England and Wales waters, foreign waters or international waters, a ship without nationality in England and Wales waters or international waters, a foreign ship in England and Wales waters, or a ship, registered under the law of a relevant territory, in England and Wales waters. The authority of the Secretary of State is required, in certain circumstances (see subss. (3)–(7)), before a constable or an enforcement officer may exercise these powers. In Schedule 2, paragraph 2 provides for the power to stop, board, divert and detain a ship where a constable or an enforcement officer has reasonable grounds to suspect that an offence under section 1 or 2 is being, or has been, committed on the ship, or the ship is otherwise being used in connection with the commission of an offence under either of those sections. Additionally, in particular, paragraph 3 provides for a power to search and obtain information, paragraph 4 provides for a power of arrest and seizure, and paragraph 5 provides that the Secretary of State must issue a code of practice for constables or law enforcement officers exercising the power of arrest set out in paragraph 4. Under paragraph 10(1), a person commits an offence where he intentionally obstructs a constable or an enforcement officer in the performance of functions under this part of this schedule, or fails without reasonable excuse to

comply with a requirement made by a constable or an enforcement officer in the performance of those functions. Under paragraph 10(2), a person who provides information in response to a requirement made by a constable or an enforcement officer in the performance of functions under this part commits an offence if the information is false in a material particular, and the person either knows it is or is reckless as to whether it is, or the person intentionally fails to disclose any material particular. Both offences under paragraph 10 are triable summarily only and, on conviction, the defendant is liable to a fine. Sections 36 and 37 relate to Scotland and Northern Ireland. Section 38 provides for powers of hot pursuit, where law enforcement officers seek to pursue a suspected vessel between waters adjacent to different jurisdictions within the United Kingdom or between United Kingdom and international waters. Section 39 is an interpretation provision for Part 3.

Protection of victims (Pt 5 (ss.45–53))

★**19-446**   Section 45(1) provides that a person is not guilty of an offence where he is aged 18 or over when he does the act that constitutes the offence, he does that act because he is compelled to (see subs. (2)), the compulsion is attributable to slavery or to relevant exploitation (see subs. (3)), and a reasonable person in the same situation as the person and having his relevant characteristics would have no realistic alternative to doing that act. Subsection (4) provides that a person is not guilty of an offence where he is under the age of 18 when he does the act that constitutes the offence, he does that act as a direct consequence of being, or having been, a victim of slavery or a victim of relevant exploitation (see subs. (5)), and a reasonable person in the same situation as the person and having the person's relevant characteristics (see subs. (5)) would do that act. However, subsections (1) and (4) do not apply to any of the long list of offences in Schedule 4 (which includes all the principal offences of violence and sexual offences and many others). Section 46 makes consequential amendments to the YJCEA 1999, ss.17(4), 25(4)(a), and 33(6)(d) (as to which, see *ante*, §§ 8-75, 8-86 and 8-98). Sections 49 to 52 make further provision in relation to suspected victims of slavery or human trafficking (including their identification and support for them), and section 53 concerns protection for overseas domestic workers.

Miscellaneous and general (Pt 7 (ss.55–62))

★**19-447**   Section 56 relates to interpretation. Part 7 (except s.57(1) and Sched. 5) came into force on Royal Assent (s.61(3)). Section 48(7) came into force on May 26, 2015 (s.61(2)). All remaining provisions come into force on a day to be appointed: s.61(1).

CHAPTER 20

SEXUAL OFFENCES

II. OFFENCES

A. GENERAL INTERPRETATION

(2) "Sexual"

Sexual Offences Act 2003, s.78

"Sexual"

★**20-17**   As from a day to be appointed, the SCA 2015, s.85(1), and Sched. 4, para. 63, amend section 78 of the 2003 Act, so as to substitute "except sections 15A and 71" for "except section 71".

F. CHILD SEX OFFENCES

(6) Arranging or facilitating commission of a child sex offence

(d) Sentence

★**20-88**   As to the repeal of section 76 of the SOCPA 2005, see *ante*, § 5-1212.

(7) Meeting a child following sexual grooming

(a) *Statute*

Sexual Offences Act 2003, s.15

Meeting a child following sexual grooming, etc.

As from April 13, 2015 (Criminal Justice and Courts Act 2015 (Commencement No. 1, Saving **★20-91** and Transitional Provisions) Order 2015 (S.I. 2015 No. 778)), the Criminal Justice and Courts Act 2015, s.36(1), amended section 15(1)(a) of the 2003 Act, so as to substitute the words "on one or more occasions" for "on at least two occasions". Section 36(2) of the 2015 Act provides that in a case in which person A met or communicated with person B only once before the event mentioned in section 15(1)(a)(i) to (iii), an offence under that section is committed only if the meeting or communication took place after section 36 comes into force.

(e) *Elements of the offence*

As to the amendment of section 15(1)(a) of the 2003 Act (see the main work), see *ante*, § 25-91.   **20-95**

(8) Sexual communication with a child

As from a day to be appointed, a new section 15A is inserted into the 2003 Act by the SCA **★20-95a** 2015, s.67, as follows—

"Sexual communication with a child
    15A.—(1) A person aged 18 or over (A) commits an offence if—
        (a) for the purpose of obtaining sexual gratification, A intentionally communicates with another person (B),
        (b) the communication is sexual or is intended to encourage B to make (whether to A or to another) a communication that is sexual, and
        (c) B is under 16 and A does not reasonably believe that B is 16 or over.
    (2) For the purposes of this section, a communication is sexual if—
        (a) any part of it relates to sexual activity, or
        (b) a reasonable person would, in all the circumstances but regardless of any person's purpose, consider any part of the communication to be sexual;
and in paragraph (a) 'sexual activity' means an activity that a reasonable person would, in all the circumstances but regardless of any person's purpose, consider to be sexual.
    (3) A person guilty of an offence under this section is liable—
        (a) on summary conviction, to imprisonment for a term not exceeding 12 months or a fine or both;
        (b) on conviction on indictment, to imprisonment for a term not exceeding 2 years.".

There is transitional provision to the effect that, in relation to an offence committed before the **★** commencement of section 154(1) of the CJA 2003 (§ 5-461 in the main work), the reference to 12 months in section 15A(3)(a) is to be read as a reference to six months: 2015 Act, s.86(14)(a).

(9) Possession of paedophile manual

With effect from May 3, 2015 (Serious Crime Act 2015 (Commencement No. 1) Regulations **★20-95b** 2015 (S.I. 2015 No. 820)), section 69 of the SCA 2015 created an offence of being in possession of a paedophile manual, as follows—

"Possession of paedophile manual
    69.—(1) It is an offence to be in possession of any item that contains advice or guidance about abusing children sexually.
    (2) It is a defence for a person (D) charged with an offence under this section—
        (a) to prove that D had a legitimate reason for being in possession of the item;
        (b) to prove that—
            (i) D had not read, viewed or (as appropriate) listened to the item, and
            (ii) D did not know, and had no reason to suspect, that it contained advice or guidance about abusing children sexually; or
        (c) to prove that—
            (i) the item was sent to D without any request made by D or on D's behalf, and
            (ii) D did not keep it for an unreasonable time.
    (3) A person guilty of an offence under this section is liable—

(a) on summary conviction in England and Wales, to imprisonment for a term not exceeding 12 months or to a fine, or to both;

(b) on summary conviction in Northern Ireland, to imprisonment for a term not exceeding 6 months or to a fine not exceeding the statutory maximum, or to both;

(c) on conviction on indictment, to imprisonment for a term not exceeding 3 years or to a fine, or to both.

(4) Proceedings for an offence under this section may be brought—

(a) in England and Wales, only by or with the consent of the Director of Public Prosecutions;

(b) in Northern Ireland, only by or with the consent of the Director of Public Prosecutions for Northern Ireland.

(5) In England and Wales, the following provisions of the Protection of Children Act 1978 apply in relation to prohibited items as they apply in relation to indecent photographs of children (within the meaning of that Act)—

(a) section 4 (entry, search and seizure);

(b) the Schedule (forfeiture of photographs).

(6) [*Northern Ireland.*]

(7) Schedule 3 makes special provision in connection with the operation of subsection (1) in relation to persons providing information society services within the meaning of that Schedule.

(8) In this section—

'abusing children sexually' means doing anything that constitutes—

(a) an offence under Part 1 of the Sexual Offences Act 2003, or under Part 2, 3 or 4 of the Sexual Offences (Northern Ireland) Order 2008 (S.I. 2008/1769 (N.I. 2)), against a person under 16, or

(b) an offence under section 1 of the Protection of Children Act 1978, or under Article 3 of the Protection of Children (Northern Ireland) Order 1978, involving indecent photographs (but not pseudo-photographs),

or doing anything outside England and Wales or Northern Ireland that would constitute such an offence if done in England and Wales or Northern Ireland;

'item' includes anything in which information of any description is recorded;

'prohibited item' means an item within subsection (1).".

★ There is transitional provision to the effect that, in relation to an offence committed before the commencement of section 154(1) of the CJA 2003 (§ 5-461 in the main work), the reference to 12 months in section 69(3)(a) is to be read as a reference to six months: 2015 Act, s.86(14)(b).

★ Schedule 3 to the 2015 Act makes special provision in connection with the operation of section 69(1) in relation to persons providing information society services within the meaning of that schedule.

L. Abuse of Children through Prostitution and Pornography

(1) Paying for sexual services of a child

(a) *Statute*

Sexual Offences Act 2003, s.47

Paying for sexual services of a child

★**20-155** With effect from May 3, 2015 (Serious Crime Act 2015 (Commencement No. 1) Regulations 2015 (S.I. 2015 No. 820)), the SCA 2015, s.68(1) and (2), substituted "Sexual exploitation of children" for the heading above section 47 of the 2003 Act.

(2) Causing, inciting, facilitating, etc., child prostitution or pornography

(a) *Statute*

Sexual Offences Act 2003, ss.48, 50, 51

Causing or inciting child prostitution or pornography

★**20-160** With effect from May 3, 2015 (Serious Crime Act 2015 (Commencement No. 1) Regulations 2015 (S.I. 2015 No. 820)), the SCA 2015, s.68(1) and (3), amended section 48 of the 2003 Act so as (i) in the heading, to substitute "sexual exploitation of a child" for "child prostitution or pornography", and (ii) in subsection (1)(a), to substitute "to be sexually exploited" for "to become a prostitute, or to be involved in pornography".

Arranging or facilitating child prostitution or pornography

With effect from May 3, 2015 (Serious Crime Act 2015 (Commencement No. 1) Regulations ★**20-161**
2015 (S.I. 2015 No. 820)), the SCA 2015, s.68(1) and (5), amended section 50 of the 2003 Act so
as (i) in the heading, to substitute "sexual exploitation of a child", for "child prostitution or
pornography", and (ii) in subsection (1)(a), to substitute "sexual exploitation" for "prostitution or
involvement in pornography".

Sections 48 to 50: interpretation

With effect from May 3, 2015 (Serious Crime Act 2015 (Commencement No. 1) Regulations ★**20-162**
2015 (S.I. 2015 No. 820)), the SCA 2015, s.68(1) and (6), amended section 51 of the 2003 Act so
as (i) to omit subsection (1), and (ii) to substitute a new subsection (2), as follows—

> "(2) For the purposes of sections 48 to 50, a person (B) is sexually exploited if—
> > (a) on at least one occasion and whether or not compelled to do so, B offers or provides
> > sexual services to another person in return for payment or a promise of payment to B or a
> > third person, or
> > (b) an indecent image of B is recorded;
> and 'sexual exploitation' is to be interpreted accordingly.".

(b) *Indictment*

As to the amendment of section 48(1) of the 2003 Act, see *ante*, § 20-160. ★**20-163**

(d) *Sentence*

As to the repeal of section 76 of the SOCPA 2005, see *ante*, § 5-1212. ★**20-165**

(e) *Elements of the offences*

As to the amendment of section 51 of the 2003 Act, see *ante*, § 20-162. ★**20-166**

(3) **Controlling a child prostitute or a child involved in pornography**

(a) *Statute*

Sexual Offences Act, s.49

Controlling a child prostitute or a child involved in pornography

With effect from May 3, 2015 (Serious Crime Act 2015 (Commencement No. 1) Regulations ★**20-167**
2015 (S.I. 2015 No. 820)), the SCA 2015, s.68(1) and (4), amended section 49 of the 2003 Act so
as (i) in the heading, to substitute "in relation to sexual exploitation" for "prostitute or a child
involved in pornography", and (ii) in subsection (1)(a), to substitute "sexual exploitation" for
"prostitution or involvement in pornography".

(b) *Indictment*

As to the amendment of section 49 of the 2003 Act, see *ante*, § 20-167. ★**20-168**

(d) *Sentence*

As to the repeal of section 76 of the SOCPA 2005, see *ante*, § 5-1212. ★**20-170**

(e) *Elements of the offence*

As to the amendment of section 51 of the 2003 Act, see *ante*, § 20-162. ★**20-171**

M. EXPLOITATION OF PROSTITUTION

(1) **Statute**

Sexual Offences Act 2003, ss.52–54

Sections 51A to 53A: interpretation

With effect from May 3, 2015 (Serious Crime Act 2015 (Commencement No. 1) Regulations ★**20-174**
2015 (S.I. 2015 No. 820)), the SCA 2015, s.85(1), and Sched. 4, para. 62, amended section 54 of
the 2003 Act so as to substitute new subsections (2) and (3), as follows—

> "(2) In sections 51A, 52, 53 and 53A 'prostitute' means a person (A) who, on at least one occasion

and whether or not compelled to do so, offers or provides sexual services to another person in return for payment or a promise of payment to A or a third person; and 'prostitution' is to be interpreted accordingly.

(3) In subsection (2) and section 53A, 'payment' means any financial advantage, including the discharge of an obligation to pay or the provision of goods or services (including sexual services) gratuitously or at a discount.".

(4) Sentence

★20-177 As to the repeal of section 76 of the SOCPA 2005, see *ante*, § 5-1212.

(5) Elements of the offences

★20-178 As to the amendment of section 51 of the 2003 Act, see *ante*, § 20-162.

N. TRAFFICKING

(1) Statute

Sexual Offences Act 2003, ss.59A–60C

Trafficking people for sexual exploitation

★20-179 As from a day to be appointed, the Modern Slavery Act 2015, s.57(1), and Sched. 5, para. 5(1) and (2), repeal sections 59A to 60C of the 2003 Act.

Section 59A: interpretation

★20-182 As to the repeal of section 60 of the 2003 Act, see *ante*, § 20-179.

Forfeiture of land vehicle, ship or aircraft

★20-182a As to the repeal of section 60A of the 2003 Act, see *ante*, § 20-179.

Detention of land vehicle, ship or aircraft

★20-182b As to the repeal of section 60B of the 2003 Act, see *ante*, § 20-179.

Sections 60A to 60B: interpretation

★20-182c As to the repeal of section 60C of the 2003 Act, see *ante*, § 20-179.

Q. OTHER STATUTORY OFFENCES

(2) Voyeurism

(e) *Elements of the offence*

★20-217 For a case considering *R. v. B. (M.)*, see *R. v. Wells*; *R. v. Masud*; *R. v. Hone*; *R. v. Kail, ante*, § 4-237.

(6) Suppression of brothels

(d) *Sentence*

★20-232 As to the repeal of section 76 of the SOCPA 2005, see *ante*, § 5-1212.

(7) Soliciting, kerb-crawling, etc.

★20-237 With effect from May 3, 2015 (Serious Crime Act 2015 (Commencement No. 1) Regulations 2015 (S.I. 2015 No. 820)), the SCA 2015, s.68(1) and (7), further amended section 1 of the Street Offences Act 1959 so as to provide that the offence can only be committed by persons aged 18 or over. There is transitional provision (s.86(11) (into force on Royal Assent)) to the effect that the amendment does not apply to proceedings which are started before the commencement of the amendment.

(8) Disclosing a private sexual photograph or film

Criminal Justice and Courts Act 2015, ss.33–35

Disclosing private sexual photographs and films with intent to cause distress

20-237a 33.—(1) It is an offence for a person to disclose a private sexual photograph or film if the disclosure is made—

    (a)   without the consent of an individual who appears in the photograph or film, and

    (b)   with the intention of causing that individual distress.

  (2) But it is not an offence under this section for the person to disclose the photograph or film to the individual mentioned in subsection (1)(a) and (b).

  (3) It is a defence for a person charged with an offence under this section to prove that he or she reasonably believed that the disclosure was necessary for the purposes of preventing, detecting or investigating crime.

  (4) It is a defence for a person charged with an offence under this section to show that—

    (a)   the disclosure was made in the course of, or with a view to, the publication of journalistic material, and

    (b)   he or she reasonably believed that, in the particular circumstances, the publication of the journalistic material was, or would be, in the public interest.

  (5) It is a defence for a person charged with an offence under this section to show that—

    (a)   he or she reasonably believed that the photograph or film had previously been disclosed for reward, whether by the individual mentioned in subsection (1)(a) and (b) or another person, and

    (b)   he or she had no reason to believe that the previous disclosure for reward was made without the consent of the individual mentioned in subsection (1)(a) and (b).

  (6) A person is taken to have shown the matters mentioned in subsection (4) or (5) if—

    (a)   sufficient evidence of the matters is adduced to raise an issue with respect to it, and

    (b)   the contrary is not proved beyond reasonable doubt.

  (7) For the purposes of subsections (1) to (5)—

    (a)   "consent" to a disclosure includes general consent covering the disclosure, as well as consent to the particular disclosure, and

    (b)   "publication" of journalistic material means disclosure to the public at large or to a section of the public.

  (8) A person charged with an offence under this section is not to be taken to have disclosed a photograph or film with the intention of causing distress merely because that was a natural and probable consequence of the disclosure.

  (9) A person guilty of an offence under this section is liable—

    (a)   on conviction on indictment, to imprisonment for a term not exceeding 2 years or a fine (or both), and

    (b)   on summary conviction, to imprisonment for a term not exceeding 12 months or a fine (or both).

  (10) Schedule 8 makes special provision in connection with the operation of this section in relation to persons providing information society services.

  (11) In relation to an offence committed before section 154(1) of the Criminal Justice Act 2003 comes into force, the reference in subsection (9)(b) to 12 months is to be read as a reference to 6 months.

  (12) In relation to an offence committed before section 85 of the Legal Aid, Sentencing and Punishment of Offenders Act 2012 comes into force, the reference in subsection (9)(b) to a fine is to be read as a reference to a fine not exceeding the statutory maximum.

As to the commencement of sections 33 to 35 of the 2015 Act, see *post*, § 20-237c.

Meaning of "disclose" and "photograph or film"

  34.—(1) The following apply for the purposes of section 33, this section and section 35.   **20-237b**

  (2) A person "discloses" something to a person if, by any means, he or she gives or shows it to the person or makes it available to the person.

  (3) Something that is given, shown or made available to a person is disclosed—

    (a)   whether or not it is given, shown or made available for reward, and

    (b)   whether or not it has previously been given, shown or made available to the person.

  (4) "Photograph or film" means a still or moving image in any form that—

    (a)   appears to consist of or include one or more photographed or filmed images, and

    (b)   in fact consists of or includes one or more photographed or filmed images.

  (5) The reference in subsection (4)(b) to photographed or filmed images includes photographed or filmed images that have been altered in any way.

  (6) "Photographed or filmed image" means a still or moving image that—

    (a)   was originally captured by photography or filming, or

    (b)   is part of an image originally captured by photography or filming.

  (7) "Filming" means making a recording, on any medium, from which a moving image may be produced by any means.

(8) References to a photograph or film include—

(a)   a negative version of an image described in subsection (4), and

(b)   data stored by any means which is capable of conversion into an image described in subsection (4).

Meaning of "private" and "sexual"

20-237c   **35.**—(1) The following apply for the purposes of section 33.

(2) A photograph or film is "private" if it shows something that is not of a kind ordinarily seen in public.

(3) A photograph or film is "sexual" if—

(a)   it shows all or part of an individual's exposed genitals or pubic area,

(b)   it shows something that a reasonable person would consider to be sexual because of its nature, or

(c)   its content, taken as a whole, is such that a reasonable person would consider it to be sexual.

(4) Subsection (5) applies in the case of —

(a)   a photograph or film that consists of or includes a photographed or filmed image that has been altered in any way,

(b)   a photograph or film that combines two or more photographed or filmed images, and

(c)   a photograph or film that combines a photographed or filmed image with something else.

(5) The photograph or film is not private and sexual if—

(a)   it does not consist of or include a photographed or filmed image that is itself private and sexual,

(b)   it is only private or sexual by virtue of the alteration or combination mentioned in subsection (4), or

(c)   it is only by virtue of the alteration or combination mentioned in subsection (4) that the person mentioned in section 33(1)(a) and (b) is shown as part of, or with, whatever makes the photograph or film private and sexual.

Sections 33 to 35 of the 2015 Act came into force on April 13, 2015 (Criminal Justice and Courts Act 2015 (Commencement No. 1, Saving and Transitional Provisions) Order 2015 (S.I. 2015 No. 778)). Schedule 8 to the 2015 Act (s.33(10)) makes special provision in connection with the operation of section 33 in relation to persons providing information society services. The provisions of Schedule 8 correspond broadly to those of the Electronic Commerce Directive (Hatred against Persons on Religious Grounds or the Grounds of Sexual Orientation) Regulations 2010 (S.I. 2010 No. 894) (as to which, see § 29-77 in the main work).

III. ANONYMITY OF VICTIMS

Sexual Offences (Amendment) Act 1992, ss.1–4

Offences to which this Act applies

★**20-258**   As from a day to be appointed, the Modern Slavery Act 2015, s.57(1), and Sched. 5, para. 4, amend section 2(1) of the 1992 Act so as: (i) after paragraph (da), to insert "(db) any offence under section 2 of the Modern Slavery Act 2015 (human trafficking);"; and (ii) in paragraph (e), to substitute "(db)" for "(da)".

IV. NOTIFICATION AND ORDERS

A. NOTIFICATION REQUIREMENTS

(3) Legislation

Sexual Offences Act 2003, ss.87–91

Method of notification and related matters

20-272   With effect from February 25, 2015, the Sexual Offences Act 2003 (Prescribed Police Stations) Regulations 2015 (S.I. 2015 No. 82) revoke and replace the Sexual Offences Act 2003 (Prescribed Police Stations) Regulations 2013 (S.I. 2013 No. 300), and prescribe the police stations listed in the schedule for the purposes of section 87(1)(a) of the 2003 Act.

Section 87: interpretation
    With effect from March 8, 2015 (Anti-social Behaviour, Crime and Policing Act 2014 (Commencement No. 8, Saving and Transitional Provisions) Order 2015 (S.I. 2015 No. 373)), section 181(1) of, and paragraphs 51 to 82 of Schedule 11 to, the 2014 Act were brought into force. ★20-273

Young offenders: parental directions
    As to the commencement of section 181(1) of, and paragraph 57 of Schedule 11 to, the Anti-social Behaviour, Crime and Policing Act 2014, see *ante*, § 20-273. ★20-274

Review of notification requirements

    As to the commencement of section 181(1) of, and paragraph 58 of Schedule 11 to, the Anti-social Behaviour, Crime and Policing Act 2014, see *ante*, § 20-273. ★20-276a

    A challenge to a decision of a magistrates' court to dismiss an appeal under section 91E of the SOA 2003 should be pursued by way of appeal by way of case stated, rather than by way of an application for judicial review: *R. (N.E.) v. Birmingham Magistrates' Court*; *R. (N.E. and N.M.) v. Birmingham Magistrates' Court and Chief Constable of West Midlands Police*, 179 J.P. 187, DC. ★

Sexual Offences Act 2003, Sched. 3

    As from a day to be appointed, the SCA 2015, s.85(1), and Sched. 4, para. 66(1) and (2), insert a new paragraph 24A into Schedule 3 to the 2003 Act, as follows— ★20-301a

    "24A. An offence under section 15A of this Act (sexual communication with a child).".

    With effect from May 3, 2015 (Serious Crime Act 2015 (Commencement No. 1) Regulations 2015 (S.I. 2015 No. 820)), the SCA 2015, s.85(1), and Sched. 4, para. 66(1) and (3), inserted a new paragraph 35C into Schedule 3 to the 2003 Act, as follows— ★20-312c

    "35C. An offence under section 69 of the Serious Crime Act 2015 (possession of paedophile manual) if the offender—
    (a) was 18 or over, or
    (b) is sentenced in respect of the offence to imprisonment for a term of at least 12 months.".

    As from a day to be appointed, the Serious Crime Act 2015, s.85(1), and Sched. 4, para. 66(1) and (4), insert a new paragraph 92Y is inserted into Schedule 3 to the 2003 Act (in identical terms to new para. 35C (as to which, see *ante*, § 20-312c)). ★20-314

B. Entry and Search of Home Address

Sexual Offences Act 2003, s.96B

Power of entry and search of relevant offender's home address
    The decision of the Divisional Court in *M. v. Chief Constable of Hampshire* (see the main work) that section 96B of the 2003 Act is compatible with the ECHR (*ibid.*, § 16-137) has been upheld: see *R. (M.) v. Chief Constable of Hampshire (Secretary of State for the Home Department intervening)*, [2015] 1 Cr.App.R. 20, CA (Civ. Div.) (where argument was confined to Art. 8). 20-321a

D. Sexual Harm Prevention Orders

    With effect from March 8, 2015 (Anti-social Behaviour, Crime and Policing Act 2014 (Commencement No. 8, Saving and Transitional Provisions) Order 2015 (S.I. 2015 No. 373)), section 113 of, and Schedule 5 to, the 2014 Act were brought into force. ★20-322a

E. Sexual Offences Prevention Orders

(1) Introduction

Replacement of sexual offences prevention orders
    As to the commencement of section 113 of, and Schedule 5 to, the Anti-social Behaviour, Crime and Policing Act 2014, see *ante*, § 20-322a. ★20-323a

Saving and transitional
    With effect from March 8, 2015 (Anti-social Behaviour, Crime and Policing Act 2014 (Com- ★20-323b

mencement No. 8, Saving and Transitional Provisions) Order 2015 (S.I. 2015 No. 373)), section 114 of the the 2014 Act was brought into force.

(2) Legislation
Sexual Offences Act 2003, ss.104, 106–110, 113

Sexual offences prevention orders: applications and grounds

20-325   *R. v. Terrell* (as to which, see the main work) was distinguished in *R. v. Cheshire* [2014] 2 Cr.App.R.(S.) 53, CA, where it was held that the dangerous offender provisions in the CJA 2003 (§§ 5-495 *et seq.* in the main work) were satisfied for offences of downloading indecent images of children. On the facts of the case, the court found that the sheer persistence and scale of the defendant's offending (convictions for sexual offences, including contact offences, stretching back over 35 years), the extreme lengths to which he was prepared to go to to hide his offending, and his failure to engage with the processes designed to help him overcome his criminality justified the conclusion that there was a serious risk that he would revert to the commission of further contact offences, given the opportunity.

SOPOs: effect

20-328   As to whether *R. v. Smith* (see the main work) can be relied on as a basis for making an application for an extension of time in which to appeal an order made prior to *Smith* and which does not comply with what was said in *Smith*, or, in the alternative, as a basis for making an application to vary such an order under section 108 of the 2003 Act (*ibid.*, § 20-329), see *R. v. Spencer (Adam Kenneth Victor)*, *post*, § 20-332.

★   For the Court of Appeal's decision upholding the decision of the Divisional Court in *R. (Richards) v. Teesside Magistrates Court and Chief Constable of Cleveland*, see *R. (Richards) v. Teesside Magistrates' Court* [2015] 1 W.L.R. 1695, CA (Civ. Div.).

SOPOs and interim SOPOs: appeals

20-332   In *R. v. Spencer (Adam Kenneth Victor)* [2014] 2 Cr.App.R.(S.) 18, CA, it was held that it was important that an application under section 108 of the 2003 Act (§ 20-329 in the main work) was supported by evidence so that, where the application was made on the papers, it would normally be appropriate for it to be supported by a witness statement. The court said that an applicant would accordingly be well advised to set out in detail what had happened since the order was originally made to justify making the application, which would most commonly be some change in the applicant's own circumstances. As had been said in *R. v. Hoath*; *R. v. Standage* (see the main work), if the applicant relied on particular and unanticipated difficulties arising from the order, they should be identified promptly and with particularity. Furthermore, the court added, the fresh guidance given in *R. v. Smith* (§ 20-328 in the main work), as to what should or should not be contained in such an order, did not provide a basis for challenging an order made before the *Smith* guidance and which did not comply with it, either by way of an out-of-time appeal against the original order or by way of an application to vary under section 108.

Other offences for purposes of Part 2

★**20-336**   As from a day to be appointed, the Modern Slavery Act 2015, s.57(1), and Sched. 5, para. 5(1) and (3), amend Schedule 5 to the SOA 2003, so as to insert a reference to an offence under section 2 of the 2015 Act (human trafficking (as to which, see *ante*, § 19-441)).

F. Foreign Travel Orders

★**20-337**   As to the commencement of sections 113 and 114 of, and Schedule 5 to, the Anti-social Behaviour, Crime and Policing Act 2014, see *ante*, §§ 20-322a, 20-323b.

G. Sexual Risk Orders

★**20-337a**   As to the commencement of section 113 of, and Schedule 5 to, the Anti-social Behaviour, Crime and Policing Act 2014, see *ante*, § 20-322a.

H. Risk of Sexual Harm Orders

★**20-338**   As to the commencement of sections 113 and 114 of, and Schedule 5 to, the Anti-social Behaviour, Crime and Policing Act 2014, see *ante*, §§ 20-322a, 20-323b.

I. Interpretation, etc. of Part 2

Sexual Offences Act 2003, ss.131–136

Part 2: general interpretation

As to the commencement of section 181(1) of, and paragraph 76 of Schedule 11 to, the Anti-social Behaviour, Crime and Policing Act 2014, see *ante*, § 20-273.

★**20-341**

J. Application of Orders

As to the commencement of section 113 of, and Schedule 5 to, the Anti-social Behaviour, Crime and Policing Act 2014, see *ante*, § 20-322a.

★**20-345**

V. CLOSURE OF PREMISES

With effect from March 8, 2015 (Anti-social Behaviour, Crime and Policing Act 2014 (Commencement No. 8, Saving and Transitional Provisions) Order 2015 (S.I. 2015 No. 373)), section 115 of, and Schedule 6 to, the 2014 Act were brought into force.

★**20-346**

With effect from May 3, 2015 (Serious Crime Act 2015 (Commencement No. 1) Regulations 2015 (S.I. 2015 No. 820)), the SCA 2015, s.85(1), and Sched. 4, paras 64 and 65, amended section 136A of the SOA 2003 so as to vary the references to sections 48, 49 and 50 of the 2003 Act in the list of "specified prostitution offences" and "specified pornography offences" to reflect the drafting changes to those sections (as to which, see *ante*, §§ 20-160, 20-161, 20-167).

★

Chapter 21

OFFENCES UNDER THE THEFT AND FRAUD ACTS

I. INTRODUCTION

Financial reporting orders and serious crime prevention orders

As to the repeal of section 76 of the SOCPA 2005, see *ante*, § 5-1212.

★**21-4b**

II. THEFT

(5) Elements of the offence of theft

(d) *"Property"*

Intangible property

For a New Zealand case in which it was held that digital files did not fall within a definition of "property" in a New Zealand statute that was similar to the definition in section 4 of the Theft Act 1968 (§ 21-48 in the main work)), see *Dixon v. The Queen* [2014] 3 N.Z.L.R. 504, New Zealand Court of Appeal ([2014] NZCA 329).

21-51

(e) *"Belonging to another"*

"Any proprietary right or interest"

Secret profits

F.H.R. European Ventures LLP v. Cedar Capital Partners LLC is now reported at [2015] A.C. 250.

★**21-69**

III. ROBBERY AND ASSAULT WITH INTENT TO ROB

A. Robbery

(2) Indictment

For a case considering whether defective particulars in an indictment alleging a conspiracy to rob rendered it a nullity, see *R. v. Clarke (Dean)*, *ante*, § 1-190.

★**21-86**

(4) Sentence

Guideline cases

21-90   The Sentencing Council for England and Wales has issued a consultation guideline on robbery. The consultation period closed on January 23, 2015.

IX. FALSE ACCOUNTING

(4) Sentence

★**21-231**   As to the repeal of section 76 of the SOCPA 2005, see *ante*, § 5-1212.

XII. BLACKMAIL

(4) Sentence

★**21-259**   As to the repeal of section 76 of the SOCPA 2005, see *ante*, § 5-1212.

XVIII. FRAUD ACT 2006

A. Fraud

(4) Sentence

Financial reporting orders

★**21-367**   As to the repeal of section 76 of the SOCPA 2005, see *ante*, § 5-1212.

(5) The elements of the offence

(b) *Fraud by false representation*

Implied representations

Withdrawal slips

★**21-379**   The correct name for the case cited as *"R. v. Harrison"* in the main work is *"R. v. Hamilton (Winston)"*.

C. Obtaining Services Dishonestly

(4) Sentence

★**21-406**   As to the repeal of section 76 of the SOCPA 2005, see *ante*, § 5-1212.

Chapter 22

FORGERY, PERSONATION AND CHEATING

I. FORGERY

A. Forgery and Counterfeiting Act 1981

(8) Custody or control of certain false instruments and manufacture, custody or control of equipment or materials with which such instruments may be made

Forgery and Counterfeiting Act 1981, s.5

Offences relating to money orders, share certificates, passports, etc.

22-31   With effect from December 16, 2014, section 5 of the 1981 Act was amended by the Marriage

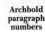
(Same Sex Couples) Act 2013 (Consequential and Contrary Provisions and Scotland) and Marriage and Civil Partnership (Scotland) Act 2014 (Consequential Provisions) Order 2014 (S.I. 2014 No. 3168), art. 2, and Sched., para. 10, so as (i) to insert ", conversions" after the words "civil partnerships" in subsection (5)(l), and (ii) to insert a new subsection (6A), as follows—

"(6A) In subsection (5)(l) above, 'conversion' means the conversion of a civil partnership into a marriage under section 9 of the Marriage (Same Sex Couples) Act 2013 and regulations made under that section.".

B. Miscellaneous Offences Akin to Forgery

(2) Identity documents

(a) *Offences*

Identity Documents Act 2010, ss.4–6

Possession of false identity documents etc. with improper intention

An application by the claimant for permission to appeal from the decision of the civil division **22-45a** of the Court of Appeal in *S.X.H. v. CPS* has been allowed: see [2015] 1 W.L.R. 559, SC.

(10) Supplying specialist printing equipment

With effect from May 26, 2015, the Specialist Printing Equipment and Materials (Offences) Act ★**22-60a** 2015, s.1, created an offence of supplying specialist printing equipment knowing that it will be used for criminal purposes, as follows—

"**1.**—(1) A person commits an offence if—
    (a) the person supplies any specialist printing equipment, and
    (b) in making the supply, the person knows that the equipment will be or is intended to be used for the purposes of criminal conduct.
  (2) 'Criminal conduct' means conduct which constitutes—
    (a) an offence under the law of England and Wales, or
    (b) an offence under the law of a country outside England and Wales which, if it took place in England and Wales, would constitute an offence in England and Wales.
  (3) An individual guilty of an offence under this section is liable on conviction on indictment to imprisonment for a term not exceeding 10 years, or to a fine, or to both.
  (4) Any other person guilty of an offence under this section is liable on conviction on indictment to a fine.
  (5) It is a defence for a person charged with an offence under this section to prove that the person's conduct was necessary for a purpose related to the prevention or detection of crime.".

Section 2 defines "specialist printing equipment" as any equipment that is designed or adapted for, or is otherwise capable of being used for, the making of "relevant documents" (s.2(1)), which include, *inter alia*, travel and identity documents, money, driving licences, debit and credit cards, and security passes or tickets to sporting or other events (s.2(2)–(5)).

CHAPTER 23

CRIMINAL DAMAGE AND KINDRED OFFENCES

II. MALICIOUS DAMAGE ACT 1861

Mode of trial and classification of offences

As to the commencement of section 85 of the LASPOA 2012 (see the main work), see *ante*, § ★**23-59** 1-125.

III. EXPLOSIVE SUBSTANCES ACT 1883

Explosive Substances Act 1883, s.2

Sentence

In *Att.-Gen.'s References (Nos 74, 75, 76, 77 and 78 of 2014) (R v. Cassidy)* [2015] 1 Cr.App.R.(S.) **23-64**

30, it was held that, given the increasing vogue nationwide for explosive attacks on banks' automated teller machines, deterrent sentences should be passed for offences contrary to sections 2 and 3 of the 1883 Act, and that it would be good practice to make sentences for such offences consecutive to those for any other offences committed at the same time (such as, on the facts of the instant case, burglary).

Explosive Substances Act 1883, s.3

Sentence

23-68   See *Att.-Gen.'s References (Nos 74, 75, 76, 77 and 78 of 2014) (R v. Cassidy)*, *ante*, § 23-64.

Explosive Substances Act 1883, s.4

Making or possession of explosive under suspicious circumstances

★23-72   As from April 13, 2015 (Criminal Justice and Courts Act 2015 (Commencement No. 1, Saving and Transitional Provisions) Order 2015 (S.I. 2015 No. 778)), section 4 of the 1883 Act is amended by the Criminal Justice and Courts Act 2015, s.1(1), so as: (i) in subsection (1), to substitute, for the words from "guilty" to the end, the words "guilty of an offence"; and (ii) to insert two new subsections (1A) and (1B), as follows—

> "(1A) A person who is guilty of an offence under subsection (1) is liable, on conviction on indictment, to imprisonment for life.
> (1B) Where a person is convicted of an offence under subsection (1) the explosive substance is to be forfeited.".

The amendments made by section 1 of the 2015 Act apply only in relation to an offence committed on or after the day on which they come into force: s.1(4). Where an offence is found to have been committed over a period of two or more days, or at some time during a period of two or more days, it must be taken for the purposes of subsection (4) to have been committed on the last of those days: s.1(5).

Sentence

23-74   As to the increase of the maximum penalty to life imprisonment as from a day to be appointed, see *ante*, § 23-72.

IV. COMPUTER MISUSE ACT 1990

A. COMPUTER MISUSE OFFENCES

Computer Misuse Act 1990, s.1

Unauthorised access to computer material

★23-87   As to an offence under section 1 of the 1990 Act becoming a specified serious offence within Schedule 1 to the SCA 2007, see *ante*, § 5-1192.

Computer Misuse Act 1990, ss.2, 3, 3A

Unauthorised access with intent to commit or facilitate commission of further offences

★23-88   As to an offence under section 2 of the 1990 Act becoming a specified serious offence within Schedule 1 to the SCA 2007, see *ante*, § 5-1192.

Unauthorised acts with intent to impair, or with recklessness as to impairing, operation of computer, etc.

★23-89   As to an offence under section 3 of the 1990 Act becoming a specified serious offence within Schedule 1 to the SCA 2007, see *ante*, § 5-1192.

★   With effect from May 3, 2015 (Serious Crime Act 2015 (Commencement No. 1) Regulations 2015 (S.I. 2015 No. 820)), a new section 3ZA was inserted into the 1990 Act (after s.3) by the SCA 2015, s.41(1) and (2), as follows—

> *"Unauthorised acts causing, or creating risk of, serious damage*
> **3ZA.**—(1) A person is guilty of an offence if—

(a) the person does any unauthorised act in relation to a computer;

(b) at the time of doing the act the person knows that it is unauthorised;

(c) the act causes, or creates a significant risk of, serious damage of a material kind; and

(d) the person intends by doing the act to cause serious damage of a material kind or is reckless as to whether such damage is caused.

(2) Damage is of a "material kind" for the purposes of this section if it is—

(a) damage to human welfare in any place;

(b) damage to the environment of any place;

(c) damage to the economy of any country; or

(d) damage to the national security of any country.

(3) For the purposes of subsection (2)(a) an act causes damage to human welfare only if it causes—

(a) loss to human life;

(b) human illness or injury;

(c) disruption of a supply of money, food, water, energy or fuel;

(d) disruption of a system of communication;

(e) disruption of facilities for transport; or

(f) disruption of services relating to health.

(4) It is immaterial for the purposes of subsection (2) whether or not an act causing damage—

(a) does so directly;

(b) is the only or main cause of the damage.

(5) In this section—

(a) a reference to doing an act includes a reference to causing an act to be done;

(b) 'act' includes a series of acts;

(c) a reference to a country includes a reference to a territory, and to any place in, or part or region of, a country or territory.

(6) A person guilty of an offence under this section is (unless subsection (7) applies) liable, on conviction on indictment, to imprisonment for a term not exceeding 14 years, or to a fine, or to both.

(7) Where an offence under this section is committed as a result of an act causing or creating a significant risk of—

(a) serious damage to human welfare of the kind mentioned in subsection (3)(a) or (3)(b), or

(b) serious damage to national security,

a person guilty of the offence is liable, on conviction on indictment, to imprisonment for life, or to a fine, or to both.".

As to an offence under section 3ZA of the 1990 Act becoming a specified serious offence within ★ Schedule 1 to the SCA 2007, see *ante*, § 5-1192.

Making, supplying or obtaining articles for use in offence under section 1 or 3

With effect from May 3, 2015 (Serious Crime Act 2015 (Commencement No. 1) Regulations ★**23-89a** 2015 (S.I. 2015 No. 820)), the heading of section 3A of the 1990 Act was amended by the SCA 2015, s.85(1), and Sched. 4, para. 8, so as to substitute, for the words "section 1 or 3", the words "section 1, 3 or 3ZA".

With effect from May 3, 2015 (Serious Crime Act 2015 (Commencement No. 1) Regulations ★ 2015 (S.I. 2015 No. 820)), section 3A of the 1990 Act was amended by the SCA 2015, ss.41(1) and (3), and 42, so as: (i) in subsections (1) to (3), to substitute, for the words "section 1 or 3", the words "section 1, 3 or 3ZA"; and (ii) in subsection (3), to substitute, for the words "article with a view to", the words—

"article—

(a) intending to use it to commit, or to assist in the commission of, an offence under section 1, 3 or 3ZA, or

(b) with a view to.".

This latter amendment is subject to section 86(5) of the 2015 Act, which provides that an of- ★ fence is not committed under section 3A(3) of the 1990 Act by virtue of the amendment made by section 42 unless every act or other event proof of which is required for conviction of the offence takes place after section 42 came into force.

As to an offence under section 3A of the 1990 Act becoming a specified serious offence within Schedule 1 to the SCA 2007, see *ante*, § 5-1192.

B. Jurisdiction

Computer Misuse Act 1990, ss.4–9

Territorial scope of offences under sections 1 to 3

★**23-90**   With effect from May 3, 2015 (Serious Crime Act 2015 (Commencement No. 1) Regulations 2015 (S.I. 2015 No. 820)), the heading of section 4 of the 1990 Act was amended by the SCA 2015, s.85(1), and Sched. 4, para. 9, so as to substitute, for the words "sections 1 to 3", the words "this Act".

★   With effect from May 3, 2015 (Serious Crime Act 2015 (Commencement No. 1) Regulations 2015 (S.I. 2015 No. 820)), section 4 of the 1990 Act was amended by the SCA 2015, s.43(1) to (3), so as: (i) in subsection (1), to substitute, for the words "section 1 or 3", the words "section 1, 3 or 3ZA"; and (ii) to insert, after subsection (4), a new subsection (4A), as follows—

"(4A) It is immaterial for the purposes of an offence under section 3A whether the accused was in the home country concerned at the time of any act or other event proof of which is required for conviction of the offence if there is a significant link with domestic jurisdiction in relation to the offence.".".

★   This latter amendment is subject to section 86(10) of the 2015 Act, which provides that the amendments made by section 43 of the 2015 Act apply only in cases where every act or other event proof of which is required for conviction of the offence in question takes place after section 43 came into force.

Significant links with domestic jurisdiction

★**23-91**   With effect from May 3, 2015 (Serious Crime Act 2015 (Commencement No. 1) Regulations 2015 (S.I. 2015 No. 820)), section 5 of the 1990 Act was amended by the SCA 2015, s.43(1), (4) and (5), so as: (i) to insert, after subsection (1), new subsections (1A) and (1B), as follows—

"(1A) In relation to an offence under section 1, 3, 3ZA or 3A, where the accused was in a country outside the United Kingdom at the time of the act constituting the offence there is a significant link with domestic jurisdiction if—
    (a) the accused was a United Kingdom national at that time; and
    (b) the act constituted an offence under the law of the country in which it occurred.
(1B) In subsection (1A)—
    'country' includes territory;
    'United Kingdom national' means an individual who is—
    (a) a British citizen, a British overseas territories citizen, a British National (Overseas) or a British Overseas citizen;
    (b) a person who under the British Nationality Act 1981 is a British subject; or
    (c) a British protected person within the meaning of that Act.";"

and (ii) to insert, after subsection (3), a new subsection (3A), as follows—

"(3A) In relation to an offence under section 3ZA, any of the following is also a significant link with domestic jurisdiction—
    (a) that the accused was in the home country concerned at the time when he did the unauthorised act (or caused it to be done);
    (b) that the unauthorised act was done in relation to a computer in the home country concerned;
    (c) that the unauthorised act caused, or created a significant risk of, serious damage of a material kind (within the meaning of that section) in the home country concerned.".".

★   These amendments are subject to section 86(10) of the 2015 Act, which provides that the amendments made by section 43 of the 2015 Act apply only in cases where every act or other event proof of which is required for conviction of the offence in question takes place after section 43 came into force.

Territorial scope of inchoate offences related to offences under sections 1 to 3

★**23-92**   With effect from May 3, 2015 (Serious Crime Act 2015 (Commencement No. 1) Regulations 2015 (S.I. 2015 No. 820)), section 6 of the 1990 Act was amended by the SCA 2015, s.85(1), and Sched. 4, para. 10, so as: (i) in the heading, to substitute, for the words "sections 1 to 3", the words "this Act"; (ii) in subsection (1), to substitute, for the words "section 1, 2 or 3 above", the words "this Act"; and (iii) in subsection (2), to substitute, for the words "section 3 above", the words "this Act".

These amendments are subject to section 86(6) of the 2015 Act, which provides that they apply,   ★
in relation to any offence of conspiracy to commit an offence under the 1990 Act or of attempting to commit such an offence, only where every act or other event proof of which is required for conviction of the conspiracy or attempt offence takes place after section 43 of the 2015 Act came into force.

British citizenship immaterial

With effect from May 3, 2015 (Serious Crime Act 2015 (Commencement No. 1) Regulations   **★23-95**
2015 (S.I. 2015 No. 820)), section 9 of the 1990 Act was amended by the SCA 2015, s.85(1), and Sched. 4, para. 11, so as: (i) in subsection (1), at the beginning, to insert the words "Except as provided by section 5(1A),"; (ii) in subsection (2)(a), to substitute, for the words "section 1, 2 or 3 above", the words "this Act "; and (iii) in subsection (2)(c), to substitute, for the words "section 3 above", the words "this Act".

C. MISCELLANEOUS AND GENERAL

Computer Misuse Act 1990, ss.10, 17

Saving for certain law enforcement powers

With effect from May 3, 2015 (Serious Crime Act 2015 (Commencement No. 1) Regulations   **★23-96**
2015 (S.I. 2015 No. 820)), the heading of section 10 of the 1990 Act was amended by the SCA 2015, s.85(1), and Sched. 4, para. 12, so as to substitute the word "Savings".

With effect from May 3, 2015 (Serious Crime Act 2015 (Commencement No. 1) Regulations   ★
2015 (S.I. 2015 No. 820)), section 10 of the 1990 Act was amended by the SCA 2015, s.44(1) and (2), so as: (i) to substitute, for the words "Section 1(1) above has", the words "Sections 1 to 3A have"; (ii) in paragraph (a), to insert, after the word "seizure", the words "or of any other enactment by virtue of which the conduct in question is authorised or required"; (iii) to substitute, for the words "the said section 1(1)", the words "any of those sections"; and (iv) to substitute, for the words "In this section 'enforcement officer' means", the following words—

"In this section—
　　'enactment' means any enactment, whenever passed or made, contained in—
　　(a) an Act of Parliament;
　　(b) an Act of the Scottish Parliament;
　　(c) a Measure or Act of the National Assembly for Wales;
　　(d) an instrument made under any such Act or Measure;
　　(e) any other subordinate legislation (within the meaning of the Interpretation Act 1978);
　　'enforcement officer' means".

CHAPTER 24

FIREARMS AND OFFENSIVE WEAPONS

I. FIREARMS

A. FIREARMS ACT 1968

(2) Offences relating to firearms certificates

Firearms Act 1968, s.1

Sentence

As to an offence under section 1(1) of the 1968 Act becoming a specified serious offence within   **★24-7**
Schedule 1 to the SCA 2007, see *ante*, § 5-1192.

Firearms Act 1968, s.2

Sentence

★**24-15**   As to an offence under section 2(1) of the 1968 Act becoming a specified serious offence within Schedule 1 to the SCA 2007, see *ante*, § 5-1192.

Firearms Act 1968, s.3

Sentence

★**24-19**   As to the repeal of section 76 of the SOCPA 2005 (see the main work), see ante, § 5-1212.

★   As to an offence under section 3(1) of the 1968 Act becoming a specified serious offence within Schedule 1 to the SCA 2007, see *ante*, § 5-1192.

(4) Prohibited weapons and ammunition

★**24-24**   For a case considering the inter-relationship of sections 1(1) and (2) (§ 24-4 in the main work) and 5(1)(aba) of the 1968 Act and section 3 of the Firearms (Amendment) Act 1997 (*ibid.*, § 24-34), see *R. v. Shahabi-Shack*, *post*, § 24-32.

Sentence

★**24-29**   As to an offence under section 5(1), (1A) or (2A) of the 1968 Act becoming a specified serious offence within Schedule 1 to the SCA 2007, see *ante*, § 5-1192.

Where an arsenal of firearms and ammunition were found in three separate stashes at the appellant's house during a search that took place on a single day, consecutive sentences which (together) exceeded the statutory maximum for possession of prohibited firearms, contrary to section 5 of the Firearms Act 1968 (§ 24-24 in the main work) were neither excessive nor wrong in principle: *R. v. Gribbin* [2014] 2 Cr.App.R.(S.) 28, CA. The court considered *Att.-Gen.'s Reference (No. 57 of 2009) (R. v. Ralphs)* (see the main work), in which it was said that it was not permissible to impose consecutive sentences for offences committed at the same time in order to evade a statutory maximum. However, it was held that since the appellant had said in interview that he had been given two lots of weaponry on separate occasions to mind, that he had been minding them for one to two years at two separate addresses, and that he had done so in exchange for money, and in the absence of any basis of plea explaining how the weaponry was acquired, the judge was fully justified in distinguishing *Ralphs* and in concluding that the appellant had played a significant role in the preservation, storage, maintenance and issuing of weapons so that they could be used by the criminal classes.

Att.-Gen.'s Reference (No. 57 of 2009) (R. v. Ralphs) (see the main work and *ante*) was followed, and *R. v. Gribbin*, *ante*, was distinguished, in *R. v. Lewis* 1 Cr.App.R.(S.) 38, where the police found weapons in different rooms of the house jointly occupied by the appellant and his co-accused; the judge, having accepted the prosecution's case that the two accused were a team and were jointly responsible for all of the weapons, was not entitled to pass consecutive sentences totalling in excess of the 10-year-maximum for possessing a single prohibited weapon; the case was indistinguishable from *Ralphs*, and differed from *Gribbin* in that there was no evidence that the weapons came into the appellant's possession on different occasions. For a suggestion that the solution in such cases may be to charge the offender under section 16 of the 1968 Act (see § 24-51 in the main work), *i.e.* possession of firearms with intent to endanger life, see the commentary at CLW/15/06/8.

Prohibited weapon

★**24-31**   In *R. v. Rhodes* [2015] Crim.L.R. 445, CA, it was held that blank firing pistols, described as "front venting multi-purpose pistols with partially blocked barrels", which would not permit the passage of a bullet but would allow irritant gases and hot burning gases fired from either a blank or a gas cartridge to pass through them, came within section 5(1)(b) of the 1968 Act; this was so even if, when originally manufactured, the pistols had been incapable of firing a gas cartridge but had only been able to do so once the manufacturers had developed a gas cartridge of the same calibre, so as to allow it to fit the pre-existing design; a pistol which has the design capability and must have the deliberate design capability of discharging gas cartridges comes within the section; if the appellant's submission were correct, a pistol specifically designed so it can discharge gas cartridges would be caught, but not one for which gas cartridges were later specifically developed so that they could be fired, even though in both instances the gun and the cartridge would be identical. For submissions to the effect that the last observation went too far, if the court really intended to rule that the lawful possession of a weapon can become unlawful overnight by dint of a manufacturer designing ammunition that could be used in the weapon, and that the case of *R. v. Law* (see the main work), partially relied upon by the court, could be distinguished, see the commentary at CLW/15/18/7.

Special exemptions from prohibition of small firearms

In *R. v. Shahabi-Shack* [2015] 1 Cr.App.R. 25, CA, the defendant's firearm certificate was varied ★**24-32** to authorise possession of a revolver for the purpose of humanely dispatching injured deer, provided that the gun was restricted to two shots. The gun as originally sold to the defendant complied with this requirement, but was then crudely altered in such a way that it could quickly and easily be made to fire more than two shots (by poking out some steel plugs). The defendant's conviction under section 5(1)(aba) of the 1968 Act was upheld. Although as sold the revolver was not prohibited, because it came within the exemption contained in section 3 of the Firearms (Amendment) Act 1997 (§ 24-34 in the main work), when subsequently altered it no longer complied with the condition in the firearms certificate and thus no longer came within the exemption, there being an important distinction to be drawn between conditions that relate to the nature and functioning of the firearm itself and to other conditions relating, for example, to the use or secure storage of the firearm; the question of whether any plug or restriction in the barrel amounted to a restriction so as to satisfy the condition of the firearms certificate was a question of fact and degree depending on all the circumstances of the case; and the jury had been entitled to conclude that the revolver as altered did not comply with the condition in the firearms certificate.

Firearms (Amendment) Act 1997, ss.2–8

Firearms used for humane killing of animals
See *R. v. Shahabi-Shack, ante,* § 24-32.   ★**24-34**

(6) Prevention of crime and preservation of public safety

(a) *Possession with intent to endanger life*

Firearms Act 1968, s.16

Sentence

Where seven offenders, during the riots in Birmingham in August, 2011, were part of a group **24-53** that broke into a public house, set fire to it, discharged 12 rounds from four different firearms in the direction of the police which did not strike anybody, and fired at least one further shot at a police helicopter, where six of them were convicted of riot, possession of a firearm with intent to endanger life and arson being reckless as to whether life was endangered (the seventh was not convicted of arson), and where two of them were additionally convicted of possession of a prohibited firearm and possession of ammunition without authority (on separate occasions), (i) the judge had been entitled to conclude that the offending was more serious than in a case of attempted murder (considering *R. v. Sheen and Sheen* (see the main work)), (ii) sentences ranging from 12 to 30 years' imprisonment were appropriate, having regard to the sentencing guidance in *R. v. Avis* (see the main work and *ibid.,* § 24-116 (as supplemented by *Sheen and Sheen*)), the Sentencing Guidelines Council's guideline on attempted murder (*post,* Appendix K-221 *et seq.*), and the aggravated seriousness of individual offences that arise out of widespread lawlessness (*R. v. Blackshaw* (§ 29-8 in the main work)), and (iii) concurrent terms were appropriate given that firearms were not used to facilitate some ulterior offending, but consituted the dominant purpose of what had been planned: *R. v. Lewis* [2014] 2 Cr.App.R.(S.) 27, CA.

Ingredients

R. v. Smith (Owen) is now reported at [2015] 1 Cr.App.R. 13.   **24-54**

(c) Use of firearms to resist arrest

Offences to which section 17(2) applies

24-59   As from March 20, 2015 (Criminal Justice and Courts Act 2015 (Commencement No. 1, Saving and Transitional Provisions) Order 2015 (S.I. 2015 No. 778)), Schedule 1 to the Firearms Act 1968 (see the main work) is amended by the Criminal Justice and Courts Act 2015, s.39, and Sched. 10, para. 30, so as to insert a new paragraph 6A, referring to an offence under paragraph 14 or 24 of Schedule 10 to the 2015 Act (assaulting a secure college custody officer).

Indicting and sentencing practice

24-64   *R. v. Guy, R. v. Eubank*, and *R. v. Murphy* (as to all of which, see the main work) were referred to in *R. v. Yusuf* [2015] 1 Cr.App.R.(S.) 4, CA, in which the proposition for which they are authority (where there is a dispute as to the use of a firearm in the course of a robbery, there should be a separate count under the Firearms Act 1968), was extended to the situation where there was never any dispute about the presence and use of a firearm in the course of a robbery, but where one defendant fell to be sentenced only for conspiracy to rob (on his plea of guilty), but had consistently denied that he knew that his co-conspirators had a firearm with them. His three co-defendants had been convicted of murder as a result of the use of the firearm in the course of the robbery, but he had been acquitted. It was held that it had not been open to the judge to sentence him for the conspiracy to rob on the basis that he must have known of the presence of the firearm in the car as the four of them drove to the scene of the robbery. By doing so, the judge was effectively convicting him of an offence under at least section 17(2) of the 1968 Act (§ 24-58 in the main work). There could and should have been a count under that provision, if he was to be sentenced on that basis.

(g) Possession of firearms by persons previously convicted of crime

Firearms Act 1968, s.21

24-80   With effect from September 19, 2014, section 21(6) of the 1968 Act is amended by the Antisocial Behaviour, Crime and Policing Act 2014 (Consequential Amendments) Order 2014 (S.I. 2014 No. 2522) so as to insert, "(2C), " before "(3)".

D. Firearms (Amendment) Act 1997

(3) Regulation of firearms and ammunition

Firearms (Amendment) Act 1997, ss.32–36

★24-162   With effect from April 16, 2015, section 39 of the 1997 Act (summarised in the main work) is amended by the Firearms Regulations 2015 (S.I. 2015 No. 860). The register created by section 39 is now described as computerised.

II. OFFENSIVE WEAPONS, BLADED ARTICLES, KNIVES

A. Having An Offensive Weapon In Public Place

(1) Statute

Prevention of Crime Act 1953, s.1

24-165   As from a day to be appointed, section 1 of the 1953 Act is amended by the Criminal Justice and Courts Act 2015, s.28(1) and (2), so as to insert, after subsection (2), new subsections (2A) to (2G), as follows—

"(2A) Subsection (2B) applies where—
    (a) a person is convicted of an offence under subsection (1) committed after this subsection is commenced, and
    (b) when the offence was committed, the person was aged 16 or over and had at least one relevant conviction (see section 1ZA).
(2B) Where this subsection applies, the court must impose an appropriate custodial sentence (with or without a fine) unless the court is of the opinion that there are particular circumstances which—

(a) relate to the offence, to the previous offence or to the offender, and

(b) would make it unjust to do so in all the circumstances.

(2C) In this section 'appropriate custodial sentence' means—

(a) in the case of a person who is aged 18 or over when convicted, a sentence of imprisonment for a term of at least 6 months;

(b) in the case of a person who is aged at least 16 but under 18 when convicted, a detention and training order of at least 4 months.

(2D) In considering whether it is of the opinion mentioned in subsection (2B) in the case of a person aged 16 or 17, the court must have regard to its duty under section 44 of the Children and Young Persons Act 1933 (general considerations).

(2E) Where—

(a) an appropriate custodial sentence has been imposed on a person under subsection (2B), and

(b) a relevant conviction without which subsection (2B) would not have applied has been subsequently set aside on appeal,

notice of appeal against the sentence may be given at any time within 28 days from the date on which the conviction was set aside (despite anything in section 18 of the Criminal Appeal Act 1968 (initiating procedure)).

(2F) Where an offence is found to have been committed over a period of two or more days, or at some time during a period of two or more days, it shall be taken for the purposes of this section to have been committed on the last of those days.

(2G) In relation to times before the coming into force of paragraph 180 of Schedule 7 to the Criminal Justice and Court Services Act 2000, the reference in subsection (2C)(a) to a sentence of imprisonment, in relation to an offender aged under 21 at the time of conviction, is to be read as a reference to a sentence of detention in a young offender institution.".

As from a day to be appointed, the 1953 Act is amended by the Criminal Justice and Courts Act **24-165a** 2015, s.28(1) and (3), so as to insert a new section 1ZA.

Prevention of Crime Act 1953, s.1ZA

Offence under section 1: previous relevant convictions

1ZA.—(1) For the purposes of section 1, "relevant conviction" means—

(a) a conviction for an offence under—

(i) section 1 or 1A of this Act, or

(ii) section 139, 139A or 139AA of the Criminal Justice Act 1988,

(a "relevant offence"), whenever committed,

(b) a conviction in Scotland, Northern Ireland or a member State other than the United Kingdom for a civilian offence, whenever committed, which would have constituted a relevant offence if committed in England and Wales at the time of that conviction,

(c) a conviction for an offence under section 42 of the Armed Forces Act 2006, whenever committed, in respect of which the corresponding offence under the law of England and Wales (within the meaning of that section) is a relevant offence,

(d) a conviction for an offence under section 70 of the Army Act 1955 , section 70 of the Air Force Act 1955 or section 42 of the Naval Discipline Act 1957, whenever committed, in respect of which the corresponding civil offence (within the meaning of the Act in question) is a relevant offence, and

(e) a conviction for a member State service offence, whenever committed, which would have constituted a relevant offence if committed in England and Wales at the time of conviction.

(2) In this section—

"civilian offence" means an offence other than—

(a) an offence under an enactment mentioned in subsection (1)(c) or (d), or

(b) a member State service offence;

"conviction" includes—

(a) in relation to an offence under section 42 of the Armed Forces Act 2006, anything which by virtue of section 376(1) and (2) of that Act is to be treated as a conviction and

(b) in relation to an offence under section 42 of the Naval Discipline Act 1957 and a member State service offence, a finding of guilt in respect of the person;

"member State service offence" means an offence which was the subject of proceedings under the law of a member state, other than the United Kingdom, governing all or any of the naval, military or air forces of that state.

(3) For the purposes of subsection (1)(c) and (d), where the offence was committed by aiding, abetting, counselling or procuring, it must be assumed that the act aided, abetted, counselled or procured was done in England and Wales.

(4) Sentence

24-168   *R. v. Gomes-Monteiro* is now reported at [2014] 2 Cr.App.R.(S.) 62, *sub nom. R. v. Gomes Monteiro.*

C. HAVING ARTICLE WITH BLADE OR POINT IN PUBLIC PLACE

Criminal Justice Act 1988, s.139

24-195   As from a day to be appointed, section 139 of the 1988 Act is amended by the Criminal Justice and Courts Act 2015, s.28(4) and (5), so as to insert, after subsection (6), new subsections (6A) to (6G), as follows—

> "(6A) Subsection (6B) applies where—
>> (a) a person is convicted of an offence under subsection (1) by a court in England and Wales,
>> (b) the offence was committed after this subsection is commenced, and
>> (c) when the offence was committed, the person was aged 16 or over and had at least one relevant conviction (see section 139AZA).
>
> (6B)–(6G) [*Identical to the Prevention of Crime Act 1953, s.1(2B)–(2G), ante, § 24-165, save that references to subss. (2B) and (2C) in s.1 of the 1953 Act are references to subss. (6B) and (6C) in s.139 of the 1988 Act.*]".

As to what constitutes a "relevant conviction", see *post*, § 24-199a.

D. HAVING ARTICLE WITH BLADE OR POINT OR OFFENSIVE WEAPON ON SCHOOL PREMISES

Criminal Justice Act 1988, s.139A

24-199   As from a day to be appointed, section 139A of the 1988 Act is amended by the Criminal Justice and Courts Act 2015, s.28(4) and (6), so as to insert, after subsection (5), new subsections (5A) to (5G), as follows—

> "(5A) Subsection (5B) applies where—
>> (a) a person is convicted of an offence under subsection (1) or (2) by a court in England and Wales,
>> (b) the offence was committed after this subsection is commenced, and
>> (c) when the offence was committed, the person was aged 16 or over and had at least one relevant conviction (see section 139AZA).
>
> (5B)–(5G) [*Identical to the Prevention of Crime Act 1953, s.1(2B)–(2G), ante, § 24-165, save that references to subss. (2B) and (2C) in s.1 of the 1953 Act are references to subss. (5B) and (5C) in s.139A of the 1988 Act.*]".

As to what constitutes a "relevant conviction", see *post*, § 24-199a.

Criminal Justice Act 1988, s.139AZA

24-199a   As from a day to be appointed, the 1988 Act is amended by the Criminal Justice and Courts Act 2015, s.28(4) and (7), so as to insert a new section 139AZA, in almost identical terms to section 1ZA of the 1953 Act, *ante*, § 24-165a (the only differences being minor changes in the wording of subs. (1)).

CHAPTER 25

OFFENCES AGAINST THE CROWN AND GOVERNMENT

III. TERRORISM

A. TERRORISM ACT 2000

Terrorism Act 2000, s.1

Terrorism: interpretation

25-13   *R. v. Gul (Mohammed)* is now reported at [2014] A.C. 1260.

Terrorism Act 2000, ss.15–23B

With effect from February 12, 2015, a new section 17A was inserted into the Terrorism Act 2000 by the Counter-Terrorism and Security Act 2015, s.42(1).

Insurance against payments made in response to terrorist demands

17A.—(1) The insurer under an insurance contract commits an offence if—

    (a) the insurer makes a payment under the contract, or purportedly under it,

    (b) the payment is made in respect of any money or other property that has been, or is to be, handed over in response to a demand made wholly or partly for the purposes of terrorism, and

    (c) the insurer or the person authorising the payment on the insurer's behalf knows or has reasonable cause to suspect that the money or other property has been, or is to be, handed over in response to such a demand.

(2) If an offence under this section committed by a body corporate is proved to have been committed with the consent or connivance of, or to be attributable to any neglect on the part of—

    (a) a director, manager, secretary or other similar officer of the body corporate, or

    (b) any person who was purporting to act in any such capacity,

that person, as well as the body corporate, is guilty of the offence and liable to be proceeded against and punished accordingly.

(3) The reference in subsection (2) to a director, in relation to a body corporate whose affairs are managed by its members, is a reference to a member of the body corporate.

(4) If an offence under this section is committed by a Scottish partnership and is proved to have been committed with the consent or connivance of, or to be attributable to any neglect on the part of—

    (a) a partner, or

    (b) any person who was purporting to act in that capacity,

that person, as well as the partnership, is guilty of the offence and liable to be proceeded against and punished accordingly.

(5) In this section "insurance contract" means a contract under which one party accepts significant insurance risk from another party ("the policyholder") by agreeing to compensate the policyholder if a specified uncertain future event adversely affects the policyholder.

Section 17A applies to any payment made by an insurer on or after February 12, 2015, even if made (a) under (or purportedly under) a contract entered into before that day, or (b) (subject to subsection (4)) in respect of money or other property handed over before that day: 2015 Act, s.42(3). It does not apply to a payment made in respect of money or other property handed over before November 27, 2014: 2015 Act, s.42(4).

Money laundering

As to the repeal of section 76 of the SOCPA 2005, see *ante*, § 5-1212.   ★**25-24**

Disclosure of information: duty

With effect from January 1, 2016, Schedule 3A to the 2000 Act is further amended by the   ★**25-26** Solvency 2 Regulations 2015 (S.I. 2015 No. 575).

Forfeiture: terrorist property offences

With effect from February 12, 2015, section 23 of the Terrorism Act 2000 was amended by the   **25-42** Counter-Terrorism and Security Act 2015, s.42(2), so as to insert a new subsection (5A), as follows—

"(5A) Where a person is convicted of an offence under section 17A the court may order the forfeiture of the amount paid under, or purportedly under, the insurance contract.".

Terrorism Act 2000, ss.54–58

Weapons training

As from April 13, 2015 (Criminal Justice and Courts Act 2015 (Commencement No. 1, Saving   ★**25-63** and Transitional Provisions) Order 2015 (S.I. 2015 No. 778)), the Criminal Justice and Courts Act 2015, s.1(2), amended section 54(6)(a) of the 2000 Act, so as to substitute the words "imprisonment for life" for the words "imprisonment for a term not exceeding ten years". The amendment applies only in relation to an offence committed on or after the day on which it came into force (s.1(4)). Where an offence is found to have been committed over a period of two or more days, or at some point during a period of two or more days, it must be taken for the purposes of subsection (4) to have been committed on the last of those days (s.1(5)).

Directing terrorist organisation

★**25-65**   As to the repeal of section 76 of the SOCPA 2005, see *ante*, § 5-1212.

Terrorism Act 2000, Sched. 2

25-91   With effect from November 28, 2014, "Ansar al-Sharia-Benghazi (Partisans of Islamic Law)", "Ajnad Misr (Soldiers of Egypt)" and "Jaysh al Khalifatu Islamiya (Army of the Islamic Caliphate) (Majahideen of the Caucasus and the Levant)" were added to the list of proscribed organisations in Schedule 2 to the 2000 Act: Terrorism Act 2000 (Proscribed Organisations) (Amendment) (No. 3) Order 2014 (S.I. 2014 No. 3189).

With effect from January 23, 2015, "Jund Al-Aqsa (Soldiers of Al-Aqsa)" and "Jund al Khalifa-Algeria (Soldiers of the Caliphate in Algeria)" were added to the list of proscribed organisations in Schedule 2 to the 2000 Act: Terrorism Act 2000 (Proscribed Organisations) (Amendment) Order 2015 (S.I. 2015 No. 55).

★   With effect from March 27, 2015, "Jamaat ul-Ahrar" and "The Haqqani Network" were added to the list of proscribed organisations in Schedule 2 to the 2000 Act: Terrorism Act 2000 (Proscribed Organisations) (Amendment) (No. 2) Order 2015 (S.I. 2015 No. 959).

Terrorism Act 2000, Sched. 4

Proceedings for an offence: timing

★**25-96**   As from April 13, 2015 (Criminal Justice and Courts Act 2015 (Commencement No. 1, Saving and Transitional Provisions) Order 2015 (S.I. 2015 No. 778)), the Criminal Justice and Courts Act 2015, s.50, and Sched. 11, para. 17, amended paragraph 11 of Schedule 4 to the 2000 Act.

Enforcement of orders made elsewhere

25-97   With effect from December 3, 2014 (Crime (International Co-operation) Act 2003 (Commencement No. 6) Order 2014 (S.I. 2014 No. 3192)), section 90 of, and paragraph 3 of Schedule 4 to, the 2003 Act (see the main work) were brought into force.

Terrorism Act 2000, Sched. 5

★**25-111**   With effect from May 26, 2015 (Deregulation Act 2015 (Commencement No. 1 and Transitional and Saving Provisions) Order 2015 (S.I. 2015 No. 994)), paragraph 11 of Schedule 5 to the 2000 Act was amended by the 2015 Act, s.82(4), so as to insert a new sub-paragraph (5), as follows—

> "(5) Criminal Procedure Rules may make provision about proceedings relating to a warrant under this paragraph.".

Terrorism Act 2000, Sched. 7

Searches

25-125   With effect from February 12, 2015, paragraph 9 of Schedule 7 to the 2000 Act was amended by the Counter-Terrorism and Security Act 2015, s.43, and Sched. 8, para. 1, so as to insert new paragraphs (2A) to (2E), and to substitute paragraphs (3) and (4), as follows—

> "(2A) The reference in sub-paragraph (2)(a) to goods which are about to leave Great Britain or Northern Ireland on a ship includes goods which—
>> (a) are held at premises operated by a sea cargo agent, and
>> (b) are to be delivered to a place in Great Britain or Northern Ireland for carriage on a ship.
> (2B) The reference in sub-paragraph (2)(b) to goods which are about to leave any place in Great Britain or Northern Ireland on an aircraft includes goods which—
>> (a) are held at premises operated by an air cargo agent, and
>> (b) are to be delivered to a place in Great Britain or Northern Ireland for carriage on an aircraft.
> (2C) An examination under this paragraph may be carried out only—

    (a) at a port;
    (b) at premises operated by a sea cargo agent or an air cargo agent;
    (c) at a transit shed;
    (d) at a location designated by the Secretary of State under sub-paragraph (2D) (a 'designated examination location').
    (2D) The Secretary of State may designate a location for the purposes of sub-paragraph (2C)(d) only if the Secretary of State reasonably believes that it is necessary to designate that location in order for examining officers to be able to exercise their functions under this paragraph.
    (2E) The Secretary of State must maintain and publish a list of designated examination locations.
    (3) In this paragraph—
    (a) 'air cargo agent' has the meaning given by section 21F(1) of the Aviation Security Act 1982;
    (b) 'goods' includes property of any description, and containers;
    (c) 'sea cargo agent' has the meaning given by section 41(1) of the Aviation and Maritime Security Act 1990;
    (d) 'transit shed' has the meaning given by section 25A of the Customs and Excise Management Act 1979.
    (4) For the purposes of determining whether to carry out an examination under this paragraph an examining officer may—
    (a) board a ship or aircraft;
    (b) enter a vehicle;
    (c) enter premises operated by a sea cargo agent or an air cargo agent;
    (d) enter a transit shed;
    (e) enter a designated examination location.".

Possession of passenger information

    With effect from February 12, 2015, paragraph 17(6) of Schedule 7 to the 2000 Act was amended by the Counter-Terrorism and Security Act 2015, s.25, and Sched. 5, para. 4, so as to substitute ", 27B or 27BA" for "or 27B. **25-130**

Terrorism Act 2000, Sched. 8

    For subsequent proceedings in the European Court of Human Rights in *R. v. Ibrahim* (see the main work) in which it was held that there had been no violation of the defendants' rights under Article 6(1) and (3) of the ECHR (*ibid.*, § 16-72) where statements made in interviews at a time when they were being denied access to legal advice (pursuant to Sched. 8, para. 8, to the 2000 Act (*ibid.*, § 25-138)) were admitted at trial, and where the wrong caution was given on some occasions, see *Ibrahim v. U.K.*, *The Times*, February 2, 2015, ECtHR. **25-139**

Terrorism Act 2000, Sched. 14

    With effect from March 25, 2015, the Terrorism Act 2000 (Code of Practice for Examining Officers and Review Officers) Order 2015 (S.I. 2015 No. 906) brought into operation a revised code of practice issued under the 2000 Act, Sched. 14, para. 6(1) and (4), to replace the code of practice referred to in the main work. The new code takes account of the amendment of paragraph 9 of Schedule 7 to the 2000 Act (as to which, see *ante*, § 25-125), and of other relevant enactments, by the Counter-Terrorism and Security Act 2015. These amendments make provision for the locations where the power to examine goods under Schedule 7, para. 9, may be exercised, and clarify that the power may be exercised in respect of postal items. ★**25-167**

C. Terrorism Act 2006

(2) Preparation of terrorist acts and training
Terrorism Act 2006, ss.5–8

Preparation of terrorist acts

    As to the commission of an offence under section 5 of the 2006 Act abroad, see *post*, § 25-205. ★**25-191**

Training for terrorism

    As from April 13, 2015 (Criminal Justice and Courts Act 2015 (Commencement No. 1, Saving and Transitional Provisions) Order 2015 (S.I. 2015 No. 778)), the Criminal Justice and Courts Act 2015, s.1(3), amended section 6(5)(a) of the 2006 Act, so as to substitute the words "imprisonment **25-193** for life" for the words "imprisonment for a term not exceeding 10 years". The amendment applies only in relation to an offence committed on or after the day on which it comes into force (s.1(4)). Where an offence is found to have been committed over a period of two or more days, or at some point during a period of two or more days, it must be taken for the purposes of subsection (4) to have been committed on the last of those days (s.1(5)).

★   As to the commission of an offence under section 6 of the 2006 Act abroad, see *post*, § 25-205.

(4) Jurisdiction, procedure, etc.
Terrorism Act 2006, ss.17–19

Commission of offences abroad

★25-205   With effect from March 3, 2015, section 17(2)(b) of the 2006 Act was amended by the SCA 2015, s.81, so as to insert the words "section 5 or 6 or" after the words "an offence under". Section 86(10) of the 2015 Act provides that this amendment applies only in cases where every act or other event proof of which is required for conviction of the offence in question takes place after the amendment came into force.

★   With effect from the same date, section 17 was further amended by the 2015 Act, s.85(1), and Sched. 4, para. 74, so as to omit "or 6" and ", instruction or training" from subsection (2)(a).

I. AVIATION SECURITY ACT 1982

(1) Introduction

25-244   With effect from February 12, 2015, Part II of the 1982 Act was extensively amended by the Counter-Terrorism and Security Act 2015, s.25, and Sched. 5.

(3) Miscellaneous and general
Aviation Security Act 1982, ss.37, 38

Interpretation, etc.

25-254   With effect from February 12, 2015, section 38(1) of the 1982 Act was amended by the Counter-Terrorism and Security Act 2015, s.25, and Sched. 5, para. 9(6), so as to substitute the words "a flight any part of which is" for the words from "flights" to "aerodromes" in paragraph (b) of the definition of "aircraft registered or operating in the United Kingdom".

★25-255   As to the commencement of section 85(1), (2) and (4) of the LASPOA 2012, see *ante*, § 1-125.

J. AVIATION AND MARITIME SECURITY ACT 1990

(1) Introduction

25-257   As from a day to be appointed, sections 19, 21, 26 and 45 of the 1990 Act are amended by the Counter-Terrorism and Security Act 2015, s.25, and Sched. 5, para. 12.

IV. IMMIGRATION

25-280   With effect from February 12, 2015, section 27 of the Immigration Act 1971 was amended by the Counter-Terrorism and Security Act 2015, s.25, and Sched. 5, para. 2.

Immigration and Asylum Act 1999, s.31

Defences based on Article 31(1) of the Refugee Convention

25-285   An application by the claimant for permission to appeal from the decision of the civil division of the Court of Appeal in *S.X.H. v. CPS* has been allowed: see [2015] 1 W.L.R. 559, SC.

Immigration Act 1971, ss.25–25C

Assisting unlawful immigration to member state

★25-286   For a further case considering the ambit of section 25 of the 1971 Act, see *R. v. Ali (Nazakat)*, *post*, § 25-291.

Forfeiture of vehicle, ship or aircraft

As from a day to be appointed, section 25C of the 1971 Act is amended by the Modern Slavery ★**25-289**
Act 2015, s.57(1), and Sched. 5, para. 2, so as to substitute, for the words, in subsections (9)(b),
(10)(b) and (11), from "a passenger" to the end, the words "the victim of conduct which constitutes
an offence under section 2 of the Modern Slavery Act 2015 (human trafficking)".

As to the repeal of section 76 of the SOCPA 2005, see *ante*, § 5-1212. ★**25-290**

R. v. Bina is now reported at [2014] 2 Cr.App.R. 30.

On a prosecution under section 25(1) of the 1971 Act (§ 25-286 in the main work), it is not ★**25-291**
necessary to prove that any actual breach of immigration law occurred; and the word "facilitates"
in section 25 requires no elaboration as to its meaning by the judge in summing up: *R. v. Ali
(Nazakat)* [2015] 1 Cr.App.R. 32, CA (considering, *inter alia, R. v. Javaherifard and Miller* (as to
which, see the main work)). For critical consideration of the court's conclusion on the first point,
see CLW/15/19/2.

Asylum and Immigration (Treatment of Claimants, etc.) Act 2004, ss.4, 5(3), (4)

Trafficking people for exploitation

As from a day to be appointed, section 4 of the 2004 Act is repealed by the Modern Slavery Act ★**25-292a**
2015, s.57(1), and Sched. 5, para. 6(1) and (2).

As from a day to be appointed, section 5(3) and (4) of the 2004 Act are repealed by the Modern ★**25-292b**
Slavery Act 2015, s.57(1), and Sched. 5, para. 6(1) and (3).

VI. COINAGE OFFENCES

G. PENALTIES, PROCEDURE, ETC., UNDER PART II

Forgery and Counterfeiting Act 1981, s.22

Penalties for offences under Part II

As to the repeal of section 76 of the SOCPA 2005, see *ante*, § 5-1212. ★**25-316**

XI. OFFENCES RELATING TO POSTS AND TELECOMMUNICATIONS

C. REGULATION OF INVESTIGATORY POWERS ACT 2000

Introduction

With effect from March 3, 2015, section 71 of the 2000 Act was amended by the SCA 2015, s.83 ★**25-384**
(in relation, in particular, to powers and duties under Pt I of the Act and the public interest in
protecting the confidentiality of journalistic sources). There is transitional provision (s.86(12)).

A minor consequential amendment to section 71(8) effected by the 2015 Act, s.85(1), and ★
Sched. 4, para. 18, was brought into force on May 3, 2015 (Serious Crime Act 2015 (Commencement No. 1) Regulations 2015 (S.I. 2015 No. 820)).

With effect from April 13, 2015 (Data Retention and Investigatory Powers Act 2014 (Com- ★
mencement) Order 2015 (S.I. 2015 No. 929)), section 1(6) of the 2014 Act was brought into force.

Codes of practice

With effect from March 25, 2015, the Regulation of Investigatory Powers (Acquisition and ★**25-385**
Disclosure of Communications Data: Code of Practice) Order 2015 (S.I. 2015 No. 927) brought
into force a revised code of practice relating to the acquisition and disclosure of communications
data under Chapter II of Part I of the 2000 Act.

With effect from the same date, the Retention of Communications Data (Code of Practice) ★
Order 2015 (S.I. 2015 No. 926) brought into force a code of practice prepared under the 2000
Act, s.71 (as modified by the Data Retention Regulations 2014 (S.I. 2014 No. 2042) (as to which,
see § 25-384 in the main work)) on the retention of communications data.

Regulation of Investigatory Powers Act 2000, ss.1–5

Lawful interception without an interception warrant

With effect from February 12, 2015, section 3 of the 2000 Act was amended by the Counter- **25-388**

Terrorism and Security Act 2015, s.43, and Sched. 8, para. 2, so as to insert a new subsection (3B), as follows—

"(3B) Conduct consisting in the interception of a communication in the course of its transmission by means of a public postal service is authorised by this section if it is conduct under paragraph 9 of Schedule 7 to the Terrorism Act 2000 (port and border controls).".

Regulation of Investigatory Powers Act 2000, ss.15–19

Exceptions to section 17

25-396
With effect from February 12, 2015, section 18 of the 2000 Act was amended by the Counter-Terrorism and Security Act 2015, s.15(3), so as (i) to insert a new paragraph (de) in subsection (1), as follows—

"(de) any TEO proceedings (within the meaning given by paragraph 1 of Schedule 3 to the Counter-Terrorism and Security Act 2015 (temporary exclusion orders: proceedings)) or any proceedings arising out of such proceedings;";

and (ii) to insert a new paragraph (zd) in subsection (2), as follows—

"(zd) in the case of proceedings falling within paragraph (de), to—
(i) a person, other than the Secretary of State, who is or was a party to the proceedings, or
(ii) any person who for the purposes of the proceedings (but otherwise than by virtue of appointment as a special advocate under Schedule 3 to the Counter-Terrorism and Security Act 2015) represents a person falling within sub-paragraph (i);".

Regulation of Investigatory Powers Act 2000, ss.21–23B

Obtaining and disclosing communications data

25-400
For the case that prompted the United Kingdom to enact the Data Retention and Investigatory Powers Act 2014 (see the main work), see *Digital Rights Ireland Ltd v. Minister for Communications, Marine and Natural Resources (Irish Human Rights Commission intervening); Proceedings brought by Kärtner Landesregierung (Joined cases C-293/12 and C-594/12)* [2015] Q.B. 127, ECJ.

With effect from February 12, 2015, the Regulation of Investigatory Powers (Communications Data) (Amendment) Order 2015 (S.I. 2015 No. 228) further amends the Regulation of Investigatory Powers (Communications Data) Order 2010 (S.I. 2010 No. 480) (see the main work, and see § 25-402 in the main work for previous amending measures) so as, *inter alia*, to add a further purpose for which communications data may be acquired (in addition to those already specified in the principal order, and in s.22(2) of the 2000 Act).

Regulation of Investigatory Powers Act 2000, s.25

Interpretation of Part II

25-402
With effect from February 12, 2015, the Regulation of Investigatory Powers (Communications Data) (Amendment) Order 2015 (S.I. 2015 No. 228) further amends the Regulation of Investigatory Powers (Communications Data) Order 2010 (S.I. 2010 No. 480).

XII. MISCONDUCT IN JUDICIAL OR PUBLIC OFFICE

Misfeasance

★**25-403**
In *R. v. A.B.C., E.F.G. and I.J.K.; R. v. Sabey* [2015] 4 *Archbold Review* 2, CA, it was held that, whereas the four elements of the offence of misconduct in public office are (a) a public officer acting as such, (b) wilfully neglecting to perform his duty and/ or wilfully misconducting himself, (c) to such a degree as to amount to an abuse of the public's trust in him, (d) without reasonable excuse or justification, no exact form of words was necessary to direct the jury as to what is required by (c), but any direction must take into account the misconduct's context; where the context was information being supplied to the media by holders of public office, it was necessary, first, to make clear that a simple breach of duty or trust *vis-à-vis* their employers or superiors was insufficient, and, secondly, it was necessary to explain to the jury how they should approach the

question whether the misconduct was sufficiently serious as to amount to an abuse of the public's trust for this purpose; as to the latter point, in the context in question, the jury should be told to consider objectively whether the provision by the office holder of information to the media in deliberate breach of his duty had the effect of harming the public interest; if not, then no offence is committed; (ii) in the case of a non-office holder defendant (A) who was charged with aiding and abetting the offence of the office holder (P), the judge had correctly directed the jury that what had to be proved was (a) that A encouraged and assisted, and intended to encourage and assist P in providing information, (b) that when A received the information from P, he knew that P's actions amounted to wilful misconduct by him, and (c) that, in the circumstances of which A was aware, P's misconduct was so serious as to amount to an abuse of the public's trust in P as the holder of a public office and for which P had no reasonable excuse or justification; it was not necessary for A to have actual knowledge that the misconduct was or would be so serious that it amounted to criminal misconduct within (i), *ante* (considering *Johnson v. Youden* (as to which, see § 17-69 in the main work)); (iii) in the case of a non-office holder defendant (C) who was charged with conspiring with the office holder (P) to commit the offence, the judge had correctly directed the jury that what had to be proved was (a) that C agreed with P and that P provided information for payment for inclusion in a newspaper, intending that he would do so, (b) that C knew, when he did so, that P was a public official, (c) that, when he did so, C knew that P's selling the information to newspapers amounted to wilful misconduct by him, and (d) that, in the circumstances of which C was aware, P's misconduct was so serious as to amount to an abuse of the public's trust in him as the holder of public office and for which P had no reasonable excuse or justification; it was not necessary for C to have intended or known that P's conduct would meet the requisite threshold; whether the misconduct reaches the threshold of seriousness is not a "fact or circumstance" necessary for the commission of the offence (knowledge of which would have to be proved against an alleged conspirator: s.1(2) of the CLA 1977 (§ 33-2 in the main work)); rather, it is an evaluative exercise to be conducted by the jury (considering *R. v. Saik* (as to which, see § 33-4 in the main work)).

Statutory offences of bribery

See section 26 of the Criminal Justice and Courts Act 2015, *post*, § 31-200. **25-407**

XIII. REVENUE AND CUSTOMS OFFENCES
A. CHEATING THE PUBLIC REVENUE

Indictment

As to the repeal of section 76 of the SOCPA 2005, see *ante*, § 5-1212. ★**25-410**

B. CUSTOMS AND EXCISE MANAGEMENT ACT 1979

(1) Introduction

The functions and powers of the Commissioners and officers of Her Majesty's Revenue and Customs

Section 63 of the Policing and Crime Act 2009 came into force on June 1, 2015 (save to a ★**25-411** limited extent relevant only to Northern Ireland): Policing and Crime Act 2009 (Commencement No. 10, Transitional Provision and Savings) Order 2015 (S.I. 2015 No. 983).

(4) Illegal importation
Customs and Excise Management Act 1979, s.50

Penalty for improper importation of goods

With effect from March 12, 2015, section 50 of the 1979 Act was amended by the Legal Aid, ★**25-430** Sentencing and Punishment of Offenders Act 2012 (Fines on Summary Conviction) Regulations 2015 (S.I. 2015 No. 664), so as to substitute "£20,000" as the maximum fine for "the prescribed sum" in subsection (4)(a), and for "the statutory maximum" in subsection (5B)(a).

★**25-431**   As to the repeal of section 76 of the SOCPA 2005, see *ante*, § 5-1212.

(5) Illegal exportation
Customs and Excise Management Act 1979, s.68

Offences in relation to exportation of prohibited or restricted goods

★**25-435**   With effect from March 12, 2015, section 68 of the 1979 Act was amended by the Legal Aid, Sentencing and Punishment of Offenders Act 2012 (Fines on Summary Conviction) Regulations 2015 (S.I. 2015 No. 664), so as to substitute "£20,000" for "the prescribed sum" in subsection (3)(a).

★**25-436**   As to the repeal of section 76 of the SOCPA 2005, see *ante*, § 5-1212.

★   As to an offence under section 68 of the 1979 Act, if committed in connection with a firearm or ammunition, becoming a specified serious offence within Schedule 1 to the SCA 2007, see *ante*, § 5-1212.

With effect from November 29, 2014, the Export Control (Russia, Crimea and Sevastopol Sanctions) Order 2014 (S.I. 2014 No. 2357) (see the main work) was amended by the Export Control (Russia, Crimea and Sevastopol Sanctions) (Amendment) Order 2014 (S.I. 2014 No. 2932) so as to provide for the enforcement of certain new trade restrictions against Russia specified in Council Regulation (EU) No. 960/2014, which amends Council Regulation (EU) No. 833/2014 concerning restrictive measures in view of Russia's actions in Ukraine. The effect was to include a reference to article 2a(1) of the latter regulation in the list of prohibitions on exportation, breach of which attracts enhanced penalties.

With effect from February 24, 2015, the Export Control (Various Amendments) Order 2015 (S.I. 2015 No. 97) further amended, *inter alia*, the Export Control (Syria Sanctions) Order 2013 (S.I. 2013 No. 2012) (see the main work) and S.I. 2014 No. 2357 (see the main work and *ante*). In S.I. 2013 No. 2012, the effect was to add to the list of specified articles of Council Regulation (EU) No. 36/2012, contravention of which attracts an increased penalty in the case of an offence contrary to section 68 of the 1979 Act. In S.I. 2014 No. 2357, the effect was to substitute a reference to Article 2b(1) of Council Regulation (EU) No. 825/2014 for the reference to Article 2(c).

(8) Powers of arrest
Customs and Excise Management Act 1970, s.138

Provisions as to arrest of persons

★**25-442**   With effect from April 16, 2015, Schedule 3 to both the Channel Tunnel (International Arrangements) Order 1993 (S.I. 1993 No. 1813) and the Channel Tunnel (Miscellaneous Provisions) Order 1994 (S.I. 1994 No. 1405) were amended by the Channel Tunnel (International Arrangements) and Channel Tunnel (Miscellaneous Provisions) (Amendment) Order 2015 (S.I. 2015 No. 856). It should be noted that, as a result of the amendments made by this order, the opening words of the final paragraph in the main work should now read "For powers of arrest and detention in a control zone".

(11) General powers of examination and search
Customs and Excise Management Act 1979, s.159

Power to examine and take account of goods

★**25-460**   With effect from March 12, 2015, section 159 of the 1979 Act was amended by the Legal Aid, Sentencing and Punishment of Offenders Act 2012 (Fines on Summary Conviction) Regulations 2015 (S.I. 2015 No. 664), so as to substitute "£20,000" for "the prescribed sum" in subsection (7)(a).

(12) Untrue declarations and falsifying documents
Customs and Excise Management Act 1979, s.167

Untrue declarations, etc.

★**25-470**   With effect from March 12, 2015, section 167 of the 1979 Act was amended by the Legal Aid, Sentencing and Punishment of Offenders Act 2012 (Fines on Summary Conviction) Regulations 2015 (S.I. 2015 No. 664), so as to substitute "£20,000" for "the prescribed sum" in subsection (2)(a).

Customs and Excise Management Act 1979, s.168

Counterfeiting documents, etc.

With effect from March 12, 2015, section 168 of the 1979 Act was amended by the Legal Aid, **★25-472**
Sentencing and Punishment of Offenders Act 2012 (Fines on Summary Conviction) Regulations
2015 (S.I. 2015 No. 664), so as to substitute "£20,000" for "the prescribed sum" in subsection
(2)(a).

(13) Fraudulent evasion offences

Customs and Excise Management Act 1979, s.170

Penalty for fraudulent evasion of duty, etc.

With effect from March 12, 2015, section 170 of the 1979 Act was amended by the Legal Aid, **★25-474**
Sentencing and Punishment of Offenders Act 2012 (Fines on Summary Conviction) Regulations
2015 (S.I. 2015 No. 664), so as to substitute "£20,000" as the maximum fine for "the prescribed
sum" in subsection (3)(a), and for "the statutory maximum" in subsection (4B)(a).

As to the repeal of section 76 of the SOCPA 2005, see *ante*, § 5-1212.   **★25-475**

As to an offence under section 170 of the 1979 Act, if committed in connection with a firearm **★**
or ammunition, becoming a specified serious offence within Schedule 1 to the SCA 2007, see *ante*,
§ 5-1192.

Evasion of excise duty

(ii) *Dutiable goods imported to the U.K. from within the Single Market*

With effect from April 1, 2015, the Excise Goods (Holding, Movement and Duty Point) Regula- **★25-503**
tions 2010 (S.I. 2010 No. 593) were amended by the Excise Goods (Aircraft and Ship's Stores)
Regulations 2015 (S.I. 2015 No. 368).

Taking steps to evade excise duty

Customs and Excise Management Act 1979, s.170B

Offence of taking preparatory steps for evasion of excise duty

With effect from March 12, 2015, section 170B of the 1979 Act was amended by the Legal Aid, **★25-505**
Sentencing and Punishment of Offenders Act 2012 (Fines on Summary Conviction) Regulations
2015 (S.I. 2015 No. 664), so as to substitute "£20,000" for "the prescribed sum" in subsection
(1)(a).

(14) Penalties and sentencing

Customs and Excise Management Act 1979, Sched. 1

With effect from March 12, 2015, paragraph (a) of the substituted text in paragraph 1 of **★25-508**
Schedule 1 to the 1979 Act was amended by the Legal Aid, Sentencing and Punishment of Offenders Act 2012 (Fines on Summary Conviction) Regulations 2015 (S.I. 2015 No. 664), so as to
substitute "£20,000" for "the prescribed sum".

C. Criminal Justice (International Co-operation) Act 1990

(2) Manufacture and supply of scheduled substances

Criminal Justice (International Co-operation) Act 1990, s.12

Sentence

As to the repeal of section 76 of the SOCPA 2005, see *ante*, § 5-1212.   **★25-515**

(3) Offences at sea

(a) *Offences*

Criminal Justice (International Co-operation) Act 1990, s.19

As to the repeal of section 76 of the SOCPA 2005, see *ante*, § 5-1212.   **★25-522**

D. Value Added Tax Offences

(2) Offences and penalties

Value Added Tax Act 1994, s.72

Offences

★**25-532**　With effect from March 12, 2015, section 72 of the 1994 Act was amended by the Legal Aid, Sentencing and Punishment of Offenders Act 2012 (Fines on Summary Conviction) Regulations 2015 (S.I. 2015 No. 664), so as to substitute "£20,000" for "the statutory maximum" in subsections (1)(a), (3)(i) and (8)(a), and for "level 5 on the standard scale" in subsections (10) and (11).

Sentence

★**25-538**　As to the repeal of section 76 of the SOCPA 2005, see *ante*, § 5-1212.

CHAPTER 26

MONEY LAUNDERING OFFENCES

I. PROCEEDS OF CRIME ACT 2002

B. Offences

(4) Legislation

Proceeds of Crime Act 2002, s.327

Concealing, etc., criminal property

26-11　*R. v. Rogers* is now reported at [2014] 2 Cr.App.R. 32, *sub nom. R. v. Rogers (Bradley)*.

★　As to the laying of charges under section 327 of the 2002 Act, see *R. v. G.H.*, *post*, § 26-12.

Proceeds of Crime Act 2002, s.328

Arrangements

★**26-12**　In *R. v. G.H.* [2015] 1 W.L.R. 2126, SC, it was held: (i) "criminal property" in the PCA 2002, ss.327 (concealing, etc., criminal property (§ 26-11 in the main work)), 328 (arrangements (see the main work) and 329 (acquisition, use and possession of criminal property (*ibid.*, § 26-13)) means property that already has the quality of being criminal property, as defined in section 340(3) (*ibid.*, § 26-40)), by reason of criminal conduct distinct from the conduct alleged to constitute the *actus reus* of the money laundering offence itself; this accords with the natural meaning of the sections and the purpose underlying them; (ii) here, where pursuant to an arrangement with a fraudster ("B"), the defendant ("H") opened two bank accounts and gave him the associated bank cards and documentation, whereupon B committed a series of frauds by setting up and operating four bogus car insurance websites, as a result of which money was transferred from the victims' respective bank accounts into the accounts opened by H, whilst H had not facilitated the "acquisition" of B's criminal property as it only became criminal property once it arrived in the bank accounts, it was perfectly possible to say that he had been party to an arrangement that facilitated the "retention, use or control" of B's criminal property (contrary to s.328(1)); it did not matter whether the criminal property existed when the arrangement was first hatched; what mattered was that the property should be criminal at a time when the arrangement operated on it; here, the character of the money (lawful property in the hands of the victims at the moment they paid it into the accounts) changed on being paid into the bank accounts, becoming criminal property in the hands of B because it was obtained through fraud perpetrated on the victims; (iii) whilst the same reasoning applied to sections 327 and 329, the ambit of those sections being wide, it would be bad practice for the prosecution to add additional counts under these sections to substantive counts unless there was a proper public purpose in doing so; further, the courts should be willing to use their powers to discourage the inappropriate use of the provisions of the 2002 Act to prosecute conduct that is sufficiently covered by substantive offences. The court distinguished *R. v. Geary* (as to which, see the main work).

Proceeds of Crime Act 2002, s.329

As to the laying of charges under section 327 of the 2002 Act, see *R. v. G.H.*, *ante*, § 26-12. ★26-13

The regulated sector and supervisory authorities

With effect from January 1, 2016, Schedule 9 to the 2002 Act is further amended by the Solvency 2 Regulations 2015 (S.I. 2015 No. 575). ★26-16

C. Appropriate Consent, Protected and Authorised Disclosures, Form and Manner of Disclosures

(1) Summary

As to the amendment of section 338 of the 2002 Act (see the main work), see *post*, § 26-36. ★26-30

(2) Legislation

Proceeds of Crime Act 2002, s.338

Authorised disclosures

With effect from June 1, 2015 (Serious Crime Act 2015 (Commencement No. 1) Regulations 2015 (S.I. 2015 No. 820)), section 338 of the 2002 Act was amended by the SCA 2015, s.37, so as to insert a new subsection (4A), as follows— ★26-36

"(4A) Where an authorised disclosure is made in good faith, no civil liability arises in respect of the disclosure on the part of the person by or on whose behalf it is made.".

D. Interpretation

Proceeds of Crime Act 2002, ss.339A, 340

Interpretation

R. v. Rogers is now reported at [2014] 2 Cr.App.R. 32, *sub nom. R. v. Rogers (Bradley)*. 26-41

E. Sentence

Proceeds of Crime Act 2002, s.334

Penalties

As to the repeal of section 76 of the SOCPA 2005, see *ante*, § 5-1212. ★26-42

II. MONEY LAUNDERING REGULATIONS 2007

With effect from February 6, 2015, the Money Laundering (Amendment) Regulations 2015 (S.I. 2015 No. 11) amended Schedule 3 to the Money Laundering Regulations 2007 (S.I. 2007 No. 2157). 26-45

With effect from January 1, 2016, the 2007 regulations are further amended by the Solvency 2 Regulations 2015 (S.I. 2015 No. 575). ★

Chapter 27

HARMFUL OR DANGEROUS DRUGS

A. Introduction

(3) Definition of a "controlled drug"

Misuse of Drugs Act 1971, s.2

Temporary class drug orders

With effect from April 10, 2015, the Misuse of Drugs Act 1971 (Temporary Class Drug) Order ★27-5a

2015 (S.I. 2015 No. 1027), specifies the following substances and products as drugs subject to temporary control—

> "1. The following substances, namely—
> 3,4-Dichloromethylphenidate (3,4-DCMP)
> Ethylphenidate
> Isopropylphenidate (IPP or IPPD)
> Methylnaphthidate (HDMP-28)
> Propylphenidate
> 2. Any stereoisomeric form of a substance specified in paragraph 1.
> 3. Any preparation or other product containing a substance specified in paragraph 1 or 2."

The order stipulates that the provisions of the Misuse of Drugs (Safe Custody) Regulations 1973 (S.I. 1973 No. 798) (see § 27-91 in the main work) apply to these substances and products, and that the Misuse of Drugs Regulations 2001 (S.I. 2001 No. 3998) (see § 27-83 in the main work) are to apply to them as if they were specified as controlled drugs to which Schedule 1 to those regulations applied. The substances and products specified will cease to be subject to temporary control after one year, or, if earlier, upon the coming into force of an order under section 2(2) listing them in Schedule 2 to the 1971 Act (s.2A(6) of the 1971 Act).

(4) Classification of controlled drugs

Misuse of Drugs Act 1971, Sched. 2

Class A drugs

27-6   With effect from January 7, 2015, the Misuse of Drugs Act 1971 (Amendment) (No. 2) Order 2014 (S.I. 2014 No. 3271) amends paragraph 1(a) of Part I of Schedule 2 to the 1971 Act so as (i) to insert—

> "(6aR,9R)-4-acetyl-N,N-diethyl-7-methyl-4,6,6a,7,8,9-hexahydroindolo[4,3-fg]quinoline-9-carboxamide(ALD-52)"

after "Trimeperidine", (ii) to insert—

> "3,4-dichloro-N-[[1-(dimethylamino)cyclohexyl]methyl]benzamide (AH-7921)
> (6aR,9R)-N,N-diethyl-7-allyl-4,6,6a,7,8,9-hexahydroindolo[4,3-fg]quinoline-9-carboxamide (AL-LAD)
> (6aR,9R)-N,N-diethyl-7-ethyl-4,6,6a,7,8,9-hexahydroindolo[4,3-fg]quinoline-9-carboxamide (ETH-LAD)
> (6aR,9R)-N,N-diethyl-7-propyl-4,6,6a,7,8,9-hexahydroindolo[4,3-fg]quinoline-9-carboxamide (PRO-LAD)"

after "4-Cyano-1-methyl-4-phenyl-piperidine", and (iii) to insert—

> "2,4-dimethylazetidinyl{6aR,9R)-7-methyl-4,6,6a,7,8,9-hexahydroindolo[4,3-fg]quinolin-9-yl}methanone(LSZ)"

after "N,N-Diethyltryptamine".

With effect from January 7, 2015, S.I. 2014 No. 3271 (*ante*) substitutes a new paragraph 1(b) of Part I of Schedule 2 to the 1971 Act, as follows—

> "(b) any compound (not being a compound for the time being specified in sub-paragraph (a) above) structurally derived from tryptamine or from a ring-hydroxy tryptamine by modification in any of the following ways, that is to say—
> (i) by substitution at the nitrogen atom of the side chain to any extent with alkyl or alkenyl substituents, or by inclusion of the nitrogen atom of the side chain (and no other atoms of the side chain) in a cyclic structure;
> (ii) by substitution at the carbon atom adjacent to the nitrogen atom of the side chain with alkyl or alkenyl substituents;
> (iii) by substitution in the 6-membered ring to any extent with alkyl, alkoxy, haloalkyl, thioalkyl, alkylenedioxy, or halide substituents;
> (iv) by substitution at the 2-position of the tryptamine ring system with an alkyl substituent;".

With effect from March 11, 2015, the Misuse of Drugs Act 1971 (Amendment) Order 2015 (S.I. 2015 No. 215) amends paragraph 1(a) of Part I of Schedule 2 to the 1971 Act so as (i) to insert

"1-Cyclohexyl-4-(1,2-diphenylethyl)piperazine (MT-45)" after "4-Cyano-1-methyl-4-phenyl-
piperidine", and (ii) to insert "4-Methyl-5-(4-methylphenyl)-4,5-dihydrooxazol-2-amine (4,4'-
DMAR)" after "4-Mehtyl-aminorex".

C. RESTRICTION OF PRODUCTION AND SUPPLY OF CONTROLLED DRUGS

(2) Production

(b) *Mode of trial, class of offence and sentence*

As to the repeal of section 76 of the SOCPA 2005, see *ante*, § 5-1212.   ★**27-31**

(3) Supply

(c) *Ingredients of the offences*

Being "concerned in"

In *R. v. Martin and Brimecome* [2015] 1 Cr.App.R. 11, CA, it was held that on a prosecution for   **27-41**
being concerned in the supply of a controlled drug, contrary to section 4(3)(b) of the Misuse of
Drugs Act 1971 (§ 27-28 in the main work), there was no need to prove an actual supply. The
sole issue was whether the evidence was sufficient to constitute evidence of "supply to another".
The word "supply" is a broad term and is not confined to "actual supply" or "past supply" but
refers to the entire process of supply. For criticism of this decision, to the effect that it
misrepresents the decision in *R. v. Hughes (R.)* (as to which, see the main work) and does considerable violence to the language of the statute, see CLW/14/45/17.

D. RESTRICTION OF POSSESSION OF CONTROLLED DRUGS

(3) Mode of trial, class of offence and sentence

As to the repeal of section 76 of the SOCPA 2005, see *ante*, § 5-1212.   ★**27-53**

E. RESTRICTION OF CULTIVATION OF CANNABIS PLANT

Misuse of Drugs Act 1971, s.6

Mode of trial, class of offence and sentence

As to an offence under section 6 of the 1971 Act becoming a specified serious offence within   ★**27-79**
Schedule 1 to the SCA 2007, enabling the court to make a serious crime prevention order under
section 19 on conviction, see *ante*, § 5-1192.

F. AUTHORISATION OF ACTIVITIES OTHERWISE UNLAWFUL UNDER SECTIONS 3 TO 6

Misuse of Drugs Act 1971, ss.7, 7A

The Misuse of Drugs Regulations 2001 (S.I. 2001 No. 3998) (see the main work) are further   ★**27-83**
amended by the Misuse of Drugs (Amendment No. 3) (England, Wales and Scotland) Regulations
2014 (S.I. 2014 No. 3277), with effect from January 7, 2015; by the Misuse of Drugs (Amendment) (England, Wales and Scotland) Regulations 2015 (S.I. 2015 No. 231), with effect from
March 11, 2015; and by the Misuse of Drugs (Amendment) (No. 2) (England, Wales and Scotland)
Regulations 2015 (S.I. 2015 No. 891), with effect from June 1, 2015, July 1, 2015, and November
30, 2015.

As to the application of the 2001 regulations to the substances and products subject to the   ★
Misuse of Drugs Act 1971 (Temporary Class Drug) Order 2015 (S.I. 2015 No. 1027), see article
3(2) of that order, *ante*, § 27-5a.

The Misuse of Drugs (Designation) Order 2001 (S.I. 2001 No. 3997) (see the main work) was
further amended by the Misuse of Drugs (Designation) (Amendment) (No. 3) (England, Wales
and Scotland) Order 2014 (S.I. 2014 No. 3276), with effect from January 7, 2015; and by the
Misuse of Drugs (Designation) (Amendment) (England, Wales and Scotland) Order 2015 (S.I.
2015 No. 232), with effect from March 11, 2015.

★   With effect from May 31, 2015, S.I. 2001 No. 3997 and its amending instruments (including, *inter alia*, S.I. 2014 No. 3276, *ante*, and S.I. 2015 No. 232, *ante*) were revoked and replaced by the Misuse of Drugs (Designation) (England, Wales and Scotland) Order 2015 (S.I. 2015 No. 704).

G. Occupiers of Premises

Mode of trial, class of offence and sentence

★**27-85**   As to the repeal of section 76 of the SOCPA 2005, see *ante*, § 5-1212.

J. Powers of Secretary of State for Preventing Misuse of Controlled Drugs

Misuse of Drugs Act 1971, s.10

★**27-91**   As to the application of the Misuse of Drugs (Safe Custody) Regulations 1973 (S.I. 1973 No. 798) to the substances and products subject to the Misuse of Drugs Act 1971 (Temporary Class Drug) Order 2015 (S.I. 2015 No. 1027), see article 3(1) of that order, *ante*, § 27-5a.

O. Participating in Offences Outside the United Kingdom

Mode of trial, class of offence and sentence

★**27-97**   As to the repeal of section 76 of the SOCPA 2005, see *ante*, § 5-1212.

R. Law Enforcement and Punishment of Offences

(1) Search and seizure

★**27-105b**   Part 4 (ss.52–65) of the SCA 2015 (into force on May 3, 2015 (Serious Crime Act 2015 (Commencement No. 1) Regulations 2015 (S.I. 2015 No. 820))) concerns the seizure and forfeiture of drug-cutting agents. Section 52 provides that a justice of the peace may issue a warrant authorising a police or customs officer to enter premises and to search them for substances that appear to be intended for use as drug-cutting agents, where he is satisfied that there are reasonable grounds to suspect that a substance intended for such use is on the premises. Such a warrant may relate to any premises occupied or controlled by a person specified in the warrant (an "all-premises warrant"), or only to premises specified in the warrant (a "specific-premises warrant"). Section 53 contains supplementary provision in relation to such warrants. Schedule 2 (given effect by s.54(1)) makes provision in respect of the execution of such warrants. An entry on, or search of, premises under a warrant will be unlawful unless it complies with Schedule 2 (s.54(2)). Reasonable force may be used for the purpose of entering premises under a warrant and obstruction, without reasonable excuse, of an officer executing a warrant is a summary offence (level 3) (s.54(3)–(5)). Section 55 provides for the seizure of any substance on the premises that the officer has reasonable grounds to suspect is intended for use as a drug-cutting agent. Section 56 provides that where an officer, who is lawfully on premises, finds such substances he may seize them without a warrant. Section 58 provides for the seizure of containers holding such substances. Sections 59 to 63 provide for the initial and continued retention, forfeiture, and disposal or return of seized substances.

(2) Procedure and penalties

Sentencing guidelines

Conspiracy

27-109   *R. v. Khan (Kazim Ali), Khan (Umar), Khan (Mohammed Arfan) and Khan (Mohammed Ahsan)* (as to which, see the main work) and the issue of the extent to which the guideline of the Sentencing Council applies to conspiracies to import, supply or produce controlled drugs were further considered in *R. v. Pitts, post*, Appendix K-626a.

CHAPTER 28

OFFENCES AGAINST PUBLIC JUSTICE

III. CONTEMPT OF COURT

B. COMMON LAW

(2) Civil and criminal contempts

Director of the Serious Fraud Office v. O'Brien is now reported at [2014] A.C. 1246. **28-33**

(7) Contempt by jurors

As from April 13, 2015, many instances of contempt by jurors will be offences under the Juries ★**28-40**
Act 1974, ss.20A–20C (*post*, §§ 28-41a *et seq.*). However, section 22(A1) of the Juries Act 1974 Act
(inserted, as from April 13, 2015 (Criminal Justice and Courts Act 2015 (Commencement No. 1,
Saving and Transitional Provisions) Order 2015 (S.I. 2015 No. 778)), by the Criminal Justice and
Courts Act 2015, s.77(2)), provides that "nothing in section 20A, 20B or 20C affects what
constitutes contempt at common law."

Juries Act 1974, s.20

Offences

As from April 13, 2015 (Criminal Justice and Courts Act 2015 (Commencement No. 1, Saving ★**28-41**
and Transitional Provisions) Order 2015 (S.I. 2015 No. 778)), the heading to section 20 of the
1974 Act is amended by the Criminal Justice and Courts Act 2015, s.70(1) and (2), so as to
substitute "Offences: failure to attend, serving while disqualified etc".

As from April 13, 2015 (Criminal Justice and Courts Act 2015 (Commencement No. 1, Saving ★**28-41a**
and Transitional Provisions) Order 2015 (S.I. 2015 No. 778)), the 1974 Act is amended by the
Criminal Justice and Courts Act 2015, ss.71(1) and (3) (so as to insert a new s.20A), 72 (so as to
insert a new s.20B), 73 (so as to insert a new s.20C) and 74(1) (so as to insert new ss.20D to 20G).

Juries Act 1974, ss.20A–20G

Offence: research by jurors

20A.—(1) It is an offence for a member of a jury that tries an issue in a case before a court to
research the case during the trial period, subject to the exceptions in subsections (6) and (7).

(2) A person researches a case if (and only if) the person—

    (a) intentionally seeks information, and

    (b) when doing so, knows or ought reasonably to know that the information is or may be
relevant to the case.

(3) The ways in which a person may seek information include—

    (a) asking a question,

    (b) searching an electronic database, including by means of the internet,

    (c) visiting or inspecting a place or object,

    (d) conducting an experiment, and

    (e) asking another person to seek the information.

(4) Information relevant to the case includes information about—

    (a) a person involved in events relevant to the case,

    (b) the judge dealing with the issue,

    (c) any other person involved in the trial, whether as a lawyer, a witness or otherwise,

    (d) the law relating to the case,

    (e) the law of evidence, and

    (f) court procedure.

(5) "The trial period", in relation to a member of a jury that tries an issue, is the period—

    (a) beginning when the person is sworn to try the issue, and

(b) ending when the judge discharges the jury or, if earlier, when the judge discharges the person.

(6) It is not an offence under this section for a person to seek information if the person needs the information for a reason which is not connected with the case.

(7) It is not an offence under this section for a person—

(a) to attend proceedings before the court on the issue;

(b) to seek information from the judge dealing with the issue;

(c) to do anything which the judge dealing with the issue directs or authorises the person to do;

(d) to seek information from another member of the jury, unless the person knows or ought reasonably to know that the other member of the jury contravened this section in the process of obtaining the information;

(e) to do anything else which is reasonably necessary in order for the jury to try the issue.

(8) A person guilty of an offence under this section is liable, on conviction on indictment, to imprisonment for a term not exceeding 2 years or a fine (or both).

(9) Proceedings for an offence under this section may only be instituted by or with the consent of the Attorney General.

Offence: sharing research with other jurors

28-41b

20B.—(1) It is an offence for a member of a jury that tries an issue in a case before a court intentionally to disclose information to another member of the jury during the trial period if—

(a) the member contravened section 20A in the process of obtaining the information, and

(b) the information has not been provided by the court.

(2) Information has been provided by the court if (and only if) it has been provided as part of—

(a) evidence presented in the proceedings on the issue, or

(b) other information provided to the jury or a juror during the trial period by, or with the permission of, the judge dealing with the issue.

(3) A person guilty of an offence under this section is liable, on conviction on indictment, to imprisonment for a term not exceeding 2 years or a fine (or both).

(4) Proceedings for an offence under this section may not be instituted except by or with the consent of the Attorney General.

(5) In this section, "the trial period" has the same meaning as in section 20A.

Offence: jurors engaging in other prohibited conduct

28-41c

20C.—(1) It is an offence for a member of a jury that tries an issue in a case before a court intentionally to engage in prohibited conduct during the trial period, subject to the exceptions in subsections (4) and (5).

(2) "Prohibited conduct" means conduct from which it may reasonably be concluded that the person intends to try the issue otherwise than on the basis of the evidence presented in the proceedings on the issue.

(3) An offence under this section is committed whether or not the person knows that the conduct is prohibited conduct.

(4) It is not an offence under this section for a member of the jury to research the case (as defined in section 20A(2) to (4)).

(5) It is not an offence under this section for a member of the jury to disclose information to another member of the jury.

(6)–(8) [*Identical to s.20B(3)–(5), ante, § 28-41b.*]

Offence: disclosing jury's deliberations

28-41d

20D.—(1) It is an offence for a person intentionally—

(a) to disclose information about statements made, opinions expressed, arguments advanced or votes cast by members of a jury in the course of their deliberations in proceedings before a court, or

(b) to solicit or obtain such information,

subject to the exceptions in sections 20E to 20G.

(2), (3) [*Identical to s.20A(8), (9), ante, § 28-41a.*]

Offence of disclosing jury's deliberations: initial exceptions

28-41e

20E.—(1) It is not an offence under section 20D for a person to disclose information in the proceedings mentioned in section 20D(1) for the purposes of enabling the jury to arrive at their verdict or in connection with the delivery of that verdict.

(2) It is not an offence under section 20D for the judge dealing with those proceedings to disclose information—

    (a) for the purposes of dealing with the case, or

    (b) for the purposes of an investigation by a relevant investigator into whether an offence or contempt of court has been committed by or in relation to a juror in the proceedings mentioned in section 20D(1).

(3) It is not an offence under section 20D for a person who reasonably believes that a disclosure described in subsection (2)(b) has been made to disclose information for the purposes of the investigation.

(4) It is not an offence under section 20D to publish information disclosed as described in subsection (1) or (2)(a) in the proceedings mentioned in section 20D(1).

(5) In this section—

"publish" means make available to the public or a section of the public;

"relevant investigator" means—

    (a) a police force;

    (b) the Attorney General;

    (c) any other person or class of person specified by the Lord Chancellor for the purposes of this section by regulations made by statutory instrument.

(6) The Lord Chancellor must obtain the consent of the Lord Chief Justice before making regulations under this section.

(7) A statutory instrument containing regulations under this section is subject to annulment in pursuance of a resolution of either House of Parliament.

Offence of disclosing jury's deliberations: further exceptions

20F.—(1) It is not an offence under section 20D for a person to disclose information to a person **28-41f** listed in subsection (2) if—

    (a) the disclosure is made after the jury in the proceedings mentioned in section 20D(1) has been discharged, and

    (b) the person making the disclosure reasonably believes that—

        (i) an offence or contempt of court has been, or may have been, committed by or in relation to a juror in connection with those proceedings, or

        (ii) conduct of a juror in connection with those proceedings may provide grounds for an appeal against conviction or sentence.

(2) Those persons are—

    (a) a member of a police force;

    (b) a judge of the Court of Appeal;

    (c) the registrar of criminal appeals;

    (d) a judge of the court where the proceedings mentioned in section 20D(1) took place;

    (e) a member of staff of that court who would reasonably be expected to disclose the information only to a person mentioned in paragraphs (b) to (d).

(3) It is not an offence under section 20D for a member of a police force to disclose information for the purposes of obtaining assistance in deciding whether to submit the information to a judge of the Court of Appeal or the registrar of criminal appeals, provided that the disclosure does not involve publishing the information.

(4) It is not an offence under section 20D for a judge of the Court of Appeal or the registrar of criminal appeals to disclose information for the purposes of an investigation by a relevant investigator into—

    (a) whether an offence or contempt of court has been committed by or in relation to a juror in connection with the proceedings mentioned in section 20D(1), or

    (b) whether conduct of a juror in connection with those proceedings may provide grounds for an appeal against conviction or sentence.

(5) It is not an offence under section 20D for a judge of the Court of Appeal or the registrar of criminal appeals to disclose information for the purposes of enabling or assisting—

    (a) a person who was the defendant in the proceedings mentioned in section 20D(1), or

    (b) a legal representative of such a person,

to consider whether conduct of a juror in connection with those proceedings may provide grounds for an appeal against conviction or sentence.

(6) It is not an offence under section 20D for a person who reasonably believes that a disclosure described in subsection (4) or (5) has been made to disclose information for the purposes of the investigation or consideration in question.

(7) It is not an offence under section 20D for a person to disclose information in evidence in—

    (a) proceedings for an offence or contempt of court alleged to have been committed by or in relation to a juror in connection with the proceedings mentioned in section 20D(1),

(b) proceedings on an appeal, or an application for leave to appeal, against a decision in the proceedings mentioned in section 20D(1) where an allegation relating to conduct of or in relation to a juror forms part of the grounds of appeal, or

(c) proceedings on any further appeal or reference arising out of proceedings mentioned in paragraph (a) or (b).

(8) It is not an offence under section 20D for a person to disclose information in the course of taking reasonable steps to prepare for proceedings described in subsection (7)(a) to (c).

(9) It is not an offence under section 20D to publish information disclosed as described in subsection (7).

(10) In this section—

"publish" means make available to the public or a section of the public;

"relevant investigator" means—

(a) a police force;

(b) the Attorney General;

(c) the Criminal Cases Review Commission;

(d) the Crown Prosecution Service;

(e) any other person or class of person specified by the Lord Chancellor for the purposes of this section by regulations made by statutory instrument.

(11) [*Identical to s.20E(6), (7), ante.*]

Offence of disclosing jury's deliberations: exceptions for soliciting disclosures or obtaining information

28-41g 20G.—(1) It is not an offence under section 20D to solicit a disclosure described in section 20E(1) to (4) or section 20F(1) to (9).

(2) It is not an offence under section 20D to obtain information—

(a) by means of a disclosure described in section 20E(1) to (4) or section 20F(1) to (9), or

(b) from a document that is available to the public or a section of the public.

(13) Publication of matter relating to proceedings in private

28-51 The Administration of Justice Act 1960, s.12(1)(c) ("(1) The publication of information relating to proceedings before any court sitting in private shall not of itself be contempt of court except in the following cases, that is to say...(c) where the court sits in private for reasons of national security during that part of the proceedings about which the information in question is published"), justified a court ordering that sensitive information heard *in camera* not be deployed on an appeal to the European Court of Human Rights; the concept of "publication" in the 1960 Act, which is not defined, extends to any circumstance where the prohibited information is made available to persons who would have been excluded from the court during the *in camera* proceedings; such persons include the staff and judges of the Strasbourg court; and the court also would have the power to make the order under its inherent jurisdiction, and under section 11 of the Contempt of Court Act 1981 (§ 28-79 in the main work): *R. (Wang Yam) v. Central Criminal Court* [2015] 1 Cr.App.R. 10, DC. As to this case, see also *ante*, §§ 4-3, 16-127; and *post*, §§ 28-56, 28-79.

(14) Disobedience to an order of the court

28-52 An advocate's wilful and deliberate disobedience of an order to attend court can amount to a contempt: *Re West (Ian Stuart) (a barrister)* [2014] 2 Cr.App.R. 28, CA. As to this case, see also *ante*, § 4-112; and *post*, §§ 28-85, 28-92, 28-98.

As to the amendment of section 39 of the CYPA 1933 (see the main work), see *ante*, § 4-24.

C. Contempt of Court Act 1981

(2) The strict liability rule

Contempt of Court Act 1981, ss.1, 2

Limitation of the scope of strict liability

28-56 The staff and judges of the European Court of Human Rights can properly be described as "any section of the public" within the meaning of section 2(1) of the 1981 Act: *R. (Wang Yam) v. Central Criminal Court* [2015] 1 Cr.App.R. 10, DC. As to this case, see also *ante*, §§ 4-3, 16-127, 28-51; and *post*, § 28-79.

Defences and power to order postponement of reporting

Contempt of Court Act 1981, ss.3, 4

28-66 As to the amendment of section 39 of the CYPA 1933 (see the main work), see *ante*, § 4-24.

(3) Miscellaneous offences
Contempt of Court Act 1981, s.8

Confidentiality of jury's deliberations

As from April 13, 2015 (Criminal Justice and Courts Act 2015 (Commencement No. 1, Saving ★**28-73**
and Transitional Provisions) Order 2015 (S.I. 2015 No. 778)), section 8 of the 1981 Act is repealed
in England and Wales, and the text and heading are amended to the extent that the section applies in Scotland and Northern Ireland: Criminal Justice and Courts Act 2015, s.74(2)–(4). Section
8 is effectively replaced in England and Wales by the Juries Act 1974, s.20D, *ante*, § 28-41d.

Criminal Procedure Rules 2014 (S.I. 2014 No. 1610), r.16.10

Forfeiture of unauthorised sound recording

As to the replacement of S.I. 2014 No. 1610 by the Criminal Procedure Rules 2015 (S.I. 2015 ★**28-76**
No. 1490), see *ante*, § 4-47.

(5) Restriction of publication of matters exempted from disclosure
Contempt of Court Act 1981, s.11

Publication of matters exempted from disclosure in court

A. *v. BBC (Secretary of State for the Home Department intervening)* is now reported at [2015] A.C. ★**28-79**
588.

A court has jurisdiction under section 11 of the 1981 Act to order that sensitive information
heard *in camera* not be deployed for the purposes of an application to the European Court of Human Rights; "publication" in section 11 is defined in section 19 (§ 28-83 in the main work) as having the meaning assigned by section 2(1) (§ 28-56 in the main work and *ante*): *R. (Wang Yam) v.
Central Criminal Court* [2015] 1 Cr.App.R. 10, DC. As to this case, see also *ante*, §§ 4-3, 7-11, 16-
127, 28-51, 28-56.

D. Summary Powers to Deal with Contempt
(2) Contempt "in the face of the court"
(a) General

R. v. Izoura and *Weston v. Central Criminal Court Courts Administrator* (both cited in the main **28-85**
work, albeit the second is incorrectly cited as *Weston v. Central Criminal Courts Administrator*) were
distinguished in *Re West (Ian Stuart) (a barrister)* [2014] 2 Cr.App.R. 28, CA. As to this case, see also
ante, §§ 4-112, 28-52; and *post*, §§ 28-92, 28-98.

(4) Procedure, etc.

General

Where contempt is alleged, the provisions of the Criminal Procedure Rules cannot be waived **28-92**
by the parties or the court: *Re West (Ian Stuart) (a barrister)* [2014] 2 Cr.App.R. 28, CA (in the
context of non-compliance with r.62.7 of the 2014 rules (§ 28-107 in the main work)). As to this
case, see also *ante*, §§ 4-112, 28-52, 28-85; and *post*, § 28-98.

(6) Consideration of the contempt by another judge

Where a judge had taken the view that the appellant (a barrister acting for the defendant in **28-98**
criminal proceedings) had been "highly impertinent" to him and had "deliberately thwarted" his
efforts at case management by a "deliberate act of defiance" in failing to attend court when
ordered to do so, thereby undermining "the dignity and authority of the court", it was not merely
the words uttered (which could be read on the transcript) but also the way in which the exchange
occurred that was relevant; only the judge was in a position to assess that feature; his decision to
deal with the contempt himself was properly made: *Re West (Ian Stuart) (a barrister)* [2014] 2
Cr.App.R. 28, CA (considering r.62.8(5) of the Criminal Procedure Rules 2014 (see § 28-108 in
the main work)). As to this case, see also *ante*, §§ 4-112, 28-52, 28-85, 28-92.

E. Procedural Rules

(1) Applications to magistrates' courts, the Crown Court and the Court of Appeal

Criminal Procedure Rules 2014 (S.I. 2014 No. 1610), Pt 62

Replacement of 2014 rules by 2015 rules

★**28-101**   With effect from October 5, 2015, the Criminal Procedure Rules 2015 (S.I. 2015 No. 1490) replace S.I. 2014 No. 1610. Part 62 of the 2014 rules is replaced by Part 48 of the 2015 rules (see *post*, Appendix P-516 *et seq.*), with several changes of substance.

Postponement of enquiry

28-107   For a case considering whether compliance with rule 62.7 of the 2014 rules (see the main work) may be waived, see *Re West (Ian Stuart) (a barrister)*, *ante*, § 28-92.

Procedure on enquiry

28-108   For a case considering whether compliance with r.62.8(5) of the 2014 rules (see the main work) may be waived, see *Re West (Ian Stuart) (a barrister)*, *ante*, § 28-98.

(3) Practice direction

★**28-129a**   A practice direction (*Practice Direction: Committal for Contempt of Court: Open Court* [2015] 1 W.L.R. 2195 (Lord Thomas C.J.) has been issued that is applicable to all proceedings for committal for contempt of court, including contempt in the face of the court, whether arising under any statutory or inherent jurisdiction. It supplements various sets of procedural rules, including the Criminal Procedure Rules 2014 (S.I. 2014 No. 1610) (see the main work, §§ 28-101 *et seq.*). It applies in all courts.

The general rule is that contempt proceedings are to be conducted in public, derogation from such rule being permissible only exceptionally and when strictly necessary to secure the proper administration of justice. Provision is made as to how committal applications and hearings are to be listed in the public court list.

Where the court is considering derogating from the general rule to any extent, it shall, before the hearing takes place, notify the media of the fact of the hearing and the nature of the proposed derogation, and it shall hear submissions at the outset from the parties and the media as to the appropriateness of any derogation. The fact that the hearing may involve the disclosure of material that ought not to be published does not, of itself, justify hearing the application in private if such publication can be restrained by order. Where the court does order some derogation from the general rule, it shall, before it continues in private, sit in public to give a reasoned judgment for its decision. An order for a committal hearing to be heard in private shall not be granted by consent of the parties.

In all cases, irrespective of whether the hearing was in public or private, where the court finds a person guilty of contempt, it shall state in public the person's name, the general nature of the contempt, and the punishment, and it shall provide these details to the national media and to the Judicial Office. The court shall also, in respect of all committal decisions, either produce a written judgment setting out its reasons or ensure that any oral judgment is transcribed, such transcription to be ordered the same day as the judgment is given and prepared on an expedited basis. Copies are then to be provided to the media, the Judicial Office and BAILII.

Advocates and the judge should be robed for all committal proceedings other than proceedings before a magistrates' court.

IV. INTIMIDATION OF WITNESSES, JURORS AND OTHERS

Criminal Justice and Public Order Act 1994, s.51

★**28-132**   As from April 13, 2015 (Criminal Justice and Courts Act 2015 (Commencement No. 1, Saving and Transitional Provisions) Order 2015 (S.I. 2015 No. 778)), section 51 of the 1994 Act is amended by the Criminal Justice and Courts Act 2015, s.50, and Sched. 11, para. 14, so as: (i) in subsection (9), (a) to substitute, for the words "'public prosecutor'", the words "'relevant prosecutor'", and (b) to insert, after the word "'requisition'", the words ", 'single justice procedure notice'"; and (ii) in subsection (10)(a)(ia), (a) to substitute, for the words "public prosecutor", the words "relevant prosecutor", and (b) to insert, after the words "and requisition", the words "or single justice procedure notice".

VI. OFFENCES AKIN TO PERJURY

A. FALSE STATEMENTS ON OATH AND DECLARATIONS

Perjury Act 1911, s.3

False statements, etc., with reference to marriage

With effect from December 16, 2014, section 3 of the 1911 Act is amended by the Marriage   **28-152**
(Same Sex Couples) Act 2013 (Consequential and Contrary Provisions and Scotland) and Marriage and Civil Partnership (Scotland) Act 2014 (Consequential Provisions) Order 2014 (S.I. 2014 No. 3168), art. 2, and Sched., para. 2, so as: (i) in subsection (1)(b), to insert the words "or register of conversions" after the words "register of marriage", and to insert the words "or any civil partnership which is to be converted into a marriage" after the word "marriage", in the second place it occurs; and (ii) to insert a new subsection (3), as follows—

"(3) In subsection (1)(b), 'register of conversions' means the register of conversions of civil partnerships into marriages kept by the Registrar General in accordance with section 9 of the Marriage (Same Sex Couples) Act 2013 and regulations made under that section.".

VII. PRISON SECURITY

A. ESCAPE

(1) Common law

As to the amendment of the Prisoners (Return to Custody) Act 1995, s.1 (see the main work),   **28-166**
by the Criminal Justice and Courts Act 2015, see *post*, § 28-170a.

(2) Statute

Prison Act 1952, ss.13(2), 39

As from March 20, 2015 (Criminal Justice and Courts Act 2015 (Commencement No. 1, Saving   **★28-168**
and Transitional Provisions) Order 2015 (S.I. 2015 No. 778)), in relation to a directly managed secure college, the phrase "an officer of the prison" in section 13(2) of the 1952 Act (§ 28-167 in the main work), as it applies to secure colleges, includes a reference to a secure college custody officer performing custodial duties at the secure college which have been contracted out: Criminal Justice and Courts Act 2015, s.39, and Sched. 10, para. 22.

As to the application of section 39 (and other sections) of the 1952 Act (as to which, see the   **★**
main work) to young offender institutions, secure training centres and secure colleges, see section 43 of that Act, as substituted by section 38(1) of the 2015 Act (as from March 20, 2015 (S.I. 2015 No. 778 (*ante*)).

Prison Act 1952, s.8

Powers of prison officers

As from March 20, 2015 (Criminal Justice and Courts Act 2015 (Commencement No. 1, Saving   **★28-169**
and Transitional Provisions) Order 2015 (S.I. 2015 No. 778)), section 8 is disapplied in relation to officers of a contracted-out secure college (but this does not affect the powers of an officer of a directly managed secure college who is temporarily attached to a contracted-out secure college): Criminal Justice and Courts Act 2015, s.39, and Sched. 10, para. 6. The powers and duties of secure college custody officers performing custodial duties at a contracted-out secure college, or carrying out contracted-out functions at a directly managed secure college, are provided for by *ibid.*, paras 8 to 11 and 21.

Remaining unlawfully at large after recall

As from April 13, 2015 (Criminal Justice and Courts Act 2015 (Commencement No. 1, Saving   **★28-170a** and Transitional Provisions) Order 2015 (S.I. 2015 No. 778)), section 12 of the Criminal Justice and Courts Act 2015 inserts a new section 32ZA after section 32 of the C(S)A 1997 (recall of life prisoners) and a new section 255ZA (*ante*, § 5-658a) after section 255 of the CJA 2003 (recall of prisoners). The effect of the two new sections is the same. A person recalled to prison, who has been notified of the recall either orally or in writing, commits an offence if, while unlawfully at large, he fails, without reasonable excuse, to take all necessary steps to return to prison as soon as possible. The offences are triable either way, with a maximum penalty on conviction on indictment of two years' imprisonment, or a fine, or both. By section 12(3) of the 2015 Act, the new sections apply in relation to a person recalled to prison before or after section 12 comes into force.

★ The Prisoners (Return to Custody) Act 1995, s.1, creates a summary offence of remaining at large after temporary release. It is amended by the Criminal Justice and Courts Act 2015, as follows: (i) the offence's application is extended to secure colleges (2015 Act, s.38(3), and Sched. 9, para. 11); and (ii) it is made triable either way, with a maximum penalty on conviction on indictment of two years' imprisonment, or a fine, or both (s.13(1)–(3)), but this does not apply where the period of temporary release expired, or the order of recall was made, before section 13 comes into force (s.13(4)). Section 13 of the 2015 Act came into force on April 13, 2015; and section 38(3) of, and Schedule 9 to, that Act came into force on March 20, 2015: S.I. 2015 No. 778 (*ante*).

E. SMUGGLING AND UNAUTHORISED PHOTOGRAPHY, ETC.

Prison Act 1952, ss.40A–40E

★**28-195a** With effect from June 1, 2015 (Serious Crime Act 2015 (Commencement No. 1) Regulations 2015 (S.I. 2015 No. 820), a new section 40CA was inserted into the 1952 Act, after section 40C, by the SCA 2015, s.78, as follows—

"Unauthorised possession in prison of knife or offensive weapon

40CA.—(1) A person who, without authorisation, is in possession of an article specified in subsection (2) inside a prison is guilty of an offence.

(2) The articles referred to in subsection (1) are—

(a) any article that has a blade or is sharply pointed;

(b) any other offensive weapon (as defined in section 1(9) of the Police and Criminal Evidence Act 1984).

(3) In proceedings for an offence under this section it is a defence for the accused to show that—

(a) he reasonably believed that he had authorisation to be in possession of the article in question, or

(b) in all the circumstances there was an overriding public interest which justified his being in possession of the article.

(4) A person guilty of an offence under this section is liable—

(a) on conviction on indictment, to imprisonment for a term not exceeding four years or to a fine (or both);

(b) on summary conviction, to imprisonment for a term not exceeding 12 months or to a fine (or both).

(5) In this section 'authorisation' means authorisation given for the purposes of this section; and subsections (1) to (3) of section 40E apply in relation to authorisations so given as they apply to authorisations given for the purposes of section 40D.".

★ Subsection 4(b) is subject to a transitional provision (s.86(14)(f) of the 2015 Act) in that the reference to 12 months should be read as a reference to six months in relation to an offence committed before section 154(1) of the CJA 2003 (§ 5-461 in the main work) comes into force.

★**28-195b** With effect from June 1, 2015 (Serious Crime Act 2015 (Commencement No. 1) Regulations 2015 (S.I. 2015 No. 820), a new section 40CB was inserted into the 1952 Act, after section 40CA, *ante*, § 28-195a, by the SCA 2015, s.79, as follows—

"Throwing articles into prisons

40CB.—(1) A person who, without authorisation, throws any article or substance into a prison is guilty of an offence.

(2) For the purposes of subsection (1)—

(a) the reference to an article or substance does not include a reference to a List A article, a List B article or a List C article (as defined by section 40A);

(b) the reference to "throwing" an article or substance into a prison includes a reference to doing anything from outside the prison that results in the article or substance being

projected or conveyed over or through a boundary of the prison so as to land inside the
prison.
(3) In proceedings for an offence under this section it is a defence for the accused to show that—
  (a) he reasonably believed that he had authorisation to do the act in respect of which the
proceedings are brought, or
  (b) in all the circumstances there was an overriding public interest which justified the doing of
that act.
(4), (5) [*Identical to s.40CA(4), (5)*, ante, *§ 28-195a*.]".

Subsection 4(b) is subject to a transitional provision (s.86(14)(g) of the 2015 Act) to the same ef- ★
fect as that applying to section 40CA(4)(b), *ante*, § 28-195a.

Chapter 29

PUBLIC ORDER OFFENCES

I. PUBLIC ORDER ACT 1986

B. Offences (Pt I (ss.1–10))

(5) Harassment, alarm or distress
Public Order Act 1986, s.4A

The repeated arrest, prosecution, conviction and imprisonment of the applicant for public   **29-44**
order offences on account of his being naked in public did not violate his rights under either
Article 8 (right to privacy and family life (§ 16-137 in the main work)) or 10 (freedom of expression (§ 16-157 in the main work)) of the ECHR: *Gough v. U.K., The Times*, December 3, 2014,
ECtHR. The court said that to the extent that there had been interference with his exercise of his
rights, such interference was justified. It added that his imprisonment was the consequence of his
repeated violation of the criminal law in full knowledge of the consequences, through conduct
which he knew full well not only went against the standards of accepted public behaviour in any
modern democratic country, but also was liable to be alarming and morally and otherwise offensive to other, unwarned members of the public going about their ordinary business. Further,
the measures adopted by the police, the prosecuting authorities and the courts met a pressing
social need in response to repeated anti-social conduct by the applicant; and it could not be said
that they were disproportionate to the legitimate aim being pursued, namely the prevention of
disorder and crime.

Chapter 30

COMMERCE, FINANCIAL MARKETS AND INSOLVENCY

I. FRAUDULENT TRADING, ETC.

A. Fraudulent Trading

(5) The nature of the offence

For the Supreme Court's decision upholding the decision of the Court of Appeal that the civil   **★30-6**
equivalent of section 993 of the Companies Act 2006 has extra-territorial effect, see *Bilta (U.K.)
Ltd (in liquidation) v. Nazir (No. 2)* [2015] 2 W.L.R. 1168, SC.

III. INSIDER DEALING

(5) The ingredients of the offence

Inside information

For a civil case considering "inside information" in the context of the FSMA 2000, s.118C, and   **30-58**

241

in particular the meaning of the words "likely" and "precise" (both of which appear in s.56 of the CJA 1991), see *Hannam v. Financial Conduct Authority* [2014] Lloyd's Rep. F.C. 704, Upper Tribunal (Tax and Chancery Chamber). The tribunal's approach to "precise" dovetails with that of the High Court of Australia in *R. v. Mansfield; R. v. Kizon* (cited in the main work and now reported at 293 A.L.R. 1).

★ For a case considering what information may be considered as "precise" for the purposes of legislation prohibiting insider dealing (see the 1991 Act, s.56(1)(d) (§ 30-38 in the main work) for the relevant domestic legislation), see *Lafonta v Authorite des marches financiers*, unreported, March 11, 2015, ECJ, where it was said that it is not the case that information is only "precise" for the purposes of legislation prohibiting insider dealing if it is information that makes it possible to determine the likely direction of change in the prices of the financial instruments concerned; the only information that may be regarded as imprecise is information that is vague or general, from which it is impossible to draw a conclusion as regards its possible effect on the prices of the instruments concerned.

Spread betting

30-64 The Court of Appeal decision in *Patel v. Mirza* is now reported at [2015] Ch. 271.

IV. OFFENCES BY BANKRUPTS, ETC.

A. Insolvency Act 1986

(2) Investigation of a bankrupt's affairs

Insolvency Act 1986, ss.288–291

Statement of affairs

★**30-71** As from a day to be appointed, section 288 of the 1986 Act is amended by the Deregulation Act 2015, s.19, and Sched. 6, para. 15, so as: (i) in subsection (1), to substitute, for the words from "the bankrupt shall submit" to the end of the subsection, the words "the official receiver may at any time before the discharge of the bankrupt require the bankrupt to submit to the official receiver a statement of affairs"; (ii) to insert, after subsection (2), a new subsection (2A), as follows—

"(2A) Where a bankrupt is required under subsection (1) to submit a statement of affairs to the official receiver, the bankrupt shall do so (subject to subsection (3)) before the end of the period of 21 days beginning with the day after that on which the prescribed notice of the requirement is given to the bankrupt by the official receiver.";

(iii) in subsection (3)(a), to substitute, for the words "the bankrupt from his duty", the words "a bankrupt from an obligation imposed on the bankrupt"; (iv) to substitute, for subsection (3)(b), a new paragraph (b), as follows—

"(b) either when giving the notice mentioned in subsection (2A) or subsequently, extend the period mentioned in that subsection,";

and (iv) in subsection (4)(a), to substitute, for the words "the obligation imposed by" (the main work erroneously reads "the obligation imposed under"), the words "an obligation imposed under".

Duties of a bankrupt in relation to official receiver

★**30-74** As from a day to be appointed, section 291 of the 1986 Act is amended by the Small Business, Enterprise and Employment Act 2015, s.133(2), and Sched. 10, paras 1 and 4, so as to omit subsections (1) to (3).

(3) General provisions of the Act applying to investigations

Insolvency Act 1986, s.433

Admissibility in evidence of statements of affairs, etc.

★**30-85** As from a day to be appointed, section 433(3)(a) of the 1986 Act is amended by the Small Business, Enterprise and Employment Act 2015, s.126, and Sched. 9, paras 1 and 56, so as: (i) to omit the words "98(6),"; and (ii) to substitute, for the words "99(3)(a)", the words "99(3)".

(5) **Bankruptcy offences**

(b) *Offences*

Insolvency Act 1986, ss.355–358

False statements

As from a day to be appointed, section 356(2)(c) of the 1986 Act is amended by the Small Business, Enterprise and Employment Act 2015, s.126, and Sched. 9, paras 1 and 85, so as: (i) to substitute, for the words "at any meeting of his creditors", the words "in connection with any creditors' decision procedure or deemed consent procedure"; and (ii) to substitute, for the words "at such a meeting", the words ""in connection with such a procedure".

★30-106

B. COMPANY DIRECTORS DISQUALIFICATION ACT 1986

Company Directors Disqualification Act 1986, s.11

Undischarged bankrupts

As from a day to be appointed, section 11 of the 1986 Act is amended by the Small Business, Enterprise and Employment Act 2015, s.113(1), so as to substitute, for subsections (1) and (2), new subsections (1), (2) and (2A), as follows—

★30-118

"(1) It is an offence for a person to act as director of a company or directly or indirectly to take part in or be concerned in the promotion, formation or management of a company, without the leave of the court, at a time when any of the circumstances mentioned in subsection (2) apply to the person.

(2) The circumstances are—
(a) the person is an undischarged bankrupt—
(i) in England and Wales or Scotland, or
(ii) in Northern Ireland,
(b) a bankruptcy restrictions order or undertaking is in force in respect of the person under—
(i) the Bankruptcy (Scotland) Act 1985 or the Insolvency Act 1986, or
(ii) the Insolvency (Northern Ireland) Order 1989,
(c) a debt relief restrictions order or undertaking is in force in respect of the person under—
(i) the Insolvency Act 1986, or
(ii) the Insolvency (Northern Ireland) Order 1989,
(d) a moratorium period under a debt relief order applies in relation to the person under—
(i) the Insolvency Act 1986, or
(ii) the Insolvency (Northern Ireland) Order 1989.
(2A) In subsection (1) 'the court' means—
(a) for the purposes of subsection (2)(a)(i)—
(i) the court by which the person was adjudged bankrupt, or
(ii) in Scotland, the court by which sequestration of the person's estate was awarded or, if awarded other than by the court, the court which would have jurisdiction in respect of sequestration of the person's estate,
(b) for the purposes of subsection (2)(b)(i)—
(i) the court which made the order,
(ii) in Scotland, if the order has been made other than by the court, the court to which the person may appeal against the order, or
(iii) the court to which the person may make an application for annulment of the undertaking,
(c) for the purposes of subsection (2)(c)(i)—
(i) the court which made the order, or
(ii) the court to which the person may make an application for annulment of the undertaking,
(d) for the purposes of subsection (2)(d)(i), the court to which the person would make an application under section 251M(1) of the Insolvency Act 1986 (if the person were dissatisfied as mentioned there),
(e) for the purposes of paragraphs (a)(ii), (b)(ii), (c)(ii) and (d)(ii) of subsection (2), the High Court of Northern Ireland.".

Company Directors Disqualification Act 1986, s.22

Interpretation

As from a day to be appointed, section 22 of the 1986 Act is amended by the Small Business,

★30-123

Enterprise and Employment Act 2015, s.111, and Sched. 7, paras 1 and 17, so as to insert, after subsection (2), a new subsection (2A), as follows—

"(2A) An 'overseas company' is a company incorporated or formed outside Great Britain.".

★**30-124**   As from a day to be appointed, sections 22A to 22F of the 1986 Act are amended by the Small Business, Enterprise and Employment Act 2015, s.111, and Sched. 7, paras 1 and 18 to 23, so as, *inter alia*, to omit section 22D.

CHAPTER 31

OFFENCES AGAINST PUBLIC MORALS AND POLICY

I. OFFENCES RELATING TO MARRIAGE

A. BIGAMY

(6) Evidence

Marriages in England and abroad

31-19   With effect from December 11, 2014, the Consular Marriages and Marriages under Foreign Law Order 2014 (S.I. 2014 No. 1110) is revoked and replaced (with some technical amendments) by the Consular Marriages and Marriages under Foreign Law (No. 2) Order 2014 (S.I. 2014 No. 3265).

Foreign marriages

31-21   As to the replacement of S.I. 2014 No. 1110, see *ante*, § 31-19.

II. PUBLIC NUISANCE

A. STATUTE

(2) Dangerous Dogs Act 1991

Dangerous Dogs Act 1991, s.3(1)–(4A)

Sentence

★**31-37b**   The Sentencing Council for England and Wales issued a consultation guideline on the offences contrary to sections 1 and 3 of the 1991 Act following amendments to that Act by the Anti-social Behaviour, Crime and Policing Act 2014, ss.106 and 107. The consultation closed on June 9, 2015 and a definitive guideline will then be issued. For the full text of the consultation guideline, see www.sentencingcouncil.org.uk. For the current guideline, see *post*, K-291 *et seq.*

Dangerous Dogs Act 1991, s.4(1)–(7)

Destruction and disqualification orders

31-38   As to the revocation and replacement of S.I. 1991 No. 1744, see *post*, § 31-38b.

Dangerous Dogs Act 1991, s.4A

Contingent destruction orders

31-38b   With effect from March 3, 2015, the Dangerous Dogs Exemption Schemes (England and Wales) Order 2015 (S.I. 2015 No. 138) revokes and replaces the Dangerous Dogs Compensation and Exemption Schemes Order 1991 (S.I. 1991 No. 1744) (as to which, see the main work).

★   Where a contingent destruction order is made under section 4B(3), and a dog is exempted within the requisite period, the destruction order is not revived if the dog ceases thereafter to be exempt; and it followed that the police had acted unlawfully in arranging for the destruction of a dog which had become exempt when it had later ceased to be exempt: *R. (Ali) v. Chief Constable of Merseyside Police*, unreported, December 9, 2014, QBD (King J.) ([2014] EWHC 4772 (Admin.)). As to the submission that this case serves to illustrate the poor drafting of the 1991 Act, see the commentary at CLW/15/17/3.

III. OBSCENE OR INDECENT PUBLICATIONS AND DISPLAYS, ETC.

B. STATUTE

(4) Protection of Children Act 1978

Protection of Children Act 1978, ss.1–1B

Ingredients of the offence

The question whether images are indecent for the purposes of section 1 of the 1978 Act is to be decided by the jury and not by any pre-conceived categorisation of images into various levels, which is only useful for sentencing purposes: *R. v. Miles* [2015] 3 *Archbold Review* 3, CA. **★31-108a**

(6) Criminal Justice and Immigration Act 2008

Criminal Justice and Immigration Act 2008, ss.63–68

Possession of extreme pornographic images

As from April 13, 2015 (Criminal Justice and Courts Act 2015 (Commencement No. 1, Saving and Transitional Provisions) Order 2015 (S.I. 2015 No. 778)), section 63 of the 2008 Act was amended by the Criminal Justice and Courts Act 2015, s.37(1) and (2), so as: (i) to insert new subsection (5A), as follows— **★31-120**

"(5A) In relation to possession of an image in England and Wales, an 'extreme image' is an image which—
  (a) falls within subsection (7) or (7A), and
  (b) is grossly offensive, disgusting or otherwise of an obscene character.";

(ii) to substitute the words "In relation to possession of an image in Northern Ireland, an" for the word "An" in subsection (6); and (iii) to insert new subsections (7A) and (7B), as follows—

"(7A) An image falls within this subsection if it portrays, in an explicit and realistic way, either of the following—
  (a) an act which involves the non-consensual penetration of a person's vagina, anus or mouth by another with the other person's penis, or
  (b) an act which involves the non-consensual sexual penetration of a person's vagina or anus by another with a part of the other person's body or anything else,
and a reasonable person looking at the image would think that the persons were real.
  (7B) For the purposes of subsection (7A)—
  (a) penetration is a continuing act from entry to withdrawal;
  (b) 'vagina' includes vulva.".

The amendments effected by section 37 of the 2015 Act do not apply to possession of an image that occurred before April 13, 2015: S.I. 2015 No. 778 (*ante*), art. 4, and Sched. 2, para. 1. **★**

Defence: participation in consensual acts

As from April 13, 2015 (Criminal Justice and Courts Act 2015 (Commencement No. 1, Saving and Transitional Provisions) Order 2015 (S.I. 2015 No. 778)), section 66 of the 2008 Act was amended by the Criminal Justice and Courts Act 2015, s.37(1) and (3), so as: (i) to insert new subsections (A1) and (A2) before subsection (1), as follows— **★31-123**

"(A1) Subsection (A2) applies where in England and Wales—
  (a) a person ('D') is charged with an offence under section 63, and
  (b) the offence relates to an image that portrays an act or acts within subsection (7)(a) to (c) or (7A) of that section (but does not portray an act within subsection (7)(d) of that section).

(A2) It is a defence for D to prove—
  (a) that D directly participated in the act or any of the acts portrayed, and
  (b) that the act or acts did not involve the infliction of any non-consensual harm on any person, and
  (c) if the image portrays an act within section 63(7)(c), that what is portrayed as a human corpse was not in fact a corpse, and
  (d) if the image portrays an act within section 63(7A), that what is portrayed as non-consensual penetration was in fact consensual.";

and (ii) in subsection (1), to substitute the words "Subsection (2)" for "This section" and to insert the words "in Northern Ireland" after "where".

★   The amendments effected by section 37 of the 2015 Act do not apply to possession of an image that occurred before April 13, 2015: S.I. 2015 No. 778 (*ante*), art. 4, and Sched. 2, para. 1.

Penalties etc. for possession of extreme pornographic images

★31-124   As from April 13, 2015 (Criminal Justice and Courts Act 2015 (Commencement No. 1, Saving and Transitional Provisions) Order 2015 (S.I. 2015 No. 778)), section 67 of the 2008 Act was amended by the Criminal Justice and Courts Act 2015, s.37(1) and (4), so as: (i) to substitute the words "If the offence relates to an image that portrays any relevant act (with or without other acts)" for the words "Except where subsection (3) applies to the offence" in subsection (2); (ii) to substitute the words "relevant act" for the words "act within section 63(7)(a) or (b)" in subsection 3; and (iii) to insert a new subsection (5), as follows—

"(5) In this section 'relevant act' means—
  (a) in relation to England and Wales, an act within section 63(7)(a) or (b) or (7A)(a) or (b);
  (b) in relation to Northern Ireland, an act within section 63(7)(a) or (b).".

★   The amendments effected by section 37 of the 2015 Act do not apply to possession of an image that occurred before April 13, 2015: S.I. 2015 No. 778 (*ante*), art. 4, and Sched. 2, para. 1.

★31-127   As from April 13, 2015 (Criminal Justice and Courts Act 2015 (Commencement No. 1, Saving and Transitional Provisions) Order 2015 (S.I. 2015 No. 778)), Schedule 14 to the 2008 Act was amended by the Criminal Justice and Courts Act 2015, s.37(1) and (5), to take account of the fact that the amendments of section 63 of the 2008 Act (as to which, see *ante*, § 31-120), effected by the 2015 Act, do not apply in Northern Ireland. The amendments effected by section 37 of the 2015 Act do not apply to possession of an image that occurred before April 13, 2015: S.I. 2015 No. 778 (*ante*), art. 4, and Sched. 2, para. 1.

IV. BRIBERY AND CORRUPTION

B. STATUTE

(3) Bribery Act 2010

(c) Statute

Bribery Act 2010, s.11

★31-181   As to the repeal of section 76 of the SOCPA 2005, see *ante*, § 5-1212.

(5) Criminal Justice and Courts Act 2015

Criminal Justice and Courts Act 2015, s.26

Corrupt or other improper exercise of police powers and privileges

31-200   **26.**—(1) A police constable listed in subsection (3) commits an offence if he or she—
  (a) exercises the powers and privileges of a constable improperly, and
  (b) knows or ought to know that the exercise is improper.
  (2) A police constable guilty of an offence under this section is liable, on conviction on indictment, to imprisonment for a term not exceeding 14 years or a fine (or both).
  (3) The police constables referred to in subsection (1) are—
  (a) a constable of a police force in England and Wales;
  (b) a special constable for a police area in England and Wales;

(c) a constable or special constable of the British Transport Police Force;

(d) a constable of the Civil Nuclear Constabulary;

(e) a constable of the Ministry of Defence Police;

(f) a National Crime Agency officer designated under section 9 or 10 of the Crime and Courts Act 2013 as having the powers and privileges of a constable.

(4) For the purposes of this section, a police constable exercises the powers and privileges of a constable improperly if—

(a) he or she exercises a power or privilege of a constable for the purpose of achieving—

(i) a benefit for himself or herself, or

(ii) a benefit or a detriment for another person, and

(b) a reasonable person would not expect the power or privilege to be exercised for the purpose of achieving that benefit or detriment.

(5) For the purposes of this section, a police constable is to be treated as exercising the powers and privileges of a constable improperly in the cases described in subsections (6) and (7).

(6) The first case is where—

(a) the police constable fails to exercise a power or privilege of a constable,

(b) the purpose of the failure is to achieve a benefit or detriment described in subsection (4)(a), and

(c) a reasonable person would not expect a constable to fail to exercise the power or privilege for the purpose of achieving that benefit or detriment.

(7) The second case is where—

(a) the police constable threatens to exercise, or not to exercise, a power or privilege of a constable,

(b) the threat is made for the purpose of achieving a benefit or detriment described in subsection (4)(a), and

(c) a reasonable person would not expect a constable to threaten to exercise, or not to exercise, the power or privilege for the purpose of achieving that benefit or detriment.

(8) An offence is committed under this section if the act or omission in question takes place in the United Kingdom or in United Kingdom waters.

(9) In this section—

"benefit" and "detriment" mean any benefit or detriment, whether or not in money or other property and whether temporary or permanent;

"United Kingdom waters" means the sea and other waters within the seaward limits of the United Kingdom's territorial sea.

(10) References in this section to exercising, or not exercising, the powers and privileges of a constable include performing, or not performing, the duties of a constable.

(11) Nothing in this section affects what constitutes the offence of misconduct in public office at common law in England and Wales or Northern Ireland.

Section 26 of the 2015 Act came into force on April 13, 2015: Criminal Justice and Courts Act ★ 2015 (Commencement No. 1, Saving and Transitional Provisions) Order 2015 (S.I. 2015 No. 778).

CHAPTER 32

MOTOR VEHICLE OFFENCES

II. DRIVING OFFENCES

B. CAUSING SERIOUS INJURY BY DANGEROUS DRIVING

(5) Sentence

Maximum

It was held in *R. v. Ellis* [2014] 2 Cr.App.R.(S.) 50, CA, that, when considering the proper ap- **32-29** proach to disqualification and the related issue of culpability for the relatively new offence of causing serious injury by dangerous driving (RTA 1988, s.1A (§ 32-25 in the main work)), assistance could be obtained from the Sentencing Guidelines Council's guideline on causing death by driving (*post*, Appendix K-185 *et seq.*), but making due allowance for the fact that the consequences of the driving will be different and the standard of driving being considered may differ. In that case an eight-year disqualification (in addition to two years' imprisonment) on a guilty plea was reduced to five years, where the offender (24/ no convictions/ clean licence/ had obtained the "pass plus" certificate and undertaken a further 30 hours of voluntary tuition after passing his driving test), had collided with another car when driving late at night like "a boy racer", causing the driver of the other car to suffer life-changing injuries.

For a further case where regard was had to the guideline on causing death by dangerous driving, and where it was said that it was not a helpful exercise to consider the very worst imaginable type of case which would attract a sentence at the maximum, see *R. v. Dewdney* [2015] 1 Cr.App.R.(S.) 5, CA.

★   In *R. v. Buckle* [2015] 1 Cr.App.R.(S.) 68, CA, it was held that the accumulation of aggravating factors justified a starting point at the maximum, notwithstanding that it was not a "near-death" case.

Concurrent/consecutive

★**32-30a**   In *R. v. Jenkins* [2015] 1 Cr.App.R.(S.) 70, CA, it was held to be wrong in principle to impose consecutive sentences for two counts of causing serious injury by dangerous driving arising out of the same incident (following *R. v. Noble*, § 5-588 in the main work, *Att.-Gen.'s Reference (No. 57 of 2009) (R. v. Ralphs)* (*ibid.*, § 24-29), and the Sentencing Council's guideline on totality (*post*, Appendix K-280 *et seq.*)).

F. Causing Death by Careless Driving when Under the Influence

(1) Statute
Road Traffic Act 1988, s.3A

Causing death by careless driving when under influence of drink or drugs

32-62   With effect from March 2, 2015 (Crime and Courts Act 2013 (Commencement No. 1) (England and Wales) Order 2014 (S.I. 2014 No. 3268)), section 56 of, and Schedule 22 to, the 2013 Act are brought into force.

G. Causing Death by Driving: Unlicensed, Disqualified or Uninsured Drivers

(1) Statute
Road Traffic Act 1988, s.3ZB

Causing death by driving: unlicensed, disqualified or uninsured drivers

★**32-71**   As from April 13, 2015 (Criminal Justice and Courts Act 2015 (Commencement No. 1, Saving and Transitional Provisions) Order 2015 (S.I. 2015 No. 778)), section 3ZB of the 1988 Act is amended by the Criminal Justice and Courts Act 2015, s.29(4), and Sched. 6, para. 1, to omit: (i) paragraph (b) (but not the word "or"); and (ii) ", disqualified" in the heading. The amendments made by section 29 and Schedule 6 have effect only in relation to driving which occurs after they come into force: 2015 Act, s.29(5).

GA. Causing Death by Driving: Disqualified Drivers

(1) Statute

★**32-76a**   As from April 13, 2015 (Criminal Justice and Courts Act 2015 (Commencement No. 1, Saving and Transitional Provisions) Order 2015 (S.I. 2015 No. 778)), the 1988 Act is amended by the Criminal Justice and Courts Act 2015, s.29(1), so as to insert new sections 3ZC and 3ZD. The amendments made by section 29 and Schedule 6 have effect only in relation to driving which occurs after they come into force: 2015 Act, s.29(5).

Road Traffic Act 1988, ss.3ZC, 3ZD

Causing death by driving: disqualified drivers
   3ZC. A person is guilty of an offence under this section if he or she—

(a) causes the death of another person by driving a motor vehicle on a road, and

(b) at that time, is committing an offence under section 103(1)(b) of this Act (driving while disqualified).

Causing serious injury by driving: disqualified drivers

3ZD.—(1) A person is guilty of an offence under this section if he or she—

(a) causes serious injury to another person by driving a motor vehicle on a road, and

(b) at that time, is committing an offence under section 103(1)(b) of this Act (driving while disqualified).

(2) In this section "serious injury" means—

(a) in England and Wales, physical harm which amounts to grievous bodily harm for the purposes of the Offences against the Person Act 1861, and

(b) [*Scotland*].

(2) Indictment

Counts alleging section 3ZC and 3ZD offences can be adapted from the precedent at § 32-72 in the main work.

32-76b

(3) Mode of trial

The section 3ZC offence is triable only on indictment; the section 3ZD offence is triable either way: see the RTOA 1988, s.9, and Sched. 2, Pt 1, as amended, as from April 13, 2015 (Criminal Justice and Courts Act 2015 (Commencement No. 1, Saving and Transitional Provisions) Order 2015 (S.I. 2015 No. 778)), by the Criminal Justice and Courts Act 2015, s.29(2). The amendments made by section 29 and Schedule 6 have effect only in relation to driving which occurs after they come into force: 2015 Act, s.29(5).

★32-76c

(4) Alternative verdicts

As to alternative verdicts generally, see the main work, §§ 4-524 *et seq.*

Driving while disqualified is a specific alternative verdict available for both sections 3ZC and 3ZD: see the RTOA 1988, s.24, *post*, § 32-224.

32-76d

(5) Sentence

The section 3ZC offence carries a maximum term of imprisonment of 10 years, or a fine, or both; the section 3ZD offence, on conviction on indictment, carries a maximum term of four years' imprisonment, or a fine, or both, and on summary conviction, imprisonment not exceeding 12 months (six months if committed before s.154(1) of the CJA 2003 comes into force: see s.29(3)(a) of the 2015 Act), or a fine, or both: RTOA 1988, s.33, and Sched. 2, Pt I, as amended, as from April 13, 2015 (Criminal Justice and Courts Act 2015 (Commencement No. 1, Saving and Transitional Provisions) Order 2015 (S.I. 2015 No. 778)), by the Criminal Justice and Courts Act 2015, s.29(2). Disqualification and endorsement are obligatory; and the offences carry 3 to 11 penalty points: RTOA 1988, ss.28, 34, 44 and Sched. 2, Pt 1, as amended, as from April 13, 2015 (S.I. 2015 No. 778 (*ante*)), by the 2015 Act, s.29(2). In addition an offender convicted of either offence must be disqualified until he passes an extended driving test: RTOA 1988, s.36, *post*, § 32-273. The amendments made by section 29 and Schedule 6 have effect only in relation to driving which occurs after they come into force: 2015 Act, s.29(5).

★32-76e

(6) Ingredients of the offences

See § 32-76 in the main work. The only additional ingredient is "serious injury", which is defined in section 3ZD(2), *ante*, § 32-76a, and, as to which, see § 19-258 in the main work.

32-76f

H. Driving, Being in Charge, Whilst Unfit

(6) Ingredients of the offence

Drink or drugs

As to the commencement of section 56 of the Crime and Courts Act 2013, see *ante*, § 32-62.

32-84

I. Driving, Being in Charge, Whilst Above the Prescribed Limit

(7) Evidence

Specimen of breath, blood or urine

★**32-101**   As to the repeal of section 8(2) of the RTA 1988, see *post*, § 32-139.

J. Driving, Being in Charge, with Concentration of Specified Controlled Drug above Specified Limit

(1) Statute

Road Traffic Act 1988, s.5A

[Driving or being in charge of a motor vehicle with concentration of specified controlled drug above specified limit

32-105   As to the commencement of section 56 of the Crime and Courts Act 2013, which inserts section 5A into the 1988 Act, see *ante*, § 32-62.

★   With effect from March 2, 2015, the Drug Driving (Specified Limits) (England and Wales) Regulations 2014 (S.I. 2014 No. 2868), as amended by the Drug Driving (Specified Limits) (England and Wales) (Amendment) Regulations 2015 (S.I. 2015 No. 911) (with effect from April 14, 2015), specify the controlled drugs, and the limit for each expressed as a concentration in blood, for the purposes of section 5A of the 1988 Act. The specified drugs are either listed in their own right in Schedule 2 to the Misuse of Drugs Act 1971 (§§ 27-6 *et seq.* in the main work), or else they come within the terms of Schedule 2, *e.g.* because they are an ester or ether of a drug which is listed in that schedule.

★   The drugs and the limits, expressed as microgrammes per litre of blood, are as follows: Amphetamine 250; Benzoylecgonine 50; Clonazepam 50; Cocaine 10; Delta-9-Tetrahydrocannabinol 2; Diazepam 550; Flunitrazepam 300; Ketamine 20; Lorazepam 100; Lysergic Acid Diethylamide 1; Methadone 500; Methylamphetamine 10; Methylenedioxymethamphetamine 10; 6-Monoacetylmorphine 5; Morphine 80; Oxazepam 300; Temazepam 1000.

K. Failure to Co-operate with Preliminary Test

(1) Statute

Road Traffic Act 1988, ss.6–6E

Preliminary drug test

32-116   As to the commencement of section 56 of the Crime and Courts Act 2013, see *ante*, § 32-62.

Arrest

32-117   As to the commencement of section 56 of the Crime and Courts Act 2013, see *ante*, § 32-62.

L. Failing to Provide Evidential Specimen

(1) Statute

Road Traffic Act 1988, s.7

Provision of specimens for analysis

32-126   As to the commencement of section 56 of the Crime and Courts Act 2013, see *ante*, § 32-62.

★   With effect from April 10, 2015 (Deregulation Act 2015 (Commencement No. 1 and Transitional and Saving Provisions) Order 2015 (S.I. 2015 No. 994)), section 7 of the 1988 Act is amended by the 2015 Act, s.52, and Sched. 11, paras 3 and 5, so as: (i) to substitute a new subsection (2), as follows—

"(2) A constable may make a requirement under this section to provide specimens of breath only if—

(a) the requirement is made at a police station or a hospital,
(b) the requirement is imposed in circumstances where section 6(5) of this Act applies, or
(c) the constable is in uniform.";

(ii) to omit subsections (2A) and (2B); (iii) to insert a new subsection (2CA) after subsection (2C), as follows—

"(2CA) For the purposes of subsection (2C) 'a relevant breath test' is a procedure involving the provision by the person concerned of a specimen of breath to be used for the purpose of obtaining an indication whether the proportion of alcohol in his breath or blood is likely to exceed the prescribed limit.";

(iv) in subsection (3)(c), to insert, after the words "advised by a medical practitioner", the words "or a registered health care professional"; and (v) to insert, after subsection (5), a new subsection (5A), as follows—

"(5A) A constable may arrest a person without warrant if—
(a) the person fails to provide a specimen of breath when required to do so in pursuance of this section, and
(b) the constable reasonably suspects that the person has alcohol in his body.".

(5) Procedure

Samples other than breath

Urine samples

With effect from April 10, 2015 (Deregulation Act 2015 (Commencement No. 1 and Transitional and Saving Provisions) Order 2015 (S.I. 2015 No. 994)), section 11(4) of the RTOA 1988 is amended by the 2015 Act, s.52, and Sched. 11, paras 3 and 9, so as to omit the words "by a medical practitioner or, if it is taken in a police station,". ★32-138

Choice of specimens of breath

With effect from April 10, 2015 (Deregulation Act 2015 (Commencement No. 1 and Transitional and Saving Provisions) Order 2015 (S.I. 2015 No. 994)), subsections (2) and (2A) of section 8 of the RTA 1988 are repealed by the 2015 Act, s.52, and Sched. 11, para. 1(1) to (3). ★32-139

Detention until fit

As to the commencement of section 56 of the Crime and Courts Act 2013, see *ante*, § 32-62. 32-140

(6) Ingredients of the offence

"without reasonable excuse"

Legal advice

For a Canadian case to the effect that the denial of legal advice to a person arrested on suspicion of impaired driving causing bodily harm meant that a blood sample taken from him while he was in custody (which constituted the evidence upon which he was convicted) was inadmissible evidence, see *R. v. Taylor*, unreported, July 18, 2014, Supreme Court of Canada (2014 SCC 50). 32-145

M. Failing to Give Permission for Laboratory Test

(1) Statute

Road Traffic Act 1988, s.7A

Specimens of blood taken from persons incapable of consenting

With effect from April 10, 2015 (Deregulation Act 2015 (Commencement No. 1 and Transitional and Saving Provisions) Order 2015 (S.I. 2015 No. 994)), section 7A of the 1988 Act is amended by the 2015 Act, s.52, and Sched. 11, paras 3 and 8, so as: (i) in subsections (1) and (2)(a), to substitute, for the words "a medical practitioner", the words "a medical or health care practitioner"; (ii) in subsection (2)(b), to substitute, for the words "a medical practitioner other than a police medical practitioner", the words "a practitioner other than a police medical or health care practitioner"; (iii) in subsection (2)(b)(i), to substitute, for the words "to made to a police medical practitioner", the words "to be made to a police medical or health care ★32-147 practitioner"; (iv) in subsection (2)(b)(ii), to omit the word "medical"; (v) in subsection (3), to substitute, for the words "a medical practitioner", the words "a medical or health care practitioner"; and (vi) to substitute a new subsection (7), as follows—

"(7) In this section—
'medical or health care practitioner' means a medical practitioner or a registered health care professional;
'police medical or health care practitioner' means a medical practitioner, or a registered health care professional, who is engaged under any agreement to provide medical or health care services for purposes connected with the activities of a police force.".

O. Driving Without a Licence

(4) Interpretation

Road Traffic Act 1988, s.108

32-157 With effect from December 29, 2014, section 108 of the 1988 Act was amended by the Road Traffic Act 1988 and Motor Vehicles (Driving Licences) (Amendment) Regulations 2014 (S.I. 2014 No. 3190), reg. 10(1) and (4), so as to insert subsections (1B) to (1E), as follows—

"(1B) For the purposes of this Part a person is normally resident in Great Britain if—
(a) the person lives in Great Britain for at least 185 days in each calendar year because of—
(i) personal and occupational ties, or
(ii) close personal ties, or
(b) the person has personal ties in Great Britain and occupational ties in another place in the EEA and consequently lives in turn in Great Britain and that other place.
(1C) For the purposes of this Part a person is normally resident in the United Kingdom if—
(a) the person lives in the United Kingdom for at least 185 days in each calendar year because of—
(i) personal and occupational ties, or
(ii) close personal ties, or
(b) the person has personal ties in the United Kingdom and occupational ties in another place in the EEA and consequently lives in turn in the United Kingdom and that other place.
(1D) In order to be normally resident in Great Britain or the United Kingdom by virtue of subsection (1B)(b) or (1C)(b) a person must return there regularly, except when the person is living in another place in the EEA in order to carry out a task of a definite duration.
(1E) For the purposes of subsections (1B) and (1C) attendance at a university or school is not a personal or occupational tie.".

★ With effect from June 8, 2015 (Road Safety Act 2006 (Commencement No. 11 and Transitional Provisions) Order 2015 (S.I. 2015 No. 560)), the provisions of the 2006 Act referred to in the main work were brought into force.

(5) Grant and form of licences

Road Traffic Act 1988, s.97

Grant of licences

★32-159 With effect from June 8, 2015 (Road Safety Act 2006 (Commencement No. 11 and Transitional Provisions) Order 2015 (S.I. 2015 No. 560)), section 10 of, paragraphs 2 and 6 (apart from para. 6(2)(b) and (3)) of Schedule 3 to, and Schedule 7(4) (apart from paragraphs (b) and (d) of the entry relating to the RTA 1988, s.97) (and s.59 in so far as it relates thereto) to, the 2006 Act (see the main work) were brought into force. The provisions that have not been brought into force relate to the repeal of the italicised words in subsections (1)(c)(ia) and (1AA) of section 97. There are transitional provisions, as to which, see in particular, articles 4 and 5 of the commencement order.

★ With effect from June 8, 2015, section 97 was further amended by the Road Safety Act 2006 (Consequential Amendments) Order 2015 (S.I. 2015 No. 583) so as: (i) in subsection (1)(c)(ia), to substitute, for the words "and its counterpart (if any) issued to him under this Part of this Act", the words "(if any)"; (ii) in subsection (1AA), to substitute, for the words "counterparts mentioned in that sub-paragraph", the words "counterpart (if any)"; and (iii) in subsection (1AA)(b), to insert, after the words "Northern Ireland counterpart", the words "(if any)".

The Motor Vehicles (Driving Licences) Regulations 1999 (S.I. 1999 No. 2864) were further **★32-160** amended by S.I. 2014 No. 3190, *ante*, § 32-157, with effect from December 29, 2014; by the Motor Vehicles (Driving Licences) (Amendment) (No. 3) Regulations 2015 (S.I. 2015 No. 719) with effect from March 26, 2015; and by S.I. 2015 No. 583 (*ante*, § 32-159), with effect from June 8, 2015.

With effect from December 29, 2014, section 97A of the 1988 Act is amended by S.I. 2014 No. **32-161** 3190, *ante*, § 32-157.

Road Traffic Act 1988, s.98

Form of licence

With effect from June 8, 2015 (Road Safety Act 2006 (Commencement No. 11 and Transitional **★32-162** Provisions) Order 2015 (S.I. 2015 No. 560)), the provisions of the 2006 Act referred to in the main work (other than s.38(3)) were brought into force. Section 38(3) omits the words "in the case of a provisional licence" and substitutes "any" for "the" in subsection (1)(c).

S. FAILING TO GIVE INFORMATION AS TO IDENTITY OF DRIVER

(1) Statute
Road Traffic Act 1988, s.172

Duty to give information as to identity of driver etc. in certain circumstances

With effect from April 12, 2015, section 172(2)(a) of the 1988 Act is amended by the **32-185** Infrastructure Act 2015, s.22(2), so as to insert the words "or the Chief Constable of the British Transport Police Force" after the words "chief officer of police".

T. POLICE POWERS

(2) Power to require production of licence

(a) *Statute*

Road Traffic Act 1988, s.164

Power of constables to require production of driving licence and in certain cases statement of date of birth

With effect from June 8, 2015 (Road Safety Act 2006 (Commencement No. 11 and Transitional **★32-194** Provisions) Order 2015 (S.I. 2015 No. 560)), the provisions of the 2006 Act referred to in the main work were brought into force. There are transitional provisions, as to which, see in particular, article 9 of the commencement order.

(4) Power to seize, etc. vehicles driven without licence or insurance

With effect from June 8, 2015, section 165A of the RTA 1988 was amended by the Road Safety **★32-204** Act 2006 (Consequential Amendments) Order 2015 (S.I. 2015 No. 583), so as, *inter alia*, to omit the words "and its counterpart".

U. PROCEDURE AND EVIDENCE

(1) Notice of intended prosecution
Road Traffic Offenders Act 1988, s.2

Requirement of warning, etc: supplementary

With effect from June 8, 2015, section 2(2)(b) of the RTOA 1988 was amended by the Road **★32-211** Safety Act 2006 (Consequential Amendments) Order 2015 (S.I. 2015 No. 583), so as to substitute, for the words "54(4)", the words "54(5)".

(3) Duty of accused to provide licence
Road Traffic Offenders Act 1988, s.7

Duty of accused to provide licence

As from April 13, 2015 (Criminal Justice and Courts Act 2015 (Commencement No. 1, Saving **★32-214** and Transitional Provisions) Order 2015 (S.I. 2015 No. 778)), the RTOA 1988, s.7, is amended by the Criminal Justice and Courts Act 2015, s.50, and Sched. 11, paras 8 and 9, so as: (i) after subsection (1), to insert new subsections (1A) to (1C), as follows—

> "(1A) Subsection (1B) applies where—
>> (a) proceedings in relation to an offence involving obligatory or discretionary disqualification are instituted by a written charge and a single justice procedure notice,
>> (b) the person prosecuted is the holder of a licence, and
>> (c) after being convicted in proceedings conducted in accordance with section 16A of the Magistrates' Courts Act 1980, the person is given the opportunity to make representations or further representations under section 16C(2)(a) of that Act.
> (1B) Where this subsection applies, the person must (instead of complying with subsection (1))—
>> (a) cause the licence to be delivered to the designated officer specified in the single justice procedure notice within such period as the person is allowed for indicating a wish to make such representations,
>> (b) post it, at such time that in the ordinary course of post it would be delivered within that period, in a letter duly addressed to that officer and either registered or sent by the recorded delivery service, or
>> (c) if the person indicates a wish to make such representations, have the licence with him at the hearing appointed to be held because of that indication.
> (1C) Subsection (1B) does not apply (and subsection (1) applies instead) if, before the period mentioned in subsection (1B)(a) comes to an end, a summons is issued under section 16B(3)(b) or 16C(3)(b) of the Magistrates' Courts Act 1980.";

and (ii) to revise the text of subsection (2) so that it will read as follows—

> "(2) In this section
> 'proper officer' means—
>> (a) in relation to a magistrates' court in England and Wales, the designated officer for the court, and
>> (b) in relation to any other court, the clerk of the court,
> 'single justice procedure notice' and 'written charge' have the same meaning as in section 29 of the Criminal Justice Act 2003.".

★   With effect from June 8, 2015 (Road Safety Act 2006 (Commencement No. 11 and Transitional Provisions) Order 2015 (S.I. 2015 No. 560)), the provisions of the 2006 Act referred to in the main work were brought into force. There are transitional provisions, as to which, see in particular, article 9 of the commencement order.

(5) Evidence
Road Traffic Offenders Act 1988, ss.13, 15, 16

Use of specimens in proceedings for an offence under [section 4 or 5] [[any of sections 3A to 5A] of the Road Traffic Act

32-219   As to the commencement of section 56 of the Crime and Courts Act 2013, see *ante*, § 32-62.
★   With effect from April 10, 2015 (Deregulation Act 2015 (Commencement No. 1 and Transitional and Saving Provisions) Order 2015 (S.I. 2015 No. 994)), section 15(4) of the RTOA 1988 was amended by the 2015 Act, s.52, and Sched. 11, para. 10, so as: (i) in paragraph (a), to substitute, for the words from "and either" to the end of the paragraph, the words "by a medical practitioner or a registered health care professional"; and (ii) in paragraph (b), to insert, after the words "medical practitioner", the words "or a registered health care professional".

(7) Alternative verdicts
Road Traffic Offenders Act 1988, s.24

Alternative verdicts: general

32-224   As to the commencement of section 56 of the Crime and Courts Act 2013, see *ante*, § 32-62.
★   As from April 13, 2015 (Criminal Justice and Courts Act 2015 (Commencement No. 1, Saving and Transitional Provisions) Order 2015 (S.I. 2015 No. 778)), the RTOA 1988, s.24, is amended by the Criminal Justice and Courts Act 2015, s.29(4), and Sched. 6, paras 2 and 3, so as: (i) after subsection (A2)(b), to insert new paragraphs (ba) and (bb), as follows—

> "(ba) an offence under section 3ZC of that Act (causing death by driving: disqualified drivers),

(bb) an offence under section 3ZD of that Act (causing serious injury by driving: disqualified
drivers),";

and (ii) in the Table in subsection (1), at the appropriate place, entries relating to sections 3ZC
and 3ZD (as to which, see *ante*, § 32-76a) are inserted, specifying in relation to each that driving
while disqualified contrary to section 103(1)(b) of the RTA 1988 is an available alternative verdict.
The amendments made by section 29 and Schedule 6 have effect only in relation to driving which
occurs after they come into force: 2015 Act, s.29(5).

(8) Offences to which sections 1, 6, 11 and 12 apply
Road Traffic Offenders Act 1988, Sched. 1

As to the commencement of section 56 of the Crime and Courts Act 2013, see *ante*, § 32-62.   **32-226**

As from April 13, 2015 (Criminal Justice and Courts Act 2015 (Commencement No. 1, Saving   ★
and Transitional Provisions) Order 2015 (S.I. 2015 No. 778)), the RTOA 1988, Sched. 1, is
amended by the Criminal Justice and Courts Act 2015, s.29(4), and Sched. 6, paras 2 and 8, so as:
(i) to omit ", disqualified" in the entry for section 3ZB of the RTA 1988; and (ii) after that entry,
to insert entries for sections 3ZC and 3ZD of the RTA 1988, specifying, in relation to section 3ZC,
that section 11 of the RTOA 1988 is applicable, and that, in relation to section 3ZD, sections 11
and 12(1) of the RTOA 1988 are applicable. The amendments made by section 29 and Schedule
6 have effect only in relation to driving which occurs after they come into force: 2015 Act, s.29(5).

V. Disqualification and Endorsement
(4) Penalty points

It was contrary to the RTOA 1988, s.44(1) (§ 32-292 in the main work), for a court to direct the   **32-231**
endorsement of a driving licence, or its counterpart, with penalty points at the same time as
imposing a disqualification: *R. v. Usaceva* [2015] R.T.R. 17, CA (following *R. v. Kent* (see §§ 32-227
et seq. in the main work)) and approving the note at this paragraph in the main work).

(5) Statutory provisions—general
Road Traffic Offenders Act 1988, ss.27, 28

Production of licence

As from April 13, 2015 (Criminal Justice and Courts Act 2015 (Commencement No. 1, Saving   **32-235**
and Transitional Provisions) Order 2015 (S.I. 2015 No. 778)), the RTOA 1988, s.27, is amended
by the Criminal Justice and Courts Act 2015, s.50, and Sched. 11, paras 8 and 11, so as: (i) after
subsection (4), to insert a new subsection (4A), as follows—

"(4A) Subsection (3) does not apply where section 7(1B) applies in relation to the proceedings and
the holder of the licence—
> (a) has caused a current receipt for the licence issued under section 56 to be delivered to the
> designated officer specified in the single justice procedure notice within the period
> described in section 7(1B)(a),
> (b) has posted it to that officer within that period in such manner as is described in section
> 7(1B)(b), or
> (c) surrenders such a receipt to the court at the hearing described in section 7(1B)(c),
and produces the licence to the court immediately on its return.";

and (ii) to revise the text of subsection (5) so that it will read as follows—

"(5) In this section
> 'proper officer' means—
> (a) in relation to a magistrates' court in England and Wales, the designated officer for the
> court, and
> (b) in relation to any other court, the clerk of the court,
> 'single justice procedure notice' and 'written charge' have the same meaning as in section 29 of
> the Criminal Justice Act 2003.".

With effect from June 8, 2015 (Road Safety Act 2006 (Commencement No. 11 and Transitional   ★
Provisions) Order 2015 (S.I. 2015 No. 560)), the provisions of the 2006 Act referred to in the
main work were brought into force. There are transitional provisions, as to which, see in
particular, article 9 of the commencement order.

Penalty points to be attributed to an offence

★**32-236**   With effect from June 8, 2015 (Road Safety Act 2006 (Commencement No. 11 and Transitional Provisions) Order 2015 (S.I. 2015 No. 560)), the uncommenced provisions of the 2006 Act referred to in the main work were brought into force.

Road Traffic Offenders Act 1988, s.29

Penalty points to be taken into account on conviction

★**32-238**   With effect from June 8, 2015 (Road Safety Act 2006 (Commencement No. 11 and Transitional Provisions) Order 2015 (S.I. 2015 No. 560)), the uncommenced provisions of the 2006 Act referred to in the main work (other than s.34(1) and (2)) were brought into force. There are transitional provisions, as to which, see in particular, article 6 of the commencement order.

Road Traffic Offenders Act 1988, s.30

Penalty points: modification where fixed penalty also in question

★**32-240**   With effect from June 8, 2015 (Road Safety Act 2006 (Commencement No. 11 and Transitional Provisions) Order 2015 (S.I. 2015 No. 560)), the uncommenced provisions of the 2006 Act referred to in the main work were brought into force.

Road Traffic Offenders Act 1988, s.31

Court may take particulars endorsed into consideration

★**32-245**   With effect from June 8, 2015 (Road Safety Act 2006 (Commencement No. 11 and Transitional Provisions) Order 2015 (S.I. 2015 No. 560)), the uncommenced provisions of the 2006 Act referred to in the main work were brought into force. There are transitional provisions, as to which, see in particular, article 6 of the commencement order.

Road Traffic Offenders Act 1988, s.34

Disqualification for certain offences

32-249   As to the commencement of section 56 of the Crime and Courts Act 2013, see *ante*, § 32-62.

★   As from April 13, 2015 (Criminal Justice and Courts Act 2015 (Commencement No. 1, Saving and Transitional Provisions) Order 2015 (S.I. 2015 No. 778)), the RTOA 1988, s.34(4)(a), is amended by the Criminal Justice and Courts Act 2015, s.29(4), and Sched. 6, paras 2 and 4, so as, after sub-paragraph (iia), to insert new sub-paragraphs (iib) and (iic), as follows—

> "(iib) an offence under section 3ZC of that Act (causing death by driving: disqualified drivers), or
>
> (iic) an offence under section 3ZD of that Act (causing serious injury by driving: disqualified drivers), or".

The amendments made by section 29 and Schedule 6 have effect only in relation to driving which occurs after they come into force: 2015 Act, s.29(5).

Length of disqualification

32-251   As to the appropriate length of disqualification for a case of causing serious injury by dangerous driving (RTA 1988, s.1A (§ 32-25 in the main work)), see *R. v. Ellis, ante*, § 32-29.

(8) Extension of disqualification where custodial sentence also imposed

★**32-269**   With effect from April 13, 2015 (Coroners and Justice Act 2009 (Commencement No. 17) Order 2015 (S.I. 2015 No. 819)), the provisions of the 2009 Act referred to in the main work were brought into force.

Road Traffic Offenders Act 1988, ss.35A, 35B

[Extension of disqualification where custodial sentence also imposed

★**32-270**   As from April 13, 2015 (Criminal Justice and Courts Act 2015 (Commencement No. 1, Saving and Transitional Provisions) Order 2015 (S.I. 2015 No. 778)), the RTOA 1988, s.35A, is amended by the Criminal Justice and Courts Act 2015, s.30(1), so as to omit: (i) the words "calculated after that term has been reduced by any relevant discount" in subsection (4)(e) and (f); (ii) the words "calculated after that sentence has been reduced by any relevant discount" in subsection (4)(h); and (iii) subsection (6) (definition of "relevant discount"). In consequence, the LASPOA 2012, Sched. 13, para. 8, is repealed (s.30(3)).

As from April 13, 2015 (S.I. 2015 No. 778 (*ante*)), the RTOA 1988, s.35A(4), is further amended ★
by the Criminal Justice and Courts Act 2015, s.6(2)(c), and Sched. 1, para. 11, so as: (i) in
paragraph (e), to substitute the words "the Criminal Justice Act 2003" for the words "that Act",
where they first appear; and (ii) to insert, after paragraph (f), a new paragraph (fa), as follows—

> "(fa) in the case of a sentence under section 236A of that Act (special custodial sentence for
> certain offenders of particular concern), a period equal to half of the term imposed pursu-
> ant to section 236A(2)(a) of that Act;".

(9) Interim disqualification
Road Traffic Offenders Act 1988, s.26

Interim disqualification
  With effect from June 8, 2015 (Road Safety Act 2006 (Commencement No. 11 and Transitional ★**32-272**
Provisions) Order 2015 (S.I. 2015 No. 560)), the provisions of the 2006 Act referred to in the
main work are brought into force. There are transitional provisions, as to which, see in particular,
article 9 of the commencement order.

(10) Disqualification until test is passed
Road Traffic Offenders Act 1988, s.36

Disqualification until test is passed
  As from April 13, 2015 (Criminal Justice and Courts Act 2015 (Commencement No. 1, Saving ★**32-273**
and Transitional Provisions) Order 2015 (S.I. 2015 No. 778)), the RTOA 1988, s.36(2), is amended
by the Criminal Justice and Courts Act 2015, s.29(4), and Sched. 6, paras 2 and 5, so as: (i) to
omit the word "or" at the end of paragraph (a); and (ii), to substitute, for paragraph (b), new
paragraphs (b) to (f), as follows—

> "(b) an offence under section 1 of the Road Traffic Act 1988 (causing death by dangerous
>   driving),
>   (c) an offence under section 1A of that Act (causing serious injury by dangerous driving),
>   (d) an offence under section 2 of that Act (dangerous driving),
>   (e) an offence under section 3ZC of that Act (causing death by driving: disqualified drivers), or
>   (f) an offence under section 3ZD of that Act (causing serious injury by driving: disqualified
>   drivers)".

  The amendments made by section 29 and Schedule 6 have effect only in relation to driving
which occurs after they come into force: 2015 Act, s.29(5).
  With effect from June 8, 2015 (Road Safety Act 2006 (Commencement No. 11 and Transitional ★
Provisions) Order 2015 (S.I. 2015 No. 560)), section 10 of, paragraphs 30 and 39 of Schedule 3
to, and Schedule 7(4) (and s.59 in so far as it relates thereto) to, the 2006 Act were brought into
force. These provisions effect the repeal of subsection (10) of section 36. It should further be
noted that the insertion of subsection (10A) of section 36 (by s.9 of, and Sched. 2, para. 7, to, the
2006 Act), took effect on April 1, 2009: Road Safety Act 2006 (Commencement No. 5) Order 2008
(S.I. 2008 No. 3164).

(13) Rehabilitation courses for drink-drive offenders

  With effect from April 6, 2015, the Rehabilitation Courses (Relevant Drink Offences) Regula- ★**32-282**
tions 2012 (S.I. 2012 No. 2939) were amended by the Rehabilitation Courses (Relevant Drink Offences) (Amendment) Regulations 2015 (S.I. 2015 No. 366).

(15) Removal of disqualification
Road Traffic Offenders Act 1988, s.42

Removal of disqualification
  With effect from June 8, 2015 (Road Safety Act 2006 (Commencement No. 11 and Transitional ★**32-289**
Provisions) Order 2015 (S.I. 2015 No. 560)), the uncommenced provisions of the 2006 Act
referred to in the main work are brought into force.

(16) Endorsement
Road Traffic Offenders Act 1988, s.44

Orders for endorsement
  With effect from June 8, 2015 (Road Safety Act 2006 (Commencement No. 11 and Transitional ★**32-292**

Provisions) Order 2015 (S.I. 2015 No. 560)), the uncommenced provisions of the 2006 Act referred to in the main work are brought into force. There are transitional provisions, as to which, see, in particular, article 7 of the commencement order.

32-293   As to not endorsing penalty points on a licence at the same time as imposing disqualification, see *R. v. Usaceva, ante*, § 32-231.

Road Traffic Offenders Act 1988, s.45

Effect of endorsement of counterparts

★**32-295**   As from April 13, 2015 (Criminal Justice and Courts Act 2015 (Commencement No. 1, Saving and Transitional Provisions) Order 2015 (S.I. 2015 No. 778)), the RTOA 1988, s.45, was amended by the Criminal Justice and Courts Act 2015, s.29(4), and Sched. 6, paras 2 and 6, so as to substitute a new subsection (6), as follows—

> "(6) Where the offence was under one of the following sections of the Road Traffic Act 1988, the endorsement remains effective until four years have elapsed since the conviction—
>
>   (a) section 1 (causing death by dangerous driving),
>   (b) section 1A (causing serious injury by dangerous driving),
>   (c) section 2 (dangerous driving),
>   (d) section 3ZC (causing death by driving: disqualified drivers), or
>   (e) section 3ZD (causing serious injury by driving: disqualified drivers).".

The amendments made by section 29 and Schedule 6 have effect only in relation to driving which occurs after they come into force: 2015 Act, s.29(5).

★   With effect from April 7, 2015, section 45(7)(a) of the RTOA 1988 was amended by the Crime and Courts Act 2013 (Consequential Amendments) (No. 2) Order 2015 (S.I. 2015 No. 733), so as to substitute, for the words "or (5)(1)(a)", the words ", 5(1)(a) or 5A(1)(a) and (2)".

★   With effect from June 8, 2015 (Road Safety Act 2006 (Commencement No. 11 and Transitional Provisions) Order 2015 (S.I. 2015 No. 560)), the uncommenced provisions of the 2006 Act referred to in the main work were brought into force, *i.e.* section 45 is repealed. There are transitional provisions, as to which, see, in particular, articles 6 and 7 of the commencement order.

Road Traffic Offenders Act 1988, s.45A

Effect of endorsement on driving records

★**32-296**   As from April 13, 2015 (Criminal Justice and Courts Act 2015 (Commencement No. 1, Saving and Transitional Provisions) Order 2015 (S.I. 2015 No. 778)), the RTOA 1988, s.45A, is amended by the Criminal Justice and Courts Act 2015, s.29(4), and Sched. 6, paras 2 and 7, so as to substitute a new subsection (4), which is identical to section 45(6), *ante*, § 32-295. The amendments made by section 29 and Schedule 6 have effect only in relation to driving which occurs after they come into force: 2015 Act, s.29(5).

★   With effect from April 7, 2015, section 45A(5)(a) of the RTOA 1988 was amended by the Crime and Courts Act 2013 (Consequential Amendments) (No. 2) Order 2015 (S.I. 2015 No. 733), so as to substitute, for the words "or (5)(1)(a)", the words ", 5(1)(a) or 5A(1)(a) and (2)".

★   With effect from June 8, 2015 (Road Safety Act 2006 (Commencement No. 11 and Transitional Provisions) Order 2015 (S.I. 2015 No. 560)), the uncommenced provisions of the 2006 Act referred to in the main work were brought into force. There are transitional provisions, as to which, see, in particular, article 6 of the commencement order.

(17) New drivers
Road Traffic (New Drivers) Act 1995, ss.1–3

Surrender of licence

★**32-299**   With effect from June 8, 2015 (Road Safety Act 2006 (Commencement No. 11 and Transitional Provisions) Order 2015 (S.I. 2015 No. 560)), the uncommenced provisions of the 2006 Act referred to in the main work were brought into force. There are transitional provisions, as to which, see, in particular, article 5 of the commencement order.

Revocation of licences

★**32-300**   With effect from June 8, 2015 (Road Safety Act 2006 (Commencement No. 11 and Transitional

Provisions) Order 2015 (S.I. 2015 No. 560)), the uncommenced provisions of the 2006 Act referred to in the main work were brought into force.

(18) Miscellaneous and general

Road Traffic Offenders Act 1988, ss.46, 47, 49

Combination of disqualification and endorsement with prohibition orders and orders for discharge

With effect from June 8, 2015 (Road Safety Act 2006 (Commencement No. 11 and Transitional ★**32-302** Provisions) Order 2015 (S.I. 2015 No. 560)), the uncommenced provisions of the 2006 Act referred to in the main work were brought into force. There are transitional provisions, as to which, see, in particular, article 6 of the commencement order.

Supplementary provisions as to disqualifications and endorsements

With effect from April 13, 2015 (Coroners and Justice Act 2009 (Commencement No. 17) ★**32-303** Order 2015 (S.I. 2015 No. 819)), paragraphs 30 and 33 of Schedule 22 to the 2009 Act were brought into force.

With effect from June 8, 2015 (Road Safety Act 2006 (Commencement No. 11 and Transitional ★ Provisions) Order 2015 (S.I. 2015 No. 560)), the uncommenced provisions of the 2006 Act referred to in the main work were brought into force. There are transitional provisions, as to which, see, in particular, articles 7 and 9 of the commencement order.

(20) Procedural rules

Criminal Procedure Rules 2014 (S.I. 2014 No. 1610), rr.55.1, 55.2, 55.4

Replacement of 2014 rules by 2015 rules

With effect from October 5, 2015, the Criminal Procedure Rules 2015 (S.I. 2015 No. 1490) ★**32-308** replace S.I. 2014 No. 1610. Part 55 of the 2014 rules is replaced by Part 29 of the 2015 rules (see *post*, Appendix P-264 *et seq.*), with several changes of substance.

W. Prosecution and Punishment of Offences

Road Traffic Offenders Act 1988, Sched. 2

As to the commencement of section 56 of the Crime and Courts Act 2013, see *ante*, § 32-62. **32-312**

As from April 13, 2015 (Criminal Justice and Courts Act 2015 (Commencement No. 1, Saving ★ and Transitional Provisions) Order 2015 (S.I. 2015 No. 778)), the RTOA 1988, Sched. 2, is amended by the Criminal Justice and Courts Act 2015, s.29(2) and (4), and Sched. 6, paras 2 and 9, so as: (i) in the entry relating to section 3ZB of the RTA 1988, in column 2, to omit ", disqualified"; and (ii) at the appropriate place, to insert entries relating to sections 3ZC and 3ZD, the details of which are summarised at §§ 32-76c, 32-76e, *ante*. The amendments made by section 29 and Schedule 6 have effect only in relation to driving which occurs after they come into force: 2015 Act, s.29(5).

With effect from April 7, 2015, Schedule 2 to the RTOA 1988 is amended by the Crime and ★ Courts Act 2013 (Consequential Amendments) (No. 2) Order 2015 (S.I. 2015 No. 733), art. 3, so as to insert the words "or proportion of a specified controlled drug" in the entries relating to sections 7 and 7A of the RTA 1988 in column (4) after the word "alcohol".

With effect from June 8, 2015 (Road Safety Act 2006 (Commencement No. 11 and Transitional ★ Provisions) Order 2015 (S.I. 2015 No. 560)), section 10 of, paragraphs 30 and 63(3) and (4) of Schedule 3 to, and Schedule 7(4) (and s.59 in so far as it relates thereto) to, the 2006 Act are brought into force (these provisions effecting the repeal of the words "and counterpart etc." in the entry relating to s.164 of the RTA 1988, and the words "counterparts of Community licences" in the entry relating to s.173 of that Act). There are transitional provisions, as to which, see, in particular, article 9 of the commencement order.

III. DOCUMENT OFFENCES

D. ROAD TRAFFIC ACT 1988

(1) Statute

Road Traffic Act 1988, ss.173, 174

Forgery of documents, etc.

★**32-316**   With effect from June 8, 2015 (Road Safety Act 2006 (Commencement No. 11 and Transitional Provisions) Order 2015 (S.I. 2015 No. 560)), section 10 of, paragraphs 2 and 28 (apart from para. 28(3)) of Schedule 3 to, and Schedule 7(4) (and s.59 in so far as it relates thereto) to, the 2006 Act were brought into force. Note that the statement in the main work that the whole of s.173(4) of the 1988 Act was repealed by the 2006 Act is incorrect; but see *post*. It should also be noted that the repeal effected by Schedule 7(10) to the 2006 Act (which is not being brought into force) consists of the omission of the word "and" at the end of subs. (2)(l) (the commencement of this provision is plainly linked to the commencement of the insertion of subs. (2)(n)).

★   With effect from June 8, 2015, section 173(4) of the 1988 Act (as to which, see *ante*) was repealed by the Road Safety Act 2006 (Consequential Amendments) Order 2015 (S.I. 2015 No. 583).

★   With effect from June 8, 2015, paragraph 29 of Schedule 5 to the Crime (International Co-operation) Act 2003 was repealed, and paragraph 32 of Schedule 1 to the Driving Licence (Community Driving Licence) Regulations 1996 (S.I. 1996 No. 1974) was revoked, by the Road Safety Act 2006 (Consequential Amendments) Order 2015 (S.I. 2015 No. 583). It was paragraph 32 of Schedule 1 to the 1996 regulations that effected the amendments made by those regulations to section 173 of the 1988 Act.

(5) Power to seize articles

Road Traffic Act 1988, s.176

Power to seize articles in respect of which offences under sections 173 to 175 may have been committed

★**32-321**   With effect from June 8, 2015 (Road Safety Act 2006 (Commencement No. 11 and Transitional Provisions) Order 2015 (S.I. 2015 No. 560)), the provisions of the 2006 Act referred to in the main work were brought into force.

★   With effect from June 8, 2015, paragraph 30 of Schedule 5 to the Crime (International Co-operation) Act 2003 was repealed, and paragraph 33 of Schedule 1 to the Driving Licence (Community Driving Licence) Regulations 1996 (S.I. 1996 No. 1974) was revoked, by the Road Safety Act 2006 (Consequential Amendments) Order 2015 (S.I. 2015 No. 583). It was paragraph 33 of Schedule 1 to the 1996 regulations that effected the amendments made by those regulations to section 176 of the 1988 Act.

CHAPTER 33

CONSPIRACY, ENCOURAGEMENT AND ATTEMPT TO COMMIT CRIME

I. CONSPIRACY

C. SAVING OF CERTAIN CONSPIRACIES AT COMMON LAW, ETC.

(2) Conspiracy to defraud

Sentence

★**33-40**   As to the repeal of section 76 of the SOCPA 2005, see *ante*, § 5-1212.

D. Pleading, Evidence and Practice

(2) The indictment

Duplicity and "rolled-up charges"

R. v. Shillam (see the main work) and *R. v. Mehta* (§ 33-73 in the main work) were considered in *Serious Fraud Office v. Papachristos* [2015] Lloyd's Rep. F.C. 88, CA, where it was held that the trial judge had erred in allowing a count to be added to the indictment alleging a conspiracy narrower in scope to that alleged in the original indictment. The new count alleged the same offence as the original count. The Court of Appeal said that its addition to the indictment was unnecessary and confusing; if the jury were satisfied as to the existence of the conspiracy and as to the participation of the defendants, it would have been open to them to convict on the original count notwithstanding that they were not satisfied that it was as far-reaching as originally alleged.

II. SOLICITING OR INCITING CRIME

(1) Common law

(a) *Introduction*

Definition

To solicit or incite another to commit a crime was indictable at common law. A person was guilty of incitement to commit an offence or offences if (a) he incited another to do or cause to be done an act or acts which, if done, would involve the commission of an offence or offences by the other; and (b) he intended or believed that the other, if he acted as incited, should or would do so with the fault required for the offence or offences: *DPP v. Armstrong (Andrew)* [2000] Crim.L.R. 379, DC; *R. v. Claydon* [2006] 1 Cr.App.R. 20, CA (approving, in both cases, the Law Commission's definition (*Criminal Law: A Criminal Code*, Law Com. No. 177, 1989)). In *Invicta Plastics Ltd v. Clare* [1976] R.T.R. 251, the Divisional Court adopted *dicta* of Lord Denning M.R. in *Race Relations Board v. Applin* [1973] 1 Q.B. 815 at 825, CA (Civ. Div.), to the effect that "to incite" was not limited to urging or spurring on by advice, encouragement or persuasion but included inciting another to do an act by threats or by pressure. Incitement also included an offer of a bribe to a person to commit an offence: *Wade v. Broughton* (1814) 3 V. & B. 172.

It was irrelevant whether the solicitation or incitement was effective: *Armstrong, ante*; or whether the principal offence existed under the common law or was created by statute: see 1 Russ.Cr. 12th ed., 176. However, the offence had to be one which was capable of being committed by the person incited: *R. v. Claydon, ante*.

Agents provocateurs

See §§ 15-452 *et seq.* in the main work, and see *R. v. Anderson* [1986] 1 A.C. 27 at 38, HL, and *R. v. Jones (James)* (§ 27-37a in the main work).

Mens rea

A person accused of incitement must be shown to have intended or believed that the person incited would, if he acted as incited to do, do so with the *mens rea* appropriate to the offence (*ante*, § 33-75). As with conspiracy (§ 33-15 in the main work), it is submitted that laudable ulterior motives are irrelevant. To the extent that *R. v. Shaw* [1994] Crim.L.R. 365, CA (93 05976 W2) is authority to the contrary, it is submitted that it is wrong (see the commentary in the *Criminal Law Review*); and it was disapproved in *Claydon, ante*, § 33-75. The explanation for the decision (that a person charged with inciting an offence of dishonesty had to be proved to have been dishonest himself) may lie in the fact that the prosecution had so put their case (transcript p.7F).

In *R. v. Curr*, 51 Cr.App.R. 113, CA, it was held that a person could only be convicted of incitement if the person incited knew that the conduct incited amounted to an offence. This was also disapproved of in *R. v. Claydon, ante*, where it was said that the actual knowledge or state of mind of the person incited was irrelevant. Albeit that this was *obiter*, it is submitted that this view is to be preferred, the offence being concerned with the state of mind of the incitor, not of the incitee.

(b) *Jurisdiction*

33-78   The common law jurisdiction in respect of incitement appears to be the same as that for conspiracy, as to which see §§ 33-21 *et seq.* in the main work. In *R. v. Tompkins* [2007] Crim.L.R. 235, CA, it was assumed that the courts of England and Wales have jurisdiction to try an allegation of incitement where the incitor was at all material times within the jurisdiction and the incitee was at all material times without the jurisdiction, provided that the *actus reus* of the offence was to occur, at least in part, within the jurisdiction.

As to the extended jurisdiction of the courts in relation to allegations of incitement to commit certain sexual acts outside the United Kingdom, see the Sexual Offences (Conspiracy and Incitement) Act 1996, s.2 (§ 2-36b in the main work); and as to their extended jurisdiction in relation to incitement to commit fraud and related offences, see Part I of the CJA 1993 (§§ 2-37 *et seq.* in the main work).

(c) *Indictment*

Statement of Offence

33-79   *Incitement to steal.*

Particulars of Offence

A B, on the _____ *day of* _____, *20__, unlawfully incited J N to steal property belonging to Y Z.*

Penalty—fine and/or imprisonment: *R. v. Higgins*, 2 East 5.

(d) *Particular offences*

To conspire or to incite

33-80   Section 5(7) of the CLA 1977 (§ 33-35 in the main work) abolished the offence of incitement to conspire.

In the course of giving the Court of Appeal's judgment in *R. v. Sirat*, 83 Cr.App.R. 41, Parker L.J. said:

> "There is no doubt that at comm on law incitement to commit a crime is an offence. This being so, it follows logically that if A incites B to incite C to commit a crime, *e.g.* to wound D, A is guilty of incitement to commit a crime, namely, incitement" (at p. 43).

Later in the judgment, however, his Lordship said, having read out the terms of section 5(7) of the 1977 Act:

> "If, therefore, A incites B to agree with C that C will wound D, A's incitement of B is by statute not an offence ... . Where however the facts are that the accused's incitement of B is actually to enter into an agreement with C for the commission of a crime, it would in our judgment be impossible to hold that the accused can be guilty of incitement, on the ground that B must of necessity propose the crime to C on the way to making the agreement. Whether other forms of incitement to incite survive will fall for decision when the question arises. It may appear to be absurd that, where a person is inciting actual agreement to be made for the commission of a crime, he should be guilty of no offence, but that where he does not seek actual agreement but mere encouragement he should be guilty. This however is not necessarily absurd, for there may well be circumstances where there is no question of an agreement being sought but where the particular form of incitement is more effective than any attempt to secure agreement" (at pp. 44–45).

To attempt, and attempt to incite

33-81   On an indictment charging the defendants with inciting, counselling and procuring a pregnant woman to administer to herself a noxious thing, namely an abortifacient, with intent to procure a miscarriage (see the Offences against the Person Act 1861, s.58 (§ 19-203 in the main work)), and with conspiracy to incite her to do the same, it was held (a) that if the woman, believing that she was taking a noxious thing within the meaning of the statute, did, with intent to procure her own abortion, take a thing in fact harmless, she was guilty of an attempt to commit an offence against section 58; but (b) that if the defendants in supplying the drug to the woman, though they well knew that she would take it in the belief that it was an abortifacient did not themselves believe that it was capable of procuring her own abortion, they could not be convicted of inciting her to commit the said offence, although if they had so believed it would have been otherwise: *R. v. Brown*, 63 J.P. 790.

In logic, it would seem that an incitement to attempt to commit an offence must necessarily be an incitement to commit that offence.

Where a letter was sent soliciting and inciting the addressee to commit a crime, but was not proved to have reached the intended recipient, the sender could properly be convicted of an attempt to incite the commission of the crime: *R. v. Banks* (1873) 12 Cox 393; *R. v. Ransford* (1874) 13 Cox 9; *R. v. Krause*, 66 J.P. 121; *R. v. Cope*, 16 Cr.App.R. 77, which may be distinguished from *R. v. Woods*, 22 Cr.App.R. 41, because in the former case the intended recipient of the letter would, if he had received it, have understood that he was being instigated to the commission of a crime, whereas in the latter case he would not; and *R. v. Goldman* [2001] Crim.L.R. 822, CA (defendant guilty of attempt to incite addressee to distribute indecent photographs of children, even where he was responding to an offer made by the addressee).

To do the impossible

A person cannot be convicted of incitement to commit a particular offence if the person incited was incapable as a matter of law of committing the offence: *R. v. Claydon* [2006] 1 Cr.App.R. 20, CA. Nor can a person be convicted of incitement to commit a particular offence if its commission is factually impossible: see *R. v. Fitzmaurice* [1983] Q.B. 1083, 76 Cr.App.R. 17, CA (giving as an example incitement to murder a person who turned out to have been dead at the time of the incitement). Where it is contended that the offence incited was factually impossible, it is necessary to analyse the evidence with care to decide the precise offence which the defendant is alleged to have incited: *ibid.* At common law, the position was the same for conspiracy and attempts, but see now the CLA 1977, s.1(1)(b) (§ 33-2 in the main work), and the Criminal Attempts Act 1981, s.1(2) (§ 33-128 in the main work). **33-82**

To commit a summary offence

Incitement to commit a summary offence was a summary offence, punishable as for the offence incited: MCA 1980, s.45(1), (3). **33-83**

To commit an offence triable either way

See the MCA 1980, s.17(1), and Sched. 1, paras 33 and 35. The effect is that incitement to commit an offence triable either way is generally itself triable either way. Note that whilst paragraph 35 of Schedule 1 to the 1980 Act was repealed by the SCA 2007, ss.63(2) and 92, Sched. 6, para. 55(1) and (4), and Sched. 14, its effect has been preserved in relation to pre-commencement offences by the 2007 Act, s.91(1), and Sched. 13, para. 5(1)(b) (§ 33-116 in the main work). **33-84**

(e) *Evidence*

Prove the soliciting or inciting as alleged in the indictment. Prove it in the same manner as the offence of being a counsellor and procurer would be proved, except that this offence is committed even though the offence solicited was not in fact committed. It is no defence to the above indictment that the person incited purposely submitted himself to the incitement with intent to betray the inciter: *R. v. Quail* (1866) 4 F. & F. 1076. **33-85**

On a charge of inciting a person to receive stolen goods it is no defence that at the time of the incitement there did not exist stolen goods of the type mentioned: *R. v. McDonough*, 47 Cr.App.R. 37, CCA.

A charge of incitement to distribute indecent photographs of children could be founded on the defendant's entering the website of a commercial child pornography business and paying the required entrance fee with his credit card; it mattered not that the process was entirely automated by the computer; the computer merely facilitated the business, and it was irrelevant to say that only the computer was incited; someone lay behind the computer: *R. (O.) v. Coventry Magistrates' Court* [2004] Crim.L.R. 948, DC.

III. ENCOURAGING OR ASSISTING CRIME

(2) Legislation

(a) *Inchoate offences*

Listed offences

★**33-100**   With effect from May 3, 2015 (Serious Crime Act 2015 (Commencement No. 1) Regulations 2015 (S.I. 2015 No. 820)), Schedule 3 to the 2007 Act is amended by the SCA 2015, s.85(1), and Sched. 4, para. 82, so as to include an offence under section 45 of the 2015 Act (as to which, see *ante*, § 18-33a).

(d) *Jurisdiction and procedure*

Serious Crime Act 2007, ss.52–58

Penalties

33-110   For a further case (see also *R. v. Woodford* (in the main work)) in which it was held that where a person is convicted of assisting a crime contrary to section 46 of the 2007 Act (here, the supply of Class A drugs), the maximum penalty being the same as the maximum penalty for the "reference offence" (or the reference offence carrying the longest maximum: see s.58(1)-(6)), a judge should use any relevant sentencing guideline for the reference offence to assist him, see *R. v. Hall* [2014] 2 Cr.App.R.(S.) 20, CA.

(4) Compatibility with the European Convention on Human Rights

★**33-125**   *R. (Nicklinson) v. Ministry of Justice (C.N.K. Alliance Ltd intervening); R. (A.M.) v. DPP (Same intervening)* is now reported at [2015] A.C. 657.

APPENDIX A
Codes of Practice and Attorney-General's Guidelines

I. CODES OF PRACTICE

A. UNDER THE POLICE AND CRIMINAL EVIDENCE ACT 1984

(1) Introduction

The Police and Criminal Evidence Act 1984 makes provision for the issuing by the Secretary of **A-1** State of codes of practice in connection with the tape-recording of interviews (s.60, § 15-173 in the main work), the visual recording of interviews (s.60A, § 15-177 in the main work), the exercise by police officers of statutory powers of "stop and search" (s.66(1)(a)(i) and (ii), § 15-2 in the main work), the exercise by police officers of statutory powers to arrest a person (s.66(1)(a)(iii), § 15-2 in the main work) the detention, treatment, questioning and identification of persons by police officers (s.66(1)(b), § 15-2 in the main work), and searches of premises and seizure of property (s.66(1)(c) and (d), § 15-2 in the main work).

There are eight extant codes: Code A (stop and search); Code B (search and seizure); Code C (detention, treatment and questioning of persons), Code D (identification), Code E (tape-recording of interviews), Code F (visual recording of interviews), Code G (arrest) and Code H (detention, treatment and questioning of persons under section 41 of, and Schedule 8 to, the Terrorism Act 2000).

Code D came into force on March 7, 2011: Police and Criminal Evidence Act 1984 (Codes of Practice) (Revision of Codes A, B and D) Order 2011 (S.I. 2011 No. 412). Code G came into force on November 12, 2012: Police and Criminal Evidence Act 1984 (Codes of Practice) (Revision of Codes C, G and H) Order 2012 (S.I. 2012 No. 1798).

The Police and Criminal Evidence Act 1984 (Codes of Practice) (Revisions to Codes A, B, C, E, F and H) Order 2013 (S.I. 2013 No. 2685) brought revised Codes A, B, C, E, F and H into force on October 27, 2013. The revisions were required in order to give effect to (i) the United Kingdom's obligations under European Parliament and Council Directive 2010/64/EU on the right to interpretation and translation in criminal proceedings, and (ii) the decision of the Divisional Court in *R. (C.) v. Secretary of State for the Home Department* (as to which, see §§ 15-6, 15-165, 15-204, 16-141 in the main work).

The Police and Criminal Evidence Act 1984 (Codes of Practice) (Revisions to Codes C and H) Order 2014 (S.I. 2014 No. 1237) brought revised Codes C and H into force on June 2, 2014. The revisions implemented obligations under European Parliament and Council Directive 2012/13/EU, in relation to the right to information in criminal proceedings. In particular, every detainee must be given a revised written notice setting out his rights and entitlements whilst in custody, which has been updated to reflect the new substantive rights conferred by the 2012 directive.

The Police and Criminal Evidence Act 1984 (Revision of Code A) Order 2015 (S.I. 2015 No. 418) brought a revised Code A into force on March 19, 2015. The main changes were intended to make clear what constitutes "reasonable grounds for suspicion". The revised code also emphasises that where officers are not using their powers properly they will be subject to formal performance or disciplinary proceedings.

For further details of the various versions of the codes and their revisions, see §§ 15-5, 15-6 in the main work. For further details in relation to the codes generally, see the main work at §§ 15-2 *et seq.* (primary legislation), § 15-5 (commencement), § 15-7 (status of codes), § 15-8 (who is bound by the codes), § 15-10 (admissibility), and § 15-11 (breaches).

It should be noted that the original text of the codes has a series of errors. Only in the most obvious cases has any change been made to the wording, but the punctuation, use of case, use of number and paragraphing have been amended with a view to injecting consistency and intelligibility.

(2) Stop and search

A. CODE OF PRACTICE FOR THE EXERCISE BY: POLICE OFFICERS OF STATUTORY POWERS OF STOP AND SEARCH; POLICE OFFICERS AND POLICE STAFF OF REQUIREMENTS TO RECORD PUBLIC ENCOUNTERS

Commencement—transitional arrangements

This code applies to any search by a police officer and the recording of public encounters taking place after 00.00 on 19 March 2015.

A:1.0 General

A-2   A:1.01 This code of practice must be readily available at all police stations for consultation by police officers, police staff, detained persons and members of the public.

A:1.02 The notes for guidance included are not provisions of this code, but are guidance to police officers and others about its application and interpretation. Provisions in the annexes to the code are provisions of this code.

A:1.03 This code governs the exercise by police officers of statutory powers to search a person or a vehicle without first making an arrest. The main stop and search powers to which this code applies are set out in Annex A, but that list should not be regarded as definitive [see *Note 1*]. In addition, it covers requirements on police officers and police staff to record encounters not governed by statutory powers (see paras 2.11 and 4.12). This code does not apply to:

    (a) the powers of stop and search under:

        (i) the Aviation Security Act 1982, s.27(2), and

        (ii) the Police and Criminal Evidence Act 1984, s.6(1) (which relates specifically to powers of constables employed by statutory undertakers on the premises of the statutory undertakers);

    (b) searches carried out for the purposes of examination under Schedule 7 to the Terrorism Act 2000 and to which the code of practice issued under paragraph 6 of Schedule 14 to the Terrorism Act 2000 applies;

    (c) the powers to search persons and vehicles and to stop and search in specified locations to which the code of practice issued under section 47AB of the Terrorism Act 2000 applies.

A:1 Principles governing stop and search

A-3   A:1.1 Powers to stop and search must be used fairly, responsibly, with respect for people being searched and without unlawful discrimination. Under the Equality Act 2010, s.149, when police officers are carrying out their functions, they also have a duty to have due regard to the need to eliminate unlawful discrimination, harassment and victimisation, to advance equality of opportunity between people who share a relevant protected characteristic and people who do not share it, and to take steps to foster good relations between those persons. [See *Notes 1* and *1A*.] The Children Act 2004, s.11, also requires chief police officers and other specified persons and bodies to ensure that in the discharge of their functions they have regard to the need to safeguard and promote the welfare of all persons under the age of 18.

A:1.2 The intrusion on the liberty of the person stopped or searched must be brief and detention for the purposes of a search must take place at or near the location of the stop.

A:1.3 If these fundamental principles are not observed the use of powers to stop and search may be drawn into question. Failure to use the powers in the proper manner reduces their effectiveness. Stop and search can play an important role in the detection and prevention of crime, and using the powers fairly makes them more effective.

A:1.4 The primary purpose of stop and search powers is to enable officers to allay or confirm suspicions about individuals without exercising their power of arrest. Officers may be required to justify the use or authorisation of such powers, in relation both to individual searches and the overall pattern of their activity in this regard, to their supervisory officers or in court. Any misuse of the powers is likely to be harmful to policing and lead to mistrust of the police. Officers must also be able to explain their actions to the member of the public searched. The misuse of these powers can lead to disciplinary action (see paras 5.5 and 5.6).

A:1.5 An officer must not search a person, even with his or her consent, where no power to search is applicable. Even where a person is prepared to submit to a search voluntarily, the person must not be searched unless the necessary legal power exists, and the search must be in accordance with the relevant power and the provisions of this code. The only exception, where an officer does not require a specific power, applies to searches of persons entering sports grounds or other premises carried out with their consent given as a condition of entry.

A:1.6 Evidence obtained from a search to which this code applies may be open to challenge if the provisions of this code are not observed.

A:2 Types of stop and search powers

A:2.1 This code applies, subject to paragraph 1.03, to powers of stop and search as follows: **A-4**

- (a) powers which require reasonable grounds for suspicion, before they may be exercised; that articles unlawfully obtained or possessed are being carried such as section 1 of PACE for stolen and prohibited articles and section 23 of the Misuse of Drugs Act 1971 for controlled drugs;
- (b) authorised under section 60 of the Criminal Justice and Public Order Act 1994, based upon a reasonable belief that incidents involving serious violence may take place or that people are carrying dangerous instruments or offensive weapons within any locality in the police area, or that it is expedient to use the powers to find such instruments or weapons that have been used in incidents of serious violence;
- (c) [*not used*];
- (d) the powers in Schedule 5 to the Terrorism Prevention and Investigation Measures (TPIM) Act 2011 to search an individual who has not been arrested, conferred by:
  - (i) paragraph 6(2)(a) at the time of serving a TPIM notice;
  - (ii) paragraph 8(2)(a) under a search warrant for compliance purposes; and
  - (iii) paragraph 10 for public safety purposes; see paragraph 2.18A;
- (e) powers to search a person who has not been arrested in the exercise of a power to search premises (see Code B, para. 2.4).

(a) Stop and search powers requiring reasonable grounds for suspicion – explanation

General

A:2.2 Reasonable grounds for suspicion is the legal test which a police officer must satisfy before **A-5** they can stop and detain individuals or vehicles to search them under powers such as section 1 of PACE (to find stolen or prohibited articles) and section 23 of the Misuse of Drugs Act 1971 (to find controlled drugs). This test must be applied to the particular circumstances in each case and is in two parts:

- (i) firstly, the officer must have formed a genuine suspicion in their own mind that they will find the object for which the search power being exercised allows them to search (see Annex A, second column, for examples); and
- (ii) secondly, the suspicion that the object will be found must be reasonable. This means that there must be an objective basis for that suspicion based on facts, information and/or intelligence which are relevant to the likelihood that the object in question will be found, so that a reasonable person would be entitled to reach the same conclusion based on the same facts and information and/or intelligence.

Officers must therefore be able to explain the basis for their suspicion by reference to intelligence or information about, or some specific behaviour by, the person concerned (see paras 3.8(d), 4.6 and 5.5).

A:2.2A The exercise of these stop and search powers depends on the likelihood that the person searched is in possession of an item for which they may be searched; it does not depend on the person concerned being suspected of committing an offence in relation to the object of the search. A police officer who has reasonable grounds to suspect that a person is in innocent possession of a stolen or prohibited article, controlled drug or other item for which the officer is empowered to search, may stop and search the person even though there would be no power of arrest. This would apply when a child under the age of criminal responsibility (10 years) is suspected of carrying any such item, even if they knew they had it. (See *Notes 1B* and *1BA*.)

Personal factors can never support reasonable grounds for suspicion

A:2.2B Reasonable suspicion can never be supported on the basis of personal factors. This means **A-5a** that unless the police have information or intelligence which provides a description of a person suspected of carrying an article for which there is a power to stop and search, the following cannot be used, alone or in combination with each other, or in combination with any other factor, as the reason for stopping and searching any individual, including any vehicle which they are driving or are being carried in:

(a) a person's physical appearance with regard, for example, to any of the "relevant protected characteristics" set out in the Equality Act 2010, s.149, which are age, disability, gender reassignment, pregnancy and maternity, race, religion or belief, sex and sexual orientation (see para. 1.1 and *Note 1A*), or the fact that the person is known to have a previous conviction; and

(b) generalisations or stereotypical images that certain groups or categories of people are more likely to be involved in criminal activity.

A:2.3 [*Not used.*]

Reasonable grounds for suspicion based on information and/or intelligence

A-5b

A:2.4 Reasonable grounds for suspicion should normally be linked to accurate and current intelligence or information, relating to articles for which there is a power to stop and search, being carried by individuals or being in vehicles in any locality. This would include reports from members of the public or other officers describing:

• a person who has been seen carrying such an article or a vehicle in which such an article has been seen;

• crimes committed in relation to which such an article would constitute relevant evidence, for example, property stolen in a theft or burglary, an offensive weapon or bladed or sharply pointed article used to assault or threaten someone or an article used to cause criminal damage to property.

A:2.4A Searches based on accurate and current intelligence or information are more likely to be effective. Targeting searches in a particular area at specified crime problems not only increases their effectiveness but also minimises inconvenience to law-abiding members of the public. It also helps in justifying the use of searches both to those who are searched and to the public. This does not, however, prevent stop and search powers being exercised in other locations where such powers may be exercised and reasonable suspicion exists.

A:2.5 [*Not used.*]

Reasonable grounds for suspicion and searching groups

A-5c

A:2.6 Where there is reliable information or intelligence that members of a group or gang habitually carry knives unlawfully or weapons or controlled drugs, and wear a distinctive item of clothing or other means of identification in order to identify themselves as members of that group or gang, that distinctive item of clothing or other means of identification may provide reasonable grounds to stop and search any person believed to be a member of that group or gang. [See *Note 9.*]

A:2.6A A similar approach would apply to particular organised protest groups where there is reliable information or intelligence:

(a) that the group in question arranges meetings and marches to which one or more members bring articles intended to be used to cause criminal damage and/or injury to others in support of the group's aims;

(b) that at one or more previous meetings or marches arranged by that group, such articles have been used and resulted in damage and/or injury; and

(c) that on the subsequent occasion in question, one or more members of the group have brought with them such articles with similar intentions.

These circumstances may provide reasonable grounds to stop and search any members of the group to find such articles (see *Note 9A*). See also paragraphs 2.12 to 2.18, "Searches authorised under section 60 of the Criminal Justice and Public Order Act 1994", when serious violence is anticipated at meetings and marches.

Reasonable grounds for suspicion based on behaviour, time and location

A-5d

A:2.6B Reasonable suspicion may also exist without specific information or intelligence and on the basis of the behaviour of a person. For example, if an officer encounters someone on the street at night who is obviously trying to hide something, the officer may (depending on the other surrounding circumstances) base such suspicion on the fact that this kind of behaviour is often linked to stolen or prohibited articles being carried. An officer who forms the opinion that a person is acting suspiciously or that they appear to be nervous must be able to explain, with reference to specific aspects of the person's behaviour or conduct which they have observed, why they formed that opinion (see paras 3.8(d) and 5.5). A hunch or instinct which cannot be explained or justified to an objective observer can never amount to reasonable grounds.

A:2.7 [*Not used.*]

A:2.8 [*Not used.*]

Securing public confidence and promoting community relations

A:2.8A All police officers must recognise that searches are more likely to be effective, legitimate   **A-5e**
and secure public confidence when their reasonable grounds for suspicion are based on a range of objective factors. The overall use of these powers is more likely to be effective when up-to-date and accurate intelligence or information is communicated to officers and they are well-informed about local crime patterns. Local senior officers have a duty to ensure that those under their command who exercise stop and search powers have access to such information, and the officers exercising the powers have a duty to acquaint themselves with that information (see paras 5.1 to 5.6).

Questioning to decide whether to carry out a search

A:2.9 An officer who has reasonable grounds for suspicion may detain the person concerned in   **A-5f**
order to carry out a search. Before carrying out the search the officer may ask questions about the person's behaviour or presence in circumstances which gave rise to the suspicion. As a result of questioning the detained person, the reasonable grounds for suspicion necessary to detain that person may be confirmed or, because of a satisfactory explanation, be dispelled. [See *Notes 2* and *3.*] Questioning may also reveal reasonable grounds to suspect the possession of a different kind of unlawful article from that originally suspected. Reasonable grounds for suspicion however cannot be provided retrospectively by such questioning during a person's detention or by refusal to answer any questions asked.

A:2.10 If, as a result of questioning before a search, or other circumstances which come to the attention of the officer, there cease to be reasonable grounds for suspecting that an article of a kind for which there is a power to stop and search is being carried, no search may take place. [See *Note 3.*] In the absence of any other lawful power to detain, the person is free to leave at will and must be so informed.

A:2.11 There is no power to stop or detain a person in order to find grounds for a search. Police officers have many encounters with members of the public which do not involve detaining people against their will and do not require any statutory power for an officer to speak to a person (see para. 4.12 and *Note 1*). However, if reasonable grounds for suspicion emerge during such an encounter, the officer may detain the person to search them, even though no grounds existed when the encounter began. As soon as detention begins, and before searching, the officer must inform the person that they are being detained for the purpose of a search and take action in accordance with paragraphs 3.8 to 3.11 under "*Steps to be taken prior to a search*".

(b) Searches authorised under section 60 of the Criminal Justice and Public Order Act 1994

A:2.12 Authority for a constable in uniform to stop and search under section 60 of the Criminal   **A-5g**
Justice and Public Order Act 1994 may be given if the authorising officer reasonably believes:

    (a) that incidents involving serious violence may take place in any locality in the officer's police area, and it is expedient to use these powers to prevent their occurrence;

    (b) that persons are carrying dangerous instruments or offensive weapons without good reason in any locality in the officer's police area; or

    (c) that an incident involving serious violence has taken place in the officer's police area, a dangerous instrument or offensive weapon used in the incident is being carried by a person in any locality in that police area, and it is expedient to use these powers to find that instrument or weapon.

A:2.13 An authorisation under section 60 may only be given by an officer of the rank of inspector or above and in writing, or orally if paragraph 2.12(c) applies and it is not practicable to give the authorisation in writing. The authorisation (whether written or oral) must specify the grounds on which it was given, the locality in which the powers may be exercised and the period of time for which they are in force. The period authorised shall be no longer than appears reasonably necessary to prevent, or seek to prevent incidents of serious violence, or to deal with the problem of carrying dangerous instruments or offensive weapons or to find a dangerous instrument or offensive weapon that has been used. It may not exceed 24 hours. An oral authorisation given where paragraph 2.12(c) applies must be recorded in writing as soon as practicable. [See *Notes 10–13.*]

A:2.14 An inspector who gives an authorisation must, as soon as practicable, inform an officer of or above the rank of superintendent. This officer may direct that the authorisation shall be extended for a further 24 hours, if violence or the carrying of dangerous instruments or offensive weapons has occurred, or is suspected to have occurred, and the continued use of the powers is considered necessary to prevent or deal with further such activity or to find a dangerous instrument or offensive weapon that has been used. That direction must be given in writing unless it is not practicable to do so, in which case it must be recorded in writing as soon as practicable afterwards. [*See Note 12.*]

A:2.14A The selection of persons and vehicles under section 60 to be stopped and, if appropriate, searched should reflect an objective assessment of the nature of the incident or weapon in question and the individuals and vehicles thought likely to be associated with that incident or those weapons [*see Notes 10 and 11*]. The powers must not be used to stop and search persons and vehicles for reasons unconnected with the purpose of the authorisation. When selecting persons and vehicles to be stopped in response to a specific threat or incident, officers must take care not to discriminate unlawfully against anyone on the grounds of any of the protected characteristics set out in the Equality Act 2010 (see paragraph 1.1).

A:2.14B The driver of a vehicle which is stopped under section 60 and any person who is searched under section 60 are entitled to a written statement to that effect if they apply within twelve months from the day the vehicle was stopped or the person was searched. This statement is a record which states that the vehicle was stopped or (as the case may be) that the person was searched under section 60 and it may form part of the search record or be supplied as a separate record.

Powers to require removal of face coverings

A-6

A:2.15 Section 60AA of the Criminal Justice and Public Order Act 1994 also provides a power to demand the removal of disguises. The officer exercising the power must reasonably believe that someone is wearing an item wholly or mainly for the purpose of concealing identity. There is also a power to seize such items where the officer believes that a person intends to wear them for this purpose. There is no power to stop and search for disguises. An officer may seize any such item which is discovered when exercising a power of search for something else, or which is being carried, and which the officer reasonably believes is intended to be used for concealing anyone's identity. This power can only be used if an authorisation given under section 60, or under section 60AA, is in force. [*See Note 4.*]

A:2.16 Authority under section 60AA for a constable in uniform to require the removal of disguises and to seize them may be given if the authorising officer reasonably believes that activities may take place in any locality in the officer's police area that are likely to involve the commission of offences and it is expedient to use these powers to prevent or control these activities.

A:2.17 An authorisation under section 60AA may only be given by an officer of the rank of inspector or above, in writing, specifying the grounds on which it was given, the locality in which the powers may be exercised and the period of time for which they are in force. The period authorised shall be no longer than appears reasonably necessary to prevent, or seek to prevent the commission of offences. It may not exceed 24 hours. [*See Notes 10–13.*]

A:2.18 An inspector who gives an authorisation must, as soon as practicable, inform an officer of or above the rank of superintendent. This officer may direct that the authorisation shall be extended for a further 24 hours, if crimes have been committed, or are suspected to have been committed, and the continued use of the powers is considered necessary to prevent or deal with further such activity. This direction must also be given in writing at the time or as soon as practicable afterwards. [*See Note 12.*]

(c) [Not used]

(d) Searches under Schedule 5 to the Terrorism Prevention and Investigation Measures Act 2011

A-7

A:2.18A Paragraph 3 of Schedule 5 to the TPIM Act 2011 allows a constable to detain an individual to be searched under the following powers:

(i) paragraph 6(2)(a) when a TPIM notice is being, or has just been, served on the individual for the purpose of ascertaining whether there is anything on the individual that contravenes measures specified in the notice;

(ii) paragraph 8(2)(a) in accordance with a warrant to search the individual issued by a justice of the peace in England and Wales, a sheriff in Scotland or a lay magistrate in Northern Ireland who is satisfied that a search is necessary for the purpose of determining whether an individual in respect of whom a TPIM notice is in force is complying with measures specified in the notice (see para. 2.20); and

(iii) paragraph 10 to ascertain whether an individual in respect of whom a TPIM notice is in force is in possession of anything that could be used to threaten or harm any person.

See paragraph 2.1(e).

A:2.19 The exercise of the powers mentioned in paragraph 2.18A does not require the constable to have reasonable grounds to suspect that the individual:

    (a) has been, or is, contravening any of the measures specified in the TPIM notice; or

    (b) has on them anything which:

- in the case of the power in sub-paragraph (i), contravenes measures specified in the TPIM notice;
- in the case of the power in sub-paragraph (ii) is not complying with measures specified in the TPIM notice; or
- in the case of the power in sub-paragraph (iii), could be used to threaten or harm any person.

A:2.20 A search of an individual on warrant under the power mentioned in paragraph 2.18A(ii) must carried [*sic*] out within 28 days of the issue of the warrant and:

- the individual may be searched on one occasion only within that period;
- the search must take place at a reasonable hour unless it appears that this would frustrate the purposes of the search.

A:2.21–2.25 [*Not used.*]

A:2.26 The powers under Schedule 5 allow a constable to conduct a search of an individual only for specified purposes relating to a TPIM notice as set out above. However, anything found may be seized and retained if there are reasonable grounds for believing that it is or it contains evidence of any offence for use at a trial for that offence or to prevent it being concealed, lost, damaged, altered, or destroyed. However, this would not prevent a search being carried out under other search powers if, in the course of exercising these powers, the officer formed reasonable grounds for suspicion.

(e) Powers to search persons in the exercise of a power to search premises

A:2.27 The following powers to search premises also authorise the search of a person, not under **A-8** arrest, who is found on the premises during the course of the search:

    (a) section 139B of the Criminal Justice Act 1988 under which a constable may enter school premises and search the premises and any person on those premises for any bladed or pointed article or offensive weapon;

    (b) under a warrant issued under section 23(3) of the Misuse of Drugs Act 1971 to search premises for drugs or documents but only if the warrant specifically authorises the search of persons found on the premises; and

    (c) under a search warrant or order issued under paragraph 1, 3 or 11 of Schedule 5 to the Terrorism Act 2000 to search premises and any person found there for material likely to be of substantial value to a terrorist investigation.

A:2.28 Before the power under section 139B of the Criminal Justice Act 1988 may be exercised, the constable must have reasonable grounds to suspect that an offence under section 139A or 139AA of the Criminal Justice Act 1988 (having a bladed or pointed article or offensive weapon on school premises) has been or is being committed. A warrant to search premises and persons found therein may be issued under section 23(3) of the Misuse of Drugs Act 1971 if there are reasonable grounds to suspect that controlled drugs or certain documents are in the possession of a person on the premises.

A:2.29 The powers in paragraph 2.27 do not require prior specific grounds to suspect that the person to be searched is in possession of an item for which there is an existing power to search. However, it is still necessary to ensure that the selection and treatment of those searched under these powers is based upon objective factors connected with the search of the premises, and not upon personal prejudice.

A:3 Conduct of searches

A:3.1 All stops and searches must be carried out with courtesy, consideration and respect for the **A-9** person concerned. This has a significant impact on public confidence in the police. Every reasonable effort must be made to minimise the embarrassment that a person being searched may experience. [See *Note 4.*]

A:3.2 The co-operation of the person to be searched must be sought in every case, even if the person initially objects to the search. A forcible search may be made only if it has been established that the person is unwilling to co-operate or resists. Reasonable force may be used as a last resort if necessary to conduct a search or to detain a person or vehicle for the purposes of a search.

As to this paragraph, see *James v. DPP* (§ 15-41 in the main work).

A:3.3 The length of time for which a person or vehicle may be detained must be reasonable and kept to a minimum. Where the exercise of the power requires reasonable suspicion, the thoroughness and extent of a search must depend on what is suspected of being carried, and by whom. If the suspicion relates to a particular article which is seen to be slipped into a person's pocket, then, in the absence of other grounds for suspicion or an opportunity for the article to be moved elsewhere, the search must be confined to that pocket. In the case of a small article which can readily be concealed, such as a drug, and which might be concealed anywhere on the person, a more extensive search may be necessary. In the case of searches mentioned in paragraph 2.1(b) and (d), which do not require reasonable grounds for suspicion, officers may make any reasonable search to look for items for which they are empowered to search. [See *Note 5.*]

A:3.4 The search must be carried out at or near the place where the person or vehicle was first detained. [See *Note 6.*]

A:3.5 There is no power to require a person to remove any clothing in public other than an outer coat, jacket or gloves, except under section 60AA of the Criminal Justice and Public Order Act 1994 (which empowers a constable to require a person to remove any item worn to conceal identity). [See *Notes 4* and *6.*] A search in public of a person's clothing which has not been removed must be restricted to superficial examination of outer garments. This does not, however, prevent an officer from placing his or her hand inside the pockets of the outer clothing, or feeling round the inside of collars, socks and shoes if this is reasonably necessary in the circumstances to look for the object of the search or to remove and examine any item reasonably suspected to be the object of the search. For the same reasons, subject to the restrictions on the removal of headgear, a person's hair may also be searched in public (see paragraphs 3.1 and 3.3).

A:3.6 Where on reasonable grounds it is considered necessary to conduct a more thorough search (*e.g.* by requiring a person to take off a T-shirt), this must be done out of public view, for example, in a police van unless paragraph 3.7 applies, or police station if there is one nearby. [See *Note 6.*] Any search involving the removal of more than an outer coat, jacket, gloves, headgear or footwear, or any other item concealing identity, may only be made by an officer of the same sex as the person searched and may not be made in the presence of anyone of the opposite sex unless the person being searched specifically requests it. [See Code C, Annex L and *Notes 4* and *7.*]

A:3.7 Searches involving exposure of intimate parts of the body must not be conducted as a routine extension of a less thorough search, simply because nothing is found in the course of the initial search. Searches involving exposure of intimate parts of the body may be carried out only at a nearby police station or other nearby location which is out of public view (but not a police vehicle). These searches must be conducted in accordance with paragraph 11 of Annex A to Code C except that an intimate search mentioned in paragraph 11(f) of Annex A to Code C may not be authorised or carried out under any stop and search powers. The other provisions of Code C do not apply to the conduct and recording of searches of persons detained at police stations in the exercise of stop and search powers. [See *Note 7.*]

Steps to be taken prior to a search

A-10

A:3.8 Before any search of a detained person or attended vehicle takes place the officer must take reasonable steps, if not in uniform (see para. 3.9), to show their warrant card to the person to be searched or in charge of the vehicle to be searched and, whether or not in uniform, to give that person the following information:

(a) that they are being detained for the purposes of a search;
(b) the officer's name (except in the case of enquiries linked to the investigation of terrorism, or otherwise where the officer reasonably believes that giving their name might put them in danger, in which case a warrant or other identification number shall be given) and the name of the police station to which the officer is attached;
(c) the legal search power which is being exercised; and
(d) a clear explanation of:
  (i) the object of the search in terms of the article or articles for which there is a power to search; and
  (ii) in the case of:
    • the power under section 60 of the Criminal Justice and Public Order Act 1994 (see para. 2.1(b)), the nature of the power, the authorisation and the fact that it has been given;
    • the powers under Schedule 5 to the Terrorism Prevention and Investigation Measures Act 2011 (see paras 2.1(e) and 2.18A):
      – the fact that a TPIM notice is in force or (in the case of para. 6(2)(a)) that a TPIM notice is being served;
      – the nature of the power being exercised (for a search under para. 8 of Schedule 5, the warrant must be produced and the person provided with a copy of it);

- all other powers requiring reasonable suspicion (see para. 2.1(a)), the grounds for that suspicion (this means explaining the basis for the suspicion by reference to information and/or intelligence about, or some specific behaviour by, the person concerned (see para. 2.2));

(e) that they are entitled to a copy of the record of the search if one is made (see section 4 below) if they ask within 3 months from the date of the search and:

    (i) if they are not arrested and taken to a police station as a result of the search and it is practicable to make the record on the spot, that immediately after the search is completed they will be given, if they request, either:

- a copy of the record, or
- a receipt which explains how they can obtain a copy of the full record or access to an electronic copy of the record; or

    (ii) if they are arrested and taken to a police station as a result of the search, that the record will be made at the station as part of their custody record and they will be given, if they request, a copy of their custody record which includes a record of the search as soon as practicable whilst they are at the station. [See *Note 16*.]

A:3.9 Stops and searches under the power mentioned in paragraph 2.1(b) may be undertaken only by a constable in uniform.

A:3.10 The person should also be given information about police powers to stop and search and the individual's rights in these circumstances.

A:3.11 If the person to be searched, or in charge of a vehicle to be searched, does not appear to understand what is being said, or there is any doubt about the person's ability to understand English, the officer must take reasonable steps to bring information regarding the person's rights and any relevant provisions of this code to his or her attention. If the person is deaf or cannot understand English and is accompanied by someone, then the officer must try to establish whether that person can interpret or otherwise help the officer to give the required information.

A:4 Recording requirements

(a) Searches which do not result in an arrest

A:4.1 When an officer carries out a search in the exercise of any power to which this code applies **A-11** and the search does not result in the person searched or person in charge of the vehicle searched being arrested and taken to a police station, a record must be made of it, electronically or on paper, unless there are exceptional circumstances which make this wholly impracticable (*e.g.* in situations involving public disorder or when the recording officer's presence is urgently required elsewhere). If a record is to be made, the officer carrying out the search must make the record on the spot unless this is not practicable, in which case the officer must make the record as soon as practicable after the search is completed. [See *Note 16.*]

A:4.2 If the record is made at the time, the person who has been searched or who is in charge of the vehicle that has been searched must be asked if they want a copy and if they do, they must be given immediately, either:

- a copy of the record, or
- a receipt which explains how they can obtain a copy of the full record or access to an electronic copy of the record.

A:4.2A An officer is not required to provide a copy of the full record or a receipt at the time if they are called to an incident of higher priority. [See *Note 21.*]

(b) Searches which result in an arrest

A:4.2B If a search in the exercise of any power to which this code applies results in a person being **A-11a** arrested and taken to a police station, the officer carrying out the search is responsible for ensuring that a record of the search is made as part of their custody record. The custody officer must then ensure that the person is asked if they want a copy of the record and if they do, that they are given a copy as soon as practicable. [See *Note 16.*]

(c) Record of search

A:4.3 The record of a search must always include the following information: **A-11b**

    (a) a note of the self-defined ethnicity, and if different, the ethnicity as perceived by the officer making the search, of the person searched or of the person in charge of the vehicle searched (as the case may be) [see *Note 18*];

    (b) the date, time and place the person or vehicle was searched [see *Note 6*];

   (c) the object of the search in terms of the article or articles for which there is a power to
      search;

   (d) in the case of:

- the power under section 60 of the Criminal Justice and Public Order Act 1994 (see paragraph 2.1(b)), the nature of the power, the authorisation and the fact that it has been given [see *Note 17*];
- the powers under Schedule 5 to the Terrorism Prevention and Investigation Measures Act 2011 (see paras 2.1(e) and 2.18A):
  – the fact that a TPIM notice is in force or (in the case of para. 6(2)(a)) that a TPIM notice is being served;
  – the nature of the power, and
  – for a search under paragraph 8, the date the search warrant was issued, the fact that the warrant was produced and a copy of it provided and the warrant must also be endorsed by the constable executing it to state whether anything was found and whether anything was seized, and
- all other powers requiring reasonable suspicion (see para. 2.1(a)), the grounds for that suspicion;

   (e) subject to paragraph 3.8(b), the identity of the officer carrying out the search. [See *Note 15*.]

A:4.3A For the purposes of completing the search record, there is no requirement to record the name, address and date of birth of the person searched or the person in charge of a vehicle which is searched. The person is under no obligation to provide this information and they should not be asked to provide it for the purpose of completing the record.

A:4.4 Nothing in paragraph 4.3 requires the names of police officers to be shown on the search record or any other record required to be made under this code in the case of enquiries linked to the investigation of terrorism or otherwise where an officer reasonably believes that recording names might endanger the officers. In such cases the record must show the officers' warrant or other identification number and duty station.

A:4.5 A record is required for each person and each vehicle searched. However, if a person is in a vehicle and both are searched, and the object and grounds of the search are the same, only one record need be completed. If more than one person in a vehicle is searched, separate records for each search of a person must be made. If only a vehicle is searched, the self-defined ethnic background of the person in charge of the vehicle must be recorded, unless the vehicle is unattended.

A:4.6 The record of the grounds for making a search must, briefly but informatively, explain the reason for suspecting the person concerned, by reference to information and/or intelligence about, or some specific behaviour by, the person concerned (see para. 2.2).

A:4.7 Where officers detain an individual with a view to performing a search, but the need to search is eliminated as a result of questioning the person detained, a search should not be carried out and a record is not required. [See paragraph 2.10, *Notes 3* and *22A*.]

A:4.8 After searching an unattended vehicle, or anything in or on it, an officer must leave a notice in it (or on it, if things on it have been searched without opening it) recording the fact that it has been searched.

A:4.9 The notice must include the name of the police station to which the officer concerned is attached and state where a copy of the record of the search may be obtained and how (if applicable) an electronic copy may be accessed and where any application for compensation should be directed.

A:4.10 The vehicle must if practicable be left secure.

Recording of encounters not governed by statutory powers

A:4.11 [*Not used.*]

A-11d   A:4.12 There is no national requirement for an officer who requests a person in a public place to account for themselves, *i.e.* their actions, behaviour, presence in an area or possession of anything, to make any record of the encounter or to give the person a receipt. [See para. 2.11 and *Notes 22A* and *22B*.]

A:5 Monitoring and supervising the use of stop and search powers

General

A-12   A:5.1 Any misuse of stop and search powers is likely to be harmful to policing and lead to mistrust of the police by the local community and by the public in general. Supervising officers must monitor the use of stop and search powers and should consider in particular whether there is any evidence that they are being exercised on the basis of stereotyped images or inappropriate generalisations. Supervising officers must satisfy themselves that the practice of officers under their supervision in stopping, searching and recording is fully in accordance with this code. Supervisors must also examine whether the records reveal any trends or patterns which give cause for concern, and if so take appropriate action to address this. (See para. 2.8A.)

A:5.2 Senior officers with area or force-wide responsibilities must also monitor the broader use of stop and search powers and, where necessary, take action at the relevant level.

A:5.3 Supervision and monitoring must be supported by the compilation of comprehensive statistical records of stops and searches at force, area and local level. Any apparently disproportionate use of the powers by particular officers or groups of officers or in relation to specific sections of the community should be identified and investigated.

A:5.4 In order to promote public confidence in the use of the powers, forces in consultation with police and crime commissioners must make arrangements for the records to be scrutinised by representatives of the community, and to explain the use of the powers at a local level. [See *Note 19.*]

Suspected misuse of powers by individual officers

A:5.5 Police supervisors must monitor the use of stop and search powers by individual officers to **A-12a** ensure that they are being applied appropriately and lawfully. Monitoring takes many forms, such as direct supervision of the exercise of the powers, examining stop and search records (particularly examining the officer's documented reasonable grounds for suspicion) and asking the officer to account for the way in which they conducted and recorded particular searches or through complaints about a stop and search that an officer has carried out.

A:5.6 Where a supervisor identifies issues with the way that an officer has used a stop and search power, the facts of the case will determine whether the standards of professional behaviour as set out in the Code of Ethics (see http://www.college.police.uk/en/20972.htm) have been breached and which formal action is pursued. Improper use might be a result of poor performance or a conduct matter, which will require the supervisor to take appropriate action such as performance or misconduct procedures. It is imperative that supervisors take both timely and appropriate action to deal with all such cases that come to their notice.

Notes for Guidance

Officers exercising stop and search powers

A:1 *This code does not affect the ability of an officer to speak to or question a person in the ordinary course of* **A-13** *the officer's duties without detaining the person or exercising any element of compulsion. It is not the purpose of the code to prohibit such encounters between the police and the community with the co-operation of the person concerned and neither does it affect the principle that all citizens have a duty to help police officers to prevent crime and discover offenders. This is a civic rather than a legal duty; but when a police officer is trying to discover whether, or by whom, an offence has been committed he or she may question any person from whom useful information might be obtained, subject to the restrictions imposed by Code C. A person's unwillingness to reply does not alter this entitlement, but in the absence of a power to arrest, or to detain in order to search, the person is free to leave at will and cannot be compelled to remain with the officer.*

A:1A *In paragraphs 1.1 and 2.2B(a), the "relevant protected characteristics" are: age, disability, gender reassignment, pregnancy and maternity, race, religion or belief, sex and sexual orientation.*

A:1B *Innocent possession means that the person does have [sic] the guilty knowledge that they are carrying an unlawful item which is required before an arrest on suspicion that the person has committed an offence in respect of the item sought (if arrest is necessary – see PACE Code G) and/or a criminal prosecution) can be considered. It is not uncommon for children under the age of criminal responsibility to be used by older children and adults to carry stolen property, drugs and weapons and, in some cases, firearms, for the criminal benefit of others, either:*

- *in the hope that police may not suspect they are being used for carrying the items; or*
- *knowing that if they are suspected of being couriers and are stopped and searched, they cannot be arrested or prosecuted for any criminal offence.*

Stop and search powers therefore allow the police to intervene effectively to break up criminal gangs and groups that use young children to further their criminal activities.

A:1BA *Whenever a child under 10 is suspected of carrying unlawful items for someone else, or is found in circumstances which suggest that their welfare and safety may be at risk, the facts should be reported and actioned in accordance with established force safeguarding procedures. This will be in addition to treating them as a potentially vulnerable or intimidated witness in respect of their status as a witness to the serious criminal offence(s) committed by those using them as couriers. Safeguarding considerations will also apply to other persons aged under 18 who are stopped and searched under any of the powers to which this code applies. See paragraph 1.1 with regard to the requirement under the Children Act 2004, s.11, for chief police officers and other specified persons and bodies, to ensure that in the discharge of their functions, they have regard to the need to safeguard and promote the welfare of all persons under the age of 18.*

A:2 *In some circumstances preparatory questioning may be unnecessary, but in general a brief conversation or exchange will be desirable not only as a means of avoiding unsuccessful searches, but to explain the grounds for the stop/search, to gain cooperation and reduce any tension there might be surrounding the stop/ search.*

A:3 *Where a person is lawfully detained for the purpose of a search, but no search in the event takes place, the detention will not thereby have been rendered unlawful.*

A:4 *Many people customarily cover their heads or faces for religious reasons—for example, Muslim women, Sikh men, Sikh or Hindu women, or Rastafarian men or women. A police officer cannot order the removal of a head or face covering except where there is reason to believe that the item is being worn by the individual wholly or mainly for the purpose of disguising identity, not simply because it disguises identity. Where there may be religious sensitivities about ordering the removal of such an item, the officer should permit the item to be removed out of public view. Where practicable, the item should be removed in the presence of an officer of the same sex as the person and out of sight of anyone of the opposite sex (see Code C, Annex L).*

A:5 *A search of a person in public should be completed as soon as possible.*

A:6 *A person may be detained under a stop and search power at a place other than where the person was first detained, only if that place, be it a police station or elsewhere, is nearby. Such a place should be located within a reasonable travelling distance using whatever mode of travel (on foot or by car) is appropriate. This applies to all searches under stop and search powers, whether or not they involve the removal of clothing or exposure of intimate parts of the body (see paragraphs 3.6 and 3.7) or take place in or out of public view. It means, for example, that a search under the stop and search power in section 23 of the Misuse of Drugs Act 1971 which involves the compulsory removal of more than a person's outer coat, jacket or gloves cannot be carried out unless a place which is both nearby the place they were first detained and out of public view, is available. If a search involves exposure of intimate parts of the body and a police station is not nearby, particular care must be taken to ensure that the location is suitable in that it enables the search to be conducted in accordance with the requirements of paragraph 11 of Annex A to Code C.*

A:7 *A search in the street itself should be regarded as being in public for the purposes of paragraphs 3.6 and 3.7 above, even though it may be empty at the time a search begins. Although there is no power to require a person to do so, there is nothing to prevent an officer from asking a person voluntarily to remove more than an outer coat, jacket or gloves in public.*

A:8 [Not used.]

A:9 *Other means of identification might include jewellery, insignias, tattoos or other features which are known to identify members of the particular gang or group.*

A:9A *A decision to search individuals believed to be members of a particular group or gang must be judged on a case by case basis according to the circumstances applicable at the time of the proposed searches and in particular, having regard to:*

   (a) *the number of items suspected of being carried;*

   (b) *the nature of those items and the risk they pose; and*

   (c) *the number of individuals to be searched.*

A group search will only be justified if it is a necessary and proportionate approach based on the facts and having regard to the nature of the suspicion in these cases. The extent and thoroughness of the searches must not be excessive.

The size of the group and the number of individuals it is proposed to search will be a key factor and steps should be taken to identify those who are to be searched to avoid unnecessary inconvenience to unconnected members of the public who are also present.

The onus is on the police to be satisfied and to demonstrate that their approach to the decision to search is in pursuit of a legitimate aim, necessary and proportionate.

Authorising officers

A-14   A:10 *The powers under section 60 are separate from and additional to the normal stop and search powers which require reasonable grounds to suspect an individual of carrying an offensive weapon (or other article). Their overall purpose is to prevent serious violence and the widespread carrying of weapons which might lead to persons being seriously injured by disarming potential offenders or finding weapons that have been used in circumstances where other powers would not be sufficient. They should not therefore be used to replace or circumvent the normal powers for dealing with routine crime problems. A particular example might be an authorisation to prevent serious violence or the carrying of offensive weapons at a sports event by rival team supporters when the expected general appearance and age range of those likely to be responsible, alone, would not be sufficiently distinctive to support reasonable suspicion (see paragraph 2.6). The purpose of the powers under section 60AA is to prevent those involved in intimidatory or violent protests using face coverings to disguise identity.*

A:11 *Authorisations under section 60 require a reasonable belief on the part of the authorising officer. This must have an objective basis, for example: intelligence or relevant information such as a history of antagonism* and violence between particular groups; previous incidents of violence at, or connected with, particular events or locations; a significant increase in knife-point robberies in a limited area; reports that individuals are regularly carrying weapons in a particular locality; information following an incident in which weapons were used about where the weapons might be found or in the case of section 60AA previous incidents of crimes being committed while wearing face coverings to conceal identity.

A:12 It is for the authorising officer to determine the period of time during which the powers mentioned in paragraph 2.1(b) may be exercised. The officer should set the minimum period he or she considers necessary to deal with the risk of violence, the carrying of knives or offensive weapons, or to find dangerous instruments or weapons that have been used. A direction to extend the period authorised under the powers mentioned in paragraph 2.1(b) may be given only once. Thereafter further use of the powers requires a new authorisation.

A:13 It is for the authorising officer to determine the geographical area in which the use of the powers is to be authorised. In doing so the officer may wish to take into account factors such as the nature and venue of the anticipated incident or the incident which has taken place, the number of people who may be in the immediate area of that incident, their access to surrounding areas and the anticipated or actual level of violence. The officer should not set a geographical area which is wider than that he or she believes necessary for the purpose of preventing anticipated violence, the carrying of knives or offensive weapons, or for finding a dangerous instrument or weapon that has been used or, in the case of section 60AA, the prevention of commission of offences. It is particularly important to ensure that constables exercising such powers are fully aware of the locality within which they may be used. The officer giving the authorisation should therefore specify either the streets which form the boundary of the locality or a divisional boundary if appropriate within the force area. If the power is to be used in response to a threat or incident that straddles police force areas, an officer from each of the forces concerned will need to give an authorisation.

A:14 [Not used.]

Recording

A:15 Where a stop and search is conducted by more than one officer the identity of all the officers engaged in **A-15** the search must be recorded on the record. Nothing prevents an officer who is present but not directly involved in searching from completing the record during the course of the encounter.

A:16 When the search results in the person searched or in charge of a vehicle which is searched being arrested, the requirement to make the record of the search as part of the person's custody record does not apply if the person is granted "street bail" after arrest (see section 30A of PACE) to attend a police station and is not taken in custody to the police station. An arrested person's entitlement to a copy of the search record which is made as part of their custody record does not affect their entitlement to a copy of their custody record or any other provisions of PACE Code C section 2 (custody records).

A:17 It is important for monitoring purposes to specify when authority is given for exercising the stop and search power under section 60 of the Criminal Justice and Public Order Act 1994.

A:18 Officers should record the self-defined ethnicity of every person stopped according to the categories used in the 2001 census question listed in Annex B. The person should be asked to select one of the five main categories representing broad ethnic groups and then a more specific cultural background from within this group. The ethnic classification should be coded for recording purposes using the coding system in Annex B. An additional "Not stated" box is available but should not be offered to respondents explicitly. Officers should be aware and explain to members of the public, especially where concerns are raised, that this information is required to obtain a true picture of stop and search activity and to help improve ethnic monitoring, tackle discriminatory practice, and promote effective use of the powers. If the person gives what appears to the officer to be an "incorrect" answer (e.g. a person who appears to be white states that they are black), the officer should record the response that has been given and then record their own perception of the person's ethnic background by using the PNC classification system. If the "Not stated" category is used the reason for this must be recorded on the form.

A:19 Arrangements for public scrutiny of records should take account of the right to confidentiality of those stopped and searched. Anonymised forms and/or statistics generated from records should be the focus of the examinations by members of the public. The groups that are consulted should always include children and young persons.

A:20 [Not used.]

A:21 In situations where it is not practicable to provide a written copy of the record or immediate access to an electronic copy of the record or a receipt of the search at the time (see paragraph 4.2A above), the officer should consider giving the person details of the station which they may attend for a copy of the record. A receipt may take the form of a simple business card which includes sufficient information to locate the record should the person ask for copy [sic], for example, the date and place of the search, and a reference number or the name of the officer who carried out the search (unless paragraph 4.4 applies).

A:22 [Not used.]

A:22A Where there are concerns which make it necessary to monitor any local disproportionality, forces have discretion to direct officers to record the self-defined ethnicity of persons they request to account for themselves in a public place or who they detain with a view to searching but do not search. Guidance should be provided locally and efforts made to minimise the bureaucracy involved. Records should be closely monitored and supervised in line with paragraphs 5.1 to 5.6, and forces can suspend or re-instate recording of these encounters as appropriate.

A:22B *A person who is asked to account for themselves should, if they request, be given information about how they can report their dissatisfaction about how they have been treated.*

Definition of offensive weapon

A:23 *"Offensive weapon" is defined as "any article made or adapted for use by him for causing injury to the person, or intended by the person having it with him for such use or by someone else". There are three categories of offensive weapons: those made for causing injury to the person; those adapted for such a purpose; and those not so made or adapted, but carried with the intention of causing injury to the person. A firearm, as defined by section 57 of the Firearms Act 1968, would fall within the definition of offensive weapon if any of the criteria above apply.*

ANNEX A

Summary of main stop and search powers to which Code A applies

This table relates to stop and search powers only. Individual statutes below may contain other police powers of entry, search and seizure.

Power	Object of search	Extent of Search	Where Exercisable
Unlawful articles general			
1. Public Stores Act 1875, s.6	HM Stores stolen or unlawfully obtained	Persons, vehicles and vessels	Anywhere where the constabulary powers are exercisable
2. Firearms Act 1968, s.47	Firearms	Persons and vehicles	A public place, or anywhere in the case of reasonable suspicion of offences of carrying rearms with criminal intent or trespassing with firearms
3. Misuse of Drugs Act 1971, s.23	Controlled drugs	Persons and vehicles	Anywhere
4. Customs and Excise Management Act 1979, s.163	Goods: (a) on which duty has not been paid; (b) being unlawfully removed, imported or exported; (c) otherwise liable to forfeiture to HM Revenue and Customs	Vehicles and vessels only	Anywhere
5. Aviation Security Act 1982, s.24B *Note: This power applies throughout the UK but the provisions of this code will apply only when the power is exercised at an aerodrome situated in England and Wales.*	Stolen articles or articles made, adapted or intended for use in the course of/in connection with conduct which constitutes an offence in the part of the UK where the aerodrome is situated or would do so, if it occurred there.	Persons, vehicles, aircraft. Anything in or on a vehicle or aircraft	Any part of an aerodrome
6. Police and Criminal Evidence Act 1984, s.1	Stolen goods;	Persons and vehicles	Where there is public access
	Articles made, adapted or intended for use in the course of or in connection with, certain offences under the Theft Act 1968, Fraud Act and Criminal Damage Act 1971;	Persons and vehicles	Where there is public access
	Offensive weapons, bladed or sharply-pointed articles (except folding pocket knives with a blade cutting edge not exceeding 3 inches);	Persons and vehicles	Where there is public access

Power	Object of search	Extent of Search	Where Exercisable
	Fireworks: category 4 (display grade) fireworks if possession prohibited, adult fireworks in possession of a person under 18 in a public place.	Persons and vehicles	Where there is public access
7. Sporting Events (Control of Alcohol etc.) Act 1985, s.7	Intoxicating liquor	Persons, coaches and trains	Designated sports grounds or coaches and trains travelling to or from a designated sporting event.
8. Crossbows Act 1987, s.4	Crossbows or parts of crossbows (except crossbows with a draw weight of less than 1.4 kilograms)	Persons and vehicles	Anywhere except dwellings
9. Criminal Justice Act 1988 s.139B	Offensive weapons, bladed or sharply pointed article	Persons	School premises
Evidence of game and wildlife offences			
10. Poaching Prevention Act 1862, s.2	Game or poaching equipment	Persons and vehicles	A public place
11. Deer Act 1991, s.12	Evidence of offences under the Act	Persons and vehicles	Anywhere except dwellings
12. Conservation of Seals Act 1970, s.4	Seals or hunting equipment	Vehicles only	Anywhere
13. Protection of Badgers Act 1992, s.11	Evidence offences under the Act	Persons and vehicles	Anywhere
14. Wildlife and Countryside Act 1981, s.19	Evidence of wildlife offences	Persons and vehicles	Anywhere except dwellings
Other			
15. Paragraphs 6 & 8 of Schedule 5 to the Terrorism Prevention and Investigation Measures Act 2011	Anything that contravenes measures specied in a TPIM notice.	Persons in respect of whom a TPIM notice is being served or is in force	Anywhere
16. Paragraph 10 of Schedule 5 to the Terrorism Prevention and Investigation Measures Act 2011	Anything that could be used to threaten or harm any person.	Persons in respect of whom a TPIM notice is in force.	Anywhere
17. [Not used.]			
18. [Not used.]			
19. Section 60 Criminal Justice and Public Order Act 1994	Offensive weapons or dangerous instruments to prevent incidents of serious violence or to deal with the carrying of such items or nd such items which have been used in incidents of serious violence	Persons and vehicles	Anywhere within a locality authorised under subsection (1)

ANNEX B

Self-defined ethnic classification categories

White	**W**
A. White—British	W1
B. White—Irish	W2
C. Any other White background	W9
Mixed	**M**
D. White and Black Caribbean	M1
E. White and Black African	M2
F. White and Asian	M3
G. Any other Mixed background	M9
Asian/ Asian—British	**A**
H. Asian—Indian	A1
I. Asian—Pakistani	A2
J. Asian—Bangladeshi	A3
K. Any other Asian background	A9
Black / Black—British	**B**
L. Black—Caribbean	B1
M. Black African	B2
N. Any other Black background	B9
Other	**O**
O. Chinese	O1
P. Any other	O9
Not stated	**NS**

A-17a

ANNEX C

Summary of powers of community support officers to search and seize

The following is a summary of the search and seizure powers that may be exercised by a community support officer (CSO) who has been designated with the relevant powers in accordance with Part 4 of the Police Reform Act 2002. When exercising any of these powers, a CSO must have regard to any relevant provisions of this code, including section 3 governing the conduct of searches and the steps to be taken prior to a search.

1. [*Not used.*]

2. Powers to search requiring the consent of the person and seizure

A CSO may detain a person using reasonable force where necessary as set out in Part 1 of Schedule 4 to the Police Reform Act 2002. If the person has been lawfully detained, the CSO may search the person provided that person gives consent to such a search in relation to the following:

Designation	Powers conferred	Object of Search	Extent of Search	Where Exercisable
Police Reform Act 2002, Schedule 4, paragraphs 7 and 7A	(a) Criminal Justice and Police Act 2001, s.12(2)	(a) Alcohol or a container for alcohol	(a) Persons	(a) Designated public place
	(b) Confiscation of Alcohol (Young Persons) Act 1997, s.1	(b) Alcohol	(b) Persons under 18 years old	(b) Public place
	(c) Children and Young Persons Act 1933, s.7(3)	(c) Tobacco or cigarette papers	(c) Persons under 16 years old found smoking	(c) Public place

3. Powers to search not requiring the consent of the person and seizure

A CSO may detain a person using reasonable force where necessary as set out in Part 1 of Schedule 4 to the Police Reform Act 2002. If the person has been lawfully detained, the CSO may search the person without the need for that person's consent in relation to the following:

Designation	Power conferred	Object of Search	Extent of Search	Where Exercisable
Police Reform Act 2002, Schedule 4, paragraph 2A	Police and Criminal Evidence Act 1984, s.32	(a) Objects that might be used to cause physical injury to the person or the CSO. (b) Items that might be used to assist escape.	Persons made subject to a requirement to wait.	Any place where the requirement to wait has been made.

4. Powers to seize without consent

This power applies when drugs are found in the course of any search mentioned above.

Designation	Power conferred	Object of Seizure	Where Exercisable
Police Reform Act 2002, Schedule 4, paragraph 7B	Police Reform Act 2002, Schedule 4, paragraph 7B	Controlled drugs in a person's possession.	Any place where the person is in possession of the drug.

Annex D—Deleted
Annex E—Deleted

ANNEX F

Establishing gender of persons for the purpose of searching

See Code C, Annex L.   **A-17b**

(3) Search and seizure

The text that follows is of the version of the code that came into force on October 27, 2013: see **A-18**
ante, Appendix A-1.

For authorities in relation to Code B, see, in particular, § 15-126 in the main work.

B. CODE OF PRACTICE FOR SEARCHES OF PREMISES BY POLICE OFFICERS AND THE SEIZURE OF PROPERTY FOUND BY POLICE OFFICERS ON PERSONS OR PREMISES

Commencement—transitional arrangements

This code applies to applications for warrants made after 00.00 on 27 October 2013 and to **A-19**
searches and seizures taking place after 00.00 on 27 October 2013.

B:1 Introduction

B:1.1 This code of practice deals with police powers to: **A-20**
- search premises
- seize and retain property found on premises and persons.

B:1.1A These powers may be used to find:
- property and material relating to a crime
- wanted persons
- children who abscond from local authority accommodation where they have been remanded or committed by a court.

B:1.2 A justice of the peace may issue a search warrant granting powers of entry, search and seizure, *e.g.* warrants to search for stolen property, drugs, firearms and evidence of serious offences. Police also have powers without a search warrant. The main ones provided by the Police and Criminal Evidence Act 1984 (PACE) include powers to search premises:
- to make an arrest
- after an arrest.

B:1.3 The right to privacy and respect for personal property are key principles of the Human Rights Act 1998. Powers of entry, search and seizure should be fully and clearly justified before use because they may significantly interfere with the occupier's privacy. Officers should consider if the necessary objectives can be met by less intrusive means.

B:1.3A Powers to search and seize must be used fairly, responsibly, with respect for people who occupy premises being searched or are in charge of property being seized and without unlawful discrimination. Under the Equality Act 2010, s.149, when police officers are carrying out their functions, they also have a duty to have due regard to the need to eliminate unlawful discrimination, harassment and victimisation, to advance equality of opportunity between people who share a relevant protected characteristic and people who do not share it, and to take steps to foster good relations between those persons. [See *Note 1A*.]

B:1.4 In all cases, police should therefore:
- exercise their powers courteously and with respect for persons and property
- only use reasonable force when this is considered necessary and proportionate to the circumstances.

B:1.5 If the provisions of PACE and this code are not observed, evidence obtained from a search may be open to question.

Notes for guidance

B:1A *In paragraph 1.3A, "relevant protected characteristic" includes: age, disability, gender reassignment, pregnancy and maternity, race, religion/belief, sex and sexual orientation.*

B:2 General

B:2.1 This code must be readily available at all police stations for consultation by:

- police officers
- police staff
- detained persons
- members of the public.

B:2.2 The *Notes for Guidance* included are not provisions of this code.

B:2.3 This code applies to searches of premises:

(a) by police for the purposes of an investigation into an alleged offence, with the occupier's consent, other than:

- routine scene of crime searches;
- calls to a fire or burglary made by or on behalf of an occupier or searches following the activation of fire or burglar alarms or discovery of insecure premises;
- searches when paragraph 5.4 applies;
- bomb threat calls;

(b) under powers conferred on police officers by PACE, ss.17, 18 and 32;

(c) undertaken in pursuance of search warrants issued to and executed by constables in accordance with PACE, ss.15 and 16 [see *Note 2A*];

(d) subject to paragraph 2.6, under any other power given to police to enter premises with or without a search warrant for any purpose connected with the investigation into an alleged or suspected offence. [See *Note 2B*.]

For the purposes of this code, "premises" as defined in PACE, s.23, includes any place, vehicle, vessel, aircraft, hovercraft, tent or movable structure and any offshore installation as defined in the Mineral Workings (Offshore Installations) Act 1971, s.1. [See *Note 2D*.]

B:2.4 A person who has not been arrested but is searched during a search of premises should be searched in accordance with Code A. [See *Note 2C*.]

B:2.5 This code does not apply to the exercise of a statutory power to enter premises or to inspect goods, equipment or procedures if the exercise of that power is not dependent on the existence of grounds for suspecting that an offence may have been committed and the person exercising the power has no reasonable grounds for such suspicion.

B:2.6 This code does not affect any directions or requirements of a search warrant, order or other power to search and seize lawfully exercised in England or Wales that any item or evidence seized under that warrant, order or power be handed over to a police force, court, tribunal, or other authority outside England or Wales. For example, warrants and orders issued in Scotland or Northern Ireland [see *Note 2B(f)*] and search warrants and powers provided for in sections 14 to 17 of the Crime (International Co-operation) Act 2003.

B:2.7 When this code requires the prior authority or agreement of an officer of at least inspector or superintendent rank, that authority may be given by a sergeant or chief inspector authorised to perform the functions of the higher rank under PACE, s.107.

B:2.8 Written records required under this code not made in the search record shall, unless otherwise specified, be made:

- in the recording officer's pocket book ("pocket book" includes any official report book issued to police officers), or
- on forms provided for the purpose.

B:2.9 Nothing in this code requires the identity of officers, or anyone accompanying them during a search of premises, to be recorded or disclosed:

(a) in the case of enquiries linked to the investigation of terrorism; or

(b) if officers reasonably believe recording or disclosing their names might put them in danger.

In these cases officers should use warrant or other identification numbers and the name of their police station. Police staff should use any identification number provided to them by the police force. [See *Note 2E*.]

B:2.10 The "officer in charge of the search" means the officer assigned specific duties and responsibilities under this code. Whenever there is a search of premises to which this code applies one officer must act as the officer in charge of the search. [See *Note 2F*.]

B:2.11 In this code:

(a) "designated person" means a person other than a police officer, designated under the Police Reform Act 2002, Pt 4 who has specified powers and duties of police officers conferred or imposed on them [see Note 2G];

(b) any reference to a police officer includes a designated person acting in the exercise or performance of the powers and duties conferred or imposed on them by their designation;

(c) a person authorised to accompany police officers or designated persons in the execution of a warrant has the same powers as a constable in the execution of the warrant and the search and seizure of anything related to the warrant. These powers must be exercised in the company and under the supervision of a police officer. [See *Note 3C.*]

B:2.12 If a power conferred on a designated person:

(a) allows reasonable force to be used when exercised by a police officer, a designated person exercising that power has the same entitlement to use force;

(b) includes power to use force to enter any premises, that power is not exercisable by that designated person except:

(i) in the company and under the supervision of a police officer; or

(ii) for the purpose of:

- saving life or limb; or
- preventing serious damage to property.

B:2.13 Designated persons must have regard to any relevant provisions of the codes of practice.

Notes for guidance

B:2A *PACE ss.15 and 16 apply to all search warrants issued to and executed by constables under any enact-* **A-22** *ment, e.g. search warrants issued by a:*

(a) *justice of the peace under the:*

- *Theft Act 1968, s.26—stolen property;*
- *Misuse of Drugs Act 1971, s.23—controlled drugs;*
- *PACE, s.8—evidence of an indictable offence;*
- *Terrorism Act 2000, Sched. 5, para. 1;*
- *Terrorism Prevention and Investigation Measures Act 2011, Sched. 5, para. 8(2)(b)— search of premises for compliance purposes (see para. 10.1);*

(b) *circuit judge under:*

- *PACE, Sched. 1;*
- *Terrorism Act 2000, Sched. 5, para. 11.*

B:2B *Examples of the other powers in paragraph 2.3(d) include:*

(a) *Road Traffic Act 1988, s.6E(1) giving police power to enter premises under section 6E(1) to:*

- *require a person to provide a specimen of breath; or*
- *arrest a person following:*
  - *a positive breath test;*
  - *failure to provide a specimen of breath;*

(b) *Transport and Works Act 1992, s.30(4) giving police powers to enter premises mirroring the powers in (a) in relation to specified persons working on transport systems to which the Act applies;*

(c) *Criminal Justice Act 1988, s.139B giving police power to enter and search school premises for offensive weapons, bladed or pointed articles;*

(d) *Terrorism Act 2000, Sched. 5, paras 3 and 15 empowering a superintendent in urgent cases to give written authority for police to enter and search premises for the purposes of a terrorist investigation;*

(e) *Explosives Act 1875, s.73(b) empowering a superintendent to give written authority for police to enter premises, examine and search them for explosives;*

(f) *search warrants and production orders or the equivalent issued in Scotland or Northern Ireland endorsed under the Summary Jurisdiction (Process) Act 1881 or the Petty Sessions (Ireland) Act 1851 respectively for execution in England and Wales;*

(g) *Terrorism Prevention and Investigation Measures Act 2011, Sched. 5, paras 5(1), 6(2)(b) and 7(2), searches relating to TPIM notices (see para. 10.1).*

B:2C *The Criminal Justice Act 1988, s.139B provides that a constable who has reasonable grounds to suspect an offence under the Criminal Justice Act 1988, s.139A or 139AA has or is being committed may enter school premises and search the premises and any persons on the premises for any bladed or pointed article or offensive weapon. Persons may be searched under a warrant issued under the Misuse of Drugs Act 1971, s.23(3) to search premises for drugs or documents only if the warrant specifically authorises the search of persons on the premises. Powers to search premises under certain terrorism provisions also authorise the search of persons on the premises, for example, under paragraphs 1, 2, 11 and 15 of Schedule 5 to the Terrorism Act 2000 and section 52 of the Anti-terrorism, Crime and Security Act 2001.*

B:2D *The Immigration Act 1971, Pt III and Sched. 2 gives immigration officers powers to enter and search premises, seize and retain property, with and without a search warrant. These are similar to the powers available to police under search warrants issued by a justice of the peace and without a warrant under PACE, ss.17, 18, 19 and 32 except they only apply to specified offences under the Immigration Act 1971 and immigration control powers. For certain types of investigations and enquiries these powers avoid the need for the Immigration Service to rely on police officers becoming directly involved. When exercising these powers, immigration officers are required by the Immigration and Asylum Act 1999, s.145 to have regard to this code's corresponding provisions. When immigration officers are dealing with persons or property at police stations, police officers should give appropriate assistance to help them discharge their specific duties and responsibilities.*

B:2E The purpose of paragraph 2.9(b) is to protect those involved in serious organised crime investigations or arrests of particularly violent suspects when there is reliable information that those arrested or their associates may threaten or cause harm to the officers or anyone accompanying them during a search of premises. In cases of doubt, an officer of inspector rank or above should be consulted.

B:2F For the purposes of paragraph 2.10, the officer in charge of the search should normally be the most senior officer present. Some exceptions are:

    (a) *a supervising officer who attends or assists at the scene of a premises search may appoint an officer of lower rank as officer in charge of the search if that officer is:*

        • *more conversant with the facts;*

        • *a more appropriate officer to be in charge of the search;*

    (b) *when all officers in a premises search are the same rank. The supervising officer if available, must make sure one of them is appointed officer in charge of the search, otherwise the officers themselves must nominate one of their number as the officer in charge;*

    (c) *a senior officer assisting in a specialist role. This officer need not be regarded as having a general supervisory role over the conduct of the search or be appointed or expected to act as the officer in charge of the search.*

Except in (c), nothing in this note diminishes the role and responsibilities of a supervisory officer who is present at the search or knows of a search taking place.

B:2G An officer of the rank of inspector or above may direct a designated investigating officer not to wear a uniform for the purposes of a specific operation.

B:3 Search warrants and production orders

(a) *Before making an application*

A-23   B:3.1 When information appears to justify an application, the officer must take reasonable steps to check the information is accurate, recent and not provided maliciously or irresponsibly. An application may not be made on the basis of information from an anonymous source if corroboration has not been sought. See *Note 3A.*

B:3.2 The officer shall ascertain as specifically as possible the nature of the articles concerned and their location.

B:3.3 The officer shall make reasonable enquiries to:

    (i) establish if:

        • anything is known about the likely occupier of the premises and the nature of the premises themselves;

        • the premises have been searched previously and how recently;

    (ii) obtain any other relevant information.

B:3.4 An application:

    (a) to a justice of the peace for a search warrant or to a circuit judge for a search warrant or production order under PACE, Sched. 1 must be supported by a signed written authority from an officer of inspector rank or above; [Note: if the case is an urgent application to a justice of the peace and an inspector or above is not readily available, the next most senior officer on duty can give the written authority];

    (b) to a circuit judge under the Terrorism Act 2000, Sched. 5 for:

        • a production order;

        • search warrant; or

        • an order requiring an explanation of material seized or produced under such a warrant or production order,

    must be supported by a signed written authority from an officer of superintendent rank or above.

B:3.5 Except in a case of urgency, if there is reason to believe a search might have an adverse effect on relations between the police and the community, the officer in charge shall consult the local police/community liaison officer:

- before the search; or
- in urgent cases, as soon as practicable after the search.

(b) *Making an application*

B:3.6 A search warrant application must be supported in writing, specifying:
(a) the enactment under which the application is made [see *Note 2A*];
(b) (i) whether the warrant is to authorise entry and search of:
- one set of premises; or
- if the application is under PACE, s.8, or Sched. 1, para. 12, more than one set of specified premises or all premises occupied or controlled by a specified person, and
(ii) the premises to be searched;
(c) the object of the search [see *Note 3B*];
(d) the grounds for the application, including, when the purpose of the proposed search is to find evidence of an alleged offence, an indication of how the evidence relates to the investigation;
(da) where the application is under PACE, s.8, or Sched. 1, para. 12 for a single warrant to enter and search:
(i) more than one set of specified premises, the officer must specify each set of premises which it is desired to enter and search;
(ii) all premises occupied or controlled by a specified person, the officer must specify:
- as many sets of premises which it is desired to enter and search as it is reasonably practicable to specify;
- the person who is in occupation or control of those premises and any others which it is desired to search;
- why it is necessary to search more premises than those which can be specified;
- why it is not reasonably practicable to specify all the premises which it is desired to enter and search;
(db) whether an application under PACE, s.8 is for a warrant authorising entry and search on more than one occasion, and if so, the officer must state the grounds for this and whether the desired number of entries authorised is unlimited or a specified maximum;
(e) that there are no reasonable grounds to believe the material to be sought, when making application to a:
(i) justice of the peace or a circuit judge consists of or includes items subject to legal privilege;
(ii) justice of the peace, consists of or includes excluded material or special procedure material;
[Note: this does not affect the additional powers of seizure in the Criminal Justice and Police Act 2001, Pt 2 covered in paragraph 7.7 [see *Note 3B*]];
(f) if applicable, a request for the warrant to authorise a person or persons to accompany the officer who executes the warrant [see *Note 3C*].

B:3.7 A search warrant application under PACE, Sched. 1, para. 12(a), shall if appropriate indicate why it is believed service of notice of an application for a production order may seriously prejudice the investigation. Applications for search warrants under the Terrorism Act 2000, Schedule 5, paragraph 11 must indicate why a production order would not be appropriate.

B:3.8 If a search warrant application is refused, a further application may not be made for those premises unless supported by additional grounds.

Notes for guidance

B:3A *The identity of an informant need not be disclosed when making an application, but the officer should be* **A-24** *prepared to answer any questions the magistrate or judge may have about:*
- *the accuracy of previous information from that source, and*
- *any other related matters.*

B:3B *The information supporting a search warrant application should be as specific as possible, particularly in relation to the articles or persons being sought and where in the premises it is suspected they may be found. The meaning of "items subject to legal privilege", "excluded material" and "special procedure material" are defined by PACE, ss.10, 11 and 14 respectively.*

B:3C *Under PACE, s.16(2), a search warrant may authorise persons other than police officers to accompany the constable who executes the warrant. This includes, e.g. any suitably qualified or skilled person or an expert in a particular field whose presence is needed to help accurately identify the material sought or to advise where certain evidence is most likely to be found and how it should be dealt with. It does not give them any right to force entry, but it gives them the right to be on the premises during the search and to search for or seize property without the occupier's permission.*

B:4 Entry without warrant—particular powers

(a) *Making an arrest etc*

A-25   B:4.1 The conditions under which an officer may enter and search premises without a warrant are set out in PACE, s.17. It should be noted that this section does not create or confer any powers of arrest. See other powers in *Note 2B(a)*.

(b) *Search of premises where arrest takes place or the arrested person was immediately before arrest*

B:4.2 When a person has been arrested for an indictable offence, a police officer has power under PACE, s.32 to search the premises where the person was arrested or where the person was immediately before being arrested.

(c) *Search of premises occupied or controlled by the arrested person*

B:4.3 The specific powers to search premises which are occupied or controlled by a person arrested for an indictable offence are set out in PACE, s.18. They may not be exercised, except if section 18 (5) applies, unless an officer of inspector rank or above has given written authority. That authority should only be given when the authorising officer is satisfied that the premises are occupied or controlled by the arrested person and that the necessary grounds exist. If possible the authorising officer should record the authority on the Notice of Powers and Rights and, subject to paragraph 2.9, sign the notice. The record of the grounds for the search and the nature of the evidence sought as required by section 18(7) of the Act should be made in:

- the custody record if there is one, otherwise
- the officer's pocket book, or
- the search record.

B:5 Search with consent

A-26   B:5.1 Subject to paragraph 5.4, if it is proposed to search premises with the consent of a person entitled to grant entry the consent must, if practicable, be given in writing on the Notice of Powers and Rights before the search. The officer must make any necessary enquiries to be satisfied the person is in a position to give such consent. [See *Notes 5A* and *5B*.]

B:5.2 Before seeking consent the officer in charge of the search shall state the purpose of the proposed search and its extent. This information must be as specific as possible, particularly regarding the articles or persons being sought and the parts of the premises to be searched. The person concerned must be clearly informed they are not obliged to consent, that any consent given can be withdrawn at any time, including before the search starts or while it is under way and anything seized may be produced in evidence. If at the time the person is not suspected of an offence, the officer shall say this when stating the purpose of the search.

B:5.3 An officer cannot enter and search or continue to search premises under paragraph 5.1 if consent is given under duress or withdrawn before the search is completed.

B:5.4 It is unnecessary to seek consent under paragraphs 5.1 and 5.2 if this would cause disproportionate inconvenience to the person concerned. [See *Note 5C*.]

Notes for guidance

A-27   B:5A *In a lodging house, hostel or similar accommodation, every reasonable effort should be made to obtain the consent of the tenant, lodger or occupier. A search should not be made solely on the basis of the landlord's consent.*

B:5B *If the intention is to search premises under the authority of a warrant or a power of entry and search without warrant, and the occupier of the premises co-operates in accordance with paragraph 6.4, there is no need to obtain written consent.*

B:5C *Paragraph 5.4 is intended to apply when it is reasonable to assume innocent occupiers would agree to, and expect, police to take the proposed action, e.g. if:*

- *a suspect has fled the scene of a crime or to evade arrest and it is necessary quickly to check surrounding gardens and readily accessible places to see if the suspect is hiding, or*
- *police have arrested someone in the night after a pursuit and it is necessary to make a brief check of gardens along the pursuit route to see if stolen or incriminating articles have been discarded.*

B:6 Searching premises—general considerations

(a) *Time of searches*

A-28

B:6.1 Searches made under warrant must be made within three calendar months of the date the warrant is issued or within the period specified in the enactment under which the warrant is issued if this is shorter.

B:6.2 Searches must be made at a reasonable hour unless this might frustrate the purpose of the search.

B:6.3 When the extent or complexity of a search mean it is likely to take a long time, the officer in charge of the search may consider using the seize and sift powers referred to in section 7.

B:6.3A A warrant under PACE, s.8 may authorise entry to and search of premises on more than one occasion if, on the application, the justice of the peace is satisfied that it is necessary to authorise multiple entries in order to achieve the purpose for which the warrant is issued. No premises may be entered or searched on any subsequent occasions without the prior written authority of an officer of the rank of inspector who is not involved in the investigation. All other warrants authorise entry on one occasion only.

B:6.3B Where a warrant under PACE, s.8, or Sched. 1, para. 12 authorises entry to and search of all premises occupied or controlled by a specified person, no premises which are not specified in the warrant may be entered and searched without the prior written authority of an officer of the rank of inspector who is not involved in the investigation.

(b) *Entry other than with consent*

B:6.4 The officer in charge of the search shall first try to communicate with the occupier, or any other person entitled to grant access to the premises, explain the authority under which entry is sought and ask the occupier to allow entry, unless:

   (i) the search premises are unoccupied;

   (ii) the occupier and any other person entitled to grant access are absent;

   (iii) there are reasonable grounds for believing that alerting the occupier or any other person entitled to grant access would frustrate the object of the search or endanger officers or other people.

B:6.5 Unless sub-paragraph 6.4(iii) applies, if the premises are occupied the officer, subject to paragraph 2.9, shall, before the search begins:

   (i) identify him or herself, show their warrant card (if not in uniform) and state the purpose of, and grounds for, the search; and

   (ii) identify and introduce any person accompanying the officer on the search (such persons should carry identification for production on request) and briefly describe that person's role in the process.

B:6.6 Reasonable and proportionate force may be used if necessary to enter premises if the officer in charge of the search is satisfied the premises are those specified in any warrant, or in exercise of the powers described in paragraph 4.1 to 4.3, and if:

   (i) the occupier or any other person entitled to grant access has refused entry;

   (ii) it is impossible to communicate with the occupier or any other person entitled to grant access; or

   (iii) any of the provisions of paragraph 6.4 apply.

(c) *Notice of powers and rights*

B:6.7 If an officer conducts a search to which this code applies the officer shall, unless it is impracticable to do so, provide the occupier with a copy of a notice in a standard format: **A-29**

   (i) specifying if the search is made under warrant, with consent, or in the exercise of the powers described in paragraphs 4.1 to 4.3. Note: the notice format shall provide for authority or consent to be indicated (see paragraphs 4.3 and 5.1);

   (ii) summarising the extent of the powers of search and seizure conferred by PACE and other relevant legislation as appropriate;

   (iii) explaining the rights of the occupier and the owner of the property seized;

   (iv) explaining compensation may be payable in appropriate cases for damages [*sic*] caused entering and searching premises, and giving the address to send a compensation application [see *Note 6A*]; and

   (v) stating this code is available at any police station.

B:6.8 If the occupier is:

   • present, copies of the notice and warrant shall, if practicable, be given to them before the search begins, unless the officer in charge of the search reasonably believes this would frustrate the object of the search or endanger officers or other people;

- not present, copies of the notice and warrant shall be left in a prominent place on the premises or appropriate part of the premises and endorsed, subject to paragraph 2.9 with the name of the officer in charge of the search, the date and time of the search. The warrant shall be endorsed to show this has been done.

(d) *Conduct of searches*

B:6.9 Premises may be searched only to the extent necessary to achieve the purpose of the search, having regard to the size and nature of whatever is sought.

B:6.9A A search may not continue under:

- a warrant's authority once all the things specified in that warrant have been found;
- any other power once the object of that search has been achieved.

B:6.9B No search may continue once the officer in charge of the search is satisfied whatever is being sought is not on the premises [see *Note 6B*]. This does not prevent a further search of the same premises if additional grounds come to light supporting a further application for a search warrant or exercise or further exercise of another power. For example, when, as a result of new information, it is believed articles previously not found or additional articles are on the premises.

B:6.10 Searches must be conducted with due consideration for the property and privacy of the occupier and with no more disturbance than necessary. Reasonable force may be used only when necessary and proportionate because the co-operation of the occupier cannot be obtained or is insufficient for the purpose. [See *Note 6C*.]

B:6.11 A friend, neighbour or other person must be allowed to witness the search if the occupier wishes unless the officer in charge of the search has reasonable grounds for believing the presence of the person asked for would seriously hinder the investigation or endanger officers or other people. A search need not be unreasonably delayed for this purpose. A record of the action taken should be made on the premises search record including the grounds for refusing the occupier's request.

B:6.12 A person is not required to be cautioned prior to being asked questions that are solely necessary for the purpose of furthering the proper and effective conduct of a search, see Code C, paragraph 10.1(c). For example, questions to discover the occupier of specified premises, to find a key to open a locked drawer or cupboard or to otherwise seek co-operation during the search or to determine if a particular item is liable to be seized.

B:6.12A If questioning goes beyond what is necessary for the purpose of the exemption in Code C, the exchange is likely to constitute an interview as defined by Code C, paragraph 11.1A and would require the associated safeguards included in Code C, section 10.

(e) *Leaving premises*

A-30

B:6.13 If premises have been entered by force, before leaving the officer in charge of the search must make sure they are secure by:

- arranging for the occupier or their agent to be present;
- any other appropriate means.

(f) *Searches under PACE, Schedule 1 or the Terrorism Act 2000, Schedule 5*

B:6.14 An officer shall be appointed as the officer in charge of the search (see paragraph 2.10), in respect of any search made under a warrant issued under PACE Act 1984, Sched. 1 or the Terrorism Act 2000, Sched. 5. They are responsible for making sure the search is conducted with discretion and in a manner that causes the least possible disruption to any business or other activities carried out on the premises.

B:6.15 Once the officer in charge of the search is satisfied material may not be taken from the premises without their knowledge, they shall ask for the documents or other records concerned. The officer in charge of the search may also ask to see the index to files held on the premises, and the officers conducting the search may inspect any files which, according to the index, appear to contain the material sought. A more extensive search of the premises may be made only if:

- the person responsible for them refuses to:
  - produce the material sought, or
  - allow access to the index;
- it appears the index is:
  - inaccurate, or
  - incomplete;

- for any other reason the officer in charge of the search has reasonable grounds for believing such a search is necessary in order to find the material sought.

Notes for guidance

B:6A *Whether compensation is appropriate depends on the circumstances in each case. Compensation for damage caused when effecting entry is unlikely to be appropriate if the search was lawful, and the force used can be shown to be reasonable, proportionate and necessary to effect entry. If the wrong premises are searched by mistake everything possible should be done at the earliest opportunity to allay any sense of grievance and there should normally be a strong presumption in favour of paying compensation.*   **A-31**

B:6B *It is important that, when possible, all those involved in a search are fully briefed about any powers to be exercised and the extent and limits within which it should be conducted.*

B:6C *In all cases the number of officers and other persons involved in executing the warrant should be determined by what is reasonable and necessary according to the particular circumstances.*

B:7 Seizure and retention of property

(a) *Seizure*

B:7.1 Subject to paragraph 7.2, an officer who is searching any person or premises under any   **A-32**
statutory power or with the consent of the occupier may seize anything:
  (a) covered by a warrant;
  (b) the officer has reasonable grounds for believing is evidence of an offence or has been obtained in consequence of the commission of an offence but only if seizure is necessary to prevent the items being concealed, lost, disposed of, altered, damaged, destroyed or tampered with;
  (c) covered by the powers in the Criminal Justice and Police Act 2001, Pt 2 allowing an officer to seize property from persons or premises and retain it for sifting or examination elsewhere.
See *Note 7B.*

B:7.2 No item may be seized which an officer has reasonable grounds for believing to be subject to legal privilege, as defined in PACE, s.10, other than under the Criminal Justice and Police Act 2001, Pt 2.

B:7.3 Officers must be aware of the provisions in the Criminal Justice and Police Act 2001, s.59, allowing for applications to a judicial authority for the return of property seized and the subsequent duty to secure in section 60 (see paragraph 7.12(iii)).

B:7.4 An officer may decide it is not appropriate to seize property because of an explanation from the person holding it but may nevertheless have reasonable grounds for believing it was obtained in consequence of an offence by some person. In these circumstances, the officer should identify the property to the holder, inform the holder of their suspicions and explain the holder may be liable to civil or criminal proceedings if they dispose of, alter or destroy the property.

B:7.5 An officer may arrange to photograph, image or copy, any document or other article they have the power to seize in accordance with paragraph 7.1. This is subject to specific restrictions on the examination, imaging or copying of certain property seized under the Criminal Justice and Police Act 2001, Pt 2. An officer must have regard to their statutory obligation to retain an original document or other article only when a photograph or copy is not sufficient.

B:7.6 If an officer considers information stored in any electronic form and accessible from the premises could be used in evidence, they may require the information to be produced in a form:
  - which can be taken away and in which it is visible and legible; or
  - from which it can readily be produced in a visible and legible form.

(b) *Criminal Justice and Police Act 2001: specific procedures for seize and sift powers*

B:7.7 The Criminal Justice and Police Act 2001, Pt 2 gives officers limited powers to seize property   **A-33**
from premises or persons so they can sift or examine it elsewhere. Officers must be careful they only exercise these powers when it is essential and they do not remove any more material than necessary. The removal of large volumes of material, much of which may not ultimately be retainable, may have serious implications for the owners, particularly when they are involved in business or activities such as journalism or the provision of medical services. Officers must carefully consider if removing copies or images of relevant material or data would be a satisfactory alternative to removing originals. When originals are taken, officers must be prepared to facilitate the provision of copies or images for the owners when reasonably practicable. [See *Note 7C.*]

B:7.8 Property seized under the Criminal Justice and Police Act 2001, s.50 or 51 must be kept securely and separately from any material seized under other powers. An examination under section

53 to determine which elements may be retained must be carried out at the earliest practicable time, having due regard to the desirability of allowing the person from whom the property was seized, or a person with an interest in the property, an opportunity of being present or represented at the examination.

B:7.8A All reasonable steps should be taken to accommodate an interested person's request to be present, provided the request is reasonable and subject to the need to prevent harm to, interference with, or unreasonable delay to the investigatory process. If an examination proceeds in the absence of an interested person who asked to attend or their representative, the officer who exercised the relevant seizure power must give that person a written notice of why the examination was carried out in those circumstances. If it is necessary for security reasons or to maintain confidentiality officers may exclude interested persons from decryption or other processes which facilitate the examination but do not form part of it. [See *Note 7D.*]

B:7.9 It is the responsibility of the officer in charge of the investigation to make sure property is returned in accordance with sections 53 to 55. Material which there is no power to retain must be:

- separated from the rest of the seized property; and
- returned as soon as reasonably practicable after examination of all the seized property.

B:7.9A Delay is only warranted if very clear and compelling reasons exist, for example:

- the unavailability of the person to whom the material is to be returned; or
- the need to agree a convenient time to return a large volume of material.

B:7.9B Legally privileged, excluded or special procedure material which cannot be retained must be returned:

- as soon as reasonably practicable; and
- without waiting for the whole examination.

B:7.9C As set out in section 58, material must be returned to the person from whom it was seized, except when it is clear some other person has a better right to it. [See *Note 7E.*]

B:7.10 When an officer involved in the investigation has reasonable grounds to believe a person with a relevant interest in property seized under section 50 or 51 intends to make an application under section 59 for the return of any legally privileged, special procedure or excluded material, the officer in charge of the investigation should be informed as soon as practicable and the material seized should be kept secure in accordance with section 61. [See *Note 7C.*]

B:7.11 The officer in charge of the investigation is responsible for making sure property is properly secured. Securing involves making sure the property is not examined, copied, imaged or put to any other use except at the request, or with the consent, of the applicant or in accordance with the directions of the appropriate judicial authority. Any request, consent or directions must be recorded in writing and signed by both the initiator and the officer in charge of the investigation. [See *Notes 7F* and *7G.*]

B:7.12 When an officer exercises a power of seizure conferred by sections 50 or 51 they shall provide the occupier of the premises or the person from whom the property is being seized with a written notice:

- (i) specifying what has been seized under the powers conferred by that section;
- (ii) specifying the grounds for those powers;
- (iii) setting out the effect of sections 59 to 61 covering the grounds for a person with a relevant interest in seized property to apply to a judicial authority for its return and the duty of officers to secure property in certain circumstances when an application is made; and
- (iv) specifying the name and address of the person to whom:
  - notice of an application to the appropriate judicial authority in respect of any of the seized property must be given;
  - an application may be made to allow attendance at the initial examination of the property.

B:7.13 If the occupier is not present but there is someone in charge of the premises, the notice shall be given to them. If no suitable person is available, so the notice will easily be found it should either be:

- left in a prominent place on the premises; or
- attached to the exterior of the premises.

(c) *Retention*

B:7.14 Subject to paragraph 7.15, anything seized in accordance with the above provisions may be   **A-34**
retained only for as long as is necessary. It may be retained, among other purposes:

    (i) for use as evidence at a trial for an offence;

    (ii) to facilitate the use in any investigation or proceedings of anything to which it is
inextricably linked [see *Note 7H*];

    (iii) for forensic examination or other investigation in connection with an offence;

    (iv) in order to establish its lawful owner when there are reasonable grounds for believing it
has been stolen or obtained by the commission of an offence.

B:7.15 Property shall not be retained under paragraph 7.14(i), (ii) or (iii) if a copy or image would
be sufficient.

(d) *Rights of owners etc*

B:7.16 If property is retained, the person who had custody or control of it immediately before
seizure must, on request, be provided with a list or description of the property within a reasonable
time.

B:7.17 That person or their representative must be allowed supervised access to the property to
examine it or have it photographed or copied, or must be provided with a photograph or copy, in
either case within a reasonable time of any request and at their own expense, unless the officer in
charge of an investigation has reasonable grounds for believing this would:

    (i) prejudice the investigation of any offence or criminal proceedings; or

    (ii) lead to the commission of an offence by providing access to unlawful material such as
pornography.

A record of the grounds shall be made when access is denied.

Notes for guidance

B:7A *Any person claiming property seized by the police may apply to a magistrates' court under the Police*   **A-35**
(Property) Act 1897 for its possession and should, if appropriate, be advised of this procedure.

B:7B *The powers of seizure conferred by PACE, ss.18(2) and 19(3) extend to the seizure of the whole premises
when it is physically possible to seize and retain the premises in their totality and practical considerations make
seizure desirable. For example, police may remove premises such as tents, vehicles or caravans to a police station
for the purpose of preserving evidence.*

B:7C *Officers should consider reaching agreement with owners and/or other interested parties on the procedures
for examining a specific set of property, rather than awaiting the judicial authority's determination. Agreement
can sometimes give a quicker and more satisfactory route for all concerned and minimise costs and legal
complexities.*

B:7D *What constitutes a relevant interest in specific material may depend on the nature of that material and
the circumstances in which it is seized. Anyone with a reasonable claim to ownership of the material and anyone
entrusted with its safe keeping by the owner should be considered.*

B:7E *Requirements to secure and return property apply equally to all copies, images or other material created
because of seizure of the original property.*

B:7F *The mechanics of securing property vary according to the circumstances; "bagging up", i.e. placing
material in sealed bags or containers and strict subsequent control of access is the appropriate procedure in many
cases.*

B:7G *When material is seized under the powers of seizure conferred by PACE, the duty to retain it under the
code of practice issued under the Criminal Procedure and Investigations Act 1996 is subject to the provisions on
retention of seized material in PACE, s.22.*

B:7H *Paragraph 7.14(ii) applies if inextricably linked material is seized under the Criminal Justice and
Police Act 2001, s.50 or 51. Inextricably linked material is material it is not reasonably practicable to separate
from other linked material without prejudicing the use of that other material in any investigation or proceedings.
For example, it may not be possible to separate items of data held on computer disk without damaging their
evidential integrity. Inextricably linked material must not be examined, imaged, copied or used for any purpose
other than for proving the source and/or integrity of the linked material.*

B:8 Action after searches

B:8.1 If premises are searched in circumstances where this code applies, unless the exceptions in   **A-36**
paragraph 2.3(a) apply, on arrival at a police station the officer in charge of the search shall make or
have made a record of the search, to include:

    (i) the address of the searched premises;

    (ii) the date, time and duration of the search;

(iii) the authority used for the search:
  * if the search was made in exercise of a statutory power to search premises without warrant, the power which was used for the search:
  * if the search was made under a warrant or with written consent;
    – a copy of the warrant and the written authority to apply for it, see paragraph 3.4; or
    – the written consent;

  shall be appended to the record or the record shall show the location of the copy warrant or consent;

(iv) subject to paragraph 2.9, the names of:
  * the officer(s) in charge of the search;
  * all other officers and any authorised persons who conducted the search;

(v) the names of any people on the premises if they are known;

(vi) any grounds for refusing the occupier's request to have someone present during the search, see paragraph 6.11;

(vii) a list of any articles seized or the location of a list and, if not covered by a warrant, the grounds for their seizure;

(viii) whether force was used, and the reason;

(ix) details of any damage caused during the search, and the circumstances;

(x) if applicable, the reason it was not practicable:
  (a) to give the occupier a copy of the notice of powers and rights, see paragraph 6.7;
  (b) before the search to give the occupier a copy of the notice, see paragraph 6.8;

(xi) when the occupier was not present, the place where copies of the notice of powers and rights and search warrant were left on the premises, see paragraph 6.8.

B:8.2 On each occasion when premises are searched under warrant, the warrant authorising the search on that occasion shall be endorsed to show:

  (i) if any articles specified in the warrant were found and the address where found;
  (ii) if any other articles were seized;
  (iii) the date and time it was executed and if present, the name of the occupier or if the occupier is not present the name of the person in charge of the premises;
  (iv) subject to paragraph 2.9, the names of the officers who executed it and any authorised persons who accompanied them; and
  (v) if a copy, together with a copy of the notice of powers and rights was:
    * handed to the occupier; or
    * endorsed as required by paragraph 6.8; and left on the premises and where.

B:8.3 Any warrant shall be returned within three calendar months of its issue or sooner on completion of the search(es) authorised by that warrant, if it was issued by a:

  * justice of the peace, to the designated officer for the local justice area in which the justice was acting when issuing the warrant; or
  * judge, to the appropriate officer of the court concerned.

B:9 Search registers

A-37

B:9.1 A search register will be maintained at each sub-divisional or equivalent police station. All search records required under paragraph 8.1 shall be made, copied, or referred to in the register. [See *Note 9A.*]

Note for guidance

B:9A *Paragraph 9.1 also applies to search records made by immigration officers. In these cases, a search register must also be maintained at an immigration office.* [See also Note 2D.]

B:10 Searches under Schedule 5 to the Terrorism Prevention and Investigation Measures Act 2011

A-37a

B:10.1 This code applies to the powers of constables under Schedule 5 to the Terrorism Prevention and Investigation Measures Act 2011 relating to TPIM notices to enter and search premises subject to the modifications in the following paragraphs.

B:10.2 In paragraph 2.3(d), the reference to the investigation into an alleged or suspected offence include [*sic*] the enforcement of terrorism prevention and investigation measures which may be imposed on an individual by a TPIM notice in accordance with the Terrorism Prevention and Investigation Measures Act 2011.

B:10.3 References to the purpose and object of the entry and search of premises, the nature of articles sought and what may be seized and retained include (as appropriate):

    (a) in relation to the power to search without a search warrant in paragraph 5 (for purposes of serving TPIM notice), finding the individual on whom the notice is to be served;

    (b) in relation to the power to search without a search warrant in paragraph 6 (at time of serving TPIM notice), ascertaining whether there is anything in the premises, that contravenes measures specified in the notice [see *Note 10A*];

    (c) in relation to the power to search without a search warrant under paragraph 7 (suspected absconding), ascertaining whether a person has absconded or if there is anything on the premises which will assist in the pursuit or arrest of an individual in respect of whom a TPIM notice is force who is reasonably suspected of having absconded;

    (d) in relation to the power to search under a search warrant issued under paragraph 8 (for compliance purposes), determining whether an individual in respect of whom a notice is in force is complying with measures specified in the notice [see *Note 10A*].

Note for guidance

    B:10A *Searches of individuals under Schedule 5, paras 6(2)(a) (at time of serving TPIM notice) and 8(2)(a) (for compliance purposes) must be conducted and recorded in accordance with Code A. See Code A, para. 2.18A for details.*

(4) Detention, treatment and questioning of persons

The text that follows is of the version of the code that came into force on June 2, 2014: see **A-38** *ante*, A-1.

For authorities in relation to Code C, see, in particular, §§ 15-167 *et seq.* (right of access to solicitor), § 15-204 (general), § 15-311 (confessions), § 15-372 (sufficient evidence for prosecution to succeed), §§ 15-401 *et seq.* (discretionary exclusion of evidence) in the main work.

C. CODE OF PRACTICE FOR THE DETENTION, TREATMENT AND QUESTIONING OF PERSONS BY POLICE OFFICERS

Commencement—transitional arrangements

This code applies to people in police detention after 00.00 on 2 June 2014, notwithstanding that **A-39** their period of detention may have commenced before that time.

C:1 General

C:1.0 The powers and procedures in this code must be used fairly, responsibly, with respect for **A-40** the people to whom they apply and without unlawful discrimination. Under the Equality Act 2010, s.149, when police officers are carrying out their functions, they also have a duty to have due regard to the need to eliminate unlawful discrimination, harassment and victimisation, to advance equality of opportunity between people who share a relevant protected characteristic and people who do not share it, and to take steps to foster good relations between those persons. See *Notes 1A* and *1AA*.

C:1.1 All persons in custody must be dealt with expeditiously, and released as soon as the need for detention no longer applies.

C:1.1A A custody officer must perform the functions in this code as soon as practicable. A custody officer will not be in breach of this code if delay is justifiable and reasonable steps are taken to prevent unnecessary delay. The custody record shall show when a delay has occurred and the reason. See *Note 1H*.

C:1.2 This code of practice must be readily available at all police stations for consultation by:

- police officers;
- police staff;
- detained persons;
- members of the public.

C:1.3 The provisions of this code:

- include the *Annexes*;
- do not include the *Notes for Guidance*.

C:1.4 If an officer has any suspicion, or is told in good faith, that a person of any age may be mentally disordered or otherwise mentally vulnerable, in the absence of clear evidence to dispel that suspicion, the person shall be treated as such for the purposes of this code. See *Note 1G*.

C:1.5 If anyone appears to be under 17, they shall in the absence of clear evidence that they are older, be treated as a juvenile for the purposes of this code and any other code.

C:1.5A If anyone appears to have attained the age of 17 and to be under the age of 18, they shall in the absence of clear evidence that they are older, be treated as a 17-year-old for the purposes of this and any other code. The provisions and *Notes for Guidance* which in accordance with paragraph 1.5 apply to a juvenile and the way they are to be treated shall also apply to them, except as described in sub-paragraphs (a) and (b) below:

(a) the statutory provisions in section 38 of PACE (detention after charge) which apply only to an arrested juvenile as defined in section 37(15) of PACE and to which paragraphs 16.7 and 16.10 and *Note 16D* of this code relate, shall not apply to a person who appears to have attained the age of 17 for the purposes of:

(i) the grounds to keep them in police detention after charge; and

(ii) the requirement to transfer a person who has been kept in police detention after charge to local authority accommodation and the power of the local authority to detain them pending appearance at court;

(b) the statutory provisions in section 65(1) of PACE (appropriate consent) which require appropriate consent for a person who has not attained the age of 17 to be given by them and their parent or guardian shall not apply to a person who appears to have attained the age of 17 and whose consent alone shall be sufficient. In this code, section 65(1) applies to Annex A, paras 2(b) and 2B (intimate searches), and Annex K, paras 1(b) and 3 (X-Ray and ultrasound scan), and in Code D (identification), to para. 2.12 and *Note 2A* with regards to taking fingerprints, samples, footwear impressions, photographs and evidential searches and examinations.

See *Notes 1L* and *1M.*

C:1.6 If a person appears to be blind, seriously visually impaired, deaf, unable to read or speak or has difficulty orally because of a speech impediment, they shall be treated as such for the purposes of this code in the absence of clear evidence to the contrary.

C:1.7 The "appropriate adult" means, in the case of a:

(a) juvenile:

(i) the parent, guardian or, if the juvenile is in the care of a local authority or voluntary organisation, a person representing that authority or organisation (see *Note 1B*);

(ii) a social worker of a local authority (see *Note 1C*);

(iii) failing these, some other responsible adult aged 18 or over who is not a police officer or employed by the police;

note: paragraph 1.5A extends sub-paragraph (a) to the person called to fulfil the role of the appropriate adult for a 17-year-old detainee [*sic*];

(b) person who is mentally disordered or mentally vulnerable (see *Note 1D*);

(i) a relative, guardian or other person responsible for their care or custody;

(ii) someone experienced in dealing with mentally disordered or mentally vulnerable people but who is not a police officer or employed by the police;

(iii) failing these, some other responsible adult aged 18 or over who is not a police officer or employed by the police.

C:1.8 If this code requires a person be given certain information, they do not have to be given it if at the time they are incapable of understanding what is said, are violent or may become violent or in urgent need of medical attention, but they must be given it as soon as practicable.

C:1.9 References to a custody officer include any police officer who for the time being, is performing the functions of a custody officer.

C:1.9A When this code requires the prior authority or agreement of an officer of at least inspector or superintendent rank, that authority may be given by a sergeant or chief inspector authorised to perform the functions of the higher rank under the Police and Criminal Evidence Act 1984 (PACE), s.107.

C:1.10 Subject to paragraph 1.12, this code applies to people in custody at police stations in England and Wales, whether or not they have been arrested, and to those removed to a police station as a place of safety under the Mental Health Act 1983, ss.135 and 136, as a last resort (see paragraph 3.16). Section 15 applies solely to people in police detention, *e.g.* those brought to a police station under arrest or arrested at a police station for an offence after going there voluntarily.

C:1.11 No part of this code applies to a detained person:

(a) to whom PACE Code H applies because:

• they are detained following arrest under section 41 of the Terrorism Act 2000 (TACT) and not charged; or

• an authorisation has been given under section 22 of the Counter-Terrorism Act 2008 (CTACT) (post-charge questioning of terrorist suspects) to interview them;

(b) to whom the code of practice issued under paragraph 6 of Schedule 14 to TACT applies because they are detained for examination under Schedule 7 to TACT.

C:1.12 This code does not apply to people in custody:

(i) arrested by officers under the Criminal Justice and Public Order Act 1994, s.136(2), on warrants issued in Scotland, or arrested or detained without warrant under section 137(2) by officers from a police force in Scotland; in these cases, police powers and duties and the person's rights and entitlements whilst at a police station in England or Wales are the same as those in Scotland;

(ii) arrested under the Immigration and Asylum Act 1999, s.142(3), in order to have their fingerprints taken;

(iii) whose detention is authorised under Schedules 2 or 3 to the Immigration Act 1971 or section 62 of the Nationality, Immigration and Asylum Act 2002;

(iv) who are convicted or remanded prisoners held in police cells on behalf of the Prison Service under the Imprisonment (Temporary Provisions) Act 1980;

(v) [*not used*];

(vi) detained for searches under stop and search powers except as required by Code A.

The provisions on conditions of detention and treatment in sections 8 and 9 must be considered as the minimum standards of treatment for such detainees.

C:1.13 In this code:

(a) "designated person" means a person other than a police officer, designated under the Police Reform Act 2002, Pt 4, who has specified powers and duties of police officers conferred or imposed on them;

(b) reference to a police officer includes a designated person acting in the exercise or performance of the powers and duties conferred or imposed on them by their designation;

(c) where a search or other procedure to which this code applies may only be carried out or observed by a person of the same sex as the detainee, the gender of the detainee and other parties present should be established and recorded in line with Annex L of this code.

C:1.14 Designated persons are entitled to use reasonable force as follows:— **A-42**

(a) when exercising a power conferred on them which allows a police officer exercising that power to use reasonable force, a designated person has the same entitlement to use force; and

(b) at other times when carrying out duties conferred or imposed on them that also entitle them to use reasonable force, for example:

• when at a police station carrying out the duty to keep detainees for whom they are responsible under control and to assist any police officer or designated person to keep any detainee under control and to prevent their escape;

• when securing, or assisting any police officer or designated person in securing, the detention of a person at a police station;

• when escorting, or assisting any police officer or designated person in escorting, a detainee within a police station;

• for the purpose of saving life or limb; or

• preventing serious damage to property.

C:1.15 Nothing in this code prevents the custody officer, or other officer given custody of the detainee, from allowing police staff who are not designated persons to carry out individual procedures or tasks at the police station if the law allows. However, the officer remains responsible for making sure the procedures and tasks are carried out correctly in accordance with the codes of practice (see *Note 3F*). Any such person must be:

(a) a person employed by a police force and under the direction and control of the chief officer of that force; or

(b) employed by a person with whom a police force has a contract for the provision of services relating to persons arrested or otherwise in custody.

C:1.16 Designated persons and other police staff must have regard to any relevant provisions of the codes of practice.

C:1.17 References to pocket books include any official report book issued to police officers or other police staff.

Notes for guidance

A-43

C:1A *Although certain sections of this code apply specifically to people in custody at police stations, those there voluntarily to assist with an investigation should be treated with no less consideration, e.g. offered refreshments at appropriate times, and enjoy an absolute right to obtain legal advice or communicate with anyone outside the police station.*

C:1AA *In paragraph 1.0, "relevant protected characteristic" includes: age, disability, gender reassignment, pregnancy and maternity, race, religion/belief, sex and sexual orientation.*

C:1B *A person, including a parent or guardian, should not be an appropriate adult if they:*

- *are*
  - *suspected of involvement in the offence;*
  - *the victim;*
  - *a witness;*
  - *involved in the investigation;*
- *received admissions prior to attending to act as the appropriate adult.*

Note: if a juvenile's parent is estranged from the juvenile, they should not be asked to act as the appropriate adult if the juvenile expressly and specifically objects to their presence.

Note: Paragraph 1.5A applies this note to 17-year-old detainees.

C:1C *If a juvenile admits an offence to, or in the presence of, a social worker or member of a youth offending team other than during the time that person is acting as the juvenile's appropriate adult, another appropriate adult should be appointed in the interest of fairness.*

Note: Paragraph 1.5A applies this note to 17-year-old detainees.

C:1D *In the case of people who are mentally disordered or otherwise mentally vulnerable, it may be more satisfactory if the appropriate adult is someone experienced or trained in their care rather than a relative lacking such qualifications. But if the detainee prefers a relative to a better qualified stranger or objects to a particular person their wishes should, if practicable, be respected.*

C:1E *A detainee should always be given an opportunity, when an appropriate adult is called to the police station, to consult privately with a solicitor in the appropriate adult's absence if they want. An appropriate adult is not subject to legal privilege.*

C:1F *A solicitor or independent custody visitor present at the police station in that capacity may not be the appropriate adult.*

C:1G *"Mentally vulnerable" applies to any detainee who, because of their mental state or capacity, may not understand the significance of what is said, of questions or of their replies. "Mental disorder" is defined in the Mental Health Act 1983, s.1(2), as "any disorder or disability of mind". When the custody officer has any doubt about the mental state or capacity of a detainee, that detainee should be treated as mentally vulnerable and an appropriate adult called.*

C:1H *Paragraph 1.1A is intended to cover delays which may occur in processing detainees, e.g. if:*

- *a large number of suspects are brought into the station simultaneously to be placed in custody;*
- *interview rooms are all being used;*
- *there are difficulties contacting an appropriate adult, solicitor or interpreter.*

C:1I *The custody officer must remind the appropriate adult and detainee about the right to legal advice and record any reasons for waiving it in accordance with section 6.*

C:1J *[Not used.]*

C:1K *This code does not affect the principle that all citizens have a duty to help police officers to prevent crime and discover offenders. This is a civic rather than a legal duty; but when police officers are trying to discover whether, or by whom, offences have been committed they are entitled to question any person from whom they think useful information can be obtained, subject to the restrictions imposed by this code. A person's declaration that they are unwilling to reply does not alter this entitlement.*

C:1L *Paragraph 1.5A does not amend section 37(15) of PACE which defines the term "arrested juvenile" for the purposes of sections 34 to 51 of PACE, or provisions in any other enactment which expressly refer and apply to persons under the age of 17. Until amended by Parliament, these statutory provisions alone do not extend to persons who have attained the age of 17.*

C:1M *The purpose of paragraph 1.5A is to extend the safeguards for juveniles to 17-year-olds unless this is precluded by any statutory provisions. Sub-paragraphs 1.5A(a) and (b) identify the provisions of sections 38 and 65 of PACE concerning detention after charge and appropriate consent which for this reason do not extend to 17-year-olds. All other safeguards in this and other codes are extended and the requirements which are indicated in the relevant provisions and Notes for Guidance are as follows:*

(a) *under paragraph 3.13 of this code, to identify and inform someone responsible for the welfare of a 17-year-old which is in addition to their right in section 5 of this code not to be held incommunicado;*

(b) *under paragraph 3.14 of this code to notify a person who has statutory responsibility under a court order to supervise or monitor a 17-year-old;*

(c) *under paragraph 8.8 with regard to cell accommodation and keeping 17-year-old detainees separate from adults;*

(d) *to call a person described by paragraph 1.7(a) or Note 17G in relation to testing for the presence of Class A drugs, to fulfil the role of the appropriate adult for the purposes of this or any other code to support and assist a 17-year-old:*

　(i) *by being present when:*

- *they are informed of their rights and entitlements and the grounds for their detention (see paras 3.17 and 3.18);*
- *they are cautioned or given a special warning (see paras 10.12 and 10.11A);*
- *they are being interviewed in accordance with this code (see sections 11 and 12) or Codes E or F unless paragraph 11.15 of this code allows the interview to go ahead without the adult being present;*
- *their detention is being reviewed or an extension is being considered (see paras 15.3(c) and 15.3C(a)):*
- *they are charged and related action is taken (see paras 16.1, 16.3, 16.4A and 16.6);*
- *samples to test for Class A drugs are requested from a person who has not attained the age of 18 (see para. 17.7);*
- *an intimate search is carried out (see Annex A, paras 2A, 2B and 5);*
- *a strip search is carried out (see Annex A, para. 11(c));*
- *an x-ray or ultrasound scan is carried out (see Annex K, paras 2 and 3);*
- *procedures in Code D involving witness identification, taking fingerprints, samples, footwear impressions and photographs and when evidential searches and examinations are carried out (see paras 2.14 and 2.15).*

　(ii) *by allowing:*

- *the adult to inspect their custody record and to have a copy of their record (see paras 2.4, 2.4A and 2.5);*
- *a 17-year-old to consult the adult in private (see para. 3.18);*
- *the adult to request legal advice on their behalf to advise and assist them (see paras 3.19, 6.5A and 11.17).*

C:2 Custody records

C:2.1A When a person:

- is brought to a police station under arrest
- is arrested at the police station having attended there voluntarily or
- attends a police station to answer bail

they must be brought before the custody officer as soon as practicable after their arrival at the station or if applicable, following their arrest after attending the police station voluntarily. This applies to both designated and non-designated police stations. A person is deemed to be "at a police station" for these purposes if they are within the boundary of any building or enclosed yard which forms part of that police station.

C:2.1 A separate custody record must be opened as soon as practicable for each person brought to a police station under arrest or arrested at the station having gone there voluntarily or attending a police station in answer to street bail. All information recorded under this code must be recorded as soon as practicable in the custody record unless otherwise specified. Any audio or video recording made in the custody area is not part of the custody record.

C:2.2 If any action requires the authority of an officer of a specified rank, subject to paragraph 2.6A, their name and rank must be noted in the custody record.

C:2.3 The custody officer is responsible for the custody record's accuracy and completeness and for making sure the record or copy of the record accompanies a detainee if they are transferred to another police station. The record shall show the:

- time and reason for transfer;
- time a person is released from detention.

C:2.3A If a person is arrested and taken to a police station as a result of a search in the exercise of any stop and search power to which PACE Code A (stop and search) or the "search powers code" issued under TACT applies, the officer carrying out the search is responsible for ensuring that the record of that stop and search, is made as part of the person's custody record. The custody officer must then ensure that the person is asked if they want a copy of the search record and if they do, that they are given a copy as soon as practicable. The person's entitlement to a copy of the search record which is made as part of their custody record is in addition to, and does not affect, their entitlement to a copy of their custody record or any other provisions of section 2 (custody records) of this code. (See Code A, para. 4.2B, and the TACT search powers code, para. 5.3.5.)

A-44

C:2.4 The detainee's solicitor and appropriate adult must be permitted to inspect the whole of the detainee's custody record as soon as practicable after their arrival at the station and at any other time on request, whilst the person is detained. This includes the following specific records relating to the reasons for the detainee's arrest and detention and the offence concerned, to which paragraph 3.1(b) refers:

> (a) the information about the circumstances and reasons for the detainee's arrest as recorded in the custody record in accordance with paragraph 4.3 of Code G; this applies to any further offences for which the detainee is arrested whilst in custody;
> (b) the record of the grounds for each authorisation to keep the person in custody; the authorisations to which this applies are the same as those described at items (i)(a) to (d) in the table in paragraph 2 of Annex M [*sic*] of this code.

Access to the records in sub-paragraphs (a) and (b) is in addition to the requirements in paragraphs 3.4(b), 11.1A, 15.0, 15.7A(c) and 16.7A to make certain documents and materials available and to provide information about the offence and the reasons for arrest and detention.

Access to the custody record for the purposes of this paragraph must be arranged and agreed with the custody officer and may not unreasonably interfere with the custody officer's duties. A record shall be made when access is allowed and whether it includes the records described in sub-paragraphs (a) and (b) above.

Note: paragraph 1.5A extends this paragraph to the person called to fulfil the role of the appropriate adult for a 17-year-old detainee.

C:2.4A When a detainee leaves police detention or is taken before a court they, their legal representative or appropriate adult shall be given, on request, a copy of the custody record as soon as practicable. This entitlement lasts for 12 months after release.

Note: paragraph 1.5A extends this paragraph to the person called to fulfil the role of the appropriate adult for a 17-year-old detainee.

C:2.5 The detainee, appropriate adult or legal representative shall be permitted to inspect the original custody record after the detainee has left police detention provided they give reasonable notice of their request. Any such inspection shall be noted in the custody record.

Note: paragraph 1.5A extends this paragraph to the person called to fulfil the role of the appropriate adult for a 17-year-old detainee.

C:2.6 Subject to paragraph 2.6A, all entries in custody records must be timed and signed by the maker. Records entered on computer shall be timed and contain the operator's identification.

C:2.6A Nothing in this code requires the identity of officers or other police staff to be recorded or disclosed:

> (a) [*not used*];
> (b) if the officer or police staff reasonably believe recording or disclosing their name might put them in danger.

In these cases, they shall use their warrant or other identification numbers and the name of their police station. See *Note 2A*.

C:2.7 The fact and time of any detainee's refusal to sign a custody record, when asked in accordance with this code, must be recorded.

Note for guidance

A-45   C:2A *The purpose of paragraph 2.6A(b) is to protect those involved in serious organised crime investigations or arrests of particularly violent suspects when there is reliable information that those arrested or their associates may threaten or cause harm to those involved. In cases of doubt, an officer of inspector rank or above should be consulted.*

C:3 Initial action

(a) Detained persons—normal procedure

A-46   C:3.1 When a person is brought to a police station under arrest or arrested at the station having gone there voluntarily, the custody officer must make sure the person is told clearly about:

> (a) the following continuing rights, which may be exercised at any stage during the period in custody:
>> (i) their right to consult privately with a solicitor and that free independent legal advice is available as in section 6;
>> (ii) their right to have someone informed of their arrest as in section 5;
>> (iii) their right to consult the codes of practice (see *Note 3D*); and
>> (iv) if applicable, their right to interpretation and translation (see para. 3.12) and their

right to communicate with their high commission, embassy or consulate (see para. 3.12A).

(b) their right to be informed about the offence and (as the case may be) any further offences for which they are arrested whilst in custody and why they have been arrested and detained in accordance with paragraphs 2.4, 3.4(a) and 11.1A of this code and paragraph 3.3 of Code G.

C:3.2 The detainee must also be given a written notice, which contains information:

(a) setting out:

(i) their rights under paragraph 3.1, paragraph 3.12 and 3.12A;

(ii) the arrangements for obtaining legal advice, see section 6;

(iii) their right to a copy of the custody record as in paragraph 2.4A;

(iv) their right to remain silent as set out in the caution in the terms prescribed in section 10;

(v) their right to have access to materials and documents which are essential to effectively challenging the lawfulness of their arrest and detention for any offence and (as the case may be) any further offences for which they are arrested whilst in custody, in accordance with paragraphs 3.4(b), 15.0, 15.7A(c) and 16.7A of this code;

(vi) the maximum period for which they may be kept in police detention without being charged, when detention must be reviewed and when release is required;

(vii) their right to medical assistance in accordance with section 9 of this code;

(viii) their right, if they are prosecuted, to have access to the evidence in the case before their trial in accordance with the Criminal Procedure and Investigations Act 1996, the Attorney General's Guidelines on Disclosure, the common law and the Criminal Procedure Rules;

(b) briefly setting out their other entitlements while in custody, by:

(i) mentioning:

– the provisions relating to the conduct of interviews;

– the circumstances in which an appropriate adult should be available to assist the detainee and their statutory rights to make representations whenever the need for their detention is reviewed;

(ii) listing the entitlements in this code, concerning:

– reasonable standards of physical comfort;

– adequate food and drink;

– access to toilets and washing facilities, clothing, medical attention, and exercise when practicable.

See *Note 3A*.

C:3.2A The detainee must be given an opportunity to read the notice and shall be asked to sign the custody record to acknowledge receipt of the notice. Any refusal to sign must be recorded on the custody record.

C:3.3 [*Not used.*]

C:3.3A An "easy read" illustrated version should also be provided if available (see *Note 3A*).

C:3.4 (a) The custody officer shall:

• record the offence(s) that the detainee has been arrested for and the reason(s) for the arrest on the custody record (see para. 10.3 and Code G, paras 2.2 and 4.3);

• note on the custody record any comment the detainee makes in relation to the arresting officer's account but shall not invite comment; if the arresting officer is not physically present when the detainee is brought to a police station, the arresting officer's account must be made available to the custody officer remotely or by a third party on the arresting officer's behalf; if the custody officer authorises a person's detention, subject to paragraph 1.8, that officer must record the grounds for detention in the detainee's presence and at the same time, inform them of the grounds; the detainee must be informed of the grounds for their detention before they are questioned about any offence;

• note any comment the detainee makes in respect of the decision to detain them but shall not invite comment;

• not put specific questions to the detainee regarding their involvement in any offence, nor in respect of any comments they may make in response to the arresting officer's account or the decision to place them in detention; such an exchange is likely to constitute an interview as in paragraph 11.1A and require the associated safeguards in section 11.

Note: this sub-paragraph also applies to any further offences and grounds for detention which come to light whilst the person is detained.

See paragraph 11.13 in respect of unsolicited comments.

(b) Documents and materials which are essential to effectively challenging the lawfulness of the detainee's arrest and detention must be made available to the detainee or their solicitor. Documents and materials will be "essential" for this purpose if they are capable of undermining the reasons and grounds which make the detainee's arrest and detention necessary. The decision about whether particular documents or materials must be made available for the purpose of this requirement therefore rests with the custody officer who determines whether detention is necessary, in consultation with the investigating officer who has the knowledge of the documents and materials in a particular case necessary to inform that decision. A note should be made in the detainee's custody record of the fact that documents or materials have been made available under this sub-paragraph and when. The investigating officer should make a separate note of what is made available and how it is made available in a particular case. This sub-paragraph also applies (with modifications) for the purposes of sections 15 (reviews and extensions of detention) and 16 (charging detained persons). See *Note 3ZA* and paragraphs 15.0 and 16.7A.

C:3.5 The custody officer or other custody staff as directed by the custody officer shall:

(a) ask the detainee, whether at this time, they:
  (i) would like legal advice, see paragraph 6.5;
  (ii) want someone informed of their detention, see section 5;

(b) ask the detainee to sign the custody record to confirm their decisions in respect of (a);

(c) determine whether the detainee:
  (i) is, or might be, in need of medical treatment or attention, see section 9;
  (ii) requires:
    • an appropriate adult (see paras 1.4, 1.5, 1.5A and 3.15);
    • help to check documentation (see para. 3.20);
    • an interpreter (see para. 3.12 and *Note 13B*);

(d) record the decision in respect of (c).

Where any duties under this paragraph have been carried out by custody staff at the direction of the custody officer, the outcomes shall, as soon as practicable, be reported to the custody officer who retains overall responsibility for the detainee's care and treatment and ensuring that it complies with this code. See *Note 3F*.

C:3.6 When these needs are determined, the custody officer is responsible for initiating an assessment to consider whether the detainee is likely to present specific risks to custody staff or themselves. Such assessments should always include a check on the Police National Computer, to be carried out as soon as practicable, to identify any risks highlighted in relation to the detainee. Although such assessments are primarily the custody officer's responsibility, it may be necessary for them to consult and involve others, *e.g.* the arresting officer or an appropriate healthcare professional, see paragraph 9.13. Reasons for delaying the initiation or completion of the assessment must be recorded.

C:3.7 Chief officers should ensure that arrangements for proper and effective risk assessments required by paragraph 3.6 are implemented in respect of all detainees at police stations in their area.

C:3.8 Risk assessments must follow a structured process which clearly defines the categories of risk to be considered and the results must be incorporated in the detainee's custody record. The custody officer is responsible for making sure those responsible for the detainee's custody are appropriately briefed about the risks. If no specific risks are identified by the assessment, that should be noted in the custody record. See *Note 3E* and paragraph 9.14.

C:3.8A The content of any risk assessment and any analysis of the level of risk relating to the person's detention is not required to be shown or provided to the detainee or any person acting on behalf of the detainee. But information should not be withheld from any person acting on the detainee's behalf, for example, an appropriate adult, solicitor or interpreter, if to do so might put that person at risk.

C:3.9 The custody officer is responsible for implementing the response to any specific risk assessment, *e.g.*:

• reducing opportunities for self harm;
• calling an appropriate healthcare professional;
• increasing levels of monitoring or observation;
• reducing the risk to those who come into contact with the detainee.

See *Note 3E*.

C:3.10 Risk assessment is an ongoing process and assessments must always be subject to review if circumstances change.

C:3.11 If video cameras are installed in the custody area, notices shall be prominently displayed showing cameras are in use. Any request to have video cameras switched off shall be refused.

(b) *Detained persons—special groups*

C:3.12 If the detainee appears to be someone who does not speak or understand English or who **A-47** has a hearing or speech impediment, the custody officer must ensure:

(a) that without delay, an interpreter is called for assistance in the action under paragraphs 3.1 to 3.5; if the person appears to have a hearing or speech impediment, the reference to "interpreter" includes appropriate assistance necessary to comply with paragraphs 3.1 to 3.5 (see para. 13.1C if the detainee is in Wales) (see section 13 and *Note 13B*);

(b) that in addition to the continuing rights set out in paragraph 3.1(a)(i) to (iv), the detainee is told clearly about their right to interpretation and translation;

(c) that the written notice given to the detainee in accordance with paragraph 3.2 is in a language the detainee understands and includes the right to interpretation and translation together with information about the provisions in section 13 and Annex M, which explain how the right applies (see *Note 3A*); and

(d) that if the translation of the notice is not available, the information in the notice is given through an interpreter and a written translation provided without undue delay.

C:3.12A If the detainee is a citizen of an independent Commonwealth country or a national of a foreign country, including the Republic of Ireland, the custody officer must ensure that in addition to the continuing rights set out in paragraph 3.1(a)(i) to (iv), they are informed as soon as practicable about their rights of communication with their high commission, embassy or consulate set out in section 7. This right must be included in the written notice given to the detainee in accordance with paragraph 3.2.

C:3.13 If the detainee is a juvenile, the custody officer must, if it is practicable, ascertain the identity of a person responsible for their welfare. That person:

*   may be:
    *   the parent or guardian;
    *   if the juvenile is in local authority or voluntary organisation care, or is otherwise being looked after under the Children Act 1989, a person appointed by that authority or organisation to have responsibility for the juvenile's welfare;
    *   any other person who has, for the time being, assumed responsibility for the juvenile's welfare;
*   must be informed as soon as practicable that the juvenile has been arrested, why they have been arrested and where they are detained. This right is in addition to the juvenile's right in section 5 not to be held incommunicado. See *Note 3C*.

Note: paragraph 1.5A extends the obligations in this paragraph to 17-year-old detainees.

C:3.14 If a juvenile is known to be subject to a court order under which a person or organisation is given any degree of statutory responsibility to supervise or otherwise monitor them, reasonable steps must also be taken to notify that person or organisation (the "responsible officer"). The responsible officer will normally be a member of a youth offending team, except for a curfew order which involves electronic monitoring when the contractor providing the monitoring will normally be the responsible officer.

Note: paragraph 1.5A extends the obligations in this paragraph to 17-year-old detainees.

C:3.15 If the detainee is a juvenile, mentally disordered or otherwise mentally vulnerable, the custody officer must, as soon as practicable:

*   inform the appropriate adult, who in the case of a juvenile may or may not be a person responsible for their welfare, as in paragraph 3.13, of:
    *   the grounds for their detention;
    *   their whereabouts;
*   ask the adult to come to the police station to see the detainee.

Note: paragraph 1.5A extends the obligation to call someone to fulfil the role of the appropriate adult to 17-year-old detainees.

C:3.16 It is imperative that a mentally disordered or otherwise mentally vulnerable person, detained under the Mental Health Act 1983, s.136, be assessed as soon as possible. A police station should only be used as a place of safety as a last resort but if that assessment is to take place at the police station, an approved mental health professional and a registered medical practitioner shall be called to the station as soon as possible to carry it out. See *Note 9D*. The appropriate adult has no role in the assessment process and their presence is not required. Once the detainee has been assessed and suitable arrangements made for their treatment or care, they can no longer be detained under section 136. A detainee must be immediately discharged from detention under section 136 if a registered medical practitioner, having examined them, concludes they are not mentally disordered within the meaning of the Act.

C:3.17 If the appropriate adult is:

- already at the police station, the provisions of paragraphs 3.1 to 3.5 must be complied with in the appropriate adult's presence;
- not at the station when these provisions are complied with, they must be complied with again in the presence of the appropriate adult when they arrive,

and a copy of the notice given to the detainee in accordance with paragraph 3.2, shall also be given to the appropriate adult.

Note: paragraph 1.5A extends the obligations in this paragraph to 17-year-old detainees.

C:3.18 The detainee shall be advised that:

- the duties of the appropriate adult include giving advice and assistance;
- they can consult privately with the appropriate adult at any time.

Note: paragraph 1.5A extends the obligations in this paragraph to 17-year-old detainees.

C:3.19 If the detainee, or appropriate adult on the detainee's behalf, asks for a solicitor to be called to give legal advice, the provisions of section 6 apply.

Note: paragraph 1.5A extends the obligations in this paragraph to 17-year-old detainees.

C:3.20 If the detainee is blind, seriously visually impaired or unable to read, the custody officer shall make sure their solicitor, relative, appropriate adult or some other person likely to take an interest in them and not involved in the investigation is available to help check any documentation. When this code requires written consent or signing the person assisting may be asked to sign instead, if the detainee prefers. This paragraph does not require an appropriate adult to be called solely to assist in checking and signing documentation for a person who is not a juvenile, or mentally disordered or otherwise mentally vulnerable (see para. 3.15 and *Note 13C*).

(c) *Persons attending a police station or elsewhere voluntarily*

A-48

C:3.21 Anybody attending a police station or other location (see para. 3.22) voluntarily to assist police with the investigation of an offence may leave at will unless arrested. See *Note 1K*. The person may only be prevented from leaving at will if their arrest on suspicion of committing the offence is necessary in accordance with Code G. See Code G, *Note 2G*.

(a) If during an interview it is decided that their arrest is necessary, they must:

- be informed at once that they are under arrest and of the grounds and reasons as required by Code G, and
- be brought before the custody officer at the police station where they are arrested or, as the case may be, at the police station to which they are taken after being arrested elsewhere. The custody officer is then responsible for making sure that a custody record is opened and that they are notified of their rights in the same way as other detainees as required by this code.

(b) If they are not arrested but are cautioned as in section 10, the person who gives the caution must, at the same time, inform them they are not under arrest, they are not obliged to remain at the station or other location but if they agree to remain, they may obtain free and independent legal advice if they want. They shall also be given a copy of the notice explaining the arrangements for obtaining legal advice and told that the right to legal advice includes the right to speak with a solicitor on the telephone and be asked if they want advice. If advice is requested, the interviewer is responsible for securing its provision without delay by contacting the defence solicitor call centre. The interviewer must ensure that other provisions of this code and Codes E and F concerning the conduct and recording of interviews of suspects and the rights and entitlements and safeguards for suspects who have been arrested and detained are followed insofar as they can be applied to suspects who are not under arrest. This includes:

- informing them of the offence and, as the case may be, any further offences, they are suspected of and the grounds and reasons for that suspicion and their right to be so informed (see para. 3.1(b));
- the caution as required in section 10;
- determining whether they require an appropriate adult and help to check documentation (see para. 3.5(c)(ii)); and
- determining whether they require an interpreter and the provision of interpretation and translation services and informing them of that right (see paras 3.1(a)(iv), 3.5(c)(ii) and 3.12, *Note 6B* and section 13),

but does not include any requirement to provide a written notice in addition to that above which concerns the arrangements for obtaining legal advice.

C:3.22 If the other location mentioned in paragraph 3.21 is any place or premises for which the interviewer requires the person's informed consent to remain, for example, the person's home, then the references that the person is "not obliged to remain" and that they "may leave at will" mean that the person may also withdraw their consent and require the officer to leave.

(d) *Documentation*

C:3.23 The grounds for a person's detention shall be recorded, in the person's presence if practicable. See paragraph 1.8.

C:3.24 Action taken under paragraphs 3.12 to 3.20 shall be recorded.

(e) *Persons answering street bail*

C:3.25 When a person is answering street bail, the custody officer should link any documentation held in relation to arrest with the custody record. Any further action shall be recorded on the custody record in accordance with paragraphs 3.23 and 3.24 above.

(f) *Requirements for suspects to be informed of certain rights*

C:3.26 The provisions of this section identify the information which must be given to suspects who have been cautioned in accordance with section 10 of this code according to whether or not they have been arrested and detained. It includes information required by EU Directive 2012/13 on the right to information in criminal proceedings. If a complaint is made by or on behalf of such a suspect that the information and (as the case may be) access to records and documents has not been provided as required, the matter shall be reported to an inspector to deal with as a complaint for the purposes of paragraph 9.2, or paragraph 12.9 if the challenge is made during an interview. This would include, for example:

    (a) in the case of a detained suspect:
- not informing them of their rights (see para. 3.1);
- not giving them a copy of the notice (see para. 3.2(a));
- not providing an opportunity to read the notice (see para. 3.2A);
- not providing the required information (see paras 3.2(a), 3.12(b) and, 3.12A);
- not allowing access to the custody record (see para. 2.4);
- not providing a translation of the notice (see para. 3.12(c) and (d)); and

    (b) in the case of a suspect who is not detained:
- not informing them of their rights or providing the required information (see para. 3.21(b)).

Notes for guidance

C:3ZA *For the purposes of paragraphs 3.4(b) and 15.0:*   **A-49**

    (a) *investigating officers are responsible for bringing to the attention of the officer who is responsible for authorising the suspect's detention or (as the case may be) continued detention (before or after charge), any documents and materials in their possession or control which appear to undermine the need to keep the suspect in custody; in accordance with Part IV of PACE, this officer will be either the custody officer, the officer reviewing the need for detention before or after charge (PACE, s.40), or the officer considering the need to extend detention without charge from 24 to 36 hours (PACE, s.42) who is then responsible for determining, which, if any, of those documents and materials are capable of undermining the need to detain the suspect and must therefore be made available to the suspect or their solicitor;*

    (b) *the way in which documents and materials are "made available", is a matter for the investigating officer to determine on a case by case basis and having regard to the nature and volume of the documents and materials involved: for example, they may be made available by supplying a copy or allowing supervised access to view; however, for view only access, it will be necessary to demonstrate that sufficient time is allowed for the suspect and solicitor to view and consider the documents and materials in question.*

C:3A *For access to currently available notices, including "easy-read" versions, see https://www.gov.uk/notice-of-rights-and-entitlements-a-persons-rights-in-police-detention.*

C:3B [*Not used.*]

C:3C *If the juvenile is in local authority or voluntary organisation care but living with their parents or other adults responsible for their welfare, although there is no legal obligation to inform them, they should normally be contacted, as well as the authority or organisation unless they are suspected of involvement in the offence concerned. Even if the juvenile is not living with their parents, consideration should be given to informing them.*

C:3D *The right to consult the codes of practice does not entitle the person concerned to delay unreasonably any necessary investigative or administrative action whilst they do so. Examples of action which need not be delayed unreasonably include:*

- *procedures requiring the provision of breath, blood or urine specimens under the Road Traffic Act 1988 or the Transport and Works Act 1992;*
- *searching detainees at the police station;*
- *taking fingerprints, footwear impressions or non-intimate samples without consent for evidential purposes.*

C:3E *The Detention and Custody Authorised Professional Practice (APP) produced by the College of Policing (see http://www.app.college.police.uk) provides more detailed guidance on risk assessments and identifies key risk areas which should always be considered.*

C:3F *A custody officer or other officer who, in accordance with this code, allows or directs the carrying out of any task or action relating to a detainee's care, treatment, rights and entitlements to another officer or any police staff must be satisfied that the officer or police staff concerned are suitable, trained and competent to carry out the task or action in question.*

C:4 Detainee's property

(a) *Action*

A-50   C:4.1 The custody officer is responsible for:

    (a) ascertaining what property a detainee:

        (i) has with them when they come to the police station, whether on:

- arrest or re-detention on answering to bail;
- commitment to prison custody on the order or sentence of a court;
- lodgement at the police station with a view to their production in court from prison custody;
- transfer from detention at another station or hospital;
- detention under the Mental Health Act 1983, s.135 or 136;
- remand into police custody on the authority of a court;

        (ii) might have acquired for an unlawful or harmful purpose while in custody;

    (b) the safekeeping of any property taken from a detainee which remains at the police station.

The custody officer may search the detainee or authorise their being searched to the extent they consider necessary, provided a search of intimate parts of the body or involving the removal of more than outer clothing is only made as in Annex A. A search may only be carried out by an officer of the same sex as the detainee. See *Note 4A* and Annex L.

C:4.2 Detainees may retain clothing and personal effects at their own risk unless the custody officer considers they may use them to cause harm to themselves or others, interfere with evidence, damage property, effect an escape or they are needed as evidence. In this event the custody officer may withhold such articles as they consider necessary and must tell the detainee why.

C:4.3 Personal effects are those items a detainee may lawfully need, use or refer to while in detention but do not include cash and other items of value.

(b) *Documentation*

C:4.4 It is a matter for the custody officer to determine whether a record should be made of the property a detained person has with him or had taken from him on arrest. Any record made is not required to be kept as part of the custody record but the custody record should be noted as to where such a record exists. Whenever a record is made the detainee shall be allowed to check and sign the record of property as correct. Any refusal to sign shall be recorded.

C:4.5 If a detainee is not allowed to keep any article of clothing or personal effects, the reason must be recorded.

Notes for guidance

A-51   C:4A *PACE, s.54(1), and paragraph 4.1 require a detainee to be searched when it is clear the custody officer will have continuing duties in relation to that detainee or when that detainee's behaviour or offence makes an inventory appropriate. They do not require every detainee to be searched, e.g. if it is clear a person will only be detained for a short period and is not to be placed in a cell, the custody officer may decide not to search them. In such a case the custody record will be endorsed "not searched", paragraph 4.4 will not apply, and the detainee will be invited to sign the entry. If the detainee refuses, the custody officer will be obliged to ascertain what property they have in accordance with paragraph 4.1.*

C:4B *Paragraph 4.4 does not require the custody officer to record on the custody record property in the detainee's possession on arrest if, by virtue of its nature, quantity or size, it is not practicable to remove it to the police station.*

C:4C *Paragraph 4.4 does not require items of clothing worn by the person to be recorded unless withheld by the custody officer as in paragraph 4.2.*

C:5 Right not to be held incommunicado

(a) *Action*

C:5.1 Subject to paragraph 5.7B, any person arrested and held in custody at a police station or **A-52** other premises may, on request, have one person known to them or likely to take an interest in their welfare informed at public expense of their whereabouts as soon as practicable. If the person cannot be contacted the detainee may choose up to two alternatives. If they cannot be contacted, the person in charge of detention or the investigation has discretion to allow further attempts until the information has been conveyed. See *Notes 5C* and *5D.*

C:5.2 The exercise of the above right in respect of each person nominated may be delayed only in accordance with Annex B.

C:5.3 The above right may be exercised each time a detainee is taken to another police station.

C:5.4 If the detainee agrees, they may at the custody officer's discretion, receive visits from friends, family or others likely to take an interest in their welfare, or in whose welfare the detainee has an interest. See *Note 5B.*

C:5.5 If a friend, relative or person with an interest in the detainee's welfare enquires about their whereabouts, this information shall be given if the suspect agrees and Annex B does not apply. See *Note 5D.*

C:5.6 The detainee shall be given writing materials, on request, and allowed to telephone one person for a reasonable time, see *Notes 5A* and *5E.* Either or both of these privileges may be denied or delayed if an officer of inspector rank or above considers sending a letter or making a telephone call may result in any of the consequences in:

    (a) Annex B, paragraphs 1 and 2 and the person is detained in connection with an indictable offence;

    (b) [*Not used.*]

Nothing in this paragraph permits the restriction or denial of the rights in paragraphs 5.1 and 6.1.

C:5.7 Before any letter or message is sent, or telephone call made, the detainee shall be informed that what they say in any letter, call or message (other than in a communication to a solicitor) may be read or listened to and may be given in evidence. A telephone call may be terminated if it is being abused. The costs can be at public expense at the custody officer's discretion.

C:5.7A Any delay or denial of the rights in this section should be proportionate and should last no longer than necessary.

C:5.7B In the case of a person in police custody for specific purposes and periods in accordance with a direction under the Crime (Sentences) Act 1997, Sched. 1 (productions from prison etc.), the exercise of the rights in this section shall be subject to any additional conditions specified in the direction for the purpose of regulating the detainee's contact and communication with others whilst in police custody. See *Note 5F.*

(b) *Documentation*

C:5.8 A record must be kept of any:

    (a) request made under this section and the action taken;

    (b) letters, messages or telephone calls made or received or visit received;

    (c) refusal by the detainee to have information about them given to an outside enquirer. The detainee must be asked to countersign the record accordingly and any refusal recorded.

Notes for guidance

C:5A *A person may request an interpreter to interpret a telephone call or translate a letter.* **A-53**

C:5B *At the custody officer's discretion and subject to the detainee's consent, visits should be allowed when possible, subject to having sufficient personnel to supervise a visit and any possible hindrance to the investigation.*

C:5C *If the detainee does not know anyone to contact for advice or support or cannot contact a friend or relative, the custody officer should bear in mind any local voluntary bodies or other organisations who might be able to help. Paragraph 6.1 applies if legal advice is required.*

C:5D *In some circumstances it may not be appropriate to use the telephone to disclose information under paragraphs 5.1 and 5.5.*

C:5E *The telephone call at paragraph 5.6 is in addition to any communication under paragraphs 5.1 and 6.1.*

C:5F *Prison Service Instruction 26/2012 (Production of Prisoners at the Request of Warranted Law Enforcement Agencies) provides detailed guidance and instructions for police officers and governors and directors of prisons regarding applications for prisoners to be transferred to police custody and their safe custody and treatments while in police custody.*

C:6 Right to legal advice

(a) *Action*

A-54   C:6.1 Unless Annex B applies, all detainees must be informed that they may at any time consult and communicate privately with a solicitor, whether in person, in writing or by telephone, and that free independent legal advice is available. See paragraph 3.1, *Notes 1I, 6B* and *6J.*

C:6.2 [*Not used.*]

C:6.3 A poster advertising the right to legal advice must be prominently displayed in the charging area of every police station. See *Note 6H.*

C:6.4 No police officer should, at any time, do or say anything with the intention of dissuading any person who is entitled to legal advice in accordance with this code, whether or not they have been arrested and are detained, from obtaining legal advice. See *Note 6ZA.*

C:6.5 The exercise of the right of access to legal advice may be delayed only as in Annex B. Whenever legal advice is requested, and unless Annex B applies, the custody officer must act without delay to secure the provision of such advice. If the detainee has the right to speak to a solicitor in person but declines to exercise the right the officer should point out that the right includes the right to speak with a solicitor on the telephone. If the detainee continues to waive this right, or a detainee whose right to free legal advice is limited to telephone advice from the Criminal Defence Service (CDS) Direct (see *Note 6B*) declines to exercise that right, the officer should ask them why and any reasons should be recorded on the custody record or the interview record as appropriate. Reminders of the right to legal advice must be given as in paragraphs 3.5, 11.2, 15.4, 16.4, 16.5, 2B of Annex A, 3 of Annex K and 5 of Annex M of this code and Code D, paragraphs 3.17(ii) and 6.3. Once it is clear a detainee does not want to speak to a solicitor in person or by telephone they should cease to be asked their reasons. See *Note 6K.*

C:6.5A In the case of a person who is a juvenile or is mentally disordered or otherwise mentally vulnerable, an appropriate adult should consider whether legal advice from a solicitor is required. If the person indicates that they do not want legal advice, the appropriate adult has the right to ask for a solicitor to attend if this would be in the best interests of the person. However, the person cannot be forced to see the solicitor if they are adamant that they do not wish to do so.

Note: paragraph 1.5A applies this paragraph to 17-year-old detainees.

C:6.6 A detainee who wants legal advice may not be interviewed or continue to be interviewed until they have received such advice unless:

(a) Annex B applies, when the restriction on drawing adverse inferences from silence in Annex C will apply because the detainee is not allowed an opportunity to consult a solicitor; or

(b) an officer of superintendent rank or above has reasonable grounds for believing that:

(i) the consequent delay might:

- lead to interference with, or harm to, evidence connected with an offence;
- lead to interference with, or physical harm to, other people;
- lead to serious loss of, or damage to, property;
- lead to alerting other people suspected of having committed an offence but not yet arrested for it;
- hinder the recovery of property obtained in consequence of the commission of an offence; see *Note 6A*;

(ii) when a solicitor, including a duty solicitor, has been contacted and has agreed to attend, awaiting their arrival would cause unreasonable delay to the process of investigation;

note: in these cases the restriction on drawing adverse inferences from silence in Annex C will apply because the detainee is not allowed an opportunity to consult a solicitor;

(c) the solicitor the detainee has nominated or selected from a list:

(i) cannot be contacted;

(ii) has previously indicated they do not wish to be contacted; or

(iii) having been contacted, has declined to attend; and

- the detainee has been advised of the duty solicitor scheme but has declined to ask for the duty solicitor;

- in these circumstances the interview may be started or continued without further
delay provided an officer of inspector rank or above has agreed to the interview
proceeding;

note: the restriction on drawing adverse inferences from silence in Annex C will not apply because the detainee is allowed an opportunity to consult the duty solicitor;

(d) the detainee changes their mind about wanting legal advice or (as the case may be) about
wanting a solicitor present at the interview and states that they no longer wish to speak to
a solicitor; in these circumstances, the interview may be started or continued without
delay provided that:

(i) an officer of inspector rank or above:

- speaks to the detainee to enquire about the reasons for their change of mind (see
Note 6K), and
- makes, or directs the making of, reasonable efforts to ascertain the solicitor's
expected time of arrival and to inform the solicitor that the suspect has stated that
they wish to change their mind and the reason (if given);

(ii) the detainee's reason for their change of mind (if given) and the outcome of the action
in (i) are recorded in the custody record;

(iii) the detainee, after being informed of the outcome of the action in (i) above, confirms
in writing that they want the interview to proceed without speaking or further speaking to a solicitor or (as the case may be) without a solicitor being present and do not
wish to wait for a solicitor by signing an entry to this effect in the custody record;

(iv) an officer of inspector rank or above is satisfied that it is proper for the interview to
proceed in these circumstances and:

- gives authority in writing for the interview to proceed and, if the authority is not
recorded in the custody record, the officer must ensure that the custody record
shows the date and time of authority and where it is recorded, and
- takes, or directs the taking of, reasonable steps to inform the solicitor that the
authority has been given and the time when the interview is expected to commence and records or causes to be recorded, the outcome of this action in the
custody record;

(v) when the interview starts and the interviewer reminds the suspect of their right to
legal advice (see paragraph 11.2, Code E, paragraph 4.5, and Code F, paragraph 4.5),
the interviewer shall then ensure that the following is recorded in the written interview
record or the interview record made in accordance with Code E or F:

- confirmation that the detainee has changed their mind about wanting legal advice
or (as the case may be) about wanting a solicitor present and the reasons for it if
given;
- the fact that authority for the interview to proceed has been given and, subject to
paragraph 2.6A, the name of the authorising officer;
- that if the solicitor arrives at the station before the interview is completed, the
detainee will be so informed without delay and a break will be taken to allow them
to speak to the solicitor if they wish, unless paragraph 6.6(a) applies; and
- that at any time during the interview, the detainee may again ask for legal advice
and that if they do, a break will be taken to allow them to speak to the solicitor, unless paragraph 6.6(a), (b), or (c) applies;

note: in these circumstances, the restriction on drawing adverse inferences from silence in
Annex C will not apply because the detainee is allowed an opportunity to consult a solicitor if they wish.

C:6.7 If paragraph 6.6(a) applies, where the reason for authorising the delay ceases to apply, there **A-55**
may be no further delay in permitting the exercise of the right in the absence of a further authorisation unless paragraph 6.6(b), (c) or (d) applies. If paragraph 6.6(b)(i) applies, once sufficient information has been obtained to avert the risk, questioning must cease until the detainee has received legal
advice unless paragraph 6.6(a), (b)(ii), (c) or (d) applies.

C:6.8 A detainee who has been permitted to consult a solicitor shall be entitled on request to have
the solicitor present when they are interviewed unless one of the exceptions in paragraph 6.6
applies.

C:6.9 The solicitor may only be required to leave the interview if their conduct is such that the
interviewer is unable properly to put questions to the suspect. See *Notes 6D* and *6E*.

C:6.10 If the interviewer considers a solicitor is acting in such a way, they will stop the interview
and consult an officer not below superintendent rank, if one is readily available, and otherwise an officer not below inspector rank not connected with the investigation. After speaking to the solicitor,

the officer consulted will decide if the interview should continue in the presence of that solicitor. If they decide it should not, the suspect will be given the opportunity to consult another solicitor before the interview continues and that solicitor given an opportunity to be present at the interview. See *Note 6E.*

C:6.11 The removal of a solicitor from an interview is a serious step and, if it occurs, the officer of superintendent rank or above who took the decision will consider if the incident should be reported to the Solicitors Regulation Authority. If the decision to remove the solicitor has been taken by an officer below superintendent rank, the facts must be reported to an officer of superintendent rank or above who will similarly consider whether a report to the Solicitors Regulation Authority would be appropriate. When the solicitor concerned is a duty solicitor, the report should be both to the Solicitors Regulation Authority and to the Legal Aid Agency.

C:6.12 "Solicitor" in this code means:

- a solicitor who holds a current practising certificate;
- an accredited or probationary representative included on the register of representatives maintained by the Legal Aid Agency.

C:6.12A An accredited or probationary representative sent to provide advice by, and on behalf of, a solicitor shall be admitted to the police station for this purpose unless an officer of inspector rank or above considers such a visit will hinder the investigation and directs otherwise. Hindering the investigation does not include giving proper legal advice to a detainee as in *Note 6D.* Once admitted to the police station, paragraphs 6.6 to 6.10 apply.

C:6.13 In exercising their discretion under paragraph 6.12A, the officer should take into account in particular:

- whether:
  - the identity and status of an accredited or probationary representative have been satisfactorily established;
  - they are of suitable character to provide legal advice, *e.g.* a person with a criminal record is unlikely to be suitable unless the conviction was for a minor offence and not recent;
- any other matters in any written letter of authorisation provided by the solicitor on whose behalf the person is attending the police station. See *Note 6F.*

C:6.14 If the inspector refuses access to an accredited or probationary representative or a decision is taken that such a person should not be permitted to remain at an interview, the inspector must notify the solicitor on whose behalf the representative was acting and give them an opportunity to make alternative arrangements. The detainee must be informed and the custody record noted.

C:6.15 If a solicitor arrives at the station to see a particular person, that person must, unless Annex B applies, be so informed whether or not they are being interviewed and asked if they would like to see the solicitor. This applies even if the detainee has declined legal advice or, having requested it, subsequently agreed to be interviewed without receiving advice. The solicitor's attendance and the detainee's decision must be noted in the custody record.

(b) *Documentation*

C:6.16 Any request for legal advice and the action taken shall be recorded.

C:6.17 A record shall be made in the interview record if a detainee asks for legal advice and an interview is begun either in the absence of a solicitor or their representative, or they have been required to leave an interview.

Notes for guidance

C:6ZA *No police officer or police staff shall indicate to any suspect, except to answer a direct question, that period for which they are liable to be detained, or if not detained, the time taken to complete the interview, might be reduced:*

- *if they do not ask for legal advice or do not want a solicitor present when they are interviewed; or*
- *if they have asked for legal advice or (as the case may be) asked for a solicitor to be present when they are interviewed but change their mind and agree to be interviewed without waiting for a solicitor.*

C:6A *In considering if paragraph 6.6(b) applies, the officer should, if practicable, ask the solicitor for an estimate of how long it will take to come to the station and relate this to the time detention is permitted, the time of day (e.g. whether the rest period under paragraph 12.2 is imminent) and the requirements of other investigations. If the solicitor is on their way or is to set off immediately, it will not normally be appropriate to begin an interview before they arrive. If it appears necessary to begin an interview before the solicitor's arrival, they should be given an indication of how long the police would be able to wait before 6.6(b) applies so there is an opportunity to make arrangements for someone else to provide legal advice.*

C:6B *A detainee has a right to free legal advice and to be represented by a solicitor. This note for guidance explains the arrangements which enable detainees to obtain legal advice. An outline of these arrangements is also included in the Notice of Rights and Entitlements given to detainees in accordance with paragraph 3.2. The arrangements also apply, with appropriate modifications, to persons attending a police station or other location voluntarily who are cautioned prior to being interviewed. See paragraph 3.21.*

When a detainee asks for free legal advice, the Defence Solicitor Call Centre (DSCC) must be informed of the request.

Free legal advice will be limited to telephone advice provided by CDS Direct if a detainee is:

- *detained for a non-imprisonable offence;*
- *arrested on a bench warrant for failing to appear and being held for production at court (except where the solicitor has clear documentary evidence available that would result in the client being released from custody);*
- *arrested for drink driving (driving/in charge with excess alcohol, failing to provide a specimen, driving/in charge whilst unfit through drink); or*
- *detained in relation to breach of police or court bail conditions;*

unless one or more exceptions apply, in which case the DSCC should arrange for advice to be given by a solicitor at the police station, for example:

- *the police want to interview the detainee or carry out an eye-witness identification procedure;*
- *the detainee needs an appropriate adult;*
- *the detainee is unable to communicate over the telephone;*
- *the detainee alleges serious misconduct by the police;*
- *the investigation includes another offence not included in the list;*
- *the solicitor to be assigned is already at the police station.*

When free advice is not limited to telephone advice, a detainee can ask for free advice from a solicitor they know or if they do not know a solicitor or the solicitor they know cannot be contacted, from the duty solicitor.

To arrange free legal advice, the police should telephone the DSCC. The call centre will decide whether legal advice should be limited to telephone advice from CDS Direct, or whether a solicitor known to the detainee or the duty solicitor should speak to the detainee.

When a detainee wants to pay for legal advice themselves:

- *the DSCC will contact a solicitor of their choice on their behalf;*
- *they may, when free advice is only available by telephone from CDS Direct, still speak to a solicitor of their choice on the telephone for advice, but the solicitor would not be paid by legal aid and may ask the person to pay for the advice;*
- *they should be given an opportunity to consult a specific solicitor or another solicitor from that solicitor's firm; if this solicitor is not available, they may choose up to two alternatives; if these alternatives are not available, the custody officer has discretion to allow further attempts until a solicitor has been contacted and agreed to provide advice;*
- *they are entitled to a private consultation with their chosen solicitor on the telephone or the solicitor may decide to come to the police station;*
- *if their chosen solicitor cannot be contacted, the DSCC may still be called to arrange free legal advice.*

Apart from carrying out duties necessary to implement these arrangements, an officer must not advise the suspect about any particular firm of solicitors.

C:6C *[Not used.]*

C:6D *The solicitor's only role in the police station is to protect and advance the legal rights of their client. On occasions this may require the solicitor to give advice which has the effect of the client avoiding giving evidence which strengthens a prosecution case. The solicitor may intervene in order to seek clarification, challenge an improper question to their client or the manner in which it is put, advise their client not to reply to particular questions, or if they wish to give their client further legal advice. Paragraph 6.9 only applies if the solicitor's approach or conduct prevents or unreasonably obstructs proper questions being put to the suspect or the suspect's response being recorded. Examples of unacceptable conduct include answering questions on a suspect's behalf or providing written replies for the suspect to quote.*

C:6E *An officer who takes the decision to exclude a solicitor must be in a position to satisfy the court the decision was properly made. In order to do this they may need to witness what is happening.*

C:6F *If an officer of at least inspector rank considers a particular solicitor or firm of solicitors is persistently sending probationary representatives who are unsuited to provide legal advice, they should inform an officer of at least superintendent rank, who may wish to take the matter up with the Solicitors Regulation Authority.*

C:6G *Subject to the constraints of Annex B, a solicitor may advise more than one client in an investigation if* **A-57**
they wish. Any question of a conflict of interest is for the solicitor under their professional code of conduct. If, however, waiting for a solicitor to give advice to one client may lead to unreasonable delay to the interview with another, the provisions of paragraph 6.6(b) may apply.

C:6H *In addition to a poster in English, a poster or posters containing translations into Welsh, the main minority ethnic languages and the principal European languages should be displayed wherever they are likely to be helpful and it is practicable to do so.*

C:6I *[Not used.]*

C:6J *Whenever a detainee exercises their right to legal advice by consulting or communicating with a solicitor, they must be allowed to do so in private. This right to consult or communicate in private is fundamental. If the requirement for privacy is compromised because what is said or written by the detainee or solicitor for the purpose of giving and receiving legal advice is overheard, listened to, or read by others without the informed consent of the detainee, the right will effectively have been denied. When a detainee speaks to a solicitor on the telephone, they should be allowed to do so in private unless this is impractical because of the design and layout of the custody area or the location of telephones. However, the normal expectation should be that facilities will be available, unless they are being used, at all police stations to enable detainees to speak in private to a solicitor either face to face or over the telephone.*

C:6K *A detainee is not obliged to give reasons for declining legal advice and should not be pressed to do so.*

C:7 Citizens of independent Commonwealth countries or foreign nationals

(a) *Action*

C:7.1 A detainee who is a citizen of an independent Commonwealth country or a national of a foreign country, including the Republic of Ireland, has the right, upon request, to communicate at any time with the appropriate high commission, embassy or consulate. That detainee must be informed as soon as practicable of this right and asked if they want to have their high commission, embassy or consulate told of their whereabouts and the grounds for their detention. Such a request should be acted upon as soon as practicable. See *Note 7A.*

C:7.2 A detainee who is a citizen of a country with which a bilateral consular convention or agreement is in force requiring notification of arrest, must also be informed that subject to paragraph 7.4, notification of their arrest will be sent to the appropriate high commission, embassy or consulate as soon as practicable, whether or not they request it. A list of the countries to which this requirement currently applies and contact details for the relevant high commissions, embassies and consulates can be obtained from the Consular Directorate of the Foreign and Commonwealth Office (FCO) as follows:

- from the FCO web pages:
  - https://gov.uk/government/publications/table-of-consular-conventions-and-mandatory-notification-obligations, and
  - https://www.gov.uk/government/publications/foreign-embassies-in-the-uk
- by telephone to 020 7008 3100,
- by email to fcocorrespondence@fco.gov.uk.
- or by letter to the Foreign and Commonwealth Office, King Charles Street, London, SW1A 2AH.

C:7.3 Consular officers may, if the detainee agrees, visit one of their nationals in police detention to talk to them and, if required, to arrange for legal advice. Such visits shall take place out of the hearing of a police officer.

C:7.4 Notwithstanding the provisions of consular conventions, if the detainee claims that they are a refugee or have applied or intend to apply for asylum, the custody officer must ensure that the UK Visas and Immigration (UKVI) (formerly the UK Border Agency) is informed as soon as practicable of the claim. UKVI will then determine whether compliance with relevant international obligations requires notification of the arrest to be sent and will inform the custody officer as to what action police need to take.

(b) *Documentation*

C:7.5 A record shall be made:
- when a detainee is informed of their rights under this section and of any requirement in paragraph 7.2;
- of any communications with a high commission, embassy or consulate; and
- of any communications with UKVI about a detainee's claim to be a refugee or to be seeking asylum and the resulting action taken by police.

Note for guidance

C:7A *The exercise of the rights in this section may not be interfered with even though Annex B applies.*

C:8 Conditions of detention

(a) *Action*

C:8.1 So far as it is practicable, not more than one detainee should be detained in each cell. See *Note 8C.*

C:8.2 Cells in use must be adequately heated, cleaned and ventilated. They must be adequately lit, subject to such dimming as is compatible with safety and security to allow people detained overnight to sleep. No additional restraints shall be used within a locked cell unless absolutely necessary and then only restraint equipment, approved for use in that force by the chief officer, which is reasonable and necessary in the circumstances having regard to the detainee's demeanour and with a view to ensuring their safety and the safety of others. If a detainee is deaf, mentally disordered or otherwise mentally vulnerable, particular care must be taken when deciding whether to use any form of approved restraints.

C:8.3 Blankets, mattresses, pillows and other bedding supplied shall be of a reasonable standard and in a clean and sanitary condition. See *Note 8A.*

C:8.4 Access to toilet and washing facilities must be provided.

C:8.5 If it is necessary to remove a detainee's clothes for the purposes of investigation, for hygiene, health reasons or cleaning, replacement clothing of a reasonable standard of comfort and cleanliness shall be provided. A detainee may not be interviewed unless adequate clothing has been offered.

C:8.6 At least two light meals and one main meal should be offered in any 24-hour period. See *Note 8B.* Drinks should be provided at meal times and upon reasonable request between meals. Whenever necessary, advice shall be sought from the appropriate healthcare professional, see *Note 9A,* on medical and dietary matters. As far as practicable, meals provided shall offer a varied diet and meet any specific dietary needs or religious beliefs the detainee may have. The detainee may, at the custody officer's discretion, have meals supplied by their family or friends at their expense. See *Note 8A.*

C:8.7 Brief outdoor exercise shall be offered daily if practicable.

C:8.8 A juvenile shall not be placed in a police cell unless no other secure accommodation is available and the custody officer considers it is not practicable to supervise them if they are not placed in a cell or that a cell provides more comfortable accommodation than other secure accommodation in the station. A juvenile may not be placed in a cell with a detained adult.

Note: paragraph 1.5A extends these requirements to 17-year-old detainees.

(b) *Documentation*

C:8.9 A record must be kept of replacement clothing and meals offered.

C:8.10 If a juvenile is placed in a cell, the reason must be recorded.

Note: paragraph 1.5A extends this requirement to 17-year-old detainees.

C:8.11 The use of any restraints on a detainee whilst in a cell, the reasons for it and, if appropriate, the arrangements for enhanced supervision of the detainee whilst so restrained, shall be recorded. See paragraph 3.9.

Notes for guidance

C:8A *The provisions in paragraph 8.3 and 8.6 respectively are of particular importance in the case of a person likely to be detained for an extended period. In deciding whether to allow meals to be supplied by family or friends, the custody officer is entitled to take account of the risk of items being concealed in any food or package and the officer's duties and responsibilities under food handling legislation.*

C:8B *Meals should, so far as practicable, be offered at recognised meal times, or at other times that take account of when the detainee last had a meal.*

C:8C *The Detention and Custody Authorised Professional Practice (APP) produced by the College of Policing (see http://www.app.college.police.uk) provides more detailed guidance on matters concerning detainee healthcare and treatment and associated f orensic issues which should be read in conjunction with sections 8 and 9 of this code.*

C:9 Care and treatment of detained persons

(a) *General*

A-64   C:9.1 Nothing in this section prevents the police from calling an appropriate healthcare professional to examine a detainee for the purposes of obtaining evidence relating to any offence in which the detainee is suspected of being involved. See *Notes 9A* and *8C*.

C:9.2 If a complaint is made by, or on behalf of, a detainee about their treatment since their arrest, or it comes to notice that a detainee may have been treated improperly, a report must be made as soon as practicable to an officer of inspector rank or above not connected with the investigation. If the matter concerns a possible assault or the possibility of the unnecessary or unreasonable use of force, an appropriate healthcare professional must also be called as soon as practicable.

C:9.3 Detainees should be visited at least every hour. If no reasonably foreseeable risk was identified in a risk assessment, see paragraphs 3.6–3.10, there is no need to wake a sleeping detainee. Those suspected of being under the influence of drink or drugs or both or of having swallowed drugs, see *Note 9CA*, or whose level of consciousness causes concern must, subject to any clinical directions given by the appropriate healthcare professional, see paragraph 9.13:

- be visited and roused at least every half hour;
- have their condition assessed as in Annex H;
- and clinical treatment arranged if appropriate.

See *Notes 9B, 9C* and *9H*.

C:9.4 When arrangements are made to secure clinical attention for a detainee, the custody officer must make sure all relevant information which might assist in the treatment of the detainee's condition is made available to the responsible healthcare professional. This applies whether or not the healthcare professional asks for such information. Any officer or police staff with relevant information must inform the custody officer as soon as practicable.

(b) *Clinical treatment and attention*

A-65   C:9.5 The custody officer must make sure a detainee receives appropriate clinical attention as soon as reasonably practicable if the person:

(a) appears to be suffering from physical illness; or
(b) is injured; or
(c) appears to be suffering from a mental disorder; or
(d) appears to need clinical attention.

C:9.5A This applies even if the detainee makes no request for clinical attention and whether or not they have already received clinical attention elsewhere. If the need for attention appears urgent, *e.g.* when indicated as in Annex H, the nearest available healthcare professional or an ambulance must be called immediately.

C:9.5B The custody officer must also consider the need for clinical attention as set out in *Note for Guidance 9C* in relation to those suffering the effects of alcohol or drugs.

C:9.6 Paragraph 9.5 is not meant to prevent or delay the transfer to a hospital if necessary of a person detained under the Mental Health Act 1983, s.136. See *Note 9D*. When an assessment under that Act is to take place at a police station, see paragraph 3.16, the custody officer must consider whether an appropriate healthcare professional should be called to conduct an initial clinical check on the detainee. This applies particularly when there is likely to be any significant delay in the arrival of a suitably qualified medical practitioner.

C:9.7 If it appears to the custody officer, or they are told, that a person brought to a station under arrest may be suffering from an infectious disease or condition, the custody officer must take reasonable steps to safeguard the health of the detainee and others at the station. In deciding what action to take, advice must be sought from an appropriate healthcare professional. See *Note 9E*. The custody officer has discretion to isolate the person and their property until clinical directions have been obtained.

A-66   C:9.8 If a detainee requests a clinical examination, an appropriate healthcare professional must be called as soon as practicable to assess the detainee's clinical needs. If a safe and appropriate care plan cannot be provided, the appropriate healthcare professional's advice must be sought. The detainee may also be examined by a medical practitioner of their choice at their expense.

C:9.9 If a detainee is required to take or apply any medication in compliance with clinical directions prescribed before their detention, the custody officer must consult the appropriate healthcare professional before the use of the medication. Subject to the restrictions in paragraph 9.10, the custody officer is responsible for the safekeeping of any medication and for making sure the detainee is given the opportunity to take or apply prescribed or approved medication. Any such consultation and its outcome shall be noted in the custody record.

C:9.10 No police officer may administer or supervise the self-administration of medically prescribed controlled drugs of the types and forms listed in the Misuse of Drugs Regulations 2001, Sched. 2 or 3. A detainee may only self-administer such drugs under the personal supervision of the registered medical practitioner authorising their use or other appropriate healthcare professional. The custody officer may supervise the self-administration of, or authorise other custody staff to supervise the self-administration of, drugs listed in Schedule 4 or 5 if the officer has consulted the appropriate healthcare professional authorising their use and both are satisfied self-administration will not expose the detainee, police officers or anyone else to the risk of harm or injury.

C:9.11 When appropriate healthcare professionals administer drugs or authorise the use of other medications, supervise their self-administration or consult with the custody officer about allowing self-administration of drugs listed in Schedule 4 or 5, it must be within current medicines legislation and the scope of practice as determined by their relevant statutory regulatory body.

C:9.12 If a detainee has in their possession, or claims to need, medication relating to a heart condition, diabetes, epilepsy or a condition of comparable potential seriousness then, even though paragraph 9.5 may not apply, the advice of the appropriate healthcare professional must be obtained.

C:9.13 Whenever the appropriate healthcare professional is called in accordance with this section to examine or treat a detainee, the custody officer shall ask for their opinion about:

- any risks or problems which police need to take into account when making decisions about the detainee's continued detention;
- when to carry out an interview if applicable; and
- the need for safeguards.

C:9.14 When clinical directions are given by the appropriate healthcare professional, whether orally or in writing, and the custody officer has any doubts or is in any way uncertain about any aspect of the directions, the custody officer shall ask for clarification. It is particularly important that directions concerning the frequency of visits are clear, precise and capable of being implemented. See *Note 9F.*

(c) *Documentation*

C:9.15 A record must be made in the custody record of: **A-67**

(a) the arrangements made for an examination by an appropriate healthcare professional under paragraph 9.2 and of any complaint reported under that paragraph together with any relevant remarks by the custody officer;

(b) any arrangements made in accordance with paragraph 9.5;

(c) any request for a clinical examination under paragraph 9.8 and any arrangements made in response;

(d) the injury, ailment, condition or other reason which made it necessary to make the arrangements in (a) to (c); see *Note 9G;*

(e) any clinical directions and advice, including any further clarifications, given to police by a healthcare professional concerning the care and treatment of the detainee in connection with any of the arrangements made in (a) to (c); see *Notes 9E* and *9F;*

(f) if applicable, the responses received when attempting to rouse a person using the procedure in Annex H. See *Note 9H.*

C:9.16 If a healthcare professional does not record their clinical findings in the custody record, the record must show where they are recorded. See *Note 9G.* However, information which is necessary to custody staff to ensure the effective ongoing care and well-being of the detainee must be recorded openly in the custody record, see paragraph 3.8 and Annex G, paragraph 7.

C:9.17 Subject to the requirements of section 4, the custody record shall include:

- a record of all medication a detainee has in their possession on arrival at the police station;
- a note of any such medication they claim to need but do not have with them.

Notes for guidance

C:9A *A "healthcare professional" means a clinically qualified person working within the scope of practice as* **A-68** *determined by their relevant statutory regulatory body. Whether a healthcare professional is "appropriate" depends on the circumstances of the duties they carry out at the time.*

C:9B *Whenever possible juveniles and mentally vulnerable detainees should be visited more frequently. Note: paragraph 1.5A extends this note to 17-year-old detainees.*

C:9C *A detainee who appears drunk or behaves abnormally may be suffering from illness, the effects of drugs or may have sustained injury, particularly a head injury which is not apparent. A detainee needing or dependent on certain drugs, including alcohol, may experience harmful effects within a short time of being deprived of their supply. In these circumstances, when there is any doubt, police should always act urgently to call an appropriate healthcare professional or an ambulance. Paragraph 9.5 does not apply to minor ailments or injuries which do not need attention. However, all such ailments or injuries must be recorded in the custody record and any doubt must be resolved in favour of calling the appropriate healthcare professional.*

C:9CA *Paragraph 9.3 would apply to a person in police custody by order of a magistrates' court under the Criminal Justice Act 1988, s.152 (as amended by the Drugs Act 2005, s.8) to facilitate the recovery of evidence after being charged with drug possession or drug trafficking and suspected of having swallowed drugs. In the case of the healthcare needs of a person who has swallowed drugs, the custody officer subject to any clinical directions, should consider the necessity for rousing every half hour. This does not negate the need for regular visiting of the suspect in the cell.*

C:9D *Whenever practicable, arrangements should be made for persons detained for assessment under the Mental Health Act 1983, s.136 to be taken to a hospital. Chapter 10 of the Mental Health Act 1983 Code of Practice (as revised) provides more detailed guidance about arranging assessments under section 136 and transferring detainees from police stations to other places of safety.*

C:9E *It is important to respect a person's right to privacy and information about their health must be kept confidential and only disclosed with their consent or in accordance with clinical advice when it is necessary to protect the detainee's health or that of others who come into contact with them.*

C:9F *The custody officer should always seek to clarify directions that the detainee requires constant observation or supervision and should ask the appropriate healthcare professional to explain precisely what action needs to be taken to implement such directions.*

C:9G *Paragraphs 9.15 and 9.16 do not require any information about the cause of any injury, ailment or condition to be recorded on the custody record if it appears capable of providing evidence of an offence.*

C:9H *The purpose of recording a person's responses when attempting to rouse them using the procedure in Annex H is to enable any change in the individual's consciousness level to be noted and clinical treatment arranged if appropriate.*

C:10 Cautions

(a) *When a caution must be given*

C:10.1 A person whom there are grounds to suspect of an offence, see *Note 10A*, must be cautioned before any questions about an offence, or further questions if the answers provide the grounds for suspicion, are put to them if either the suspect's answers or silence (*i.e.* failure or refusal to answer or answer satisfactorily) may be given in evidence to a court in a prosecution. A person need not be cautioned if questions are for other necessary purposes, *e.g.*:

    (a) solely to establish their identity or ownership of any vehicle;

    (b) to obtain information in accordance with any relevant statutory requirement, see paragraph 10.9;

    (c) in furtherance of the proper and effective conduct of a search, *e.g.* to determine the need to search in the exercise of powers of stop and search or to seek co-operation while carrying out a search; or

    (d) to seek verification of a written record as in paragraph 11.13.

C:10.2 Whenever a person not under arrest is initially cautioned, or reminded they are under caution, that person must at the same time be told they are not under arrest and informed of the provisions of paragraph 3.21 which explain how they may obtain legal advice according to whether they are at a police station or elsewhere. See *Note 10C*.

C:10.3 A person who is arrested, or further arrested, must be informed at the time if practicable or, if not, as soon as it becomes practicable thereafter, that they are under arrest and of the grounds and reasons for their arrest, see paragraph 3.4, *Note 10B* and Code G, paragraphs 2.2 and 4.3.

C:10.4 As required by Code G, section 3, a person who is arrested, or further arrested, must also be cautioned unless:

    (a) it is impracticable to do so by reason of their condition or behaviour at the time;

    (b) they have already been cautioned immediately prior to arrest as in paragraph 10.1.

(b) *Terms of the cautions*

C:10.5 The caution which must be given on:

    (a) arrest; or

    (b) all other occasions before a person is charged or informed they may be prosecuted; see section 16,

should, unless the restriction on drawing adverse inferences from silence applies, see Annex C, be in the following terms:

*"You do not have to say anything. But it may harm your defence if you do not mention when questioned
something which you later rely on in court. Anything you do say may be given in evidence.".*

Where the use of the Welsh language is appropriate, a constable may provide the caution directly
in Welsh in the following terms:

*"Does dim rhaid i chi ddweud dim byd. Ond gall niweidio eich amddiffyniad os na fyddwch chi'n sôn, wrth
gael eich holi, am rywbeth y byddwch chi'n dibynnu arno nes ymlaen yn y Llys. Gall unrhyw beth yr ydych yn ei
ddweud gael ei roi fel tystiolaeth.".*

See *Note 10G.*

C:10.6 Annex C, paragraph 2, sets out the alternative terms of the caution to be used when the   **A-70**
restriction on drawing adverse inferences from silence applies.

C:10.7 Minor deviations from the words of any caution given in accordance with this code do not
constitute a breach of this code, provided the sense of the relevant caution is preserved. See *Note
10D.*

C:10.8 After any break in questioning under caution, the person being questioned must be made
aware they remain under caution. If there is any doubt the relevant caution should be given again in
full when the interview resumes. See *Note 10E.*

C:10.9 When, despite being cautioned, a person fails to co-operate or to answer particular questions which may affect their immediate treatment, the person should be informed of any relevant
consequences and that those consequences are not affected by the caution. Examples are when a
person's refusal to provide:

- their name and address when charged may make them liable to detention;
- particulars and information in accordance with a statutory requirement, *e.g.* under the
  Road Traffic Act 1988, may amount to an offence or may make the person liable to a
  further arrest.

(c) *Special warnings under the Criminal Justice and Public Order Act 1994, ss.36 and 37*

C:10.10 When a suspect interviewed at a police station or authorised place of detention after ar-   **A-71**
rest fails or refuses to answer certain questions, or to answer satisfactorily, after due warning, see *Note
10F,* a court or jury may draw such inferences as appear proper under the Criminal Justice and
Public Order Act 1994, ss.36 and 37. Such inferences may only be drawn when:

(a) the restriction on drawing adverse inferences from silence, see Annex C, does not apply;
  and
(b) the suspect is arrested by a constable and fails or refuses to account for any objects, marks
  or substances, or marks on such objects found:
  - on their person;
  - in or on their clothing or footwear;
  - otherwise in their possession; or
  - in the place they were arrested;
(c) the arrested suspect was found by a constable at a place at or about the time the offence
  for which that officer has arrested them is alleged to have been committed, and the
  suspect fails or refuses to account for their presence there.

When the restriction on drawing adverse inferences from silence applies, the suspect may still be
asked to account for any of the matters in (b) or (c) but the special warning described in paragraph
10.11 will not apply and must not be given.

C: 10.11 For an inference to be drawn when a suspect fails or refuses to answer a question about
one of these matters or to answer it satisfactorily, the suspect must first be told in ordinary language:

(a) what offence is being investigated;
(b) what fact they are being asked to account for;
(c) this fact may be due to them taking part in the commission of the offence;
(d) a court may draw a proper inference if they fail or refuse to account for this fact; and
(e) a record is being made of the interview and it may be given in evidence if they are
  brought to trial.

(d) *Juveniles and persons who are mentally disordered or otherwise mentally vulnerable*

C:10.11A The information required in paragraph 10.11 must not be given to a suspect who is a
juvenile or who is mentally disordered or otherwise mentally vulnerable unless the appropriate adult
is present.

C:10.12 If a juvenile or a person who is mentally disordered or otherwise mentally vulnerable is cautioned in the absence of the appropriate adult, the caution must be repeated in the adult's presence.

C:10.12A Paragraph 1.5A extends the requirements in paragraphs 10.11A and 10.12 to 17-year-old detainees.

(e) *Documentation*

C:10.13 A record shall be made when a caution is given under this section, either in the interviewer's pocket book or in the interview record.

Notes for guidance

C:10A *There must be some reasonable, objective grounds for the suspicion, based on known facts or information which are relevant to the likelihood the offence has been committed and the person to be questioned committed it.*

C:10B *An arrested person must be given sufficient information to enable them to understand that they have been deprived of their liberty and the reason they have been arrested,* e.g. *when a person is arrested on suspicion of committing an offence they must be informed of the suspected offence's nature, when and where it was committed. The suspect must also be informed of the reason or reasons why the arrest is considered necessary. Vague or technical language should be avoided.*

C:10C *The restriction on drawing inferences from silence, see Annex C, paragraph 1, does not apply to a person who has not been detained and who therefore cannot be prevented from seeking legal advice if they want, see paragraph 3.21.*

C:10D *If it appears a person does not understand the caution, the person giving it should explain it in their own words.*

C:10E *It may be necessary to show to the court that nothing occurred during an interview break or between interviews which influenced the suspect's recorded evidence. After a break in an interview or at the beginning of a subsequent interview, the interviewing officer should summarise the reason for the break and confirm this with the suspect.*

C:10F *The Criminal Justice and Public Order Act 1994, ss.36 and 37, apply only to suspects who have been arrested by a constable or an officer of Revenue and Customs and are given the relevant warning by the police or Revenue and Customs officer who made the arrest or who is investigating the offence. They do not apply to any interviews with suspects who have not been arrested.*

C:10G *Nothing in this code requires a caution to be given or repeated when informing a person not under arrest they may be prosecuted for an offence. However, a court will not be able to draw any inferences under the Criminal Justice and Public Order Act 1994, s.34, if the person was not cautioned.*

C:11 Interviews—general

(a) *Action*

C:11.1A An interview is the questioning of a person regarding their involvement or suspected involvement in a criminal offence or offences which, under paragraph 10.1, must be carried out under caution. Before a person is interviewed, they and, if they are represented, their solicitor must be given sufficient information to enable them to understand the nature of any such offence, and why they are suspected of committing it (see paras 3.4(a) and 10.3), in order to allow for the effective exercise of the rights of the defence. However, whilst the information must always be sufficient for the person to understand the nature of any offence (see *Note 11ZA*), this does not require the disclosure of details at a time which might prejudice the criminal investigation. The decision about what needs to be disclosed for the purpose of this requirement therefore rests with the investigating officer who has sufficient knowledge of the case to make that decision. The officer who discloses the information shall make a record of the information disclosed and when it was disclosed. This record may be made in the interview record, in the officer's pocket book or other form provided for this purpose. Procedures under the Road Traffic Act 1988, s.7, or the Transport and Works Act 1992, s.31, do not constitute interviewing for the purpose of this code.

C:11.1 Following a decision to arrest a suspect, they must not be interviewed about the relevant offence except at a police station or other authorised place of detention, unless the consequent delay would be likely to:

    (a) lead to:
- interference with, or harm to, evidence connected with an offence;
- interference with, or physical harm to, other people; or
- serious loss of, or damage to, property;

    (b) lead to alerting other people suspected of committing an offence but not yet arrested for it; or

(c) hinder the recovery of property obtained in consequence of the commission of an offence. Interviewing in any of these circumstances shall cease once the relevant risk has been averted or the necessary questions have been put in order to attempt to avert that risk.

C:11.2 Immediately prior to the commencement or re-commencement of any interview at a police station or other authorised place of detention, the interviewer should remind the suspect of their entitlement to free legal advice and that the interview can be delayed for legal advice to be obtained, unless one of the exceptions in paragraph 6.6 applies. It is the interviewer's responsibility to make sure all reminders are recorded in the interview record.

C:11.3 [*Not used.*]

C:11.4 At the beginning of an interview the interviewer, after cautioning the suspect, see section 10, shall put to them any significant statement or silence which occurred in the presence and hearing of a police officer or other police staff before the start of the interview and which have not been put to the suspect in the course of a previous interview. See *Note 11A*. The interviewer shall ask the suspect whether they confirm or deny that earlier statement or silence and if they want to add anything.

C:11.4A A significant statement is one which appears capable of being used in evidence against the suspect, in particular a direct admission of guilt. A significant silence is a failure or refusal to answer a question or answer satisfactorily when under caution, which might, allowing for the restriction on drawing adverse inferences from silence, see Annex C, give rise to an inference under the Criminal Justice and Public Order Act 1994, Pt III.

C:11.5 No interviewer may try to obtain answers or elicit a statement by the use of oppression. Except as in paragraph 10.9, no interviewer shall indicate, except to answer a direct question, what action will be taken by the police if the person being questioned answers questions, makes a statement or refuses to do either. If the person asks directly what action will be taken if they answer questions, make a statement or refuse to do either, the interviewer may inform them what action the police propose to take provided that action is itself proper and warranted.

C:11.6 The interview or further interview of a person about an offence with which that person has not been charged or for which they have not been informed they may be prosecuted, must cease when:

    (a) the officer in charge of the investigation is satisfied all the questions they consider relevant to obtaining accurate and reliable information about the offence have been put to the suspect, this includes allowing the suspect an opportunity to give an innocent explanation and asking questions to test if the explanation is accurate and reliable, *e.g.* to clear up ambiguities or clarify what the suspect said;

    (b) the officer in charge of the investigation has taken account of any other available evidence; and

    (c) the officer in charge of the investigation, or in the case of a detained suspect, the custody officer, see paragraph 16.1, reasonably believes there is sufficient evidence to provide a realistic prospect of conviction for that offence. See *Note 11B*.

This paragraph does not prevent officers in revenue cases or acting under the confiscation provisions of the Criminal Justice Act 1988 or the Drug Trafficking Act 1994 from inviting suspects to complete a formal question and answer record after the interview is concluded.

(b) *Interview records*

C:11.7 (a) An accurate record must be made of each interview, whether or not the interview takes place at a police station.   **A-74**

    (b) The record must state the place of interview, the time it begins and ends, any interview breaks and, subject to paragraph 2.6A, the names of all those present; and must be made on the forms provided for this purpose or in the interviewer's pocket book or in accordance with Codes of Practice E or F.

    (c) Any written record must be made and completed during the interview, unless this would not be practicable or would interfere with the conduct of the interview, and must constitute either a verbatim record of what has been said or, failing this, an account of the interview which adequately and accurately summarises it.

C:11.8 If a written record is not made during the interview it must be made as soon as practicable after its completion.

C:11.9 Written interview records must be timed and signed by the maker.

C:11.10 If a written record is not completed during the interview the reason must be recorded in the interview record.

C:11.11 Unless it is impracticable, the person interviewed shall be given the opportunity to read the interview record and to sign it as correct or to indicate how they consider it inaccurate. If the person interviewed cannot read or refuses to read the record or sign it, the senior interviewer present shall read it to them and ask whether they would like to sign it as correct or make their mark or to indicate how they consider it inaccurate. The interviewer shall certify on the interview record itself what has occurred. See *Note 11E.*

C:11.12 If the appropriate adult or the person's solicitor is present during the interview, they should also be given an opportunity to read and sign the interview record or any written statement taken down during the interview.

Note: paragraph 1.5A extends the requirement in this paragraph to interviews of 17-year-old suspects.

C:11.13 A written record shall be made of any comments made by a suspect, including unsolicited comments, which are outside the context of an interview but which might be relevant to the offence. Any such record must be timed and signed by the maker. When practicable the suspect shall be given the opportunity to read that record and to sign it as correct or to indicate how they consider it inaccurate. See *Note 11E.*

C:11.14 Any refusal by a person to sign an interview record when asked in accordance with this code must itself be recorded.

(c) *Juveniles and mentally disordered or otherwise mentally vulnerable people*

A-75

C:11.15 A juvenile or person who is mentally disordered or otherwise mentally vulnerable must not be interviewed regarding their involvement or suspected involvement in a criminal offence or offences, or asked to provide or sign a written statement under caution or record of interview, in the absence of the appropriate adult unless paragraphs 11.1, 11.18 to 11.20 apply. See *Note 11C.*

Note: paragraph 1.5A extends the requirement in this paragraph to 17-year-old suspects.

C:11.16 Juveniles may only be interviewed at their place of education in exceptional circumstances and only when the principal or their nominee agrees. Every effort should be made to notify the parent(s) or other person responsible for the juvenile's welfare and the appropriate adult, if this is a different person, that the police want to interview the juvenile and reasonable time should be allowed to enable the appropriate adult to be present at the interview. If awaiting the appropriate adult would cause unreasonable delay, and unless the juvenile is suspected of an offence against the educational establishment, the principal or their nominee can act as the appropriate adult for the purposes of the interview.

Note: paragraph 1.5A extends the requirement in this paragraph to 17-year-old suspects.

C:11.17 If an appropriate adult is present at an interview, they shall be informed:

- that they are not expected to act simply as an observer; and
- that the purpose of their presence is to:
  - advise the person being interviewed;
  - observe whether the interview is being conducted properly and fairly; and
  - facilitate communication with the person being interviewed.

(d) *Vulnerable suspects—urgent interviews at police stations*

C:11.18 The following interviews may take place only if an officer of superintendent rank or above considers delaying the interview will lead to the consequences in paragraph 11.1(a) to (c), and is satisfied the interview would not significantly harm the person's physical or mental state (see Annex G):

- (a) an interview of a juvenile or person who is mentally disordered or otherwise mentally vulnerable without the appropriate adult being present (note: paragraph 1.5A extends this requirement to 17-year-old detainees);
- (b) an interview of anyone other than in (a) who appears unable to:
  - appreciate the significance of questions and their answers; or
  - understand what is happening because of the effects of drink, drugs or any illness, ailment or condition;
- (c) an interview, without an interpreter being present, of a person whom the custody officer has determined requires an interpreter (see paras 3.5(c)(ii) and 3.12) which is carried out by an interviewer speaking the suspect's own language or (as the case may be) otherwise establishing effective communication which is sufficient to enable the necessary questions to be asked and answered in order to avert the consequences. See paragraphs 13.2 and 13.5.

C:11.19 These interviews may not continue once sufficient information has been obtained to avert the consequences in paragraph 11.1(a) to (c).

C:11.20 A record shall be made of the grounds for any decision to interview a person under paragraph 11.18.

Notes for guidance

C:11ZA *The requirement in paragraph 11.1A for a suspect to be given sufficient information about the offence*   **A-76**
applies prior to the interview and whether or not they are legally represented. What is sufficient will depend on the circumstances of the case, but it should normally include, as a minimum, a description of the facts relating to the suspected offence that are known to the officer, including the time and place in question. This aims to avoid suspects being confused or unclear about what they are supposed to have done and to help an innocent suspect to clear the matter up more quickly.

C:11A *Paragraph 11.4 does not prevent the interviewer from putting significant statements and silences to a suspect again at a later stage or a further interview.*

C:11B *The Criminal Procedure and Investigations Act 1996 code of practice, paragraph 3.5 states "In conducting an investigation, the investigator should pursue all reasonable lines of enquiry, whether these point towards or away from the suspect. What is reasonable will depend on the particular circumstances." Interviewers should keep this in mind when deciding what questions to ask in an interview.*

C:11C *Although juveniles or people who are mentally disordered or otherwise mentally vulnerable are often capable of providing reliable evidence, they may, without knowing or wishing to do so, be particularly prone in certain circumstances to provide information that may be unreliable, misleading or self-incriminating. Special care should always be taken when questioning such a person, and the appropriate adult should be involved if there is any doubt about a person's age, mental state or capacity. Because of the risk of unreliable evidence it is also important to obtain corroboration of any facts admitted whenever possible. Paragraph 1.5A extends this note to 17-year-old suspects.*

C:11D *Juveniles should not be arrested at their place of education unless this is unavoidable. When a juvenile is arrested at their place of education, the principal or their nominee must be informed. Paragraph 1.5A extends this note to 17-year-old suspects.*

C:11E *Significant statements described in paragraph 11.4 will always be relevant to the offence and must be recorded. When a suspect agrees to read records of interviews and other comments and sign them as correct, they should be asked to endorse the record with, e.g. "I agree that this is a correct record of what was said" and add their signature. If the suspect does not agree with the record, the interviewer should record the details of any disagreement and ask the suspect to read these details and sign them to the effect that they accurately reflect their disagreement. Any refusal to sign should be recorded.*

C:12 Interviews in police stations

(a) *Action*

C:12.1 If a police officer wants to interview or conduct enquiries which require the presence of a   **A-77**
detainee, the custody officer is responsible for deciding whether to deliver the detainee into the officer's custody. An investigating officer who is given custody of a detainee takes over responsibility for the detainee's care and safe custody for the purposes of this code until they return the detainee to the custody officer when they must report the manner in which they complied with the code whilst having custody of the detainee.

C:12.2 Except as below, in any period of 24 hours a detainee must be allowed a continuous period of at least 8 hours for rest, free from questioning, travel or any interruption in connection with the investigation concerned. This period should normally be at night or other appropriate time which takes account of when the detainee last slept or rested. If a detainee is arrested at a police station after going there voluntarily, the period of 24 hours runs from the time of their arrest and not the time of arrival at the police station. The period may not be interrupted or delayed, except:

  (a) when there are reasonable grounds for believing not delaying or interrupting the period would:

    (i) involve a risk of harm to people or serious loss of, or damage to, property;

    (ii) delay unnecessarily the person's release from custody; or

    (iii) otherwise prejudice the outcome of the investigation;

  (b) at the request of the detainee, their appropriate adult or legal representative;

  (c) when a delay or interruption is necessary in order to:

    (i) comply with the legal obligations and duties arising under section 15; or

    (ii) to take action required under section 9 or in accordance with medical advice.

If the period is interrupted in accordance with (a), a fresh period must be allowed. Interruptions under (b) and (c) do not require a fresh period to be allowed.

C:12.3 Before a detainee is interviewed the custody officer, in consultation with the officer in charge of the investigation and appropriate healthcare professionals as necessary, shall assess whether the detainee is fit enough to be interviewed. This means determining and considering the risks to the detainee's physical and mental state if the interview took place and determining what safeguards are needed to allow the interview to take place. See Annex G. The custody officer shall not allow a detainee to be interviewed if the custody officer considers it would cause significant harm to the detainee's physical or mental state. Vulnerable suspects listed at paragraph 11.18 shall be treated as always being at some risk during an interview and these persons may not be interviewed except in accordance with paragraphs 11.18 to 11.20.

C:12.4 As far as practicable interviews shall take place in interview rooms which are adequately heated, lit and ventilated.

C:12.5 A suspect whose detention without charge has been authorised under PACE because the detention is necessary for an interview to obtain evidence of the offence for which they have been arrested may choose not to answer questions but police do not require the suspect's consent or agreement to interview them for this purpose. If a suspect takes steps to prevent themselves being questioned or further questioned, *e.g.* by refusing to leave their cell to go to a suitable interview room or by trying to leave the interview room, they shall be advised their consent or agreement to interview is not required. The suspect shall be cautioned as in section 10, and informed if they fail or refuse to co-operate, the interview may take place in the cell and that their failure or refusal to co-operate may be given in evidence. The suspect shall then be invited to co-operate and go into the interview room.

C:12.6 People being questioned or making statements shall not be required to stand.

A-78

C:12.7 Before the interview commences each interviewer shall, subject to paragraph 2.6A, identify themselves and any other persons present to the interviewee.

C:12.8 Breaks from interviewing should be made at recognised meal times or at other times that take account of when an interviewee last had a meal. Short refreshment breaks shall be provided at approximately two hour intervals, subject to the interviewer's discretion to delay a break if there are reasonable grounds for believing it would:

(i) involve a:
- risk of harm to people;
- serious loss of, or damage to, property;
(ii) unnecessarily delay the detainee's release; or
(iii) otherwise prejudice the outcome of the investigation.

See *Note 12B*.

C:12.9 If during the interview a complaint is made by or on behalf of the interviewee concerning the provisions of any of the codes, or it comes to the interviewer's notice that the interviewee may have been treated improperly, the interviewer should:

(i) record the matter in the interview record; and
(ii) inform the custody officer, who is then responsible for dealing with it as in section 9.

(b) *Documentation*

A-79

C:12.10 A record must be made of the:
- time a detainee is not in the custody of the custody officer, and why;
- reason for any refusal to deliver the detainee out of that custody.

C:12.11 A record shall be made of:

(a) the reasons it was not practicable to use an interview room; and
(b) any action taken as in paragraph 12.5.

The record shall be made on the custody record or in the interview record for action taken whilst an interview record is being kept, with a brief reference to this effect in the custody record.

C:12.12 Any decision to delay a break in an interview must be recorded, with reasons, in the interview record.

C:12.13 All written statements made at police stations under caution shall be written on forms provided for the purpose.

C:12.14 All written statements made under caution shall be taken in accordance with Annex D. Before a person makes a written statement under caution at a police station, they shall be reminded about the right to legal advice. See *Note 12A*.

Notes for guidance

A-80

C:12A *It is not normally necessary to ask for a written statement if the interview was recorded in writing and the record signed in accordance with paragraph 11.11 or audibly or visually recorded in accordance with Code E or F. Statements under caution should normally be taken in these circumstances only at the person's express wish. A person may however be asked if they want to make such a statement.*

C:12B *Meal breaks should normally last at least 45 minutes and shorter breaks after two hours should last at least 15 minutes. If the interviewer delays a break in accordance with paragraph 12.8 and prolongs the interview, a longer break should be provided. If there is a short interview and another short interview is contemplated, the length of the break may be reduced if there are reasonable grounds to believe this is necessary to avoid any of the consequences in paragraph 12.8(i) to (iii).*

C:13 Interpreters

(a) *General*

C:13.1 Chief officers are responsible for making arrangements to provide appropriately qualified **A-81** independent persons to act as interpreters and to provide translations of essential documents for:

- detained suspects who, in accordance with paragraph 3.5(c)(ii), the custody officer has determined require an interpreter, and
- suspects who are not under arrest but are cautioned as in section 10 who, in accordance with paragraph 3.21, the interviewer has determined require an interpreter. In these cases, the responsibilities of the custody officer are, if appropriate, assigned to the interviewer. An interviewer who has any doubts about whether an interpreter is required or about how the provisions of this section should be applied to a suspect who is not under arrest should seek advice from an officer of the rank of sergeant or above.

If the suspect has a hearing or speech impediment, references to "interpreter" and "interpretation" in this code include appropriate assistance necessary to establish effective communication with that person. See paragraph 13.1C below if the person is in Wales.

C:13.1A The arrangements must comply with the minimum requirements set out in Directive 2010/64/EU of the European Parliament and of the Council of 20 October 2010 on the right to interpretation and translation in criminal proceedings (see *Note 13A*). The provisions of this code implement the requirements for those to whom this code applies. These requirements include the following:

- that the arrangements made and the quality of interpretation and translation provided shall be sufficient to "*safeguard the fairness of the proceedings, in particular by ensuring that suspected or accused persons have knowledge of the cases against them and are able to exercise their right of defence*"; this term which is used by the directive means that the suspect must be able to understand their position and be able to communicate effectively with police officers, interviewers, solicitors and appropriate adults as provided for by this and any other code in the same way as a suspect who can speak and understand English and who does not have a hearing or speech impediment and who would therefore not require an interpreter;
- the provision of a written translation of all documents considered essential for the person to exercise their right of defence and to "*safeguard the fairness of the proceedings*" as described above; for the purposes of this code, this includes any decision to authorise a person to be detained and details of any offence(s) with which the person has been charged or for which they have been told they may be prosecuted, see Annex M;
- procedures to help determine:
  - whether a suspect can speak and understand English and needs the assistance of an interpreter, see paragraph 13.1 and *Notes 13B* and *13C*; and
  - whether another interpreter should be called or another translation should be provided when a suspect complains about the quality of either or both, see paragraphs 13.10A and 13.10C.

C:13.1B All reasonable attempts should be made to make the suspect understand that interpretation and translation will be provided at public expense.

C:13.1C With regard to persons in Wales, nothing in this or any other code affects the application of the Welsh language schemes produced by police and crime commissioners in Wales in accordance with the Welsh Language Act 1993: see paragraphs 3.12 and 13.1.

(b) *Interviewing suspects—foreign languages*

C:13.2 Unless paragraphs 11.1 or 11.18(c) apply, a suspect who for the purposes of this code requires an interpreter because they do not appear to speak or understand English (see paras 3.5(c)(ii) and 3.12) must not be interviewed in the absence of a person capable of interpreting.

C:13.2A An interpreter should also be called if a juvenile is interviewed and their parent or guardian, present as the appropriate adult, does not appear to speak or understand English, unless the interview is urgent and paragraphs 11.1 or 11.18(c) apply.

Note: paragraph 1.5A extends the requirement in this paragraph to interviews of 17-year-old suspects.

C:13.3 When a written record of the interview is made (see para. 11.7), the interviewer shall make sure the interpreter makes a note of the interview at the time in the person's language for use in the event of the interpreter being called to give evidence, and certifies its accuracy. The interviewer should allow sufficient time for the interpreter to note each question and answer after each is put, given and interpreted. The person should be allowed to read the record or have it read to them and sign it as correct or indicate the respects in which they consider it inaccurate. If an audio or visual record of the interview is made, the arrangements in Code E or F shall apply.

C:13.4 In the case of a person making a statement under caution to a police officer or other police staff other than in English:

(a) the interpreter shall record the statement in the language it is made;

(b) the person shall be invited to sign it;

(c) an official English translation shall be made in due course.

(c) *Interviewing suspects who have a hearing or speech impediment*

A-82

C:13.5 Unless paragraphs 11.1 or 11.18(c) (urgent interviews) apply, a suspect who for the purposes of this code requires an interpreter or other appropriate assistance to enable effective communication with them because they appear to have a hearing or speech impediment (see paras 3.5(c)(ii) and 3.12) must not be interviewed in the absence of an independent person capable of interpreting or without that assistance.

C:13.6 An interpreter should also be called if a juvenile is interviewed and their parent or guardian, present as the appropriate adult, appears to have a hearing or speech impediment, unless the interview is urgent and paragraphs 11.1 or 11.18(c) apply.

Note: paragraph 1.5A extends the requirement in this paragraph to interviews of 17-year-old suspects.

C:13.7 The interviewer shall make sure the interpreter is allowed to read the interview record and certify its accuracy in the event of the interpreter being called to give evidence. If the interview is audibly recorded or visually recorded, the arrangements in Code E or F apply.

(d) *Additional rules for detained persons*

C:13.8 [*Not used.*]

C:13.9 If paragraph 6.1 applies and the detainee cannot communicate with the solicitor because of language, hearing or speech difficulties, an interpreter must be called. A police officer or any other police staff may not be used for this purpose.

C:13.10 After the custody officer has determined that a detainee requires an interpreter (see para. 3.5(c)(ii)) and following the initial action in paragraphs 3.1 to 3.5, arrangements must also be made for an interpreter to:

• explain the grounds and reasons for any authorisation for their continued detention, before or after charge and any information about the authorisation given to them by the authorising officer and which is recorded in the custody record (see paras 15.3, 15.4 and 15.16(a) and (b));

• be present at the magistrates' court for the hearing of an application for a warrant of further detention or any extension or further extension of such warrant to explain any grounds and reasons for the application and any information about the authorisation of their further detention given to them by the court (see PACE, ss.43 and 44 and paras 15.2 and 15.16(c)), and

• explain any offence with which the detainee is charged or for which they are informed they may be prosecuted and any other information about the offence given to them by or on behalf of the custody officer (see paras 16.1 and 16.3).

C:13.10A If a detainee complains that they are not satisfied with the quality of interpretation, the custody officer or (as the case may be) the interviewer, is responsible for deciding whether a different interpreter should be called in accordance with the procedures set out in the arrangements made by the chief officer (see para. 13.1A).

(e) *Translations of essential documents*

C:13.10B Written translations, oral translations and oral summaries of essential documents in a language the detainee understands shall be provided in accordance with Annex M (translations of documents and records).

C:13.10C If a detainee complains that they are not satisfied with the quality of the translation, the custody officer or (as the case may be) the interviewer, is responsible for deciding whether a further translation should be provided in accordance with the procedures set out in the arrangements made by the chief officer (see para. 13.1A).

(f) *Decisions not to provide interpretation and translation.*

C:13.10D If a suspect challenges a decision:

- made by the custody officer or (as the case may be) by the interviewer, in accordance with this code (see paras 3.5(c)(ii) and 3.21) that they do not require an interpreter; or
- made in accordance with paragraphs 13.10A, 13.10B or 13.10C not to provide a different interpreter or another translation or not to translate a requested document,

the matter shall be reported to an inspector to deal with as a complaint for the purposes of paragraph 9.2 or paragraph 12.9 if the challenge is made during an interview.

(g) *Documentation*

C:13.11 The following must be recorded in the custody record or, as applicable, the interview record:

- (a) action taken to call an interpreter;
- (b) action taken when a detainee is not satisfied about the standard of interpretation or translation provided (see paras 13.10A and 13.10C);
- (c) when an urgent interview is carried out in accordance with paragraph 13.2 or 13.5 in the absence of an interpreter;
- (d) when a detainee has been assisted by an interpreter for the purpose of providing or being given information or being interviewed;
- (e) action taken in accordance with Annex M when:
  - a written translation of an essential document is provided;
  - an oral translation or oral summary of an essential document is provided instead of a written translation and the authorising officer's reason(s) why this would not prejudice the fairness of the proceedings (see Annex M, para. 3);
  - a suspect waives their right to a translation of an essential document (see Annex M, para. 4);
  - when representations that a document which is not included in the table is essential and that a translation should be provided are refused and the reason for the refusal (see Annex M, para. 8).

Notes for guidance

C:13A *Chief officers have discretion when determining the individuals or organisations they use to provide interpretation and translation services for their forces provided that these are compatible with the requirements of the directive. One example which chief officers may wish to consider is the Ministry of Justice framework agreement for interpretation and translation services.*

C:13B *A procedure for determining whether a person needs an interpreter might involve a telephone interpreter service or using cue cards or similar visual aids which enable the detainee to indicate their ability to speak and understand English and their preferred language. This could be confirmed through an interpreter who could also assess the extent to which the person can speak and understand English.*

C:13C *There should also be a procedure for determining whether a suspect who requires an interpreter requires assistance in accordance with paragraph 3.20 to help them check and, if applicable, sign any documentation.*

C:14 Questioning—special restrictions

C:14.1 If a person is arrested by one police force on behalf of another and the lawful period of **A-83** detention in respect of that offence has not yet commenced in accordance with PACE, s.41, no questions may be put to them about the offence while they are in transit between the forces except to clarify any voluntary statement they make.

C:14.2 If a person is in police detention at a hospital, they may not be questioned without the agreement of a responsible doctor. See *Note 14A.*

Note for guidance

C:14A *If questioning takes place at a hospital under paragraph 14.2, or on the way to or from a hospital, the* **A-84** *period of questioning concerned counts towards the total period of detention permitted.*

C:15 Reviews and extensions of detention

(a) *Persons detained under PACE*

A-85   C:15.0 The requirement in paragraph 3.4(b) that documents and materials essential to challenging the lawfulness of the detainee's arrest and detention must be made available to the detainee or their solicitor, applies for the purposes of this section as follows:

> (a) the officer reviewing the need for detention without charge (PACE, s.40), or (as the case may be) the officer considering the need to extend detention without charge from 24 to 36 hours (PACE, s.42), is responsible, in consultation with the investigating officer, for deciding which documents and materials are essential and must be made available;
>
> (b) when paragraph 15.7A applies (application for a warrant of further detention or extension of such a warrant), the officer making the application is responsible for deciding which documents and materials are essential and must be made available before the hearing. See *Note 3ZA*.

C:15.1 The review officer is responsible under PACE, s.40, for periodically determining if a person's detention, before or after charge, continues to be necessary. This requirement continues throughout the detention period and, except as in paragraph 15.10, the review officer must be present at the police station holding the detainee. See *Notes 15A* and *15B*.

C:15.2 Under PACE, s.42, an officer of superintendent rank or above who is responsible for the station holding the detainee may give authority any time after the second review to extend the maximum period the person may be detained without charge by up to 12 hours. Further detention without charge may be authorised only by a magistrates' court in accordance with PACE, ss.43 and 44. See *Notes 15C, 15D* and *15E*.

C:15.2A An authorisation under section 42(1) of PACE extends the maximum period of detention permitted before charge for indictable offences from 24 hours to 36 hours. Detaining a juvenile or mentally vulnerable person for longer than 24 hours will be dependent on the circumstances of the case and with regard to the person's:

> (a) special vulnerability;
>
> (b) the legal obligation to provide an opportunity for representations to be made prior to a decision about extending detention;
>
> (c) the need to consult and consider the views of any appropriate adult; and
>
> (d) any alternatives to police custody.

Note: paragraph 1.5A extends sub-paragraph (c) to 17-year-old detainees.

C:15.3 Before deciding whether to authorise continued detention the officer responsible under paragraph 15.1 or 15.2 shall give an opportunity to make representations about the detention to:

> (a) the detainee, unless in the case of a review as in paragraph 15.1, the detainee is asleep;
>
> (b) the detainee's solicitor if available at the time; and
>
> (c) the appropriate adult if available at the time.

Note: paragraph 1.5A extends the requirement in sub-paragraph (c) to 17-year-old detainees. See *Note 15CA*.

C:15.3A Other people having an interest in the detainee's welfare may also make representations at the authorising officer's discretion.

C:15.3B Subject to paragraph 15.10, the representations may be made orally in person or by telephone or in writing. The authorising officer may, however, refuse to hear oral representations from the detainee if the officer considers them unfit to make representations because of their condition or behaviour. See *Note 15C*.

C:15.3C The decision on whether the review takes place in person or by telephone or by video conferencing (see *Note 15G*) is a matter for the review officer. In determining the form the review may take, the review officer must always take full account of the needs of the person in custody. The benefits of carrying out a review in person should always be considered, based on the individual circumstances of each case with specific additional consideration if the person is:

> (a) a juvenile (and the age of the juvenile); or (note: para. 1.5A extends this sub-paragraph to 17-year-old detainees)
>
> (b) suspected of being mentally vulnerable; or
>
> (c) in need of medical attention for other than routine minor ailments; or
>
> (d) subject to presentational or community issues around their detention.

A-86   C:15.4 Before conducting a review or determining whether to extend the maximum period of detention without charge, the officer responsible must make sure the detainee is reminded of their entitlement to free legal advice, see paragraph 6.5, unless in the case of a review the person is asleep.

C:15.5 If, after considering any representations, the review officer under paragraph 15.1 decides to keep the detainee in detention or the superintendent under paragraph 15.2 extends the maximum period for which they may be detained without charge, then any comment made by the detainee shall be recorded. If applicable, the officer shall be informed of the comment as soon as practicable. See also paragraphs 11.4 and 11.13.

C:15.6 No officer shall put specific questions to the detainee:
- regarding their involvement in any offence; or
- in respect of any comments they may make:
  - when given the opportunity to make representations; or
  - in response to a decision to keep them in detention or extend the maximum period of detention.

Such an exchange could constitute an interview as in paragraph 11.1A and would be subject to the associated safeguards in section 11 and, in respect of a person who has been charged, paragraph 16.5. See also paragraph 11.13.

C:15.7 A detainee who is asleep at a review, see paragraph 15.1, and whose continued detention is authorised must be informed about the decision and reason as soon as practicable after waking.

C:15.7A When an application is made to a magistrates' court under PACE, s.43, for a warrant of further detention to extend detention without charge of a person arrested for an indictable offence, or under section 44, to extend or further extend that warrant, the detainee:
- (a) must be brought to court for the hearing of the application;
- (b) is entitled to be legally represented if they wish, in which case, Annex B cannot apply;
- (c) must be given a copy of the information which supports the application and states:
  - (i) the nature of the offence for which the person to whom the application relates has been arrested;
  - (ii) the general nature of the evidence on which the person was arrested;
  - (iii) what inquiries about the offence have been made and what further inquiries are proposed;
  - (iv) the reasons for believing continued detention is necessary for the purposes of the further inquiries.

Note: a warrant of further detention can only be issued or extended if the court has reasonable grounds for believing that the person's further detention is necessary for the purpose of obtaining evidence of an indictable offence for which the person has been arrested and that the investigation is being conducted diligently and expeditiously.

See paragraph 15.0(b).

C:15.8 [*Not used.*]

(b) *Review of detention by telephone and video conferencing facilities*

C:15.9 PACE, s.40A, provides that the officer responsible under section 40 for reviewing the deten- **A-87** tion of a person who has not been charged, need not attend the police station holding the detainee and may carry out the review by telephone.

C:15.9A PACE, s.45A(2), provides that the officer responsible under section 40 for reviewing the detention of a person who has not been charged, need not attend the police station holding the detainee and may carry out the review by video conferencing facilities. (See *Note 15G.*)

C:15.9B A telephone review is not permitted where facilities for review by video conferencing exist and it is practicable to use them.

C:15.9C The review officer can decide at any stage that a telephone review or review by video conferencing should be terminated and that the review will be conducted in person. The reasons for doing so should be noted in the custody record. See *Note 15F.*

C:15.10 When a review is carried out by telephone or by video conferencing facilities, an officer at the station holding the detainee shall be required by the review officer to fulfil that officer's obligations under PACE, s.40, and this code by:
- (a) making any record connected with the review in the detainee's custody record;
- (b) if applicable, making the record in (a) in the presence of the detainee; and
- (c) for a review by telephone, giving the detainee information about the review.

C:15.11 When a review is carried out by telephone or by video conferencing facilities, the requirement in paragraph 15.3 will be satisfied:
- (a) if facilities exist for the immediate transmission of written representations to the review officer, *e.g.* fax or email message, by allowing those who are given the opportunity to make representations, to make their representations:
  - (i) orally by telephone or (as the case may be) by means of the video conferencing facilities; or

(ii) in writing using the facilities for the immediate transmission of written representations; and

(b) in all other cases, by allowing those who are given the opportunity to make representations, to make their representations orally by telephone or by means of the video conferencing facilities.

(c) *Documentation*

C:15.12 It is the officer's responsibility to make sure all reminders given under paragraph 15.4 are noted in the custody record.

C:15.13 The grounds for, and extent of, any delay in conducting a review shall be recorded.

C:15.14 When a review is carried out by telephone or video conferencing facilities, a record shall be made of:

(a) the reason the review officer did not attend the station holding the detainee;

(b) the place the review officer was;

(c) the method representations, oral or written, were made to the review officer, see paragraph 15.11.

C:15.15 Any written representations shall be retained.

C:15.16 A record shall be made as soon as practicable of:

(a) the outcome of each review of detention before or after charge, and if paragraph 15.7 applies, of when the person was informed and by whom;

(b) the outcome of any determination under PACE, s.42, by a superintendent whether to extend the maximum period of detention without charge beyond 24 hours from the relevant time; if an authorisation is given, the record shall state the number of hours and minutes by which the detention period is extended or further extended;

(c) the outcome of each application under PACE, s.43, for a warrant of further detention or under section 44, for an extension or further extension of that warrant; if a warrant for further detention is granted under section 43 or extended or further extended under 44, the record shall state the detention period authorised by the warrant and the date and time it was granted or (as the case may be) the period by which the warrant is extended or further extended.

Note: any period during which a person is released on bail does not count towards the maximum period of detention without charge allowed under PACE, ss.41 to 44.

Notes for guidance

A-88

C:15A *Review officer for the purposes of:*

- *PACE, ss.40, 40A and 45A means, in the case of a person arrested but not charged, an officer of at least inspector rank not directly involved in the investigation and, if a person has been arrested and charged, the custody officer.*

C:15B *The detention of persons in police custody not subject to the statutory review requirement in paragraph 15.1 should still be reviewed periodically as a matter of good practice. Such reviews can be carried out by an officer of the rank of sergeant or above. The purpose of such reviews is to check the particular power under which a detainee is held continues to apply, any associated conditions are complied with and to make sure appropriate action is taken to deal with any changes. This includes the detainee's prompt release when the power no longer applies, or their transfer if the power requires the detainee be taken elsewhere as soon as the necessary arrangements are made. Examples include persons:*

(a) *arrested on warrant because they failed to answer bail to appear at court;*

(b) *arrested under the Bail Act 1976, s.7(3), for breaching a condition of bail granted after charge;*

(c) *in police custody for specific purposes and periods under the Crime (Sentences) Act 1997, Sched. 1;*

(d) *convicted, or remand prisoners, held in police stations on behalf of the Prison Service under the Imprisonment (Temporary Provisions) Act 1980, s.6;*

(e) *being detained to prevent them causing a breach of the peace;*

(f) *detained at police stations on behalf of Immigration Enforcement (formerly the UK Immigration Service);*

(g) *detained by order of a magistrates' court under the Criminal Justice Act 1988, s.152 (as amended by the Drugs Act 2005, s.8) to facilitate the recovery of evidence after being charged with drug possession or drug trafficking and suspected of having swallowed drugs.*

The detention of persons remanded into police detention by order of a court under the Magistrates' Courts Act 1980, s.128, is subject to a statutory requirement to review that detention. This is to make sure the detainee is taken back to court no later than the end of the period authorised by the court or when the need for their detention by police ceases, whichever is the sooner.

C:15C *In the case of a review of detention, but not an extension, the detainee need not be woken for the review. However, if the detainee is likely to be asleep, e.g. during a period of rest allowed as in paragraph 12.2, at the latest time a review or authorisation to extend detention may take place, the officer should, if the legal obligations and time constraints permit, bring forward the procedure to allow the detainee to make representations. A detainee not asleep during the review must be present when the grounds for their continued detention are recorded and must at the same time be informed of those grounds unless the review officer considers the person is incapable of understanding what is said, violent or likely to become violent or in urgent need of medical attention.*

C:15CA *In paragraph 15.3(b) and (c), "available" includes being contactable in time to enable them to make representations remotely by telephone or other electronic means or in person by attending the station. Reasonable efforts should therefore be made to give the solicitor and appropriate adult sufficient notice of the time the decision is expected to be made so that they can make themselves available.*

C:15D *An application to a magistrates' court under PACE, s.43 or 44, for a warrant of further detention or its extension should be made between 10am and 9pm, and if possible during normal court hours. It will not usually be practicable to arrange for a court to sit specially outside the hours of 10am to 9pm. If it appears a special sitting may be needed outside normal court hours but between 10am and 9pm, the clerk to the justices should be given notice and informed of this possibility, while the court is sitting if possible.*

C:15E *In paragraph 15.2, the officer responsible for the station holding the detainee includes a superintendent or above who, in accordance with their force operational policy or police regulations, is given that responsibility on a temporary basis whilst the appointed long-term holder is off duty or otherwise unavailable.*

C:15F *The provisions of PACE, s.40A, allowing telephone reviews do not apply to reviews of detention after charge by the custody officer. When video conferencing is not required, they allow the use of a telephone to carry out a review of detention before charge. The procedure under PACE, s.42, must be done in person.*

C:15G *Video conferencing facilities means any facilities (whether a live television link or other facilities) by means of which the review can be carried out with the review officer, the detainee concerned and the detainee's solicitor all being able to both see and to hear each other. The use of video conferencing facilities for decisions about detention under section 45A of PACE is subject to regulations made by the Secretary of State being in force.*

C:16 Charging detained persons

(a) *Action*

C:16.1 When the officer in charge of the investigation reasonably believes there is sufficient **A-89** evidence to provide a realistic prospect of conviction for the offence (see paragraph 11.6), they shall without delay, and subject to the following qualification, inform the custody officer who will be responsible for considering whether the detainee should be charged. See *Notes 11B* and *16A*. When a person is detained in respect of more than one offence it is permissible to delay informing the custody officer until the above conditions are satisfied in respect of all the offences, but see paragraph 11.6. If the detainee is a juvenile, mentally disordered or otherwise mentally vulnerable, any resulting action shall be taken in the presence of the appropriate adult if they are present at the time.

Note: paragraph 1.5A requires someone to fulfil the role of the appropriate adult to be present when the action applies to a 17-year-old detainee.

See *Notes 16B* and *16C*.

C:16.1A Where guidance issued by the Director of Public Prosecutions under PACE, s.37A, is in force the custody officer must comply with that guidance in deciding how to act in dealing with the detainee. See *Notes 16AA* and *16AB*.

C:16.1B Where in compliance with the DPP's guidance the custody officer decides that the case should be immediately referred to the CPS to make the charging decision, consultation should take place with a crown prosecutor as soon as is reasonably practicable. Where the crown prosecutor is unable to make the charging decision on the information available at that time, the detainee may be released without charge and on bail (with conditions if necessary) under section 37(7)(a). In such circumstances, the detainee should be informed that they are being released to enable the Director of Public Prosecutions to make a decision under section 37B.

C:16.2 When a detainee is charged with or informed they may be prosecuted for an offence, see *Note 16B*, they shall, unless the restriction on drawing adverse inferences from silence applies, see Annex C, be cautioned as follows:

"You do not have to say anything. But it may harm your defence if you do not mention now something which you later rely on in court. Anything you do say may be given in evidence.".

Where the use of the Welsh language is appropriate, a constable may provide the caution directly in Welsh in the following terms:

"Does dim rhaid i chi ddweud dim byd. Ond gall niweidio eich amddiffyniad os na fyddwch chi'n sôn, yn awr, am rywbeth y byddwch chi'n dibynnu arno nes ymlaen yn y llys. Gall unrhyw beth yr ydych yn ei ddweud gael ei

roi fel tystiolaeth.".

Annex C, paragraph 2, sets out the alternative terms of the caution to be used when the restriction on drawing adverse inferences from silence applies.

C:16.3 When a detainee is charged they shall be given a written notice showing particulars of the offence and, subject to paragraph 2.6A, the officer's name and the case reference number. As far as possible the particulars of the charge shall be stated in simple terms, but they shall also show the precise offence in law with which the detainee is charged. The notice shall begin:

"You are charged with the offence(s) shown below." Followed by the caution.

If the detainee is a juvenile, mentally disordered or otherwise mentally vulnerable, a copy of the notice should also be given to the appropriate adult.

Note: paragraph 1.5A provides that a copy of the notice should be given to the person called to fulfil the role of the appropriate adult when a 17-year-old detainee is charged.

C:16.4 If, after a detainee has been charged with or informed they may be prosecuted for an offence, an officer wants to tell them about any written statement or interview with another person relating to such an offence, the detainee shall either be handed a true copy of the written statement or the content of the interview record brought to their attention. Nothing shall be done to invite any reply or comment except to:

(a) caution the detainee, *"You do not have to say anything, but anything you do say may be given in evidence.";*

where the use of the Welsh Language is appropriate, caution the detainee in the following terms:

"Does dim rhaid i chi ddweud dim byd, ond gall unrhyw beth yr ydych yn ei ddweud gael ei roi fel tystiolaeth."; and

(b) remind the detainee about their right to legal advice.

C:16.4A If the detainee:

- cannot read, the document may be read to them;
- is a juvenile, mentally disordered or otherwise mentally vulnerable, the appropriate adult shall also be given a copy, or the interview record shall be brought to their attention.

Note: paragraph 1.5A requires a copy of the record to be given to, or brought to the attention of, the person called to fulfil the role of the appropriate adult for a 17-year-old detainee.

C:16.5 A detainee may not be interviewed about an offence after they have been charged with, or informed they may be prosecuted for it, unless the interview is necessary:

- to prevent or minimise harm or loss to some other person, or the public;
- to clear up an ambiguity in a previous answer or statement;
- in the interests of justice for the detainee to have put to them, and have an opportunity to comment on, information concerning the offence which has come to light since they were charged or informed they might be prosecuted.

Before any such interview, the interviewer shall:

(a) caution the detainee, *"You do not have to say anything, but anything you do say may be given in evidence.";*

where the use of the Welsh language is appropriate, the interviewer shall caution the detainee: *"Does dim rhaid i chi ddweud dim byd, ond gall unrhyw beth yr ydych yn ei ddweud gael ei roi fel tystiolaeth.";*

(b) remind the detainee about their right to legal advice.

See *Note 16B.*

C:16.6 The provisions of paragraphs 16.2 to 16.5 must be complied with in the appropriate adult's presence if they are already at the police station. If they are not at the police station then these provisions must be complied with again in their presence when they arrive unless the detainee has been released. See *Note 16C.*

Note: Paragraph 1.5A extends the requirement in this paragraph to 17-year-old detainees.

C:16.7 When a juvenile is charged with an offence and the custody officer authorises their continued detention after charge, the custody officer must make arrangements for the juvenile to be taken into the care of a local authority to be detained pending appearance in court unless the custody officer certifies in accordance with PACE, s.38(6), that:

(a) for any juvenile, it is impracticable to do so; or

(b) in the case of a juvenile of at least 12 years old, no secure accommodation is available and other accommodation would not be adequate to protect the public from serious harm from that juvenile. See *Note 16D.*

Note: the 16-year-old maximum age limit for transfer to local authority accommodation, the power of the local authority to detain the person transferred and take over responsibility for that person from the police are determined by section 38 of PACE. For this reason, this paragraph and *Note 16D* do <u>not</u> apply to detainees who appear to have attained the age of 17 (see para. 1.5A(a)).

C:16.7A The requirement in paragraph 3.4(b) that documents and materials essential to effectively challenging the lawfulness of the detainee's arrest and detention must be made available to the detainee and, if they are represented, their solicitor, applies for the purposes of this section and a person's detention after charge. This means that the custody officer making the bail decision (PACE, s.38) or reviewing the need for detention after charge (PACE, s.40), is responsible for determining what, if any, documents or materials are essential and must be made available to the detainee or their solicitor. See *Note 3ZA.*

(b) *Documentation*

C:16.8 A record shall be made of anything a detainee says when charged.

C:16.9 Any questions put in an interview after charge and answers given relating to the offence shall be recorded in full during the interview on forms for that purpose and the record signed by the detainee or, if they refuse, by the interviewer and any third parties present. If the questions are audibly recorded or visually recorded the arrangements in Code E or F apply.

C:16.10 If arrangements for a juvenile's transfer into local authority care as in paragraph 16.7 are not made, the custody officer must record the reasons in a certificate which must be produced before the court with the juvenile. See *Note 16D.*

Notes for guidance

C:16A *The custody officer must take into account alternatives to prosecution under the Crime and Disorder Act* **A-91**
1998 applicable to persons under 18, and in national guidance on the cautioning of offenders applicable to persons aged 18 and over.

C:16AA *When a person is arrested under the provisions of the Criminal Justice Act 2003 which allow a person to be re-tried after being acquitted of a serious offence which is a qualifying offence specified in Schedule 5 to that Act and not precluded from further prosecution by virtue of section 75(3) of that Act the detention provisions of PACE are modified and make an officer of the rank of superintendent or above who has not been directly involved in the investigation responsible for determining whether the evidence is sufficient to charge.*

C:16AB *Where guidance issued by the Director of Public Prosecutions under section 37B is in force, a custody officer who determines in accordance with that guidance that there is sufficient evidence to charge the detainee, may detain that person for no longer than is reasonably necessary to decide how that person is to be dealt with under PACE, s.37(7)(a) to (d), including, where appropriate, consultation with the duty prosecutor. The period is subject to the maximum period of detention before charge determined by PACE, ss.41 to 44. Where in accordance with the guidance the case is referred to the CPS for decision, the custody officer should ensure that an officer involved in the investigation sends to the CPS such information as is specified in the guidance.*

C:16B *The giving of a warning or the service of the notice of intended prosecution required by the Road Traffic Offenders Act 1988, s.1 does not amount to informing a detainee they may be prosecuted for an offence and so does not preclude further questioning in relation to that offence.*

C:16C *There is no power under PACE to detain a person and delay action under paragraphs 16.2 to 16.5 solely to await the arrival of the appropriate adult. Reasonable efforts should therefore be made to give the appropriate adult sufficient notice of the time the decision (charge etc.) is to be implemented so that they can be present. If the appropriate adult is not, or cannot be, present at that time, the detainee should be released on bail to return for the decision to be implemented when the adult is present, unless the custody officer determines that the absence of the appropriate adult makes the detainee unsuitable for bail for this purpose. After charge, bail cannot be refused, or release on bail delayed, simply because an appropriate adult is not available, unless the absence of that adult provides the custody officer with the necessary grounds to authorise detention after charge under PACE, s.38.*

C:16D *Except as in paragraph 16.7, neither a juvenile's behaviour nor the nature of the offence provides grounds for the custody officer to decide it is impracticable to arrange the juvenile's transfer to local authority care. Impracticability concerns the transport and travel requirements and the lack of secure accommodation which is provided for the purposes of restricting liberty does not make it impracticable to transfer the juvenile. The availability of secure accommodation is only a factor in relation to a juvenile aged 12 or over when other local authority accommodation would not be adequate to protect the public from serious harm from them. The obligation to transfer a juvenile to local authority accommodation applies as much to a juvenile charged during the daytime as to a juvenile to be held overnight, subject to a requirement to bring the juvenile before a court under PACE, s.46.*
This note does not apply to 17-year-old detainees (see para. 16.7).

C:17 Testing persons for the presence of specified Class A drugs

(a) Action

C:17.1 This section of Code C applies only in selected police stations in police areas where the provisions for drug testing under section 63B of PACE (as amended by section 5 of the Criminal Justice Act 2003 and section 7 of the Drugs Act 2005) are in force and in respect of which the Secretary of State has given a notification to the relevant chief officer of police that arrangements for the taking of samples have been made. Such a notification will cover either a police area as a whole or particular stations within a police area. The notification indicates whether the testing applies to those arrested or charged or under the age of 18 as the case may be and testing can only take place in respect of the persons so indicated in the notification. Testing cannot be carried out unless the relevant notification has been given and has not been withdrawn. See *Note 17F*.

C:17.2 A sample of urine or a non-intimate sample may be taken from a person in police detention for the purpose of ascertaining whether they have any specified Class A drug in their body only where they have been brought before the custody officer and:

    (a) either the arrest condition, see paragraph 17.3, or the charge condition, see paragraph 17.4, is met;

    (b) the age condition, see paragraph 17.5, is met;

    (c) the notification condition is met in relation to the arrest condition, the charge condition, or the age condition, as the case may be (testing on charge and/or arrest must be specifically provided for in the notification for the power to apply; in addition, the fact that testing of under 18s is authorised must be expressly provided for in the notification before the power to test such persons applies); see paragraph 17.1; and

    (d) a police officer has requested the person concerned to give the sample (the request condition).

C:17.3 The arrest condition is met where the detainee:

    (a) has been arrested for a trigger offence, see *Note 17E*, but not charged with that offence; or

    (b) has been arrested for any other offence but not charged with that offence and a police officer of inspector rank or above, who has reasonable grounds for suspecting that their misuse of any specified Class A drug caused or contributed to the offence, has authorised the sample to be taken.

C:17.4 The charge condition is met where the detainee:

    (a) has been charged with a trigger offence; or

    (b) has been charged with any other offence and a police officer of inspector rank or above, who has reasonable grounds for suspecting that the detainee's misuse of any specified Class A drug caused or contributed to the offence, has authorised the sample to be taken.

C:17.5 The age condition is met where:

    (a) in the case of a detainee who has been arrested but not charged as in paragraph 17.3, they are aged 18 or over;

    (b) in the case of a detainee who has been charged as in paragraph 17.4, they are aged 14 or over.

C:17.6 Before requesting a sample from the person concerned, an officer must:

    (a) inform them that the purpose of taking the sample is for drug testing under PACE; this is to ascertain whether they have a specified Class A drug present in their body;

    (b) warn them that if, when so requested, they fail without good cause to provide a sample they may be liable to prosecution;

    (c) where the taking of the sample has been authorised by an inspector or above in accordance with paragraph 17.3(b) or 17.4(b) above, inform them that the authorisation has been given and the grounds for giving it;

    (d) remind them of the following rights, which may be exercised at any stage during the period in custody:

        (i) the right to have someone informed of their arrest [see section 5];

        (ii) the right to consult privately with a solicitor and that free independent legal advice is available [see section 6]; and

        (iii) the right to consult these codes of practice [see section 3].

C:17.7 In the case of a person who has not attained the age of 17—

    (a) the making of the request for a sample under paragraph 17.2(d) above;

    (b) the giving of the warning and the information under paragraph 17.6 above; and

    (c) the taking of the sample,

may not take place except in the presence of an appropriate adult. See *Note 17G*.

Note: paragraph 1.5A requires someone to fulfil the role of the appropriate adult to be present if the person to be tested appears to be under the age of 18.

C:17.8 Authorisation by an officer of the rank of inspector or above within paragraph 17.3(b) or 17.4(b) may be given orally or in writing but, if it is given orally, it must be confirmed in writing as soon as practicable.

C:17.9 If a sample is taken from a detainee who has been arrested for an offence but not charged with that offence as in paragraph 17.3, no further sample may be taken during the same continuous period of detention. If during that same period the charge condition is also met in respect of that detainee, the sample which has been taken shall be treated as being taken by virtue of the charge condition, see paragraph 17.4, being met.

C:17.10 A detainee from whom a sample may be taken may be detained for up to six hours from the time of charge if the custody officer reasonably believes the detention is necessary to enable a sample to be taken. Where the arrest condition is met, a detainee whom the custody officer has decided to release on bail without charge may continue to be detained, but not beyond 24 hours from the relevant time (as defined in section 41(2) of PACE), to enable a sample to be taken.

C:17.11 A detainee in respect of whom the arrest condition is met, but not the charge condition, see paragraphs 17.3 and 17.4, and whose release would be required before a sample can be taken had they not continued to be detained as a result of being arrested for a further offence which does not satisfy the arrest condition, may have a sample taken at any time within 24 hours after the arrest for the offence that satisfies the arrest condition.

(b) *Documentation*

C:17.12 The following must be recorded in the custody record:
 (a) if a sample is taken following authorisation by an officer of the rank of inspector or above, the authorisation and the grounds for suspicion;
 (b) the giving of a warning of the consequences of failure to provide a sample;
 (c) the time at which the sample was given; and
 (d) the time of charge or, where the arrest condition is being relied upon, the time of arrest and, where applicable, the fact that a sample taken after arrest but before charge is to be treated as being taken by virtue of the charge condition, where that is met in the same period of continuous detention. See paragraph 17.9.

(c) *General*

C:17.13 A sample may only be taken by a prescribed person. See *Note 17C*.

C:17.14 Force may not be used to take any sample for the purpose of drug testing.

C:17.15 The terms "Class A drug" and "misuse" have the same meanings as in the Misuse of Drugs Act 1971. "Specified" (in relation to a Class A drug) and "trigger offence" have the same meanings as in Part III of the Criminal Justice and Court Services Act 2000.

C:17.16 Any sample taken:
 (a) may not be used for any purpose other than to ascertain whether the person concerned has a specified Class A drug present in his body; and
 (b) can be disposed of as clinical waste unless it is to be sent for further analysis in cases where the test result is disputed at the point when the result is known, including on the basis that medication has been taken, or for quality assurance purposes.

(d) *Assessment of misuse of drugs*

C:17.17 Under the provisions of Part 3 of the Drugs Act 2005, where a detainee has tested positive for a specified Class A drug under section 63B of PACE a police officer may, at any time before the person's release from the police station, impose a requirement on the detainee to attend an initial assessment of their drug misuse by a suitably qualified person and to remain for its duration. Where such a requirement is imposed, the officer must, at the same time, impose a second requirement on the detainee to attend and remain for a follow-up assessment. The officer must inform the detainee that the second requirement will cease to have effect if, at the initial assessment they are informed that a follow-up assessment is not necessary. These requirements may only be imposed on a person if:
 (a) they have reached the age of 18;
 (b) notification has been given by the Secretary of State to the relevant chief officer of police that arrangements for conducting initial and follow-up assessments have been made for those from whom samples for testing have been taken at the police station where the detainee is in custody.

C:17.18 When imposing a requirement to attend an initial assessment and a follow-up assessment the police officer must:

(a) inform the person of the time and place at which the initial assessment is to take place;

(b) explain that this information will be confirmed in writing; and

(c) warn the person that they may be liable to prosecution if they fail without good cause to attend the initial assessment and remain for its duration and if they fail to attend the follow-up assessment and remain for its duration (if so required).

C:17.19 Where a police officer has imposed a requirement to attend an initial assessment and a follow-up assessment in accordance with paragraph 17.17, he must, before the person is released from detention, give the person notice in writing which:

(a) confirms their requirement to attend and remain for the duration of the assessments; and

(b) the information and repeats the warning referred to in paragraph 17.18.

C:17.20 The following must be recorded in the custody record:

(a) that the requirement to attend an initial assessment and a follow-up assessment has been imposed; and

(b) the information, explanation, warning and notice given in accordance with paragraphs 17.17 and 17.19.

C:17.21 Where a notice is given in accordance with paragraph 17.19, a police officer can give the person a further notice in writing which informs the person of any change to the time or place at which the initial assessment is to take place and which repeats the warning referred to in paragraph 17.18(c).

C:17.22 Part 3 of the Drugs Act 2005 also requires police officers to have regard to any guidance issued by the Secretary of State in respect of the assessment provisions.

Notes for guidance

C:17A *When warning a person who is asked to provide a urine or non-intimate sample in accordance with paragraph 17.6(b), the following form of words may be used:*

"*You do not have to provide a sample, but I must warn you that if you fail or refuse without good cause to do so, you will commit an offence for which you may be imprisoned, or fined, or both*".

Where the Welsh language is appropriate, the following form of words may be used:

"*Does dim rhaid i chi roi sampl, ond mae'n rhaid i mi eich rhybuddio y byddwch chin cyflawni trosedd os byddwch chi'n methu neu yn gwrthod gwneud hynny heb reswm da, ac y gellir, oherwydd hynny, eich carcharu, eich dirwyo, neu'r ddau.*"

C:17B *A sample has to be sufficient and suitable. A sufficient sample is sufficient in quantity and quality to enable drug-testing analysis to take place. A suitable sample is one which by its nature, is suitable for a particular form of drug analysis.*

C:17C *A prescribed person in paragraph 17.13 is one who is prescribed in regulations made by the Secretary of State under section 63B(6) of the Police and Criminal Evidence Act 1984. [The regulations are currently contained in regulation S.I. 2001 No. 2645, the Police and Criminal Evidence Act 1984 (Drug Testing Persons in Police Detention) (Prescribed Persons) Regulations 2001.]*

C:17D *Samples, and the information derived from them, may not be subsequently used in the investigation of any offence or in evidence against the persons from whom they were taken.*

C:17E *Trigger offences are:*

1. *Offences under the following provisions of the Theft Act 1968:*

section 1	*(theft)*
section 8	*(robbery)*
section 9	*(burglary)*
section 10	*(aggravated burglary)*
section 12	*(taking a motor vehicle or other conveyance without authority)*
section 12A	*(aggravated vehicle-taking)*
section 22	*(handling stolen goods)*
section 25	*(going equipped for stealing, etc.).*

2. *Offences under the following provisions of the Misuse of Drugs Act 1971, if committed in respect of a specified Class A drug:*

section 4	*(restriction on production and supply of controlled drugs)*

section 5(2)   *(possession of a controlled drug)*

section 5(3)   *(possession of a controlled drug with intent to supply).*

3. *Offences under the following provisions of the Fraud Act 2006:*

section 1   *(fraud)*

section 6   *(possession etc. of articles for use in frauds)*

section 7   *(making or supplying articles for use in frauds).*

3A. *An offence under section 1(1) of the Criminal Attempts Act 1981 if committed in respect of an offence under:*

(a) any of the following provisions of the Theft Act 1968:

section 1   *(theft)*

section 8   *(robbery)*

section 9   *(burglary)*

section 22   *(handling stolen goods)*

(b) section 1 of the Fraud Act 2006 (fraud).

4. *Offences under the following provisions of the Vagrancy Act 1824:*

section 3   *(begging)*

section 4   *(persistent begging).*

C:17F *The power to take samples is subject to notification by the Secretary of State that appropriate arrangements for the taking of samples have been made for the police area as a whole or for the particular police station concerned for whichever of the following is specified in the notification:*

(a) *persons in respect of whom the arrest condition is met;*

(b) *persons in respect of whom the charge condition is met;*

(c) *persons who have not attained the age of 18.*

Note: notification is treated as having been given for the purposes of the charge condition in relation to a police area, if testing (on charge) under section 63B(2) of PACE was in force immediately before section 7 of the Drugs Act 2005 was brought into force; and for the purposes of the age condition, in relation to a police area or police station, if immediately before that day, notification that arrangements had been made for the taking of samples from persons under the age of 18 (those aged 14-17) had been given and had not been withdrawn.

C:17G *Appropriate adult in paragraph 17.7 means the person's—*

(a) *parent or guardian or, if they are in the care of a local authority or voluntary organisation, a person representing that authority or organisation; or*

(b) *a social worker of a local authority; or*

(c) *if no person falling within (a) or (b) above is available, any responsible person aged 18 or over who is not a police officer or a person employed by the police.*

Note: paragraph 1.5A extends this note to the person called to fulfil the role of the appropriate adult for a 17-year-old detainee for the purposes of paragraph 17.7.

ANNEX A

Intimate and strip searches

A *Intimate search*

C:1. An intimate search consists of the physical examination of a person's body orifices other than the mouth. The intrusive nature of such searches means the actual and potential risks associated with intimate searches must never be underestimated.   **A-92**

(a) Action

C:2. Body orifices other than the mouth may be searched only: **A-93**

(a) if authorised by an officer of inspector rank or above who has reasonable grounds for believing that the person may have concealed on themselves:

(i) anything which they could and might use to cause physical injury to themselves or others at the station; or

(ii) a Class A drug which they intended to supply to another or to export;

and the officer has reasonable grounds for believing that an intimate search is the only means of removing those items; and

(b) if the search is under paragraph 2(a)(ii) (a drug offence search), the detainee's appropriate consent has been given in writing.

C:2A. Before the search begins, a police officer or designated detention officer, must tell the detainee:

> (a) that the authority to carry out the search has been given;
>
> (b) the grounds for giving the authorisation and for believing that the article cannot be removed without an intimate search.

Note: paragraph 1.5A of this code requires someone to fulfil the role of the appropriate adult to be present when a 17-year-old is told about the authority and grounds for an intimate search.

C:2B. Before a detainee is asked to give appropriate consent to a search under paragraph 2(a)(ii) (a drug offence search) they must be warned that if they refuse without good cause their refusal may harm their case if it comes to trial, see *Note A6*. This warning may be given by a police officer or member of police staff. In the case of juveniles, mentally vulnerable or mentally disordered suspects the seeking and giving of consent must take place in the presence of the appropriate adult. A juvenile's consent is only valid if their parent's or guardian's consent is also obtained unless the juvenile is under 14, when their parent's or guardian's consent is sufficient in its own right. A detainee who is not legally represented must be reminded of their entitlement to have free legal advice, see Code C, paragraph 6.5, and the reminder noted in the custody record.

Note: paragraph 1.5A of this code requires someone to fulfil the role of the appropriate adult to be present when the warning is given to a 17-year-old and their consent to a drug offence search is sought and given but the consent of their parent or guardian is not required.

C:3. An intimate search may only be carried out by a registered medical practitioner or registered nurse, unless an officer of at least inspector rank considers this is not practicable and the search is to take place under paragraph 2(a)(i), in which case a police officer may carry out the search. See *Notes A1 to A5*.

C:3A. Any proposal for a search under paragraph 2(a)(i) to be carried out by someone other than a registered medical practitioner or registered nurse must only be considered as a last resort and when the authorising officer is satisfied the risks associated with allowing the item to remain with the detainee outweigh the risks associated with removing it. See *Notes A1 to A5*.

C:4. An intimate search under:

> • paragraph 2(a)(i) may take place only at a hospital, surgery, other medical premises or police station;
>
> • paragraph 2(a)(ii) may take place only at a hospital, surgery or other medical premises and must be carried out by a registered medical practitioner or a registered nurse.

C:5. An intimate search at a police station of a juvenile or mentally disordered or otherwise mentally vulnerable person may take place only in the presence of an appropriate adult of the same sex (see Annex L), unless the detainee specifically requests a particular adult of the opposite sex who is readily available. In the case of a juvenile, the search may take place in the absence of the appropriate adult only if the juvenile signifies in the presence of the appropriate adult they do not want the adult present during the search and the adult agrees. A record shall be made of the juvenile's decision and signed by the appropriate adult.

Note: paragraph 1.5A of this code extends the requirement in this paragraph to an intimate search of a 17-year-old.

C:6. When an intimate search under paragraph 2(a)(i) is carried out by a police officer, the officer must be of the same sex as the detainee (see Annex L). A minimum of two people, other than the detainee, must be present during the search. Subject to paragraph 5, no person of the opposite sex who is not a medical practitioner or nurse shall be present, nor shall anyone whose presence is unnecessary. The search shall be conducted with proper regard to the sensitivity and vulnerability of the detainee.

(b) Documentation

A-94   C:7. In the case of an intimate search, the following shall be recorded as soon as practicable in the detainee's custody record:

> (a) for searches under paragraphs 2(a)(i) and (ii);
>
> > • the authorisation to carry out the search;
> >
> > • the grounds for giving the authorisation;
> >
> > • the grounds for believing the article could not be removed without an intimate search;
> >
> > • which parts of the detainee's body were searched;
> >
> > • who carried out the search;
> >
> > • who was present;

- the result;

(b) for searches under paragraph 2(a)(ii):

  - the giving of the warning required by paragraph 2B;
  - the fact that the appropriate consent was given or (as the case may be) refused, and if refused, the reason given for the refusal (if any).

C:8. If an intimate search is carried out by a police officer, the reason why it was impracticable for a registered medical practitioner or registered nurse to conduct it must be recorded.

B *Strip search*

C:9. A strip search is a search involving the removal of more than outer clothing. In this code, **A-95** outer clothing includes shoes and socks.

(a) Action

C:10. A strip search may take place only if it is considered necessary to remove an article which a **A-96** detainee would not be allowed to keep and the officer reasonably considers the detainee might have concealed such an article. Strip searches shall not be routinely carried out if there is no reason to consider that articles are concealed.

The conduct of strip searches

C:11. When strip searches are conducted:

(a) a police officer carrying out a strip search must be the same sex as the detainee (see Annex L);

(b) the search shall take place in an area where the detainee cannot be seen by anyone who does not need to be present, nor by a member of the opposite sex (see Annex L) except an appropriate adult who has been specifically requested by the detainee;

(c) except in cases of urgency, where there is risk of serious harm to the detainee or to others, whenever a strip search involves exposure of intimate body parts, there must be at least two people present other than the detainee, and if the search is of a juvenile or mentally disordered or otherwise mentally vulnerable person, one of the people must be the appropriate adult; except in urgent cases as above, a search of a juvenile may take place in the absence of the appropriate adult only if the juvenile signifies in the presence of the appropriate adult that they do not want the adult to be present during the search and the adult agrees; a record shall be made of the juvenile's decision and signed by the appropriate adult; the presence of more than two people, other than an appropriate adult, shall be permitted only in the most exceptional circumstances (note: para. 1.5A of this code extends the requirement in this sub-paragraph to a strip search of a 17-year-old);

(d) the search shall be conducted with proper regard to the sensitivity and vulnerability of the detainee in these circumstances and every reasonable effort shall be made to secure the detainee's co-operation and minimise embarrassment; detainees who are searched shall not normally be required to remove all their clothes at the same time, *e.g.* a person should be allowed to remove clothing above the waist and redress before removing further clothing;

(e) if necessary to assist the search, the detainee may be required to hold their arms in the air or to stand with their legs apart and bend forward so a visual examination may be made of the genital and anal areas provided no physical contact is made with any body orifice;

(f) if articles are found, the detainee shall be asked to hand them over; if articles are found within any body orifice other than the mouth, and the detainee refuses to hand them over, their removal would constitute an intimate search, which must be carried out as in Part A;

(g) a strip search shall be conducted as quickly as possible, and the detainee allowed to dress as soon as the procedure is complete.

(b) Documentation

C:12. A record shall be made on the custody record of a strip search including the reason it was **A-97** considered necessary, those present and any result.

Notes for guidance

A-98

C:A1 *Before authorising any intimate search, the authorising officer must make every reasonable effort to persuade the detainee to hand the article over without a search. If the detainee agrees, a registered medical practitioner or registered nurse should whenever possible be asked to assess the risks involved and, if necessary, attend to assist the detainee.*

C:A2 *If the detainee does not agree to hand the article over without a search, the authorising officer must carefully review all the relevant factors before authorising an intimate search. In particular, the officer must consider whether the grounds for believing an article may be concealed are reasonable.*

C:A3 *If authority is given for a search under paragraph 2(a)(i), a registered medical practitioner or registered nurse shall be consulted whenever possible. The presumption should be that the search will be conducted by the registered medical practitioner or registered nurse and the authorising officer must make every reasonable effort to persuade the detainee to allow the medical practitioner or nurse to conduct the search.*

C:A4 *A constable should only be authorised to carry out a search as a last resort and when all other approaches have failed. In these circumstances, the authorising officer must be satisfied the detainee might use the article for one or more of the purposes in paragraph 2(a)(i) and the physical injury likely to be caused is sufficiently severe to justify authorising a constable to carry out the search.*

C:A5 *If an officer has any doubts whether to authorise an intimate search by a constable, the officer should seek advice from an officer of superintendent rank or above.*

C:A6 *In warning a detainee who is asked to consent to an intimate drug offence search, as in paragraph 2B, the following form of words may be used:*

"You do not have to allow yourself to be searched, but I must warn you that if you refuse without good cause, your refusal may harm your case if it comes to trial.".

Where the use of the Welsh language is appropriate, the following form of words may be used:

"Nid oes rhaid i chi roi caniatâd i gael eich archwilio, ond mae'n rhaid i mi eich rhybuddio os gwrthodwch heb reswm da, y gallai eich penderfyniad i wrthod wneud niwed i'ch achos pe bai'n dod gerbron llys.".

ANNEX B

Delay in notifying arrest or allowing access to legal advice

A *Persons detained under PACE*

A-99

C:1. The exercise of the rights in section 5 or section 6, or both, may be delayed if the person is in police detention, as in PACE, section 118(2), in connection with an indictable offence, has not yet been charged with an offence and an officer of superintendent rank or above, or inspector rank or above only for the rights in section 5, has reasonable grounds for believing their exercise will:

   (i) lead to:
- interference with, or harm to, evidence connected with an indictable offence; or
- interference with, or physical harm to, other people; or

   (ii) lead to alerting other people suspected of having committed an indictable offence but not yet arrested for it; or

   (iii) hinder the recovery of property obtained in consequence of the commission of such an offence.

C:2. These rights may also be delayed if the officer has reasonable grounds to believe that:

   (i) the person detained for an indictable offence has benefited from their criminal conduct (decided in accordance with Part 2 of the Proceeds of Crime Act 2002); and

   (ii) the recovery of the value of the property constituting that benefit will be hindered by the exercise of either right.

C:3. Authority to delay a detainee's right to consult privately with a solicitor may be given only if the authorising officer has reasonable grounds to believe the solicitor the detainee wants to consult will, inadvertently or otherwise, pass on a message from the detainee or act in some other way which will have any of the consequences specified under paragraphs 1 or 2. In these circumstances, the detainee must be allowed to choose another solicitor. See *Note B3*.

C:4. If the detainee wishes to see a solicitor, access to that solicitor may not be delayed on the grounds they might advise the detainee not to answer questions or the solicitor was initially asked to attend the police station by someone else. In the latter case, the detainee must be told the solicitor has come to the police station at another person's request, and must be asked to sign the custody record to signify whether they want to see the solicitor.

C:5. The fact the grounds for delaying notification of arrest may be satisfied does not automatically mean the grounds for delaying access to legal advice will also be satisfied.

C:6. These rights may be delayed only for as long as grounds exist and in no case beyond 36 hours after the relevant time as in PACE, s.41. If the grounds cease to apply within this time, the detainee must, as soon as practicable, be asked if they want to exercise either right, the custody record must be noted accordingly, and action taken in accordance with the relevant section of the code.

C:7. A detained person must be permitted to consult a solicitor for a reasonable time before any court hearing.

B [*Not used.*]

C *Documentation*

C:13. The grounds for action under this annex shall be recorded and the detainee informed of **A-100** them as soon as practicable.

C:14. Any reply given by a detainee under paragraphs 6 or 11 must be recorded and the detainee asked to endorse the record in relation to whether they want to receive legal advice at this point.

D *Cautions and special warnings*

C:15. When a suspect detained at a police station is interviewed during any period for which access to legal advice has been delayed under this annex, the court or jury may not draw adverse inferences from their silence.

Notes for guidance

C:B1 *Even if Annex B applies in the case of a juvenile, or a person who is mentally disordered or otherwise* **A-101** *mentally vulnerable, action to inform the appropriate adult and the person responsible for a juvenile's welfare if that is a different person, must nevertheless be taken as in paragraph 3.13 and 3.15.*

Note: paragraph 1.5A of this code extends this note to 17-year-old detainees.

C:B2 *In the case of Commonwealth citizens and foreign nationals, see Note 7A.*

C:B3 *A decision to delay access to a specific solicitor is likely to be a rare occurrence and only when it can be shown the suspect is capable of misleading that particular solicitor and there is more than a substantial risk that the suspect will succeed in causing information to be conveyed which will lead to one or more of the specified consequences.*

ANNEX C

Restriction on drawing adverse inferences from silence and terms of the caution when the restriction applies

(a) *The restriction on drawing adverse inferences from silence*

C:1. The Criminal Justice and Public Order Act 1994, ss.34, 36 and 37 as amended by the Youth **A-102** Justice and Criminal Evidence Act 1999, s.58 describe the conditions under which adverse inferences may be drawn from a person's failure or refusal to say anything about their involvement in the offence when interviewed, after being charged or informed they may be prosecuted. These provisions are subject to an overriding restriction on the ability of a court or jury to draw adverse inferences from a person's silence. This restriction applies:

    (a) to any detainee at a police station, see *Note 10C*, who, before being interviewed, see section 11, or being charged or informed they may be prosecuted, see section 16, has:

        (i) asked for legal advice, see section 6, paragraph 6.1;

        (ii) not been allowed an opportunity to consult a solicitor, including the duty solicitor, as in this code; and

        (iii) not changed their mind about wanting legal advice, see section 6, paragraph 6.6(d);

            – [note the condition in (ii) will

                – apply when a detainee who has asked for legal advice is interviewed before speaking to a solicitor as in section 6, paragraph 6.6(a) or (b);

                – not apply if the detained person declines to ask for the duty solicitor, see section 6, paragraphs 6.6(c) and (d)];

    (b) to any person charged with, or informed they may be prosecuted for, an offence who:

        (i) has had brought to their notice a written statement made by another person or the content of an interview with another person which relates to that offence, see section 16, paragraph 16.4;

        (ii) is interviewed about that offence, see section 16, paragraph 16.5; or

(iii) makes a written statement about that offence, see Annex D paragraphs 4 and 9.

(b) *Terms of the caution when the restriction applies*

C:2. When a requirement to caution arises at a time when the restriction on drawing adverse inferences from silence applies, the caution shall be:

"You do not have to say anything, but anything you do say may be given in evidence.".

Where the use of the Welsh language is appropriate, the caution may be used directly in Welsh in the following terms:

"Does dim rhaid i chi ddweud dim byd, ond gall unrhyw beth yr ydych chi'n ei ddweud gael ei roi fel tystiolaeth.".

C:3. Whenever the restriction either begins to apply or ceases to apply after a caution has already been given, the person shall be re-cautioned in the appropriate terms. The changed position on drawing inferences and that the previous caution no longer applies shall also be explained to the detainee in ordinary language. See *Note C2.*

Notes for guidance

C:C1 *The restriction on drawing inferences from silence does not apply to a person who has not been detained and who therefore cannot be prevented from seeking legal advice if they want to, see paragraphs 10.2 and 3.15.*

C:C2 *The following is suggested as a framework to help explain changes in the position on drawing adverse inferences if the restriction on drawing adverse inferences from silence:*

(a) *begins to apply:*

"The caution you were previously given no longer applies. This is because after that caution:
   (i) *you asked to speak to a solicitor but have not yet been allowed an opportunity to speak to a solicitor;" see paragraph 1(a); or*
"(ii) you have been charged with/informed you may be prosecuted." See paragraph 1(b).
"This means that from now on, adverse inferences cannot be drawn at court and your defence will not be harmed just because you choose to say nothing. Please listen carefully to the caution I am about to give you because it will apply from now on. You will see that it does not say anything about your defence being harmed.";

(b) *ceases to apply before or at the time the person is charged or informed they may be prosecuted, see paragraph 1(a);*

"The caution you were previously given no longer applies. This is because after that caution you have been allowed an opportunity to speak to a solicitor. Please listen carefully to the caution I am about to give you because it will apply from now on. It explains how your defence at court may be affected if you choose to say nothing.".

ANNEX D

Written statements under caution

(a) *Written by a person under caution*

A-103   C:1. A person shall always be invited to write down what they want to say.

C:2. A person who has not been charged with, or informed they may be prosecuted for, any offence to which the statement they want to write relates, shall:

(a) unless the statement is made at a time when the restriction on drawing adverse inferences from silence applies, see Annex C, be asked to write out and sign the following before writing what they want to say:

"I make this statement of my own free will. I understand that I do not have to say anything but that it may harm my defence if I do not mention when questioned something which I later rely on in court. This statement may be given in evidence.";

(b) if the statement is made at a time when the restriction on drawing adverse inferences from silence applies, be asked to write out and sign the following before writing what they want to say;

"I make this statement of my own free will. I understand that I do not have to say anything. This statement may be given in evidence.".

C:3. When a person, on the occasion of being charged with or informed they may be prosecuted for any offence, asks to make a statement which relates to any such offence and wants to write it they shall:

    (a) unless the restriction on drawing adverse inferences from silence, see Annex C, applied when they were so charged or informed they may be prosecuted, be asked to write out and sign the following before writing what they want to say:

        "I make this statement of my own free will. I understand that I do not have to say anything but that it may harm my defence if I do not mention when questioned something which I later rely on in court. This statement may be given in evidence.";

    (b) if the restriction on drawing adverse inferences from silence applied when they were so charged or informed they may be prosecuted, be asked to write out and sign the following before writing what they want to say:

        "I make this statement of my own free will. I understand that I do not have to say anything. This statement may be given in evidence.".

C:4. When a person who has already been charged with or informed they may be prosecuted for any offence asks to make a statement which relates to any such offence and wants to write it, they shall be asked to write out and sign the following before writing what they want to say:

"I make this statement of my own free will. I understand that I do not have to say anything. This statement may be given in evidence.".

C:5. Any person writing their own statement shall be allowed to do so without any prompting except a police officer or police staff may indicate to them which matters are material or question any ambiguity in the statement.

(b) *Written by a police officer or other police staff*

C:6. If a person says they would like someone to write the statement for them, a police officer, or **A-104** other police staff shall write the statement.

C:7. If the person has not been charged with, or informed they may be prosecuted for, any offence to which the statement they want to make relates they shall, before starting, be asked to sign, or make their mark, to the following:

    (a) unless the statement is made at a time when the restriction on drawing adverse inferences from silence applies, see Annex C:

        "I, ..., wish to make a statement. I want someone to write down what I say. I understand that I do not have to say anything but that it may harm my defence if I do not mention when questioned something which I later rely on in court. This statement may be given in evidence.";

    (b) if the statement is made at a time when the restriction on drawing adverse inferences from silence applies:

        "I, ..., wish to make a statement. I want someone to write down what I say. I understand that I do not have to say anything. This statement may be given in evidence.".

C:8. If, on the occasion of being charged with or informed they may be prosecuted for any offence, the person asks to make a statement which relates to any such offence they shall before starting be asked to sign, or make their mark to, the following:

    (a) unless the restriction on drawing adverse inferences from silence applied, see Annex C, when they were so charged or informed they may be prosecuted:

        "I, ..., wish to make a statement. I want someone to write down what I say. I understand that I do not have to say anything but that it may harm my defence if I do not mention when questioned something which I later rely on in court. This statement may be given in evidence.";

    (b) if the restriction on drawing adverse inferences from silence applied when they were so charged or informed they may be prosecuted:

        "I, ..., wish to make a statement. I want someone to write down what I say. I understand that I do not have to say anything. This statement may be given in evidence.".

C:9. If, having already been charged with or informed they may be prosecuted for any offence, a person asks to make a statement which relates to any such offence they shall before starting, be asked to sign, or make their mark to:

"I, ..., wish to make a statement. I want someone to write down what I say. I understand that I do

not have to say anything. This statement may be given in evidence.".

C:10. The person writing the statement must take down the exact words spoken by the person making it and must not edit or paraphrase it. Any questions that are necessary, *e.g.* to make it more intelligible, and the answers given must be recorded at the same time on the statement form.

C:11. When the writing of a statement is finished the person making it shall be asked to read it and to make any corrections, alterations or additions they want. When they have finished reading they shall be asked to write and sign or make their mark on the following certificate at the end of the statement:

"I have read the above statement, and I have been able to correct, alter or add anything I wish. This statement is true. I have made it of my own free will.".

C:12. If the person making the statement cannot read, or refuses to read it, or to write the above mentioned certificate at the end of it or to sign it, the person taking the statement shall read it to them and ask them if they would like to correct, alter or add anything and to put their signature or make their mark at the end. The person taking the statement shall certify on the statement itself what has occurred.

ANNEX E

Summary of provisions relating to mentally disordered and otherwise mentally vulnerable people

A-105

C:1. If an officer has any suspicion, or is told in good faith, that a person of any age may be mentally disordered or otherwise mentally vulnerable, or mentally incapable of understanding the significance of questions or their replies that person shall be treated as mentally disordered or otherwise mentally vulnerable for the purposes of this code. See paragraph 1.4 and *Note E4*.

C:2. In the case of a person who is mentally disordered or otherwise mentally vulnerable, "the appropriate adult" means:

    (a) a relative, guardian or other person responsible for their care or custody;

    (b) someone experienced in dealing with mentally disordered or mentally vulnerable people but who is not a police officer or employed by the police;

    (c) failing these, some other responsible adult aged 18 or over who is not a police officer or employed by the police.

See paragraph 1.7(b) and *Note 1D*.

C:3. If the custody officer authorises the detention of a person who is mentally vulnerable or appears to be suffering from a mental disorder, the custody officer must as soon as practicable inform the appropriate adult of the grounds for detention and the person's whereabouts, and ask the adult to come to the police station to see them. If the appropriate adult:

    • is already at the station when information is given as in paragraphs 3.1 to 3.5 the information must be given in their presence;

    • is not at the station when the provisions of paragraph 3.1 to 3.5 are complied with these provisions must be complied with again in their presence once they arrive.

See paragraphs 3.15 to 3.17.

C:4. If the appropriate adult, having been informed of the right to legal advice, considers legal advice should be taken, the provisions of section 6 apply as if the mentally disordered or otherwise mentally vulnerable person had requested access to legal advice. See paragraph 3.19 and *Note E1*.

C:5. The custody officer must make sure a person receives appropriate clinical attention as soon as reasonably practicable if the person appears to be suffering from a mental disorder or in urgent cases immediately call the nearest appropriate healthcare professional or an ambulance. It is not intended these provisions delay the transfer of a detainee to a place of safety under the Mental Health Act 1983, s.136, if that is applicable. If an assessment under that Act is to take place at a police station, the custody officer must consider whether an appropriate healthcare professional should be called to conduct an initial clinical check on the detainee. See paragraph 9.5 and 9.6.

C:6. It is imperative a mentally disordered or otherwise mentally vulnerable person detained under the Mental Health Act 1983, s.136, be assessed as soon as possible. A police station should only be used as a place of safety as a last resort but if that assessment is to take place at the police station, an approved social worker and registered medical practitioner shall be called to the station as soon as possible to carry it out. Once the detainee has been assessed and suitable arrangements been made for their treatment or care, they can no longer be detained under section 136. A detainee should be immediately discharged from detention if a registered medical practitioner having examined them, concludes they are not mentally disordered within the meaning of the Act. See paragraph 3.16.

C:7. If a mentally disordered or otherwise mentally vulnerable person is cautioned in the absence of the appropriate adult, the caution must be repeated in the appropriate adult's presence. See paragraph 10.12.

C:8. A mentally disordered or otherwise mentally vulnerable person must not be interviewed or asked to provide or sign a written statement in the absence of the appropriate adult unless the provisions of paragraphs 11.1 or 11.18 to 11.20 apply. Questioning in these circumstances may not continue in the absence of the appropriate adult once sufficient information to avert the risk has been obtained. A record shall be made of the grounds for any decision to begin an interview in these circumstances. See paragraphs 11.1, 11.15 and 11.18 to 11.20.

C:9. If the appropriate adult is present at an interview, they shall be informed they are not expected to act simply as an observer and the purposes of their presence are to:

- advise the interviewee;
- observe whether or not the interview is being conducted properly and fairly;
- facilitate communication with the interviewee.

See paragraph 11.17.

C:10. If the detention of a mentally disordered or otherwise mentally vulnerable person is **A-106** reviewed by a review officer or a superintendent, the appropriate adult must, if available at the time, be given an opportunity to make representations to the officer about the need for continuing detention. See paragraph 15.3.

C:11. If the custody officer charges a mentally disordered or otherwise mentally vulnerable person with an offence or takes such other action as is appropriate when there is sufficient evidence for a prosecution this must be carried out in the presence of the appropriate adult if they are at the police station. A copy of the written notice embodying any charge must also be given to the appropriate adult. See paragraphs 16.1 to 16.4A.

C:12. An intimate or strip search of a mentally disordered or otherwise mentally vulnerable person may take place only in the presence of the appropriate adult of the same sex, unless the detainee specifically requests the presence of a particular adult of the opposite sex. A strip search may take place in the absence of an appropriate adult only in cases of urgency when there is a risk of serious harm to the detainee or others. See Annex A, paragraphs 5 and 11(c).

C:13. Particular care must be taken when deciding whether to use any form of approved restraints on a mentally disordered or otherwise mentally vulnerable person in a locked cell. See paragraph 8.2.

Notes for guidance

C:E1 *The purpose of the provision at paragraph 3.19 is to protect the rights of a mentally disordered or* **A-107** *otherwise mentally vulnerable detained person who does not understand the significance of what is said to them. If the detained person wants to exercise the right to legal advice, the appropriate action should be taken and not delayed until the appropriate adult arrives. A mentally disordered or otherwise mentally vulnerable detained person should always be given an opportunity, when an appropriate adult is called to the police station, to consult privately with a solicitor in the absence of the appropriate adult if they want.*

C:E2 *Although people who are mentally disordered or otherwise mentally vulnerable are often capable of providing reliable evidence, they may, without knowing or wanting to do so, be particularly prone in certain circumstances to provide information that may be unreliable, misleading or self-incriminating. Special care should always be taken when questioning such a person, and the appropriate adult should be involved if there is any doubt about a person's mental state or capacity. Because of the risk of unreliable evidence, it is important to obtain corroboration of any facts admitted whenever possible.*

C:E3 *Because of the risks referred to in Note E2, which the presence of the appropriate adult is intended to minimise, officers of superintendent rank or above should exercise their discretion to authorise the commencement of an interview in the appropriate adult's absence only in exceptional cases, if it is necessary to avert an immediate risk of serious harm. See paragraphs 11.1, 11.18 to 11.20.*

C:E4 *There is no requirement for an appropriate adult to be present if a person is detained under section 136 of the Mental Health Act 1983 for assessment.*

ANNEX F

[*Not used.*] **A-108**

ANNEX G

Fitness to be interviewed

C:1. This annex contains general guidance to help police officers and health care professionals as- **A-109** sess whether a detainee might be at risk in an interview.

C:2. A detainee may be at risk in an interview if it is considered that:

(a) conducting the interview could significantly harm the detainee's physical or mental state;

(b) anything the detainee says in the interview about their involvement or suspected involvement in the offence about which they are being interviewed **might** be considered unreliable in subsequent court proceedings because of their physical or mental state.

C:3. In assessing whether the detainee should be interviewed, the following must be considered:

(a) how the detainee's physical or mental state might affect their ability to understand the nature and purpose of the interview, to comprehend what is being asked and to appreciate the significance of any answers given and make rational decisions about whether they want to say anything;

(b) the extent to which the detainee's replies may be affected by their physical or mental condition rather than representing a rational and accurate explanation of their involvement in the offence;

(c) how the nature of the interview, which could include particularly probing questions, might affect the detainee.

A-110   C:4. It is essential health care professionals who are consulted consider the functional ability of the detainee rather than simply relying on a medical diagnosis, *e.g.* it is possible for a person with severe mental illness to be fit for interview.

C:5. Health care professionals should advise on the need for an appropriate adult to be present, whether reassessment of the person's fitness for interview may be necessary if the interview lasts beyond a specified time, and whether a further specialist opinion may be required.

C:6. When health care professionals identify risks they should be asked to quantify the risks. They should inform the custody officer:

- whether the person's condition:
  - is likely to improve;
  - will require or be amenable to treatment; and
- indicate how long it may take for such improvement to take effect.

C:7. The role of the health care professional is to consider the risks and advise the custody officer of the outcome of that consideration. The health care professional's determination and any advice or recommendations should be made in writing and form part of the custody record.

C:8. Once the health care professional has provided that information, it is a matter for the custody officer to decide whether or not to allow the interview to go ahead and if the interview is to proceed, to determine what safeguards are needed. Nothing prevents safeguards being provided in addition to those required under the code. An example might be to have an appropriate health care professional present during the interview, in addition to an appropriate adult, in order constantly to monitor the person's condition and how it is being affected by the interview.

ANNEX H

Detained person: observation list

A-111   C:1. If any detainee fails to meet any of the following criteria, an appropriate health care professional or an ambulance must be called.

C:2. When assessing the level of rousability, consider:

Rousability—can they be woken?

- go into the cell
- call their name
- shake gently

Response to questions—can they give appropriate answers to questions such as:

- What's your name?
- Where do you live?
- Where do you think you are?

Response to commands—can they respond appropriately to commands such as:

- Open your eyes!
- Lift one arm, now the other arm!

C:3. Remember to take into account the possibility or presence of other illnesses, injury, or mental condition; a person who is drowsy and smells of alcohol may also have the following:

- Diabetes
- Epilepsy
- Head injury
- Drug intoxication or overdose
- Stroke

ANNEX I

[*Not used.*]

ANNEX J

[*Not used.*]

ANNEX K

X-rays and ultrasound scans

(a) *Action*

C:1. PACE, s.55A allows a person who has been arrested and is in police detention to have an **A-111a** x-ray taken of them or an ultrasound scan to be carried out on them (or both) if:

    (a) authorised by an officer of inspector rank or above who has reasonable grounds for believing that the detainee:
        (i) may have swallowed a Class A drug; and
        (ii) was in possession of that Class A drug with the intention of supplying it to another or to export; and
    (b) the detainee's appropriate consent has been given in writing.

C:2. Before an x-ray is taken or an ultrasound scan carried out, a police officer or designated detention officer must tell the detainee:

    (a) that the authority has been given; and
    (b) the grounds for giving the authorisation.

Note: paragraph 1.5A in this code requires someone to fulfil the role of the appropriate adult to be present when a 17-year-old is told about the authority and grounds for an x-ray and ultrasound scan.

C:3. Before a detainee is asked to give appropriate consent to an x-ray or an ultrasound scan, they must be warned that if they refuse without good cause their refusal may harm their case if it comes to trial, see *Notes K1* and *K2*. This warning may be given by a police officer or member of police staff. In the case of juveniles, mentally vulnerable or mentally disordered suspects the seeking and giving of consent must take place in the presence of the appropriate adult. A juvenile's consent is only valid if their parent's or guardian's consent is also obtained unless the juvenile is under 14, when their parent's or guardian's consent is sufficient in its own right. A detainee who is not legally represented must be reminded of their entitlement to have free legal advice, see Code C, paragraph 6.5, and the reminder noted in the custody record.

Note: paragraph 1.5A in this code requires someone to fulfil the role of the appropriate adult to be present when the warning is given to a 17-year-old and their consent to an x-ray or ultrasound scan is sought and given but the consent of their parent or guardian is not required.

C:4. An x-ray may be taken, or an ultrasound scan may be carried out, only by a registered medical practitioner or registered nurse, and only at a hospital, surgery or other medical premises.

(b) *Documentation*

C:5. The following shall be recorded as soon as practicable in the detainee's custody record:

    (a) the authorisation to take the x-ray or carry out the ultrasound scan (or both);
    (b) the grounds for giving the authorisation;
    (c) the giving of the warning required by paragraph 3; and
    (d) the fact that the appropriate consent was given or (as the case may be) refused, and if refused, the reason given for the refusal (if any); and
    (e) if an x-ray is taken or an ultrasound scan carried out:
        • where it was taken or carried out;
        • who took it or carried it out;
        • who was present;
        • the result.

Notes for guidance

C:K1 *If authority is given for an x-ray to be taken or an ultrasound scan to be carried out (or both),* **A-111b** *consideration should be given to asking a registered medical practitioner or registered nurse to explain to the detainee what is involved and to allay any concerns the detainee might have about the effect which taking an x-ray or carrying out an ultrasound scan might have on them. If appropriate consent is not given, evidence of the* *explanation may, if the case comes to trial, be relevant to determining whether the detainee had a good cause for refusing.*

C:K2 In warning a detainee who is asked to consent to an x-ray being taken or an ultrasound scan being carried out (or both), as in paragraph 3, the following form of words may be used:

> "You do not have to allow an x-ray of you to be taken or an ultrasound scan to be carried out on you, but I must warn you that if you refuse without good cause, your refusal may harm your case if it comes to trial.".

Where the use of the Welsh language is appropriate, the following form of words may be provided in Welsh:

> "Does dim rhaid i chi ganiatáu cymryd sgan uwchsain neu belydr-x (neu'r ddau) arnoch, ond mae'n rhaid i mi eich rhybuddio os byddwch chin gwrthod gwneud hynny heb reswm da, fe allai hynny niweidio eich achos pe bai'n dod gerbron llys.".

ANNEX L

Establishing gender of persons for the purpose of searching

A-111c

C:1. 1. Certain provisions of this and other PACE codes explicitly state that searches and other procedures may only be carried out by, or in the presence of, persons of the same sex as the person subject to the search or other procedure. See *Note L1.*

C:2. All searches and procedures must be carried out with courtesy, consideration and respect for the person concerned. Police officers should show particular sensitivity when dealing with transgender individuals (including transsexual persons) and transvestite persons (see *Notes L2, L3* and *L4*).

(a) Consideration

A-111d

C:3. In law, the gender (and accordingly the sex) of an individual is their gender as registered at birth unless they have been issued with a gender recognition certificate (GRC) under the Gender Recognition Act 2004 (GRA), in which case the person's gender is their acquired gender. This means that if the acquired gender is the male gender, the person's sex becomes that of a man and, if it is the female gender, the person's sex becomes that of a woman and they must be treated as their acquired gender.

C:4. When establishing whether the person concerned should be treated as being male or female for the purposes of these searches and procedures, the following approach which is designed to minimise embarrassment and secure the person's co-operation should be followed:

   (a) the person must not be asked whether they have a GRC (see paragraph 8);

   (b) if there is no doubt as to as to whether the person concerned should be treated as being male or female, they should be dealt with as being of that sex;

   (c) if at any time (including during the search or carrying out the procedure) there is doubt as to whether the person should be treated, or continue to be treated, as being male or female:

      (i) the person should be asked what gender they consider themselves to be; if they express a preference to be dealt with as a particular gender, they should be asked to indicate and confirm their preference by signing the custody record or, if a custody record has not been opened, the search record or the officer's notebook; subject to (ii) below, the person should be treated according to their preference;

      (ii) if there are grounds to doubt that the preference in (i) accurately reflects the person's predominant lifestyle, for example, if they ask to be treated as a woman but documents and other information make it clear that they live predominantly as a man, or vice versa, they should be treated according to what appears to be their predominant lifestyle and not their stated preference;

      (iii) if the person is unwilling to express a preference as in (i) above, efforts should be made to determine their predominant lifestyle and they should be treated as such; for example, if they appear to live predominantly as a woman, they should be treated as being female; or

      (iv) if none of the above apply, the person should be dealt with according to what reasonably appears to have been their sex as registered at birth.

C:5. Once a decision has been made about which gender an individual is to be treated as, each officer responsible for the search or procedure should where possible be advised before the search or procedure starts of any doubts as to the person's gender and the person informed that the doubts have been disclosed. This is important so as to maintain the dignity of the person and any officers concerned.

(b) *Documentation*

C:6. The person's gender as established under paragraph 4(c)(i) to (iv) above must be recorded in   **A-111e**
the person's custody record or, if a custody record has not been opened, on the search record or in
the officer's notebook.

C:7. Where the person elects which gender they consider themselves to be under paragraph
4(b)(i) but, following 4(b)(ii) is not treated in accordance with their preference, the reason must be
recorded in the search record, in the officer's notebook or, if applicable, in the person's custody
record.

(c) *Disclosure of information*

C:8. Section 22 of the GRA defines any information relating to a person's application for a GRC or   **A-111f**
to a successful applicant's gender before it became their acquired gender as "protected information".
Nothing in this annex is to be read as authorising or permitting any police officer or any police staff
who has acquired such information when acting in their official capacity to disclose that information
to any other person in contravention of the GRA. Disclosure includes making a record of "protected
information" which is read by others.

Notes for guidance

C:L1 *Provisions to which paragraph 1 applies include:*   **A-111g**

- *in Code C; paragraph 4.1 and Annex A, paragraphs 5, 6 and 11 (searches, strip and intimate
  searches of detainees under sections 54 and 55 of PACE);*
- *in Code A; paragraphs 2.8 and 3.6 and Note 4;*
- *in Code D; paragraph 5.5 and Note 5F (searches, examinations and photographing of detainees
  under section 54A of PACE) and paragraph 6.9 (taking samples);*
- *in Code H; paragraph 4.1 and Annex A, paragraphs 6, 7 and 12 (searches, strip and intimate
  searches under sections 54 and 55 of PACE of persons arrested under section 41 of the Terrorism
  Act 2000).*

C:L2 *While there is no agreed definition of transgender (or trans), it is generally used as an umbrella term to
describe people whose gender identity (self-identification as being a woman, man, neither or both) differs from the
sex they were registered as at birth. The term includes, but is not limited to, transsexual people.*

C:L3 *Transsexual means a person who is proposing to undergo, is undergoing or has undergone a process (or
part of a process) for the purpose of gender reassignment, which is a protected characteristic under the Equality
Act 2010 (see paragraph 1.0) by changing physiological or other attributes of their sex. This includes aspects of
gender such as dress and title. It would apply to a woman making the transition to being a man and a man making the transition to being a woman, as well as to a person who has only just started out on the process of gender
reassignment and to a person who has completed the process. Both would share the characteristic of gender reassignment with each having the characteristics of one sex, but with certain characteristics of the other sex.*

C:L4 *Transvestite means a person of one gender who dresses in the clothes of a person of the opposite gender.
However, a transvestite does not live permanently in the gender opposite to their birth sex.*

C:L5 *Chief officers are responsible for providing corresponding operational guidance and instructions for the
deployment of transgender officers and staff under their direction and control to duties which involve carrying out,
or being present at, any of the searches and procedures described in paragraph 1. The guidance and instructions
must comply with the Equality Act 2010 and should therefore complement the approach in this annex.*

ANNEX M

Documents and records to be translated

C:1. For the purposes of Directive 2010/64/EU of the European Parliament and of the Council of   **A-111h**
20 October 2010 and this code, essential documents comprise records required to be made in accordance with this code which are relevant to decisions to deprive a person of their liberty, to any charge
and to any record considered necessary to enable a detainee to defend themselves in criminal
proceedings and to safeguard the fairness of the proceedings. Passages of essential documents which
are not relevant need not be translated. See *Note M1.*

C:2. The table below lists the documents considered essential for the purposes of this code and
when (subject to paras 3 to 7) written translations must be created and provided.

Table of essential documents:

A-111i

	Essential documents for the purposes of this code	When translation to be created	When translation to be provided.
(i)	The grounds for each of the following authorisations to keep the person in custody as they are described and referred to in the custody record: (a) authorisation for detention before and after charge given by the custody o cer and by the review officer, see Code C, paras 3.4 and 15.16(a); (b) authorisation to extend detention without charge beyond 24 hours given by a superintendent, see Code C, para. 15.16(b); (c) a warrant of further detention issued by a magistrates court and any extension(s) of the warrant, see Code C, para. 15.16(c); (d) an authority to detain in accordance with the directions in a warrant of arrest issued in connection with criminal proceedings including the court issuing the warrant.	As soon as practicable after each authorisation has been recorded in the custody record.	As soon as practicable after the translation has been created, whilst the person is detained or after they have been released (see *Note M3*).
(ii)	Written notice showing particulars of the offence charged required by Code C, para. 16.3, or the offence for which the suspect has been told they may be prosecuted.	As soon as practicable after the person has been charged or reported.	
(iii)	Written interview records: Code C:11.11, 13.3, 13.4 & Code E4.7 Written statement under caution: Code C, Annex D.	To be created contemporaneously by the interpreter for the person to check and sign.	As soon as practicable after the person has been charged or told they may be prosecuted.

C:3. The custody officer may authorise an oral translation or oral summary of documents (i) to (ii) in the table (but not (iii)) to be provided (through an interpreter) instead of a written translation. Such an oral translation or summary may only be provided if it would not prejudice the fairness of the proceedings by in any way adversely affecting or otherwise undermining or limiting the ability of the suspect in question to understand their position and to communicate effectively with police officers, interviewers, solicitors and appropriate adults with regard to their detention and the investigation of the offence in question and to defend themselves in the event of criminal proceedings. The quantity and complexity of the information in the document should always be considered and specific additional consideration given if the suspect is mentally disordered or otherwise mentally vulnerable or is a juvenile or a 17-year-old (see Code C, para. 1.5A). The reason for the decision must be recorded (see para. 13.11(e))

C:4. Subject to paragraphs 5 to 7 below, a suspect may waive their right to a written translation of the essential documents described in the table but only if they do so voluntarily after receiving legal advice or having full knowledge of the consequences and give their unconditional and fully informed consent in writing (see para. 9).

C:5. The suspect may be asked if they wish to waive their right to a written translation and before giving their consent, they must be reminded of their right to legal advice and asked whether they wish to speak to a solicitor.

C:6. No police officer or police staff should do or say anything with the intention of persuading a suspect who is entitled to a written translation of an essential document to waive that right. See *Notes M2* and *M3*.

C:7. For the purpose of the waiver:

(a) the consent of a person who is mentally disordered or otherwise mentally vulnerable person is only valid if the information about the circumstances under which they can waive the right and the reminder about their right to legal advice mentioned in paragraphs 3 to 5 and their consent is given in the presence of the appropriate adult (note: para. 1.5A in Code C requires someone to fulfil the role of the appropriate adult to be present when a 17-year-old is given the information and reminder mentioned in sub-para. (a) above and gives their consent to waive their right; the consent of their parent or guardian is not required);

(b) the consent of a juvenile is only valid if their parent's or guardian's consent is also obtained unless the juvenile is under 14, when their parent's or guardian's consent is sufficient in its own right and the information and reminder mentioned in sub-paragraph (a) above and their consent is also given in the presence of the appropriate adult (who may or may not be a parent or guardian).

C:8. The detainee, their solicitor or appropriate adult may make representations to the custody officer that a document which is not included in the table is essential and that a translation should be provided. The request may be refused if the officer is satisfied that the translation requested is not essential for the purposes described in paragraph 1 above.

C:9. If the custody officer has any doubts about—

* providing an oral translation or summary of an essential document instead of a written translation (see para. 3),
* whether the suspect fully understands the consequences of waiving their right to a written translation of an essential document (see para. 4), or
* about refusing to provide a translation of a requested document (see para. 7),

the officer should seek advice from an inspector or above.

Documentation

C:10. Action taken in accordance with this annex shall be recorded in the detainee's custody **A-111j** record or interview record as appropriate (see Code C, para. 13.11(e)).

Notes for guidance

C:M1 *It is not necessary to disclose information in any translation which is capable of undermining or* **A-111k** *otherwise adversely affecting any investigative processes, for example, by enabling the suspect to fabricate an innocent explanation or to conceal lies from the interviewer.*

C:M2 *No police officer or police staff shall indicate to any suspect, except to answer a direct question, whether the period for which they are liable to be detained or if not detained, the time taken to complete the interview, might be reduced:*

* *if they do not ask for legal advice before deciding whether they wish to waive their right to a written translation of an essential document; or*
* *if they decide to waive their right to a written translation of an essential document.*

C:M3 *There is no power under PACE to detain a person or to delay their release solely to create and provide a written translation of any essential document.*

(5) Identification

The text that follows is of the version of the code that came into force on March 7, 2011: see **A-112** *ante*, Appendix A-1.

In connection with Code D, see also §§ 14-39 *et seq.* (application of code), §§ 14-45 *et seq.* (identification procedures), § 14-54 (group identification, confrontation and video identification), §§ 14-57 *et seq.* (effect of breaches), §§ 14-60 *et seq.* (photographs), § 14-62 (video recordings), and § 15-199 (photographs) in the main work.

D. CODE OF PRACTICE FOR THE IDENTIFICATION OF PERSONS BY POLICE OFFICERS

Commencement—Transitional arrangements

A-113   This code has effect in relation to any identification procedure carried out after midnight on 6 March 2011.

D:1 Introduction

A-114   D:1.1 This code of practice concerns the principal methods used by police to identify people in connection with the investigation of offences and the keeping of accurate and reliable criminal records. The powers and procedures in this code must be used fairly, responsibly, with respect for the people to whom they apply and without unlawful discrimination. The Equality Act 2010 makes it unlawful for police officers to discriminate against, harass or victimise any person on the grounds of the "protected characteristics" of age, disability, gender reassignment, race, religion or belief, sex and sexual orientation, marriage and civil partnership, pregnancy and maternity when using their powers. When police forces are carrying out their functions they also have a duty to have regard to the need to eliminate unlawful discrimination, harassment and victimisation and to take steps to foster good relations.

D:1.2 In this code, identification by an eye-witness arises when a witness who has seen the offender committing the crime and is given an opportunity to identify a person suspected of involvement in the offence in a video identification, identification parade or similar procedure. These eyewitness identification procedures (see Part A of section 3 below) are designed to:

- test the witness's ability to identify the suspect as the person they saw on a previous occasion;
- provide safeguards against mistaken identification.

While this code concentrates on visual identification procedures, it does not preclude the police making use of aural identification procedures such as a "voice identification parade", where they judge that appropriate.

D:1.2A In this code, separate provisions in Part B of section 3 below apply when any person, including a police officer, is asked if they recognise anyone they see in an image as being someone they know and to test their claim that they recognise that person as someone who is known to them. Except where stated, these separate provisions are not subject to the eye-witnesses identification procedures described in paragraph 1.2.

D:1.3 Identification by fingerprints applies when a person's fingerprints are taken to:

- compare with fingerprints found at the scene of a crime;
- check and prove convictions;
- help to ascertain a person's identity.

D:1.3A Identification using footwear impressions applies when a person's footwear impressions are taken to compare with impressions found at the scene of a crime.

D:1.4 Identification by body samples and impressions includes taking samples such as blood or hair to generate a DNA profile for comparison with material obtained from the scene of a crime, or a victim.

D:1.5 Taking photographs of arrested people applies to recording and checking identity and locating and tracing persons who:

- are wanted for offences;
- fail to answer their bail.

D:1.6 Another method of identification involves searching and examining detained suspects to find, *e.g.*, marks such as tattoos or scars which may help establish their identity or whether they have been involved in committing an offence.

D:1.7 The provisions of the Police and Criminal Evidence Act 1984 (PACE) and this code are designed to make sure fingerprints, samples, impressions and photographs are taken, used and retained, and identification procedures carried out, only when justified and necessary for preventing, detecting or investigating crime. If these provisions are not observed, the application of the relevant procedures in particular cases may be open to question.

D:2 General

A-115   D:2.1 This code must be readily available at all police stations for consultation by:

- police officers and police staff;
- detained persons;
- members of the public.

D:2.2 The provisions of this code:

- include the Annexes;
- do not include the *Notes for guidance*.

D:2.3 Code C, paragraph 1.4, regarding a person who may be mentally disordered or otherwise mentally vulnerable and the *Notes for guidance* applicable to those provisions apply to this code.

D:2.4 Code C, paragraph 1.5, regarding a person who appears to be under the age of 17 applies to this code.

D:2.5 Code C, paragraph 1.6, regarding a person who appears to be blind, seriously visually impaired, deaf, unable to read or speak or has difficulty communicating orally because of a speech impediment applies to this code.

D:2.6 In this code:

- "appropriate adult" means the same as in Code C, paragraph 1.7;
- "solicitor" means the same as in Code C, paragraph 6.12;
  and the *Notes for guidance* applicable to those provisions apply to this code;
- where a search or other procedure under this code may only be carried out or observed by a person of the same sex as the person to whom the search or procedure applies, the gender of the detainee and other persons present should be established and recorded in line with Annex F of Code A.

D:2.7 References to custody officers include those performing the functions of custody officer, see paragraph 1.9 of Code C.

D:2.8 When a record of any action requiring the authority of an officer of a specified rank is made under this code, subject to paragraph 2.18, the officer's name and rank must be recorded.

D:2.9 When this code requires the prior authority or agreement of an officer of at least inspector or superintendent rank, that authority may be given by a sergeant or chief inspector who has been authorised to perform the functions of the higher rank under PACE, s.107.

D:2.10 Subject to paragraph 2.18, all records must be timed and signed by the maker.

D:2.11 Records must be made in the custody record, unless otherwise specified. References to "pocket book" include any official report book issued to police officers or police staff.

D:2.12 If any procedure in this code requires a person's consent, the consent of a:

- mentally disordered or otherwise mentally vulnerable person is only valid if given in the presence of the appropriate adult;
- juvenile is only valid if their parent's or guardian's consent is also obtained unless the juvenile is under 14, when their parent's or guardian's consent is sufficient in its own right. If the only obstacle to an identification procedure in section 3 is that a juvenile's parent or guardian refuses consent or reasonable efforts to obtain it have failed, the identification officer may apply the provisions of paragraph 3.21. See *Note 2A*.

D:2.13 If a person is blind, seriously visually impaired or unable to read, the custody officer or identification officer shall make sure their solicitor, relative, appropriate adult or some other person likely to take an interest in them and not involved in the investigation is available to help check any documentation. When this code requires written consent or signing, the person assisting may be asked to sign instead, if the detainee prefers. This paragraph does not require an appropriate adult to be called solely to assist in checking and signing documentation for a person who is not a juvenile, or mentally disordered or otherwise mentally vulnerable (see *Note 2B* and Code C, paragraph 3.15).

D:2.14 If any procedure in this code requires information to be given to or sought from a suspect, it must be given or sought in the appropriate adult's presence if the suspect is mentally disordered, otherwise mentally vulnerable or a juvenile. If the appropriate adult is not present when the information is first given or sought, the procedure must be repeated in the presence of the appropriate adult when they arrive. If the suspect appears deaf or there is doubt about their hearing or speaking ability or ability to understand English, and effective communication cannot be established, the information must be given or sought through an interpreter.

D:2.15 Any procedure in this code involving the participation of a suspect who is mentally disordered, otherwise mentally vulnerable or a juvenile must take place in the presence of the appropriate adult. See Code C, paragraph 1.4.

D:2.15A Any procedure in this code involving the participation of a witness who is or appears to be mentally disordered, otherwise mentally vulnerable or a juvenile should take place in the presence of a pre-trial support person unless the witness states that they do not want a support person to be present. A support person must not be allowed to prompt any identification of a suspect by a witness. See *Note 2AB*.

D:2.16 References to:

- "taking a photograph", include the use of any process to produce a single, still or moving, visual image;
- "photographing a person", should be construed accordingly;
- "photographs", "films", "negatives" and "copies" include relevant visual images recorded, stored, or reproduced through any medium;

- "destruction" includes the deletion of computer data relating to such images or making access to that data impossible.

D:2.17 Except as described, nothing in this code affects the powers and procedures:

(i) for requiring and taking samples of breath, blood and urine in relation to driving offences, etc, when under the influence of drink, drugs or excess alcohol under the:
- Road Traffic Act 1988, ss.4 to 11;
- Road Traffic Offenders Act 1988, ss.15 and 16;
- Transport and Works Act 1992, ss.26 to 38;

(ii) under the Immigration Act 1971, Sched. 2, para. 18, for taking photographs and fingerprints from persons detained under that Act, Schedule 2, paragraph 16 (administrative controls as to control on entry etc.); for taking fingerprints in accordance with the Immigration and Asylum Act 1999, ss.141 and 142(3), or other methods for collecting information about a person's external physical characteristics provided for by regulations made under that Act, section 144;

(iii) under the Terrorism Act 2000, Sched. 8, for taking photographs, fingerprints, skin impressions, body samples or impressions from people:
- arrested under that Act, section 41,
- detained for the purposes of examination under that Act, Schedule 7, and to whom the code of practice issued under that Act, Schedule 14, paragraph 6, applies ("the terrorism provisions"); see *Note 2C*;

(iv) for taking photographs, fingerprints, skin impressions, body samples or impressions from people who have been:
- arrested on warrants issued in Scotland, by officers exercising powers under the Criminal Justice and Public Order Act 1994, s.136(2);
- arrested or detained without warrant by officers from a police force in Scotland exercising their powers of arrest or detention under the Criminal Justice and Public Order Act 1994, s.137(2) (cross border powers of arrest etc.).

Note: in these cases, police powers and duties and the person's rights and entitlements whilst at a police station in England and Wales are the same as if the person had been arrested in Scotland by a Scottish police officer.

D:2.18 Nothing in this code requires the identity of officers or police staff to be recorded or disclosed:

(a) in the case of enquiries linked to the investigation of terrorism;
(b) if the officers or police staff reasonably believe recording or disclosing their names might put them in danger.

In these cases, they shall use warrant or other identification numbers and the name of their police station. See *Note 2D*.

A-118   D:2.19 In this code:

(a) "designated person" means a person other than a police officer, designated under the Police Reform Act 2002, Pt 4, who has specified powers and duties of police officers conferred or imposed on them;
(b) any reference to a police officer includes a designated person acting in the exercise or performance of the powers and duties conferred or imposed on them by their designation.

D:2.20 If a power conferred on a designated person:

(a) allows reasonable force to be used when exercised by a police officer, a designated person exercising that power has the same entitlement to use force;
(b) includes power to use force to enter any premises, that power is not exercisable by that designated person except:
    (i) in the company, and under the supervision, of a police officer; or
    (ii) for the purpose of:
        - saving life or limb; or
        - preventing serious damage to property.

D:2.21 Nothing in this code prevents the custody officer, or other officer given custody of the detainee, from allowing police staff who are not designated persons to carry out individual procedures or tasks at the police station if the law allows. However, the officer remains responsible for making sure the procedures and tasks are carried out correctly in accordance with the codes of practice. Any such person must be:

(a) a person employed by a police authority maintaining a police force and under the control and direction of the chief officer of that force;
(b) employed by a person with whom a police authority has a contract for the provision of services relating to persons arrested or otherwise in custody.

D:2.22 Designated persons and other police staff must have regard to any relevant provisions of the codes of practice.

Notes for guidance

D:2A *For the purposes of paragraph 2.12, the consent required from a parent or guardian may, for a juvenile* **A-119** *in the care of a local authority or voluntary organisation, be given by that authority or organisation. In the case of a juvenile, nothing in paragraph 2.12 requires the parent, guardian or representative of a local authority or voluntary organisation to be present to give their consent, unless they are acting as the appropriate adult under paragraphs 2.14 or 2.15. However, it is important that a parent or guardian not present is fully informed before being asked to consent. They must be given the same information about the procedure and the juvenile's suspected involvement in the offence as the juvenile and appropriate adult. The parent or guardian must also be allowed to speak to the juvenile and the appropriate adult if they wish. Provided the consent is fully informed and is not withdrawn, it may be obtained at any time before the procedure takes place.*

D:2AB *The Youth Justice and Criminal Evidence Act 1999 guidance "Achieving Best Evidence in Criminal Proceedings" indicates that a pre-trial support person should accompany a vulnerable witness during any identification procedure unless the witness states that they do not want a support person to be present. It states that this support person should not be (or not be likely to be) a witness in the investigation.*

D:2B *People who are seriously visually impaired or unable to read may be unwilling to sign police documents. The alternative,* i.e. *their representative signing on their behalf, seeks to protect the interests of both police and suspects.*

D:2C *Photographs, fingerprints, samples and impressions may be taken from a person detained under the terrorism provisions to help determine whether they are, or have been, involved in terrorism, as well as when there are reasonable grounds for suspecting their involvement in a particular offence.*

D:2D *The purpose of paragraph 2.18(b) is to protect those involved in serious organised crime investigations or arrests of particularly violent suspects when there is reliable information that those arrested or their associates may threaten or cause harm to the officers. In cases of doubt, an officer of inspector rank or above should be consulted.*

D:3 Identification and recognition of suspects

(a) *Identification of a suspect by an eye-witness*

D:3.0 This part applies when an eye-witness has seen the offender committing the crime or in any **A-120** other circumstances which tend to prove or disprove the involvement of the person they saw in the crime, for example, close to the scene of the crime, immediately before or immediately after it was committed. It sets out the procedures to be used to test the ability of that eye-witness to identify a person suspected of involvement in the offence as the person they saw on the previous occasion. Except where stated, this part does not apply to the procedures described in Part B and *Note 3AA*.

D:3.1 A record shall be made of the suspect's description as first given by a potential witness. This record must:

(a) be made and kept in a form which enables details of that description to be accurately produced from it, in a visible and legible form, which can be given to the suspect or the suspect's solicitor in accordance with this code; and

(b) unless otherwise specified, be made before the witness takes part in any identification procedures under paragraphs 3.5 to 3.10, 3.21 or 3.23.

A copy of the record shall where practicable, be given to the suspect or their solicitor before any procedures under paragraphs 3.5 to 3.10, 3.21 or 3.23 are carried out. See *Note 3E*.

(a) Cases when the suspect's identity is not known

D:3.2 In cases when the suspect's identity is not known, a witness may be taken to a particular neighbourhood or place to see whether they can identify the person they saw on a previous occasion. Although the number, age, sex, race, general description and style of clothing of other people present at the location and the way in which any identification is made cannot be controlled, the principles applicable to the formal procedures under paragraphs 3.5 to 3.10 shall be followed as far as practicable. For example:

(a) where it is practicable to do so, a record should be made of the witness's description of the suspect, as in paragraph 3.1(a), before asking the witness to make an identification;

(b) care must be taken not to direct the witness's attention to any individual unless, taking into account all the circumstances, this cannot be avoided; however, this does not prevent a witness being asked to look carefully at the people around at the time or to look towards a group or in a particular direction, if this appears necessary to make sure that the witness does not overlook a possible suspect simply because the witness is looking in the opposite direction and also to enable the witness to make comparisons between any suspect and others who are in the area; see *Note 3F*;

(c) where there is more than one witness, every effort should be made to keep them separate and witnesses should be taken to see whether they can identify a person independently;

(d) once there is sufficient information to justify the arrest of a particular individual for suspected involvement in the offence, *e.g.*, after a witness makes a positive identification, the provisions set out from paragraph 3.4 onwards shall apply for any other witnesses in relation to that individual;

(e) the officer or police staff accompanying the witness must record, in their pocket book, the action taken as soon as, and in as much detail, as possible. The record should include: the date, time and place of the relevant occasion the witness claims to have previously seen the suspect; where any identification was made; how it was made and the conditions at the time (*e.g.* the distance the witness was from the suspect, the weather and light); if the witness's attention was drawn to the suspect; the reason for this; and anything said by the witness or the suspect about the identification or the conduct of the procedure.

D:3.3 A witness must not be shown photographs, computerised or artist's composite likenesses or similar likenesses or pictures (including "E-fit" images) if the identity of the suspect is known to the police and the suspect is available to take part in a video identification, an identification parade or a group identification. If the suspect's identity is not known, the showing of such images to a witness to obtain identification evidence must be done in accordance with Annex E.

(b) Cases when the suspect is known and available

D:3.4 If the suspect's identity is known to the police and they are available, the identification procedures set out in paragraphs 3.5 to 3.10 may be used. References in this section to a suspect being "known" mean there is sufficient information known to the police to justify the arrest of a particular person for suspected involvement in the offence. A suspect being "available" means they are immediately available or will be within a reasonably short time and willing to take an effective part in at least one of the following which it is practicable to arrange:

- video identification;
- identification parade; or
- group identification.

Video identification

D:3.5 A "video identification" is when the witness is shown moving images of a known suspect, together with similar images of others who resemble the suspect. Moving images must be used unless:

- the suspect is known but not available (see paragraph 3.21 of this code); or
- in accordance with paragraph 2A of Annex A of this code, the identification officer does not consider that replication of a physical feature can be achieved or that it is not possible to conceal the location of the feature on the image of the suspect.

The identification officer may then decide to make use of video identification but using **still** images.

D:3.6 Video identifications must be carried out in accordance with Annex A.

Identification parade

D:3.7 An "identification parade" is when the witness sees the suspect in a line of others who resemble the suspect.

D:3.8 Identification parades must be carried out in accordance with Annex B.

Group identification

D:3.9 A "group identification" is when the witness sees the suspect in an informal group of people.

D:3.10 Group identifications must be carried out in accordance with Annex C.

Arranging identification procedures

D:3.11 Except for the provisions in paragraph 3.19, the arrangements for, and conduct of, the identification procedures in paragraphs 3.5 to 3.10 and circumstances in which an identification procedure must be held shall be the responsibility of an officer not below inspector rank who is not involved with the investigation, "the identification officer". Unless otherwise specified, the identification officer may allow another officer or police staff, see paragraph 2.21, to make arrangements for, and conduct, any of these identification procedures. In delegating these procedures, the identification officer must be able to supervise effectively and either intervene or be contacted for advice. No officer or any other person involved with the investigation of the case against the suspect, beyond the extent required by these procedures, may take any part in these procedures or act as the identification officer. This does not prevent the identification officer from consulting the officer in charge of the investigation to determine which procedure to use. When an identification procedure is required, in the interest of fairness to suspects and witnesses, it must be held as soon as practicable.

Circumstances in which an eye-witness identification procedure must be held

D:3.12 Whenever:

(i) an eye witness has identified a suspect or purported to have identified them prior to any identification procedure set out in paragraphs 3.5 to 3.10 having been held; or

(ii) there is a witness available who expresses an ability to identify the suspect, or where there is a reasonable chance of the witness being able to do so, and they have not been given an opportunity to identify the suspect in any of the procedures set out in paragraphs 3.5 to 3.10,

and the suspect disputes being the person the witness claims to have seen, an identification procedure shall be held unless it is not practicable or it would serve no useful purpose in proving or disproving whether the suspect was involved in committing the offence, for example:

- where the suspect admits being at the scene of the crime and gives an account of what took place and the eye-witness does not see anything which contradicts that;
- when it is not disputed that the suspect is already known to the witness who claims to have recognised them when seeing them commit the crime.

D:3.13 An eye-witness identification procedure may also be held if the officer in charge of the investigation considers it would be useful.

Selecting an identification procedure

D:3.14 If, because of paragraph 3.12, an identification procedure is to be held, the suspect shall initially be offered a video identification unless:

(a) a video identification is not practicable; or

(b) an identification parade is both practicable and more suitable than a video identification; or

(c) paragraph 3.16 applies.

The identification officer and the officer in charge of the investigation shall consult each other to determine which option is to be offered. An identification parade may not be practicable because of factors relating to the witnesses, such as their number, state of health, availability and travelling requirements. A video identification would normally be more suitable if it could be arranged and completed sooner than an identification parade. Before an option is offered the suspect must also be reminded of their entitlement to have free legal advice, see Code C, paragraph 6.5.

D:3.15 A suspect who refuses the identification procedure first offered shall be asked to state their reason for refusing and may get advice from their solicitor and/or if present, their appropriate adult. The suspect, solicitor and/or appropriate adult shall be allowed to make representations about why another procedure should be used. A record should be made of the reasons for refusal and any representations made. After considering any reasons given, and representations made, the identification officer shall, if appropriate, arrange for the suspect to be offered an alternative which the officer considers suitable and practicable. If the officer decides it is not suitable and practicable to offer an alternative identification procedure, the reasons for that decision shall be recorded.

D:3.16 A group identification may initially be offered if the officer in charge of the investigation considers it is more suitable than a video identification or an identification parade and the identification officer considers it practicable to arrange.

Notice to suspect

D:3.17 Unless paragraph 3.20 applies, before a video identification, an identification parade or **A-123** group identification is arranged, the following shall be explained to the suspect:

(i) the purposes of the video identification, identification parade or group identification;

(ii) their entitlement to free legal advice; see Code C, paragraph 6.5;

(iii) the procedures for holding it, including their right to have a solicitor or friend present;

(iv) that they do not have to consent to or co-operate in a video identification, identification parade or group identification;

(v) that if they do not consent to, and co-operate in, a video identification, identification parade or group identification, their refusal may be given in evidence in any subsequent trial and police may proceed covertly without their consent or make other arrangements to test whether a witness can identify them, see paragraph 3.21;

(vi) whether, for the purposes of the video identification procedure, images of them have previously been obtained, see paragraph 3.20, and if so, that they may co-operate in providing further, suitable images to be used instead;

(vii) if appropriate, the special arrangements for juveniles;

(viii) if appropriate, the special arrangements for mentally disordered or otherwise mentally vulnerable people;

(ix) that if they significantly alter their appearance between being offered an identification procedure and any attempt to hold an identification procedure, this may be given in evidence if the case comes to trial, and the identification officer may then consider other forms of identification, see paragraph 3.21 and *Note 3C*;

(x) that a moving image or photograph may be taken of them when they attend for any identification procedure;

(xi) whether, before their identity became known, the witness was shown photographs, a computerised or artist's composite likeness or similar likeness or image by the police, see *Note 3B*;

(xii) that if they change their appearance before an identification parade, it may not be practicable to arrange one on the day or subsequently and, because of the appearance change, the identification officer may consider alternative methods of identification, see *Note 3C*;

(xiii) that they or their solicitor will be provided with details of the description of the suspect as first given by any witnesses who are to attend the video identification, identification parade, group identification or confrontation, see paragraph 3.1.

D:3.18 This information must also be recorded in a written notice handed to the suspect. The suspect must be given a reasonable opportunity to read the notice, after which, they should be asked to sign a second copy to indicate if they are willing to co-operate with the making of a video or take part in the identification parade or group identification. The signed copy shall be retained by the identification officer.

D:3.19 The duties of the identification officer under paragraphs 3.17 and 3.18 may be performed by the custody officer or other officer not involved in the investigation if:

(a) it is proposed to release the suspect in order that an identification procedure can be arranged and carried out and an inspector is not available to act as the identification officer, see paragraph 3.11, before the suspect leaves the station; or

(b) it is proposed to keep the suspect in police detention whilst the procedure is arranged and carried out and waiting for an inspector to act as the identification officer, see paragraph 3.11, would cause unreasonable delay to the investigation.

The officer concerned shall inform the identification officer of the action taken and give them the signed copy of the notice. See *Note 3C*.

D:3.20 If the identification officer and officer in charge of the investigation suspect, on reasonable grounds that if the suspect was given the information and notice as in paragraphs 3.17 and 3.18, they would then take steps to avoid being seen by a witness in any identification procedure, the identification officer may arrange for images of the suspect suitable for use in a video identification procedure to be obtained before giving the information and notice. If suspect's [*sic*] images are obtained in these circumstances, the suspect may, for the purposes of a video identification procedure, co-operate in providing new images which if suitable, would be used instead, see paragraph 3.17(vi).

(c) Cases when the suspect is known but not available

A-124

D:3.21 When a known suspect is not available or has ceased to be available, see paragraph 3.4, the identification officer may make arrangements for a video identification (see Annex A). If necessary, the identification officer may follow the video identification procedures but using still images. Any suitable moving or still images may be used and these may be obtained covertly if necessary. Alternatively, the identification officer may make arrangements for a group identification. See *Note 3D*. These provisions may also be applied to juveniles where the consent of their parent or guardian is either refused or reasonable efforts to obtain that consent have failed (see paragraph 2.12).

D:3.22 Any covert activity should be strictly limited to that necessary to test the ability of the witness to identify the suspect.

D:3.23 The identification officer may arrange for the suspect to be confronted by the witness if none of the options referred to in paragraphs 3.5 to 3.10 or 3.21 are practicable. A "confrontation" is when the suspect is directly confronted by the witness. A confrontation does not require the suspect's consent. Confrontations must be carried out in accordance with Annex D.

D:3.24 Requirements for information to be given to, or sought from, a suspect or for the suspect to be given an opportunity to view images before they are shown to a witness, do not apply if the suspect's lack of co-operation prevents the necessary action.

(d) Documentation

D:3.25 A record shall be made of the video identification, identification parade, group identifica- **A-125** tion or confrontation on forms provided for the purpose.

D:3.26 If the identification officer considers it is not practicable to hold a video identification or identification parade requested by the suspect, the reasons shall be recorded and explained to the suspect.

D:3.27 A record shall be made of a person's failure or refusal to co-operate in a video identification, identification parade or group identification and, if applicable, of the grounds for obtaining images in accordance with paragraph 3.20.

(e) Showing films and photographs of incidents and information released to the media

D:3.28 Nothing in this code inhibits showing films, photographs or other images to the public **A-126** through the national or local media, or to police officers for the purposes of recognition and tracing suspects. However, when such material is shown to obtain evidence of recognition, the procedures in Part B will apply. See *Note 3AA*.

D:3.29 When a broadcast or publication is made, see paragraph 3.28, a copy of the relevant material released to the media for the purposes of recognising or tracing the suspect, shall be kept. The suspect or their solicitor shall be allowed to view such material before any eye-witness identification procedures under paragraphs 3.5 to 3.10, 3.21 or 3.23 of Part A are carried out, provided it is practicable and would not unreasonably delay the investigation. Each eye-witness involved in the procedure shall be asked, after they have taken part, whether they have seen any film, photograph or image relating to the offence or any description of the suspect which has been broadcast or published in any national or local media or on any social networking site and if they have, they should be asked to give details of the circumstances, such as the date and place as relevant. Their replies shall be recorded. This paragraph does not affect any separate requirement under the Criminal Procedure and Investigations Act 1996 to retain material in connection with criminal investigations.

(f) Destruction and retention of photographs taken or used in eye-witness identification procedures

D:3.30 PACE, s.64A, see paragraph 5.12, provides powers to take photographs of suspects and allows these photographs to be used or disclosed only for purposes related to the prevention or detection of crime, the investigation of offences or the conduct of prosecutions by, or on behalf of, police or other law enforcement and prosecuting authorities inside and outside the United Kingdom or the enforcement of a sentence. After being so used or disclosed, they may be retained but can only be used or disclosed for the same purposes.

D:3.31 Subject to paragraph 3.33, the photographs (and all negatives and copies), of suspects not taken in accordance with the provisions in paragraph 5.12 which are taken for the purposes of, or in connection with, the identification procedures in paragraphs 3.5 to 3.10, 3.21 or 3.23 must be destroyed unless the suspect:

    (a) is charged with, or informed they may be prosecuted for, a recordable offence;

    (b) is prosecuted for a recordable offence;

    (c) is cautioned for a recordable offence or given a warning or reprimand in accordance with the Crime and Disorder Act 1998 for a recordable offence; or

    (d) gives informed consent, in writing, for the photograph or images to be retained for purposes described in paragraph 3.30.

D:3.32 When paragraph 3.31 requires the destruction of any photograph, the person must be given an opportunity to witness the destruction or to have a certificate confirming the destruction if they request one within five days of being informed that the destruction is required.

D:3.33 Nothing in paragraph 3.31 affects any separate requirement under the Criminal Procedure and Investigations Act 1996 to retain material in connection with criminal investigations.

(b) *Evidence of recognition by showing films, photographs and other images*

D:3.34 This part of this section applies when, for the purposes of obtaining evidence of recogni- **A-126a** tion, any person, including a police officer:

    (a) views the image of an individual in a film, photograph or any other visual medium; and

    (b) is asked whether they recognise that individual as someone who is known to them.

See *Notes 3AA* and *3G*.

D:3.35 The films, photographs and other images shall be shown on an individual basis to avoid any possibility of collusion and to provide safeguards against mistaken recognition (see *Note 3G*), the showing shall as far as possible follow the principles for video identification if the suspect is known, see Annex A, or identification by photographs if the suspect is not known, see Annex E.

D:3.36 A record of the circumstances and conditions under which the person is given an opportunity to recognise the individual must be made and the record must include:

(a) whether the person knew or was given information concerning the name or identity of any suspect;

(b) what the person has been told *before* the viewing about the offence, the person(s) depicted in the images or the offender and by whom;

(c) how and by whom the witness was asked to view the image or look at the individual;

(d) whether the viewing was alone or with others and if with others, the reason for it;

(e) the arrangements under which the person viewed the film or saw the individual and by whom those arrangements were made;

(f) whether the viewing of any images was arranged as part of a mass circulation to police and the public or for selected persons;

(g) the date time and place images were viewed or further viewed or the individual was seen;

(h) the times between which the images were viewed or the individual was seen;

(i) how the viewing of images or sighting of the individual was controlled and by whom;

(j) whether the person was familiar with the location shown in any images or the place where they saw the individual and if so, why;

(k) whether or not on this occasion, the person claims to recognise any image shown, or any individual seen, as being someone known to them, and if they do:

(i) the reason;

(ii) the words of recognition;

(iii) any expressions of doubt;

(iv) what features of the image or the individual triggered the recognition.

D:3.37 The record under paragraph 3.36 may be made by:

• the person who views the image or sees the individual and makes the recognition;

• the officer or police staff in charge of showing the images to the person or in charge of the conditions under which the person sees the individual.

Notes for guidance

D:3AA *The eye-witness identification procedures in Part A should not be used to test whether a witness can recognise a person as someone they know and would be able to give evidence of recognition along the lines that "On (describe date, time location) I saw an image of an individual who I recognised as AB." In these cases, the procedures in Part B shall apply.*

D:3A *Except for the provisions of Annex E, paragraph 1, a police officer who is a witness for the purposes of this part of the code is subject to the same principles and procedures as a civilian witness.*

D:3B *When a witness attending an identification procedure has previously been shown photographs, or been shown or provided with computerised or artist's composite likenesses, or similar likenesses or pictures, it is the officer in charge of the investigation's responsibility to make the identification officer aware of this.*

D:3C *The purpose of paragraph 3.19 is to avoid or reduce delay in arranging identification procedures by enabling the required information and warnings, see sub-paragraphs 3.17(ix) and 3.17(xii), to be given at the earliest opportunity.*

D:3D *Paragraph 3.21 would apply when a known suspect deliberately makes themselves "unavailable" in order to delay or frustrate arrangements for obtaining identification evidence. It also applies when a suspect refuses or fails to take part in a video identification, an identification parade or a group identification, or refuses or fails to take part in the only practicable options from that list. It enables any suitable images of the suspect, moving or still, which are available or can be obtained, to be used in an identification procedure. Examples include images from custody and other CCTV systems and from visually recorded interview records, see Code F, Note for Guidance 2D.*

D:3E *When it is proposed to show photographs to a witness in accordance with Annex E, it is the responsibility of the officer in charge of the investigation to confirm to the officer responsible for supervising and directing the showing, that the first description of the suspect given by that witness has been recorded. If this description has not been recorded, the procedure under Annex E must be postponed. See Annex E, paragraph 2.*

D:3F *The admissibility and value of identification evidence obtained when carrying out the procedure under paragraph 3.2 may be compromised if:*

(a) *before a person is identified, the witness's attention is specifically drawn to that person; or*

(b) *the suspect's identity becomes known before the procedure.*

D:3G *The admissibility and value of evidence of recognition obtained when carrying out the procedures in Part B may be compromised if before the person is recognised, the witness who has claimed to know them is given or is made, or becomes aware of, information about the person which was not previously known to them personally but which they have purported to rely on to support their claim that the person is in fact known to them.*

D:4 Identification by fingerprints and footwear impressions

(a) *Taking fingerprints in connection with a criminal investigation*

(a) General

D:4.1 References to "fingerprints" means any record, produced by any method, of the skin pattern and other physical characteristics or features of a person's: **A-128**
  (i) fingers; or
  (ii) palms.

(b) Action

D:4.2 A person's fingerprints may be taken in connection with the investigation of an offence only with their consent or if paragraph 4.3 applies. If the person is at a police station consent must be in writing.

D:4.3 PACE, s.61, provides powers to take fingerprints without consent from any person over the age of ten years:
  (a) under section 61(3), from a person detained at a police station in consequence of being arrested for a recordable offence, see *Note 4A*, if they have not had their fingerprints taken in the course of the investigation of the offence unless those previously taken fingerprints are not a complete set or some or all of those fingerprints are not of sufficient quality to allow satisfactory analysis, comparison or matching;
  (b) under section 61(4), from a person detained at a police station who has been charged with a recordable offence, see *Note 4A*, or informed they will be reported for such an offence if they have not had their fingerprints taken in the course of the investigation of the offence unless those previously taken fingerprints are not a complete set or some or all of those fingerprints are not of sufficient quality to allow satisfactory analysis, comparison or matching;
  (c) under section 61(4A), from a person who has been bailed to appear at a court or police station if the person:
    (i) has answered to bail for a person whose fingerprints were taken previously and there are reasonable grounds for believing they are not the same person; or
    (ii) who has answered to bail claims to be a different person from a person whose fingerprints were previously taken;
    and in either case, the court or an officer of inspector rank or above, authorises the fingerprints to be taken at the court or police station (an inspector's authority may be given in writing or orally and confirmed in writing, as soon as practicable);
  (ca) under section 61(5A) from a person who has been arrested for a recordable offence and released if the person:
    (i) is on bail and has not had their fingerprints taken in the course of the investigation of the offence; or
    (ii) has had their fingerprints taken in the course of the investigation of the offence, but they do not constitute a complete set or some, or all, of the fingerprints are not of sufficient quality to allow satisfactory analysis, comparison or matching;
  (cb) under section 61(5B) from a person not detained at a police station who has been charged with a recordable offence or informed they will be reported for such an offence if they have not had their fingerprints taken in the course of the investigation or their fingerprints have been taken in the course of the investigation of the offence, but they do not constitute a complete set or some, or all, of the fingerprints are not of sufficient quality to allow satisfactory analysis, comparison or matching;
  (d) under section 61(6), from a person who has been:
    (i) convicted of a recordable offence;
    (ii) given a caution in respect of a recordable offence which, at the time of the caution, the person admitted; or
    (iii) warned or reprimanded under the Crime and Disorder Act 1998, s.65, for a recordable offence, if, since their conviction, caution, warning or reprimand their fingerprints

have not been taken or their fingerprints which have been taken since then do not constitute a complete set or some, or all, of the fingerprints are not of sufficient quality to allow satisfactory analysis, comparison or matching, and in either case, an officer of inspector rank or above, is satisfied that taking the fingerprints is necessary to assist in the prevention or detection of crime and authorises the taking;

(e) under section 61(6A) from a person a constable reasonably suspects is committing or attempting to commit, or has committed or attempted to commit, any offence if either:

- the person's name is unknown and cannot be readily ascertained by the constable; or
- the constable has reasonable grounds for doubting whether a name given by the person is their real name; note: fingerprints taken under this power are not regarded as having been taken in the course of the investigation of an offence; [see *Note 4C*];

(f) under section 61(6D) from a person who has been convicted outside England and Wales of an offence which if committed in England and Wales would be a qualifying offence as defined by PACE, s.65A [see *Note 4AB*] if:

(i) the person's fingerprints have not been taken previously under this power or their fingerprints have been so taken on a previous occasion but they do not constitute a complete set or some, or all, of the fingerprints are not of sufficient quality to allow satisfactory analysis, comparison or matching; and

(ii) a police officer of inspector rank or above is satisfied that taking fingerprints is necessary to assist in the prevention or detection of crime and authorises them to be taken.

D:4.4 PACE, s.63A(4), and Sched. 2A, provide powers to:

(a) make a requirement (in accordance with Annex G) for a person to attend a police station to have their fingerprints taken in the exercise of certain powers in paragraph 4.3 above when that power applies at the time the fingerprints would be taken in accordance with the requirement; those powers are:

(i) section 61(5A)—persons arrested for a recordable offence and released, see paragraph 4.3(ca): the requirement may not be made more than six months from the day the investigating officer was informed that the fingerprints previously taken were incomplete or below standard;

(ii) section 61(5B)—persons charged etc. with a recordable offence, see paragraph 4.3(cb): the requirement may not be made more than six months from:

- the day the person was charged or reported if fingerprints have not been taken since then; or
- the day the investigating officer was informed that the fingerprints previously taken were incomplete or below standard;

(iii) section 61(6)—person convicted, cautioned, warned or reprimanded for a recordable offence in England and Wales, see paragraph 4.3(d): where the offence for which the person was convicted etc is also a qualifying offence (see *Note 4AB*), there is no time limit for the exercise of this power; where the conviction etc. is for a recordable offence which is <u>not</u> a qualifying offence, the requirement may not be made more than two years from:

- the day the person was convicted, cautioned, warned or reprimanded, or the day Schedule 2A comes into force (if later), if fingerprints have not been taken since then; or
- the day an officer from the force investigating the offence was informed that the fingerprints previously taken were incomplete or below standard or the day Schedule 2A comes into force (if later);

(v) [*sic*] section 61(6D)—a person who has been convicted of a qualifying offence (see *Note 4AB*) outside England and Wales, see paragraph 4.3(g): there is no time limit for making the requirement;

note: a person who has had their fingerprints taken under any of the powers in section 61 mentioned in paragraph 4.3 on two occasions in relation to any offence may not be required under Schedule 2A to attend a police station for their fingerprints to be taken again under section 61 in relation to that offence, unless authorised by an officer of inspector rank or above; the fact of the authorisation and the reasons for giving it must be recorded as soon as practicable;

(b) arrest, without warrant, a person who fails to comply with the requirement.

D:4.5 A person's fingerprints may be taken, as above, electronically.

D:4.6 Reasonable force may be used, if necessary, to take a person's fingerprints without their consent under the powers as in paragraphs 4.3 and 4.4.

D:4.7 Before any fingerprints are taken:

(a) without consent under any power mentioned in paragraphs 4.3 and 4.4 above, the person must be informed of:

    (i) the reason their fingerprints are to be taken;

    (ii) the power under which they are to be taken; and

    (iii) the fact that the relevant authority has been given if any power mentioned in paragraph 4.3(c), (d) or (f) applies;

(b) with or without consent at a police station or elsewhere, the person must be informed:

    (i) that their fingerprints may be subject of a speculative search against other fingerprints, see *Note 4B*; and

    (ii) that their fingerprints may be retained in accordance with Annex F, Part (a) unless they were taken under the power mentioned in paragraph 4.3(e) when they must be destroyed after they have being [*sic*] checked (see *Note 4C*).

(c) Documentation

D:4.8A A record must be made as soon as practicable after the fingerprints are taken, of:

- the matters in paragraph 4.7(a)(i) to (iii) and the fact that the person has been informed of those matters; and
- the fact that the person has been informed of the matters in paragraph 4.7(b)(i) and (ii).

The record must be made in the person's custody record if they are detained at a police station when the fingerprints are taken.

D:4.8 If force is used, a record shall be made of the circumstances and those present.

D:4.9 [*Not used.*]

(b) Taking fingerprints in connection with immigration enquiries

Action

D:4.10 A person's fingerprints may be taken and retained for the purposes of immigration law **A-129** enforcement and control in accordance with powers and procedures other than under PACE and for which the UK Border Agency (not the police) are responsible. Details of these powers and procedures which are under the Immigration Act 1971, Sched. 2 and Immigration and Asylum Act 1999, s.141, including modifications to the *PACE Codes of Practice* are contained in Chapter 24 of the operational instructions and guidance manual which is published by the UK Border Agency (see *Note 4D*).

D:4.11–15 [*Not used.*]

(c) Taking footwear impressions in connection with a criminal investigation

(a) Action

D:4.16 Impressions of a person's footwear may be taken in connection with the investigation of an offence only with their consent or if paragraph 4.17 applies. If the person is at a police station consent must be in writing.

D:4.17 PACE, s.61A, provides power for a police officer to take footwear impressions without consent from any person over the age of ten years who is detained at a police station:

(a) in consequence of being arrested for a recordable offence, see *Note 4A*; or if the detainee has been charged with a recordable offence, or informed they will be reported for such an offence; and

(b) the detainee has not had an impression of their footwear taken in the course of the investigation of the offence unless the previously taken impression is not complete or is not of sufficient quality to allow satisfactory analysis, comparison or matching (whether in the case in question or generally).

D:4.18 Reasonable force may be used, if necessary, to take a footwear impression from a detainee without consent under the power in paragraph 4.17.

D:4.19 Before any footwear impression is taken with, or without, consent as above, the person must be informed:

(a) of the reason the impression is to be taken;

(b) that the impression may be retained and may be subject of a speculative search against other impressions, see *Note 4B*, unless destruction of the impression is required in accordance with Annex F, Part (a); and

(c) that if their footwear impressions are required to be destroyed, they may witness their destruction as provided for in Annex F, Part (a).

(b) Documentation

D:4.20 A record must be made as soon as possible, of the reason for taking a person's footwear impressions without consent. If force is used, a record shall be made of the circumstances and those present.

D:4.21 A record shall be made when a person has been informed under the terms of paragraph 4.19(b), of the possibility that their footwear impressions may be subject of a speculative search.

Notes for guidance

D:4A *References to "recordable offences" in this code relate to those offences for which convictions, cautions, reprimands and warnings may be recorded in national police records: see PACE, s.27(4). The recordable offences current at the time when this code was prepared, are any offences which carry a sentence of imprisonment on conviction (irrespective of the period, or the age of the offender or actual sentence passed) as well as the non-imprisonable offences under the Vagrancy Act 1824, ss.3 and 4 (begging and persistent begging), the Street Offences Act 1959, s.1 (loitering or soliciting for purposes of prostitution), the Road Traffic Act 1988, s.25 (tampering with motor vehicles), the Criminal Justice and Public Order Act 1994, s.167 (touting for car hire services) and others listed in the National Police Records (Recordable Offences) Regulations 2000 as amended.*

D:4AB *A qualifying offence is one of the offences specified in PACE, s.65A. These indictable offences which concern the use or threat of violence or unlawful force against persons, sexual offences and offences against children include, for example, murder, manslaughter, false imprisonment, kidnapping and other offences such as:*

- *sections 4, 16, 18, 20 to 24 or 47 of the Offences Against the Person Act 1861;*
- *sections 16 to 18 of the Firearms Act 1968;*
- *sections 9 or 10 of the Theft Act 1968 or under section 12A of that Act involving an accident which caused a person's death;*
- *section 1 of the Criminal Damage Act 1971 required to be charged as arson;*
- *section 1 of the Protection of Children Act 1978 and;*
- *sections 1 to 19, 25, 26, 30 to 41, 47 to 50, 52, 53, 57 to 59, 61 to 67, 69 and 70 of the Sexual Offences Act 2003.*

D:4B *Fingerprints, footwear impressions or a DNA sample (and the information derived from it) taken from a person arrested on suspicion of being involved in a recordable offence, or charged with such an offence, or informed they will be reported for such an offence, may be subject of a speculative search. This means the fingerprints, footwear impressions or DNA sample may be checked against other fingerprints, footwear impressions and DNA records held by, or on behalf of, the police and other law enforcement authorities in, or outside, the UK, or held in connection with, or as a result of, an investigation of an offence inside or outside the UK. Fingerprints, footwear impressions and samples taken from a person suspected of committing a recordable offence but not arrested, charged or informed they will be reported for it, may be subject to a speculative search only if the person consents in writing. The following is an example of a basic form of words:*

"I consent to my fingerprints, footwear impressions and DNA sample and information derived from it being retained and used only for purposes related to the prevention and detection of a crime, the investigation of an offence or the conduct of a prosecution either nationally or internationally.

I understand that my fingerprints, footwear impressions or DNA sample may be checked against other fingerprint, footwear impressions and DNA records held by or on behalf of relevant law enforcement authorities, either nationally or internationally.

I understand that once I have given my consent for my fingerprints, footwear impressions or DNA sample to be retained and used I cannot withdraw this consent."

See Annex F regarding the retention and use of fingerprints and footwear impressions taken with consent for elimination purposes.

D:4C *The power under section 61(6A) of PACE described in paragraph 4.3(e) allows fingerprints of a suspect who has not been arrested to be taken in connection with any offence (whether recordable or not) using a mobile device and then checked on the street against the database containing the national fingerprint collection. Fingerprints taken under this power cannot be retained after they have been checked. The results may make an arrest for the suspected offence based on the name condition unnecessary (see code G, paragraph 2.9(a)) and enable the offence to be disposed of without arrest, for example, by summons/charging by post, penalty notice or words of advice. If arrest for a non-recordable offence is necessary for any other reasons, this power may also be exercised at the station. Before the power is exercised, the officer should:*

- *inform the person of the nature of the suspected offence and why they are suspected of committing it;*
- *give them a reasonable opportunity to establish their real name before deciding that their name is unknown and cannot be readily ascertained or that there are reasonable grounds to doubt that a name they have given is their real name;*
- *as applicable, inform the person of the reason why their name is not known and cannot be readily ascertained or of the grounds for doubting that a name they have given is their real name, including, for example, the reason why a particular document the person has produced to verify their real name, is not sufficient.*

D:4D *Powers to take fingerprints without consent for immigration purposes are given to police and immigration officers under the:*

    (a) *Immigration Act 1971, Sched. 2, para. 18(2), when it is reasonably necessary for the purposes of identifying a person detained under the Immigration Act 1971, Sched. 2, para. 16 (detention of person liable to examination or removal), and*

    (b) *Immigration and Asylum Act 1999, s.141(7) when a person:*

- *fails without reasonable excuse to produce, on arrival, a valid passport with a photograph or some other document satisfactorily establishing their identity and nationality;*
- *is refused entry to the UK but is temporarily admitted if an immigration officer reasonably suspects the person might break a residence or reporting condition;*
- *is subject to directions for removal from the UK;*
- *has been arrested under the Immigration Act 1971, Sched. 2, para. 17;*
- *has made a claim for asylum;*
- *is a dependant of any of the above.*

The Immigration and Asylum Act 1999, s.142(3), also gives police and immigration officers power to arrest without warrant a person who fails to comply with a requirement imposed by the Secretary of State to attend a specified place for fingerprinting.

D:5 Examinations to establish identity and the taking of photographs

(a) *Detainees at police stations*

(a) Searching or examination of detainees at police stations

D:5.1 PACE, s.54A(1), allows a detainee at a police station to be searched or examined or both, to **A-130** establish:

    (a) whether they have any marks, features or injuries that would tend to identify them as a person involved in the commission of an offence and to photograph any identifying marks, see paragraph 5.5; or

    (b) their identity, see *Note 5A*.

A person detained at a police station to be searched under a stop and search power, see Code A, is not a detainee for the purposes of these powers.

D:5.2 A search and/or examination to find marks under section 54A(1)(a) may be carried out without the detainee's consent, see paragraph 2.12, only if authorised by an officer of at least inspector rank when consent has been withheld or it is not practicable to obtain consent, see *Note 5D*.

D:5.3 A search or examination to establish a suspect's identity under section 54A(1)(b) may be carried out without the detainee's consent, see paragraph 2.12, only if authorised by an officer of at least inspector rank when the detainee has refused to identify themselves or the authorising officer has reasonable grounds for suspecting the person is not who they claim to be.

D:5.4 Any marks that assist in establishing the detainee's identity, or their identification as a person involved in the commission of an offence, are identifying marks. Such marks may be photographed with the detainee's consent, see paragraph 2.12; or without their consent if it is withheld or it is not practicable to obtain it, see *Note 5D*.

D:5.5 A detainee may only be searched, examined and photographed under section 54A, by a police officer of the same sex.

D:5.6 Any photographs of identifying marks, taken under section 54A, may be used or disclosed only for purposes related to the prevention or detection of crime, the investigation of offences or the conduct of prosecutions by, or on behalf of, police or other law enforcement and prosecuting authorities inside, and outside, the UK. After being so used or disclosed, the photograph may be retained but must not be used or disclosed except for these purposes, see *Note 5B*.

D:5.7 The powers, as in paragraph 5.1, do not affect any separate requirement under the Criminal Procedure and Investigations Act 1996 to retain material in connection with criminal investigations.

D:5.8 Authority for the search and/or examination for the purposes of paragraphs 5.2 and 5.3 may be given orally or in writing. If given orally, the authorising officer must confirm it in writing as soon as practicable. A separate authority is required for each purpose which applies.

D:5.9 If it is established a person is unwilling to co-operate sufficiently to enable a search and/or examination to take place or a suitable photograph to be taken, an officer may use reasonable force to:

    (a) search and/or examine a detainee without their consent; and

    (b) photograph any identifying marks without their consent.

D:5.10 The thoroughness and extent of any search or examination carried out in accordance with the powers in section 54A must be no more than the officer considers necessary to achieve the required purpose. Any search or examination which involves the removal of more than the person's outer clothing shall be conducted in accordance with Code C, Annex A, paragraph 11.

D:5.11 An intimate search may not be carried out under the powers in section 54A.

(b) Photographing detainees at police stations and other persons elsewhere than at a police station

A-131
D:5.12 Under PACE, s.64A, an officer may photograph:

(a) any person whilst they are detained at a police station; and

(b) any person who is elsewhere than at a police station and who has been:

(i) arrested by a constable for an offence;

(ii) taken into custody by a constable after being arrested for an offence by a person other than a constable;

(iii) made subject to a requirement to wait with a community support officer under paragraph 2(3) or (3B) of Schedule 4 to the Police Reform Act 2002;

(iiia) given a direction by a constable under section 27 of the Violent Crime Reduction Act 2006;

(iv) given a penalty notice by a constable in uniform under Chapter 1 of Part 1 of the Criminal Justice and Police Act 2001, a penalty notice by a constable under section 444A of the Education Act 1996, or a fixed penalty notice by a constable in uniform under section 54 of the Road Traffic Offenders Act 1988;

(v) given a notice in relation to a relevant fixed penalty offence (within the meaning of paragraph 1 of Schedule 4 to the Police Reform Act 2002) by a community support officer by virtue of a designation applying that paragraph to him;

(vi) given a notice in relation to a relevant fixed penalty offence (within the meaning of paragraph 1 of Schedule 5 to the Police Reform Act 2002) by an accredited person by virtue of accreditation specifying that that paragraph applies to him; or

(vii) given a direction to leave and not return to a specified location for up to 48 hours by a police constable (under section 27 of the Violent Crime Reduction Act 2006).

D:5.12A Photographs taken under PACE, s.64A:

(a) may be taken with the person's consent, or without their consent if consent is withheld or it is not practicable to obtain their consent, see *Note 5E*; and

(b) may be used or disclosed only for purposes related to the prevention or detection of crime, the investigation of offences or the conduct of prosecutions by, or on behalf of, police or other law enforcement and prosecuting authorities inside and outside the United Kingdom or the enforcement of any sentence or order made by a court when dealing with an offence. After being so used or disclosed, they may be retained but can only be used or disclosed for the same purposes. See *Note 5B*.

D:5.13 The officer proposing to take a detainee's photograph may, for this purpose, require the person to remove any item or substance worn on, or over, all, or any part of, their head or face. If they do not comply with such a requirement, the officer may remove the item or substance.

D:5.14 If it is established the detainee is unwilling to co-operate sufficiently to enable a suitable photograph to be taken and it is not reasonably practicable to take the photograph covertly, an officer may use reasonable force, see *Note 5F*:

(a) to take their photograph without their consent; and

(b) for the purpose of taking the photograph, remove any item or substance worn on, or over, all, or any part of, the person's head or face which they have failed to remove when asked.

D:5.15 For the purposes of this code, a photograph may be obtained without the person's consent by making a copy of an image of them taken at any time on a camera system installed anywhere in the police station.

(c) Information to be given

A-132
D:5.16 When a person is searched, examined or photographed under the provisions as in paragraph 5.1 and 5.12, or their photograph obtained as in paragraph 5.15, they must be informed of the:

(a) purpose of the search, examination or photograph;

(b) grounds on which the relevant authority, if applicable, has been given; and

(c) purposes for which the photograph may be used, disclosed or retained.

This information must be given before the search or examination commences or the photograph is taken, except if the photograph is:

(i) to be taken covertly;

(ii) obtained as in paragraph 5.15, in which case the person must be informed as soon as practicable after the photograph is taken or obtained.

(d) Documentation

D:5.17 A record must be made when a detainee is searched, examined, or a photograph of the person, or any identifying marks found on them, are [*sic*] taken. The record must include the:

    (a) identity, subject to paragraph 2.18, of the officer carrying out the search, examination or taking the photograph;

    (b) purpose of the search, examination or photograph and the outcome;

    (c) detainee's consent to the search, examination or photograph, or the reason the person was searched, examined or photographed without consent;

    (d) giving of any authority as in paragraphs 5.2 and 5.3, the grounds for giving it and the authorising officer.

D:5.18 If force is used when searching, examining or taking a photograph in accordance with this section, a record shall be made of the circumstances and those present.

(b) *Persons at police stations not detained*

D:5.19 When there are reasonable grounds for suspecting the involvement of a person in a   **A-133** criminal offence, but that person is at a police station *voluntarily* and not detained, the provisions of paragraphs 5.1 to 5.18 should apply, subject to the modifications in the following paragraphs.

D:5.20 References to the "person being detained" and to the powers mentioned in paragraph 5.1 which apply only to detainees at police stations shall be omitted.

D:5.21 Force may not be used to:

    (a) search and/or examine the person to:

        (i) discover whether they have any marks that would tend to identify them as a person involved in the commission of an offence; or

        (ii) establish their identity, see *Note 5A*;

    (b) take photographs of any identifying marks, see paragraph 5.4; or

    (c) take a photograph of the person.

D:5.22 Subject to paragraph 5.24, the photographs of persons or of their identifying marks which are not taken in accordance with the provisions mentioned in paragraphs 5.1 or 5.12, must be destroyed (together with any negatives and copies) unless the person:

    (a) is charged with, or informed they may be prosecuted for, a recordable offence;

    (b) is prosecuted for a recordable offence;

    (c) is cautioned for a recordable offence or given a warning or reprimand in accordance with the Crime and Disorder Act 1998 for a recordable offence; or

    (d) gives informed consent, in writing, for the photograph or image to be retained as in paragraph 5.6.

D:5.23 When paragraph 5.22 requires the destruction of any photograph, the person must be given an opportunity to witness the destruction or to have a certificate confirming the destruction provided they so request the certificate within five days of being informed the destruction is required.

D:5.24 Nothing in paragraph 5.22 affects any separate requirement under the Criminal Procedure and Investigations Act 1996 to retain material in connection with criminal investigations.

Notes for guidance

D:5A *The conditions under which fingerprints may be taken to assist in establishing a person's identity, are*   **A-134** *described in section 4.*

D:5B *Examples of purposes related to the prevention or detection of crime, the investigation of offences or the conduct of prosecutions include:*

    (a) *checking the photograph against other photographs held in records or in connection with, or as a result of, an investigation of an offence to establish whether the person is liable to arrest for other offences;*

    (b) *when the person is arrested at the same time as other people, or at a time when it is likely that other people will be arrested, using the photograph to help establish who was arrested, at what time and where;*

    (c) *when the real identity of the person is not known and cannot be readily ascertained or there are reasonable grounds for doubting a name and other personal details given by the person are their real name and personal details; in these circumstances, using or disclosing the photograph to help to establish or verify their real identity or determine whether they are liable to arrest for some other offence, e.g. by checking it against other photographs held in records or in connection with, or as a result of, an investigation of an offence;*

(d) *when it appears any identification procedure in section 3 may need to be arranged for which the person's photograph would assist;*

(e) *when the person's release without charge may be required, and if the release is:*

   (i) *on bail to appear at a police station, using the photograph to help verify the person's identity when they answer their bail and if the person does not answer their bail, to assist in arresting them; or*

   (ii) *without bail, using the photograph to help verify their identity or assist in locating them for the purposes of serving them with a summons to appear at court in criminal proceedings;*

(f) *when the person has answered to bail at a police station and there are reasonable grounds for doubting they are the person who was previously granted bail, using the photograph to help establish or verify their identity;*

(g) *when the person arrested on a warrant claims to be a different person from the person named on the warrant and a photograph would help to confirm or disprove their claim;*

(h) *when the person has been charged with, reported for, or convicted of, a recordable offence and their photograph is not already on record as a result of (a) to (f) or their photograph is on record but their appearance has changed since it was taken and the person has not yet been released or brought before a court.*

D:5C *There is no power to arrest a person convicted of a recordable offence solely to take their photograph. The power to take photographs in this section applies only where the person is in custody as a result of the exercise of another power, e.g. arrest for fingerprinting under PACE, s.27.*

D:5D *Examples of when it would not be practicable to obtain a detainee's consent, see paragraph 2.12, to a search, examination or the taking of a photograph of an identifying mark include:*

(a) *when the person is drunk or otherwise unfit to give consent;*

(b) *when there are reasonable grounds to suspect that if the person became aware a search or examination was to take place or an identifying mark was to be photographed, they would take steps to prevent this happening, e.g. by violently resisting, covering or concealing the mark etc and it would not otherwise be possible to carry out the search or examination or to photograph any identifying mark;*

(c) *in the case of a juvenile, if the parent or guardian cannot be contacted in sufficient time to allow the search or examination to be carried out or the photograph to be taken.*

D:5E *Examples of when it would not be practicable to obtain the person's consent, see paragraph 2.12, to a photograph being taken include:*

(a) *when the person is drunk or otherwise unfit to give consent;*

(b) *when there are reasonable grounds to suspect that if the person became aware a photograph, suitable to be used or disclosed for the use and disclosure described in paragraph 5.6, was to be taken, they would take steps to prevent it being taken, e.g. by violently resisting, covering or distorting their face etc, and it would not otherwise be possible to take a suitable photograph;*

(c) *when, in order to obtain a suitable photograph, it is necessary to take it covertly; and*

(d) *in the case of a juvenile, if the parent or guardian cannot be contacted in sufficient time to allow the photograph to be taken.*

D:5F *The use of reasonable force to take the photograph of a suspect elsewhere than at a police station must be carefully considered. In order to obtain a suspect's consent and co-operation to remove an item of religious headwear to take their photograph, a constable should consider whether in the circumstances of the situation the removal of the headwear and the taking of the photograph should be by an officer of the same sex as the person. It would be appropriate for these actions to be conducted out of public view.*

D:6 Identification by body samples and impressions

(a) General

A-135   D:6.1 References to:

(a) an "intimate sample" mean a dental impression or sample of blood, semen or any other tissue fluid, urine, or pubic hair, or a swab taken from any part of a person's genitals or from a person's body orifice other than the mouth;

(b) a "non-intimate sample" means:

   (i) a sample of hair, other than pubic hair, which includes hair plucked with the root, see Note 6A;

   (ii) a sample taken from a nail or from under a nail;

   (iii) a swab taken from any part of a person's body other than a part from which a swab taken would be an intimate sample;

   (iv) saliva;

   (v) a skin impression which means any record, other than a fingerprint, which is a record, in any form and produced by any method, of the skin pattern and other physical characteristics or features of the whole, or any part of, a person's foot or of any other part of their body.

(b) Action

(a) Intimate samples

D:6.2 PACE, s.62, provides that intimate samples may be taken under: **A-136**

  (a) section 62(1), from a person in police detention only:

    (i) if a police officer of inspector rank or above has reasonable grounds to believe such an impression or sample will tend to confirm or disprove the suspect's involvement in a recordable offence, see *Note 4A*, and gives authorisation for a sample to be taken; and

    (ii) with the suspect's written consent;

  (b) section 62(1A), from a person not in police detention but from whom two or more non-intimate samples have been taken in the course of an investigation of an offence and the samples, though suitable, have proved insufficient if:

    (i) a police officer of inspector rank or above authorises it to be taken; and

    (ii) the person concerned gives their written consent; see *Notes 6B* and *6C*;

  (c) section 62(2A), from a person convicted outside England and Wales of an offence which if committed in England and Wales would be qualifying offence [*sic*] as defined by PACE, s.65A (see *Note 4AB*) from whom two or more non-intimate samples taken under section 63(3E) (see paragraph 6.6(h)) have proved insufficient if:

    (i) a police officer of inspector rank or above is satisfied that taking the sample is necessary to assist in the prevention or detection of crime and authorises it to be taken; and

    (ii) the person concerned gives their written consent.

D:6.2A PACE, s.63A(4), and Sched. 2A, provide powers [*sic*] to:

  (a) [*sic*] make a requirement (in accordance with Annex G) for a person to attend a police station to have an intimate sample taken in the exercise of one of the following powers in paragraph 6.2 when that power applies at the time the sample is to be taken in accordance with the requirement or after the person's arrest if they fail to comply with the requirement:

    (i) section 62(1A)—persons from whom two or more non-intimate samples have been taken and proved to be insufficient, see paragraph 6.2(b); there is no time limit for making the requirement;

    (ii) section 62(2A)—persons convicted outside England and Wales from whom two or more non-intimate samples taken under section 63(3E) (see paragraph 6.6(h)) have proved insufficient, see paragraph 6.2(c); there is no time limit for making the requirement.

D:6.3 Before a suspect is asked to provide an intimate sample, they must be:

  (a) informed:

    (i) of the reason, including the nature of the suspected offence (except if taken under paragraph 6.2(c) from a person convicted outside England and Wales;

    (ii) that authorisation has been given and the provisions under which given;

    (iii) that a sample taken at a police station may be subject of a speculative search;

  (b) warned that if they refuse without good cause their refusal may harm their case if it comes to trial, see *Note 6D*. If the suspect is in police detention and not legally represented, they must also be reminded of their entitlement to have free legal advice, see Code C, paragraph 6.5, and the reminder noted in the custody record. If paragraph 6.2(b) applies and the person is attending a station voluntarily, their entitlement to free legal advice as in Code C, paragraph 3.21 shall be explained to them.

D:6.4 Dental impressions may only be taken by a registered dentist. Other intimate samples, except for samples of urine, may only be taken by a registered medical practitioner or registered nurse or registered paramedic.

(b) Non-intimate samples

D:6.5 A non-intimate sample may be taken from a detainee only with their written consent or if **A-137** paragraph 6.6 applies.

D:6.6 A non-intimate sample may be taken from a person without the appropriate consent in the following circumstances:

    (a) under section 63(2A) from a person who is in police detention as a consequence of being arrested for a recordable offence and who has not had a non-intimate sample of the same type and from the same part of the body taken in the course of the investigation of the offence by the police or they have had such a sample taken but it proved insufficient;

    (b) under section 63(3) from a person who is being held in custody by the police on the authority of a court if an officer of at least the rank of inspector authorises it to be taken; an authorisation may be given:

        (i) if the authorising officer has reasonable grounds for suspecting the person of involvement in a recordable offence and for believing that the sample will tend to confirm or disprove that involvement; and

        (ii) in writing or orally and confirmed in writing, as soon as practicable; but an authorisation may not be given to take from the same part of the body a further non-intimate sample consisting of a skin impression unless the previously taken impression proved insufficient;

    (c) under section 63(3ZA) from a person who has been arrested for a recordable offence and released if the person:

        (i) is on bail and has not had a sample of the same type and from the same part of the body taken in the course of the investigation of the offence; or

        (ii) has had such a sample taken in the course of the investigation of the offence, but it proved unsuitable or insufficient;

    (d) under section 63(3A), from a person (whether or not in police detention or held in custody by the police on the authority of a court) who has been charged with a recordable offence or informed they will be reported for such an offence if the person:

        (i) has not had a non-intimate sample taken from them in the course of the investigation of the offence;

        (ii) has had a sample so taken, but it proved unsuitable or insufficient, see *Note 6B*; or

        (iii) has had a sample taken in the course of the investigation of the offence and the sample has been destroyed and in proceedings relating to that offence there is a dispute as to whether a DNA profile relevant to the proceedings was derived from the destroyed sample;

    (e) under section 63(3B), from a person who has been:

        (i) convicted of a recordable offence;

        (ii) given a caution in respect of a recordable offence which, at the time of the caution, the person admitted; or

        (iii) warned or reprimanded under the Crime and Disorder Act 1998, s.65, for a recordable offence,

    if, since their conviction, caution, warning or reprimand a non-intimate sample has not been taken from them or a sample which has been taken since then has proved to be unsuitable or insufficient and in either case, an officer of inspector rank or above, is satisfied that taking the fingerprints [*sic*] is necessary to assist in the prevention or detection of crime and authorises the taking;

    (f) under section 63(3C) from a person to whom section 2 of the Criminal Evidence (Amendment) Act 1997 applies (persons detained following acquittal on grounds of insanity or finding of unfitness to plead);

    (g) under section 63(3E) from a person who has been convicted outside England and Wales of an offence which if committed in England and Wales would be a qualifying offence as defined by PACE, s.65A (see *Note 4AB*) if:

        (i) a non-intimate sample has not been taken previously under this power or unless a sample was so taken but was unsuitable or insufficient; and

        (ii) a police officer of inspector rank or above is satisfied that taking a sample is necessary to assist in the prevention or detection of crime and authorises it to be taken.

D:6.6A PACE, s.63A(4), and Sched. 2A, provide powers to:

    (a) make a requirement (in accordance with Annex G) for a person to attend a police station to have a non-intimate sample taken in the exercise of one of the following powers in paragraph 6.6 when that power applies at the time the sample would be taken in accordance with the requirement:

        (i) section 63(3ZA)—persons arrested for a recordable offence and released, see paragraph 6.6(c); the requirement may not be made more than six months from the day the investigating officer was informed that the sample previously taken was unsuitable or insufficient;

(ii) section 63(3A)—persons charged etc. with a recordable offence, see paragraph 6.6(d); the requirement may not be made more than six months from:

- the day the person was charged or reported if a sample has not been taken since then; or
- the day the investigating officer was informed that the sample previously taken was unsuitable or insufficient;

(iii) section 63(3B)—person convicted, cautioned, warned or reprimanded for a recordable offence in England and Wales, see paragraph 6.6(e); where the offence for which the person was convicted etc is also a qualifying offence (see *Note 4AB*), there is no time limit for the exercise of this power; where the conviction etc was for a recordable offence that is not a qualifying offence, the requirement may not be made more than two years from:

- the day the person was convicted, cautioned, warned or reprimanded, or the day Schedule 2A comes into force (if later), if a samples [*sic*] has not been taken since then; or
- the day an officer from the force investigating the offence was informed that the sample previously taken was unsuitable or insufficient or the day Schedule 2A comes into force (if later);

(iv) section 63(3E)—a person who has been convicted of qualifying offence (see *Note 4AB*) outside England and Wales, see paragraph 6.6(h); there is no time limit for making the requirement;

note: a person who has had a non-intimate sample taken under any of the powers in section 63 mentioned in paragraph 6.6 on two occasions in relation to any offence may not be required under Schedule 2A to attend a police station for a sample to be taken again under section 63 in relation to that offence, unless authorised by an officer of inspector rank or above; the fact of the authorisation and the reasons for giving it must be recorded as soon as practicable;

(b) arrest, without warrant, a person who fails to comply with the requirement.

D:6.7 Reasonable force may be used, if necessary, to take a non-intimate sample from a person without their consent under the powers mentioned in paragraph 6.6.

D:6.8 Before any non-intimate sample is taken:

(a) without consent under any power mentioned in paragraphs 6.6 and 6.6A, the person must be informed of:

(i) the reason for taking the sample;

(ii) the power under which the sample is to be taken;

(iii) the fact that the relevant authority has been given if any power mentioned in paragraph 6.6(b), (e) or (h) applies;

(b) with or without consent at a police station or elsewhere, the person must be informed:

(i) that their sample or information derived from it may be subject of a speculative search against other samples and information derived from them, see *Note 6E*; and

(ii) that their sample and the information derived from it may be retained in accordance with Annex F, Part (a).

D:6.9 When clothing needs to be removed in circumstances likely to cause embarrassment to the person, no person of the opposite sex who is not a registered medical practitioner or registered health care professional shall be present (unless in the case of a juvenile, mentally disordered or mentally vulnerable person, that person specifically requests the presence of an appropriate adult of the opposite sex who is readily available), nor shall anyone whose presence is unnecessary. However, in the case of a juvenile, this is subject to the overriding proviso that such a removal of clothing may take place in the absence of the appropriate adult only if the juvenile signifies in their presence, that they prefer the adult's absence and they agree.

(c) Documentation

D:6.10 A record must be made as soon as practicable after the sample is taken of:

- the matters in paragraph 6.8(a)(i) to (iii) and the fact that the person has been informed of those matters; and
- the fact that the person has been informed of the matters in paragraph 6.8(b)(i) and (ii).

D:6.10A If force is used, a record shall be made of the circumstances and those present.

D:6.11 A record must be made of a warning given as required by paragraph 6.3.

A-138   D:6A *When hair samples are taken for the purpose of DNA analysis (rather than for other purposes such as making a visual match), the suspect should be permitted a reasonable choice as to what part of the body the hairs are taken from. When hairs are plucked, they should be plucked individually, unless the suspect prefers otherwise and no more should be plucked than the person taking them reasonably considers necessary for a sufficient sample.*

> (a) *An insufficient sample is one which is not sufficient either in quantity or quality to provide information for a particular form of analysis, such as DNA analysis. A sample may also be insufficient if enough information cannot be obtained from it by analysis because of loss, destruction, damage or contamination of the sample or as a result of an earlier, unsuccessful attempt at analysis.*

> (b) *An unsuitable sample is one which, by its nature, is not suitable for a particular form of analysis.*

D:6C *Nothing in paragraph 6.2 prevents intimate samples being taken for elimination purposes with the consent of the person concerned but the provisions of paragraph 2.12 relating to the role of the appropriate adult, should be applied. Paragraph 6.2(b) does not, however, apply where the non-intimate samples were previously taken under the Terrorism Act 2000, Sched. 8, para. 10.*

D:6D *In warning a person who is asked to provide an intimate sample as in paragraph 6.3, the following form of words may be used:*

> *"You do not have to provide this sample/allow this swab or impression to be taken, but I must warn you that if you refuse without good cause, your refusal may harm your case if it comes to trial."*

D:6E *Fingerprints or a DNA sample and the information derived from it taken from a person arrested on suspicion of being involved in a recordable offence, or charged with such an offence, or informed they will be reported for such an offence, may be subject of a speculative search. This means they may be checked against other fingerprints and DNA records held by, or on behalf of, the police and other law enforcement authorities in or outside the UK or held in connection with, or as a result of, an investigation of an offence inside or outside the UK. Fingerprints and samples taken from any other person, e.g. a person suspected of committing a recordable offence but who has not been arrested, charged or informed they will be reported for it, may be subject to a speculative search only if the person consents in writing to their fingerprints being subject of such a search. The following is an example of a basic form of words:*

> *"I consent to my fingerprints/DNA sample and information derived from it being retained and used only for purposes related to the prevention and detection of a crime, the investigation of an offence or the conduct of a prosecution either nationally or internationally.*

> *I understand that this sample may be checked against other fingerprint/DNA records held by or on behalf of relevant law enforcement authorities, either nationally or internationally.*

> *I understand that once I have given my consent for the sample to be retained and used I cannot withdraw this consent."*

See Annex F regarding the retention and use of fingerprints and samples taken with consent for elimination purposes.

D:6F *Samples of urine and non-intimate samples taken in accordance with sections 63B and 63C of PACE may not be used for identification purposes in accordance with this code. See Code C note for guidance 17D.*

ANNEX A

Video identification

(a) *General*

A-139   D:1 The arrangements for obtaining and ensuring the availability of a suitable set of images to be used in a video identification must be the responsibility of an identification officer, who has no direct involvement with the case.

D:2 The set of images must include the suspect and at least eight other people who, so far as possible, resemble the suspect in age, general appearance and position in life. Only one suspect shall appear in any set unless there are two suspects of roughly similar appearance, in which case they may be shown together with at least twelve other people.

D:2A If the suspect has an unusual physical feature, *e.g.* a facial scar, tattoo or distinctive hairstyle or hair colour which does not appear on the images of the other people that are available to be used, steps may be taken to:

> (a) conceal the location of the feature on the images of the suspect and the other people; or

> (b) replicate that feature on the images of the other people.

For these purposes, the feature may be concealed or replicated electronically or by any other method which is practicable to use to ensure that the images of the suspect and other people resemble each other. The identification officer has discretion to choose whether to conceal or replicate the feature and the method to be used. If an unusual physical feature has been described by the witness, the identification officer should, if practicable, have that feature replicated. If it has not been described, concealment may be more appropriate.

D:2B If the identification officer decides that a feature should be concealed or replicated, the reason for the decision and whether the feature was concealed or replicated in the images shown to any witness shall be recorded.

D:2C If the witness requests to view an image where an unusual physical feature has been concealed or replicated without the feature being concealed or replicated, the witness may be allowed to do so.

D:3 The images used to conduct a video identification shall, as far as possible, show the suspect and other people in the same positions or carrying out the same sequence of movements. They shall also show the suspect and other people under identical conditions unless the identification officer reasonably believes:

    (a) because of the suspect's failure or refusal to co-operate or other reasons, it is not practicable for the conditions to be identical; and

    (b) any difference in the conditions would not direct a witness's attention to any individual image.

D:4 The reasons identical conditions are not practicable shall be recorded on forms provided for the purpose.

D:5 Provision must be made for each person shown to be identified by number.

D:6 If police officers are shown, any numerals or other identifying badges must be concealed. If a prison inmate is shown, either as a suspect or not, then either all, or none of, the people shown should be in prison clothing.

D:7 The suspect or their solicitor, friend, or appropriate adult must be given a reasonable op- **A-140** portunity to see the complete set of images before it is shown to any witness. If the suspect has a reasonable objection to the set of images or any of the participants, the suspect shall be asked to state the reasons for the objection. Steps shall, if practicable, be taken to remove the grounds for objection. If this is not practicable, the suspect and/or their representative shall be told why their objections cannot be met and the objection, the reason given for it and why it cannot be met shall be recorded on forms provided for the purpose.

D:8 Before the images are shown in accordance with paragraph 7, the suspect or their solicitor shall be provided with details of the first description of the suspect by any witnesses who are to attend the video identification. When a broadcast or publication is made, as in paragraph 3.28, the suspect or their solicitor must also be allowed to view any material released to the media by the police for the purpose of recognising or tracing the suspect, provided it is practicable and would not unreasonably delay the investigation.

D:9 The suspect's solicitor, if practicable, shall be given reasonable notification of the time and place the video identification is to be conducted so a representative may attend on behalf of the suspect. The suspect may not be present when the images are shown to the witness(es). In the absence of the suspect's solicitor, the viewing itself shall be recorded on video. No unauthorised people may be present.

(b) *Conducting the video identification*

D:10 The identification officer is responsible for making the appropriate arrangements to make **A-141** sure, before they see the set of images, witnesses are not able to communicate with each other about the case, see any of the images which are to be shown, see, or be reminded of, any photograph or description of the suspect or be given any other indication as to the suspect's identity, or overhear a witness who has already seen the material. There must be no discussion with the witness about the composition of the set of images and they must not be told whether a previous witness has made any identification.

D:11 Only one witness may see the set of images at a time. Immediately before the images are shown, the witness shall be told that the person they saw on a specified earlier occasion may, or may not, appear in the images they are shown and that if they cannot make a positive identification, they should say so. The witness shall be advised that at any point, they may ask to see a particular part of the set of images or to have a particular image frozen for them to study. Furthermore, it should be pointed out to the witness that there is no limit on how many times they can view the whole set of images or any part of them. However, they should be asked not to make any decision as to whether the person they saw is on the set of images until they have seen the whole set at least twice.

D:12 Once the witness has seen the whole set of images at least twice and has indicated that they do not want to view the images, or any part of them, again, the witness shall be asked to say whether the individual they saw in person on a specified earlier occasion has been shown and, if so, to identify them by number of the image. The witness will then be shown that image to confirm the identification, see paragraph 17.

D:13 Care must be taken not to direct the witness's attention to any one individual image or give any indication of the suspect's identity. Where a witness has previously made an identification by photographs, or a computerised or artist's composite or similar likeness, the witness must not be reminded of such a photograph or composite likeness once a suspect is available for identification by other means in accordance with this code. Nor must the witness be reminded of any description of the suspect.

D:14 After the procedure, each witness shall be asked whether they have seen any broadcast or published films or photographs, or any descriptions of suspects relating to the offence and their reply shall be recorded.

(c) *Image security and destruction*

D:15 Arrangements shall be made for all relevant material containing sets of images used for specific identification procedures to be kept securely and their movements accounted for. In particular, no-one involved in the investigation shall be permitted to view the material prior to it being shown to any witness.

D:16 As appropriate, paragraph 3.30 or 3.31 applies to the destruction or retention of relevant sets of images.

(d) *Documentation*

D:17 A record must be made of all those participating in, or seeing, the set of images whose names are known to the police.

D:18 A record of the conduct of the video identification must be made on forms provided for the purpose. This shall include anything said by the witness about any identifications or the conduct of the procedure and any reasons it was not practicable to comply with any of the provisions of this code governing the conduct of video identifications.

ANNEX B

Identification parades

(a) *General*

A-142   D:1 A suspect must be given a reasonable opportunity to have a solicitor or friend present, and the suspect shall be asked to indicate on a second copy of the notice whether or not they wish to do so.

D:2 An identification parade may take place either in a normal room or one equipped with a screen permitting witnesses to see members of the identification parade without being seen. The procedures for the composition and conduct of the identification parade are the same in both cases, subject to paragraph 8 (except that an identification parade involving a screen may take place only when the suspect's solicitor, friend or appropriate adult is present or the identification parade is recorded on video).

D:3 Before the identification parade takes place, the suspect or their solicitor shall be provided with details of the first description of the suspect by any witnesses who are attending the identification parade. When a broadcast or publication is made as in paragraph 3.28, the suspect or their solicitor should also be allowed to view any material released to the media by the police for the purpose of recognising or tracing the suspect, provided it is practicable to do so and would not unreasonably delay the investigation.

(b) *Identification parades involving prison inmates*

D:4 If a prison inmate is required for identification, and there are no security problems about the person leaving the establishment, they may be asked to participate in an identification parade or video identification.

D:5 An identification parade may be held in a Prison Department establishment but shall be conducted, as far as practicable under normal identification parade rules. Members of the public shall make up the identification parade unless there are serious security, or control, objections to their admission to the establishment. In such cases, or if a group or video identification is arranged within the establishment, other inmates may participate. If an inmate is the suspect, they are not required to wear prison clothing for the identification parade unless the other people taking part are other inmates in similar clothing, or are members of the public who are prepared to wear prison clothing for the occasion.

(c) *Conduct of the identification parade*

D:6 Immediately before the identification parade, the suspect must be reminded of the procedures **A-143**
governing its conduct and cautioned in the terms of Code C, paragraphs 10.5 or 10.6, as appropriate.

D:7 All unauthorised people must be excluded from the place where the identification parade is
held.

D:8 Once the identification parade has been formed, everything afterwards, in respect of it, shall
take place in the presence and hearing of the suspect and any interpreter, solicitor, friend or appropriate adult who is present (unless the identification parade involves a screen, in which case
everything said to, or by, any witness at the place where the identification parade is held, must be
said in the hearing and presence of the suspect's solicitor, friend or appropriate adult or be recorded
on video).

D:9 The identification parade shall consist of at least eight people (in addition to the suspect) who,
so far as possible, resemble the suspect in age, height, general appearance and position in life. Only
one suspect shall be included in an identification parade unless there are two suspects of roughly
similar appearance, in which case they may be paraded together with at least twelve other people. In
no circumstances shall more than two suspects be included in one identification parade and where
there are separate identification parades, they shall be made up of different people.

D:10 If the suspect has an unusual physical feature, *e.g.*, a facial scar, tattoo or distinctive hairstyle
or hair colour which cannot be replicated on other members of the identification parade, steps may
be taken to conceal the location of that feature on the suspect and the other members of the identification parade if the suspect and their solicitor, or appropriate adult, agree. For example, by use of a
plaster or a hat, so that all members of the identification parade resemble each other in general
appearance.

D:11 When all members of a similar group are possible suspects, separate identification parades
shall be held for each unless there are two suspects of similar appearance when they may appear on
the same identification parade with at least twelve other members of the group who are not suspects.
When police officers in uniform form an identification parade any numerals or other identifying
badges shall be concealed.

D:12 When the suspect is brought to the place where the identification parade is to be held, they
shall be asked if they have any objection to the arrangements for the identification parade or to any
of the other participants in it and to state the reasons for the objection. The suspect may obtain
advice from their solicitor or friend, if present, before the identification parade proceeds. If the
suspect has a reasonable objection to the arrangements or any of the participants, steps shall, if
practicable, be taken to remove the grounds for objection. When it is not practicable to do so, the
suspect shall be told why their objections cannot be met and the objection, the reason given for it and
why it cannot be met, shall be recorded on forms provided for the purpose.

D:13 The suspect may select their own position in the line, but may not otherwise interfere with
the order of the people forming the line. When there is more than one witness, the suspect must be
told, after each witness has left the room, that they can, if they wish, change position in the line. Each
position in the line must be clearly numbered, whether by means of a number laid on the floor in
front of each identification parade member or by other means.

D:14 Appropriate arrangements must be made to make sure, before witnesses attend the identifica- **A-144**
tion parade, they are not able to:

    (i) communicate with each other about the case or overhear a witness who has already seen
       the identification parade;

    (ii) see any member of the identification parade;

    (iii) see, or be reminded of, any photograph or description of the suspect or be given any
       other indication as to the suspect's identity; or

    (iv) see the suspect before or after the identification parade.

D:15 The person conducting a witness to an identification parade must not discuss with them the
composition of the identification parade and, in particular, must not disclose whether a previous witness has made any identification.

D:16 Witnesses shall be brought in one at a time. Immediately before the witness inspects the
identification parade, they shall be told the person they saw on a specified earlier occasion may, or
may not, be present and if they cannot make a positive identification, they should say so. The witness
must also be told they should not make any decision about whether the person they saw is on the
identification parade until they have looked at each member at least twice.

D:17 When the officer or police staff (see paragraph 3.11) conducting the identification procedure
is satisfied the witness has properly looked at each member of the identification parade, they shall ask
the witness whether the person they saw on a specified earlier occasion is on the identification parade
and, if so, to indicate the number of the person concerned, see paragraph 28.

D:18 If the witness wishes to hear any identification parade member speak, adopt any specified posture or move, they shall first be asked whether they can identify any person(s) on the identification parade on the basis of appearance only. When the request is to hear members of the identification parade speak, the witness shall be reminded that the participants in the identification parade have been chosen on the basis of physical appearance only. Members of the identification parade may then be asked to comply with the witness's request to hear them speak, see them move or adopt any specified posture.

A-145

D:19 If the witness requests that the person they have indicated remove anything used for the purposes of paragraph 10 to conceal the location of an unusual physical feature, that person may be asked to remove it.

D:20 If the witness makes an identification after the identification parade has ended, the suspect and, if present, their solicitor, interpreter or friend shall be informed. When this occurs, consideration should be given to allowing the witness a second opportunity to identify the suspect.

D:21 After the procedure, each witness shall be asked whether they have seen any broadcast or published films or photographs or any descriptions of suspects relating to the offence and their reply shall be recorded.

D:22 When the last witness has left, the suspect shall be asked whether they wish to make any comments on the conduct of the identification parade.

(d) *Documentation*

D:23 A video recording must normally be taken of the identification parade. If that is impracticable, a colour photograph must be taken. A copy of the video recording or photograph shall be supplied, on request, to the suspect or their solicitor within a reasonable time.

D:24 As appropriate, paragraph 3.30 or 3.31, should apply to any photograph or video taken as in paragraph 23.

D:25 If any person is asked to leave an identification parade because they are interfering with its conduct, the circumstances shall be recorded.

D:26 A record must be made of all those present at an identification parade whose names are known to the police.

D:27 If prison inmates make up an identification parade, the circumstances must be recorded.

D:28 A record of the conduct of any identification parade must be made on forms provided for the purpose. This shall include anything said by the witness or the suspect about any identifications or the conduct of the procedure, and any reasons it was not practicable to comply with any of this code's provisions.

ANNEX C

Group identification

(a) *General*

A-146

D:1 The purpose of this annex is to make sure, as far as possible, group identifications follow the principles and procedures for identification parades so the conditions are fair to the suspect in the way they test the witness's ability to make an identification.

D:2 Group identifications may take place either with the suspect's consent and co-operation or covertly without their consent.

D:3 The location of the group identification is a matter for the identification officer, although the officer may take into account any representations made by the suspect, appropriate adult, their solicitor or friend.

D:4 The place where the group identification is held should be one where other people are either passing by or waiting around informally, in groups such that the suspect is able to join them and be capable of being seen by the witness at the same time as others in the group. For example people leaving an escalator, pedestrians walking through a shopping centre, passengers on railway and bus stations, waiting in queues or groups or where people are standing or sitting in groups in other public places.

D:5 If the group identification is to be held covertly, the choice of locations will be limited by the places where the suspect can be found and the number of other people present at that time. In these cases, suitable locations might be along regular routes travelled by the suspect, including buses or trains or public places frequented by the suspect.

A-147

D:6 Although the number, age, sex, race and general description and style of clothing of other people present at the location cannot be controlled by the identification officer, in selecting the location the officer must consider the general appearance and numbers of people likely to be present. In particular, the officer must reasonably expect that over the period the witness observes the group, they will be able to see, from time to time, a number of others whose appearance is broadly similar to that of the suspect.

D:7 A group identification need not be held if the identification officer believes, because of the unusual appearance of the suspect, none of the locations it would be practicable to use, satisfy the requirements of paragraph 6 necessary to make the identification fair.

D:8 Immediately after a group identification procedure has taken place (with or without the suspect's consent), a colour photograph or video should be taken of the general scene, if practicable, to give a general impression of the scene and the number of people present. Alternatively, if it is practicable, the group identification may be video recorded.

D:9 If it is not practicable to take the photograph or video in accordance with paragraph 8, a photograph or film of the scene should be taken later at a time determined by the identification officer if the officer considers it practicable to do so.

D:10 An identification carried out in accordance with this code remains a group identification even though, at the time of being seen by the witness, the suspect was on their own rather than in a group.

D:11 Before the group identification takes place, the suspect or their solicitor shall be provided with details of the first description of the suspect by any witnesses who are to attend the identification. When a broadcast or publication is made, as in paragraph 3.28, the suspect or their solicitor should also be allowed to view any material released by the police to the media for the purposes of recognising or tracing the suspect, provided that it is practicable and would not unreasonably delay the investigation.

D:12 After the procedure, each witness shall be asked whether they have seen any broadcast or published films or photographs or any descriptions of suspects relating to the offence and their reply recorded.

(b) *Identification with the consent of the suspect*

D:13 A suspect must be given a reasonable opportunity to have a solicitor or friend present. They **A-148** shall be asked to indicate on a second copy of the notice whether or not they wish to do so.

D:14 The witness, the person carrying out the procedure and the suspect's solicitor, appropriate adult, friend or any interpreter for the witness, may be concealed from the sight of the individuals in the group they are observing, if the person carrying out the procedure considers this assists the conduct of the identification.

D:15 The person conducting a witness to a group identification must not discuss with them the forthcoming group identification and, in particular, must not disclose whether a previous witness has made any identification.

D:16 Anything said to, or by, the witness during the procedure about the identification should be said in the presence and hearing of those present at the procedure.

D:17 Appropriate arrangements must be made to make sure, before witnesses attend the group identification, they are not able to:

    (i) communicate with each other about the case or overhear a witness who has already been given an opportunity to see the suspect in the group;

    (ii) see the suspect; or

    (iii) see, or be reminded of, any photographs or description of the suspect or be given any other indication of the suspect's identity.

D:18 Witnesses shall be brought one at a time to the place where they are to observe the group. Immediately before the witness is asked to look at the group, the person conducting the procedure shall tell them that the person they saw may, or may not, be in the group and that if they cannot make a positive identification, they should say so. The witness shall be asked to observe the group in which the suspect is to appear. The way in which the witness should do this will depend on whether the group is moving or stationary.

Moving group

D:19 When the group in which the suspect is to appear is moving, *e.g.* leaving an escalator, the **A-149** provisions of paragraphs 20 to 24 should be followed.

D:20 If two or more suspects consent to a group identification, each should be the subject of separate identification procedures. These may be conducted consecutively on the same occasion.

D:21 The person conducting the procedure shall tell the witness to observe the group and ask them to point out any person they think they saw on the specified earlier occasion.

D:22 Once the witness has been informed as in paragraph 21 the suspect should be allowed to take whatever position in the group they wish.

D:23 When the witness points out a person as in paragraph 21 they shall, if practicable, be asked to take a closer look at the person to confirm the identification. If this is not practicable, or they cannot confirm the identification, they shall be asked how sure they are that the person they have indicated is the relevant person.

D:24 The witness should continue to observe the group for the period which the person conducting the procedure reasonably believes is necessary in the circumstances for them to be able to make comparisons between the suspect and other individuals of broadly similar appearance to the suspect as in paragraph 6.

Stationary groups

A-150

D:25 When the group in which the suspect is to appear is stationary, *e.g.* people waiting in a queue, the provisions of paragraphs 26 to 29 should be followed.

D:26 If two or more suspects consent to a group identification, each should be subject to separate identification procedures unless they are of broadly similar appearance when they may appear in the same group. When separate group identifications are held, the groups must be made up of different people.

D:27 The suspect may take whatever position in the group they wish. If there is more than one witness, the suspect must be told, out of the sight and hearing of any witness, that they can, if they wish, change their position in the group.

D:28 The witness shall be asked to pass along, or amongst, the group and to look at each person in the group at least twice, taking as much care and time as possible according to the circumstances, before making an identification. Once the witness has done this, they shall be asked whether the person they saw on the specified earlier occasion is in the group and to indicate any such person by whatever means the person conducting the procedure considers appropriate in the circumstances. If this is not practicable, the witness shall be asked to point out any person they think they saw on the earlier occasion.

D:29 When the witness makes an indication as in paragraph 28, arrangements shall be made, if practicable, for the witness to take a closer look at the person to confirm the identification. If this is not practicable, or the witness is unable to confirm the identification, they shall be asked how sure they are that the person they have indicated is the relevant person.

All cases

A-151

D:30 If the suspect unreasonably delays joining the group, or having joined the group, deliberately conceals themselves [*sic*] from the sight of the witness, this may be treated as a refusal to co-operate in a group identification.

D:31 If the witness identifies a person other than the suspect, that person should be informed what has happened and asked if they are prepared to give their name and address. There is no obligation upon any member of the public to give these details. There shall be no duty to record any details of any other member of the public present in the group or at the place where the procedure is conducted.

D:32 When the group identification has been completed, the suspect shall be asked whether they wish to make any comments on the conduct of the procedure.

D:33 If the suspect has not been previously informed, they shall be told of any identifications made by the witnesses.

(c) *Identification without the suspect's consent*

A-152

D:34 Group identifications held covertly without the suspect's consent should, as far as practicable, follow the rules for conduct of group identification by consent.

D:35 A suspect has no right to have a solicitor, appropriate adult or friend present as the identification will take place without the knowledge of the suspect.

D:36 Any number of suspects may be identified at the same time.

(d) *Identifications in police stations*

D:37 Group identifications should only take place in police stations for reasons of safety, security or because it is not practicable to hold them elsewhere.

D:38 The group identification may take place either in a room equipped with a screen permitting witnesses to see members of the group without being seen, or anywhere else in the police station that the identification officer considers appropriate.

D:39 Any of the additional safeguards applicable to identification parades should be followed if the identification officer considers it is practicable to do so in the circumstances.

(e) Identifications involving prison inmates

D:40 A group identification involving a prison inmate may only be arranged in the prison or at a **A-153** police station.

D:41 When a group identification takes place involving a prison inmate, whether in a prison or in a police station, the arrangements should follow those in paragraphs 37 to 39. If a group identification takes place within a prison, other inmates may participate. If an inmate is the suspect, they do not have to wear prison clothing for the group identification unless the other participants are wearing the same clothing.

(f) Documentation

D:42 When a photograph or video is taken as in paragraph 8 or 9, a copy of the photograph or video shall be supplied on request to the suspect or their solicitor within a reasonable time.

D:43 Paragraph 3.30 or 3.31, as appropriate, shall apply when the photograph or film taken in accordance with paragraph 8 or 9 includes the suspect.

D:44 A record of the conduct of any group identification must be made on forms provided for the purpose. This shall include anything said by the witness or suspect about any identifications or the conduct of the procedure and any reasons why it was not practicable to comply with any of the provisions of this code governing the conduct of group identifications.

ANNEX D

Confrontation by a witness

D:1 Before the confrontation takes place, the witness must be told that the person they saw may, **A-154** or may not, be the person they are to confront and that if they are not that person, then the witness should say so.

D:2 Before the confrontation takes place the suspect or their solicitor shall be provided with details of the first description of the suspect given by any witness who is to attend. When a broadcast or publication is made, as in paragraph 3.28, the suspect or their solicitor should also be allowed to view any material released to the media for the purposes of recognising or tracing the suspect, provided it is practicable to do so and would not unreasonably delay the investigation.

D:3 Force may not be used to make the suspect's face visible to the witness.

D:4 Confrontation must take place in the presence of the suspect's solicitor, interpreter or friend unless this would cause unreasonable delay.

D:5 The suspect shall be confronted independently by each witness, who shall be asked "Is this the person?". If the witness identifies the person but is unable to confirm the identification, they shall be asked how sure they are that the person is the one they saw on the earlier occasion.

D:6 The confrontation should normally take place in the police station, either in a normal room or one equipped with a screen permitting a witness to see the suspect without being seen. In both cases, the procedures are the same except that a room equipped with a screen may be used only when the suspect's solicitor, friend or appropriate adult is present or the confrontation is recorded on video.

D:7 After the procedure, each witness shall be asked whether they have seen any broadcast or published films or photographs or any descriptions of suspects relating to the offence and their reply shall be recorded.

ANNEX E

Showing photographs

(a) Action

D:1 An officer of sergeant rank or above shall be responsible for supervising and directing the **A-155** showing of photographs. The actual showing may be done by another officer or police staff, see paragraph 3.11.

D:2 The supervising officer must confirm the first description of the suspect given by the witness has been recorded before they are shown the photographs. If the supervising officer is unable to confirm the description has been recorded they shall postpone showing the photographs.

D:3 Only one witness shall be shown photographs at any one time. Each witness shall be given as much privacy as practicable and shall not be allowed to communicate with any other witness in the case.

D:4 The witness shall be shown not less than twelve photographs at a time, which shall, as far as possible, all be of a similar type.

D:5 When the witness is shown the photographs, they shall be told the photograph of the person they saw may, or may not, be amongst them and if they cannot make a positive identification, they should say so. The witness shall also be told they should not make a decision until they have viewed at least twelve photographs. The witness shall not be prompted or guided in any way but shall be left to make any selection without help.

D:6 If a witness makes a positive identification from photographs, unless the person identified is otherwise eliminated from enquiries or is not available, other witnesses shall not be shown photographs. But both they, and the witness who has made the identification, shall be asked to attend a video identification, an identification parade or group identification unless there is no dispute about the suspect's identification.

A-156

D:7 If the witness makes a selection but is unable to confirm the identification, the person showing the photographs shall ask them how sure they are that the photograph they have indicated is the person they saw on the specified earlier occasion.

D:8 When the use of a computerised or artist's composite or similar likeness has led to there being a known suspect who can be asked to participate in a video identification, appear on an identification parade or participate in a group identification, that likeness shall not be shown to other potential witnesses.

D:9 When a witness attending a video identification, an identification parade or group identification has previously been shown photographs or computerised or artist's composite or similar likeness (and it is the responsibility of the officer in charge of the investigation to make the identification officer aware that this is the case), the suspect and their solicitor must be informed of this fact before the identification procedure takes place.

D:10 None of the photographs shown shall be destroyed, whether or not an identification is made, since they may be required for production in court. The photographs shall be numbered and a separate photograph taken of the frame or part of the album from which the witness made an identification as an aid to reconstituting it.

(b) *Documentation*

A-157

D:11 Whether or not an identification is made, a record shall be kept of the showing of photographs on forms provided for the purpose. This shall include anything said by the witness about any identification or the conduct of the procedure, any reasons it was not practicable to comply with any of the provisions of this code governing the showing of photographs and the name and rank of the supervising officer.

D:12 The supervising officer shall inspect and sign the record as soon as practicable.

ANNEX F

Fingerprints, footwear impressions and samples—destruction and speculative searches

(a) *Fingerprints, footwear impressions and samples taken in connection with a criminal investigation from a person suspected of committing the offence under investigation*

A-158

D:1 The retention and destruction of fingerprints, footwear impressions and samples taken in connection with a criminal investigation from a person suspected of committing the offence under investigation is subject to PACE, s.64.

(b) *Fingerprints, footwear impressions and samples taken in connection with a criminal investigation from a person not suspected of committing the offence under investigation*

D:2 When fingerprints, footwear impressions or DNA samples are taken from a person in connection with an investigation and the person is not suspected of having committed the offence, see *Note F1*, they must be destroyed as soon as they have fulfilled the purpose for which they were taken unless:

> (a) they were taken for the purposes of an investigation of an offence for which a person has been convicted; and
> (b) fingerprints, footwear impressions or samples were also taken from the convicted person for the purposes of that investigation.

However, subject to paragraph 2, the fingerprints, footwear impressions and samples, and the information derived from samples, may not be used in the investigation of any offence or in evidence against the person who is, or would be, entitled to the destruction of the fingerprints, footwear impressions and samples, see *Note F2*.

D:3 The requirement to destroy fingerprints, footwear impressions and DNA samples, and information derived from samples, and restrictions on their retention and use in paragraph 1 do not

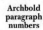

apply if the person gives their written consent for their fingerprints, footwear impressions or sample to be retained and used after they have fulfilled the purpose for which they were taken, see *Note F1*.

D:4 When a person's fingerprints, footwear impressions or sample are to be destroyed:

    (a) any copies of the fingerprints and footwear impressions must also be destroyed;

    (b) the person may witness the destruction of their fingerprints, footwear impressions or copies if they ask to do so within five days of being informed destruction is required;

    (c) access to relevant computer fingerprint data shall be made impossible as soon as it is practicable to do so and the person shall be given a certificate to this effect within three months of asking; and

    (d) neither the fingerprints, footwear impressions, the sample, or any information derived from the sample, may be used in the investigation of any offence or in evidence against the person who is, or would be, entitled to its destruction.

D:5 Fingerprints, footwear impressions or samples, and the information derived from samples, taken in connection with the investigation of an offence which are not required to be destroyed, may be retained after they have fulfilled the purposes for which they were taken but may be used only for purposes related to the prevention or detection of crime, the investigation of an offence or the conduct of a prosecution in, as well as outside, the UK and may also be subject to a speculative search. This includes checking them against other fingerprints, footwear impressions and DNA records held by, or on behalf of, the police and other law enforcement authorities in, as well as outside, the UK.

(b) [*sic*] *Fingerprints taken in connection with Immigration Service enquiries*

D:6 See paragraph 4.10.   **A-159**

Notes for guidance

D:F1 *Fingerprints, footwear impressions and samples given voluntarily for the purposes of elimination play an*   **A-160**
important part in many police investigations. It is, therefore, important to make sure innocent volunteers are not deterred from participating and their consent to their fingerprints, footwear impressions and DNA being used for the purposes of a specific investigation is fully informed and voluntary. If the police or volunteer seek to have the fingerprints, footwear impressions or samples retained for use after the specific investigation ends, it is important the volunteer's consent to this is also fully informed and voluntary.

  Examples of consent for:

    • *DNA/fingerprints/footwear impressions—to be used only for the purposes of a specific investigation;*

    • *DNA/fingerprints/footwear impressions—to be used in the specific investigation and retained by the police for future use.*

To minimise the risk of confusion, each consent should be physically separate and the volunteer should be asked to sign **each consent**.

    (a) *DNA:*

        (i) *DNA sample taken for the purposes of elimination or as part of an intelligence-led screening and to be used only for the purposes of that investigation and destroyed afterwards:*

          "I consent to my DNA/mouth swab being taken for forensic analysis. I understand that the sample will be destroyed at the end of the case and that my profile will only be compared to the crime stain profile from this enquiry. I have been advised that the person taking the sample may be required to give evidence and/or provide a written statement to the police in relation to the taking of it.".

        (ii) *DNA sample to be retained on the National DNA database and used in the future:*

          "I consent to my DNA sample and information derived from it being retained and used only for purposes related to the prevention and detection of a crime, the investigation of an offence or the conduct of a prosecution either nationally or internationally.

          I understand that this sample may be checked against other DNA records held by, or on behalf of, relevant law enforcement authorities, either nationally or internationally.

          I understand that once I have given my consent for the sample to be retained and used I cannot withdraw this consent.".

    (b) *Fingerprints:*

        (i) *Fingerprints taken for the purposes of elimination or as part of an intelligence-led screening and to be used only for the purposes of that investigation and destroyed afterwards:*

          "I consent to my fingerprints being taken for elimination purposes. I understand that the fingerprints will be destroyed at the end of the case and that my fingerprints will only be compared

381

to the fingerprints from this enquiry. I have been advised that the person taking the fingerprints may be required to give evidence and/or provide a written statement to the police in relation to the taking of it.".

(ii) *Fingerprints to be retained for future use:*

"*I consent to my fingerprints being retained and used only for purposes related to the prevention and detection of a crime, the investigation of an offence or the conduct of a prosecution either nationally or internationally.*

I understand that my fingerprints may be checked against other records held by, or on behalf of, relevant law enforcement authorities, either nationally or internationally.

I understand that once I have given my consent for my fingerprints to be retained and used I cannot withdraw this consent.".

(c) *Footwear impressions:*

(i) *Footwear impressions taken for the purposes of elimination or as part of an intelligence-led screening and to be used only for the purposes of that investigation and destroyed afterwards:*

"*I consent to my footwear impressions being taken for elimination purposes. I understand that the footwear impressions will be destroyed at the end of the case and that my footwear impressions will only be compared to the footwear impressions from this enquiry. I have been advised that the person taking the footwear impressions may be required to give evidence and/or provide a writtens statement to the police in relation to the taking of it.*".

(ii) *Footwear impressions to be retained for future use:*

"*I consent to my footwear impressions being retained and used only for purposes related to the prevention and detection of a crime, the investigation of an offence or the conduct of a prosecution, either nationally or internationally.*

I understand that my footwear impressions may be checked against other records held by, or on behalf of, relevant law enforcement authorities, either nationally or internationally.

I understand that once I have given my consent for my footwear impressions to be retained and used I cannot withdraw this consent.".

A-161   D:F2 *The provisions for the retention of fingerprints, footwear impressions and samples in paragraph 1 allow for all fingerprints, footwear impressions and samples in a case to be available for any subsequent miscarriage of justice investigation.*

ANNEX G

Requirement for a person to attend a police station for fingerprints and samples

A-161a   D:1 A requirement under Schedule 2A for a person to attend a police station to have fingerprints or samples taken:

(a) must give the person a period of at least seven days within which to attend the police station; and

(b) may direct them to attend at a specified time of day or between specified times of day.

D:2 When specifying the period and times of attendance, the officer making the requirements must consider whether the fingerprints or samples could reasonably be taken at a time when the person is required to attend the police station for any other reason. See *Note G1.*

D:3 An officer of the rank of inspector or above may authorise a period shorter than 7 days if there is an urgent need for person's fingerprints or sample for the purposes of the investigation of an offence. The fact of the authorisation and the reasons for giving it must be recorded as soon as practicable.

D:4 The constable making a requirement and the person to whom it applies may agree to vary it so as to specify any period within which, or date or time at which, the person is to attend. However, variation shall not have effect for the purposes of enforcement, unless it is confirmed by the constable in writing.

Notes for guidance

A-161b   D:G1 *The specified period within which the person is to attend need not fall within the period allowed (if applicable) for making the requirement.*

D:G2 *To justify the arrest without warrant of a person who fails to comply with a requirement, (see paragraph 4.4(b) above), the officer making the requirement, or confirming a variation, should be prepared to explain how, when and where the requirement was made or the variation was confirmed and what steps were taken to ensure the person understood what to do and the consequences of not complying with the requirement.*

(6) Tape-recording of interviews

The text that follows is of the version of the code that came into force on October 27, 2013: see **A-162** *ante*, Appendix A-1.

For further details of the application of the code, and as to commencement of the governing legislation, see § 15-174, *ante*.

E. CODE OF PRACTICE ON AUDIO RECORDING INTERVIEWS WITH SUSPECTS

Commencement—transitional arrangements

This code applies to interviews carried out after 00.00 on 27 October 2013 notwithstanding that **A-162a** the interview may have commenced before that time.

E:1 General

E:1.0 The procedures in this code must be used fairly, responsibly, with respect for the people to **A-163** whom they apply and without unlawful discrimination. Under the Equality Act 2010, s.149, when police officers are carrying out their functions, they also have a duty to have due regard to the need to eliminate unlawful discrimination, harassment and victimisation, to advance equality of opportunity between people who share a relevant protected characteristic and people who do not share it, and to take steps to foster good relations between those persons. See *Note 1B*.

E:1.1 This code of practice must be readily available for consultation by:

- police officers;
- police staff;
- detained persons;
- members of the public.

E:1.2 The *Notes for Guidance* included are not provisions of this code.

E:1.3 Nothing in this code shall detract from the requirements of Code C, the code of practice for the detention, treatment and questioning of persons by police officers.

E:1.4 The interviews to which this code applies are described in section 3.

E:1.5 The term:

- "appropriate adult" has the same meaning as in Code C, para. 1.7, and in the case of a 17-year-old suspect, includes the person called to fulfil that role in accordance with paragraph 1.5A of Code C;
- "solicitor" has the same meaning as in Code C, para. 6.12;
- "interview" has the same meaning as in Code C, para. 11.1A.

E:1.5A Recording of interviews shall be carried out openly to instil confidence in its reliability as an impartial and accurate record of the interview.

E:1.6 In this code: **A-164**

- (aa) "recording media" means any removable, physical audio recording medium (such as magnetic tape, optical disc or solid state memory) which can be played and copied;
- (a) "designated person" means a person other than a police officer, designated under the Police Reform Act 2002, Pt 4, who has specified powers and duties of police officers conferred or imposed on them;
- (b) any reference to a police officer includes a designated person acting in the exercise or performance of the powers and duties conferred or imposed on them by their designation; and
- (c) "secure digital network" is a computer network system which enables an original interview recording to be stored as a digital multi media file or a series of such files, on a secure file server which is accredited by the National Accreditor for Police Information Systems in accordance with the UK Government Protective Marking Scheme. (See section 7 of this code.).

E:1.7 Sections 2 to 6 of this code set out the procedures and requirements which apply to all interviews together with the provisions which apply only to interviews recorded using removable media. Section 7 sets out the provisions which apply to interviews recorded using a secure digital network and specifies the provisions in sections 2 to 6 which do not apply to secure digital network recording.

E:1.8 Nothing in this code prevents the custody officer, or other officer given custody of the **A-165** detainee, from allowing police staff who are not designated persons to carry out individual procedures or tasks at the police station if the law allows. However, the officer remains responsible for making sure the procedures and tasks are carried out correctly in accordance with this code. Any such police staff must be:

(a) a person employed by a police force and under the control and direction of the chief officer of that force; or

(b) employed by a person with whom a police force has a contract for the provision of services relating to persons arrested or otherwise in custody.

E:1.9 Designated persons and other police staff must have regard to any relevant provisions of the codes of practice.

E:1.10 References to pocket book [*sic*] include any official report book issued to police officers or police staff.

E:1.11 References to a custody officer include those performing the functions of a custody officer as in paragraph 1.9 of Code C.

E:1.12 In the application of this code to the conduct and recording of an interview of a suspect who has not been arrested:

(a) references to the "custody officer" include references to an officer of the rank of sergeant or above who is not directly involved in the investigation of the offence(s);

(b) if the interview takes place elsewhere than at a police station, references to "interview room" include any place or location which the interviewer is satisfied will enable the interview to be conducted and recorded in accordance with this code and where the suspect is present voluntarily (see Note 1A); and

(c) provisions in addition to those which expressly apply to these interviews shall be followed insofar as they are relevant and can be applied in practice.

Notes for guidance

E:1A *An interviewer who is not sure, or has any doubt, about the suitability of a place or location of an interview to be carried out elsewhere than at a police station, should consult an officer of the rank of sergeant or above for advice.*

E:1B *In paragraph 1.0, "relevant protected characteristic" includes: age, disability, gender reassignment, pregnancy and maternity, race, religion/belief, sex and sexual orientation.*

E:2 Recording and sealing master recordings

A-166

E:2.1 [*Not used.*]

E:2.2 One recording, the master recording, will be sealed in the suspect's presence. A second recording will be used as a working copy. The master recording is any of the recordings made by a multi-deck/drive machine or the only recording made by a single deck/drive machine. The working copy is one of the other recordings made by a multi-deck/drive machine or a copy of the master recording made by a single deck/drive machine. (See *Note 2A*.)

[This paragraph does not apply to interviews recorded using a secure digital network, see paras 7.4 to 7.6.]

E:2.3 Nothing in this code requires the identity of officers or police staff conducting interviews to be recorded or disclosed:

(a) [*not used*];

(b) if the interviewer reasonably believes recording or disclosing their name might put them in danger.

In these cases interviewers should use warrant or other identification numbers and the name of their police station. Such instances and the reasons for them shall be recorded in the custody record or the interviewer's pocket book. See *Note 2C*.

Notes for guidance

A-167

E:2A *The purpose of sealing the master recording before it leaves the suspect's presence is to establish their confidence that the integrity of the recording is preserved. If a single deck/drive machine is used the working copy of the master recording must be made in the suspect's presence and without the master recording leaving their sight. The working copy shall be used for making further copies if needed.*

E:2B [*Not used.*]

E:2C *The purpose of paragraph 2.3(b) is to protect those involved in serious organised crime investigations or arrests of particularly violent suspects when there is reliable information that those arrested or their associates may threaten or cause harm to those involved. In cases of doubt, an officer of inspector rank or above should be consulted.*

E:3 Interviews to be audio recorded

A-168

E:3.1 Subject to paragraphs 3.3 and 3.4, audio recording shall be used for any interview:

(a) with a person cautioned under Code C, section 10 in respect of any indictable offence, which includes any offence triable either way, except where that person has been arrested and the interview takes place elsewhere than at a police station in accordance with Code C, para. 11.1, for which a written record would be required (see *Note 3A*);

(b) which takes place as a result of an interviewer exceptionally putting further questions to a suspect about an offence described in paragraph 3.1(a) after they have been charged with, or told they may be prosecuted for, that offence, see Code C, para. 16.5;

(c) when an interviewer wants to tell a person, after they have been charged with, or informed they may be prosecuted for, an offence described in paragraph 3.1(a), about any written statement or interview with another person, see Code C, para. 16.4.

E:3.2 The Terrorism Act 2000 and the Counter-Terrorism Act 2008 make separate provisions for a code of practice for the video recording with sound of:

- interviews of persons detained under section 41 of, or Schedule 7 to, the 2000 Act; and
- post-charge questioning of persons authorised under section 22 or 23 of the 2008 Act.

The provisions of this code do not apply to such interviews. (See *Note 3C*.)

E:3.3 If the conditions in paragraph 3.3A are satisfied, authority not to audio record an interview to which paragraph 3.1 applies may be given by:

(a) the custody officer in the case of a detained suspect, or

(b) an officer of the rank of sergeant or above in the case of a suspect who has not been arrested and to whom paragraphs 3.21 and 3.22 of Code C (persons attending a police station or elsewhere voluntarily) apply.

E:3.3A The conditions referred to in paragraph 3.3 are:

(a) it is not reasonably practicable to audio record, or as the case may be, continue to audio record, the interview because of equipment failure or the unavailability of a suitable interview room or recording equipment; and

(b) the authorising officer considers, on reasonable grounds, that the interview or continuation of the interview should not be delayed until the failure has been rectified or until a suitable room or recording equipment becomes available.

In these cases:

- the interview must be recorded or continue to be recorded in writing in accordance with Code C, section 11; and
- the authorising officer shall record the specific reasons for not audio recording and the interviewer is responsible for ensuring that the written interview record shows the date and time of the authority, the authorising officer and where the authority is recorded. (See *Note 3B*.)

E:3.4 If a detainee refuses to go into or remain in a suitable interview room, see Code C, paragraph 12.5, and the custody officer considers, on reasonable grounds, that the interview should not be delayed the interview may, at the custody officer's discretion, be conducted in a cell using portable recording equipment or, if none is available, recorded in writing as in Code C, section 11. The reasons for this shall be recorded.

E:3.5 The whole of each interview shall be audio recorded, including the taking and reading back of any statement.

E:3.6 A sign or indicator which is visible to the suspect must show when the recording equipment is recording.

Notes for guidance

E:3A *Nothing in this code is intended to preclude audio recording at police discretion of interviews at police stations or elsewhere with people cautioned in respect of offences not covered by paragraph 3.1, or responses made by persons after they have been charged with, or told they may be prosecuted for, an offence, provided this code is complied with.*

A-169

E:3B *A decision not to audio record an interview for any reason may be the subject of comment in court. The authorising offcer should be prepared to justify that decision.*

E:3C *If, during the course of an interview under this code, it becomes apparent that the interview should be conducted under the terrorism code for the video recording with sound of interviews, the interview should only continue in accordance with that code.*

E:3D *Attention is drawn to the provisions set out in Code C about the matters to be considered when deciding whether a detained person is fit to be interviewed.*

E:3E *Code C sets out the circumstances in which a suspect may be questioned about an offence after being charged with it.*

E:3F *Code C sets out the procedures to be followed when a person's attention is drawn after charge, to a statement made by another person. One method of bringing the content of an interview with another person to the notice of a suspect may be to play them a recording of that interview.*

E:4 The interview

(a) *General*

E:4.1 The provisions of Code C:

- sections 10 and 11, and the applicable *Notes for Guidance* apply to the conduct of interviews to which this code applies;
- paragraphs 11.7 to 11.14 apply only when a written record is needed.

E:4.2 Code C, paragraphs 10.10, 10.11 and Annex C describe the restriction on drawing adverse inferences from an arrested suspect's failure or refusal to say anything about their involvement in the offence when interviewed or after being charged or informed they may be prosecuted, and how it affects the terms of the caution and determines if and by whom a special warning under sections 36 and 37 of the Criminal Justice and Public Order Act 1994 can be given.

(b) *Commencement of interviews*

E:4.3 When the suspect is brought into the interview room the interviewer shall, without delay but in the suspect's sight, load the recorder with new recording media and set it to record. The recording media must be unwrapped or opened in the suspect's presence.

[This paragraph does not apply to interviews recorded using a secure digital network, see paras 7.4 and 7.5.]

E:4.4 The interviewer should tell the suspect about the recording process and point out the sign or indicator which shows that the recording equipment is activated and recording. See paragraph 3.6. The interviewer shall:

- (a) explain that the interview is being audibly recorded;
- (b) subject to paragraph 2.3, give their name and rank and that of any other interviewer present;
- (c) ask the suspect and any other party present, *e.g.* the appropriate adult, a solicitor or interpreter, to identify themselves;
- (d) state the date, time of commencement and place of the interview; and
- (e) state the suspect will be given a notice about what will happen to the recording. [This sub-paragraph does not apply to interviews recorded using a secure digital network, see paras 7.4 and 7.6 to 7.7.]

See *Note 4A*.

E:4.4A Any person entering the interview room after the interview has commenced shall be invited by the interviewer to identify themselves for the purpose of the audio recording and state the reason why they have entered the interview room.

E:4.5 The interviewer shall:

- caution the suspect, see Code C, section 10; and
- if they are detained, remind them of their entitlement to free legal advice, see Code C, para. 11.2; or
- if they are not detained under arrest, explain this and their entitlement to free legal advice, see Code C, para. 3.21.

E:4.6 The interviewer shall put to the suspect any significant statement or silence, see Code C, paragraph 11.4.

(c) *Interviews with suspects who appear to have a hearing impediment*

E:4.7 If the suspect appears to have a hearing impediment, the interviewer shall make a written note of the interview in accordance with Code C, at the same time as audio recording it in accordance with this code. (See *Notes 4B* and *4C*.)

(d) *Objections and complaints by the suspect*

E:4.8 If the suspect or an appropriate adult on their behalf objects to the interview being audibly recorded either at the outset, during the interview or during a break, the interviewer shall explain that the interview is being audibly recorded and that this code requires the objections to be recorded on the audio recording. When any objections have been audibly recorded or the suspect or appropriate adult have refused to have their objections recorded, the interviewer shall say they are turning off the recorder, give their reasons and turn it off. The interviewer shall then make a written record of the interview as in Code C, section 11. If, however, the interviewer reasonably considers they may proceed to question the suspect with the audio recording still on, the interviewer may do so. This procedure also applies in cases where the suspect has previously objected to the interview being visually recorded, see Code F, para. 4.8, and the investigating officer has decided to audibly record the interview. (See *Note 4D*.)

E:4.9 If in the course of an interview a complaint is made by or on behalf of the person being questioned concerning the provisions of this or any other codes, or it comes to the interviewer's notice that the person may have been treated improperly, the interviewer shall act as in Code C, para. 12.9. (See *Notes 4E* and *4F*.)

E:4.10 If the suspect indicates they want to tell the interviewer about matters not directly connected with the offence of which they are suspected and they are unwilling for these matters to be audio recorded, the suspect should be given the opportunity to tell the interviewer about these matter [*sic*] after the conclusion of the formal interview.

(e) *Changing recording media*

E:4.11 When the recorder shows the recording media only has a short time left to run, the interviewer shall so inform the person being interviewed and round off that part of the interview. If the interviewer leaves the room for a second set of recording media, the suspect shall not be left unattended. The interviewer will remove the recording media from the recorder and insert the new recording media which shall be unwrapped or opened in the suspect's presence. The recorder should be set to record on the new media. To avoid confusion between the recording media, the interviewer shall mark the media with an identification number immediately after it is removed from the recorder.

[This paragraph does not apply to interviews recorded using a secure digital network as this does not use removable media, see paras 1.6(c), 7.4 and 7.14 to 7.15.]

(f) *Taking a break during interview*

E:4.12 When a break is taken, the fact that a break is to be taken, the reason for it and the time **A-172** shall be recorded on the audio recording.

E:4.12A When the break is taken and the interview room vacated by the suspect, the recording media shall be removed from the recorder and the procedures for the conclusion of an interview followed, see paragraph 4.18.

E:4.13 When a break is a short one and both the suspect and an interviewer remain in the interview room, the recording may be stopped. There is no need to remove the recording media and when the interview recommences the recording should continue on the same recording media. The time the interview recommences shall be recorded on the audio recording.

E:4.14 After any break in the interview the interviewer must, before resuming the interview, remind the person being questioned of their right to legal advice if they have not exercised it and that they remain under caution or, if there is any doubt, give the caution in full again. (See *Note 4G*.)

[Paragraphs 4.12 to 4.14 do not apply to interviews recorded using a secure digital network, see paras 7.4 and 7.8 to 7.10.]

(g) *Failure of recording equipment*

E:4.15 If there is an equipment failure which can be rectified quickly, *e.g.* by inserting new recording media, the interviewer shall follow the appropriate procedures as in paragraph 4.11. When the recording is resumed the interviewer shall explain what happened and record the time the interview recommences. If, however, it will not be possible to continue recording on that recorder and no replacement recorder is readily available, the interview may continue without being audibly recorded. If this happens, the interviewer shall seek the authority as in paragraph 3.3 of the custody officer, or as applicable, a sergeant or above. (See *Note 4H*.)

[This paragraph does not apply to interviews recorded using a secure digital network, see paras 7.4 and 7.11.]

(h) *Removing recording media from the recorder*

E:4.16 Recording media which is removed from the recorder during the interview shall be retained and the procedures in paragraph 4.18 followed.

[This paragraph does not apply to interviews recorded using a secure digital network as this does not use removable media, see 1.6(c), 7.4 and 7.14 to 7.15.]

(i) *Conclusion of interview*

E:4.17 At the conclusion of the interview, the suspect shall be offered the opportunity to clarify anything they have said and asked if there is anything they want to add.

E:4.18 At the conclusion of the interview, including the taking and reading back of any written statement, the time shall be recorded and the recording shall be stopped. The interviewer shall seal the master recording with a master recording label and treat it as an exhibit in accordance with force standing orders. The interviewer shall sign the label and ask the suspect and any third party present during the interview to sign it. If the suspect or third party refuse to sign the label an officer of at least the rank of inspector, or if not available the custody officer, or if the suspect has not been arrested, a sergeant, shall be called into the interview room and asked, subject to paragraph 2.3, to sign it.

E:4.19 The suspect shall be handed a notice which explains:
- how the audio recording will be used;
- the arrangements for access to it;
- that if they are charged or informed they will be prosecuted, a copy of the audio recording will be supplied as soon as practicable or as otherwise agreed between the suspect and the police or on the order of the court.

[Paragraphs 4.17 to 4.19 do not apply to interviews recorded using a secure digital network, see paras 7.4 and 7.12 to 7.13.]

Notes for guidance

A-173   E:4A *For the purpose of voice identification the interviewer should ask the suspect and any other people present to identify themselves.*

E:4B *This provision is to give a person who is deaf or has impaired hearing equivalent rights of access to the full interview record as far as this is possible using audio recording.*

E:4C *The provisions of Code C on interpreters for suspects who do not appear to speak or understand English, or who appear to have a hearing or speech impediment, continue to apply.*

E:4D *The interviewer should remember that a decision to continue recording against the wishes of the suspect may be the subject of comment in court.*

E:4E *If the custody officer, or in the case of a person who has not been arrested, a sergeant, is called to deal with the complaint, the recorder should, if possible, be left on until the officer has entered the room and spoken to the person being interviewed. Continuation or termination of the interview should be at the interviewer's discretion pending action by an inspector under Code C, paragraph 9.2.*

A-174   E:4F *If the complaint is about a matter not connected with this code or Code C, the decision to continue is at the interviewer's discretion. When the interviewer decides to continue the interview, they shall tell the suspect that at the conclusion of the interview, the complaint will be brought to the attention of the custody officer, or in the case of a person who has not been arrested, a sergeant. When the interview is concluded the interviewer must, as soon as practicable, inform the custody officer or, as the case may be, the sergeant, about the existence and nature of the complaint made.*

E:4G *In considering whether to caution again after a break, the interviewer should bear in mind that they may have to satisfy a court that the person understood that they were still under caution when the interview resumed. The interviewer should also remember that it may be necessary to show to the court that nothing occurred during a break or between interviews which influenced the suspect's recorded evidence. After a break or at the beginning of a subsequent interview, the interviewer should consider summarising on the record the reason for the break and confirming this with the suspect.*

E:4H *Where the interview is being recorded and the media or the recording equipment fails, the interviewer should stop the interview immediately. Where part of the interview is unaffected by the error and is still accessible on the media, that part shall be copied and sealed in the suspect's presence as a master copy and the interview recommenced using new equipment/media as required. Where the content of the interview has been lost in its entirety, the media should be sealed in the suspect's presence and the interview begun again. If the recording equipment cannot be fixed or no replacement is immediately available, the interview should be recorded in accordance with Code C, section 11.*

E:5 After the interview

A-175   E:5.1 The interviewer shall make a note in their pocket book that the interview has taken place and that it was audibly recorded, the time it commenced, its duration and date and identification number of the master recording.

E:5.2 If no proceedings follow in respect of the person whose interview was recorded, the recording media must be kept securely as in paragraph 6.1 and *Note 6A.*

[This section (paras 5.1, 5.2 and Note 5A) does not apply to interviews recorded using a secure digital network, see paras 7.4 and 7.14 to 7.15.]

E:5A *Any written record of an audio recorded interview should be made in accordance with current national* **A-176** *guidelines for police officers, police staff and CPS prosecutors concerned with the preparation, processing and submission of prosecution files.*

E:6 Master recording security

(a) *General*

E:6.1 The officer in charge of each police station at which interviews with suspects are recorded or **A-177** as the case may be, where recordings of interviews carried out elsewhere than at a police station are held, shall make arrangements for master recordings to be kept securely and their movements accounted for on the same basis as material which may be used for evidential purposes, in accordance with force standing orders. (See *Note 6A*.)

(b) *Breaking master recording seal for criminal proceedings*

E:6.2 A police officer has no authority to break the seal on a master recording which is required for criminal trial or appeal proceedings. If it is necessary to gain access to the master recording, the police officer shall arrange for its seal to be broken in the presence of a representative of the Crown Prosecution Service. The defendant or their legal adviser should be informed and given a reasonable opportunity to be present. If the defendant or their legal representative is present they shall be invited to re-seal and sign the master recording. If either refuses or neither is present this should be done by the representative of the Crown Prosecution Service. (See *Notes 6B* and *6C*.)

(c) *Breaking master recording seal: other cases*

E:6.3 The chief officer of police is responsible for establishing arrangements for breaking the seal of the master copy where no criminal proceedings result, or the criminal proceedings to which the interview relates have been concluded and it becomes necessary to break the seal. These arrangements should be those which the chief officer considers are reasonably necessary to demonstrate to the person interviewed and any other party who may wish to use or refer to the interview record that the master copy has not been tampered with and that the interview record remains accurate. (See *Note 6D*.)

E:6.3A Subject to paragraph 6.3C, a representative of each party must be given a reasonable opportunity to be present when the seal is broken and the master recording copied and resealed.

E:6.3B If one or more of the parties is not present when the master copy seal is broken because they cannot be contacted or refuse to attend or paragraph 6.6 applies, arrangements should be made for an independent person such as a custody visitor, to be present. Alternatively, or as an additional safeguard, arrangement should be made for a film or photographs to be taken of the procedure.

E:6.3C Paragraph 6.3A does not require a person to be given an opportunity to be present when:

    (a) it is necessary to break the master copy seal for the proper and effective further investigation of the original offence or the investigation of some other offence; and

    (b) the officer in charge of the investigation has reasonable grounds to suspect that allowing an opportunity might prejudice any such an investigation or criminal proceedings which may be brought as a result or endanger any person. (See *Note 6E*.)

(d) *Documentation*

E:6.4 When the master recording seal is broken, a record must be made of the procedure followed, including the date, time, place and persons present.

[This section (paras 6.1 to 6.4 and *Notes 6A* to *6E*) does not apply to interviews recorded using a secure digital network, see paras 7.4 and 7.14 to 7.15.]

E:6A *This section is concerned with the security of the master recording sealed at the conclusion of the* **A-178** *interview. Care must be taken of working recordings because their loss or destruction may lead unnecessarily to the need to access master recordings.*

E:6B *If the master recording has been delivered to the Crown Court for their keeping after committal for trial the crown prosecutor will apply to the chief clerk of the Crown Court centre for the release of the recording for unsealing by the crown prosecutor.*

E:6C *Reference to the Crown Prosecution Service or to the crown prosecutor in this part of the code should be* **A-179** *taken to include any other body or person with a statutory responsibility for the proceedings for which the police recorded interview is required.*

E:6D *The most common reasons for needing access to master copies that are not required for criminal proceedings arise from civil actions and complaints against police and civil actions between individuals arising out of allegations of crime investigated by police.*

E:6E *Paragraph 6.3C could apply, for example, when one or more of the outcomes or likely outcomes of the investigation might be: (i) the prosecution of one or more of the original suspects; (ii) the prosecution of someone previously not suspected, including someone who was originally a witness; and (iii) any original suspect being treated as a prosecution witness and when premature disclosure of any police action, particularly through contact with any parties involved, could lead to a real risk of compromising the investigation and endangering witnesses.*

E:7 Recording of interviews by secure digital network

A-179a

E:7.1 A secure digital network does not use removable media and this section specifies the provisions which will apply when a secure digital network is used.

E:7.2 [*Not used.*]

E:7.3 The following requirements are solely applicable to the use of a secure digital network for the recording of interviews.

(a) *Application of sections 1 to 6 of Code E*

A-179b

E:7.4 Sections 1 to 6 of CodeE above apply except for the following paragraphs:
- paragraph 2.2 under "Recording and sealing of master recordings";
- paragraph 4.3 under "(b) Commencement of interviews";
- paragraph 4.4 (e) under "(b) Commencement of interviews";
- paragraphs 4.11 to 4.19 under "(e) Changing recording media", "(f) Taking a break during interview", "(g) Failure of recording equipment", "(h) Removing recording media from the recorder" and (i) "Conclusion of the interview"; and
- paragraphs 6.1 to 6.4 and *Notes 6A to 6C* under "Media security".

(b) *Commencement of interviews*

A-179c

E:7.5 When the suspect is brought into the interview room, the interviewer shall without delay and in the sight of the suspect, switch on the recording equipment and enter the information necessary to log on to the secure network and start recording.

E:7.6 The interviewer must then inform the suspect that the interview is being recorded using a secure digital network and that recording has commenced.

E:7.7 In addition to the requirements of paragraph 4.4(a) to (d) above, the interviewer must inform the person that:
- they will be given access to the recording of the interview in the event that they are charged or informed that they will be prosecuted but if they are not charged or informed that they will be prosecuted they will only be given access as agreed with the police or on the order of a court; and
- they will be given a written notice at the end of the interview setting out their rights to access the recording and what will happen to the recording.

(c) *Taking a break during interview*

A-179d

E:7.8 When a break is taken, the fact that a break is to be taken, the reason for it and the time shall be recorded on the audio recording. The recording shall be stopped and the procedures in paragraphs 7.12 and 7.13 for the conclusion of an interview followed.

E:7.9 When the interview recommences the procedures in paragraphs 7.5 to 7.7 for commencing an interview shall be followed to create a new file to record the continuation of the interview. The time the interview recommences shall be recorded on the audio recording.

E:7.10 After any break in the interview the interviewer must, before resuming the interview, remind the person being questioned that they remain under caution or, if there is any doubt, give the caution in full again. (See *Note 4G*.)

(d) *Failure of recording equipment*

A-179e

E:7.11 If there is an equipment failure which can be rectified quickly, *e.g.* by commencing a new secure digital network recording, the interviewer shall follow the appropriate procedures as in paragraphs 7.8 to 7.10. When the recording is resumed the interviewer shall explain what happened and record the time the interview recommences. If, however, it is not possible to continue recording on the secure digital network the interview should be recorded on removable media as in paragraph 4.3 unless the necessary equipment is not available. If this happens the interview may continue without being audibly recorded and the interviewer shall seek the authority of the custody officer or a sergeant as in paragraph 3.3(a) or (b). (See *Note 4H*.)

(e) *Conclusion of interview*

E:7.12 At the conclusion of the interview, the suspect shall be offered the opportunity to clarify anything he or she has said and asked if there is anything they want to add.

E:7.13 At the conclusion of the interview, including the taking and reading back of any written statement:

    (a) the time shall be orally recorded;

    (b) the suspect shall be handed a notice (see *Note 7A*) which explains:

- how the audio recording will be used,
- the arrangements for access to it,
- that if they are charged or informed that they will be prosecuted, they will be given access to the recording of the interview either electronically or by being given a copy on removable recording media, but if they are not charged or informed that they will prosecuted, they will only be given access as agreed with the police or on the order of a court;

    (c) the suspect must be asked to confirm that he or she has received a copy of the notice at sub-paragraph (b) above; if the suspect fails to accept or to acknowledge receipt of the notice, the interviewer will state for the recording that a copy of the notice has been provided to the suspect and that he or she has refused to take a copy of the notice or has refused to acknowledge receipt;

    (d) the time shall be recorded and the interviewer shall notify the suspect that the recording is being saved to the secure network. The interviewer must save the recording in the presence of the suspect. The suspect should then be informed that the interview is terminated.

(f) *After the interview*

E:7.14 The interviewer shall make a note in their pocket book that the interview has taken place and that it was audibly recorded, the time it commenced, its duration and date and the identification number of the original recording.

E:7.15 If no proceedings follow in respect of the person whose interview was recorded, the recordings must be kept securely as in paragraphs 7.16 and 7.17. (See *Note 5A*.)

(g) *Security of secure digital network interview records*

E:7.16 Interview record files are stored in read only format on non-removable storage devices, for example, hard disk drives, to ensure their integrity. The recordings are first saved locally to a secure non-removable device before being transferred to the remote network device. If for any reason the network connection fails, the recording remains on the local device and will be transferred when the network connections are restored.

E:7.17 Access to interview recordings, including copying to removable media, must be strictly controlled and monitored to ensure that access is restricted to those who have been given specific permission to access for specified purposes when this is necessary. For example, police officers and CPS lawyers involved in the preparation of any prosecution case, persons interviewed if they have been charged or informed they may be prosecuted and their legal representatives.

Note for guidance

E:7A *The notice at paragraph 7.13 above should provide a brief explanation of the secure digital network and how access to the recording is strictly limited. The notice should also explain the access rights of the suspect, his or her legal representative, the police and the prosecutor to the recording of the interview. Space should be provided on the form to insert the date and the file reference number for the interview.*

(7) Visual recording of interviews

The text that follows is of the version of the code that came into force on October 27, 2013: see *ante*, Appendix A-1.

As at July 1, 2015, there was no requirement on any police force to make visual recordings of interviews, but police officers who choose to make such recordings will still be required to have regard to the provisions of this code.

F. CODE OF PRACTICE ON VISUAL RECORDINGS WITH SOUND OF INTERVIEWS WITH SUSPECTS

Commencement—transitional arrangements

A-180a   The contents of this code should be considered if an interviewer decides to make a visual recording with sound of an interview with a suspect after 00.00 on 27 October 2013. There is no statutory requirement under *PACE* to visually record interviews.

F:1 General

A-181   F:1.0 The procedures in this code must be used fairly, responsibly, with respect for the people to whom they apply and without unlawful discrimination. Under the Equality Act 2010, section 149, when police officers are carrying out their functions, they also have a duty to have due regard to the need to eliminate unlawful discrimination, harassment and victimisation, to advance equality of opportunity between people who share a relevant protected characteristic and people who do not share it, and to take steps to foster good relations between those persons. [See *Note 1C*.]

F:1.1 This code of practice must be readily available for consultation by police officers and other police staff, detained persons and members of the public.

F:1.2 The notes for guidance included are not provisions of this code. They form guidance to police officers and others about its application and interpretation.

F:1.3 Nothing in this code shall be taken as detracting in any way from the requirements of the Code of Practice for the Detention, Treatment and Questioning of Persons by Police Officers (Code C). [See *Note 1A*.]

F:1.4 The interviews to which this code applies are described in section 3.

F:1.5 In this code, the term "appropriate adult", "solicitor" and "interview" have the same meaning as those set out in Code C and in the case of a 17-year-old suspect, "appropriate adult" includes the person called to fulfil that role in accordance with paragraph 1.5A of Code C. The corresponding provisions and *Notes for Guidance* in Code C applicable to those terms shall also apply where appropriate.

F:1.5A The visual recording of interviews shall be carried out openly to instil confidence in its reliability as an impartial and accurate record of the interview.

F:1.6 Any reference in this code to visual recording shall be taken to mean visual recording with sound and in this code:

  (aa) "recording media" means any removable, physical audio recording medium (such as magnetic tape, optical disc or solid state memory) which can be played and copied;

  (a) "designated person" means a person other than a police officer, designated under the Police Reform Act 2002, Pt 4, who has specified powers and duties of police officers conferred or imposed on them;

  (b) any reference to a police officer includes a designated person acting in the exercise or performance of the powers and duties conferred or imposed on them by their designation;

  (c) "secure digital network" is a computer network system which enables an original interview recording to be stored as a digital multi media file or a series of such files, on a secure file server which is accredited by the National Accreditor for Police Information Systems in accordance with the UK Government Protective Marking Scheme. See paragraph 1.6A and section 7 of this code.

F:1.6A Section 7 below sets out the provisions which apply to interviews visually recorded using a secure digital network by reference to Code E and by excluding provisions of sections 1 to 6 of this code which relate or apply only to removable media.

F:1.7 References to "pocket book" in this code include any official report book issued to police officers.

F:1.8 In the application of this code to the conduct and visual recording of an interview of a suspect who has not been arrested:

  (a) references to the "custody officer" include references to an officer of the rank of sergeant or above who is not directly involved in the investigation of the offence(s);

  (b) if the interview takes place elsewhere than at a police station, references to "interview room" include any place or location which the interviewer is satisfied will enable the interview to be conducted and recorded in accordance with this code and where the suspect is present voluntarily [see *Note 1B*]; and

  (c) provisions in addition to those which expressly apply to these interviews shall be followed insofar as they are relevant and can be applied in practice.

Notes for guidance

F:1A *As in paragraph 1.9 of Code C, references to custody officers include those carrying out the functions of a custody officer.*

F:1B *An interviewer who is not sure, or has any doubt, about the suitability of a place or location of an interview to be carried out elsewhere than at a police station, should consult an officer of the rank of sergeant or above for advice.*

F:1C *In paragraph 1.0, "relevant protected characteristic" includes: age, disability, gender reassignment, pregnancy and maternity, race, religion/belief, sex and sexual orientation.*

F:2 Recording and sealing of master recordings

F:2.1 [*Not used.*]

F:2.2 The camera(s) shall be placed in the interview room so as to ensure coverage of as much of the room as is practicably possible whilst the interviews are taking place. [See *Note 2A.*]

F:2.3 When the recording medium is placed in the recorder and it is switched on to record, the correct date and time, in hours, minutes and seconds will be superimposed automatically, second by second, during the whole recording, see *Note 2B*. See section 7 regarding the use of a secure digital network to record the interview.

F:2.4 One recording, referred to in this code as the master recording copy, will be sealed before it leaves the presence of the suspect. A second recording will be used as a working copy. [See *Notes 2C and 2D.*]

F:2.5 Nothing in this code requires the identity of an officer or police staff to be recorded or disclosed:

    (a) [*not used*];

    (b) if the interviewer reasonably believes that recording or disclosing their name might put them in danger.

In these cases, the interviewer will have their back to the camera and shall use their warrant or other identification number and the name of the police station to which they are attached. Such instances and the reasons for them shall be recorded in the custody record or the interviewer's pocket book. [See *Note 2E.*]

Notes for guidance

F:2A *Interviewers will wish to arrange that, as far as possible, visual recording arrangements are unobtrusive. It must be clear to the suspect, however, that there is no opportunity to interfere with the recording equipment or the recording media.*

F:2B *In this context, the recording medium should be capable of having an image of the date and time superimposed as the interview is recorded.*

F:2C *The purpose of sealing the master recording before it leaves the presence of the suspect is to establish their confidence that the integrity of the recording is preserved.*

F:2D *The visual recording of the interview may be used for identification procedures in accordance with paragraph 3.21 or Annex E of Code D.*

F:2E *The purpose of the [sic] paragraph 2.5(b) is to protect police officers and others involved in the investigation of serious organised crime or the arrest of particularly violent suspects when there is reliable information that those arrested or their associates may threaten or cause harm to the officers, their families or their personal property. In cases of doubt, an officer of inspector rank should be consulted.*

F:3 Interviews to be visually recorded

F:3.1 Subject to paragraph 3.2 below, when an interviewer is deciding whether to make a visual recording, these are the areas where it might be appropriate:

    (a) with a suspect in respect of an indictable offence (including an offence triable either way) [see *Notes 3A* and *3B*];

    (b) which takes place as a result of an interviewer exceptionally putting further questions to a suspect about an offence described in sub-paragraph (a) above after they have been charged with, or informed they may be prosecuted for, that offence [see *Note 3C*];

    (c) in which an interviewer wishes to bring to the notice of a person, after that person has been charged with, or informed they may be prosecuted for an offence described in subparagraph (a) above, any written statement made by another person, or the content of an interview with another person [see *Note 3D*];

    (d) with, or in the presence of, a deaf or deaf/blind or speech impaired person who uses sign language to communicate;

(e) with, or in the presence of anyone who requires an "appropriate adult"; or

(f) in any case where the suspect or their representative requests that the interview be recorded visually.

A-185   F:3.2 The Terrorism Act 2000 and the Counter-Terrorism Act 2008 make separate provisions for a code of practice for the video recording with sound of:

• interviews of persons detained under section 41 of, or Schedule 7 to, the 2000 Act; and

• post-charge questioning of persons authorised under section 22 or 23 of the 2008 Act.

The provisions of this code do not therefore apply to such interviews. [See *Note 3E*.]

F:3.3 Following a decision by an interviewer to visually record any interview mentioned in paragraph 3.1 above, the custody officer in the case of a detained person, or a sergeant in the case of a suspect who has not been arrested, may authorise the interviewer not to make a visual record and for the purpose of this code (F), the provisions of Code E, paras 3.1, 3.2, 3.3, 3.3A and 3.4 shall apply as appropriate. However, authority not to make a visual recording does not detract in any way from the requirement for audio recording. This would require a further authorisation not to make in accordance with Code E. [See *Note 3F*.]

F:3.4 [*Not used.*]

F:3.5 The whole of each interview shall be recorded visually, including the taking and reading back of any statement.

F:3.6 A sign or indicator which is visible to the suspect must show when the visual recording equipment is recording.

Notes for guidance

A-186   F:3A *Nothing in the code is intended to preclude visual recording at police discretion of interviews at police stations or elsewhere with people cautioned in respect of offences not covered by paragraph 3.1, or responses made by persons after they have been charged with or informed they may be prosecuted for, an offence, provided that this code is complied with.*

F:3B *Attention is drawn to the provisions set out in Code C about the matters to be considered when deciding whether a detained person is fit to be interviewed.*

F:3C *Code C sets out the circumstances in which a suspect may be questioned about an offence after being charged with it.*

F:3D *Code C sets out the procedures to be followed when a person's attention is drawn after charge, to a statement made by another person. One method of bringing the content of an interview with another person to the notice of a suspect may be to play them a recording of that interview.*

F:3E *If during the course of an interview under this code, it becomes apparent that the interview should be conducted under the terrorism code for the video recording with sound of interviews, the interview should only continue in accordance with that code.*

F:3F *A decision not to record an interview visually for any reason may be the subject of comment in court. The authorising officer should therefore be prepared to justify their decision in each case.*

F:4 The interview

(a) *General*

A-187   F:4.1 The provisions of Code C in relation to cautions and interviews and the Notes for Guidance applicable to those provisions shall apply to the conduct of interviews to which this code applies.

F:4.2 Particular attention is drawn to those parts of Code C that describe the restrictions on drawing adverse inferences from an arrested suspect's failure or refusal to say anything about their involvement in the offence when interviewed, or after being charged or informed they may be prosecuted and how those restrictions affect the terms of the caution and determine whether a special warning under sections 36 and 37 of the Criminal Justice and Public Order Act 1994 can be given.

(b) *Commencement of interviews*

A-188   F:4.3 When the suspect is brought into the interview room the interviewer shall without delay, but in sight of the suspect, load the recording equipment and set it to record. The recording media must be unwrapped or otherwise opened in the presence of the suspect. [See *Note 4A*.]

F:4.4 The interviewer shall then tell the suspect formally about the visual recording and point out the sign or indicator which shows that the recording equipment is activated and recording. See paragraph 3.6. The interviewer shall:

(a) explain that the interview is being visually recorded;

(b) subject to paragraph 2.5, give their name and rank, and that of any other interviewer present;

(c) ask the suspect and any other party present (*e.g.* the appropriate adult, a solicitor or interpreter) to identify themselves;

(d) state the date, time of commencement and place of the interview; and

(e) state that the suspect will be given a notice about what will happen to the recording.

[See *Note 4AA.*]

F:4.4A Any person entering the interview room after the interview has commenced shall be invited by the interviewer to identify themselves for the purpose of the recording and state the reason why they have entered the interview room.

F:4.5 The interviewer shall then caution the suspect, see Code C, section 10, and:

- if they are detained, remind them of their entitlement to free legal advice, see Code C, para. 11.2, or
- if they are not detained under arrest, explain this and their entitlement to free legal advice, see Code C, para. 3.21.

F:4.6 The interviewer shall then put to the suspect any significant statement or silence, see Code C, para. 11.4.

(c) *Interviews with suspects who appear to require an interpreter*

F:4.7 The provisions of Code C on interpreters for suspects who do not appear to speak or **A-189** understand English, or who appear to have a hearing or speech impediment, continue to apply.

(d) *Objections and complaints by the suspect*

F:4.8 If the suspect or an appropriate adult on their behalf, objects to the interview being visually **A-190** recorded either at the outset or during the interview or during a break in the interview, the interviewer shall explain that the interview is being visually recorded and that this code requires the objections to be recorded on the visual recording. When any objections have been recorded or the suspect or the appropriate adult have refused to have their objections recorded, the interviewer shall say that they are turning off the visual recording, give their reasons and turn it off. If a separate audio recording is being maintained, the interviewer shall ask the person to record the reasons for refusing to agree to the interview being visually recorded. Paragraph 4.8 of Code E will apply if the person also objects to the interview being audio recorded. If the interviewer reasonably considers they may proceed to question the suspect with the visual recording still on, the interviewer may do so. [See *Note 4G.*]

F:4.9 If in the course of an interview a complaint is made by the person being questioned, or on their behalf, concerning the provisions of this or any other code, or it comes to the interviewer's notice that the person may have been treated improperly, then the interviewer shall act as in Code C, para. 12.9. [See *Notes 4B* and *4C.*]

F:4.10 If the suspect indicates that they wish to tell the interviewer about matters not directly connected with the offence of which they are suspected and that they are unwilling for these matters to be visually recorded, the suspect should be given the opportunity to tell the interviewer about these matters after the conclusion of the formal interview.

(e) *Changing the recording media*

F:4.11 In instances where the recording medium is not of sufficient length to record all of the **A-191** interview with the suspect, further certified recording medium will be used. When the recording equipment indicates that the recording medium has only a short time left to run, the interviewer shall advise the suspect and round off that part of the interview. If the interviewer wishes to continue the interview but does not already have further certified recording media with him, they shall obtain a set. The suspect should not be left unattended in the interview room. The interviewer will remove the recording media from the recording equipment and insert the new ones which have been unwrapped or otherwise opened in the suspect's presence. The recording equipment shall then be set to record. Care must be taken, particularly when a number of sets of recording media have been used, to ensure that there is no confusion between them. This could be achieved by marking the sets of recording media with consecutive identification numbers.

(f) *Taking a break during the interview*

F:4.12 When a break is taken, the fact that a break is to be taken, the reason for it and the time **A-192** shall be recorded on the visual record.

F:4.12A When the break is taken and the interview room vacated by the suspect, the recording media shall be removed from the recorder and the procedures for the conclusion of an interview followed. (See para. 4.18.)

F:4.13 When a break is a short one and both the suspect and an interviewer remain in the interview room, the recording may be stopped. There is no need to remove the recording media and when the interview recommences the recording should continue on the same recording media. The time at which the interview recommences shall be recorded.

F:4.14 After any break in the interview the interviewer must, before resuming the interview, remind the person being questioned of their right to legal advice if they have not exercised it and that they remain under caution or, if there is any doubt, give the caution in full again. [See *Notes 4D* and *4E*.]

(g) *Failure of recording equipment*

A-193

F:4.15 If there is a failure of equipment which can be rectified quickly, the appropriate procedures set out in paragraph 4.12 shall be followed. When the recording is resumed the interviewer shall explain what has happened and record the time the interview recommences. If, however, it is not possible to continue recording on that particular recorder and no alternative equipment is readily available, the interview may continue without being recorded visually. In such circumstances, the procedures set out in paragraph 3.3 of this code for seeking the authority of the custody officer or a sergeant will be followed. [See *Note 4F*.]

(h) *Removing used recording media from recording equipment*

A-194

F:4.16 Where used recording media are removed from the recording equipment during the course of an interview, they shall be retained and the procedures set out in paragraph 4.18 below followed.

(i) *Conclusion of interview*

A-195

F:4.17 Before the conclusion of the interview, the suspect shall be offered the opportunity to clarify anything he or she has said and asked if there is anything that they wish to add.

F:4.18 At the conclusion of the interview, including the taking and reading back of any written statement, the time shall be recorded and the recording equipment switched off. The master recording shall be removed from the recording equipment, sealed with a master recording label and treated as an exhibit in accordance with the force standing orders. The interviewer shall sign the label and also ask the suspect and any third party present during the interview to sign it. If the suspect or third party refuses to sign the label, an officer of at least the rank of inspector, or if one is not available, the custody officer or, if the suspect has not been arrested, a sergeant, shall be called into the interview room and asked, subject to paragraph 2.5, to sign it.

F:4.19 The suspect shall be handed a notice which explains the use which will be made of the recording and the arrangements for access to it. The notice will also advise the suspect that a copy of the tape shall be supplied as soon as practicable if the person is charged or informed that he will be prosecuted.

Notes for guidance

A-196

F:4AA *For the purpose of voice identification the interviewer should ask the suspect and any other people present to identify themselves.*

F:4A *The interviewer should attempt to estimate the likely length of the interview and ensure that an appropriate quantity of certified recording media and labels with which to seal the master copies are available in the interview room.*

F:4B *Where the custody officer, or in the case of a person who has not been arrested, a sergeant, is called to deal with the complaint, wherever possible the recorder should be left to run until the officer has entered the interview room and spoken to the person being interviewed. Continuation or termination of the interview should be at the discretion of the interviewer pending action by an inspector under Code C, para.9.2.*

F:4C *Where the complaint is about a matter not connected with this code or Code C, the decision to continue with the interview is at the interviewer's discretion. Where the interviewer decides to continue with the interview, the person being interviewed shall be told that at the conclusion of the interview, the complaint will be brought to the attention of the custody officer, or in the case of a person who has not been arrested, a sergeant. When the interview is concluded, the interviewer must, as soon as practicable, inform the custody officer or the sergeant of the existence and nature of the complaint made.*

F:4D *In considering whether to caution again after a break, the interviewer should bear in mind that they may have to satisfy a court that the person understood that they were still under caution when the interview resumed.*

F:4E *The officer should bear in mind that it may be necessary to satisfy the court that nothing occurred during a break in an interview or between interviews which influenced the suspect's recorded evidence. On the recommencement of an interview, the interviewer should consider summarising on the record the reason for the break and confirming this with the suspect.*

F:4F *Where the interview is being recorded and the media or the recording equipment fails, the interviewer should stop the interview immediately. Where part of the interview is unaffected by the error and is still accessible on the media, that part shall be copied and sealed in the suspect's presence as a master copy and the interview recommenced using new equipment/media as required. Where the content of the interview has been lost in its entirety, the media should be sealed in the suspect's presence and the interview begun again. If the recording equipment cannot be fixed or no replacement is immediately available, the interview should be audio recorded in accordance with Code E.*

F:4G *The interviewer should be aware that a decision to continue recording against the wishes of the suspect may be the subject of comment in court.*

F:5 After the interview

F:5.1 The interviewer shall make a note in his or her pocket book of the fact that the interview has taken place and has been recorded, its time, duration and date and the identification number of the master copy of the recording media. **A-197**

F:5.2 Where no proceedings follow in respect of the person whose interview was recorded, the recording media must nevertheless be kept securely in accordance with paragraph 6.1 and *Note 6A.*

Note for guidance

F:5A *Any written record of a recorded interview shall be made in accordance with current national guidelines for police officers, police staff and CPS prosecutors concerned with the preparation, processing and submission of files.*

F:6 Master recording security

(a) *General*

F:6.1 The officer in charge of the police station at which interviews with suspects are recorded or as the case may be, where recordings of interviews carried out elsewhere than at a police station are held, shall make arrangements for the master copies to be kept securely and their movements accounted for on the same basis as other material which may be used for evidential purposes, in accordance with force standing orders. [See *Note 6A.*] **A-198**

(b) *Breaking master recording seal for criminal proceedings*

F:6.2 A police officer has no authority to break the seal on a master copy which is required for criminal trial or appeal proceedings. If it is necessary to gain access to the master copy, the police officer shall arrange for its seal to be broken in the presence of a representative of the Crown Prosecution Service. The defendant or their legal adviser shall be informed and given a reasonable opportunity to be present. If the defendant or their legal representative is present they shall be invited to reseal and sign the master copy. If either refuses or neither is present, this shall be done by the representative of the Crown Prosecution Service. [See *Notes 6B* and *6C.*] **A-199**

(c) *Breaking master recording seal: other cases*

F:6.3 The chief officer of police is responsible for establishing arrangements for breaking the seal of the master copy where no criminal proceedings result, or the criminal proceedings, to which the interview relates, have been concluded and it becomes necessary to break the seal. These arrangements should be those which the chief officer considers are reasonably necessary to demonstrate to the person interviewed and any other party who may wish to use or refer to the interview record that the master copy has not been tampered with and that the interview record remains accurate. [See *Note 6D.*] **A-200**

F:6.4 Subject to paragraph 6.6, a representative of each party must be given a reasonable opportunity to be present when the seal is broken and the master recording copied and re-sealed.

F:6.5 If one or more of the parties is not present when the master copy seal is broken because they cannot be contacted or refuse to attend or paragraph 6.6 applies, arrangements should be made for an independent person such as a custody visitor, to be present. Alternatively, or as an additional safeguard, arrangement should be made for a film or photographs to be taken of the procedure.

F:6.6 Paragraph 6.4 does not require a person to be given an opportunity to be present when:

    (a) it is necessary to break the master copy seal for the proper and effective further investigation of the original offence or the investigation of some other offence; and

    (b) the officer in charge of the investigation has reasonable grounds to suspect that allowing an opportunity might prejudice any such an investigation or criminal proceedings which may be brought as a result or endanger any person. [See *Note 6E.*]

(d) Documentation

A-201 F:6.7 When the master copy seal is broken, copied and re-sealed, a record must be made of the procedure followed, including the date time and place and persons present.

Notes for guidance

A-202 F:6A *This section is concerned with the security of the master recordings which will have been sealed at the conclusion of the interview. Care should, however, be taken of working recordings since their loss or destruction may lead unnecessarily to the need to have access to master copies.*

F:6B *If the master recording has been delivered to the Crown Court for their keeping after committal for trial the crown prosecutor will apply to the chief clerk of the Crown Court centre for its release for unsealing by the crown prosecutor.*

F:6C *Reference to the Crown Prosecution Service or to the crown prosecutor in this part of the code shall be taken to include any other body or person with a statutory responsibility for prosecution for whom the police conduct any recorded interviews.*

F:6D *The most common reasons for needing access to master recordings that are not required for criminal proceedings arise from civil actions and complaints against police and civil actions between individuals arising out of allegations of crime investigated by police.*

F:6E *Paragraph 6.6 could apply, for example, when one or more of the outcomes or likely outcomes of the investigation might be: (i) the prosecution of one or more of the original suspects; (ii) the prosecution of someone previously not suspected, including someone who was originally a witness; and (iii) any original suspect being treated as a prosecution witness and when premature disclosure of any police action, particularly through contact with any parties involved, could lead to a real risk of compromising the investigation and endangering witnesses.*

F:7 Visual recording of interviews by secure digital network

A-202a F:7.1 This section applies if an officer wishes to make a visual recording with sound of an interview mentioned in section 3 of this code using a secure digital network which does not use removable media (see paragraph 1.6(c) above).

F:7.3 [*sic*] The provisions of sections 1 to 6 of this code which relate or apply only to removable media will not apply to a secure digital network recording.

F:7.4 The statutory requirement and provisions for the audio recording of interviews using a secure digital network set out in section 7 of Code E should be applied to the visual recording with sound of interviews mentioned in section 3 of this code as if references to audio recordings of interviews include visual recordings with sound.

(8) Statutory power of arrest

A-203 The first version of Code G came into force on January 1, 2006, to coincide with the commencement of the substantial changes to the provisions of the PACE Act 1984 relating to the powers of arrest of police constables. As from that date, all offences became arrestable offences, but the lawfulness of an arrest by a constable for an offence became dependent on the constable having "reasonable grounds for believing that for any of the reasons mentioned in subsection (5) [of section 24] it is necessary to arrest the person in question". For the substituted section 24, see § 15-131 in the main work.

A revised code G came into force on November 12, 2012 (see *ante*, A-1).

G. CODE OF PRACTICE FOR THE STATUTORY POWER OF ARREST BY POLICE OFFICERS

Commencement

A-203a This code applies to any arrest made by a police officer after 00.00 on 12 November 2012.

G:1 Introduction

A-204 G:1.1 This code of practice deals with statutory power of police to arrest a person who is involved, or suspected of being involved, in a criminal offence. The power of arrest must be used fairly, responsibly, with respect for people suspected of committing offences and without unlawful discrimination. The Equality Act 2010 makes it unlawful for police officers to discriminate against, harass or victimise any person on the grounds of the "protected characteristics" of age, disability, gender reassignment, race, religion or belief, sex and sexual orientation, marriage and civil partnership, pregnancy and maternity when using their powers. When police forces are carrying out their functions they also have a duty to have regard to the need to eliminate unlawful discrimination, harassment and victimisation and to take steps to foster good relations.

G:1.2 The exercise of the power of arrest represents an obvious and significant interference with the right to liberty and security under Article 5 of the European Convention on Human Rights set out in Part I of Schedule 1 to the Human Rights Act 1998.

G:1.3 The use of the power must be fully justified and officers exercising the power should consider if the necessary objectives can be met by other, less intrusive means. Absence of justification for exercising the power of arrest may lead to challenges should the case proceed to court. It could also lead to civil claims against police for unlawful arrest and false imprisonment. When the power of arrest is exercised it is essential that it is exercised in a non-discriminatory and proportionate manner which is compatible with the right to liberty under Article 5. See *Note 1B*.

G:1.4 Section 24 of the Police and Criminal Evidence Act 1984 (as substituted by section 110 of the Serious Organised Crime and Police Act 2005) provides the statutory power for a constable to arrest without warrant for all offences. If the provisions of the Act and this code are not observed, both the arrest and the conduct of any subsequent investigation may be open to question.

G:1.5 This code of practice must be readily available at all police stations for consultation by police officers and police staff, detained persons and members of the public.

G:1.6 The notes for guidance are not provisions of this code.

G:2 Elements of arrest under section 24 PACE

G:2.1 A lawful arrest requires two elements: **A-205**

a person's involvement or suspected involvement or attempted involvement in the commission of a criminal offence; and

reasonable grounds for believing that the person's arrest is necessary.

Both elements must be satisfied, and it can never be necessary to arrest a person unless there are reasonable grounds to suspect them of committing an offence.

G:2.2 The arrested person must be informed that they have been arrested, even if this fact is obvious, and of the relevant circumstances of the arrest in relation to both the above elements. The custody officer must be informed of these matters on arrival at the police station. See paragraphs 2.9, 3.3 and *Note 3* and Code C, para. 3.4.

(a) *"Involvement in the commission of an offence"*

G:2.3 A constable may arrest without warrant in relation to any offence (see *Notes 1* and *1A*) **A-206** anyone:

- who is about to commit an offence or is in the act of committing an offence;
- whom the officer has reasonable grounds for suspecting is about to commit an offence or to be committing an offence;
- whom the officer has reasonable grounds to suspect of being guilty of an offence which he or she has reasonable grounds for suspecting has been committed;
- anyone [*sic*] who is guilty of an offence which has been committed or anyone whom the officer has reasonable grounds for suspecting to be guilty of that offence.

G:2.3A There must be some reasonable, objective grounds for the suspicion, based on known facts and information which are relevant to the likelihood the offence has been committed and the person liable to arrest committed it. See *Notes 2* and *2A*.

(b) *Necessity criteria*

G:2.4 The power of arrest is only exercisable if the constable has reasonable grounds for believing **A-207** that it is necessary to arrest the person. The statutory criteria for what may constitute necessity are set out in paragraph 2.9 and it remains an operational decision at the discretion of the constable to decide:

- which one or more of the necessity criteria (if any) applies to the individual; and
- if any of the criteria do apply, whether to arrest, grant street bail after arrest, report for summons or for charging by post, issue a penalty notice or take any other action that is open to the officer.

G:2.5 In applying the criteria, the arresting officer has to be satisfied that at least one of the reasons supporting the need for arrest is satisfied.

G:2.6 Extending the power of arrest to all offences provides a constable with the ability to use that power to deal with any situation. However, applying the necessity criteria requires the constable to examine and justify the reason or reasons why a person needs to be arrested or (as the case may be) further arrested, for an offence for the custody officer to decide whether to authorise their detention for that offence. See *Note 2C*.

G:2.7 The criteria in paragraph 2.9 below which are set out in section 24 of PACE, as substituted by section 110 of the Serious Organised Crime and Police Act 2005, are exhaustive. However, the circumstances that may satisfy those criteria remain a matter for the operational discretion of individual officers. Some examples are given to illustrate what those circumstances might be and what officers might consider when deciding whether arrest is necessary.

G:2.8 In considering the individual circumstances, the constable must take into account the situation of the victim, the nature of the offence, the circumstances of the suspect and the needs of the investigative process.

A-208

G:2.9 When it is practicable to tell a person why their arrest is necessary (as required by paragraphs 2.2, 3.3 and *Note 3*), the constable should outline the facts, information and other circumstances which provide the grounds for believing that their arrest is necessary and which the officer considers satisfy one or more of the statutory criteria in sub-paragraphs (a) to (f), namely:

(a) to enable the name of the person in question to be ascertained (in the case where the constable does not know, and cannot readily ascertain, the person's name, or has reasonable grounds for doubting whether a name given by the person as his name is his real name):

an officer might decide that a person's name cannot be readily ascertained if they fail or refuse to give it when asked, particularly after being warned that failure or refusal is likely to make their arrest necessary (see *Note 2D*); grounds to doubt a name given may arise if the person appears reluctant or hesitant when asked to give their name or to verify the name they have given;

where mobile fingerprinting is available and the suspect's name cannot be ascertained or is doubted, the officer should consider using the power under section 61(6A) of PACE (see Code D, para. 4.3(e)) to take and check the fingerprints of a suspect as this may avoid the need to arrest solely to enable their name to be ascertained;

(b) correspondingly as regards the person's address:

an officer might decide that a person's address cannot be readily ascertained if they fail or refuse to give it when asked, particularly after being warned that such a failure or refusal is likely to make their arrest necessary (see *Note 2D*); grounds to doubt an address given may arise if the person appears reluctant or hesitant when asked to give their address or is unable to provide verifiable details of the locality they claim to live in;

when considering reporting to consider summons or charging by post as alternatives to arrest, an address would be satisfactory if the person will be at it for a sufficiently long period for it to be possible to serve them with the summons or requisition and charge; or, that some other person at that address specified by the person will accept service on their behalf; when considering issuing a penalty notice, the address should be one where the person will be in the event of enforcement action if the person does not pay the penalty or is convicted and fined after a court hearing;

(c) to prevent the person in question:

(i) causing physical injury to himself or any other person; this might apply where the suspect has already used or threatened violence against others and it is thought likely that they may assault others if they are not arrested (see *Note 2D*);

(ii) suffering physical injury; this might apply where the suspect's behaviour and actions are believed likely to provoke, or have provoked, others to want to assault the suspect unless the suspect is arrested for their own protection (see *Note 2D*);

(iii) causing loss or damage to property; this might apply where the suspect is a known persistent offender with a history of serial offending against property (theft and criminal damage) and it is thought likely that they may continue offending if they are not arrested;

(iv) committing an offence against public decency (only applies where members of the public going about their normal business cannot reasonably be expected to avoid the person in question); this might apply when an offence against public decency is being committed in a place to which the public have access and is likely to be repeated in that or some other public place at a time when the public are likely to encounter the suspect (see *Note 2D*);

(v) causing an unlawful obstruction of the highway; this might apply to any offence where its commission causes an unlawful obstruction which it is believed may continue or be repeated if the person is not arrested, particularly if the person has been warned that they are causing an obstruction (see *Note 2D*);

(d) to protect a child or other vulnerable person from the person in question; this might apply when the health (physical or mental) or welfare of a child or vulnerable person is likely to be harmed or is at risk of being harmed, if the person is not arrested in cases where it is not practicable and appropriate to make alternative arrangements to prevent the suspect from having any harmful or potentially harmful contact with the child or vulnerable person;

(e) to allow the prompt and effective investigation of the offence or of the conduct of the person in question (see *Note 2E*); this may arise when it is thought likely that unless the person is arrested and then either taken in custody to the police station or granted "street bail" to attend the station later (see *Note 2J*), further action considered necessary to properly investigate their involvement in the offence would be frustrated, unreasonably delayed or otherwise hindered and therefore be impracticable; examples of such actions include:

(i) interviewing the suspect on occasions when the person's voluntary attendance is not considered to be a practicable alternative to arrest, because for example:

- it is thought unlikely that the person would attend the police station voluntarily to be interviewed;
- it is necessary to interview the suspect about the outcome of other investigative action for which their arrest is necessary, see (ii) to (v) below;
- arrest would enable the special warning to be given in accordance with Code C, paras 10.10 and 10.11 when the suspect is found:
  - in possession of incriminating objects, or at a place where such objects are found;
  - at or near the scene of the crime at or about the time it was committed;
- the person has made false statements and/or presented false evidence;
- it is thought likely that the person:
  - may steal or destroy evidence;
  - may collude or make contact with, co-suspects or conspirators;
  - may intimidate or threaten or make contact with, witnesses;

(see *Notes 2F* and *2G*);

(ii) when considering arrest in connection with the investigation of an indictable offence (see *Note 6*), there is a need:

- to enter and search without a search warrant any premises occupied or controlled by the arrested person or where the person was when arrested or immediately before arrest;
- to prevent the arrested person from having contact with others;
- to detain the arrested person for more than 24 hours before charge;

(iii) when considering arrest in connection with any recordable offence and it is necessary to secure or preserve evidence of that offence by taking fingerprints, footwear impressions or samples from the suspect for evidential comparison or matching with other material relating to that offence, for example, from the crime scene (see *Note 2H*);

(iv) when considering arrest in connection with any offence and it is necessary to search, examine or photograph the person to obtain evidence (see *Note 2H*);

(v) when considering arrest in connection with an offence to which the statutory Class A drug testing requirements in Code C, section 17, apply, to enable testing when it is thought that drug misuse might have caused or contributed to the offence (see *Note 2I*);

(f) to prevent any prosecution for the offence from being hindered by the disappearance of the person in question; this may arise when it is thought that:

- if the person is not arrested they are unlikely to attend court if they are prosecuted;
- the address given is not a satisfactory address for service of a summons or a written charge and requisition to appear at court because the person will not be at it for a sufficiently long period for the summons or charge and requisition to be served and no other person at that specified address will accept service on their behalf.

G:3 Information to be given on arrest

(a) *Cautions—when a caution must be given*

G:3.1 Code C, paras 10.1 and 10.2, set out the requirement for a person whom there are grounds **A-209** to suspect of an offence (see *Note 2*) to be cautioned before being questioned or further questioned about an offence.

G:3.2 [*Not used.*]

G:3.3 A person who is arrested, or further arrested, must be informed at the time if practicable, or if not, as soon as it becomes practicable thereafter, that they are under arrest and of the grounds and reasons for their arrest (see paragraphs [*sic*] 2.2 and *Note 3*).

G:3.4 A person who is arrested, or further arrested, must be cautioned unless:

    (a) it is impracticable to do so by reason of their condition or behaviour at the time;

    (b) they have already been cautioned immediately prior to arrest as in paragraph 3.1.

(b) *Terms of the caution (taken from Code C, section 10)*

A-210

G:3.5 The caution, which must be given on arrest, should be in the following terms:

"You do not have to say anything. But it may harm your defence if you do not mention when questioned something which you later rely on in court. Anything you do say may be given in evidence.".

Where the use of the Welsh language is appropriate, a constable may provide the caution directly in Welsh in the following terms:

"Does dim rhaid i chi ddweud dim byd. Ond gall niweidio eich amddiffyniad os na fyddwch chi'n sôn, wrth gael eich holi, am rywbeth y byddwch chi'n dibynnu arno nes ymlaen yn y Llys. Gall unrhyw beth yr ydych yn ei ddweud gael ei roi fel tystiolaeth.".

See *Note 4*.

G:3.6 Minor deviations from the words of any caution given in accordance with this code do not constitute a breach of this code, provided the sense of the relevant caution is preserved. See *Note 5*.

G:3.7 *Not used*.

G:4 Records of arrest

(a) *General*

A-211

G:4.1 The arresting officer is required to record in his pocket book or by other methods used for recording information:

    • the nature and circumstances of the offence leading to the arrest;

    • the reason or reasons why arrest was necessary;

    • the giving of the caution; and

    • anything said by the person at the time of arrest.

G:4.2 Such a record should be made at the time of the arrest unless impracticable to do. If not made at that time, the record should then be completed as soon as possible thereafter.

G:4.3 On arrival at the police station or after being first arrested at the police station, the arrested person must be brought before the custody officer as soon as practicable and a custody record must be opened in accordance with section 2 of Code C. The information given by the arresting officer on the circumstances and reason or reasons for arrest shall be recorded as part of the custody record. Alternatively, a copy of the record made by the officer in accordance with paragraph 4.1 above shall be attached as part of the custody record. See paragraph 2.2 and Code C, paras 3.4 and 10.3.

G:4.4 The custody record will serve as a record of the arrest. Copies of the custody record will be provided in accordance with paragraphs 2.4 and 2.4A of Code C and access for inspection of the original record in accordance with paragraph 2.5 of Code C.

(b) *Interviews and arrests*

G:4.5 Records of interviews, significant statements or silences will be treated in the same way as set out in sections 10 and 11 of Code C and in Codes E and F (audio and visual recording of interviews).

Notes for guidance

A-212

G:1 *For the purposes of this code, "offence" means any statutory or common law offence for which a person may be tried by a magistrates' court or the Crown Court and punished if convicted.* [The note then gives examples of statutory and common law offences.]

G:1A *This code does not apply to powers of arrest conferred on constables under any arrest warrant, for example, a warrant issued under the Magistrates' Courts Act 1980, ss.1 or 13, or the Bail Act 1976, s.7(1), or to the powers of constables to arrest without warrant other than under section 24 of PACE for an offence. These other powers to arrest without warrant do not depend on the arrested person committing any specific offence and include:*

    • *PACE, s.46A, arrest of person who fails to answer police bail to attend police station or is suspected of breaching any condition of that bail for the custody officer to decide whether they should be kept in*

police detention which applies whether or not the person commits an offence under section 6 of the
Bail Act 1976 (e.g. failing without reasonable cause to surrender to custody);

- *Bail Act 1976, s.7(3),* arrest of person bailed to attend court who is suspected of breaching, or is
  believed likely to breach, any condition of bail to take them to court for bail to be re-considered;
- *Children and Young Persons Act 1969, s.32(1A) (absconding)* – arrest to return the person to the
  place where they are required to reside;
- *Immigration Act 1971, Sched. 2,* to arrest a person liable to examination to determine their right to
  remain in the U.K.;
- *Mental Health Act 1983, s.136* to remove person suffering from mental disorder to place of safety
  for assessment;
- *Prison Act 1952, s.49,* arrest to return person unlawfully at large to the prison, etc., where they are
  liable to be detained;
- *Road Traffic Act 1988, s.6D,* arrest of driver following the outcome of a preliminary roadside test
  requirement to enable the driver to be required to provide an evidential sample;
  - common law power to stop or prevent a breach of the peace—*after arrest a person aged 18 or over
    may be brought before a justice of the peace court to show cause why they should not be bound over to
    keep the peace* – not criminal proceedings.

G:1B *Juveniles should not be arrested at their place of education unless this is unavoidable. When a juvenile
is arrested at their place of education, the principal or their nominee must be informed (from Code C, Note 11D).*

G:2 *Facts and information relevant to a person's suspected involvement in an offence should not be confined to
those which tend to indicate the person has committed or attempted to commit the offence. Before making a decision
to arrest, a constable should take account of any facts and information that are available, including claims of innocence made by the person, that might dispel the suspicion.*

G:2A *Particular examples of facts and information which might point to a person's innocence and may tend to
dispel suspicion include those which relate to the statutory defence provided by the Criminal Law Act 1967, s.3(1)
which allows the use of reasonable force in the prevention of crime or making an arrest and the common law of
self-defence. This may be relevant when a person appears, or claims, to have been acting reasonably in defence of
themselves or others or to prevent their property or the property of others from being stolen, destroyed or damaged,
particularly if the offence alleged is based on the use of unlawful force, e.g. a criminal assault. When investigating allegations involving the use of force by school staff, the power given to all school staff under the Education
and Inspections Act 2006, s.93, to use reasonable force to prevent their pupils from committing any offence, injur-
ing persons, damaging property or prejudicing the maintenance of good order and discipline may be similarly
relevant. The Association of Chief Police Officers and the Crown Prosecution Service have published joint guidance to help the public understand the meaning of reasonable force and what to expect from the police and CPS
in cases which involve claims of self-defence. Separate advice for school staff on their powers to use reasonable
force is available from the Department for Education.*

G:2B *If a constable who is dealing with an allegation of crime and considering the need to arrest becomes an
investigator for the purposes of the Code of Practice under the Criminal Procedure and Investigations Act 1996,
the officer should, in accordance with paragraph 3.5 of that code, "pursue all reasonable lines of inquiry, whether
these point towards or away from the suspect. What is reasonable in each case will depend on the particular
circumstances."*

G:2C *For a constable to have reasonable grounds for believing it necessary to arrest, he or she is not required
to be satisfied that there is no viable alternative to arrest. However, it does mean that in all cases, the officer should
consider that arrest is the practical, sensible and proportionate option in all the circumstances at the time the decision is made. This applies equally to a person in police detention after being arrested for an offence who is
suspected of involvement in a further offence and the necessity to arrest them for that further offence is being
considered.*

G:2D *Although a warning is not expressly required, officers should if practicable, consider whether a warning
which points out their offending behaviour, and explains why, if they do not stop, the resulting consequences may
make their arrest necessary. Such a warning might:*

- *if heeded, avoid the need to arrest, or*
- *if it is ignored, support the need to arrest and also help prove the mental element of certain offences,
  for example, the person's intent or awareness, or help to rebut a defence that they were acting
  reasonably.*

*A person who is warned that they may be liable to arrest if their real name and address cannot be ascertained,
should be given a reasonable opportunity to establish their real name and address before deciding that either or
both are unknown and cannot be readily ascertained or that there are reasonable grounds to doubt that a name
and address they have given is their real name and address. They should be told why their name is not known and
cannot be readily ascertained and (as the case may be) of the grounds for doubting that a name and address they
have given is their real name and address, including, for example, the reason why a particular document the
person has produced to verify their real name and/or address, is not sufficient.*

G:2E *The meaning of "prompt" should be considered on a case by case basis taking account of all the circumstances. It indicates that the progress of the investigation should not be delayed to the extent that it would adversely affect the effectiveness of the investigation. The arresting officer also has discretion to release the arrested person on "street bail" as an alternative to taking the person directly to the station (see Note 2J).*

G:2F *An officer who believes that it is necessary to interview the person suspected of committing the offence must then consider whether their arrest is necessary in order to carry out the interview. The officer is not required to interrogate the suspect to determine whether they will attend a police station voluntarily to be interviewed but they must consider whether the suspect's voluntary attendance is a practicable alternative for carrying out the interview. If it is, then arrest would not be necessary. Conversely, an officer who considers this option but is not satisfied that it is a practicable alternative, may have reasonable grounds for deciding that the arrest is necessary at the outset "on the street". Without such considerations, the officer would not be able to establish that arrest was necessary in order to interview.*

Circumstances which suggest that a person's arrest "on the street" would not be necessary to interview them might be where the officer:

- *is satisfied as to their identity and address and that they will attend the police station voluntarily to be interviewed, either immediately or by arrangement at a future date and time; and*
- *is not aware of any other circumstances which indicate that voluntary attendance would not be a practicable alternative (see paragraph 2.9(e)(i) to (v)).*

When making arrangements for the person's voluntary attendance, the officer should tell the person:

- *that to properly investigate their suspected involvement in the offence they must be interviewed under caution at the police station, but in the circumstances their arrest for this purpose will not be necessary if they attend the police station voluntarily to be interviewed;*
- *that if they attend voluntarily, they will be entitled to free legal advice before, and to have a solicitor present at, the interview;*
- *that the date and time of the interview will take account of their circumstances and the needs of the investigation; and*
- *that if they do not agree to attend voluntarily at a time which meets the needs of the investigation, or having so agreed, fail to attend, or having attended, fail to remain for the interview to be completed, their arrest will be necessary to enable them to be interviewed.*

G:2G *When the person attends the police station voluntarily for interview by arrangement as in Note 2F above, their arrest on arrival at the station prior to interview would only be justified if:*

- *new information coming to light after the arrangements were made indicates that from that time, voluntary attendance ceased to be a practicable alternative and the person's arrest became necessary; and*
- *it was not reasonably practicable for the person to be arrested before they attended the station.*

If a person who attends the police station voluntarily to be interviewed decides to leave before the interview is complete, the police would at that point be entitled to consider whether their arrest was necessary to carry out the interview. The possibility that the person might decide to leave during the interview is therefore not a valid reason for arresting them before the interview has commenced (see Code C, para. 3.21).

G:2H *The necessity criteria do not permit arrest solely to enable the routine taking, checking (speculative searching) and retention of fingerprints, samples, footwear impressions and photographs when there are no prior grounds to believe that checking and comparing the fingerprints, etc., or taking a photograph would provide relevant evidence of the person's involvement in the offence concerned or would help to ascertain or verify their real identity.*

G:2I *The necessity criteria do not permit arrest for an offence solely because it happens to be one of the statutory drug testing "trigger offences" (see Code C, Note 17E) when there is no suspicion that Class A drug misuse might have caused or contributed to the offence.*

G:2J *Having determined that the necessity criteria have been met and having made the arrest, the officer can then consider the use of street bail on the basis of the effective and efficient progress of the investigation of the offence in question. It gives the officer discretion to compel the person to attend a police station at a date/ time that best suits the overall needs of the particular investigation. Its use is not confined to dealing with child care issues or allowing officers to attend to more urgent operational duties and granting street bail does not retrospectively negate the need to arrest.*

G:3 *An arrested person must be given sufficient information to enable them to understand they have been deprived of their liberty and the reason they have been arrested, as soon as practicable after the arrest, e.g. when a person is arrested on suspicion of committing an offence they must be informed of the nature of the suspected offence and when and where it was committed. The suspect must also be informed of the reason or reasons why arrest is considered necessary. Vague or technical language should be avoided. When explaining why one or more of the arrest criteria apply, it is not necessary to disclose any specific details that might undermine or otherwise adversely affect any investigative processes. An example might be the conduct of a formal interview when prior disclosure of such details might give the suspect an opportunity to fabricate an innocent explanation or to otherwise conceal lies from the interviewer.*

G:4 *Nothing in this code requires a caution to be given or repeated when informing a person not under arrest they may be prosecuted for an offence. However, a court will not be able to draw any inferences under the Criminal Justice and Public Order Act 1994, s.34, if the person was not cautioned.*

G:5 *If it appears a person does not understand the caution, the person giving it should explain it in their own words.*

G:6 *Certain powers available as the result of an arrest - for example, entry and search of premises, detention without charge beyond 24 hours, holding a person incommunicado and delaying access to legal advice - only apply in respect of indictable offences and are subject to the specific requirements on authorisation as set out in PACE and the relevant code of practice.*

(9) Detention treatment and questioning of terrorist suspects

The Police and Criminal Evidence Act 1984 (Code of Practice C and Code of Practice H) Order   **A-213**
2006 (S.I. 2006 No. 1938) provided for a revised Code C, and for a new Code H (on detention, treatment and questioning by police officers of persons under section 41 of, and Schedule 8 to, the Terrorism Act 2000), to come into operation on July 25, 2006. The new codes were consequential upon the commencement of the provisions of the Terrorism Act 2006, which were concerned with the 28-day detention of those arrested under section 41 of the 2000 Act. Whereas Code C had previously regulated the detention, treatment and questioning of those detained following arrest under section 41, from that date onwards these matters were regulated by Code H. Code C was revised so as to remove references to detention under the 2000 Act. The new Code H largely mirrored the provisions of Code C, but with various differences.

A revised Code H came into force on July 10, 2012, and a further revision came into force on October 27, 2013. The text that follows is that of a yet further revision that came into force on June 2, 2014 (see *ante*, A-1).

H. CODE OF PRACTICE IN CONNECTION WITH THE DETENTION, TREATMENT AND QUESTIONING BY POLICE OFFICERS OF PERSONS UNDER SECTION 41 OF, AND SCHEDULE 8 TO, THE TERRORISM ACT 2000

Commencement—transitional arrangements

This code applies to people in police detention after 00.00 on 2 June 2014, notwithstanding that   **A-214**
their period of detention may have commenced before that time.

H:1 General

H:1.0 *[Identical to C1:0.]*   **A-214a**
H:1.1 This code of practice applies to, and only to:
   (a) persons in police detention after being arrested under section 41 of the Terrorism Act 2000 (TACT) and detained under section 41 of, or Schedule 8 to that Act and not charged; and
   (b) detained persons in respect of whom an authorisation has been given under section 22 of the Counter-Terrorism Act 2008 (post-charge questioning of terrorist suspects) to interview them in which case, section 15 of this code will apply.
H:1.2 The provisions in *PACE* Code C apply when a person:
   (a) is in custody otherwise than as a result of being arrested under section 41 of TACT or detained for examination under Schedule 7 to TACT (see paragraph 1.4);
   (b) is charged with an offence; or
   (c) is being questioned about any offence after being charged with that offence without an authorisation being given under section 22 of the Counter-Terrorism Act 2008.
See *Note 1N.*

H:1.3 In this code references to an offence and to a person's involvement or suspected involvement in an offence where the person has not been charged with an offence, include being concerned, or suspected of being concerned, in the commission, preparation or instigation of acts of terrorism.

H:1.4 The code of practice issued under paragraph 6 of Schedule 14 to TACT applies to persons detained for examination under Schedule 7 to TACT. See *Note 1N.*

H:1.5 All persons in custody must be dealt with expeditiously, and released as soon as the need for detention no longer applies.

H:1.6 There is no provision for bail under TACT before or after charge. See *Note 1N.*

H:1.7 An officer must perform the assigned duties in this code as soon as practicable. An officer will not be in breach of this code if delay is justifiable and reasonable steps are taken to prevent unnecessary delay. The custody record shall show when a delay has occurred and the reason. See *Note 1H*.

H:1.8–1.10 [*Identical to C:1.2 to C:1.4, respectively.*]

H:1.11 For the purposes of this code, a juvenile is any person under the age of 17. If anyone appears to be under 17, and there is no clear evidence that they are 17 or over, they shall be treated as a juvenile for the purposes of this code.

H:1.11A If anyone appears to have attained the age of 17 and to be under the age of 18, they shall in the absence of clear evidence that they are older, be treated as a 17-year-old for the purposes of this code and the provisions and *Notes for Guidance* which in accordance with paragraph 1.11 apply to a juvenile and the way they are to be treated shall also apply to them, except for the purposes of the statutory provisions in section 65(1) of PACE (appropriate consent) which by virtue of paragraph 15 of Schedule 8 to the Terrorism Act 2000, applies to the powers in paragraphs 10 to 14 of that schedule to take fingerprints, intimate and non-intimate samples. For these powers, the statutory requirement for appropriate consent for a person who has not attained the age of 17 to be given by them and their parent or guardian shall not apply to a person who appears to have attained the age of 17 and whose consent alone is sufficient. (See *Notes 10* and *1P*.)

H:1.12 [*Identical to C:1.6.*]

H:1.13 [*Identical to C:1.7, save for reference to "paragraph 1.11A" in lieu of reference to "paragraph 1.5A".*]

H:1.14 [*Identical to C:1.8.*]

H:1.15 [*Identical to C:1.9.*]

H:1.16 When this code requires the prior authority or agreement of an officer of at least inspector or superintendent rank, that authority may be given by a sergeant or chief inspector authorised by section 107 of PACE to perform the functions of the higher rank under TACT.

H:1.17 In this code:

    (a) "designated person" means a person other than a police officer, designated under the Police Reform Act 2002, Pt 4, who has specified powers and duties of police officers conferred or imposed on them;

    (b) reference to a police officer includes a designated person acting in the exercise or performance of the powers and duties conferred or imposed on them by their designation;

    (c) where a search or other procedure to which this code applies may only be carried out or observed by a person of the same sex as the detainee, the gender of the detainee and other parties present should be established and recorded in line with Annex I of this code.

H:1.18 [*Identical to C:1.14.*]

H:1.19 [*Identical to C:1.15.*]

H:1.20 Designated persons and other police staff must have regard to any relevant provisions of this code.

H:1.21 [*Identical to C:1.17.*]

Notes for guidance

H:1A *Although certain sections of this code apply specifically to people in custody at police stations, those there voluntarily to assist with an investigation should be treated with no less consideration, e.g. offered refreshments at appropriate times, and enjoy an absolute right to obtain legal advice or communicate with anyone outside the police station.*

H:1AA [*Identical to C:1AA.*]

H:1B *A person, including a parent or guardian, should not be an appropriate adult if they:*

    • *are:*

        – *suspected of involvement in the offence or involvement in the commission, preparation or instigation of acts of terrorism;*

        – *the victim;*

        – *a witness;*

        – *involved in the investigation;*

    • *received admissions prior to attending to act as the appropriate adult.*

Note: if a juvenile's parent is estranged from the juvenile, they should not be asked to act as the appropriate adult if the juvenile expressly and specifically objects to their presence.

Note: Paragraph 1.11A applies this note to 17-year-old detainees.

H:1C *If a juvenile admits an offence to, or in the presence of, a social worker or member of a youth offending team other than during the time that person is acting as the juvenile's appropriate adult, another appropriate adult should be appointed in the interest of fairness.*

Note: Paragraph 1.11A applies this note to 17-year-old detainees.

H:1D–1G [*Identical to C:1D–G.*]

H:1H *Paragraph 1.7 is intended to cover delays which may occur in processing detainees* e.g. *if:*

- *a large number of suspects are brought into the station simultaneously to be placed in custody;*
- *interview rooms are all being used;*
- *there are difficulties contacting an appropriate adult, solicitor or interpreter.*

H:1I–1K [*Identical to C:1I to C:1K, respectively.*]

H:1L *If a person is moved from a police station to receive medical treatment, or for any other reason, the period of detention is still calculated from the time of arrest under section 41 of TACT (or, if a person was being detained under TACT, Sched. 7, when arrested, from the time at which the examination under Schedule 7 began).*

H:1M *Under paragraph 1 of Schedule 8 to TACT, all police stations are designated for detention of persons arrested under section 41 of TACT. Paragraph 4 of Schedule 8 requires that the constable who arrests a person under section 41 takes him as soon as practicable to the police station which the officer considers is "most appropriate".*

H:1N *The powers under Part IV of PACE to detain and release on bail (before or after charge) a person arrested under section 24 of PACE for any offence (see PACE Code G (Arrest)) do not apply to persons whilst they are detained under the terrorism powers following their arrest/detention under section 41 of, or Schedule 7 to, TACT. If when the grounds for detention under these powers cease the person is arrested under section 24 of PACE for a specific offence, the detention and bail provisions of PACE will apply and must be considered from the time of that arrest.*

H:1O *Paragraph 1.11A does not amend the provisions in any enactment which expressly refer and apply to persons under the age of 17. Until amended by Parliament, these statutory provisions alone do not extend to persons who have attained the age of 17.*

H:1P *The purpose of paragraph 1.11A is to extend the safeguards for juveniles to 17-year-olds unless this is precluded by any statutory provisions. The exception identifies section 65 of PACE which by virtue of paragraph 15 of Schedule 8 to the Terrorism Act 2000, is applied to the powers under that schedule to take fingerprints and samples. All other safeguards in this code are extended and the requirements which are indicated in the relevant provisions and Notes for Guidance are as follows:*

(a) *under paragraph 3.15 of this code, to identify and inform someone responsible for the welfare of a 17-year-old which is in addition to their right in section 5 of this code not to be held incommunicado;*

(b) *under paragraph 3.16 of this code to notify a person who has statutory responsibility under a court order to supervise or monitor a 17-year-old;*

(c) *under paragraph 8.9 with regard to cell accommodation and keeping 17-year-old detainees separate from adults;*

(d) *to call a person described by paragraph 1.13(a) to fulfil the role of the appropriate adult for the purposes of this or any other code to support and assist a 17-year-old:*

   (i) *by being present when:*

- *they are informed of their rights and entitlements and the grounds for their detention (see paras 3.17 and 3.18);*
- *they are cautioned or given a special warning (see paras 10.10 and 10.11A);*
- *they are being interviewed unless paragraph 11.11 of this code allows the interview to go ahead without the adult being present;*
- *an intimate search is carried out (see Annex A, paras 3 and 6);*
- *a strip search is carried out (see Annex A, para. 12);*

   (ii) *by allowing:*

- *the adult to inspect their custody record and to have a copy of their record (see paras 2.5, 2.6 and 2.7);*
- *a 17-year-old to consult the adult in private (see para. 3.19);*
- *the adult to request legal advice on their behalf to advise and assist them (see paras 3.20, 6.6 and 11.10).*

H:2 Custody records

H:2.1 When a person is:

A-215

- brought to a police station following arrest under TACT, s.41;
- arrested under TACT, s.41 at a police station having attended there voluntarily;
- brought to a police station and there detained to be questioned in accordance with an authorisation under section 22 of the Counter-Terrorism Act 2008 (post-charge questioning) (see *Notes 15A and 15B*); or

- at a police station and there detained when authority for post-charge questioning is given under section 22 of the Counter-Terrorism Act 2008 (see *Notes 15A* and *15B*),

they should be brought before the custody officer as soon as practicable after their arrival at the station or, if appropriate, following the authorisation of post-charge questioning or following arrest after attending the police station voluntarily: see *Note 3H*. A person is deemed to be "at a police station" for these purposes if they are within the boundary of any building or enclosed yard which forms part of that police station.

H:2.2 A separate custody record must be opened as soon as practicable for each person described in paragraph 2.1. All information recorded under this code must be recorded as soon as practicable in the custody record unless otherwise specified. Any audio or video recording made in the custody area is not part of the custody record.

H:2.3 If any action requires the authority of an officer of a specified rank, this must be noted in the custody record, subject to paragraph 2.8.

H:2.3A If a person is arrested under TACT, s.41, and taken to a police station as a result of a search in the exercise of any stop and search power to which PACE Code A (stop and search) or the "search powers code" issued under TACT applies, the officer carrying out the search is responsible for ensuring that the record of that stop and search is made as part of the person's custody record. The custody officer must then ensure that the person is asked if they want a copy of the search record and if they do, that they are given a copy as soon as practicable. The person's entitlement to a copy of the search record which is made as part of their custody record is in addition to, and does not affect, their entitlement to a copy of their custody record or any other provisions of section 2 (custody records) of this code. See Code A, para. 4.2B, and the TACT search powers code para. 5.3.5.

H:2.4 [*Identical to C:2.3.*]

H:2.5 The detainee's solicitor and appropriate adult must be permitted to inspect the whole of the detainee's custody record as soon as practicable after their arrival at the station and at any other time on request whilst the person is detained. This includes the following specific records relating to the reasons for the detainee's arrest and detention and the offence concerned to which paragraph 3.1(b) refers:

    (a) the information about the circumstances and reasons for the detainee's arrest as recorded in the custody record in accordance with paragraph 3.4; this applies to any further reasons which come to light and are recorded whilst the detainee is detained;

    (b) the record of the grounds for each authorisation to keep the person in custody; the authorisations to which this applies are the same as those described in paragraph 2 of Annex M [*sic*] of this code.

Access to the records in sub-paragraphs (a) and (b) is in addition to the requirements in paragraphs 3.4(b), 11.1 and 14.0 (to make certain documents and materials available and to provide information about the reasons for arrest and detention) and in paragraph 14.4A to provide written information about the grounds for continued detention when an application for a warrant of further detention (or for an extension of such a warrant) is made.

Access to the custody record for the purposes of this paragraph must be arranged and agreed with the custody officer and may not unreasonably interfere with the custody officer's duties or the justifiable needs of the investigation. A record shall be made when access is allowed and whether it includes the records described in sub-paragraphs (a) and (b) above.

Note: paragraph 1.11A extends this paragraph to the person called to fulfil the role of the appropriate adult for a 17-year-old detainee.

H:2.6 [*Identical to C:2.4A, save for reference to "paragraph 1.11A" in lieu of reference to "paragraph 1.5A".*]

H:2.7 The detainee, appropriate adult or legal representative shall be permitted to inspect the original custody record once the detained person is no longer being held under the provisions of TACT, s.41, and Sched. 8, or being questioned after charge as authorised under section 22 of the Counter-Terrorism Act 2008 (see section 15), provided they give reasonable notice of their request. Any such inspection shall be noted in the custody record.

Note: paragraph 1.11A extends this paragraph to the person called to fulfil the role of the appropriate adult for a 17-year-old detainee.

H:2.8 All entries in custody records must be timed and identified by the maker. Nothing in this code requires the identity of officers or other police staff to be recorded or disclosed in the case of enquiries linked to the investigation of terrorism. In these cases, they shall use their warrant or other identification numbers and the name of their police station: see *Note 2A*. Records entered on computer shall be timed and contain the operator's identification.

H:2.9 [*Identical to C:2.7.*]

Note for guidance

H:2A *The purpose of paragraph 2.8 is to protect those involved in terrorist investigations or arrests of terrorist*   **A-215a**
*suspects from the possibility that those arrested, their associates or other individuals or groups may threaten or
cause harm to those involved.*

H:3 Initial action

(a) *Detained persons—normal procedure*

H:3.1 When a person to whom paragraph 2.1 applies is at a police station, the custody officer must   **A-215b**
make sure the person is told clearly about:

- (a) the following continuing rights which may be exercised at any stage during the period in
custody:
  - (i) their right to consult privately with a solicitor and that free independent legal advice is
available as in section 6;
  - (ii) their right to have someone informed of their arrest as in section 5;
  - (iii) the right to consult this code of practice (see *Note 3D*); and
  - (iv) if applicable, their right to interpretation and translation (see para. 3.14) and their
right to communicate with their high commission, embassy or consulate (see para.
3.14A);
- (b) their right to be informed about why they have been arrested and detained on suspicion
of being involved in the commission, preparation or instigation of acts of terrorism in accordance with paragraphs 2.5, 3.4(a) and 11.1A of this code.

H:3.2 The detainee must also be given a written notice, which contains information:

- (a) setting out:
  - (i) their rights under paragraphs 3.1, 3.14 and 3.14A;
  - (ii) the arrangements for obtaining legal advice, see section 6;
  - (iii) their right to a copy of the custody record as in paragraph 2.6;
  - (iv) their right to remain silent as set out in the caution in the terms prescribed in section
10;
  - (v) their right to have access to records and documents which are essential to effectively
challenging the lawfulness of their arrest and detention as required in accordance with
paragraphs 3.4(b) and 14.0 of this code;
  - (vi) the maximum period for which they may be kept in police detention without being
charged, when detention must be reviewed and when release is required;
  - (vii) their right to medical assistance in accordance with section 9 of this code;
  - (viii) their right, if they are prosecuted, to have access to the evidence in the case before
their trial in accordance with the Criminal Procedure and Investigations Act 1996, the
Attorney General's Guidelines on Disclosure, the common law and the Criminal
Procedure Rules;
- (b) briefly setting out their other entitlements while in custody, by:
  - (i) mentioning:
    - the provisions relating to the conduct of interviews;
    - the circumstances in which an appropriate adult should be available to assist the
detainee and their statutory rights to make representations whenever the need for
their detention is reviewed;
  - (ii) listing the entitlements in this code, concerning:
    - reasonable standards of physical comfort;
    - adequate food and drink;
    - access to toilets and washing facilities, clothing, medical attention, and exercise
when practicable.

See *Note 3A.*

H:3.2A The detainee must be given an opportunity to read the notice and shall be asked to sign
the custody record to acknowledge receipt of these notices. Any refusal must be recorded on the
custody record.

H:3.3 [*Not used.*]

H:3.3A [*Identical to C:3.3A.*]

H:3.4

- (a) The custody officer shall:
  - • record that the person was arrested under section 41 of TACT and the reason(s) for
the arrest on the custody record (see para. 10.2 and *Note 3G*);

- note on the custody record any comment the detainee makes in relation to the arresting officer's account but shall not invite comment; if the arresting officer is not physically present when the detainee is brought to a police station, the arresting officer's account must be made available to the custody officer remotely or by a third party on the arresting officer's behalf;

- note any comment the detainee makes in respect of the decision to detain them but shall not invite comment;

- not put specific questions to the detainee regarding their involvement in any offence (see para. 1.3), nor in respect of any comments they may make in response to the arresting officer's account or the decision to place them in detention (see paras 14.1 and 14.2 and *Notes 3H, 14A* and *14B*); such an exchange is likely to constitute an interview as in paragraph 11.1 and require the associated safeguards in section 11.

Note: this sub-paragraph also applies to any further reasons and grounds for detention which come to light whilst the person is detained.

See paragraph 11.8A in respect of unsolicited comments.

If the first review of detention is carried out at this time, see paragraphs 14.1 and 14.2, and Part II of Schedule 8 to the Terrorism Act 2000 in respect of action by the review officer.

(b) Any available documents and materials which are essential to effectively challenging the lawfulness the detainee's arrest and detention must be made available to the detainee or their solicitor. Documents and material will be "essential" for this purpose if they are capable of undermining the reasons and grounds which make the detainee's arrest and detention necessary. The decision about whether particular documents or materials must made [*sic*] available for the purpose of this requirement rests with the officer responsible under Schedule 8 to the Terrorism Act 2000 for determining whether detention is necessary, in consultation with the investigating officer who has the knowledge of the documents and materials in a particular case necessary to inform that decision (see *Note 3G*). A note should be made in the detainee's custody record of the fact that documents or materials have been made available under this sub-paragraph and when. The investigating officer should make a separate note of what is made available in a particular case. This sub-paragraph also applies for the purposes of section 14 (reviews and extensions of detention under the Terrorism Act 2000). See *Note 3ZA* and paragraph 14.0.

H:3.5 The custody officer or other custody staff as directed by the custody officer shall:

(a) ask the detainee, whether at this time, they:

(i) would like legal advice, see paragraph 6.4;

(ii) want someone informed of their detention, see section 5;

(b) ask the detainee to sign the custody record to confirm their decisions in respect of (a);

(c) determine whether the detainee:

(i) is, or might be, in need of medical treatment or attention, see section 9;

(ii) requires:

- an appropriate adult (see paras 1.10, 1.11A, and 3.15);
- help to check documentation (see para. 3.21);
- an interpreter (see para. 3.14 and *Note 13B*).

(d) record the decision in respect of (c).

Where any duties under this paragraph have been carried out by custody staff at the direction of the custody officer, the outcomes shall, as soon as practicable, be reported to the custody officer who retains overall responsibility for the detainee's care and safe custody and ensuring it complies with this code. See *Note 3I*.

H:3.6 When these needs are determined, the custody officer is responsible for initiating an assessment to consider whether the detainee is likely to present specific risks to custody staff, any individual who may have contact with the detainee (*e.g.* legal advisers, medical staff), or themselves. Such assessments should always include a check on the Police National Computer, to be carried out as soon as practicable, to identify any risks highlighted in relation to the detainee. Although such assessments are primarily the custody officer's responsibility, it will be necessary to obtain information from other sources, especially the investigation team (see *Note 3E*), the arresting officer or an appropriate healthcare professional (see paragraph 9.15). Reasons for delaying the initiation or completion of the assessment must be recorded.

H:3.7 [*Identical to C:3.7.*]

H:3.8 Risk assessments must follow a structured process which clearly defines the categories of risk to be considered and the results must be incorporated in the detainee's custody record. The custody officer is responsible for making sure those responsible for the detainee's custody are appropriately briefed about the risks. The content of any risk assessment and any analysis of the level of risk relating to the person's detention is not required to be shown or provided to the detainee or any person acting on behalf of the detainee. If no specific risks are identified by the assessment, that should be noted in the custody record. See *Note 3F* and paragraph 9.15.

H:3.8A The content of any risk assessment and any analysis of the level of risk relating to the person's detention is not required to be shown or provided to the detainee or any person acting on behalf of the detainee. But information should not be withheld from any person acting on the detainee's behalf, for example, an appropriate adult, solicitor or interpreter, if to do so might put that person at risk.

H:3.9 Custody officers are responsible for implementing the response to any specific risk assessment, which should include for example:

- reducing opportunities for self harm;
- calling a health care professional;
- increasing levels of monitoring or observation;
- reducing the risk to those who come into contact with the detainee.

See *Note 3F*.

H:3.10, 3.11 [*Identical to C:3.10 and C:3.11, respectively.*]

H:3.12 A constable, prison officer or other person authorised by the Secretary of State may take any steps which are reasonably necessary for—

- (a) photographing the detained person,
- (b) measuring the person, or
- (c) identifying the person.

H:3.13 Paragraph 3.12 concerns the power in TACT, Sched. 8, para. 2. The power in TACT, Sched. 8, para. 2, does not cover the taking of fingerprints, intimate samples or non-intimate samples, which is covered in TACT, Sched. 8, paras 10–15.

(b) *Detained persons—special groups*

H:3.14 [*Identical to C:3.12, save for reference to "Annex K" in lieu of reference to "Annex M".*]

H:3.14A [*Identical to C:3.12A.*]

H:3.15, 3.16 [*Identical to C:3.13 and C:3.14 respectively, save for references to "paragraph 1.11A" in lieu of references to "paragraph 1.5A".*]

H:3.17 [*Identical to C:3.15, save for references to "paragraph 3.15" and "paragraph 1.11A" in lieu of references to "paragraph 3.13" and "paragraph 1.5A" respectively.*]

H:3.18–3.20 [*Identical to C:3.17 to C:3.19 respectively, save for references to "paragraph 1.11A" in lieu of references to "paragraph 1.5A".*]

H:3.21 [*Identical to C:3.20, save for reference to "paragraph 3.17" in lieu of reference to "paragraph 3.15".*]

(d) [*sic*] *Documentation*

H:3.22 The grounds for a person's detention shall be recorded, in the person's presence if practicable.

H:3.23 Action taken under paragraphs 3.14 to 3.22 shall be recorded.

(e) *Requirements for suspects to be informed of certain rights*

H:3.24 The provisions of this section identify the information which must be given to suspects who have been arrested under section 41 of the Terrorism Act and cautioned in accordance with section 10 of this code. It includes information required by EU Directive 2012/13 on the right to information in criminal proceedings. If a complaint is made by or on behalf of such a suspect that the information and (as the case may be) access to records and documents has not been provided as required, the matter shall be reported to an inspector to deal with as a complaint for the purposes of paragraph 9.3, or paragraph 12.10 if the challenge is made during an interview. This would include, for example:

- not informing them of their rights (see para. 3.1);
- not giving them a copy of the notice (see para. 3.2(a));
- not providing an opportunity to read the notice (see para. 3.2A);
- not providing the required information (see paras 3.2(a), 3.14(b) and, 3.14A);
- not allowing access to the custody record (see para. 2.5);
- not providing a translation of the notice (see para. 3.14(c) and (d)).

Notes for guidance

A-216   H:3ZA *For the purposes of paragraphs 3.4(b) and 14.0:*

   (a) *investigating officers are responsible for bringing to the attention of the officer who is responsible for authorising the suspect's detention or (as the case may be) continued detention, any documents and materials in their possession or control which appear to undermine the need to keep the suspect in custody; in accordance with Part II of Schedule 8 to the Terrorism Act 2000, this officer will be either the inspector or superintendent reviewing the need for detention; this officer is then responsible for determining which, if any, of those documents and materials are capable of undermining the need to detain the suspect and must therefore be made available to the suspect or their solicitor;*

   (b) *the way in which documents and materials are "made available", is a matter for the investigating officer to determine on a case by case basis and having regard to the nature and volume of the documents and materials involved; for example, they may be made available by supplying a copy or allowing supervised access to view; however, for view only access, it will be necessary to demonstrate that sufficient time is allowed for the suspect and solicitor to view and consider the documents and materials in question.*

H:3A *[Identical to C:3A.]*

H:3B *[Not used.]*

H:3C *[Identical to C:3C.]*

H:3D *The right to consult this or other relevant codes of practice does not entitle the person concerned to delay unreasonably any necessary investigative or administrative action whilst they do so. Examples of action which need not be delayed unreasonably include:*

   • *searching detainees at the police station;*

   • *taking fingerprints or non-intimate samples without consent for evidential purposes.*

H:3E *The investigation team will include any officer involved in questioning a suspect, gathering or analysing evidence in relation to the offences of which the detainee is suspected of having committed. Should a custody officer require information from the investigation team, the first point of contact should be the officer in charge of the investigation.*

H:3F *Home Office Circular 32/2000 provides more detailed guidance on risk assessments and identifies key risk areas which should always be considered.*

H:3G *Arrests under TACT, s.41, can only be made where an officer has reasonable grounds to suspect that the individual concerned is a "terrorist". This differs from the PACE power of arrest in that it need not be linked to a specific offence. There may also be circumstances where an arrest under TACT is made on the grounds of sensitive information which cannot be disclosed. In such circumstances, the grounds for arrest may be given in terms of the interpretation of a "terrorist" set out in TACT, s.40(1)(a) or (b).*

H:3H *For the purpose of arrests under TACT, s.41, the review officer is responsible for authorising detention (see paragraphs 14.1 and 14.2, and Notes for Guidance 14A and 14B). The review officer's role is explained in TACT, Sched. 8, Pt II. A person may be detained after arrest pending the first review, which must take place as soon as practicable after the person's arrest.*

H:3I *A custody officer or other officer who, in accordance with this code, allows or directs the carrying out of any task or action relating to a detainee's care, treatment, rights and entitlements by another officer or any police staff must be satisfied that the officer or police staff concerned are suitable, trained and competent to carry out the task or action in question.*

H:4 Detainee's property

(a) *Action*

A-216a   H:4.1 The custody officer is responsible for:

   (a) ascertaining what property a detainee:

   (i) has with them when they come to the police station, either on first arrival at the police station or any subsequent arrivals at a police station in connection with that detention;

   (ii) might have acquired for an unlawful or harmful purpose while in custody;

   (b) the safekeeping of any property taken from a detainee which remains at the police station.

The custody officer may search the detainee or authorise their being searched to the extent they consider necessary, provided a search of intimate parts of the body or involving the removal of more than outer clothing is only made as in Annex A. A search may only be carried out by an officer of the same sex as the detainee. See *Note 4A* and Annex I.

H:4.2, 4.3 *[Identical to C:4.2 and C:4.3, respectively.]*

(b) *Documentation*

H:4.4 It is a matter for the custody officer to determine whether a record should be made of the property a detained person has with him or had taken from him on arrest [see *Note 4D*]. Any record made is not required to be kept as part of the custody record but the custody record should be noted as to where such a record exists. Whenever a record is made the detainee shall be allowed to check and sign the record of property as correct. Any refusal to sign shall be recorded.

H:4.5 [*Identical to C:4.5.*]

Notes for guidance

H:4A–4C [*Identical to C:4A to C:4C, respectively.*] **A-216b**

H:4D *Section 43(2) of TACT allows a constable to search a person who has been arrested under section 41 to discover whether they have anything in their possession that may constitute evidence that they are a terrorist.*

H:5 Right not to be held incommunicado

(a) *Action*

H:5.1 Any person to whom this code applies who is held in custody at a police station or other **A-217** premises may, on request, have one named person who is a friend, relative or a person known to them who is likely to take an interest in their welfare informed at public expense of their whereabouts as soon as practicable. If the person cannot be contacted the detainee may choose up to two alternatives. If they cannot be contacted, the person in charge of detention or the investigation has discretion to allow further attempts until the information has been conveyed. See *Notes 5D* and *5E*.

H:5.2 [*Identical to C:5.2.*]

H:5.3 The above right may be exercised each time a detainee is taken to another police station or returned to a police station having been previously transferred to prison. This code does not afford such a right to a person on transfer to a prison, where a detainee's rights will be governed by prison rules [see paragraph 14.8].

H:5.4 If the detainee agrees, they may at the custody officer's discretion receive visits from friends, family or others likely to take an interest in their welfare, or in whose welfare the detainee has an interest. Custody officers should liaise closely with the investigation team [see *Note 3E*] to allow risk assessments to be made where particular visitors have been requested by the detainee or identified themselves to police. In circumstances where the nature of the investigation means that such requests cannot be met, consideration should be given, in conjunction with a representative of the relevant scheme, to increasing the frequency of visits from independent visitor schemes. See *Notes 5B* and *5C*.

H:5.5 [*Identical to C:5.5, save for reference to "Note 5E" in lieu of reference to "Note 5D".*]

H:5.6 The detainee shall be given writing materials, on request, and allowed to telephone one person for a reasonable time, see *Notes 5A* and *5F*. Either or both these privileges may be denied or delayed if an officer of inspector rank or above considers sending a letter or making a telephone call may result in any of the consequences in Annex B, paras 1 and 2, particularly in relation to the making of a telephone call in a language which an officer listening to the call [see paragraph 5.7] does not understand. See *Note 5G*.

Nothing in this paragraph permits the restriction or denial of the rights in paragraphs 5.1 and 6.1.

H:5.7 Before any letter or message is sent, or telephone call made, the detainee shall be informed that what they say in any letter, call or message (other than in a communication to a solicitor) may be read or listened to and may be given in evidence. A telephone call may be terminated if it is being abused [see *Note 5G*]. The costs can be at public expense at the custody officer's discretion.

H:5.8 [*Identical to C:5.7A.*]

(b) *Documentation*

H:5.9 A record must be kept of any:

(a) request made under this section and the action taken;

(b) letters, messages or telephone calls made or received or visit received;

(c) refusal by the detainee to have information about them given to an outside enquirer, or any refusal to see a visitor. The detainee must be asked to countersign the record accordingly and any refusal recorded.

Notes for guidance

A-217a

H:5A *A person may request an interpreter to interpret a telephone call or translate a letter.*

H:5B *At the custody officer's discretion (and subject to the detainee's consent), visits should be allowed when possible, subject to sufficient personnel being available to supervise a visit and any possible hindrance to the investigation. Custody officers should bear in mind the exceptional nature of prolonged TACT detention and consider the potential benefits that visits may bring to the health and welfare of detainees who are held for extended periods.*

H:5C *Official visitors should be given access following consultation with the officer who has overall responsibility for the investigation provided the detainee consents, and they do not compromise safety or security or unduly delay or interfere with the progress of an investigation. Official visitors should still be required to provide appropriate identification and subject to any screening process in place at the place of detention. Official visitors may include:*

- *an accredited faith representative;*
- *Members of either House of Parliament;*
- *public officials needing to interview the prisoner in the course of their duties;*
- *other persons visiting with the approval of the officer who has overall responsibility for the investigation;*
- *consular officials visiting a detainee who is a national of the country they represent subject to section 7 of this code.*

Visits from appropriate members of the Independent Custody Visitors Scheme should be dealt with in accordance with the separate Code of Practice on Independent Custody Visiting.

H:5D *If the detainee does not know anyone to contact for advice or support or cannot contact a friend or relative, the custody officer should bear in mind any local voluntary bodies or other organisations that might be able to help. Paragraph 6.1 applies if legal advice is required.*

H:5E *In some circumstances it may not be appropriate to use the telephone to disclose information under paragraphs 5.1 and 5.5.*

H:5F *The telephone call at paragraph 5.6 is in addition to any communication under paragraphs 5.1 and 6.1. Further calls may be made at the custody officer's discretion.*

H:5G *The nature of terrorism investigations means that officers should have particular regard to the possibility of suspects attempting to pass information which may be detrimental to public safety, or to an investigation.*

H:6 Right to legal advice

(a) *Action*

A-217b

H:6.1 Unless Annex B applies, all detainees must be informed that they may at any time consult and communicate privately with a solicitor, whether in person, in writing or by telephone, and that free independent legal advice is available from the duty solicitor. Where an appropriate adult is in attendance, they must also be informed of this right. See paragraph 3.1, *Note 1I*, *Notes 6B* and *6J*.

H:6.2 A poster advertising the right to legal advice must be prominently displayed in the charging area of every police station. See *Note 6G*.

H:6.3 [*Identical to C:6.4.*]

H:6.4 The exercise of the right of access to legal advice may be delayed exceptionally only as in Annex B. Whenever legal advice is requested, and unless Annex B applies, the custody officer must act without delay to secure the provision of such advice. If, on being informed or reminded of this right, the detainee declines to speak to a solicitor in person, the officer should point out that the right includes the right to speak with a solicitor on the telephone (see paragraph 5.6). If the detainee continues to waive this right the officer should ask them why and any reasons should be recorded on the custody record or the interview record as appropriate. Reminders of the right to legal advice must be given as in paragraphs 3.5, 11.3 and 5 of Annex K [*sic*] of this code and *PACE* Code D on the Identification of Persons by Police Officers, paragraphs 3.17(ii) and 6.3. Once it is clear a detainee does not want to speak to a solicitor in person or by telephone they should cease to be asked their reasons. See *Note 6J*.

H:6.5 An officer of the rank of commander or assistant chief constable or above may give a direction under TACT, Sched. 8, para. 9, that a detainee may only consult a solicitor within the sight and hearing of a qualified officer. Such a direction may only be given if the officer has reasonable grounds to believe that if it were not, it may result in one of the consequences set out in TACT, Sched. 8, para. 8(4) or (5)(c). See Annex B, para. 3, and *Note 6I*. A "qualified officer" means a police officer who:

    (a) is at least the rank of inspector;

    (b) is of the uniformed branch of the force of which the officer giving the direction is a member; and

(c) in the opinion of the officer giving the direction, has no connection with the detained person's case.

Officers considering the use of this power should first refer to Home Office *Circular 40/2003*.

H:6.6 [*Identical to C:6.5A, save for reference to "paragraph 1.11A" in lieu of reference to "paragraph 1.5A".*]

H:6.7 A detainee who wants legal advice may not be interviewed or continue to be interviewed until they have received such advice unless:

(a) [*identical to C:6.6(a)*];

(b) [*identical to C:6.6(b)*];

(c) [*identical to C:6.6(c)*];

(d) the detainee changes their mind, about wanting legal advice or (as the case may be) about wanting a solicitor present at the interview, and states that they no longer wish to speak to a solicitor; in these circumstances the interview may be started or continued without delay provided that:

    (i) an officer of inspector rank or above:

- speaks to the detainee to enquire about the reasons for their change of mind (see *Note 6J*); and
- makes, or directs the making of, reasonable efforts to ascertain the solicitor's expected time of arrival and to inform the solicitor that the suspect has stated that they wish to change their mind and the reason (if given);

    (ii) the detainee's reason for their change of mind (if given) and the outcome of the action in (i) are recorded in the custody record;

    (iii) the detainee, after being informed of the outcome of the action in (i) above, confirms in writing that they want the interview to proceed without speaking or further speaking to a solicitor or (as the case may be) without a solicitor being present and do not wish to wait for a solicitor by signing an entry to this effect in the custody record;

    (iv) an officer of inspector rank or above is satisfied that it is proper for the interview to proceed in these circumstances and:

- gives authority in writing for the interview to proceed and if the authority is not recorded in the custody record, the officer must ensure that the custody record shows the date and time of authority and where it is recorded; and
- takes or directs the taking of, reasonable steps to inform the solicitor that the authority has been given and the time when the interview is expected to commence and records or causes to be recorded, the outcome of this action in the custody record;

    (v) when the interview starts and the interviewer reminds the suspect of their right to legal advice (see paragraph 11.3) and the code of practice issued under paragraph 3 of Schedule 8 to the Terrorism Act 2000 for the video recording with sound of interviews, the interviewer shall then ensure that the following is recorded in the interview record made in accordance with that code:

- confirmation that the detainee has changed their mind about wanting legal advice or (as the case may be) about wanting a solicitor present and the reasons for it if given;
- the fact that authority for the interview to proceed has been given and, subject to paragraph 2.8, the name of the authorising officer;
- that if the solicitor arrives at the station before the interview is completed, the detainee will be so informed without delay and a break will be taken to allow them to speak to the solicitor if they wish, unless paragraph 6.7(a) applies; and
- that at any time during the interview, the detainee may again ask for legal advice and that if they do, a break will be taken to allow them to speak to the solicitor, unless paragraph 6.7(a), (b) or (c) applies.

    Note: in these circumstances the restriction on drawing adverse inferences from silence in Annex C will not apply because the detainee is allowed an opportunity to consult a solicitor if they wish.

H:6.8 If paragraph 6.7(a) applies, where the reason for authorising the delay ceases to apply, there may be no further delay in permitting the exercise of the right in the absence of a further authorisation unless paragraph 6.7(b), (c) or (d) applies. If paragraph 6.7(b)(i) applies, once sufficient information has been obtained to avert the risk, questioning must cease until the detainee has received legal advice unless paragraph 6.7(a), (b)(ii), (c) or (d) applies.

H:6.9 [*Identical to C:6.8, save for reference to "paragraph 6.7" in lieu of reference to "paragraph 6.6".*]

H:6.10 The solicitor may only be required to leave the interview if their conduct is such that the interviewer is unable properly to put questions to the suspect. See *Notes 6C* and *6D*.

H:6.11 [*Identical to C:6.10, save for reference to "Note 6D" in lieu of reference to "Note 6E".*]

H:6.12 [*Identical to C:6.11.*]

H: 6.13 [*Identical to C:6.12.*]

H:6.14 [*Identical to C:6.12A, save for references to "Note 6C" and to "paragraphs 6.7 to 6.11" in lieu of references to "Note 6D" and "paragraphs 6.6. to 6.10".*]

H:6.15 In exercising their discretion under paragraph 6.14, the officer should take into account in particular:

- whether:
    - the identity and status of an accredited or probationary representative have been satisfactorily established;
    - they are of suitable character to provide legal advice,
- any other matters in any written letter of authorisation provided by the solicitor on whose behalf the person is attending the police station. See *Note 6E*.

H:6.16 If the inspector refuses access to an accredited or probationary representative or a decision is taken that such a person should not be permitted to remain at an interview, the inspector must notify the solicitor on whose behalf the representative was acting and give them an opportunity to make alternative arrangements. The detainee must be informed and the custody record noted.

H:6.17 If a solicitor arrives at the station to see a particular person, that person must, unless Annex B applies, be so informed whether or not they are being interviewed and asked if they would like to see the solicitor. This applies even if the detainee has declined legal advice or, having requested it, subsequently agreed to be interviewed without receiving advice. The solicitor's attendance and the detainee's decision must be noted in the custody record.

(b) *Documentation*

H:6.18, 6.19 [*Identical to C:6.16 and C:6.17, respectively.*]

Notes for guidance

A-218

H:6ZA *No police officer or police staff shall indicate to any suspect, except to answer a direct question, that period for which they are liable to be detained, or the time taken to complete the interview, might be reduced:*

- *if they do not ask for legal advice or do not want a solicitor present when they are interviewed; or*
- *if after asking for legal advice, they change their mind about wanting it or (as the case may be) wanting a solicitor present when they are interviewed and agree to be interviewed without waiting for a solicitor.*

H:6A *In considering if paragraph 6.7(b) applies, the officer should, if practicable, ask the solicitor for an estimate of how long it will take to come to the station and relate this to the time detention is permitted, the time of day (i.e. whether the rest period under paragraph 12.2 is imminent) and the requirements of other investigations. If the solicitor is on their way or is to set off immediately, it will not normally be appropriate to begin an interview before they arrive. If it appears necessary to begin an interview before the solicitor's arrival, they should be given an indication of how long the police would be able to wait so there is an opportunity to make arrangements for someone else to provide legal advice. Nothing within this section is intended to prevent police from ascertaining immediately after the arrest of an individual whether a threat to public safety exists (see paragraph 11.2).*

H:6B *A detainee has a right to free legal advice and to be represented by a solicitor. This note for guidance explains the arrangements which enable detainees to whom this code applies to obtain legal advice. An outline of these arrangements is also included in the Notice of Rights and Entitlements given to detainees in accordance with paragraph 3.2.*

The detainee can ask for free advice from a solicitor they know or if they do not know a solicitor or the solicitor they know cannot be contacted, from the duty solicitor.

To arrange free legal advice, the police should telephone the Defence Solicitor Call Centre (DSCC). The call centre will contact either the duty solicitor or the solicitor requested by the detainee as appropriate.

When a detainee wants to pay for legal advice themselves:

- *the DSCC will contact a solicitor of their choice on their behalf;*
- *they should be given an opportunity to consult a specific solicitor or another solicitor from that solicitor's firm; if this solicitor is not available, they may choose up to two alternatives; if these alternatives are not available, the custody officer has discretion to allow further attempts until a solicitor has been contacted and agreed to provide advice;*
- *they are entitled to a private consultation with their chosen solicitor on the telephone or the solicitor may decide to come to the police station;*
- *if their chosen solicitor cannot be contacted, the DSCC may still be called to arrange free legal advice.*

Apart from carrying out duties necessary to implement these arrangements, an officer must not advise the suspect about any particular firm of solicitors.

H:6C [*Identical to C:6D.*]

H:6D [*Identical to C:6E.*]

H:6E [*Identical to C:6F.*]

H:6F [*Identical to C:6G, save for reference to "paragraph 6.7(b)" in lieu of reference to "paragraph 6.6(b)".*]

H:6G [*Identical to C:6H.*]

H:6H [*Not used.*]

H:6I *Whenever a detainee exercises their right to legal advice by consulting or communicating with a solicitor, they must be allowed to do so in private. This right to consult or communicate in private is fundamental. Except as allowed by the Terrorism Act 2000, Sched. 8, para. 9, if the requirement for privacy is compromised because what is said or written by the detainee or solicitor for the purpose of giving and receiving legal advice is overheard, listened to, or read by others without the informed consent of the detainee, the right will effectively have been denied. When a detainee speaks to a solicitor on the telephone, they should be allowed to do so in private unless a direction under Schedule 8, paragraph 9 of the Terrorism Act 2000 has been given or this is impractical because of the design and layout of the custody area, or the location of telephones. However, the normal expectation should be that facilities will be available, unless they are being used, at all police stations to enable detainees to speak in private to a solicitor either face to face or over the telephone.*

H:6J [*Identical to C:6K.*]

H:7 Citizens of independent Commonwealth countries or foreign nationals

[*Identical to C:7 (apart from use of "are" instead of "is" in paragraph 7.4).*]

A-218a

H:8 Conditions of detention

(a) *Action*

H:8.1, 8.2 [*Identical to C:8.1, save for omission of reference to Note 8C, and C:8.2, respectively.*]

A-218b

H:8.3 [*Identical to C:8.3, save for omission of reference to Note 8A.*]

H:8.4, 8.5 [*Identical to C:8.4 and C:8.5, respectively.*]

H:8.6 At least two light meals and one main meal should be offered in any 24-hour period. See *Note 8B*. Drinks should be provided at meal times and upon reasonable request between meals. Whenever necessary, advice shall be sought from the appropriate health care professional, see *Note 9A*, on medical and dietary matters. As far as practicable, meals provided shall offer a varied diet and meet any specific dietary needs or religious beliefs the detainee may have. Detainees should also be made aware that the meals offered meet such needs. The detainee may, at the custody officer's discretion, have meals supplied by their family or friends at their expense. See *Note 8A*.

H:8.7 Brief outdoor exercise shall be offered daily if practicable. Where facilities exist, indoor exercise shall be offered as an alternative if outside conditions are such that a detainee cannot be reasonably expected to take outdoor exercise (*e.g.*, in cold or wet weather) or if requested by the detainee or for reasons of security. See *Note 8C*.

H:8.8 Where practicable, provision should be made for detainees to practice [*sic*] religious observance. Consideration should be given to providing a separate room which can be used as a prayer room. The supply of appropriate food and clothing, and suitable provision for prayer facilities, such as uncontaminated copies of religious books, should also be considered. See *Note 8D*.

H:8.9 A juvenile shall not be placed in a cell unless no other secure accommodation is available and the custody officer considers it is not practicable to supervise them if they are not placed in a cell or that a cell provides more comfortable accommodation than other secure accommodation in the station. A juvenile may not be placed in a cell with a detained adult.

Note: paragraph 1.11A extends these requirements to 17-year-old detainees.

H:8.10 Police stations should keep a reasonable supply of reading material available for detainees, including but not limited to, the main religious texts. See *Note 8D*. Detainees should be made aware that such material is available and reasonable requests for such material should be met as soon as practicable unless to do so would:

    (i) interfere with the investigation; or

    (ii) prevent or delay an officer from discharging his statutory duties, or those in this code.

If such a request is refused on the grounds of (i) or (ii) above, this should be noted in the custody record and met as soon as possible after those grounds cease to apply.

(b) *Documentation*

H:8.11, 8.12 [*Identical to C:8.9 and C:8.11, respectively.*]

Notes for guidance

A-219   H:8A *In deciding whether to allow meals to be supplied by family or friends, the custody officer is entitled to take account of the risk of items being concealed in any food or package and the officer's duties and responsibilities under food handling legislation. If an officer needs to examine food or other items supplied by family and friends before deciding whether they can be given to the detainee, he should inform the person who has brought the item to the police station of this and the reasons for doing so.*

H:8B [*Identical to C:8B.*]

H:8C *In light of the potential for detaining individuals for extended periods of time, the overriding principle should be to accommodate a period of exercise, except where to do so would hinder the investigation, delay the detainee''s release or charge, or it is declined by the detainee.*

H:8D *Police forces should consult with representatives of the main religious communities to ensure the provision for religious observance is adequate, and to seek advice on the appropriate storage and handling of religious texts or other religious items.*

H:9 Care and treatment of detained persons

(a) *General*

A-219a   H:9.1 Notwithstanding other requirements for medical attention as set out in this section, detainees who are held for more than 96 hours must be visited by an appropriate healthcare professional at least once every 24 hours.

H:9.2, 9.3 [*Identical to C:9.1, save for omission of reference to Note 8C, and C:9.2, respectively.*]

H:9.4 [*Identical to C:9.3, save for references to "Note 9C", "paragraph 9.15" and "Note 9G" in lieu of references to "Note 9CA", "paragraph 9.13" and "Note 9H", respectively.*]

H:9.5 [*Identical to C:9.4.*]

(b) *Clinical treatment and attention*

H:9.6, 9.7, 9.8 [*Identical to C:9.5, C:9.5A and C: 9.5B, respectively.*]

H:9.9 [*Identical to C:9.7, save for reference to "Note 9D" in lieu of reference to "Note 9E".*]

H:9.10 [*Identical to C:9.8.*]

H:9.11 [*Identical to C:9.9, save for reference to "paragraph 9.12" in lieu of reference to "paragraph 9.10".*]

H:9.12 No police officer may administer or supervise the self-administration of medically prescribed controlled drugs of the types and forms listed in the Misuse of Drugs Regulations 2001, Sched. 2 or 3. A detainee may only self-administer such drugs under the personal supervision of the registered medical practitioner authorising their use or other appropriate healthcare professional. The custody officer may supervise the self-administration of, or authorise other custody staff to supervise the self-administration of, drugs listed in Schedule 4 or 5 if the officer has consulted the appropriate healthcare professional authorising their use and both are satisfied self-administration will not expose the detainee, police officers or anyone else to the risk of harm or injury.

H:9.13 When appropriate healthcare professionals administer drugs or authorise the use of other medications, or consult with the custody officer about allowing self-administration of drugs listed in Schedule 4 or 5, it must be within current medicines legislation and the scope of practice as determined by their relevant regulatory body.

H:9.14 [*Identical to C:9.12, save for reference to "paragraph 9.6" in lieu of reference to "paragraph 9.5".*]

H:9.15 [*Identical to C:9.13.*]

H:9.16 [*Identical to C:9.14, save for reference to "Note 9E" in lieu of reference to "Note 9F".*]

(c) *Documentation*

H:9.17 [*Identical to C:9.15, save for references to "paragraph 9.3", "paragraph 9.6", "paragraph 9.10", "Note 9F", "Notes 9D and 9E" and "Note 9G" in lieu of references to "paragraph 9.2", "paragraph 9.5", "paragraph 9.8", "Note 9G", "Notes 9E and 9F" and "Note 9H", respectively.*]

H:9.18 [*Identical to C:9.16, save for reference to "Note 9F" in lieu of reference to "Note 9G".*]

H:9.19 [*Identical to C:9.17.*]

Notes for guidance

H:9A, 9B [*Identical to C:9A and C:9B (save for reference to "paragraph 1.11A" in lieu of reference to "paragraph 1:5A"), respectively.*]

H:9C [*Identical to C:9C, save for reference to "Paragraph 9.6" in lieu of reference to "Paragraph 9.5".*]

H:9D, 9E [*Identical to C:9E and C:9F, respectively.*]

H:9F [*Identical to C:9G, save for reference to "Paragraphs 9.17 and 9.18" in lieu of reference to "Paragraphs 9.15 and 9.16".*]

H:9G [*Identical to C:9H.*]

H:10 Cautions

(a) *When a caution must be given*

H:10.1 A person whom there are grounds to suspect of an offence, see *Note 10A*, must be cautioned before any questions about an offence, or further questions if the answers provide the grounds for suspicion, are put to them if either the suspect's answers or silence (*i.e.* failure or refusal to answer or answer satisfactorily) may be given in evidence to a court in a prosecution.

H:10.2 A person who is arrested, or further arrested, must be informed at the time if practicable or, if not, as soon as it becomes practicable thereafter, that they are under arrest and of the grounds and reasons for their arrest, see paragraph 3.4, *Note 3G* and *Note 10B*.

H:10.3 [*Effectively identical to C:10.4.*]

(b) *Terms of the cautions*

H:10.4 The caution which must be given:

(a) on arrest;

(b) on all other occasions before a person is charged or informed they may be prosecuted; see PACE, Code C, section 16; and

(c) before post-charge questioning under section 22 of the Counter-Terrorism Act 2008 (see section 15.9);

should, unless the restriction on drawing adverse inferences from silence applies, see Annex C, be in the following terms:

"*You do not have to say anything. But it may harm your defence if you do not mention when questioned something which you later rely on in court. Anything you do say may be given in evidence.*".

Where the use of the Welsh language is appropriate, a constable may provide the caution directly in Welsh in the following terms:

"*Does dim rhaid i chi ddweud dim byd. Ond gall niweidio eich amddiffyniad os na fyddwch chi'n sôn, wrth gael eich holi, am rywbeth y byddwch chi'n dibynnu arno nes ymlaen yn y Llys. Gall unrhyw beth yr ydych yn ei ddweud gael ei roi fel tystiolaeth.*".

See *Note 10F.*

H:10.5 [*Identical to C:10.6.*]

H:10.6 [*Identical to C:10.7, save for reference to "Note 10C" in lieu of reference to "Note 10D".*]

H:10.7 [*Identical to C:10.8, save for reference to "Note 10D" in lieu of reference to "Note 10E".*]

H: 10.8 [*Identical to C:10.9, but the words following "statutory requirement" have been omitted.*]

(c) *Special warnings under the Criminal Justice and Public Order Act 1994, sections 36 and 37*

H:10.9 [*Identical to C:10.10, save for references to "Note 10E" and "paragraph 10.10" in lieu of references to "Note 10F" and "paragraph 10.11", respectively.*]

H:10.10 [*Identical to C:10.11.*]

(d) *Juveniles and persons who are mentally disordered or otherwise mentally vulnerable*

H:10.10A [*Identical to C:10.11A, save for reference to "paragraph 10.10" in lieu of reference to "paragraph 10.11".*]

H:10.11 [*Identical to C:10.12.*]

H:10.11A Paragraph 1.11A extends the requirements in paragraphs 10.10A and 10.11 to 17-year-old detainees.

(e) *Documentation*

H:10.12 [*Identical to C:10.13.*]

Notes for guidance

H:10A [*Identical to C:10A.*]

H:10B [*Identical to C:10B, save for inclusion of reference to "Note 3G" after the word "committed".*]

H:10C–10F [*Identical to C:10D to C:10G.*]

H:11 Interviews—general

(a) *Action*

H:11.1 An interview in this code is the questioning of a person arrested on suspicion of being a terrorist which, under paragraph 10.1, must be carried out under caution. Before a person is interviewed they and, if they are represented, their solicitor must be informed of the grounds for arrest, and given sufficient information to enable them to understand the nature of their suspected involvement in the commission, preparation or instigation of acts of terrorism (see para. 3.4(a)) in order to allow for the effective exercise of the rights of the defence. However, whilst the information must always be sufficient information for the person to understand the nature of their suspected involvement in the commission, preparation or instigation of acts of terrorism, this does not require the disclosure of details at a time which might prejudice the investigation (see *Notes 3G* and *11ZA*). The decision about what needs to be disclosed for the purpose of this requirement therefore rests with the investigating officer who has sufficient knowledge of the case to make that decision. The officer who discloses the information shall make a record of the information disclosed and when it was disclosed. This record may be made in the interview record, in the officer's pocket book or other form provided for this purpose.

H:11.2 Following the arrest of a person under section 41 TACT, that person must not be interviewed about the relevant offence except at a place designated for detention under Schedule 8, paragraph 1, of the Terrorism Act 2000, unless the consequent delay would be likely to:

    (a) lead to:

- interference with, or harm to, evidence connected with an offence;
- interference with, or physical harm to, other people; or
- serious loss of, or damage to, property;

    (b) lead to alerting other people suspected of committing an offence but not yet arrested for it; or

    (c) hinder the recovery of property obtained in consequence of the commission of an offence. Interviewing in any of these circumstances shall cease once the relevant risk has been averted or the necessary questions have been put in order to attempt to avert that risk.

H:11.3 Immediately prior to the commencement or re-commencement of any interview at a designated place of detention, the interviewer should remind the suspect of their entitlement to free legal advice and that the interview can be delayed for legal advice to be obtained, unless one of the exceptions in paragraph 6.7 applies. It is the interviewer's responsibility to make sure all reminders are recorded in the interview record.

H:11.4, 11.5 [*Identical to C:11.4 and C:11.4A.*]

H:11.6 [*Identical to C:11.5, save for reference "paragraph 10.8" in lieu of reference to "paragraph 10.9".*]

H:11.7 [*Identical to C:11.6, but with the omission of the final sub-paragraph of that paragraph.*]

(b) *Interview records*

H:11.8 Interviews of a person detained under section 41 of, or Schedule 8 to, TACT must be video recorded with sound in accordance with the code of practice issued under paragraph 3 of Schedule 8 to the Terrorism Act 2000, or in the case of post-charge questioning authorised under section 22 of the Counter-Terrorism Act 2008, the code of practice issued under section 25 of that Act.

H:11.8A [*Identical to C:11.13.*]

(c) *Juveniles and mentally disordered or otherwise mentally vulnerable people*

H:11.9 [*Identical to C:11.15, save for reference to "paragraphs 11.2, 11.11 to 11.13" in lieu of reference to "paragraphs 11.1, 11.18 to 11.20", and to "paragraph 1.11A" in lieu of reference to "paragraph 1.5A".*]

H:11.10 If an appropriate adult is present at an interview, they shall be informed:

- that they are not expected to act simply as an observer; and

- that the purpose of their presence is to:
  - advise the person being interviewed;
  - observe whether the interview is being conducted properly and fairly;
  - facilitate communication with the person being interviewed.

The appropriate adult may be required to leave the interview if their conduct is such that the interviewer is unable properly to put questions to the suspect. This will include situations where the appropriate adult's approach or conduct prevents or unreasonably obstructs proper questions being put to the suspect or the suspect's responses being recorded. If the interviewer considers an appropriate adult is acting in such a way, they will stop the interview and consult an officer not below superintendent rank, if one is readily available, and otherwise an officer not below inspector rank not connected with the investigation. After speaking to the appropriate adult, the officer consulted will decide if the interview should continue without the attendance of that appropriate adult. If they decide it should not, another appropriate adult should be obtained before the interview continues, unless the provisions of paragraph 11.11 below apply.

(d) *Vulnerable suspects—urgent interviews at police stations*

H:11.11–11.13 [*Identical to C:11.18 to C:11.20, save for references to "paragraph 11.2(a) to (c)", "paragraph 1.11A", "paragraph 3.14" and "paragraph 11.11", in lieu of references to "paragraph 11.1(a) to (c)", "paragraph 1.5A", paragraph "3.12" and "paragraph 11.18", respectively.*]

Notes for guidance

H:11ZA *The requirement in paragraph 11.1A for a suspect to be given sufficient information about the nature*   **A-221**
of their suspected involvement in the commission, preparation or instigation of acts of terrorism applies prior to the interview and whether or not they are legally represented. What is sufficient will depend on the circumstances of the case, but it should normally include, as a minimum, enough to avoid suspects being confused or unclear about what they are supposed to have done and to help an innocent suspect to clear the matter up more quickly.

H:11A–11C [*Identical to C:11A (save for an erroneous reference to para. 3.4 of code of practice under 1996 Act) to C:11C (save for reference to "paragraph 1.11A" in lieu of reference to "paragraph 1.5A"), respectively.*]

H:11B *The Criminal Procedure and Investigations Act 1996 Code of Practice, paragraph 3.4 states 'In conducting an investigation, the investigator should pursue all reasonable lines of enquiry, whether these point towards or away from the suspect. What is reasonable will depend on the particular circumstances.' Interviewers should keep this in mind when deciding what questions to ask in an interview.*

H:11C *Although juveniles or people who are mentally disordered or otherwise mentally vulnerable are often capable of providing reliable evidence, they may, without knowing or wishing to do so, be particularly prone in certain circumstances to provide information that may be unreliable, misleading or self-incriminating. Special care should always be taken when questioning such a person, and the appropriate adult should be involved if there is any doubt about a person's age, mental state or capacity. Because of the risk of unreliable evidence it is also important to obtain corroboration of any facts admitted whenever possible. Paragraph 1.11A extends this note to 17-year-old suspects.*

H:11D *Consideration should be given to the effect of extended detention on a detainee and any subsequent information they provide, especially if it relates to information on matters that they have failed to provide previously in response to similar questioning: see Annex G.*

H:11E [*Identical to C:11E.*]

H:12 Interviews in police stations

(a) *Action*

H:12.1 If a police officer wants to interview or conduct enquiries which require the presence of a   **A-221a**
detainee, the custody officer is responsible for deciding whether to deliver the detainee into the officer's custody. An investigating officer who is given custody of a detainee takes over responsibility for the detainee's care and treatment for the purposes of this code until they return the detainee to the custody officer when they must report the manner in which they complied with the code whilst having custody of the detainee.

H:12.2 Except as below, in any period of 24 hours a detainee must be allowed a continuous period of at least 8 hours for rest, free from questioning, travel or any interruption in connection with the investigation concerned. This period should normally be at night or other appropriate time which takes account of when the detainee last slept or rested. If a detainee is arrested at a police station after going there voluntarily, the period of 24 hours runs from the time of their arrest (or, if a person was being detained under TACT, Sched. 7, when arrested, from the time at which the examination under Schedule 7 began) and not the time of arrival at the police station. The period may not be interrupted or delayed, except:

(a) when there are reasonable grounds for believing not delaying or interrupting the period would:

(i) involve a risk of harm to people or serious loss of, or damage to, property;

(ii) delay unnecessarily the person's release from custody; or

(iii) otherwise prejudice the outcome of the investigation;

(b) at the request of the detainee, their appropriate adult or legal representative;

(c) when a delay or interruption is necessary in order to:

(i) comply with the legal obligations and duties arising under section 14; or

(ii) to take action required under section 9 or in accordance with medical advice.

If the period is interrupted in accordance with (a), a fresh period must be allowed. Interruptions under (b) and (c), do not require a fresh period to be allowed.

H:12.3 [*Identical to C:12.3, save that there is no reference to "Annex G" and the references to "paragraph 11.18" and "paragraphs 11.18 to 11.20" are replaced by references to "paragraph 11.11" and "paragraphs 11.11 to 11.13".*]

H:12.4 [*Identical to C:12.4.*]

H:12.5 A suspect whose detention without charge has been authorised under TACT, Sched. 8, because the detention is necessary for an interview to obtain evidence of the offence for which they have been arrested, may choose not to answer questions but police do not require the suspect's consent or agreement to interview them for this purpose. If a suspect takes steps to prevent themselves being questioned or further questioned, *e.g.* by refusing to leave their cell to go to a suitable interview room or by trying to leave the interview room, they shall be advised their consent or agreement to interview is not required. The suspect shall be cautioned as in section 10, and informed if they fail or refuse to co-operate, the interview may take place in the cell and that their failure or refusal to co-operate may be given in evidence. The suspect shall then be invited to co-operate and go into the interview room.

H:12.6 People being questioned or making statements shall not be required to stand.

H:12.7 Before the interview commences each interviewer shall, subject to the qualification at paragraph 2.8, identify themselves and any other persons present to the interviewee.

H:12.8 [*Effectively identical to C:12.8.*]

H:12.9 During extended periods where no interviews take place, because of the need to gather further evidence or analyse existing evidence, detainees and their legal representative shall be informed that the investigation into the relevant offence remains ongoing. If practicable, the detainee and legal representative should also be made aware in general terms of any reasons for long gaps between interviews. Consideration should be given to allowing visits, more frequent exercise, or for reading or writing materials to be offered: see paragraph 5.4, section 8 and *Note 12C.*

H:12.10 [*Identical to C:12.9.*]

(b) *Documentation*

H:12.11-12.15 [*Identical to C:12.10 to C:12.14, respectively.*]

Notes for guidance

A-221b
H:12A *It is not normally necessary to ask for a written statement if the interview was recorded in accordance with the code of practice issued under TACT, Sched. 8, para. 3. Statements under caution should normally be taken in these circumstances only at the person's express wish. A person may however be asked if they want to make such a statement.*

H:12B [*Identical to C:12B.*]

H:12C *Consideration should be given to the matters referred to in paragraph 12.9 after a period of over 24 hours without questioning. This is to ensure that extended periods of detention without an indication that the investigation remains ongoing do not contribute to a deterioration of the detainee's well-being.*

H:13 Interpreters

(a) *General*

H:13.1 Chief officers are responsible for making arrangements to provide appropriately qualified independent persons to act as interpreters and to provide translations of essential documents for detained suspects who, in accordance with paragraph 3.5(c)(ii), the custody officer has determined require an interpreter.

If the suspect has a hearing or speech impediment, references to "interpreter" and "interpretation" in this code include appropriate assistance necessary to establish effective communication with that person. See paragraph 13.1C if the detainee is in Wales.

H:13.1A [*Identical to C:13.1A, save for reference to "Annex K" in lieu of reference to "Annex M".*]

H:13.1B [*Identical to C:13.1B.*]

H:13.1C [*Identical to C:13.1C, save for reference to paragraph "3.14" in lieu of reference to paragraph "3.12".*]

(b) *Interviewing suspects—foreign languages*

H:13.2 Unless paragraphs 11.2 or 11.11(c) apply, a suspect who for the purposes of this code requires an interpreter because they do not appear to speak or understand English (see paras 3.5(c)(ii) and 3.14) must not be interviewed in the absence of a person capable of interpreting.

H:13.3 An interpreter should also be called if a juvenile is interviewed and their parent or guardian, present as the appropriate adult, does not appear to speak or understand English, unless the interview is urgent and paragraphs 11.2 or 11.11(c) apply.

Note: paragraph 1.11A extends the requirement in this paragraph to interviews of 17-year-old suspects.

H:13.4 [*Identical to C:13.4.*]

(c) *Interviewing suspects who have a hearing or speech impediment*

H:13.5 [*Identical to C:13.5, save for reference to paragraph "3.14" in lieu of reference to paragraph "3.12".*]

H:13.6 An interpreter should also be called if a juvenile is interviewed and their parent or guardian present as the appropriate adult appears to have a hearing or speech impediment, unless the interview is urgent and paragraphs 11.2 or 11.11(c) apply.

Note: paragraph 1.11A extends the requirement in this paragraph to interviews of 17-year-old suspects.

H:13.7 [*Not used.*]

(d) *Additional rules for detained persons*

H:13.8 [*Not used.*]

H:13.9 [*Identical to C:13.9.*]

H:13.10 After the custody officer has determined that a detainee requires an interpreter (see para. 3.5(c)(ii)) and following the initial action in paragraphs 3.1 to 3.5, arrangements must also be made for an interpreter to explain:

- the grounds and reasons for any authorisation of their detention under the provisions of the Terrorism Act 2000 or the Counter Terrorism Act 2008 (post-charge questioning) to which this code applies, and
- any information about the authorisation given to them by the authorising officer or (as the case may be) the court and which is recorded in the custody record.

See sections 14 and 15 of this code.

H:13.10A [*Identical to C:13.10A.*]

(e) *Translations of essential documents*

H:13.10B [*Identical to C:13.10B, save for reference to "Annex K" in lieu of reference to "Annex M".*]

H:13.10C [*Identical to C:13.10C.*]

(f) *Decisions not to provide interpretation and translation.*

H:13.10D If a suspect challenges a decision:

- made by the custody officer in accordance with this code (see para. 3.5(c)(ii)) that they do not require an interpreter, or
- made in accordance with paragraphs 13.10A, 13.10B or 13.10C not to provide a different interpreter or another translation or not to translate a requested document,

the matter shall be reported to an inspector to deal with as a complaint for the purposes of paragraph 9.3 or 12.10 if the challenge is made during an interview.

(g) *Documentation*

H:13.11 [*Identical to C:13.11, save for references to "Annex K" in lieu of references to "Annex M".*]

Notes for guidance

H:13A–13C [*Identical to C:13A to C:13C, respectively.*]

H:14 Reviews and extensions of detention under the Terrorism Act 2000

(a) *General*

A-222   H:14.0 The requirement in paragraph 3.4(b) that documents and materials essential to challenging the lawfulness of the detainee's arrest and detention must be made available to the detainee or their solicitor, applies for the purposes of this section as follows:

(a) the officer reviewing the need for detention (TACT, Sched. 8) is responsible, in consultation with the investigating officer, for deciding which documents and materials are essential and must be made available;

(b) when an application is to be made for a warrant as described in paragraph 14.3, the person making the application is responsible for deciding which documents and materials are essential and must be made available before the hearing. See *Note 3ZA.*

H:14.1 The powers and duties of the review officer are in the Terrorism Act 2000, Sched. 8, Pt II. See *Notes 14A* and *14B*. A review officer should carry out their duties at the police station where the detainee is held, and be allowed such access to the detainee as is necessary to exercise those duties.

H:14.2 For the purposes of reviewing a person's detention, no officer shall put specific questions to the detainee:

- regarding their involvement in any offence; or
- in respect of any comments they may make:
  - when given the opportunity to make representations; or
  - in response to a decision to keep them in detention or extend the maximum period of detention.

Such an exchange could constitute an interview as in paragraph 11.1 and would be subject to the associated safeguards in section 11.

H:14.3 If detention is necessary for longer than 48 hours from the time of arrest or, if a person was being detained under TACT, Sched. 7, from the time at which the examination under Schedule 7 began), a police officer of at least superintendent rank, or a crown prosecutor may apply for a warrant of further detention or for an extension or further extension of such a warrant under paragraph 29 or (as the case may be) 36 of Part III of Schedule 8 to the Terrorism Act 2000. See paragraph 14.0(b) and *Note 14C*.

H:14.4 When an application is made for a warrant as described in paragraph 14.3, the detained person and their representative must be informed of their rights in respect of the application. These include:

(i) the right to a written notice of the application (see para. 14.4 [*sic*]);

(ii) the right to make oral or written representations to the judicial authority/High Court judge about the application;

(iii) the right to be present and legally represented at the hearing of the application, unless specifically excluded by the judicial authority/High Court judge;

(iv) their right to free legal advice (see section 6 of this code).

H:14.4A TACT, Sched. 8, para. 31, requires the notice of the application for a warrant of further detention to be provided before the judicial hearing of the application for that warrant and that the notice must include:

(a) notification that the application for a warrant has been made;

(b) the time at which the application was made;

(c) the time at which the application is to be heard;

(d) the grounds on which further detention is sought.

A notice must also be provided each time an application is made to extend or further extend an existing warrant.

(b) *Transfer of persons detained for more than 14 days to prison*

H:14.5 If the *Detention of Terrorists Suspects (Temporary Extension) Bill* is enacted and in force, a High Court judge may extend or further extend a warrant of further detention to authorise a person to be detained beyond a period of 14 days from the time of their arrest (or if they were being detained under TACT, Sched. 7, from the time at which their examination under Schedule 7 began). The provisions of Annex J will apply when a warrant of further detention is so extended or further extended.

H:14.6–14.10 [*Not used.*]

(c) *Documentation*

H:14.11 It is the responsibility of the officer who gives any reminders as at paragraph 14.4, to ensure that these are noted in the custody record, as well any comments made by the detained person upon being told of those rights.

H:14.12 The grounds for, and extent of, any delay in conducting a review shall be recorded.

H:14.13 Any written representations shall be retained.

H:14.14 A record shall be made as soon as practicable about the outcome of each review and, if applicable, the grounds on which the review officer authorises continued detention. A record shall also be made as soon as practicable about the outcome of an application for a warrant of further detention or its extension.

H:14.15 [*Not used.*]

Notes for guidance

H:14A *TACT, Sched. 8, Pt II, sets out the procedures for review of detention up to 48 hours from the time of* **A-222a** *arrest under TACT, s.41 (or if a person was being detained under TACT, Sched. 7, from the time at which the examination under Schedule 7 began). These include provisions for the requirement to review detention, postponing a review, grounds for continued detention, designating a review officer, representations, rights of the detained person and keeping a record. The review officer's role ends after a warrant has been issued for extension of detention under Part III of Schedule 8.*

H:14B *A review officer may authorise a person's continued detention if satisfied that detention is necessary—*

    (a) *to obtain relevant evidence whether by questioning the person or otherwise;*

    (b) *to preserve relevant evidence;*

    (c) *while awaiting the result of an examination or analysis of relevant evidence;*

    (d) *for the examination or analysis of anything with a view to obtaining relevant evidence;*

    (e) *pending a decision to apply to the Secretary of State for a deportation notice to be served on the detainee, the making of any such application, or the consideration of any such application by the Secretary of State;*

    (f) *pending a decision to charge the detainee with an offence.*

H:14C *Applications for warrants to extend detention beyond 48 hours, may be made for periods of 7 days at a time (initially under TACT, Sched. 8, para. 29, and extensions thereafter under TACT, Sched. 8, para. 36), up to a maximum period of 14 days (or 28 days if the Detention of Terrorists Suspects (Temporary Extension) Bill is enacted and in force) from the time of their arrest (or if they were being detained under TACT, Sched. 7, from the time at which their examination under Schedule 7 began). Applications may be made for shorter periods than 7 days, which must be specified. The judicial authority or High Court judge may also substitute a shorter period if they feel a period of 7 days is inappropriate.*

H:14D *Unless Note 14F applies, applications for warrants that would take the total period of detention up to 14 days or less should be made to a judicial authority, meaning a District Judge (Magistrates' Court) designated by the Lord Chief Justice to hear such applications.*

H:14E *If by virtue of the relevant provisions described in Note 14C being enacted the maximum period of detention is extended to 28 days, any application for a warrant which would take the period of detention beyond 14 days from the time of arrest (or if a person was being detained under TACT, Sched. 7, from the time at which the examination under Schedule 7 began), must be made to a High Court Judge.*

H:14F *If, when the Detention of Terrorists Suspects (Temporary Extension) Bill is enacted and in force, an application is made to a High Court judge for a warrant which would take detention beyond 14 days and the High Court judge instead issues a warrant for a period of time which would not take detention beyond 14 days, further applications for extension of detention must also be made to a High Court judge, regardless of the period of time to which they refer.*

H:14G [*Not used.*]

H:14H *An offcer applying for an order under TACT, Sched. 8, para. 34, to withhold specified information on which they intend to rely when applying for a warrant of further detention or the extension or further extension of such a warrant, may make the application for the order orally or in writing. The most appropriate method of application will depend on the circumstances of the case and the need to ensure fairness to the detainee.*

H:14I *After hearing any representations by or on behalf of the detainee and the applicant, the judicial authority or High Court judge may direct that the hearing relating to the extension of detention under Part III of Schedule 8 is to take place using video conferencing facilities. However, if the judicial authority requires the detained person to be physically present at any hearing, this should be complied with as soon as practicable. Paragraph 33(4) to (9) of TACT, Sched. 8, govern the hearing of applications via video-link or other means.*

H:14J [*Not used.*]

H:14K [*Not used.*]

H:15 Charging and post-charge questioning in terrorism cases

(a) *Charging*

A-222b H:15.1 Charging of detained persons is covered by PACE and guidance issued under PACE by the Director of Public Prosecutions. Decisions to charge persons to whom this code (H) applies, the charging process and related matters are subject to section 16 of PACE Code C.

(b) *Post-charge questioning*

A-222c H:15.2 Under section 22 of the Counter-Terrorism Act 2008, a judge of the Crown Court may authorise the questioning of a person about an offence for which they have been charged, informed that they may be prosecuted or sent for trial, if the offence:

- is a terrorism offence as set out in section 27 of the Counter-Terrorism Act 2008; or
- is an offence which appears to the judge to have a terrorist connection (see *Note 15C*).

The decision on whether to apply for such questioning will be based on the needs of the investigation. There is no power to detain a person solely for the purposes of post-charge questioning. A person can only be detained whilst being so questioned (whether at a police station or in prison) if they are already there in lawful custody under some existing power. If at a police station the contents of sections 8 and 9 of this code must be considered the minimum standards of treatment for such detainees.

H:15.3 The Crown Court judge may authorise the questioning if they are satisfied that:

- further questioning is necessary in the interests of justice;
- the investigation for the purposes of which the further questioning is being proposed is being conducted diligently and expeditiously; and
- the questioning would not interfere unduly with the preparation of the person's defence to the charge or any other criminal charge that they may be facing.

See *Note 15E*.

H:15.4 The judge authorising questioning may specify the location of the questioning.

H:15.5 The judge may only authorise a period up to a maximum of 48 hours before further authorisation must be sought. The 48 hour period would run continuously from the commencement of questioning. This period must include breaks in questioning in accordance with paragraphs 8.6 and 12.2 of this code (see *Note 15B*).

H:15.6 Nothing in this code shall be taken to prevent a suspect seeking a voluntary interview with the police at any time.

H:15.7 For the purposes of this section, any reference in sections 6, 10, 11, 12 and 13 of this code to:

- "suspect" means the person in respect of whom an authorisation has been given under section 22 of the Counter-Terrorism Act 2008 (post-charge questioning of terrorist suspects) to interview them;
- "interview" means post-charge questioning authorised under section 22 of the CounterTerrorism Act 2008;
- "offence" means an offence for which the person has been charged, informed that they may be prosecuted or sent for trial and about which the person is being questioned; and
- "place of detention" means the location of the questioning specified by the judge (see paragraph 15.4),

and the provisions of those sections apply (as appropriate), to such questioning (whether at a police station or in prison) subject to the further modifications in the following paragraphs:

Right to legal advice

H:15.8 In section 6 of this code, for the purposes of post-charge questioning:

- access to a solicitor may not be delayed under Annex B; and
- paragraph 6.5 (direction that a detainee may only consult a solicitor within the sight and hearing of a qualified officer) does not apply.

Cautions

H:15.9 In section 10 of this code, unless the restriction on drawing adverse inferences from silence applies (see paragraph 15.10), for the purposes of post-charge questioning, the caution must be given in the following terms before any such questions are asked:

"You do not have to say anything. But it may harm your defence if you do not mention when questioned

something which you later rely on in court. Anything you do say may be given in evidence.".

Where the use of the Welsh language is appropriate, a constable may provide the caution directly in Welsh in the following terms:

"Does dim rhaid i chi ddweud dim byd. Ond gall niweidio eich amddiffyniad os na fyddwch chi'n sôn, yn awr, am rywbeth y byddwch chi'n dibynnu arno nes ymlaen yn y llys. Gall unrhyw beth yr ydych yn ei ddweud gael ei roi fel tystiolaeth.".

H:15.10 The only restriction on drawing adverse inferences from silence, see Annex C, applies in those situations where a person has asked for legal advice and is questioned before receiving such advice in accordance with paragraph 6.7(b).

Interviews

H:15.11 In section 11, for the purposes of post-charge questioning, whenever a person is questioned, they must be informed of the offence for which they have been charged or informed that they may be prosecuted, or that they have been sent for trial and about which they are being questioned.

H:15.12 Paragraph 11.2 (place where questioning may take place) does not apply to postcharge questioning.

Recording post-charge questioning

H:15.13 All interviews must be video recorded with sound in accordance with the separate code of practice issued under section 25 of the Counter-Terrorism Act 2008 for the video recording with sound of post-charge questioning authorised under section 22 of the Counter-Terrorism Act 2008 (see paragraph 11.8).

Notes for guidance

H:15A *If a person is detained at a police station for the purposes of post-charge questioning, a custody record*   **A-222d**
must be opened in accordance with section 2 of this code. The custody record must note the power under which the person is being detained, the time at which the person was transferred into police custody, their time of arrival at the police station and their time of being presented to the custody officer.

H:15B *The custody record must note the time at which the interview process commences. This shall be regarded as the relevant time for any period of questioning in accordance with paragraph 15.5 of this code.*

H:15C *Where reference is made to "terrorist connection" in paragraph 15.2, this is determined in accordance with section 30 of the Counter-Terrorism Act 2008. Under section 30 of that Act a court must in certain circumstances determine whether an offence has a terrorist connection. These are offences under general criminal law which may be prosecuted in terrorism cases (for example explosives-related offences and conspiracy to murder). An offence has a terrorist connection if the offence is, or takes place in the course of, an act of terrorism or is committed for the purposes of terrorism (section 98 of the Act). Normally the court will make the determination during the sentencing process, however for the purposes of post-charge questioning, a Crown Court judge must determine whether the offence could have a terrorist connection.*

H:15D *The powers under section 22 of the Counter-Terrorism Act 2008 are separate from and additional to the normal questioning procedures within this code. Their overall purpose is to enable the further questioning of a terrorist suspect after charge. They should not therefore be used to replace or circumvent the normal powers for dealing with routine questioning.*

H:15E *Post-charge questioning has been created because it is acknowledged that terrorist investigations can be large and complex and that a great deal of evidence can come to light following the charge of a terrorism suspect. This can occur, for instance, from the translation of material or as the result of additional investigation. When considering an application for post-charge questioning, the police must "satisfy" the judge on all three points under paragraph 15.3. This means that the judge will either authorise or refuse an application on the balance of whether the conditions in paragraph 15.3 are all met. It is important therefore, when making the application, to consider the following questions:*

- *What further evidence is the questioning expected to provide?*
- *Why was it not possible to obtain this evidence before charge?*
- *How and why was the need to question after charge first recognised?*
- *How is the questioning expected to contribute further to the case?*
- *To what extent could the time and place for further questioning interfere with the preparation of the person's defence (for example if authorisation is sought close to the time of a trial)?*
- *What steps will be taken to minimise any risk that questioning might interfere with the preparation of the person's defence?*

This list is not exhaustive but outlines the type of questions that could be relevant to any asked by a judge in considering an application.

H:16 Testing persons for the presence of specified Class A drugs

A-223   H:16.1 The provisions for drug testing under section 63B of PACE (as amended by section 5 of the Criminal Justice Act 2003 and section 7 of the Drugs Act 2005), do not apply to persons to whom this code applies. Guidance on these provisions can be found in section 17 of PACE Code C.

ANNEX A

Intimate and strip searches

A *Intimate search*

A-223a   H:1. [*Identical to Code C, Annex A, para. 1.*]

(a) Action

H:2. Body orifices other than the mouth may be searched if authorised by an officer of inspector rank or above who has reasonable grounds for believing that the person may have concealed on themselves anything which they could and might use to cause physical injury to themselves or others at the station and the officer has reasonable grounds for believing that an intimate search is the only means of removing those items.

H:3. [*Identical to Code C, Annex A, para. 2A, save for reference to "paragraph 1.11A" in lieu of reference to "paragraph 1.5A".*]

H:4. An intimate search may only be carried out by a registered medical practitioner or registered nurse, unless an officer of at least inspector rank considers this is not practicable, in which case a police officer may carry out the search. See *Notes A1 to A5.*

H:5. Any proposal for a search under paragraph 2 to be carried out by someone other than a registered medical practitioner or registered nurse must only be considered as a last resort and when the authorising officer is satisfied the risks associated with allowing the item to remain with the detainee outweigh the risks associated with removing it. See *Notes A1 to A5.*

H:6. An intimate search at a police station of a juvenile or mentally disordered or otherwise mentally vulnerable person may take place only in the presence of an appropriate adult of the same sex (see Annex I), unless the detainee specifically requests a particular adult of the opposite sex who is readily available. In the case of a juvenile the search may take place in the absence of the appropriate adult only if the juvenile signifies in the presence of the appropriate adult they do not want the adult present during the search and the adult agrees. A record shall be made of the juvenile's decision and signed by the appropriate adult.

Note: paragraph 1.11A of this code extends the requirement in this paragraph to an intimate search of a 17-year-old.

H:7. When an intimate search under paragraph 2 is carried out by a police officer, the officer must be of the same sex as the detainee (see Annex I). A minimum of two people, other than the detainee, must be present during the search. Subject to paragraph 6, no person of the opposite sex who is not a medical practitioner or nurse shall be present, nor shall anyone whose presence is unnecessary. The search shall be conducted with proper regard to the sensitivity and vulnerability of the detainee.

(b) Documentation

H:8. In the case of an intimate search under paragraph 2, the following shall be recorded as soon as practicable, in the detainee's custody record:
- the authorisation to carry out the search;
- the grounds for giving the authorisation;
- the grounds for believing the article could not be removed without an intimate search;
- which parts of the detainee's body were searched;
- who carried out the search;
- who was present;
- the result.

H:9. [*Identical to Code C, Annex A, para. 8.*]

B *Strip search*

H:10. [*Identical to Code C, Annex A, para. 9.*]

(a) Action

H:11. [*Identical to Code C, Annex A, para. 10.*]

The conduct of strip searches

H:12. [*Identical to Code C, Annex A, para. 11, save for references to "Annex I" in lieu of references to "Annex L", and reference to "paragraph 1.11A" in lieu of reference to "paragraph 1.5A".*]

(b) Documentation

H:13. [*Identical to Code C, Annex A, para. 12.*]

Notes for guidance

H:A1 [*Identical to Code C, Annex A, A1.*]

H:A2 [*Identical to Code C, Annex A, A2.*]

H:A3 [*Identical to Code C, Annex A, A3, save for reference to "paragraph 2" in lieu of reference to "paragraph 2(a)(i)".*]

H:A4 [*Identical to Code C, Annex A, A4, save for reference to "paragraph 2" in lieu of reference to "paragraph 2(a)(i)".*]

H:A5 [*Identical to Code C, Annex A, A5.*]

A-223b

ANNEX B

Delay in notifying arrest or allowing access to legal advice for persons detained under the Terrorism Act 2000

H:1. The rights as in sections 5 or 6, may be delayed if the person is detained under the Terror-   **A-224**
ism Act 2000, s.41, has not yet been charged with an offence and an officer of superintendent rank or above has reasonable grounds for believing the exercise of either right will have one of the following consequences:

- (a) interference with or harm to evidence of a serious offence;
- (b) interference with or physical injury to any person;
- (c) the alerting of persons who are suspected of having committed a serious offence but who have not been arrested for it;
- (d) the hindering of the recovery of property obtained as a result of a serious offence or in respect of which a forfeiture order could be made under section 23;
- (e) interference with the gathering of information about the commission, preparation or instigation of acts of terrorism;
- (f) the alerting of a person and thereby making it more difficult to prevent an act of terrorism; or
- (g) the alerting of a person and thereby making it more difficult to secure a person's apprehension, prosecution or conviction in connection with the commission, preparation or instigation of an act of terrorism.

H:2. These rights may also be delayed if the officer has reasonable grounds for believing that:

- (a) the detained person has benefited from his criminal conduct (to be decided in accordance with Part 2 of the Proceeds of Crime Act 2002); and
- (b) the recovery of the value of the property constituting the benefit will be hindered by—
  - (i) informing the named person of the detained person's detention (in the case of an authorisation under paragraph 8(1)(a) of Schedule 8 to TACT); or
  - (ii) the exercise of the right under paragraph 7 (in the case of an authorisation under paragraph 8(1)(b) of Schedule 8 to TACT).

H:3. Authority to delay a detainee's right to consult privately with a solicitor may be given only if the authorising officer has reasonable grounds to believe the solicitor the detainee wants to consult will, inadvertently or otherwise, pass on a message from the detainee or act in some other way which will have any of the consequences specified under paragraph 8 of Schedule 8 to the Terrorism Act 2000. In these circumstances, the detainee must be allowed to choose another solicitor. See *Note B3*.

H:4. [*Identical to Code C, Annex B, para. 4.*]

H:5. [*Identical to Code C, Annex B, para. 5.*]

H:6. These rights may be delayed only for as long as is necessary but not beyond 48 hours from the time of arrest (or if a person was being detained under TACT, Sched. 7, from the time at which the examination under Schedule 7 began). If the above grounds cease to apply within this time the detainee must as soon as practicable be asked if they wish to exercise either right, the custody record noted accordingly, and action taken in accordance with the relevant section of this code.

H:7. A person must be allowed to consult a solicitor for a reasonable time before any court hearing.

Documentation

H:8. [*Identical to Code C, Annex B, para. 13.*]

H:9. [*Identical to Code C, Annex B, para. 14, save for reference to "paragraph 6" in lieu of reference to "paragraphs 6 or 11".*]

Cautions and special warnings

H:10. [*Identical to Code C, Annex B, para. 15.*]

Notes for guidance

A-224a

H:B1 [*Identical to Code C, Annex B, B1, save for reference to "paragraph 3.15 and 3.17" in lieu of reference to "paragraph 3.13 and 3.15" and reference to "paragraph 1.11A" in lieu of reference to "paragraph 1.5A".*]

H:B2 [*Identical to Code C, Annex B, B2.*]

H:B3 [*Identical to Code C, Annex B, B3.*]

ANNEX C

Restriction on drawing adverse inferences from silence and terms of the caution when the restriction applies

(a) *The restriction on drawing adverse inferences from silence*

A-224b

H:1. The Criminal Justice and Public Order Act 1994, ss.34, 36 and 37 as amended by the Youth Justice and Criminal Evidence Act 1999, s.58 describe the conditions under which adverse inferences may be drawn from a person's failure or refusal to say anything about their involvement in the offence when interviewed, after being charged or informed they may be prosecuted. These provisions are subject to an overriding restriction on the ability of a court or jury to draw adverse inferences from a person's silence. This restriction applies:

(a) to any detainee at a police station who, before being interviewed, see section 11 or being charged or informed they may be prosecuted, see section 15, has:

  (i) asked for legal advice, see section 6, paragraph 6.1;

  (ii) not been allowed an opportunity to consult a solicitor, including the duty solicitor, as in this code; and

  (iii) not changed their mind about wanting legal advice, see section 6, paragraph 6.7(d); Note the condition in (ii) will:

  – apply when a detainee who has asked for legal advice is interviewed before speaking to a solicitor as in section 6, paragraph 6.6(a) or (b);

  – not apply if the detained person declines to ask for the duty solicitor, see section 6, paragraphs 6.7(b) and (c);

(b) to any person who has been charged with, or informed they may be prosecuted for, an offence who:

  (i) has had brought to their notice a written statement made by another person or the content of an interview with another person which relates to that offence, see PACE Code C, section 16, paragraph 16.4;

  (ii) is interviewed about that offence, see *PACE* Code C, section 16, paragraph 16.5; or

  (iii) makes a written statement about that offence, see Annex D, paragraphs 4 and 9, unless post-charge questioning has been authorised in accordance with section 22 of the Counter-Terrorism Act 2008, in which case the restriction will apply only if the person has asked for legal advice, see section 6, paragraph 6.1, and is questioned before receiving such advice in accordance with paragraph 6.7(b). See paragraph 15.11.

(b) *Terms of the caution when the restriction applies*

H:2. [*Identical to Code C, Annex C, para. 2.*]

H:3. [*Identical to Code C, Annex C, para. 3, save for reference to "Note C1" in lieu of reference to "Note C2".*]

Notes for guidance

H:C1 [*Identical to Code C, Annex C, C2.*]   **A-225**

ANNEX D

Written statements under caution

[*Identical to Annex D to Code C.*]   **A-225a**

ANNEX E

Summary of provisions relating to mentally disordered and otherwise mentally vulnerable people

H:1. [*Identical to Code C, Annex E, para. 1, save for reference to "paragraph 1.10" in lieu of reference to* **A-225b** *"paragraph 1.4" and absence of any reference to Note E4.*]

H:2. [*Identical to Code C, Annex E, para. 2, save for reference to "paragraph 1.13(b)" in lieu of reference to "paragraph 1.7(b)".*]

H:3. If the detention of a person who is mentally vulnerable or appears to be suffering from a mental disorder is authorised by the review officer (see paragraphs 14.1 and 14.2 and *Notes for Guidance 14A and 14B*), the custody officer must as soon as practicable inform the appropriate adult of the grounds for detention and the person's whereabouts, and ask the adult to come to the police station to see them. If the appropriate adult:

- is already at the station when information is given as in paragraphs 3.1 to 3.5 the information must be given in their presence
- is not at the station when the provisions of paragraph 3.1 to 3.5 are complied with these provisions must be complied with again in their presence once they arrive.

See paragraphs 3.15 to 3.16.

H:4. [*Identical to Code C, Annex E, para. 4, save for reference to "paragraph 3.20" in lieu of reference to "paragraph 3.19".*]

H:5. [*Identical to Code C, Annex E, para. 5, save for reference to "paragraph 9.6 and 9.8" in lieu of reference to "paragraph 9.5 and 9.6".*]

H:6. If a mentally disordered or otherwise mentally vulnerable person is cautioned in the absence of the appropriate adult, the caution must be repeated in the appropriate adult's presence. See paragraph 10.11.

H:7. A mentally disordered or otherwise mentally vulnerable person must not be interviewed or asked to provide or sign a written statement in the absence of the appropriate adult unless the provisions of paragraphs 11.2 or 11.11 to 11.13 apply. Questioning in these circumstances may not continue in the absence of the appropriate adult once sufficient information to avert the risk has been obtained. A record shall be made of the grounds for any decision to begin an interview in these circumstances. See paragraphs 11.2, 11.9 and 11.11 to 11.13.

H:8. If the appropriate adult is present at an interview, they shall be informed they are not expected to act simply as an observer and the purposes of their presence are to:

- advise the interviewee;
- observe whether or not the interview is being conducted properly and fairly;
- facilitate communication with the interviewee.

See paragraph 11.10.

H:9. If the custody officer charges a mentally disordered or otherwise mentally vulnerable person with an offence or takes such other action as is appropriate when there is sufficient evidence for a prosecution this must be carried out in the presence of the appropriate adult if they are at the police station. A copy of the written notice embodying any charge must be given to the appropriate adult. See *PACE* Code C, section 16.

H:10. [*Identical to Code C, Annex E, para. 12, save for reference to "paragraphs 6 and 12(c)" in lieu of reference to "paragraphs 5 and 11(c)".*]

H:11. [*Identical to Code C, Annex E, para. 13.*]

Notes for guidance

H:E1 [*Identical to Code C, Annex E, E1, save for reference to "paragraph 3.20" in lieu of reference to* **A-226** *"paragraph 3.19".*]

H:E2 [*Identical to Code C, Annex E, E2.*]

H:E3 [*Identical to Code C, Annex E, E3, save for reference to "paragraphs 11.2, 11.11 to 11.13" in lieu of reference to "paragraphs 11.1, 11.18 to 11.20".*]

ANNEX F

A-226a   [*Not used.*]

ANNEX G

Fitness to be interviewed

A-226b   [*Identical to Annex G to Code C.*]

ANNEX H

Detained person: observation list

A-227   [*Identical to Annex H to Code C.*]

ANNEX I

Establishing gender of persons for the purpose of searching

A-228   [*Identical to Annex L to Code C, save that the references to notes are to Note I1, I2 and so on, rather than to Note L1, L2 and so on.*]

ANNEX J

Transfer of persons detained for more than 14 days to prison

A-229   H:1. When a warrant of further detention is extended or further extended by a High Court judge to authorise a person's detention beyond a period of 14 days from the time of their arrest (or if they were being detained under TACT, Sched. 7, from the time at which their examination under Schedule 7 began), the person must be transferred from detention in a police station to detention in a designated prison as soon as is practicable after the warrant is issued, unless:

> (a) the detainee specifically requests to remain in detention at a police station and that request can be accommodated; or
>
> (b) there are reasonable grounds to believe that transferring the detainee to a prison would:
>> (i) significantly hinder a terrorism investigation;
>> (ii) delay charging of the detainee or their release from custody; or
>> (iii) otherwise prevent the investigation from being conducted diligently and expeditiously.

Any grounds in (b)(i) to (iii) above which are relied upon for not transferring the detainee to prison must be presented to the senior judge as part of the application for the extension or further extension of the warrant. See *Note J1*.

H:2 If at any time during which a person remains in detention at a police station under the warrant, the grounds at (b)(i) to (iii) cease to apply, the person must be transferred to a prison as soon as practicable.

H:3 Police should maintain an agreement with the National Offender Management Service (NOMS) that stipulates named prisons to which individuals may be transferred under this paragraph. This should be made with regard to ensuring detainees are moved to the most suitable prison for the purposes of the investigation and their welfare, and should include provision for the transfer of male, female and juvenile detainees. Police should ensure that the governor of a prison to which they intend to transfer a detainee is given reasonable notice of this. Where practicable, this should be no later than the point at which a warrant is applied for that would take the period of detention beyond 14 days.

H:4 Following a detainee's transfer to a designated prison, their detention will be governed by the terms of Schedule 8 to TACT 2000 and the *Prison Rules* and this code of practice will not apply during any period that the person remains in prison detention. The code will once more apply if the person is transferred back from prison detention to police detention. In order to enable the governor to arrange for the production of the detainee back into police custody, police should give notice to the governor of the relevant prison as soon as possible of any decision to transfer a detainee from prison back to a police station. Any transfer between a prison and a police station should be conducted by police and this code will be applicable during the period of transit. See *Note 2J*. A detainee should only remain in police custody having been transferred back from a prison, for as long as is necessary for the purpose of the investigation.

H:5 The investigating team and custody officer should provide as much information as necessary to enable the relevant prison authorities to provide appropriate facilities to detain an individual. This should include, but not be limited to:

    (i) medical assessments;

    (ii) security and risk assessments;

    (iii) details of the detained person's legal representatives;

    (iv) details of any individuals from whom the detained person has requested visits, or who have requested to visit the detained person.

H:6 Where a detainee is to be transferred to prison, the custody officer should inform the detainee's legal adviser beforehand that the transfer is to take place (including the name of the prison). The custody officer should also make all reasonable attempts to inform:

- family or friends who have been informed previously of the detainee's detention; and
- the person who was initially informed of the detainee's detention in accordance with paragraph 5.1.

H:7 Any decision not to transfer a detained person to a designated prison under paragraph 1, must be recorded, along with the reasons for this decision. If a request under paragraph 1(a) is not accommodated, the reasons for this should also be recorded.

Notes for guidance

H:J1 *Transfer to prison is intended to ensure that individuals who are detained for extended periods of time are held in a place designed for longer periods of detention than police stations. Prison will provide detainees with a greater range of facilities more appropriate to longer detention periods.* **A-230**

H:J2 *This code will only apply as is appropriate to the conditions of detention during the period of transit. There is obviously no requirement to provide such things as bed linen or reading materials for the journey between prison and police station.*

ANNEX K

Documents and records to be translated

H:1. [*Identical to Code C, Annex M, para. 1.*] **A-230a**

H:2. The documents considered essential for the purposes of this code and for which (subject to paragraphs 3 to 7) written translations must be created are the records made in accordance with this code of the grounds and reasons for any authorisation of a suspect's detention under the provisions of the Terrorism Act 2000 or the Counter Terrorism Act 2008 (post-charge questioning) to which this code applies as they are described and referred to in the suspect's custody record. Translations should be created as soon as practicable after the authorisation has been recorded and provided as soon as practicable thereafter, whilst the person is detained or after they have been released (see *Note K3*).

H:3. [*Identical to Code C, Annex M, para. 3, save for reference to "Code H, paragraph 1.11A" in lieu of reference to "Code C, paragraph 1.5A".*]

H:4. [*Identical to Code C, Annex M, para. 4 (but note that there is no table in Annex K (unlike Annex M to Code C)).*]

H:5. [*Identical to Code C, Annex M, para. 5.*]

H:6. [*Identical to Code C, Annex M, para. 6, save for reference to "Notes K2 and K3" in lieu of reference to "Notes M2 and M3".*]

H:7. For the purpose of the waiver:

    (a) the consent of a person who is mentally disordered or otherwise mentally vulnerable person is only valid if the information about the circumstances under which they can waive the right and the reminder about their right to legal advice mentioned in paragraphs 3 to 5 and their consent is given in the presence of the appropriate adult, and the appropriate adult also agrees;

    (b) the consent of a juvenile is only valid if their parent's or guardian's consent is also obtained unless the juvenile is under 14, when their parent's or guardian's consent is sufficient in its own right and the information and reminder mentioned in sub-paragraph (a) above and their consent is also given in the presence of the appropriate adult (who may or may not be a parent or guardian).

Note: paragraph 1.11A in Code C [*sic*] requires someone to fulfil the role of the appropriate adult to be present when a 17-year-old is given the information and reminder mentioned in sub paragraph (a) above and gives their consent to waive their right. The consent of their parent or guardian is not required.

H:8. [*Identical to Code C, Annex M, para. 8 (but note that there is no table in Annex K (unlike Annex M to Code C)).*]

H:9. [*Identical to Code C, Annex M, para. 9.*]

Documentation

H:10. [*Identical to Code C, Annex M, para. 10, save for reference to "Code H" in lieu of reference to "Code C".*]

Note for guidance

H:K1–K3 [*Identical to Code C, Annex M, M1–M3, save for reference to 2000 Act in lieu of reference to 1984 Act.*]

B. UNDER THE CRIMINAL PROCEDURE AND INVESTIGATIONS ACT 1996

(1) As to the recording and retention by the police of material obtained during an investigation and its supply to the prosecutor

Introduction

A-231   Pursuant to sections 23 and 25 of the 1996 Act (§§ 12-97, 12-98 in the main work), the Secretary of State has prepared and published three codes of practice governing the action the police must take in recording and retaining material obtained in the course of a criminal investigation and regulating its supply to the prosecutor for a decision on disclosure.

★   The first code came into force on the day appointed for the purpose of Part I of the 1996 Act, namely April 1, 1997 (S.I. 1997 No. 1033). A second code came into force on April 4, 2005: Criminal Procedure and Investigations Act 1996 (Code of Practice) Order 2005 (S.I. 2005 No. 985). The third code (set out *post*) came into force on March 19, 2015: Criminal Procedure and Investigations Act 1996 (Code of Practice) Order 2015 (S.I. 2015 No. 861).

In connection with this code, see also § 12-96 in the main work (meaning of "investigation").

As to the significance of the code of practice in relation to material held overseas, outside the European Union, by entities not subject to the jurisdiction of the United Kingdom, see *R. v. Flook* [2010] 1 Cr.App.R. 30, CA (§ 12-53 in the main work).

CRIMINAL PROCEDURE AND INVESTIGATIONS ACT 1996 CODE OF PRACTICE UNDER PART II

Preamble

★A-232   This code of practice is issued under Part II of the Criminal Procedure and Investigations Act 1996 ("the Act"). It sets out the manner in which police officers are to record, retain and reveal to the prosecutor material obtained in a criminal investigation and which may be relevant to the investigation, and related matters.

1. Introduction

★A-232a   1.1 This code of practice applies in respect of criminal investigations conducted by police officers which begin on or after the day on which this code comes into effect. Persons other than police officers who are charged with the duty of conducting an investigation as defined in the Act are to have regard to the relevant provisions of the code, and should take these into account in applying their own operating procedures.

1.2 This code does not apply to persons who are not charged with the duty of conducting an investigation as defined in the Act.

1.3 Nothing in this code applies to material intercepted in obedience to a warrant issued under section 2 of the Interception of Communications Act 1985 or section 5 of the Regulation of Investigatory Powers Act 2000, or to any copy of that material as defined in section 10 of the 1985 Act or section 15 of the 2000 Act.

1.4 This code extends only to England and Wales.

2. Definitions

★A-233   2.1 In this code:
- a criminal investigation is an investigation conducted by police officers with a view to it being ascertained whether a person should be charged with an offence, or whether a person charged with an offence is guilty of it. This will include:
  - investigations into crimes that have been committed;
  - investigations whose purpose is to ascertain whether a crime has been committed, with a view to the possible institution of criminal proceedings; and

- investigations which begin in the belief that a crime may be committed, for example when the police keep premises or individuals under observation for a period of time, with a view to the possible institution of criminal proceedings;
- charging a person with an offence includes prosecution by way of summons or postal requisition;
- an investigator is any police officer involved in the conduct of a criminal investigation. All investigators have a responsibility for carrying out the duties imposed on them under this code, including in particular recording information, and retaining records of information and other material;
- the officer in charge of an investigation is the police officer responsible for directing a criminal investigation. He is also responsible for ensuring that proper procedures are in place for recording information, and retaining records of information and other material, in the investigation;
- the disclosure officer is the person responsible for examining material retained by the police during the investigation; revealing material to the prosecutor during the investigation and any criminal proceedings resulting from it, and certifying that he has done this; and disclosing material to the accused at the request of the prosecutor;
- the prosecutor is the authority responsible for the conduct, on behalf of the Crown, of criminal proceedings resulting from a specific criminal investigation;
- material is material of any kind, including information and objects, which is obtained or inspected in the course of a criminal investigation and which may be relevant to the investigation. This includes not only material coming into the possession of the investigator (such as documents seized in the course of searching premises) but also material generated by him (such as interview records);
- material may be relevant to the investigation if it appears to an investigator, or to the officer in charge of an investigation, or to the disclosure officer, that it has some bearing on any offence under investigation or any person being investigated, or on the surrounding circumstances of the case, unless it is incapable of having any impact on the case;
- sensitive material is material, the disclosure of which, the disclosure officer believes, would give rise to a real risk of serious prejudice to an important public interest;
- references to prosecution disclosure are to the duty of the prosecutor under sections 3 and 7A of the Act to disclose material which is in his possession or which he has inspected in pursuance of this code, and which might reasonably be considered capable of undermining the case against the accused, or of assisting the case for the accused;
- references to the disclosure of material to a person accused of an offence include references to the disclosure of material to his legal representative;
- references to police officers and to the chief officer of police include those employed in a police force as defined in section 3(3) of the Prosecution of Offences Act 1985.

As to the meaning of "criminal investigation", see *DPP v. Metten*, unreported, January 22, 1999, DC (§ 12-96 in the main work).

3. General responsibilities

3.1 The functions of the investigator, the officer in charge of an investigation and the disclosure officer are separate. Whether they are undertaken by one, two or more persons will depend on the complexity of the case and the administrative arrangements within each police force. Where they are undertaken by more than one person, close consultation between them is essential to the effective performance of the duties imposed by this code. **★A-234**

3.2 In any criminal investigation, one or more deputy disclosure officers may be appointed to assist the disclosure officer, and a deputy disclosure officer may perform any function of a disclosure officer as defined in paragraph 2.1.

3.3 The chief officer of police for each police force is responsible for putting in place arrangements to ensure that in every investigation the identity of the officer in charge of an investigation and the disclosure officer is recorded. The chief officer of police for each police force shall ensure that disclosure officers and deputy disclosure officers have sufficient skills and authority, commensurate with the complexity of the investigation, to discharge their functions effectively. An individual must not be appointed as disclosure officer, or continue in that role, if that is likely to result in a conflict of interest, for instance, if the disclosure officer is the victim of the alleged crime which is the subject of the investigation. The advice of a more senior officer must always be sought if there is doubt as to whether a conflict of interest precludes an individual acting as disclosure officer. If thereafter the doubt remains, the advice of a prosecutor should be sought.

3.4 The officer in charge of an investigation may delegate tasks to another investigator, to civilians employed by the police force, or to other persons participating in the investigation under arrangements for joint investigations, but he remains responsible for ensuring that these have been carried out and for accounting for any general policies followed in the investigation. In particular, it is an essential part of his duties to ensure that all material which may be relevant to an investigation is retained, and either made available to the disclosure officer or (in exceptional circumstances) revealed directly to the prosecutor.

3.5 In conducting an investigation, the investigator should pursue all reasonable lines of inquiry, whether these point towards or away from the suspect. What is reasonable in each case will depend on the particular circumstances. For example, where material is held on computer, it is a matter for the investigator to decide which material on the computer it is reasonable to inquire into, and in what manner.

3.6 If the officer in charge of an investigation believes that other persons may be in possession of material that may be relevant to the investigation, and if this has not been obtained under paragraph 3.5 above, he should ask the disclosure officer to inform them of the existence of the investigation and to invite them to retain the material in case they receive a request for its disclosure. The disclosure officer should inform the prosecutor that they may have such material. However, the officer in charge of an investigation is not required to make speculative enquiries of other persons; there must be some reason to believe that they may have relevant material. That reason may come from information provided to the police by the accused or from other inquiries made or from some other source.

3.7 If, during a criminal investigation, the officer in charge of an investigation or disclosure officer for any reason no longer has responsibility for the functions falling to him, either his supervisor or the police officer in charge of criminal investigations for the police force concerned must assign someone else to assume that responsibility. That person's identity must be recorded, as with those initially responsible for these functions in each investigation.

As to the meaning of "criminal investigation", see *DPP v. Metten*, unreported, January 22, 1999, DC (§ 12-96 in the main work).

Where, in the run-up to an election, there was an arrangement that a local electoral office would notify the police of any suspected fraudulent applications for postal votes, where that office submitted 1,600 suspected fraudulent applications to the police (out of a total of 10,000 applications), where the criminal investigation that ensued resulted in the prosecution of the appellants for conspiracy to defraud the electoral officer, and where complaint was made about the non-disclosure of the 8,400 postal vote applications that had been examined by the electoral office, but had not been submitted to the police, there was no duty of disclosure on the electoral office as either a delegate of the investigator or as a joint investigator within paragraph 3.4; the role of the electoral office was in the nature of an examination by a complainant of suspicious documents subsequently handed to the police, comparable to that of a bank handing over suspicious cheques to the police: *R. v. Khan* [2011] L.S. Gazette, October 20, 23, CA ([2011] EWCA Crim. 2240).

4. Recording of information

★**A-235**   4.1 If material which may be relevant to the investigation consists of information which is not recorded in any form, the officer in charge of an investigation must ensure that it is recorded in a durable or retrievable form (whether in writing, on video or audio tape, or on computer disk).

4.2 Where it is not practicable to retain the initial record of information because it forms part of a larger record which is to be destroyed, its contents should be transferred as a true record to a durable and more easily-stored form before that happens.

4.3 Negative information is often relevant to an investigation. If it may be relevant it must be recorded. An example might be a number of people present in a particular place at a particular time who state that they saw nothing unusual.

4.4 Where information which may be relevant is obtained, it must be recorded at the time it is obtained or as soon as practicable after that time. This includes, for example, information obtained in house-to-house enquiries, although the requirement to record information promptly does not require an investigator to take a statement from a potential witness where it would not otherwise be taken.

5. Retention of material

(a) Duty to retain material

★**A-236**   5.1 The investigator must retain material obtained in a criminal investigation which may be relevant to the investigation. Material may be photographed, video-recorded, captured digitally or otherwise retained in the form of a copy rather than the original at any time, if the original is perishable; the original was supplied to the investigator rather than generated by him and is to be returned to its owner; or the retention of a copy rather than the original is reasonable in all the circumstances.

5.2 Where material has been seized in the exercise of the powers of seizure conferred by the Police and Criminal Evidence Act 1984, the duty to retain it under this code is subject to the provisions on the retention of seized material in section 22 of that Act.

5.3 If the officer in charge of an investigation becomes aware as a result of developments in the case that material previously examined but not retained (because it was not thought to be relevant) may now be relevant to the investigation, he should, wherever practicable, take steps to obtain it or ensure that it is retained for further inspection or for production in court if required.

5.4 The duty to retain material includes in particular the duty to retain material falling into the following categories, where it may be relevant to the investigation:

- crime reports (including crime report forms, relevant parts of incident report books or police officer's notebooks);
- custody records;
- records which are derived from tapes of telephone messages (for example, 999 calls) containing descriptions of an alleged offence or offender;
- final versions of witness statements (and draft versions where their content differs from the final version), including any exhibits mentioned (unless these have been returned to their owner on the understanding that they will be produced in court if required);
- interview records (written records, or audio or video tapes, of interviews with actual or potential witnesses or suspects);
- communications between the police and experts such as forensic scientists, reports of work carried out by experts, and schedules of scientific material prepared by the expert for the investigator, for the purposes of criminal proceedings;
- records of the first description of a suspect by each potential witness who purports to identify or describe the suspect, whether or not the description differs from that of subsequent descriptions by that or other witnesses;
- any material casting doubt on the reliability of a witness.

5.5 The duty to retain material, where it may be relevant to the investigation, also includes in particular the duty to retain material which may satisfy the test for prosecution disclosure in the Act, such as:

- information provided by an accused person which indicates an explanation for the offence with which he has been charged;
- any material casting doubt on the reliability of a confession;
- any material casting doubt on the reliability of a prosecution witness.

5.6 The duty to retain material falling into these categories does not extend to items which are purely ancillary to such material and possess no independent significance (for example, duplicate copies of records or reports).

(b) Length of time for which material is to be retained

5.7 All material which may be relevant to the investigation must be retained until a decision is ★**A-236a** taken whether to institute proceedings against a person for an offence.

5.8 If a criminal investigation results in proceedings being instituted, all material which may be relevant must be retained at least until the accused is acquitted or convicted or the prosecutor decides not to proceed with the case.

5.9 Where the accused is convicted, all material which may be relevant must be retained at least until:

- the convicted person is released from custody, or discharged from hospital, in cases where the court imposes a custodial sentence or a hospital order;
- six months from the date of conviction, in all other cases.

If the court imposes a custodial sentence or hospital order and the convicted person is released from custody or discharged from hospital earlier than six months from the date of conviction, all material which may be relevant must be retained at least until six months from the date of conviction.

5.10 If an appeal against conviction is in progress when the release or discharge occurs, or at the end of the period of six months specified in paragraph 5.9, all material which may be relevant must be retained until the appeal is determined. Similarly, if the Criminal Cases Review Commission is considering an application at that point in time, all material which may be relevant must be retained at least until the Commission decides not to refer the case to the court.

6. Preparation of material for prosecutor

(a) Introduction

★A-237   6.1 The officer in charge of the investigation, the disclosure officer or an investigator may seek advice from the prosecutor about whether any particular item of material may be relevant to the investigation.

6.2 Material which may be relevant to an investigation, which has been retained in accordance with this code, and which the disclosure officer believes will not form part of the prosecution case, must be listed on a schedule. This process will differ depending on whether the case is likely to be heard in the magistrates' court or the Crown Court.

(b) Magistrates' Court

Anticipated guilty pleas

★A-237a   6.3 If the accused is charged with a summary offence or an either-way offence that is likely to remain in the magistrates' court, and it is considered that he is likely to plead guilty (*e.g.* because he has admitted the offence), a schedule or streamlined disclosure certificate is not required. However, the common law duty to disclose material which may assist the defence at bail hearings or in the early preparation of their case remains, and where there is such material the certification on the Police Report (MG5/SDF) must be completed. Where there is no such material, a certificate to that effect must be completed in like form to that attached at the Annex.

6.4 If, contrary to the expectation of a guilty plea being entered, the accused pleads not guilty at the first hearing, the disclosure officer must ensure that the streamlined disclosure certificate is prepared and submitted as soon as is reasonably practicable after that happens.

Anticipated not guilty pleas

★A-237b   6.5 If the accused is charged with a summary offence or an either-way offence that is likely to remain in the magistrates' court, and it is considered that he is likely to plead not guilty, a streamlined disclosure certificate must be completed in like form to that attached at the Annex.

Material which may assist the defence

★A-237c   6.6 In every case, irrespective of the anticipated plea, if there is material known to the disclosure officer that might assist the defence with the early preparation of their case or at a bail hearing (for example, a key prosecution witness has relevant previous convictions or a witness has withdrawn his or her statement), a note must be made on the MG5 (or other format agreed under the National File Standards). The material must be disclosed to the prosecutor who will disclose it to the defence if he thinks it meets this common law test.

No undermining or assisting material and sensitive material – magistrates' court cases

★A-237d   6.7 If there is no material which might fall to be disclosed as undermining the prosecution case or assisting the defence, the officer should complete the appropriate entry on the streamlined disclosure certificate. If there is any sensitive unused material the officer should complete a sensitive material schedule (MG6D or similar) and attach it to the prosecution file. In exceptional circumstances, when its existence is so sensitive that it cannot be listed, it should be revealed to the prosecutor separately.

(c) Crown Court

★A-237e   6.8 For cases to be held in the Crown Court, the unused material schedules (MG6 series) are used.

6.9 The disclosure officer must ensure that a schedule is prepared in the following circumstances:
- the accused is charged with an offence which is triable only on indictment;
- the accused is charged with an offence which is triable either way, and it is considered that the case is likely to be tried on indictment.

6.10 Material which the disclosure officer does not believe is sensitive must be listed on a schedule of non-sensitive material. The schedule must include a statement that the disclosure officer does not believe the material is sensitive.

Way in which material is to be listed on schedule

★A-237f   6.11 For indictable only cases or either-way cases sent to the Crown Court, schedules MG6 C, D and E should be completed to facilitate service of the MG6C with the prosecution case, wherever possible. The disclosure officer should ensure that each item of material is listed separately on the schedule, and is numbered consecutively. The description of each item should make clear the nature of the item and should contain sufficient detail to enable the prosecutor to decide whether he needs to inspect the material before deciding whether or not it should be disclosed.

6.12 In some enquiries it may not be practicable to list each item of material separately. For example, there may be many items of a similar or repetitive nature. These may be listed in a block and described by quantity and generic title.

6.13 Even if some material is listed in a block, the disclosure officer must ensure that any items among that material which might satisfy the test for prosecution disclosure are listed and described individually.

(d) Sensitive material – Crown Court

6.14 Any material which is believed to be sensitive either must be listed on a schedule of sensitive material or, in exceptional circumstances where its existence is so sensitive that it cannot be listed, it should be revealed to the prosecutor separately. If there is no sensitive material, the disclosure officer must record this fact on a schedule of sensitive material, or otherwise so indicate. ★A-237g

6.15 Subject to paragraph 6.16 below, the disclosure officer must list on a sensitive schedule any material the disclosure of which he believes would give rise to a real risk of serious prejudice to an important public interest, and the reason for that belief. The schedule must include a statement that the disclosure officer believes the material is sensitive. Depending on the circumstances, examples of such material may include the following among others:

- material relating to national security;
- material received from the intelligence and security agencies;
- material relating to intelligence from foreign sources which reveals sensitive intelligence gathering methods;
- material given in confidence;
- material relating to the identity or activities of informants, or undercover police officers, or witnesses, or other persons supplying information to the police who may be in danger if their identities are revealed;
- material revealing the location of any premises or other place used for police surveillance, or the identity of any person allowing a police officer to use them for surveillance;
- material revealing, either directly or indirectly, techniques and methods relied upon by a police officer in the course of a criminal investigation, for example covert surveillance techniques, or other methods of detecting crime;
- material whose disclosure might facilitate the commission of other offences or hinder the prevention and detection of crime;
- material upon the strength of which search warrants were obtained;
- material containing details of persons taking part in identification parades;
- material supplied to an investigator during a criminal investigation which has been generated by an official of a body concerned with the regulation or supervision of bodies corporate or of persons engaged in financial activities, or which has been generated by a person retained by such a body;
- material supplied to an investigator during a criminal investigation which relates to a child or young person and which has been generated by a local authority social services department, an Area Child Protection Committee or other party contacted by an investigator during the investigation;
- material relating to the private life of a witness.

6.16 In exceptional circumstances, where an investigator considers that material is so sensitive that its revelation to the prosecutor by means of an entry on the sensitive schedule is inappropriate, the existence of the material must be revealed to the prosecutor separately. This will apply only where compromising the material would be likely to lead directly to the loss of life, or directly threaten national security.

6.17 In such circumstances, the responsibility for informing the prosecutor lies with the investigator who knows the detail of the sensitive material. The investigator should act as soon as is reasonably practicable after the file containing the prosecution case is sent to the prosecutor. The investigator must also ensure that the prosecutor is able to inspect the material so that he can assess whether it is disclosable and, if so, whether it needs to be brought before a court for a ruling on disclosure.

7. Revelation of material to prosecutor

7.1 Certain unused material must be disclosed to the accused at common law if it would assist the ★A-238 defence with the early preparation of their case or at a bail hearing. This material may consist of items such as a previous relevant conviction of a key prosecution witness or the withdrawal of support for the prosecution by a witness. This material must be revealed to the prosecutor for service on the defence with the initial details of the prosecution case.

7.1A In anticipated not guilty plea cases for hearing in the magistrates' court the disclosure officer must give the streamlined disclosure certificate to the prosecutor at the same time as he gives the prosecutor the file containing the material for the prosecution case.

7.1B In cases sent to the Crown Court, wherever possible, the disclosure officer should give the schedules concerning unused material to the prosecutor at the same time as the prosecution file in preparation for the first hearing and any case management that the judge may wish to conduct at that stage.

7.2 The disclosure officer should draw the attention of the prosecutor to any material an investigator has retained (including material to which paragraph 6.13 applies) which may satisfy the test for prosecution disclosure in the Act, and should explain why he has come to that view.

N.B. The reference to paragraph 6.13 (a leftover from the previous version of the code) should have been updated to refer to paragraph 6.16.

7.3 At the same time as complying with the duties in paragraphs 7.1 and 7.2, the disclosure officer must give the prosecutor a copy of any material which falls into the following categories (unless such material has already been given to the prosecutor as part of the file containing the material for the prosecution case):

- information provided by an accused person which indicates an explanation for the offence with which he has been charged;
- any material casting doubt on the reliability of a confession;
- any material casting doubt on the reliability of a prosecution witness;
- any other material which the investigator believes may satisfy the test for prosecution disclosure in the Act;

7.4 If the prosecutor asks to inspect material which has not already been copied to him, the disclosure officer must allow him to inspect it. If the prosecutor asks for a copy of material which has not already been copied to him, the disclosure officer must give him a copy. However, this does not apply where the disclosure officer believes, having consulted the officer in charge of the investigation, that the material is too sensitive to be copied and can only be inspected.

7.5 If material consists of information which is recorded other than in writing, whether it should be given to the prosecutor in its original form as a whole, or by way of relevant extracts recorded in the same form, or in the form of a transcript, is a matter for agreement between the disclosure officer and the prosecutor.

8. Subsequent action by disclosure officer

★**A-239** 8.1 At the time when a streamlined disclosure certificate is prepared for magistrates' court cases, or a schedule of non-sensitive material is prepared for Crown Court cases, the disclosure officer may not know exactly what material will form the case against the accused. In addition, the prosecutor may not have given advice about the likely relevance of particular items of material. Once these matters have been determined, the disclosure officer must give the prosecutor, where necessary, an amended certificate or schedule listing any additional material:

- which may be relevant to the investigation;
- which does not form part of the case against the accused;
- which is not already listed on the schedule; and
- which he believes is not sensitive,

unless he is informed in writing by the prosecutor that the prosecutor intends to disclose the material to the defence.

8.2 Section 7A of the Act imposes a continuing duty on the prosecutor, for the duration of criminal proceedings against the accused, to disclose material which satisfies the test for disclosure (subject to public interest considerations). To enable him to do this, any new material coming to light should be treated in the same way as the earlier material.

8.3 In particular, after a defence statement has been given, or details of the issues in dispute have been recorded on the effective trial preparation form, the disclosure officer must look again at the material which has been retained and must draw the attention of the prosecutor to any material which might reasonably be considered capable of undermining the case for the prosecution against the accused or of assisting the case for the accused; and he must reveal it to him in accordance with paragraphs 7.4 and 7.5 above.

9. Certification by disclosure officer

★**A-240** 9.1 The disclosure officer must certify to the prosecutor that, to the best of his knowledge and belief, all relevant material which has been retained and made available to him has been revealed to the prosecutor in accordance with this code. He must sign and date the certificate. It will be necessary to certify not only at the time when the schedule and accompanying material is submitted to the prosecutor, and when relevant material which has been retained is reconsidered after the accused has given a defence statement, but also whenever a schedule is otherwise given or material is otherwise revealed to the prosecutor.

10. Disclosure of material to accused

10.1 Other than early disclosure under common law, in the magistrates' court the streamlined certificate at the Annex (and any relevant unused material to be disclosed under it) must be disclosed to the accused either: ★A-240a

- at the hearing where a not guilty plea is entered, or
- as soon as possible following a formal indication from the accused or representative that a not guilty plea will be entered at the hearing.

10.1A If material has not already been copied to the prosecutor, and he requests its disclosure to the accused on the ground that:

- it satisfies the test for prosecution disclosure, or
- the court has ordered its disclosure after considering an application from the accused,

the disclosure officer must disclose it to the accused.

10.2 If material has been copied to the prosecutor, and it is to be disclosed, whether it is disclosed by the prosecutor or the disclosure officer is a matter of agreement between the two of them.

10.3 The disclosure officer must disclose material to the accused either by giving him a copy or by allowing him to inspect it. If the accused person asks for a copy of any material which he has been allowed to inspect, the disclosure officer must give it to him, unless in the opinion of the disclosure officer that is either not practicable (for example because the material consists of an object which cannot be copied, or because the volume of material is so great), or not desirable (for example because the material is a statement by a child witness in relation to a sexual offence).

10.4 If material which the accused has been allowed to inspect consists of information which is recorded other than in writing, whether it should be given to the accused in its original form or in the form of a transcript is a matter for the discretion of the disclosure officer. If the material is transcribed, the disclosure officer must ensure that the transcript is certified to the accused as a true record of the material which has been transcribed.

10.5 If a court concludes that an item of sensitive material satisfies the prosecution disclosure test and that the interests of the defence outweigh the public interest in withholding disclosure, it will be necessary to disclose the material if the case is to proceed. This does not mean that sensitive documents must always be disclosed in their original form: for example, the court may agree that sensitive details still requiring protection should be blocked out, or that documents may be summarised, or that the prosecutor may make an admission about the substance of the material under section 10 of the Criminal Justice Act 1967.

ANNEX

The annex to the code is not set out in this work. ★A-241

(2) As to the practice for arranging and conducting interviews of witnesses notified by the accused

Introduction

As from May 1, 2010, a new code of practice entitled "Code of Practice for Arranging and Conducting Interviews of Witnesses Notified by the Accused", which was prepared under section 21A of the CPIA 1996, was brought into force by the Criminal Procedure and Investigations Act 1996 (Code of Practice for Interviews of Witnesses Notified by Accused) Order 2010 (S.I. 2010 No. 1223). A-241a

CODE OF PRACTICE FOR ARRANGING AND CONDUCTING INTERVIEWS OF WITNESSES NOTIFIED BY THE ACCUSED

Preamble

A-241b   This code of practice is issued under section 21A of the Criminal Procedure and Investigations Act 1996 ("the Act"). It sets out guidance that police officers and other persons charged with investigating offences must follow if they arrange or conduct interviews of proposed witnesses whose details are disclosed to the prosecution by an accused person pursuant to the disclosure provisions in Part I of the Act.

Introduction

A-241c   1.1 Part I of the Act sets out rules governing disclosure of information in the course of criminal proceedings by both the prosecution and persons accused of offences to which that Part of the Act applies.

1.2. Sections 5 and 6 of the Act provide for accused persons to give defence statements to the prosecution and to the court and section 6A sets out what those defence statements must contain. Section 6A(2) requires that any defence statement that discloses an alibi must give particulars of it, including prescribed details of any witness who the accused believes is able to give evidence in support of the alibi and any information the accused has which may assist in identifying or finding such a witness.

1.3. Section 6C of the Act requires the accused to give to the prosecutor and the court a notice indicating whether he intends to call any witnesses at trial and giving details of those witnesses.

1.4. This code of practice sets out guidance that police officers and other persons charged with investigating offences must have regard to when they are arranging and conducting interviews of proposed witnesses identified in a defence statement given under section 6A(2) of the Act or a notice given under section 6C of the Act.

Definitions

A-241d   2. In this code:—
  – *the accused* means a person mentioned in section 1(1) or (2) of the Act;
  – "an appropriate person" means:
    (a) in the case of a witness under the age of 18:
      (i) the parent, guardian or, if the witness is in local authority or voluntary organisation care, or is otherwise being looked after under the Children Act 1989, a person representing that authority or organisation; or
      (ii) a social worker of a local authority; or
      (iii) failing these, some other responsible person aged 18 or over who is not a police officer or employed by the police; and
    (b) in the case of a witness who is mentally disordered or mentally vulnerable:
      (i) a relative, guardian or other person responsible for the witness's care or custody; or
      (ii) someone experienced in dealing with mentally disordered or mentally vulnerable people but who is not a police officer or employed by the police; or
      (iii) failing these, some other responsible person aged 18 or over who is not a police officer or employed by the police.
  – *an investigator* is a police officer or any other person charged with the duty of investigating offences.
  – *a witness* is a potential witness identified by an accused person either:
    – in a defence statement under section 6A(2) of the Act as being a witness that he believes is able to give evidence in support of an alibi disclosed in the statement; or
    – in a notice given to the court and the prosecutor under section 6C of the Act as being a person that he intends to call as a witness at his trial.

Arrangement of the interview

Information to be provided to the witness before any interview may take place

A-241e   3.1. If an investigator wishes to interview a witness, the witness must be asked whether he consents to being interviewed and informed that:
  • an interview is being requested following his identification by the accused as a proposed witness under section 6A(2) or section 6C of the Act;
  • he is not obliged to attend the proposed interview;
  • he is entitled to be accompanied by a solicitor at the interview (but nothing in this code of

practice creates any duty on the part of the Legal Services Commission to provide funding for any such attendance); and
- a record will be made of the interview and he will subsequently be sent a copy of the record.

3.2. If the witness consents to being interviewed, the witness must be asked:
- whether he wishes to have a solicitor present at the interview;
- whether he consents to a solicitor attending the interview on behalf of the accused, as an observer; and
- whether he consents to a copy of the record being sent to the accused. If he does not consent, the witness must be informed that the effect of disclosure requirements in criminal proceedings may nevertheless require the prosecution to disclose the record to the accused (and any co-accused) in the course of the proceedings.

Information to be provided to the accused before any interview may take place

4.1. The investigator must notify the accused or, if the accused is legally represented in the **A-241f**
proceedings, the accused's representatives:
- that the investigator requested an interview with the witness;
- whether the witness consented to the interview; and
- if the witness consented to the interview, whether the witness also consented to a solicitor attending the interview on behalf of the accused, as an observer.

4.2. If the accused is not legally represented in the proceedings, and if the witness consents to a solicitor attending the interview on behalf of the accused, the accused must be offered the opportunity, a reasonable time before the interview is held, to appoint a solicitor to attend it.

Identification of the date, time and venue for the interview

5. The investigator must nominate a reasonable date, time and venue for the interview and notify **A-241g**
the witness of them and any subsequent changes to them.

Notification to the accused's solicitor of the date, time and venue of the interview

6. If the witness has consented to the presence of the accused's solicitor, the accused's solicitor **A-241h**
must be notified that the interview is taking place, invited to observe, and provided with reasonable notice of the date, time and venue of the interview and any subsequent changes.

Conduct of the interview

The investigator conducting the interview

7. The identity of the investigator conducting the interview must be recorded. That person must **A-241i**
have sufficient skills and authority, commensurate with the complexity of the investigation, to discharge his functions effectively. That person must not conduct the interview if that is likely to result in a conflict of interest, for instance, if that person is the victim of the alleged crime which is the subject of the proceedings. The advice of a more senior officer must always be sought if there is doubt as to whether a conflict of interest precludes an individual conducting the interview. If thereafter the doubt remains, the advice of a prosecutor must be sought.

Attendance of the accused's solicitor

8.1. The accused's solicitor may only attend the interview if the witness has consented to his pres- **A-241j**
ence as an observer. Provided that the accused's solicitor was given reasonable notice of the date, time and place of the interview, the fact that the accused's solicitor is not present will not prevent the interview from being conducted. If the witness at any time withdraws consent to the accused's solicitor being present at the interview, the interview may continue without the presence of the accused's solicitor.

8.2. The accused's solicitor may attend only as an observer.

Attendance of the witness's solicitor

9. Where a witness has indicated that he wishes to appoint a solicitor to be present, that solicitor **A-241k**
must be permitted to attend the interview.

Attendance of any other appropriate person

A-241l   10. A witness under the age of 18 or a witness who is mentally disordered or otherwise mentally vulnerable must be interviewed in the presence of an appropriate person.

Recording of the interview

A-241m   11.1. An accurate record must be made of the interview, whether it takes place at a police station or elsewhere. The record must be made, where practicable, by audio recording or by visual recording with sound, or otherwise in writing. Any written record must be made and completed during the interview, unless this would not be practicable or would interfere with the conduct of the interview, and must constitute either a verbatim record of what has been said or, failing this, an account of the interview which adequately and accurately summarises it. If a written record is not made during the interview it must be made as soon as practicable after its completion. Written interview records must be timed and signed by the maker.

11.2 A copy of the record must be given, within a reasonable time of the interview, to:

     (a) the witness; and

     (b) if the witness consents, to the accused or the accused's solicitor.

II. ATTORNEY-GENERAL'S GUIDELINES

A. DISCLOSURE

Introduction

A-242   On December 3, 2013, the Attorney-General published revised guidelines on disclosure, replacing the 2005 guidelines, and also the supplementary guidelines on digital material issued in 2011, which are now annexed to the new guidelines. The new guidelines should be read together with the revised protocol on the disclosure of unused material in criminal cases (*post*, Appendix N-52 *et seq.*), and are not designed to be a substitute for a thorough understanding of the relevant legislation, codes of practice, case law and procedure. They have immediate effect (para. 73).

Paragraphs 1 to 3 emphasise the importance of disclosure and a "timely dialogue between the prosecution, defence and the court", and are a shortened version of the introductory section to the 2005 guidelines. Paragraphs 4 to 14 relate to general principles and incorporate most of the corresponding section in the 2005 guidelines, but also stress the role the defence have to play in ensuring that the prosecution are directed towards appropriate material, the importance of communication within the prosecution team and the role of the reviewing lawyer. Paragraphs 15 to 27 relate to the duties on investigators and disclosure officers, incorporating a shortened version of the corresponding section in the 2005 guidelines. They underline that thought must be given to defining and limiting the scope of investigations under the guidance of the reviewing lawyer and prosecutor where appropriate, the need to keep full records of meetings and decisions taken and that, whilst there will be some cases where detailed examination of all material seized will be necessary, there will be others where this is impossible. Paragraphs 28 to 34 set out the disclosure duties on prosecutors, again incorporating a shortened version of the corresponding section in the 2005 guidelines, and also highlighting that prosecutors should challenge the lack of, or inadequate, defence statements in writing, copying the document to the court. Paragraphs 35 to 37 set out the disclosure duties on prosecution advocates, incorporating a shortened version of the corresponding section in the 2005 guidelines, and make clear the duty to keep disclosure under review, whenever possible in consultation with the reviewing prosecutor. Paragraphs 39 to 43 deal with the defence, and emphasise the importance of early and meaningful defence engagement and defence statements, including in the magistrates' courts.

Paragraphs 44 to 47 relate to disclosure obligations in magistrates' courts where a not guilty plea is entered. Paragraphs 48 and 49 relate to the Crown Court, particularly cases which involve digital material. Paragraphs 50 to 52 deal with large and complex cases in the Crown Court. Paragraphs 53 to 55 relate to material held by government departments and third parties and paragraphs 56 and 57 to material held by other domestic bodies. Both largely replicate the corresponding sections in the 2005 guidelines. Paragraphs 59 to 64 concern material held overseas (and correspond to paras 58-63 of the 2011 supplementary guidelines on digital material). Paragraphs 65 to 69 deal with applications for non-disclosure in the public interest and largely reproduce the corresponding section in the 2005 guidelines. Finally, paragraphs 70 to 72 ("other disclosure", "material relevant to sentence" and "post-conviction") correspond to the sections relating to material relevant to sentence and the post-conviction period in the 2005 guidelines.

As to the significance of the guidelines in relation to material held overseas, outside the European Union, by entities not subject to the jurisdiction of the United Kingdom, see *R. v. Flook* [2010] 1 Cr.App.R. 30, CA (§§ 12-53, 12-101 in the main work).

Foreword

We are pleased to publish a revised judicial protocol and revised guidance on the disclosure of   **A-242a** unused material in criminal cases. Proper disclosure of unused material, made through a rigorous and carefully considered application of the law, remains a crucial part of a fair trial, and essential to avoiding miscarriages of justice. These new documents are intended to clarify the procedures to be followed and to encourage the active participation of all parties.

They have been prepared following the recommendations of Lord Justice Gross in his September 2011 "Review of Disclosure in Criminal Proceedings" and take account of Lord Justice Gross and Lord Justice Treacy's "Further review of disclosure in criminal proceedings: sanctions for disclosure failure", published in November 2012.

There are important roles for the prosecution, the defence and the court in ensuring that disclosure is conducted properly, including on the part of the investigating, case progression and disclosure officers, as well as the lawyers and advocates. Lord Justice Gross particularly recommended that the guidance on disclosure of unused material in criminal cases should be consolidated and abbreviated. Given all of those involved in this process have separate constitutional roles, the judiciary and the Attorney-General have worked together to produce complementary guidance that is shorter than the previous iterations, but remains comprehensive. The two documents are similarly structured for ease of reference and should be read together.

The Rt. Hon. Dominic Grieve Q.C. M.P., Attorney General

The Rt. Hon. The Lord Thomas, Lord Chief Justice of England and Wales

Introduction

These guidelines are issued by the Attorney General for investigators, prosecutors and defence   **A-243** practitioners on the application of the disclosure regime contained in the Criminal Procedure and Investigations Act 1996 ("CPIA"). The guidelines emphasise the importance of prosecution-led disclosure and the importance of applying the CPIA regime in a "thinking manner", tailored, where appropriate, to the type of investigation or prosecution in question.

The guidelines do not contain the detail of the disclosure regime; they outline the high level principles which should be followed when the disclosure regime is applied.

These guidelines replace the existing Attorney General's Guidelines on Disclosure issued in 2005 and the Supplementary Guidelines on Digital Material issued in 2011, which is an annex to the general guidelines.

The guidelines are intended to operate alongside the Judicial Protocol on the Disclosure of Unused Material in Criminal Cases. They are not designed to be an unequivocal statement of the law at any one time, nor are they a substitute for a thorough understanding of the relevant legislation, codes of practice, case law and procedure.

Readers should note that a review of disclosure in the magistrates' courts is currently being undertaken by H.H.J. Kinch Q.C. and the Chief Magistrate, on behalf of Lord Justice Gross, the Senior Presiding Judge. Amendments may therefore be made to these documents following the recommendations of that review, and in accordance with other forthcoming changes to the criminal justice system.

The importance of disclosure

1. The statutory framework for criminal investigations and disclosure is contained in the Criminal   **A-244** Procedure and Investigations Act 1996 (the CPIA) and the *CPIA Code of Practice*. The CPIA aims to ensure that criminal investigations are conducted in a fair, objective and thorough manner, and requires prosecutors to disclose to the defence material which has not previously been disclosed to the accused and which might reasonably be considered capable of undermining the case for the prosecution against the accused or of assisting the case for the accused. The CPIA requires a timely dialogue between the prosecution, defence and the court to enable the prosecution properly to identify such material.

2. Every accused person has a right to a fair trial, a right long embodied in our law and guaranteed by Article 6 of the European Convention on Human Rights (ECHR). A fair trial is the proper object and expectation of all participants in the trial process. Fair disclosure to the accused is an inseparable

part of a fair trial. A fair trial should not require consideration of irrelevant material and should not involve spurious applications or arguments which serve to divert the trial process from examining the real issues before the court.

3. Properly applied, the CPIA should ensure that material is not disclosed which overburdens the participants in the trial process, diverts attention from the relevant issues, leads to unjustifiable delay, and is wasteful of resources. Consideration of disclosure issues should be an integral part of a good investigation and not something that exists separately.

Disclosure: general principles

A-245   4. Disclosure refers to providing the defence with copies of, or access to, any prosecution material which might reasonably be considered capable of undermining the case for the prosecution against the accused, or of assisting the case for the accused, and which has not previously been disclosed (s.3 CPIA).

5. Prosecutors will only be expected to anticipate what material might undermine their case or strengthen the defence in the light of information available at the time of the disclosure decision, and they may take into account information revealed during questioning.

6. In deciding whether material satisfies the disclosure test, consideration should be given amongst other things to:

    a. the use that might be made of it in cross-examination;

    b. its capacity to support submissions that could lead to:

      (i) the exclusion of evidence;

      (ii) a stay of proceedings, where the material is required to allow a proper application to be made;

      (iii) a court or tribunal finding that any public authority had acted incompatibly with the accused's rights under the ECHR;

    c. its capacity to suggest an explanation or partial explanation of the accused's actions;

    d. the capacity of the material to have a bearing on scientific or medical evidence in the case.

7. It should also be borne in mind that while items of material viewed in isolation may not be reasonably considered to be capable of undermining the prosecution case or assisting the accused, several items together can have that effect.

8. Material relating to the accused's mental or physical health, intellectual capacity, or to any ill treatment which the accused may have suffered when in the investigator's custody is likely to fall within the test for disclosure set out in paragraph 4 above.

9. Disclosure must not be an open-ended trawl of unused material. A critical element to fair and proper disclosure is that the defence play their role to ensure that the prosecution are directed to material which might reasonably be considered capable of undermining the prosecution case or assisting the case for the accused. This process is key to ensuring prosecutors make informed determinations about disclosure of unused material. The defence statement is important in identifying the issues in the case and why it is suggested that the material meets the test for disclosure.

10. Disclosure should be conducted in a thinking manner and never be reduced to a box-ticking exercise[1]; at all stages of the process, there should be consideration of **why** the CPIA disclosure regime requires a particular course of action and what should be done to achieve that aim.

11. There will always be a number of participants in prosecutions and investigations: senior investigation officers, disclosure officers, investigation officers, reviewing prosecutors, leading counsel, junior counsel, and sometimes disclosure counsel. Communication within the "prosecution team" is vital to ensure that all matters which could have a bearing on disclosure issues are given sufficient attention by the right person. This is especially so given many reviewing lawyers will be unable to sit behind the trial advocate throughout the trial. In practice, this is likely to mean that a full log of disclosure decisions (with reasons) must be kept on the file and made available as appropriate to the prosecution team.

12. The role of the reviewing lawyer will be central to ensuring all members of the prosecution team are aware of, and carry out, their duties and role(s). Where this involves counsel or more than one reviewing lawyer, this should be done by giving clear written instructions and record keeping.

13. The centrality of the reviewing lawyer does not mean that he or she has to do all the work personally; on the contrary, it will often mean effective delegation. Where the conduct of a prosecution is assigned to more than one prosecutor, steps must be taken to ensure that all involved in the case properly record their decisions. Subsequent prosecutors must be able to see and understand previous disclosure decisions before carrying out their continuous review function.

14. Investigators must always be alive to the potential need to reveal and prosecutors to the

---

[1] *R. v. Olu, Wilson and Brooks* [2010] EWCA Crim. 2975, [2011] 1 Cr.App.R. 33, CA (at [42]).

potential need to disclose material, in the interests of justice and fairness in the particular circumstances of any case, after the commencement of proceedings but before their duty arises under the Act. For instance, disclosure ought to be made of significant information that might affect a bail decision. This is likely to depend on what the defence chooses to reveal at that stage.

Investigators and disclosure officers

15. Investigators and disclosure officers must be fair and objective and must work together with **A-246** prosecutors to ensure that disclosure obligations are met. Investigators and disclosure officers should be familiar with the CPIA Code of Practice, in particular their obligations to **retain** and **record** relevant material, to **review** it and to **reveal** it to the prosecutor.

16. Whether a case is a summary only matter or a long and complex trial on indictment, it is important that investigators and disclosure officers should approach their duties in a "thinking manner" and not as a box ticking exercise. Where necessary, the reviewing lawyer should be consulted. It is important that investigators and disclosure officers are deployed on cases which are commensurate with their training, skills and experience. The conduct of an investigation provides the foundation for the entire case, and may even impact the conduct of linked cases. It is vital that there is always consideration of disclosure matters at the outset of an investigation, regardless of its size.

17. A fair investigation involves the pursuit of material following all reasonable lines of enquiry, whether they point towards or away from the suspect. What is "reasonable" will depend on the context of the case. A fair investigation does not mean an endless investigation: investigators and disclosure officers must give thought to defining, and thereby limiting, the scope of their investigations, seeking the guidance of the prosecutor where appropriate.

18. Where there are a number of disclosure officers assigned to a case, there should be a lead disclosure officer who is the focus for enquiries and whose responsibility it is to ensure that the investigator's disclosure obligations are complied with. Where appropriate, regular case conferences and other meetings should be held to ensure prosecutors are apprised of all relevant developments in investigations. Full records should be kept of such meetings.

19. The *CPIA Code of Practice* encourages investigators and disclosure officers to seek advice from prosecutors about whether any particular item of material may be relevant to the investigation, and if so, how. Investigators and disclosure officers should record key decisions taken on these matters and be prepared to account for their actions later. An identical approach is not called for in each and every case.

20. Investigators are to approach their task seeking to establish what actually happened. They are to be fair and objective.

21. Disclosure officers (or their deputies) must inspect, view, listen to or search all relevant material that has been retained by the investigator and the disclosure officer must provide a personal declaration to the effect that this task has been undertaken. In some cases, a detailed examination of all material seized may be required. In others, however, a detailed examination of every item of material seized would be virtually impossible: see the **Annex**.

22. Prosecutors only have knowledge of matters which are revealed to them by investigators and disclosure officers, and the schedules are the written means by which that revelation takes place. Whatever the approach taken by investigators or disclosure officers to examining the material gathered or generated in the course of an investigation, it is crucial that disclosure officers record their reasons for a particular approach in writing.

23. In meeting the obligations in paragraph 6.9 and 8.1 of the code, schedules must be completed in a form which not only reveals sufficient information to the prosecutor, but which demonstrates a transparent and thinking approach to the disclosure exercise, to command the confidence of the defence and the court. Descriptions on non-sensitive schedules must be clear and accurate, and must contain sufficient detail to enable the prosecutor to make an informed decision on disclosure. The use of abbreviations and acronyms can be problematic and lead to difficulties in appreciating the significance of the material.

24. Sensitive schedules must contain sufficiently clear descriptions to enable the prosecutor to make an informed decision as to whether or not the material itself should be viewed, to the extent possible without compromising the confidentiality of the information.

25. It may become apparent to an investigator that some material obtained in the course of an investigation, either because it was considered to be potentially relevant, or because it was inextricably linked to material that was relevant, is, in fact, incapable of impact. It is not necessary to retain such material, although the investigator should err on the side of caution in reaching that conclusion and should be particularly mindful of the fact that some investigations continue over some time and that what is incapable of impact may change over time. The advice of the prosecutor should be sought where appropriate.

26. Disclosure officers must specifically draw material to the attention of the prosecutor for consideration where they have any doubt as to whether it might reasonably be considered capable of undermining the prosecution case or of assisting the case for the accused.

27. Disclosure officers must seek the advice and assistance of prosecutors when in doubt as to their responsibility as early as possible. They must deal expeditiously with requests by the prosecutor for further information on material, which may lead to disclosure.

Prosecutors

28. Prosecutors are responsible for making proper disclosure in consultation with the disclosure officer. The duty of disclosure is a continuing one and disclosure should be kept under review. In addition, prosecutors should ensure that advocates in court are properly instructed as to disclosure issues. Prosecutors must also be alert to the need to provide advice to, and where necessary probe actions taken by, disclosure officers to ensure that disclosure obligations are met. There should be no aspects of an investigation about which prosecutors are unable to ask probing questions.

29. Prosecutors must review schedules prepared by disclosure officers thoroughly and must be alert to the possibility that relevant material may exist which has not been revealed to them or material included which should not have been. If no schedules have been provided, or there are apparent omissions from the schedules, or documents or other items are inadequately described or are unclear, the prosecutor must at once take action to obtain properly completed schedules. Likewise schedules should be returned for amendment if irrelevant items are included. If prosecutors remain dissatisfied with the quality or content of the schedules they must raise the matter with a senior investigator to resolve the matter satisfactorily.

30. Where prosecutors have reason to believe that the disclosure officer has not discharged the obligation in paragraph 21 to inspect, view, listen to or search relevant material, they must at once raise the matter with the disclosure officer and request that it be done. Where appropriate the matter should be raised with the officer in the case or a senior officer.

31. Prosecutors should copy the defence statement to the disclosure officer and investigator as soon as reasonably practicable and prosecutors should advise the investigator if, in their view, reasonable and relevant lines of further enquiry should be pursued. If the defence statement does point to other reasonable lines of enquiry, further investigation is required and evidence obtained as a result of these enquiries may be used as part of the prosecution case or to rebut the defence.

32. It is vital that prosecutors consider defence statements thoroughly. Prosecutors cannot comment upon, or invite inferences to be drawn from, failures in defence disclosure otherwise than in accordance with section 11 of the CPIA. Prosecutors may cross-examine the accused on differences between the defence case put at trial and that set out in his or her defence statement. In doing so, it may be appropriate to apply to the judge under section 6E of the CPIA for copies of the statement to be given to a jury, edited if necessary to remove inadmissible material. Prosecutors should examine the defence statement to see whether it points to other lines of enquiry.

33. Prosecutors should challenge the lack of, or inadequate, defence statements in writing, copying the document to the court and the defence and seeking directions from the court to require the provision of an adequate statement from the defence.

34. If the material does not fulfil the disclosure test there is no requirement to disclose it. For this purpose, the parties' respective cases should not be restrictively analysed but must be carefully analysed to ascertain the specific facts the prosecution seek to establish and the specific grounds on which the charges are resisted.

Prosecution advocates

35. Prosecution advocates should ensure that all material which ought to be disclosed under the Act is disclosed to the defence. However, prosecution advocates cannot be expected to disclose material if they are not aware of its existence. As far as is possible, prosecution advocates must place themselves in a fully informed position to enable them to make decisions on disclosure.

36. Upon receipt of instructions, prosecution advocates should consider as a priority all the information provided regarding disclosure of material. Prosecution advocates should consider, in every case, whether they can be satisfied that they are in possession of all relevant documentation and that they have been fully instructed regarding disclosure matters. If as a result the advocate considers that further information or action is required, written advice should promptly be provided setting out the aspects that need clarification or action.

37. The prosecution advocate must keep decisions regarding disclosure under review until the conclusion of the trial, whenever possible in consultation with the reviewing prosecutor. The prosecution advocate must in every case specifically consider whether he or she can satisfactorily discharge the duty of continuing review on the basis of the material supplied already, or whether it is necessary

to inspect further material or to reconsider material already inspected. Prosecution advocates must not abrogate their responsibility under the CPIA by disclosing material which does not pass the test for disclosure, set out in paragraph 4, above.

38. There remains no basis in practice or law for counsel to counsel disclosure.

Defence

39. Defence engagement must be early and meaningful for the CPIA regime to function as intended. Defence statements are an integral part of this and are intended to help focus the attention of the prosecutor, court and co-defendants on the relevant issues in order to identify exculpatory unused material. Defence statements should be drafted in accordance with the relevant provisions of the CPIA. **A-249**

40. Defence requests for further disclosure should ordinarily only be answered by the prosecution if the request is relevant to and directed to an issue identified in the defence statement. If it is not, then a further or amended defence statement should be sought by the prosecutor and obtained before considering the request for further disclosure.

41. In some cases that involve extensive unused material that is within the knowledge of a defendant, the defence will be expected to provide the prosecution and the court with assistance in identifying material which is suggested to pass the test for disclosure.

42. The prosecution's continuing duty to keep disclosure under review is crucial, and particular attention must be paid to understanding the significance of developments in the case on the unused material and earlier disclosure decisions. Meaningful defence engagement will help the prosecution to keep disclosure under review. The continuing duty of review for prosecutors is less likely to require the disclosure of further material to the defence if the defence have clarified and articulated their case, as required by the CPIA.

43. In the magistrates' courts, where the provision of a defence statement is not mandatory, early identification of the material issues by the defence, whether through a defence statement, case management form or otherwise, will help the prosecution to focus its preparation of the case and allow any defence disclosure queries to be dealt with promptly and accurately.

Magistrates' courts (including the youth court)

44. The majority of criminal cases are heard in the magistrates' court. The requirement for the prosecution to provide initial disclosure only arises after a not guilty plea has been entered but prosecutors should be alert to the possibility that material may exist which should be disclosed to the defendant prior to the CPIA requirements applying to the case.[2] **A-250**

45. Where a not guilty plea is entered in the magistrates' court, prosecutors should ensure that any issues of dispute which are raised are noted on the file. They should also seek to obtain a copy of any Magistrates' Court Trial Preparation Form. Consideration of the issues raised in court and on the trial preparation form will assist in deciding what material undermines the prosecution case or assists the defendant.

46. Where a matter is set down for trial in the magistrates' court, prosecutors should ensure that the investigator is requested to supply any outstanding disclosure schedules as a matter of urgency. Prosecutors should serve initial disclosure in sufficient time to ensure that the trial date is effective.

47. There is no requirement for a defence statement to be served in the magistrates' court but it should be noted that if none is given the court has no power to hear an application for further prosecution disclosure under section 8 of the CPIA and the Criminal Procedure Rules.

Cases in the Crown Court

48. The exponential increase in the use of technology in society means that many routine Crown Court cases are increasingly likely to have to engage with digital material of some form. It is not only in large and complex cases that there may be large quantities of such material. Where such investigations involve digital material, it will be virtually impossible for investigators (or prosecutors) to examine every item of such material individually and there should be no expectation that such material will be so examined. Having consulted with the prosecution as appropriate, disclosure officers should determine what their approach should be to the examination of the material. Investigators or disclosure officers should decide how best to pursue a reasonable line of enquiry in relation to the relevant digital material, and ensure that the extent and manner of the examination are commensurate with the issues in the case. **A-251**

49. Consideration should be given to any local or national agreements in relation to disclosure in "Early Guilty Plea Scheme" cases.

---

[2] See for example *R. v. DPP, ex p. Lee* [1999] 2 Cr.App.R. 304, DC.

Large and complex cases in the Crown Court

A-252   50. The particular challenges presented by large and complex criminal prosecutions require an approach to disclosure which is specifically tailored to the needs of such cases. In these cases more than any other is the need for careful thought to be given to prosecution-led disclosure matters from the very earliest stage. It is essential that the prosecution takes a grip on the case and its disclosure requirements from the very outset of the investigation, which must continue throughout all aspects of the case preparation.

Disclosure management documents

A-253   51. Accordingly, investigations and prosecutions of large and complex cases should be carefully defined and accompanied by a clear investigation and prosecution strategy. The approach to disclosure in such cases should be outlined in a document which should be served on the defence and the court at an early stage. Such documents, sometimes known as disclosure management documents, will require careful preparation and presentation, tailored to the individual case. They may include:

    a. where prosecutors and investigators operate in an integrated office, an explanation as to how the disclosure responsibilities have been managed;

    b. a brief summary of the prosecution case and a statement outlining how the prosecutor's general approach will comply with the CPIA regime, these guidelines and the Judicial Protocol on the Disclosure of Unused Material in Criminal Cases;

    c. the prosecutor's understanding of the defence case, including information revealed during interview;

    d. an outline of the prosecution's general approach to disclosure, which may include detail relating to:

       (i) digital material: explaining the method and extent of examination, in accordance with the **Annex** to these guidelines;

       (ii) video footage;

       (iii) linked investigations: explaining the nexus between investigations, any memoranda of understanding or disclosure agreements between investigators;

       (iv) third party and foreign material, including steps taken to obtain the material;

       (v) reasonable lines of enquiry: a summary of the lines pursued, particularly those that point away from the suspect, or which may assist the defence;

       (vi) credibility of a witness: confirmation that witness checks, including those of professional witnesses have, or will be, carried out.

52. Thereafter the prosecution should follow the disclosure management document. They are living documents and should be amended in light of developments in the case; they should be kept up to date as the case progresses. Their use will assist the court in its own case management and will enable the defence to engage from an early stage with the prosecution's proposed approach to disclosure.

Material not held by the prosecution

Involvement of other agencies: material held by other government departments and third parties

A-254   53. Where it appears to an investigator, disclosure officer or prosecutor that a government department or other Crown body has material that may be relevant to an issue in the case, reasonable steps should be taken to identify and consider such material. Although what is reasonable will vary from case to case, the prosecution should inform the department or other body of the nature of its case and of relevant issues in the case in respect of which the department or body might possess material, and ask whether it has any such material.

54. It should be remembered that investigators, disclosure officers and prosecutors cannot be regarded to be in constructive possession of material held by government departments or Crown bodies simply by virtue of their status as government departments or Crown bodies.

55. Where, after reasonable steps have been taken to secure access to such material, access is denied, the investigator, disclosure officer or prosecutor should consider what if any further steps might be taken to obtain the material or inform the defence. The final decision on any further steps will be for the prosecutor.

Third party material: other domestic bodies

A-255   56. There may be cases where the investigator, disclosure officer or prosecutor believes that a third party (for example, a local authority, a social services department, a hospital, a doctor, a school, a provider of forensic services) has material or information which might be relevant to the prosecution case. In such cases, investigators, disclosure officers and prosecutors should take reasonable steps to identify, secure and consider material held by any third party where it appears to the investigator, disclosure officer or prosecutor that (a) such material exists and (b) that it may be relevant to an issue in the case.

57. If the investigator, disclosure officer or prosecutor seeks access to the material or information but the third party declines or refuses to allow access to it, the matter should not be left. If despite any reasons offered by the third party it is still believed that it is reasonable to seek production of the material or information, and the requirements of section 2 of the Criminal Procedure (Attendance of Witnesses) Act 1965 or as appropriate section 97 of the Magistrates' Courts Act 1980 are satisfied (or any other relevant power), then the prosecutor or investigator should apply for a witness summons causing a representative of the third party to produce the material to the court.

58. Sometimes, for example through multi-agency working arrangements, investigators, disclosure officers or prosecutors may become aware of the content or nature of material held by a third party. Consultation with the relevant third party must always take place before disclosure is made; there may be public interest reasons to apply to the court for an order for non-disclosure in the public interest, in accordance with the procedure outlined in paragraph 65 and following.

International matters

59. The obligations under the CPIA Code to pursue all reasonable lines of enquiry apply to material held overseas. **A-256**

60. Where it appears that there is relevant material, the prosecutor must take reasonable steps to obtain it, either informally or making use of the powers contained in the Crime (International Co-operation) Act 2003 and any EU and international conventions. See CPS Guidance "Obtaining Evidence and Information from Abroad".

61. There may be cases where a foreign state or a foreign court refuses to make the material available to the investigator or prosecutor. There may be other cases where the foreign state, though willing to show the material to investigators, will not allow the material to be copied or otherwise made available and the courts of the foreign state will not order its provision.

62. It is for these reasons that there is no absolute duty on the prosecutor to disclose relevant material held overseas by entities not subject to the jurisdiction of the courts in England and Wales. However consideration should be given to whether the type of material believed to be held can be provided to the defence.

63. The obligation on the investigator and prosecutor under the CPIA is to take reasonable steps. Where investigators are allowed to examine files of a foreign state but are not allowed to take copies or notes or list the documents held, there is no breach by the prosecution in its duty of disclosure by reason of its failure to obtain such material, provided reasonable steps have been taken to try and obtain the material. Prosecutors have a margin of consideration as to what steps are appropriate in the particular case but prosecutors must be alive to their duties and there may be some circumstances where these duties cannot be met. Whether the prosecutor has taken reasonable steps is for the court to determine in each case if the matter is raised.

64. In these circumstances it is important that the position is clearly set out in writing so that the court and the defence know what the position is. Investigators and prosecutors must record and explain the situation and set out, insofar as they are permitted by the foreign state, such information as they can and the steps they have taken.

Applications for non-disclosure in the public interest

65. The CPIA allows prosecutors to apply to the court for an order to withhold material which would otherwise fall to be disclosed if disclosure would give rise to a real risk of serious prejudice to an important public interest. Before making such an application, prosecutors should aim to disclose as much of the material as they properly can (for example, by giving the defence redacted or edited copies or summaries). Neutral material or material damaging to the defendant need not be disclosed and there is no need to bring it to the attention of the court. Only in truly borderline cases should the prosecution seek a judicial ruling on whether material in its possession should be disclosed. **A-257**

66. Prior to the hearing, the prosecutor and the prosecution advocate must examine all material which is the subject matter of the application and make any necessary enquiries of the investigator. The investigator must be frank with the prosecutor about the full extent of the sensitive material. Prior to or at the hearing, the court must be provided with full and accurate information about the material.

67. The prosecutor (or representative) and/or investigator should attend such applications. Section 16 of the CPIA allows a person claiming to have an interest in the sensitive material to apply to the court for the opportunity to be heard at the application.

68. The principles set out at paragraph 36 of *R. v. H.* [2004] 2 A.C. 134, [2004] UKHL 3, should be applied rigorously, firstly by the prosecutor and then by the court considering the material. It is essential that these principles are scrupulously adhered to, to ensure that the procedure for examination of material in the absence of the accused is compliant with Article 6.

69. If prosecutors conclude that a fair trial cannot take place because material which satisfies the test for disclosure cannot be disclosed, and that this cannot be remedied by the above procedure; how the case is presented; or by any other means, they should not continue with the case.

Other disclosure

A-258   70. Disclosure of any material that is made outside the ambit of CPIA will attract confidentiality by virtue of *Taylor v. Serious Fraud Office* [1999] 2 A.C. 177, HL.

Material relevant to sentence

A-259   71. In all cases the prosecutor must consider disclosing in the interests of justice any material which is relevant to sentence (*e.g.* information which might mitigate the seriousness of the offence or assist the accused to lay blame in part upon a co-accused or another person).

Post-conviction

A-260   72. Where, after the conclusion of the proceedings, material comes to light, that might cast doubt upon the safety of the conviction, the prosecutor must consider disclosure of such material.

Applicability of these guidelines

A-261   73. These guidelines shall have immediate effect.

Annex: Attorney General's Guidelines on Disclosure: Supplementary Guidelines on Digitally Stored Material (2011)

A-262   A1. The guidelines are intended to supplement the Attorney General's Guidelines on Disclosure.

A2. As a result of the number of cases now involving digitally stored material and the scale of the digital material that may be involved, more detailed guidance is considered to be needed. The objective of these guidelines is to set out how material satisfying the tests for disclosure can best be identified and disclosed to the defence without imposing unrealistic or disproportionate demands on the investigator and prosecutor.

A3. The approach set out in these guidelines is in line with existing best practice, in that:

    a. investigating and prosecuting agencies, especially in large and complex cases, will apply their respective case management and disclosure strategies and policies and be transparent with the defence and the courts about how the prosecution has approached complying with its disclosure obligations in the context of the individual case; and,

    b. the defence will be expected to play their part in defining the real issues in the case. In this context, the defence will be invited to participate in defining the scope of the reasonable searches that may be made of digitally stored material by the investigator to identify material that might reasonably be expected to undermine the prosecution case or assist the defence.

A4. Only if this approach is followed can the courts be in a position to use their case management powers effectively and to determine applications for disclosure fairly.

A5. The Attorney General's Guidelines are not detailed operational guidelines. They are intended to set out a common approach to be adopted in the context of digitally stored material.

Types of digital material

A-263   A6. Digital material falls into two categories: the first category is material which is created natively within an electronic environment (*e.g.* email, office files, system files, digital photographs, audio, etc.); the second category is material which has been digitised from an analogue form (*e.g.* scanned copy of a document, scanned photograph, a faxed document). Irrespective of the way in which technology changes, the categorisation of digital material will remain the same.

A7. Digital material is usually held on one of the three types of media. Optical media (*e.g.* CD, DVD, Blu-ray) and solid-state media (*e.g.* removable memory cards, solid-state music players or mobile devices, etc.) cater for usually lower volume storage. Magnetic media (*e.g.* disk drives and back up tapes) usually cater for high volume storage.

General principles for investigators

A8. The general principles[3] to be followed by investigators in handling and examining digital   **A-264**
material are:

    a. no action taken by investigators or their agents should change data held on a computer
or storage media which may subsequently be relied upon in court;

    b. in circumstances where a person finds it necessary to access original data held on
computer or storage media, that person must be competent to do so and be able to give
evidence explaining the relevance and implications of their actions;

    c. an audit trail or other record of all processes applied to computer-based electronic
evidence should be created and preserved; an independent third party should be able to
examine those processes (see further the sections headed "Record keeping" and "Scheduling" below); and

    d. the person in charge of the investigation has overall responsibility for ensuring that the
law and these principles are followed.

A9. Where an investigator has reasonable grounds for believing that digital material may contain
material subject to legal professional privilege, very strong legal constraints apply. No digital material
may be seized which an investigator has reasonable grounds for believing to be subject to legal
privilege, other than where the provisions of the Criminal Justice and Police Act 2001 apply. Strict
controls need to be applied where privileged material is seized. See the more detailed section on
legal professional privilege starting at paragraph A28, below.

Seizure, relevance and retention

A10. The legal obligations are to be found in a combination of the Police and Criminal Evidence   **A-265**
Act 1984 (PACE), the Criminal Justice and Police Act 2001 (CJPA 2001) and the Criminal Procedure
and Investigations Act 1996 (the CPIA 1996).

A11. These guidelines also apply to digital material seized or imaged under other statutory
provisions. For example, the Serious Fraud Office has distinct powers of seizure under warrant
obtained under section 2(4) of the Criminal Justice Act 1987. In cases concerning indecent images of
children and obscene material, special provisions apply to the handling, storage and copying of such
material. Practitioners should refer to specific guidance on the application of those provisions.

Seizure

A12. Before searching a suspect's premises where digital evidence is likely to be found, considera-   **A-266**
tion must be given to what sort of evidence is likely to be found and in what volume, whether it is
likely to be possible to view and copy, if relevant, the material at the location (it is not uncommon
with the advent of cloud computing for digital material to be hosted by a third party) and to what
should be seized. Business and commercial premises will often have very substantial amounts of
digital material stored on computers and other media. Investigators will need to consider the
practicalities of seizing computer hard drives and other media, the effect this may have on the business and, where it is not feasible to obtain an image of digital material, the likely timescale for returning seized items.

A13. In deciding whether to seize and retain digital material it is important that the investigator
either complies with the procedure under the relevant statutory authority, relying either on statutory
powers or a search warrant, or obtains the owner's consent. In particular, investigators need to be
aware of the constraints applying to legally privileged material.

A14. A computer hard drive or single item of media, such as a back up tape, is a single storage
entity. This means that if any digital material found on the hard drive or other media can lawfully be
seized the computer hard drive or single item of media may, if appropriate, be seized or imaged. In
some circumstances investigators may wish to image specific folders, files or categories of data where
it is feasible to do so without seizing the hard drive or other media, or instead of taking an image of
all data on the hard drive or other media. In practice, the configuration of most systems means that
data may be contained across a number of hard drives and more than one hard drive or item of
media may be required in order to access the information sought.

A15. Digital material must not be seized if an investigator has reasonable grounds for believing it
is subject to legal professional privilege, other than where sections 50 or 51 of the CJPA 2001 apply.
If such material is seized it must be isolated from other seized material and any other investigation
material in the possession of the investigating authority.

---

[3] Based on: Association of Chief Police Officers: Good Practice Guide for Computer Based Electronic Evidence Version
0.1.4.

The Police and Criminal Evidence Act 1984

A-267

A16. PACE 1984 provides powers to seize and retain anything for which the search has been authorised or after arrest, other than items attracting legal professional privilege.[4] In addition, there is a general power to seize anything which is on the premises if there are reasonable grounds to believe that it has been obtained in the commission of an offence, or that it is evidence and that it is necessary to seize it to prevent it being concealed, lost, altered or destroyed.[5] There is another related power to require information which is stored in any electronic form and is accessible from the premises to be produced in a form in which it can be taken away and in which it is visible and legible or from which it can readily be produced in a visible and legible form.[6]

A17. An image (a forensically sound copy) of the digital material may be taken at the location of the search. Where the investigator makes an image of the digital material at the location, the original need not be seized. Alternatively, when originals are taken, investigators must be prepared to copy or image the material for the owners when reasonably practicable in accordance with PACE 1984, Code B 7.17.

A18. Where it is not possible or reasonably practicable to image the computer or hard drive, it will need to be removed from the location or premises for examination elsewhere. This allows the investigator to seize and sift material for the purpose of identifying that which meets the tests for retention in accordance with the 1984 PACE.[7]

The Criminal Justice and Police Act 2001

A-268

A19. The additional powers of seizure in sections 50 and 51 of the CJPA 2001 Act [*sic*] only extend the scope of existing powers of search and seizure under the PACE and other specified statutory authorities[8] where the relevant conditions and circumstances apply.

A20. Investigators must be careful only to exercise powers under the CJPA 2001 when it is necessary and not to remove any more material than is justified. The removal of large volumes of material, much of which may not ultimately be retainable, may have serious consequences for the owner of the material, particularly when they are involved in business or other commercial activities.

A21. A written notice must be given to the occupier of the premises where items are seized under sections 50 and 51.[9]

A22. Until material seized under the CJPA 2001 has been examined, it must be kept securely and separately from any material seized under other powers. Any such material must be examined as soon as reasonably practicable to determine which elements may be retained and which should be returned. Regard must be had to the desirability of allowing the person from whom the property was seized — or a person with an interest in the property — an opportunity of being present or represented at the examination.

Retention

A-269

A23. Where material is seized under the powers conferred by PACE the duty to retain it under the code of practice issued under the CPIA is subject to the provisions on retention under section 22 of PACE. Material seized under sections 50 and 51 of the CJPA 2001 may be retained or returned in accordance with sections 53–58 of that Act.

A24. Retention is limited to evidence and relevant material (as defined in the code of practice issued under the CPIA). Where either evidence or relevant material is inextricably linked to nonrelevant material which is not reasonably practicable to separate, that material can also be retained. Inextricably linked material is material that is not reasonably practicable to separate from other linked material without prejudicing the use of that other material in any investigation or proceedings.

A25. However, inextricably linked material must not be examined, imaged, copied or used for any purpose other than for providing the source of or the integrity of the linked material.

A26. There are four categories of material that may be retained:

    a. material that is evidence or potential evidence in the case; where material is retained for evidential purposes there will be a strong argument that the whole thing (or an authenticated image or copy) should be retained for the purpose of proving provenance and continuity;

---

[4] By warrant under s.8, and Sched. 1 and s.18.
[5] S.19.
[6] S.20.
[7] Special provision exists for investigations conducted by Her Majesty's Revenue and Customs in the application of their powers under PACE — see s.114(2)(b) — and the CJPA 2001.
[8] Sched. 1 to the CJPA 2001.
[9] S.52.

b. where evidential material has been retained, inextricably linked non-relevant material which is not reasonably practicable to separate can also be retained (PACE, Code B, para. 7);

c. an investigator should retain material that is relevant to the investigation and required to be scheduled as unused material; this is broader than but includes the duty to retain material which may satisfy the test for prosecution disclosure; the general duty to retain relevant material is set out in the CPIA code at paragraph 5; or

d. material which is inextricably linked to relevant unused material which of itself may not be relevant material; such material should be retained (PACE, Code B, para. 7).

A27. The balance of any digital material should be returned in accordance with sections 53–55 of the CJPA 2001 if seized under that Act.

Legal professional privilege (LPP)

A28. No digital material may be seized which an investigator has reasonable grounds for believing **A-270** to be subject to LPP, other than under the additional powers of seizure in the CJPA 2001.

A29. The CJPA 2001 enables an investigator to seize relevant items which contain LPP material where it is not reasonably practicable on the search premises to separate LPP material from non-LPP material.

A30. Where LPP material or material suspected of containing LPP is seized, it must be isolated from the other material which has been seized in the investigation. The mechanics of securing property vary according to the circumstances; "bagging up", *i.e.* placing materials in sealed bags or containers, and strict subsequent control of access, is the appropriate procedure in many cases.

A31. Where material has been identified as potentially containing LPP it must be reviewed by a lawyer independent of the prosecuting authority. No member of the investigative or prosecution team involved in either the current investigation or, if the LPP material relates to other criminal proceedings, in those proceedings should have sight of or access to the LPP material.

A32. If the material is voluminous, search terms or other filters may have to be used to identify the LPP material. If so this will also have to be done by someone independent and not connected with the investigation.

A33. It is essential that anyone dealing with LPP material maintains proper records showing the way in which the material has been handled and those who have had access to it as well as decisions taken in relation to that material.

A34. LPP material can only be retained in specific circumstances in accordance with section 54 of the CJPA 2001, *i.e.* where the property which comprises the LPP material has been lawfully seized and it is not reasonably practicable for the item to be separated from the rest of the property without prejudicing the use of the rest of the property. LPP material which cannot be retained must be returned as soon as practicable after the seizure without waiting for the whole examination of the seized material.

Excluded and special procedure material

A35. Similar principles to those that apply to LPP material apply to excluded or special procedure **A-271** material, as set out in section 55 of the CJPA 2001.[10]

Encryption

A36. Part III of the Regulation of Investigatory Powers Act 2000 (RIPA) and the *Investigation of* **A-272** *Protected Electronic Information Code of Practice* govern encryption. See the CPS's Guidance RIPA, Part III.

A37. RIPA enables specified law enforcement agencies to compel individuals or companies to provide passwords or encryption keys for the purpose of rendering protected material readable. Failure to comply with RIPA, Part III orders is a criminal offence. The code of practice provides guidance when exercising powers under RIPA, to require disclosure of protected electronic data in an intelligible form or to acquire the means by which protected electronic data may be accessed or put in an intelligible form.

Sifting/examination

A38. In complying with its duty of disclosure, the prosecution should follow the procedure as **A-273** outlined below.

A39. Where digital material is examined, the extent and manner of inspecting, viewing or listening will depend on the nature of the material and its form.

---

[10] Special provision exists for investigations conducted by Her Majesty's Revenue and Customs in the application of their powers under PACE — see s.114(2)(b) — and the CJPA.

A40. It is important for investigators and prosecutors to remember that the duty under the CPIA code of practice is to "pursue all reasonable lines of enquiry including those that point away from the suspect". Lines of enquiry, of whatever kind, should be pursued only if they are reasonable in the context of the individual case. It is not the duty of the prosecution to comb through all the material in its possession – *e.g.* every word or byte of computer material – on the look out for anything which might conceivably or speculatively assist the defence. The duty of the prosecution is to disclose material which might reasonably be considered capable of undermining its case or assisting the case for the accused which they become aware of, or to which their attention is drawn.

A41. In some cases the sift may be conducted by an investigator/disclosure officer manually assessing the content of the computer or other digital material from its directory and determining which files are relevant and should be retained for evidence or unused material.

A42. In other cases such an approach may not be feasible. Where there is an enormous volume of material it is perfectly proper for the investigator/disclosure officer to search it by sample, key words, or other appropriate search tools or analytical techniques to locate relevant passages, phrases and identifiers.

A43. In cases involving very large quantities of data, the person in charge of the investigation will develop a strategy setting out how the material should be analysed or searched to identify categories of data. Where search tools are used to examine digital material it will usually be appropriate to provide the accused and his or her legal representative with a copy of reasonable search terms used, or to be used, and invite them to suggest any further reasonable search terms. If search terms are suggested which the investigator or prosecutor believes will not be productive – for example because of the use of common words that are likely to identify a mass of irrelevant material, the investigator or prosecutor is entitled to open a dialogue with the defence representative with a view to agreeing sensible refinements. The purpose of this dialogue is to ensure that reasonable and proportionate searches can be carried out.

A44. It may be necessary to carry out sampling and searches on more than one occasion, especially as there is a duty on the prosecutor to keep duties of disclosure under review. To comply with this duty it may be appropriate (and should be considered) where further evidence or unused material is obtained in the course of the investigation; the defence statement is served on the prosecutor; the defendant makes an application under section 8 of the CPIA for disclosure; or the defendant requests that further sampling or searches be carried out (provided it is a reasonable line of enquiry).

Record keeping

A45. A record or log must be made of all digital material seized or imaged and subsequently retained as relevant to the investigation.

A46. In cases involving very large quantities of data where the person in charge of the investigation has developed a strategy setting out how the material should be analysed or searched to identify categories of data, a record should be made of the strategy and the analytical techniques used to search the data. The record should include details of the person who has carried out the process and the date and time it was carried out. In such cases the strategy should record the reasons why certain categories have been searched for (such as names, companies, dates, etc).

A47. In any case it is important that any searching or analytical processing of digital material, as well as the data identified by that process, is properly recorded. So far as practicable, what is required is a record of the terms of the searches or processing that has been carried out. This means that in principle the following details may be recorded:

  a. a record of all searches carried out, including the date of each search and the person(s) who conducted it;

  b. a record of all search words or terms used on each search; however where it is impracticable to record each word or terms (such as where Boolean searches or search strings or conceptual searches are used) it will usually be sufficient to record each broad category of search;

  c. a log of the key judgements made while refining the search strategy in the light of what is found, or deciding not to carry out further searches; and

  d. where material relating to a "hit" is not examined, the decision not to examine should be explained in the record of examination or in a statement; for instance, a large number of "hits" may be obtained in relation to a particular search word or term, but material relating to the "hits" is not examined because they do not appear to be relevant to the investigation; any subsequent refinement of the search terms and further hits should also be noted and explained as above.

A48. Just as it is not necessary for the investigator or prosecutor to produce records of every search made of hard copy material, it is not necessary to produce records of what may be many hundreds of searches or analyses that have been carried out on digitally stored material, simply to demonstrate that these have been done. It should be sufficient for the prosecution to explain how the disclosure exercise has been approached and to give the accused or suspect's legal representative an opportunity to participate in defining the reasonable searches to be made, as described in the section on sifting/examination.

Scheduling

A49. The disclosure officer should ensure that scheduling of relevant material is carried out in ac-   **A-275**
cordance with the CPIA code of practice. This requires each item of unused material to be listed separately on the unused material schedule and numbered consecutively. The description of each item should make clear the nature of the item and should contain sufficient detail to enable the prosecutor to decide whether he needs to inspect the material before deciding whether or not it should be disclosed (see para. A24).

A50. In some enquiries it may not be practicable to list each item of material separately. If so, these may be listed in a block and described by quantity and generic title. Even if the material is listed in a block, the search terms used and any items of material which might satisfy the disclosure test are listed and described separately. In practical terms this will mean, where appropriate, cross referencing the schedules to your disclosure management document.

A51. The remainder of any computer hard drive/media containing material which is not responsive to search terms or other analytical technique or not identified by any "hits", and material identified by "hits" but not examined, is unused material and should be recorded (if appropriate by a generic description) and retained.

A52. Where continuation sheets of the unused material schedule are used, or additional schedules are sent subsequently, the item numbering must be, where possible, sequential to all other items on earlier schedules.

Third party material

A53. Third party material is material held by a person, organisation, or government department   **A-275a**
other than the investigator and prosecutor within the UK or outside the UK.

Within the UK

A54. The CPIA code and the AG's Guidelines make clear the obligation on the prosecution to   **A-275b**
pursue all reasonable lines of enquiry in relation to material held by third parties within the UK.

A55. If as a result of the duty to pursue all reasonable lines of enquiry, the investigator or prosecutor obtains or receives the material from the third party, then it must be dealt with in accordance with the CPIA, *i.e.* the prosecutor must disclose material if it meets the disclosure tests, subject to any public interest immunity claim. The person who has an interest in the material (the third party) may make representations to the court concerning public interest immunity (see s.16 of the CPIA 1996).

A56. Material not in the possession of an investigator or prosecutor falls outside the CPIA. In such cases the Attorney General's Guidelines on Disclosure prescribe the approach to be taken to disclosure of material held by third parties as does the judicial disclosure protocol.

B. ACCEPTANCE OF PLEAS

Introduction

The Attorney-General issued revised guidelines on the acceptance of pleas, which came into   **A-276**
force on December 1, 2009. The principal changes were to Part C (basis of plea). Paragraph C.1 now makes it clear that in multi-handed cases, any bases of plea must be factually consistent with each other. Paragraph C.2 now states that a defence advocate must reduce an acceptable basis of plea to writing in all cases save for those in which the defendant has indicated that the guilty plea has been or will be tendered on the basis of the prosecution case (previously this was not necessary in cases where the issue was "simple"). Paragraph C.4 now additionally provides that, where the basis of plea differs in its implications for sentencing or the making of ancillary orders from the case originally outlined by the prosecution, the prosecution advocate must ensure that such differences are accurately reflected in the written record prior to showing it to the prosecuting authority. New paragraph C.6 provides that in all cases where it is likely to assist the court where the sentencing issues are complex or unfamiliar, the prosecution must add to the written outline of the case served upon the court a summary of the key considerations, taking the form of brief

notes on (a) any statutory limitations, (b) any relevant sentencing authorities or guidelines, (c) the scope for any ancillary orders, and (d) the age of the defendant and information regarding any outstanding offences. Paragraph C.7 was new and clarifies that the prosecution are able to provide further written information where they think that it is likely to assist the judge or where the judge requests it. Old paragraph C.7 became new paragraph C.8, and was amended to ensure that the procedure to be followed where the prosecution advocate takes issue with all or part of the written basis of plea is in line with the then consolidated criminal practice direction. Old paragraph C.8 is now paragraph C.11. For the relevant provisions of *Criminal Practice Direction (Sentence) B* [2013] 1 W.L.R. 3164, see §§ 4-175 and 5-91 *et seq.* in the main work; and *post*, A-299 *et seq.*

ATTORNEY-GENERAL'S GUIDELINES ON THE ACCEPTANCE OF PLEAS AND THE PROSECUTOR'S ROLE IN THE SENTENCING EXERCISE

A. Foreword

A-277
A:1. Prosecutors have an important role in protecting the victim's interests in the criminal justice process, not least in the acceptance of pleas and the sentencing exercise. The basis of plea, particularly in a case that is not contested, is the vehicle through which the victim's voice is heard. Factual inaccuracies in pleas in mitigation cause distress and offence to victims, the families of victims and witnesses. This can take many forms but may be most acutely felt when the victim is dead and the family hears inaccurate assertions about the victim's character or lifestyle. Prosecution advocates are reminded that they are required to adhere to the standards set out in the Victim's Charter, which places the needs of the victim at the heart of the criminal justice process, and that they are subject to a similar obligation in respect of the Code of Practice for Victims of Crime.

A:2. The principle of fairness is central to the administration of justice. The implementation of Human Rights Act 1998 [*sic*] in October 2000 incorporated into domestic law the principle of fairness to the accused articulated in the European Convention on Human Rights. Accuracy and reasonableness of plea plays an important part in ensuring fairness both to the accused and to the victim.

A:3. The Attorney General's Guidelines on the Acceptance of Pleas issued on December 7, 2000 highlighted the importance of transparency in the conduct of justice. The basis of plea agreed by the parties in a criminal trial is central to the sentencing process. An illogical or unsupported basis of plea can lead to an unduly lenient sentence being passed and has a consequential effect where consideration arises as to whether to refer the sentence to the Court of Appeal under section 36 of the Criminal Justice Act 1988.

A:4. These Guidelines, which replace the Guidelines issued in October 2005, give guidance on how prosecutors should meet these objectives of protection of victims' interests and of securing fairness and transparency in the process. They take into account paragraphs IV.45.4 and following of the consolidated criminal practice direction, amended May 2009, and the guidance issued by the Court of Appeal (Criminal) Division [*sic*] in *R. v. Beswick* [1996] 1 Cr.App.R. 343, *R. v. Tolera* [1999] 1 Cr.App.R. 25 and *R. v. Underwood* [2005] 1 Cr.App.R 13. They complement the Bar Council Guidance on Written Standards for the Conduct of Professional Work issued with the 7th edition of the Code of Conduct for the Bar of England and Wales and the Law Society's Professional Conduct Rules. When considering the acceptance of a guilty plea prosecution advocates are also reminded of the need to apply "The Farquharson Guidelines on The Role and Responsibilities of the Prosecution Advocate".

A:5. The Guidelines should be followed by all prosecutors and those persons designated under section 7 of the Prosecution of Offences Act 1985 (designated caseworkers) and apply to prosecutions conducted in England and Wales.

B. General Principles

A-278
B:1. Justice in this jurisdiction, save in the most exceptional circumstances, is conducted in public. This includes the acceptance of pleas by the prosecution and sentencing.

B:2. The Code for Crown Prosecutors governs the prosecutor's decision-making prior to the commencement of the trial hearing and sets out the circumstances in which pleas to a reduced number of charges, or less serious charges, can be accepted.

B:3. When a case is listed for trial and the prosecution form the view that the appropriate course is to accept a plea before the proceedings commence or continue, or to offer no evidence on the indictment or any part of it, the prosecution should whenever practicable speak to the victim or the victim's family, so that the position can be explained. The views of the victim or the family may assist in informing the prosecutor's decision as to whether it is the [*sic*] public interest, as defined by the

Code for Crown Prosecutors, to accept or reject the plea. The victim or victim's family should then be kept informed and decisions explained once they are made at court.

B:4. The appropriate disposal of a criminal case after conviction is as much a part of the criminal justice process as the trial of guilt or innocence. The prosecution advocate represents the public interest, and should be ready to assist the court to reach its decision as to the appropriate sentence. This will include drawing the court's attention to:

> — any victim personal statement or other information available to the prosecution advocate as to the impact of the offence on the victim;
>
> — where appropriate, to any evidence of the impact of the offending on a community;
>
> — any statutory provisions relevant to the offender and the offences under consideration;
>
> — any relevant sentencing guidelines and guideline cases; and
>
> — the aggravating and mitigating factors of the offence under consideration.

The prosecution advocate may also offer assistance to the court by making submissions, in the light of all these factors, as to the appropriate sentencing range.

In all cases, it is the prosecution advocate's duty to apply for appropriate ancillary orders, such as anti-social behaviour orders and confiscation orders. When considering which ancillary orders to apply for, prosecution advocates must always have regard to the victim's needs, including the question of his or her future protection.

C. The Basis of Plea

C:1. The basis of a guilty plea must not be agreed on a misleading or untrue set of facts and must **A-279** take proper account of the victim's interests. An illogical or insupportable basis of plea will inevitably result in the imposition of an inappropriate sentence and is capable of damaging public confidence in the criminal justice system. In cases involving multiple defendants the bases of plea for each defendant must be factually consistent with each other.

C:2. When the defendant indicates an acceptable plea, the defence advocate should reduce the basis of the plea to writing. This must be done in all cases save for those in which the defendant has indicated that the guilty plea has been or will be tendered on the basis of the prosecution case.

C:3. The written basis of plea must be considered with great care, taking account of the position of any other relevant defendant where appropriate. The prosecution should not lend itself to any agreement whereby a case is presented to the sentencing judge on a misleading or untrue set of facts or on a basis that is detrimental to the victim's interests. There will be cases where a defendant seeks to mitigate on the basis of assertions of fact which are outside the scope of the prosecution's knowledge. A typical example concerns the defendant's state of mind. If a defendant wishes to be sentenced on this basis, the prosecution advocate should invite the judge not to accept the defendant's version unless he or she gives evidence on oath to be tested in cross-examination. Paragraph IV.45.14 of the consolidated criminal practice direction states that in such circumstances the defence advocate should be prepared to call the defendant and, if the defendant is not willing to testify, subject to any explanation that may be given, the judge may draw such inferences as appear appropriate.

C:4. The prosecution advocate should show the prosecuting authority any written record relating to the plea and agree with them the basis on which the case will be opened to the court. If, as may well be the case, the basis of plea differs in its implications for sentencing or the making of ancillary orders from the case originally outlined by the prosecution, the prosecution advocate must ensure that such differences are accurately reflected in the written record prior to showing it to the prosecuting authority.

C:5. It is the responsibility of the prosecution advocate thereafter to ensure that the defence advocate is aware of the basis on which the plea is accepted by the prosecution and the way in which the prosecution case will be opened to the court.

C:6. In all cases where it is likely to assist the court where the sentencing issues are complex or unfamiliar the prosecution must add to the written outline of the case which is served upon the court a summary of the key considerations. This should take the form of very brief notes on:

> — any relevant statutory limitations;
>
> — the names of any relevant sentencing authorities or guidelines;
>
> — the scope for any ancillary orders (*e.g.* concerning anti-social behaviour, confiscation or deportation will need to be considered.

The outline should also include the age of the defendant and information regarding any outstanding offences.

C:7. It remains open to the prosecutor to provide further written information (for example to supplement and update the analysis at later stages of the case) where he or she thought that likely to assist the court, or if the judge requests it.

C:8. When the prosecution advocate has agreed the written basis of plea submitted by the defence advocate, he or she should endorse the document accordingly. If the prosecution advocate takes issue with all or part of the written basis of plea, the procedure set out in the consolidated criminal practice direction (and in Part 37.10(5) of the Criminal Procedure Rules) should be followed. The defendant's basis of plea must be set out in writing identifying what is in dispute; the court may invite the parties to make representations about whether the dispute is material to sentence; and if the court decides that it is a material dispute, the court will invite further representations or evidence as it may require and decide the dispute in accordance with the principles set out in *R. v. Newton*, 77 Cr.App.R.13, CA. The signed original document setting out the disputed factual matters should be made available to the trial judge and thereafter lodged with the court papers, as it will form part of the record of the hearing.

C:9. Where the basis of plea cannot be agreed and the discrepancy between the two accounts is such as to have a potentially significant effect on the level of sentence, it is the duty of the defence advocate so to inform the court before the sentencing process begins. There remains an overriding duty on the prosecution advocate to ensure that the sentencing judge is made aware of the discrepancy and of the consideration which must be given to holding a *Newton* hearing to resolve the issue. The court should be told where a derogatory reference to a victim, witness or third party is not accepted, even though there may be no effect on sentence.

C:10. As emphasised in paragraph IV.45.10 of the consolidated criminal practice direction, whenever an agreement as to the basis of plea is made between the prosecution and defence, any such agreement will be subject to the approval of the trial judge, who may of his or her own motion disregard the agreement and direct that a *Newton* hearing should be held to determine the proper basis on which sentence should be passed.

C:11. Where a defendant declines to admit an offence that he or she previously indicated should be taken into consideration, the prosecution advocate should indicate to the defence advocate and the court that, subject to further review, the offence may now form the basis of a new prosecution.

D. Sentence Indications

A-280

D:1. Only in the Crown Court may sentence indications be sought. Advocates there are reminded that indications as to sentence should not be sought from the trial judge unless issues between the prosecution and defence have been addressed and resolved. Therefore, in difficult or complicated cases, no less than seven days notice in writing of an intention to seek an indication should normally be given to the prosecution and the court. When deciding whether the circumstances of a case require such notice to be given, defence advocates are reminded that prosecutors should not agree a basis of plea unless and until the necessary consultation has taken place first with the victim and/or the victim's family and second, in the case of an independent prosecution advocate, with the prosecuting authority.

D:2. If there is no final agreement about the plea to the indictment, or the basis of plea, and the defence nevertheless proceeds to seek an indication of sentence, which the judge appears minded to give, the prosecution advocate should remind him or her of the guidance given in *R. v. Goodyear (Karl)* [2005] EWCA 888 [*sic*] that normally speaking an indication of sentence should not be given until the basis of the plea has been agreed or the judge has concluded that he or she can properly deal with the case without the need for a trial of the issue.

D:3. If an indication is sought, the prosecution advocate should normally enquire whether the judge is in possession of or has access to all the evidence relied on by the prosecution, including any victim personal statement, as well as any information about relevant previous convictions recorded against the defendant.

D:4. Before the judge gives the indication, the prosecution advocate should draw the judge's attention to any minimum or mandatory statutory sentencing requirements. Where the prosecution advocate would be expected to offer the judge assistance with relevant guideline cases or the views of the Sentencing Guidelines Council, he or she should invite the judge to allow them to do so. Where it applies, the prosecution advocate should remind the judge that the position [*sic*] of the Attorney General to refer any sentencing decision as unduly lenient is unaffected. In any event, the prosecution advocate should not say anything which may create the impression that the sentence indication has the support or approval of the Crown.

E. Pleas in Mitigation

A-281

E:1. The prosecution advocate must challenge any assertion by the defence in mitigation which is derogatory to a person's character (for instance, because it suggests that his or her conduct is or has been criminal, immoral or improper) and which is either false or irrelevant to proper sentencing considerations. If the defence advocate persists in that assertion, the prosecution advocate should invite the court to consider holding a *Newton* hearing to determine the issue.

E:2. The defence advocate must not submit in mitigation anything that is derogatory to a person's character without giving advance notice in writing so as to afford the prosecution advocate the opportunity to consider their position under paragraph E:1. When the prosecution advocate is so notified they must take all reasonable steps to establish whether the assertions are true. Reasonable steps will include seeking the views of the victim. This will involve seeking the views of the victim's family if the victim is deceased, and the victim's parents or legal guardian where the victim is a child. Reasonable steps may also include seeking the views of the police or other law enforcement authority, as appropriate. An assertion which is derogatory to a person's character will rarely amount to mitigation unless it has a causal connection to the circumstances of the offence or is otherwise relevant to proper sentencing considerations.

E:3. Where notice has not been given in accordance with paragraph E:2, the prosecution advocate must not acquiesce in permitting mitigation which is derogatory to a person's character. In such circumstances, the prosecution advocate should draw the attention of the court to the failure to give advance notice and seek time, and if necessary, an adjournment to investigate the assertion in the same way as if proper notice had been given. Where, in the opinion of the prosecution advocate, there are substantial grounds for believing that such an assertion is false or irrelevant to sentence, he or she should inform the court of their opinion and invite the court to consider making an order under section 58(8) of the Criminal Procedure and Investigations Act 1996, preventing publication of the assertion.

E:4. Where the prosecution advocate considers that the assertion is, if true, relevant to sentence, or the court has so indicated, he or she should seek time, and if necessary an adjournment, to establish whether the assertion is true. If the matter cannot be resolved to the satisfaction of the parties, the prosecution advocate should invite the court to consider holding a *Newton* hearing to determine the issue.

C. Jury Checks

Introduction

For the background to these guidelines, see § 4-275 in the main work. They were updated in November 2012. **A-282**

Attorney-General's Guidelines: Jury checks, unreported, November 27, 2012

1. The principles which are generally to be observed are: **A-283**
   (a) that members of a jury should be selected at random from the panel,
   (b) the Juries Act 1974 identifies those classes of persons who alone are either disqualified from or ineligible for service on a jury; no other class of person may be treated as disqualified or ineligible,
   (c) the correct way for the Crown to seek to exclude a member of the panel from sitting as a juror is by the exercise in open court of the right to request a stand by or, if necessary, to challenge for cause.

2. Parliament has provided safeguards against jurors who may be corrupt or biased. In addition to the provision for majority verdicts, there is the sanction of a criminal offence for a disqualified person to serve on a jury. The omission of a disqualified person from the panel is a matter for court officials—they will check criminal records for the purpose of ascertaining whether or not a potential juror is a disqualified person.

3. There are, however, certain exceptional types of case of public importance for which the provisions as to majority verdicts and the disqualification of jurors may not be sufficient to ensure the proper administration of justice. In such cases it is in the interests of both justice and the public that there should be further safeguards against the possibility of bias and in such cases checks which go beyond the investigation of criminal records may be necessary. **A-284**

4. These classes of case may be defined broadly as (a) cases in which national security is involved and part of the evidence is likely to be heard *in camera*, and (b) security and terrorist cases in which a juror's extreme beliefs could prevent a fair trial.

5. The particular aspects of these cases which may make it desirable to seek extra precautions are:
   (a) in security cases a danger that a juror, either voluntarily or under pressure, may make an improper use of evidence which, because of its sensitivity, has been given in camera,
   (b) in both security and terrorist cases the danger that a juror's personal beliefs are so biased as to go beyond normally reflecting the broad spectrum of views and interests in the community to reflect the extreme views of sectarian interest or pressure group to a degree which might interfere with his fair assessment of the facts of the case or lead him to exert improper pressure on his fellow jurors.

6. In order to ascertain whether in exceptional circumstances of the above nature either of these factors might seriously influence a potential juror's impartial performance of his duties or his respecting the secrecy of evidence given *in camera*, it may be necessary to conduct a limited investigation of the panel. In general, such further investigation beyond one of criminal records made for disqualifications may only be made with the records of the police. However, a check may, additionally, be made against the records of the Security Service. No checks other than on these sources and no general inquiries are to be made save to the limited extent that they may be needed to confirm the identity of a juror about whom the initial check has raised serious doubts.

7. No further investigation, as described in paragraph 6 above, should be made save with the personal authority of the Attorney-General on the application of the Director of Public Prosecutions and such checks are hereafter referred to as "authorised checks". When a chief officer of police or the prosecutor has reason to believe that it is likely that an authorised check may be desirable and proper in accordance with these guidelines, he should refer the matter to the Director of Public Prosecutions. In those cases in which the Director of Public Prosecutions believes authorised checks are both proportionate and necessary, the Director will make an application to the Attorney-General.

8. The Director of Public Prosecutions will provide the Attorney-General with all relevant information in support of the requested authorised checks. The Attorney-General will consider personally the request and, if appropriate, authorise the check.

9. The result of any authorised check will be sent to the Director of Public Prosecutions. The Director will then decide, having regard to the matters set out in paragraph 5 above, what information ought to be brought to the attention of prosecuting counsel. The Director will also provide the Attorney-General with the result of the authorised check.

10. Although the right of stand by and the decision to authorise checks are wholly within the discretion of the Attorney-General, when the Attorney-General has agreed to an authorised check being conducted, the Director of Public Prosecutions will write to the presiding judge for the area to advise him that this is being done.

11. No right of stand by should be exercised by counsel for the Crown on the basis of information obtained as a result of an authorised check save with the personal authority of the Attorney-General and unless the information is such as, having regard to the facts of the case and the offences charged, to afford strong reason for believing that a particular juror might be a security risk, be susceptible to improper approaches or be influenced in arriving at a verdict for the reasons given above.

12. Information revealed in the course of an authorised check must be considered in line with the normal rules on disclosure.

13. A record is to be kept by the Director of Public Prosecutions of the use made by counsel of the information passed to him and of the jurors stood by or challenged by the parties to the proceedings. A copy of this record is to be forwarded to the Attorney-General for the sole purpose of enabling him to monitor the operation of these guidelines.

14. No use of the information obtained as a result of an authorised check is to be made except as may be necessary in direct relation to or arising out of the trial for which the check was authorised. The information may, however, be used for the prevention of crime or as evidence in a future criminal prosecution, save that material obtained from the Security Service may only be used in those circumstances with the authority of the Security Service.

D. PROSECUTION'S RIGHT OF STAND BY

For the background to these guidelines, see §§ 4-304, 4-305 in the main work. They were updated in November, 2012.

Attorney-General's Guidelines on the Exercise by the Crown of its Right of Stand By, unreported, November 27, 2012

1. Although the law has long recognised the right of the Crown to exclude a member of a jury panel from sitting as a juror by the exercise in open court of the right to request a stand by or, if necessary, by challenge for cause, it has been customary for those instructed to prosecute on behalf of the Crown to assert that right only sparingly and in exceptional circumstances. It is generally accepted that the prosecution should not use its right in order to influence the overall composition of a jury or with a view to tactical advantage.

2. The approach outlined above is founded on the principles that:

(a) the members of a jury should be selected at random from the panel subject to any rule of law as to right of challenge by the defence, and

(b) the Juries Act 1974 identifies those classes of persons who alone are disqualified from or ineligible for service on a jury. No other class of person may be treated as disqualified or ineligible.

3. The enactment by Parliament of section 118 of the Criminal Justice Act 1988 abolishing the right of defendants to remove jurors by means of peremptory challenge makes it appropriate that the Crown should assert its right to stand by only on the basis of clearly defined and restrictive criteria. Derogation from the principle that members of a jury should be selected at random should be permitted only where it is essential.

4. Primary responsibility for ensuring that an individual does not serve on a jury if he is not competent to discharge properly the duties of a juror rests with the appropriate court officer and, ultimately the trial judge. Current legislation provides, in sections 9 to 10 of the Juries Act 1974, fairly wide discretion to excuse, defer or discharge jurors.

5. The circumstances in which it would be proper for the Crown to exercise its right to stand by a member of a jury panel are:

  (a) where a jury check authorised in accordance with the Attorney-General's guidelines on jury checks reveals information justifying exercise of the right to stand by in accordance with paragraph 11 of the guidelines ... and the Attorney-General personally authorises the exercise of the right to stand by; or

  (b) where a person is about to be sworn as a juror who is manifestly unsuitable and the defence agree that, accordingly, the exercise by the prosecution of the right to stand by would be appropriate. An example of the sort of exceptional circumstances which might justify stand by is where it becomes apparent that, despite the provisions mentioned in paragraph 4 above, a juror selected for service to try a complex case is in fact illiterate.

E. Conspiracy to Defraud

The Attorney-General has issued guidance to prosecuting authorities in relation to charging a **A-290** common law conspiracy to defraud instead of a substantive offence, contrary to the Fraud Act 2006, or a statutory conspiracy to commit a substantive offence, contrary to section 1 of the CLA 1977 (§ 33-2 in the main work); the prosecutor should consider (i) whether the conduct alleged falls within the ambit of a statutory offence, and (ii) whether such a charge or charges would adequately reflect the gravity of the alleged offending; as to (i), non-exhaustive examples of circumstances falling outside of the range of statutory offences, but within the ambit of the common law offence, are: (a) the dishonest obtaining of land or other property which cannot be stolen; (b) the dishonest infringement of another's right (*e.g.* the dishonest exploitation of another's patent); (c) an agreement involving an intention that the final offence be committed by someone outside the conspiracy; and (d) an agreement where the conspirators cannot be proved to have had the necessary degree of knowledge for the substantive offence to be perpetrated; as to (ii), prosecution for the common law offence may be more effective where the interests of justice can only be served by presenting an overall picture which could not be achieved by charging a series of substantive offences or statutory conspiracies (because of a large number of counts and/or the possibility of severed trials and evidence on one count being deemed inadmissible on another); where a case lawyer proposes to charge the common law offence, he must consider, and set out in the review note, how much such a charge would add to the amount of evidence likely to be called by the parties, the justification for using the charge, and why specific statutory offences are inadequate or otherwise inappropriate; a supervising lawyer experienced in fraud cases must also specifically approve the charge: *Attorney-General's guidance on the use of the common law offence of conspiracy to defraud*, unreported, January 9, 2007.

F. Prosecutor's Role in Applications for Witness Anonymity Orders

On July 21, 2008, the Attorney-General issued guidelines on the overarching principles which **A-291** a prosecutor must consider when deciding whether to apply for witness anonymity orders under the Criminal Evidence (Witness Anonymity) Act 2008 (now the Coroners and Justice Act 2009, ss.86–97 (§§ 8-151 *et seq.* in the main work)).

The guidance is in four parts (Part A (foreword), Part B (prosecutor's duties), Part C (applications by defendants) and Part D (appointment and role of special counsel)), and, to a large extent, highlights various provisions of the Act and restates elementary aspects of fairness at trial. Paragraph A2 makes clear that, given that the defendant's right to confront and challenge those who accuse him is an important aspect of a fair trial, making a witness anonymity order is a serious step which must only be taken where there are genuine grounds to believe that the conditions set out in the Act have been satisfied, which must be evaluated with care on the facts of each case. Paragraph B3 sets out the prosecutor's role, which prosecutors must approach in light of their overriding duties to be fair, independent and objective, and which includes a duty: (a) to examine with care and probe where appropriate, the material provided in support of the application and the evidential basis for it, and (b) to put before the court and to disclose to the defendant all material relevant to the application and the defence, including material which may undermine or qualify the prosecution case. Any such material is particularly relevant if credibility is in issue, for example, if there is a known link between the witness and defendant or a co-accused. Paragraph B4 explains that applications should only be authorised by prosecutors of an appropriately senior level. Paragraph D5 explains that a prosecutor making an application for an order must always be prepared to assist the court to consider whether the circumstances are such that exceptionally the appointment of special counsel may be called for, and, where appropriate, should draw to the attention of the court any aspect of the application which may be relevant to such appointment. Where the court decides to invite the Attorney-General to appoint special counsel, the prosecutor should (regardless of any steps taken by the court or any defendant) ensure that the Attorney-General's office is promptly notified and receives all information needed to take a decision as to whether to make such appointment. If special counsel is appointed, the prosecutor should then provide special counsel with open material made available to the accused regarding the application, and any other open material requested by special counsel. Closed or unredacted material which has been provided to the court should only be given to special counsel after open material has been provided and after special counsel has subsequently sought instructions from the defendant and his legal representative.

G. Plea Discussions in Cases of Serious or Complex Fraud

(1) Guidelines

A-292   On March 18, 2009, the Attorney-General issued guidelines setting out the process by which a prosecutor may discuss allegations of serious or complex fraud with a person whom he is prosecuting or expecting to prosecute.

ATTORNEY GENERAL'S GUIDELINES ON PLEA DISCUSSIONS IN CASES OF SERIOUS OR COMPLEX FRAUD

A. Foreword

A-293   A:1 These guidelines set out a process by which a prosecutor may discuss an allegation of serious or complex fraud with a person who he or she is prosecuting or expects to prosecute, or with that person's legal representative. They come into force on the 5th day of May 2009 and apply to plea discussions initiated on or after that date.

A:2 The guidelines will be followed by all prosecutors in England and Wales when conducting plea discussions in cases of serious or complex fraud. For the purposes of the guidelines, fraud means any financial, fiscal or commercial misconduct or corruption which is contrary to the criminal law. Fraud may be serious or complex if at least two of the following factors are present:

- the amount obtained or intended to be obtained is alleged to exceed £500,000;
- there is a significant international dimension;
- the case requires specialised knowledge of financial, commercial, fiscal or regulatory matters such as the operation of markets, banking systems, trusts or tax regimes;
- the case involves allegations of fraudulent activity against numerous victims;
- the case involves an allegation of substantial and significant fraud on a public body;
- the case is likely to be of widespread public concern;
- the alleged misconduct endangered the economic well-being of the United Kingdom, for example by undermining confidence in financial markets.

Taking account of these matters, it is for the prosecutor to decide whether or not a case is one of fraud, and whether or not it is serious or complex.

A:3 The decision whether a person should be charged with a criminal offence rests with the prosecutor. In selecting the appropriate charge or charges, the prosecutor applies principles set out in the Code for Crown Prosecutors ("the code"). Charges should reflect the seriousness and extent of the offending, give the court adequate sentencing powers and enable the case to be presented in a clear and simple way. The code also states that prosecutors should not go ahead with more charges to encourage a defendant to plead guilty to a few; equally, prosecutors should not charge a more serious offence to encourage a defendant to plead to a less serious one.

A:4 Once proceedings are instituted, the accused may plead guilty to all of the charges selected. If the defendant will plead guilty to some, but not all, of the charges or to a different, possibly less serious charge, the code states that a prosecutor is entitled to accept such pleas if he or she assesses that the court could still pass an adequate sentence. In taking these decisions the prosecutor also applies the Attorney General's Guidelines on the Acceptance of Pleas and the Prosecutor's Role in the Sentencing Exercise ("the acceptance of pleas guidelines") [*ante*, A-259 *et seq.*].

A:5 The purpose of plea discussions is to narrow the issues in the case with a view to reaching a just outcome at the earliest possible time, including the possibility of reaching an agreement about acceptable pleas of guilty and preparing a joint submission as to sentence.

A:6 The potential benefits of plea discussions are that:

- early resolution of the case may reduce the anxiety and uncertainty for victims and witnesses, and provide earlier clarity for accused persons who admit their guilt (subject to the court's power to reject the agreement);
- the issues in dispute may be narrowed so that even if the case proceeds to trial, it can be managed more efficiently in accordance with rule 3.2 of the Criminal Procedure Rules 2005. If pleas are agreed, litigation can be kept to a minimum.

A:7 Where plea discussions take place prior to the commencement of proceedings, the charges brought by the prosecutor will reflect those agreed, rather than those that the prosecutor would necessarily have preferred if no agreement had been reached. Also, any criminal investigation may not be complete when these discussions take place. For these reasons it is important that the procedures followed should command public and judicial confidence; that any agreement reached is reasonable, fair and just; that there are safeguards to ensure that defendants are not under improper pressure to make admissions; and that there are proper records of discussions that have taken place.

A:8 The guidelines are not intended to prevent or discourage existing practices by which prosecutors and prosecuting advocates discuss cases with defence legal representatives after charge, in order to narrow the issues or to agree a basis of plea. Neither do they affect the existing practice of judicial sentence indications at the plea and case management hearing or later in accordance with the guidance in *R. v. Goodyear* [2005] 2 Cr.App.R. 20 (§ 5-110 in the main work) (see also the acceptance of pleas guidelines). They complement, and do not detract from or replace, the code and the acceptance of pleas guidelines, or any other relevant guidance such as the Prosecutor's Pledge, the Victim's Charter and the Code of Practice for Victims of Crime.

A:9 Where a plea agreement is reached, it remains entirely a matter for the court to decide how to deal with the case.

B. General Principles

B:1 In conducting plea discussions and presenting a plea agreement to the court, the prosecutor **A-294** must act openly, fairly and in the interests of justice.

B:2 Acting in the interests of justice means ensuring that the plea agreement reflects the seriousness and extent of the offending, gives the court adequate sentencing powers, and enables the court, the public and the victims to have confidence in the outcome. The prosecutor must consider carefully the impact of a proposed plea or basis of plea on the community and the victim, and on the prospects of successfully prosecuting any other person implicated in the offending. The prosecutor must not agree to a reduced basis of plea which is misleading, untrue or illogical.

B:3 Acting fairly means respecting the rights of the defendant and of any other person who is being or may be prosecuted in relation to the offending. The prosecutor must not put improper pressure on a defendant in the course of plea discussions, for example by exaggerating the strength of the case in order to persuade the defendant to plead guilty, or to plead guilty on a particular basis.

B:4 Acting openly means being transparent with the defendant, the victim and the court. The prosecutor must:

- ensure that a full and accurate record of the plea discussions is prepared and retained;
- ensure that the defendant has sufficient information to enable him or her to play an informed part in the plea discussions;
- communicate with the victim before accepting a reduced basis of plea, wherever it is practicable to do so, so that the position can be explained; and
- ensure that the plea agreement placed before the court fully and fairly reflects the matters agreed. The prosecutor must not agree additional matters with the defendant which are not recorded in the plea agreement and made known to the court.

C. Initiating Plea Discussions

When and with whom discussions should be initiated and conducted

A-295   C:1 Where he or she believes it advantageous to do so, the prosecutor may initiate plea discussions with any person who is being prosecuted or investigated with a view to prosecution in connection with a serious or complex fraud, and who is legally represented. The prosecutor will not initiate plea discussions with a defendant who is not legally represented. If the prosecutor receives an approach from such a defendant, he or she may enter into discussions if satisfied that it is appropriate to do so.

C:2 Where proceedings have not yet been instituted, the prosecutor should not initiate plea discussions until he or she and the investigating officer are satisfied that the suspect's criminality is known. This will not usually be the case until after the suspect has been interviewed under caution.

C:3 The prosecutor should be alert to any attempt by the defendant to use plea discussions as a means of delaying the investigation or prosecution, and should not initiate or continue discussions where the defendant's commitment to the process is in doubt. The prosecutor should ensure that the position is preserved during plea discussions by, for example, restraining assets in anticipation of the making of a confiscation order. Where a defendant declines to take part in plea discussions, the prosecutor should not make a second approach unless there is a material change in circumstances.

Invitation letter

C:4 In order to initiate the plea discussions, the prosecutor will send the defendant's representatives a letter which:

- asks whether the defence wish to enter into discussions in accordance with these guidelines; and
- sets a deadline for a response from the defence.

Terms and conditions letter

C:5 Where the defence agree to engage in plea discussions, the prosecutor should send them a letter setting out the way in which the discussions will be conducted. This letter should deal with:

- the confidentiality of information provided by the prosecutor and defendant in the course of the plea discussions;
- the use which may be made by the prosecutor of information provided by the defendant; and
- the practical means by which the discussions will be conducted.

Confidentiality and use of information

C:6 In relation to confidentiality, the prosecutor will indicate that he or she intends to provide an undertaking to the effect that the fact that the defendant has taken part in the plea discussions, and any information provided by the defence in the course of the plea discussions will be treated as confidential and will not be disclosed to any other party other than for the purposes of the plea discussions and plea agreement (applying these guidelines), or as required by law. The undertaking will make it clear that the law in relation to the disclosure of unused material may require the prosecutor to provide information about the plea discussions to another defendant in criminal proceedings.

C:7 The prosecutor will require the defendant's legal representative to provide an undertaking to the effect that information provided by the prosecutor in the course of the plea discussions will be treated as confidential and will not be disclosed to any other party, other than for the purposes of the plea discussion and plea agreement or as required by law.

C:8 In relation to the use of information, the prosecutor will indicate that he or she intends to undertake not to rely upon the fact that the defendant has taken part in the plea discussions, or any information provided by the defendant in the course of the discussions, as evidence in any prosecution of that defendant for the offences under investigation, should the discussions fail. However, this undertaking will make it clear that the prosecutor is not prevented from:

- relying upon a concluded and signed plea agreement as confession evidence or as admissions;
- relying upon any evidence obtained from enquiries made as a result of the provision of information by the defendant;
- relying upon information provided by the defendant as evidence against him or her in any prosecution for an offence other than the fraud which is the subject of the plea discussion and any offence which is consequent upon it, such as money laundering; and
- relying upon information provided by the defendant in a prosecution of any other person for any offence (so far as the rules of evidence allow).

C:9 In exceptional circumstances the prosecutor may agree to different terms regarding the confidentiality and use of information. However, the prosecutor must not surrender the ability to rely upon a concluded and signed plea agreement as evidence against the defendant. The prosecutor may reserve the right to bring other charges (additional to those to which the defendant has indicated a willingness to plead guilty) in specific circumstances, for example if substantial new information comes to light at a later stage, the plea agreement is rejected by the court, or the defendant fails to honour the agreement.

C:10 Until the issues of confidentiality and use of information have been agreed to the satisfaction of both parties, and the agreement reflected in signed undertakings, the prosecutor must not continue with the substantive plea discussions.

D. Conducting Plea Discussions

Statement of case

D:1 Where plea discussions take place prior to proceedings being instituted, the prosecutor will **A-296** provide a statement of case to the defence. This is a written summary of the nature of the allegation against the suspect and the evidence which has been obtained, or is expected to be obtained, to support it. The statement of case should include a list of the proposed charges. Material in support of the statement of case may also be provided, whether or not in the form of admissible evidence. However, the prosecutor is not obliged to reveal to the suspect all of the information or evidence supporting his case, provided that this does not mislead the suspect to his or her prejudice.

D:2 Where plea discussions are initiated after proceedings have been commenced, but before the prosecutor has provided the defence with a case summary or opening note, the prosecutor may provide a statement of case to assist the defendant in understanding the evidence and identifying the issues.

Unused material

D:3 These guidelines do not affect the prosecutor's existing duties in relation to the disclosure of unused material. Where plea discussions take place prior to the institution of proceedings, the prosecutor should ensure that the suspect is not misled as to the strength of the prosecution case. It will not usually be necessary to provide copies of unused material in order to do this.

Conducting and recording the discussions

D:4 Having provided the defence with the statement of case and supporting material, the parties will then be in a position to conduct the plea discussion proper. Whether this is done by correspondence, by face-to-face meetings or by a combination of the two is a matter for the parties to decide in the individual case.

D:5 It is essential that a full written record is kept of every key action and event in the discussion process, including details of every offer or concession made by each party, and the reasons for every decision taken by the prosecutor. Meetings between the parties should be minuted and the minutes agreed and signed. Particular care should be taken where the defendant is not legally represented. The prosecutor should only meet with a defendant who is not legally represented if the defendant agrees to the meeting being recorded, or to the presence of an independent third party.

Queen's evidence

D:6 If the defendant offers at any stage to provide information, or to give evidence about the criminal activities of others, any such offer will be dealt with in accordance with sections 71 to 75 of the Serious Organised Crime and Police Act 2005 ("SOCPA"), the judgment of the Court of Appeal in *R. v. P.; R. v. Blackburn* [2008] 2 Cr.App.R.(S.) 5 (§ 5-137 in the main work) and the guidance agreed and issued by the Director of Public Prosecutions, the Director of the Serious Fraud Office and the Director of Revenue and Customs Prosecutions.

Discussion of pleas

D:7 In deciding whether or not to accept an offer by the defendant to plead guilty, the prosecutor will follow sections 7 and 10 of the code relating to the selection of charges and the acceptance of guilty pleas. The prosecutor should ensure that:
- the charges reflect the seriousness and extent of the offending;
- they give the court adequate powers to sentence and impose appropriate post-conviction orders;
- they enable the case to be presented in a clear and simple way (bearing in mind that many cases of fraud are necessarily complex);

- the basis of plea enables the court to pass a sentence that matches the seriousness of the offending, particularly if there are aggravating features;
- the interests of the victim, and where possible any views expressed by the victim, are taken into account when deciding whether it is in the public interest to accept the plea; and
- the investigating officer is fully appraised of developments in the plea discussions and his or her views are taken into account.

D:8 In reaching an agreement on pleas, the parties should resolve any factual issues necessary to allow the court to sentence the defendant on a clear, fair and accurate basis. Before agreeing to proposed pleas, the prosecutor should satisfy him or herself that the full code test as set out in the code will be made out in respect of each charge. In considering whether the evidential stage of the test will be met, the prosecutor should assume that the offender will sign a plea agreement amounting to an admission to the charge.

Discussion of sentence

D:9 Where agreement is reached as to pleas, the parties should discuss the appropriate sentence with a view to presenting a joint written submission to the court. This document should list the aggravating and mitigating features arising from the agreed facts, set out any personal mitigation available to the defendant, and refer to any relevant sentencing guidelines or authorities. In the light of all of these factors, it should make submissions as to the applicable sentencing range in the relevant guideline. The prosecutor must ensure that the submissions are realistic, taking full account of all relevant material and considerations.

D:10 The prosecutor should bear in mind all of the powers of the court, and seek to include in the joint submission any relevant ancillary orders. It is particularly desirable that measures should be included that achieve redress for victims (such as compensation orders) and protection for the public (such as directors' disqualification orders, serious crime prevention orders or financial reporting orders).

D:11 Due regard should be had to the court's asset recovery powers and the desirability of using these powers both as a deterrent to others and as a means of preventing the defendant from benefiting from the proceeds of crime or funding future offending. The Proceeds of Crime Act 2002 requires the Crown Court to proceed to the making of a confiscation order against a convicted defendant who has benefited from his criminal conduct where the prosecutor asks the court to do so, or the court believes that it is appropriate to do so. Fraud is an acquisitive crime, and the expectation in a fraud case should be that a confiscation order will be sought by the prosecutor reflecting the full benefit to the defendant. However, in doing so it is open to the prosecutor to take a realistic view of the likely approach of the court to the determination of any points in dispute (such as the interest of a third party in any property).

D:12 In the course of the plea discussions the prosecutor must make it clear to the defence that the joint submission as to sentence (including confiscation) is not binding on the court.

Liaison with another prosecutor or regulator

D:13 The prosecutor may become aware that another prosecuting authority or regulatory body (either in England and Wales or elsewhere) has an interest in the defendant. The prosecutor should liaise with the other agency, in accordance with the Prosecutors' Convention and any other relevant agreement or guidance. The other agency may wish to take part in the plea discussions, or they may authorise the prosecutor to discuss with the defendant the matters which they are interested in, with a view to resolving all matters in one plea agreement. The prosecutor should warn the defendant that a plea agreement will not bind any other agency which is not a party to it.

E. The Written Plea Agreement

A-297

E:1 All matters agreed between the prosecutor and the defence must be reduced to writing as a plea agreement and signed by both parties. The plea agreement will include:
- a list of the charges;
- a statement of the facts; and
- a declaration, signed by the defendant personally, to the effect that he or she accepts the stated facts and admits he or she is guilty of the agreed charges.

E:2 Any agreement under the SOCPA regarding the giving of assistance to the prosecutor by the defendant should be in a separate document accompanying the plea agreement.

E:3 Once a plea agreement is signed in a case where proceedings have not yet been commenced, the prosecutor will review the case in accordance with the code and, assuming the evidential stage of the full code test is satisfied on the basis of the signed plea agreement and the other available evidence, will arrange for proceedings to be instituted by summons or charge.

E:4 In advance of the defendant's first appearance in the Crown Court, the prosecutor should send the court sufficient material to allow the judge to understand the facts of the case and the history of the plea discussions, to assess whether the plea agreement is fair and in the interests of justice, and to decide the appropriate sentence. This will include:

- the signed plea agreement;
- a joint submission as to sentence and sentencing considerations;
- any relevant sentencing guidelines or authorities;
- all of the material provided by the prosecution to the defendant in the course of the plea discussions;
- any material provided by the defendant to the prosecution, such as documents relating to personal mitigation; and
- the minutes of any meetings between the parties and any correspondence generated in the plea discussions.

E:5 It will then be for the court to decide how to deal with the plea agreement. In particular, the court retains an absolute discretion as to whether or not it sentences in accordance with the joint submission from the parties.

F. Failure of Plea Discussions

F:1 There are several circumstances in which plea discussions may result in an outcome other **A-298** than the defendant pleading guilty in accordance with a plea agreement. The prosecutor or the defendant may break off the discussions. They may be unable to reach an agreement. They may reach an agreement, but intervening events may lead the prosecutor to decide that proceedings should not be instituted. Proceedings may be instituted but the court may reject the plea agreement. The defendant may decline to plead guilty in accordance with the plea agreement, either as a result of a sentence indication given under the procedure set out in *R. v. Goodyear*, or for some other reason.

F:2 If any of these situations arises, the prosecutor may wish for further enquiries to be made with a view to bringing or completing proceedings against the defendant. If proceedings have already been instituted, the prosecutor will use the appropriate means to delay them - either discontinuing under section 23 or 23A of the Prosecution of Offences Act 1985 or (if the indictment has already been preferred) applying for an adjournment or stay of the proceedings. The prosecutor and the defendant's representatives will continue to be bound by the preliminary undertakings made in relation to the confidentiality and use of information provided in the course of the plea discussions.

F:3 Where plea discussions have broken down for any reason, it will be rare that the prosecutor will wish to re-open them, but he or she may do so if there is a material change in circumstances which warrants it.

(2) Practice

Paragraphs IV.45.18 to IV.45.28 of the consolidated criminal practice direction, as inserted by **A-299** *Practice Direction (Criminal proceedings: substituted and additional provisions)* [2009] 1 W.L.R. 1396, with effect from May 14, 2009, made provision as to the practice to be followed where a plea agreement has been reached and a joint sentencing submission is to be placed before the court. Paragraph IV.45 of the consolidated criminal practice direction has now been revoked (*Criminal Practice Direction (General matters) A2* [2013] 1 W.L.R. 3164), with paragraphs IV.45.18 to IV.45.28 being superseded by paragraphs B.17 to B.27 of *Criminal Practice Direction (Sentencing) B* [2013] 1 W.L.R. 3164.

Criminal Practice Direction (Sentencing) B, paras B.17–27 [2013] 1 W.L.R. 3164

B.17 In this part— **A-300**
- (a) "a plea agreement" means a written basis of plea agreed between the prosecution and defendant(s) in accordance with the principles set out in *R. v. Underwood* [see § 5-90 in the main work, and *ante*, A-277], supported by admissible documentary evidence or admissions under section 10 of the Criminal Justice Act 1967;
- (b) "a sentencing submission" means sentencing submissions made jointly by the prosecution and defence as to the appropriate sentencing authorities and applicable sentencing range in the relevant sentencing guideline relating to the plea agreement;
- (c) "serious or complex fraud" includes, but is not limited to, allegations of fraud where two or more of the following are present [list as per the guidelines, *ante*, A-293]:

Procedure

B.18 The procedure regarding agreed bases of plea outlined above [§§ 5-91 *et seq.* in the main **A-301**

work], applies with equal rigour to the acceptance of pleas under this procedure. However, because under this procedure the parties will have been discussing the plea agreement and the charges from a much earlier stage, it is vital that the judge is fully informed of all relevant background to the discussions, charges and the eventual basis of plea.

B.19 Where the defendant has not yet appeared before the Crown Court, the prosecutor must send full details of the plea agreement and sentencing submission(s) to the court, at least 7 days in advance of the defendant's first appearance. Where the defendant has already appeared before the Crown Court, the prosecutor must notify the court as soon as is reasonably practicable that a plea agreement and sentencing submissions under the Attorney-General's Plea Discussion Guidelines are to be submitted. The court should set a date for the matter to be heard, and the prosecutor must send full details of the plea agreement and sentencing submission(s) to the court as soon as practicable, or in accordance with the directions of the court.

B.20 The provision to the judge of full details of the plea agreement requires sufficient information to be provided to allow the judge to understand the facts of the case and the history of the plea discussions, to assess whether the plea agreement is fair and in the interests of justice, and to decide the appropriate sentence. This will include, but is not limited to: (i) the plea agreement; (ii) the sentencing submission(s); (iii) all of the material provided by the prosecution to the defendant in the course of the plea discussions; (iv) relevant material provided by the defendant, for example documents relating to personal mitigation; and (v) the minutes of any meetings between the parties and any correspondence generated in the plea discussions. The parties should be prepared to provide additional material at the request of the court.

B.21 The court should at all times have regard to the length of time that has elapsed since the date of the occurrence of the events giving rise to the plea discussions, the time taken to interview the defendant, the date of charge and the prospective trial date (if the matter were to proceed to trial) so as to ensure that its consideration of the plea agreement and sentencing submissions does not cause any unnecessary further delay.

Status of plea agreement and joint sentencing submissions

A-302

B.22 Where a plea agreement and joint sentencing submissions are submitted, it remains entirely a matter for the court to decide how to deal with the case. The judge retains the absolute discretion to refuse to accept the plea agreement and to sentence otherwise than in accordance with the sentencing submissions made under the Attorney-General's Plea Discussion Guidelines.

B.23 Sentencing submissions should draw the court's attention to any applicable range in any relevant guideline, and to any ancillary orders that may be applicable. Sentencing submissions should not include a specific sentence or agreed range other than the ranges set out in sentencing guidelines or authorities.

B.24 Prior to pleading guilty in accordance with the plea agreement, the defendant(s) may apply to the court for an indication of the likely maximum sentence [in accordance with *R. v. Goodyear*, as to which, see § 5-110 in the main work].

B.25 In the event that the judge indicates a sentence or passes a sentence which is not within the submissions made on sentencing, the plea agreement remains binding.

B.26 If the defendant does not plead guilty in accordance with the plea agreement or if a defendant who has pleaded guilty in accordance with a plea agreement successfully applies to withdraw his plea under rule 39.3 of the Criminal Procedure Rules, the signed plea agreement may be treated as confession evidence, and may be used against the defendant at a later stage in these or any other proceedings. Any credit for a timely guilty plea may be lost. The court may exercise its discretion under section 78 of the Police and Criminal Evidence Act 1984 to exclude any such evidence ... .

B.27 Where a defendant has failed to plead guilty in accordance with a plea agreement, the case is unlikely to be ready for trial immediately. The prosecution may have been commenced earlier than it otherwise would have been, in reliance upon the defendant's agreement to plead guilty. This is likely to be a relevant consideration for the court in deciding whether or not to grant an application to adjourn or stay the proceedings to allow the matter to be prepared for trial in accordance with the protocol on the Control and Management of Heavy Fraud and other Complex Criminal Cases, or as required.

(3) Authorities

A-303

As to the limitations on prosecuting authorities' power to enter into agreements (with overseas authorities or a potential accused) as to how a case should be disposed of, see *R. v. Innospec Ltd*, § 1-369 in the main work. As to this case, see also § 5-804 in the main work.

In *R. v. Dougall* [2011] 1 Cr.App.R.(S.) 37, CA, it was said that a joint submission as to sentence pursuant to the Attorney-General's Guidelines on Plea Discussions in Cases of Serious or Complex

Fraud, *ante*, should recognise that it is the court alone that decides on sentence, should avoid advocacy of a particular outcome, and should confine itself to the appropriate range within which it is said the sentence should fall. As to this case, see also § 5-138 in the main work.

H. Asset Recovery Powers of Prosecuting Authorities

The Attorney-General and the Home Secretary have issued joint guidance under section 2A of **A-304** the PCA 2002 to the National Crime Agency, the DPP, the Director of Revenue and Customs Prosecutions, the Director of the Serious Fraud Office and the DPP for Northern Ireland directing them to consider using their civil asset recovery powers under the 2002 Act wherever proceeds of crime have been identified but it is not feasible to secure a conviction, or a conviction has been secured but no confiscation order made (para. 2). They must also consider whether the public interest might be better served by using these powers, rather than by instituting a criminal investigation or prosecution, whilst applying the principle that a criminal disposal will generally make the best contribution to the reduction of crime (para. 3). Paragraph 4 states that the factors listed in the Code for Crown Prosecutors (*post*, Appendix E-6) as being relevant to the question whether a prosecution would be in the public interest might also be relevant when considering at any stage whether or not the civil recovery powers should be used; but it is emphasised that a potential defendant should not be able to escape an appropriate prosecution by the simple device of agreeing to a civil recovery order. Paragraph 5 contains a non-exhaustive list of circumstances in which use of the powers might be appropriate because it is not feasible to secure a conviction and paragraph 6 contains an equivalent list for where a conviction is feasible but where the public interest might be better served by use of these powers. Paragraph 8 sets out the ways in which the relevant authorities should seek to minimise any potential prejudice to a related or potential criminal investigation or proceedings, including through the disclosure of relevant information. Paragraph 9 confirms that the guidance does not prohibit (i) a criminal investigation being carried out by a law enforcement authority at the same time as a civil recovery and/or a tax investigation; (ii) civil recovery and/or tax proceedings being instituted where a criminal investigation by a law enforcement authority is being carried out at the same time into unrelated criminality (subjectto the duty set out in para. 8, *ante*); or (iii) criminal proceedings being instituted or carried on by a prosecuting authority at the same time as a civil recovery and/or tax investigation is being carried out. However, paragraph 10 prohibits in all circumstances criminal and civil/tax proceedings being carried on at the same time in relation to the same criminality. Where criminal proceedings have been stayed by a court, or cannot progress (*e.g.* because the defendant has absconded), they are not being "carried on" for the purposes of this prohibition. Paragraph 11 sets out the circumstances in which a relevant authority may agree to accept a reduced sum in satisfaction of a civil recovery claim. For the full text of the guidance, see http://www.attorneygen eral.gov.uk/Publications/Pages/AttorneyGeneralsGuidelines.aspx.

APPENDIX B
Interpretation Act 1978

General provisions as to enactment and operation

Words of enactment
1. Every section of an Act takes effect as a substantive enactment without introductory words.　**B-1**

Amendment or repeal in same Session
2. Any Act may be amended or repealed in the Session of Parliament in which it is passed.　**B-2**

Judicial notice
3. Every Act is a public Act to be judicially noticed as such, unless the contrary is expressly **B-3** provided by the Act.

Time of commencement
4. An Act or provision of an Act comes into force—　**B-4**
    (a) where provision is made for it to come into force on a particular day, at the beginning of that day;
    (b) where no provision is made for its coming into force, at the beginning of the day on which the Act receives the Royal Assent.

Interpretation and construction

Definitions
5. In any Act, unless the contrary intention appears, words and expressions listed in Schedule 1 to **B-5** this Act are to be construed according to that Schedule.

Gender and number
6. In any Act, unless the contrary intention appears,—　**B-6**
    (a) words importing the masculine gender include the feminine;
    (b) words importing the feminine gender include the masculine;
    (c) words in the singular include the plural and words in the plural include the singular.

References to service by post
7. Where an Act authorises or requires any document to be served by post (whether the expres- **B-7** sion "serve" or the expression "give" or "send" or any other expression is used) then, unless the contrary intention appears, the service is deemed to be effected by properly addressing, prepaying and posting a letter containing the document and, unless the contrary is proved, to have been effected at the time at which the letter would be delivered in the ordinary course of post.

References to distance
8. In the measurement of any distance for the purposes of an Act, that distance shall, unless the **B-8** contrary intention appears, be measured in a straight line on a horizontal plane.

References to time of day
9. Subject to section 3 of the Summer Time Act 1972 (construction of references to points of time **B-9** during the period of summer time), whenever an expression of time occurs in an Act, the time referred to shall, unless it is otherwise specifically stated, be held to be Greenwich mean time.

References to Sovereign
10. In any Act a reference to the Sovereign reigning at the time of the passing of the Act is to be **B-10** construed, unless the contrary intention appears, as a reference to the Sovereign for the time being.

Construction of subordinate legislation
11. Where an Act confers power to make subordinate legislation, expressions used in that legisla- **B-11** tion have, unless the contrary intention appears, the meaning which they bear in the Act.

Statutory powers and duties

Continuity of powers and duties
12.—(1) Where an Act confers a power or imposes a duty it is implied, unless the contrary inten- **B-12** tion appears, that the power may be exercised, or the duty is to be performed, from time to time as occasion requires.
(2) Where an Act confers a power or imposes a duty on the holder of an office as such, it is implied, unless the contrary intention appears, that the power may be exercised, or the duty is to be performed, by the holder for the time being of the office.

Anticipatory exercise of powers
13. Where an Act which (or any provision of which) does not come into force immediately on its **B-13**

passing confers power to make subordinate legislation, or to make appointments, give notices, prescribe forms or do any other thing for the purposes of the Act, then, unless the contrary intention appears, the power may be exercised, and any instrument made thereunder may be made so as to come into force, at any time after the passing of the Act so far as may be necessary or expedient for the purpose—

  (a) of bringing the Act or any provision of the Act into force; or

  (b) of giving full effect to that Act or any such provision at or after the time when it comes into force.

Implied power to amend

B-14 14. Where an Act confers power to make—

  (a) rules, regulations or byelaws; or

  (b) Orders in Council, orders or other subordinate legislation to be made by statutory instrument,

it implies, unless the contrary intention appears, a power exercisable in the same manner and subject to the same conditions or limitations, to revoke, amend or re-enact any instrument made under the power.

Power to include sunset and review provisions in subordinate legislation

B-14a 14A.—(1) This section applies where an Act confers a power or a duty on a person to make subordinate legislation except to the extent that—

  (a) the power or duty is exercisable by the Scottish Ministers, or

  (b) the power or duty is exercisable by any other person within devolved competence (within the meaning of the Scotland Act 1998).

(2) The subordinate legislation may include—

  (a) provision requiring the person to review the effectiveness of the legislation within a specified period or at the end of a specified period;

  (b) provision for the legislation to cease to have effect at the end of a specified day or a specified period;

  (c) if the power or duty is being exercised to amend other subordinate legislation, provision of the kind mentioned in paragraph (a) or (b) in relation to that other legislation.

(3) The provision that may be made by virtue of subsection (2)(a) includes provision requiring the person to consider whether the objectives which it was the purpose of the legislation to achieve remain appropriate and, if so, whether they could be achieved in another way.

(4) Subordinate legislation including provision of a kind mentioned in subsection (2) may make such provision generally or only in relation to specified provisions of the legislation or specified cases or circumstances.

(5) Subordinate legislation including provision of a kind mentioned in subsection (2) may make transitional, consequential, incidental or supplementary provision or savings in connection with such provision.

(6) In this section "specified" means specified in the subordinate legislation.

[This section was inserted by the Enterprise and Regulatory Reform Act 2013, s.59(1) and (2).]

Repealing enactments

Repeal of repeal

B-15 15. Where an Act repeals a repealing enactment, the repeal does not revive any enactment previously repealed unless words are added reviving it.

General savings

B-16 16.—(1) Without prejudice to section 15, where an Act repeals an enactment, the repeal does not, unless the contrary intention appears,—

  (a) revive anything not in force or existing at the time at which the repeal takes effect;

  (b) affect the previous operation of the enactment repealed or anything duly done or suffered under that enactment;

  (c) affect any right, privilege, obligation or liability acquired, accrued or incurred under that enactment;

  (d) affect any penalty, forfeiture or punishment incurred in respect of any offence committed against that enactment;

  (e) affect any investigation, legal proceeding or remedy in respect of any such right, privilege, obligation, liability, penalty, forfeiture or punishment;

and any such investigation, legal proceeding or remedy may be instituted, continued or enforced, and any such penalty, forfeiture or punishment may be imposed, as if the repealing Act had not been passed.

(2) This section applies to the expiry of a temporary enactment as if it were repealed by an Act.

[Considered in *R. v. West London Stipendiary Magistrate, ex p. Simeon* [1983] A.C. 234, HL. See also *Hough v. Windus* (1884) 12 Q.B.D. 224, and *R. v. Fisher (Charles)* [1969] 1 W.L.R. 8, CA.]

Repeal and re-enactment

17.—(1) Where an Act repeals a previous enactment and substitutes provisions for the enactment **B-17** repealed, the repealed enactment remains in force until the substitute provisions come into force.

(2) Where an Act repeals and re-enacts, with or without modification, a previous enactment then, unless the contrary intention appears,—

    (a) any reference in any other enactment to the enactment so repealed shall be construed as a reference to the provision re-enacted;

    (b) in so far as any subordinate legislation made or other thing done under the enactment so repealed, or having effect as if so made or done, could have been made or done under the provision re-enacted, it shall have effect as if made or done under that provision.

Miscellaneous

Duplicated offences

18. Where an act or omission constitutes an offence under two or more Acts, or both under an Act **B-18** and at common law, the offender shall, unless the contrary intention appears, be liable to be prosecuted and punished under either or any of those Acts or at common law, but shall not be liable to be punished more than once for the same offence.

See in the main work, § 4-189.

Citation of other Acts

19. Where an Act cites another Act by year, statute, session or chapter, or a section or other por- **B-19** tion of another Act by number or letter, the reference shall, unless the contrary intention appears, be read as referring—

    (a) in the case of Acts included in any revised edition of the statutes printed by authority, to that edition;

    (b) in the case of Acts not so included but included in the edition prepared under the direction of the Record Commission, to that edition;

    (c) in any other case, to the Acts printed by the Queen's Printer, or under the superintendence or authority of Her Majesty's Stationery Office.

(2) An Act may continue to be cited by the short title authorised by any enactment notwithstanding the repeal of that enactment.

References to other enactments

20.—(1) Where an Act describes or cites a portion of an enactment by referring to words, sections **B-20** or other parts from or to which or from and to which the portion extends, the portion described or cited includes the words, sections or other parts referred to unless the contrary intention appears.

(2) Where an Act refers to an enactment, the reference unless the contrary intention appears, is a reference to that enactment as amended, and includes a reference thereto as extended or applied, by or under any other enactment, including any other provision of that Act.

References to EU instruments

20A. Where an Act passed after the commencement of this section refers to a EU instrument that **B-20a** has been amended, extended or applied by another such instrument, the reference, unless the contrary intention appears, is a reference to that instrument as so amended, extended or applied.

[This section was inserted by the Legislative and Regulatory Reform Act 2006, s.25(1). It is printed as amended by the European Union (Amendment) Act 2008, s.3, and Sched., Pt 2.]

Supplementary

Interpretation, etc.

B-21   **21.**—(1) In this Act "Act" includes a local and personal or private Act; and "subordinate legisla-tion" means Orders in Council, orders, rules, regulations, schemes, warrants, byelaws and other instruments made or to be made under any Act.

(2) This Act binds the Crown.

Application to Acts and Measures

B-22   **22.**—(1) This Act applies to itself, to any Act passed after the commencement of this Act (subject, in the case of section 20A, to the provision made in that section) and, to the extent specified in Part I of Schedule 2, to Acts passed before the commencement of this Act.

(2) In any of the foregoing provisions of this Act a reference to an Act is a reference to an Act to which that provision applies; but this does not affect the generality of references to enactments or of the references in section 19(1) to other Acts.

(3) This Act applies to Measures of the General Synod of the Church of England (and, so far as it relates to Acts passed before the commencement of this Act, to Measures of the Church Assembly passed after May 28, 1925) as it applies to Acts.

[This section is printed as amended by the Legislative and Regulatory Reform Act 2006, s.25(2).]

Application to other instruments

B-23   **23.**—(1) The provisions of this Act, except sections 1 to 3 and 4(b), apply, so far as applicable and unless the contrary intention appears, to subordinate legislation made after the commencement of this Act and, to the extent specified in Part II of Schedule 2, to subordinate legislation made before the commencement of this Act, as they apply to Acts.

(2) In the application of this Act to Acts passed or subordinate legislation made after the com-mencement of this Act, all references to an enactment include an enactment comprised in subordinate legislation whenever made, and references to the passing or repeal of an enactment are to be construed accordingly.

(3) Sections 9 and 19(1) also apply to deeds and other instruments and documents as they apply to Acts and subordinate legislation; and in the application of section 17(2)(a) to Acts passed or subordinate legislation made after the commencement of this Act, the reference to any other enact-ment includes any deed or other instrument or document.

(4) Subsections (1) and (2) of this section do not apply to Orders in Council made under section 5 of the Statutory Instruments Act 1946, section 1(3) of the Northern Ireland (Temporary Provisions) Act 1972 or Schedule 1 to the Northern Ireland Act 1974.

B-23a   **23A.** [*Acts of the Scottish Parliament,*] etc.
B-23b   **23B.** [*Measures and Acts of the National Assembly for Wales,*] etc.
B-24   **24.** [*Application to Northern Ireland.*]

Repeals and savings

B-25   **25.**—(1) The enactments described in Schedule 3 are repealed to the extent specified in the third column of that Schedule.

(2) Without prejudice to section 17(2)(a), a reference to the Interpretation Act 1889, to any provi-sion of that Act or to any other enactment repealed by this Act whether occurring in another Act, in subordinate legislation, in Northern Ireland legislation or in any deed or other instrument or docu-ment, shall be construed as referring to this Act, or to the corresponding provision of this Act, as it applies to Acts passed at the time of the reference.

(3) The provisions of this Act relating to Acts passed after any particular time do not affect the construction of Acts passed before that time, though continued or amended by Acts passed thereafter.

B-26   **26.** [*Commencement.*]
B-27   **27.** [*Short title.*]

SCHEDULES

SCHEDULE 1

WORDS AND EXPRESSIONS DEFINED

B-28   *Note*: The years or dates which follow certain entries in this Schedule are relevant for the purposes of paragraph 4 of Schedule 2 (application to existing enactments).

Definitions

... .

"Bank of England" means, as the context requires, the Governor and Company of the Bank of England or the bank of the Governor and Company of the Bank of England.

... .

"British Islands" means the United Kingdom, the Channel Islands and the Isle of Man. [1889]

"British possession" means any part of Her Majesty's dominions outside the United Kingdom; and where parts of such dominions are under both a central and local legislature, all parts under the central legislature are deemed, for the purposes of this definition, to be one British possession. [1889]

... .

"Central funds", in an enactment providing in relation to England and Wales for the payment of costs out of central funds, means money provided by Parliament.

... .

"Civil partnership" means a civil partnership which exists under or by virtue of the Civil Partnership Act 2004 (and any reference to a civil partner is to be read accordingly).

[This definition is inserted by the Civil Partnership Act 2004, s.261(1), and Sched. 27, para. 59.]

"Colonial legislature", and "legislature" in relation to a British possession, mean the authority, other than the Parliament of the United Kingdom or Her Majesty in Council, competent to make laws for the possession. [1889]

"Colony" means any part of Her Majesty's dominions outside the British Islands except—

    (a) countries having fully responsible status within the Commonwealth;

    (b) territories for whose external relations a country other than the United Kingdom is responsible;

    (c) associated states; and where parts of such dominions are under both a central and a local legislature, all parts under the central legislature are deemed for the purposes of this definition to be one colony. [1889]

"Commencement", in relation to an Act or enactment, means the time when the Act or enactment comes into force.

"The EU", or "the EU Treaties" and other expressions defined by section 1 of and Schedule 1 to the European Communities Act 1972 have the meanings prescribed by that Act.

[This definition is printed as amended by the European Union (Amendment) Act 2008, s.3, and Sched., Pt 2.]

... .

"Consular officer" has the meaning assigned by Article 1 of the Vienna Convention set out in Schedule 1 to the Consular Relations Act 1968.

... .

"County Court" means—

    (a) in relation to England and Wales, the County Court established under section A1 of the County Courts Act 1984;

    (b) [*Northern Ireland*].

[This definition is printed as amended by the County Courts Act 1984, Sched. 2; and the Crime and Courts Act 2013, s.17(5), and Sched. 9. para. 94.]

"Court of Appeal" means—

    (a) in relation to England and Wales, Her Majesty's Court of Appeal in England;

    (b) in relation to Northern Ireland, Her Majesty's Court of Appeal in Northern Ireland.

"Court of summary jurisdiction", "summary conviction" and "Summary Jurisdiction Acts", in relation to Northern Ireland, have the same meanings as in Measures of the Northern Ireland Assembly and Acts of the Parliament of Northern Ireland.

"Crown Court" means—

    (a) in relation to England and Wales, the Crown Court constituted by section 4 of the Courts Act 1971;

    (b) [*Northern Ireland*].

... .

"EEA agreement" means the agreement on the European Economic Area signed at Oporto on 2nd

May 1992, together with the Protocol adjusting that Agreement signed at Brussels on 17th March 1993, as modified or supplemented from time to time. [The date of the coming into force of this paragraph.]

"EEA state", in relation to any time, means—

    (a) a state which at that time is a member State; or

    (b) any other state which at that time is a party to the EEA agreement. [The date of the coming into force of this paragraph.]

[These two definitions were inserted, as from January 8, 2007, by the Legislative and Regulatory Reform Act 2006, s.26(1).]

"England" means, subject to any alteration of boundaries under Part IV of the Local Government Act 1972, the area consisting of the counties established by section 1 of that Act, Greater London and the Isles of Scilly. [1st April 1974]

... .

"Governor-General" includes any person who for the time being has the powers of the Governor-General, and "Governor", in relation to any British possession, includes the officer for the time being administering the government of that possession. [1889]

"Her Majesty's Revenue and Customs" has the meaning given by section 4 of the Commissioners for Revenue and Customs Act 2005.

[This definition was inserted by the Commissioners for Revenue and Customs Act 2005, s.4(3).]

"High Court" means—

    (a) in relation to England and Wales, Her Majesty's High Court of Justice in England;

    (b) in relation to Northern Ireland, Her Majesty's High Court of Justice in Northern Ireland.

... .

"Land" includes buildings and other structures, land covered with water, and any estate, interest, easement, servitude or right in or over land. [1st January 1979]

... .

"Local policing body" has the meaning given by section 101(1) of the Police Act 1996.

[This definition was inserted by the Police Reform and Social Responsibility Act 2011, s.97(1) and (2).]

"London borough" means a borough described in Schedule 1 to the London Government Act 1963, "inner London borough" means one of the boroughs so described and numbered from 1 to 12 and "outer London borough" means one of the boroughs so described and numbered 13 to 32, subject (in each case) to any alterations made under Part IV of the Local Government Act 1972 or Part II of the Local Government Act 1992.

[This definition is printed as amended by the Local Government Act 1992, s.27(1), and Sched. 3, para. 21.]

"Lord Chancellor" means the Lord High Chancellor of Great Britain.

"Magistrates' court" has the meaning assigned to it—

    (a) in relation to England and Wales, by section 148 of the Magistrates' Courts Act 1980;

    (b) [*Northern Ireland*].

[This definition is printed as amended by the MCA 1980, s.154, and Sched. 7, para. 169.]

"Month" means calendar month. [1850]

... .

"Oath" and "affidavit" include affirmation and declaration, and "swear" includes affirm and declare.

"Officer of Revenue and Customs" has the meaning given by section 2(1) of the Commissioners for Revenue and Customs Act 2005.

[This definition was inserted by the Commissioners for Revenue and Customs Act 2005, s.2(7).]

"Ordnance Map" means a map made under powers conferred by the Ordnance Survey Act 1841 or the Boundary Survey (Ireland) Act 1854.

"Parliamentary Election" means the election of a Member to serve in Parliament for a constituency. [1889]

"Person" includes a body of persons corporate or unincorporate. [1889]

"Police and crime commissioner" means a police and crime commissioner established under section 1 of the Police Reform and Social Responsibility Act 2011.

[This definition was inserted by the Police Reform and Social Responsibility Act 2011, s.97(1) and (3).]

"Police area" ... and other expressions relating to the police have the meaning or effect described—
    (a) in relation to England and Wales, by section 101(1) of the Police Act 1996; ...

[This definition is printed as amended by the Police Act 1996, Sched. 7, para. 32; the Police Reform and Social Responsibility Act 2011, s.97(1) and (4); and the Police and Fire Reform (Scotland) Act 2012 (Consequential Provisions and Modifications) Order 2013 (S.I. 2013 No. 602).]

"The Privy Council" means the Lords and others of Her Majesty's Most Honourable Privy Council.
"Registered" in relation to nurses, midwives and health visitors, means registered in the register maintained by the United Kingdom Central Council for Nursing, Midwifery and Health Visiting by virtue of qualifications in nursing, midwifery or health visiting, as the case may be.

[This definition was inserted by the Nurses, Midwives and Health Visitors Act 1979, s.23(4), and Sched. 7, para. 30.]

"Registered medical practitioner" means a fully registered person within the meaning of the Medical Act 1983 who holds a licence to practise under that Act. [1st January 1979]

[This definition is printed as amended by the Medical Act 1983, s.56(1), and Sched. 5, para. 18; and the Medical Act 1983 (Amendment) Order 2002 (S.I 2002 No. 3135), Sched.1, para. 10.]

"Rules of Court" in relation to any court means rules made by the authority having power to make rules or orders regulating the practice and procedure of that court, and in Scotland includes Acts of Adjournal and Acts of Sederunt; and the power of the authority to make rules of court (as above defined) includes power to make such rules for the purpose of any Act which directs or authorises anything to be done by rules of court. [1889]
"Secretary of State" means one of Her Majesty's Principal Secretaries of State.
"Senior Courts" means the Senior Courts of England and Wales.

[This definition was inserted by the Constitutional Reform Act 2005, s.59(5), and Sched. 11, para. 24.]

"Sent for trial" means, in relation to England and Wales, sent by a magistrates' court to the Crown Court for trial pursuant to section 51 or 51A of the Crime and Disorder Act 1998.

[This definition was inserted by the CJA 2003, s.41, and Sched. 3, para. 49(b).]

... .
"The standard scale", with reference to a fine or penalty for an offence triable only summarily,—
    (a) in relation to England and Wales, has the meaning given by section 37 of the Criminal Justice Act 1982;
    (b) [*Scotland*];
    (c) [*Northern Ireland*].

[This definition was inserted by the CJA 1988, s.170(1), and Sched. 15, para. 58(a). (For s.37 of the 1982 Act, see the main work, § 5-683.)]

"Statutory declaration" means a declaration made by virtue of the Statutory Declarations Act 1835.
"Statutory maximum", with reference to a fine or penalty on summary conviction for an offence—
    (a) in relation to England and Wales, means the prescribed sum within the meaning of section 32 of the Magistrates' Courts Act 1980;
    (b) [*Scotland*]; and
    (c) [*Northern Ireland*].

[This definition was inserted by the CJA 1988, s.170(1), and Sched. 15, para. 58(b). (For s.32 of the 1980 Act, see the main work, § 1-123.)]

"Supreme Court" means the Supreme Court of the United Kingdom.

[This definition is printed as amended by the Constitutional Reform Act 2005, s.59(5), and Sched. 11, para. 24.]

"The Treasury" means the Commissioners of Her Majesty's Treasury.
"United Kingdom" means Great Britain and Northern Ireland. [12th April 1927]
"Wales" means the combined area of the counties which were created by section 20 of the Local

Government Act 1972, as originally enacted, but subject to any alteration made under section 73 of that Act (consequential alteration of boundary following alteration of watercourse) [1st April 1974]

[This definition was substituted by the Local Government (Wales) Act 1994, Sched. 2, para. 9.]

... .

"Writing" includes typing, printing, lithography, photography and other modes of representing or reproducing words in avisible form, and expressions referring to writing are construed accordingly.

Construction of certain expressions relating to offences

In relation to England and Wales—
    (a) "indictable offence" means an offence which, if committed by an adult, is triable on indictment, whether it is exclusively so triable or triable either way;
    (b) "summary offence" means an offence which, if committed by an adult, is triable only summarily;
    (c) "offence triable either way" means an offence, other than an offence triable on indictment only by virtue of Part V of the Criminal Justice Act 1988 which, if committed by an adult, is triable either on indictment or summarily;
and the terms "indictable", "summary" and "triable either way", in their application to offences are to be construed accordingly.

In the above definitions references to the way or ways in which an offence is triable are to be construed without regard to the effect, if any, of section 22 of the Magistrates' Courts Act 1980 on the mode of trial in a particular case.

[This para. is printed as amended by the MCA 1980, Sched. 7; and the CJA 1988, Sched. 15, para. 59.]

Construction of certain references to relationships

In relation to England and Wales—
    (a) references (however expressed) to any relationship between two persons;
    (b) references to a person whose father and mother were or were not married to each other at the time of his birth; and
    (c) references cognate with references falling within paragraph (b) above,
shall be construed in accordance with section 1 of the Family Law Reform Act 1987. [The date of the coming into force of that section.]

[This para. was added by Schedule 2 to the Family Law Reform Act 1987.]

Construction of certain expressions relating to the police: Scotland

In relation to Scotland—
    (a) references to a police force include references to the Police Service of Scotland;
    (b) references to a chief officer of police include references to the chief constable of the Police Service of Scotland;
    (c) "police authority" means the Scottish Police Authority;
    (d) the "police area" of the Police Service of Scotland is Scotland and references to a police force or police authority for any area include references to the Police Service of Scotland or, as the case may be, the Scottish Police Authority;
    (e) references to a constable or chief constable of, or appointed for, any area are to be construed as references to a constable or, as the case may be, the chief constable of, or appointed for, the Police Service of Scotland.

[This para. was added by the Police and Fire Reform (Scotland) Act 2012 (Consequential Provisions and Modifications) Order 2013 (S.I. 2013 No. 602).]

NOTE: the definitions of the following expressions have been omitted: "Associated state", "Bank of Ireland", "Building regulations", "Charity Commissioners", "Comptroller and Auditor General", "Consular officer", "The Corporation Tax Acts", "Crown Estate Commissioners", "Financial year", "The Income Tax Acts", "Lands Clauses Act", "National Debt Commissioners",

"Northern Ireland legislation", "Sewerage undertaker", "Sheriff", "The Tax Acts" and "Water undertaker".

SCHEDULE 2

APPLICATION OF ACT TO EXISTING ENACTMENTS

PART I

ACTS

1. The following provisions of this Act apply to Acts whenever passed:—   **B-29**

   Section 6(a) and (c) so far as applicable to enactments relating to offences punishable on indictment or on summary conviction

   Section 9

   Section 10

   Section 11 so far as it relates to subordinate legislation made after the year 1889

   Section 14A

   Section 18

   Section 19(2).

[Para. 1 is printed as amended by the Enterprise and Regulatory Reform Act 2013, s.59(1) and (3).]

2. The following apply to Acts passed after the year 1850:—

   Section 1

   Section 2

   Section 3

   Section 6(a) and (c) so far as not applicable to such Acts by virtue of paragraph 1

   Section 15

   Section 17(1).

3. The following apply to Acts passed after the year 1889:—

   Section 4

   Section 7

   Section 8

   Section 12

   Section 13

   Section 14 so far as it relates to rules, regulations or byelaws

   Section 16(1)

   Section 17(2)(a)

   Section 19(1)

   Section 20(1).

4.—(1) Subject to the following provisions of this paragraph—

   (a) paragraphs of Schedule 1 at the end of which a year or date is specified or described apply, so far as applicable, to Acts passed on or after the date, or after the year, so specified or described; and

   (b) paragraphs of that Schedule at the end of which no year or date is specified or described apply, so far as applicable, to Acts passed at any time.

(2) The definition of "British Islands", in its application to Acts passed after the establishment of the Irish Free State but before the commencement of this Act, includes the Republic of Ireland.

(3) The definition of "colony", in its application to an Act passed at any time before the commencement of this Act, includes—

   (a) any colony within the meaning of section 18(3) of the Interpretation Act 1889 which was excluded, but in relation only to Acts passed at a later time, by any enactment repealed by this Act;

   (b) any country or territory which ceased after that time to be part of Her Majesty's dominions but subject to a provision for the continuation of existing law as if it had not so ceased;

and paragraph (b) of the definition does not apply.

(4) The definition of "Lord Chancellor" does not apply to Acts passed before 1st October 1921 in which that expression was used in relation to Ireland only.

(5) The definition of "person", so far as it includes bodies corporate, applies to any provision of an Act whenever passed relating to an offence punishable on indictment or on summary conviction.

(6) This paragraph applies to the National Health Service Reorganisation Act 1973 and the Water Act 1973 as if they were passed after 1st April 1974.

[Para. 4 is printed as amended by the Family Law Reform Act 1987, Scheds 2 and 4.]

5. The following definitions shall be treated as included in Schedule 1 for the purposes specified in this paragraph—

    (a) in any Act passed before 1st April 1974, a reference to England includes Berwick upon Tweed and Monmouthshire and, in the case of an Act passed before the Welsh Language Act 1967, Wales;

    (b) in any Act passed before the commencement of this Act and after the year 1850, "land" includes messuages, tenements and hereditaments, houses and buildings of any tenure;

    (c) [*Scotland*].

PART II

SUBORDINATE LEGISLATION

B-30

6. Sections 4(a), 9 and 19(1), and so much of Schedule 1 as defines the following expressions, namely—

    England;

    Local land charges register and appropriate local land charges register;

    in relation to Scotland, expressions relating to the police;

    United Kingdom;

    Wales;

apply to subordinate legislation made at any time before the commencement of this Act as they apply to Acts passed at that time.

[Para. 6 is printed as amended by the British Nationality Act 1981, Sched. 9; and the Police and Fire Reform (Scotland) Act 2012 (Consequential Provisions and Modifications) Order 2013 (S.I. 2013 No. 602).]

7. The definition in Schedule 1 of "county court", in relation to England and Wales, applies to Orders in Council made after the year 1846.

APPENDIX C
The Duties of Advocates

I. CODE OF CONDUCT

The first edition of the Bar Standards Board Handbook came into force on January 6, 2014. It   **C-1**
contains (in Part 2) the ninth edition of the Code of Conduct for the Bar of England and Wales.
Part 1 of the handbook is an introduction. Parts 3 and 4 contain the scope of practice rules and
the qualification rules. Part 5 comprises the enforcement regulations and Part 6 provides for the
interpretation of terms used throughout the handbook.

Within the code, there are "core duties", "outcomes", "rules" and "guidance". The significance
of each is explained in the introductory section of the handbook. Thus the core duties (italicised
words and expressions are defined in Part 6)—

> "underpin the entire regulatory framework and set the mandatory standards that all *BSB regulated
> persons* are required to meet. They also define the core elements of professional conduct.
> Disciplinary proceedings may be taken against a *BSB regulated person* if the *Bar Standards Board*
> believes there has been a breach by that person of the Core Duties set out in this *Handbook* and
> that such action would be in accordance with the *Enforcement Policy*."

The outcomes—

> "explain the reasons for the regulatory scheme and what it is designed to achieve. They are
> derived from the *regulatory objectives* as defined in the *LSA* and the risks which must be managed if
> those objectives are to be achieved. They are not themselves mandatory rules, but they are factors
> which *BSB regulated persons* should have in mind when considering how the Core Duties, Conduct
> Rules or Qualification Rules (as appropriate) should be applied in particular circumstances. The
> *Bar Standards Board* will take into account whether or not an Outcome has, or might have been,
> adversely affected when considering how to respond to alleged breaches of the Core Duties,
> Conduct Rules or Qualification Rules."

The conduct rules (*i.e.* those in the code of conduct)—

> "supplement the Core Duties and are mandatory. Disciplinary proceedings may be taken against a
> *BSB regulated person* if the *Bar Standards Board* believes there has been a breach by that person of
> the Conduct Rules set out in Part 2 of this *Handbook* and that it would be in accordance with the
> *Enforcement policy* to take such action. However, the Conduct Rules are not intended to be
> exhaustive. In any situation where no specific Rule applies, reference should be made to the Core
> Duties. In situations where specific Rules do apply, it is still necessary to consider the Core Duties,
> since compliance with the Rules alone will not necessarily be sufficient to comply with the Core
> Duties."

The guidance is self-explanatory, its principal purpose being to assist in the interpretation of
the core duties and rules.

The code of conduct itself is divided into four sections: A - Application, B - The Core Duties, C   **C-2**
- The Conduct Rules, and D - Rules Applying to Particular Groups of Regulated Persons. The
conduct rules are themselves divided into five sections, *viz.* C1 "You and the court", C2 "Behaving ethically", C3 "You and your client", C4 "You and your regulator" and C5 "You and your
practice". So far as practice in court is concerned, the most important rules are contained in section C1. These, together with the core duties, are set in full, *post.* The handbook runs to a total of
277 pages and space precludes the inclusion of more detail. However it should be noted that C2
(behaving ethically) contains provisions relating to honesty, integrity and independence, referral
fees, undertakings, discrimination and foreign work, and that C3 (you and your client) has rules
relating to "best interests of each client, provision of a competent standard of work, and
confidentiality", "not misleading clients and potential clients", "personal responsibility", "accepting instructions", "defining terms or basis on which instructions are accepted", "returning instructions", "requirement not to discriminate", "the 'cab-rank rule'" and the "quality assurance scheme
for advocates rules".

Core duties

CD1	You must observe your duty to the court in the administration of justice.	
CD2	You must act in the best interests of each client.	
CD3	You must act with honesty and integrity.	
CD4	You must maintain your independence.	
CD5	You must not behave in a way which is likely to diminish the trust and confidence which the public places in you or in the profession.	
CD6	You must keep the affairs of each client confidential.	
CD7	You must provide a competent standard of work and service to each client.	
CD8	You must not discriminate unlawfully against any person.	
CD9	You must be open and co-operative with your regulators.	
CD10	You must take reasonable steps to manage your practice, or carry out your role within your practice, competently and in such a way as to achieve compliance with your legal and regulatory obligations.	

Guidance to the core duties

gC1 The Core Duties are not presented in order of precedence, subject to the following:

.1 CD1 overrides any other core duty, if and to the extent the two are inconsistent. Rules C3.5 and C4 deal specifically with the relationship between CD1, CD2 and CD6 and you should refer to those rules and to the related Guidance;

.2 in certain other circumstances set out in this Code of Conduct one Core Duty overrides another. Specifically, Rule C16 provides that CD2 (as well as being subject to CD1) is subject to your obligations under CD3, CD4 and CD8.

gC2 Your obligation to take reasonable steps to manage your *practice*, or carry out your role within your *practice*, competently and in such a way as to achieve compliance with your legal and regulatory obligations (CD10) includes an obligation to take all reasonable steps to mitigate the effects of any breach of those legal and regulatory obligations once you become aware of the same.

The Conduct Rules

C.1 You and the court

Outcomes

oC1 The *court* is able to rely on information provided to it by those conducting litigation and by advocates who appear before it.

oC2 The proper administration of justice is served.

oC3 The interests of *clients* are protected to the extent compatible with outcomes oC1 and oC2 and the Core Duties.

oC4 Both those who appear before the *court* and *clients* understand clearly the extent of the duties owed to the *court* by advocates and those conducting litigation and the circumstances in which duties owed to *clients* will be overridden by the duty owed to the *court*.

oC5 *The public* has confidence in the administration of justice and in those who serve it.

Rules

rC3 You owe a duty to the *court* to act with independence in the interests of justice. This duty overrides any inconsistent obligations which you may have (other than obligations under the criminal law). It includes the following specific obligations which apply whether you are acting as an advocate or are otherwise involved in the conduct of litigation in whatever role (with the exception of Rule C3.1 below, which applies when acting as an advocate):

.1 you must not knowingly or recklessly mislead or attempt to mislead the *court*;

.2 you must not abuse your role as an advocate;

.3 you must take reasonable steps to avoid wasting the *court's* time;

.4 you must take reasonable steps to ensure that the *court* has before it all relevant decisions and legislative provisions;

.5 you must ensure that your ability to act independently is not compromised.

rC4 Your duty to act in the best interests of each *client* is subject to your duty to the *court*.

rC5 Your duty to the *court* does not require you to act in breach of your duty to keep the affairs of each *client* confidential.

Not misleading the court

rC6 Your duty not to mislead the *court* or to permit the *court* to be misled will include the following obligations: **C-7**

    .1 you must not:

        .a make submissions, representations or any other statement; or

        .b ask questions which suggest facts to witnesses

        which you know, or are instructed, are untrue or misleading.

    .2 you must not call witnesses to give evidence or put affidavits or witness statements to the *court* which you know, or are *instructed*, are untrue or misleading, unless you make clear to the *court* the true position as known by or instructed to you.

Not abusing your role as an advocate

rC7 Where you are acting as an advocate, your duty not to abuse your role includes the following obligations: **C-8**

    .1 you must not make statements or ask questions merely to insult, humiliate or annoy a witness or any other person;

    .2 you must not make a serious allegation against a witness whom you have had an opportunity to cross-examine unless you have given that witness a chance to answer the allegation in cross-examination;

    .3 you must not make a serious allegation against any person, or suggest that a person is guilty of a crime with which your *client* is charged unless:

        .a you have reasonable grounds for the allegation; and

        .b the allegation is relevant to your *client's* case or the credibility of a witness; and

        .c where the allegation relates to a third party, you avoid naming them in open *court* unless this is reasonably necessary.

    .4 you must not put forward to the *court* a personal opinion of the facts or the law unless you are invited or required to do so by the *court* or by law.

Guidance

Guidance on Rules C3 - C6 and relationship to CD1 and CD2

gC3 Rules C3 - C6 set out some specific aspects of your duty to the *court* (CD1). See CD1 and associated Guidance at gC1. **C-9**

gC4 Knowingly misleading the *court* includes inadvertently misleading the *court* if you later realise that you have misled the *court*, and you fail to correct the position. Recklessness means being indifferent to the truth, or not caring whether something is true or false. The duty continues to apply for the duration of the case.

gC5 Your duty under Rule C3.3 includes drawing to the attention of the *court* any decision or provision which may be adverse to the interests of your *client*. It is particularly important where you are appearing against a litigant who is not legally represented.

gC6 You are obliged by CD2 to promote and to protect your *client's* interests so far as that is consistent with the law and with your overriding duty to the *court* under CD1. Your duty to the *court* does not prevent you from putting forward your *client's* case simply because you do not believe that the facts are as your *client* states them to be (or as you, on your *client's* behalf, state them to be), as long as any positive case you put forward accords with your *instructions* and you do not mislead the *court*. Your role when acting as an advocate or conducting litigation is to present your *client's* case, and it is not for you to decide whether your *client's* case is to be believed.

gC7 For example, you are entitled and it may often be appropriate to draw to the witness's attention other evidence which appears to conflict with what the witness is saying and you are entitled to indicate that a *court* may find a particular piece of evidence difficult to accept. But if the witness maintains that the evidence is true, it should be recorded in the witness statement and you will not be misleading the *court* if you call the witness to confirm their witness statement. Equally, there may be circumstances where you call a hostile witness whose evidence you are instructed is untrue. You will not be in breach of Rule C6 if you make the position clear to the *court*. See further the guidance at gC14.

gC8 As set out in Rule C4, your duty to the *court* does not permit or require you to disclose confidential information which you have obtained in the course of your *instructions* and which your *client* has not authorised you to disclose to the *court*. However, Rule C6 requires you not knowingly to mislead the *court* or to permit the *court* to be misled. There may be situations where you have obligations under both these rules.

gC9 Rule C3.5 makes it clear that your duty to act in the best interests of your *client* is subject to your duty to the *court*. For example, if your *client* were to tell you that he had committed the crime with which he was charged, in order to be able to ensure compliance with Rule C4 on the one hand and Rule C3 and Rule C6 on the other:

  .1 you would not be entitled to disclose that information to the *court* without your *client's* consent; and

  .2 you would not be misleading the *court* if, after your *client* had entered a plea of "not guilty", you were to test in cross-examination the reliability of the evidence of the prosecution witnesses and then address the jury to the effect that the prosecution had not succeeded in making them sure of your *client's* guilt.

gC10 However, you would be misleading the *court* and would therefore be in breach of Rules C3 and C6 if you were to set up a positive case inconsistent with the confession, as for example by:

  .1 suggesting to prosecution witnesses, calling your *client* or your witnesses to show; or submitting to the *jury*, that your *client* did not commit the crime; or

  .2 suggesting that someone else had done so; or

  .3 putting forward an alibi.

gC11 If there is a risk that the *court* will be misled unless you disclose confidential information which you have learned in the course of your *instructions*, you should ask the client for permission to disclose it to the *court*. If your *client* refuses to allow you to make the disclosure you must cease to act, and return your *instructions*: see Rules C25 to C27 below. In these circumstances you must not reveal the information to the *court*.

gC12 For example, if your *client* tells you that he has previous *convictions* of which the prosecution is not aware, you may not disclose this without his consent. However, in a case where mandatory sentences apply, the non-disclosure of the previous *convictions* will result in the *court* failing to pass the sentence that is required by law. In that situation, you must advise your *client* that if consent is refused to your revealing the information you will have to cease to act. In situations where mandatory sentences do not apply, and your *client* does not agree to disclose the previous *convictions*, you can continue to represent your *client* but in doing so must not say anything that misleads the *court*. This will constrain what you can say in mitigation. For example, you could not advance a positive case of previous good character knowing that there are undisclosed prior *convictions*. Moreover, if the *court* asks you a direct question you must not give an untruthful answer and therefore you would have to withdraw if, on your being asked such a question, your *client* still refuses to allow you to answer the question truthfully. You should explain this to your *client*.

gC13 Similarly, if you become aware that your *client* has a document which should be disclosed but has not been disclosed, you cannot continue to act unless your *client* agrees to the disclosure of the document. In these circumstances you must not reveal the existence or contents of the document to the *court*.

[The next paragraph is C-20.]

II. BAR COUNCIL GUIDANCE

Written standards of work

C-20   The Bar Council issued written standards for the conduct of professional work together with the eighth edition of the code of conduct. They did not form part of the code, but paragraph 701(d) obliged a barrister "to have regard to any relevant written standards." They can still be found on the website of the Bar Standards Board, but it does not appear that they are intended to have any continuing effect as there is a statement at the top of the page to the effect that, as from January 6, 2014, barristers should refer to the board's handbook (as to which, see *ante*, C-1) for rules and guidance on their conduct as such.

[The next paragraph is C-45.]

Criticism of previous counsel

In consequence of observations made by the Court of Appeal in *R. v. Clarke and Jones, The* **C-45** *Times,* August 19, 1994, and *R. v. Bowler, The Times,* May 9, 1995, the following guidance was approved by Lord Taylor C.J. and the Bar Council. It is still to be found on the website of the Bar Council, but it is emphasised there that it is not "guidance" for the purposes of the Bar Standards Board's handbook (as to which, see *ante*, C-1)), and it is accompanied by a disclaimer to the effect that it does not constitute legal advice and a statement to the effect that it was prepared by the Bar Council to assist barristers on matters of professional conduct and ethics.

1. Allegations against former counsel may receive substantial publicity whether accepted or rejected by the court. Counsel should not settle or sign grounds of appeal unless he is satisfied that they are reasonable, have some real prospect of success and are such that he is prepared to argue before the court (Guide to Proceedings in the Court of Appeal Criminal Division, para. A2-6 [*post*, Appendix J-5]). When such allegations are properly made however, in accordance with the Code of Conduct counsel newly instructed must promote and protect fearlessly by all proper and lawful means his lay client's best interests without regard to others, including fellow members of the legal profession (Code, para. 303(a)).

2. When counsel newly instructed is satisfied that such allegations are made, and a waiver of privilege is necessary, he should advise the lay client fully about the consequences of waiver and should obtain a waiver of privilege in writing signed by the lay client relating to communications with, instructions given to and advice given by former counsel. The allegations should be set out in the Grounds of Application for Leave of Appeal. Both waiver and grounds should be lodged without delay; the grounds may be perfected if necessary in due course.

3. On receipt of the waiver and grounds, the Registrar of Criminal Appeals will send both to former counsel with an invitation on behalf of the court to respond to the allegations made.

4. If former counsel wishes to respond and considers the time for doing so insufficient, he should ask the Registrar for further time. The court will be anxious to have full information and to give counsel adequate time to respond.

5. The response should be sent to the Registrar. On receipt, he will send it to counsel newly instructed who may reply to it. The grounds and the responses will go before the single judge.

6. The Registrar may have received grounds of appeal direct from the applicant, and obtained a waiver of privilege before fresh counsel is assigned. In those circumstances, when assigning counsel, the Registrar will provide copies of the waiver, the grounds of appeal and any response from former counsel.

7. This guidance covers the formal procedures to be followed. It is perfectly proper for counsel newly instructed to speak to former counsel as a matter of courtesy before grounds are lodged to inform him of the position.

As to the need to follow the Bar Council's guidance, see *R. v. Nasser, The Times,* February 19, 1998, CA.

Preparation of defence statements

As to guidance regarding the duties of counsel in relation to the preparation of defence state- **C-46** ments, see § 12-122 in the main work.

III. MISCELLANEOUS AUTHORITIES ON DUTIES OF ADVOCATES

(1) Return of brief or instructions

Members of the criminal bar have a personal responsibility for compliance with provisions of **C-47** the Code of Conduct relating to the return of instructions, of which their clerks should be aware. It is open to a court concerned with a problem caused by a late return of a brief to send a complaint to the Professional Conduct Committee of the Bar Council: *R. v. Sutton JJ., ex p. DPP,* 95 Cr.App.R. 180, DC, *per* Brooke J., at p. 186 (decided in relation to paragraphs 507 and 508 of the fifth edition of the Code of Conduct).

The absence of what counsel would regard as sufficient time for preparation does not constitute an exception to the cab-rank rule requiring him to act for his client: see *R. v. Ulcay* (§ 4-67 in the main work).

(2) Duty not to accept certain instructions

C-48   Counsel should not appear for the prosecution in a case where the defendant is a person he has previously represented; para. 501(f) of the Code of Conduct for the Bar (6th ed.) referred to the risk that the barrister might have considential information or special knowledge disadvantageous to the defendant, his former client; it is contrary to the spirit of the code that a barrister should put himself in a position where such a risk might be perceived: *R. v. Dann* [1997] Crim.L.R. 46, CA. As to *Dann*, see further *Re T. and A. (Children) (Risk of Disclosure)* [2002] 1 F.L.R. 859, CA (Civ.Div.).

(3) Duty in relation to the giving of advice and taking of instructions

C-48a   Although not laid down in prescriptive form in the codes of conduct governing barristers and solicitors, solicitors and counsel should make a brief note of the advice given and the instructions received in conference on important issues as to the conduct of the defence (such as discussions relating to strategy, including as to whether the defendant should give evidence); such a note would be to the benefit of the client, in that it will serve to ensure that he has been given the appropriate advice; it would also serve to protect the advocate and his instructing solicitors from criticism based on assertions made after the event by a dissatisfied client: *R. v. Anderson, The Times,* December 23, 2010, CA.

(4) Duty of counsel to acquaint themselves with the terms of the indictment

C-49   See *R. v. Peckham*, 25 Cr.App.R. 125, CCA (prosecution), and *R. v. Olivo*, 28 Cr.App.R. 173, CCA (defence).

(5) Duty concerning recent legislation

C-50   In *R. v. Isaacs, The Times,* February 9, 1990, the Court of Appeal said that when presenting cases at first instance or in appellate courts, counsel have a positive duty to inform the court of all relevant commencement dates of recent legislation.

(6) Duty of counsel to inform themselves of the sentencing powers of the court

C-51   The Court of Appeal has repeatedly emphasised the duty of both counsel to inform themselves before the commencement of proceedings in the Crown Court of the sentencing powers of the court, including powers in relation to ancillary orders, such as costs, compensation, etc. The starting point is *R. v. Clarke (R.W.W.)*, 59 Cr.App.R. 298, CA. Lawton L.J. concluded the judgment of the court with the following general observations and guidance. His Lordship's remarks are even more apposite today than when they were made: legislation in relation to sentence has become ever more complex. Sections 28 and 29 of the MCA 1952 were replaced by sections 37 and 38 respectively of the MCA 1980, which have themselves since been subject to extensive amendment. Section 37 was eventually repealed by the CDA 1998, and section 38 was repealed and replaced by section 3 of the PCC(S)A 2000.

> "We adjudge that counsel as a matter of professional duty to the Court, and in the case of defending counsel to their client, should always before starting a criminal case satisfy themselves as to what the maximum sentence is. There can be no excuse for counsel not doing this and they should remember that the performance of this duty is particularly important in a case where a man has been committed to the Crown Court for sentencing pursuant to the provisions of sections 28 and 29 of the Magistrates' Courts Act 1952, and section 56 of the Criminal Justice Act 1967. Those statutory provisions are pregnant with dangers for court and for counsel and above all for accused persons...
>
> Secondly, those who administer the Crown Court should act as follows. Before the Crown Court came into existence..., it was the practice of many clerks of assize and many clerks of the peace to make a note on the documents put before the trial judge of the maximum sentence which could be passed and of the paragraphs in *Archbold's Criminal Pleading, Evidence and Practice* which dealt with the offence. In some Crown Courts this former practice has been followed. On the other hand it is clear from this case and from inquiries which we have made that it is not

always followed. It should be; and it is particularly important that it should be when judges are asked to deal with cases committed for sentence under the statutory provisions to which I have already referred" (at pp. 301–302).

A reminder of the duty of counsel for both sides to ensure that sentences imposed, and orders made, are within the powers of the court, and to invite the court to vary a sentence if on subsequent consideration it appears to be unlawful, was given in *R. v. Komsta and Murphy*, 12 Cr.App.R.(S.) 63. Turner J. commented that it could not be too clearly understood that there was positive obligation on counsel, both for the prosecution and the defence, to ensure that no order was made that the court had no power to make. The PCC(S)A 2000, s. 155(1) (see § 5-1289 in the main work) allowed the Crown Court to alter or vary any sentence or order, within the period of 28 [now 56] days of the making of the order. If it appeared to either counsel that the order was one which the court had no power to make, counsel should not hesitate to invite the court to exercise such powers.

See also *R. v. Richards, The Times*, April 1, 1993, CA, *R. v. Hartrey* [1993] Crim.L.R. 230, CA, *R. v. Johnstone (D.), The Times*, June 18, 1996, CA, *R. v. Bruley* [1996] Crim.L.R. 913, CA, *R. v. McDonnell* [1996] Crim.L.R. 914, CA, *R. v. Street*, 161 J.P. 28, CA, *R. v. Blight* [1999] Crim.L.R. 426, CA and, most recently, *R. v. Cain* [2007] 2 Cr.App.R.(S.) 25, CA. In *Blight*, it was said that counsel do not discharge their duty simply by having a copy of *Archbold* "to hand"; it is the duty of both counsel to be aware in advance of the powers of the court so that any error may be recited immediately; as to the defence counsel, it was said to be very difficult to see how mitigation can be done properly without having in the very front of the mind the powers within which the judge must exercise his duty. In *R. v. Cain*, it was said that defence advocates should ascertain and be prepared to assist the judge with any relevant legal restrictions on sentence, and the prosecution advocate should ensure that the sentencer does not, through inadvertence, impose an unlawful sentence; in particular, prosecution advocates should always be ready to assist the court by drawing attention to any statutory provisions that govern the court's sentencing powers and to any sentencing guidelines or guideline decisions of the Court of Appeal.

In *R. v. Reynolds* [2007] 2 Cr.App.R.(S.) 87, CA, it was said that prosecuting and defence **C-52** advocates must ensure that they are fully aware of the potential impact of the provisions of the dangerous offender provisions in Chapter 5 of Part 12 of the CJA 2003 (§§ 5-495 *et seq.* in the main work), that they are able to assist the sentencer in that respect and are alert to any mistakes made in passing sentence so that any problem can be resolved before it is too late.

(7) Defendant absconding

See generally, §§ 3-222 *et seq.* in the main work, and *R. v. Shaw*, 70 Cr.App.R. 313, CA (§ 7-87 **C-53** in the main work).

(8) Defendant not giving evidence

In *R. v. Bevan*, 98 Cr.App.R. 354, CA, it was held that where a defendant decides not to give **C-54** evidence, it should be the invariable practice of counsel to record that decision and to cause the defendant to sign that record, indicating clearly first, that he has, of his own free will, decided not to give evidence and, secondly, that he has so decided bearing in mind the advice given to him by counsel. In the light of section 35 of the CJPOA 1994 (§ 4-377 in the main work), the advice of the Court of Appeal in *Bevan* is likely to become of greater importance than at the time of the decision. As to this, see also *Ebanks (Kurt) v. The Queen* [2006] 1 W.L.R. 1827, PC (§ 4-382 in the main work).

(9) Duties in relation to cross-examination

See §§ 8-216, 8-219 *et seq.* in the main work and, in relation to defence counsel's duty when **C-55** cross-examining a co-defendant, see *R. v. Fenlon*, 71 Cr.App.R. 307, CA, see § 8-297 in the main work.

(10) Duties in relation to the summing up

See §§ 4-433 *et seq.* in the main work. **C-56**

(11) Duties in relation to appeal

As to the duty to advise in relation to the possibility of an appeal against conviction or sentence, **C-57** see §§ 7-165 *et seq.* in the main work.

As to counsel's general duty in relation to the drafting of grounds of appeal, see § 7-168 in the main work. As to criticism of former counsel, see § 7-83 in the main work and *ante*, and § C-45, *ante*.

As to the duty of counsel for the prosecution, see § 7-201 in the main work.

The duty of a barrister to present his client's case before the Court of Appeal could not extend to advancing the client's assertion, unsubstantiated by any evidence, that the trial judge was corrupt or biased. A barrister's duty in such circumstances is either to decline to comply with the instructions or to withdraw from the case: *Thatcher v. Douglas, The Times*, January 8, 1996, CA (Civ. Div.).

(12) Duties of prosecuting counsel

C-58   Apart from the matters mentioned above, see also (a) *The Role and Responsibilities of the Prosecution Advocate, post*, E-15 *et seq.*; (b) *R. v. Herbert*, 94 Cr.App.R. 230, CA (§ 4-173 in the main work) and *R. v. Richards and Stober*, 96 Cr.App.R. 258, CA (§ 19-103 in the main work), in relation to "plea-bargaining" and the acceptance of pleas, with particular reference to cases where there are two or more defendants; (c) §§ 4-342 *et seq.* in the main work, in relation to the opening of a case generally, and *R. v. Hobstaff*, 14 Cr.App.R.(S.) 605, CA, in relation to opening the facts on a plea of guilty; and (d) the Attorney-General's guidelines on the acceptance of pleas and the prosecutor's role in the sentencing exercise (*ante*, Appendix A-276 *et seq.*).

(13) Advocate as witness

C-59   In *R. v. Jacquith (or Jaquith) and Emode* [1989] Crim.L.R. 508 and 563, CA, junior counsel for one defendant has been called on his behalf to rebut a suggestion of recent invention made against him. The Court of Appeal said that the evidence on this point was admissible but it was very undesirable for counsel to give evidence on this point in court. In addition to the effect on the jury it caused embarrassment and difficulty to other members of the Bar who had to set about cross-examining a colleague.

May L.J. said that the suggestion had been made that the court give some indication of its views concerning evidence given by counsel and also where a client alleged an attempt to pervert the court of justice by a co-defendant. their Lordships considered, however, that the right course would be to list points for consideration by the Bar Council and the Law Society. It was not sought to lay these maters down as ones of principle; their Lordships merely thought they deserved consideration.

1. No advocate should ever give evidence if that could possibly be avoided. 2. Where it was not possible for an advocate to avoid giving evidence, he should take no further part in the case. It necessarily followed that, if he was not being led, the trial must stop and a retrial be ordered. 3. There was a duty on counsel to anticipate circumstances in which he might be called upon to give evidence. Experienced counsel ought to be able to anticipate whether such a situation might arise. Where such a situation was anticipated, or envisaged even as a possibility, he should withdraw from the case. 4. Where it came to the notice of a legal adviser, through an accused person, that one of his co-defendants had attempted to pervert the court of justice, there was a duty on the legal adviser, usually the instructing solicitor, to take a detailed proof at once to provide a record and for further investigation. 5. Where the giving of evidence by an advocate caused real embarrassment or inhibition or difficulty regarding cross-examination by other advocates, the judge should exercise his discretion to discharge the jury and order a retrial.

(14) Co-habiting counsel

C-60   It is generally undesirable for husband and wife, or other partners living together, to appear as counsel on opposite sides in the same criminal matter since it might give rise to an apprehension that the proper conduct of the case had been in some way affected by that personal relationship: *R. v. Batt, The Times*, May 30, 1996, CA. See also *Re L. (Minors) (Care Proceedings: Solicitors)* [2001] 1 W.L.R. 100, Fam D. (Wilson J.).

APPENDIX D
Forms for use at Preliminary Hearings and Plea and Case Management Hearings

CROWN COURT

CASE PROGRESSION

PRELIMINARY HEARING

Date of hearing: / /　　　　　　　　　Judge:

Prosecution advocate:		
D1	[bail][custody] represented by:	
D2	[bail][custody] represented by:	
D3	[bail][custody] represented by:	
D4	[bail][custody] represented by:	
D5	[bail][custody] represented by:	

No. of case in Crown Court:　　　　　　　　URN:

Has the defendant been advised about credit for pleading guilty?	D1	D2	D3	D4	D5
Has the defendant been warned that if he is on bail and fails to attend, the proceedings may continue in his absence?					

1) TRIAL JUDGE

Should the future management of the case be under the supervision of the trial judge or a
nominated judge?　　　　　　　　　　　　　　　　　　　　　YES/NO

2) PLEA

a.	Is it likely that the case can be concluded by the defendant pleading guilty?	D1	D2	D3	D4	D5

b. If yes and if the defendant cannot be sentenced at the preliminary hearing, go to 3) and/or
4) as appropriate

3) LIKELY GUILTY PLEA

a. *The defendant will be sentenced on:　 / /　 or at the plea and case management hearing*

b. *The directions made by the magistrates' court when the case was sent shall apply subject to
the following amendments:*

c. *The pre-sentence report (if required) to be received by the Crown Court and made
available to the defence and the prosecution by:*

d. *The defence to serve any material which it wishes the court to consider when sentencing
by:*

e.	Does the defence intend to make "derogatory assertions" against a person's character in the course of mitigation?	D1	D2	D3	D4	D5

f. *If yes, the court orders:*

g. Are there any other matters against a defendant which should be dealt with at the same time as the proceedings in this case (other offences/TIC's)?

D1	D2	D3	D4	D5

h. If yes, give brief details:

i. *If there are other matters, the court orders:*

j. *Further orders (e.g. orders re medical, psychiatric reports, confiscation proceedings or Newton hearings):*

4) DIRECTIONS FOR PLEA AND CASE MANAGEMENT HEARING
  a. *The directions made by the Magistrates' Court when the case was sent shall apply subject to the following amendments:*

  b. *Further orders:*

5) EXPERT EVIDENCE
  a. **Is this a case in which the parties will rely on expert evidence?**

P	D1	D2	D3	D4	D5

  b. *If yes, the court orders:*

6) TRIAL
  a. **Can the date of the trial or the period during which the trial will take place be fixed now?**

      YES/NO

  b. *If yes, the trial will take place on:*
      or within the period of:
      and it is estimated that it will last:

CROWN COURT
CASE PROGRESSION
PRELIMINARY HEARING
<u>GUIDANCE NOTES</u>

General notes

These notes accompany the preliminary hearing form.

The parties must ensure that the Court has a copy of the "CASE SENT TO THE CROWN COURT UNDER SECTION 51 OF THE CRIME AND DISORDER ACT 1998" form completed in the Magistrates' Court.

The answers to the questions in bold must be filled in before the hearing. The proposed italicised orders should be filled in before the hearing, if possible (if there are more than five defendants, a further form should be filled in only so far as necessary).

Except where otherwise required, a direction in the form to "serve" material means serve on the other party(ies) and file with the Crown Court.

Notes relevant to specific sections

1) TRIAL JUDGE OR NOMINATED JUDGE

If the case is due to last for more than 4 weeks or if it seems likely that a preparatory hearing will be ordered, the future case management should normally be under the supervision of the trial judge or a nominated judge. It may also be desirable for the future case management to be under the supervision of the trial judge or a nominated judge in other cases where, for example there are difficult issues of law to be considered or where the prosecution intends to make a public interest immunity application.

If the case fits into this category, the court should normally make the necessary directions for the plea and case management hearing and then direct that the case be considered by the Resident Judge.

2) PLEA

If it is likely that the case can be concluded by all the defendants pleading guilty then 3) should be completed and there should be no need to make any orders under 4). Otherwise any appropriate orders under 3) should be made in respect of those defendants likely to plead guilty and 4) should be completed.

3) LIKELY GUILTY PLEA

3b. The Crown Court has a greater power to vary the time limits than the magistrates' court.

3c. A pre-sentence report will not be required in every case.

3e. Advance notice of the fact that such an assertion is going to be made should be given to the prosecution to enable it to decide whether to challenge the assertion and to enable the sentencing court to consider whether to make an order restricting the publication of the assertion under sections 58-61 of the Criminal Procedure and Investigations Act 1996 ("CPIA").

3i. If the defendant is facing charges in other courts give brief details of offence, court and court number.

4) DIRECTIONS FOR PLEA AND CASE MANAGEMENT HEARING

4a. The Crown Court has a greater power to vary the time limits than the Magistrates' Court.

5) EXPERT EVIDENCE

The court should identify any issues in relation to which it is appropriate to call expert evidence and set a timetable for obtaining, serving, and (if possible) agreeing such evidence or identifying the issues in dispute. See also paragraph 15 of the guidance notes to the PCMH form.

The parties should consider whether orders being considered by the court will involve costs being incurred which may not be met by the Legal Services Commission.

7) TRIAL

The court should consider whether it is possible and desirable to set the trial date or period because, for example, of the health, vulnerability or availability of a witness or the defendant or because the defendant falls within the definition of a persistent young offender, or because experts and/or leading counsel may have to be instructed and, before any such instructions can be expected, it is necessary to know the date.

The Crown Court	
CC Case Number D1	
Date of trial	
Fixed	☐
Warned	☐

Plea and Case Management Hearing

Advocates' Questionnaire

■ Parties must complete this form.

■ This form is to be used at all Crown Court Centres, without local variation.

There is an electronic version of the form on the Ministry of Justice website, at:

www.justice.gov.uk/courts/procedure-rules/criminal/formspage

PART ONE
(Questions 1 to 15 are to be completed in all cases, together with question 37 'Witness List')

1   Date of trial and custody time limits

1.1

Date of PCMH

PTI URN

Judge

Estimated length of trial

1.2   What are the custody time limit expiry dates as agreed between the parties? *(If different custody time limits attach to different offences or defendants, please give details.)*

1.3   Can an application to extend any custody time limit be made today?   ☐ No   ☐ Yes

2   Parties

Prosecuting authority		Advocate	
P			

Defendant's name	Age	Remand status	Trial Advocate	PCMH Advocate (if different)
D1		C ☐ B ☐		

Plea and Case Management Hearing, Criminal Procedure Rules – March 2013

3   Contact details

3.1   Parties

     P   Office

Name	Phone
Email	

       Advocate

Name	Phone
Email	

    D1   Solicitor

Name	Phone
Email	

       Advocate

Name	Phone
Email	

3.2   Case progression officers

     P

Name	Phone
Email	

     D1

Name	Phone
Email	

    Court

Name	Phone
Email	

4   Readiness for PCMH

4.1   Which, if any, of the orders made at the magistrates' court have not been complied with?

     P

    D1

4.2   Are the parties ready for the PCMH? If not, why not?

     P

    D1

5   Has the defendant been advised that he or she will receive credit for a guilty plea?

    D1   ☐ No   ☐ Yes

6   Has the defendant been warned that the case may proceed in his or her absence?

    D1   ☐ No   ☐ Yes

7   What guilty plea(s) (if any) is the defendant offering?

    D1

8   Should the case be referred to the Resident Judge for a trial judge to be allocated?   ☐ No   ☐ Yes

9   Give details of any issues relating to the defendant's fitness to plead or to stand trial.

D1

10   Prosecution evidence

10.1   Has the prosecution served the principal evidence on which the prosecution case relies, and if so when (give the date)? If not, why not?

P

10.2   What further evidence (if any) does the prosecution expect to serve? By when is it reasonably practicable to serve it (give the date)?

P

10.3   Defence comments (if any) on the prosecution replies to 10.1 and 10.2:

D1

11   Disclosure, defence statement and defence witness notice

11.1   Has the prosecution made statutory disclosure and if so when (give the date)? If not, why not?

P

11.2   When does / did the time expire for service of a defence statement and witness notice (give the date)?

P

11.3   Defence comments (if any) on the prosecution replies to 11.1 and 11.2:

D1

11.4   Has the defence served (a) a defence statement and (b) a witness notice, and if so when (give the date(s))? If not, why not?

D1

11.5   Do the defence statement and witness notice comply with the statutory requirements?

P   *Prosecution comments (if any):*

11.6   Has the defendant been warned of the consequences of any failure to serve a defence statement and witness notice (a) within the time prescribed and (b) complying with the statutory requirements?   ☐ No   ☐ Yes

11.7   If the defendant has served a defence statement, does the defendant expect to apply for further prosecution disclosure?   ☐ No   ☐ Yes

11.8   If not clear from the defence statement, what are the real issues?

D1

P   *Prosecution comments (if any):*

12   Expert evidence

12.1   Give details of any expert evidence likely to be relied upon, including why it is required and by when it is reasonably practicable to serve this.

P

D1

12.2   Is a note of agreement / disagreement required?

13   Witnesses

13.1   Have the parties completed the Witness List (see **37**)?   ☐ No ☐ Yes

13.2   Are the parties satisfied that all the listed witnesses are needed (see **37**)?   ☐ No ☐ Yes
If 'no', give details.

13.3   Are the parties satisfied that the time estimates for questioning witnesses are realistic (see **37**)?   ☐ No ☐ Yes
If 'no', give details.

13.4   Is any witness summons necessary?   ☐ No ☐ Yes
If 'yes', give particulars:

13.5   Can a timetable be fixed now for the calling of witnesses?   ☐ No ☐ Yes
If 'no', why not?

14   Timetabling of the trial

14.1   Are there matters which need to be determined at the start of the trial, which may affect the timetable?   ☐ No ☐ Yes
If so, when will (1) the jury and (2) the witnesses be required?

What timetable can now be set for the conduct of the trial (see rule 3.10)?

The indictment

14.2

15

15.1   Has the indictment been signed and dated as required by Part 14 of the CrimPR?   ☐ No ☐ Yes

15.2   Is any amendment of the indictment required?   ☐ No ☐ Yes

---

PART TWO
Question 37 (Witness list) is to be completed in every case
Answer the remaining questions only where relevant

---

16   Admissions and agreed facts

What matters can usefully be admitted or put into schedules, diagrams, visual aids etc.?

17   Case summary

P   Is it proposed to serve a case summary or note of opening?   ☐ No ☐ Yes

18   Measures to assist witnesses and defendants in giving evidence

18A   **Measures to assist a witness in giving evidence.**

Each of these issues must be addressed separately in respect of each young vulnerable or intimidated witness who is or may be required to give evidence in person. (If completed electronically, the form will expand to deal with each separate witness separately. If completed manually, attach separate sheets if necessary.)

Name and age of witness:

Name: Age:

What arrangements have been made for a pre-trial visit?

What arrangements have been made to ensure that the witness sees the video of their evidence BEFORE the trial (i.e. not immediately before giving their evidence over the live link)?

Has the witness been offered a 'supporter'?　　　　　　　　　　　　　　　　☐ No　　☐ Yes
If 'yes', give particulars:

Does the witness need an intermediary?　　　　　　　　　　　　　　　　　☐ No　　☐ Yes
If 'yes', give particulars:

What arrangements have been made for the witness to access the court building other than by the main public entrance?

What are the arrangements to ensure that this witness can give evidence without waiting or at least by reducing waiting to a minimum (*e.g. by ensuring that the opening and any preliminary points will be finished before the time appointed for the witness to attend or by agreeing and fixing a timed witness order in advance*)?

Have the views of the witness been sought and, if so, has s/he expressed any particular view or concerns?　　　　　　　　　　　　　　　　　　　　　　　　　☐ No　　☐ Yes

If 'yes', give particulars:

If views not sought, why not?

What material (if any) needs to be available to the witness in the video suite?

18B　　Defendant's evidence direction

Is any defendant's evidence direction to be sought?	☐ No	☐ Yes
If so, has the necessary application been made, complying with Section 4 of CrimPR Part 29?	☐ No	☐ Yes

If so, give details

18C   **Witness anonymity order**

Is any witness anonymity order sought / to be made?   ☐ No   ☐ Yes

If so, has an application been made, complying with Section 5 of CrimPR Part 29?   ☐ No   ☐ Yes

If so give details (subject to the restrictions in Section 5 of CrimPR Part 29).

19   **Young or vulnerable defendants**

Are any other arrangements needed for any young or vulnerable defendants?

D1

20   **Reporting restrictions**

State type and grounds of any reporting restriction sought.

P

D1

21   **Third party material**

Is any application to be made for the production of third party material?   ☐ No   ☐ Yes

22   **Defendant's interview(s)**

22.1   Specify any issue relating to the admissibility of all or any part of the defendant's interview(s). Can the issue be resolved now ? If not, when ? Are skeleton arguments needed and, if so, when ?

22.2   By how much can the interview(s) be shortened by editing / summary for trial ? Give a timetable for the service of any proposed summary by the prosecution and agreement / counter-proposal by the defence.

22.3   Specify any other issues concerning the defendant's interview(s).

23   Witnesses giving evidence by video or DVD interview

23.1   Is there video or DVD evidence of any young / vulnerable / intimidated witness yet to be served?

23.2   Has each video been transcribed?

23.3   Is there an issue in relation to the accuracy / admissibility / quality / length of any video or transcript?

24   Witness interview(s)

24.1   Are there any videos / audio tapes of witness interviews which, if they meet the disclosure test, are yet to be disclosed as unused material?

24.2   If so, is any application made for that video / audio tape to be transcribed and, if so, why?

25   CCTV evidence

25.1   Are there any outstanding issues in relation to service or disclosure of CCTV footage? *If the material is in the possession of a third party, complete 21 instead.*

25.2 Is an edited version to be served / used?

26 Electronic equipment

26.1 Give details of any special equipment (e.g. CCTV, live link, audio recordings, DVD) required in the trial courtroom.

P

D1

26.2 Is the evidence in its present form compatible with the equipment in court?

27 Cross-examination on sexual history

If an application has not already been made, does the defence intend to make an application under section 41 of the Youth Justice and Criminal Evidence Act 1999 to cross-examine a witness about his or her sexual history?

D1

28 Bad character

Are any directions necessary in relation to bad character applications? Are there to be any further applications?

P

D1

29   Hearsay

Are any directions necessary in relation to hearsay applications? Are there to be any further applications?

P

D1

30   Admissibility and legal issues

What points on admissibility / other legal issues are to be taken? Is it necessary for any to be resolved before trial?

P

D1

31   Public interest immunity

Is any 'on notice' public interest immunity application to be made?

P

32   Jury bundle

What proposals do the prosecution make for a jury bundle?

P

33   Concurrent family proceedings

Give details of any concurrent family proceedings.

Plea and Case Management Hearing, Criminal Procedure Rules – March 2013   10

34 **Other special arrangements**

Give details of any special arrangements (e.g., interpreter, intermediary, wheelchair access, hearing loop system, breaks) needed for anyone attending the trial.

35 **Linked criminal proceedings**

Are there other criminal proceedings against the defendant or otherwise linked?

36 **Additional orders**

Are any additional orders required?

37 **Witness List** (see table for completion, over page)

511

37   Witness List

The parties should indicate here which prosecution witnesses are required to give evidence at trial. The attendance of any witness is subject to the judge's direction.

Name of witness	Page No.	Required by	What is the relevant, disputed issue?	Estimated time for questioning	
				Chief	X - exam

Plea and Case Management Hearing Form: Guidance Notes

The need for an effective PCMH

i. The public, and all those concerned in or affected by a criminal case, have a right to expect that the business of the courts will be conducted fairly but also efficiently and effectively. Delays cost money and adversely impact on the quality of justice. The Plea and Case Management Hearing offers the best, and often the only, opportunity for the judge properly and effectively to manage the case before it is listed for trial. Other hearings – formerly called 'mentions' – are expensive and should actively be discouraged; nearly everything formerly done at a 'mention' can – and should – be done in some other way (usually by telephone or on paper or by an exchange of email, as permitted by CrimPR 3.5(2)(d)). An effective PCMH is therefore vital.

ii. Advocates should attend the hearing fully prepared to deal with the issues that are likely to arise, and the listing officer should consider reasonable requests to list the PCMH to enable trial counsel to attend.

iii. Since an effective PCMH can only take place after the defence have had a proper opportunity to consider the papers, it is suggested that at least four weeks should elapse between the service of the prosecution case papers and listing of the PCMH.

iv. The short guidance given here is intended to be followed in every case but, of course, it is not possible to cover exhaustively all the situations which may be relevant to achieving an effective PCMH. See also Consolidated Criminal Practice Direction (CCPD), paragraph IV.41, Management of Cases to be Heard in the Crown Court; and paragraph V.56, Case Management in Magistrates' Courts.

How to use the form

v. The parties should complete only one form for each case. **The form should be used in every Crown Court centre, without any local exception or variation**.

vi. The form may be completed in manuscript or electronically.

vii. Questions 1 to 15 (in Part I) must be answered in every case.

viii. Questions 16-36 (in Part II) need only be answered if they are relevant.

ix. Question 37, at the end of the form, (the witness list) must be completed in every case.

x. The advocate may be asked by the court to expand upon or explain an entry, or to account for the absence of an entry, where one is required. The judge will record on the judicial orders template, or on the PCMH form, any orders made and, if practicable, issue a copy to the parties before the hearing ends. The parties must obtain a copy of that record and comply with the orders made by the date given.

Accessing the form

xi.   The current version of the form is available on the Ministry of Justice website at www.justice.gov.uk/guidance/courts-and-tribunals/courts/procedure-rules/criminal/formspage.htm

Transmitting the form

xii.   If you complete the form on the screen, it can still be printed off and used in hard copy. Alternatively, it can be emailed as an attachment.

Contents of the form

(The following commentary is to assist with the completion of the questions so numbered on the PCMH form.)

1 Date of trial and custody time limits

The date of trial should normally be fixed at the PCMH (or before). Any application to extend the Custody Time Limit is best dealt with at the PCMH, when the reasons for fixing a case beyond the time limits will be clear; otherwise there will be the avoidable expense of another hearing.

2 and 3 Details of case and parties

This section must be fully completed. The parties must be able to contact one another as must case progression officers and the court. Any change in the details must immediately be notified to the other parties and to the court. See CrimPR 3.4.

4 Compliance with the directions given by magistrates' courts

The standard / specific directions given by magistrates' courts should be complied with (CrimPR 3.5(3)). The court will need to know which orders have not been complied with, and why.

5 Credit for guilty plea

Defendants are entitled to be given the advice that credit is given for guilty pleas and the earlier the plea is entered, the greater is the credit given. The judge needs to know that this advice has been given.

6 Trial in absence

Defendants need to be warned that if they waive their right to attend, the trial may proceed in their absence. No one can engineer an adjournment simply by absconding. Those who claim to be ill must support that claim by medical evidence to the effect that they are unfit to attend their trial; it is unlikely that a medical certificate merely suggesting that they are unfit to work will be sufficient. See CCPD, I.13; CrimPR 3.8(2)(a).

7 The pleas which the defendant is offering

Recording in writing pleas offered to alternative offences which the prosecution are initially unwilling to accept will be advantageous to the defendant if the prosecution subsequently changes its position. In such circumstances, it will be easier for a defendant to claim maximum credit if that offer has been recorded. Pleas offered to counts on the indictment must similarly be recorded before credit is claimed.

8 Allocation of the case

Most courts have a system to identify before the PCMH those cases which require allocation to a particular judge; this question is intended to seek out those cases which have been missed.

9 Fitness to plead

This is self explanatory, but the judge will need assistance to fix a timetable for the service of experts' reports and for the issue to be tried.

10 Disclosure, the defence statement and notification of defence witnesses

The parties must identify any outstanding disclosure points. See Part 22 of The Criminal Procedure Rules 2010. The defence must serve a detailed defence statement setting out the issues in the trial; any failure to do so may be the subject of adverse comment at the trial and the judge may issue a warning to this effect, under section 11(3) of the Criminal Procedure and Investigations Act 1996. Pending service of a defence statement, question 10.4 allows the defence to give some notification of the defence. The practice of appending long 'shopping lists' to vague and unspecific defence statements has no legal foundation; any application for further disclosure should be made by way of formal application under section 8 of the Criminal Procedure and Investigations Act 1996 (as amended). The judge will expect compliance with the relevant Practice Directions, Guidelines and Protocols.

Pursuant to section 6C of the Criminal Procedure and Investigations Act 1996, the defence must notify the prosecution and the court whether he intends to call any witnesses at trial, and if so, give their names, addresses and dates of birth. The Practice Direction sets out a form for use by the defence when giving this notice (see rule 22.4). It may be that the time limit for notification has not expired when the PCMH is held but even so the defence might usefully be reminded of their responsibilities under that provision; if even as early as the PCMH the defence can comply, then they should be encouraged to do so.

11 and 12 Timetable of further evidence and expert evidence

Advocates should have available proper information as to what remains to be served, together with a realistic timetable for compliance. Parties should be prepared to provide realistic time estimates and not rely on a standard time period of, for example, 28 days if this has little bearing on the true amount of time likely to be required. The court needs detailed and accurate information as to when the evidence will be available. These enquiries should be made before the hearing. Failure to do so is likely to cause unnecessary adjournments. Consideration should be given to CrimPR 33.6 and whether (now or later) the experts should be asked to confer, to identify the real areas of dispute.

13 (and 37) Witness list

The mere fact of warning a witness to attend may cause him or her anxiety. Furthermore, the warning of witnesses is time consuming and expensive. When completing the witness list at paragraph 37, it is important to identify the relevant disputed issues to which the evidence of any particular witness is necessary, so that the judge can decide whether their attendance is necessary. The court may decline to order the attendance of witnesses unless their presence is really necessary. Consideration should therefore also be given to those witnesses in respect of whom a summons is required. See CrimPR Part 28 for rules on witness summonses. Thought should always be given to the staggering of witnesses to eliminate or reduce waiting times. The witnesses' availability must be known at the PCMH to ensure that the trial date is convenient.

14 Timetabling of the trial

Part 3.10 CrimPR requires the judge to consider timetabling in every case, with a view to improving efficiency; these matters require consideration throughout the trial; it may be possible to make some orders even at the PCMH.

If there are to be preliminary points taken, then consideration must be given to when a jury will be required and arrangements made to stagger the attendance of witnesses. No one should be asked to attend for a 10.30 am start only to find that there is a lengthy legal argument before the case can even be opened.

15 The Indictment

CrimPR 14.1(3)(a) requires the indictment to be signed by the court officer. Any amendment to the indictment must be ordered by the court.

16 Admissions and agreed facts

Admissions, sometimes more accurately called agreed facts, take time to draft but they can save a great deal of court time and thereby reduce costs. This applies not only to formal evidence (for example of continuity or of the captions to photographs) but also to many other types of evidence, of which these are but examples: lengthy police interviews are often better summarised and agreed; witness statements which are agreed to be read can often be summarised; expert evidence, including medical evidence, is often easier to understand if it is summarised by way of agreement rather than being read; this applies with particular force to evidence of telephone traffic and to cell site analysis; bad character evidence, if admissible, is also often better agreed.

17 Case Summary

Case Summaries should have been provided before the PCMH in all Class 1 cases and in any other case of complexity, but they may be needed in other cases as well.

18 Measures to assist witnesses and defendants in giving evidence

In accordance with CrimPR Part 29, special measures applications should have been made by the parties and considered by the court before the PCMH. This question addresses other points:

> **Question 18A** serves to remind advocates and judges of the needs of vulnerable and intimidated witnesses and of the measures which now exist to assist them in giving evidence;

> **Question 18B** serves a similar purpose in relation to defendants, who may require assistance in giving evidence;

> **Question 18C** alerts the judge to applications to be made in relation to anonymous witnesses, which are likely to require a separate hearing, ideally before the trial judge.

19 Young or vulnerable defendants

Question 18B addresses the assistance which a defendant may need to facilitate giving evidence. This question seeks to identify any other needs of defendants who are children or young people or adults who are 'vulnerable' in that they suffer from a mental disorder or from some other significant impairment of intelligence or social function and for whom special arrangements must be made so that they can effectively understand and participate in the proceedings (as to which see generally paragraph III.30 of the CCPD).

20 Reporting restrictions

Reporting restrictions need to be carefully considered and balanced against the rights of the press and other interested parties. The judge is likely to require assistance before making any order. See CCPD I.3. and the JSB and Society of Editors publication, *Reporting Restrictions in the Criminal Courts*, url
hhtp://www.judiciary.gov.uk/Resources/JCO/Documents/crown court reporting restrictions 021009.pdf.)

21 Third party material

Such applications must comply with CrimPR Part 28. Careful thought needs to go into identifying the witness to be served, the material sought and the reason that it is said to be relevant to an issue in the case. Any person whose right of confidentiality might be adversely affected must also be identified and information provided as to how and by whom they are to be notified, how they are to be permitted to make representations and when and by whom any rulings are to be made. It is important that such applications are made no later than the PCMH to avoid adjournments at a later stage arising out of delayed applications. Any such application is better made using the appropriate form set out in the Practice Direction for use in connection with an application under Part 28, which directs the applicant and the judge to the relevant criteria.

22 Defendant's interviews

Inaccuracies within transcriptions and likely submissions as to admissibility must be identified. Furthermore, the police may interview suspects at length, producing bundles of transcripts, the volume of which may make them unsuitable to put before a jury. The parties must consider producing summaries. The production of the first draft is primarily the responsibility of the advocate for the prosecution. If practicable, interviews should be available in electronic form, so that editing, pagination and copying can be done without delay. Further guidance is given in CCPD IV.43.

23 Witnesses giving evidence by video or DVD interview

These questions, each of which raises a separate point, are self-explanatory but failure to address them is a frequent source of adjournments. The quality of the recording, the accuracy of the transcript and the admissibility of the interview (or any particular part or parts of it) are separate points, each of which needs to be addressed at the PCMH.

Any editing of the tape (or disc) takes time. Particular care must be taken to ensure that any editing of the tapes has not diminished its sound quality and that any editing of the tape is precisely reflected in editing to the transcript; again this takes time. It should not be done on the morning of the trial or the day beforehand.

Only if these issues are addressed in advance can young and vulnerable witnesses be called as soon as they arrive at court. It is unacceptable to prolong the anxiety of young and vulnerable witnesses simply because these issues have not been resolved at PCMH. See also CrimPR Part 29 for rules on special measures directions; and CCPD IV.40.

Furthermore, the extreme and unnecessary length of many of these interviews is becoming a matter of great concern. Judges have a responsibility to eliminate undue repetition and may require interviews to be reduced in length, so as to reduce the burden on the jury, and on the witness, whilst not disadvantaging the defendant.

24 Witness interviews

The issues raised in this question differ from those raised in question 23. There is a growing practice of recording interviews with witnesses before setting out their evidence in a written witness statement. If this is done, then, subject to the disclosure test, the video or audio recording should be disclosed as unused material. The prosecution advocate therefore needs to know if any witness was interviewed in this way (which may not be clear from the papers served). It will normally suffice for the video or audio recording itself to be disclosed. Transcripts are expensive and any claim for a transcript needs to be justified.

25 and 26 CCTV evidence and electronic equipment

Subject to the duties of the prosecution properly to investigate the case under the relevant Guidelines, the prosecution only have duties to consider disclosure of CCTV footage in their possession. If the defence seek footage from third parties, it is for them to do so, rather than the prosecution. Furthermore, much CCTV footage is in a format (e.g. multiplex) which is unsuitable for showing in court without adaptation or editing. This must be sorted out before the trial. Many courts have simple VHS video and DVD playback facilities and the parties must ensure that the material which they want to play is compatible with the court equipment (if not, they must provide their own).

27 Cross-examination on sexual history

Section 41 of the Youth Justice and Criminal Evidence Act 1999 enacts an important principle and compliance with its requirements is vital to ensure that those who complain that they are victims of rape (and other sexual offences) receive the protection which the law affords to them. In accordance with CrimPR Part 36, applications should be made and considered – by the trial judge if possible – at or before the PCMH. Applications made on the day of the trial are strongly to be discouraged.

28 and 29 Bad character and hearsay

CrimPR at Parts 34 (Hearsay) and 35 (Evidence of bad character) provide for detailed applications to be made in the prescribed forms. Questions 28 and 29 therefore only seek to identify any outstanding issues (or potential future applications).

30 Admissibility and legal issues

Issues of admissibility and legal issues should, where possible, be identified before the trial, so that the parties can exchange skeleton arguments and the judge can properly prepare for the hearing. See also section 7 of the Criminal Justice Act 1987; and sections 31 and 40 of the Criminal Procedure and Investigations Act 1996.

31 Public Interest Immunity claims

If a claim is to be made on notice, then the necessary arrangements must be made. See CrimPR 22.3.

Revised 2011

6

32 Jury bundle

If a jury bundle will be needed at the trial, then its content will need to be agreed before the trial. Any outstanding issues need to be identified.

33 Concurrent family proceedings

It is important to identify those cases where there are concurrent family proceedings, so that the Designated Family Judge can be alerted.

34 Special arrangements

Any requirements for an interpreter or for those with a disability must be identified in advance, so that proper arrangements can be made. See CrimPR 10.5(1)(h) and 12.1(1)(e).

35 Linked criminal proceedings

These need to be identified, if possible with the court reference numbers.

36 Additional orders

It is important to identify additional orders which may be required.

37 Witness List

See the note in paragraph 13, above.

Forms for use in cases with two or more defendants

D-3   An expanded version of the plea and case management hearing form, for use in connection with cases involving up to 10 defendants is available on the Ministry of Justice website (http://www.justice.gov.uk/courts/procedure-rules/criminal/formspage).

Criminal practice directions

D-4   The consolidated criminal practice direction has now been revoked: *Criminal Practice Direction (General matters) A2* [2013] 1 W.L.R. 3164. For paragraph I.3 of that practice direction (referred to in para. 20 of the guidance notes), see now *Criminal Practice Direction (Preliminary proceedings) 16B* [2013] 1 W.L.R. 3164; for paragraph I.13 of that practice direction (para. 6), see now *Criminal Practice Direction (Custody and bail) 19B* [2013] 1 W.L.R. 3164; for paragraph III.30 of that practice direction (para. 19), see now *Criminal Practice Direction (General matters) 3G* [2013] 1 W.L.R. 3164; for paragraph IV.40 of that practice direction (para. 23), see now *Criminal Practice Direction (Evidence) 27B* [2013] 1 W.L.R. 3164; for paragraph IV.41 of that practice direction (para. (iv)), see now *Criminal Practice Direction (General matters) 3A and 3B* [2013] 1 W.L.R. 3164; for paragraph IV.43 of that practice direction (para. 22), see now *Criminal Practice Direction (Evidence) 27C* [2013] 1 W.L.R. 3164; and for paragraph V.56 of that practice direction (para. (iv)), see now *Criminal Practice Direction (General matters) 3A* [2013] 1 W.L.R. 3164.

APPENDIX E
Crown Prosecution Service

I. CODE FOR CROWN PROSECUTORS

A. INTRODUCTION

The Crown Prosecution Service is the principal public prosecuting authority for England and **E-1** Wales and is headed by the Director of Public Prosecutions, who is to discharge his functions under the superintendence of the Attorney-General (Prosecution of Offences Act 1985, s.3(1)). The Attorney-General is accountable to Parliament for the Service.

The Crown Prosecution Service is a national organisation consisting of 42 areas. Each area is headed by a Chief Crown Prosecutor and corresponds to a single police force area, with one for London. It was set up in 1986 to prosecute cases investigated by the police.

Although the Crown Prosecution Service works closely with the police, it is independent of them. The independence of crown prosecutors is of fundamental constitutional importance. Casework decisions taken with fairness, impartiality and integrity help deliver justice for victims, witnesses, defendants and the public.

The Crown Prosecution Service co-operates with the investigating and prosecuting agencies of other jurisdictions.

The Director of Public Prosecutions is responsible for issuing a Code for Crown Prosecutors under section 10 of the Prosecution of Offences Act 1985, giving guidance on the general principles to be applied when making decisions about prosecutions. This is the seventh edition of the code and replaces all earlier versions. It was issued on January 28, 2013.

B. THE CODE

1. INTRODUCTION

1.1 The Code for Crown Prosecutors (the code) is issued by the Director of Public Prosecutions **E-2** (DPP) under section 10 of the Prosecution of Offences Act 1985. This is the seventh edition of the code and replaces all earlier versions.

1.2 The DPP is the head of the Crown Prosecution Service (CPS), which is the principal public prosecution service for England and Wales. The DPP operates independently, under the superintendence of the Attorney-General who is accountable to Parliament for the work of the CPS.

1.3 The code gives guidance to prosecutors on the general principles to be applied when making decisions about prosecutions. The code is issued primarily for prosecutors in the CPS, but other prosecutors follow the code either through convention or because they are required to do so by law.

1.4 In this code, the term "suspect" is used to describe a person who is not yet the subject of formal criminal proceedings; the term "defendant" is used to describe a person who has been charged or summonsed; and the term "offender" is used to describe a person who has admitted his or her guilt to a police officer or other investigator or prosecutor, or who has been found guilty in a court of law.

2. GENERAL PRINCIPLES

2.1 The decision to prosecute or to recommend an out-of-court disposal is a serious step that af- **E-3** fects suspects, victims, witnesses and the public at large and must be undertaken with the utmost care.

2.2 It is the duty of prosecutors to make sure that the right person is prosecuted for the right offence and to bring offenders to justice wherever possible. Casework decisions taken fairly, impartially and with integrity help to secure justice for victims, witnesses, defendants and the public. Prosecutors must ensure that the law is properly applied; that relevant evidence is put before the court; and that obligations of disclosure are complied with.

2.3 Although each case must be considered on its own facts and on its own merits, there are general principles that apply in every case.

2.4 Prosecutors must be fair, independent and objective. They must not let any personal views about the ethnic or national origin, gender, disability, age, religion or belief, political views, sexual orientation, or gender identity of the suspect, victim or any witness influence their decisions. Neither must prosecutors be affected by improper or undue pressure from any source. Prosecutors must always act in the interests of justice and not solely for the purpose of obtaining a conviction.

2.5 The CPS is a public authority for the purposes of current, relevant equality legislation. Prosecutors are bound by the duties set out in this legislation.

2.6 Prosecutors must apply the principles of the European Convention on Human Rights, in accordance with the Human Rights Act 1998, at each stage of a case. Prosecutors must also comply with any guidelines issued by the Attorney-General; with the *Criminal Procedure Rules* currently in force; and have regard to the obligations arising from international conventions. They must follow the policies and guidance of the CPS issued on behalf of the DPP and available for the public to view on the CPS website.

3. THE DECISION WHETHER TO PROSECUTE

E-4

3.1 In more serious or complex cases, prosecutors decide whether a person should be charged with a criminal offence and, if so, what that offence should be. They make their decisions in accordance with this code and the DPP's guidance on charging. The police apply the same principles in deciding whether to start criminal proceedings against a person in those cases for which they are responsible.

3.2 The police and other investigators are responsible for conducting enquiries into any alleged crime and for deciding how to deploy their resources. This includes decisions to start or continue an investigation and on the scope of the investigation. Prosecutors often advise the police and other investigators about possible lines of inquiry and evidential requirements, and assist with pre-charge procedures. In large scale investigations the prosecutor may be asked to advise on the overall investigation strategy, including decisions to refine or narrow the scope of the criminal conduct and the number of suspects under investigation. This is to assist the police and other investigators to complete the investigation within a reasonable period of time and to build the most effective prosecution case. However, prosecutors cannot direct the police or other investigators.

3.3 Prosecutors should identify and, where possible, seek to rectify evidential weaknesses, but, subject to the threshold test (see section 5), they should swiftly stop cases which do not meet the evidential stage of the full code test (see section 4) and which cannot be strengthened by further investigation, or where the public interest clearly does not require a prosecution (see section 4). Although prosecutors primarily consider the evidence and information supplied by the police and other investigators, the suspect or those acting on his or her behalf may also submit evidence or information to the prosecutor via the police or other investigators, prior to charge, to help inform the prosecutor's decision.

3.4 Prosecutors must only start or continue a prosecution when the case has passed both stages of the full code test (see section 4). The exception is when the threshold test (see section 5) may be applied where it is proposed to apply to the court to keep the suspect in custody after charge, and the evidence required to apply the full code test is not yet available.

3.5 Prosecutors should not start or continue a prosecution which would be regarded by the courts as oppressive or unfair and an abuse of the court's process.

3.6 Prosecutors review every case they receive from the police or other investigators. Review is a continuing process and prosecutors must take account of any change in circumstances that occurs as the case develops, including what becomes known of the defence case. Wherever possible, they should talk to the investigator when thinking about changing the charges or stopping the case. Prosecutors and investigators work closely together, but the final responsibility for the decision whether or not a case should go ahead rests with the CPS.

3.7 Parliament has decided that a limited number of offences should only be taken to court with the agreement of the DPP. These are called consent cases. In such cases the DPP, or prosecutors acting on his or her behalf, apply the code in deciding whether to give consent to a prosecution. There are also certain offences that should only be taken to court with the consent of the Attorney-General. Prosecutors must follow current guidance when referring any such cases to the Attorney-General. Additionally, the Attorney-General will be kept informed of certain cases as part of his or her superintendence of the CPS and accountability to Parliament for its actions.

4. THE FULL CODE TEST

E-5

4.1 The full code test has two stages: (i) the evidential stage; followed by (ii) the public interest stage.

4.2 In most cases, prosecutors should only decide whether to prosecute after the investigation has been completed and after all the available evidence has been reviewed. However there will be cases where it is clear, prior to the collection and consideration of all the likely evidence, that the public interest does not require a prosecution. In these instances, prosecutors may decide that the case should not proceed further.

4.3 Prosecutors should only take such a decision when they are satisfied that the broad extent of the criminality has been determined and that they are able to make a fully informed assessment of the public interest. If prosecutors do not have sufficient information to take such a decision, the investigation should proceed and a decision taken later in accordance with the full code test set out in this section.

The evidential stage

4.4 Prosecutors must be satisfied that there is sufficient evidence to provide a realistic prospect of **E-6** conviction against each suspect on each charge. They must consider what the defence case may be, and how it is likely to affect the prospects of conviction. A case which does not pass the evidential stage must not proceed, no matter how serious or sensitive it may be.

4.5 The finding that there is a realistic prospect of conviction is based on the prosecutor's objective assessment of the evidence, including the impact of any defence and any other information that the suspect has put forward or on which he or she might rely. It means that an objective, impartial and reasonable jury or bench of magistrates or judge hearing a case alone, properly directed and acting in accordance with the law, is more likely than not to convict the defendant of the charge alleged. This is a different test from the one that the criminal courts themselves must apply. A court may only convict if it is sure that the defendant is guilty.

4.6 When deciding whether there is sufficient evidence to prosecute, prosecutors should ask themselves the following:

Can the evidence be used in court?

Prosecutors should consider whether there is any question over the admissibility of certain evidence. In doing so, prosecutors should assess:

    (a) the likelihood of that evidence being held as inadmissible by the court; and

    (b) the importance of that evidence in relation to the evidence as a whole.

Is the evidence reliable?

Prosecutors should consider whether there are any reasons to question the reliability of the evidence, including its accuracy or integrity.

Is the evidence credible?

Prosecutors should consider whether there are any reasons to doubt the credibility of the evidence.

The public interest stage

4.7 In every case where there is sufficient evidence to justify a prosecution, prosecutors must go **E-7** on to consider whether a prosecution is required in the public interest.

4.8 It has never been the rule that a prosecution will automatically take place once the evidential stage is met. A prosecution will usually take place unless the prosecutor is satisfied that there are public interest factors tending against prosecution which outweigh those tending in favour. In some cases the prosecutor may be satisfied that the public interest can be properly served by offering the offender the opportunity to have the matter dealt with by an out-of-court disposal rather than bringing a prosecution.

4.9 When deciding the public interest, prosecutors should consider each of the questions set out below in paragraphs 4.12(a) to (g) so as to identify and determine the relevant public interest factors tending for and against prosecution. These factors, together with any public interest factors set out in relevant guidance or policy issued by the DPP, should enable prosecutors to form an overall assessment of the public interest.

4.10 The explanatory text below each question in paragraphs 4.12(a) to (g) provides guidance to prosecutors when addressing each particular question and determining whether it identifies public interest factors for or against prosecution. The questions identified are not exhaustive, and not all the questions may be relevant in every case. The weight to be attached to each of the questions, and the factors identified, will also vary according to the facts and merits of each case.

4.11 It is quite possible that one public interest factor alone may outweigh a number of other factors which tend in the opposite direction. Although there may be public interest factors tending against prosecution in a particular case, prosecutors should consider whether nonetheless a prosecution should go ahead and those factors put to the court for consideration when sentence is passed.

4.12 Prosecutors should consider each of the following questions:

(a) *How serious is the offence committed?*

The more serious the offence, the more likely it is that a prosecution is required. When deciding the level of seriousness of the offence committed, prosecutors should include amongst the factors for consideration the suspect's culpability and the harm to the victim by asking themselves the questions at (b) and (c).

(b) *What is the level of culpability of the suspect?*

The greater the suspect's level of culpability, the more likely it is that a prosecution is required. Culpability is likely to be determined by the suspect's level of involvement; the extent to which the offending was premeditated and/or planned; whether they have previous criminal convictions and/or out-of-court disposals and any offending whilst on bail or whilst subject to a court order; whether the offending was or is likely to be continued, repeated or escalated; and the suspect's age or maturity (see paragraph (d) below for suspects under 18). Prosecutors should also have regard when considering culpability as to whether the suspect is, or was at the time of the offence, suffering from any significant mental or physical ill-health as in some circumstances this may mean that it is less likely that a prosecution is required. However, prosecutors will also need to consider how serious the offence was, whether it is likely to be repeated and the need to safeguard the public or those providing care to such persons.

(c) *What are the circumstances of and the harm caused to the victim?*

The circumstances of the victim are highly relevant. The greater the vulnerability of the victim, the more likely it is that a prosecution is required. This includes where a position of trust or authority exists between the suspect and victim. A prosecution is also more likely if the offence has been committed against a victim who was at the time a person serving the public. Prosecutors must also have regard to whether the offence was motivated by any form of discrimination against the victim's ethnic or national origin, gender, disability, age, religion or belief, sexual orientation or gender identity; or the suspect demonstrated hostility towards the victim based on any of those characteristics. The presence of any such motivation or hostility will mean that it is more likely that prosecution is required. In deciding whether a prosecution is required in the public interest, prosecutors should take into account the views expressed by the victim about the impact that the offence has had. In appropriate cases, this may also include the views of the victim's family. Prosecutors also need to consider if a prosecution is likely to have an adverse effect on the victim's physical or mental health, always bearing in mind the seriousness of the offence. If there is evidence that prosecution is likely to have an adverse impact on the victim's health it may make a prosecution less likely, taking into account the victim's views. However, the CPS does not act for victims or their families in the same way as solicitors act for their clients, and prosecutors must form an overall view of the public interest.

(d) *Was the suspect under the age of 18 at the time of the offence?*

The criminal justice system treats children and young people differently from adults and significant weight must be attached to the age of the suspect if they are a child or young person under 18. The best interests and welfare of the child or young person must be considered including whether a prosecution is likely to have an adverse impact on his or her future prospects that is disproportionate to the seriousness of the offending. Prosecutors must have regard to the principal aim of the youth justice system which is to prevent offending by children and young people. Prosecutors must also have regard to the obligations arising under the United Nations 1989 Convention on the Rights of the Child. As a starting point, the younger the suspect, the less likely it is that a prosecution is required. However, there may be circumstances which mean that notwithstanding the fact that the suspect is under 18, a prosecution is in the public interest. These include where the offence committed is serious, where the suspect's past record suggests that there are no suitable alternatives to prosecution, or where the absence of an admission means that out-of-court disposals which might have addressed the offending behaviour are not available.

(e) *What is the impact on the community?*

The greater the impact of the offending on the community, the more likely it is that a prosecution is required. In considering this question, prosecutors should have regard to how community is an inclusive term and is not restricted to communities defined by location.

(f) *Is prosecution a proportionate response?*

Prosecutors should also consider whether prosecution is proportionate to the likely outcome, and in so doing the following may be relevant to the case under consideration:

- the cost to the CPS and the wider criminal justice system, especially where it could be regarded as excessive when weighed against any likely penalty (prosecutors should not decide the public interest on the basis of this factor alone; it is essential that regard is also given to the public interest factors identified when considering the other questions in paragraphs 4.12(a) to (g), but cost is a relevant factor when making an overall assessment of the public interest);
- cases should be capable of being prosecuted in a way that is consistent with principles of effective case management; for example, in a case involving multiple suspects, prosecution might be reserved for the main participants in order to avoid excessively long and complex proceedings.

(g) *Do sources of information require protecting?*

In cases where public interest immunity does not apply, special care should be taken when proceeding with a prosecution where details may need to be made public that could harm sources of information, international relations or national security. It is essential that such cases are kept under continuing review.

5. The Threshold Test

5.1 The threshold test may only be applied where the suspect presents a substantial bail risk and   **E-8** not all the evidence is available at the time when he or she must be released from custody unless charged.

When the threshold test may be applied

5.2 Prosecutors must determine whether the following conditions are met: **E-8a**
   (a) there is insufficient evidence currently available to apply the evidential stage of the full code test; and
   (b) there are reasonable grounds for believing that further evidence will become available within a reasonable period; and
   (c) the seriousness or the circumstances of the case justifies the making of an immediate charging decision; and
   (d) there are continuing substantial grounds to object to bail in accordance with the Bail Act 1976 and in all the circumstances of the case it is proper to do so.

5.3 Where any of the above conditions is not met, the threshold test cannot be applied and the suspect cannot be charged. The custody officer must determine whether the person may continue to be detained or be released on bail, with or without conditions.

5.4 There are two parts to the evidential consideration of the threshold test.

The first part of the threshold test—is there reasonable suspicion?

5.5 Prosecutors must be satisfied that there is at least a reasonable suspicion that the person to be charged has committed the offence.

5.6 In determining this, prosecutors must consider the evidence then available. This may take the form of witness statements, material or other information, provided the prosecutor is satisfied that:
   (a) it is relevant; and
   (b) it is capable of being put into an admissible format for presentation in court; and
   (c) it would be used in the case.

5.7 If satisfied on this the prosecutor should then consider the second part of the threshold test.

The second part of the threshold test – can further evidence be gathered to provide a realistic prospect of conviction?

5.8 Prosecutors must be satisfied that there are reasonable grounds for believing that the continuing investigation will provide further evidence, within a reasonable period of time, so that all the evidence together is capable of establishing a realistic prospect of conviction in accordance with the full code test.

5.9 The further evidence must be identifiable and not merely speculative.

5.10 In reaching this decision prosecutors must consider:
   (a) the nature, extent and admissibility of any likely further evidence and the impact it will have on the case;
   (b) the charges that all the evidence will support;
   (c) the reasons why the evidence is not already available;

(d) the time required to obtain the further evidence and whether any consequential delay is reasonable in all the circumstances.

5.11 If both parts of the threshold test are satisfied, prosecutors must apply the public interest stage of the full code test based on the information available at that time.

Reviewing the threshold test

E-9
5.12 A decision to charge under the threshold test must be kept under review. The evidence must be regularly assessed to ensure that the charge is still appropriate and that continued objection to bail is justified. The full code test must be applied as soon as is reasonably practicable and in any event before the expiry of any applicable custody time limit.

6. SELECTION OF CHARGES

E-10
6.1 Prosecutors should select charges which:

(a) reflect the seriousness and extent of the offending supported by the evidence;

(b) give the court adequate powers to sentence and impose appropriate post-conviction orders; and

(c) enable the case to be presented in a clear and simple way.

6.2 This means that prosecutors may not always choose or continue with the most serious charge where there is a choice.

6.3 Prosecutors should never go ahead with more charges than are necessary just to encourage a defendant to plead guilty to a few. In the same way, they should never go ahead with a more serious charge just to encourage a defendant to plead guilty to a less serious one.

6.4 Prosecutors should not change the charge simply because of the decision made by the court or the defendant about where the case will be heard.

6.5 Prosecutors must take account of any relevant change in circumstances as the case progresses after charge.

7. OUT-OF-COURT DISPOSALS

E-11
7.1 An out-of-court disposal may take the place of a prosecution in court if it is an appropriate response to the offender and/or the seriousness and consequences of the offending.

7.2 Prosecutors must follow any relevant guidance when asked to advise on or authorise a simple caution, a conditional caution, any appropriate regulatory proceedings, a punitive or civil penalty, or other disposal. They should ensure that the appropriate evidential standard for the specific out-of-court disposal is met including, where required, a clear admission of guilt, and that the public interest would be properly served by such a disposal.

8. MODE OF TRIAL

E-12
8.1 Prosecutors must have regard to the current guidelines on sentencing and allocation when making submissions to the magistrates' court about where the defendant should be tried.

8.2 Speed must never be the only reason for asking for a case to stay in the magistrates' court. But prosecutors should consider the effect of any likely delay if a case is sent to the Crown Court, and the possible effect on any victim or witness if the case is delayed.

Venue for trial in cases involving youths

8.3 Prosecutors must bear in mind that youths should be tried in the youth court wherever possible. It is the court which is best designed to meet their specific needs. A trial of a youth in the Crown Court should be reserved for the most serious cases or where the interests of justice require a youth to be jointly tried with an adult.

9. ACCEPTING GUILTY PLEAS

E-12a
9.1 Defendants may want to plead guilty to some, but not all, of the charges. Alternatively, they may want to plead guilty to a different, possibly less serious, charge because they are admitting only part of the crime.

9.2 Prosecutors should only accept the defendant's plea if they think the court is able to pass a sentence that matches the seriousness of the offending, particularly where there are aggravating features. Prosecutors must never accept a guilty plea just because it is convenient.

9.3 In considering whether the pleas offered are acceptable, prosecutors should ensure that the interests and, where possible, the views of the victim, or in appropriate cases the views of the victim's family, are taken into account when deciding whether it is in the public interest to accept the plea. However, the decision rests with the prosecutor.

9.4 It must be made clear to the court on what basis any plea is advanced and accepted. In cases where a defendant pleads guilty to the charges but on the basis of facts that are different from the prosecution case, and where this may significantly affect sentence, the court should be invited to hear evidence to determine what happened, and then sentence on that basis.

9.5 Where a defendant has previously indicated that he or she will ask the court to take an offence into consideration when sentencing, but then declines to admit that offence at court, prosecutors will consider whether a prosecution is required for that offence. Prosecutors should explain to the defence advocate and the court that the prosecution of that offence may be subject to further review, in consultation with the police or other investigators wherever possible.

9.6 Particular care must be taken when considering pleas which would enable the defendant to avoid the imposition of a mandatory minimum sentence. When pleas are offered, prosecutors must also bear in mind the fact that ancillary orders can be made with some offences but not with others.

10. RECONSIDERING A PROSECUTION DECISION

10.1 People should be able to rely on decisions taken by the CPS. Normally, if the CPS tells a   **E-12b** suspect or defendant that there will not be a prosecution, or that the prosecution has been stopped, the case will not start again. But occasionally there are reasons why the CPS will overturn a decision not to prosecute or to deal with the case by way of an out-of-court disposal or when it will restart the prosecution, particularly if the case is serious.

10.2 These reasons include:

    (a) cases where a new look at the original decision shows that it was wrong and, in order to maintain confidence in the criminal justice system, a prosecution should be brought despite the earlier decision;

    (b) cases which are stopped so that more evidence which is likely to become available in the fairly near future can be collected and prepared; in these cases, the prosecutor will tell the defendant that the prosecution may well start again;

    (c) cases which are stopped because of a lack of evidence but where more significant evidence is discovered later; and

    (d) cases involving a death in which a review following the findings of an inquest concludes that a prosecution should be brought, notwithstanding any earlier decision not to prosecute.

© Crown Copyright 2013

C. AUTHORITIES

Charging of youths

Whereas the code for crown prosecutors requires consideration to be given to the interests of a   **E-12c** child or young person when deciding whether it is in the public interest to prosecute (see now para. 4.12(d), *ante*, E-7), there is no requirement that a crown prosecutor should obtain a risk assessment from the youth offending services or that he should contact the potential defendant's school: *R. (A.) v. South Yorkshire Police and CPS*, 171 J.P. 465, DC.

In *D. and B. v. Commr of Police for the Metropolis, CPS, Croydon JJ.* [2008] A.C.D. 47, DC, it was held that it was permissible for a crown prosecutor to decide that the combination of the seriousness of an offence and the public interest warranted prosecution, despite the fact that the particular circumstances of the offence would normally, in accordance with the guidance issued under section 65 of the CDA 1998, be such as to justify only a final warning.

Charging victims of human trafficking

What follows will have to be considered in the light of the defence provided by section 45 of   **★E-12d** the Modern Slavery Act 2015 (*ante*, § 19-445), as and when that provision comes into force.

Where it is possible that a defendant or potential defendant is a victim of human trafficking, a prosecutor should take cognisance of the CPS guidance on (i) the prosecution of defendants charged with immigration offences who might be victims of trafficking, and (ii) the prosecution of young offenders charged with offences who might be such victims; in particular, under (i), when deciding whether to prosecute, or to continue to prosecute, a "credible trafficked victim" for immigration offences, prosecutors should consider whether this would serve the public interest; and under (ii), a case should be discontinued on evidential grounds where there is clear evidence that a youth has a credible defence of duress, but, if the evidence is less certain, further details should be sought from the police and youth offender teams; the defence, on the other hand, should make inquiries wherever there is credible material showing that the defendant might have been a trafficked victim, especially if the client is young; as a signatory to the Council of Europe Convention on Action against Trafficking in Human Beings, the United Kingdom is required to identify and protect victims of trafficking, and, whereas the CPS guidance supports the purpose of the convention, a trial which had failed to have proper regard to it was not fair, either under the principles of the common law or under the principles enshrined in the ECHR: *R. v. O.*, *The Times*, October 2, 2008, CA ([2008] EWCA Crim. 2835).

R. v. O. and the issues arising from it were further considered in *R. v. M. (L.), B. (M.) and G. (D.); R. v. Tabot; R. v. Tijani* [2011] 1 Cr.App.R. 12, CA. It was held that one way in which the duty under Article 26 of the Council of Europe Convention (to avoid the imposition of penalties on victims of human trafficking for their involvement in unlawful activities to the extent that they were compelled to become so involved) is met in England and Wales, is by means of the guidance given to prosecutors considering whether charges should be brought against those who are or may be victims of trafficking (the court pointed out that whilst the guidance is now set out in the context of immigration offences only, it should be taken to apply whatever the nature of the allegation). The effect of the CPS's guidance, according to the court, is to require of prosecutors a three-stage exercise, asking, first, whether there is reason to believe that the person has been trafficked, secondly, whether there is clear evidence of a common law defence (in which case, any proceedings will be discontinued on evidential grounds) and, thirdly, where there is no such evidence, but the offence may have been committed as a result of compulsion arising from the trafficking, whether the public interest requires a prosecution. It was said that Article 26 does not require a blanket immunity from prosecution for trafficked victims, and that there will normally be no reason not to prosecute a victim of trafficking if the offence appears to have been committed out-with any reasonable nexus of compulsion occasioned by the trafficking. The court said that material considerations for the prosecutor when deciding whether to pursue a prosecution will be the gravity of the offence, the degree of continuing compulsion and the alternatives reasonably available to the defendant. As to this case, see also § 17-119 in the main work.

R. v. O. and *R. v. M. (L.), B. (M.) and G. (D.); R. v. Tabot; R. v. Tijani* were further considered in *R. v. N. (A.); R. v. Le* [2012] 1 Cr.App.R. 35, CA. It was held that: (i) implementation of Article 26 is normally achieved by the proper exercise of the prosecutorial discretion which enables the Crown, however strong the evidence, to decide that it would be inappropriate to prosecute, or to continue with the prosecution of, a defendant who is unable to advance duress as a defence, but who falls within the protective ambit of that article; this requires a judgment to be made in the light of all the available evidence; the responsibility is not that of the court but of the prosecution; but the court may intervene if its process is abused by using the "ultimate sanction" of a stay; the burden of establishing an improper exercise of the discretion rests on the defendant; that the context is the United Kingdom's convention obligation does not involve the creation of any new principles; apart from the specific jurisdiction to stay proceedings, the court may also, in the exercise of its sentencing responsibilities, implement Article 26 in the language of the article itself, by discharging the defendant absolutely or conditionally; (ii) the only publication likely to be relevant to an inquiry into an alleged abuse is the CPS's guidance on human trafficking and smuggling as it was in force at the time when the relevant decisions were made; unless it is to be argued that the guidance itself is open to question because it has failed to keep itself regularly updated in light of developing knowledge, for the purposes of the court considering an alleged abuse for which the prosecution are responsible, it is that guidance that should be the starting, and in the overwhelming majority of cases, the finishing point; (iii) expert evidence is unlikely to assist on the issue of the correctness of the decision to prosecute; (iv) a defendant has one opportunity to give his instructions to his legal advisers; it is only most exceptionally that the court would, on appeal, consider it appropriate to allow a defendant to advance fresh instructions about the facts; and there is no special category of exceptionality in the context of Article 26; and (v) an abuse argument founded on the convention that is advanced long after conviction is most unlikely to succeed on the basis that subsequent events show that, if the decision whether to prosecute were to be taken now, the result might have been different from the decision actually taken in the light of the standards and guidance existing at the time it was taken.

These issues were further considered in *R. v. L. (C.); R. v. N. (H.V.); R. v. N. (T.H.); R. v. T. (H.D.) (Children's Commr for England and Equality and Human Rights Commission Intervening)* [2013] 2 Cr.App.R. 23, CA. It was held that: (i) whereas Article 8 of European Parliament and Council Directive 2011/36/EU obliges member states to "take the necessary measures to ensure that competent national authorities are entitled not to prosecute or impose penalties on victims of trafficking ... for their involvement in criminal activities which they have been compelled to commit as a direct consequence of being subjected" to trafficking, the courts will give effect to this obligation by reviewing decisions to prosecute, staying inappropriate prosecutions and discharging defendants where prosecution was appropriate but punishment inappropriate; as to the review of the decision to prosecute, this is no mere *Wednesbury* review (*Associated Picture Houses Ltd v. Wednesbury Corporation* [1948] 1 K.B. 223, CA); the court must reach its own conclusion on the evidence presented to it; (ii) if it is found that the defendant is a victim of trafficking, the next question is the extent to which the offences with which he is charged were integral to, or consequent on, the exploitation of which he was the victim; in some cases the facts will show that he was under levels of compulsion that mean that, in reality, culpability was extinguished; if so, a stay is likely to be granted; in other cases, more likely in the case of a defendant who is no longer a child (18 plus), culpability may be diminished but nevertheless be significant; for these individuals, prosecution may well be appropriate, with due allowance to be made in any sentencing decision for their diminished culpability; in yet other cases, the fact that the defendant was a victim of trafficking will provide no more than a colourable excuse for criminality that is unconnected to and does not arise from their victimisation; (iii) as to the question whether the defendant was indeed a victim of trafficking, where there has been a referral to one of the two competent authorities (the U.K. Border Agency and the U.K. Human Tracking Centre), if their conclusion is that the defendant is a victim of trafficking, the court is likely to adopt that view although it is not bound by it, as it is the court that has the ultimate responsibility for making the decision with all the relevant evidence bearing on the issues of trafficking, exploitation, age and culpability being addressed; while there is no obligation to seek assistance from experts in the field, the court may adjourn for further information on the subject, and indeed may require the assistance of various authorities; and (iv) where the defendant is under 18, his best interests are not the only consideration, but they are a primary consideration; and where there is any doubt about whether or not the defendant is under that age, "due inquiry" must be made (CYPA 1933, s.99(1) (§ 19-412 in the main work)); this requires much more than superficial observation of the defendant in the dock; the court must be provided with all the relevant evidence that bears on the issue of age; if, at the end of the inquiry, his age remains in doubt and there are reasons to believe that he is under the age of 18, he must be presumed to be under that age.

The full code test/evidential stage

When applying the "realistic prospect of conviction" test, a prosecutor should adopt a "merits **E-12e** based" approach, imagining himself to be the fact finder and asking himself, whether, on balance, the evidence is sufficient to merit a conviction, taking into account what he knows about the defence case, rather than a predictive "bookmaker's" approach, based on past experience of similar cases; questions of how a jury are likely to see a case are not relevant at this stage but at a later stage, under the public interest test in paragraphs 5.6 to 5.13 of the code: *R. (F.B.) v. DPP* [2009] 1 Cr.App.R. 38, DC. As to this case, see also §§ 1-337, 16-48 in the main work.

II. LEGAL GUIDANCE AND CHARGING STANDARDS

Apart from the code for crown prosecutors, the CPS has prepared legal guidance to prosecu- **E-13** tors and caseworkers in relation to many criminal offences and procedural issues. It has never been suggested that such guidance has the force of law, or even parity of standing with the code. It is merely, in the words of the CPS website (where it is available to the public), "an aid to guide crown prosecutors and associate prosecutors in the use of their discretion in making decisions in cases", which "does not create any rights enforceable at law, in any legal proceedings", and is subject to the principles as set out in the code for crown prosecutors.

Incorporated within the guidance are various "charging standards" for various offences or **E-14** groups of offences, such as offences against the person, driving offences, drug offences, public order offences and theft. They contain a mixture of propositions of law (as to the ingredients of the various offences, maximum penalties, available alternative verdicts, etc.) and guidance as to the various factors that should be taken into consideration in deciding which offence to charge. The standards emphasise that they:

(a) are not to be used in the determination of any pre-charge decision, such as the decision to arrest;

(b) do not override any guidance issued on the use of appropriate alternative forms of disposal short of charge, such as cautioning;

(c) do not override the principles set out in the code for crown prosecutors;

(d) do not override the need for consideration to be given in every case as to whether a charge or prosecution is in the public interest;

(e) do not override particular policy guidance involving hate crimes; and

(f) do not remove the need for each case to be considered on its individual merits or fetter the discretion of the police to charge and the CPS to prosecute the most appropriate offence depending on the particular facts of the case in question.

The following recitation of general charging principles is common to all the standards:

(a) the charge or charges preferred should accurately reflect the extent of the defendant's involvement and responsibility, thereby allowing the courts the discretion to sentence appropriately;

(b) the choice of charges should ensure the clear and simple presentation of the case, particularly where there is more than one defendant;

(c) it is wrong to encourage a defendant to plead guilty to a few charges by selecting more charges than are necessary;

(d) it is wrong to select a more serious charge which is not supported by the evidence in order to encourage a plea of guilty to a lesser allegation.

III. THE ROLE AND RESPONSIBILITIES OF THE PROSECUTION ADVOCATE

Foreword

E-15   The prosecution advocate plays an important public role and as such may be considered a cornerstone of an open and fair criminal justice system. The principles so well articulated by Farquharson L.J. and his committee as to the role of the prosecution advocate have served us well since they were published in 1986. However, the time has come for new guidance which, whilst building on the established principles, reflects the changes that have occurred in the criminal courts, at the Bar and within the Crown Prosecution Service over recent years.

I welcome and commend the new Guidelines which, whilst not legally binding unless expressly approved by the Court of Appeal, nonetheless provide important practical guidance for practitioners involved in the prosecution process.

Lord Woolf C.J.

Introduction

E-16   The work undertaken in 1986 by the committee chaired by Farquharson L.J. has, for over 15 years, provided valuable guidance as to role [*sic*] of the prosecution advocate and their relationship with the Crown Prosecution Service (CPS).

However, the ever-evolving criminal justice system, changes at the Bar and developments in the CPS brought about by the implementation of Sir Iain Glidewell's Review, mean that the environment in which we all operate has radically changed since the original report was published.

Whilst the principles established by Farquharson L.J.'s committee have been enormously helpful and will continue to apply, the time has come for new guidance that reflects the changes and emphasises the new relationship that is developing between CPS Areas and the local Bar.

The new Guidelines have therefore been developed to take account of the changes and are the result of the Bar and CPS working in partnership and in consultation with the judiciary, Bar Council and Law Society.

We commend the Guidelines as providing valuable guidance and a framework within which the Bar and the CPS can work effectively together.

Lord Goldsmith Q.C., Attorney General

David Calvert-Smith Q.C., Director of Public Prosecutions

1. Pre-trial preparation

Farquharson

(a) *It is the duty of prosecution counsel to read the Instructions delivered to him expeditiously and to advise or confer with those instructing him on all aspects of the case well before its commencement.* **E-17**

1.1 The Crown Prosecution Service (CPS) will deliver instructions at a stage in the proceedings **E-18** that allows sufficient time for the prosecution advocate adequately to consider, prepare and advise on the evidence before the court hearing or draft/agree the indictment.

1.2 Where a CPS higher court advocate represents the prosecution at a Plea and Directions Hearing (PDH), the CPS will deliver instructions to the trial advocate no later than 10 working days after the date of the PDH.

1.3 The CPS will deliver instructions which:

    i. address the issues in the case including any strategic decisions that have been or may need to be made;

    ii. identify relevant case law;

    iii. explain the basis and rationale of any decision made in relation to the disclosure of unused material;

    iv. where practical, provide specific guidance or indicate parameters on acceptable plea(s); and

    v. where a case is an appeal either to the Crown Court from the magistrates' court or is before the Court of Appeal, Divisional Court or House of Lords, address the issues raised in the notice of appeal, case stated, application for judicial review or petition.

Action on receipt of instructions

1.4 On receipt of instructions the prosecution advocate will consider the papers and advise the **E-19** CPS, ordinarily in writing, or orally in cases of urgency where:

    i. the prosecution advocate forms a different view to that expressed by the CPS (or where applicable a previous prosecution advocate) on acceptability of plea;

    ii. the indictment as preferred requires amendment;

    iii. additional evidence is required;

    iv. there is an evidential deficiency (which cannot be addressed by the obtaining of further evidence) and, applying the Code for Crown Prosecutors, there is no longer a realistic prospect of conviction; or the prosecution advocate believes that it is not in the public interest to continue the prosecution;

    v. in order to expedite and simplify proceedings certain formal admissions should be made;

    vi. the prosecution advocate, having reviewed previous disclosure decisions, disagrees with a decision that has been made; or is not satisfied that he or she is in possession of all relevant documentation; or considers that he or she has not been fully instructed regarding disclosure matters;

    vii. a case conference is required (particularly where there is a sensitive issue, *e.g.* informant/ PII/ disclosure etc);

    viii. the presentation of the case to the court requires special preparation of material for the jury or presentational aids.

1.5 The prosecution advocate will endeavour to respond within five working days of receiving **E-20** instructions, or within such period as may be specified or agreed where the case is substantial or the issues complex.

1.6 Where the prosecution advocate is to advise on a specific aspect of the case other than 1.4 (i-viii), the advocate should contact the CPS and agree a realistic timescale within which advice is to be provided.

1.7 The prosecution advocate will inform the CPS without delay where the advocate is unlikely to be available to undertake the prosecution or advise within the relevant timescale.

1.8 When returning a brief, the advocate originally instructed must ensure that the case is in good order and should discuss outstanding issues or potential difficulties with the advocate receiving the brief. Where the newly instructed advocate disagrees with a decision or opinion reached by the original advocate, the CPS should be informed so that the matter can be discussed.

Case summaries

E-21

1.9 When a draft case summary is prepared by the CPS, the prosecution advocate will consider the summary and either agree the contents or advise the CPS of any proposed amendment.

1.10 In cases where the prosecution advocate is instructed to settle the case summary or schedules, the document(s) will be prepared and submitted to the CPS without delay.

Case management plan

E-22

1.11 On receipt of a case management plan the prosecution advocate, having considered the papers, will contact the Crown Prosecutor within seven days, or such period as may be specified or agreed where the case is substantial or the issues complex, to discuss and agree the plan. The plan will be maintained and regularly reviewed to reflect the progress of the case.

Keeping the prosecution advocate informed

E-23

1.12 The CPS will inform the prosecution advocate of developments in the case without delay and, where a decision is required which may materially affect the conduct and presentation of the case, will consult with the prosecution advocate prior to that decision.

1.3 Where the CPS is advised by the defence of a plea(s) of guilty or there are developments which suggest that offering no evidence on an indictment or count therein is an appropriate course, the matter should always be discussed with the prosecution advocate without delay unless to do so would be wholly impracticable.

Victims and witnesses

E-24

1.14 When a decision whether or not to prosecute is based on the public interest, the CPS will always consider the consequences of that decision for the victim and will take into account any views expressed by the victim or the victim's family.

1.15 The prosecution advocate will follow agreed procedures and guidance on the care and treatment of victims and witnesses, particularly those who may be vulnerable or have special needs.

Appeals

E-25

1.16 Where the prosecution advocate forms a different view to that expressed by the CPS on the conduct/approach to the appeal, the advocate should advise the CPS within FIVE working days of receiving instructions or such period as may be specified or agreed where the case is substantial or the issues complex.

PDH and other preliminary hearings

E-26

1.17 The principles and procedures applying to trials as set out in the following paragraphs will be equally applicable where the prosecution advocate is conducting a PDH or other preliminary hearing.

2. Withdrawal of instructions

Farquharson

E-27

(b) *A solicitor who has briefed counsel to prosecute may withdraw his instructions before the commencement of the trial up to the point when it becomes impracticable to do so, if he disagrees with the advice given by Counsel or for any other proper professional reason.*

2.1 The CPS will consult and take all reasonable steps to resolve any issue or disagreement and will only consider withdrawing instructions from a prosecution advocate as a last resort.

2.2 If the prosecution advocate disagrees with any part of his or her instructions the advocate should contact the responsible Crown Prosecutor to discuss the matter. Until the disagreement has been resolved the matter will remain confidential and must not be discussed by the prosecution advocate with any other party to the proceedings.

"Proper professional reason"

E-28

2.3 The prosecution advocate will keep the CPS informed of any personal concerns, reservations or ethical issues that the advocate considers have the potential to lead to possible conflict with his or her instructions.

2.4 Where the CPS identifies the potential for professional embarrassment or has concerns about the prosecution advocate's ability or experience to present the case effectively to the court, the CPS reserves the right to withdraw instructions.

Timing

2.5 It is often difficult to define when, in the course of a prosecution it becomes impracticable to **E-29** withdraw instructions as circumstances will vary according to the case. The nature of the case, its complexity, witness availability and the view of the court will often be factors that will influence the decision.

2.6 In the majority of prosecutions it will not be practicable to withdraw instructions once the judge has called the case before the court as a preliminary step to the swearing of the jury.

2.7 If instructions are withdrawn, the prosecution advocate will be informed in writing and reasons will be given.

2.8 Instructions may only be withdrawn by or with the consent of the Chief Crown Prosecutor, Assistant Chief Crown Prosecutor, Head of a CPS Trials Unit or, in appropriate cases, Head of a CPS Criminal Justice Unit.

2.9 In relation to cases prosecuted by the CPS Casework Directorate, the decision may only be taken by the Director Casework or Head of Division.

3. Presentation and conduct

Farquharson

(c) *While he remains instructed it is for counsel to take all necessary decisions in the presentation and general* **E-30** *conduct of the prosecution.*

3.1 The statement at 3(c) applies when the prosecution advocate is conducting the trial, PDH or any other preliminary hearing, but is subject to the principles and procedures relating to matters of policy set out in section 4 below.

Disclosure of material

3.2 Until the conclusion of the trial the prosecution advocate and CPS have a continuing duty to **E-31** keep under review decisions regarding disclosure. The prosecution advocate should in every case specifically consider whether he or she can satisfactorily discharge the duty of continuing review on the basis of the material supplied already, or whether it is necessary to inspect further material or to reconsider material already inspected.

3.3 Disclosure of material must always follow the established law and procedure. Unless consultation is impracticable or cannot be achieved without a delay to the hearing, it is desirable that the CPS, and where appropriate the disclosure officer are consulted over disclosure decisions.

4. Policy decisions

Farquharson

(d) *Where matters of policy[1] fall to be decided after the point indicated in (b) above (including offering no* **E-32** *evidence on the indictment or on a particular count, or on the acceptance of pleas to lesser counts), it is the duty of Counsel to consult his Instructing Solicitor/Crown Prosecutor whose views at this stage are of crucial importance.*

(e) *In the rare case where counsel and his instructing solicitor are unable to agree on a matter of policy, it is, subject to (g) below, for prosecution counsel to make the necessary decisions.*

Policy issues arising at trial

4.1 The prosecution advocate should alert the CPS at the first opportunity if a matter of policy is **E-33** likely to arise.

4.2 The prosecution advocate must not give an indication or undertaking which binds the prosecution without first discussing the issue with the CPS.

CPS representation at Crown Court

4.3 Whenever possible, an experienced Crown Prosecutor will be available at the Crown Court to **E-34** discuss and agree any issue involving the conduct or progress of the case.

---

[1] "Policy" decisions should be understood as referring to non-evidential decisions on: the acceptance of pleas of guilty to lesser counts or groups of counts or available alternatives; offering no evidence on particular counts; consideration of a retrial; whether to lodge an appeal; certification of a point of law; and the withdrawal of the prosecution as a whole.

4.4 When it is not possible to provide a Crown Prosecutor at court, an experienced caseworker will attend and facilitate communication between the prosecution advocate and the Crown Prosecutor having responsibility for the case.

4.5 In exceptional circumstances where it is not possible to contact a Crown Prosecutor, the prosecution advocate should ask the court to adjourn the hearing for a realistic period in order to consult with the CPS. Where an adjournment is refused, the prosecution advocate may make the decision but should record his or her reasons in writing.

Referral to senior CPS representative

E-35

4.6 Where an issue remains unresolved following consultation with a Crown Prosecutor; or where the case/issue under consideration is substantial, sensitive or complex; or the prosecution advocate disagrees with the advice of the Crown Prosecutor, the matter may be referred to the Chief Crown Prosecutor, the Director Casework or to a senior Crown Prosecutor with delegated authority to act on their behalf.

4.7 In order to ensure consultation takes place at the highest level appropriate to the circumstances and nature of the case, the court should be asked to adjourn if necessary. When an adjournment is sought, the facts leading to the application should be placed before the court only in so far as they are relevant to that application.

4.8 Where a Chief Crown Prosecutor has been directly involved in the decision making process and the issue remains unresolved, the matter may be referred to the Director of Public Prosecutions.

Farquharson

E-36

(f) *Where counsel has taken a decision on a matter of policy with which his Instructing Solicitor has not agreed, then it would be appropriate for the Attorney General to require Counsel to submit to him a written report of all the circumstances, including his reasons for disagreeing with those who instruct him.*

4.9 It will only be in exceptional circumstances that the Attorney General will require a written report. The prosecution advocate will first discuss the decision with the Chief Crown Prosecutor or the Director, Casework. Where, by agreement, the issue remains one that either party considers should be drawn to the attention of the Director of Public Prosecutions the prosecution advocate will, on request, provide a written report for submission to the Director of Public Prosecutions. If he considers it appropriate to do so, the Director of Public Prosecutions may refer the matter to the Attorney General.

4.10 Where there has been a disagreement on a matter of policy, provided that the CPS is satisfied that the prosecution advocate followed the principles set out in this document, the professional codes of conduct and was not *Wednesbury* unreasonable, the CPS will not apply sanctions in respect of any future work solely as a result of the decision in a particular case.

5. Change of advice

Farquharson

E-37

(g) *When counsel has had the opportunity to prepare his brief and to confer with those instructing him, but at the last moment before trial unexpectedly advises that the case should not proceed or that pleas to lesser offences should be accepted, and his Instructing Solicitor does not accept such advice, counsel should apply for an adjournment if instructed so to do.*

E-38

5.1 The CPS and the prosecution advocate should agree a period of adjournment that would allow a newly instructed advocate to prepare for trial. The period should be realistic and acknowledge that in such circumstances a case conference will usually be required.

5.2 The facts leading to the application for the adjournment should be placed before the court only in so far as they are relevant to that application.

6. Prosecution advocate's role in decision making at trial

Farquharson

E-39

(h) *Subject to the above, it is for prosecution counsel to decide whether to offer no evidence on a particular count or on the indictment as a whole and whether to accept pleas to a lesser count or counts.*

6.1 The prosecution advocate may ask the defence advocate as to whether a plea will be forthcoming but at this initial stage should not suggest or indicate a plea that might be considered acceptable to the prosecution before a plea is offered.

6.2 Where the defence advocate subsequently offers details of a plea, the prosecution advocate may discuss the matter with a view to establishing an acceptable plea that reflects the defendant's criminality and provides the court with sufficient powers to sentence appropriately.

Responsibility of prosecution advocate to consult

6.3 Where the prosecution advocate forms the view that the appropriate course is to accept a plea   **E-40**
before proceedings commence or continue, or to offer no evidence on the indictment or any part of
it, the prosecution advocate should:

    i. whenever practicable, speak with the victim or victim's family attending court to explain
    the position;

    ii. ensure that the interests of the victim or any views expressed by the victim or victim's
    family are taken into account as part of the decision making process; and

    iii. keep the victim or victim's family attending court informed and explain decisions as they
    are made.

6.4 Where appropriate the prosecution advocate may seek an adjournment of the court hearing in
order to facilitate discussion with the victim or victim's family.

6.5 The prosecution advocate should always comply with paragraph 6.3 and, where practicable,
discuss the matter with the CPS before informing the defence advocate or the court that a plea is
acceptable.

6.6 Where the defendant indicates an acceptable plea, unless the issue is simple, the defence
should reduce the basis of the plea to writing. The prosecution advocate should show the CPS any
written record relating to the plea and agree with the CPS the basis on which the case will be opened
to the court.

6.7 It is the responsibility of the prosecution advocate to ensure that the defence advocate is aware
of the basis on which the plea is accepted by the prosecution and the way in which the prosecution
case will be opened to the court.

6.8 It will not be necessary for the prosecution advocate to consult the CPS where the plea or
course of action accords with the written instructions received from the CPS, although paragraph 6.3
may still apply.

Prosecution advocate's role in sentencing

6.9 The prosecution advocate should always draw the court's attention to any matters, including   **E-41**
aggravating or mitigating features, that might affect sentence. Additionally, the advocate should be in
a position to assist the court, if requested, with any statutory provisions or sentencing guidelines and
should always draw attention to potential sentencing errors.

6.10 Where a discussion on plea and sentence takes place, the prosecution advocate must adhere
to the Attorney General's Guidelines on the Acceptance of Pleas published on 7 December 2000.

7. Seeking judicial approval

Farquharson

(i) *If prosecution counsel invites the Judge to approve the course he is proposing to take, then he must abide by*   **E-42**
the judge's decision.

7.1 A discussion with the judge about the acceptability of a plea or conduct of the case should be
held in the presence of the defendant unless exceptional circumstances apply.[2]

7.2 In exceptional circumstances, where the prosecution advocate considers it appropriate to communicate with the judge or seek the judge's view in chambers, the CPS should be consulted before
such a step is taken.

7.3 Where discussions take place in chambers it is the responsibility of the prosecution advocate to
remind the judge, if necessary, that an independent record must always be kept.

7.4 The prosecution advocate should also make a full note of such an event, recording all decisions
and comments. This note should be made available to the CPS.

Farquharson

(j) *If prosecution counsel does not invite the judge's approval of his decision it is open to the judge to express*   **E-43**

[2] For the purposes of these guidelines, "exceptional circumstances" would include the following:

    (i) Where there is material or information which should not be made public, *e.g.* a police text, or for some
    other compelling reason such as a defendant or witness suffering, unknown to them, from a serious or
    terminal illness; or

    (ii) There are sensitivities surrounding a prosecution decision or proposed action which need to be explained
    in chambers with a view to obtaining judicial approval. Such approval may be given in open court where it
    is necessary to explain a prosecution decision or action in order to maintain public confidence in the
    criminal justice system.

his dissent with the course proposed and invite counsel to reconsider the matter with those instructing him, but having done so, the final decision remains with counsel.

7.5 Where a judge expresses a view based on the evidence or public interest, the CPS will carry out a further review of the case.

7.6 The prosecution advocate will inform the CPS in a case where the judge has expressed a dissenting view and will agree the action to be taken. Where there is no CPS representative at court, the prosecution advocate will provide a note of the judge's comments.

7.7 The prosecution advocate will ensure that the judge is aware of all factors that have a bearing on the prosecution decision to adopt a particular course. Where there is a difference of opinion between the prosecution advocate and the CPS the judge will be informed as to the nature of the disagreement.

Farquharson

E-44

(k) *In an extreme case where the judge is of the opinion that the course proposed by counsel would lead to serious injustice, he may decline to proceed with the case until counsel has consulted with either the Director or the Attorney General as may be appropriate.*

7.8 As a preliminary step, the prosecution advocate will discuss the judge's observations with the Chief Crown Prosecutor in an attempt to resolve the issue. Where the issue remains unresolved the Director of Public Prosecutions will be consulted. In exceptional circumstances the Director of Public Prosecutions may consult the Attorney General.

E-45

Note: These Guidelines are subject to the Code of Conduct of the Bar of England and Wales (barrister advocates) and The Law Society's The Guide to the Professional Conduct of Solicitors (solicitor advocates). Whilst reference is made in the guidelines to the CPS and levels of authority within the Service, the guidelines may be adopted as best practice, with consequential amendments to levels of authority, by other prosecuting authorities.

These Guidelines may be amended at any time and copyright is waived.

These Guidelines are also available on the CPS Website: www.cps.gov.uk.

APPENDIX F
The Listing and Allocation of Criminal Cases

Introduction

The practice directions relating to the listing and allocation of criminal cases that are set out **F-1** below, whilst signed off by the Lord Chief Justice, are clearly the product of the Ministry of Justice, albeit with judicial input, and they are largely administrative in nature (see para. B.1, *post*, F-6). As such, they are more appropriately included in an appendix, rather than in the main work (where their predecessor provisions were to be found).

Practice Direction (Criminal Proceedings: Various Changes) [2014] 1 W.L.R. 3001

CPD LISTING AND ALLOCATION

These practice directions on listing and allocation replace sections III.21, IV.31, IV.32, IV.33, **F-2** IV.38 and IV.41.9 and Annex F of *Practice Direction (Criminal Proceedings: Consolidation)* [2002] 1 W.L.R. 2870 ... Additionally, they consolidate "Deployment and Allocation in Criminal Cases in Class 1, 2 and 3: Guidance for all Resident Judges" issued by the Senior Presiding Judge on 26 May 2005, incorporate parts of the guidance issued by the Senior Presiding Judge and by HMCTS on custody time limits in May 2012 and replace the guidance on transfer of cases to other Crown Courts for sentence issued by the Senior Presiding Judge in March 2009. Reference is made to recommendations from the Magistrates' Courts Disclosure Review May 2014. Annex 1 incorporates the relevant operational parts of the "Protocol to Support Judicial Deployment in the Magistrates' Courts" issued in November 2012. Annex 2 subsumes the "Sexual Offences Protocol in the Youth Court" issued by the Senior Presiding Judge in March 2010.

CPD LISTING A: JUDICIAL RESPONSIBILITY FOR LISTING AND KEY PRINCIPLES

Listing as a judicial responsibility and function

A.1 Listing is a judicial responsibility and function. The purpose is to ensure that all cases are **F-3** brought to a hearing or trial in accordance with the interests of justice, that the resources available for criminal justice are deployed as effectively as possible, and that cases are heard by an appropriate judge or bench with the minimum of delay.

A.2 The agreement reached between the Lord Chief Justice and the Secretary of State for Constitutional Affairs and Lord Chancellor set out in a statement to the House of Lords on 26 January 2004 ("the Concordat"), states that judges, working with HMCTS, are responsible for deciding on the assignment of cases to particular courts and the listing of those cases before particular judges. Therefore:

(a) The presiding judges of each circuit have the overall responsibility for listing at all courts, Crown and magistrates', on their circuit.

(b) Subject to the supervision of the presiding judges, the resident judge at each Crown Court has the general responsibility within his or her court centre for the allocation of criminal judicial work, to ensure the just and efficient despatch of the business of the court or group of courts. This includes overseeing the deployment of allocated judges at the court or group, including the distribution of work between all the judges allocated to that court. A resident judge must appoint a deputy or deputies to exercise his or her functions when he or she is absent from his or her court centre. See also paragraph A.5: Discharge of judicial responsibilities.

(c) The listing officer in the Crown Court is responsible for carrying out the day-to-day operation of listing practice under the direction of the resident judge. The listing officer at each Crown Court centre has one of the most important functions at that Crown Court and makes a vital contribution to the efficient running of that Crown Court and to the efficient operation of the administration of criminal justice.

(d) In the magistrates' courts, the Judicial Business Group, subject to the supervision of the presiding judges of the circuit, is responsible for determining the listing practice in that area. The day-to-day operation of that listing practice is the responsibility of the justices' clerk with the assistance of the listing officer.

Key principles of listing

A.3 When setting the listing practice, the resident judge or the Judicial Business Group should **F-4** take into account principles (a)–(j):

(a) Ensure the timely trial of cases and resolution of other issues (such as confiscation) so that justice is not delayed. The following factors are relevant: (i) In general, each case should be tried within as short a time of its arrival in the court as is consistent with the interests of justice, the needs of victims and witnesses, and with the proper and timely preparation by the prosecution and defence of their cases in accordance with the directions and timetable set. (ii) Priority should be accorded to the trial of young defendants, and cases where there are vulnerable or young witnesses. In *R. v. B.* [2010] EWCA Crim. 4; *The Times*, 5 February 2010, Lord Judge C.J. highlighted "the importance to the trial and investigative process of keeping any delay in a case involving a child complainant to an irreducible minimum". (iii) Custody time limits ("CTLs") should be observed: see CPD Listing F. (iv) Every effort must be made to avoid delay in cases in which the defendant is on bail.

(b) Ensure that in the magistrates' court unless impracticable, non-custody anticipated guilty plea cases are listed 14 days after charge, and non-custody anticipated not guilty pleas are listed 28 days after charge.

(c) Provide, when possible, for certainty and/or as much advance notice as possible, of the trial date; and take all reasonable steps to ensure that the trial date remains fixed.

(d) Ensure that a judge or bench with any necessary authorisation and of appropriate experience is available to try each case and, wherever desirable and practicable, there is judicial continuity, including in relation to post-trial hearings.

(e) Strike an appropriate balance in the use of resources, by taking account of: (i) the efficient deployment of the judiciary in the Crown Court and the magistrates' courts taking into account relevant sitting requirements for magistrates (see Annex 1 for information to support judicial deployment in the magistrates' courts); (ii) the proper use of the courtrooms available at the court; (iii) the provision in long and/or complex cases for adequate reading time for the judiciary; (iv) the facilities in the available courtrooms, including the security needs (such as a secure dock), size and equipment, such as video and live link facilities; (v) the proper use of those who attend the Crown Court as jurors; (vi) the availability of legal advisers in the magistrates' courts; (vii) the need to return those sentenced to custody as soon as possible after the sentence is passed, and to facilitate the efficient operation of the prison escort contract.

(f) Provide where practicable: (i) the defendant and the prosecution with the advocate of their choice where this does not result in any delay to the trial of the case; and, (ii) for the efficient deployment of advocates, lawyers and associate prosecutors of the Crown Prosecution Service, and other prosecuting authorities, and of the resources available to the independent legal profession, for example by trying to group certain cases together.

(g) Meet the need for special security measures for category A and other high-risk defendants.

(h) Ensure that proper time (including judicial reading time) is afforded to hearings in which the court is exercising powers that impact on the rights of individuals, such as applications for investigative orders or warrants.

(i) Consider the significance of ancillary proceedings, such as confiscation hearings, and the need to deal with such hearings promptly and, where possible, for such hearings to be conducted by the trial judge.

(j) Provide for government initiatives or projects approved by the Lord Chief Justice.

A.4 Although the listing practice at each Crown Court centre and magistrates' court will take these principles into account, the listing practice adopted will vary from court to court depending particularly on the number of courtrooms and the facilities available, the location and the workload, its volume and type.

Discharge of judicial responsibilities

F-5   **A.5** The resident judge of each court is responsible for: (i) ensuring that good practice is implemented throughout the court, such that all hearings commence on time; (ii) ensuring that the causes of trials that do not proceed on the date originally fixed are examined to see if there is any systemic issue; (iii) monitoring the general performance of the court and the listing practices; (iv) monitoring the timeliness of cases and reporting any cases of serious concern to the presiding judge; (v) maintaining and reviewing annually a list of recorders, qualifying judge advocates and deputy circuit judges authorised to hear appeals from the magistrates' courts unless such a list is maintained by the presiding judge.

A.6 The Judicial Business Group for each clerkship subject to the overall jurisdiction of the presiding judge is responsible for: (i) monitoring the workload and anticipated changes which may impact on listing policies; (ii) ensuring that any listing practice meets the needs of the system as a whole.

CPD LISTING B: CLASSIFICATION

F-6   **B.1** The classification structure outlined below is solely for the purposes of trial in the Crown Court. The structure has been devised to accommodate practical administrative functions and is not intended to reflect a hierarchy of the offences therein. Offences are classified as follows:

Class 1: A:

(i) Murder; (ii) attempted murder; (iii) manslaughter; (iv) infanticide; (v) child destruction (section 1(1) of the Infant Life (Preservation) Act 1929); (vi) abortion (section 58 of the Offences against the Person Act 1861); (vii) assisting a suicide; (viii) cases including section 5 of the Domestic Violence, Crime and Victims Act 2004, as amended (if a fatality has resulted); (ix) soliciting, inciting, encouraging or assisting, attempting or conspiring to commit any of the above offences or assisting an offender having committed such an offence.

Class 1: B:

(i) Genocide; (ii) torture, hostage-taking and offences under the War Crimes Act 1991; (iii) offences under sections 51 and 52 of the International Criminal Court Act 2001; (iv) an offence under section 1 of the Geneva Conventions Act 1957; (v) terrorism offences (where offence charged is indictable only and took place during an act of terrorism or for the purposes of terrorism as defined in section 1 of the Terrorism Act 2000); (vi) piracy, under the Merchant Shipping and Maritime Security Act 1997; (vii) treason; (viii) an offence under the Official Secrets Acts; (ix) incitement to disaffection; (x) soliciting, inciting, encouraging or assisting, attempting or conspiring to commit any of the above offences or assisting an offender having committed such an offence.

Class 1: C:

(i) Prison mutiny, under the Prison Security Act 1992; (ii) riot in the course of serious civil disturbance; (iii) serious gang related crime resulting in the possession or discharge of firearms, particularly including a campaign of firebombing or extortion, especially when accompanied by allegations of drug trafficking on a commercial scale; (iv) complex sexual offence cases in which there are many complainants (often under age, in care or otherwise particularly vulnerable) and/or many defendants who are alleged to have systematically groomed and abused them, often over a long period of time; (v) cases involving people trafficking for sexual, labour or other exploitation and cases of human servitude; (vi) soliciting, inciting, encouraging or assisting, attempting or conspiring to commit any of the above offences or assisting an offender having committed such an offence.

Class 1: D:

(i) Causing death by dangerous driving; (ii) causing death by careless driving; (iii) causing death by unlicensed, disqualified or uninsured driving; (iv) any health and safety case resulting in a fatality or permanent serious disability; (v) any other case resulting in a fatality or permanent serious disability; (vi) soliciting, inciting, encouraging or assisting, attempting or conspiring to commit any of the above offences or assisting an offender having committed such an offence.

Class 2: A:

(i) Arson with intent to endanger life or reckless as to whether life was endangered; (ii) cases in which explosives, firearms or imitation firearms are used or carried or possessed; (iii) kidnapping or false imprisonment (without intention to commit a sexual offence but charged on the same indictment as a serious offence of violence such as under section 18 or section 20 of the Offences against the Person Act 1861); (iv) cases in which the defendant is a police officer, member of the legal profession or a high profile or public figure; (v) cases in which the complainant or an important witness is a high profile or public figure; (vi) riot otherwise than in the course of serious civil disturbance; (vii) child cruelty; (viii) cases including section 5 of the Domestic Violence, Crime and Victims Act 2004, as amended (if no fatality has resulted); (ix) soliciting, inciting, encouraging or assisting, attempting or conspiring to commit any of the above offences or assisting an offender having committed such an offence.

Class 2: B:

(i) Any sexual offence, with the exception of those included in Class 1C; (ii) kidnapping or false imprisonment (with intention to commit a sexual offence or charged on the same indictment as a sexual offence); (iii) soliciting, inciting, encouraging or assisting, attempting or conspiring to commit any of the above offences or assisting an offender having committed such an offence.

Class 2: C:

(i) Serious, complex fraud; (ii) serious and/or complex money laundering; (iii) serious and/or complex bribery; (iv) corruption; (v) complex cases in which the defendant is a corporation (including cases for sentence as well as for trial); (vi) any case in which the defendant is a corporation with a turnover in excess of £1 billion (including cases for sentence as well as for trial); (vii) soliciting, inciting, encouraging or assisting, attempting or conspiring to commit any of the above offences or assisting an offender having committed such an offence.

Class 3: All other offences not listed in the classes above.

Deferred prosecution agreements

B.2 Cases coming before the court under section 45 of and Schedule 17 to the Crime and Courts **F-7** Act 2013 must be referred to the President of the Queen's Bench Division who will allocate the matter to a judge from a list of judges approved by the Lord Chief Justice. Only the allocated judge may thereafter hear any matter or make any decision in relation to that case.

Criminal Cases Review Commission

B.3 Where the Criminal Cases Review Commission refers a case upon conviction from the **F-8** magistrates' courts to the Crown Court, this shall be dealt with at a Crown Court centre designated by the Senior Presiding Judge.

CPD LISTING C: REFERRAL OF CASES IN THE CROWN COURT TO THE RESIDENT JUDGE AND TO THE PRESIDING JUDGES

5-9   **C.1** This practice direction specifies: (a) cases which must be referred to a presiding judge for release; and (b) cases which must be referred to the resident judge before being assigned to a judge, recorder or qualifying judge advocate to hear. It is applicable to all Crown Courts, but its application may be modified by the Senior Presiding Judge or the presiding judges, with the approval of the Senior Presiding Judge, through the provision of further specific guidance to resident judges in relation to the allocation and management of the work at their court.

    C.2 This practice direction does not prescribe the way in which the resident judge gives directions as to listing policy to the listing officer; its purpose is to ensure that there is appropriate judicial control over the listing of cases. However, the resident judge must arrange with the listing officers a satisfactory means of ensuring that all cases listed at their court are listed before judges, recorders or qualifying judge advocates of suitable seniority and experience, subject to the requirements of this practice direction. The resident judge should ensure that listing officers are made aware of the contents and importance of this practice direction, and that listing officers develop satisfactory procedures for referral of cases to him or her.

    C.3 In order to assist the resident judge and the listing officer, all cases sent to the Crown Court should where possible include a brief case summary prepared by the prosecution. The prosecutor should ensure that any factors that make the case complex, or would lead it to be referred to the resident judge or a presiding judge are highlighted. The defence may also send submissions to the court, again highlighting any areas of complexity or any other factors that might assist in the case being allocated to an appropriate judge.

Cases in the Crown Court to be referred to the resident judge

F-10   **C.4** All cases in Class 1A, 1B, 1C, 1D, 2A and 2C must be referred to the resident judge as must any case which appears to raise particularly complex, sensitive or serious issues.

    C.5 Resident judges should give guidance to the judges and staff of their respective courts as to which Class 2B cases should be referred to them following consultation with the Senior Presiding Judge. This will include any cases that may be referred to the presiding judge, see below. Class 2B cases to be referred to the resident judge are likely to be identified by the list officer, or by the judge at the first hearing in the Crown Court.

    C.6 Once a case has been referred to the resident judge, the resident judge should refer the case to the presiding judge, following the guidance below, or allocate the case to an appropriate category of judge, and if possible to a named judge.

Cases in the Crown Court to be referred to a presiding judge

F-11   **C.7** All cases in Class 1A, 1B and 1C must be referred by the resident judge to a presiding judge, as must a case in any class which is: (i) an usually grave or complex case or one in which a novel and important point of law is to be raised; (ii) a case where it is alleged that the defendant caused more than one fatality; (iii) a non-fatal case of baby shaking where serious injury resulted; (iv) a case where the defendant is a police officer, or a member of the legal profession or a high profile figure; (v) a case which for any reason is likely to attract exceptional media attention; (vi) a case where a large organisation or corporation may, if convicted, be ordered to pay a very large fine; (vii) any case likely to last more than three months.

    C.8 Resident judges are encouraged to refer any other case if they think it is appropriate to do so.

    C.9 Presiding judges and resident judges should agree a system for the referral of cases to the presiding judge, ideally by electronic means. The system agreed should include provision for the resident judge to provide the presiding judge with a brief summary of the case, a clear recommendation by the resident judge about the judges available to try the case and any other comments. A written record of the decision and brief reasons for it must be made and retained.

    C.10 Once a case has been referred to the presiding judge, the presiding judge may retain the case for trial by a High Court judge, or release the case back to the resident judge, either for trial by a named judge, or for trial by an identified category of judges, to be allocated by the resident judge.

CPD LISTING D: AUTHORISATION OF JUDGES

F-12   **D.1** Judges must be authorised by the Lord Chief Justice before they may hear certain types of case.

    D.2 Judges (other than High Court judges) to hear Class 1A cases must be authorised to hear such cases. Any judge previously granted a "Class 1" or "murder" authorisation is authorised to hear Class 1A cases. Judges previously granted an "attempted murder" (including soliciting, incitement or conspiracy thereof) authorisation can only deal with these cases within Class 1A.

    D.3 Judges (other than High Court judges) to hear sexual offences cases in Class 1C or any case within Class 2B must be authorised to hear such cases. Any judge previously granted a "Class 2" or "serious sex offences" authorisation is authorised to hear sexual offences cases in Class 1C or 2B. It is a condition of the authorisation that it does not take effect until the judge has attended the relevant Judicial College course; the resident judge should check in the case of newly authorised judges that they have attended the course. Judges who have been previously authorised to try such cases should make every effort to ensure their training is up-to-date and maintained by by attending the Serious Sexual Offences Seminar at least once every three years. See Annex 2 for guidance in dealing with sexual offences in the youth court.

D.4 Cases in the magistrates' courts involving the imposition of very large fines

(i) Where a defendant appears before a magistrates' court for an either way offence, to which CPD XIII Annex 3 applies the case must be dealt with by a district judge (magistrates' courts) who has been authorised to deal with such cases by the Chief Magistrate.

(ii) The authorised district judge (magistrates' courts) must first consider whether such cases should be allocated to the Crown Court or, where the defendant pleads guilty, committed for sentence under section 3 of the Powers of Criminal Courts (Sentencing) Act 2000, and must do so when the district judge (magistrates' courts) considers the offence or combination of offences so serious that the Crown Court should deal with the defendant had they been convicted on indictment.

(iii) If an authorised district judge (magistrates' courts) decides not to commit such a case the reasons must be recorded in writing to be entered onto the court register.

CPD LISTING E: ALLOCATION OF BUSINESS WITHIN THE CROWN COURT

E.1 Cases in Class 1A may only be tried by: (i) a High Court judge, or (ii) a circuit judge, or **F-13** deputy High Court judge, authorised to try such cases and provided that the presiding judge has released the case for trial by such a judge.

E.2 Cases in Class 1B may only be tried by: (i) a High Court judge, or (ii) a circuit judge, or a deputy High Court judge, provided that the presiding judge has released the case for trial by such a judge.

E.3 Cases in Class 1C may only be tried by: (i) a High Court judge, or (ii) a circuit judge, or a deputy High Court judge, or deputy circuit judge, authorised to try such cases (if the case requires the judge to be authorised to hear sexual offences cases), provided that the presiding judge has released the case for trial by such a judge, or, if the case is a sexual offence, the presiding judge has assigned the case to that named judge. See also *CPD Listing* C.10.

E.4 Cases in Class 1D and 2A may be tried by: (i) a High Court judge, or (ii) a circuit judge, or deputy High Court judge, or deputy circuit judge, or a recorder or a qualifying judge advocate, provided that either the presiding judge has released the case or the resident judge has allocated the case for trial by such a judge; with the exception that Class 2A(i) cases may not be tried by a recorder or qualifying judge advocate.

E.5 Cases in Class 2B may be tried by: (i) a High Court judge, or (ii) a circuit judge, or deputy High Court judge, or deputy circuit judge, or a recorder or a qualifying judge advocate, authorised to try such cases and provided that either the presiding judge has released the case or the resident judge has allocated the case for trial by such a judge.

E.6 Cases in Class 2C may be tried by: (i) a High Court judge, or (ii) a circuit judge, or deputy High Court judge, or deputy circuit judge, or a recorder or a qualifying judge advocate, with suitable experience (for example, with company accounts or other financial information) and provided that either the presiding judge has released the case or the resident judge has allocated the case for trial by such a judge.

E.7 Cases in Classes 1D, 2A and 2C will usually be tried by a circuit judge.

E.8 Cases in Class 3 may be tried by a High Court judge, or a circuit judge, a deputy circuit judge, a recorder or a qualifying judge advocate. A case in Class 3 shall not be listed for trial by a High Court judge except with the consent of a presiding judge.

E.9 If a case has been allocated to a judge, recorder or qualifying judge advocate, the preliminary hearing should be conducted by the allocated judge if practicable, and if not, if possible by a judge of at least equivalent standing. PCMHs should only be heard by recorders or qualifying judge advocates with the approval of the resident judge.

E.10 For cases in Class 1A, 1B or 1C, or any case that has been referred to the presiding judge, the preliminary hearing and PCMH must be conducted by a High Court judge; by a circuit judge; or by a judge authorised by the presiding judges to conduct such hearings. In the event of a guilty plea before such an authorised judge, the case will be adjourned for sentencing and will immediately be referred to the presiding judge who may retain the case for sentence by a High Court judge, or release the case back to the resident judge, either for sentence by a named judge, or for sentence by an identified category of judges, to be allocated by the resident judge.

E.11 Appeals from decisions of magistrates' courts shall be heard by: (i) a resident judge, or (ii) a circuit judge, nominated by the resident judge, who regularly sits at the Crown Court centre, or (iii) a recorder or qualifying judge advocate or a deputy circuit judge listed by the presiding judge to hear such appeals; or, if there is no such list nominated by the resident judge to hear such appeals; (iv) and, no less than two and no more than four justices of the peace, none of whom took part in the decision under appeal; (v) where no circuit judge or recorder or qualifying judge advocate satisfying the requirements above is available, by a circuit judge, recorder, qualifying judge advocate or deputy circuit judge selected by the resident judge to hear a specific case or cases listed on a specific day.

E.12 Allocation or committal for sentence following breach (such as a matter in which a community order has been made, or a suspended sentence passed), should, where possible, be listed before the judge who originally dealt with the matter or, if not, before a judge of the same or higher level.

E.13 Applications for removal of a driving disqualification should be made to the location of the Crown Court where the order of disqualification was made. Where possible, the matter should be listed before the judge who originally dealt with the matter or, if not, before a judge of the same or higher level.

CPD LISTING F: LISTING OF TRIALS, CUSTODY TIME LIMITS AND TRANSFER OF CASES

Estimates of trial length

F-14

F.1 Under the regime set out in the Crim PR, the parties will be expected to provide an accurate estimate of the length of trial at the hearing where the case is to be managed based on a detailed estimate of the time to be taken with each witness to be called, and accurate information about the availability of witnesses.

F.2 At the hearing the judge will ask the prosecution to clarify any custody time limit ("CTL") dates. The court clerk must ensure the CTL date is marked clearly on the court file or electronic file. When a case is subject to a CTL all efforts must be made at the first hearing to list the case within the CTL and the judge should seek to ensure this. Further guidance on listing CTL cases can be found below.

Cases that should usually have fixed trial dates

F-15

F.3 The cases where fixtures should be given will be set out in the listing practice applicable at the court, but should usually include the following: (i) cases in classes 1A, 1B, 1C, 2B and 2C; (ii) cases involving vulnerable and intimidated witnesses (including domestic violence cases), whether or not special measures have been ordered by the court; (iii) cases where the witnesses are under 18 or have to come from overseas; (iv) cases estimated to last more than a certain time—the period chosen will depend on the size of the centre and the available judges; (v) cases where a previous fixed hearing has not been effective; (vi) retrials; and, (vii) cases involving expert witnesses.

Custody time limits

F-16

F.4 Every effort must be made to list cases for trial within the CTL limits set by Parliament. The guiding principles are: (i) At the first hearing in the Crown Court, prosecution will inform the court when the CTL lapses. The CTL may only be extended in accordance with section 22 of the Prosecution of Offences Act 1985 and the (S.I. 1987 No. 299). (iii) If suitable, given priority and listed on a date not less than two weeks before the CTL expires, the case may be placed in a warned list. (iv) The CTL must be kept under continual review by the parties, HMCTS and the resident judge. (v) If the CTL is at risk of being exceeded, an additional hearing should take place and should be listed before the resident judge or trial judge or other judge nominated by the resident judge. (vi) An application to extend the CTL in any case listed outside the CTL must be considered by the court whether or not it was listed with the express consent of the defence. (vii) Any application to extend CTLs must be considered as a matter of urgency. The reasons for needing the extension must be ascertained and fully explained to the court. (viii) Where courtroom or judge availability is an issue, the court must itself list the case to consider the extension of any CTL. The delivery director of the circuit must provide a statement setting out in detail what has been done to try to accommodate the case within the CTL. (ix) Where courtroom or judge availability is not in issue, but all parties and the court agree that the case will not be ready for trial before the expiration of the CTL, a date may be fixed outside the CTL. This may be done without prejudice to any application to extend the CTLs or with the express consent of the defence; this must be noted on the papers.

F.5 As legal argument may delay the swearing in of a jury, it is desirable to extend the CTL to a date later than the first day of the trial.

Retrials ordered by the Court of Appeal

F-17

F.6 The Crown Court must comply with the directions of the Court of Appeal and cannot vary those directions without reference to the Court of Appeal.

F.7 In cases where a retrial is ordered by the Court of Appeal the CTL is 112 days starting from the date that the new indictment is preferred, ie from the date that the indictment is delivered to the Crown Court. Court centres should check that CREST has calculated the dates correctly and that it has not used 182 days on cases that have previously been "sent".

Changes to the date of fixed cases

F.8 Once a trial date or window is fixed, it should not be vacated or moved without good reason. **F-18** Under the Crim PR, parties are expected to be ready by the trial date.

F.9 The listing officer may, in circumstances determined by the resident judge, agree to the movement of the trial to a date to which the defence and prosecution both consent, provided the timely hearing of the case is not delayed. The prosecution will be expected to have consulted the witnesses before agreeing to any change.

F.10 In all other circumstances, requests to adjourn or vacate fixtures or trial windows must be referred to the resident judge for his or her personal attention; the resident judge may delegate the decision to a named deputy.

Transferring cases to another court

F.11 Transfer between courts on the same circuit must be agreed by the resident judges of each **F-19** court, subject to guidance from the presiding judges of the circuit.

F.12 Transfer of trials between circuits must be agreed between the presiding judges and delivery directors of the respective circuits.

F.13 Transfers may be agreed either in specific cases or in accordance with general principles agreed between those cited above.

CPD Listing G: Listing of Hearings other than Trials

G.1 In addition to trials, the court's listing practice will have to provide court time for shorter matters, such as those listed below. These hearings are important, often either for setting the necessary **F-20** case management framework for the proper and efficient preparation of cases for trial, or for determining matters that affect the rights of individuals. They must be afforded the appropriate level of resource that they require to be considered properly, and this may include judicial reading time as well as an appropriate length of hearing.

G.2 The applicant is responsible for notifying the court, and the other party if appropriate, and ensuring that the papers are served in good time, including a time estimate for judicial reading time and for the hearing. The applicant must endeavour to complete the application within the time estimate provided unless there are exceptional circumstances.

G.3 Hearings other than trials include the following: (i) applications for search warrants and production orders, sufficient reading time must be provided: see G.8 below; (ii) bail applications; (iii) applications to vacate or adjourn hearings; (iv) applications for dismissal of charges; (v) preliminary hearings; (vi) preparatory hearings; (vii) plea and case management hearings; (viii) applications for disclosure of further unused material under section 8 of the Criminal Procedure and Investigations Act 1996; (ix) case progression or case management hearings; (x) applications in respect of sentence indications not sought at the PCMH; (xi) sentences; (xii) civil applications under the Anti-social Behaviour, Crime and Policing Act 2014; (xiii) appeals from the magistrates' court: it is essential in all cases where witnesses are likely to be needed on the appeal to check availability before a date is fixed.

G.4 Short hearings should not generally be listed before a judge such that they may delay the start or continuation of a trial at the Crown Court. It is envisaged that any such short hearing will be completed by 10.30 am or start after 4.30 pm.

G.5 Each Crown Court equipped with a video link with a prison must have in place arrangements for the conduct of PCMHs, other pre-trial hearings and sentencing hearings by video link.

Notifying sureties of hearing dates

G.6 Where a surety has entered into a recognisance in the magistrates' court in respect of a case **F-21** allocated or sent to the Crown Court and where the bail order or recognisance refers to attendance at the first hearing in the Crown Court, the defendant should be reminded by the listing officer that the surety should attend the first hearing in the Crown Court in order to provide further recognisance. If attendance is not arranged, the defendant may be remanded in custody pending the recognisance being provided.

G.7 The court should also notify sureties of the dates of the hearing at the Crown Court at which the defendant is ordered to appear in as far in advance as possible: see the observations of Parker LJ in *R. v. Reading Crown Court, ex p. Bello*, 92 Cr.App.R. 303, CA (Civ. Div.) [§ 3-192 in the main work].

Applications for production orders and search warrants

G.8 The use of production orders and search warrants involve the use of intrusive state powers **F-22**

that affect the rights and liberties of individuals. It is the responsibility of the court to ensure that those powers are not abused. To do so, the court must be presented with a properly completed application, on the appropriate form, which includes a summary of the investigation to provide the context for the order, a clear explanation of how the statutory requirements are fulfilled, and full and frank disclosure of anything that might undermine the basis for the application. Further directions on the proper making and consideration of such applications will be provided by practice direction. However, the complexity of the application must be taken into account in listing it such that the judge is afforded appropriate reading time and the hearing is given sufficient time for the issues to be considered thoroughly, and a short judgment given.

Confiscation and related hearings

F-23

G.9 Applications for restraint orders should be determined by the resident judge, or a judge nominated by the resident judge, at the Crown Court location at which they are lodged.

G.10 In order to prevent possible dissipation of assets of significant value, applications under the Proceeds of Crime Act 2002 should be considered urgent when lists are being fixed. In order to prevent potential prejudice, applications for the variation and discharge of orders, for the appointment of receivers, and applications to punish alleged breaches of orders as a contempt of court should similarly be treated as urgent and listed expeditiously.

Confiscation hearings

F-24

G.11 It is important that confiscation hearings take place in good time after the defendant is convicted or sentenced.

CPD Listing: Annex 1: General Principles for the Deployment of the Judiciary in the Magistrates' Court

F-25

This distils the full deployment guidance issued in November 2012. The relevant sections dealing specifically with the allocation of work within the magistrates' court have been incorporated into this practice direction. It does not seek to replace the guidance in its entirety.

Presumptions

F-26

1 The presumptions which follow are intended to provide an acceptable and flexible framework establishing the deployment of the district judges (magistrates' courts) and magistrates. The system must be capable of adaptation to meet particular needs, whether of locality or caseload. In any event, the presumptions which follow are illustrative not exhaustive.

2 District judges (magistrates' courts) should generally (not invariably) be deployed in accordance with the following presumptions ("the presumptions"): (a) Cases involving complex points of law and evidence; (b) cases involving complex procedural issues; (c) long cases (included on grounds of practicality); (d) interlinked cases (given the need for consistency, together with their likely complexity and novelty); (e) cases for which armed police officers are required in court, such as high end firearms cases; (f) a share of the more routine business of the court, including case management and pre-trial reviews, (for a variety of reasons, including the need for district judges (magistrates' courts) to have competence in all areas of work and the desirability of an equitable division of work between magistrates and district judges (magistrates' courts), subject always to the interests of the administration of justice); (g) where appropriate, in supporting the training of magistrates; (h) occasionally, in mixed benches of district judges (magistrates' courts) and magistrates (with a particular view both to improving the case management skills of magistrates and to improving the culture of collegiality); (i) in the short-term tackling of particular local backlogs ("backlog busting"), sometimes in combination with magistrates from the local or (with the Senior Presiding Judge's approval) adjoining benches.

3 In accordance with current arrangements certain classes of cases necessarily require district judges (magistrates' courts) and have therefore been excluded from the above presumptions; these are as follows: (a) extradition; (b) terrorism; (c) prison adjudications; (d) sex cases in the youth court as per Annex 2; (e) cases where the defendant is likely to be sentenced to a very large fine: see Annex 3; (f) the special jurisdiction of the Chief Magistrate.

4 In formulating the presumptions, the following considerations have been taken into account:

(a) The listing of cases is here, as elsewhere, a judicial function: see *CPD Listing* A.1. In the magistrates' courts the Judicial Business Group, subject to the supervision of the presiding judges of the circuit, is responsible for determining the day-to-day listing practice in that area. The day-to-day operation of that listing practice is the responsibility of the justices' clerk with the assistance of the listing officer.

(b) Equally, providing the training of magistrates is a responsibility of justices' clerks.

(c) It is best not to treat "high profile" cases as a separate category but to consider their listing in the light of the principles and presumptions. The circumstances surrounding high profile cases do not permit ready generalisation, save that they are likely to require especially sensitive handling. Listing decisions involving such cases will often benefit from good communication at a local level between the justices' clerk, the district judge (magistrates' courts) and the bench chairman.

(d) Account must be taken of the need to maintain the competences of all members of the judiciary sitting in the magistrates' court.

CPD LISTING: ANNEX 2: SEXUAL OFFENCES IN THE YOUTH COURT

Introduction

1 This annex sets out the procedure to be applied in the youth court in all cases involving allegations of sexual offences which are capable of being sent for trial at the Crown Court under the grave crime provisions. **F-27**

2 This applies to all cases involving such charges, irrespective of the gravity of the allegation, the age of the defendant and/or the antecedent history of the defendant. (So, for example, every allegation of sexual touching, under section 3 of the Sexual Offences Act 2003, is covered by this protocol.)

3 This does not alter the test (set out in the Sentencing Guidelines Council's definitive guideline, entitled "Overarching Principles—Sentencing Youths", published by the Sentencing Guidelines Council in November 2009) that the youth court must apply when determining whether a case is a "grave crime".

4 In the Crown Court, cases involving allegations of sexual offences frequently involve complex and sensitive issues and only those circuit judges and recorders who have been specifically authorised and who have attended the appropriate Judicial College course may try this type of work.

5 A number of district judges (magistrates' courts) have now undertaken training in dealing with these difficult cases and have been specifically authorised to hear cases involving serious sexual offences which fall short of requiring to be sent to the Crown Court ("an authorised district judge (magistrates' courts)"). As such, a procedure similar to that of the Crown Court will now apply to allegations of sexual offences in the youth court.

Procedure

6 The determination of venue in the youth court is governed by section 51 of the Crime and Disorder Act 1998, which provides that the youth must be tried summarily unless charged with such a grave crime that long-term detention is a realistic possibility (section 24(1) of the Magistrates' Courts Act 1980), or that one of the other exceptions to this presumption arises. **F-28**

7 Wherever possible such cases should be listed before an authorised district judge (magistrates' courts), to decide whether the case falls within the grave crime provisions and should therefore be sent for trial. If jurisdiction is retained and the allegation involves actual, or attempted, penetrative activity, the case must be tried by an authorised district judge (magistrates' courts). In all other cases, the authorised district judge (magistrates' courts) must consider whether the case is so serious and/or complex that it must be tried by an authorised district judge (magistrates' courts), or whether the case can be heard by any district judge (magistrates' courts) or any youth court bench.

8 If it is not practicable for an authorised district judge (magistrates' courts) to determine venue, any district judge (magistrates' courts) or any youth court bench may consider that issue. If jurisdiction is retained, appropriate directions may be given but the case papers, including a detailed case summary and a note of any representations made by the parties, must be sent to an authorised district judge (magistrates' courts) to consider. As soon as possible the authorised district judge (magistrates' courts) must decide whether the case must be tried by an authorised district judge (magistrates' courts) or whether the case is suitable to be heard by any district judge (magistrates' courts) or any youth court bench; however, if the case involves actual, or alleged, penetrative activity, the trial must be heard by an authorised district judge (magistrates' courts).

9 Once an authorised district judge (magistrates' courts) has decided that the case is one which must be tried by an authorised district judge (magistrates' courts), and in all cases involving actual or alleged penetrative activity, all further procedural hearings should, so far as practicable, be heard by an authorised district judge (magistrates' courts).

10 All cases which are remitted for sentence from the Crown Court to the youth court should be listed for sentence before an authorised district judge (magistrates' courts).

Arrangements for an authorised district judge (magistrates' courts) to be appointed

11 Where a case is to be tried by an authorised district judge (magistrates' courts) but no such judge is available, the bench legal adviser should contact the Chief Magistrate's Office for an authorised district judge (magistrates' courts) to be assigned. **F-29**

CPD LISTING: ANNEX 3: CASES INVOLVING VERY LARGE FINES IN THE MAGISTRATES' COURT

1 This Annex applies when section 85 of the Legal Aid, Sentencing and Punishment of Offenders **F-30**

Act 2012 comes into force and the magistrates' court has the power to impose a maximum fine of any amount.

2 An authorised district judge (magistrates' courts) must deal with any allocation decision, trial and sentencing hearing in the following types of cases which are triable either way: (a) cases involving death or significant, life changing injury or a high risk of death or significant, life-changing injury; (b) cases involving substantial environmental damage or polluting material of a dangerous nature; (c) cases where major adverse effect on human health or quality of life, animal health or flora has resulted; (d) cases where major costs through clean-up, site restoration or animal rehabilitation have been incurred; (e) cases where the defendant corporation has a turnover in excess of £10m but does not exceed £250m, and has acted in a deliberate, reckless or negligent manner; (f) cases where the defendant corporation has a turnover in excess of £250m; (g) cases where the court will be expected to analyse complex company accounts; (h) high profile cases or ones of an exceptionally sensitive nature.

3 The prosecution agency must notify the justices' clerk where practicable of any case of the type mentioned in paragraph 2 of this Annex, no less than seven days before the first hearing to ensure that an authorised district judge (magistrates' courts) is available at the first hearing.

4 The justices' clerk shall contact the Office of the Chief Magistrate to ensure that an authorised district judge (magistrates' courts) can be assigned to deal with such a case if there is not such a person available in the courthouse. The justices' clerk shall also notify a presiding judge of the circuit that such a case has been listed.

5 Where an authorised district judge (magistrates' courts) is not appointed at the first hearing the court shall adjourn the case. The court shall ask the accused for an indication of his plea, but shall not allocate the case nor, if the accused indicates a guilty plea, sentence him, commit him for sentence, ask for a pre-sentence report or give any indication as to likely sentence that will be imposed. The justices' clerk shall ensure an authorised district judge (magistrates' courts) is appointed for the following hearing and notify the presiding judge of the circuit that the case has been listed.

6 When dealing with sentence, section 3 of the Powers of Criminal Courts (Sentencing) Act 2000 can be invoked where, despite the magistrates' court having maximum fine powers available to it, the offence or combination of offences make it so serious that the Crown Court should deal with it as though the person had been convicted on indictment.

7 An authorised district judge (magistrates' courts) should consider allocating the case to the Crown Court or committing the accused for sentence.

CPD LISTING: ANNEX 4: THE MANAGEMENT OF TERRORISM CASES

(as inserted by Practice Direction (Criminal Proceedings: Various Amendments) [2015] 1 W.L.R. 1643)

★**F-31**   This annex replaces the protocol on the case management of terrorism cases issued in December 2006 by the President of the Queen's Bench Division.

Application

★**F-32**   **1** This annex applies to "terrorism cases". For the purposes of this annex a case is a "terrorism case" where:

  (a) one of the offences charged against any of the defendants is indictable only and it is alleged by the prosecution that there is evidence that it took place during an act of terrorism or for the purposes of terrorism as defined in s.1 of the Terrorism Act 2000; this may include, but is not limited to:

     (i) murder;
     (ii) manslaughter;
     (iii) an offence under section 18 of the Offences against the Person Act 1861 (wounding with intent);
     (iv) an offence under section 23 or 24 of that Act (administering poison etc);
     (v) an offence under section 28 or 29 of that Act (explosives);
     (vi) an offence under section 2, 3 or 5 of the Explosive Substances Act 1883 (causing explosions);
     (vii) an offence under section 1 (2) of the Criminal Damage Act 1971 (endangering life by damaging property);
     (viii) an offence under section 1 of the Biological Weapons Act 1974 (biological weapons);
     (ix) an offence under section 2 of the Chemical Weapons Act 1996 (chemical weapons);
     (x) an offence under section 56 of the Terrorism Act 2000 (directing a terrorist organisation);

    (xi) an offence under section 59 of that Act (inciting terrorism overseas);

    (xii) offences under (v), (vii) and (viii) above given jurisdiction by virtue of section 62 of that Act (terrorist bombing overseas); and

    (xiii) an offence under section 5 of the Terrorism Act 2006 (preparation of terrorism acts);

(b) one of the offences charged is indictable only and includes an allegation by the prosecution of serious fraud that took place during an act of terrorism or for the purposes of terrorism as defined in s.1 of the Terrorism Act 2000 and meets the test to be transferred to the Crown Court under section 4 of the Criminal Justice Act 1987;

(c) one of the offences charged is indictable only, which includes an allegation that a defendant conspired, incited or attempted to commit an offence under sub-paragraphs (1)(a) or (b) above; or

(d) it is a case (which can be indictable only or triable either way) that a judge of the terrorism cases list (see paragraph 2(a) below) considers should be a terrorism case.

In deciding whether a case not covered by sub-paragraphs (1)(a), (b) or (c) above should be a terrorism case, the judge may hear representations from the Crown Prosecution Service.

The terrorism cases list

2 (a) All terrorism cases, wherever they originate in England and Wales, will be managed in a list known as the "terrorism cases list" by such judges of the High Court as are nominated by the President of the Queen's Bench Division.   ★**F-33**

(b) Such cases will be tried, unless otherwise directed by the President of the Queen's Bench Division, by a judge of the High Court as nominated by the President of the Queen's Bench Division.

3 The judges managing the terrorism cases referred to in paragraph 2(a) will be supported by the London and South Eastern Regional Co-ordinator's Office (the "Regional Co-ordinator's Office"). An official of that office or an individual nominated by that office will act as the case progression officer for cases in that list for the purposes of rule 3.4 of the Criminal Procedure Rules.

Procedure after charge

4 Immediately after a person has been charged in a terrorism case, anywhere in England and Wales, a representative of the Crown Prosecution Service will notify the person on the 24-hour rota for special jurisdiction matters at Westminster Magistrates' Court of the following information: ★**F-34**

(a) the full name of each defendant and the name of his solicitor of other legal representative, if known;

(b) the charges laid;

(c) the name and contact details of the Crown Prosecutor with responsibility for the case, if known; and

(d) confirmation that the case is a terrorism case.

5 The person on the 24-hour rota will then ensure that all terrorism cases wherever they are charged in England and Wales are listed before the Chief Magistrate or other District Judge designated under the Terrorism Act 2000. Unless the Chief Magistrate or other District Judge designated under the Terrorism Act 2000 directs otherwise, the first appearance of all defendants accused of terrorism offences will be listed at Westminster Magistrates' Court.

6 In order to comply with section 46 of the Police and Criminal Evidence Act 1984, if a defendant in a terrorism case is charged at a police station within the local justice area in which Westminster Magistrates' Court is situated, the defendant must be brought before Westminster Magistrates' Court as soon as is practicable and in any event not later than the first sitting after he is charged with the offence. If a defendant in a terrorism case is charged in a police station outside the local justice area in which Westminster Magistrates' Court is situated, unless the Chief Magistrate or other designated judge directs otherwise, the defendant must be removed to that area as soon as is practicable. He must then be brought before Westminster Magistrates' Court as soon as is practicable after his arrival in the area and in any event not later than the first sitting of Westminster Magistrates' Court after his arrival in that area.

7 As soon as is practicable after charge a representative of the Crown Prosecution Service will also provide the Regional Listing Co-ordinator's Office with the information listed in paragraph 4 above.

8 The Regional Co-ordinator's Office will then ensure that the Chief Magistrate and the Legal Aid Agency have the same information.

Cases to be sent to the Crown Court under section 51 of the Crime and Disorder Act 1998

9 A preliminary hearing should normally be ordered by the magistrates' court in a terrorism case. The court should ordinarily direct that the preliminary hearing should take place about 14 days after charge.   ★**F-35**

10 The sending magistrates' court should contact the Regional Listing Co-ordinator's Office who will be responsible for notifying the magistrates' court as to the relevant Crown Court to which to send the case.

11 In all terrorism cases, the magistrates' court case progression form for cases sent to the Crown Court under section 51 of the Crime and Disorder Act 1998 should not be used. Instead of the automatic directions set out in that form, the magistrates' court shall make the following directions to facilitate the preliminary hearing at the Crown Court:

    (a) three days prior to the preliminary hearing in the terrorism cases list, the prosecution must serve upon each defendant and the Regional Listing Co-ordinator:

        (i) a preliminary summary of the case;

        (ii) the names of those who are to represent the prosecution, if known;

        (iii) an estimate of the length of the trial;

        (iv) a suggested provisional timetable which should generally include:

- the general nature of further enquiries being made by the prosecution,
- the time needed for the completion of such enquiries,
- the time required by the prosecution to review the case,
- a timetable for the phased service of the evidence,
- the time for the provision by the Attorney General for his consent if necessary,
- the time for service of the detailed defence case statement,
- the date for the case management hearing, and
- the estimated trial date;

        (v) a preliminary statement of the possible disclosure issues setting out the nature and scale of the problem, including the amount of unused material, the manner in which the prosecution seeks to deal with these matters and a suggested timetable for discharging their statutory duty; and

        (vi) any information relating to bail and custody time limits;

    (b) one day prior to the preliminary hearing in the terrorist cases list, each defendant must serve in writing on the Regional Listing Co-ordinator and the prosecution:

        (i) the proposed representation;

        (ii) observations on the timetable; and

        (iii) an indication of plea and the general nature of the defence.

Cases to be transferred to the Crown Court under section 4(1) of the Criminal Justice Act 1987

★**F-36**
    12 If a terrorism case is to be transferred to the Crown Court the magistrates' court should proceed as if it is being sent to the Crown Court, as in paragraphs 9-11 above.

13 When a terrorism case is so sent or transferred the case will go into the terrorism list and be managed by a judge as described in paragraph 2(a) above.

The preliminary hearing at the Crown Court

★**F-37**
    14 At the preliminary hearing, the judge will determine whether the case is one to remain in the terrorism list and if so, give directions setting the provisional timetable.

15 The Legal Aid Agency must attend the hearing by an authorised officer to assist the court.

Use of video links

★**F-38**
    16 Unless a judge otherwise directs, all Crown Court hearings prior to the trial will be conducted by video link for all defendants in custody.

Security

★**F-39**
    17 The police service and the prison service will provide the Regional Listing Co-ordinator's Office with an initial joint assessment of the security risks associated with any court appearance by the defendants within 14 days of charge. Any subsequent changes in circumstances or the assessment of risk which have the potential to impact upon the choice of trial venue will be notified to the Regional Listing Co-ordinator's Office immediately.

CPD LISTING: ANNEX 5: MANAGEMENT OF CASES FROM THE ORGANISED CRIME DIVISION
OF THE CROWN PROSECUTION SERVICE

(as inserted by Practice Direction (Criminal Proceedings: Various Amendments) [2015] 1 W.L.R. 1643)

★**F-40**
    This annex replaces the guidance issued by the Senior Presiding Judge in January 2014.

★**F-41**
    1 The Organised Crime Division (OCD) of the CPS is responsible for prosecution of cases from the

National Crime Agency (NCA). Typically, these cases involve more than one defendant, are voluminous and raise complex and specialised issues of law. It is recognised that if not closely managed, such cases have the potential to cost vast amounts of public money and take longer than necessary.

2 This annex applies to all cases handled by the OCD.

Designated court centres

3 Subject to the overriding discretion of the presiding judges of the circuit, OCD cases should ★**F-42** normally be heard at Designated Court Centres (DCC). The process of designating court centres for this purpose has taken into account geographical factors and the size, security and facilities of those court centres. The designated court centres are:

(a) Northern Circuit: Manchester, Liverpool and Preston;

(b) North Eastern Circuit: Leeds, Newcastle and Sheffield;

(c) Western Circuit: Bristol and Winchester;

(d) South Eastern Circuit (not including London): Reading, Luton, Chelmsford, Ipswich, Maidstone, Lewes and Hove;

(e) South Eastern Circuit (London only): Southwark, Blackfriars, Kingston, Woolwich, Croydon and the Central Criminal Court;

(f) Midland Circuit: Birmingham, Leicester and Nottingham;

(g) Wales Circuit: Cardiff, Swansea and Mold.

Selection of designated court centres

4 If arrests are made in different parts of the country and the OCD seeks to have all defendants ★**F-43** tried by one Crown Court, the OCD will, at the earliest opportunity, write to the cluster manager with a recommendation as to the appropriate designated court centre, requesting that the decision be made by the relevant presiding judges. In the event that the designated court centre within one region is unable to accommodate a case, for example, as a result of a custody time limit expiry date, consideration may be given to transferring the case to a DCC in another region with the consent of the relevant presiding judges.

5 There will be a single point of contact person at the OCD for each HMCTS region, to assist listing co-ordinators.

6 The single contact person for each HMCTS region will be the cluster manager, with the exception of the South Eastern Circuit, where the appropriate point will be the Regional Listing Co-ordinator.

Designation of the trial judge

7 The trial judge will be assigned by the Presiding Judge at the earliest opportunity, and in ac- ★**F-44** cordance with CPD XIII Listing E: Allocation of Business within the Crown Court. Where the trial judge is unable to continue with the case, all further pre-trial hearings should be by a single judge until a replacement has been assigned.

Procedure after charge

8 Within 24 hours of the laying of a charge, a representative of the OCD will notify the cluster ★**F-45** manager of the following information to enable an agreement to be reached between the cluster manager and the reviewing CPS lawyer before the first appearance as to the DCC to which the case should be sent or committed:

(a) the full name of each defendant and the name of his legal representatives, if known;

(b) the charges laid; and

(c) the name and contact details of the Crown Prosecutor with responsibility for the case.

Exceptions

9 Where it is not possible to have a case dealt with at a DCC, the OCD should liaise closely with ★**F-46** the relevant cluster manager and the presiding judges to ensure that the cases are sent to the most appropriate court centre. This will, among other things, take into account the location of the likely source of the case, convenience of the witnesses, travelling distance for OCD staff and facilities at the court centres.

10 In the event that it is allocated to a non-designated court centre, the OCD should be permitted to make representations in writing to the presiding judges within 14 days as to why the venue is not suitable. The presiding judges will consider the reasons and, if necessary, hold a hearing. The CPS may renew their request at any stage where further reasons come to light that may affect the original decision on venue.

11 Nothing in this protocol should be taken to remove the right of the defence to make representations as to the venue.

APPENDIX G
Guidelines on Claims for Fees under a Crown Court Representation Order and in the Court of Appeal

A. SUMMARY OF SOURCE MATERIAL

Legislation

As from April 2, 2001 the relevant provisions of the Legal Aid in Criminal and Care Proceed- **G-1** ings (Costs) Regulations 1989 (S.I. 1989 No. 343), as amended, were superseded, virtually unamended, by the Criminal Defence Service (Funding) Order 2001 (S.I. 2001 No. 855) ("the Funding Order 2001"). This was significantly amended by a series of amending orders until it was revoked and replaced, in relation to representation orders granted on or after April 30, 2007, by the Criminal Defence Service (Funding) Order 2007 (S.I. 2007 No. 1174). The 2007 order was itself amended on many occasions over the following six years, until it lapsed on April 1, 2013, with the commencement of the repeal of its enabling legislation by the LASPOA 2012, s.39(1), and Sched. 5, para. 39. Full details of all the amending instruments for both the 2001 order and the 2007 order may be found in the second supplement to the 2013 edition of this work, together with the full text of the 2007 order (as amended).

The Criminal Legal Aid (Remuneration) Regulations 2013 (S.I. 2013 No. 435) (set out in full, *post*, G-6 *et seq.*) came into force on April 1, 2013. The substance of the 2013 regulations is almost identical to that of the 2007 order as it read at the time it lapsed, and many, if not all, the authorities that related to the 2007 order at that time will simply carry across. Where they are referred to *post* in this appendix, references to provisions of the former legislation have simply been updated to refer to the corresponding provision of the 2013 regulations.

As to the transitional arrangements in connection with the repeal of the relevant provisions of the Access to Justice Act 1999 and the commencement of the relevant provisions of the 2012 Act, see *ante*, § 6-173.

A challenge to the 8.75 per cent reduction in litigators' fees effected by amendments to Schedules 2, 3 and 4 to S.I. 2013 No. 435 (*ante*) in the Criminal Legal Aid (Remuneration) (Amendment) Regulations 2014 (S.I. 2013 No. 415) (as to which, see *post*, G-71, G-71a, G-72, G-72a, G-73, G-75a, G-80, G-86, G-92a) was rejected in *R. (London Criminal Courts Solicitors' Association) v. Lord Chancellor* [2015] Costs L.R. 7, QBD (Burnett J.).

The current regimes

Apart from a handful of historical cases which will be governed by the former provisions for *ex* **G-2** *post facto* taxation (as to which see Appendix G-200 *et seq.* in the supplements to the 2010 edition of this work), advocates' fees in the Crown Court effectively fall into one of two regimes:

(i) *Graduated fees.* These were first introduced in 1997 for trials lasting up to 10 days, appeals and other minor Crown Court business: Legal Aid in Criminal and Care Proceedings (Costs) Regulations 1989 (S.I. 1989 No. 343), Sched. 3. The scheme was then extended to cover trials of up to 25 days and, as from 2005, of trials up to 40 days. As from April 30, 2007, it was intended that the scheme would cover all Crown Court work save for those cases contracted under the Very High Costs Case provisions: Criminal Defence Service (Funding) Order 2007 (S.I. 2007 No. 1174), art. 3(6A), and Sched. 1, para. 2(1). The 2007 scheme is sometimes referred to as the Revised Advocacy Graduated Fee Scheme (RAGFS). The details were contained in Schedule 1 to the 2007 order, which replaced Schedule 4 to the Criminal Defence Service (Funding) Order 2001 (S.I. 2001 No. 855). The 2007 scheme (as amended) is now to be found in Schedule 1 to the Criminal Legal Aid (Remuneration) Regulations 2013 (S.I. 2013 No. 435).

(ii) *Very High Cost Cases (VHCC).* This regime came into effect on October 29, 2001. All cases estimated to last more than 24 days are capable of being subject to a VHCC contract. As to the current VHCC regime, see *post,* G-181 *et seq.*

Notes for guidance

(a) Graduated fees

G-3   The Ministry of Justice's *Graduated Fee Scheme Guidance (GFSG)* is updated at regular intervals. In addition, guidance notes have been issued by the Criminal Bar Association, and are available on both the Criminal Bar Association's and the Courts Service's National Taxing Team's websites. The GFSG includes references to costs judges' decisions which are given and commonly referred to and indexed by their "X" references. For convenience these references are used hereafter. The guidance may be cited by advocates when asking for a re-determination: GFSG, Preface. However, while interesting and instructive, it is simply the department's gloss on the wording of the regulations, and does not bind costs judges: *R. v. Phillips,* X1, SCTO 594/97.

The Bar Council has also introduced a *Graduated Fee Payment Protocol.* This is an essential part of the mechanism by which advocates will be remunerated in future, and sets out arrangements to ensure that substitute advocates are paid by instructed advocates. The protocol falls outside the immediate scope of this work. It is available on both the Bar Council's and the Criminal Bar Association's websites.

(b) Very High Cost Cases

G-4   Very High Cost Cases are governed by the Very High Cost (Crime) Cases Arrangements 2013 (see *post,* G-181 *et seq.*). Additional guidance is contained in the 2013 VHCC Guidance (published by the Legal Aid Agency, an executive agency of the Ministry of Justice).

Contract Appeals Committee decisions

G-5   Summaries of decisions of the Contract Appeals Committee have been collated and appear on the website of the Legal Aid Agency's section of the Ministry of Justice's website.

B. THE REMUNERATION REGULATIONS

Criminal Legal Aid (Remuneration) Regulations 2013 (S.I. 2013 No. 435)

Citation and commencement

G-6   **1.** These Regulations may be cited as the Criminal Legal Aid (Remuneration) Regulations 2013 and shall come into force on 1st April 2013.

Interpretation

★G-7   **2.**—(1) In these Regulations—

"the Act" means the Legal Aid, Sentencing and Punishment of Offenders Act 2012;

"advocate" means a barrister, a solicitor advocate or a solicitor who is exercising their automatic rights of audience in the Crown Court;

"appropriate officer" means—

(a) in the case of proceedings in the civil division of the Court of Appeal, the head of the civil appeals office;

(b) in the case of proceedings in the criminal division of the Court of Appeal, the registrar of criminal appeals;

(c) in the case of proceedings in the Crown Court, the Lord Chancellor;

(d) in respect of advice or assistance as to an appeal from the Crown Court to the Court of Appeal (except in the case of an appeal under section 9(11) of the Criminal Justice Act 1987 (preparatory hearings)) where, on the advice of any representative instructed, notice of appeal is given, or application for leave to appeal is made, whether or not such appeal is later abandoned, the registrar of criminal appeals;

    (e) in respect of advice or assistance as to an appeal to the Courts-Martial Appeal Court, the registrar of criminal appeals;

    (f) in respect of advice or assistance as to an appeal from the Court of Appeal to the Supreme Court, where the appeal is not lodged with the Supreme Court, the registrar of criminal appeals; and

    (g) in any other case, the Lord Chancellor,

and, in any case, includes an officer designated by the person who is the appropriate officer by virtue of paragraphs (a) to (g) to act on his behalf for the purposes of these Regulations;

"assisted person" means an individual in whose favour a section 16 determination has been made;

"fee earner" means a litigator, or person employed by a litigator, who undertakes work on a case;

"instructed advocate" means—

    (a) where the section 16 determination provides for representation by a single advocate, the first barrister or solicitor advocate instructed in the case, who has primary responsibility for the case; or

    (b) where the section 16 determination provides for representation by more than one advocate, each of—

        (i) the leading instructed advocate; and

        (ii) the led instructed advocate;

"leading instructed advocate" means the first leading barrister or solicitor advocate instructed in the case who has primary responsibility for those aspects of a case undertaken by a leading advocate;

"led instructed advocate" means the first led barrister or solicitor advocate instructed in the case who has primary responsibility for those aspects of the case undertaken by a led advocate;

"litigator" means the person referred to in the representation order as representing an assisted person, being a solicitor, firm of solicitors or other appropriately qualified person.

"main hearing" means—

    (a) in relation to a case which goes to trial, the trial;

    (b) in relation to a guilty plea (within the meaning of Schedule 1), the hearing at which pleas are taken or, where there is more than one such hearing, the last such hearing;

    (c) in relation to a cracked trial (within the meaning of Schedule 1), the hearing at which—

        (i) the case becomes a cracked trial by meeting the conditions in the definition of a cracked trial, whether or not any pleas were taken at that hearing; or

        (ii) a formal verdict of not guilty was entered as a result of the prosecution offering no evidence, whether or not the parties attended the hearing;

    (d) in relation to an appeal against conviction or sentence in the Crown Court, the hearing of the appeal;

    (e) in relation to proceedings arising out of a committal for sentence in the Crown Court, the sentencing hearing; and

    (f) in relation to proceedings arising out of an alleged breach of an order of the Crown Court, the hearing at which those proceedings are determined;

"related proceedings" means—

    (a) two or more sets of proceedings involving the same defendant which are prepared, heard or dealt with together; or

    (b) proceedings involving more than one defendant which arise out of the same incident, so that the defendants are charged, tried or disposed of together;

"representation order" means a document which records a section 16 determination;

"representative" means a litigator or an advocate including, where appropriate, an instructed advocate or trial advocate;

"section 16 determination" means a determination made under section 16 of the Act that an individual qualities for representation for the purposes of criminal proceedings;

"senior solicitor" means a solicitor who, in the judgement of the appropriate officer, has the skill, knowledge and experience to deal with the most difficult and complex cases;

"solicitor advocate" means a solicitor who has obtained a higher courts advocacy qualification in accordance with regulations and rules of conduct of the Law Society;

"solicitor, legal executive or fee earner of equivalent experience" means a solicitor, Fellow of the Institute of Legal Executives or equivalent senior fee earner who, in the judgement of the appropriate officer, has good knowledge and experience of the conduct of criminal cases;

"trainee solicitor or fee earner of equivalent experience" means a trainee solicitor or other fee earner who is not a Fellow of the Institute of Legal Executives, who, in the judgement of the appropriate officer, carries out the routine work on a case;

"trial advocate" means, unless otherwise provided, an advocate instructed pursuant to a section 16 determination to represent the assisted person at the main hearing in any case;

"Very High Cost Case" means a case in which a section 16 determination has been made and which the Director classifies as a Very High Cost Case on the grounds that—

    (a) in relation to fees claimed by litigators—

        (i) if the case were to proceed to trial, the trial would in the opinion of the Director be likely to last for more than 40 days and the Director considers that there are no exceptional circumstances which make it unsuitable to be dealt with under an individual case contract for Very High Cost Cases made by the Lord Chancellor under section 2(1) of the Act; or

        (ii) if the case were to proceed to trial, the trial would in the opinion of the Director be likely to last no fewer than 25 and no more than 40 days and the Director considers that there are circumstances which make it suitable to be dealt with under an individual case contract for Very High Cost Cases made by the Lord Chancellor under section 2(1) of the Act;

    (b) in relation to fees claimed by advocates, if the case were to proceed to trial, the trial would in the opinion of the Director be likely to last for more than 60 days and the Director considers that there are no exceptional circumstances which make it unsuitable to be dealt with under an individual case contract for Very High Cost Cases made by the Lord Chancellor under section 2(1) of the Act;

"Very High Cost Case contract" means the 2013 VHCC contract between the Lord Chancellor and a representative for the provision of representation under section 16 of the Act (criminal legal aid).

(2) The fees and rates set out in the Schedules to these Regulations are exclusive of value added tax.

(3) A function of the Lord Chancellor or Director under these Regulations may be exercised by, or by an employee of, a person authorised for that purpose by the Lord Chancellor or Director respectively.

[This regulation is printed as amended (insertion of definition of "Very High Cost Case contract") by the Criminal Legal Aid (Remuneration) (Amendment) Regulations 2013 (S.I. 2013 No. 2803), reg. 3(1) and (3). The amendment applies in relation to fees for work undertaken on or after December 2, 2013: *ibid.*, reg. 4. It is also printed as further amended by the Criminal Legal Aid (Remuneration) (Amendment) Regulations 2015 (S.I. 2015 No. 882), reg. 2(1) and (2) (insertion of definitions of "main hearing" and "trial advocate", and inclusion of words "or trial advocate" at the end of the definition of "representative"). The amendments apply to criminal proceedings in the Crown Court in which a determination under the LASPOA 2012, s.16 (§ 6-212 in the main work) is made on or after May 5, 2015.]

Scope

★G-8
    3.—(1) Regulations 5(2), 10 and 14(1) apply to proceedings in magistrates' courts and to proceedings in the Crown Court.

(2) Regulation 8 and Schedule 4 apply to proceedings in magistrates' courts, to proceedings in the County Court, to proceedings in the Crown Court and to proceedings in the High Court.

(3) Regulations 16 and 31 and Schedule 5 apply to proceedings in magistrates' courts, to proceedings in the Crown Court and to proceedings in the Court of Appeal.

(4) Regulations 4, 5(1) and (3) to (8), 13, 14(2) to (9), 15, 17 to 24 and 28 to 30 and Schedules 1 and 2 apply to proceedings in the Crown Court only.

(5) Regulations 9, 11 and 25 to 27, apply to proceedings in the Crown Court and to proceedings in the Court of Appeal.

(6) Regulation 6 and Schedule 3 apply to proceedings in the Court of Appeal only.

(7) Regulation 7 applies to proceedings in the Supreme Court only.

(8) With the exception of regulations 12 and 12A and paragraphs 13(8) and (9) of Schedule 2 and Schedule 6, these Regulations do not apply to Very High Cost Cases.

(9) For the purpose of these Regulations, any reference to the Court of Appeal includes as appropriate a reference to—

    (a) the criminal division of the Court of Appeal;

   (b)   the civil division of the Court of Appeal;

   (c)   the Courts-Martial Appeal Court; and

   (d)   a Divisional Court of the High Court.

[This regulation is printed as amended (insertion of references to reg. 12A and Sched. 6) by the Criminal Legal Aid (Remuneration) (Amendment) Regulations 2013 (S.I. 2013 No. 2803), reg. 3(1) and (4). The amendment applies in relation to fees for work undertaken on or after December 2, 2013: *ibid.*, reg. 4. It is also printed as further amended by the Civil and Criminal Legal Aid (Remuneration) (Amendment) Regulations 2015 (S.I. 2015 No. 325), reg. 3(1) and (2).]

[The next paragraph is G-10.]

Claims for fees by advocates—Crown Court

   4.—(1) Claims for fees by a trial advocate in proceedings in the Crown Court must be made and **★G-10** determined in accordance with the provisions of Schedule 1 to these Regulations.

   (2) A claim for fees under this regulation and Schedule 1 must be made by each trial advocate.

   (3) Subject to regulation 31, a claim by a trial advocate for fees in respect of work done pursuant to a section 16 determination must not be entertained unless the trial advocate submits it within three months of the conclusion of the proceedings to which it relates.

   (4) A trial advocate must submit a claim for fees to the appropriate officer in such form and manner as the appropriate officer may direct.

   (5) A trial advocate must supply such further information and documents as the appropriate officer may require.

   (6) Where a confiscation hearing under Part 2 of the Proceeds of Crime Act 2002 (confiscation: England and Wales), section 2 of the Drug Trafficking Act 1994 (confiscation orders) or section 71 of the Criminal Justice Act 1988 (confiscation orders) is to be held more than 28 days after—

     (a)   the conclusion of the trial to which the section 16 determination relates; or

     (b)   the entering of a guilty plea,

a trial advocate may submit any claim for fees in respect of the trial or guilty plea as soon as the trial has concluded or the guilty plea has been entered.

   (7) Where the section 16 determination provides for representation by—

     (a)   a single advocate other than a QC; or

     (b)   two or more advocates other than QC,

and a QC agrees to appear as the single advocate or as a leading junior, that QC must be treated for all the purposes of these Regulations as having been instructed in relation to that determination, and the remuneration of that QC must be determined as if the advocate were not a QC.

   (8) In this regulation, where the main hearing is a trial, "trial advocate" means an advocate who—

     (a)   is instructed pursuant to a section 16 determination to represent the assisted person at the trial, and

     (b)   attends the first day of the trial.

[This regulation is printed as amended, with effect from May 5, 2015, by the Criminal Legal Aid (Remuneration) (Amendment) Regulations 2015 (S.I. 2015 No. 882), reg. 2(3)(a), (4)(a), (5)(a), (6)(a) and (7). For the transitional provision, see *ante*, G-7.]

Claims for fees and disbursements by litigators—Crown Court

   5.—(1) Claims for fees by litigators in proceedings in the Crown Court must be made and **G-11** determined in accordance with the provisions of Schedule 2 to these Regulations.

   (2) Claims for disbursements by litigators in proceedings in the Crown Court or in proceedings in a magistrates' court which are subsequently committed or sent for trial to the Crown Court must be made and determined in accordance with the provisions of regulations 14 to 17.

   (3) Subject to regulation 31, a claim by a litigator for fees in respect of work done pursuant to a section 16 determination must not be entertained unless the litigator submits it within three months of the conclusion of the proceedings to which it relates.

   (4) Subject to paragraph (5), a claim by a litigator for fees in proceedings in the Crown Court must be submitted to the appropriate officer in such form and manner as the appropriate officer may direct and must be accompanied by the representation order and any receipts or other documents in support of any disbursement claimed.

   (5) A claim under paragraph 20 or 26 of Schedule 2 to these Regulations must—

(a) summarise the items of work done by a fee earner in respect of which fees are claimed according to the classes specified in paragraph 26(2) of Schedule 2;

(b) state, where appropriate, the dates on which the items of work were done, the time taken, the sums claimed and whether the work was done for more than one assisted person;

(c) specify, where appropriate, the level of fee earner who undertook each of the items of work claimed; and

(d) give particulars of any work done in relation to more than one indictment or a retrial.

(6) Where the litigator claims that paragraph 29 of Schedule 2 applies in relation to an item of work, the litigator must give full particulars in support of the claim.

(7) The litigator must specify any special circumstances which the litigator considers should be drawn to the attention of the appropriate officer.

(8) The litigator must supply such further information and documents as the appropriate officer may require.

[The next paragraph is G-13.]

Proceedings in the Court of Appeal

G-13   6. Claims for fees by representatives in proceedings in the Court of Appeal must be made and determined in accordance with the provisions of Schedule 3 to these Regulations.

Proceedings in the Supreme Court

G-14   7.—(1) In proceedings in the Supreme Court, the fees payable to a representative in respect of advice and assistance or representation made available to an individual in accordance with sections 15 or 16 of the Act must be determined by such officer as may be prescribed by order of the Supreme Court.

(2) Subject to paragraph (1), these Regulations do not apply to proceedings in the Supreme Court.

Claims for fees for certain categories of work to which the Standard Crime Contract applies

G-15   8.—(1) This regulation applies to—

(a) advice and assistance provided pursuant to a determination made under section 13 or section 15 of the Act;

(b) representation in proceedings in a magistrates' court pursuant to a section 16 determination;

(c) representation pursuant to a section 16 determination in proceedings prescribed as criminal proceedings under section 14(h) of the Act; and

(d) representation in appeals by way of case stated to the High Court.

(2) Claims for fees in cases to which this regulation applies must—

(a) be made and determined in accordance with the 2010 Standard Crime Contract; and

(b) be paid in accordance with the rates set out in Schedule 4.

(3) In this regulation and in Schedule 4, "2010 Standard Crime Contract" means the contract so named between the Lord Chancellor and a person with whom the Lord Chancellor has made an arrangement under section 2(1) of the Act for the provision of advice, assistance and representation made available under sections 13, 15 and 16 of the Act.

Payments from other sources

G-16   9. Where representation is provided in respect of any proceedings, the representative, whether acting pursuant to a section 16 determination or otherwise, must not receive or be a party to the making of any payment for work done in connection with those proceedings, except such payments as may be made—

(a) by the Lord Chancellor; or

(b) in respect of any expenses or fees incurred in—

(i) preparing, obtaining or considering any report, opinion or further evidence, whether provided by an expert witness or otherwise; or

(ii) obtaining any transcripts or recordings,

where an application under regulation 13 for an authority to incur such fees or expenses has been refused by a committee appointed under arrangements made by the Lord Chancellor to deal with, amongst other things, appeals of, or review of, assessment of costs.

In connection with regulation 9, see *R. v. Banfield, ante,* § 7-165.

Cases committed or sent for trial to the Crown Court

10.—(1) Where a case is committed or sent for trial or transferred to the Crown Court, the payment in relation to work carried out in the magistrates' court is included within the applicable fee payable under Schedule 1 or Schedule 2.   **G-17**

(2) Paragraph (1) does not apply where the case is remitted to a magistrates' court.

Proceedings for contempt

11. Where representation is provided in proceedings referred to in section 14(g) of the Act   **G-18**
(proceedings for contempt in the face of a court), the Lord Chancellor may only pay remuneration for services in accordance with Schedules 1, 2 and 3.

Notification of Very High Cost Cases

12.—(1) A litigator who has conduct of a case which is, or is likely to be classified as, a Very High   **G-18a**
Cost Case, must notify the Lord Chancellor in writing as soon as practicable.

(2) Where a litigator fails to comply with this regulation without good reason, and as a result there is a loss to public funds, the Lord Chancellor may refuse payment of the litigator's costs up to the extent of such loss.

(3) The Lord Chancellor must not refuse payment under paragraph (2) unless the litigator has been given a reasonable opportunity to show why the payment should not be refused.

Fees in Very High Cost Cases

12A. Where services consisting of representation made available under section 16 of the Act (criminal legal aid) are provided in a case which is the subject of a Very High Cost Case contract, fees for that case must be paid—

(a)   in accordance with the terms of that contract; and

(b)   at the rates set out for the appropriate category and level of representative set out in Schedule 6 to these Regulations.

[This regulation was inserted by the Criminal Legal Aid (Remuneration) (Amendment) Regulations 2013 (S.I. 2013 No. 2803), reg. 3(1) and (5). It applies in relation to fees for work undertaken on or after December 2, 2013: *ibid.*, reg. 4.]

Authorisation of expenditure

13.—(1) Where it appears to a litigator necessary for the proper conduct of proceedings in the   **★G-18b**
Crown Court for costs to be incurred in relation to representation by taking any of the following steps—

(a)   obtaining a written report or opinion of one or more experts;

(b)   employing a person to provide a written report or opinion (otherwise than as an expert);

(c)   obtaining any transcripts or recordings; or

(d)   performing an act which is either unusual in its nature or involves unusually large expenditure,

the litigator may apply to the Lord Chancellor for prior authority to do so.

(2) Where the Lord Chancellor authorises the taking of any step referred to in paragraph (1), the Lord Chancellor shall also authorise the maximum to be paid in respect of that step.

(3) A representative assigned to an assisted person in any proceedings in the Crown Court may apply to the Lord Chancellor for prior authority for the incurring of travelling and accommodation expenses in order to attend at the main hearing in those proceedings.

[This regulation is printed as amended, with effect from May 5, 2015, by the Criminal Legal Aid (Remuneration) (Amendment) Regulations 2015 (S.I. 2015 No. 882), reg. 2(8). For the transitional provision, see *ante*, G-7.]

The following authorities were decided under the corresponding provisions in earlier legal aid legislation: see, in particular, regulation 54 of the Legal Aid in Criminal and Care Proceedings (General) Regulations 1989 (S.I. 1989 No. 344).

In *R. v. Silcott, Braithwaite and Raghip*, *The Times*, December 9, 1991, the Court of Appeal said that all members of the legal profession were under a duty not to involve the legal aid fund in unnecessary expenditure. If an expert consulted by the defence was hostile to the accused's case or his solicitor considered the opinion to be wrong or defective it was most unlikely that legal aid authority would be given on application by the solicitor to consult more than one expert and certainly no more than two. In the instant case, the opinions of two experts had been obtained on behalf of one defendant. They were adverse to the defendant. Neither expert was called, but both changed their views in the light of the opinion of a third expert, who had been consulted after the trial's conclusion. This demonstrated that a third opinion had been necessary in the interests of justice. "Expert shopping" was to be discouraged, but there were exceptional cases where the need for a further expert opinion could be demonstrated. In such cases counsel should be asked to advise on evidence in support of an extension of the legal aid certificate, if he thought it right to do so. The courts and those responsible for the legal aid fund must rely on proper professional standards being observed by all the lawyers concerned.

A judge has no power to authorise the incurring of costs under a legal aid order for an expert witness, although he may express his opinion as to the desirability of legal aid being so extended: *R. v. Donnelly* [1998] Crim.L.R. 131, CA.

G-19

14.—(1) A litigator may submit a claim to the appropriate officer for payment of a disbursement for which the litigator has incurred liability in proceedings in the Crown Court, or in proceedings in a magistrates' court which are subsequently committed or sent for trial or transferred to the Crown Court, in accordance with the provisions of this regulation.

(2) A claim for payment under paragraph (1) may be made where—

(a) a litigator has obtained prior authority to incur expenditure of £100 or more under regulation 13; and

(b) the litigator has incurred such a liability.

(3) Without prejudice to regulation 17(4) and (5) a claim for payment under paragraph (1) must not exceed the maximum amount authorised under the prior authority.

(4) A claim for payment under paragraph (1) may be made at any time before the litigator submits a claim for fees under regulation 5.

(5) A claim for payment under paragraph (1) must be submitted to the appropriate officer in such form and manner as the appropriate officer may direct and must be accompanied by the authority to incur expenditure and any invoices or other documents in support of the claim.

(6) Subject to regulation 16, the appropriate officer must allow the disbursement subject to the limit in paragraph (3) if it appears to have been reasonably incurred in accordance with the prior authority.

(7) The appropriate officer must notify the litigator and, where the disbursement claimed includes the fees or charges of any person, may notify that person of the appropriate officer's decision.

(8) Where the appropriate officer allows the disbursement, the appropriate officer must notify the litigator and, where the disbursement includes the fees or charges of any person, may notify that person, of the amount payable, and must authorise payment to the litigator accordingly.

(9) Regulations 28 to 30 do not apply to a payment under this regulation.

Interim disbursements and final determination of fees

G-20

15.—(1) On a final determination of fees, regulations 5(2) and 17 apply notwithstanding that a payment has been made under regulation 14.

(2) Where the amount found to be due under regulation 17 in respect of a disbursement is less than the amount paid under regulation 14 ("the interim payment"), the appropriate officer must deduct the difference from the sum otherwise payable to the litigator on the determination of fees, and where the amount due under regulation 17 exceeds the interim payment, the appropriate officer must add the difference to the amount otherwise payable to the litigator.

Expert services

G-20a

16.—(1) Subject to paragraph (2), the Lord Chancellor may provide for the payment of expert services only at the fixed fees or at rates not exceeding the rates set out in Schedule 5.

(2) The appropriate officer may, in relation to a specific claim, increase the fixed fees or rates set out in Schedule 5 if that officer considers it reasonable to do so in exceptional circumstances.

(3) For the purposes of paragraph (2), exceptional circumstances are where the expert's evidence is key to the client's case and either—

(a) the complexity of the material is such that an expert with a high level of seniority is required; or

(b) the material is of such a specialised and unusual nature that only very few experts are available to provide the necessary evidence.

Determination of litigators' disbursements

G-21

17.—(1) Subject to paragraphs (2) to (5), the appropriate officer must allow such disbursements claimed under regulation 5(2) as appear to the appropriate officer to have been reasonably incurred.

(2) If the disbursements claimed are abnormally large by reason of the distance of the court or the assisted person's residence or both from the litigator's place of business, the appropriate officer may limit reimbursement of the disbursements to what otherwise would, having regard to all the circumstances, be a reasonable amount.

(3) No question as to the propriety of any step or act in relation to which prior authority has been obtained under regulation 13 may be raised on any determination of disbursements, unless the litigator knew or ought reasonably to have known that the purpose for which the authority was given had failed or had become irrelevant or unnecessary before the disbursements were incurred.

(4) Where disbursements are reasonably incurred in accordance with and subject to the limit imposed by a prior authority given under regulation 13, no question may be raised on any determination of fees as to the amount of the payment to be allowed for the step or act in relation to which the authority was given.

(5) Where disbursements are incurred in taking any steps or doing any act for which authority may be given under regulation 13, without such authority having been given or in excess of any fee so authorised, payment in respect of those disbursements may nevertheless be allowed on a determination of disbursements payable under regulation 5.

(6) Paragraph (7) applies where the Lord Chancellor receives a request for funding of an expert service of a type not listed in Schedule 5.

(7) In considering the rate at which to fund the expert service the Lord Chancellor—

    (a)   must have regard to the rates set out in Schedule 5; and

    (b)   may require more than one quotation for provision of the service to be submitted to the Lord Chancellor.

Interim payment of litigators' fees

17A.—(1) A litigator may make a claim to the appropriate officer for an interim payment of the **G-21a** litigator's fees, in relation to proceedings in the Crown Court, in accordance with this regulation.

(2) Subject to paragraphs (3) to (6), a litigator may make a claim for an interim payment under this regulation in relation to one or more of the following stages in the proceedings—

    (a)   after a plea and case management hearing at which directions for trial are given;

    (b)   where representation is transferred to the litigator following the ordering of a retrial, after the date for the retrial has been set; and

    (c)   after commencement of a trial which is listed for 10 days or more.

(3) A litigator may not make a claim for an interim payment under paragraph (2)(a) or (b) in relation to a case committed or sent for trial to the Crown Court on the election of a defendant where the magistrates' court has determined the case to be suitable for summary trial.

(4) Subject to paragraphs (5) and (6), a litigator may make only one claim in relation to each of the stages in the proceedings set out in paragraph (2).

(5) A litigator may not make a claim for an interim payment under paragraph (2)(a) or (b) at the same time as, or after, that litigator has made a claim for an interim payment under paragraph (2)(c).

(6) A litigator may not make a claim for an interim payment under paragraph (2)(c) if the trial in question is a retrial and the litigator was the litigator for the first or a previous trial.

(7) A litigator may not make a claim for an interim payment at the same time as, or after, that litigator has made a claim under regulation 5.

(8) A litigator must make a claim for an interim payment to the appropriate officer in such form and manner as the appropriate officer may direct.

(9) A litigator must supply such information and documents as the appropriate officer may require to determine the claim for interim payment.

(10) Where a claim for an interim payment is made in accordance with this regulation, the appropriate officer must authorise payment.

(11) Where the claim is made under paragraph (2)(a) the amount of the interim payment is the sum of—

    (a)   the fee which, on a final determination of fees, would be paid to the litigator if paragraph 13 of Schedule 2 and the scenario "Before trial transfer (original litigator)" set out in the table following that paragraph applied; and

    (b)   any additional payments which, on a final determination of fees, would be paid to the litigator under paragraph 12 of Schedule 2.

(12) Where the claim is made under paragraph (2)(b), the amount of the interim payment is the sum of—

    (a)   the fee which, on a final determination of fees, would be paid to the litigator under paragraph 13 of Schedule 2 and the scenario "Transfer before cracked retrial (new litigator)" set out in the table following that paragraph; and

    (b) any additional payments which, on a final determination of fees, would be paid to the litigator under paragraph 12 of Schedule 2.

(13) Where the claim is made under paragraph (2)(c), the amount of the interim payment is—

    (a) the sum of—

        (i) the fee determined in accordance with paragraph (14) on the basis that the trial length is one day; and

        (ii) any additional payments which, on a final determination of fees, must be paid to the litigator under paragraph 12 of Schedule 2;

    (b) less any amount paid to the litigator, in the proceedings in question, for a claim under paragraph (2)(a) or (b).

(14) The fee referred to in paragraph (13)(a)(i) is—

    (a) where the number of pages of prosecution evidence is less than or equal to the PPE Cut-off specified in the table following paragraph 5(2) of Schedule 2, the basic fee specified in the table following paragraph 7(2) of that Schedule;

    (b) where the pages of prosecution evidence exceeds the PPE Cut-off specified in the table following paragraph 5(2) of Schedule 2, the final fee as calculated in accordance with paragraph 9(2) of that Schedule.

(15) For purposes of paragraphs (11) to (14)—

    (a) the number of defendants;

    (b) the number of pages of prosecution evidence served on the court; and

    (c) the offence with which the assisted person is charged are determined as at the date of the claim for the interim payment.

(16) Where a litigator has received a hardship payment under regulation 21, the amount of that hardship payment must be deducted from any interim payment payable to that litigator under this regulation.

(17) Where a litigator has already received one or more interim payments under this regulation, the amount to be deducted under paragraph (16) excludes any hardship payment already deducted from any earlier interim payment.

(18) Regulations 28 to 30 do not apply to a payment under this regulation.

(19) In this regulation, "PPE Cut-off" has the meaning given in Schedule 2.

[This regulation was inserted by the Criminal Legal Aid (Remuneration) (Amendment) (No. 2) Regulations 2014 (S.I. 2014 No. 2422), reg. 2(3), and Sched., with effect from October 2, 2014. The amendments made by these regulations apply to criminal proceedings in which a determination under the LASPOA 2012, s.16 (§ 6-212 in the main work) was made on or after October 2 2014: reg. 3.]

Interim payments in cases awaiting determination of fees

★G-22   **18.**—(1) The appropriate officer must authorise an interim payment in respect of a claim for fees in proceedings in the Crown Court in accordance with this regulation.

(2) Entitlement to a payment arises in respect of a claim for fees by a trial advocate, where—

    (a) the graduated fee claimed in accordance with Schedule 1 is £4,000 or more (exclusive of value added tax); and

    (b) the claim for fees is for less than the amount mentioned in sub-paragraph (a) but is related to any claim for fees falling under sub-paragraph (a).

(3) For the purposes of this regulation, the following claims for fees are related to each other—

    (a) the claims of trial advocates acting in the same proceedings for a defendant; and

    (b) the claims of any instructed advocate acting for any assisted person in related proceedings.

(4) Entitlement to a payment under paragraph (1) does not arise until three months have elapsed from the earlier of—

    (a) the date on which the claim for fees is received by the appropriate officer for determination, except that where there are related claims for fees, the date on which the last claim is received by the appropriate officer; or

    (b) three months after the conclusion of the last of any related proceedings.

(5) A trial advocate may submit a claim for an interim payment under this regulation where—

    (a) no payment has been made under paragraph (1); and

    (b) six months have elapsed from the conclusion of the proceedings against the assisted person.

(6) Subject to regulation 31, payment must not be made under this regulation unless the trial advocate has submitted a claim for fees in accordance with regulation 4(3).

(7) In this regulation, where the main hearing is a trial, "trial advocate" means an advocate who—

    (a) is instructed pursuant to a section 16 determination to represent the assisted person at the trial, and

    (b) attends the first day of the trial.

[This regulation is printed as amended, with effect from May 5, 2015, by the Criminal Legal Aid (Remuneration) (Amendment) Regulations 2015 (S.I. 2015 No. 882), reg. 2(3)(b), (4)(b), (5)(b) and (9). For the transitional provision, see *ante*, G-7.]

Amount of interim payments in cases awaiting determination of fees

19.—(1) Where entitlement to an interim payment arises under regulation 18, the amount payable **G-23** is 40% of the total claim for fees, less any sum already paid.

(2) Regulations 28 to 30 do not apply to an interim payment under this regulation.

Staged payments in long Crown Court proceedings

20.—(1) An instructed advocate may submit a claim to the appropriate officer for a staged pay- **G-24** ment of the instructed advocate's fees in relation to proceedings in the Crown Court.

(2) Where a claim is submitted in accordance with this regulation, a staged payment must be allowed where the appropriate officer is satisfied—

    (a) that the claim relates to fees for a period of preparation of 100 hours or more, for which the instructed advocate will, subject to final determination of the fees payable, be entitled to be paid in accordance with Schedule 1; and

    (b) that the period from committal, or sending for trial or transfer (or from the date of the section 16 determination, if later) to the conclusion of the Crown Court proceedings is likely to exceed 12 months, having regard, amongst other matters, to the number of defendants, the anticipated pleas and the weight and complexity of the case.

(3) In this regulation, "preparation" means—

    (a) reading the papers in the case;

    (b) contact with prosecutors;

    (c) written or oral advice on plea;

    (d) researching the law, preparation for examination of witnesses and preparation of oral submissions;

    (e) viewing exhibits or undisclosed material at police stations;

    (f) written advice on evidence;

    (g) preparation of written submissions, notices or other documents for use at the trial;

    (h) attendance at views at the scene of the alleged offence,

and is limited to preparation done before the trial, except in proceedings in which a preparatory hearing has been ordered under section 8 of the Criminal Justice Act 1987 (commencement of trial and arraignment), in which case it is limited to preparation done before the date on which the jury is sworn (or on which it became certain, by reason of pleas of guilty or otherwise, that the matter would not proceed to trial).

(4) The amount allowed for preparation falling within paragraph (3) must be determined by reference to the number of hours of preparation which it appears to the appropriate officer, without prejudice to the final determination of the fees payable, has been reasonably done, multiplied by the hourly rate for special preparation as set out in the table following paragraph 24 of Schedule 1, as appropriate to the category of advocate.

(5) A claim for staged payment of fees under this regulation must be made to the appropriate officer in such form and manner as the appropriate officer may direct, including such case plan as the appropriate officer may require for the purposes of paragraph (2)(a).

(6) An instructed advocate may claim further staged payments in accordance with this regulation in respect of further periods of preparation exceeding 100 hours which were not included in an earlier claim.

(7) Regulations 28 to 30 do not apply to a payment under this regulation.

[The next paragraph is G-26.]

Hardship payments

21.—(1) Subject to paragraphs (5) and (6), the appropriate officer may allow a hardship payment **★G-26** to a representative in the circumstances set out in paragraph (2).

(2) Those circumstances are that the representative—

  (a) represents the assisted person in proceedings in the Crown Court;

  (b) applies for such payment, in such form and manner as the appropriate officer may direct, not less than six months after the representative was first instructed in those proceedings, or in related proceedings if the representative was instructed in those proceedings earlier than in the proceedings to which the application relates;

  (c) is unlikely to receive final payment in respect of the proceedings, as determined under Schedule 1 or 2, within the three months following the application for the hardship payment; and

  (d) satisfies the appropriate officer that, by reason of the circumstance in sub-paragraph (c), the representative is likely to suffer financial hardship.

(3) Every application for a hardship payment by an advocate must be accompanied by such information and documents as the appropriate officer may require as evidence of—

  (a) the work done by the advocate in relation to the proceedings up to the date of the application; and

  (b) the likelihood of financial hardship.

(4) Every application for a hardship payment by a litigator must be accompanied by such information and documents as the appropriate officer may require as evidence of—

  (a) the Class of Offence with which the assisted person is charged, in accordance with Part 7 of Schedule 1;

  (b) the length of trial, where appropriate;

  (c) the number of pages of prosecution evidence, determined in accordance with paragraph 1(2) of Schedule 2;

  (d) the total number of defendants in the proceedings who are represented by the litigator;

  (e) the likelihood of financial hardship.

(5) The amount of any hardship payment is at the discretion of the appropriate officer, but must not exceed such sum as would be reasonable remuneration for the work done by the representative in the proceedings up to the date of the application.

(6) A hardship payment must not be made if it appears to the appropriate officer that the sum which would be reasonable remuneration for the representative, or the sum required to relieve the representative's financial hardship, is less than £5,000 (excluding value added tax).

(7) Subject to paragraphs (9) and (10) where the appropriate officer allows a hardship payment under paragraph (1), the appropriate officer must authorise payment accordingly.

(8) Where the application for a hardship payment is made by an advocate other than a trial advocate, and the appropriate officer allows a hardship payment under paragraph (1)—

  (a) payment must be made to the—

    (i) appropriate trial advocate who attends the first day of trial, where the trial has commenced;

    (ii) appropriate trial advocate, where a trial has not commenced, or

    (iii) appropriate instructed advocate, where there is no trial advocate, and;

  (b) the appropriate officer must notify the advocate who made the application that payment has been made to the appropriate trial advocate or the appropriate instructed advocate.

(9) Where a litigator has received an interim payment under regulation 17A, the amount of that interim payment must be deducted from any hardship payment payable to that litigator under this regulation.

(10) Where a litigator has already received one or more hardship payments under this regulation, the amount deducted under paragraph (9) excludes any interim payment already deducted from any earlier hardship payment.

(11) In paragraph (8)—

"appropriate instructed advocate" means—

  (a) where the section 16 determination provides for representation by a single advocate, the instructed advocate, or

  (b) where the section 16 determination provides for representation by more than one advocate, the leading instructed advocate or the led instructed advocate, as appropriate, and

"appropriate trial advocate" means—

  (a) where the section 16 determination provides for representation by a single advocate, the trial advocate, or

  (b) where the section 16 determination provides for representation by more than one advocate, the leading trial advocate or the led trial advocate, as appropriate.

[This regulation is printed as amended by S.I. 2014 No. 2422 (*ante*, G-21a). For the transitional provision, see *ante*, G-21a. It is also printed as further amended, with effect from May 5, 2015, by the Criminal Legal Aid (Remuneration) (Amendment) Regulations 2015 (S.I. 2015 No. 882), reg. 2(3)(c) and (10). For the transitional provision, see *ante*, G-7.]

Computation of final claim where an interim payment has been made

22.—(1) At the conclusion of a case in which one or more payments have been made to an instructed advocate, a trial advocate or a litigator under regulations 17A to 21, the trial advocate or litigator must submit a claim under regulation 4 or 5 for the determination of the overall remuneration, whether or not such a claim will result in any payment additional to those already made. ★**G-27**

(2) In the determination of the amount payable to a trial advocate or litigator under regulation 4 or 5—

    (a) the appropriate officer must deduct the amount of any payment made under regulations 17A to 21 in respect of the same case from the amount that would otherwise be payable; and

    (b) if the amount of the interim payment is greater than the amount that would otherwise be payable, the appropriate officer may recover the amount of the difference, either by way of repayment by the trial advocate or litigator or by way of deduction from any other amount that may be due to the trial advocate or litigator.

(3) In this regulation, where the main hearing is a trial, "trial advocate" means an advocate who—

    (a) is instructed pursuant to a section 16 determination to represent the assisted person at the trial, and

    (b) attends the first day of the trial.

[This regulation is printed as amended by S.I. 2014 No. 2422 (*ante*, G-21a). For the transitional provision, see *ante*, G-21a. It is also printed as further amended, with effect from May 5, 2015, by the Criminal Legal Aid (Remuneration) (Amendment) Regulations 2015 (S.I. 2015 No. 882), reg. 2(3)(d), (6)(b) and (11). For the transitional provision, see *ante*, G-7.]

Payment of fees to advocates—Crown Court

23.—(1) Having determined the fees payable to each trial advocate, in accordance with Schedule 1, the appropriate officer must notify each trial advocate of the fees payable and authorise payment accordingly. ★**G-28**

(2) Where, as a result of any redetermination or appeal made or brought pursuant to regulations 28 to 30, the fees payable under paragraph (1) are altered—

    (a) if they are increased, the appropriate officer must authorise payment of the increase; or

    (b) if they are decreased, the trial advocate must repay the amount of such decrease.

(3) Where the payment of any fees of a trial advocate is ordered under regulation 29(12) or regulation 30(8), the appropriate officer must authorise payment.

(4) In this regulation, where the main hearing is a trial, "trial advocate" means an advocate who—

    (a) is instructed pursuant to a section 16 determination to represent the assisted person at the trial, and

    (b) attends the first day of the trial.

[This regulation is printed as amended, with effect from May 5, 2015, by the Criminal Legal Aid (Remuneration) (Amendment) Regulations 2015 (S.I. 2015 No. 882), reg. 2(3)(e), (5)(c), (6)(c) and (12). For the transitional provision, see *ante*, G-7.]

Payment of fees to litigators—Crown Court

24.—(1) Having determined the fees payable to a litigator in accordance with Schedule 2, the appropriate officer must authorise payment accordingly. **G-29**

(2) Where the appropriate officer determines that the fees payable under paragraph (1) are greater than or less than the amount claimed by the litigator under regulation 5(1), the appropriate officer must notify the litigator of the amount the appropriate officer has determined to be payable.

(3) Where, as a result of any redetermination or appeal made or brought pursuant to regulations 28 to 30, the fees payable under paragraph (1) are altered—

    (a) if they are increased, the appropriate officer must authorise payment of the increase; or

    (b) if they are decreased, the litigator must repay the amount of such decrease.

(4) Where the payment of any fees of the litigator is ordered under regulation 29(12) or regulation 30(8), the appropriate officer must authorise payment.

[The next paragraph is G-31.]

Recovery of overpayments

★**G-31**   **25.**—(1) This regulation applies where a representative is entitled to be paid a certain sum ("the amount due") by virtue of the provisions of Schedule 1, 2 or 3 and, for whatever reason, the representative is paid an amount greater than that sum.

(2) Where this regulation applies, the appropriate officer may—

(a) require immediate repayment of the amount in excess of the amount due ("the excess amount"); or

(b) deduct the excess amount from any other sum which is or becomes payable to the representative by virtue of the provisions of Schedule 1, 2 or 3,

and where sub-paragraph (a) applies the representative must repay the excess amount to the appropriate officer.

(3) The appropriate officer may proceed under paragraph (2)(b) without first proceeding under paragraph (2)(a).

(4) Paragraph (2) applies notwithstanding that the representative to whom the excess amount was paid is exercising, or may exercise, a right under regulations 28 to 30.

(5) In this regulation, where the main hearing is a trial, "trial advocate" means, for the purposes of the meaning of "representative", the advocate who—

(a) is instructed pursuant to a section 16 determination to represent the assisted person at the trial, and

(b) attends the first day of the trial.

[This regulation is printed as amended, with effect from May 5, 2015, by the Criminal Legal Aid (Remuneration) (Amendment) Regulations 2015 (S.I. 2015 No. 882), reg. 2(13). For the transitional provision, see *ante*, G-7.]

Adverse observations

G-32   **26.**—(1) Where in any proceedings to which Schedule 1, 2 or 3 applies, the court makes adverse observations concerning a representative's conduct of the proceedings, the appropriate officer may reduce any fee which would otherwise be payable in accordance with Schedule 1, 2 or 3 by such proportion as the appropriate officer considers reasonable.

(2) Before reducing the fee payable to a representative in accordance with the provisions of paragraph (1), the appropriate officer must give the representative the opportunity to make representations about whether it is appropriate to reduce the fee and the extent to which the fee should be reduced.

Wasted costs orders

G-33   **27.**—(1) Subject to paragraph (2), where the court has disallowed the whole or any part of any wasted costs under section 19A of the Prosecution of Offences Act 1985 (costs against legal representatives *etc*), the appropriate officer, in determining fees in respect of work done by the representative against whom the wasted costs order was made, may deduct the amount in the wasted costs order from the amount otherwise payable in accordance with these Regulations.

(2) Where the appropriate officer, in accordance with this regulation, is minded to disallow any amount of a claim for work done to which the wasted costs order relates, the appropriate officer must disallow that amount or the amount of the wasted costs order, whichever is the greater.

Redetermination of fees by appropriate offcer

★**G-34**   **28.**—(1) Where—

(a) an advocate in proceedings in the Crown Court is dissatisfied with the decision not to allow any of the following fees, or with the number of hours allowed in the calculation of such a fee, namely—

(i)   a special preparation fee under paragraph 17 of Schedule 1; or

(ii) a wasted preparation fee under paragraph 18 of Schedule 1; or

(b) a trial advocate in proceedings in the Crown Court is dissatisfied with—

(i)   the decision not to allow an hourly fee in respect of attendance at conferences or views at the scene of the alleged offence under paragraph 19 of Schedule 1, or with the number of hours allowed in the calculation of such a fee;

(ii) the calculation by the appropriate officer of the fee payable to the trial advocate in accordance with Schedule 1; or

(iii) the decision of the appropriate officer under paragraph 3(3) of Schedule 1 (reclassification of an offence not specifically listed in the relevant Table of Offences and so deemed to fall within Class H); or

   (c)   a litigator is dissatisfied with—

       (i)   the calculation by the appropriate officer of the fee payable to the litigator in accordance with Schedule 2; or

      (ii)   the decision of the appropriate officer under paragraph 3(3) of Schedule 2 (reclassification of an offence not specifically listed in the relevant Table of Offences and so deemed to fall within Class H),

the advocate, trial advocate or litigator, as the case may be, may apply to the appropriate officer to redetermine those fees, to review that decision or to reclassify the offence, as appropriate.

(2) An application under paragraph (1) may not challenge the quantum of any of the fees set out in Schedule 1 or Schedule 2.

(3) Subject to regulation 31, an application under paragraph (1), or paragraph 11(1) of Schedule 3, must be made—

   (a)   within 21 days of the receipt of the fees payable under regulation 23, regulation 24 or paragraph 10 of Schedule 3, as appropriate;

   (b)   by giving notice in writing to the appropriate officer, specifying the matters in respect of which the application is made and the grounds of objection; and

   (c)   in such form and manner as the appropriate officer may direct.

(4) The notice of application must be accompanied by the information and documents supplied under regulation 4, regulation 5 or Schedule 3, as appropriate.

(5) The notice of application must state whether the applicant wishes to appear or to be represented and, if the applicant so wishes, the appropriate officer must notify the applicant of the hearing date and time.

(6) The applicant must supply such further information and documents as the appropriate officer may require.

(7) The appropriate officer must, in the light of the objections made by the applicant or on behalf of the applicant—

   (a)   redetermine the fees, whether by way of confirmation, or increase or decrease in the amount previously determined;

   (b)   confirm the classification of the offence within Class H; or

   (c)   reclassify the offence,

as the case may be, and must notify the applicant of his decision.

(8) Where the applicant so requests, the appropriate officer must give reasons in writing for the appropriate officer's decision.

(9) Subject to regulation 31, any request under paragraph (8) must be made within 21 days of receiving notification of the appropriate officer's decision under paragraph (7).

(10) In this regulation, where the main hearing is a trial, "trial advocate" means an advocate who—

   (a)   is instructed pursuant to a section 16 determination to represent the assisted person at the trial, and

   (b)   attends the first day of the trial.

[This regulation is printed as amended, with effect from May 5, 2015, by the Criminal Legal Aid (Remuneration) (Amendment) Regulations 2015 (S.I. 2015 No. 882), reg. 2(14). For the transitional provision, see *ante*, G-7.]

Appeals to a costs judge

29.—(1) Where the appropriate officer has given his reasons for his decision under regulation 28(8), a representative who is dissatisfied with that decision may appeal to a costs judge.   **G-35**

(2) Subject to regulation 31, an appeal under paragraph (1) or paragraph 11(2) of Schedule 3 must be instituted within 21 days of the receipt of the appropriate officer's reasons, by giving notice in writing to the Senior Costs Judge.

(3) The appellant must send a copy of any notice of appeal given under paragraph (2) to the appropriate officer.

(4) The notice of appeal must be accompanied by—

   (a)   a copy of any written representations given under regulation 28(3);

   (b)   the appropriate officer's reasons for the appropriate officer's decision given under regulation 28(8); and

   (c)   the information and documents supplied to the appropriate officer under regulation 28.

(5) The notice of appeal must—

   (a)   be in such form as the Senior Costs Judge may direct;

(b) specify separately each item appealed against, showing (where appropriate) the amount claimed for the item, the amount determined and the grounds of the objection to the determination; and

(c) state whether the appellant wishes to appear or to be represented or whether the appellant will accept a decision given in the appellant's absence.

(6) The Senior Costs Judge may, and if so directed by the Lord Chancellor either generally or in a particular case must, send to the Lord Chancellor a copy of the notice of appeal together with copies of such other documents as the Lord Chancellor may require.

(7) With a view to ensuring that the public interest is taken into account, the Lord Chancellor may arrange for written or oral representations to be made on the Lord Chancellor's behalf and, if the Lord Chancellor intends to do so, the Lord Chancellor must inform the Senior Costs Judge and the appellant.

(8) Any written representations made on behalf of the Lord Chancellor under paragraph (7) must be sent to the Senior Costs Judge and the appellant and, in the case of oral representations, the Senior Costs Judge and the appellant must be informed of the grounds on which such representations will be made.

(9) The appellant must be permitted a reasonable opportunity to make representations in reply.

(10) The costs judge must inform the appellant (or the person representing him) and the Lord Chancellor, where representations have been or are to be made on the Lord Chancellor's behalf, of the date of any hearing and, subject to the provisions of this regulation, may give directions as to the conduct of the appeal.

(11) The costs judge may consult the trial judge or the appropriate officer and may require the appellant to provide any further information which the costs judge requires for the purpose of the appeal and, unless the costs judge otherwise directs, no further evidence may be received on the hearing of the appeal and no ground of objection may be raised which was not raised under regulation 28.

(12) The costs judge has the same powers as the appropriate officer under these Regulations and, in the exercise of such powers, may alter the redetermination of the appropriate officer in respect of any sum allowed, whether by increasing or decreasing it, as the costs judge thinks fit.

(13) The costs judge must communicate his decision and the reasons for it in writing to the appellant, the Lord Chancellor and the appropriate officer.

(14) Where the costs judge increases the sums redetermined under regulation 28, the costs judge may allow the appellant a sum in respect of part or all of any reasonable costs incurred by the appellant in connection with the appeal (including any fee payable in respect of an appeal).

Appeals to the High Court

G-36   30.—(1) A representative who is dissatisfied with the decision of a costs judge on an appeal under regulation 29 may apply to a costs judge to certify a point of principle of general importance.

(2) Subject to regulation 31, an application under paragraph (1) or paragraph 11(3) of Schedule 3 must be made within 21 days of receiving notification of a costs judge's decision under regulation 29(13).

(3) Where a costs judge certifies a point of principle of general importance the appellant may appeal to the High Court against the decision of a costs judge on an appeal under regulation 29, and the Lord Chancellor must be a respondent to such an appeal.

(4) Subject to regulation 31, an appeal under paragraph (3) must be instituted within 21 days of receiving notification of a costs judge's certificate under paragraph (1).

(5) Where the Lord Chancellor is dissatisfied with the decision of a costs judge on an appeal under regulation 29, the Lord Chancellor may, if no appeal has been made by an appellant under paragraph (3), appeal to the High Court against that decision, and the appellant must be a respondent to the appeal.

(6) Subject to regulation 31, an appeal under paragraph (5) must be instituted within 21 days of receiving notification of the costs judge's decision under regulation 29(13).

(7) An appeal under paragraph (3) or (5) must—

(a) be brought in the Queen's Bench Division;

(b) subject to paragraph (4), follow the procedure set out in Part 52 of the Civil Procedure Rules 1998; and

(c) be heard and determined by a single judge whose decision will be final.

(8) The judge has the same powers as the appropriate officer and a costs judge under these Regulations and may reverse, affirm or amend the decision appealed against or make such other order as the judge thinks fit.

Time limits

31.—(1) Subject to paragraph (2), the time limit within which any act is required or authorised to   ★**G-37**
be done under these Regulations may, for good reason, be extended—

    (a) in the case of acts required or authorised to be done under regulations 29 or 30, by a costs
        judge or the High Court as the case may be; and

    (b) in the case of acts required or authorised to be done by a representative under any other
        regulation, by the appropriate officer.

(2) Where a representative without good reason has failed (or, if an extension were not granted,
would fail) to comply with a time limit, the appropriate officer, a costs judge or the High Court, as
the case may be, may, in exceptional circumstances, extend the time limit and must consider whether
it is reasonable in the circumstances to reduce the fees payable to the representative under regulations 4, 5 or 6, provided that the fees must not be reduced unless the representative has been allowed a reasonable opportunity to show cause orally or in writing why the fees should not be
reduced.

(3) A representative may appeal to a costs judge against a decision made under this regulation by
an appropriate officer and such an appeal must be instituted within 21 days of the decision being
given by giving notice in writing to the Senior Costs Judge specifying the grounds of appeal.

(4) In this regulation, where the main hearing is a trial, "trial advocate" means, for the purposes of
the meaning of "representative", the advocate who—

    (a) is instructed pursuant to a section 16 determination to represent the assisted person at the
        trial, and

    (b) attends the first day of the trial.

[This regulation is printed as amended, with effect from May 5, 2015, by the Criminal Legal
Aid (Remuneration) (Amendment) Regulations 2015 (S.I. 2015 No. 882), reg. 2(15). For the
transitional provision, see *ante*, G-7.]

[The next paragraph is G-39.]

Regulation 4   SCHEDULE 1

ADVOCATES' GRADUATED FEE SCHEME

PART 1

DEFINITIONS AND SCOPE

Interpretation

1.—(1) In this Schedule—   ★**G-39**

    "case" means proceedings in the Crown Court against any one assisted person—

        (a) on one or more counts of a single indictment;

        (b) arising out of a single notice of appeal against conviction or sentence, or a single
            committal for sentence, whether on one or more charges; or

        (c) arising out of a single alleged breach of an order of the Crown Court,

    and a case falling within paragraph (c) must be treated as a separate case from the proceed-
    ings in which the order was made;

    "cracked trial" means a case on indictment in which—

        (a) a plea and case management hearing takes place and—

            (i) the case does not proceed to trial (whether by reason of pleas of guilty or for other
                reasons) or the prosecution offers no evidence; and

           (ii) either—

               (aa) in respect of one or more counts to which the assisted person pleaded guilty,
                     the assisted person did not so plead at the plea and case management hear-
                     ing; or

               (bb) in respect of one or more counts which did not proceed, the prosecution did
                     not, before or at the plea and case management hearing, declare an inten-
                     tion of not proceeding with them; or

        (b) the case is listed for trial without a plea and case management hearing taking place;

    "guilty plea" means a case on indictment which—

        (a) is disposed of without a trial because the assisted person pleaded guilty to one or
            more counts; and

   (b) is not a cracked trial;

"*Newton* hearing" means a hearing at which evidence is heard for the purpose of determining the sentence of a convicted person in accordance with the principles of *R. v. Newton* (1982) 77 Cr.App.R. 13;

"standard appearance" means an appearance by the trial advocate or substitute advocate in any of the following hearings which do not form part of the main hearing—

   (a) a plea and case management hearing, except the first plea and case management hearing;

   (b) a pre-trial review;

   (c) the hearing of a case listed for plea which is adjourned for trial;

   (d) any hearing (except a trial, a plea and case management hearing, a pre-trial review or a hearing referred to in paragraph 2(1)(b)) which is listed but cannot proceed because of the failure of the assisted person or a witness to attend, the unavailability of a pre-sentence report or other good reason;

   (e) custody time limit applications;

   (f) bail and other applications (except where any such applications take place in the course of a hearing referred to in paragraph 2(1)(b));

   (g) the hearing of the case listed for mention only, including applications relating to the date of the trial (except where an application takes place in the course of a hearing referred to in paragraph 2(1)(b));

   (h) a sentencing hearing other than one falling within paragraph 2(1)(b)(ii), paragraph 15(1) or paragraph 34;

   (i) a preliminary hearing; or

   (j) a hearing, whether contested or not, relating to breach of bail, failure to surrender to bail or execution of a bench warrant,

provided that a fee is not payable elsewhere under this Schedule in respect of the hearing;

"substitute advocate" means an advocate who is not an instructed advocate or the trial advocate but who undertakes work on the case; ... .

(2) For the purposes of this Schedule, the number of pages of prosecution evidence served on the court must be determined in accordance with sub-paragraphs (3) to (5).

(3) The number of pages of prosecution evidence includes all—

   (a) witness statements;

   (b) documentary and pictorial exhibits;

   (c) records of interviews with the assisted person; and

   (d) records of interviews with other defendants,

which form part of the committal or served prosecution documents or which are included in any notice of additional evidence.

(4) Subject to sub-paragraph (5), a document served by the prosecution in electronic form is included in the number of pages of prosecution evidence.

(5) A documentary or pictorial exhibit which—

   (a) has been served by the prosecution in electronic form; and

   (b) has never existed in paper form,

is not included within the number of pages of prosecution evidence unless the appropriate officer decides that it would be appropriate to include it in the pages of prosecution evidence taking into account the nature of the document and any other relevant circumstances.

(6) In proceedings on indictment in the Crown Court initiated otherwise than by committal for trial, the appropriate officer must determine the number of pages of prosecution evidence in accordance with sub-paragraphs (2) to (5) or as nearly in accordance with those sub-paragraphs as possible as the nature of the case permits.

(7) A reference to the Table of Offences in this Schedule is to the Table of Offences in Part 7 and a reference to a Class of Offence in this Schedule is to the Class in which that offence is listed in the Table of Offences.

[This paragraph is printed as amended, with effect from May 5, 2015, by the Criminal Legal Aid (Remuneration) (Amendment) Regulations 2015 (S.I. 2015 No. 882), reg. 2(16)(a). For the transitional provision, see *ante*, G-7.]

Application

G-40   2.—(1) Subject to sub-paragraphs (2) to (11), this Schedule applies to—

   (a) every case on indictment; and

   (b) the following proceedings in the Crown Court—

    (i)   an appeal against conviction or sentence;

    (ii)   a sentencing hearing following a committal for sentence to the Crown Court; and

    (iii)   proceedings arising out of an alleged breach of an order of the Crown Court (whether or not this Schedule applies to the proceedings in which the order was made).

  (2) Sub-paragraphs (3) and (4) apply where, following a trial, an order is made for a new trial and the same trial advocate appears at both trials where—

    (a)   the defendant is an assisted person at both trials; or

    (b)   the defendant is an assisted person at the new trial only; or

    (c)   the new trial is a cracked trial or guilty plea.

  (3) Subject to sub-paragraph (4), in respect of a new trial, or if the trial advocate so elects, in respect of the first trial, the graduated fee payable to the trial advocate must be calculated in accordance with Part 2 or Part 3, as appropriate, except that the fee must be reduced by—

    (a)   30%, where the new trial started within one month of the conclusion of the first trial;

    (b)   20%, where the new trial did not start within one month of the conclusion of the first trial;

    (c)   40%, where the new trial becomes a cracked trial or guilty plea within one month of the conclusion of the first trial; or

    (d)   25% where the new trial becomes a cracked trial or guilty plea more than one month after the conclusion of the first trial.

  (4) Where—

    (a)   in relation to the first trial, the case was committed or sent for trial to the Crown Court on the election of a defendant where the magistrates' court had determined the case to be suitable for summary trial; and

    (b)   the new trial becomes a cracked trial or guilty plea,

the fee payable to the trial advocate must be—

        (i)   the graduated fee calculated in accordance with Part 2, in respect of the first trial; and

        (ii)   the fixed fee set out in paragraph 10 in respect of the new trial.

  (5) Sub-paragraphs (6) and (7) apply in the circumstances set out in sub-paragraph (2) but where a different trial advocate appears for the assisted person at each trial.

  (6) Subject to sub-paragraph (7), in respect of each trial, the graduated fee payable to the trial advocate must be calculated in accordance with Part 2 or Part 3 as appropriate.

  (7) Where—

    (a)   in relation to the first trial, the case was committed or sent for trial to the Crown Court on the election of a defendant where the magistrates' court had determined the case to be suitable for summary trial; and

    (b)   the new trial becomes a cracked trial or guilty plea,

the fee payable to the trial advocate at the first trial must be the graduated fee, calculated in accordance with Part 2 and the fee payable to the trial advocate at the new trial must be the fixed fee set out in paragraph 10.

  (8) Where following a case on indictment a *Newton* hearing takes place—

    (a)   for the purposes of this Schedule the case is to be treated as having gone to trial;

    (b)   the length of the trial is to be taken to be the combined length of the main hearing and the *Newton* hearing;

    (c)   the provisions of this Schedule relating to cracked trials and guilty pleas do not apply; and

    (d)   no fee is payable under paragraph 15 in respect of the *Newton* hearing.

  (9) Sub-paragraph (10) applies where proceedings are—

    (a)   sent for trial to the Crown Court; or

    (b)   transferred to the Crown Court under—

        (i)   section 4 of the Criminal Justice Act 1987 (transfer of serious fraud cases); or

        (ii)   section 53 of the Criminal Justice Act 1991 (transfer of certain cases involving children).

  (10) Where, at any time after proceedings are sent or transferred to the Crown Court as referred to in sub-paragraph (9), they are—

    (a)   discontinued by a notice served under section 23A of the Prosecution of Offences Act 1985 (discontinuance of proceedings after accused has been sent for trial); or

    (b)   dismissed pursuant to—

        (i)   paragraph 2 of Schedule 3 to the Crime and Disorder Act 1998 (applications for dismissal);

        (ii)   section 6 of the Criminal Justice Act 1987 (applications for dismissal); or

(iii)   paragraph 5 of Schedule 6 to the Criminal Justice Act 1991 (applications for dismissal),
the provisions of paragraph 22 apply.

(11) For the purposes of this Schedule, a case on indictment which discontinues at or before the
plea and case management hearing otherwise than—

(a) by reason of a plea of guilty being entered; or

(b) in accordance with sub-paragraph (10),

must be treated as a guilty plea.

Class of offences

G-41   3.—(1) For the purposes of this Schedule—

(a) every indictable offence falls within the Class under which it is listed in the Table of Offences and, subject to sub-paragraph (2), indictable offences not specifically so listed are
deemed to fall within Class H;

(b) conspiracy to commit an indictable offence contrary to section 1 of the Criminal Law Act
1977 (the offence of conspiracy), incitement to commit an indictable offence and attempts
to commit an indictable offence contrary to section 1 of the Criminal Attempts Act 1981 (attempting to commit an offence) fall within the same Class as the substantive offence to
which they relate;

(c) where the Table of Offences specifies that the Class within which an offence falls depends
on whether the value involved exceeds a stated limit, the value must be presumed not to
exceed that limit unless the advocate making the claim under regulation 4 proves otherwise
to the satisfaction of the appropriate officer;

(d) where more than one count of the indictment is for an offence in relation to which the
Class depends on the value involved, that value must be taken to be the total value involved
in all those offences, but where two or more counts relate to the same property, the value
of that property must be taken into account once only;

(e) where an entry in the Table of Offences specifies an offence as being contrary to a statutory
provision, then subject to any express limitation in the entry that entry includes every offence contrary to that statutory provision whether or not the words of description in the
entry are appropriate to cover all such offences;

(f) where in a case on indictment there is a hearing to determine the question of whether an
assisted person is unfit to plead or unfit to stand trial, the trial advocate must elect whether
that hearing falls within the same Class as the indictable offence to which it relates or within
Class D; and

(g) where in a case on indictment a restriction order is made under section 41 of the Mental
Health Act 1983 (power of higher courts to restrict discharge from hospital), the offence
falls within Class A, regardless of the Class under which the offence would be listed in the
Table of Offences but for this paragraph.

(2) Where an advocate in proceedings in the Crown Court is dissatisfied with the classification
within Class H of an indictable offence not listed in the Table of Offences, the advocate may apply to
the appropriate officer when lodging the claim for fees to reclassify the offence.

(3) The appropriate officer must, in light of the objections made by the advocate—

(a) confirm the classification of the offence within Class H; or

(b) reclassify the offence,

and must notify the advocate of the decision.

As to this paragraph, see *post*, G-119.

Part 2

Graduated Fees for Trial

Calculation of graduated fees

G-42   4. The amount of the graduated fee for a single trial advocate representing one assisted person being tried on one indictment in the Crown Court in a trial lasting one to 40 days must be calculated in
accordance with the following formula—

$$G = B + (d \times D) + (e \times E) + (w \times W)$$

Where—

• **G** is the amount of the graduated fee;

• **B** is the basic fee specified in the table following paragraph 5 as appropriate to the offence for
which the assisted person is tried and the category of trial advocate;

• **d** is the number of days or parts of a day on which the advocate attends at court by which the
trial exceeds 2 days but does not exceed 40 days;

- **D** is the fee payable in respect of daily attendance at court for the number of days by which the trial exceeds 2 days but does not exceed 40 days, as appropriate to the offence for which the assisted person is tried and the category of trial advocate;
- **e** is the number of pages of prosecution evidence excluding the first 50, up to a maximum of 10,000;
- **E** is the evidence uplift specified in the table following paragraph 5 as appropriate to the offence for which the assisted person is tried and the category of trial advocate;
- **w** is the number of prosecution witnesses excluding the first 10;
- **W** is the witness uplift specified in the table following paragraph 5 as appropriate to the offence for which the assisted person is tried and the category of trial advocate.

Table of fees

5. For the purposes of paragraph 4 the basic fee (B), the daily attendance fee (D), the evidence **G-43** uplift (E) and the witness uplift (W) appropriate to any offence are those specified in the table following this paragraph in accordance with the Class within which that offence falls.

TABLE OF FEES AND UPLIFTS

Class of Offence	Basic Fee (B) (£)	Daily attendance fee (D) (£)	Evidence uplift (E) (£)	Witness uplift (W) (£)
QC				
A	2,856	979	1.63	6.53
B	2,529	857	1.63	6.53
C	1,968	816	1.63	6.53
D	2,284	816	1.63	6.53
E	1,514	612	1.63	6.53
F	1,514	612	1.63	6.53
G	1,514	612	1.63	6.53
H	1,903	816	1.63	6.53
I	2,122	816	1.63	6.53
J	2,856	979	1.63	6.53
K	2,856	979	1.63	6.53
Leading Junior				
A	2,142	734	1.23	4.9
B	1,897	643	1.23	4.9
C	1,476	612	1.23	4.9
D	1,714	612	1.23	4.9
E	1,136	459	1.23	4.9
F	1,136	459	1.23	4.9
G	1,136	459	1.23	4.9
H	1,427	612	1.23	4.9
I	1,592	612	1.23	4.9
J	2,142	734	1.23	4.9
K	2,142	734	1.23	4.9
Led Junior				
A	1,632	490	0.81	3.26
B	1,265	428	0.81	3.26
C	898	408	0.81	3.26
D	1,125	408	0.81	3.26
E	694	306	0.81	3.26
F	694	306	0.81	3.26
G	694	306	0.81	3.26

Class of Offence	Basic Fee (B) (£)	Daily attendance fee (D) (£)	Evidence uplift (E) (£)	Witness uplift (W) (£)
H	816	408	0.81	3.26
I	979	408	0.81	3.26
J	1,632	490	0.81	3.26
K	1,428	490	0.81	3.26
Junior alone				
A	1,632	530	0.98	4.9
B	1,305	469	0.98	4.9
C	898	408	0.98	4.9
D	1,125	408	0.98	4.9
E	653	326	0.98	4.9
F	694	326	0.98	4.9
G	694	326	0.98	4.9
H	816	408	0.98	4.9
I	979	408	0.98	4.9
J	1,632	530	0.98	4.9
K	1,632	530	0.98	4.9

PART 3

GRADUATED FEES FOR GUILTY PLEAS AND CRACKED TRIALS

Scope of Part 3

G-44   6.—(1) Subject to sub-paragraph (2) and to paragraph 22, this Part does not apply to a case committed or sent for trial to the Crown Court on the election of a defendant where the magistrates' court has determined the case to be suitable for a summary trial.

(2) This Part applies in all cases where the trial is a cracked trial because the prosecution offer no evidence on all counts against a defendant and the judge directs that a not guilty verdict be entered.

[This paragraph was substituted by S.I. 2014 No. 2422 (*ante*, G-21a). For the transitional provision, see *ante*, G-21a.]

Calculation of graduated fees in guilty pleas and cracked trials

G-44a   7.—(1) The amount of the graduated fee for a single trial advocate representing one assisted person in a guilty plea or cracked trial is—

    (a) where the case is a guilty plea or a trial which cracks in the first third—

        (i) the basic fee specified in Table A following paragraph 8 as appropriate to the offence with which the assisted person is charged, and the category of trial advocate; and

        (ii) the evidence uplift, as appropriate to the number of pages of prosecution evidence, calculated in accordance with that table; and

    (b) where the case is a trial which cracks in the second or last third—

        (i) the basic fee specified in Table B following paragraph 8 as appropriate to the offence with which the assisted person is charged and the category of trial advocate; and

        (ii) the evidence uplift, as appropriate to the number of pages of prosecution evidence, calculated in accordance with that table.

    (2) Where—

    (a) the trial of a case does not commence on the date first fixed; or

    (b) the case is not taken and disposed of from the first warned list in which it is entered,

the basic fee and evidence uplift for the offence are those specified for the last third in Table B following paragraph 8.

(3) In this paragraph, and in the tables following paragraph 8, references to the first, second and last third are references to the first, second and last third—

    (a) where a case is first listed for trial on a fixed date, of the period of time beginning with the day after the date on which the case is so listed and ending with the day before the date so fixed;

    (b) where the case is first placed in a warned list, of the period of time beginning with the day

after the date on which the case is so placed and ending with the day before the date of the
     start of that warned list,

and where the number of days in this period of time cannot be divided by three equally, any days
remaining after such division must be added to the last third.

(4) Where a graduated fee is calculated in accordance with this Part for the purposes of paragraph
2(3), the fee must be calculated as if the trial had cracked in the last third.

Tables of fees

8. Subject to paragraph 7, the basic fee and evidence uplift appropriate to any offence are specified   **G-45**
in the tables following this paragraph in accordance with the Class within which that offence falls, the
category of trial advocate and whether the case is a guilty plea, a trial which cracks in the first third
or a trial which cracks in the second or last third.

TABLE A: FEES AND UPLIFTS IN GUILTY PLEAS AND TRIALS WHICH CRACK IN THE FIRST THIRD

Class of Offence	Basic fee (£)	Evidence uplift per page of prosecution evidence (pages 1 to 1,000) (£)	Evidence uplift per page of prosecution evidence (1,001 to 10,000) (£)
QC			
A	1,714	2.85	1.43
B	1,305	1.8	0.9
C	1,224	1.28	0.64
D	1,305	2.85	1.43
E	1,081	0.92	0.46
F	1,081	1.2	0.61
G	1,081	1.2	0.61
H	1,224	1.65	0.82
I	1,224	1.61	0.8
J	1,714	2.85	1.43
K	1,714	1.59	0.8
Leading Junior			
A	1,285	2.15	1.07
B	979	1.35	0.67
C	918	0.96	0.48
D	979	2.15	1.07
E	811	0.69	0.35
F	811	0.9	0.46
G	811	0.9	0.46
H	918	1.24	0.61
I	918	1.21	0.6
J	1,285	2.15	1.07
K	1,285	1.19	0.6
Led Junior			
A	857	1.43	0.72
B	653	0.9	0.45
C	612	0.64	0.32
D	653	1.43	0.72
E	541	0.46	0.23
F	541	0.61	0.3
G	541	0.61	0.3
H	612	0.83	0.42

Class of Offence	Basic fee (£)	Evidence uplift per page of prosecution evidence (pages 1 to 1,000) (£)	Evidence uplift per page of prosecution evidence (1,001 to 10,000) (£)
I	612	0.8	0.4
J	857	1.43	0.72
K	857	0.8	0.4
Junior Alone			
A	979	1.19	0.59
B	694	0.81	0.41
C	449	0.6	0.3
D	694	1.19	0.59
E	408	0.35	0.17
F	408	0.54	0.27
G	408	0.54	0.27
H	490	0.54	0.28
I	571	0.42	0.22
J	979	1.19	0.59
K	979	1.02	0.51

TABLE B: FEES AND UPLIFTS IN TRIALS WHICH CRACK IN THE SECOND OR FINAL THIRD

Class of Offence	Basic Fee (£)	Evidence uplift per page of prosecution evidence (pages 1 to 250) (£)	Evidence up lift per page of prosecutionevidence (pages 251-1000) (£)	Evidence uplift per page of prosecution evidence (pages 1,001 to 10,000) (£)
QC				
A	2,324	5.07	1.27	1.68
B	1,743	3.2	0.8	1.06
C	1,520	2.27	0.57	0.75
D	1,743	5.07	1.27	1.68
E	1,232	1.63	0.41	0.54
F	1,232	2.14	0.54	0.71
G	1,232	2.14	0.54	0.71
H	1,540	2.93	0.73	0.96
I	1,598	2.87	0.71	0.94
J	2,324	5.07	1.27	1.68
K	2,324	2.83	0.71	0.94
Leading Junior				
A	1,744	3.8	0.95	1.26
B	1,307	2.4	0.6	0.8
C	1,140	1.7	0.43	0.56
D	1,307	3.8	0.95	1.26
E	924	1.22	0.31	0.41
F	924	1.6	0.41	0.53
G	924	1.6	0.41	0.53
H	1,155	2.2	0.54	0.72
I	1,198	2.14	0.53	0.71
J	1,744	3.8	0.95	1.26

Class of Offence	Basic Fee (£)	Evidence uplift per page of prosecution evidence (pages 1 to 250) (£)	Evidence up lift per page of prosecutionevidence (pages 251-1000) (£)	Evidence uplift per page of prosecution evidence (pages 1,001 to 10,000) (£)
K	1,744	2.13	0.53	0.71
Led Junior				
A	1162	2.54	0.64	0.84
B	871	1.6	0.4	0.53
C	760	1.14	0.28	0.37
D	871	2.54	0.64	0.84
E	616	0.82	0.2	0.27
F	616	1.07	0.27	0.36
G	616	1.07	0.27	0.36
H	770	1.46	0.37	0.48
I	798	1.43	0.36	0.48
J	1162	2.54	0.64	0.84
K	1162	1.42	0.36	0.47
Junior alone				
A	1307	4.52	2.1	0.69
B	908	3.11	1.45	0.48
C	581	2.31	1.07	0.36
D	808	4.52	2.1	0.69
E	508	1.34	0.63	0.2
F	508	2.08	0.96	0.32
G	508	2.08	0.96	0.32
H	618	2.08	0.97	0.32
I	726	1.63	0.76	0.25
J	1307	4.52	2.1	0.69
K	1234	3.91	1.82	0.60

PART 4

FIXED FEE FOR GUILTY PLEAS AND CRACKED TRIALS

Scope of Part 4

9.—(1) Subject to sub-paragraph (2), this Part applies to a case committed or sent for trial to the **G-46** Crown Court on the election of a defendant where the magistrates' court has determined the case to be suitable for summary trial.

(2) This Part does not apply where the trial is a cracked trial because the prosecution offer no evidence on all counts against a defendant and the judge directs that a not guilty verdict be entered.

[This paragraph was substituted by S.I. 2014 No. 2422 (*ante*, G-21a). For the transitional provision, see *ante*, G-21a.]

Fixed fee for guilty pleas or cracked trials

10. The fee payable to an advocate in relation to a guilty plea or cracked trial to which this Part applies is £194 per proceedings.

PART 5

FIXED FEES

General provisions

11.—(1) All work undertaken by an advocate in a case to which Part 4 applies is included within **G-46a** the fee set out in paragraph 10 except for attendance at a confiscation hearing to which paragraph 14 applies.

(2) Except as provided under this Part, all work undertaken by an advocate in a case to which Part 3 applies is included within the basic fee (B) specified in the table following paragraph 5, or that following paragraph 8, as appropriate to—

    (a) the offence for which the assisted person is tried;

    (b) the category of advocate; and

    (c) whether the case is a cracked trial, guilty plea or trial.

Fees for plea and case management hearings and standard appearance

G-47
    12.—(1) The fee payable in respect of—

    (a) an appearance by the trial advocate or substitute advocate at the first plea and case management hearing or pre-trial review; and

    (b) up to four standard appearances by the trial advocate or substitute advocate,

is included within the basic fee (B) specified in the table following paragraph 5, or that following paragraph 8, as appropriate to the offence for which the assisted person is tried and the category of trial advocate.

(2) The fee payable in respect of an appearance by the trial advocate or substitute advocate at a plea and case management hearing or standard appearance not included in sub-paragraph (1) is specified in the table following paragraph 24 as appropriate to the category of trial advocate or substitute advocate.

(3) The fee payable for preparing and filing the plea and case management questionnaire where no oral hearing takes place is specified in the table following paragraph 24 as appropriate to the category of trial advocate or substitute advocate.

(4) This paragraph does not apply to a standard appearance which is or forms part of the main hearing in a case or to a hearing for which a fee is payable elsewhere under this Schedule.

As to whether any appearances can be remunerated under paragraph 12(2) where no basic fee is payable, see *R. v. Metcalf* and *R. v. Muoka, post,* G-129.

Fees for abuse of process, disclosure, admissibility and withdrawal of plea hearings

G-48
    13.—(1) This paragraph applies to—

    (a) the hearing of an application to stay the case on indictment or any count on the ground that the proceedings constitute an abuse of the process of the court;

    (b) any hearing relating to the question of whether any material should be disclosed by the prosecution to the defence or the defence to the prosecution (whether or not any claim to public interest immunity is made);

    (c) the hearing of an application under section 2(1) of the Criminal Procedure (Attendance of Witnesses) Act 1965 (issue of witness summons on application to Crown Court) for disclosure of material held by third parties;

    (d) any hearing relating to the question of the admissibility as evidence of any material; and

    (e) the hearing of an application to withdraw a plea of guilty where the application is—

        (i) made by an advocate other than the advocate who appeared at the hearing at which the plea of guilty was entered; and

        (ii) unsuccessful.

(2) Where a hearing to which this paragraph applies is held on any day of the main hearing of a case on indictment, no separate fee is payable in respect of attendance at the hearing, but the hearing is included in the length of the main hearing for the purpose of calculating the fees payable.

(3) Where a hearing to which this paragraph applies is held prior to the first or only day of the main hearing, it is not included in the length of the main hearing for the purpose of calculating the fees payable and the trial advocate or substitute advocate must be remunerated for attendance at such a hearing—

    (a) in respect of any day where the hearing begins before and ends after the luncheon adjournment, at the daily rate set out in the table following paragraph 24 as appropriate to the category of trial advocate or substitute advocate; or

    (b) in respect of any day where the hearing begins and ends before the luncheon adjournment, or begins after the luncheon adjournment, at the half-daily rate set out in the table following paragraph 24 as appropriate to the category of trial advocate or substitute advocate.

Fees for confiscation hearings

G-49
    14.—(1) This paragraph applies to—

    (a) a hearing under Part 2 of the Proceeds of Crime Act 2002 (confiscation: England and Wales);

(b) a hearing under section 2 of the Drug Trafficking Act 1994 (confiscation orders); and

(c) a hearing under section 71 of the Criminal Justice Act 1988 (confiscation orders).

(2) A hearing to which this paragraph applies is not included in the length of the main hearing or of any sentencing hearing for the purpose of calculating the fees payable, and the trial advocate or substitute advocate must be remunerated in respect of such a hearing—

(a) where the number of pages of evidence is fewer than 51, for attendance—

  (i) in respect of any day when the hearing begins before and ends after the luncheon adjournment, at the daily rate set out in the first section of the table following this sub-paragraph; or

  (ii) in respect of any day when the hearing begins and ends before the luncheon adjournment, or begins after the luncheon adjournment, at the half-daily rate set out in the first section of that table,

  as appropriate to the category of trial advocate or substitute advocate;

(b) where the number of pages of evidence is between 51 and 1000—

  (i) at the rates for the relevant number of pages set out in the second section of the table following this sub-paragraph; and

  (ii) where the hearing lasts for more than one day, for attendance on subsequent days or half-days at the daily rate or half-daily rate set out in the first section of that table,

  as appropriate to the category of trial advocate or substitute advocate; or

(c) where the number of pages of evidence exceeds 1000—

  (i) at the rates for 751 to 1000 pages set out in the second section of the table following this sub-paragraph;

  (ii) with such fee as the appropriate officer considers reasonable for preparation in respect of the pages in excess of 1000, at the hourly rates for preparation set out in the third section of that table; and

  (iii) where the hearing lasts for more than one day, for attendance on subsequent days or half-days at the daily rate or half-daily rate set out in the first section of that table,

  as appropriate to the category of trial advocate or substitute advocate.

FEES FOR CONSFISCATION HEARINGS

	Fee for QC (£)	Fee for leading junior (£)	Fee for junior alone (£)	Fee for led junior (£)
1. Daily and half-daily rates				
Half-daily rate	260	195	130	130
Daily rate	497	346	238	238
2. Pages of evidence				
51-250	649	541	433	324
251–500	973	811	649	486
501–750	1,298	1,081	865	649
751–1000	1,946	1,622	1,298	973
3. Preparation				
Hourly rates	74	56	39	39

(3) In sub-paragraph (2) "evidence" means—

(a) the statement of information served under section 16 of the Proceeds of Crime Act 2002 and relied on by the prosecution for the purposes of a hearing under Part 2 of that Act, or a similar statement served and so relied on for the purposes of a hearing under section 2 of the Drug Trafficking Act 1994 or under section 71 of the Criminal Justice Act 1988 and, in each case, any attached annexes and exhibits;

(b) any other document which—

  (i) is served as a statement or an exhibit for the purposes of the trial;

  (ii) is specifically referred to in, but not served with, a statement mentioned in paragraph (a); and

  (iii) the prosecution state that they intend to rely on in the hearing; and

(c) any written report of an expert obtained with the prior authority of the Lord Chancellor under regulation 13 or allowed by the appropriate officer under these Regulations, and any attached annexes and exhibits, other than documents contained in such annexes or exhibits which have also been served under paragraph (a) or (b) or which consist of financial records or similar data.

Fees for sentencing hearings

G-50   15.—(1) This paragraph applies to a sentencing hearing following a case on indictment to which this Schedule applies, where sentence has been deferred under section 1 of the Powers of Criminal Courts (Sentencing) Act 2000 (deferment of sentence).

(2) The fee payable to an advocate for appearing at a hearing to which this paragraph applies is that set out in the table following paragraph 24 as appropriate to the category of trial advocate or substitute advocate and the circumstances of the hearing.

Fees for ineffective trials

G-51   16. The fee set out in the table following paragraph 24 as appropriate to the category of trial advocate is payable in respect of each day on which the case was listed for trial but did not proceed on the day for which it was listed, for whatever reason.

Fees for special preparation

★G-52   17.—(1) This paragraph applies where, in any case on indictment in the Crown Court in respect of which a graduated fee is payable under Part 2 or Part 3—

   (a) it has been necessary for an advocate to do work by way of preparation substantially in excess of the amount normally done for cases of the same type because the case involves a very unusual or novel point of law or factual issue;

   (b) the number of pages of prosecution evidence, as defined in paragraph 1(2), exceeds 10,000 and the appropriate officer considers it reasonable to make a payment in excess of the graduated fee payable under this Schedule; or

   (c) a documentary or pictorial exhibit is served by the prosecution in electronic form where—
      (i)   the exhibit has never existed in paper form; and
      (ii) the appropriate officer—
         (aa) does not consider it appropriate to include the exhibit in the pages of prosecution evidence; and
         (bb) considers it reasonable to make a payment in respect of the exhibit in excess of the graduated fee.

(2) Where this paragraph applies, a special preparation fee may be paid, in addition to the graduated fee payable under Part 2 or Part 3.

(3) The amount of the special preparation fee must be calculated—

   (a) where sub-paragraph (1)(a) applies, from the number of hours preparation in excess of the amount the appropriate officer considers reasonable for cases of the same type;

   (b) where sub-paragraph (1)(b) applies, from the number of hours which the appropriate officer considers reasonable to read the excess pages; and

   (c) where sub-paragraph (1)(c) applies, from the number of hours which the appropriate officer considers reasonable to view the prosecution evidence,

and in each case using the hourly fee rates set out in the table following paragraph 24 as appropriate to the category of trial advocate.

(4) Any claim for a special preparation fee under this paragraph must be made by a trial advocate, whether or not the trial advocate did the work claimed for.

(5) A trial advocate claiming a special preparation fee must supply such information and documents as may be required by the appropriate officer in support of the claim.

(6) In determining a claim under this paragraph, the appropriate officer must take into account all the relevant circumstances of the case, including, where special preparation work has been undertaken by more than one advocate, the benefit of such work to the trial advocate.

(7) In sub-paragraphs (4) and (5), where the main hearing is a trial, "trial advocate" means the advocate who—

   (a) is instructed pursuant to a section 16 determination to represent the assisted person at the trial, and

   (b) attends the first day of the trial.

[This paragraph is printed as amended, with effect from May 5, 2015, by the Criminal Legal Aid (Remuneration) (Amendment) Regulations 2015 (S.I. 2015 No. 882), reg. 2(3)(f), (4)(c), (6)(d), and (16)(b). For the transitional provision, see *ante*, G-7.]

Fees for wasted preparation

★G-53   18.—(1) A wasted preparation fee may be claimed where a trial advocate in any case to which this paragraph applies is prevented from representing the assisted person in the main hearing by any of the following circumstances—

(a) the trial advocate is instructed to appear in other proceedings at the same time as the main hearing in the case and has been unable to secure a change of date for either the main hearing or the other proceedings;

(b) the date fixed for the main hearing is changed by the court despite the trial advocate's objection;

(c) the trial advocate has withdrawn from the case with the leave of the court because of the trial advocate's professional code of conduct or to avoid embarrassment in the exercise of the trial advocate's profession;

(d) the trial advocate has been dismissed by the assisted person or the litigator; or

(e) the trial advocate is obliged to attend at any place by reason of a judicial office held by the trial advocate or other public duty.

(2) This paragraph applies to every case on indictment to which this Schedule applies provided that—

(a) the case goes to trial, and the trial lasts for five days or more; or

(b) the case is a cracked trial, and the number of pages of prosecution evidence exceeds 150.

(3) The amount of the wasted preparation fee must be calculated from the number of hours of preparation reasonably carried out by the trial advocate, using the hourly fee rates set out in the table following paragraph 24 as appropriate to the category of trial advocate, but no such fee is payable unless the number of hours of preparation is eight or more.

(4) Any claim for a wasted preparation fee under this paragraph must be made by a trial advocate, whether or not the trial advocate did the work claimed for.

(5) A trial advocate claiming a wasted preparation fee must supply such information and documents as may be required by the appropriate officer as proof of the circumstances in which the advocate was prevented from representing the assisted person and of the number of hours of preparation.

(6) In sub-paragraphs (4) and (5), where the main hearing is a trial, "trial advocate" means an advocate who—

(a) is instructed pursuant to a section 16 determination to represent the assisted person at the trial, and

(b) attends the first day of the trial.

[This paragraph is printed as amended, with effect from May 5, 2015, by the Criminal Legal Aid (Remuneration) (Amendment) Regulations 2015 (S.I. 2015 No. 882), reg. 2(4)(c), (6)(d) and (16)(c). For the transitional provision, see *ante*, G-7.]

Fees for conferences and views

19.—(1) This paragraph applies to the following types of work—   **G-54**

(a) attendance by the trial advocate at pre-trial conferences with prospective or actual expert witnesses not held at court;

(b) attendance by the trial advocate at views at the scene of the alleged offence;

(c) attendance by the trial advocate at pre-trial conferences with the assisted person not held at court;

(d) reasonable travelling time by the trial advocate for the purpose of attending a view at the scene of the alleged offence; or

(e) reasonable travelling time by the trial advocate for the purpose of attending a pre-trial conference with the assisted person or prospective or actual expert witness, where the appropriate officer is satisfied that the assisted person or prospective or actual expert witness was unable or could not reasonably have been expected to attend a conference at the trial advocate's chambers or office.

(2) The fees payable in respect of attendance at the first three pre-trial conferences or views, as set out in sub-paragraph (1)(a) to (c), are included in the basic fee (B) specified in the table following paragraph 5, or that following paragraph 8, as appropriate to the offence for which the assisted person is tried, the category of trial advocate and whether the case is a guilty plea, cracked trial or trial, provided that the trial advocate satisfies the appropriate officer that the work was reasonably necessary.

(3) The fee specified in the table following paragraph 24 as appropriate to the category of trial advocate is payable in the following circumstances, provided that the trial advocate satisfies the appropriate officer that the work was reasonably necessary—

(a) for trials lasting not less than 21 and not more than 25 days, and cracked trials where it was accepted by the court at the plea and case management hearing that the trial would last not less than 21 days and not more than 25 days, one further pre-trial conference or view not exceeding two hours;

(b) for trials lasting not less than 26 and not more than 35 days, and cracked trials where it was accepted by the court at the plea and case management hearing that the trial would last not less than 26 days and not more than 35 days, two further pre-trial conferences or views each not exceeding two hours; and

(c) for trials lasting not less than 36 days, and cracked trials where it was accepted by the court at the plea and case management hearing that the trial would last not less than 36 days and not more than 40 days, three further pre-trial conferences or views each not exceeding two hours.

(4) Travel expenses must be paid for all conferences and views set out in sub-paragraph (1)(a) to (c), provided that the trial advocate satisfies the appropriate officer that they were reasonably incurred.

(5) Travelling time must be paid for all conferences and views set out in sub-paragraph (1)(a) to (c), provided that the trial advocate satisfies the appropriate officer that it was reasonable.

Fees for appeals, committals for sentence and breach hearings

G-55

20.—(1) Subject to sub-paragraphs (4) and (5) and paragraph 26 the fee payable to a trial advocate in any of the hearings referred to in paragraph 2(1)(b) is the fixed fee specified in the table following paragraph 24.

(2) Where a hearing referred to in paragraph 2(1)(b) is listed but cannot proceed because of the failure of the assisted person or a witness to attend, the unavailability of a pre-sentence report, or other good reason, the fee payable to the advocate is the fixed fee specified in the table following paragraph 24.

(3) Where—

(a) a bail application;

(b) a mention hearing; or

(c) any other application,

takes place in the course of a hearing referred to in paragraph 2(1)(b), the fee payable to the advocate is the fixed fee specified in the table following paragraph 24.

(4) Where it appears to the appropriate officer that the fixed fee allowed under sub-paragraph (1) would be inappropriate taking into account all of the relevant circumstances of the case the appropriate officer may instead allow fees of such amounts as appear to the appropriate officer to be reasonable remuneration for the relevant work in accordance with sub-paragraph (5).

(5) The appropriate officer may allow any of the following classes of fees to an advocate in respect of work allowed by the appropriate officer under this paragraph—

(a) a fee for preparation including, where appropriate, the first day of the hearing including, where they took place on that day—

(i) short conferences;

(ii) consultations;

(iii) applications and appearances (including bail applications);

(iv) views at the scene of the alleged offence; and

(v) any other preparation;

(b) a refresher fee for any day or part of a day for which a hearing continued, including, where they took place on that day—

(i) short conferences;

(ii) consultations;

(iii) applications and appearances (including bail applications);

(iv) views at the scene of the alleged offence; and

(v) any other preparation; and

(c) subsidiary fees for—

(i) attendance at conferences, consultations and views at the scene of the alleged offence not covered by paragraph (a) or (b);

(ii) written advice on evidence, plea, appeal, case stated or other written work; and

(iii) attendance at applications and appearances (including bail applications and adjournments for sentence) not covered by paragraph (a) or (b).

Fees for contempt proceedings

G-55a

21.—(1) Subject to sub-paragraph (2), remuneration for advocates in proceedings referred to in section 14(g) of the Act in the Crown Court must be at the rates specified in the table following this sub-paragraph.

Category of advocate	Payment rates (£ per day)
QC	300
Leading junior	225
Led junior or junior acting alone	150

(2) Where an advocate and a litigator are instructed in proceedings referred to in section 14(g) of the Act, remuneration must be at the rates specified in the table following this sub-paragraph, as appropriate to the category of advocate.

Category of advocate	Payment rates (£ per day)
QC	175
Leading junior	125
Led junior or junior acting alone	100

Discontinuance or dismissal of sent or transferred proceedings

22.—(1) This paragraph applies to proceedings which are—

(a) sent for trial to the Crown Court; or

(b) transferred to the Crown Court under—

    (i)   section 4 of the Criminal Justice Act 1987 (transfer of serious fraud cases); or

    (ii) section 53 of the Criminal Justice Act 1991 (transfer of certain cases involving children).

(2) Where proceedings referred to in sub-paragraph (1) are discontinued by a notice served under section 23A of the Prosecution of Offences Act 1985 (discontinuance of proceedings after accused has been sent for trial) at any time before the prosecution serves its evidence in accordance with the Crime and Disorder Act 1998 (Service of Prosecution Evidence) Regulations 2005 the advocate must be paid 50% of the basic fee (B) for a guilty plea, as specified in the table following paragraph 8 as appropriate to the offence for which the assisted person is charged and the category of advocate.

(3) Where proceedings referred to in sub-paragraph (1) are discontinued by a notice served under section 23A of the Prosecution of Offences Act 1985 (discontinuance of proceedings after accused has been sent for trial) at any time after the prosecution serves its evidence in accordance with the Crime and Disorder Act 1998 (Service of Prosecution Evidence) Regulations 2005, the advocate must be paid a graduated fee calculated in accordance with paragraph 7, as appropriate for representing an assisted person in a guilty plea.

(4) Sub-paragraph (5) applies to—

(a) a plea and case management hearing that takes place after the prosecution serves its evidence; and

(b) any other hearing that takes place before a plea and case management hearing has taken place but after the prosecution has served its evidence.

(5) Where, at a hearing to which this sub-paragraph applies—

(a) the prosecution offers no evidence and the assisted person is discharged; or

(b) the case is remitted to the magistrates' court in accordance with paragraph 10(3)(a), 13(2) or 15(3)(a) of Schedule 3 to the Crime and Disorder Act 1998,

the advocate instructed in the proceedings must be paid a graduated fee calculated in accordance with paragraph 7, as appropriate for representing an assisted person in a guilty plea.

(6) Where an application for dismissal is made under paragraph 2 of Schedule 3 to the Crime and Disorder Act 1998, section 6 of the Criminal Justice Act 1987 or paragraph 5 of Schedule 6 to the Criminal Justice Act 1991 (applications for dismissal), the advocate must be remunerated for attendance at the hearing of the application for dismissal—

(a) in respect of any day where the hearing begins before and ends after the luncheon adjournment, at the daily rate set out in the table following paragraph 24 as appropriate to the category of advocate; or

(b) in respect of any day where the hearing begins and ends before the luncheon adjournment, or begins after the luncheon adjournment, at the half-daily rate set out in that table as appropriate to the category of advocate,

provided that a fee is not payable elsewhere under this Schedule in respect of any day of the hearing.

(7) Where an application for dismissal is made under paragraph 2 of Schedule 3 to the Crime and Disorder Act 1998, section 6 of the Criminal Justice Act 1987 or paragraph 5 of Schedule 6 to the Criminal Justice Act 1991, and—

(a) the charge, or charges, are dismissed and the assisted person is discharged; or

(b) the case is remitted to the magistrates' court in accordance with paragraph 10(3)(a), 13(2) or 15(3)(a) of Schedule 3 to the Crime and Disorder Act 1998,

in respect of the first day of the hearing of the application to dismiss, the advocate instructed in the proceedings must be paid a graduated fee calculated in accordance with paragraph 7, as appropriate for representing an assisted person in a guilty plea.

(8) Where an advocate represents more than one assisted person in proceedings referred to in sub-paragraph (1), the advocate must be paid a fixed fee of 20% of—

(a) the fee specified in sub-paragraph (2) where that sub-paragraph applies; or

(b) the basic fee (B) specified in the table following paragraph 8 where sub-paragraph (3), (4) or (5) applies, as appropriate for the circumstances set out in the relevant sub-paragraph,

in respect of each additional assisted person the advocate represents.

Noting brief fees

G-57   23. The fee payable to an advocate retained solely for the purpose of making a note of any hearing must be the daily fee set out in the table following paragraph 24.

Fixed fees

G-57a   24. The table following this paragraph sets out the fixed fees payable in relation to the category of work specified in the first column of the table.

FIXED FEES

Category of work	Paragraph providing for fee	Fee for QC £	Fee for leading junior £	Fee for led junior or junior alone £
Standard appearance	9(2)	173 per day	130 per day	87 per day
Paper plea and case management hearing	9(3)	26 per case	26 per case	26 per case
Abuse of process hearing	10(1)(a)	260 Half day	195 Half day	130 Half day
		497 Full day	346 Full day	238 Full day
Hearings relating to disclosure	10(1)(b) and (c)	260 Half day	195 Half day	130 Half day
		497 Full day	346 Full day	238 Full day
Hearings relating to the admissibility of evidence	10(1)(d)	260 Half day	195 Half day	130 Half day
		497 Full day	346 Full day	238 Full day
Hearings on withdrawal of guilty plea	10(1)(e)	260 Half day	195 Half day	130 Half day
		497 Full day	346 Full day	238 Full day
Deferred sentencing hearing	12(1)(a)	324 per day	238 per day	173 per day
Ineffective trial payment	13	281 per day	195 per day	130 per day
Special preparation	14	74 per hour	56 per hour	39 per hour
Wasted preparation	15	74 per hour	56 per hour	39 per hour
Conferences and views	16	74 per hour	56 per hour	39 per hour
Appeals to the Crown Court against conviction	17(1)	260 per day	195 per day	130 per day

Category of work	Paragraph providing for fee	Fee for QC £	Fee for leading junior £	Fee for led junior or junior alone £
Appeals to the Crown Court against sentence	17(1)	216 per day	151 per day	108 per day
Proceedings relating to breach of an order of the Crown Court	17(1)	216 per day	151 per day	108 per day
Committal for sentence	17(1)	260 per day	195 per day	130 per day
Adjourned appeals, committals for sentence and breach hearings	17(2)	173 per day	130 per day	87 per day
Bail applications, mentions and other applications in appeals, committals for sentence and breach hearings	17(3)	173 per day	130 per day	87 per day
Second and subsequent days of an application to dismiss	18(6)	260 Half day	195 Half day	130 Half day
		497 Full day	346 Full day	238 Full day
Noting brief	19	—	—	108 per day
Hearing for mitigation of sentence	29	260 per day	173 per day	108 per day

PART 6

MISCELLANEOUS

Identity of instructed advocate

25.—(1) Where an instructed advocate is appointed before the plea and case management hear- **G-58** ing, the instructed advocate must notify the Court in writing as soon as the appointment is made and, where appropriate, must confirm whether the instructed advocate is the leading instructed advocate or the led instructed advocate.

(2) Where the section 16 determination provides for representation by a single advocate and no instructed advocate has been notified to the Court in accordance with sub-paragraph (1)—

(a) the barrister or solicitor advocate who attends the plea and case management hearing is deemed to be the instructed advocate; and

(b) the Court must make a written record of this fact.

(3) Where the section 16 determination provides for representation by a single advocate and no barrister or solicitor advocate attends the plea and case management hearing—

(a) the barrister or solicitor advocate who attends the next hearing in the case is deemed to be the instructed advocate; and

(b) the Court must make a written record of this fact.

(4) Where the section 16 determination provides for representation by more than one advocate, and no leading instructed advocate has been notified to the Court in accordance with sub-paragraph (1), the leading advocate who attends—

(a) the plea and case management hearing; or

(b) where no leading advocate attends the plea and case management hearing, the next hearing in the case attended by a leading advocate,

is deemed to be the leading instructed advocate, and the Court must make a written record of this fact.

(5) Where the section 16 determination provides for representation by more than one advocate, and no led instructed advocate has been notified to the Court in accordance with sub-paragraph (1), the led advocate who attends—

(a) the plea and case management hearing; or

(b) where no led advocate attends the plea and case management hearing, the next hearing in the case attended by a led advocate,

is deemed to be the led instructed advocate, and the Court must make a written record of this fact.

(6) Where a section 16 determination is amended after the plea and case management hearing to provide for representation by more than one advocate—

(a) the additional instructed advocate must notify the Court in writing of the additional instructed advocate's appointment within 7 days of the date on which the section 16 determination is amended; and

(b) each instructed advocate must notify the Court whether that instructed advocate is the leading instructed advocate or the led instructed advocate.

(7) Where no additional instructed advocate has been notified to the Court in accordance with sub-paragraph (6)(a), the advocate who attends the next hearing in the case is deemed to be an instructed advocate and the Court must record in writing whether that instructed advocate is the leading instructed advocate or the led instructed advocate, as appropriate to the circumstances of the case.

(8) Where—

(a) a case ceases to be a Very High Cost Case (in relation to fees claimed by advocates); and

(b) none of sub-paragraphs (1) to (7) applies,

the instructed advocate must notify the Court in writing of the instructed advocate's appointment within 7 days of the case ceasing to be a Very High Cost Case.

(9) The Court must attach—

(a) any notice received under sub-paragraph (1), (6) or (8); and

(b) any record made by it under sub-paragraph (2), (3), (4), (5) or (7),

to the representation order.

(10) An instructed advocate must remain as instructed advocate at all times, except where—

(a) a date for trial is fixed at or before the plea and case management hearing and the instructed advocate is unable to conduct the trial due to the instructed advocate's other pre-existing commitments;

(b) the instructed advocate is dismissed by the assisted person or the litigator; or

(c) the instructed advocate is required to withdraw because of his professional code of conduct.

(11) Where, in accordance with sub-paragraph (10), an instructed advocate withdraws, the instructed advocate must—

(a) immediately notify the court of the withdrawal—

(i) in writing; or

(ii) where the withdrawal takes place at a plea and case management hearing, orally; and

(b) within 7 days of the date of the withdrawal, notify the court in writing of the identity of a replacement instructed advocate, who must fulfil all the functions of an instructed advocate in accordance with these Regulations.

(12) This paragraph does not apply to a claim for fees under paragraph 32, 33 or 34.

Payment of fees to trial advocate

★**G-59** 26.—(1) In accordance with regulation 23 the appropriate officer must notify each trial advocate of the total fees payable and authorise payment to the trial advocate accordingly.

(2) Payment of the fees in accordance with sub-paragraph (1) must be made to each trial advocate.

(3) Where the section 16 determination provides for representation by a single advocate, the trial advocate is responsible for arranging payment of fees to the instructed advocate and any substitute advocate who has undertaken work on the case.

(4) Where there are two trial advocates for an assisted person, payment must be made to each trial advocate individually, and—

(a) the leading trial advocate is responsible for arranging payment of fees to the instructed advocate and any substitute advocate who have undertaken work on the case of a type for which a leading advocate is responsible; and

(b) the led trial advocate is responsible for arranging payment of fees to the instructed advocate and any substitute advocate who have undertaken work on the case of a type for which a led advocate is responsible.

(4A) In this paragraph, where the main hearing is a trial, "trial advocate" means an advocate who—

(a) is instructed pursuant to a section 16 determination to represent the assisted person at the trial, and

(b) attends the first day of the trial.

(5) This paragraph does not apply to a claim for fees under paragraph 32, 33 or 34.

[This paragraph is printed as amended, with effect from May 5, 2015, by the Criminal Legal Aid (Remuneration) (Amendment) Regulations 2015 (S.I. 2015 No. 882), reg. 2(5)(d) and (16)(d). For the transitional provision, see *ante*, G-7.]

Additional charges and additional cases

27.—(1) Where an assisted person is charged with more than one offence on one indictment, the **G-60** fee payable to the trial advocate under this Schedule must be based on whichever of those offences the trial advocate selects.

(2) Where two or more cases to which this Schedule applies involving the same trial advocate are heard concurrently (whether involving the same or different assisted persons)—

- (a) the trial advocate must select one case ("the principal case"), which must be treated for the purposes of remuneration in accordance with this Schedule;
- (b) in respect of the main hearing in each of the other cases the trial advocate must be paid a fixed fee of 20% of—
    - (i) the basic fee (B) specified in the table following paragraph 5 or that following paragraph 8, as appropriate, for the principal case, where that is a case falling within paragraph 2(1)(a); or
    - (ii) the fixed fee for the principal case, where that is a case falling within paragraph 2(1)(b) or paragraph 10.

(3) Nothing in sub-paragraphs (4) to (6) permits a fixed fee under Part 5, other than one to which paragraph 14 applies, to be paid in a case to which Part 4 applies.

(4) Where a trial advocate or substitute advocate appears at a hearing specified in paragraph 12, 13, 14, 15 or 16, forming part of two or more cases involving different assisted persons, the trial advocate or substitute advocate must be paid—

- (a) in respect of the first such case, the fixed fee for that hearing specified in the table following paragraph 24; and
- (b) in respect of each of the other cases, 20% of that fee.

(5) Subject to sub-paragraphs (1) to (4), where a trial advocate or substitute advocate appears at a hearing forming part of two or more cases, the trial advocate or substitute advocate must be paid the fixed fee for that hearing specified in the table following paragraph 24 in respect of one such case, without any increase in respect of the other cases.

(6) Where a trial advocate selects—

- (a) one offence, in preference to another offence, under sub-paragraph (1); or
- (b) one case as the principal case, in preference to another case, under sub-paragraph (2),

that selection does not affect the trial advocate's right to claim any of the fees set out in the table following paragraph 24 to which the trial advocate would otherwise have been entitled.

Multiple advocates

28. Where a section 16 determination provides for representation by three advocates in a case the **G-61** provisions of this Schedule apply, and the fees payable to the led juniors in accordance with Part 2 or Part 3 are payable to each led junior who is instructed in the case.

Non-local appearances

29. Where an advocate is instructed to appear in a court which is not within 40 kilometres of the **G-62** advocate's office or chambers, the appropriate officer may allow an amount for travelling and other expenses incidental to that appearance, provided that the amount must not be greater than the amount, if any, which would be payable to a trial advocate from the nearest local Bar or the nearest advocate's office (whichever is the nearer) unless the advocate instructed to appear has obtained prior approval under regulation 13 for the incurring of such expenses or can justify the attendance having regard to all the relevant circumstances of the case.

Trials lasting over 40 days

30. Where a trial exceeds 40 days, the trial advocate must be paid a fee as set out in the table fol- **G-63** lowing this paragraph, as appropriate to the category of trial advocate and the Class of Offence, for each day by which the trial exceeds 40 days on which the trial advocate attends at court.

DAILY RATES PAYABLE WHERE A TRIAL LASTS OVER 40 DAYS

Class of Offence	Daily rate payable for days 41 to 50 (£)	Daily rate payable for days 51 and over (£)
QC		
A–K	387	414
Leading Junior		
A–K	331	356
Led Junior		

Class of Offence	Daily rate payable for days 41 to 50 (£)	Daily rate payable for days 51 and over (£)
A–K	221	237
Junior Acting Alone		
A	266	285
B	247	265
C	247	265
D	266	285
E	225	241
F	225	241
G	225	241
H	247	265
I	247	265
J	266	285
K	266	285

Assisted person unfit to plead or stand trial

G-64   31. Where in any case a hearing is held to determine the question of whether the assisted person is unfit to plead or to stand trial (a "fitness hearing")—

    (a) if a trial on indictment is held, or continues, at any time thereafter, the length of the fitness hearing is included in determining the length of the trial for the calculation of the graduated fee in accordance with Part 2 or Part 3;

    (b) if a trial on indictment is not held, or does not continue, thereafter by reason of the assisted person being found unfit to plead or to stand trial, the trial advocate must be paid—

        (i) a graduated fee calculated in accordance with paragraph 4 as appropriate to the combined length of—

            (aa) the fitness hearing; and

            (bb) any hearing under section 4A of the Criminal Procedure (Insanity) Act 1964 (finding that the accused did the act or made the omission charged against him); or

        (ii) a graduated fee calculated in accordance with paragraph 7 as appropriate for representing an assisted person in a cracked trial,

    whichever the trial advocate elects; and

    (c) if at any time the assisted person pleads guilty to the indictable offence, the trial advocate must be paid either—

        (i) a graduated fee calculated in accordance with paragraph 4 as appropriate to the length of the fitness hearing; or

        (ii) a graduated fee calculated in accordance with paragraph 7 as appropriate for representing an assisted person in a guilty plea,

    whichever the trial advocate elects.

Cross examination of witness

G-65   32.—(1) Where in any case on indictment an advocate is retained solely for the purpose of cross-examining a witness under section 38 of the Youth Justice and Criminal Evidence Act 1999 (defence representation for purposes of cross-examination), the advocate must be paid a graduated fee calculated in accordance with paragraph 4.

(2) For the purposes of this paragraph the daily attendance fee (D) is as set out in the table following paragraph 5 as appropriate to the number of days of attendance at court by the advocate.

Provision of written or oral advice

G-66   33.—(1) Where in any case on indictment an advocate is assigned pursuant to a section 16 determination solely for the purpose of providing written or oral advice, the advocate must be paid for the reasonable number of hours of preparation for that advice using the hourly fee rates for special preparation set out in the table following paragraph 24 as appropriate to the category of trial advocate.

(2) An advocate claiming a fee for advice under this paragraph may apply to the appropriate officer to redetermine the fee under regulation 28 and the advocate must supply such information and documents as may be required by the appropriate officer as proof of the number of hours of preparation.

Mitigation of sentence

34.—(1) Where in any case on indictment an advocate is assigned pursuant to a section 16 **G-67** determination to appear at a sentencing hearing solely for the purpose of applying to the court to mitigate the assisted person's sentence, the advocate must be paid in respect of that appearance the fee specified in the table following paragraph 24 together with a fee calculated from the reasonable number of hours of preparation for that appearance using the hourly fee rates for special preparation set out in the table following paragraph 24 as appropriate to the category of trial advocate.

(2) An advocate claiming an hourly preparation fee under this paragraph may apply to the appropriate officer to redetermine such hourly fee under regulation 28 and the advocate must supply such information and documents as may be required by the appropriate officer as proof of the number of hours of preparation.

Table of offences

At the end of Schedule 1 to the regulations (in Pt 7), there is a table of offences. For the effect **G-68** thereof, see *post*, G-119, G-168 *et seq.*

Regulation 5 SCHEDULE 2

LITIGATORS' GRADUATED FEE SCHEME

PART 1

DEFINITION AND SCOPE

Interpretation

1.—(1) In this Schedule— **G-69**
"case" means proceedings in the Crown Court against any one assisted person—
    (a) on one or more counts of a single indictment;
    (b) arising out of a single notice of appeal against conviction or sentence, or a single committal for sentence, whether on one or more charges; or
    (c) arising out of a single alleged breach of an order of the Crown Court,
    and a case falling within paragraph (c) must be treated as a separate case from the proceedings in which the order was made;
"cracked trial" means a case on indictment in which—
    (a) a plea and case management hearing takes place and
        (i) the case does not proceed to trial (whether by reason of pleas of guilty or for other reasons) or the prosecution offers no evidence; and
        (ii) either—
            (aa) in respect of one or more counts to which the assisted person pleaded guilty, the assisted person did not so plead at the plea and case management hearing; or
            (bb) in respect of one or more counts which did not proceed, the prosecution did not, before or at the plea and case management hearing, declare an intention of not proceeding with them; or
    (b) the case is listed for trial without a plea and case management hearing taking place;
"guilty plea" means a case on indictment which—
    (a) is disposed of without a trial because the assisted person pleaded guilty to one or more counts; and
    (b) is not a cracked trial;
"main hearing" means—
    (a) in relation to a case which goes to trial, the trial;
    (b) in relation to a guilty plea, the hearing at which pleas are taken or, where there is more than one such hearing, the last such hearing;
    (c) in relation to a cracked trial, the hearing at which—
        (i) the case becomes a cracked trial by meeting the conditions in the definition of a cracked trial, whether or not any pleas were taken at that hearing; or
        (ii) a formal verdict of not guilty was entered as a result of the prosecution offering no evidence, whether or not the parties attended the hearing;
    (d) in relation to an appeal against conviction or sentence in the Crown Court, the hearing of the appeal;
    (e) in relation to proceedings arising out of a committal for sentence in the Crown Court, the sentencing hearing; and

(f) in relation to proceedings arising out of an alleged breach of an order of the Crown Court, the hearing at which those proceedings are determined;

"*Newton* hearing" means a hearing at which evidence is heard for the purpose of determining the sentence of a convicted person in accordance with the principles of *R. v. Newton* (1982) 77 Cr.App.R. 13;

"PPE Cut-off" means the minimum number of pages of prosecution evidence for use in calculating the fee payable to a litigator under this Schedule, as set out in the tables following paragraph 5(1) and (2).

(2) For the purposes of this Schedule, the number of pages of prosecution evidence served on the court must be determined in accordance with sub-paragraphs (3) to (5).

(3) The number of pages of prosecution evidence includes all—

(a) witness statements;

(b) documentary and pictorial exhibits;

(c) records of interviews with the assisted person; and

(d) records of interviews with other defendants,

which form part of the committal or served prosecution documents or which are included in any notice of additional evidence.

(4) Subject to sub-paragraph (5), a document served by the prosecution in electronic form is included in the number of pages of prosecution evidence.

(5) A documentary or pictorial exhibit which—

(a) has been served by the prosecution in electronic form; and

(b) has never existed in paper form,

is not included within the number of pages of prosecution evidence unless the appropriate officer decides that it would be appropriate to include it in the pages of prosecution evidence taking into account the nature of the document and any other relevant circumstances.

(6) In proceedings on indictment in the Crown Court initiated otherwise than by committal for trial, the appropriate officer must determine the number of pages of prosecution evidence in accordance with sub-paragraphs (2) to (5) or as nearly in accordance with those sub-paragraphs as possible as the nature of the case permits.

(7) A reference to the Table of Offences in this Schedule is to the Table of Offences in Part 7 of Schedule 1 and a reference to a Class of Offence in this Schedule is to the Class in which that offence is listed in the Table of Offences.

Application

G-69a

2.—(1) Subject to sub-paragraphs (2) to (7), this Schedule applies to—

(a) every case on indictment;

(b) the following proceedings in the Crown Court—

(i) an appeal against conviction or sentence from the magistrates' court;

(ii) a sentencing hearing following a committal for sentence to the Crown Court;

(iii) proceedings arising out of an alleged breach of an order of the Crown Court (whether or not this Schedule applies to the proceedings in which the order was made);

(c) a sentencing hearing following a case on indictment to which this Schedule applies, where sentence has been deferred under section 1 of the Powers of Criminal Courts (Sentencing) Act 2000 (deferment of sentence);

(d) any other post-sentence hearing.

(2) Sub-paragraph (3) applies where proceedings are—

(a) sent for trial to the Crown Court; or

(b) transferred to the Crown Court under—

(i) section 4 of the Criminal Justice Act 1987 (transfer of serious fraud cases); or

(ii) section 53 of the Criminal Justice Act 1991 (transfer of certain cases involving children).

(3) Where, at any time after proceedings are sent or transferred to the Crown Court as referred to in sub-paragraph (2), they are—

(a) discontinued by a notice served under section 23A of the Prosecution of Offences Act 1985 (discontinuance of proceedings after accused has been sent for trial); or

(b) dismissed pursuant to—

(i) paragraph 2 of Schedule 3 to the Crime and Disorder Act 1998 (applications for dismissal);

(ii) section 6 of the Criminal Justice Act 1987 (applications for dismissal); or

(iii) paragraph 5 of Schedule 6 to the Criminal Justice Act 1991 (applications for dismissal), the provisions of paragraphs 21 and 22 apply.

(4) Where, following a case on indictment, a *Newton* hearing takes place—

    (a) for the purposes of this Schedule the case is to be treated as having gone to trial;

    (b) the length of the trial is to be taken to be the combined length of the main hearing and the *Newton* hearing; and

    (c) the provisions of this Schedule relating to cracked trials and guilty pleas will not apply.

(5) For the purposes of this Schedule, a case on indictment which discontinues at or before the plea and case management hearing otherwise than—

    (a) by reason of a plea of guilty being entered; or

    (b) in accordance with sub-paragraph (3),

must be treated as a guilty plea.

(6) For the purposes of this Schedule, where a trial that is not a Very High Cost Case (in relation to fees claimed by litigators) lasts over 200 days, it must be treated as if it had lasted 200 days.

(7) For the purposes of this Schedule, where the number of pages of prosecution evidence in a case which is not a Very High Cost Case (in relation to fees claimed by litigators) exceeds—

    (a) the PPE Cut-off figure specified in the table following paragraph 5(2) as appropriate to the offence for which the assisted person is to be tried and the length of trial; and

    (b) 10,000,

the case must be treated as though it had 10,000 pages of prosecution evidence.

Class of offences

3.—(1) For the purposes of this Schedule—   **G-70**

    (a) every indictable offence falls within the Class under which it is listed in the Table of Offences and, subject to sub-paragraph (2), indictable offences not specifically so listed are deemed to fall within Class H;

    (b) conspiracy to commit an indictable offence contrary to section 1 of the Criminal Law Act 1977 (the offence of conspiracy), incitement to commit an indictable offence and attempts to commit an indictable offence contrary to section 1 of the Criminal Attempts Act 1981 (attempting to commit an offence) fall within the same Class as the substantive offence to which they relate;

    (c) where the Table of Offences specifies that the Class within which an offence falls depends on whether the value involved exceeds a stated limit, the value must be presumed not to exceed that limit unless the litigator making the claim under regulation 5 proves otherwise to the satisfaction of the appropriate officer;

    (d) where more than one count of the indictment is for an offence in relation to which the Class depends on the value involved, that value must be taken to be the total value involved in all those offences, but where two or more counts relate to the same property, the value of that property must be taken into account once only;

    (e) where an entry in the Table of Offences specifies an offence as being contrary to a statutory provision, then subject to any express limitation in the entry that entry includes every offence contrary to that statutory provision whether or not the words of description in the entry are appropriate to cover all such offences;

    (f) where in a case on indictment there is a hearing to determine the question of whether an assisted person is unfit to plead or unfit to stand trial, the litigator must elect whether that hearing falls within the same Class as the indictable offence to which it relates or within Class D;

    (g) where in a case on indictment a restriction order is made under section 41 of the Mental Health Act 1983 (power of higher courts to restrict discharge from hospital), the offence falls within Class A, regardless of the Class under which the offence would be listed in the Table of Offences, but for this paragraph.

(2) Where a litigator in proceedings in the Crown Court is dissatisfied with the classification within Class H of an indictable offence not listed in the Table of Offences, the litigator may apply to the appropriate officer, when lodging the claim for fees, to reclassify the offence.

(3) The appropriate officer must, in light of the objections made by the litigator—

    (a) confirm the classification of the offence within Class H; or

    (b) reclassify the offence,

and must notify the litigator of the decision.

As to this paragraph, see *post*, G-119.

PART 2

GRADUATED FEES FOR GUILTY PLEAS, CRACKED TRIALS AND TRIALS

Scope

G-70a   4.—(1) Subject to sub-paragraph (2) and to paragraph 21, this Part does not apply to a guilty plea or cracked trial in a case committed or sent for trial to the Crown Court on the election of a defendant where the magistrates' court has determined the case to be suitable for summary trial.

(2) This Part applies in all cases where the trial is a cracked trial because the prosecution offer no evidence on all counts against a defendant and the judge directs that a not guilty verdict be entered.

[This paragraph was substituted by S.I. 2014 No. 2422 (*ante*, G-21a). For the transitional provision, see *ante*, G-21a.]

Pages of prosecution evidence

G-70b   5.—(1) For the purposes of this Part, the PPE Cut-off figures in a cracked trial or guilty plea are specified in the table following this sub-paragraph, as appropriate to the offence with which the assisted person is charged.

PPE CUT-OFF FIGURES IN CRACKED TRIALS AND GUILTY PLEAS

Type of case	Class of offence										
	A	B	C	D	E	F	G	H	I	J	K
Cracked trial or guilty plea	80	70	40	80	40	50	50	40	40	80	120

(2) For the purposes of this Part, the PPE Cut-off figures in a trial are specified in the table following this sub-paragraph, as appropriate to the offence for which the assisted person is tried and the length of trial.

PPE Cut-off figures in trials

Trial length in days	PPE Cut off A	PPE Cut off B	PPE Cut off C	PPE Cut off D	PPE Cut off E	PPE Cut off F	PPE Cut off G	PPE Cut off H	PPE Cut off I	PPE Cut off J	PPE Cut off K
1	80	70	40	80	40	50	50	40	40	80	120
2	80	70	40	80	40	50	50	40	40	80	120
3	95	105	81	95	120	138	138	122	134	95	186
4	126	139	120	126	158	173	173	157	185	126	252
5	156	170	157	156	195	206	206	191	232	156	314
6	186	203	193	186	229	240	240	225	281	186	372
7	218	238	230	218	265	276	276	260	329	218	433
8	257	274	267	257	301	310	310	301	376	257	495
9	293	306	301	293	333	342	342	338	420	293	550
10	330	338	339	330	365	373	373	374	464	330	606
11	367	370	378	367	399	405	405	412	509	367	663
12	404	402	417	404	433	437	437	449	554	404	721
13	440	434	455	440	467	470	470	486	598	440	779
14	477	465	493	477	500	501	501	523	642	477	836
15	514	497	531	514	532	533	533	559	686	514	894
16	551	535	569	551	565	564	564	596	730	551	951
17	587	573	607	587	598	596	596	637	774	587	1,007
18	624	611	646	624	646	627	627	687	818	624	1,063
19	661	649	684	661	696	659	659	736	862	661	1,119
20	697	687	722	697	746	690	690	786	907	697	1,174
21	742	722	753	742	787	720	720	826	943	742	1,230
22	786	757	785	786	828	752	752	867	980	786	1,286
23	830	792	819	830	868	784	784	908	1,017	830	1,341
24	874	826	857	874	908	816	816	948	1,053	874	1,396
25	917	860	894	917	948	848	848	988	1,088	917	1,451
26	961	895	931	961	988	880	880	1,028	1,124	961	1,505

Trial length in days	PPE Cut off A	PPE Cut off B	PPE Cut off C	PPE Cut off D	PPE Cut off E	PPE Cut off F	PPE Cut off G	PPE Cut off H	PPE Cut off I	PPE Cut off J	PPE Cut off K
27	1,005	935	967	1,005	1,028	912	912	1,068	1,160	1,005	1,560
28	1,049	975	1,004	1,049	1,068	944	944	1,107	1,196	1,049	1,615
29	1,099	1,016	1,041	1,099	1,108	976	976	1,147	1,231	1,099	1,670
30	1,150	1,057	1,077	1,150	1,148	1,007	1,007	1,187	1,267	1,150	1,725
31	1,200	1,098	1,114	1,200	1,188	1,039	1,039	1,226	1,303	1,200	1,780
32	1,251	1,138	1,151	1,251	1,228	1,070	1,070	1,266	1,349	1,251	1,835
33	1,301	1,179	1,187	1,301	1,268	1,102	1,102	1,307	1,394	1,301	1,889
34	1,352	1,220	1,224	1,352	1,308	1,133	1,133	1,357	1,439	1,352	1,944
35	1,402	1,261	1,262	1,402	1,347	1,165	1,165	1,407	1,485	1,402	1,999
36	1,453	1,302	1,303	1,453	1,435	1,196	1,196	1,457	1,530	1,453	2,054
37	1,503	1,348	1,345	1,503	1,526	1,228	1,228	1,507	1,575	1,503	2,109
38	1,554	1,395	1,386	1,554	1,617	1,259	1,259	1,557	1,621	1,554	2,164
39	1,604	1,441	1,428	1,604	1,708	1,291	1,291	1,607	1,666	1,604	2,219
40	1,652	1,484	1,444	1,652	1,745	1,314	1,314	1,629	1,704	1,652	2,271
41	1,700	1,527	1,461	1,700	1,782	1,338	1,338	1,651	1,742	1,700	2,324
42	1,748	1,570	1,477	1,748	1,820	1,361	1,361	1,673	1,780	1,748	2,377
43	1,796	1,613	1,494	1,796	1,857	1,384	1,384	1,695	1,818	1,796	2,430
44	1,844	1,656	1,511	1,844	1,895	1,410	1,410	1,716	1,856	1,844	2,483
45	1,892	1,699	1,527	1,892	1,932	1,440	1,440	1,738	1,894	1,892	2,536
46	1,939	1,742	1,544	1,939	1,970	1,470	1,470	1,760	1,932	1,939	2,589
47	1,987	1,785	1,560	1,987	2,007	1,501	1,501	1,782	1,970	1,987	2,642
48	2,039	1,828	1,577	2,039	2,045	1,531	1,531	1,804	2,008	2,039	2,695
49	2,091	1,871	1,594	2,091	2,082	1,561	1,561	1,826	2,046	2,091	2,749
50	2,144	1,914	1,610	2,144	2,120	1,591	1,591	1,848	2,084	2,144	2,802
51	2,196	1,957	1,627	2,196	2,158	1,622	1,622	1,870	2,122	2,196	2,855
52	2,249	2,000	1,644	2,249	2,195	1,652	1,652	1,892	2,160	2,249	2,908
53	2,301	2,043	1,660	2,301	2,233	1,682	1,682	1,914	2,198	2,301	2,962
54	2,354	2,086	1,677	2,354	2,271	1,712	1,712	1,936	2,236	2,354	3,015

Trial length in days	PPE Cut off A	PPE Cut off B	PPE Cut off C	PPE Cut off D	PPE Cut off E	PPE Cut off F	PPE Cut off G	PPE Cut off H	PPE Cut off I	PPE Cut off J	PPE Cut off K
55	2,406	2,129	1,694	2,406	2,308	1,743	1,743	1,958	2,275	2,406	3,068
56	2,459	2,172	1,710	2,459	2,346	1,773	1,773	1,980	2,313	2,459	3,121
57	2,512	2,215	1,727	2,512	2,384	1,803	1,803	2,002	2,351	2,512	3,175
58	2,564	2,258	1,744	2,564	2,422	1,833	1,833	2,024	2,389	2,564	3,228
59	2,617	2,301	1,760	2,617	2,459	1,864	1,864	2,046	2,427	2,617	3,281
60	2,669	2,345	1,777	2,669	2,497	1,894	1,894	2,068	2,465	2,669	3,335
61	2,722	2,388	1,794	2,722	2,535	1,924	1,924	2,090	2,503	2,722	3,388
62	2,775	2,431	1,811	2,775	2,572	1,959	1,959	2,112	2,542	2,775	3,442
63	2,827	2,474	1,827	2,827	2,610	2,020	2,020	2,134	2,580	2,827	3,495
64	2,880	2,517	1,844	2,880	2,648	2,081	2,081	2,156	2,618	2,880	3,549
65	2,933	2,561	1,861	2,933	2,686	2,141	2,141	2,178	2,656	2,933	3,602
66	2,985	2,604	1,877	2,985	2,723	2,202	2,202	2,200	2,694	2,985	3,656
67	3,038	2,647	1,894	3,038	2,761	2,263	2,263	2,222	2,776	3,038	3,709
68	3,091	2,690	1,911	3,091	2,799	2,323	2,323	2,244	2,865	3,091	3,763
69	3,144	2,734	1,927	3,144	2,836	2,384	2,384	2,266	2,954	3,144	3,816
70	3,196	2,777	1,944	3,196	2,874	2,445	2,445	2,288	3,043	3,196	3,870
71	3,249	2,820	1,961	3,249	2,912	2,506	2,506	2,310	3,132	3,249	3,923
72	3,302	2,864	1,978	3,302	2,950	2,566	2,566	2,332	3,221	3,302	3,977
73	3,355	2,907	1,994	3,355	2,987	2,627	2,627	2,354	3,310	3,355	4,031
74	3,407	2,950	2,016	3,407	3,025	2,688	2,688	2,376	3,399	3,407	4,084
75	3,460	2,994	2,040	3,460	3,063	2,749	2,749	2,398	3,488	3,460	4,138
76	3,513	3,037	2,064	3,513	3,101	2,809	2,809	2,420	3,577	3,513	4,192
77	3,566	3,080	2,089	3,566	3,138	2,870	2,870	2,442	3,666	3,566	4,245
78	3,619	3,124	2,113	3,619	3,176	2,931	2,931	2,464	3,755	3,619	4,299
79	3,672	3,167	2,137	3,672	3,214	2,992	2,992	2,486	3,844	3,672	4,353
80	3,724	3,211	2,161	3,724	3,251	3,052	3,052	2,508	3,933	3,724	4,406
81	3,777	3,254	2,185	3,777	3,289	3,113	3,113	2,530	4,023	3,777	4,460
82	3,830	3,297	2,210	3,830	3,327	3,174	3,174	2,552	4,112	3,830	4,514

Trial length in days	PPE Cut off A	PPE Cut off B	PPE Cut off C	PPE Cut off D	PPE Cut off E	PPE Cut off F	PPE Cut off G	PPE Cut off H	PPE Cut off I	PPE Cut off J	PPE Cut off K
83	3,883	3,341	2,234	3,883	3,365	3,235	3,235	2,575	4,201	3,883	4,568
84	3,936	3,384	2,258	3,936	3,402	3,295	3,295	2,597	4,290	3,936	4,622
85	3,989	3,428	2,282	3,989	3,440	3,356	3,356	2,619	4,379	3,989	4,675
86	4,042	3,471	2,307	4,042	3,478	3,417	3,417	2,641	4,469	4,042	4,729
87	4,095	3,515	2,331	4,095	3,516	3,478	3,478	2,663	4,558	4,095	4,783
88	4,148	3,558	2,355	4,148	3,553	3,539	3,539	2,685	4,647	4,148	4,837
89	4,201	3,602	2,379	4,201	3,591	3,599	3,599	2,707	4,737	4,201	4,891
90	4,254	3,645	2,404	4,254	3,629	3,660	3,660	2,729	4,826	4,254	4,945
91	4,307	3,689	2,428	4,307	3,666	3,721	3,721	2,751	4,915	4,307	4,999
92	4,360	3,733	2,452	4,360	3,704	3,782	3,782	2,774	5,005	4,360	5,053
93	4,413	3,776	2,477	4,413	3,742	3,843	3,843	2,796	5,094	4,413	5,107
94	4,466	3,820	2,501	4,466	3,780	3,903	3,903	2,818	5,183	4,466	5,161
95	4,519	3,863	2,525	4,519	3,817	3,964	3,964	2,840	5,273	4,519	5,215
96	4,572	3,907	2,549	4,572	3,855	4,025	4,025	2,862	5,362	4,572	5,269
97	4,625	3,951	2,574	4,625	3,893	4,086	4,086	2,884	5,452	4,625	5,323
98	4,679	3,994	2,598	4,679	3,930	4,147	4,147	2,906	5,541	4,679	5,377
99	4,732	4,038	2,622	4,732	3,968	4,207	4,207	2,929	5,631	4,732	5,431
100	4,785	4,082	2,647	4,785	4,006	4,268	4,268	2,951	5,720	4,785	5,485
101	4,838	4,125	2,671	4,838	4,044	4,329	4,329	2,973	5,810	4,838	5,539
102	4,891	4,169	2,695	4,891	4,081	4,390	4,390	2,995	5,899	4,891	5,593
103	4,944	4,213	2,720	4,944	4,119	4,451	4,451	3,032	5,989	4,944	5,647
104	4,997	4,257	2,744	4,997	4,157	4,512	4,512	3,073	6,079	4,997	5,702
105	5,051	4,300	2,768	5,051	4,195	4,573	4,573	3,114	6,168	5,051	5,756
106	5,104	4,344	2,793	5,104	4,232	4,633	4,633	3,155	6,258	5,104	5,810
107	5,157	4,388	2,817	5,157	4,270	4,694	4,694	3,196	6,348	5,157	5,864
108	5,210	4,432	2,841	5,210	4,308	4,755	4,755	3,237	6,437	5,210	5,918
109	5,264	4,475	2,866	5,264	4,345	4,816	4,816	3,278	6,527	5,264	5,973
110	5,317	4,519	2,890	5,317	4,383	4,877	4,877	3,319	6,617	5,317	6,027

Trial length in days	PPE Cut off A	PPE Cut off B	PPE Cut off C	PPE Cut off D	PPE Cut off E	PPE Cut off F	PPE Cut off G	PPE Cut off H	PPE Cut off I	PPE Cut off J	PPE Cut off K
111	5,370	4,563	2,914	5,370	4,421	4,938	4,938	3,361	6,706	5,370	6,081
112	5,423	4,607	2,939	5,423	4,459	4,999	4,999	3,402	6,796	5,423	6,135
113	5,477	4,650	2,963	5,477	4,496	5,059	5,059	3,443	6,886	5,477	6,189
114	5,530	4,694	2,987	5,530	4,534	5,120	5,120	3,484	6,976	5,530	6,244
115	5,583	4,738	3,012	5,583	4,572	5,181	5,181	3,525	7,066	5,583	6,298
116	5,637	4,782	3,036	5,637	4,610	5,242	5,242	3,566	7,155	5,637	6,352
117	5,690	4,826	3,060	5,690	4,647	5,303	5,303	3,607	7,245	5,690	6,406
118	5,743	4,869	3,085	5,743	4,685	5,364	5,364	3,648	7,335	5,743	6,460
119	5,797	4,913	3,109	5,797	4,723	5,425	5,425	3,689	7,425	5,797	6,514
120	5,850	4,957	3,133	5,850	4,760	5,486	5,486	3,730	7,515	5,850	6,569
121	5,904	5,001	3,158	5,904	4,798	5,547	5,547	3,771	7,605	5,904	6,623
122	5,956	5,044	3,182	5,956	4,836	5,607	5,607	3,812	7,693	5,956	6,677
123	6,009	5,088	3,206	6,009	4,874	5,668	5,668	3,853	7,782	6,009	6,731
124	6,061	5,131	3,230	6,061	4,911	5,729	5,729	3,895	7,871	6,061	6,785
125	6,114	5,175	3,254	6,114	4,949	5,789	5,789	3,936	7,959	6,114	6,839
126	6,167	5,218	3,278	6,167	4,987	5,850	5,850	3,977	8,048	6,167	6,892
127	6,219	5,261	3,302	6,219	5,025	5,911	5,911	4,017	8,137	6,219	6,945
128	6,272	5,304	3,326	6,272	5,062	5,971	5,971	4,058	8,225	6,272	6,999
129	6,324	5,347	3,350	6,324	5,100	6,032	6,032	4,098	8,314	6,324	7,052
130	6,377	5,390	3,374	6,377	5,138	6,093	6,093	4,139	8,403	6,377	7,106
131	6,430	5,433	3,398	6,430	5,175	6,153	6,153	4,179	8,491	6,430	7,159
132	6,482	5,476	3,422	6,482	5,213	6,214	6,214	4,219	8,580	6,482	7,212
133	6,535	5,520	3,446	6,535	5,251	6,274	6,274	4,260	8,669	6,535	7,266
134	6,588	5,563	3,470	6,588	5,289	6,335	6,335	4,300	8,757	6,588	7,319
135	6,640	5,606	3,494	6,640	5,326	6,396	6,396	4,341	8,846	6,640	7,373
136	6,693	5,649	3,518	6,693	5,364	6,456	6,456	4,381	8,935	6,693	7,426
137	6,745	5,692	3,542	6,745	5,402	6,517	6,517	4,422	9,023	6,745	7,479
138	6,798	5,735	3,566	6,798	5,439	6,578	6,578	4,462	9,112	6,798	7,533

Trial length in days	PPE Cut off A	PPE Cut off B	PPE Cut off C	PPE Cut off D	PPE Cut off E	PPE Cut off F	PPE Cut off G	PPE Cut off H	PPE Cut off I	PPE Cut off J	PPE Cut off K
139	6,851	5,778	3,590	6,851	5,477	6,638	6,638	4,503	9,201	6,851	7,586
140	6,903	5,821	3,614	6,903	5,515	6,699	6,699	4,543	9,289	6,903	7,639
141	6,956	5,864	3,638	6,956	5,553	6,760	6,760	4,584	9,378	6,956	7,693
142	7,008	5,908	3,662	7,008	5,590	6,820	6,820	4,624	9,467	7,008	7,746
143	7,061	5,951	3,686	7,061	5,628	6,881	6,881	4,664	9,555	7,061	7,800
144	7,114	5,994	3,709	7,114	5,666	6,942	6,942	4,705	9,644	7,114	7,853
145	7,166	6,037	3,733	7,166	5,704	7,002	7,002	4,745	9,733	7,166	7,906
146	7,219	6,080	3,757	7,219	5,741	7,063	7,063	4,786	9,821	7,219	7,960
147	7,272	6,123	3,781	7,272	5,779	7,124	7,124	4,826	9,910	7,272	8,013
148	7,324	6,166	3,805	7,324	5,817	7,184	7,184	4,867	9,999	7,324	8,067
149	7,377	6,209	3,829	7,377	5,854	7,245	7,245	4,907	10,087	7,377	8,120
150	7,429	6,252	3,853	7,429	5,892	7,305	7,305	4,948	10,176	7,429	8,173
151	7,482	6,296	3,877	7,482	5,930	7,366	7,366	4,988	10,265	7,482	8,227
152	7,535	6,339	3,901	7,535	5,968	7,427	7,427	5,029	10,353	7,535	8,280
153	7,587	6,382	3,925	7,587	6,005	7,487	7,487	5,069	10,442	7,587	8,333
154	7,640	6,425	3,949	7,640	6,043	7,548	7,548	5,110	10,531	7,640	8,387
155	7,692	6,468	3,973	7,692	6,081	7,609	7,609	5,150	10,619	7,692	8,440
156	7,745	6,511	3,997	7,745	6,119	7,669	7,669	5,190	10,708	7,745	8,494
157	7,798	6,554	4,021	7,798	6,156	7,730	7,730	5,231	10,797	7,798	8,547
158	7,850	6,597	4,045	7,850	6,194	7,791	7,791	5,271	10,885	7,850	8,600
159	7,903	6,641	4,069	7,903	6,232	7,851	7,851	5,312	10,974	7,903	8,654
160	7,956	6,684	4,093	7,956	6,269	7,912	7,912	5,352	11,063	7,956	8,707
161	8,008	6,727	4,117	8,008	6,307	7,973	7,973	5,393	11,151	8,008	8,760
162	8,061	6,770	4,141	8,061	6,345	8,033	8,033	5,433	11,240	8,061	8,814
163	8,113	6,813	4,165	8,113	6,383	8,094	8,094	5,474	11,329	8,113	8,867
164	8,166	6,856	4,189	8,166	6,420	8,155	8,155	5,514	11,417	8,166	8,921
165	8,219	6,899	4,213	8,219	6,458	8,215	8,215	5,555	11,506	8,219	8,974
166	8,271	6,942	4,237	8,271	6,496	8,276	8,276	5,595	11,595	8,271	9,027

Trial length in days	PPE Cut off A	PPE Cut off B	PPE Cut off C	PPE Cut off D	PPE Cut off E	PPE Cut off F	PPE Cut off G	PPE Cut off H	PPE Cut off I	PPE Cut off J	PPE Cut off K
167	8,324	6,985	4,261	8,324	6,534	8,337	8,337	5,636	11,683	8,324	9,081
168	8,376	7,029	4,285	8,376	6,571	8,397	8,397	5,676	11,772	8,376	9,134
169	8,429	7,072	4,309	8,429	6,609	8,458	8,458	5,716	11,861	8,429	9,188
170	8,482	7,115	4,333	8,482	6,647	8,518	8,518	5,757	11,949	8,482	9,241
171	8,534	7,158	4,357	8,534	6,684	8,579	8,579	5,797	12,038	8,534	9,294
172	8,587	7,201	4,380	8,587	6,722	8,640	8,640	5,838	12,127	8,587	9,348
173	8,639	7,244	4,404	8,639	6,760	8,700	8,700	5,878	12,215	8,639	9,401
174	8,692	7,287	4,428	8,692	6,798	8,761	8,761	5,919	12,304	8,692	9,454
175	8,745	7,330	4,452	8,745	6,835	8,822	8,822	5,959	12,393	8,745	9,508
176	8,797	7,373	4,476	8,797	6,873	8,882	8,882	6,000	12,481	8,797	9,561
177	8,850	7,417	4,500	8,850	6,911	8,943	8,943	6,040	12,570	8,850	9,615
178	8,903	7,460	4,524	8,903	6,948	9,004	9,004	6,081	12,659	8,903	9,668
179	8,955	7,503	4,548	8,955	6,986	9,064	9,064	6,121	12,747	8,955	9,721
180	9,008	7,546	4,572	9,008	7,024	9,125	9,125	6,162	12,836	9,008	9,775
181	9,060	7,589	4,596	9,060	7,062	9,186	9,186	6,202	12,925	9,060	9,828
182	9,113	7,632	4,620	9,113	7,099	9,246	9,246	6,242	13,013	9,113	9,881
183	9,166	7,675	4,644	9,166	7,137	9,307	9,307	6,283	13,102	9,166	9,935
184	9,218	7,718	4,668	9,218	7,174	9,368	9,368	6,323	13,191	9,218	9,988
185	9,271	7,762	4,692	9,271	7,211	9,428	9,428	6,364	13,279	9,271	10,042
186	9,323	7,805	4,716	9,323	7,248	9,489	9,489	6,404	13,368	9,323	10,095
187	9,376	7,848	4,740	9,376	7,285	9,549	9,549	6,445	13,457	9,376	10,148
188	9,429	7,891	4,764	9,429	7,322	9,610	9,610	6,485	13,545	9,429	10,202
189	9,481	7,934	4,788	9,481	7,360	9,671	9,671	6,526	13,634	9,481	10,255
190	9,534	7,977	4,812	9,534	7,397	9,731	9,731	6,566	13,723	9,534	10,309
191	9,587	8,020	4,836	9,587	7,434	9,792	9,792	6,607	13,811	9,587	10,362
192	9,639	8,063	4,860	9,639	7,471	9,853	9,853	6,647	13,900	9,639	10,415
193	9,692	8,106	4,884	9,692	7,508	9,913	9,913	6,687	13,988	9,692	10,469
194	9,744	8,150	4,908	9,744	7,545	9,974	9,974	6,728	14,077	9,744	10,522

Trial length in days	PPE Cut off A	PPE Cut off B	PPE Cut off C	PPE Cut off D	PPE Cut off E	PPE Cut off F	PPE Cut off G	PPE Cut off H	PPE Cut off I	PPE Cut off J	PPE Cut off K
195	9,797	8,193	4,932	9,797	7,582	10,035	10,035	6,768	14,166	9,797	10,575
196	9,850	8,236	4,956	9,850	7,620	10,095	10,095	6,809	14,254	9,850	10,629
197	9,902	8,279	4,980	9,902	7,657	10,156	10,156	6,849	14,343	9,902	10,682
198	9,955	8,322	5,004	9,955	7,694	10,217	10,217	6,890	14,432	9,955	10,736
199	10,007	8,365	5,028	10,007	7,731	10,277	10,277	6,930	14,520	10,007	10,789
200	10,060	8,408	5,051	10,060	7,768	10,338	10,338	6,971	14,609	10,060	10,842

Cracked trial or guilty plea where the number of pages of prosecution evidence is less than or equal to the PPE Cut-off

6.—(1) Where in a cracked trial or guilty plea the number of pages of prosecution evidence is less **G-71** than or equal to the PPE Cut-off specified in the table following paragraph 5(1) as appropriate to the Class of Offence with which the assisted person is charged, the total fee payable to the litigator is—

  (a) the basic fee, calculated in accordance with the table following sub-paragraph (2) of this paragraph;

  (b) the defendant uplift, if any, calculated in accordance with the table following paragraph 12; and

  (c) the adjustment for transfers and retrials, if any, calculated in accordance with paragraph 13.

(2) For the purposes of sub-paragraph (1), the basic fee appropriate to a cracked trial or a guilty plea is specified in the table following this sub-paragraph, in accordance with the type of case and Class of Offence with which the assisted person is charged.

BASIC FEES FOR CRACKED TRIALS AND GUILTY PLEAS (£)

Type of case	Class of Offence										
	A	B	C	D	E	F	G	H	I	J	K
Cracked trial	904.58	707.32	524.83	859.35	233.03	224.23	224.23	237.00	253.67	904.58	773.86
Guilty plea	680.39	556.11	442.91	646.36	184.70	195.81	195.81	190.97	174.60	680.39	640.84

[The table following para. 6(2) is printed as substituted by the Criminal Legal Aid (Remuneration) (Amendment) Regulations 2014 (S.I. 2014 No. 415). The amendments made by S.I. 2014 No. 415 apply to matters in which a determination under section 13 (advice or assistance for individuals in custody (as to which, see § 6-209 in the main work)), 15 (advice or assistance for criminal proceedings (§ 6-211 in the main work)) or 16 (representation for criminal proceedings (§ 6-212 in the main work)) of the LASPOA 2012 is made on or after March 20, 2014: S.I. 2014 No. 415, reg. 3.]

Trial where the number of pages of prosecution evidence is less than or equal to the PPE Cut-off

7.—(1) Where in a trial the number of pages of prosecution evidence is less than or equal to the **G-71a** PPE Cut-off specified in the table following paragraph 5(2) as appropriate to the offence for which the assisted person is tried and the length of trial, the total fee payable to the litigator is—

  (a) the basic fee, calculated in accordance with the table following sub-paragraph (2);

  (b) the length of trial proxy, if any, calculated in accordance with the table following subparagraph (3);

  (c) the defendant uplift, if any, calculated in accordance with the table following paragraph 12; and

  (d) the adjustment for transfers and retrials, if any, calculated in accordance with paragraph 13.

(2) For the purposes of sub-paragraph (1), the basic fee appropriate to a trial is specified in the table following this sub-paragraph, in accordance with the offence for which the assisted person is tried.

BASIC FEES FOR TRIALS (£)

Type of case	Class of Offence										
	A	B	C	D	E	F	G	H	I	J	K
Trial	1,467.58	1,097.66	739.59	1,394.20	352.72	357.60	357.60	357.75	357.44	1,467.58	1,031.82

(3) For the purposes of sub-paragraph (1), the length of trial proxy is specified in the table following this sub-paragraph, in accordance with the offence for which the assisted person is tried and the length   of   trial.

LENGTH OF TRIAL PROXY

Trial length in Days	Trial length proxy A	Trial length proxy B	Trial length proxy C	Trial length proxy D	Trial length proxy E	Trial length proxy F	Trial length proxy G	Trial length proxy H	Trial length proxy I	Trial length proxy J	Trial length proxy K
1	0.00	0.00	0.00	0.00	0.00	0.00	0.00	0.00	0.00	0.00	0.00
2	0.00	0.00	0.00	0.00	0.00	0.00	0.00	0.00	0.00	0.00	0.00
3	252.54	452.88	432.51	239.92	716.58	644.94	644.94	703.69	862.39	252.54	574.13
4	769.79	879.65	843.33	731.30	1,033.65	898.77	898.77	1,009.83	1,320.93	769.79	1,140.63
5	1,261.16	1,285.08	1,233.61	1,198.10	1,334.86	1,139.90	1,139.90	1,300.64	1,756.54	1,261.16	1,678.81
6	1,761.17	1,695.98	1,621.20	1,673.12	1,617.11	1,386.43	1,386.43	1,589.05	2,200.59	1,761.17	2,181.04
7	2,253.87	2,102.22	2,011.03	2,141.18	1,915.45	1,632.83	1,632.83	1,879.51	2,637.65	2,253.87	2,713.26
8	2,746.56	2,508.44	2,400.87	2,609.24	2,213.79	1,875.25	1,875.25	2,169.97	3,074.70	2,746.56	3,245.48
9	3,210.92	2,874.04	2,751.71	3,050.38	2,482.29	2,093.45	2,093.45	2,431.38	3,473.43	3,210.92	3,724.49
10	3,675.29	3,239.65	3,102.56	3,491.52	2,750.81	2,311.64	2,311.64	2,692.79	3,872.17	3,675.29	4,203.48
11	4,143.10	3,605.74	3,462.93	3,935.94	3,031.66	2,536.06	2,536.06	2,961.38	4,279.02	4,143.10	4,703.99
12	4,607.74	3,971.38	3,823.47	4,377.35	3,312.59	2,760.47	2,760.47	3,229.64	4,686.22	4,607.74	5,204.80
13	5,072.39	4,337.02	4,175.80	4,818.77	3,593.15	2,983.98	2,983.98	3,492.07	5,086.28	5,072.39	5,705.63
14	5,537.03	4,702.67	4,528.13	5,260.19	3,865.07	3,203.34	3,203.34	3,754.51	5,486.32	5,537.03	6,206.43
15	6,001.68	5,068.31	4,880.46	5,701.59	4,136.15	3,422.69	3,422.69	4,016.95	5,886.37	6,001.68	6,707.21
16	6,466.32	5,433.96	5,232.79	6,143.00	4,407.26	3,642.05	3,642.05	4,279.39	6,286.42	6,466.32	7,207.20
17	6,930.96	5,799.60	5,585.12	6,584.42	4,678.35	3,861.41	3,861.41	4,541.82	6,686.47	6,930.96	7,693.86
18	7,395.60	6,165.24	5,937.45	7,025.83	4,949.45	4,080.76	4,080.76	4,804.26	7,086.52	7,395.60	8,180.52
19	7,860.25	6,530.88	6,289.77	7,467.24	5,220.54	4,300.12	4,300.12	5,066.69	7,486.57	7,860.25	8,667.17
20	8,324.89	6,896.53	6,642.11	7,908.66	5,491.63	4,519.48	4,519.48	5,329.13	7,886.63	8,324.89	9,153.84
21	8,798.40	7,234.27	6,931.61	8,358.47	5,715.66	4,698.94	4,698.94	5,544.96	8,215.37	8,798.40	9,640.50
22	9,271.81	7,571.99	7,221.19	8,808.22	5,939.70	4,878.48	4,878.48	5,760.90	8,544.12	9,271.81	10,127.16
23	9,737.21	7,909.69	7,510.79	9,250.36	6,157.06	5,058.02	5,058.02	5,976.83	8,872.90	9,737.21	10,613.82
24	10,202.62	8,239.72	7,800.39	9,692.49	6,374.43	5,237.57	5,237.57	6,192.76	9,198.07	10,202.62	11,100.48
25	10,668.04	8,569.74	8,088.48	10,134.63	6,591.80	5,417.10	5,417.10	6,405.21	9,519.15	10,668.04	11,587.14

Trial length in Days	Trial length proxy A	Trial length proxy B	Trial length proxy C	Trial length proxy D	Trial length proxy E	Trial length proxy F	Trial length proxy G	Trial length proxy H	Trial length proxy I	Trial length proxy J	Trial length proxy K
26	11,133.44	8,899.77	8,371.53	10,576.78	6,809.17	5,596.65	5,596.65	6,615.99	9,840.24	11,133.44	12,073.81
27	11,598.84	9,229.80	8,654.60	11,018.90	7,026.53	5,776.19	5,776.19	6,826.76	10,161.33	11,598.84	12,560.46
28	12,064.25	9,559.83	8,937.65	11,461.05	7,243.91	5,955.73	5,955.73	7,037.54	10,482.41	12,064.25	13,047.13
29	12,529.67	9,889.86	9,220.70	11,903.18	7,461.27	6,133.18	6,133.18	7,248.30	10,803.51	12,529.67	13,533.78
30	12,995.07	10,219.88	9,503.75	12,345.31	7,678.63	6,309.59	6,309.59	7,459.07	11,124.59	12,995.07	14,020.44
31	13,460.48	10,549.91	9,786.81	12,787.46	7,896.01	6,486.01	6,486.01	7,669.85	11,445.67	13,460.48	14,507.11
32	13,925.88	10,879.95	10,069.87	13,229.59	8,113.38	6,662.43	6,662.43	7,880.61	11,766.76	13,925.88	14,993.76
33	14,391.30	11,209.97	10,352.92	13,671.73	8,330.74	6,838.84	6,838.84	8,091.39	12,087.84	14,391.30	15,480.43
34	14,856.70	11,540.00	10,635.97	14,113.87	8,548.11	7,015.26	7,015.26	8,302.16	12,408.93	14,856.70	15,967.09
35	15,322.11	11,870.03	10,919.03	14,556.01	8,765.48	7,191.68	7,191.68	8,512.93	12,730.02	15,322.11	16,453.75
36	15,787.52	12,200.05	11,202.09	14,998.14	8,982.84	7,368.10	7,368.10	8,723.70	13,051.10	15,787.52	16,940.41
37	16,252.93	12,530.09	11,485.14	15,440.28	9,200.22	7,544.51	7,544.51	8,934.48	13,372.19	16,252.93	17,427.07
38	16,718.33	12,860.11	11,768.20	15,882.42	9,417.58	7,720.93	7,720.93	9,145.25	13,693.28	16,718.33	17,913.73
39	17,183.74	13,190.13	12,051.25	16,324.55	9,634.94	7,897.35	7,897.35	9,356.02	14,014.36	17,183.74	18,400.40
40	17,622.38	13,492.13	12,163.57	16,741.26	9,722.09	8,027.76	8,027.76	9,447.16	14,282.00	17,622.38	18,865.89
41	18,063.40	13,796.43	12,277.13	17,160.24	9,811.54	8,158.44	8,158.44	9,539.40	14,551.22	18,063.40	19,334.83
42	18,504.54	14,100.82	12,390.73	17,579.32	9,901.04	8,289.12	8,289.12	9,631.68	14,820.51	18,504.54	19,803.93
43	18,945.79	14,405.31	12,504.33	17,998.51	9,990.58	8,419.82	8,419.82	9,723.97	15,089.84	18,945.79	20,273.20
44	19,387.15	14,709.89	12,617.96	18,417.79	10,080.16	8,550.52	8,550.52	9,816.28	15,359.23	19,387.15	20,742.61
45	19,828.61	15,014.56	12,731.61	18,837.18	10,169.77	8,681.22	8,681.22	9,908.63	15,628.69	19,828.61	21,212.18
46	20,270.18	15,319.32	12,845.28	19,256.68	10,259.43	8,811.94	8,811.94	10,000.97	15,898.19	20,270.18	21,681.91
47	20,711.85	15,624.18	12,958.98	19,676.26	10,349.13	8,942.66	8,942.66	10,093.35	16,167.76	20,711.85	22,151.80
48	21,153.65	15,929.14	13,072.69	20,095.97	10,438.87	9,073.39	9,073.39	10,185.75	16,437.38	21,153.65	22,621.84
49	21,595.54	16,234.19	13,186.44	20,515.76	10,528.64	9,204.12	9,204.12	10,278.16	16,707.05	21,595.54	23,092.04
50	22,037.53	16,539.33	13,300.19	20,935.66	10,618.45	9,334.88	9,334.88	10,370.61	16,976.79	22,037.53	23,562.39
51	22,479.65	16,844.56	13,413.98	21,355.67	10,708.32	9,465.63	9,465.63	10,463.06	17,246.59	22,479.65	24,032.91
52	22,921.86	17,149.88	13,527.78	21,775.77	10,798.21	9,596.40	9,596.40	10,555.54	17,516.43	22,921.86	24,503.58

Trial length in Days	Trial length proxy A	Trial length proxy B	Trial length proxy C	Trial length proxy D	Trial length proxy E	Trial length proxy F	Trial length proxy G	Trial length proxy H	Trial length proxy I	Trial length proxy J	Trial length proxy K
53	23,364.19	17,455.30	13,641.60	22,195.99	10,888.15	9,727.16	9,727.16	10,648.04	17,786.33	23,364.19	24,974.41
54	23,806.62	17,760.82	13,755.44	22,616.29	10,978.13	9,857.94	9,857.94	10,740.56	18,056.29	23,806.62	25,445.40
55	24,249.16	18,066.42	13,869.31	23,036.69	11,068.14	9,988.72	9,988.72	10,833.10	18,326.31	24,249.16	25,916.54
56	24,691.80	18,372.13	13,983.20	23,457.22	11,158.20	10,119.52	10,119.52	10,925.66	18,596.39	24,691.80	26,387.85
57	25,134.56	18,677.92	14,097.11	23,877.83	11,248.29	10,250.32	10,250.32	11,018.24	18,866.52	25,134.56	26,859.31
58	25,577.42	18,983.81	14,211.04	24,298.55	11,338.39	10,381.13	10,381.13	11,110.84	19,136.71	25,577.42	27,330.92
59	26,020.39	19,289.79	14,325.00	24,719.38	11,428.49	10,511.95	10,511.95	11,203.47	19,406.96	26,020.39	27,802.70
60	26,463.47	19,595.86	14,438.97	25,140.29	11,518.59	10,642.77	10,642.77	11,296.10	19,677.26	26,463.47	28,274.63
61	26,906.66	19,902.03	14,552.97	25,561.32	11,608.70	10,773.60	10,773.60	11,388.77	19,947.62	26,906.66	28,746.72
62	27,349.94	20,208.30	14,666.99	25,982.45	11,698.80	10,904.44	10,904.44	11,481.46	20,218.04	27,349.94	29,218.96
63	27,793.35	20,514.64	14,781.02	26,403.69	11,788.90	11,035.28	11,035.28	11,574.16	20,488.52	27,793.35	29,691.37
64	28,236.86	20,821.10	14,895.09	26,825.02	11,879.00	11,166.14	11,166.14	11,666.89	20,759.04	28,236.86	30,163.93
65	28,680.48	21,127.63	15,009.17	27,246.45	11,969.10	11,297.01	11,297.01	11,759.62	21,029.63	28,680.48	30,636.65
66	29,124.20	21,434.28	15,123.28	27,667.99	12,059.20	11,427.88	11,427.88	11,852.39	21,300.28	29,124.20	31,109.52
67	29,568.03	21,741.01	15,237.40	28,089.63	12,149.30	11,558.76	11,558.76	11,945.17	21,570.97	29,568.03	31,582.55
68	30,011.97	22,047.83	15,351.55	28,511.37	12,239.40	11,689.65	11,689.65	12,037.98	21,841.73	30,011.97	32,055.74
69	30,456.02	22,354.74	15,465.72	28,933.21	12,329.50	11,820.54	11,820.54	12,130.81	22,112.55	30,456.02	32,529.08
70	30,900.17	22,661.76	15,579.91	29,355.16	12,419.60	11,951.45	11,951.45	12,223.66	22,383.42	30,900.17	33,002.60
71	31,344.44	22,968.86	15,694.12	29,777.22	12,509.70	12,082.36	12,082.36	12,316.53	22,654.35	31,344.44	33,476.26
72	31,788.81	23,276.06	15,808.35	30,199.37	12,599.80	12,213.28	12,213.28	12,409.42	22,925.33	31,788.81	33,950.08
73	32,233.28	23,583.35	15,922.61	30,621.63	12,689.90	12,344.21	12,344.21	12,502.32	23,196.37	32,233.28	34,424.05
74	32,677.87	23,890.74	16,036.89	31,043.98	12,780.00	12,475.14	12,475.14	12,595.26	23,467.47	32,677.87	34,898.19
75	33,122.56	24,198.21	16,151.19	31,466.43	12,870.10	12,606.09	12,606.09	12,688.21	23,738.63	33,122.56	35,372.48
76	33,567.36	24,505.78	16,265.50	31,889.00	12,960.20	12,737.03	12,737.03	12,781.18	24,009.84	33,567.36	35,846.92
77	34,012.28	24,813.45	16,379.85	32,311.66	13,050.30	12,867.99	12,867.99	12,874.16	24,281.10	34,012.28	36,321.53
78	34,457.29	25,121.21	16,494.21	32,734.43	13,140.40	12,998.95	12,998.95	12,967.17	24,552.43	34,457.29	36,796.30
79	34,902.42	25,429.06	16,608.60	33,157.30	13,230.50	13,129.94	13,129.94	13,060.21	24,823.82	34,902.42	37,271.22

Trial length in Days	Trial length proxy A	Trial length proxy B	Trial length proxy C	Trial length proxy D	Trial length proxy E	Trial length proxy F	Trial length proxy G	Trial length proxy H	Trial length proxy I	Trial length proxy J	Trial length proxy K
80	35,347.65	25,737.00	16,723.00	33,580.26	13,320.60	13,260.92	13,260.92	13,153.27	25,095.26	35,347.65	37,746.29
81	35,792.99	26,045.04	16,837.42	34,003.35	13,410.70	13,391.90	13,391.90	13,246.34	25,366.75	35,792.99	38,221.52
82	36,238.43	26,353.17	16,951.88	34,426.52	13,500.80	13,522.90	13,522.90	13,339.43	25,638.30	36,238.43	38,696.92
83	36,683.99	26,661.40	17,066.35	34,849.80	13,590.90	13,653.90	13,653.90	13,432.55	25,909.92	36,683.99	39,172.47
84	37,129.65	26,969.72	17,180.83	35,273.17	13,681.01	13,784.93	13,784.93	13,525.68	26,181.58	37,129.65	39,648.18
85	37,575.42	27,278.13	17,295.35	35,696.65	13,771.11	13,915.94	13,915.94	13,618.83	26,453.30	37,575.42	40,124.04
86	38,021.30	27,586.64	17,409.90	36,120.24	13,861.21	14,046.97	14,046.97	13,712.01	26,725.09	38,021.30	40,600.06
87	38,467.29	27,895.23	17,524.45	36,543.93	13,951.31	14,178.01	14,178.01	13,805.21	26,996.93	38,467.29	41,076.24
88	38,913.39	28,203.93	17,639.03	36,967.72	14,041.41	14,309.06	14,309.06	13,898.42	27,268.82	38,913.39	41,552.58
89	39,359.59	28,512.71	17,753.63	37,391.61	14,131.51	14,440.10	14,440.10	13,991.66	27,540.77	39,359.59	42,029.07
90	39,805.90	28,821.60	17,868.25	37,815.60	14,221.61	14,571.17	14,571.17	14,084.91	27,812.78	39,805.90	42,505.73
91	40,252.32	29,130.57	17,982.89	38,239.70	14,311.71	14,702.24	14,702.24	14,178.20	28,084.84	40,252.32	42,982.53
92	40,698.83	29,439.63	18,097.56	38,663.90	14,401.81	14,833.32	14,833.32	14,271.49	28,356.97	40,698.83	43,459.49
93	41,145.47	29,748.80	18,212.24	39,088.20	14,491.91	14,964.40	14,964.40	14,364.81	28,629.15	41,145.47	43,936.62
94	41,592.21	30,058.05	18,326.95	39,512.60	14,582.01	15,095.49	15,095.49	14,458.15	28,901.38	41,592.21	44,413.90
95	42,039.06	30,367.40	18,441.68	39,937.10	14,672.11	15,226.59	15,226.59	14,551.52	29,173.67	42,039.06	44,891.33
96	42,486.02	30,676.84	18,556.44	40,361.72	14,762.22	15,357.69	15,357.69	14,644.89	29,446.03	42,486.02	45,368.93
97	42,933.08	30,986.38	18,671.21	40,786.43	14,852.32	15,488.81	15,488.81	14,738.25	29,718.43	42,933.08	45,846.68
98	43,380.25	31,296.01	18,786.00	41,211.24	14,942.42	15,619.94	15,619.94	14,831.63	29,990.89	43,380.25	46,324.60
99	43,827.53	31,605.73	18,900.82	41,636.15	15,032.52	15,751.07	15,751.07	14,925.00	30,263.42	43,827.53	46,802.66
100	44,274.91	31,915.55	19,015.65	42,061.17	15,122.62	15,882.21	15,882.21	15,018.37	30,535.98	44,274.91	47,280.88
101	44,722.41	32,225.46	19,130.51	42,486.29	15,212.72	16,013.36	16,013.36	15,111.74	30,808.63	44,722.41	47,759.26
102	45,170.01	32,535.45	19,245.39	42,911.51	15,302.82	16,144.51	16,144.51	15,205.11	31,081.31	45,170.01	48,237.80
103	45,617.73	32,845.55	19,360.30	43,336.84	15,392.92	16,275.67	16,275.67	15,298.48	31,354.06	45,617.73	48,716.50
104	46,065.54	33,155.74	19,475.21	43,762.27	15,483.02	16,406.84	16,406.84	15,391.85	31,626.86	46,065.54	49,195.35
105	46,513.46	33,466.03	19,590.12	44,187.79	15,573.12	16,538.02	16,538.02	15,485.22	31,899.72	46,513.46	49,674.36
106	46,961.50	33,776.40	19,705.04	44,613.42	15,663.22	16,669.21	16,669.21	15,578.59	32,172.64	46,961.50	50,153.43

Trial length in Days	Trial length proxy A	Trial length proxy B	Trial length proxy C	Trial length proxy D	Trial length proxy E	Trial length proxy F	Trial length proxy G	Trial length proxy H	Trial length proxy I	Trial length proxy J	Trial length proxy K
107	47,409.64	34,086.84	19,819.95	45,039.15	15,753.32	16,800.40	16,800.40	15,671.96	32,445.62	47,409.64	50,632.48
108	47,857.89	34,397.27	19,934.87	45,465.00	15,843.43	16,931.60	16,931.60	15,765.33	32,718.65	47,857.89	51,111.54
109	48,306.24	34,707.71	20,049.78	45,890.93	15,933.53	17,062.82	17,062.82	15,858.70	32,991.74	48,306.24	51,590.60
110	48,754.70	35,018.15	20,164.69	46,316.97	16,023.63	17,194.03	17,194.03	15,952.07	33,264.88	48,754.70	52,069.66
111	49,203.28	35,328.59	20,279.60	46,743.12	16,113.73	17,325.26	17,325.26	16,045.44	33,538.08	49,203.28	52,548.71
112	49,651.95	35,639.02	20,394.51	47,169.36	16,203.83	17,456.49	17,456.49	16,138.81	33,811.34	49,651.95	53,027.77
113	50,100.74	35,949.45	20,509.43	47,595.72	16,293.93	17,587.73	17,587.73	16,232.18	34,084.66	50,100.74	53,506.84
114	50,549.63	36,259.89	20,624.34	48,022.16	16,384.03	17,718.99	17,718.99	16,325.55	34,358.03	50,549.63	53,985.89
115	50,998.64	36,570.33	20,739.25	48,448.70	16,474.13	17,850.24	17,850.24	16,418.92	34,631.46	50,998.64	54,464.95
116	51,447.75	36,880.77	20,854.17	48,875.36	16,564.23	17,981.51	17,981.51	16,512.29	34,904.94	51,447.75	54,944.01
117	51,896.97	37,191.20	20,969.08	49,302.12	16,654.33	18,112.78	18,112.78	16,605.66	35,178.49	51,896.97	55,423.07
118	52,346.29	37,501.64	21,083.99	49,728.98	16,744.43	18,244.06	18,244.06	16,699.03	35,452.09	52,346.29	55,902.12
119	52,795.73	37,812.07	21,198.91	50,155.94	16,834.53	18,375.35	18,375.35	16,792.40	35,725.74	52,795.73	56,381.19
120	53,245.27	38,122.51	21,313.82	50,583.00	16,924.63	18,506.65	18,506.65	16,885.77	35,999.46	53,245.27	56,860.25
121	53,694.91	38,432.95	21,428.73	51,010.17	17,014.73	18,637.95	18,637.95	16,979.14	36,273.23	53,694.91	57,339.30
122	54,137.91	38,743.38	21,543.64	51,431.02	17,104.83	18,768.69	18,768.69	17,072.51	36,543.17	54,137.91	57,818.36
123	54,580.90	39,053.82	21,658.55	51,851.87	17,194.93	18,899.43	18,899.43	17,165.88	36,813.11	54,580.90	58,297.42
124	55,023.91	39,360.61	21,771.79	52,272.71	17,285.03	19,030.16	19,030.16	17,259.25	37,083.05	55,023.91	58,775.55
125	55,466.90	39,666.39	21,884.98	52,693.55	17,375.13	19,160.90	19,160.90	17,352.62	37,353.00	55,466.90	59,247.42
126	55,909.89	39,972.16	21,998.17	53,114.41	17,465.23	19,291.63	19,291.63	17,445.93	37,622.93	55,909.89	59,719.29
127	56,352.90	40,277.95	22,111.36	53,535.25	17,555.33	19,422.37	19,422.37	17,537.91	37,892.88	56,352.90	60,191.17
128	56,795.89	40,583.73	22,224.55	53,956.10	17,645.43	19,553.11	19,553.11	17,629.88	38,162.82	56,795.89	60,663.04
129	57,238.88	40,889.51	22,337.74	54,376.94	17,735.53	19,683.85	19,683.85	17,721.85	38,432.76	57,238.88	61,134.92
130	57,681.88	41,195.29	22,450.92	54,797.79	17,825.63	19,814.58	19,814.58	17,813.82	38,702.70	57,681.88	61,606.79
131	58,124.87	41,501.07	22,564.12	55,218.63	17,915.74	19,945.32	19,945.32	17,905.79	38,972.65	58,124.87	62,078.65
132	58,567.87	41,806.85	22,677.30	55,639.48	18,005.84	20,076.06	20,076.06	17,997.76	39,242.58	58,567.87	62,550.53
133	59,010.87	42,112.63	22,790.49	56,060.32	18,095.94	20,206.79	20,206.79	18,089.73	39,512.53	59,010.87	63,022.41

Trial length in Days	Trial length proxy A	Trial length proxy B	Trial length proxy C	Trial length proxy D	Trial length proxy E	Trial length proxy F	Trial length proxy G	Trial length proxy H	Trial length proxy I	Trial length proxy J	Trial length proxy K
134	59,453.86	42,418.40	22,903.68	56,481.17	18,186.04	20,337.53	20,337.53	18,181.70	39,782.47	59,453.86	63,494.28
135	59,896.86	42,724.19	23,016.87	56,902.01	18,276.14	20,468.27	20,468.27	18,273.66	40,052.42	59,896.86	63,966.15
136	60,339.86	43,029.97	23,130.07	57,322.86	18,366.24	20,599.01	20,599.01	18,365.63	40,322.36	60,339.86	64,438.02
137	60,782.85	43,335.75	23,243.25	57,743.70	18,456.34	20,729.74	20,729.74	18,457.60	40,592.30	60,782.85	64,909.90
138	61,225.85	43,641.53	23,356.44	58,164.56	18,546.44	20,860.48	20,860.48	18,549.57	40,862.24	61,225.85	65,381.77
139	61,668.84	43,947.30	23,469.63	58,585.40	18,636.54	20,991.22	20,991.22	18,641.54	41,132.19	61,668.84	65,853.64
140	62,111.84	44,253.09	23,582.82	59,006.25	18,726.64	21,121.95	21,121.95	18,733.52	41,402.13	62,111.84	66,325.52
141	62,554.83	44,558.86	23,696.01	59,427.09	18,816.74	21,252.69	21,252.69	18,825.48	41,672.07	62,554.83	66,797.38
142	62,997.82	44,864.65	23,809.20	59,847.94	18,906.84	21,383.43	21,383.43	18,917.46	41,942.01	62,997.82	67,269.26
143	63,440.83	45,170.43	23,922.38	60,268.79	18,996.95	21,514.17	21,514.17	19,009.43	42,211.96	63,440.83	67,741.13
144	63,883.82	45,476.21	24,035.58	60,689.64	19,087.05	21,644.90	21,644.90	19,101.39	42,481.89	63,883.82	68,213.00
145	64,326.82	45,781.99	24,148.77	61,110.47	19,177.15	21,775.64	21,775.64	19,193.36	42,751.84	64,326.82	68,684.88
146	64,769.82	46,087.77	24,261.95	61,531.33	19,267.25	21,906.38	21,906.38	19,285.32	43,021.78	64,769.82	69,156.75
147	65,212.81	46,393.55	24,375.15	61,952.17	19,357.35	22,037.11	22,037.11	19,377.30	43,291.72	65,212.81	69,628.62
148	65,655.81	46,699.32	24,488.33	62,373.03	19,447.45	22,167.85	22,167.85	19,469.27	43,561.66	65,655.81	70,100.49
149	66,098.81	47,005.10	24,601.52	62,793.86	19,537.55	22,298.59	22,298.59	19,561.24	43,831.61	66,098.81	70,572.37
150	66,541.80	47,310.89	24,714.71	63,214.71	19,627.65	22,429.33	22,429.33	19,653.21	44,101.54	66,541.80	71,044.25
151	66,984.79	47,616.67	24,827.90	63,635.56	19,717.75	22,560.06	22,560.06	19,745.18	44,371.49	66,984.79	71,516.11
152	67,427.79	47,922.44	24,941.09	64,056.41	19,807.85	22,690.80	22,690.80	19,837.15	44,641.43	67,427.79	71,987.98
153	67,870.78	48,228.23	25,054.28	64,477.25	19,897.95	22,821.54	22,821.54	19,929.12	44,911.37	67,870.78	72,459.86
154	68,313.78	48,534.00	25,167.46	64,898.10	19,988.05	22,952.27	22,952.27	20,021.09	45,181.32	68,313.78	72,931.73
155	68,756.78	48,839.79	25,280.66	65,318.94	20,078.16	23,083.01	23,083.01	20,113.05	45,451.26	68,756.78	73,403.61
156	69,199.78	49,145.56	25,393.84	65,739.79	20,168.26	23,213.74	23,213.74	20,205.02	45,721.20	69,199.78	73,875.48
157	69,642.77	49,451.34	25,507.03	66,160.63	20,258.36	23,344.49	23,344.49	20,297.00	45,991.14	69,642.77	74,347.34
158	70,085.77	49,757.13	25,620.22	66,581.48	20,348.46	23,475.22	23,475.22	20,388.96	46,261.09	70,085.77	74,819.22
159	70,528.77	50,062.91	25,733.41	67,002.33	20,438.56	23,605.96	23,605.96	20,480.93	46,531.02	70,528.77	75,291.10
160	70,971.76	50,368.69	25,846.61	67,423.17	20,528.66	23,736.70	23,736.70	20,572.91	46,800.97	70,971.76	75,762.97

Trial length in Days	Trial length proxy A	Trial length proxy B	Trial length proxy C	Trial length proxy D	Trial length proxy E	Trial length proxy F	Trial length proxy G	Trial length proxy H	Trial length proxy I	Trial length proxy J	Trial length proxy K
161	71,414.76	50,674.46	25,959.79	67,844.02	20,618.76	23,867.43	23,867.43	20,664.87	47,070.91	71,414.76	76,234.84
162	71,857.75	50,980.24	26,072.98	68,264.86	20,708.86	23,998.17	23,998.17	20,756.85	47,340.85	71,857.75	76,706.71
163	72,300.74	51,286.02	26,186.17	68,685.72	20,798.96	24,128.91	24,128.91	20,848.82	47,610.79	72,300.74	77,178.59
164	72,743.74	51,591.80	26,299.36	69,106.56	20,889.06	24,259.64	24,259.64	20,940.78	47,880.74	72,743.74	77,650.46
165	73,186.74	51,897.59	26,412.55	69,527.40	20,979.16	24,390.38	24,390.38	21,032.75	48,150.67	73,186.74	78,122.33
166	73,629.73	52,203.37	26,525.74	69,948.25	21,069.26	24,521.12	24,521.12	21,124.72	48,420.62	73,629.73	78,594.21
167	74,072.73	52,509.14	26,638.92	70,369.10	21,159.36	24,651.85	24,651.85	21,216.69	48,690.56	74,072.73	79,066.07
168	74,515.73	52,814.93	26,752.12	70,789.95	21,249.46	24,782.59	24,782.59	21,308.66	48,960.50	74,515.73	79,537.95
169	74,958.72	53,120.70	26,865.30	71,210.79	21,339.56	24,913.33	24,913.33	21,400.63	49,230.44	74,958.72	80,009.83
170	75,401.72	53,426.48	26,978.49	71,631.63	21,429.66	25,044.06	25,044.06	21,492.60	49,500.39	75,401.72	80,481.69
171	75,844.72	53,732.26	27,091.68	72,052.49	21,519.76	25,174.81	25,174.81	21,584.57	49,770.33	75,844.72	80,953.57
172	76,287.71	54,038.04	27,204.87	72,473.33	21,609.86	25,305.54	25,305.54	21,676.54	50,040.28	76,287.71	81,425.44
173	76,730.70	54,343.83	27,318.06	72,894.18	21,699.96	25,436.28	25,436.28	21,768.51	50,310.22	76,730.70	81,897.32
174	77,173.70	54,649.60	27,431.25	73,315.02	21,790.06	25,567.02	25,567.02	21,860.48	50,580.16	77,173.70	82,369.19
175	77,616.70	54,955.38	27,544.44	73,735.87	21,880.16	25,697.75	25,697.75	21,952.44	50,850.10	77,616.70	82,841.06
176	78,059.69	55,261.16	27,657.63	74,156.71	21,970.26	25,828.49	25,828.49	22,044.41	51,120.05	78,059.69	83,312.94
177	78,502.69	55,566.94	27,770.82	74,577.56	22,060.36	25,959.23	25,959.23	22,136.39	51,389.98	78,502.69	83,784.80
178	78,945.69	55,872.72	27,884.00	74,998.40	22,150.47	26,089.96	26,089.96	22,228.35	51,659.93	78,945.69	84,256.68
179	79,388.68	56,178.50	27,997.20	75,419.25	22,240.57	26,220.70	26,220.70	22,320.32	51,929.87	79,388.68	84,728.55
180	79,831.68	56,484.28	28,110.38	75,840.09	22,330.67	26,351.44	26,351.44	22,412.30	52,199.81	79,831.68	85,200.42
181	80,274.68	56,790.07	28,223.58	76,260.94	22,420.77	26,482.17	26,482.17	22,504.26	52,469.75	80,274.68	85,672.30
182	80,717.67	57,095.84	28,336.77	76,681.78	22,510.87	26,612.91	26,612.91	22,596.24	52,739.70	80,717.67	86,144.17
183	81,160.67	57,401.62	28,449.95	77,102.64	22,599.68	26,743.65	26,743.65	22,688.21	53,009.63	81,160.67	86,616.04
184	81,603.66	57,707.40	28,563.15	77,523.48	22,688.43	26,874.38	26,874.38	22,780.17	53,279.58	81,603.66	87,087.91
185	82,046.65	58,013.18	28,676.33	77,944.32	22,777.18	27,005.13	27,005.13	22,872.14	53,549.52	82,046.65	87,559.79
186	82,489.66	58,318.96	28,789.52	78,365.17	22,865.93	27,135.86	27,135.86	22,964.11	53,819.46	82,489.66	88,031.67
187	82,932.65	58,624.74	28,902.71	78,786.02	22,954.68	27,266.60	27,266.60	23,056.08	54,089.40	82,932.65	88,503.53

Trial length in Days	Trial length proxy A	Trial length proxy B	Trial length proxy C	Trial length proxy D	Trial length proxy E	Trial length proxy F	Trial length proxy G	Trial length proxy H	Trial length proxy I	Trial length proxy J	Trial length proxy K
188	83,375.65	58,930.52	29,015.90	79,206.87	23,043.43	27,397.34	27,397.34	23,148.05	54,359.35	83,375.65	88,975.40
189	83,818.64	59,236.30	29,129.09	79,627.71	23,132.18	27,528.06	27,528.06	23,240.02	54,629.29	83,818.64	89,447.28
190	84,261.64	59,542.08	29,242.28	80,048.55	23,220.93	27,658.81	27,658.81	23,331.99	54,899.23	84,261.64	89,919.15
191	84,704.64	59,847.86	29,355.46	80,469.41	23,309.68	27,789.55	27,789.55	23,423.96	55,169.18	84,704.64	90,391.03
192	85,147.63	60,153.64	29,468.66	80,890.25	23,398.43	27,920.28	27,920.28	23,515.94	55,439.11	85,147.63	90,862.90
193	85,590.63	60,459.41	29,581.84	81,311.10	23,487.18	28,051.02	28,051.02	23,607.90	55,709.06	85,590.63	91,334.76
194	86,033.62	60,765.20	29,695.03	81,731.94	23,575.92	28,181.76	28,181.76	23,699.87	55,979.00	86,033.62	91,806.64
195	86,476.61	61,070.98	29,808.22	82,152.79	23,664.67	28,312.49	28,312.49	23,791.84	56,248.94	86,476.61	92,278.52
196	86,919.61	61,376.76	29,921.41	82,573.64	23,753.42	28,443.23	28,443.23	23,883.80	56,518.88	86,919.61	92,750.39
197	87,362.61	61,682.54	30,034.60	82,994.48	23,842.17	28,573.96	28,573.96	23,975.78	56,788.83	87,362.61	93,222.26
198	87,805.60	61,988.32	30,147.79	83,415.33	23,930.92	28,704.70	28,704.70	24,067.75	57,058.76	87,805.60	93,694.13
199	88,248.61	62,294.10	30,260.97	83,836.17	24,019.67	28,835.45	28,835.45	24,159.72	57,328.71	88,248.61	94,166.01
200	88,691.60	62,599.87	30,374.17	84,257.02	24,108.42	28,966.17	28,966.17	24,251.69	57,598.65	88,691.60	94,637.88

[The tables following sub-paras 7(2) and (3) are printed as substituted by the Criminal Legal Aid (Remuneration) (Amendment) Regulations 2014 (S.I. 2014 No. 415). As to their application, see *ante*, G-71.]

Cracked trials and guilty pleas where the number of pages of prosecution evidence exceeds the PPE Cut-off

G-72   8.—(1) Where in a cracked trial or guilty plea the number of pages of prosecution evidence exceeds the PPE Cut-off specified in the table following paragraph 5(1) as appropriate to the offence with which the assisted person is charged, the total fee payable to the litigator is—

   (a) the final fee, calculated in accordance with sub-paragraph (2) of this paragraph;

   (b) the defendant uplift, if any, calculated in accordance with the table following paragraph 12; and

   (c) the adjustment for transfers and retrials, if any, calculated in accordance with paragraph 13.

(2) For the purposes of sub-paragraph (1), the final fee payable to a litigator in a cracked trial or guilty plea is calculated in accordance with the following formula—

$$F = I + (D \times i)$$

Where—

• **F** is the amount of the final fee;

• **I** is the initial fee specified in the tables following this paragraph, as appropriate to the type of case, the offence with which the assisted person is charged and the number of pages of prosecution evidence;

• **D** is the difference between—

   (i) the number of pages of prosecution evidence in the case; and

   (ii) the lower number in the PPE range as specified in the tables following this paragraph, as appropriate to the type of case, the offence with which the assisted person is charged and the number of pages of prosecution evidence in the case;

• **i** is the incremental fee per page of prosecution evidence specified in the tables following this paragraph, as appropriate to the type of case, the offence with which the assisted person is charged and the number of pages of prosecution evidence in the case.

TABLE OF FINAL FEES IN CRACKED TRIALS

Class of Offence	PPE Range	Initial fee (£)	Incremental fee per page of prosecution evidence (£)
A and J	0–79	904.58	0
A and J	80–249	904.58	10.70
A and J	250–999	2,722.89	6.71
A and J	1000–2799	7,757.90	3.92
A and J	2800–4599	14,820.75	3.92
A and J	4600–6399	21,883.61	3.11
A and J	6400–8199	27,490.35	3.11
A and J	8200–9999	33,097.09	3.11
A and J	10,000	38,700.71	0
B	0–69	709.15	0
B	70–249	709.15	7.83
B	250–999	2,117.67	3.66
B	1000–2799	4,864.56	2.44
B	2800–4599	9,255.51	2.44
B	4600–6399	13,646.46	2.05
B	6400–8199	17,338.49	2.05
B	8200–9999	21,030.50	2.05
B	10,000	24,720.46	0
C	0–39	524.84	0
C	40–249	524.84	3.92

Class of Offence	PPE Range	Initial fee (£)	Incremental fee per page of prosecution evidence (£)
C	250–999	1,348.77	2.25
C	1000–2799	3,033.06	1.43
C	2800–4599	5,607.48	1.43
C	4600–6399	8,181.89	1.43
C	6400–8199	10,756.31	1.43
C	8200–9999	13,330.74	1.43
C	10,000	15,903.73	0
D	0–79	859.35	0
D	80–249	859.35	10.14
D	250–999	2,582.50	6.11
D	1000–2799	7,163.76	3.61
D	2800–4599	13,655.74	3.61
D	4600–6399	20,147.71	2.96
D	6400–8199	25,474.79	2.96
D	8200–9999	30,801.87	2.96
D	10,000	36,125.98	0
E	0–39	233.03	0
E	40–249	233.03	4.60
E	250–999	1,199.43	1.46
E	1000–2799	2,291.54	0.61
E	2800–4599	3,390.26	0.61
E	4600–6399	4,488.97	0.61
E	6400–8199	5,587.69	0.61
E	8200–9999	6,686.41	0.61
E	10,000	7,784.51	0
F and G	0–49	224.22	0
F and G	50–249	224.22	4.42
F and G	250–999	1,107.53	1.79
F and G	1000–2799	2,450.39	0.70
F and G	2800–4599	3,704.67	0.70
F and G	4600–6399	4,958.94	0.70
F and G	6400–8199	6,213.21	0.70
F and G	8200–9999	7,467.49	0.70
F and G	10,000	8,721.06	0
H	0–39	237.00	0
H	40–249	237.00	4.26
H	250–999	1,131.61	1.56
H	1000–2799	2,298.20	0.70
H	2800–4599	3,550.79	0.70
H	4600–6399	4,803.37	0.70
H	6400–8199	6,055.96	0.70
H	8200–9999	7,308.55	0.70
H	10,000	8,560.44	0

Class of Offence	PPE Range	Initial fee (£)	Incremental fee per page of prosecution evidence (£)
I	0–39	253.68	0
I	40–249	253.68	5.92
I	250–999	1,496.80	2.31
I	1000–2799	3,231.91	0.90
I	2800–4599	4,847.36	0.90
I	4600–6399	6,462.79	0.90
I	6400–8199	8,078.23	0.90
I	8200–9999	9,693.67	0.90
I	10,000	11,308.20	0
K	0–119	773.86	0
K	120–249	773.86	6.55
K	250–999	1,624.85	5.02
K	1000–2799	5,388.98	4.39
K	2800–4599	13,299.04	4.39
K	4600–6399	21,209.12	3.75
K	6400–8199	27,954.29	3.75
K	8200–9999	34,699.46	3.75
K	10,000	41,440.89	0

TABLE OF FINAL FEES IN GUILTY PLEAS

Class of Offence	PPE Range	Initial fee (£)	Incremental fee per page of prosecution evidence (£)
A and J	0–79	680.39	0
A and J	80–399	680.39	5.62
A and J	400–999	2,478.29	2.96
A and J	1000–2799	4,256.09	1.89
A and J	2800–4599	7,666.89	1.89
A and J	4600–6399	11,077.68	1.12
A and J	6400–8199	13,090.60	1.12
A and J	8200–9999	15,103.53	1.12
A and J	10,000	17,115.33	0
B	0–69	556.11	0
B	70–399	556.11	4.52
B	400–999	2,046.59	2.28
B	1000–2799	3,411.75	1.45
B	2800–4599	6,025.92	1.45
B	4600–6399	8,640.11	1.06
B	6400–8199	10,555.35	1.06
B	8200–9999	12,470.60	1.06
B	10,000	14,384.78	0
C	0–39	442.91	0
C	40–399	442.91	2.66
C	400–999	1,401.88	1.46

Class of Offence	PPE Range	Initial fee (£)	Incremental fee per page of prosecution evidence (£)
C	1000–2799	2,276.27	0.79
C	2800–4599	3,699.93	0.79
C	4600–6399	5,123.61	0.79
C	6400–8199	6,547.28	0.79
C	8200–9999	7,970.95	0.79
C	10,000	9,393.82	0
D	0–79	646.36	0
D	80–399	646.36	5.23
D	400–999	2,320.66	2.75
D	1000–2799	3,968.37	1.71
D	2800–4599	7,046.20	1.71
D	4600–6399	10,124.03	1.06
D	6400–8199	12,036.98	1.06
D	8200–9999	13,949.91	1.06
D	10,000	15,861.79	0
E	0–39	184.70	0
E	40–399	184.70	2.92
E	400–999	1,237.24	1.25
E	1000–2799	1,989.07	0.46
E	2800–4599	2,819.70	0.46
E	4600–6399	3,650.33	0.46
E	6400–8199	4,480.96	0.46
E	8200–9999	5,311.59	0.46
E	10,000	6,141.75	0
F and G	0–49	195.81	0
F and G	50–399	195.81	2.83
F and G	400–999	1,187.73	0.99
F and G	1000–2799	1,781.21	0.32
F and G	2800–4599	2,354.07	0.32
F and G	4600–6399	2,926.93	0.32
F and G	6400–8199	3,499.78	0.32
F and G	8200–9999	4,072.64	0.32
F and G	10,000	4,645.18	0
H	0–39	190.97	0
H	40–399	190.97	2.79
H	400–999	1,196.59	0.99
H	1000–2799	1,790.74	0.32
H	2800–4599	2,359.85	0.32
H	4600–6399	2,928.98	0.32
H	6400–8199	3,498.10	0.32
H	8200–9999	4,067.22	0.32
H	10,000	4,636.00	0
I	0–39	174.60	0

Class of Offence	PPE Range	Initial fee (£)	Incremental fee per page of prosecution evidence (£)
I	40–399	174.60	3.12
I	400–999	1,298.52	1.36
I	1000–2799	2,116.29	0.51
I	2800–4599	3,033.02	0.51
I	4600–6399	3,949.75	0.51
I	6400–8199	4,866.48	0.51
I	8200–9999	5,783.22	0.51
I	10,000	6,699.45	0
K	0–119	640.84	0
K	120–399	640.84	5.26
K	400–999	2,113.13	2.93
K	1000–2799	3,869.24	2.73
K	2800–4599	8,775.55	2.73
K	4600–6399	13,681.86	2.08
K	6400–8199	17,423.28	2.08
K	8200–9999	21,164.71	2.08
K	10,000	24,904.04	0

[The tables in para. 8 are printed as substituted by the Criminal Legal Aid (Remuneration) (Amendment) Regulations 2014 (S.I. 2014 No. 415). As to their application, see *ante*, G-71.]

Trials where the number of pages of prosecution evidence exceeds the PPE Cut-off

G-72a   9.—(1) Where in a trial the number of pages of prosecution evidence exceeds the PPE Cut-off figure specified in the table following paragraph 5(2) as appropriate to the offence for which the assisted person is tried and the length of trial, the total fee payable to the litigator is—

(a) the final fee, calculated in accordance with sub-paragraph (2) of this paragraph;

(b) the defendant uplift, if any, calculated in accordance with the table following paragraph 12; and

(c) the adjustment for transfers and retrials, if any, calculated in accordance with paragraph 13.

(2) For the purposes of sub-paragraph (1), the final fee is calculated in accordance with the following formula—

$$F = I + (D \times i)$$

Where—

• **F** is the amount of the final fee;

• **I** is the initial fee specified in the table following this paragraph as appropriate to the offence for which the assisted person is tried and the number of pages of prosecution evidence;

• **D** is the difference between—

(i) the number of pages of prosecution evidence in the case; and

(ii) the lower number in the PPE range as specified in the table following this paragraph, as appropriate to the offence for which the assisted person is tried and the number of pages of prosecution evidence in the case;

• **i** is the incremental fee per page of prosecution evidence specified in the table following this paragraph, as appropriate to the offence for which the assisted person is tried and the number of pages of prosecution evidence in the case.

TABLE OF FINAL FEES IN TRIALS

Offence Class	PPE Range	Initial Fee	Incremental fee per page
A and J	0–79	1,467.58	0
A and J	80–209	1,467.58	16.58

Offence Class	PPE Range	Initial Fee	Incremental fee per page
A and J	210–699	3,622.54	12.66
A and J	700–1049	9,824.91	10.62
A and J	1050–1999	13,543.42	9.21
A and J	2000–3599	22,295.42	8.42
A and J	3600–5199	35,767.03	8.42
A and J	5200–6799	49,238.64	8.42
A and J	6800–8399	62,710.26	8.42
A and J	8400–9999	76,181.87	8.42
A and J	10,000	89,645.06	0
B	0–69	1,097.66	0
B	70–199	1,097.66	12.81
B	200–499	2,762.60	11.44
B	500–899	6,195.38	9.63
B	900–1299	10,048.21	8.09
B	1300–1999	13,285.03	7.09
B	2000–3299	18,249.51	7.09
B	3300–4999	27,469.24	7.09
B	5000–5999	39,525.82	7.09
B	6000–7999	46,617.93	7.09
B	8000–8999	60,802.14	7.09
B	9000–9999	67,894.24	7.09
B	10,000	74,979.26	0
C	0–39	739.59	0
C	40–299	739.59	10.57
C	300–799	3,486.54	9.23
C	800–1249	8,101.74	7.73
C	1250–1999	11,578.09	6.83
C	2000–3199	16,700.93	4.72
C	3200–4559	22,368.79	4.72
C	4560–5919	28,792.38	4.72
C	5920–7279	35,215.96	4.72
C	7280–8639	41,639.54	4.72
C	8640–9999	48,063.12	4.72
C	10,000	54,482.00	0
D	0–79	1,394.20	0
D	80–209	1,394.20	15.75
D	210–699	3,441.41	12.03
D	700–1049	9,333.67	10.09
D	1050–1999	12,866.25	8.75
D	2000–3599	21,180.65	8.00
D	3600–5199	33,978.67	8.00
D	5200–6799	46,776.70	8.00
D	6800–8399	59,574.74	8.00
D	8400–9999	72,372.77	8.00
D	10,000	85,162.80	0

Offence Class	PPE Range	Initial Fee	Incremental fee per page
E	0–39	352.72	0
E	40–69	352.72	9.52
E	70–129	638.20	8.57
E	130–599	1,152.58	8.29
E	600–1349	5,049.74	5.44
E	1350–2999	9,131.96	2.39
E	3000–4749	13,072.77	2.39
E	4750–6499	17,252.41	2.39
E	6500–8249	21,432.04	2.39
E	8250–9999	25,611.69	2.39
E	10,000	29,788.93	0
F and G	0–49	357.60	0
F and G	50–229	357.60	7.31
F and G	230–699	1,673.21	6.96
F and G	700–1399	4,946.64	5.60
F and G	1400–1949	8,865.80	4.32
F and G	1950–3549	11,242.37	2.16
F and G	3550–5149	14,691.41	2.16
F and G	5150–6749	18,140.45	2.16
F and G	6750–8349	21,589.49	2.16
F and G	8350–9999	25,038.53	2.16
F and G	10,000	28,593.21	0
H	0–39	357.75	0
H	40–249	357.75	8.60
H	250–619	2,162.92	7.15
H	620–1299	4,807.79	5.31
H	1300–2999	8,418.74	4.21
H	3000–4999	15,583.59	2.27
H	5000–5999	20,129.84	2.27
H	6000–6999	22,402.90	2.27
H	7000–7999	24,676.03	2.27
H	8000–8999	26,949.15	2.27
H	9000–9999	29,222.28	2.27
H	10,000	31,493.13	0
I	0–39	357.44	0
I	40–369	357.44	9.14
I	370–799	3,373.66	9.09
I	800–1299	7,282.43	8.99
I	1300–2699	11,779.02	7.08
I	2700–4199	21,697.63	3.04
I	4200–5359	26,264.52	3.04
I	5360–6519	29,796.25	3.04
I	6520–7679	33,327.97	3.04
I	7680–8839	36,859.71	3.04
I	8840–9999	40,391.43	3.04

Offence Class	PPE Range	Initial Fee	Incremental fee per page
I	10,000	43,920.11	0
K	0–119	1,031.82	0
K	120–734	1,031.82	8.66
K	735-1289	6,356.06	8.72
K	1290–2399	11,193.67	8.87
K	2400–4499	21,042.53	8.84
K	4500–7999	39,605.74	8.84
K	8000–8399	70,544.40	8.84
K	8400–8799	74,080.24	8.84
K	8800–9199	77,616.08	8.84
K	9200–9599	81,151.94	8.84
K	9600–9999	84,687.78	8.84
K	10,000	88,214.79	0

[The table in para. 9 is printed as substituted by the Criminal Legal Aid (Remuneration) (Amendment) Regulations 2014 (S.I. 2014 No. 415). As to its application, see *ante*, G-71.]

PART 3

FIXED FEE FOR GUILTY PLEAS AND CRACKED TRIALS

Scope of Part 3

G-73

10.—(1) Subject to sub-paragraph (2), this Part applies to a case committed or sent for trial to the Crown Court on the election of a defendant where the magistrates' court has determined the case to be suitable for summary trial.

(2) This Part does not apply where the trial is a cracked trial because the prosecution offer no evidence on all counts against a defendant and the judge directs that a not guilty verdict be entered.

[This paragraph was substituted by S.I. 2014 No. 2422 (*ante*, G-21a). For the transitional provision, see *ante*, G-21a.]

Fixed fee for guilty pleas or cracked trials

11. The fee payable to a litigator in relation to a guilty plea or cracked trial to which this Part applies is £330.33 per proceedings.

[Para. 11 is printed as amended by the Criminal Legal Aid (Remuneration) (Amendment) Regulations 2014 (S.I. 2014 No. 415). As to the application of this amendment, see *ante*, G-71.]

PART 4

DEFENDANT UPLIFTS, RETRIALS AND TRANSFERS

Defendant uplifts

G-73a

12.—(1) The defendant uplift payable to a litigator is calculated in accordance with the table following this paragraph.

(2) Only one defendant uplift is payable in each case.

(3) In the table following this paragraph, the total fee means—

(a) in a cracked trial or guilty plea where the number of pages of prosecution evidence does not exceed the PPE Cut-off specified in the table following paragraph 5(1), the basic fee specified in the table following paragraph 6(2);

(b) in a trial where the number of pages of prosecution evidence does not exceed the PPE Cut-off specified in the table following paragraph 5(2), the basic fee specified in the table following paragraph 7(2) plus the length of trial proxy specified in the table following paragraph 7(3);

(c) in a cracked trial or guilty plea where the number of pages of prosecution evidence exceeds the PPE Cut-off specified in the table following paragraph 5(1), the final fee, as calculated in accordance with paragraph 8(2); and

(d) in a trial where the number of pages of prosecution evidence exceeds the PPE Cut-off specified in the table following paragraph 5(2), the final fee, as calculated in accordance with paragraph 9(2);

(e)   where appropriate, the fee set out in paragraph 11.

(4) In a case where the representation of one defendant would attract a fixed fee under Part 3 and the representation of one or more of the other defendants would attract a graduated fee under Part 2, the total fee is the fee falling within whichever of paragraphs (a) to (d) of sub-paragraph (3) is appropriate.

Defendant Uplifts

Total number of defendants represented by litigator	Percentage uplift to total fee
2–4	20%
5+	30%

Retrials and transfers

13.—(1) Where following a trial an order is made for a retrial and the same litigator acts for the assisted person at both trials the fee payable to that litigator is—

(a)   in respect of the first trial, a fee calculated in accordance with the provisions of this Schedule; and

(b)   in respect of the retrial, 25% of the fee, as appropriate to the circumstances of the retrial, in accordance with the provisions of this Schedule.

(2) Where—

(a)   a case is transferred to a new litigator; or

(b)   a retrial is ordered and a new litigator acts for the assisted person at the retrial,

the fee payable to the original litigator and the new litigator is a percentage of the total fee, calculated in accordance with the table following this paragraph, as appropriate to the circumstances and timing of the retrial, transfer or withdrawal of the section 16 determination.

(3) In sub-paragraph (2), "transfer" includes the making of a section 16 determination in favour of an individual who, immediately before the making of the section 16 determination—

(a)   had represented themselves; or

(b)   had been represented (otherwise than pursuant to a section 16 determination) by the litigator named in the order,

and for the purposes of that sub-paragraph the litigator is to be treated as a new litigator.

(4) For the purposes of sub-paragraph (2), a case is not transferred to a new litigator where—

(a)   a firm of solicitors is named as litigator in the representation order and the solicitor or other appropriately qualified person with responsibility for the case moves to another firm;

(b)   a firm of solicitors is named as litigator in the representation order and the firm changes (whether by merger or acquisition or in some other way), but so that the new firm remains closely related to the firm named in the order; or

(c)   a solicitor or other appropriately qualified person is named as litigator in the representation order and responsibility for the case is transferred to another solicitor or appropriately qualified person in the same firm or a closely related firm.

(5) For the purposes of sub-paragraph (2), where a case which has been transferred to a new litigator is transferred again, that new litigator—

(a)   must be treated as the original litigator, where the transfer takes place at any time before the trial or any retrial;

(b)   must be treated as a new litigator, where the transfer takes place during the trial or any retrial; and

(c)   must not receive any fee, where the transfer takes place after the trial or any retrial but before the sentencing hearing.

(6) Where a section 16 determination is withdrawn before the case ends, a litigator must receive a percentage of the total fee, in accordance with the table following this paragraph, as appropriate to the circumstances and timing of a transfer.

(7) In the table following this paragraph, the total fee means—

(a)   in a cracked trial or guilty plea in a case to which Part 2 applies, where the number of pages of prosecution evidence is less than or equal to the PPE Cut-off specified in the table following paragraph 5(1), the basic fee as set out in the table following paragraph 6(2);

(b)   in a trial where the number of pages of prosecution evidence is less than or equal to the PPE Cut-off specified in the table following paragraph 5(2), the basic fee specified in the table following paragraph 7(2) plus the length of trial proxy specified in the table following paragraph 7(3);

(c)   in a cracked trial or guilty plea in a case to which Part 2 applies, where the number of pages of prosecution evidence exceeds the PPE Cut-off specified in the table following paragraph 5(1), the final fee as calculated in accordance with paragraph 8(2);

(d) in a trial where the number of pages of prosecution evidence exceeds the PPE Cut-off specified in the table following paragraph 5(2), the final fee, as calculated in accordance with paragraph 9(2);

(e) in a cracked trial or guilty plea in a case to which Part 3 applies, the fixed fee set out in paragraph 11.

(8) Where a case becomes a Very High Cost Case after a section 16 determination has been made and is transferred from the litigator named on the representation order to a new litigator—

(a) the original litigator must be remunerated in accordance with the individual Very High Cost Case contract entered into by that litigator; and

(b) the new litigator must be remunerated in accordance with the individual Very High Cost Case contract entered into by that litigator.

(9) Where a case becomes a Very High Cost Case after a section 16 determination has been made and the section 16 determination is withdrawn before the end of the case, the litigator must be remunerated in accordance with the table following this paragraph as appropriate to the circumstances and timing of the withdrawal.

(10) Sub-paragraph (11) applies where—

(a) the case is a case to which Part 3 would apply if it resulted in a cracked trial or guilty plea; and

(b) at the time the case is transferred to a new litigator in accordance with sub-paragraph (2) it is not known whether the case would result in a cracked trial or guilty plea or whether it would proceed to trial.

(11) Where this sub-paragraph applies—

(a) for the purpose of a claim by the original litigator at the time of the transfer of the case, "total fee" in the table following this paragraph, means the fixed fee set out in paragraph 11;

(b) the original litigator may, if the case proceeds to trial, claim the difference between the payment received at the time of transfer of the case and the payment that would have been due at that time if that payment had been based on the case proceeding to trial.

(12) A litigator may not be treated both as an original litigator and as a new litigator in a case.

RETRIALS AND TRANSFERS

Scenario	Percentage of the total fee	Case type used to determine total fee	Claim period
Cracked trial before retrial, where there is no change of litigator	25%	Cracked trial	—
Retrial, where there is no change of litigator	25%	Trial	—
Up to and including plea and case management hearing transfer (original litigator)	25%	Cracked trial	—
Up to and including plea and case management hearing transfer — guilty plea (new litiga-tor)	100%	Guilty plea	—
Up to and including plea and case management hearing transfer — cracked trial (new litigator)	100%	Cracked trial	—
Up to and including plea and case management hearing transfer — trial (new litigator)	100%	Trial	—
Before trial transfer (original litigator)	75%	Cracked trial	—
Before trial transfer — cracked trial (new litigator)	100%	Cracked trial	—
Before trial transfer — trial (new litigator)	100%	Trial	—

Scenario	Percentage of the total fee	Case type used to determine total fee	Claim period
During trial transfer (original litigator)	100%	Trial	Claim up to and including the day before the transfer
During trial transfer (new litigator)	50%	Trial	Claim for the full trial length
Transfer after trial or guilty plea and before sentencing hearing (original litigator)	100%	Trial, cracked trial or guilty plea as appropriate	Claim for the full trial length, excluding the length of the sentencing hearing
Transfer after trial or guilty plea and before sentencing hearing (new litigator)	10%	Trial	Claim for one day, or for the length of the sentencing hearing if longer than one day
Transfer before retrial (original litigator)	25%	Cracked trial	—
Transfer before cracked retrial (new litigator)	50%	Cracked trial	
Transfer before retrial (new litigator)	50%	Trial	Claim for the full retrial length
Transfer during retrial (original litigator)	25%	Trial	Claim up to and including the day before the transfer
Transfer during retrial (new litigator)	50%	Trial	Claim for the full retrial length
Transfer after retrial or cracked retrial and before sentencing hearing (original litigator)	25%	Trial or cracked trial as appropriate	Claim for the full retrial length, excluding the length of the sentencing hearing
Transfer after retrial or cracked retrial and before sentencing hearing (new litigator)	10%	Trial	Claim for one day, or for the length of the sentencing hearing if longer than one day

PART 5

FIXED FEES

General provisions

G-74   14.—(1) All work undertaken by a litigator in a case to which Part 3 applies is included within the fee set out in paragraph 11 except for a defendant uplift as provided for in paragraph 22.

(2) Except as provided under this Part, remuneration for all work undertaken by a litigator in a case to which Part 2 applies is included within the fee set out in Part 2 of this Schedule as appropriate to—

    (a)   the offence for which the assisted person is charged or tried;

    (b)   whether the case is a cracked trial, guilty plea or trial; and

    (c)   the number of pages of prosecution evidence.

Fees for appeals and committals for sentence hearings

G-74a   15. The fee payable to a litigator instructed in—

    (a)   an appeal against conviction from a magistrates' court;

    (b)   an appeal against sentence from a magistrates' court; or

    (c)   a sentencing hearing following a committal for sentence to the Crown Court,

is that set out in the table following paragraph 19.

Fees for hearing subsequent to sentence

16.—(1) The fee payable to a litigator instructed in relation to a hearing under an enactment listed   **G-74b**
in sub-paragraph (2) is that set out in the table following paragraph 19.

(2) The enactments are—

(a) section 1CA of the Crime and Disorder Act 1998 (variation and discharge of orders under
section 1C);

(b) section 155 of the Powers of Criminal Courts (Sentencing) Act 2000 (alteration of Crown
Court sentence);

(c) section 74 of the Serious Organised Crime and Police Act 2005 (assistance by defendant:
review of sentence).

Fees for contempt proceedings

17.—(1) This paragraph applies to proceedings referred to in section 14(g) of the Act in the   **G-75**
Crown Court.

(2) Where, in proceedings to which this paragraph applies, the contempt is alleged to have been
committed by a person other than a defendant in a case to which this Schedule applies, remuneration for litigators must be at the rate set out in the table following paragraph 19.

(3) Where, in proceedings to which this paragraph applies, the contempt is alleged to have been
committed by the defendant in a case to which this Schedule applies, all work undertaken by the
litigator is included within—

(a) the fee payable under Part 2 of this Schedule, or

(b) in proceedings under paragraph 15 or paragraph 18, the fixed fee set out in the table following paragraph 19.

Fees for alleged breaches of a Crown Court order

18.—(1) This paragraph applies to proceedings in the Crown Court against one assisted person   **G-75a**
arising out of a single alleged breach of an order of the Crown Court.

(3) The fee payable to the litigator in respect of the proceedings to which this paragraph applies is
that set out in the table following paragraph 19.

Fixed Fees

19. The table following this paragraph sets out the fixed fees payable in relation to the category of
work specified in the first column of the table.

FIXED FEES

Type of proceedings	*Paragraph providing for free*	*Fee payable (£ per proceedings)*
Appeal against sentence from a magistrates' Court	15	155.32
Appeal against conviction from a magistrates' Court	15	349.47
Committal for sentence	15	232.98
Hearing subsequent to sentence	16	155.32
Contempt proceedings (where contempt is alleged to have been committed by a person other than the defendant)	17(2)	116.49
Alleged breach of a Crown Court order	18(2)	77.66

[The table in para. 19 is printed as substituted by the Criminal Legal Aid (Remuneration)
(Amendment) Regulations 2014 (S.I. 2014 No. 415). As to its application, see *ante*, G-71.]

Fees for special preparation

20.—(1) This paragraph applies in any case on indictment in the Crown Court—   **G-76**

(a) where a documentary or pictorial exhibit is served by the prosecution in electronic form
and—

(i)   the exhibit has never existed in paper form; and

(ii) the appropriate officer does not consider it appropriate to include the exhibit in the
pages of prosecution evidence; or

(b) in respect of which a fee is payable under Part 2 (other than paragraph 7), where the
number of pages of prosecution evidence, as so defined, exceeds 10,000,

and the appropriate officer considers it reasonable to make a payment in excess of the fee payable
under Part 2.

(2) Where this paragraph applies, a special preparation fee may be paid, in addition to the fee payable under Part 2.

(3) The amount of the special preparation fee must be calculated from the number of hours which the appropriate officer considers reasonable—

(a)   where sub-paragraph (1)(a) applies, to view the prosecution evidence; and

(b)   where sub-paragraph (1)(b) applies, to read the excess pages,

and in each case using the rates specified in the table following paragraph 27.

(4) A litigator claiming a special preparation fee must supply such information and documents as may be required by the appropriate officer in support of the claim.

(5) In determining a claim under this paragraph, the appropriate officer must take into account all the relevant circumstances of the case.

Discontinuance or dismissal of sent or transferred proceedings

G-76a   21.—(1) This paragraph applies to proceedings which are—

(a)   sent for trial to the Crown Court; or

(b)   transferred to the Crown Court under—

(i)   section 4 of the Criminal Justice Act 1987 (transfer of serious fraud cases); or

(ii)   section 53 of the Criminal Justice Act 1991 (transfer of certain cases involving children).

(2) Where proceedings to which this paragraph applies are discontinued by a notice served under section 23A of the Prosecution of Offences Act 1985 (discontinuance of proceedings after accused has been sent for trial) at any time before the prosecution serves its evidence in accordance with the Crime and Disorder Act 1998 (Service of Prosecution Evidence) Regulations 2005 the litigator must be paid 50% of the basic fee for a guilty plea, as specified in the table following paragraph 6, as appropriate to the offence for which the assisted person is charged.

(3) Where proceedings to which this paragraph applies are discontinued by a notice served under section 23A of the Prosecution of Offences Act 1985 (discontinuance of proceedings after accused has been sent for trial) at any time after the prosecution serves its evidence in accordance with the Crime and Disorder Act 1998 (Service of Prosecution Evidence) Regulations 2005, the litigator must be paid a fee calculated in accordance with paragraph 6, or, where appropriate, paragraph 8, as appropriate for representing an assisted person in a guilty plea.

(4) Where an application for dismissal is made under paragraph 2 of Schedule 3 to the Crime and Disorder Act 1998, section 6 of the Criminal Justice Act 1987 or paragraph 5 of Schedule 6 to the Criminal Justice Act 1991, and—

(a)   the charge, or charges are dismissed and the assisted person is discharged; or

(b)   the case is remitted to the magistrates' court in accordance with paragraph 10(3)(a), 13(2) or 15(3)(a) of Schedule 3 to the Crime and Disorder Act 1998,

the litigator instructed in the proceedings must be paid a fee calculated in accordance with paragraph 6, or where appropriate, paragraph 8, as appropriate for representing an assisted person in a guilty plea.

(5) Sub-paragraph (6) applies to—

(a)   a plea and case management hearing that takes place after the prosecution serves its evidence; and

(b)   any other hearing that takes place before a plea and case management hearing has taken place, but after the prosecution has served its evidence.

(6) Where, at a hearing to which this paragraph applies—

(a)   the prosecution offers no evidence and the assisted person is discharged; or

(b)   the case is remitted to the magistrates' court in accordance with paragraph 10(3)(a), 13(2) or 15(3)(a) of Schedule 3 to the Crime and Disorder Act 1998,

the litigator must be paid a fee calculated in accordance with paragraph 6 or where appropriate paragraph 8, as appropriate for representing an assisted person in a guilty plea.

Defendant uplifts

G-77   22.—(1) Where a litigator represents more than one assisted person in proceedings referred to in paragraph 21(2), (3), (4) or (5), a defendant uplift is payable.

(2) The defendant uplift must be calculated in accordance with the table following this paragraph.

(3) In the table following this paragraph, the total fee means—

(a)   the fee specified in sub-paragraph (2) of paragraph 21 where that sub-paragraph applies;

(b)   the basic fee (B) specified in the table following paragraph 6, or, where appropriate, the initial fee specified in paragraph 8, where paragraph 21(3), (4) or (5) applies, as appropriate for the circumstances set out in that sub-paragraph; or

    (c) where appropriate the fee set out in paragraph 11.

    (4) In a case where the representation of one defendant would attract a fixed fee under Part 3 and the representation of one or more of the other defendants would attract a graduated fee under Part 2, the total fee in the table following this paragraph means the fee falling within sub-paragraph (3)(b).

DEFENDANT UPLIFTS

Total number of defendants represented by litigator	Percentage uplift to total fee
2–4	20%
5+	30%

Warrant for arrest

    23.—(1) This paragraph applies where—   **G-77a**

    (a) the assisted person fails to attend a hearing;

    (b) at that hearing the court issues a warrant for the arrest of the assisted person, pursuant to section 7(1) of the Bail Act 1976 ("the warrant"); and

    (c) the case does not proceed in the absence of the assisted person.

    (2) Where in a case on indictment the warrant is not executed within three months of the date on which it was issued, the fee payable to the litigator is—

    (a) where the warrant is issued at or before the plea and case management hearing, the fee payable for a guilty plea in accordance with paragraph 6 or where appropriate paragraph 8;

    (b) where the warrant is issued after the plea and case management hearing but before the trial, the fee payable for a cracked trial in accordance with paragraph 6 or where appropriate paragraph 8, as appropriate to the Class of Offence with which the assisted person is charged; and

    (c) where the warrant is issued during the trial, and the trial is aborted as a result, the fee payable for a trial as if the trial had ended on the day the warrant was issued.

    (3) Where the warrant is issued during the course of proceedings referred to in paragraph 15 or 18 the fee payable to the litigator is the fee set out in the table following paragraph 19, as appropriate to the type of proceedings.

    (4) Sub-paragraph (5) applies where—

    (a) a fee has been paid, or is payable, to the litigator in accordance with sub-paragraph (2);

    (b) the warrant is executed within 15 months of the date on which it was issued;

    (c) the case proceeds after the warrant has been executed; and

    (d) the litigator submits a claim for fees for the determination of the litigator's overall remuneration in the case, in accordance with regulation 5.

    (5) Where this sub-paragraph applies—

    (a) the appropriate officer must deduct the amount paid or payable in accordance with sub-paragraph (2) from the amount payable to the litigator on the final determination of fees in the case; and

    (b) if the fee paid or payable in accordance with sub-paragraph (2) is greater than the amount payable to the litigator on the final determination of fees in the case, the appropriate officer may recover the amount of the difference by way of repayment by the litigator.

PART 6

MISCELLANEOUS

Additional charges

    24.—(1) Where an assisted person is charged with more than one offence on one indictment, the   **G-78** fee payable to the litigator under this Schedule must be based on whichever of those offences the litigator selects.

    (2) Where a litigator selects one offence, in preference to another offence, under sub-paragraph (1) that selection does not affect the litigator's right to claim any of the fees provided for in Part 5 of this Schedule to which the litigator would otherwise have been entitled.

Assisted person unfit to plead or stand trial

    25. Where in any case a hearing is held to determine the question of whether the assisted person   **G-78a** is unfit to plead or to stand trial (a "fitness hearing")—

    (a) if a trial on indictment is held, or continues, at any time thereafter, the length of the fitness hearing is included in determining the length of the trial for the calculation of the fee in accordance with Part 2;

   (b) if a trial on indictment is not held, or does not continue, thereafter by reason of the assisted person being found unfit to plead or to stand trial, the litigator must be paid—

      (i) a fee calculated in accordance with paragraph 7 or where appropriate paragraph 9, as appropriate to the combined length of—

         (aa) the fitness hearing; and

         (bb) any hearing under section 4A of the Criminal Procedure (Insanity) Act 1964 (finding that the accused did the act or made the omission charged against him); or

      (ii) a fee calculated in accordance with paragraph 6, or where appropriate paragraph 8, as appropriate, for representing an assisted person in a cracked trial,

     whichever the litigator elects; and

   (c) if at any time the assisted person pleads guilty to the indictable offence, the litigator must be paid either—

      (i) a fee calculated in accordance with paragraph 7 or, where appropriate, paragraph 9, as appropriate to the length of the fitness hearing; or

      (ii) a fee calculated in accordance with paragraph 6 or, where appropriate, paragraph 8, as appropriate for representing an assisted person in a guilty plea,

     whichever the litigator elects.

Fees for confiscation proceedings

G-79   26.—(1) This paragraph applies to—

   (a) proceedings under Part 2 of the Proceeds of Crime Act 2002 (confiscation: England and Wales);

   (b) proceedings under section 2 of the Drug Trafficking Act 1994 (confiscation orders); and

   (c) proceedings under section 71 of the Criminal Justice Act 1988 (confiscation orders).

(2) Where this paragraph applies, the appropriate officer may allow work done in the following classes by a litigator—

   (a) preparation, including taking instructions, interviewing witnesses, ascertaining the prosecution case, preparing and perusing documents, dealing with letters and telephone calls, instructing an advocate and expert witnesses, conferences, consultations and work done in connection with advice on appeal;

   (b) attending at court where an advocate is instructed, including conferences with the advocate at court;

   (c) travelling and waiting; and

   (d) writing routine letters and dealing with routine telephone calls.

(3) The appropriate officer must consider the claim, any further particulars, information or documents submitted by the litigator under regulation 5 and any other relevant information and must allow such work as appears to him to have been reasonably done in the proceedings.

(4) Subject to sub-paragraph (3), the appropriate officer must allow fees under this paragraph in accordance with paragraph 27.

(5) The appropriate officer must allow fees in accordance with paragraphs 27 to 29 as appropriate to such of the following grades of fee earner as the appropriate officer considers reasonable—

   (a) senior solicitor;

   (b) solicitor, legal executive or fee earner of equivalent experience; or

   (c) trainee or fee earner of equivalent experience.

Prescribed fee rates

G-80   27. Subject to paragraphs 28 and 29, for proceedings in the Crown Court to which paragraph 26 applies the appropriate officer must allow fees for work under paragraph 26(2) at the following prescribed rates—

TABLE 1

Class of work	Grade of fee earner	Rate	Variations
Preparation	Senior solicitor	£48.36 per hour	£50.87 per hour for a fee earner whose office is situated within the City of

Class of work	Grade of fee earner	Rate	Variations
			London or a London borough
	Solicitor, legal executive or fee earner of equivalent experience	£41.06 per hour	£43.12 per hour for a fee earner whose office is situated within the City of London or a London borough
	Trainee or fee earner of equivalent experience	£27.15 per hour	£31.03 per hour for a fee earner whose office is situated within the City of London or a London borough
Attendance at court where more than one representative instructed	Senior solicitor	£38.55 per hour	
	Solicitor, legal executive or fee earner of equivalent experience	£31.03 per hour	
	Trainee or fee earner of equivalent experience	£18.71 per hour	
Travelling and waiting	Senior solicitor	£22.58 per hour	
	Solicitor, legal executive or fee earner of equivalent experience	£22.58 per hour	
	Trainee or fee earner of equivalent experience	£11.41 per hour	

[The table in para. 27 is printed as substituted by the Criminal Legal Aid (Remuneration) (Amendment) Regulations 2014 (S.I. 2014 No. 415). As to its application, see *ante*, G-71.]

Allowing fees at less than the prescribed rates

G-81

28. In respect of any item of work, the appropriate officer may allow fees at less than the relevant prescribed rate specified in paragraph 27 where it appears to the appropriate officer reasonable to do so having regard to the competence and despatch with which the work was done.

Allowing fees at more than the prescribed rates

G-81a

29.—(1) Upon a determination the appropriate officer may, subject to the provisions of this paragraph, allow fees at more than the relevant prescribed rate specified in paragraph 27 for preparation, attendance at court where more than one representative is instructed, routine letters written and routine telephone calls, in respect of offences in Class A, B, C, D, G, I, J or K in the Table of Offences.

(2) The appropriate officer may allow fees at more than the prescribed rate where it appears to the appropriate officer, taking into account all the relevant circumstances of the case, that—

(a) the work was done with exceptional competence, skill or expertise;

(b) the work was done with exceptional despatch; or

(c) the case involved exceptional complexity or other exceptional circumstances.

(3) Paragraph 3 of Schedule 1 applies to litigators in respect of proceedings in the Crown Court as it applies to advocates.

(4) Where the appropriate officer considers that any item or class of work should be allowed at more than the prescribed rate, the appropriate officer must apply to that item or class of work a percentage enhancement in accordance with the following provisions of this paragraph.

(5) In determining the percentage by which fees should be enhanced above the prescribed rate the appropriate officer must have regard to—

    (a) the degree of responsibility accepted by the fee earner;

    (b) the care, speed and economy with which the case was prepared; and

    (c) the novelty, weight and complexity of the case.

(6) The percentage above the relevant prescribed rate by which fees for work may be enhanced must not exceed 100%.

(7) The appropriate officer may have regard to the generality of proceedings to which these Regulations apply in determining what is exceptional within the meaning of this paragraph.

G-81b   In *R. v. Farrell and Selby* [2007] Costs L.R. 495, it was held in relation to the provisions of paragraph 4 of Part 1 of Schedule 2 to the Criminal Defence Service (Funding) Order 2001 (S.I. 2001 No. 855) for paying enhanced rates to solicitors, (i) it was open to a determining officer to apply different rates of enhancement to different items of work; since a determining officer was required, in deciding on the rate of enhancement, to have regard, *inter alia*, to the "degree of responsibility accepted by the solicitor and his staff", it was permissible for a determining officer to apply a lesser rate of enhancement to work of a routine nature done by Grade B fee earners than that applied to the senior fee earners to whom they reported; (ii) when enhancement was appropriate, a determining officer should first assess what enhanced rate would have been applied if legal aid had been granted prior to October 1, 1994 (the date of commencement of the revised rules as to enhancement introduced by the Legal Aid in Criminal and Care Proceedings (Costs) (Amendment) (No. 3) Regulations 1994 (S.I. 1994 No. 2218)), *viz.* the hourly broad average direct cost rate plus an appropriate uplift for care and conduct, and then he should adjust the resulting figure upwards to allow for subsequent inflation; he should then decide on a rate of enhancement such as would match this figure; where, however, the figure exceeded the maximum enhanced rate under the 2001 order, then the determining officer should apply the maximum enhanced rate. Since the provisions under consideration corresponded to those of paragraph 6 of Schedule 2 to the Criminal Defence Service (Funding) Order 2007 (S.I. 2007 No. 1174) (prior to amendment), it could safely be taken that this decision carried across to that order (prior to amendment) with the effect—as in this case—that, wherever enhanced rates are appropriate, the rate of enhancement is always going to be 100 per cent because the 1994 hourly direct cost plus uplift for care and attention, plus uplift for inflation is always going to exceed twice the current hourly rates, which have remained unchanged for many years. This was confirmed in *R. v. Bowles* [2007] Costs L.R. 514. Whilst the provision for payment at enhanced rates under the 2013 regulations relates only to fees payable under paragraph 26, the provisions of paragraph 29 correspond to paragraph 6 of the unamended Schedule 2, and it would appear that the decision in *Farrell and Selby* will carry across to this paragraph in the same way that it carried across to paragraph 6.

Regulation 6   **SCHEDULE 3**

PROCEEDINGS IN THE COURT OF APPEAL

General provisions

G-82   1.—(1) The provisions of this Schedule apply to proceedings in the Court of Appeal.

(2) In determining fees the appropriate officer must, subject to the provisions of this Schedule—

    (a) take into account all the relevant circumstances of the case including the nature, importance, complexity or difficulty of the work and the time involved; and

    (b) allow a reasonable amount in respect of all work actually and reasonably done.

Claims for fees and disbursements by litigators

2.—(1) Subject to regulation 31, no claim by a litigator for fees and disbursements in respect of work done in proceedings in the Court of Appeal pursuant to a section 16 determination must be entertained unless the litigator submits it within three months of the conclusion of the proceedings to which it relates.

(2) Subject to sub-paragraph (3), a claim for fees in proceedings in the Court of Appeal must be submitted to the appropriate officer in such form and manner as the appropriate officer may direct and must be accompanied by the representation order and any receipts or other documents in support of any disbursement claimed.

(3) A claim must—

    (a) summarise the items of work done by a fee earner in respect of which fees are claimed according to the classes specified in paragraph 3(1);

(b) state, where appropriate, the dates on which the items of work were done, the time taken, the sums claimed and whether the work was done for more than one assisted person;

(c) specify, where appropriate, the level of fee earner who undertook each of the items of work claimed;

(d) give particulars of any work done in relation to more than one indictment or a retrial; and

(e) specify any disbursements claimed, the circumstances in which they were incurred and the amounts claimed in respect of them.

(4) Where the litigator claims that paragraph 8(1) applies in relation to an item of work, the litigator must give full particulars in support of the claim.

(5) The litigator must specify any special circumstances which the litigator considers should be drawn to the attention of the appropriate officer.

(6) The litigator must supply such further information and documents as the appropriate officer may require.

(7) Where a retrospective section 16 determination has been made under regulations made under section 19 of the Act in respect of any proceedings where an appellant has been successful on appeal and granted a defendant's costs order under section 16(4) of the Prosecution of Offences Act 1985 (defence costs), the litigator must certify that no claim for fees incurred before the retrospective section 16 determination was made has been or will be made from central funds in relation to that work.

Determination of litigators' fees

3.—(1) The appropriate officer may allow work done in the following classes by fee earners—   **G-83**

(a) preparation, including taking instructions, interviewing witnesses, ascertaining the prosecution case, advising on plea and mode of trial, preparing and perusing documents, dealing with letters and telephone calls which are not routine, preparing for advocacy, instructing an advocate and expert witnesses, conferences, consultations, views and work done in connection with advice on appeal;

(b) advocacy, including applications for bail and other applications to the court;

(c) attending at court where an advocate is assigned, including conferences with the advocate at court;

(d) travelling and waiting; and

(e) writing routine letters and dealing with routine telephone calls.

(2) The appropriate officer must consider the claim, any further information or documents submitted by the fee earner under paragraph 2 and any other relevant information and must allow—

(a) such work as appears to the appropriate officer to have been reasonably done pursuant to the section 16 determination (including any representation or advice which is deemed to be work done pursuant to that determination) by a fee earner, classifying such work according to the classes specified in sub-paragraph (1) as the appropriate officer considers appropriate; and

(b) such time in each class of work allowed by him (other than routine letters written and routine telephone calls) as the appropriate officer considers reasonable.

(3) The fees allowed in accordance with this Schedule are those appropriate to such of the following grades of litigator as the appropriate officer considers reasonable—

(a) senior solicitor;

(b) solicitor, legal executive or fee earner of equivalent experience; or

(c) trainee or fee earner of equivalent experience.

Determination of litigators' disbursements

4. The appropriate officer must allow such disbursements claimed under paragraph 2 as appear to   **G-84** the appropriate officer to have been reasonably incurred, provided that—

(a) if they are abnormally large by reason of the distance of the court or the assisted person's residence or both from the litigator's place of business, the appropriate officer may limit reimbursement of the disbursements to what otherwise would, having regard to all the circumstances, be a reasonable amount; and

(b) the cost of a transcript, or any part thereof, of the proceedings in the court from which the appeal lies obtained otherwise than through the registrar must not be allowed except where the appropriate officer considers that it is reasonable in all the circumstances for such disbursement to be allowed.

Claims for fees by advocates

5.—(1) Subject to regulation 31, a claim by an advocate for fees for work done in proceedings in the Court of Appeal pursuant to a section 16 determination must not be entertained unless the advocate submits it within three months of the conclusion of the proceedings to which the section 16 determination relates.

(2) Where the advocate claims that paragraph 9(4) applies in relation to an item of work the advocate must give full particulars in support of his claim.

(3) Subject to sub-paragraph (4), a claim for fees by an advocate in proceedings in the Court of Appeal must be submitted to the appropriate officer in such form and manner as the appropriate officer may direct.

(4) A claim must—

    (a)   summarise the items of work done by an advocate in respect of which fees are claimed according to the classes specified in paragraph 6(2);

    (b)   state, where appropriate, the dates on which the items of work were done, the time taken, the sums claimed and whether the work was done for more than one assisted person; and

    (c)   give particulars of any work done in relation to more than one indictment or a retrial.

(5) The advocate must specify any special circumstances which the advocate considers should be drawn to the attention of the appropriate officer.

(6) The advocate must supply such further information and documents as the appropriate officer may require.

Determination of advocate's fees

G-85

6.—(1) The appropriate officer must consider the claim, any further particulars and information submitted by an advocate under paragraph 5 and any other relevant information and must allow such work as appears to the appropriate officer to have been reasonably done.

(2) The appropriate officer may allow any of the following classes of fee to an advocate in respect of work allowed by him under this paragraph—

    (a)   a basic fee for preparation including preparation for a pre-trial review and, where appropriate, the first day's hearing including, where they took place on that day, short conferences, consultations, applications and appearances (including bail applications), views and any other preparation;

    (b)   a refresher fee for any day or part of a day during which a hearing continued, including, where they took place on that day, short conferences, consultations, applications and appearances (including bail applications), views at the scene of the alleged offence and any other preparation;

    (c)   subsidiary fees for—

        (i)   attendance at conferences, consultations and views at the scene of the alleged offence not covered by paragraph (a) or (b);

        (ii)   written advice on evidence, plea or appeal or other written work; and

        (iii)   attendance at pre-trial reviews, applications and appearances (including bail applications and adjournments for sentence) not covered by paragraph (a) or (b).

(3) Where a section 16 determination provides for representation by—

    (a)   a single advocate other than a QC; or

    (b)   two advocates other than QC,

and a QC agrees to appear as the single advocate or as a leading junior, that QC must be treated for all the purposes of this Schedule as having been instructed pursuant to that section 16 determination, and the remuneration of the QC must be determined as if the advocate were not a QC.

In connection with this paragraph, see *R. v. Bromige, post,* G-160.

Litigators' fees for proceedings in the Court of Appeal

G-86

7.—(1) For proceedings in the Court of Appeal the appropriate officer must allow fees for work by litigators at the following prescribed rates

Class of work	Grade of fee earner	Rate	Variations
Preparation	Senior solicitor	£48.36 per hour	£50.87 per hour for a litigator whose office is situated within the City of London or a London borough
	Solicitor, legal executive or fee earner	£41.06 per hour	£43.12 per hour for a litigator whose office is

Class of work	Grade of fee earner	Rate	Variations
	of equivalent experience		situated within the City of London or a London borough
	Trainee or fee earner of equivalent experience	£26.46 per hour	£31.03 per hour for a litigator whose office is situated within the City of London or a London borough
Advocacy	Senior solicitor	£58.40 per hour	
	Solicitor	£51.10 per hour	
Attendance at court where more than one representative assigned	Senior solicitor	£38.55 per hour	
	Solicitor, legal executive or fee earner of equivalent experience	£31.03 per hour	
	Trainee or fee earner of equivalent experience	£18.71 per hour	
Travelling and waiting	Senior solicitor	£22.58 per hour	
	Solicitor, legal executive or fee earner of equivalent experience	£22.58 per hour	
	Trainee or fee earner of equivalent experience	£11.41 per hour	
Routine letters written and routine telephone calls		£3.15 per item	£3.29 per item for a litigator whose office is situated within the City of London or a London borough

(2) In respect of any item of work, the appropriate officer may allow fees at less than the relevant prescribed rate specified in the table following sub-paragraph (1) where it appears to the appropriate officer reasonable to do so having regard to the competence and despatch with which the work was done.

[The table in para. 7 is printed as substituted by the Criminal Legal Aid (Remuneration) (Amendment) Regulations 2014 (S.I. 2014 No. 415). As to its application, see *ante*, G-71.]

Allowance of litigators' fees at more than the prescribed rate

8.—(1) Upon a determination of fees the appropriate officer may, subject to the provisions of this **G-87** paragraph, allow fees at more than the relevant prescribed rate specified in paragraph 7 for preparation, advocacy, attendance at court where more than one representative is assigned, routine letters written and routine telephone calls, in respect of offences in Class A, B, C, D, G, I, J or K in the Table of Offences in Part 7 of Schedule 1.

(2) The appropriate officer may allow fees at more than the prescribed rate where it appears to the appropriate officer, taking into account all the relevant circumstances of the case, that—

   (a)   the work was done with exceptional competence, skill or expertise;

   (b)   the work was done with exceptional despatch; or

   (c)   the case involved exceptional complexity or other exceptional circumstances.

(3) Paragraph 3 of Schedule 1 applies to litigators in respect of proceedings in the Court of Appeal as it applies to advocates.

(4) Where the appropriate officer considers that any item or class of work should be allowed at more than the prescribed rate, the appropriate officer must apply to that item or class of work a percentage enhancement in accordance with the following provisions of this paragraph.

(5) In determining the percentage by which fees should be enhanced above the prescribed rate the appropriate officer may have regard to—

    (a)   the degree of responsibility accepted by the fee earner;

    (b)   the care, speed and economy with which the case was prepared; and

    (c)   the novelty, weight and complexity of the case.

(6) The percentage above the relevant prescribed rate by which fees for work may be enhanced must not exceed 100%.

(7) The appropriate officer may have regard to the generality of proceedings to which these Regulations apply in determining what is exceptional within the meaning of this paragraph.

Advocates' fees for proceedings in the Court of Appeal

G-88
    9.—(1) Subject to sub-paragraph 9(4), for proceedings in the Court of Appeal the appropriate officer must allow fees for work by advocates at the following prescribed rates—

JUNIOR COUNSEL

Type of proceedings	Basic fee	Full day refresher	Subsidiary fees		
			Attendance at consultation, conferences and views	Written work	Attendance at pretrial reviews, applications and other appearances
All appeals	Maximum amount: £545.00 per case	Maximum amount: £178.75 per day	£33.50 per hour, minimum amount: £16.75	Maximum amount: £58.25 per item	Maximum amount: £110 per appearance

QC

Type of proceedings	Basic fee	Full day refresher	Subsidiary fees		
			Attendance at consultation, conferences and views	Written work	Attendance at pretrial reviews, applications and other appearances
All appeals	Maximum amount: £5,400.00 per case	Maximum amount: £330.50 per day	£62.50 per hour, minimum amount: £32.00	Maximum amount: £119.50 per item	Maximum amount: £257.50 per appearance

(2) Where an hourly rate is specified in the table following sub-paragraph (1), the appropriate officer must determine any fee for such work in accordance with that hourly rate, provided that the fee determined must not be less than the minimum amount specified.

(3) Where a refresher fee is claimed in respect of less than a full day, the appropriate officer must allow such fee as appears to the appropriate officer reasonable having regard to the fee which would be allowable for a full day.

(4) Where it appears to the appropriate officer, taking into account all the relevant circumstances of the case, that owing to the exceptional circumstances of the case the amount payable by way of fees in accordance with the table following sub-paragraph (1) would not provide reasonable remuneration for some or all of the work the appropriate officer has allowed, the appropriate officer may allow such amounts as appear to the appropriate officer to be reasonable remuneration for the relevant work.

[The next paragraph is G-91.]

Payment of fees

G-91
    10.—(1) Having determined the fees payable to a representative in accordance with the terms of this Schedule, the appropriate officer must notify the representative of the fees payable and authorise payment accordingly.

(2) Where, as a result of any redetermination or appeal made or brought pursuant to paragraph 11, the fees payable under paragraph (1) are altered—

(a) if they are increased, the appropriate officer must authorise payment of the increase; and

(b) if they are decreased, the representative must repay the amount of such decrease.

(3) Where the payment of any fees of the representative is ordered under regulation 29(12) or regulation 30(8), the appropriate officer must authorise payment.

Redeterminations and appeals

11.—(1) Where a representative is dissatisfied with—   **G-92**

(a) the fees determined in accordance with the provisions of this Schedule; or

(b) the decision of the appropriate officer under paragraph 3(3) of Schedule 1,

he may apply to the appropriate officer to redetermine those fees or reclassify the offence, in accordance with the provisions of regulation 28(3) to (9).

(2) Where—

(a) a representative has made an application to the appropriate officer under sub-paragraph (1); and

(b) the appropriate officer has given his reasons for a decision under regulation 28(7),

a representative who is dissatisfied with that decision may appeal to a costs judge, in accordance with the provisions of regulation 29(2) to (14).

(3) A representative who is dissatisfied with the decision of a costs judge on an appeal under subparagraph (2) may apply to a costs judge to certify a point of principle of general importance, and the provisions of regulation 30(2) to (8) apply.

Regulation 8   SCHEDULE 4

RATES PAYABLE FOR THE CLAIMS SPECIFIED IN REGULATION 8

[*Sets out the rates payable for proceedings in a magistrates' court and certain other work to which the 2010*   ★**G-92a**
Standard Crime Contract applies (para. 11 was amended by the Criminal Legal Aid (Remuneration) (Amendment) Regulations 2013 (S.I. 2013 No. 2803), reg. 3(1) and (6); paras 3 to 12 were amended by the Criminal Legal Aid (Remuneration) (Amendment) Regulations 2014 (S.I. 2014 No. 415), reg. 2(4), and Sched. 3 (as to which, see ante, *G-71)); and paras 1, 5, 7 and 10 were amended, and para. 5A was inserted, by the Civil and Criminal Legal Aid (Remuneration) (Amendment) Regulations 2015 (S.I. 2015 No. 325), reg. 3(1) and (4) to (9).*]

Regulation 16   SCHEDULE 5

EXPERTS' FEES AND RATES

                                                   G-92b

Expert	Non-London – hourly rate unless stated to be a fixed fee	London – hourly rate unless stated to be a fixed fee
A&E consultant	£100.80	£108
Accident reconstruction	£72	£54.40
Accountant	£64	£64
Accountant (general staff)	£40	£40
Accountant (manager)	£86.40	£86.40
Accountant (partner)	£115.20	£115.20
Anaesthetist	£108	£72
Architect	£79.20	£72
Back calculations	£144 fixed fee	£151.20 fixed fee
Benefit expert	£72	£72
Cardiologist	£115.20	£72
Cell telephone site analysis	£72	£72
Child psychiatrist	£108	£72
Child psychologist	£100.80	£72
Computer expert	£72	£72
Consultant engineer	£72	£54.40
Dentist	£93.60	£72
Dermatologist	£86.40	£72
Disability consultant	£54.40	£54.40

Expert	Non-London – hourly rate unless stated to be a fixed fee	London – hourly rate unless stated to be a fixed fee
DNA (testing of sample)	£252 per test	£252 per test
DNA (preparation of report)	£72	£72
Doctor (GP)	£79.20	£72
Drug expert	£72	£72
Employment consultant	£54.40	£54.40
Enquiry agent	£25.60	£18.40
ENT surgeon	£100.80	£72
Facial mapping	£108	£72
Fingerprint expert	£72	£37.60
Fire investigation	£72	£54.40
Firearm expert	£72	£72
Forensic scientist	£90.40	£72
General surgeon	£108	£72
Geneticist	£86.40	£72
GP (records report)	£50.40 fixed fee	£72 fixed fee
Gynaecologist	£108	£72
Haematologist	£97.60	£72
Handwriting expert	£72	£72
Interpreter	£28	£25
Lip reader/Signer	£57.60	£32.80
Mediator	£100.80	£100.80
Medical consultant	£108	£72
Medical microbiologist	£108	£72
Medical report	£79.20	£72
Meteorologist	£100.80	£144 fixed fee
Midwife	£72	£72
Neonatologist	£108	£72
Neurologist	£122.40	£72
Neuropsychiatrist	£126.40	£72
Neuroradiologist	£136.80	£72
Neurosurgeon	£136.80	£72
Nursing expert	£64.80	£64.80
Obstetrician	£108	£72
Occupational therapist	£54.40	£54.40
Oncologist	£112	£72
Orthopaedic surgeon	£115.20	£72
Paediatrician	£108	£72
Pathologist	£122.40	£432 fixed fee
Pharmacologist	£97.60	£72
Photographer	£25.60	£18.40
Physiotherapist	£64.80	£64.80
Plastic surgeon	£108	£72
Process server	£25.60	£18.40
Psychiatrist	£108	£72

Expert	Non-London – hourly rate unless stated to be a fixed fee	London – hourly rate unless stated to be a fixed fee
Psychologist	£93.60	£72
Radiologist	£108	£72
Rheumatologist	£108	£72
Risk assessment expert	£50.40	£50.40
Speech therapist	£79.20	£72
Surgeon	£108	£72
Surveyor	£40	£40
Telecoms expert	£72	£72
Toxicologist	£108	£72
Urologist	£108	£72
Vet	£72	£72
Voice recognition	£93.60	£72

[Schedule 5 is printed as substituted by the Criminal Legal Aid (Remuneration) (Amendment) Regulations 2013 (S.I. 2013 No. 2803), reg. 3(1) and (7), and Sched. 1.]

SCHEDULE 6

FEES IN VERY HIGH COST CASES

PART 1

INTERPRETATION AND APPLICATION

Interpretation

1.—(1) In this Schedule—   **G-92c**

(a) a reference to a level is a reference to that level as defined in the Very High Cost Case contract;

(b) a reference to a category is a reference to that category as defined in that contract;

(c) the standard rates apply to work as described in the Very High Cost Case contract Guide; and

(d) the preliminary hearing, half day and full day rates apply as described in the Very High Cost Case contract Guide.

(2) In this Part—

(a) "Task List" has the meaning given in the Very High Cost Case contract;

(b) "parties" means the representative who has signed the Very High Cost Case contract and the Lord Chancellor.

(3) In Table 2, a junior may be either a barrister or a solicitor-advocate.

Application

2.—(1) This paragraph makes provision in relation to the application of this Schedule to work **G-92d** done in a case which is the subject of a Very High Cost Case contract signed by the parties before 2nd December 2013.

(2) Part 2 of this Schedule applies to work done pursuant to any Task List agreed between the parties before 2nd December 2013.

(3) Subject to sub-paragraph (4), Part 3 of this Schedule applies to work done pursuant to any Task List agreed between the parties on or after 2nd December 2013.

(4) Part 2 of this Schedule applies to work done in a case in which—

(a) the court has set a trial date before 2nd December 2013; and

(b) that trial date is on or before 31st March 2014.

(5) For the purpose of sub-paragraph (4), any adjournment or postponement of a trial which takes place after the trial date is set must be disregarded.

3. Part 3 of this Schedule applies to work done in a case which is the subject of a Very High Cost Case contract signed by the parties on or after 2nd December 2013.

PART 2

TABLE 1: PREPARATION (HOURLY RATES)

	Category 1 (£)	Category 2 (£)	Category 3 (£)	Category 4 (£)	Standard Rates (£)
Litigator					
Level A	145.00	113.00	91.00	91.00	55.75
Level B	127.00	100.00	79.00	79.00	47.25
Level C	84.00	65.00	51.00	51.00	34.00
Pupil/junior	45.00	36.00	30.00	30.00	
Barrister					
QC	145.00	113.00	91.00	91.00	
Leading junior	127.00	100.00	79.00	79.00	
Led junior	91.00	73.00	61.00	61.00	
Junior alone	100.00	82.00	70.00	70.00	
2nd Led junior	63.00	50.00	43.00	43.00	
Solicitor Advocate					
Leading level A	145.00	113.00	91.00	91.00	
Led level A	127.00	100.00	79.00	79.00	
Leading level B	127.00	100.00	79.00	79.00	
Led level B	104.00	86.00	66.00	66.00	
Level A alone	131.00	109.00	88.00	88.00	
Level B alone	113.00	95.00	75.00	75.00	
Second advocate	63.00	50.00	43.00	43.00	

TABLE 2: ADVOCACY RATES

	Preliminary hearing (£)	Half day (£)	Full day (£)
QC	113.00	238.00	476.00
Leading junior	86.00	195.00	390.00
Led junior	58.00	126.00	252.00
Junior alone	67.00	143.00	285.00
2nd Led junior	34.00	64.00	128.00
Noting junior	29.00	55.00	109.00

TABLE 3: ATTENDANCE AT COURT WITH ADVOCATE (HOURLY RATES FOR LITIGATORS)

	£
Level A	42.25
Level B	34.00
Level C	20.50

TABLE 4: TRAVELLING, WAITING AND MILEAGE

	£
Travelling (hourly rates)	25.00 (up to a maximum of 4 hours in one day)
Waiting (hourly rates)	25.00
Mileage	00.45 per mile

PART 3

TABLE 1: PREPARATION (HOURLY RATES)

	Category 1 (£)	Category 2 (£)	Category 3 (£)	Category 4 (£)	Standard Rates (£)
Litigator					
Level A	101.50	79.10	63.70	63.70	39.03
Level B	88.90	70.00	55.30	55.30	33.08
Level C	58.80	45.50	35.70	35.70	24.50
Pupil/junior	31.50	25.20	21.00	21.00	
Barrister					
QC	101.50	79.10	63.70	63.70	
Leading junior	88.90	70.00	55.30	55.30	
Led junior	63.70	51.10	42.70	42.70	
Junior alone	70.00	57.40	49.00	49.00	
2nd Led junior	44.10	35.00	30.10	30.10	
Solicitor Advocate					
Leading level A	101.50	79.10	63.70	63.70	
Led level A	88.90	70.00	55.30	55.30	
Leading level B	88.90	70.00	55.30	55.30	
Led level B	72.80	60.20	46.20	46.20	
Level A alone	91.70	76.30	61.60	61.60	
Level B alone	79.10	66.50	52.50	52.50	
Second advocate	44.10	35.00	30.10	30.10	

TABLE 2: ADVOCACY RATES

	Preliminary hearing (£)	Half day (£)	Full day (£)
QC	79.10	166.60	333.20
Leading junior	60.20	136.50	273.00
Led junior	40.60	88.20	176.40
Junior alone	46.90	100.10	199.50
2nd Led junior	23.80	44.80	89.60
Noting junior	20.30	38.50	76.30

TABLE 3: ATTENDANCE AT COURT WITH ADVOCATE (HOURLY RATES FOR LITIGATORS)

	£
Level A	29.58
Level B	23.80
Level C	14.35

TABLE 4: TRAVELLING, WAITING AND MILEAGE

	£
Travelling (hourly rates)	25.00 (up to a maximum of 4 hours in one day)
Waiting (hourly rates)	25.00
Mileage	00.45 per mile

[Schedule 6 was inserted by the Criminal Legal Aid (Remuneration) (Amendment) Regulations 2013 (S.I. 2013 No. 2803), reg. 3(1) and (8), and Sched. 2. It applies in relation to fees for work undertaken on or after December 2, 2013: *ibid.*, reg. 4.]

C. REPRESENTATION ORDERS

G-93   Representatives are entitled to claim and be remunerated only for work done in respect of Crown Court proceedings in accordance with the provisions of the schedules to the remuneration regulations: S.I. 2013 No. 435, regs 4, 5 and 9.

Existence of a valid representation order

G-94   Payment can only be made for work done under a representation order. There is no power under the legislation to make a payment in respect of work actually and reasonably undertaken by counsel in the genuine but mistaken belief that the appropriate order was in existence.

Solicitors are obliged to enclose a copy of the representation order with counsel's instructions, and to inform counsel of any subsequent amendments: *General Criminal Contract: Contract Specification*, Part B, para. 5.4. It is, however, incumbent upon counsel to check whether the appropriate order exists. If it is not with his instructions, then it is his duty, if he seeks to look to the legal aid fund thereafter for remuneration, to see that the appropriate authority is obtained and supplied to him: *Hunt v. East Dorset Health Authority* [1992] 1 W.L.R. 785 at 788 (Hobhouse J.); and *R. v. Welsby* [1998] 1 Cr.App.R. 197, Crown Court (Ebsworth J.) (counsel has a professional duty to ensure that he is covered by appropriate certificate).

Determining the effective date of a representation order

G-95   The effective date of a representation order for the purposes of determining which regulations apply is the date upon which representation was first granted to counsel's instructing solicitors and not the date of the later representation order under which they instructed counsel: *R. v. Hadley* [2005] Costs L.R. 548.

Orders made ultra vires

G-96   Representation orders assigning solicitors or counsel which are made *ultra vires* are invalid, and work done under such an order cannot be remunerated. However, where it is possible to construe an order as *intra vires*, that construction should be adopted: *R. v. O'Brien and Oliffe*, 81 Cr.App.R. 25 at 30 (Hobhouse J.). There is no power to backdate a representation order: *R. v. Welsby, ante*; *R. v. Conroy* [2004] Costs L.R. 182.

Representation by an advocate

G-97   As to when a representation order may include representation by one or more advocates or by a Queen's Counsel, see regulations 16 to 20 of the Criminal Legal Aid (Determinations by a Court and Choice of Representative) Regulations 2013 (S.I. 2013 No. 614) (*ante*, §§ 6-263f *et seq.*).

It is submitted that a leading junior would not be entitled to any remuneration where he acts under a certificate granted for Queen's Counsel. A leading junior who acted under an unamended legal aid certificate granted to cover Queen's Counsel was not covered by the certificate and could not be remunerated under the order or by a defendant's costs order under section 16 of the Prosecution of Offences Act 1985: *R. v. Liverpool Crown Court, ex p. The Lord Chancellor, The Times*, April 22, 1993, DC. However, a Queen's Counsel must be remunerated at the appropriate rate for junior counsel where he agrees to act as a sole advocate or as a leading junior: S.I. 2013 No. 435, reg. 4(7).

[The next paragraph is G-100.]

Orders for Queen's Counsel acting alone

G-100   Where prior authority has been obtained to instruct a Queen's Counsel alone, the propriety of the order may not be challenged on the determination of Queen's Counsel's fees unless the solicitor knew or ought reasonably to have known that the purpose for which the authority had been given had failed or become irrelevant or unnecessary before the fees were incurred: S.I. 2013 No. 435, reg. 17(3).

Work done under the order

The work claimed for must have been done under the order. Work done before the date of **G-101** commencement of the representation order cannot be claimed or allowed: *R. v. Clarke* (1991) Costs L.R. 496. An order cannot be backdated in respect of proceedings in the Crown Court: *R. v. North Staffordshire JJ., ex p. O'Hara* [1994] C.O.D. 248, DC; *R. v. Welsby* [1998] 1 Cr.App.R. 197, Crown Court (Ebsworth J.).

"Topping up"

An assisted person's solicitor or advocate is prohibited from receiving or being party to the **G-102** making of any payment for work done in connection with the proceedings in respect of which the representation order was made other than payments by the Lord Chancellor or in respect of various specified disbursements: S.I. 2013 No. 435, reg. 9. These provisions are designed to prevent "topping" up of fees, rather than to prevent counsel from receiving payment for private fees incurred before the representation order was granted or *ex gratia* payments from solicitors who wrongly instructed counsel in the mistaken belief that he was covered by a representation order. However, once a representation order has been granted, the prohibition applies to all solicitors and advocates and not merely those persons acting under the representation order: *R. v. Grant* [2006] Costs L.R. 173.

D. Reasonable Remuneration

The basic principle of remuneration under the former *ex post facto* regime was that counsel **G-103** should receive reasonable remuneration for work actually and reasonably undertaken by him. Assessment of the work undertaken and the remuneration claimed was made in each case after the event by experienced officers appointed by the Lord Chancellor's department and subject to the appellate and expert supervision of costs judges and the High Court.

Graduated fees are calculated by reference to pre-determined fixed fees. Although allowances **G-104** are made for different classes of case and for the length and size of each case, the scheme necessarily embraces a "swings and roundabouts" principle. Save in exceptional cases, graduated fees draw no distinction between straightforward and complex cases of the same length, class and size.

When they were introduced in 1997, it was intended that they would be cost neutral. The extension of fees to cover 25 to 40 day cases represented a diminution in fees for defence work, balanced by an increase in the fees of prosecution counsel who are now subject to a similar scheme. The further extension of the scheme in 2007 to all trials on indictment save for those covered by VHCC contracts was a far remove from its original ambit, and may give rise to some serious underfunding of cases or aspects of cases.

Very High Cost Cases are remunerated by an hourly preparation fee and refreshers which fall within prescribed bands. The categorisation of the class of case, rates of remuneration, refreshers and the number of hours of preparation allowed to counsel must be agreed before the work is undertaken.

E. Interim Fees and other Pre-assessment Payments

(1) Staged payments for preparation in long cases

Where the period from sending to the Crown Court to the conclusion of the proceedings is **G-105** likely to exceed 12 months, a legal representative may apply for staged payments (*i.e.* interim fees for the preparation of a case) in respect of each period of preparation of 100 hours or more undertaken before trial or, in serious fraud cases, before the empanelling of a jury. Preparation in this context is widely defined and includes, *inter alia*, conferences with the defendant, written advice on evidence or plea, legal research and preparation for oral or written submissions: S.I. 2013 No. 435, reg. 20.

[The next paragraph is G-110.]

(2) Interim payment of expenses

G-110   A litigator may make a claim for an interim payment of disbursements in accordance with the provisions of regulation 14 of S.I. 2013 No. 435.

(3) Interim payment pending determination

Entitlement

G-111   In certain circumstances, an advocate may claim an interim payment of 40 per cent of the total claim less any sum already paid: S.I. 2013 No. 435, reg. 19(1). Such payments may only be made where, (a) the basic fee claimed by counsel, or the total costs claimed by a solicitor in a related claim, or the basic fee claimed by counsel in a related claim, exceeds £4,000 (exclusive of VAT); and (b) three months have elapsed from either the date on which the bill is ready to tax or, if earlier, three months after the conclusion of the last of any related proceedings. A bill is deemed to be ready to tax on the date of receipt of the last bill in a related claim. Related claims are claims for costs of solicitors and counsel in the same proceedings acting for the same defendant or acting in related proceedings. Related proceedings are those involving the same defendant which are prepared, heard, or dealt with together, or proceedings involving more than one defendant arising out of the same incident so that the defendants are charged, tried, or disposed of together: S.I. 2013 No. 435, reg. 18.

There is no right of re-determination or appeal against the interim award: S.I. 2013 No. 435, reg. 19(2).

Claims

G-112   An advocate may submit a claim for interim payment where, (a) he is entitled to such payment; (b) no payment has been made; (c) six months have elapsed since the conclusion of the proceedings against the defendant he represented; and (d) counsel has submitted a proper claim under regulation 4(3) (three-month time limit for the submission of claims): S.I. 2013 No. 435, reg. 18(2)–(6).

(4) Hardship payments

G-113   A discretionary hardship payment may be made on proof of the likelihood of financial hardship. The proof required is left to the discretion of taxing officers. Counsel are advised to contact their circuit representative, before submitting a claim, to determine the form of proof likely to be acceptable. The sum paid cannot exceed the amount which is likely to be eventually paid, but payment will not be made for sums less than £5,000. Claims may only be made, (a) at least six months after the legal representative was first instructed, and (b) where final payment is unlikely to be made within the next three months by reason of which the applicant is likely to suffer financial hardship: S.I. 2013 No. 435, reg. 21.

(5) Obligations to submit claims

G-114   Any person who has received a staged, interim or hardship payment must submit a claim under the appropriate regulation for final determination of his overall remuneration: S.I. 2013 No. 435, reg. 22(1). Any such payment will be set off against the overall remuneration on final determination and excess payments can be recovered: *ibid.*, reg. 22(2).

F. Graduated Fees

(1) Introduction

G-115   As to the introduction of the scheme for graduated fees, see *ante*, G-2.

The scheme determines the taxation and payment of fees for advocacy and preparation in something of a mechanistic or formulaic way: *Meeke and Taylor v. Secretary of State for Constitutional Affairs* [2006] Costs L.R. 1. It is a comprehensive scheme which must be applied by examining the particular wording of the legislation: *R. v. Kemp*, X15 363/99. There is no "equity" in the regulations; they have to be construed and given effect however hard the result might be: *R. v. Riddell*, X3, SCCO 319/98, even where payment is morally due: see *R. v. Dhaliwal* [2004] Costs L.R. 689. Conversely, as was pointed out in *R. v. Chubb* [2002] Costs L.R. 333:

"As has often been said, when the graduated fee system was introduced, it was on a principle which was expressed as being 'swings and roundabouts'. It is perfectly reasonable where the system operates against the Lord Chancellor's Department, that an appeal should be launched. There are many occasions, in my experience, when the graduated fee system has operated very much to the disadvantage of members of the bar and there is no reason why the bar should not take advantage when it operates in their favour."

References within this section to paragraphs are references to paragraphs in Schedule 1 to S.I. 2013 No. 435 (unless otherwise stated).

[The next paragraph is G-118.]

(2) Cases on indictment

Scheduled offences

A "case" includes proceedings in the Crown Court against any one assisted person on one or more counts of a single indictment: S.I. 2013 No. 435, Sched. 1, para. 1(1). Where counts or defendants are severed and dealt with separately, then each separate indictment is a separate case. Conversely, indictments which are joined should be treated as one case: GFSG: A1, A2: *R. v. Chubb* [2002] Costs L.R. 333. A "case" should not be confused with a trial; there may be two trials in one case: *R. v. Bond* [2005] Costs L.R. 533.

G-118

All cases on indictment now fall within the scheme unless specifically excluded: S.I. 2013 No. 435, Sched. 1, para. 2. As to pre-indictment hearings, see *post*, G-121a.

In *R. v. Hussain* [2011] Costs L.R. 689, after one defendant was committed for trial and a plea and case management hearing was conducted in relation to a single-count indictment, a second defendant was committed for trial, as a result of which a second indictment was preferred which included the allegation against the first defendant in the single-count indictment, and the defendants were in due course tried on the second indictment. It was held that: (i) whereas paragraph 1(1) of Schedule 2 to S.I. 2013 No. 435 (*ante*, G-69) provides that "'case' means proceedings in the Crown Court against any one assisted person—(a) on one or more counts of a single indictment ...", there were two "cases"; (ii) in respect of the second indictment, the solicitors were entitled to a graduated fee for trial, together with the appropriate uplift for representing more than one defendant; and (iii) in respect of the first indictment, they were entitled to a graduated fee for a cracked trial. The costs judge observed that whilst it might be thought that the solicitors had obtained something of a windfall for, in layman's terms, this was really only one case, the regulations must be applied mechanistically.

Table of offences

The table of offences in Schedule 1 to S.I. 2013 No. 435 contains offences listed by statute with a description set out only for convenience. The statutory reference includes every offence contrary to that reference, whether or not the description of the offence is apt to describe the offence actually charged: S.I. 2013 No. 435, Sched. 1, para. 3(1)(e). Cases which do not appear in the table of offences are deemed to fall within Class H: S.I. 2013 No. 435, Sched. 1, para. 3(1)(a). An advocate who is dissatisfied with that deemed classification may apply to the appropriate officer to reclassify the offence: S.I. 2013 No. 435, Sched. 1, para. 3(2).

G-119

The offences are divided into the following classes:

Class A	Homicide and related grave offences
Class B	Offences involving serious violence or damage and serious drug offences
Class C	Lesser offences involving violence or damage, and less serious drug offences
Class D	Sexual offences and offences against children
Class E	Burglary and going equipped

Class F	Other offences of dishonesty including those where the value does not exceed £30,000
Class G	Other more serious offences of dishonesty including those where the value exceeds £30,000 but does not exceed £100,000
Class H	Miscellaneous lesser offences
Class I	Offences against public justice and similar offences
Class J	Serious sexual offences
Class K	The most serious offences of dishonesty and other offences where the value exceeds £100,000

Where counts of differing classes appear in the same indictment, the fee is based upon the class selected by the advocate: S.I. 2013 No. 435, Sched. 1, para. 27(1). Once counsel has chosen which count to use as the basis of a claim, that choice is irrevocable: *R. v. Buoniauto*, X25, SCCO 483/ 2000. Where an indictment is drafted in such a way that the offence charged could fall into either of two different classes in the table of offences, the advocate may choose the class to which the case is to be assigned for the purpose of calculating the fees payable: *Lord Chancellor v. Ahmed* [2014] Costs L.R. 21, QBD (Andrews J.). Where two or more advocates appear for the same defendant, the grounds of each claim must be the same: *R. v. Powell*, X8, SCTO 336/98.

The offences are summarised and listed alphabetically by statute: *post*, G-168 *et seq.*

G-120 Conspiracy, incitement or attempt to commit an offence fall within the same class as the substantive offence: S.I. 2013 No. 435, Sched. 1, para. 3(1)(b). Conspiracy to defraud at common law does not appear in the table of offences. It will accordingly fall within Class H: S.I. 2013 No. 435, Sched. 1, para. 3(1)(a). Where the appropriate class depends upon a value, the lower value is presumed unless the claimant "proves otherwise to the satisfaction of the appropriate authority": S.I. 2013 No. 435, Sched. 1, para. 3(1)(c). This may be done by extracts from the indictment or witness statements. Values relating to offences taken into consideration should be excluded from the computation: GFSG: E10. The proof required is proof on a balance of probabilities, and the appropriate officer must take a common sense approach in deciding whether the burden has been discharged: *R. v. Garness* [2014] Costs L.R. 201.

In *R. v. O'Donnell and Fawley* [2012] Costs L.R. 431, it was held that the scheme is mechanistic and that there is no discretion for the court to say that, because the defendants may have been shown to have committed offences in a different class, which would attract a higher fee, it is permissible to reclassify the offence actually charged accordingly.

The calculation of values

G-121 The property values of each count falling within the same class may be aggregated, provided the same property is not counted twice: S.I. 2013 No. 435, Sched. 1, para. 3(1)(d). However, offences taken into consideration are excluded from the calculation, even where it is agreed that the counts on the indictment are to be treated merely as sample counts: *R. v. Knight*, X35, SCCO 34/ 2003.

In *R. v. Wei* [2010] Costs L.R. 846, it was held that "value", for the purposes of paragraph 3 of Schedule 2 to S.I. 2013 No. 435 and the table of offences in Part 7 of Schedule 1 (*ante*, G-68, G-70; *post*, G-168 *et seq.*), must, in the context of an offence of dishonesty, such as possession of articles for use in fraud, mean the value of the dishonest enterprise, and not the value of the particular articles. The court said that the obvious intention was to provide greater remuneration for more complex and lengthy cases within the confines of the formulaic graduated fee system.

Preliminary hearings

G-121a In *Lord Chancellor v. Shapiro* [2010] Costs L.R. 769, QBD (Sweeney J.), it was held that for a first hearing in the Crown Court of a case sent for trial under section 51 of the CDA 1998 (§ 1-25 in the main work) to fall within the graduated fee scheme there must be an indictment in existence at the time. It was said that since the order makes no specific provision for such hearings, it follows that they fall to be remunerated as part of the basic fee if there is an indictment in existence at the time, and, if there is not, there is no provision for payment; in particular, the order making

no provision for *ex post facto* taxation (except in strictly limited circumstances), there is no power
to make a payment on an *ex post facto* basis. For criticism of this decision, see the commentary in
CLW/10/38/8.

Pleas and directions hearings and pre-trial reviews

Pleas and directions hearings are not defined under the regulations. Accordingly if a matter is   **G-122**
listed as a pleas and directions hearing, it will be so treated. There is nothing to prevent a pleas
and directions hearing from being adjourned, or there being more than one or even a series of
such hearings: *R. v. Beecham*, X11, QBD (Ebsworth J.). However, the listing of the case is not
necessarily determinative. For example, although a case may be listed as a pleas and directions
hearing, if a defendant pleads at that hearing and is sentenced, it cannot be said that a pleas and
directions hearing has taken place: *R. v. Johnson*, SCCO 51/06. Pleas and directions hearings
(other than those which form part of the main hearing) and pre-trial reviews are payable at a
fixed rate. Any pre-trial hearings to determine, for example, the admissibility of evidence, fall
outside the main hearing and are remunerated as standard appearance fees: *R. v. Rahman*, X21,
SCCO 119/2000; *R. v. Carter*, X18, SCCO 384/99.

Fees are payable for preparing and filing a plea and case management questionnaire where no
oral hearing takes place: S.I. 2013 No. 435, Sched. 1, para. 12(3). Fees for oral hearings which fall
within the definition of a standard appearance are deemed to be included in the basic fee: see
post, G-129. Plea and case management hearings which are not standard appearances are
remunerated according to the fees set out in the table following paragraph 24: S.I. 2013 No. 435,
Sched. 1, para. 12(2). As to standard appearances, see *post*, G-129.

The start of the main hearing

In *Lord Chancellor v. Ian Henery Solicitors Ltd* [2012] Costs L.R. 205, QBD (Spencer J.), it was   **G-123**
held that when considering the question whether, and if so on what date, a case has proceeded to
trial, the following principles apply: (i) whether or not a jury have been sworn is not conclusive;
(ii) there can be no doubt that a trial will have begun if the jury have been sworn, the case has
been opened, and evidence has been called; (iii) a trial will also have begun if the jury have been
sworn and the case has been opened to any extent, even if only for a few minutes (*Meeke and
Taylor v. Secretary of State for Constitutional Affairs* [2006] Costs L.R. 1, QBD (David Clarke J.)); (iv) a
trial will not have begun, even if the jury have been sworn (and whether or not the defendant has
been put in the charge of the jury), if there has been no trial in a meaningful sense, *e.g.* because,
before the case can be opened, the defendant pleads guilty (*R. v. Brook* [2004] Costs L.R. 178, *R.
v. Baker and Fowler* [2004] Costs L.R. 693, and *R. v. Sanghera* [2008] Costs L.R. 823); (v) a trial will
have begun, even if there has been no empanelment of a jury, if submissions have begun in a
continuous process resulting in the empanelling of a jury, the opening of the case, and the leading of evidence (considering *R. v. Wembo* [2011] Costs L.R. 926, *R. v. Bullingham* [2011] Costs L.R.
1078, and an unreported decision of Mitting J. in December, 2005, in the case of *R. v. Smith*); (vi)
if, in accordance with modern practice in long cases, a jury have been selected but not sworn,
then provided the court is dealing with substantial matters of case management it may well be
that the trial has begun in a meaningful sense; and (vii) where there is likely to be any difficulty in
deciding whether a trial has begun, and if so when it began, the judge should be prepared, upon
request, to indicate his view on the matter for the benefit of the parties and the determining officer, in the light of these principles.

In *R. v. Budai* [2011] Costs L.R. 1073, the costs judge acknowledged the principle in (v), *ante*,
but held that this did not cover a case where, on the day listed for trial, all that was done was that
interpreters were sworn, a potential panel of 18 jurors was selected (prior to their being sent
away until the following day to assess their availability for a lengthy trial) and there was a direction made regarding the amendment of the indictment. On the other side of the line are *R. v.
Wembo, ante* (where, immediately prior to a jury being empanelled, counsel had attended two days
of hearings that related to a witness anonymity order, those days had formed part of the trial for
the purposes of calculating the graduated fee); and *R. v. Bullingham, ante* (where a jury had not
been empanelled, but the judge directed that there should be a *voire dire* to determine the admissibility of evidence which the prosecution wanted to open to the jury, and there was such a *voire
dire* at which evidence was called, the trial started with the giving of that direction even though

the effect of the ruling on the *voire dire* was that the prosecution decided to accept pleas to lesser offences in consequence of which the defendant pleaded guilty and there was no requirement for a jury). The reasoning in *Bullingham* was expressly approved in *Lord Chancellor v. Ian Henery Solicitors Ltd*, *ante*, but it is submitted that the result is difficult to justify, not least for its failure to give effect to the obvious purpose of paragraph 13 of Schedule 1 (*ante*, § G-48), which the costs judge did not even refer to. Sub-paragraph (1)(d) expressly contemplates that a hearing as to the admissibility of evidence may take place before the main hearing of a case (trial or cracked trial), and if it does, it is to be remunerated in accordance with that paragraph. The decision of the costs judge effectively emasculates this by converting the admissibility hearing into the main hearing. See also the commentary in CLW/12/01/14.

The start of a preparatory hearing is the commencement of the trial for the purposes of the regulations: *R. v. Jones*, X17, SCCO 527/99: GFSG: B8, B8A.

Calculating the length of the main hearing

G-124   Length of the main hearing means the number of days of the main hearing together with the number of days of any *Newton* hearing in relation to the assisted person whose trial is under consideration: S.I. 2013 No. 435, reg. 2(1), and Sched. 1, para. 2(8). Thus, where counsel successfully submits that there is no case to answer, the main hearing ceases, despite the fact that the trial may continue against the co-defendants: *Secretary of State for Constitutional Affairs v. Stork*, *The Times*, October 7, 2005, QBD (Gray J.). This can lead to harsh anomalies, as where a defendant pleads guilty shortly after a jury have been sworn during an estimated three-week trial; despite preparation for a three-week trial, counsel will be remunerated as for a one day trial: *Meeke and Taylor v. Secretary of State for Constitutional Affairs*, *ante*. Non-sitting days cannot be included: *R. v. Nassir*, X13, SCCO 703/98. Where a jury are sworn, but discharged the same day for some reason other than the private or professional convenience of counsel, with a new jury sworn the following day, there may be sufficient continuity to conclude that the trial did in fact proceed, and start of the trial is the date on which the first jury were sworn: *R. v. Gussman*, X14, SCTO 40/99, but part of a day counts as a whole day: S.I. 2013 No. 435, Sched. 1, para. 4. Applications relating to abuse of process, disclosure and witness summonses are to be treated as part of the main hearing where they are heard during the main hearing: S.I. 2013 No. 435, Sched. 1, para. 13(2). The length of a fitness hearing which precedes a trial on indictment must also be included in determining the length of the trial: S.I. 2013 No. 435, Sched. 1, para. 31(a). Confiscation proceedings are excluded from the computation: S.I. 2013 No. 435, Sched. 1, para. 14(2).

Where, during the currency of a trial, there had been a day when one juror could not attend, but the judge had directed all counsel to attend in order that agreement should be reached as to how to reduce one section of the evidence, counsel was not entitled to count that day as a day of the trial; although the judge had indicated he would be available in case there was some issue on which agreement could not be reached, it had not been necessary to involve the judge and the case had not been called on in court; counsel was, however, entitled to a non-effective hearing fee for that day (under Sched. 1, para. 16 (*ante*, G-51)); the case was listed for that day, counsel had been obliged to attend, but in fact the trial did not proceed on that day: *R. v. Budai*, *ante*.

Fees for contested trials

G-125   The calculation of any graduated fee involves arcane formulae: S.I. 2013 No. 435, Sched. 1, para. 4. To calculate the correct fee, the appropriate figures should be substituted from the tables of fees and uplifts: S.I. 2013 No. 435, Sched. 1, para. 5.

[The next paragraph is G-129.]

Standard appearances

G-129   Standard appearances are defined in S.I. 2013 No. 435 as appearances which do not form part of the main hearing, and constitute (i) plea and case management hearings (other than the first such hearing); (ii) pre-trial reviews; (iii) the hearing of a case listed for plea which is adjourned for trial; (iv) custody time limit, bail and other applications; (v) mentions, including applications relating to the date of trial; (vi) a sentencing hearing other than one following a committal for sentence to the Crown Court, or one where sentence has been deferred under the PCC(S)A 2000, s.1, or one where the advocate has been instructed solely for the purposes of entering a plea in mitigation under paragraph 34 of Schedule 1; (vii) a hearing, whether contested or not, relating to breach of bail, failure to surrender to bail or execution of a bench warrant; and (viii) any hearing (except a trial, plea and case management hearing, appeal against conviction or sentence, sentencing hearing following a committal for sentence to the Crown Court, or proceedings arising out of an alleged breach of an order of the Crown Court) which is listed but cannot proceed because of the failure of the assisted person or a witness to attend, the unavailability of a pre-sentence report or other good reason: Sched. 1, para. 1(1). Under S.I. 2013 No. 435, an advocate's fees payable for the first plea and case management hearing or pre-trial review and up to four standard appearances are deemed to be included in the basic fee and are not subject to separate remuneration: Sched. 1, para. 12 (*ante*, G-47). The fifth and subsequent standard appearances are remunerated as set out in the table following paragraph 24: *ibid.*, para. 12(2).

Where an advocate made three appearances at non-effective hearings, the first two of which had been listed as a plea and case management hearing and the third of which had been listed for an anticipated plea of guilty to be taken, where the third hearing was ineffective because the defendant had absconded, and where a bench warrant had been issued which remained outstanding, paragraph 12(1) did not apply as no basic fee had become payable (and thus it did not prevent payment in respect of the three appearances); payment could be made under paragraph 12(2); there was no authority in the legislation for a statement in the graduated fee scheme guidance that suggested that no fee could be paid so long as a bench warrant was outstanding: *R. v. Metcalf* [2010] Costs L.R. 646; and, to similar effect, see *R. v. Muoka* [2013] Costs L.R. 523.

Trial of Bail Act offences

G-130   The trial of any Bail Act 1976 offence in the Crown Court entitles counsel who attends to apply for a new "trial" fee for the contested trial or plea: *R. v. Shaw* [2005] Costs L.R. 326; *R. v. Despres* [2005] Costs L.R. 750.

Sendings to the Crown Court

G-131   Where cases are sent to the Crown Court under the CDA 1998, s.51, and are discontinued before the prosecution serve their evidence, the advocate is entitled to 50 per cent of the fee calculated on the basis of a guilty plea: S.I. 2013 No. 435, Sched. 1, para. 22(2), together with an additional 20 per cent of that fee for each additional person represented: para. 22(8)(a). Once the prosecution have served their evidence, discontinuance, the offering of no evidence at a pleas and case management hearing, or the remitting of the case to the magistrates' court at such hearing because the indictment contains no indictable offence, is treated for the purposes of calculating the relevant fee as if each was a guilty plea: *ibid.*, para. 22(3) and (5). An advocate representing more than one person in the latter circumstances is entitled to 20 per cent of the appropriate basic fee for each additional person he represents: para. 22(8)(b).

Dismissal hearings

G-132   Where a successful application for dismissal is made under the CDA 1998, Sched. 3, para. 2, with the result that the case is dismissed or remitted back to the magistrates' court, the fee is calculated as if the matter had been disposed of by a guilty plea, together with an attendance fee based upon the total number of days and half days occupied by the hearing: S.I. 2013 No. 435, Sched. 1, para. 22(6) and (7). A full day's hearing is any court day which begins before and ends after the luncheon adjournment: para. 22(6)(a). An advocate representing more than one person in such circumstances is entitled to 20 per cent of the appropriate basic fee for each additional person he represents: para. 22(8)(b).

Transfers

G-133   A case will be "transferred" to a new litigator for the purposes of paragraph 13(2)(a) of Schedule 2 to the Criminal Legal Aid (Remuneration) Regulations 2013 (S.I. 2013 No. 435) (*ante*, G-73b) where the representation order has been amended to substitute the new litigator and the new litigator has agreed to accept the instructions and has carried out a conflicts check; an amended representation order will not be effective to transfer a case to a new litigator who has not carried out a conflicts check because it is incumbent upon any firm of solicitors to carry out such a check before accepting instructions and, therefore, in such circumstances, it cannot be said that the new litigator has been "instructed" until that duty has been discharged: *Tuckers Solicitors v. Lord Chancellor* [2014] Costs L.R. 29, QBD (Andrews J.) (considering a corresponding provision in the Criminal Defence Service (Funding) Order 2007 (S.I. 2007 No. 1174), and observing that, in practice, it would be desirable if, when the Crown Court sends information to the putative new litigator, it were to include the indictment, witness list and, if available, the case summary, rather than leaving it to the former solicitors to do so).

In *R. v. Rayan* [2010] Costs L.R. 969, it was held that, for the purposes of paragraph 13(2) of Schedule 2 to S.I. 2013 No. 435 (*ante*, G-73b), which provides that where a case is transferred from one litigator to another, the original litigator is entitled to 25 per cent of the cracked trial fee where the transfer took place "up to and including plea and case management hearing" or a fee of 75 per cent of the cracked trial fee for a "before trial transfer", the reference to a "plea and case management hearing" must be taken to be a reference to an effective such hearing. An effective hearing, it was held, requires there to have been a plea, and for case management directions of sufficient substance to have been made such that the hearing could be described as a plea and case management hearing.

Retrials

G-134   A standard graduated fee is paid for retrials, where the same advocate appears, subject to the following discounts based upon the time elapsed from the conclusion of the first trial to the start of the retrial: S.I. 2013 No. 435, para. 2(3):

30 per cent	retrial starts within one month
20 per cent	retrial starts after one month
40 per cent	retrial is cracked or becomes a guilty plea within one month
25 per cent	retrial is cracked or becomes a guilty plea after one month.

No discounts are applied where the advocate who conducts the retrial is not the advocate who conducted the original trial: *ibid.*, para. 2(5) and (6).

In *R. v. Connors* [2014] Costs L.R. 942 it was held that under the graduated fee scheme for advocates as set out in Schedule 1 to the Criminal Defence Service (Funding) Order 2007 (S.I. 2007 No. 1174), where there is a trial followed by a retrial with the same advocate acting in both trials, the advocate does not have to wait until the conclusion of the second trial to claim payment for the first trial. Furthermore, an advocate need not wait until the conclusion of the second trial before electing to have the reduced fee applied to the first trial under paragraph 2(4) of Schedule 1 to the 2007 order (now under Sched. 1, para. 2(2) and (3), to S.I. 2013 No. 435 (*ante*, G-40)). If it turned out that there should have been a greater reduction than the one actually applied, the Legal Aid Agency could recoup any excess payment via article 26 of the 2007 order (now via reg. 25 of S.I. 2013 No. 435 (Appendix G-31)): *ibid.*

Where the case was sent to the Crown Court on the election of the defendant where the magistrates' court had determined the case to be suitable for summary trial, and the new trial becomes a cracked trial or guilty plea, the advocate will receive a graduated fee for the first trial and a fixed fee for the second trial: S.I. 2013 No. 435, Sched. 1, para. 2(4). This also applies where the trial advocate is different at the second trial: S.I. 2013 No. 435, Sched. 1, para. 2(5) and (7).

G-134a   Where a defence advocate was initially retained privately but, the jury at the first trial having been unable to agree on a verdict, was then instructed for the retrial under a representation order, the defendant having run out of money, and where the defendant was acquitted at the retrial with a defendant's costs order being made in his favour, no payment could be made under the defendant's costs order out of central funds in respect of work done in preparation for the retrial between the date of the first trial and the grant of the representation order; the graduated fee payable for a retrial under the Criminal Defence Service (Funding) Order 2001 (S.I. 2001 No. 855) was intended to allow for all preparation carried out for that retrial; to have authorised the payment would have resulted in a double payment out of public funds effectively in respect of the same work: *R. v. Long* [2009] Costs L.R. 151. The result would be the same under S.I. 2013 No. 435.

In *Lord Chancellor v. Purnell and McCarthy* [2010] Costs L.R. 81, QBD (Sir Christopher Holland), where a full trial had been conducted in which the jury had acquitted the defendant on the main charge of murder, but had been unable to agree on an alternative charge of manslaughter and on another count of violent disorder, where a date for a retrial had been fixed, where the prosecution eventually decided to offer no evidence, and where it was clear that counsel had not, meanwhile, been standing by awaiting a decision by the prosecution whether to proceed (it was not the case that the matter had been adjourned after trial to allow the prosecution time to decide whether they intended to proceed further) but, on the contrary, had begun preparing for the retrial, it was held that counsel were entitled to a graduated fee for a "cracked trial". They had every reason to expect and prepare for a retrial, as the case was serious and had so far featured a finding by at least three jurors that manslaughter had been proved against the defendant to the criminal standard. Under the 2001 order, there was no provision for any percentage reduction of the fee in such cases. This, however, has since been remedied: see now S.I. 2013 No. 435, Sched. 1, para. 2(2) and (3) (*ante*, G-40).

In *R. v. Seivwright* [2011] Costs L.R. 327, it was held that paragraph 13(1) of Schedule 2 to S.I. 2013 No. 435 (*ante*, G-73b) applies only where the retrial follows a trial and an order has been made for a retrial following appeal or where a jury have failed to reach a verdict, and that "retrial" for this purpose means a new trial which is not part of the same procedural and temporal matrix as the first trial. It was said that whilst this conclusion might be thought to conflict with the Litigator Graduated Fee Scheme Guidance published by the Legal Services Commission, that was merely guidance and not a source of law that was binding. On the facts, it was held that where the trial had commenced on a Monday, the jury had been discharged on the Thursday, the matter was listed for mention on the Friday when it was agreed that a new jury would be empanelled on the following Monday, and where they were so empanelled, there was but one trial.

In *R. v. Nettleton* [2014] Costs L.R. 387, it was held that where the question arises whether "an order [was] made for a retrial", this is not to be confined to cases where one jury are discharged following a disagreement and an order for a new trial is made before a different jury, but it does not extend to every interruption to the trial process, even if it involves the discharge of one jury and the empanelment of a fresh jury. The question is whether the new proceeding was part of the same procedural and temporal matrix as the prior proceeding (see *Seivwright, ante*). If there is a continuous process, even a long gap will not necessarily render the second proceeding a "retrial", and the fact that additional evidence has been served by the prosecution, including from one or more new witnesses, will not *per se* render the new proceeding a retrial. In this case, it was held that it was clear that there had been a trial and a retrial where the jury at the original hearing had been discharged following the arrest of the judge, and there had then been a four-month gap before the second proceeding began with a new judge, new jury and, in the case of some defendants, new counsel.

Guilty pleas

S.I. 2013 No. 435 defines a guilty plea as a case on indictment which is disposed of without trial **G-135** because of the guilty plea, and is not a cracked trial: Sched. 1, para. 1(1). Cases which result in a *Newton* hearing are excluded: *ibid.*, para. 2(8)(c); and see *post*, G-147.

The graduated fee for guilty pleas is calculated by reference to the basic fee, together with the appropriate evidence uplift per page as set out in the table of fees and uplifts: S.I. 2013 No. 435, Sched. 1, paras 7 and 8 (and Table A).

Graduated fees for guilty pleas under Part 3 of Schedule 1 to S.I. 2013 No. 435 no longer apply to cases committed to the Crown Court on the election of the defendant where the magistrates' court determined that the case was suitable for summary trial: S.I. 2013 No. 435, Sched. 1, para. 6.

In *R. v. Agbobu* [2009] Costs L.R. 374, it was held that even though a case may not be a "guilty plea" within the definition in paragraph 1(1) of Schedule 2 to S.I. 2013 No. 435 (*ante*, G-69), paragraph 21(4) of Part 3 of that schedule (*ante*, G-76a) nevertheless provides that "where an application for dismissal is made ... and—(a) the charge, or charges are dismissed and the assisted person is discharged; ... the litigator instructed in the proceedings must be paid a fee calculated in accordance with paragraph 6, or where appropriate, paragraph 8, as appropriate for representing an assisted person in a guilty plea". Accordingly, the fee payable for a litigator representing a defendant against whom charges were dismissed was that payable for a guilty plea and not a cracked trial.

Cracked trials

G-136   A cracked trial is a case on indictment in which (a) a plea and case management hearing takes place and (i) the case does not proceed to trial (whether by reason of pleas of guilty or for other reasons) or the prosecution offer no evidence; and (ii) either (aa) in respect of one or more counts to which the assisted person pleaded guilty, he did not so plead at the plea and case management hearing; or (bb) in respect of one or more counts which did not proceed, the prosecution did not, before or at the plea and case management hearing, declare an intention of not proceeding with them; or (b) the case is listed for trial without a plea and case management hearing taking place: S.I. 2013 No. 435, Sched. 1, para. 1(1) (the definition is defective in that in (b) there is no reference to the case not proceeding to trial (read literally it would cover cases that go to trial where no plea and case management hearing took place)). The rationale for the cracked trial fee is that it provides some element of compensation for the loss of refreshers and trial length increments which otherwise would have been payable: *R. v. Frampton* [2005] Costs L.R. 527. Graduated fees for guilty pleas under Part 3 of Schedule 1 to S.I. 2013 No. 435 no longer apply to cases committed to the Crown Court on the election of the defendant where the magistrates' court determined that the case was suitable for summary trial: S.I. 2013 No. 435, Sched. 1, para. 6.

The essence of a cracked trial is that after the conclusion of a pleas and directions hearing there are still counts on which the prosecution and defence do not agree so that a trial remains a real possibility: *R. v. Minster*, X23, SCTO 647/99; *R. v. Mohammed*, X27, SCCO 210/2000. A case listed for a plea and directions hearing is ultimately defined by what actually happens at that hearing. If a defendant pleads guilty at what is listed as a plea and directions hearing, the plea obviates the need for such a hearing. Accordingly, an advocate is entitled to a fee for a cracked trial: *R. v. Johnson* [2006] Costs L.R. 852 (*sed quaere*, as this flies in the face of the definition of a "cracked trial": see (a), *ante*). Where an indictment containing two counts was listed for trial following a plea and directions hearing, but the defendant pleaded guilty to one count, which was acceptable to the prosecution, whereupon the case was put back for sentence, and where, at the adjourned hearing, a formal not guilty verdict was entered on the other count and where the defendant was represented by different counsel on the two occasions, it was counsel who represented him on the first occasion who was entitled to the "cracked trial" fee as what happened on that occasion came within the definition of a "cracked trial" (*viz.* case was one in which a plea and directions hearing took place, the case did not proceed to trial, but the guilty plea was not entered at that hearing): *R. v. Johnson (Craig)* [2007] Costs L.R. 316. Once a meaningful trial has started, a change of plea cannot convert the trial into a cracked trial: *R. v. Maynard*, X19, SCCO 461/99; *R. v. Karra*, X19A, SCCO 375/99; and *Meeke and Taylor v. Secretary of State for Constitutional Affairs* [2006] Costs L.R. 1, QBD (David Clarke J.). Where a jury were discharged on the second day of a trial on a three count indictment, and on the following working day the prosecution added a new lesser count, and, before a new jury were sworn, the defendant offered sufficient pleas to the indictment, counsel was entitled to a fee for the first (abortive) trial, and a cracked trial fee for the later hearing at which pleas were tendered: *Frampton, ante.*

Cracked trial fees do not apply where a person pleads not guilty at a pleas and directions hearing, but later the same day changes his plea; a guilty plea fee is appropriate: *R. v. Baxter*, X22, SCCO 375/99.

The fee for a cracked trial is calculated by reference to when the case cracked, *i.e.* in the first, second or third part of a period calculated from the date when the court first fixed the date of trial or first ordered that the case should be placed into a warned list, to the date of that first fixture or the date of the start of that warned list. The fact that the fixture might later be broken, or the case moved to another warned list is immaterial and does not affect the calculation. Where the number of days in the period cannot be equally divided by three, the remainder is simply added to the last third of the period: S.I. 2013 No. 435, Sched. 1, paras 7 and 8. The fee is payable to the advocate who appeared at the hearing where pleas were entered or the last such hearing if there was more than one: *R. v. Faulkner*, X33, SCCO 201/02.

In *R. v. Carty* [2009] Costs L.R. 500, it was held that where the prosecution of one of several defendants was stayed, the case fell within the definition of a "cracked trial". The fact that the defendant's advocate had not been present on the occasion of the stay (which had been ordered at a hearing when the principal defendant, being before the court on a separate indictment, had then entered acceptable pleas to the indictment in question) did not preclude payment. Moreover, since 1996, there had been an administrative practice which permitted the prosecution to offer no evidence and an acquittal to be pronounced in open court without the legal representatives being present, and paragraph F.11 of the Graduated Fee Guidance Manual permitted a cracked trial fee to be paid in such circumstances. For this purpose, there was no reason to differentiate between a cracked trial arising from the prosecution offering no evidence and one arising from a stay.

In *R. v. Harris* [2009] Costs L.R. 507, where the defendant had pleaded guilty at a pleas and directions hearing to various offences, but where his "benefit" for the purpose of confiscation proceedings under the CJA 1988 had not yet been agreed, and where sentence and those proceedings had therefore been adjourned, the matter was held not to fall within the definition of a "cracked trial" in paragraph 9(3) of Schedule 4 to the Criminal Defence Service (Funding) Order 2001 (S.I. 2001 No. 855) (which corresponds to the current definition), and the hearing at which the confiscation order was eventually made was said not to fall within the definition of a *Newton* hearing (*R. v. Newton*, 77 Cr.App.R. 13, CA) under paragraph 1(1) (corresponding to the definition in para. 1(1) of Sched. 1 to S.I. 2013 No. 435) for the purposes of paragraph 2(6) (see now para. 2(6) of Sched. 1 to S.I. 2013 No. 435, *ante*, G-40). The prosecution had accepted the basis of the defendant's guilty plea, but in the knowledge that it would take further time, and in all likelihood another hearing, to work out the defendant's benefit. The matter, therefore, fell within the definition of "guilty plea" under paragraph 9(5).

As to the distinction between a "trial" and a "cracked trial", see also *ante*, G-123.

Calculating the pages of prosecution evidence

Prosecution evidence includes all witness statements, documentary and pictorial exhibits and **G-137** records of interview with any defendant served on the defence pursuant to the Crime and Disorder Act 1998 (Service of Prosecution Evidence) Regulations 2005 (S.I. 2005 No. 902) (§§ 1-47, 1-48 in the main work), or included in any notice of additional evidence, and now includes documents served in electronic form, except for a documentary or pictorial exhibit which has never existed in paper form, unless the appropriate officer decides that it would be appropriate to include it in the page count taking into account the nature of the document and any other relevant circumstances: S.I. 2013 No. 435, Sched. 1, para. 1(2) to (5), and Sched. 2, para. 1(2) to (5). The first 50 pages must be excluded for the purposes of the calculation: S.I. 2013 No. 435, Sched. 1, para. 4. Additional documents cannot be included in the computation unless accompanied by a written notice of additional evidence: *R. v. Sturdy*, X9, December 18, 1998, SCTO 714/98; *R. v. Gkampos* [2011] Costs L.R. 142 (pages of antecedent materials relating to the defendant); and *R. v. Ward* [2012] Costs L.R. 605; but see *R. v. Qu* [2012] Costs L.R. 599 (evidence served by prosecution during trial and on which they intended to rely to be included in page count, though not accompanied by formal notice of additional evidence (see CLW/12/26/12 for the suggestion that the costs judge arrived at the correct result, but not necessarily for the right reasons)). Where one or more notices of additional evidence have been served, a page count should include the contents of all such notices, unless all sides are agreed that service of a particular notice was an administrative error; and it is irrelevant when a notice was served, or whether it was requested by the defence or prosecution: *R. v. Taylor* [2005] Costs L.R. 712 (notice served on day jury retired). A prosecution notice of intention to adduce bad character evidence does not fall within the term "any notice of additional evidence": *R. v. McCall* [2011] Costs L.R. 914 (but for a critique of the reasoning, see CLW/11/40/5). Where the Crown have exhibited and served tapes of interview, and defence counsel considers that a transcript of the interview is necessary, the pages of transcript should be included in the computation: *R. v. Brazier*, X5, SCTO 810/97. Taxing officers have been directed to include the fullest transcript produced, together with the version in the transfer bundle (if shorter), and also to include any video evidence transcripts requested by the judge: GFSG A4, A4A. Taxing officers have been directed to exclude title and separator pages: GFSG: A4A; and any additional edited versions of transcripts placed before a jury: GFSG: A5. Fax front sheets which are no more than title pages, duplicate witness statements, whether typed or hand-written, and very short lists of (*e.g.* two) exhibits should not be counted: *R. v. El Treki*, X26, SCCO 431/2000. And nor should pages comprising admissions and a jury bundle consisting of, *inter alia*, an index and details of the defendants: *R. v. Wei* [2010] Costs L.R. 846. No allowance is made for small or large typefaces or for line spacing. Unused material is also excluded.

Whereas paragraph 1(3) of Schedule 2 to S.I. 2013 No. 435 (*ante*, G-69) lists the documents that may be included when calculating the "pages of prosecution evidence" for the purposes of determining a litigator's fee under the graduated fee scheme, the list is to be taken to be exhaustive, notwithstanding that it does not include documents which will have to be read in most cases or even referred to in court (such as the indictment, custody records, correspondence, crime reports, and unused material): *R. v. Tucker* [2010] Costs L.R. 850.

In *R. v. Jalibaghodelehzi* [2014] Costs L.R. 781, it was held that when deciding whether a documentary or pictorial exhibit fell within paragraph 1(2C) of Schedule 1 to the Criminal Defence Service (Funding) Order 2007 (S.I. 2007 No. 1174) (see now the corresponding provision in paragraph 1(5) of Schedules 1 and 2 to S.I. 2013 No. 435 (*ante*, G-39, G-69)), such exhibits should be included if they required a similar degree of consideration to evidence served on paper. Thus, if thousands of pages of raw telephone data were served and the task of the defence lawyers was simply to see whether their client's mobile phone number appeared anywhere (a task more easily done by electronic search), it would be difficult to conclude that the pages should be treated as part of the page count. However, if the evidence served electronically was an important part of the prosecution case, it would be difficult to conclude that the pages should not be included in the page count.

A submission that *R. v. Jalibaghodelehzi* (*ante*) was wrongly decided was rejected in *R. v. Napper* [2014] Costs L.R. 947. In that case it was held that any documentary or pictorial exhibit served electronically is to be included in the page count where it previously existed in paper form. Where it had not previously existed in paper form, or it was impossible to determine whether it had previously existed in paper form, then determining officers are required to consider the nature of the documents and all the relevant circumstances, including the significance of the documents in the case as a whole. The court said that the task of a determining officer under paragraph 1(2C) of Schedule 1 to the 2007 order (*ante*) was not merely to make a determination as to whether such evidence would in practice have been served in paper form prior to the amendments made by the Criminal Defence Service (Funding) (Amendment) Order 2012 (S.I. 2012 No. 750). However, where the litigator and the advocate are one and the same person, this is a circumstance to be taken into account. It was stated that in such a case, if it is appropriate to include exhibits falling within paragraph (2C) in the page count for the purposes of calculating the litigator's fee, it will not be appropriate to include them again when calculating the fee payable under Schedule 1.

R. v. Jalibaghodelehzi and *R. v. Napper* (*ante*) were approved and followed in *R. v. Dodd* [2014] Costs L.R. 1131; and the factual narrative revealed in *R. v. Sana* [2014] Costs L.R. 1143, suggests that, in that case at least, the Legal Aid Agency had accepted and applied the approach in *R. v. Jalibaghodelehzi* and *R. v. Napper*. In *R. v. Furniss* [2015] Costs L.R. 151, Crown Court at Nottingham, Haddon-Cave J. (i) approved *R. v. Jalibaghodelehzi*, (ii) said that cell site, telephone, and similar material served by the prosecution in digital form must be included as pages of prosecution evidence for graduated fee purposes, irrespective of how important or central it is to the prosecution case (thus going further than the costs judges in *R. v. Jalibaghodelehzi, R. v. Napper* and *R. v. Dodd*), and (iii) opined that the page-count limit of 10,000 pages in the graduated fee scheme for advocates constituted an artificial cap on their remuneration irrespective of the work actually done, and that, whilst it was possible to divine a pragmatic reason for a rough-and-ready cap where the actual page count was not significantly above the maximum (say 20–30 per cent), where it vastly exceeded 10,000 pages, such a restriction was manifestly disproportionate and could not rationally have been intended to apply. However, it appears that no argument to the contrary was advanced (and certainly none on behalf of the Lord Chancellor), and it is submitted that his Lordship's remarks (which included gratuitous suggestions as to the computation of the page count in confiscation proceedings and as to costs against the Legal Aid Agency on an indemnity basis if advocates have to bring further appeals on these points to costs judges), made in the context of a Crown Court trial and wholly outside the legislative framework for the determination of legal aid fees, are of doubtful authoritative status (as to which, see the commentary in CLW/15/05/8).

It was held in *R. v. Thompson* [2015] Costs L.R. 173 that *R. v. Furniss* (*ante*) is binding on costs ★
judges. However, it was further held that *Furniss* was only concerned with cases in which the representation order was granted before April 1, 2012 (the date on which the amendments to the Criminal Defence Service (Funding) Order 2007 (S.I. 2007 No. 1174) effected by the Criminal Defence Service (Funding) (Amendment) Order 2012 (S.I. 2012 No. 750), came into force), and that where a representation order was granted before that date (as in the instant case), costs judges had no discretion to include the material referred to in *Furniss* in the page count. In the instant appeal, the Lord Chancellor did not appear but made a written submission in which he pointed out that, on any view, *Furniss* did not apply to the case, and more generally, he took issue with the status of *Furniss*.

In *R. v Manning*, unreported, April 3, 2015, Crown Court at Manchester (H.H. Judge Mansell ★
Q.C.), the judge found that *R. v. Furniss* was not only not binding on the Crown Court, but that the reasoning was flawed for the reasons given in the commentary in CLW/15/05/8. The judge further found that it is no part of the function of a trial judge to dictate to the prosecution how to serve their evidence or to direct them to make agreements with the defence so as to affect the calculation of defence graduated fees (or to dictate to the determining officer how fees are to be calculated under the Criminal Legal Aid (Remuneration) Regulations 2013 (S.I. 2013 No. 435) (*ante*, G-6 *et seq.*) in any given case).

The decisions of the costs judges in *R. v. O'Cuneff* [2010] Costs L.R. 476, *R. v. Burbidge* [2010] Costs L.R. 639, and *R. v. Ibefune*, unreported, June 24, 2010, evidence a conflict as between them and the Legal Services Commission as to the weight to be given to the number of pages of prosecution evidence agreed between the parties and the Crown Court at the end of the case. The commission's stance of not accepting this figure without additional objective evidence has now, however, been fully vindicated by *Criminal Practice Direction (General matters) 3B* [2013] 1 W.L.R. 3164. This inserts new requirements relating to the pagination and indexing of served evidence (as to which, see § 4-344 in the main work). It was plainly no coincidence that, in doing so, the practice direction adopted the (then) definition of "pages of prosecution evidence" contained in the Criminal Defence Service (Funding) Order 2007 (S.I. 2007 No. 1174). Compliance with the requirements of the new provisions by the prosecution will supply the commission (and costs judges) with an objective measure of the number of pages of prosecution evidence.

In *R. v. Greenwood* [2010] Costs L.R. 268, it was held that whereas paragraph 13(2) of Schedule 2 to S.I. 2013 No. 435 (*ante*, G-73b) provides that "where …a case is transferred to a new litigator … the fee payable to the original litigator and the new litigator is a percentage of the total fee, calculated in accordance with the table following this paragraph, as appropriate to the circumstances and timing of the … transfer", and whereas the table provides that where a case is transferred prior to the plea and case management hearing the original litigator should receive 25 per cent of a cracked trial fee, in calculating that fee, the number of pages of prosecution evidence should be taken to be the number of such pages served on the court as at the date of transfer.

Images and photographs

See now paragraphs 1(2) to (5) of Schedules 1 and 2 to S.I. 2013 No. 435. For authorities on   **G-138**
the former provision, which will still apply where the representation order was granted before April 1, 2012, see *R. v. Rigelsford* [2006] Costs L.R. 518, and *R. v. Austin* [2006] Costs L.R. 857.

Fees for leading and junior counsel

Under S.I. 2013 No. 435, fees payable to Queen's Counsel, leading juniors and led juniors are   **G-139**
not directly related, and are calculated from the relevant tables: see, for example, the tables following paragraphs 5 and 8 of Schedule 1. Where two or more led juniors are instructed in the same case, each is paid as if they were the sole junior: Sched. 1, para. 28.

In *R. v. Newport* [2009] Costs L.R. 983, where two juniors appeared for the defendant when the   **G-140**
representation order authorised instruction of junior counsel and Queen's Counsel, it was held that whilst a strict approach would lead to the conclusion that the leading junior was entitled to

no payment, such an outcome would be unjust. Justice demanded that some payment should be made, especially given that the representation order had contemplated payment of two counsel. However, it was said that payment should be at the rate applicable to a leading junior. As to this case, see also *post*, G-269.

Advocates instructed for limited purposes

G-141   Advocates retained for a limited purpose are remunerated according to the specific provisions of S.I. 2013 No. 435. The limited purposes are:

  (a) the cross-examination of witnesses under the YJCEA 1999, s.38, which is remunerated as if for trial, save that the daily attendance fee is calculated by reference to the number of days the advocate actually attended court, instead of the number of days of the trial itself: S.I. 2013 No. 435, Sched. 1, para. 32;

  (b) the provision of written or oral advice: see *post*, G-160;

  (c) mitigation of sentence on indictment, which is remunerated as for a sentencing hearing together with a fee based on the fixed hourly special preparation rate according to the "reasonable number of hours" taken: S.I. 2013 No. 435, Sched. 1, para. 34(1); and an advocate who is discontented with the fee paid may seek a redetermination: para. 34(2).

[The next paragraph is G-143.]

Instructed and substitute advocates

G-143   An instructed advocate is the first advocate instructed in the case who has primary responsibility for the case, or, where a representation order provides for more than one advocate, it means both the first advocate instructed who has primary responsibility for those aspects of a case undertaken by a leading advocate and the first advocate instructed who has primary responsibility for those aspects of a case undertaken by a led advocate: S.I. 2013 No. 435, reg. 2(1).

The new scheme (RAGFS) places great emphasis on continuity of representation. It seeks to achieve this partly by identifying an "instructed advocate" who is responsible for advocacy services and partly by paying the total fee for advocacy to the instructed advocate. An instructed advocated remains an instructed advocate at all times, although provision is made for the instructed advocate to be changed, where, for example, he is unable to conduct the trial because of a clash of commitments, is dismissed by the client, or professionally embarrassed: see Sched. 1, para. 25(10). If the instructed advocate cannot attend a preliminary hearing, and sends a substitute advocate, he nevertheless remains responsible both for the conduct of the case and the ultimate payment of the substitute advocate.

Instructed advocates appointed before the pleas and directions hearing must in writing inform the court of their appointment as soon as they are appointed, otherwise the advocate who attends the pleas and directions hearing will be deemed to be the instructed advocate. If no advocate attends the plea and directions hearing, the advocate who attends the next hearing will be deemed to be and will be recorded by the court as the instructed advocate: see Sched. 1, para. 25(1)–(6). Where the representation order is amended after a plea and case management hearing to include a second advocate, each advocate must notify the court in writing whether they are the led or leading advocate. Where no additional instructed advocate is notified to the court in writing within seven days of the plea and case management hearing, the advocate to appear at the next hearing is deemed to be the instructed advocate and the court will record in writing whether he is the leading instructed advocate or the led instructed advocate, as appropriate to the circumstances of the case: *ibid.*, para. 25(7).

To give effect to the scheme, emphasise the continuity of representation, and ensure that all substitute advocates are paid for any RAGFS work they undertake, the Bar Council has introduced a *Graduated Fee Payment Protocol*. The protocol is an essential part of the mechanism by which advocates will be remunerated in future, but it falls outside the immediate scope of this work. It is available on both the Bar Council's and the Criminal Bar Association's websites.

Sentencing hearings in cases on indictment

G-144   Any person appearing at a sentencing hearing in a case on indictment is entitled to a fixed fee where sentence has been deferred: S.I. 2013 No. 435, Sched. 1, para. 15.

A contested application for an anti-social behaviour order at a sentencing hearing does not attract a separate or additional fee: *R. v. Brinkworth* [2006] Costs L.R. 512.

Under S.I. 2013 No. 435, an advocate instructed solely for the purpose of mitigation shall be paid the fee payable under paragraph 15 together with a fee calculated by reference to the reasonable number of hours of preparation for that appearance multiplied by the hourly rate set out in the table following paragraph 24 which is appropriate to the category of trial advocate: Sched. 1, para. 34(1). The advocate may apply for redetermination of such fee and shall supply such information and documents as may be required by the appropriate officer as proof of the number of hours of preparation: *ibid.*, para. 34(2).

Fitness hearings

A fitness hearing is a hearing to determine whether a defendant is fit to plead or stand trial: **G-145** S.I. 2013 No. 435, Sched. 1, para. 31. If there is a trial on indictment at any time thereafter, the length of the fitness hearing shall be included in determining the length of the trial: *ibid.*, para. 31(a). Where a person pleads guilty at any time after a fitness hearing is held, the advocate may elect to be paid either as if the fitness hearing was a trial or for the guilty plea: *ibid.*, para. 31(c). Where a person is found to be unfit, the trial advocate may elect to treat the fitness hearing either as a trial or as a cracked trial: *ibid.*, para. 31(b).

Cross-examination of vulnerable witnesses

Where an advocate is retained solely for the purpose of cross-examining a vulnerable witness **G-146** under section 38 of the YJCEA 1999, the graduated fee shall be assessed as though the matter was a trial, with the length of trial uplift and refresher calculated by reference to the number of days the advocate attended court: S.I. 2013 No. 435, Sched. 1, para. 32.

Newton hearings

Where a *Newton* hearing takes place following a trial on indictment the provisions relating to **G-147** cracked trials, guilty pleas and sentencing hearings do not apply. The hearing is remunerated as for a contested trial. For the purposes of computation, the length of the *Newton* hearing is added to the main hearing: S.I. 2013 No. 435, Sched. 1, para. 2(8). Thus the main hearing starts on the day the plea is entered, even if this occurred during a pleas and directions hearing: *R. v. Gemeskel*, X2, SCTO 180/98. The advocate who attended the main hearing should claim the whole fee and remunerate the other advocate (if any) who attended the *Newton* hearing: GFSG: B12, 13.

Where a *Newton* hearing does not take place because the basis of plea was subsequently agreed, the case reverts to a guilty plea or cracked trial as appropriate: *R. v. Riddell*, X3, SCTO 318/98. If the hearing is aborted, the usual rules apply: see *post*, G-162, and *R. v. Ayres* [2002] Costs L.R. 330.

In *R. v. Newton*, 77 Cr.App.R. 13, the Court of Appeal clearly envisaged circumstances in which a sentencing judge could reach a conclusion without hearing evidence. However, the regulations define a *Newton* hearing as one at which evidence is heard for the purpose of determining the sentence of a convicted person in accordance with the *Newton* principles. Accordingly, a *Newton* hearing at which no evidence is called can only be remunerated by a standard appearance fee as it is not a *Newton* hearing for the purposes of the regulations: *R. v. Hunter-Brown*, X29, SCCO, 164/2001.

Where a *Newton* hearing is held on a committal for sentence, the only fee payable under Schedule 2 to S.I. 2013 No. 435 is the fixed fee payable for a committal for sentence: *R. v. Holden* [2010] Costs L.R. 851.

Adverse judicial comment and reduction of graduated or fixed fees

Where a trial judge makes adverse observations concerning an advocate's conduct of a gradu- **G-148** ated or fixed fee case, the appropriate authority may reduce the fee by such proportion as it "considers reasonable", having first given the advocate the opportunity to make representations about the extent of the reduction: S.I. 2013 No. 435, reg. 26. See also *post*, G-220.

(3) Additional fees

Confiscation proceedings

Hearings under section 2 of the DTA 1994, section 71 of the CJA 1988 or Part 2 of the PCA **G-149**

2002 are excluded from the length computation of the main hearing and are remunerated separately as work for which a daily or half-daily fee is payable: S.I. 2013 No. 435, Sched. 1, para. 14(1) and (2). Entitlement to the daily fee arises where the hearing begins before but ends after the luncheon adjournment; a half-daily fee is paid where the hearing ends before or begins after the luncheon adjournment: S.I. 2013 No. 435, Sched. 1, para. 14(2). The appropriate rates are set out in the table following paragraph 14(2).

Abuse of process, disclosure and witness summonses' etc.

G-150   Applications relating to abuse of process, disclosure or witness summonses heard before the main hearing are paid at the daily rates set out in the table following paragraph 24: S.I. 2013 No. 435, Sched. 1, para. 13(2). As to remuneration for such applications where they take place as part of the main hearing, see *ante*, G-124. A hearing merely relating to the failure of the prosecution to comply with an earlier disclosure order attracts only a standard appearance fee: GFSG: 12.

In respect of representation orders granted on or after April 30, 2007, these provisions were extended to include applications relating to the admissibility of evidence, and an unsuccessful application to withdraw a guilty plea made by an advocate other than the advocate who appeared at the hearing where the plea was tendered: see now S.I. 2013 No. 435, Sched. 1, para. 13(1)(d) and (e).

[The next paragraph is G-152.]

Conferences and views

G-152   The first three pre-trial conferences or views are not separately remunerated; the fees are deemed to be included in the basic fee: Sched. 1, para. 19(2). Thereafter, the permitted number of further conferences or views (each not exceeding two hours) is as follows:

1 conference	trials of more than 20 but less than 26 days
2 conferences	trials of more than 25 days but less than 36 days
3 conferences	trials of more than 35 days

The number of further conferences allowed in respect of cracked trials is similar, save that the anticipated length of trial is that accepted by the court at the plea and case management hearing (save that, on a literal reading of the legislation, three conferences will only be paid for where it was accepted that the trial would last not more than 40 days): Sched. 1, para. 19(3).

G-153   Conferences include conferences with expert witnesses: S.I. 2013 No. 435, Sched. 1, para. 19(1)(a). Travel expenses and the time taken in travelling, including time taken to travel to a conference with a defendant who could not reasonably be expected to attend counsel's chambers, are remunerated at the specified hourly rate: *ibid.*, para. 19(5). Where such fees are allowed, reasonable travelling expenses may also be claimed: *ibid.*, para. 19(4). The local bar rule has no application to such fees: *R. v. Carlyle* [2002] Costs L.R. 192.

[The next paragraph is G-156.]

Special preparation

G-156   Special preparation is preparation substantially in excess of the amount normally done for cases of the type in question and undertaken because the case involves "a very unusual or novel point of law or factual issue": S.I. 2013 No. 435, Sched. 1, para. 17(1)(a). "Very" qualifies both "unusual" and "novel" and the phrase "very unusual or novel" qualifies both the expressions "point of law" and "factual issue": *Meeke and Taylor v. Secretary of State for Constitutional Affairs* [2006] Costs L.R. 1, QBD (David Clarke J.). Remuneration is calculated at an hourly rate for "the number of hours preparation in excess of the amount the appropriate officer considers reasonable for cases of the same type": S.I. 2013 No. 435, Sched. 1, para. 17(3)(a); and with no enhancement under paragraph 29 of Schedule 2: *Lord Chancellor v. McLarty & Co. Solicitors* [2012] Costs L.R. 190, QBD (Burnett J.).

What falls to be compensated is the extra work caused by the unusual or novel point by comparison with the sort of case involved without the unusual or novel point; as the term is used in relation to the quantification of fees, "type" in this context should be defined as an indication of weight; but the exercise does not include any consideration of the reasonableness of the time claimed; thus, once the determining officer has resolved that the case qualifies for a special preparation fee, he must assess the number of hours worked in excess of the norm and compensate for those hours at the prescribed hourly rate: *R. v. Goodwin* [2008] Costs L.R. 497.

R. v. Goodwin, ante, was considered in *R. v. Kholi* [2010] Costs L.R. 982, in which it was held that under paragraph 52(i) of the Guidance Manual for the CPS Graduated Fee Scheme (which is in materially identical terms to para. 17(1)(a) of Sched. 1 to S.I. 2013 No. 435 (*ante*, G-53)), it is only those hours of work attributable to the unusual or novel point of law or factual issue which was involved, which fall to be remunerated as special preparation; it is not the case that all time spent by the advocate in preparation over and above the norm for the type of case should be so remunerated.

The concept of "normal preparation" done for a case of the same type is wholly artificial. Other than in routine cases of burglary and theft, in virtually all other crimes in the criminal calendar, the circumstances vary infinitely: *R. v. Briers* [2005] Costs L.R. 146. The test is "What is the normal preparation for this offence?" not "What is the normal preparation for a case exhibiting these particular facts": *Briers, ante; R. v. Ward-Allen* [2005] Costs L.R. 745.

It is for counsel to differentiate between what he considers to be the normal preparation for a case of that type and the actual preparation that he has carried out: *Briers, ante; R. v. Marandola* [2006] Costs L.R. 184.

Very unusual or novel points of law have an obvious meaning, namely a point of law which either has never been raised or decided (novel) or which is outwith the usual professional experience (very unusual): *R. v. Ward-Allen, ante*. Some further assistance can be found in *Perry v. Lord Chancellor*, *The Times*, May 26, 1994, although it should be noted that that case was not concerned with these regulations.

Very unusual or novel factual issues have a similar meaning, namely a factual issue which either has never been raised or which is outwith the usual professional experience: *R. v. Ward-Allen, ante*. Such issues might cover extremely rare medical conditions, such as Munchausen's Syndrome by Proxy or "pubic symphysitis dysfunction", the exceptional, if not unique, nature of which was held in *R. v. Bishop* [2008] Costs L.R. 808, to justify a special preparation fee where it had contributed to prosecution material of over 600 pages (not served as part of the page count); novel issues might, for example have included DNA fingerprinting when it was introduced, but it would not qualify now. A case involving "shaken baby syndrome" does not necessarily attract a special preparation fee, unless there are additional medical complications: *R. v. Khair* [2005] Costs L.R. 542. A special preparation fee was allowed in *R. v. Thompson* [2006] Costs L.R. 668 where the defendant was accused of murdering her husband 10 years earlier. Counsel had to consider not only pathology and toxicology reports, but also a psychiatric profile on the husband prepared by a psychiatrist who had never met him, and issues arising in diabetology and physiology. Transcripts of the original coroner's inquest and the defendant's previous trials for theft and attempted murder of another husband were also served.

The novelty of the bad character provisions of the CJA 2003 did not provide grounds for claiming a special preparation fee; the criminal law is constantly changing: *R. v. Christie* [2010] 4 Costs L.R. 634.

A special preparation fee would be reasonable where counsel had to check a sample of over 33,000 original photographs of which the prosecution had only copied a representative fraction for use at trial: *R. v. Rigelsford* [2006] Costs L.R. 523; and see *ante*, G-138. But the mere fact that preparation properly undertaken for a complex three-week rape trial was "wasted" because the defendant decided to plead guilty during the prosecution opening did not justify a special preparation fee: *Meeke and Taylor v. Secretary of State for Constitutional Affairs, ante*.

A large quantity of unused material does not of itself give rise to a novel or unusual factual issue even where it is accepted that detailed examination of the material was necessary: *R. v. Lawrence* [2007] Costs L.R. 138; and even where the trial judge has extended a representation order to allow two juniors to peruse such material: *R. v. Dhaliwal* [2004] Costs L.R. 689. Such work is not remunerated under the graduated fee scheme or indeed at all: *ibid*. Nor does the mere failure of the scheme to accommodate unused material amount to a breach of the principle of equality of arms: *R. v. Marandola, ante.*

An advocate can also claim a special preparation fee where the prosecution evidence exceeds 10,000 pages and the appropriate officer considers that it is reasonable to make a payment in excess of the graduated fee which would otherwise be payable; the fee is calculated by reference to the number of hours which the appropriate officer considers reasonable to read the excess pages, using the current hourly fee rate: S.I. 2013 No. 435, Sched. 1, para. 17(1)(b), (2) and (3)(b).

An advocate making a claim for special preparation should provide the Legal Aid Agency with dates, times and descriptions of the work completed, and the page count of any material considered, and any documents produced as a result of the special preparation should be annexed to the claim form, and the claim should relate each item of special preparation to the very unusual or novel point of law or fact that gave rise to the need for special preparation in the first place: *R. v. French* [2014] Costs L.R. 786.

An advocate's failure to keep a contemporaneous work log may result in rejection of a claim for a special preparation fee: *R. v. Dunne* [2013] Costs L.R. 1031 (considering the corresponding provision in the Criminal Defence Service (Funding) Order 2007 (S.I. 2007 No. 1174).

Evidence served electronically

G-157   A special preparation fee may also be claimed where a documentary or pictorial exhibit, which has never existed in paper form, is served by the prosecution in electronic form, and the appropriate officer does not consider it appropriate to include it in the pages of prosecution evidence; and such fee may be paid if the appropriate officer considers it reasonable to make a payment in excess of the fee otherwise payable under the graduated fee scheme, with the amount of the payment depending on the number of hours which the appropriate officer considers reasonable to view the exhibit: see Sched. 1, para. 17(1)(c) and (2), and Sched. 2, para. 20(1)(a) and (2). The drafting of these provisions in the two schedules is slightly different, but it is submitted that the intent is the same. As to the drafting, this – taken at face value – gives the appropriate officer a discretion whether to make a payment even where he considers it reasonable to do so. It is submitted, however, that the legislation is unlikely to be so construed: if the appropriate officer considers it reasonable to make a payment, then it is likely to be held that he should do so. The revised wording of these provisions (introduced by the Criminal Defence Service (Funding) (Amendment) Order 2001 (S.I. 2012 No. 750)) was doubtless intended to avoid the difficulties caused by the former wording and which gave rise to a series of decisions, such as *R. v. Rigelsford* [2006] Costs L.R. 518, *R. v. Austin* [2006] Costs L.R. 857, *Lord Chancellor v. Michael J. Reed Ltd* [2010] Costs L.R. 72, QBD (Penry-Davey J.), *Lord Chancellor v. McLarty & Co. Solicitors* [2012] Costs L.R. 190, QBD (Burnett J.), and *R. v. Jones* [2010] Costs L.R. 469. For details of these authorities, which will still have application to cases in which a representation order was granted before April 1, 2012, see previous supplements.

Lord Chancellor v. Michael J. Reed Ltd (ante) was followed in *R. v. Osoteko* [2014] Costs L.R. 190, but the costs judge certified a point of principle of general importance, *viz.* whether that case had created too narrow a definition of pages of prosecution evidence. The appeal to the High Court (see *Maclaverty Cooper Atkins v. Lord Chancellor* [2014] Costs L.R. 629, QBD (Akenhead J.)) was dismissed, the court approving and following *Lord Chancellor v. Michael J. Reed Ltd.*

[The next paragraph is G-159.]

Listening to or viewing tapes

G-159   There is now no provision for any separate payment for listening to or viewing tapes. These are now treated as being rolled up within the whole of the graduated fee.

Provision of written or oral advice

G-160   Any advocate instructed solely to provide written or oral advice shall be paid a fee calculated from the reasonable number of hours of preparation for that advice using the appropriate hourly rate in the table following paragraph 24 of Schedule 1 to S.I. 2013 No. 435: see Sched. 1, para. 33(1). The advocate may apply for re-determination of such fee under regulation 28, and he shall supply such information and documents as may be required by the appropriate officer as proof of the number of hours of preparation: *ibid.*, para. 33(2).

As to whether a solicitor may properly instruct counsel other than counsel who appeared at trial to advise on the question of appeal where trial counsel has advised in the negative, see *R. v. Umezie*, § 7-165 in the main work.

R. v. Umezie was considered in *R. v. Bromige* [2011] Costs L.R. 145, in which it was held that where solicitors, on receipt of trial counsel's negative advice as to the prospects of a successful appeal against sentence, instructed fresh counsel to advise on the question, trial counsel's negative advice (whether written or oral) did not terminate the representation order; paragraph A1–2 of the Guide to Commencing Proceedings in the Court of Appeal (Criminal Division) (*post*, Appendix J-4) did not preclude payment of a fee for subsequent advice given by fresh counsel in relation to the appeal, because that paragraph was only concerned with the amendment of representation orders, and no amendment to the representation order granted by the magistrates' court was necessary to instruct fresh counsel to advise; however, fresh counsel's claim for a fee for his advice could only fall within paragraph 6 of Schedule 3 to S.I. 2013 No. 435 (*ante*, G-85), which provides, that upon the determination of an advocate's fees in proceedings in the Court of Appeal, "the appropriate officer must consider the claim ... and must allow such work as appears to him to have been reasonably done"; as a general principle it will not be reasonable to obtain advice on a point that has already been the subject of advice, with the obvious exceptions to this principle being if the initial advice is incompetent or ambiguous, or if there is a change in circumstances or if new evidence has come to light; the reason given in this case for seeking further advice, *viz.* that the solicitors were not convinced as to the correctness of the negative oral advice from trial counsel, was not sufficient; therefore the work done by fresh counsel was not reasonably done for the purposes of paragraph 6 because no good reason had been shown for instructing him to give advice on a point that had already been the subject of advice. For the submission that the costs judge's reliance on paragraph 6 of Schedule 3 is unsustainable, see CLW/11/08/45.

(4) Acting for more than one defendant, or in more than one "case"

The definition of "case" in paragraph 1(1) of Schedule 2 (*ante*, G-69) could not possibly lead to the conclusion that if a litigator represents more than one defendant charged and tried on the same indictment that litigator is then entitled to be paid on the basis that there are as many cases as there are defendants: *Lord Chancellor v. Eddowes Perry and Osbourne Ltd* [2011] Costs L.R. 498, QBD (Spencer J.). As to this case, see also *post*, G-273.   **G-161**

An uplift of one-fifth for each additional defendant represented may only be claimed where the regulations so provide: S.I. 2013 No. 435, Sched. 1, para. 27(2). Where an advocate acts for more than one defendant, the advocate must select the case on which remuneration is to be based (the principal case). Claims for such uplifts may be made for pleas and directions hearings, some aborted hearings, main hearings, appeals against conviction, committals for sentence, proceedings for a breach of a Crown Court order, disclosure, abuse and witness summons hearings, and confiscation proceedings: S.I. 2013 No. 435, Sched. 1, para. 27(4). But no uplifts for these hearings, with the exception of confiscation proceedings, are payable in cases that were committed to the Crown Court on the election of the defendant, where the magistrates' court had determined that the case was suitable for summary trial: *ibid.*, para. 27(3). In respect of a trial, the uplift is limited to one-fifth of the basic fee and not the basic fee enhanced by reference to the prosecution evidence, witnesses and length of trial uplift: ibid., para. 27(2)(b), *i.e.* where the main hearing in each case was heard concurrently: *R. v. Fletcher*, X6, SCTO 815/97.

The above provisions also apply where the advocate conducts two or more cases concurrently: S.I. 2013 No. 435, Sched. 1, para. 27(2). Proceedings arising out of a single notice of appeal against conviction or sentence, or single committal for sentence, constitute a separate "case": para. 1(1) of Schedule 1 to S.I. 2013 No. 435. However, a committal for sentence together with a committal for breach of a community service order constituted two separate "cases" as the latter was a committal for breach of an earlier order: *R. v. Hines*, X24, SCCO 337/2000. As a case means proceedings on one or more counts of a single indictment, it is submitted that two trials arising from a severed indictment give rise to two separate graduated fees, as the trials are not heard concurrently.

In *R. v. Fury* [2011] Costs L.R. 919, it was said that if a hearing deals with one case then another, independently of each other, it will be hearing them consecutively; hearings will be concurrent only if they are combined or conjoined or somehow interlinked; this will be so where the main hearings of a number of cases against the same defendant are listed together and the defendant either pleads guilty or is to be sentenced in all of the cases; the cases will impact on each other either as to the directions that are given for sentencing or as to the sentences that are imposed; they will not be considered independently of each other. For criticism of the actual decision in this case (cases were not heard concurrently where, as part of an agreed package, defendant pleaded guilty to one indictment and prosecution offered no evidence on the other, all counts having originally been in the same indictment), see CLW/11/40/3.

In *R. v. Sturmer and Lewis* [2009] Costs L.R. 364, it was said that the combined effect of paragraph 15 and the table in paragraph 19 of Schedule 2 to S.I. 2013 No. 435 (*ante*, G-74a, G-75a) is that where a litigator is "instructed in ... a sentencing hearing following a committal for sentence to the Crown Court", the "fee payable ... is that set out in the table" (para. 15), *i.e.* "£212.77" per proceedings (the table). "Proceedings" can involve more than one defendant and, if there is only one "proceedings", only one fee will be payable, however many defendants are represented by the litigator.

[The next paragraph is G-163.]

(5) Abortive hearings

G-163   The payment of fixed fees for abortive hearings is limited to ineffective trials: see Sched. 1, para. 16. As to this, see *R. v. Budai*, *ante*, G-124.

(6) Wasted preparation

G-164   Wasted preparation occurs where an advocate does not represent his client because of (a) a clash of listings and the advocate has been unable to secure a change of date for either hearing; or (b) a fixture for a main hearing is altered by the court despite the advocate's objection; or (c) the advocate withdraws with leave of the court because of professional embarrassment; or (d) the advocate is dismissed by the client; or (e) the advocate is obliged to undertake judicial or other public duties: S.I. 2013 No. 435, Sched. 1, para. 18(1). A representation order replacing a single junior with Queen's Counsel acting alone does not entitle junior counsel to claim a wasted preparation fee in respect of the preparation reasonably and properly undertaken; counsel has no redress under the scheme: *R. v. Schultz*, X10, SCTO 552/98. The hourly fee may be claimed only where eight or more hours of preparation have been undertaken, and (a) the trial lasted for five days or more, or (b) in the case of a cracked trial, there are more than 150 pages of prosecution evidence: S.I. 2013 No. 435, Sched. 1, para. 18(2). The wasted preparation fee is calculated by reference to the number of hours of preparation reasonably carried out by the advocate, who must supply such information and documents in support of the claim as may be required: S.I. 2013 No. 435, Sched. 1, para. 18(3) and (5).

The requirements of paragraph 18(1) were satisfied where, following the vacation of the trial date by the trial judge and his proposal of a new date, counsel had written objecting to the new date (on the grounds that he had booked and paid for a holiday abroad that started within 10 days of the new date), but where, despite that objection, the trial had gone ahead on the proposed date, with the result that counsel had had to return the brief: *R. v. Ghaffar* [2009] Costs L.R. 980. The fact that counsel's objection was to the new date, and not to the vacation of the original fixture, was not a valid ground for refusing a wasted preparation fee in respect of the substantial preparation done by counsel prior to the vacation of the original fixture. Changing a fixture is a process and an objection to part of that process is therefore an objection to the change. There was nothing in paragraph 18(1)(b) that restricted it to counsel's professional commitments.

(7) Appeals, pleas before venue, committals and other fees

G-165   Graduated fixed fees are also payable in respect of committals for sentence (which include plea before venue cases), appeals from magistrates' courts and breach of Crown Court orders: S.I. 2013 No. 435, Sched. 1, para. 20; noting briefs: *ibid.*, para. 23; bail and other applications, and mentions when not forming part of a main hearing or other hearing for which a fixed fee is provided: *ibid.*, para. 20(3). The appropriate rate is that listed in the table following paragraph 24. After the Crown Court is seized of a case, any bail applications, or executions of bench warrants made in a magistrates' court are remunerated as if made in the Crown Court: *R. v. Bailey*, X16, 378/99. As to trials of Bail Act 1976 offences, see *ante*, G-130.

(8) Contempt proceedings

Remuneration for proceedings for contempt in the face of the court is fixed at discrete daily **G-166** rates: S.I. 2013 No. 435, reg. 11, and Sched. 1, para. 21. The fees are fixed and there is no discretion to allow *ex post facto* payment, however regrettable and unfair the result may be: *R. v. Russell* [2006] Costs L.R. 841. Such payments do not fall within the graduated fee scheme and, therefore, such hearings do not form part of the main hearing or the sentencing hearing.

(9) Travel expenses

Travel and hotel expenses may be claimed subject to the usual 40 kilometre local bar rule: S.I. **G-167** 2013 No. 435, Sched. 1, para. 29 (see generally *post*, G-253). Expenses should not be paid in respect of conferences for which advocates are not entitled to be remunerated, unless the conference was abortive due to circumstances beyond the advocate's control: *R. v. Pickett*, X39.

(10) Table of offences

The effect of the table of offences at the end of Schedule 1 to S.I. 2013 No. 435 (as amended by **G-168** the Protection of Freedoms Act 2012 (Consequential Amendments) Order 2013 (S.I. 2013 No. 862)) is set out in the following paragraphs. Offences are divided into those below £30,000, those where the value is £30,000 or more, but less than £100,000, and those where the value involved is £100,000 or more. As to the method of calculation for the purposes of determining value, see *ante*, G-121. As to conspiracy, incitement and attempt, see *ante*, G-120. It should be noted that there are various errors in the table: for example, it refers to section 39 (rather than section 139) of the CJA 1988 (this has been corrected below) and it refers to various measures that have been repealed and replaced, including the Post Office Act 1953, the Merchant Shipping Act 1970 and the Air Navigation Order 2005 (S.I. 2005 No. 1970)).

An "armed robbery" (see the Theft Act 1968 entries) arises where the offender was armed with a firearm or imitation firearm, or was thought by the victim to have been so armed, or was armed with an offensive weapon: *R. v. Stables*, X12, SCTO 102/99.

Where a judge proposes to try an offence under the Bail Act 1976, s.6, in respect of a defendant who is first brought up before him for non-attendance, then there is a trial or guilty plea under the graduated fee scheme: *R. v. Shaw* [2005] Costs L.R. 326.

As several statutes are listed under more than one class, the following is a list of the statutes **G-169** and orders featured in the table, with the classes in which they appear—

Air Navigation Order 2005 (S.I. 2005 No. 1970)	H
Aviation Security Act 1982	B
Bail Act 1976	H
Bribery Act 2010	I
Child Abduction Act 1984	C
Children and Young Persons Act 1933	B, J
Cremation Act 1902	I
Crime and Disorder Act 1998	B, C, H
Criminal Damage Act 1971	B, C
Criminal Justice Act 1961	C
Criminal Justice Act 1967	I
Criminal Justice Act 1988	H

Criminal Justice Act 1991	B
Criminal Justice (International Co-operation) Act 1990	B
Criminal Justice (Terrorism and Conspiracy) Act 1998	I
Criminal Justice and Public Order Act 1994	I
Criminal Law Act 1967	I
Criminal Law Act 1977	C
Customs and Excise Management Act 1979	B, C, F, G, H, K
Dangerous Dogs Act 1991	C
Disorderly Houses Act 1751	H
Domestic Violence, Crime and Victims Act 2004	B
Drug Trafficking Act 1994	B, I
Drug Trafficking Offences Act 1986	C
European Communities Act 1972	I
Explosive Substances Act 1883	A, B
Firearms Act 1968	B, C
Firearms (Amendment) Act 1988	C
Forgery Act 1861	F, I
Forgery and Counterfeiting Act 1981	F, G, K
Fraud Act 2006	F, G, K
Hallmarking Act 1973	F, G, K
Identity Cards Act 2006	F
Immigration Act 1971	C
Indecency with Children Act 1960	J
Indecent Displays (Control) Act 1981	H
Infant Life (Preservation) Act 1929	A
Infanticide Act 1938	A
Insolvency Act 1986	G
Magistrates' Courts Act 1980	I
Malicious Damage Act 1861	H
Mental Health Act 1959	J
Mental Health Act 1983	D
Merchant Shipping Act 1970	H
Misuse of Drugs Act 1971	B, C, H
Nuclear Material (Offences) Act 1983	B
Obscene Publications Act 1959	H
Offences against the Person Act 1861	A, B, C, H
Perjury Act 1911	I
Post Office Act 1953	H
Prevention of Corruption Act 1906	I
Prevention of Crime Act 1953	H
Prison Act 1952	C
Prison Security Act 1992	B
Proceeds of Crime Act 2002	B
Prohibition of Female Circumcision Act 1985	C

Protection from Eviction Act 1977	H
Protection from Harassment Act 1997	H
Protection of Children Act 1978	J
Public Bodies Corrupt Practices Act 1889	I
Public Order Act 1986	B, C, H
Public Passenger Vehicles Act 1981	H
Road Traffic Act 1960	H
Road Traffic Act 1988	B, H
Road Traffic Regulation Act 1984	H
Sexual Offences Act 1956	D, H, J
Sexual Offences Act 1967	D, H
Sexual Offences Act 2003	D, J
Sexual Offences (Amendment) Act 2000	D
Stamp Duties Management Act 1891	F, G, K
Submarine Telegraph Act 1885	C
Suicide Act 1961	B
Taking of Hostages Act 1982	B
Terrorism Act 2000	B, C
Theatres Act 1968	H
Theft Act 1968	B, C, E, F, G, H, K
Theft Act 1978	F, G, H, K
Trade Descriptions Act 1968	H, I
Treason Act 1842	C
Value Added Tax Act 1994	F, G, K
Vehicle Excise and Registration Act 1994	H

Class A: homicide and related grave offences

(i) *Common law offences*
Murder and manslaughter   **G-170**

(ii) *Offences created by primary or secondary legislation*
Those contrary to the following provisions:
Explosive Substances Act 1883, ss.2 and 3;
Infant Life (Preservation) Act 1929, s.1(1);
Infanticide Act 1938, s.1(1);
Offences against the Person Act 1861, s.4.

Class B: offences involving serious violence or damage, and serious drugs offences

(i) *Common law offences*
Kidnapping and false imprisonment   **G-171**

(ii) *Offences created by primary or secondary legislation*
Those contrary to the following provisions:
Aviation Security Act 1982, s.2(1)(b);
Crime and Disorder Act 1998, s.30(1);
Children and Young Persons Act 1933, s.1;
Criminal Damage Act 1971, s.1(2) and (where the value exceeds £30,000) s.1(3);

Criminal Justice Act 1991, s.90;

Criminal Justice (International Co-operation) Act 1990, ss.12 and 18;

Customs and Excise Management Act 1979, s.50 (Class A or B drugs), s.85, s.170(2)(b) or (c) (in relation to Class A or B drugs);

Domestic Violence, Crime and Victims Act 2004, s.5;

Drug Trafficking Act 1994, ss.49, 50, 51, 52 and 53;

Explosive Substances Act 1883, s.4(1);

Firearms Act 1968, ss.5, 16, 17 and 18;

Misuse of Drugs Act 1971, s.4 (Class A or B drug), s.5(3) (Class A or B drug), ss.6, 8, 9, 12 and 13;

Nuclear Material (Offences) Act 1983, s.2;

Offences against the Person Act 1861, ss.16, 17, 18, 21, 22, 23, 28, 29, 30, 32, 33, 34 and 58;

Prison Security Act 1992, s.1;

Proceeds of Crime Act 2002, ss.327, 328, 329, 330, 331, 332, 333, 339(1A);

Public Order Act 1986, ss.1, 2 and 38;

Road Traffic Act 1988, ss.1, 3A and 22A;

Suicide Act 1961, s.2;

Taking of Hostages Act 1982, s.1;

Terrorism Act 2000, ss.11, 12, 13, 15, 16, 17, 18, 39, 54, 56, 57, 58 and 59;

Theft Act 1968, s.8(1) (if "armed"), s.8(2) (if "with weapon"), s.10, s.12A (if resulting in death) and 21.

Class C: lesser offences involving violence or damage, and less serious drugs offences

(i) *Common law offences*

G-172   Permitting an escape, rescue, breach of prison and escaping from lawful custody without force

(ii) *Offences created by primary or secondary legislation*

Those contrary to the following provisions:

Child Abduction Act 1984, ss.1 and 2;

Crime and Disorder Act 1998, ss.29(1) and 30(1);

Criminal Damage Act 1971, s.1(1) and, where the offence does not also fall within section 1(2) and where the value of the damage is less than £30,000, s.1(3), s.2 and s.3;

Criminal Justice Act 1961, s.22;

Criminal Law Act 1977, s.51;

Customs and Excise Management Act 1979, s.50 (in relation to Class C drugs), s.68A(1) and (2), s.86, s.170(2)(b), (c) (in relation to Class C drugs);

Dangerous Dogs Act 1991, s.3;

Drug Trafficking Offences Act 1986, ss.26B and 26C;

Firearms Act 1968, ss.1, 2, 3, 4, 19, 20, 21(4), 21(5) and 42;

Firearms (Amendment) Act 1988, s.6(1);

Immigration Act 1971, s.25;

Misuse of Drugs Act 1971, s.4 (Class C drug), s.5(2) (Class A drug), s.5(3) (Class C drug);

Offences against the Person Act 1861, ss.20, 24, 26, 27, 31, 37, 47, 59, 60 and 64;

Prison Act 1952, s.39;

Prohibition of Female Circumcision Act 1985, s.1;

Public Order Act 1986, ss.18 to 23;

Submarine Telegraph Act 1885, s.3;

Terrorism Act 2000, s.19;

Theft Act 1968, s.8(1) (other than when "armed");

Treason Act 1842, s.2.

Class D: sexual offences and offences against children

Offences created by primary or secondary legislation
    Those contrary to the following provisions: **G-173**
        Criminal Law Act 1977, s.54;
        Mental Health Act 1983, s.127;
        Sexual Offences Act 1956, s.4, s.9, s.10 (other than by man with girl under 13), s.11, s.13 (between male aged 21 or over and male under 16), ss.14, 15, 19, 21, 23, 27, 29, 30 and 31;
        Sexual Offences Act 1967, s.5;
        Sexual Offences Act 2003, s.3, s.4 (without penetration), ss.11 to 13, 15 to 19, 32, 33, 36, 37, 40, 41, 52, 53, 61 to 67, 69 and 70;
        Sexual Offences (Amendment) Act 2000, s.3.

Class E: burglary, etc.

Offences created by primary or secondary legislation
    Those contrary to the following provisions: **G-174**
        Theft Act 1968, ss.9 and 25

Classes F, G and K: other offences of dishonesty (offences always in Class F)

Offences created by primary or secondary legislation
    Those contrary to the following provisions: **G-175**
        Forgery Act 1861, ss.36, 37;
        Identity Cards Act 2006, s.25(1), (3) and (5).

Classes F, G and K: other offences of dishonesty (offences always in Class G)

Offences created by primary or secondary legislation
    Those contrary to the following provisions: **G-176**
        Customs and Excise Management Act 1979, s.50 (counterfeit notes or coins), s.170(2)(b) or (c) (counterfeit notes or coins);
        Forgery and Counterfeiting Act 1981, ss.14 to 17;
        Insolvency Act 1986, s.360.

Classes F, G and K: other offences of dishonesty (offences in Class G if value exceeds £30,000, in Class K if value exceeds £100,000 and otherwise in Class F)

Offences created by primary or secondary legislation
    Those contrary to the following provisions: **G-177**
        Customs and Excise Management Act 1979, s.50 (to the extent not specified elsewhere), s.168, s.170(1)(b), s.170(2)(b), (c) (to the extent not specified elsewhere);
        Forgery and Counterfeiting Act 1981, ss.1 to 5;
        Fraud Act 2006, ss.2, 3, 4, 6, 7, 9 and 11;
        Hallmarking Act 1973, s.6;
        Stamp Duties Management Act 1891, s.13;
        Theft Act 1968, ss.1, 11, 13, 15, 16, 17 and 22;
        Theft Act 1978, ss.1 and 2;
        Value Added Tax Act 1994, s.72(1)–(8).

Class H: miscellaneous other offences

(i) *Common law offences*
        Keeping a disorderly house, outraging public decency   **G-178**

(ii) *Offences created by primary or secondary legislation*
Those contrary to the following provisions:
>Air Navigation Order 2005 (S.I. 2005 No. 1970), art. 75;
>Bail Act 1976, s.9(1);
>Crime and Disorder Act 1998, ss.1(10), 2(8), 31(1) and 32(1);
>Criminal Justice Act 1988, s.139;
>Customs and Excise Management Act 1979, ss.13 and 16;
>Disorderly Houses Act 1751, s.8;
>Indecent Displays (Control) Act 1981, s.1;
>Malicious Damage Act 1861, s.36;
>Merchant Shipping Act 1970, s.27;
>Misuse of Drugs Act 1971, s.5(2) (Class B or C drug); s.11;
>Obscene Publications Act 1959, ss.1 and 2;
>Offences against the Person Act 1861, ss.35 and 38;
>Post Office Act 1953, s.11;
>Prevention of Crime Act 1953, s.1;
>Protection from Eviction Act 1977, s.1;
>Protection from Harassment Act 1997, ss.3(6), 4(1) and 5(5);
>Public Order Act 1986, s.3;
>Public Passenger Vehicles Act 1981, s.65;
>Road Traffic Act 1960, s.233;
>Road Traffic Act 1988, ss.2 and 173;
>Road Traffic Regulation Act 1984, s.115;
>Sexual Offences Act 1956, ss.2, 3, 12, 13 (other than where one participant over 21 and the other under 16), 22, 24 and 32;
>Sexual Offences Act 1967, s.4;
>Theatres Act 1968, s.2;
>Theft Act 1968, s.12A (but not where death results);
>Theft Act 1978, s.3;
>Trade Descriptions Act 1968, ss.1, 8, 9, 12, 13 and 14;
>Vehicle Excise and Registration Act 1994, s.44.

Class I: offences against public justice and similar offences

(i) *Common law offences*

G-179   Embracery, fabrication of evidence with intent to mislead tribunal, perverting the course of justice and personation of jurors

(ii) *Offences created by primary or secondary legislation*
Those contrary to the following provisions:
>Bribery Act 2010, ss.1, 2 and 6;
>Cremation Act 1902, s.8(2);
>Criminal Justice Act 1967, s.89;
>Criminal Justice (Terrorism and Conspiracy) Act 1998, s.5;
>Criminal Justice and Public Order Act 1994, ss.51(1) and (2), 75(1) and (2);
>Criminal Law Act 1967, ss.4(1) and 5;
>Drug Trafficking Act 1994, s.58(1);
>European Communities Act 1972, s.11;
>Forgery Act 1861, s.34;
>Magistrates' Courts Act 1980, s.106;
>Perjury Act 1911, ss.1 to 7(2);
>Prevention of Corruption Act 1906, s.1;
>Public Bodies Corrupt Practices Act 1889, s.1;

Trade Descriptions Act 1968, s.29(2).

Class J: serious sexual offences

Offences created by primary or secondary legislation

Those contrary to the following provisions: **G-180**

Children and Young Persons Act 1933, ss.25, 26;

Indecency with Children Act 1960, s.1(1);

Protection of Children Act 1978, s.1;

Sexual Offences Act 1956, ss.1(1), 5, 6, 7, 10, 12 (of person under 16), 16, 17, 20, 25, 26
and 28;

Sexual Offences Act 2003, ss.1, 2, 4 (activity involving penetration), 5 to 10, 14, 25, 26, 30,
31, 34, 35, 38, 39, 47 to 50 and 57 to 59A.

G. Very High Cost Cases

Definition

For the definition of a "Very High Cost Case", see regulation 2 of S.I. 2013 No. 435 (*ante*, G-7). **G-181**
Regulation 3(8) (*ante*, G-8) provides that the regulations (with the exception of reg. 12 and para.
13(8) and (9) of Schedule 2) do not apply to Very High Costs Cases.

Background

Unlike the former scheme for the *ex post facto* taxation of fees (as to which, see Appendix G in **G-182**
the supplements to the 2010 edition of this work) and the graduated fee scheme, the Very High
Cost Case ("VHCC") regime is not concerned with fee assessment after the completion of a case.
VHCCs operate under a contract-based system where litigators' and advocates' tasks and the time
allotted for each task are agreed or determined before the work is undertaken. They are managed by the Complex Crime Unit of the Legal Aid Agency (an executive agency of the Ministry of
Justice).

Notification and classification

Litigators (referred to by the Legal Aid Agency as "organisations") are required to notify the **G-183**
Legal Aid Agency of any case which is, or is likely to be, a VHCC: S.I. 2013 No. 435, reg. 12.
Notification is effected by submitting a VHCC Notification Request Form 2013, which is available
on the agency's website. If a case qualifies, or if an organisation is in any doubt about this, the
organisation should make the notification within five business days of the earliest hearing at which
the court sets a trial estimate, or the organisation identifying that the case will be or is likely to be
a VHCC, or the organisation receiving a VHCC notification request form 2013 from the agency.
If the notification requirements are not met, and the agency is likely to or will suffer financial loss
as a result, it may, in discharging its functions under the LASPOA 2012: (a) impose any sanction
on the organisation in accordance with any other legal aid agreement or contract; (b) exclude the
organisation from undertaking VHCC work or Individual Case Contract work on the case that it
failed to notify; (c) where it persistently breaches this duty, exclude the organisation from
undertaking future VHCC work or Individual Case Contract Work or reduce or refuse any payment to the organisation in relation to the case.

Part A of the current (2013) arrangements sets out the obligations and processes for notification
and classification for all cases which may be classified as VHCCs on or after April 1, 2013. Part B
applies to cases which fall to be classified on or after that date and where the trial would in the
opinion of the Director of Legal Aid Casework be likely to last for more than 60 days (para. 1.4).
Part C applies to cases which fall to be classified on or after that date where the case satisfies the
definition of a Very High Cost Case (in reg. 2(1) of S.I. 2013 No. 435 (*ante*, G-7)) and the trial
would in the opinion of the agency be likely to last for less than 61 days. Paragraph 5.4 of the arrangements states that where it is the opinion of the agency that a case will last no fewer than 25
days and no more than 40 days, it will only be classified as a Very High Cost Case if it is prosecuted
by the Serious Fraud Office or it is a terrorism case.

Where a case satisfies the definition of a VHCC for organisations, the agency will issue a VHCC decision letter. If the case is one which in the director's opinion will last more than 60 days, the agency will issue a 2013 VHCC Contract (for organisations). In other cases, the agency will issue a 2013 Individual Case Contract (for organisations).

Where the case satisfies the definition of a VHCC for advocates, and a self-employed advocate has been instructed, the agency will issue a VHCC decision letter and a 2013 VHCC contract (for self-employed advocates) to the self-employed advocate. Exceptional circumstances apart, organisations and advocates must meet the eligibility criteria set out in the arrangements before they can undertake work on a Very High Cost Case.

For information as to the working of earlier arrangements, see the second supplement to the 2013 edition of this work.

Paragraph 13(9) of Schedule 2 is not to be construed literally; where, therefore, a very high cost case panel firm was instructed under the representation order prior to the case being classified as a very high cost case, where it continued to act after such classification and where, after the defendant had pleaded guilty and been put back for sentence, the representation order was withdrawn (apparently on the application of the solicitors) by order of the court, solicitors and counsel fell to be remunerated under the very high cost cases regime, not the graduated fee regime; paragraph 13(9) had no application to this situation; rather, it was intended to deal with the remuneration of a non-panel firm where a case is reclassified as a very high cost case whereupon the representation order is withdrawn (rather than being transferred to another litigator, in which case para. 13(8) is engaged): *Lord Chancellor v. Alexander Johnson & Co. Solicitors and McCarthy* [2011] Costs L.R. 987, QBD (Davis J.).

[The next paragraph is G-187.]

Remuneration

G-187   Once a case is classified as a VHCC, the Legal Aid Agency will assign it to one of four categories against the criteria contained in clause 4.21 of the VHCC Specification (see also §§ 4.12 *et seq.* in the VHCC Guidance). For this purpose, the contracted organisation is required to submit a completed VHCC category assessment sheet within 15 business days of the decision letter: Arrangements, para. 8.2(c). The category to which the case is assigned determines the hourly rate payable for preparatory work undertaken by litigators. Advocacy rates are non-category specific.

Self-employed advocates are remunerated directly by the Legal Aid Agency: clause 5.21 of the VHCC Specification (for organisations). Where the VHCC has been classified both as a VHCC for organisations and for advocates, self-employed advocates must claim under their VHCC contract. Where the case is a VHCC for organisations but has not been classified as a VHCC for advocates, any self-employed advocate must claim under the advocates' graduated fee scheme. Employed advocates must claim payment through their organisation, whether under the graduated fee scheme (where the VHCC has not been classified as a VHCC for advocates) or under the VHCC scheme (where the VHCC is a VHCC in relation to both organisations and advocates).

As to rates of payments, these are now determined by regulation 12A of, and Schedule 6 (*ante*, G-18a, G-92c, *et seq.*) to the Criminal Legal Aid (Remuneration) Regulations 2013 (S.I. 2013 No. 435) for cases subject to the 2013 VHCC contract, and by the provisions of the Criminal Defence Service (Very High Cost Cases) (Funding) Order 2013 (S.I. 2013 No. 2804) for work undertaken on or after December 2, 2013 (unless the trial date was set before that date and is before April, 2014), in a "pre-commencement case" (as to which, see the Legal Aid, Sentencing and Punishment of Offenders Act 2012 (Consequential, Transitional and Saving Provisions) Regulations 2013 (S.I. 2013 No. 534), reg. 2) that was the subject of a contract made between the Legal Services Commission and members of the (now abolished) Very High Cost Case (Crime) Panel (art. 3 and Sched. 1) or was the subject of a 2010 VHCC contract (art. 4 and Sched. 2). S.I. 2013 No. 2804 also amended paragraph 25 (Very High Cost Cases) of Schedule 2 (litigators' graduated fee scheme) to the Criminal Defence Service (Funding) Order 2007 (S.I. 2007 No. 1174) (which was revoked by the Criminal Defence Service (Funding) (Amendment) Order 2011 (S.I. 2011 No. 2065) in relation to proceedings in which a representation order was granted on or after October 3, 2011) to provide for reduced fees for work done on or after December 2, 2013 (unless the trial date was set before that date and is before April, 2014), in a Very High Costs Case where a litigator instructed an advocate who was not a member of the Very High Cost Case (Crime) Panel.

[The next paragraph is G-195.]

H. Preparation and Submission of Claims

(1) The preparation of claims

There is no mandatory graduated fee form. The use of computer-generated forms is permitted **G-195** and this allows only the relevant data to be submitted. As to graduated fees generally, see *ante*, G-115 *et seq.*

(2) Time limits for the submission of claims

No claim by an advocate for fees for work done shall be entertained unless submitted within **G-196** three months of the conclusion of the proceedings to which it relates: S.I. 2013 No. 435, reg. 4(3). However, where a confiscation hearing under section 2 of the DTA 1994, section 71 of the CJA 1988 or Part 2 of the PCA 2002 is held more than 28 days after a person has been found or pleaded guilty, a graduated fee claim can be submitted despite the fact that the proceedings have not yet been completed: *ibid.*, reg. 4(6). The time limit may be extended for "good reason": *ibid.*, reg. 31(1); for example, where the claim is particularly complicated and difficult to prepare, where a co-defendant's case is awaiting disposal, or because there is a genuine misunderstanding about the submission of a claim. Extensions should be sought before the time limit expires.

Where there are no good reasons, the time may be extended in "exceptional circumstances", in **G-197** which case the appropriate authority shall consider whether it is reasonable to reduce the fee: S.I. 2013 No. 435, reg. 31(2). An advocate should be given a reasonable opportunity to show cause why his costs should not be reduced (*ibid.*). Any reduction may be challenged by appeal to the taxing master: *post*, G-269. As to what may constitute "good reason" or "exceptional circumstances", see *post*, G-269.

Notwithstanding that a representation order may be expressed to cover proceedings in the Crown Court "and in the event of [the defendant] being convicted or sentenced ..., advice and assistance in regard to the making of an appeal", the legislation is clear as to the need for a claim in relation to work done in the Crown Court to be submitted within three months of the conclusion of the proceedings in that court, rather than within three months of the date on which an application for leave to appeal to the Court of Appeal was refused: *R. v. White* [2008] Costs L.R. 479.

In *R. v. Dumbaya* [2012] Costs L.R. 976, the costs judge took a different view and held that since "representation" for the purposes of Part I of the Access to Justice Act 1999, "includes ... subject to any time limits which may be prescribed, advice and assistance as to any appeal" (the 1999 Act, s.26), proceedings should not be regarded as "concluded" until any such advice or assistance has been given. For corresponding provision in the LASPOA 2012, see section 42(1).

The Legal Services Commission disagreed with the judge in *Dumbaya*. Its November, 2012, guidance provides that (i) the "conclusion of the proceedings" for litigators is the date on which the defendant was acquitted or sentenced; where confiscation proceedings follow sentence, these will be treated as separate proceedings; (ii) the "conclusion of the proceedings" for advocates is the date on which the defendant was acquitted or sentenced or on which confiscation proceedings are concluded; (iii) the commission is currently seeking clarification (in light of conflicting authorities) on whether the time taken, following conviction, to obtain and provide advice on appeal can be taken into account when determining when proceedings conclude, but, pending clarification, proposes to use the date of sentence or acquittal as the conclusion of proceedings; advocates or litigators who risk not meeting the three-month time limit as a result of obtaining or providing advice on appeal should contact the commission for an extension; (iv) bereavement, serious illness, burglary, and flooding in an office, are examples of what are likely to constitute "good reason", but delay in obtaining evidence (including prosecution page counts) and administrative errors will not; (v) those who believe that they are unlikely to meet the time limit should email requesting an extension as soon as possible with grounds; advocates, if appropriate, should provide the name of any firm that is refusing to provide relevant documents; (vi) while the disallowance of the entirety of a claim might constitute a disproportionate sanction and, accordingly, an "exceptional" circumstance, as might the length of the delay and the amount of money involved, a rigid framework for imposing financial penalties is not suitable, and claims must instead be assessed on a case-by-case basis; (vii) accordingly, litigators and advocates who submit claims out of time without "good reason" should provide an explanation as to the impact on them of a total disallowance or reduction of fees for the specific case; although the amount of detail need not be equivalent to that provided when asking for payments to be expedited on hardship grounds, it must be sufficient to enable the determining officer to understand the impact of any decision to disallow or reduce fees.

It is submitted that the commission's stance that proceedings conclude upon acquittal or sentence is to be preferred to the approach of the costs judge in *Dumbaya, ante*. As there is no provision under the 2007 order for payment for advice or assistance on appeal, there seems little point in delaying the date on which the proceedings may be said to have concluded. Any other view also introduces uncertainty.

(3) Submitting an amended claim

G-198   Where a genuine error is made in submitting a graduated fee claim, counsel should not be precluded for all time from submitting an amended claim where the refusal to permit him to do so could result in his being deprived of fees to which he would have been entitled had the claim been advanced correctly in the first place: *R. v. Hann* [2009] Costs L.R. 833. Where, therefore, counsel, as a result of a genuine error, had submitted a claim for a cracked trial where the case was disposed of as a guilty plea (albeit there had been a long delay between plea and sentence, throughout which it had been on the cards that a *Newton* hearing (*R. v. Newton*, 77 Cr.App.R. 13, CA) would eventually be required), it was held that counsel (who had been paid the appropriate graduated fee for a guilty plea) should be granted an extension of time in which to submit an amended claim for a guilty plea plus a special preparation fee (under what is now S.I. 2013 No. 435, Sched. 1 para. 17). See also *R. v. Lafayette* [2010] 4 Costs L.R. 650 (there is no good reason why a lawyer who has submitted a claim should not be permitted to amend it before it has been determined).

[The next paragraph is G-251.]

I. Disbursements and Expenses

(1) Disbursements

G-251   A barrister is not entitled to claim for disbursements or expenses other than those permitted under S.I. 2013 No. 435.

For an example of the Legal Services Commission successfully questioning, pursuant to regulation 17 of S.I. 2013 No. 435 (*ante*, G-21), the propriety of incurring costs where the defence had sought, and obtained, prior authority to incur those costs, see *R. v. Ward* [2012] Costs L.R. 605. The costs related to the printing of a large quantity of documentation that had been contained on two computer discs and a memory stick. The solicitors had obtained authority on the ground that the files were inaccessible electronically, or that the software would corrupt their own network or that specialist software was needed to download and read the material. However, this only applied to the documents on the memory stick, and when the decision was taken not to print off the material on the memory stick, the solicitors "knew or ought reasonably to have known that the purpose for which authority had been given had failed or had become irrelevant or unnecessary before the disbursements were incurred." It had not been reasonable to incur the considerable costs when the prosecution did not intend to print the material off, and when there was no real difficulty in accessing it electronically. However, it was held that the purchase of a hard drive used by a computer expert instructed to analyse computers that had been seized was reasonable; it was inevitable that the contents would have to be copied on to a new drive, rather than a previously used drive, to avoid contamination, and such a purchase would not be part of the expert's overheads because once the drive was used, it could not be re-used for the same purpose.

(2) Travelling and accommodation expenses

Entitlement under the regulations

Travel and other expenses incidental to appearance at court may be claimed provided the   **G-252**
court is not within 40 kilometres of the advocate's office or chambers. Unless prior approval for
the expenditure has been obtained under the regulations, or unless the advocate can justify his
attendance having regard to all the relevant circumstances of the case, the amount payable shall
not be greater than that, if any, payable to a trial advocate from the nearest local Bar or the nearest advocate's office (whichever is the nearer): S.I. 2013 No. 435, Sched. 1, para. 29. As to interim
payment of travel and accommodation expenses, see *ante*, G-110.

Local bars

In *R. v. Comer* [2009] Costs L.R. 972, it was said that in paragraph 29 of Schedule 1 to S.I. 2013   **G-253**
No. 435 (*ante*, G-62), the juxtaposition of the phrase "local Bar" with the phrase "advocate's office" suggests that a fairly modest number of practitioners can constitute a local bar. The existence
of a bar mess is not a prerequisite, and whether the barristers based in an area constitute a local
bar will be a question of feel. In this case, the view of the resident judge that "there is a healthy
local bar" was considered to be the best evidence of such a bar. As to this case, see also *post*,
G-258.

An advocate may be able to justify his attendance in a distant court which is usually serviced by
a local bar where:

   (a) the instruction of local counsel might lead to suspicion of prejudice, lack of independence
       or lack of objectivity (*e.g.* cases of local notoriety involving public figures or officials);
   (b) there are insufficient local counsel whom instructing solicitors consider are sufficiently
       experienced to undertake the case in question so as to give the client a reasonable choice;
   (c) the services of an advocate who has specialised experience and knowledge of the type of
       case of an unusual or technical nature are required;
   (d) the advocate has previously been instructed in related matters which would assist him in
       the presentation or preparation of the case in question: *R. v. Conboy* (1990) Costs L.R. 493;
       and see *R. v. Gussman*, X14, SCTO 40/99 (counsel had represented his client seven years
       earlier on a charge of murder; his knowledge of his client's earlier medical condition was
       relevant to the current charges of rape, and this amounted to special circumstances justify-
       ing his attendance).

It is submitted that a further justification arises where an advocate is forced to follow a particular
judge on circuit who is seized of his case and it was not reasonable to instruct another local
advocate for that particular hearing. Where an advocate is instructed from outside a local bar for
any of the above reasons it is advisable that he obtains a letter from his instructing solicitor
explaining why he was instructed, and for his clerk to obtain prior approval for incurring such
expenses from the court. This applies also to Queen's Counsel practising off-circuit: *post*, G-256.

[The next paragraph is G-256.]

Queen's Counsel and local bars

Queen's Counsel should not be regarded as being "local" to any particular bar, even though his   **G-256**
chambers are in one particular place. Where Queen's Counsel practises on circuit, he should as a
general rule receive an amount in respect of travelling and hotel expenses actually and reasonably incurred and necessarily and exclusively attributable to his attendance at a court on the
circuit on which he practises: *R. v. Thomas*; *R. v. Davidson*; *R. v. Hutton* (1985) Costs L.R. 469.
Where Queen's Counsel practises outside his circuit, the "local bar" rules apply: *ante*, G-253.

Expenses reasonably incurred

The reasonableness of an advocate's claim for travel and hotel expenses should be judged not   **G-257**
by reference to the expenses incurred by other advocates in the same case, but in relation to the

demands upon the advocate in putting forward his lay client's case and his own particular circumstances in relation to the conduct of the trial: *R. v. Plews* (1984) Costs L.R. 466; *post*, G-260.

The regulations refer to expenditure "reasonably incurred", whereas earlier regulations referred to expenses "actually and reasonably incurred". In *R. v. Conboy* (1990) Costs L.R. 493, the taxing master observed that the current wording is wider. It is submitted that the alteration acknowledges an advocate's entitlement to recover a reasonable amount in respect of expenses necessarily and exclusively attributable to attendance at court. Thus, where the expense incurred was reasonable, an advocate should recover in full. Where the travel undertaken or accommodation used was reasonable but the cost incurred was excessive, an advocate may only claim for and recover a reasonable amount being a sum no greater than that which he would have incurred had his expenses been reasonable.

Travel to court

G-258   In determining what is actually and reasonably incurred the relevant travel is that between court and an advocate's chambers: *R. v. Khan*, January 1989, TC C/13. Actual expenses incurred in travelling from an advocate's home to court will only be allowed if his home is nearer to court than his chambers, otherwise his journey is deemed to start from chambers: *R. v. Slessor* (1984) Costs L.R. 438. And, in such a case, he will only be entitled to travelling expenses actually incurred, *i.e.* from home to court: *R. v. Comer* [2009] Costs L.R. 972 (as to which, see also *ante*, G-253).

(i) *Public transport expenses*

G-259   Where expenses are recoverable, travel costs are generally limited to the cost of public transport actually incurred, together with the expense incurred in getting from the starting point to the railhead or coach station and the expense incurred from getting from the terminal to the court: *Slessor, ante*.

(ii) *Car expenses*

G-260   Where an advocate chooses to journey by car, the expenses allowed will not exceed the equivalent cost of public transport: *Slessor, ante*; *Conboy, ante*. The expenses of travel by car will be allowed where public transport is not available or is not reasonably convenient. What is "not reasonably convenient" is a matter for the discretion of the taxing officer. What may be convenient in one case may not be convenient in another. The time spent in getting from the starting point to the railhead, and from the terminus to court is always relevant: if it is considerable, the use of a car may be justified. Taxing officers have been urged to adopt a flexible and broad approach to the problem: *Slessor, ante*. Where the case papers are heavy and bulky, an advocate may be justified in using a car (an example given by the taxing officer in argument in *Conboy, ante*). In *R. v. Plews* (1984) Costs L.R. 466, counsel would have had to catch a 7.15 a.m. train from London to allow him to arrive at court in sufficient time to robe, see his client and solicitor, and to hold any pre-hearing discussions. It was therefore reasonable for counsel, bearing in mind that he had to travel from his home to the station and was faced with a full day in court, to travel by car.

(iii) *Expenses for reasonable travel by car*

G-261   In *Plews, ante*, counsel's claim, based on a mileage rate less than that prescribed for medical practitioners in regulations then current, was considered reasonable, the taxing master observing that a claim based upon the equivalent rate would have been allowed. The usual means of estimating the expenses of travel by car is the standard mileage rate which is calculated by reference to the average cost of running a motor car, including such matters as depreciation, insurance, maintenance, *etc.*, which are referable to the running of a car of the relevant engine capacity. Although the rate is not a precise measure of the actual cost of a particular form of transport, it is intended to provide a mechanism for reimbursing expenses incurred when travelling by car: *Conboy, ante*. Where it is reasonable to incur the expense of travelling by car it must also be reasonable to incur necessary and consequential costs of car parking (if any).

The Legal Services Commission announced an increase in its rates for civil solicitors from 36p per mile to 45p per mile as from April 2, 2001. It is submitted that it is reasonable that similar rates should apply to criminal advocates.

Accommodation expenses

G-262   Hotel or accommodation expenses cannot be divorced from travelling expenses. They should be paid instead of travelling expenses where an advocate reasonably chooses, or by reason of distance is obliged, to stay near a court distant from his chambers rather than travel daily. If travelling expenses are not payable then neither are hotel or accommodation expenses: *R. v. Khan*, January 1989, TC C/13. Where an advocate claims expenses for overnight accommodation and the cost equals or is less than that of the daily travel for which he would be entitled to be reimbursed, such expenses should be allowed. Where the hotel expenses are more than the cost of daily travel, they should be allowed if, having regard to the demands of the case on an advocate, including the need for conferences after court and overnight preparation, the advocate could not have returned home at a reasonable hour: *Plews, ante.*

Conference travel expenses and travel time

Travel expenses reasonably incurred and necessarily and exclusively attributable to attending a **G-263** conference should be reimbursed where an advocate attends a conference in prison where the authorities will only produce the client at the place of detention; the same principle applies when the client is a patient in a psychiatric hospital: *R. v. Hindle* (1987) Costs L.R. 486.

J. PROCEEDINGS IN THE COURT OF APPEAL

General principles

Payment for proceedings in the Court of Appeal is governed by Schedule 3 to S.I. 2013 No. **G-264** 435 (*ante*, G-82 *et seq.*), which provides for *ex post facto* taxation, the overriding principles being that the appropriate officer should, in determining fees, allow a "reasonable amount" in respect of all work "actually and reasonably done".

Advice on appeal

As to this, see, in particular, *R. v. Umezie*, § 7-165 in the main work, and *R. v. Bromige, ante*, **G-265** G-160.

Solicitor advocates

In *R. v. Mansell* [2011] Costs L.R. 531, it was held that: (i) under S.I. 2013 No. 435, the fees of **G-266** a solicitor advocate in the Court of Appeal fall to be determined under Schedule 3 as if he were an advocate, and not a litigator; (ii) a solicitor advocate is an "advocate" for all proceedings covered by S.I. 2013 No. 435, including in the Court of Appeal (see the definition of "advocate" in reg. 2, *ante*, G-7); and (iii) that paragraph 3 of Schedule 3 (determination of litigators' fees (*ante*, G-83)), which permits payment of advocacy by litigators, does not mean that all advocacy by solicitors is payable under that paragraph.

K. DETERMINATIONS AND APPEALS

(1) The taxing authorities

Graduated fee claims are determined by Crown Court taxing officers and should usually be **G-267** paid within 10 working days of receipt of the claim.

Applications for re-determination are addressed to the chief clerk of the Crown Court or the regional taxation director as appropriate. The re-determination does not have to be carried out by the original officer, although this is usually the case. Where difficult points of principle arise or large sums are in dispute the matter is referred to the regional taxation director or his assistant. Appeals from re-determinations are heard by costs judges appointed by the Lord Chancellor.

(2) Guide to the process of determination and appeal

A brief outline of the various stages of the determination of an advocate's fees is set out below. **G-268** The regulations referred to are those of S.I. 2013 No. 435 (*ante*, §§ G-6 *et seq.*). The table below is merely intended as a guide to the relevant procedures.

As to the circumstances in which an advocate or a litigator may apply to the appropriate officer for a redetermination of his fees, for a review of specified decisions or for an offence to be reclassified, see regulation 28 of S.I. 2013 No. 435 (*ante*, G-34).

The references in the last column in the tables below are references to regulations of S.I. 2013 No. 435.

Stage	Description	reg.
Submission of Claim		4
Time limit	Within 3 months of conclusion of proceedings (see *ante*, G-196)	4(3)
Particulars submitted in all cases	In the form and manner directed by the appropriate officer	4(3)
Interim payments (40% of total claim less any sum paid)		19
Definition	Payable where:	18
	(a) the basic fee claimed by any counsel in any related proceedings exceeds £4,000, and	18(2)
	(b) 3 months have elapsed from the date of the conclusion of related proceedings or the date on which the bill is ready to tax, whichever is earlier.	18(4)
Related proceedings	Proceedings involving the same defendant heard or dealt with together or proceedings involving more than one defendant arising out of the same incident so that defendants are charged, tried or disposed of together.	18(3)
When the bill is ready to tax	Date of receipt of last bill in related proceedings.	18(4)
Entitlement	Where counsel is entitled to an interim payment but no interim payment has been made and counsel has submitted his claim.	18(4), (5)
Time limit	6 months after the conclusion of proceedings against the defendant represented.	18(5)
Determination and notification of costs; authorisation of payment		
	Costs determined in accordance with Schedule 1.	23(1)
	Counsel notified of costs payable and payment authorised.	23(1)
Re-calculation of graduated fee or re-determination of decision to allow special or wasted preparation fee, or classification of offence		
Time limit	Within 21 days of receipt or notification of costs payable.	28(3)
Particulars to be submitted	(a) Written notice specifying matters in respect of which application is made, grounds of objection and whether counsel wishes to appear or to be represented.	28(3), (5)
	(b) Documents and information supplied with submission of claim.	28(4)
	(c) Further information, particulars and documents as required by the appropriate officer.	28(6)
Re-determination of decision not to allow conference fee (time limit and particulars as above)		28(1)(b)
Re-determination by the appropriate officer		28(7)
Application for written reasons		28(8)
Time limit	21 days of notification of the decision	28(8), (9)

Stage	Description	reg.
Appeal to costs judge		29(1)
Time limit	21 days of receipt of written reasons.	29(2)
Particulars to be submitted to costs judge and appropriate officer	(a) Copy of written representations on application for re-determination. (b) Appropriate officer's written reasons. (c) All documents supplied hereto.	29(4)
Form of notice of appeal	(a) As directed by the costs judge. (b) Specifying separately each item appealed against, showing amount claimed and determined for each item and the ground of objection. (c) Stating whether appellant wishes to appear or to be represented.	29(5)
Lord Chancellor's written representations	Where the Lord Chancellor makes written representations, counsel shall have a reasonable opportunity to make representations in reply.	29(9)
Notification of hearing	The costs judge shall inform counsel of hearing date and give directions as to conduct of appeal.	29(10)
No further evidence	Unless costs judge otherwise directs no other evidence shall be raised at the hearing nor objection taken which was not raised at redetermination.	29(11)
Notification of costs judge's decision		29(13)
Costs	Costs may be awarded where the appeal is allowed.	29(14)
Appeals to the High Court		30
Right of appeal	Right of appeal to single QBD judge from costs judge's decision on a point of principle of public importance.	30(7)
Application for costs judge's certificate	Counsel may apply to the costs judge to certify a point of principle of general importance.	30(1)
Time limit for application	Within 21 days of notification of costs judge's decision.	30(2)
Time limit for appeal	Within 21 days from receipt of costs judge's certificate.	
Appeal by Lord Chancellor	Within 21 days of notification of costs judge's decision, the Lord Chancellor may appeal the decision if counsel does not do so.	30(5)

(3) The enforcement and extension of time limits

Time limits may be extended for good reason by the appropriate authority, *i.e.* the appropriate **G-269** officer, costs judge, or the High Court: S.I. 2013 No. 435, reg. 31(1). Where for no good reason the time limit is not adhered to, the appropriate authority may in exceptional circumstances extend the time limit and shall consider whether it is reasonable in the circumstances to reduce the costs, subject to granting the advocate a reasonable opportunity to state either orally or in writing why the costs should not be reduced: *ibid.*, reg. 31(2). A decision not to extend time, or to reduce costs for claims out of time may be appealed by notice in writing to the senior costs judge specifying the grounds of appeal. The appeal must be instituted within 21 days of the decision being given: *ibid.*, reg. 31(3); and see *ante*, G-198. For the latest guidance from the Legal Services Commission on the submission of late claims and what may or may not be treated as "good reason" or "exceptional circumstances", see *ante*, G-197.

It was held in *R. v. Mahmood* [2008] Costs L.R. 326, that where a 10 per cent penalty was imposed following a delay of over two months in submitting a claim for costs, but where the representative had only received a notice, prior to the case being tried, stating that all late claims would be the subject of a penalty unless there was a good reason, this did not constitute notice to show cause why the claim should not be reduced. The determining officer had clearly not considered the circumstances of the particular case on its own merits.

In *R. v. Roberts* [2008] Costs L.R. 323, the oversight of two fee earners, the holiday of one of those fee-earners (even if well-deserved), and a subsequent systematic firm-wide failure did not constitute "good reason" or "exceptional circumstances" so as to justify an extension of time, following a delay of 17 months in submitting a claim for costs. Nor did previous good character constitute "exceptional circumstances", although it was said that it might amount to mitigating circumstances when considering the extent of any reduction in costs (were an extension to be granted). This was the case despite a general softening in the attitude to the delay.

A misunderstanding of the legislation cannot amount to "good reason", but could amount to "exceptional circumstances" where the evidence was that other bills that had been submitted late for like reason in the past had been accepted: *R. v. White* [2008] Costs L.R. 479. But a simple failure to follow up a case could rarely constitute "good reason" or "exceptional circumstances", and it made no difference that the firm in question had generally had a good record for submitting claims in time: *R. v. Johnson* [2008] Costs L.R. 983.

Neither "mere oversight" on the part of leading counsel nor a mistaken belief on the part of junior counsel that leading counsel's clerk was dealing with their fees could amount to "good reason" for not submitting their claims on time; but disallowance of fees *in toto* may be so disproportionate as to amount to "exceptional circumstances": see *R. v. Lafayette* [2010] 4 Costs L.R. 650.

In *R. v. Griffin* [2008] Costs L.R. 483, leading counsel had been under the mistaken impression that his junior was going to prepare a taxation note to be agreed between them before submission. However, in the event, his junior submitted his own claim independently and sent a copy of his taxation note to his leader, such note making it plain that he had submitted a claim and asserting, mistakenly, that leading counsel had already submitted his own claim. It was held that as this was already seven months out of time, and leading counsel only submitted his own claim after a further two years, neither the misunderstanding as between leader and junior, nor extreme pressure of work plus some personal pressure over the two years that followed discovery of the fact that his junior had submitted his own claim, could amount to "good reason" for the failure to submit the claim within the three-month time limit; nor could they amount to "exceptional circumstances" so as to justify an extension of time despite the absence of good reason. There had been no obligation on the determining officer to remind counsel that his claim was late and the absence, at the time, of published criteria to be applied to the submission of late claims, did not avail counsel. What was critical to the outcome was the fact that two years before his eventual submission of his claim, he had been alerted by his junior's note to the fact that he would need to submit his own claim and he had failed then to take any steps to address the situation.

G-270 In *R. v. Islami* [2009] Costs L.R. 988, following a ruling that total disallowance of a claim by solicitors for £58,060.13 (including disbursements and travelling expenses) due to delay (of three years and nine months) would be so disproportionate (because of the substantial effect that this would have on the firm's profits) as to amount to "exceptional circumstances" and that the claim should be re-submitted, albeit that a five per cent penalty should be applied to the sum ultimately allowed, it was held that the fact that an administrative officer at the firm had then not complied with her instructions to submit the relevant documents for taxation, and the fact that this was only discovered during her ensuing extensive sick leave, did not amount to a "good reason" for a further delay of nine months in re-submitting the claim. In these circumstances, total disallowance of the claim, and the ensuing effect on the firm's profits, was no longer a disproportionate penalty sufficient to constitute "exceptional circumstances". Had the sum been needed with the urgency suggested at the original hearing, the firm would have ensured that the claim was re-submitted immediately and carefully tracked. Instead, the administrative problems identified at the original hearing had clearly not been resolved. However, it was said that this conclusion should be applied only to the profit costs and that the claim, so far as it related to disbursements (which had long since been paid out by the firm), should still be determined (without penalty), provided that the necessary papers were lodged within 14 days.

A reduction of an out-of-time claim to zero is not automatically to be regarded as so disproportionate as to give rise to "exceptional circumstances", but the shortness of the delay, the amount of money involved and the impact on the advocate or litigator involved are capable of constituting exceptional circumstances; each case must, however, turn on its own facts; there can be no hard and fast rules or pre-set scales: *R. v. Grigoropolou* [2012] Costs L.R. 982.

In *R. v. Newport* [2009] Costs L.R. 983, it was said that, although it has often been stated that **G-271** barristers must have suitable systems in place to ensure that claims for fees and requests for redeterminations are made within the relevant time limits, and although the delay in this particular case was significant (over three years after the determining officer had refused payment), "exceptional circumstances" for extending the time to apply for a redetermination had been made out where counsel had trusted his senior clerk to ensure that the claim and any appeal procedure was appropriately and punctually concluded, but where he had been deliberately misled by the clerk, who failed, despite counsel's regular enquiries, to inform counsel that his claim had been refused *in toto*. This was found to be a rare and regrettable situation and not akin to an argument that "pressures of work" constituted exceptional circumstances (which would not be successful).

(4) Re-determinations and appeals

Graduated fees

An advocate may only seek re-determination or appeal in respect of graduated fees where, (a) **G-272** the issue is either whether the graduated fee scheme applied to the relevant proceedings, or (b) complaint is made as to the calculation of the remuneration payable, or (c) where the advocate is dissatisfied with a refusal to allow a special preparation fee or the number of hours allowed in the calculation of such fee; or (d) where the advocate is dissatisfied with the classification of an offence which does not appear in the Table of offences: S.I. 2013 No. 435, reg. 28(3). Under S.I. 2013 No. 435 a re-determination may also be sought in respect of a decision not to allow an hourly fee in respect of attendance at conferences or views at the scene of the alleged offence, or of the number of hours allowed in the calculation of such a fee: see reg. 28(1)(b)(i).

Re-determination

On an application for re-determination an advocate shall specify the grounds of his objection to **G-273** all or any part of the determination (S.I. 2013 No. 435, reg. 28(3)(b)) and may appear in person or through another to make representations: S.I. 2013 No. 435, reg. 28(5). An advocate is not obliged to provide fresh information or material to assist the determining officer in the redetermination. If no additional information is provided, the determining officer has a duty to redetermine on the basis of the information already supplied: *R. v. O'Brien* [2003] Costs L.R. 625. Many appeals which might otherwise have succeeded have failed because the representations made to the appropriate officer have been perfunctory and inexplicit: *R. v. Davies* (1985) Costs L.R. 472.

As from January 1, 1994, the General Council of the Bar has agreed that all requests for fees to be re-determined or for written reasons to be provided should be signed by counsel personally.

Re-determination should, where possible, be carried out by the officer who determined costs. Where cases are cited in support of the re-determination, sufficient references must be given to allow an advocate to identify and look them up: *R. v. Pelepenko*, X27A, SCCO 186/2001.

Where the Legal Aid Agency makes a decision to recover an overpayment of fees pursuant to regulation 25 of S.I. 2013 No. 435 (*ante*, G-31) and the litigator requests a review, a subsequent confirmation by the commission of its decision to recoup constitutes a redetermination within the meaning of regulation 28 (*ante*, G-34), so as to allow the litigator to appeal to a costs judge pursuant to regulation 29(1) (*ante*, G-35): *Lord Chancellor v. Eddowes Perry and Osbourne Ltd* [2011] Costs L.R. 498, QBD (Spencer J.) (disapproving *R. v. Charlery*; *R. v. Small* [2011] Costs L.R. 331). As to this case, see also *ante*, G-161.

Further evidence on appeal and supplemental written reasons

On appeal before a costs judge no further evidence shall be received and no ground of objec- **G-274** tion shall be valid which was not raised on the application for re-determination unless the costs judge otherwise directs: S.I. 2013 No. 435, reg. 29(11). These provisions are strictly applied. A costs judge will rarely accede to a request to adduce further evidence or allow a fresh objection to be raised. Where written reasons do not address a point raised in the claim, counsel cannot pursue the matter in the appeal. The proper method of dealing with such an omission is to seek supplemental written reasons from the appropriate officer.

Appeals

G-275   The right of appeal to a costs judge is effectively limited in that no appeal lies against a determination unless the advocate has applied for a re-determination and, thereafter, for written reasons under S.I. 2013 No. 435, reg. 29(1).

An advocate wishing to appeal must have regard to, and be familiar with, the provisions of Part 5 of the *Practice Direction (Criminal Proceedings: Costs)* [2013] 1 W.L.R. 3255 (§§ 6-146 *et seq.* in the main work).

Representation, costs and expenses of appeal

G-276   For the purposes of an appeal to a costs judge, an advocate is treated as the appellant and can elect to be represented at the hearing. A successful appellant may be awarded a sum in respect of part or all of any reasonable costs incurred in connection with the appeal: S.I. 2013 No. 435, reg. 29(14); and see *R. v. Boswell; R. v. Halliwell* [1987] 1 W.L.R. 705 (Leggatt J.).

A barrister without the intervention of a solicitor may accept a brief or instructions, with or without fee, directly from, and represent, another barrister on that other barrister's appeal as to his fees before a costs judge: see *Code of Conduct*, 8th ed., para. 401 (Appendix C-7, *ante*). A professional fee payable by one barrister to another for conducting the former's appeal is capable of constituting part of the costs incurred by the appellant counsel: *R. v. Boswell; R. v. Halliwell, ante.* In assessing such costs the costs judge is entitled to take account of time and skill expended by the appellant or his counsel in the drawing of grounds and preparation of the appeal, and the conduct of the hearing, and travel and subsidence costs: *ibid.* Costs incurred in instructing other counsel are clearly reasonable where there is some technical question on the applicability of some part of the regulations or other issue which legitimately deserves the attention of specialist costs counsel. Costs are not reasonably incurred if trial counsel is available, could easily have represented himself and the only real issue is the weight of the case or the value of a particular item of work undertaken: *Jackson v. Lord Chancellor* [2003] Costs L.R. 395; and *R. v. Martin* [2007] Costs L.R. 128. A successful appellant will ordinarily be entitled to the return of the fee payable in respect of the appeal.

Appeals to the single judge

G-277   As to appeals from a costs judge to the High Court, see S.I. 2013 No. 435, reg. 30. The ambit of an appeal is strictly limited to the point of principle certified by the costs judge as being of general importance (such certificate being a pre-condition to an appeal): *Patten v. Lord Chancellor*, 151 N.L.J. 851, QBD (Leveson J.), not following *Harold v. Lord Chancellor* [1999] Costs L.R. 14. Although *Patten* was concerned with the interpretation of regulation 16 of the Legal Aid in Criminal and Care Proceedings (Costs) Regulations 1989 (S.I. 1989 No. 343), regulation 29 of S.I. 2013 No. 435 is worded in almost identical terms. A refusal of a costs judge to certify that the matter raises a point of principle of general importance is not susceptible to judicial review: *R. v. Supreme Court Taxing Office, exp. John Singh & Co* [1997] 1 Costs L.R. 49, CA (Civ. Div). As to the limited scope for a challenge, by way of judicial review, to the substantive decision of a costs judge where a certificate has been refused, see § 6-75 in the main work.

(5) Recovery of overpayment

G-278   Where an advocate receives a sum in excess of his entitlement, the taxing authority may either require immediate repayment of that excess, or deduct the excess from any other sum payable to the advocate under the regulations: S.I. 2013 No. 435, reg. 25. These provisions apply notwithstanding the fact that a re-determination or appeal has been or may be requested: S.I. 2013 No. 435, reg. 25(4).

(6) Appeals under VHCCs

G-279   Under the arrangements that came into force on April 1, 2013 (*ante*, G-181 *et seq.*), both the VHCC Specification for organisations and that for advocates provide for a right of appeal to the

VHCC Appeals Panel. The details are set out in paragraph 6 of the specifications, with paragraph 6.4 listing the issues in relation to which there is a right of appeal (*e.g.* the category to which a case has been assigned) and paragraph 6.5 listing those issues in relation to which there is no right of appeal. The appeal process, including time limits, is provided for by paragraphs 6.6 to 6.30. The appeal will normally be determined by a single adjudicator but may be referred to an appeals committee. The decision of the adjudicator or committee is final (para. 6.28), but is binding only in relation to the particular appeal (para. 6.29). Anonymised versions of decisions will be published on the Legal Aid Agency's website (para. 6.30).

APPENDIX H
Sexual Offences (The Law as at April 30, 2004)

A. Introduction

The history of the sexual offences legislation since 1956 is set out in detail at §§ 20-1 *et seq.* in **H-1** the main work. All the statutory provisions contained in this appendix were repealed with effect from May 1, 2004, by the SOA 2003, but, as stated in the main work, they have continuing effect in relation to conduct occurring prior to that date. It should be borne in mind that this appendix states the law as at April 30, 2004, and that, therefore, there may yet be prosecutions for offences committed prior to even earlier material changes in the law: see, in particular, the amendments effected by the SOA 1985 and the CJPOA 1994 (summarised at §§ 20-2, 20-3 in the main work).

B. Sexual Offences Act 1956

(1) Rape

(a) *Introduction*

Section 1 of the 1956 Act made rape an offence. Section 1(1) of the Sexual Offences (Amend- **H-2** ment) Act 1976 provided a statutory definition of rape in terms designed to give effect to the Report of the Advisory Group on the Law of Rape (Cmnd. 6352) and the views expressed by the House of Lords in *DPP v. Morgan* [1976] A.C. 182. Section 1(1) was repealed by the CJPOA 1994, which also substituted a new section 1 in the 1956 Act. The effect of this was to adopt the 1976 definition, but to extend it so as to cover anal intercourse with a woman or a man. In addition, the new provision referred simply to "sexual intercourse" whereas the 1976 Act referred to "unlawful sexual intercourse". The omission of the word "unlawful" made clear Parliament's adoption of the decision of the House of Lords in *R. v. R.* [1992] A.C. 599, that a man may rape his wife.

Section 7(2) of the 1976 Act (as amended by the CJA 1988, s.158(1) and (6)) provided that in that Act "a rape offence":

> "means any of the following, namely rape, attempted rape, aiding, abetting, counselling and procuring rape or attempted rape, incitement to commit rape, conspiracy to rape and burglary with intent to rape."

(b) *Statute*

Sexual Offences Act 1956, s.1

Rape of woman or man

1.—(1) It is an offence for a man to rape a woman or another man.   **H-3**

(2) A man commits rape if—

   (a) he has sexual intercourse with a person (whether vaginal or anal) who at the time of the intercourse does not consent to it; and

   (b) at the time he knows that the person does not consent to the intercourse or is reckless as to whether that person consents to it.

(3) A man also commits rape if he induces a married woman to have sexual intercourse with him by impersonating her husband.

(4) Subsection (2) applies for the purposes of any enactment.

[This section is printed as substituted (from November 3, 1994) by the CJPOA 1994, s.142.]

Sexual Offences (Amendment) Act 1976, s.1

1.—(1) [*Repealed by Criminal Justice and Public Order Act 1994, s.168(3) and Sched. 11.*]   **H-4**

(2) It is hereby declared that if at a trial for a rape offence the jury has to consider whether a man believed that a woman or man was consenting to sexual intercourse, the presence or absence of reasonable grounds for such a belief is a matter to which the jury is to have regard, in conjunction with any other relevant matters, in considering whether he so believed.

[Subs. (2) is printed as amended by the CJPOA 1994, s.168(2), and Sched. 10, para. 35(1), (2).]

As to the use of the words "man" and "woman", see *post*, H-222. As to the meaning of "a rape offence", see *ante*, H-2.

In the case of a summary trial or a trial by court-martial, the references to the jury in section 1(2) of the 1976 Act are to be construed as references to the court: *ibid.*, s.7(3).

(c) *Anonymity*

H-5   See §§ 20-257 *et seq.* in the main work.

(d) *Indictment*

Statement of Offence

H-6   *Rape, contrary to section 1(1) of the Sexual Offences Act 1956.*

Particulars of Offence

A B on the ____ day of ____, 20__, had sexual intercourse with C D who at the time of the said intercourse did not consent to it, the said A B either knowing that the said C D did not so consent or being reckless as to whether she [or he] so consented.

Where the victim is a woman, the intercourse may be vaginal or anal: s.1(1) of the 1956 Act, *ante*, H-3. It is unnecessary to specify in the indictment whether the allegation is of vaginal or anal intercourse, but there will be cases where it is of assistance to do so. This can be done by adding the words "*per vaginam*" or "*per anum*" after the words "sexual intercourse". The addition of these words will be particularly useful where it is alleged that a woman was raped both vaginally and anally; the counts will reflect this and will ensure, in the event of a conviction on one count only, that the court is aware of the basis of the jury's verdict. As to where it is unclear on the evidence whether penetration was of the vagina or the anus, see *R. v. K. (Robert)* [2009] 1 Cr.App.R. 24, CA (§ 20-20 in the main work).

Good practice does not require that, where the prosecution rely on recklessness as an alternative to knowledge, there should be separate counts (alleging respectively knowledge and recklessness): *R. v. Flitter* [2001] Crim.L.R. 328, CA.

Allegation of joint offence

H-7   Where a person has been raped by more than one man on the same occasion, all the accused should be charged in one count of rape, with no mention of aiders and abettors: see the direction of the House of Lords in *DPP v. Merriman* [1973] A.C. 584. This enables the jury to be told that it matters not whether an individual accused physically committed the act of rape, or assisted or encouraged someone else to; thus, several accused may be convicted where the jury is satisfied only that each played a guilty part, but not as to who committed the physical act.

(e) *Mode of trial and class of offence*

H-8   This offence and an attempt to commit it are triable on indictment only: SOA 1956, s.37(2), and Sched. 2, para. 1. As to the classification of offences, see *ante*, Appendix F-6.

(f) *Alternative verdicts*

H-9   On a count of rape, the accused may be convicted of procurement of a woman by threats (s.2) or false pretences (s.3) or of administering drugs to obtain or facilitate intercourse (s.4): SOA 1956, s.37(4), and Sched. 2, para. 1.

As to alternative verdicts generally, see §§ 4-524 *et seq.* in the main work. Where the alleged victim was a girl under 16 years of age, then whether or not her age is averred in the indictment, a jury may not convict the accused under section 6(3) of the CLA 1967 (§ 4-525 in the main work) of an offence contrary to section 6 of the SOA 1956 (unlawful intercourse with a girl under 16): *R.*

v. Fisher [1969] 2 Q.B. 114, Assizes (Cusack J.); *R. v. Mochan*, 54 Cr.App.R. 5, Assizes (Cusack J.), approved in *R. v. Hodgson* [1973] Q.B. 565, 57 Cr.App.R. 502, CA.

As every charge of rape contains the essential ingredients of indecent assault (*viz.* an assault and indecency), it follows that where a man is acquitted of rape on the ground of the victim's consent, it is open to the jury to convict him where the victim is under 16, of indecent assault, because the consent which provided a defence to a charge of rape cannot, by virtue of the SOA 1956, ss.14(2) and 15(2), provide a defence to a charge of indecent assault. Age is not an ingredient of, nor an essential averment in the framing of a count of indecent assault: *R. v. Hodgson, ante.*

In *R. v. Timmins* [2006] 1 Cr.App.R. 18, CA, it was held that the effect of the decision in *R. v. J.* [2005] 1 A.C. 562, HL (on a true construction of the 1956 Act, it was impermissible to prosecute a charge of indecent assault under section 14(1) (*post*, H-117) in circumstances where the only conduct upon which the charge was based was an act of unlawful sexual intercourse with a girl under the age of 16 in respect of which no prosecution could be commenced under section 6(1) (*post*, H-50) by virtue of the time bar contained in section 37(2) of, and Schedule 2 to, the Act) was not such as to preclude a judge from leaving it to a jury to convict of indecent assault as an alternative to a charge of rape, under section 6(3) of the CLA 1967 (*ante*), where they were satisfied as to the act of sexual intercourse and as to the fact that the girl was under 16 at the time, and where they acquitted of rape on the ground that they were not satisfied as to lack of consent, and this was so notwithstanding that the proceedings for rape had been begun over 12 months after the alleged offence; the decision in *J.* had turned on the words of Schedule 2 to the 1956 Act, which provided that "A prosecution may not be commenced more than 12 months after the offence charged."; leaving a possible alternative verdict to a jury could not be described as a "commencement" of proceedings for the offence; but it would be an abuse of process to bring a charge of rape against a person against whom there was no evidence whatever of rape (in particular lack of consent) in order to circumvent a time limit.

In the earlier case of *R. v. Rabbitts* (2005) 149 S.J. 890, CA, it was held that, *R. v. J.* having decided that, as a matter of statutory construction, it was not open to the prosecution to bring a charge of indecent assault where the conduct on which the prosecution was based was an act of consensual sexual intercourse with a girl under 16, and where the purpose was to circumvent the statutory time limit of 12 months on prosecutions for unlawful sexual intercourse with a girl of that age, it made no difference that the count of indecent assault was included in the indictment as an alternative to a charge of rape to cater for the possibility that the jury would not be satisfied as to lack of consent.

In *R. v. Cottrell; R. v. Fletcher* [2008] 1 Cr.App.R. 7, CA, it was said that to the extent that *Timmins* and *Rabbitts* were inconsistent, they should be followed as they apply to the facts of the individual case. As to the flawed nature of the decision in *Timmins*, see CLW/05/43/4.

(g) *Autrefois acquit and convict*

For the general principles, see §§ 4-183 *et seq.* in the main work. **H-10**

An acquittal upon an indictment for rape was held to be no bar to a subsequent indictment on the same facts for a common assault: *R. v. Dungey* (1864) 4 F. & F. 99 (and see now s.6(3A) of the CLA 1967 (§ 4-525 in the main work), reversing the effect of *R. v. Mearns* [1991] 1 Q.B. 82, 91 Cr.App.R. 312, CA).

An acquittal on an indictment for rape cannot be successfully pleaded as a bar to a subsequent indictment for assault with intent to commit rape: *R. v. Gisson* (1847) 2 C. & K. 781, or, in certain circumstances, to a subsequent indictment for attempted rape, see *R. v. Hearn* [1970] Crim.L.R. 175, CA (§ 4-203 in the main work).

However, it should be noted that there was (as at April 30, 2004), in all probability, no longer an offence of assault with intent to rape, contrary to common law. It did not survive the creation of an identical statutory offence in the Offences against the Person Act 1861, s.38, which was in turn abolished by virtue of section 10 of, and Schedule 3 to, the Criminal Law Act 1967: *R. v. P.* [1990] Crim.L.R. 323, Crown Court (Pill J.) (but note the commentary and reference, by Professor J. C. Smith, to the opposite view expressed by Turner J. in *R. v. J.*, unreported, June 9, 1986). *Cf.* section 16 of the 1956 Act (assault with intent to commit buggery), *post*, H-138.

(h) *Sentence*

Maximum

H-11   Rape: life imprisonment—SOA 1956, s.37(3), and Sched. 2, para. 1(a).

Attempted rape: life imprisonment—SOA 1956, s.37(3), and Sched. 2, para. 1(a) (as amended by the SOA 1985, s.3).

Guidelines

H-12   See *post*, Appendix K-83 *et seq.*

In *R. v. H.* [2012] 2 Cr.App.R.(S.) 21, CA, it was said that in the search for principle, it is impossible to reconcile all the authorities that purport to provide guidance on sentencing for historic sexual offending; that the following considerations, derived from statute (general provisions about sentencing in the CJA 2003, Pt 12, Chap. 1 (ss.142–176), and the Coroners and Justice Act 2009, s.125 (sentencing guidelines: duty of court (§ 5-149 in the main work))) and case law, should be treated as guidance; and that reference to earlier decisions (with the exception of *R. v. Millberry*; *R. v. Morgan*; *R. v. Lackenby*, *post*, Appendix K-83) is unlikely to be helpful and is to be discouraged. First, sentence will be imposed on the basis of the legislative provisions current at the time of sentence, and by measured reference to any definitive sentencing guidelines relevant to the situation revealed by the established facts. Secondly, although sentence must be limited to the maximum permissible at the date when the offence was committed, it is wholly unrealistic to attempt an assessment of sentence by seeking to identify today what the sentence was likely to have been if the offence had come to light at or shortly after its commission. Thirdly, the particular circumstances in which the offence was committed and its seriousness must be the main focus; due allowance for the passage of time may be appropriate; the date may have a considerable bearing on the offender's culpability; for example, if he was young and immature at the time, that remains a continuing feature of the sentencing decision; similarly, if the allegations had come to light many years earlier, and the offender admitted them, but, for whatever reason, the complaint had not been drawn to the attention of, or investigated by, the police, or had been investigated but had not then been pursued to trial, these too would be relevant matters. Fourthly, careful judgment of the harm done to the victim is always a critical feature of the sentencing decision; simultaneously, equal care needs to be taken to assess the true extent of the offender's criminality by reference to what he actually did and the circumstances in which he did it. Fifthly, the passing of the years may demonstrate aggravating features if, for example, the offender has continued to commit sexual crime or he represents a continuing risk to the public; on the other hand, mitigation may be found in an unblemished life over the intervening years, particularly if accompanied by evidence of positive good character. Sixthly, early admissions and a guilty plea are of particular importance in historic cases; given that it is tempting to lie about events long ago, it is greatly to the offender's credit if he makes early admissions; even more powerful mitigation is available to the offender who, out of a sense of guilt and remorse, reports himself to the authorities. The court considered, *inter alia*, *R. v. Bowers* [1999] 2 Cr.App.R.(S.) 97, CA, *R. v. Fowler* [2002] 2 Cr.App.R.(S.) 99, CA, *Att.-Gen.'s References (Nos 37, 38, 44, 54, 51, 53, 35, 40, 43, 45, 41 and 42 of 2003)* [2004] 1 Cr.App.R.(S.) 84, CA, *R. v. McKendrick* [2005] 2 Cr.App.R.(S.) 68, CA, *R. v. Patterson* [2006] 2 Cr.App.R.(S.) 48, CA, *Att.-Gen.'s Reference (No. 39 of 2006) (R. v. J. (Rodney Clive))* [2007] 1 Cr.App.R.(S.) 34, CA, *R. v. Moon* [2011] 1 Cr.App.R.(S.) 34, CA, *R. v. Hartley (Practice Note)* [2012] 1 Cr.App.R. 7, CA, and *Att.-Gen.'s Reference (No. 78 of 2010)* [2011] 2 Cr.App.R.(S.) 109, CA.

This approach to sentencing historic sexual offences has been specifically endorsed by the Sentencing Council for England and Wales: see Annex B to its definitive guideline on sexual offences (*post*, Appendix K-84).

For a case considering *R. v. H.* (*ante*) see *R. v. Clifford*, *post*, H-120.

(i) *Ingredients of the offence*

A "man"

H-13   The common law presumption that a boy under the age of 14 was incapable of sexual intercourse was abolished (for both natural and unnatural intercourse) by the SOA 1993, ss.1, 2(2), (3).

A woman may be convicted as an aider and abettor: *R. v. Ram* (1893) 17 Cox 609 at 610n.

A man may be convicted of raping his wife: *R. v. R.* [1992] 1 A.C. 599, HL (confirmed by the revised definition of "rape" introduced by the CJPOA 1994, *ante*, § H-3).

Sexual intercourse

Where it is necessary to prove sexual intercourse (whether natural or unnatural), it shall not be **H-14** necessary to prove the completion of the intercourse by the emission of seed, but it shall be deemed complete upon proof of penetration only: SOA 1956, s.44 (*post*, § H-219). "Unnatural" intercourse in section 44 means buggery (including bestiality): *R. v. Gaston*, 73 Cr.App.R. 164, CA.

The amendment of section 1 of the 1956 Act by the 1994 Act (§ 20-3 in the main work, and *ante*, H-3) did not alter the law (whereunder even the slightest penetration would be sufficient: see *R. v. R'Rue* (1838) 8 C. & P. 641; *R. v. Allen* (1839) 9 C. & P. 31) so as to make penetration of the vagina, properly so-called, an essential ingredient of "vaginal" rape; it is sufficient that there was any degree of penetration by the penis within the labia of the pudendum of the complainant; the word "vaginal" in section 1 is used in comparison with, or in addition to, "anal", and not so as to indicate that the word is being used in the medical sense, rather than the general sense of the female genitalia: *R. v. J.F.*, unreported, December 16, 2002, CA ([2002] EWCA Crim. 2936).

Sexual intercourse is a continuing act; it follows that consensual intercourse will become rape if the woman (or man) ceases to consent during the intercourse, and the man (other man), with the necessary *mens rea*, continues the act: *Kaitamaki v. R.* [1985] A.C. 147, PC (decided on the corresponding New Zealand legislation). It should be noted that these were not the facts in *Kaitamaki*; the facts were that the defendant claimed he only realised the woman was not consenting after intercourse had begun. As to this aspect of the decision, see *post*, H-20. However, the foregoing proposition appears to follow as a matter of logic from the Board's decision on the narrower point.

Absence of consent

General

It must be proved that the accused had sexual intercourse with the complainant without her or **H-15** his consent: s.1(2)(a) of the 1956 Act, *ante*, H-3. This applies even where the offence is alleged to have been committed on a person under the age of 16, though sometimes in such a case the prosecution will not need to prove much more than the age of the victim: *R. v. Harling*, 26 Cr.App.R. 127, CCA. It is not, however, necessary to support a charge of rape that there is evidence that the complainant demonstrated her lack of consent or communicated it to the accused; the minimum requirement is evidence of lack of consent in fact, which might take many forms; the most obvious is the complainant's simple assertion, which may or may not be backed up by evidence of force or threats; alternatively, it may consist of evidence that by reason of drink, drugs, sleep, age or mental handicap the complainant was unaware of what was occurring and/or incapable of giving consent; or it may consist of evidence that the complainant was deceived as to the identity of the man with whom she had intercourse: *R. v. Malone* [1998] 2 Cr.App.R. 447, CA. As to intercourse with a woman known to be asleep, see *R. v. Mayers* (1872) 12 Cox 311; *R. v. Young* (1878) 14 Cox 114.

Lack of consent will have been established if the jury are satisfied that although the complainant did not dissent, her understanding and lack of knowledge were such, whether on account of age, the consumption of drink or drugs or mental handicap, that she was incapable of giving consent or of exercising any judgment on the matter: see *R. v. Howard*, 50 Cr.App.R. 56, CCA (age); *R. v. Lang*, 62 Cr.App.R. 50, CA (drink); *R. v. Fletcher* (1859) Bell 63; *R. v. Ryan* (1846) 2 Cox 115; *R. v. Fletcher* (1866) L.R. 1 C.C.R. 39; *R. v. Barratt* (1873) L.R. 2 C.C.R. 81; *R. v. Pressy* (1867) 10 Cox 635, CCR (mental handicap). To the extent that they suggest that where no force, threat or deceit was used, there must be evidence of some resistance on the part of the complainant, *Howard* and *Lang* should no longer be taken to represent the law: *Malone, ante*.

Evidence of resistance may, of course, be highly relevant to the separate issue of the defendant's knowledge or recklessness in relation to the lack of consent.

H-16   Although juries should be told that "consent" in the context of the offence of rape is a word which must be given its ordinary meaning, it is sometimes necessary for the judge to go further. For example, he should point out, if necessary, that there is a difference between consent and submission (as to which, see also § 20-10 in the main work). In cases where intercourse took place after threats not involving violence, or the fear of it, a jury should be directed to concentrate on the state of mind of the victim immediately before the act of intercourse. The jury should be reminded too of the wide spectrum of states of mind which consent could comprehend and that where a dividing line had to be drawn between real consent and mere submission they should apply their combined good sense, experience and knowledge of human nature and modern behaviour to all the relevant facts of the case: *R. v. Olugboja*, 73 Cr.App.R. 344, CA (*cf. R. v. McAllister* [1997] Crim.L.R. 233, CA, *post*, H-124). The word "want" should not be used in directing a jury on the issue of consent, there being a clear difference between "wanting" to have intercourse and "consenting" to it: *R. v. T. (D.)* [2000] 7 *Archbold News* 3, CA.

As to evidence about the lack of sexual experience of a complainant, see § 20-11 in the main work.

As to intercourse with a defective, see also the SOA 1956, ss.7 and 45 (*post*, H-64, H-68).

Intercourse by false pretences

H-17   The only types of fraud which vitiate consent for the purposes of the law of rape are frauds as to the nature of the act or as to the identity of the person doing the act: *R. v. Linekar* [1995] 2 Cr.App.R. 49, CA. As to frauds as to the nature of the act, see *R. v. Case* (1850) 1 Den. 580, and *R. v. Flattery* (1877) 2 Q.B.D. 410, where the consent was induced by the pretence that the act of intercourse was a form of medical treatment, and *R. v. Williams* [1923] 1 K.B. 340, 17 Cr.App.R. 56, CCA, where a choirmaster pretended to be testing a girl's breathing powers with an instrument. As to fraud as to the identity of the perpetrator of the Act, section 1(3) of the SOA 1956 (*ante*, H-3) makes express provision for the case of a man inducing a married woman to have sexual intercourse with him by impersonating her husband. This provision was first introduced by the Criminal Law Amendment Act 1885 for the purpose of reversing the decision in *R. v. Barrow* (1868) L.R. 1 C.C.R. 156. As to other instances of impersonation, it is possible that the principle in *Barrow* will still prevail; but it was dissented from in *R. v. Dee* (1884) 15 Cox C.C. 57, and doubt about the correctness of the decision was expressed in *Flattery*. What was said in *Linekar* as to fraud as to identity vitiating consent was *obiter*, the case not concerning mistake as to identity at all, but it is submitted that the view of the Court of Appeal represents the modern and better view.

See also section 3 of the SOA 1956 (*post*, H-27) in relation to false pretences of a less fundamental character; and *R. v. Tabassum* [2000] 2 Cr.App.R. 328, CA (*post*, H-124) in which it was held that a deception as to the quality of the act vitiated consent in a case of indecent assault.

Recent complaint

H-18   See § 20-12 in the main work.

Distress of victim

H-19   See § 20-13 in the main work.

Mens rea

General

H-20   It must be proved that at the time of the non-consensual intercourse, the defendant either knew that the victim was not consenting or that he was reckless as to whether she or he was consenting: see s.1(2)(b) of the SOA 1956, *ante*, H-3. If the tribunal of fact has to consider whether the defendant believed that a person was consenting to intercourse, the presence or absence of reasonable grounds for such a belief is a matter to which the tribunal is to have regard, in conjunction with any other relevant matters, in considering whether he so believed: Sexual Offences (Amendment) Act 1976, s.1(2), *ante*, H-4.

Sexual intercourse is a continuing act, which ends upon withdrawal. If, therefore, a man becomes aware that the other person is not consenting after intercourse has commenced and he does not desist, he will be guilty of rape from the moment that he realises that she or he is not consenting: *Kaitamaki v. R.* [1985] A.C. 147, PC. This case was decided on sections 127 and 128 of the New Zealand Crimes Act 1961, which are to the same effect as section 44 of the 1956 Act (*post*, H-219) and section 1 of the 1956 Act (*ante*, H-3). As to the situation where the victim was in fact consenting at the outset, but ceases to consent, see *ante*, H-14. This will also be rape provided that the man was aware of the change or was reckless in respect thereof.

Recklessness

Substantive offences. In *R. v. Satnam and Kewal*, 78 Cr.App.R. 149, CA, earlier confusion was **H-21** resolved. The authorities having been reviewed, it was held that any direction as to the definition of rape should be based upon section 1 of the Sexual Offences (Amendment) Act 1976 (see now s.1(2) of the SOA 1956, *ante*, H-3) and upon *DPP v. Morgan* [1976] A.C. 182, HL (§ 17-10 in the main work). The court suggested that a practical definition of recklessness in sexual cases had been given in *R. v. Kimber*, 77 Cr.App.R. 225, CA (a case of indecent assault), namely if the jury were sure that the defendant had been indifferent to the feelings and wishes of the victim, aptly described colloquially as "couldn't care less" then that in law was "reckless". Thus (see pp. 154-155), in summing up a case of rape which involves the issue of consent, the judge should, in dealing with the state of mind of the defendant, direct the jury that before they can convict, the Crown must have proved either that he knew the woman did not consent to sexual intercourse, or that he was reckless as to whether she consented. If the jury are sure he knew she did not consent, they will find him guilty of rape knowing there to be no consent. If they are not sure about that, they will go on to consider reckless rape. If he may genuinely have believed that she did consent, even though he was mistaken in that belief he must be acquitted: see s.1(2) of the 1976 Act, *ante*, H-4. In considering whether his belief may have been genuine, the jury should take into account all the relevant circumstances (including presence or absence of reasonable grounds: see s.1(2)). If, after considering them, the jury are sure that the defendant had no genuine belief that the woman consented to have intercourse, then they will convict. He will be guilty because that finding of fact would mean that his mental state was such that either he knew she was not consenting or he was reckless as to whether she was consenting. If the jury are sure that he could not have cared less whether she wanted to have sexual intercourse or not, but pressed on regardless, then he would have been reckless and could not have believed that she wanted to.

In *R. v. Taylor (Robert)*, 80 Cr.App.R. 327, CA, Lord Lane C.J. said (at p. 332) that in rape, the defendant is reckless if he does not believe the woman is consenting and could not care less whether she is consenting or not but presses on regardless. *Taylor* was followed and applied in *R. v. Adkins* [2000] 2 All E.R. 185, CA, where it was held to be unnecessary to give a direction as to honest belief in every case where consent is in issue; such a direction is only required when, on the evidence in the case, there is room for the possibility of a genuine mistaken belief that the victim had consented; equally, the question of honest belief does not necessarily arise where reckless rape is in issue, for the defendant might have failed to address his mind to the question whether or not there was consent, or have been indifferent as to whether or not there was consent, in circumstances where, if he had addressed his mind to the question, he could not genuinely have believed that there was consent; where, therefore, the defence case was not merely that the complainant consented but that she actively facilitated intercourse, there was no scope for a genuine, but mistaken, belief as to consent.

Attempts. In *R. v. Khan*, 91 Cr.App.R. 29, the Court of Appeal held that precisely the same **H-22** analysis can be made of the offence of attempted rape as that of the full offence, namely: (a) the intention of the offender is to have sexual intercourse with another person; (b) the offence is committed if, but only if, the circumstances are that: (i) the other person does not consent; *and* (ii) the defendant knows that he or she is not consenting or is reckless as to that fact.

Drunkenness and mistake of fact

It is clear from both *DPP v. Majewski* [1977] A.C. 443, HL (§ 17-107 in the main work) and *R.* **H-23** *v. Caldwell* [1982] A.C. 341, HL (§ 17-112 in the main work) that "recklessness" as a consequence of voluntarily induced intoxication cannot amount to a defence.

If the accused was, or may have been, genuinely mistaken as to fact (see generally, §§ 17-10 *et seq.* in the main work, and H-21, *ante*), for example, if he thought or may have thought that the complainant was consenting to sexual intercourse, and the jury are sure that that mistake was a consequence of intoxication, what then is the position? It appears to be this: implicit in such a finding is the finding that but for the voluntary consumption of drink the jury are sure that the accused would have known either that the complainant was not consenting or, at the very least, that there was a risk that she was not consenting. Whatever the true scope of the meaning of "reckless" in the context of sexual offences, it is plain (see *ante*, H-21) that to proceed knowing that there was a risk that the complainant was not consenting and not caring whether she consented or not is to act recklessly. It therefore follows that if the jury are sure that by virtue of drink (or drugs) the accused was not alerted, at the very least to the existence of that risk, that in itself constitutes the necessary recklessness for the purposes of the offence, see *Majewski* (§ 17-109 in the main work); and a genuine mistake as to fact in such circumstances constitutes no defence. This approach is borne out by the decision of the Court of Appeal in *R. v. Woods (W.),* 74 Cr.App.R. 312. It was conceded on behalf of W that, but for section 1(2) of the Sexual Offences (Amendment) Act 1976 (*ante*, H-4), the principles in *Majewski* and *Caldwell* (as to the relevance of drink to recklessness) would apply and that accordingly a genuine mistake as to fact as a consequence of drink could found no defence. However, it was argued that section 1(2) of the 1976 Act permitted the jury to take into account a defendant's drunken state as a possible reasonable ground for his belief that a woman was consenting to intercourse. The submission was roundly rejected. "Relevant" in that subsection means "*legally* relevant". W's drunkenness was not a matter that the jury were entitled to take into consideration in deciding whether or not reasonable grounds existed for W's belief that the woman consented to intercourse.

The question was considered again in *R. v. Fotheringham,* 88 Cr.App.R. 206, CA, in which the defendant was charged with rape. His defence was that he was so drunk at the time that he believed he was having intercourse with his wife. Applying *Majewski, Caldwell, Woods, ante,* and *R. v. O'Grady* [1987] Q.B. 995, 85 Cr.App.R. 315, CA (§ 17-16 in the main work), the court held that "in rape, self-induced intoxication is no defence, whether the issue be intention, consent or, as here, mistake as to the identity of the victim" (at p. 212).

(j) *Liability of accessories*

H-24   As to indicting accessories to rape, see *ante*, H-7; and as to their liability to conviction, notwithstanding the acquittal of the alleged principal, see *R. v. Cogan and Leak* [1976] Q.B. 217, 61 Cr.App.R. 217, CA (§ 20-26 in the main work).

(k) *Attempts*

H-25   See § 20-27 in the main work, and, in relation to the *mens rea* of an attempt, see *ante*, H-22.

(2) Procurement of intercourse by threats or false pretences

(a) *Statute*

Sexual Offences Act 1956, ss.2, 3

H-26   2.—(1) It is an offence for a person to procure a woman, by threats or intimidation, to have ... sexual intercourse in any part of the world.

(2) [*Repealed by CJPOA 1994, s.33(1).*]

[Subs. (1) is printed as repealed in part by the CJPOA 1994, s.168(1) and (3), and Scheds 9, para. 2, and 11.]

H-27   3.—(1) It is an offence for a person to procure a woman, by false pretences or false representations, to have ... sexual intercourse in any part of the world.

(2) [*Repealed by Criminal Justice and Public Order Act 1994, s.33(1).*]

[Subs. (1) is printed as repealed in part by the CJPOA 1994, s.168(1) and (3), and Scheds 9, para. 2, and 11.]

As to the meaning of "sexual intercourse", see *post*, H-219; as to the use of the word "woman", see *post*, H-222.

For anonymity provisions, see §§ 20-257 *et seq.* in the main work.

(b) *Indictment*

Statement of Offence

Procuration, contrary to section 3(1) of the Sexual Offences Act 1956.

Particulars of Offence

A B, on the _____ day of _____, 20__, procured J N, a woman, to have sexual intercourse with himself [or *with E F, as the case may be*] *by falsely pretending or representing to her that* [state in ordinary language the false pretence or representation].

The false pretences must be set out: *R. v. Field* (1892) 116 CCC Sess.Pap. 1891–1892, 757; but they need not be expressly negatived: *R. v. Clarke*, 59 J.P. 248.

An indictment for an offence contrary to section 2 may easily be framed from the above specimen.

(c) *Mode of trial and classification of offences*

The offence contrary to section 2 and an attempt to commit it are triable on indictment only: **H-29**
SOA 1956, s.37(2), and Sched. 2, para. 7(a), (b).

The offence contrary to section 3 is triable on indictment only: SOA 1956, s.37(2), and Sched. 2, para. 8.

As to the classification of offences, see *ante*, Appendix F-6.

(d) *Alternative verdicts*

As to the possibility of a conviction of either of these offences on a charge of rape, see *ante*, H-9.   **H-30**

(e) *Sentence*

Either offence, or an attempt to commit the offence contrary to section 2: imprisonment not   **H-31**
exceeding two years—SOA 1956, s.37(3), and Sched. 2, paras 7(a), (b), and 8.

(f) *Ingredients of the offences*

"Procure"

See *post*, H-171.   **H-32**

False pretences

Seduction by a married man of a woman under promise of marriage by false representation   **H-33**
was held to be within section 3(2) of the Criminal Law Amendment Act 1885 (*rep.*), of which section 3(1) of the Act of 1956 was a replacement: *R. v. Williams*, 62 J.P. 310. It is immaterial whether the intercourse was procured with the defendant or with another: *ibid.*, and see *R. v. Jones* [1896] 1 Q.B. 4.

(3) **Administering drugs to obtain or facilitate intercourse**

(a) *Statute*

Sexual Offences Act 1956, s.4

4.—(1) It is an offence for a person to apply or administer to, or cause to be taken by, a woman   **H-34**
any drug, matter or thing with intent to stupefy or overpower her so as thereby to enable any man to have unlawful sexual intercourse with her.

(2) [*Repealed by Criminal Justice and Public Order Act 1994, s.33(1).*]

As to the meaning of "sexual intercourse", see *post*, H-219; as to the use of the words "man" and "woman", see *post*, H-222.

For anonymity provisions, see *post*, §§ 20-257 *et seq.* in the main work.

(b) *Mode of trial and class of offence*

This offence is triable only on indictment: SOA 1956, s.37(2), and Sched. 2, para. 9. As to the   **H-35**
classification of offences, see *ante*, Appendix F-6.

(c) Alternative verdicts

H-36 As to the possibility of a conviction of this offence on a charge of rape, see *ante*, H-9.

(d) Sentence

H-37 Imprisonment not exceeding two years: SOA 1956, s.37(3), and Sched. 2, para. 9.

(e) Ingredients of the offence

H-38 "Unlawful" sexual intercourse means illicit sexual intercourse, *i.e.* outside the bond of marriage:
R. v. Chapman [1959] 1 Q.B. 100, 42 Cr.App.R. 257, CCA (considering s.19 of the 1956 Act, *post*,
H-148).

The essence of the offence is the administering of the drug. If there has been only one
administration, there can be only one offence, even though the intention of the administration
was to enable more than one man to have intercourse with the woman: *R. v. Shillingford and
Vanderwall*, 52 Cr.App.R. 188, CA.

(4) Sexual intercourse with girl under 13

(a) Statute

Sexual Offences Act 1956, s.5

H-39 **5.** It is an offence for a man to have unlawful sexual intercourse with a girl under the age of
thirteen.

[This section is printed as effectively amended by the CLA 1967, s.12(5)(a).]

As to the meaning of "sexual intercourse", see *post*, H-219; as to the use of the words "man"
and "girl", see *post*, H-222.

For anonymity provisions, see §§ 20-257 *et seq.* in the main work.

(b) Indictment

Statement of Offence

H-40 *Sexual intercourse with a girl under 13, contrary to section 5 of the Sexual Offences Act 1956.*

Particulars of Offence

A B, on the _____ day of _____, 20__, had sexual intercourse with J N, a girl under the age of 13 years.

(c) Mode of trial and classification of offences

H-41 This offence and an attempt to commit it are triable only on indictment: SOA 1956, s.37(2),
and Sched. 2, para. 2(a), (b). As to the classification of offences, see *ante*, Appendix F-6.

(d) Alternative verdicts

H-42 Indecent assault, contrary to section 14(1) of the 1956 Act (*post*, H-117): *R. v. McCormack* [1969]
2 Q.B. 442, 53 Cr.App.R. 514, CA. As to alternative verdicts generally, see §§ 4-524 *et seq.* in the
main work.

(e) Sentence

H-43 The full offence: life imprisonment—SOA 1956, s.37(2), and Sched. 2, para. 2(a).

Attempt: imprisonment not exceeding seven years—*ibid.*, para. 2(b).

Custodial sentences are normally imposed, unless the offender is psychologically abnormal or
of limited intelligence (see in particular *Att.-Gen.'s Reference (No. 20 of 1994)*, 16 Cr.App.R.(S.) 578,
CA.). Some guidance may be obtained from the guideline of the Sentencing Council in relation to
offences under the SOA 2003 (*post*, Appendix K-84 *et seq.*); and for guidance as to how to sentence
historic offences, see *R. v. H.*, *ante*, H-12.

(f) Ingredients of the offence

Man

H-44 As to the abolition of the presumption that a boy under 14 is incapable of sexual intercourse,
see *ante*, H-13.

Consent immaterial

The evidence is the same as in rape, with the exception that it is immaterial whether the act **H-45** was done with or without the consent of the girl. If it was in fact without her consent, an indictment for rape will lie, notwithstanding the age of the child: *R. v. Dicken* (1877) 14 Cox 8; *R. v. Harling*, 26 Cr.App.R. 127, CCA; *R. v. Howard*, 50 Cr.App.R. 56, CCA, *ante*, H-15. So, where the defendant was indicted for an attempt to commit the offence, and the evidence was that he had attempted to have sexual intercourse with the girl, but that she had consented to the attempt, it was held that the fact of her consent was immaterial, and that the defendant was properly convicted: *R. v. Beale* (1865) L.R. 1 C.C.R. 10.

Knowledge of age immaterial

A mistake as to the age of the girl, even if based on reasonable grounds, will not avail a **H-46** defendant: *R. v. Prince* (1875) L.R. 2 C.C.R. 154 (*post*, H-161); *R. v. K.* [2002] 1 A.C. 462, HL; and see the specific defence provided by section 6(3) in relation to the less serious offence of intercourse with a girl under 16 (*post*, H-50).

(g) *Evidence*

Recent complaint

See § 20-12 in the main work. **H-47**

Distress of victim

See § 20-13 in the main work. **H-48**

Age

The provisions of section 99(2) of the CYPA 1933 (§ 19-412 in the main work), as to presump- **H-49** tion and determination of age do not apply: see the proviso to Schedule 1 to the 1933 Act (whilst the proviso was repealed by the SOA 2003 (see § 19-412 in the main work), its effect in relation to any prosecution for an offence under the 1956 Act will be saved by virtue of the Interpretation Act 1978, s.16 (*ante*, Appendix B-16)). The girl must be proved to have been under 13 years of age when the offence was committed. The best way of doing this is to produce a duly certified copy of the certificate of birth, coupled with evidence of identity; but the age may be proved by any other legal means: *R. v. Cox* [1898] 1 Q.B. 179 (age could be proved by persons who had seen the child and by a teacher at an elementary school which the child attended). Where a certificate of birth is put in, there must be evidence of identity as well: see *R. v. Nicholls* (1867) 10 Cox 476; *R. v. Bellis*, 6 Cr.App.R. 283, CCA; *R. v. Rogers*, 10 Cr.App.R. 276, CCA.

In the case of an adopted child, the date of birth may be proved by a certified copy of an entry in the Adopted Children Register: Adoption and Children Act 2002, s.77(5).

(5) Sexual intercourse with a girl under 16

(a) *Statute*

Sexual Offences Act 1956, s.6

6.—(1) It is an offence, subject to the exceptions mentioned in this section, for a man to have **H-50** unlawful sexual intercourse with a girl ... under the age of sixteen.

(2) Where a marriage is invalid under section two of the Marriage Act 1949, or section one of the Age of Marriage Act 1929 (the wife being a girl under the age of sixteen), the invalidity does not make the husband guilty of an offence under this section because he has sexual intercourse with her, if he believes her to be his wife, and has reasonable cause for the belief.

(3) A man is not guilty of an offence under this section because he has unlawful sexual intercourse with a girl under the age of sixteen, if he is under the age of twenty-four and has not previously been charged with a like offence, and he believes her to be of the age of sixteen or over and has reasonable cause for the belief.

In this subsection "a like offence" means an offence under this section or an attempt to commit one, or an offence under paragraph (1) of section five of the Criminal Law Amendment Act 1885 (the provision replaced for England and Wales by this section).

[This section is printed as repealed in part by the CLA 1967, s.10(1), and Sched. 2, para. 14.]

As to the meaning of "sexual intercourse", see *post*, H-219; as to the use of the words "man" and "girl", see *post*, H-222.

As to the proof of exceptions, see the SOA 1956, s.47, *post*, H-225.

For anonymity provisions, see §§ 20-257 *et seq.* in the main work.

Marriage Act 1949, s.2

Marriages of persons under sixteen

H-51   **2.** A marriage solemnized between persons either of whom is under the age of sixteen shall be void.

(b) *Indictment*

Statement of Offence

H-52   *Sexual intercourse with a girl under 16, contrary to section 6(1) of the Sexual Offences Act 1956.*

Particulars of Offence

A B, on the _____ day of _____, 20___, had sexual intercourse with J N, a girl under the age of 16 years.

(c) *Mode of trial and classification of offences*

H-53   This offence and an attempt to commit it are triable either way: MCA 1980, s.17(1), and Sched. 1 (§ 1-130 in the main work). As to the classification of offences, see *ante*, Appendix F-6.

(d) *Alternative verdicts*

H-54   Indecent assault, contrary to section 14(1) of the 1956 Act (*post*, H-117): *R. v. McCormack* [1969] 2 Q.B. 442, 53 Cr.App.R. 514, CA. As to alternative verdicts generally, see §§ 4-524 *et seq.* in the main work.

(e) *Time limit on prosecutions*

H-55   Prosecutions for an offence under section 6 or an attempt to commit such offence may not be commenced more than 12 months after the offence charged: SOA 1956, s.37(2), and Sched. 2, para. 10(a), (b).

As to what is a commencement of the prosecution, see *R. v. West* [1898] 1 Q.B. 174; *R. v. Wakely* [1920] 1 K.B. 688, 14 Cr.App.R. 121, CCA.

In appropriate circumstances, evidence of prior offences by the defendant against the same girl committed outside the 12 months' time limit will be admissible: *R. v. Shellaker* [1914] 1 K.B. 414, 9 Cr.App.R. 240, CCA; *cf. R. v. Hewitt*, 19 Cr.App.R. 64, CCA; *R. v. Adams*, *The Times*, April 8, 1993, CA.

As to the impropriety of bringing a prosecution for indecent assault, based on an act of consensual sexual intercourse, where a prosecution under section 6 is time barred, see *R. v. J.*, *post*, H-118.

(f) *Sentence*

H-56   The full offence, or an attempt to commit it: imprisonment not exceeding two years' SOA 1956, s.37(3), and Sched. 2, para. 10(a), (b). The penalty on summary conviction is governed by section 32 of the MCA 1980 (§ 1-125 in the main work).

In *R. v. Taylor*, 64 Cr.App.R. 182, CA, the court laid down guidelines for the sentencing of persons convicted of having unlawful sexual intercourse with a girl under the age of 16. Lawton L.J. distinguished between cases where "virtuous friendship" between young people of about the same age ended in sexual intercourse, and cases where a man in a supervisory capacity set out to seduce a girl under 16 who was in his charge. In the first type of case, sentences of a punitive nature were not required; in the second, sentences near the maximum of two years should be passed.

In *R. v. Bayliss* [2000] 1 Cr.App.R.(S.) 412, CA, it was said that attitudes to teenage prostitution had changed since *Taylor*, and that there was a greater appreciation that this offence and that of taking indecent photographs of children, contrary to the Protection of Children Act 1978 (§§ 31-107 *et seq.* in the main work), had been put on the statute book for the protection of children, including against themselves.

(g) *Ingredients of the offence*

Man

As to the abolition of the presumption that a boy under 14 is incapable of sexual intercourse, see *ante*, H-13.   **H-57**

A girl under 16 cannot be indicted for "abetting" or "inciting" a man to have unlawful sexual intercourse with herself: *R. v. Tyrrell* [1894] 1 Q.B. 710.

As to doctors who prescribe contraceptive pills to girls under 16, see *Gillick v. West Norfolk and Wisbech Area Health Authority* [1986] A.C. 112, HL, *post*, H-196.

Consent immaterial

See *ante*, H-45, and *R. v. Ratcliffe* (1882) 10 Q.B.D. 74.   **H-58**

"Unlawful" sexual intercourse

See *R. v. Chapman, ante*, H-38.   **H-59**

(h) *Evidence*

Recent complaint

See § 20-12 in the main work.   **H-60**

Distress of victim

See § 20-13 in the main work.   **H-61**

Age

See *ante*, H-49, the contents of which apply, *mutatis mutandis*, to the offence under section 6.   **H-62**

(i) *Defences*

In the case of a man under the age of 24, the presence of reasonable cause to believe that the girl was over the age of 16 years is a valid defence provided that the defendant has not previously been charged with a like offence: SOA 1956, s.6(3) (*ante*, H-50). As to the meaning of the expression "a like offence", see *ibid.* The defence is not incompatible with Article 6 (right to fair trial (§ 16-72 in the main work)) or 14 (prohibition on discrimination (§ 16-177 in the main work)) of the ECHR as being discriminatory on the grounds that, (a) a woman who had sexual intercourse with a boy under 16 would, if prosecuted, be charged with indecent assault, in relation to which she would have a defence, whatever her age, of genuine belief that the boy was 16 or more, and (b) it was restricted to men under the age of 24; as to (b), even though the choice of age was arbitrary, it did not introduce an element of disproportionality into the offence: *R. v. Kirk and Russell* [2002] Crim.L.R. 756, CA.   **H-63**

In *R. v. Rider*, 37 Cr.App.R. 209, Assizes, Streatfeild J. had to construe the wording of the Criminal Law Amendment Act 1922. The proviso to section 2 of that Act gave a man under 24 years of age a defence to a charge of unlawful sexual intercourse with a girl under 16 years of age if at the time of the intercourse he had reasonable cause to believe that the girl was over the age of 16; but the defence was only available "on the first occasion on which he is charged with" such an offence. It was held that "charged" in this context meant "appeared before a court with jurisdiction to deal with the matter". The defendant had been committed for trial on two separate occasions in respect of like allegations relating to different girls. Both allegations were joined in the same indictment and it was held that appearance before the assize was the first occasion on which he appeared before a court with jurisdiction to deal with the matter and, therefore, the defence was available in respect of both counts. Streatfeild J. said, however, that had the magistrates refused to commit for trial in respect of the first matter, the appearance at the assize on the second matter would have been the second occasion. This result seems illogical. It should be borne in mind that at the time of *Rider*, the offence in question could be tried only on indictment. It is now triable either way and it is respectfully submitted that the defence should only be available to a person who at the time of the alleged offence has not been before a court (magistrates' court, whether or not the matter is to be tried summarily, Crown Court or service court) on a charge of such an offence. This gives due effect to the actual decision in *Rider* to the revised formulation of the defence in the 1956 Act and to the changes in the legislation relating to mode of trial. It is also consistent with the rationale underlying the restriction on the defence, *viz.* that once the serious nature of such conduct has been brought to the attention of a man, he can legitimately be expected to be more careful about a girl's age.

To constitute a defence under this proviso, where it applies, the defendant must have reasonable cause to believe, and, in fact, must have believed that the girl was over the age of 16 years: *R. v. Banks* [1916] 2 K.B. 621, 12 Cr.App.R. 74, CCA; *R. v. Harrison*, 26 Cr.App.R. 166, CCA. The question of the existence of reasonable cause to believe is one for the jury: *R. v. Forde* [1923] 2 K.B. 400, 17 Cr.App.R. 99, CCA.

The defence is available not only where intercourse has taken place, but also where it has been merely attempted: *R. v. Collier* [1960] Crim.L.R. 204, Assizes (Streatfeild J.).

As to the burden of proof of the "exceptions" (defences) in subsections (2) and (3) of section 6, see section 47 of the 1956 Act, *post*, H-225.

(6) Intercourse with defectives

(a) *Statute*

Sexual Offences Act 1956, ss.7, 9

Intercourse with defective

H-64   **7.**—(1) It is an offence, subject to the exception mentioned in this section, for a man to have unlawful sexual intercourse with a woman who is a defective.

(2) A man is not guilty of an offence under this section because he has unlawful sexual intercourse with a woman if he does not know and has no reason to suspect her to be a defective.

[This section is printed as substituted by the MHA 1959, s.127(1)(a).]

Procurement of defective

H-65   **9.**—(1) It is an offence, subject to the exception mentioned in this section, for a person to procure a woman who is a defective to have unlawful sexual intercourse in any part of the world.

(2) A person is not guilty of an offence under this section because he procures a defective to have unlawful sexual intercourse, if he does not know and has no reason to suspect her to be a defective.

As to the meaning of "sexual intercourse", see *post*, H-219 as to the use of the words "man" and "woman", see *post*, H-222; as to the meaning of "defective", see *post*, H-68.

For anonymity provisions, see §§ 20-257 *et seq.* in the main work.

As to the burden of proof in relation to the exception in subsection (2) of both sections, see section 47 of the Act, *post*, H-225.

(b) *Mode of trial and classification of offences*

H-66   Offences against sections 7 and 9, and attempts to commit them, are triable only on indictment: SOA 1956, s.37(2), and Sched. 2, paras 11(a), (b), and 13(a), (b). As to the classification of offences, see *ante*, Appendix F-6.

(c) *Sentence*

H-67   Offences against sections 7 and 9, and attempts to commit them: imprisonment not exceeding two years—SOA 1956, s.37(3), and Sched. 2, paras 11(a), (b), and 13(a), (b). For an illustrative example, see *R. v. Adcock* [2000] 1 Cr.App.R.(S.) 563, CA.

(d) *Ingredients of the offences*

"Defective"

Sexual Offences Act 1956, s.45

Meaning of defective

45. In this Act "defective" means a person suffering from a state of arrested or incomplete develop- **H-68** ment of mind which includes severe impairment of intelligence and social functioning.

[This section is printed as substituted by the MHA 1959, s.127(1); and as amended by the Mental Health (Amendment) Act 1982, Sched. 3.]

The words "severe impairment of intelligence and social functioning" are ordinary English words and not words of art; they were inserted in the definition to protect women, if defectives, from exploitation. Severe impairment is to be measured against the standards of normal persons: *R. v. Hall (J.H.)*, 86 Cr.App.R. 159, CA. The trial judge's direction that it was for them to decide on all the evidence whether the victim was severely impaired within the ordinary meaning of those words was correct.

"Unlawful" sexual intercourse

See *R. v. Chapman, ante*, H-38. **H-69**

"Procure"

See *post*, H-171. **H-70**

(7) Incest by a man

(a) *Statute*

Sexual Offences Act 1956, s.10

10.—(1) It is an offence for a man to have sexual intercourse with a woman whom he knows to be **H-71** his grand-daughter, daughter, sister or mother.

(2) In the foregoing subsection "sister" includes half-sister and for the purposes of that subsection any expression importing a relationship between two people shall be taken to apply notwithstanding that the relationship is not traced through lawful wedlock.

As to the meaning of "sexual intercourse", see *post*, H-219; as to the use of the words "man" and "woman", see *post*, § H-222.

For anonymity provisions, see §§ 20-257 *et seq.* in the main work.

(b) *Indictment*

Statement of Offence

Incest, contrary to section 10(1) of the Sexual Offences Act 1956. **H-72**

Particulars of Offence

A B, being a male person, on the _____ day of _____, 20___, had sexual intercourse with J N, whom he knew to be his daughter [if under the age of 13, add her age].

An indictment which charged the offence as having been committed "on divers days" between two specified dates was held to be bad for duplicity: *R. v. Thompson* [1914] 2 K.B. 99, 9 Cr.App.R. 252, CCA.

Where a brother and sister were charged in separate counts of the same indictment with committing incest and were tried separately, with the result that the brother was convicted and the sister acquitted, it was held that the acquittal of the sister did not make the conviction of the brother bad: *R. v. Gordon*, 19 Cr.App.R. 20, CCA. As to inconsistent verdicts generally, see §§ 7-70 *et seq.* in the main work.

(c) *Mode of trial and classification of offences*

This offence, and an attempt to commit it, are triable only on indictment: SOA 1956, s.37(2), **H-73** and Sched. 2, para. 14(a), (b). As to the classification of offences, see *ante*, Appendix F-6.

(d) *Alternative verdicts*

H-74   On a charge of the full offence, unlawful sexual intercourse with a girl under 13 (s.5) or with a girl under 16 (s.6): SOA 1956, s.37(4), and Sched. 2, para. 14(a). Where the girl is under 16, indecent assault (whether or not the indictment avers her age): *R. v. Rogina*, 64 Cr.App.R. 79, CA. This possibility arises by virtue of the combination of section 37(5) (*post*, H-226) and the specific provision in Schedule 2 for a conviction of an offence under either section 5 or 6 (indecent assault being an alternative on an indictment charging either of those offences, *ante*, H-42, H-54).

(e) *Restriction on prosecution*

H-75   A prosecution for this offence, or an attempt to commit it, may not be commenced except by or with the consent of the DPP: SOA 1956, s.37(2), and Sched. 2, para. 14(a), (b).

(f) *Sentence*

Maximum

H-76   The full offence and an attempt to commit it: if with a girl under 13, and so charged in the indictment, life imprisonment, otherwise imprisonment not exceeding seven years— SOA 1956, s.37(3), and Sched. 2, para. 14(a), (b).

Basis of sentence

H-77   See *R. v. Huchison*, 56 Cr.App.R. 307, CA.

Guidelines

H-78   In *Att.-Gen.'s Reference (No. 1 of 1989)*, 90 Cr.App.R. 141, the Court of Appeal laid down guidelines for sentencing in cases of incest by a father against a daughter. The court made the following suggestions "as a broad guide" to the level of sentence for various categories of the crime of incest. All were on the assumption that there had been no plea of guilty. They should be read subject to *Practice Statement (Crime: Sentencing)* [1992] 1 W.L.R. 948. See, in particular, paragraph 10 thereof.

(i) *Girl aged over 16 years*

H-79   A range from three years' imprisonment down to a nominal penalty would be appropriate depending in particular on the one hand whether force was used and the degree of harm if any, to the girl, and, on the other, the desirability where it existed of keeping family disruption to a minimum. The older the girl the greater the possibility that she might have been willing or even the instigating party, a factor which would be reflected in the sentence.

(ii) *Girl aged from 13 to 16 years*

H-80   A sentence between about five years' and three years' imprisonment would be appropriate. Much the same principles would apply as in the case of the girl over 16 years, though the likelihood of corruption increased in inverse proportion to the age of the girl.

(iii) *Girl aged under 13 years*

H-81   It was here that the widest range of sentences was likely to be found. If any case of incest could properly be described as the "ordinary" type of case, it would be one where the sexual relationship between husband and wife had broken down; the father had probably resorted to excessive drinking and the eldest daughter was gradually, by way of familiarities, indecent acts and suggestions made the object of the father's frustrated inclinations. If the girl was not far short of her thirteenth birthday and there were no particularly adverse or favourable features, a term of about six years' imprisonment would seem to be appropriate. The younger the girl when the sexual approach was started, the more likely it would be that the girl's will was overborne and, accordingly, the more serious would be the crime.

(iv) *Aggravating factors*

H-82   Whatever the age of the girl, the following, *inter alia*, would aggravate the offence:

(a) physical or psychological suffering from the offence;
(b) the incest taking place at frequent intervals or over a long period;
(c) the use of threats or violence, or the girl being otherwise terrified of her father;
(d) the incest being accompanied by perversions abhorrent to the girl, such as buggery or *fellatio*;
(e) the girl becoming pregnant; and
(f) the commission of similar offences against more than one girl.

(v) *Mitigating features*

Possible mitigating features were, *inter alia*: **H-83**

(a) a plea of guilty;
(b) genuine affection on the defendant's part rather than the intention to use the girl simply as an outlet for his sexual inclinations;
(c) previous sexual experience by the girl; and
(d) deliberate attempts at seduction by the girl.

In relation to a plea of guilty, the court said that such a plea was seldom not entered and it should be met by an appropriate discount, depending on the usual considerations, that is, how promptly the defendant confessed, the degree of contrition and so on. The court also said that occasionally a shorter term of imprisonment than would otherwise be imposed might be justified as being of benefit to the victim and the family.

For cases illustrating the application of these guidelines, see CSP B4–2. For cases of incest by a brother with a sister, see *ibid.*, B4–2.3D; for a case of incest by a mother with her young son, see *ibid.*, B4–2.3E.

(g) *Effect of adoption*

The prohibition contained in section 10(1) applies notwithstanding the adoption of one of the **H-84** parties: Adoption and Children Act 2002, s.74(1)(b) (whilst this provision was amended to substitute a reference to sections 64 and 65 of the SOA 2003 for the references to sections 10 and 11 of the 1956 Act, its previous operation will be saved by virtue of section 16 of the Interpretation Act 1978 (*ante*, Appendix B-16)).

(h) *Ingredients of the offence*

If a man makes a genuine mistake as to the identity of the person with whom he has intercourse, **H-85** he will not commit the offence: *R. v. Baillie-Smith*, 64 Cr.App.R. 76, CA (intercourse with daughter, thinking her to be his wife).

As to the abolition of the common law presumption that a boy under 14 is incapable of sexual intercourse, see *ante*, H-13.

(i) *Evidence*

The relationship between the parties may be proved by oral evidence or by certificates of mar- **H-86** riage and birth, coupled with identification. An admission by the defendant that the person with whom the offence had been committed was his daughter may be sufficient evidence of the relationship: *R. v. Jones (Evan)*, 24 Cr.App.R. 55, CCA.

Evidence tending to show pre-existent sexual passion between the parties is admissible: *R. v. Ball* [1911] A.C. 47, HL.

The defendant was charged with incest with S, who was alleged to be his daughter. His defence was that he had no knowledge that S *was* his daughter. He desired to give evidence:

(a) that he had been told by his first wife (the mother of S) that S had been begotten by another man and that he believed that statement to be true;
(b) that he had told his second wife that he was not the father of S;
(c) explaining statements which he had made on certain occasions acknowledging S to be his daughter.

It was held (on appeal) that this evidence was relevant to the issue whether the defendant *knew* that S was his daughter and that he was entitled to give any evidence relevant to that issue, including evidence of an admission by his first wife: *R. v. Carmichael* [1940] 1 K.B. 630, 27 Cr.App.R. 183, CCA.

(8) Incitement to incest of girls under 16

H-87   See the CLA 1977, s.54, *post*, H-239.

(9) Incest by a woman

(a) *Statute*

Sexual Offences Act 1956, s.11

H-88   11.—(1) It is an offence for a woman of the age of sixteen or over to permit a man whom she knows to be her grandfather, father, brother or son to have sexual intercourse with her by her consent.

(2) In the foregoing subsection "brother" includes half-brother, and for the purposes of that subsection any expression importing a relationship between two people shall be taken to apply notwithstanding that the relationship is not traced through lawful wedlock.

As to the meaning of "sexual intercourse", see *post*, H-219; as to the use of the words "woman" and "man", see *post*, H-222.

For anonymity provisions, see §§ 20-257 *et seq.* in the main work.

(b) *Indictment*

Statement of Offence

H-89   *Incest, contrary to section 11(1) of the Sexual Offences Act 1956.*

Particulars of Offence

A B, being a female person of the age of 18, on the _____ day of _____, 20__, with her consent permitted J N, whom she knew to be her father, to have sexual intercourse with her.

As to the form of the indictment, see also *R. v. Thompson*, *ante*, H-72.

(c) *Mode of trial and classification of offences*

H-90   This offence, and an attempt to commit it, are triable only on indictment: SOA 1956, s.37(2), and Sched. 2, para. 15(a), (b). As to the classification of offences, see *ante*, Appendix F-6.

(d) *Restriction on prosecution*

H-91   A prosecution for this offence or an attempt to commit it may not be commenced except by or with the consent of the DPP: SOA 1956, s.37(2), and Sched. 2, para. 15(a), (b).

(e) *Sentence*

H-92   The full offence: imprisonment not exceeding seven years—SOA 1956, s.37(3), and Sched. 2, para. 15(a).

Attempt: imprisonment not exceeding two years—*ibid.*, para. 15(b).

(f) *Effect of adoption*

H-93   The prohibition contained in section 11(1) applies notwithstanding the adoption of one of the parties: Adoption and Children Act 2002, s.74(1)(b) (as to which, see *ante*, H-84).

(g) *Ingredients of offence*

H-94   The common law presumption as to incapacity in relation to boys under 14 years of age (*ante*, H-13) had no application where a woman was charged with committing incest with such a boy: *R. v. Pickford* [1995] 1 Cr.App.R. 420, CA.

(10) Buggery

(a) *Introduction*

H-95   The SOA 1956 contains two "unnatural offences", namely buggery (with a person or with an animal) and gross indecency between men. There are time limits and requirements as to the consent of the DPP in respect of both offences in certain circumstances.

The SOA 1967 amended the law by providing, in particular, that consenting men over the age of 21 (reduced to 18 by the CJPOA 1994, and to 16 by the Sexual Offences (Amendment) Act 2000) who commit buggery or gross indecency in private, do not commit an offence (s.1, *post*, H-97). There are different rules regarding the lawfulness of procuration of buggery and gross indecency (s.4, *post*, H-236). Section 11(3) provides that section 46 of the 1956 Act (use of words "man", "boy" and other expressions) shall apply for the purposes of the provisions of the 1967 Act as it applies for the purposes of the provisions of that Act. For section 46, see *post*, H-222.

The CJPOA 1994 effected further changes in the law. Apart from reducing the age of consent for homosexual acts to 18 (*ante*), it redefined the offence of rape to include non-consensual anal intercourse with a man or a woman (*ante*, H-3). Non-consensual buggery should, therefore, be charged as rape. Consensual buggery between two people will not be an offence if the act takes place in private and both parties have achieved the age of 16.

As to the offences of indecent assault on a man and assault with intent to commit buggery, which may be on a man or a woman (categorised in the 1956 Act as "assault" offences rather than as "unnatural offences"), see sections 15, *post*, H-127, and 16, *post*, H-138.

(b) *Statute*

Sexual Offences Act 1956, s.12

12.—(1) It is an offence for a person to commit buggery with another person otherwise than in the circumstances first described in subsection (1A) or (1AA) below or with an animal. **H-96**

(1A) The circumstances referred to in subsection (1) are that the act of buggery takes place in private and both parties have attained the age of sixteen.

(1AA) The other circumstances so referred to are that the person is under the age of sixteen and the other person has attained that age.

(1B) An act of buggery by one man with another shall not be treated as taking place in private if it takes place—

(a) when more than two persons take part or are present; or

(b) in a lavatory to which the public have or are permitted to have access, whether on payment or otherwise.

(1C) In any proceedings against a person for buggery with another person it shall be for the prosecutor to prove that the act of buggery took place otherwise than in private or that one of the parties to it had not attained the age of sixteen.

(2), (3) [*Repealed by Police and Criminal Evidence Act 1984, Sched. 7.*]

[Subs. (1) is printed as amended by the CLA 1967, s.12(5)(a); the CJPOA 1994, s.143(1), (2); and the Sexual Offences (Amendment) Act 2000, s.2(1)(a) and (b); subss. (1A), (1B) and (1C) were inserted by the 1994 Act, s.143(1), (3); and are printed as amended by the 2000 Act, s.1(1); subs. (1AA) was inserted by the 2000 Act, s.2(1)(c).]

For anonymity provisions, see §§ 20-257 *et seq.* in the main work.

As to conspiracy or incitement to commit this offence, see *R. v. Boulton* (1871) 12 Cox 87.

Sexual Offences Act 1967, s.1

Amendment of law relating to homosexual acts in private

1.—(1) Notwithstanding any statutory or common law provision, ... **H-97**

(a) a homosexual act in private shall not be an offence provided that the parties consent thereto and have attained the age of sixteen years; and

(b) a homosexual act by any person shall not be an offence if he is under the age of sixteen and the other party has attained that age.

(2) An act which would otherwise be treated for the purposes of this Act as being done in private shall not be so treated if done—

(a) when more than two persons take part or are present; or

(b) in a lavatory to which the public have or are permitted to have access, whether on payment or otherwise.

(3) A man who is suffering from severe mental handicap cannot in law give any consent which, by

virtue of subsection (1) of this section, would prevent a homosexual act from being an offence, but a person shall not be convicted, on account of the incapacity of such a man to consent, of an offence consisting of such an act if he proves that he did not know and had no reason to suspect that man to be suffering from severe mental handicap.

(3A) In subsection (3) of this section "severe mental handicap" means a state of arrested or incomplete development of mind which includes severe impairment of intelligence and social functioning.

(4) Section 128 of the Mental Health Act 1959 (prohibition on men on the staff of a hospital, or otherwise having responsibility for mental patients, having sexual intercourse with women patients) shall have effect as if any reference therein to having unlawful sexual intercourse with a woman included a reference to committing buggery or an act of gross indecency with another man.

(5) [*Repealed by CJPOA 1994, s.168(3) and Sched. 11.*]

(6) It is hereby declared that where in any proceedings it is charged that a homosexual act is an offence the prosecutor shall have the burden of proving that the act was done otherwise than in private or otherwise than with the consent of the parties or that any of the parties had not attained the age of sixteen years.

(7) For the purposes of this section a man shall be treated as doing a homosexual act if, and only if, he commits buggery with another man or commits an act of gross indecency with another man or is a party to the commission by a man of such an act.

[This section is printed as amended and repealed in part by the Mental Health (Amendment) Act 1982, s.65(1), (2), and Scheds 3, para. 34, and 4; the CJPOA 1994, ss.146(1) and 168(3), and Sched. 11; and the Sexual Offences (Amendment) Act 2000, ss.1(2)(a) and 2(3)(a) and (b).]

As to the use of the word "man", see *post*, H-222.
For section 128 of the MHA 1959, see *post*, H-228.

(c) Indictment for buggery with a person

Statement of Offence

H-98 *Buggery, contrary to section 12(1) of the Sexual Offences Act 1956.*

Particulars of Offence

A B, a person of [or over] the age of 21 years, on the _____ day of _____, 20__, committed buggery with J N, a person under the age of 18 years.

Because the penalty provisions have the effect of creating a number of separate offences (see *post*, H-103), the particulars should be clear as to which offence is alleged; in the specimen set out above, it is a five year offence that is alleged. Alternative counts may be laid, where appropriate: see *R. v. Reakes* [1974] Crim.L.R. 615, CA.

As to the correct practice where old offences are charged, see *R. v. R.* [1993] Crim.L.R. 541, CA; *R. v. B.*, *ibid.* As to the need for special caution where extremely old offences are alleged, *i.e.* dating back to the period prior to the passing of the SOA 1967 (July 27, 1967), see *R. v. D.* [1993] Crim.L.R. 542, CA.

As to the particulars which need to be averred on a charge of attempted buggery, see *R. v. D.*, *ante*. The principles are the same as for the full offence.

(d) Indictment for buggery with an animal (bestiality)

Statement of Offence

H-99 *Buggery, contrary to section 12(1) of the Sexual Offences Act 1956.*

Particulars of Offence

A B, a person of [or over] the age of 21 years, on the _____ day of _____, 20__, committed buggery with a cow [or as the case may be].

(e) Mode of trial and classification of offences

H-100 This offence, and an attempt to commit it, are triable only on indictment: SOA 1956, s.37(2), and Sched. 2, para. 3(a), (b). As to the classification of offences, see *ante*, Appendix F-6.

(f) *Time limits*

Sexual Offences Act 1967, s.7

7.—(1) No proceedings for an offence to which this section applies shall be commenced after the **H-101**
expiration of twelve months from the date on which that offence was committed.

(2) This section applies to—

    (a) any offence under section 13 of the Act of 1956 (gross indecency between men);

    (b) [*repealed by Criminal Law Act 1977, Sched. 13*];

    (c) any offence of buggery by a man with another man not amounting to an assault on that
other man and not being an offence by a man with a boy under the age of 16.

For section 13 of the 1956 Act, see *post*, H-107.

Where it was unclear upon the evidence given at the trial whether the offence charged had
been committed within the 12 month period prior to the commencement of proceedings for the
offence, the court quashed the conviction: *R. v. Lewis*, 68 Cr.App.R. 310, CA. A judge need not in
every case to which section 7(1) applies direct the jury that they must be sure the offence was
committed within the prescribed period. However, he must do so where an issue under the
subsection is raised by the defence, or where it clearly arises on the evidence given at the trial:
ibid.

(g) *Restriction on prosecutions*

Sexual Offences Act 1967, s.8

8. No proceedings shall be instituted except by or with the consent of the Director of Public **H-102**
Prosecutions against any man for the offence of buggery with, or gross indecency with, another man
... or for aiding, abetting, counselling, procuring or commanding its commission where either of
those men was at the time of its commission under the age of sixteen.

[This section is printed as amended by the Sexual Offences (Amendment) Act 2000, s.1(2)(b);
and as repealed in part by the Criminal Jurisdiction Act 1975, s.14(5), and Sched. 6, Pt I; and the
Criminal Attempts Act 1981, s.10, and Sched., Pt I.]

Failure to obtain the consent of the DPP will lead to the quashing of the conviction: *R. v. Angel*,
52 Cr.App.R. 280, CA; *Secretary of State for Defence v. Warn* [1970] A.C. 394, HL (proceedings
before court-martial).

Section 8 does not apply to proceedings under the Indecency with Children Act 1960 (*post*,
H-230): CJA 1972, s.48.

(h) *Sentence*

Maximum

The full offence, or an attempt to commit it: if with a person under the age of 16 or with an **H-103**
animal, life imprisonment; if the accused is of or over the age of 21 and the other person is under
the age of 18, imprisonment not exceeding five years; otherwise, imprisonment not exceeding two
years—SOA 1956, s.37(3), and Sched. 2, para. 3(a), (b) (as substituted by the CJPOA 1994,
s.144(1), (2)). (For an offence of non-consensual buggery with a male over 15 committed before
the commencement of the amendments effected by the 1994 Act (November 3, 1994), the
maximum remains at 10 years: *Att.-Gen.'s Reference (No. 48 of 1994) (R. v. Jeffrey)*, 16 Cr.App.R.(S.)
980, CA.)

The effect of the different penalty provisions is to create distinct offences: see *R. v. Courtie*
[1984] A.C. 463, HL.

Absence of consent not being an ingredient of the offence, it is not open to a judge to sentence
on the basis that there was lack of consent; if lack of consent is alleged, there should be a charge
of rape: *R. v. Davies* [1998] 1 Cr.App.R.(S.) 380, CA; *R. v. D. (Anthony)* [2000] 1 Cr.App.R.(S.) 120,
CA.

Guidelines

The bracket of sentencing in cases of homosexual offences against boys with neither aggravat- **H-104** ing nor mitigating factors was set out in *R. v. Willis*, 60 Cr.App.R. 146, CA, as being from three to five years. The court in that case also identified the principal aggravating and mitigating features. In *R. v. A. and W.* [2001] 2 Cr.App.R. 18, CA, the court specifically said that the guidelines in *Willis* remained the starting point. In *R. v. Patterson* [2006] 2 Cr.App.R.(S.) 48, however, the Court of Appeal said that sentences in historic cases of buggery should now be determined as if the offence were one of rape in accordance with the guidelines in *R. v. Millberry; R. v. Morgan; R. v. Lackenby* [2003] 1 Cr.App.R. 25, CA, instead of by reference to the *Willis* guidelines. The court said that it is important that the sentence should reflect the gravity of the offence rather than the particular label attached to it, and since there is no distinction in principle or in essential gravity made in the *Millberry* guidelines between rape of a male and rape of a female, it would be wrong for a sentence of buggery to be imposed on any other basis. This approach was taken further in *R. v. Kearns* [2009] 1 Cr.App.R.(S.) 107, CA, where it was applied to what was apparently a case of consensual buggery of a 15-year-old boy. For criticism of the *Patterson/Kearns* approach, see the commentaries at CLW/06/34/24 and CLW/09/16/8. Whilst this criticism remains valid, sentencers dealing with historic offending should now be guided, as to general principles, by the judgment of the Court of Appeal in *R. v. H.*, ante, H-12.

(i) *Ingredients of the offence*

H-105   The definition of the offence derives from the common law. It consists of sexual intercourse (*per anum—R. v. Jacobs* (1817) R. & R. 331) by man with man or, in the same manner, by man with woman (*R. v. Wiseman* (1718) Fortescue K.B. 91; Fost. 91), or by man or woman in any manner (*R. v. Bourne*, 36 Cr.App.R. 125, CCA) with beast (also referred to as bestiality): see 1 Hale 669; 1 Hawk. c. 4; 1 East P.C. 480; 1 Russ. Cr., 12th ed., 735. Once penetration is proved, both parties (if consenting) are equally guilty.

Penetration, without emission, is sufficient: *R. v. Reekspear* (1832) 1 Mood. 342.

As to the abolition of the common law presumption that a boy under 14 is incapable of sexual intercourse, see *ante*, H-13.

The offence of bestiality does not depend on consent but on the commission of a particular act: *R. v. Bourne, ante* (defendant convicted of aiding and abetting his wife to commit buggery with a dog, it being assumed that she would have been entitled to an acquittal on the ground of duress).

The following direction on the question of privacy (1967 Act, s.1, *ante*) has been approved by the Court of Appeal: "you look at all the circumstances, the time of night, the nature of the place including such matters as lighting and you consider further the likelihood of a third person coming upon the scene": *R. v. Reakes* [1974] Crim.L.R. 615.

In relation to subsection (3A) of section 1 of the 1967 Act, it is open to the prosecution to prove severe mental handicap without calling medical evidence but by inviting the jury to observe the behaviour and reactions of the complainant and to draw what they consider to be an appropriate inference: *R. v. Robbins* [1988] Crim.L.R. 744, CA.

(j) *Evidence*

H-106   The rule as to the admissibility of recent complaints was held to apply in the case of buggery with a youth of 19: *R. v. Wannell*, 17 Cr.App.R. 53, CCA.

(11) **Gross indecency**

(a) *Statute*

Sexual Offences Act 1956, s.13

H-107   **13.** It is an offence for a man to commit an act of gross indecency with another man otherwise than in the circumstances described below, whether in public or private, or to be a party to the commission by a man of an act of gross indecency with another man, or to procure the commission by a man of an act of gross indecency with another man.

The circumstances referred to above are that the man is under the age of sixteen and the other man has attained that age.

[This section is printed as amended by the Sexual Offences (Amendment) Act 2000, s.2(2)(a) and (b).]

Gross indecency is no longer an offence where the act takes place in private and both parties consent thereto and both have attained the age of 16: see SOA 1967, s.1 (as amended by the Sexual Offences (Amendment) Act 2000, s.1(2)(a)), *ante,* H-97.

Furthermore, it is not an offence under this section for a man to procure the commission by another man of an act of gross indecency with himself which by reason of section 1 of the 1967 Act is not an offence under this section: see section 4(3) of the 1967 Act, *post,* H-236. As to procuration of gross indecency, see further H-113, *post.*

As to the use of the word "man", see *post,* H-222.

(b) *Indictment*

Statement of Offence

Gross indecency, contrary to section 13 of the Sexual Offences Act 1956.   **H-108**

Particulars of Offence

A B, on the _____ day of _____, 20__, being a male person, committed an act of gross indecency with J N, a male person otherwise than in private [or with J N, a male person under the age of 18 years, namely, of the age of _____ years].

(c) *Mode of trial and classification of offences*

Offences contrary to section 13, and an attempt to procure the commission by a man of an act **H-109** of gross indecency with another man, are triable either way: MCA 1980, s.17(1), and Sched. 1 (§ 1-130 in the main work). As to the classification of offences, see *ante,* Appendix F-6.

(d) *Time limits and restrictions on prosecutions*

See *ante,* H-101, H-102.   **H-110**

(e) *Sentence*

Offences contrary to section 13: if by a man of or over the age of 21 with a man under the age **H-111** of 16, imprisonment not exceeding five years, otherwise two years—SOA 1956, s.37(3), and Sched. 2, para. 16(a) (as amended by the CJPOA 1994, s.144(1), (3), and the Sexual Offences (Amendment) Act 2000, s.1(1)).

An attempt to procure the commission by a man of an act of gross indecency with another man: as for the full offences—SOA 1956, s.37(3), and Sched. 2, para. 16(b) (as amended by the CJPOA 1994, s.144(1), (3), and the Sexual Offences (Amendment) Act 2000, s.1(1)).

Penalties on summary conviction are provided for by the MCA 1980, s.32 (§ 1-125 in the main work).

An attempt to commit any other offence than the one specifically provided for by the 1956 Act will be punishable in accordance with the Criminal Attempts Act 1981, ss.1 and 4 (§§ 33-128 *et seq.* in the main work).

(f) *Ingredients of the offences*

Gross indecency

If there is an agreement whereby two male persons act in concert to behave in a grossly **H-112** indecent manner, as, for example, to make a grossly indecent exhibition, the offence is committed even though there has been no actual physical contact: *R. v. Hunt,* 34 Cr.App.R. 135, CCA.

An offence of indecency between men is not committed unless both men participate in the indecency. "With another man" in section 13 cannot be construed as meaning "against" or "directed towards" a person who did not consent: *R. v. Preece and Howells* [1977] Q.B. 370, 63 Cr.App.R. 28, CA, and see *R. v. Hornby and Peaple,* 32 Cr.App.R. 1, CCA, and *R. v. Hunt, ante.*

Where two persons are jointly indicted for an offence under the section, one may be convicted and the other acquitted: *R. v. Jones* [1896] 1 Q.B. 4; *R. v. Pearce,* 35 Cr.App.R. 17, CCA; but see *R. v. Batten, The Times,* March 16, 1990, CA, where two men were charged with committing an act of gross indecency with each other. The jury convicted one defendant, but failed to agree in respect of the other and were discharged. The Court of Appeal quashed the conviction: the issue was the same in the case of both men and it was not a case where there was some evidence such as a confession, implicating one man but not the other. If both are to be convicted, it is important that the jury should be directed that, to establish the offence, it must be proved that there was an act of gross indecency by the one defendant with the other and that the two defendants were acting in concert: *R. v. Hornby and Peaple, ante.*

A conviction for attempting to commit an act of gross indecency may be maintained where one of the persons implicated alone has been charged and the other has not been charged but has been called as a witness for the prosecution and swears that he did not consent to any act of indecency: *R. v. Pearce, ante.*

Procuring gross indecency

H-113   It is an offence within section 13 for a male person to procure the commission with himself of an act of gross indecency by another male person: *R. v. Jones, ante; R. v. Cope*, 16 Cr.App.R. 77, CCA. But, if the act itself is not an offence by virtue of section 1 of the SOA 1967, the procuration thereof will not be an offence either: *ibid.*, s.4(3). See *ante*, H-97, and *post*, H-236.

If a male person persuades, or attempts to persuade, a boy to handle him indecently, such person alone may be charged and convicted under this section. In a case where indecent assault may be difficult or impossible to prove, because no threat or hostile act by the defendant towards the boy can easily be established, the proper charge is that of procuring or attempting to procure (as the case may be) an act of gross indecency with the defendant himself: *R. v. Burrows*, 35 Cr.App.R. 180, CCA.

On a charge of incitement to procure an act of gross indecency, it is not necessary that there should be, at the time of the incitement, an ascertained person with whom the act was to be committed: *R. v. Bentley* [1923] 1 K.B. 403, CCA.

As to the meaning of "procure", see also *post*, H-171.

Attempting to procure an act of gross indecency

H-114   Procuring the commission of an act of gross indecency under section 13 of the 1956 Act is itself a substantive offence. Section 1(4)(b) of the Criminal Attempts Act 1981 (§ 33-128 in the main work) does not preclude the charging of an attempt to procure an act of gross indecency under section 1(1) of the 1981 Act because section 1(4)(b) applies in circumstances when the alleged procurement is additional to and not part of the substantive offence: *Chief Constable of Hampshire v. Mace*, 84 Cr.App.R. 40, DC. (The penalty for such attempt is specifically provided for by the 1956 Act: see *ante*, H-111.)

What conduct will be sufficient to constitute an attempt will depend on the application of the formula in section 1(1) of the 1981 Act: was what was done "more than merely preparatory to the commission of the offence"?

Authorities decided prior to the 1981 Act can be no more than illustrative: see *R. v. Cope, ante; R. v. Woods*, 22 Cr.App.R. 41, CCA; *R. v. Miskell*, 37 Cr.App.R. 214, Ct-MAC.

(g) *Evidence*

Guilty plea by one defendant

H-115   See *R. v. Mattison* [1990] Crim.L.R. 117, CA (§ 9-90 in the main work).

Recent complaint

H-116   The rule as to admissibility of recent complaints was held not to apply to this offence on the ground that consent of the other male person is immaterial: *R. v. Hoodless*, 64 J.P. 282.

(12) Indecent assault on a woman

(a) *Statute*

Sexual Offences Act 1956, s.14

Indecent assault on a woman

H-117   **14.**—(1) It is an offence, subject to the exception mentioned in subsection (3) of this section, for a person to make an indecent assault on a woman.

(2) A girl under the age of sixteen cannot in law give any consent which would prevent an act being an assault for the purposes of this section.

(3) Where a marriage is invalid under section two of the Marriage Act 1949, or section one of the Age of Marriage Act 1929 (the wife being a girl under the age of sixteen), the invalidity does not make the husband guilty of any offence under this section by reason of her incapacity to consent while under that age, if he believes her to be his wife and has reasonable cause for the belief.

(4) A woman who is a defective cannot in law give any consent which would prevent an act being an assault for the purposes of this section, but a person is only to be treated as guilty of an indecent assault on a defective by reason of that incapacity to consent, if that person knew or had reason to suspect her to be a defective.

As to the use of the words "woman" and "girl", see *post*, H-222.

As to the meaning of "defective", see *ante*, H-68.

For the Marriage Act 1949, s.2, see *ante*, H-51.

For the burden of proof of exceptions, see section 47 of the 1956 Act, *post*, H-225.

For anonymity provisions, see *post*, §§ 20-257 *et seq.* in the main work.

(b) *Indictment*

Statement of Offence

Indecent assault, contrary to section 14(1) of the Sexual Offences Act 1956.   **H-118**

Particulars of Offence

A B, on the _____ day of _____, 20__, indecently assaulted J N, a woman.

Age is not an essential ingredient of, nor an essential averment in, the framing of a count under section 14(1): *R. v. Hodgson* [1973] Q.B. 565, 57 Cr.App.R. 502, CA. As to the need, however, to specify the age of the girl in certain old cases, see *post*, H-120.

Where the prosecution case leaves it open to the jury to convict on either of two distinct factual bases, it will be necessary for the judge to direct them as to the need for unanimity as to the basis of any verdict of guilty: see *R. v. Turner* [2000] Crim.L.R. 325, CA, and *R. v. D.* [2001] 1 Cr.App.R. 13, CA.

In *R. v. J.* [2005] 1 A.C. 562, HL, it was held that, on a true construction of the SOA 1956, it is impermissible to prosecute a charge of indecent assault under section 14(1) in circumstances where the only conduct upon which that charge was based was an act of unlawful sexual intercourse with a girl under the age of 16 in respect of which no prosecution might be commenced under section 6(1) (*ante*, H-50) by virtue of the time bar of 12 months contained in section 37(2) of, and Schedule 2, para. 10, to, the Act (as to which, see *ante*, H-55). Their Lordships held that the court was under a duty to give effect to a statute which was plain and unambiguous; it must have been intended that the prohibition in paragraph 10 would have some meaningful effect, otherwise there would have been no possible purpose in prohibiting prosecution under section 6 after a lapse of 12 months if exactly the same conduct could thereafter be prosecuted, with exposure to the same penalty (at the time of enactment), under section 14; but this did not prevent a prosecution being properly founded on independent acts other than sexual intercourse itself or conduct inherent in or forming part of it. As to the effect of this decision in relation to indecent assault as a possible alternative verdict on a charge of rape, see the cases cited at H-9, *ante*.

(c) *Mode of trial and class of offence*

This offence is triable either way: MCA 1980, s.17(1), and Sched. 1 (§ 1-130 in the main work).   **H-119**
As to the classification of offences, see *ante*, Appendix F-6.

(d) *Sentence*

Imprisonment, not exceeding 10 years: SOA 1956, s.37, and Sched. 2, para. 17 (as amended by   **H-120**
the SOA 1985, s.3(3)). The 1985 amendment took effect on September 16, 1985: prior to that, the maximum penalty was two years' imprisonment, save where the girl was under 13 and was so stated in the indictment, in which case the maximum was five years' imprisonment. In relation to cases where the facts date back beyond September 16, 1985, see *R. v. R.* [1993] Crim.L.R. 541, CA; *R. v. B., ibid.*

Where a defendant charged with rape of a girl under 16 is acquitted of rape, but convicted of indecent assault on the basis that consent is no defence, the sentence should not exceed the maximum for an offence of unlawful sexual intercourse with a girl under 16 (as to which, see *ante*, H-56): *R. v. Iles* [1998] 2 Cr.App.R.(S.) 63, CA.

The fact that the victim had been abused on a previous occasion does not reduce, but might increase, the gravity of further offending by an adult thereafter. If, however, by reason of being corrupted or precocious, or both, the victim instigated offences against herself, that was an aspect which the judge was entitled to take into account. But it was mitigation only in a negative sense, namely that the child was not being treated in a way which she was personally resisting or found repugnant: *Att.-Gen.'s Reference (No. 36 of 1995) (R. v. Dawson)* [1996] 2 Cr.App.R.(S.) 50, CA.

There is no sentencing principle which precludes the imposition of a custodial sentence on a first conviction of a persistent indecent assault (on a female on an underground train): *R. v. Townsend*, 16 Cr.App.R.(S.) 553, CA, *R. v. Tanyildiz* [1998] 1 Cr.App.R.(S.) 362, CA, and *R. v. Diallo* [2000] 1 Cr.App.R.(S.) 426, CA (not following *R. v. Neem*, 14 Cr.App.R.(S.) 18, CA).

Cases decided prior to the increase in the statutory maximum effected by the SOA 1985 could not be regarded as authoritative in relation to the tariff after the increase; the conclusion in *R. v. Demel* [1997] 2 Cr.App.R.(S.) 5, CA, that the upper end of the tariff for a single incident involving a breach of trust following a trial was in the range of 13 to 18 months' imprisonment should not be followed as the authorities relied on were decided in relation to a different statutory framework or had been decided without apparent appreciation of the effect of the 1985 Act: *R. v. L.* [1999] 1 Cr.App.R. 117, CA (two years' imprisonment following trial for "grave" breach of trust by 52-year-old man on nine-year-old girl upheld; declining to issue guidelines, but observing that in most cases the personal circumstances of the offender would have to take second place to the duty of the court to protect victims). See also *R. v. Wellman* [1999] 2 Cr.App.R.(S.) 162, CA.

For cases of indecent assault, see CSP B4–6.

As to the non-applicability of the Sentencing Guidelines Council's guideline on sexual offences to offences under the 1956 Act, see *Att.-Gen.'s Reference (No. 78 of 2010)* [2011] 2 Cr.App.R.(S.) 109, CA (pointing out that offences under the SOA 2003 are differently defined and have different (more severe) maximum penalties); but see *R. v. H., ante*, H-12, as to the approach to sentencing for historic offences generally.

In *R. v. Clifford* [2015] 1 Cr.App.R.(S.) 32, CA, the appellant (71/ no convictions) was convicted on eight counts of indecent assault, contrary to section 14(1) of the 1956 Act, in respect of four victims, in relation to offences committed between 1977 and 1984 when the statutory maximum was two years' imprisonment. It was held (considering *R. v. H., ante*) that the judge had been entitled in the course of his sentencing remarks to observe that some of the offending would now be charged as rape or assault by penetration, and had been entitled to impose consecutive sentences to reflect the overall criminality involved according to modern standards and attitudes (as reflected in the Sentencing Council for England and Wales's guideline on sexual offences (*post*, Appendix K-84 *et seq.*)). However, the judge had been wrong to take into account when passing sentence the appellant's assertions of innocence (which did not directly impugn the victims (by way of distinction from *Att.-Gen.'s Reference (No. 38 of 2013) (R. v. Hall)* [2014] 1 Cr.App.R.(S.) 61, CA)), his vehement complaints about the fact that the victims were entitled to anonymity, and the fact that he had stood behind a television reporter on camera outside the court, mimicking the reporter's actions (where there was no evidence that the victims were aware of this conduct and the matter had not been dealt with as a contempt of court).

(e) *Ingredients of the offence*

General

H-121   For a full exposition of the elements of the offence, see *R. v. Court* [1989] A.C. 28, HL.

(a) Most indecent assaults will be clearly of a sexual nature. Some may have only sexual undertones. The jury must decide whether "right-minded persons would consider the conduct indecent or not". The test is whether what occurred was so offensive to contemporary standards of modesty and privacy as to be indecent.

(b) If the circumstances of the assault are *incapable* of being regarded as indecent, then the undisclosed intention of the accused could not make the assault an indecent one: see *R. v. George* [1956] Crim.L.R. 52, Assizes (Streatfeild J.).

(c) The victim need not be aware of the circumstances of indecency or apprehended indecency.

(d) Cases which ordinarily present no problem are those in which the facts, *devoid of explanation*, will give rise to the irresistible inference that the defendant intended to assault his victim in a manner which right-minded persons would clearly think was indecent. Where the circumstances are such as only to be *capable* of constituting an indecent assault, in order to determine whether or not right-minded persons might think that the assault was indecent the following factors are relevant:

(i) the relationship of the defendant to the victim (relative, friend, stranger);

(ii) how the defendant had come to embark on this conduct and why he was so behaving. Such information helps a jury to answer the vital question: are we sure that the defendant not only intended to commit an assault but an assault which was indecent? Any evidence which tends to explain the reason for the defendant's conduct is relevant to establish whether or not he intended to commit not only an assault but an indecent one.

(e) The prosecution must prove: (i) that the accused intentionally assaulted the victim; (ii) that the assault, or the assault and the circumstances accompanying it, are capable of being considered by right-minded persons as indecent; and (iii) that the accused intended to commit such an assault as is referred to in (ii) above.

The above propositions are founded upon Lord Ackner's speech (at p.36), with which the other members of the House concurred, except Lord Goff, who dissented from the decision. It follows that no offence will be committed where the man believes that the woman is consenting to his conduct, whether his belief is based on reasonable grounds or not: this was the effect of the earlier Court of Appeal decision in *R. v. Kimber*, 77 Cr.App.R. 225.

R. v. Court was considered in *R. v. C.* [1992] Crim.L.R. 642, CA, in which it was held that where an assault was indecent in itself, it was unnecessary to establish a specific indecent intent. In *Court*, the issue of whether or not what had occurred amounted to an indecent assault turned on motive and, therefore, specific intent had been necessary to the verdict. Where there was no question whether what had occurred was indecent or not, the basic intent of assault was sufficient. The law before *Court* remained the law and indecent assault remained an offence of basic intent; self-induced voluntary intoxication is not a defence. See also *DPP v. H.* [1992] C.O.D. 266, an earlier decision of the Divisional Court to the same effect.

Court and *George, ante*, were referred to in *R. v. Price* [2004] 1 Cr.App.R. 12, CA, in which it was held that stroking a woman's legs over trousers and below the knee was capable of amounting to an indecent assault.

In *R. v. Kumar* (2006) 150 S.J. 1053, CA, it was said that whilst *Court* was authority for the proposition that a doctor who obtained sexual satisfaction from a necessary medical examination properly conducted was not guilty of indecent assault where the prosecution case was limited to an allegation that he had carried out a medical examination in appropriate circumstances but in an inappropriate way and as a cloak for his own sexual gratification, where the issue had been as to the manner in which the defendant had carried out the examination (*i.e.* in an appropriate way in the presence of a chaperon or in an inappropriate way in the absence of a chaperon), there had been no need to direct the jury as to the remote theoretical possibility suggested in *Court*.

Person

A woman may be guilty of an offence under this section: *R. v. Hare* [1934] 1 K.B. 354, 24 **H-122** Cr.App.R. 108, CCA.

Assault

As to this, see generally, §§ 19-221 *et seq.* in the main work. **H-123**

In *Fairclough v. Whipp*, 35 Cr.App.R. 138, DC, the respondent exposed himself in the presence of a girl aged nine and invited her to touch his exposed person, which she did. *Held*, an invitation to another person to touch the invitor could not amount to an assault on the invitee, and that therefore there had been no assault and consequently no indecent assault by the respondent: applied in *DPP v. Rogers*, 37 Cr.App.R. 137, DC; but *cf. Beal v. Kelley*, 35 Cr.App.R. 128, DC, and *R. v. Sargeant*, 161 J.P. 127, CA, *post*, H-133. See also *R. v. Sutton*, 66 Cr.App.R. 21, CA, *post*, H-134, and the Indecency with Children Act 1960, *post*, H-230 *et seq.*

If a man inserts his finger into the vagina of a girl under 16, this is an indecent assault, however willing or co-operative the girl may be: *R. v. McCormack* [1969] 2 Q.B. 442, 53 Cr.App.R. 514, CA.

Consent

H-124 If the person assaulted is under 16, her consent is no defence: SOA 1956, s.14(2) (*ante*, H-117).

Where the woman's consent was procured by fraud as to the nature (*R. v. Case* (1850) 4 Cox 220) or quality (*R. v. Tabassum* [2000] 2 Cr.App.R. 328, CA) of the act, such consent constitutes no defence. See also § 19-233 in the main work, and *ante*, H-17.

Where a jury asked for the difference between consent and submission to be defined, it was not incumbent on the judge to direct the jury that reluctant acquiescence amounted to consent; it was for the jury to decide whether there was consent and their good sense and experience should lead them to the right conclusion: *R. v. McAllister* [1997] Crim.L.R. 233, CA (*cf. R. v. Olugboja*, 73 Cr.App.R. 344, CA, *ante*, H-16).

Consent cannot be a defence where the indecent assault consists in the infliction of blows intended or likely to cause bodily harm: *R. v. Donovan* [1934] 2 K.B. 498, 25 Cr.App.R. 1, CCA; approved and applied by the House of Lords in *R. v. Brown (Anthony)* [1994] 1 A.C. 212. (As to *Brown*, see also § 19-233 in the main work.) *Donovan* was also referred to in *R. v. Boyea* [1992] Crim.L.R. 574, CA, in which it was held that an assault which was intended or likely to cause bodily harm, and which was accompanied by indecency, constituted the offence of indecent assault regardless of consent, provided that the injury was not "transient or trifling". However, the tribunal of fact must take account of changing social attitudes, particularly in the field of sexual relations between adults. As a generality, the level of vigour in sexual congress which was generally acceptable, and therefore the voluntarily accepted risk of incurring some injury was probably higher now than in 1934, when *Donovan* was decided. It followed that the phrase "transient or trifling" must be understood in the light of current conditions. *Boyea* was approved in *Brown (Anthony)*, *ante*. (See also *R. v. Wilson (A.)* [1996] 2 Cr.App.R. 241, CA (§ 19-235 in the main work).)

Bona fide belief as to age of girl

H-125 Where the complainant was under the age of 16 at the time of the alleged offence, the defendant's genuine belief that she was in fact 16 or over at the time will negative criminal liability if the complainant in fact consented or the defendant genuinely believed that she was consenting: *R. v. K.* [2002] 1 A.C. 462, HL.

Indecent assault within marriage

H-126 A man may be guilty of indecent assault upon his wife: *R. v. Kowalski*, 86 Cr.App.R. 339, CA.

(13) Indecent assault on a man

(a) *Statute*

Sexual Offences Act 1956, s.15

H-127 **15.**—(1) It is an offence for a person to make an indecent assault on a man.

(2) A boy under the age of sixteen cannot in law give any consent which would prevent an act being an assault for the purposes of this section.

(3) A man who is a defective cannot in law give any consent which would prevent an act being an assault for the purposes of this section, but a person is only to be treated as guilty of an indecent assault on a defective by reason of that incapacity to consent, if that person knew or had reason to suspect him to be a defective.

(4), (5) [*Repealed by Police and Criminal Evidence Act 1984, Sched. 7.*]

As to the use of the words "man" and "boy", see *post*, H-222.

As to the meaning of "defective", see *ante*, H-68.

For anonymity provisions, see §§ 20-257 *et seq.* in the main work.

(b) *Indictment*

Statement of Offence

Indecent assault on male person, contrary to section 15(1) of the Sexual Offences Act 1956.   **H-128**

Particulars of Offence

A B, on the _____ day of _____, 20__, indecently assaulted J N, a male person.

In practice, the age of the alleged victim, if he was under the age of 16, was usually averred.

(c) *Mode of trial and class of offence*

This offence is triable either way: MCA 1980, s.17(1), and Sched. 1 (§ 1-130 in the main work).   **H-129**
As to the classification of offences, see *ante*, Appendix F-6.

(d) *Sentence*

Imprisonment not exceeding 10 years: SOA 1956, s.37(3), and Sched. 2, para. 18.   **H-130**
As to the approach to sentencing for historic offences, see *R. v. H.*, *ante*, H-12.

(e) *Ingredients of the offence*

General

See *R. v. Court* and *R. v. C.*, *ante*, H-121, which, it is submitted, apply equally to this offence.   **H-131**

Person

A woman may be guilty of this offence: *R. v. Hare*, *ante*, H-122.   **H-132**

Assault

As to assaults generally, see §§ 19-221 *et seq.* in the main work.   **H-133**

An offence under section 15 is committed when a woman immediately prior to having sexual intercourse with a 14-year-old boy holds his penis. The act alleged to constitute the assault is an indecent act, consent is therefore no defence (s.15(2)—see *R. v. Sutton*, 66 Cr.App.R. 21, CA): *Faulkner v. Talbot*, 74 Cr.App.R. 1, DC.

Semble, an allegation of sexual intercourse by a woman with a boy under 16, *per se* connotes an allegation of indecent assault: see *R. v. McCormack* [1969] 2 Q.B. 442, 53 Cr.App.R. 514, CA; *Faulkner v. Talbot*, *ante*.

If there is an assault committed in circumstances of indecency, then there need not be an indecent touching: see *Beal v. Kelly*, 35 Cr.App.R. 128, DC (when boy refused to touch defendant's penis when asked to do so, defendant pulled boy towards him, but let him go); and *R. v. Sargeant*, 161 J.P. 127, CA (grabbed boy, then used threat of further force to compel boy to masturbate himself). *Cf. Fairclough v. Whipp*, *ante*, H-123.

In order to constitute an assault against a child under 16, the act complained of either must   **H-134** itself be inherently indecent or it must be one that is hostile or threatening or an act which the child is demonstrably reluctant to accept (see *DPP v. Rogers*, 37 Cr.App.R. 137, DC, and *Williams v. Gibbs* [1958] Crim.L.R. 127, DC). Although sections 14(2) and 15(2) of the 1956 Act bar the child's consent from preventing an act being an indecent assault, consent does avail to prevent the act being an assault if the act is not inherently indecent. The proper course where there is an act which could not conceivably be called an assault but which takes place in an indecent situation, is to prosecute under the Indecency with Children Act 1960 (*post*, H-230 *et seq.*): *R. v. Sutton*, 66 Cr.App.R. 21, CA. The defendant photographed partially clothed and unclothed boys, intending to sell the photographs to magazines. In order to arrange poses, he touched the boys on the hands, legs and torso; the actions were not threatening or hostile and the boys consented to them. His convictions under section 15(1) were quashed: touching merely to indicate a pose was not of itself indecent and was consented to. Consent did therefore avail to prevent the acts having been assaults and the question of indecency did not arise.

Consent

Consent is a defence as it negatives the assault: see *R. v. Wollaston* (1872) 12 Cox 180, CCR. See   **H-135** also *ante*, H-124.

A boy under the age of 16 cannot in law give any consent which would prevent an act being an assault for the purposes of the section: s.15(2), *ante*, H-127; but see the cases cited in the previous paragraph.

Bona fide belief as to age of boy

H-136 See *R. v. K.* [2002] 1 A.C. 462, HL, *ante*, H-125; and *R. v. Fernandez*, *The Times*, June 26, 2002, CA (confirming that the decision of the House of Lords applies equally to this offence).

(f) *Evidence*

H-137 The rule as to the admissibility of recent complaints (§§ 8-207 *et seq.* in the main work) was held to apply in the case of an indecent assault upon a boy of 15: *R. v. Camelleri* [1922] 2 K.B. 122, 16 Cr.App.R. 162, CCA.

(14) Assault with intent to commit buggery

(a) *Statute*

Sexual Offences Act 1956, s.16

H-138 **16.**—(1) It is an offence for a person to assault another person with intent to commit buggery.
(2)–(3) [*Repealed by Police and Criminal Evidence Act 1984, Sched. 7.*]

As to the offence of buggery, see *ante*, H-96 *et seq.*
As to assault, see generally, §§ 19-221 *et seq.* in the main work.
For anonymity provisions, see §§ 20-257 *et seq.* in the main work.

(b) *Indictment*

Statement of Offence

H-139   *Assault with intent to commit buggery, contrary to section 16(1) of the Sexual Offences Act 1956.*

Particulars of Offence

A B, on the _____ day of _____, 20__, assaulted J N with intent to commit buggery with the said J N.

(c) *Mode of trial and class of offence*

H-140 This offence is triable only on indictment: SOA 1956, s.37(2), and Sched. 2, para. 19. As to the classification of offences, see *ante*, Appendix F-6.

(d) *Sentence*

H-141 Imprisonment not exceeding 10 years: SOA 1956, s.37(3), and Sched. 2, para. 19.

(e) *Effect of Criminal Justice and Public Order Act 1994*

H-142 It seems that no thought could have been given to the effect on this offence of the redefinition of rape to include non-consensual anal intercourse. The logical solution would have been to substitute "rape" for "buggery" at the end of subsection (1). The offence consisting of an assault allied to a specific intent suggests non-consensual buggery, but because of the bizarre nature of the amendments to section 12, not all nonconsensual buggery (*e.g.* both parties over 18 and the act takes place in private) constitutes the *offence* of buggery, although it will always be rape. It is submitted that the proper interpretation is that an offence under section 16 is committed where there is an assault accompanied by the requisite intent regardless of whether or not the act itself, if completed, would constitute the offence of buggery. This does, of course, lead to anomalous results; it would be an offence contrary to this provision to assault a woman intending to have anal intercourse with her but it would not be an offence to do so intending to have vaginal intercourse, although both acts, if completed, would constitute rape. The alternative interpretation would be to confine the offence to the commission of an assault with intent to commit buggery in circumstances which would make the act, if completed, an offence contrary to section 12. Because of the assault ingredient, this would effectively confine the offence to assaults on persons

under 18. This seems to be an unwarranted restriction of the scope of the offence; Parliament
having, if anything, deemed non-consensual buggery to be a more serious offence than it was
previously, it would be an extremely curious result of the legislation if someone who committed
an assault with the intention of committing that more serious offence should no longer be guilty
of an offence under section 16.

As to whether there was a common law offence of assault with intent to rape, see *ante,* H-10.

(15) Abduction of woman by force or for the sake of her property

(a) *Statute*

Sexual Offences Act 1956, s.17

17.—(1) It is an offence for a person to take away or detain a woman against her will with the   **H-143**
intention that she shall marry or have unlawful sexual intercourse with that or any other person, if
she is so taken away or detained either by force or for the sake of her property or expectations of
property.

(2) In the foregoing subsection, the reference to a woman's expectations of property relates only to
property of a person to whom she is next of kin or one of the next of kin, and "property" includes
any interest in property.

[This section is printed as effectively amended by the CLA 1967, s.12(5)(a).]

As to the meaning of "sexual intercourse", see *post,* H-219; as to the use of the word "woman",
see *post,* H-222.

(b) *Indictment*

Statement of Offence

Abduction, contrary to section 17(1) of the Sexual Offences Act 1956.   **H-144**

Particulars of Offence

A B, on the _____ day of _____, 20__, took away [or *detained*] *J N against her will and by force* [or *for the
sake of her property or expectations of property*] *with the intention that she should have unlawful sexual
intercourse with him the said A B or with another* [or *with the intention that she should marry him the said A B
or another*].

(c) *Mode of trial and class of offence*

This offence is triable on indictment only: SOA 1956, s.37(2), and Sched. 2, para. 4. As to the   **H-145**
classification of offences, see *ante,* Appendix F-6.

(d) *Sentence*

Imprisonment not exceeding 14 years: SOA 1956, s.37(3), and Sched. 2, para. 4.   **H-146**

(e) *Ingredients of the offence*

As to the meaning of "unlawful" sexual intercourse, see *ante,* H-38.   **H-147**

If the woman is taken away with her own consent, but afterwards refuses to continue further
with the offender, and is forcibly detained by him, this is within the statute: see 1 Hawk. c.41
(*Forcible Marriage*), s.7.

(16) Abduction of unmarried girl under 18 from parent or guardian

(a) *Statute*

Sexual Offences Act 1956, s.19

19.—(1) It is an offence, subject to the exception mentioned in this section, for a person to take an   **H-148**
unmarried girl under the age of eighteen out of the possession of her parent or guardian against his

will, if she is taken with the intention that she shall have unlawful sexual intercourse with men or with a particular man.

(2) A person is not guilty of an offence under this section because he takes such a girl out of the possession of her parent or guardian as mentioned above, if he believes her to be of the age of eighteen or over and has reasonable cause for the belief.

(3) In this section "guardian" means any person having the parental responsibility for or care of the girl.

[This section is printed as amended by the Children Act 1989, s.108(4), and Sched. 12, para. 11.]

As to the meaning of "sexual intercourse", see *post*, H-219; as to the use of the words "girl" and "man", see *post*, H-222; as to the meaning of "parental responsibility", see *post*, H-224.

For the burden of proof of exceptions, see section 47 of the 1956 Act, *post*, H-225.

(b) *Indictment*

Statement of Offence

H-149   *Abduction of girl, contrary to section 19(1) of the Sexual Offences Act 1956.*

Particulars of Offence

A B, on the _____ day of _____, 20__, unlawfully took or caused to be taken J N, an unmarried girl under the age of 18, out of the possession and against the will of her father [or mother or of C D then having parental responsibility for or care of her] with an intent unlawfully to have sexual intercourse with her [or that she should have unlawful sexual intercourse with E F or generally].

(c) *Mode of trial and class of offence*

H-150   This offence is triable on indictment only: SOA 1956, s.37(2), and Sched. 2, para. 20. As to the classification of offences, see *ante*, Appendix F-6.

(d) *Sentence*

H-151   Imprisonment not exceeding two years: SOA 1956, s.37(3), and Sched. 2, para. 20.

(e) *Ingredients of the offence*

H-152   For the evidence necessary to support this indictment, see *post*, H-157 *et seq.*, *mutatis mutandis*.

As to the meaning of "unlawful" sexual intercourse, see *ante*, H-38.

Upon an indictment under this section for taking a girl out of the possession of her father, it was proved that at the time of the commission of the alleged offence she was employed by another person as barmaid at a distance from her father's home. It was held that she was under the lawful charge of her employer and not in the possession of her father, and that therefore the defendant could not be convicted of the offence with which he was charged: *R. v. Henkers* (1886) 16 Cox 257. The age of the girl must be proved by the prosecution, as *ante*, H-49. The presumption of the CYPA 1933, s.99, does not apply to this offence: see the proviso to Schedule 1 to the 1933 Act (as to which see *ante*, H-49).

(17) Abduction of unmarried girl under 16 from parent or guardian

(a) *Statute*

Sexual Offences Act 1956, s.20

H-153   **20.**—(1) It is an offence for a person acting without lawful authority or excuse to take an unmarried girl under the age of sixteen out of the possession of her parent or guardian against his will.

(2) In the foregoing subsection "guardian" means any person having parental responsibility for or care of the girl.

[This section is printed as amended by the Children Act 1989, s.108(4), and Sched. 12, para. 12.]

As to the use of the word "girl", see *post*, H-222; as to the meaning of "parental responsibility", see *post*, H-224.

See now section 2 of the Child Abduction Act 1984 (§ 19-397 in the main work) which covers much the same ground and is not limited to the abduction of girls.

(b) *Indictment*

Statement of Offence

Abduction of a girl, contrary to section 20(1) of the Sexual Offences Act 1956.　　　**H-154**

Particulars of Offence

A B, on the _____ day of _____, 20__, unlawfully took or caused to be taken J N, an unmarried girl aged 14, out of the possession and against the will of her father [or *mother or of E F then having parental responsibility for or care of her*].

(c) *Mode of trial and class of offence*

This offence is triable on indictment only: SOA 1956, s.37(2), and Sched. 2, para. 21. As to the　**H-155** classification of offences, see *ante*, Appendix F-6.

(d) *Sentence*

Imprisonment not exceeding two years: SOA 1956, s.37(3), and Sched. 2, para. 21.　　**H-156**

(e) *Ingredients of the offence*

That the girl was in the possession of her father, etc.

This is a question for the jury: *R. v. Mace*, 50 J.P. 776. A girl will still be in the possession of her　**H-157** parent/guardian even while she is away from home if she intends to return; and if, when so out of the house, the defendant induces her to run away with him, he is guilty: *R. v. Mycock* (1871) 12 Cox 28. See also *R. v. Baillie* (1859) 8 Cox 238; *R. v. Green* (1862) 3 F. & F. 274; and *R. v. Miller* (1876) 13 Cox 179.

The taking

The taking need not be by force, either actual or constructive, and it is immaterial whether the　**H-158** girl consents or not: *R. v. Manktelow* (1853) 6 Cox 143, and see *R. v. Kipps* (1850) 4 Cox 167; *R. v. Booth* (1872) 12 Cox 231; and *R. v. Robins* (1844) 1 C. & K. 456 (where the girl positively encouraged the defendant).

The words "taking out of the possession and against the will" of the parent mean some conduct amounting to a substantial interference with the possessory relationship of parent and child: *R. v. Jones (J.W.)* [1973] Crim.L.R. 621 (Swanwick J.)—attempt to take girls (aged 10) for a walk with a view to indecently assaulting them held not to constitute an attempt to commit the offence. (*Cf. R. v. Leather*, 98 Cr.App.R. 179, CA, decided on the Child Abduction Act 1984 (§ 19-398 in the main work).)

It is no defence that the defendant acted in concert with the girl and had no intention of keeping her away from her home permanently: *R. v. Timmins* (1860) 8 Cox 401; *R. v. Frazer and Norman*, *ibid.* at 446. See also *R. v. Baillie*, *ibid.* at 238.

Instead of a taking, it can be shown that a girl left her parent or guardian, in consequence of some persuasion, inducement or blandishment held out to her by the defendant: *R. v. Henkers* (1886) 16 Cox 257, following *R. v. Olifier* (1866) 10 Cox 402.

Where a man induces a girl, by promise of what he will do for her, to leave her father's house　**H-159** and live with him, he may be convicted, although he is not actually present or assisting her at the time when she leaves her father's roof: *R. v. Robb* (1864) 4 F. & F. 59. If the girl leaves her father, without any persuasion, inducement or blandishment held out to her by the defendant, so that she has got fairly away from home, and then goes to him, although it may be his moral duty to return her to her father's custody, yet his not doing so is no infringement of this statute, for the statute does not say he shall restore, but only that he shall not take her away: *R. v. Olifier, ante*, and this is so even though it be proved that before she so left he had taken her about to places of amusement and had intercourse with her: *R. v. Kauffman*, 68 J.P. 189. If the suggestion to go away with the defendant comes from the girl only, and he takes merely the passive part of yield-ing to her suggestion, he is entitled to an acquittal: *R. v. Jarvis* (1903) 20 Cox 249. It is submitted that the ruling to the contrary in *R. v. Biswell* (1847) 2 Cox 279 is not law. For a discussion of the authorities, see *R. v. Mackney* (1903) 29 Vict.L.R. 22, where the English cases are considered.

Against the will, etc.

H-160 If the defendant induced the parents, by false and fraudulent representations, to allow him to take the child away, this is an abduction: *R. v. Hopkins* (1842) C. & Mar. 254.

Where the girl's mother had encouraged her in a lax course of life, by permitting her to go out alone at night and dance at public-houses, from one of which she went away with the defendant, Cockburn C.J. ruled that she could not be said to be taken away against her mother's will: *R. v. Primelt* (1858) 1 F. & F. 50.

To prove this element of the offence, it has been said that the parent or guardian must be called: *R. v. Nash*, *The Times*, July 2, 1903. *Sed quaere.*

Under 16, etc.

H-161 Prove that she was under the age of 16 years and unmarried. As to the power of a court to presume her age from her appearance, see the CYPA 1933, s.99(2) (§ 19-412 in the main work) and Sched. 1 (§ 19-408 in the main work (prior to its repeal by the SOA 2003, the proviso to Sched. 1 stipulated that s.99(2) did apply to offences under s.20)). It is no defence that the defendant did not know her to be under 16, or might suppose from her appearance that she was older: *R. v. Olifier*, *ante*; *R. v. Mycock*, *ante*; *R. v. Booth*, *ante*; or even that the defendant bona fide believed and had reasonable grounds for believing that she was over 16: *R. v. Prince* (1875) L.R. 2 C.C.R. 154. Doubts about *Prince* were expressed by the House of Lords in *B. (a Minor) v. DPP* [2000] 2 A.C. 428 (*post*, H-235) and *R. v. K.* [2002] 1 A.C. 462 (*ante*, H-125), but its correctness did not fall to be decided upon. Those expressions of doubt are likely to found a challenge to *Prince*, but it is submitted that the express provision of a defence based on mistake as to age in relation to the offence contrary to section 19 (*ante*, H-148) makes it abundantly clear that Parlia-ment intended that there should be no corresponding defence in relation to the abduction of a girl under 16.

Mens rea

H-162 The act of abduction is positively prohibited, and therefore the absence of a corrupt motive is no answer to the charge: see *R. v. Booth*, *ante*.

If the defendant, at the time he took the girl away, did not know, and had no reason to know, that she was subject to the parental responsibility and care of her father, mother or some other person, he is not guilty of this offence: *R. v. Hibbert* (1869) L.R. 1 C.C.R. 184.

Without lawful authority or excuse

H-163 The defendant must show that he had either lawful authority or a lawful excuse; motive is irrelevant: *R. v. Tegerdine*, 75 Cr.App.R. 298, CA (statutory history reviewed). It is submitted that the burden on the defendant is merely an evidential one, which is discharged if there is sufficient evidence to raise an issue on the matter: *cf.* the specific provision in section 47 (*post*, H-225) in relation to "exceptions" under the Act. And see generally, §§ 4-444 *et seq.* in the main work.

(18) Abduction of defective from parent or guardian

(a) *Statute*

Sexual Offences Act 1956, s.21

H-164   21.—(1) It is an offence, subject to the exception mentioned in this section, for a person to take a woman who is a defective out of the possession of her parent or guardian against his will, if she is so taken with the intention that she shall have unlawful sexual intercourse with men or with a particular man.

(2) A person is not guilty of an offence under this section because he takes such a woman out of the possession of her parent or guardian as mentioned above, if he does not know and has no reason to suspect her to be a defective.

(3) In this section "guardian" means any person having parental responsibility for or care of the woman.

[This section is printed as amended by the Children Act 1989, s.108(4), and Sched. 12, para. 13.]

As to the meaning of "sexual intercourse", see *post*, H-219; as to the meaning of "unlawful" sexual intercourse, see *ante*, H-38; as to the use of the words "man" and "woman", see *post*, H-222; as to the meaning of "defective", see *ante*, H-68; as to the meaning of "parental responsibility", see *post*, H-224.

For the burden of proof of exceptions, see section 47 of the 1956 Act, *post*, H-225.

(b) *Mode of trial and class of offence*

This offence is triable on indictment only: SOA 1956, s.37(2), and Sched. 2, para. 22. As to the **H-165** classification of offences, see *ante*, Appendix F-6.

(c) *Sentence*

Imprisonment not exceeding two years: SOA 1956, s.37(3), and Sched. 2, para. 22.   **H-166**

(19) Causing prostitution of women

(a) *Statute*

Sexual Offences Act 1956, s.22

22.—(1) It is an offence for a person—   **H-167**
    (a) to procure a woman to become, in any part of the world, a common prostitute; or
    (b) to procure a woman to leave the United Kingdom, intending her to become an inmate of or frequent a brothel elsewhere; or
    (c) to procure a woman to leave her usual place of abode in the United Kingdom, intending her to become an inmate of or frequent a brothel in any part of the world for the purposes of prostitution.

(2) [*Repealed by Criminal Justice and Public Order Act 1994, s.33(1).*]

As to the use of the word "woman", see *post*, H-222.

(b) *Indictment*

Statement of Offence

Procuring a woman to become a common prostitute, contrary to section 22(1)(a) of the   **H-168**
Sexual Offences Act 1956.

Particulars of Offence

A B, on or about the _____ day of _____, 20__, at _____ procured C D, a woman, to become a common prostitute.

(c) *Mode of trial and classification of offences*

This offence, and an attempt to commit it, are triable on indictment only: SOA 1956, s.37(2),   **H-169** and Sched. 2, para. 23(a), (b). As to the classification of offences, see *ante*, Appendix F-6.

(d) *Sentence*

The full offence, and an attempt to commit it: imprisonment not exceeding two years: SOA   **H-170** 1956, s.37(3), and Sched. 2, para. 23(a), (b).

(e) *Ingredients of the offence*

"Procure"

As to the meaning of the word "procure" in general, see §§ 18-22, 18-23 in the main work, and   **H-171** see *Att.-Gen.'s Reference (No. 1 of 1975)* [1975] Q.B. 773, 61 Cr.App.R. 118, CA; *Re Royal Victoria*

Pavilion, Ramsgate [1961] Ch. 581, Ch D, and *Blakely v. DPP* [1991] R.T.R. 405, DC. In the first of these authorities, Lord Widgery C.J. said that to procure, "means to produce by endeavour. You procure a thing by setting out to see that it happens and taking the appropriate steps to produce that happening" (at pp.779, 121). In *Re Royal Victoria Pavilion, Ramsgate*, Pennycuick J. (at p.587) defined "to procure" as "to obtain by care and effort" or "to see to it".

In *R. v. Broadfoot*, 64 Cr.App.R. 71, CA, the court described *Att.-Gen's Reference (No. 1 of 1975)*, *ante*, as a useful guide. Whilst saying that the interpretation of the word was a matter of common sense for the jury to determine in the light of the particular facts, the court appears to have approved (see p.74) the suggestion of Shaw L.J., during argument, that it could be regarded as bringing about a course of conduct which the woman in question would not have embarked upon of her own volition. *R. v. Christian* (1913) 23 Cox 541, was distinguished. It was there held that procuration could be negatived by evidence showing the girl was not really procured, because she needed no procuring, and acted of her own free will.

If a woman is already a common prostitute she cannot become one and accordingly cannot be procured to become one. It follows that if there is evidence of procuration but "the woman" is a police officer it is a good defence to a charge of attempting to procure a woman to become a prostitute contrary to section 1(1) of the Criminal Attempts Act 1981, that the defendant thought that "the woman" he was attempting to procure was already a prostitute. If he believed (or might have believed) that, it could not be said that he was trying to procure her to become that which he believed she already was. Section 1(3) of the 1981 Act (§ 33-128 in the main work) is concerned with the converse case where the woman is a common prostitute but the defendant believes she is not. In such circumstances, he may be convicted of an attempt even though the commission of the offence is impossible: *R. v. Brown (R.A.)*, 80 Cr.App.R. 36, CA.

As to "attempting to do the impossible", see also § 33-137 in the main work.

"Common prostitute"

H-172   This includes a woman who offers her body commonly for acts of lewdness for payment although there is no act or offer of an act of ordinary sexual intercourse: *R. v. De Munck* [1918] 1 K.B. 635, 13 Cr.App.R. 113, CCA. The word "common" in the term "common prostitute" is not mere surplusage—a common prostitute is any woman who offers herself commonly for lewdness for reward. Whether or not the performance by a woman of a single act of lewdness with a man on one occasion for reward constitutes the woman a prostitute, it plainly does not make her a woman who offers herself commonly for lewdness. That must be someone who is prepared for reward to engage in acts of lewdness with all and sundry or with anyone who may hire her for that purpose: *R. v. Morris-Lowe*, 80 Cr.App.R. 114, CA, applying *R. v. De Munck, ante*.

It is not necessary that she should have submitted to acts of lewdness in a passive way. Active acts of indecency by the woman herself, *e.g.* masturbation by her of clients when acting as a masseuse will fall within the section: *R. v. Webb* [1964] 1 Q.B. 357, 47 Cr.App.R. 265, CCA.

In *R. v. McFarlane* [1994] Q.B. 419, 99 Cr.App.R. 8, CA, it was held in relation to a prosecution under section 30 of the 1956 Act (*post*, H-197) that the essence of prostitution is the making of an offer of sexual services for reward, and that it is immaterial that the person making the offer does not intend to perform them and does not do so. It is obviously desirable that "prostitution" is given the same meaning wherever it appears in a statute; accordingly, this decision is likely to be applied to section 22. For a criticism of this decision, see the 1996 edition of this work.

(20) Procuration of girl under 21

(a) *Statute*

Sexual Offences Act 1956, s.23

H-173   23.—(1) It is an offence for a person to procure a girl under the age of twenty-one to have unlawful sexual intercourse in any part of the world with a third person.

(2) [*Repealed by Criminal Justice and Public Order Act 1994, s.33(1).*]

As to the meaning of "sexual intercourse", see *post*, H-219; as to the use of the word "girl", see *post*, H-222.

(b) *Mode of trial and classification of offences*

This offence, and an attempt to commit it, are triable on indictment only: SOA 1956, s.37(2), **H-174**
and Sched. 2, para. 24(a), (b). As to the classification of offences, see *ante*, Appendix F-6.

(c) *Sentence*

The full offence, and an attempt to commit it: imprisonment not exceeding two years; SOA **H-175**
1956, s.37(3), and Sched. 2, para. 24(a), (b).

(d) *Ingredients of the offence*

As to the meaning of "procure", see *ante*, H-171. As to the meaning of "unlawful" sexual **H-176**
intercourse, see *ante*, H-38.

Before the defendant can be found guilty of an offence contrary to this section, it is necessary
to prove that unlawful sexual intercourse did take place; if intercourse is not proved to have
taken place but procurement with the intention that it should take place is proved, there may be
a conviction of an attempt to commit the full offence: *R. v. Johnson* [1964] 2 Q.B. 404, 48 Cr.App.R.
25, CCA. As to the difference between an attempt and an intention, see *R. v. Landow*, 8 Cr.App.R.
218, CCA. As to conspiracy with the procurer, see *R. v. Mackenzie and Higginson*, 6 Cr.App.R. 64,
CCA.

(21) Detention of a woman in brothel or other premises

(a) *Statute*

Sexual Offences Act 1956, s.24

24.—(1) It is an offence for a person to detain a woman against her will on any premises with the **H-177**
intention that she shall have unlawful sexual intercourse with men or with a particular man, or to
detain a woman against her will in a brothel.

(2) Where a woman is on any premises for the purpose of having unlawful sexual intercourse or is
in a brothel, a person shall be deemed for the purpose of the foregoing subsection to detain her
there if, with the intention of compelling or inducing her to remain there, he either withholds from
her her clothes or any other property belonging to her or threatens her with legal proceedings in the
event of her taking away clothes provided for her by him or on his directions.

(3) A woman shall not be liable to any legal proceedings, whether civil or criminal, for taking away
or being found in possession of any clothes she needed to enable her to leave premises on which she
was for the purpose of having unlawful sexual intercourse or to leave a brothel.

As to the meaning of "sexual intercourse", see *post*, H-219; as to the use of the words "man"
and "woman", see *post*, H-222.

(b) *Indictment*

Statement of Offence

Detaining a woman against her will for unlawful sexual intercourse [or *in a brothel*], **H-178**
contrary to section 24(1) of the Sexual Offences Act 1956.

Particulars of Offence

A B, on or about the _____ *day of* _____, *20__, detained C D, a woman, against her will at* _____
intending her to have unlawful sexual intercourse with men [or *with E F, a man*] [or *detained C D, a woman,*
against her will at _____, *a brothel*].

(c) *Mode of trial and class of offence*

This offence is triable on indictment only: SOA 1956, s.37(2), and Sched. 2, para. 25. As to the **H-179**
classification of offences, see *ante*, Appendix F-6.

(d) *Sentence*

Imprisonment not exceeding two years: SOA 1956, s.37(3), and Sched. 2, para. 25. **H-180**

(e) *Ingredients of offence*

Unlawful sexual intercourse

See *ante*, H-38. **H-181**

"Brothel"

H-182   See §§ 20-233 *et seq.* in the main work.

(f) *Evidence*

H-183   See § 20-235 in the main work.

(22) Allowing premises to be used for intercourse

(a) *Statute*

Sexual Offences Act 1956, ss.25, 26, 27

Permitting girl under thirteen to use premises for intercourse

H-184   **25.** It is an offence for a person who is the owner or occupier of any premises, or who has, or acts or assists in, the management or control of any premises, to induce or knowingly suffer a girl under the age of thirteen to resort to or be on those premises for the purpose of having unlawful sexual intercourse with men or with a particular man.

[This section is printed as effectively amended by the CLA 1967, s.12(5)(a).]

Permitting girl between thirteen and sixteen to use premises for intercourse

H-185   **26.** It is an offence for a person who is the owner or occupier of any premises, or who has, or acts or assists in, the management or control of any premises, to induce or knowingly suffer a girl ... under the age of sixteen, to resort to or be on those premises for the purpose of having unlawful sexual intercourse with men or with a particular man.

[The words omitted were repealed by the CLA 1967, s.10(1), and Sched. 2, para. 14. This repeal renders the marginal note misleading.]

Permitting defective to use premises for intercourse

H-186   **27.**—(1) It is an offence, subject to the exception mentioned in this section, for a person who is the owner or occupier of any premises, or who has, or acts or assists in, the management or control of any premises, to induce or knowingly suffer a woman who is a defective to resort to or be on those premises for the purpose of having unlawful sexual intercourse with men or with a particular man.

(2) A person is not guilty of an offence under this section because he induces or knowingly suffers a defective to resort to or be on any premises for the purpose mentioned, if he does not know and has no reason to suspect her to be a defective.

As to the meaning of "sexual intercourse", see *post*, H-219; as to the use of the words "man", "woman" and "girl", see *post*, H-222; as to the meaning of "defective", see *ante*, H-68.

For the burden of proof of exceptions, see section 47 of the 1956 Act, *post*, H-225.

(b) *Mode of trial and classification of offences*

H-187   Section 25— this offence is triable only on indictment: SOA 1956, s.37(2), and Sched. 2, para. 6.

Section 26—this offence is triable either way: MCA 1980, s.17(1), and Sched. 1 (§ 1-130 in the main work).

Section 27—this offence is triable only on indictment: SOA 1956, s.37(2), and Sched. 2, para. 27.

As to the classification of offences, see *ante*, Appendix F-6.

(c) *Sentence*

H-188   Section 25—life imprisonment: SOA 1956, s.37(3), and Sched. 2, para. 6.

Section 26—imprisonment not exceeding two years: SOA 1956, s.37(3), and Sched. 2, para. 26. The penalty on summary conviction is provided for by the MCA 1980, s.32 (§ 1-125 in the main work).

Section 27—imprisonment not exceeding two years: SOA 1956, s.37(3), and Sched. 2, para. 27.

(d) *Ingredients of the offences*

"Management", "assists in the management"

H-189   See the following cases, decided in relation to section 33 of the 1956 Act ("assisting in the management of a brothel"): *Abbott v. Smith* [1965] 2 Q.B. 662, DC (meaning of "management"); *Gorman v. Standen*; *Palace-Clark v. Standen* [1964] 1 Q.B. 294, 48 Cr.App.R. 30, DC; *Jones and Wood v. DPP*, 96 Cr.App.R. 130, DC; and *Elliott v. DPP*; *Dublides v. DPP*, *The Times*, January 19, 1989, DC ("assisting in the management"). In the last of these cases, the court appears to have accepted a distinction between assisting in the management of premises and assisting the management of premises.

"Unlawful" sexual intercourse

See *ante*, H-38.   **H-190**

"Knowingly suffer"

In *R. v. Webster* (1885) 16 Q.B.D. 134, it was held that the words "knowingly suffer" mean that **H-191** the defendant knew of the girl's purpose in being on the premises and did not prevent the unlawful sexual intercourse from occurring when it was in his power to do so. The girl was the defendant's daughter, and the premises were her home, where she resided with the defendant. But see *R. v. Merthyr Tydfil JJ.* (1894) 10 T.L.R. 375, where a mother was held not within the section, who for the purposes of obtaining conclusive evidence against a man who had seduced her daughter, permitted him to come to her house to repeat his unlawful intercourse.

(23) Causing or encouraging prostitution, etc.

(a) *Statute*

Sexual Offences Act 1956, ss.28, 29

Causing or encouraging prostitution of, intercourse with, or indecent assault on, girl under sixteen

28.—(1) It is an offence for a person to cause or encourage the prostitution of, or the commission **H-192** of unlawful sexual intercourse with, or of an indecent assault on, a girl under the age of sixteen for whom he is responsible.

(2) Where a girl has become a prostitute, or has had unlawful sexual intercourse, or has been indecently assaulted, a person shall be deemed for the purposes of this section to have caused or encouraged it, if he knowingly allowed her to consort with, or to enter or continue in the employment of, any prostitute or person of known immoral character.

(3) The persons who are to be treated for the purposes of this section as responsible for a girl are (subject to subsection (4) of this section)—

    (a)   her parents;

    (b)   any person who is not a parent of hers but who has parental responsibility for her; and

    (c)   any person who has care of her.

(4) An individual falling within subsection (3)(a) or (b) of this section is not to be treated as responsible for a girl if—

    (a)   a residence order under the Children Act 1989 is in force with respect to her and he is not named in the order as the person with whom she is to live; *or*

    (aa) a special guardianship order under that Act is in force with respect to her and he is not her special guardian; or

    (b)   a care order under that Act is in force with respect to her.

(5) If, on a charge of an offence against a girl under this section, the girl appears to the court to have been under the age of sixteen at the time of the offence charged, she shall be presumed for the purposes of this section to have been so, unless the contrary is proved.

[This section is printed as amended by the Children Act 1989, s.108(4), and Sched. 12, para. 14; and the Adoption and Children Act 2002, s.139(1), and Sched. 3, para. 8.]

Causing or encouraging prostitution of defective

29.—(1) It is an offence, subject to the exception mentioned in this section, for a person to cause **H-193** or encourage the prostitution in any part of the world of a woman who is a defective.

(2) A person is not guilty of an offence under this section because he causes or encourages the prostitution of such a woman, if he does not know and has no reason to suspect her to be a defective.

As to the meaning of "sexual intercourse", see *post*, H-219; as to the use of the words "woman" and "girl", see *post*, H-222; as to the meaning of "parental responsibility", see *post*, H-224; as to the meaning of "defective", see *ante*, H-68.

For the burden of proof of exceptions, see section 47 of the 1956 Act, *post*, § H-225.

(b) *Mode of trial and classification of offences*

H-194   These offences are triable only on indictment: SOA 1956, s.37(2), and Sched. 2, paras 28 and 29. As to the classification of offences, see *ante*, Appendix F-6.

(c) *Sentence*

H-195   Sections 28 and 29—imprisonment not exceeding two years: SOA 1956, s.37(3), and Sched. 2, paras 28 and 29.

(d) *Ingredients of the offences*

H-196   As to what constitutes "causing" or "encouraging", see *R. v. Ralphs*, 9 Cr.App.R. 86, CCA; *R. v. Chainey* [1914] 1 K.B. 137, 9 Cr.App.R. 175, CCA.

In *R. v. Drury*, 60 Cr.App.R. 195, CA, it was held that there was evidence on which it could be held that a girl (aged 14) was in the care of the defendant where, at the time of the assault by a friend of the defendant, she was babysitting for him. The case was decided on the original wording of section 28(3)(c), *viz.* "any other person who has the custody, charge or care of her". The 1989 amendment (*ante*) would not appear to affect this point. As to encouragement, the court said that there must be encouragement in fact and an intention to encourage.

A doctor who in the exercise of his clinical judgment gives contraceptive advice and treatment to a girl under 16 without her parents' consent does not commit an offence under section 6 or 28 of the 1956 Act, because the bona fide exercise by the doctor of his clinical judgment negates the *mens rea* which is an essential ingredient of those offences: *Gillick v. West Norfolk and Wisbech Area Health Authority* [1986] A.C. 112, HL.

As to the meaning of "unlawful" sexual intercourse, see *ante*, H-38.

(24) Man living on earnings of prostitution

(a) *Statute*

Sexual Offences Act 1956, s.30

H-197   **30.**—(1) It is an offence for a man knowingly to live wholly or in part on the earnings of prostitution.

(2) For the purposes of this section a man who lives with or is habitually in the company of a prostitute, or who exercises control, direction or influence over a prostitute's movements in a way which shows he is aiding, abetting or compelling her prostitution with others, shall be presumed to be knowingly living on the earnings of prostitution, unless he proves the contrary.

As to the use of the word "man", see *post*, H-222.

(b) *Indictment*

Statement of Offence

H-198   *Living on prostitution, contrary to section 30(1) of the Sexual Offences Act 1956.*

Particulars of Offence

A B, being a man, on the _____ day of _____, 20__, and on other days between that date and the _____ day of _____, 20__, knowingly lived wholly or in part on the earnings of the prostitution of J N.

In an indictment for this offence a person may be charged with having committed the offence on one specified day only: *R. v. Hill*, 10 Cr.App.R. 56, CCA. Evidence is admissible to show what the defendant's relations with the woman in question had been either before or after the day specified in the indictment: *ibid*.

As to the application of the alibi notice provisions to this offence, see *R. v. Hassan*, 54 Cr.App.R. 56, CA (§ 12-66 in the main work).

(c) *Mode of trial and class of offence*

H-199   This offence is triable either way: SOA 1956, s.37(2), and Sched. 2, para. 30. As to the classification of offences, see *ante*, Appendix F-6.

(d) *Sentence*

Maximum

On conviction on indictment, imprisonment not exceeding seven years; on summary convic- **H-200**
tion, six months, or a fine not exceeding £5,000: SOA 1956, s.37(3), and Sched. 2, para. 30 (as
amended by the Street Offences Act 1959, s.4), and the MCA 1980, ss.32, 34(3)(a).

Guidelines

A sentence exceeding two years should be reserved for cases where there is some evidence of **H-201**
physical or mental coercion of the prostitutes involved, or of corruption. The existence of such
coercion or corruption is the crucial sentencing factor: *R. v. Farrugia*, 69 Cr.App.R. 108, CA. See
also *R. v. Thomas*, 5 Cr.App.R.(S.) 138, CA; *R. v. El-Gazzar*, 8 Cr.App.R.(S.) 182, CA; *R. v. Malik*
[1998] 1 Cr.App.R.(S.) 115, CA; and CSP B5–1.

(e) *Ingredients of the offence*

"Man"

In *R. v. Tan* [1983] Q.B. 1053, 76 Cr.App.R. 300, CA, it was held that a person who was born a **H-202**
man and who remained biologically a man was a man for all purposes although he had undergone
hormone treatment and surgical treatment consisting of sex-change operations and had become
philosophically or psychologically female (applying *Corbett v. Corbett* [1971] P. 83).

Prostitution

As to what constitutes "prostitution", see *ante*, H-172. As to proving that at the material time **H-203**
the woman was a prostitute, see § 20-235 in the main work, and *R. v. Wilson (D.T.)*, 78 Cr.App.R.
247, CA, in which *Woodhouse v. Hall*, 72 Cr.App.R. 39, DC, was applied in the context of a
prosecution under section 30.

Knowingly living on earnings of prostitution

There are three distinct foundations upon which the prosecution can rely in order to raise a **H-204**
presumption that an offence has been committed under section 30(2) (*ante*, H-197):
  (a) proof that the accused was at the material time living with the prostitute;
  (b) proof that he was habitually at the material time in her company;
  (c) proof that he exercised control, direction or influence over her movements in a way which
      showed him to be aiding or abetting her prostitution.
Once evidence giving rise to the presumption has been led, it then has two facets: (a) it is
presumed that he is living on immoral earnings; and (b) it is presumed that he is doing so
knowingly: *R. v. Clarke*, 63 Cr.App.R. 16, CA. It is not necessary to prove that he was living with
or habitually in the company of such a prostitute in a way which showed that he was aiding, abetting or compelling her prostitution with others: *ibid.* See also *R. v. Lawrence*, *post*, H-206.

In *R. v. Stewart*, 83 Cr.App.R. 327, CA, the court was referred to *R. v. Silver*, 40 Cr.App.R. 32, **H-205**
CCC (Judge Maude); *R. v. Thomas*, 41 Cr.App.R. 121, CCA; *Shaw v. DPP* [1962] A.C. 220, HL; *R.
v. Calderhead and Bidney*, 68 Cr.App.R. 37, CA; and *R. v. Wilson (D.T.)*, *ante*. Mustill L.J. said, in
giving the court's judgment:

> "What we collect from them is as follows: according to the literal meaning of the section any
> person who supplies goods or services to a prostitute is in one sense living off the earnings of
> prostitution: for in part he earns his livelihood from payments which the woman would not be
> able to make but for her trade. This cannot be the right view. There has to be a closer connection
> between the receipt of money and the trade before the recipient commits an offence. We doubt
> whether it is possible to devise a definition of the type and closeness of the necessary connection
> which will deal with all the circumstances which may arise; and, indeed, it is dangerous to treat
> words or phrases from judgments delivered in relation to one set of facts, as if they provided a
> statutory gloss which can be reliably applied to facts of a quite different nature … .
>   Subject to this reservation, we believe that an approach which will often be useful is to identify
> for the jury the flavour of the words 'living off', and then to express this general concept in the

shape of guidance more directly referable to the case in hand. In our judgment, the word 'parasite' (to be found in the speech of Lord Reid in *Shaw v. DPP* ...), or some expanded equivalent, provides a useful starting point for this exercise, and does express a concept which accounts for all the reported cases except for *Silver*.

Adopting this general approach, and dealing specifically with a defendant who supplies goods or services to a prostitute, a good working test, sufficient to deal with many cases, is whether the fact of supply means that the supplier and the prostitute were engaged in the business of prostitution together: and 'the fact of supply' will include the scale of supply, the price charged and the nature of the goods or services. It will be impossible to say in advance that certain categories of supplies must necessarily fall outside the section, any more than that other categories must be within it, but the idea of participation in the prostitute's business will enable the jury to distinguish readily between (say) the supplier of groceries on the one hand and the publisher of prostitutes' advertisements on the other. There will remain a residue of more difficult cases, and these include the situation where premises are let at a market rent with knowledge of the purpose to which they are to be put. We see no room here for any rule of thumb distinction between premises which are or are not let at abnormally high rates. Certainly, the jury will find it easier to infer in the former case that the lessor participates in the woman's earnings. ... We can, however, see no logic in the suggestion that the lessor cannot be convicted unless the rent is exorbitant and indeed the judgment of Ashworth J. in *Shaw v. DPP* (at p.230) and the speech of Lord Simonds in the same case (at p.265 ... see the words 'whatever the rent') are authority for the view that the presence or absence of this factor is not conclusive. Nor in our opinion is the question whether the premises are occupied or capable of occupation as residential premises to be taken as the touchstone.

Instead, the judge must bear in mind when framing his direction the distinction between the offence under section 30(1), and the offences under sections 34, 35 and 36, and must not allow the jury to believe that knowledge of use to which the premises are put will be sufficient in itself to found a conviction. He must draw the attention of the jury to whatever factors are material to the individual case. These will often include, but not be limited to, the nature and location of the premises, the involvement of the lessor in adapting, furnishing or outfitting the premises for prostitution, the duration of the letting, the hours during which the premises are occupied, the rent at which they are let, the method of payment of rent, the fact that the prostitute does or does not live as well as work at the premises, the presence or absence of a personal relationship between the lessor and the lessee, the steps taken by the lessor to remove the prostitutes from his premises, and the steps taken by the lessor to disguise his relationship with the premises and the persons working there. Having presented the facts to the jury, the judge will invite them to consider whether they are sure that the lessor was involved together with the prostitute in the business of prostitution" (at pp.332–333).

H-206   Mustill L.J. then said that in the opinion of the court, the judge's direction, that where a letting was referable to prostitution and nothing else it was immaterial whether the letting was at a higher than normal rent, was correct, and to the extent that *Silver, ante*, is a decision to the contrary, it should not be followed.

It is essential that a jury should receive a clear and careful direction with regard to this offence and the burden of proof in relation to it. In particular, where the prosecution rely on subsection (2) (*ante*, H-197), the jury's attention should be directed to the various alternatives contained in the subsection, and to any evidence relating to any of those alternatives: *R. v. Lawrence*, 47 Cr.App.R. 72, CCA.

In *R. v. Howard*, 94 Cr.App.R. 89, CA, Lord Lane C.J. said that what is required is a simple direction based primarily on what was said in *Shaw v. DPP, ante*, and *Stewart, ante*, adjusted to the facts of the particular case.

(f) *Evidence*

H-207   That the defendant knowingly lived wholly or in part on the earnings of prostitution is usually proved by evidence that the prostitute paid the rent of rooms where both were living together, or paid for his food, or supplied him with money, or paid for drink consumed by him in public-houses, or the like. Whether conversation and association with a prostitute amounts to proof that the defendant was habitually in her company is a question of fact for the jury: *R. v. Ptohopoulos*, 52 Cr.App.R. 47, CA.

There need not be proof that the prostitute handed money to the defendant if the evidence establishes that what the defendant received was earned by the prostitute (see *Calvert v. Mayes* [1954] 1 Q.B. 242, approved in *Shaw*). Nor, as was held in *R. v. Ansell* [1975] Q.B. 215, 60

Cr.App.R. 45, CA, if the money comes from the men with whom the prostitutes are dealing and not from the prostitutes themselves, does that fact in law prevent the money being the earnings of prostitution: see, for example, *R. v. Farrugia*, 69 Cr.App.R. 108, CA.

(25) Woman exercising control over prostitute

(a) *Statute*

Sexual Offences Act 1956, s.31

31. It is an offence for a woman for purposes of gain to exercise control, direction or influence **H-208** over a prostitute's movements in a way which shows she is aiding, abetting or compelling her prostitution.

As to the use of the word "woman", see *post*, H-222. As to the meaning of "prostitution", see *ante*, H-172.

(b) *Mode of trial and class of offence*

This offence is triable either way: SOA 1956, s.37(2), and Sched. 2, para. 31. As to the classifica- **H-209** tion of offences, see *ante*, Appendix F-6.

(c) *Sentence*

On conviction on indictment, imprisonment not exceeding seven years; on summary convic- **H-210** tion, six months, or a fine not exceeding £5,000: SOA 1956, s.37(3), and Sched. 2, para. 31 (as amended by the Street Offences Act 1959, s.4), and the MCA 1980, ss.32, 34(3)(a).

(26) Solicitation for immoral purposes

(a) *Statute*

Sexual Offences Act 1956, s.32

32. It is an offence for a man persistently to solicit or importune in a public place for immoral **H-211** purposes.

As to the use of the word "man", see *post*, H-222.

(b) *Mode of trial and class of offence*

This offence is triable either way: SOA 1956, s.37(2), and Sched. 2, para. 32. As to the classifica- **H-212** tion of offences, see *ante*, Appendix F-6.

(c) *Sentence*

On conviction on indictment, imprisonment not exceeding two years; on summary conviction, **H-213** six months, or a fine not exceeding £5,000: SOA 1956, s.37(3), and Sched. 2, para. 32, and the MCA 1980, ss.32, 34(3)(a).

(d) *Ingredients of the offence*

"persistently"

Two separate acts of importuning within the period named in the information or indictment **H-214** are sufficient to render the importuning persistent: *Dale v. Smith* [1967] 1 W.L.R. 700, DC (justices entitled to treat the use of the word "Hello" by the defendant to a youth in a public lavatory as an act of importuning, in view of the fact that the same word had been used by the defendant to another youth on the previous evening and had been followed by an undoubted act of importuning, *viz.* an invitation to look at indecent photographs).

"solicit"

In *Behrendt v. Burridge*, 63 Cr.App.R. 202, DC, the defendant was observed for about 50 **H-215** minutes sitting on a high stool in the bay window of a house. She sat silent and motionless, dressed in a low cut top and mini-skirt. The bay window was illuminated by a red light. She was charged with soliciting for the purpose of prostitution, contrary to section 1 of the Street Offences Act 1959. The Divisional Court said that the fact that her behaviour could be described as an explicit form of advertising was not decisive in her favour: advertising and soliciting are not mutually exclusive. It was clear that she was soliciting in the sense of tempting or allowing prospective customers to come in for the purposes of prostitution.

See also *Horton v. Mead* [1913] 1 K.B. 154, DC, and *Burge v. DPP* [1962] 1 W.L.R. 265, DC.

"importune"

H-216   See *Dale v. Smith, ante,* H-214.

"public place"

H-217   No definition appears in the 1956 Act, but it is a frequently used expression in legislation: see, for example, the Public Order Act 1936, s.9 (§ 25-329 in the main work), the Prevention of Crime Act 1953, s.1(4) (§ 24-165 in the main work) and the Firearms Act 1968, s.57(4) (§ 24-120 in the main work).

"for immoral purposes"

H-218   An immoral purpose within section 32 has to be some kind of sexual activity: *Crook v. Edmondson* [1966] 2 Q.B. 81, DC; *R. v. Kirkup,* 96 Cr.App.R. 352, CA.

Section 32 applies both to heterosexual and homosexual behaviour: *R. v. Goddard,* 92 Cr.App.R. 185, CA.

Although section 1 of the SOA 1967 (*ante,* H-97) prevents homosexual practices in private between consenting parties who have attained the age of 16 from being a criminal offence, the 1967 Act did not change the law to the extent of preventing approaches for such purposes from being the offence of persistently importuning for "immoral purposes": *R. v. Ford,* 66 Cr.App.R. 46, CA. The judge correctly ruled that the conduct complained of could amount to an offence and correctly left the jury to decide whether the conduct was or was not immoral.

Similarly, in *R. v. Goddard, ante,* the unchallenged evidence of two young women was that they had had explicit sexual invitations made to them by G. It was held: (a) that it did not matter that the proposed sexual activity may be within the law; and (b) that it was a matter for the jury to decide, whether the invitations were for sexually immoral purposes, considering the circumstances in which the overtures were made and the nature of the overtures. This decision effectively overruled that part of the majority decision in *Crook v. Edmondson, ante,* which had held that "immoral purposes" was to be confined to purposes declared to be offences under other provisions of the 1956 Act.

The correct procedure is for the trial judge to rule whether the acts complained of could amount to an offence and, provided they are so capable, to leave it to the jury to decide whether the conduct, in fact, involved an immoral purpose, applying contemporary standards of morality: *R. v. Goddard, ante.*

(27) Interpretation

(a) *Meaning of "sexual intercourse"*

Sexual Offences Act 1956, s.44

H-219   **44.** Where, on the trial of any offence under this Act, it is necessary to prove sexual intercourse (whether natural or unnatural), it shall not be necessary to prove the completion of the intercourse by the emission of seed, but the intercourse shall be deemed complete upon proof of penetration only.

See further, *ante,* H-14.

Boys under the age of 14

H-220   As to the abolition of the common law presumption that a boy under the age of 14 is incapable of sexual intercourse, see *ante,* H-13. The presumption did not apply to a charge of aiding and abetting the commission of an offence: 1 Hale 630; *R. v. Williams* [1893] 1 Q.B. 320. Nor would it apply where the boy was not the defendant: see *R. v. Pickford* [1995] 1 Cr.App.R. 420, CA (*ante*, H-94).

(b) *Meaning of "defective"*

See section 45 of the SOA 1956, *ante*, H-68. **H-221**

(c) *Use of words "man", "boy", "woman" and "girl"*

Sexual Offences Act 1956, s.46

46. The use in any provision of this Act of the word "man" without the addition of the word "boy", **H-222** or *vice versa*, shall not prevent the provision applying to any person to whom it would have applied if both words had been used, and similarly with the words "woman" and "girl".

As to the use of the word "man", see *R. v. Tan* [1983] Q.B. 1053, 76 Cr.App.R. 300, CA, *ante*, H-202.

Section 46 applies for the purposes of the provisions of the SOA 1967 as it applies for the purposes of the provisions of the 1956 Act: SOA 1967, s.11(3). It also has effect as if the reference to the 1956 Act included a reference to the Sexual Offences (Amendment) Act 1976: Sexual Offences (Amendment) Act 1976, s.7(2).

(d) *Meaning of "parental responsibility"*

Sexual Offences Act 1956, s.46A

46A. In this Act "parental responsibility" has the same meaning as in the Children Act 1989. **H-223**

[This section was inserted by the Children Act 1989, s.108(4), and Sched. 12, para. 17.]

Section 105(1) of the Act of 1989 provides that in that Act "parental responsibility" has the meaning given by section 3.

Children Act 1989, s.3

3.—(1) In this Act "parental responsibility" means all the rights, duties, powers, responsibilities **H-224** and authority which by law a parent of a child has in relation to the child and his property.

(2) It also includes the rights, powers and duties which a guardian of the child's estate (appointed, before the commencement of section 5, to act generally) would have had in relation to the child and his property.

(3) The rights referred to in subsection (2) include, in particular, the right of the guardian to receive or recover in his own name, for the benefit of the child, property of whatever description and wherever situated which the child is entitled to receive or recover.

(4) The fact that a person has, or does not have, parental responsibility for a child shall not affect—

    (a) any obligation which he may have in relation to the child (such as a statutory duty to maintain the child); or

    (b) any rights which, in the event of the child's death, he (or any other person) may have in relation to the child's property.

(5) A person who—

    (a) does not have parental responsibility for a particular child; but

    (b) has care of the child,

may (subject to the provisions of this Act) do what is reasonable in all the circumstances of the case for the purpose of safeguarding or promoting the child's welfare.

Further reference may need to be made to sections 2 (parental responsibility for children) and 12 (residence orders and parental responsibility) of the 1989 Act.

(28) Proof of exceptions

Sexual Offences Act 1956, s.47

H-225   47. Where in any of the foregoing sections the description of an offence is expressed to be subject to exceptions mentioned in the section, proof of the exception is to lie on the person relying on it.

(29) Powers and procedure for dealing with offenders

Sexual Offences Act 1956, s.37

Prosecution and punishment of offences

H-226   37.—(1) The Second Schedule to this Act shall have effect, subject to and in accordance with the following provisions of this section, with respect to the prosecution and punishment of the offences listed in the first column of the Schedule, being the offences under this Act and attempts to commit certain of those offences.

(2) The second column in the Schedule shows, for any offence, if it may be prosecuted on indictment or summarily, or either ... and what special restrictions (if any) there are on the commencement of a prosecution.

(3) The third column in the Schedule shows, for any offence, the punishments which may be imposed on conviction on indictment or on summary conviction, a reference to a period giving the maximum term of imprisonment and a reference to a sum of money the maximum fine.

(4) The fourth column in the Schedule contains provisions which are either supplementary to those in the second or third column or enable a person charged on indictment with the offence specified in the first column to be found guilty of another offence if the jury are not satisfied that he is guilty of the offence charged or of an attempt to commit it, but are satisfied that he is guilty of the other offence.

(5) A provision in the fourth column of the Schedule enabling the jury to find the accused guilty of an offence specified in that provision authorises them, if not satisfied that he is guilty of the offence so specified, to find him guilty of any other offence of which they could find him guilty if he had been indicted for the offence so specified.

(6) Where in the Schedule there is used a phrase descriptive of an offence or group of offences followed by a reference to a section by its number only, the reference is to a section of this Act, and the phrase shall be taken as referring to any offence under the section mentioned.

(7) Nothing in this section or in the Second Schedule to this Act shall exclude the application to any of the offences referred to in the first column of the Schedule—

(a) of section 24 of the Magistrates' Courts Act 1980 (which relates to the summary trial of young offenders for indictable offences); or

(b) of subsection (5) of section 121 of the Magistrates' Courts Act 1980 (which limits the punishment which may be imposed by a magistrates' court sitting in an occasional courthouse); or

(c) of any enactment or rule of law restricting a court's power to imprison; or

(d) of any enactment or rule of law authorising an offender to be dealt with in a way not authorised by the enactments specially relating to his offence; or

(e) of any enactment or rule of law authorising a jury to find a person guilty of an offence other than that with which he is charged.

[This section is printed as amended by the MCA 1980, Sched. 7, para. 17; and as repealed in part by the Courts Act 1971, s.56(4), and Sched. 11, Pt IV.]

Subsection (5) was considered in *R. v. Rogina*, 64 Cr.App.R. 79, CA, *ante*, H-74.

Attempts

H-227   Schedule 2 to the 1956 Act is not set out in this appendix. All relevant provisions thereof are referred to in the context of the individual offences, *ante*. Some of the paragraphs in the Schedule specifically refer to an attempt to commit a particular offence (sometimes with a different penalty to the full offence, sometimes with the same penalty). Wherever there is specific reference to an attempt in the schedule, this is referred to in the text in relation to the offence in question; where there is no such reference in the text, this is because there is no separate reference to an attempt in the schedule. In such cases, the Criminal Attempts Act 1981 will exclusively determine liability to prosecution and punishment for an attempt: for the 1981 Act, see §§ 33-128 *et seq.* in the main work.

C. MENTAL HEALTH ACT 1959

Mental Health Act 1959, s.128

Sexual intercourse with patients

128.—(1) Without prejudice to section seven of the Sexual Offences Act 1956, it shall be an of-   **H-228**
fence, subject to the exception mentioned in this section,—

  (a) for a man who is an officer on the staff of or is otherwise employed in, or is one of the
       managers of, a hospital independent hospital or care home to have unlawful sexual
       intercourse with a woman who is for the time being receiving treatment for mental disorder
       in that hospital or home, or to have such intercourse on the premises of which the hospital
       or home forms part with a woman who is for the time being receiving such treatment there
       as an outpatient;

  (b) for a man to have unlawful sexual intercourse with a woman who is a mentally disordered
       patient and who is subject to his guardianship under the Mental Health Act 1983 or is
       otherwise in his custody or care under the Mental Health Act 1983 or in pursuance of ar-
       rangements under ... Part III of the National Assistance Act 1948 ... or the National
       Health Service Act 1977, or as a resident in a care home.

  (2) It shall not be an offence under this section for a man to have sexual intercourse with a woman
if he does not know and has no reason to suspect her to be a mentally disordered patient.

  (3) Any person guilty of an offence under this section shall be liable on conviction on indictment to
imprisonment for a term not exceeding two years.

  (4) No proceedings shall be instituted for an offence under this section except by or with the
consent of the Director of Public Prosecutions.

  (5) This section shall be construed as one with the Sexual Offences Act 1956; and section 47 of that
Act (which relates to the proof of exceptions) shall apply to the exception mentioned in this section.

  (6) In this section "independent hospital" and "care home" have the same meaning as in the Care
Standards Act 2000.

[This section is printed as amended by the National Health Service Act 1977, s.129, Sched. 15,
para. 29, and Sched. 16; the MHA 1983, s.148, and Sched. 3, para. 15; the Registered Homes Act
1984, s.57, and Sched. 1, para. 2; and the Care Standards Act 2000, s.116, and Sched. 4, para. 2.]

As to the meaning of "sexual intercourse", see *ante*, H-219; as to the meaning of "unlawful"   **H-229**
sexual intercourse, see *R. v. Chapman*, *ante*, H-38; as to the use of the words "man" and "woman",
see *ante*, H-222.

For anonymity provisions, see §§ 20-257 *et seq.* in the main work.

For section 47 of the 1956 Act (burden of proof of exceptions), see *ante*, H-225.

By section 1(4) of the Sexual Offences Act 1967, section 128 is to have effect as if any reference
therein to having unlawful sexual intercourse with a woman included a reference to committing
buggery or an act of gross indecency with another man.

In connection with the offences created by this section, see *R. v. Davies and Poolton* [2000]
Crim.L.R. 297, CA (§ 19-363 in the main work), decided in relation to the similarly worded section 127 of the 1959 Act.

D. INDECENCY WITH CHILDREN ACT 1960

(1) Statute

Indecency with Children Act 1960, s.1(1)

  1.—(1) Any person who commits an act of gross indecency with or towards a child under the age   **H-230**
of sixteen, or who incites a child under that age to such an act with him or another, shall be liable on
conviction on indictment to imprisonment for a term not exceeding ten years, or on summary
conviction to imprisonment for a term not exceeding six months, to a fine not exceeding the
prescribed sum, or to both.

  (2) [*Repealed by Police and Criminal Evidence Act 1984, Sched. 7.*]

  (3) References in the Children and Young Persons Act 1933 ... to the offences mentioned in the
First Schedule to that Act shall include offences under this section.

  (4) offences under this section shall be deemed to be offences against the person for the purpose of
section three of the Visiting Forces Act 1952 (which restricts the trial by United Kingdom courts of
offenders connected with visiting forces).

[Subs. (1) is printed as amended by the C(S)A 1997, s.52 (substitution of "ten" for "two"); and the CJCSA 2000, s.39 (substitution of "sixteen" for "fourteen"). The first of these amendments took effect on October 1, 1997, but does not apply to offences committed before that date: Crime (Sentences) Act (Commencement No. 2 and Transitional Provisions) Order 1997 (S.I. 1997 No. 2200). The second amendment took effect on January 11, 2001: Criminal Justice and Court Services Act 2000 (Commencement No. 1) Order 2000 (S.I. 2000 No. 3302).]

As to Schedule 1 to the CYPA 1933, see § 19-408 in the main work.

For anonymity provisions, see §§ 20-257 *et seq.* in the main work.

(2) Indictment

Statement of Offence

H-231

Indecency with a child, contrary to section 1(1) of the Indecency with Children Act 1960.

Particulars of offence

A B, on the _____ day of _____, 20__, committed an act of gross indecency with [or towards] J N, a child of the age of 10 years [or incited J N, a child of the age of 10 years to commit an act of gross indecency with him the said A B (or with Y Z)].

It is a prerequisite of a conviction contrary to section 1 that the child was under the age of 16 at the time of the act or incitement: the child's age is an ingredient of the offence about which the jury must be satisfied and, unless age is admitted, calls for an appropriate direction from the judge: see *R. v. Goss and Goss*, 90 Cr.App.R. 400, CA, and *R. v. Radcliffe* [1990] Crim.L.R. 524, CA.

As to the propriety of preferring a charge of outraging public decency although the facts are covered by section 1(1), see *R. v. May (J.)*, 91 Cr.App.R. 157, CA (§ 20-238 in the main work).

(3) Mode of trial and class of offence

H-232

This offence is triable either way: s.1(1), *ante*. As to the classification of offences, see *ante*, Appendix F-6.

(4) Sentence

H-233

See section 1(1), *ante*. As to "the prescribed sum", see section 32 of the MCA 1980 (§ 1-125 in the main work).

(5) Consent of Director of Public Prosecutions

H-234

Section 8 of the SOA 1967 (no proceedings shall be instituted except by or with the consent of the Director against any man for gross indecency or certain other offences where any person involved is under 21) shall not apply to proceedings under the Indecency with Children Act 1960: CJA 1972, s.48.

(6) Ingredients of the offence

H-235

In *R. v. Speck*, 65 Cr.App.R. 161, CA, it was held that section 1 was contravened where S passively permitted a child to keep her hand on his penis for so long (in this case about five minutes) that his inactivity amounted to an invitation to her to continue the activity. If such an invitation could properly be inferred, it would constitute an "act" within section 1(1). Apart from allowing the child's hand to remain where she had placed it, S did nothing to encourage the child. A proper direction to the jury in such circumstances would be that the defendant's conduct might constitute an offence under section 1(1) if it amounted to an invitation from the defendant to the child to continue the activity in question. If they took that view (*i.e.* that there had been an "act") then they should go on to determine whether the act was an act of gross indecency. See also *R. v. B.* [1999] Crim.L.R. 594, CA.

Section 1(1) creates one offence of gross indecency, namely, the committing of an act of gross indecency involving a child; that is, "with or towards a child" is to be read as a phrase: *DPP v. Burgess* [1971] Q.B. 432, DC; *R. v. Francis*, 88 Cr.App.R. 127, CA. In *Francis*, the court considered the circumstances in which a man contravened section 1(1) if he masturbated in the presence of a child: the act had to be directed towards the child, the offender at the very least deriving satisfaction from the knowledge that the child was watching what he was doing.

As to the age of the victim being an essential ingredient of the offence, see *ante*, H-220; and it is necessary for the prosecution to prove the absence of a genuine belief on the part of the defendant that the victim was 16 years or above: *B. (a Minor) v. DPP* [2000] 2 A.C. 428, HL. The presence or absence of reasonable grounds for such belief goes only to whether such belief was genuinely held: *ibid.*

E. Sexual Offences Act 1967

(1) Procuring others to commit homosexual acts

Sexual Offences Act 1967, s.4

4.—(1) A man who procures another man to commit with a third man an act of buggery which by   H-236
reason of section 1 of this Act is not an offence shall be liable on conviction on indictment to imprisonment for a term not exceeding two years.

(2) [*Repealed by Criminal Law Act 1977, Sched. 13.*]

(3) It shall not be an offence under section 13 of the Act of 1956 for a man to procure the commission by another man of an act of gross indecency with the first-mentioned man which by reason of section 1 of this Act is not an offence under the said section 13.

The offence under subsection (1) is triable either way: MCA 1980, s.17(1), and Sched. 1 (§ 1-125 in the main work).

As to the use of the word "man", see *ante*, H-222.

As to the offence of buggery, see *ante*, H-95 *et seq.*

For section 13 of the 1956 Act, see *ante*, H-107.

As to "procures", see *ante*, H-171.

(2) Living on earnings of male prostitution

Sexual Offences Act 1967, s.5

5.—(1) A man or woman who knowingly lives wholly or in part on the earnings of prostitution of   H-237
another man shall be liable—

    (a) on summary conviction to imprisonment for a term not exceeding six months, or

    (b) on conviction on indictment to imprisonment for a term not exceeding seven years.

(2) [*Repealed by Criminal Law Act 1977, Sched. 13.*]

(3) Anyone may arrest without a warrant a person found committing an offence under this section.

As to the use of the words "man" and "woman", see *ante*, H-222 and—in relation to "man"—   H-238
see *R. v. Tan* [1983] Q.B. 1053, 76 Cr.App.R. 300, CA, *ante*, H-202.

The offence is a class 3 offence (§ 2-17 in the main work).

Subsection (3) has ceased to have effect by virtue of the PACE Act 1984, s.26(1) (§ 15-133 in the main work).

F. Criminal Law Act 1977

Criminal Law Act 1977, s.54

Incitement of girls under 16

54.—(1) It is an offence for a man to incite to have sexual intercourse with him a girl under the   H-239
age of sixteen whom he knows to be his grand-daughter, daughter or sister.

(2) In the preceding subsection "man" includes boy, "sister" includes half-sister, and for the purposes of that subsection any expression importing a relationship between two people shall be taken to apply notwithstanding that the relationship is not traced through lawful wedlock.

(3) The following provisions of section 1 of the Indecency with Children Act 1960, namely—

...

    subsection (3) (references in Children and Young Persons Act 1933 to the offences mentioned in Schedule 1 to that Act to include offences under that section);

    subsection (4) (offences under that section to be deemed offences against the person for the purpose of section 3 of the Visiting Forces Act 1952),

shall apply in relation to offences under this section.

(4) A person guilty of an offence under this section shall be liable—

    (a) on summary conviction, to imprisonment for a term not exceeding six months or to a fine not exceeding the prescribed sum or both;

(b) on conviction on indictment to imprisonment for a term not exceeding two years.

[This section is printed as effectively amended by the MCA 1980, s.32(2) (substitution of reference to "the prescribed sum"); and as repealed in part by the PACE Act 1984, Sched. 7.]

H-240   As to Schedule 1 to the CYPA 1933, see § 19-408 in the main work.

As to "the prescribed sum", see the MCA 1980, s.32(2) and (9) (§ 1-125 in the main work).

For anonymity provisions, see §§ 20-257 *et seq.* in the main work.

Section 54 filled a *lacuna* in the law, identified in *R. v. Whitehouse* [1977] Q.B. 868, 65 Cr.App.R. 33, CA.

As to incitement at common law, see *ante*, §§ 33-74 *et seq.*

G. Sexual Offences (Amendment) Act 2000

(1) Statute

Sexual Offences (Amendment) Act 2000, ss.3, 4

Abuse of position of trust

H-241   **3.**—(1) Subject to subsections (2) and (3) below, it shall be an offence for a person aged 18 or over—

(a) to have sexual intercourse (whether vaginal or anal) with a person under that age; or

(b) to engage in any other sexual activity with or directed towards such a person,

if (in either case) he is in a position of trust in relation to that person.

(2) Where a person ("A") is charged with an offence under this section of having sexual intercourse with, or engaging in any other sexual activity with or directed towards, another person ("B"), it shall be a defence for A to prove that, at the time of the intercourse or activity—

(a) he did not know, and could not reasonably have been expected to know, that B was under 18;

(b) he did not know, and could not reasonably have been expected to know, that B was a person in relation to whom he was in a position of trust; or

(c) he was lawfully married to B.

(3) It shall not be an offence under this section for a person ("A") to have sexual intercourse with, or engage in any other sexual activity with or directed towards, another person ("B") if immediately before the commencement of this Act—

(a) A was in a position of trust in relation to B; and

(b) a sexual relationship existed between them.

(4) A person guilty of an offence under this section shall be liable—

(a) on summary conviction, to imprisonment for a term not exceeding six months, or to a fine not exceeding the statutory maximum, or to both;

(b) on conviction on indictment, to imprisonment for a term not exceeding five years, or to a fine, or to both.

(5) In this section, "sexual activity"—

(a) does not include any activity which a reasonable person would regard as sexual only with knowledge of the intentions, motives or feelings of the parties; but

(b) subject to that, means any activity which such a person would regard as sexual in all the circumstances.

As to "the commencement of this Act", see the Sexual Offences (Amendment) Act 2000 (Commencement No. 1) Order 2000 (S.I. 2000 No. 3303), which brought the Act into force on January 8, 2001.

Meaning of "position of trust"

H-242   **4.**—(1) For the purposes of section 3 above, a person aged 18 or over ("A") is in a position of trust in relation to a person under that age ("B") if any of the four conditions set out below, or any condition specified in an order made by the Secretary of State by statutory instrument, is fulfilled.

(2) The first condition is that A looks after persons under 18 who are detained in an institution by virtue of an order of a court or under an enactment, and B is so detained in that institution.

(3) The second condition is that A looks after persons under 18 who are resident in a home or other place in which—

(a) accommodation and maintenance are provided by an authority under section 23(2) of the Children Act 1989 or Article 27(2) of the Children (Northern Ireland) Order 1995;

  (b) accommodation is provided by a voluntary organisation under section 59(1) of that Act or
      Article 75(1) of that Order; or

  (c) accommodation is provided by an authority under section 26(1) of the Children (Scotland)
      Act 1995,

and B is resident, and is so provided with accommodation and maintenance or accommodation, in
that place.

(4) The third condition is that A looks after persons under 18 who are accommodated and cared
for in an institution which is—

  (a) a hospital;

  (b) a residential care home, nursing home, mental nursing home or private hospital;

  (c) a community home, voluntary home, children's home or residential establishment; or

  (d) a home provided under section 82(5) of the Children Act 1989,

and B is accommodated and cared for in that institution.

(5) The fourth condition is that A looks after persons under 18 who are receiving full-time education at an educational institution, and B is receiving such education at that institution.

(6) No order shall be made under subsection (1) above unless a draft of the order has been laid
before and approved by a resolution of each House of Parliament.

(7) A person looks after persons under 18 for the purposes of this section if he is regularly
involved in caring for, training, supervising or being in sole charge of such persons.

(8) For the purposes of this section a person receives full-time education at an educational institution if—

  (a) he is registered or otherwise enrolled as a full-time pupil or student at the institution; or

  (b) he receives education at the institution under arrangements with another educational
      institution at which he is so registered or otherwise enrolled.

(9) In this section, except where the context otherwise requires—

"authority" means—

    (a) in relation to Great Britain, a local authority; and

    (b) [*Northern Ireland*];

"children's home" has—

    (a) in relation to England and Wales, the meaning which would be given by subsection
       (3) of section 63 of the Children Act 1989 if the reference in paragraph (a) of that
       subsection to more than three children were a reference to one or more children;
       and

    (b) [*Northern Ireland*];

"community home" has the meaning given by section 53(1) of the Children Act 1989;

"hospital" has—

    (a) in relation to England and Wales, the meaning given by section 128(1) of the National
       Health Service Act 1977;

    (b) [*Scotland*]; and

    (c) [*Northern Ireland*];

"mental nursing home" has, in relation to England and Wales, the meaning given by section
    22(1) of the Registered Homes Act 1984

"nursing home"—

    (a) in relation to England and Wales, has the meaning given by section 21(1) of the
       Registered Homes Act 1984;

    (b) [*Scotland*];

    (c) [*Northern Ireland*];

"private hospital" has—

    (a) [*Scotland*]; and

    (b) [*Northern Ireland*];

"residential care home"—

    (a) in relation to England and Wales, has the meaning given by section 1(2) of the
       Registered Homes Act 1984;

    (b) [*Scotland*]; and

    (c) [*Northern Ireland*];

"residential establishment" has the meaning given by section 93(1) of the Children (Scotland)
    Act 1995 as the meaning of that expression in Scotland;

"voluntary home" has—

    (a) in relation to England and Wales, the meaning given by section 60(3) of the Children
       Act 1989; and

(b) [*Northern Ireland*].

(2) Indictment

Statement of Offence

H-243   *Abuse of a position of trust, contrary to section 3(1)(a) of the Sexual Offences (Amendment) Act 2000.*

Particulars of Offence

A B, on the _____ day of _____, 20__, being a person of the age of at least 18 years, had sexual intercourse with J N, being a person under the age of 18 years, and being at the time in a position of trust in relation to J N, in that at the time he looked after persons under the age of 18 years who were receiving full-time education at _____ school, and J N was at the time in receipt of such education at the aforesaid school.

(3) Mode of trial and class of offence

H-244   This offence is triable either way: s.3(4), *ante*. As to the classification of offences, see *ante*, Appendix F-6.

(4) Sentence

H-245   See s.3(4), *ante*.

The setting out of the various positions of trust in section 4(2) to (5) is not to be taken as indicative of descending seriousness: *R. v. Hubbard* [2002] 2 Cr.App.R.(S.) 101, CA.

APPENDIX J
A Guide to Commencing Proceedings in the Court of Appeal (Criminal Division)

NOTE: the text of the guide that follows has been subjected to some editorial revision (in relation to such matters as punctuation, use of upper and lower case, abbreviations, manner of citation of legislative references and authorities, and in order to correct a small number of obvious, minor errors). None of these revisions has any effect on the sense of the guide.

A GUIDE TO COMMENCING PROCEEDINGS IN THE COURT OF APPEAL (CRIMINAL DIVISION)

Foreword by the Lord Chief Justice of England and Wales

In recent years the Court of Appeal Criminal Division has faced increased complexity in appeals, not only against conviction but also against sentence, particularly in the light of the plethora of recent sentencing legislation. Additionally, the jurisdiction of the court has expanded to encompass a variety of diverse applications and appeals by the defence, the Crown and other interested parties. **J-1**

This guide provides invaluable advice as to the initial steps for commencing proceedings in the Court of Appeal Criminal Division generally and in relation to perhaps unfamiliar provisions.

The first and most important step is, of course, the preparation of the grounds of appeal. The rules prescribe the form and content of the Notice and Grounds of Appeal. Practitioners are also required to summarise the facts and outline their arguments concisely. Well drafted grounds of appeal assist the single judge when considering leave and serve to shorten any hearing before the full court. Ill-prepared and prolix documents necessarily lead to wasted time spent on preparation and unnecessarily protracted hearings.

It is important that we all take seriously our responsibility to ensure the effective progression of cases and keep delay to a minimum. Once an application or appeal is commenced, the responsible officer at the Criminal Appeal Office will be available to assist with any queries on practice or procedure.

The court could not deal with this volume of work efficiently without the support of the Registrar and his staff in the Criminal Appeal Office. Their experience and expertise is invaluable and can always be relied on by those who use the court, not least those who are unfamiliar with its practice and procedures.

Judge C.J.

October 2008

Introduction

Since the publication of the last Guide to Proceedings in the Court of Appeal (Criminal Division), the court's jurisdiction has increased. It hears appeals not only against conviction and sentence, but also against various interlocutory rulings, as well as other appeals and applications. **J-2**

This guide provides practical information about how to commence and conduct proceedings before the court. Once proceedings are commenced, an application will have its own unique reference number and a case progression officer who can help with any difficulties or queries about procedure.

The guide is set out as follows:

    A. General principles of practice and procedure when applying for leave to appeal conviction and sentence.

    B. Guidance on appeals against rulings made in preparatory hearings.

    C. Guidance on prosecution appeals against 'terminating' rulings.

    D. Brief guidance on other appeals in bullet point form showing:
- the type of appeal,
- the relevant section of the statute
- the relevant Criminal Procedure Rules
- who can apply
- the forms to be used and time limits
- respondents' notices,
- whether representation orders are available
- whether leave to appeal is required

E. Guidance on applications for a retrial for a serious offence.

A list of all up to date forms referred to in this guide may be accessed from the HMCS website at www.hmcourts-service.gov.uk or the Criminal Procedure Rules Committee website at www.justice.gov.uk/criminal/procrules. Where the Criminal Procedure Rules do not provide for a specific form, this guide indicates the appropriate form to be used.

This guide was prepared under my direction by the staff of the Criminal Appeal Office, but principally by Ms Alix Beldam and Ms Susan Holdham. It describes the law and practice of the Court as at 1st October 2008.

Master Venne

Registrar of Criminal Appeals

Terminology

J-3
The Criminal Appeal Act 1968 refers to "leave to appeal". This is now referred to as "permission to appeal" in the Criminal Procedure Rules 2007. This guide keeps to the terminology used by the Act.

Also consistently with the Act, an "appellant" is referred to without distinction, but it should be borne in mind that it is the accepted practice of the Criminal Appeal Office (CAO) to refer to a person who has served notice of appeal but not been granted leave to appeal as an "applicant" and use the term "appellant" to refer to a person who has been granted leave to appeal.

Any reference to counsel should be read as including a solicitor advocate as appropriate.

A. GENERAL PRINCIPLES OF PRACTICE AND PROCEDURE WHEN APPLYING FOR LEAVE TO APPEAL CONVICTION AND

SENTENCE

A1 Advice and assistance

J-4
A1-1 Provision for advice or assistance on appeal is included in the trial representation order issued by the Crown Court. Solicitors should not wait to be asked for advice by the defendant. Immediately following the conclusion of the case, the legal representatives should see the defendant and counsel should express orally his final view as to the prospects of a successful appeal (whether against conviction or sentence or both). If there are no reasonable grounds of appeal, that should be confirmed in writing and a copy provided then, or as soon as practicable thereafter, to the defendant by the solicitor. If there are reasonable grounds, grounds of appeal should be drafted, signed and sent to instructing solicitors as soon as possible. Solicitors should immediately send a copy of the documents received from counsel to the defendant.

A1-2 Prior to the lodging of the notice and grounds of appeal by service of Form NG, the Registrar has no power to grant a representation order. Also, the Crown Court can only amend a representation order in favour of fresh legal representatives if advice on appeal has not been given by trial legal representatives and it is necessary and reasonable for another legal representative to be instructed. Where advice on appeal has been given by trial legal representatives, application for funding may only be made to the Legal Services Commission (LSC).

A1-3 Once the Form NG has been lodged, the Registrar is the authority for decisions about representation orders, in accordance with the principle that the court before which there are proceedings is the court with power to grant a right to representation (Access to Justice Act 1999, Sched. 3, affirmed by regulation 10 of the Criminal Defence Service (General) (No. 2) Regulations 2001 (S.I. 2001 No. 1437)).

A1-4 Where, in order to settle grounds of appeal, work of an exceptional nature is contemplated or where the expense will be great, legal representatives should submit a Form NG with provisional grounds of appeal and with a note to the Registrar requesting a representation order to cover the specific work considered necessary to enable proper grounds of appeal to be settled.

A2 Form NG and grounds of appeal

J-5
A2-1 Where counsel has advised an appeal, solicitors should forward the signed grounds of appeal to the Crown Court accompanied by Form NG and such other forms as may be appropriate. It should be noted that Form NG and grounds of appeal are required to be served within the relevant time limit in all cases, whether or not leave to appeal is required (*e.g.* where a trial judge's certificate has been granted). However, on a reference by the Criminal Cases Review Commission (CCRC), if no Form NG and grounds are served within the required period, then the reference shall be treated as the appeal notice: rule 68.5(2).

A2-2 Grounds must be settled with sufficient particularity to enable the Registrar, and subsequently the court, to identify clearly the matters relied upon. A mere formula such as "the conviction is unsafe" or "the sentence is in all the circumstances too severe" will be ineffective as grounds and time will continue to run against the defendant.

A2-3 Rule 68.3(1) sets out the information that must be contained in the appeal notice. The notice must ... [*see § 7-382 in the main work*].

A2-4 There is now a requirement for the grounds of appeal to set out the relevant facts and nature of the proceedings concisely in one all encompassing document, not separate grounds and advice. The intended readership of this document is the court and not the lay or professional client. Its purpose is to enable the single judge to grasp quickly the facts and issues in the case. In appropriate cases, draft grounds of appeal may be perfected before submission to the single judge (*see further below para. A5*).

A2-5 Any document mentioned in the grounds should be identified clearly, by exhibit number or otherwise. Similarly, if counsel requires an original exhibit or shorthand writer's tape recording, he should say so well in advance of any determination or hearing.

A2-6 Counsel should not settle or sign grounds unless they are reasonable, have some real prospect of success and are such that he is prepared to argue them before the court. Counsel should not settle grounds he cannot support because he is "instructed" to do so by a defendant.

A2-7 Procedure in relation to particular grounds of appeal

A2-7.1 *Applications to call fresh evidence*

A Form W and a statement from the witness in the form prescribed by section 9 of the CJA 1967 should be lodged in respect of each witness it is proposed to call. The Form W should indicate whether there is an application for a witness order. The Registrar or the single judge may direct the issue of a witness order, but only the court hearing the appeal may give leave for a witness to be called.

The court will require a cogent explanation for the failure to adduce the evidence at trial. A supporting witness statement or affidavit from the appellant's solicitor should be lodged in this regard (*R. v. Gogana, The Times,* July 12, 1999).

If there is to be an application to adduce hearsay and/or evidence of bad character or for special measures, then the appropriate forms should be lodged: rule 68.7(1).

A2-7.2 *Complaints against trial counsel as a ground of appeal*

Where a ground of appeal explicitly criticises trial counsel and/or trial solicitors, the Registrar will institute the "waiver of privilege" procedure. The appellant will be asked to "waive privilege" in respect of instructions to and advice at trial from legal representatives. If he does waive privilege, the grounds of appeal are sent to the appropriate trial representative(s) and they are invited to respond. Any response will be sent to the appellant or his fresh legal representatives for comment. All these documents will be sent to the single judge when considering the application for leave. The single judge may draw inferences from any failure to participate in the process. "Waiver of privilege" is a procedure that should be instigated by the Registrar and not by fresh legal representatives, who should go no further than obtaining a waiver of privilege from the appellant: *R. v. Doherty and McGregor* [1997] 2 Cr.App.R. 218.

A2-7.3 *Insufficient weight given to assistance to prosecution authorities*

Where a ground of appeal against sentence is that the judge has given insufficient weight to the assistance given to the prosecution authorities, the "text" which had been prepared for the sentencing judge is obtained by the Registrar. Grounds of appeal should be drafted in an anodyne form with a note to the Registrar alerting him to the existence of a "text". The single judge will have seen the "text" when considering leave as will the full court before the appeal hearing and it need not be alluded to in open court.

A3 Time limits

A3-1 Notice and grounds should reach the Crown Court within 28 days from the date of the conviction in the case of an application for leave to appeal against conviction and within 28 days from the date of sentence in the case of an application for leave to appeal against sentence [CAA 1968, s.18 and rule 68.2(1)]. On a reference by the CCRC, Form NG and grounds should be served on the Registrar not more than 56 days after the Registrar has served notice that the CCRC has referred a conviction and not more than 28 days in the case of a sentence referral: rule 68.2(2). **J-6**

A3-2 A confiscation order (whether made under the CJA 1988, the DTA 1994 or the PCA 2002) is a sentence [CAA 1968, s.50]. Where sentences are passed in separate proceedings on different dates there may be two appeals against sentence. Thus, there may be an appeal against the custodial part of a sentence and an appeal against a confiscation order (*R. v. Neal* [1999] 2 Cr.App.R.(S.) 352).

A3-3 An application for extension of the 28 day period in which to give notice of application for leave to appeal or notice of appeal must always be supported by reasons why the application for leave was not submitted in time. It is not enough merely to tick the relevant box on Form NG.

A3-4 Such an application should be submitted when the application for leave to appeal against either conviction or sentence is made and not in advance. Notwithstanding the terms of section 18(3) of the CAA 1968, it has long been the practice of the Registrar to require the extension of time application to be made at the time of service of the notice and grounds of appeal. This practice is now reflected by Criminal Procedure Rule 65.4.

A4 Transcript and notes of evidence

A4-1 In conviction cases, transcripts of the summing up and proceedings up to and including verdict are obtained as a matter of course. Similarly, the transcript of the prosecution opening of facts on a guilty plea and the judge's observations on passing sentence are usually obtained in sentence cases. There is now an obligation under rule 68.3(2) for counsel to identify any further transcript which counsel considers the court will need and to provide a note of names, dates and times to enable an order to be placed with the shorthand writers. Whether or not any further transcript is required is a matter for the judgment of the Registrar or his staff.

A4-2 Transcript should only be requested if it is essential for the proper conduct of the appeal in the light of the grounds. If the Registrar and counsel are unable to agree the extent of the transcript to be obtained, the Registrar may refer that matter to a judge. In some cases the Registrar may propose that counsel agree a note in place of transcript.

A4-3 In certain circumstances the costs of unnecessary transcript could be ordered to be paid by the appellant. Where transcript is obtained otherwise than through the Registrar, he may disallow the cost on taxation of public funding.

A5 Perfection of grounds of appeal

A5-1 The purpose of perfection is (a) to save valuable judicial time by enabling the court to identify at once the relevant parts of the transcript and (b) to give counsel the opportunity to reconsider his original grounds in the light of the transcript. Perfected grounds should consist of a fresh document which supersedes the original grounds of appeal and contains *inter alia* references by page number and letter (or paragraph number) to all relevant passages in the transcript.

A5-2 In conviction or confiscation cases, the Registrar will almost certainly invite counsel to perfect grounds in the light of the transcript obtained, to assist the single judge or full court. Where counsel indicates a wish to perfect grounds of appeal against sentence, the Registrar will consider the request and will only invite perfection where he considers it necessary for the assistance of the single judge or full court.

A5-3 If perfection is appropriate, counsel will be sent a copy of the transcript and asked to perfect his grounds within 14 days. In the absence of any response from counsel, the existing notice and grounds of appeal will be placed before the single judge or the court without further notice. If counsel does not wish to perfect his grounds, the transcript should be returned with a note to that effect.

A5-4 If, having considered the transcript, counsel is of opinion that there are no valid grounds, he should set out his reasons in a further advice and send it to his instructing solicitors. He should inform the Registrar that he has done so, but should not send him a copy of that advice. Solicitors should send a copy to the appellant and obtain instructions, at the same time explaining that if the appellant persists with his application the court may consider whether to make a loss of time order (*see further below A-13*).

A6 Respondent's notice

A6-1 The Criminal Procedure Rules 2005 provide for the service of a respondent's notice. Under rule 68.6(1) the Registrar may serve the appeal notice on any party directly affected by the appeal (usually the prosecution) and must do so in a CCRC case. That party may then serve a respondent's notice if it wishes to make representations and must do so if the Registrar so directs: rule 68.6(2). The respondent's notice should be served within 14 days (rule 68.6(4)) on the appellant, the Registrar and any other party on whom the Registrar served the appeal notice (rule 68.6(3)). The respondent's notice must be in the specified form [Form RN], in which a respondent should set out the grounds of opposition (rule 68.6(5)) and which must include the information set out in rule 68.6(6).

A6-2 In practice, this procedure primarily applies prior to consideration of leave by the single judge in both conviction and sentence cases. The Attorney General and the Registrar, following consultation with representatives from the Crown Prosecution Service (CPS) and the Revenue and Customs Prosecution Office (RCPO), have agreed guidance on types of cases and/or issues where the Registrar should consider whether to serve an appeal notice and direct or invite a party to serve a respondent's notice before the consideration of leave by the single judge. Examples of when the Registrar might **direct** a respondent's notice include where the grounds concern matters which were the subject of public interest immunity (PII), allegations of jury irregularity, criticism of the conduct of the judge and complex frauds. Cases where it might be appropriate for the Registrar to **invite** a respondent's notice include, for example, homicide offences, serious sexual offences, cases with national profile or high media interest, cases of violence or domestic violence.

A6-3 In conviction cases where leave has been granted or where the application for leave has been referred to the full court, the Crown is briefed to attend the hearing and required to submit a respondent's notice/skeleton argument. In relation to sentence cases where leave has been granted, referred or an appellant is represented on a renewed application, the sentence protocol set out in paragraph II.1 of the consolidated criminal practice direction [see now *Criminal Practice Direction (Appeal) 68A* [2013] 1 W.L.R. 3164 (§ 7-203 in the main work)] will apply. In those cases, a respondent's notice/skeleton argument will have to be served when the Crown indicates a wish to attend or when the Registrar invites or directs the Crown to attend.

A7 Referral by the Registrar

A7-1 Leave to appeal is required in all cases except where the trial judge or sentencing judge has   **J-10** certified that the case is fit for appeal (CAA 1968, ss.1(2) and 11(1A)) or where the case has been referred by the CCRC. The appellant must obtain leave to pursue grounds not related to the Commission's reasons for referral: CAA 1995, s.14(4B).

A7-2 Where leave to appeal is required and the Registrar has obtained the necessary documents, he will refer the application(s) either (a) to a single judge for decision under section 31 of the CAA 1968 or (b) directly to the full court, in which case a representation order is usually granted for the hearing. However, the Registrar will not grant a representation order when the presence of counsel is not required, *e.g.* where the application refers solely to an amendment of the number of days to be credited as "remand time" and the figure is agreed by the parties. Where an application is referred to the full court by the Registrar because an unlawful sentence has been passed or other procedural error identified, a representation order will ordinarily be granted, but counsel should be aware that the court may make observations for the attention of the determining officer that a full fee should not be allowed on taxation.

A7-3 Where leave to appeal is not required, *e.g.* on appeal by certificate of the trial judge, the Registrar will usually grant a representation order for the hearing. On a reference from the CCRC, it is the Registrar's usual practice to grant a representation order in the first instance, to solicitors for them to nominate and instruct counsel to settle grounds of appeal. Once counsel's details are known, a further representation order will be granted to cover the preparation (including settling grounds) and presentation of the appeal by counsel and further work by solicitors, as necessary in light of the grounds.

A8 Bail pending appeal

A8-1 Bail may be granted (a) by a single judge or the full court or (b) by a trial or sentencing   **J-11** judge who has certified the case fit for appeal. In the latter case, bail can only be granted within 28 days of the conviction or sentence which is the subject of the appeal and may not be granted if an application for bail has already been made to the Court of Appeal.

A8-2 An application to the Court of Appeal for bail must be supported by a completed Form B, whether or not the application is made at the same time as the notice and grounds are served. The completed Form B must be served on the Registrar <u>and the prosecution</u> at least 24 hours before any application is made to enable the Crown to make representations (either written or oral) about the application and any conditions.

A8-3 An application for bail will not be considered by a single judge or the court until notice of application for leave to appeal or notice of appeal has first been given. In practice, judges will also require the relevant transcripts to be available so they may take a view as to the merits of the substantive application.

A8-4 It is the practice of the court, if bail is granted, to require a condition of residence. An application for variation of conditions of bail may be determined by the Registrar (if unopposed) or a single judge.

A9 Consideration of the applications by single judge

A9-1 Normally a single judge will consider the application for leave to appeal together with any   **J-12** ancillary applications, *e.g.* for bail or representation order, without hearing oral argument. Counsel may request an oral hearing, but it is only in very rare circumstances that the Registrar would consider it appropriate to grant a representation order for the proceedings before a single judge at an oral hearing, but counsel may appear to argue the applications before the single judge where instructed to do so, usually appearing either *pro bono* or privately funded. Oral applications for leave and bail are usually heard at 9.30 a.m. before the normal court sittings. Counsel appears unrobed. If counsel considers that an application may take longer than 20 minutes, the Registrar must be informed.

A10 Powers of the single judge

J-13   A10-1 The single judge may grant the application for leave, refuse it or refer it to the full court. In conviction cases and in sentence cases where appropriate, the single judge may grant limited leave, *i.e.* leave to argue some grounds but not others. If the grounds upon which leave has been refused are to be renewed before the full court, counsel must notify the Registrar within 14 days. In the absence of any notification of renewal, it will be assumed that the grounds upon which leave was refused will not be pursued.

The single judge may also grant, refuse or refer any ancillary application.

A11 Grant of leave or reference to full court

J-14   A11-1 Where the single judge grants leave or refers an application to the court, it is usual to grant a representation order for the preparation and presentation of the appeal. This is usually limited to the services of counsel only, in which event counsel will be assigned by the Registrar. In such a case the Registrar will provide a brief but does not act as an appellant's solicitor. Counsel who settled grounds of appeal will usually be assigned. However, the Registrar may assign one counsel to represent more than one appellant if appropriate. If it is considered that a representation order for two counsel and/or solicitors is required, counsel should notify the Registrar and provide written justification in accordance with the Criminal Defence Service (General) (No. 2) Regulations 2001.

A11-2 If solicitors are assigned, it should be noted that by virtue of regulation 13 of the Criminal Defence Service (General) (No. 2) Regulations 2001, a representation order can only be issued to a solicitor if he holds a General Criminal Contract (Crime Franchise) with the LSC. A solicitor not holding such a franchise may apply to the LSC for an individual case contract (by virtue of which the solicitor is employed on behalf of the LSC to represent an appellant in a given case). Such a contract is sufficient for the purposes of regulation 13.

A11-3 In some circumstances, the Registrar may refer an application to the full court. This may be because there is a novel point of law or because in a sentence case, the sentence passed is unlawful and regardless of the merits, the sentence should be amended. A representation order for counsel is usually granted. Counsel for the prosecution usually attends a Registrar's referral.

A12 Refusal by the single judge

J-15   A12-1 Where the single judge refuses leave to appeal, the Registrar sends a notification of the refusal, including any observations which the judge may have made, to the appellant, who is informed that he may require the application to be considered by the court by serving a renewal notice [Form SJ-Renewal] upon the Registrar within 14 days from the date on which the notice of refusal was served on him.

A12-2 A refused application which is not renewed within 14 days lapses. An appellant may apply for an extension of time in which to renew his application for leave: CAA 1968, s.31, and rule 65.5(2). The Registrar will normally refer such an application to the court to be considered at the same time as the renewed application for leave to appeal. An application for extension for time in which to renew must be supported by cogent reasons.

A12-3 If it is intended that counsel should represent the appellant at the hearing of the renewed application for leave to appeal, whether privately instructed or on a *pro bono* basis, such intention must be communicated to the CAO in writing as soon as that decision has been made. Whilst a representation order is not granted by the Registrar in respect of a renewed application for leave, counsel may apply at the hearing to the court for a representation order to cover that appearance. In practice, this is only granted where the application for leave is successful.

A13 Directions for loss of time

J-16   A13-1 The CAA 1968, s. 29, empowers the court to direct that time spent in custody as an appellant shall not count as part of the term of any sentence to which the appellant is for the time being subject. The court will do so where it considers that an application is wholly without merit. Such an order may not be made where leave to appeal or a trial judge's certificate has been granted, on a reference by the CCRC or where an appeal has been abandoned.

A13-2 The mere fact that counsel has advised that there are grounds of appeal will not be a sufficient answer to the question as to whether or not an application has indeed been brought which was wholly without merit: *R. v. Hart; R. v. George; R. v. Clarke; R. v. Brown* [2007] 1 Cr.App.R. 31.

A13-3 The Form SJ, on which the single judge records his decisions, and the reverse of which is used by appellants to indicate their wish to renew, includes:

- a box for the single judge to initial to indicate that that the full court should consider loss of time if the application is renewed and
- a box for the applicant to give reasons why such an order should not be made, whether or not an indication has been given by a single judge.

A14 Abandonment

A14-1 An appeal or application may be abandoned at any time before the hearing without leave by **J-17** completing and lodging Form A. An oral instruction or letter indicating a wish to abandon is insufficient.

A14-2 At the hearing, an application or appeal can only be abandoned with the permission of the court: rule 65.13(2). An appeal or application which is abandoned is treated as having been dismissed or refused by the full court, as the case may be: rule 65.13(4)(c).

A14-3 A notice of abandonment cannot be withdrawn nor can it be conditional. A person who wants to reinstate an application or appeal after abandonment must apply in writing with reasons: rule 65.13(5). The court has power to allow reinstatement only where the purported abandonment can be treated as a nullity (see *R. v. Medway*, 62 Cr.App.R. 85; *R. v. Burt, The Independent*, December 3, 2004; *R. v. Grant* (2005) 149 S.J. 1186).

A15 Case management duties

A15-1 Rule 65.2 gives the court and parties the same powers and duties of case management as in **J-18** Part 3 of the rules. In accordance with those duties, for each application received, the Registrar nominates a case progression officer (the "responsible officer"). There is also a duty on the parties actively to assist the court to progress cases. Close contact between counsel and solicitors and the responsible officer is encouraged in order to facilitate the efficient preparation and listing of appeals, especially in complex cases and those involving witnesses.

A15-2 Powers exercisable by the single judge and the Registrar are contained in the CAA 1968, s.31. These powers include the power to make procedural directions for the efficient and effective preparation of an application or appeal and the power to make an order under section 23(1)(a) of the 1968 Act for the production of evidence etc. necessary for the determination of the case.

A15-3 Procedural directions given by the Registrar may be appealed to a single judge. Those given by a single judge, including a single Lord Justice, are final.

B. Interlocutory Appeals against Rulings in Preparatory Hearings

Appeal against a ruling under section 9 of the Criminal Justice Act 1987 or a decision under section 35 of the Criminal Procedure and Investigations Act 1996 [Part 66 Criminal Procedure Rules 2007]

B1 Where a judge has ordered a preparatory hearing, he may make a ruling as to the admissibil- **J-19** ity of evidence; any other question of law relating to the case or any question as to the severance or joinder of charges. (s.9(3)(b), (c) and (d) of the 1987 Act/s.31(3)(a), (b) and (c) of the 1996 Act)

B2 Under section 9(11) of the 1987 Act/section 35(1) of the 1996 Act the defence or the prosecution may appeal to the CACD (and ultimately to the House of Lords) against such a ruling, but only with the leave of the trial judge, single judge or the full court. As to the scope of a judge's powers in relation to a preparatory hearing and thus the extent of appeal rights, see *R. v. H* (§ 7-310 in the main work).

B3 If the trial date is imminent and the application is urgent, the Registrar should be notified so that he may consider referring the application directly to the full court and make arrangements for listing.

B4 If an application for leave to appeal is made to the trial judge, it should be made orally immediately after the ruling, or within two business days by serving a notice of an application on the appropriate officer of the Crown Court and all parties directly affected: rule 66.4. Notice of appeal or application for leave to appeal [Form NG (Prep)] is to be served on the Registrar, the Crown Court and the parties within five business days of the ruling or the trial judge's decision whether to grant leave: rule 66.2.

B5 The notice and grounds of appeal having been served on the other parties, grounds of opposition should be served in a respondent's notice [Form RN (Prep)] within five business days of service of the appeal notice: rule 66.5.

B6 Defence representatives are usually covered by the Crown Court representation order if one is in force (Access to Justice Act 1999, Sched. 3, para. 2(2)).

B7 If the relevant time limits are not complied with, the court has power to grant an extension of time, but cogent grounds in support of the application will be required. Where a single judge refuses leave to appeal or an extension of time within which to serve a notice, the application may be renewed for determination by the full court by serving the notice of refusal, appropriately completed, upon the Registrar within five business days of the refusal being served (rule 66.7).

C. Appeals by a Prosecutor Against a "Terminating" Ruling

Criminal Justice Act 2003, s.58 [Part 67 Criminal Procedure Rules 2007]

J-20   C1 Section 58 of the 2003 Act gives the prosecution a right of appeal in relation to a "terminating" ruling: in effect where the prosecution agrees to the defendant's acquittal if the appeal against the ruling is not successful (*R. v. Y.* [2008] 1 Cr.App.R. 34). This is wide enough to encompass a case management decision (*R. v. Clarke* [2008] 1 Cr.App.R. 33).

C2 There is no right of appeal in respect of a ruling that the jury be discharged or a ruling in respect of which there is a right of appeal to the Court of Appeal by virtue of another enactment (s.57(2)). The prosecution should therefore consider whether there is a right of appeal under section 9 of the CJA 1987 or section 35 of the CPIA 1996.

C3 The prosecution must inform the court that it intends to appeal or request an adjournment to consider whether to appeal (s.58(4)), which will be until the next business day (rule 67.2(2)). The judge has a discretion to adjourn for longer if there is a real reason for doing so (*R. v. H.* [2008] EWCA Crim. 483). The prosecution can then ask the trial judge to grant leave to appeal (rule 67.5), although leave to appeal can be granted by the trial judge, the single judge or the full court. The Crown must give the undertaking (as to the defendant's acquittal if the appeal is abandoned or leave to appeal is not obtained) at the time when it informs the court of its intention to appeal. The failure to give it then is fatal to an application to the Court of Appeal for leave: s.58(8); *R. v. Arnold* [2008] R.T.R. 25.

C4 Whether or not leave is granted, the trial judge must then decide if the appeal is to be expedited and if so, adjourn the case. If he decides that the appeal should not be expedited, then he can adjourn the case or discharge the jury (s.59). Leave should be granted only where the trial judge considers there is a real prospect of success and not in an attempt to speed up the hearing of the appeal (*R. v. J.G.* [2006] EWCA Crim. 3276).

C5 Whether the appeal is expedited or not affects the time limits for service of the notice of appeal [Form NG (Pros)] and respondent's notice [Form RN (Pros)]. If expedited, the appeal notice must be served the next business day after the decision, if not expedited, it must be served within five business days. Similar time limits apply to the service of the respondent's notice. Defence representatives are usually covered by the Crown Court representation order if one is in force (such proceedings being considered incidental within the Access to Justice Act 1999, Sched. 3, para. 2(2)). If the relevant time limits are not complied with, the court has power to grant an extension of time.

C6 Expedition does not impose time limits on the Registrar or Court of Appeal. However, if leave has not been granted by the trial judge, the application may be referred to the full court by the Registrar to enable the application and appeal to be heard together to ensure that the matter is dealt with quickly.

C7 The Registrar endeavours to list prosecution appeals where a jury has not been discharged as quickly as possible. He is unlikely to be able to list an appeal in less than a week from the ruling because it is necessary for the prosecution to obtain transcripts, papers to be copied and the judges to read their papers. It is of great assistance if it is anticipated that there is to be an appeal against a ruling where the jury has not been discharged, that a telephone call is made to the Registrar or CAO general office (020 7947 6011) notifying the office even before the appeal notice is sent, so that the list office may be put on notice. The listing of an urgent appeal invariably means that other cases have to be removed from the list.

D. Other Appeals

D1 Prosecution appeal against the making of a confiscation order or where the court declines to make one (save on reconsideration of benefit)

J-21
- S.31 of the PCA 2002.
- Parts 71 and 72 of the Criminal Procedure Rules.
- From April 1, 2008 only the prosecution can appeal
- Proceedings are commenced by serving a Form PoCA 1 on the defendant and the Crown Court within 28 days of the decision appealed against. [Proceeds of Crime Act (Appeals under Part 2) Order 2003, art. 3(2)(a).]

- A respondent's notice PoCA 2 is to be served on the Registrar of Criminal Appeals and the appellant not later than 14 days after receiving PoCA 1.
- An undischarged Crown Court representation order will cover advice and assistance on the merits of opposing the appeal and drafting the respondent's notice, otherwise an application for a representation order can be made to the Registrar [Access to Justice Act 1999, ss.12(2)(b), 26]. In any event, where an application for a representation order is made on PoCA 2, the Registrar will consider a representation order for the hearing.
- Leave to appeal can be granted by a single judge or the full court.

D2 Appeal in relation to a restraint order
- S.43 of the PCA 2002.   **J-22**
- Parts 71 and 73 of the Criminal Procedure Rules.
- The prosecution or an accredited financial investigator can appeal a refusal to make a restraint order. A person who applied for an order or who is affected by the order can apply to the Crown Court to vary or discharge the order and then appeal that decision to the Court of Appeal.
- Proceedings are commenced by serving a form PoCA 3 on the Crown Court within 14 days of the decision being appealed. PoCA 3 must then be served on any respondent, and on any person who holds realisable property to which the appeal relates, or is affected by the appeal, not later than seven days after the form is lodged at the Crown Court. The documents which are to be served with PoCA 3 are set out in rule 73.2(3).
- A respondent's notice PoCA 4 is to be served on the Registrar not later than 14 days after the respondent is notified that the appellant has leave to appeal or notified that the application for leave and any appeal are to be heard together. PoCA 4 is then to be served on the appellant and any other respondent as soon as is practicable and not later than seven days after it was served on the Registrar.
- An application for a restraint order can be made as soon as a criminal investigation has begun. The proposed defendant may not have been charged: PCA 2002, s.40. This affects the type of public funding.
- If a defendant has been charged with a criminal offence connected to the restraint order then the restraint proceedings are regarded as incidental to the criminal proceedings and are treated as criminal proceedings for funding purposes [Criminal Defence Service (General) (No. 2) Regulations 2001, reg.3(3)(c)] and the Registrar can grant a representation order if a defendant appeals a decision on an application to vary or discharge the restraint order.
- If the prosecution apply for a restraint order in the Crown Court before the subject of the restraint order has been charged with a criminal offence and the subject of that order wishes to appeal a decision on an application to vary or discharge the restraint order then civil legal aid may be available as these proceedings fall within the Access to Justice Act 1999, Sched. 2, para. 3. The Legal Services Commission should be contacted for funding within the Community Legal Service scheme.
- Similarly, a person affected by the order who wishes to appeal a decision on an application to vary or discharge the restraint order should apply to the Legal Services Commission for funding within the Community Legal Service scheme.
- Leave to appeal can be granted by a single judge or full court.

D3 Appeal in relation to a receivership order
- S.65 of the PCA 2002.   **J-23**
- Parts 71 and 73 of the Criminal Procedure Rules.
- An appeal can be brought by:
  (a) the person who applied for the order,
  (b) a person who is affected by the order or,
  (c) the receiver.
  The orders against which an appeal will lie are:
  (1) the appointment or non-appointment of a receiver,
  (2) the powers of a receiver,
  (3) an order giving a direction to a receiver, and
  (4) the variation or discharge of a receivership order.
- Proceedings are commenced by serving a Form PoCA 3 on the Crown Court within 14 days of the decision being appealed. PoCA 3 must then be served on any respondent and

on any person who holds realisable property to which the appeal relates, or is affected by the appeal, not later than seven days after the form is lodged at the Crown Court. The documents which are to be served with PoCA 3 are set out in rule 73.2(3).

- A respondent's notice PoCA 4 is to be served on the Registrar not later than 14 days after the respondent is notified that the appellant has leave to appeal or is notified that the application for leave and any appeal are to be heard together. PoCA 4 is then to be served on the appellant and any other respondent as soon as is practicable and not later than seven days after it was served on the Registrar.
- If a defendant has been charged with a criminal offence connected to a receivership order then the receivership proceedings are regarded as incidental to the criminal proceedings and are treated as criminal proceedings for funding purposes [Criminal Defence Service (General) (No. 2) Regulations 2001, reg.3(3)(c)] and the Registrar can grant a representation order if a defendant appeals a decision relating to a receivership order.
- If a management receivership order or an application for such an order is made in the Crown Court before a criminal offence has been charged and a person affected by the order (including the proposed defendant) wishes to appeal a decision then civil legal aid may be available as these proceedings fall within Access to Justice Act 1999, Sched. 2, para. 3. The Legal Services Commission should be contacted for funding within the Community Legal Service scheme.
- Leave to appeal can be granted by a single judge or the full court.

D4 Appeal against an order of the Crown Court in the exercise of its jurisdiction to punish for contempt – usually a finding of contempt or sentence for contempt

J-24
- S.13 of the Administration of Justice Act 1960.
- Part 68 of the Criminal Procedure Rules.
- Anyone dealt with by the Crown Court for contempt may appeal.
- Proceedings are commenced by lodging a Form NG at the Crown Court not more than 28 days after the order to be appealed.
- The Registrar may direct a respondent's notice Form RN or the Crown may serve one if they wish to make representations to the court.
- An undischarged Crown Court representation order will cover advice and assistance on appeal. The Registrar will usually grant a representation order for the hearing: Access to Justice Act 1999, s.12(2)(b).
- No leave to appeal is required. The appeal is as of right.
- Appeals occur most frequently when an appellant wishes to appeal a sentence for failing to appear at the Crown Court as the failing to appear is dealt with as if it were contempt.

D5 Appeal against a minimum term set or reviewed by a High Court judge

J-25
- Para. 14 of Schedule 22 to the CJA 2003
- Part 68 of the Criminal Procedure Rules
- A defendant with a mandatory life sentence imposed before December 18, 2003 who has had his minimum term set or reviewed by a High Court judge can appeal.
- Proceedings are commenced by service of Form NG (MT) on the Registrar not more than 28 days after the decision.
- The Registrar may direct a respondent's notice Form RN or the Crown may serve one if they wish to make representations to the court.
- An application for a representation order can be made to the Registrar [Access to Justice Act 1999, s.12(2)(b)].
- Leave to appeal is required and can be granted by the full court or a single judge: Criminal Justice Act 2003 (Mandatory Life Sentences: Appeals in Transitional Cases) Order 2005 (S.I. 2005 No. 2798), art. 8.

D6 Attorney General's reference of an unduly lenient sentence

J-26
- S.36 of the CJA 1988.
- Part 70 of the Criminal Procedure Rules.
- The Attorney General can refer sentences only in relation to specific offences or sentences [CJA 1988, ss.35, 36, and Criminal Justice Act 1988 (Reviews of Sentencing) Order 2006] including a minimum term, set or reviewed by a High Court judge [CJA 2003, Sched. 22, para. 15].

- Although rule 70.3(1) implies there is a specific form to commence proceedings, in practice a standard letter with supporting documents is sent by the Attorney General's office no more than 28 days after sentence.
- If the defendant wishes to make representations to the court he must serve a respondent's notice within 14 days of the Registrar serving the application upon him. Again, there is no specific form designated.
- Representation orders are not issued to respond to an Attorney General's reference but a defendant who appears by counsel is entitled to his reasonable costs from central funds. The cost of instructing leading counsel in addition to or instead of junior counsel is generally not considered reasonable unless there is a compelling reason. It is advisable to consult with the Registrar before leading counsel is instructed.
- The leave of the Court of Appeal is required.

D7 Attorney General's reference of a point of law on an acquittal

J-27

- S.36 of the CJA 1972.
- Part 70 of the Criminal Procedure Rules.
- The Attorney General can refer a point of law to the Court of Appeal for an opinion on the acquittal on indictment of the defendant.
- Although rule 70.3(1) implies there is a specific form to commence proceedings, there is no such form and rule 70.3 sets out what should be included in the reference. The defendant should not be identified.
- There is no time limit.
- If the defendant wishes to make representations to the court he must serve a respondent's notice within 28 days of the Registrar serving the application upon him. Again there is no specific form.
- Representation orders are not issued to respond to an Attorney General's reference but a defendant who appears by counsel is entitled to his reasonable costs from central funds.
- Leave is not required.

D8 Appeal against a finding of unfitness to plead or a finding that the accused did the act or made the omission charged

J-28

- S.15 of the CAA 1968.
- Part 68 of the Criminal Procedure Rules.
- The accused can appeal (by the person appointed to represent the accused) against
  — a finding of unfitness to plead (but not fitness to plead as the defendant can appeal any subsequent conviction in the usual way on the basis he was not fit to plead) or
  — that he did the act or made the omission charged or
  — both findings.
  The appeal does not lie until both findings have been made.
- Proceedings are commenced by the service of Form NG on the Crown Court not more than 28 days after the finding made which the accused wishes to appeal.
- The Crown should serve a respondent's notice Form RN if directed by the Registrar or if they wish to make representations to the court.
- There does not appear to be any statutory provision empowering the grant of a representation order. The Prosecution of Offences Act 1985, s.19, refers to costs from central funds being available to cover the fees of a person appointed by the Crown Court under section 4A of the Criminal Procedure (Insanity) Act 1964. In *R. v. Antoine* ([1999] 2 Cr.App.R 225, CA) this was interpreted to include the costs of an appeal. The Prosecution of Offences Act 1985, s.16(4) provides that where the Court of Appeal allows an appeal under Part 1 of the CAA 1968 against a finding under the Criminal Procedure (Insanity) Act 1964 that the appellant is under a disability, or that he did the act or made the omission charged against him the court may make a defendant's costs order in favour of the accused.
- Leave to appeal may be granted by the Crown Court judge, a single judge or the full court.

D9 Appeal against a verdict of not guilty by reason of insanity

J-29

- S.12 of the CAA 1968.
- Part 68 of the Criminal Procedure Rules.
- The defendant can appeal a verdict of not guilty by reason of insanity.

- Proceedings are commenced by the service of Form NG on the Crown Court not more than 28 days after the verdict.
- The Crown should serve a respondent's notice Form RN if directed by the Registrar or if they wish to make representations to the court.
- There does not appear to be any statutory provision empowering the grant of a representation order. The Prosecution of Offences Act 1985, s.16(4), provides that where the Court of Appeal <u>allows an appeal</u> then the court may make a defendant's costs order. If the appeal is not allowed costs from central funds should be available on the same basis as was allowed in *Antoine* (*ante*) in the absence of any statutory provision.
- Leave to appeal may be granted by the Crown Court judge, a single judge or the full court.

D10 Appeal against the order following a verdict of not guilty by reason of insanity or a finding of unfitness to plead

J-30
- S.16A of the CAA 1968.
- Part 68 of the Criminal Procedure Rules.
- An accused who, as a result of a verdict of not guilty by reason of insanity or a finding of fitness to plead has a hospital order, interim hospital order or supervision order made against him may appeal against the order.
- Proceedings are commenced by the service of Form NG on the Crown Court not more than 28 days after the order.
- [As D9, *ante*.]
- [As D9, *ante*.]
- [As D9, *ante*.]

D11 Appeal against review of sentence

J-31
- S.74(8) of the SOCPA 2005.
- Part 68 of the Criminal Procedure Rules.
- A defendant or specified prosecutor may appeal.
- Proceedings are commenced by serving a Form NG (RD) on the Crown Court not more than 28 days after the review.
- A respondent's notice Form RN should be served if directed by the Registrar or if the respondent wishes to make representations to the Court.
- An application for a representation order can be made to the Registrar: Access to Justice Act 1999, s.12(2)(b).
- Leave to appeal can be granted by the single judge or full court [Serious Organised Crime and Police Act 2005 (Appeals under section 74) Order 2006 (S.I. 2006 No. 2135)].

D12 Appeal against an order for trial by jury of sample counts

J-32
- S.18 of the Domestic Violence, Crime and Victims Act 2004.
- Part 66 of the Criminal Procedure Rules.
- The defendant can appeal.
- An application for the jury to try some counts as sample counts and the judge to try the remainder if the jury convict, must be determined at a preparatory hearing and section 18 confers rights of interlocutory appeal. A Form NG (Prep) must be served on the Crown Court, the Registrar and any party directly affected not more than five business days after the order or the Crown Court judge granting or refusing leave. (*For applications to the Crown Court judge, see Part B above.*)
- A respondent's notice Form RN (Prep) should be served if the court directs or the Crown (or any party affected) wants to make representations to the court.
- Defence representatives are usually covered by the Crown Court representation order if one is in force [Access to Justice Act 1999, Sched. 3, para. 2(2)].
- The Crown Court Judge, single judge or full court can grant leave to appeal.

D13 Appeal against an order relating to a trial to be conducted without a jury where there is a danger of jury tampering

J-33
- S.9(11) of the CJA 1987 and s.35(1) of the CPIA 1996.
- Part 66 of the Criminal Procedure Rules.
- The prosecution can appeal the refusal to make an order; the defence can appeal the making of an order.

- A Form NG (Prep) must be served on the Crown Court, the Registrar and any party directly affected not more than five business days after the order or the Crown Court judge grants or refuses leave. (*For applications to the Crown Court judge, see Part B above.*)
- A respondent's notice Form RN (Prep) should be served if the court directs or the Crown (or any party affected) wants to make representations to the court.
- Defence representatives are usually covered by the Crown Court representation order if one is in force [Access to Justice Act 1999, Sched. 3, para.2 (2)].
- Leave is required. The Crown Court judge, single judge or full court can grant leave to appeal.

D14 Appeal against an order that a trial should continue without a jury or a new trial take place without a jury after jury tampering

- S.47 of the CJA 2003.   **J-34**
- Part 66 of the Criminal Procedure Rules (relating to appeals against an order made in a preparatory hearing notwithstanding the ruling will not have been in the context of a preparatory hearing).
- The defendant can appeal.
- As D13, *ante*
- As D13, *ante*
- As D13, *ante*
- As D13, *ante*

D15 Appeal against orders restricting or preventing reports or restricting public access

- S.159 of the CJA 1988   **J-35**
- Part 69 of the Criminal Procedure Rules
- A person aggrieved may appeal.
- Applications against orders restricting reporting shall be made within 10 business days after the date on which the order was made by serving Form NG (159) on the Registrar, the Crown Court, the prosecutor and defendant and any other affected person. Applications against orders to restrict public access must be made the next business day after the order was made. If advance notice of an order restricting public access is given, then advance notice of an intention to appeal may be made not more than five business days after the advance notice is displayed.
- A person on whom an appeal notice is served should serve a respondent's notice Form RN (159) within three business days if he wishes to make representations to the court or the court so directs.
- The court may make such order as to costs as it thinks fit (CJA 1988, s.159(5)(c)), but not out of central funds - *Holden v. CPS (No. 2)* [1994] 1 A.C. 22, HL.
- A single judge or the full court can grant leave to appeal: CAA 1968, s.31(2B).
- Applications for leave to appeal and appeals in relation to reporting restrictions may be heard in private (rule 65.6 (1)). Applications for leave to appeal and appeals relating to restricting public access must be determined without a hearing (rule 65.6(3)).

D16 Appeal against a wasted costs order and appeal against a third party costs order

- Regulation 3C (costs wasted) and 3E (third party costs) of the Costs in Criminal Cases **J-36** (General) Regulations 1986.
- A legal or other representative against whom a wasted costs order has been made in the Crown Court or a third party against whom a third party costs order has been made may appeal.
- Notice of appeal should be served on the Crown Court within 21 days of the order being made. There is no specific form. The notice should be served on any interested party (including, if appropriate, the Ministry of Justice).
- Any interested party can make representations orally or in writing.
- There is no power to grant a representation order or to order costs out of central funds as these proceedings are civil in nature.
- Leave to appeal is not required.

D17 Appeal relating to serious crime prevention orders

- S.24 of the SCA 2007.   **J-37**

- Part 68 of the Criminal Procedure Rules.
- A person subject to the order, an applicant authority or anyone given the opportunity to make representations at the Crown Court about the making, refusal to make, variation or non-variation of an order may appeal.
- Proceedings are commenced by the service of Form NG (SCPO) on the Crown Court not more than 28 days after the order.
- A respondent's notice Form RN (SCPO) should be served if directed by the Registrar or if the respondent wishes to make representations to the court.
- Proceedings before the Crown Court or the Court of Appeal relating to serious crime prevention orders and arising by virtue of section 19, 20, 21 or 24 of the SCA 2007 are criminal proceedings for the purposes of section 12(2)(g) of the Access to Justice Act 1999 [see the Criminal Defence Service (General) (No. 2) (Amendment) Regulations (S.I. 2008 No. 725)]. Accordingly, the Registrar may grant a representation order to a person subject to the order. A person who made representations at the Crown Court can apply to the LSC for funding. The court has discretion to order costs as it thinks fit [Serious Crime Act 2007 (Appeals under section 24) Order 2008 (S.I. 2008 No. 1863), Pt 3].
- Leave to appeal can be granted by the Crown Court judge, full court or single judge [S.I. 2008 No. 1863, art. 9].

D18 Appeal against the non-making of a football banning order

J-38
- S.14A(5A) of the Football Spectators Act 1989.
- Part 68 of the Criminal Procedure Rules.
- The prosecution can appeal.
- The appeal notice should be served on the Crown Court within 28 days of the decision not to make an order. However, there is no designated form.
- A respondent's notice should be served if directed by the Registrar or if the respondent wishes to make representations to the court. However, again there is no designated form.
- An application for a representation order may be made to the Registrar - Access to Justice Act 1999, s.12(2)(b).
- Currently, the Court of Appeal has been given no powers to deal with these appeals.

E. Application for a Retrial for a Serious Offence

E1 Application by a prosecutor to quash an acquittal and seek a retrial for a qualifying offence

S.76(1) of the Criminal Justice Act 2003 [Part 41 of the Criminal Procedure Rules]

J-39   E1-1 There must be new and compelling evidence and it must be in the interests of justice for the acquitted person to be retried for a qualifying offence as listed in the CJA 2003, Sched. 5, Pt 1 (CJA 2003, ss.78, 79: see *R. v. Dunlop* [2007] 1 Cr.App.R. 8, and *R. v. Miell* [2008] 1 Cr.App.R. 23).

E1-2 Proceedings can begin in one of two ways.

(1) By serving notice of the application under section 76 on the Court of Appeal and within two days serving the notice on the acquitted person (s.80). This notice charges him with the offence. It requires the personal written consent of the Director of Public Prosecutions (DPP) (s.76(3)). If the acquitted person is not in custody the prosecution can ask the Crown Court to issue:

(i) a summons for the acquitted person to appear before the Court of Appeal for the hearing of the application or

(ii) a warrant for his arrest (s.89(3)).

Once arrested on the warrant the acquitted person must be brought before the Crown Court within 48 hours (s.89(6)).

(2) An acquitted person may be charged with the offence before an application under section 76 has been made. This may be after an arrest in an investigation authorised by the DPP (s.85(2)) or where no authorisation has been given, after arrest under a warrant issued by a justice of the peace (s.87(1)). Having been charged, the acquitted person must be brought before the Crown Court to consider bail within 24 hours (s.88(2)). He can then be remanded in custody or on bail for 42 days whilst an application under s.76 is prepared: s.88(6) unless an extension is granted under subsection (8). Once a notice of application under section 76 has been served, stating that the acquitted person has previously been charged with the offence, the acquitted person must be brought before the Crown Court to consider bail within 48 hours of the notice being given to the Registrar, if the acquitted person is already in custody under secton 88 (*ante*) (s.89(2)).

E1-3 Thus in either case, bail is dealt with largely by the Crown Court. The Court of Appeal only considers bail on the adjournment of the hearing of the application under section 76 (s.90(1)).

E1-4 The notice ["Notice of a s.76 application required by s.80(1) Criminal Justice Act 2003"] should where practicable be accompanied by the witness statements which are relied on as the new and compelling evidence, the original witness statements, unused statements, indictment, paper exhibits from the original trial, any relevant transcripts from the original trial and any other documents relied on: rule 41.2(2).

E1-5 An acquitted person who wants to oppose a section 76 application must serve a response ["Response of the acquitted person under s.80 Criminal Justice Act 2003"] not more than 28 days after receiving the notice: rule 41.3(2).

E2 Application by a prosecutor for a determination whether a foreign acquittal is a bar to a trial and if so, an order that it not be a bar

S.76(2) of the Criminal Justice Act 2003 [Part 41 of the Criminal Procedure Rules]

E2-1 The prosecution can apply, with the personal written consent of the DPP (s.76(3)) for a **J-40** determination whether an acquittal outside the UK is a bar to the acquitted person being tried in England and Wales and if it is found to be so, an order that the acquittal not be a bar. Proceedings can begin in the same way as for an application under section 76(1).

E3 Application for restrictions on publication relating to an application under section 76

S.82 of the Criminal Justice Act 2003 [Part 41 of the Criminal Procedure Rules]

E3-1 An application can be made by the DPP for reporting restrictions. This can be made after a **J-41** notice of an application for a retrial has been made and may also be made by the court of its own motion (s.82(5)). An application can also be made by the DPP for reporting restrictions *before* a notice of an application for a retrial if an investigation has been commenced: s.82(6). The application for reporting restrictions must be served on the Registrar ["Application for restrictions on publication under s.82 Criminal Justice Act 2003"] and (usually) the acquitted person (rule 41.8(1)).

E3-2 A party who wants to vary or revoke an order for restrictions on publication under section 82(7) may apply to the Court of Appeal in writing at any time after the order was made (rule 41.9(1)).

E4 Representation orders

E4-1 The Registrar will usually grant a representation order to the acquitted person for solicitors **J-42** and counsel to respond to any of the above applications.

APPENDIX K

Guidelines issued by the
Sentencing Guidelines Council
and by the Sentencing Council
for England and Wales

I. GUIDELINES

A. REDUCTION IN SENTENCE FOR A GUILTY PLEA

GUIDELINE

CONTENTS

FOREWORD

K-2   One of the first guidelines to be issued by the Sentencing Guidelines Council related to the statutory obligation to take account of any guilty plea when determining sentence. As set out in the foreword to that guideline,[1] the intention was "to promote consistency in sentencing by providing clarity for courts, court users and victims so that everyone knows exactly what to expect". Prior to that guideline there had been different understandings of the purpose of the reduction and the extent of any reduction given.

Since the guideline was issued, there has been much greater clarity but there still remain concerns about some of the content of the guideline and about the extent to which the guideline has been consistently applied. Accordingly the council has undertaken a review of the guideline (in accordance with the statutory obligation placed upon it to do so from time to time[2]); it has also requested that the Judicial Studies Board consider further ways in which judicial training can incorporate the guideline.

The council is extremely grateful to the Sentencing Advisory Panel for the speed and thoroughness with which it has prepared its advice following extensive consultation. The council has accepted almost all the recommendations of the panel; the issues and arguments are set out fully in the panel's advice (see www.sentencing-guidelines.gov.uk). This revised guideline applies to all cases sentenced on or after 23 July 2007.

The council has agreed with the panel that the general approach of the guideline is correct in setting out clearly the purpose of the reduction for a guilty plea, in settling for a reduction no greater than one third (with lower levels of reduction where a plea is entered other than at the first reasonable opportunity) and in continuing to provide for a special approach when fixing the minimum term for a life sentence imposed following conviction for murder.

The council has agreed with the panel that some discretion should be introduced to the approach where the prosecution case is "overwhelming".

The council has not accepted the panel's recommendation in relation to circumstances where a magistrates' court is sentencing an offender for a number of offences where the overall maximum imprisonment is six months. The council continues to consider that there must be some incentive to plead guilty in such circumstances; this is consistent with other aspects of the guideline.

The council has not accepted the panel's recommendation in relation to the "capping" of the effect of reduction on very large fines. The number of such fines is very low and the council was not convinced that the arguments were strong enough to justify a departure from the general approach in the guideline not to "cap" the effect of the reduction. In addition, the revised guideline provides guidance as to when the "first reasonable opportunity" is likely to occur in relation to indictable only offences; emphasises that remorse and material assistance provided to prosecuting authorities are separate issues from those to which the guideline applies and makes clear that the approach to calculation of the reduction where an indeterminate sentence is imposed (other than that following conviction for murder) should be the same as that for determinate sentences.

---

[1] Published December 2004.
[2] Criminal Justice Act 2003, s.170(4).

Since the guideline was issued in 2004, there have been changes in the statutory provisions governing the reduction for guilty plea and in those relating to sentences for public protection. The review has provided an opportunity to bring the guideline up to date and those changes have been incorporated.

The council published a draft guideline in accordance with section 170(8) of the Criminal Justice Act 2003 inviting responses by 14 March 2007. A response has been received from the Home Affairs Committee, a response has been received from the Attorney General and seven other responses have been received. A summary of the responses and the decisions of the council has been published separately.

Chairman of the Council
July 2007

A. Statutory Provisions

Section 144 Criminal Justice Act 2003 provides [the guideline here sets out the text of section 144   **K-3** of the 2003 Act, set out in the main work at § 5-107].

Section 174(2) Criminal Justice Act 2003 provides [the guideline here sets out the text of section 174(2)(d) of the 2003 Act, set out in the main work at § 5-165].

1.1 This guideline applies whether a case is dealt with in a magistrates' court or in the Crown Court and whenever practicable in the youth court (taking into account legislative restrictions such as those relevant to the length of detention and training orders).

1.2 The application of this guideline to sentencers when arriving at the appropriate minimum term for the offence of murder is set out in Section F.

1.3 This guideline can also be found at www.sentencing-guidelines.gov.uk or can be obtained from the Council's Secretariat at 4th Floor, 8–10 Great George Street, London SW1P 3AE.

B. Statement of Purpose

2.1 When imposing a custodial sentence, statute requires that a court must impose the shortest   **K-4** term that is commensurate with the seriousness of the offence(s)[3]. Similarly, when imposing a community order, the restrictions on liberty must be commensurate with the seriousness of the offence(s)[4]. Once that decision is made, a court is required to give consideration to the reduction for any guilty plea. As a result, the final sentence after the reduction for a guilty plea will be less than the seriousness of the offence requires.

2.2 A reduction in sentence is appropriate because a guilty plea avoids the need for a trial (thus enabling other cases to be disposed of more expeditiously), shortens the gap between charge and sentence, saves considerable cost, and, in the case of an early plea, saves victims and witnesses from the concern about having to give evidence. The reduction principle derives from the need for the effective administration of justice and not as an aspect of mitigation.

2.3 Where a sentencer is in doubt as to whether a custodial sentence is appropriate, the reduction attributable to a guilty plea will be a relevant consideration. Where this is amongst the factors leading to the imposition of a non-custodial sentence, there will be no need to apply a further reduction on account of the guilty plea. A similar approach is appropriate where the reduction for a guilty plea is amongst the factors leading to the imposition of a financial penalty or discharge instead of a community order.

2.4 When deciding the most appropriate length of sentence, the sentencer should address separately the issue of remorse, together with any other mitigating features, before calculating the reduction for the guilty plea. Similarly, assistance to the prosecuting or enforcement authorities is a separate issue which may attract a reduction in sentence under other procedures; care will need to be taken to ensure that there is no "double counting".

2.5 The implications of other offences that an offender has asked to be taken into consideration should be reflected in the sentence before the reduction for guilty plea has been applied.

2.6 A reduction in sentence should only be applied to the punitive elements of a penalty[5]. The guilty plea reduction has no impact on sentencing decisions in relation to ancillary orders, including orders of disqualification from driving.

C. Application of the Reduction Principle

3.1 Recommended approach   **K-5**

---

[3] Criminal Justice Act 2003, s.153(2).
[4] Criminal Justice Act 2003, s.148(2).
[5] Where a court imposes an indeterminate sentence for public protection, the reduction principle applies in the normal way to the determination of the minimum term (see para. 5.1, footnote and para. 7 below) but release from custody requires the authorisation of the Parole Board once that minimum term has been served.

> The court decides sentence for the offence(s) taking into account aggravating and mitigating factors and any other offences that have been formally admitted (TICs)
>
> ⇩
>
> The court selects the amount of the reduction by reference to the sliding scale
>
> ⇩
>
> The court applies the reduction
>
> ⇩
>
> When pronouncing sentence the court should usually state what the sentence would have been if there had been no reduction as a result of the guilty plea.

D. Determining the Level of Reduction

K-6

4.1 The level of reduction should be *a proportion of the total sentence* imposed, with the proportion calculated by reference to the circumstances in which the guilty plea was indicated, in particular the stage in the proceedings. The greatest reduction will be given where the plea was indicated at the "first reasonable opportunity".

4.2 Save where section 144(2) of the 2003 Act applies[6], the level of the reduction will be gauged on a *sliding scale* ranging from a recommended *one third* (where the guilty plea was entered at the first reasonable opportunity in relation to the offence for which sentence is being imposed), reducing to a recommended *one quarter* (where a trial date has been set) and to a recommended *one tenth* (for a guilty plea entered at the 'door of the court' or after the trial has begun). *See diagram below.*

4.3 The level of reduction should reflect the stage at which the offender indicated a *willingness to admit guilt* to the offence for which he is eventually sentenced:

(i) the largest recommended reduction will not normally be given unless the offender indicated willingness to admit guilt at the first reasonable opportunity; when this occurs will vary from case to case (see *Annex 1 for illustrative examples*);

(ii) where the admission of guilt comes later than the first reasonable opportunity, the reduction for guilty plea will normally be less than one third;

(iii) where the plea of guilty comes very late, it is still appropriate to give some reduction;

(iv) if after pleading guilty there is a *Newton* hearing and the offender's version of the circumstances of the offence is rejected, this should be taken into account in determining the level of reduction;

(v) if the not guilty plea was entered and maintained for tactical reasons (such as to retain privileges whilst on remand), a late guilty plea should attract very little, if any, discount.

---

[6] See section A above.

In each category, there is a presumption that the recommended reduction will be given unless there are good reasons for a lower amount.

First reasonable opportunity	After a trial date is set	Door of the court/ after trial has begun

======= | ============ | ============ |

recommended 1/3   recommended 1/4   recommended 1/10

E. Witholding a Reduction

On the basis of dangerousness

5.1   Where a sentence for a "dangerous offender" is imposed under the provisions in the Criminal **K-7** Justice Act 2003, whether the sentence requires the calculation of a minimum term or is an extended sentence, the approach will be the same as for any other determinate sentence (see also section G below)[7].

Where the prosecution case is overwhelming

5.2   The purpose of giving credit is to encourage those who are guilty to plead at the earliest opportunity. Any defendant is entitled to put the prosecution to proof and so every defendant who is guilty should be encouraged to indicate that guilt at the first reasonable opportunity.

5.3   Where the prosecution case is overwhelming, it may not be appropriate to give the full reduction that would otherwise be given. Whilst there is a presumption in favour of the full reduction being given where a plea has been indicated at the first reasonable opportunity, the fact that the prosecution case is overwhelming without relying on admissions from the defendant may be a reason justifying departure from the guideline.

5.4   Where a court is satisfied that a lower reduction should be given for this reason, a recommended reduction of 20% is likely to be appropriate where the guilty plea was indicated at the first reasonable opportunity.

5.5   A court departing from a guideline must state the reasons for doing so[8].

Where the maximum penalty for the offence is thought to be too low

5.6   The sentencer is bound to sentence for the offence with which the offender has been charged, and to which he has pleaded guilty. The sentencer cannot remedy perceived defects (for example an inadequate charge or maximum penalty) by refusal of the appropriate discount.

Where jurisdictional issues arise

(i) Where sentencing powers are limited to six months' imprisonment despite multiple offences

5.7 When the total sentence for both or all of the offences is six months' imprisonment, a court may determine to impose consecutive sentences which, even allowing for a reduction for a guilty plea where appropriate on each offence, would still result in the imposition of the maximum sentence available. In such circumstances, in order to achieve the purpose for which the reduction principle has been established[9], some modest allowance should normally be given against the total sentence for the entry of a guilty plea.

(ii) Where a maximum sentence might still be imposed

5.8 Despite a guilty plea being entered which would normally attract a reduction in sentence, a magistrates' court may impose a sentence of imprisonment of 6 months for a single either-way offence where, but for the plea, that offence would have been committed to the Crown Court for sentence.

---

[7] There will be some cases arising from offences committed before the commencement of the relevant provisions of the Criminal Justice Act 2003 in which a court will determine that a longer than commensurate, extended, or indeterminate sentence is required for the protection of the public. In such a case, the minimum custodial term (but not the protection of public element of the sentence) should be reduced to reflect the plea.

[8] Criminal Justice Act 2003, s.174(2)(a).

[9] See section B above.

5.9 Similarly, a detention and training order of 24 months may be imposed on an offender aged under 18 if the offence is one which would but for the plea have attracted a sentence of long-term detention in excess of 24 months under the Powers of Criminal Courts (Sentencing) Act 2000, s.91.

F. Application to Sentencing for Murder

K-8   6.1 Murder has always been regarded as the most serious criminal offence and the sentence prescribed is different from other sentences. By law, the sentence for murder is imprisonment (detention) for life and an offender will remain subject to the sentence for the rest of his/her life.

6.2 The decision whether to release the offender from custody during this sentence will be taken by the Parole Board which will consider whether it is safe to release the offender on licence. The court that imposes the sentence is required by law to set a minimum term that has to be served before the Parole Board may start to consider whether to authorise release on licence. If an offender is released, the licence continues for the rest of the offender's life and recall to prison is possible at any time.

6.3 Uniquely, Parliament has set starting points[10] (based on the circumstances of the killing) which a court will apply when it fixes the minimum term. Parliament has further prescribed that, having identified the appropriate starting point, the court must then consider whether to increase or reduce it in the light of aggravating or mitigating factors, some of which are listed in statute. Finally, Parliament specifically provides[11] that the obligation to have regard to any guilty plea applies to the fixing of the minimum term, by making the same statutory provisions that apply to other offences apply to murder without limiting the court's discretion (as it did with other sentences under the Powers of Criminal Courts (Sentencing) Act 2000).

6.4 There are important differences between the usual fixed term sentence and the minimum term set following the imposition of the mandatory life sentence for murder. The most significant of these, from the sentencer's point of view, is that a reduction for a plea of guilty in the case of murder will have double the effect on time served in custody when compared with a determinate sentence. This is because a determinate sentence will provide (in most circumstances) for the release of the offender[12] on licence half way through the total sentence whereas in the case of murder a minimum term is the period in custody before consideration is given by the Parole Board to whether release is appropriate.

6.5 Given this difference, the special characteristic of the offence of murder and the unique statutory provision of starting points, careful consideration will need to be given to the extent of any reduction and to the need to ensure that the minimum term properly reflects the seriousness of the offence. Whilst the general principles continue to apply (both that a guilty plea should be encouraged and that the extent of any reduction should reduce if the indication of plea is later than the first reasonable opportunity), the process of determining the level of reduction will be different.

6.6 Approach

K-9   1. Where a court determines that there should be a whole life minimum term, there will be no reduction for a guilty plea.

    2. In other circumstances,

        (a) the court will weigh carefully the overall length of the minimum term taking into account other reductions for which the offender may be eligible so as to avoid a combination leading to an inappropriately short sentence;

        (b) where it is appropriate to reduce the minimum term having regard to a plea of guilty, the reduction will not exceed one sixth and will never exceed five years;

        (c) the sliding scale will apply so that, where it is appropriate to reduce the minimum term on account of a guilty plea, the maximum reduction (one sixth or five years whichever is the less) is only available where there has been an indication of willingness to plead guilty at the first reasonable opportunity, with a recommended 5% for a late guilty plea;

        (d) the court should then review the sentence to ensure that the minimum term accurately reflects the seriousness of the offence taking account of the statutory starting point, all aggravating and mitigating factors and any guilty plea entered.

---

[10] Criminal Justice Act 2003, Schedule 21.
[11] Criminal Justice Act 2003, Schedule 1, para 12(c).
[12] In accordance with the provisions of the Criminal Justice Act 2003.

G. Application to other Indeterminate Sentences

7.1 There are other circumstances in which an indeterminate sentence will be imposed. This may **K-10** be a discretionary life sentence or imprisonment for public protection.

7.2 As with the mandatory life sentence imposed following conviction for murder, the court will be obliged to fix a minimum term to be served before the Parole Board is able to consider whether the offender can be safely released.

7.3 However, the process by which that minimum term is fixed is different from that followed in relation to the mandatory life sentence and requires the court first to determine what the equivalent determinate sentence would have been. Accordingly, the approach to the calculation of the reduction for any guilty plea should follow the process and scale adopted in relation to determinate sentences, as set out in section D above.

ANNEX 1

First reasonable opportunity

1. The critical time for determining the maximum reduction for a guilty plea is the first reason- **K-11** able opportunity for the defendant to have indicated a willingness to plead guilty. This opportunity will vary with a wide range of factors and the court will need to make a judgement on the particular facts of the case before it.

2. The key principle is that the purpose of giving a reduction is to recognise the benefits that come from a guilty plea not only for those directly involved in the case in question but also in enabling courts more quickly to deal with other outstanding cases.

3. This Annex seeks to help courts to adopt a consistent approach by giving examples of circumstances where a determination will have to be made:

(a) the first reasonable opportunity may be the first time that a defendant appears before the court and has the opportunity to plead guilty;

(b) but the court may consider that it would be reasonable to have expected an indication of willingness even earlier, perhaps whilst under interview;

Note: For (a) and (b) to apply, the court will need to be satisfied that the defendant (and any legal adviser) would have had sufficient information about the allegations

(c) where an offence triable either way is committed to the Crown Court for trial and the defendant pleads guilty at the first hearing in that court, the reduction will be less than if there had been an indication of a guilty plea given to the magistrates' court (recommended reduction of one third) but more than if the plea had been entered after a trial date had been set (recommended reduction of one quarter), and is likely to be in the region of 30%;

(d) where an offence is triable only on indictment, it may well be that the first reasonable opportunity would have been during the police station stage; where that is not the case, the first reasonable opportunity is likely to be at the first hearing in the Crown Court;

(e) where a defendant is convicted after pleading guilty to an alternative (lesser) charge to that to which he/she had originally pleaded not guilty, the extent of any reduction will be determined by the stage at which the defendant first formally indicated to the court willingness to plead guilty to the lesser charge and the reason why that lesser charge was proceeded with in preference to the original charge.

[The next paragraph is K-13.]

B. Overarching Principles: Seriousness

GUIDELINE

Contents

    D   Assessment of culpability and harm

          (i) Aggravating factors

          (ii) Mitigating factors

          (iii) Personal mitigation

          (iv) Reduction for a guilty plea

    E   The sentencing thresholds

          The custody threshold

          The threshold for community sentences

    F   Prevalence

FOREWORD

K-14   In accordance with the provisions of section 170(9) Criminal Justice Act 2003, the Sentencing Guidelines Council issues this guideline as a definitive guideline. By virtue of section 172 of the Act, every court must have regard to a relevant guideline.

The Council was created in 2004 in order to frame Guidelines to assist Courts as they deal with criminal cases across the whole of England and Wales.

The Council has stated that it intends to follow a principled approach to the formulation of guidelines to assist sentencers which will include consideration of overarching and general principles relating to the sentencing of offenders. Following the planned implementation of many of the sentencing provisions in the 2003 Act in April 2005, this guideline deals with the general concept of seriousness in the light of those provisions and considers how sentencers should determine when the respective sentencing thresholds have been crossed when applying the provisions of the Act.

This guideline applies only to sentences passed under the sentencing framework applicable to those aged 18 or over although there are some aspects that will assist courts assessing the seriousness of offences committed by those under 18. The Council has commissioned separate advice from the Sentencing Advisory Panel on the sentencing of young offenders.

This is the first time that it has been possible to produce definitive guidelines not only before new provisions come into force but also before much of the training of judiciary and practitioners.

The Council has appreciated greatly the work of the Sentencing Advisory Panel in preparing the advice on which this guideline has been based and for the many organisations and individuals who have responded so thoughtfully to the consultation of both the Panel and the Council. The advice and this guideline are available on www.sentencing-guidelines.gov.uk or from the Sentencing Guidelines Secretariat. A summary of the responses to the Council's consultation also appears on the website.

Chairman of the Council

December 2004

SERIOUSNESS

A. STATUTORY PROVISION

K-15   1.1 In every case where the offender is aged 18 or over at the time of conviction, the court must have regard to the five purposes of sentencing contained in section 142(1) Criminal Justice Act 2003:

          (a) the punishment of offenders

          (b) the reduction of crime (including its reduction by deterrence)

          (c) the reform and rehabilitation of offenders

          (d) the protection of the public

          (e) the making of reparation by offenders to persons affected by their offence

1.2 The Act does not indicate that any one purpose should be more important than any other and in practice they may all be relevant to a greater or lesser degree in any individual case—the sentencer has the task of determining the manner in which they apply.

1.3 The sentencer must start by considering the seriousness of the offence, the assessment of which will:

      • determine which of the sentencing thresholds has been crossed;

      • indicate whether a custodial, community or other sentence is the most appropriate;

      • be the key factor in deciding the length of a custodial sentence, the onerousness of requirements to be incorporated in a community sentence and the amount of any fine imposed.

762

1.4 A court is required to pass a sentence that is commensurate with the seriousness of the offence. The seriousness of an offence is determined by two main parameters; the **culpability** of the offender and the **harm** caused or risked being caused by the offence

1.5 Section 143(1) Criminal Justice Act 2003 provides [see § 5-67 in the main work].

B. CULPABILITY

1.6 Four levels of criminal culpability can be identified for sentencing purposes: **K-16**

1.7 Where the offender;

    (i) has the **intention** to cause harm, with the highest culpability when an offence is planned. The worse the harm intended, the greater the seriousness.

    (ii) is **reckless** as to whether harm is caused, that is, where the offender appreciates at least some harm would be caused but proceeds giving no thought to the consequences even though the extent of the risk would be obvious to most people.

    (iii) has **knowledge** of the specific risks entailed by his actions even though he does not intend to cause the harm that results.

    (iv) is guilty of **negligence**.

Note: *There are offences where liability is strict and no culpability need be proved for the purposes of obtaining a conviction, but the degree of culpability is still important when deciding sentence. The extent to which reckless-ness, knowledge or negligence are involved in a particular offence will vary.*

C. HARM

1.8 The relevant provision is widely drafted so that it encompasses those offences where harm is **K-17** caused but also those where neither individuals nor the community suffer harm but a risk of harm is present.

To individual victims

1.9 The types of harm caused or risked by different types of criminal activity are diverse and victims may suffer physical injury, sexual violation, financial loss, damage to health or psychological distress. There are gradations of harm within all of these categories.

1.10 The nature of harm will depend on personal characteristics and circumstances of the victim and the court's assessment of harm will be an effective and important way of taking into consideration the impact of a particular crime on the victim.

1.11 In some cases no actual harm may have resulted and the court will be concerned with assessing the relative dangerousness of the offender's conduct; it will consider the likelihood of harm occurring and the gravity of the harm that could have resulted.

To the community

1.12 Some offences cause harm to the community at large (instead of or as well as to an individual victim) and may include economic loss, harm to public health, or interference with the administration of justice.

Other types of harm

1.13 There are other types of harm that are more difficult to define or categorise. For example, cruelty to animals certainly causes significant harm to the animal but there may also be a human victim who also suffers psychological distress and/or financial loss.

1.14 Some conduct is criminalised purely by reference to public feeling or social mores. In addition, public concern about the damage caused by some behaviour, both to individuals and to society as a whole, can influence public perception of the harm caused, for example, by the supply of prohibited drugs.

D. THE ASSESSMENT OF CULPABILITY AND HARM

1.15 Section 143(1) makes clear that the assessment of the seriousness of any individual offence **K-18** must take account not only of any harm actually caused by the offence, but also of any harm that was intended to be caused or might foreseeably be caused by the offence.

1.16 Assessing seriousness is a difficult task, particularly where there is an imbalance between culpability and harm:

    • sometimes the harm that actually results is greater than the harm intended by the offender;

- in other circumstances, the offender's culpability may be at a higher level than the harm resulting from the offence

1.17 Harm must always be judged in the light of culpability. The precise level of culpability will be determined by such factors as motivation, whether the offence was planned or spontaneous or whether the offender was in a position of trust.

Culpability will be greater if:

- an offender deliberately causes more harm than is necessary for the commission of the offence, or
- where an offender targets a vulnerable victim (because of their old age or youth, disability or by virtue of the job they do).

1.18 Where unusually serious harm results and was unintended and beyond the control of the offender, culpability will be significantly influenced by the extent to which the harm could have been foreseen.

1.19 If much **more** harm, or much **less** harm has been caused by the offence than the offender intended or foresaw, the culpability of the offender, depending on the circumstances, may be regarded as carrying greater or lesser weight as appropriate.

The culpability of the offender in the particular circumstances of an individual case should be the initial factor in determining the seriousness of an offence.

(i) Aggravating factors

K-19   1.20 Sentencing guidelines for a particular offence will normally include a list of aggravating features which, if present in an individual instance of the offence, would indicate *either* a higher than usual level of culpability on the part of the offender, *or* a greater than usual degree of harm caused by the offence (or sometimes both).

1.21 The lists below bring together the most important aggravating features with potential application to more than one offence or class of offences. They include some factors (such as the vulnerability of victims or abuse of trust) which are integral features of certain offences; in such cases, the presence of the aggravating factor is already reflected in the penalty for the offence and **cannot be used as justification for increasing the sentence further**. The lists are not intended to be comprehensive and the aggravating factors are not listed in any particular order of priority. On occasions, two or more of the factors listed will describe the same feature of the offence and care needs to be taken to avoid "double counting". Those factors starred with an asterisk are statutory aggravating factors where the statutory provisions are in force. Those marked with a hash are yet to be brought into force but as factors in an individual case are still relevant and should be taken into account.

1.22 **Factors indicating higher culpability:**

- Offence committed whilst on bail for other offences
- Failure to respond to previous sentences
- Offence was racially or religiously aggravated
- Offence motivated by, or demonstrating, hostility to the victim based on his or her sexual orientation (or presumed sexual orientation)
- Offence motivated by, or demonstrating, hostility based on the victim's disability (or presumed disability)
- Previous conviction(s), particularly where a pattern of repeat offending is disclosed
- Planning of an offence
- An intention to commit more serious harm than actually resulted from the offence
- Offenders operating in groups or gangs
- "Professional" offending
- Commission of the offence for financial gain (where this is not inherent in the offence itself)
- High level of profit from the offence
- An attempt to conceal or dispose of evidence
- Failure to respond to warnings or concerns expressed by others about the offender's behaviour
- Offence committed whilst on licence
- Offence motivated by hostility towards a minority group, or a member or members of it
- Deliberate targeting of vulnerable victim(s)
- Commission of an offence while under the influence of alcohol or drugs
- Use of a weapon to frighten or injure victim

- Deliberate and gratuitous violence or damage to property, over and above what is needed to carry out the offence
- Abuse of power
- Abuse of a position of trust

1.23 **Factors indicating a more than usually serious degree of harm:**
- Multiple victims
- An especially serious physical or psychological effect on the victim, even if unintended
- A sustained assault or repeated assaults on the same victim
- Victim is particularly vulnerable
- Location of the offence (for example, in an isolated place)
- Offence is committed against those working in the public sector or providing a service to the public
- Presence of others *e.g.* relatives, especially children or partner of the victim
- Additional degradation of the victim (*e.g.* taking photographs of a victim as part of a sexual offence)
- In property offences, high value (including sentimental value) of property to the victim, or substantial consequential loss (*e.g.* where the theft of equipment causes serious disruption to a victim's life or business)

(ii) Mitigating factors

1.24 Some factors may indicate that an offender's culpability is **unusually** low, or that the harm **K-20** caused by an offence is less than usually serious.

1.25 **Factors indicating significantly lower culpability:**
- A greater degree of provocation than normally expected
- Mental illness or disability
- Youth or age, where it affects the responsibility of the individual defendant
- The fact that the offender played only a minor role in the offence

(iii) Personal mitigation

1.26 Section 166(1) Criminal Justice Act 2003 makes provision for a sentencer to take account of **K-21** any matters that "in the opinion of the court, are relevant in mitigation of sentence".

1.27 When the court has formed an initial assessment of the seriousness of the offence, then it should consider any offender mitigation. The issue of remorse should be taken into account at this point along with other mitigating features such as admissions to the police in interview.

(iv) Reduction for a guilty plea

1.28 Sentencers will normally reduce the severity of a sentence to reflect an early guilty plea. **K-22** This subject is covered by a separate guideline and provides a sliding scale reduction with a normal maximum one-third reduction being given to offenders who enter a guilty plea at the first reasonable opportunity.

1.29 Credit may also be given for ready co-operation with the authorities. This will depend on the particular circumstances of the individual case.

E. THE SENTENCING THRESHOLDS

1.30 Assessing the seriousness of an offence is only the first step in the process of determining the **K-23** appropriate sentence in an individual case. Matching the offence to a type and level of sentence is a separate and complex exercise assisted by the application of the respective threshold tests for custodial and community sentences.

The custody threshold

1.31 Section 152(2) Criminal Justice Act 2003 provides [see § 5-458 in the main work]. **K-24**

1.32 In applying the threshold test, sentencers should note: the clear intention of the threshold test is to reserve prison as a punishment for the most serious offences;
- it is impossible to determine definitively which features of a particular offence make it serious enough to merit a custodial sentence;
- passing the custody threshold does not mean that a custodial sentence should be deemed inevitable, and custody can still be avoided in the light of personal mitigation or where there is a suitable intervention in the community which provides sufficient restriction (by

way of punishment) while addressing the rehabilitation of the offender to prevent future crime. For example, a prolific offender who currently could expect a short custodial sentence (which, in advance of custody plus, would have no provision for supervision on release) might more appropriately receive a suitable community sentence.

1.33 The approach to the imposition of a custodial sentence under the new framework should be as follows:

(a) has the custody threshold been passed?

(b) if so, is it unavoidable that a custodial sentence be imposed?

(c) if so, can that sentence be suspended? (sentencers should be clear that they would have imposed a custodial sentence if the power to suspend had not been available)

(d) if not, can the sentence be served intermittently?

(e) if not, impose a sentence which takes immediate effect for the term commensurate with the seriousness of the offence.

The threshold for community sentences

K-25

1.34 Section 148(1) Criminal Justice Act 2003 provides [see § 5-248 in the main work].

1.35 In addition, the threshold for a community sentence can be crossed even though the seriousness criterion is not met. Section 151 Criminal Justice Act 2003 provides that, in relation to an offender aged 16 or over on whom, on three or more previous occasions, sentences had been passed consisting only of a fine, a community sentence may be imposed (if it is in the interests of justice) despite the fact that the seriousness of the current offence (and others associated with it) might not warrant such a sentence.

1.36 Sentencers should consider all of the disposals available (within or below the threshold passed) at the time of sentence before reaching the provisional decision to make a community sentence, so that, even where the threshold for a community sentence has been passed, a financial penalty or discharge may still be an appropriate penalty.

Summary

K-26

1.37 It would not be feasible to provide a form of words or to devise any formula that would provide a general solution to the problem of where the custody threshold lies. Factors vary too widely between offences for this to be done. It is the task of guidelines for individual offences to provide more detailed guidance on what features within that offence point to a custodial sentence, and also to deal with issues such as sentence length, the appropriate requirements for a community sentence or the use of appropriate ancillary orders.

Having assessed the seriousness of an individual offence, sentencers must consult the sentencing guidelines for an offence of that type for guidance on the factors that are likely to indicate whether a custodial sentence or other disposal is most likely to be appropriate.

F. PREVALENCE

K-27

1.38 The seriousness of an individual case should be judged on its own dimensions of harm and culpability rather than as part of a collective social harm. It is legitimate for the overall approach to sentencing levels for particular offences to be guided by their cumulative effect. However, it would be wrong to further penalise individual offenders by increasing sentence length for committing an individual offence of that type.

1.39 There may be exceptional local circumstances that arise which may lead a court to decide that prevalence should influence sentencing levels. The pivotal issue in such cases will be the harm being caused to the community. It is essential that sentencers both have supporting evidence from an external source (for example the local Criminal Justice Board) to justify claims that a particular crime is prevalent in their area and are satisfied that there is a compelling need to treat the offence more seriously than elsewhere.

The key factor in determining whether sentencing levels should be enhanced in response to prevalence will be the level of harm being caused in the locality. Enhanced sentences should be exceptional and in response to exceptional circumstances. Sentencers must sentence within the sentencing guidelines once the prevalence has been addressed. Having assessed the seriousness of an individual offence, sentencers must consult the sentencing guidelines for an offence of that type for guidance on the factors that are likely to indicate whether a custodial sentence or other disposal is most likely to be appropriate.

C. New Sentences: Criminal Justice Act 2003

GUIDELINE

Foreword

In accordance with the provisions of section 170(9) Criminal Justice Act 2003, the Sentencing **K-28**
Guidelines Council issues this guideline as a definitive guideline. By virtue of section 172 of the Act, every court must have regard to a relevant guideline.

The Council was created in 2004 in order to frame Guidelines to assist Courts as they deal with criminal cases across the whole of England and Wales.

This guideline relates to the new sentencing framework introduced by the Criminal Justice Act 2003, which affects the nature of community and custodial sentences. Only those sentences and related provisions which are expected to come into force by April 2005 are dealt with in this guideline. It will be followed by further guidelines in due course. This is an unusual guideline since it covers a range of sentences outside the context of individual offences and does so in readiness for the coming into force of the statutory provisions creating the sentences. It is designed with the object of ensuring a consistent approach when the sentences become available.

This guideline applies only to sentences passed under the sentencing framework applicable to those aged 18 or over.

The guideline is divided into two sections:
  * Sections 1 covers the practical aspects of implementing the non-custodial powers namely the new community sentence and the new form of deferred sentence;
  * Section 2 deals with the new custodial sentence provisions relating to suspended sentences, prison sentences of 12 months or more, and intermittent custody.[13]

The Act also contains an extensive range of provisions to protect the public from dangerous offenders. These will be dealt with separately.

The Advice of the Sentencing Advisory Panel to the Council (published on 20th September 2004) has been broadly accepted by the Council and forms the basis of this guideline. Further information on the issues covered in this guideline can be found in that Advice or in the discussion document that preceded it. All these documents are available on www.sentencing-guidelines.gov.uk or from the Sentencing Guidelines Secretariat.

Chairman of the Council
December 2004

Contents

[13] References to the Probation Service reflect current roles and responsibilities. By the time these provisions come into force, some or all of those roles and responsibilities may be those of the National Offender Management Service (NOMS).

SECTION 1 PART 1—COMMUNITY SENTENCES

A. Statutory Provisions

(i) The thresholds for community sentence

K-30   1.1.1   Seriousness—Section 148 Criminal Justice Act 2003 [sets out subsection (1), as to which, see § 5-248 in the main work].

1.1.2   Persistent offenders—Section 151 Criminal Justice Act 2003 [sets out subsections (1) and (2), as to which, see § 5-252 in the main work].

(ii) The sentences available

K-31   1.1.3   Meaning of community sentence—Section 147 Criminal Justice Act 2003 [sets out subsection (1), as to which, see § 5-247 in the main work].

1.1.4   Offenders aged 16 or over—Section 177 Criminal Justice Act 2003 [sets out subsections (1) to (4), as to which, see § 5-253 in the main work].

(iii) Determining which orders to make & requirements to include

K-32   1.1.5   Suitability—Section 148 Criminal Justice Act 2003 [sets out subsection (2), as to which see § 5-248 in the main work].

1.1.6   Restrictions on liberty—Section 148 Criminal Justice Act 2003 [sets out subsection (1), as to which see § 5-248 in the main work].

1.1.7   Compatibility—Section 177 Criminal Justice Act 2003 [sets out subsection (6), as to which see § 5-253 in the main work].

(iv) Electronic monitoring

K-33   1.1.8   Section 177 Criminal Justice Act 2003 [sets out subsections (3) and (4), as to which see § 5-253 in the main work].

B. Imposing a Community Sentence—The Approach

K-34   1.1.9 On pages 8 and 9 of the seriousness guideline the two thresholds for the imposition of a community sentence are considered. Sentencers must consider all of the disposals available (within or below the threshold passed) at the time of sentence, and reject them before reaching the provisional decision to make a community sentence, so that even where the threshold for a community sentence has been passed a financial penalty or discharge may still be an appropriate penalty. Where an offender has a low risk of reoffending, particular care needs to be taken in the light of evidence that indicates that there are circumstances where inappropriate intervention can increase the risk of reoffending rather than decrease it. In addition, recent improvements in enforcement of financial penalties make them a more viable sentence in a wider range of cases.

1.1.10 Where an offender is being sentenced for a non-imprisonable offence or offences, great care will be needed in assessing whether a community sentence is appropriate since failure to comply could result in a custodial sentence.

1.1.11 Having decided (in consultation with the Probation Service where appropriate) that a community sentence is justified, the court must decide which requirements should be included in the community order. The requirements or orders imposed will have the effect of restricting the offender's liberty, whilst providing punishment in the community, rehabilitation for the offender, and/or ensuring that the offender engages in reparative activities.

The key issues arising are:
- **(i) which requirements to impose;**
- **(ii) how to make allowance for time spent on remand; and**
- **(iii) how to deal with breaches.**

(i) Requirements

1.1.12 When deciding which requirements to include, the court must be satisfied on three matters— **K-35**

- (i) that the **restriction on liberty is commensurate with the seriousness** of the offence(s);[14]
- (ii) that the **requirements are the most suitable** for the offender;[15] and
- (iii) that, where there are two or more requirements included, they are **compatible with each other**.[16]

1.1.13 Sentencers should have the possibility of breach firmly in mind when passing sentence for the original offence. If a court is to reflect the seriousness of an offence, there is little value in setting requirements as part of a community sentence that are not demanding enough for an offender. on the other hand, there is equally little value in imposing requirements that would "set an offender up to fail" and almost inevitably lead to sanctions for a breach.

In community sentences, the guiding principles are proportionality and suitability. Once a court has decided that the offence has crossed the community sentence threshold and that a community sentence is justified, the initial factor in defining which requirements to include in a community sentence should be the seriousness of the offence committed.

1.1.14 This means that "seriousness" is an important factor in deciding whether the court chooses the low, medium or high range (see below) but, having taken that decision, selection of the content of the order within the range will be determined by a much wider range of factors.

- **Sentencing ranges must remain flexible enough to take account of the suitability of the offender, his or her ability to comply with particular requirements and their availability in the local area.**
- **The justification for imposing a community sentence in response to persistent petty offending is the persistence of the offending behaviour rather than the seriousness of the offences being committed. The requirements imposed should ensure that the restriction on liberty is proportionate to the seriousness of the offending, to reflect the fact that the offences, of themselves, are not sufficiently serious to merit a community sentence.**

(a) Information for sentencers

1.1.15 In many cases, a pre-sentence report[17] will be pivotal in helping a sentencer decide **K-36** whether to impose a custodial sentence or whether to impose a community sentence and, if so, whether particular requirements, or combinations of requirements, are suitable for an individual offender. The court must always ensure (especially where there are multiple requirements) that the restriction on liberty placed on the offender is proportionate to the seriousness of the offence committed.[18] The court must also consider the likely effect of one requirement on another, and that they do not place conflicting demands upon the offender.[19]

1.1.16 The council supports the approach proposed by the panel at paragraph 78 of its advice that, having reached the provisional view that a community sentence is the most appropriate disposal, the sentencer should request a pre-sentence report, indicating which of the three sentencing ranges is relevant and the purpose(s) of sentencing that the package of requirements is required to fulfil. Usually the most helpful way for the court to do this would be to produce a written note for the report writer, copied on the court file. If it is known that the same tribunal and defence advocate will

---

[14] Criminal Justice Act 2003 section 148(2)(b).

[15] *ibid.*, section 148(2)(a).

[16] *ibid.*, section 177(6).

[17] Under the Act, a pre-sentence report includes a full report following adjournment, a specific sentence report, a short format report or an oral report. The type of report supplied will depend on the level of information requested. Wherever it appears, the term "pre-sentence report" includes all these types of report.

[18] Criminal Justice Act 2003 section 148(2).

[19] *ibid.*, section 177(6).

be present at the sentencing hearing and a probation officer is present in court when the request for a report is made, it may not be necessary to commit details of the request to writing. However, events may change during the period of an adjournment and it is good practice to ensure that there is a clear record of the request for the court. These two factors will guide the Probation Service in determining the nature and combination of requirements that may be appropriate and the onerousness and intensity of those requirements. A similar procedure should apply when ordering a pre-sentence report when a custodial sentence is being considered.

1.1.17   There will be occasions when any type of report may be unnecessary despite the intention to pass a community sentence though this is likely to be infrequent. A court could consider dispensing with the need to obtain a pre-sentence report for adult offenders—

- where the offence falls within the LOW range of seriousness (see pp.9-10); and
- where the sentencer was minded to impose a single requirement, such as an exclusion requirement (where the circumstances of the case mean that this would be an appropriate disposal without electronic monitoring); and
- where the sentence will not require the involvement of the Probation Service, for example an electronically monitored curfew (subject to the court being satisfied that there is an appropriate address at which the curfew can operate).

(b) Ranges of sentence within the community sentence band

K-37   1.1.18   To enable the court to benefit from the flexibility that community sentences provide and also to meet its statutory obligations, any structure governing the use of community requirements must allow the courts to choose the most appropriate sentence for each individual offender.

1.1.19   Sentencers have a statutory obligation to pass sentences that are commensurate with the seriousness of an offence. However, within the range of sentence justified by the seriousness of the offence(s), courts will quite properly consider those factors that heighten the risk of the offender committing further offences or causing further harm with a view to lessening that risk. The extent to which requirements are imposed must be capable of being varied to ensure that the restriction on liberty is commensurate with the seriousness of the offence.

1.1.20   The council recognises that it would be helpful for sentencers to have a framework to help them decide on the most appropriate use of the new community sentence. While there is no single guiding principle, the seriousness of the offence that has been committed is an important factor. Three sentencing ranges (low, medium and high) within the community sentence band can be identified. It is not possible to position particular types of offence at firm points within the three ranges because the seriousness level of an offence is largely dependent upon the culpability of the offender and this is uniquely variable. The difficulty is particularly acute in relation to the medium range where it is clear that requirements will need to be tailored across a relatively wide range of offending behaviour.

1.1.21   In general terms, the lowest range of community sentence would be for those offenders whose offence was relatively minor within the community sentence band and would include persistent petty offenders whose offences only merit a community sentence by virtue of failing to respond to the previous imposition of fines. Such offenders would merit a 'light touch' approach, for example, normally a single requirement such as a short period of unpaid work, or a curfew, or a prohibited activity requirement or an exclusion requirement (where the circumstances of the case mean that this would be an appropriate disposal without electronic monitoring).

1.1.22   The top range would be for those offenders who have only just fallen short of a custodial sentence and for those who have passed the threshold but for whom a community sentence is deemed appropriate.

1.1.23   In all three ranges there must be sufficient flexibility to allow the sentence to be varied to take account of the suitability of particular requirements for the individual offender and whether a particular requirement or package of requirements might be more effective at reducing any identified risk of re-offending. It will fall to the sentencer to ensure that the sentence strikes the right balance between proportionality and suitability.

There should be three sentencing ranges (low, medium and high) within the community sentence band based upon seriousness.

It is not intended that an offender necessarily progress from one range to the next on each sentencing occasion. The decision as to the appropriate range each time is based upon the seriousness of the new offence(s).

The decision on the nature and severity of the requirements to be included in a community sentence should be guided by:

   (i) the assessment of offence seriousness (low, medium or high);

   (ii) the purpose(s) of sentencing the court wishes to achieve;

(iii) **the risk of re-offending;**

(iv) **the ability of the offender to comply, and**

(v) **the availability of requirements in the local area.**

The resulting restriction on liberty must be a proportionate response to the offence that was committed.

1.1.24 Below we set out a non-exhaustive description of examples of requirements that might be appropriate in the three sentencing ranges. These examples focus on punishment in the community, although it is recognised that not all packages will necessarily need to include a punitive requirement. There will clearly be other requirements of a rehabilitative nature, such as a treatment requirement or an accredited programme, which may be appropriate depending on the specific needs of the offender and assessment of suitability. Given the intensity of such interventions, it is expected that these would normally only be appropriate at medium and high levels of seriousness, and where assessed as having a medium or high risk of re-offending. In addition, when passing sentence in any one of the three ranges, the court should consider whether a rehabilitative intervention such as a programme requirement, or a restorative justice intervention might be suitable as an additional or alternative part of the sentence.

Low

1.1.25 For offences only just crossing the community sentence threshold (such as persistent petty **K-38** offending, some public order offences, some thefts from shops, or interference with a motor vehicle, where the seriousness of the offence or the nature of the offender's record means that a discharge or fine is inappropriate).

1.1.26 Suitable requirements might include:

- 40 to 80 hours of unpaid work; or
- a curfew requirement within the lowest range (*e.g.* up to 12 hours per day for a few weeks); or
- an exclusion requirement (where the circumstances of the case mean that this would be an appropriate disposal without electronic monitoring) lasting a few months; or
- a prohibited activity requirement; or
- an attendance centre requirement (where available).

1.1.27 Since the restriction on liberty must be commensurate with the seriousness of the offence, particular care needs to be taken with this band to ensure that this obligation is complied with. In most cases, only one requirement will be appropriate and the length may be curtailed if additional requirements are necessary.

Medium

1.1.28 For offences that obviously fall within the community sentence band such as handling **K-39** stolen goods worth less than £1000 acquired for resale or somewhat more valuable goods acquired for the handler's own use, some cases of burglary in commercial premises, some cases of taking a motor vehicle without consent, or some cases of obtaining property by deception.

1.1.29 Suitable requirements might include:

- a greater number (*e.g.* 80 to 150) of hours of unpaid work; or
- an activity requirement in the middle range (20 to 30 days); or
- a curfew requirement within the middle range (*e.g.* up to 12 hours for 2–3 months); or
- an exclusion requirement lasting in the region of six months or
- a prohibited activity requirement.

1.1.30 Since the restriction on liberty must be commensurate with the seriousness of the offence, particular care needs to be taken with this band to ensure that this obligation is complied with.

High

1.1.31 For offences that only just fall below the custody threshold or where the custody threshold **K-40** is crossed but a community sentence is more appropriate in all the circumstances, for example some cases displaying the features of a standard domestic burglary committed by a first-time offender.

1.1.32 More intensive sentences which combine two or more requirements may be appropriate at this level. Suitable requirements might include an unpaid work order of between 150 and 300 hours; an activity requirement up to the maximum 60 days; an exclusion order lasting in the region of 12 months; a curfew requirement of up to 12 hours a day for 4–6 months.

(c) Electronic monitoring

K-41   1.1.33   The court must also consider whether an electronic monitoring requirement[20] should be imposed which is mandatory[21] in some circumstances.

Electronic monitoring should be used with the primary purpose of promoting and monitoring compliance with other requirements, in circumstances where the punishment of the offender and/or the need to safeguard the public and prevent re-offending are the most important concerns.

(d) Recording the sentence imposed

K-42   1.1.34   Under the new framework there is only one (generic) community sentence provided by statute. This does not mean that offenders who have completed a community sentence and have then re-offended should be regarded as ineligible for a second community sentence on the basis that this has been tried and failed. Further community sentences, perhaps with different requirements, may well be justified.

1.1.35   Those imposing sentence will wish to be clear about the 'purposes' that the community sentence is designed to achieve when setting the requirements. Sharing those purposes with the offender and Probation Service will enable them to be clear about the goals that are to be achieved.

1.1.36   Any future sentencer must have full information about the requirements that were inserted by the court into the previous community sentence imposed on the offender (including whether it was a low/medium/high level order) and also about the offender's response. This will enable the court to consider the merits of imposing the same or different requirements as part of another community sentence. The requirements should be recorded in such a way as to ensure that they can be made available to another court if another offence is committed.

When an offender is required to serve a community sentence, the court records should be clearly annotated to show which particular requirements have been imposed.

(ii) Time spent on remand

K-43   1.1.37   The court will need to consider whether to give any credit for time spent in custody on remand.[22] (For further detail from the Panel's Advice, see Annex A.)

The court should seek to give credit for time spent on remand (in custody or equivalent status) in all cases. It should make clear, when announcing sentence, whether or not credit for time on remand has been given (bearing in mind that there will be no automatic reduction in sentence once section 67 of the Criminal Justice Act 1967 is repealed) and should explain its reasons for not giving credit when it considers either that this is not justified, would not be practical, or would not be in the best interests of the offender.

1.1.38   Where an offender has spent a period of time in custody on remand, there will be occasions where a custodial sentence is warranted but the length of the sentence justified by the seriousness of the offence would mean that the offender would be released immediately. Under the present framework, it may be more appropriate to pass a community sentence since that will ensure supervision on release.

1.1.39   However, given the changes in the content of the second part of a custodial sentence of 12 months or longer, a court in this situation where the custodial sentence would be 12 months or more should, under the new framework, pass a custodial sentence in the knowledge that licence requirements will be imposed on release from custody. This will ensure that the sentence imposed properly reflects the seriousness of the offence.

1.1.40   Recommendations made by the court at the point of sentence will be of particular importance in influencing the content of the licence. This will properly reflect the gravity of the offence(s) committed.

(iii) Breaches

K-44   1.1.41   Where an offender fails, without reasonable excuse, to comply with one or more requirements, the 'responsible officer'[23] can either give a warning or initiate breach proceedings. Where the offender fails to comply without reasonable excuse for the second time within a 12-month period, the 'responsible officer' must initiate proceedings.

---

[20] *ibid.*, section 177(3) and (4).
[21] Unless the necessary facilities are not available or, in the particular circumstances of the case, the court considers it inappropriate.
[22] Criminal Justice Act 2003 section 149.
[23] Criminal Justice Act 2003 Schedule 8, paragraphs 5–6.

1.1.42   In such proceedings the court must[24] either **increase the severity of the existing sentence** (*i.e.* impose more onerous conditions including requirements aimed at enforcement, such as a curfew or supervision requirement) or **revoke the existing sentence and proceed as though sentencing for the original offence**. The court is required to take account of the circumstances of the breach,[25] which will inevitably have an impact on its response.

1.1.43   In certain circumstances (where an offender has wilfully and persistently failed to comply with an order made in respect of an offence that is not itself punishable by imprisonment), the court can **impose a maximum of 51 weeks custody**.[26]

1.1.44   When increasing the onerousness of requirements, the court must consider the impact on the offender's ability to comply and the possibility of precipitating a custodial sentence for further breach. For that reason, and particularly where the breach occurs towards the end of the sentence, the court should take account of compliance to date and may consider that extending the supervision or operational periods will be more sensible; in other cases it might choose to add punitive or rehabilitative requirements instead. In making these changes the court must be mindful of the legislative restrictions on the overall length of community sentences and on the supervision and operational periods allowed for each type of requirement.

1.1.45   The court dealing with breach of a community sentence should have as its primary objective ensuring that the requirements of the sentence are finished, and this is important if the court is to have regard to the statutory purposes of sentencing. A court that imposes a custodial sentence for breach without giving adequate consideration to alternatives is in danger of imposing a sentence that is not commensurate with the seriousness of the original offence and is solely a punishment for breach. This risks undermining the purposes it has identified as being important. Nonetheless, courts will need to be vigilant to ensure that there is a realistic prospect of the purposes of the order being achieved.

Having decided that a community sentence is commensurate with the seriousness of the offence, the primary objective when sentencing for breach of requirements is to ensure that those requirements are completed.

1.1.46   A court sentencing for breach must take account of the extent to which the offender has complied with the requirements of the community order, the reasons for breach and the point at which the breach has occurred. Where a breach takes place towards the end of the operational period and the court is satisfied that the offender's appearance before the court is likely to be sufficient in itself to ensure future compliance, then given that it is not open to the court to make no order, an approach that the court might wish to adopt could be to re-sentence in a way that enables the original order to be completed properly—for example, a differently constructed community sentence that aims to secure compliance with the purposes of the original sentence.

1.1.47   If the court decides to increase the onerousness of an order, it must give careful consideration, with advice from the Probation Service, to the offender's ability to comply. A custodial sentence should be the last resort, where all reasonable efforts to ensure that an offender completes a community sentence have failed.

- **The Act allows for a custodial sentence to be imposed in response to breach of a community sentence. Custody should be the last resort, reserved for those cases of deliberate and repeated breach where all reasonable efforts to ensure that the offender complies have failed.**

- **Before increasing the onerousness of requirements, sentencers should take account of the offender's ability to comply and should avoid precipitating further breach by overloading the offender with too many or conflicting requirements.**

- **There may be cases where the court will need to consider re-sentencing to a differently constructed community sentence in order to secure compliance with the purposes of the original sentence, perhaps where there has already been partial compliance or where events since the sentence was imposed have shown that a different course of action is likely to be effective.**

---

[24] *ibid.*, paragraphs 9-10.
[25] *ibid.*, paragraph 9(2).
[26] *ibid.*, paragraph 9(1)(c).

SECTION 1 PART 2—DEFERRED SENTENCES

A. Statutory Provisions

K-45   1.2.1 Under the existing legislation,[27] a court can defer a sentence for up to six months, provided the offender consents and the court considers that deferring the sentence is in the interests of justice.

1.2.2 The new provisions[28] continue to require the consent of the offender and that the court be satisfied that the making of such a decision is in the interests of justice. However, it is also stated that the power to defer sentence can only be exercised where:

> "the offender undertakes to comply with any requirements as to his conduct during the period of the deferment that the court considers it appropriate to impose;".[29]

1.2.3 This enables the court to impose a wide variety of conditions (including a residence requirement).[30] The Act allows the court to appoint the probation service or other responsible person to oversee the offender's conduct during this period and prepare a report for the court at the point of sentence *i.e.* the end of the deferment period.

1.2.4 As under the existing legislation, if the offender commits another offence during the deferment period the court may have the power to sentence for both the original and the new offence at once. Sentence cannot be deferred for more than six months and, in most circumstances, no more than one period of deferment can be granted.[31]

1.2.5 A significant change is the provision enabling a court to deal with an offender before the end of the period of deferment.[32] For example if the court is satisfied that the offender has failed to comply with one or more requirements imposed in connection with the deferment, the offender can be brought back before the court and the court can proceed to sentence.

B. Use of Deferred Sentences

K-46   1.2.6 Under the new framework, there is a wider range of sentencing options open to the courts, including the increased availability of suspended sentences, and deferred sentences are likely to be used in very limited circumstances. A deferred sentence enables the court to review the conduct of the defendant before passing sentence, having first prescribed certain requirements. It also provides several opportunities for an offender to have some influence as to the sentence passed—

    (a) it tests the commitment of the offender not to re-offend;

    (b) it gives the offender an opportunity to do something where progress can be shown within a short period;

    (c) it provides the offender with an opportunity to behave or refrain from behaving in a particular way that will be relevant to sentence.

1.2.7 Given the new power to require undertakings and the ability to enforce those undertakings before the end of the period of deferral, the decision to defer sentence should be predominantly for a small group of cases at either the custody threshold or the community sentence threshold where the sentencer feels that there would be particular value in giving the offender the opportunities listed because, if the offender complies with the requirements, a different sentence will be justified at the end of the deferment period. This could be a community sentence instead of a custodial sentence or a fine or discharge instead of a community sentence. It may, rarely, enable a custodial sentence to be suspended rather than imposed immediately.

> **The use of deferred sentences should be predominantly for a small group of cases close to a significant threshold where, should the defendant be prepared to adapt his behaviour in a way clearly specified by the sentencer, the court may be prepared to impose a lesser sentence.**

1.2.8 A court may impose any conditions during the period of deferment that it considers appropriate.[33] These could be specific requirements as set out in the provisions for community sentences,[34] or requirements that are drawn more widely. These should be specific, measurable conditions so that the offender knows exactly what is required and the court can assess compliance; the restriction on liberty should be limited to ensure that the offender has a reasonable expectation of being able to comply whilst maintaining his or her social responsibilities.

---

[27] Powers of Criminal Courts (Sentencing) Act 2000 sections 1 and 2.
[28] Criminal Justice Act 2003 schedule 23 repealing and replacing sections 1 and 2 of the 2000 Act.
[29] *ibid.*, new section 1(3)(b) as inserted by Schedule 23 to the Criminal Justice Act 2003.
[30] *ibid.*, new section 1A(1).
[31] *ibid.*, new section 1(4).
[32] *ibid.*, new section 1B.
[33] *ibid.*, new section 1 (3)(b) as inserted by Schedule 23 to the Criminal Justice Act 2003.
[34] Criminal Justice Act 2003 section 177.

1.2.9 Given the need for clarity in the mind of the offender and the possibility of sentence by another court, the court should give a clear indication (and make a written record) of the type of sentence it would be minded to impose if it had not decided to defer and ensure that the offender understands the consequences of failure to comply with the court's wishes during the deferral period.

When deferring sentence, the sentencer must make clear the consequence of not complying with any requirements and should indicate the type of sentence it would be minded to impose. Sentencers should impose specific, measurable conditions that do not involve a serious restriction on liberty.

SECTION 2—CUSTODIAL SENTENCES PART 1—CUSTODIAL SENTENCES OF 12 MONTHS OR MORE

A. Statutory Provisions

2.1.1 Under existing legislation: **K-47**
  • an adult offender receiving a custodial sentence of at least 12 months and below 4 years will automatically be released at the halfway point and will then be supervised under licence until the three-quarter point of the sentence. [For some, the actual release date may be earlier as a result of release on home detention curfew (HDC).]
  • an adult offender receiving a determinate sentence of 4 years or above will be eligible for release from the halfway point and, if not released before, will automatically be released at the two-thirds point. After release, the offender will be supervised under licence until the three-quarter point of the sentence.

2.1.2 Under the new framework, the impact of a custodial sentence will be more severe since the period in custody and under supervision will be for the whole of the sentence term set by the court. Additionally, separate provisions for the protection of the public will be introduced for those offenders designated as "dangerous" under the Act which are designed to ensure that release only occurs when it is considered safe to do so.

2.1.3 Where a prison sentence of 12 months or more is imposed on an offender who is not classified as "dangerous", that offender will be entitled to be released from custody after completing half of the sentence. The whole of the second half of the sentence will be subject to licence requirements. These requirements will be set shortly before release by the Secretary of State (with advice from the Governor responsible for authorising the prisoner's release in consultation with the Probation Service) but a court will be able to make recommendations at the sentencing stage on the content of those requirements.[35] The conditions that the Secretary of State may attach to a licence are to be prescribed by order.[36]

2.1.4 The Act requires that a custodial sentence for a fixed term should be for the shortest term that is commensurate with the seriousness of the offence.[37]

B. Imposition of Custodial Sentences of 12 Months or More

(i) Length of sentence

2.1.5 The requirement that the second half of a prison sentence will be served in the community   **K-48** subject to conditions imposed prior to release is a major new development and will require offenders to be under supervision for the full duration of the sentence prescribed by the court. The Probation Service will be able to impose a number of complementary requirements on the offender during the second half of a custodial sentence and these are expected to be more demanding and involve a greater restriction on liberty than current licence conditions.

2.1.6 As well as restricting liberty to a greater extent, the new requirements will last until the very end of the sentence, rather than to the three-quarter point as at present, potentially making a custodial sentence significantly more demanding than under existing legislation. Breach of these requirements at any stage is likely to result in the offender being returned to custody and this risk continues, therefore, for longer under the new framework than under the existing legislation.

Transitional arrangements

2.1.7 In general, a fixed term custodial sentence of 12 months or more under the new framework   **K-49** will increase the sentence actually served (whether in custody or in the community) since it continues to the end of the term imposed. Existing guidelines issued since 1991 have been based on a different

---

[35] Criminal Justice Act 2003 section 238(1).
[36] *ibid.*, section 250.
[37] *ibid.*, section 153(2).

framework and so, in order to maintain consistency between the lengths of sentence under the current and the new framework, there will need to be some adjustment to the starting points for custodial sentences contained in those guidelines (subject to the special sentences under the 2003 Act where the offender is a "dangerous" offender).

2.1.8   This aspect of the guideline will be temporary to overcome the short-term situation where sentencing guidelines (issued since implementation of the reforms to custodial sentences introduced by the Criminal Justice Act 1991) are based on a different framework and the new framework has made those sentences more demanding. As new guidelines are issued they will take into account the new framework in providing starting points and ranges of appropriate sentence lengths for offences and an adjustment will not be necessary.

2.1.9   Since there are so many factors that will vary, it is difficult to calculate precisely how much more demanding a sentence under the new framework will be. The council's conclusion is that the sentencer should seek to achieve the best match between a sentence under the new framework and its equivalent under the old framework so as to maintain the same level of punishment. As a guide, the Council suggests the sentence length should be reduced by in the region of 15%.

2.1.10   The changes in the nature of a custodial sentence will require changes in the way the sentence is announced. Sentencers will need to continue[38] to spell out the practical implications of the sentence being imposed so that offenders, victims and the public alike all understand that the sentence does not end when the offender is released from custody. The fact that a breach of the requirements imposed in the second half of the sentence is likely to result in a return to custody should also be made very clear at the point of sentence.

- **When imposing a fixed term custodial sentence of 12 months or more under the new provisions, courts should consider reducing the overall length of the sentence that would have been imposed under the current provisions by in the region of 15%.**
- **When announcing sentence, sentencers should explain the way in which the sentence has been calculated, how it will be served and the implications of non-compliance with licence requirements. In particular, it needs to be stated clearly that the sentence is in two parts, one in custody and one under supervision in the community.**
- **This proposal does not apply to sentences for dangerous offenders, for which separate provision has been made in the Act.**

(ii) Licence conditions

K-50   2.1.11   Under the Act, a court imposing a prison sentence of 12 months or more may recommend conditions that should be imposed by the Secretary of State (with advice from the governor responsible for authorising the prisoner's release in consultation with the Probation Service) on release from custody.[39] Recommendations do not form part of the sentence and they are not binding on the Secretary of State.[40]

2.1.12   When passing such a sentence, the court will not know with any certainty to what extent the offender's behaviour may have been addressed in custody or what the offender's health and other personal circumstances might be on release and so it will be extremely difficult, especially in the case of longer custodial sentences, for sentencers to make an informed judgement about the most appropriate licence conditions to be imposed on release. However, in most cases, it would be extremely helpful for sentencers to indicate areas of an offender's behaviour about which they have the most concern and to make suggestions about the types of intervention whether this, in practice, takes place in prison or in the community.

2.1.13   The involvement of the Probation Service at the pre-sentence stage will clearly be pivotal. A recommendation on the likely post-release requirements included in a presentence report will assist the court with the decision on overall sentence length, although any recommendation would still have to be open to review when release is being considered. A curfew, exclusion requirement or prohibited activity requirement might be suitable conditions to recommend for the licence period. A court might also wish to suggest that the offender should complete a rehabilitation programme, for example for drug abuse, anger management, or improving skills such as literacy and could recommend that this should be considered as a licence requirement if the programme has not been undertaken or completed in custody.

2.1.14   The governor responsible for authorising the prisoner's release, in consultation with the Probation Service, is best placed to make recommendations at the point of release; this is the case at present and continues to be provided for in the Act. Specific court recommendations will only generally be appropriate in the context of relatively short sentences, where it would not be unreasonable

---

[38] Having reference to the *Consolidated Criminal Practice Direction* [2002] 2 Cr App R 533, Annex C, as suitably amended.
[39] Criminal Justice Act 2003 section 238(1).
[40] *ibid.*, section 250.

for the sentencer to anticipate the relevance of particular requirements at the point of release. Making recommendations in relation to longer sentences (other than suggestions about the types of intervention that might be appropriate at some point during the sentence) would be unrealistic. The governor and Probation Service should have due regard to any recommendations made by the sentencing court and the final recommendation to the Secretary of State on licence conditions will need to build upon any interventions during the custodial period and any other changes in the offender's circumstances.

- **A court may sensibly suggest interventions that could be useful when passing sentence, but should only make specific recommendations about the requirements to be imposed on licence when announcing short sentences and where it is reasonable to anticipate their relevance at the point of release. The governor and Probation Service should have due regard to any recommendations made by the sentencing court but its decision should be contingent upon any changed circumstances during the custodial period.**
- **The court should make it clear, at the point of sentence, that the requirements to be imposed on licence will ultimately be the responsibility of the Governor and Probation Service and that they are entitled to review any recommendations made by the court in the light of any changed circumstances.**

SECTION 2 PART 2—SUSPENDED SENTENCES OF IMPRISONMENT

A. Statutory Provisions

2.2.1 Section 189 Criminal Justice Act 2003 [sets out full text of section 189, as to which, see § 5-547 in the main work].　**K-51**

2.2.2 Imposition of requirements—Section 190 Criminal Justice Act 2003 [sets out full text of section 190, as to which, see § 5-550 in the main work].　**K-52**

2.2.3 Power to provide for review—Section 191 Criminal Justice Act 2003 [sets out full text of section 191, as to which, see § 5-551 in the main work].　**K-53**

2.2.4 Periodic reviews—Section 192 Criminal Justice Act 2003 [sets out full text of section 192, as to which, see § 5-552 in the main work].　**K-54**

2.2.5 Breach, revocation or amendment of orders, and effect of further conviction—Section 193 Criminal Justice Act 2003 [sets out full text of section 193, as to which, see § 5-554 in the main work].　**K-55**

B. Imposing A Suspended Sentence

2.2.6 A suspended sentence is a sentence of imprisonment. it is subject to the same criteria as a sentence of imprisonment which is to commence immediately. in particular, this requires a court to be satisfied that the custody threshold has been passed and that the length of the term is the shortest term commensurate with the seriousness of the offence.　**K-56**

2.2.7 A court which passes a prison sentence of less than 12 months may suspend it for between six months and two years (the operational period).[41] During that period, the court can impose one or more requirements for the offender to undertake in the community. The requirements are identical to those available for the new community sentence.

2.2.8 The period during which the offender undertakes community requirements is "the supervision period" when the offender will be under the supervision of a "responsible officer"; this period may be shorter than the operational period. The court may periodically review the progress of the offender in complying with the requirements and the reviews will be informed by a report from the responsible officer.

2.2.9 If the offender fails to comply with a requirement during the supervision period, or commits a further offence during the operational period, the suspended sentence can be activated in full or in part or the terms of the supervision made more onerous. There is a presumption that the suspended sentence will be activated either in full or in part.

(i) The decision to suspend

2.2.10　There are many similarities between the suspended sentence and the community sentence. in both cases, requirements can be imposed during the supervision period and the court can respond to breach by sending the offender to custody. The crucial difference is that the suspended sentence is a prison sentence and is appropriate only for an offence that passes the custody threshold and for which imprisonment is the only option. A community sentence may also be imposed for an offence that passes the custody threshold where the court considers that to be appropriate.　**K-57**

---

[41] The power to suspend a sentence is expected to come into force earlier than the provisions implementing "custody plus" and transitional provisions are expected to enable any sentence of imprisonment of under 12 months to be suspended. This guideline therefore is written in the language of the expected transitional provisions.

2.2.11 The full decision making process for imposition of custodial sentences under the new framework (including the custody threshold test) is set out in paragraphs 1.31-1.33 of the seriousness guideline. For the purposes of suspended sentences the relevant steps are:

(a) has the custody threshold been passed?

(b) if so, is it unavoidable that a custodial sentence be imposed?

(c) if so, can that sentence be suspended? (sentencers should be clear that they would have imposed a custodial sentence if the power to suspend had not been available)

(d) if not, can the sentence be served intermittently?

(e) if not, impose a sentence which takes immediate effect for the term commensurate with the seriousness of the offence.

(ii) Length of sentence

K-58 2.2.12 Before making the decision to suspend sentence, the court must already have decided that a prison sentence is justified and should also have decided the length of sentence that would be the shortest term commensurate with the seriousness of the offence if it were to be imposed immediately. The decision to suspend the sentence should not lead to a longer term being imposed than if the sentence were to take effect immediately.

A prison sentence that is suspended should be for the same term that would have applied if the offender were being sentenced to immediate custody.

2.2.13 When assessing the length of the operational period of a suspended sentence, the court should have in mind the relatively short length of the sentence being suspended and the advantages to be gained by retaining the opportunity to extend the operational period at a later stage (see below).

The operational period of a suspended sentence should reflect the length of the sentence being suspended. As an approximate guide, an operational period of up to 12 months might normally be appropriate for a suspended sentence of up to 6 months and an operational period of up to 18 months might normally be appropriate for a suspended sentence of up to 12 months.

(iii) Requirements

K-59 2.2.14 The court will set the requirements to be complied with during the supervision period. Whilst the offence for which a suspended sentence is imposed is generally likely to be more serious than one for which a community sentence is imposed, the imposition of the custodial sentence is a clear punishment and deterrent. In order to ensure that the overall terms of the sentence are commensurate with the seriousness of the offence, it is likely that the requirements to be undertaken during the supervision period would be less onerous than if a community sentence had been imposed. These requirements will need to ensure that they properly address those factors that are most likely to reduce the risk of re-offending.

Because of the very clear deterrent threat involved in a suspended sentence, requirements imposed as part of that sentence should generally be less onerous than those imposed as part of a community sentence. A court wishing to impose onerous or intensive requirements on an offender should reconsider its decision to suspend sentence and consider whether a community sentence might be more appropriate.

C. Breaches

K-60 2.2.15 The essence of a suspended sentence is to make it abundantly clear to an offender that failure to comply with the requirements of the order or commission of another offence will almost certainly result in a custodial sentence. Where an offender has breached any of the requirements without reasonable excuse for the first time, the responsible officer must either give a warning or initiate breach proceedings.[42] Where there is a further breach within a twelve-month period, breach proceedings must be initiated.[43]

2.2.16 Where proceedings are brought the court has several options, including extending the operational period. However, the presumption (which also applies where breach is by virtue of the commission of a further offence) is that the suspended prison sentence will be activated (either with its original custodial term or a lesser term) unless the court takes the view that this would, in all the

[42] Criminal Justice Act 2003 schedule 12, para. 4.
[43] *ibid.*, para. 5.

circumstances, be unjust. In reaching that decision, the court may take into account both the extent to which the offender has complied with the requirements and the facts of the new offence.[44]

2.2.17 Where a court considers that the sentence needs to be activated, it may activate it in full or with a reduced term. Again, the extent to which the requirements have been complied with will be very relevant to this decision.

2.2.18 If a court amends the order rather than activating the suspended prison sentence, it must either make the requirements more onerous, or extend the supervision or operational periods (provided that these remain within the limits defined by the Act).[45] In such cases, the court must state its reasons for not activating the prison sentence,[46] which could include the extent to which the offender has complied with requirements or the facts of the subsequent offence.

2.2.19 If an offender near the end of an operational period (having complied with the requirements imposed) commits another offence, it may be more appropriate to amend the order rather than activate it.

2.2.20 If a new offence committed is of a less serious nature than the offence for which the suspended sentence was passed, it may justify activating the sentence with a reduced term or amending the terms of the order.

2.2.21 It is expected that any activated suspended sentence will be consecutive to the sentence imposed for the new offence.

2.2.22 If the new offence is non-imprisonable, the sentencer should consider whether it is appropriate to activate the suspended sentence at all.

Where the court decides to amend a suspended sentence order rather than activate the custodial sentence, it should give serious consideration to extending the supervision or operational periods (within statutory limits) rather than making the requirements more onerous.

ANNEX A

Time spent on remand—Sentencing Advisory Panel's advice

The Act makes provision for a sentencer to give credit for time spent on remand in custody where   **K-70** a custodial sentence is passed.[47] It also empowers the court to have regard to time spent on remand in custody when determining the restrictions on liberty to be imposed by a community order or youth community order.[48] Where an offender has spent several weeks in custody, this may affect the nature of the offence that is passed. For example, where the court decides that a custodial sentence is justified some sentencers may decide to pass a community sentence instead, on the basis that the offender has already completed the equivalent of a punitive element in a sentence. The Panel takes the view that, given the changes in the content of the second part of a custodial sentence, in such cases it will be more appropriate to pass a custodial sentence knowing that licence requirements will be imposed on release from custody (which may be immediate). Recommendations made by the court at the point of sentence will then be of particular importance in influencing the content of the licence. This will help to ensure that the record clearly shows the assessment of seriousness of the offending behaviour.

Whereas the Act clearly states that time spent on remand is to be regarded as part of a custodial sentence unless the Court considers it unjust,[49] it states that sentencers passing a community sentence may have regard to time spent on remand, but no further information is given on how this discretion should be exercised. The Panel recognises that giving credit for time spent on remand is likely to be easier to apply in relation to punitive requirements rather than the rehabilitative elements of a community sentence. For example, reducing the number of unpaid work hours could be fairly easy, whereas reducing the length of a rehabilitation programme might not be appropriate as it could undermine its effectiveness. Where an offender has been kept on remand, one could take the view that this action was justified by the bail provisions and that the sentencer should not, therefore, feel obliged to adjust the terms of the community sentence. However, in principle, the Panel recommends that the court should seek to give credit for time spent on remand in all cases and should explain its reasons for not doing so when it considers either that this is not justified, would not be practical, or would not be in the best interests of the offender.

The court should seek to give credit for time spent on remand in all cases. It should make clear, when announc-

---

[44] *ibid.*, para. 8(4).
[45] *ibid.*, section 189(3) and (4).
[46] *ibid.*, schedule 12, para. 8(3).
[47] Criminal Justice Act 2003 section 240.
[48] *ibid.*, section 149.
[49] *ibid.*, section 240 (which will, at a future date, replace Criminal Justice Act 1967, section 67, by which such period is now deducted automatically).

ing sentence, whether or not credit for time on remand has been given and should explain its reasons for not giving credit when it considers either that this is not justified, would not be practical, or would not be in the best interests of the offender.

Where, following a period of time spent in custody on remand, the court decides that a custodial sentence is justified then, given the changes in the content of the second part of a custodial sentence, the court should pass a custodial sentence in the knowledge that licence requirements will be imposed on release from custody. Recommendations made by the court at the point of sentence will be of particular importance in influencing the content of the licence.[50]

D. Manslaughter by Reason of Provocation

GUIDELINE

Foreword

K-71   In accordance with section 170(9) of the Criminal Justice Act 2003, the Sentencing Guidelines Council issues this guideline as a definitive guideline. By virtue of section 172 of the Act, every court must have regard to a relevant guideline. This guideline applies to offenders convicted of manslaughter by reason of provocation who are sentenced after 28 November 2005.

This guideline stems from a reference from the Home Secretary for consideration of the issue of sentencing where provocation is argued in cases of homicide, and, in particular, domestic violence homicides. For the purpose of describing "domestic violence", the Home Secretary adopted the Crown Prosecution Service definition.[51] The guideline applies to sentencing of an adult offender for this offence in whatever circumstances it occurs. it identifies the widely varying features of both the provocation and the act of retaliation and sets out the approach to be adopted in deciding both the sentencing range and the starting point within that range.

This guideline is for use where the conviction for manslaughter is clearly founded on provocation alone. There will be additional, different and more complicated matters to be taken into account where the other main partial defence, diminished responsibility, is a factor.

The Council's Guideline *New Sentences: Criminal Justice Act 2003* recognised the potentially more demanding nature of custodial sentences of 12 months or longer imposed under the new framework introduced by the Criminal Justice Act 2003. Consequently the sentencing ranges and starting points in this guideline take that principle into account.

Guidelines are created following extensive consultation. The Sentencing Advisory Panel first consults widely on the basis of a thoroughly researched consultation paper, then provides the Council with advice. Having considered the advice, the Council prepares a draft guideline on which there is further consultation with Parliament, with the Home Secretary and with Ministers of other relevant Government Departments. This guideline is the culmination of that process.

The Council has appreciated greatly the work of the Sentencing Advisory Panel in preparing the advice on which this guideline has been based and for those who have responded so thoughtfully to the consultation of both the Panel and the Council.

The advice and this guideline are available on www.sentencing-guidelines.gov.uk or from the Sentencing Guidelines Secretariat at 85 Buckingham Gate, London SW1E 6PD. A summary of the responses to the Council's consultation also appears on the website.

Chairman of the Council

November 2005

Contents

K-72   Foreword

---

[50] This recommendation only applies to sentences of 12 months and above pending the implementation of 'custody plus'.

[51] "Any criminal offence arising out of physical, sexual, psychological, emotional or financial abuse by one person against a current or former partner in a close relationship, or against a current or former family member." A new definition of domestic violence was agreed in 2004 (and appears in the CPS Policy on Prosecuting cases of Domestic Violence, 2005) "any incident of threatening behaviour, violence or abuse [psychological, physical, sexual, financial or emotional] between adults who are or have been intimate partners or family members, regardless of gender or sexuality".

MANSLAUGHTER BY REASON OF PROVOCATION

A. Statutory Provision

1.1 Murder and manslaughter are common law offences and there is no complete statutory defini- **K-73** tion of either. 'Provocation' is one of the partial defences by which an offence that would otherwise be murder may be reduced to manslaughter.

1.2 Before the issue of provocation can be considered, the Crown must have proved beyond reasonable doubt that all the elements of murder were present, including the necessary intent (*i.e.* the offender must have intended either to kill the victim or to cause grievous bodily harm). The court must then consider section 3 of the Homicide Act 1957, which provides:

Where on a charge of murder there is evidence on which the jury can find that the person charged was provoked (whether by things done or by things said or by both together) to lose his self-control, the question whether the provocation was enough to make a reasonable man do as he did shall be left to be determined by the jury; and in determining that question the jury shall take into account everything both done and said according to the effect which, in their opinion, it would have on a reasonable man.

Although both murder and manslaughter result in death, the difference in the level of culpability creates offences of a distinctively different character. Therefore the approach to sentencing in each should start from a different basis.

B. Establishing the Basis for Sentencing

2.1 The Court of Appeal in *Attorney General's References (Nos. 74, 95 and 118 of 2002) (Suratan and* **K-74** *others)*,[52] set out a number of assumptions that a judge must make in favour of an offender found not guilty of murder but guilty of manslaughter by reason of provocation. The assumptions are required in order to be faithful to the verdict and should be applied equally in all cases whether conviction follows a trial or whether the Crown has accepted a plea of guilty to manslaughter by reason of provocation:

- first, that the offender had, at the time of the killing, lost self-control; mere loss of temper or jealous rage is not sufficient
- second, that the offender was caused to lose self-control by things said or done, normally by the person killed
- third, that the offender's loss of control was reasonable in all the circumstances, even bearing in mind that people are expected to exercise reasonable control over their emotions and that, as society advances, it ought to call for a higher measure of self-control
- fourth, that the circumstances were such as to make the loss of self-control sufficiently excusable to reduce the gravity of the offence from murder to manslaughter.

[52] [2003] 2 Cr.App.R.(S.) 42.

> Bearing in mind the loss of life caused by manslaughter by reason of
> provocation, the starting point for sentencing should be a custodial sentence.
> Only in a very small number of cases involving very exceptional mitigating
> factors should a judge consider that a on-custodial sentence is justified.
>
> The same general sentencing principles should apply in all cases of
> manslaughter by reason of provocation irrespective of whether or not the
> killing takes place in a domestic context.

C. Factors Influencing Sentence

K-75   3.1 A number of elements must be considered and balanced by the sentencer. Some of these are common to all types of manslaughter by reason of provocation; others have a particular relevance in cases of manslaughter in a domestic context.

3.2 **The degree of provocation as shown by its nature and duration**—An assessment of the *degree* of the provocation as shown by its nature and duration is the critical factor in the sentencing decision.

(a) In assessing the *degree* of provocation, account should be taken of the following factors:

- if the provocation (which does not have to be a wrongful act) involves gross and extreme conduct on the part of the victim, it is a more significant mitigating factor than conduct which, although significant, is not as extreme
- the fact that the victim presented a threat not only to the offender, but also to children in his or her care
- the offender's previous experiences of abuse and/or domestic violence either by the victim or by other people
- any mental condition which may affect the offender's perception of what amounts to provocation
- the nature of the conduct, the period of time over which it took place and its cumulative effect
- discovery or knowledge of the fact of infidelity on the part of a partner does not necessarily amount to *high* provocation. The gravity of such provocation depends entirely on all attendant circumstances.

(b) Whether the provocation was suffered over a *long or short* period is important to the assessment of gravity. The following factors should be considered:

- the impact of provocative behaviour on an offender can build up over a period of time
- consideration should not be limited to acts of provocation that occurred immediately before the victim was killed. For example, in domestic violence cases, cumulative provocation may eventually become intolerable, the latest incident seeming all the worse because of what went before.

(c) When looking at the *nature* of the provocation the court should consider both the type of provocation and whether, in the particular case, the actions of the victim would have had a particularly marked effect on the offender:

- actual (or anticipated) violence from the victim will generally be regarded as involving a higher degree of provocation than provocation arising from abuse, infidelity or offensive words unless that amounts to psychological bullying
- in cases involving actual or anticipated violence, the culpability of the offender will therefore generally be less than in cases involving verbal provocation
- where the offender's actions were motivated by fear or desperation, rather than by anger, frustration, resentment or a desire for revenge, the offender's culpability will generally be lower.

3.3 **The extent and timing of the retaliation**—It is implicit in the verdict of manslaughter by reason of provocation that the killing was the result of a loss of self-control because of things said and/or done. The intensity, extent and nature of that loss of control must be assessed in the context of the provocation that preceded it.

3.4 The *circumstances of the killing* itself will be relevant to the offender's culpability, and hence to the appropriate sentence:

- in general, the offender's violent response to provocation is likely to be less culpable the shorter the time gap between the provocation (or the last provocation) and the killing—as evidenced, for example, by the use of a weapon that happened to be available rather than by one that was carried for that purpose or prepared for use in advance
- conversely, it is not necessarily the case that greater culpability will be found where there has been a significant lapse of time between the provocation (or the last provocation) and the killing. Where the provocation is cumulative, and particularly in those circumstances where the offender is found to have suffered domestic violence from the victim over a significant period of time, the required loss of self-control may not be sudden as some experience a "slow-burn" reaction and appear calm
- choosing or taking advantage of favourable circumstances for carrying out the killing (so that the victim was unable to resist, such as where the victim was not on guard, or was asleep) may well be an aggravating factor—unless this is mitigated by the circumstances of the offender, resulting in the offender being the weaker or vulnerable party.

3.5 The *context of the relationship* between the offender and the victim must be borne in mind when **K-76** assessing the nature and degree of the provocation offered by the victim before the crime and the length of time over which the provocation existed. In cases where the parties were still in a relationship at the time of the killing, it will be necessary to examine the balance of power between one party and the other and to consider other family members who may have been drawn into, or been victims of, the provocative behaviour.

Although there will usually be less culpability when the retaliation to provocation is sudden, it is not always the case that greater culpability will be found where there has been a significant lapse of time between the provocation and the killing.

It is for the sentencer to consider the impact on an offender of provocative behaviour that has built up over a period of time.

An offence should be regarded as aggravated where it is committed in the presence of a child or children or other vulnerable family member, whether or not the offence takes place in a domestic setting.

3.6 **Post-offence behaviour**—The behaviour of the offender after the killing can be relevant to sentence:

- immediate and genuine remorse may be demonstrated by the summoning of medical assistance, remaining at the scene, and co-operation with the authorities
- concealment or attempts to dispose of evidence or dismemberment of the body may aggravate the offence.

Post-offence behaviour is relevant to the sentence. It may be an aggravating or mitigating factor. When sentencing, the judge should consider the motivation behind the offender's actions.

3.7 **Use of a weapon**

(a) In relation to this offence, as in relation to many different types of offence, the carrying and use of a weapon is an aggravating factor. Courts must consider the type of weapon used and, importantly, whether it was to hand or carried to the scene and who introduced it to the incident.

(b) The use or not of a weapon is a factor heavily influenced by the gender of the offender. Whereas men can and do kill using physical strength alone, women often cannot and thus resort to using a weapon. The issue of key importance is whether the weapon was to hand or carried deliberately to the scene, although the circumstances in which the weapon was brought to the scene will need to be considered carefully.

The use of a weapon should not necessarily move a case into another sentencing bracket.

In cases of manslaughter by reason of provocation, use of a weapon may reflect the imbalance in strength between the offender and the victim and how that weapon came to hand is likely to be far more important than the use of the weapon itself.

It will be an aggravating factor where the weapon is brought to the scene in contemplation of use *before* the loss of self-control (which may occur some time before the fatal incident).

D. Sentence Ranges and Starting Points

K-77   4.1 **Manslaughter is a "serious offence" for the purposes of the provisions in the Criminal Justice Act 2003**[53] **for dealing with dangerous offenders. It is possible that a court will be required to use the sentences for public protection prescribed in the Act when sentencing an offender convicted of the offence of manslaughter by reason of provocation. An alternative is a discretionary life sentence. In accordance with normal practice, when setting the minimum term to be served within an indeterminate sentence under these provisions, that term will usually be half the equivalent determinate sentence.**

4.1 **Identifying sentence ranges**—The key factor that will be relevant in every case is the nature and the duration of the provocation.

(a) The process to be followed by the court will be:

identify the sentence range by reference to the degree of provocation

adjust the starting point within the range by reference to the length of time over which the provocation took place

take into consideration the circumstances of the killing (e.g. the length of time that had elapsed between the provocation and the retaliation and the circumstances in which any weapon was used)

(b) This guideline establishes that:
- there are three sentencing ranges defined by the **degree of provocation**—low, substantial and high
- within the three ranges, the starting point is based on provocation taking place over **a short period of time**.
- the court will move from the starting point (based upon the degree of provocation) by considering the length of time over which the provocation has taken place, and by reference to any **aggravating and mitigating factors**

Manslaughter by Reason of Provocation

Factors to take into consideration

K-78   1. The sentences for public protection <u>must</u> be considered in all cases of manslaughter.

2. The presence of any of the general aggravating factors identified in the Council's Guideline *Overarching Principles: Seriousness* or any of the additional factors identified in this Guideline will indicate a sentence above the normal starting point.

3. This offence will not be an initial charge but will arise following a charge of murder. The

[53] Sections 224–230.

Council Guideline *Reduction in Sentence for a Guilty Plea* will need to be applied with this in mind. In particular, consideration will need to be given to the time at which it was indicated that the defendant would plead guilty to manslaughter by reason of provocation.

4. An assessment of the *degree* of the provocation as shown by its nature and duration is the critical factor in the sentencing decision.

5. The intensity, extent and nature of the loss of control must be assessed in the context of the provocation that preceded it.

6. Although there will usually be less culpability when the retaliation to provocation is sudden, it is not always the case that greater culpability will be found where there has been a significant lapse of time between the provocation and the killing.

7. It is for the sentencer to consider the impact on an offender of provocative behaviour that has built up over a period of time.

8. The use of a weapon should not necessarily move a case into another sentencing bracket.

9. Use of a weapon may reflect the imbalance in strength between the offender and the victim and how that weapon came to hand is likely to be far more important than the use of the weapon itself.

10. It will be an aggravating factor where the weapon is brought to the scene in contemplation of use *before* the loss of self-control (which may occur some time before the fatal incident).

11. Post-offence behaviour is relevant to the sentence. It may be an aggravating or mitigating factor. When sentencing, the judge should consider the motivation behind the offender's actions.

MANSLAUGHTER BY REASON OF PROVOCATION

This is a serious offence for the purposes of section 224 of the Criminal Justice Act 2003

Maximum penalty: **Life imprisonment**   **K-79**

Type/Nature of Activity	Sentence Ranges & Starting Points
Low degree of provocation: A low degree of provocation occurring over a short period	Sentence Range: 10 years – life Starting Point – 12 years custody
Substantial degree of provocation: A substantial degree of provocation occurring over a short period	Sentence Range: 4 – 9 years Starting Point – 8 years custody
High degree of provocation: A high degree of provocation occurring over a short period	Sentence Range: if custody is necessary, up to 4 years Starting Point – 3 years custody

Additional aggravating factors	Additional mitigating factors
1. Concealment or attempts to dispose of evidence* 2. Dismemberment or mutilation of the body* 3. Offence committed in the presence of a child/ children or other vulnerable family member *subject to para 3.6 above.	1. The offender was acting to protect another 2. Spontaneity and lack of premeditation 3. Previous experiences of abuse and/or domestic violence 4. Evidence that the victim presented an ongoing danger to the offender or another 5. Actual (or reasonably anticipated) violence from the victim

The Council Guideline New Sentences: Criminal Justice Act 2003 recognised the potentially more demanding nature of custodial sentences of 12 months or longer imposed under the new framework introduced by the Criminal Justice Act 2003. The sentencing ranges and starting points in the above guideline take account of this.

E. ROBBERY

The Sentencing Guidelines Council has issued a definitive guideline on robbery (Theft Act **K-80** 1968, s.8(1) (§ 21-84 in the main work)). It deals with offenders sentenced on or after August 1, 2006. The drafting of the guideline is inconsistent and repetitious. It lacks a coherent structure, and consists, in large part, of a series of lists and bullet points. Accordingly, it is not set out in full here. The following is a summary of its essential contents, but for those wishing to refer to the original, it may be located at www.sentencingguidelines.gov.uk.

The foreword states that robbery will usually merit a custodial sentence, but that exceptional circumstances may justify a non-custodial penalty for an adult and, more frequently, for a young offender; that the guideline is not, therefore, intended to mark a significant shift in sentencing practice; and that the sentencing ranges and starting points in the guideline take into account the more demanding nature of custodial sentences of 12 months or more under the CJA 2003. The guideline only provides guidance in relation to street robberies, robberies of small businesses, and less sophisticated commercial robberies. No guidance is provided in relation to violent personal robberies in the home and professionally planned commercial robberies.

The sentences suggested by the guideline are determined by the identification of one of three levels of seriousness. These are themselves determined by reference to the type of activity which characterises the offence, and the degree of force or threat present. Level 1 involves a threat and/or minimal use of force. Level 2 involves use of a weapon to threaten and/or use of significant force. Level 3 involves use of a weapon and/or significant force, and the causing of serious injury. Where the offence will fall within a particular level is determined by the presence of one or more aggravating features. However, exceptionally serious aggravating features may have the effect of moving the case to the next level. Aggravating factors which are particularly relevant to the assessment of seriousness are:

(a) the nature and degree of any force or violence used or threatened;

(b) the nature of any weapon carried or used, or the use of which is threatened;

(c) the vulnerability of the victim;

(d) the number of offenders involved and their roles;

(e) the value of the property taken;

(f) the fact that the offence was committed at night or in the hours of darkness; and

(g) the wearing of a disguise.

Mitigating factors which are particularly relevant are:

(a) an unplanned or opportunistic offence;

(b) a peripheral involvement in the offence; and

(c) the voluntary return of the property taken.

Where an offence is committed by a young offender, sentencers should additionally take into account age and immaturity and any group pressure under which the offender may have been acting. Further, in relation to such an offender, the guideline requires that where there is evidence that the offence was committed to fund a drug habit and that treatment might help tackle offending behaviour, the court should consider a drug treatment requirement as part of a supervision order or action plan. In all cases, the court should consider making a restitution or compensation order; in cases where a non-custodial order is made, the court may consider making an anti-social behaviour order.

Starting points and sentencing ranges are prescribed depending on whether the offender is an adult or a young offender. In each case, the starting point is based upon a first time offender who has pleaded not guilty, and who has not been assessed as being dangerous for the purposes of the dangerous offender provisions under the CJA 2003, Pt 12, Chap. 5 (ss.224 *et seq.*) (§§ 5-495 *et seq.* in the main work). In the case of young offenders, the starting points are based on a 17-year-old. Sentencers are required to consider whether a lower starting point is justified on account of the offender's age or immaturity. In the case of an adult offender, the starting point for a level 1 offence is 12 months' custody and the sentence range is from a community order (in exceptional circumstances, as stated in the foreword) to three years' custody. The starting point for a level 2 offence is four years' custody and the sentence range is two to seven years. The starting point for a level 3 offence is eight years' custody and the sentence range is seven to 12 years. In the case of the notional young offender, the starting point for a level 1 offence is a community order and the sentence range is from a community order to a 12-month detention and training order. The starting point for a level 2 offence is three years' detention and the sentence range is one to six years' detention. The starting point for a level 3 offence is seven years' detention and the sentence range is six to 10 years' detention.

F. BREACH OF A PROTECTIVE ORDER

K-81   The Sentencing Guidelines Council has issued a definitive guideline relating to the sentencing of offenders who have breached either a restraining order under the Protection from Harassment

Act 1997, s.5 (§ 19-350 in the main work), or a non-molestation order imposed under section 42 of the Family Law Act 1996 (breach being made an offence by section 42A, which is inserted, as from a day to be appointed, by the Domestic Violence, Crime and Victims Act 2004, s.1). It deals with offenders sentenced on or after December 18, 2006.

Paragraph 2 points out that the facts constituting the breach may amount to a substantive offence in their own right. It advises that in such cases it is desirable that there should be separate counts, and, where necessary, there should be consecutive sentences to reflect the seriousness of the counts and to achieve the appropriate totality. It continues, however, by saying that where there is only the one count, the overall sentence should not generally be affected. If the sole count is the breach, the sentence should reflect the nature of the breach; and if the substantive offence alone has been charged, the fact that it constituted a breach of a court order should be regarded as a matter of aggravation. Where no substantive offence was involved, the sentence should reflect the circumstances of the breach, including whether it was an isolated breach, or part of a course of conduct in breach of the order; whether it was planned or spontaneous; and any consequences of the breach, including psychiatric injury or distress to the person protected by the order.

Paragraph 3 is headed "Factors influencing sentencing". It says that since the order will have been made for the purpose of protecting an individual from harm, the main aim of the sentencer should be to achieve future compliance with the order where that is realistic. The nature of the original conduct or offence is relevant in so far as it allows a judgment to be made on the level of harm caused to the victim by the breach and the extent to which that harm was intended by the offender (para. 3.5). However, sentence following a breach is for the breach alone and must avoid punishing the offender again for the offence or conduct as a result of which the order was made (para. 3.7).

When dealing with a breach, a court will need to consider the extent to which the conduct amounting to the breach put the victim at risk of harm (para. 3.8). Where the order is breached by the use of physical violence, the starting point should normally be a custodial sentence (para. 3.9). Non-violent behaviour and/or indirect contact can also cause (or be intended to cause) a high degree of harm and anxiety. In such circumstances, it is likely that the custody threshold will have been crossed (para. 3.10). Where an order was made in civil proceedings, its purpose may have been to cause the subject of the order to modify behaviour rather than to imply that the conduct was especially serious. If so, it is likely to be disproportionate to impose a custodial sentence for a breach of the order if the breach did not involve threats or violence (para. 3.11). In some cases where a breach might result in a short custodial sentence but the court is satisfied that the offender genuinely intends to reform his behaviour and there is a real prospect of rehabilitation, the court may consider it appropriate to impose a sentence that will allow this. This may mean imposing a suspended sentence order or a community order (where appropriate with a requirement to attend an accredited domestic violence programme) (para. 3.12).

Paragraph 4 deals with matters of aggravation and mitigation. The matters of aggravation mirror those in the guideline on domestic violence (*post*, Appendix K-82), but there is added the fact that the breach was a further breach following previous breach proceedings or that it was committed shortly after the order was made. The matters of mitigation that are listed are that the breach followed a long period of compliance, or that the victim initiated contact.

At the end of the guideline there is a table with suggested starting points. The premise is that the "activity has either been prosecuted separately as an offence or is not of a character sufficient to justify prosecution of it as an offence in its own right". The first column is headed "Nature of activity" and the second column is headed "Starting points". There are five entries in the first column, "Breach (whether one or more) involving significant physical violence and significant physical or psychological harm to the victim", "More than one breach involving some violence and/or significant physical or psychological harm to the victim", "Single breach involving some violence and/or significant physical or psychological harm to the victim", "More than one breach involving no/ minimal contact or some direct contact" and "Single breach involving no/ minimal direct contact". The corresponding entries in the second column are, "More than 12 months. The length of the … sentence will depend on the nature and seriousness of the breaches.", "26–39 weeks' custody [Medium/High Custody Plus order] (when the relevant provisions of the CJA 2003 are in force)", "13-26 weeks' custody [Low/Medium Custody Plus order] (when the relevant provisions of the CJA 2003 are in force)", "Medium range community order" and "Low range community order".

G. Domestic Violence

K-82   The Sentencing Guidelines Council has issued a definitive guideline for use in all cases that fall within the Crown Prosecution Service definition of "domestic violence", *viz.* "Any incident of threatening behaviour, violence or abuse [psychological, physical, sexual, financial or emotional] between adults who are or have been intimate partners or family members, regardless of gender or sexuality." It deals with offenders sentenced on or after December 18, 2006. The guideline makes clear that offences committed in a domestic context should be regarded as being no less serious than offences committed in a non-domestic context. Indeed, because an offence has been committed in a domestic context, there are likely to be aggravating factors present that make it more serious. The foreword, signed by Lord Phillips C.J., as chairman of the council, states that in many situations of domestic violence, the circumstances require the sentence to demonstrate clearly that the conduct is unacceptable, but that there will be cases where all parties genuinely and realistically wish the relationship to continue as long as the violence stops. In such cases, and where the violence is towards the lower end of the scale of seriousness, it is likely to be appropriate for the court to impose a sentence that provides the necessary support.

Paragraph 1 defines "domestic violence" for the purposes of the guideline (*ante*). Paragraph 2 relates to the assessment of seriousness and says nothing new. Paragraph 3 is concerned with matters of aggravation and mitigation. By way of preamble it is stated that the history of the relationship will be relevant to the assessment of seriousness. There follows a non-exhaustive list of aggravating matters, *viz.* abuse of trust or power, that the victim is particularly vulnerable, the exposure of children to an offence (directly or indirectly), using contact arrangements with a child to instigate an offence, a proven history of violence or threats by the offender in a domestic setting, a history of disobedience to court orders and conduct which has forced the victim to leave home. The two matters of mitigation that are listed are positive good character and provocation, but, as to the former, the point is made that the perpetrator of domestic violence may have two personae, and that good character in relation to conduct outside the home should generally be of no relevance where there is a proven pattern of behaviour.

Paragraph 4 deals with the relevance of the wishes of the victim to the sentence. As a matter of general principle, the sentence should be determined by the seriousness of the offence, not by the expressed wishes of the victim. The guideline states that it is particularly important that this principle should be observed in this context, as (a) it is undesirable that a victim should feel a responsibility for the sentence imposed; (b) there is a risk that a plea for mercy made by a victim will be induced by threats made by, or by a fear of, the offender; and (c) the risk of such threats will be increased if it is generally believed that the severity of the sentence may be affected by the wishes of the victim. However, there may be cases in which the court can properly mitigate a sentence to give effect to the expressed wish of the victim that the relationship should be permitted to continue. The court must, however, be confident that such a wish is genuine, and that giving effect to it will not expose the victim to a real risk of further violence. Up-to-date information in a pre-sentence report and victim personal statement will be of vital importance. Either the offender or the victim (or both) may ask the court to take into consideration the interests of any children and to impose a less severe sentence. The court will wish to have regard not only to the effect on the children if the relationship is disrupted but also to the likely effect on the children of any further incidents of domestic violence.

The final section of the guideline is headed "Factors to Take into Consideration". It contains nothing new, save that it advises that where "the custody threshold is only just crossed, so that if a custodial sentence is imposed it will be a short sentence, the court will wish to consider whether the better option is a suspended sentence order or a community order, including in either case a requirement to attend an accredited domestic violence programme. Such an option will only be appropriate where the court is satisfied that the offender genuinely intends to reform his ... behaviour and that there is a real prospect of rehabilitation being successful. Such a situation is unlikely to arise where there has been a pattern of abuse."

H. Sexual Offences

(1) Sentencing Guidelines Council

K-83   The Sentencing Guidelines Council issued a definitive guideline on sexual offences, which applied to offenders sentenced on or after May 14, 2007. For the great majority of sexual offences, this will be overtaken, in relation to offenders sentenced on or after April 1, 2014, by the definitive guideline issued by the Sentencing Council for England and Wales (*post*, K-84 *et seq.*). Those wishing to consult the full detail of the former guideline should refer to the first supplement to this edition.

The new guideline does not cover three offences that were covered by the former guideline, and, since the new guideline does not purport to "revoke" its predecessor, it would appear that the former guideline will still hold sway in relation to those three offences.

At §§ K-83d, K-83e, *post*, Section 7 (sentencing young offenders - offences with a lower statutory maximum) of the Sentencing Guidelines Council's sexual offences guideline is set out. As to the reason for this, see § 20-9c in the main work.

Intercourse with an animal (s.69 of the SOA 2003)

For a basic offence assuming no aggravating or mitigating factors, the recommended starting point was a community order and the range was an "appropriate non-custodial sentence". The one specified aggravating feature was "recording activity and circulating pictures/video", and the one specified mitigating factor was "symptom of isolation rather than depravity". **K-83a**

Sexual penetration of a corpse (s.70 of the SOA 2003)

For a basic offence assuming no aggravating or mitigating factors, the recommended starting point was a community order and the range was an "appropriate non-custodial sentence". For a case of repeat offending or one accompanied by aggravating factors, the range was four weeks' to 18 months' custody, with a starting point of 26 weeks' custody. There were four aggravating factors that were specifically identified, *viz.* distress caused to relatives or friends of the deceased, physical damage caused to the body of the deceased, corpse was that of a child, and offence was committed in a funeral home or a mortuary. **K-83b**

Sexual activity in a public lavatory (s.71 of the SOA 2003)

For a basic offence assuming no aggravating or mitigaging factors, the recommended starting point was a fine, and the range was an "appropriate non-custodial sentence". For a case of repeat offending or one accompanied by aggravating factors, the range was the same but the starting point was a community order. The one aggravating factor specifically identified was "intimidating behaviour/threats of violence to member(s) of the public". **K-83c**

Part 7: Sentencing young offenders—offences with a lower statutory maximum

The guidelines in this part are intended for cases where the court considers that the facts found by the court justify the involvement of the criminal law, which findings may be different from those on which a decision to prosecute was made. The guidelines relate to sentencing on conviction of a first time offender. Where a young offender pleads guilty to one of the offences dealt with in this part, a youth court may impose an absolute discharge, a mental health disposal, a custodial sentence, or make a referral order. Where a custodial sentence is imposed in the Crown Court, it may be a detention and training order, or detention under section 91 of the PCC(S)A 2000 for a period up to the maximum for the offence. **K-83d**

The guideline (as originally drafted) referred to the offences in this part as being contrary to sections 9, 10, 11, 12, 25 and 26 of the 2003 Act. These can be split into two, as slightly different considerations apply to sections 9 to 12 as compared with sections 25 and 26.

As to sections 9 to 12, the guideline was in error in its premise that a person under 18 can commit one of these offences. Each of those offences is defined in such a way that it can only be committed by a person aged 18 or over. If a person under that age does an act proscribed by any of those sections, he does not offend against them. Section 13(1) (not mentioned in the guideline as originally drafted), however, provides that "(1) A person under 18 commits an offence if he does anything which would be an offence under any of sections 9 to 12 if he were aged 18.", and subsection (2) provides for a lesser maximum penalty. A person under 18 who does that which is prohibited by any of those sections would commit an offence under section 13, and should be charged as having committed an offence "contrary to section 13". The guideline has now been corrected in this respect. An offence contrary to section 13 is a specified offence, but not a serious offence for the purposes of Chapter 5 of Part 12 of the CJA 2003.

With sections 25 and 26, the position is less clear-cut. It is subsection (1) in each case that creates the offence and age is not an ingredient of the offence; but subsections (4) and (5) contain different penalty provisions according to whether the offender is aged 18 or over or under 18. Where the offender is under 18, the maximum is five years' custody. Taking the section as a whole, it is submitted, on the basis of *R. v. Courtie* [1984] A.C. 463, HL (the effect of the varying penalty provisions in the SOA 1956, according to the circumstances of an act of buggery, was to create separate offences), that sections 25 and 26 create distinct offences for those under 18. If this is correct, then these offences are specified offences, but not serious offences, because they carry a maximum of five years' custody and they cannot—by definition—be committed by an 18-year-old. The separate listing of these offences in section 91 of the PCC(S)A 2000 (§ 5-610 in the main work) supports this view: an offence under section 25 or 26 committed by an adult carries 14 years' imprisonment and there would have been no need to make special mention of it if there were only one offence.

This view was not accepted by the Sentencing Guidelines Council as the guideline still shows (as it appears on the website of the Sentencing Council (as to which, see § 20-9c in the main work)) the offences contrary to sections 25 and 26, when committed by an under 18-year-old, as "serious offences". It is submitted that the better view is that they are "specified", but not "serious" offences.

Key to table of starting points, etc., for parts 6B to 6D

| † | Denotes that an offence is a "specified offence" for the purposes of section 224 of the Criminal Justice Act 2003 |
| ‡ | Denotes that an offence is a "serious offence" for the purposes of section 224 of the Criminal Justice Act 2003 |

Aggravating factors.

A2:	Background of intimidation or coercion
A3:	Use of drugs, alcohol or other substance to facilitate the offence
A4:	Threats to prevent victim reporting the incident
A5:	Abduction or detention
A6:	Offender aware that he or she is suffering from a sexually transmitted infection
A10:	Images of violent activity

Mitigating factors

M5:	Youth and immaturity of offender
M7:	Offender intervenes to prevent incited offence from taking place
M8:	Small disparity in age between victim and offender
M9:	Relationship of genuine affection

OFFENCE	TYPE/ NATURE OF ACTIVITY	STARTING POINTS (AND SENTENCING RANGES)	AGG. & MIT. FACTORS
Sexual activity with a child 13(9) (intentional sexual touching of a person under 16) (offender under 18) †	Offence involving penetration where one or more aggravating factors exist or where there is a substantial age gap between the parties	12-month detention and training order (6- to 24-month detention and training order)	A2, A3, A4, A5, A6 M9, M5
	Any form of sexual activity (non–penetrative or penetrative) not involving any aggravating factors	Community order (appropriate non–custodial sentence)	
Causing or inciting a child to engage in sexual activity 13(10) (causing or inciting a child to engage in sexual activity) (offender under 18) †	Offence involving penetration where one or more aggravating factors exist or where there is a substantial age gap between the parties	12-month detention and training order (6- to 24-month detention and training order)	A2, A3, A4, A5, A6 M9, M7, M5
	Any form of sexual activity (non–penetrative or penetrative) not involving any aggravating factors	Community order (appropriate non-custodial sentence)	
Engaging in sexual activity in the presence of a child 13(11) (engaging in sexual activity in the presence of a child) (offender under 18) †	Sexual activity involving penetration where one or more aggravating factors exist	12-month detention and training order (6- to 24-month detention and training order)	A2, A3, A4, A5 M5
	Any form of sexual activity (non–penetrative or penetrative) not involving any aggravating factors	Community order (appropriate non-custodial sentence)	
Causing a child to watch a sexual act 13(12) (causing a child to watch a sexual act) (offender under 18) †	Live sexual activity	8-month detention and training order (6- to 12-month detention and training order)	A2, A3, A4, A5, A10 M5
	Moving or still images of people engaged in sexual acts involving penetration	Community order (appropriate non-custodial sentence)	
	Moving or still images of people engaged in sexual acts other than penetration	Community order (appropriate non-custodial sentence)	

OFFENCE	TYPE/ NATURE OF ACTIVITY	STARTING POINTS (AND SENTENCING RANGES)	AGG. & MIT. FACTORS
Sexual activity with a child family member and inciting a child family member to engage in sexual activity 25 (sexual activity with a child family member) (offender under 18) ‡ 26 (inciting a child family member to engage in sexual activity) (offender under 18) ‡	Offence involving penetration where one or more aggravating factors exist or where there is a substantial age gap between the parties	18-month detention and training order (6- to 24-month detention and training order)	A2, A3, A4, A6 M8, M9, M5
	Any form of sexual activity that does not involve any aggravating factors	Community order (appropriate non-custodial sentence)	
N.B.: As to whether these offences are "serious offences", see ante.			

(2) Sentencing Council for England and Wales

The Sentencing Council for England and Wales has issued a definitive guideline covering the   **K-84**
sexual offences set out at I to XXXIII, *post*, applying to all offenders aged 18 or over who are
sentenced on or after April 1, 2014.

The guideline sets out nine steps to be followed (in order) when sentencing for these offences,
which correspond broadly to the steps set out in the guideline on offences against the person
(*post*, K-113 *et seq.*). The offence in XVIII, *post*, only has eight steps (missing out the step requiring
the court to consider whether an offender meets the dangerousness criteria).

In particular, step one requires the court to determine the offence category, based on harm
and culpability. In determining the harm and culpability, the court should refer only to the
indicators set out for each offence (*post*) (although this is not specified for XVI, *post*). Step two
requires the court to use the starting point identified for the relevant category to reach a sentence
within the category range (*post*). The starting point applies to all offenders irrespective of plea or
previous convictions. The court should then consider adjustment within the category range for
aggravating or mitigating features set out for each offence, *post*, which contain a non-exhaustive
list of additional factual elements providing the context of the offence and factors relating to the
offender. A case of particular gravity, reflected by multiple features of culpability or harm in step
one, could merit upward adjustment of the starting point before further adjustment for aggravating or mitigating features. Having considered all factors, it might be appropriate to move outside
the identified category range.

Annex A contains further information about ancillary orders and provisions that apply
automatically by operation of law, Annex B describes the approach to sentencing for historic
sexual offences (see *R. v. H.*, *ante*, Appendix H-12), Annex C lists the various historic offences and
Annex D sets out fine bands, and a non-exhaustive description of examples of requirements that
might be appropriate for low, medium and high level community orders, corresponding to those
in the guideline on offences against the person (*ante*).

Key to factors indicating varying levels of harm and culpability (step one)

Harm factors

           K-84a

1. Severe psychological or physical harm
2. Pregnancy or STI as a consequence of offence
3. Additional degradation/humiliation
4. Abduction
5. Prolonged detention/sustained incident
6. Violence or threats of violence (beyond what is inherent in the offence, where relevant)
7. Forced/uninvited entry into victim's home or residence
8. Victim is particularly vulnerable due to personal circumstances and/or (offences against victims under 13) extreme youth
9. Penetration using large or dangerous object(s)
10. Touching of naked genitalia or naked breasts
11. Penetration of vagina or anus (using body or object) by, or of, the victim
12. Penile penetration of mouth by, or of, the victim
13. Touching, or exposure, of naked genitalia or naked breasts by, or of, the victim
14. Other sexual activity
15. Touching of naked genitalia or naked breasts by, or of, the victim
16. Causing victim to view extreme pornography
17. Causing victim to view indecent/prohibited images of children

18. Engaging in, or causing a victim to view live, sexual activity involving sadism/violence/ sexual activity with an animal/child

19. Engaging in, or causing a victim to view images of or view live, sexual activity involving penetration of vagina or anus (using body or object) or penile penetration of the mouth or masturbation

20. Continued contact despite victim's attempts to terminate contact

21. Sexual images exchanged

22. Victim exposed to extreme sexual content (*e.g.* extreme pornography)

23. Abduction/detention

24. Sustained and systematic psychological abuse

25. Individual(s)/those working in brothel forced or coerced to participate in unsafe/ degrading sexual activity

26. Individual(s)/those working in brothel forced or coerced into seeing many "customers"

27. Individual(s)/ those working in brothel forced/coerced/deceived into prostitution

28. Under 18-year-olds working in brothel

29. Established evidence of community impact

30. Victims involved in penetrative activity

31. Victim(s) participated in unsafe/ degrading sexual activity beyond that which is inherent in the offence

32. Victim(s) passed around by the offender to other "customers" and/or moved to other brothels

33. Victim subjected to unsafe/degrading sexual activity (beyond that which is inherent in the offence)

34. Victim(s) under 18

35. Victim(s) forced/coerced into prostitution

36. Victim(s) tricked/deceived as to purpose of visit

37. Victim followed/pursued

38. Offender masturbated

39. Image(s) available to be viewed by others

40. Victim observed or recorded in their own home or residence

41. Child conceived

42. Offence committed in victim's home

Culpability factors

K-84b

43. Significant degree of planning

44. Acting with others to commit offence

45. Use of alcohol/drugs on victim to facilitate the offence

46. Abuse of trust

47. Previous violence against victim

48. Offence committed in course of burglary

49. Recording of the offence

50. Commercial exploitation and/or motivation

51. Offence racially or religiously aggravated

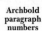

52. Offence motivated by, or demonstrating, hostility to the victim based on his sexual orientation (or presumed sexual orientation) or transgender identity (or presumed transgender identity)

53. Offence motivated by, or demonstrating, hostility to the victim based on his disability (or presumed disability)

54. Grooming behaviour used against victim

55. Sexual images of victim recorded, retained, solicited or shared

56. Deliberate isolation of victim

57. Use of threats (including blackmail)

58. Specific targeting of a particularly vulnerable child/victim

59. Offender lied about age

60. Significant disparity in age

61. Communication indicates penetrative sexual activity is intended

62. Offender lied about persona

63. Use of gifts, bribes

64. Abduction/detention

65. Causing, inciting or controlling prostitution/ keeping brothel/ directing or organising child prostitution or pornography/ directing or organising trafficking on significant commercial basis

66. Expectation of significant financial or other gain

67. Exploitation of those known to be trafficked

68. Significant involvement in limiting the freedom of prostitute(s)/ those working in brothel/ victims of child prostitution or pornography/ significant influence over others in trafficking organisation/ hierarchy

69. Grooming of individual(s) to enter prostitution/ child pornography/ work in brothel, including through cultivation of a dependency on drugs or alcohol

70. Close involvement with prostitute(s)/ those working in brothel, *e.g.* control of finances, choice of clients, working conditions, etc., or with inciting, controlling, arranging or facilitating child prostitution or pornography (where offender's involvement is not as a result of coercion)

71. Performs limited function under direction

72. Close involvement but engaged by coercion/intimidation/ exploitation

73. Involvement in keeping a number of brothels

74. Keeping/ managing premises

75. Use of alcohol/ drugs on victim

76. Blackmail or other threats made

77. Offender aware that he has a sexually transmitted disease

78. Offender aware victim has been trafficked

79. Significant influence over others in trafficking organisation/ hierarchy

80. Operational or management function within hierarchy

81. Involves others in operation whether by coercion/ intimidation/ exploitation or reward (and offender's involvement is not as a result of coercion)

82. Specific or previous targeting of a particularly vulnerable victim

83. Image(s) recorded

84. Intended sexual offence carries a statutory maximum of life imprisonment

85. Possession of weapon or other item to frighten or injure

Key to aggravating and mitigating factors (step two)

Statutory aggravating factors

86. Previous convictions (CJA 2003, s.143(2) (§ 5-67 in the main work))

87. Offence committed whilst on bail (*ibid.*, s.143(3))

Other aggravating factors

88. Specific targeting of a particularly vulnerable victim

89. Ejaculation (where not taken into account at step one)

90. Blackmail or other threats made (where not taken into account at step one)

91. Location of offence

92. Timing of offence

93. Use of weapon or other item to frighten or injure

94. Victim compelled to leave their home, institution, school, etc.

95. Failure to comply with current court orders

96. Offence committed whilst on licence

97. Exploiting contact arrangements with a child to commit an offence

98. Presence of others, especially children

99. Any steps taken to prevent the reporting of an incident, obtaining assistance and/ or from assisting or supporting the prosecution

100. Attempts to dispose of or conceal evidence

101. Commission of offence whilst under the influence of alcohol or drugs

102. Victim encouraged to recruit others

103. Pregnancy or STI as a consequence of offence

104. Failure of offender to respond to previous warnings

105. Period over which offence committed/ operation has been run

106. Severe psychological or physical harm

107. Age and/ or vulnerability of the child depicted (this should be given significant weight; in cases where the actual age is difficult to determine, sentencers should consider the development of the child – infant, pre-pubescent, post-pubescent)

108. Discernible pain or distress suffered by child depicted

109. High volume of images possessed, distributed or produced

110. Placing images where there is the potential for a high volume of viewers

111. Collection includes moving images

112. Abuse of trust

113. Child depicted known to offender

114. Active involvement in a network or process that facilitates or commissions the creation or sharing of indecent images of children

115. Commercial exploitation and/ or motivation

116. Deliberate or systematic searching for images portraying young children, category A images or the portrayal of familial sexual abuse

117. Large number of different victims

118. Child depicted intoxicated or drugged

119. Deliberate isolation of victim(s)/ prostitute(s)/ those working in brothel

120. Threats made to expose victim(s)/ prostitute(s)/ those working in brothel to the authorities (*e.g.* immigration or police), family/ friends or others

121. Harm threatened against the family/ friends of victim(s)/ prostitute(s)/ those working in brothel

122. Passport/ identity documents removed

123. Victim(s)/ prostitute(s)/ those working in brothel prevented from seeking medical treatment

124. Food withheld

125. Earnings withheld/ kept by offender or evidence of excessive wage reduction or debt bondage, inflated travel or living expenses or unreasonable interest rates

126. Prostitute/ those working in brothel forced or coerced into pornography

127. Those working in brothel passed around by offender and moved to other brothels

128. Vulnerability of victim(s)

129. Victim prevented from attending school

130. Children of victim(s) left in home country due to trafficking

131. Exploitation of victim(s) from particularly vulnerable backgrounds

132. Victim(s) previously trafficked/ sold/ passed around

133. Use of drugs/ alcohol or other substance to secure victim's compliance

134. Distribution of images, whether or not for gain

135. Placing images where there is the potential for a high volume of viewers

136. Period over which victim observed

137. Period over which images were made or distributed

Mitigating factors

K-84e

138. No previous convictions or no relevant/recent convictions

139. Remorse

140. Previous good character and/ or exemplary conduct (but the more serious the offence the less weight should be attributed to this factor, particularly where it has been used to facilitate the offence, when it may well be an aggravating factor; where this number is followed by a *, the factor should not normally be given any significant weight or justify a reduction in what would otherwise be the appropriate sentence)

141. Age and/ or lack of maturity where it affects the responsibility of the offender

142. Mental disorder or learning disability, particularly where linked to the commission of the offence

143. Demonstration of steps taken to address offending behaviour

144. Sexual activity was incited but no activity took place because the offender voluntarily desisted or intervened to prevent it

Consideration of custody threshold

K-84f

In the following sections, where there is a sufficient prospect of rehabilitation, a community order with a sex offender treatment programme requirement can be a proper alternative to a short or moderate custodial sentence: II to IV, VII, IX to XI, XIV, and XV to XXX.

When sentencing for some or all of the categories within the various offences, it is sometimes indicated that the court should consider whether the custody threshold has been passed, if so, whether it is unavoidable that a custodial sentence be imposed, and, if so, whether that sentence can be suspended, or whether the community order threshold has been passed. The categories for which these should be considered, if at all, are indicated at the end of step two for each section, *e.g.*, as follows:

Consideration of custody threshold: category 2 or 3

Consideration of community order threshold: category 3

I. Rape (SOA 2003, s.1 (§ 20-19 in the main work))

K-85   Offences here may be of such severity, for example including a campaign of rape, that sentences of 20 years and above may be appropriate.

Factors indicating harm and culpability (step one)

> *Harm*
>
> > Category 1:   The extreme nature of one or more category 2 factors or the extreme impact caused by a combination of category 2 factors **may** elevate to category 1
> >
> > Category 2:   Factors 1–8
> >
> > Category 3:   Factor(s) in categories 1 and 2 not present

> *Culpability*
>
> > Category A: Factors 43–53
> >
> > Category B: Factor(s) in category A not present

Starting point and category range (step two)

	A	**B**
Category 1	**Starting point** 15 years **Range** 13 – 19 years	**Starting point** 12 years **Range** 10 – 15 years
Category 2	**Starting point** 10 years **Range** 9 – 13 years	**Starting point** 8 years **Range** 7 – 9 years
Category 3	**Starting point** 7 years **Range** 6 – 9 years	**Starting point** 5 years **Range** 4 – 7 years

Aggravating and mitigating factors

> Aggravating factors: Factors 86-101
> Mitigating factors: Factors 138, 139, 140*, 141, 142

II. Assault by penetration (2003 Act, s.2 (ibid., § 20-28))

Factors indicating harm and culpability (step one)

K-85b   *Harm*

> > Category 1:   The extreme nature of one or more category 2 factors or the extreme impact caused by a combination of category 2 factors **may** elevate to category 1
> >
> > Category 2:   Factors 1, 3–9
> >
> > Category 3:   Factor(s) in categories 1 and 2 not present

> *Culpability*
>
> > Same as I (*ante*)

Starting point and category range (step two)

	A	B
Category 1	**Starting point** 15 years **Range** 13 – 19 years	**Starting point** 12 years **Range** 10 – 15 years
Category 2	**Starting point** 8 years **Range** 5 – 13 years	**Starting point** 6 years **Range** 4 – 9 years
Category 3	**Starting point** 4 years **Range** 2 – 6 years	**Starting point** 2 years **Range** high level community order – 4 years

Consideration of custody threshold: category 3

Aggravating and mitigating factors

Aggravating factors:	Factors 86–88, 90–101
Mitigating factors:	Factors 138, 139, 140*, 141, 142

III. Sexual assault (2003 Act, s.3 (ibid., § 20-29))

Factors indicating harm and culpability (step one)

Harm   **K-85c**

Category 1:   Factors 1, 4, 6, 7

Category 2:   Factors 3, 5, 8, 10

Category 3:   Factor(s) in categories 1 and 2 not present

Culpability

Same as I (*ante*)

Starting point and category range (step two)

	A	B
Category 1	**Starting point** 4 years **Range** 3 – 7 years	**Starting point** 2.5 years **Range** 2 – 4 years
Category 2	**Starting point** 2 years **Range** 1 – 4 years	**Starting point** 1 year **Range** high level community order – 2 years
Category 3	**Starting point** 26 weeks **Range** high level community order – 1 year	**Starting point** high level community order **Range** medium level community order – 26 weeks

Consideration of custody threshold: category 2 or 3

Aggravating and mitigating factors

Aggravating factors:	Factors 86–88, 90–101
Mitigating factors:	Factors 138-143

IV. Causing a person to engage in sexual activity without consent (2003 Act, s.4 (ibid., § 20-40))

Factors indicating harm and culpability (step one)

Harm   **K-86**

Category 1: The extreme nature of one or more category 2 factors or the extreme impact caused by a combination of category 2 factors **may** elevate to category 1

Category 2: Factors 1–9

Category 3: Factor(s) in categories 1 and 2 not present

Culpability

Same as I (*ante*)

Starting point and category range (step two)

Where offence involved penetration: same as II (*ante*)

Where offence did not involve penetration: same as III (*ante*)

Consideration of custody threshold: category 2 or 3

Aggravating and mitigating factors

Same as I (*ante*)

V. Rape of a child under 13 (2003 Act, s.5 (ibid., § 20-49))

K-87   Offences here may be of such severity, for example including a campaign of rape, that sentences of 20 years and above may be appropriate. Sentencers should have particular regard to the fact that these offences are not only committed through force or fear of force but may include exploitative behaviour towards a child, that should be considered to indicate high culpability. This guideline is designed to deal with the majority of offending behaviour but there may be exceptional cases where a lengthy community order with a requirement to participate in a sex of-fender treatment programme may be the best way of changing the offender's behaviour and of protecting the public by preventing any repetition of the offence.

This guideline may not be appropriate where the sentencer is satisfied that on the available evidence, and in the absence of exploitation, a young or particularly immature defendant genuinely believed, on reasonable grounds, that the victim was aged 16 or over and that they were engaging in lawful sexual activity.

Factors indicating harm and culpability (step one)

Harm

Same as I (*ante*)

Culpability

Category A: Factors 43–48, 50–56

Category B: Factor(s) in category A not present

Starting point and category range (step two)

	A	B
Category 1	**Starting point** 16 years **Range** 13 – 19 years	**Starting point** 13 years **Range** 11 – 17 years
Category 2	**Starting point** 13 years **Range** 11 – 17 years	**Starting point** 10 years **Range** 8 – 13 years
Category 3	**Starting point** 10 years **Range** 8 – 13 years	**Starting point** 8 years **Range** 6 – 11 years

Aggravating and mitigating factors

    Aggravating factors: Factors 86–102

    Mitigating factors: Factors 138, 139, 140*, 141, 142

VI. Assault of a child under 13 by penetration (2003 Act, s.6 (ibid., § 20-50))

Factors indicating harm and culpability (step one)

Harm   **K-87a**

    Same as II (*ante*)

Culpability

    Same as V (*ante*)

Starting point and category range (step two)

	A	B
Category 1	**Starting point** 16 years **Range** 13 – 19 years	**Starting point** 13 years **Range** 11 – 17 years
Category 2	**Starting point** 11 years **Range** 7 – 15 years	**Starting point** 8 years **Range** 5 – 13 years
Category 3	**Starting point** 6 years **Range** 4 – 9 years	**Starting point** 4 years **Range** 2 – 6 years

Aggravating and mitigating factors

    Aggravating factors: Factors 86–88, 90–102

    Mitigating factors: Factors 138, 139, 140*, 141, 142

VII. Sexual assault of a child under 13 (2003 Act, s.7 (ibid., § 20-51))

Factors indicating harm and culpability (step one)

Harm   **K-87b**

    Same as III (*ante*)

Culpability

    Same as V (*ante*)

Starting point and category range (step two)

	A	B
Category 1	**Starting point** 6 years **Range** 4 – 9 years	**Starting point** 4 years **Range** 3 – 7 years
Category 2	**Starting point** 4 years **Range** 3 – 7 years	**Starting point** 2 years **Range** 1 – 4 years
Category 3	**Starting point** 1 year **Range** 26 weeks – 2 years	**Starting point** 26 weeks **Range** high level community order – 1 year

Aggravating and mitigating factors

> Same as VI (*ante*)

VIII. Causing or inciting a child under 13 to engage in sexual activity (2003 Act, s.8 (ibid., § 20-52))

Factors indicating harm and culpability (step one)

K-87c   *Harm*

> Category 1: The extreme nature of one or more category 2 factors or the extreme impact caused by a combination of category 2 factors **may** elevate to category 1
>
> Category 2: Factors 1, 3–8, 11, 12
>
> Category 3: Factor(s) in categories 1 and 2 not present

> *Culpability*
>
> Same as V (*ante*)

Starting point and category range (step two)

	A	B
Category 1	**Starting point** 13 years **Range** 11 – 17 years	**Starting point** 11 years **Range** 10 – 15 years
Category 2	**Starting point** 8 years **Range** 5 – 10 years	**Starting point** 6 years **Range** 3 – 9 years
Category 3	**Starting point** 5 years **Range** 3 – 8 years	**Starting point** 2 years **Range** 1 – 4 years

Aggravating and mitigating factors

> Aggravating factors: Factors 86–103
>
> Mitigating factors: Factors 138, 139, 140*, 141, 142, 144

IX. Sexual activity with a child (2003 Act, s.9 (ibid., § 20-58)); causing or inciting a child to engage in sexual activity (2003 Act, s.10 (ibid., § 20-64))

Factors indicating harm and culpability (step one)

K-88   *Harm*

> Category 1: Factors 11, 12
>
> Category 2: Factor 13
>
> Category 3: Factor 14

> *Culpability*
>
> Category A: Factors 43–46, 50–55, 57–60
>
> Category B: Factor(s) in category A not present

Starting point and category range (step two)

	A	B
Category 1	**Starting point** 5 years **Range** 4 – 10 years	**Starting point** 1 year **Range** high level community order – 2 years
Category 2	**Starting point** 3 years **Range** 2 – 6 years	**Starting point** 26 weeks **Range** high level community order – 1 year
Category 3	**Starting point** 26 weeks **Range** high level community order – 3 years	**Starting point** medium level community order **Range** low level – high level community order

Consideration of custody threshold: category 2 or 3

Aggravating and mitigating factors

Aggravating factors: Factors 86, 87, 89, 91, 92, 94–106

Mitigating factors: Factors 138, 139, 140*, 141, 142, 144

X. Sexual activity with a child family member (2003 Act, s.25 (ibid., § 20-110)); inciting a child family member to engage in sexual activity (2003 Act, s.26 (ibid., § 20-111))

It should be assumed that the greater the trust, the more serious the offence.   **K-89**

Factors indicating harm and culpability (step one)

Harm

     Category 1:   Factors 11, 12

     Category 2:   Factor 15

     Category 3:   Factor 14

Culpability

     Category A: Factors 43–45, 50–55, 57, 58, 60

     Category B: Factor(s) in category A not present

Starting point and category range (step two)

	A	B
Category 1	**Starting point** 6 years **Range** 4 – 10 years	**Starting point** 3.5 years **Range** 2.5 – 5 years
Category 2	**Starting point** 4 years **Range** 2 – 6 years	**Starting point** 18 months **Range** 26 weeks – 2.5 years
Category 3	**Starting point** 1 year **Range** high level community order – 3 years	**Starting point** medium level community order **Range** low level – high level community order

Consideration of custody threshold: category 3

Aggravating and mitigating factors

Same as IX (*ante*)

XI. Engaging in sexual activity in the presence of a child (2003 Act, s.11 (ibid., § 20-69)); causing a child to watch a sexual act (2003 Act, s.12 (ibid., § 20-74))

Factors indicating harm and culpability (step one)

K-90   *Harm*

Category 1:	Factors 16–18
Category 2:	Factor 19
Category 3:	Factor(s) in categories 1 and 2 not present

Culpability

Category A:	Factors 43–46, 50–54, 57, 58, 60
Category B:	Factor(s) in category A not present

Starting point and category range (step two)

	A	B
Category 1	**Starting point** 4 years **Range** 3 – 6 years	**Starting point** 2 years **Range** 1 – 3 years
Category 2	**Starting point** 2 years **Range** 1 – 3 years	**Starting point** 1 year **Range** high level community order – 18 months
Category 3	**Starting point** 26 weeks **Range** high level community order – 1 year	**Starting point** medium level community order **Range** low level – high level community order

Consideration of custody threshold: category 2 or 3

Aggravating and mitigating factors

Aggravating factors:	Factors 86, 87, 91, 92, 94–102, 104
Mitigating factors:	Factors 138–143

XII. Arranging or facilitating the commission of a child sex offence (2003 Act, s.14 (ibid., § 20-85))

K-90a   Sentencers should refer to the guideline for the applicable, substantive offences under sections IX and XI. The level of harm should be determined by reference to the type of activity arranged or facilitated. For offences involving significant commercial exploitation and/ or an international element, it may, in the interests of justice, be appropriate to increase a sentence to a point above the category range. In exceptional cases, such as where a vulnerable offender performed a limited role, having been coerced or exploited by others, sentences below the starting point and range may be appropriate.

XIII. Meeting a child following sexual grooming (2003 Act, s.15 (ibid., § 20-91))

Factors indicating harm and culpability (step one)

Category 1:   Raised harm **and** raised culpability   **K-90b**
Category 2:   Raised harm **or** raised culpability
Category 3:   Grooming **without** raised harm or culpability factors present

   Where an offence does not fall squarely into a category, individual factors may require a degree of weighting before making an overall assessment and determining the appropriate offence category.

Indicators of raised harm
      Factors 8, 20–22

Indicators of raised culpability
      Factors 44, 46, 50–53, 57–59, 61–64

Starting point and category range (step two)

Category 1	**Starting point** 4 years **Range** 3 – 7 years
Category 2	**Starting point** 2 years **Range** 1 – 4 years
Category 3	**Starting point** 18 months **Range** 1 – 2.5 years

Aggravating and mitigating factors

Aggravating factors: Factors 86, 87, 95, 96, 99, 100, 102
Mitigating factors: Factors 138–143

XIV. Abuse of position of trust: sexual activity with a child (2003 Act, s.16 (ibid., § 20-96)); abuse of position of trust: causing a child to engage in sexual activity (2003 Act, s.17 (ibid., § 20-97))

Factors indicating harm and culpability (step one)

Harm   **K-90c**
      Category 1:   Factors 11, 12
      Category 2:   Factor 13
      Category 3:   Factor(s) in categories 1 and 2 not present

Culpability
      Category A: Factors 43–45, 50–55, 57, 58
      Category B: Factor(s) in category A not present

Starting point and category range (step two)

	A	B
Category 1	**Starting point** 18 months **Range** 1 – 2 years	**Starting point** 1 year **Range** 26 weeks – 18 months

| Category 2 | **Starting point** 1 year
Range 26 weeks – 18 months | **Starting point** 26 weeks
Range high level community order – 1 year |
| Category 3 | **Starting point** 26 weeks
Range high level community order – 1 year | **Starting point** medium level community order
Range low level – high level community order |

Consideration of custody threshold: category 2 or 3

Aggravating and mitigating factors

Aggravating factors: Factors 86, 87, 89, 91, 92, 94–96, 98–104

Mitigating factors: Factors 138–144

XV. Abuse of position of trust: sexual activity in the presence of a child (2003 Act, s.18 (ibid., § 20-98)); abuse of position of trust: causing a child to watch a sexual act (2003 Act, s.19 (ibid., § 20-99))

Factors indicating harm and culpability (step one)

K-90d   *Harm*

Same as XI (*ante*)

Culpability

Category A: Factors 43–45, 50–54, 57, 58

Category B: Factor(s) in category A not present

Starting point and category range (step two)

Same as XIV (*ante*)

Consideration of custody threshold: category 2 or 3

Aggravating and mitigating factors

Aggravating factors: Factors 86, 87, 91, 92, 94–96, 98–102, 104

Mitigating factors: Factors 138–143

XVI. Possession of indecent photograph of child (CJA 1988, s.160 (ibid., § 31-115)); indecent photographs of children (Protection of Children Act 1978, s.1 (ibid., § 31-107))

Factors indicating harm and culpability (step one)

K-91

	Possession	**Distribution**	**Production**
Category A	Of images involving penetrative sexual activity	Sharing such images	Creating such images
	Of images involving sexual activity with an animal or sadism	Sharing such images	Creating such images

| Category B | Of images involving non-penetrative sexual activity | Sharing such images | Creating such images |
| Category C | Of other indecent images not falling within categories A or B | Sharing such images | Creating such images |

Distribution includes possession with a view to distributing or sharing images. Production includes the taking or making of any image at source, for instance the original image. Making an image by simple downloading should be treated as possession for the purposes of sentencing.

In most cases the intrinsic character of the most serious of the offending images will initially determine the appropriate category. If, however, the most serious images are unrepresentative of the offender's conduct, a lower category may be appropriate. A lower category will not, however, be appropriate if the offender has produced or taken (*e.g.* photographed) images of a higher category.

Starting point and category range (step two)

	Possession	Distribution	Production
Category A	**Starting point** 1 year **Range** 26 weeks – 3 years	**Starting point** 3 years **Range** 2 – 5 years	**Starting point** 6 years **Range** 4 – 9 years
Category B	**Starting point** 26 weeks **Range** high level community order – 18 months	**Starting point** 1 year **Range** 26 weeks – 2 years	**Starting point** 2 years **Range** 1 – 4 years
Category C	**Starting point** high level community order **Range** medium level community order – 26 weeks	**Starting point** 13 weeks **Range** high level community order – 26 weeks	**Starting point** 18 months **Range** 1 – 3 years

Consideration of custody threshold: category 2 or 3

Aggravating and mitigating factors

Aggravating factors: Factors 86, 87, 95, 96, 100, 105, 107–118

Mitigating factors: Factors 138–143

XVII. Causing or inciting prostitution for gain (2003 Act, s.52 (ibid., § 20–172)); controlling prostitution for gain (2003 Act, s.53 (ibid., § 20–173))

Factors indicating harm and culpability (step one)

Harm   **K-92**

    Category 1:   Factors 6, 23–27

    Category 2:   Factor(s) in category 1 not present

Culpability

    Category A: Factors 46, 65–69

    Category B: Factor 70

    Category C: Factors 71, 72

Starting point and category range (step two)

	A	B	C
Category 1	**Starting point** 4 years **Range** 3 – 6 years	**Starting point** 2.5 years **Range** 2 – 4 years	**Starting point** 1 year **Range** 26 weeks – 2 years
Category 2	**Starting point** 2.5 years **Range** 2 – 5 years	**Starting point** 1 year **Range** high level community order – 2 years	**Starting point** medium level community order **Range** low level – high level community order

Consideration of custody threshold: category 2 or 3

Aggravating and mitigating factors

Aggravating factors: Factors 86, 87, 95, 96, 99, 100, 105, 119–126
Mitigating factors: Factors 138–143

XVIII. Keeping a brothel used for prostitution (SOA 1956, s.33A (ibid., § 20-229))

Factors indicating harm and culpability (step one)

K-92a   *Harm*

Category 1:   Factors 6, 23–29
Category 2:   Factor(s) in category 1 not present

Culpability

Category A: Factors 46, 65–69, 73
Category B: Factors 70, 74
Category C: Factors 71, 72

Starting point and category range (step two)

	A	B	C
Category 1	**Starting point** 5 years **Range** 3 – 6 years	**Starting point** 3.5 years **Range** 2 – 5 years	**Starting point** 1 year **Range** high level community order – 18 months
Category 2	**Starting point** 3 years **Range** 2 – 5 years	**Starting point** 1 year **Range** 26 weeks – 2 years	**Starting point** medium level community order **Range** low level – high level community order

Consideration of custody threshold: category 1

Aggravating and mitigating factors

Aggravating factors: Factors 86, 87, 95, 96, 99, 100, 105, 119–127

Mitigating factors: Factors 138–143

XIX. Causing or inciting child prostitution or pornography (2003 Act, s.48 (ibid., § 20-160)); controlling a child prostitute or child involved in pornography (2003 Act, s.49 (ibid., § 20-167)); arranging or facilitating child prostitution or pornography (2003 Act, s.50 (ibid., § 20-161))

Factors indicating harm and culpability (step one)

Harm   **K-92b**

     Category 1:   Factors 6, 23, 24, 30–32

     Category 2:   Factor(s) in category 1 not present

Culpability

     Same as XVII (*ante*)

Starting point and category range (step two)

	Age of victim	A	B	C
Category 1	U13	**Starting point** 10 years **Range** 8 – 13 years	**Starting point** 8 years **Range** 6 – 11 years	**Starting point** 5 years **Range** 2 – 6 years
	13–15	**Starting point** 8 years **Range** 6 – 11 years	**Starting point** 5 years **Range** 4 – 8 years	**Starting point** 2.5 years **Range** 1 – 4 years
	16–17	**Starting point** 4 years **Range** 3 – 7 years	**Starting point** 2 years **Range** 1 – 4 years	**Starting point** 1 year **Range** 26 weeks – 2 years
Category 2	U13	**Starting point** 8 years **Range** 6 – 11 years	**Starting point** 6 years **Range** 4 – 9 years	**Starting point** 2 years **Range** 1 – 4 years
	13–15	**Starting point** 6 years **Range** 4 – 9 years	**Starting point** 3 years **Range** 2 – 5 years	**Starting point** 1 year **Range** 26 weeks – 2 years
	16–17	**Starting point** 3 years **Range** 2 – 5 years	**Starting point** 1 year **Range** 26 weeks – 2 years	**Starting point** 26 weeks **Range** high level community order – 1 year

Consideration of custody threshold: category 2

Aggravating and mitigating factors

Aggravating factors: Factors 86, 87, 95, 96, 99, 100, 105, 119-125, 128, 129

Mitigating factors: Factors 138, 139, 140*, 141, 142

XX. Paying for the sexual services of a child (2003 Act, s.47 (ibid., § 20-155))

K-92c   This guideline should only be used where the victim was aged 16 or 17.

Factors indicating harm and culpability (step one)

> *Harm*
>> Category 1:   Factors 6, 11, 12, 33
>>
>> Category 2:   Factor 15
>>
>> Category 3:   Factor 14

> *Culpability*
>> Category A: Factors 44, 46, 47, 55, 64, 75–78
>>
>> Category B: Factor(s) in category A not present

Starting point and category range (step two)

	A	B
Category 1	**Starting point** 4 years **Range** 2 – 5 years	**Starting point** 2 years **Range** 1 – 4 years
Category 2	**Starting point** 3 years **Range** 1 – 4 years	**Starting point** 1 year **Range** 26 weeks – 2 years
Category 3	**Starting point** 1 year **Range** 26 weeks – 2 years	**Starting point** 26 weeks **Range** high level community order – 1 year

Consideration of custody threshold: category 3

Aggravating and mitigating factors

> Aggravating factors: Factors 86, 87, 89, 95, 96, 99, 100
>
> Mitigating factors: Factors 138–143

XXI. Trafficking people for sexual exploitation (2003 Act, s.59A (ibid., § 20-179)) (and also ss.57–59 before their replacement by s.59A)

Factors indicating harm and culpability (step one)

K-93   *Harm*
>> Category 1:   Factors 6, 23–25, 34–36
>>
>> Category 2:   Factor(s) in category 1 not present

> *Culpability*
>> Category A: Factors 46, 65, 66, 68
>>
>> Category B: Factors 80, 81
>>
>> Category C: Factors 71, 72

Starting point and category range (step two)

	A	B	C
Category 1	**Starting point** 8 years **Range** 6 – 12 years	**Starting point** 6 years **Range** 4 – 8 years	**Starting point** 18 months **Range** 26 weeks – 2 years
Category 2	**Starting point** 6 years **Range** 4 – 8 years	**Starting point** 4 years **Range** 2 – 6 years	**Starting point** 26 weeks **Range** high level community order – 18 months

Consideration of custody threshold: category 2

Aggravating and mitigating factors

Aggravating factors:	Factors 86, 87, 95, 96, 99, 100, 105, 119–125, 131–133
Mitigating factors:	Factors 138, 139, 140*, 141, 142

XXII. Sexual activity with a person with a mental disorder impeding choice (2003 Act, s.30 (ibid., § 20-125)); causing or inciting such a person to engage in a sexual activity (2003 Act, s.31 (ibid., § 20-126))

Factors indicating harm and culpability (step one)

Harm **K-94**

Category 1:	The extreme nature of one or more category 2 factors or the extreme impact caused by a combination of category 2 factors **may** elevate to category 1
Category 2:	Factors 1–7
Category 3:	Factor(s) in categories 1 and 2 not present

Culpability

Category A:	Factors 43–48, 50–56
Category B:	Factor(s) in category A not present

Starting point and category range (step two)

Where offence involved penetration: same as V (*ante*)

Where offence did not involve penetration: same as VII (*ante*)

Consideration of custody threshold: when appropriate

Aggravating and mitigating factors

Aggravating factors:	Factors 86, 87, 89, 90–96, 98–101
Mitigating factors:	Factors 138, 139, 140*, 141, 142, 144

XXIII. Engaging in sexual activity in the presence of a person with a mental disorder impeding choice (2003 Act, s.32 (ibid., § 20-127)); causing such a person to watch a sexual act (2003 Act, s.33 (ibid., § 20-128))

Factors indicating harm and culpability (step one)

K-95   *Harm*

Same as XI (*ante*)

Culpability

Category A: Factors 43–46, 50–54, 57

Category B: Factor(s) in category A not present

Starting point and category range (step two)

Same as XI (*ante*)

Consideration of custody threshold: category 2 or 3

Aggravating and mitigating factors

Aggravating factors: Factors 86, 87, 91, 92, 95, 96, 99–101

Mitigating factors: Factors 138–143

XXIV. Inducement, threat or deception to procure sexual activity with a person with a mental disorder (2003 Act, s.34 (ibid., § 20-134)); causing such a person to engage in or agree to engage in sexual activity by inducement, threat or deception (2003 Act, s.35 (ibid., § 20-135))

Factors indicating harm and culpability (step one)

K-96   *Harm*

Same as IX (*ante*)

Culpability

Category A: Factors 43–46, 50–53, 55

Category B: Factor(s) in category A not present

Starting point and category range (step two)

Same as IX (*ante*)

Consideration of custody threshold: category 2 or 3

Aggravating and mitigating factors

Aggravating factors: Factors 86, 87, 89, 91, 92, 94–96, 99–101, 103, 106

Mitigating factors: Factors 138, 139, 140*, 141, 142

XXV. Engaging in sexual activity in the presence, procured by inducement, threat or deception, of a person with a mental disorder (2003 Act, s.36 (ibid., § 20-136)); causing such a person to watch a sexual act by inducement, threat or deception (2003 Act, s.37 (ibid., § 20-137))

Factors indicating harm and culpability (step one)

Harm **K-97**

 Same as XI (*ante*)

Culpability

Category A:	Factors 43–46, 50–53
Category B:	Factor(s) in category A not present

Starting point and category range (step two)

 Same as XI (*ante*)

 Consideration of custody threshold: category 2 or 3

Aggravating and mitigating factors

Aggravating factors:	Factors 86, 87, 91, 92, 95, 96, 99–101
Mitigating factors:	Factors 138–143

XXVI. Care workers: sexual activity with a person with a mental disorder (2003 Act, s.38 (ibid., § 20-143)); care workers: causing or inciting sexual activity (2003 Act, s.39 (ibid., § 20-144))

Factors indicating harm and culpability (step one)

Harm **K-98**

 Same as XIV (*ante*)

Culpability

Category A:	Factors 43–45, 50–55, 57
Category B:	Factor(s) in category A not present

Starting point and category range (step two)

	A	B
Category 1	**Starting point** 5 years **Range** 4 – 10 years	**Starting point** 18 months **Range** 1 – 2 years
Category 2	**Starting point** 3 years **Range** 2 – 6 years	**Starting point** 26 weeks **Range** medium level community order – 1 year
Category 3	**Starting point** 26 weeks **Range** high level community order – 3 years	**Starting point** medium level community order **Range** low level – high level community order

Consideration of custody threshold: category 2 or 3

Aggravating and mitigating factors

    Aggravating factors: Factors 86, 87, 89, 91, 92, 94–96, 99–101, 103, 104

    Mitigating factors: Factors 138, 139, 140*, 141, 142, 144

XXVII. Care workers: sexual activity in the presence of a person with a mental disorder (2003 Act, s.40 (ibid., § 20-145)); care workers: causing such a person to watch a sexual act (2003 Act, s.41 (ibid., § 20-146))

Factors indicating harm and culpability (step one)

K-99   *Harm*

          Same as XI (*ante*)

      Culpability

          Category A: Factors 43–45, 50–54, 57

          Category B: Factor(s) in category A not present

Starting point and category range (step two)

          Same as XIV (*ante*)

      Consideration of custody threshold: category 2 or 3

Aggravating and mitigating factors

    Aggravating factors: Factors 86, 87, 91, 92, 95, 96, 99–101, 104

    Mitigating factors: Factors 138–143

XXVIII. Exposure (2003 Act, s.66 (ibid., § 20-208))

Factors indicating harm and culpability (step one)

K-100   Category 1:   Raised harm **and** raised culpability

          Category 2:   Raised harm **or** raised culpability

          Category 3:   Exposure **without** raised harm or culpability factors present

    Where an offence does not fall squarely into a category, individual factors may require a degree of weighting before making an overall assessment and determining the appropriate offence category.

      Indicators of raised harm

          Factors 37, 38

      Indicators of raised culpability

          Factors 46, 51–53, 57, 82

Starting point and category range (step two)

Category 1	**Starting point** 26 weeks **Range** 12 weeks – 1 year
Category 2	**Starting point** high level community order **Range** medium level community order – 26 weeks

| Category 3 | **Starting point** medium level community order |
| | **Range** band A fine – high level community order |

Consideration of custody threshold: category 2
Consideration of community order threshold: category 3

Aggravating and mitigating factors

| Aggravating factors: | Factors 86, 87, 91, 92, 95, 96, 98, 99, 101 |
| Mitigating factors: | Factors 138–143 |

XXIX. Voyeurism (2003 Act, s.67 (ibid., § 20-212))

Factors indicating harm and culpability (step one)

Category 1:   Raised harm **and** raised culpability   **K-101**

Category 2:   Raised harm **or** raised culpability

Category 3:   Voyeurism **without** raised harm or culpability factors present

   Where an offence does not fall squarely into a category, individual factors may require a degree of weighting before making an overall assessment and determining the appropriate offence category.

   Indicators of raised harm
      Factors 39, 40

   Indicators of raised culpability
      Factors 43, 46, 50–53, 82, 83

Starting point and category range (step two)

Category 1	**Starting point** 26 weeks
	Range 12 weeks – 18 months
Category 2	**Starting point** high level community order
	Range medium level community order – 26 weeks
Category 3	**Starting point** medium level community order
	Range band A fine – high level community order

Consideration of custody threshold: category 2
Consideration of community order threshold: category 3

Aggravating and mitigating factors

| Aggravating factors: | Factors 86, 87, 91, 92, 95, 96, 99, 100, 134–137 |
| Mitigating factors: | Factors 138–143 |

XXX. Sex with an adult relative: penetration (2003 Act, s.64 (ibid., § 20-202)); sex with an adult relative: consenting to penetration (2003 Act, s.65 (ibid., § 20-203))

Factors indicating harm and culpability (step one)

Category 1:   Raised harm **and** raised culpability   **K-102**

815

Category 2:   Raised harm **or** raised culpability

Category 3:   Sex with an adult relative **without** raised harm or culpability factors
                 present

Where an offence does not fall squarely into a category, individual factors may require a degree
of weighting before making an overall assessment and determining the appropriate offence
category.

Indicators of raised harm
      Factors 8, 41

Indicators of raised culpability
      Factors 54, 57

Starting point and category range (step two)

Category 1	**Starting point** 1 year **Range** 26 weeks – 2 years
Category 2	**Starting point** high level community order **Range** medium level community order – 1 year
Category 3	**Starting point** medium level community order **Range** band A fine – high level community order

Consideration of custody threshold: category 2
Consideration of community order threshold: category 3

Aggravating and mitigating factors

Aggravating factors: Factors 86, 87, 95, 96, 99, 100, 104

Mitigating factors: Factors 138–143

XXXI. Administering a substance with intent (2003 Act, s.61 (ibid., § 20-187))

Factors indicating harm and culpability (step one)

K-103   Category 1:   Raised harm **and** raised culpability

                   Category 2:   Raised harm **or** raised culpability

                   Category 3:   Administering a substance with intent **without** raised harm or culpabil-
                                    ity factors present

Where an offence does not fall squarely into a category, individual factors may require a degree
of weighting before making an overall assessment and determining the appropriate offence
category. Where no substantive sexual offence has been committed the main consideration for the
court will be the offender's conduct as a whole including, but not exclusively, the offender's
intention.

Indicators of raised harm
      Factors 1, 3, 5

Indicators of raised culpability
      Factors 43, 44, 46, 49–53, 58, 84

Starting point and category range (step two)

Category 1	**Starting point** 6 years **Range** 4 – 9 years
Category 2	**Starting point** 4 years **Range** 3 – 7 years
Category 3	**Starting point** 2 years **Range** 1 – 5 years

Aggravating and mitigating factors

Aggravating factors: Factors 86, 87, 91, 92, 95, 96, 99, 100

Mitigating factors: Factors 138–143

XXXII. Committing an offence with intent to commit a sexual offence (2003 Act, s.62 (ibid., § 20-192))

The starting point and range should be commensurate with that for the preliminary offence actually committed, but with an enhancement to reflect the intention to commit a sexual offence. This will vary depending on the nature and seriousness of the intended sexual offence, but two years is suggested as a suitable enhancement where the intent was to commit rape or assault by penetration. **K-104**

XXXIII. Trespass with intent to commit a sexual offence (2003 Act, s.63 (ibid., § 20-197))

Factors indicating harm and culpability (step one)

Category 1:	Raised harm **and** raised culpability	**K-105**
Category 2:	Raised harm **or** raised culpability	
Category 3:	Trespass with intent to commit a sexual offence **without** raised harm or culpability factors present	

Where an offence does not fall squarely into a category, individual factors may require a degree of weighting before making an overall assessment and determining the appropriate offence category. Where no substantive sexual offence has been committed the main consideration for the court will be the offender's conduct as a whole including, but not exclusively, the offender's intention.

Indicators of raised harm

Factors 3, 5, 42

Indicators of raised culpability

Factors 43, 44, 46, 50–53, 58, 84, 85

Starting point and category range (step two)

Same as XXXI (*ante*)

Aggravating and mitigating factors

Same as XXXI (*ante*)

Errors

In XXVII, the starting point for a category 1A offence is given as 18 years' custody. It has been **K-106**

assumed that this should be 18 months. In XI, XXIII and XXV, the top of the range for a
category 3B offence is given as a medium level community order (the same as the starting point),
and thus it has been assumed that the top of the range should be a high level community order.

I. Failing to Surrender to Bail

K-107   The Sentencing Guidelines Council has issued a definitive guideline on failing to surrender to
bail (Bail Act 1976, s.6(1) and (2) (§ 3-31 in the main work)). It deals with offenders sentenced on
or after December 10, 2007, and only relates to the sentencing of those aged 18 or over.

Assessment of seriousness

K-108   The seriousness of an offence is to be determined by: (a) the offender's culpability (in particular,
whether the failure to surrender was intended to cause harm and, if so, what level of harm), and
(b) any harm which the offence caused, was intended to cause or might foreseeably have caused
(in particular, to what extent the failure to surrender impeded the course of justice), and "harm"
includes not only harm caused to victims and witnesses but also the consequential drain on the
police and the courts and the wider negative impact on public confidence in the criminal justice
system. The same approach to sentencing should be adopted for offences under both section 6(1)
and (2), though the seriousness is likely to be less for an offence under subsection (2). The assessment of culpability requires consideration of the immediate reason why the defendant failed to
appear, which can range from forgetfulness or fear of the outcome of the hearing to a deliberate
act, and where the failure to surrender was deliberate, it will be relevant whether it was designed
to disrupt the system to the defendant's advantage or whether the defendant simply gave no
thought at all to the consequences. Failure to surrender will always cause some degree of harm,
will inevitably delay justice, and will almost always waste public money. The circumstances of an
offence, and the harm likely to be caused, will range from failure to appear for a first hearing but
attending shortly afterwards (where the only harm caused is likely to be financial and procedural),
to failure to appear for trial or sentence, especially where the trial does not proceed in the
defendant's absence (where the harm caused may extend to the prevention of justice). Generally,
the same approach should be taken whether the failure to surrender is to a court or to a police
station, but the harm caused is likely to be less in the case of a police station, and there are also
circumstances where the culpability may be less. Where sentence is passed in advance of the offence in respect of which bail was granted, the seriousness of that offence should not affect the assessment of seriousness, but the nature of that offence may affect the degree or likelihood of harm
caused, such as where it is a violent or sexual offence, and an acquittal for that offence will not affect the seriousness of the failure to surrender.

  Aggravating factors that are particularly relevant to the assessment of seriousness are: (a)
repeated offences under section 6; (b) the absence of the offender causing a lengthy delay to the
administration of justice; and (c) a determined effort to avoid the jurisdiction of the court or to
undermine the course of justice. Mitigating factors that are particularly relevant are: (a) prompt
voluntary surrender (if initiated by the offender); (b) misunderstanding (which must be differenti-
ated from a mistake on the part of the offender); (c) a failure to comprehend the requirements or
significance of bail; and (d) caring responsibilities (where these are the cause of the failure to
surrender). The fact that the offender has a disorganised or chaotic lifestyle (which may be due to
dependence on drugs or alcohol) does not mitigate the seriousness of the offence (though it may
amount to personal mitigation).

Procedural issues

K-109   *As to when to sentence*, the key principle is stated to be that a court should deal with a defendant
who fails to surrender as soon as it is practicable, even if the trial or other hearing for the offence
in respect of which bail was granted is adjourned. Relevant factors when deciding what is
practicable include: (a) when the proceedings in respect of which bail was granted are expected to
conclude; (b) the seriousness of that offence; and (c) the type of penalty that might be imposed for
that offence and for the failure to surrender. Liability for the section 6 offence should be
determined as soon as possible, since it will be central to the issue of whether bail should be
renewed; accordingly, a trial should be held on the first appearance after arrest or surrender, un-

less an adjournment is necessary. Occasions on which it may be more appropriate to sentence both offences together include circumstances where the totality of sentence may affect sentence type and where the harm caused cannot be assessed at an earlier stage.

As to sentencing, the alternatives to immediate custody are a community order, including an **K-110** electronically monitored curfew requirement and, perhaps, a supervision or activity requirement, and, in more serious cases, a suspended sentence. Where custodial sentences are imposed both for the section 6 offence and for the substantive offence, they should normally be consecutive, but should be concurrent where otherwise the overall sentence would be disproportionate to the combined seriousness of the offences.

As to trial in the defendant's absence, where it has proved possible to proceed to trial or conclude **K-111** proceedings in the absence of the defendant, this should have no bearing on culpability, but may be relevant to the assessment of harm, if the harm caused by the failure to attend has been reduced or avoided by such a course.

Sentencing ranges and starting points

The sentencing ranges and starting points relate to persons convicted following a plea of not **K-112** guilty, and who do not have a conviction which, by virtue of the CJA 2003, s.143(2) (§ 5-67 in the main work), must be treated as an aggravating factor. A court should identify the description that most nearly matches the facts of the offence and this will identify a starting point, from which a provisional sentence can be reached. The sentencing range is the bracket into which the provisional sentence will fall after consideration of aggravating or mitigating factors (although particular circumstances, particular matters of aggravation or mitigation or the reduction for a guilty plea may require a sentence outside of that range). A court should give reasons for imposing a sentence of a different kind or outside the range provided in the guideline.

For a deliberate failure to attend causing delay and/or interference with the administration of justice, the starting point is 14 days' custody, and the range, in a magistrates' court, should be from a community order (low) to 10 weeks' custody, and in the Crown Court, should be from a community order (medium) to 40 weeks' custody, with the type and degree of harm actually caused affecting where in the range the case falls. For a negligent or non-deliberate failure to attend causing delay and/or interference with the administration of justice, the starting point should be a fine, and the range (regardless of court) should be from a fine to a community order (medium). Where the defendant surrenders late, but the case proceeds as planned, the starting point and the range should be a fine.

J. Assault and Other Offences Against the Person

The Sentencing Council for England and Wales has issued a definitive guideline on non-fatal **K-113** offences against the person, applying to all offenders aged 18 or over who are sentenced on or after June 13, 2011, regardless of the date of their offence. The offences covered are: (A) causing grievous bodily harm, or wounding, with intent to do grievous bodily harm (Offences against the Person Act 1861, s.18 (§ 19-251 in the main work)), (B) inflicting grievous bodily harm or unlawful wounding (1861 Act, s.20 (*ibid.*, § 19-252)) and racially or religiously aggravated grievous bodily harm or unlawful wounding (CDA 1998, s.29 (*ibid.*, § 19-266)), (C) assault occasioning actual bodily harm (1861 Act, s.47 (*ibid.*, § 19-242)) and racially or religiously aggravated actual bodily harm (1998 Act, s.29), (D) assault with intent to resist arrest (1861 Act, s.38 (*ibid.*, § 19-316)), (E) assault on a police constable in execution of his duty (Police Act 1996, s.89), and (F) common assault (CJA 1988, s.39) and racially or religiously aggravated common assault (1998 Act, s.29).

The guideline sets out eight to nine steps to be followed (in order) when sentencing for these **K-114** offences, which are as follows, subject to any modifications set out in the specific sections relating to each group (*post*).

Step one requires the court to determine within which of three categories reflecting various degrees of seriousness the offence falls. Category 1 requires greater harm and higher culpability, category 2 requires either greater harm and lower culpability or lesser harm and higher culpability, and category 3 requires lesser harm and lower culpability. In determining the offender's culpability and the harm caused (or intended), the court should refer only to the factors indicating harm and culpability set out in the specific sections relating to A to F, *post*, which comprise the principal factual elements of the offence.

Step two requires the court to use the starting point identified for the relevant category (as to which, see also the specific sections relating to A-F, *post*) to reach a sentence within the category range (*post*). The starting point applies to all offenders irrespective of plea or previous convictions. A case of particular gravity, reflected by multiple features of culpability in step one, could merit upward adjustment from the starting point before further adjustment is made for the aggravating or mitigating factors increasing or reducing seriousness or reflecting personal mitigation set out in the specific sections relating to A to F, post, which contain a non-exhaustive list of additional factual elements providing the context of the offence and factors relating to the offender. Having considered all these, and other relevant factors, it might be appropriate to move outside the identified category range.

At step three, the court should take into account sections 73 and 74 of the SOCPA 2005 (assistance by defendants: reduction or review of sentence (*ibid.*, §§ 5-132, 5-133)), and any other rule of law by virtue of which an offender may receive a discounted sentence in consequence of assistance given (or offered) to the prosecutor or investigator.

At step four, the court should take account of any potential reduction for a guilty plea in accordance with section 144 of the CJA 2003 (*ibid.*, § 5-107) and the revised guideline on reductions in sentence for guilty pleas (*ante*, Appendix K-1 *et seq.*).

At step five, which does not apply to the offence in E (assault on a police constable in execution of his duty), the court will consider whether the offender meets the dangerousness criteria for a life sentence or imprisonment for public protection (in respect of those offences which are serious offences within the meaning of the 2003 Act, Ch. 5 (*ibid.*, §§ 5-495 *et seq.*), in which case the notional determinate sentence should be used as the basis for setting the minimum term) or an extended sentence (in respect of those offences which are specified offences within the meaning of the 2003 Act, Ch. 5).

At step six (or five), the court should apply the totality principle, step seven (or six), consider whether to make compensation or other ancillary orders or both, step eight (or seven), give its reasons for, and explain the effect of, the sentence (2003 Act, s.174 (*ibid.*, § 5-165)), and step nine (or eight) take into account any time spent on remand in custody or on bail (2003 Act, ss.240 and 240A (*ibid.*, §§ 5-640, 5-645)).

For offences under the 1998 Act, s.29, only, the court should determine the appropriate sentence for the offence without taking account of the element of aggravation, and then make an addition to the sentence, considering the level of aggravation involved. It may be appropriate to move outside the identified category range, taking into account the increased statutory maximum.

Key to factors indicating greater harm and higher or lower culpability (step one)

Factors indicating greater harm

K-115
    a. Injury (which includes disease transmission and/ or psychological harm) which is serious in the context of the offence (must normally be present).

    b. Victim is particularly vulnerable because of personal circumstances.

    c. Sustained or repeated assault on the same victim.

    d. Injury or fear of injury which is serious in the context of the offence (must normally be present).

Factors indicating higher culpability

K-116 Statutory aggravating factors:

    e. offence racially or religiously aggravated.

    f. offence motivated by, or demonstrating, hostility to the victim based on his or her sexual orientation (or presumed sexual orientation).

    g. offence motivated by, or demonstrating, hostility to the victim based on the victim's disability (or presumed disability).

Other aggravating factors:

    h. A significant degree of premeditation.

    i. Use of weapon or weapon equivalent (*e.g.* shod foot, headbutting, use of acid, use of animal).

    j. Threatened use of weapon or weapon equivalent.

k. Intention to commit more serious harm than actually resulted from the offence.
l. Deliberately causes more harm than is necessary for commission of offence.
m. Deliberate targeting of vulnerable victim.
n. Leading role in group or gang.
o. Offence motivated by, or demonstrating, hostility based on the victim's age, sex, gender identity (or presumed gender identity).

Factors indicating lower culpability

p. Subordinate role in group or gang.   **K-117**
q. A greater degree of provocation than normally expected.
r. Lack of premeditation.
s. Mental disorder or learning disability, where linked to commission of the offence.
t. Excessive self defence.

Key to factors increasing or reducing seriousness or reflecting personal mitigation (step 2)

Factors increasing seriousness

Statutory aggravating factors: **K-118**
u. Previous convictions (in accordance with the 2003 Act, s.143(2) (§ 5-67 in the main work)).
v. Offence committed whilst on bail (2003 Act, s.143(3)).

Other aggravating factors include:

w. Location of the offence.
x. Timing of the offence.
y. Continuing effect upon the victim.
z. Offence committed against those working in the public sector or providing a service to the public.
aa. Presence of others including relatives, especially children or partner of the victim.
bb. Gratuitous degradation of victim.
cc. In domestic violence cases, victim forced to leave home.
dd. Failure to comply with current court orders.
ee. Offence committed whilst on licence.
ff. An attempt to conceal or dispose of evidence.
gg. Failure to respond to warnings or concerns expressed by others about the offender's behaviour.
hh. Commission of offence whilst under the influence of alcohol or drugs.
ii. Abuse of power and/ or position of trust.
jj. Exploiting contact arrangements with a child to commit an offence.
kk. Any steps taken to prevent the victim reporting an incident, obtaining assistance and/ or from assisting or supporting the prosecution.
ll. Offences taken into consideration.

Factors reducing seriousness or reflecting personal mitigation

mm. No previous convictions or no relevant/ recent convictions.   **K-119**
nn. Single blow.
oo. Remorse.
pp. Good character and/ or exemplary conduct.
qq. Determination and/ or demonstration of steps taken to address addiction or offending behaviour.
rr. serious medical conditions requiring urgent, intensive or long-term treatment.
ss. isolated incident.
tt. Age and/ or lack of maturity where it affects the responsibility of the offender.
uu. Lapse of time since the offence where this is not the fault of the offender.
vv. Mental disorder or learning disability, where not linked to the commission of the offence.
ww. Sole or primary carer for dependent relatives.

Fine bands

Fine band	Starting point (applicable to all offenders)	Category range (applicable to all offenders)
band A	50% of relevant weekly income	25 – 75% of relevant weekly income
band B	100% of relevant weekly income	75 – 125% of relevant weekly income
band C	150% of relevant weekly income	125 – 175% of relevant weekly income

Community orders

K-121   The following table sets out a non-exhaustive description of examples of requirements that might be appropriate for low, medium and high level community orders (respectively). Where two or more requirements are ordered, they must be compatible with each other.

Low	Medium	High
In general, only one requirement will be appropriate and the length may be curtailed if additional requirements are necessary		More intensive sentences which combine two or more requirements may be appropriate
Suitable requirements might include: • 40 – 80 hours unpaid work • curfew requirement within the lowest range (*e.g.* up to 12 hours per day for a few weeks) • exclusion requirement, without electronic monitoring, for a few months • prohibited activity requirement • attendance centre requirement (where available)	Suitable requirements might include: • greater number of hours of unpaid work (*e.g.* 80 – 150 hours) • an activity requirement in the middle range (20 – 30 days) • curfew requirement within the middle range (*e.g.* up to 12 hours for two – three months) • exclusion requirement, lasting in the region of six months • prohibited activity requirement	Suitable requirements might include: • 150 – 300 hours unpaid work • activity requirement up to the maximum of 60 days • curfew requirement up to 12 hours per day for four – six months • exclusion order lasting in the region of 12 months

A. Causing grievous bodily harm, or wounding, with intent to do grievous bodily harm

K-122   In assessing whether there has been greater harm for the purposes of determining the offence category in respect of these offences, serious injury must normally be present.

Factors indicating harm and culpability (step one)
>   Greater harm: a–c
>   Lesser harm: injury which is less serious in the context of the offence
>   Higher culpability: e–i, k–o
>   Lower culpability: p–t

Starting point and category range (step two)

Offence category		Starting point (applicable to all offenders)	Category range (applicable to all offenders)
category 1		12 years' custody	nine – 16 years' custody
category 2		six years' custody	five – nine years' custody
category 3		four years' custody	three – five years' custody

Factors increasing or reducing seriousness or reflecting personal mitigation
      Factors increasing seriousness: u–z, aa–ll
      Factors reducing seriousness or reflecting personal mitigation: mm–ww

B. Inflicting grievous bodily harm or unlawful wounding and racially or religiously aggravated grievous bodily harm or unlawful wounding

In assessing whether there has been greater harm for the purposes of determining the offence **K-123** category in respect of these offences, serious injury must normally be present.

Factors indicating harm and culpability (step one)
      Greater harm: a–c
      Lesser harm: injury which is less serious in the context of the offence
      Higher culpability: f–i, k–o
      Lower culpability: p–t

Starting point and category range (step two)

Offence category	Starting point (applicable to all offenders)	Category range (applicable to all offenders)
category 1	three years' custody	30 months' – four years' custody
category 2	18 months' custody	one – three years' custody
category 3	high level community order	low level community order – 51 weeks' custody

When sentencing for category three offences, the court should consider whether the custody threshold has been passed, if so, whether it is unavoidable that a custodial sentence be imposed and, if so, whether that sentence can be suspended.

Factors increasing or reducing seriousness or reflecting personal mitigation
      Same as for A, *ante.*

C. Assault occasioning actual bodily harm and racially or religiously aggravated actual bodily harm

In assessing whether there has been "greater harm" for the purposes of determining the of- **K-124** fence category in respect of these offences, serious injury must normally be present.

Factors indicating harm and culpability (step one)
      Same as for B, *ante.*

Starting point and category range (step two)

Offence category	Starting point (applicable to all offenders)	Category range (applicable to all offenders)
category 1	18 months' custody	one – three years' custody
category 2	26 weeks' custody	low level community order – 51 weeks' custody
category 3	medium level community order	band A fine – high level community order

When sentencing for category two offences, the court should consider whether the custody threshold has been passed, if so, whether it is unavoidable that a custodial sentence be imposed and, if so, whether that sentence can be suspended; and in sentencing for category three offences, the court should also consider whether the community order threshold has been passed.

Factors increasing or reducing seriousness or reflecting personal mitigation
>Same as for A and B, *ante.*

D. Assault with intent to resist arrest

Factors indicating harm and culpability (step one)

K-125
>Greater harm: c
>Lesser harm: injury which is less serious in the context of the offence
>Higher culpability: e–i, k–l, n, o
>Lower culpability: p, r, s

Starting point and category range (step two)

Offence category	Starting point (applicable to all offenders)	Category range (applicable to all offenders)
category 1	26 weeks' custody	12 – 51 weeks' custody
category 2	medium level community order	low level community order – high level community order
category 3	band B fine	band A fine – band C fine

When sentencing for category one offences, the court should consider whether the sentence can be suspended.

Factors increasing or reducing seriousness or reflecting personal mitigation
>Factors increasing seriousness: u–y, bb, dd–hh, kk, ll
>Factors reducing seriousness or reflecting personal mitigation: mm–tt, vv, ww

E. Assault on a police constable in execution of his duty

Factors indicating harm and culpability (step one)

K-126
>Same as for D, *ante.*

Starting point and category range (step two)

Offence category	Starting point (applicable to all offenders)	Category range (applicable to all offenders)
category 1	12 weeks' custody	low level community order – 26 weeks' custody
category 2	medium level community order	low level community order – high level community order
category 3	band B fine	band A fine – band C fine

When sentencing for category one offences, the court should consider whether the custody
threshold has been passed, if so, whether it is unavoidable that a custodial sentence be imposed
and, if so, whether that sentence can be suspended.

Factors increasing or reducing seriousness or reflecting personal mitigation
　　Factors increasing seriousness: u–y, bb, dd–hh, kk, ll
　　Factors reducing seriousness or reflecting personal mitigation: mm–ww

F. Common assault and racially or religiously aggravated common assault

In assessing whether there has been "greater harm" for the purposes of determining the of-　**K-127**
fence category in respect of these offences, injury or fear of injury must normally be present.

Factors indicating harm and culpability (step one)
　　Greater harm: b–d
　　Lesser harm: injury which is less serious in the context of the offence
　　Higher culpability: f–o
　　Lower culpability: p–t

Starting point and category range (step two)

Offence category	Starting point (applicable to all offenders)	Category range (applicable to all offenders)
category 1	high level community order	low level community order – 26 weeks' custody
category 2	medium level community order	band A fine – high level community order
category 3	band A fine	discharge – band C fine

When sentencing for category one offences, the court should consider whether the custody
threshold has been passed, if so, whether it is unavoidable that a custodial sentence be imposed
and, if so, whether that sentence can be suspended. When sentencing for category two offences,
the court should consider whether the community order threshold has been crossed.

Factors increasing or reducing seriousness or reflecting personal mitigation
　　Same as for A, B and C, *ante*.

[The next paragraph is K-131.]

K. Assaults on Children and Cruelty to a Child

The Sentencing Guidelines Council has issued a definitive guideline (i) supplementing the　**K-131**
guideline on assaults and other offences against the person (*ante*, K-113 *et seq.*) by detailing additional principles which apply where the victim of the offence was aged 15 or under and (ii) on
the offence of cruelty to a child (CYPA 1933, s.1(1)). It deals with offenders sentenced on or after
March 3, 2008, and only relates to the sentencing of those aged 18 or over.

Part 1: Assaults on children: general principles

Assessing seriousness

The seriousness of an offence is to be determined by (a) the culpability of the offender and (b)　**K-132**
the harm caused, intended or reasonably foreseeable, and guidance on whether sentencing
thresholds have been reached is provided by the guideline on seriousness. Where an offender has
previous convictions, the court must consider whether it should treat any of them as an aggravating factor, having regard to the nature and relevance of each offence and the time that has
elapsed since the conviction. The fact that the victim is a child is likely to aggravate the seriousness of the offence where the offender is an adult.

Aggravation

K-133   The fact that the victim of an assault is a child will often mean that the offence involves a particularly vulnerable victim. The most relevant aggravating factors are: (i) the victim is particularly vulnerable; (ii) an abuse of power; (iii) an abuse of a position of trust; (iv) an especially serious physical or psychological effect on the victim, even if unintended; (v) the presence of others, *e.g.* relatives, especially other children; and (vi) additional degradation of the victim. Additional aggravating factors are: (i) sadistic behaviour; (ii) the making of threats to prevent the victim reporting the offence; (iii) the deliberate concealment of the victim from the authorities; and (iv) a failure to seek medical help. The location and particular circumstances of the offence may also be relevant aggravating factors.

Mitigation

K-134   The defence of lawful chastisement is only available on a charge of common assault, and where that defence is not available or is not made out, sentencing for the offence should normally be approached in the same way as for any other assault, even where an offender held a genuine belief that his actions amounted to no more than a legitimate form of physical punishment. However, if an offender has been charged with assault occasioning actual bodily harm and the court has found that he only intended to administer lawful chastisement to the child, and that the injury that was inflicted was neither intended nor foreseen by him, there should be a substantial reduction in sentence and a custodial sentence should not normally be imposed. Where the injury was neither intended nor foreseen, and was not even reasonably foreseeable, then a discharge might be appropriate.

Other factors relevant to sentencing

Adverse effect of the sentence on the victim

K-135   Imposition of a custodial sentence will often protect a victim from further harm and anguish, and some children will be less traumatised once they are no longer living with an abusive carer, but where imprisonment of the offender deprives a child victim of his sole or main carer (and may result in the child being taken into care), it may punish and re-victimise the child. Imposing a custodial sentence on the offender may be the only option, but where other sentencing options remain open, the court should take into account the impact that a custodial sentence for the offender might have on the victim. The court also needs to be aware of the progress of any concurrent family proceedings.

Offenders who have primary care responsibilities

K-136   Where the offender is the sole or primary carer of the victim or other dependants, this should potentially be taken into account for sentencing purposes, regardless of whether the offender is male or female. In such cases, an immediate custodial sentence may not be appropriate and, subject to a risk assessment, the offender may be able to resume care of or have contact with the victim.

Part 2: Cruelty to a child

Assessing seriousness

K-137   One category of child cruelty is not automatically more serious than another and, in order properly to assess the seriousness of an offence, its precise nature must be established before consideration is given to a range of contingent factors, including the defendant's intent, the length of time over which the cruelty took place, and the degree of physical and psychological harm suffered by the victim.

Culpability

K-138   Culpability should be the initial factor in determining the seriousness of an offence. An offence may be the consequence of a wide range of factors including: (i) sadism; (ii) violence resulting from any number of causes; (iii) a reduced ability to protect a child in the face of aggression from an overbearing partner; (iv) indifference or apathy resulting from low intelligence or induced by alcohol or drug dependence; (v) immaturity or social deprivation resulting in an inability to cope with the pressures of caring for children; and (vi) psychiatric illness. It might also arise as the result of a momentary lack of control by an otherwise responsible and loving carer. The extent to which any of these factors might have contributed to the commission of an offence will be important in determining the culpability of the offender. A court must strike a balance between the need to reflect the serious view which society takes of the ill-treatment of young children and the need to protect those children, and also the pressures upon immature and inadequate parents attempting to cope with the problems of infancy, and the extent to which remorse should influence sentence will always have to be judged in the light of all the circumstances. The normal starting point should be a custodial sentence, the length of which should be influenced by the circumstances surrounding the offence.

Harm

It is helpful if the indictment clearly states the nature of the offender's conduct, but even where **K-139** this is clear, difficulties arise in determining the relative seriousness of the different forms of child cruelty. There is, however, a significant distinction between cases of wilful ill-treatment which usually involve positive acts of abuse and physical violence, and cases of neglect which are typified by the absence of actions. There is also a distinction between cases involving physical injury, whether resulting directly from an assault or ill-treatment or resulting from a period of abandonment or neglect, and cases where the harm occasioned is exposure to the risk of harm or lack of proper care, attention or supervision. In addition, whether one form of cruelty is worse than another will depend not only on the degree to which the victim suffers as a result but also on the motivation and culpability of the offender.

Aggravating and mitigating factors

The guideline refers to the guideline on seriousness for general aggravating and mitigating **K-140** factors. In particular, care should be taken to avoid "double-counting" when an essential element of an offence might, in other circumstances, be an aggravating factor, and the abuse of trust or abuse of power inherent in the offence have been built into the guideline and should not be treated as aggravating factors. Relevant aggravating factors are targeting one particular child from the family and the four additional aggravating factors listed under "Assaults on children: general principles" (*ante*). The sole relevant mitigating factor is seeking medical help or bringing the situation to the notice of the authorities.

Other factors relevant to sentencing

Long-term psychological harm

The starting points have been calculated to reflect the likelihood of psychological harm and this **K-141** cannot be treated as an aggravating factor. Where there is an especially serious physical or psychological effect on the victim, even if unintended, this should result in an increased sentence.

Adverse effect of the sentence on the victim

As in Part 1, *ante*. **K-142**

Offenders who have primary care responsibilities

As in Part 1, *ante*. **K-143**

Personal mitigation

The most relevant areas of personal mitigation are likely to be: (i) mental illness/ depression; **K-144** (ii) inability to cope with the pressures of parenthood; (iii) lack of support; (iv) sleep deprivation; (v) domination of the offender by an abusive or stronger partner; (vi) extreme behavioural difficulties in the child, often coupled with a lack of support; and (vii) inability to secure assistance or support services in spite of every effort having been made by the offender. However, some of these factors could be regarded as an inherent part of caring for children, especially with young children, and so before they are accepted in mitigation, there must be evidence that these factors were present to a high degree and had an identifiable and significant impact on the offender's behaviour.

Factors to take into consideration

Dangerous offenders: the offence is a "specified offence" within the CJA 2003, s.224, and so a **K-145** court must consider the imposition of a sentence for public protection. The guideline only applies to offenders who have not been classed as dangerous.

Categories of offence: the same starting point applies regardless of which of the various ways in which the offence can be committed is in point, and it already assumes an abuse of trust or power and the likelihood of psychological harm, and is designed to reflect the seriousness with which society as a whole regards these offences.

Additional factors: only additional aggravating and mitigating factors specifically relevant to this offence are included in the guideline, and a court must always take into account the full list of factors in the guideline on seriousness.

Sentencing ranges and starting points

K-146   The sentencing ranges and starting points relate to persons convicted following a plea of not guilty, and who do not have a conviction which, by virtue of the 2003 Act, s.143(2) (§ 5-67 in the main work), must be treated as an aggravating factor. A court should identify the description that most nearly matches the facts of the offence and this will identify a starting point, from which a provisional sentence can be reached. The sentencing range is the bracket into which the provisional sentence will fall after consideration of aggravating or mitigating factors (although particular circumstances, particular matters of aggravation or mitigation, or the reduction for a guilty plea may require a sentence outside of that range). The provisional sentence may then be reduced by matters of personal mitigation, which may also take it outside the appropriate sentencing range. A court should give reasons for imposing a sentence of a different kind or outside the range provided in the guideline.

Where there has been (i) serious cruelty over a period of time, (ii) serious long-term neglect, or (iii) a failure to protect a child from either of these, the starting point is six years' custody and the sentencing range is five to nine years' custody.

Where there has been (i) a series of assaults (the more serious the individual assaults and the longer the period over which they are perpetrated, the more serious the offence), (ii) protracted neglect or ill-treatment (the longer the period of ill-treatment or neglect and the longer the period over which it takes place, the more serious the offence), or (iii) a failure to protect a child from either of these, the starting point is three years' custody and the sentencing range is two to five years' custody.

Where there has been (i) an assault resulting in injuries consistent with assault occasioning actual bodily harm, (ii) more than one incident of neglect or ill-treatment (but not amounting to long-term behaviour), (iii) a single incident of long-term abandonment or regular incidents of short-term abandonment (the longer the period of long-term abandonment or the greater the number of incidents of short-term abandonment, the more serious the offence), or (iv) a failure to protect a child from any of these, the starting point is 36 weeks' custody and the sentencing range is 26 weeks' to two years' custody.

Where there has been (i) short-term neglect or ill-treatment, (ii) a single incident of shortterm abandonment, or (iii) a failure to protect a child from any of these, the starting point is 12 weeks' custody and the sentencing range is a community order (low) to 26 weeks' custody.

L. Sentencing in Magistrates' Courts

Introduction

K-147   The Sentencing Guidelines Council has issued a guideline on offences for which sentence is frequently imposed in magistrates' courts when dealing with adult offenders, which replaces the guidelines which were effective from January 1, 2004. The foreword and introduction state that they are to apply to all relevant cases appearing for allocation (mode of trial) or for sentence on or after August 4, 2008, not only in magistrates' courts, but also in the Crown Court when dealing with appeals against sentence and when sentencing for summary only offences. The guideline should be consulted when dealing with an either-way offence for which there is no plea or an indication of a not guilty plea, since it will be relevant to the mode of trial decision. The guideline will also be relevant to decisions as to committal for sentence.

There have been 12 updates to these guidelines. An update that took effect on January 5, 2009, made changes to Parts 1 (indices), 3 (offence guidelines) and 5 (explanatory material). The effect of the changes to Part 3 was (i) to include extracts from the guideline on breach of an anti-social behaviour order (*post*, K-196 *et seq.*) and the guideline on theft and burglary in a building other than a dwelling (*post*, K-209 *et seq.*) in these guidelines in the appropriate places, and (ii) to make a clarificatory amendment to the existing guideline for burglary in a dwelling. Consequential amendments were made to the section in Part 5 that relates to ancillary orders, in respect of anti-social behaviour orders, and an amendment was also made to that section in respect of orders disqualifying an offender from driving, to reflect recent case law.

An update implemented on August 4, 2008, made equivalent changes to Part 3 in relation to the guideline on causing death by driving (*post*, K-185 *et seq.*) and modified Part 5 in respect of explanatory material relating to dangerous offenders (to take account of changes made by the CJIA 2008).

The third update was published on October 13, 2009. This included new guidelines for statutory offences of fraud (reflective of the guideline for such offences (*post*, K-228 *et seq.*). In addition, supplementary guidance was provided in relation to sentencing for health and safety offences following changes to the maximum penalty for certain offences effected by the Health and Safety (Offences) Act 2008 and which came into effect on January 16, 2009.

As from June 13, 2011, a fourth update will apply to all offenders aged 18 or over who are sentenced on or after that date, regardless of the date of their offence, with the effect that the new guideline on offences against the person (as to which, see *ante*, K-113 *et seq.*) is imported, except for those parts dealing with indictable-only offences, with the imposition of sentences which magistrates are not entitled to impose, and with sections 73 and 74 of the SOCPA 2005 (§§ 5-132, 5-133 in the main work), since they apply only in the Crown Court.

A fifth update was issued on October 13, 2011, and applies to all offenders aged 18 or over who are sentenced on or after January 16, 2012, regardless of the date of their offence. The effect is to import the guidelines on domestic and non-domestic burglary (but not aggravated burglary, which is an indictable-only offence) (as to which, see *post*, K-259 *et seq.*), except that, at step three, there is no mention of sections 73 and 74 of the SOCPA 2005 (§§ 5-132, 5-133 in the main work), since they apply only in the Crown Court. The starting points and category ranges apply to all offenders in all cases, irrespective of plea or previous convictions.

A sixth update was issued on January 24, 2012. This applies to all offenders aged 18 or over who are sentenced on or after February 27, 2012, regardless of the date of their offence. The effect is to import the guidelines on drug offences (*post*, K-271 *et seq.*).

As from June 11, 2012, a seventh update applies to all offenders aged 18 or over who are sentenced on or after that date, regardless of the date of their offence, with the effect that a new definitive guideline on the allocation of offences (see *ante*, § 1-97) and a guideline on offences taken into consideration (*ante*, §§ 5-160 *et seq.*) and totality (*post*, K-280 *et seq.*) are imported. It also corrects an error in one of the drug offence guidelines (importation) issued in the sixth update (this correction has been incorporated into the supplement at K-275, *post*).

As from August 20, 2012, an eighth update applies to all offenders aged 18 or over who are sentenced on or after that date, regardless of the date of their offence, with the effect that a new definitive guideline on dangerous dog offences (*post*, K-291 *et seq.*) is imported into the guideline.

A ninth update makes alterations to Part 5 (explanatory material) to reflect changes made to the victim surcharge by the Criminal Justice Act 2003 (Surcharge) Order 2012 (S.I. 2012 No. 1696) (see §§ 5-1300 *et seq.* in the main work) and amendments (not yet in force) to sentencing legislation effected by the LASPOA 2012. As to the latter, the new material deals, in particular, with the new requirements (foreign travel prohibition and alcohol abstinence and monitoring) that may be attached to a community sentence or a suspended sentence, the new law relating to suspended sentences (their length and the necessity or otherwise to attach community requirements) and the making of hostility based on transgender identity a statutory aggravating factor.

The Sentencing Council issued a tenth update, applying to all offenders aged 18 or over who are sentenced on or after April 1, 2014. The principal effect was to replace the incorporation of the previous Sentencing Guideline's Council guideline on sexual offences with the new Sentencing Council's guideline on sexual offences (*ante*, K-84 *et seq.*), save for such parts thereof as can only have any application in the Crown Court. The starting points apply in all cases, irrespective of previous convictions or plea.

The update also revised the explanatory material in Part 5 relating to road traffic offences. The starting point when considering disqualification from driving in a defendant's absence is now that disqualification should be imposed in an offender's absence if there is no reason to believe that the defendant is unaware of the proceedings and where the statutory notice has been served pursuant to the MCA 1980, s.11(4). It should not be imposed in the absence of the offender where there is evidence that there is an acceptable reason for the defendant's absence or where there are reasons to believe it would be contrary to the interests of justice.

As from July 1, 2014, an eleventh update to the sentencing guidelines for magistrates' courts applies to all offenders aged 18 or over who are sentenced on or after that date, the principal effect of which was to incorporate the Sentencing Council's guideline on environmental offences (as to which, see § 5-147 in the main work), and to expand the explanatory material relating to health and safety offences to include environmental offences. The update also corrects an error in the section of the tenth update (*ante*) relating to indecent photographs of children.

As from October 1, 2014, a twelfth update to the sentencing guidelines for magistrates' courts applies to all offenders aged 18 or over who are sentenced on or after that date. The principal effect is to incorporate the Sentencing Council's guideline on fraud, money laundering and bribery offences (*post*, Appendix K-297 *et seq.*), but the opportunity has also been taken to bring up to date the table of offences for which fixed penalty notices are available and the amount of such penalties in Annex B to the explanatory material.

Recommendations

K-148   The following recommendations are sentence recommendations where the starting points are based on a first time offender who has pleaded not guilty. However, the guideline makes plain that they are to be used by magistrates in making decisions as to whether or not an offender should be tried or sentenced in the magistrates' court or the Crown Court. What is set out below is confined to that which is material to the latter decision. It follows, therefore, that the full range of recommendations is not necessarily set out. For example, in the case of burglary of a dwelling, for a case involving an unforced entry with property of low value being stolen and no aggravating features, the top end of the recommended range is 12 weeks' custody, which is well within the maximum available to a magistrates' court. Any description of offence which is of a less serious nature than the descriptions set out below may, therefore, be taken to be suitable for summary trial.

Whilst the guideline itself lists aggravating and mitigating features for all the offences, these are only set out below where the presence or absence of such features is relevant to the decision as to the appropriate court for trial or sentence.

Burglary in a dwelling

K-149   The guideline recommends—
    (i) a starting point of 12 weeks' custody and a range of sentence from a high level community order to sentence in the Crown Court for a case of forced entry where the goods stolen were not of high value and without aggravating features;
    (ii) sentence in the Crown Court where the goods stolen were of high value and any aggravating feature was present.

K-150   Particular aggravating features mentioned are: (*as indicating higher culpability*) ransacking, professionalism, a victim deliberately targeted, *e.g.* out of spite, the carrying of housebreaking implements or weapons; (*as indicating greater degree of harm*) occupier at home or returning home during burglary, goods stolen being of sentimental value.

As to aggravating features, see *R. v. Saw, post*, § K-441.

For offences for which sentence is passed on or after January 16, 2012, see now the guideline issued by the Sentencing Council for England and Wales, *post*, K-259 *et seq.*

Handling stolen goods

K-151   The guideline recommends—
    (i) a starting point of 12 weeks' custody and a range of sentence from six weeks' custody to sentence in the Crown Court for sophisticated offending or the presence of at least two aggravating features;

(ii) sentence in the Crown Court where the offence was committed in the context of a business, the offender acts as an organiser/ distributor of the proceeds of crime, the offender makes himself available to other criminals as willing to handle the proceeds of thefts or burglaries, the offending was highly organised or professional, or the original offence was particularly serious, *e.g.* armed robbery.

Particular aggravating features mentioned are: (*as indicating higher culpability*) closeness of of-   **K-152**
fender to primary offence, which may be geographical (arising from presence at or near the
primary offence) or temporal (where offender instigated primary offence or, soon after, provided
safe haven or route for disposal), high level of profit made or expected; (*as indicating greater degree
of harm*) seriousness of the primary offence, including domestic burglary, high (including
sentimental) value of goods; threats of violence or abuse of power by offender over others, such as
an adult commissioning criminal activity by children or a drug dealer pressurising addicts to steal
to fund their habit.

Going equipped for theft

The guideline recommends a starting point of a high level community order and a range of a   **K-153**
medium level community order to sentence in the Crown Court in the case of possession of items
for burglary or robbery.

False statements/representations to obtain social security benefits

For offences under the Social Security Administration Act 1992, s.111A, see the fraud guideline,   **K-154**
post, K-297 *et seq.*

Vehicle licence/registration fraud (Vehicle Excise and Registration Act 1994, s.44)

The guideline recommends sentence in the Crown Court in the case of (a) use of number   **K-155**
plates from another vehicle, or (b) the forging or altering of licence/ number plates for sale to
another.

Assault occasioning actual bodily harm and racially/religiously aggravated versions

The guideline recommends—   **K-156**
- (i) a starting point of 24 weeks' custody and a range of 12 weeks' custody to sentence in the Crown Court for a pre-meditated assault resulting in minor, non-permanent injury;
- (ii) sentence in the Crown Court for a pre-meditated assault either resulting in relatively serious injury or involving the use of a weapon.

Inflicting grievous bodily harm/wounding and racially/religiously aggravated versions

The guideline recommends—   **K-157**
- (i) a starting point of 24 weeks' custody and a range of a high level community order to sentence in the Crown Court for "other assault" where no weapon has been used;
- (ii) a starting point of sentence in the Crown Court and a range of 24 weeks' custody to sentence in the Crown Court for a pre-meditated assault where no weapon has been used;
- (iii) sentence in the Crown Court for a pre-meditated assault where a weapon has been used or for any other assault where particularly grave injury results or a weapon has been used.

Assault with intent to resist arrest

The guideline recommends a starting point of sentence in the Crown Court and a range from   **K-158**
24 weeks' custody to sentence in the Crown Court.

Threats to kill

The guideline recommends sentence in the Crown Court for repeated threats or a threat ac-   **K-159**
companied by a visible weapon.

Firearm, carrying in public place (Firearms Act 1968, s.19)

The guideline recommends (but note that certain offences under this section are triable only on   **K-160** indictment (not mentioned in the guideline) and certain offences are triable only summarily, as to which, see § 24-72 in the main work)—

  (i) a starting point of a high level community order and a range of a medium level community order to sentence in the Crown Court for the carrying of an imitation firearm or an unloaded shot gun without ammunition;
  (ii) sentence in the Crown Court for the carrying of a loaded shot gun or for the carrying of a shot gun or any other firearm together with ammunition for it.

Bladed article/offensive weapon (possession of)

K-161   The guideline recommends—

  (i) a starting point of six weeks' custody and a range of a high level community order to sentence in the Crown Court where the weapon was not used to threaten or cause fear but the offence was committed in dangerous circumstances;
  (ii) sentence in the Crown Court where the weapon was used to threaten or cause fear and the offence was committed in dangerous circumstances.

Cruelty to a child

K-162   The guideline recommends—

  (i) a starting point of sentence in the Crown Court and a range of 26 weeks' custody to sentence in the Crown Court for an assault (assaults) resulting in injuries consistent with actual bodily harm, more than one incident of neglect or ill-treatment (but not amounting to long-term behaviour), a single incident of long-term abandonment or regular incidents of short-term abandonment (the longer the period of abandonment or the greater the number of incidents of short-term abandonment, the more serious the offence) or failure to protect a child from any of the foregoing;
  (ii) sentence in the Crown Court for a series of assaults, protracted neglect or ill- treatment, serious cruelty over a period of time or failure to protect a child from any of the foregoing.

Affray

K-163   The guideline recommends 18 weeks' custody as a starting point and a range of 12 weeks' custody to sentence in the Crown Court in the case of a fight involving a weapon or the throwing of objects or conduct causing risk of serious injury.

Harassment (putting people in fear of violence) (Protection from Harassment Act 1997, s.4), and the racially/religiously aggravated version

K-164   The guideline recommends—

  (i) a starting point of 18 weeks' custody and a range of 12 weeks' custody to sentence in the Crown Court for a case involving deliberate threats or persistent action over a longer period or an intention to cause a fear of violence;
  (ii) sentence in the Crown Court for "sexual threats, vulnerable person targeted".

Breach of a protective order (other than in a domestic context)

K-165   The guideline recommends—

  (i) a starting point of sentence in the Crown Court and a range of 26 weeks' custody to sentence in the Crown Court for more than one breach involving some violence and/or significant physical or psychological harm to the victim;
  (ii) sentence in the Crown Court for a breach (one or more) involving significant physical violence and significant physical or psychological harm to the victim.

Witness intimidation

K-166   The guideline recommends—

  (i) a starting point of 18 weeks' custody and a range of 12 weeks' custody to sentence in the Crown Court for conduct amounting to a threat, staring at, approaching or following witnesses, talking about the case, trying to alter or stop evidence;

(ii) sentence in the Crown Court for threats of violence to witnesses and/or their families or for deliberately seeking out witnesses.

Sexual assault (SOA 2003, ss.3, 7)

See Sections III and VII of the sexual offences guideline, *ante*, K-85c, K-87b. **K-167**

Child prostitution and pornography

The guideline recommends that these offences should normally be dealt with in the Crown **K-168** Court but that there may be rare cases of non-penetrative activity involving a victim aged 16 or 17 where the offender's involvement is minimal and not for gain in which a custodial sentence within the power of a magistrates' court may be appropriate.

Exploitation of prostitution (SOA 2003, ss.52, 53)

See Section XVII of the sexual offences guideline, *ante*, K-92. **K-169**

Exposure (SOA 2003, s.66)

See Section XXVIII of the sexual offences guideline, *ante*, K-100. **K-170**

Voyeurism (SOA 2003, s.67)

See Section XXIX of the sexual offences guideline, *ante*, K-101. **K-171**

Keeping a brothel used for prostitution (SOA 1956, s.33A)

See Section XVIII of the sexual offences guideline, *ante*, K-92a. **K-172**

Indecent photographs of children

See Section XVI of the sexual offences guideline, *ante*, K-91. **K-173**

Failure to comply with the notification requirements applicable to sex offenders

The guideline recommends a starting point of 18 weeks' custody and a range of six weeks' **K-174** custody to sentence in the Crown Court for a deliberate failure to comply or the supply of information known to be false accompanied by long-period of non-compliance or attempts to avoid detection.

Drugs

See *ante*, K-147; and *post*, K-271 *et seq.* **K-175**

[The next paragraph is K-179.]

Dangerous driving

The guideline recommends sentence in the Crown Court for (a) prolonged bad driving involv- **K-179** ing deliberate disregard for the safety of others, (b) incidents involving excessive speed or showing off, especially on busy roads or in a built up area, by a disqualified driver, or while driver was being pursued by the police.

Aggravated vehicle-taking (damage to property other than the vehicle taken in accident or to the vehicle)

The guideline recommends sentence in the Crown Court if the vehicle was taken as part of a **K-180** burglary or from private premises and the damage caused was valued at in excess of £5,000.

Aggravated vehicle-taking (dangerous driving or accident causing injury)

The guideline recommends sentence in the Crown Court if there was a course of prolonged **K-181** bad driving involving deliberate disregard for the safety of others.

Arson

K-182   The guideline recommends sentence in the Crown Court in the case of "significant" damage.

Criminal damage (not arson) and racially/religiously aggravated version of offence

K-183   The guideline recommends sentence in the Crown Court if the value of the damage done was in excess of £10,000.

Identity documents (possession of false or of another's improperly obtained) (Identity Cards Act 2006, s.25(5))

K-184   The guideline recommends—

(i) a starting point of 12 weeks' custody and a range of a six weeks' custody to sentence in the Crown Court for a small number of documents where there is no evidence of dealing;

(ii) sentence in the Crown Court for "considerable number of documents possessed, evidence of involvement in larger operation".

M. Causing Death by Driving

K-185   The Sentencing Guidelines Council has issued a guideline on the offences of causing death by dangerous driving (RTA 1988, s.1), causing death by careless driving when under the influence of drink or drugs or having failed without reasonable excuse either to provide a specimen for analysis or to permit the analysis of a blood sample (*ibid.*, s.3A), causing death by careless or inconsiderate driving (*ibid.*, s.2B) and causing death by driving while unlicensed, disqualified or uninsured (*ibid.*, s.3ZB). The guideline applies to offenders aged 18 or over who are sentenced on or after August 4, 2008, and is based on first-time offenders convicted after trial.

The guideline has an introduction and four parts. Part A sets out factors relating to the assessment of seriousness, Part B relates to ancillary orders, Part C contains explanatory material relating to sentencing ranges and starting points, and a description of the decision making process, and Part D contains the offence guidelines. The introduction also refers to Annex A which sets out the statutory definitions of dangerous driving, careless driving and inconsiderate driving, and gives examples.

The introduction makes plain that since the causing of death is common to all offences covered by the guideline, the factor that is going to have the greatest weight in determining a starting point for any particular offence will be the culpability of the offender and, accordingly, the primary task for the court (apart from s.3ZB cases) will be an evaluation of the quality of the driving involved and the degree of danger that it foreseeably created. The degree of intoxication must also be considered where this is an element of the offence. The introduction further points out that the guideline draws a distinction between those factors of an offence that are intrinsic to the quality of the driving ("determinants of seriousness") and those which, while they aggravate the offence (*e.g.* more than one death), are not.

Part A: Assessing seriousness

Determinants of seriousness

K-186   There are five determinants of seriousness, for each of which the guideline sets out examples: (i) the offender's awareness of risk (*e.g.* typified by a prolonged, persistent and deliberate course of bad driving), (ii) where the presence of alcohol or drugs is not an element of the offence, the effect of consumption of any alcohol or drugs (which includes a failure to supply a specimen for analysis (unless inherent in the offence or charged separately) and the consumption of legal drugs where this impaired the offender's ability to drive and the offender knew or should have known about the likelihood of impairment), (iii) whether the offender was driving at an inappropriate speed, (iv) whether the offender behaved in a seriously culpable manner, and (v) the identity of the victim (*e.g.* failing to have regard to, and to take extra care when driving near, vulnerable road users such as cyclists, motorcyclists, horse riders, pedestrians and those working in the road).

Examples of (iv), *ante*, are aggressive driving, driving whilst using a hand-held mobile telephone, driving whilst the driver's attention is avoidably distracted (*e.g.* reading or adjusting the controls of electronic equipment), driving when knowingly suffering from a medical or physical condition that significantly impairs the offender's driving skills (including failure to take prescribed medication), driving when knowingly deprived of adequate sleep or rest, particularly where this is caused by commercial concerns, and driving a poorly maintained or dangerously loaded vehicle, again, particularly where this is caused by commercial concerns. A distinction is drawn between ordinary avoidable distractions and gross avoidable distractions (*e.g.* reading or composing a text message over a period of time), but where the degree of impairment is so serious that it is used to determine whether the offence is based on dangerous or careless driving, care must be taken to avoid double counting.

Aggravating and mitigating factors

Once the court has considered the determinants of seriousness, it must then consider whether **K-187** any aggravating or mitigating factors affect culpability so as to increase or decrease the starting point, or move the offence into a different sentencing range. When assessing seriousness, the court should have regard to the full list of aggravating and mitigating factors set out in the guideline on seriousness (*ante*, § K-13) and the particular aggravating and mitigating factors applicable to each offence, a key to which is set out, *post*:

Key to aggravating factors:

1	Previous convictions for motoring offences, particularly offences that involve bad driving or the consumption of excessive alcohol or drugs before driving.
2	Previous convictions for motoring offences, particularly offences that involve bad driving.
3	Previous convictions for motoring offences, whether involving bad driving or an offence of the same kind that forms part of the present conviction.
4	More than one person killed as a result of the offence. Where the number of deaths is high and that was reasonably foreseeable, this is likely to provide sufficient justification for moving an offence into the next highest sentencing range.
5	Serious injury to one or more victims, in addition to the death(s).
6	Disregard of warnings.
7	Other offences committed at the same time, such as driving other than in accordance with the terms of a valid licence, driving while disqualified, etc.
8	Irresponsible behaviour such as failing to stop, falsely claiming that one of the victims was responsible, or trying to throw the victim off the car by swerving in order to escape.
9	Irresponsible behaviour such as failing to stop or falsely claiming that one of the victims was responsible for the collision.
10	Driving off in an attempt to avoid detection or apprehension.

K-188

Key to mitigating factors:

11	Alcohol or drugs consumed unwittingly.
12	Offender was seriously injured in the collision, but the greater the driver's fault, the less effect this factor should have on mitigation.
13	The victim was a close friend or relative, but the greater the driver's fault, the less effect this factor should have on mitigation.
14	Actions of the victim or a third party contributed significantly to the likelihood of a collision occurring and/ or death resulting.
15	Actions of the victim or a third party contributed to the commission of the offence.
16	The offender's lack of driving experience contributed significantly to the likelihood of a collision occurring and/ or death resulting.

K-189

17 The offender's lack of driving experience contributed to the commission of the offence.

18 The driving was in response to a proven and genuine emergency falling short of a defence.

19 The offender genuinely believed that he or she was insured or licensed to drive.

Personal mitigation

K-190 If the offender can show that he previously had a good driving record, or can demonstrate remorse or that he provided direct and positive assistance to a victim at the scene of the accident, this may justify a reduction in sentence.

Part B: Ancillary orders

K-191 An order disqualifying an offender from driving is usually a mandatory requirement when sentencing for these offences. In principle, the minimum period of disqualification should either equate to the length of the custodial sentence imposed or the relevant statutory minimum disqualification period, whichever results in the longer period of disqualification.

The court may also consider whether to impose an order depriving the offender of property, *e.g.*, a vehicle.

Part D: Offence guidelines

Causing death by dangerous driving

K-192 There are three levels of seriousness which relate predominantly to the standard of driving.

Level 1 (starting point 8 years, sentencing range of 7–14 years): driving that involved a deliberate decision to ignore (or a flagrant disregard for) the rules of the road and an apparent disregard for the great danger being caused to others. Determinants of seriousness (as identified *ante*) that will fix a case at this level include (a) a prolonged, persistent and deliberate course of bad driving, (b) consumption of substantial amounts of alcohol or drugs leading to gross impairment, and/or (c) a group of determinants of seriousness which in isolation or smaller number would place the offence in level 2. The presence of both (a) and (b), particularly if accompanied by aggravating factors will move the offence towards the top of the sentencing range.

Level 2 (starting point 5 years, sentencing range of 4–7 years): driving that created a *substantial* risk of danger. Determinants of seriousness that will fix a case at this level include greatly excessive speed, racing or competitive driving, gross avoidable distraction, driving whilst ability to drive is impaired as a result of consumption of alcohol or drugs, failing to take prescribed medication or a known medical condition, or a group of determinants of seriousness which in isolation or smaller number would place the offence in level 3.

Level 3 (starting point 3 years, sentencing range of 2–5 years): driving that created a *significant* risk of danger. Relevant determinants of seriousness include driving above the speed limit or at a speed that is inappropriate for the prevailing conditions, driving when knowingly deprived of adequate sleep or rest or knowing that the vehicle has a dangerous defect or is poorly maintained or is dangerously loaded, a brief but obvious danger arising from a seriously dangerous manoeuvre, driving whilst avoidably distracted, or failing to have proper regard to vulnerable road users. Where the driving is markedly less serious than this level, reference should be made to the starting point for the most serious level of causing death by careless driving.

Additional aggravating and mitigating factors applicable to sentencing for this offence: 1, 4–8, 10-13, 16, 17 (as to which, see the key, *ante*).

Causing death by careless driving when under the influuence of drink or drugs etc.

K-193

The legal limit of alcohol is 35µg breath (80mg in blood and 107mg in urine)	Careless/ inconsiderate driving arising from momentary inattention with no aggravating factors	Other cases of careless/ inconsiderate driving	Careless/ inconsiderate driving falling not far short of dangerousness
Level 1 71µg or above of alcohol/ high quantity of drugs OR deliberate non-provision of specimen where evidence of serious impairment	Starting point 6 years Sentencing range 5–10 years	Starting point 7 years Sentencing range 6–12 years	Starting point 8 years Sentencing range 7–14 years
Level 2 51–70µg of alcohol/ moderate quantity of drugs OR deliberate non-provision of specimen	Starting point 4 years Sentencing range 3–7 years	Starting point 5 years Sentencing range 4–8 years	Starting point 6 years Sentencing range 5–9 years
Level 3 35–50µg of alcohol/ minimum quantity of drugs OR test refused because of honestly held but unreasonable belief	Starting point 18 months Sentencing range 26 weeks–4 years	Starting point 3 years Sentencing range 2–5 years	Starting point 4 years Sentencing range 3–6 years

Additional aggravating and mitigating factors applicable to sentencing for this offence: 1, 4, 5, 7, 9, 11–14, 18 (as to which, see the key, *ante*).

Causing death by careless or inconsiderate driving

K-194

There are three levels of seriousness defined by the degree of carelessness involved in the standard of driving. A fine is unlikely to be an appropriate sentence for this offence. The most likely requirements to be included in a community order are unpaid work requirements, activity requirements, programme requirements and curfew requirements.

Level 1 (starting point 15 months, sentencing range of 36 weeks–3 years): careless or inconsiderate driving falling not far short of dangerous driving.

Level 2 (starting point 36 weeks, sentencing range of community order (high)–2 years): other cases of careless or inconsiderate driving.

Level 3 (starting point community order (medium), sentencing range of community order (low)-community order (high)): careless or inconsiderate driving arising from momentary inattention with no aggravating features. Examples include misjudging the speed of a vehicle or turning without seeing an oncoming vehicle because of restricted visibility.

Additional aggravating and mitigating factors applicable to sentencing for this offence: 2, 4, 5, 7, 9, 11, 12, 14, 15, 17 (as to which, see the key, *ante*).

Causing death by driving while unlicensed, disqualified or uninsured

K-195

A fine is unlikely to be an appropriate sentence for this offence.

Level 1 (starting point 12 months, sentencing range of 36 weeks–2 years): (i) the offender was disqualified from driving or (ii) the offender was unlicensed or uninsured and there are two or more aggravating features from the list, *post*.

Level 2 (starting point 26 weeks, sentencing range of community order (high)–36 weeks): the offender was unlicensed or uninsured and there was at least one aggravating factor from the list, *post*.

Level 3 (starting point community order (medium), sentencing range of community order (low)-community order (high)): the offender was unlicensed or uninsured, with no aggravating factors.

Additional aggravating and mitigating factors applicable to sentencing for this offence: 3, 4, 5, 9, 11, 12, 17, 19 (as to which, see the key, *ante*).

N. Breach of an Anti-Social Behaviour Order

Summary

K-196   The Sentencing Guidelines Council issued a guideline on the sentencing of offenders convicted of breaching an anti-social behaviour order. It applies to the sentencing of adult and young offenders, who are sentenced on or after January 5, 2009, and is based on first-time offenders (*i.e.* in respect of adult offenders, those who do not have a previous conviction for breach of an anti-social behaviour order and, in respect of young offenders, to have its usual meaning) convicted after trial. Since the sentencing framework for offenders under 18 is significantly different from that for older offenders, the guidance for young offenders is in the form of principles (see Part E, *post*). It is noted that regard should also be had to the approach to sentencing for breaches of orders set out in the guideline on new sentences (*ante*, K-28 *et seq.*) and the guideline on breach of a protective order (*ante*, K-81).

The guideline is in five parts. Part A sets out section 1(10), and summarises the effect of section 1(11) of the CDA 1998 (§ 5-1199 in the main work), Part B is an introduction, Part C sets out factors relating to the assessment of seriousness, Part D contains explanatory material relating to sentencing ranges and starting points, a description of the decision making process, and the sentencing guideline for adult offenders, and Part E sets out sentencing principles in relation to young offenders.

Anti-social behaviour orders in criminal proceedings have now been replaced by criminal behaviour orders: see §§ 5-1198a *et seq.*, §§ 5-1210a *et seq.* in the main work and *ante*. As there are few, if any, significant differences between the old and the new orders, there seems to be no reason why this guideline should not be applied to breaches of criminal behaviour orders.

Part B: introduction

K-197   The main aim of sentencing for breach of an order is to achieve the purpose of the order. When sentencing, the primary consideration should therefore be to reflect the harassment, alarm or distress involved, with the fact that it constituted a breach of a court order (and the consequent harm caused by the undermining of public confidence in the effective administration of justice) being a secondary consideration.

Part C: assessing seriousness

K-198   This must be assessed by considering the offender's culpability in committing the offence and the harm which the offence caused, was intended to cause, or might foreseeably have caused. In order properly to assess the seriousness of a breach, a court needs to be aware of the purpose of the order and the context in which it was made. To this end, Annex A summarises the key principles and considerations applicable when making an order. Whereas a breach may be of one or more prohibitions in an order, the approach to sentencing should be based on an assessment of the seriousness of the harm arising from the breach (or intended by the offender) rather than the number of prohibitions not complied with.

Culpability and harm

K-199   When determining the seriousness of a breach, the court will need to consider (a) the degree to which the offender intended to breach the order, and (b) the degree to which the offender intended to cause the harm that resulted (or could have resulted).

Relevance of the originating conduct

K-200   As stated in previous guidelines, the original conduct that led to the making of an order is relevant in so far as it indicates the level of harm caused and whether this was intended. High culpability and/ or harm may be indicated if the breach continues a pattern of behaviour against an identifiable victim, but the offence may be less serious if there is little connection between the breach and the behaviour that the order was aimed at. The court should examine the prohibitions of the order itself (particularly those in older orders made without the benefit of the guidance set out in Annex A), and their necessity and reasonableness in the circumstances.

Breach of an interim order

Breach of such an order is as serious as breach of a final order, and the same approach to sentencing should be taken. If the hearing regarding the final order can be brought forward, this should be done so that the two issues can be considered together, but sentencing for the interim breach should not be delayed for this purpose and should take place as soon as possible. The court should also consider the extent to which an urgent need for specific interim prohibitions was originally demonstrated, or if the interim order was sought principally in order to obtain additional time to prepare a case for the full hearing.

K-201

Breach that also constitutes another criminal offence

If the substantive offence only has been charged, the fact that it also constitutes breach of an anti-social behaviour order should be treated as an aggravating factor.

K-202

If breach of the order only has been charged, the sentence should reflect the full circumstances of the breach, which will include the conduct that could have been charged as a substantive offence.

Where breach of the order also constitutes another offence with a lower maximum penalty, that penalty is an element to be considered in the interests of proportionality, although the court will not be limited by it.

Aggravating and mitigating factors

For ease of reference, Annex B sets out the aggravating and mitigating factors in the guideline on seriousness (*ante*, K-13 *et seq.*) that might increase or mitigate the seriousness of an offence. Additional aggravating and mitigating factors are identified in the guideline (*post*).

K-203

Personal mitigation

This is particularly relevant to breach of an anti-social behaviour order, since compliance depends on an ability to understand its terms and make rational decisions. Sentence may be mitigated where the offender has a lower level of understanding due to mental health issues or learning difficulties, was acting under the influence of an older or more experienced offender or has complied with an individual support order or intervention order imposed at the same time as the anti-social behaviour order.

K-204

Part D: sentencing guideline—adult offenders

There are three levels of seriousness:

K-205

   (i) *serious harm caused or intended*: examples may involve the use of violence, significant threats or intimidation, or the targeting of individuals or groups of people in a manner that leads to a fear of violence;

   (ii) *lesser degree of harm intended or likely*: examples may include lesser degrees of threats or intimidation, the use of seriously abusive language or causing more than minor damage to property;

   (iii) *no harm caused or intended*: examples may involve being drunk or begging, the prohibited use of public transport, or entry into a prohibited area, provided there is no evidence that harassment, alarm or distress was caused or intended.

The suggested starting points, *post*, are based on the assumption that the offender had the highest level of culpability (*i.e.* he intended the breach). Care needs to be taken to ensure that there is no double counting when an element of the breach determines the level of seriousness where it might in other circumstances be an aggravating factor. In the most serious cases involving repeat offending and a breach causing serious harassment, together with the presence of several aggravating factors such as the use of violence, a sentence beyond the highest range will be justified.

K-206

A conditional discharge is not available as a sentence for this offence.

Nature of failure and harm	Starting point	Sentencing range
Serious harassment, alarm or distress has been caused or where such harm was intended	26 weeks' custody	Custody threshold–2 years' custody
Lesser degree of harassment, alarm or distress, where such harm was intended, or where it would have been likely if the offender had not been apprehended	6 weeks' custody	Community order (medium)–26 weeks' custody
No harassment, alarm or distress was actually caused by the breach and none was intended by the offender	Community order (low)	Fine (Band B)–community order (medium)

K-207 Additional aggravating factors:

   (i) offender has a history of disobedience to court orders;

   (ii) breach was committed immediately or shortly after the order was made;

   (iii) breach was committed subsequent to earlier breach proceedings arising from the same order;

   (iv) targeting of a person the order was made to protect or a witness in the original proceedings.

Additional mitigating factors:

   (i) breach occurred after a long period of compliance;

   (ii) the prohibition(s) breached was/were not fully understood, especially where an interim order was made without notice.

Part E: sentencing guideline—young offenders

K-208 It is noted that the principles covered in Part C apply equally to young offenders.

Apart from those cases where the court is bound to make a referral order, in less serious cases, such as where the breach has not involved any harassment, alarm or distress, a fine may be appropriate if it will be paid by the offender; otherwise a reparation order. In most cases, however, the appropriate sentence will be a community sentence. The custody threshold should be set at a significantly higher level than for adults, and will usually not be crossed unless the breach involves serious harassment alarm or distress (as to which, see the levels of seriousness, *ante*). Exceptionally, the custody threshold may also be crossed where a youth is being sentenced for more than one offence of breach (committed on separate occasions within a short period) involving a lesser but substantial degree of harassment, alarm or distress. Even where the custody threshold is crossed, the court should normally impose a community sentence in preference to a detention and training order and custody should be used only as a last resort. Where custody is unavoidable, the starting point for sentencing should be four months' detention, with a range of up to 12 months. Where the youth is being sentenced for more than one breach involving serious harassment, alarm or distress, however, the sentence may go beyond that range.

Factors likely to aggravate or mitigate a breach are the same as the additional factors listed in the guideline for adult offenders (*ante*) and the principles relating to personal mitigation (*ante*) also apply. In addition, peer pressure and lack of parental support may justify mitigation of sentence.

When imposing a community sentence, a court must consider what requirements will best prevent further offending and the individual circumstances of the offender, including his particular stage of intellectual or emotional maturity. Any requirements imposed must be compatible both with each other and with the prohibitions of the anti-social behaviour order, if it remains in force, and the combination of both must not be so onerous as to make further breaches likely.

O. THEFT AND BURGLARY IN A BUILDING OTHER THAN A DWELLING

Summary

The Sentencing Guidelines Council has issued a guideline on these offences. The guideline ap- **K-209**
plies only to the sentencing of offenders aged 18 and over, who are sentenced on or after January
5, 2009, and is based on first-time offenders convicted after trial (but as to offences of burglary for
which sentence is to be passed on or after January 16, 2012, see *post*, K-259 *et seq.*).

The guideline is in five parts. Part A sets out the statutory provisions relating to the offences,
Part B sets out factors relating to the assessment of seriousness, Part C relates to ancillary orders,
Part D contains explanatory material relating to sentencing ranges and starting points, and a
description of the decision making process, and Part E contains the offence guidelines.

Part A: statutory provisions

In addition to setting out the relevant statutory provisions, the mode of trial and the maximum **K-210**
penalties, Part A states that (i) in relation to burglary, the guideline relates solely to cases in which
an offender enters a building other than a dwelling as a trespasser with intent to steal or, having
entered a building as a trespasser, actually goes on to steal, and (ii) the forms of theft covered by
the guideline are theft in breach of trust, theft in a dwelling, theft from persons, and theft from
shops; but that (iii) the principles in Parts B and C are of general application and likely to be of
assistance where a court is sentencing for any other form of theft.

Part B: assessing seriousness

This must be assessed by considering the offender's culpability in committing the offence and **K-211**
the harm which the offence caused, was intended to cause, or might foreseeably have caused.
When assessing the harm caused, the starting point should be the loss suffered by the victim.
However, the monetary value might not reflect the full extent of the harm and the court should
take into account the impact of the offence on the particular victim (*e.g.* where the value of the
loss is high in proportion to the victim's financial circumstances), any harm to a person other than
the immediate victim, and any harm in the form of public concern or erosion of public confidence.

Aggravating and mitigating factors which may affect the seriousness of the offence must be
considered, including those identified in the guideline on seriousness (*ante*, K-13 *et seq.*) (and set
out in Annex A) and the additional factors identified in each offence guideline. Since the suggested starting points and sentencing ranges are based on the assumption that the offender was
motivated by greed or a desire to live beyond his means, in order to avoid double counting, such
a motivation should not be treated as a factor that increases culpability. The aggravating factors
from the seriousness guideline most relevant to these offences are planning, offenders operating
in groups or gangs and deliberate targeting of vulnerable victims, and the most relevant aggravating factors indicating a more than usually serious degree of harm are particularly vulnerable
victims, high levels of gain and the high value (including sentimental value) of property to the
victim or substantial consequential loss.

The court must also consider the following matters of personal mitigation: return of stolen
property (depending on voluntariness and timeliness of return), whether the offender has been
motivated by addiction (in which case, while seriousness will not be mitigated, it may be appropriate to impose a drug rehabilitation requirement, alcohol treatment requirement or activity or
supervision requirement, as part of a community or suspended sentence order), and whether the
offender has been motivated by desperation or need (which may count as personal mitigation in
exceptional circumstances).

Part C: ancillary orders

The ancillary orders which a court must consider are restitution (PCC(S)A 2000, s.148 (§ 5-711 **K-212**
in the main work)), compensation (*ibid.*, s.130 (§ 5-691 in the main work)), deprivation (*ibid.*, s.143
(§ 5-726 in the main work)) and confiscation (PCA 2002, s.6 (§ 5-805 in the main work)). Neither
restitution nor compensation orders should normally impact or influence the choice of sentence.
However, where an offender has acted (as opposed to offered) to free assets in order to pay
compensation, this is akin to making voluntary restitution and may be regarded as personal

mitigation. In making compensation orders, consideration should be given to the wishes of the victim and, where it is difficult to ascertain the full amount of the loss suffered, the making of an order for an amount representing the agreed or likely loss.

Part D: offence guidelines

Theft in breach of trust

K-213   While the seriousness of the offence will generally increase in line with the level of trust breached, the extent to which the nature and degree of trust placed in an offender should be regarded as increasing seriousness will depend on a careful assessment of the circumstances of each individual case, including the type and terms of the relationship between the offender and victim. A court should also consider whether a suspended sentence would be appropriate, particularly where this may allow reparation to be made either to the victim or to the community at large.

Type/ nature of activity	Starting point	Sentencing range
Theft of £125,000 or more **or** theft of £20,000 or more in breach of a high degree of trust	3 years' custody	2–6 years' custody
Theft of £20,000 or more but less than £125,000 **or** theft of £2,000 or more but less than £20,000 in breach of a high degree of trust	2 years' custody	12 months–3 years' custody
Theft of £2,000 or more but less than £20,000 **or** theft of less than £2,000 in breach of a high degree of trust	18 weeks' custody	Community order (high)–12 months' custody
Theft of less than £2,000	Community order (medium)	Fine–26 weeks' custody

K-214   Additional aggravating factors:
  (i) long course of offending;
  (ii) suspicion deliberately thrown on others;
  (iii) offender motivated by intention to cause harm or out of revenge.
Additional mitigating factors:
  (i) offender has been given inappropriate degree of trust or responsibility;
  (ii) genuine cessation of offending before discovery (particularly where evidence of remorse);
  (iii) offender reports undiscovered offending;
  (iv) other than in the most exceptional of circumstances, loss of employment and any consequential hardship should *not* constitute personal mitigation.

Theft in a dwelling

K-215   It is noted that the guideline does not apply where the offender has been convicted of a burglary.

For the purposes of the table, post, property should generally be regarded as having a high monetary value if it is worth more than £2,000 and a victim is vulnerable if he is targeted by the offender because it is anticipated that he will be unlikely or unable to resist the theft.

Type/ nature of activity	Starting point	Sentencing range
Where the effect on the victim is particularly severe, the stolen property is of high value (see ante), or substantial consequential loss (e.g. serious disruption to victim's life or business) results, a sentence higher than the range into which the offence otherwise would fall may be appropriate		

Type/ nature of activity	Starting point	Sentencing range
Theft from a vulnerable victim (see *ante*) involving intimidation or the use or threat of force (falling short of robbery) or the use of deception	18 months' custody	12 months–3 years' custody
Theft from a vulnerable victim	18 weeks' custody	Community order (high)–12 months' custody
Theft not involving vulnerable victim	Community order (medium)	Fine–18 weeks' custody

Additional aggravating factors:

   (i) offender motivated by intention to cause harm or out of revenge;

  (ii) intimidation or face-to-face confrontation with victim (except where this takes the offence into a higher sentencing range);

 (iii) use of force, or threat of force, against victim (not amounting to robbery) (except where this takes the offence into a higher sentencing range);

 (iv) use of deception (except where this takes the offence into a higher sentencing range);

  (v) offender takes steps to prevent the victim from reporting the crime or seeking help.

K-216

Theft from the person

   It is noted that the guideline does not apply where the offender has been convicted of robbery (the guideline for which is set out *ante*, K-80 *et seq.*). As to the approach, to issues of local prevalence, see the seriousness guideline (*ante*, K-27). Issues of national prevalence should *not* be used by sentencers to justify including a deterrent element as this is already taken into account in these and other guidelines.

   For the purposes of the table, post, property should generally be regarded as having a high monetary value if it is worth more than £2,000 and a victim is vulnerable if he is targeted by the offender because it is anticipated that he will be unlikely or unable to resist the theft (*e.g.* because of youth or age or disability).

K-216a

Type/ nature of activity	Starting point	Sentencing range
Where the effect on the victim is particularly severe, the stolen property is of high value (see ante), or substantial consequential loss (e.g. serious disruption to victim's life or business) results, a sentence higher than the range into which the offence otherwise would fall may be appropriate		
Theft from a vulnerable victim (see *ante*) involving intimidation or the use or threat of force (falling short of robbery)	18 months' custody	12 months–3 years' custody
Theft from a vulnerable victim	18 weeks' custody	Community order (high)–12 months' custody
Theft not involving vulnerable victim	Community order (medium)	Fine–18 weeks' custody

Additional aggravating factors:

   (i) offender motivated by intention to cause harm or out of revenge;

  (ii) intimidation or face-to-face confrontation with victim (except where this takes the offence into a higher sentencing range);

 (iii) use of force, or threat of force, against victim (not amounting to robbery) (except where this takes the offence into a higher sentencing range);

 (iv) high level of inconvenience caused to victim, *e.g.* replacing house keys, credit cards, etc., or where the victim is a tourist.

K-216b

Theft from a shop

K-217   When assessing the level of harm, the circumstances of the retailer (*e.g.* size) are a proper
consideration. However, the seriousness of an individual case must be judged on its own dimension of harm and culpability and the sentence on an individual offender should not be increased
to reflect the harm caused to retailers in general by the totality of this type of offending (*e.g.*
higher insurance premiums, cost of preventative security measures). Whereas the seriousness
guideline requires the value of goods to be taken into account in property offences, where this is
associated with other aggravating factors such as the degree of planning and/or operating in a
group, care will need to be taken to avoid double counting.

When taking previous convictions into account, if the offender demonstrates a level of persistent
or seriously persistent offending, the community and custody thresholds may be crossed even
though the other characteristics of the offence would otherwise warrant a lesser sentence.

Type/ nature of activity	Starting point	Sentencing range
Organised gang/ group **and** intimidation or the use or threat of force (short of robbery)	12 months' custody	36 weeks–4 years' custody
Significant intimidation or threats **or** use of force resulting in slight injury **or** very high level of planning **or** significant related damage	6 weeks' custody	Community order (high)–36 weeks' custody
Low level intimidation or threats **or** some planning, *e.g.* a session of stealing on the same day or going equipped **or** some related damage	Community order (low)	Fine–community order (medium)
Little or no planning or sophistication **and** goods stolen of low value	Fine	Conditional discharge–community order (low)

K-218   Additional aggravating factors:
  (i) child accompanying offender where child is involved or aware of theft;
 (ii) offender is subject to a banning order that includes the store targeted (care to be taken to
      avoid double counting where offender also being sentenced for breach of order);
(iii) offender motivated by intention to cause harm or out of revenge;
 (iv) professional offending;
  (v) victim particularly vulnerable (*e.g.* small, independent shop);
 (vi) offender targeted high value goods;
(vii) intimidation, threat or use of force (falling short of robbery) and additional damage to
      property.

[The next paragraph is K-221.]

P. ATTEMPTED MURDER

K-221   The Sentencing Guidelines Council has issued a guideline which applies only to the sentencing
of offenders aged 18 and over, who are sentenced on or after July 27, 2009, and is based on first-
time offenders convicted after trial. The guideline is not intended to provide for an offence found
to be based on a genuine belief that murder would be an act of mercy, although the approach to
assessing the seriousness in such cases might be similar.

Part A: Assessing seriousness

K-222   This must be assessed, first, by considering the offender's culpability in committing the offence.

While an offender convicted of an offence of attempted murder will have already demonstrated a high level of culpability (intention to kill), the precise level of culpability will vary in line with the circumstances of the offence (*e.g.* whether a weapon was used) and whether it was planned or spontaneous.

Next, the court must consider the harm caused. Since there is a potential imbalance between culpability and harm, the degree of (or lack of) physical or psychological harm suffered by a victim may generally influence sentence, in particular where the degree of harm actually caused to the victim is negligible.

Aggravating and mitigating factors will also affect the seriousness of the offence. The court should consider (i) the specific factors identified in Part D (*post*), which follow those set out in the CJA 2003, Sched. 21 (§ 5-425 in the main work), (ii) the factors identified in the guideline on seriousness (*ante*, K-13 *et seq.*), although, here, care needs to be taken to ensure that there is no double counting where an essential element of the offence charged might, in other circumstances, be an aggravating factor, and (iii) the additional statutory aggravating factor introduced by the Counter-Terrorism Act 2008, s.30 (§ 25-213 in the main work) and Sched. 2 (offence having a terrorist connection).

Part B: ancillary orders

A court must consider making a compensation order. **K-223**

Part C: sentencing ranges and starting points

Part C contains explanatory material relating to sentencing ranges and starting points, and a **K-224** description of the decision making process. This is largely repetitious of material that appears in previous guidelines (see, in particular, the guideline on the assessment of seriousness, *ante*, K-13 *et seq.*, and, in relation to sexual offences, *ante*, K-85).

Part D: offence guidelines

K-225

Nature of offence	Starting point	Sentencing range
Level 1		
The most serious offences including those which (if the charge had been murder) would come within the 2003 Act, Sched. 21, paras 4 and 5		
Serious and long term physical or psychological harm	30 years' custody	27–35 years' custody
Some physical or psychological harm	20 years" custody	17–25 years' custody
Little or no physical or psychological harm	15 years' custody	12–20 years' custody
Level 2		
Other planned attempt to kill		
Serious and long term physical or psychological harm	20 years' custody	17–25 years' custody
Some physical or psychological harm	15 years' custody	12–20 years' custody
Little or no physical or psychological harm	10 years' custody	7–15 years' custody
Level 3		
Other spontaneous attempt to kill		
Serious and long term physical or psychological harm	15 years' custody	12–20 years' custody
Some physical or psychological harm	12 years' custody	9–17 years' custody
Little or no physical or psychological harm	9 years' custody	6–14 years' custody

Specific aggravating factors: **K-226**
   (i) the fact that the victim was particularly vulnerable, *e.g.*, because of age or disability;

    (ii) mental or physical suffering inflicted on the victim;

    (iii) the abuse of a position of trust;

    (iv) the use of duress or threats against another person to facilitate the commission of the offence;

    (v) the fact that the victim was providing a public service or performing a public duty.

K-227   Specific mitigating factors:

    (i) the fact that the offender suffered from any mental disorder or mental disability which lowered his degree of culpability;

    (ii) the fact that the offender was provoked (for example, by prolonged stress);

    (iii) the fact that the offender acted to any extent in self-defence;

    (iv) the age of the offender.

[The next paragraph is K-240.]

Q. SENTENCING YOUTHS

K-240   The Sentencing Guidelines Council issued a definitive guideline in relation to the sentencing of offenders who are under 18 years of age. It applies to any sentence imposed on or after November 30, 2009. The foreword states that the offence-specific guidelines for youths convicted of offences under the SOA 2003 which have a lower maximum penalty when committed by a person under the age of 18 (*ante*, K-83 *et seq.*), and of robbery (*ante*, K-80), continue to apply and are not superseded by these guidelines. As with other guidelines issued by the council, there is a great deal of repetition both within the guideline itself and of material from other guidelines.

General approach

Statutory provisions

K-241   As well as summarising key statutory provisions, this section reminds sentencers that they must be aware of a range of international conventions which emphasise the importance of avoiding "criminalisation" of young people while ensuring that they are held responsible for their actions and, where possible, take part in repairing the damage that they have caused, the intention being to establish responsibility and to promote re-integration rather than to impose retribution.

Sentencing principles

K-242   The approach will be individualistic, with the response varying significantly according to the actual age and maturity of the offender. Sentences must remain proportionate (except in the case of dangerous offenders), with particular care needing to be taken where a young person has committed a relatively less serious offence but there is a high risk of re-offending. Whilst a court is sometimes required to treat the seriousness of an offence as aggravated where there are previous convictions (CJA 2003, s.143(2) (§ 5-67 in the main work)), a sentence that follows re-offending does not need to be more severe than a previous sentence solely because of the previous conviction.

    As to the CDA 1998, s.37 (principal aim of the youth justice system is to prevent offending by children and young people (§ 5-63 in the main work)), the guideline points out that, in relation to the offender, this incorporates the need to demonstrate that his conduct is not acceptable in a way that makes an impact on him whilst also identifying and seeking to address any other factors that make offending more likely; and that, for any victim and society as a whole, it incorporates the need to demonstrate that the law is being effectively enforced and to sustain confidence in the rule of law. Overall, the emphasis should be on approaches that seem most likely to be effective in realising the aim set out in section 37.

    As to the duty to have regard to the welfare of the offender (CYPA 1933, s.44 (§ 5-64 in the main work)), a court should ensure that it is alert to—

    (i) the high incidence of mental health problems and learning difficulties or disabilities amongst young people in the criminal justice system;

    (ii) the effect that speech and language difficulties might have on the ability of the young person (or any adult with them) to communicate with the court, to understand the sanction imposed or to fulfil the obligations resulting from that sanction;

(iii) the extent to which young people anticipate that they will be discriminated against by those in authority and the effect that it has on the way that they conduct themselves during court proceedings;

(iv) the vulnerability of young people to self harm, particularly within a custodial environment;

(v) the extent to which the changes which take place during adolescence can lead to experimentation; and

(vi) the effect on young people of experiences of loss or abuse.

Effect on sentence of the offender being a young person

There is an expectation that, generally, a youth will be dealt with less severely than an adult, **K-243** although the distinction diminishes as the offender approaches the age of 18. Factors which govern the approach to the sentencing of young people who offend (compared with the approach for adult offenders), and which will affect the sentence imposed in individual cases, include:

(i) offending by a young person is frequently a phase which passes fairly rapidly and therefore the reaction to it needs to be kept well balanced in order to avoid alienating the young person from society;

(ii) a criminal conviction at this stage of a person's life may have a disproportionate impact on the ability of the offender to gain meaningful employment and play a worthwhile role in society;

(iii) the impact of punishment is felt more heavily by young people in the sense that any sentence will seem far longer in comparison with their relative age than a like sentence imposed on an adult;

(iv) young people may be receptive to changing the way they conduct themselves and should be able to respond more quickly to interventions;

(v) young people should be given greater opportunity to learn from their mistakes; and

(vi) young people will be no less vulnerable than adults to the contaminating influences that can be expected within a custodial context and probably more so.

Having taken account of all relevant considerations, the court should, within a disposal that is no more restrictive of liberty than is proportionate to the seriousness of the offence(s), impose a sentence which:

(i) confronts the young offender with the consequences of the offending (either for the offender himself, his family, the victim(s) or the community), and helps him to develop a sense of personal responsibility;

(ii) tackles the particular factors (personal, family, social, educational or health) that put the young person at risk of offending;

(iii) strengthens those factors that reduce the risk that the young person will continue to offend;

(iv) encourages reparation; and

(v) defines, agrees and reinforces the responsibilities of the parents.

Crossing a significant age threshold between commission of an offence and sentence

Where an increase in the age of an offender results in the maximum sentence on the date of **K-244** conviction being greater than that available on the date on which the offence was committed, a court should take as its starting point the sentence likely to have been imposed on the date on which the offence was committed. It would be rare for a court to have to consider passing a sentence more severe than the maximum it would have had jurisdiction to pass at the time the offence was committed even where the offender has subsequently attained the age of 18. However, a sentence at or close to the maximum may be appropriate, especially where a serious offence was committed by an offender close to the age threshold.

Persistent offenders

Whereas certain sentences are available only where the offender is a "persistent offender", in **K-245** determining whether a young person is a persistent offender for these purposes a court should consider simply whether he is someone who persists in offending. A finding of persistence may be derived from previous convictions but may also arise from other orders or disposals which require an admission or finding of guilt. A finding of persistence is likely where an offender has been convicted of, or made subject of a pre-court disposal that involved an admission or finding of guilt in relation to, imprisonable offences on at least three occasions in a 12-month period.

Enforcing the responsibilities of parents and guardians

K-246   In considering whether to make a parenting order under the CDA 1998, s.8(6) (§ 5-1282 in the main work), a court must consider the strength of familial relationships and any diversity issues, in particular relating to sexual orientation or race, which might impact on the achievement of the purpose of the order.

Particular sentences and orders

Referral orders

K-247   A court should be prepared to use the full range of periods allowed; in general, orders of 10 to 12 months should be made only for more serious offences. Typically, the length of an order should be three to five months, five to seven months or seven to nine months according to whether the court assesses the seriousness of the offending to be relatively low, of medium seriousness or relatively high.

Financial orders

K-248   It will rarely be appropriate to take an education maintenance allowance or a similar means-related provision into account as a resource from which a young person may pay a financial penalty, especially where the recipient is a young person who is living independently or as part of a household primarily dependent on state benefit.

Youth rehabilitation orders

K-249   From the commencement (on November 30, 2009) of section 1 of the CJIA 2008 (§ 5-314 in the main work), youth rehabilitation orders have been the sole available community sentence for young offenders. Where a court is considering sentence for an offence for which a custodial sentence is justified, a guilty plea may be one of the factors that persuades a court that it can properly impose a youth rehabilitation order instead, and in those circumstances no further adjustment to that sentence would need to be made in order to fulfil the obligation to give credit for the plea. Where, however, the provisional sentence is already a youth rehabilitation order, the necessary reduction for a guilty plea should apply to those requirements within the order that are primarily punitive rather than those which are primarily rehabilitative.

K-249a   **Determining the requirements and the length of an order:** where a court concludes that a youth rehabilitation order is appropriate, taking account of the assessment in the presentence report, the court should consider (i) the requirements that are most suitable for the offender, (ii) what period is necessary to ensure that all requirements may be satisfactorily completed, and (iii) whether the restrictions on liberty that result from those requirements are commensurate with the seriousness of the offence.

K-249b   **Orders with intensive supervision and surveillance:** when imposing a youth rehabilitation order with intensive supervision and surveillance a court must ensure that the requirements are not so onerous as to make the likelihood of a breach almost inevitable.

K-249c   **Orders with a fostering requirement:** it is unlikely that the statutory criteria, contained in Schedule 1, para. 4, to the 2008 Act (§ 5-315 in the main work), will be met in many cases; where they are met and the court is considering making an order, care should be taken to ensure that there is a well developed plan for the care and support of the young person throughout the period of the order and following conclusion of the order.

K-249d   **Breaches:** the primary objective when dealing with a breach of an order is to ensure that the young person completes the requirements imposed by the court. Where the failure arises primarily from non-compliance with reporting or other similar obligations, if a sanction is necessary, the most appropriate one is likely to be the inclusion of, or increase in, a primarily punitive requirement. A court must ensure that it has sufficient information to enable it to understand why the order has been breached and that all steps have been taken by relevant authorities to give the young person appropriate opportunity and support. This will be particularly important if the court is considering imposing a custodial sentence as a result of the breach. Where a court is considering whether a young person has "wilfully and persistently" breached an order, it should apply the same approach as when determining whether an offender is a "persistent offender" (as to which, see *ante*). In particular, a young person almost certainly will have "persistently" breached an order where there have been three breaches (each resulting in an appearance before the court) demonstrating a lack of willingness to comply with the order.

Custodial sentences

Threshold and approach: a pre-sentence report must be considered in all cases before a **K-250** custodial sentence is imposed. Even where the custody threshold (*viz.* that the youth cannot properly be dealt with by a fine alone or by a youth rehabilitation order) has been crossed, a court is not required to impose a custodial sentence. This is likely only to be the case where a custodial sentence will be more effective in preventing offending by children and young persons. The obligation to have regard to the welfare of the offender will require the court to take account of a wide range of issues including those relating to mental health, capability and maturity.

Length of sentence (offenders aged 15, 16 or 17): where the offender is aged 15, 16 or 17, the **K-250a** court will need to consider the maturity of the offender as well as age. Where there is no offence-specific guideline it may be appropriate, depending on maturity, to consider a starting point from half to three-quarters of that which would have been identified for an adult offender. The closer the offender was to being 18 when the offence was committed, and the greater the maturity of the offender, or the sophistication of the offence, the closer the starting point is likely to be to that appropriate for an adult. For younger offenders, greater flexibility is required to reflect the potentially wider range of culpability. Where an offence shows considerable planning or sophistication, a court may need to adjust this approach upwards; conversely, where an offender is particularly immature, the approach may need to be adjusted downwards. It will be particularly important to consider maturity when the court has to sentence multiple offenders. When the offenders are of different ages, including when one or more is over 18, the court will also need to have proper regard to parity between their sentences.

Length of sentence (offenders aged under 15): where the offender is under 15, sentence **K-250b** should normally be imposed in a youth court, and the length of sentence will normally be shorter than for an older offender convicted of the same offence. An offender should be sentenced to detention under the PCC(S)A 2000, s.91 (§ 5-610 in the main work), only where necessary for the protection of the public, either because of the risk of harm from future offending or the persistence of the offending behaviour, or, exceptionally, because the seriousness of the offence alone warrants such a disposal.

Length of sentence (detention and training orders): in determining the term of a detention **K-250c** and training order the proper approach to taking account of any period for which the offender has been remanded in custody or on bail subject to a qualifying curfew condition and electronic monitoring (see s.101(8) of the Act of 2000 (*ibid.*, § 5-598)) is to reduce, if possible, the length of the part of the sentence that is to be served in custody from what would otherwise have been appropriate, in order to reflect that period.

Trial and sentencing of cases in the Crown Court

A youth will appear for trial and sentence in the Crown Court only when charged with **K-251** homicide, when subject to a statutory minimum sentence, when charged with a "grave crime" and a youth court has determined that, if convicted, its powers of sentence would be insufficient, or when charged together with an adult offender who has been sent to the Crown Court and it has been determined that the cases should be kept together. Where a sentence under the "dangerous offender" provisions is likely to be needed the youth may be committed for trial or for sentence.

"Grave crimes"

The power of a youth court to commit a young person charged with a "grave crime" for trial **K-251a** (MCA 1980, s.24 (§ 1-110 in the main work)) should be exercised sparingly, since (i) it is the general policy of Parliament that those under 18 should be tried in a youth court wherever possible, (ii) trial in the Crown Court should be reserved for the most serious cases, recognising the greater formality of the proceedings and the greatly increased number of people involved, and (iii) offenders aged under 15 will rarely attract a period of detention under the "grave crimes" provision, and those under 12 even more rarely. A child aged 10 or 11 (or aged 12 to 14 but not a persistent offender) should be committed to the Crown Court only when charged with an offence of such gravity that, despite the normal prohibition on a custodial sentence for a person of that age, a sentence exceeding two years is a realistic possibility. A young person aged 12 to 17 (for whom a detention and training order could have been imposed) should be committed to the Crown Court only when charged with an offence of such gravity that a sentence substantially beyond the two year maximum for a detention and training order is a realistic possibility.

Dangerous offenders

K-251b   A sentence under the dangerous offender provisions of the CJA 2003 (§§ 5-497, 5-499 in the main work) may be imposed only where an equivalent determinate sentence of at least four years would have been imposed. Criteria relating to future offending and the risk of serious harm must be assessed in light of the maturity of the offender, the possibility of change in a much shorter time than would apply for an adult, and the wider circumstances of a young person. Where a young person charged with a specified offence would not otherwise be committed or sent to the Crown Court for trial, it is generally preferable for the decision whether to commit under these provisions to be taken after conviction.

Remittal from the Crown Court

K-251c   Where a child or young person is convicted before the Crown Court of an offence other than homicide there is an obligation to remit to a youth court for sentence unless it would be undesirable to do so. In considering whether remittal is undesirable, a court should balance the need for expertise in the sentencing of young offenders with the benefits of sentence being imposed by the court which has determined guilt. Particular attention should be given to the obligation to remit where a young person appears before the Crown Court only because he was jointly charged with an adult.

For the full text of the guidelines, see www.sentencing-guidelines.gov.uk/guidelines/council/final.html.

R. Corporate Manslaughter and Health and Safety Offences Causing Death

K-252   The Sentencing Guidelines Council has issued a definitive guideline in relation to corporate manslaughter and health and safety offences causing death. It applies to the sentencing of organisations on or after February 15, 2010.

K-253   The guidelines are in nine parts (elements of the offences; factors likely to affect seriousness; financial information — size and nature of the organisation; level of fines; compensation; costs; publicity orders; remedial orders; summary of approach to sentence) and there is an annex (financial information expected to be provided to the court). Part B emphasises that the guideline only applies to corporate manslaughter and to those health and safety offences where the offence is shown to have been a significant cause of the death. The approach to the assessment of seriousness requires the court to consider the foreseeability of serious injury, how far short of the applicable standard the defendant fell, how common the kind of breach in the organisation was, and at what level the organisation was at fault. There is a non-exhaustive list of aggravating factors (more than one death/ grave injury in addition to death/ failure to heed warnings or advice/ cost-cutting/ deliberate failure to obtain or comply with relevant licences/ injury to vulnerable persons), and a similar list of mitigating factors (prompt acceptance of responsibility/ high level of co-operation with investigation beyond that which will always be expected/ genuine efforts to remedy defect/ good record/ responsible attitude). Paragraph 9 states that it is unlikely, in relation to an offence of corporate manslaughter (having regard to the definition of the offence), that the unauthorised act of an employee will significantly reduce the culpability of the defendant, whereas paragraph 10 advises that, where a health and safety offence is established solely by reference to the unauthorised act of an employee, an assessment of the culpability of the organisation itself must be undertaken.

K-254   Part C states that there is no direct correlation between size and culpability. Size is, however, relevant, as the means of any defendant are relevant to the fine (which is the principal available

penalty for organisations) that is to be imposed in any case. Paragraph 14 states that the court
should require information about the financial circumstances of the defendant, and that the best
practice in such circumstances would be to call for the relevant information for a three year
period including the year of the offence, so as to avoid any risk of atypical figures in a single year.
The financial information ordinarily expected to be provided to the court is set out in Annex A. A
fixed correlation between turnover and fine is not appropriate (para. 15). Paragraph 19 sets out a
non-exhaustive list of factors which may or may not be relevant when the court is assessing the
financial consequences of a fine. The effect on the employment of the innocent may be relevant;
the effect on shareholders, directors or prices will not normally be relevant, save in the case of the
prices of a monopoly supplier of public services; the effect on the provision of services to the
public will be relevant; liability to pay civil compensation and the cost of meeting any remedial
work will ordinarily be irrelevant; whether the fine will have the effect of putting the defendant
out of business will be relevant, although in bad cases, this may be an acceptable consequence.
Although in the case of a large organisation payment of any fine should be required within 28
days, it is permissible, in the case of a smaller or financially stretched organisation, to require payment to be spread over a much longer period. Where commission of the offence resulted in a
broadly quantifiable saving, it will be appropriate to ensure that the fine is such as to remove the
profit and impose an additional penalty.

Part D states that the level of fine will vary considerably, but that any fine must be punitive and   **K-255**
sufficient to have an impact on the defendant. For an offence of corporate manslaughter the appropriate fine will seldom be less than £500,000 and may be measured in millions of pounds. For
health and safety offences, the range of seriousness is greater, but the appropriate fine will seldom
be less than £100,000 and may be measured in hundreds of thousands of pounds or more. Part E
states that, in the great majority of cases, the court should conclude that compensation should be
dealt with in a civil court, and should say that no order is made for that reason. Part F provides
that the defendant ought ordinarily (subject to means) to be ordered to pay the properly incurred
costs of the prosecution.

Part G concerns publicity orders, which are available under the Corporate Manslaughter and   **K-256**
Corporate Homicide Act 2007, s.10 (§ 19-149 in the main work), and which should ordinarily be
imposed in such cases. The order should particularise the matters to be published, the place
where the public announcement is to be made, the size of any notice and the number of inser-
tions (if to be made in a newspaper). The prosecution should serve a draft order on the court and
the defendant and the judge should personally endorse the final form of the order. The order
may stipulate that any comment placed by the defendant alongside the required announcement
should be separated from it and clearly identified as such. Since a publicity order is part of the
penalty, the cost of compliance should be kept in mind when fixing the fine.

Part H concerns remedial orders under section 9 of the 2007 Act (§ 19-148 in the main work)   **K-257**
and section 42 of the Health and Safety at Work etc. Act 1974. Where appropriate remedial action has not already been taken, such an order should be imposed, provided that it can be made
sufficiently specific to be enforceable.

Annex A says that for companies, partnerships and "third sector" organisations, audited ac-   **K-258**
counts should be produced. In the case of the first two, particular attention should be paid to
turnover, profit before tax, directors' remuneration (partners' drawings), loan accounts and pen-
sion provision, and assets, as disclosed by the balance sheet. Where such information is not
produced, an inference may properly be made that the defendant can afford any appropriate
fine. For local authorities, police and fire authorities and similar public bodies, it is said that reference should be made to their annual revenue budget. For health trusts, reference should be
made to the quarterly reports and annual figures as to their financial strength and stability
published by Monitor, their regulator. This will reveal their annual income.

S. Aggravated Burglary and Burglary

On October 13, 2011, the Sentencing Council for England and Wales issued a definitive   **K-259**
guideline on burglary, applying to all offenders aged 18 or over who are sentenced on or after
January 16, 2012, regardless of the date of their offence. The offences covered are: (A) aggravated
burglary (Theft Act 1968, s.10 (§ 21-129 in the main work)), (B) domestic burglary (1968 Act, s.9
(*ibid.*, § 21-108)) and (C) non-domestic burglary (1968 Act, s.9).

The guideline sets out nine steps to be followed (in order) when sentencing for these offences, which correspond to the steps set out in the guideline on assault and other offences against the person (*ante*, K-114), subject to the modifications set out in the specific sections A to C relating to each offence (*post*).

In particular, step one requires the court to determine within which of three categories reflecting various degrees of seriousness the offence falls. Category 1 requires greater harm and higher culpability, category 2 requires either greater harm and lower culpability or lesser harm and higher culpability, and category 3 requires lesser harm and lower culpability. In determining the offender's culpability and the harm caused or intended, the court should refer only to the factors indicating harm and culpability set out in the specific sections relating to A to C, *post*, which comprise the principal factual elements of the offence. Where an offence does not fall squarely into a category, individual factors may require a degree of weighting before making an overall assessment and determining the appropriate offence category.

Step two requires the court to use the starting point identified for the relevant category (as to which, see also the specific sections relating to A-C, *post*) to reach a sentence within the category range (*post*). The starting point applies to all offenders irrespective of plea or previous convictions. A case of particular gravity, reflected by multiple features of culpability in step one, could merit upward adjustment from the starting point before further adjustment is made for the aggravating or mitigating factors increasing or reducing seriousness or reflecting personal mitigation set out in the specific sections A to C, *post*, which contain a non-exhaustive list of additional factual elements providing the context of the offence and factors relating to the offender. In particular, relevant recent convictions are likely to result in an upward adjustment. Having considered all these, and other relevant factors, it might be appropriate to move outside the identified category range.

Fine bands, and a non-exhaustive description of examples of requirements that might be appropriate for low, medium and high level community orders, correspond to those set out in the guideline on assaults and other offences against the person (*ante*), and are set out in the annex to the guideline.

Key to factors indicating greater or lesser harm and higher or lower culpability (step one)

K-260   A number of the following factors may apply when determining the offence category for aggravated burglary, and domestic and non-domestic burglary. As to which factors may apply to each type of offence, see the specific sections A–C, *post*.

(a) *Factors indicating greater harm*

K-261   i. Theft of/damage to property causing a significant degree of loss to the victim (whether economic, sentimental or personal).

       ii. Soiling, ransacking or vandalism of property.

       iii. Occupier and/or victim at home or on the premises (or returns) while offender present.

       iv. Significant physical or psychological injury or other significant trauma to the victim.

       v. Violence used or threatened against victim (particularly, in relation to offences of aggravated burglary, involving a weapon).

       vi. Context of general public disorder.

       vii. Trauma to the victim, beyond the normal inevitable consequence of intrusion and theft.

(b) *Factors indicating lesser harm*

K-262   i. No physical or psychological injury or other significant trauma to the victim.

       ii. No violence used or threatened and a weapon is not produced.

       iii. Nothing stolen or only property of very low value to the victim (whether economic, sentimental or personal).

       iv. Limited damage or disturbance to property.

(c) *Factors indicating higher culpability*

K-263   i. Victim or premises deliberately targeted (for example, due to vulnerability or hostility based on disability, race, sexual orientation, and, in relation to offences of non-domestic burglary, to include a pharmacy or doctor's surgery).

  ii. A significant degree of planning or organisation.

  iii. Equipped for burglary (for example, implements carried and/or use of vehicle).

  iv. Weapon present on entry.

  v. Member of a group or gang.

  vi. Knife or other weapon carried (where not charged separately).

(d) *Factors indicating lower culpability*

  i. Offender exploited by others. **K-264**

  ii. Mental disorder or learning disability, where linked to the commission of the offence.

  iii. Offence committed on impulse, with limited intrusion into property.

Key to factors increasing or reducing seriousness or reflecting personal mitigation (step 2)

  A number of the following factors may apply when determining the sentence within the **K-265**
category range for offences of aggravated burglary, and domestic and non-domestic burglary. As
to which factors may apply to each type of offence, see the specific sections A-C, *post.*

(e) *Factors increasing seriousness*

  Statutory aggravating factors:

  i. Previous convictions (in accordance with the Criminal Justice Act 2003, s.143(2) (*ibid.*, § **K-266**
    5-67)).

  ii. Offence committed whilst on bail (2003 Act, s.143(3)).

  Other aggravating factors include:

  iii. Child at home (or returns home) when offence committed.

  iv. Offence committed at night (particularly, in relation to offences of non-domestic burglary,
    where staff are, or are likely to be, present).

  v. Abuse of power and/or position of trust.

  vi. Gratuitous degradation of victim.

  vii. Any steps taken to prevent the victim reporting the incident or obtaining assistance and/or
    from assisting or supporting the prosecution.

  viii. Victim compelled to leave home (in particular victims of domestic violence).

  ix. Established evidence of community impact.

  x. Commission of offence whilst under the influence of alcohol or drugs.

  xi. Failure to comply with current court orders.

  xii. Offence committed whilst on licence.

  viii. Offences taken into consideration.

(f) *Factors reducing seriousness or reflecting personal mitigation*

  i. Subordinate role in a group or gang. **K-267**

  ii. Injuries caused recklessly.

  iii. Nothing stolen or only property of low value to the victim (whether economic, com-
    mercial, sentimental or personal).

  iv. Offender has made voluntary reparation to the victim.

  v. No previous convictions or no relevant/recent convictions.

  vi. Remorse.

  vii. Good character and/or exemplary conduct.

  viii. Determination, and/or demonstration of steps taken to address addiction or offending
    behaviour.

  ix. Serious medical condition requiring urgent, intensive or long-term treatment.

  x. Age and/or lack of maturity where it affects the responsibility of the offender.

  xi. Lapse of time since the offence where this is not the fault of the offender.

  xii. Mental disorder or learning disability, where not linked to the commission of the offence.

  xiii Sole or primary carer for dependent relatives.

A. Aggravated burglary

Factors indicating harm and culpability (step one)

K-268

Greater harm *list (a)*	i–vi
Lesser harm *list (b)*	i, ii
Higher culpability *list (c)*	i–iii, v, vi
Lower culpability *list (d)*	i–iii

Starting point and category range (step two)

Offence category	Starting point (applicable to all offenders)	Category range (applicable to all offenders)
category 1	10 years' custody	nine –13 years' custody
category 2	six years' custody	four –nine years' custody
category 3	two years' custody	one –four years' custody

Factors increasing or reducing seriousness or reflecting personal mitigation

Factors increasing seriousness *list (e)*	i–xiii
Factors reducing seriousness or reflecting personal mitigation *list (f)*	i–xiii

B. Domestic burglary

Factors indicating harm and culpability (step one)

K-269

Greater harm *list (a)*	i–iii, v–vii
Lesser harm *list (b)*	iii, iv
Higher culpability *list (c)*	i–iii, v, vi
Lower culpability *list (d)*	i–iii

Starting point and category range (step two)

Offence category	Starting point (applicable to all offenders)	Category range (applicable to all offenders)
category 1	three years' custody	two –six years' custody
category 2	one year's custody	high level community order –two years' custody

Offence category	Starting point (applicable to all offenders)	Category range (applicable to all offenders)
category 3	high level community order	low level community order –26 weeks' custody

Where the defendant is dependent on, or has a propensity to misuse, drugs and there is sufficient prospect of success, a community order with a drug rehabilitation requirement under section 209 of the 2003 Act (*ibid.*, § 5-275) may be a proper alternative to a short or moderate custodial sentence.

When sentencing for category 2 or 3 offences, the court should consider whether the custody threshold has been passed, if so, whether it is unavoidable that a custodial sentence be imposed and, if so, whether that sentence can be suspended.

Factors increasing or reducing seriousness or reflecting personal mitigation

Factors increasing seriousness list (e)	i–iv, vi–xiii
Factors reducing seriousness or reflecting personal mitigation list (f)	i, iv–xiii

C. Non-domestic burglary

Factors indicating harm and culpability (step one)
As for B, *ante*.

K-270

Starting point and category range (step two)

Offence category	Starting point (applicable to all offenders)	Category range (applicable to all offenders)
category 1	two years' custody	one –five years' custody
category 2	18 weeks' custody	low level community order –51 weeks' custody
category 3	medium level community order	band B fine –18 weeks' custody

Where the defendant is dependent on, or has a propensity to misuse, drugs and there is sufficient prospect of success, a community order with a drug rehabilitation requirement under section 209 of the 2003 Act may be a proper alternative to a short or moderate custodial sentence.

When sentencing for category 2 or 3 offences, the court should consider whether the custody threshold has been passed, if so, whether it is unavoidable that a custodial sentence be imposed and, if so, whether that sentence can be suspended; and in sentencing for category three offences, the court should also consider whether the community order threshold has been passed.

Factors increasing or reducing seriousness or reflecting personal mitigation

Factors increasing seriousness list (e)	i, ii, iv–vii, ix–xiii
Factors reducing seriousness or reflecting personal mitigation list (f)	i, iv–xiii

T. DRUG OFFENCES

On January 24, 2012, the Sentencing Council for England and Wales issued a definitive **K-271** guideline, applying to all offenders aged 18 or over who are sentenced on or after February 27, 2012, regardless of the date of their offence. The offences covered are:

    I. fraudulent evasion of a prohibition on the importation or exportation of a controlled drug (CEMA 1979, s.170(2) (§ 25-474 in the main work));

    II. supplying or offering to supply such a drug (Misuse of Drugs Act 1971, s.4(3) (*ibid.*, § 27-28)) and possession of such a drug with intent to supply it to another (1971 Act, s.5(3) (*ibid.*, § 27-50));

    III. production of such a drug (1971 Act, s.4(2)(a) or (b)) and cultivation of a cannabis plant (1971 Act, s.6(2) (*ibid.*, § 27-79));

    IV. permitting premises to be used (1971 Act, s.8 (*ibid.*, § 27-84)); and

    V. possession of a controlled drug (1971 Act, s.5(2)).

The guideline sets out eight steps to be followed (in order), which broadly correspond to the steps set out in the guideline on offences against the person (*ante*, Appendix K-113 *et seq.*), except that there is no step requiring the court to consider whether an offender meets the dangerousness criteria.

Step one requires the court to determine the offence category based on varying factors set out in the specific sections I to V (*post*).

Step two requires the court to use the starting point identified for the relevant category (as to which, see also the specific sections relating to I-V, *post*) to reach a sentence within the category range (*post*) dependent on whether the offence in question relates to a Class A, B or C drug. The starting point applies to all offenders. The court should then consider adjustment within the category range for aggravating or mitigating features set out in the specific sections I to V, *post*, which contain a non-exhaustive list of additional factual elements providing the context of the offence and factors relating to the offender. Having considered all these, and other relevant factors, it might be appropriate to move outside the identified category range. In cases where the offender is regarded as being at the very top of a "leading role" (which does not apply to section IV and V offences), it may be justifiable for the court to depart from the guideline. Where the defendant is dependent on, or has a propensity to misuse, drugs and there is a sufficient prospect of success, a community order with a drug rehabilitation requirement under the CJA 2003, s.209 (§ 5-275 in the main work), can be a proper alternative to a short or moderate length custodial sentence. As with previous guidelines, the council emphasises that, where appropriate, courts should consider whether community or custodial thresholds have been passed and, if the latter threshold has been passed, whether it is unavoidable that a custodial sentence be imposed and, if so, whether that sentence can be suspended. The guidelines are subject to section 110 of the PC-C(S)A 2000 (minimum sentences for third drug trafficking offence (*ibid.*, § 5-443)).

In addition to considering whether to make ancillary orders, step six also requires the court, except for section V offences, to consider confiscation where the Crown invokes the process or where it considers it appropriate.

Fine bands, and a non-exhaustive description of examples of requirements that might be appropriate for low, medium and high level community orders, correspond to those in the guideline on offences against the person (*ante*), and are set out in the annex to the guideline.

Key to factors increasing or reducing seriousness or reflecting personal mitigation (step two)

K-272   A number of the following factors may apply when determining the sentence within the category range. As to which factors may apply to each type of offence, see the specific sections I to V, *post*.

(a) *Factors increasing seriousness*

    Statutory aggravating factors:

K-273   (i) Previous convictions (CJA 2003, s.143(2) (§ 5-67 in the main work)).

    (ii) using or permitting a person under 18 to deliver a controlled drug to a third person (1971 Act, s.4A (*ibid.*, § 27-28a)).

    (iii) Supplying or offering to supply a drug on, or in the vicinity of, school premises (1971 Act, s.4A).

(iv) Offence committed on bail (2003 Act, s.143(3)).

Other aggravating factors include:

(v) Targeting of any premises to locate vulnerable individuals or supply to such individuals and/ or supply to those under 18.

(vi) Nature of any likely supply.

(vii) Level of any profit element.

(viii) Use of premises accompanied by unlawful access to electricity/ other utility supply.

(ix) Continuing/ large scale operation as evidenced by presence and nature of specialist equipment.

(x) Exposure of others to more than usual danger, *e.g.* drugs cut with harmful substances.

(xi) Length of time over which premises used for drug activity.

(xii) Volume of drug activity permitted.

(xiii) Premises adapted to facilitate drug activity.

(xiv) Location of premises, *e.g.* proximity to school.

(xv) Attempts to conceal or dispose of evidence, where not charged separately.

(xvi) Possession of drug in prison or in a school or licensed premises.

(xvii) Presence of others, especially children and/ or non-users.

(xviii) Presence of weapon(s), where not charged separately.

(xix) Charged as importation of a very small amount.

(xx) High purity or high potential yield.

(xxi) Failure to comply with current court orders or offence committed on licence.

(xxii) Established evidence of community impact.

b) Factors reducing seriousness or reflecting personal mitigation

(i) Involvement due to pressure, intimidation or coercion, except where already taken into **K-274** account at step one.

(ii) Supply only of drug to which offender addicted.

(iii) Mistaken belief as to type of drug, taking into account the reasonableness of such belief.

(iv) Isolated incident.

(v) Low purity.

(vi) No previous convictions or no relevant or recent convictions.

(vii) Offender's vulnerability was exploited.

(viii) Remorse.

(ix) Good character and/ or exemplary conduct.

(x) Offender is using cannabis to help with a diagnosed medical condition.

(xi) Determination and/ or demonstration of steps having been taken to address addiction or offending behaviour.

(xii) Serious medical conditions requiring urgent, intensive or long-term treatment.

(xiii) Age and/ or lack of maturity where it affects the responsibility of the offender.

(xiv) Mental disorder or learning disability.

(xv) Sole or primary carer for dependent relatives.

I. Fraudulent evasion of a prohibition on importation or exportation

Determining the offence category (step one)

The court should determine the weight of the drugs involved and the offender's culpability **K-275** demonstrated by his role, by reference to the tables below. Where there are characteristics present that fall under different role categories, the court should balance them to reach a fair assessment of the offender's culpability.

Culpability demonstrated by offender's role
One or more of these characteristics may demonstrate the offender's role. These lists are not exhaustive.

LEADING role:
• directing or organising buying and selling on a commercial scale; • substantial links to, and influence on, others in a chain; • close links to original source; • expectation of substantial financial gain; • use of business as cover; • abuse of a position of trust or responsibility.

SIGNIFICANT role:
• operational or management function within a chain; • involvement of others whether by pressure, influence, intimidation or reward; • motivated by financial or other advantage, whether or not operating alone; • some awareness and understanding of scale of operation.

LESSER role:
• performance of limited function under direction; • engaged by pressure, coercion, intimidation; • involvement through naïvety/ exploitation; • no influence on those above in a chain; • little, if any, awareness or understanding of the scale of operation; • if own operation, solely for own use (considering reasonableness of account).

Category of harm
Indicative quantity of drug concerned (upon which the starting point is based):
Category 1 - heroin, cocaine - 5 kg; Ecstasy - 10,000 tablets; LSD - 250,000 squares; amphetamine - 20 kg; cannabis - 200 kg; ketamine - 5 kg.
Category 2 - heroin, cocaine - 1 kg; Ecstasy - 2,000 tablets; LSD - 25,000 squares; amphetamine - 4 kg; cannabis - 40 kg; ketamine - 1 kg.
Category 3 - heroin, cocaine - 150g; Ecstasy - 300 tablets; LSD - 2,500 squares; amphetamine - 750g; cannabis - 6 kg; ketamine - 150g.
Category 4 - heroin, cocaine - 5g; Ecstasy - 20 tablets; LSD - 170 squares; amphetamine - 20g; cannabis - 100g; ketamine - 5g.

Where the operation is on the most serious and commercial scale, involving a quantity of drugs significantly higher than category 1, sentences of 20 years and above may be appropriate, depending on the role of the offender.

Starting point and category range (step two)

Class A	Leading role	Significant role	Lesser role
Category 1	*Starting point* 14 years *Category range* 12 –16 years	*Starting point* 10 years *Category range* 9 –12 years	*Starting point* 8 years *Category range* 6 –9 years
Category 2	*Starting point* 11 years *Category range* 9 –13 years	*Starting point* 8 years *Category range* 6.5 –10 years	*Starting point* 6 years *Category range* 5 –7 years

Category 3	Starting point 8.5 years Category range 6.5 –10 years	Starting point 6 years Category range 5 –7 years	Starting point 4.5 years Category range 3.5 –5 years
Category 4	Where the quantity falls below the indicative amount set out for category 4 in the "category of harm" table (*ante*), first identify the role for the importation offence, then refer to the starting point and ranges for possession or supply offences, depending on intent. Where the quantity is significantly larger than the indicative amounts for category 4 but below category 3 amounts, refer to the category 3 ranges above.		

Class B	**Leading role**	**Significant role**	**Lesser role**
Category 1	Starting point 8 years Category range 7 –10 years	Starting point 5.5 years Category range 5 –7 years	Starting point 4 years Category range 2.5 –5 years
Category 2	Starting point 6 years Category range 4.5 –8 years	Starting point 4 years Category range 2.5 –5 years	Starting point 2 years Category range 1.5 –3 years
Category 3	Starting point 4 years Category range 2.5 –5 years	Starting point 2 years Category range 1.5 –3 years	Starting point 1 year Category range 12 weeks –18 months
Category 4	As for "Category 4" Class A offences, *ante*.		

Class C	**Leading role**	**Significant role**	**Lesser role**
Category 1	Starting point 5 years Category range 4 –8 years	Starting point 3 years Category range 2 –5 years	Starting point 1.5 years Category range 1 –3 years
Category 2	Starting point 3.5 years Category range 2 –5 years	Starting point 1.5 years Category range 1 –3 years	Starting point 26 weeks Category range 12 weeks –18 months
Category 3	Starting point 1.5 years Category range 1 –3 years	Starting point 26 weeks Category range 12 weeks – 18 months	Starting point high level community order Category range medium level community order – 12 weeks
Category 4	As for "Category 4" class A offences, *ante*.		

Factors increasing or reducing seriousness or reflecting personal mitigation

Factors increasing seriousness	i, iv, xi–xv, xvii, xviii, xx–xxii
Factors reducing seriousness or reflecting personal mitigation	i, iv–ix, xi–xv

II. Supplying, offering to supply, possession with intent to supply

Determining the offence category (step one)

K-276　　The court should determine the weight of the drugs and the offender's culpability demonstrated by his role, by reference to the tables below. Where there are characteristics present that fall under different role categories, the court should balance them to reach a fair assessment of the offender's culpability.

Culpability demonstrated by offender's role
One or more of these characteristics may demonstrate the offender's role. These lists are not exhaustive.
LEADING role:
As for "Leading role" in section I, *ante*.
SIGNIFICANT role:
As for "Significant role" in section I, *ante*, but also:
supply, other than by a person in a position of responsibility, to a prisoner for gain without coercion.
LESSER role:
As for "Lesser role" in section I, *ante*, save that:
if own operation, absence of any financial gain, *e.g.* joint purchase for no profit, or sharing minimal quantity between peers on non-commercial basis.

Category of harm
Indicative quantity of drug concerned (upon which the starting point is based):
Category 1
As for "Category 1" in section I, *ante*.
Category 2
As for "Category 2" in section I, *ante*.
Category 3
As for "Category 3" in section I, *ante*.
OR
supplying drugs in prison by a prison employee or "street dealing", *i.e.* selling directly to users (including test purchase officers).
Category 4
As for "Category 4" in section I, *ante*,

Where the operation is on the most serious and commercial scale, involving a quantity of drugs significantly higher than category 1, sentences of 20 years and above may be appropriate, depending on the role of the offender.

Starting point and category range (step two)

Class A	**Leading role**	**Significant role**	**Lesser role**
Category 1	*Starting point* 14 years *Category range* 12 – 16 years	*Starting point* 10 years *Category range* 9 – 12 years	*Starting point* 7 years Category range 6 – 9 years

Category 2	Starting point 11 years Category range 9 – 13 years	Starting point 8 years Category range 6.5 – 10 years	Starting point 5 years Category range 3.5 – 7 years
Category 3	Starting point 8.5 years Category range 6.5 – 10 years	Starting point 4.5 years Category range 3.5 – 7 years	Starting point 3 years Category range 2 – 4.5 years
Category 4	Starting point 5.5 years Category range 4.5 – 7.5 years	Starting point 3.5 years Category range 2 – 5 years	Starting point 1.5 years Category range high level community order – 3 years

Class B	Leading role	Significant role	Lesser role
Category 1	Starting point 8 years Category range 7 – 10 years	Starting point 5.5 years Category range 5 – 7 years	Starting point 3 years Category range 2.5 – 5 years
Category 2	Starting point 6 years Category range 4.5 – 8 years	Starting point 4 years Category range 2.5 – 5 years	Starting point 1 year Category range 26 weeks – 3 years
Category 3	Starting point 4 years Category range 2.5 – 5 years	Starting point 1 year Category range 26 weeks – 3 years	Starting point high level community order Category range low level community order – 26 weeks
Category 4	Starting point 1.5 years Category range 26 weeks – 3 years	Starting point high level community order Category range medium level community order – 26 weeks	Starting point low level community order Category range band B fine – medium level community order

Class C	Leading role	Significant role	Lesser role
Category 1	Starting point 5 years Category range 4 – 8 years	Starting point 3 years Category range 2 – 5 years	Starting point 1.5 years Category range 1 – 3 years
Category 2	Starting point 3.5 years Category range 2 – 5 years	Starting point 1.5 years Category range 1 – 3 years	Starting point 26 years Category range 12 weeks – 1.5 years

| Category 3 | Starting point 1.5 years Category range 1 – 3 years | Starting point 26 years Category range 12 weeks – 1.5 years | Starting point high level community order Category range low level community-order – 12 weeks |
| Category 4 | Starting point 26 years Category range high level community order – 1.5 years | Starting point high level community order Category range low level community order – 12 weeks | Starting point low level community order Category range band A fine – medium level community order |

Factors increasing or reducing seriousness or reflecting personal mitigation

| Factors increasing seriousness | i–v, x, xv, xvii–xxii |
| Factors reducing seriousness or reflecting personal mitigation | i–ix, xi–xv |

III. Production of a controlled drug OR cultivation of a cannabis plant

Determining the offence category (step one)

K-277   The court should determine the offender's culpability demonstrated by his role and the output or potential output based on the weight of the product or number of plants/ scale of operation, by reference to the tables below. Where there are characteristics present that fall under different role categories, the court should balance them to reach a fair assessment of the offender's culpability.

| **Culpability demonstrated by offender's role** |
| One or more of these characteristics may demonstrate the offender's role. These lists are not exhaustive. |
| **LEADING role:** |
| As for "Leading role" in section I, *ante*, save that there is no reference here to closeness to the original source. |
| **SIGNIFICANT role:** |
| As for "Significant role" in section I, *ante*. |
| **LESSER role:** |
| As for "Lesser role" in section I, *ante*. |
| **Category of harm** Indicative quantity of drug concerned (upon which the starting point is based): |
| **Category 1** As for "Category 1" in section I, *ante*, except that the quantity specified for cannabis is an operation capable of producing industrial quantities for commercial use. |
| **Category 2** As for "Category 2" in section I, *ante*, except that the quantity specified for cannabis is an operation capable of producing significant quantities for commercial use. |
| **Category 3** As for "Category 3" in section I, *ante*, except that the quantity specified for cannabis is 28 plants (with an assumed yield of 40g per plant). |

> **Category 4**
> As for "Category 4" in section I, *ante*, except that the quantity specified for cannabis is nine plants (with an assumed yield of 40g per plant) (domestic operation).

Where the operation is on the most serious and commercial scale, involving a quantity of drugs significantly higher than category 1, sentences of 20 years and above may be appropriate, depending on the role of the offender.

Starting point and category range (step two)

For Class A offences, as for "Class A" in section II, *ante*, except for category 3:

Class A	Leading role	Significant role	Lesser role
Category 3	*Starting point* 8.5 years *Category range* 6.5 – 10 years	*Starting point* 5 years *Category range* 3.5 – 7 years	*Starting point* 3.5 years *Category range* 2 – 5 years

For Class B offences, as for "Class B" in section II, *ante*, except for category 4:

Class B	Leading role	Significant role	Lesser role
Category 4	*Starting point* 1 year *Category range* high level community order – 3 years	*Starting point* high level community order *Category range* medium level community order – 26 weeks	*Starting point* band C fine *Category range* discharge – medium level community order

Class C	Leading role	Significant role	Lesser role
Category 1	*Starting point* 5 years *Category range* 4 – 8 years	*Starting point* 3 years *Category range* 2 – 5 years	*Starting point* 1.5 years *Category range* 1 – 3 years
Category 2	*Starting point* 3.5 years *Category range* 2 – 5 years	*Starting point* 1.5 years *Category range* 1 – 3 years	*Starting point* 26 weeks *Category range* high level community order – 1.5 years
Category 3	*Starting point* 1.5 years *Category range* 1 – 3 years	*Starting point* 26 weeks *Category range* high level community order – 1.5 years	*Starting point* high level community order *Category range* low level community order – 12 weeks
Category 4	*Starting point* 26 weeks *Category range* high level community order – 1.5 years	*Starting point* high level community order *Category range* low level community order – 12 weeks	*Starting point* band C fine *Category range* discharge – medium level community order

Factors increasing or reducing seriousness or reflecting personal mitigation

Factors increasing seriousness	i, iv, vi–x, xv, xvii, xviii, xx–xxii
Factors reducing seriousness or reflecting personal mitigation	i, iv–ix, xi–xv

IV. Permitting premises to be used

Determining the offence category (step one)

K-278   The court should determine into which of three categories the offence falls by reference to the offender's culpability and the harm caused (which will be based on the extent of the activity and/ or the quantity of drugs). Category 1 requires greater harm and higher culpability, category 2 requires either greater harm and lower culpability or lesser harm and higher culpability, and category 3 requires lesser harm and lower culpability.

Factors indicating higher culpability (non-exhaustive):
- Premises used primarily for drug activity, *e.g.* crack house.
- Expectation of substantial financial gain.
- Use of legitimate business premises to aid and/ or conceal illegal activity, *e.g.* public house or club.

Factors indicating lower culpability (non-exhaustive):
- Limited or no financial gain.
- No active role in any supply taking place.
- Involvement through naivety.

Factors indicating greater harm (non-exhaustive):
- Regular drug-related activity.
- Higher quantity of drugs, *e.g.* more than 5g of heroin or cocaine or more than 50g or cannabis.

Factors indicating lesser harm (non-exhaustive):
- Infrequent drug-related activity.
- Lower quantity of drugs.

Starting point and category range (step two)

Class A	Starting point	Category range
Category 1	2.5 years	1.5 – 4 year
Category 2	36 weeks	high level community order – 1.5 years
Category 3	medium level community order	low level community order – high level community order

Class B	Starting point	Category range
Category 1	1 year	26 weeks – 1.5 years
Category 2	high level community order	low level community order – 26 weeks
Category 3	band C fine	band A fine – low level community order

Class C	Starting point	Category range
Category 1	12 weeks	high level community order – 26 weeks (3 months if tried summarily)
Category 2	low level community order	band C fine – high level community order
Category 3	band A fine	discharge – band C fine

Factors increasing or reducing seriousness or reflecting personal mitigation

Factors increasing seriousness	i, iv, xi–xv, xvii, xviii, xx–xxii
Factors reducing seriousness or reflecting personal mitigation	i, iv–ix, xi–xv

V. Possession of a controlled drug

Determining the offence category (step one)

The court should determine the offence category based on the class of drug involved.   **K-279**

Starting point and category range (step two)

Offence category	Starting point	Category range
Category 1 (Class A)	band C fine	band A fine – 51 weeks
Category 2 (Class B)	band B fine	discharge – 26 weeks
Category 3 (Class C)	band A fine	discharge – medium level community order

Factors increasing or reducing seriousness or reflecting personal mitigation

Factors increasing seriousness	i, iv, xv–xvii, xix, xxi, xxii
Factors reducing seriousness or reflecting personal mitigation	iv, vi, viii–xv

U. Offences Taken into Consideration and Totality

The Sentencing Council issued a guideline on the related topics of taking offences into **K-280** consideration (TICs) and totality, applying to all offenders whose cases are dealt with on or after June 11, 2012. In addition to setting out the applicable principles to be gleaned from legislation and case-law, the guideline covers the following.

A. Offences taken into consideration

See §§ 5-160 *et seq.* in the main work.   **K-281**

B. Totality

This part of the guideline applies to the sentencing of an offender for multiple offences or **K-282** when he is serving an existing sentence. The principle of totality comprises two elements: (i) all courts when sentencing for more than a single offence should pass a just and proportionate total sentence that reflects all the offending behaviour, whether the sentences are structured as concurrent or consecutive (in respect of which there is no inflexible rule); (ii) it is usually impossible to arrive at a just and proportionate total sentence simply by adding together notional single sentences - it is necessary to address the offending behaviour, together with the factors personal to the offender, as a whole.

The general approach (as applied to determinate custodial sentences) consists of four steps:

  (i) consider the sentence for each individual offence;

 (ii) determine whether the case calls for concurrent or consecutive sentences;

(iii) test the overall sentence against the requirement that it should be just and proportionate; and

(iv) consider whether the sentence is structured in a way that will be best understood by all concerned with it.

As to (ii), concurrent sentences will ordinarily be appropriate where the offences arise out of the same incident or facts or where there is a series of offences of the same or similar kind, especially when committed against the same person, with examples of both being set out in the guideline. Consecutive offences will be appropriate where the offences arise out of unrelated facts or incidents, where the offences are of the same or similar kind, but where the overall criminality will not sufficiently be reflected by concurrent sentences, or where one or more offence qualifies for a statutory minimum sentence and concurrent sentences would improperly undermine that minimum. Examples are again set out, including ways in which the court can reach a just and proportionate sentence where this is not achieved by simply aggregating the consecutive sentences (*e.g.* with offences of a similar level of severity, by reducing all of the sentences proportionately or by identifying the most serious principal offence and reducing the remainder proportionately; with offences of differing levels of seriousness, by recording lesser offences as "no separate penalty" or by ordering the lesser sentences to run concurrently).

Tables follow the guideline, setting out the approach to be taken when applying the totality principle in specified circumstances (this is in large part based on existing legislation and case-law).

Determinate custodial sentence to be passed

K-283   a. where the offender is serving an existing custodial determinate sentence: if the new offence was committed before the imposition of that sentence, the court should consider what sentence would have been imposed if the court had dealt with the offences at the same time; if it was committed after that sentence, then generally the sentence will be consecutive;

b. where the offender is serving a custodial determinate sentence, but had been released from custody prior to being recalled, the court should follow *R. v. Costello* [2010] 2 Cr.App.R.(S.) 94, CA (§ 5-669 in the main work);

c. where the offender is liable to be returned to custody under the PCC(S)A 2000, s.116, see subsection (6)(c);

d. where the offender is in breach of a suspended sentence, the additional sentence will generally be consecutive to the activated suspended sentence;

Extended sentences

K-284   e. when using multiple offences to calculate the requisite determinate term (in accordance with *R. v. Joyce; R. v. Pinnell* [2011] 2 Cr.App.R.(S.) 30, CA (§ 5-523 in the main work)), the custodial period must be adjusted for totality in the same way as determinate sentences would be;

Indeterminate sentences

K-285   f. when imposing multiple indeterminate sentences and using multiple offences to calculate the minimum term for an indeterminate sentence, assess the notional determinate term for all offences (serious, specified or otherwise) in the usual way, adjusting for totality, and then, normally, impose the indeterminate sentence on all serious specified offences concurrently;

g. where the offender is already serving an existing determinate sentence, the court should order the sentence to run concurrently but adjust the minimum term to reflect half of any period still remaining to be served under the existing sentence; where the offender is already serving an existing indeterminate sentence, the court may order the sentence to run consecutively to the existing sentence (*R. v. Hills* [2009] 1 Cr.App.R.(S.) 75, CA (§ 5-523 in the main work)), but the aggregate minimum terms should be adjusted if this is not just and proportionate;

h. when ordering a determinate sentence to run consecutively to an indeterminate sentence, the court should consider the total sentence that the offender will serve before becoming eligible for consideration for release, achieving justice and proportionality, if necessary, by reducing the length of the determinate sentence or, alternatively, ordering the second sentence to be served concurrently;

Multiple fines for non-imprisonable offences

K-286   i. where the offender has been convicted of more than one offence where a fine is appropriate, there are various ways in which the court can achieve a just and proportionate fine if this is not achieved by simply totting up the fines; the court should also consider *R. v. John Pointon & Sons Ltd* [2008] 2 Cr.App.R.(S.) 82, CA (as to the need to avoid double counting);

Fines in combination with other sentences

    j. a fine may be imposed in addition to any other sentence (subject to statutory exceptions), **K-287** but combining a fine with an immediate custodial sentence is only likely to be justifiable if a confiscation order is not contemplated, there is no obvious victim to receive compensation and the offender has the means to pay;

Community orders

    k. multiple offences that do not individually cross the custody threshold may do so when **K-288** taken in combination;

    l. where there is more than one offence, with one meriting immediate custody and one meriting a community order, the custodial sentence should be enhanced by virtue of the associated offence or no separate penalty should be imposed for the lesser offence;

    m. where the offender has been convicted of more than one offence where a community order is appropriate, the court should generally impose a single community order that reflects the overall criminality of the offending behaviour; where it is necessary to impose more than one community order, these should be ordered to run concurrently and, for ease of administration, each of the orders should be identical;

    n. where the offender is convicted of an offence while serving a community order, the court should consider if the overall seriousness of the offending behaviour justifies a custodial sentence; if not, it should impose a single community order reflecting the overall totality of criminality; and it should take into account the extent to which the offender complied with the requirements of the previous order;

Disqualifications from driving

    o. where the offender has been convicted of two or more obligatory disqualification offences, **K-289** the court should take into account all offences when determining the disqualification periods and should generally impose like periods for each offence (which have to be concurrent);

    p. where the offender has been convicted of two or more offences and is liable to disqualification under the "totting up" provisions of the RTOA 1988, s.35 (§ 32-264 in the main work), the guideline simply sets out the effect of subsection (3);

    q. where the offender has otherwise been convicted of two or more offences involving discretionary disqualification, it is generally desirable for the court to impose a single disqualification order that reflects the overall criminality of the offending behaviour;

Compensation orders

    r. a global compensation order should not be made unless the offences were committed **K-290** against the same victim; where there are competing claims for limited funds, the amount available should normally be apportioned on a *pro rata* basis;

    s. compensation may be combined with a fine (with priority to compensation), a confiscation order, a community order, a suspended sentence or an immediate custodial sentence (where the offender is clearly able to pay or has good prospects of employment on release).

V. DANGEROUS DOG OFFENCES

The Sentencing Council for England and Wales issued a definitive guideline, applying to all of- **K-291** fenders aged 18 or over who were sentenced on or after August 20, 2012, regardless of the date of the offence. The offences covered are: (A) owning or being in charge of a dog that injures a person whilst dangerously out of control in a public place (Dangerous Dogs Act 1991, s.3(1) (§ 31-35 in the main work)), and allowing a dog to enter a private place where the dog is not permitted to be, where it then injures any person (1991 Act, s.3(3)(a)), (B) owning or being in charge of a dog dangerously out of control in a public place (1991 Act, s.3(1)), and allowing a dog to enter a private place where the dog is not permitted to be, and, while it is there, there are grounds for reasonable apprehension that it will injure any person (1991 Act, s.3(3)(b)), and (C) possession of a prohibited dog (1991 Act, s.1(3)), and breeding, selling, exchanging or advertising a prohibited dog (1991 Act, s.1(2)).

In view of the legislative changes made to the 1991 Act by the Anti-social Behaviour, Crime and Policing Act 2014, including by way of abolishing the offences under section 3(3), extending the offence under section 3(1) to private places as well as public places, and increasing the penalties for aggravated offences under section 3(1), the guideline now needs to be approached with considerable caution.

The guideline sets out eight steps to be followed (in order), which broadly correspond to the steps set out in the guideline on offences against the person (*ante*, K-113 *et seq.*), except that there is no step requiring the court to consider whether an offender meets the dangerousness criteria, and consideration of compensation and/ or ancillary orders is step five (as to which, see the specific sections relating to A to C, *post*), preceding consideration of the totality principle (now step six).

Step one requires the court to determine within which of three categories reflecting various degrees of seriousness the offence falls. In determining the offender's culpability and the harm caused (or intended), the court should refer only to the factors indicating harm and culpability set out in the specific sections relating to A to C, *post*, which comprise the principal factual elements of the offence.

Step two requires the court to use the starting point identified for the relevant category (as to which, see also the specific sections relating to A to C, *post*) to reach a sentence within the category range. The starting point applies to all offenders irrespective of plea or previous convictions. The court should then consider adjustment within the category range for aggravating or mitigating features set out in the specific sections A to C, *post*, which contain a non-exhaustive list of additional factual elements providing the context of the offence and factors relating to the offender. Having considered all these, and other relevant factors, it might be appropriate to move outside the identified category range. As with previous guidelines, the council emphasises that, where appropriate, courts should consider whether community or custodial thresholds have been passed and, if the latter threshold has been passed, whether it is unavoidable that a custodial sentence be imposed and, if so, whether that sentence can be suspended.

Fine bands, and a non-exhaustive description of examples of requirements that might be appropriate for low, medium and high level community orders, correspond to those in the guideline on offences against the person (*ante*), and are set out in the annex to the guideline.

★   As to a new consultation guideline on dangerous dog offences, see *ante*, § 31-37b.

Key to factors increasing or reducing seriousness or reflecting personal mitigation (step two)

K-292   A number of the following factors may apply when determining the sentence within the category range. As to which factors may apply to each type of offence, see the specific sections A to C, *post*.

(a) *Factors increasing seriousness*

   Statutory aggravating factors:

   i. Previous convictions.

   ii. Offence committed on bail.

   Other aggravating factors include:

   iii. Injury to other animal(s).

   iv. Location of offence.

   v. Continuing effect upon victim and/ or others.

   vi. Failure to take adequate precautions to prevent dog escaping.

   vii. Allowing insufficiently experienced or trained person to be in charge of dog.

   viii. Presence of children or others who are vulnerable because of personal circumstances.

   ix. Ill-treatment or failure to ensure welfare needs of dog, where not charged separately.

   x. Dog known to be prohibited.

   xi. Lack or loss of control of dog due to influence of alcohol or drugs.

   xii. Offence committed against those working in the public sector or providing a service to the public.

xiii. Established evidence of community impact.

xiv. Failure to comply with current court orders or offence committed on licence.

(b) *Factors reducing seriousness or reflecting personal mitigation*

    i. No previous convictions or no relevant/ recent convictions.

    ii. Isolated incident.

    iii. No previous complaints against, or incidents involving, the dog.

    iv. Unaware that dog was prohibited type despite reasonable efforts to identify type.

    v. Evidence of safety or control measures having been taken by owner.

    vi. Prosecution results from owner notification.

    vii. Remorse.

    viii. Good character and/ or exemplary conduct.

    ix. Evidence of responsible ownership.

    x. Determination, and/ or demonstration of steps taken, to address addiction or offending behaviour.

    xi. Serious medical condition requiring urgent, intensive or long-term treatment.

    xii. Age and/ or lack of maturity where it affects the responsibility of the offender.

    xiii. Lapse of time since the offence where this was not the fault of the offender.

    xiv. Mental disorder or learning disability (for offences in sections A and B only, where not linked to commission of the offence).

    xv. Sole or primary carer for dependent relatives.

A. Dog dangerously out of control in a public place, injuring any person, or allowing a dog to enter a private place where the dog is not permitted to be, where it then injures any person

Determining the offence category (step one)

Category 1 requires greater harm and higher culpability, category 2 requires either greater   **K-293**
harm and lower culpability or lesser harm and higher culpability, and category 3 requires lesser harm and lower culpability.

Factors indicating greater harm

- Serious injury (including disease transmission and/ or psychological harm)
- Sustained or repeated attack
- Victim is a child or otherwise vulnerable because of personal circumstances

Factors indicating lesser harm

- Minor injury

Factors indicating higher culpability

Statutory aggravating factors:

- Offence racially or religiously aggravated
- Offence motivated by, or demonstrating, hostility to the victim based on sexual orientation or disability (or presumed sexual orientation or disability)

Other aggravating factors:

- Failure to respond to others' warnings or concerns about dog's behaviour
- Goading, or allowing goading, of dog
- Dog used as weapon to intimidate victim
- Offence motivated by, or demonstrating, hostility to the victim based on age, sex, or (presumed) gender identity

Factors indicating lower culpability

- Attempts made to regain control of dog and/ or intervene
- Provocation of dog without fault of offender

- Evidence of safety or control measures taken
- Mental disorder or disability, where linked to the commission of the offence

Starting point and category range (step two)

Offence category	Starting point (applicable to all offenders)	Category range (applicable to all offenders)
category 1	six months' custody	medium level community order - 18 months' custody
category 2	medium level community order	band B fine - six months' custody
category 3	band B fine	discharge - band C fine

Factors increasing or reducing seriousness or reflecting personal mitigation

Factors increasing seriousness: i-vii, ix-xiv

Factors reducing seriousness or reflecting personal mitigation: i-iii, vii-xii, xiv, xv

Compensation and ancillary orders (step five)

The court should consider whether to make a compensation order and/ or other ancillary orders. The court may disqualify the offender from having custody of a dog, the test being whether the offender is a fit and proper person to have custody of a dog. The court shall make a destruction order (after giving the owner, where not the offender, an opportunity to be present and make representations) unless satisfied that the dog would not constitute a danger to public safety. In reaching a decision, the court should consider the relevant circumstances, which include (i) the incident — what degree of harm was caused by the dog's behaviour, (ii) past behaviour of the dog — whether this was an isolated incident or whether there have been previous warnings or incidents, and (iii) the owner's character — whether the owner is a fit and proper person to own the particular dog. If satisfied that the dog would not constitute a danger to public safety, the court shall make a contingent destruction order imposing certain conditions. Where the court makes a destruction order, it may order the offender to pay reasonable expenses.

B. Dog dangerously out of control in a public place, or allowing a dog to enter a private place where the dog is not permitted to be, where there are grounds for reasonable apprehension that it will injure any person

Determining the offence category (step one)

K-294   Same categories as for A, *ante*.

Factors indicating greater harm

- Presence of children or others who are vulnerable because of personal circumstances
- Injury to another animal(s)

Factors indicating lesser harm

- Low risk to the public

Factors indicating higher culpability

- Same as for A, *ante*

Factors indicating lower culpability

- Same as for A, *ante*

Starting point and category range (step two)

Offence category	Starting point (applicable to all offenders)	Category range (applicable to all offenders)
category 1	medium level community order	band C fine - six months' custody
category 2	band B fine	band A fine - low level community order
category 3	band A fine	discharge - band B fine

Factors increasing or reducing seriousness or reflecting personal mitigation

  Factors increasing seriousness: i, ii, iv-vii, ix-xiv

  Factors reducing seriousness or reflecting personal mitigation: i-iii, vii-xii, xiv, xv

Compensation and ancillary orders (step five)

 Same as for A, *ante*, except the court is permitted (rather than required) to make a destruction order or contingent destruction order. In reaching a decision, the court should consider the relevant circumstances, which include those set out in section A, *ante*.

C. Possession of a prohibited dog, or breeding, selling, exchanging or advertising a prohibited dog

Determining the offence category (step one)

 Category 1 requires greater harm and higher culpability, category 2 requires either greater **K-295** harm or higher culpability, and category 3 requires that there be neither greater harm nor higher culpability.

Factors indicating greater harm

- Injury to person
- Injury to another animal(s)

Factors indicating higher culpability

- Dog known to be prohibited
- Offence committed for gain
- Dog used to threaten or intimidate
- Permitting fighting
- Training and/ or possession of paraphernalia for dog fighting

Starting point and category range (step two)

Offence category	Starting point (applicable to all offenders)	Category range (applicable to all offenders)
category 1	medium level community order	band C fine - six months' custody
category 2	band C fine	band A fine - medium level community order
category 3	band A fine	discharge - band B fine

Factors increasing or reducing seriousness or reflecting personal mitigation

  Factors increasing seriousness: i, ii, viii, ix, xiii, xiv

  Factors reducing seriousness or reflecting personal mitigation: i, iv-xv.

Ancillary orders (step five)

 The court may disqualify the offender from having custody of a dog, the test being whether the **K-296** offender is a fit and proper person to have custody of a dog. The court shall make a destruction order unless satisfied that the dog would not constitute a danger to public safety. In reaching a decision, the court should consider the relevant circumstances, which include those set out in section A, *ante*. If the court does not make a destruction order, the court shall make a contingent destruction order providing that unless the dog is exempted from the prohibition within two months it shall be destroyed. Where the offender is the owner of the dog, it would not normally be appropriate to make a contingent destruction order in conjunction with a disqualification order. Further, the court must not transfer ownership of the dog to another. Where the court makes a destruction order, it may order the offender to pay reasonable expenses.

W. Fraud, Bribery and Money Laundering

K-297   The Sentencing Council for England and Wales has issued a definitive guideline for offences of fraud, money laundering and bribery falling to be sentenced on or after October 1, 2014. The guideline is in seven sections, the seventh of which relates to corporate offenders and incorporates an earlier guideline issued by the Sentencing Council.

Each section (apart from Section VII, which is dealt with separately, *post*) describes eight steps to be gone through.

Step 1 (determining the offence category)

K-298   This involves determination of the offence category by reference to the tables in each section. In order to do this, the court should make an assessment of culpability and harm. The level of culpability is determined by weighing up all the factors of the case to determine the offender's role and the extent to which the offending was planned and the sophistication with which it was carried out.

The following indicators of culpability are used throughout the guideline (apart from Section VII, which is dealt with separately (*post*)).

Higher culpability (A)

HC1:	A leading role where offending is part of a group activity
HC2:	Involvement of others through pressure, influence
HC3:	Abuse of position of power, trust or responsibility
HC4:	Sophisticated nature of offence/ significant planning
HC5:	Fraudulent activity conducted over sustained period of time
HC6:	Large number of victims
HC7:	Deliberate targeting of victim on basis of vulnerability
HC8:	Articles deliberately designed to target victims on basis of vulnerability
HC9:	Criminal activity/ offending conducted over sustained period of time
HC10:	Intended corruption (directly or indirectly) of a senior official performing a public function or of a law enforcement officer
HC11:	Motivated by expectation of substantial financial, commercial or political gain

Medium culpability (B)

MC1:	Other cases where characteristics for categories A or C are not present
MC2:	A significant role where offending is part of a group activity
MC3:	Claim not fraudulent from outset

Lesser culpability (C)

LC1:	Involved through coercion, intimidation or exploitation
LC2:	Not motivated by personal gain

LC3: Peripheral role in organised fraud

LC4: Opportunistic "one-off" offence

LC5: Limited awareness or understanding of the extent of the fraudulent activity

LC6: Performed limited function under direction

Where there are characteristics present that fall under different levels of culpability, the court hould balance them to reach a fair assessment of the offender's culpability.

As to the assessment of harm, see the individual sections.

Step 2 (starting point and category range)

Having determined the category, the court should use the appropriate starting point to reach a **K-299** entence within the category range in the tables. The starting points apply to all offenders irespective of plea and previous convictions. Where the starting point is based on a particular alue (as in Sections I, III, IV and V), this should be adjusted upwards or downwards according o the actual value involved. Where the value greatly exceeds the amount of the starting point for category 1 case, it may be appropriate to move outside the identified range.

The tables of starting points and category ranges in each section are followed by a "nonexhaustive list of additional factual elements providing the context of the offence and factors elating to the offender." The court is then to identify whether any combination of these or other elevant factors should result in an upward or downward adjustment from the sentence arrived at pased on culpability and harm alone. In each section, it is also stated that consecutive sentences or multiple offences may be appropriate where large sums are involved.

The following aggravating and mitigating factors are used throughout the guideline (apart rom Section VII, which is dealt with separately (*post*)).

Aggravating factors

A1: Previous convictions, having regard to (a) the nature of the offence to which the conviction relates and its relevance to the current offence; and (b) the time that has elapsed since the conviction

A2: Offence committed whilst on bail

A3: Steps taken to prevent the victim reporting or obtaining assistance and/ or from assisting or supporting the prosecution

A4: Attempts to conceal/ dispose of evidence

A5: Established evidence of community/ wider impact

A6: Failure to comply with current court orders

A7: Offence committed on licence

A8: Offences taken into consideration

A9: Failure to respond to warnings about behaviour

A10: Offences committed across borders

A11: Blame wrongly placed on others

A12: Involves multiple frauds

A13: Number of false declarations

A14: Damage to third party (*e.g.* as a result of identity theft, or loss of employment to legitimate employees)

A15: Dealing with goods with an additional health risk

A16: Disposing of goods to under age purchasers

A17: Claim fraudulent from outset

A18: Proceeds of fraud funded lavish lifestyle

A19: Length of time over which offending was committed

A20:   Pressure exerted on another party

A21:   Offence committed to facilitate other criminal activity

Mitigating factors

M1:   No previous convictions or no relevant/ recent convictions

M2:   Remorse

M3:   Good character and/ or exemplary conduct

M4:   Little or no prospect of success

M5:   Serious medical conditions requiring urgent, intensive or long-term treatment

M6:   Age and/ or lack of maturity where it affects the responsibility of the offender

M7:   Lapse of time since apprehension where this does not arise from the conduct of the offender

M8:   Mental disorder or learning disability

M9:   Sole or primary carer for dependent relatives

M10:   Offender co-operated with investigation, made early admissions and/ or voluntarily reported offending

M11:   Determination and/ or demonstration of steps having been taken to address addiction or offending behaviour

M12:   Activity originally legitimate

M13:   Legitimate entitlement to benefits not claimed

M14:   Offender experiencing significant financial hardship or pressure at time fraud was committed due to exceptional circumstances

Steps 3–8

K-300   These are standard steps in guidelines issued by the Sentencing Council. They require the court to consider the SOCPA 2005, ss.73 and 74 (assistance by defendants; reduction or review of sentence (§§ 5-132, 5-133 in the main work)), credit for a guilty plea, the totality principle, the question of confiscation, compensation and any appropriate ancillary orders, the need to give reasons and to make any appropriate allowance for time spent on bail (CJA 2003, s.240A (§ 5-645 in the main work)).

I. Fraud

K-301   This section covers fraud (Fraud Act 2006, s.1, (§ 21-356 in the main work)), conspiracy to defraud (§§ 33-37 *et seq.* in the main work) and false accounting (Theft Act 1968, s.17 (§ 21-226 in the main work)), but none of these if the fraud is a revenue or benefit fraud (as to which, see Sections III and IV, *post*).

Step 1: determine the level of culpability and the harm category (and see generally, ante)
   Culpability

High culpability (HC)	Medium culpability (MC)	Lesser culpability (LC)
HC1–HC7	MC1, MC2	LC1–LC5

Harm

This is initially assessed by the actual, intended or risked loss that may arise from the offence. The values in the table below are to be used for actual or intended loss only. Intended loss relates to offences where circumstances prevent the actual loss that is intended to be caused by the fraudulent activity. Risk of loss (*e.g.* in mortgage frauds) involves consideration of the likelihood of harm occurring and its extent if it does, and is less serious than actual or intended loss. Where the offence has caused risk of loss but no (or much less) actual loss, the normal approach is to move down to the corresponding point in the next category. This may be inappropriate if the likelihood or extent of risked loss is particularly high.

Category 1	£500k or more	Starting point based on £1m
Category 2	£100k–£500k or risk of category 1 harm	Starting point based on £300k
Category 3	£20k–£100k or risk of category 2 harm	Starting point based on £50k
Category 4	£5k–20k or risk of category 3 harm	Starting point based on £12.5k
Category 5	Less than £5k or risk of category 4 harm	Starting point based on £2.5k

If there is risk of category 5 harm, the court should move further down the range within the category.

Harm B — Victim impact

The court should then take into account the level of harm caused to the victim or others to determine whether it warrants the sentence being moved up to the corresponding point in the next category or further up the range of the initial category.

| **High impact** — move up a category; if in category 1 move up the range
• Serious detrimental effect on the victim whether financial or otherwise, *e.g.* substantial damage to credit rating.
• Victim particularly vulnerable (due to factors including, but not limited to, age, financial circumstances and mental capacity). |
| **Medium impact** — move upwards within the category range
• Considerable detrimental effect on the victim, financial or otherwise. |
| **Lesser impact** — no adjustment
• Some detrimental impact on victim, financial or otherwise. |

Step 2: use the following tables to reach a provisional sentence (and see generally, ante)

Table 1 (fraud and conspiracy to defraud)

Harm	Culpability (A)	Culpability (B)	Culpability (C)
	Starting points and ranges	*Starting points and ranges*	*Starting points and ranges*
Category 1	7 years 5–8 years	5 years 3–6 years	3 years 1.5–4 years
Category 2	5 years 3–6 years	3 years 1.5–4 years	1.5 years 26 weeks–3 years
Category 3	3 years 1.5–4 years	1.5 years 26 weeks–3 years	26 weeks Medium level community order–12 months
Category 4	1.5 years 26 weeks–3 years	26 weeks Medium level community order–12 months	Medium level community order Band B fine–high level community order

Harm	Culpability (A)	Culpability (B)	Culpability (C)
	Starting points and ranges	*Starting points and ranges*	*Starting points and ranges*
Category 5	36 weeks' custody High level community order–12 months	Medium level community order Band B fine–26 weeks	Band B fine Discharge–medium level community order

Table 2 (false accounting)

Harm	Culpability (A)	Culpability (B)	Culpability (C)
	Starting points and ranges	*Starting points and ranges*	*Starting points and ranges*
Category 1	5.5 years 4–6.5 years	4 years 2.5–5 years	2.5 years 15 months–3.5 years
Category 2	4 years 2.5–5 years	2.5 years 15 months–3.5 years	15 months 26 weeks–2.5 years
Category 3	2.5 years 15 months–3.5 years	15 months High level community order–2.5 years	High level community order Low level community order–36 weeks
Category 4	15 months High level community order–2.5 years	High level community order Low level community order–36 weeks	Low level community order Band B fine–medium level community order
Category 5	26 weeks Medium level community order–36 weeks	Low level community order Band B fine–medium level community order	Band B fine Discharge–low level community order

Adjust the provisional sentence according to the presence of the following factors:

Factors increasing seriousness	Factors reducing seriousness or reflecting personal mitigation
A1–A11	M1–M12

Steps 3–8: see *ante*

II. Possessing, making or supplying articles for use in fraud

K-302   This section covers the offences contrary to sections 6 and 7 of the Fraud Act 2006 (§§ 21-390, 21-391 in the main work)).

Step 1: determine the level of culpability and the harm category (and see generally, ante).
Culpability

High culpability (A)	Medium culpability (B)	Lesser culpability (C)
HC1–HC5, HC8	MC1, MC2	LC1, LC2, LC4–LC6

Harm
The level of harm is determined by weighing up all the factors to determine the harm that would be caused if the article(s) was (were) used to commit a substantive offence.

Greater harm
• Large number of articles created/ supplied/ in possession.
• Article has potential to facilitate fraudulent acts affecting large number of victims.
• Article has potential to facilitate fraudulent acts involving significant sums.

| • Use of third party identities.
| • Offender making considerable gain as result of the offence. |

Lesser harm
• All other offences.

Step 2: use the following tables to reach a provisional sentence (and see generally, ante).
Table 1 (possessing articles for use in fraud (2006 Act, s.6))

Harm	Culpability (A)	Culpability (B)	Culpability (C)
Greater	*Starting points and ranges* 1.5 years 36 weeks–3 years	*Starting points and ranges* 36 weeks High level community order–2 years	*Starting points and ranges* High level community order Medium level community order–26 weeks
Lesser	26 weeks High level community order–1.5 years	Medium level community order Low level community order–26 weeks	Band B fine Band A fine–medium level community order

Table 2 (making, adapting or supplying articles for use in fraud (2006 Act, s.7))

Harm	Culpability (A)	Culpability (B)	Culpability (C)
Greater	*Starting points and ranges* 4.5 years 3–7 years	*Starting points and ranges* 2.5 years 1.5–5 years	*Starting points and ranges* 12 months High level community order–3 years
Lesser	2 years 26 weeks–4 years	36 weeks Low level community order–2 years	Medium level community order Band C fine–26 weeks

The table of additional factual elements providing the context of the offence and factors relating to the offender is the same as in Section I (*ante*).
Steps 3–8: see *ante*.

III. Revenue fraud

This section covers the same offences as in Section I, plus cheating the public revenue and of- **K-303**
fences under the Taxes Management Act 1970, s.106A (fraudulent evasion of income tax), the
CEMA 1979, ss.50, 170 and 170B (fraudulent evasion of duty; improper importation of goods (§§
25-430, 25-474, 25-505 in the main work)), and the Value Added Tax Act 1994, s.72 (§ 25-532 in
the main work).

Step 1: determine the level of culpability and the harm category (and see generally, ante).
Culpability

High culpability (A)	Medium culpability (B)	Lesser culpability (C)
HC1–HC5	MC1, MC2	LC1, LC2, LC4–LC6

Harm
Gain or intended gain, or loss or intended loss.

877

Category 1	£50m or more	Starting point based on £80m
Category 2	£10m–£50m	Starting point based on £30m
Category 3	£2m–£10m	Starting point based on £5m
Category 4	£500k–£2m	Starting point based on £1m
Category 5	£100k–£500k	Starting point based on £300k
Category 6	£20k–100k	Starting point based on £50k
Category 7	Less than £20k	Starting point based on £12.5k

Step 2: use the following tables to reach a provisional sentence (and see generally, ante).

Table 1 (2006 Act, s.1, conspiracy to defraud)

Where the value of the fraud is over £2 million, the court should refer to the corresponding category in Table 3, subject to the maximum sentence of 10 years for these offences.

Harm	*Culpability (A)*	*Culpability (B)*	*Culpability (C)*
	Starting points and ranges	*Starting points and ranges*	*Starting points and ranges*
Category 4	7 years 5–8 years	5 years 3–6 years	3 years 1.5–4 years
Category 5	5 years 3–6 years	3 years 1.5–4 years	1.5 years 26 weeks–3 years
Category 6	3 years 1.5–4 years	1.5 years 26 weeks–3 years	26 weeks Medium level community order–12 months
Category 7	1.5 years 36 weeks–3 years	36 weeks Medium level community order–18 months	Medium level community order Low–high level community order

Table 2 (1968 Act, s.17, 1970 Act, s.106(a), 1979 Act, ss.50(1)(a) and (2), 170(1)(a)(i) and (ii), (1)(b), and (2)(a), and 170B, and 1994 Act, s.72(1), (3) and (8))

Harm	*Culpability (A)*	*Culpability (B)*	*Culpability (C)*
	Starting points and ranges	*Starting points and ranges*	*Starting points and ranges*
Category 4	5.5 years 4–6.5 years	4 years 2.5–5 years	2.5 years 15 months–3.5 years
Category 5	4 years 2.5–5 years	2.5 years 15 months–3.5 years	15 months 26 weeks–2.5 years
Category 6	2.5 years 15 months–3.5 years	15 months High level community order–2.5 years	High level community order Low level community order–36 weeks
Category 7	15 months 26 weeks–2.5 years	26 weeks Medium level community order–15 months	Medium level community order Band C fine–high level community order

Table 3 (cheating the revenue)

Where the offending is on the most serious scale, involving sums significantly higher than the starting point in category 1, sentences of 15 years and above may be appropriate. In cases involving sums below £2 million, the court should refer to Table 1.

Harm	Culpability (A)	Culpability (B)	Culpability (C)
	Starting points and ranges	*Starting points and ranges*	*Starting points and ranges*
Category 1	12 years 10–17 years	8 years 7–12 years	6 years 4–8 years
Category 2	10 years 8–13 years	7 years 5–9 years	5 years 3–6 years
Category 3	8 years 6–10 years	6 years 4–7 years	4 years 3–5 years

Adjust the provisional sentence according to the presence of the following factors:

Factors increasing seriousness	*Factors reducing seriousness or reflecting personal mitigation*
A1, A2, A4, A6–A9, A11–A16	M1–M12

Steps 3–8: see *ante*.

IV. Benefit fraud

This section covers the offences in Section I, plus offences under the Social Security Administra- **K-304** tion Act 1992, ss.111A (dishonest representations for obtaining benefit, *etc.*) and 112 (false representations for obtaining benefit, *etc.*), and the Tax Credits Act 2002, s.35 (tax credit fraud).

Step 1: determine the level of culpability and the harm category (and see generally, ante).
Culpability

High culpability (A)	Medium culpability (B)	Lesser culpability (C)
HC1-HC4	MC1-MC3	LC1, LC6

Harm
Amount obtained or intended to be obtained:

Category 1	£500k–£2m [*sic*]	Starting point based on £1m
Category 2	£100k–£500k	Starting point based on £300k
Category 3	£50k–£100k	Starting point based on £75k
Category 4	£10k–£50k	Starting point based on £30k
Category 5	£2.5k–£10k	Starting point based on £5k
Category 6	Less than £2.5k	Starting point based on £1k

Step 2: use the following tables to reach a provisional sentence (and see generally, ante).
Table 1 (1968 Act, s.17, 1992 Act, s.111A, 2002 Act, s.35)

Harm	Culpability (A)	Culpability (B)	Culpability (C)
	Starting points and ranges	*Starting points and ranges*	*Starting points and ranges*
Category 1 £500k or more [*sic*]	5.5 years 4–6.5 years	4 years 2.5–5 years	2.5 years 15 months–3.5 years
Category 2	4 years 2.5–5 years	2.5 years 15 months–3.5 years	12 months 26 weeks–2.5 years
Category 3	2.5 years 2–3.5 years	12 months 26 weeks–2.5 years	26 weeks High level community order–36 weeks

Harm	Culpability (A)	Culpability (B)	Culpability (C)
	Starting points and ranges	*Starting points and ranges*	*Starting points and ranges*
Category 4	1.5 years 36 weeks–2.5 years	36 weeks Medium level community order–21 months	Medium level community order Low level community order–26 weeks
Category 5	36 weeks Medium level community order–1.5 years	Medium level community order Low level community order–26 weeks	Low level community order Band B fine–medium level community order
Category 6	Medium level community order Low level community order–26 weeks	Low level community order Band A fine–medium level community order	Band A fine Discharge–band B fine

Table 2 (1992 Act, s.112)

Harm	Culpability (A)	Culpability (B)	Culpability (C)
	Starting points and ranges	*Starting points and ranges*	*Starting points and ranges*
Category 5 Above £2.5k Starting point based on £5k	High level community order Medium level community order–12 weeks	Medium level community order Band B fine–high level community order	Low level community order Band A fine–medium level community order
Category 6 Less than £2.5k Starting point based on £1k	Medium level community order Low–high level community order	Band B fine Band A–band C fine	Band A fine Discharge–band B fine

Table 3 (2006 Act, s.1, conspiracy to defraud)

Harm	Culpability (A)	Culpability (B)	Culpability (C)
	Starting points and ranges	*Starting points and ranges*	*Starting points and ranges*
Category 1 £500k or more [*sic*] Starting point based on £1m	7 years 5–8 years	5 years 3–6 years	3 years 1.5–4 years
Category 2	5 years 3–6 years	3 years 1.5–4 years	15 months 26 weeks–3 years
Category 3	3 years 2.5–4 years	15 months 36 weeks–3 years	36 weeks 26 weeks–12 months
Category 4	21 months 12 months–3 years	12 months High level community order–2 years	High level community order Low level community order–26 weeks
Category 5	12 months	High level community order	Medium level community order

Harm	Culpability (A)	Culpability (B)	Culpability (C)
	Starting points and ranges	*Starting points and ranges*	*Starting points and ranges*
	High level community order–2 years	Low level community order–26 weeks	Band C fine–high level community order
Category 6	High level community order	Low level community order	Band B fine
	Low level community order–26 weeks	Band B fine–medium level community order	Discharge–band C fine

Adjust the provisional sentence according to the presence of the following factors:

Factors increasing seriousness	Factors reducing seriousness or reflecting personal mitigation
A1, A2, A4, A6–A9, A11, A13, A14, A17–A19	M1–M11, M13, M14

Steps 3–8: see *ante*.

V. Money laundering

This section covers offences contrary to the PCA 2002, ss.327–329 (§§ 26-11 *et seq.* in the main **K-305** work).

Step 1: determine the level of culpability and the harm category (and see generally, ante).
Culpability

High culpability (A)	Medium culpability (B)	Lesser culpability (C)
HC1–HC4, HC9	MC1, MC2	LC1, LC2, LC4–LC6

Harm A
Harm is initially assessed by the value of the money laundered.

Category 1	£10m or more	Starting point based on £30m
Category 2	£2m–£10m	Starting point based on £5m
Category 3	£500k–£2m	Starting point based on £1m
Category 4	£100k–£500k	Starting point based on £300k
Category 5	£10k–£100k	Starting point based on £50k
Category 6	Less than £10k	Starting point based on £5k

Harm B
To complete the assessment of harm, the court should take into account the level of harm associated with the underlying offence to determine whether it warrants upward adjustment of the starting point within the range, or in appropriate cases, outside the range. Where it is possible to identify the underlying offence, the court should have regard to the relevant sentencing levels for that offence.

Step 2: use the following table to reach a provisional sentence (and see generally, ante).

Harm	Culpability (A)	Culpability (B)	Culpability (C)
	Starting points and ranges	*Starting points and ranges*	*Starting points and ranges*
Category 1	10 years	7 years	4 years
	8–13 years	5–10 years	3–6 years
Category 2	8 years	5 years	3.5 years
	6–9 years	3.5–7 years	2–5 years
Category 3	7 years	5 years	3 years
	5–8 years	3–6 years	1.5–4 years

Harm	Culpability (A)	Culpability (B)	Culpability (C)
	Starting points and ranges	*Starting points and ranges*	*Starting points and ranges*
Category 4	5 years 3–6 years	3 years 1.5–4 years	1.5 years 26 weeks–3 years
Category 5	3 years 1.5–4 years	1.5 years 26 weeks–3 years	26 weeks Medium level community order–12 months
Category 6	12 months 26 weeks–2 years	High level community order Low level community order–12 months	Low level community order Band B fine–medium level community order

Adjust the provisional sentence according to the presence of the following factors:

Factors increasing seriousness	Factors reducing seriousness or reflecting personal mitigation
A1, A2, A4–A11, A14.	M1–M12

Steps 3–8: see *ante*.

VI. Bribery

K-306   This section covers offences under sections 1, 2 and 6 of the Bribery Act 2010 (§§ 31-171, 31-172, 31-176 in the main work).

Step 1: determine the level of culpability and the harm category (and see generally, ante).
Culpability

High culpability (A)	Medium culpability (B)	Lesser culpability (C)
HC1–HC4, HC9–HC11	MC1, MC2	LC1–LC5

Harm is to be assessed in relation to any impact caused by the offending (whether to identifiable victims or in a wider context) and the actual or intended gain to the offender, and it is demonstrated by one or more of the following factors:

Category 1	• Serious detrimental effect on individuals (*e.g.* by provision of sub-standard goods or services resulting from the corrupt behaviour). • Serious environmental impact. • Serious undermining of the proper function of local or national government, business or public services. • Substantial actual or intended financial gain to offender or another or loss caused to others.
Category 2	• Significant detrimental effect on individuals. • As 2–4 in Category 1, but with substitution of "Significant" for "Serious" (2 & 3) and "Substantial" (4) • Risk of category 1 harm.
Category 3	• Limited detrimental impact on individuals, the environment, government, business or public services. • Risk of category 2 harm.
Category 4	• Risk of category 3 harm.

Step 2: use the following table to reach a provisional sentence (and see generally, ante).

Harm	Culpability (A)	Culpability (B)	Culpability (C)
	Starting points and ranges	*Starting points and ranges*	*Starting points and ranges*
Category 1	7 years 5–8 years	5 years 3–6 years	3 years 1.5–4 years
Category 2	5 years 3–6 years	3 years 1.5–4 years	1.5 years 26 weeks–3 years
Category 3	3 years 1.5–4 years	1.5 years 26 weeks–3 years	26 weeks Medium level community order–12 months
Category 4	1.5 years 26 weeks–3 years	26 weeks Medium level community order–12 months	Medium level community order Band B fine–high level community order

Adjust the provisional sentence according to the presence of the following factors:

Factors increasing seriousness	Factors reducing seriousness or reflecting personal mitigation
A1, A2, A3–A11, A20, A21	M1–M10

Steps 3–8: see *ante*.

VII. Corporate offenders

This section applies to corporate offenders and covers the offences in Sections I, II, V and VI **K-307** plus cheating the public revenue, fraudulent evasion of value added tax (Value Added Tax Act 1994, s.72 (§ 25-532 in the main work)), fraudulent evasion of duty (CEMA 1979, s.170 (§ 25-474 in the main work)), and failure of commercial organisations to prevent bribery (Bribery Act 2010, s.7 (§ 31-177 in the main work)).

The guideline sets out 10 steps to be followed when sentencing for these offences. Step one **K-308** requires the court to consider making a compensation order. Step two requires the court to consider confiscation. Step three requires the court to determine the level of culpability and the harm caused or intended. Where there are characteristics present that fall under different categories, the court should balance them to reach a fair assessment of the offender's culpability. The culpability attaching to the offender's role and motivation may be demonstrated by one or more of the following non-exhaustive characteristics:

High culpability (A)	Medium culpability (B)	Lesser culpability (C)
Plays a leading role in organised, planned activity (whether acting alone or with others). Wilful obstruction of detection (*e.g.* destruction of evidence, misleading investigators, suborning employees).	Plays a significant role in activity organised by others. Activity not unlawful from the outset. Recklessness in making false statement (1994 Act, s.72).	Plays a minor, peripheral role in activity organised by others. Some effort made to put bribery prevention measures in place but insufficient to amount to a defence (2010 Act, s.7).
Involving others through pressure or coercion (*e.g.* employees or suppliers). Targeting of vulnerable victims or large number of victims.	All other cases where characteristics for categories A or C are not present.	Involvement through coercion, intimidation or exploitation.

High culpability (A)	Medium culpability (B)	Lesser culpability (C)
Corruption of local or national government officials or ministers, or of law enforcement officials. Abuse of dominant market position or position of trust or responsibility. Offending committed over a sustained period of time. Culture of wilful disregard of offences by employees or agents with no effort to put effective systems in place (2010 Act, s.7, only).		

K-309 Harm is represented by a financial sum calculated by reference to the table below:

Fraud	For fraud, conspiracy to defraud, cheating the Revenue and fraudulent evasion of duty or value added tax, harm will normally be the actual or intended gross gain to the offender.
Bribery	The appropriate figure will normally be the gross profit from the contract obtained, retained or sought as a result of the offending. An alternative measure for offences under s.7 may be the likely cost avoided by failing to put in place appropriate measures to prevent bribery.
Money laundering	The appropriate figure will normally be the amount laundered or, alternatively, the likely cost avoided by failing to put in place an effective anti-money laundering programme if this is higher.
General	Where the actual or intended gain cannot be established, the appropriate measure will be the amount that the court considers was likely to be achieved in all the circumstances. In the absence of sufficient evidence of the amount that was likely to be obtained, 10–20 per cent of the relevant revenue (*e.g.* 10–20 per cent of the worldwide revenue derived from the product or business area to which the offence relates for the period of the offending) may be an appropriate measure. There may be large cases in which the true harm is to commerce or markets generally. That may justify adopting a harm figure beyond the normal measures here set out.

K-310 Having determined the culpability level, step four requires the court to determine the starting point within the category range using the table below. The harm figure from step three is multiplied by the relevant percentage figure representing culpability.

	A (high)	B (medium)	C (low)
Harm figure multiplier	Starting point 300% Category range 250% to 400%	Starting point 200% Category range 100% to 300%	Starting point 100% Category range 20% to 150%

K-311 After determining the appropriate starting point, the court should then consider adjustment within the category range for aggravating or mitigating features. In some cases it may be appropriate to move outside the identified category range. The following is a non-exhaustive list of aggravating and mitigating factors:

Increasing seriousness	*Reducing seriousness or reflecting mitigation*
Previous relevant convictions or subject to previous relevant civil or regulatory enforcement action.	No previous relevant convictions or previous relevant civil or regulatory enforcement action.
Corporation or subsidiary set up to commit fraudulent activity.	Victims voluntarily reimbursed/compensated. No actual loss to victims.
Fraudulent activity endemic within corporation.	Corporation co-operated with investigation, made early admissions and/or voluntarily reported offending.
Attempts made to conceal misconduct.	Offending committed under previous director(s)/manager(s).
Substantial harm (whether financial or otherwise) suffered by victims of offending or by third parties affected by offending.	Little or no actual gain to corporation from offending.
Risk of harm greater than actual or intended harm (*e.g.* in banking/credit fraud).	
Substantial harm to integrity or confidence of markets.	
Substantial harm to integrity of local or national governments.	
Serious nature of underlying criminal activity (money laundering offences).	
Offence committed across borders or jurisdictions.	

K-312   The court should determine the appropriate level of fine in accordance with the CJA 2003, s.164 (§ 5-674 in the main work). Where the offender fails to provide comprehensive accounts for the last three years, or where the court is not satisfied that it has been given sufficiently reliable information, the court will be entitled to draw reasonable inferences as to the offender's means from evidence it has heard and from all the circumstances of the case. The information that should be examined in relation to different companies and bodies is then set out (this coincides with the guidance in the Sentencing Guidelines Council's guideline on corporate manslaughter and health and safety offences causing death (*ante*, K-258)).

K-313   Under step five, the court should consider the overall effect of its orders and whether there are any further factors that require an adjustment in the level of the fine. The combination of orders ought to achieve the removal of all gain, appropriate additional punishment and deterrence. The court may adjust the fine to ensure that these objectives are met in a fair way, and should consider any further factors relevant to the setting of the fine to ensure that it is proportionate, with regard to the seriousness of the offence and the size and financial position of the organisation. The fine must be substantial enough to have a real economic impact. Whether the fine will put the offender out of business will be relevant, and in some bad cases this may be an acceptable consequence. The court should consider whether the level of fine would cause unacceptable harm to third parties (bearing in mind that the payment of any compensation should take priority over any fine). Below is a non-exhaustive list of additional factual elements to consider in adjusting the level of fine:

- whether it fulfils the objectives of punishment, deterrence and removal of gain;
- the offender's value, worth or available means;
- whether the fine impairs the offender's ability to make restitution to the victims;
- the fine's impact on the offender's ability to implement effective compliance programmes;
- the fine's impact on the employment of staff, service users, customers and the local economy (but not shareholders);
- the fine's impact on the performance of public or charitable functions.

K-314   At step six, the court should take into account the SOCPA 2005, ss.73 (assistance by defendant: reduction of sentence (§ 5-132 in the main work)) and 74 (assistance by defendant: review of sentence (*ibid.*, § 5-133)), and any other rule of law by virtue of which an offender may receive a discounted sentence in consequence of assistance given (or offered) to the prosecutor or investigator. At step seven, the court should take into account any potential reduction for a guilty plea. At step eight, the court must consider whether to make any ancillary orders, and at step nine, if sentencing the offender for more than one offence, it must consider the totality principle. At step 10, the court must give reasons for and explain the effect of the sentence.

[The next paragraph is K-350.]

II. AUTHORITIES ON OFFICIAL GUIDELINES

A. REDUCTION IN SENTENCE FOR GUILTY PLEA

Introduction

K-350   The purpose of this section of this appendix is to give details of authorities considering particular aspects of final guidelines issued by the Sentencing Guidelines Council and which are set out in full or summarised in the previous section of this appendix. There is, however, a fine line that divides cases specifically on some aspect of a guideline from those considering a statutory provision or some more general aspect of sentencing. Accordingly, practitioners looking for authorities on sentencing in relation to one of the guideline subjects should also make reference to the relevant paragraphs of the main work.

Relevant main work references

K-351   For sentencing guidelines generally, see section 125 of the Coroners and Justice Act 2009 (§ 5-149 in the main work); and for the reduction in sentence for a guilty plea, see section 144 of that Act (*ibid.*, § 5-107), and the authorities set out at §§ 5-109 *et seq.*, and, in particular, §§ 5-115, 5-118.

First reasonable opportunity

K-351a   See *R. v. Caley*, § 5-114 in the main work.

Credit in overwhelming cases

K-352   Even in overwhelming cases, a plea of guilty was a distinct public benefit and the earlier it was put forward the better it was for everyone; where, therefore, the judge had given no credit for a plea of guilty on the basis that the evidence was such that the offender had had no option but to plead guilty, and where no specific feature of the case required the Sentencing Guidelines Council's guidance on credit for pleas of guilty (*ante*, K-7) to be disapplied, it was appropriate to vary the sentence to allow limited credit; it would be productive ultimately of chaos, and would undermine consistency in sentencing and the value of a guilty plea to the criminal justice system, if an existing guideline could be disregarded, unless it was possible to find that the interests of justice required its disapplication; it was important to underline that part of the advice that would be given to a defendant was that a guilty plea, even in an extreme case, would attract some discount: *R. v. Wilson* [2012] 2 Cr.App.R.(S.) 77, CA.

Wilson, ante, was considered in *R. v. Caley*, § 5-115 in the main work.

★   In *R. v. Walter* [2015] 1 Cr.App.R.(S.) 22, CA, it was held that a judge had been entitled to take the view that the evidence was overwhelming and, in consequence, to reduce the standard discount for a plea of guilty to one of 20 per cent in accordance with the Sentencing Guidelines Council's guideline, notwithstanding that, at the preliminary hearing at which the defendant had indicated a wish to plead guilty, there had been no indictment, the prosecution indicating that they were awaiting an expert report before finalising the indictment (which was not the principal evidence).

★   *Walter, ante,* was a case of causing death by dangerous driving (RTA 1988, s.1 (§ 32-2 in the main work)). For two cases of causing serious injury by dangerous driving (RTA 1988, s.1A (§ 32-25 in the main work)), where the evidence was said to have been overwhelming, see *R. v.*

enkins [2015] 1 Cr.App.R.(S.) 70, CA (discount should have been limited to 20 per cent), and *R.
. Buckle* [2015] 1 Cr.App.R.(S.) 68, CA (discount of 30 per cent was "generous").

[The next paragraph is K-360.]

B. Overarching Principles: Seriousness

ntroduction

As to the purpose of this section of this appendix, see *ante*, K-350. **K-360**

Relevant main work references

For sentencing guidelines generally, see section 125 of the Coroners and Justice Act 2009 (§ **K-361**
-149 in the main work); and for the determination of the seriousness of an offence, see section
43 of that Act (*ibid.*, § 5-67).

Vulnerability of victim

It had not been open to the Crown Court to sentence on the basis that the victim of a domestic **K-362**
ssault was particularly vulnerable where none of the features of vulnerability mentioned in
paragraph 1.17 of the guideline on overarching principles (*ante*, K-18) or in paragraph 3 of the
domestic violence guideline (*ante*, K-82 *et seq.*) were present, with the finding instead being based
n the complainant's timid demeanour when giving evidence: *Barnard v. DPP* [2011] A.C.D. 108,
C.

C. New Sentences: Criminal Justice Act 2003

ntroduction

As to the purpose of this section of this appendix, see *ante*, K-350. **K-370**

Relevant main work references

For sentencing guidelines generally, see section 125 of the Coroners and Justice Act 2009 (§ **K-371**
-149 in the main work). As to community sentences generally, see § 5-185 *et seq.* in the main
vork; as to the restrictions on the imposition of such sentences, see *ibid.*, § 5-248; as to community
rders generally, see *ibid.*, §§ 5-253 *et seq.*; as to the requirements that may be included in a com-
nunity order, see *ibid.*, §§ 5-265 *et seq.*; as to the misleading terminology adopted in this guideline,
ee *ibid.*, § 5-288.

Transitional arrangements

In *R. v. Whittle* (2007) 151 S.J. 398, CA, it was said that whereas paragraph 2.1.9 suggests that **K-372**
ny sentence of 12 months or more should be reduced by in the region of 15 per cent to reflect
he more onerous nature of the release on licence regime under the CJA 2003, where an offender
s sentenced to a term of four years or more, the sentencer may be entitled not to reduce the
entence to the full extent or at all; in relation to such sentences, the increased onerousness of the
icence conditions would be more or less in balance with the fact that the offender would be
entitled to release at the half way point under the new regime instead of at the two-thirds point
under the pre-existing regime.

D. Manslaughter by Reason of Provocation

Introduction

As to the purpose of this section of this appendix, see *ante*, K-350. **K-380**

Relevant main work references

For sentencing guidelines generally, see section 125 of the Coroners and Justice Act 2009 (§ **K-381**
-149 in the main work); and for provocation as a defence to a charge of murder generally, see

ante, §§ 19-65 *et seq.* For "loss of control" as a defence to murder, see §§ 19-54 *et seq.* in the main work. It is submitted that pending the issuing of any new guideline, the existing guideline may be applied to the new defence, with appropriate caution to take account of the differing ingredients of the two defences.

Approach to guideline

K-382   Referring to heightened and justifiable public concern about cases involving the stabbing of one teenager by another, the court in *R. v. Daley* [2008] 2 Cr.App.R.(S.) 95, CA, said that the guideline had not been intended to lay down fixed or rigid boundaries.

In *Att.-Gen.'s Reference (No. 8 of 2011) (R. v. Edwards)* [2012] 1 Cr.App.R.(S.) 53, CA, the court emphasised that the guideline on manslaughter by reason of provocation should be approached with caution. It did not reflect the impact on sentencing for murder of Schedule 21 to the CJA 2003 (§§ 5-425 *et seq.* in the main work); and, in a series of cases, it had now been recognised that the upward shift in sentencing for murder required a corresponding upward shift in sentencing for manslaughter (see, in particular, *R. v. Thornley*, *post*, K-383). The court commented that the apparently higher threshold for the loss of control defence under the Coroners and Justice Act 2009 (§§ 19-55, 19-56 in the main work), as compared with the common law defence of provocation, may impact on sentencing both for murder and for manslaughter.

For a case considering *Att.-Gen.'s Reference (No. 8 of 2011) (R. v. Edwards)*, and its significance for manslaughter by reason of loss of control, see *R. v. Ward* (§ 19-64 in the main work).

Use of a knife

K-383   Just as sentencing guidelines are not tramlines, nor are they ring-fenced; the interests of justice require that consideration be given to any subsequent thinking of the Court of Appeal and the legislature on sentencing issues which may impact on any definitive guideline; since the guideline on manslaughter by reason of provocation was issued, there had been at least four developments relevant to the sentencing of manslaughter by provocation using a knife (*viz.* (a) the Court of Appeal had, in *R. v. Povey* (§ 24-168 in the main work), addressed the issue of knife crime generally, and the need for the courts to be alert on appropriate occasions to impose deterrent sentences on those who carry knives, (b) the court had come to appreciate the impact of Schedule 21 to the CJA 2003 (*ibid.*, §§ 5-425 *et seq.*) on cases of manslaughter because of the need for there to be a proportionate relationship with sentences for murder, (c) a specific provision relating to the use of a knife as a murder weapon had been introduced into Schedule 21, and (d) the entire law on provocation had been changed by legislation); as to (a) and (b), the weight to be attached to decisions of the Court of Appeal on sentencing issues or policy was undiminished by the issue of guidelines; as to (c) and (d), these changes could not be ignored on the basis of a guideline issued in 2005; accordingly, the use of a knife should now be regarded as a more significant feature of aggravation than it was when the guideline was published: *R. v. Thornley* [2011] 2 Cr.App.R.(S.) 62, CA.

E. ROBBERY

Introduction

K-390   As to the purpose of this section of this appendix, see *ante*, K-350.

Relevant main work references

K-391   For sentencing guidelines generally, see section 125 of the Coroners and Justice Act 2009 (§ 5-149 in the main work)). As to this guideline, see, in particular, § 21-93 in the main work; as to sentencing for armed robbery, for robbery in the course of burglary and for the hijacking of cars, see *ibid.*, §§ 21-91, 21-92 and 21-94a respectively. For examples of the application of the dangerous offender provisions of the 2003 Act to cases of robbery, see *ibid.*, § 5-520.

Dangerous offenders

K-391a   The guideline is unequivocal (see para. G.1) about its non-applicability to offenders who have been assessed as dangerous. However, since section 226A(5) and (6) of the CJA 2003 (§ 5-498 in

he main work) require the custodial element of an extended sentence to be fixed by reference to
he term that would have been passed had the offender not been found to be dangerous, it would
seem that the sentencer is bound to have regard to the guideline where an extended sentence is
to be imposed: see, for example, *R. v. Greaves* [2009] 2 Cr.App.R.(S.) 88, CA.

"less sophisticated commercial robbery"

In *Att.-Gen.'s References (Nos 32, 33 and 34 of 2007) (R. v. Bate)* [2008] 1 Cr.App.R.(S.) 35, CA, it   **K-392**
was held that for the purposes of the guideline on robbery, (i) the boundary between a "less
sophisticated commercial robbery" falling within the guideline and a "professionally planned
commercial robbery" falling without the guideline is not a hard and fast one (to like effect, see *R.
v. Lafferty* [2012] 2 Cr.App.R.(S.) 93, CA, and *R. v. O'Bryan* [2013] 2 Cr.App.R.(S.) 16, CA (a case
which fell on or just over the borderline)) and many cases would properly be regarded as falling
on either side of the line; and a judge had been entitled to regard as falling within the guideline
(and to regard the case as a level 1 case) two robberies during normal working hours (involving
prior reconnaissance or information and the use of a stolen car) in which the three unarmed
defendants, wearing masks and using a stolen car, had intercepted unaccompanied lorry drivers
making deliveries of cigarettes to shops; and (ii) whereas "vulnerability of the victim" as an aggravating factor is expressly stated to be "targeting the elderly, the young, those with disabilities
and persons performing a service to the public, especially outside normal working hours", there
was nonetheless a low level of vulnerability (and hence aggravation) where the targets of the robberies were delivery drivers working alone, albeit delivering to shops where there were people to
receive them.

Whilst the CJA 2003, s.172, required a court to have regard to a relevant sentencing guideline
(see now the Coroners and Justice Act 2009, s.125 (§ 5-149 in the main work)), a guideline is only
a guideline and the guideline on robbery cannot cover each and every category because of the
immense variety of circumstances in which offences of robbery are committed, and as such there
is a wide spectrum of offences that fall between "less sophisticated commercial robberies" and
"professionally-planned commercial robberies", as described in the guideline; where, therefore,
four men had "swiftly" robbed the driver of a delivery van in a robbery that was "cynically and
callously planned" with one of the men persuading him to drive with them to a secluded place
whilst wearing a mask and rubber gloves and being armed with a knife, the case did not fall
neatly and cleanly within the category of the "less sophisticated commercial robbery" (which has
an indicated starting point of four years' custody) and instead fell within a range of six to 10 years
(possibly more for a ring leader); and, in the case of the respondent (40), who acted as the driver
of the robbers' vehicle, three years' imprisonment on conviction was unduly lenient given that,
although he was not a prime mover and did not wield the knife, it must have been within his
contemplation that some degree of threat or force would be used on the victim; taking account,
however, of the fact that he suffered from Asperger's syndrome, which made him vulnerable to
being manipulated by more sophisticated offenders, the appropriate bracket was six to eight
years' imprisonment: *Att.-Gen.'s Reference (No. 147 of 2006) (R. v. Gunner)* [2008] 1 Cr.App.R.(S.)
9(2), CA (substituting six years).

As to there being a category of case that falls between the "less sophisticated commercial robbery" and the "professionally planned commercial robbery", see also *R. v. Eccleston* [2008] 2
Cr.App.R.(S.) 56, CA.

In *R. v. Yarboi* [2010] 2 Cr.App.R.(S.) 40, CA, one of the defendants snatched a cash box
containing £11,530 from a security guard who was attempting to deliver it to a cash machine. He
ran to a car (the number plates of which had been removed) being driven by another of the
defendants and, after half a mile, they abandoned the car and got into a third vehicle driven by a
further defendant. The Court of Appeal found that the case did not fit easily within any of the
categories within the Sentencing Guidelines Council's guideline (see *ante*, K-80), being close to the
border between "less sophisticated commercial robberies" and "professionally planned robberies".
The most aggravating feature was that the robbery had been pre-planned, although cases could
come within the least serious category even where there had been some pre-planning. The
removal of the first car's number plates, and the use of a second "clean" getaway car, however,
made the case rather more unusual, and showed a significant degree of planning. On the other
hand, the force used was minimal, being only that which was necessary in order to snatch the

container from the security guard, there was only a single robber involved at that stage, and there was no intimidation from a group, no weapon, no threat of force, and no disguises were used. The court said that whilst the planning, therefore, might have taken the case out of the least serious category, it was difficult to conclude that it was of such sophistication as to justify a starting point of double the maximum for that category. In all the circumstances, it was decided that the proper starting point was four-and-a-half years.

"vulnerability of the victim"

K-393   See *Att.-Gen.'s References (Nos 32, 33 and 34 of 2007) (R. v. Bate)*, ante, § K-392.

Ranges

K-394   For an example of a sentence that was significantly above the recommended range being upheld on account of "additional aggravating features", albeit that most of them are foreshadowed in the guideline, see *R. v. Sheller* [2010] 1 Cr.App.R.(S.) 107, CA.

In *R. v. Taylor (Shaun)* [2012] 2 Cr.App.R.(S.) 98, CA, it was held that the judge had been wrong to sentence on the basis that the guideline sentences were out of date and that it had been "almost a different world when they came into force"; when appropriate, the court added, it is of course open to a judge to sentence outside guidelines and to support such a course by giving reasons for doing so; but personal disagreement with a guideline will not furnish a good reason for departing from them; and the guideline was not out of date.

F. BREACH OF A PROTECTIVE ORDER

Introduction

K-400   As to the purpose of this section of this appendix, see *ante*, K-350.

Relevant main work references

K-401   For sentencing guidelines generally, see section 125 of the Coroners and Justice Act 2009 (§ 5-149 in the main work); for breach of a restraining order under the Protection from Harassment Act 1997, see *ibid.*, § 19-357; and for breach of a sexual offences prevention order, see *ibid.*, § 20-334. As to breach of an anti-social behaviour order, see *ante*, K-196 *et seq.*

Taking the original offence into account

K-401a   As to the importance of avoiding sentencing again for the original offence when sentencing for a breach, and as to the need to reserve the maximum sentence for the most serious of breaches, see *R. v. McDonald* [2013] 1 Cr.App.R.(S.) 3, CA.

Repeated breaches

K-402   For a case in which a sentence substantially outside the guidelines was upheld where there had been repeated (low-level) breaches of a restraining order over a long period, see *R. v. Todd* [2013] 1 Cr.App.R.(S.) 89, CA.

G. DOMESTIC VIOLENCE

Introduction

K-410   As to the purpose of this section of this appendix, see *ante*, K-350.

Relevant main work references

K-411   For sentencing guidelines generally, see section 125 of the Coroners and Justice Act 2009 (§ 5-149 in the main work); and for breach of a restraining order under the Protection from Harassment Act 1997, see § 19-357 in the main work.

Attitude of victim

K-412   In *R. v. Fazli*, unreported, April 24, 2009, CA ([2009] EWCA Crim. 939), the court emphasised that the principle (see para. 4 of the guideline) that a sentence should not be determined by the expressed wishes of the victim, was of particular importance in cases of domestic violence. The court said that, in the case with which it was concerned, the victim (the defendant's wife) had been made to feel responsible for his incarceration, and that such feelings on the part of the victim were a familiar consequence of controlling and intimidating behaviour such as that of the offender. The responsibility for what had happened to him lay entirely with him.

Vulnerability of victim

See *Barnard v. DPP, ante*, K-362. **K-413**

Aggravating factors

In *R. v. Caceres* [2014] 1 Cr.App.R.(S.) 23, CA, it was said that whilst the guideline stressed that **K-414** violence in the home was no less serious than violence elsewhere simply because it was committed in the home, and whilst this was correct in so far as it went, where someone is put in constant peril and fear in their own home as a result of repetitive domestic abuse, that was potentially a substantial aggravating factor. The court said that the aggravation is compounded where the perpetrator is in reality controlling the victim and abusing his position in the home, and the victim is, in the domestic context, vulnerable; and a further aggravating feature is where the victim is effectively forced to leave home as a consequence of the abuse.

H. Sexual Offences

Introduction

As to the purpose of this section of this appendix, see *ante*, K-350. **K-420**

Relevant main work references

For sentencing guidelines generally, see section 125 of the Coroners and Justice Act 2009 (§ **K-421** 5-149 in the main work).

Gender

Sentencing guidelines for sexual offences are gender-neutral: *Att.-Gen.'s Reference (No. 85 of* **★K-421a** *2014) (R. v. A.)* [2015] 1 Cr.App.R.(S.) 14, CA. As to this case, see also *ante*, § 5-110.

Historic offences

See *R. v. H., ante*, H-12 *et seq.* **K-422**
For a case considering the application of the Sentencing Council's guideline on sexual offences to historic offences, see *R. v. Clifford, ante*, Appendix H-120.

Rehabilitation

In *R. v. Jones (David William)* [2015] 1 Cr.App.R.(S.) 9, CA, a community order with a sex of- **K-423** fender treatment programme requirement was considered a proper alternative to a moderate custodial sentence in accordance with the guideline of the Sentencing Council (see Appendix K-84f). The 64-year-old offender (who had previously served a short prison sentence for similar offences but had received no treatment) had pleaded guilty to making (Protection of Children Act 1978, s.1(1)(a) (§ 31-107 in the main work)) and possessing (CJA 1988, s.160(1) (*ibid.*, § 31-115)) indecent photographs of a child. Reports before the judge suggested that there was little likelihood of the offender moving on to contact offences, and that he would be likely to benefit from a sex offender treatment programme. It was held that the public would be better protected by a disposal that might prevent further offending than by a short sentence that was unlikely to have that result.

Rape

It was held in *R. v. O. (D.)* [2015] 1 Cr.App.R.(S.) 41, CA, that not every case of rape within an **★K-423a** established relationship should be treated as an "abuse of trust" for the purposes of the guideline (*ante*, K-84).

★   For an example of a case falling within the rubric in the guideline (*ante*, K-85), *viz.* that "Offences may be of such severity, for example involving a campaign of rape, that sentences of 20 years and above may be appropriate.", see *R. v. J.H.* [2015] 1 Cr.App.R.(S.) 59, CA (appellant convicted of a number of sexual offences, including rape, against his daughter, aged 11 to 15 at the time, committed over a prolonged period, "in gross breach of trust", involving planning emotional and sometimes physical pressure, plus an element of degradation and humiliation).

Rape of a child under 13

K-424   In *R. v. Watkins* [2015] 1 Cr.App.R.(S.) 6, CA, total sentences of 29 years' imprisonment (15 years for two attempted rapes, plus an extended sentence of 20 years (14 + 6) for sexual assault and conspiracy to rape a child under 13 (including concurrent lesser sentences on other related counts)) for the first defendant (lead singer of a rock band), and 17 years' imprisonment (14 years and four months for assault by penetration and conspiracy to rape, plus two years and eight months for sexual assault) for the second defendant, were upheld where the second defendant and another woman (who did not appeal her sentence), acting independently of one another, allowed the first defendant to abuse their own infant children (including the almost completed oral and anal rape of one child) and to abuse them themselves with his encouragement and also to participate in his filming of these activities and the planning of further such activities.

Sexual activity with a child

K-425   In *Att.-Gen.'s Reference (No. 53 of 2013) (R. v. Wilson)* [2014] 2 Cr.App.R.(S.) 1, CA, it was said that the fact that the complainant had initiated the activity was an aggravating rather than mitigating factor; it has long been clear that Parliament's purpose in passing legislation making it a crime to have sexual relations with those under 16 was to protect those under 16; to reduce the punishment on the basis that the person needing protection encouraged the offence is simply wrong; an under-age person who encourages sexual relations with herself needs more not less protection.

I. Failing to Surrender to Bail

Introduction

K-430   As to the purpose of this section of this appendix, see *ante*, K-350.

Relevant main work references

K-431   For sentencing guidelines generally, see section 125 of the Coroners and Justice Act 2009 (§ 5-149 in the main work); for *Criminal Practice Direction (Custody and bail) 19C* [2013] 1 W.L.R. 3164 (which covers the same ground), see §§ 3-37 *et seq.* in the main work.

Sentencing outside recommended range

K-432   For a case where the imposition of the maximum sentence, outside the recommended range in the guideline, was upheld on appeal, see *R. v. Chowdhury* [2014] 1 Cr.App.R.(S.) 27, CA (defendant had been at large for 13 years; trial of the substantive offence had become impossible as a result of the delay).

   In *R. v. Armaselu* [2014] 2 Cr.App.R.(S.) 65, CA, six months' imprisonment for failing to surrender after the offender had been at large for 15 months was upheld. The court said that whilst it was aware of the Sentencing Guidelines Council's guideline (*ante*, K-107 *et seq.*), the Court of Appeal had on a number of occasions since then upheld sentences in the range of six months' custody for absences of 18 months to two years.

J. Assault and Other Offences Against the Person

Introduction

K-433   As to the purpose of this section of this appendix, see *ante*, K-350.

Relevant main work references

K-434   For sentencing guidelines generally, see section 125 of the Coroners and Justice Act 2009 (§ 5-149 in the main work).

Use in case of young offenders

In *R. v. Bowley* [2009] 1 Cr.App.R.(S.) 79, CA, where a 17-year-old pleaded guilty to causing **K-434a** grievous bodily harm with intent after stabbing a rival gang member, the court said (i) that the judge had been entitled to look to the guideline of the Sentencing Guidelines Council for assistance, even though it did not apply to offenders under 18 and (ii) in making use of it, the judge need not have been unduly constrained by the particular sentencing brackets set out therein, because the case was one where an element of deterrence was an essential ingredient of the sentencing decision.

Ranges

Where an offence of assault occasioning actual bodily harm fell within category 2 as being one **K-434b** of lesser harm and greater culpability, the judge had been entitled to go outside the category range where there were present six factors from the non-exhaustive list of 18 factors that are capable of increasing the seriousness of the offence and there was just one factor reducing its seriousness: *R. v. Nelson, The Times,* October 27, 2011, CA.

As to departure from the guidelines when sentencing those convicted of an offence committed during the widespread public disorder of the kind seen in the riots that occurred around the country in August, 2011, and as to the appropriateness of sentences beyond the range set out in those guidelines, see *R. v. Blackshaw,* § 29-8 in the main work.

"particularly vulnerable"

It was held in *R. v. Halane* [2014] 2 Cr.App.R.(S.) 46, CA that, in a case of assault, a victim's **K-434c** state of intoxication may be such that he may properly be regarded as being "particularly vulnerable" for the purposes of the Sentencing Council's guideline (Appendix K-113 *et seq.*), and where such a person struck the first blow, that did not necessarily mean that he could no longer be treated as having been particularly vulnerable.

Section 18

Use of a knife

In *R. v. Fadairo* [2013] 1 Cr.App.R.(S.) 66, CA, a case of "wounding" (not "causing grievous **K-434d** bodily harm") in which "lesser harm" was caused but with higher culpability, the court said that a starting point above the category two range was justified because of the use of a knife. Parliament had dictated, the court said, in enacting section 18 of the 1861 Act, that assaults with a knife or other bladed weapon should be regarded and punished more seriously than assaults without a weapon or with another kind of weapon; and there was a need for deterrence. For critical consideration of this approach to the guideline, see CLW/12/27/3.

Sections 18 and 20 ("particularly grave injury")

A fractured ankle and torn knee ligaments were not injuries constituting "greater harm" within **K-434e** the Sentencing Council's guideline (*ante*, K-113 *et seq.*), but were to be classified as being injuries of the normal level that constituted grievous bodily harm: *R. v. McIntosh* [2014] 2 Cr.App.R.(S.) 64, CA.

K. Assaults on Children and Cruelty to a Child

Introduction

As to the purpose of this section of this appendix, see *ante*, K-350. **K-436**

Relevant main work references

For sentencing guidelines generally, see section 125 of the Coroners and Justice Act 2009 (§ **K-437** 5-149 in the main work).

The four categories of seriousness

In *R. v. S. (Will)* [2009] 1 Cr.App.R.(S.) 40, CA, the offender (30/good character/no previous **K-438** parenting experience) subjected a "challenging" five-year-old, one of the four children of his (now ex-)partner, to a particularly harsh regime of discipline. She was shouted at, made to feel unwanted, and sent to her room for long periods (sometimes day after day). No violence was used except on one occasion, when the offender put masking tape over her mouth (for which he later expressed regret). At school, it was noticed that the child, from being a relatively happy child, became tearful and unsettled. On pleas of guilty to two counts of "causing cruelty to a child", 30 months' imprisonment was held to be manifestly and grossly excessive. The court found that it was clear that the offender's actions were not those of a gratuitous bully, but of an inexperienced parent, at the end of his tether, who, together with the mother, was doing what he mistakenly believed to be the right thing in respect of what he saw as an ill-behaved child. In particular, it was said that the judge had wrongly identified the case as falling within the second of the four categories of seriousness in the guideline, which, the court noted, should more properly be reserved for cases of actual abuse, either through physical violence or deprivation of food, clothing, shelter or attendance. A community order with a supervision requirement (to include a parenting course) was substituted.

It had been open to a judge to place the offender's intense neglect of her child into the category of "protracted" neglect (*ante*, Appendix K-146), where it took place over a period that adults might regard as a relatively short period (a few days): *R. v. Sutherland* [2011] 1 Cr.App.R.(S.) 90, CA.

L. SENTENCING IN MAGISTRATES' COURTS

Introduction

K-439   As to the purpose of this section of this appendix, see *ante*, K-350.

Relevant main work references

K-440   For sentencing guidelines generally, see section 125 of the Coroners and Justice Act 2009 (§ 5-149 in the main work); for general mode of trial considerations, see *Criminal Practice Direction (Preliminary proceedings) 9A* [2013] 1 W.L.R. 3164 (§ 1-119 in the main work).

M. CAUSING DEATH BY DRIVING

Introduction

K-442   As to the purpose of this section of this appendix, see *ante*, K-350.

Relevant main work references

K-443   For sentencing guidelines generally, see section 125 of the Coroners and Justice Act 2009 (§ 5-149 in the main work). For the penalty provisions relating to the offences covered by this guideline, see § 32-6 (causing death by dangerous driving); § 32-50 (causing death by careless or inconsiderate driving); § 32-66 (causing death by careless driving when under the influence of drink or drugs or having failed without reasonable excuse either to provide a specimen for analysis or to permit the analysis of a blood sample) and § 32-75 (causing death by driving while unlicensed, disqualified or uninsured). As to disqualification and endorsement, see §§ 32-227 *et seq.*

Aggravating and mitigating factors

K-444   As to the importance of taking care to ensure that factors which put an offence into a particular category are not then double-counted as matters of aggravation, see *R. v. Watson* [2010] 1 Cr.App.R.(S.) 29, CA.

In *R. v. Lawes* [2010] 2 Cr.App.R.(S.) 43, CA, it was held that the potentially aggravating feature, identified in the guideline, of more than one death was not intended to apply to the case of a pregnant mother and her unborn child.

Borderline between careless and dangerous driving

K-445   For a case of dangerous driving that was close to the borderline with careless driving, see *R. v.*

Foster [2010] 1 Cr.App.R.(S.) 36, CA. A 64-year-old man had been driving his wife, who suffered from motor neurone disease, home from the hospital, where she had been told that her condition had deteriorated to the point that her treatment should no longer be continued, when he crossed onto the wrong side of the road and collided with a motorcyclist. The central issue at trial had been whether the defendant had crossed onto the wrong side of the road because he had "blacked out"; in passing sentence, the judge proceeded on the basis that the defendant had convinced himself that that was what had happened. On appeal, the court reduced a sentence of 18 months' imprisonment to 12 months' imprisonment suspended for two years, on the basis that the appellant was distracted for a "matter of seconds at most" and, importantly, when his emotions as a result of the hospital visit must have made him susceptible to distraction. The court pointed out that the guideline on causing death by driving states (see *ante*, K-192) that where the driving is markedly less culpable than for the lowest of the three categories for the offence of causing death by dangerous driving, reference should be made to the starting point for the most serious level of causing death by careless driving (starting point 15 months' imprisonment, range of 36 weeks to three years) and that, having regard to this, and to the other mitigation, in particular the appellant's character and his deep and genuine remorse, that starting point could be reduced. The court concluded that if it be a merciful sentence to suspend the term of imprisonment, this was a proper case for mercy.

In *R. v. Crew* [2010] 2 Cr.App.R.(S.) 23, CA, a 52-year-old, the day after an overnight flight from the United States (where he lived), fell asleep momentarily at the wheel of his car while travelling along a long straight road in daylight hours. It was likely that, on waking, he instinctively over-corrected the car's direction of travel as he was used to driving on the opposite side of the road, and in so doing he collided with an oncoming car. A sentence of 14 months' imprisonment on a plea of guilty, entered at the earliest opportunity, was upheld by the Court of Appeal. It was said that the case fell into the most serious category identified in the Sentencing Guidelines Council's guideline (*ante*, Appendix K-194), and that the carelessness had bordered on dangerous driving. The offender had had no more than five hours' sleep in the previous 24 hours, during which he had twice been disturbed to take his young son to the lavatory, and, as an experienced traveller, he must have known the risk he was taking, so his culpability was accordingly high.

Causing death by careless or inconsiderate driving

In *R. v. Campbell (Karl)* [2010] 2 Cr.App.R.(S.) 28, CA, the court said that whereas the guideline (*ante*, K-194) identified three categories of case, the most serious being cases where the driving was not far short of dangerous driving and the least serious comprising cases of momentary inattention with no aggravating features, the guideline provided no assistance as to the intermediate category of "other cases", but this could include cases of single misjudgments, such as a failure to see a vehicle approaching from the right when emerging from a minor road and when the visibility permitted the vehicle to have been seen in good time.
    K-446

Campbell (Karl) was considered in *R. v. Odedara* [2010] 2 Cr.App.R.(S.) 51, CA, in which the court said of a case of momentary inattention with no aggravating features and some mitigating features, that it did not pass the custody threshold on a plea of guilty and probably would not have done so on conviction.

Ranges

In *R. v. Shepherd* [2010] 2 Cr.App.R.(S.) 54, CA, it was pointed out that since the recommended range for the most serious of the three categories of cases of causing death by careless driving tops short (at four years' custody) of the statutory maximum (five years), there must be cases in which a judge will be entitled to go above the recommended range. **K-447**

Where the offender, despite being aware that the braking system of the coach he was driving was not operating satisfactorily, drove the coach in terrain where there were regular hills, the driving created a "substantial risk of danger" such that the case fell within level 2, rather than a "significant risk of danger" such that the case would fall within level 3, of the guideline relating to causing death by dangerous driving (*ante*, K-192): *R. v. Oughton* [2011] 1 Cr.App.R.(S.) 62, CA.

Foreign drivers

Where a fatal accident is caused by a person driving on the wrong side of the road at night, the **K-448** culpability involved will be a good deal lower for a person who is used to driving on the right-hand side of the road, and who has only just arrived in this country: *R. v. Fleury* [2014] 2 Cr.App.R.(S.) 14, CA.

N. Breach of an Anti-Social Behaviour Order

Introduction

K-450   As to the purpose of this section of this appendix, see *ante*, K-350.

Relevant main work references

K-451   For sentencing guidelines generally, see section 125 of the Coroners and Justice Act 2009 (§ 5-149 in the main work). For the power to make an anti-social behaviour order on conviction, see section 1C of the CDA 1998 (§ 5-1198 in the main work). For authorities considering the imposition of an anti-social behaviour order, see § 5-1202 in the main work.

As to the replacement of anti-social behaviour orders by criminal behaviour orders, see *ante*, K-196.

Ranges

K-452   In *R. v. Fagan* [2011] 1 Cr.App.R.(S.) 105, CA, the court upheld a sentence that was above the upper bracket for the most serious category in the guideline (*ante*, K-206), even though it was accepted that the case fell within the intermediate category. Referring to the maximum permissible sentence of five years' imprisonment, the court said that it followed that the guideline (which recommended a maximum of two years for a single offence) was not appropriate in the case of a persistent offender such as the appellant.

O. Theft and Burglary in a Building Other Than a Dwelling

Introduction

K-475   As to the purpose of this section of this appendix, see *ante*, K-350.

Relevant main work references

K-476   For sentencing guidelines generally, see section 125 of the Coroners and Justice Act 2009 (§ 5-149 in the main work). For previous guidelines in relation to various types of theft, see §§ 21-4c *et seq.* in the main work.

Theft in breach of trust

K-477   In *R. v. Hakimzadeh* [2010] 1 Cr.App.R.(S.) 8, CA, the appellant was a 61-year-old American of Iranian origin, who was an expert on cultural relations between Iran and the western world. He owned an extensive collection of materials relating to that topic and considered his library to be the fourth most significant in the world. Over a substantial period, in order to improve his personal library, he stole maps and illustrations from books and some books themselves from the British and Bodleian libraries. The court said that whilst the guideline did not specifically address such cases, the section on theft in breach of trust provided some relevant basis of comparison; the offender was able to access the books in the manner that he did partly because of his reputation and partly because he was trusted to treat them in the way that scholars should treat such important resources. See also § 5-1267 in the main work.

R. v. Hakimzadeh, ante, was considered in *R. v. Jacques* [2011] 2 Cr.App.R.(S.) 39, CA, a case that involved the theft of a set of 13 rare books from The Linley, the public library of the Royal Horticultural Society, which were valued at £40,000 for insurance purposes (but could have been sold for £27,000). The offender had gained access using a reader's card under an assumed name and was found to be in possession of a list of 70 other books and their valuations. The court held that the case was wholly different to *R. v. Hakimzadeh, ante*, because none of what was regarded as exceptional mitigation in that case applied here. As to the guideline, it was said that this provided an inadequate foundation for identifying the appropriate level of sentence in a case such as this;

o categorise this case as a breach of trust was a poor guide to the gravity of this type of offending, which constituted a deliberate attack undermining the importance of libraries.

Theft from the person

In *R. v. De Weever* [2010] 1 Cr.App.R.(S.) 3, CA, the appellant had pushed a woman as she **K-478** boarded a tube train and stolen a purse from her shoulder bag. The Court of Appeal found that the offence fell into the bottom level of seriousness identified in the Sentencing Guidelines Council's guidelines on theft from the person (see *ante*, K-215). However, they considered that there were a number of grave aggravating factors (*viz.* the offence was clearly planned and was carried out in a highly professional manner, it involved the use of force (a push) short of robbery and resulted in a high level of inconvenience to the victim, the offender had a number of like convictions, albeit from many years ago, and he had failed to respond to his most recent sentences) which took the offence out of the lowest level in the guideline, and to the top of the level above it, where the starting point would be 12 months' imprisonment.

De Weever (*ante*) was considered in *R. v. Sayed* [2014] 2 Cr.App.R.(S.) 39, CA, where it was held that the reference to a victim being "vulnerable" in the guideline on theft from the person referred to the personal characteristics of the victim, rather than circumstances in which a victim was vulnerable to theft.

In *R. v. Bond* [2014] 2 Cr.App.R.(S) 3, CA, the court upheld a sentence of four years' imprisonment for a professional thief with an "appalling criminal record" who had stolen luggage, while operating with accomplices, from victims at Heathrow Airport on two occasions. The court said that it was clear from the narrative accompanying the guideline on "theft from the person" (*ante*, K-216a) that it did not provide for circumstances such as those in the present case where the court was sentencing a defendant for crimes involving a high degree of planning and sophistication, where the victims were targeted because they were likely to be travelling with considerable amounts of money or highly valuable property, and where the defendant had a criminal background of persistent and grave offending, frequently carried out in circumstances identical to the offences before the court.

Offences occurring in the context of widespread public disorder

As to departure from the guidelines when sentencing those convicted of theft and burglary in **K-479** the context of widespread public disorder of the kind seen in the riots that occurred around the country in August, 2011, and as to the appropriateness of sentences beyond the range set out in those guidelines, see *R. v. Blackshaw*, § 29-8 in the main work.

P. ATTEMPTED MURDER

Introduction

As to the purpose of this section of this appendix, see *ante*, § K-350. **K-500**

Relevant main work references

For sentencing guidelines generally, see section 125 of the Coroners and Justice Act 2009 (§ **K-501** 5-149 in the main work). For the statutory guidelines on fixing the minimum term in a case of murder, see Schedule 21 to the CJA 2003 (§§ 5-425 *et seq.* in the main work).

Conspiracy to murder

It was correct for the judge to have considered the Sentencing Guidelines Council's guideline **K-502** on attempted murder in a case charged as a conspiracy to murder but in which the facts would have supported a charge of attempted murder: *R. v. Jolie* [2011] 1 Cr.App.R.(S.) 87, CA.

Ranges

The Sentencing Guidelines Council's guideline had no application to the scale of criminality **K-503** involved in a "hideous" case where the offender woke the lone female victim at night, stole from her and subjected her to rape, beatings, stabbings and set fire to her clothes and her home after tying her up, see *Att.-Gen.'s Reference (No. 37 of 2011) (R. v. Parsons)* [2012] 1 Cr.App.R.(S.) 84, CA.

An indeterminate sentence with a minimum term which reflected a notional determinate term that was way above the top of the recommended range for a determinate sentence was justified where the term was intended to reflect a course of violent offending (including a second attempted murder and two offences of wounding with intent to cause grievous bodily harm): *R. v. Onyenaychi* [2013] 1 Cr.App.R.(S.) 59, CA.

Use of a knife or other weapon

K-504   Although the guideline was published prior to the insertion of paragraph 5A (taking a knife or other weapon to the scene/25-year starting point) in Schedule 21 to the 2003 Act (*ante*), given the way the guideline was constructed with direct reference to Schedule 21, it was incumbent on a judge to take account of the amendment of the law in relation to knives in a case involving the use of a knife: *R. v. Barnaby* [2013] 1 Cr.App.R.(S.) 53, CA; and, to similar effect, see *R. v. Gayzer-Tomlinson* [2013] 1 Cr.App.R.(S.) 98, CA.

[The next paragraph is K-550.]

Q. Sentencing Youths

Introduction

K-550   As to the purpose of this section of this appendix, see *ante*, K-350.

Relevant main work references

K-551   As to the aim of the youth justice system, see section 37 of the CDA 1998 (§ 5-63 in the main work); as to the requirement for a court to have regard to the welfare of a child or young person, see section 44 of the CYPA 1933 (*ibid.*, § 5-64); as to the purposes of sentencing when dealing with young offenders, see section 142A of the CJA 2003 (*ibid.*, § 5-66) (not in force as at October 17, 2014); as to youth rehabilitation orders, see §§ 5-314 *et seq.* in the main work; as to the enforcement of such orders, see §§ 5-380 *et seq.* in the main work; as to detention and training orders, see sections 100 to 107 of the PCC(S)A 2000 (§§ 5-597 *et seq.* in the main work); and as to the detention of young offenders convicted of certain grave crimes, see section 91 of the 2000 Act (*ibid.*, § 5-610).

For sentencing guidelines generally, see section 125 of the Coroners and Justice Act 2009 (§ 5-149 in the main work).

R. Corporate Manslaughter and Health and Safety Offences Causing Death

Introduction

K-575   As to the purpose of this section of this appendix, see *ante*, K-350.

Relevant main work references

K-576   For sentencing guidelines generally, see section 125 of the Coroners and Justice Act 2009 (§ 5-149 in the main work). As to the offence of corporate manslaughter, see §§ 19-138 *et seq.* in the main work. For the maximum sentence, for the power to order the taking of remedial action and for the power to order a conviction to be publicised, see sections 1(2), 9 and 10 of the Corporate Manslaughter and Corporate Homicide Act 2007 respectively (§§ 19-138, 19-148, 19-149 in the main work). For decisions of the Court of Appeal considering the proper approach to determining the amount of a fine, see § 5-685 in the main work.

S. Aggravated Burglary and Burglary

Introduction

K-600   As to the purpose of this section of this appendix, see *ante*, K-350.

Relevant main work references

K-601   For sentencing guidelines generally, see section 125 of the Coroners and Justice Act 2009 (§

5-149 in the main work). For section 9 of the Theft Act 1968 (burglary), see § 21-108 in the main work; and for section 10 of the 1968 Act (aggravated burglary, see § 21-129 in the main work).

Harm

Whereas one of the factors indicative of greater harm is "theft of/damage to property causing a significant degree of loss to the victim (whether economic, sentimental or personal value)", this is primarily addressing the position at the time of the theft or damage; subsequent recovery of the property, particularly if it is through voluntary reparation, may be a mitigating factor, but it does not change the character of the offence: *R. v. Franks* [2013] 1 Cr.App.R.(S.) 65, CA. **K-602**

Distraction burglaries

In *R. v. Dance* [2014] 1 Cr.App.R.(S.) 51, CA, the court held that while courts must apply the guideline when passing sentence for distraction burglaries, judges are entitled to have regard to previous decisions of the Court of Appeal, provided that they bear in mind that those cases were decided before the guideline came into force. The earlier authorities provided a useful reminder that distraction burglaries targeted at vulnerable victims are a very serious crime, despite the fact that they may involve no violence to person or property. Such offences may well merit a sentence higher than the top of the range in the guidelines, particularly if there is a pattern of repeat offending of this kind. **K-603**

"group" or "gang"

It was held in *R. v. Blaydes* [2014] 2 Cr.App.R.(S.) 55, CA, that where two people take part in a dwelling-house burglary, that is a clear and substantial aggravating feature for the purposes of the guideline, and it was not necessary to go into the semantics of whether two people amount to a "group" or "gang" (a factor indicating higher culpability in the guideline (see *ante*, K-263)). See also *R. v. Taylor* [2014] 2 Cr.App.R.(S.) 85, CA, where it was held that two persons acting together in committing a burglary do constitute a "group" for the purposes of the guideline. **K-604**

T. DRUG OFFENCES

Introduction

As to the purpose of this section of this appendix, see *ante*, K-350. **K-625**

Relevant main work references

For sentencing guidelines generally, see section 125 of the Coroners and Justice Act 2009 (§ 5-149). For section 170 of the CEMA 1979, see § 25-474; and for the penalty provisions in Schedule 1 to that Act, see § 25-508; for section 4 of the Misuse of Drugs Act 1971 (restriction of production and supply of controlled drugs), see § 27-28; for section 4A of the 1971 Act (aggravation of offence of supply of controlled drug), see § 27-28a; for section 5 of the 1971 Act (restriction of possession of controlled drug), see § 27-50; for section 6 of the 1971 Act (restriction of cultivation of cannabis plant), see § 27-79; for section 8 of the 1971 Act (occupiers of premises), see § 27-84; for section 25 of the 1971 Act (prosecution and punishment of offences), see § 27-105; for the sentencing guidelines of the Court of Appeal, see §§ 27-107 *et seq.*; and for the table of maximum penalties under the 1971 Act (and mode of trial provisions), see § 27-130. **K-626**

Scope of the guideline

The Sentencing Council's guideline on drug offences does not cover the offence of taking a prohibited article into prison, contrary to the Prison Act 1952, s.40B (§ 28-194 in the main work), where the article in question is a controlled drug and it is supplied to, or intended for supply to, a prisoner: *R. v. Simmons* [2013] 1 Cr.App.R.(S.) 109, CA. For critical consideration of this approach, see CLW/13/20/4. **K-626a**

The guideline should be applied to an offence of conspiracy to supply a controlled drug, but it should be approached with a degree of common sense and flexibility; whilst a judge should reflect the individual's culpability in the sentence passed, perhaps by adjusting the category to one better reflecting the reality, the fact of involvement in a conspiracy is an aggravating feature, since each conspirator playing his part gives comfort and assistance to others knowing that he is doing so, and the greater his awareness of the scale of the enterprise in which he is assisting, the greater his culpability: *R. v. Khan (Kazim Ali), Khan (Umar), Khan (Mohammed Arfan) and Khan (Mohammed Ahsan)* [2014] 1 Cr.App.R.(S.) 10, CA. The court also held that a judge was not confined to category 3 of the guideline because the end point activity of a conspiracy was street dealing; the words in the guideline "Where the offence is street dealing ... the quantity of the product is less indicative of the harm caused and therefore the starting point is not based on quantity." were plainly intended to move what would otherwise be category 4 offending into category 3; and it did not follow that those involved in street dealing of quantities which in aggregate went far beyond the amounts shown in category 4 can limit themselves to category 3 no matter what the scale of their dealing. As to street dealing, see also *R. v. Dyer, post,* § K-629.

R. v. Khan, ante, was referred to in *R. v. Pitts* [2014] Crim.L.R. 834, CA, where it was said that while the parameters of the guideline do not explicitly encompass the offences of conspiracy to import, supply or produce drugs, there was no error in the judge seeking to derive some assistance as to starting points by reference to the weights of drugs recovered, but this was subject to recognition that the criminality of a conspiracy is not necessarily thereby confined. The court emphasised that the degree of participation in the illegal agreement and its scope must also be considered. It added that the broad brush of defining leading, significant and lesser roles may be a helpful indicator as to participation, but these categories would be likely to be subject to further refinement on the facts. The court also warned against a slavish following of the guidelines on the basis of weights of drugs discovered at the conclusion of a surveillance operation when sentencing for drugs conspiracies. As to *Pitts*, see also *post,* K-632.

Prospective or retrospective

K-627   The guideline is not retrospective: *R. v. Boakye and other cases* [2013] 1 Cr.App.R.(S.) 2, CA.

Categorisation of role

K-628   In *Att.-Gen.'s References (Nos 15, 16 and 17 of 2012) (R. v. Lewis)* [2013] 1 Cr.App.R.(S.) 52, CA, it was said that there may be a misunderstanding as to how to categorise the role of an offender; the essential nature of a drugs hierarchy remains the same even if the terminology in the guideline ("leading", "significant" and "lesser" roles) has changed; the guideline provides a list of characteristics to guide the judge in his task, but the list is not exhaustive, and it is not necessary for an offender to possess every characteristic before he can be described as fulfilling any particular role; there may be a tendency to focus on the "non-exhaustive" list of characteristics provided and to give them far too strict a meaning; the words chosen have a broad meaning and judges should be astute not to place offenders in a lower category than is appropriate; the judge should declare his conclusions on step one in his sentencing remarks, for the benefit of the offender, those advising the offender, and the Court of Appeal; at step two, having determined the offender's role and the category of harm, the judge should "use the corresponding starting point to reach a sentence within the category ranges" which follow, and then factor in any aggravating or mitigating features.

It is not the case that a "leading role" should be reserved for cases where there is an operational hierarchy and a chain of employees, and that a "significant role" should apply to an organiser where there is no such chain: *R. v. Descombre and Thomas* [2013] 2 Cr.App.R.(S.) 51, CA (considering *R. v. Healey, post,* K-630).

Categorisation of harm

K-628a   For a case applying the principle that the quantities of drug listed in the categories of harm in the drugs guideline are not thresholds but indicative quantities, see *R. v. Henry* [2014] 1 Cr.App.R.(S.) 55, CA.

Community impact

K-628b   Where the offender, having installed a sophisticated cannabis cultivation set-up at his home, fell to be sentenced for an offence of production of a controlled drug, the judge had been entitled to take the case to the top of the relevant bracket having regard to the evidence provided by a community impact statement of a detective inspector, which dealt with the effect of drugs in the South Yorkshire area, and which noted that there was a significant risk of harm to communities from associated crime, namely, violence directed at cannabis producers in order to "tax" them ("taxing" being the street term used to describe the taking of drugs and other assets from those engaged in crime), and that innocent victims were also sometimes the target of "taxing" due to mistaken identity: *R. v. Wicks* [2014] 1 Cr.App.R.(S.) 57, CA.

Supply

In *R. v. Dyer* [2014] 2 Cr.App.R.(S.) 11, CA, it was held: (i) against the background of the **K-629** Sentencing Council's definitive guideline, earlier authorities have limited, if any, relevance, and further reliance on *R. v. Afonso*; *R. v. Sajid*; *R. v. Andrews* [2005] 1 Cr.App.R.(S.) 99, CA (sentencing of unemployed drug addicts), is inappropriate; (ii) in relation to selling directly to users ("street dealing"), harm is not categorised by quantity in the guideline; the fact of street dealing is sufficient to put the offending into Category 3 irrespective of the quantity involved; street dealing will inevitably be in quantities far smaller than those listed in the guideline (but see *R. v. Khan (Kazim Ali), Khan (Umar), Khan (Mohammed Arfan) and Khan (Mohammed Ahsan)*, *ante*, K-626a); (iii) the fact that drugs have been supplied to a test purchase or undercover officer is not a reason to reduce the category; (iv) whereas "lesser role" in the guideline includes "if own operation, absence of any financial gain, for example joint purchase for no profit, or sharing minimal quantity between peers on non-commercial basis", street dealers funding their own habit, or perhaps an extremely meagre living, are motivated by financial and other advantage and are not the same as those who, for example, are funded by friends to buy drugs for the group without any question of financial or other reward; and (v) as street dealing is always likely to be at a low level and the category is fixed, the descriptors "some awareness and understanding of the scale of the operation" in relation to "significant role", and "very little, if any, awareness or understanding of the scale of the operation" in relation to "lesser role", are of far greater relevance to those being sentenced on the basis of the quantity of the drug concerned (*e.g.* a courier or low-level participant in a substantial drug dealing operation). As to this case, see also *ante*, §§ 5-141, 5-159.

Att.-Gen.'s References (Nos 82–96 and 104–109 of 2011) (R. v. Page) [2012] 2 Cr.App.R.(S.) 56, CA, was a pre-guideline case. However, the court's general observations as to the assessment of roles would seem to carry over to sentencing under the guideline (*Dyer*, *ante*, notwithstanding). The court said that all dealers are not the same; on the whole, the greater the quantity, the longer the period over which supplies were made, and the greater the profit, the more serious the offence is likely to be, with wholesale supply likely to be more serious than retail supply because of the quantity involved; and just as dealers vary, so do transporters or "couriers"; some people fulfilling the role of transporting drugs may in fact be very close to the central organisers of the trade, the "entrepreneurs"; other couriers, however, are little more than hired hands, operating under the direction of the entrepreneurs, and are likely to be paid per task; when sentencing, therefore, it is necessary to ensure that couriers or other handlers of drugs are placed in the right relationship with the entrepreneurs, especially the principals (those responsible for large scale purchase and sale), but also the entrepreneurs who are dealers, wholesale or retail.

R. v. Kelly [2014] 2 Cr.App.R.(S.) 70, CA, was a conspiracy to supply case to which the guidelines had no direct application. However, it was held that the judge had been entitled to take account of the purity of the drugs found, first, in assigning roles to the defendants and, secondly, in deciding into which harm category to place the case, despite the guideline stating (see Appendix K-276) that quantity alone is to be assessed at step 1 (when the decision as to category of harm should be taken) and purity should be taken into account only as a potentially aggravating feature at step 2.

In *R. v. Williams* [2014] 2 Cr.App.R.(S.) 58, CA, it was held that a judge had been entitled to place an offence of possession of a Class A drug (heroin) with intent to supply into category 3 of the guideline (*ante*, K-275) where the offender was found in possession of 54 grammes of powder containing diamorphine mixed with caffeine and paracetamol, being enough to be divided into 288 separate deals, and where he entered his plea on the basis that he was storing the goods for his supplier to whom he was in debt. The court said that whilst the indicative quantity for category 3 was 150 grammes, category 3 also embraced "street dealing", in which case the starting point was not based on a quantity of drugs. Whilst the appellant was not street dealing himself, the court found that his involvement was, if anything, higher up the chain, given that he was fully aware that he was holding a stock of heroin which would be used to supply street dealers.

In *R. v. Sanchez-Canadas* [2013] 1 Cr.App.R.(S.) 114, CA, it was said that the judge had been wrong to elevate a case from category 4 to category 3 on the ground that the supply was to a prisoner; as to culpability, however, the court said that the supply of drugs into a prison ought normally to be regarded as best fitting the description of "significant role"; and it will ordinarily demand a prison sentence, even when there is no commercial motive, and even where the supplier has come under some moral pressure.

Where the person supplied dies as a result of taking the drug supplied, this had to be treated as a substantial aggravating feature notwithstanding that it was not intended, it was not anticipated, it was greatly regretted, and there was no reason for the offender to consider that it would result, except for the fact that any supply of Class A drugs carries risks: *R. v. Harrod* [2014] 1 Cr.App.R.(S.) 76, CA.

In *R. v. Bush* [2014] 1 Cr.App.R.(S.) 40, CA, the court held that anyone involved in selling drugs at summer music festivals, even on a relatively low level basis, must expect an immediate custodial sentence; such festivals are an increasingly important part of the popular culture and teenagers, who are often away from direct parental control for the first time, attend them in groups and are thus particularly vulnerable to those trying to sell them drugs.

Where the drug being sold turns out to be Class A, not Class B, as the seller believed, this should not lead to the seller being sentenced as if he were selling a Class B drug; however, a genuine misunderstanding as to the nature of a drug was relevant, because it is more culpable to sell a Class A drug, knowing it to be Class A, than to sell a Class A drug, reasonably believing it to be Class B: *R. v. Bird* [2014] 1 Cr.App.R.(S.) 77, CA.

In *R. v. Tumara and Wheaton* [2014] 8 *Archbold Review* 3, CA, it was held that where offences of supply and importation of cannabis were committed at a time when cannabis had been re-classified as a Class C drug from a Class B drug (between 2004 and 2009), a judge was not required to impose sentences in accordance with the guideline for a Class C offence. When cannabis was first classified as a Class C drug in 2004 the maximum sentences for the supply and importation of Class C drugs were increased to 14 years' imprisonment (CJA 2003, s.284, and Sched. 28) which brought them into line with the maximum for Class B drugs. Parliament had thus intended the penalty to be the same for both classes of drugs.

Cultivation and production

K-630   In *R. v. Healey* [2013] 1 Cr.App.R.(S.) 33, CA, it was said that whereas the guideline uses pictorial boxes to describe the broad categories of offence, adjacent boxes are not mutually exclusive; there is an inevitable overlap between the scenarios described; the guideline sets out to describe such sliding scales and graduations as occur in real-life offending; the quantities which appear in the boxes as broad indicators of harm are neither fixed points nor thresholds; they are "indicative" quantities designed to enable the experienced judge to put the case into the right context on the sliding scale. In production cases, the court continued, it is the output or the potential output that counts, and the number of plants is to be considered only as a route to the more fundamental question of output or potential output; there may be evidence that the yield per plant is higher than the assumption used in the guideline, in which case the application of the guideline must be adjusted accordingly. It was held that those who create a purpose-built room in their loft, cellar or garage, or who dedicate a bedroom to cultivating cannabis, having invested substantially in professional equipment for watering, for lighting and/or for electronically controlled timing, can perfectly properly be described as being at the next level up (*viz.* having a "significant role") from those who are at the lowest level; and where there is a real likelihood of additional wider circulation, in other words supply, whether for money or not, they are to be positioned higher up in the "significant role" category; as the quantity of cannabis increases, the likelihood of it being intended for the sole consumption of the defendant reduces; and a judge faced with a defendant who asserts that an improbably large quantity of cannabis is entirely for his own use should indicate that he is not presently inclined to accept that assertion, and give the defendant and his counsel the opportunity to give evidence about it if he wishes; what a judge is not entitled to do is to say that he accepts the assertion that the drug cultivation was all for the defendant's own use and yet sentence on the basis that there is likely to be a supply to somebody else. As to this case, and what was said about guidelines generally, see also §§ 5-152, 5-153 in the main work. *Healey* (which was considered in *R. v. Descombre and Thomas, ante,* K-628) may be contrasted with *R. v. Bamford* [2013] 1 Cr.App.R.(S.) 4, CA, which was decided a month earlier, where the defendant had converted a bedroom into a professionally-equipped small cannabis farm. The court said that, as it was accepted that it was all for his own use, he was properly to be described as having a "lesser role".

In *R. v. Wiseman* [2014] 2 Cr.App.R.(S.) 23, CA, it was held that whilst the Sentencing Council's definitive guideline in relation to the production of a controlled drug or cultivation of cannabis (*ante,* K-277 *et seq.*), did not provide any indicative weight or quantity of plants to assist the sentencer in the descriptions of cases that may fall into category 1 ("operation capable of producing industrial quantities for commercial use") or category 2 ("operation capable of producing significant quantities for commercial use"), a comparison with the guidelines for the importation (*ante,* K-275) and supply (*ante,* K-276) of drugs, where indicative weight was listed, was not appropriate. There was a crucial distinction between the offences of importation and supply on the one hand, and production of drugs on the other. When a controlled drug was imported or supplied, the charge in most cases related to an identified quantity of that drug where a particular seizure has been made or a particular sale and purchase has been intercepted. In contrast, many offences involving the production of a controlled drug did not involve a specific quantity that was never going to be exceeded.

It was held in *R. v. Dang* [2014] 2 Cr.App.R.(S.) 49, CA, (i) that a judge was not permitted to sentence according to his personal opinion that the starting points and ranges for cannabis offences in the guideline on drugs offences (*ante,* K-271 *et seq.*) were in general too low for "skunk" offences, and that "the distinction to be drawn between cultivated skunk and Class A drugs is not a large one", and (ii) that the above average potency of the particular drugs seized was properly to be regarded as an aggravating factor.

The guideline does not require "slide-rule sentencing": *R. v. Soloman* [2015] 1 Cr.App.R.(S.) 57, ★ CA (judge had been entitled to sentence on the basis that the case was more akin to category 3 than category 4 where the evidence suggested that the anticipated yield from the cannabis operation that the appellant was involved in setting up was closer to category 3 than category 4, and where it was more akin to a commercial, than to a domestic operation).

Importation

In *R. v. Jaramillo* [2013] 1 Cr.App.R.(S.) 110, CA, the court considered what is said in the **K-631** guideline about a starting point of 20 years (*ante,* K-275), but said that such a starting point is likely to be reserved for cases of commercial importation where the amount of drugs involved is enormous, the offender is an organiser, he has taken part in more than one importation, or he has a record of serious drug dealing.

It was held in *R. v. Sidlauskas* [2015] Crim.L.R. 297, CA, that importing 14.5 kilogrammes of ★ khat (Class C) (representing a potential 140 deals) was enough to put the offence into category 3 of the guideline (despite it containing no indicative weights for khat).

Cannabis

As the sentencing of cannabis offences committed at a time when cannabis had been re-classified **K-631a** as a Class C drug, see *R. v. Tumara and Wheaton, ante,* K-629; and as to whether it was legitimate to align "skunk cannabis" with Class A drugs, see *R. v. Dang, ante,* § K-630.

MDPV and M-Kat

In determining the category of harm into which an offence falls, the harm associated with the **K-632** synthetic Class B drug methylenedioxypyrovalerone (or "MDPV"), a derivative of cathinone, is to be treated as commensurate to the harm associated with amphetamine, and the potential of a particular quantity of MDPV for causing harm is to be taken to be the same as the potential for the same quantity of amphetamine; the purity of any given quantity was to be taken into account at step 2, that is when determining where in the range the sentence should be positioned: *R. v. Brown* [2014] 1 Cr.App.R.(S.) 84, CA.

R. v. Brown, ante, was considered in *R. v. Pitts* [2014] Crim.L.R. 834, CA (as to which, see also *ante*, K-626a), where it was similarly held that, in the case of mephedrone (or M-Kat), a Class B drug that, along with its associated cathinone derivatives, is not explicitly covered by the guideline, the correct weight comparator for deciding the entry point into the guideline is amphetamine and not cannabis.

U. OFFENCES TAKEN INTO CONSIDERATION AND TOTALITY

Introduction

K-650   As to the purpose of this section of this appendix, see *ante*, K-350.

Relevant main work references

K-651   For sentencing guidelines generally, see section 125 of the Coroners and Justice Act 2009 (§ 5-149).

As to offences taken into consideration, see §§ 5-160 *et seq.*

As to "totality" and consecutive or concurrent sentences, see the CJA 2003, ss.166(3)(b) (§ 5-126) and 265 (§ 5-668); and for the existing case law, see §§ 5-585 *et seq.*

V. DANGEROUS DOG OFFENCES

Introduction

K-675   As to the purpose of this section of this appendix, see *ante*, K-350.

Relevant main work references

K-676   For sentencing guidelines generally, see section 125 of the Coroners and Justice Act 2009 (§ 5-149). For sections 3, 4 and 4A of the Dangerous Dogs Act 1991, see §§ 31-35, 31-38 and 31-38a respectively (and *ante*).

W. FRAUD, BRIBERY AND MONEY LAUNDERING

Introduction

K-700   As to the purpose of this section of this appendix, see *ante*, K-350.

Relevant main work references

K-701   For sentencing guidelines generally, see section 125 of the Coroners and Justice Act 2009 (§ 5-149). For conspiracy to defraud, see §§ 33-37 *et seq.*; for false accounting (Theft Act 1968, s.17), see § 21-226; for possession, etc., of articles for use in fraud (2006 Act, s.6), see § 21-390; for making or supplying articles for use in fraud (2006 Act, s.7), see § 21-391; for fraudulent evasion of value added tax (Value Added Tax Act 1994, s.72), see § 25-532, for improper importation of goods (CEMA 1979, s.50), see § 25-430; for fraudulent evasion of duty (CEMA 1979, s.170), see § 25-474; for taking steps to evade duty (CEMA 1979, s.170B), see § 25-505; for cheating the public revenue, see §§ 25-409 *et seq.*; for money laundering (PCA 2002, ss.327 to 329), see §§ 26-11 *et seq*; for bribery (Bribery Act 2010, ss.1, 2 and 6), see §§ 31-171, 31-172, 31-176; and for failure of commercial organisations to prevent bribery (2010 Act, s.7), see § 31-177.

III. COMPENDIUM OF GUIDELINE CASES

K-1000   The Sentencing Guidelines Council has published a compendium of those cases that it regards as constituting considered guidance and issued over the past 30 years. The list is in two parts, "Generic sentencing principles" and "Offences". It has been updated five times, with some cases having been removed from the original list.

As at October, 8, 2014, there was a note on the website of the Sentencing Council stating that the case compendium is no longer being updated and should be referred to for reference only.

In the first list are: *R. v. Martin (Selina)* [2007] 1 Cr.App.R.(S.) 3 (**approach to sentencing**); *Att.-Gen.'s Reference (No. 4 of 1989) (R. v. Brunt)*, 11 Cr.App.R.(S.) 517 (**Attorney-General's references**); *R. v. Montgomery*, 16 Cr.App.R.(S.) 274 (**contempt**); *R. v. Bernard* [1997] 1 Cr.App.R.(S.)

135 (**health of the offender**); *R. v. Goodyear* [2005] 3 All E.R. 117; *R. v. Kulah* [2008] 1 Cr.App.R.(S.) 85 (**indication of sentence**); *R. v. Buckland* [2000] 1 W.L.R. 1262 (**automatic life sentences**); *R. v. Hodgson*, 52 Cr.App.R. 113; *R. v. Chapman* [2000] 1 Cr.App.R. 77; *R. v. McNee, Gunn and Russell* [2008] 1 Cr.App.R.(S.) 24; *R. v. Kehoe* [2009] 1 Cr.App.R.(S.) 9; *R. v. Davies* [2009] 1 Cr.App.R.(S.) 15 (**discretionary life sentences**); *R. v. M. (Discretionary Life Sentence)*; *R. v. L.* [1999] 1 W.L.R. 485; *R. v. Szczerba* [2002] 2 Cr.App.R.(S.) 86 (**life sentence—specified period**); *R. v. McLean*, 6 Cr.App.R. 26; *R. v. Simons*, 37 Cr.App.R. 120; *R. v. Walsh*, unreported, March 8, 1973 (**taking offences into consideration**); *Att.-Gen.'s Reference (No. 52 of 2003) (R. v. Webb)* [2004] Crim.L.R. 306 (**prosecution duty**); *R. v. Kelly and Donnelly* [2001] 2 Cr.App.R.(S.) 73; *R. v. McGillivray* [2005] 2 Cr.App.R.(S.) 60; *R. v. O'Callaghan* [2005] 2 Cr.App.R.(S.) 83 (**racially aggravated offences**); *R. v. A. and B.* [1999] 1 Cr.App.R.(S.) 52; *R. v. Guy* [1999] 2 Cr.App.R.(S.) 24; *R. v. X. (No. 2)* [1999] 2 Cr.App.R.(S.) 294; *R. v. R. (Informer: Reduction in sentence)*, *The Times*, February 18, 2002; *R. v. P.*; *R. v. Blackburn* [2008] 2 Cr.App.R.(S.) 5 (**discount on account of assistance given to the police**); *R. v. Bird*, 9 Cr.App.R.(S.) 77; *R. v. Tiso*, 12 Cr.App.R.(S.) 122 (**discount on account of lapse of time since offence**); *R. v. Bibi* [1980] 1 W.L.R. 1193; *R. v. Ollerenshaw* [1999] 1 Cr.App.R.(S.) 65; *R. v. Kefford* [2002] 2 Cr.App.R.(S.) 106 (**length of custodial sentences**); *R. v. Nelson* [2002] 1 Cr.App.R.(S.) 134; *R. v. Cornelius* [2002] 2 Cr.App.R.(S.) 69; *R. v. Pepper* [2006] 1 Cr.App.R.(S.) 20 (**length of extended sentences**); *R. v. Lang* [2006] 2 Cr.App.R.(S.) 3; *R. v. S.*; *R. v. Burt* [2006] 2 Cr.App.R.(S.) 35; *CPS v. South East Surrey Youth Court* [2006] 2 Cr.App.R.(S.) 26 (**dangerousness**); *R. v. Reynolds* [2007] 2 Cr.App.R.(S.) 87; *R. v. Johnson* [2007] 1 Cr.App.R.(S.) 112; *R. v. O'Brien* [2007] 1 Cr.App.R.(S.) 75; *R. v. O'Halloran*, unreported, November 14, 2006 ([2006] EWCA Crim. 3148) (**dangerousness: imprisonment for public protection**); *R. v. Brown and Butterworth* [2007] 1 Cr.App.R.(S.) 77; *R. v. Lay* [2007] 2 Cr.App.R.(S.) 4; *R. v. C.*; *R. v. Bartley* [2007] 2 Cr.App.R.(S.) 98 (**dangerousness: extended sentences**); *Att.-Gen.'s Reference (No. 101 of 2006) (R. v. P.)*, unreported, December 8, 2006 ([2006] EWCA Crim. 3335) (**deferment of sentence**); *R. v. Cain* [2007] 2 Cr.App.R.(S.) 25 (**prosecution and defence duty to assist at sentencing**); *R. v. Seed; R. v. Stark* [2007] 2 Cr.App.R.(S.) 69 (**sentence length: custodial sentences**); *R. (Stellato) v. Secretary of State for the Home Department* [2007] 2 A.C. 70 (**sentence length: licence period**); *Att.-Gen.'s Reference (No. 6 of 2006) (R. v. Farish)* [2007] 1 Cr.App.R.(S.) 12 (**sentence length: minimum sentences**); *R. v. Gordon* [2007] 2 All E.R. 768 (**sentence length: time spent in custody on remand**); *R. v. Tyre*, 6 Cr.App.R.(S.) 247 (**sentence length: joint conviction with a juvenile offender**); *R. v. Davies* [2009] 1 Cr.App.R.(S.) 15 (**sentence length: standard of proof**); *R. v. Raza* [2010] 1 Cr.App.R.(S.) 56, CA (**sentence length: discounts; totality and mandatory minimum sentences**); *R. v. Round; R. v. Dunn* [2010] 2 Cr.App.R.(S.) 45, CA (**sentence length: early release provisions**); *Att.-Gen.'s Reference (No. 55 of 2008) (R. v. C.)* [2009] 2 Cr.App.R.(S.) 22, CA (**sentence length: imprisonment for public protection**); *R. v. Costello* [2010] 2 Cr.App.R.(S.) 94, CA (**sentence length: offence committed whilst on licence**); *R. v. McGrath* [2005] 2 Cr.App.R.(S.). 85; *R. v. Morrison* [2006] 1 Cr.App.R.(S.) 85; *R. v. Lamb* [2006] 2 Cr.App.R.(S.) 11 (**anti-social behaviour orders**); *R. v. P. (Shane Tony)* [2004] 2 Cr.App.R.(S.) 63 (**anti-social behaviour order imposed with custody**); *R. v. Sullivan* [2003] EWCA Crim. 1736 (**compensation with custody**); *R. v. Robinson* [2002] 2 Cr.App.R.(S.) 95; *Att.-Gen.'s Reference (No. 64 of 2003)* [2004] 2 Cr.App.R.(S.) 22; *R. v. Woods and Collins* [2006] 1 Cr.App.R.(S.) 83 (**drug treatment and testing orders**); *R. v. Richards* [2007] 1 Cr.App.R.(S.) 120 (**sexual offences prevention orders**); *R. v. Kidd; R. v. Canavan; R. v. Shaw (Dennis)* [1998] 1 W.L.R. 604; *R. v. Tovey; R. v. Smith* [2005] 2 Cr.App.R.(S.) 100 (**specimen offences**); *R. v. Perks* [2001] 1 Cr.App.R.(S.) 66; *R. v. Ismail* [2005] 2 Cr.App.R.(S.) 88 (**victim's wishes**); *R. v. Danga*, 13 Cr.App.R.(S.) 408 (**age for purpose of sentencing**); *R. (W.) v. Southampton Youth Court; R. (K.) v. Wirral Borough Magistrates' Court* [2003] 1 Cr.App.R.(S.) 87 (**venue for trial**); *R. v. Sharma* [2006] 2 Cr.App.R.(S.) 63 (**confiscation orders**); *R. v. Oshungbure and Odewale* [2005] 2 Cr.App.R.(S.) 102 (**confiscation proceedings following sentence**); *R. v. Richards (Michael)* [2005] 2 Cr.App.R.(S.) 97 (**confiscation order: obtaining social security benefits by false representations**); *R. v. Debnath* [2006] 2 Cr.App.R.(S.) 25 (**restraining orders**); *R. v. Lees-Wolfenden* [2007] 1 Cr.App.R.(S.) 119 (**suspended sentence orders**); *R. v. Sheppard* [2008] 2 Cr.App.R.(S.) 93, CA; *R. v. Chalmers*, unreported, August 7, 2009, CA ([2009] EWCA Crim. 1814) (**activation of suspended sentences**).

In the second list are:—

    affray—*R. v. Fox and Hicks* [2006] 1 Cr.App.R.(S.) 17;

    breach of licence—*R. v. Pick and Dillon* [2006] 1 Cr.App.R.(S.) 61;

burglary (domestic)—*R. v. McInerney; R. v. Keating* [2003] 1 All E.R. 1089; *R. v. Saw* [2009] 2 Cr.App.R.(S.) 54, CA [but see now *R. v. Dance, ante,* K-603];

counterfeiting and forgery—*R. v. Howard,* 7 Cr.App.R.(S.) 320 (dealing in counterfeit currency); *R. v. Crick,* 3 Cr.App.R.(S.) 275 (counterfeiting coins); *R. v. Kolawole* [2005] 2 Cr.App.R.(S.) 14; *R. v. Mutede* [2006] 2 Cr.App.R.(S.) 22; *Att.-Gen.'s Reference (Nos 1 and 6 of 2008) (R. v. Dziruni and Laby)* [2008] 2 Cr.App.R.(S.) 99; *R. v. Mabengo, Lomoka, Salang and Birindwa, The Times,* July 17, 2008, CA; and *R. v. Ovieriakhi* [2009] 2 Cr.App.R.(S.) 91, CA (false passports);

drugs—[for a listing of the cases included in the compendium, see the first supplement to this edition; they have not been included here in light of the observations of the Court of Appeal in *R. v. Dyer, ante,* K-629 about the citation of pre-guideline authorities];

explosive offences—*R. v. Martin* [1999] 1 Cr.App.R.(S.) 477;

firearms offences—*R. v. Avis; R. v. Barton; R. v. Thomas; R. v. Torrington; R. v. Marquez; R. v. Goldsmith* [1998] 1 Cr.App.R. 420; *Att.-Gen.'s Reference (No. 43 of 2009) (R. v. Bennett); R. v. Wilkinson* [2010] 1 Cr.App.R.(S.) 100; *R. v. Rehman; R. v. Wood* [2006] 1 Cr.App.R.(S.) 77 (exceptional circumstances);

fraud—*R. v. Feld* [1999] 1 Cr.App.R.(S.) 1 (company management); *R. v. Palk and Smith* [1997] 2 Cr.App.R.(S.) 167 (fraudulent trading); *R. v. Roach* [2002] 1 Cr.App.R.(S.) 12 (obtaining money transfer by deception);

handling stolen goods—*R. v. Webbe* [2002] 1 Cr.App.R.(S.) 22;

health and safety offences—*R. v. F. Howe and Son (Engineers) Ltd* [1999] 2 All E.R. 249; *R. v. Rollco Screw and Rivet Co Ltd* [1999] 2 Cr.App.R.(S.) 436; *R. v. Balfour Beatty Infrastructure Ltd* [2007] 1 Cr.App.R.(S.) 65;

immigration—*R. v. Le and Stark* [1999] 1 Cr.App.R.(S.) 422; *R. v. Ai (Lu Zhu)* [2006] 1 Cr.App.R.(S.) 5 (failing to produce an immigration document);

incest—*Att.-Gen.'s Reference (No. 1 of 1989),* 11 Cr.App.R.(S.) 409;

indecent assault—*Att.-Gen.'s References (Nos 120, 91 and 119 of 2002)* [2003] 2 All E.R. 955 (general); *R. v. Lennon* [1999] 1 Cr.App.R. 117 (on male);

insider dealing—*R. v. McQuoid* [2010] 1 Cr.App.R.(S.) 43, CA;

intimidation of witness—*R. v. Williams* [1997] 2 Cr.App.R.(S.) 221; *R. v. Chinery* [2002] 2 Cr.App.R.(S.) 244(55);

kidnapping—*R. v. Spence and Thomas,* 5 Cr.App.R.(S.) 413;

manslaughter—*R. v. Chambers,* 5 Cr.App.R.(S.) 190 (diminished responsibility); *R. v. Furby* [2006] 2 Cr.App.R.(S.) 8; *Att.-Gen.'s Reference (No. 60 of 2009) (R. v. Appleby)* [2010] 2 Cr.App.R.(S.) 46, CA ("single punch"); *Att.-Gen.'s Reference (No. 111 of 2006) (R. v. Hussain)* [2007] 2 Cr.App.R.(S.) 26 ("motor"); *R. v. Wood* [2010] 1 Cr.App.R.(S.) 2, CA (diminished responsibility);

money laundering—*R. v. Basra* [2002] 2 Cr.App.R.(S.) 100; *R. v. Gonzalez and Sarmineto* [2003] 2 Cr.App.R.(S.) 9 (general); *R. v. El-Delbi* [2003] 7 *Archbold News* 1 (proceeds of drug trafficking);

murder—*R. v. Jones* [2006] 2 Cr.App.R.(S.) 19; *R. v. Barot* [2008] 1 Cr.App.R.(S.) 31; *R. v. McNee, Gunn and Russell* [2008] 1 Cr.App.R.(S.) 24 (conspiracy); *R. v. Davies* [2009] 1 Cr.App.R.(S.) 15 (minimum term); *R. v. Javed* [2008] 2 Cr.App.R.(S.) 12 (soliciting); *R. v. M.; R. v. A.M.; R. v. Kika* [2010] 2 Cr.App.R.(S.) 19, CA (with a knife);

offensive weapons—*R. v. Poulton; R. v. Celaire* [2003] 4 All E.R. 869; *R. v. Povey* [2009] 1 Cr.App.R.(S.) 42;

perjury—*R. v. Archer* [2003] 1 Cr.App.R.(S.) 86;

perverting the course of justice—*R. v. Walsh and Nightingale,* 14 Cr.App.R.(S.) 671; *R. v. Tunney* [2007] 1 Cr.App.R.(S.) 91, CA;

pornography—*R. v. Holloway,* 4 Cr.App.R.(S.) 128 (having obscene articles for publication for gain); *R. v. Nooy and Schyff,* 4 Cr.App.R.(S.) 308 (importation of indecent or obscene publications);

prison breaking (escape)—*R. v. Coughtrey* [1997] 2 Cr.App.R.(S.) 269;

public nuisance—*R. v. Kavanagh* [2008] 2 Cr.App.R.(S.) 86;

riot—*R. v. Najeeb* [2003] 2 Cr.App.R.(S.) 69;

robbery—*R. v. Snowden, The Times,* November 11, 2002 (hijacking of cars);

sex offenders' register—*Att.-Gen.'s Reference (No. 50 of 1997) (R. v. V.)* [1998] 2 Cr.App.R.(S.) 155;

theft—*R. v. Evans* [1996] 1 Cr.App.R.(S.) 105 ("ringing" stolen cars);

trafficking women for prostitution—*Att.-Gen.'s Reference (No. 6 of 2004) (R. v. Plakici)* [2005] 1 Cr.App.R.(S.) 19;

violent disorder—*R. v. Chapman* (2002) 146 S.J. (LB 242);

APPENDIX N
Protocols

A. CONTROL AND MANAGEMENT OF HEAVY FRAUD AND OTHER COMPLEX CRIMINAL CASES

A protocol issued by the Lord Chief Justice of England and Wales   **N-1**

22 March 2005

Introduction

The investigation

> The role of the prosecuting authority and the judge
>
> Interviews
>
> The prosecution and defence teams
>
> Initial consideration of the length of a case
>
> Notification of cases likely to last more than 8 weeks
>
> Notification of cases likely to last more than 8 weeks
>
> Venue

Designation of the trial judge

> The assignment of a judge

Case management

> Objectives
>
> The assignment of a judge

Case management

> Objectives
>
> Fixing the trial date
>
> The first hearing for the giving of initial directions
>
> The first Case Management Hearing
>
> Further Case Management Hearings
>
> Consideration of the length of the trial
>
> The exercise of the powers
>
> Fixing the trial date
>
> The first hearing for the giving of initial directions
>
> The first Case Management Hearing
>
> Further Case Management Hearings
>
> Consideration of the length of the trial
>
> The exercise of the powers
>
> Expert Evidence
>
> Surveillance Evidence

Disclosure

Abuse of process

The trial

> The particular hazard of heavy fraud trials
>
> Judicial mastery of the case
>
> The order of the evidence
>
> Case management sessions

Introduction

N-2   There is a broad consensus that the length of fraud and trials of other complex crimes must be controlled within proper bounds in order:

(i) To enable the jury to retain and assess the evidence which they have heard. If the trial is so long that the jury cannot do this, then the trial is not fair either to the prosecution or the defence.

(ii) To make proper use of limited public resources: see *Jisl* [2004] EWCA Crim. 696 at [113]-[121].

There is also a consensus that no trial should be permitted to exceed a given period, save in exceptional circumstances; some favour 3 months, others an outer limit of 6 months. Whatever view is taken, it is essential that the current length of trials is brought back to an acceptable and proper duration.

This Protocol supplements the Criminal Procedure Rules and summarises good practice which experience has shown may assist in bringing about some reduction in the length of trials of fraud and other crimes that result in complex trials. Flexibility of application of this Protocol according to the needs of each case is essential; it is designed to inform but not to proscribe.

This Protocol is primarily directed towards cases which are likely to last eight weeks or longer. It should also be followed, however, in all cases estimated to last more than four weeks. This Protocol applies to trials by jury, but many of the principles will be applicable if trials without a jury are permitted under s.43 of the Criminal Justice Act 2003.

The best handling technique for a long case is continuous management by an experienced Judge nominated for the purpose.

It is intended that this Protocol be kept up to date; any further practices or techniques found to be successful in the management of complex cases should be notified to the office of the Lord Chief Justice.

1. The investigation

(i) The role of the prosecuting authority and the judge

N-3   (a) Unlike other European countries, a judge in England and Wales does not directly control the investigation process; that is the responsibility of the Investigating Authority, and in turn the Prosecuting Authority and the prosecution advocate. Experience has shown that a prosecution lawyer (who must be of sufficient experience and who will be a member of the team at trial) and the prosecution advocate, if different, should be involved in the investigation as soon as it appears that a heavy fraud trial or other complex criminal trial is likely to ensue. The costs that this early preparation will incur will be saved many times over in the long run.

(b) The judge can and should exert a substantial and beneficial influence by making it clear that, generally speaking, trials should be kept within manageable limits. In most cases 3 months should be the target outer limit, but there will be cases where a duration of 6 months, or in exceptional circumstances, even longer may be inevitable.

(ii) Interviews

(a) At present many interviews are too long and too unstructured. This has a knock-on effect **N-4** on the length of trials. Interviews should provide an opportunity for suspects to respond to the allegations against them. They should not be an occasion to discuss every document in the case. It should become clear from judicial rulings that interviews of this kind are a waste of resources.

(b) The suspect must be given sufficient information before or at the interview to enable them to meet the questions fairly and answer them honestly; the information is not provided to give him the opportunity to manufacture a false story which fits undisputable facts.

(c) It is often helpful if the principal documents are provided either in advance of the interview or shown as the interview progresses; asking detailed questions about events a considerable period in the past without reference to the documents is often not very helpful.

(iii) The prosecution and defence teams

(a) **The Prosecution Team**

While instructed it is for the lead advocate for the prosecution to take all necessary deci- **N-5** sions in the presentation and general conduct of the prosecution case. The prosecution lead advocate will be treated by the court as having that responsibility.

However, in relation to policy decisions the lead advocate for the prosecution must not give an indication or undertaking which binds the prosecution without first discussing the issue with Director of the Prosecuting authority or other senior officer.

"Policy" decisions should be understood as referring to non-evidential decisions on: the acceptance of pleas of guilty to lesser counts or groups of counts or available alternatives: offering no evidence on particular counts; consideration of a re-trial; whether to lodge an appeal; certification of a point of law; and the withdrawal of the prosecution as a whole (for further information see the "Farquharson Guidelines" on the role and responsibilities of the prosecution advocate).

(b) **The Defence Team**

In each case, the lead advocate for the defence will be treated by the court as having responsibility to the court for the presentation and general conduct of the defence case.

(c) In each case, a case progression officer must be assigned by the court, prosecution and defence from the time of the first hearing when directions are given (as referred to in paragraph 3(iii)) until the conclusion of the trial.

(d) In each case where there are multiple defendants, the LSC will need to consider carefully the extent and level of representation necessary.

(iv) Initial consideration of the length of a case

If the prosecutor in charge of the case from the Prosecuting Authority or the lead advocate for the **N-6** prosecution consider that the case as formulated is likely to last more than 8 weeks, the case should be referred in accordance with arrangements made by the Prosecuting Authority to a more senior prosecutor. The senior prosecutor will consider whether it is desirable for the case to be prosecuted in that way or whether some steps might be taken to reduce its likely length, whilst at the same time ensuring that the public interest is served.

Any case likely to last 6 months or more must be referred to the Director of the Prosecuting Authority so that similar considerations can take place.

(v) Notification of cases likely to last more than 8 weeks

Special arrangements will be put in place for the early notification by the CPS and other Prosecut- **N-7** ing Authorities, to the LSC and to a single designated officer of the Court in each Region (Circuit) of any case which the CPS or other Prosecuting Authority consider likely to last over 8 weeks.

(vi) Venue

The court will allocate such cases and other complex cases likely to last 4 weeks or more to a **N-8** specific venue suitable for the trial in question, taking into account the convenience to witnesses, the parties, the availability of time at that location, and all other relevant considerations.

2. Designation of the trial judge

The assignment of a judge

N-9

(a) In any complex case which is expected to last more than four weeks, the trial judge will be assigned under the direction of the Presiding Judges at the earliest possible moment.

(b) Thereafter the assigned judge should manage that case "from cradle to grave"; it is essential that the same judge manages the case from the time of his assignment and that arrangements are made for him to be able to do so. It is recognised that in certain court centres with a large turnover of heavy cases (*e.g.* Southwark) this objective is more difficult to achieve. But in those court centres there are teams of specialist judges, who are more readily able to handle cases which the assigned judge cannot continue with because of unexpected events; even at such courts, there must be no exception to the principle that one judge must handle all the pre-trial hearings until the case is assigned to another judge.

3. Case management

(i) Objectives

N-10

(a) The number, length and organisation of case management hearings will, of course, depend critically on the circumstances and complexity of the individual case. However, thorough, well-prepared and extended case management hearings will save court time and costs overall.

(b) Effective case management of heavy fraud and other complex criminal cases requires the judge to have a much more detailed grasp of the case than may be necessary for many other Plea and Case Management Hearings (PCMHs). Though it is for the judge in each case to decide how much pre-reading time he needs so that the judge is on top of the case, it is not always a sensible use of judicial time to allocate a series of reading days, during which the judge sits alone in his room, working through numerous boxes of ring binders.

See paragraph 3(iv)(e) below

(ii) Fixing the trial date

N-11

Although it is important that the trial date should be fixed as early as possible, this may not always be the right course. There are two principal alternatives:

(a) The trial date should be fixed at the first opportunity—*i.e.* at the first (and usually short) directions hearing referred to in The first hearing for the giving of initial directions. From then on everyone must work to that date. All orders and pre-trial steps should be timetabled to fit in with that date. All advocates and the judge should take note of this date, in the expectation that the trial will proceed on the date determined.

(b) The trial date should not be fixed until the issues have been explored at a full case management hearing (referred to in The first Case Management Hearing), after the advocates on both sides have done some serious work on the case. Only then can the length of the trial be estimated.

Which is apposite must depend on the circumstances of each case, but the earlier it is possible to fix a trial date, by reference to a proper estimate and a timetable set by reference to the trial date, the better.

It is generally to be expected that once a trial is fixed on the basis of the estimate provided, that it will not be **increased** if, and only if, the party seeking to extend the time justifies why the original estimate is no longer appropriate.

(iii) The first hearing for the giving of initial directions

N-12

At the first opportunity the assigned judge should hold a short hearing to give initial directions. The directions on this occasion might well include:

(a) That there should be a full case management hearing on, or commencing on, a specified future date by which time the parties will be properly prepared for a meaningful hearing and the defence will have full instructions.

(b) That the prosecution should provide an outline written statement of the prosecution case at least one week in advance of that case management hearing, outlining in simple terms:

(i) the key facts on which it relies;

(ii) the key evidence by which the prosecution seeks to prove the facts.

The statement must be sufficient to permit the judge to understand the case and for the defence to appreciate the basic elements of its case against each defendant. The prosecution may be invited to highlight the key points of the case orally at the case management hearing by way of a short mini-opening. The outline statement should not be considered binding, but it will serve the essential purpose in telling the judge, and everyone else, what the case is really about and identifying the key issues.

(c) That a core reading list and core bundle for the case management hearing should be delivered at least one week in advance.

(d) Preliminary directions about disclosure: see paragraph 4.

(iv) The first case management hearing

(a) At the first case management hearing: **N-13**

  (1) the prosecution advocate should be given the opportunity to highlight any points from the prosecution outline statement of case (which will have been delivered at least a week in advance;

  (2) each defence advocate should be asked to outline the defence.

If the defence advocate is not in a position to say what is in issue and what is not in issue, then the case management hearing can be adjourned for a short and limited time and to a fixed date to enable the advocate to take instructions; such an adjournment should only be necessary in exceptional circumstances, as the defence advocate should be properly instructed by the time of the first case management hearing and in any event is under an obligation to take sufficient instructions to fulfil the obligations contained in sections 33–39 of Criminal Justice Act 2003.

(b) There should then be a real dialogue between the judge and all advocates for the purpose of identifying:

  (i) the focus of the prosecution case;

  (ii) the common ground;

  (iii) the real issues in the case. (Rule 3.2 of the Criminal Procedure Rules.)

(c) The judge will try to generate a spirit of co-operation between the court and the advocates on all sides. The expeditious conduct of the trial and a focussing on the real issues must be in the interests of **all** parties. It cannot be in the interests of any defendant for his good points to become lost in a welter of uncontroversial or irrelevant evidence.

(d) In many fraud cases the primary facts are not seriously disputed. The real issue is what each defendant knew and whether that defendant was dishonest. Once the judge has identified what is in dispute and what is not in dispute, the judge can then discuss with the advocate how the trial should be structured, what can be dealt with by admissions or agreed facts, what uncontroversial matters should be proved by concise oral evidence, what timetabling can be required under Rule 3.10 Criminal Procedure Rules, and other directions.

(e) In particularly heavy fraud or complex cases the judge may possibly consider it necessary to allocate a whole week for a case management hearing. If that week is used wisely, many further weeks of trial time can be saved. In the gaps which will inevitably arise during that week (for example while the advocates are exploring matters raised by the judge) the judge can do a substantial amount of informed reading. The case has come "alive" at this stage. Indeed, in a really heavy fraud case, if the judge fixes one or more case management hearings on this scale, there will be need for fewer formal reading days. Moreover a huge amount can be achieved in the pre-trial stage, if all trial advocates are gathered in the same place, focussing on the case **at the same time**, for several days consecutively.

(f) Requiring the defence to serve proper case statements may enable the court to identify

  (i) what is common ground and

  (ii) the real issues.

It is therefore important that proper defence case statements be provided as required by the Criminal Procedure Rules; judges will use the powers contained in ss.28–34 of the Criminal Proceedings and Evidence Act 1996 [*sic*] (and the corresponding provisions of the CJA 1987, ss.33 and following of the Criminal Justice Act 2003) and the Criminal Procedure Rules to ensure that realistic defence case statements are provided.

(g) Likewise this objective may be achieved by requiring the prosecution to serve draft admissions by a specified date and by requiring the defence to respond within a specified number of weeks.

(v) Further case management hearings

(a) The date of the next case management hearing should be fixed at the conclusion of the **N-14** hearing so that there is no delay in having to fix the date through listing offices, clerks and others.

(b) If one is looking at a trial which threatens to run for months, pre-trial case management on an intensive scale is essential.

(vi) Consideration of the length of the trial

N-15

(a) Case management on the above lines, the procedure set out in paragraph 1(iv), may still be insufficient to reduce the trial to a manageable length; generally a trial of 3 months should be the target, but there will be cases where a duration of 6 months or, in exceptional circumstances, even longer may be inevitable.

(b) If the trial is not estimated to be within a manageable length, it will be necessary for the judge to consider what steps should be taken to reduce the length of the trial, whilst still ensuring that the prosecution has the opportunity of placing the full criminality before the court.

(c) To assist the judge in this task,

(i) the lead advocate for the prosecution should be asked to explain why the prosecution have rejected a shorter way of proceeding; they may also be asked to divide the case into sections of evidence and explain the scope of each section and the need for each section;

(ii) the lead advocates for the prosecution and for the defence should be prepared to put forward in writing, if requested, ways in which a case estimated to last more than three months can be shortened, including possible severance of counts or defendants, exclusions of sections of the case or of evidence or areas of the case where admissions can be made.

(d) One course the judge may consider is pruning the indictment by omitting certain charges and/or by omitting certain defendants. The judge must not usurp the function of the prosecution in this regard, and he must bear in mind that he will, at the outset, know less about the case than the advocates. The aim is achieve [*sic*] fairness to all parties

(e) Nevertheless, the judge does have two methods of pruning available for use in appropriate circumstances:

(i) persuading the prosecution that it is not worthwhile pursuing certain charges and/or certain defendants;

(ii) severing the indictment. Severance for reasons of case management alone is perfectly proper, although judges should have regard to any representations made by the prosecution that severance would weaken their case. Indeed the judge's hand will be strengthened in this regard by rule 1.1(2)(g) of the Criminal Procedure Rules. However, before using what may be seen as a blunt instrument, the judge should insist on seeing full defence statements of all affected defendants. Severance may be unfair to the prosecution if, for example, there is a cut-throat defence in prospect. For example, the defence of the principal defendant may be that the defendant relied on the advice of his accountant or solicitor that what was happening was acceptable. The defence of the professional may be that he gave no such advice. Against that background, it might be unfair to the prosecution to order separate trials of the two defendants.

(vii) The exercise of the powers

N-16

(a) The Criminal Procedure Rules require the court to take a more active part in case management. These are salutary provisions which should bring to an end interminable criminal trials of the kind which the Court of Appeal criticised in *Jisl* [2004] EWCA 696 at [113]-[121].

(b) Nevertheless these salutary provisions do not have to be used on every occasion. Where the advocates have done their job properly, by narrowing the issues, pruning the evidence and so forth, it may be quite inappropriate for the judge to "weigh in" and start cutting out more evidence or more charges of his own volition. It behoves the judge to make a careful assessment of the degree of judicial intervention which is warranted in each case.

(c) The note of caution in the previous paragraph is supported by certain experience which has been gained of the Civil Procedure Rules (on which the Criminal Procedure Rules are based). The CPR contain valuable and efficacious provisions for case management by the judge on his own initiative which have led to huge savings of court time and costs. Surveys by the Law Society have shown that the CPR have been generally welcomed by court users and the profession, but there have been reported to have been isolated instances in which the parties to civil litigation have faithfully complied with both the letter and the spirit of the CPR, and have then been aggrieved by what was perceived to be unnecessary intermeddling by the court.

(viii) Expert evidence

(a) Early identification of the subject matter of expert evidence to be adduced by the prosecution and the defence should be made as early as possible, preferably at the directions hearing.   **N-17**

(b) Following the exchange of expert evidence, any areas of disagreement should be identified and a direction should generally be made requiring the experts to meet and prepare, after discussion, a joint statement identifying points of agreement and contention and areas where the prosecution is put to proof on matters of which a positive case to the contrary is not advanced by the defence. After the statement has been prepared it should be served on the court, the prosecution and the defence. In some cases, it might be appropriate to provide that to the jury.

(ix) Surveillance evidence

(a) Where a prosecution is based upon many months' observation or surveillance evidence and it appears that it is capable of effective presentation based on a shorter period, the advocate should be required to justify the evidence of such observations before it is permitted to be adduced, either substantially or in its entirety.   **N-18**

(b) Schedules should be provided to cover as much of the evidence as possible and admissions sought.

4. Disclosure

[Replaced by the 2013 judicial protocol on disclosure: see post, N-52 et seq.]   **N-19**

5. Abuse of process

(i) Applications to stay or dismiss for abuse of process have become a normal feature of heavy and complex cases. Such applications may be based upon delay and the health of defendants.   **N-20**

(ii) Applications in relation to absent special circumstances *[sic]* tend to be unsuccessful and not to be pursued on appeal. For this reason there is comparatively little Court of Appeal guidance: but see: *Harris and Howells* [2003] EWCA Crim. 486. It should be noted that abuse of process is not there to discipline the prosecution or the police.

(iii) The arguments on both sides must be reduced to writing. Oral evidence is seldom relevant.

(iv) The judge should direct full written submissions (rather than "skeleton arguments") on any abuse application in accordance with a timetable set by him; these should identify any element of prejudice the defendant is alleged to have suffered.

(v) The judge should normally aim to conclude the hearing within an absolute maximum limit of one day, if necessary in accordance with a timetable. The parties should therefore prepare their papers on this basis and not expect the judge to allow the oral hearing to be anything more than an occasion to highlight concisely their arguments and answer any questions the court may have of them; applications will not be allowed drag on.

6. The trial

(i) The particular hazard of heavy fraud trials

A heavy fraud or other complex trial has the potential to lose direction and focus. This is a disaster for three reasons: **N-21**

(a) the jury will lose track of the evidence, thereby prejudicing both prosecution and defence;

(b) the burden on the defendants, the judge and indeed all involved will become intolerable;

(c) scarce public resources are wasted. Other prosecutions are delayed or—worse—may never happen. Fraud which is detected but not prosecuted (for resource reasons) undermines confidence.

(ii) Judicial mastery of the case

(a) It is necessary for the judge to exercise firm control over the conduct of the trial at all stages.   **N-22**

(b) In order to do this the judge must read the witness statements and the documents, so that the judge can discuss case management issues with the advocates on—almost—an equal footing.

(c) To this end, the judge should not set aside weeks or even days for pre-reading (see paragraph 3(i)(b)). Hopefully the judge will have gained a good grasp of the evidence during the case management hearings. Nevertheless, realistic reading time must be provided for the judge in advance of trial.

(d) The role of the judge in a heavy fraud or other complex criminal trial is different from his/ her role in a "conventional" criminal trial. So far as possible, the judge should be freed from other duties and burdens, so that he/she can give the high degree of commitment which a heavy fraud trial requires. This will pay dividends in terms of saving weeks or months of court time.

(iii) The order of the evidence

N-23

(a) By the outset of the trial at the latest (and in most cases very much earlier) the judge must be provided with a schedule, showing the sequence of prosecution (and in an appropriate case defence) witnesses and the dates upon which they are expected to be called. This can only be prepared by discussion between prosecution and defence which the judge should expect, and say he/she expects, to take place: See: Criminal Procedure Rule 3.10. The schedule should, in so far as it relates to prosecution witnesses, be developed in consultation with the witnesses, via the witness care units, and with consideration given to their personal needs. Copies of the schedule should be provided for the Witness Service.

(b) The schedule should be kept under review by the trial judge and by the parties. If a case is running behind or ahead of schedule, each witness affected must be advised by the party who is calling that witness at the earliest opportunity.

(c) If an excessive amount of time is allowed for any witness, the judge can ask why. The judge may probe with the advocates whether the time envisaged for the evidence-in-chief or cross-examination (as the case may be) of a particular witness is really necessary.

(iv) Case management sessions

N-24

(a) The order of the evidence may have legitimately to be departed from. It will, however, be a useful for tool for monitoring the progress of the case. There should be periodic case management sessions, during which the judge engages the advocates upon a stock-taking exercise: asking, amongst other questions, "where are we going?" and "what is the relevance of the next three witnesses?". This will be a valuable means of keeping the case on track. Rule 3.10 of the Criminal Procedure Rules will again assist the judge.

(b) The judge may wish to consider issuing the occasional use of "case management notes" to the advocates, in order to set out the judge's tentative views on where the trial may be going off track, which areas of future evidence are relevant and which may have become irrelevant (*e.g.* because of concessions, admissions in cross-examination and so forth). Such notes from the judge plus written responses from the advocates can, cautiously used, provide a valuable focus for debate during the periodic case management reviews held during the course of the trial.

(v) Controlling prolix cross-examination

N-25

(a) Setting **rigid** time limits in advance for cross-examination is rarely appropriate—as experience has shown in civil cases; but a timetable is essential so that the judge can exercise control and so that there is a clear target to aim at for the completion of the evidence of each witness. Moreover the judge can and should indicate when cross-examination is irrelevant, unnecessary or time wasting. The judge may limit the time for further cross-examination of a particular witness.

(vi) Electronic presentation of evidence

N-26

(a) Electronic presentation of evidence (EPE) has the potential to save huge amounts of time in fraud and other complex criminal trials and should be used more widely.

(b) HMCS is providing facilities for the easier use of EPE with a standard audio visual facility. Effectively managed, the savings in court time achieved by EPE more than justify the cost.

(c) There should still be a core bundle of those documents to which frequent reference will be made during the trial. The jury may wish to mark that bundle or to refer back to particular pages as the evidence progresses. EPE can be used for presenting all documents not contained in the core bundle.

(d) Greater use of other modern forms of graphical presentations should be made wherever possible.

(vii) Use of interviews

The judge should consider extensive editing of self serving interviews, even when the defence **N-27** want the jury to hear them in their entirety; such interviews are not evidence of the truth of their contents but merely of the defendant's reaction to the allegation.

(viii) Jury management

(a) The jury should be informed as early as possible in the case as to what the issues are in a **N-28** manner directed by the Judge.
(b) The jury must be regularly updated as to the trial timetable and the progress of the trial, subject to warnings as to the predictability of the trial process.
(c) Legal argument should be heard at times that causes the least inconvenience to jurors.
(d) It is useful to consider with the advocates whether written directions should be given to the jury and, if so, in what form.

(ix) Maxwell hours

(a) Maxwell hours should only be permitted after careful consideration and consultation with **N-29** the Presiding Judge.
(b) Considerations in favour include:
  (i) legal argument can be accommodated without disturbing the jury;
  (ii) there is a better chance of a representative jury;
  (iii) time is made available to the judge, advocates and experts to do useful work in the afternoons
(c) Considerations against include:
  (i) the lengthening of trials and the consequent waste of court time;
  (ii) the desirability of making full use of the jury once they have arrived at court;
  (iii) shorter trials tend to diminish the need for special provisions *e.g.* there are fewer difficulties in empanelling more representative juries;
  (iv) they are unavailable if any defendant is in custody.
(d) It may often be the case that a maximum of one day of Maxwell hours a week is sufficient; if so, it should be timetabled in advance to enable all submissions by advocates, supported by skeleton arguments served in advance, to be dealt with in the period after 1:30 pm on that day.

(x) Livenote

If Livenote is used, it is important that all users continue to take a note of the evidence, otherwise **N-30** considerable time is wasted in detailed reading of the entire daily transcript.

7. Other issues

(i) Defence representation and defence costs

(a) Applications for change in representation in complex trials need special consideration; **N-31** the ruling of HH Judge Wakerley QC (as he then was) in *Asghar Ali* has been circulated by the JSB.
(b) Problems have arisen when the Legal Services Commission have declined to allow advocates or solicitors to do certain work; on occasions the matter has been raised with the judge managing or trying the case.
(c) The Legal Services Commission has provided guidance to judges on how they can obtain information from the LSC as to the reasons for their decisions; further information in relation to this can be obtained from *Nigel Field, Head of the Complex Crime Unit, Legal Services Commission, 29–37 Red Lion Street, London, WC1R 4PP.*

(ii) Assistance to the judge

Experience has shown that in some very heavy cases, the judge's burden can be substantially offset **N-32** with the provision of a judicial assistant or other support and assistance.

[The next paragraph is N-52.]

B. Disclosure of Unused Material in Criminal Cases

Foreword

N-52   [*Identical to the foreword to the Attorney-General's guidelines*: ante, § A-242a.]

Introduction

N-53   This protocol is prescribed for use by CPD IV Disclosure 22A: Disclosure of Unused Material. It is applicable in all the criminal courts of England and Wales, including the Crown Court, the Court Martial[1] and the magistrates' courts. It replaces the previous judicial document 'Disclosure: a Protocol for the Control and Management of Unused Material in the Crown Court'[2] and it also replaces section 4 'Disclosure' of the Lord Chief Justice's Protocol on the Control and Management of Heavy Fraud and Other Complex Criminal Cases, dated 22 March 2005.[3]

This protocol is intended to provide a central source of guidance for the judiciary, although that produced by the Attorney General also requires attention.

In summary, this judicial protocol sets out the principles to be applied to, and the importance of, disclosure; the expectations of the court and its role in disclosure, in particular in relation to case management; and the consequences if there is a failure by the prosecution or defence to comply with their obligations.

Readers should note that a review of disclosure in the magistrates' courts is currently being undertaken by H.H.J. Kinch Q.C. and the Chief Magistrate, on behalf of Lord Justice Gross, the Senior Presiding Judge. Amendments may therefore be made following the recommendations of that review, and in accordance with other forthcoming changes to the criminal justice system.

The importance of disclosure for fair trials

N-54   1. Disclosure remains one of the most important – as well as one of the most misunderstood and abused – of the procedures relating to criminal trials. Lord Justice Gross' review has reemphasised the need for all those involved to understand the statutory requirements and to undertake their roles with rigour, in a timely manner.

2. The House of Lords stated in *R. v. H.* [2004] UKHL 3; [2004] 2 A.C. 134; [2004] 2 Cr.App.R. 10:

> "Fairness ordinarily requires that any material held by the prosecution which weakens its case or strengthens that of the defendant, if not relied on as part of its formal case against the defendant, should be disclosed to the defence. Bitter experience has shown that miscarriages of justice may occur where such material is withheld from disclosure. The golden rule is that full disclosure of such material should be made" ([2004] 2 A.C. 134, at 147).

The Criminal Cases Review Commission has recently noted that failure to disclose material to the defence to which they were entitled remains the biggest single cause of miscarriages of justice.

3. However, it is also essential that the trial process is not overburdened or diverted by erroneous and inappropriate disclosure of unused prosecution material or by misconceived applications. Although the drafters of the Criminal Procedure and Investigations Act 1996 ('CPIA 1996') cannot have anticipated the vast increase in the amount of electronic material that has been generated in recent years, nevertheless the principles of that Act still hold true. Applications by the parties or decisions by judges based on misconceptions of the law or a general laxity of approach (however well-intentioned) which result in an improper application of the disclosure regime have, time and again, proved unnecessarily costly and have obstructed justice. As Lord Justice Gross noted, the burden of disclosure must not be allowed to render the prosecution of cases impracticable.

4. The overarching principle is that unused prosecution material will fall to be disclosed if, and only if, it satisfies the test for disclosure applicable to the proceedings in question, subject to any over-

---

[1] The timetables given here may vary in the Court Martial and reference should be made to the Criminal Procedure and Investigations Act 1996 (Application to the Armed Forces) Order 2009 and to any practice note issued by the Judge Advocate General.
[2] The previous judicial protocol was endorsed by the Court of Appeal in *R. v. K.* [2006] EWCA Crim. 724; [2006] 2 All ER 552 (Note).
[3] This protocol also replaces the Protocol for the Provision of Advance Information, Prosecution Evidence and Disclosure of Unused Material in the Magistrates' Courts, dated 12 May 2006, which was adopted as part of the Stop Delaying Justice initiative.

riding public interest considerations. The test for disclosure will depend on the date the criminal investigation in question commenced, as this will determine whether the common law disclosure regime applies, or either of the two disclosure regimes under the CPIA 1996.

5. The test for disclosure under section 3 of the CPIA 1996 as amended will be applicable in nearly every case and all those involved in the process will need to be familiar with it. Material fulfils the test if – but only if – it "might reasonably be considered capable of undermining the case for the prosecution … or of assisting the case for the accused."

6. The disclosure process must be led by the prosecution so as to trigger comprehensive defence engagement, supported by robust judicial case management. Active participation by the court in the disclosure process is a critical means of ensuring that delays and adjournments are avoided, given failures by the parties to comply with their obligations may disrupt and (in some cases) frustrate the course of justice.

Disclosure of unused material in criminal cases

7. The court should keep the timetable for prosecution and defence disclosure under review from **N-55** the first hearing. Judges should as a matter of course ask the parties to identify the issues in the case, and invite the parties to indicate whether further disclosure is sought, and on what topics. For example, it is not enough for the judge to rely on the content of the PCMH form. Proper completion of the disclosure process is a vital part of case preparation, and it may well affect the progress of the case. The court will expect disclosure to have been considered from the outset; the prosecution and defence advocates need to be aware of any potential problems and substantive difficulties should be explained to the judge; and the parties should propose a sensible timetable. Realism is preferable to optimistic but unachievable deadlines which may dislocate the court schedule and imperil the date of trial. It follows that judges should not impose deadlines for service of the case papers or disclosure until they are confident that the prosecution advocate has taken instructions from the individuals who are best placed to evaluate the work to be undertaken.

8. The advocates – both prosecution and defence – must be kept fully informed throughout the course of the proceedings as to any difficulties which may prevent them from complying with their disclosure obligations. When problems arise or come to light after directions have been given, the advocates should notify the court and the other party (or parties) immediately rather than waiting until the date set by the court for the service of the material is imminent or has passed, and they must provide the court with a suggested timetable in order to resolve the problem. The progress of the disclosure process should be reviewed at every hearing. There remains no basis in practice or law for counsel to counsel disclosure.

9. If there is a preliminary hearing the judge should seize the opportunity to impose an early timetable for disclosure and to identify any likely problems including as regards third party material and material that will require an application to the Family Court. In an appropriate case the court should consider holding a joint criminal/care directions hearing. See "Material held by Third Parties", from paragraph 44 below.

10. For the PCMH to be effective, the defence must have a proper opportunity to review the case papers and consider initial disclosure, with a view to preparing a properly completed defence statement which will inform the judge's conduct of the PCMH, and inform the prosecution of the matters required by sections 5, 6A and 6C of the CPIA. As the Court of Appeal noted in *R. v. Newell* [2012] EWCA Crim. 650; [2012] 2 Cr.App.R. 10, "a typed defence statement must be provided before the PCMH. If there is no defence statement by the time of the PCMH, then a judge will usually require the trial advocate to see that such a statement is provided and not proceed with the PCMH until that is done. In the ordinary case the trial advocate will be required to do that at the court and the PCMH resumed later in the day to avoid delay". There may be some instances when there will be a well-founded defence application to extend the 28-day time limit for serving a proper defence statement. In a proper case (but never routinely), it may be appropriate to put the PCMH back by a week or more, to enable an appropriate defence statement to be filed.

11. The defence statement can be admitted into evidence under section 6E(4) of the CPIA 1996. However, information included on the PCMH form (which is primarily an administrative form) will not usually be admitted in evidence when the defence advocate has complied with the letter and the spirit of the Criminal Procedure Rules.[4] Introducing the PCMH form (or part of it) during the trial is likely to be an exceptional event. The status of the trial preparation form in the magistrates' court is somewhat different, as discussed below.

12. The court should not extend time lightly or as a matter of course. If an extension is sought, it ought to be accompanied by an appropriate explanation. For instance, it is not sufficient for the prosecutor merely to say that the investigator has delivered the papers late: the underlying reasons

---

[4] *R. v. Newell* [2012] EWCA Crim. 650; [2012] 2 Cr.App.R. 10.

are to be provided to the court. The same applies if the defence statement is delayed. Whichever party is at fault, realistic proposals for service are to be set out.

13. Judges should not allow the prosecution to avoid their statutory responsibility for reviewing the unused material by the expedient of permitting the defence to have access to (or providing the defence with copies of) the material listed in the schedules of non-sensitive unused prosecution material irrespective of whether it satisfies, wholly or in part, the relevant test for disclosure. Additionally, it is for the prosecutor to decide on the manner of disclosure, and it does not have to mirror the form in which the information was originally recorded. Rose L.J. gave guidance on case management issues in this context in *R. v. CPS (Interlocutory Application under sections 35/36 CPIA)* [2005] EWCA Crim. 2342. Allowing the defence to inspect items that fulfil the disclosure test is also a valid means of providing disclosure.

14. The larger and more complex the case, the more important it is for the prosecution to adhere to the overarching principle and ensure that sufficient prosecution attention and resources are allocated to the task. Handing the defendant the "keys to the warehouse" has been the cause of many gross abuses in the past, resulting in considerable expenditure by the defence without any material benefit to the course of justice. The circumstances relating to large and complex cases are outlined below.

15. The court will require the defence to engage and assist in the early identification of the real issues in the case and, particularly in the larger and more complex cases, to contribute to the search terms to be used for, and the parameters of, the review of any electronically held material (which can be very considerable). Any defence criticisms of the prosecution approach to disclosure should be timely and reasoned; there is no place for disclosure "ambushes" or for late or uninformative defence statements. Admissions should be used so far as possible to narrow the real issues in dispute.

16. A constructive approach to disclosure is a necessary part of professional best practice, for the defence and prosecution. This does not undermine the defendant's legitimate interests, it accords with his or her obligations under the rules and it ensures that all the relevant material is provided. Delays and failures by the prosecution and the defence are equally damaging to a timely, fair and efficient trial, and judges should be vigilant in preventing and addressing abuses. Accordingly, whenever there are potential failings by either the defence or the prosecution, judges, in exercising appropriate oversight of disclosure, should carefully investigate the suggested default and give timely directions.

17. In the Crown Court, the defence statement is to be served within 28 days of the date when the prosecution complies with its duty of initial disclosure (or purports to do so) and whenever section 5(5) of the CPIA applies to the proceedings, and the defence statement must comply with section 6A of the CPIA. Service of the defence statement is a most important stage in the disclosure process, and timely service is necessary to facilitate proper consideration of the disclosure issues well in advance of the trial date. Judges expect a defence statement to contain a clear and detailed exposition of the issues of fact and law. Defence statements that merely rehearse the suggestion that the defendant is innocent do not comply with the requirements of the CPIA.

18. The prosecutor should consider the defence statement carefully and promptly provide a copy to the disclosure officer, to assist the prosecution in its continuing disclosure obligations. The court expects the Crown to identify any suggested deficiencies in the defence statement, and to draw these to the attention of the defence and the court; in particular in large and complex cases, it will assist the court if this is in writing. Although the prosecution's ability to request, and the court's jurisdiction to give, an adverse inference direction under section 11 of CPIA is not contingent on the prosecution having earlier identified any suggested deficiencies, nevertheless the prosecutor must provide a timely written explanation of its position.

19. Judges should examine the defence statement with care to ensure that it complies with the formalities required by the CPIA. As stated in *R. v. H.* (*supra*) (para. 35):

> "If material does not weaken the prosecution case or strengthen that of the defendant, there is no requirement to disclose it. For this purpose the parties' respective cases should not be restrictively analysed. But they must be carefully analysed, to ascertain the specific facts the prosecution seek to establish and the specific grounds on which the charges are resisted. The trial process is not well served if the defence are permitted to make general and unspecified allegations and then seek far-reaching disclosure in the hope that material may turn up to make them good. Neutral material or material damaging to the defendant need not be disclosed and should not be brought to the attention of the court."

20. If no defence statement – or an inadequate defence statement – is served within the relevant time limits, the judge should investigate the position. At every PCMH where there is no defence statement, including those where an extension has been given, or the time for filing has not yet expired, the defence should be warned in appropriate terms that pursuant to section 6E(2) of the

CPIA an adverse inference may be drawn during the trial, and this result is likely if there is no justification for the deficiency. The fact that a warning has been given should be noted.

21. An adverse inference may be drawn under section 11 of the CPIA if the accused fails to discharge his or her disclosure obligations. Whenever the amended CPIA regime applies, the prosecution may comment on any failure in defence disclosure (except where the failure relates to a point of law) without leave of the court, but counsel should use a measure of judgment as to whether it is wise to embark on cross-examination about such a failure.[5] If the accused is cross-examined about discrepancies between his evidence and his defence statement, or if adverse comment is made, the judge must give appropriate guidance to the jury.[6]

22. In order to secure a fair trial, it is vital that the prosecution is mindful of its continuing duty of disclosure. Once the defence statement has been received, the Crown must review disclosure in the light of the issues identified in the defence statement. In cases of complexity, the following steps are then likely to be necessary:

    i. service by the prosecution of any further material due to the defence following receipt of the defence statement;

    ii. any defence request to the prosecution for service of additional specific items; as discussed below, these requests must be justified by reference to the defence statement and they should be submitted on the section 8 form;

    iii. prosecution response to the defence request;

    iv. if the defence considers that disclosable items are still outstanding, a section 8 application should be made using the appropriate form.

23. It follows that all requests by the defence to the prosecution for disclosure should be made on the section 8 application form, even if no hearing is sought in the first instance. Discussion and co-operation between the parties outside of court is encouraged in order to ensure that the court is only asked to issue a ruling when strictly necessary. However, use of the section 8 form will ensure that focussed requests are clearly set out in one place.

24. The judge should set a date as part of the timetabling exercise by which any application under section 8 is to be made, if this appears to be a likely eventuality.

25. The court will require the section 8 application to be served on the prosecution well in advance of the hearing – indeed, prior to requesting the hearing – to enable the Crown to identify and serve any items that meet the test for disclosure.

26. Service of a defence statement is an essential precondition for an application under section 8, and applications should not be heard or directions for disclosure issued in the absence of a properly completed statement (see Part 22 of the Criminal Procedure Rules). In particular, blanket orders in this context are inconsistent with the statutory framework for disclosure laid down by the CPIA and the decision of the House of Lords in *R. v. H.* (*supra*). It follows that defence requests for disclosure of particular pieces of unused prosecution material which are not referable to any issue in the case identified in the defence statement should be rejected.

27. Judges must ensure that defendants are not prejudiced on account of the failures of their lawyers, and, when necessary, the professions should be reminded that if justice is to be done, and if disclosure is to be dealt with fairly in accordance with the law, a full and careful defence statement and a reasoned approach to section 8 applications are essential. In exploring the adequacy of the defence statement, a judge should always ask what the issues are and upon what matters of fact the defendant intends to rely[7] and on what matters of fact the defendant takes issue.

Listing

28. Sufficient time is necessary for the judge properly to undertake the PCMH, and this is a **N-56** paramount consideration when listing cases. Unless the court is able to sit early, judges who are part heard on trials are probably not best placed to conduct PCMHs.

29. Cases that raise particularly difficult issues of disclosure should be referred to the resident judge for directions (unless a trial judge has been allocated) and, for trials of real complexity, the trial judge should be identified at an early stage, prior to the PCMH if possible. Listing officers, working in consultation with the resident judge and, if allocated, the trial judge, should ensure that sufficient time is allowed for judges to prepare and deal with prosecution and defence applications relating to disclosure, particularly in the more complex cases.

Magistrates' courts (including the youth court)

30. The principles relating to disclosure apply equally in the magistrates' courts. It follows that **N-57**

---

[5] *R. v. Essa* [2009] EWCA Crim. 43, para. 22.
[6] *R. v. Hanyes* [2011] EWCA Crim. 3281.
[7] *R. v. Rochford* [2010] EWCA Crim. 1928; [2011] 1 Cr.App.R. 11.

whilst disclosure of unused material in compliance with the statutory test is undoubtedly essential in order to achieve justice, it is critical that summary trials are not delayed or made over-complicated by misconceived applications for, or inappropriate disclosure of, prosecution material.

31. Magistrates will rely on their legal advisers for guidance, and the latter should draw the attention of the parties and the court to the statutory provisions and the applicable case law. Cases raising disclosure issues of particular complexity should be referred to a District Judge (Magistrates' Courts), if available.

32. Although service of a defence statement is voluntary for summary trials (s.6 CPIA), the defendant cannot make an application for specific disclosure under section 8 CPIA, and the court cannot make any orders in this regard, unless a proper defence statement has been provided. It follows that although providing a defence statement is not mandatory, it remains a critical stage in the disclosure process. If disclosure issues are to be raised by the defence, a defence statement must be served well in advance of the trial date. Any section 8 application must be made in strict compliance with the rules.

33. The case-management forms used in the magistrates' courts fulfil some of the functions of a defence statement, and the prosecution must take into account the information provided as to the defence case when conducting its on-going review of unused material. As the Court of Appeal noted in *R. v. Newell (supra)*, admissions can be made in the trial preparation form and the defence is able to identify the matters that are not in issue. Admissions made in these circumstances may be admissible during the trial. However, other information on the form that does not come within the section relating to admissions should be treated in the same way as the contents of a PCMH form in the Crown Court and it should not generally be introduced as part of the evidence at trial. However, the contents of the trial preparation form do not replace the need to serve a defence statement if the defendant seeks to apply for disclosure under section 8 CPIA.

34. The standard directions require that any defence statement is to be served within 14 days of the date upon which the prosecution has complied with, or purported to comply with, the duty to provide initial disclosure. There may be some instances when there will be a wellfounded defence application to extend the 14-day time limit for serving the defence statement. These applications must be made in accordance with the Criminal Procedure Rules, in writing and before the time limit expires.

35. Although CCTV footage frequently causes difficulties, it is to be treated as any other category of unused material and it should only be disclosed if the material meets the appropriate test for disclosure under the CPIA. The defence should either be provided with copies of the sections of the CCTV or afforded an opportunity to view them. If the prosecution refuses to disclose CCTV material that the defence considers to be discloseable, the courts should not make standard or general directions requiring the prosecutor to disclose material of this kind in the absence of an application under section 8. When potentially relevant CCTV footage is not in the possession of the police, the guidance in relation to third party material will apply, although the police remain under a duty to pursue all reasonable lines of inquiry, including those leading away from a suspect, whether or not defence requests are made.

36. The previous convictions of witnesses and any disciplinary findings against officers in the case are frequently discloseable and care should be taken to disclose them as appropriate. Documents such as crime reports or records of emergency calls should not be provided on a routine basis, for instance as part of a bundle of disclosed documents, irrespective of whether the material satisfies the appropriate test for disclosure. Defence advocates should not request this material in standard or routine correspondence, and instead focussed consideration should be given to the circumstances of the particular case. Unjustified requests for disclosure of material of this kind are routinely made, frequently leading to unnecessary delays and adjournments. The prosecution should always consider whether the request is properly made out.

37. The supervisory role of the courts is critical in this context, and magistrates must guard against granting unnecessary adjournments and issuing unjustified directions.

Large and complex cases in the Crown Court

38. Disclosure is a particular problem with the larger and more complex cases, which require a scrupulous approach by the parties and robust case management by the judiciary. If possible, the trial judge should be identified at the outset.

39. The legal representatives need to fulfil their duties in this context with care and efficiency; they should co-operate with the other party (or parties) and the court; and the judge and the other party (or parties) are to be informed of any difficulties, as soon as they arise. The court should be provided with an up-to-date timetable for disclosure whenever there are material changes in this regard. A disclosure-management document, or similar, prepared by the prosecution will be of particular assistance to the court in large and complex cases.

40. Judges should be prepared to give early guidance as to the prosecution's approach to disclosure, thereby ensuring early engagement by the defence.

41. Cases of this nature frequently include large volumes of digitally stored material. The Attorney General's 2011 guidance (now included as an annex to the Attorney General's Guidelines on Disclosure 2013) is of particular relevance and assistance in this context.

42. Applications for witness anonymity orders require particular attention; as the Court of Appeal noted in *R. v. Mayers* [2008] EWCA Crim. 2989; [2009] 1 Cr.App.R. 30, in making such an application, the prosecution's obligations of disclosure "go much further than the ordinary duties of disclosure".

43. If the judge considers that there are reasonable grounds to doubt the good faith of the investigation, he or she will be concerned to see that there has been independent and effective appraisal of the documents contained in the disclosure schedule and that its contents are adequate. In appropriate cases where this issue has arisen and there are grounds which show there is a real issue, consideration should be given to receiving evidence on oath from the senior investigating officer at an early case management hearing.

Material held by third parties

44. Where material is held by a third party such as a local authority, a social services department, **N-59** hospital or business, the investigators and the prosecution may need to make enquiries of the third party, with a view to inspecting the material and assessing whether the relevant test for disclosure is met and determining whether any or all of the material should be retained, recorded and, in due course, disclosed to the accused. If access by the prosecution is granted, the investigators and the prosecution will need to establish whether the custodian of the material intends to raise PII issues, as a result of which the material may have to be placed before the court for a decision. This does not obviate the need for the defence to conduct its own enquiries as appropriate. Speculative enquiries without any proper basis in relation to third party material – whether by the prosecution or the defence – are to be discouraged, and, in appropriate cases, the court will consider making an order for costs where an application is clearly unmeritorious and misconceived.

45. The 2013 Protocol and Good Practice Model on Disclosure of Information in Cases of Alleged Child Abuse and Linked Criminal and Care Directions Hearings has recently been published. It provides a framework and timetable for the police and CPS to obtain discloseable material from local authorities, and for applications to be made to the Family Court. It is applicable to all cases of alleged child abuse where the child is aged 17 years or under. It is not binding on local authorities, but it does represent best practice and therefore should be consulted in all such cases. Delays in obtaining this type of material have led to unacceptable delays to trials involving particularly vulnerable witnesses and every effort must be made to ensure that all discloseable material is identified at an early stage so that any necessary applications can be made and the defence receive material to which they are entitled in good time.

46. There is no specific procedure for disclosure of material held by third parties in criminal proceedings, although the procedure established under section 2 of the Criminal Procedure (Attendance of Witnesses) Act 1965 or section 97 of the Magistrates' Courts Act 1980 is often used for this purpose. Where the third party in question declines to allow inspection of the material, or requires the prosecution to obtain an order before providing copies, the prosecutor will need to consider whether it is appropriate to obtain a witness summons under either section 2 of the Criminal Procedure (Attendance of Witnesses) Act 1965 or section 97 of the Magistrates' Courts Act 1980. Part 28 of the Criminal Procedure Rules and paragraphs 3.5 and 3.6 of the Code of Practice under the CPIA 1996 should be followed.

47. Applications for third party disclosure must identify the documents that are sought and provide full details of why they are discloseable. This is particularly relevant when access is sought to the medical records of those who allege they are victims of crime. It should be appreciated that a duty to assert confidentiality may arise when a third party receives a request for disclosure, or the right to privacy may be claimed under Article 8 of the ECHR (see in particular Crim. P.R., Pt 28.6). Victims do not waive the confidentiality of their medical records, or their right to privacy under Article 8 of the ECHR, by making a complaint against the accused. The court, as a public authority, must ensure that any interference with the right to privacy under Article 8 is in accordance with the law, and is necessary in pursuit of a legitimate public interest. General and unspecified requests to trawl through such records should be refused. Confidentiality rests with the subject of the material, not with the authority holding it. The subject is entitled to service of the application and has the right to make representations: Criminal Procedure Rule 22.3 and *R. (B.) v. Stafford Combined Court* [2006] EWHC 1645 (Admin.); [2006] 2 Cr.App.R. 34. The 2013 Protocol and Good Practice Model at paragraph 13 should be followed. It is likely that the judge will need to issue directions when issues of this kind are raised (*e.g.* whether enquiries with the third party are likely to be appropriate; who is to make the request; what material is to be sought, and from whom; and a timetable should be set).

48. The judge should consider whether to take any steps if a third party fails, or refuses, to comply with a request for disclosure, including suggesting that either of the parties pursue the request and if necessary, make an application for a witness summons. In these circumstances, the court will need to set an appropriate timetable for compliance with Part 28 of the rules. Any failure to comply with the timetable must immediately be referred back to the court for further directions, although a hearing will not always be necessary. Generally, it may be appropriate for the defence to pursue requests of this kind when the prosecution, for good reason, decline to do so and the court will need to ensure that this procedure does not delay the trial.

49. There are very limited circumstances in which information relating to Family Court proceedings (*e.g.* where there have been care proceedings in relation to a child who has complained to the police of mistreatment) may be communicated without a court order: see the Family Procedure Rules 12.73. Reference should be made to the 2013 Protocol and Good Practice Model. In most circumstances, a court order will be required and paragraph 11 of the Protocol which sets out how an application should be made should be followed.

Other government departments

N-60
50. Material held by other government departments or other Crown agencies will not be prosecution material for the purposes of section 3(2) or section 8(4) of the CPIA if it has not been inspected, recorded and retained during the course of the relevant criminal investigation. The *CPIA Code of Practice and the Attorney General's Guidelines on Disclosure*, however, impose a duty upon the investigators and the prosecution to pursue all reasonable lines of inquiry and that may involve seeking disclosure from the relevant body.

International matters

N-61
51. The obligations of the Crown in relation to relevant third-party material held overseas are as set out in *R. v. Flook* [2009] EWCA Crim. 682; [2010] 1 Cr.App.R. 30: the Crown must pursue reasonable lines of enquiry and if it appears there is relevant material, all reasonable steps must be taken to obtain it, whether formally or otherwise. To a great extent, the success of these enquiries will depend on the laws of the country where the material is held and the facts of the individual case. It needs to be recognised that when the material is held in a country outside of the European Union, the power of the Crown and the courts of England and Wales to obtain third-party material may well be limited. If informal requests are unsuccessful, the avenues are limited to the Crime (International Co-operation) Act 2003 and any applicable international conventions. It cannot, in any sense, be guaranteed that a request to a foreign government, court or body will produce the material sought. Additionally, some foreign authorities may be prepared to show the material in question to the investigating officers, whilst refusing to allow the material to be copied or otherwise made available.

52. As the Court of Appeal observed in *R. v. Khyam* [2008] EWCA Crim. 1612; [2009] 1 Cr.App.R.(S.) 77:

"The prosecuting authorities in this jurisdiction simply cannot compel authorities in a foreign country to acknowledge, let alone comply with, our disclosure principles" (at [37]).

The obligation is therefore to take reasonable steps. Whether the Crown has complied with that obligation is for the courts to judge in each case.

53. It is, therefore, important that the prosecution sets out the position clearly in writing, including any inability to inspect or retrieve any material that potentially ought to be disclosed, along with the steps that have been taken.

Applications for non-disclosure in the public interest

N-62
54. Applications in this context, whenever possible, should be considered by the trial judge. The House of Lords in *R. v. H.* (*supra*) has provided useful guidance as to the proper approach to be applied (para. [36]):

"When any issue of derogation from the golden rule of full disclosure comes before it, the court must address a series of questions:

(1) What is the material which the prosecution seek to withhold? This must be considered by the court in detail.

(2) Is the material such as may weaken the prosecution case or strengthen that of the defence? If No, disclosure should not be ordered. If Yes, full disclosure should (subject to (3), (4) and (5) below) be ordered.

(3) Is there a real risk of serious prejudice to an important public interest (and, if so, what) if full disclosure of the material is ordered? If No, full disclosure should be ordered.

(4) If the answer to (2) and (3) is Yes, can the defendant's interest be protected without disclosure or disclosure be ordered to an extent or in a way which will give adequate protection to the public interest in question and also afford adequate protection to the interests of the defence?

> This question requires the court to consider, with specific reference to the material which the prosecution seek to withhold and the facts of the case and the defence as disclosed, whether the prosecution should formally admit what the defence seek to establish or whether disclosure short of full disclosure may be ordered. This may be done in appropriate cases by the preparation of summaries or extracts of evidence, or the provision of documents in an edited or anonymised form, provided the documents supplied are in each instance approved by the judge. In appropriate cases the appointment of special counsel may be a necessary step to ensure that the contentions of the prosecution are tested and the interests of the defendant protected (see para. [22] above). In cases of exceptional difficulty the court may require the appointment of special counsel to ensure a correct answer to questions (2) and (3) as well as (4).

(5) Do the measures proposed in answer to (4) represent the minimum derogation necessary to protect the public interest in question? If No, the court should order such greater disclosure as will represent the minimum derogation from the golden rule of full disclosure.

(6) If limited disclosure is ordered pursuant to (4) or (5), may the effect be to render the trial process, viewed as a whole, unfair to the defendant? If Yes, then fuller disclosure should be ordered even if this leads or may lead the prosecution to discontinue the proceedings so as to avoid having to make disclosure.

(7) If the answer to (6) when first given is No, does that remain the correct answer as the trial unfolds, evidence is adduced and the defence advanced?

It is important that the answer to (6) should not be treated as a final, once-and-for-all, answer but as a provisional answer which the court must keep under review."

55. In this context, the following matters are to be emphasised:

    a. the procedure for making applications to the court is set out in the Criminal Procedure Rules, Pt 22;

    b. when the PII application is a Type 1 or Type 2 application, proper notice to the defence is necessary to enable the accused to make focused submissions to the court and the notice should be as specific as the nature of the material allows; it is appreciated that in some cases only the generic nature of the material can be identified; in some wholly exceptional cases (Type 3 cases) it may be justified to give no notice at all; the judge should always ask the prosecution to justify the form of notice (or the decision to give no notice at all);

    c. the prosecution should be alert to the possibility of disclosing a statement in a redacted form by, for example, simply removing personal details; this may obviate the need for a PII application, unless the redacted material satisfies the test for disclosure;

    d. except when the material is very short (for instance only a few sheets), or for reasons of sensitivity, the prosecution should supply securely sealed copies to the judge in advance, together with a short statement explaining the relevance of each document, how it satisfies the disclosure test and why it is suggested that disclosure would result in a real risk of serious prejudice to an important public interest; in undertaking this task, the use of merely formulaic expressions is to be discouraged; in any case of complexity a schedule of the material should be provided, identifying the particular objection to disclosure in relation to each item, and leaving a space for the judge's decision;

    e. the application, even if held in private or in secret, should be recorded; the judge should give some short statement of reasons; this is often best done document by document as the hearing proceeds;

    f. the recording, copies of the judge's orders (and any copies of the material retained by the court) should be clearly identified, securely sealed and kept in the court building in a safe or locked cabinet consistent with its security classification, and there should be a proper register of the contents; arrangements should be made for the return of the material to the prosecution once the case is concluded and the time for an appeal has elapsed.

Conclusion

56. Historically, disclosure was viewed essentially as being a matter to be resolved between the par- **N-63**

ties, and the court only became engaged if a particular issue or complaint was raised. That perception is now wholly out of date. The regime established under the Criminal Justice Act 2003 and the Criminal Procedure Rules gives judges the power – indeed, it imposes a duty on the judiciary – actively to manage disclosure in every case. The efficient, effective and timely resolution of these issues is a critical element in meeting the overriding objective of the Criminal Procedure Rules of dealing with cases justly.

APPENDIX P
The Criminal Procedure Rules 2015

Introduction

In accordance with the Criminal Procedure Rule Committee's previously stated intention (as to which, see § 2-205 in the main work), the Criminal Procedure Rules 2015 (S.I. 2015 No. 1490) consolidate the Criminal Procedure Rules 2014 (S.I. 2015 No. 1610), as amended by the Criminal Procedure (Amendment) Rules 2015 (S.I. 2015 No. 13) and the Criminal Procedure (Amendment No. 2) Rules 2015 (S.I. 2015 No. 646), introduce further amendments and rearrange the rules into a more logical order and with no missing parts, so that the parts are now numbered 1 to 50, rather than 1 to 76 as they were in the 2014 rules, but with a number of "empty" parts. The 2015 rules come into force on October 5, 2015, and they are set out below (apart from Parts 7, 13, 30 and 50). The following table shows where parts of the 2014 rules are now to be found, but it should be noted that new Parts 23 and 27 have been substantially revised as compared with their predecessor provisions. ★**P-1**

2014 rules Part number	*2015 rules Part number*
1	1
2	2 & 46
3	3
4	4
5	5
6	47
7	7
8	12
9	9
10	8
12	11
14	10
16	6
17	50
18	13
19	14
22	15
27	16
28	17
29	18
31	23
32	49
33	19
34	20
35	21
36	22
37	24
38	25
39	26
40	27
41	27
42	28
44	32

Criminal Procedure Rules 2015 (S.I. 2015 No. 1490)

ARRANGEMENT OF RULES

Parts

General matters

Costs

45. Costs

Other proceedings

46. Representatives

47. Investigation of orders and warrants

48. Contempt of court

49. International co-operation

50. Extradition

PART 1

THE OVERRIDING OBJECTIVE

The overriding objective

★**P-3**   **1.1.**—(1) The overriding objective of this procedural code is that criminal cases be dealt with justly.
(2) Dealing with a criminal case justly includes—

(a) acquitting the innocent and convicting the guilty;

(b) dealing with the prosecution and the defence fairly;

(c) recognising the rights of a defendant, particularly those under Article 6 of the European Convention on Human Rights;

(d) respecting the interests of witnesses, victims and jurors and keeping them informed of the progress of the case;

(e) dealing with the case efficiently and expeditiously;

(f) ensuring that appropriate information is available to the court when bail and sentence are considered; and

(g) dealing with the case in ways that take into account—

(i) the gravity of the offence alleged,

(ii) the complexity of what is in issue,

(iii) the severity of the consequences for the defendant and others affected, and

(iv) the needs of other cases.

The duty of the participants in a criminal case

★**P-4**   **1.2.**—(1) Each participant, in the conduct of each case, must—

(a) prepare and conduct the case in accordance with the overriding objective;

(b) comply with these rules, practice directions and directions made by the court; and

(c) at once inform the court and all parties of any significant failure (whether or not that participant is responsible for that failure) to take any procedural step required by these rules, any practice direction or any direction of the court. A failure is significant if it might hinder the court in furthering the overriding objective.

(2) Anyone involved in any way with a criminal case is a participant in its conduct for the purposes of this rule.

The application by the court of the overriding objective

★**P-5**   **1.3.** The court must further the overriding objective in particular when—

(a) exercising any power given to it by legislation (including these rules);

(b) applying any practice direction; or

(c) interpreting any rule or practice direction.

PART 2

UNDERSTANDING AND APPLYING THE RULES

When the rules apply

★**P-6**   **2.1.**—(1) In general, Criminal Procedure Rules apply—

(a) in all criminal cases in magistrates' courts and in the Crown Court;

(b) in extradition cases in the High Court; and

(c)   in all cases in the criminal division of the Court of Appeal.

(2) If a rule applies only in one or some of those courts, the rule makes that clear.

(3) These rules apply on and after 5th October, 2015, but—

(a)   unless the court otherwise directs, they do not affect a right or duty existing under the Criminal Procedure Rules 2014; and

(b)   unless the High Court otherwise directs, Section 3 of Part 50 (extradition - appeal to the High Court) does not apply to a case in which notice of an appeal was given before 6th October, 2014.

(4) In a case in which a request for extradition was received by a relevant authority in the United Kingdom on or before 31st December, 2003—

(a)   the rules in Part 50 (extradition) do not apply; and

(b)   the rules in Part 17 of the Criminal Procedure Rules 2012 (extradition) continue to apply as if those rules had not been revoked.

Definitions

2.2.—(1) In these rules, unless the context makes it clear that something different is meant: ★**P-7**

"advocate" means a person who is entitled to exercise a right of audience in the court under section 13 of the Legal Services Act 2007;

"business day" means any day except Saturday, Sunday, Christmas Day, Boxing Day, Good Friday, Easter Monday or a bank holiday;

"court" means a tribunal with jurisdiction over criminal cases. It includes a judge, recorder, District Judge (Magistrates' Court), lay justice and, when exercising their judicial powers, the Registrar of Criminal Appeals, a justices' clerk or assistant clerk;

"court officer" means the appropriate member of the staff of a court;

"justices' legal adviser" means a justices' clerk or an assistant to a justices' clerk;

"legal representative" means:

(i)   the person for the time being named as a party's representative in any legal aid representation order made under section 16 of the Legal Aid, Sentencing and Punishment of Offenders Act 2012, or

(ii)   subject to that, the person named as a party's representative in any notice for the time being given under rule 46.2 (notice of appointment or change of legal representative), provided that person is entitled to conduct litigation in the court under section 13 of the Legal Services Act 2007;

"live link" means an arrangement by which a person can see and hear, and be seen and heard by, the court when that person is not in court;

"Practice Direction" means the Lord Chief Justice's Criminal Practice Directions, as amended, and "Criminal Costs Practice Direction" means the Lord Chief Justice's Practice Direction (Costs in Criminal Proceedings), as amended;

"public interest ruling" means a ruling about whether it is in the public interest to disclose prosecution material under sections 3(6), 7A(8) or 8(5) of the Criminal Procedure and Investigations Act 1996; and

"Registrar" means the Registrar of Criminal Appeals or a court officer acting with the Registrar's authority.

(2) Definitions of some other expressions are in the rules in which they apply.

References to legislation, including these rules

2.3.—(1) In these rules, where a rule refers to an Act of Parliament or to subordinate legislation by   ★**P-8**
title and year, subsequent references to that Act or to that legislation in the rule are shortened: so, for example, after a reference to the Criminal Procedure and Investigations Act 1996 that Act is called "the 1996 Act"; and after a reference to the Criminal Procedure and Investigations Act 1996 (Defence Disclosure Time Limits) Regulations 2011 those Regulations are called "the 2011 Regulations".

(2) In the courts to which these rules apply—

(a)   unless the context makes it clear that something different is meant, a reference to the Criminal Procedure Rules, without reference to a year, is a reference to the Criminal Procedure Rules in force at the date on which the event concerned occurs or occurred;

(b)   a reference to the Criminal Procedure Rules may be abbreviated to "CrimPR"; and

(c)   a reference to a part or rule in the Criminal Procedure Rules may be abbreviated to, for example, "CrimPR Part 3" or "CrimPR 3.5".

PART 3

CASE MANAGEMENT

General Rules

When this part applies

★P-9   **3.1.**—(1) Rules 3.1 to 3.12 apply to the management of each case in a magistrates' court and in the Crown Court (including an appeal to the Crown Court) until the conclusion of that case.

(2) Rules 3.13 to 3.26 apply where—

    (a) the defendant is sent to the Crown Court for trial;

    (b) a High Court or Crown Court judge gives permission to serve a draft indictment; or

    (c) the Court of Appeal orders a retrial.

The duty of the court

★P-10   **3.2.**—(1) The court must further the overriding objective by actively managing the case.

(2) Active case management includes—

    (a) the early identification of the real issues;

    (b) the early identification of the needs of witnesses;

    (c) achieving certainty as to what must be done, by whom, and when, in particular by the early setting of a timetable for the progress of the case;

    (d) monitoring the progress of the case and compliance with directions;

    (e) ensuring that evidence, whether disputed or not, is presented in the shortest and clearest way;

    (f) discouraging delay, dealing with as many aspects of the case as possible on the same occasion, and avoiding unnecessary hearings;

    (g) encouraging the participants to co-operate in the progression of the case; and

    (h) making use of technology.

(3) The court must actively manage the case by giving any direction appropriate to the needs of that case as early as possible.

The duty of the parties

★P-11   **3.3.**—(1) Each party must—

    (a) actively assist the court in fulfilling its duty under rule 3.2, without or if necessary with a direction; and

    (b) apply for a direction if needed to further the overriding objective.

(2) Active assistance for the purposes of this rule includes—

    (a) at the beginning of the case, communication between the prosecutor and the defendant at the first available opportunity and in any event no later than the beginning of the day of the first hearing;

    (b) after that, communication between the parties and with the court officer until the conclusion of the case;

    (c) by such communication establishing, among other things—

        (i) whether the defendant is likely to plead guilty or not guilty,

        (ii) what is agreed and what is likely to be disputed,

        (iii) what information, or other material, is required by one party of another, and why, and

        (iv) what is to be done, by whom, and when (without or if necessary with a direction); and

    (d) reporting on that communication to the court—

        (i) at the first hearing, and

        (ii) after that, as directed by the court.

Case progression officers and their duties

★P-12   **3.4.**—(1) At the beginning of the case each party must, unless the court otherwise directs—

    (a) nominate someone responsible for progressing that case; and

    (b) tell other parties and the court who that is and how to contact that person.

(2) In fulfilling its duty under rule 3.2, the court must where appropriate—

    (a) nominate a court officer responsible for progressing the case; and

    (b) make sure the parties know who that is and how to contact that court officer.

(3) In this part a person nominated under this rule is called a case progression officer.

(4) A case progression officer must—

    (a) monitor compliance with directions;

    (b) make sure that the court is kept informed of events that may affect the progress of that case;

    (c) make sure that he or she can be contacted promptly about the case during ordinary business hours;

    (d) act promptly and reasonably in response to communications about the case; and

    (e) if he or she will be unavailable, appoint a substitute to fulfil his or her duties and inform the other case progression officers.

The court's case management powers

3.5.—(1) In fulfilling its duty under rule 3.2 the court may give any direction and take any step ★**P-13** actively to manage a case unless that direction or step would be inconsistent with legislation, including these rules.

(2) In particular, the court may—

    (a) nominate a judge, magistrate or justices' legal adviser to manage the case;

    (b) give a direction on its own initiative or on application by a party;

    (c) ask or allow a party to propose a direction;

    (d) for the purpose of giving directions, receive applications and representations by letter, by telephone or by any other means of electronic communication, and conduct a hearing by such means;

    (e) give a direction—

        (i) at a hearing, in public or in private, or

        (ii) without a hearing;

    (f) fix, postpone, bring forward, extend, cancel or adjourn a hearing;

    (g) shorten or extend (even after it has expired) a time limit fixed by a direction;

    (h) require that issues in the case should be—

        (i) identified in writing,

        (ii) determined separately, and decide in what order they will be determined; and

    (i) specify the consequences of failing to comply with a direction.

(3) A magistrates' court may give a direction that will apply in the Crown Court if the case is to continue there.

(4) The Crown Court may give a direction that will apply in a magistrates' court if the case is to continue there.

(5) Any power to give a direction under this part includes a power to vary or revoke that direction.

(6) If a party fails to comply with a rule or a direction, the court may—

    (a) fix, postpone, bring forward, extend, cancel or adjourn a hearing;

    (b) exercise its powers to make a costs order; and

    (c) impose such other sanction as may be appropriate.

Application to vary a direction

3.6.—(1) A party may apply to vary a direction if— ★**P-14**

    (a) the court gave it without a hearing;

    (b) the court gave it at a hearing in that party's absence; or

    (c) circumstances have changed.

(2) A party who applies to vary a direction must—

    (a) apply as soon as practicable after becoming aware of the grounds for doing so; and

    (b) give as much notice to the other parties as the nature and urgency of the application permits.

Agreement to vary a time limit fixed by a direction

3.7.—(1) The parties may agree to vary a time limit fixed by a direction, but only if— ★**P-15**

    (a) the variation will not—

        (i) affect the date of any hearing that has been fixed, or

        (ii) significantly affect the progress of the case in any other way;

    (b) the court has not prohibited variation by agreement; and

    (c) the court's case progression officer is promptly informed.

(2) The court's case progression officer must refer the agreement to the court if in doubt that the condition in paragraph (1)(a) is satisfied.

Court's power to vary requirements under this part

★**P-16**   3.8.—(1) The court may—

(a)   shorten or extend (even after it has expired) a time limit set by this part; and

(b)   allow an application or representations to be made orally.

(2) A person who wants an extension of time must—

(a)   apply when serving the application or representations for which it is needed; and

(b)   explain the delay.

Case preparation and progression

★**P-17**   3.9.—(1) At every hearing, if a case cannot be concluded there and then the court must give directions so that it can be concluded at the next hearing or as soon as possible after that.

(2) At every hearing the court must, where relevant—

(a)   if the defendant is absent, decide whether to proceed nonetheless;

(b)   take the defendant's plea (unless already done) or if no plea can be taken then find out whether the defendant is likely to plead guilty or not guilty;

(c)   set, follow or revise a timetable for the progress of the case, which may include a timetable for any hearing including the trial or (in the Crown Court) the appeal;

(d)   in giving directions, ensure continuity in relation to the court and to the parties' representatives where that is appropriate and practicable; and

(e)   where a direction has not been complied with, find out why, identify who was responsible, and take appropriate action.

(3) In order to prepare for the trial, the court must take every reasonable step—

(a)   to encourage and to facilitate the attendance of witnesses when they are needed; and

(b)   to facilitate the participation of any person, including the defendant.

(4) Facilitating the participation of the defendant includes finding out whether the defendant needs interpretation because—

(a)   the defendant does not speak or understand English; or

(b)   the defendant has a hearing or speech impediment.

(5) Where the defendant needs interpretation—

(a)   the court officer must arrange for interpretation to be provided at every hearing which the defendant is due to attend;

(b)   interpretation may be by an intermediary where the defendant has a speech impediment, without the need for a defendant's evidence direction;

(c)   on application or on its own initiative, the court may require a written translation to be provided for the defendant of any document or part of a document, unless—

(i)   translation of that document, or part, is not needed to explain the case against the defendant, or

(ii)   the defendant agrees to do without and the court is satisfied that the agreement is clear and voluntary and that the defendant has had legal advice or otherwise understands the consequences;

(d)   on application by the defendant, the court must give any direction which the court thinks appropriate, including a direction for interpretation by a different interpreter, where—

(i)   no interpretation is provided,

(ii)   no translation is ordered or provided in response to a previous application by the defendant, or

(iii) the defendant complains about the quality of interpretation or of any translation.

(6) Facilitating the participation of any person includes giving directions for the appropriate treatment and questioning of a witness or the defendant, especially where the court directs that such questioning is to be conducted through an intermediary.

(7) Where directions for appropriate treatment and questioning are required, the court must—

(a)   invite representations by the parties and by any intermediary; and

(b)   set ground rules for the conduct of the questioning, which rules may include—

(i)   a direction relieving a party of any duty to put that party's case to a witness or a defendant in its entirety,

(ii)   directions about the manner of questioning,

(iii) directions about the duration of questioning,

    (iv) if necessary, directions about the questions that may or may not be asked,

    (v) where there is more than one defendant, the allocation among them of the topics about which a witness may be asked, and

    (vi) directions about the use of models, plans, body maps or similar aids to help communicate a question or an answer.

Readiness for trial or appeal

3.10.—(1) This rule applies to a party's preparation for trial or appeal, and in this rule and rule 3.11 "trial" includes any hearing at which evidence will be introduced. ★P-18

  (2) In fulfilling the duty under rule 3.3, each party must—

    (a) comply with directions given by the court;

    (b) take every reasonable step to make sure that party's witnesses will attend when they are needed;

    (c) make appropriate arrangements to present any written or other material; and

    (d) promptly inform the court and the other parties of anything that may—

      (i) affect the date or duration of the trial or appeal, or

      (ii) significantly affect the progress of the case in any other way.

  (3) The court may require a party to give a certificate of readiness.

Conduct of a trial or an appeal

3.11. In order to manage a trial or an appeal, the court— ★P-19

    (a) must establish, with the active assistance of the parties, what are the disputed issues;

    (b) must consider setting a timetable that—

      (i) takes account of those issues and of any timetable proposed by a party, and

      (ii) may limit the duration of any stage of the hearing;

    (c) may require a party to identify—

      (i) which witnesses that party wants to give evidence in person,

      (ii) the order in which that party wants those witnesses to give their evidence,

      (iii) whether that party requires an order compelling the attendance of a witness,

      (iv) what arrangements are desirable to facilitate the giving of evidence by a witness,

      (v) what arrangements are desirable to facilitate the participation of any other person, including the defendant,

      (vi) what written evidence that party intends to introduce,

      (vii) what other material, if any, that person intends to make available to the court in the presentation of the case, and

      (viii) whether that party intends to raise any point of law that could affect the conduct of the trial or appeal; and

    (d) may limit—

      (i) the examination, cross-examination or re-examination of a witness, and

      (ii) the duration of any stage of the hearing.

Duty of court officer

3.12. The court officer must— ★P-20

    (a) where a person is entitled or required to attend a hearing, give as much notice as reasonably practicable to—

      (i) that person, and

      (ii) that person's custodian (if any);

    (b) where the court gives directions, promptly make a record available to the parties.

Preparation for Trial in the Crown Court

Pre-trial hearings: general rules

3.13.—(1) The Crown Court— ★P-21

    (a) may, and in some cases must, conduct a preparatory hearing where rule 3.14 applies;

    (b) must conduct a plea and trial preparation hearing;

    (c) may conduct a further pre-trial case management hearing (and if necessary more than one such hearing) only where—

      (i) the court anticipates a guilty plea,

      (ii) it is necessary to conduct such a hearing in order to give directions for an effective trial, or

(iii) such a hearing is required to set ground rules for the conduct of the questioning of a witness or defendant.

(2) A pre-trial case management hearing—

(a) must be in public, as a general rule, but all or part of the hearing may be in private if the court so directs; and

(b) must be recorded, in accordance with rule 5.5 (recording and transcription of proceedings in the Crown Court).

(3) Where the court determines a pre-trial application in private, it must announce its decision in public.

Preparatory hearing

★**P-22**   **3.14.**—(1) This rule applies where the Crown Court—

(a) can order a preparatory hearing, under—

(i) section 7 of the Criminal Justice Act 1987 (cases of serious or complex fraud), or

(ii) section 29 of the Criminal Procedure and Investigations Act 1996 (other complex, serious or lengthy cases);

(b) must order such a hearing, to determine an application for a trial without a jury, under—

(i) section 44 of the Criminal Justice Act 2003 (danger of jury tampering), or

(ii) section 17 of the Domestic Violence, Crime and Victims Act 2004 (trial of sample counts by jury, and others by judge alone);

(c) must order such a hearing, under section 29 of the 1996 Act, where section 29(1B) or (1C) applies (cases in which a terrorism offence is charged, or other serious cases with a terrorist connection).

(2) The court may decide whether to order a preparatory hearing—

(a) on an application or on its own initiative;

(b) at a hearing (in public or in private), or without a hearing;

(c) in a party's absence, if that party—

(i) applied for the order, or

(ii) has had at least 14 days in which to make representations.

Application for preparatory hearing

★**P-23**   **3.15.**—(1) A party who wants the court to order a preparatory hearing must—

(a) apply in writing—

(i) as soon as reasonably practicable, and in any event

(ii) not more than 14 days after the defendant pleads not guilty;

(b) serve the application on—

(i) the court officer, and

(ii) each other party.

(2) The applicant must—

(a) if relevant, explain what legislation requires the court to order a preparatory hearing;

(b) otherwise, explain—

(i) what makes the case complex or serious, or makes the trial likely to be long,

(ii) why a substantial benefit will accrue from a preparatory hearing, and

(iii) why the court's ordinary powers of case management are not adequate.

(3) A prosecutor who wants the court to order a trial without a jury must explain—

(a) where the prosecutor alleges a danger of jury tampering—

(i) what evidence there is of a real and present danger that jury tampering would take place,

(ii) what steps, if any, reasonably might be taken to prevent jury tampering, and

(iii) why, notwithstanding such steps, the likelihood of jury tampering is so substantial as to make it necessary in the interests of justice to order such a trial; or

(b) where the prosecutor proposes trial without a jury on some counts on the indictment—

(i) why a trial by jury involving all the counts would be impracticable,

(ii) how the counts proposed for jury trial can be regarded as samples of the others, and

(iii) why it would be in the interests of justice to order such a trial.

Application for non-jury trial containing information withheld from a defendant

★**P-24**   **3.16.**—(1) This rule applies where—

(a) the prosecutor applies for an order for a trial without a jury because of a danger of jury tampering; and

(b) the application includes information that the prosecutor thinks ought not be revealed to a defendant.

(2) The prosecutor must—

(a) omit that information from the part of the application that is served on that defendant;

(b) mark the other part to show that, unless the court otherwise directs, it is only for the court; and

(c) in that other part, explain why the prosecutor has withheld that information from that defendant.

(3) The hearing of an application to which this rule applies—

(a) must be in private, unless the court otherwise directs; and

(b) if the court so directs, may be, wholly or in part, in the absence of a defendant from whom information has been withheld.

(4) At the hearing of an application to which this rule applies—

(a) the general rule is that the court will receive, in the following sequence—

(i) representations first by the prosecutor and then by each defendant, in all the parties' presence, and then

(ii) further representations by the prosecutor, in the absence of a defendant from whom information has been withheld; but

(b) the court may direct other arrangements for the hearing.

(5) Where, on an application to which this rule applies, the court orders a trial without a jury—

(a) the general rule is that the trial will be before a judge other than the judge who made the order; but

(b) the court may direct other arrangements.

Representations in response to application for preparatory hearing

3.17.—(1) This rule applies where a party wants to make representations about— ★P-25

(a) an application for a preparatory hearing;

(b) an application for a trial without a jury.

(2) Such a party must—

(a) serve the representations on—

(i)   the court officer, and

(ii) each other party;

(b) do so not more than 14 days after service of the application;

(c) ask for a hearing, if that party wants one, and explain why it is needed.

(3) Where representations include information that the person making them thinks ought not be revealed to another party, that person must—

(a) omit that information from the representations served on that other party;

(b) mark the information to show that, unless the court otherwise directs, it is only for the court; and

(c) with that information include an explanation of why it has been withheld from that other party.

(4) Representations against an application for an order must explain why the conditions for making it are not met.

Commencement of preparatory hearing

3.18. At the beginning of a preparatory hearing, the court must— ★P-26

(a) announce that it is such a hearing; and

(b) take the defendant's plea under rule 3.24 (arraigning the defendant on the indictment), unless already done.

Defence trial advocate

3.19.—(1) The defendant must notify the court officer of the identity of the intended defence trial ★P-27
advocate—

(a) as soon as practicable, and in any event no later than the day of the plea and trial preparation hearing;

(b) in writing, or orally at that hearing.

(2) The defendant must notify the court officer in writing of any change in the identity of the

intended defence trial advocate as soon as practicable, and in any event not more than 5 business days after that change.

Application to stay case for abuse of process

★**P-28**   **3.20.**—(1) This rule applies where a defendant wants the Crown Court to stay the case on the grounds that the proceedings are an abuse of the court, or otherwise unfair.

(2) Such a defendant must—

   (a) apply in writing—

      (i) as soon as practicable after becoming aware of the grounds for doing so,

      (ii) at a pre-trial hearing, unless the grounds for the application do not arise until trial, and

      (iii) in any event, before the defendant pleads guilty or the jury (if there is one) retires to consider its verdict at trial;

   (b) serve the application on—

      (i) the court officer, and

      (ii) each other party; and

   (c) in the application—

      (i) explain the grounds on which it is made,

      (ii) include, attach or identify all supporting material,

      (iii) specify relevant events, dates and propositions of law, and

      (iv) identify any witness the applicant wants to call to give evidence in person.

(3) A party who wants to make representations in response to the application must serve the representations on—

   (a) the court officer; and

   (b) each other party,

not more than 14 days after service of the application.

Application for joint or separate trials, etc.

★**P-29**   **3.21.**—(1) This rule applies where a party wants the Crown Court to order—

   (a) the joint trial of—

      (i) offences charged by separate indictments, or

      (ii) defendants charged in separate indictments;

   (b) separate trials of offences charged by the same indictment;

   (c) separate trials of defendants charged in the same indictment; or

   (d) the deletion of a count from an indictment.

(2) Such a party must—

   (a) apply in writing—

      (i) as soon as practicable after becoming aware of the grounds for doing so, and

      (ii) before the trial begins, unless the grounds for the application do not arise until trial;

   (b) serve the application on—

      (i) the court officer, and

      (ii) each other party; and

   (c) in the application—

      (i) specify the order proposed, and

      (ii) explain why it should be made.

(3) A party who wants to make representations in response to the application must serve the representations on—

   (a) the court officer; and

   (b) each other party,

not more than 14 days after service of the application.

Order for joint or separate trials, or amendment of the indictment

★**P-30**   **3.22.**—(1) This rule applies where the Crown Court makes an order—

   (a) on an application under rule 3.21 applies (application for joint or separate trials, etc.); or

   (b) amending an indictment in any other respect.

(2) Unless the court otherwise directs, the court officer must endorse any paper copy of each affected indictment made for the court with—

   (a) a note of the court's order; and

(b) the date of that order.

Application for indication of sentence
  3.23.—(1) This rule applies where a defendant wants the Crown Court to give an indication of the   ★**P-31**
maximum sentence that would be passed if a guilty plea were entered when the indication is sought.
  (2) Such a defendant must—
    (a) apply in writing as soon as practicable; and
    (b) serve the application on—
      (i) the court officer, and
      (ii) the prosecutor.
  (3) The application must—
    (a) specify—
      (i) the offence or offences to which it would be a guilty plea, and
      (ii) the facts on the basis of which that plea would be entered; and
    (b) include the prosecutor's agreement to, or representations on, that proposed basis of plea.
  (4) The prosecutor must—
    (a) provide information relevant to sentence, including—
      (i) any previous conviction of the defendant, and the circumstances where relevant,
      (ii) any statement of the effect of the offence on the victim, the victim's family or others;
      and
    (b) identify any other matter relevant to sentence, including—
      (i) the legislation applicable,
      (ii) any sentencing guidelines, or guideline cases, and
      (iii) aggravating and mitigating factors.
  (5) The hearing of the application—
    (a) may take place in the absence of any other defendant;
    (b) must be attended by—
      (i) the applicant defendant's legal representatives (if any), and
      (ii) the prosecution advocate.

Arraigning the defendant on the indictment
  3.24.—(1) In order to take the defendant's plea, the Crown Court must—   ★**P-32**
    (a) ensure that the defendant is correctly identified by the indictment;
    (b) in respect of each count in the indictment—
      (i) read the count aloud to the defendant, or arrange for it to be read aloud or placed
      before the defendant in writing,
      (ii) ask whether the defendant pleads guilty or not guilty to the offence charged by that
      count, and
      (iii) take the defendant's plea.
  (2) Where a count is read which is substantially the same as one already read aloud, then only the
materially different details need be read aloud.
  (3) Where a count is placed before the defendant in writing, the court must summarise its gist
aloud.
  (4) In respect of each count in the indictment—
    (a) if the defendant declines to enter a plea, the court must treat that as a not guilty plea un-
    less rule 25.11 applies (defendant unfit to plead);
    (b) if the defendant pleads not guilty to the offence charged by that count but guilty to another
    offence of which the court could convict on that count—
      (i) if the prosecutor and the court accept that plea, the court must treat the plea as one
      of guilty of that other offence, but
      (ii) otherwise, the court must treat the plea as one of not guilty;
    (c) if the defendant pleads a previous acquittal or conviction of the offence charged by that
    count—
      (i) the defendant must identify that acquittal or conviction in writing, explaining the
      basis of that plea, and
      (ii) the court must exercise its power to decide whether that plea disposes of that count.

Place of trial
  3.25.—(1) Unless the court otherwise directs, the court officer must arrange for the trial to take   ★**P-33**
place in a courtroom provided by the Lord Chancellor.

(2) The court officer must arrange for the court and the jury (if there is one) to view any place required by the court.

Use of Welsh language at trial

★P-34

3.26. Where the trial will take place in Wales and a participant wishes to use the Welsh language—

    (a) that participant must serve notice on the court officer, or arrange for such a notice to be served on that participant's behalf—

        (i) at or before the plea and trial preparation hearing, or

        (ii) in accordance with any direction given by the court; and

    (b) if such a notice is served, the court officer must arrange for an interpreter to attend.

PART 4

SERVICE OF DOCUMENTS

When this part applies

★P-35

4.1.—(1) The rules in this part apply—

    (a) to the service of every document in a case to which these rules apply; and

    (b) for the purposes of section 12 of the Road Traffic Offenders Act 1988, to the service of a requirement to which that section applies.

(2) The rules apply subject to any special rules in other legislation (including other parts of these rules) or in the Practice Direction.

Methods of service

★P-36

4.2.—(1) A document may be served by any of the methods described in rules 4.3 to 4.6 (subject to rules 4.7 and 4.10), or in rule 4.8.

(2) Where a document may be served by electronic means under rule 4.6, the general rule is that the person serving it must use that method.

Service by handing over a document

★P-37

4.3.—(1) A document may be served on—

    (a) an individual by handing it to him or her;

    (b) a corporation by handing it to a person holding a senior position in that corporation;

    (c) an individual or corporation who is legally represented in the case by handing it to that legal representative;

    (d) the prosecution by handing it to the prosecutor or to the prosecution representative;

    (e) the court officer by handing it to a court officer with authority to accept it at the relevant court office; and

    (f) the Registrar of Criminal Appeals by handing it to a court officer with authority to accept it at the Criminal Appeal Office.

(2) If an individual is under 18, a copy of a document served under paragraph (1)(a) must be handed to his or her parent, or another appropriate adult, unless no such person is readily available.

(3) Unless the court otherwise directs, for the purposes of paragraph (1)(c) or (d) (service by handing a document to a party's representative) "representative" includes an advocate appearing for that party at a hearing.

(4) In this rule, "the relevant court office" means—

    (a) in relation to a case in a magistrates' court or in the Crown Court, the office at which that court's business is administered by court staff;

    (b) in relation to an extradition appeal case in the High Court, the Administrative Court Office of the Queen's Bench Division of the High Court.

Service by leaving or posting a document

★P-38

4.4.—(1) A document may be served by addressing it to the person to be served and leaving it at the appropriate address for service under this rule, or by sending it to that address by first class post or by the equivalent of first class post.

(2) The address for service under this rule on—

    (a) an individual is an address where it is reasonably believed that he or she will receive it;

    (b) a corporation is its principal office, and if there is no readily identifiable principal office then any place where it carries on its activities or business;

    (c) an individual or corporation who is legally represented in the case is that legal representative's office;

    (d)   the prosecution is the prosecutor's office;

    (e)   the court officer is the relevant court office; and

    (f)   the Registrar of Criminal Appeals is the Criminal Appeal Office, Royal Courts of Justice, Strand, London WC2A 2LL.

  (3) In this rule, "the relevant court office" means—

    (a)   in relation to a case in a magistrates' court or in the Crown Court, the office at which that court's business is administered by court staff;

    (b)   in relation to an extradition appeal case in the High Court, the Administrative Court Office, Royal Courts of Justice, Strand, London WC2A 2LL.

Service by document exchange

4.5.—(1) This rule applies where—   ★**P-39**

    (a)   the person to be served—

        (i)   has given a document exchange (DX) box number, and

        (ii)   has not refused to accept service by DX; or

    (b)   the person to be served is legally represented in the case and the legal representative has given a DX box number.

  (2) A document may be served by—

    (a)   addressing it to that person or legal representative, as appropriate, at that DX box number; and

    (b)   leaving it at—

        (i)   the document exchange at which the addressee has that DX box number, or

        (ii)   a document exchange at which the person serving it has a DX box number.

Service by electronic means

4.6.—(1) This rule applies where—   ★**P-40**

    (a)   the person to be served—

        (i)   has given an electronic address and has not refused to accept service at that address, or

        (ii)   is given access to an electronic address at which a document may be deposited and has not refused to accept service by the deposit of a document at that address; or

    (b)   the person to be served is legally represented in the case and the legal representative—

        (i)   has given an electronic address, or

        (ii)   is given access to an electronic address at which a document may be deposited.

  (2) A document may be served—

    (a)   by sending it by electronic means to the address which the recipient has given; or

    (b)   by depositing it at an address to which the recipient has been given access and—

        (i)   in every case, making it possible for the recipient to read the document, or view or listen to its content, as the case may be,

        (ii)   unless the court otherwise directs, making it possible for the recipient to make and keep an electronic copy of the document, and

        (iii)   notifying the recipient of the deposit of the document (which notice may be given by electronic means).

  (3) Where a document is served under this rule the person serving it need not provide a paper copy as well.

Documents that must be served by specified methods

4.7.—(1) An application or written statement, and notice, under rule 48.9 alleging contempt of ★**P-41**
court may be served—

    (a)   on an individual, only under rule 4.3(1)(a) (by handing it to him or her);

    (b)   on a corporation, only under rule 4.3(1)(b) (by handing it to a person holding a senior position in that corporation).

  (2) For the purposes of section 12 of the Road Traffic Offenders Act 1988, a notice of a requirement under section 172 of the Road Traffic Act 1988 or under section 112 of the Road Traffic Regulation Act 1984 to identify the driver of a vehicle may be served—

    (a)   on an individual, only by post under rule 4.4(1) and (2)(a);

    (b)   on a corporation, only by post under rule 4.4(1) and (2)(b).

Service by person in custody

4.8.—(1) A person in custody may serve a document by handing it to the custodian addressed to ★**P-42**
the person to be served.

(2) The custodian must—

    (a) endorse it with the time and date of receipt;

    (b) record its receipt; and

    (c) forward it promptly to the addressee.

Service by another method

★P-43   **4.9.**—(1) The court may allow service of a document by a method—

    (a) other than those described in rules 4.3 to 4.6 and in rule 4.8;

    (b) other than one specified by rule 4.7, where that rule applies.

  (2) An order allowing service by another method must specify—

    (a) the method to be used; and

    (b) the date on which the document will be served.

Documents that may not be served on a legal representative

★P-44   **4.10.** Unless the court otherwise directs, service on a party's legal representative of any of the following documents is not service of that document on that party—

    (a) a summons, requisition, single justice procedure notice or witness summons;

    (b) notice of an order under section 25 of the Road Traffic Offenders Act 1988;

    (c) a notice of registration under section 71(6) of that Act;

    (d) notice of a hearing to review the postponement of the issue of a warrant of detention or imprisonment under section 77(6) of the Magistrates' Courts Act 1980;

    (e) notice under section 86 of that Act of a revised date to attend a means inquiry;

    (f) any notice or document served under Part 14 (bail and custody time limits);

    (g) notice under rule 24.16(a) of when and where an adjourned hearing will resume;

    (h) notice under rule 28.5(3) of an application to vary or discharge a compensation order;

    (i) notice under rule 28.10(2)(c) of the location of the sentencing or enforcing court;

    (j) a collection order, or notice requiring payment, served under rule 30.2(a); or

    (k) an application or written statement, and notice, under rule 48.9 alleging contempt of court.

Date of service

★P-45   **4.11.**—(1) A document served under rule 4.3 or rule 4.8 is served on the day it is handed over.

  (2) Unless something different is shown, a document served on a person by any other method is served—

    (a) in the case of a document left at an address, on the next business day after the day on which it was left;

    (b) in the case of a document sent by first class post or by the equivalent of first class post, on the second business day after the day on which it was posted or despatched;

    (c) in the case of a document served by document exchange, on the second business day after the day on which it was left at a document exchange allowed by rule 4.5;

    (d) in the case of a document served by electronic means—

      (i) on the day on which it is sent under rule 4.6(2)(a), if that day is a business day and if it is sent by no later than 2.30pm that day,

      (ii) on the day on which notice of its deposit is given under rule 4.6(2)(b), if that day is a business day and if that notice is given by no later than 2.30pm that day, or

      (iii) otherwise, on the next business day after it was sent or such notice was given; and

    (e) in any case, on the day on which the addressee responds to it, if that is earlier.

  (3) Unless something different is shown, a document produced by a computer system for dispatch by post is to be taken as having been sent by first class post, or by the equivalent of first class post, to the addressee on the business day after the day on which it was produced.

  (4) Where a document is served on or by the court officer, "business day" does not include a day on which the court office is closed.

Proof of service

★P-46   **4.12.** The person who serves a document may prove that by signing a certificate explaining how and when it was served.

Court's power to give directions about service

★P-47   **4.13.**—(1) The court may specify the time as well as the date by which a document must be—

(a) served under rule 4.3 (service by handing over a document) or rule 4.8 (service by person in custody); or

(b) sent or deposited by electronic means, if it is served under rule 4.6.

(2) The court may treat a document as served if the addressee responds to it even if it was not served in accordance with the rules in this part.

PART 5

FORMS AND COURT RECORDS

Forms

Applications, etc. by forms or electronic means

5.1.—(1) This rule applies where a rule, a practice direction or the court requires a person to— **★P-48**

(a) make an application or give a notice;

(b) supply information for the purposes of case management by the court; or

(c) supply information needed for other purposes by the court.

(2) Unless the court otherwise directs, such a person must—

(a) use such electronic arrangements as the court officer may make for that purpose, in accordance with those arrangements; or

(b) if no such arrangements have been made, use the appropriate form set out in the Practice Direction or the Criminal Costs Practice Direction, in accordance with those Directions.

Forms in Welsh

5.2.—(1) Any Welsh language form set out in the Practice Direction, or in the Criminal Costs **★P-49** Practice Direction, is for use in connection with proceedings in courts in Wales.

(2) Both a Welsh form and an English form may be contained in the same document.

(3) Where only a Welsh form, or only the corresponding English form, is served—

(a) the following words in Welsh and English must be added:

"Darperir y ddogfen hon yn Gymraeg / Saesneg os bydd arnoch ei heisiau. Dylech wneud cais yn ddi-oed i (swyddog y llys) (rhodder yma'r cyfeiriad)

This document will be provided in Welsh / English if you require it. You should apply immediately to (the court officer) (address)"; and

(b) the court officer, or the person who served the form, must, on request, supply the corresponding form in the other language to the person served.

Signature of forms

5.3.—(1) This rule applies where a form provides for its signature. **★P-50**

(2) Unless other legislation otherwise requires, or the court otherwise directs, signature may be by any written or electronic authentication of the form by, or with the authority of, the signatory.

Court Records

Duty to make records

5.4.—(1) For each case, as appropriate, the court officer must record, by such means as the Lord **★P-51** Chancellor directs—

(a) each charge or indictment against the defendant;

(b) the defendant's plea to each charge or count;

(c) each acquittal, conviction, sentence, determination, direction or order;

(d) each decision about bail;

(e) the power exercised where the court commits or adjourns the case to another court—

(i) for sentence, or

(ii) for the defendant to be dealt with for breach of a community order, a deferred sentence, a conditional discharge, or a suspended sentence of imprisonment, imposed by that other court;

(f) the court's reasons for a decision, where legislation requires those reasons to be recorded;

(g) any appeal;

(h) each party's presence or absence at each hearing;

(i) any consent that legislation requires before the court can proceed with the case, or proceed to a decision;

    (j)   in a magistrates' court—
        (i)   any indication of sentence given in connection with the allocation of a case for trial, and
        (ii)   the registration of a fixed penalty notice for enforcement as a fine, and any related endorsement on a driving record;
    (k)   in the Crown Court, any request for assistance or other communication about the case received from a juror;
    (l)   the identity of—
        (i)   the prosecutor,
        (ii)   the defendant,
        (iii)   any other applicant to whom these rules apply,
        (iv)   any interpreter or intermediary,
        (v)   the parties' legal representatives, if any, and
        (vi)   the judge, magistrate or magistrates, justices' legal adviser or other person who made each recorded decision;
    (m)   where a defendant is entitled to attend a hearing, any agreement by the defendant to waive that right; and
    (n)   where interpretation is required for a defendant, any agreement by that defendant to do without the written translation of a document.
  (2) Such records must include—
    (a)   each party's and representative's address, including any electronic address and telephone number available;
    (b)   the defendant's date of birth, if available; and
    (c)   the date of each event and decision recorded.

Recording and transcription of proceedings in the Crown Court

★P-52   **5.5.**—(1) Where someone may appeal to the Court of Appeal, the court officer must—
    (a)   arrange for the recording of the proceedings in the Crown Court, unless the court otherwise directs; and
    (b)   arrange for the transcription of such a recording if—
        (i)   the Registrar wants such a transcript, or
        (ii)   anyone else wants such a transcript (but that is subject to the restrictions in paragraph (2)).
  (2) Unless the court otherwise directs, a person who transcribes a recording of proceedings under such arrangements—
    (a)   must not supply anyone other than the Registrar with a transcript of a recording of—
        (i)   a hearing in private, or
        (ii)   information to which reporting restrictions apply;
    (b)   subject to that, must supply any person with any transcript for which that person asks—
        (i)   in accordance with the transcription arrangements made by the court officer, and
        (ii)   on payment by that person of any fee prescribed.
  (3) A party who wants to hear a recording of proceedings must—
    (a)   apply—
        (i)   in writing to the Registrar, if an appeal notice has been served where Part 36 applies (appeal to the Court of Appeal: general rules), or
        (ii)   orally or in writing to the Crown Court officer;
    (b)   explain the reasons for the request; and
    (c)   pay any fee prescribed.
  (4) If the Crown Court or the Registrar so directs, the Crown Court officer must allow that party to hear a recording of—
    (a)   a hearing in public;
    (b)   a hearing in private, if the applicant was present at that hearing.

Custody of case materials

★P-53   **5.6.** Unless the court otherwise directs, in respect of each case the court officer may—
    (a)   keep any evidence, application, representation or other material served by the parties; or
    (b)   arrange for the whole or any part to be kept by some other appropriate person, subject to—
        (i)   any condition imposed by the court, and

(ii) the rules in Part 34 (appeal to the Crown Court) and Part 36 (appeal to the Court of Appeal: general rules) about keeping exhibits pending any appeal.

Supply to a party of information or documents from records or case materials

5.7.—(1) This rule applies where— ★**P-54**

(a) a party wants information, or a copy of a document, from records or case materials kept by the court officer (for example, in case of loss, or to establish what is retained); or

(b) a person affected by an order made, or warrant issued, by the court wants such information or such a copy.

(2) Such a party or person must—

(a) apply to the court officer;

(b) specify the information or document required; and

(c) pay any fee prescribed.

(3) The application—

(a) may be made orally, giving no reasons, if paragraph (4) requires the court officer to supply the information or document requested;

(b) must be in writing, unless the court otherwise permits, and must explain for what purpose the information is required, in any other case.

(4) The court officer must supply to the applicant party or person—

(a) a copy of any document served by, or on, that party or person (but not of any document not so served);

(b) by word of mouth, or in writing, as requested—

(i) information that was received from that party or person in the first place,

(ii) information about the terms of any direction or order directed to that party or person, or made on an application by that party or person, or at a hearing in public,

(iii) information about the outcome of the case.

(5) If the court so directs, the court officer must supply to the applicant party or person, by word of mouth or in writing, as requested, information that paragraph (4) does not require the court officer to supply.

(6) Where the information requested is about the grounds on which an order was made, or a warrant was issued, in the absence of the party or person applying for that information—

(a) that party or person must also serve the request on the person who applied for the order or warrant;

(b) if the person who applied for the order or warrant objects to the supply of the information requested, that objector must—

(i) give notice of the objection not more than 14 days after service of the request (or within any longer period allowed by the court),

(ii) serve that notice on the court officer and on the party or person requesting the information, and

(iii) if the objector wants a hearing, explain why one is needed;

(c) the court may determine the application for information at a hearing (which must be in private unless the court otherwise directs), or without a hearing;

(d) the court must not permit the information requested to be supplied unless the person who applied for the order or warrant has had at least 14 days (or any longer period allowed by the court) in which to make representations.

(7) A notice of objection under paragraph (6) must explain—

(a) whether the objection is to the supply of any part of the information requested, or only to the supply of a specified part, or parts, of it;

(b) whether the objection is to the supply of the information at any time, or only to its supply before a date or event specified by the objector; and

(c) the grounds of the objection.

(8) Where a notice of objection under paragraph (6) includes material that the objector thinks ought not be revealed to the party or person applying for information, the objector must—

(a) omit that material from the notice served on that party or person;

(b) mark the material to show that it is only for the court; and

(c) with that material include an explanation of why it has been withheld.

(9) Where paragraph (8) applies—

(a) a hearing of the application may take place, wholly or in part, in the absence of the party or person applying for information;

(b) at any such hearing, the general rule is that the court must consider, in the following sequence—

   (i) representations first by the party or person applying for information and then by the objector, in the presence of both, and then

   (ii) further representations by the objector, in the absence of that party or person

but the court may direct other arrangements for the hearing.

Supply to the public, including reporters, of information about cases

★**P-55**   **5.8.**—(1) This rule—

(a) applies where a member of the public, including a reporter, wants information about a case from the court officer;

(b) requires the court officer to publish information about cases due to be heard.

(2) A person who wants information about a case from the court officer must—

(a) apply to the court officer;

(b) specify the information requested; and

(c) pay any fee prescribed.

(3) The application—

(a) may be made orally, giving no reasons, if paragraph (4) requires the court officer to supply the information requested;

(b) must be in writing, unless the court otherwise permits, and must explain for what purpose the information is required, in any other case.

(4) The court officer must supply to the applicant—

(a) any information listed in paragraph (6), if—

   (i) the information is available to the court officer,

   (ii) the supply of the information is not prohibited by a reporting restriction, and

   (iii) the trial has not yet concluded, or the verdict was not more than 6 months ago; and

(b) details of any reporting or access restriction ordered by the court.

(5) The court officer must supply that information—

(a) by word of mouth; or

(b) by such other arrangements as the Lord Chancellor directs.

(6) The information that paragraph (4) requires the court officer to supply is—

(a) the date of any hearing in public, unless any party has yet to be notified of that date;

(b) each alleged offence and any plea entered;

(c) the court's decision at any hearing in public, including any decision about—

   (i) bail, or

   (ii) the committal, sending or transfer of the case to another court;

(d) whether the case is under appeal;

(e) the outcome of any trial and any appeal; and

(f) the identity of—

   (i) the prosecutor,

   (ii) the defendant,

   (iii) the parties' representatives, including their addresses, and

   (iv) the judge, magistrate or magistrates, or justices' legal adviser by whom a decision at a hearing in public was made.

(7) If the court so directs, the court officer must—

(a) supply to the applicant, by word of mouth, other information about the case; or

(b) allow the applicant to inspect or copy a document, or part of a document, containing information about the case.

(8) The court may determine an application to which paragraph (7) applies—

(a) at a hearing, in public or in private; or

(b) without a hearing.

(9) The court officer must publish the information listed in paragraph (11) if—

(a) the information is available to the court officer;

(b) the hearing to which the information relates is due to take place in public; and

(c) the publication of the information is not prohibited by a reporting restriction.

(10) The court officer must publish that information—

(a) by notice displayed somewhere prominent in the vicinity of the court room in which the hearing is due to take place;

(b) by such other arrangements as the Lord Chancellor directs, including arrangements for publication by electronic means; and

(c) for no longer than 2 business days.

(11) The information that paragraph (9) requires the court officer to publish is—

(a) the date, time and place of the hearing;

(b) the identity of the defendant; and

(c) such other information as it may be practicable to publish concerning—

(i) the type of hearing,

(ii) the identity of the court,

(iii) the offence or offences alleged, and

(iv) whether any reporting restriction applies.

Supply of written certificate or extract from records

5.9.—(1) This rule applies where legislation— ★**P-56**

(a) allows a certificate of conviction or acquittal, or an extract from records kept by the court officer, to be introduced in evidence in criminal proceedings; or

(b) requires such a certificate or extract to be supplied by the court officer to a specified person for a specified purpose.

(2) A person who wants such a certificate or extract must—

(a) apply in writing to the court officer;

(b) specify the certificate or extract required;

(c) explain under what legislation and for what purpose it is required; and

(d) pay any fee prescribed.

(3) If the application satisfies the requirements of that legislation, the court officer must supply the certificate or extract requested—

(a) to a party;

(b) unless the court otherwise directs, to any other applicant.

PART 6

REPORTING, ETC. RESTRICTIONS

General Rules

When this part applies

6.1.—(1) This part applies where the court can— ★**P-57**

(a) impose a restriction on—

(i) reporting what takes place at a public hearing, or

(ii) public access to what otherwise would be a public hearing;

(b) vary or remove a reporting or access restriction that is imposed by legislation;

(c) withhold information from the public during a public hearing;

(d) order a trial in private;

(e) allow there to take place during a hearing—

(i) sound recording, or

(ii) communication by electronic means.

(2) This part does not apply to arrangements required by legislation, or directed by the court, in connection with—

(a) sound recording during a hearing, or the transcription of such a recording; or

(b) measures to assist a witness or defendant to give evidence.

Exercise of court's powers to which this part applies

6.2.—(1) When exercising a power to which this part applies, as well as furthering the overriding ★**P-58** objective, in accordance with rule 1.3, the court must have regard to the importance of—

(a) dealing with criminal cases in public; and

(b) allowing a public hearing to be reported to the public.

(2) The court may determine an application or appeal under this part—

(a) at a hearing, in public or in private; or

(b) without a hearing.

(3) But the court must not exercise a power to which this part applies unless each party and any other person directly affected—

  (a) is present; or

  (b) has had an opportunity—

    (i) to attend, or

    (ii) to make representations.

Court's power to vary requirements under this part

★P-59

6.3.—(1) The court may—

  (a) shorten or extend (even after it has expired) a time limit under this part;

  (b) require an application to be made in writing instead of orally;

  (c) consider an application or representations made orally instead of in writing;

  (d) dispense with a requirement to—

    (i) give notice, or

    (ii) serve a written application.

(2) Someone who wants an extension of time must—

  (a) apply when making the application or representations for which it is needed; and

  (b) explain the delay.

Reporting and Access Restrictions

Reporting and access restrictions

★P-60

6.4.—(1) This rule applies where the court can—

  (a) impose a restriction on—

    (i) reporting what takes place at a public hearing, or

    (ii) public access to what otherwise would be a public hearing;

  (b) withhold information from the public during a public hearing.

(2) Unless other legislation otherwise provides, the court may do so—

  (a) on application by a party; or

  (b) on its own initiative.

(3) A party who wants the court to do so must—

  (a) apply as soon as reasonably practicable;

  (b) notify—

    (i) each other party, and

    (ii) such other person (if any) as the court directs;

  (c) specify the proposed terms of the order, and for how long it should last;

  (d) explain—

    (i) what power the court has to make the order, and

    (ii) why an order in the terms proposed is necessary;

  (e) where the application is for a reporting direction under section 45A of the Youth Justice and Criminal Evidence Act 1999 (power to restrict reporting of criminal proceedings for lifetime of witnesses and victims under 18), explain—

    (i) how the circumstances of the person whose identity is concerned meet the conditions prescribed by that section, having regard to the factors which that section lists; and

    (ii) why such a reporting direction would be likely to improve the quality of any evidence given by that person, or the level of co-operation given by that person to any party in connection with the preparation of that party's case, taking into account the factors listed in that section;

  (f) where the application is for a reporting direction under section 46 of the Youth Justice and Criminal Evidence Act 1999 (power to restrict reports about certain adult witnesses in criminal proceedings), explain—

    (i) how the witness is eligible for assistance, having regard to the factors listed in that section, and

    (ii) why such a reporting direction would be likely to improve the quality of the witness' evidence, or the level of co-operation given by the witness to the applicant in connection with the preparation of the applicant's case, taking into account the factors which that section lists.

Varying or removing restrictions

★P-61

6.5.—(1) This rule applies where the court can vary or remove a reporting or access restriction.

(2) Unless other legislation otherwise provides, the court may do so—

   (a) on application by a party or person directly affected; or

   (b) on its own initiative.

(3) A party or person who wants the court to do so must—

   (a) apply as soon as reasonably practicable;

   (b) notify—

     (i) each other party, and

     (ii) such other person (if any) as the court directs;

   (c) specify the restriction;

   (d) explain, as appropriate, why it should be varied or removed.

(4) A person who wants to appeal to the Crown Court under section 141F of the Education Act 2002 must—

   (a) serve an appeal notice on—

     (i) the Crown Court officer, and

     (ii) each other party;

   (b) serve on the Crown Court officer, with the appeal notice, a copy of the application to the magistrates' court;

   (c) serve the appeal notice not more than 21 days after the magistrates' court's decision against which the appellant wants to appeal; and

   (d) in the appeal notice, explain, as appropriate, why the restriction should be maintained, varied or removed.

(5) Rule 34.11 (constitution of the Crown Court) applies on such an appeal.

Trial in private

6.6.—(1) This rule applies where the court can order a trial in private.   ★**P-62**

(2) A party who wants the court to do so must—

   (a) apply in writing not less than 5 business days before the trial is due to begin; and

   (b) serve the application on—

     (i) the court officer, and

     (ii) each other party.

(3) The applicant must explain—

   (a) the reasons for the application;

   (b) how much of the trial the applicant proposes should be in private; and

   (c) why no measures other than trial in private will suffice, such as—

     (i) reporting restrictions,

     (ii) an admission of facts,

     (iii) the introduction of hearsay evidence,

     (iv) a direction for a special measure under section 19 of the Youth Justice and Criminal Evidence Act 1999,

     (v) a witness anonymity order under section 86 of the Coroners and Justice Act 2009, or

     (vi) arrangements for the protection of a witness.

(4) Where the application includes information that the applicant thinks ought not be revealed to another party, the applicant must—

   (a) omit that information from the part of the application that is served on that other party;

   (b) mark the other part to show that, unless the court otherwise directs, it is only for the court; and

   (c) in that other part, explain why the applicant has withheld that information from that other party.

(5) The court officer must at once—

   (a) display notice of the application somewhere prominent in the vicinity of the courtroom; and

   (b) give notice of the application to reporters by such other arrangements as the Lord Chancellor directs.

(6) The application must be determined at a hearing which—

   (a) must be in private, unless the court otherwise directs;

   (b) if the court so directs, may be, wholly or in part, in the absence of a party from whom information has been withheld; and

   (c) in the Crown Court, must be after the defendant is arraigned but before the jury is sworn.

(7) At the hearing of the application—

    (a) the general rule is that the court must consider, in the following sequence—
        (i) representations first by the applicant and then by each other party, in all the parties presence, and then
        (ii) further representations by the applicant, in the absence of a party from whom information has been withheld; but
    (b) the court may direct other arrangements for the hearing.
  (8) The court must not hear a trial in private until—
    (a) the business day after the day on which it orders such a trial, or
    (b) the disposal of any appeal against, or review of, any such order, if later.

Representations in response

★P-63   **6.7.**—(1) This rule applies where a party, or person directly affected, wants to make representations about an application or appeal.
  (2) Such a party or person must—
    (a) serve the representations on—
        (i) the court officer,
        (ii) the applicant,
        (iii) each other party, and
        (iv) such other person (if any) as the court directs;
    (b) do so as soon as reasonably practicable after notice of the application; and
    (c) ask for a hearing, if that party or person wants one, and explain why it is needed.
  (3) Representations must—
    (a) explain the reasons for any objection;
    (b) specify any alternative terms proposed.

Order about restriction or trial in private

★P-64   **6.8.**—(1) This rule applies where the court—
    (a) orders, varies or removes a reporting or access restriction; or
    (b) orders a trial in private.
  (2) The court officer must—
    (a) record the court's reasons for the decision; and
    (b) as soon as reasonably practicable, arrange for notice of the decision to be—
        (i) displayed somewhere prominent in the vicinity of the courtroom, and
        (ii) communicated to reporters by such other arrangements as the Lord Chancellor directs.

Sound Recording and Electronic Communication

Sound recording and electronic communication

★P-65   **6.9.**—(1) This rule applies where the court can give permission to—
    (a) bring into a hearing for use, or use during a hearing, a device for—
        (i) recording sound, or
        (ii) communicating by electronic means; or
    (b) publish a sound recording made during a hearing.
  (2) The court may give such permission—
    (a) on application; or
    (b) on its own initiative.
  (3) A person who wants the court to give such permission must—
    (a) apply as soon as reasonably practicable;
    (b) notify—
        (i) each party, and
        (ii) such other person (if any) as the court directs; and
    (c) explain why the court should permit the use or publication proposed.
  (4) As a condition of the applicant using such a device, the court may direct arrangements to minimise the risk of its use—
    (a) contravening a reporting restriction;
    (b) disrupting the hearing; or
    (c) compromising the fairness of the hearing, for example by affecting—

      (i)   the evidence to be given by a witness, or

      (ii) the verdict of a jury.

(5) Such a direction may require that the device is used only—

    (a) in a specified part of the courtroom;

    (b) for a specified purpose;

    (c) for a purpose connected with the applicant's activity as a member of a specified group, for example representatives of news-gathering or reporting organisations;

    (d) at a specified time, or in a specified way.

Forfeiture of unauthorised sound recording

6.10.—(1) This rule applies where someone without the court's permission—   ★**P-66**

    (a) uses a device for recording sound during a hearing; or

    (b) publishes a sound recording made during a hearing.

(2) The court may exercise its power to forfeit the device or recording—

    (a) on application by a party, or on its own initiative;

    (b) provisionally, despite rule 6.2(3), to allow time for representations.

(3) A party who wants the court to forfeit a device or recording must—

    (a) apply as soon as reasonably practicable;

    (b) notify—

      (i)   as appropriate, the person who used the device, or who published the recording, and

      (ii) each other party; and

    (c) explain why the court should exercise that power.

7. [*Starting a prosecution in a magistrates' court*]   ★**P-67**

PART 8

INITIAL DETAILS OF THE PROSECUTION CASE

When this part applies

8.1. This part applies in a magistrates' court.   ★**P-68**

Providing initial details of the prosecution case

8.2.—(1) The prosecutor must serve initial details of the prosecution case on the court officer—   ★**P-69**

    (a) as soon as practicable; and

    (b) in any event, no later than the beginning of the day of the first hearing.

(2) Where a defendant requests those details, the prosecutor must serve them on the defendant—

    (a) as soon as practicable; and

    (b) in any event, no later than the beginning of the day of the first hearing.

(3) Where a defendant does not request those details, the prosecutor must make them available to the defendant at, or before, the beginning of the day of the first hearing.

Content of initial details

8.3. Initial details of the prosecution case must include—   ★**P-70**

    (a) where, immediately before the first hearing in the magistrates' court, the defendant was in police custody for the offence charged—

      (i)   a summary of the circumstances of the offence, and

      (ii) the defendant's criminal record, if any;

    (b) where paragraph (a) does not apply—

      (i)   a summary of the circumstances of the offence,

      (ii) any account given by the defendant in interview, whether contained in that summary or in another document,

      (iii) any written witness statement or exhibit that the prosecutor then has available and considers material to plea, or to the allocation of the case for trial, or to sentence,

      (iv) the defendant's criminal record, if any, and

      (v) any available statement of the effect of the offence on a victim, a victim's family or others.

PART 9

ALLOCATION AND SENDING FOR TRIAL

General Rules

When this part applies

★**P-71**   **9.1.**—(1) This part applies to the allocation and sending of cases for trial under—

(a) sections 17A to 26 of the Magistrates' Courts Act 1980; and

(b) sections 50A to 52 of the Crime and Disorder Act 1998.

(2) Rules 9.6 and 9.7 apply in a magistrates' court where the court must, or can, send a defendant to the Crown Court for trial, without allocating the case for trial there.

(3) Rules 9.8 to 9.14 apply in a magistrates' court where the court must allocate the case to a magistrates' court or to the Crown Court for trial.

(4) Rules 9.15 and 9.16 apply in the Crown Court, where a defendant is sent for trial there.

Exercise of magistrates' court's powers

★**P-72**   **9.2.**—(1) This rule applies to the exercise of the powers to which rules 9.6 to 9.14 apply.

(2) The general rule is that the court must exercise its powers at a hearing in public, but it may exercise any power it has to—

(a) withhold information from the public; or

(b) order a hearing in private.

(3) The general rule is that the court must exercise its powers in the defendant's presence, but it may exercise the powers to which the following rules apply in the defendant's absence on the conditions specified—

(a) where rule 9.8 (adult defendant: request for plea), rule 9.9 (adult defendant: guilty plea) or rule 9.13 (young defendant) applies, if—

(i) the defendant is represented, and

(ii) the defendant's disorderly conduct makes his or her presence in the courtroom impracticable;

(b) where rule 9.10 (adult defendant: not guilty plea) or rule 9.11 (adult defendant: allocation for magistrates' court trial) applies, if—

(i) the defendant is represented and waives the right to be present, or

(ii) the defendant's disorderly conduct makes his or her presence in the courtroom impracticable.

(4) The court may exercise its power to adjourn—

(a) if either party asks; or

(b) on its own initiative.

(5) Where the court on the same occasion deals with two or more offences alleged against the same defendant, the court must deal with those offences in the following sequence—

(a) any to which rule 9.6 applies (prosecutor's notice requiring Crown Court trial);

(b) any to which rule 9.7 applies (sending for Crown Court trial, without allocation there), in this sequence—

(i) any the court must send for trial, then

(ii) any the court can send for trial; and

(c) any to which rule 9.14 applies (allocation and sending for Crown Court trial).

(6) Where the court on the same occasion deals with two or more defendants charged jointly with an offence that can be tried in the Crown Court then in the following sequence—

(a) the court must explain, in terms each defendant can understand (with help, if necessary) that if the court sends one of them to the Crown Court for trial then the court must send for trial in the Crown Court, too, any other of them—

(i) who is charged with the same offence as the defendant sent for trial, or with an offence which the court decides is related to that offence,

(ii) who does not wish to plead guilty to each offence with which he or she is charged and

(iii) (if that other defendant is under 18, and the court would not otherwise have sent him or her for Crown Court trial) where the court decides that sending is necessary in the interests of justice

even if the court by then has decided to allocate that other defendant for magistrates' court trial; and

(b) the court may ask the defendants questions to help it decide in what order to deal with them.

(7) After following paragraph (5), if it applies, where the court on the same occasion—

(a) deals with two or more defendants charged jointly with an offence that can be tried in the Crown Court;

(b) allocates any of them to a magistrates' court for trial; and

(c) then sends another one of them to the Crown Court for trial,

the court must deal again with each one whom, on that occasion, it has allocated for magistrates' court trial.

Matters to be specified on sending for trial

9.3.—(1) Where the court sends a defendant to the Crown Court for trial, it must specify—   **★P-73**

(a) each offence to be tried;

(b) in respect of each, the power exercised to send the defendant for trial for that offence; and

(c) the Crown Court centre at which the trial will take place.

(2) In a case in which the prosecutor serves a notice to which rule 9.6(1)(a) applies (notice requiring Crown Court trial in a case of serious or complex fraud), the court must specify the Crown Court centre identified by that notice.

(3) In any other case, in deciding the Crown Court centre at which the trial will take place, the court must take into account—

(a) the convenience of the parties and witnesses;

(b) how soon a suitable courtroom will be available; and

(c) the directions on the allocation of Crown Court business contained in the Practice Direction.

Duty of justices' legal adviser

9.4.—(1) This rule applies—   **★P-74**

(a) only in a magistrates' court; and

(b) unless the court—

(i) includes a District Judge (Magistrates' Courts), and

(ii) otherwise directs.

(2) On the court's behalf, a justices' legal adviser may—

(a) read the allegation of the offence to the defendant;

(b) give any explanation and ask any question required by the rules in this part;

(c) make any announcement required by the rules in this part, other than an announcement of—

(i) the court's decisions about allocation and sending,

(ii) any indication by the court of likely sentence, or

(iii) sentence.

(3) A justices' legal adviser must—

(a) assist an unrepresented defendant;

(b) give the court such advice as is required to enable it to exercise its powers;

(c) if required, attend the members of the court outside the courtroom to give such advice, but inform the parties of any advice so given.

Duty of magistrates' court officer

9.5.—(1) The magistrates' court officer must—   **★P-75**

(a) serve notice of a sending for Crown Court trial on—

(i) the Crown Court officer, and

(ii) the parties;

(b) in that notice record—

(i) the matters specified by the court under rule 9.3 (matters to be specified on sending for trial),

(ii) any indication of intended guilty plea given by the defendant under rule 9.7 (sending for Crown Court trial),

(iii) any decision by the defendant to decline magistrates' court trial under rule 9.11 (adult defendant: allocation to magistrates' court for trial), and

(iv) the date on which any custody time limit will expire;

(c) record any indication of likely sentence to which rule 9.11 applies; and

(d) give the court such other assistance as it requires.

(2) The magistrates' court officer must include with the notice served on the Crown Court officer—

    (a)   the initial details of the prosecution case served by the prosecutor under rule 8.2;

    (b)   a record of any—

        (i)   listing or case management direction affecting the Crown Court,

        (ii)   direction about reporting restrictions,

        (iii)   decision about bail, for the purposes of section 5 of the Bail Act 1976,

        (iv)   recognizance given by a surety, or

        (v)   representation order; and

    (c)   if relevant, any available details of any—

        (i)   interpreter,

        (ii)   intermediary, or

        (iii)   other supporting adult, where the defendant is assisted by such a person.

Sending without Allocation for Crown Court Trial

Prosecutor's notice requiring Crown Court trial

★P-76   **9.6.**—(1) This rule applies where a prosecutor with power to do so requires a magistrates' court to send for trial in the Crown Court—

    (a)   a case of serious or complex fraud; or

    (b)   a case which will involve a child witness.

(2) The prosecutor must serve written notice of that requirement—

    (a)   on the magistrates' court officer and on the defendant; and

    (b)   before trial in a magistrates' court begins under Part 24 (trial and sentence in a magistrates' court).

(3) The notice must identify—

    (a)   the power on which the prosecutor relies; and

    (b)   the Crown Court centre at which the prosecutor wants the trial to take place.

(4) The prosecutor—

    (a)   must, when choosing a Crown Court centre, take into account the matters listed in rule 9.3(3) (court deciding to which Crown Court centre to send a case); and

    (b)   may change the centre identified before the case is sent for trial.

Sending for Crown Court trial

★P-77   **9.7.**—(1) This rule applies where a magistrates' court must, or can, send a defendant to the Crown Court for trial without first allocating the case for trial there.

(2) The court must read the allegation of the offence to the defendant.

(3) The court must explain, in terms the defendant can understand (with help, if necessary)—

    (a)   the allegation, unless it is self-explanatory;

    (b)   that the offence is one for which the court, as appropriate—

        (i)   must send the defendant to the Crown Court for trial because the offence is one which can only be tried there or because the court for some other reason is required to send that offence for trial,

        (ii)   may send the defendant to the Crown Court for trial if the magistrates' court decides that the offence is related to one already sent for trial there, or

        (iii)   (where the offence is low-value shoplifting and the defendant is 18 or over) must send the defendant to the Crown Court for trial if the defendant wants to be tried there;

    (c)   that reporting restrictions apply, which the defendant may ask the court to vary or remove

(4) In the following sequence, the court must then—

    (a)   invite the prosecutor to—

        (i)   identify the court's power to send the defendant to the Crown Court for trial for the offence, and

        (ii)   make representations about any ancillary matters, including bail and directions for the management of the case in the Crown Court;

    (b)   invite the defendant to make representations about—

        (i)   the court's power to send the defendant to the Crown Court, and

        (ii)   any ancillary matters;

    (c)   (where the offence is low-value shoplifting and the defendant is 18 or over) offer the defendant the opportunity to require trial in the Crown Court; and

    (d)   decide whether or not to send the defendant to the Crown Court for trial.

(5) If the court sends the defendant to the Crown Court for trial, it must—

    (a) ask whether the defendant intends to plead guilty in the Crown Court and—

        (i) if the answer is "yes", make arrangements for the Crown Court to take the defendant's plea as soon as possible, or

        (ii) if the defendant does not answer, or the answer is "no", make arrangements for a case management hearing in the Crown Court; and

    (b) give any other ancillary directions.

Allocation for Magistrates' Court or Crown Court Trial

Adult defendant: request for plea

9.8.—(1) This rule applies where—   ★**P-78**

    (a) the defendant is 18 or over; and

    (b) the court must decide whether a case is more suitable for trial in a magistrates' court or in the Crown Court.

(2) The court must read the allegation of the offence to the defendant.

(3) The court must explain, in terms the defendant can understand (with help, if necessary)—

    (a) the allegation, unless it is self-explanatory;

    (b) that the offence is one which can be tried in a magistrates' court or in the Crown Court;

    (c) that the court is about to ask whether the defendant intends to plead guilty;

    (d) that if the answer is "yes", then the court must treat that as a guilty plea and must sentence the defendant, or commit the defendant to the Crown Court for sentence;

    (e) that if the defendant does not answer, or the answer is "no", then—

        (i) the court must decide whether to allocate the case to a magistrates' court or to the Crown Court for trial,

        (ii) the value involved may require the court to order trial in a magistrates' court (where the offence is one to which section 22 of the Magistrates' Courts Act 1980 applies), and

        (iii) if the court allocates the case to a magistrates' court for trial, the defendant can nonetheless require trial in the Crown Court (unless the offence is one to which section 22 of the Magistrates' Courts Act 1980 applies and the value involved requires magistrates' court trial); and

    (f) that reporting restrictions apply, which the defendant may ask the court to vary or remove.

(4) The court must then ask whether the defendant intends to plead guilty.

Adult defendant: guilty plea

9.9.—(1) This rule applies where—   ★**P-79**

    (a) rule 9.8 applies; and

    (b) the defendant indicates an intention to plead guilty.

(2) The court must exercise its power to deal with the case—

    (a) as if the defendant had just pleaded guilty at a trial in a magistrates' court; and

    (b) in accordance with rule 24.11 (procedure if the court convicts).

Adult defendant: not guilty plea

9.10.—(1) This rule applies where—   ★**P-80**

    (a) rule 9.8 applies; and

    (b) the defendant—

        (i) indicates an intention to plead not guilty, or

        (ii) gives no indication of intended plea.

(2) In the following sequence, the court must then—

    (a) where the offence is one to which section 22 of the Magistrates' Courts Act 1980 applies, explain in terms the defendant can understand (with help, if necessary) that—

        (i) if the court decides that the value involved clearly is less than £5,000, the court must order trial in a magistrates' court,

        (ii) if the court decides that it is not clear whether that value is more or less than £5,000, then the court will ask whether the defendant agrees to be tried in a magistrates' court, and

        (iii) if the answer to that question is "yes", then the court must order such a trial and if the defendant is convicted then the maximum sentence is limited;

    (b) invite the prosecutor to—

        (i) identify any previous convictions of which it can take account, and

        (ii) make representations about how the court should allocate the case for trial, including representations about the value involved, if relevant;

    (c) invite the defendant to make such representations;

    (d) where the offence is one to which section 22 of the Magistrates' Courts Act 1980 applies—

        (i) if it is not clear whether the value involved is more or less than £5,000, ask whether the defendant agrees to be tried in a magistrates' court,

        (ii) if the defendant's answer to that question is "yes", or if that value clearly is less than £5,000, order a trial in a magistrates' court,

        (iii) if the defendant does not answer that question, or the answer is "no", or if that value clearly is more than £5,000, apply paragraph (2)(e);

    (e) exercise its power to allocate the case for trial, taking into account—

        (i) the adequacy of a magistrates' court's sentencing powers,

        (ii) any representations by the parties, and

        (iii) any allocation guidelines issued by the Sentencing Council.

Adult defendant: allocation for magistrates' court trial

★P-81   **9.11.**—(1) This rule applies where—

    (a) rule 9.10 applies; and

    (b) the court allocates the case to a magistrates' court for trial.

    (2) The court must explain, in terms the defendant can understand (with help, if necessary) that—

    (a) the court considers the case more suitable for trial in a magistrates' court than in the Crown Court;

    (b) if the defendant is convicted at a magistrates' court trial, then in some circumstances the court may commit the defendant to the Crown Court for sentence;

    (c) if the defendant does not agree to a magistrates' court trial, then the court must send the defendant to the Crown Court for trial; and

    (d) before deciding whether to accept magistrates' court trial, the defendant may ask the court for an indication of whether a custodial or non-custodial sentence is more likely in the event of a guilty plea at such a trial, but the court need not give such an indication.

    (3) If the defendant asks for such an indication of sentence and the court gives such an indication—

    (a) the court must then ask again whether the defendant intends to plead guilty;

    (b) if, in answer to that question, the defendant indicates an intention to plead guilty, then the court must exercise its power to deal with the case—

        (i) as if the defendant had just pleaded guilty to an offence that can be tried only in a magistrates' court, and

        (ii) in accordance with rule 24.11 (procedure if the court convicts);

    (c) if, in answer to that question, the defendant indicates an intention to plead not guilty, or gives no indication of intended plea, in the following sequence the court must then—

        (i) ask whether the defendant agrees to trial in a magistrates' court,

        (ii) if the defendant's answer to that question is "yes", order such a trial,

        (iii) if the defendant does not answer that question, or the answer is "no", apply rule 9.14.

    (4) If the defendant asks for an indication of sentence but the court gives none, or if the defendant does not ask for such an indication, in the following sequence the court must then—

    (a) ask whether the defendant agrees to trial in a magistrates' court;

    (b) if the defendant's answer to that question is "yes", order such a trial;

    (c) if the defendant does not answer that question, or the answer is "no", apply rule 9.14.

Adult defendant: prosecutor's application for Crown Court trial

★P-82   **9.12.**—(1) This rule applies where—

    (a) rule 9.11 applies;

    (b) the defendant agrees to trial in a magistrates' court; but

    (c) the prosecutor wants the court to exercise its power to send the defendant to the Crown Court for trial instead.

    (2) The prosecutor must—

    (a) apply before trial in a magistrates' court begins under Part 24 (trial and sentence in a magistrates' court); and

(b) notify—
   (i) the defendant, and
   (ii) the magistrates' court officer.

(3) The court must determine an application to which this rule applies before it deals with any other pre-trial application.

Young defendant

9.13.—(1) This rule applies where— ★P-83
   (a) the defendant is under 18; and
   (b) the court must decide whether to send the defendant for Crown Court trial instead of ordering trial in a youth court.

(2) The court must read the allegation of the offence to the defendant.

(3) The court must explain, in terms the defendant can understand (with help, if necessary)—
   (a) the allegation, unless it is self-explanatory;
   (b) that the offence is one which can be tried in the Crown Court instead of in a youth court;
   (c) that the court is about to ask whether the defendant intends to plead guilty;
   (d) that if the answer is "yes", then the court must treat that as a guilty plea and must sentence the defendant, or commit the defendant to the Crown Court for sentence;
   (e) that if the defendant does not answer, or the answer is "no", then the court must decide whether to send the defendant for Crown Court trial instead of ordering trial in a youth court; and
   (f) that reporting restrictions apply, which the defendant may ask the court to vary or remove.

(4) The court must then ask whether the defendant intends to plead guilty.

(5) If the defendant's answer to that question is "yes", the court must exercise its power to deal with the case—
   (a) as if the defendant had just pleaded guilty at a trial in a youth court; and
   (b) in accordance with rule 24.11 (procedure if the court convicts).

(6) If the defendant does not answer that question, or the answer is "no", in the following sequence the court must then—
   (a) invite the prosecutor to make representations about whether Crown Court or youth court trial is more appropriate;
   (b) invite the defendant to make such representations;
   (c) exercise its power to allocate the case for trial, taking into account—
      (i) the offence and the circumstances of the offence,
      (ii) the suitability of a youth court's sentencing powers,
      (iii) where the defendant is jointly charged with an adult, whether it is necessary in the interests of justice for them to be tried together in the Crown Court, and
      (iv) any representations by the parties.

Allocation and sending for Crown Court trial

9.14.—(1) This rule applies where— ★P-84
   (a) under rule 9.10 or rule 9.13, the court allocates the case to the Crown Court for trial;
   (b) under rule 9.11, the defendant does not agree to trial in a magistrates' court; or
   (c) under rule 9.12, the court grants the prosecutor's application for Crown Court trial.

(2) In the following sequence, the court must—
   (a) invite the prosecutor to make representations about any ancillary matters, including bail and directions for the management of the case in the Crown Court;
   (b) invite the defendant to make any such representations; and
   (c) exercise its powers to—
      (i) send the defendant to the Crown Court for trial, and
      (ii) give any ancillary directions.

Crown Court Initial Procedure after Sending for Trial

Service of prosecution evidence

9.15.—(1) This rule applies where— ★P-85
   (a) a magistrates' court sends the defendant to the Crown Court for trial; and
   (b) the prosecutor serves on the defendant copies of the documents containing the evidence on which the prosecution case relies.

(2) The prosecutor must at the same time serve copies of those documents on the Crown Court officer.

Application to dismiss offence sent for Crown Court trial

★P-86   **9.16.**—(1) This rule applies where a defendant wants the Crown Court to dismiss an offence sent for trial there.

(2) The defendant must—

    (a) apply in writing—

        (i) not more than 28 days after service of the prosecution evidence, and

        (ii) before the defendant's arraignment;

    (b) serve the application on—

        (i) the Crown Court officer, and

        (ii) each other party;

    (c) in the application—

        (i) explain why the prosecution evidence would not be sufficient for the defendant to be properly convicted,

        (ii) ask for a hearing, if the defendant wants one, and explain why it is needed,

        (iii) identify any witness whom the defendant wants to call to give evidence in person, with an indication of what evidence the witness can give,

        (iv) identify any material already served that the defendant thinks the court will need to determine the application, and

        (v) include any material not already served on which the defendant relies.

(3) A prosecutor who opposes the application must—

    (a) serve notice of opposition, not more than 14 days after service of the defendant's notice, on—

        (i) the Crown Court officer, and

        (ii) each other party;

    (b) in the notice of opposition—

        (i) explain the grounds of opposition,

        (ii) ask for a hearing, if the prosecutor wants one, and explain why it is needed,

        (iii) identify any witness whom the prosecutor wants to call to give evidence in person, with an indication of what evidence the witness can give,

        (iv) identify any material already served that the prosecutor thinks the court will need to determine the application, and

        (v) include any material not already served on which the prosecutor relies.

(4) The court may determine an application under this rule—

    (a) at a hearing, in public or in private, or without a hearing;

    (b) in the absence of—

        (i) the defendant who made the application,

        (ii) the prosecutor, if the prosecutor has had at least 14 days in which to serve notice opposing the application.

(5) The court may—

    (a) shorten or extend (even after it has expired) a time limit under this rule;

    (b) allow a witness to give evidence in person even if that witness was not identified in the defendant's application or in the prosecutor's notice.

PART 10

THE INDICTMENT

Service of indictment

★P-87   **10.1.**—(1) The prosecutor must serve a draft indictment on the Crown Court officer not more than 28 days after—

    (a) service on the defendant and on the Crown Court officer of copies of the documents containing the evidence on which the charge or charges are based, in a case where the defendant is sent for trial;

    (b) a High Court judge gives permission to serve a draft indictment;

    (c) the Court of Appeal orders a retrial.

(2) The Crown Court may extend the time limit, even after it has expired.

(3) Unless the Crown Court otherwise directs, the court officer must—

    (a) endorse any paper copy of the indictment made for the court with—

        (i) a note to identify it as the indictment served under this rule, and

        (ii) the date on which the draft indictment was served on the court officer; and

    (b) serve a copy of the indictment on all parties.

Form and content of indictment

10.2.—(1) An indictment must be in one of the forms set out in the Practice Direction and must   **★P-88**
contain, in a paragraph called a "count"—

    (a) a statement of the offence charged that—

        (i) describes the offence in ordinary language, and

        (ii) identifies any legislation that creates it; and

    (b) such particulars of the conduct constituting the commission of the offence as to make clear
what the prosecutor alleges against the defendant.

(2) More than one incident of the commission of the offence may be included in a count if those
incidents taken together amount to a course of conduct having regard to the time, place or purpose
of commission.

(3) An indictment may contain more than one count if all the offences charged—

    (a) are founded on the same facts; or

    (b) form or are a part of a series of offences of the same or a similar character.

(4) The counts must be numbered consecutively.

(5) An indictment may contain—

    (a) any count charging substantially the same offence as one specified in the notice of the of-
fence or offences for which the defendant was sent for trial; and

    (b) any other count based on the prosecution evidence already served which the Crown Court
may try.

Part 11

Deferred Prosecution Agreements

When this part applies

11.1.—(1) This part applies to proceedings in the Crown Court under Schedule 17 to the Crime   **★P-89**
and Courts Act 2013.

(2) In this part—

    (a) "agreement" means a deferred prosecution agreement under paragraph 1 of that Schedule;

    (b) "prosecutor" means a prosecutor designated by or under paragraph 3 of that Schedule;
and

    (c) "defendant" means the corporation, partnership or association with whom the prosecutor
proposes to enter, or enters, an agreement.

Exercise of court's powers

11.2.—(1) The court must determine an application to which this part applies at a hearing,   **★P-90**
which—

    (a) must be in private, under rule 11.3 (application to approve a proposal to enter an
agreement);

    (b) may be in public or private, under rule 11.4 (application to approve the terms of an agree-
ment), rule 11.6 (application to approve a variation of the terms of an agreement) or rule
11.9 (application to postpone the publication of information by the prosecutor);

    (c) must be in public, under rule 11.5 (application on breach of agreement) or rule 11.7 (ap-
plication to lift suspension of prosecution), unless the court otherwise directs.

(2) If at a hearing in private to which rule 11.4 or rule 11.6 applies the court approves the agreement or the variation proposed, the court must announce its decision and reasons at a hearing in
public.

(3) The court must not determine an application under rule 11.3, rule 11.4 or rule 11.6 unless—

    (a) both parties are present;

    (b) the prosecutor provides the court with a written declaration that, for the purposes of the
application—

        (i) the investigator enquiring into the alleged offence or offences has certified that no
information has been supplied which the investigator knows to be inaccurate, misleading or incomplete, and

963

    (ii) the prosecutor has complied with the prosecution obligation to disclose material to
     the defendant; and
  (c) the defendant provides the court with a written declaration that, for the purposes of the
    application—
    (i) the defendant has not supplied any information which the defendant knows to be
     inaccurate, misleading or incomplete, and
    (ii) the individual through whom the defendant makes the declaration has made reason-
     able enquiries and believes the defendant's declaration to be true.
 (4) The court must not determine an application under rule 11.5 or rule 11.7—
  (a) in the prosecutor's absence; or
  (b) in the absence of the defendant, unless the defendant has had at least 28 days in which to
    make representations.
 (5) If the court approves a proposal to enter an agreement—
  (a) the general rule is that any further application to which this part applies must be made to
    the same judge; but
  (b) the court may direct other arrangements.
 (6) The court may adjourn a hearing—
  (a) if either party asks, or on its own initiative;
  (b) in particular, if the court requires more information about—
    (i) the facts of an alleged offence,
    (ii) the terms of a proposal to enter an agreement, or of a proposed agreement or varia-
     tion of an agreement, or
    (iii) the circumstances in which the prosecutor wants the court to decide whether the
     defendant has failed to comply with the terms of an agreement.
 (7) The court may—
  (a) hear an application under rule 11.4 immediately after an application under rule 11.3, if
    the court approves a proposal to enter an agreement;
  (b) hear an application under rule 11.7 immediately after an application under rule 11.5, if
    the court terminates an agreement.

Application to approve a proposal to enter an agreement

★P-91 **11.3.**—(1) This rule applies where a prosecutor wants the court to approve a proposal to enter an
agreement.
 (2) The prosecutor must—
  (a) apply in writing after the commencement of negotiations between the parties but before
    the terms of agreement have been settled; and
  (b) serve the application on—
    (i) the court officer, and
    (ii) the defendant.
 (3) The application must—
  (a) identify the parties to the proposed agreement;
  (b) attach a proposed indictment setting out such of the offences listed in Part 2 of Schedule 17
    to the Crime and Courts Act 2013 as the prosecutor is considering;
  (c) include or attach a statement of facts proposed for inclusion in the agreement, which must
    give full particulars of each alleged offence, including details of any alleged financial gain
    or loss;
  (d) include any information about the defendant that would be relevant to sentence in the
    event of conviction for the offence or offences;
  (e) specify the proposed expiry date of the agreement;
  (f) describe the proposed terms of the agreement, including details of any—
    (i) monetary penalty to be paid by the defendant, and the time within which any such
     penalty is to be paid,
    (ii) compensation, reparation or donation to be made by the defendant, the identity of
     the recipient of any such payment and the time within which any such payment is to
     be made,
    (iii) surrender of profits or other financial benefit by the defendant, and the time within
     which any such sum is to be surrendered,
    (iv) arrangement to be made in relation to the management or conduct of the defendant's
     business,
    (v) co-operation required of the defendant in any investigation related to the offence or
     offences,

   (vi)   other action required of the defendant,

  (vii)   arrangement to monitor the defendant's compliance with a term,

 (viii)   consequence of the defendant's failure to comply with a term, and

  (ix)   prosecution costs to be paid by the defendant, and the time within which any such costs are to be paid;

 (g) in relation to those terms, explain how they comply with—

    (i)   the requirements of the code issued under paragraph 6 of Schedule 17 to the Crime and Courts Act 2013, and

   (ii)   any sentencing guidelines or guideline cases which apply;

 (h) contain or attach the defendant's written consent to the proposal; and

 (i) explain why—

    (i)   entering into an agreement is likely to be in the interests of justice, and

   (ii)   the proposed terms of the agreement are fair, reasonable and proportionate.

(4) If the proposed statement of facts includes assertions that the defendant does not admit, the application must—

 (a) specify the facts that are not admitted; and

 (b) explain why that is immaterial for the purposes of the proposal to enter an agreement.

Application to approve the terms of an agreement

11.4.—(1) This rule applies where— ★**P-92**

 (a) the court has approved a proposal to enter an agreement on an application under rule 11.3; and

 (b) the prosecutor wants the court to approve the terms of the agreement.

(2) The prosecutor must—

 (a) apply in writing as soon as practicable after the parties have settled the terms; and

 (b) serve the application on—

    (i)   the court officer, and

   (ii)   the defendant.

(3) The application must—

 (a) attach the agreement;

 (b) indicate in what respect, if any, the terms of the agreement differ from those proposed in the application under rule 11.3;

 (c) contain or attach the defendant's written consent to the agreement;

 (d) explain why—

    (i)   the agreement is in the interests of justice, and

   (ii)   the terms of the agreement are fair, reasonable and proportionate;

 (e) attach a draft indictment, charging the defendant with the offence or offences the subject of the agreement; and

 (f) include any application for the hearing to be in private.

(4) If the court approves the agreement and the draft indictment, the court officer must—

 (a) endorse any paper copy of the indictment made for the court with—

    (i)   a note to identify it as the indictment approved by the court, and

   (ii)   the date of the court's approval; and

 (b) treat the case as if it had been suspended by order of the court.

Application on breach of agreement

11.5.—(1) This rule applies where— ★**P-93**

 (a) the prosecutor believes that the defendant has failed to comply with the terms of an agreement; and

 (b) the prosecutor wants the court to decide—

    (i)   whether the defendant has failed to comply, and

   (ii)   if so, whether to terminate the agreement, or to invite the parties to agree proposals to remedy that failure.

(2) The prosecutor must—

 (a) apply in writing, as soon as practicable after becoming aware of the grounds for doing so; and

 (b) serve the application on—

    (i)   the court officer, and

   (ii)   the defendant.

(3) The application must—

    (a) specify each respect in which the prosecutor believes the defendant has failed to comply with the terms of the agreement, and explain the reasons for the prosecutor's belief; and

    (b) attach a copy of any document containing evidence on which the prosecutor relies.

(4) A defendant who wants to make representations in response to the application must serve the representations on—

    (a) the court officer; and

    (b) the prosecutor,

not more than 28 days after service of the application.

Application to approve a variation of the terms of an agreement

★P-94   **11.6.**—(1) This rule applies where the parties have agreed to vary the terms of an agreement because—

    (a) on an application under rule 11.5 (application on breach of agreement), the court has invited them to do so; or

    (b) variation of the agreement is necessary to avoid a failure by the defendant to comply with its terms in circumstances that were not, and could not have been, foreseen by either party at the time the agreement was made.

(2) The prosecutor must—

    (a) apply in writing, as soon as practicable after the parties have settled the terms of the variation; and

    (b) serve the application on—

      (i) the court officer, and

      (ii) the defendant.

(3) The application must—

    (a) specify each variation proposed;

    (b) contain or attach the defendant's written consent to the variation;

    (c) explain why—

      (i) the variation is in the interests of justice, and

      (ii) the terms of the agreement as varied are fair, reasonable and proportionate; and

    (d) include any application for the hearing to be in private.

Application to lift suspension of prosecution

★P-95   **11.7.**—(1) This rule applies where—

    (a) the court terminates an agreement before its expiry date; and

    (b) the prosecutor wants the court to lift the suspension of the prosecution that applied when the court approved the terms of the agreement.

(2) The prosecutor must—

    (a) apply in writing, as soon as practicable after the termination of the agreement; and

    (b) serve the application on—

      (i) the court officer, and

      (ii) the defendant.

(3) A defendant who wants to make representations in response to the application must serve the representations on—

    (a) the court officer; and

    (b) the prosecutor,

not more than 28 days after service of the application.

Notice to discontinue prosecution

★P-96   **11.8.**—(1) This rule applies where an agreement expires—

    (a) on its expiry date, or on a date treated as its expiry date; and

    (b) without having been terminated by the court.

(2) The prosecutor must—

    (a) as soon as practicable give notice in writing discontinuing the prosecution on the indictment approved by the court under rule 11.4 (application to approve the terms of an agreement); and

    (b) serve the notice on—

      (i) the court officer, and

      (ii) the defendant.

Application to postpone the publication of information by the prosecutor

11.9.—(1) This rule applies where the prosecutor—

    (a) makes an application under rule 11.4 (application to approve the terms of an agreement), rule 11.5 (application on breach of agreement) or rule 11.6 (application to approve a variation of the terms of an agreement);

    (b) decides not to make an application under rule 11.5, despite believing that the defendant has failed to comply with the terms of the agreement; or

    (c) gives a notice under rule 11.8 (notice to discontinue prosecution).

(2) A party who wants the court to order that the publication of information by the prosecutor about the court's or the prosecutor's decision should be postponed must—

    (a) apply in writing, as soon as practicable and in any event before such publication occurs;

    (b) serve the application on—

        (i) the court officer, and

        (ii) the other party; and

    (c) in the application—

        (i) specify the proposed terms of the order, and for how long it should last, and

        (ii) explain why an order in the terms proposed is necessary.

★P-97

Duty of court officer, etc.

11.10.—(1) Unless the court otherwise directs, the court officer must—

    (a) arrange for the recording of proceedings on an application to which this part applies;

    (b) arrange for the transcription of such a recording if—

        (i) a party wants such a transcript, or

        (ii) anyone else wants such a transcript (but that is subject to the restrictions in paragraph (2)).

(2) Unless the court otherwise directs, a person who transcribes a recording of proceedings under such arrangements—

    (a) must not supply anyone other than a party with a transcript of a recording of—

        (i) a hearing in private, or

        (ii) a hearing in public to which reporting restrictions apply;

    (b) subject to that, must supply any person with any transcript for which that person asks—

        (i) in accordance with the transcription arrangements made by the court officer, and

        (ii) on payment by that person of any fee prescribed.

(3) The court officer must not identify either party to a hearing in private under rule 11.3 (application to approve a proposal to enter an agreement) or rule 11.4 (application to approve the terms of an agreement)—

    (a) in any notice displayed in the vicinity of the courtroom; or

    (b) in any other information published by the court officer.

★P-98

Court's power to vary requirements under this part

11.11.—(1) The court may—

    (a) shorten or extend (even after it has expired) a time limit under this part;

    (b) allow there to be made orally—

        (i) an application under rule 11.4 (application to approve the terms of an agreement), or

        (ii) an application under rule 11.7 (application to lift suspension of prosecution)

    where the court exercises its power under rule 11.2(7) to hear one application immediately after another.

(2) A party who wants an extension of time must—

    (a) apply when serving the application or notice for which it is needed; and

    (b) explain the delay.

★P-99

PART 12

DISCONTINUING A PROSECUTION

When this part applies

12.1.—(1) This part applies where—

    (a) the Director of Public Prosecutions can discontinue a case in a magistrates' court, under section 23 of the Prosecution of Offences Act 1985;

★P-100

    (b)　the Director of Public Prosecutions, or another public prosecutor, can discontinue a case sent for trial in the Crown Court, under section 23A of the Prosecution of Offences Act 1985.

(2) In this part, "prosecutor" means one of those authorities.

Discontinuing a case

★P-101　　**12.2.**—(1) A prosecutor exercising a power to which this part applies must serve notice on—

    (a)　the court officer;

    (b)　the defendant; and

    (c)　any custodian of the defendant.

(2) Such a notice must—

    (a)　identify—

        (i)　the defendant and each offence to which the notice relates,

        (ii)　the person serving the notice, and

        (iii)　the power that that person is exercising;

    (b)　explain—

        (i)　in the copy of the notice served on the court officer, the reasons for discontinuing the case,

        (ii)　that the notice brings the case to an end,

        (iii)　if the defendant is in custody for any offence to which the notice relates, that the defendant must be released from that custody, and

        (iv)　if the notice is under section 23 of the 1985 Act, that the defendant has a right to require the case to continue.

(3) Where the defendant is on bail, the court officer must notify—

    (a)　any surety; and

    (b)　any person responsible for monitoring or securing the defendant's compliance with a condition of bail.

Defendant's notice to continue

★P-102　　**12.3.**—(1) This rule applies where a prosecutor serves a notice to discontinue under section 23 of the 1985 Act.

(2) A defendant who wants the case to continue must serve notice—

    (a)　on the court officer; and

    (b)　not more than 35 days after service of the notice to discontinue.

(3) If the defendant serves such a notice, the court officer must—

    (a)　notify the prosecutor; and

    (b)　refer the case to the court.

★P-103　　**13.** [*Warrants for arrest, detention or imprisonment*]

PART 14

BAIL AND CUSTODY TIME LIMITS

General Rules

When this part applies

★P-104　　**14.1.**—(1) This part applies where—

    (a)　a magistrates' court or the Crown Court can—

        (i)　grant or withhold bail, or impose or vary a condition of bail, and

        (ii)　where bail has been withheld, extend a custody time limit;

    (b)　a magistrates' court can monitor and enforce compliance with a supervision measure imposed in another European Union member State.

(2) In this part, "defendant" includes a person who has been granted bail by a police officer.

Exercise of court's powers to which this part applies

★P-105　　**14.2.**—(1) The court must not make a decision to which this part applies unless—

    (a)　each party to the decision and any surety directly affected by the decision—

        (i)　is present, in person or by live link, or

        (ii)　has had an opportunity to make representations;

    (b)　on an application for bail by a defendant who is absent and in custody, the court is satisfied that the defendant—

      (i) has waived the right to attend, or

      (ii) was present when a court withheld bail in the case on a previous occasion and has been in custody continuously since then;

  (c) on a prosecutor's appeal against a grant of bail, application to extend a custody time limit or appeal against a refusal to extend such a time limit—

      (i) the court is satisfied that a defendant who is absent has waived the right to attend, or

      (ii) the court is satisfied that it would be just to proceed even though the defendant is absent.

(2) The court may make a decision to which this part applies at a hearing, in public or in private.

(3) The court may determine without a hearing an application to vary a condition of bail if—

  (a) the parties to the application have agreed the terms of the variation proposed; or

  (b) on an application by a defendant, the court determines the application no sooner than the fifth business day after the application was served.

(4) The court may adjourn a determination to which this part applies, if that is necessary to obtain information sufficient to allow the court to make the decision required.

(5) At any hearing at which the court makes one of the following decisions, the court must announce in terms the defendant can understand (with help, if necessary) its reasons for—

  (a) withholding bail, or imposing or varying a bail condition;

  (b) granting bail, where the prosecutor opposed the grant; or

  (c) where the defendant is under 18—

      (i) imposing or varying a bail condition when ordering the defendant to be detained in local authority accommodation, or

      (ii) ordering the defendant to be detained in youth detention accommodation.

(6) At any hearing at which the court grants bail, the court must—

  (a) tell the defendant where and when to surrender to custody; or

  (b) arrange for the court officer to give the defendant, as soon as practicable, notice of where and when to surrender to custody.

Duty of justices' legal adviser

14.3.—(1) This rule applies—   ★**P-106**

  (a) only in a magistrates' court; and

  (b) unless the court—

      (i) includes a District Judge (Magistrates' Courts), and

      (ii) otherwise directs.

(2) A justices' legal adviser must—

  (a) assist an unrepresented defendant;

  (b) give the court such advice as is required to enable it to exercise its powers;

  (c) if required, attend the members of the court outside the courtroom to give such advice, but inform the parties of any advice so given.

General duties of court officer

14.4.—(1) The court officer must arrange for a note or other record to be made of—   ★**P-107**

  (a) the parties' representations about bail; and

  (b) the court's reasons for a decision—

      (i) to withhold bail, or to impose or vary a bail condition, or

      (ii) to grant bail, where the prosecutor opposed the grant.

(2) The court officer must serve notice of a decision about bail on—

  (a) the defendant (but, in the Crown Court, only where the defendant's legal representative asks for such a notice, or where the defendant has no legal representative);

  (b) the prosecutor (but only where the court granted bail, the prosecutor opposed the grant, and the prosecutor asks for such a notice);

  (c) a party to the decision who was absent when it was made;

  (d) a surety who is directly affected by the decision;

  (e) the defendant's custodian, where the defendant is in custody and the decision requires the custodian—

      (i) to release the defendant (or will do so, if a requirement ordered by the court is met), or

      (ii) to transfer the defendant to the custody of another custodian;

  (f) the court officer for any other court at which the defendant is required by that decision to surrender to custody.

(3) Where the court postpones the date on which a defendant who is on bail must surrender to custody, the court officer must serve notice of the postponed date on—

    (a) the defendant; and

    (b) any surety.

(4) Where a magistrates' court withholds bail in a case to which section 5(6A) of the Bail Act 1976 applies (remand in custody after hearing full argument on an application for bail), the court officer must serve on the defendant a certificate that the court heard full argument.

Bail

Prosecutor's representations about bail

★P-108   **14.5.**—(1) This rule applies whenever the court can grant or withhold bail.

(2) The prosecutor must provide the court with all the information in the prosecutor's possession which is material to what the court must decide.

(3) A prosecutor who opposes the grant of bail must specify—

    (a) each exception to the general right to bail on which the prosecutor relies; and

    (b) each consideration that the prosecutor thinks relevant.

(4) A prosecutor who wants the court to impose a condition on any grant of bail must—

    (a) specify each condition proposed; and

    (b) explain what purpose would be served by such a condition.

Reconsideration of police bail by magistrates' court

★P-109   **14.6.**—(1) This rule applies where a party wants a magistrates' court to reconsider a bail decision by a police officer.

(2) An application under this rule must be made to—

    (a) the magistrates' court to whose custody the defendant is under a duty to surrender, if any; or

    (b) any magistrates' court acting for the police officer's local justice area, in any other case.

(3) The applicant party must—

    (a) apply in writing; and

    (b) serve the application on—

        (i) the court officer,

        (ii) the other party, and

        (iii) any surety affected or proposed.

(4) The application must—

    (a) specify—

        (i) the decision that the applicant wants the court to make,

        (ii) each offence charged, or for which the defendant was arrested, and

        (iii) the police bail decision to be reconsidered and the reasons given for it;

    (b) explain, as appropriate—

        (i) why the court should grant bail itself, or withdraw it, or impose or vary a condition, and

        (ii) if the applicant is the prosecutor, what material information has become available since the police bail decision was made;

    (c) propose the terms of any suggested condition of bail; and

    (d) if the applicant wants an earlier hearing than paragraph (7) requires, ask for that, and explain why it is needed.

(5) A prosecutor who applies under this rule must serve on the defendant, with the application, notice that the court has power to withdraw bail and, if the defendant is absent when the court makes its decision, order the defendant's arrest.

(6) A party who opposes an application must—

    (a) so notify the court officer and the applicant at once; and

    (b) serve on each notice of the reasons for opposition.

(7) Unless the court otherwise directs, the court officer must arrange for the court to hear the application as soon as practicable and in any event—

    (a) if it is an application to withdraw bail, no later than the second business day after it was served;

    (b) in any other case, no later than the fifth business day after it was served.

(8) The court may—

(a) vary or waive a time limit under this rule;

(b) allow an application to be in a different form to one set out in the Practice Direction;

(c) if rule 14.2 allows, determine without a hearing an application to vary a condition.

Notice of application to consider bail

14.7.—(1) This rule applies where—

★P-110

(a) in a magistrates' court—

  (i) a prosecutor wants the court to withdraw bail granted by the court, or to impose or vary a condition of such bail, or

  (ii) a defendant wants the court to reconsider such bail before the next hearing in the case;

(b) in the Crown Court—

  (i) a party wants the court to grant bail that has been withheld, or to withdraw bail that has been granted, or to impose a new bail condition or to vary a present one, or

  (ii) a prosecutor wants the court to consider whether to grant or withhold bail, or impose or vary a condition of bail, under section 88 or section 89 of the Criminal Justice Act 2003 (bail and custody in connection with an intended application to the Court of Appeal to which Part 27 (retrial after acquittal) applies).

(2) Such a party must—

(a) apply in writing;

(b) serve the application on—

  (i) the court officer,

  (ii) the other party, and

  (iii) any surety affected or proposed; and

(c) serve the application not less than 2 business days before any hearing in the case at which the applicant wants the court to consider it, if such a hearing is already due.

(3) The application must—

(a) specify—

  (i) the decision that the applicant wants the court to make,

  (ii) each offence charged, and

  (iii) each relevant previous bail decision and the reasons given for each;

(b) if the applicant is a defendant, explain—

  (i) as appropriate, why the court should not withhold bail, or why it should vary a condition, and

  (ii) what further information or legal argument, if any, has become available since the most recent previous bail decision was made;

(c) if the applicant is the prosecutor, explain—

  (i) as appropriate, why the court should withdraw bail, or impose or vary a condition, and

  (ii) what material information has become available since the most recent previous bail decision was made;

(d) propose the terms of any suggested condition of bail; and

(e) if the applicant wants an earlier hearing than paragraph (6) requires, ask for that, and explain why it is needed.

(4) A prosecutor who applies under this rule must serve on the defendant, with the application, notice that the court has power to withdraw bail and, if the defendant is absent when the court makes its decision, order the defendant's arrest.

(5) A party who opposes an application must—

(a) so notify the court officer and the applicant at once; and

(b) serve on each notice of the reasons for opposition.

(6) Unless the court otherwise directs, the court officer must arrange for the court to hear the application as soon as practicable and in any event—

(a) if it is an application to grant or withdraw bail, no later than the second business day after it was served;

(b) if it is an application to impose or vary a condition, no later than the fifth business day after it was served.

(7) The court may—

(a) vary or waive a time limit under this rule;

(b) allow an application to be in a different form to one set out in the Practice Direction, or to be made orally;

(c) if rule 14.2 allows, determine without a hearing an application to vary a condition.

Defendant's application or appeal to the Crown Court after magistrates' court bail decision

★**P-111**   **14.8.**—(1) This rule applies where a defendant wants to—

    (a) apply to the Crown Court for bail after a magistrates' court has withheld bail; or

    (b) appeal to the Crown Court after a magistrates' court has refused to vary a bail condition as the defendant wants.

(2) The defendant must—

    (a) apply to the Crown Court in writing as soon as practicable after the magistrates' court's decision; and

    (b) serve the application on—

        (i) the Crown Court officer,

        (ii) the magistrates' court officer,

        (iii) the prosecutor, and

        (iv) any surety affected or proposed.

(3) The application must—

    (a) specify—

        (i) the decision that the applicant wants the Crown Court to make, and

        (ii) each offence charged;

    (b) explain—

        (i) as appropriate, why the Crown Court should not withhold bail, or why it should vary the condition under appeal, and

        (ii) what further information or legal argument, if any, has become available since the magistrates' court's decision;

    (c) propose the terms of any suggested condition of bail;

    (d) if the applicant wants an earlier hearing than paragraph (6) requires, ask for that, and explain why it is needed; and

    (e) on an application for bail, attach a copy of the certificate of full argument served on the defendant under rule 14.4(4).

(4) The magistrates' court officer must as soon as practicable serve on the Crown Court officer—

    (a) a copy of the note or record made under rule 14.4(1) in connection with the magistrates' court's decision; and

    (b) the date of the next hearing, if any, in the magistrates' court.

(5) A prosecutor who opposes the application must—

    (a) so notify the Crown Court officer and the defendant at once; and

    (b) serve on each notice of the reasons for opposition.

(6) Unless the Crown Court otherwise directs, the court officer must arrange for the court to hear the application or appeal as soon as practicable and in any event no later than the business day after it was served.

(7) The Crown Court may vary a time limit under this rule.

Prosecutor's appeal against grant of bail

★**P-112**   **14.9.**—(1) This rule applies where a prosecutor wants to appeal—

    (a) to the Crown Court against a grant of bail by a magistrates' court, in a case in which the defendant has been charged with, or convicted of, an offence punishable with imprisonment; or

    (b) to the High Court against a grant of bail—

        (i) by a magistrates' court, in an extradition case, or

        (ii) by the Crown Court, in a case in which the defendant has been charged with, or convicted of, an offence punishable with imprisonment (but not in a case in which the Crown Court granted bail on an appeal to which paragraph (1)(a) applies).

(2) The prosecutor must tell the court which has granted bail of the decision to appeal—

    (a) at the end of the hearing during which the court granted bail; and

    (b) before the defendant is released on bail.

(3) The court which has granted bail must exercise its power to remand the defendant in custody pending determination of the appeal.

(4) The prosecutor must serve an appeal notice—

    (a) on the court officer for the court which has granted bail and on the defendant;

    (b) not more than 2 hours after telling that court of the decision to appeal.

(5) The appeal notice must specify—
    (a) each offence with which the defendant is charged;
    (b) the decision under appeal;
    (c) the reasons given for the grant of bail; and
    (d) the grounds of appeal.

(6) On an appeal to the Crown Court, the magistrates' court officer must, as soon as practicable, serve on the Crown Court officer—
    (a) the appeal notice;
    (b) a copy of the note or record made under rule 14.4(1) (record of bail decision); and
    (c) notice of the date of the next hearing in the court which has granted bail.

(7) If the Crown Court so directs, the Crown Court officer must arrange for the defendant to be assisted by the Official Solicitor in a case in which the defendant—
    (a) has no legal representative; and
    (b) asks for such assistance.

(8) On an appeal to the Crown Court, the Crown Court officer must arrange for the court to hear the appeal as soon as practicable and in any event no later than the second business day after the appeal notice was served.

(9) The prosecutor—
    (a) may abandon an appeal to the Crown Court without the court's permission, by serving a notice of abandonment, signed by or on behalf of the prosecutor, on—
        (i) the defendant,
        (ii) the Crown Court officer, and
        (iii) the magistrates' court officer
        before the hearing of the appeal begins; but
    (b) after the hearing of the appeal begins, may only abandon the appeal with the Crown Court's permission.

(10) The court officer for the court which has granted bail must instruct the defendant's custodian to release the defendant on the bail granted by that court, subject to any condition or conditions of bail imposed, if—
    (a) the prosecutor fails to serve an appeal notice within the time to which paragraph (4) refers; or
    (b) the prosecutor serves a notice of abandonment under paragraph (9).

Consideration of bail in a murder case

14.10.—(1) This rule applies in a case in which—   ★**P-113**
    (a) the defendant is charged with murder; and
    (b) the Crown Court has not yet considered bail.

(2) The magistrates' court officer must arrange with the Crown Court officer for the Crown Court to consider bail as soon as practicable and in any event no later than the second business day after—
    (a) a magistrates' court sends the defendant to the Crown Court for trial; or
    (b) the first hearing in the magistrates' court, if the defendant is not at once sent for trial.

Condition of residence

14.11.—(1) The defendant must notify the prosecutor of the address at which the defendant will   ★**P-114**
live and sleep if released on bail with a condition of residence—
    (a) as soon as practicable after the institution of proceedings, unless already done; and
    (b) as soon as practicable after any change of that address.

(2) The prosecutor must help the court to assess the suitability of an address proposed as a condition of residence.

Electronic monitoring requirements

14.12.—(1) This rule applies where the court imposes electronic monitoring requirements, where   ★**P-115**
available, as a condition of bail.

(2) The court officer must—
    (a) inform the person responsible for the monitoring ("the monitor") of—
        (i) the defendant's name, and telephone number if available,
        (ii) each offence with which the defendant is charged,
        (iii) details of the place at which the defendant's presence must be monitored,
        (iv) the period or periods during which the defendant's presence at that place must be monitored, and

(v)   if fixed, the date on which the defendant must surrender to custody;

(b)   inform the defendant and, where the defendant is under 16, an appropriate adult, of the monitor's identity and the means by which the monitor may be contacted; and

(c)   notify the monitor of any subsequent—

    (i)   variation or termination of the electronic monitoring requirements, or

    (ii)   fixing or variation of the date on which the defendant must surrender to custody.

Accommodation or support requirements

★P-116   **14.13.**—(1) This rule applies where the court imposes as a condition of bail a requirement, where available, that the defendant must—

(a)   reside in accommodation provided for that purpose by, or on behalf of, a public authority;

(b)   receive bail support provided by, or on behalf of, a public authority.

(2) The court officer must—

(a)   inform the person responsible for the provision of any such accommodation or support ("the service provider") of—

    (i)   the defendant's name, and telephone number if available,

    (ii)   each offence with which the defendant is charged,

    (iii)   details of the requirement,

    (iv)   any other bail condition, and

    (v)   if fixed, the date on which the defendant must surrender to custody;

(b)   inform the defendant and, where the defendant is under 16, an appropriate adult, of—

    (i)   the service provider's identity and the means by which the service provider may be contacted, and

    (ii)   the address of any accommodation in which the defendant must live and sleep; and

(c)   notify the service provider of any subsequent—

    (i)   variation or termination of the requirement,

    (ii)   variation or termination of any other bail condition, and

    (iii)   fixing or variation of the date on which the defendant must surrender to custody.

Requirement for a surety or payment, etc.

★P-117   **14.14.**—(1) This rule applies where the court imposes as a condition of bail a requirement for—

(a)   a surety;

(b)   a payment;

(c)   the surrender of a document or thing.

(2) The court may direct how such a condition must be met.

(3) Unless the court otherwise directs, if any such condition or direction requires a surety to enter into a recognizance—

(a)   the recognizance must specify—

    (i)   the amount that the surety will be required to pay if the purpose for which the recognizance is entered is not fulfilled, and

    (ii)   the date, or the event, upon which the recognizance will expire;

(b)   the surety must enter into the recognizance in the presence of—

    (i)   the court officer,

    (ii)   the defendant's custodian, where the defendant is in custody, or

    (iii)   someone acting with the authority of either; and

(c)   the person before whom the surety enters into the recognizance must at once serve a copy on—

    (i)   the surety, and

    (ii)   as appropriate, the court officer and the defendant's custodian.

(4) Unless the court otherwise directs, if any such condition or direction requires someone to make a payment, or surrender a document or thing—

(a)   that payment, document or thing must be made or surrendered to—

    (i)   the court officer,

    (ii)   the defendant's custodian, where the defendant is in custody, or

    (iii)   someone acting with the authority of either; and

(b)   the court officer or the custodian, as appropriate, must serve immediately on the other a statement that the payment, document or thing has been made or surrendered.

(5) The custodian must release the defendant when each requirement ordered by the court has been met.

Forfeiture of a recognizance given by a surety

14.15.—(1) This rule applies where the court imposes as a condition of bail a requirement that a surety enter into a recognizance and, after the defendant is released on bail,— ★**P-118**

    (a) the defendant fails to surrender to custody as required, or

    (b) it appears to the court that the surety has failed to comply with a condition or direction.

(2) The court officer must serve notice on—

    (a) the surety; and

    (b) each party to the decision to grant bail,

of the hearing at which the court will consider the forfeiture of the recognizance.

(3) The court must not forfeit the recognizance less than 5 business days after service of notice under paragraph (2).

Bail condition to be enforced in another European Union member State

14.16.—(1) This rule applies where the court can impose as a condition of bail pending trial a requirement— ★**P-119**

    (a) with which the defendant must comply while in another European Union member State; and

    (b) which that other member State can monitor and enforce.

(2) The court—

    (a) must not exercise its power to impose such a requirement until the court has decided what, if any, condition or conditions of bail to impose while the defendant is in England and Wales;

    (b) subject to that, may exercise its power to make a request for the other member State to monitor and enforce that requirement.

(3) Where the court makes such a request, the court officer must—

    (a) issue a certificate requesting the monitoring and enforcement of the defendant's compliance with that requirement, in the form required by EU Council Framework Decision 2009/829/JHA;

    (b) serve on the relevant authority of the other member State—

        (i) the court's decision or a certified copy of that decision,

        (ii) the certificate, and

        (iii) a copy of the certificate translated into an official language of the other member State, unless English is such a language or the other member State has declared that it will accept a certificate in English; and

    (c) report to the court—

        (i) any request for further information returned by the competent authority in the other member State, and

        (ii) that authority's decision.

(4) Where the competent authority in the other member State agrees to monitor and enforce the requirement—

    (a) the court—

        (i) may exercise its power to withdraw the request (where it can), but

        (ii) whether or not it does so, must continue to exercise the powers to which this part applies in accordance with the rules in this part;

    (b) the court officer must immediately serve notice on that authority if—

        (i) legal proceedings are brought in relation to the requirement being monitored and enforced

        (ii) the court decides to vary or revoke that requirement, or to issue a warrant for the defendant's arrest; and

    (c) the court officer must promptly report to the court any information and any request received from that authority.

Enforcement of measure imposed in another European Union member State

14.17.—(1) This rule applies where the Lord Chancellor serves on the court officer a certificate requesting the monitoring and enforcement of a defendant's compliance with a supervision measure imposed by an authority in another European Union member State. ★**P-120**

(2) The court officer must arrange for the court to consider the request—

    (a) as a general rule—

        (i) within 20 business days of the date on which the Lord Chancellor received it from the requesting authority, or

     (ii)   within 40 business days of that date, if legal proceedings in relation to the supervision measure are brought within the first 20 business days;

   (b) exceptionally, later than that, but in such a case the court officer must immediately serve on the requesting authority—

     (i)   an explanation for the delay, and

     (ii)   an indication of when the court's decision is expected.

(3) On consideration of the request by the court, the court officer must—

   (a) without delay serve on the requesting authority—

     (i)   notice of any further information required by the court, and

     (ii)   subject to any such requirement and any response, notice of the court's decision; and

   (b) where the court agrees to monitor the supervision measure, serve notice of the court's decision on any supervisor specified by the court.

(4) Where the court agrees to monitor the supervision measure—

   (a) the court officer must immediately serve notice on the requesting authority if there is reported to the court—

     (i)   a breach of the measure, or

     (ii)   any other event that might cause the requesting authority to review its decision;

   (b) the court officer must without delay serve notice on the requesting authority if—

     (i)   legal proceedings are brought in relation to the decision to monitor compliance with the bail condition,

     (ii)   there is reported to the court a change of the defendant's residence, or

     (iii)   the court decides (where it can) to stop monitoring the defendant's compliance with the measure.

Custody Time Limits

Application to extend a custody time limit

★P-121   **14.18.**—(1) This rule applies where the prosecutor gives notice of application to extend a custody time limit.

(2) The court officer must arrange for the court to hear that application as soon as practicable after the expiry of—

   (a) 5 days from the giving of notice, in the Crown Court; or

   (b) 2 days from the giving of notice, in a magistrates' court.

(3) The court may shorten a time limit under this rule.

Appeal against custody time limit decision

★P-122   **14.19.**—(1) This rule applies where—

   (a) a defendant wants to appeal to the Crown Court against a decision by a magistrates' court to extend a custody time limit;

   (b) a prosecutor wants to appeal to the Crown Court against a decision by a magistrates' court to refuse to extend a custody time limit.

(2) The appellant must serve an appeal notice—

   (a) on—

     (i)   the other party to the decision,

     (ii)   the Crown Court officer, and

     (iii)   the magistrates' court officer;

   (b) in a defendant's appeal, as soon as practicable after the decision under appeal;

   (c) in a prosecutor's appeal—

     (i)   as soon as practicable after the decision under appeal, and

     (ii)   before the relevant custody time limit expires.

(3) The appeal notice must specify—

   (a) each offence with which the defendant is charged;

   (b) the decision under appeal;

   (c) the date on which the relevant custody time limit will expire;

   (d) on a defendant's appeal, the date on which the relevant custody time limit would have expired but for the decision under appeal; and

   (e) the grounds of appeal.

(4) The Crown Court officer must arrange for the Crown Court to hear the appeal as soon as practicable and in any event no later than the second business day after the appeal notice was served.

(5) The appellant—

    (a) may abandon an appeal without the Crown Court's permission, by serving a notice of abandonment, signed by or on behalf of the appellant, on—

        (i) the other party,

        (ii) the Crown Court officer, and

        (iii) the magistrates' court officer

    before the hearing of the appeal begins; but

    (b) after the hearing of the appeal begins, may only abandon the appeal with the Crown Court's permission.

PART 15

DISCLOSURE

When this part applies

15.1. This part applies—

    (a) in a magistrates' court and in the Crown Court;

    (b) where Parts I and II of the Criminal Procedure and Investigations Act 1996 apply.

★P-123

Prosecution disclosure

15.2.—(1) This rule applies where, under section 3 of the Criminal Procedure and Investigations Act 1996, the prosecutor—

    (a) discloses prosecution material to the defendant; or

    (b) serves on the defendant a written statement that there is no such material to disclose.

(2) The prosecutor must at the same time so inform the court officer.

★P-124

Prosecutor's application for public interest ruling

15.3.—(1) This rule applies where—

    (a) without a court order, the prosecutor would have to disclose material; and

    (b) the prosecutor wants the court to decide whether it would be in the public interest to disclose it.

(2) The prosecutor must—

    (a) apply in writing for such a decision; and

    (b) serve the application on—

        (i) the court officer,

        (ii) any person who the prosecutor thinks would be directly affected by disclosure of the material, and

        (iii) the defendant, but only to the extent that serving it on the defendant would not disclose what the prosecutor thinks ought not be disclosed.

(3) The application must—

    (a) describe the material, and explain why the prosecutor thinks that—

        (i) it is material that the prosecutor would have to disclose,

        (ii) it would not be in the public interest to disclose that material, and

        (iii) no measure such as the prosecutor's admission of any fact, or disclosure by summary, extract or edited copy, adequately would protect both the public interest and the defendant's right to a fair trial;

    (b) omit from any part of the application that is served on the defendant anything that would disclose what the prosecutor thinks ought not be disclosed (in which case, paragraph (4) of this rule applies); and

    (c) explain why, if no part of the application is served on the defendant.

(4) Where the prosecutor serves only part of the application on the defendant, the prosecutor must—

    (a) mark the other part, to show that it is only for the court; and

    (b) in that other part, explain why the prosecutor has withheld it from the defendant.

(5) Unless already done, the court may direct the prosecutor to serve an application on—

    (a) the defendant;

    (b) any other person who the court considers would be directly affected by the disclosure of the material.

(6) The court must determine the application at a hearing which—

    (a) must be in private, unless the court otherwise directs; and

★P-125

Archbold
paragraph
numbers

P-125

Archbold's Criminal Pleading—2015 ed.

    (b) if the court so directs, may take place, wholly or in part, in the defendant's absence.

(7) At a hearing at which the defendant is present—

    (a) the general rule is that the court must consider, in the following sequence—

        (i) representations first by the prosecutor and any other person served with the application, and then by the defendant, in the presence of them all, and then

        (ii) further representations by the prosecutor and any such other person in the defendant's absence; but

    (b) the court may direct other arrangements for the hearing.

(8) The court may only determine the application if satisfied that it has been able to take adequate account of—

    (a) such rights of confidentiality as apply to the material; and

    (b) the defendant's right to a fair trial.

(9) Unless the court otherwise directs, the court officer—

    (a) must not give notice to anyone other than the prosecutor—

        (i) of the hearing of an application under this rule, unless the prosecutor served the application on that person, or

        (ii) of the court's decision on the application;

    (b) may—

        (i) keep a written application or representations, or

        (ii) arrange for the whole or any part to be kept by some other appropriate person, subject to any conditions that the court may impose.

Defence disclosure

★**P-126**   **15.4.**—(1) This rule applies where—

    (a) under section 5 or 6 of the Criminal Procedure and Investigations Act 1996, the defendant gives a defence statement;

    (b) under section 6C of the 1996 Act, the defendant gives a defence witness notice.

(2) The defendant must serve such a statement or notice on—

    (a) the court officer; and

    (b) the prosecutor.

Defendant's application for prosecution disclosure

★**P-127**   **15.5.**—(1) This rule applies where the defendant—

    (a) has served a defence statement given under the Criminal Procedure and Investigations Act 1996; and

    (b) wants the court to require the prosecutor to disclose material.

(2) The defendant must serve an application on—

    (a) the court officer; and

    (b) the prosecutor.

(3) The application must—

    (a) describe the material that the defendant wants the prosecutor to disclose;

    (b) explain why the defendant thinks there is reasonable cause to believe that—

        (i) the prosecutor has that material, and

        (ii) it is material that the Criminal Procedure and Investigations Act 1996 requires the prosecutor to disclose; and

    (c) ask for a hearing, if the defendant wants one, and explain why it is needed.

(4) The court may determine an application under this rule—

    (a) at a hearing, in public or in private; or

    (b) without a hearing.

(5) The court must not require the prosecutor to disclose material unless the prosecutor—

    (a) is present; or

    (b) has had at least 14 days in which to make representations.

Review of public interest ruling

★**P-128**   **15.6.**—(1) This rule applies where the court has ordered that it is not in the public interest to disclose material that the prosecutor otherwise would have to disclose, and—

    (a) the defendant wants the court to review that decision; or

    (b) the Crown Court reviews that decision on its own initiative.

(2) Where the defendant wants the court to review that decision, the defendant must—

(a) serve an application on—
    (i) the court officer, and
    (ii) the prosecutor; and
(b) in the application—
    (i) describe the material that the defendant wants the prosecutor to disclose, and
    (ii) explain why the defendant thinks it is no longer in the public interest for the prosecutor not to disclose it.
(3) The prosecutor must serve any such application on any person who the prosecutor thinks would be directly affected if that material were disclosed.
(4) The prosecutor, and any such person, must serve any representations on—
(a) the court officer; and
(b) the defendant, unless to do so would in effect reveal something that either thinks ought not be disclosed.
(5) The court may direct—
(a) the prosecutor to serve any such application on any person who the court considers would be directly affected if that material were disclosed;
(b) the prosecutor and any such person to serve any representations on the defendant.
(6) The court must review a decision to which this rule applies at a hearing which—
(a) must be in private, unless the court otherwise directs; and
(b) if the court so directs, may take place, wholly or in part, in the defendant's absence.
(7) At a hearing at which the defendant is present—
(a) the general rule is that the court must consider, in the following sequence—
    (i) representations first by the defendant, and then by the prosecutor and any other person served with the application, in the presence of them all, and then
    (ii) further representations by the prosecutor and any such other person in the defendant's absence; but
(b) the court may direct other arrangements for the hearing.
(8) The court may only conclude a review if satisfied that it has been able to take adequate account of—
(a) such rights of confidentiality as apply to the material; and
(b) the defendant's right to a fair trial.

Defendant's application to use disclosed material
15.7.—(1) This rule applies where a defendant wants the court's permission to use disclosed **★P-129** prosecution material—
(a) otherwise than in connection with the case in which it was disclosed; or
(b) beyond the extent to which it was displayed or communicated publicly at a hearing.
(2) The defendant must serve an application on—
(a) the court officer; and
(b) the prosecutor.
(3) The application must—
(a) specify what the defendant wants to use or disclose; and
(b) explain why.
(4) The court may determine an application under this rule—
(a) at a hearing, in public or in private; or
(b) without a hearing.
(5) The court must not permit the use of such material unless—
(a) the prosecutor has had at least 28 days in which to make representations; and
(b) the court is satisfied that it has been able to take adequate account of any rights of confidentiality that may apply to the material.

Unauthorised use of disclosed material
15.8.—(1) This rule applies where a person is accused of using disclosed prosecution material in **★P-130** contravention of section 17 of the Criminal Procedure and Investigations Act 1996.
(2) A party who wants the court to exercise its power to punish that person for contempt of court must comply with the rules in Part 48 (contempt of court).
(3) The court must not exercise its power to forfeit material used in contempt of court unless—
(a) the prosecutor; and
(b) any other person directly affected by the disclosure of the material,
is present, or has had at least 14 days in which to make representations.

★**P-131**   **15.9.** The court may—
    (a) shorten or extend (even after it has expired) a time limit under this part;
    (b) allow a defence statement, or a defence witness notice, to be in a different written form to
        one set out in the Practice Direction, as long as it contains what the Criminal Procedure
        and Investigations Act 1996 requires;
    (c) allow an application under this part to be in a different form to one set out in the Practice
        Direction, or to be presented orally; and
    (d) specify the period within which—
        (i) any application under this part must be made, or
        (ii) any material must be disclosed, on an application to which rule 15.5 applies
           (defendant's application for prosecution disclosure).

PART 16

WRITTEN WITNESS STATEMENTS

When this part applies
★**P-132**   **16.1.** This part applies where a party wants to introduce a written witness statement in evidence
under section 9 of the Criminal Justice Act 1967.

Content of written witness statement
★**P-133**   **16.2.** The statement must contain—
    (a) at the beginning—
        (i) the witness' name, and
        (ii) the witness' age, if under 18;
    (b) a declaration by the witness that—
        (i) it is true to the best of the witness' knowledge and belief, and
        (ii) the witness knows that if it is introduced in evidence, then it would be an offence wil-
           fully to have stated in it anything that the witness knew to be false or did not believe
           to be true;
    (c) if the witness cannot read the statement, a signed declaration by someone else that that
        person read it to the witness; and
    (d) the witness' signature.

Reference to exhibit
★**P-134**   **16.3.** Where the statement refers to a document or object as an exhibit—
    (a) the statement must contain such a description of that exhibit as to identify it clearly; and
    (b) the exhibit must be labelled or marked correspondingly, and the label or mark signed by
        the maker of the statement.

Written witness statement in evidence
★**P-135**   **16.4.**—(1) A party who wants to introduce in evidence a written witness statement must—
    (a) before the hearing at which that party wants to introduce it, serve a copy of the statement
        on—
        (i) the court officer, and
        (ii) each other party; and
    (b) at or before that hearing, serve on the court officer the statement or an authenticated copy.
    (2) If that party relies on only part of the statement, that party must mark the copy in such a way
as to make that clear.
    (3) A prosecutor must serve on a defendant, with the copy of the statement, a notice—
    (a) of the right to object to the introduction of the statement in evidence instead of the witness
        giving evidence in person;
    (b) of the time limit for objecting under this rule; and
    (c) that if the defendant does not object in time, the court—
        (i) can nonetheless require the witness to give evidence in person, but
        (ii) may decide not to do so.
    (4) A party served with a written witness statement who objects to its introduction in evidence
must—
    (a) serve notice of the objection on—

    (i)   the party who served it, and

    (ii)   the court officer; and

  (b) serve the notice of objection not more than 7 days after service of the statement unless—

    (i)   the court extends that time limit, before or after the statement was served,

    (ii)   rule 24.8 (written guilty plea: special rules) applies, in which case the time limit is the later of 7 days after service of the statement or 7 days before the hearing date, or

    (iii)   rule 24.9 (single justice procedure: special rules) applies, in which case the time limit is 21 days after service of the statement.

(5) The court may exercise its power to require the witness to give evidence in person—

  (a) on application by any party; or

  (b) on its own initiative.

(6) A party entitled to receive a copy of a statement may waive that entitlement by so informing—

  (a) the party who would have served it; and

  (b) the court.

PART 17

WITNESS SUMMONSES, WARRANTS AND ORDERS

When this part applies

17.1.—(1) This part applies in magistrates' courts and in the Crown Court where—   ★**P-136**

  (a) a party wants the court to issue a witness summons, warrant or order under—

    (i)   section 97 of the Magistrates' Courts Act 1980,

    (ii)   paragraph 4 of Schedule 3 to the Crime and Disorder Act 1998,

    (iii)   section 2 of the Criminal Procedure (Attendance of Witnesses) Act 1965, or

    (iv)   section 7 of the Bankers' Books Evidence Act 1879;

  (b) the court considers the issue of such a summons, warrant or order on its own initiative as if a party had applied; or

  (c) one of those listed in rule 17.7 wants the court to withdraw such a summons, warrant or order.

(2) A reference to a "witness" in this part is a reference to a person to whom such a summons, warrant or order is directed.

Issue etc. of summons, warrant or order with or without a hearing

17.2.—(1) The court may issue or withdraw a witness summons, warrant or order with or without   ★**P-137**
a hearing.

(2) A hearing under this part must be in private unless the court otherwise directs.

Application for summons, warrant or order: general rules

17.3.—(1) A party who wants the court to issue a witness summons, warrant or order must apply   ★**P-138**
as soon as practicable after becoming aware of the grounds for doing so.

(2) The party applying must—

  (a) identify the proposed witness;

  (b) explain—

    (i)   what evidence the proposed witness can give or produce,

    (ii)   why it is likely to be material evidence, and

    (iii)   why it would be in the interests of justice to issue a summons, order or warrant as appropriate.

(3) The application may be made orally unless—

  (a) rule 17.5 applies; or

  (b) the court otherwise directs.

Written application: form and service

17.4.—(1) An application in writing under rule 17.3 must be in the form set out in the Practice   ★**P-139**
Direction, containing the same declaration of truth as a witness statement.

(2) The party applying must serve the application—

  (a) in every case, on the court officer and as directed by the court; and

  (b) as required by rule 17.5, if that rule applies.

Application for summons to produce a document, etc.: special rules

17.5.—(1) This rule applies to an application under rule 17.3 for a witness summons requiring the   ★**P-140**
proposed witness—

   (a) to produce in evidence a document or thing; or

   (b) to give evidence about information apparently held in confidence,

that relates to another person.

(2) The application must be in writing in the form required by rule 17.4.

(3) The party applying must serve the application—

   (a) on the proposed witness, unless the court otherwise directs; and

   (b) on one or more of the following, if the court so directs—

      (i) a person to whom the proposed evidence relates,

      (ii) another party.

(4) The court must not issue a witness summons where this rule applies unless—

   (a) everyone served with the application has had at least 14 days in which to make representations, including representations about whether there should be a hearing of the application before the summons is issued; and

   (b) the court is satisfied that it has been able to take adequate account of the duties and rights, including rights of confidentiality, of the proposed witness and of any person to whom the proposed evidence relates.

(5) This rule does not apply to an application for an order to produce in evidence a copy of an entry in a banker's book.

Application for summons to produce a document, etc.: court's assessment of relevance and confidentiality

★**P-141**   **17.6.**—(1) This rule applies where a person served with an application for a witness summons requiring the proposed witness to produce in evidence a document or thing objects to its production on the ground that—

   (a) it is not likely to be material evidence; or

   (b) even if it is likely to be material evidence, the duties or rights, including rights of confidentiality, of the proposed witness or of any person to whom the document or thing relates, outweigh the reasons for issuing a summons.

(2) The court may require the proposed witness to make the document or thing available for the objection to be assessed.

(3) The court may invite—

   (a) the proposed witness or any representative of the proposed witness; or

   (b) a person to whom the document or thing relates or any representative of such a person,

to help the court assess the objection.

Application to withdraw a summons, warrant or order

★**P-142**   **17.7.**—(1) The court may withdraw a witness summons, warrant or order if one of the following applies for it to be withdrawn—

   (a) the party who applied for it, on the ground that it no longer is needed;

   (b) the witness, on the grounds that—

      (i) he was not aware of any application for it, and

      (ii) he cannot give or produce evidence likely to be material evidence, or

      (iii) even if he can, his duties or rights, including rights of confidentiality, or those of any person to whom the evidence relates, outweigh the reasons for the issue of the summons, warrant or order; or

   (c) any person to whom the proposed evidence relates, on the grounds that—

      (i) he was not aware of any application for it, and

      (ii) that evidence is not likely to be material evidence, or

      (iii) even if it is, his duties or rights, including rights of confidentiality, or those of the witness, outweigh the reasons for the issue of the summons, warrant or order.

(2) A person applying under the rule must—

   (a) apply in writing as soon as practicable after becoming aware of the grounds for doing so, explaining why he wants the summons, warrant or order to be withdrawn; and

   (b) serve the application on the court officer and as appropriate on—

      (i) the witness,

      (ii) the party who applied for the summons, warrant or order, and

      (iii) any other person who he knows was served with the application for the summons, warrant or order.

(3) Rule 17.6 applies to an application under this rule that concerns a document or thing to be produced in evidence.

Court's power to vary requirements under this part

★**P-143**   **17.8.**—(1) The court may—

   (a) shorten or extend (even after it has expired) a time limit under this part; and

(b)   where a rule or direction requires an application under this part to be in writing, allow that application to be made orally instead.

(2) Someone who wants the court to allow an application to be made orally under paragraph (1)(b) of this rule must—

(a)   give as much notice as the urgency of his application permits to those on whom he would otherwise have served an application in writing; and

(b)   in doing so explain the reasons for the application and for wanting the court to consider it orally.

PART 18

MEASURES TO ASSIST A WITNESS OR DEFENDANT TO GIVE EVIDENCE

General Rules

When this part applies

18.1. This part applies—   **★P-144**

(a)   where the court can give a direction (a "special measures direction"), under section 19 of the Youth Justice and Criminal Evidence Act 1999, on an application or on its own initiative, for any of the following measures—

   (i)   preventing a witness from seeing the defendant (section 23 of the 1999 Act),

   (ii)   allowing a witness to give evidence by live link (section 24 of the 1999 Act),

   (iii) hearing a witness' evidence in private (section 25 of the 1999 Act),

   (iv)   dispensing with the wearing of wigs and gowns (section 26 of the 1999 Act),

   (v)   admitting video recorded evidence (sections 27 and 28 of the 1999 Act),

   (vi)   questioning a witness through an intermediary (section 29 of the 1999 Act),

   (vii) using a device to help a witness communicate (section 30 of the 1999 Act);

(b)   where the court can vary or discharge such a direction, under section 20 of the 1999 Act;

(c)   where the court can give, vary or discharge a direction (a "defendant's evidence direction") for a defendant to give evidence—

   (i)   by live link, under section 33A of the 1999 Act, or

   (ii)   through an intermediary, under sections 33BA and 33BB of the 1999 Act;

(d)   where the court can—

   (i)   make a witness anonymity order, under section 86 of the Coroners and Justice Act 2009, or

   (ii)   vary or discharge such an order, under section 91, 92 or 93 of the 2009 Act;

(e)   where the court can give or discharge a direction (a "live link direction"), on an application or on its own initiative, for a witness to give evidence by live link under—

   (i)   section 32 of the Criminal Justice Act 1988, or

   (ii)   sections 51 and 52 of the Criminal Justice Act 2003;

(f)   where the court can exercise any other power it has to give, vary or discharge a direction for a measure to help a witness give evidence.

Meaning of "witness"

18.2. In this part, "witness" means anyone (other than a defendant) for whose benefit an applica-   **★P-145** tion, direction or order is made.

Making an application for a direction or order

18.3. A party who wants the court to exercise its power to give or make a direction or order   **★P-146** must—

(a)   apply in writing as soon as reasonably practicable, and in any event not more than—

   (i)   28 days after the defendant pleads not guilty, in a magistrates' court, or

   (ii)   14 days after the defendant pleads not guilty, in the Crown Court; and

(b)   serve the application on—

   (i)   the court officer, and

   (ii)   each other party.

Decisions and reasons

18.4.—(1) A party who wants to introduce the evidence of a witness who is the subject of an ap-   **★P-147** plication, direction or order must—

(a) inform the witness of the court's decision as soon as reasonably practicable; and

(b) explain to the witness the arrangements that as a result will be made for him or her to give evidence.

(2) The court must announce, at a hearing in public before the witness gives evidence, the reasons for a decision—

(a) to give, make, vary or discharge a direction or order; or

(b) to refuse to do so.

Court's power to vary requirements under this part

★P-148 18.5.—(1) The court may—

(a) shorten or extend (even after it has expired) a time limit under this part; and

(b) allow an application or representations to be made in a different form to one set out in the Practice Direction, or to be made orally.

(2) A person who wants an extension of time must—

(a) apply when serving the application or representations for which it is needed; and

(b) explain the delay.

Custody of documents

★P-149 18.6. Unless the court otherwise directs, the court officer may—

(a) keep a written application or representations; or

(b) arrange for the whole or any part to be kept by some other appropriate person, subject to any conditions that the court may impose.

Declaration by intermediary

★P-150 18.7.—(1) This rule applies where—

(a) a video recorded interview with a witness is conducted through an intermediary;

(b) the court directs the examination of a witness or defendant through an intermediary.

(2) An intermediary must make a declaration—

(a) before such an interview begins;

(b) before the examination begins (even if such an interview with the witness was conducted through the same intermediary).

(3) The declaration must be in these terms—

"I solemnly, sincerely and truly declare [or I swear by Almighty God] that I will well and faithfully communicate questions and answers and make true explanation of all matters and things as shall be required of me according to the best of my skill and understanding."

Special Measures Directions

Exercise of court's powers

★P-151 18.8. The court may decide whether to give, vary or discharge a special measures direction—

(a) at a hearing, in public or in private, or without a hearing;

(b) in a party's absence, if that party—

(i) applied for the direction, variation or discharge, or

(ii) has had at least 14 days in which to make representations.

Special measures direction for a young witness

★P-152 18.9.—(1) This rule applies where, under section 21 or section 22 of the Youth Justice and Criminal Evidence Act 1999, the primary rule requires the court to give a direction for a special measure to assist a child witness or a qualifying witness—

(a) on an application, if one is made; or

(b) on the court's own initiative, in any other case.

(2) A party who wants to introduce the evidence of such a witness must as soon as reasonably practicable—

(a) notify the court that the witness is eligible for assistance;

(b) provide the court with any information that the court may need to assess the witness' views, if the witness does not want the primary rule to apply; and

(c) serve any video recorded evidence on—

(i) the court officer, and

(ii) each other party.

Content of application for a special measures direction

18.10. An applicant for a special measures direction must—   **★P-153**

(a) explain how the witness is eligible for assistance;

(b) explain why special measures would be likely to improve the quality of the witness' evidence;

(c) propose the measure or measures that in the applicant's opinion would be likely to maximise, so far as practicable, the quality of that evidence;

(d) report any views that the witness has expressed about—

  (i) his or her eligibility for assistance,

  (ii) the likelihood that special measures would improve the quality of his or her evidence, and

  (iii) the measure or measures proposed by the applicant;

(e) in a case in which a child witness or a qualifying witness does not want the primary rule to apply, provide any information that the court may need to assess the witness' views;

(f) in a case in which the applicant proposes that the witness should give evidence by live link—

  (i) identify someone to accompany the witness while the witness gives evidence,

  (ii) name that person, if possible, and

  (iii) explain why that person would be an appropriate companion for the witness, including the witness' own views;

(g) in a case in which the applicant proposes the admission of video recorded evidence, identify—

  (i) the date and duration of the recording,

  (ii) which part the applicant wants the court to admit as evidence, if the applicant does not want the court to admit all of it;

(h) attach any other material on which the applicant relies; and

(i) if the applicant wants a hearing, ask for one, and explain why it is needed.

Application to vary or discharge a special measures direction

18.11.—(1) A party who wants the court to vary or discharge a special measures direction must—   **★P-154**

(a) apply in writing, as soon as reasonably practicable after becoming aware of the grounds for doing so; and

(b) serve the application on—

  (i) the court officer, and

  (ii) each other party.

(2) The applicant must—

(a) explain what material circumstances have changed since the direction was given (or last varied, if applicable);

(b) explain why the direction should be varied or discharged; and

(c) ask for a hearing, if the applicant wants one, and explain why it is needed.

Application containing information withheld from another party

18.12.—(1) This rule applies where—   **★P-155**

(a) an applicant serves an application for a special measures direction, or for its variation or discharge; and

(b) the application includes information that the applicant thinks ought not be revealed to another party.

(2) The applicant must—

(a) omit that information from the part of the application that is served on that other party;

(b) mark the other part to show that, unless the court otherwise directs, it is only for the court; and

(c) in that other part, explain why the applicant has withheld that information from that other party.

(3) Any hearing of an application to which this rule applies—

(a) must be in private, unless the court otherwise directs; and

(b) if the court so directs, may be, wholly or in part, in the absence of a party from whom information has been withheld.

(4) At any hearing of an application to which this rule applies—

(a) the general rule is that the court must consider, in the following sequence—

(i)   representations first by the applicant and then by each other party, in all the parties' presence, and then

(ii) further representations by the applicant, in the absence of a party from whom information has been withheld; but

(b) the court may direct other arrangements for the hearing.

Representations in response

★**P-156**   **18.13.**—(1) This rule applies where a party wants to make representations about—

(a) an application for a special measures direction;

(b) an application for the variation or discharge of such a direction; or

(c) a direction, variation or discharge that the court proposes on its own initiative.

(2) Such a party must—

(a) serve the representations on—

(i)   the court officer, and

(ii) each other party;

(b) do so not more than 14 days after, as applicable—

(i)   service of the application, or

(ii) notice of the direction, variation or discharge that the court proposes; and

(c) ask for a hearing, if that party wants one, and explain why it is needed.

(3) Where representations include information that the person making them thinks ought not be revealed to another party, that person must—

(a) omit that information from the representations served on that other party;

(b) mark the information to show that, unless the court otherwise directs, it is only for the court; and

(c) with that information include an explanation of why it has been withheld from that other party.

(4) Representations against a special measures direction must explain, as appropriate—

(a) why the witness is not eligible for assistance;

(b) if the witness is eligible for assistance, why—

(i)   no special measure would be likely to improve the quality of the witness' evidence,

(ii) the proposed measure or measures would not be likely to maximise, so far as practicable, the quality of the witness' evidence, or

(iii) the proposed measure or measures might tend to inhibit the effective testing of that evidence;

(c) in a case in which the admission of video recorded evidence is proposed, why it would not be in the interests of justice for the recording, or part of it, to be admitted as evidence.

(5) Representations against the variation or discharge of a special measures direction must explain why it should not be varied or discharged.

Defendant's Evidence Directions

Exercise of court's powers

★**P-157**   **18.14.** The court may decide whether to give, vary or discharge a defendant's evidence direction—

(a) at a hearing, in public or in private, or without a hearing;

(b) in a party's absence, if that party—

(i)   applied for the direction, variation or discharge, or

(ii) has had at least 14 days in which to make representations.

Content of application for a defendant's evidence direction

★**P-158**   **18.15.** An applicant for a defendant's evidence direction must—

(a) explain how the proposed direction meets the conditions prescribed by the Youth Justice and Criminal Evidence Act 1999;

(b) in a case in which the applicant proposes that the defendant give evidence by live link—

(i)   identify a person to accompany the defendant while the defendant gives evidence, and

(ii) explain why that person is appropriate;

(c) ask for a hearing, if the applicant wants one, and explain why it is needed.

Application to vary or discharge a defendant's evidence direction

★**P-159**   **18.16.**—(1) A party who wants the court to vary or discharge a defendant's evidence direction must—

    (a) apply in writing, as soon as reasonably practicable after becoming aware of the grounds for doing so; and

    (b) serve the application on—

        (i) the court officer, and

        (ii) each other party.

(2) The applicant must—

    (a) on an application to discharge a live link direction, explain why it is in the interests of justice to do so;

    (b) on an application to discharge a direction for an intermediary, explain why it is no longer necessary in order to ensure that the defendant receives a fair trial;

    (c) on an application to vary a direction for an intermediary, explain why it is necessary for the direction to be varied in order to ensure that the defendant receives a fair trial; and

    (d) ask for a hearing, if the applicant wants one, and explain why it is needed.

Representations in response

18.17.—(1) This rule applies where a party wants to make representations about—   ★P-160

    (a) an application for a defendant's evidence direction;

    (b) an application for the variation or discharge of such a direction; or

    (c) a direction, variation or discharge that the court proposes on its own initiative.

(2) Such a party must—

    (a) serve the representations on—

        (i) the court officer, and

        (ii) each other party;

    (b) do so not more than 14 days after, as applicable—

        (i) service of the application, or

        (ii) notice of the direction, variation or discharge that the court proposes; and

    (c) ask for a hearing, if that party wants one, and explain why it is needed.

(3) Representations against a direction, variation or discharge must explain why the conditions prescribed by the Youth Justice and Criminal Evidence Act 1999 are not met.

Witness Anonymity Orders

Exercise of court's powers

18.18.—(1) The court may decide whether to make, vary or discharge a witness anonymity order—   ★P-161

    (a) at a hearing (which must be in private, unless the court otherwise directs), or without a hearing (unless any party asks for one);

    (b) in the absence of a defendant.

(2) The court must not exercise its power to make, vary or discharge a witness anonymity order, or to refuse to do so—

    (a) before or during the trial, unless each party has had an opportunity to make representations;

    (b) on an appeal by the defendant to which applies Part 34 (appeal to the Crown Court) or Part 39 (appeal to the Court of Appeal about conviction or sentence), unless in each party's case—

        (i) that party has had an opportunity to make representations, or

        (ii) the appeal court is satisfied that it is not reasonably practicable to communicate with that party;

    (c) after the trial and any such appeal are over, unless in the case of each party and the witness—

        (i) each has had an opportunity to make representations, or

        (ii) the court is satisfied that it is not reasonably practicable to communicate with that party or witness.

Content and conduct of application for a witness anonymity order

18.19.—(1) An applicant for a witness anonymity order must—   ★P-162

    (a) include in the application nothing that might reveal the witness' identity;

    (b) describe the measures proposed by the applicant;

    (c) explain how the proposed order meets the conditions prescribed by section 88 of the Coroners and Justice Act 2009;

    (d) explain why no measures other than those proposed will suffice, such as—

        (i)   an admission of the facts that would be proved by the witness,

        (ii) an order restricting public access to the trial,

        (iii) reporting restrictions, in particular under sections 45, 45A or 46 of the Youth Justice and Criminal Evidence Act 1999,

        (iv) a direction for a special measure under section 19 of the Youth Justice and Criminal Evidence Act 1999,

        (v) introduction of the witness' written statement as hearsay evidence, under section 116 of the Criminal Justice Act 2003, or

        (vi) arrangements for the protection of the witness;

    (e) attach to the application—

        (i)   a witness statement setting out the proposed evidence, edited in such a way as not to reveal the witness' identity,

        (ii) where the prosecutor is the applicant, any further prosecution evidence to be served, and any further prosecution material to be disclosed under the Criminal Procedure and Investigations Act 1996, similarly edited, and

        (iii) any defence statement that has been served, or as much information as may be available to the applicant that gives particulars of the defence; and

    (f) ask for a hearing, if the applicant wants one.

  (2) At any hearing of the application, the applicant must—

    (a) identify the witness to the court, unless at the prosecutor's request the court otherwise directs; and

    (b) present to the court, unless it otherwise directs—

        (i)   the unedited witness statement from which the edited version has been prepared,

        (ii) where the prosecutor is the applicant, the unedited version of any further prosecution evidence or material from which an edited version has been prepared, and

        (iii) such further material as the applicant relies on to establish that the proposed order meets the conditions prescribed by section 88 of the 2009 Act.

  (3) At any such hearing—

    (a) the general rule is that the court must consider, in the following sequence—

        (i)   representations first by the applicant and then by each other party, in all the parties' presence, and then

        (ii) information withheld from a defendant, and further representations by the applicant, in the absence of any (or any other) defendant; but

    (b) the court may direct other arrangements for the hearing.

  (4) Before the witness gives evidence, the applicant must identify the witness to the court—

    (a) if not already done;

    (b) without revealing the witness' identity to any other party or person; and

    (c) unless at the prosecutor's request the court otherwise directs.

Duty of court officer to notify the Director of Public Prosecutions

★P-163   **18.20.** The court officer must notify the Director of Public Prosecutions of an application, unless the prosecutor is, or acts on behalf of, a public authority.

Application to vary or discharge a witness anonymity order

★P-164   **18.21.**—(1) A party who wants the court to vary or discharge a witness anonymity order, or a witness who wants the court to do so when the case is over, must—

    (a) apply in writing, as soon as reasonably practicable after becoming aware of the grounds for doing so; and

    (b) serve the application on—

        (i)   the court officer, and

        (ii) each other party.

  (2) The applicant must—

    (a) explain what material circumstances have changed since the order was made (or last varied, if applicable);

    (b) explain why the order should be varied or discharged, taking account of the conditions for making an order; and

    (c) ask for a hearing, if the applicant wants one.

  (3) Where an application includes information that the applicant thinks might reveal the witness' identity, the applicant must—

    (a) omit that information from the application that is served on a defendant;

    (b) mark the information to show that it is only for the court and the prosecutor (if the prosecutor is not the applicant); and

    (c) with that information include an explanation of why it has been withheld.

(4) Where a party applies to vary or discharge a witness anonymity order after the trial and any appeal are over, the party who introduced the witness' evidence must serve the application on the witness.

Representations in response

18.22.—(1) This rule applies where a party or, where the case is over, a witness, wants to make representations about—   ★**P-165**

    (a) an application for a witness anonymity order;

    (b) an application for the variation or discharge of such an order; or

    (c) a variation or discharge that the court proposes on its own initiative.

(2) Such a party or witness must—

    (a) serve the representations on—

        (i) the court officer, and

        (ii) each other party;

    (b) do so not more than 14 days after, as applicable—

        (i) service of the application, or

        (ii) notice of the variation or discharge that the court proposes; and

    (c) ask for a hearing, if that party or witness wants one.

(3) Where representations include information that the person making them thinks might reveal the witness' identity, that person must—

    (a) omit that information from the representations served on a defendant;

    (b) mark the information to show that it is only for the court (and for the prosecutor, if relevant); and

    (c) with that information include an explanation of why it has been withheld.

(4) Representations against a witness anonymity order must explain why the conditions for making the order are not met.

(5) Representations against the variation or discharge of such an order must explain why it would not be appropriate to vary or discharge it, taking account of the conditions for making an order.

(6) A prosecutor's representations in response to an application by a defendant must include all information available to the prosecutor that is relevant to the conditions and considerations specified by sections 88 and 89 of the Coroners and Justice Act 2009.

Live Link Directions

Exercise of court's powers

18.23. The court may decide whether to give or discharge a live link direction—   ★**P-166**

    (a) at a hearing, in public or in private, or without a hearing;

    (b) in a party's absence, if that party—

        (i) applied for the direction or discharge, or

        (ii) has had at least 14 days in which to make representations in response to an application by another party.

Content of application for a live link direction

18.24. An applicant for a live link direction must—   ★**P-167**

    (a) unless the court otherwise directs, identify the place from which the witness will give evidence;

    (b) if that place is in the United Kingdom, explain why it would be in the interests of the efficient or effective administration of justice for the witness to give evidence by live link;

    (c) if the applicant wants the witness to be accompanied by another person while giving evidence—

        (i) name that person, if possible, and

        (ii) explain why it is appropriate for the witness to be accompanied;

    (d) ask for a hearing, if the applicant wants one, and explain why it is needed.

Application to discharge a live link direction

18.25.—(1) A party who wants the court to discharge a live link direction must—   ★**P-168**

    (a) apply in writing, as soon as reasonably practicable after becoming aware of the grounds for doing so; and

989

   (b) serve the application on—
        (i)   the court officer, and
        (ii) each other party.
(2) The applicant must—
   (a) explain what material circumstances have changed since the direction was given;
   (b) explain why it is in the interests of justice to discharge the direction; and
   (c) ask for a hearing, if the applicant wants one, and explain why it is needed.

Representations in response

★P-169   **18.26.**—(1) This rule applies where a party wants to make representations about an application for a live link direction or for the discharge of such a direction.
(2) Such a party must—
   (a) serve the representations on—
        (i)   the court officer, and
        (ii) each other party;
   (b) do so not more than 14 days after service of the application; and—
   (c) ask for a hearing, if that party wants one, and explain why it is needed.
(3) Representations against a direction or discharge must explain, as applicable, why the conditions prescribed by the Criminal Justice Act 1988 or the Criminal Justice Act 2003 are not met.

PART 19

EXPERT EVIDENCE

When this part applies

★P-170   **19.1.**—(1) This part applies where a party wants to introduce expert opinion evidence.
(2) A reference to an "expert" in this part is a reference to a person who is required to give or prepare expert evidence for the purpose of criminal proceedings, including evidence required to determine fitness to plead or for the purpose of sentencing.

Expert's duty to the court

★P-171   **19.2.**—(1) An expert must help the court to achieve the overriding objective—
   (a) by giving opinion which is—
        (i)   objective and unbiased, and
        (ii) within the expert's area or areas of expertise; and
   (b) by actively assisting the court in fulfilling its duty of case management under rule 3.2, in particular by—
        (i)   complying with directions made by the court, and
        (ii) at once informing the court of any significant failure (by the expert or another) to take any step required by such a direction.
(2) This duty overrides any obligation to the person from whom the expert receives instructions or by whom the expert is paid.
(3) This duty includes obligations—
   (a) to define the expert's area or areas of expertise—
        (i)   in the expert's report, and
        (ii) when giving evidence in person;
   (b) when giving evidence in person, to draw the court's attention to any question to which the answer would be outside the expert's area or areas of expertise; and
   (c) to inform all parties and the court if the expert's opinion changes from that contained in a report served as evidence or given in a statement.

Introduction of expert evidence

★P-172   **19.3.**—(1) A party who wants another party to admit as fact a summary of an expert's conclusions must serve that summary—
   (a) on the court officer and on each party from whom that admission is sought;
   (b) as soon as practicable after the defendant whom it affects pleads not guilty.
(2) A party on whom such a summary is served must—
   (a) serve a response stating—
        (i)   which, if any, of the expert's conclusions are admitted as fact, and

      (ii)   where a conclusion is not admitted, what are the disputed issues concerning that conclusion; and

  (b) serve the response—

      (i)   on the court officer and on the party who served the summary,

      (ii) as soon as practicable, and in any event not more than 14 days after service of the summary.

(3) A party who wants to introduce expert evidence otherwise than as admitted fact must—

  (a) serve a report by the expert which complies with rule 19.4 (content of expert's report) on—

      (i)   the court officer, and

      (ii) each other party;

  (b) serve the report as soon as practicable, and in any event with any application in support of which that party relies on that evidence;

  (c) serve with the report notice of anything of which the party serving it is aware which might reasonably be thought capable of detracting substantially from the credibility of that expert;

  (d) if another party so requires, give that party a copy of, or a reasonable opportunity to inspect—

      (i)   a record of any examination, measurement, test or experiment on which the expert's findings and opinion are based, or that were carried out in the course of reaching those findings and opinion, and

      (ii) anything on which any such examination, measurement, test or experiment was carried out.

(4) Unless the parties otherwise agree or the court directs, a party may not—

  (a) introduce expert evidence if that party has not complied with paragraph (3);

  (b) introduce in evidence an expert report if the expert does not give evidence in person.

Content of expert's report

19.4. Where rule 19.3(3) applies, an expert's report must—   ★**P-173**

  (a) give details of the expert's qualifications, relevant experience and accreditation;

  (b) give details of any literature or other information which the expert has relied on in making the report;

  (c) contain a statement setting out the substance of all facts given to the expert which are material to the opinions expressed in the report, or upon which those opinions are based;

  (d) make clear which of the facts stated in the report are within the expert's own knowledge;

  (e) say who carried out any examination, measurement, test or experiment which the expert has used for the report and—

      (i)   give the qualifications, relevant experience and accreditation of that person,

      (ii) say whether or not the examination, measurement, test or experiment was carried out under the expert's supervision, and

      (iii) summarise the findings on which the expert relies;

  (f) where there is a range of opinion on the matters dealt with in the report—

      (i)   summarise the range of opinion, and

      (ii) give reasons for the expert's own opinion;

  (g) if the expert is not able to give an opinion without qualification, state the qualification;

  (h) include such information as the court may need to decide whether the expert's opinion is sufficiently reliable to be admissible as evidence;

  (i) contain a summary of the conclusions reached;

  (j) contain a statement that the expert understands an expert's duty to the court, and has complied and will continue to comply with that duty; and

  (k) contain the same declaration of truth as a witness statement.

Expert to be informed of service of report

19.5. A party who serves on another party or on the court a report by an expert must, at once, ★**P-174**
inform that expert of that fact.

Pre-hearing discussion of expert evidence

19.6.—(1) This rule applies where more than one party wants to introduce expert evidence. ★**P-175**

(2) The court may direct the experts to—

(a) discuss the expert issues in the proceedings; and

(b) prepare a statement for the court of the matters on which they agree and disagree, giving their reasons.

(3) Except for that statement, the content of that discussion must not be referred to without the court's permission.

(4) A party may not introduce expert evidence without the court's permission if the expert has not complied with a direction under this rule.

Court's power to direct that evidence is to be given by a single joint expert

★**P-176**   **19.7.**—(1) Where more than one defendant wants to introduce expert evidence on an issue at trial, the court may direct that the evidence on that issue is to be given by one expert only.

(2) Where the co-defendants cannot agree who should be the expert, the court may—

(a) select the expert from a list prepared or identified by them; or

(b) direct that the expert be selected in another way.

Instructions to a single joint expert

★**P-177**   **19.8.**—(1) Where the court gives a direction under rule 19.7 for a single joint expert to be used, each of the co-defendants may give instructions to the expert.

(2) A co-defendant who gives instructions to the expert must, at the same time, send a copy of the instructions to each other co-defendant.

(3) The court may give directions about—

(a) the payment of the expert's fees and expenses; and

(b) any examination, measurement, test or experiment which the expert wishes to carry out.

(4) The court may, before an expert is instructed, limit the amount that can be paid by way of fees and expenses to the expert.

(5) Unless the court otherwise directs, the instructing co-defendants are jointly and severally liable for the payment of the expert's fees and expenses.

Court's power to vary requirements under this part

★**P-178**   **19.9.**—(1) The court may extend (even after it has expired) a time limit under this part.

(2) A party who wants an extension of time must—

(a) apply when serving the report, summary or notice for which it is required; and

(b) explain the delay.

PART 20

HEARSAY EVIDENCE

When this part applies

★**P-179**   **20.1.** This part applies—

(a) in a magistrates' court and in the Crown Court;

(b) where a party wants to introduce hearsay evidence, within the meaning of section 114 of the Criminal Justice Act 2003.

Notice to introduce hearsay evidence

★**P-180**   **20.2.**—(1) This rule applies where a party wants to introduce hearsay evidence for admission under any of the following sections of the Criminal Justice Act 2003—

(a) section 114(1)(d) (evidence admissible in the interests of justice);

(b) section 116 (evidence where a witness is unavailable);

(c) section 117(1)(c) (evidence in a statement prepared for the purposes of criminal proceedings);

(d) section 121 (multiple hearsay).

(2) That party must—

(a) serve notice on—

(i) the court officer, and

(ii) each other party;

(b) in the notice—

(i) identify the evidence that is hearsay,

(ii) set out any facts on which that party relies to make the evidence admissible,

(iii) explain how that party will prove those facts if another party disputes them, and

(iv) explain why the evidence is admissible; and

(c) attach to the notice any statement or other document containing the evidence that has not already been served.

(3) A prosecutor who wants to introduce such evidence must serve the notice not more than—

(a) 28 days after the defendant pleads not guilty, in a magistrates' court; or

(b) 14 days after the defendant pleads not guilty, in the Crown Court.

(4) A defendant who wants to introduce such evidence must serve the notice as soon as reasonably practicable.

(5) A party entitled to receive a notice under this rule may waive that entitlement by so informing—

(a) the party who would have served it; and

(b) the court.

Opposing the introduction of hearsay evidence

20.3.—(1) This rule applies where a party objects to the introduction of hearsay evidence.   ★**P-181**

(2) That party must—

(a) apply to the court to determine the objection;

(b) serve the application on—

(i) the court officer, and

(ii) each other party;

(c) serve the application as soon as reasonably practicable, and in any event not more than 14 days after—

(i) service of notice to introduce the evidence under rule 20.2,

(ii) service of the evidence to which that party objects, if no notice is required by that rule, or

(iii) the defendant pleads not guilty

whichever of those events happens last; and

(d) in the application, explain—

(i) which, if any, facts set out in a notice under rule 20.2 that party disputes,

(ii) why the evidence is not admissible, and

(iii) any other objection to the evidence.

(3) The court—

(a) may determine an application—

(i) at a hearing, in public or in private, or

(ii) without a hearing;

(b) must not determine the application unless the party who served the notice—

(i) is present, or

(ii) has had a reasonable opportunity to respond;

(c) may adjourn the application; and

(d) may discharge or vary a determination where it can do so under—

(i) section 8B of the Magistrates' Courts Act 1980 (ruling at pre-trial hearing in a magistrates' court), or

(ii) section 9 of the Criminal Justice Act 1987, or section 31 or 40 of the Criminal Procedure and Investigations Act 1996 (ruling at preparatory or other pre-trial hearing in the Crown Court).

Unopposed hearsay evidence

20.4.—(1) This rule applies where—   ★**P-182**

(a) a party has served notice to introduce hearsay evidence under rule 20.2; and

(b) no other party has applied to the court to determine an objection to the introduction of the evidence.

(2) The court must treat the evidence as if it were admissible by agreement.

Court's power to vary requirements under this part

20.5.—(1) The court may—   ★**P-183**

(a) shorten or extend (even after it has expired) a time limit under this part;

(b) allow an application or notice to be in a different form to one set out in the Practice Direction, or to be made or given orally;

(c) dispense with the requirement for notice to introduce hearsay evidence.

(2) A party who wants an extension of time must—

    (a) apply when serving the application or notice for which it is needed; and

    (b) explain the delay.

PART 21

EVIDENCE OF BAD CHARACTER

When this part applies

★P-184   **21.1.** This part applies—

    (a) in a magistrates' court and in the Crown Court;

    (b) where a party wants to introduce evidence of bad character, within the meaning of section 98 of the Criminal Justice Act 2003.

Content of application or notice

★P-185   **21.2.**—(1) A party who wants to introduce evidence of bad character must—

    (a) make an application under rule 21.3, where it is evidence of a non-defendant's bad character;

    (b) give notice under rule 21.4, where it is evidence of a defendant's bad character.

(2) An application or notice must—

    (a) set out the facts of the misconduct on which that party relies,

    (b) explain how that party will prove those facts (whether by certificate of conviction, other official record, or other evidence), if another party disputes them, and

    (c) explain why the evidence is admissible.

Application to introduce evidence of a non-defendant's bad character

★P-186   **21.3.**—(1) This rule applies where a party wants to introduce evidence of the bad character of a person other than the defendant.

(2) That party must serve an application to do so on—

    (a) the court officer; and

    (b) each other party.

(3) The applicant must serve the application—

    (a) as soon as reasonably practicable; and in any event

    (b) not more than 14 days after the prosecutor discloses material on which the application is based (if the prosecutor is not the applicant).

(4) A party who objects to the introduction of the evidence must—

    (a) serve notice on—

        (i) the court officer, and

        (ii) each other party

    not more than 14 days after service of the application; and

    (b) in the notice explain, as applicable—

        (i) which, if any, facts of the misconduct set out in the application that party disputes,

        (ii) what, if any, facts of the misconduct that party admits instead,

        (iii) why the evidence is not admissible, and

        (iv) any other objection to the application.

(5) The court—

    (a) may determine an application—

        (i) at a hearing, in public or in private, or

        (ii) without a hearing;

    (b) must not determine the application unless each party other than the applicant—

        (i) is present, or

        (ii) has had at least 14 days in which to serve a notice of objection;

    (c) may adjourn the application; and

    (d) may discharge or vary a determination where it can do so under—

        (i) section 8B of the Magistrates' Courts Act 1980 (ruling at pre-trial hearing in a magistrates' court), or

        (ii) section 9 of the Criminal Justice Act 1987, or section 31 or 40 of the Criminal Procedure and Investigations Act 1996 (ruling at preparatory or other pre-trial hearing in the Crown Court).

Notice to introduce evidence of a defendant's bad character

21.4.—(1) This rule applies where a party wants to introduce evidence of a defendant's bad   **★P-187**
character.

(2) That party must serve notice on—

    (a) the court officer; and

    (b) each other party.

(3) A prosecutor who wants to introduce such evidence must serve the notice not more than—

    (a) 28 days after the defendant pleads not guilty, in a magistrates' court; or

    (b) 14 days after the defendant pleads not guilty, in the Crown Court.

(4) A co-defendant who wants to introduce such evidence must serve the notice—

    (a) as soon as reasonably practicable; and in any event

    (b) not more than 14 days after the prosecutor discloses material on which the notice is based.

(5) A party who objects to the introduction of the evidence must—

    (a) apply to the court to determine the objection;

    (b) serve the application on—

        (i) the court officer, and

        (ii) each other party

    not more than 14 days after service of the notice; and

    (c) in the application explain, as applicable—

        (i) which, if any, facts of the misconduct set out in the notice that party disputes,

        (ii) what, if any, facts of the misconduct that party admits instead,

        (iii) why the evidence is not admissible,

        (iv) why it would be unfair to admit the evidence, and

        (v) any other objection to the notice.

(6) The court—

    (a) may determine an application—

        (i) at a hearing, in public or in private, or

        (ii) without a hearing;

    (b) must not determine the application unless the party who served the notice—

        (i) is present, or

        (ii) has had a reasonable opportunity to respond;

    (c) may adjourn the application; and

    (d) may discharge or vary a determination where it can do so under—

        (i) section 8B of the Magistrates' Courts Act 1980 (ruling at pre-trial hearing in a magistrates' court), or

        (ii) section 9 of the Criminal Justice Act 1987, or section 31 or 40 of the Criminal Procedure and Investigations Act 1996 (ruling at preparatory or other pre-trial hearing in the Crown Court).

(7) A party entitled to receive a notice may waive that entitlement by so informing—

    (a) the party who would have served it; and

    (b) the court.

Reasons for decisions

21.5. The court must announce at a hearing in public (but in the absence of the jury, if there is   **★P-188**
one) the reasons for a decision—

    (a) to admit evidence as evidence of bad character, or to refuse to do so; or

    (b) to direct an acquittal or a retrial under section 107 of the Criminal Justice Act 2003.

Court's power to vary requirements under this part

21.6.—(1) The court may—   **★P-189**

    (a) shorten or extend (even after it has expired) a time limit under this part;

    (b) allow an application or notice to be in a different form to one set out in the Practice Direction, or to be made or given orally;

    (c) dispense with a requirement for notice to introduce evidence of a defendant's bad character.

(2) A party who wants an extension of time must—

    (a) apply when serving the application or notice for which it is needed; and

    (b) explain the delay.

PART 22

EVIDENCE OF A COMPLAINANT'S PREVIOUS SEXUAL BEHAVIOUR

When this part applies

★**P-190**   **22.1.** This part applies in magistrates' courts and in the Crown Court where a defendant wants to—

(a)   introduce evidence; or

(b)   cross-examine a witness,

about a complainant's sexual behaviour despite the prohibition in section 41 of the Youth Justice and Criminal Evidence Act 1999.

Application for permission to introduce evidence or cross-examine

★**P-191**   **22.2.** The defendant must apply for permission to do so—

(a)   in writing; and

(b)   not more than 28 days after the prosecutor has complied or purported to comply with section 3 of the Criminal Procedure and Investigations Act 1996 (disclosure by prosecutor).

Content of application

★**P-192**   **22.3.** The application must—

(a)   identify the issue to which the defendant says the complainant's sexual behaviour is relevant;

(b)   give particulars of—

(i)   any evidence that the defendant wants to introduce, and

(ii)   any questions that the defendant wants to ask;

(c)   identify the exception to the prohibition in section 41 of the Youth Justice and Criminal Evidence Act 1999 on which the defendant relies; and

(d)   give the name and date of birth of any witness whose evidence about the complainant's sexual behaviour the defendant wants to introduce.

Service of application

★**P-193**   **22.4.** The defendant must serve the application on the court officer and all other parties.

Reply to application

★**P-194**   **22.5.** A party who wants to make representations about an application under rule 22.2 must—

(a)   do so in writing not more than 14 days after receiving it; and

(b)   serve those representations on the court officer and all other parties.

Application for special measures

★**P-195**   **22.6.** If the court allows an application under rule 22.2 then—

(a)   a party may apply not more than 14 days later for a special measures direction or for the variation of an existing special measures direction; and

(b)   the court may shorten the time for opposing that application.

Court's power to vary requirements under this part

★**P-196**   **22.7.** The court may shorten or extend (even after it has expired) a time limit under this part.

PART 23

RESTRICTION ON CROSS-EXAMINATION BY A DEFENDANT

General Rules

When this part applies

★**P-197**   **23.1.** This part applies where—

(a)   a defendant may not cross-examine in person a witness because of section 34 or section 35 of the Youth Justice and Criminal Evidence Act 1999 (complainants in proceedings for sexual offences; child complainants and other child witnesses);

(b)   the court can prohibit a defendant from cross-examining in person a witness under section 36 of that Act (direction prohibiting accused from cross-examining particular witness).

Appointment of advocate to cross-examine witness

23.2.—(1) This rule applies where a defendant may not cross-examine in person a witness in ★**P-198** consequence of—

    (a) the prohibition imposed by section 34 or section 35 of the Youth Justice and Criminal Evidence Act 1999; or

    (b) a prohibition imposed by the court under section 36 of the 1999 Act.

(2) The court must, as soon as practicable, explain in terms the defendant can understand (with help, if necessary)—

    (a) the prohibition and its effect;

    (b) that the defendant is entitled to arrange for a lawyer with a right of audience in the court to cross-examine the witness on his or her behalf;

    (c) that the defendant must notify the court officer of the identity of any such lawyer, with details of how to contact that person, by no later than a date set by the court;

    (d) that if the defendant does not want to make such arrangements, or if the defendant gives no such notice by that date, then—

        (i) the court must decide whether it is necessary in the interests of justice to appoint such a lawyer to cross-examine the witness for the defendant, and

        (ii) if the court decides that that is necessary, the court will appoint a lawyer chosen by the court.

(3) Having given those explanations, the court must—

    (a) ask whether the defendant wants to arrange for a lawyer to cross-examine the witness, and set a date by when the defendant must notify the court officer of the identity of that lawyer if the answer to that question is "yes";

    (b) if the answer to that question is "no", or if by the date set the defendant has given no such notice—

        (i) decide whether it is necessary in the interests of justice for the witness to be cross-examined by an advocate appointed to represent the defendant's interests, and

        (ii) if the court decides that that is necessary, give directions for the appointment of such an advocate.

(4) Where an advocate is appointed by the court—

    (a) the directions that the court gives under paragraph (3)(b)(ii) must provide for the material to be supplied to that advocate, including by whom and when it must be supplied; and

    (b) the appointment terminates at the conclusion of the cross-examination of the witness.

(5) The court may give the explanations and ask the questions required by this rule—

    (a) at a hearing, in public or in private; or

    (b) without a hearing, by written notice to the defendant.

(6) The court may extend (even after it has expired) the time limit that it sets under paragraph (3)(a)—

    (a) on application by the defendant; or

    (b) on its own initiative.

Application to Prohibit Cross-Examination

Exercise of court's powers

23.3.—(1) The court may decide whether to impose or discharge a prohibition against cross- ★**P-199** examination under section 36 of the Youth Justice and Criminal Evidence Act 1999—

    (a) at a hearing, in public or in private, or without a hearing;

    (b) in a party's absence, if that party—

        (i) applied for the prohibition or discharge, or

        (ii) has had at least 14 days in which to make representations.

(2) The court must announce, at a hearing in public before the witness gives evidence, the reasons for a decision—

    (a) to impose or discharge such a prohibition; or

    (b) to refuse to do so.

Application to prohibit cross-examination

23.4.—(1) This rule applies where under section 36 of the Youth Justice and Criminal Evidence ★**P-200** Act 1999 the prosecutor wants the court to prohibit the cross-examination of a witness by a defendant in person.

(2) The prosecutor must—

(a) apply in writing, as soon as reasonably practicable after becoming aware of the grounds for doing so; and

(b) serve the application on—

(i) the court officer,

(ii) the defendant who is the subject of the application, and

(iii) any other defendant, unless the court otherwise directs.

(3) The application must—

(a) report any views that the witness has expressed about whether he or she is content to be cross-examined by the defendant in person;

(b) identify—

(i) the nature of the questions likely to be asked, having regard to the issues in the case,

(ii) any relevant behaviour of the defendant at any stage of the case, generally and in relation to the witness,

(iii) any relationship, of any nature, between the witness and the defendant,

(iv) any other defendant in the case who is subject to such a prohibition in respect of the witness, and

(v) any special measures direction made in respect of the witness, or for which an application has been made;

(c) explain why the quality of evidence given by the witness on cross-examination—

(i) is likely to be diminished if no such prohibition is imposed, and

(ii) would be likely to be improved if it were imposed; and

(d) explain why it would not be contrary to the interests of justice to impose the prohibition.

Application to discharge prohibition imposed by the court

★**P-201**　　**23.5.**—(1) A party who wants the court to discharge a prohibition against cross-examination which the court imposed under section 36 of the Youth Justice and Criminal Evidence Act 1999 must—

(a) apply in writing, as soon as reasonably practicable after becoming aware of the grounds for doing so; and

(b) serve the application on—

(i) the court officer, and

(ii) each other party.

(2) The applicant must—

(a) explain what material circumstances have changed since the prohibition was imposed; and

(b) ask for a hearing, if the applicant wants one, and explain why it is needed.

Application containing information withheld from another party

★**P-202**　　**23.6.**—(1) This rule applies where—

(a) an applicant serves an application for the court to impose a prohibition against cross-examination, or for the discharge of such a prohibition; and

(b) the application includes information that the applicant thinks ought not be revealed to another party.

(2) The applicant must—

(a) omit that information from the part of the application that is served on that other party;

(b) mark the other part to show that, unless the court otherwise directs, it is only for the court; and

(c) in that other part, explain why the applicant has withheld that information from that other party.

(3) Any hearing of an application to which this rule applies—

(a) must be in private, unless the court otherwise directs; and

(b) if the court so directs, may be, wholly or in part, in the absence of a party from whom information has been withheld.

(4) At any hearing of an application to which this rule applies—

(a) the general rule is that the court must consider, in the following sequence—

(i) representations first by the applicant and then by each other party, in all the parties' presence, and then

(ii) further representations by the applicant, in the absence of a party from whom information has been withheld; but

(b) the court may direct other arrangements for the hearing.

Representations in response

23.7.—(1) This rule applies where a party wants to make representations about—   ★**P-203**

    (a) an application under rule 23.4 for a prohibition against cross-examination;

    (b) an application under rule 23.5 for the discharge of such a prohibition; or

    (c) a prohibition or discharge that the court proposes on its own initiative.

(2) Such a party must—

    (a) serve the representations on—

        (i) the court officer, and

        (ii) each other party;

    (b) do so not more than 14 days after, as applicable—

        (i) service of the application, or

        (ii) notice of the prohibition or discharge that the court proposes; and

    (c) ask for a hearing, if that party wants one, and explain why it is needed.

(3) Representations against a prohibition must explain in what respect the conditions for imposing it are not met.

(4) Representations against the discharge of a prohibition must explain why it should not be discharged.

(5) Where representations include information that the person making them thinks ought not be revealed to another party, that person must—

    (a) omit that information from the representations served on that other party;

    (b) mark the information to show that, unless the court otherwise directs, it is only for the court; and

    (c) with that information include an explanation of why it has been withheld from that other party.

Court's power to vary requirements

23.8.—(1) The court may—   ★**P-204**

    (a) shorten or extend (even after it has expired) a time limit under rule 23.4 (application to prohibit cross-examination), rule 23.5 (application to discharge prohibition imposed by the court) or rule 23.7 (representations in response); and

    (b) allow an application or representations required by any of those rules to be made in a different form to one set out in the Practice Direction, or to be made orally.

(2) A person who wants an extension of time must—

    (a) apply when serving the application or representations for which it is needed; and

    (b) explain the delay.

Part 24

Trial and Sentence in a Magistrates' Court

When this part applies

24.1.—(1) This part applies in a magistrates' court where—   ★**P-205**

    (a) the court tries a case;

    (b) the defendant pleads guilty;

    (c) under section 14 or section 16E of the Magistrates' Courts Act 1980, the defendant makes a statutory declaration of not having found out about the case until after the trial began;

    (d) under section 142 of the 1980 Act, the court can—

        (i) set aside a conviction, or

        (ii) vary or rescind a costs order, or an order to which Part 31 applies (behaviour orders).

(2) Where the defendant is under 18, in this part—

    (a) a reference to convicting the defendant includes a reference to finding the defendant guilty of an offence; and

    (b) a reference to sentence includes a reference to an order made on a finding of guilt.

General rules

24.2.—(1) Where this part applies—   ★**P-206**

    (a) the general rule is that the hearing must be in public; but

    (b) the court may exercise any power it has to—

        (i) impose reporting restrictions,

  (ii) withhold information from the public, or

  (iii) order a hearing in private; and

 (c) unless the court otherwise directs, only the following may attend a hearing in a youth court—

  (i) the parties and their legal representatives,

  (ii) a defendant's parents, guardian or other supporting adult,

  (iii) a witness,

  (iv) anyone else directly concerned in the case, and

  (v) a representative of a news-gathering or reporting organisation.

(2) Unless already done, the justices' legal adviser or the court must—

 (a) read the allegation of the offence to the defendant;

 (b) explain, in terms the defendant can understand (with help, if necessary)—

  (i) the allegation, and

  (ii) what the procedure at the hearing will be;

 (c) ask whether the defendant has been advised about the potential effect on sentence of a guilty plea;

 (d) ask whether the defendant pleads guilty or not guilty; and

 (e) take the defendant's plea.

(3) The court may adjourn the hearing—

 (a) at any stage, to the same or to another magistrates' court; or

 (b) to a youth court, where the court is not itself a youth court and the defendant is under 18.

(4) Paragraphs (1) and (2) of this rule do not apply where the court tries a case under rule 24.9 (single justice procedure: special rules).

Procedure on plea of not guilty

★P-207 **24.3.**—(1) This rule applies—

 (a) if the defendant has—

  (i) entered a plea of not guilty, or

  (ii) not entered a plea; or

 (b) if, in either case, it appears to the court that there may be grounds for making a hospital order without convicting the defendant.

(2) If a not guilty plea was taken on a previous occasion, the justices' legal adviser or the court must ask the defendant to confirm that plea.

(3) In the following sequence—

 (a) the prosecutor may summarise the prosecution case, identifying the relevant law and facts;

 (b) the prosecutor must introduce the evidence on which the prosecution case relies;

 (c) at the conclusion of the prosecution case, on the defendant's application or on its own initiative, the court—

  (i) may acquit on the ground that the prosecution evidence is insufficient for any reasonable court properly to convict, but

  (ii) must not do so unless the prosecutor has had an opportunity to make representations;

 (d) the justices' legal adviser or the court must explain, in terms the defendant can understand (with help, if necessary)—

  (i) the right to give evidence, and

  (ii) the potential effect of not doing so at all, or of refusing to answer a question while doing so;

 (e) the defendant may introduce evidence;

 (f) a party may introduce further evidence if it is then admissible (for example, because it is in rebuttal of evidence already introduced);

 (g) the prosecutor may make final representations in support of the prosecution case, where—

  (i) the defendant is represented by a legal representative, or

  (ii) whether represented or not, the defendant has introduced evidence other than his or her own; and

 (h) the defendant may make final representations in support of the defence case.

(4) Where a party wants to introduce evidence or make representations after that party's opportunity to do so under paragraph (3), the court—

 (a) may refuse to receive any such evidence or representations; and

 (b) must not receive any such evidence or representations after it has announced its verdict.

(5) If the court—

(a) convicts the defendant; or

(b) makes a hospital order instead of doing so,

it must give sufficient reasons to explain its decision.

  (6) If the court acquits the defendant, it may—

(a) give an explanation of its decision; and

(b) exercise any power it has to make—

(i) a behaviour order,

(ii) a costs order.

Evidence of a witness in person

  24.4.—(1) This rule applies where a party wants to introduce evidence by calling a witness to give ★**P-208**
that evidence in person.

  (2) Unless the court otherwise directs—

(a) a witness waiting to give evidence must not wait inside the courtroom, unless that witness
is—

(i) a party, or

(ii) an expert witness;

(b) a witness who gives evidence in the courtroom must do so from the place provided for that
purpose; and

(c) a witness' address must not be announced unless it is relevant to an issue in the case.

  (3) Unless other legislation otherwise provides, before giving evidence a witness must take an oath
or affirm.

  (4) In the following sequence—

(a) the party who calls a witness must ask questions in examination-in-chief;

(b) every other party may ask questions in cross-examination;

(c) the party who called the witness may ask questions in re-examination.

  (5) If other legislation so permits, at any time while giving evidence a witness may refer to a record
of that witness' recollection of events.

  (6) The justices' legal adviser or the court may—

(a) ask a witness questions; and in particular

(b) where the defendant is not represented, ask any question necessary in the defendant's
interests.

Evidence of a witness in writing

  24.5.—(1) This rule applies where a party wants to introduce in evidence the written statement of ★**P-209**
a witness to which applies—

(a) Part 16 (written witness statements);

(b) Part 19 (expert evidence); or

(c) Part 20 (hearsay evidence).

  (2) If the court admits such evidence—

(a) the court must read the statement; and

(b) unless the court otherwise directs, if any member of the public, including any reporter, is
present, each relevant part of the statement must be read or summarised aloud.

Evidence by admission

  24.6.—(1) This rule applies where—   ★**P-210**

(a) a party introduces in evidence a fact admitted by another party; or

(b) parties jointly admit a fact.

  (2) Unless the court otherwise directs, a written record must be made of the admission.

Procedure on plea of guilty

  24.7.—(1) This rule applies if—   ★**P-211**

(a) the defendant pleads guilty; and

(b) the court is satisfied that the plea represents a clear acknowledgement of guilt.

  (2) The court may convict the defendant without receiving evidence.

Written guilty plea: special rules

  24.8.—(1) This rule applies where—   ★**P-212**

(a) the offence alleged—

(i) can be tried only in a magistrates' court, and

      (ii) is not one specified under section 12(1)(a) of the Magistrates' Courts Act 1980;

  (b) the defendant is at least 16 years old;

  (c) the prosecutor has served on the defendant—

      (i) the summons or requisition,

      (ii) the material listed in paragraph (2) on which the prosecutor relies to set out the facts of the offence,

      (iii) the material listed in paragraph (3) on which the prosecutor relies to provide the court with information relevant to sentence,

      (iv) a notice that the procedure set out in this rule applies, and

      (v) a notice for the defendant's use if the defendant wants to plead guilty without attending court; and

  (d) the prosecutor has served on the court officer—

      (i) copies of those documents, and

      (ii) a certificate of service of those documents on the defendant.

(2) The material that the prosecutor must serve to set out the facts of the offence is—

  (a) a summary of the evidence on which the prosecution case is based;

  (b) any—

      (i) written witness statement to which Part 16 (written witness statements) applies, or

      (ii) document or extract setting out facts; or

  (c) any combination of such a summary, statement, document or extract.

(3) The material that the prosecutor must serve to provide information relevant to sentence is—

  (a) details of any previous conviction of the defendant which the prosecutor considers relevant, other than any conviction listed in the defendant's driving record;

  (b) if applicable, a notice that the defendant's driving record will be made available to the court;

  (c) a notice containing or describing any other information about the defendant, relevant to sentence, which will be made available to the court.

(4) A defendant who wants to plead guilty without attending court must, before the hearing date specified in the summons or requisition—

  (a) serve a notice of guilty plea on the court officer; and

  (b) include with that notice—

      (i) any representations that the defendant wants the court to consider, and

      (ii) a statement of the defendant's assets and other financial circumstances.

(5) A defendant who wants to withdraw such a notice must notify the court officer in writing before the hearing date.

(6) If the defendant does not withdraw the notice before the hearing date, then on or after that date—

  (a) to establish the facts of the offence and other information about the defendant relevant to sentence, the court may take account only of—

      (i) information contained in a document served by the prosecutor under paragraph (1),

      (ii) any previous conviction listed in the defendant's driving record, where the offence is under the Road Traffic Regulation Act 1984, the Road Traffic Act 1988, the Road Traffic (Consequential Provisions) Act 1988 or the Road Traffic (Driver Licensing and Information Systems) Act 1989,

      (iii) any other information about the defendant, relevant to sentence, of which the prosecutor served notice under paragraph (1), and

      (iv) any representations and any other information served by the defendant under paragraph (4)

    and rule 24.11(3) to (9) inclusive must be read accordingly;

  (b) unless the court otherwise directs, the prosecutor need not attend; and

  (c) the court may accept such a guilty plea and pass sentence in the defendant's absence.

(7) With the defendant's agreement, the court may deal with the case in the same way as under paragraph (6) where the defendant is present and—

  (a) has served a notice of guilty plea under paragraph (4); or

  (b) pleads guilty there and then.

Single justice procedure: special rules

★P-213
    24.9.—(1) This rule applies where—

  (a) the offence alleged—

    (i)   can be tried only in a magistrates' court, and

    (ii)   is not one punishable with imprisonment;

  (b) the defendant is at least 18 years old;

  (c) the prosecutor has served on the defendant—

    (i)   a written charge,

    (ii)   the material listed in paragraph (2) on which the prosecutor relies to set out the facts of the offence,

    (iii)   the material listed in paragraph (3) on which the prosecutor relies to provide the court with information relevant to sentence,

    (iv)   a notice that the procedure set out in this rule applies,

    (v)   a notice for the defendant's use if the defendant wants to plead guilty,

    (vi)   a notice for the defendant's use if the defendant wants to plead guilty but wants the case dealt with at a hearing by a court comprising more than one justice, and

    (vii)   a notice for the defendant's use if the defendant wants to plead not guilty; and

  (d) the prosecutor has served on the court officer—

    (i)   copies of those documents, and

    (ii)   a certificate of service of those documents on the defendant.

(2) The material that the prosecutor must serve to set out the facts of the offence is—

  (a) a summary of the evidence on which the prosecution case is based;

  (b) any—

    (i)   written witness statement to which Part 16 (written witness statements) applies, or

    (ii)   document or extract setting out facts; or

  (c) any combination of such a summary, statement, document or extract.

(3) The material that the prosecutor must serve to provide information relevant to sentence is—

  (a) details of any previous conviction of the defendant which the prosecutor considers relevant, other than any conviction listed in the defendant's driving record;

  (b) if applicable, a notice that the defendant's driving record will be made available to the court;

  (c) a notice containing or describing any other information about the defendant, relevant to sentence, which will be made available to the court.

(4) Not more than 21 days after service on the defendant of the documents listed in paragraph (1)(c)—

  (a) a defendant who wants to plead guilty must serve a notice to that effect on the court officer and include with that notice—

    (i)   any representations that the defendant wants the court to consider, and

    (ii)   a statement of the defendant's assets and other financial circumstances;

  (b) a defendant who wants to plead guilty but wants the case dealt with at a hearing by a court comprising more than one justice must serve a notice to that effect on the court officer;

  (c) a defendant who wants to plead not guilty must serve a notice to that effect on the court officer.

(5) If within 21 days of service on the defendant of the documents listed in paragraph (1)(c) the defendant serves a notice to plead guilty under paragraph (4)(a)—

  (a) the court officer must arrange for the court to deal with the case in accordance with that notice; and

  (b) the time for service of any other notice under paragraph (4) expires at once.

(6) If within 21 days of service on the defendant of the documents listed in paragraph (1)(c) the defendant wants to withdraw a notice which he or she has served under paragraph (4)(b) (notice to plead guilty at a hearing) or under paragraph (4)(c) (notice to plead not guilty), the defendant must—

  (a) serve notice of that withdrawal on the court officer; and

  (b) serve any substitute notice under paragraph (4).

(7) Paragraph (8) applies where by the date of trial the defendant has not—

  (a) served notice under paragraph (4)(b) or (c) of wanting to plead guilty at a hearing, or wanting to plead not guilty; or

  (b) given notice to that effect under section 16B(2) of the Magistrates' Courts Act 1980.

(8) Where this paragraph applies—

  (a) the court may try the case in the parties' absence and without a hearing;

  (b) the court may accept any guilty plea of which the defendant has given notice under paragraph (4)(a);

    (c)   to establish the facts of the offence and other information about the defendant relevant to sentence, the court may take account only of—

        (i)   information contained in a document served by the prosecutor under paragraph (1),

        (ii)   any previous conviction listed in the defendant's driving record, where the offence is under the Road Traffic Regulation Act 1984, the Road Traffic Act 1988, the Road Traffic (Consequential Provisions) Act 1988 or the Road Traffic (Driver Licensing and Information Systems) Act 1989,

        (iii)   any other information about the defendant, relevant to sentence, of which the prosecutor served notice under paragraph (1), and

        (iv)   any representations and any other information served by the defendant under paragraph (4)(a)

    and rule 24.11(3) to (9) inclusive must be read accordingly.

   (9) Paragraph (10) applies where—

    (a)   the defendant serves on the court officer a notice under paragraph (4)(b) or (c); or

    (b)   the court which tries the defendant under paragraph (8) adjourns the trial for the defendant to attend a hearing by a court comprising more than one justice.

   (10) Where this paragraph applies, the court must exercise its power to issue a summons and—

    (a)   the rules in Part 7 apply (starting a prosecution in a magistrates' court) as if the prosecutor had just served an information in the same terms as the written charge;

    (b)   the rules in Part 8 (initial details of the prosecution case) apply as if the documents served by the prosecutor under paragraph (1) had been served under that part;

    (c)   except for rule 24.8 (written guilty plea: special rules) and this rule, the rules in this part apply.

Application to withdraw a guilty plea

★P-214   **24.10.**—(1) This rule applies where the defendant wants to withdraw a guilty plea.

   (2) The defendant must apply to do so—

    (a)   as soon as practicable after becoming aware of the reasons for doing so; and

    (b)   before sentence.

   (3) Unless the court otherwise directs, the application must be in writing and the defendant must serve it on—

    (a)   the court officer; and

    (b)   the prosecutor.

   (4) The application must—

    (a)   explain why it would be unjust not to allow the defendant to withdraw the guilty plea;

    (b)   identify—

        (i)   any witness that the defendant wants to call, and

        (ii)   any other proposed evidence; and

    (c)   say whether the defendant waives legal professional privilege, giving any relevant name and date.

Procedure if the court convicts

★P-215   **24.11.**—(1) This rule applies if the court convicts the defendant.

   (2) The court—

    (a)   may exercise its power to require—

        (i)   a statement of the defendant's assets and other financial circumstances,

        (ii)   a pre-sentence report; and

    (b)   may (and in some circumstances must) remit the defendant to a youth court for sentence where—

        (i)   the defendant is under 18, and

        (ii)   the convicting court is not itself a youth court.

   (3) The prosecutor must—

    (a)   summarise the prosecution case, if the sentencing court has not heard evidence;

    (b)   identify any offence to be taken into consideration in sentencing;

    (c)   provide information relevant to sentence, including any statement of the effect of the offence on the victim, the victim's family or others; and

    (d)   where it is likely to assist the court, identify any other matter relevant to sentence, including—

        (i)   the legislation applicable,

        (ii)   any sentencing guidelines, or guideline cases,

    (iii) aggravating and mitigating features affecting the defendant's culpability and the harm which the offence caused, was intended to cause or might forseeably have caused, and

    (iv) the effect of such of the information listed in paragraph (2)(a) as the court may need to take into account.

(4) The defendant must provide details of financial circumstances—

  (a) in any form required by the court officer;

  (b) by any date directed by the court or by the court officer.

(5) Where the defendant pleads guilty but wants to be sentenced on a different basis to that disclosed by the prosecution case—

  (a) the defendant must set out that basis in writing, identifying what is in dispute;

  (b) the court may invite the parties to make representations about whether the dispute is material to sentence; and

  (c) if the court decides that it is a material dispute, the court must—

    (i) invite such further representations or evidence as it may require, and

    (ii) decide the dispute.

(6) Where the court has power to order the endorsement of the defendant's driving record, or power to order the defendant to be disqualified from driving—

  (a) if other legislation so permits, a defendant who wants the court not to exercise that power must introduce the evidence or information on which the defendant relies;

  (b) the prosecutor may introduce evidence; and

  (c) the parties may make representations about that evidence or information.

(7) Before the court passes sentence—

  (a) the court must—

    (i) give the defendant an opportunity to make representations and introduce evidence relevant to sentence, and

    (ii) where the defendant is under 18, give the defendant's parents, guardian or other supporting adult, if present, such an opportunity as well; and

  (b) the justices' legal adviser or the court must elicit any further information relevant to sentence that the court may require.

(8) If the court requires more information, it may exercise its power to adjourn the hearing for not more than—

  (a) 3 weeks at a time, if the defendant will be in custody; or

  (b) 4 weeks at a time.

(9) When the court has taken into account all the evidence, information and any report available, the court must—

  (a) as a general rule, pass sentence there and then;

  (b) when passing sentence, explain the reasons for deciding on that sentence, unless neither the defendant nor any member of the public, including any reporter, is present;

  (c) when passing sentence, explain to the defendant its effect, the consequences of failing to comply with any order or pay any fine, and any power that the court has to vary or review the sentence, unless—

    (i) the defendant is absent, or

    (ii) the defendant's ill-health or disorderly conduct makes such an explanation impracticable;

  (d) give any such explanation in terms the defendant, if present, can understand (with help, if necessary); and

  (e) consider exercising any power it has to make a costs or other order.

(10) Despite the general rule—

  (a) the court must adjourn the hearing if the defendant is absent, the case started with a summons, requisition or single justice procedure notice, and either—

    (i) the court considers passing a custodial sentence (where it can do so), or

    (ii) the court considers imposing a disqualification (unless it has already adjourned the hearing to give the defendant an opportunity to attend);

  (b) the court may exercise any power it has to—

    (i) commit the defendant to the Crown Court for sentence (and in some cases it must do so), or

    (ii) defer sentence for up to 6 months.

Procedure where a party is absent

  24.12.—(1) This rule—   ★**P-216**

  (a) applies where a party is absent; but

  (b) does not apply where—

    (i) the defendant has served a notice of guilty plea under rule 24.8 (written guilty plea: special rules), or

    (ii) the court tries a case under rule 24.9 (single justice procedure: special rules).

 (2) Where the prosecutor is absent, the court may—

  (a) if it has received evidence, deal with the case as if the prosecutor were present; and

  (b) in any other case—

    (i) enquire into the reasons for the prosecutor's absence, and

    (ii) if satisfied there is no good reason, exercise its power to dismiss the allegation.

 (3) Where the defendant is absent—

  (a) the general rule is that the court must proceed as if the defendant—

    (i) were present, and

    (ii) had pleaded not guilty (unless a plea already has been taken)

  and the court must give reasons if it does not do so; but

  (b) the general rule does not apply if the defendant is under 18;

  (c) the general rule is subject to the court being satisfied that—

    (i) any summons or requisition was served on the defendant a reasonable time before the hearing, or

    (ii) in a case in which the hearing has been adjourned, the defendant had reasonable notice of where and when it would resume;

  (d) the general rule is subject also to rule 24.11(10)(a) (restrictions on passing sentence in the defendant's absence).

 (4) Where the defendant is absent, the court—

  (a) must exercise its power to issue a warrant for the defendant's arrest, if it passes a custodial sentence; and

  (b) may exercise its power to do so in any other case, if it does not apply the general rule in paragraph (3)(a) of this rule about proceeding in the defendant's absence.

Provision of documents for the court

★P-217 **24.13.**—(1) A party who introduces a document in evidence, or who otherwise uses a document in presenting that party's case, must provide a copy for—

  (a) each other party;

  (b) any witness that party wants to refer to that document;

  (c) the court; and

  (d) the justices' legal adviser.

 (2) Unless the court otherwise directs, on application or on its own initiative, the court officer must provide for the court—

  (a) any copy received under paragraph (1) before the hearing begins; and

  (b) a copy of the court officer's record of—

    (i) information supplied by each party for the purposes of case management, including any revision of information previously supplied,

    (ii) each pre-trial direction for the management of the case,

    (iii) any pre-trial decision to admit evidence,

    (iv) any pre-trial direction about the giving of evidence, and

    (v) any admission to which rule 24.6 applies.

 (3) Where rule 24.8 (written guilty plea: special rules) applies, the court officer must provide for the court—

  (a) each document served by the prosecutor under rule 24.8(1)(d);

  (b) the defendant's driving record, where the offence is under the Road Traffic Regulation Act 1984, the Road Traffic Act 1988, the Road Traffic (Consequential Provisions) Act 1988 or the Road Traffic (Driver Licensing and Information Systems) Act 1989;

  (c) any other information about the defendant, relevant to sentence, of which the prosecutor served notice under rule 24.8(1); and

  (d) the notice of guilty plea and any representations and other information served by the defendant under rule 24.8(4).

 (4) Where the court tries a case under rule 24.9 (single justice procedure: special rules), the court officer must provide for the court—

  (a) each document served by the prosecutor under rule 24.9(1)(d);

  (b) the defendant's driving record, where the offence is under the Road Traffic Regulation Act

1984, the Road Traffic Act 1988, the Road Traffic (Consequential Provisions) Act 1988 or the Road Traffic (Driver Licensing and Information Systems) Act 1989;

(c) any other information about the defendant, relevant to sentence, of which the prosecutor served notice under rule 24.9(1); and

(d) any notice, representations and other information served by the defendant under rule 24.9(4)(a).

Place of trial
24.14.—(1) The hearing must take place in a courtroom provided by the Lord Chancellor, un-   ★**P-218**
less—

(a) the court otherwise directs; or

(b) the court tries a case under rule 24.9 (single justice procedure: special rules).

(2) Where the hearing takes place in Wales—

(a) any party or witness may use the Welsh language; and

(b) if practicable, at least one member of the court must be Welsh-speaking.

Duty of justices' legal adviser
24.15.—(1) A justices' legal adviser must attend the court and carry out the duties listed in this   ★**P-219**
rule, as applicable, unless the court—

(a) includes a District Judge (Magistrates' Courts); and

(b) otherwise directs.

(2) A justices' legal adviser must—

(a) before the hearing begins, by reference to what is provided for the court under rule 24.13 (provision of documents for the court) draw the court's attention to—

   (i) what the prosecutor alleges,

   (ii) what the parties say is agreed,

   (iii) what the parties say is in dispute, and

   (iv) what the parties say about how each expects to present the case, especially where that may affect its duration and timetabling;

(b) whenever necessary, give the court legal advice and—

   (i) if necessary, attend the members of the court outside the courtroom to give such advice, but

   (ii) inform the parties (if present) of any such advice given outside the courtroom; and

(c) assist the court, where appropriate, in the formulation of its reasons and the recording of those reasons.

(3) A justices' legal adviser must—

(a) assist an unrepresented defendant;

(b) assist the court by—

   (i) making a note of the substance of any oral evidence or representations, to help the court recall that information,

   (ii) if the court rules inadmissible part of a written statement introduced in evidence, marking that statement in such a way as to make that clear,

   (iii) ensuring that an adequate record is kept of the court's decisions and the reasons for them, and

   (iv) making any announcement, other than of the verdict or sentence.

(4) Where the defendant has served a notice of guilty plea to which rule 24.8 (written guilty plea: special rules) applies, a justices' legal adviser must—

(a) unless the court otherwise directs, if any member of the public, including any reporter, is present, read aloud to the court—

   (i) the material on which the prosecutor relies to set out the facts of the offence and to provide information relevant to sentence (or summarise any written statement included in that material, if the court so directs), and

   (ii) any written representations by the defendant;

(b) otherwise, draw the court's attention to—

   (i) what the prosecutor alleges, and any significant features of the material listed in paragraph (4)(a)(i), and

   (ii) any written representations by the defendant.

(5) Where the court tries a case under rule 24.9 (single justice procedure: special rules), a justices' legal adviser must draw the court's attention to—

(a) what the prosecutor alleges, and any significant features of the material on which the prosecutor relies to prove the alleged offence and to provide information relevant to sentence; and

(b) any representations served by the defendant.

Duty of court officer

★P-220   **24.16.** The court officer must—

(a) serve on each party notice of where and when an adjourned hearing will resume, unless—

(i)   the party was present when that was arranged,

(ii) the defendant has served a notice of guilty plea to which rule 24.8 (written guilty plea: special rules) applies, and the adjournment is for not more than 4 weeks, or

(iii) the court tries a case under rule 24.9 (single justice procedure: special rules), and the adjourned trial will resume under that rule;

(b) if the reason for the adjournment was to postpone sentence, include that reason in any such notice to the defendant;

(c) unless the court otherwise directs, make available to the parties any written report to which rule 24.11 (procedure if the court convicts) applies;

(d) where the court has ordered a defendant to provide information under section 25 of the Road Traffic Offenders Act 1988, serve on the defendant notice of that order unless the defendant was present when it was made;

(e) serve on the prosecutor—

(i)   any notice of guilty plea to which rule 24.8 (written guilty plea: special rules) applies,

(ii) any declaration served under rule 24.17 (statutory declaration of ignorance of proceedings) that the defendant did not know about the case;

(f) serve on the prosecutor notice of any hearing date arranged in consequence of such a declaration, unless—

(i)   the prosecutor was present when that was arranged, or

(ii) the court otherwise directs;

(g) serve on the prosecutor—

(i)   notice of any hearing date arranged in consequence of the issue of a summons under rule 37.9 (single justice procedure: special rules), and in that event

(ii) any notice served by the defendant under rule 37.9(2)(b) or (c);

(h) record the court's reasons for not proceeding in the defendant's absence where rule 24.12(3)(a) applies; and

(i) give the court such other assistance as it requires.

Statutory declaration of ignorance of proceedings

★P-221   **24.17.**—(1) This rule applies where—

(a) the case started with—

(i)   an information and summons,

(ii) a written charge and requisition, or

(iii) a written charge and single justice procedure notice; and

(b) under section 14 or section 16E of the Magistrates' Courts Act 1980, the defendant makes a statutory declaration of not having found out about the case until after the trial began.

(2) The defendant must—

(a) serve such a declaration on the court officer—

(i)   not more than 21 days after the date of finding out about the case, or

(ii) with an explanation for the delay, if serving it more than 21 days after that date;

(b) serve with the declaration one of the following, as appropriate, if the case began with a written charge and single justice procedure notice—

(i)   a notice under rule 24.9(4)(a) (notice of guilty plea), with any representations that the defendant wants the court to consider and a statement of the defendant's assets and other financial circumstances, as required by that rule,

(ii) a notice under rule 24.9(4)(b) (notice of intention to plead guilty at a hearing before a court comprising more than one justice), or

(iii) a notice under rule 24.9(4)(c) (notice of intention to plead not guilty).

(3) The court may extend that time limit, even after it has expired—

(a) at a hearing, in public or in private; or

(b) without a hearing.

(4) Where the defendant serves such a declaration, in time or with an extension of time in which to do so, and the case began with a summons or requisition—

(a) the court must treat the summons or requisition and all subsequent proceedings as void (but not the information or written charge with which the case began);

(b) if the defendant is present when the declaration is served, the rules in this part apply as if the defendant had been required to attend the court on that occasion;

(c) if the defendant is absent when the declaration is served—

    (i) the rules in Part 7 apply (starting a prosecution in a magistrates' court) as if the prosecutor had just served an information in the same terms as the original information or written charge;

    (ii) the court may exercise its power to issue a summons in accordance with those rules; and

    (iii) except for rule 24.8 (written guilty plea: special rules), the rules in this part then apply.

(5) Where the defendant serves such a declaration, in time or with an extension of time in which to do so, and the case began with a single justice procedure notice—

(a) the court must treat the single justice procedure notice and all subsequent proceedings as void (but not the written charge with which the case began);

(b) rule 24.9 (single justice procedure: special rules) applies as if the defendant had served the notice required by paragraph (2)(b) of this rule within the time allowed by rule 24.9(4); and

(c) where that notice is under rule 24.9(4)(b) (notice of intention to plead guilty at a hearing before a court comprising more than one justice) or under rule 24.9(4)(c) (notice of intention to plead not guilty), then—

    (i) if the defendant is present when the declaration is served, the rules in this part apply as if the defendant had been required to attend the court on that occasion,

    (ii) if the defendant is absent when the declaration is served, paragraph (6) of this rule applies.

(6) Where this paragraph applies, the court must exercise its power to issue a summons and—

(a) the rules in Part 7 apply (starting a prosecution in a magistrates' court) as if the prosecutor had just served an information in the same terms as the written charge;

(b) except for rule 24.8 (written guilty plea: special rules) and rule 24.9 (single justice procedure: special rules), the rules in this part apply.

Setting aside a conviction or varying a costs etc. order

24.18.—(1) This rule applies where under section 142 of the Magistrates' Courts Act 1980, the ★**P-222** court can—

(a) set aside a conviction, or

(b) vary or rescind—

    (i) a costs order, or

    (ii) an order to which Part 31 applies (behaviour orders).

(2) The court may exercise its power—

(a) on application by a party, or on its own initiative;

(b) at a hearing, in public or in private, or without a hearing.

(3) The court must not exercise its power in a party's absence unless—

(a) the court makes a decision proposed by that party;

(b) the court makes a decision to which that party has agreed in writing; or

(c) that party has had an opportunity to make representations at a hearing (whether or not that party in fact attends).

(4) A party who wants the court to exercise its power must—

(a) apply in writing as soon as reasonably practicable after the conviction or order that that party wants the court to set aside, vary or rescind;

(b) serve the application on—

    (i) the court officer, and

    (ii) each other party; and

(c) in the application—

    (i) explain why, as appropriate, the conviction should be set aside, or the order varied or rescinded,

    (ii) specify any variation of the order that the applicant proposes,

    (iii) identify any witness that the defendant wants to call, and any other proposed evidence,

    (iv) say whether the defendant waives legal professional privilege, giving any relevant name and date, and

(v)   if the application is late, explain why.
(5) The court may—
    (a)   extend (even after it has expired) the time limit under paragraph (4), unless the court's power to set aside the conviction, or vary the order, can no longer be exercised;
    (b)   allow an application to be made orally.

PART 25

TRIAL AND SENTENCE IN THE CROWN COURT

When this part applies

★P-223   **25.1.** This part applies in the Crown Court where—
    (a)   the court tries a case; or
    (b)   the defendant pleads guilty.

General powers and requirements

★P-224   **25.2.**—(1) Where this part applies, the general rule is that—
    (a)   the trial must be in public, but that is subject to the court's power to—
        (i)   impose a restriction on reporting what takes place at a public hearing, or public access to what otherwise would be a public hearing,
        (ii)   withhold information from the public during a public hearing, or
        (iii)   order a trial in private;
    (b)   the court must not proceed if the defendant is absent, unless the court is satisfied that—
        (i)   the defendant has waived the right to attend, and
        (ii)   the trial will be fair despite the defendant's absence;
    (c)   the court must not sentence the defendant to imprisonment or detention unless—
        (i)   the defendant has a legal representative,
        (ii)   the defendant has been sentenced to imprisonment or detention on a previous occasion in the United Kingdom, or
        (iii)   the defendant could have been represented under legal aid but is not because section 83(3) of the Powers of Criminal Courts (Sentencing) Act 2000 applies to him or her.
(2) The court may adjourn the trial at any stage.

Application for ruling on procedure, evidence or other question of law

★P-225   **25.3.**—(1) This rule applies to an application—
    (a)   about—
        (i)   case management, or any other question of procedure, or
        (ii)   the introduction or admissibility of evidence, or any other question of law;
    (b)   that has not been determined before the trial begins.
(2) The application is subject to any other rule that applies to it (for example, as to the time and form in which the application must be made).
(3) Unless the court otherwise directs, the application must be made, and the court's decision announced, in the absence of the jury (if there is one).

Procedure on plea of guilty

★P-226   **25.4.**—(1) This rule applies if—
    (a)   the defendant pleads guilty to an offence; and
    (b)   the court is satisfied that the plea represents a clear acknowledgement of guilt.
(2) The court need not receive evidence unless rule 25.16(4) applies (determination of facts for sentencing).

Application to vacate a guilty plea

★P-227   **25.5.**—(1) This rule applies where a party wants the court to vacate a guilty plea.
(2) Such a party must—
    (a)   apply in writing—
        (i)   as soon as practicable after becoming aware of the grounds for doing so, and
        (ii)   in any event, before the final disposal of the case, by sentence or otherwise; and
    (b)   serve the application on—
        (i)   the court officer, and
        (ii)   the prosecutor.

(3) Unless the court otherwise directs, the application must—

    (a)   explain why it would be unjust for the guilty plea to remain unchanged;

    (b)   indicate what, if any, evidence the applicant wishes to call;

    (c)   identify any proposed witness; and

    (d)   indicate whether legal professional privilege is waived, specifying any material name and date.

Selecting the jury

25.6.—(1) This rule—   **★P-228**

    (a)   applies where—

        (i)   the defendant pleads not guilty,

        (ii)   the defendant declines to enter a plea and the court treats that as a not guilty plea, or

        (iii)   the court determines that the defendant is not fit to be tried;

    (b)   does not apply where—

        (i)   the court orders a trial without a jury because of a danger of jury tampering or where jury tampering appears to have taken place, or

        (ii)   the court tries without a jury counts on an indictment after a trial of sample counts with a jury.

(2) The court must select a jury to try the case from the panel, or part of the panel, of jurors summoned by the Lord Chancellor to attend at that time and place.

(3) Where it appears that too few jurors to constitute a jury will be available from among those so summoned, the court—

    (a)   may exercise its own power to summon others in the court room, or in the vicinity, up to the number likely to be required, and add their names to the panel summoned by the Lord Chancellor; but

    (b)   must inform the parties, if they are absent when the court exercises that power.

(4) The court must select the jury by drawing at random each juror's name from among those so summoned and—

    (a)   announcing each name so drawn; or

    (b)   announcing an identifying number assigned by the court officer to that person, where the court is satisfied that that is necessary.

(5) If too few jurors to constitute a jury are available from the panel after all their names have been drawn, the court may—

    (a)   exercise its own power to summon others in the court room, or in the vicinity, up to the number required; and

    (b)   announce—

        (i)   the name of each person so summoned, or

        (ii)   an identifying number assigned by the court officer to that person, where the court is satisfied that that is necessary.

(6) The jury the court selects—

    (a)   must comprise no fewer than 12 jurors;

    (b)   may comprise as many as 14 jurors to begin with, where the court expects the trial to last for more than 4 weeks.

(7) Where the court selects a jury comprising more than 12 jurors, the court must explain to them that—

    (a)   the purpose of selecting more than 12 jurors to begin with is to fill any vacancy or vacancies caused by the discharge of any of the first 12 before the prosecution evidence begins;

    (b)   any such vacancy or vacancies will be filled by the extra jurors in order of their selection from the panel;

    (c)   the court will discharge any extra juror or jurors remaining by no later than the beginning of the prosecution evidence; and

    (d)   any juror who is discharged for that reason then will be available to be selected for service on another jury, during the period for which that juror has been summoned.

(8) Each of the 12 or more jurors the court selects—

    (a)   must take an oath or affirm; and

    (b)   becomes a full jury member until discharged.

(9) The oath or affirmation must be in these terms, or in any corresponding terms that the juror declares to be binding on him or her—

      "I swear by Almighty God [*or* I do solemnly, sincerely and truly declare and affirm] that I will faithfully try the defendant and give a true verdict according to the evidence."

Discharging jurors

★**P-229**   **25.7.**—(1) The court may exercise its power to discharge a juror at any time—

    (a) after the juror completes the oath or affirmation; and

    (b) before the court discharges the jury.

(2) No later than the beginning of the prosecution evidence, if the jury then comprises more than 12 jurors the court must discharge any in excess of 12 in reverse order of their selection from the panel.

(3) The court may exercise its power to discharge the jury at any time—

    (a) after each juror has completed the oath or affirmation; and

    (b) before the jury has delivered its verdict on each offence charged in the indictment.

(4) The court must exercise its power to discharge the jury when, in respect of each offence charged in the indictment, either—

    (a) the jury has delivered its verdict on that offence; or

    (b) the court has discharged the jury from reaching a verdict.

Objecting to jurors

★**P-230**   **25.8.**—(1) A party who objects to the panel of jurors must serve notice explaining the objection on the court officer and on the other party before the first juror's name or number is drawn.

(2) A party who objects to the selection of an individual juror must—

    (a) tell the court of the objection—

        (i) after the juror's name or number is announced, and

        (ii) before the juror completes the oath or affirmation; and

    (b) explain the objection.

(3) A prosecutor who exercises the prosecution right without giving reasons to prevent the court selecting an individual juror must announce the exercise of that right before the juror completes the oath or affirmation.

(4) The court must determine an objection under paragraph (1) or (2)—

    (a) at a hearing, in public or in private; and

    (b) in the absence of the jurors, unless the court otherwise directs.

Procedure on plea of not guilty

★**P-231**   **25.9.**—(1) This rule applies where—

    (a) the defendant pleads not guilty; or

    (b) the defendant declines to enter a plea and the court treats that as a not guilty plea.

(2) In the following sequence—

    (a) where there is a jury, the court must—

        (i) inform the jurors of each offence charged in the indictment to which the defendant pleads not guilty, and

        (ii) explain to the jurors that it is their duty, after hearing the evidence, to decide whether the defendant is guilty or not guilty of each offence;

    (b) the prosecutor may summarise the prosecution case;

    (c) the prosecutor must introduce the evidence on which the prosecution case relies;

    (d) subject to paragraph (3), at the end of the prosecution evidence, on the defendant's application or on its own initiative, the court—

        (i) may direct the jury (if there is one) to acquit on the ground that the prosecution evidence is insufficient for any reasonable court properly to convict, but

        (ii) must not do so unless the prosecutor has had an opportunity to make representations;

    (e) subject to paragraph (4), at the end of the prosecution evidence, the court must ask whether the defendant intends to give evidence in person and, if the answer is "no", then the court must satisfy itself that there has been explained to the defendant, in terms the defendant can understand (with help, if necessary)—

        (i) the right to give evidence in person, and

        (ii) that if the defendant does not give evidence in person, or refuses to answer a question while giving evidence, the court may draw such inferences as seem proper;

    (f) the defendant may summarise the defence case, if he or she intends to call at least one witness other than him or herself to give evidence in person about the facts of the case;

    (g) in this order (or in a different order, if the court so directs) the defendant may—

        (i) give evidence in person,

        (ii) call another witness, or witnesses, to give evidence in person, and

        (iii) introduce any other evidence;

(h) a party may introduce further evidence if it is then admissible (for example, because it is in rebuttal of evidence already introduced);

(i) the prosecutor may make final representations, where—

  (i) the defendant has a legal representative,

  (ii) the defendant has called at least one witness, other than the defendant him or herself, to give evidence in person about the facts of the case, or

  (iii) the court so permits; and

(j) the defendant may make final representations.

(3) Paragraph (2)(d) does not apply in relation to a charge of murder, manslaughter, attempted murder, or causing harm contrary to section 18 or 20 of the Offences against the Person Act 1861 until the court has heard all the evidence (including any defence evidence), where the defendant is charged with—

(a) any of those offences; and

(b) an offence of causing or allowing a child or vulnerable adult to die or to suffer serious physical harm, contrary to section 5 of the Domestic Violence, Crime and Victims Act 2004.

(4) Paragraph (2)(e) does not apply where it appears to the court that, taking account of all the circumstances, the defendant's physical or mental condition makes it undesirable for the defendant to give evidence in person.

(5) Where there is more than one defendant, this rule applies to each in the order their names appear in the indictment, or in an order directed by the court.

(6) Unless the jury (if there is one) has retired to consider its verdict, the court may allow a party to introduce evidence, or make representations, after that party's opportunity to do so under paragraph (2).

(7) Unless the jury has already reached a verdict on a count, the court may exercise its power to—

(a) discharge the jury from reaching a verdict on that count;

(b) direct the jury to acquit the defendant on that count; or

(c) invite the jury to convict the defendant, if the defendant pleads guilty to the offence charged by that count.

Defendant unfit to plead

25.10.—(1) This rule applies where—   **★P-232**

(a) it appears to the court, on application or on its own initiative, that the defendant may not be fit to be tried; and

(b) the defendant has not by then been acquitted of each offence charged by the indictment.

(2) The court—

(a) must exercise its power to decide, without a jury, whether the defendant is fit to be tried;

(b) may postpone the exercise of that power until immediately before the opening of the defence case.

(3) Where the court determines that the defendant is not fit to be tried—

(a) the court must exercise its power to appoint a person to put the case for the defence, taking account of all the circumstances and in particular—

  (i) the willingness and suitability (including the qualifications and experience) of that person,

  (ii) the nature and complexity of the case,

  (iii) any advantage of continuity of representation, and

  (iv) the defendant's wishes and needs;

(b) the court must select a jury, if none has been selected yet; and

(c) rule 25.9 (procedure on plea of not guilty) applies, if the steps it lists have not already been taken, except that—

  (i) everything which that rule requires to be done by the defendant may be done instead by the person appointed to put the case for the defence,

  (ii) under rule 25.9(2)(a), the court must explain to the jurors that their duty is to decide whether or not the defendant did the act or made the omission charged as an offence, not whether the defendant is guilty of that offence, and

  (iii) rule 25.9(2)(e) does not apply (warning of consequences of defendant not giving evidence).

Evidence of a witness in person

25.11.—(1) This rule applies where a party wants to introduce evidence by calling a witness to give   **★P-233**
that evidence in person.

(2) Unless the court otherwise directs—

 (a) a witness waiting to give evidence must not wait inside the courtroom, unless that witness is—

  (i) a party, or

  (ii) an expert witness;

 (b) a witness who gives evidence in the courtroom must do so from the place provided for that purpose; and

 (c) a witness' address—

  (i) must not be given in public unless the address is relevant to an issue in the case,

  (ii) may be given in writing to the court, parties and jury.

(3) Unless other legislation otherwise provides, before giving evidence a witness must take an oath or affirm.

(4) In the following sequence—

 (a) the party who calls a witness may ask questions in examination-in-chief;

 (b) if the witness gives evidence for the prosecution—

  (i) the defendant, if there is only one, may ask questions in cross-examination, or

  (ii) subject to the court's directions, each defendant, if there is more than one, may ask such questions, in the order their names appear in the indictment or as directed by the court;

 (c) if the witness gives evidence for a defendant—

  (i) subject to the court's directions, each other defendant, if there is more than one, may ask questions in cross-examination, in the order their names appear in the indictment or as directed by the court, and

  (ii) the prosecutor may ask such questions;

 (d) the party who called the witness may ask questions in re-examination arising out of any cross-examination.

(5) If other legislation so permits, at any time while giving evidence a witness may refer to a record of that witness' recollection of events.

(6) The court may—

 (a) ask a witness questions; and in particular

 (b) where the defendant is not represented, ask a witness any question necessary in the defendant's interests.

Evidence of a witness in writing

★P-234

25.12.—(1) This rule applies where a party wants to introduce in evidence the written statement of a witness to which applies—

 (a) Part 16 (written witness statements);

 (b) Part 19 (expert evidence); or

 (c) Part 20 (hearsay evidence).

(2) If the court admits such evidence—

 (a) the court and the jury (if there is one) must read the statement;

 (b) the gist of the statement must be summarised aloud; and

 (c) unless the court otherwise directs, if any member of the public, including any reporter, is present, each relevant part of the statement must be read or summarised aloud.

Evidence by admission

★P-235

25.13.—(1) This rule applies where—

 (a) a party introduces in evidence a fact admitted by another party; or

 (b) parties jointly admit a fact.

(2) Unless the court otherwise directs, a written record must be made of the admission.

Directions to the jury and taking the verdict

★P-236

25.14.—(1) This rule applies where there is a jury.

(2) The court must give the jury directions about the relevant law at any time at which to do so will assist jurors to evaluate the evidence.

(3) After following the sequence in rule 25.9 (procedure on plea of not guilty), the court must—

 (a) summarise for the jury, to such extent as is necessary, the evidence relevant to the issues they must decide;

 (b) give the jury such questions, if any, as the court invites jurors to answer in coming to a verdict;

(c)   direct the jury to retire to consider its verdict;

(d)   if necessary, recall the jury to answer jurors' questions;

(e)   if appropriate, recall the jury to give directions for a verdict by a majority; and

(f)   recall the jury when it informs the court that it has reached a verdict.

(4) The court may give the jury directions, questions or other assistance in writing.

(5) When the court recalls the jury to deliver its verdict, the court must ask the foreman chosen by the jury, in respect of each count—

(a)   whether the jury has reached a verdict on which all the jurors agree;

(b)   if so, whether that verdict is guilty or not guilty;

(c)   if not, where the jury has deliberated for at least 2 hours and if the court decides to invite a majority verdict, then—

    (i)   whether at least 10 (of 11 or 12 jurors), or 9 (of 10 jurors), agreed on a verdict,

    (ii)   if so, is that verdict guilty or not guilty, and

    (iii)   if (and only if) such a verdict is guilty, how many jurors agreed to that verdict and how many disagreed.

(6) Where evidence has been given that the defendant was insane, so as not to be responsible for the act or omission charged as the offence, then under paragraph (4)(b) the court must ask whether the jury's verdict is guilty, not guilty, or not guilty by reason of insanity.

Conviction or acquittal without a jury

25.15.—(1) This rule applies where—   ★**P-237**

(a)   the court tries the case without a jury; and

(b)   after following the sequence in rule 25.9 (procedure on plea of not guilty).

(2) In respect of each count, the court must give reasons for its decision to convict or acquit.

Procedure if the court convicts

25.16.—(1) This rule applies where, in respect of any count in the indictment—   ★**P-238**

(a)   the defendant pleads guilty; or

(b)   the court convicts the defendant.

(2) The court may exercise its power—

(a)   if the defendant is an individual—

    (i)   to require a pre-sentence report,

    (ii)   to request a medical report,

    (iii)   to require a statement of the defendant's assets and other financial circumstances;

(b)   if the defendant is a corporation, to require such information as the court directs about the defendant's corporate structure and financial resources;

(c)   to adjourn sentence pending—

    (i)   receipt of any such report, statement or information,

    (ii)   the verdict in a related case.

(3) The prosecutor must—

(a)   summarise the prosecution case, if the sentencing court has not heard evidence;

(b)   identify in writing any offence that the prosecutor proposes should be taken into consideration in sentencing;

(c)   provide information relevant to sentence, including—

    (i)   any previous conviction of the defendant, and the circumstances where relevant,

    (ii)   any statement of the effect of the offence on the victim, the victim's family or others; and

(d)   identify any other matter relevant to sentence, including—

    (i)   the legislation applicable,

    (ii)   any sentencing guidelines, or guideline cases,

    (iii)   aggravating and mitigating features affecting the defendant's culpability and the harm which the offence caused, was intended to cause or might foreseeably have caused, and

    (iv)   the effect of such of the information listed in paragraph (2) as the court may need to take into account.

(4) Where the defendant pleads guilty, the court may give directions for determining the facts on the basis of which sentence must be passed if—

(a)   the defendant wants to be sentenced on a basis agreed with the prosecutor; or

(b)   in the absence of such agreement, the defendant wants to be sentenced on the basis of different facts to those disclosed by the prosecution case.

(5) Where the court has power to order the endorsement of the defendant's driving record, or power to order the defendant to be disqualified from driving—

    (a) if other legislation so permits, a defendant who wants the court not to exercise that power must introduce the evidence or information on which the defendant relies;

    (b) the prosecutor may introduce evidence; and

    (c) the parties may make representations about that evidence or information.

(6) Before passing sentence—

    (a) the court must give the defendant an opportunity to make representations and introduce evidence relevant to sentence;

    (b) where the defendant is under 18, the court may give the defendant's parents, guardian or other supporting adult, if present, such an opportunity as well; and

    (c) if the court requires more information, it may exercise its power to adjourn the hearing.

(7) When the court has taken into account all the evidence, information and any report available, the court must—

    (a) as a general rule, pass sentence at the earliest opportunity;

    (b) when passing sentence—

        (i) explain the reasons,

        (ii) explain to the defendant its effect, the consequences of failing to comply with any order or pay any fine, and any power that the court has to vary or review the sentence, unless the defendant is absent or the defendant's ill-health or disorderly conduct makes such an explanation impracticable, and

        (iii) give any such explanation in terms the defendant, if present, can understand (with help, if necessary); and

    (c) deal with confiscation, costs and any behaviour order.

(8) The general rule is subject to the court's power to defer sentence for up to 6 months.

Provision of documents for the court

★**P-239**   **25.17.**—(1) Unless the court otherwise directs, a party who introduces a document in evidence, or who otherwise uses a document in presenting that party's case, must provide a copy for—

    (a) each other party;

    (b) any witness that party wants to refer to the document; and

    (c) the court.

(2) If the court so directs, a party who introduces or uses a document for such a purpose must provide a copy for the jury.

(3) Unless the court otherwise directs, on application or on its own initiative, the court officer must provide for the court—

    (a) any copy received under paragraph (1) before the trial begins; and

    (b) a copy of the court officer's record of—

        (i) information supplied by each party for the purposes of case management, including any revision of information previously supplied,

        (ii) each pre-trial direction for the management of the case,

        (iii) any pre-trial decision to admit evidence,

        (iv) any pre-trial direction about the giving of evidence, and

        (v) any admission to which rule 25.13 (Evidence by admission) applies; and

    (c) any other document served on the court officer for the use of the court.

Duty of court officer

★**P-240**   **25.18.** The court officer must—

    (a) serve on each party notice of where and when an adjourned hearing will resume, unless that party was present when that was arranged;

    (b) if the reason for the adjournment was to postpone sentence, include that reason in any such notice to the defendant;

    (c) unless the court otherwise directs, make available to the parties any written report to which rule 25.16(2) applies (pre-sentence and medical reports);

    (d) where the court has ordered a defendant to provide information under section 25 of the Road Traffic Offenders Act 1988, serve on the defendant notice of that order unless the defendant was present when it was made;

    (e) give the court such other assistance as it requires, including—

        (i) selecting jurors from the panel summoned by the Lord Chancellor, under rule 25.6 (selecting the jury),

(ii) taking the oaths or affirmations of jurors and witnesses, under rules 25.6 and 25.11 (evidence of a witness in person),

(iii) informing the jurors of the offence or offences charged in the indictment, and of their duty, under rule 25.9 (procedure on plea of not guilty),

(iv) recording the date and time at which the court gives the jury oral directions under rule 25.14(2) (directions about the law),

(v) recording the date and time at which the court gives the jury any written directions, questions or other assistance under rule 25.14(4), and

(vi) asking the jury foreman to deliver the verdict, under rule 25.14(5).

PART 26

JURORS

Appeal against officer's refusal to excuse or postpone jury service

26.1.—(1) This rule applies where a person summoned for jury service in the Crown Court, the **★P-241** High Court or the county court wants to appeal against a refusal by an officer on the Lord Chancellor's behalf—

(a) to excuse that person from such service; or

(b) to postpone the date on which that person is required to attend for such service.

(2) The appellant must appeal to the court to which the appellant has been summoned.

(3) The appellant must—

(a) apply in writing, as soon as reasonably practicable; and

(b) serve the application on the court officer.

(4) The application must—

(a) attach a copy of—

(i) the jury summons, and

(ii) the refusal to excuse or postpone which is under appeal; and

(b) explain why the court should excuse the appellant from jury service, or postpone its date, as appropriate.

(5) The court to which the appeal is made—

(a) may extend the time for appealing, and may allow the appeal to be made orally;

(b) may determine the appeal at a hearing in public or in private, or without a hearing;

(c) may adjourn any hearing of the appeal;

(d) must not determine an appeal unless the appellant has had a reasonable opportunity to make representations in person.

Excusal from jury service by court

26.2. At any time before a juror completes the oath or affirmation, the court may exercise its **★P-242** power to excuse him or her from jury service for lack of capacity to act effectively as a juror because of an insufficient understanding of English—

(a) on the court's own initiative, or where the court officer refers the juror to the court; and

(b) after enquiry of the juror.

Provision of information for jurors

26.3. The court officer must arrange for each juror to receive— **★P-243**

(a) by such means as the Lord Chancellor directs, general information about jury service and about a juror's responsibilities;

(b) written notice of the prohibitions against—

(i) research by a juror into the case,

(ii) disclosure by a juror of any such research to another juror during the trial,

(iii) conduct by a juror which suggests that that juror intends to try the case otherwise than on the evidence,

(iv) disclosure by a juror of the deliberations of the jury;

(c) written warning that breach of those prohibitions is an offence, for which the penalty is imprisonment or a fine or both, and may be a contempt of court.

Assessment of juror's availability for long trial, etc.

26.4.—(1) The court may invite each member of a panel of jurors to provide such information, by **★P-244** such means and at such a time as the court directs, about—

(a) that juror's availability to try a case expected to last for longer than the juror had expected to serve;

(b) any association of that juror with, or any knowledge by that juror of—

    (i)   a party or witness, or

    (ii) any other person, or any place, of significance to the case.

(2) Where jurors provide information under this rule, the court may postpone the selection of the jury to try a case to allow each juror an opportunity to review and amend that information before that selection.

(3) Using that information, the court may exercise its power to excuse a juror from selection as a member of the jury to try a case, but the court must not—

(a) excuse a juror without allowing the parties an opportunity to make representations; or

(b) refuse to excuse a juror without allowing that juror such an opportunity.

Surrender of electronic communication devices by jurors

★P-245

26.5.—(1) This rule applies where the court can order the members of a jury to surrender for a specified period any electronic communication devices that they possess.

(2) The court may make such an order—

(a) on application; or

(b) on its own initiative.

(3) A party who wants the court to make such an order must—

(a) apply as soon as reasonably practicable;

(b) notify each other party;

(c) specify for what period any device should be surrendered; and

(d) explain why—

    (i)   the proposed order is necessary or expedient in the interest of justice, and

    (ii) the terms of the proposed order are a proportionate means of safeguarding those interests.

PART 27

RETRIAL AFTER ACQUITTAL

General

When this part applies

★P-246

27.1.—(1) Rule 27.2 applies where, under section 54 of the Criminal Procedure and Investigations Act 1996, the Crown Court or a magistrates' court can certify for the High Court that interference or intimidation has been involved in proceedings leading to an acquittal.

(2) Rules 27.3 to 27.7 apply where, under section 77 of the Criminal Justice Act 2003, the Court of Appeal can—

(a) quash an acquittal for a serious offence and order a defendant to be retried; or

(b) order that an acquittal outside the United Kingdom is no bar to the defendant being tried in England and Wales,

if there is new and compelling evidence and it is in the interests of justice to make the order.

Application for Certificate to Allow Order for Retrial

Application for certificate

★P-247

27.2.—(1) This rule applies where—

(a) a defendant has been acquitted of an offence;

(b) a person has been convicted of one of the following offences involving interference with or intimidation of a juror or a witness (or potential witness) in any proceedings which led to the defendant's acquittal—

    (i)   perverting the course of justice,

    (ii) intimidation etc. of witnesses, jurors and others under section 51(1) of the Criminal Justice and Public Order Act 1994, or

    (iii) aiding, abetting, counselling, procuring, suborning or inciting another person to commit an offence under section 1 of the Perjury Act 1911; and

(c) the prosecutor wants the court by which that person was convicted to certify for the High Court that there is a real possibility that, but for the interference or intimidation, the defendant would not have been acquitted.

(2) The prosecutor must—
  (a) apply in writing as soon as practicable after that person's conviction; and
  (b) serve the application on—
    (i)   the court officer, and
    (ii) the defendant who was acquitted, if the court so directs.
(3) The application must—
  (a) give details, with relevant facts and dates, of—
    (i)   the conviction for interference or intimidation, and
    (ii) the defendant's acquittal; and
  (b) explain—
    (i)   why there is a real possibility that, but for the interference or intimidation, the defendant would not have been acquitted, and
    (ii) why it would not be contrary to the interests of justice to prosecute the defendant again for the offence of which he or she was acquitted, despite any lapse of time or other reason.
(4) The court may—
  (a) extend the time limit under paragraph (2);
  (b) allow an application to be in a different form to one set out in the Practice Direction, or to be made orally;
  (c) determine an application under this rule—
    (i)   at a hearing, in private or in public; or
    (ii) without a hearing.
(5) If the court gives a certificate, the court officer must serve it on—
  (a) the prosecutor; and
  (b) the defendant who was acquitted.

Application to Court of Appeal to Quash Acquittal and Order Retrial

Application for reporting restriction pending application for order for retrial

27.3.—(1) This rule applies where—   **★P-248**
  (a) no application has been made under rule 27.4 (application for order for retrial);
  (b) an investigation by officers has begun into an offence with a view to an application under that rule; and
  (c) the Director of Public Prosecutions wants the Court of Appeal to make, vary or remove an order for a reporting restriction under section 82 of the Criminal Justice Act 2003 (restrictions on publication in the interests of justice).
(2) The Director must—
  (a) apply in writing;
  (b) serve the application on—
    (i)   the Registrar, and
    (ii) the defendant, unless the court otherwise directs.
(3) The application must, as appropriate—
  (a) explain why the Director wants the court to direct that it need not be served on the defendant until the application under rule 27.4 is served;
  (b) specify the proposed terms of the order, and for how long it should last;
  (c) explain why an order in the terms proposed is necessary;
  (d) explain why an order should be varied or removed.

Application for order for retrial

27.4.—(1) This rule applies where—   **★P-249**
  (a) a defendant has been acquitted—
    (i)   in the Crown Court, or on appeal from the Crown Court, of an offence listed in Part 1 of Schedule 5 to the Criminal Justice Act 2003 (qualifying offences),
    (ii) in proceedings elsewhere than in the United Kingdom of an offence under the law of that place, if what was alleged would have amounted to or included one of those listed offences;
  (b) with the Director of Public Prosecutions' written consent, a prosecutor wants the Court of Appeal to make an order, as the case may be—
    (i)   quashing the acquittal in the Crown Court and ordering the defendant to be retried for the offence, or

    (ii) declaring whether the acquittal outside the United Kingdom is a bar to the defendant's trial in England and Wales and, if it is, whether that acquittal shall not be such a bar.

(2) Such a prosecutor must—

    (a) apply in writing;

    (b) serve the application on the Registrar;

    (c) not more than 2 business days later serve on the defendant who was acquitted—

        (i) the application, and

       (ii) a notice charging the defendant with the offence, unless the defendant has already been arrested and charged under section 87 of the Criminal Justice Act 2003 (arrest under warrant or otherwise, and charge).

(3) The application must—

    (a) give details, with relevant facts and dates, of the defendant's acquittal;

    (b) explain—

        (i) what new and compelling evidence there is against the defendant, and

       (ii) why in all the circumstances it would be in the interests of justice for the court to make the order sought;

    (c) include or attach any application for the following, with reasons—

        (i) an order under section 80(6) of the Criminal Justice Act 2003 (procedure and evidence) for the production of any document, exhibit or other thing which in the prosecutor's opinion is necessary for the determination of the application,

       (ii) an order under that section for the attendance before the court of any witness who would be a compellable witness at the trial the prosecutor wants the court to order,

      (iii) an order for a reporting restriction under section 82 of the Criminal Justice Act 2003 (restrictions on publication in the interests of justice); and

    (d) attach—

        (i) written witness statements of the evidence on which the prosecutor relies as new and compelling evidence against the defendant,

       (ii) relevant documents from the trial at which the defendant was acquitted, including a record of the offence or offences charged and of the evidence given, and

      (iii) any other document or thing that the prosecutor thinks the court will need to decide the application.

Respondent's notice

★P-250

    27.5.—(1) A defendant on whom a prosecutor serves an application may serve a respondent's notice, and must do so if the defendant wants to make representations to the court.

(2) Such a defendant must serve the respondent's notice on—

    (a) the Registrar; and

    (b) the prosecutor,

not more than 28 days after service of the application.

(3) The respondent's notice must—

    (a) give the date on which the respondent was served with the prosecutor's application;

    (b) summarise any relevant facts not contained in that application;

    (c) explain the defendant's grounds for opposing that application;

    (d) include or attach any application for the following, with reasons—

        (i) an extension of time within which to serve the respondent's notice,

       (ii) bail pending the hearing of the prosecutor's application, if the defendant is in custody,

      (iii) a direction to attend in person any hearing that the defendant could attend by live link, if the defendant is in custody,

      (iv) an order under section 80(6) of the Criminal Justice Act 2003 (procedure and evidence) for the production of any document, exhibit or other thing which in the defendant's opinion is necessary for the determination of the prosecutor's application,

       (v) an order under that section for the attendance before the court of any witness who would be a compellable witness at the trial the prosecutor wants the court to order; and

    (e) attach or identify any other document or thing that the defendant thinks the court will need to decide the application.

Application to Crown Court for summons or warrant

27.6.—(1) This rule applies where— ★**P-251**

    (a) the prosecutor has served on the Registrar an application under rule 27.4 (application for order for retrial);

    (b) the defendant is not in custody as a result of arrest under section 88 of the Criminal Justice Act 2003 (bail and custody before application); and

    (c) the prosecutor wants the Crown Court to issue—

        (i) a summons requiring the defendant to appear before the Court of Appeal at the hearing of the prosecutor's application, or

        (ii) a warrant for the defendant's arrest

      under section 89 of the 2003 Act (bail and custody before hearing).

(2) The prosecutor must—

    (a) apply in writing; and

    (b) serve the application on the Crown Court officer.

(3) The application must—

    (a) explain what the case is about, including a brief description of the defendant's acquittal, the new evidence and the stage that the application to the Court of Appeal has reached;

    (b) specify—

        (i) the decision that the prosecutor wants the Crown Court to make,

        (ii) each offence charged, and

        (iii) any relevant previous bail decision and the reasons given for it;

    (c) propose the terms of any suggested condition of bail.

Application of other rules about procedure in the Court of Appeal

27.7. On an application under rule 27.4 (application for order for retrial)— ★**P-252**

    (a) the rules in Part 36 (appeal to the Court of Appeal: general rules) apply with the necessary modifications;

    (b) rules 39.8, 39.9 and 39.10 (bail and bail conditions in the Court of Appeal) apply as if the references in those rules to appeal included references to an application under rule 27.4; and

    (c) rule 39.14 (renewal or setting aside of order for retrial) applies as if the reference to section 7 of the Criminal Appeal Act 1968 were a reference to section 84 of the Criminal Justice Act 2003 (retrial).

PART 28

SENTENCING PROCEDURES IN SPECIAL CASES

Reasons for not following usual sentencing requirements

28.1.—(1) This rule applies where the court decides— ★**P-253**

    (a) not to follow a relevant sentencing guideline;

    (b) not to make, where it could—

        (i) a reparation order (unless it passes a custodial or community sentence),

        (ii) a compensation order,

        (iii) a slavery and trafficking reparation order, or

        (iv) a travel restriction order;

    (c) not to order, where it could—

        (i) that a suspended sentence of imprisonment is to take effect,

        (ii) the endorsement of the defendant's driving record, or

        (iii) the defendant's disqualification from driving, for the usual minimum period or at all;

    (d) to pass a lesser sentence than it otherwise would have passed because the defendant has assisted, or has agreed to assist, an investigator or prosecutor in relation to an offence.

(2) The court must explain why it has so decided, when it explains the sentence that it has passed.

(3) Where paragraph (1)(d) applies, the court must arrange for such an explanation to be given to the defendant and to the prosecutor in writing, if the court thinks that it would not be in the public interest to explain in public.

Notice of requirements of suspended sentence and community, etc. orders

28.2.—(1) This rule applies where the court— ★**P-254**

    (a) makes a suspended sentence order;

    (b) imposes a requirement under—

        (i) a community order,

        (ii) a youth rehabilitation order, or

        (iii) a suspended sentence order; or

    (c) orders the defendant to attend meetings with a supervisor.

(2) The court officer must notify—

    (a) the defendant of—

        (i) the length of the sentence suspended by a suspended sentence order, and

        (ii) the period of the suspension;

    (b) the defendant and, where the defendant is under 14, an appropriate adult, of—

        (i) any requirement or requirements imposed, and

        (ii) the identity of any responsible officer or supervisor, and the means by which that person may be contacted;

    (c) any responsible officer or supervisor, and, where the defendant is under 14, the appropriate qualifying officer (if that is not the responsible officer), of—

        (i) the defendant's name, address and telephone number (if available),

        (ii) the offence or offences of which the defendant was convicted, and

        (iii) the requirement or requirements imposed; and

    (d) the person affected, where the court imposes a requirement—

        (i) for the protection of that person from the defendant, or

        (ii) requiring the defendant to reside with that person.

(3) If the court imposes an electronic monitoring requirement, the monitor of which is not the responsible officer, the court officer must—

    (a) notify the defendant and, where the defendant is under 16, an appropriate adult, of the monitor's identity, and the means by which the monitor may be contacted; and

    (b) notify the monitor of—

        (i) the defendant's name, address and telephone number (if available),

        (ii) the offence or offences of which the defendant was convicted,

        (iii) the place or places at which the defendant's presence must be monitored,

        (iv) the period or periods during which the defendant's presence there must be monitored, and

        (v) the identity of the responsible officer, and the means by which that officer may be contacted.

Notification requirements

★**P-255**   **28.3.**—(1) This rule applies where, on a conviction, sentence or order, legislation requires the defendant—

    (a) to notify information to the police; or

    (b) to be included in a barred list.

(2) The court must tell the defendant that such requirements apply, and under what legislation.

Variation of sentence

★**P-256**   **28.4.**—(1) This rule—

    (a) applies where a magistrates' court or the Crown Court can vary or rescind a sentence or order, other than an order to which rule 24.18 applies (setting aside a conviction or varying a costs etc. order); and

    (b) authorises the Crown Court, in addition to its other powers, to do so within the period of 56 days beginning with another defendant's acquittal or sentencing where—

        (i) defendants are tried separately in the Crown Court on the same or related facts alleged in one or more indictments, and

        (ii) one is sentenced before another is acquitted or sentenced.

(2) The court may exercise its power—

    (a) on application by a party, or on its own initiative;

    (b) at a hearing, in public or in private, or without a hearing.

(3) A party who wants the court to exercise that power must—

    (a) apply in writing as soon as reasonably practicable after—

        (i) the sentence or order that that party wants the court to vary or rescind, or

        (ii) where paragraph (1)(b) applies, the other defendant's acquittal or sentencing;

    (b) serve the application on—
        (i)   the court officer, and
        (ii) each other party; and
    (c) in the application—
        (i)   explain why the sentence should be varied or rescinded,
        (ii) specify the variation that the applicant proposes, and
        (iii) if the application is late, explain why.
  (4) The court must not exercise its power in the defendant's absence unless—
    (a) the court makes a variation—
        (i)   which is proposed by the defendant, or
        (ii) the effect of which is that the defendant is no more severely dealt with under the sentence as varied than before; or
    (b) the defendant has had an opportunity to make representations at a hearing (whether or not the defendant in fact attends).
  (5) The court may—
    (a) extend (even after it has expired) the time limit under paragraph (3), unless the court's power to vary or rescind the sentence cannot be exercised;
    (b) allow an application to be made orally.

Application to vary or discharge a compensation, etc. order
28.5.—(1) This rule applies where on application by the defendant a magistrates' court can vary or   ★**P-257** discharge—
    (a) a compensation order; or
    (b) a slavery and trafficking reparation order.
  (2) A defendant who wants the court to exercise that power must—
    (a) apply in writing as soon as practicable after becoming aware of the grounds for doing so;
    (b) serve the application on the magistrates' court officer;
    (c) where the order was made in the Crown Court, serve a copy of the application on the Crown Court officer; and
    (d) in the application, specify the order that the defendant wants the court to vary or discharge and explain (as applicable)—
        (i)   what civil court finding shows that the injury, loss or damage was less than it had appeared to be when the order was made,
        (ii) in what circumstances the person for whose benefit the order was made has recovered the property for the loss of which it was made,
        (iii) why a confiscation order, unlawful profit order or slavery and trafficking reparation order makes the defendant now unable to pay compensation or reparation in full, or
        (iv) in what circumstances the defendant's means have been reduced substantially and unexpectedly, and why they seem unlikely to increase for a considerable period.
  (3) The court officer must serve a copy of the application on the person for whose benefit the order was made.
  (4) The court must not vary or discharge the order unless—
    (a) the defendant, and the person for whose benefit it was made, each has had an opportunity to make representations at a hearing (whether or not either in fact attends); and
    (b) where the order was made in the Crown Court, the Crown Court has notified its consent.

Application to remove, revoke or suspend a disqualification or restriction
28.6.—(1) This rule applies where, on application by the defendant, the court can remove, revoke   ★**P-258** or suspend a disqualification or restriction included in a sentence (except a disqualification from driving).
  (2) A defendant who wants the court to exercise such a power must—
    (a) apply in writing, no earlier than the date on which the court can exercise the power;
    (b) serve the application on the court officer; and
    (c) in the application—
        (i)   specify the disqualification or restriction, and
        (ii) explain why the defendant wants the court to remove, revoke or suspend it.
  (3) The court officer must serve a copy of the application on the chief officer of police for the local justice area.

Application for a restitution order by the victim of a theft
28.7.—(1) This rule applies where, on application by the victim of a theft, the court can order a   ★**P-259** defendant to give that person goods obtained with the proceeds of goods stolen in that theft.

(2) A person who wants the court to exercise that power if the defendant is convicted must—

    (a) apply in writing as soon as practicable (without waiting for the verdict);

    (b) serve the application on the court officer; and

    (c) in the application—

        (i) identify the goods, and

        (ii) explain why the applicant is entitled to them.

(3) The court officer must serve a copy of the application on each party.

(4) The court must not determine the application unless the applicant and each party has had an opportunity to make representations at a hearing (whether or not each in fact attends).

(5) The court may —

    (a) extend (even after it has expired) the time limit under paragraph (2); and

    (b) allow an application to be made orally.

Requests for medical reports, etc.

★P-260   **28.8.**—(1) This rule applies where the court—

    (a) requests a medical examination of the defendant and a report; or

    (b) requires information about the arrangements that could be made for the defendant where the court is considering—

        (i) a hospital order, or

        (ii) a guardianship order.

(2) Unless the court otherwise directs, the court officer must, as soon as practicable, serve on each person from whom a report or information is sought a note that—

    (a) specifies the power exercised by the court;

    (b) explains why the court seeks a report or information from that person; and

    (c) sets out or summarises any relevant information available to the court.

Information to be supplied on admission to hospital or guardianship

★P-261   **28.9.**—(1) This rule applies where the court—

    (a) orders the defendant's detention and treatment in hospital; or

    (b) makes a guardianship order.

(2) Unless the court otherwise directs, the court officer must, as soon as practicable, serve on (as applicable) the hospital or the guardian—

    (a) a record of the court's order;

    (b) such information as the court has received that appears likely to assist in treating or otherwise dealing with the defendant, including information about—

        (i) the defendant's mental condition,

        (ii) the defendant's other circumstances, and

        (iii) the circumstances of the offence.

Information to be supplied on committal for sentence, etc.

★P-262   **28.10.**—(1) This rule applies where a magistrates' court or the Crown Court convicts the defendant and—

    (a) commits or adjourns the case to another court—

        (i) for sentence, or

        (ii) for the defendant to be dealt with for breach of a deferred sentence, a conditional discharge, or a suspended sentence of imprisonment, imposed by that other court;

    (b) deals with a deferred sentence, a conditional discharge, or a suspended sentence of imprisonment, imposed by another court; or

    (c) makes an order that another court is, or may be, required to enforce.

(2) Unless the convicting court otherwise directs, the court officer must, as soon as practicable—

    (a) where paragraph (1)(a) applies, arrange the transmission from the convicting to the other court of a record of any relevant—

        (i) certificate of conviction,

        (ii) magistrates' court register entry,

        (iii) decision about bail, for the purposes of section 5 of the Bail Act 1976,

        (iv) note of evidence,

        (v) statement or other document introduced in evidence,

        (vi) medical or other report,

        (vii) representation order or application for such order, and

(viii)   interim driving disqualification;
(b)   where paragraph (1)(b) or (c) applies, arrange—
  (i)   the transmission from the convicting to the other court of notice of the convicting court's order, and
  (ii)   the recording of that order at the other court;
(c)   in every case, notify the defendant and, where the defendant is under 14, an appropriate adult, of the location of the other court.

Application to review sentence because of assistance given or withheld
28.11.—(1) This rule applies where the Crown Court can reduce or increase a sentence on ap- ★**P-263**
plication by a prosecutor in a case in which—
(a)   since being sentenced, the defendant has assisted, or has agreed to assist, an investigator or prosecutor in relation to an offence; or
(b)   since receiving a reduced sentence for agreeing to give such assistance, the defendant has failed to do so.
(2) A prosecutor who wants the court to exercise that power must—
(a)   apply in writing as soon as practicable after becoming aware of the grounds for doing so;
(b)   serve the application on—
  (i)   the court officer, and
  (ii)   the defendant; and
(c)   in the application—
  (i)   explain why the sentence should be reduced, or increased, as appropriate, and
  (ii)   identify any other matter relevant to the court's decision, including any sentencing guideline or guideline case.
(3) The general rule is that the application must be determined by the judge who passed the sentence, unless that judge is unavailable.
(4) The court must not determine the application in the defendant's absence unless the defendant has had an opportunity to make representations at a hearing (whether or not the defendant in fact attends).

PART 29

ROAD TRAFFIC PENALTIES

Representations about obligatory disqualification or endorsement
29.1.—(1) This rule applies—   ★**P-264**
(a)   where the court—
  (i)   convicts the defendant of an offence involving obligatory disqualification from driving and section 34(1) of the Road Traffic Offenders Act 1988 (disqualification for certain offences) applies,
  (ii)   convicts the defendant of an offence where section 35 of the 1988 Act (disqualification for repeated offences) applies, or
  (iii)   convicts the defendant of an offence involving obligatory endorsement of the defendant's driving record and section 44 of the 1988 Act (orders for endorsement) applies;
(b)   unless the defendant is absent.
(2) The court must explain, in terms the defendant can understand (with help, if necessary)—
(a)   where paragraph (1)(a)(i) applies (obligatory disqualification under section 34)—
  (i)   that the court must order the defendant to be disqualified from driving for a minimum of 12 months (or 2 or 3 years, as the case may be, according to the offence and the defendant's driving record), unless the court decides that there are special reasons to order disqualification for a shorter period, or not to order disqualification at all, and
  (ii)   if applicable, that the period of disqualification will be reduced by at least 3 months if, by no later than 2 months before the end of the reduced period, the defendant completes an approved driving course;
(b)   where paragraph (1)(a)(ii) applies (disqualification under section 35)—
  (i)   that the court must order the defendant to be disqualified from driving for a minimum of 6 months (or 1 or 2 years, as the case may be, according to the defendant's driving record), unless, having regard to all the circumstances, the court decides to order disqualification for a shorter period, or not to order disqualification at all, and

  (ii) that circumstances of which the court cannot take account in making its decision are any that make the offence not a serious one; hardship (other than exceptional hardship); and any that during the last 3 years already have been taken into account by a court when ordering disqualification for less than the usual minimum period, or not at all, for repeated driving offences;

 (c) where paragraph (1)(a)(iii) applies (obligatory endorsement), that the court must order the endorsement of the defendant's driving record unless the court decides that there are special reasons not to do so;

 (d) in every case, as applicable—

  (i) that the court already has received representations from the defendant about whether any such special reasons or mitigating circumstances apply and will take account of them, or

  (ii) that the defendant may make such representations now, on oath or affirmation.

(3) Unless the court already has received such representations from the defendant, before it applies rule 24.11 (magistrates' court procedure if the court convicts) or rule 25.16 (Crown Court procedure if the court convicts), as the case may be, the court must—

 (a) ask whether the defendant wants to make any such representations; and

 (b) if the answer to that question is "yes", require the defendant to take an oath or affirm and make them.

Application to remove a disqualification from driving

★P-265 **29.2.**—(1) This rule applies where, on application by the defendant, the court can remove a disqualification from driving.

(2) A defendant who wants the court to exercise that power must—

 (a) apply in writing, no earlier than the date on which the court can exercise the power;

 (b) serve the application on the court officer; and

 (c) in the application—

  (i) specify the disqualification, and

  (ii) explain why the defendant wants the court to remove it.

(3) The court officer must serve a copy of the application on the chief officer of police for the local justice area.

Information to be supplied on order for endorsement of driving record, etc.

★P-266 **29.3.**—(1) This rule applies where the court—

 (a) convicts the defendant of an offence involving obligatory endorsement, and orders there to be endorsed on the defendant's driving record (and on any counterpart licence, if other legislation requires)—

  (i) particulars of the conviction,

  (ii) particulars of any disqualification from driving that the court imposes, and

  (iii) the penalty points to be attributed to the offence;

 (b) disqualifies the defendant from driving for any other offence; or

 (c) suspends or removes a disqualification from driving.

(2) The court officer must, as soon as practicable, serve on the Secretary of State notice that includes details of—

 (a) where paragraph (1)(a) applies—

  (i) the local justice area in which the court is acting,

  (ii) the dates of conviction and sentence,

  (iii) the offence, and the date on which it was committed,

  (iv) the sentence, and

  (v) the date of birth, and sex, of the defendant, where those details are available;

 (b) where paragraph (1)(b) applies—

  (i) the date and period of the disqualification,

  (ii) the power exercised by the court;

 (c) where paragraph (1)(c) applies—

  (i) the date and period of the disqualification,

  (ii) the date and terms of the order for its suspension or removal,

  (iii) the power exercised by the court, and

  (iv) where the court suspends the disqualification pending appeal, the court to which the defendant has appealed.

Statutory declaration to avoid fine after fixed penalty notice

29.4.—(1) This rule applies where—　　　　　　　　　　　　　　　　★**P-267**

(a) a chief officer of police, or the Secretary of State, serves on the magistrates' court officer a certificate registering, for enforcement as a fine, a sum payable by a defendant after failure to comply with a fixed penalty notice;

(b) the court officer notifies the defendant of the registration; and

(c) the defendant makes a statutory declaration with the effect that—

　(i)　the fixed penalty notice, or any associated notice sent to the defendant as owner of the vehicle concerned, and

　(ii)　the registration and any enforcement proceedings

become void.

(2) The defendant must serve that statutory declaration not more than 21 days after service of notice of the registration, unless the court extends that time limit.

(3) The court officer must—

(a) serve a copy of the statutory declaration on the person by whom the certificate was registered;

(b) cancel any endorsement on the defendant's driving record (and on any counterpart licence, if other legislation requires); and

(c) notify the Secretary of State of any such cancellation.

Application for declaration about a course or programme certificate decision

29.5.—(1) This rule applies where the court can declare unjustified—　　　　★**P-268**

(a) a course provider's failure or refusal to give a certificate of the defendant's satisfactory completion of an approved course; or

(b) a programme provider's giving of a certificate of the defendant's failure fully to participate in an approved programme.

(2) A defendant who wants the court to exercise that power must—

(a) apply in writing, not more than 28 days after—

　(i)　the date by which the defendant was required to complete the course, or

　(ii)　the giving of the certificate of failure fully to participate in the programme;

(b) serve the application on the court officer; and

(c) in the application, specify the course or programme and explain (as applicable)—

　(i)　that the course provider has failed to give a certificate,

　(ii)　where the course provider has refused to give a certificate, why the defendant disagrees with the reasons for that decision, or

　(iii)　where the programme provider has given a certificate, why the defendant disagrees with the reasons for that decision.

(3) The court officer must serve a copy of the application on the course or programme provider.

(4) The court must not determine the application unless the defendant, and the course or programme provider, each has had an opportunity to make representations at a hearing (whether or not either in fact attends).

Appeal against recognition of foreign driving disqualification

29.6.—(1) This rule applies where—　　　　　　　　　　　　　　　　★**P-269**

(a) a Minister gives a disqualification notice under section 57 of the Crime (International Co-operation) Act 2003; and

(b) the person to whom it is given wants to appeal under section 59 of the Act to a magistrates' court.

(2) That person ("the appellant") must serve an appeal notice on—

(a) the court officer, at a magistrates' court in the local justice area in which the appellant lives; and

(b) the Minister, at the address given in the disqualification notice.

(3) The appellant must serve the appeal notice within the period for which section 59 of the 2003 Act provides.

(4) The appeal notice must—

(a) attach a copy of the disqualification notice;

(b) explain which of the conditions in section 56 of the 2003 Act is not met, and why section 57 of the Act therefore does not apply; and

(c) include any application to suspend the disqualification, under section 60 of the Act.

(5) The Minister may serve a respondent's notice, and must do so if—

    (a) the Minister wants to make representations to the court; or

    (b) the court so directs.

(6) The Minister must—

    (a) unless the court otherwise directs, serve any such respondent's notice not more than 14 days after—

        (i) the appellant serves the appeal notice, or

        (ii) a direction to do so;

    (b) in any such respondent's notice—

        (i) identify the grounds of opposition on which the Minister relies,

        (ii) summarise any relevant facts not already included in the disqualification and appeal notices, and

        (iii) identify any other document that the Minister thinks the court will need to decide the appeal (and serve any such document with the notice).

(7) Where the court determines an appeal, the general rule is that it must do so at a hearing (which must be in public, unless the court otherwise directs).

(8) The court officer must serve on the Minister—

    (a) notice of the outcome of the appeal;

    (b) notice of any suspension of the disqualification; and

    (c) the appellant's driving licence, if surrendered to the court officer.

★**P-270**   **30.** [*Enforcement of fines and other orders for payment*]

PART 31

BEHAVIOUR ORDERS

When this part applies

★**P-271**   **31.1.**—(1) This part applies where—

    (a) a magistrates' court or the Crown Court can make, vary or revoke a civil order—

        (i) as well as, or instead of, passing a sentence, or in any other circumstances in which other legislation allows the court to make such an order, and

        (ii) that requires someone to do, or not do, something;

    (b) a magistrates' court or the Crown Court can make a European protection order;

    (c) a magistrates' court can give effect to a European protection order made in another European Union member State.

(2) A reference to a "behaviour order" in this part is a reference to any such order.

(3) A reference to "hearsay evidence" in this part is a reference to evidence consisting of hearsay within the meaning of section 1(2) of the Civil Evidence Act 1995.

Behaviour orders: general rules

★**P-272**   **31.2.**—(1) The court must not make a behaviour order unless the person to whom it is directed has had an opportunity—

    (a) to consider—

        (i) what order is proposed and why, and

        (ii) the evidence in support; and

    (b) to make representations at a hearing (whether or not that person in fact attends).

(2) That restriction does not apply to making—

    (a) an interim behaviour order, but unless other legislation otherwise provides such an order has no effect unless the person to whom it is directed—

        (i) is present when it is made, or

        (ii) is handed a document recording the order not more than 7 days after it is made;

    (b) a restraining order that gives effect to a European protection order, where rule 31.10 applies (giving effect to a European protection order made in another EU member State).

(3) Where the court decides not to make, where it could—

    (a) a football banning order; or

    (b) a parenting order, after a person under 16 is convicted of an offence,

the court must announce, at a hearing in public, the reasons for its decision.

(4) Where the court makes an order which imposes one or more of the prohibitions or restrictions listed in rule 31.9(1), the court must arrange for someone to explain to the person who benefits from that protection—

    (a) that that person may apply for a European protection order, if he or she decides to reside or stay in another European Union member State;

(b)   the basic conditions for making such an application; and

(c)   that it is advisable to make any such application before leaving the United Kingdom.

Application for behaviour order and notice of terms of proposed order: special rules
    31.3.—(1) This rule applies where— ★**P-273**
      (a)   a prosecutor wants the court to make—
        (i)   an anti-social behaviour order (but this rule does not apply to an application for an interim anti-social behaviour order),
        (ii)   a serious crime prevention order, or
        (iii)   a criminal behaviour order; or
      (b)   a prosecutor proposes, on the prosecutor's initiative or at the court's request a sexual harm prevention order,
if the defendant is convicted.
    (2) Where paragraph (1)(a) applies, the prosecutor must serve a notice of intention to apply for such an order on—
      (a)   the court officer;
      (b)   the defendant against whom the prosecutor wants the court to make the order; and
      (c)   any person on whom the order would be likely to have a significant adverse effect,
as soon as practicable (without waiting for the verdict).
    (3) A notice under paragraph (2) must—
      (a)   summarise the relevant facts;
      (b)   identify the evidence on which the prosecutor relies in support;
      (c)   attach any written statement that the prosecutor has not already served; and
      (d)   specify the order that the prosecutor wants the court to make.
    (4) A defendant served with a notice under paragraph (2) must—
      (a)   serve written notice of any evidence on which the defendant relies on—
        (i)   the court officer, and
        (ii)   the prosecutor,
      as soon as practicable (without waiting for the verdict); and
      (b)   in the notice, identify that evidence and attach any written statement that has not already been served.
    (5) Where paragraph (1)(b) applies, the prosecutor must—
      (a)   serve a draft order on the court officer and on the defendant not less than 2 business days before the hearing at which the order may be made;
      (b)   in a case in which a sexual harm prevention order is proposed, in the draft order specify those prohibitions which the prosecutor proposes as necessary for the purpose of—
        (i)   protecting the public or any particular members of the public from sexual harm from the defendant, or
        (ii)   protecting children or vulnerable adults generally, or any particular children or vulnerable adults, from sexual harm from the defendant outside the United Kingdom.
    (6) Where the prosecutor wants the court to make an anti-social behaviour order or a criminal behaviour order, the rules about special measures directions in Part 18 (measures to assist a witness or defendant to give evidence) apply, but—
      (a)   the prosecutor must apply when serving a notice under paragraph (2); and
      (b)   the time limits in rule 18.3(a) do not apply.

Evidence to assist the court: special rules
    31.4.—(1) This rule applies where the court can make on its own initiative— ★**P-274**
      (a)   a football banning order;
      (b)   a restraining order; or
      (c)   an anti-social behaviour order.
    (2) A party who wants the court to take account of evidence not already introduced must—
      (a)   serve notice in writing on—
        (i)   the court officer, and
        (ii)   every other party,
      as soon as practicable (without waiting for the verdict); and
      (b)   in the notice, identify that evidence; and
      (c)   attach any written statement containing such evidence.

Application to vary or revoke behaviour order
    31.5.—(1) The court may vary or revoke a behaviour order if— ★**P-275**
      (a)   the legislation under which it is made allows the court to do so; and

    (b) one of the following applies—
        (i)   the prosecutor,
        (ii) the person to whom the order is directed,
        (iii) any other person protected or affected by the order,
        (iv) the relevant authority or responsible officer,
        (v) the relevant Chief Officer of Police,
        (vi) the Director of Public Prosecutions, or
        (vii) the Director of the Serious Fraud Office.
  (2) A person applying under this rule must—
    (a) apply in writing as soon as practicable after becoming aware of the grounds for doing so, explaining—
        (i)   what material circumstances have changed since the order was made, and
        (ii) why the order should be varied or revoked as a result; and
    (b) serve the application on—
        (i)   the court officer,
        (ii) as appropriate, the prosecutor or defendant, and
        (iii) any other person listed in paragraph (1)(b), if the court so directs.
  (3) A party who wants the court to take account of any particular evidence before making its decision must, as soon as practicable—
    (a) serve notice in writing on—
        (i)   the court officer,
        (ii) as appropriate, the prosecutor or defendant, and
        (iii) any other person listed in paragraph (1)(b) on whom the court directed the application to be served; and
    (b) in that notice identify the evidence and attach any written statement that has not already been served.
  (4) The court may decide an application under this rule with or without a hearing.
  (5) But the court must not—
    (a) dismiss an application under this rule unless the applicant has had an opportunity to make representations at a hearing (whether or not the applicant in fact attends); or
    (b) allow an application under this rule unless everyone required to be served, by this rule or by the court, has had at least 14 days in which to make representations, including representations about whether there should be a hearing.
  (6) The court officer must—
    (a) serve the application on any person, if the court so directs; and
    (b) give notice of any hearing to—
        (i)   the applicant, and
        (ii) any person required to be served, by this rule or by the court.

Notice of hearsay evidence

★P-276   **31.6.**—(1) A party who wants to introduce hearsay evidence must—
    (a) serve a notice in writing on—
        (i)   the court officer, and
        (ii) every other party directly affected; and
    (b) in that notice—
        (i)   explain that it is a notice of hearsay evidence,
        (ii) identify that evidence,
        (iii) identify the person who made the statement which is hearsay, or explain why if that person is not identified, and
        (iv) explain why that person will not be called to give oral evidence.
  (2) A party may serve one notice under this rule in respect of more than one notice and more than one witness.

Cross-examination of maker of hearsay statement

★P-277   **31.7.**—(1) This rule applies where a party wants the court's permission to cross-examine a person who made a statement which another party wants to introduce as hearsay.
  (2) The party who wants to cross-examine that person must—
    (a) apply in writing, with reasons, not more than 7 days after service of the notice of hearsay evidence; and

   (b)   serve the application on—
      (i)   the court officer,
     (ii)   the party who served the hearsay evidence notice, and
    (iii)   every party on whom the hearsay evidence notice was served.

(3) The court may decide an application under this rule with or without a hearing.

(4) But the court must not—

   (a)   dismiss an application under this rule unless the applicant has had an opportunity to make representations at a hearing (whether or not the applicant in fact attends); or

   (b)   allow an application under this rule unless everyone served with the application has had at least 7 days in which to make representations, including representations about whether there should be a hearing.

Credibility and consistency of maker of hearsay statement

31.8.—(1) This rule applies where a party wants to challenge the credibility or consistency of a   **★P-278** person who made a statement which another party wants to introduce as hearsay.

(2) The party who wants to challenge the credibility or consistency of that person must—

   (a)   serve a written notice of intention to do so on—
      (i)   the court officer, and
     (ii)   the party who served the notice of hearsay evidence
     not more than 7 days after service of that hearsay evidence notice; and

   (b)   in the notice, identify any statement or other material on which that party relies.

(3) The party who served the hearsay notice—

   (a)   may call that person to give oral evidence instead; and

   (b)   if so, must serve a notice of intention to do so on—
      (i)   the court officer, and
     (ii)   every party on whom the hearsay notice was served
     not more than 7 days after service of the notice under paragraph (2).

European protection order to be given effect in another EU member State

31.9.—(1) This rule applies where—   **★P-279**

   (a)   a person benefits from the protection of one or more of the following prohibitions or restrictions imposed on another person by an order of a court in England and Wales when dealing with a criminal cause or matter—
      (i)   a prohibition from entering certain localities, places or defined areas where the protected person resides or visits,
     (ii)   a prohibition or restriction of contact with the protected person by any means (including by telephone, post, facsimile transmission or electronic mail),
    (iii)   a prohibition or restriction preventing the other person from approaching the protected person whether at all or to within a particular distance; and either

   (b)   that protected person wants the Crown Court or a magistrates' court to make a European protection order to supplement such an order; or

   (c)   the court varies or revokes such a prohibition or restriction in such an order and correspondingly amends or revokes a European protection order already made.

(2) Such a protected person—

   (a)   may apply orally or in writing to the Crown Court at the hearing at which the order imposing the prohibition or restriction is made by that court; or

   (b)   in any other case, must apply in writing to a magistrates' court and serve the application on the court officer.

(3) The application must—

   (a)   identify the prohibition or restriction that the European protection order would supplement;

   (b)   identify the date, if any, on which that prohibition or restriction will expire;

   (c)   specify the European Union member State in which the applicant has decided to reside or stay, or in which he or she already is residing or staying;

   (d)   indicate the length of the period for which the applicant intends to reside or stay in that member State;

   (e)   explain why the applicant needs the protection of that measure while residing or staying in that member State; and

   (f)   include any other information of which the applicant wants the court to take account.

(4) Where the court makes or amends a European protection order, the court officer must—

(a)   issue an order in the form required by Directive 2011/99/EU;

(b)   serve on the competent authority of the European Union member State in which the protected person has decided to reside or stay—

(i)   a copy of that form, and

(ii)   a copy of the form translated into an official language of that member State, or into an official language of the European Union if that member State has declared that it will accept a translation in that language.

(5) Where the court revokes a European protection order, the court officer must without delay so inform that authority.

(6) Where the court refuses to make a European protection order, the court officer must arrange for the protected person to be informed of any available avenue of appeal or review against the court's decision.

Giving effect to a European protection order made in another EU member State

★P-280   31.10.—(1) This rule applies where the Lord Chancellor serves on the court officer—

(a)   a request by an authority in another European Union member State to give effect to a European protection order;

(b)   a request by such an authority to give effect to a variation of such an order; or

(c)   notice by such an authority of the revocation or withdrawal of such an order.

(2) In the case of a request to which paragraph (1) refers, the court officer must, without undue delay—

(a)   arrange for the court to consider the request;

(b)   serve on the requesting authority—

(i)   notice of any further information required by the court, and

(ii)   subject to any such requirement and any response, notice of the court's decision;

(c)   where the court gives effect to the European protection order—

(i)   include in the notice served on the requesting authority the terms of the restraining order made by the court,

(ii)   serve notice of those terms, and of the potential legal consequences of breaching them, on the person restrained by the order made by the court and on the person protected by that order, and

(iii)   serve notice on the Lord Chancellor of any breach of the restraining order which is reported to the court;

(d)   where the court refuses to give effect to the European protection order—

(i)   include in the notice served on the requesting authority the grounds for the refusal,

(ii)   where appropriate, inform the protected person, or any representative or guardian of that person, of the possibility of applying for a comparable order under the law of England and Wales, and

(iii)   arrange for that person, representative or guardian to be informed of any available avenue of appeal or review against the court's decision.

(3) In the case of a notice to which paragraph (1) refers, the court officer must, as soon as possible, arrange for the court to act on that notice.

(4) Unless the court otherwise directs, the court officer must omit from any notice served on a person against whom a restraining order may be, or has been, made the address or contact details of the person who is the object of the European protection order.

Court's power to vary requirements under this part

★P-281   31.11. Unless other legislation otherwise provides, the court may—

(a)   shorten a time limit or extend it (even after it has expired);

(b)   allow a notice or application to be given in a different form, or presented orally.

PART 32

BREACH, REVOCATION AND AMENDMENT OF COMMUNITY AND OTHER ORDERS

When this part applies

★P-282   32.1. This part applies where—

(a)   the person responsible for a defendant's compliance with an order to which applies—

(i)   Schedule 3, 5, 7 or 8 to the Powers of Criminal Courts (Sentencing) Act 2000,

(ii)   Schedule 8 or 12 to the Criminal Justice Act 2003,

    (iii)   Schedule 2 to the Criminal Justice and Immigration Act 2008, or

    (iv)   the Schedule to the Street Offences Act 1959

wants the court to deal with that defendant for failure to comply;

    (b)   one of the following wants the court to exercise any power it has to revoke or amend such an order—

        (i)   the responsible officer or supervisor,

        (ii)   the defendant, or

        (iii)   where the legislation allows, a person affected by the order; or

    (c)   the court considers exercising on its own initiative any power it has to revoke or amend such an order.

Application by responsible officer or supervisor

★P-283

32.2.—(1) This rule applies where—

    (a)   the responsible officer or supervisor wants the court to—

        (i)   deal with a defendant for failure to comply with an order to which this part applies, or

        (ii)   revoke or amend such an order; or

    (b)   the court considers exercising on its own initiative any power it has to—

        (i)   revoke or amend such an order, and

        (ii)   summon the defendant to attend for that purpose.

(2) Rules 7.2 to 7.4, which deal, among other things, with starting a prosecution in a magistrates' court by information and summons, apply—

    (a)   as if—

        (i)   a reference in those rules to an allegation of an offence included a reference to an allegation of failure to comply with an order to which this part applies, and

        (ii)   a reference to the prosecutor included a reference to the responsible officer or supervisor; and

    (b)   with the necessary consequential modifications.

Application by defendant or person affected

★P-284

32.3.—(1) This rule applies where—

    (a)   the defendant wants the court to exercise any power it has to revoke or amend an order to which this part applies; or

    (b)   where the legislation allows, a person affected by such an order wants the court to exercise any such power.

(2) That defendant, or person affected, must—

    (a)   apply in writing, explaining why the order should be revoked or amended; and

    (b)   serve the application on—

        (i)   the court officer,

        (ii)   the responsible officer or supervisor, and

        (iii)   as appropriate, the defendant or the person affected.

Procedure on application by responsible officer or supervisor

★P-285

32.4.—(1) Except for rules 24.8 (written guilty plea: special rules) and 24.9 (single justice procedure: special rules), the rules in Part 24, which deal with the procedure at a trial in a magistrates' court, apply—

    (a)   as if—

        (i)   a reference in those rules to an allegation of an offence included a reference to an allegation of failure to comply with an order to which this part applies,

        (ii)   a reference to the court's verdict included a reference to the court's decision to revoke or amend such an order, or to exercise any other power it has to deal with the defendant, and

        (iii)   a reference to the court's sentence included a reference to the exercise of any such power; and

    (b)   with the necessary consequential modifications.

(2) The court officer must serve on each party any order revoking or amending an order to which this part applies.

PART 33

CONFISCATION AND RELATED PROCEEDINGS

General Rules

Interpretation

★P-286   **33.1.** In this part:

"document" means anything in which information of any description is recorded;

"hearsay evidence" means evidence consisting of hearsay within the meaning of section 1(2) of the Civil Evidence Act 1995;

"restraint proceedings" means proceedings under sections 42 and 58(2) and (3) of the Proceeds of Crime Act 2002;

"receivership proceedings" means proceedings under sections 48, 49, 50, 51, 54(4), 59(2) and (3), 62 and 63 of the 2002 Act;

"witness statement" means a written statement signed by a person which contains the evidence, and only that evidence, which that person would be allowed to give orally; and words and expressions used have the same meaning as in Part 2 of the 2002 Act.

Calculation of time

★P-287   **33.2.**—(1) This rule shows how to calculate any period of time for doing any act which is specified by this part for the purposes of any proceedings under Part 2 of the Proceeds of Crime Act 2002 or by an order of the Crown Court in restraint proceedings or receivership proceedings.

(2) A period of time expressed as a number of days shall be computed as clear days.

(3) In this rule "clear days" means that in computing the number of days—

(a)   the day on which the period begins; and

(b)   if the end of the period is defined by reference to an event, the day on which that event occurs,

are not included.

(4) Where the specified period is 5 days or less and includes a day which is not a business day that day does not count.

Court office closed

★P-288   **33.3.** When the period specified by this part, or by an order of the Crown Court under Part 2 of the Proceeds of Crime Act 2002, for doing any act at the court office falls on a day on which the office is closed, that act shall be in time if done on the next day on which the court office is open.

Application for registration of Scottish or Northern Ireland order

★P-289   **33.4.**—(1) This rule applies to an application for registration of an order under article 6 of the Proceeds of Crime Act 2002 (enforcement in different parts of the United Kingdom) Order 2002.

(2) The application may be made without notice.

(3) The application must be in writing and may be supported by a witness statement which must—

(a)   exhibit the order or a certified copy of the order; and

(b)   to the best of the witness's ability, give full details of the realisable property located in England and Wales in respect of which the order was made and specify the person holding that realisable property.

(4) If the court registers the order, the applicant must serve notice of the registration on—

(a)   any person who holds realisable property to which the order applies; and

(b)   any other person whom the applicant knows to be affected by the order.

(5) The permission of the Crown Court under rule 33.10 (service outside the jurisdiction) is not required to serve the notice outside England and Wales.

Application to vary or set aside registration

★P-290   **33.5.**—(1) An application to vary or set aside registration of an order under article 6 of the Proceeds of Crime Act 2002 (enforcement in different parts of the United Kingdom) Order 2002 may be made to the Crown Court by—

(a)   any person who holds realisable property to which the order applies; and

(b)   any other person affected by the order.

(2) The application must be in writing and may be supported by a witness statement.

(3) The application and any witness statement must be lodged with the Crown Court.

(4) The application must be served on the person who applied for registration at least 7 days before the date fixed by the court for hearing the application, unless the Crown Court specifies a shorter period.

(5) No property in England and Wales may be realised in pursuance of the order before the Crown Court has decided the application.

Register of orders

33.6.—(1) The Crown Court must keep, under the direction of the Lord Chancellor, a register of the orders registered under article 6 of the Proceeds of Crime Act 2002 (enforcement in different parts of the United Kingdom) Order 2002. ★**P-291**

(2) The register must include details of any variation or setting aside of a registration under rule 33.5 and of any execution issued on a registered order.

(3) If the person who applied for registration of an order which is subsequently registered notifies the Crown Court that the court which made the order has varied or discharged the order, details of the variation or discharge, as the case may be, must be entered in the register.

Statements of truth

33.7.—(1) Any witness statement required to be served by this part must be verified by a statement of truth contained in the witness statement. ★**P-292**

(2) A statement of truth is a declaration by the person making the witness statement to the effect that the witness statement is true to the best of his knowledge and belief and that he made the statement knowing that, if it were tendered in evidence, he would be liable to prosecution if he wilfully stated in it anything which he knew to be false or did not believe to be true.

(3) The statement of truth must be signed by the person making the witness statement.

(4) If the person making the witness statement fails to verify the witness statement by a statement of truth, the Crown Court may direct that it shall not be admissible as evidence.

Use of witness statements for other purposes

33.8.—(1) Except as provided by this rule, a witness statement served in proceedings under Part 2 of the Proceeds of Crime Act 2002 may be used only for the purpose of the proceedings in which it is served. ★**P-293**

(2) Paragraph (1) does not apply if and to the extent that—
    (a) the witness gives consent in writing to some other use of it;
    (b) the Crown Court gives permission for some other use; or
    (c) the witness statement has been put in evidence at a hearing held in public.

Service of documents

33.9.—(1) Rule 49.1 (notice required to accompany process served outside the United Kingdom and translations) shall not apply in restraint proceedings and receivership proceedings. ★**P-294**

(2) An order made in restraint proceedings or receivership proceedings may be enforced against the defendant or any other person affected by it notwithstanding that service of a copy of the order has not been effected in accordance with Part 4 if the Crown Court is satisfied that the person had notice of the order by being present when the order was made.

Service outside the jurisdiction

33.10.—(1) Where this part requires a document to be served on someone who is outside England and Wales, it may be served outside England and Wales with the permission of the Crown Court. ★**P-295**

(2) Where a document is to be served outside England and Wales it may be served by any method permitted by the law of the country in which it is to be served.

(3) Nothing in this rule or in any court order shall authorise or require any person to do anything in the country where the document is to be served which is against the law of that country.

(4) Where this part requires a document to be served a certain period of time before the date of a hearing and the recipient does not appear at the hearing, the hearing must not take place unless the Crown Court is satisfied that the document has been duly served.

Certificates of service

33.11.—(1) Where this part requires that the applicant for an order in restraint proceedings or receivership proceedings serve a document on another person, the applicant must lodge a certificate of service with the Crown Court within 7 days of service of the document. ★**P-296**

(2) The certificate must state—

    (a) the method of service;

    (b) the date of service; and

    (c) if the document is served under rule 4.9 (service by another method), such other information as the court may require when making the order permitting service by that method.

    (3) Where a document is to be served by the Crown Court in restraint proceedings and receivership proceedings and the court is unable to serve it, the court must send a notice of non-service stating the method attempted to the party who requested service.

External requests and orders

★**P-297**   **33.12.**—(1) The rules in this part and in Part 42 (appeal to the Court of Appeal in confiscation and related proceedings) apply with the necessary modifications to proceedings under the Proceeds of Crime Act 2002 (External Requests and Orders) Order 2005 in the same way that they apply to corresponding proceedings under Part 2 of the Proceeds of Crime Act 2002.

    (2) This table shows how provisions of the 2005 Order correspond with provisions of the 2002 Act.

Article of the Proceeds of Crime Act 2002 (External Requests and Orders) Order 2005	Section of the Proceeds of Crime Act 2002
8	41
9	42
10	43
11	44
15	48
16	49
17	58
23	31
27	50
28	51
41	62
42	63
44	65
45	66

Confiscation Proceedings

Statements in connection with confiscation orders

★**P-298**   **33.13.**—(1) This rule applies where—

    (a) the court can make a confiscation order; and

    (b) the prosecutor asks the court to make such an order, or the court decides to make such an order on its own initiative.

    (2) Within such periods as the court directs—

    (a) if the court so orders, the defendant must give such information, in such manner, as the court directs;

    (b) the prosecutor must serve a statement of information relevant to confiscation on the court officer and the defendant;

    (c) if the court so directs—

      (i) the defendant must serve a response notice on the court officer and the prosecutor, and

      (ii) the parties must identify what is in dispute.

    (3) Where it appears to the court that a person other than the defendant holds, or may hold, an interest in property held by the defendant which property is likely to be realised or otherwise used to satisfy a confiscation order—

    (a) the court must not determine the extent of the defendant's interest in that property unless that other person has had a reasonable opportunity to make representations; and

    (b) the court may order that other person to give such information, in such manner and within such a period, as the court directs.

    (4) The court may—

   (a) shorten or extend a time limit which it has set;

   (b) vary, discharge or supplement an order which it has made;

   (c) postpone confiscation proceedings without a hearing.

(5) A prosecutor's statement of information must—

   (a) identify the maker of the statement and show its date;

   (b) identify the defendant in respect of whom it is served;

   (c) specify the conviction which gives the court power to make the confiscation order, or each conviction if more than one;

   (d) if the prosecutor believes the defendant to have a criminal lifestyle, include such matters as the prosecutor believes to be relevant in connection with deciding—

      (i) whether the defendant has such a lifestyle,

     (ii) whether the defendant has benefited from his or her general criminal conduct,

     (iii) the defendant's benefit from that conduct, and

     (iv) whether the court should or should not make such assumptions about the defendant's property as legislation permits;

   (e) if the prosecutor does not believe the defendant to have a criminal lifestyle, include such matters as the prosecutor believes to be relevant in connection with deciding—

      (i) whether the defendant has benefited from his or her particular criminal conduct, and

     (ii) the defendant's benefit from that conduct;

   (f) in any case, include such matters as the prosecutor believes to be relevant in connection with deciding—

      (i) whether to make a determination about the extent of the defendant's interest in property in which another person holds, or may hold, an interest, and

     (ii) what determination to make, if the court decides to make one.

(6) A defendant's response notice must—

   (a) indicate the extent to which the defendant accepts the allegations made in the prosecutor's statement of information; and

   (b) so far as the defendant does not accept an allegation, give particulars of any matters on which the defendant relies,

in any manner directed by the court.

(7) The court must satisfy itself that there has been explained to the defendant, in terms the defendant can understand (with help, if necessary)—

   (a) that if the defendant accepts to any extent an allegation in a prosecutor's statement of information, then the court may treat that as conclusive for the purposes of deciding whether the defendant has benefited from general or particular criminal conduct, and if so by how much;

   (b) that if the defendant fails in any respect to comply with a direction to serve a response notice, then the court may treat that as acceptance of each allegation to which the defendant has not replied, except the allegation that the defendant has benefited from general or particular criminal conduct; and

   (c) that if the defendant fails without reasonable excuse to comply with an order to give information, then the court may draw such inference as it believes is appropriate.

Application for compliance order

33.14.—(1) This rule applies where—   ★**P-299**

   (a) the prosecutor wants the court to make a compliance order after a confiscation order has been made;

   (b) the prosecutor or a person affected by a compliance order wants the court to vary or discharge the order.

(2) Such a prosecutor or person must—

   (a) apply in writing; and

   (b) serve the application on—

      (i) the court officer, and

     (ii) as appropriate, the prosecutor and any person who is affected by the compliance order (or who would be affected if it were made), unless the court otherwise directs.

(3) The application must—

   (a) specify—

      (i) the confiscation order,

     (ii) the compliance order, if it is an application to vary or discharge that order;

    (b) if it is an application for a compliance order—

        (i) specify each measure that the prosecutor proposes to ensure that the confiscation order is effective, including in particular any restriction or prohibition on the defendant's travel outside the United Kingdom, and

        (ii) explain why each such measure is appropriate;

    (c) if it is an application to vary or discharge a compliance order, as appropriate—

        (i) specify any proposed variation, and

        (ii) explain why it is appropriate for the order to be varied or discharged;

    (d) attach any material on which the applicant relies;

    (e) propose the terms of the order; and

    (f) ask for a hearing, if the applicant wants one, and explain why it is needed.

(4) A person who wants to make representations about the application must—

    (a) serve the representations on—

        (i) the court officer, and

        (ii) the applicant;

    (b) do so as soon as reasonably practicable after service of the application;

    (c) attach any material on which that person relies; and

    (d) ask for a hearing, if that person wants one, and explain why it is needed.

(5) The court—

    (a) may determine the application at a hearing (which must be in private unless the court otherwise directs), or without a hearing;

    (b) may dispense with service on any person of a prosecutor's application for a compliance order if, in particular—

        (i) the application is urgent, or

        (ii) there are reasonable grounds for believing that to give notice of the application would cause the dissipation of property that otherwise would be available to satisfy the confiscation order.

Application for reconsideration

★P-300   **33.15.**—(1) This rule applies where the prosecutor wants the court, in view of fresh evidence—

    (a) to consider making a confiscation order where the defendant was convicted but no such order was considered;

    (b) to reconsider a decision that the defendant had not benefited from criminal conduct;

    (c) to reconsider a decision about the amount of the defendant's benefit.

(2) The application must be in writing and give details of—

    (a) the name of the defendant;

    (b) the date on which and the place where any relevant conviction occurred;

    (c) the date on which and the place where any relevant confiscation order was made or varied;

    (d) any slavery and trafficking reparation order made by virtue of any relevant confiscation order;

    (e) the grounds for the application; and

    (f) an indication of the evidence available to support the application.

(3) The application must be served on the court officer.

(4) The application must be served on the defendant at least 7 days before the date fixed by the court for hearing the application, unless the court specifies a shorter period.

Application for new calculation of available amount

★P-301   **33.16.**—(1) This rule applies where the prosecutor or a receiver wants the court to make a new calculation of the amount available for confiscation.

(2) The application—

    (a) must be in writing and may be supported by a witness statement; and

    (b) must identify any slavery and trafficking reparation order made by virtue of the confiscation order.

(3) The application and any witness statement must be served on the court officer.

(4) The application and any witness statement must be served on—

    (a) the defendant;

    (b) the receiver, if the prosecutor is making the application and a receiver has been appointed; and

(c)   the prosecutor, if the receiver is making the application,

at least 7 days before the date fixed by the court for hearing the application, unless the court specifies a shorter period.

Variation of confiscation order due to inadequacy of available amount

33.17.—(1) This rule applies where the defendant, the prosecutor or a receiver wants the court to   ★P-302
vary a confiscation order because the amount available is inadequate.

(2) The application—

(a)   must be in writing and may be supported by a witness statement; and

(b)   must identify any slavery and trafficking reparation order made by virtue of the confiscation order.

(3) The application and any witness statement must be served on the court officer.

(4) The application and any witness statement must be served on—

(a)   the prosecutor;

(b)   the defendant, if the receiver is making the application; and

(c)   the receiver, if the defendant is making the application and a receiver has been appointed,

at least 7 days before the date fixed by the court for hearing the application, unless the court specifies a shorter period.

Application by magistrates' court officer to discharge confiscation order

33.18.—(1) This rule applies where a magistrates' court officer wants the court to discharge a   ★P-303
confiscation order because the amount available is inadequate or the sum outstanding is very small.

(2) The application must be in writing and give details of—

(a)   the confiscation order;

(b)   any slavery and trafficking reparation order made by virtue of the confiscation order;

(c)   the amount outstanding under the order; and

(d)   the grounds for the application.

(3) The application must be served on—

(a)   the defendant;

(b)   the prosecutor; and

(c)   any receiver.

(4) The court may determine the application without a hearing unless a person listed in paragraph (3) indicates, within 7 days after the application was served, that he or she would like to make representations.

(5) If the court makes an order discharging the confiscation order, the court officer must, at once, send a copy of the order to—

(a)   the magistrates' court officer who applied for the order;

(b)   the defendant;

(c)   the prosecutor; and

(d)   any receiver.

Application for variation of confiscation order made against an absconder

33.19.—(1) This rule applies where the defendant wants the court to vary a confiscation order   ★P-304
made while the defendant was an absconder.

(2) The application must be in writing and supported by a witness statement which must give details of—

(a)   the confiscation order;

(b)   any slavery and trafficking reparation order made by virtue of the confiscation order;

(c)   the circumstances in which the defendant ceased to be an absconder;

(d)   the defendant's conviction of the offence or offences concerned; and

(e)   the reason why the defendant believes the amount required to be paid under the confiscation order was too large.

(3) The application and witness statement must be served on the court officer.

(4) The application and witness statement must be served on the prosecutor at least 7 days before the date fixed by the court for hearing the application, unless the court specifies a shorter period.

Application for discharge of confiscation order made against an absconder

33.20.—(1) This rule applies where the defendant wants the court to discharge a confiscation   ★P-305
order made while the defendant was an absconder and—

(a) the defendant since has been tried and acquitted of each offence concerned; or

(b) the prosecution has not concluded or is not to proceed.

(2) The application must be in writing and supported by a witness statement which must give details of—

(a) the confiscation order;

(b) the date on which the defendant ceased to be an absconder;

(c) the acquittal of the defendant if he or she has been acquitted of the offence concerned; and

(d) if the defendant has not been acquitted of the offence concerned—

(i) the date on which the defendant ceased to be an absconder,

(ii) the date on which the proceedings taken against the defendant were instituted and a summary of steps taken in the proceedings since then, and

(iii) any indication that the prosecutor does not intend to proceed against the defendant.

(3) The application and witness statement must be served on the court officer.

(4) The application and witness statement must be served on the prosecutor at least 7 days before the date fixed by the court for hearing the application, unless the court specifies a shorter period.

(5) If the court orders the discharge of the confiscation order, the court officer must serve notice on any other court responsible for enforcing the order.

Application for increase in term of imprisonment in default

★P-306

33.21.—(1) This rule applies where—

(a) a court varies a confiscation order; and

(b) the prosecutor wants the court in consequence to increase the term of imprisonment to be served in default of payment.

(2) The application must be made in writing and give details of—

(a) the name and address of the defendant;

(b) the confiscation order;

(c) the grounds for the application; and

(d) the enforcement measures taken, if any.

(3) On receipt of the application, the court officer must—

(a) at once, send to the defendant and any other court responsible for enforcing the order, a copy of the application; and

(b) fix a time, date and place for the hearing and notify the applicant and the defendant of that time, date and place.

(4) If the court makes an order increasing the term of imprisonment in default, the court officer must, at once, send a copy of the order to—

(a) the applicant;

(b) the defendant;

(c) where the defendant is in custody at the time of the making of the order, the person having custody of the defendant; and

(d) any other court responsible for enforcing the order.

Compensation – general

★P-307

33.22.—(1) This rule applies where a person who held realisable property wants the court to award compensation for loss suffered in consequence of anything done in relation to that property in connection with confiscation proceedings.

(2) The application must be in writing and may be supported by a witness statement.

(3) The application and any witness statement must be served on the court officer.

(4) The application and any witness statement must be served on—

(a) the person alleged to be in default; and

(b) the person or authority by whom the compensation would be payable,

at least 7 days before the date fixed by the court for hearing the application, unless the court directs otherwise.

Compensation – confiscation order made against absconder

★P-308

33.23.—(1) This rule applies where—

(a) the court varies or discharges a confiscation order made against an absconder;

(b) a person who held realisable property suffered loss as a result of the making of that confiscation order; and

(c) that person wants the court to award compensation for that loss.

(2) The application must be in writing and supported by a witness statement which must give details of—

    (a) the confiscation order;

    (b) the variation or discharge of the confiscation order;

    (c) the realisable property to which the application relates; and

    (d) the loss suffered by the applicant as a result of the confiscation order.

(3) The application and witness statement must be served on the court officer.

(4) The application and witness statement must be served on the prosecutor at least 7 days before the date fixed by the court for hearing the application, unless the court specifies a shorter period.

Payment of money in bank or building society account in satisfaction of confiscation order

    33.24.—(1) An order under section 67 of the Proceeds of Crime Act 2002 requiring a bank or   ★**P-309**
building society to pay money to a magistrates' court officer ("a payment order") shall—

    (a) be directed to the bank or building society in respect of which the payment order is made;

    (b) name the person against whom the confiscation order has been made;

    (c) state the amount which remains to be paid under the confiscation order;

    (d) state the name and address of the branch at which the account in which the money ordered to be paid is held and the sort code of that branch, if the sort code is known;

    (e) state the name in which the account in which the money ordered to be paid is held and the account number of that account, if the account number is known;

    (f) state the amount which the bank or building society is required to pay to the court officer under the payment order;

    (g) give the name and address of the court officer to whom payment is to be made; and

    (h) require the bank or building society to make payment within a period of 7 days beginning on the day on which the payment order is made, unless it appears to the court that a longer or shorter period would be appropriate in the particular circumstances.

(2) In this rule "confiscation order" has the meaning given to it by section 88(6) of the Proceeds of Crime Act 2002.

Application to realise seized property

    33.25.—(1) This rule applies where—   ★**P-310**

    (a) property is held by a defendant against whom a confiscation order has been made;

    (b) the property has been seized by or produced to an officer; and

    (c) an officer who is entitled to apply wants a magistrates' court—

        (i) to make an order under section 67A of the Proceeds of Crime Act 2002 authorising the realisation of the property towards satisfaction of the confiscation order, or

        (ii) to determine any storage, insurance or realisation costs in respect of the property which may be recovered under section 67B of the 2002 Act.

(2) Such an officer must—

    (a) apply in writing; and

    (b) serve the application on—

        (i) the court officer, and

        (ii) any person whom the applicant believes would be affected by an order.

(3) The application must—

    (a) specify the property;

    (b) explain—

        (i) the applicant's entitlement to apply,

        (ii) how the proposed realisation meets the conditions prescribed by section 67A of the 2002 Act, and

        (iii) how any storage, etc. costs have been calculated;

    (c) attach any material on which the applicant relies; and

    (d) propose the terms of the order.

(4) The court may—

    (a) determine the application at a hearing, or without a hearing;

    (b) consider an application made orally instead of in writing;

    (c) consider an application which has not been served on a person likely to be affected by an order.

(5) If the court authorises the realisation of the property, the applicant must—

    (a) notify any person affected by the order who was absent when it was made; and

(b) serve on the court officer a list of those so notified.

Appeal about decision on application to realise seized property

★**P-311**   **33.26.**—(1) This rule applies where on an application under rule 33.25 for an order authorising the realisation of property—

(a) a magistrates' court decides not to make such an order and an officer who is entitled to apply wants to appeal against that decision to the Crown Court, under section 67C(1) of the Proceeds of Crime Act 2002;

(b) a magistrates' court makes such an order and a person who is affected by that decision, other than the defendant against whom the confiscation order was made, wants to appeal against it to the Crown Court, under section 67C(2) of the 2002 Act;

(c) a magistrates' court makes a decision about storage, etc. costs and an officer who is entitled to apply wants to appeal against that decision to the Crown Court, under section 67C(4) of the 2002 Act.

(2) The appellant must serve an appeal notice—

(a) on the Crown Court officer and on any other party;

(b) not more than 21 days after the magistrates' court's decision, or, if applicable, service of notice under rule 33.25(5).

(3) The appeal notice must—

(a) specify the decision under appeal;

(b) where paragraph (1)(a) applies, explain why the property should be realised;

(c) in any other case, propose the order that the appellant wants the court to make, and explain why.

(4) Rule 34.11 (constitution of the Crown Court) applies on such an appeal.

Application for direction about surplus proceeds

★**P-312**   **33.27.**—(1) This rule applies where—

(a) on an application under rule 33.25, a magistrates' court has made an order authorising an officer to realise property;

(b) an officer so authorised holds proceeds of that realisation;

(c) the confiscation order has been fully paid; and

(d) the officer, or a person who had or has an interest in the property represented by the proceeds, wants a magistrates' court or the Crown Court to determine under section 67D of the Proceeds of Crime Act 2002—

(i) to whom the remaining proceeds should be paid, and

(ii) in what amount or amounts.

(2) Such a person must—

(a) apply in writing; and

(b) serve the application on—

(i) the court officer, and

(ii) as appropriate, the officer holding the proceeds, or any person to whom such proceeds might be paid.

(3) The application must—

(a) specify the property which was realised;

(b) explain the applicant's entitlement to apply;

(c) describe the distribution proposed by the applicant and explain why that is proposed;

(d) attach any material on which the applicant relies; and

(e) ask for a hearing, if the applicant wants one, and explain why it is needed.

(4) A person who wants to make representations about the application must—

(a) serve the representations on—

(i) the court officer,

(ii) the applicant, and

(iii) any other person to whom proceeds might be paid;

(b) do so as soon as reasonably practicable after service of the application;

(c) attach any material on which that person relies; and

(d) ask for a hearing, if that person wants one, and explain why it is needed.

(5) The court—

(a) must not determine the application unless the applicant and each person on whom it was served—

    (i)   is present, or

    (ii) has had an opportunity to attend or to make representations;

  (b) subject to that, may determine the application—

    (i)   at a hearing (which must be in private unless the court otherwise directs), or without a hearing,

    (ii) in the absence of any party to the application.

Seizure and Detention Proceedings

Application for approval to seize property or to search

33.28.—(1) This rule applies where an officer who is entitled to apply wants the approval of a ★**P-313** magistrates' court, under section 47G of the Proceeds of Crime Act 2002—

  (a) to seize property, under section 47C of that Act;

  (b) to search premises or a person or vehicle for property to be seized, under section 47D, 47E or 47F of that Act.

(2) Such an officer must—

  (a) apply in writing; and

  (b) serve the application on the court officer.

(3) The application must—

  (a) explain—

    (i)   the applicant's entitlement to apply, and

    (ii) how the proposed seizure meets the conditions prescribed by sections 47B, 47C and, if applicable, 47D, 47E or 47F of the 2002 Act;

  (b) if applicable, specify any premises, person or vehicle to be searched;

  (c) attach any material on which the applicant relies; and

  (d) propose the terms in which the applicant wants the court to give its approval.

(4) The court—

  (a) must determine the application—

    (i)   at a hearing, which must be in private unless the court otherwise directs, and

    (ii) in the applicant's presence;

  (b) may consider an application made orally instead of in writing.

Application to extend detention period

33.29.—(1) This rule applies where an officer who is entitled to apply, or the prosecutor, wants a ★**P-314** magistrates' court to make an order, under section 47M of the Proceeds of Crime Act 2002, extending the period for which seized property may be detained.

(2) Such an officer or prosecutor must—

  (a) apply in writing; and

  (b) serve the application on—

    (i)   the court officer, and

    (ii) any person whom the applicant believes would be affected by an order.

(3) The application must—

  (a) specify—

    (i)   the property to be detained, and

    (ii) whether the applicant wants it to be detained for a specified period or indefinitely;

  (b) explain—

    (i)   the applicant's entitlement to apply, and

    (ii) how the proposed detention meets the conditions prescribed by section 47M of the 2002 Act;

  (c) attach any material on which the applicant relies; and

  (d) propose the terms of the order.

(4) The court—

  (a) must determine the application—

    (i)   at a hearing, which must be in private unless the court otherwise directs, and

    (ii) in the applicant's presence;

  (b) may—

    (i)   consider an application made orally instead of in writing,

    (ii) require service of the application on the court officer after it has been heard, instead of before.

(5) If the court extends the period for which the property may be detained, the applicant must—

    (a) notify any person affected by the order who was absent when it was made; and

    (b) serve on the court officer a list of those so notified.

Application to vary or discharge order for extended detention

★P-315   **33.30.**—(1) This rule applies where an officer who is entitled to apply, the prosecutor, or a person affected by an order to which rule 33.29 applies, wants a magistrates' court to vary or discharge that order, under section 47N of the Proceeds of Crime Act 2002.

(2) Such a person must—

    (a) apply in writing; and

    (b) serve the application on—

        (i) the court officer, and

        (ii) as appropriate, the applicant for the order, or any person affected by the order.

(3) The application must—

    (a) specify the order and the property detained;

    (b) explain—

        (i) the applicant's entitlement to apply,

        (ii) why it is appropriate for the order to be varied or discharged,

        (iii) if applicable, on what grounds the court must discharge the order;

    (c) attach any material on which the applicant relies;

    (d) if applicable, propose the terms of any variation; and

    (e) ask for a hearing, if the applicant wants one, and explain why it is needed.

(4) A person who wants to make representations about the application must—

    (a) serve the representations on—

        (i) the court officer, and

        (ii) the applicant;

    (b) do so as soon as reasonably practicable after service of the application;

    (c) attach any material on which that person relies; and

    (d) ask for a hearing, if that person wants one, and explain why it is needed.

(5) The court—

    (a) must not determine the application unless the applicant and each person on whom it was served—

        (i) is present, or

        (ii) has had an opportunity to attend or to make representations;

    (b) subject to that, may determine the application—

        (i) at a hearing (which must be in private unless the court otherwise directs), or without a hearing,

        (ii) in the absence of any party to the application.

Appeal about property detention decision

★P-316   **33.31.**—(1) This rule applies where—

    (a) on an application under rule 33.29 for an order extending the period for which property may be detained—

        (i) a magistrates' court decides not to make such an order, and

        (ii) an officer who is entitled to apply for such an order, or the prosecutor, wants to appeal against that decision to the Crown Court under section 47O(1) of the Proceeds of Crime Act 2002;

    (b) on an application under rule 33.30 to vary or discharge an order under rule 33.29—

        (i) a magistrates' court determines the application, and

        (ii) a person who is entitled to apply under that rule wants to appeal against that decision to the Crown Court under section 47O(2) of the 2002 Act.

(2) The appellant must serve an appeal notice—

    (a) on the Crown Court officer and on any other party;

    (b) not more than 21 days after the magistrates' court's decision, or, if applicable, service of notice under rule 33.29(5).

(3) The appeal notice must—

    (a) specify the decision under appeal;

    (b) where paragraph (1)(a) applies, explain why the detention period should be extended;

    (c)   where paragraph (1)(b) applies, propose the order that the appellant wants the court to make, and explain why.

(4) Rule 34.11 (constitution of the Crown Court) applies on such an appeal.

Restraint and Receivership Proceedings: Rules that Apply Generally

Taking control of goods and forfeiture

33.32.—(1) This rule applies to applications under sections 58(2) and (3) and 59(2) and (3) of the Proceeds of Crime Act 2002 for leave of the Crown Court to take control of goods or levy distress against property, or to exercise a right of forfeiture by peaceable re-entry in relation to a tenancy, in circumstances where the property or tenancy is the subject of a restraint order or a receiver has been appointed in respect of the property or tenancy.   **★P-317**

(2) The application must be made in writing to the Crown Court.

(3) The application must be served on—

    (a)   the person who applied for the restraint order or the order appointing the receiver; and

    (b)   any receiver appointed in respect of the property or tenancy,

at least 7 days before the date fixed by the court for hearing the application, unless the Crown Court specifies a shorter period.

Joining of applications

33.33. An application for the appointment of a management receiver or enforcement receiver under rule 33.56 may be joined with—   **★P-318**

    (a)   an application for a restraint order under rule 33.51; and

    (b)   an application for the conferral of powers on the receiver under rule 33.57.

Applications to be dealt with in writing

33.34. Applications in restraint proceedings and receivership proceedings are to be dealt with without a hearing, unless the Crown Court orders otherwise.   **★P-319**

Business in chambers

33.35. Restraint proceedings and receivership proceedings may be heard in chambers.   **★P-320**

Power of court to control evidence

33.36.—(1) When hearing restraint proceedings and receivership proceedings, the Crown Court may control the evidence by giving directions as to—   **★P-321**

    (a)   the issues on which it requires evidence;

    (b)   the nature of the evidence which it requires to decide those issues; and

    (c)   the way in which the evidence is to be placed before the court.

(2) The court may use its power under this rule to exclude evidence that would otherwise be admissible.

(3) The court may limit cross-examination in restraint proceedings and receivership proceedings.

Evidence of witnesses

33.37.—(1) The general rule is that, unless the Crown Court orders otherwise, any fact which needs to be proved in restraint proceedings or receivership proceedings by the evidence of a witness is to be proved by their evidence in writing.   **★P-322**

(2) Where evidence is to be given in writing under this rule, any party may apply to the Crown Court for permission to cross-examine the person giving the evidence.

(3) If the Crown Court gives permission under paragraph (2) but the person in question does not attend as required by the order, his evidence may not be used unless the court gives permission.

Witness summons

33.38.—(1) Any party to restraint proceedings or receivership proceedings may apply to the Crown Court to issue a witness summons requiring a witness to—   **★P-323**

    (a)   attend court to give evidence; or

    (b)   produce documents to the court.

(2) Rule 17.3 (application for summons, warrant or order: general rules) applies to an application under this rule as it applies to an application under section 2 of the Criminal Procedure (Attendance of Witnesses) Act 1965.

Hearsay evidence

33.39. Section 2(1) of the Civil Evidence Act 1995 (duty to give notice of intention to rely on hearsay evidence) does not apply to evidence in restraint proceedings and receivership proceedings.   **★P-324**

Disclosure and inspection of documents

★P-325   **33.40.**—(1) This rule applies where, in the course of restraint proceedings or receivership proceedings, an issue arises as to whether property is realisable property.

(2) The Crown Court may make an order for disclosure of documents.

(3) Part 31 of the Civil Procedure Rules 1998 as amended from time to time shall have effect as if the proceedings were proceedings in the High Court.

Court documents

★P-326   **33.41.**—(1) Any order which the Crown Court issues in restraint proceedings or receivership proceedings must—

    (a)   state the name and judicial title of the person who made it;

    (b)   bear the date on which it is made; and

    (c)   be sealed by the Crown Court.

(2) The Crown Court may place the seal on the order—

    (a)   by hand; or

    (b)   by printing a facsimile of the seal on the order whether electronically or otherwise.

(3) A document purporting to bear the court's seal shall be admissible in evidence without further proof.

Consent orders

★P-327   **33.42.**—(1) This rule applies where all the parties to restraint proceedings or receivership proceedings agree the terms in which an order should be made.

(2) Any party may apply for a judgment or order in the terms agreed.

(3) The Crown Court may deal with an application under paragraph (2) without a hearing.

(4) Where this rule applies—

    (a)   the order which is agreed by the parties must be drawn up in the terms agreed;

    (b)   it must be expressed as being "By Consent"; and

    (c)   it must be signed by the legal representative acting for each of the parties to whom the order relates or by the party if he is a litigant in person.

(5) Where an application is made under this rule, then the requirements of any other rule as to the procedure for making an application do not apply.

Slips and omissions

★P-328   **33.43.**—(1) The Crown Court may at any time correct an accidental slip or omission in an order made in restraint proceedings or receivership proceedings.

(2) A party may apply for a correction without notice.

Supply of documents from court records

★P-329   **33.44.**—(1) No document relating to restraint proceedings or receivership proceedings may be supplied from the records of the Crown Court for any person to inspect or copy unless the Crown Court grants permission.

(2) An application for permission under paragraph (1) must be made on notice to the parties to the proceedings.

Disclosure of documents in criminal proceedings

★P-330   **33.45.**—(1) This rule applies where—

    (a)   proceedings for an offence have been started in the Crown Court and the defendant has not been either convicted or acquitted on all counts; and

    (b)   an application for a restraint order under section 42(1) of the Proceeds of Crime Act 2002 has been made.

(2) The judge presiding at the proceedings for the offence may be supplied from the records of the Crown Court with documents relating to restraint proceedings and any receivership proceedings.

(3) Such documents must not otherwise be disclosed in the proceedings for the offence.

Preparation of documents

★P-331   **33.46.**—(1) Every order in restraint proceedings or receivership proceedings must be drawn up by the Crown Court unless—

    (a)   the Crown Court orders a party to draw it up;

    (b)   a party, with the permission of the Crown Court, agrees to draw it up; or

(c)   the order is made by consent under rule 33.42.

(2) The Crown Court may direct that—

(a)   an order drawn up by a party must be checked by the Crown Court before it is sealed; or

(b)   before an order is drawn up by the Crown Court, the parties must lodge an agreed statement of its terms.

(3) Where an order is to be drawn up by a party—

(a)   he must lodge it with the Crown Court no later than 7 days after the date on which the court ordered or permitted him to draw it up so that it can be sealed by the Crown Court; and

(b)   if he fails to lodge it within that period, any other party may draw it up and lodge it.

(4) Nothing in this rule shall require the Crown Court to accept a document which is illegible, has not been duly authorised, or is unsatisfactory for some other similar reason.

Order for costs

33.47.—(1) This rule applies where the Crown Court is deciding whether to make an order for costs in restraint proceedings or receivership proceedings.   ★**P-332**

(2) The court has discretion as to—

(a)   whether costs are payable by one party to another;

(b)   the amount of those costs; and

(c)   when they are to be paid.

(3) If the court decides to make an order about costs—

(a)   the general rule is that the unsuccessful party must be ordered to pay the costs of the successful party; but

(b)   the court may make a different order.

(4) In deciding what order (if any) to make about costs, the court must have regard to all of the circumstances, including—

(a)   the conduct of all the parties; and

(b)   whether a party has succeeded on part of an application, even if he has not been wholly successful.

(5) The orders which the court may make include an order that a party must pay—

(a)   a proportion of another party's costs;

(b)   a stated amount in respect of another party's costs;

(c)   costs from or until a certain date only;

(d)   costs incurred before proceedings have begun;

(e)   costs relating to particular steps taken in the proceedings;

(f)   costs relating only to a distinct part of the proceedings; and

(g)   interest on costs from or until a certain date, including a date before the making of an order.

(6) Where the court would otherwise consider making an order under paragraph (5)(f), it must instead, if practicable, make an order under paragraph (5)(a) or (c).

(7) Where the court has ordered a party to pay costs, it may order an amount to be paid on account before the costs are assessed.

Assessment of costs

33.48.—(1) Where the Crown Court has made an order for costs in restraint proceedings or receivership proceedings it may either—   ★**P-333**

(a)   make an assessment of the costs itself; or

(b)   order assessment of the costs under rule 45.11.

(2) In either case, the Crown Court or the assessing authority, as the case may be, must—

(a)   only allow costs which are proportionate to the matters in issue; and

(b)   resolve any doubt which it may have as to whether the costs were reasonably incurred or reasonable and proportionate in favour of the paying party.

(3) The Crown Court or the assessing authority, as the case may be, is to have regard to all the circumstances in deciding whether costs were proportionately or reasonably incurred or proportionate and reasonable in amount.

(4) In particular, the Crown Court or the assessing authority must give effect to any orders which have already been made.

(5) The Crown Court or the assessing authority must also have regard to—

(a)   the conduct of all the parties, including in particular, conduct before, as well as during, the proceedings;

    (b)   the amount or value of the property involved;

    (c)   the importance of the matter to all the parties;

    (d)   the particular complexity of the matter or the difficulty or novelty of the questions raised;

    (e)   the skill, effort, specialised knowledge and responsibility involved;

    (f)   the time spent on the application; and

    (g)   the place where and the circumstances in which work or any part of it was done.

Time for complying with an order for costs

★**P-334**   **33.49.** A party to restraint proceedings or receivership proceedings must comply with an order for the payment of costs within 14 days of—

    (a)   the date of the order if it states the amount of those costs;

    (b)   if the amount of those costs is decided later under rule 45.11, the date of the assessing authority's decision; or

    (c)   in either case, such later date as the Crown Court may specify.

Application of costs rules

★**P-335**   **33.50.** Rules 33.47, 33.48 and 33.49 do not apply to the assessment of costs in proceedings to the extent that section 11 of the Access to Justice Act 1999 applies and provisions made under that Act make different provision.

Restraint Proceedings

Application for restraint order or ancillary order

★**P-336**   **33.51.**—(1) This rule applies where the prosecutor, or an accredited financial investigator, makes an application under section 42 of the Proceeds of Crime Act 2002 for—

    (a)   a restraint order, under section 41(1) of the 2002 Act; or

    (b)   an ancillary order, under section 41(7) of that Act, for the purpose of ensuring that a restraint order is effective.

(2) The application may be made without notice if the application is urgent or if there are reasonable grounds for believing that giving notice would cause the dissipation of realisable property which is the subject of the application.

(3) An application for a restraint order must be in writing and supported by a witness statement which must—

    (a)   give the grounds for the application;

    (b)   to the best of the witness' ability, give full details of the realisable property in respect of which the applicant is seeking the order and specify the person holding that realisable property;

    (c)   include the proposed terms of the order.

(4) An application for an ancillary order must be in writing and supported by a witness statement which must—

    (a)   give the grounds for, and full details of, the application;

    (b)   include, if appropriate—

        (i)   any request for an order for disclosure of documents to which rule 33.40 applies (disclosure and inspection of documents),

        (ii)   the identity of any person whom the applicant wants the court to examine about the extent or whereabouts of realisable property,

        (iii)   a list of the main questions that the applicant wants to ask any such person, and

        (iv)   a list of any documents to which the applicant wants to refer such a person; and

    (c)   include the proposed terms of the order.

(5) An application for a restraint order and an application for an ancillary order may (but need not) be made at the same time and contained in the same documents.

(6) An application by an accredited financial investigator must include a statement that, under section 68 of the 2002 Act, the applicant has authority to apply.

Restraint and ancillary orders

★**P-337**   **33.52.**—(1) The Crown Court may make a restraint order subject to exceptions, including, but not limited to, exceptions for reasonable living expenses and reasonable legal expenses, and for the purpose of enabling any person to carry on any trade, business or occupation.

(2) But the Crown Court must not make an exception for legal expenses where this is prohibited by section 41(4) of the Proceeds of Crime Act 2002.

(3) An exception to a restraint order may be made subject to conditions.

(4) The Crown Court must not require the applicant for a restraint order to give any undertaking relating to damages sustained as a result of the restraint order by a person who is prohibited from dealing with realisable property by the restraint order.

(5) The Crown Court may require the applicant for a restraint order to give an undertaking to pay the reasonable expenses of any person, other than a person who is prohibited from dealing with realisable property by the restraint order, which are incurred in complying with the restraint order.

(6) An order must include a statement that disobedience of the order, either by a person to whom the order is addressed, or by another person, may be contempt of court and the order must include details of the possible consequences of being held in contempt of court.

(7) Unless the Crown Court otherwise directs, an order made without notice has effect until the court makes an order varying or discharging it.

(8) The applicant for an order must—

    (a) serve copies of the order and of the witness statement made in support of the application on the defendant and any person who is prohibited by the order from dealing with realisable property; and

    (b) notify any person whom the applicant knows to be affected by the order of its terms.

Application for discharge or variation of restraint or ancillary order by a person affected by the order

33.53.—(1) This rule applies where a person affected by a restraint order makes an application to the Crown Court under section 42(3) of the Proceeds of Crime Act 2002 to discharge or vary the restraint order or any ancillary order made under section 41(7) of the Act. ★**P-338**

(2) The application must be in writing and may be supported by a witness statement.

(3) The application and any witness statement must be lodged with the Crown Court.

(4) The application and any witness statement must be served on the person who applied for the restraint order and any person who is prohibited from dealing with realisable property by the restraint order (if he is not the person making the application) at least 2 days before the date fixed by the court for hearing the application, unless the Crown Court specifies a shorter period.

Application for variation of restraint or ancillary order by the person who applied for the order

33.54.—(1) This rule applies where the applicant for a restraint order makes an application under section 42(3) of the Proceeds of Crime Act 2002 to the Crown Court to vary the restraint order or any ancillary order made under section 41(7) of the 2002 Act (including where the court has already made a restraint order and the applicant is seeking to vary the order in order to restrain further realisable property). ★**P-339**

(2) The application may be made without notice if the application is urgent or if there are reasonable grounds for believing that giving notice would cause the dissipation of realisable property which is the subject of the application.

(3) The application must be in writing and must be supported by a witness statement which must—

    (a) give the grounds for the application;

    (b) where the application is for the inclusion of further realisable property in a restraint order give full details, to the best of the witness's ability, of the realisable property in respect of which the applicant is seeking the order and specify the person holding that realisable property;

    (c) where the application is to vary an ancillary order, include, if appropriate—

        (i) any request for an order for disclosure of documents to which rule 33.40 applies (disclosure and inspection of documents),

        (ii) the identity of any person whom the applicant wants the court to examine about the extent or whereabouts of realisable property,

        (iii) a list of the main questions that the applicant wants to ask any such person, and

        (iv) a list of any documents to which the applicant wants to refer such a person; and

    (d) include the proposed terms of the variation.

(4) An application by an accredited financial investigator must include a statement that, under section 68 of the 2002 Act, the applicant has authority to apply.

(5) The application and witness statement must be lodged with the Crown Court.

(6) Except where, under paragraph (2), notice of the application is not required to be served, the application and witness statement must be served on any person who is prohibited from dealing with realisable property by the restraint order at least 2 days before the date fixed by the court for hearing the application, unless the Crown Court specifies a shorter period.

(7) If the court makes an order for the variation of a restraint or ancillary order, the applicant must serve copies of the order and of the witness statement made in support of the application on—

    (a) the defendant;

    (b) any person who is prohibited from dealing with realisable property by the restraint order (whether before or after the variation); and

    (c) any other person whom the applicant knows to be affected by the order.

Application for discharge of restraint or ancillary order by the person who applied for the order

★P-340   **33.55.**—(1) This rule applies where the applicant for a restraint order makes an application under section 42(3) of the Proceeds of Crime Act 2002 to discharge the order or any ancillary order made under section 41(7) of the 2002 Act.

(2) The application may be made without notice.

(3) The application must be in writing and must state the grounds for the application.

(4) If the court makes an order for the discharge of a restraint or ancillary order, the applicant must serve copies of the order on—

    (a) the defendant;

    (b) any person who is prohibited from dealing with realisable property by the restraint order (whether before or after the discharge); and

    (c) any other person whom the applicant knows to be affected by the order.

Receivership Proceedings

Application for appointment of a management or an enforcement receiver

★P-341   **33.56.**—(1) This rule applies to an application for the appointment of a management receiver under section 48(1) of the Proceeds of Crime Act 2002 and an application for the appointment of an enforcement receiver under section 50(1) of the 2002 Act.

(2) The application may be made without notice if—

    (a) the application is joined with an application for a restraint order under rule 33.51 (application for restraint order or ancillary order);

    (b) the application is urgent; or

    (c) there are reasonable grounds for believing that giving notice would cause the dissipation of realisable property which is the subject of the application.

(3) The application must be in writing and must be supported by a witness statement which must—

    (a) give the grounds for the application;

    (b) give full details of the proposed receiver;

    (c) to the best of the witness' ability, give full details of the realisable property in respect of which the applicant is seeking the order and specify the person holding that realisable property;

    (d) where the application is made by an accredited financial investigator, include a statement that, under section 68 of the 2002 Act, the applicant has authority to apply; and

    (e) if the proposed receiver is not a person falling within section 55(8) of the 2002 Act and the applicant is asking the court to allow the receiver to act—

       (i) without giving security, or

       (ii) before he has given security or satisfied the court that he has security in place,

      explain the reasons why that is necessary.

(4) Where the application is for the appointment of an enforcement receiver, the applicant must provide the Crown Court with a copy of the confiscation order made against the defendant.

(5) The application and witness statement must be lodged with the Crown Court.

(6) Except where, under paragraph (2), notice of the application is not required to be served, the application and witness statement must be lodged with the Crown Court and served on—

    (a) the defendant;

    (b) any person who holds realisable property to which the application relates; and

    (c) any other person whom the applicant knows to be affected by the application,

at least 7 days before the date fixed by the court for hearing the application, unless the Crown Court specifies a shorter period.

(7) If the court makes an order for the appointment of a receiver, the applicant must serve copies of the order and of the witness statement made in support of the application on—

    (a) the defendant;

(b) any person who holds realisable property to which the order applies; and

(c) any other person whom the applicant knows to be affected by the order.

Application for conferral of powers on a management receiver or an enforcement receiver

33.57.—(1) This rule applies to an application for the conferral of powers on a management receiver under section 49(1) of the Proceeds of Crime Act 2002 or an enforcement receiver under section 51(1) of the 2002 Act. ★P-342

(2) The application may be made without notice if the application is to give the receiver power to take possession of property and—

(a) the application is joined with an application for a restraint order under rule 33.51 (application for restraint order or ancillary order);

(b) the application is urgent; or

(c) there are reasonable grounds for believing that giving notice would cause the dissipation of the property which is the subject of the application.

(3) The application must be made in writing and supported by a witness statement which must—

(a) give the grounds for the application;

(b) give full details of the realisable property in respect of which the applicant is seeking the order and specify the person holding that realisable property;

(c) where the application is made by an accredited financial investigator, include a statement that, under section 68 of the 2002 Act, the applicant has authority to apply; and

(d) where the application is for power to start, carry on or defend legal proceedings in respect of the property, explain—

(i) what proceedings are concerned, in what court, and

(ii) what powers the receiver will ask that court to exercise.

(4) Where the application is for the conferral of powers on an enforcement receiver, the applicant must provide the Crown Court with a copy of the confiscation order made against the defendant.

(5) The application and witness statement must be lodged with the Crown Court.

(6) Except where, under paragraph (2), notice of the application is not required to be served, the application and witness statement must be served on—

(a) the defendant;

(b) any person who holds realisable property in respect of which a receiver has been appointed or in respect of which an application for a receiver has been made;

(c) any other person whom the applicant knows to be affected by the application; and

(d) the receiver (if one has already been appointed),

at least 7 days before the date fixed by the court for hearing the application, unless the Crown Court specifies a shorter period.

(7) If the court makes an order for the conferral of powers on a receiver, the applicant must serve copies of the order on—

(a) the defendant;

(b) any person who holds realisable property in respect of which the receiver has been appointed; and

(c) any other person whom the applicant knows to be affected by the order.

Applications for discharge or variation of receivership orders, and applications for other orders

33.58.—(1) This rule applies to applications under section 62(3) of the Proceeds of Crime Act 2002 for orders (by persons affected by the action of receivers) and applications under section 63(1) of the 2002 Act for the discharge or variation of orders relating to receivers. ★P-343

(2) The application must be made in writing and lodged with the Crown Court.

(3) The application must be served on the following persons (except where they are the person making the application)—

(a) the person who applied for appointment of the receiver;

(b) the defendant;

(c) any person who holds realisable property in respect of which the receiver has been appointed;

(d) the receiver; and

(e) any other person whom the applicant knows to be affected by the application,

at least 7 days before the date fixed by the court for hearing the application, unless the Crown Court specifies a shorter period.

(4) If the court makes an order for the discharge or variation of an order relating to a receiver

under section 63(2) of the 2002 Act, the applicant must serve copies of the order on any persons whom he knows to be affected by the order.

Sums in the hands of receivers

★P-344   **33.59.**—(1) This rule applies where the amount payable under a confiscation order has been fully paid and any sums remain in the hands of an enforcement receiver.

(2) The receiver must make an application to the Crown Court for directions as to the distribution of the sums in his hands.

(3) The application and any evidence which the receiver intends to rely on in support of the application must be served on—

(a)   the defendant; and

(b)   any other person who held (or holds) interests in any property realised by the receiver,

at least 7 days before the date fixed by the court for hearing the application, unless the Crown Court specifies a shorter period.

(4) If any of the provisions listed in paragraph (5) (provisions as to the vesting of funds in a trustee in bankruptcy) apply, then the Crown Court must make a declaration to that effect.

(5) These are the provisions—

(a)   section 31B of the Bankruptcy (Scotland) Act 1985;

(b)   section 306B of the Insolvency Act 1986; and

(c)   article 279B of the Insolvency (Northern Ireland) Order 1989.

Security

★P-345   **33.60.**—(1) This rule applies where the Crown Court appoints a receiver under section 48 or 50 of the Proceeds of Crime Act 2002 and the receiver is not a person falling within section 55(8) of the 2002 Act (and it is immaterial whether the receiver is a permanent or temporary member of staff or on secondment from elsewhere).

(2) The Crown Court may direct that before the receiver begins to act, or within a specified time he must either—

(a)   give such security as the Crown Court may determine; or

(b)   file with the Crown Court and serve on all parties to any receivership proceedings evidence that he already has in force sufficient security,

to cover his liability for his acts and omissions as a receiver.

(3) The Crown Court may terminate the appointment of a receiver if he fails to—

(a)   give the security; or

(b)   satisfy the court as to the security he has in force,

by the date specified.

Remuneration

★P-346   **33.61.**—(1) This rule applies where the Crown Court appoints a receiver under section 48 or 50 of the Proceeds of Crime Act 2002 and the receiver is not a person falling within section 55(8) of the 2002 Act (and it is immaterial whether the receiver is a permanent or temporary member of staff or on secondment from elsewhere).

(2) The receiver may only charge for his services if the Crown Court—

(a)   so directs; and

(b)   specifies the basis on which the receiver is to be remunerated.

(3) Unless the Crown Court orders otherwise, in determining the remuneration of the receiver the Crown Court shall award such sum as is reasonable and proportionate in all the circumstances and which takes into account—

(a)   the time properly given by him and his staff to the receivership;

(b)   the complexity of the receivership;

(c)   any responsibility of an exceptional kind or degree which falls on the receiver in consequence of the receivership;

(d)   the effectiveness with which the receiver appears to be carrying out, or to have carried out, his duties; and

(e)   the value and nature of the subject matter of the receivership.

(4) The Crown Court may refer the determination of a receiver's remuneration to be ascertained by the taxing authority of the Crown Court and rules 45.11 (assessment and re-assessment) to 45.14 (application for an extension of time) shall have effect as if the taxing authority was ascertaining costs

(5) A receiver appointed under section 48 of the 2002 Act is to receive his remuneration by realising property in respect of which he is appointed, in accordance with section 49(2)(d) of the 2002 Act.

(6) A receiver appointed under section 50 of the 2002 Act is to receive his remuneration by apply-ing to the magistrates' court officer for payment under section 55(4)(b) of the 2002 Act.

Accounts

33.62.—(1) The Crown Court may order a receiver appointed under section 48 or 50 of the   **★P-347**
Proceeds of Crime Act 2002 to prepare and serve accounts.

(2) A party to receivership proceedings served with such accounts may apply for an order permit-ting him to inspect any document in the possession of the receiver relevant to those accounts.

(3) Any party to receivership proceedings may, within 14 days of being served with the accounts, serve notice on the receiver—

    (a) specifying any item in the accounts to which he objects;

    (b) giving the reason for such objection; and

    (c) requiring the receiver within 14 days of receipt of the notice, either—

        (i) to notify all the parties who were served with the accounts that he accepts the objec-tion, or

        (ii) if he does not accept the objection, to apply for an examination of the accounts in relation to the contested item.

(4) When the receiver applies for the examination of the accounts he must at the same time lodge with the Crown Court—

    (a) the accounts; and

    (b) a copy of the notice served on him under this section of the rule.

(5) If the receiver fails to comply with paragraph (3)(c) of this rule, any party to receivership proceedings may apply to the Crown Court for an examination of the accounts in relation to the contested item.

(6) At the conclusion of its examination of the accounts the court must certify the result.

Non-compliance by receiver

33.63.—(1) If a receiver appointed under section 48 or 50 of the Proceeds of Crime Act 2002 fails   **★P-348**
to comply with any rule, practice direction or direction of the Crown Court, the Crown Court may order him to attend a hearing to explain his non-compliance.

(2) At the hearing, the Crown Court may make any order it considers appropriate, including—

    (a) terminating the appointment of the receiver;

    (b) reducing the receiver's remuneration or disallowing it altogether; and

    (c) ordering the receiver to pay the costs of any party.

Proceedings under the Criminal Justice Act 1988 and the Drug Trafficking Act 1994

Statements, etc. relevant to making confiscation orders

33.64.—(1) Where a prosecutor or defendant?   **★P-349**

    (a) serves on the magistrates' court officer any statement or other document under section 73 of the Criminal Justice Act 1988 in any proceedings in respect of an offence listed in Schedule 4 to that Act; or

    (b) serves on the Crown Court officer any statement or other document under section 11 of the Drug Trafficking Act 1994 or section 73 of the 1988 Act in any proceedings in respect of a drug trafficking offence or in respect of an offence to which Part VI of the 1988 Act applies,

that party must serve a copy as soon as practicable on the defendant or the prosecutor, as the case may be.

(2) Any statement tendered by the prosecutor to the magistrates' court under section 73 of the 1988 Act or to the Crown Court under section 11(1) of the 1994 Act or section 73(1A) of the 1988 Act must include the following particulars—

    (a) the name of the defendant;

    (b) the name of the person by whom the statement is made and the date on which it was made;

    (c) where the statement is not tendered immediately after the defendant has been convicted, the date on which and the place where the relevant conviction occurred; and

    (d) such information known to the prosecutor as is relevant to the determination as to whether or not the defendant has benefited from drug trafficking or relevant criminal conduct and to the assessment of the value of any proceeds of drug trafficking or, as the case may be, benefit from relevant criminal conduct.

(3) Where, in accordance with section 11(7) of the 1994 Act or section 73(1C) of the 1988 Act, the defendant indicates in writing the extent to which he or she accepts any allegation contained within the prosecutor's statement, the defendant must serve a copy of that reply on the court officer.

(4) Expressions used in this rule have the same meanings as in the 1994 Act or, where appropriate, the 1988 Act.

Postponed determinations

★P-350   **33.65.**—(1) Where an application is made by the defendant or the prosecutor –

    (a) to a magistrates' court under section 72A(5)(a) of the Criminal Justice Act 1988 asking the court to exercise its powers under section 72A(4) of that Act; or

    (b) to the Crown Court under section 3(5)(a) of the Drug Trafficking Act 1994 asking the court to exercise its powers under section 3(4) of that Act, or under section 72A(5)(a) of the 1988 Act asking the court to exercise its powers under section 72A(4) of the 1988 Act,

the application must be in writing and the applicant must serve a copy on the prosecutor or the defendant, as the case may be.

(2) A party served with a copy of an application under paragraph (1) must, within 28 days of the date of service, notify the applicant and the court officer, in writing, whether or not that party opposes the application, giving reasons for any opposition.

(3) After the expiry of the period referred to in paragraph (2), the court may determine an application under paragraph (1)—

    (a) without a hearing; or

    (b) at a hearing at which the parties may be represented.

Confiscation orders - revised assessments

★P-351   **33.66.**—(1) Where the prosecutor makes an application under section 13, 14 or 15 of the Drug Trafficking Act 1994 or section 74A, 74B or 74C of the Criminal Justice Act 1988, the application must be in writing and a copy must be served on the defendant.

(2) The application must include the following particulars—

    (a) the name of the defendant;

    (b) the date on which and the place where any relevant conviction occurred;

    (c) the date on which and the place where any relevant confiscation order was made or, as the case may be, varied;

    (d) the grounds on which the application is made; and

    (e) an indication of the evidence available to support the application.

Application to the Crown Court to discharge or vary order to make material available

★P-352   **33.67.**—(1) Where an order under section 93H of the Criminal Justice Act 1988 (order to make material available) or section 55 of the Drug Trafficking Act 1994 (order to make material available) has been made by the Crown Court, any person affected by it may apply in writing to the court officer for the order to be discharged or varied, and on hearing such an application the court may discharge the order or make such variations to it as the court thinks fit.

(2) Subject to paragraph (3), where a person proposes to make an application under paragraph (1) for the discharge or variation of an order, that person must give a copy of the application, not later than 48 hours before the making of the application—

    (a) to a constable at the police station specified in the order; or

    (b) to the office of the appropriate officer who made the application, as specified in the order,

in either case together with a notice indicating the time and place at which the application for discharge or variation is to be made.

(3) The court may direct that paragraph (2) need not be complied with if satisfied that the person making the application has good reason to seek a discharge or variation of the order as soon as possible and it is not practicable to comply with that paragraph.

(4) In this rule:

    "constable" includes a person commissioned by the Commissioners for Her Majesty's Revenue and Customs;

    "police station" includes a place for the time being occupied by Her Majesty's Revenue and Customs.

Application to the Crown Court for increase in term of imprisonment in default of payment

★P-353   **33.68.**—(1) This rule applies to applications made, or that have effect as made, to the Crown Court under section 10 of the Drug Trafficking Act 1994 and section 75A of the Criminal Justice Act 1988 (interest on sums unpaid under confiscation orders).

(2) Notice of an application to which this rule applies to increase the term of imprisonment or detention fixed in default of payment of a confiscation order by a person ("the defendant") must be made by the prosecutor in writing to the court officer.

(3) A notice under paragraph (2) shall—

(a) state the name and address of the defendant;

(b) specify the grounds for the application;

(c) give details of the enforcement measures taken, if any; and

(d) include a copy of the confiscation order.

(4) On receiving a notice under paragraph (2), the court officer must—

(a) forthwith send to the defendant and the magistrates' court required to enforce payment of the confiscation order under section 140(1) of the Powers of Criminal Courts (Sentencing) Act 2000, a copy of the said notice; and

(b) notify in writing the applicant and the defendant of the date, time and place appointed for the hearing of the application.

(5) Where the Crown Court makes an order pursuant to an application mentioned in paragraph (1) above, the court officer must send forthwith a copy of the order—

(a) to the applicant;

(b) to the defendant;

(c) where the defendant is at the time of the making of the order in custody, to the person having custody of him or her; and

(d) to the magistrates' court mentioned in paragraph (4)(a).

Drug trafficking – compensation on acquittal in the Crown Court

33.69. Where the Crown Court cancels a confiscation order under section 22(2) of the Drug Traf- **★P-354** ficking Act 1994, the Crown Court officer must serve notice to that effect on the High Court officer and on the court officer of the magistrates' court which has responsibility for enforcing the order.

Contempt Proceedings

Application to punish for contempt of court

33.70.—(1) This rule applies where a person is accused of disobeying— **★P-355**

(a) a compliance order made for the purpose of ensuring that a confiscation order is effective;

(b) a restraint order; or

(c) an ancillary order made for the purpose of ensuring that a restraint order is effective.

(2) An applicant who wants the Crown Court to exercise its power to punish that person for contempt of court must comply with the rules in Part 48 (contempt of court).

PART 34

APPEAL TO THE CROWN COURT

When this part applies

34.1.—(1) This part applies where— **★P-356**

(a) a defendant wants to appeal under—

(i) section 108 of the Magistrates' Courts Act 1980,

(ii) section 45 of the Mental Health Act 1983,

(iii) paragraph 10 of Schedule 3 to the Powers of Criminal Courts (Sentencing) Act 2000, or paragraphs 9(8) or 13(5) of Schedule 8 to the Criminal Justice Act 2003,

(iv) section 42 of the Counter Terrorism Act 2008;

(b) the Criminal Cases Review Commission refers a defendant's case to the Crown Court under section 11 of the Criminal Appeal Act 1995;

(c) a prosecutor wants to appeal under—

(i) section 14A(5A) of the Football Spectators Act 1989, or

(ii) section 147(3) of the Customs and Excise Management Act 1979; or

(d) a person wants to appeal under—

(i) section 1 of the Magistrates' Courts (Appeals from Binding Over Orders) Act 1956,

(ii) section 12(5) of the Contempt of Court Act 1981,

(iii) regulation 3C or 3H of the Costs in Criminal Cases (General) Regulations 1986,

(iv) section 22 of the Football Spectators Act 1989, or

(v)   section 10(4) or (5) of the Crime and Disorder Act 1998.

(2) A reference to an "appellant" in this part is a reference to such a party or person.

Service of appeal notice

★P-357   **34.2.**—(1) An appellant must serve an appeal notice on—

(a)   the magistrates' court officer; and

(b)   every other party.

(2) The appellant must serve the appeal notice—

(a)   as soon after the decision appealed against as the appellant wants; but

(b)   not more than 21 days after—

(i)   sentence or the date sentence is deferred, whichever is earlier, if the appeal is against conviction or against a finding of guilt,

(ii)   sentence, if the appeal is against sentence, or

(iii)   the order or failure to make an order about which the appellant wants to appeal, in any other case.

(3) The appellant must serve with the appeal notice any application for the following, with reasons—

(a)   an extension of the time limit under this rule, if the appeal notice is late;

(b)   bail pending appeal, if the appellant is in custody;

(c)   the suspension of any disqualification imposed in the case, where the magistrates' court or the Crown Court can order such a suspension pending appeal.

(4) Where both the magistrates' court and the Crown Court can suspend a disqualification pending appeal, an application for its suspension must indicate by which court the appellant wants the application determined.

Form of appeal notice

★P-358   **34.3.** The appeal notice must be in writing and must—

(a)   specify—

(i)   the conviction or finding of guilt,

(ii)   the sentence, or

(iii)   the order, or the failure to make an order

about which the appellant wants to appeal;

(b)   summarise the issues;

(c)   in an appeal against conviction—

(i)   identify the prosecution witnesses whom the appellant will want to question if they are called to give oral evidence, and

(ii)   say how long the trial lasted in the magistrates' court and how long the appeal is likely to last in the Crown Court;

(d)   in an appeal against a finding that the appellant insulted someone or interrupted proceedings in the magistrates' court, attach—

(i)   the magistrates' court's written findings of fact, and

(ii)   the appellant's response to those findings;

(e)   say whether the appellant has asked the magistrates' court to reconsider the case; and

(f)   include a list of those on whom the appellant has served the appeal notice.

Duty of magistrates' court officer

★P-359   **34.4.** The magistrates' court officer must—

(a)   as soon as practicable serve on the Crown Court officer—

(i)   the appeal notice and any accompanying application served by the appellant,

(ii)   details of the parties including their addresses,

(iii)   a copy of each magistrates' court register entry relating to the decision under appeal and to any application for bail pending appeal, and

(iv)   any report received for the purposes of sentencing;

(b)   keep any document or object exhibited in the proceedings in the magistrates' court, or arrange for it to be kept by some other appropriate person, until—

(i)   6 weeks after the conclusion of those proceedings, or

(ii)   the conclusion of any proceedings in the Crown Court that begin within that 6 weeks;

(c)   provide the Crown Court with any document, object or information for which the Crown Court officer asks, within such period as the Crown Court officer may require; and

(d) arrange for the magistrates' court to hear as soon as practicable any application to that court under rule 34.2(3)(c) (suspension of disqualification pending appeal).

Duty of person keeping exhibit
34.5. A person who, under arrangements made by the magistrates' court officer, keeps a document   **★P-360**
or object exhibited in the proceedings in the magistrates' court must—
  (a) keep that exhibit until—
    (i) 6 weeks after the conclusion of those proceedings, or
    (ii) the conclusion of any proceedings in the Crown Court that begin within that 6 weeks, unless the magistrates' court or the Crown Court otherwise directs; and
  (b) provide the Crown Court with any such document or object for which the Crown Court officer asks, within such period as the Crown Court officer may require.

Reference by the Criminal Cases Review Commission
34.6.—(1) The Crown Court officer must, as soon as practicable, serve a reference by the Criminal   **★P-361**
Cases Review Commission on—
  (a) the appellant;
  (b) every other party; and
  (c) the magistrates' court officer.
  (2) The appellant may serve an appeal notice on—
  (a) the Crown Court officer; and
  (b) every other party,
not more than 21 days later.
  (3) The Crown Court must treat the reference as the appeal notice if the appellant does not serve an appeal notice.

Application to introduce further evidence
34.7.—(1) This rule applies where—   **★P-362**
  (a) a party wants to introduce evidence which was not introduced by either party in the magistrates' court; and
  (b) one of these part applies—
    (i) Part 18 (measures to assist a witness or defendant to give evidence),
    (ii) Part 20 (hearsay evidence),
    (iii) Part 21 (evidence of bad character), or
    (iv) Part 22 (evidence of a complainant's previous sexual behaviour).
  (2) Such a party must serve the notice or application to introduce evidence required by that part not more than 14 days after service of the appeal notice.

Hearings and decisions
34.8.—(1) The Crown Court as a general rule must hear in public an appeal or reference to which   **★P-363**
this part applies, but—
  (a) may order any hearing to be in private; and
  (b) where a hearing is about a public interest ruling, must hold that hearing in private.
  (2) The Crown Court officer must give as much notice as reasonably practicable of every hearing to—
  (a) the parties;
  (b) any party's custodian; and
  (c) any other person whom the Crown Court requires to be notified.
  (3) The Crown Court officer must serve every decision on—
  (a) the parties;
  (b) any other person whom the Crown Court requires to be served; and
  (c) the magistrates' court officer and any party's custodian, where the decision determines an appeal.
  (4) But where a hearing or decision is about a public interest ruling, the Crown Court officer must not—
  (a) give notice of that hearing to; or
  (b) serve that decision on,
anyone other than the prosecutor who applied for that ruling, unless the court otherwise directs.

Abandoning an appeal
34.9.—(1) The appellant—   **★P-364**
  (a) may abandon an appeal without the Crown Court's permission, by serving a notice of abandonment on—

      (i)   the magistrates' court officer,

      (ii)   the Crown Court officer, and

      (iii)   every other party

    before the hearing of the appeal begins; but

  (b)   after the hearing of the appeal begins, may only abandon the appeal with the Crown Court's permission.

(2) A notice of abandonment must be signed by or on behalf of the appellant.

(3) Where an appellant who is on bail pending appeal abandons an appeal—

  (a)   the appellant must surrender to custody as directed by the magistrates' court officer; and

  (b)   any conditions of bail apply until then.

Court's power to vary requirements under this part

★P-365   **34.10.** The Crown Court may—

  (a)   shorten or extend (even after it has expired) a time limit under this part;

  (b)   allow an appellant to vary an appeal notice that that appellant has served;

  (c)   direct that an appeal notice be served on any person;

  (d)   allow an appeal notice or a notice of abandonment to be in a different form to one set out in the Practice Direction, or to be presented orally.

Constitution of the Crown Court

★P-366   **34.11.** On the hearing of an appeal—

  (a)   the general rule is that the Crown Court must comprise—

      (i)   a judge of the High Court, a circuit judge, a recorder or a qualifying judge advocate, and

      (ii)   no less than two and no more than four justices of the peace, none of whom took part in the decision under appeal; and

  (b)   if the appeal is from a youth court—

      (i)   each justice of the peace must be qualified to sit as a member of a youth court, and

      (ii)   the Crown Court must include a man and a woman; but

  (c)   the Crown Court may include only one justice of the peace and need not include both a man and a woman if—

      (i)   the presiding judge decides that otherwise the start of the appeal hearing will be delayed unreasonably, or

      (ii)   one or more of the justices of the peace who started hearing the appeal is absent.

Part 35

Appeal to the High Court by Case Stated

When this part applies

★P-367   **35.1.** This part applies where a person wants to appeal to the High Court by case stated—

  (a)   under section 111 of the Magistrates' Courts Act 1980, against a decision of a magistrates' court; or

  (b)   under section 28 of the Senior Courts Act 1981, against a decision of the Crown Court.

Application to state a case

★P-368   **35.2.**—(1) A party who wants the court to state a case for the opinion of the High Court must—

  (a)   apply in writing, not more than 21 days after the decision against which the applicant wants to appeal; and

  (b)   serve the application on—

      (i)   the court officer, and

      (ii)   each other party.

(2) The application must—

  (a)   specify the decision in issue;

  (b)   specify the proposed question or questions of law or jurisdiction on which the opinion of the High Court will be asked;

  (c)   indicate the proposed grounds of appeal; and

  (d)   include or attach any application for the following, with reasons—

      (i)   if the application is to the Crown Court, an extension of time within which to apply to state a case,

    (ii) bail pending appeal,

    (iii) the suspension of any disqualification imposed in the case, where the court can order such a suspension pending appeal.

(3) A party who wants to make representations about the application must—

  (a) serve the representations on—

    (i) the court officer, and

    (ii) each other party; and

  (b) do so not more than 14 days after service of the application.

(4) The court may determine the application without a hearing.

(5) If the court decides not to state a case, the court officer must serve on each party—

  (a) notice of that decision; and

  (b) the court's written reasons for that decision, if not more than 21 days later the applicant asks for those reasons.

Preparation of case stated

35.3.—(1) This rule applies where the court decides to state a case for the opinion of the High   ★**P-369** Court.

(2) The court officer must serve on each party notice of—

  (a) the decision to state a case, and

  (b) any recognizance ordered by the court.

(3) Unless the court otherwise directs, not more than 21 days after the court's decision to state a case—

  (a) in a magistrates court, the court officer must serve a draft case on each party;

  (b) in the Crown Court, the applicant must serve a draft case on the court officer and each other party.

(4) The draft case must—

  (a) specify the decision in issue;

  (b) specify the question(s) of law or jurisdiction on which the opinion of the High Court will be asked;

  (c) include a succinct summary of—

    (i) the nature and history of the proceedings,

    (ii) the court's relevant findings of fact, and

    (iii) the relevant contentions of the parties;

  (d) if a question is whether there was sufficient evidence on which the court reasonably could reach a finding of fact—

    (i) specify that finding, and

    (ii) include a summary of the evidence on which the court reached that finding.

(5) Except to the extent that paragraph (4)(d) requires, the draft case must not include an account of the evidence received by the court.

(6) A party who wants to make representations about the content of the draft case, or to propose a revised draft, must—

  (a) serve the representations, or revised draft, on—

    (i) the court officer, and

    (ii) each other party; and

  (b) do so not more than 21 days after service of the draft case.

(7) The court must state the case not more than 21 days after the time for service of representations under paragraph (6) has expired.

(8) A case stated for the opinion of the High Court must—

  (a) comply with paragraphs (4) and (5); and

  (b) identify—

    (i) the court that stated it, and

    (ii) the court office for that court.

(9) The court officer must serve the case stated on each party.

Duty of justices' legal adviser

35.4.—(1) This rule applies—   ★**P-370**

  (a) only in a magistrates' court; and

  (b) unless the court—

    (i) includes a District Judge (Magistrates' Courts), and

(ii)   otherwise directs.

(2) A justices' legal adviser must—

(a)   give the court legal advice; and

(b)   if the court so requires, assist it by—

(i)   preparing and amending the draft case, and

(ii)   completing the case stated.

Court's power to vary requirements under this part

★P-371   **35.5.**—(1) The court may shorten or extend (even after it has expired) a time limit under this part.

(2) A person who wants an extension of time must—

(a)   apply when serving the application, representations or draft case for which it is needed; and

(b)   explain the delay.

PART 36

APPEAL TO THE COURT OF APPEAL: GENERAL RULES

When this part applies

★P-372   **36.1.**—(1) This part applies to all the applications, appeals and references to the Court of Appeal to which Parts 37, 38, 39, 40, 41 and 43 apply.

(2) In this part and in those, unless the context makes it clear that something different is meant "court" means the Court of Appeal or any judge of that court.

Case management in the Court of Appeal

★P-373   **36.2.**—(1) The court and the parties have the same duties and powers as under Part 3 (case management).

(2) The Registrar—

(a)   must fulfil the duty of active case management under rule 3.2; and

(b)   in fulfilling that duty may exercise any of the powers of case management under—

(i)   rule 3.5 (the court's general powers of case management),

(ii)   rule 3.10(3) (requiring a certificate of readiness), and

(iii)   rule 3.11 (requiring a party to identify intentions and anticipated requirements) subject to the directions of the court.

(3) The Registrar must nominate a case progression officer under rule 3.4.

Power to vary requirements

★P-374   **36.3.** The court or the Registrar may—

(a)   shorten a time limit or extend it (even after it has expired) unless that is inconsistent with other legislation;

(b)   allow a party to vary any notice that that party has served;

(c)   direct that a notice or application be served on any person;

(d)   allow a notice or application to be in a different form, or presented orally.

Application for extension of time

★P-375   **36.4.** A person who wants an extension of time within which to serve a notice or make an application must—

(a)   apply for that extension of time when serving that notice or making that application; and

(b)   give the reasons for the application for an extension of time.

Renewing an application refused by a judge or the Registrar

★P-376   **36.5.**—(1) This rule applies where a party with the right to do so wants to renew—

(a)   to a judge of the Court of Appeal an application refused by the Registrar; or

(b)   to the Court of Appeal an application refused by a judge of that court.

(2) That party must—

(a)   renew the application in the form set out in the Practice Direction, signed by or on behalf of the applicant;

(b)   serve the renewed application on the Registrar not more than 14 days after—

(i)   the refusal of the application that the applicant wants to renew; or

(ii)   the Registrar serves that refusal on the applicant, if the applicant was not present in person or by live link when the original application was refused.

Hearings

36.6.—(1) The general rule is that the Court of Appeal must hear in public— ★**P-377**

    (a) an application, including an application for permission to appeal; and

    (b) an appeal or reference,

but it may order any hearing to be in private.

(2) Where a hearing is about a public interest ruling, that hearing must be in private unless the court otherwise directs.

(3) Where the appellant wants to appeal against an order restricting public access to a trial, the court—

    (a) may decide without a hearing—

        (i) an application, including an application for permission to appeal, and

        (ii) an appeal; but

    (b) must announce its decision on such an appeal at a hearing in public.

(4) Where the appellant wants to appeal or to refer a case to the Supreme Court, the court—

    (a) may decide without a hearing an application—

        (i) for permission to appeal or to refer a sentencing case, or

        (ii) to refer a point of law; but

    (b) must announce its decision on such an application at a hearing in public.

(5) A judge of the Court of Appeal and the Registrar may exercise any of their powers—

    (a) at a hearing in public or in private; or

    (b) without a hearing.

Notice of hearings and decisions

36.7.—(1) The Registrar must give as much notice as reasonably practicable of every hearing to— ★**P-378**

    (a) the parties;

    (b) any party's custodian;

    (c) any other person whom the court requires to be notified; and

    (d) the Crown Court officer, where Parts 37, 38 or 40 apply.

(2) The Registrar must serve every decision on—

    (a) the parties;

    (b) any other person whom the court requires to be served; and

    (c) the Crown Court officer and any party's custodian, where the decision determines an appeal or application for permission to appeal.

(3) But where a hearing or decision is about a public interest ruling, the Registrar must not—

    (a) give notice of that hearing to; or

    (b) serve that decision on,

anyone other than the prosecutor who applied for that ruling, unless the court otherwise directs.

Duty of Crown Court officer

36.8.—(1) The Crown Court officer must provide the Registrar with any document, object or ★**P-379** information for which the Registrar asks, within such period as the Registrar may require.

(2) Where someone may appeal to the Court of Appeal, the Crown Court officer must keep any document or object exhibited in the proceedings in the Crown Court, or arrange for it to be kept by some other appropriate person, until—

    (a) 6 weeks after the conclusion of those proceedings; or

    (b) the conclusion of any appeal proceedings that begin within that 6 weeks,

unless the court, the Registrar or the Crown Court otherwise directs.

(3) Where Part 37 applies (appeal to the Court of Appeal against ruling at preparatory hearing), the Crown Court officer must as soon as practicable serve on the appellant a transcript or note of—

    (a) each order or ruling against which the appellant wants to appeal; and

    (b) the decision by the Crown Court judge on any application for permission to appeal.

(4) Where Part 38 applies (appeal to the Court of Appeal against ruling adverse to prosecution), the Crown Court officer must as soon as practicable serve on the appellant a transcript or note of—

    (a) each ruling against which the appellant wants to appeal;

    (b) the decision by the Crown Court judge on any application for permission to appeal; and

    (c) the decision by the Crown Court judge on any request to expedite the appeal.

(5) Where Part 39 applies (appeal to the Court of Appeal about conviction or sentence), the Crown Court officer must as soon as practicable serve on the Registrar—

    (a) the appeal notice and any accompanying application that the appellant serves on the Crown Court officer;

    (b) any Crown Court judge's certificate that the case is fit for appeal;

    (c) the decision on any application at the Crown Court centre for bail pending appeal;

    (d) such of the Crown Court case papers as the Registrar requires; and

    (e) such transcript of the Crown Court proceedings as the Registrar requires.

(6) Where Part 40 applies (appeal to the Court of Appeal about reporting or public access) and an order is made restricting public access to a trial, the Crown Court officer must—

    (a) immediately notify the Registrar of that order, if the appellant has given advance notice of intention to appeal; and

    (b) as soon as practicable provide the applicant for that order with a transcript or note of the application.

Duty of person transcribing proceedings in the Crown Court

★P-380　　**36.9.** A person who transcribes a recording of proceedings in the Crown Court under arrangements made by the Crown Court officer must provide the Registrar with any transcript for which the Registrar asks, within such period as the Registrar may require.

Duty of person keeping exhibit

★P-381　　**36.10.** A person who under arrangements made by the Crown Court officer keeps a document or object exhibited in the proceedings in the Crown Court must—

    (a) keep that exhibit until—

        (i) 6 weeks after the conclusion of the Crown Court proceedings, or

        (ii) the conclusion of any appeal proceedings that begin within that 6 weeks,

        unless the court, the Registrar or the Crown Court otherwise directs; and

    (b) provide the Registrar with any such document or object for which the Registrar asks, within such period as the Registrar may require.

Registrar's duty to provide copy documents for appeal or reference

★P-382　　**36.11.** Unless the court otherwise directs, for the purposes of an appeal or reference—

    (a) the Registrar must—

        (i) provide a party with a copy of any document or transcript held by the Registrar for such purposes, or

        (ii) allow a party to inspect such a document or transcript,

        on payment by that party of any charge fixed by the Treasury; but

    (b) the Registrar must not provide a copy or allow the inspection of—

        (i) a document provided only for the court and the Registrar, or

        (ii) a transcript of a public interest ruling or of an application for such a ruling.

Declaration of incompatibility with a Convention right

★P-383　　**36.12.**—(1) This rule applies where a party—

    (a) wants the court to make a declaration of incompatibility with a Convention right under section 4 of the Human Rights Act 1998; or

    (b) raises an issue that the Registrar thinks may lead the court to make such a declaration.

(2) The Registrar must serve notice on—

    (a) the relevant person named in the list published under section 17(1) of the Crown Proceedings Act 1947; or

    (b) the Treasury Solicitor, if it is not clear who is the relevant person.

(3) That notice must include or attach details of—

    (a) the legislation affected and the Convention right concerned;

    (b) the parties to the appeal; and

    (c) any other information or document that the Registrar thinks relevant.

(4) A person who has a right under the 1998 Act to become a party to the appeal must—

    (a) serve notice on—

        (i) the Registrar, and

        (ii) the other parties,

        if that person wants to exercise that right; and

    (b) in that notice—

        (i) indicate the conclusion that that person invites the court to reach on the question of incompatibility, and

        (ii) identify each ground for that invitation, concisely outlining the arguments in support.

(5) The court must not make a declaration of incompatibility—

(a) less than 21 days after the Registrar serves notice under paragraph (2); and

(b) without giving any person who serves a notice under paragraph (4) an opportunity to make representations at a hearing.

Abandoning an appeal

36.13.—(1) This rule applies where an appellant wants to—   ★**P-384**

  (a) abandon—

    (i) an application to the court for permission to appeal, or

    (ii) an appeal; or

  (b) reinstate such an application or appeal after abandoning it.

(2) The appellant—

  (a) may abandon such an application or appeal without the court's permission by serving a notice of abandonment on—

    (i) the Registrar, and

    (ii) any respondent

    before any hearing of the application or appeal; but

  (b) at any such hearing, may only abandon that application or appeal with the court's permission.

(3) A notice of abandonment must be in the form set out in the Practice Direction, signed by or on behalf of the appellant.

(4) On receiving a notice of abandonment the Registrar must—

  (a) date it;

  (b) serve a dated copy on—

    (i) the appellant,

    (ii) the appellant's custodian, if any,

    (iii) the Crown Court officer, and

    (iv) any other person on whom the appellant or the Registrar served the appeal notice; and

  (c) treat the application or appeal as if it had been refused or dismissed by the Court of Appeal.

(5) An appellant who wants to reinstate an application or appeal after abandoning it must—

  (a) apply in writing, with reasons; and

  (b) serve the application on the Registrar.

Abandoning a ground of appeal or opposition

36.14.—(1) This rule applies where a party wants to abandon—   ★**P-385**

  (a) a ground of appeal identified in an appeal notice; or

  (b) a ground of opposition identified in a respondent's notice.

(2) Such a party must give written notice to—

  (a) the Registrar; and

  (b) every other party,

before any hearing at which that ground will be considered by the court.

PART 37

APPEAL TO THE COURT OF APPEAL AGAINST RULING AT PREPARATORY HEARING

When this part applies

37.1.—(1) This part applies where a party wants to appeal under—   ★**P-386**

  (a) section 9(11) of the Criminal Justice Act 1987 or section 35(1) of the Criminal Procedure and Investigations Act 1996; or

  (b) section 47(1) of the Criminal Justice Act 2003.

(2) A reference to an "appellant" in this part is a reference to such a party.

Service of appeal notice

37.2.—(1) An appellant must serve an appeal notice on—   ★**P-387**

  (a) the Crown Court officer;

  (b) the Registrar; and

  (c) every party directly affected by the order or ruling against which the appellant wants to appeal.

(2) The appellant must serve the appeal notice not more than 5 business days after—

    (a) the order or ruling against which the appellant wants to appeal; or

    (b) the Crown Court judge gives or refuses permission to appeal.

Form of appeal notice

★**P-388**   **37.3.**—(1) An appeal notice must be in the form set out in the Practice Direction.

    (2) The appeal notice must—

    (a) specify each order or ruling against which the appellant wants to appeal;

    (b) identify each ground of appeal on which the appellant relies, numbering them consecutively (if there is more than one) and concisely outlining each argument in support;

    (c) summarise the relevant facts;

    (d) identify any relevant authorities;

    (e) include or attach any application for the following, with reasons—

        (i) permission to appeal, if the appellant needs the court's permission,

        (ii) an extension of time within which to serve the appeal notice,

        (iii) a direction to attend in person a hearing that the appellant could attend by live link, if the appellant is in custody;

    (f) include a list of those on whom the appellant has served the appeal notice; and

    (g) attach—

        (i) a transcript or note of each order or ruling against which the appellant wants to appeal,

        (ii) all relevant skeleton arguments considered by the Crown Court judge,

        (iii) any written application for permission to appeal that the appellant made to the Crown Court judge,

        (iv) a transcript or note of the decision by the Crown Court judge on any application for permission to appeal, and

        (v) any other document or thing that the appellant thinks the court will need to decide the appeal.

Crown Court judge's permission to appeal

★**P-389**   **37.4.**—(1) An appellant who wants the Crown Court judge to give permission to appeal must—

    (a) apply orally, with reasons, immediately after the order or ruling against which the appellant wants to appeal; or

    (b) apply in writing and serve the application on—

        (i) the Crown Court officer, and

        (ii) every party directly affected by the order or ruling

    not more than 2 business days after that order or ruling.

    (2) A written application must include the same information (with the necessary adaptations) as an appeal notice.

Respondent's notice

★**P-390**   **37.5.**—(1) A party on whom an appellant serves an appeal notice may serve a respondent's notice, and must do so if—

    (a) that party wants to make representations to the court; or

    (b) the court so directs.

    (2) Such a party must serve the respondent's notice on—

    (a) the appellant;

    (b) the Crown Court officer;

    (c) the Registrar; and

    (d) any other party on whom the appellant served the appeal notice.

    (3) Such a party must serve the respondent's notice not more than 5 business days after—

    (a) the appellant serves the appeal notice; or

    (b) a direction to do so.

    (4) The respondent's notice must be in the form set out in the Practice Direction.

    (5) The respondent's notice must—

    (a) give the date on which the respondent was served with the appeal notice;

    (b) identify each ground of opposition on which the respondent relies, numbering them consecutively (if there is more than one), concisely outlining each argument in support and identifying the ground of appeal to which each relates;

(c)   summarise any relevant facts not already summarised in the appeal notice;

(d)   identify any relevant authorities;

(e)   include or attach any application for the following, with reasons—

(i)   an extension of time within which to serve the respondent's notice,

(ii)   a direction to attend in person any hearing that the respondent could attend by live link, if the respondent is in custody;

(f)   identify any other document or thing that the respondent thinks the court will need to decide the appeal.

Powers of Court of Appeal judge
37.6. A judge of the Court of Appeal may give permission to appeal as well as exercising the powers given by other legislation (including these rules). ★P-391

Renewing applications
37.7. Rule 36.5 (renewing an application refused by a judge or the Registrar) applies with a time limit of 5 business days. ★P-392

Right to attend hearing
37.8.—(1) A party who is in custody has a right to attend a hearing in public. ★P-393

(2) The court or the Registrar may direct that such a party is to attend a hearing by live link.

PART 38

APPEAL TO THE COURT OF APPEAL AGAINST RULING ADVERSE TO PROSECUTION

When this part applies
38.1.—(1) This part applies where a prosecutor wants to appeal under section 58(2) of the Criminal Justice Act 2003. ★P-394

(2) A reference to an "appellant" in this part is a reference to such a prosecutor.

Decision to appeal
38.2.—(1) An appellant must tell the Crown Court judge of any decision to appeal— ★P-395

(a)   immediately after the ruling against which the appellant wants to appeal; or

(b)   on the expiry of the time to decide whether to appeal allowed under paragraph (2).

(2) If an appellant wants time to decide whether to appeal—

(a)   the appellant must ask the Crown Court judge immediately after the ruling; and

(b)   the general rule is that the judge must not require the appellant to decide there and then but instead must allow until the next business day.

Service of appeal notice
38.3.—(1) An appellant must serve an appeal notice on— ★P-396

(a)   the Crown Court officer;

(b)   the Registrar; and

(c)   every defendant directly affected by the ruling against which the appellant wants to appeal.

(2) The appellant must serve the appeal notice not later than—

(a)   the next business day after telling the Crown Court judge of the decision to appeal, if the judge expedites the appeal; or

(b)   5 business days after telling the Crown Court judge of that decision, if the judge does not expedite the appeal.

Form of appeal notice
38.4.—(1) An appeal notice must be in the form set out in the Practice Direction. ★P-397

(2) The appeal notice must—

(a)   specify each ruling against which the appellant wants to appeal;

(b)   identify each ground of appeal on which the appellant relies, numbering them consecutively (if there is more than one) and concisely outlining each argument in support;

(c)   summarise the relevant facts;

(d)   identify any relevant authorities;

(e)   include or attach any application for the following, with reasons—

(i)   permission to appeal, if the appellant needs the court's permission,

    (ii)   an extension of time within which to serve the appeal notice,

    (iii)   expedition of the appeal, or revocation of a direction expediting the appeal;

  (f)   include a list of those on whom the appellant has served the appeal notice;

  (g)   attach—

    (i)   a transcript or note of each ruling against which the appellant wants to appeal,

    (ii)   all relevant skeleton arguments considered by the Crown Court judge,

    (iii)   any written application for permission to appeal that the appellant made to the Crown Court judge,

    (iv)   a transcript or note of the decision by the Crown Court judge on any application for permission to appeal,

    (v)   a transcript or note of the decision by the Crown Court judge on any request to expedite the appeal, and

    (vi)   any other document or thing that the appellant thinks the court will need to decide the appeal; and

  (h)   attach a form of respondent's notice for any defendant served with the appeal notice to complete if that defendant wants to do so.

Crown Court judge's permission to appeal

★P-398   **38.5.**—(1) An appellant who wants the Crown Court judge to give permission to appeal must—

  (a)   apply orally, with reasons, immediately after the ruling against which the appellant wants to appeal; or

  (b)   apply in writing and serve the application on—

    (i)   the Crown Court officer, and

    (ii)   every defendant directly affected by the ruling

    on the expiry of the time allowed under rule 67.2 to decide whether to appeal.

    (2) A written application must include the same information (with the necessary adaptations) as an appeal notice.

    (3) The Crown Court judge must allow every defendant directly affected by the ruling an opportunity to make representations.

    (4) The general rule is that the Crown Court judge must decide whether or not to give permission to appeal on the day that the application for permission is made.

Expediting an appeal

★P-399   **38.6.**—(1) An appellant who wants the Crown Court judge to expedite an appeal must ask, giving reasons, on telling the judge of the decision to appeal.

    (2) The Crown Court judge must allow every defendant directly affected by the ruling an opportunity to make representations.

    (3) The Crown Court judge may revoke a direction expediting the appeal unless the appellant has served the appeal notice.

Respondent's notice

★P-400   **38.7.**—(1) A defendant on whom an appellant serves an appeal notice may serve a respondent's notice, and must do so if—

  (a)   the defendant wants to make representations to the court; or

  (b)   the court so directs.

    (2) Such a defendant must serve the respondent's notice on—

  (a)   the appellant;

  (b)   the Crown Court officer;

  (c)   the Registrar; and

  (d)   any other defendant on whom the appellant served the appeal notice.

    (3) Such a defendant must serve the respondent's notice—

  (a)   not later than the next business day after—

    (i)   the appellant serves the appeal notice, or

    (ii)   a direction to do so

    if the Crown Court judge expedites the appeal; or

  (b)   not more than 5 business days after—

    (i)   the appellant serves the appeal notice, or

    (ii)   a direction to do so

    if the Crown Court judge does not expedite the appeal.

    (4) The respondent's notice must be in the form set out in the Practice Direction.

(5) The respondent's notice must—
- (a) give the date on which the respondent was served with the appeal notice;
- (b) identify each ground of opposition on which the respondent relies, numbering them consecutively (if there is more than one), concisely outlining each argument in support and identifying the ground of appeal to which each relates;
- (c) summarise any relevant facts not already summarised in the appeal notice;
- (d) identify any relevant authorities;
- (e) include or attach any application for the following, with reasons—
    - (i) an extension of time within which to serve the respondent's notice,
    - (ii) a direction to attend in person any hearing that the respondent could attend by live link, if the respondent is in custody;
- (f) identify any other document or thing that the respondent thinks the court will need to decide the appeal.

Public interest ruling

38.8.—(1) This rule applies where the appellant wants to appeal against a public interest ruling.   ★**P-401**

(2) The appellant must not serve on any defendant directly affected by the ruling—
- (a) any written application to the Crown Court judge for permission to appeal; or
- (b) an appeal notice,

if the appellant thinks that to do so in effect would reveal something that the appellant thinks ought not be disclosed.

(3) The appellant must not include in an appeal notice—
- (a) the material that was the subject of the ruling; or
- (b) any indication of what sort of material it is,

if the appellant thinks that to do so in effect would reveal something that the appellant thinks ought not be disclosed.

(4) The appellant must serve on the Registrar with the appeal notice an annex—
- (a) marked to show that its contents are only for the court and the Registrar;
- (b) containing whatever the appellant has omitted from the appeal notice, with reasons; and
- (c) if relevant, explaining why the appellant has not served the appeal notice.

(5) Rules 38.5(3) and 38.6(2) do not apply.

Powers of Court of Appeal judge

38.9. A judge of the Court of Appeal may—   ★**P-402**
- (a) give permission to appeal;
- (b) revoke a Crown Court judge's direction expediting an appeal; and
- (c) where an appellant abandons an appeal, order a defendant's acquittal, his release from custody and the payment of his costs,

as well as exercising the powers given by other legislation (including these rules).

Renewing applications

38.10. Rule 36.5 (renewing an application refused by a judge or the Registrar) applies with a time   ★**P-403**
limit of 5 business days.

Right to attend hearing

38.11.—(1) A respondent who is in custody has a right to attend a hearing in public.   ★**P-404**

(2) The court or the Registrar may direct that such a respondent is to attend a hearing by live link.

PART 39

APPEAL TO THE COURT OF APPEAL ABOUT CONVICTION OR SENTENCE

When this part applies

39.1.—(1) This part applies where—   ★**P-405**
- (a) a defendant wants to appeal under—
    - (i) Part 1 of the Criminal Appeal Act 1968,
    - (ii) section 274(3) of the Criminal Justice Act 2003,
    - (iii) paragraph 14 of Schedule 22 to the Criminal Justice Act 2003, or
    - (iv) section 42 of the Counter Terrorism Act 2008;
- (b) the Criminal Cases Review Commission refers a case to the Court of Appeal under section 9 of the Criminal Appeal Act 1995;

(c) a prosecutor wants to appeal to the Court of Appeal under section 14A(5A) of the Football Spectators Act 1989;

(d) a party wants to appeal under section 74(8) of the Serious Organised Crime and Police Act 2005;

(e) a person found in contempt of court wants to appeal under section 13 of the Administration of Justice Act 1960 and section 18A of the Criminal Appeal Act 1968; or

(f) a person wants to appeal to the Court of Appeal under—

    (i) section 24 of the Serious Crime Act 2007, or

    (ii) regulation 3C or 3H of the Costs in Criminal Cases (General) Regulations 1986.

(2) A reference to an "appellant" in this part is a reference to such a party or person.

Service of appeal notice

★P-406   **39.2.**—(1) The general rule is that an appellant must serve an appeal notice—

(a) on the Crown Court officer at the Crown Court centre where there occurred—

    (i) the conviction, verdict, or finding,

    (ii) the sentence, or

    (iii) the order, or the failure to make an order

    about which the appellant wants to appeal; and

(b) not more than—

    (i) 28 days after that occurred, or

    (ii) 21 days after the order, in a case in which the appellant appeals against a wasted or third party costs order.

(2) But an appellant must serve an appeal notice—

(a) on the Registrar instead where—

    (i) the appeal is against a minimum term review decision under section 274(3) of, or paragraph 14 of Schedule 22 to, the Criminal Justice Act 2003, or

    (ii) the Criminal Cases Review Commission refers the case to the court; and

(b) not more than 28 days after—

    (i) the minimum term review decision about which the appellant wants to appeal, or

    (ii) the Registrar serves notice that the Commission has referred a conviction.

Form of appeal notice

★P-407   **39.3.**—(1) An appeal notice must be in the form set out in the Practice Direction.

(2) The appeal notice must—

(a) specify—

    (i) the conviction, verdict, or finding,

    (ii) the sentence, or

    (iii) the order, or the failure to make an order

    about which the appellant wants to appeal;

(b) identify each ground of appeal on which the appellant relies, numbering them consecutively (if there is more than one) and concisely outlining each argument in support;

(c) identify the transcript that the appellant thinks the court will need, if the appellant wants to appeal against a conviction;

(d) identify the relevant sentencing powers of the Crown Court, if sentence is in issue;

(e) where the Criminal Cases Review Commission refers a case to the court, explain how each ground of appeal relates (if it does) to the reasons for the reference;

(f) summarise the relevant facts;

(g) identify any relevant authorities;

(h) include or attach any application for the following, with reasons—

    (i) permission to appeal, if the appellant needs the court's permission,

    (ii) an extension of time within which to serve the appeal notice,

    (iii) bail pending appeal,

    (iv) a direction to attend in person a hearing that the appellant could attend by live link, if the appellant is in custody,

    (v) the introduction of evidence, including hearsay evidence and evidence of bad character,

    (vi) an order requiring a witness to attend court,

    (vii) a direction for special measures for a witness,

    (viii) a direction for special measures for the giving of evidence by the appellant;

(i) identify any other document or thing that the appellant thinks the court will need to decide the appeal.

Crown Court judge's certificate that case is fit for appeal

39.4.—(1) An appellant who wants the Crown Court judge to certify that a case is fit for appeal **★P-408** must—

(a) apply orally, with reasons, immediately after there occurs—
   (i) the conviction, verdict, or finding,
   (ii) the sentence, or
   (iii) the order, or the failure to make an order
   about which the appellant wants to appeal; or

(b) apply in writing and serve the application on the Crown Court officer not more than 14 days after that occurred.

(2) A written application must include the same information (with the necessary adaptations) as an appeal notice.

Reference by Criminal Cases Review Commission

39.5.—(1) The Registrar must serve on the appellant a reference by the Criminal Cases Review **★P-409** Commission.

(2) The court must treat that reference as the appeal notice if the appellant does not serve such a notice under rule 39.2.

Respondent's notice

39.6.—(1) The Registrar— **★P-410**

(a) may serve an appeal notice on any party directly affected by the appeal; and

(b) must do so if the Criminal Cases Review Commission refers a conviction, verdict, finding or sentence to the court.

(2) Such a party may serve a respondent's notice, and must do so if—

(a) that party wants to make representations to the court; or

(b) the court or the Registrar so directs.

(3) Such a party must serve the respondent's notice on—

(a) the appellant;

(b) the Registrar; and

(c) any other party on whom the Registrar served the appeal notice.

(4) Such a party must serve the respondent's notice—

(a) not more than 14 days after the Registrar serves—
   (i) the appeal notice, or
   (ii) a direction to do so; or

(b) not more than 28 days after the Registrar serves notice that the Commission has referred a conviction.

(5) The respondent's notice must be in the form set out in the Practice Direction.

(6) The respondent's notice must—

(a) give the date on which the respondent was served with the appeal notice;

(b) identify each ground of opposition on which the respondent relies, numbering them consecutively (if there is more than one), concisely outlining each argument in support and identifying the ground of appeal to which each relates;

(c) identify the relevant sentencing powers of the Crown Court, if sentence is in issue;

(d) summarise any relevant facts not already summarised in the appeal notice;

(e) identify any relevant authorities;

(f) include or attach any application for the following, with reasons—
   (i) an extension of time within which to serve the respondent's notice,
   (ii) bail pending appeal,
   (iii) a direction to attend in person a hearing that the respondent could attend by live link, if the respondent is in custody,
   (iv) the introduction of evidence, including hearsay evidence and evidence of bad character,
   (v) an order requiring a witness to attend court,
   (vi) a direction for special measures for a witness; and

(g) identify any other document or thing that the respondent thinks the court will need to decide the appeal.

Adaptation of rules about introducing evidence

★**P-411**   **39.7.**—(1) The following parts apply with such adaptations as the court or the Registrar may direct—

(a)   Part 18 (measures to assist a witness or defendant to give evidence);

(b)   Part 20 (hearsay evidence);

(c)   Part 21 (evidence of bad character); and

(d)   Part 22 (evidence of a complainant's previous sexual behaviour).

(2) But the general rule is that—

(a)   a respondent who opposes an appellant's application to which one of those parts applies must do so in the respondent's notice, with reasons;

(b)   an appellant who opposes a respondent's application to which one of those parts applies must serve notice, with reasons, on—

(i)   the Registrar, and

(ii)   the respondent

not more than 14 days after service of the respondent's notice; and

(c)   the court or the Registrar may give directions with or without a hearing.

Application for bail pending appeal or retrial

★**P-412**   **39.8.**—(1) This rule applies where a party wants to make an application to the court about bail pending appeal or retrial.

(2) That party must serve an application in the form set out in the Practice Direction on—

(a)   the Registrar, unless the application is with the appeal notice; and

(b)   the other party.

(3) The court must not decide such an application without giving the other party an opportunity to make representations, including representations about any condition or surety proposed by the applicant.

(4) This rule and rule 14.16 (bail condition to be enforced in another European Union member State) apply where the court can impose as a condition of bail pending retrial a requirement—

(a)   with which a defendant must comply while in another European Union member State; and

(b)   which that other member State can monitor and enforce.

Conditions of bail pending appeal or retrial

★**P-413**   **39.9.**—(1) This rule applies where the court grants a party bail pending appeal or retrial subject to any condition that must be met before that party is released.

(2) The court may direct how such a condition must be met.

(3) The Registrar must serve a certificate in the form set out in the Practice Direction recording any such condition and direction on—

(a)   that party;

(b)   that party's custodian; and

(c)   any other person directly affected by any such direction.

(4) A person directly affected by any such direction need not comply with it until the Registrar serves that person with that certificate.

(5) Unless the court otherwise directs, if any such condition or direction requires someone to enter into a recognizance it must be—

(a)   in the form set out in the Practice Direction and signed before—

(i)   the Registrar,

(ii)   the custodian, or

(iii)   someone acting with the authority of the Registrar or custodian;

(b)   copied immediately to the person who enters into it; and

(c)   served immediately by the Registrar on the appellant's custodian or vice versa, as appropriate.

(6) Unless the court otherwise directs, if any such condition or direction requires someone to make a payment, surrender a document or take some other step—

(a)   that payment, document or step must be made, surrendered or taken to or before—

(i)   the Registrar,

(ii)   the custodian, or

(iii)   someone acting with the authority of the Registrar or custodian;

(b)   the Registrar or the custodian, as appropriate, must serve immediately on the other a statement that the payment, document or step has been made, surrendered or taken, as appropriate.

(7) The custodian must release the appellant where it appears that any condition ordered by the court has been met.

(8) For the purposes of section 5 of the Bail Act 1976 (record of decision about bail), the Registrar must keep a copy of—

    (a) any certificate served under paragraph (3);

    (b) a notice of hearing given under rule 36.7(1); and

    (c) a notice of the court's decision served under rule 36.7(2).

(9) Where the court grants bail pending retrial the Registrar must serve on the Crown Court officer copies of the documents kept under paragraph (8).

Forfeiture of a recognizance given as a condition of bail

39.10.—(1) This rule applies where—   **★P-414**

    (a) the court grants a party bail pending appeal or retrial; and

    (b) the bail is subject to a condition that that party provides a surety to guarantee that he will surrender to custody as required; but

    (c) that party does not surrender to custody as required.

(2) The Registrar must serve notice on—

    (a) the surety; and

    (b) the prosecutor,

of the hearing at which the court may order the forfeiture of the recognizance given by that surety.

(3) The court must not forfeit a surety's recognizance—

    (a) less than 7 days after the Registrar serves notice under paragraph (2); and

    (b) without giving the surety an opportunity to make representations at a hearing.

Right to attend hearing

39.11. A party who is in custody has a right to attend a hearing in public unless—   **★P-415**

    (a) it is a hearing preliminary or incidental to an appeal, including the hearing of an application for permission to appeal; or

    (b) that party is in custody in consequence of—

        (i) a verdict of not guilty by reason of insanity, or

        (ii) a finding of disability.

Power to vary determination of appeal against sentence

39.12.—(1) This rule applies where the court decides an appeal affecting sentence in a party's absence.   **★P-416**

(2) The court may vary such a decision if it did not take account of something relevant because that party was absent.

(3) A party who wants the court to vary such a decision must—

    (a) apply in writing, with reasons;

    (b) serve the application on the Registrar not more than 7 days after—

        (i) the decision, if that party was represented at the appeal hearing, or

        (ii) the Registrar serves the decision, if that party was not represented at that hearing.

Directions about re-admission to hospital on dismissal of appeal

39.13.—(1) This rule applies where—   **★P-417**

    (a) an appellant subject to—

        (i) an order under section 37(1) of the Mental Health Act 1983 (detention in hospital on conviction), or

        (ii) an order under section 5(2) of the Criminal Procedure (Insanity) Act 1964 (detention in hospital on finding of insanity or disability)

      has been released on bail pending appeal; and

    (b) the court—

        (i) refuses permission to appeal,

        (ii) dismisses the appeal, or

        (iii) affirms the order under appeal.

(2) The court must give appropriate directions for the appellant's—

    (a) re-admission to hospital; and

    (b) if necessary, temporary detention pending re-admission.

Renewal or setting aside of order for retrial

39.14.—(1) This rule applies where—   **★P-418**

    (a) a prosecutor wants a defendant to be arraigned more than 2 months after the court ordered a retrial under section 7 of the Criminal Appeal Act 1968; or

(b) a defendant wants such an order set aside after 2 months have passed since it was made.
(2) That party must apply in writing, with reasons, and serve the application on—
    (a) the Registrar;
    (b) the other party.

PART 40

APPEAL TO THE COURT OF APPEAL ABOUT REPORTING OR PUBLIC ACCESS RESTRICTION

When this part applies

★P-419   **40.1.**—(1) This part applies where a person directly affected by an order to which section 159(1) of the Criminal Justice Act 1988 applies wants to appeal against that order.
(2) A reference to an "appellant" in this part is a reference to such a party.

Service of appeal notice

★P-420   **40.2.**—(1) An appellant must serve an appeal notice on—
    (a) the Crown Court officer;
    (b) the Registrar;
    (c) the parties; and
    (d) any other person directly affected by the order against which the appellant wants to appeal.
(2) The appellant must serve the appeal notice not later than—
    (a) the next business day after an order restricting public access to the trial;
    (b) 10 business days after an order restricting reporting of the trial.

Form of appeal notice

★P-421   **40.3.**—(1) An appeal notice must be in the form set out in the Practice Direction.
(2) The appeal notice must—
    (a) specify the order against which the appellant wants to appeal;
    (b) identify each ground of appeal on which the appellant relies, numbering them consecutively (if there is more than one) and concisely outlining each argument in support;
    (c) summarise the relevant facts;
    (d) identify any relevant authorities;
    (e) include or attach, with reasons—
      (i) an application for permission to appeal,
      (ii) any application for an extension of time within which to serve the appeal notice,
      (iii) any application for a direction to attend in person a hearing that the appellant could attend by live link, if the appellant is in custody,
      (iv) any application for permission to introduce evidence, and
      (v) a list of those on whom the appellant has served the appeal notice; and
    (f) attach any document or thing that the appellant thinks the court will need to decide the appeal.

Advance notice of appeal against order restricting public access

★P-422   **40.4.**—(1) This rule applies where the appellant wants to appeal against an order restricting public access to a trial.
(2) The appellant may serve advance written notice of intention to appeal against any such order that may be made.
(3) The appellant must serve any such advance notice—
    (a) on—
      (i) the Crown Court officer,
      (ii) the Registrar,
      (iii) the parties, and
      (iv) any other person who will be directly affected by the order against which the appellant intends to appeal, if it is made; and
    (b) not more than 5 business days after the Crown Court officer displays notice of the application for the order.
(4) The advance notice must include the same information (with the necessary adaptations) as an appeal notice.
(5) The court must treat that advance notice as the appeal notice if the order is made.

Duty of applicant for order restricting public access

★P-423   **40.5.**—(1) This rule applies where the appellant wants to appeal against an order restricting public access to a trial.

(2) The party who applied for the order must serve on the Registrar—

(a) a transcript or note of the application for the order; and

(b) any other document or thing that that party thinks the court will need to decide the appeal.

(3) That party must serve that transcript or note and any such other document or thing as soon as practicable after—

(a) the appellant serves the appeal notice; or

(b) the order, where the appellant served advance notice of intention to appeal.

Respondent's notice on appeal against reporting restriction

40.6.—(1) This rule applies where the appellant wants to appeal against an order restricting the reporting of a trial. **★P-424**

(2) A person on whom an appellant serves an appeal notice may serve a respondent's notice, and must do so if—

(a) that person wants to make representations to the court; or

(b) the court so directs.

(3) Such a person must serve the respondent's notice on—

(a) the appellant;

(b) the Crown Court officer;

(c) the Registrar;

(d) the parties; and

(e) any other person on whom the appellant served the appeal notice.

(4) Such a person must serve the respondent's notice not more than 3 business days after—

(a) the appellant serves the appeal notice; or

(b) a direction to do so.

(5) The respondent's notice must be in the form set out in the Practice Direction.

(6) The respondent's notice must—

(a) give the date on which the respondent was served with the appeal notice;

(b) identify each ground of opposition on which the respondent relies, numbering them consecutively (if there is more than one), concisely outlining each argument in support and identifying the ground of appeal to which each relates;

(c) summarise any relevant facts not already summarised in the appeal notice;

(d) identify any relevant authorities;

(e) include or attach any application for the following, with reasons—

(i) an extension of time within which to serve the respondent's notice,

(ii) a direction to attend in person any hearing that the respondent could attend by live link, if the respondent is in custody,

(iii) permission to introduce evidence; and

(f) identify any other document or thing that the respondent thinks the court will need to decide the appeal.

Renewing applications

40.7. Rule 36.5 (renewing an application refused by a judge or the Registrar) applies with a time limit of 5 business days. **★P-425**

Right to introduce evidence

40.8. No person may introduce evidence without the court's permission. **★P-426**

Right to attend hearing

40.9.—(1) A party who is in custody has a right to attend a hearing in public of an appeal against an order restricting the reporting of a trial. **★P-427**

(2) The court or the Registrar may direct that such a party is to attend a hearing by live link.

PART 41

REFERENCE TO THE COURT OF APPEAL OF POINT OF LAW OR UNDULY LENIENT SENTENCING

When this part applies

41.1. This part applies where the Attorney General wants to— **★P-428**

(a) refer a point of law to the Court of Appeal under section 36 of the Criminal Justice Act 1972; or

(b)   refer a sentencing case to the Court of Appeal under section 36 of the Criminal Justice Ac
1988.

Service of notice of reference and application for permission

★P-429   **41.2.**—(1) The Attorney General must—
(a)   serve on the Registrar—
(i)   any notice of reference, and
(ii)   any application for permission to refer a sentencing case; and
(b)   with a notice of reference of a point of law, give the Registrar details of—
(i)   the defendant affected,
(ii)   the date and place of the relevant Crown Court decision, and
(iii) the relevant verdict and sentencing.
(2) The Attorney General must serve an application for permission to refer a sentencing case no
more than 28 days after the last of the sentences in that case.

Form of notice of reference and application for permission

★P-430   **41.3.**—(1) A notice of reference and an application for permission to refer a sentencing case must
be in the appropriate form set out in the Practice Direction, giving the year and number.
(2) A notice of reference of a point of law must—
(a)   specify the point of law in issue and indicate the opinion that the Attorney General invites
the court to give;
(b)   identify each ground for that invitation, numbering them consecutively (if there is more
than one) and concisely outlining each argument in support;
(c)   exclude any reference to the defendant's name and any other reference that may identify
the defendant;
(d)   summarise the relevant facts; and
(e)   identify any relevant authorities.
(3) An application for permission to refer a sentencing case must—
(a)   give details of—
(i)   the defendant affected,
(ii)   the date and place of the relevant Crown Court decision, and
(iii) the relevant verdict and sentencing;
(b)   explain why that sentencing appears to the Attorney General unduly lenient, concisely
outlining each argument in support; and
(c)   include the application for permission to refer the case to the court.
(4) A notice of reference of a sentencing case must—
(a)   include the same details and explanation as the application for permission to refer the case;
(b)   summarise the relevant facts; and
(c)   identify any relevant authorities.
(5) Where the court gives the Attorney General permission to refer a sentencing case, it may treat
the application for permission as the notice of reference.

Registrar's notice to defendant

★P-431   **41.4.**—(1) The Registrar must serve on the defendant—
(a)   a notice of reference;
(b)   an application for permission to refer a sentencing case.
(2) Where the Attorney General refers a point of law, the Registrar must give the defendant notice
that—
(a)   the outcome of the reference will not make any difference to the outcome of the trial; and
(b)   the defendant may serve a respondent's notice.
(3) Where the Attorney General applies for permission to refer a sentencing case, the Registrar
must give the defendant notice that—
(a)   the outcome of the reference may make a difference to that sentencing, and in particular
may result in a more severe sentence; and
(b)   the defendant may serve a respondent's notice.

Respondent's notice

★P-432   **41.5.**—(1) A defendant on whom the Registrar serves a reference or an application for permission
to refer a sentencing case may serve a respondent's notice, and must do so if—

(a) the defendant wants to make representations to the court; or

(b) the court so directs.

(2) Such a defendant must serve the respondent's notice on—

(a) the Attorney General; and

(b) the Registrar.

(3) Such a defendant must serve the respondent's notice—

(a) where the Attorney General refers a point of law, not more than 28 days after—

(i) the Registrar serves the reference, or

(ii) a direction to do so;

(b) where the Attorney General applies for permission to refer a sentencing case, not more than 14 days after—

(i) the Registrar serves the application, or

(ii) a direction to do so.

(4) Where the Attorney General refers a point of law, the respondent's notice must—

(a) identify each ground of opposition on which the respondent relies, numbering them consecutively (if there is more than one), concisely outlining each argument in support and identifying the Attorney General's ground or reason to which each relates;

(b) summarise any relevant facts not already summarised in the reference;

(c) identify any relevant authorities; and

(d) include or attach any application for the following, with reasons—

(i) an extension of time within which to serve the respondent's notice,

(ii) permission to attend a hearing that the respondent does not have a right to attend,

(iii) a direction to attend in person a hearing that the respondent could attend by live link, if the respondent is in custody.

(5) Where the Attorney General applies for permission to refer a sentencing case, the respondent's notice must—

(a) say if the respondent wants to make representations at the hearing of the application or reference; and

(b) include or attach any application for the following, with reasons—

(i) an extension of time within which to serve the respondent's notice,

(ii) permission to attend a hearing that the respondent does not have a right to attend,

(iii) a direction to attend in person a hearing that the respondent could attend by live link, if the respondent is in custody.

Variation or withdrawal of notice of reference or application for permission

41.6.—(1) This rule applies where the Attorney General wants to vary or withdraw— **★P-433**

(a) a notice of reference; or

(b) an application for permission to refer a sentencing case.

(2) The Attorney General—

(a) may vary or withdraw the notice or application without the court's permission by serving notice on—

(i) the Registrar, and

(ii) the defendant

before any hearing of the reference or application; but

(b) at any such hearing, may only vary or withdraw that notice or application with the court's permission.

Right to attend hearing

41.7.—(1) A respondent who is in custody has a right to attend a hearing in public unless it is a **★P-434**
hearing preliminary or incidental to a reference, including the hearing of an application for permission to refer a sentencing case.

(2) The court or the Registrar may direct that such a respondent is to attend a hearing by live link.

Anonymity of defendant on reference of point of law

★P-435   **41.8.** Where the Attorney General refers a point of law, the court must not allow anyone to
identify the defendant during the proceedings unless the defendant gives permission.

PART 42

APPEAL TO THE COURT OF APPEAL IN CONFISCATION AND RELATED PROCEEDINGS

General Rules

Extension of time

★P-436   **42.1.**—(1) An application to extend the time limit for giving notice of application for permission to
appeal under Part 2 of the Proceeds of Crime Act 2002 must—

    (a) be included in the notice of appeal; and

    (b) state the grounds for the application.

(2) The parties may not agree to extend any date or time limit set by this part or by the Proceeds
of Crime Act 2002 (Appeals under Part 2) Order 2003.

Other applications

★P-437   **42.2.** Rule 39.3(2)(h) (form of appeal notice) applies in relation to an application—

    (a) by a party to an appeal under Part 2 of the Proceeds of Crime Act 2002 that, under article
        7 of the Proceeds of Crime Act 2002 (Appeals under Part 2) Order 2003, a witness be
        ordered to attend or that the evidence of a witness be received by the Court of Appeal; or

    (b) by the defendant to be given permission by the court to be present at proceedings for
        which permission is required under article 6 of the 2003 Order,

as it applies in relation to applications under Part I of the Criminal Appeal Act 1968 and the form in
which rule 39.3 requires notice to be given may be modified as necessary.

Examination of witness by court

★P-438   **42.3.** Rule 36.7 (notice of hearings and decisions) applies in relation to an order of the court
under article 7 of the Proceeds of Crime Act 2002 (Appeals under Part 2) Order 2003 to require a
person to attend for examination as it applies in relation to such an order of the court under Part I
of the Criminal Appeal Act 1968.

Supply of documentary and other exhibits

★P-439   **42.4.** Rule 36.11 (registrar's duty to provide copy documents for appeal or reference) applies in
relation to an appellant or respondent under Part 2 of the Proceeds of Crime Act 2002 as it applies
in relation to an appellant and respondent under Part I of the Criminal Appeal Act 1968.

Registrar's power to require information from court of trial

★P-440   **42.5.** The Registrar may require the Crown Court to provide the Court of Appeal with any assistance or information which it requires for the purposes of exercising its jurisdiction under Part 2
of the Proceeds of Crime Act 2002, the Proceeds of Crime Act 2002 (Appeals under Part 2) Order
2003 or this part.

Hearing by single judge

★P-441   **42.6.** Rule 36.6(5) (hearings) applies in relation to a judge exercising any of the powers referred to
in article 8 of the Proceeds of Crime Act 2002 (Appeals under Part 2) Order 2003 or the powers in
rules 42.12(3) and (4) (respondent's notice), 42.15(2) (notice of appeal) and 42.16(6) (respondent's
notice), as it applies in relation to a judge exercising the powers referred to in section 31(2) of the
Criminal Appeal Act 1968.

Determination by full court

★P-442   **42.7.** Rule 36.5 (renewing an application refused by a judge or the Registrar) applies where a
single judge has refused an application by a party to exercise in that party's favour any of the powers
listed in article 8 of the Proceeds of Crime Act 2002 (Appeals under Part 2) Order 2003, or the
power in rule 42.12(3) or (4) as it applies where the judge has refused to exercise the powers
referred to in section 31(2) of the Criminal Appeal Act 1968.

Notice of determination

★P-443   **42.8.**—(1) This rule applies where a single judge or the Court of Appeal has determined an application or appeal under the Proceeds of Crime Act 2002 (Appeals under Part 2) Order 2003 or
under Part 2 of the Proceeds of Crime Act 2002.

(2) The Registrar must, as soon as practicable, serve notice of the determination on all of the parties to the proceedings.

(3) Where a single judge or the Court of Appeal has disposed of an application for permission to appeal or an appeal under section 31 of the 2002 Act, the Registrar must also, as soon as practicable, serve the order on a court officer of the court of trial and any magistrates' court responsible for enforcing any confiscation order which the Crown Court has made.

Record of proceedings and transcripts

42.9. Rule 5.5 (recording and transcription of proceedings in the Crown Court) and rule 36.9 **★P-444** (duty of person transcribing proceedings in the Crown Court) apply in relation to proceedings in respect of which an appeal lies to the Court of Appeal under Part 2 of the Proceeds of Crime Act 2002 as they apply in relation to proceedings in respect of which an appeal lies to the Court of Appeal under Part I of the Criminal Appeal Act 1968.

Appeal to the Supreme Court

42.10.—(1) An application to the Court of Appeal for permission to appeal to the Supreme Court **★P-445** under Part 2 of the Proceeds of Crime Act 2002 must be made—

(a) orally after the decision of the Court of Appeal from which an appeal lies to the Supreme Court; or

(b) in the form set out in the Practice Direction, in accordance with article 12 of the Proceeds of Crime Act 2002 (Appeals under Part 2) Order 2003 and served on the Registrar.

(2) The application may be abandoned at any time before it is heard by the Court of Appeal by serving notice in writing on the Registrar.

(3) Rule 36.6(5) (hearings) applies in relation to a single judge exercising any of the powers referred to in article 15 of the 2003 Order, as it applies in relation to a single judge exercising the powers referred to in section 31(2) of the Criminal Appeal Act 1968.

(4) Rule 36.5 (renewing an application refused by a judge or the Registrar) applies where a single judge has refused an application by a party to exercise in that party's favour any of the powers listed in article 15 of the 2003 Order as they apply where the judge has refused to exercise the powers referred to in section 31(2) of the 1968 Act.

(5) The form in which rule 36.5(2) requires an application to be made may be modified as necessary.

Confiscation: Appeal by Prosecutor or by Person with Interest in Property

Notice of appeal

42.11.—(1) Where an appellant wishes to apply to the Court of Appeal for permission to appeal **★P-446** under section 31 of the Proceeds of Crime Act 2002, the appellant must serve a notice of appeal in the form set out in the Practice Direction on—

(a) the Crown Court officer; and

(b) the defendant.

(2) When the notice of a prosecutor's appeal about a confiscation order is served on the defendant, it must be accompanied by a respondent's notice in the form set out in the Practice Direction for the defendant to complete and a notice which—

(a) informs the defendant that the result of an appeal could be that the Court of Appeal would increase a confiscation order already imposed, make a confiscation order itself or direct the Crown Court to hold another confiscation hearing;

(b) informs the defendant of any right under article 6 of the Proceeds of Crime Act 2002 (Appeals under Part 2) Order 2003 to be present at the hearing of the appeal, although in custody;

(c) invites the defendant to serve any notice on the Registrar—

   (i) to apply to the Court of Appeal for permission to be present at proceedings for which such permission is required under article 6 of the 2003 Order, or

   (ii) to present any argument to the Court of Appeal on the hearing of the application or, if permission is given, the appeal, and whether the defendant wishes to present it in person or by means of a legal representative;

(d) draws to the defendant's attention the effect of rule 42.4 (supply of documentary and other exhibits); and

(e) advises the defendant to consult a solicitor as soon as possible.

(3) The appellant must provide the Crown Court officer with a certificate of service stating that the appellant has served the notice of appeal on the defendant in accordance with paragraph (1) or explaining why it has not been possible to do so.

★P-447

42.12.—(1) This rule applies where a defendant is served with a notice of appeal under rule 42.11.

(2) If the defendant wishes to oppose the application for permission to appeal, the defendant must, not more than 14 days after service of the notice of appeal, serve on the Registrar and on the appellant a notice in the form set out in the Practice Direction—

    (a) stating the date on which the notice of appeal was served;

    (b) summarising the defendant's response to the arguments of the appellant; and

    (c) specifying the authorities which the defendant intends to cite.

(3) The time for giving notice under this rule may be extended by the Registrar, a single judge or by the Court of Appeal.

(4) Where the Registrar refuses an application under paragraph (3) for the extension of time, the defendant is entitled to have the application determined by a single judge.

(5) Where a single judge refuses an application under paragraph (3) or (4) for the extension of time, the defendant is entitled to have the application determined by the Court of Appeal.

Amendment and abandonment of appeal

★P-448

42.13.—(1) The appellant may amend a notice of appeal served under rule 42.11 or abandon an appeal under section 31 of the Proceeds of Crime Act 2002—

    (a) without the permission of the court at any time before the Court of Appeal has begun hearing the appeal; and

    (b) with the permission of the court after the Court of Appeal has begun hearing the appeal,

by serving notice in writing on the Registrar.

(2) Where the appellant serves a notice abandoning an appeal under paragraph (1), the appellant must send a copy of it to—

    (a) the defendant;

    (b) a court officer of the court of trial; and

    (c) the magistrates' court responsible for enforcing any confiscation order which the Crown Court has made.

(3) Where the appellant serves a notice amending a notice of appeal under paragraph (1), the appellant must send a copy of it to the defendant.

(4) Where an appeal is abandoned under paragraph (1), the application for permission to appeal or appeal must be treated, for the purposes of section 85 of the 2002 Act (conclusion of proceedings), as having been refused or dismissed by the Court of Appeal.

Appeal About Compliance, Restraint or Receivership Order

Permission to appeal

★P-449

42.14.—(1) Permission to appeal to the Court of Appeal under section 13B, section 43 or section 65 of the Proceeds of Crime Act 2002 may only be given where—

    (a) the Court of Appeal considers that the appeal would have a real prospect of success; or

    (b) there is some other compelling reason why the appeal should be heard.

(2) An order giving permission to appeal may limit the issues to be heard and be made subject to conditions.

Notice of appeal

★P-450

42.15.—(1) Where an appellant wishes to apply to the Court of Appeal for permission to appeal under section 13B, 43 or 65 of the Proceeds of Crime Act 2002 Act, the appellant must serve a notice of appeal in the form set out in the Practice Direction on the Crown Court officer.

(2) Unless the Registrar, a single judge or the Court of Appeal directs otherwise, the appellant must serve the notice of appeal, accompanied by a respondent's notice in the form set out in the Practice Direction for the respondent to complete, on—

    (a) each respondent;

    (b) any person who holds realisable property to which the appeal relates; and

    (c) any other person affected by the appeal,

as soon as practicable and in any event not later than 5 business days after the notice of appeal is served on the Crown Court officer.

(3) The appellant must serve the following documents with the notice of appeal—

    (a) four additional copies of the notice of appeal for the Court of Appeal;

    (b) four copies of any skeleton argument;

(c) one sealed copy and four unsealed copies of any order being appealed;

(d) four copies of any witness statement or affidavit in support of the application for permission to appeal;

(e) four copies of a suitable record of the reasons for judgment of the Crown Court; and

(f) four copies of the bundle of documents used in the Crown Court proceedings from which the appeal lies.

(4) Where it is not possible to serve all of the documents referred to in paragraph (3), the appellant must indicate which documents have not yet been served and the reasons why they are not currently available.

(5) The appellant must provide the Crown Court officer with a certificate of service stating that the notice of appeal has been served on each respondent in accordance with paragraph (2) and including full details of each respondent or explaining why it has not been possible to effect service.

Respondent's notice

42.16.—(1) This rule applies to an appeal under section 13B, 43 or 65 of the Proceeds of Crime ★**P-451** Act 2002.

(2) A respondent may serve a respondent's notice on the Registrar.

(3) A respondent who—

(a) is seeking permission to appeal from the Court of Appeal; or

(b) wishes to ask the Court of Appeal to uphold the decision of the Crown Court for reasons different from or additional to those given by the Crown Court,

must serve a respondent's notice on the Registrar.

(4) A respondent's notice must be in the form set out in the Practice Direction and where the respondent seeks permission to appeal to the Court of Appeal it must be requested in the respondent's notice.

(5) A respondent's notice must be served on the Registrar not later than 14 days after—

(a) the date the respondent is served with notification that the Court of Appeal has given the appellant permission to appeal; or

(b) the date the respondent is served with notification that the application for permission to appeal and the appeal itself are to be heard together.

(6) Unless the Registrar, a single judge or the Court of Appeal directs otherwise, the respondent serving a respondent's notice must serve the notice on the appellant and any other respondent—

(a) as soon as practicable; and

(b) in any event not later than 5 business days,

after it is served on the Registrar.

Amendment and abandonment of appeal

42.17.—(1) The appellant may amend a notice of appeal served under rule 42.15 or abandon an ★**P-452** appeal under section 13B, 43 or 65 of the Proceeds of Crime Act 2002—

(a) without the permission of the court at any time before the Court of Appeal has begun hearing the appeal; and

(b) with the permission of the court after the Court of Appeal has begun hearing the appeal, by serving notice in writing on the Registrar.

(2) Where the appellant serves a notice under paragraph (1), the appellant must send a copy of it to each respondent.

Stay

42.18. Unless the Court of Appeal or the Crown Court orders otherwise, an appeal under section ★**P-453** 13B, 43 or 65 of the Proceeds of Crime Act 2002 does not operate as a stay of any order or decision of the Crown Court.

Striking out appeal notices and setting aside or imposing conditions on permission to appeal

42.19.—(1) The Court of Appeal may— ★**P-454**

(a) strike out the whole or part of a notice of appeal served under rule 42.15; or

(b) impose or vary conditions upon which an appeal under section 13B, 43 or 65 of the Proceeds of Crime Act 2002 may be brought.

(2) The Court of Appeal may only exercise its powers under paragraph (1) where there is a compelling reason for doing so.

(3) Where a party is present at the hearing at which permission to appeal was given, that party may not subsequently apply for an order that the Court of Appeal exercise its powers under paragraph (1)(b).

Hearing of appeals

★P-455   42.20.—(1) This rule applies to appeals under section 13B, 43 or 65 of the Proceeds of Crime Act 2002.

(2) Every appeal must be limited to a review of the decision of the Crown Court unless the Court of Appeal considers that in the circumstances of an individual appeal it would be in the interests of justice to hold a re-hearing.

(3) The Court of Appeal may allow an appeal where the decision of the Crown Court was—

    (a) wrong; or

    (b) unjust because of a serious procedural or other irregularity in the proceedings in the Crown Court.

(4) The Court of Appeal may draw any inference of fact which it considers justified on the evidence.

(5) At the hearing of the appeal a party may not rely on a matter not contained in that party's notice of appeal unless the Court of Appeal gives permission.

PART 43

APPEAL OR REFERENCE TO THE SUPREME COURT

When this part applies

★P-456   43.1.—(1) This part applies where—

    (a) a party wants to appeal to the Supreme Court after—

        (i) an application to the Court of Appeal to which Part 27 applies (retrial following acquittal), or

        (ii) an appeal to the Court of Appeal to which applies Part 37 (appeal to the Court of Appeal against ruling at preparatory hearing), Part 38 (appeal to the Court of Appeal against ruling adverse to prosecution), or Part 39 (appeal to the Court of Appeal about conviction or sentence); or

    (b) a party wants to refer a case to the Supreme Court after a reference to the Court of Appeal to which Part 41 applies (reference to the Court of Appeal of point of law or unduly lenient sentencing).

(2) A reference to an "appellant" in this part is a reference to such a party.

Application for permission or reference

★P-457   43.2.—(1) An appellant must—

    (a) apply orally to the Court of Appeal—

        (i) for permission to appeal or to refer a sentencing case, or

        (ii) to refer a point of law

    immediately after the court gives the reasons for its decision; or

    (b) apply in writing and serve the application on the Registrar and every other party not more than—

        (i) 14 days after the court gives the reasons for its decision if that decision was on a sentencing reference to which Part 70 applies (Attorney General's reference of sentencing case), or

        (ii) 28 days after the court gives those reasons in any other case.

(2) An application for permission to appeal or to refer a sentencing case must—

    (a) identify the point of law of general public importance that the appellant wants the court to certify is involved in the decision; and

    (b) give reasons why—

        (i) that point of law ought to be considered by the Supreme Court, and

        (ii) the court ought to give permission to appeal.

(3) An application to refer a point of law must give reasons why that point ought to be considered by the Supreme Court.

(4) An application must include or attach any application for the following, with reasons—

    (a) an extension of time within which to make the application for permission or for a reference;

    (b) bail pending appeal;

    (c) permission to attend any hearing in the Supreme Court, if the appellant is in custody.

(5) A written application must be in the form set out in the Practice Direction.

Determination of detention pending appeal, etc.

★P-458   43.3. On an application for permission to appeal, the Court of Appeal must—

    (a) decide whether to order the detention of a defendant who would have been liable to be detained but for the decision of the court; and

1080

(b) determine any application for—
(i) bail pending appeal,
(ii) permission to attend any hearing in the Supreme Court, or
(iii) a representation order.

Bail pending appeal
43.4. Rules 39.8 (application for bail pending appeal or retrial), 39.9 (conditions of bail pending   ★**P-459**
appeal or re-trial) and 39.10 (forfeiture of a recognizance given as a condition of bail) apply.

PART 44

REQUEST TO THE EUROPEAN COURT FOR A PRELIMINARY RULING

When this part applies
44.1. This part applies where the court can request the Court of Justice of the European Union   ★**P-460**
("the European Court") to give a preliminary ruling, under Article 267 of the Treaty on the Functioning of the European Union.

Preparation of request
44.2.—(1) The court may—   ★**P-461**
(a) make an order for the submission of a request—
(i) on application by a party, or
(ii) on its own initiative;
(b) give directions for the preparation of the terms of such a request.
(2) The court must—
(a) include in such a request—
(i) the identity of the court making the request,
(ii) the parties' identities,
(iii) a statement of whether a party is in custody,
(iv) a succinct statement of the question on which the court seeks the ruling of the
European Court,
(v) a succinct statement of any opinion on the answer that the court may have expressed
in any judgment that it has delivered,
(vi) a summary of the nature and history of the proceedings, including the salient facts
and an indication of whether those facts are proved, admitted or assumed,
(vii) the relevant rules of national law,
(viii) a summary of the relevant contentions of the parties,
(ix) an indication of the provisions of European Union law that the European Court is
asked to interpret, and
(x) an explanation of why a ruling of the European Court is requested;
(b) express the request in terms that can be translated readily into other languages; and
(c) set out the request in a schedule to the order.

Submission of request
44.3.—(1) The court officer must serve the order for the submission of the request on the Senior   ★**P-462**
Master of the Queen's Bench Division of the High Court.
(2) The Senior Master must—
(a) submit the request to the European Court; but
(b) unless the court otherwise directs, postpone the submission of the request until—
(i) the time for any appeal against the order has expired, and
(ii) any appeal against the order has been determined.

PART 45

COSTS

General Rules

When this part applies
45.1.—(1) This part applies where the court can make an order about costs under—   ★**P-463**

1081

(a) Part II of the Prosecution of Offences Act 1985 and Part II, IIA or IIB of The Costs in Criminal Cases (General) Regulations 1986;
(b) section 109 of the Magistrates' Courts Act 1980;
(c) section 52 of the Senior Courts Act 1981 and rule 76.6 or rule 76.7;
(d) section 8 of the Bankers Books Evidence Act 1879;
(e) section 2C(8) of the Criminal Procedure (Attendance of Witnesses) Act 1965;
(f) section 36(5) of the Criminal Justice Act 1972;
(g) section 159(5) and Schedule 3, paragraph 11, of the Criminal Justice Act 1988;
(h) section 14H(5) of the Football Spectators Act 1989;
(i) section 4(7) of the Dangerous Dogs Act 1991;
(j) Part 3 of the Serious Crime Act 2007 (Appeals under Section 24) Order 2008; or
(k) Part 1 or 2 of the Extradition Act 2003.

(2) In this part, "costs" means—
(a) the fees payable to a legal representative;
(b) the disbursements paid by a legal representative; and
(c) any other expenses incurred in connection with the case.

Costs orders: general rules

★**P-464**   45.2.—(1) The court must not make an order about costs unless each party and any other person directly affected—
(a) is present; or
(b) has had an opportunity—
   (i) to attend, or
   (ii) to make representations.

(2) The court may make an order about costs—
(a) at a hearing in public or in private; or
(b) without a hearing.

(3) In deciding what order, if any, to make about costs, the court must have regard to all the circumstances, including—
(a) the conduct of all the parties; and
(b) any costs order already made.

(4) If the court makes an order about costs, it must—
(a) specify who must, or must not, pay what, to whom; and
(b) identify the legislation under which the order is made, where there is a choice of powers.

(5) The court must give reasons if it—
(a) refuses an application for a costs order; or
(b) rejects representations opposing a costs order.

(6) If the court makes an order for the payment of costs—
(a) the general rule is that it must be for an amount that is sufficient reasonably to compensate the recipient for costs—
   (i) actually, reasonably and properly incurred, and
   (ii) reasonable in amount; but
(b) the court may order the payment of—
   (i) a proportion of that amount,
   (ii) a stated amount less than that amount,
   (iii) costs from or until a certain date only,
   (iv) costs relating only to particular steps taken, or
   (v) costs relating only to a distinct part of the case.

(7) On an assessment of the amount of costs, relevant factors include—
(a) the conduct of all the parties;
(b) the particular complexity of the matter or the difficulty or novelty of the questions raised;
(c) the skill, effort, specialised knowledge and responsibility involved;
(d) the time spent on the case;
(e) the place where and the circumstances in which work or any part of it was done; and
(f) any direction or observations by the court that made the costs order.

(8) If the court orders a party to pay costs to be assessed under rule 45.11, it may order that party to pay an amount on account.

(9) An order for the payment of costs takes effect when the amount is assessed, unless the court exercises any power it has to order otherwise.

Court's power to vary requirements

45.3.—(1) The court may— ★**P-465**

 (a) extend a time limit for serving an application or representations under rules 45.4 to 45.10, even after it has expired; and

 (b) consider an application or representations—

  (i) made in a different form to one set out in the Practice Direction, or

  (ii) made orally instead of in writing.

(2) A person who wants an extension of time must—

 (a) apply when serving the application or representations for which it is needed; and

 (b) explain the delay.

Costs Out of Central Funds

Costs out of central funds

45.4.—(1) This rule applies where the court can order the payment of costs out of central funds. ★**P-466**

(2) In this rule, costs—

 (a) include—

  (i) on an appeal, costs incurred in the court that made the decision under appeal, and

  (ii) at a retrial, costs incurred at the initial trial and on any appeal; but

 (b) do not include costs met by legal aid.

(3) The court may make an order—

 (a) on application by the person who incurred the costs; or

 (b) on its own initiative.

(4) Where a person wants the court to make an order that person must—

 (a) apply as soon as practicable; and

 (b) outline the type of costs and the amount claimed, if that person wants the court to direct an assessment; or

 (c) specify the amount claimed, if that person wants the court to assess the amount itself.

(5) The general rule is that the court must make an order, but—

 (a) the court may decline to make a defendant's costs order if, for example—

  (i) the defendant is convicted of at least one offence, or

  (ii) the defendant's conduct led the prosecutor reasonably to think the prosecution case stronger than it was; and

 (b) the court may decline to make a prosecutor's costs order if, for example, the prosecution was started or continued unreasonably.

(6) If the court makes an order—

 (a) the court may direct an assessment under, as applicable—

  (i) Part III of the Costs in Criminal Cases (General) Regulations 1986, or

  (ii) Part 3 of the Serious Crime Act 2007 (Appeals under Section 24) Order 2008;

 (b) the court may assess the amount itself in a case in which either—

  (i) the recipient agrees the amount, or

  (ii) the court decides to allow a lesser sum than that which is reasonably sufficient to compensate the recipient for expenses properly incurred in the proceedings;

 (c) an order for the payment of a defendant's costs which includes an amount in respect of fees payable to a legal representative, or disbursements paid by a legal representative, must include a statement to that effect.

(7) If the court directs an assessment, the order must specify any restriction on the amount to be paid that the court considers appropriate.

(8) If the court assesses the amount itself, it must do so subject to any restriction on the amount to be paid that is imposed by regulations made by the Lord Chancellor.

Payment of Costs by One Party to Another

Costs on conviction and sentence, etc.

45.5.—(1) This rule applies where the court can order a defendant to pay the prosecutor's costs if ★**P-467** the defendant is—

 (a) convicted or found guilty;

 (b) dealt with in the Crown Court after committal for sentence there;

 (c) dealt with for breach of a sentence; or

(d) in an extradition case—

    (i) ordered to be extradited, under Part 1 of the Extradition Act 2003,

    (ii) sent for extradition to the Secretary of State, under Part 2 of that Act, or

    (iii) unsuccessful on an appeal by the defendant to the High Court, or on an application by the defendant for permission to appeal from the High Court to the Supreme Court.

(2) The court may make an order—

    (a) on application by the prosecutor; or

    (b) on its own initiative.

(3) Where the prosecutor wants the court to make an order—

    (a) the prosecutor must—

        (i) apply as soon as practicable, and

        (ii) specify the amount claimed; and

    (b) the general rule is that the court must make an order if it is satisfied that the defendant can pay.

(4) A defendant who wants to oppose an order must make representations as soon as practicable.

(5) If the court makes an order, it must assess the amount itself.

Costs on appeal

★**P-468** **45.6.**—(1) This rule—

    (a) applies where a magistrates' court, the Crown Court or the Court of Appeal can order a party to pay another person's costs on an appeal, or an application for permission to appeal;

    (b) authorises the Crown Court, in addition to its other powers, to order a party to pay another party's costs on an appeal to that court, except on an appeal under—

        (i) section 108 of the Magistrates' Courts Act 1980, or

        (ii) section 45 of the Mental Health Act 1983.

(2) In this rule, costs include—

    (a) costs incurred in the court that made the decision under appeal; and

    (b) costs met by legal aid.

(3) The court may make an order—

    (a) on application by the person who incurred the costs; or

    (b) on its own initiative.

(4) A person who wants the court to make an order must—

    (a) apply as soon as practicable;

    (b) notify each other party;

    (c) specify—

        (i) the amount claimed, and

        (ii) against whom; and

    (d) where an appellant abandons an appeal to the Crown Court by serving a notice of abandonment—

        (i) apply in writing not more than 14 days later, and

        (ii) serve the application on the appellant and on the Crown Court officer.

(5) A party who wants to oppose an order must—

    (a) make representations as soon as practicable; and

    (b) where the application was under paragraph (4)(d), serve written representations on the applicant, and on the Crown Court officer, not more than 7 days after it was served.

(6) Where the application was under paragraph (4)(d), the Crown Court officer may—

    (a) submit it to the Crown Court; or

    (b) serve it on the magistrates' court officer, for submission to the magistrates' court.

(7) If the court makes an order, it may direct an assessment under rule 45.6, or assess the amount itself where—

    (a) the appellant abandons an appeal to the Crown Court;

    (b) the Crown Court decides an appeal, except an appeal under—

        (i) section 108 of the Magistrates' Courts Act 1980, or

        (ii) section 45 of the Mental Health Act 1983; or

    (c) the Court of Appeal decides an appeal to which Part 40 applies (appeal to the Court of Appeal about reporting or public access restriction).

(8) If the court makes an order in any other case, it must assess the amount itself.

Costs on an application

45.7.—(1) This rule—   ★**P-469**

   (a) applies where the court can order a party to pay another person's costs in a case in which—

      (i) the court decides an application for the production in evidence of a copy of a bank record,

      (ii) a magistrates' court or the Crown Court decides an application to terminate a football banning order,

      (iii) a magistrates' court or the Crown Court decides an application to terminate a disqualification for having custody of a dog,

      (iv) the Crown Court allows an application to withdraw a witness summons, or

      (v) the Crown Court decides an application relating to a deferred prosecution agreement under rule 11.5 (breach), rule 11.6 (variation) or rule 11.7 (lifting suspension of prosecution);

   (b) authorises the Crown Court, in addition to its other powers, to order a party to pay another party's costs on an application to that court under rule 11.5, 11.6 or 11.7.

(2) The court may make an order—

   (a) on application by the person who incurred the costs; or

   (b) on its own initiative.

(3) A person who wants the court to make an order must—

   (a) apply as soon as practicable;

   (b) notify each other party; and

   (c) specify—

      (i) the amount claimed, and

      (ii) against whom.

(4) A party who wants to oppose an order must make representations as soon as practicable.

(5) If the court makes an order, it may direct an assessment under rule 45.11, or assess the amount itself.

Costs resulting from unnecessary or improper act, etc.

45.8.—(1) This rule applies where the court can order a party to pay another party's costs incurred   ★**P-470**
as a result of an unnecessary or improper act or omission by or on behalf of the first party.

(2) In this rule, costs include costs met by legal aid.

(3) The court may make an order—

   (a) on application by the party who incurred such costs; or

   (b) on its own initiative.

(4) A party who wants the court to make an order must—

   (a) apply in writing as soon as practicable after becoming aware of the grounds for doing so;

   (b) serve the application on—

      (i) the court officer (or, in the Court of Appeal, the Registrar), and

      (ii) each other party;

   (c) in that application specify—

      (i) the party by whom costs should be paid,

      (ii) the relevant act or omission,

      (iii) the reasons why that act or omission meets the criteria for making an order,

      (iv) the amount claimed, and

      (v) those on whom the application has been served.

(5) Where the court considers making an order on its own initiative, it must—

   (a) identify the party against whom it proposes making the order; and

   (b) specify—

      (i) the relevant act or omission,

      (ii) the reasons why that act or omission meets the criteria for making an order, and

      (iii) with the assistance of the party who incurred the costs, the amount involved.

(6) A party who wants to oppose an order must—

   (a) make representations as soon as practicable; and

   (b) in reply to an application, serve written representations on the applicant and on the court officer (or Registrar) not more than 7 days after it was served.

(7) If the court makes an order, it must assess the amount itself.

Other Costs Orders

Costs against a legal representative

★**P-471**   **45.9.**—(1) This rule applies where—

    (a) a party has incurred costs—

        (i) as a result of an improper, unreasonable or negligent act or omission by a legal or other representative or representative's employee, or

        (ii) which it has become unreasonable for that party to have to pay because of such an act or omission occurring after those costs were incurred; and

    (b) the court can—

        (i) order the representative responsible to pay such costs, or

        (ii) prohibit the payment of costs to that representative.

(2) In this rule, costs include costs met by legal aid.

(3) The court may make an order—

    (a) on application by the party who incurred such costs; or

    (b) on its own initiative.

(4) A party who wants the court to make an order must—

    (a) apply in writing as soon as practicable after becoming aware of the grounds for doing so;

    (b) serve the application on—

        (i) the court officer (or, in the Court of Appeal, the Registrar),

        (ii) the representative responsible,

        (iii) each other party, and

        (iv) any other person directly affected;

    (c) in that application specify—

        (i) the representative responsible,

        (ii) the relevant act or omission,

        (iii) the reasons why that act or omission meets the criteria for making an order,

        (iv) the amount claimed, and

        (v) those on whom the application has been served.

(5) Where the court considers making an order on its own initiative, it must—

    (a) identify the representative against whom it proposes making that order; and

    (b) specify—

        (i) the relevant act or omission,

        (ii) the reasons why that act or omission meets the criteria for making an order, and

        (iii) with the assistance of the party who incurred the costs, the amount involved.

(6) A representative who wants to oppose an order must—

    (a) make representations as soon as practicable; and

    (b) in reply to an application, serve written representations on the applicant and on the court officer (or Registrar) not more than 7 days after it was served.

(7) If the court makes an order—

    (a) the general rule is that it must do so without waiting until the end of the case, but it may postpone making the order; and

    (b) it must assess the amount itself.

(8) Instead of making an order, the court may make adverse observations about the representative's conduct for use in an assessment where—

    (a) a party's costs are—

        (i) to be met by legal aid, or

        (ii) to be paid out of central funds; or

    (b) there is to be an assessment under rule 45.11.

Costs against a third party

★**P-472**   **45.10.**—(1) This rule applies where—

    (a) there has been serious misconduct by a person who is not a party; and

    (b) the court can order that person to pay a party's costs.

(2) In this rule, costs include costs met by legal aid.

(3) The court may make an order—

(a) on application by the party who incurred the costs; or

(b) on its own initiative.

(4) A party who wants the court to make an order must—

(a) apply in writing as soon as practicable after becoming aware of the grounds for doing so;

(b) serve the application on—

   (i) the court officer (or, in the Court of Appeal, the Registrar),

   (ii) the person responsible,

   (iii) each other party, and

   (iv) any other person directly affected;

(c) in that application specify—

   (i) the person responsible,

   (ii) the relevant misconduct,

   (iii) the reasons why the criteria for making an order are met,

   (iv) the amount claimed, and

   (v) those on whom the application has been served.

(5) Where the court considers making an order on its own initiative, it must—

(a) identify the person against whom it proposes making that order; and

(b) specify—

   (i) the relevant misconduct,

   (ii) the reasons why the criteria for making an order are met, and

   (iii) with the assistance of the party who incurred the costs, the amount involved.

(6) A person who wants to oppose an order must—

(a) make representations as soon as practicable; and

(b) in reply to an application, serve written representations on the applicant and on the court officer (or Registrar) not more than 7 days after it was served.

(7) If the court makes an order—

(a) the general rule is that it must do so at the end of the case, but it may do so earlier; and

(b) it must assess the amount itself.

Assessment of Costs

Assessment and re-assessment

45.11.—(1) This rule applies where the court directs an assessment under— **★P-473**

(a) rule 33.48 (confiscation and related proceedings – restraint and receivership proceedings: rules that apply generally – assessment of costs);

(b) rule 45.6 (costs on appeal); or

(c) rule 45.7 (costs on an application).

(2) The assessment must be carried out by the relevant assessing authority, namely—

(a) the Lord Chancellor, where the direction was given by a magistrates' court or by the Crown Court; or

(b) the Registrar, where the direction was given by the Court of Appeal.

(3) The party in whose favour the court made the costs order ("the applicant") must—

(a) apply for an assessment—

   (i) in writing, in any form required by the assessing authority, and

   (ii) not more than 3 months after the costs order; and

(b) serve the application on—

   (i) the assessing authority, and

   (ii) the party against whom the court made the costs order ("the respondent").

(4) The applicant must—

(a) summarise the work done;

(b) specify—

   (i) each item of work done, giving the date, time taken and amount claimed,

   (ii) any disbursements or expenses, including the fees of any advocate, and

   (iii) any circumstances of which the applicant wants the assessing authority to take particular account; and

(c) supply—

   (i) receipts or other evidence of the amount claimed, and

   (ii) any other information or document for which the assessing authority asks, within such period as that authority may require.

(5) A respondent who wants to make representations about the amount claimed must—

    (a) do so in writing; and

    (b) serve the representations on the assessing authority, and on the applicant, not more than 21 days after service of the application.

(6) The assessing authority must—

    (a) if it seems likely to help with the assessment, obtain any other information or document;

    (b) resolve in favour of the respondent any doubt about what should be allowed; and

    (c) serve the assessment on the parties.

(7) Where either party wants the amount allowed re-assessed—

    (a) that party must—

        (i) apply to the assessing authority, in writing and in any form required by that authority,

        (ii) serve the application on the assessing authority, and on the other party, not more than 21 days after service of the assessment,

        (iii) explain the objections to the assessment,

        (iv) supply any additional supporting information or document, and

        (v) ask for a hearing, if that party wants one; and

    (b) a party who wants to make representations about an application for re-assessment must—

        (i) do so in writing,

        (ii) serve the representations on the assessing authority, and on the other party, not more than 21 days after service of the application, and

        (iii) ask for a hearing, if that party wants one;

    (c) the assessing authority—

        (i) must arrange a hearing, in public or in private, if either party asks for one,

        (ii) subject to that, may re-assess the amount allowed with or without a hearing,

        (iii) must re-assess the amount allowed on the initial assessment, taking into account the reasons for disagreement with that amount and any other representations,

        (iv) may maintain, increase or decrease the amount allowed on the assessment,

        (v) must serve the re-assessment on the parties, and

        (vi) must serve written reasons on the parties, if not more than 21 days later either party asks for such reasons.

(8) A time limit under this rule may be extended even after it has expired—

    (a) by the assessing authority, or

    (b) by the Senior Costs Judge, if the assessing authority declines to do so.

Appeal to a costs judge

★P-474   **45.12.**—(1) This rule applies where—

    (a) the assessing authority has re-assessed the amount allowed under rule 45.11; and

    (b) either party wants to appeal against that amount.

(2) That party must—

    (a) serve an appeal notice on—

        (i) the Senior Costs Judge,

        (ii) the other party, and

        (iii) the assessing authority

    not more than 21 days after service of the written reasons for the re-assessment;

    (b) explain the objections to the re-assessment;

    (c) serve on the Senior Costs Judge with the appeal notice—

        (i) the applications for assessment and re-assessment,

        (ii) any other information or document considered by the assessing authority,

        (iii) the assessing authority's written reasons for the re-assessment, and

        (iv) any other information or document for which a costs judge asks, within such period as the judge may require; and

    (d) ask for a hearing, if that party wants one.

(3) A party who wants to make representations about an appeal must—

    (a) serve representations in writing on—

        (i) the Senior Costs Judge, and

        (ii) the applicant

    not more than 21 days after service of the appeal notice; and

(b) ask for a hearing, if that party wants one.

(4) Unless a costs judge otherwise directs, the parties may rely only on—

    (a) the objections to the amount allowed on the initial assessment; and

    (b) any other representations and material considered by the assessing authority.

(5) A costs judge—

    (a) must arrange a hearing, in public or in private, if either party asks for one;

    (b) subject to that, may determine an appeal with or without a hearing;

    (c) may—

        (i) consult the assessing authority,

        (ii) consult the court which made the costs order, and

        (iii) obtain any other information or document;

    (d) must reconsider the amount allowed by the assessing authority, taking into account the objections to the re-assessment and any other representations;

    (e) may maintain, increase or decrease the amount allowed on the re-assessment;

    (f) may provide for the costs incurred by either party to the appeal; and

    (g) must serve reasons for the decision on—

        (i) the parties, and

        (ii) the assessing authority.

(6) A costs judge may extend a time limit under this rule, even after it has expired.

Appeal to a High Court judge

45.13.—(1) This rule applies where—   **★P-475**

    (a) a costs judge has determined an appeal under rule 45.12; and

    (b) either party wants to appeal against the amount allowed.

(2) A party who wants to appeal—

    (a) may do so only if a costs judge certifies that a point of principle of general importance was involved in the decision on the review; and

    (b) must apply in writing for such a certificate and serve the application on—

        (i) the costs judge,

        (ii) the other party

    not more than 21 days after service of the decision on the review.

(3) That party must—

    (a) appeal to a judge of the High Court attached to the Queen's Bench Division as if it were an appeal from the decision of a master under Part 52 of the Civil Procedure Rules 1998; and

    (b) serve the appeal not more than 21 days after service of the costs judge's certificate under paragraph (2).

(4) A High Court judge—

    (a) may extend a time limit under this rule even after it has expired;

    (b) has the same powers and duties as a costs judge under rule 45.12; and

    (c) may hear the appeal with one or more assessors.

Application for an extension of time

45.14. A party who wants an extension of time under rule 45.11, 45.12 or 45.13 must—   **★P-476**

    (a) apply in writing;

    (b) explain the delay; and

    (c) attach the application, representations or appeal for which the extension of time is needed.

PART 46

REPRESENTATIVES

Functions of representatives and supporters

46.1.—(1) Under these rules, anything that a party may or must do may be done—   **★P-477**

    (a) by a legal representative on that party's behalf;

    (b) by a person with the corporation's written authority, where that corporation is a defendant;

    (c) with the help of a parent, guardian or other suitable supporting adult where that party is a defendant—

        (i) who is under 18, or

    (ii)   whose understanding of what the case involves is limited

unless other legislation (including a rule) otherwise requires.

    (2) A member, officer or employee of a prosecutor may, on the prosecutor's behalf—

      (a)   serve on the magistrates' court officer, or present to a magistrates' court, an information under section 1 of the Magistrates' Courts Act 1980; or

      (b)   issue a written charge and requisition, or single justice procedure notice, under section 29 of the Criminal Justice Act 2003.

Notice of appointment, etc. of legal representative: general rules

★P-478   **46.2.**—(1) This rule applies—

      (a)   in relation to a party who does not have legal aid for the purposes of a case;

      (b)   where such a party—

         (i)   appoints a legal representative for the purposes of the case, or

        (ii)   dismisses such a representative, with or without appointing another;

      (c)   where a legal representative for such a party withdraws from the case.

    (2) Where paragraph (1)(b) applies, that party must give notice of the appointment or dismissal to—

      (a)   the court officer;

      (b)   each other party; and

      (c)   where applicable, the legal representative who has been dismissed,

as soon as practicable and in any event within 5 business days.

    (3) Where paragraph (1)(c) applies, that legal representative must, as soon as practicable, give notice to—

      (a)   the court officer;

      (b)   the party whom he or she has represented; and

      (c)   each other party.

    (4) Any such notice—

      (a)   may be given orally, but only if—

         (i)   it is given at a hearing, and

        (ii)   it specifies no restriction under paragraph (5)(b) (restricted scope of appointment);

      (b)   otherwise, must be in writing.

    (5) A notice of the appointment of a legal representative—

      (a)   must identify—

         (i)   the legal representative who has been appointed, with details of how to contact that representative, and

        (ii)   all those to whom the notice is given;

      (b)   may specify a restriction, or restrictions, on the purpose or duration of the appointment; and

      (c)   if it specifies any such restriction, may nonetheless provide that documents may continue to be served on the represented party at the representative's address until—

         (i)   further notice is given under this rule, or

        (ii)   that party obtains legal aid for the purposes of the case.

    (6) A legal representative who is dismissed by a party or who withdraws from representing a party must, as soon as practicable, make available to that party such documents in the representative's possession as have been served on that party.

Application to change legal representative: legal aid

★P-479   **46.3.**—(1) This rule applies—

      (a)   in relation to a party who has legal aid for the purposes of a case;

      (b)   where such a party wants to select a legal representative in place of the representative named in the legal aid representation order.

    (2) Such a party must—

      (a)   apply in writing as soon as practicable after becoming aware of the grounds for doing so; and

      (b)   serve the application on—

         (i)   the court officer, and

        (ii)   the legal representative named in the legal aid representation order.

    (3) The application must—

      (a)   explain what the case is about, including what offences are alleged, what stage it has reached and what is likely to be in issue at trial;

(b) explain how and why the applicant chose the legal representative named in the legal aid representation order;

(c) if an advocate other than that representative has been instructed for the applicant, explain whether the applicant wishes to replace that advocate;

(d) explain, giving relevant facts and dates—

   (i) in what way, in the applicant's opinion, there has been a breakdown in the relationship between the applicant and the current representative such that neither the individual representing the applicant nor any colleague of his or hers any longer can provide effective representation, or

   (ii) what other compelling reason, in the applicant's opinion, means that neither the individual representing the applicant nor any colleague of his or hers any longer can provide effective representation;

(e) give details of any previous application by the applicant to replace the legal representative named in the legal aid representation order;

(f) state whether the applicant—

   (i) waives the legal professional privilege attaching to the applicant's communications with the current representative, to the extent required to allow that representative to respond to the matters set out in the application, or

   (ii) declines to waive that privilege and acknowledges that the court may draw such inferences as it thinks fit in consequence;

(g) explain how and why the applicant has chosen the proposed new representative;

(h) include or attach a statement by the proposed new representative which—

   (i) confirms that that representative is eligible and willing to conduct the case for the applicant,

   (ii) confirms that that representative can and will meet the current timetable for the case, including any hearing date or dates that have been set, if the application succeeds,

   (iii) explains what, if any, dealings that representative has had with the applicant before the present case; and

(i) ask for a hearing, if the applicant wants one, and explain why it is needed.

(4) The legal representative named in the legal aid representation order must—

(a) respond in writing no more than 5 business days after service of the application; and

(b) serve the response on—

   (i) the court officer,

   (ii) the applicant, and

   (iii) the proposed new representative.

(5) The response must—

(a) explain which, if any, of the matters set out in the application the current representative disputes;

(b) explain, as appropriate, giving relevant facts and dates—

   (i) whether, and if so in what way, in the current representative's opinion, there has been a breakdown in the relationship with the applicant such that neither the individual representing the applicant nor any colleague of his or hers any longer can provide effective representation,

   (ii) whether, in the current representative's opinion, there is some other compelling reason why neither the individual representing the applicant nor any colleague of his or hers any longer can provide effective representation, and if so what reason,

   (iii) whether the current representative considers there to be a duty to withdraw from the case in accordance with professional rules of conduct, and if so the nature of that duty, and

   (iv) whether the current representative no longer is able to represent the applicant through circumstances outside the representative's control, and if so the particular circumstances that render the representative unable to do so;

(c) explain what, if any, dealings the current representative had had with the applicant before the present case; and

(d) ask for a hearing, if the current representative wants one, and explain why it is needed.

(6) The court may determine the application—

(a) without a hearing, as a general rule; or

(b) at a hearing, which must be in private unless the court otherwise directs.

(7) Unless the court otherwise directs, any hearing must be in the absence of each other party and each other party's representative and advocate (if any).

(8) If the court allows the application, as soon as practicable—

    (a) the current representative must make available to the new representative such document in the current representative's possession as have been served on the applicant party; and

    (b) the new representative must serve notice of appointment on each other party.

(9) Paragraph (10) applies where—

    (a) the court refuses the application;

    (b) in response to that decision—

        (i) the applicant declines further representation by the current representative or asks for legal aid to be withdrawn, or

        (ii) the current representative declines further to represent the applicant; and

    (c) the court in consequence withdraws the applicant's legal aid.

(10) The court officer must serve notice of the withdrawal of legal aid on—

    (a) the applicant; and

    (b) the current representative.

PART 47

INVESTIGATION ORDERS AND WARRANTS

Section 1: Understanding and Applying this Part

When this part applies

★P-480   **47.1.**—(1) Sections 2 and 3 of this part apply where, for the purposes of a terrorist investigation—

    (a) a circuit judge can make, vary or discharge—

        (i) an order for the production of, or for giving access to, material, or for a statement of its location, under paragraphs 5 and 10 of Schedule 5 to the Terrorism Act 2000,

        (ii) an explanation order, under paragraphs 10 and 13 of Schedule 5 to the 2000 Act,

        (iii) a customer information order, under paragraphs 1 and 4 of Schedule 6 to the 2000 Act;

    (b) a circuit judge can make, and the Crown Court can vary or discharge, an account monitoring order, under paragraphs 2 and 4 of Schedule 6A to the 2000 Act.

(2) Sections 2 and 4 of this part apply where, for the purposes of an investigation to which Part 8 of the Proceeds of Crime Act 2002 or the Proceeds of Crime Act 2002 (External Investigations) Order 2014 applies, a Crown Court judge can make, and the Crown Court can vary or discharge—

    (a) a production order, under sections 345 and 351 of the 2002 Act or under articles 6 and 12 of the 2014 Order;

    (b) an order to grant entry, under sections 347 and 351 of the 2002 Act or under articles 8 and 12 of the 2014 Order;

    (c) a disclosure order, under sections 357 and 362 of the 2002 Act or under articles 16 and 21 of the 2014 Order;

    (d) a customer information order, under sections 363 and 369 of the 2002 Act or under articles 22 and 28 of the 2014 Order;

    (e) an account monitoring order, under sections 370, 373 and 375 of the 2002 Act or under articles 29, 32 and 34 of the 2014 Order.

(3) Rule 47.5 and Section 5 of this part apply where—

    (a) a justice of the peace can make or discharge an investigation anonymity order, under sections 76 and 80(1) of the Coroners and Justice Act 2009;

    (b) a Crown Court judge can determine an appeal against—

        (i) a refusal of such an order, under section 79 of the 2009 Act,

        (ii) a decision on an application to discharge such an order, under section 80(6) of the 2009 Act.

(4) Sections 2 and 6 of this part apply where a justice of the peace can make an order approving—

    (a) the grant or renewal of an authorisation, or the giving or renewal of a notice, under section 23A of the Regulation of Investigatory Powers Act 2000;

    (b) the grant or renewal of an authorisation under section 32A of the 2000 Act.

(5) Rule 47.5 and Section 7 of this part apply where a justice of the peace can issue a warrant under—

    (a) section 8 of the Police and Criminal Evidence Act 1984;

    (b) section 2 of the Criminal Justice Act 1987;

    (c)   other powers to which sections 15 and 16 of the Police and Criminal Evidence Act 1984 apply.

(6) Rules 47.4 and 47.5 and Section 8 of this part apply where—

    (a)   a District Judge (Magistrates' Court) can make an order under—

        (i)   section 63F(7) or 63R(6) of the Police and Criminal Evidence Act 1984, or

        (ii)   paragraph 20B(5) or 20G(6) of Schedule 8 to the Terrorism Act 2000;

    (b)   the Crown Court can determine an appeal under—

        (i)   section 63F(10) of the Police and Criminal Evidence Act 1984, or

        (ii)   paragraph 20B(8) of Schedule 8 to the Terrorism Act 2000.

Meaning of "court", "applicant" and "respondent"

47.2. In this part—   **★P-481**

    (a)   a reference to the "court" includes a reference to any justice of the peace or judge who can exercise a power to which this part applies;

    (b)   "applicant" means a person who, or an authority which, can apply for an order or warrant to which this part applies; and

    (c)   "respondent" means any person—

        (i)   against whom such an order is sought or made, or

        (ii)   on whom an application for such an order is served.

Section 2: General Rules

Exercise of court's powers

47.3.—(1) Subject to paragraphs (2) and (3), the court may determine an application for an order, **★P-482**
or to vary or discharge an order—

    (a)   at a hearing (which must be in private unless the court otherwise directs), or without a hearing; and

    (b)   in the absence of—

        (i)   the applicant,

        (ii)   the respondent (if any),

        (iii)   any other person affected by the order.

(2) The court must not determine such an application in the applicant's absence if—

    (a)   the applicant asks for a hearing; or

    (b)   it appears to the court that—

        (i)   the proposed order may infringe legal privilege, within the meaning of section 10 of the Police and Criminal Evidence Act 1984 or of section 348 or 361 of the Proceeds of Crime Act 2002,

        (ii)   the proposed order may require the production of excluded material, within the meaning of section 11 of the 1984 Act, or

        (iii)   for any other reason the application is so complex or serious as to require the court to hear the applicant.

(3) The court must not determine such an application in the absence of any respondent or other person affected, unless—

    (a)   the absentee has had at least 2 business days in which to make representations; or

    (b)   the court is satisfied that—

        (i)   the applicant cannot identify or contact the absentee,

        (ii)   it would prejudice the investigation if the absentee were present,

        (iii)   it would prejudice the investigation to adjourn or postpone the application so as to allow the absentee to attend, or

        (iv)   the absentee has waived the opportunity to attend.

(4) The court must not make, vary or discharge an order unless the applicant states, in writing or orally, that to the best of the applicant's knowledge and belief—

    (a)   the application discloses all the information that is material to what the court must decide; and

    (b)   the content of the application is true.

(5) Where the statement required by paragraph (4) is made orally—

    (a)   the statement must be on oath or affirmation, unless the court otherwise directs; and

    (b)   the court must arrange for a record of the making of the statement.

Court's power to vary requirements under this part

★P-483   **47.4.**—(1) The court may—

    (a) shorten or extend (even after it has expired) a time limit under this part;

    (b) dispense with a requirement for service under this part (even after service was required) and

    (c) consider an application made orally instead of in writing.

    (2) A person who wants an extension of time must—

    (a) apply when serving the application for which it is needed; and

    (b) explain the delay.

Documents served on the court officer

★P-484   **47.5.**—(1) Unless the court otherwise directs, the court officer may—

    (a) keep a written application; or

    (b) arrange for the whole or any part to be kept by some other appropriate person, subject to any conditions that the court may impose.

    (2) Where the court makes an order when the court office is closed, the applicant must, not more than 72 hours later, serve on the court officer—

    (a) a copy of the order; and

    (b) any written material that was submitted to the court.

    (3) Where the court issues a warrant—

    (a) the applicant must return it to the court officer as soon as practicable after it has been executed, and in any event not more than 3 months after it was issued (unless other legislation otherwise provides); and

    (b) the court officer must—

      (i) keep the warrant for 12 months after its return, and

      (ii) during that period, make it available for inspection by the occupier of the premises to which it relates, if that occupier asks to inspect it.

Section 3: Orders under the Terrorism Act 2000

Application for an order under the Terrorism Act 2000

★P-485   **47.6.**—(1) This rule applies where an applicant wants the court to make one of the orders listed in rule 47.1(1).

    (2) The applicant must—

    (a) apply in writing;

    (b) serve the application on—

      (i) the court officer, and

      (ii) the respondent (unless the court otherwise directs);

    (c) identify the respondent;

    (d) give the information required by whichever of rules 47.7 to 47.10 applies; and

    (e) serve any order made on the respondent.

Content of application for a production etc. order

★P-486   **47.7.** As well as complying with rule 47.6, an applicant who wants the court to make an order for the production of, or access to, material, or for a statement of its location, must—

    (a) describe that material;

    (b) explain why the applicant thinks the material is—

      (i) in the respondent's possession, custody or power, or

      (ii) likely to be so within 28 days of the order;

    (c) explain how the material constitutes or contains excluded material or special procedure material;

    (d) confirm that none of the material is expected to be subject to legal privilege;

    (e) explain why the material is likely to be of substantial value to the investigation;

    (f) explain why it is in the public interest for the material to be produced, or for the applicant to be given access to it, having regard to—

      (i) the benefit likely to accrue to the investigation if it is obtained, and

      (ii) the circumstances in which the respondent has the material, or is expected to have it; and

    (g) propose—

    (i)   the terms of the order, and

    (ii) the period within which it should take effect.

Content of application for an explanation order

47.8. As well as complying with rule 47.6, an applicant who wants the court to make an explanation order must—   ★**P-487**

    (a) identify the material that the applicant wants the respondent to explain;

    (b) confirm that the explanation is not expected to infringe legal privilege; and

    (c) propose—

        (i)   the terms of the order, and

        (ii) the period within which it should take effect, if 7 days from the date of the order would not be appropriate.

Content of application for a customer information order

47.9. As well as complying with rule 47.6, an applicant who wants the court to make a customer information order must—   ★**P-488**

    (a) explain why it is desirable for the purposes of the investigation to trace property said to be terrorist property within the meaning of the Terrorism Act 2000;

    (b) explain why the order will enhance the effectiveness of the investigation; and

    (c) propose the terms of the order.

Content of application for an account monitoring order

47.10. As well as complying with rule 47.6, an applicant who wants the court to make an account monitoring order must—   ★**P-489**

    (a) specify—

        (i)   the information sought,

        (ii) the period during which the applicant wants the respondent to provide that information (to a maximum of 90 days), and

        (iii) where, when and in what manner the applicant wants the respondent to provide that information;

    (b) explain why it is desirable for the purposes of the investigation to trace property said to be terrorist property within the meaning of the Terrorism Act 2000;

    (c) explain why the order will enhance the effectiveness of the investigation; and

    (d) propose the terms of the order.

Application to vary or discharge an order

47.11.—(1) This rule applies where one of the following wants the court to vary or discharge an order listed in rule 47.1(1)—   ★**P-490**

    (a) an applicant;

    (b) the respondent; or

    (c) a person affected by the order.

  (2) That applicant, respondent or person affected must—

    (a) apply in writing as soon as practicable after becoming aware of the grounds for doing so;

    (b) serve the application on—

        (i)   the court officer, and

        (ii) the respondent, applicant, or any person known to be affected, as applicable;

    (c) explain why it is appropriate for the order to be varied or discharged;

    (d) propose the terms of any variation; and

    (e) ask for a hearing, if one is wanted, and explain why it is needed.

Application containing information withheld from a respondent or other person

47.12.—(1) This rule applies where—   ★**P-491**

    (a) an applicant serves on a respondent or other person an application for one of the orders listed in rule 47.1(1), or for the variation or discharge of such an order; and

    (b) the application includes information that the applicant thinks ought not be revealed to that recipient.

  (2) The applicant must—

    (a) omit that information from the part of the application that is served on the respondent or other person;

    (b) mark the other part, to show that it is only for the court; and

    (c) in that other part, explain why the applicant has withheld it.

(3) A hearing of an application to which this rule applies may take place, wholly or in part, in the absence of the respondent and any other person.

(4) At a hearing of an application to which this rule applies—

    (a) the general rule is that the court must consider, in the following sequence—

        (i) representations first by the applicant and then by the respondent and any other person, in the presence of them all, and then

        (ii) further representations by the applicant, in the others' absence; but

    (b) the court may direct other arrangements for the hearing.

Application to punish for contempt of court

★P-492   **47.13.**—(1) This rule applies where a person is accused of disobeying—

    (a) a production etc. order made under paragraph 5 of Schedule 5 to the Terrorism Act 2000,

    (b) an explanation order made under paragraph 13 of that Schedule; or

    (c) an account monitoring order made under paragraph 2 of Schedule 6A to that Act.

(2) An applicant who wants the court to exercise its power to punish that person for contempt of court must comply with the rules in Part 48 (contempt of court).

Section 4: Orders under the Proceeds of Crime Act 2002 etc.

Application for an order under the Proceeds of Crime Act 2002 etc.

★P-493   **47.14.**—(1) This rule applies where an applicant wants the court to make one of the orders listed in rule 47.1(2).

(2) The applicant must—

    (a) apply in writing;

    (b) serve the application on—

        (i) the court officer, and

        (ii) the respondent (unless the court otherwise directs);

    (c) identify—

        (i) the respondent, and

        (ii) the person or property the subject of the investigation;

    (d) in the case of an investigation in the United Kingdom, explain why the applicant thinks that—

        (i) the person under investigation has benefited from criminal conduct, in the case of a confiscation investigation, or committed a money laundering offence, in the case of a money laundering investigation, or

        (ii) the cash involved is property obtained through unlawful conduct, or is intended to be used in unlawful conduct, in the case of a detained cash investigation;

    (e) in the case of an investigation outside the United Kingdom, explain why the applicant thinks that—

        (i) there is an investigation by an overseas authority which relates to a criminal investigation or to criminal proceedings (including proceedings to remove the benefit of a person's criminal conduct following that person's conviction), and

        (ii) the investigation is into whether property has been obtained as a result of or in connection with criminal conduct, or into the extent or whereabouts of such property;

    (f) give the additional information required by whichever of rules 47.15 to 47.19 applies; and

    (g) serve any order made on each respondent.

Content of application for a production order

★P-494   **47.15.** As well as complying with rule 47.14, an applicant who wants the court to make an order for the production of, or access to, material, must—

    (a) describe that material;

    (b) explain why the applicant thinks the material is in the respondent's possession or control;

    (c) confirm that none of the material is—

        (i) expected to be subject to legal privilege, or

        (ii) excluded material;

    (d) explain why the material is likely to be of substantial value to the investigation;

    (e) explain why it is in the public interest for the material to be produced, or for the applicant to be given access to it, having regard to—

(i) the benefit likely to accrue to the investigation if it is obtained, and

(ii) the circumstances in which the respondent has the material; and

(f) propose—

(i) the terms of the order, and

(ii) the period within which it should take effect, if 7 days from the date of the order would not be appropriate.

Content of application for an order to grant entry

47.16. An applicant who wants the court to make an order to grant entry in aid of a production **★P-495**
order must—

(a) specify the premises to which entry is sought;

(b) explain why the order is needed; and

(c) propose the terms of the order.

Content of application for a disclosure order

47.17. As well as complying with rule 47.14, an applicant who wants the court to make a disclosure **★P-496**
order must—

(a) describe in general terms the information that the applicant wants the respondent to provide;

(b) confirm that none of the information is—

(i) expected to be subject to legal privilege, or

(ii) excluded material;

(c) explain why the information is likely to be of substantial value to the investigation;

(d) explain why it is in the public interest for the information to be provided, having regard to the benefit likely to accrue to the investigation if it is obtained; and

(e) propose the terms of the order.

Content of application for a customer information order

47.18. As well as complying with rule 47.14, an applicant who wants the court to make a customer **★P-497**
information order must—

(a) explain why customer information about the person under investigation is likely to be of substantial value to that investigation;

(b) explain why it is in the public interest for the information to be provided, having regard to the benefit likely to accrue to the investigation if it is obtained; and

(c) propose the terms of the order.

Content of application for an account monitoring order

47.19. As well as complying with rule 47.14, an applicant who wants the court to make an account **★P-498**
monitoring order for the provision of account information must—

(a) specify—

(i) the information sought,

(ii) the period during which the applicant wants the respondent to provide that information (to a maximum of 90 days), and

(iii) when and in what manner the applicant wants the respondent to provide that information;

(b) explain why the information is likely to be of substantial value to the investigation;

(c) explain why it is in the public interest for the information to be provided, having regard to the benefit likely to accrue to the investigation if it is obtained; and

(d) propose the terms of the order.

Application to vary or discharge an order

47.20.—(1) This rule applies where one of the following wants the court to vary or discharge an **★P-499**
order listed in rule 47.1(2)—

(a) an applicant;

(b) the respondent; or

(c) a person affected by the order.

(2) That applicant, respondent or person affected must—

(a) apply in writing as soon as practicable after becoming aware of the grounds for doing so;

(b) serve the application on—

    (i)   the court officer, and

    (ii) the respondent, applicant, or any person known to be affected, as applicable;

  (c) explain why it is appropriate for the order to be varied or discharged;

  (d) propose the terms of any variation; and

  (e) ask for a hearing, if one is wanted, and explain why it is needed.

Application containing information withheld from a respondent or other person

★**P-500**
    47.21.—(1) This rule applies where—

  (a) an applicant serves on a respondent or other person an application for one of the order listed in rule 47.1(2), or for the variation or discharge of such an order; and

  (b) the application includes information that the applicant thinks ought not be revealed to tha recipient.

  (2) The applicant must—

  (a) omit that information from the part of the application that is served on the respondent o other person;

  (b) mark the other part, to show that it is only for the court; and

  (c) in that other part, explain why the applicant has withheld it.

  (3) A hearing of an application to which this rule applies may take place, wholly or in part, in the absence of the respondent and any other person.

  (4) At a hearing of an application to which this rule applies—

  (a) the general rule is that the court must consider, in the following sequence—

    (i)   representations first by the applicant and then by the respondent and any othe person, in the presence of them all, and then

    (ii) further representations by the applicant, in the others' absence; but

  (b) the court may direct other arrangements for the hearing.

Application to punish for contempt of court

★**P-501**
    47.22.—(1) This rule applies where a person is accused of disobeying—

  (a) a production order made under section 345 of the Proceeds of Crime Act 2002 or article 6 of the Proceeds of Crime Act 2002 (External Investigations) Order 2014; or

  (b) an account monitoring order made under section 370 of the 2002 Act or article 29 of the 2014 Order.

  (2) An applicant who wants the court to exercise its power to punish that person for contempt of court must comply with the rules in Part 48 (contempt of court).

Section 5: Orders under the Coroners and Justice Act 2009

Exercise of court's powers

★**P-502**
    47.23.—(1) The court may determine an application for an investigation anonymity order, and any appeal against the refusal of such an order—

  (a) at a hearing (which must be in private unless the court otherwise directs); or

  (b) without a hearing.

  (2) The court must determine an application to discharge an investigation anonymity order, and any appeal against the decision on such an application—

  (a) at a hearing (which must be in private unless the court otherwise directs); and

  (b) in the presence of the person specified in the order, unless—

    (i)   that person applied for the discharge of the order,

    (ii) that person has had an opportunity to make representations, or

    (iii) the court is satisfied that it is not reasonably practicable to communicate with that person.

  (3) The court may consider an application or an appeal made orally instead of in writing.

Application for an investigation anonymity order

★**P-503**
    47.24.—(1) This rule applies where an applicant wants a magistrates' court to make an investigation anonymity order.

  (2) The applicant must—

  (a) apply in writing;

  (b) serve the application on the court officer;

  (c) identify the person to be specified in the order, unless—

(i)   the applicant wants the court to determine the application at a hearing, or

(ii)   the court otherwise directs;

(d)   explain how the proposed order meets the conditions prescribed by section 78 of the Coroners and Justice Act 2009;

(e)   say if the applicant intends to appeal should the court refuse the order;

(f)   attach any material on which the applicant relies; and

(g)   propose the terms of the order.

(3) At any hearing of the application, the applicant must—

(a)   identify to the court the person to be specified in the order, unless—

(i)   the applicant has done so already, or

(ii)   the court otherwise directs; and

(b)   unless the applicant has done so already, inform the court if the applicant intends to appeal should the court refuse the order.

Application to discharge an investigation anonymity order

47.25.—(1) This rule applies where one of the following wants a magistrates' court to discharge an   **★P-504**
investigation anonymity order—

(a)   an applicant; or

(b)   the person specified in the order.

(2) That applicant or the specified person must—

(a)   apply in writing as soon as practicable after becoming aware of the grounds for doing so;

(b)   serve the application on—

(i)   the court officer, and as applicable

(ii)   the applicant for the order, and

(iii)   the specified person;

(c)   explain—

(i)   what material circumstances have changed since the order was made, or since any previous application was made to discharge it, and

(ii)   why it is appropriate for the order to be discharged; and

(d)   attach—

(i)   a copy of the order, and

(ii)   any material on which the applicant relies.

(3) A party must inform the court if that party intends to appeal should the court discharge the order.

Appeal

47.26.—(1) This rule applies where one of the following ("the appellant") wants to appeal to the   **★P-505**
Crown Court—

(a)   the applicant for an investigation anonymity order, where a magistrates' court has refused to make the order;

(b)   a party to an application to discharge such an order, where a magistrates' court has decided that application.

(2) The appellant must—

(a)   serve on the Crown Court officer a copy of the application to the magistrates' court; and

(b)   where the appeal concerns a discharge decision, notify each other party,

not more than 21 days after the decision against which the appellant wants to appeal.

(3) The Crown Court must hear the appeal without justices of the peace.

Section 6: Orders under the Regulation of Investigatory Powers Act 2000

Application for approval for authorisation or notice

47.27.—(1) This rule applies where an applicant wants a magistrates' court to make an order ap-   **★P-506**
proving—

(a)   under sections 23A and 23B of the Regulation of Investigatory Powers Act 2000—

(i)   an authorisation to obtain or disclose communications data, under section 22(3) of the 2000 Act, or

(ii)   a notice that requires a postal or telecommunications operator if need be to obtain, and in any case to disclose, communications data, under section 22(4) of the 2000 Act;

(b)   under sections 32A and 32B of the Regulation of Investigatory Powers Act 2000, an authorisation for—

    (i) the carrying out of directed surveillance, under section 28 of the 2000 Act, or

    (ii) the conduct or use of a covert human intelligence source, under section 29 of the 2000 Act.

(2) The applicant must—

    (a) apply in writing and serve the application on the court officer;

    (b) attach the authorisation or notice which the applicant wants the court to approve;

    (c) attach such other material (if any) on which the applicant relies to satisfy the court—

        (i) as required by section 23A(3) and (4) of the 2000 Act, in relation to communications data,

        (ii) as required by section 32A(3) and (4) of the 2000 Act, in relation to directed surveillance, or

        (iii) as required by section 32A(5) and (6), and, if relevant, section 43(6A), of the 2000 Act, in relation to a covert human intelligence source; and

    (d) propose the terms of the order.

Exercise of court's power to quash an authorisation or notice

★P-507
    47.28.—(1) This rule applies where, under section 23A or 32A of the Regulation of Investigatory Powers Act 2000, a magistrates' court refuses to approve the grant, giving or renewal of an authorisation or notice.

(2) The court must not exercise its power to quash that authorisation or notice unless the applicant has had at least 2 business days from the date of the refusal in which to make representations.

Section 7: Search Warrants

Exercise of court's powers

★P-508
    47.29.—(1) The court must determine an application for a warrant—

    (a) at a hearing, which must be in private unless the court otherwise directs;

    (b) in the presence of the applicant; and

    (c) in the absence of any person affected by the warrant, including any person in occupation or control of premises which the applicant wants to search.

(2) If the court so directs, the applicant may attend the hearing by live link.

(3) The court must not determine an application unless satisfied that sufficient time has been allowed for it.

(4) The court must not determine an application unless the applicant confirms, on oath or affirmation, that to the best of the applicant's knowledge and belief—

    (a) the application discloses all the information that is material to what the court must decide, including any circumstances that might reasonably be considered capable of undermining any of the grounds of the application; and

    (b) the content of the application is true.

(5) If the court requires the applicant to answer a question about an application—

    (a) the applicant's answer must be on oath or affirmation;

    (b) the court must arrange for a record of the gist of the question and reply; and

    (c) if the applicant cannot answer to the court's satisfaction, the court may—

        (i) specify the information the court requires, and

        (ii) give directions for the presentation of any renewed application.

(6) Unless to do so would be inconsistent with other legislation, on an application the court may issue—

    (a) a warrant in respect of specified premises;

    (b) a warrant in respect of all premises occupied or controlled by a specified person;

    (c) a warrant in respect of all premises occupied or controlled by a specified person which specifies some of those premises; or

    (d) more than one warrant—

        (i) each one in respect of premises specified in the warrant,

        (ii) each one in respect of all premises occupied or controlled by a person specified in the warrant (whether or not such a warrant also specifies any of those premises), or

        (iii) at least one in respect of specified premises and at least one in respect of all premises occupied or controlled by a specified person (whether or not such a warrant also specifies any of those premises).

Application for warrant under section 8 of the Police and Criminal Evidence Act 1984

★P-509
    47.30.—(1) This rule applies where an applicant wants a magistrates' court to issue a warrant or warrants under section 8 of the Police and Criminal Evidence Act 1984.

(2) The applicant must—
   (a) apply in writing;
   (b) serve the application on—
      (i) the court officer, or
      (ii) if the court office is closed, the court;
   (c) give the court an estimate of how long the court should allow—
      (i) to read and prepare for the application, and
      (ii) for the hearing of the application; and
   (d) tell the court when the applicant expects any warrant issued to be executed.

(3) The application must—
   (a) specify the offence under investigation (and see paragraph (4));
   (b) so far as practicable, identify the material sought (and see paragraph (5));
   (c) specify the premises to be searched (and see paragraphs (6) and (7));
   (d) state whether the applicant wants the premises to be searched on more than one occasion (and see paragraph (8)); and
   (e) state whether the applicant wants other persons to accompany the officers executing the warrant or warrants (and see paragraph (9)).

(4) In relation to the offence under investigation, the application must—
   (a) state whether that offence is—
      (i) an indictable offence, or
      (ii) a relevant offence as defined in section 28D of the Immigration Act 1971; and
   (b) explain the grounds for believing that the offence has been committed.

(5) In relation to the material sought, the application must explain the grounds for believing that that material—
   (a) is likely to be of substantial value to the investigation (whether by itself, or together with other material);
   (b) is likely to be admissible evidence at trial for the offence under investigation; and
   (c) does not consist of or include items subject to legal privilege, excluded material or special procedure material.

(6) In relation to premises which the applicant wants to be searched and can specify, the application must—
   (a) specify each set of premises;
   (b) in respect of each set of premises, explain the grounds for believing that material sought is on those premises; and
   (c) in respect of each set of premises, explain the grounds for believing that—
      (i) it is not practicable to communicate with any person entitled to grant entry to the premises,
      (ii) it is practicable to communicate with such a person but it is not practicable to communicate with any person entitled to grant access to the material sought,
      (iii) entry to the premises will not be granted unless a warrant is produced, or
      (iv) the purpose of a search may be frustrated or seriously prejudiced unless a constable arriving at the premises can secure immediate entry to them.

(7) In relation to premises which the applicant wants to be searched but at least some of which the applicant cannot specify, the application must—
   (a) explain the grounds for believing that—
      (i) because of the particulars of the offence under investigation it is necessary to search any premises occupied or controlled by a specified person, and
      (ii) it is not reasonably practicable to specify all the premises which that person occupies or controls which might need to be searched;
   (b) specify as many sets of premises as is reasonably practicable;
   (c) in respect of each set of premises, whether specified or not, explain the grounds for believing that material sought is on those premises; and
   (d) in respect of each specified set of premises, explain the grounds for believing that—
      (i) it is not practicable to communicate with any person entitled to grant entry to the premises,
      (ii) it is practicable to communicate with such a person but it is not practicable to communicate with any person entitled to grant access to the material sought,
      (iii) entry to the premises will not be granted unless a warrant is produced, or

(iv)   the purpose of a search may be frustrated or seriously prejudiced unless a constable arriving at the premises can secure immediate entry to them.

(8) In relation to any set of premises which the applicant wants to be searched on more than one occasion, the application must—

(a)   explain why it is necessary to search on more than one occasion in order to achieve the purpose for which the applicant wants the court to issue the warrant; and

(b)   specify any proposed maximum number of occasions.

(9) In relation to any set of premises which the applicant wants to be searched by the officers executing the warrant with other persons authorised by the court, the application must—

(a)   identify those other persons, by function or description; and

(b)   explain why those persons are required.

(10) The application must disclose anything known or reported to the applicant that might reasonably be considered capable of undermining any of the grounds of the application.

(11) Where the application includes information that the applicant thinks should be supplied only to the court, the applicant may—

(a)   set out that information in a separate document, marked accordingly; and

(b)   in that document, explain why the applicant thinks that that information ought not to be supplied to anyone other than the court.

(12) The application must include—

(a)   a declaration by the applicant that to the best of the applicant's knowledge and belief—

(i)   the application discloses all the information that is material to what the court must decide, including anything that might reasonably be considered capable of undermining any of the grounds of the application, and

(ii)   the content of the application is true; and

(b)   a declaration by an officer senior to the applicant that the senior officer has reviewed and authorised the application.

(13) The application must attach a draft warrant or warrants in the terms proposed by the applicant.

Application for warrant under section 2 of the Criminal Justice Act 1987

★**P-510**   **47.31.**—(1) This rule applies where an applicant wants a magistrates' court to issue a warrant or warrants under section 2 of the Criminal Justice Act 1987.

(2) The applicant must—

(a)   apply in writing;

(b)   serve the application on—

(i)   the court officer, or

(ii)   if the court office is closed, the court;

(c)   give the court an estimate of how long the court should allow—

(i)   to read and prepare for the application, and

(ii)   for the hearing of the application; and

(d)   tell the court when the applicant expects any warrant issued to be executed.

(3) The application must—

(a)   describe the investigation being conducted by the Director of the Serious Fraud Office and include—

(i)   an explanation of what is alleged and why, and

(ii)   a chronology of relevant events;

(b)   specify the document, documents or description of documents sought by the applicant (and see paragraphs (4) and (5)); and

(c)   specify the premises which the applicant wants to be searched (and see paragraph (6)).

(4) In relation to each document or description of documents sought, the application must—

(a)   explain the grounds for believing that each such document—

(i)   relates to a matter relevant to the investigation, and

(ii)   could not be withheld from disclosure or production on grounds of legal professional privilege; and

(b)   explain the grounds for believing that—

(i)   a person has failed to comply with a notice by the Director to produce the document or documents,

(ii)   it is not practicable to serve such a notice, or

(iii)   the service of such a notice might seriously impede the investigation.

(5) In relation to any document or description of documents which the applicant wants to be preserved but not seized under a warrant, the application must—

    (a) specify the steps for which the applicant wants the court's authority in order to preserve and prevent interference with the document or documents; and

    (b) explain why such steps are necessary.

(6) In respect of each set of premises which the applicant wants to be searched, the application must explain the grounds for believing that a document or description of documents sought by the applicant is on those premises.

(7) If the court so directs, the applicant must make available to the court material on which is based the information given under paragraph (3).

(8) The application must disclose anything known or reported to the applicant that might reasonably be considered capable of undermining any of the grounds of the application.

(9) Where the application includes information that the applicant thinks should be supplied only to the court, the applicant may—

    (a) set out that information in a separate document, marked accordingly; and

    (b) in that document, explain why the applicant thinks that that information ought not to be supplied to anyone other than the court.

(10) The application must include—

    (a) a declaration by the applicant that to the best of the applicant's knowledge and belief—

        (i) the application discloses all the information that is material to what the court must decide, including anything that might reasonably be considered capable of undermining any of the grounds of the application, and

        (ii) the content of the application is true; and

    (b) a declaration by an officer senior to the applicant that the senior officer has reviewed and authorised the application.

(11) The application must attach a draft warrant or warrants in the terms proposed by the applicant.

Application for warrant under another power to which sections 15 and 16 of the Police and Criminal Evidence Act 1984 apply

47.32.—(1) This rule applies where—   ★**P-511**

    (a) an applicant wants a magistrates' court to issue a warrant or warrants under a power to which sections 15 and 16 of the Police and Criminal Evidence Act 1984 apply; and

    (b) neither rule 47.30 nor rule 47.31 applies.

(2) The applicant must—

    (a) apply in writing;

    (b) serve the application on—

        (i) the court officer, or

        (ii) if the court office is closed, the court;

    (c) give the court an estimate of how long the court should allow—

        (i) to read and prepare for the application, and

        (ii) for the hearing of the application; and

    (d) tell the court when the applicant expects any warrant issued to be executed.

(3) The application must—

    (a) state the legislation which allows the court to issue the warrant (in this rule, described as "the main search power"; and see paragraph (4));

    (b) so far as practicable, identify the articles or persons sought (and see paragraph (5));

    (c) specify the premises to be searched (and see paragraphs (6) and (7));

    (d) state whether the applicant wants the premises to be searched on more than one occasion (and see paragraph (8)); and

    (e) state whether the applicant wants other persons to accompany the officers executing the warrant or warrants (and see paragraph (9)).

(4) The application must—

    (a) include or attach the terms of the main search power; and

    (b) explain how the circumstances satisfy any criteria prescribed by the main search power for making the application.

(5) In relation to the articles or persons sought, the application must explain how they satisfy any criteria prescribed by the main search power about such articles or persons.

(6) In relation to premises which the applicant wants to be searched and can specify, the application must—

(a) specify each set of premises; and

(b) in respect of each, explain how the circumstances satisfy any criteria prescribed by the main search power—

    (i) for thinking that the articles or persons sought are on those premises, and

    (ii) for asserting that the court can exercise its power to authorise the search of those premises.

(7) In relation to premises which the applicant wants to be searched but at least some of which the applicant cannot specify, the application must—

(a) explain how the main search power allows the court to authorise such searching;

(b) specify the person who occupies or controls such premises;

(c) specify as many sets of such premises as is reasonably practicable;

(d) explain why—

    (i) it is necessary to search more premises than those specified, and

    (ii) it is not reasonably practicable to specify all the premises which the applicant wants to be searched;

(e) in respect of each set of premises, whether specified or not, explain how the circumstances satisfy any criteria prescribed by the main search power for thinking that the articles or persons sought are on those premises; and

(f) in respect of each specified set of premises, explain how the circumstances satisfy any criteria prescribed by the main search power for asserting that the court can exercise its power to authorise the search of those premises.

(8) In relation to any set of premises which the applicant wants to be searched on more than one occasion, the application must—

(a) explain how the main search power allows the court to authorise such searching;

(b) explain why the applicant wants the premises to be searched more than once; and

(c) specify any proposed maximum number of occasions.

(9) In relation to any set of premises which the applicant wants to be searched by the officers executing the warrant with other persons authorised by the court, the application must—

(a) identify those other persons, by function or description; and

(b) explain why those persons are required.

(10) The application must disclose anything known or reported to the applicant that might reasonably be considered capable of undermining any of the grounds of the application.

(11) Where the application includes information that the applicant thinks should be supplied only to the court, the applicant may—

(a) set out that information in a separate document, marked accordingly; and

(b) in that document, explain why the applicant thinks that that information ought not to be supplied to anyone other than the court.

(12) The application must include—

(a) a declaration by the applicant that to the best of the applicant's knowledge and belief—

    (i) the application discloses all the information that is material to what the court must decide, including anything that might reasonably be considered capable of undermining any of the grounds of the application, and

    (ii) the content of the application is true; and

(b) a declaration by an officer senior to the applicant that the senior officer has reviewed and authorised the application.

(13) The application must attach a draft warrant or warrants in the terms proposed by the applicant.

Information to be included in a warrant

★P-512   **47.33.**—(1) A warrant must identify—

(a) the person or description of persons by whom it may be executed;

(b) any person who may accompany a person executing the warrant;

(c) so far as practicable, the material, documents, articles or persons to be sought;

(d) the legislation under which it was issued;

(e) the name of the applicant;

(f) the court that issued it, unless that is otherwise recorded by the court officer;

(g) the court office for the court that issued it; and

(h) the date on which it was issued.

(2) A warrant must specify—

(a) the premises to be searched, where the application specified premises;

(b) the person in occupation or control of premises to be searched, where the application specified such a person; and

(c) the number of occasions on which specified premises may be searched, if more than one.

(3) A warrant must include, by signature, initial, or otherwise, an indication that it has been approved by the court that issued it.

(4) Where a warrant comprises more than a single page, each page must include such an indication.

(5) A copy of a warrant must include a prominent certificate that it is such a copy.

Section 8: Orders for the Retention of Fingerprints, etc.

Exercise of court's powers

47.34.—(1) The court must determine an application under rule 47.35, and an appeal under rule 47.36— **★P-513**

(a) at a hearing, which must be in private unless the court otherwise directs; and

(b) in the presence of the applicant or appellant.

(2) The court must not determine such an application or appeal unless any person served under those rules—

(a) is present; or

(b) has had an opportunity—

(i) to attend, or

(ii) to make representations.

Application to extend retention period

47.35.—(1) This rule applies where a magistrates' court can make an order extending the period **★P-514** for which there may be retained material consisting of—

(a) fingerprints taken from a person—

(i) under a power conferred by Part V of the Police and Criminal Evidence Act 1984,

(ii) with that person's consent, in connection with the investigation of an offence by the police, or

(iii) under a power conferred by Schedule 8 to the Terrorism Act 2000 in relation to a person detained under section 41 of that Act;

(b) a DNA profile derived from a DNA sample so taken; or

(c) a sample so taken.

(2) A chief officer of police who wants the court to make such an order must—

(a) apply in writing—

(i) within the period of 3 months ending on the last day of the retention period, where the application relates to fingerprints or a DNA profile, or

(ii) before the expiry of the retention period, where the application relates to a sample;

(b) in the application—

(i) identify the material,

(ii) state when the retention period expires,

(iii) give details of any previous such application relating to the material, and

(iv) outline the circumstances in which the material was acquired;

(c) serve the application on the court officer, in every case; and

(d) serve the application on the person from whom the material was taken, where—

(i) the application relates to fingerprints or a DNA profile, or

(ii) the application is for the renewal of an order extending the retention period for a sample.

(3) An application to extend the retention period for fingerprints or a DNA profile must explain why that period should be extended.

(4) An application to extend the retention period for a sample must explain why, having regard to the nature and complexity of other material that is evidence in relation to the offence, the sample is likely to be needed in any proceedings for the offence for the purposes of—

(a) disclosure to, or use by, a defendant; or

(b) responding to any challenge by a defendant in respect of the admissibility of material that is evidence on which the prosecution proposes to rely.

(5) On an application to extend the retention period for fingerprints or a DNA profile, the applicant must serve notice of the court's decision on any respondent where—

(a) the court makes the order sought; and

(b) the respondent was absent when it was made.

Appeal

★**P-515**   47.36.—(1) This rule applies where, under rule 47.35, a magistrates' court determines an application relating to fingerprints or a DNA profile and—

(a) the person from whom the material was taken wants to appeal to the Crown Court against an order extending the retention period; or

(b) a chief officer of police wants to appeal to the Crown Court against a refusal to make such an order.

(2) The appellant must—

(a) serve an appeal notice—

    (i) on the Crown Court officer and on the other party, and

    (ii) not more than 21 days after the magistrates' court's decision, or, if applicable, service of notice under rule 47.35(5); and

(b) in the appeal notice, explain, as appropriate, why the retention period should, or should not, be extended.

(3) Rule 34.11 (constitution of the Crown Court) applies on such an appeal.

Part 48

Contempt of Court

General Rules

When this part applies

★**P-516**   48.1.—(1) This part applies where the court can deal with a person for conduct—

(a) in contempt of court; or

(b) in contravention of the legislation to which rules 48.5 and 48.9 refer.

(2) In this part, "respondent" means any such person.

Exercise of court's power to deal with contempt of court

★**P-517**   48.2.—(1) The court must determine at a hearing—

(a) an enquiry under rule 48.8;

(b) an allegation under rule 48.9.

(2) The court must not proceed in the respondent's absence unless—

(a) the respondent's behaviour makes it impracticable to proceed otherwise; or

(b) the respondent has had at least 14 days' notice of the hearing, or was present when it was arranged.

(3) If the court hears part of an enquiry or allegation in private, it must announce at a hearing in public—

(a) the respondent's name;

(b) in general terms, the nature of any conduct that the respondent admits, or the court finds proved; and

(c) any punishment imposed.

Notice of suspension of imprisonment by Court of Appeal or Crown Court

★**P-518**   48.3.—(1) This rule applies where—

(a) the Court of Appeal or the Crown Court suspends an order of imprisonment for contempt of court; and

(b) the respondent is absent when the court does so.

(2) The respondent must be served with notice of the terms of the court's order—

(a) by any applicant under rule 48.9; or

(b) by the court officer, in any other case.

Application to discharge an order for imprisonment

★**P-519**   48.4.—(1) This rule applies where the court can discharge an order for a respondent's imprisonment for contempt of court.

(2) A respondent who wants the court to discharge such an order must—

(a) apply in writing, unless the court otherwise directs, and serve any written application on—
  (i) the court officer, and
  (ii) any applicant under rule 48.9 on whose application the respondent was imprisoned;
(b) in the application—
  (i) explain why it is appropriate for the order for imprisonment to be discharged, and
  (ii) give details of any appeal, and its outcome; and
(c) ask for a hearing, if the respondent wants one.

Contempt of Court by Obstruction, Disruption, etc.

Initial procedure on obstruction, disruption, etc.

48.5.—(1) This rule applies where the court observes, or someone reports to the court— **★P-520**
  (a) in the Court of Appeal or the Crown Court, obstructive, disruptive, insulting or intimidating conduct, in the courtroom or in its vicinity, or otherwise immediately affecting the proceedings;
  (b) in the Crown Court, a contravention of—
    (i) section 3 of the Criminal Procedure (Attendance of Witnesses) Act 1965 (disobeying a witness summons);
    (ii) section 20 of the Juries Act 1974 (disobeying a jury summons);
    (iii) section 8 of the Contempt of Court Act 1981 (obtaining details of a jury's deliberations, etc.);
  (c) in a magistrates' court, a contravention of—
    (i) section 97(4) of the Magistrates' Courts Act 1980 (refusing to give evidence), or
    (ii) section 12 of the Contempt of Court Act 1981 (insulting or interrupting the court, etc.);
  (d) a contravention of section 9 of the Contempt of Court Act 1981 (without the court's permission, recording the proceedings, etc.);
  (e) any other conduct with which the court can deal as, or as if it were, a criminal contempt of court, except failure to surrender to bail under section 6 of the Bail Act 1976.
(2) Unless the respondent's behaviour makes it impracticable to do so, the court must—
  (a) explain, in terms the respondent can understand (with help, if necessary)—
    (i) the conduct that is in question,
    (ii) that the court can impose imprisonment, or a fine, or both, for such conduct,
    (iii) (where relevant) that the court has power to order the respondent's immediate temporary detention, if in the court's opinion that is required,
    (iv) that the respondent may explain the conduct,
    (v) that the respondent may apologise, if he or she so wishes, and that this may persuade the court to take no further action, and
    (vi) that the respondent may take legal advice; and
  (b) allow the respondent a reasonable opportunity to reflect, take advice, explain and, if he or she so wishes, apologise.
(3) The court may then—
  (a) take no further action in respect of that conduct;
  (b) enquire into the conduct there and then; or
  (c) postpone that enquiry (if a magistrates' court, only until later the same day).

Review after temporary detention

48.6.—(1) This rule applies in a case in which the court has ordered the respondent's immediate **★P-521** temporary detention for conduct to which rule 48.5 applies.
(2) The court must review the case—
  (a) if a magistrates' court, later the same day;
  (b) if the Court of Appeal or the Crown Court, no later than the next business day.
(3) On the review, the court must—
  (a) unless the respondent is absent, repeat the explanations required by rule 48.5(2)(a); and
  (b) allow the respondent a reasonable opportunity to reflect, take advice, explain and, if he or she so wishes, apologise.
(4) The court may then—
  (a) take no further action in respect of the conduct;
  (b) if a magistrates' court, enquire into the conduct there and then; or

(c) if the Court of Appeal or the Crown Court—
  (i) enquire into the conduct there and then, or
  (ii) postpone the enquiry, and order the respondent's release from such detention in the meantime.

Postponement of enquiry

★P-522   48.7.—(1) This rule applies where the Court of Appeal or the Crown Court postpones the enquiry.

(2) The court must arrange for the preparation of a written statement containing such particulars of the conduct in question as to make clear what the respondent appears to have done.

(3) The court officer must serve on the respondent—
  (a) that written statement;
  (b) notice of where and when the postponed enquiry will take place; and
  (c) a notice that—
    (i) reminds the respondent that the court can impose imprisonment, or a fine, or both, for contempt of court, and
    (ii) warns the respondent that the court may pursue the postponed enquiry in the respondent's absence, if the respondent does not attend.

Procedure on enquiry

★P-523   48.8.—(1) At an enquiry, the court must—
  (a) ensure that the respondent understands (with help, if necessary) what is alleged, if the enquiry has been postponed from a previous occasion;
  (b) explain what the procedure at the enquiry will be; and
  (c) ask whether the respondent admits the conduct in question.

(2) If the respondent admits the conduct, the court need not receive evidence.

(3) If the respondent does not admit the conduct, the court must consider—
  (a) any statement served under rule 48.7;
  (b) any other evidence of the conduct;
  (c) any evidence introduced by the respondent; and
  (d) any representations by the respondent about the conduct.

(4) If the respondent admits the conduct, or the court finds it proved, the court must—
  (a) before imposing any punishment for contempt of court, give the respondent an opportunity to make representations relevant to punishment;
  (b) explain, in terms the respondent can understand (with help, if necessary)—
    (i) the reasons for its decision, including its findings of fact, and
    (ii) the punishment it imposes, and its effect; and
  (c) if a magistrates' court, arrange for the preparation of a written record of those findings.

(5) The court that conducts an enquiry—
  (a) need not include the same member or members as the court that observed the conduct; but
  (b) may do so, unless that would be unfair to the respondent.

Contempt of Court by Failure to Comply with Court Order, etc.

Initial procedure on failure to comply with court order, etc.

★P-524   48.9.—(1) This rule applies where—
  (a) a party, or other person directly affected, alleges—
    (i) in the Crown Court, a failure to comply with an order to which applies rule 33.70 (compliance order, restraint order or ancillary order), rule 47.13 (certain investigation orders under the Terrorism Act 2000) or rule 47.22 (certain investigation orders under the Proceeds of Crime Act 2002),
    (ii) in the Court of Appeal or the Crown Court, any other conduct with which that court can deal as a civil contempt of court, or
    (iii) in the Crown Court or a magistrates' court, unauthorised use of disclosed prosecution material under section 17 of the Criminal Procedure and Investigations Act 1996;
  (b) the court deals on its own initiative with conduct to which paragraph (1)(a) applies.

(2) Such a party or person must—
  (a) apply in writing and serve the application on the court officer; and
  (b) serve on the respondent—

(i)   the application, and

(ii)   notice of where and when the court will consider the allegation (not less than 14 days after service).

(3) The application must—

(a)   identify the respondent;

(b)   explain that it is an application for the respondent to be dealt with for contempt of court;

(c)   contain such particulars of the conduct in question as to make clear what is alleged against the respondent; and

(d)   include a notice warning the respondent that the court—

(i)   can impose imprisonment, or a fine, or both, for contempt of court, and

(ii)   may deal with the application in the respondent's absence, if the respondent does not attend the hearing.

(4) A court which acts on its own initiative under paragraph (1)(b) must—

(a)   arrange for the preparation of a written statement containing the same information as an application; and

(b)   arrange for the service on the respondent of—

(i)   that written statement, and

(ii)   notice of where and when the court will consider the allegation (not less than 14 days after service).

Procedure on hearing

48.10.—(1) At the hearing of an allegation under rule 48.9, the court must—   ★**P-525**

(a)   ensure that the respondent understands (with help, if necessary) what is alleged;

(b)   explain what the procedure at the hearing will be; and

(c)   ask whether the respondent admits the conduct in question.

(2) If the respondent admits the conduct, the court need not receive evidence.

(3) If the respondent does not admit the conduct, the court must consider—

(a)   the application or written statement served under rule 48.9;

(b)   any other evidence of the conduct;

(c)   any evidence introduced by the respondent; and

(d)   any representations by the respondent about the conduct.

(4) If the respondent admits the conduct, or the court finds it proved, the court must—

(a)   before imposing any punishment for contempt of court, give the respondent an opportunity to make representations relevant to punishment;

(b)   explain, in terms the respondent can understand (with help, if necessary)—

(i)   the reasons for its decision, including its findings of fact, and

(ii)   the punishment it imposes, and its effect; and

(c)   in a magistrates' court, arrange for the preparation of a written record of those findings.

Introduction of written witness statement or other hearsay

48.11.—(1) Where rule 48.9 applies, an applicant or respondent who wants to introduce in   ★**P-526**
evidence the written statement of a witness, or other hearsay, must—

(a)   serve a copy of the statement, or notice of other hearsay, on—

(i)   the court officer, and

(ii)   the other party; and

(b)   serve the copy or notice—

(i)   when serving the application under rule 48.9, in the case of an applicant, or

(ii)   not more than 7 days after service of that application or of the court's written statement, in the case of the respondent.

(2) Such service is notice of that party's intention to introduce in evidence that written witness statement, or other hearsay, unless that party otherwise indicates when serving it.

(3) A party entitled to receive such notice may waive that entitlement.

Content of written witness statement

48.12.—(1) This rule applies to a written witness statement served under rule 48.11.   ★**P-527**

(2) Such a written witness statement must contain a declaration by the person making it that it is true to the best of that person's knowledge and belief.

Content of notice of other hearsay

48.13.—(1) This rule applies to a notice of hearsay, other than a written witness statement, served   ★**P-528**
under rule 48.11.

(2) Such a notice must—

    (a) set out the evidence, or attach the document that contains it; and

    (b) identify the person who made the statement that is hearsay.

Cross-examination of maker of written witness statement or other hearsay

★P-529
    48.14.—(1) This rule applies where a party wants the court's permission to cross-examine a person who made a statement which another party wants to introduce as hearsay.

    (2) The party who wants to cross-examine that person must—

    (a) apply in writing, with reasons; and

    (b) serve the application on—

        (i) the court officer, and

        (ii) the party who served the hearsay.

    (3) A respondent who wants to cross-examine such a person must apply to do so not more than 7 days after service of the hearsay by the applicant.

    (4) An applicant who wants to cross-examine such a person must apply to do so not more than 3 days after service of the hearsay by the respondent.

    (5) The court—

    (a) may decide an application under this rule without a hearing; but

    (b) must not dismiss such an application unless the person making it has had an opportunity to make representations at a hearing.

Credibility and consistency of maker of written witness statement or other hearsay

★P-530
    48.15.—(1) This rule applies where a party wants to challenge the credibility or consistency of a person who made a statement which another party wants to introduce as hearsay.

    (2) The party who wants to challenge the credibility or consistency of that person must—

    (a) serve a written notice of intention to do so on—

        (i) the court officer, and

        (ii) the party who served the hearsay; and

    (b) in it, identify any statement or other material on which that party relies.

    (3) A respondent who wants to challenge such a person's credibility or consistency must serve such a notice not more than 7 days after service of the hearsay by the applicant.

    (4) An applicant who wants to challenge such a person's credibility or consistency must serve such a notice not more than 3 days after service of the hearsay by the respondent.

    (5) The party who served the hearsay—

    (a) may call that person to give oral evidence instead; and

    (b) if so, must serve a notice of intention to do so on—

        (i) the court officer, and

        (ii) the other party

    as soon as practicable after service of the notice under paragraph (2).

Magistrates' courts' powers to adjourn, etc.

★P-531
    48.16.—(1) This rule applies where a magistrates' court deals with unauthorised disclosure of prosecution material under sections 17 and 18 of the Criminal Procedure and Investigations Act 1996.

    (2) The sections of the Magistrates' Courts Act 1980 listed in paragraph (3) apply as if in those sections—

    (a) "complaint" and "summons" each referred to an application or written statement under rule 48.9;

    (b) "complainant" meant an applicant; and

    (c) "defendant" meant the respondent.

    (3) Those sections are—

    (a) section 51 (issue of summons on complaint);

    (b) section 54 (adjournment);

    (c) section 55 (non-appearance of defendant);

    (d) section 97(1) (summons to witness);

    (e) section 121(1) (constitution and place of sitting of court);

    (f) section 123 (defect in process).

    (4) Section 127 of the 1980 Act (limitation of time) does not apply.

Court's power to vary requirements
48.17.—(1) The court may shorten or extend (even after it has expired) a time limit under rule ★**P-532**
48.11, 48.14 or 48.15.
(2) A person who wants an extension of time must—
(a) apply when serving the statement, notice or application for which it is needed; and
(b) explain the delay.

PART 49

INTERNATIONAL CO-OPERATION

Notice required to accompany process served outside the United Kingdom and translations
49.1.—(1) The notice which by virtue of section 3(4)(b) of the Crime (International Co-operation) ★**P-533**
Act 2003 (general requirements for service of process) must accompany any process served outside
the United Kingdom must give the information specified in paragraphs (2) and (4) below.
(2) The notice must—
(a) state that the person required by the process to appear as a party or attend as a witness can
obtain information about his rights in connection therewith from the relevant authority;
and
(b) give the particulars specified in paragraph (4) about that authority.
(3) The relevant authority where the process is served—
(a) at the request of the prosecuting authority, is that authority; or
(b) at the request of the defendant or the prosecutor in the case of a private prosecution, is the
court by which the process is served.
(4) The particulars referred to in paragraph (2) are—
(a) the name and address of the relevant authority, together with its telephone and fax
numbers and e-mail address; and
(b) the name of a person at the relevant authority who can provide the information referred to
in paragraph (2)(a), together with his telephone and fax numbers and e-mail address.
(5) The justices' clerk or Crown Court officer must send, together with any process served outside
the United Kingdom —
(a) any translation which is provided under section 3(3)(b) of the 2003 Act; and
(b) any translation of the information required to be given by this rule which is provided to
him.
(6) In this rule, "process" has the same meaning as in section 51(3) of the 2003 Act.

Proof of service outside the United Kingdom
49.2.—(1) A statement in a certificate given by or on behalf of the Secretary of State— ★**P-534**
(a) that process has been served on any person under section 4(1) of the Crime (International
Co-operation) Act 2003 (service of process otherwise than by post);
(b) of the manner in which service was effected; and
(c) of the date on which process was served;
shall be admissible as evidence of any facts so stated.
(2) In this rule, "process" has the same meaning as in section 51(3) of the 2003 Act.

Supply of copy of notice of request for assistance abroad
49.3. Where a request for assistance under section 7 of the Crime (International Co-operation) Act ★**P-535**
2003 is made by a justice of the peace or a judge exercising the jurisdiction of the Crown Court and
is sent in accordance with section 8(1) of the 2003 Act, the justices' clerk or the Crown Court officer
shall send a copy of the letter of request to the Secretary of State as soon as practicable after the
request has been made.

Persons entitled to appear and take part in proceedings before a nominated court, and exclusion of the public
49.4. A court nominated under section 15(1) of the Crime (International Co-operation) Act 2003 ★**P-536**
(nominating a court to receive evidence) may—
(a) determine who may appear or take part in the proceedings under Schedule 1 to the 2003
Act before the court and whether a party to the proceedings is entitled to be legally
represented; and
(b) direct that the public be excluded from those proceedings if it thinks it necessary to do so
in the interests of justice.

Record of proceedings to receive evidence before a nominated court
49.5.—(1) Where a court is nominated under section 15(1) of the Crime (International Co- ★**P-537**
operation) Act 2003 the justices' clerk or Crown Court officer shall enter in an overseas record—

1111

(a) details of the request in respect of which the notice under section 15(1) of the 2003 Act was given;

(b) the date on which, and place at which, the proceedings under Schedule 1 to the 2003 Act in respect of that request took place;

(c) the name of any witness who gave evidence at the proceedings in question;

(d) the name of any person who took part in the proceedings as a legal representative or an interpreter;

(e) whether a witness was required to give evidence on oath or (by virtue of section 5 of the Oaths Act 1978) after making a solemn affirmation; and

(f) whether the opportunity to cross-examine any witness was refused.

(2) When the court gives the evidence received by it under paragraph 6(1) of Schedule 1 to the 2003 Act to the court or authority that made the request or to the territorial authority for forwarding to the court or authority that made the request, the justices' clerk or Crown Court officer shall send to the court, authority or territorial authority (as the case may be) a copy of an extract of so much of the overseas record as relates to the proceedings in respect of that request.

Interpreter for the purposes of proceedings involving a television or telephone link

★P-538   **49.6.**—(1) This rule applies where a court is nominated under section 30(3) (hearing witnesses in the UK through television links) or section 31(4) (hearing witnesses in the UK by telephone) of the Crime (International Co-operation) Act 2003.

(2) Where it appears to the justices' clerk or the Crown Court officer that the witness to be heard in the proceedings under Part 1 or 2 of Schedule 2 to the 2003 Act ("the relevant proceedings") is likely to give evidence in a language other than English, he shall make arrangements for an interpreter to be present at the proceedings to translate what is said into English.

(3) Where it appears to the justices' clerk or the Crown Court officer that the witness to be heard in the relevant proceedings is likely to give evidence in a language other than that in which the proceedings of the court referred to in section 30(1) or, as the case may be, 31(1) of the 2003 Act ("the external court") will be conducted, he shall make arrangements for an interpreter to be present at the relevant proceedings to translate what is said into the language in which the proceedings of the external court will be conducted.

(4) Where the evidence in the relevant proceedings is either given in a language other than English or is not translated into English by an interpreter, the court shall adjourn the proceedings until such time as an interpreter can be present to provide a translation into English.

(5) Where a court in Wales understands Welsh—

(a) paragraph (2) does not apply where it appears to the justices' clerk or Crown Court officer that the witness in question is likely to give evidence in Welsh;

(b) paragraph (4) does not apply where the evidence is given in Welsh; and

(c) any translation which is provided pursuant to paragraph (2) or (4) may be into Welsh instead of English.

Record of television link hearing before a nominated court

★P-539   **49.7.**—(1) This rule applies where a court is nominated under section 30(3) of the Crime (International Co-operation) Act 2003.

(2) The justices' clerk or Crown Court officer shall enter in an overseas record—

(a) details of the request in respect of which the notice under section 30(3) of the 2003 Act was given;

(b) the date on which, and place at which, the proceedings under Part 1 of Schedule 2 to that Act in respect of that request took place;

(c) the technical conditions, such as the type of equipment used, under which the proceedings took place;

(d) the name of the witness who gave evidence;

(e) the name of any person who took part in the proceedings as a legal representative or an interpreter; and

(f) the language in which the evidence was given.

(3) As soon as practicable after the proceedings under Part 1 of Schedule 2 to the 2003 Act took place, the justices' clerk or Crown Court officer shall send to the external authority that made the request a copy of an extract of so much of the overseas record as relates to the proceedings in respect of that request.

Record of telephone link hearing before a nominated court

★P-540   **49.8.**—(1) This rule applies where a court is nominated under section 31(4) of the Crime (International Co-operation) Act 2003.

(2) The justices' clerk or Crown Court officer shall enter in an overseas record—

    (a) details of the request in respect of which the notice under section 31(4) of the 2003 Act was given;

    (b) the date, time and place at which the proceedings under Part 2 of Schedule 2 to the 2003 Act took place;

    (c) the name of the witness who gave evidence;

    (d) the name of any interpreter who acted at the proceedings; and

    (e) the language in which the evidence was given.

Overseas record

49.9.—(1) The overseas records of a magistrates' court shall be part of the register (within the   **★P-541** meaning of section 150(1) of the Magistrates' Courts Act 1980).

(2) The overseas records of any court shall not be open to inspection by any person except—

    (a) as authorised by the Secretary of State; or

    (b) with the leave of the court.

Overseas freezing orders

49.10.—(1) This rule applies where a court is nominated under section 21(1) of the Crime   **★P-542** (International Co-operation) Act 2003 to give effect to an overseas freezing order.

(2) Where the Secretary of State serves a copy of such an order on the court officer—

    (a) the general rule is that the court must consider the order no later than the next business day;

    (b) exceptionally, the court may consider the order later than that, but not more than 5 business days after service.

(3) The court must not consider the order unless—

    (a) it is satisfied that the chief officer of police for the area in which the evidence is situated has had notice of the order; and

    (b) that chief officer of police has had an opportunity to make representations, at a hearing if that officer wants.

(4) The court may consider the order—

    (a) without a hearing; or

    (b) at a hearing, in public or in private.

Overseas forfeiture orders

49.11.—(1) This rule applies where—   **★P-543**

    (a) the Crown Court can—

        (i) make a restraint order under article 5 of the Criminal Justice (International Co-operation) Act 1990 (Enforcement of Overseas Forfeiture Orders) Order 2005, or

        (ii) give effect to an external forfeiture order under article 19 of that Order;

    (b) the Director of Public Prosecutions or the Director of the Serious Fraud Office receives—

        (i) a request for the restraint of property to which article 3 of the 2005 Order applies, or

        (ii) a request to give effect to an external forfeiture order to which article 15 of the Order applies; and

    (c) the Director wants the Crown Court to—

        (i) make such a restraint order, or

        (ii) give effect to such a forfeiture order.

(2) The Director must—

    (a) apply in writing;

    (b) serve the application on the court officer; and

    (c) serve the application on the defendant and on any other person affected by the order, unless the court is satisfied that—

        (i) the application is urgent, or

        (ii) there are reasonable grounds for believing that to give notice of the application would cause the dissipation of the property which is the subject of the application.

(3) The application must—

    (a) identify the property the subject of the application;

    (b) identify the person who is or who may become the subject of such a forfeiture order;

    (c) explain how the requirements of the 2005 Order are satisfied, as the case may be—

        (i) for making a restraint order, or

(ii)   for giving effect to a forfeiture order;

(d)   where the application is to give effect to a forfeiture order, include an application to appoint the Director as the enforcement authority; and

(e)   propose the terms of the Crown Court order.

(4) If the court allows the application, it must—

(a)   where it decides to make a restraint order—

(i)   specify the property the subject of the order,

(ii)   specify the person or persons who are prohibited from dealing with that property,

(iii)   specify any exception to that prohibition, and

(iv)   include any ancillary order that the court believes is appropriate to ensure that the restraint order is effective;

(b)   where it decides to give effect to a forfeiture order, exercise its power to—

(i)   direct the registration of the order as an order of the Crown Court,

(ii)   give directions for notice of the order to be given to any person affected by it, and

(iii)   appoint the applicant Director as the enforcement authority.

(5) Paragraph (6) applies where a person affected by an order, or the Director, wants the court to vary or discharge a restraint order or cancel the registration of a forfeiture order.

(6) Such a person must—

(a)   apply in writing as soon as practicable after becoming aware of the grounds for doing so;

(b)   serve the application on the court officer and, as applicable—

(i)   the other party, and

(ii)   any other person who will or may be affected;

(c)   explain why it is appropriate, as the case may be—

(i)   for the restraint order to be varied or discharged, or

(ii)   for the registration of the forfeiture order to be cancelled;

(d)   propose the terms of any variation; and

(e)   ask for a hearing, if one is wanted, and explain why it is needed.

(7) The court may—

(a)   consider an application

(i)   at a hearing, which must be in private unless the court otherwise directs, or

(ii)   without a hearing;

(b)   allow an application to be made orally.

Overseas restraint orders

★P-544   **49.12.**—(1) This rule applies where—

(a)   the Crown Court can give effect to an overseas restraint order under regulation 10 of the Criminal Justice and Data Protection (Protocol No. 36) Regulations 2014;

(b)   the Director of Public Prosecutions or the Director of the Serious Fraud Office receives a request from a court or authority in another European Union member State to give effect to such an order; and

(c)   the Director serves on the Crown Court officer—

(i)   the certificate which accompanied the request for enforcement of the order,

(ii)   a copy of the order restraining the property to which that certificate relates, and

(iii)   a copy of an order confiscating the property in respect of which the restraint order was made, or an indication of when such a confiscation order is expected.

(2) On service of those documents on the court officer—

(a)   the general rule is that the Crown Court must consider the order, with a view to its registration, no later than the next business day;

(b)   exceptionally, the court may consider the order later than that, but not more than 5 business days after service.

(3) The court—

(a)   must not consider the order unless the Director—

(i)   is present, or

(ii)   has had a reasonable opportunity to make representations;

(b)   subject to that, may consider the order—

(i)   at a hearing, which must be in private unless the court otherwise directs, or

(ii)   without a hearing.

(4) If the court decides to give effect to the order, the court must—

(a)   direct its registration as an order of the Crown Court; and

(b)   give directions for notice of the order to be given to any person affected by it.

(5) Paragraph (6) applies where a person affected by the order, or the Director, wants the court to cancel the registration or vary the property to which the order applies.

(6) Such a person must—

(a)   apply in writing as soon as practicable after becoming aware of the grounds for doing so;

(b)   serve the application on the court officer and, as applicable—

(i)   the other party, and

(ii)   any other person who will or may be affected;

(c)   explain, as applicable—

(i)   when the overseas restraint order ceased to have effect in the European Union member State in which it was made,

(ii)   why continuing to give effect to that order would be impossible as a consequence of an immunity under the law of England and Wales,

(iii)   why continuing to give effect to that order would be incompatible with a Convention right within the meaning of the Human Rights Act 1998,

(iv)   why therefore it is appropriate for the registration to be cancelled or varied;

(d)   include with the application any evidence in support;

(e)   propose the terms of any variation; and

(f)   ask for a hearing, if one is wanted, and explain why it is needed.

Overseas confiscation orders

49.13.—(1) This rule applies where—   ★**P-545**

(a)   the Crown Court can give effect to an overseas confiscation order under regulation 15 of the Criminal Justice and Data Protection (Protocol No. 36) Regulations 2014;

(b)   the Director of Public Prosecutions or the Director of the Serious Fraud Office receives a request from a court or authority in another European Union member State to give effect to such an order; and

(c)   the Director serves on the Crown Court officer—

(i)   the certificate which accompanied the request for enforcement of the order, and

(ii)   a copy of the confiscation order to which that certificate relates.

(2) The court—

(a)   must not consider the order unless the Director—

(i)   is present, or

(ii)   has had a reasonable opportunity to make representations;

(b)   subject to that, may consider the order—

(i)   at a hearing, which must be in private unless the court otherwise directs, or

(ii)   without a hearing.

(3) If the court decides to give effect to the order, the court must—

(a)   direct its registration as an order of the Crown Court; and

(b)   give directions for notice of the order to be given to any person affected by it.

(4) Paragraph (5) applies where a person affected by the order, or the Director, wants the court to cancel the registration or vary the property to which the order applies.

(5) Such a person must—

(a)   apply in writing as soon as practicable after becoming aware of the grounds for doing so;

(b)   serve the application on the court officer and, as applicable—

(i)   the other party, and

(ii)   any other person who will or may be affected;

(c)   explain, as applicable—

(i)   when the overseas confiscation order ceased to have effect in the European Union member State in which it was made,

(ii)   why continuing to give effect to that order would be statute-barred, provided that the criminal conduct that gave rise to the order falls within the jurisdiction of England and Wales,

(iii)   why continuing to give effect to that order would be impossible as a consequence of an immunity under the law of England and Wales,

(iv)   why continuing to give effect to that order would be incompatible with a Convention right within the meaning of the Human Rights Act 1998,

(v)   why therefore it is appropriate for the registration to be cancelled or varied;

(d)   include with the application any evidence in support;

(e) propose the terms of any variation; and

(f) ask for a hearing, if one is wanted, and explain why it is needed.

★**P-546**   **50.** [*Extradition*]

ALMANAC

TABLE OF CONTENTS

2011

JANUARY
M	T	W	Th	F	Sa	Su
					1	2
3	4	5	6	7	8	9
10	11	12	13	14	15	16
17	18	19	20	21	22	23
24	25	26	27	28	29	30
31						

FEBRUARY
M	T	W	Th	F	Sa	Su
	1	2	3	4	5	6
7	8	9	10	11	12	13
14	15	16	17	18	19	20
21	22	23	24	25	26	27
28						

MARCH
M	T	W	Th	F	Sa	Su
	1	2	3	4	5	6
7	8	9	10	11	12	13
14	15	16	17	18	19	20
21	22	23	24	25	26	27
28	29	30	31			

APRIL
M	T	W	Th	F	Sa	Su
				1	2	3
4	5	6	7	8	9	10
11	12	13	14	15	16	17
18	19	20	21	22	23	24
25	26	27	28	29	30	

MAY
M	T	W	Th	F	Sa	Su
2	3	4	5	6	7	1
9	10	11	12	13	14	8
16	17	18	19	20	21	15
23	24	25	26	27	28	22
30	31					29

JUNE
M	T	W	Th	F	Sa	Su
		1	2	3	4	5
6	7	8	9	10	11	12
13	14	15	16	17	18	19
20	21	22	23	24	25	26
27	28	29	30			

JULY
M	T	W	Th	F	Sa	Su
				1	2	3
4	5	6	7	8	9	10
11	12	13	14	15	16	17
18	19	20	21	22	23	24
25	26	27	28	29	30	31

AUGUST
M	T	W	Th	F	Sa	Su
1	2	3	4	5	6	7
8	9	10	11	12	13	14
15	16	17	18	19	20	21
22	23	24	25	26	27	28
29	30	31				

SEPTEMBER
M	T	W	Th	F	Sa	Su
			1	2	3	4
5	6	7	8	9	10	11
12	13	14	15	16	17	18
19	20	21	22	23	24	25
26	27	28	29	30		

OCTOBER
M	T	W	Th	F	Sa	Su
					1	2
3	4	5	6	7	8	9
10	11	12	13	14	15	16
17	18	19	20	21	22	23
24	25	26	27	28	29	30
31						

NOVEMBER
M	T	W	Th	F	Sa	Su
	1	2	3	4	5	6
7	8	9	10	11	12	13
14	15	16	17	18	19	20
21	22	23	24	25	26	27
28	29	30				

DECEMBER
M	T	W	Th	F	Sa	Su
			1	2	3	4
5	6	7	8	9	10	11
12	13	14	15	16	17	18
19	20	21	22	23	24	25
26	27	28	29	30	31	

2012

JANUARY

M	T	W	Th	F	Sa	Su
2	3	4	5	6	7	1
9	10	11	12	13	14	8
16	17	18	19	20	21	15
23	24	25	26	27	28	22
30	31					29

FEBRUARY

M	T	W	Th	F	Sa	Su
6	7	1	2	3	4	5
13	14	8	9	10	11	12
20	21	15	16	17	18	19
27	28	22	23	24	25	26
		29				

MARCH

M	T	W	Th	F	Sa	Su
5	6	7	1	2	3	4
12	13	14	8	9	10	11
19	20	21	15	16	17	18
26	27	28	22	23	24	25
			29	30	31	

APRIL

M	T	W	Th	F	Sa	Su
2	3	4	5	6	7	1
9	10	11	12	13	14	8
16	17	18	19	20	21	15
23	24	25	26	27	28	22
30						29

MAY

M	T	W	Th	F	Sa	Su
7	1	2	3	4	5	6
14	8	9	10	11	12	13
21	15	16	17	18	19	20
28	22	23	24	25	26	27
	29	30	31			

JUNE

M	T	W	Th	F	Sa	Su
4	5	6	7	1	2	3
11	12	13	14	8	9	10
18	19	20	21	15	16	17
25	26	27	28	22	23	24
				29	30	

JULY

M	T	W	Th	F	Sa	Su
2	3	4	5	6	7	1
9	10	11	12	13	14	8
16	17	18	19	20	21	15
23	24	25	26	27	28	22
30	31					29

AUGUST

M	T	W	Th	F	Sa	Su
6	7	1	2	3	4	5
13	14	8	9	10	11	12
20	21	15	16	17	18	19
27	28	22	23	24	25	26
		29	30	31		

SEPTEMBER

M	T	W	Th	F	Sa	Su
3	4	5	6	7	1	2
10	11	12	13	14	8	9
17	18	19	20	21	15	16
24	25	26	27	28	22	23
					29	30

OCTOBER

M	T	W	Th	F	Sa	Su
1	2	3	4	5	6	7
8	9	10	11	12	13	14
15	16	17	18	19	20	21
22	23	24	25	26	27	28
29	30	31				

NOVEMBER

M	T	W	Th	F	Sa	Su
5	6	7	1	2	3	4
12	13	14	8	9	10	11
19	20	21	15	16	17	18
26	27	28	22	23	24	25
			29	30		

DECEMBER

M	T	W	Th	F	Sa	Su
3	4	5	6	7	1	2
10	11	12	13	14	8	9
17	18	19	20	21	15	16
24	25	26	27	28	22	23
31					29	30

2013

JANUARY

M	T	W	Th	F	Sa	Su
	1	2	3	4	5	6
7	8	9	10	11	12	13
14	15	16	17	18	19	20
21	22	23	24	25	26	27
28	29	30	31			

FEBRUARY

M	T	W	Th	F	Sa	Su
4	5	6	7	1	2	3
11	12	13	14	8	9	10
18	19	20	21	15	16	17
25	26	27	28	22	23	24

MARCH

M	T	W	Th	F	Sa	Su
4	5	6	7	1	2	3
11	12	13	14	8	9	10
18	19	20	21	15	16	17
25	26	27	28	22	23	24
				29	30	31

APRIL

M	T	W	Th	F	Sa	Su
1	2	3	4	5	6	7
8	9	10	11	12	13	14
15	16	17	18	19	20	21
22	23	24	25	26	27	28
29	30					

MAY

M	T	W	Th	F	Sa	Su
6	7	1	2	3	4	5
13	14	8	9	10	11	12
20	21	15	16	17	18	19
27	28	22	23	24	25	26
		29	30	31		

JUNE

M	T	W	Th	F	Sa	Su
3	4	5	6	7	1	2
10	11	12	13	14	8	9
17	18	19	20	21	15	16
24	25	26	27	28	22	23
					29	30

JULY

M	T	W	Th	F	Sa	Su
1	2	3	4	5	6	7
8	9	10	11	12	13	14
15	16	17	18	19	20	21
22	23	24	25	26	27	28
29	30	31				

AUGUST

M	T	W	Th	F	Sa	Su
5	6	7	1	2	3	4
12	13	14	8	9	10	11
19	20	21	15	16	17	18
26	27	28	22	23	24	25
			29	30	31	

SEPTEMBER

M	T	W	Th	F	Sa	Su
2	3	4	5	6	7	1
9	10	11	12	13	14	8
16	17	18	19	20	21	15
23	24	25	26	27	28	22
30						29

OCTOBER

M	T	W	Th	F	Sa	Su
7	1	2	3	4	5	6
14	8	9	10	11	12	13
21	15	16	17	18	19	20
28	22	23	24	25	26	27
	29	30	31			

NOVEMBER

M	T	W	Th	F	Sa	Su
4	5	6	7	1	2	3
11	12	13	14	8	9	10
18	19	20	21	15	16	17
25	26	27	28	22	23	24
				29	30	

DECEMBER

M	T	W	Th	F	Sa	Su
2	3	4	5	6	7	1
9	10	11	12	13	14	8
16	17	18	19	20	21	15
23	24	25	26	27	28	22
30	31					29

2014

JANUARY

M	T	W	Th	F	Sa	Su
		1	2	3	4	5
6	7	8	9	10	11	12
13	14	15	16	17	18	19
20	21	22	23	24	25	26
27	28	29	30	31		

FEBRUARY

M	T	W	Th	F	Sa	Su
					1	2
3	4	5	6	7	8	9
10	11	12	13	14	15	16
17	18	19	20	21	22	23
24	25	26	27	28		

MARCH

M	T	W	Th	F	Sa	Su
					1	2
3	4	5	6	7	8	9
10	11	12	13	14	15	16
17	18	19	20	21	22	23
24	25	26	27	28	29	30
31						

APRIL

M	T	W	Th	F	Sa	Su
	1	2	3	4	5	6
7	8	9	10	11	12	13
14	15	16	17	18	19	20
21	22	23	24	25	26	27
28	29	30				

MAY

M	T	W	Th	F	Sa	Su
			1	2	3	4
5	6	7	8	9	10	11
12	13	14	15	16	17	18
19	20	21	22	23	24	25
26	27	28	29	30	31	

JUNE

M	T	W	Th	F	Sa	Su
						1
2	3	4	5	6	7	8
9	10	11	12	13	14	15
16	17	18	19	20	21	22
23	24	25	26	27	28	29
30						

JULY

M	T	W	Th	F	Sa	Su
	1	2	3	4	5	6
7	8	9	10	11	12	13
14	15	16	17	18	19	20
21	22	23	24	25	26	27
28	29	30	31			

AUGUST

M	T	W	Th	F	Sa	Su
				1	2	3
4	5	6	7	8	9	10
11	12	13	14	15	16	17
18	19	20	21	22	23	24
25	26	27	28	29	30	31

SEPTEMBER

M	T	W	Th	F	Sa	Su
1	2	3	4	5	6	7
8	9	10	11	12	13	14
15	16	17	18	19	20	21
22	23	24	25	26	27	28
29	30					

OCTOBER

M	T	W	Th	F	Sa	Su
		1	2	3	4	5
6	7	8	9	10	11	12
13	14	15	16	17	18	19
20	21	22	23	24	25	26
27	28	29	30	31		

NOVEMBER

M	T	W	Th	F	Sa	Su
					1	2
3	4	5	6	7	8	9
10	11	12	13	14	15	16
17	18	19	20	21	22	23
24	25	26	27	28	29	30

DECEMBER

M	T	W	Th	F	Sa	Su
1	2	3	4	5	6	7
8	9	10	11	12	13	14
15	16	17	18	19	20	21
22	23	24	25	26	27	28
29	30	31				

2015

JANUARY

M	T	W	Th	F	Sa	Su
			1	2	3	4
5	6	7	8	9	10	11
12	13	14	15	16	17	18
19	20	21	22	23	24	25
26	27	28	29	30	31	

FEBRUARY

M	T	W	Th	F	Sa	Su
						1
2	3	4	5	6	7	8
9	10	11	12	13	14	15
16	17	18	19	20	21	22
23	24	25	26	27	28	

MARCH

M	T	W	Th	F	Sa	Su
						1
2	3	4	5	6	7	8
9	10	11	12	13	14	15
16	17	18	19	20	21	22
23	24	25	26	27	28	29
30	31					

APRIL

M	T	W	Th	F	Sa	Su
		1	2	3	4	5
6	7	8	9	10	11	12
13	14	15	16	17	18	19
20	21	22	23	24	25	26
27	28	29	30			

MAY

M	T	W	Th	F	Sa	Su
				1	2	3
4	5	6	7	8	9	10
11	12	13	14	15	16	17
18	19	20	21	22	23	24
25	26	27	28	29	30	31

JUNE

M	T	W	Th	F	Sa	Su
1	2	3	4	5	6	7
8	9	10	11	12	13	14
15	16	17	18	19	20	21
22	23	24	25	26	27	28
29	30					

JULY

M	T	W	Th	F	Sa	Su
		1	2	3	4	5
6	7	8	9	10	11	12
13	14	15	16	17	18	19
20	21	22	23	24	25	26
27	28	29	30	31		

AUGUST

M	T	W	Th	F	Sa	Su
					1	2
3	4	5	6	7	8	9
10	11	12	13	14	15	16
17	18	19	20	21	22	23
24	25	26	27	28	29	30
31						

SEPTEMBER

M	T	W	Th	F	Sa	Su
	1	2	3	4	5	6
7	8	9	10	11	12	13
14	15	16	17	18	19	20
21	22	23	24	25	26	27
28	29	30				

OCTOBER

M	T	W	Th	F	Sa	Su
			1	2	3	4
5	6	7	8	9	10	11
12	13	14	15	16	17	18
19	20	21	22	23	24	25
26	27	28	29	30	31	

NOVEMBER

M	T	W	Th	F	Sa	Su
						1
2	3	4	5	6	7	8
9	10	11	12	13	14	15
16	17	18	19	20	21	22
23	24	25	26	27	28	29
30						

DECEMBER

M	T	W	Th	F	Sa	Su
	1	2	3	4	5	6
7	8	9	10	11	12	13
14	15	16	17	18	19	20
21	22	23	24	25	26	27
28	29	30	31			

2016

JANUARY
M	T	W	Th	F	Sa	Su
				1	2	3
4	5	6	7	8	9	10
11	12	13	14	15	16	17
18	19	20	21	22	23	24
25	26	27	28	29	30	31

FEBRUARY
M	T	W	Th	F	Sa	Su
1	2	3	4	5	6	7
8	9	10	11	12	13	14
15	16	17	18	19	20	21
22	23	24	25	26	27	28
29						

MARCH
M	T	W	Th	F	Sa	Su
	1	2	3	4	5	6
7	8	9	10	11	12	13
14	15	16	17	18	19	20
21	22	23	24	25	26	27
28	29	30	31			

APRIL
M	T	W	Th	F	Sa	Su
				1	2	3
4	5	6	7	8	9	10
11	12	13	14	15	16	17
18	19	20	21	22	23	24
25	26	27	28	29	30	

MAY
M	T	W	Th	F	Sa	Su
						1
2	3	4	5	6	7	8
9	10	11	12	13	14	15
16	17	18	19	20	21	22
23	24	25	26	27	28	29
30	31					

JUNE
M	T	W	Th	F	Sa	Su
		1	2	3	4	5
6	7	8	9	10	11	12
13	14	15	16	17	18	19
20	21	22	23	24	25	26
27	28	29	30			

JULY
M	T	W	Th	F	Sa	Su
				1	2	3
4	5	6	7	8	9	10
11	12	13	14	15	16	17
18	19	20	21	22	23	24
25	26	27	28	29	30	31

AUGUST
M	T	W	Th	F	Sa	Su
1	2	3	4	5	6	7
8	9	10	11	12	13	14
15	16	17	18	19	20	21
22	23	24	25	26	27	28
29	30	31				

SEPTEMBER
M	T	W	Th	F	Sa	Su
			1	2	3	4
5	6	7	8	9	10	11
12	13	14	15	16	17	18
19	20	21	22	23	24	25
26	27	28	29	30		

OCTOBER
M	T	W	Th	F	Sa	Su
					1	2
3	4	5	6	7	8	9
10	11	12	13	14	15	16
17	18	19	20	21	22	23
24	25	26	27	28	29	30
31						

NOVEMBER
M	T	W	Th	F	Sa	Su
	1	2	3	4	5	6
7	8	9	10	11	12	13
14	15	16	17	18	19	20
21	22	23	24	25	26	27
28	29	30				

DECEMBER
M	T	W	Th	F	Sa	Su
			1	2	3	4
5	6	7	8	9	10	11
12	13	14	15	16	17	18
19	20	21	22	23	24	25
26	27	28	29	30	31	

2017

JANUARY

M	T	W	Th	F	Sa	Su
2	3	4	5	6	7	1
9	10	11	12	13	14	8
16	17	18	19	20	21	15
23	24	25	26	27	28	22
30	31					29

FEBRUARY

M	T	W	Th	F	Sa	Su
6	7	1	2	3	4	5
13	14	8	9	10	11	12
20	21	15	16	17	18	19
27	28	22	23	24	25	26

MARCH

M	T	W	Th	F	Sa	Su
6	7	1	2	3	4	5
13	14	8	9	10	11	12
20	21	15	16	17	18	19
27	28	22	23	24	25	26
		29	30	31		

APRIL

M	T	W	Th	F	Sa	Su
3	4	5	6	7	1	2
10	11	12	13	14	8	9
17	18	19	20	21	15	16
24	25	26	27	28	22	23
					29	30

MAY

M	T	W	Th	F	Sa	Su
1	2	3	4	5	6	7
8	9	10	11	12	13	14
15	16	17	18	19	20	21
22	23	24	25	26	27	28
29	30	31				

JUNE

M	T	W	Th	F	Sa	Su
5	6	7	1	2	3	4
12	13	14	8	9	10	11
19	20	21	15	16	17	18
26	27	28	22	23	24	25
			29	30		

JULY

M	T	W	Th	F	Sa	Su
3	4	5	6	7	1	2
10	11	12	13	14	8	9
17	18	19	20	21	15	16
24	25	26	27	28	22	23
31					29	30

AUGUST

M	T	W	Th	F	Sa	Su
7	1	2	3	4	5	6
14	8	9	10	11	12	13
21	15	16	17	18	19	20
28	22	23	24	25	26	27
	29	30	31			

SEPTEMBER

M	T	W	Th	F	Sa	Su
4	5	6	7	1	2	3
11	12	13	14	8	9	10
18	19	20	21	15	16	17
25	26	27	28	22	23	24
				29	30	

OCTOBER

M	T	W	Th	F	Sa	Su
2	3	4	5	6	7	1
9	10	11	12	13	14	8
16	17	18	19	20	21	15
23	24	25	26	27	28	22
30	31					29

NOVEMBER

M	T	W	Th	F	Sa	Su
6	7	1	2	3	4	5
13	14	8	9	10	11	12
20	21	15	16	17	18	19
27	28	22	23	24	25	26
		29	30			

DECEMBER

M	T	W	Th	F	Sa	Su
4	5	6	7	1	2	3
11	12	13	14	8	9	10
18	19	20	21	15	16	17
25	26	27	28	22	23	24
				29	30	31

2018

JANUARY

M	T	W	Th	F	Sa	Su
1	2	3	4	5	6	7
8	9	10	11	12	13	14
15	16	17	18	19	20	21
22	23	24	25	26	27	28
29	30	31				

FEBRUARY

M	T	W	Th	F	Sa	Su
			1	2	3	4
5	6	7	8	9	10	11
12	13	14	15	16	17	18
19	20	21	22	23	24	25
26	27	28				

MARCH

M	T	W	Th	F	Sa	Su
			1	2	3	4
5	6	7	8	9	10	11
12	13	14	15	16	17	18
19	20	21	22	23	24	25
26	27	28	29	30	31	

APRIL

M	T	W	Th	F	Sa	Su
						1
2	3	4	5	6	7	8
9	10	11	12	13	14	15
16	17	18	19	20	21	22
23	24	25	26	27	28	29
30						

MAY

M	T	W	Th	F	Sa	Su
	1	2	3	4	5	6
7	8	9	10	11	12	13
14	15	16	17	18	19	20
21	22	23	24	25	26	27
28	29	30	31			

JUNE

M	T	W	Th	F	Sa	Su
				1	2	3
4	5	6	7	8	9	10
11	12	13	14	15	16	17
18	19	20	21	22	23	24
25	26	27	28	29	30	

JULY

M	T	W	Th	F	Sa	Su
						1
2	3	4	5	6	7	8
9	10	11	12	13	14	15
16	17	18	19	20	21	22
23	24	25	26	27	28	29
30	31					

AUGUST

M	T	W	Th	F	Sa	Su
		1	2	3	4	5
6	7	8	9	10	11	12
13	14	15	16	17	18	19
20	21	22	23	24	25	26
27	28	29	30	31		

SEPTEMBER

M	T	W	Th	F	Sa	Su
					1	2
3	4	5	6	7	8	9
10	11	12	13	14	15	16
17	18	19	20	21	22	23
24	25	26	27	28	29	30

OCTOBER

M	T	W	Th	F	Sa	Su
1	2	3	4	5	6	7
8	9	10	11	12	13	14
15	16	17	18	19	20	21
22	23	24	25	26	27	28
29	30	31				

NOVEMBER

M	T	W	Th	F	Sa	Su
			1	2	3	4
5	6	7	8	9	10	11
12	13	14	15	16	17	18
19	20	21	22	23	24	25
26	27	28	29	30		

DECEMBER

M	T	W	Th	F	Sa	Su
					1	2
3	4	5	6	7	8	9
10	11	12	13	14	15	16
17	18	19	20	21	22	23
24	25	26	27	28	29	30
31						

Holidays and Notable Dates

Holiday, etc.	2011	2012	2013	2014	2015	2016	2017	2018
New Year's Day	Jan. 1	Jan. 1	Jan. 1	Jan. 1	Jan. 1	Jan. 1	Jan. 1	Jan. 1
New Year Holiday (England)	Jan. 3	Jan. 2	—	—	—	—	—	—
New Year Holiday (Scotland)	Jan. 4	Jan. 3	Jan. 2	Jan. 2	Jan. 2	Jan. 2	Jan. 2	Jan. 2
St David's Day (Wales)	Mar. 1	Mar. 1	Mar. 1	Mar. 1	Mar. 1	Mar. 1	Mar. 1	Mar. 1
St Patrick's Day (Ireland)	Mar. 17	Mar. 17	Mar. 17	Mar. 17	Mar. 17	Mar. 17	Mar. 17	Mar. 17
Good Friday	Apr. 22	Apr. 6	Apr.29	Apr. 18	Mar. 3	Apr. 25	Mar. 14	Mar. 30
Easter Monday	Apr. 25	Apr. 9	Apr.1	Apr. 21	Apr. 6	Apr. 28	Mar. 17	Apr. 2
St George's Day (England)	Apr. 23	Apr. 23	Apr. 23	Apr. 23	Apr. 23	Apr. 23	Apr. 23	Apr. 23
May Day Holiday	May 2	May 7	May 6	May 5	May 4	May 2	May 1	May 7
Queen's Diamond Jubilee	—	Jun. 4	—	—	—	—	—	—
Spring Bank Holiday	May 30	Jun. 5	May 27	May 26	May 25	May 30	May 29	May 28
August Bank Holiday	Aug. 29	Aug. 27	Aug. 26	Aug. 25	Aug. 24	Aug. 29	Aug. 28	Aug. 27
St Andrew's Day (Scotland)	Nov. 30	Nov. 30	Nov. 30	Nov. 30	Nov. 30	Nov. 30	Nov. 30	Nov. 30
Christmas Day	Dec. 25	Dec. 25	Dec. 25	Dec. 25	Dec. 25	Dec. 25	Dec. 25	Dec. 25
Boxing Day	Dec. 26	Dec. 26	Dec. 26	Dec. 26	Dec. 26	Dec. 26	Dec. 26	Dec. 26
Christmas Holiday(s)	—	—	—	—	—	Dec. 27		

Measurement Conversion Tables

The measurements set out below are based upon the following standards set by the Weights **AL-10**
and Measures Act 1985, Sched. 1, Pts I to V:

YARD = 0.9144 metre; GALLON = 4.546 09 cubic decimetres or litres; POUND = 0.453 592
37 kilograms

Measurements of Length

Imperial Units of Length	Metric Equivalents
Mil	1/1000 inch	0.0254 millimetres
Inch	1000 mils	2.54 centimetres
Link	7.92 inches	20.1168 centimetres
Foot	12 inches	0.3048 metres
Yard	3 feet	0.9144 metres
Fathom	6 feet	1.8288 metres
Cable	60 feet or 10 fathoms	18.288 metres
Chain	22 yards (100 links)	20.1168 metres
Furlong	220 yards	201.168 metres
Mile	1,760 yards (8 furlongs)	1.609344 kilometres
Nautical mile	6080 feet	1.853184 kilometres

Metric Units of Length	Imperial Equivalents
Micron	1/1000 millimetre	0.03937007 mils
Millimetre	1/1000 metre	0.03937007 inches
Centimetre	1/100 metre	0.3937 inches
Decimetre	1/10 metre	3.937 inches
Metre	Metre	1.09361329 yards
Kilometre	1000 metres	0.62137712 miles or 0.53961 nautical miles

Measurements of Area

Imperial Units of Area	Metric Equivalents
Square inch	1/144 square feet	6,4516 square centimetres
Square foot	1/9 square yard	929.0304 square centimetres
Square yard	Square yard	0.83613 square metres

Imperial Units of Area		*Metric Equivalents*
Square chain	484 square yards	404.685642 square metres
Rood	1,210 square yards	1011.714 square metres
Acre	4 roods or 4840 square yards	4046.85642 sq. ms or 40.4685642 acres
Square mile	640 acres	258.998811 hectares

Metric Units of Area		*Imperial Equivalents*
Square millimetre	1/100 square centimetre	0.00155 square inches
Square centimetre	1/100 square decimetre	0.155 square inches
Square decimetre	1/100 metre	15.5 square inches
Square metre	Square metre	1.1959 sq. yards or 10.7639 sq. ft
Are	100 square metres	119.599 sq. yds or 0.09884 roods
Dekare	10 ares	0.2471 acres
Hectare	100 ares (1,000 square metres)	2.47105 acres
Square kilometre	100 hectares	247.105 acres or 0.3861 square miles

Measurements of Volume

Imperial Units of Volume		*Metric Equivalents*
Cubic inch		16.387064 cubic centimetres
Cubic foot	1,728 cubic inches	28.3168465 decimetres
Cubic yard	27 cubic feet	0.76455485 cubic metres

Metric Units of Volume		*Imperial Equivalents*
Cubic centimetre	1,000 cubic millimetres	0.06102374 cubic inches
Cubic decimetre	1,000 cubic centimetres	0.03531466 cubic feet
Cubic metre	1,000 cubic decimetres	1.30795061 cubic yards or 35.3147 cu. ft.

Archbold
paragraph
numbers

AL-13

Archbold's Criminal Pleading—2015 ed.

AL-18

Measurements of Capacity

Imperial, Apothecaries and US Units of Capacity		Metric Equivalents
Minim		0.0591938 millilitres
Fluid Drachm	60 minims	0.35516328 centilitres
Fluid ounce	8 fluid drachms	2.84130625 centilitres
US fluid ounce	1.0408 UK fluid ounces	29.573522656 millilitres
Gill	5 fluid ounces	1.42065312 decilitres
Pint	4 gills or 20 fluid ounces	0.56826125 litres
US pint	0.8327 UK pints or 16 US fluid ounces	0.47317636 litres
Quart	2 pints or 8 gills	1.1365225 litres
Gallon	4 quarts or 1.20095 US gallons	4.54609 litres
US gallon	0.08327 UK gallons	3.7854109 litres
Peck	2 gallons or 16 pints	9.09218 litres
Bushel	4 pecks or 8 gallons	36.36872 litres
Quarter	8 bushels or 36 pecks	2.9094976 hectolitres
Chaldron	36 bushels or 4 ½ quarters	13.0927392 hectolitres

Metric Units of Capacity		Imperial Equivalents
Millilitre		0.28156064 fluid drachms
Centilitre	10 millilitres	0.35195080 fluid ounces
Decilitre	10 centilitres	0.70390160 gills
Litre	10 decilitres	1.75975398 pints or 0.21996924 UK gallons
Dekalitre	10 litres	2.196924 UK gallons
Hectolitre	10 dekalitres or 100 litres	21.996824 UK gallons

Measurements of Weight

Imperial and Apothecaries Units of Weight		Metric Equivalents
Grain	Grain	64.79891 milligrams

Imperial and Apothecaries Units of Weight		Metric Equivalents
Scruple	20 grains	1.2959782 grams
Pennyweight	24 grains	1.55517384 grams
Drachm	3 scruples or 60 grains	3.8879346 grams
Troy ounce	8 drachms or 480 grains	31.1034768 grams
Dram	1/16 ounce	1.77184519 grams
Ounce	16 drams or 437.5 grains	28.3495231 gram
Troy pound (US)	12 troy ounces or 5,760 grains	373.241721 grams
Pound	16 ounces or 7,000 grains	453.59237 grams or 0.45359237 kilograms
Stone	14 pounds	6.35029318 kilograms
Quarter	28 pounds or 2 stone	12.7005863 kilograms
Cental	100 pounds	45.359237 kilograms
Hundredweight	4 quarters or 112 pounds	50.8023454 kilograms
Short hundredweight (US)	100 pounds	45.359237 kilograms
Ton (UK or long ton)	20 cwt or 2,240 pounds	1.0160469 metric tonnes (tonne)
Ton (US or short ton)	2,000 pounds	0.90718474 metric tonnes

Metric Units of Weight		Imperial Equivalents
Milligram	.001 grams	0.012432 grains
Centigram	.01 grams	0.15432 grains
Decigram	.1 grams	1.5432 grains
Gram	1 gram	0.0327396 ounces or 0.03215 troy ounces
Dekagram	10 grams	0.35273961 ounces
Hectogram	100 grams	3.52739619 ounces
Kilogram	1,000 grams	2.20462262 pounds
Myriagram	10 kilograms	22.0462 pounds
Quintal	100 kilograms	1.9684 hundredweight
Tonne	1,000 kilograms	0.984207 UK tons or 1.10231 US tons

Measurements of Velocity

Per Hour	Per Minute	Per Second
Mile	88 feet	17.6 inches per second
1.609344 kph	26.8224 metres	44.704 centimetres per second
Kilometres	16.6667 metres	27.7778 centimetres
0.62137 mph	54.6806 feet	10.9361 inches

Système Internationale D'unites or SI Units

1. SI units are increasingly being used to report laboratory results. They have largely replaced **AL-16**
   earlier systems such as c.g.s. units (centimetre, gram, second), m.k.s. or Giorgi units
   (metre, kilogram, second), and Imperial units (yard, pound, second).
2. S.I. Units comprise 7 base units and 2 supplementary units. Other units are derived from
   these. 18 derived units are currently widely accepted.

Base SI Units

Physical Quantity	Unit	Symbol
Length	metre	m
Mass	kilogram	kg
Time	second	s
Electric current	ampere	A
Temperature	kelvin	K
Luminosity	candela	cd
Amount of substance	mole	mol
Plane angle*	radian*	rad
Solid angle*	steradian*	sr

*Supplementary Units

Derived SI Units

Physical Quantity	Unit	Symbol
Frequency	hertz	Hz
Energy	joule	J
Force	newton	N
Power	watt	W
Pressure	pascal	Pa
Electric charge	coulomb	C
Electric potential difference	volt	V
Electrical resistance	ohm	Ω
Electric conductance	siemens	S
Electric capacitance	farad	F
Magnetic flux	weber	Wb
Inductance	henry	H
Magnetic flux density	tesla	T
Luminous flux	lumen	lm
Illuminance	lux	lx
Absorbed dose	gray	Gy
Activity	becquerel	Bq
Dose Equivalence	sievert	Sv

Multiples and Subdivisions of SI Units

Prefix	Symbol	Power	Value
exa	E	10^{18}	1,000,000,000,000,000,000
peta	P	10^{15}	1,000,000,000,000,000

Prefix	Symbol	Power	Value
tera	T	10^{12}	1,000,000,000,000
giga	G	10^{9}	1,000,000,000
mega	M	10^{6}	1,000,000
kilo	k	10^{3}	1,000
hecto	h	10^{2}	100
deca	da	10	10
-			1
deci	d	10^{-1}	1/10
centi	c	10^{-2}	1/100
milli	m	10^{-3}	1/1,000
micro	μ	10^{-6}	1/1,000,000
nano	n	10^{-9}	1/1,000,000,000
pico	p	10^{-12}	1/1,000,000,000,000
femto	f	10^{-15}	1/1,000,000,000,000,000
atto	a	10^{-18}	1/1,000,000,000,000,000,000

International Time Differences

AL-20   The following time differences are based upon Greenwich Mean Time (GMT). British Summer Time (BST) is one hour in advance of GMT.

Country		Hours +/-
Algeria		+1 hour
Argentina		-3 hours
Australia	South Australia	+9½ hours
	New South Wales	+10 hours
	Tasmania	+10 hours
	Victoria	+10 hours
Austria		+1 hour
Belgium		+1 hour
Bolivia		-4 hours
Brazil		-3 hours
Bulgaria		+2 hours
Canada	Newfoundland	-3½ hours
	Atlantic	-4 hours
	Eastern	-5 hours
	Central	-6 hours
	Mountain	-7 hours
	Pacific	-8 hours
	Yukon	-9 hours
Chile		-4 hours
China		+8 hours
Columbia		-5 hours
Czech Lands		+1 hour
Denmark		+1 hour
Egypt		+2 hours
Finland		+2 hours

Country	Hours +/-
France	+1 hour
Germany	+1 hour
Ghana	
Greece	+2 hours
Holland	+1 hour
Hong Kong	+8 hours
Hungary	+1 hour
India	+5½ hours
Iraq	+3 hours
Ireland	
Israel	+2 hours
Italy	+1 hour
Jamaica	-5 hours
Japan	+9 hours
Kenya	+3 hours

Country	Hours +/-
Luxembourg	+1 hour
Malaysia	+8 hours
Malta	+1 hour
Morocco	
New Zealand	+12 hours
Nigeria	+1 hour
Norway	+1 hour
Peru	-5 hours
Philippines	+8 hours
Poland	+1 hour

Country		Hours +/-
Portugal		—
Romania		+2 hours
Russia	Moscow	+3 hours
	Vladivostok	+10 hours
Saudi Arabia		+3 hours
Serbia		+1 hours
Singapore		+8 hours
South Africa		+2 hours
Spain		+1 hour
Sri Lanka		+5½ hours
Sweden		+1 hour
Switzerland		+1 hour
Taiwan		+8 hours
Thailand		+7 hours
Tunisia		+1 hour
Turkey		+2 hours
Ukraine		+3 hours
United Arab Emirates		+4 hours
United States	Eastern	-5 hours
	Central	-6 hours
	Mountain	-7 hours
	Pacific	-8 hours
Zambia		+2 hours
Zimbabwe		+2 hours

Stopping Distances

AL-22

Speed (m.p.h.)	Stopping distance (feet)
20	40
30	75
40	120
50	175
60	240
70	315

Useful Contact Details

	Telephone	Email
Courts, etc.		
House of Lords, Judicial Office	(020) 7219 3111	
Royal Courts of Justice	(020) 7947 6000	
Registrar, Criminal Appeals	(020) 7947 6103	
Criminal Appeal Office	(020) 7947 6011	Criminalappealoffice.generaloffice@hmcourts-service.x.gsi.gov.uk
Administrative Court Office	(020) 7947 6205	
Official Bodies		
Home Office	(020) 7035 4848	public.enquiries@homeoffice.gsi.gov.uk
Serious Fraud Office	(020) 7239 7272	public.enquiries@sfo.gsi.gov.uk
H.M. Revenue and Customs	0845 010 9000	Enquiries.estn@hmrc.gsi.gov.uk This address handles all enquiries related to VAT, Excise and other duties formerly administered by HM Customs and Excise (with the exception of International Trade)
New Scotland Yard	(020) 7230 1212	new.scotland.yard@met.police.uk
City of London Police	(020) 7601 2222	postmaster@cityoflondon.police.uk
British Transport Police	0800 40 50 40	
Others		
Justice	(020) 7329 5100	admin@justice.org.uk
Liberty	(020) 7403 3888	
Bar Council	(020) 7242 0082	
Bar Council Ethical Enquiries Line	(020) 7611 1307	
Bar Standards Board	(020) 7611 1444	

	Telephone	Email
Law Society — Lawyerline	0870 606 2588	
Law Society — Practice Advice Service	0870 606 2522	

INDEX

LEGAL TAXONOMY
FROM SWEET & MAXWELL

This index has been prepared using Sweet and Maxwell's Legal Taxonomy. Main index entries conform to keywords provided by the Legal Taxonomy except where references to specific documents or non-standard terms (denoted by quotation marks) have been included. These keywords provide a means of identifying similar concepts in other Sweet & Maxwell publications and online services to which keywords from the Legal Taxonomy have been applied. Readers may find some minor differences between terms used in the text and those which appear in the index. Suggestions to *sweetandmaxwell.taxonomy@thomson.com*.

All references are to paragraph numbers.